MW01233989

Copyright © 2024 by TimelessTruth Editions

All rights reserved.

No part of this publication may be reproduced, distributed,
or transmitted in any form or by any means,
including photocopying, recording, or other electronic
or mechanical methods, without the prior written permission
of the publisher, except as permitted by U.S. copyright law.
For permission requests, contact TimelessTruth Editions.

Book Cover by Mitria Suric
Introduction by the Publisher

1st edition 2024

The Largest and Most Complete Collection

THE ULTIMATE 84-BOOK APOCRYPHA

*Featuring Enoch, Jasher, and Jubilees,
with Deuterocanon and Pseudepigrapha,
Lost Gospels, Apocalypses, and More*

CONTENTS

CONTENTS

Introduction to
"The Ultimate 84-Book Apocrypha:
The Largest and Most Complete Apocrypha Collection
of the Lost Books of the Bible"

This anthology represents the most extensive and comprehensive collection
of apocryphal and deuterocanonical books ever assembled,
offering an unparalleled insight into the theological and historical contexts
from which these texts emerge.

The term "apocrypha" traditionally denotes writings excluded from the canon of the Hebrew Bible
and the Christian Old Testament, while "deuterocanonical" refers to those scriptures accepted
as canonical in certain Christian traditions but not universally recognized.
These texts provide a window into the varied landscape of belief, tradition
and narrative that coexisted and sometimes intertwined with the recognized canonical works.

Theological Significance

From a theological standpoint, this collection presents an opportunity to delve into the diverse beliefs,
liturgical practices, and theological discourses of early Jewish and Christian communities.
Through narratives rich in wisdom, ethical discourse, divine nature, and human destiny,
the apocryphal and deuterocanonical books offer a broader spectrum for interpreting sacred scriptures.
They unveil a multitude of spiritual entities, eschatological visions, and moral teachings
that have significantly shaped religious thought.

Historical Importance

Historically, these works are invaluable to scholars and religious enthusiasts alike,
illuminating the spiritual terrain of the ancient Near East, Second Temple Judaism
and nascent Christianity. They underscore the multiplicity of religious expressions
and scriptural interpretations, highlighting the fluidity and dynamism of sacred literature.
This anthology's inclusion of martyrdom accounts, alternative gospel narratives,
apostolic acts, visionary apocalypses, epistolary teachings and wisdom literature showcases
the rich diversity of texts that flourished beyond the established canon.

Inside the Anthology

- Martyrdoms and Others: Featuring narratives of steadfast faith and sacrifice,
along with writings that explore cosmology, ethics, and the end times, this section offers
a glimpse into the spiritual and moral convictions of early believers.

- Gospels: Providing varied perspectives on Jesus Christ's life, teachings
and divine mission, these texts contribute to a deeper, multifaceted understanding
of the Christian message.

- Acts: Detailing the endeavors, trials, and divine interventions experienced by the apostles
and early Christians, these accounts document the spread of Christianity
and the foundation of the Church.

- Apocalypses: Filled with prophetic revelations, these texts offer visions of the end of days,
celestial realms, and the final judgment, enriching our eschatological understanding.

- Letters and Teachings: This section includes epistles and discourses that delve into community ethics,
theological contemplation, and spiritual practices, guiding readers toward a life of virtue.

- Deuterocanonical Books: Embraced by certain Christian traditions, these texts enhance
our appreciation of biblical wisdom, historical narratives, and prophetic declarations.

"The Ultimate 84-book Apocrypha" invites readers to embark on an exploration of these profound
and captivating texts. By making this remarkable collection available, we aim to foster a deeper
appreciation for the rich diversity of religious thought and spirituality that characterizes this significant
historical period. These texts, whether approached with scholarly interest, spiritual seeking,
or historical curiosity, offer invaluable insights, inspiration, and enlightenment.

Greek manuscript of the Book of Enoch, 4th century

MARTYRDOMS
AND OTHERS

BOOK OF ENOCH

INTRODUCTION

Section I. Chapters I-XXXVI

[Chapter 1]

[1] The words of the blessing of Enoch, wherewith he blessed the elect and righteous, who will be [2] living in the day of tribulation, when all the wicked and godless are to be removed. And he took up his parable and said - Enoch a righteous man, whose eyes were opened by God, saw the vision of the Holy One in the heavens, which the angels showed me, and from them I heard everything, and from them I understood as I saw, but not for this generation, but for a remote one which is [3] for to come. Concerning the elect I said, and took up my parable concerning them:

> The Holy Great One will come forth from His dwelling,
> [4] And the eternal God will tread upon the earth, (even) on Mount Sinai,
> [And appear from His camp]
> And appear in the strength of His might from the heaven of heavens.

> [5] And all shall be smitten with fear
> And the Watchers shall quake,
> And great fear and trembling shall seize them unto the ends of the earth.

> [6] And the high mountains shall be shaken,
> And the high hills shall be made low,
> And shall melt like wax before the flame

> [7] And the earth shall be wholly rent in sunder,
> And all that is upon the earth shall perish,
> And there shall be a judgement upon all (men).

> [8] But with the righteous He will make peace.

> And will protect the elect,
> And mercy shall be upon them.

> And they shall all belong to God,
> And they shall be prospered,
> And they shall all be blessed.

> And He will help them all,
> And light shall appear unto them,
> And He will make peace with them'.

> [9] And behold! He cometh with ten thousands of His holy ones

> To execute judgement upon all,
> And to destroy all the ungodly:
> And to convict all flesh
> Of all the works of their ungodliness which they have ungodly committed,
> And of all the hard things which ungodly sinners have spoken against Him.

[Chapter 2]

[1] Observe ye everything that takes place in the heaven, how they do not change their orbits, and the luminaries which are in the heaven, how they all rise and set in order each in its season, and [2] transgress not against their appointed order. Behold ye the earth, and give heed to the things which take place upon it from first to last, how steadfast they are, how none of the things upon earth [3] change, but all the works of God appear to you. Behold the summer and the winter, how the whole earth is filled with water, and clouds and dew and rain lie upon it.

[Chapter 3]

Observe and see how (in the winter) all the trees seem as though they had withered and shed all their leaves, except fourteen trees, which do not lose their foliage but retain the old foliage from two to three years till the new comes.

[Chapter 4]

And again, observe ye the days of summer how the sun is above the earth over against it. And you seek shade and shelter by reason of the heat of the sun, and the earth also burns with growing heat, and so you cannot tread on the earth, or on a rock by reason of its heat.

[Chapter 5]

[1] Observe ye how the trees cover themselves with green leaves and bear fruit: wherefore give ye heed and know with regard to all His works, and recognize how He that liveth for ever hath made them so. [2] And all His works go on thus from year to year for ever, and all the tasks which they accomplish for Him, and their tasks change not, but according as God hath ordained so is it done. [3] And behold how the sea and the rivers in like manner accomplish and change not their tasks from His commandments'.

> [4] But ye -ye have not been steadfast, nor done the commandments of the Lord,

> But ye have turned away and spoken proud and hard words
> With your impure mouths against His greatness.

> Oh, ye hard-hearted, ye shall find no peace.

5 Therefore shall ye execrate your days,

And the years of your life shall perish,

And the years of your destruction shall be multiplied in eternal execration,

And ye shall find no mercy.

6a In those days ye shall make your names an eternal execration unto all the righteous,

b And by you shall all who curse, curse,

And all the sinners and godless shall imprecate by you,
7c And for you the godless there shall be a curse.

6d And all the . . . shall rejoice,

e And there shall be forgiveness of sins,

f And every mercy and peace and forbearance:
g There shall be salvation unto them, a goodly light.

i And for all of you sinners there shall be no salvation,

j But on you all shall abide a curse.

7a But for the elect there shall be light and joy and peace,

b And they shall inherit the earth.

8 And then there shall be bestowed upon the elect wisdom,

And they shall all live and never again sin,

Either through ungodliness or through pride:

But they who are wise shall be humble.

9 And they shall not again transgress,

Nor shall they sin all the days of their life,

Nor shall they die of (the divine) anger or wrath,
But they shall complete the number of the days of their life.

And their lives shall be increased in peace,

And the years of their joy shall be multiplied,

In eternal gladness and peace,

All the days of their life

[Chapter 6]

1 And it came to pass when the children of men had multiplied that in those days were born unto 2 them beautiful and comely daughters. And the angels, the children of the heaven, saw and lusted after them, and said to one another: 'Come, let us choose us wives from among the children of men 3 and beget us children.' And Semjaza, who was their leader, said unto them: 'I fear ye will not 4 indeed agree to do this deed, and I alone shall have to pay the penalty of a great sin.' And they all answered him and said: 'Let us all swear an oath, and all bind ourselves by mutual imprecations 5 not to abandon this plan but to do this thing.' Then sware they all together and bound themselves 6 by mutual imprecations upon it. And they were in all two hundred; who descended in the days of Jared on the summit of Mount Hermon, and they called it Mount Hermon, because they had sworn 7 and bound themselves by mutual imprecations upon it. And these are the names of their leaders: Samlazaz, their leader, Araklba, Rameel, Kokablel, Tamlel, Ramlel, Danel, Ezeqeel, Baraqijal, 8 Asael, Armaros, Batarel, Ananel, Zaqiel, Samsapeel, Satarel, Turel, Jomjael, Sariel. These are their chiefs of tens.

[Chapter 7]

1 And all the others together with them took unto themselves wives, and each chose for himself one, and they began to go in unto them and to defile themselves with them, and they taught them charms 2 and enchantments, and the cutting of roots, and made them acquainted with plants. And they 3 became pregnant, and they bare great giants, whose height was three thousand ells: Who consumed 4 all the acquisitions of men. And when men could no longer sustain them, the giants turned against 5 them and devoured mankind. And they began to sin against birds, and beasts, and reptiles, and 6 fish, and to devour one another's flesh, and drink the blood. Then the earth laid accusation against the lawless ones.

[Chapter 8]

1 And Azazel taught men to make swords, and knives, and shields, and breastplates, and made known to them the metals of the earth and the art of working them, and bracelets, and ornaments, and the use of antimony, and the beautifying of the eyelids, and all kinds of costly stones, and all 2 colouring tinctures. And there arose much godlessness, and they committed fornication, and they 3 were led astray, and became corrupt in all their ways. Semjaza taught enchantments, and root-cuttings, 'Armaros the resolving of enchantments, Baraqijal (taught) astrology, Kokabel the constellations, Ezeqeel the knowledge of the clouds, Araqiel the signs of the earth, Shamsiel the signs of the sun, and Sariel the course of the moon. And as men perished, they cried, and their cry went up to heaven . . .

[Chapter 9]

1 And then Michael, Uriel, Raphael, and Gabriel looked down from heaven and saw much blood being 2 shed upon the earth, and all lawlessness being wrought upon the earth. And they said one to another: 'The earth made without inhabitant cries the voice of their cryingst up to the gates of heaven. 3 And now to you, the holy ones of heaven, the souls of men make their suit, saying, "Bring our cause 4 before the Most High."' And they said to the Lord of the ages: 'Lord of lords, God of gods, King of kings, and God of the ages, the throne of Thy glory (standeth) unto all the generations of the 5 ages, and Thy name holy and glorious and blessed unto all the ages! Thou hast made all things, and power over all things hast Thou: and all things are naked and open in Thy sight, and Thou seest all 6 things, and nothing can hide itself from Thee. Thou seest what Azazel hath done, who hath taught all unrighteousness on earth and revealed the eternal secrets which were (preserved) in heaven, which 7 men were striving to learn: And Semjaza, to whom Thou hast given authority to bear rule over his associates. And they have gone to the daughters of men upon the earth, and have slept with the 9 women, and have defiled themselves, and revealed to them all kinds of sins. And the women have 10 borne giants, and the whole earth has thereby been filled with blood and unrighteousness. And now, behold, the souls of those who have died are crying and making their suit to the gates of heaven, and their lamentations have ascended: and cannot cease because of the lawless deeds which are 11 wrought on the earth. And Thou knowest all things before they come to pass, and Thou seest these things and Thou dost suffer them, and Thou dost not say to us what we are to do to them in regard to these.'

[Chapter 10]

1 Then said the Most High, the Holy and Great One spake, and sent Uriel to the son of Lamech, 2 and said to him: 'Go to Noah and tell him in my name "Hide thyself!" and reveal to him the end that is approaching: that the whole earth will be destroyed, and a deluge is about to come 3 upon the whole earth, and will destroy all that is on it. And now instruct him that he may escape 4 and his seed may be preserved for all the generations of the world.' And again the Lord said to Raphael: 'Bind Azazel hand and foot, and cast him into the darkness: and make an opening 5 in the desert, which is in Dudael, and cast him therein. And place upon him rough and jagged rocks, and cover him with darkness, and let him abide there for ever, and cover his face that he may 6,7 not see light. And on the day of the great judgement he shall be cast into the fire. And heal the earth which the angels have corrupted, and proclaim the healing of the earth, that they may heal the plague, and that all the children of men may not perish through all the secret things that the 8 Watchers have disclosed and have taught their sons. And the whole earth has been corrupted 9 through the works that were taught by Azazel: to him ascribe all sin.' And to Gabriel said the Lord: 'Proceed against the bastards and the reprobates, and against the children of fornication: and destroy [the children of fornication and] the children of the Watchers from amongst men [and cause them to go forth]: send them one against the other that they may destroy each other in 10 battle: for length of days shall they not have. And no request that they (i.e. their fathers) make of thee shall be granted unto their fathers on their behalf; for they hope to live an eternal life, and 11 that each one of them will live five hundred years.' And the Lord said unto Michael: 'Go, bind Semjaza and his associates who have united themselves with women so as to have defiled themselves 12 with them in all their uncleanness. And when their sons have slain one another, and they have seen the destruction of their beloved ones, bind them fast for seventy generations in the valleys of the earth, till the day of their judgement and of their consummation, till the judgement that is 13 for ever and ever is consummated. In those days they shall be led off to the abyss of fire: and 14 to the torment and the prison in which they shall be confined for ever. And whosoever shall be condemned and destroyed will from thenceforth be bound together with them to the end of all 15 generations. And destroy all the spirits of the reprobate and the children of the Watchers, because 16 they have wronged mankind. Destroy all wrong from the face of the earth and let every evil work come to an end: and let the plant of righteousness and truth appear: and it shall prove a blessing; the works of righteousness and truth' shall be planted in truth and joy for evermore.

17 And then shall all the righteous escape,
And shall live till they beget thousands of children
And all the days of their youth and their old age
Shall they complete in peace.

18 And then shall the whole earth be tilled in righteousness, and shall all be planted with trees and 19 be full of blessing. And all desirable trees shall be planted on it, and they shall plant vines on it: and the vine which they plant thereon shall yield wine in abundance, and as for all the seed which is sown thereon each measure (of it) shall bear a thousand, and each measure of olives shall yield 20 ten presses of oil. And cleanse thou the earth from all oppression, and from all unrighteousness, and from all sin, and from all godlessness: and all the uncleanness that is wrought upon the earth 21 destroy from off the earth. And all the children of men shall become righteous, and all nations 22 shall offer adoration and shall praise Me, and all shall worship Me. And the earth shall be cleansed from all defilement, and from all sin, and from all punishment, and from all torment, and I will never again send (them) upon it from generation to generation and for ever.

[Chapter 11]

1 And in those days I will open the store chambers of blessing which are in the heaven, so as to send 2 them

down upon the earth over the work and labour of the children of men. And truth and peace shall be associated together throughout all the days of the world and throughout all the generations of men.'

[Chapter 12]

1 Before these things Enoch was hidden, and no one of the children of men knew where he was 2 hidden, and where he abode, and what had become of him. And his activities had to do with the Watchers, and his days were with the holy ones. 3 And I Enoch was blessing the Lord of majesty and the King of the ages, and lo! the Watchers 4 called me -Enoch the scribe- and said to me: 'Enoch, thou scribe of righteousness, go, declare to the Watchers of the heaven who have left the high heaven, the holy eternal place, and have defiled themselves with women, and have done as the children of earth do, and have taken unto themselves 5 wives: "Ye have wrought great destruction on the earth: And ye shall have no peace nor forgiveness 6 of sin: and inasmuch as they delight themselves in their children, The murder of their beloved ones shall they see, and over the destruction of their children shall they lament, and shall make supplication unto eternity, but mercy and peace shall ye not attain."'

[Chapter 13]

1 And Enoch went and said: 'Azazel, thou shalt have no peace: a severe sentence has gone forth 2 against thee to put thee in bonds: And thou shalt not have toleration nor request granted to thee, because of the unrighteousness which thou hast taught, and because of all the works of godlessness 3 and unrighteousness and sin which thou hast shown to men.' Then I went and spoke to them all 4 together, and they were all afraid, and fear and trembling seized them. And they besought me to draw up a petition for them that they might find forgiveness, and to read their petition in the presence 5 of the Lord of heaven. For from thenceforward they could not speak (with Him) nor lift up their 6 eyes to heaven for shame of their sins for which they had been condemned. Then I wrote out their petition, and the prayer in regard to their spirits and their deeds individually and in regard to their 7 requests that they should have forgiveness and length. And I went off and sat down at the waters of Dan, in the land of Dan, to the south of the west of Hermon: I read their petition till I fell 8 asleep. And behold a dream came to me, and visions fell down upon me, and I saw visions of chastisement, and a voice came bidding (me) I to tell it to the sons of heaven, and reprimand them. 9 And when I awaked, I came unto them, and they were all sitting gathered together, weeping in 10 'Abelsjail, which is between Lebanon and Seneser, with their faces covered. And I recounted before them all the visions which I had seen in sleep, and I began to speak the words of righteousness, and to reprimand the heavenly Watchers.

[Chapter 14]

1 The book of the words of righteousness, and of the reprimand of the eternal Watchers in accordance 2 with the command of the Holy Great One in that vision. I saw in my sleep what I will now say with a tongue of flesh and with the breath of my mouth: which the Great One has given to men to 3 converse therewith and understand with the heart. As He has created and given to man the power of understanding the word of wisdom, so hath He created me also and given me the power of reprimanding 4 the Watchers, the children of heaven. I wrote out your petition, and in my vision it appeared thus, that your petition will not be granted unto you throughout all the days of eternity, and that judgement 5 has been finally passed upon you: yea (your petition) will not be granted unto you. And from henceforth you shall not ascend into heaven unto all eternity, and in bonds of the earth the decree 6 has gone forth to bind you for all the days of the world. And (that) previously you shall have seen the destruction of your beloved sons and ye shall have no pleasure in them, but they shall fall before 7 you by the sword. And your petition on their behalf shall not be granted, nor yet on your own: even though you weep and pray and speak all the words contained in the writing which I have 8 written. And the vision was shown to me thus: Behold, in the vision clouds invited me and a mist summoned me, and the course of the stars and the lightnings sped and hastened me, and the winds in 9 the vision caused me to fly and lifted me upward, and bore me into heaven. And I went in till I drew nigh to a wall which is built of crystals and surrounded by tongues of fire: and it began to affright 10 me. And I went into the tongues of fire and drew nigh to a large house which was built of crystals: and the walls of the house were like a tesselated floor (made) of crystals, and its groundwork was 11 of crystal. Its ceiling was like the path of the stars and the lightnings, and between them were 12 fiery cherubim, and their heaven was (clear as) water. A flaming fire surrounded the walls, and its 13 portals blazed with fire. And I entered into that house, and it was hot as fire and cold as ice: there 14 were no delights of life therein: fear covered me, and trembling got hold upon me. And as I quaked 15 and trembled, I fell upon my face. And I beheld a vision, And lo! there was a second house, greater 16 than the former, and the entire portal stood open before me, and it was built of flames of fire. And in every respect it so excelled in splendour and magnificence and extent that I cannot describe to 17 you its splendour and its extent. And its floor was of fire, and above it were lightnings and the path 18 of the stars, and its ceiling also was flaming fire. And I looked and saw therein a lofty throne: its appearance was as crystal, and the wheels thereof as the shining sun, and there was the vision of 19 cherubim. And from underneath the throne came streams of flaming fire so that I could not look 20 thereon. And the Great Glory sat thereon, and His raiment shone more brightly than the sun and 21 was whiter than any snow. None of the angels could enter and could behold His face by reason 22 of the magnificence and glory and no flesh could behold Him. The flaming fire was round about Him, and a great fire

stood before Him, and none around could draw nigh Him: ten thousand times [23] ten thousand (stood) before Him, yet He needed no counselor. And the most holy ones who were [24] nigh to Him did not leave by night nor depart from Him. And until then I had been prostrate on my face, trembling: and the Lord called me with His own mouth, and said to me: ' Come hither, [25] Enoch, and hear my word.' And one of the holy ones came to me and waked me, and He made me rise up and approach the door: and I bowed my face downwards.

[Chapter 15]

[1] And He answered and said to me, and I heard His voice: 'Fear not, Enoch, thou righteous [2] man and scribe of righteousness: approach hither and hear my voice. And go, say to the Watchers of heaven, who have sent thee to intercede for them: "You should intercede" for men, and not men [3] for you: Wherefore have ye left the high, holy, and eternal heaven, and lain with women, and defiled yourselves with the daughters of men and taken to yourselves wives, and done like the children [4] of earth, and begotten giants (as your) sons? And though ye were holy, spiritual, living the eternal life, you have defiled yourselves with the blood of women, and have begotten (children) with the blood of flesh, and, as the children of men, have lusted after flesh and blood as those also do who die [5] and perish. Therefore have I given them wives also that they might impregnate them, and beget [6] children by them, that thus nothing might be wanting to them on earth. But you were formerly [7] spiritual, living the eternal life, and immortal for all generations of the world. And therefore I have not appointed wives for you; for as for the spiritual ones of the heaven, in heaven is their dwelling. [8] And now, the giants, who are produced from the spirits and flesh, shall be called evil spirits upon [9] the earth, and on the earth shall be their dwelling. Evil spirits have proceeded from their bodies; because they are born from men and from the holy Watchers is their beginning and primal origin; [10] they shall be evil spirits on earth, and evil spirits shall they be called. [As for the spirits of heaven, in heaven shall be their dwelling, but as for the spirits of the earth which were born upon the earth, on the earth shall be their dwelling.] And the spirits of the giants afflict, oppress, destroy, attack, do battle, and work destruction on the earth, and cause trouble: they take no food, but nevertheless [12] hunger and thirst, and cause offences. And these spirits shall rise up against the children of men and against the women, because they have proceeded from them.

[Chapter 16]

[1] From the days of the slaughter and destruction and death of the giants, from the souls of whose flesh the spirits, having gone forth, shall destroy without incurring judgement -thus shall they destroy until the day of the consummation, the great judgement in which the age shall be [2] consummated, over the Watchers and the godless, yea, shall be wholly consummated." And now as to the watchers who have sent thee to intercede for them, who had been aforetime in heaven, (say [3] to them): "You have been in heaven, but all the mysteries had not yet been revealed to you, and you knew worthless ones, and these in the hardness of your hearts you have made known to the women, and through these mysteries women and men work much evil on earth." [4] Say to them therefore: " You have no peace.'"

[Chapter 17]

[1] And they took and brought me to a place in which those who were there were like flaming fire, [2] and, when they wished, they appeared as men. And they brought me to the place of darkness, and to a mountain the point of whose summit reached to heaven. And I saw the places of the luminaries and the treasuries of the stars and of the thunder and in the uttermost depths, where were [4] a fiery bow and arrows and their quiver, and a fiery sword and all the lightnings. And they took [5] me to the living waters, and to the fire of the west, which receives every setting of the sun. And I came to a river of fire in which the fire flows like water and discharges itself into the great sea towards [6] the west. I saw the great rivers and came to the great river and to the great darkness, and went [7] to the place where no flesh walks. I saw the mountains of the darkness of winter and the place [8] whence all the waters of the deep flow. I saw the mouths of all the rivers of the earth and the mouth of the deep.

[Chapter 18]

[1] I saw the treasuries of all the winds: I saw how He had furnished with them the whole creation [2] and the firm foundations of the earth. And I saw the corner-stone of the earth: I saw the four [3] winds which bear [the earth and] the firmament of the heaven. And I saw how the winds stretch out the vaults of heaven, and have their station between heaven and earth: these are the pillars [4] of the heaven. I saw the winds of heaven which turn and bring the circumference of the sun and [5] all the stars to their setting. I saw the winds on the earth carrying the clouds: I saw the paths [6] of the angels. I saw at the end of the earth the firmament of the heaven above. And I proceeded and saw a place which burns day and night, where there are seven mountains of magnificent stones, [7] three towards the east, and three towards the south. And as for those towards the east, was of coloured stone, and one of pearl, and one of jacinth, and those towards the south of red stone. [8] But the middle one reached to heaven like the throne of God, of alabaster, and the summit of the [9,10] throne was of sapphire. And I saw a flaming fire. And beyond these mountains Is a region the end of the great earth: there the heavens were completed. And I saw a deep abyss, with columns of heavenly fire, and among them I saw columns of fire fall, which were beyond measure alike towards [12] the height and towards the depth. And beyond that abyss I saw a place which had no firmament of the heaven above, and no firmly founded earth beneath it: there was no water upon it, and no [13] birds, but it was a waste and horrible place. I saw there seven stars like great burning mountains, [14] and to me, when I

inquired regarding them, The angel said: 'This place is the end of heaven and earth: this has become a prison for the stars and the host of heaven. And the stars which roll over the fire are they which have transgressed the commandment of the Lord in the beginning of [16] their rising, because they did not come forth at their appointed times. And He was wroth with them, and bound them till the time when their guilt should be consummated (even) for ten thousand years.'

[Chapter 19]

[1] And Uriel said to me: 'Here shall stand the angels who have connected themselves with women, and their spirits assuming many different forms are defiling mankind and shall lead them astray into sacrificing to demons as gods, (here shall they stand,) till the day of the great judgement in [2] which they shall be judged till they are made an end of. And the women also of the angels who [3] went astray shall become sirens.' And I, Enoch, alone saw the vision, the ends of all things: and no man shall see as I have seen.

[Chapter 20]

[1,2] And these are the names of the holy angels who watch. Uriel, one of the holy angels, who is [3] over the world and over Tartarus. Raphael, one of the holy angels, who is over the spirits of men. [4,5] Raguel, one of the holy angels who takes vengeance on the world of the luminaries. Michael, one [6] of the holy angels, to wit, he that is set over the best part of mankind and over chaos. Saraqael, [7] one of the holy angels, who is set over the spirits, who sin in the spirit. Gabriel, one of the holy [8] angels, who is over Paradise and the serpents and the Cherubim. Remiel, one of the holy angels, whom God set over those who rise.

[Chapter 21]

[1,2] And I proceeded to where things were chaotic. And I saw there something horrible: I saw neither [3] a heaven above nor a firmly founded earth, but a place chaotic and horrible. And there I saw [4] seven stars of the heaven bound together in it, like great mountains and burning with fire. Then [5] I said: 'For what sin are they bound, and on what account have they been cast in hither?' Then said Uriel, one of the holy angels, who was with me, and was chief over them, and said: 'Enoch, why [6] dost thou ask, and why art thou eager for the truth? These are of the number of the stars of heaven, which have transgressed the commandment of the Lord, and are bound here till ten thousand years, [7] the time entailed by their sins, are consummated.' And from thence I went to another place, which was still more horrible than the former, and I saw a horrible thing: a great fire there which burnt and blazed, and the place was cleft as far as the abyss, being full of great descending columns of [8] fire: neither its extent or magnitude could I see, nor could I conjecture. Then I said: 'How [9] fearful is the place and how terrible to look upon!' Then Uriel answered me, one of the holy angels who was with me, and said unto me: 'Enoch, why hast

thou such fear and affright?' And [10] I answered: 'Because of this fearful place, and because of the spectacle of the pain.' And he said unto me: 'This place is the prison of the angels, and here they will be imprisoned for ever.'

[Chapter 22]

[1] And thence I went to another place, and he mountain [and] of hard rock. [2] And there was in it four hollow places, deep and wide and very smooth. How smooth are the hollow places and deep and dark to look at. [3] Then Raphael answered, one of the holy angels who was with me, and said unto me: 'These hollow places have been created for this very purpose, that the spirits of the souls of the dead should [4] assemble therein, yea that all the souls of the children of men should assemble here. And these places have been made to receive them till the day of their judgement and till their appointed period [till the period appointed], till the great judgement (comes) upon them.' I saw (the spirit of) a dead man making suit, [5] and his voice went forth to heaven and made suit. And I asked Raphael the angel who was [6] with me, and I said unto him: 'This spirit which maketh suit, whose is it, whose voice goeth forth and maketh suit to heaven?' [7] And he answered me saying: 'This is the spirit which went forth from Abel, whom his brother Cain slew, and he makes his suit against him till his seed is destroyed from the face of the earth, and his seed is annihilated from amongst the seed of men.' [8] The I asked regarding it, and regarding all the hollow places: 'Why is one separated from the other?' [9] And he answered me and said unto me: 'These three have been made that the spirits of the dead might be separated. And such a division has been make (for) the spirits of the righteous, in which there is the bright spring of [10] water. And such has been made for sinners when they die and are buried in the earth and judgement has not been executed on them in their [11] lifetime. Here their spirits shall be set apart in this great pain till the great day of judgement and punishment and torment of those who curse for ever and retribution for their spirits. There [12] He shall bind them for ever. And such a division has been made for the spirits of those who make their suit, who make disclosures concerning their destruction, when they were slain in the days [13] of the sinners. Such has been made for the spirits of men who were not righteous but sinners, who were complete in transgression, and of the transgressors they shall be companions: but their spirits shall not be slain in the day of judgement nor shall they be raised from thence.' [14] The I blessed the Lord of glory and said: 'Blessed be my Lord, the Lord of righteousness, who ruleth for ever.'

[Chapter 23]

[1,2] From thence I went to another place to the west of the ends of the earth. And I saw a burning [3] fire which ran without resting, and paused not from its course day or night but (ran) regularly. And [4] I asked saying: 'What is this which rests not?' Then Raguel, one of the holy angels who was with me, answered me and said unto me: 'This course of fire which thou hast seen is the fire in the

west which persecutes all the luminaries of heaven.'

[Chapter 24]

1 And from thence I went to another place of the earth, and he showed me a mountain range of 2 fire which burnt day and night. And I went beyond it and saw seven magnificent mountains all differing each from the other, and the stones (thereof) were magnificent and beautiful, magnificent as a whole, of glorious appearance and fair exterior: three towards the east, one founded on the other, and three towards the south, one upon the other, and deep rough ravines, no one of which 3 joined with any other. And the seventh mountain was in the midst of these, and it excelled them 4 in height, resembling the seat of a throne: and fragrant trees encircled the throne. And amongst them was a tree such as I had never yet smelt, neither was any amongst them nor were others like it: it had a fragrance beyond all fragrance, and its leaves and blooms and wood wither not for ever: 5 and its fruit is beautiful, and its fruit n resembles the dates of a palm. Then I said: 'How beautiful is this tree, and fragrant, and its leaves are fair, and its blooms very delightful in appearance.' 6 Then answered Michael, one of the holy and honoured angels who was with me, and was their leader.

[Chapter 25]

1 And he said unto me: 'Enoch, why dost thou ask me regarding the fragrance of the tree, 2 and why dost thou wish to learn the truth?' Then I answered him saying: 'I wish to 3 know about everything, but especially about this tree.' And he answered saying: 'This high mountain which thou hast seen, whose summit is like the throne of God, is His throne, where the Holy Great One, the Lord of Glory, the Eternal King, will sit, when He shall come down to visit 4 the earth with goodness. And as for this fragrant tree no mortal is permitted to touch it till the great judgement, when He shall take vengeance on all and bring (everything) to its consummation 5 for ever. It shall then be given to the righteous and holy. Its fruit shall be for food to the elect: it shall be transplanted to the holy place, to the temple of the Lord, the Eternal King.

6 Then shall they rejoice with joy and be glad,
And into the holy place shall they enter;
And its fragrance shall be in their bones,
And they shall live a long life on earth,
Such as thy fathers lived:

And in their days shall no sorrow or plague
Or torment or calamity touch them.'

7 Then blessed I the God of Glory, the Eternal King, who hath prepared such things for the righteous, and hath created them and promised to give to them.

[Chapter 26]

1 And I went from thence to the middle of the earth, and I saw a blessed place in which there were 2 trees with branches abiding and blooming [of a dismembered tree]. And there I saw a holy mountain, 3 and underneath the mountain to the east there was a stream and it flowed towards the south. And I saw towards the east another mountain higher than this, and between them a deep and narrow 4 ravine: in it also ran a stream underneath the mountain. And to the west thereof there was another mountain, lower than the former and of small elevation, and a ravine deep and dry between them: and another deep and dry ravine was at the extremities of the three mountains. And all the ravines were deep and narrow, (being formed) of hard rock, and trees were not planted upon 6 them. And I marveled at the rocks, and I marveled at the ravine, yea, I marveled very much.

[Chapter 27]

1 Then said I: 'For what object is this blessed land, which is entirely filled with trees, and this 2 accursed valley between?' Then Uriel, one of the holy angels who was with me, answered and said: 'This accursed valley is for those who are accursed for ever: Here shall all the accursed be gathered together who utter with their lips against the Lord unseemly words and of His glory speak hard things. Here shall they be gathered together, and here 3 shall be their place of judgement. In the last days there shall be upon them the spectacle of righteous judgement in the presence of the righteous for ever: here shall the merciful bless the Lord of glory, the Eternal King. 4 In the days of judgement over the former, they shall bless Him for the mercy in accordance with 5 which He has assigned them (their lot).' Then I blessed the Lord of Glory and set forth His glory and lauded Him gloriously.

[Chapter 28]

1 And thence I went towards the east, into the midst of the mountain range of the desert, and 2 I saw a wilderness and it was solitary, full of trees and plants. And water gushed forth from 3 above. Rushing like a copious watercourse [which flowed] towards the north-west it caused clouds and dew to ascend on every side.

[Chapter 29]

1 And thence I went to another place in the desert, and approached to the east of this mountain 2 range. And there I saw aromatic trees exhaling the fragrance of frankincense and myrrh, and the trees also were similar to the almond tree.

[Chapter 30]

1,2 And beyond these, I went afar to the east, and I saw another place, a valley (full) of water. And 3 therein there was a tree, the colour (?) of fragrant trees such as the mastic. And on the sides of those valleys I saw fragrant cinnamon. And beyond these I proceeded to the east.

[Chapter 31]

¹ And I saw other mountains, and amongst them were groves of trees, and there flowed forth from ² them nectar, which is named sarara and galbanum. And beyond these mountains I saw another mountain to the east of the ends of the earth, whereon were aloe-trees, and all the trees were full ³ of stacte, being like almond-trees. And when one burnt it, it smelt sweeter than any fragrant odour.

[Chapter 32]

¹ And after these fragrant odours, as I looked towards the north over the mountains I saw seven mountains full of choice nard and fragrant trees and cinnamon and pepper. ² And thence I went over the summits of all these mountains, far towards the east of the earth, and passed above the Erythraean sea and went far from it, and passed over the angel Zotiel. And I came to the Garden of Righteousness, ³ I and from afar off trees more numerous than I these trees and great-two trees there, very great, beautiful, and glorious, and magnificent, and the tree of knowledge, whose holy fruit they eat and know great wisdom. ⁴ That tree is in height like the fir, and its leaves are like (those of) the Carob tree: and its fruit ⁵ is like the clusters of the vine, very beautiful: and the fragrance of the tree penetrates afar. Then ⁶ I said: 'How beautiful is the tree, and how attractive is its look!' Then Raphael the holy angel, who was with me, answered me and said: 'This is the tree of wisdom, of which thy father old (in years) and thy aged mother, who were before thee, have eaten, and they learnt wisdom and their eyes were opened, and they knew that they were naked and they were driven out of the garden.'

[Chapter 33]

¹ And from thence I went to the ends of the earth and saw there great beasts, and each differed from the other; and (I saw) birds also differing in appearance and beauty and voice, the one differing from the other. And to the east of those beasts I saw the ends of the earth whereon the heaven ² rests, and the portals of the heaven open. And I saw how the stars of heaven come forth, and ³ I counted the portals out of which they proceed, and wrote down all their outlets, of each individual star by itself, according to their number and their names, their courses and their positions, and their ⁴ times and their months, as Uriel the holy angel who was with me showed me. He showed all things to me and wrote them down for me: also their names he wrote for me, and their laws and their companies.

[Chapter 34]

¹ And from thence I went towards the north to the ends of the earth, and there I saw a great and ² glorious device at the ends of the whole earth. And here I saw three portals of heaven open in the heaven: through each of them proceed north winds: when they blow there is cold, hail, frost, ³ snow, dew, and rain. And out of one portal they blow for good: but when they blow through the other two portals, it is with violence and affliction on the earth, and they blow with violence.

[Chapter 35]

¹ And from thence I went towards the west to the ends of the earth, and saw there three portals of the heaven open such as I had seen in the east, the same number of portals, and the same number of outlets.

[Chapter 36]

¹ And from thence I went to the south to the ends of the earth, and saw there three open portals ² of the heaven: and thence there come dew, rain, and wind. And from thence I went to the east to the ends of the heaven, and saw here the three eastern portals of heaven open and small portals ³ above them. Through each of these small portals pass the stars of heaven and run their course to the west on the path which is shown to them. And as often as I saw I blessed always the Lord of Glory, and I continued to bless the Lord of Glory who has wrought great and glorious wonders, to show the greatness of His work to the angels and to spirits and to men, that they might praise His work and all His creation: that they might see the work of His might and praise the great work of His hands and bless Him for ever.

THE PARABLES

Section II. Chapters XXXVII-LXXI

[Chapter 37]

1 The second vision which he saw, the vision of wisdom - which Enoch the son of Jared, the son 2 of Mahalalel, the son of Cainan, the son of Enos, the son of Seth, the son of Adam, saw. And this is the beginning of the words of wisdom which I lifted up my voice to speak and say to those which dwell on earth: Hear, ye men of old time, and see, ye that come after, the words of the Holy 3 One which I will speak before the Lord of Spirits. It were better to declare (them only) to the men of old time, but even from those that come after we will not withhold the beginning of wisdom. 4 Till the present day such wisdom has never been given by the Lord of Spirits as I have received according to my insight, according to the good pleasure of the Lord of Spirits by whom the lot of 5 eternal life has been given to me. Now three Parables were imparted to me, and I lifted up my voice and recounted them to those that dwell on the earth.

[Chapter 38]

1 The first Parable.

When the congregation of the righteous shall appear,
And sinners shall be judged for their sins,
And shall be driven from the face of the earth:

2 And when the Righteous One shall appear
before the eyes of the righteous,
Whose elect works hang upon the Lord of Spirits,
And light shall appear to the righteous and the elect who dwell on the earth,

Where then will be the dwelling of the sinners,

And where the resting-place of those who have denied the Lord of Spirits?
It had been good for them if they had not been born.

3 When the secrets of the righteous shall be revealed and the sinners judged,
And the godless driven from the presence of the righteous and elect,
4 From that time those that possess the earth shall no longer be powerful and exalted:
And they shall not be able to behold the face of the holy,
For the Lord of Spirits has caused His light to appear
On the face of the holy, righteous, and elect.

5 Then shall the kings and the mighty perish
And be given into the hands of the righteous and holy.
6 And thenceforward none shall seek for

themselves mercy from the Lord of Spirits
For their life is at an end.

[Chapter 39]

1 [And it shall come to pass in those days that elect and holy children will descend from the 2 high heaven, and their seed will become one with the children of men. And in those days Enoch received books of zeal and wrath, and books of disquiet and expulsion.]

And mercy shall not be accorded to them, saith the Lord of Spirits.
3 And in those days a whirlwind carried me off from the earth,
And set me down at the end of the heavens.

4 And there I saw another vision, the dwelling-places of the holy,
And the resting-places of the righteous.

5 Here mine eyes saw their dwellings with His righteous angels,
And their resting-places with the holy.
And they petitioned and interceded and prayed for the children of men,
And righteousness flowed before them as water,

And mercy like dew upon the earth:
Thus it is amongst them for ever and ever.

6a And in that place mine eyes saw the Elect One of righteousness and of faith,
7a And I saw his dwelling-place under the wings of the Lord of Spirits.
6b And righteousness shall prevail in his days,
And the righteous and elect shall be without number before Him for ever and ever.
7b And all the righteous and elect before Him shall be strong as fiery lights,
And their mouth shall be full of blessing,

And their lips extol the name of the Lord of Spirits,
And righteousness before Him shall never fail,
[And uprightness shall never fail before Him.]
8 There I wished to dwell,
And my spirit longed for that dwelling-place:
And there heretofore hath been my portion,
For so has it been established concerning me before the Lord of Spirits.

9 In those days I praised and extolled the name of the Lord of Spirits with blessings and praises, because He hath destined me for blessing and glory according to the good pleasure of the Lord of 10 Spirits. For a long time my eyes regarded that place, and I blessed Him and praised Him, saying: 'Blessed is He, and may He be blessed from the beginning and for evermore. And before Him there is no ceasing. He knows before the world was created what is for

ever and what will be from [12] generation unto generation. Those who sleep not bless Thee: they stand before Thy glory and bless, praise, and extol, saying: "Holy, holy, holy, is the Lord of Spirits: He filleth the earth with [13] spirits."' And here my eyes saw all those who sleep not: they stand before Him and bless and say: 'Blessed be Thou, and blessed be the name of the Lord for ever and ever.' And my face was changed; for I could no longer behold.

[Chapter 40]

[1] And after that I saw thousands of thousands and ten thousand times ten thousand, I saw a multitude [2] beyond number and reckoning, who stood before the Lord of Spirits. And on the four sides of the Lord of Spirits I saw four presences, different from those that sleep not, and I learnt their names: for the angel that went with me made known to me their names, and showed me all the hidden things. [3] And I heard the voices of those four presences as they uttered praises before the Lord of glory. [4,5] The first voice blesses the Lord of Spirits for ever and ever. And the second voice I heard blessing [6] the Elect One and the elect ones who hang upon the Lord of Spirits. And the third voice I heard pray and intercede for those who dwell on the earth and supplicate in the name of the Lord of Spirits. [7] And I heard the fourth voice fending off the Satans and forbidding them to come before the Lord [8] of Spirits to accuse them who dwell on the earth. After that I asked the angel of peace who went with me, who showed me everything that is hidden: 'Who are these four presences which I have [9] seen and whose words I have heard and written down?' And he said to me: 'This first is Michael, the merciful and long-suffering: and the second, who is set over all the diseases and all the wounds of the children of men, is Raphael: and the third, who is set over all the powers, is Gabriel: and the fourth, who is set over the repentance unto hope of those who inherit eternal life, is named Phanuel.' [10] And these are the four angels of the Lord of Spirits and the four voices I heard in those days.

[Chapter 41]

[1] And after that I saw all the secrets of the heavens, and how the kingdom is divided, and how the [2] actions of men are weighed in the balance. And there I saw the mansions of the elect and the mansions of the holy, and mine eyes saw there all the sinners being driven from thence which deny the name of the Lord of Spirits, and being dragged off: and they could not abide because of the punishment which proceeds from the Lord of Spirits. [3] And there mine eyes saw the secrets of the lightning and of the thunder, and the secrets of the winds, how they are divided to blow over the earth, and the secrets of the clouds and dew, and there [4] I saw from whence they proceed in that place and from whence they saturate the dusty earth. And there I saw closed chambers out of which the winds are divided, the chamber of the hail and winds, the chamber of the mist, and of the clouds, and the cloud thereof hovers over the earth from the [5] beginning of the world. And I saw the chambers of the sun and moon, whence they proceed and whither they come again, and their glorious return, and how one is superior to the other, and their stately orbit, and how they do not leave their orbit, and they add nothing to their orbit and they take nothing from it, and they keep faith with each other, in accordance with the oath by which they [6] are bound together. And first the sun goes forth and

traverses his path according to the commandment [7] of the Lord of Spirits, and mighty is His name for ever and ever. And after that I saw the hidden and the visible path of the moon, and she accomplishes the course of her path in that place by day and by night-the one holding a position opposite to the other before the Lord of Spirits.

And they give thanks and praise and rest not;
For unto them is their thanksgiving rest.
8 For the sun changes oft for a blessing or a curse,
And the course of the path of the moon is light to the righteous
And darkness to the sinners in the name of the Lord,
Who made a separation between the light and the darkness,
And divided the spirits of men,
And strengthened the spirits of the righteous,
In the name of His righteousness.

[9] For no angel hinders and no power is able to hinder; for He appoints a judge for them all and He judges them all before Him.

[Chapter 42]

[1] Wisdom found no place where she might dwell;
Then a dwelling-place was assigned her in the heavens.

[2] Wisdom went forth to make her dwelling among the children of men,
And found no dwelling-place:

Wisdom returned to her place,
And took her seat among the angels.

[3] And unrighteousness went forth from her chambers:
Whom she sought not she found,
And dwelt with them,
As rain in a desert
And dew on a thirsty land.

[Chapter 43]

[1] And I saw other lightnings and the stars of heaven, and I saw how He called them all by their [2] names and they hearkened unto Him. And I saw how they are weighed in a righteous balance according to their proportions of light: (I saw) the width of their spaces and the day of their appearing, and how their revolution produces lightning: and (I saw) their revolution according to the [3] number of the angels, and (how) they keep faith with each other. And I asked the angel who went [4] with me who showed me what was hidden: 'What are these?' And he said to me: 'The Lord of Spirits hath showed thee their parabolic meaning (lit. 'their parable'): these are the names of the holy who dwell on the earth and believe in the name of the Lord of Spirits for ever and ever.'

[Chapter 44]

Also another phenomenon I saw in regard to the lightnings: how some of the stars arise and become lightnings and cannot part with their new form.

[Chapter 45]

1 And this is the second Parable concerning those who deny the name of the dwelling of the holy ones and the Lord of Spirits.

2 And into the heaven they shall not ascend,
And on the earth they shall not come:
Such shall be the lot of the sinners
Who have denied the name of the Lord of
Spirits,
Who are thus preserved for the day of suffering
and tribulation.

3 On that day Mine Elect One shall sit on the throne of glory
And shall try their works,
And their places of rest shall be innumerable.

And their souls shall grow strong within them when they see Mine Elect Ones,
And those who have called upon My glorious name:
4 Then will I cause Mine Elect One to dwell among them.

And I will transform the heaven and make it an eternal blessing and light
5 And I will transform the earth and make it a blessing:

And I will cause Mine elect ones to dwell upon it:
But the sinners and evil-doers shall not set foot thereon.

6 For I have provided and satisfied with peace My righteous ones
And have caused them to dwell before Me:

But for the sinners there is judgement impending with Me,
So that I shall destroy them from the face of the earth.

[Chapter 46]

1 And there I saw One who had a head of days,
And His head was white like wool,
And with Him was another being whose countenance had the appearance of a man,
And his face was full of graciousness, like one of the holy angels.
2 And I asked the angel who went with me and

showed me all the hidden things, concerning that
3 Son of Man, who he was, and whence he was, (and) why he went with the Head of Days? And he answered and said unto me:
This is the son of Man who hath righteousness,
With whom dwelleth righteousness,
And who revealeth all the treasures of that which is hidden,

Because the Lord of Spirits hath chosen him,
And whose lot hath the pre-eminence before the Lord of Spirits in uprightness for ever.

4 And this Son of Man whom thou hast seen
Shall raise up the kings and the mighty from their seats,
[And the strong from their thrones]
And shall loosen the reins of the strong,
And break the teeth of the sinners.

5 [And he shall put down the kings from their thrones and kingdoms]
Because they do not extol and praise Him,
Nor humbly acknowledge whence the kingdom was bestowed upon them.
6 And he shall put down the countenance of the strong,
And shall fill them with shame.

And darkness shall be their dwelling,
And worms shall be their bed,
And they shall have no hope of rising from their beds,
Because they do not extol the name of the Lord of Spirits.
[And raise their hands against the Most High],
And tread upon the earth and dwell upon it.
And all their deeds manifest unrighteousness,
And their power rests upon their riches,
And their faith is in the gods which they have made with their hands,
And they deny the name of the Lord of Spirits,

8 And they persecute the houses of His congregations,
And the faithful who hang upon the name of the Lord of Spirits.

[Chapter 47]

1 And in those days shall have ascended the prayer of the righteous,
And the blood of the righteous from the earth before the Lord of Spirits.

2 In those days the holy ones who dwell above in the heavens
Shall unite with one voice
And supplicate and pray [and praise,
And give thanks and bless the name of the

Lord of Spirits
On behalf of the blood of the righteous which
has been shed,
And that the prayer of the righteous may not be
in vain before the Lord of Spirits,
That judgement may be done unto them,
And that they may not have to suffer for ever.

3 In those days I saw the Head of Days when
He seated himself upon the throne of His
glory,
And the books of the living were opened
before Him:
And all His host which is in heaven above and
His counselors stood before Him,

4 And the hearts of the holy were filled with
joy;
Because the number of the righteous had been
offered,
And the prayer of the righteous had been
heard,
And the blood of the righteous been required
before the Lord of Spirits.

[Chapter 48]

1 And in that place I saw the fountain of
righteousness
Which was inexhaustible:
And around it were many fountains of wisdom:
And all the thirsty drank of them,
And were filled with wisdom,
And their dwellings were with the righteous
and holy and elect.
2 And at that hour that Son of Man was named
In the presence of the Lord of Spirits,
And his name before the Head of Days.

3 Yea, before the sun and the signs were
created,
Before the stars of the heaven were made,
His name was named before the Lord of
Spirits.

4 He shall be a staff to the righteous whereon to
stay themselves and not fall,
And he shall be the light of the Gentiles,
And the hope of those who are troubled of
heart.
5 All who dwell on earth shall fall down and
worship before him,
And will praise and bless and celebrate with
song the Lord of Spirits.

6 And for this reason hath he been chosen and
hidden before Him,
Before the creation of the world and for
evermore.

7 And the wisdom of the Lord of Spirits hath

revealed him to the holy and righteous;
For he hath preserved the lot of the righteous,
Because they have hated and despised this
world of unrighteousness,
And have hated all its works and ways in the
name of the Lord of Spirits:
For in his name they are saved,
And according to his good pleasure hath it
been in regard to their life.

8 In these days downcast in countenance shall
the kings of the earth have become,
And the strong who possess the land because
of the works of their hands,
For on the day of their anguish and affliction
they shall not (be able to) save themselves.
And I will give them over into the hands of
Mine elect:
9As straw in the fire so shall they burn before
the face of the holy:
As lead in the water shall they sink before the
face of the righteous,
And no trace of them shall any more be found.

10 And on the day of their affliction there shall
be rest on the earth,
And before them they shall fall and not rise
again:
And there shall be no one to take them with his
hands and raise them:
For they have denied the Lord of Spirits and
His Anointed.
The name of the Lord of Spirits be blessed.

[Chapter 49]

1 For wisdom is poured out like water,
And glory faileth not before him for evermore.

2 For he is mighty in all the secrets of
righteousness,
And unrighteousness shall disappear as a
shadow,
And have no continuance;
Because the Elect One standeth before the
Lord of Spirits,
And his glory is for ever and ever,
And his might unto all generations.

3 And in him dwells the spirit of wisdom,
And the spirit which gives insight,
And the spirit of understanding and of might,
And the spirit of those who have fallen asleep
in righteousness.

4 And he shall judge the secret things,
And none shall be able to utter a lying word
before him;
For he is the Elect One before the Lord of
Spirits according to His good pleasure.

[Chapter 50]

[1] And in those days a change shall take place for the holy and elect,
And the light of days shall abide upon them,
And glory and honour shall turn to the holy,
[2] On the day of affliction on which evil shall have been treasured up against the sinners.

And the righteous shall be victorious in the name of the Lord of Spirits:
And He will cause the others to witness (this)
That they may repent
And forgo the works of their hands.

[3] They shall have no honour through the name of the Lord of Spirits,
Yet through His name shall they be saved,
And the Lord of Spirits will have compassion on them,
For His compassion is great.

[4] And He is righteous also in His judgement,
And in the presence of His glory
unrighteousness also shall not maintain itself:
At His judgement the unrepentant shall perish before Him.

[5] And from henceforth I will have no mercy on them, saith the Lord of Spirits.

[Chapter 51]

[1] And in those days shall the earth also give back that which has been entrusted to it,
And Sheol also shall give back that which it has received,
And hell shall give back that which it owes.

[5a] For in those days the Elect One shall arise,
[2] And he shall choose the righteous and holy from among them:
For the day has drawn nigh that they should be saved.

[3] And the Elect One shall in those days sit on My throne,
And his mouth shall pour forth all the secrets of wisdom and counsel:
For the Lord of Spirits hath given (them) to him and hath glorified him.

[4] And in those days shall the mountains leap like rams,
And the hills also shall skip like lambs satisfied with milk,
And the faces of [all] the angels in heaven shall be lighted up with joy.

[5b] And the earth shall rejoice,
[c] And the righteous shall dwell upon it,
[d] And the elect shall walk thereon.

[Chapter 52]

[1] And after those days in that place where I had seen all the visions of that which is hidden -for [2] I had been carried off in a whirlwind and they had borne me towards the west- There mine eyes saw all the secret things of heaven that shall be, a mountain of iron, and a mountain of copper, and a mountain of silver, and a mountain of gold, and a mountain of soft metal, and a mountain of lead. [3] And I asked the angel who went with me, saying, 'What things are these which I have seen in [4] secret?' And he said unto me: 'All these things which thou hast seen shall serve the dominion of His Anointed that he may be potent and mighty on the earth.' [5] And that angel of peace answered, saying unto me: 'Wait a little, and there shall be revealed unto thee all the secret things which surround the Lord of Spirits.

[6] And these mountains which thine eyes have seen,
The mountain of iron, and the mountain of copper, and the mountain of silver,
And the mountain of gold, and the mountain of soft metal, and the mountain of lead,
All these shall be in the presence of the Elect One
As wax: before the fire,
And like the water which streams down from above [upon those mountains],
And they shall become powerless before his feet.
[7] And it shall come to pass in those days that none shall be saved,
Either by gold or by silver,
And none be able to escape.
[8] And there shall be no iron for war,
Nor shall one clothe oneself with a breastplate.
Bronze shall be of no service,
And tin [shall be of no service and] shall not be esteemed,
And lead shall not be desired.
[9] And all these things shall be [denied and] destroyed from the surface of the earth,
When the Elect One shall appear before the face of the Lord of Spirits.'

[Chapter 53]

[1] There mine eyes saw a deep valley with open mouths, and all who dwell on the earth and sea and islands shall bring to him gifts and presents and tokens of homage, but that deep valley shall not become full.

[2] And their hands commit lawless deeds,
And the sinners devour all whom they lawlessly oppress:
Yet the sinners shall be destroyed before the face of the Lord of Spirits,
And they shall be banished from off the face of His earth,
And they shall perish for ever and ever.

3 For I saw all the angels of punishment abiding (there) and preparing all the instruments of Satan. 4 And I asked the angel of peace who went with me: ' For whom are they preparing these Instruments?' 5 And he said unto me: ' They prepare these for the kings and the mighty of this earth, that they may thereby be destroyed. 6 And after this the Righteous and Elect One shall cause the house of his congregation to appear: henceforth they shall be no more hindered in the name of the Lord of Spirits.

7 And these mountains shall not stand as the
earth before his righteousness,
But the hills shall be as a fountain of water,
And the righteous shall have rest from the
oppression of sinners.'

[Chapter 54]

1 And I looked and turned to another part of the earth, and saw there a deep valley with burning 2 fire. And they brought the kings and the mighty, and began to cast them into this deep valley. 3 And there mine eyes saw how they made these their instruments, iron chains of immeasurable weight. 4 And I asked the angel of peace who went with me, saying: ' For whom are these chains being prepared ? ' And he said unto me: ' These are being prepared for the hosts of Azazel, so that they may take them and cast them into the abyss of complete condemnation, and they shall cover their jaws with rough stones as the Lord of Spirits commanded. 6 And Michael, and Gabriel, and Raphael, and Phanuel shall take hold of them on that great day, and cast them on that day into the burning furnace, that the Lord of Spirits may take vengeance on them for their unrighteousness in becoming subject to Satan and leading astray those who dwell on the earth.' 7 And in those days shall punishment come from the Lord of Spirits, and he will open all the chambers of waters which are above the heavens, and of the fountains which are beneath the earth. 8 And all the waters shall be joined with the waters: that which is above the heavens is the masculine, 9 and the water which is beneath the earth is the feminine. And they shall destroy all who dwell 10 on the earth and those who dwell under the ends of the heaven. And when they have recognized their unrighteousness which they have wrought on the earth, then by these shall they perish.

[Chapter 55]

1 And after that the Head of Days repented and said: ' In vain have I destroyed all who dwell 2 on the earth.' And He sware by His great name: ' Henceforth I will not do so to all who dwell on the earth, and I will set a sign in the heaven: and this shall be a pledge of good faith between Me and them for ever, so long as heaven is above the earth. And this is in accordance with My command. 3 When I have desired to take hold of them by the hand of the angels on the day of tribulation and pain because of this, I will cause My chastisement and My wrath to abide upon them, saith 4 God, the Lord of Spirits. Ye mighty kings who dwell on the earth, ye shall have to behold Mine Elect One, how he sits on the throne of glory and judges Azazel, and all his associates, and all his hosts in the name of the Lord of Spirits.'

[Chapter 56]

1 And I saw there the hosts of the angels of punishment going, and they held scourges and chains 2 of iron and bronze. And I asked the angel of peace who went with me, saying: ' To whom are 3 these who hold the scourges going ? ' And he said unto me: ' To their elect and beloved ones, that they may be cast into the chasm of the abyss of the valley.

4 And then that valley shall be filled with their elect and beloved,
And the days of their lives shall be at an end,
And the days of their leading astray shall not thenceforward be reckoned.

5 And in those days the angels shall return
And hurl themselves to the east upon the Parthians and Medes:

They shall stir up the kings, so that a spirit of unrest shall come upon them,
And they shall rouse them from their thrones,

That they may break forth as lions from their lairs,
And as hungry wolves among their flocks.

6 And they shall go up and tread under foot the land of His elect ones
[And the land of His elect ones shall be before them a threshing-floor and a highway :]
7 But the city of my righteous shall be a hindrance to their horses.

And they shall begin to fight among themselves,
And their right hand shall be strong against themselves,

And a man shall not know his brother,
Nor a son his father or his mother,

Till there be no number of the corpses through their slaughter,
And their punishment be not in vain.
8 In those days Sheol shall open its jaws,
And they shall be swallowed up therein

And their destruction shall be at an end;
Sheol shall devour the sinners in the presence of the elect.'

[Chapter 57]

1 And it came to pass after this that I saw another host of wagons, and men riding thereon, and 2 coming on the winds from the east, and from the west to the south. And the noise of their wagons was heard, and when this turmoil took place the holy ones from heaven remarked it, and the pillars of the earth were moved from their place, and the sound thereof was heard from the one end of heaven 3 to the other, in one day. And they shall all fall down and

worship the Lord of Spirits. And this is the end of the second Parable.

[Chapter 58]

¹ And I began to speak the third Parable concerning the righteous and elect.

² Blessed are ye, ye righteous and elect,
For glorious shall be your lot.

³ And the righteous shall be in the light of the sun.
And the elect in the light of eternal life:
The days of their life shall be unending,
And the days of the holy without number.

⁴ And they shall seek the light and find righteousness with the Lord of Spirits:
There shall be peace to the righteous in the name of the Eternal Lord.

⁵ And after this it shall be said to the holy in heaven
That they should seek out the secrets of righteousness, the heritage of faith:
For it has become bright as the sun upon earth,
And the darkness is past.

⁶ And there shall be a light that never endeth,
And to a limit (lit. ' number ') of days they shall not come,
For the darkness shall first have been destroyed,
[And the light established before the Lord of Spirits]
And the light of uprightness established for ever before the Lord of Spirits.

[Chapter 59]

¹ [In those days mine eyes saw the secrets of the lightnings, and of the lights, and the judgements they execute (lit. ' their judgement '): and they lighten for a blessing or a curse as the Lord of ² Spirits willeth. And there I saw the secrets of the thunder, and how when it resounds above in the heaven, the sound thereof is heard, and he caused me to see the judgements executed on the earth, whether they be for well-being and blessing, or for a curse according to the word of the Lord of Spirits. ³ And after that all the secrets of the lights and lightnings were shown to me, and they lighten for blessing and for satisfying.]

[Chapter 60] A Fragment of the Book of Noah

¹ In the year 500, in the seventh month, on the fourteenth day of the month in the life of Enoch. In that Parable I saw how a mighty quaking made the heaven of heavens to quake, and the host of the Most High, and the angels, a thousand thousands and ten thousand times ten thousand, were ² disquieted with a great disquiet. And the Head of Days sat on the throne of His glory, and the angels and the righteous stood around Him.

³ And a great trembling seized me,
And fear took hold of me,
And my loins gave way,
And dissolved were my reins,
And I fell upon my face.

⁴ And Michael sent another angel from among the holy ones and he raised me up, and when he had raised me up my spirit returned; for I had not been able to endure the look of this host, and the ⁵ commotion and the quaking of the heaven. And Michael said unto me: ' Why art thou disquieted with such a vision? Until this day lasted the day of His mercy; and He hath been merciful and ⁶ long-suffering towards those who dwell on the earth. And when the day, and the power, and the punishment, and the judgement come, which the Lord of Spirits hath prepared for those who worship not the righteous law, and for those who deny the righteous judgement, and for those who take His name in vain-that day is prepared, for the elect a covenant, but for sinners an inquisition. ²⁵ When the punishment of the Lord of Spirits shall rest upon them, it shall rest in order that the punishment of the Lord of Spirits may not come, in vain, and it shall slay the children with their mothers and the children with their fathers. Afterwards the judgement shall take place according to His mercy and His patience.' ⁷ And on that day were two monsters parted, a female monster named Leviathan, to dwell in the ⁸ abysses of the ocean over the fountains of the waters. But the male is named Behemoth, who occupied with his breast a waste wilderness named Duidain, on the east of the garden where the elect and righteous dwell, where my grandfather was taken up, the seventh from Adam, the first ⁹ man whom the Lord of Spirits created. And I besought the other angel that he should show me the might of those monsters, how they were parted on one day and cast, the one into the abysses ¹⁰ of the sea, and the other unto the dry land of the wilderness. And he said to me: ' Thou son of man, herein thou dost seek to know what is hidden.' ¹¹ And the other angel who went with me and showed me what was hidden told me what is first and last in the heaven in the height, and beneath the earth in the depth, and at the ends of the ¹² heaven, and on the foundation of the heaven. And the chambers of the winds, and how the winds are divided, and how they are weighed, and (how) the portals of the winds are reckoned, each according to the power of the wind, and the power of the lights of the moon, and according to the power that is fitting: and the divisions of the stars according to their names, and how all the divisions ¹³ are divided. And the thunders according to the places where they fall, and all the divisions that are made among the lightnings that it may lighten, and their host that they may at once obey. ¹⁴ For the thunder has places of rest (which) are assigned (to it) while it is waiting for its peal; and the thunder and lightning are inseparable, and although not one and undivided, they both go together ¹⁵ through the spirit and separate not. For when the lightning lightens, the thunder utters its voice, and the spirit enforces a pause during the peal, and divides equally between them; for the treasury of their peals is like the sand, and each one of them as it peals is held in with a bridle, and turned back by the power of the spirit, and pushed forward according to the many quarters of the earth. ¹⁶ And the spirit of the sea is masculine and strong,

and according to the might of his strength he draws it back with a rein, and in like manner it is driven forward and disperses amid all the mountains 17 of the earth. And the spirit of the hoar-frost is his own angel, and the spirit of the hail is a good 18 angel. And the spirit of the snow has forsaken his chambers on account of his strength -There is a special spirit therein, and that which ascends from it is like smoke, and its name is frost. And the spirit of the mist is not united with them in their chambers, but it has a special chamber; for its course is glorious both in light and in darkness, and in winter and in summer, and in its chamber is an angel. 19 And the spirit of the dew has its dwelling at the ends of the heaven, and is connected with the chambers of the rain, and its course is in winter and summer: and its clouds and the clouds of the 20 mist are connected, and the one gives to the other. And when the spirit of the rain goes forth from its chamber, the angels come and open the chamber and lead it out, and when it is diffused over the whole earth it unites with the water on the earth. And whensoever it unites with the water on 21 the earth . . . For the waters are for those who dwell on the earth; for they are nourishment for the earth from the Most High who is in heaven: therefore there is a measure for the rain, 22, and the angels take it in charge. And these things I saw towards the Garden of the Righteous. 23 And the angel of peace who was with me said to me: ' These two monsters, prepared conformably to the greatness of God, shall feed . . .

[Chapter 61]

1 And I saw in those days how long cords were given to those angels, and they took to themselves wings and flew, and they went towards the north. 2 And I asked the angel, saying unto him: ' Why have those (angels) taken these cords and gone off ? ' And he said unto me: ' They have gone to measure.'

    3 And the angel who went with me said unto me:
' These shall bring the measures of the righteous,
And the ropes of the righteous to the righteous,
That they may stay themselves on the name of the Lord of Spirits for ever and ever.

    4 The elect shall begin to dwell with the elect,
And those are the measures which shall be given to faith
And which shall strengthen righteousness.

    5 And these measures shall reveal all the secrets of the depths of the earth,
And those who have been destroyed by the desert,
And those who have been devoured by the beasts,
And those who have been devoured by the fish of the sea,
That they may return and stay themselves
On the day of the Elect One;
For none shall be destroyed before the Lord of Spirits,
And none can be destroyed.

6 And all who dwell above in the heaven received a command and power and one voice and one light like unto fire.

7 And that One (with) their first words they blessed,
And extolled and lauded with wisdom,
And they were wise in utterance and in the spirit of life.

8 And the Lord of Spirits placed the Elect one on the throne of glory.
And he shall judge all the works of the holy above in the heaven,
And in the balance shall their deeds be weighed

9 And when he shall lift up his countenance
To judge their secret ways according to the word of the name of the Lord of Spirits,
And their path according to the way of the righteous judgement of the Lord of Spirits,
Then shall they all with one voice speak and bless,
And glorify and extol and sanctify the name of the Lord of Spirits.

10 And He will summon all the host of the heavens, and all the holy ones above, and the host of God, the Cherubic, Seraphin and Ophannin, and all the angels of power, and all the angels of principalities, and the Elect One, and the other powers on the earth (and) over the water On that day shall raise one voice, and bless and glorify and exalt in the spirit of faith, and in the spirit of wisdom, and in the spirit of patience, and in the spirit of mercy, and in the spirit of judgement and peace, and in the spirit of goodness, and shall all say with one voice: " Blessed is He, and may the name of the Lord of Spirits be blessed for ever and ever."

    12 All who sleep not above in heaven shall bless Him:
All the holy ones who are in heaven shall bless Him,
And all the elect who dwell in the garden of life:

And every spirit of light who is able to bless, and glorify, and extol, and hallow Thy blessed name,
And all flesh shall beyond measure glorify and bless Thy name for ever and ever.

    13 For great is the mercy of the Lord of Spirits, and He is long-suffering,
And all His works and all that He has created He has revealed to the righteous and elect
In the name of the Lord of Spirits.

[Chapter 62]

1 And thus the Lord commanded the kings and the mighty

and the exalted, and those who dwell on the earth, and said:

' Open your eyes and lift up your horns if ye are able to recognize the Elect One.'
2 And the Lord of Spirits seated him on the throne of His glory,
And the spirit of righteousness was poured out upon him,
And the word of his mouth slays all the sinners,
And all the unrighteous are destroyed from before his face.
3 And there shall stand up in that day all the kings and the mighty,
And the exalted and those who hold the earth,
And they shall see and recognize How he sits on the throne of his glory,
And righteousness is judged before him,
And no lying word is spoken before him.

4 Then shall pain come upon them as on a woman in travail,
[And she has pain in bringing forth]
When her child enters the mouth of the womb,
And she has pain in bringing forth.
5 And one portion of them shall look on the other,
And they shall be terrified,
And they shall be downcast of countenance,
And pain shall seize them,
When they see that Son of Man Sitting on the throne of his glory.

6 And the kings and the mighty and all who possess the earth shall bless and glorify and extol him who rules over all, who was hidden.

7 For from the beginning the Son of Man was hidden,
And the Most High preserved him in the presence of His might,
And revealed him to the elect.

8 And the congregation of the elect and holy shall be sown,
And all the elect shall stand before him on that day.

9 And all the kings and the mighty and the exalted and those who rule the earth
Shall fall down before him on their faces,
And worship and set their hope upon that Son of Man,
And petition him and supplicate for mercy at his hands.

10 Nevertheless that Lord of Spirits will so press them
That they shall hastily go forth from His presence,
And their faces shall be filled with shame,
And the darkness grow deeper on their faces.

11 And He will deliver them to the angels for punishment,
To execute vengeance on them because they have oppressed His children and His elect
12 And they shall be a spectacle for the righteous and for His elect:
They shall rejoice over them,
Because the wrath of the Lord of Spirits resteth upon them,
And His sword is drunk with their blood.

13 And the righteous and elect shall be saved on that day,
And they shall never thenceforward see the face of the sinners and unrighteous.

14 And the Lord of Spirits will abide over them,
And with that Son of Man shall they eat
And lie down and rise up for ever and ever.

15 And the righteous and elect shall have risen from the earth,
And ceased to be of downcast countenance.
And they shall have been clothed with garments of glory,

16 And these shall be the garments of life from the Lord of Spirits:

And your garments shall not grow old,
Nor your glory pass away before the Lord of Spirits.

[Chapter 63]

1 In those days shall the mighty and the kings who possess the earth implore (Him) to grant them a little respite from His angels of punishment to whom they were delivered, that they might fall 2 down and worship before the Lord of Spirits, and confess their sins before Him. And they shall bless and glorify the Lord of Spirits, and say:

' Blessed is the Lord of Spirits and the Lord of kings,
And the Lord of the mighty and the Lord of the rich,
And the Lord of glory and the Lord of wisdom,

3 And splendid in every secret thing is Thy power from generation to generation,
And Thy glory for ever and ever:

Deep are all Thy secrets and innumerable,
And Thy righteousness is beyond reckoning.

4 We have now learnt that we should glorify
And bless the Lord of kings and Him who is king over all kings.'
5 And they shall say:

' Would that we had rest to glorify and give
thanks
And confess our faith before His glory !

6 And now we long for a little rest but find it
not:
We follow hard upon and obtain (it) not:

And light has vanished from before us,
And darkness is our dwelling-place for ever and
ever:

7 For we have not believed before Him
Nor glorified the name of the Lord of Spirits,
[nor glorified our Lord]

But our hope was in the sceptre of our
kingdom,
And in our glory.

8 And in the day of our suffering and
tribulation He saves us not,
And we find no respite for confession

That our Lord is true in all His works, and in
His judgements and His justice,
And His judgements have no respect of
persons.

And we pass away from before His face on
account of our works,
And all our sins are reckoned up in
righteousness.'

10 Now they shall say unto themselves: ' Our souls are full
of unrighteous gain, but it does not prevent us from
descending from the midst thereof into the burden of
Sheol.'

11 And after that their faces shall be filled with
darkness
And shame before that Son of Man,
And they shall be driven from his presence,
And the sword shall abide before his face in
their midst.

12 Thus spake the Lord of Spirits: ' This is the ordinance
and judgement with respect to the mighty and the kings
and the exalted and those who possess the earth before the
Lord of Spirits.'

[Chapter 64]

1,2 And other forms I saw hidden in that place. I heard the
voice of the angel saying: ' These are the angels who
descended to the earth, and revealed what was hidden to
the children of men and seduced the children of men into
committing sin.'

[Chapter 65]

1, 2 And in those days Noah saw the earth that it had sunk
down and its destruction was nigh. And he arose from
thence and went to the ends of the earth, and cried aloud to
his grandfather Enoch: 3 and Noah said three times with an
embittered voice: Hear me, hear me, hear me.' And I said
unto him: ' Tell me what it is that is falling out on the earth
that the earth is in such evil plight 4 and shaken, lest
perchance I shall perish with it ? ' And thereupon there was
a great commotion , on the earth, and a voice was heard
from heaven, and I fell on my face. And Enoch my
grandfather came and stood by me, and said unto me: '
Why hast thou cried unto me with a bitter cry and
weeping 6 And a command has gone forth from the
presence of the Lord concerning those who dwell on the
earth that their ruin is accomplished because they have
learnt all the secrets of the angels, and all the violence of
the Satans, and all their powers -the most secret ones- and
all the power of those who practice sorcery, and the power
of witchcraft, and the power of those who make molten
images 7 for the whole earth: And how silver is produced
from the dust of the earth, and how soft metal 8 originates
in the earth. For lead and tin are not produced from the
earth like the first: it is a fountain 9 that produces them, and
an angel stands therein, and that angel is pre-eminent.' And
after that my grandfather Enoch took hold of me by my
hand and raised me up, and said unto me: ' Go, for I
have 10 asked the Lord of Spirits as touching this
commotion on the earth. And He said unto me: " Because
of their unrighteousness their judgement has been
determined upon and shall not be withheld by Me for ever.
Because of the sorceries which they have searched out and
learnt, the earth and those 11 who dwell upon it shall be
destroyed." And these-they have no place of repentance for
ever, because they have shown them what was hidden, and
they are the damned: but as for thee, my son, the Lord of
Spirits knows that thou art pure, and guiltless of this
reproach concerning the secrets.

12 And He has destined thy name to be among
the holy,
And will preserve thee amongst those who
dwell on the earth,
And has destined thy righteous seed both for
kingship and for great honours,
And from thy seed shall proceed a fountain of
the righteous and holy without number for
ever.

[Chapter 66]

1 And after that he showed me the angels of punishment
who are prepared to come and let loose all the powers of
the waters which are beneath in the earth in order to bring
judgement and destruction 2 on all who [abide and] dwell
on the earth. And the Lord of Spirits gave commandment
to the angels who were going forth, that they should not
cause the waters to rise but should hold them 3 in check;
for those angels were over the powers of the waters. And I
went away from the presence of Enoch.

[Chapter 67]

1 And in those days the word of God came unto me, and
He said unto me: ' Noah, thy lot has come 2 Up before Me,

a lot without blame, a lot of love and uprightness. And now the angels are making a wooden (building), and when they have completed that task I will place My hand upon it and preserve it, and there shall come forth from it the seed of life, and a change shall set in so that the ³ earth will not remain without inhabitant. And I will make fast thy sed before me for ever and ever, and I will spread abroad those who dwell with thee: it shall not be unfruitful on the face of the earth, but it shall be blessed and multiply on the earth in the name of the Lord.' ⁴ And He will imprison those angels, who have shown unrighteousness, in that burning valley which my grandfather Enoch had formerly shown to me in the west among the mountains of gold ⁵ and silver and iron and soft metal and tin. And I saw that valley in which there was a great ⁶ convulsion and a convulsion of the waters. And when all this took place, from that fiery molten metal and from the convulsion thereof in that place, there was produced a smell of sulphur, and it was connected with those waters, and that valley of the angels who had led astray (mankind) burned ⁷ beneath that land. And through its valleys proceed streams of fire, where these angels are punished who had led astray those who dwell upon the earth. ⁸ But those waters shall in those days serve for the kings and the mighty and the exalted, and those who dwell on the earth, for the healing of the body, but for the punishment of the spirit; now their spirit is full of lust, that they may be punished in their body, for they have denied the Lord of Spirits ⁹ and see their punishment daily, and yet believe not in His name. And in proportion as the burning of their bodies becomes severe, a corresponding change shall take place in their spirit for ever and ever; ¹⁰ for before the Lord of Spirits none shall utter an idle word. For the judgement shall come upon them, ¹¹ because they believe in the lust of their body and deny the Spirit of the Lord. And those same waters will undergo a change in those days; for when those angels are punished in these waters, these water-springs shall change their temperature, and when the angels ascend, this water of the ¹² springs shall change and become cold. And I heard Michael answering and saying: ' This judgement wherewith the angels are judged is a testimony for the kings and the mighty who possess the ¹³ earth.' Because these waters of judgement minister to the healing of the body of the kings and the lust of their body; therefore they will not see and will not believe that those waters will change and become a fire which burns for ever.

[Chapter 68]

¹ And after that my grandfather Enoch gave me the teaching of all the secrets in the book in the Parables which had been given to him, and he put them together for me in the words of the book ² of the Parables. And on that day Michael answered Raphael and said: ' The power of the spirit transports and makes me to tremble because of the severity of the judgement of the secrets, the judgement of the angels: who can endure the severe judgement which has been executed, and before ³ which they melt away ? ' And Michael answered again, and said to Raphael: ' Who is he whose heart is not softened concerning it, and whose reins are not troubled by this word of judgement ⁴ (that) has gone forth upon them because of those who have thus led them out ? ' And it came to pass when he stood before the Lord of Spirits, Michael said thus to Raphael: ' I will not take their part under the eye of the Lord; for the Lord of Spirits has been angry with them because they do ⁵ as if

they were the Lord. Therefore all that is hidden shall come upon them for ever and ever; for neither angel nor man shall have his portion (in it), but alone they have received their judgement for ever and ever.

[Chapter 69]

¹ And after this judgement they shall terrify and make them to tremble because they have shown this to those who dwell on the earth. ² And behold the names of those angels [and these are their names: the first of them is Samjaza, the second Artaqifa, and the third Armen, the fourth Kokabel, the fifth Turael, the sixth Rumjal, the seventh Danjal, the eighth Neqael, the ninth Baraqel, the tenth Azazel, the eleventh Armaros, the twelfth Batarjal, the thirteenth Busasejal, the fourteenth Hananel, the fifteenth Turel, and the sixteenth Simapesiel, the seventeenth Jetrel, the eighteenth Tumael, the nineteenth Turel, ³ the twentieth Rumael, the twenty-first Azazel. And these are the chiefs of their angels and their names, and their chief ones over hundreds and over fifties and over tens]. ⁴ The name of the first Jeqon: that is, the one who led astray [all] the sons of God, and brought them ⁵ down to the earth, and led them astray through the daughters of men. And the second was named Asbeel: he imparted to the holy sons of God evil counsel, and led them astray so that they defiled ⁶ their bodies with the daughters of men. And the third was named Gadreel: he it is who showed the children of men all the blows of death, and he led astray Eve, and showed [the weapons of death to the sons of men] the shield and the coat of mail, and the sword for battle, and all the weapons ⁷ of death to the children of men. And from his hand they have proceeded against those who dwell ⁸ on the earth from that day and for evermore. And the fourth was named Penemue: he taught the ⁹ children of men the bitter and the sweet, and he taught them all the secrets of their wisdom. And he instructed mankind in writing with ink and paper, and thereby many sinned from eternity to ¹⁰ eternity and until this day. For men were not created for such a purpose, to give confirmation ¹¹ to their good faith with pen and ink. For men were created exactly like the angels, to the intent that they should continue pure and righteous, and death, which destroys everything, could not have taken hold of them, but through this their knowledge they are perishing, and through this power ¹² it is consuming me. And the fifth was named Kasdeja: this is he who showed the children of men all the wicked smitings of spirits and demons, and the smitings of the embryo in the womb, that it may pass away, and [the smitings of the soul] the bites of the serpent, and the smitings ¹³ which befall through the noontide heat, the son of the serpent named Taba'et. And this is the task of Kasbeel, the chief of the oath which he showed to the holy ones when he dwelt high ¹⁴ above in glory, and its name is Biqa. This (angel) requested Michael to show him the hidden name, that he might enunciate it in the oath, so that those might quake before that name and oath who revealed all that was in secret to the children of men. And this is the power of this oath, for it is powerful and strong, and he placed this oath Akae in the hand of Michael.

> ¹⁶ And these are the secrets of this oath . . .
> And they are strong through his oath:
> And the heaven was suspended before the
> world was created,

And for ever

17 And through it the earth was founded upon
the water,
And from the secret recesses of the mountains
come beautiful waters,
From the creation of the world and unto
eternity.

18 And through that oath the sea was created,
And as its foundation He set for it the sand
against the time of (its) anger,
And it dare not pass beyond it from the
creation of the world unto eternity.

19 And through that oath are the depths made
fast,
And abide and stir not from their place from
eternity to eternity.

20 And through that oath the sun and moon
complete their course,
And deviate not from their ordinance from
eternity to eternity.

21 And through that oath the stars complete
their course,
And He calls them by their names,
And they answer Him from eternity to eternity.

22 [And in like manner the spirits of the water, and of the
winds, and of all zephyrs, and (their) paths 23 from all the
quarters of the winds. And there are preserved the voices
of the thunder and the light of the lightnings: and there are
preserved the chambers of the hail and the chambers of
the 24 hoarfrost, and the chambers of the mist, and the
chambers of the rain and the dew. And all these believe and
give thanks before the Lord of Spirits, and glorify (Him)
with all their power, and their food is in every act of
thanksgiving: they thank and glorify and extol the name of
the Lord of Spirits for ever and ever.]

25 And this oath is mighty over them
And through it [they are preserved and] their
paths are preserved,
And their course is not destroyed.

26 And there was great joy amongst them,
And they blessed and glorified and extolled
Because the name of that Son of Man had been
revealed unto them.

27 And he sat on the throne of his glory,
And the sum of judgement was given unto the
Son of Man,
And he caused the sinners to pass away and be
destroyed from off the face of the earth,
And those who have led the world astray.

28 With chains shall they be bound,

And in their assemblage-place of destruction
shall they be imprisoned,
And all their works vanish from the face of the
earth.

29 And from henceforth there shall be nothing
corruptible;
For that Son of Man has appeared,
And has seated himself on the throne of his
glory,
And all evil shall pass away before his face,
And the word of that Son of Man shall go forth

And be strong before the Lord of Spirits.

[Chapter 70]

1 And it came to pass after this that his name during his
lifetime was raised aloft to that Son of 2 Man and to the
Lord of Spirits from amongst those who dwell on the earth.
And he was raised aloft 3 on the chariots of the spirit and
his name vanished among them. And from that day I was
no longer numbered amongst them: and he set me between
the two winds, between the North and the 4 West, where
the angels took the cords to measure for me the place for
the elect and righteous. And there I saw the first fathers
and the righteous who from the beginning dwell in that
place.

[Chapter 71]

1 And it came to pass after this that my spirit
was translated
And it ascended into the heavens:
And I saw the holy sons of God.
They were stepping on flames of fire:
Their garments were white [and their raiment],
And their faces shone like snow.

2 And I saw two streams of fire,
And the light of that fire shone like hyacinth,
And I fell on my face before the Lord of
Spirits.

3 And the angel Michael [one of the archangels]
seized me by my right hand,
And lifted me up and led me forth into all the
secrets,
And he showed me all the secrets of
righteousness.

4 And he showed me all the secrets of the ends
of the heaven,
And all the chambers of all the stars, and all the
luminaries,
Whence they proceed before the face of the
holy ones.

5 And he translated my spirit into the heaven of
heavens,
And I saw there as it were a structure built of

crystals,
And between those crystals tongues of living
fire.

6 And my spirit saw the girdle which girt that
house of fire,
And on its four sides were streams full of living
fire,
And they girt that house.

7 And round about were Seraphin, Cherubic,
and Ophannin:
And these are they who sleep not
And guard the throne of His glory.

8 And I saw angels who could not be counted,
A thousand thousands, and ten thousand times
ten thousand,
Encircling that house.

And Michael, and Raphael, and Gabriel, and
Phanuel,
And the holy angels who are above the
heavens,
Go in and out of that house.

9 And they came forth from that house,
And Michael and Gabriel, Raphael and
Phanuel,
And many holy angels without number.

10 And with them the Head of Days,
His head white and pure as wool,
And His raiment indescribable.

11 And I fell on my face,
And my whole body became relaxed,
And my spirit was transfigured;

And I cried with a loud voice, . . .
with the spirit of power,
And blessed and glorified and extolled.

12 And these blessings which went forth out of my mouth
were well pleasing before that Head of Days. And that
Head of Days came with Michael and Gabriel, Raphael and
Phanuel, thousands and ten thousands of angels without
number.
[Lost passage wherein the Son of Man was described as
accompanying the Head of Days, and Enoch asked one of
the angels concerning the Son of Man as to who he was.]

14 And he (i.e. the angel) came to me and
greeted me with His voice, and said unto me '
This is the Son of Man who is born unto
righteousness,
And righteousness abides over him,
And the righteousness of the Head of Days
forsakes him not.'
15 And he said unto me:

' He proclaims unto thee peace in the name of
the world to come;
For from hence has proceeded peace since the
creation of the world,
And so shall it be unto thee for ever and for
ever and ever.

16 And all shall walk in his ways since
righteousness never forsaketh him:
With him will be their dwelling-places, and with
him their heritage,
And they shall not be separated from him for
ever and ever and ever.

And so there shall be length of days with that
Son of Man,
And the righteous shall have peace and an
upright way
In the name of the Lord of Spirits for ever and
ever.'

THE BOOK OF THE HEAVENLY LUMINARIES

Section III. Chapters LXXII-LXXXII

[Chapter 72]

[1] The book of the courses of the luminaries of the heaven, the relations of each, according to their classes, their dominion and their seasons, according to their names and places of origin, and according to their months, which Uriel, the holy angel, who was with me, who is their guide, showed me; and he showed me all their laws exactly as they are, and how it is with regard to all the years of the world [2] and unto eternity, till the new creation is accomplished which dureth till eternity. And this is the first law of the luminaries: the luminary the Sun has its rising in the eastern portals of the heaven, [3] and its setting in the western portals of the heaven. And I saw six portals in which the sun rises, and six portals in which the sun sets and the moon rises and sets in these portals, and the leaders of the stars and those whom they lead: six in the east and six in the west, and all following each other [4] in accurately corresponding order: also many windows to the right and left of these portals. And first there goes forth the great luminary, named the Sun, and his circumference is like the [5] circumference of the heaven, and he is quite filled with illuminating and heating fire. The chariot on which he ascends, the wind drives, and the sun goes down from the heaven and returns through the north in order to reach the east, and is so guided that he comes to the appropriate (lit. ' that ') portal and [6] shines in the face of the heaven. In this way he rises in the first month in the great portal, which [7] is the fourth [those six portals in the east]. And in that fourth portal from which the sun rises in the first month are twelve window-openings, from which proceed a flame when they are opened in [8] their season. When the sun rises in the heaven, he comes forth through that fourth portal thirty, [9] mornings in succession, and sets accurately in the fourth portal in the west of the heaven. And during this period the day becomes daily longer and the night nightly shorter to the thirtieth [10] morning. On that day the day is longer than the night by a ninth part, and the day amounts exactly to ten parts and the night to eight parts. And the sun rises from that fourth portal, and sets in the fourth and returns to the fifth portal of the east thirty mornings, and rises from it and sets in the fifth [12] portal. And then the day becomes longer by two parts and amounts to eleven parts, and the night [13] becomes shorter and amounts to seven parts. And it returns to the east and enters into the sixth [14] portal, and rises and sets in the sixth portal one-and-thirty mornings on account of its sign. On that day the day becomes longer than the night, and the day becomes double the night, and the day [15] becomes twelve parts, and the night is shortened and becomes six parts. And the sun mounts up to make the day shorter and the night longer, and the sun returns to the east and enters into the [16] sixth portal, and rises from it and sets thirty mornings. And when thirty mornings are accomplished, [17] the day decreases by exactly one part, and becomes eleven parts, and the night seven. And the sun goes forth from that sixth portal in the west, and

goes to the east and rises in the fifth portal for [18] thirty mornings, and sets in the west again in the fifth western portal. On that day the day decreases by two parts, and amounts to ten parts and the night to eight parts. And the sun goes forth from that fifth portal and sets in the fifth portal of the west, and rises in the fourth portal for one- [20] and-thirty mornings on account of its sign, and sets in the west. On that day the day is equalized with the night, [and becomes of equal length], and the night amounts to nine parts and the day to [21] nine parts. And the sun rises from that portal and sets in the west, and returns to the east and rises [22] thirty mornings in the third portal and sets in the west in the third portal. And on that day the night becomes longer than the day, and night becomes longer than night, and day shorter than day till the thirtieth morning, and the night amounts exactly to ten parts and the day to eight [23] parts. And the sun rises from that third portal and sets in the third portal in the west and returns to the east, and for thirty mornings rises [24] in the second portal in the east, and in like manner sets in the second portal in the west of the heaven. And on that day the night amounts to eleven [25] parts and the day to seven parts. And the sun rises on that day from that second portal and sets in the west in the second portal, and returns to the east into the first portal for one-and-thirty [26] mornings, and sets in the first portal in the west of the heaven. And on that day the night becomes longer and amounts to the double of the day: and the night amounts exactly to twelve parts and [27] the day to six. And the sun has (therewith) traversed the divisions of his orbit and turns again on those divisions of his orbit, and enters that portal thirty mornings and sets also in the west [28] opposite to it. And on that night has the night decreased in length by a ninth part, and the night [29] has become eleven parts and the day seven parts. And the sun has returned and entered into the second portal in the east, and returns on those his divisions of his orbit for thirty mornings, rising [30] and setting. And on that day the night decreases in length, and the night amounts to ten parts [31] and the day to eight. And on that day the sun rises from that portal, and sets in the west, and returns to the east, and rises in the third portal for one-and-thirty mornings, and sets in the west of the heaven. [32] On that day the night decreases and amounts to nine parts, and the day to nine parts, and the night [33] is equal to the day and the year is exactly as to its days three hundred and sixty-four. And the length of the day and of the night, and the shortness of the day and of the night arise-through the course [34] of the sun these distinctions are made (lit. ' they are separated '). So it comes that its course becomes [35] daily longer, and its course nightly shorter. And this is the law and the course of the sun, and his return as often as he returns sixty times and rises, i.e. the great luminary which is named the sun, for ever and ever. And that which (thus) rises is the great luminary, and is so named according to [37] its appearance, according as the Lord commanded. As he rises, so he sets and decreases not, and rests not, but runs day and night, and his light is sevenfold brighter than that of the moon; but as regards size they are both equal.

[Chapter 73]

[1] And after this law I saw another law dealing with the smaller luminary, which is named the Moon. And her circumference is like the circumference of the heaven, and her chariot in which she rides is driven by the wind, and light is given to her in (definite) measure. And her rising and setting change every month: and her days are like the days of the sun, and when her light is uniform (i.e. full) it amounts to the seventh part of the light of the sun. And thus she rises. And her first phase in the east comes forth on the thirtieth morning: and on that day she becomes visible, and constitutes for you the first phase of the moon on the thirtieth day together with the sun in the portal where the sun rises. And the one half of her goes forth by a seventh part, and her whole circumference is empty, without light, with the exception of one-seventh part of it, (and) the [6] fourteenth part of her light. And when she receives one-seventh part of the half of her light, her light [7] amounts to one-seventh part and the half thereof. And she sets with the sun, and when the sun rises the moon rises with him and receives the half of one part of light, and in that night in the beginning of her morning [in the commencement of the lunar day] the moon sets with the sun, and [8] is invisible that night with the fourteen parts and the half of one of them. And she rises on that day with exactly a seventh part, and comes forth and recedes from the rising of the sun, and in her remaining days she becomes bright in the (remaining) thirteen parts.

[Chapter 74]

[1] And I saw another course, a law for her, (and) how according to that law she performs her monthly [2] revolution. And all these Uriel, the holy angel who is the leader of them all, showed to me, and their positions, and I wrote down their positions as he showed them to me, and I wrote down their months [3] as they were, and the appearance of their lights till fifteen days were accomplished. In single seventh parts she accomplishes all her light in the east, and in single seventh parts accomplishes all her [4] darkness in the west. And in certain months she alters her settings, and in certain months she pursues [5] her own peculiar course. In two months the moon sets with the sun: in those two middle portals the [6] third and the fourth. She goes forth for seven days, and turns about and returns again through the portal where the sun rises, and accomplishes all her light: and she recedes from the sun, and in eight [7] days enters the sixth portal from which the sun goes forth. And when the sun goes forth from the fourth portal she goes forth seven days, until she goes forth from the fifth and turns back again in seven days into the fourth portal and accomplishes all her light: and she recedes and enters into the [8] first portal in eight days. And she returns again in seven days into the fourth portal from which the [9, 10] sun goes forth. Thus I saw their position -how the moons rose and the sun set in those days. And if five years are added together the sun has an overplus of thirty days, and all the days which accrue [11] to it for one of those five years, when they are full, amount to 364 days. And the overplus of the sun and of the stars amounts to six days: in 5 years 6 days every year come to 30 days: and the [12] moon falls behind the sun and stars to the number of 30 days. And the sun and the stars bring in all the years exactly, so that they do not advance or delay their position by a single day unto eternity; but complete the years with perfect justice in 364 days. In 3 years there are 1,092 days, and in 5 years 1,820 days, so that in 8 years there are 2,912 days. For the moon alone the days amount in 3 years to 1,062 days, and in 5 years she falls 50 days behind: [i.e. to the sum (of 1,770) there is 5 to be added (1,000 and) 62 days.] And in 5 years there are 1,770 days, so that for the moon the days 6 in 8 years amount to 21,832 days. [For in 8 years she falls behind to the amount of 80 days], all the 17 days she falls behind in 8 years are 80. And the year is accurately completed in conformity with their world-stations and the stations of the sun, which rise from the portals through which it (the sun) rises and sets 30 days.

[Chapter 75]

[1] And the leaders of the heads of the thousands, who are placed over the whole creation and over all the stars, have also to do with the four intercalary days, being inseparable from their office, according to the reckoning of the year, and these render service on the four days which are not [2] reckoned in the reckoning of the year. And owing to them men go wrong therein, for those luminaries truly render service on the world-stations, one in the first portal, one in the third portal of the heaven, one in the fourth portal, and one in the sixth portal, and the exactness of the year is [3] accomplished through its separate three hundred and sixty-four stations. For the signs and the times and the years and the days the angel Uriel showed to me, whom the Lord of glory hath set for ever over all the luminaries of the heaven, in the heaven and in the world, that they should rule on the face of the heaven and be seen on the earth, and be leaders for the day and the night, i.e. the sun, moon, and stars, and all the ministering creatures which make their revolution in all the chariots [4] of the heaven. In like manner twelve doors Uriel showed me, open in the circumference of the sun's chariot in the heaven, through which the rays of the sun break forth: and from them is warmth [5] diffused over the earth, when they are opened at their appointed seasons. [And for the winds and [6] the spirit of the dew when they are opened, standing open in the heavens at the ends.] As for the twelve portals in the heaven, at the ends of the earth, out of which go forth the sun, moon, and stars, [7] and all the works of heaven in the east and in the west, There are many windows open to the left and right of them, and one window at its (appointed) season produces warmth, corresponding (as these do) to those doors from which the stars come forth according as He has commanded them, [8] and wherein they set corresponding to their number. And I saw chariots in the heaven, running [9] in the world, above those portals in which revolve the stars that never set. And one is larger than all the rest, and it is that that makes its course through the entire world.

[Chapter 76]

1 And at the ends of the earth I saw twelve portals open to all the quarters (of the heaven), from 2 which the winds go forth and blow over the earth. Three of them are open on the face (i.e. the east) of the heavens, and three in the west, and three on the right (i.e. the south) of the heaven, and 3 three on the left (i.e. the north). And the three first are those of the east, and three are of the 4 north, and three [after those on the left] of the south, and three of the west. Through four of these come winds of blessing and prosperity, and from those eight come hurtful winds: when they are sent, they bring destruction on all the earth and on the water upon it, and on all who dwell thereon, and on everything which is in the water and on the land. 5 And the first wind from those portals, called the east wind, comes forth through the first portal which is in the east, inclining towards the south: from it come forth desolation, drought, heat, 6 and destruction. And through the second portal in the middle comes what is fitting, and from it there come rain and fruitfulness and prosperity and dew; and through the third portal which lies toward the north come cold and drought. 7 And after these come forth the south winds through three portals: through the first portal of 8 them inclining to the east comes forth a hot wind. And through the middle portal next to it there 9 come forth fragrant smells, and dew and rain, and prosperity and health. And through the third portal lying to the west come forth dew and rain, locusts and desolation. 10 And after these the north winds: from the seventh portal in the east come dew and rain, locusts and desolation. And from the middle portal come in a direct direction health and rain and dew and prosperity; and through the third portal in the west come cloud and hoar-frost, and snow and rain, and dew and locusts. 12 And after these [four] are the west winds: through the first portal adjoining the north come forth dew and hoar-frost, and cold and snow and frost. And from the middle portal come forth dew and rain, and prosperity and blessing; and through the last portal which adjoins the south come forth drought and desolation, and burning and destruction. And the twelve portals of the four quarters of the heaven are therewith completed, and all their laws and all their plagues and all their benefactions have I shown to thee, my son Methuselah.

[Chapter 77]

1 And the first quarter is called the east, because it is the first: and the second, the south, because the Most High will descend there, yea, there in quite a special sense will He who is blessed for ever 2 descend. And the west quarter is named the diminished, because there all the luminaries of the 3 heaven wane and go down. And the fourth quarter, named the north, is divided into three parts: the first of them is for the dwelling of men: and the second contains seas of water, and the abysses and forests and rivers, and darkness and clouds; and the third part contains the garden of righteousness. 4 I saw seven high mountains, higher than all the mountains which are on the earth: and thence 5 comes forth hoar-frost, and days, seasons, and years pass away. I saw seven rivers on the earth larger than all the rivers: one of them coming

from the west pours its waters into the Great Sea. 6 And these two come from the north to the sea and pour their waters into the Erythraean Sea in the 7 east. And the remaining, four come forth on the side of the north to their own sea, two of them to the Erythraean Sea, and two into the Great Sea and discharge themselves there [and some say: 8 into the desert]. Seven great islands I saw in the sea and in the mainland: two in the mainland and five in the Great Sea.

[Chapter 78]

1, 2 And the names of the sun are the following: the first Orjares, and the second Tomas. And the moon has four names: the first name is Asonja, the second Ebla, the third Benase, and the fourth 3 Erae. These are the two great luminaries: their circumference is like the circumference of the 4 heaven, and the size of the circumference of both is alike. In the circumference of the sun there are seven portions of light which are added to it more than to the moon, and in definite measures it is s transferred till the seventh portion of the sun is exhausted. And they set and enter the portals of the west, and make their revolution by the north, and come forth through the eastern portals 6 on the face of the heaven. And when the moon rises one-fourteenth part appears in the heaven: 7 [the light becomes full in her]: on the fourteenth day she accomplishes her light. And fifteen parts of light are transferred to her till the fifteenth day (when) her light is accomplished, according to the sign of the year, and she becomes fifteen parts, and the moon grows by (the addition of) fourteenth 8 parts. And in her waning (the moon) decreases on the first day to fourteen parts of her light, on the second to thirteen parts of light, on the third to twelve, on the fourth to eleven, on the fifth to ten, on the sixth to nine, on the seventh to eight, on the eighth to seven, on the ninth to six, on the tenth to five, on the eleventh to four, on the twelfth to three, on the thirteenth to two, on the 9 fourteenth to the half of a seventh, and all her remaining light disappears wholly on the fifteenth. And 10 in certain months the month has twenty-nine days and once twenty-eight. And Uriel showed me another law: when light is transferred to the moon, and on which side it is transferred to her by the sun. During all the period during which the moon is growing in her light, she is transferring it to herself when opposite to the sun during fourteen days [her light is accomplished in the heaven, 12 and when she is illumined throughout, her light is accomplished full in the heaven. And on the first 13 day she is called the new moon, for on that day the light rises upon her. She becomes full moon exactly on the day when the sun sets in the west, and from the east she rises at night, and the moon shines the whole night through till the sun rises over against her and the moon is seen over against the sun. On the side whence the light of the moon comes forth, there again she wanes till all the light vanishes and all the days of the month are at an end, and her circumference is empty, void of 5 light. And three months she makes of thirty days, and at her time she makes three months of twenty-nine days each, in which she accomplishes her waning in the first period of time, and in the first 6 portal for one hundred and seventy-seven days. And in the time of her going out she appears for three months (of) thirty days each, and for three months she appears (of) twenty-nine each. At night she appears like a man for twenty days each time, and by day she appears like the heaven, and there is nothing else in her save her light.

[Chapter 79]

[1] And now, my son, I have shown thee everything, and the law of all the stars of the heaven is [2] completed. And he showed me all the laws of these for every day, and for every season of bearing rule, and for every year, and for its going forth, and for the order prescribed to it every month [3] and every week: And the waning of the moon which takes place in the sixth portal: for in this [4] sixth portal her light is accomplished, and after that there is the beginning of the waning: (And the waning) which takes place in the first portal in its season, till one hundred and seventy-seven [5] days are accomplished: reckoned according to weeks, twenty-five (weeks) and two days. She falls behind the sun and the order of the stars exactly five days in the course of one period, and when [6] this place which thou seest has been traversed. Such is the picture and sketch of every luminary which Uriel the archangel, who is their leader, showed unto me.

[Chapter 80]

[1] And in those days the angel Uriel answered and said to me: ' Behold, I have shown thee everything, Enoch, and I have revealed everything to thee that thou shouldst see this sun and this moon, and the leaders of the stars of the heaven and all those who turn them, their tasks and times and departures.

[2] And in the days of the sinners the years shall be shortened,
And their seed shall be tardy on their lands and fields,
And all things on the earth shall alter,
And shall not appear in their time:
And the rain shall be kept back
And the heaven shall withhold (it).
[3] And in those times the fruits of the earth shall be backward,
And shall not grow in their time,
And the fruits of the trees shall be withheld in their time.
[4] And the moon shall alter her order,
And not appear at her time.

[5] [And in those days the sun shall be seen and he shall journey in the evening on the extremity of the great chariot in the west]

And shall shine more brightly than accords with the order of light.
[6] And many chiefs of the stars shall transgress the order (prescribed).
And these shall alter their orbits and tasks,
And not appear at the seasons prescribed to them.
[7] And the whole order of the stars shall be concealed from the sinners,
And the thoughts of those on the earth shall err concerning them,
[And they shall be altered from all their ways],
Yea, they shall err and take them to be gods.
[8] And evil shall be multiplied upon them,
And punishment shall come upon them So as to destroy all.'

[Chapter 81]

[1] And he said unto me:
' Observe, Enoch, these heavenly tablets,
And read what is written thereon,
And mark every individual fact.'

[2] And I observed the heavenly tablets, and read everything which was written (thereon) and understood everything, and read the book of all the deeds of mankind, and of all the children of flesh [3] that shall be upon the earth to the remotest generations. And forthwith I blessed the great Lord the King of glory for ever, in that He has made all the works of the world,

And I extolled the Lord because of His patience,
And blessed Him because of the children of men.

[4] And after that I said:
' Blessed is the man who dies in righteousness and goodness,
Concerning whom there is no book of unrighteousness written,
And against whom no day of judgement shall be found.'

[5] And those seven holy ones brought me and placed me on the earth before the door of my house, and said to me: ' Declare everything to thy son Methuselah, and show to all thy children that no [6] flesh is righteous in the sight of the Lord, for He is their Creator. One year we will leave thee with thy son, till thou givest thy (last) commands, that thou mayest teach thy children and record (it) for them, and testify to all thy children; and in the second year they shall take thee from their midst.

[7] Let thy heart be strong,
For the good shall announce righteousness to the good;

The righteous with the righteous shall rejoice,
And shall offer congratulation to one another.

8 But the sinners shall die with the sinners,
And the apostate go down with the apostate.

9 And those who practice righteousness shall
die on account of the deeds of men,
And be taken away on account of the doings
of the godless.'

10 And in those days they ceased to speak to me, and I
came to my people, blessing the Lord of the world.

[Chapter 82]

1 And now, my son Methuselah, all these things I am
recounting to thee and writing down for thee! and I have
revealed to thee everything, and given thee books
concerning all these: so preserve, my son Methuselah,
the books from thy father's hand, and (see) that thou
deliver them to the generations of the world.

2 I have given Wisdom to thee and to thy
children,
[And thy children that shall be to thee],
That they may give it to their children for
generations,
This wisdom (namely) that passeth their
thought.

3 And those who understand it shall not
sleep,
But shall listen with the ear that they may
learn this wisdom,
And it shall please those that eat thereof
better than good food.

4 Blessed are all the righteous, blessed are all those who
walk In the way of righteousness and sin not as the
sinners, in the reckoning of all their days in which the
sun traverses the heaven, entering into and departing
from the portals for thirty days with the heads of
thousands of the order of the stars, together with the
four which are intercalated which divide the four
portions of the year, which 5 lead them and enter with
them four days. Owing to them men shall be at fault and
not reckon them in the whole reckoning of the year: yea,
men shall be at fault, and not recognize
them 6 accurately. For they belong to the reckoning of
the year and are truly recorded (thereon) for ever, one in
the first portal and one in the third, and one in the
fourth and one in the sixth, and the year is completed in
three hundred and sixty-four days. 7 And the account
thereof is accurate and the recorded reckoning thereof
exact; for the luminaries, and months and festivals, and
years and days, has Uriel shown and revealed to me, to
whom the 8 Lord of the whole creation of the world
hath subjected the host of heaven. And he has power
over night and day in the heaven to cause the light to
give light to men -sun, moon, and stars, 9 and all the
powers of the heaven which revolve in their circular
chariots. And these are the orders of the stars, which set

in their places, and in their seasons and festivals and
months. 10 And these are the names of those who lead
them, who watch that they enter at their times, in their
orders, in their seasons, in their months, in their periods
of dominion, and in their positions. Their four leaders
who divide the four parts of the year enter first; and after
them the twelve leaders of the orders who divide the
months; and for the three hundred and sixty (days) there
are heads over thousands who divide the days; and for
the four intercalary days there are the leaders which
sunder 12 the four parts of the year. And these heads
over thousands are intercalated between 13 leader and
leader, each behind a station, but their leaders make the
division. And these are the names of the leaders who
divide the four parts of the year which are ordained:
Milki'el, Hel'emmelek, and Mel'ejal, 14 and Narel. And
the names of those who lead them: Adnar'el, and
Ijasusa'el, and 'Elome'el- these three follow the leaders of
the orders, and there is one that follows the three leaders
of the orders which follow those leaders of stations that
divide the four parts of the year. In the beginning of the
year Melkejal rises first and rules, who is named Tam'aini
and sun, and 16 all the days of his dominion whilst he
bears rule are ninety-one days. And these are the signs of
the days which are to be seen on earth in the days of his
dominion: sweat, and heat, and calms; and all the trees
bear fruit, and leaves are produced on all the trees, and
the harvest of wheat, and the rose-flowers, and all the
flowers which come forth in the field, but the trees of
the winter season become withered. And these are the
names of the leaders which are under them: Berka'el,
Zelebs'el, and another who is added a head of a
thousand, called Hilujaseph: and the days of the
dominion of this (leader) are at an end. 18 The next
leader after him is Hel'emmelek, whom one names the
shining sun, and all the days 19 of his light are ninety-one
days. And these are the signs of (his) days on the earth:
glowing heat and dryness, and the trees ripen their fruits
and produce all their fruits ripe and ready, and the sheep
pair and become pregnant, and all the fruits of the earth
are gathered in, and everything that is 20 in the fields, and
the winepress: these things take place in the days of his
dominion. These are the names, and the orders, and the
leaders of those heads of thousands: Gida'ljal, Ke'el, and
He'el, and the name of the head of a thousand which is
added to them, Asfa'el: and the days of his dominion are
at an end.

THE DREAM-VISIONS

Section IV. Chapters LXXXIII-XC.

[Chapter 83]

[1] And now, my son Methuselah, I will show thee all my visions which I have seen, recounting [2] them before thee. Two visions I saw before I took a wife, and the one was quite unlike the other: the first when I was learning to write: the second before I took thy mother, (when) I saw a terrible [3] vision. And regarding them I prayed to the Lord. I had laid me down in the house of my grandfather Mahalalel, (when) I saw in a vision how the heaven collapsed and was borne off and fell to [4] the earth. And when it fell to the earth I saw how the earth was swallowed up in a great abyss, and mountains were suspended on mountains, and hills sank down on hills, and high trees were rent [5] from their stems, and hurled down and sunk in the abyss. And thereupon a word fell into my mouth, [6] and I lifted up (my voice) to cry aloud, and said: ' The earth is destroyed.' And my grandfather Mahalalel waked me as I lay near him, and said unto me: ' Why dost thou cry so, my son, and why [7] dost thou make such lamentation?' And I recounted to him the whole vision which I had seen, and he said unto me: ' A terrible thing hast thou seen, my son, and of grave moment is thy dream- vision as to the secrets of all the sin of the earth: it must sink into the abyss and be destroyed with [8] a great destruction. And now, my son, arise and make petition to the Lord of glory, since thou art a believer, that a remnant may remain on the earth, and that He may not destroy the whole [9] earth. My son, from heaven all this will come upon the earth, and upon the earth there will be great [10] destruction. After that I arose and prayed and implored and besought, and wrote down my prayer for the generations of the world, and I will show everything to thee, my son Methuselah. And when I had gone forth below and seen the heaven, and the sun rising in the east, and the moon setting in the west, and a few stars, and the whole earth, and everything as He had known it in the beginning, then I blessed the Lord of judgement and extolled Him because He had made the sun to go forth from the windows of the east, and he ascended and rose on the face of the heaven, and set out and kept traversing the path shown unto him.

[Chapter 84]

[1] And I lifted up my hands in righteousness and blessed the Holy and Great One, and spake with the breath of my mouth, and with the tongue of flesh, which God has made for the children of the flesh of men, that they should speak therewith, and He gave them breath and a tongue and a mouth that they should speak therewith:

[2] Blessed be Thou, O Lord, King,
Great and mighty in Thy greatness,
Lord of the whole creation of the heaven,
King of kings and God of the whole world.
And Thy power and kingship and greatness
abide for ever and ever,
And throughout all generations Thy dominion;
And all the heavens are Thy throne for ever,
And the whole earth Thy footstool for ever and ever.

[3] For Thou hast made and Thou rulest all things,
And nothing is too hard for Thee,
Wisdom departs not from the place of Thy throne,
Nor turns away from Thy presence.
And Thou knowest and seest and hearest everything,
And there is nothing hidden from Thee [for Thou seest everything]
[4] And now the angels of Thy heavens are guilty of trespass,
And upon the flesh of men abideth Thy wrath until the great day of judgement.
[5] And now, O God and Lord and Great King,
I implore and beseech Thee to fulfil my prayer,
To leave me a posterity on earth,
And not destroy all the flesh of man,
And make the earth without inhabitant,
So that there should be an eternal destruction.
[6] And now, my Lord, destroy from the earth the flesh which has aroused Thy wrath,
But the flesh of righteousness and uprightness establish as a plant of the eternal seed,
And hide not Thy face from the prayer of Thy servant, O Lord.'

[Chapter 85]

[1,2] And after this I saw another dream, and I will show the whole dream to thee, my son. And Enoch lifted up (his voice) and spake to his son Methuselah: ' To thee, my son, will I speak: hear my words-incline thine ear to the dream-vision of thy father. Before I took thy mother Edna, I saw in a vision on my bed, and behold a bull came forth from the earth, and that bull was white; and after it came forth a heifer, and along with this (latter) came forth two bulls, one of them black and [4] the other red. And that black bull gored the red one and pursued him over the earth, and thereupon [5] I could no longer see that red bull. But that black bull grew and that heifer went with him, and [6] I saw that many oxen proceeded from him which resembled and followed him. And that cow, that first one, went from the presence of that first bull in order to seek that red one, but found him [7] not, and lamented with a great lamentation over him and sought him. And I looked till that first [8] bull came to her and quieted her, and from that time onward she cried no more. And after that she bore another white bull, and after him she bore many bulls and black cows. [9] And I saw in my sleep that white bull likewise grow and

become a great white bull, and from Him proceeded many white bulls, and they resembled him. And they began to beget many white bulls, which resembled them, one following the other, (even) many.

[Chapter 86]

[1] And again I saw with mine eyes as I slept, and I saw the heaven above, and behold a star fell [2] from heaven, and it arose and eat and pastured amongst those oxen. And after that I saw the large and the black oxen, and behold they all changed their stalls and pastures and their cattle, and began [3] to live with each other. And again I saw in the vision, and looked towards the heaven, and behold I saw many stars descend and cast themselves down from heaven to that first star, and they became [4] bulls amongst those cattle and pastured with them [amongst them]. And I looked at them and saw, and behold they all let out their privy members, like horses, and began to cover the cows of the oxen, [5] and they all became pregnant and bare elephants, camels, and asses. And all the oxen feared them and were affrighted at them, and began to bite with their teeth and to devour, and to gore with their [6] horns. And they began, moreover, to devour those oxen; and behold all the children of the earth began to tremble and quake before them and to flee from them.

[Chapter 87]

[1] And again I saw how they began to gore each other and to devour each other, and the earth [2] began to cry aloud. And I raised mine eyes again to heaven, and I saw in the vision, and behold there came forth from heaven beings who were like white men: and four went forth from that place [3] and three with them. And those three that had last come forth grasped me by my hand and took me up, away from the generations of the earth, and raised me up to a lofty place, and showed me [4] a tower raised high above the earth, and all the hills were lower. And one said unto me: ' Remain here till thou seest everything that befalls those elephants, camels, and asses, and the stars and the oxen, and all of them.'

[Chapter 88]

[1] And I saw one of those four who had come forth first, and he seized that first star which had fallen from the heaven, and bound it hand and foot and cast it into an abyss: now that abyss was [2] narrow and deep, and horrible and dark. And one of them drew a sword, and gave it to those elephants and camels and asses: then they began to smite each other, and the whole earth quaked [3] because of them. And as I was beholding in the vision, lo, one of those four who had come forth stoned (them) from heaven, and gathered and took all the great stars whose privy members were like those of horses, and bound them all hand and foot, and cast them in an abyss of the earth.

[Chapter 89]

[1] And one of those four went to that white bull and instructed him in a secret, without his being terrified: he was born a bull and became a man, and built for himself a great vessel and dwelt thereon; [2] and three bulls dwelt with him in that vessel and they were covered in. And again I raised mine eyes towards heaven and saw a lofty roof, with seven water torrents thereon, and those torrents [3] flowed with much water into an enclosure. And I saw again, and behold fountains were opened on the surface of that great enclosure, and that water began to swell and rise upon the surface, [4] and I saw that enclosure till all its surface was covered with water. And the water, the darkness, and mist increased upon it; and as I looked at the height of that water, that water had risen above the height of that enclosure, and was streaming over that enclosure, and it stood upon the earth. [5] And all the cattle of that enclosure were gathered together until I saw how they sank and were [6] swallowed up and perished in that water. But that vessel floated on the water, while all the oxen and elephants and camels and asses sank to the bottom with all the animals, so that I could no longer see them, and they were not able to escape, (but) perished and sank into the depths. And again I saw in the vision till those water torrents were removed from that high roof, and the chasms [8] of the earth were leveled up and other abysses were opened. Then the water began to run down into these, till the earth became visible; but that vessel settled on the earth, and the darkness [9] retired and light appeared. But that white bull which had become a man came out of that vessel, and the three bulls with him, and one of those three was white like that bull, and one of them was red as blood, and one black: and that white bull departed from them. [10] And they began to bring forth beasts of the field and birds, so that there arose different genera: lions, tigers, wolves, dogs, hyenas, wild boars, foxes, squirrels, swine, falcons, vultures, kites, eagles, and ravens; and among them was born a white bull. And they began to bite one another; but that white bull which was born amongst them begat a wild ass and a white bull with it, and the [12] wild asses multiplied. But that bull which was born from him begat a black wild boar and a white [13] sheep; and the former begat many boars, but that sheep begat twelve sheep. And when those twelve sheep had grown, they gave up one of them to the asses, and those asses again gave up that sheep to the wolves, and that sheep grew up among the wolves. And the Lord brought the eleven sheep to live with it and to pasture with it among the wolves: and they multiplied and became many flocks of sheep. And the wolves began to fear them, and they oppressed them until they destroyed their little ones, and they cast their young into a river of much water: but those sheep began to [16] cry aloud on account of their little ones, and to complain unto their Lord. And a sheep which had been saved from the wolves fled and escaped to the wild asses; and I saw the sheep how they lamented and cried, and besought their Lord with all their might, till that Lord of the sheep descended at the voice of the sheep from a lofty abode, and came to them and pastured them. And He called that sheep which had escaped the wolves, and spake with it concerning the wolves that it should [18] admonish them not to touch the sheep. And the sheep went to the wolves according to the word of the Lord, and another

sheep met it and went with it, and the two went and entered together into the assembly of those wolves, and spake with them and admonished them not to touch the [19] sheep from henceforth. And thereupon I saw the wolves, and how they oppressed the sheep [20] exceedingly with all their power; and the sheep cried aloud. And the Lord came to the sheep and they began to smite those wolves: and the wolves began to make lamentation; but the sheep became [21] quiet and forthwith ceased to cry out. And I saw the sheep till they departed from amongst the wolves; but the eyes of the wolves were blinded, and those wolves departed in pursuit of the sheep [22] with all their power. And the Lord of the sheep went with them, as their leader, and all His sheep [23] followed Him: and his face was dazzling and glorious and terrible to behold. But the wolves [24] began to pursue those sheep till they reached a sea of water. And that sea was divided, and the water stood on this side and on that before their face, and their Lord led them and placed Himself between [25] them and the wolves. And as those wolves did not yet see the sheep, they proceeded into the midst of that sea, and the wolves followed the sheep, and [those wolves] ran after them into that sea. [26] And when they saw the Lord of the sheep, they turned to flee before His face, but that sea gathered itself together, and became as it had been created, and the water swelled and rose till it covered [27] those wolves. And I saw till all the wolves who pursued those sheep perished and were drowned. [28] But the sheep escaped from that water and went forth into a wilderness, where there was no water and no grass; and they began to open their eyes and to see; and I saw the Lord of the sheep [29] pasturing them and giving them water and grass, and that sheep going and leading them. And that [30] sheep ascended to the summit of that lofty rock, and the Lord of the sheep sent it to them. And after that I saw the Lord of the sheep who stood before them, and His appearance was great and [31] terrible and majestic, and all those sheep saw Him and were afraid before His face. And they all feared and trembled because of Him, and they cried to that sheep with them [which was amongst [32] them]: ' We are not able to stand before our Lord or to behold Him.' And that sheep which led them again ascended to the summit of that rock, but the sheep began to be blinded and to wander [33] from the way which he had showed them, but that sheep wot not thereof. And the Lord of the sheep was wrathful exceedingly against them, and that sheep discovered it, and went down from the summit of the rock, and came to the sheep, and found the greatest part of them blinded and fallen [34] away. And when they saw it they feared and trembled at its presence, and desired to return to their [35] folds. And that sheep took other sheep with it, and came to those sheep which had fallen away, and began to slay them; and the sheep feared its presence, and thus that sheep brought back those [36] sheep that had fallen away, and they returned to their folds. And I saw in this vision till that sheep became a man and built a house for the Lord of the sheep, and placed all the sheep in that house. [37] And I saw till this sheep which had met that sheep which led them fell asleep: and I saw till all the great sheep perished and little ones arose in their place, and they

came to a pasture, and [38] approached a stream of water. Then that sheep, their leader which had become a man, withdrew [39] from them and fell asleep, and all the sheep sought it and cried over it with a great crying. And I saw till they left off crying for that sheep and crossed that stream of water, and there arose the two sheep as leaders in the place of those which had led them and fallen asleep (lit. ' had fallen asleep and led [40] them '). And I saw till the sheep came to a goodly place, and a pleasant and glorious land, and I saw till those sheep were satisfied; and that house stood amongst them in the pleasant land. [41] And sometimes their eyes were opened, and sometimes blinded, till another sheep arose and led them and brought them all back, and their eyes were opened. [42] And the dogs and the foxes and the wild boars began to devour those sheep till the Lord of the sheep raised up [another sheep] a ram from their [43] midst, which led them. And that ram began to butt on either side those dogs, foxes, and wild [44] boars till he had destroyed them all. And that sheep whose eyes were opened saw that ram, which was amongst the sheep, till it forsook its glory and began to butt those sheep, and trampled upon them, and behaved itself [45] unseemly. And the Lord of the sheep sent the lamb to another lamb and raised it to being a ram and leader of the sheep instead of that [46] ram which had forsaken its glory. And it went to it and spake to it alone, and raised it to being a ram, and made it the prince and leader of the sheep; but during all these things those dogs [47] oppressed the sheep. And the first ram pursued that second ram, and that second ram arose and fled before it; and I saw till those dogs pulled [48] down the first ram. And that second ram arose [49] and led the [little] sheep. And those sheep grew and multiplied; but all the dogs, and foxes, and wild boars feared and fled before it, and that ram butted and killed the wild beasts, and those wild beasts had no longer any power among the [48b] sheep and robbed them no more of ought. And that ram begat many sheep and fell asleep; and a little sheep became ram in its stead, and became prince and leader of those sheep. [50] And that house became great and broad, and it was built for those sheep: (and) a tower lofty and great was built on the house for the Lord of the sheep, and that house was low, but the tower was elevated and lofty, and the Lord of the sheep stood on that tower and they offered a full table before Him. [51] And again I saw those sheep that they again erred and went many ways, and forsook that their house, and the Lord of the sheep called some from amongst the sheep and sent them to the sheep, [52] but the sheep began to slay them. And one of them was saved and was not slain, and it sped away and cried aloud over the sheep; and they sought to slay it, but the Lord of the sheep saved it from [53] the sheep, and brought it up to me, and caused it to dwell there. And many other sheep He sent to those sheep to testify unto them and lament over them. And after that I saw that when they forsook the house of the Lord and His tower they fell away entirely, and their eyes were blinded; and I saw the Lord of the sheep how He wrought much slaughter amongst them in their herds until [55] those sheep invited that slaughter and betrayed His place. And He gave them over into the hands of the lions and tigers, and wolves and hyenas, and into the hand of the foxes, and to all the wild [56] beasts, and those wild beasts began to tear in pieces those sheep. And I saw that He forsook that their house and their tower and gave them all into the hand of the lions, to tear and devour them, [57] into the hand of all the wild beasts. And I began to cry aloud with all my power, and to appeal to the Lord of the sheep, and to represent to Him in regard to the sheep that they were devoured [58] by all the wild beasts. But He remained unmoved, though He saw it, and rejoiced that they were devoured and swallowed and robbed, and left them to be devoured in the hand of all the beasts. [59] And He called seventy shepherds, and cast those sheep to them that they might pasture them, and He spake to the shepherds and their companions: ' Let each individual of you pasture the sheep [60] henceforward, and everything that I shall command you that do ye. And I will deliver them over unto you duly numbered, and tell you which of them are to be destroyed-and them destroy ye.' And [61] He gave over unto them those sheep. And He called another and spake unto him: ' Observe and mark everything that the shepherds will do to those sheep; for they will destroy more of them than [62] I have commanded them. And every excess and the destruction which will be wrought through the shepherds, record (namely) how many they destroy according to my command, and how many according to their own caprice: record against every individual shepherd all the destruction he [63] effects. And read out before me by number how many they destroy, and how many they deliver over for destruction, that I may have this as a testimony against them, and know every deed of the shepherds, that I may comprehend and see what they do, whether or not they abide by my [64] command which I have commanded them. But they shall not know it, and thou shalt not declare it to them, nor admonish them, but only record against each individual all the destruction which [65] the shepherds effect each in his time and lay it all before me.' And I saw till those shepherds pastured in their season, and they began to slay and to destroy more than they were bidden, and they delivered [66] those sheep into the hand of the lions. And the lions and tigers eat and devoured the greater part of those sheep, and the wild boars eat along with them; and they burnt that tower and demolished [67] that house. And I became exceedingly sorrowful over that tower because that house of the sheep was demolished, and afterwards I was unable to see if those sheep entered that house. [68] And the shepherds and their associates delivered over those sheep to all the wild beasts, to devour them, and each one of them received in his time a definite number: it was written by the other [69] in a book how many each one of them destroyed of them. And each one slew and destroyed many [70] more than was prescribed; and I began to weep and lament on account of those sheep. And thus in the vision I saw that one who wrote, how he wrote down every one that was destroyed by those shepherds, day by day, and carried up and laid down and showed actually the whole book to the Lord of the sheep-(even) everything that they had done, and all that each one of them had made [71] away with, and all that they had given over to destruction. And the book was read before the Lord of the sheep, and He took the book from his hand and read it and sealed it

and laid it down. [72] And forthwith I saw how the shepherds pastured for twelve hours, and behold three of those sheep turned back and came and entered and began to build up all that had fallen down of that [73] house; but the wild boars tried to hinder them, but they were not able. And they began again to build as before, and they reared up that tower, and it was named the high tower; and they began again to place a table before the tower, but all the bread on it was polluted and not pure. [74] And as touching all this the eyes of those sheep were blinded so that they saw not, and (the eyes of) their shepherds likewise; and they delivered them in large numbers to their shepherds for [75] destruction, and they trampled the sheep with their feet and devoured them. And the Lord of the sheep remained unmoved till all the sheep were dispersed over the field and mingled with them (i.e. the [76] beasts), and they (i.e. the shepherds) did not save them out of the hand of the beasts. And this one who wrote the book carried it up, and showed it and read it before the Lord of the sheep, and implored Him on their account, and besought Him on their account as he showed Him all the doings [77] of the shepherds, and gave testimony before Him against all the shepherds. And he took the actual book and laid it down beside Him and departed.

[Chapter 90]

[1] And I saw till that in this manner thirty-five shepherds undertook the pasturing (of the sheep), and they severally completed their periods as did the first; and others received them into their [2] hands, to pasture them for their period, each shepherd in his own period. And after that I saw in my vision all the birds of heaven coming, the eagles, the vultures, the kites, the ravens; but the eagles led all the birds; and they began to devour those sheep, and to pick out their eyes and to [3] devour their flesh. And the sheep cried out because their flesh was being devoured by the birds, [4] and as for me I looked and lamented in my sleep over that shepherd who pastured the sheep. And I saw until those sheep were devoured by the dogs and eagles and kites, and they left neither flesh nor skin nor sinew remaining on them till only their bones stood there: and their bones too fell [5] to the earth and the sheep became few. And I saw until that twenty-three had undertaken the pasturing and completed in their several periods fifty-eight times. [6] But behold lambs were borne by those white sheep, and they began to open their eyes and to see, [7] and to cry to the sheep. Yea, they cried to them, but they did not hearken to what they said to [8] them, but were exceedingly deaf, and their eyes were very exceedingly blinded. And I saw in the vision how the ravens flew upon those lambs and took one of those lambs, and dashed the sheep [9] in pieces and devoured them. And I saw till horns grew upon those lambs, and the ravens cast down their horns; and I saw till there sprouted a great horn of one of those sheep, and their eyes [10] were opened. And it looked at them [and their eyes opened], and it cried to the sheep, and the [11] rams saw it and all ran to it. And notwithstanding all this those eagles and vultures and ravens and kites still kept tearing the sheep and swooping down upon them and devouring them: still the

sheep remained silent, but the rams lamented and cried out. And those ravens fought and battled with it and sought to lay low its horn, but they had no power over it. All the eagles and vultures and ravens and kites were gathered together, and there came with them all the sheep of the field, yea, they all came together, and helped each other to break that horn of the ram. 19 And I saw till a great sword was given to the sheep, and the sheep proceeded against all the beasts of the field to slay them, and all the beasts and the birds of the heaven fled before their face. And I saw that man, who wrote the book according to the command of the Lord, till he opened that book concerning the destruction which those twelve last shepherds had wrought, and showed that they had destroyed much more than their predecessors, before the Lord of the sheep. And I saw till the Lord of the sheep came unto them and took in His hand the staff of His wrath, and smote the earth, and the earth clave asunder, and all the beasts and all the birds of the heaven fell from among those sheep, and were swallowed up in the earth and it covered them. 20 And I saw till a throne was erected in the pleasant land, and the Lord of the sheep sat Himself thereon, and the other took the sealed books and opened those books before the Lord of the sheep. 21 And the Lord called those men the seven first white ones, and commanded that they should bring before Him, beginning with the first star which led the way, all the stars whose privy members 22 were like those of horses, and they brought them all before Him. And He said to that man who wrote before Him, being one of those seven white ones, and said unto him: ' Take those seventy shepherds to whom I delivered the sheep, and who taking them on their own authority slew more 23 than I commanded them.' And behold they were all bound, I saw, and they all stood before Him. 24 And the judgement was held first over the stars, and they were judged and found guilty, and went to the place of condemnation, and they were cast into an abyss, full of fire and flaming, and full 25 of pillars of fire. And those seventy shepherds were judged and found guilty, and they were cast 26 into that fiery abyss. And I saw at that time how a like abyss was opened in the midst of the earth, full of fire, and they brought those blinded sheep, and they were all judged and found guilty and 27 cast into this fiery abyss, and they burned; now this abyss was to the right of that house. And I saw those sheep burning and their bones burning. 28 And I stood up to see till they folded up that old house; and carried off all the pillars, and all the beams and ornaments of the house were at the same time folded up with it, and they carried 29 it off and laid it in a place in the south of the land. And I saw till the Lord of the sheep brought a new house greater and loftier than that first, and set it up in the place of the first which had beer folded up: all its pillars were new, and its ornaments were new and larger than those of the first, the old one which He had taken away, and all the sheep were within it. 30 And I saw all the sheep which had been left, and all the beasts on the earth, and all the birds of the heaven, falling down and doing homage to those sheep and making petition to and obeying 31 them in every thing. And thereafter those three who were clothed in white and had seized me by my hand [who had taken me up before], and the hand of

that ram also seizing hold of me, they 32 took me up and set me down in the midst of those sheep before the judgement took place. And those 33 sheep were all white, and their wool was abundant and clean. And all that had been destroyed and dispersed, and all the beasts of the field, and all the birds of the heaven, assembled in that house, and the Lord of the sheep rejoiced with great joy because they were all good and had returned to 34 His house. And I saw till they laid down that sword, which had been given to the sheep, and they brought it back into the house, and it was sealed before the presence of the Lord, and all the sheep 35 were invited into that house, but it held them not. And the eyes of them all were opened, and they 36 saw the good, and there was not one among them that did not see. And I saw that that house was large and broad and very full. 37 And I saw that a white bull was born, with large horns and all the beasts of the field and all the 38 birds of the air feared him and made petition to him all the time. And I saw till all their generations were transformed, and they all became white bulls; and the first among them became a lamb, and that lamb became a great animal and had great black horns on its head; and the Lord of the sheep 39 rejoiced over it and over all the oxen. And I slept in their midst: and I awoke and saw everything. 40 This is the vision which I saw while I slept, and I awoke and blessed the Lord of righteousness and 41 gave Him glory. Then I wept with a great weeping and my tears stayed not till I could no longer endure it: when I saw, they flowed on account of what I had seen; for everything shall come and 42 be fulfilled, and all the deeds of men in their order were shown to me. On that night I remembered the first dream, and because of it I wept and was troubled-because I had seen that vision.

A BOOK OF EXHORTATION AND PROMISED BLESSING FOR THE RIGHTEOUS AND OF MALEDICTION AND WOE FOR THE SINNERS

Section V. XCI-CIV
(i.e. XCII, XCI. 1-1O, 18-19, XCIII. 1-1O, XCI. 12-17, XCIV-CIV.).

[Chapter 92]

¹ The book written by Enoch-[Enoch indeed wrote this complete doctrine of wisdom, (which is) praised of all men and a judge of all the earth] for all my children who shall dwell on the earth. And for the future generations who shall observe uprightness and peace.

² Let not your spirit be troubled on account of the times;
For the Holy and Great One has appointed days for all things.

³ And the righteous one shall arise from sleep,
[Shall arise] and walk in the paths of righteousness,
And all his path and conversation shall be in eternal goodness and grace.

⁴ He will be gracious to the righteous and give him eternal uprightness,
And He will give him power so that he shall be (endowed) with goodness and righteousness.
And he shall walk in eternal light.

⁵ And sin shall perish in darkness for ever,
And shall no more be seen from that day for evermore.

[Chapter 91]

¹ And now, my son Methuselah, call to me all thy brothers
And gather together to me all the sons of thy mother;
For the word calls me,
And the spirit is poured out upon me,
That I may show you everything
That shall befall you for ever.'

² And there upon Methuselah went and summoned to him all his brothers and assembled his relatives.
³ And he spake unto all the children of righteousness and said:

'Hear, ye sons of Enoch, all the words of your father,
And hearken aright to the voice of my mouth;
For I exhort you and say unto you, beloved:

⁴ Love uprightness and walk therein.

And draw not nigh to uprightness with a double heart,
And associate not with those of a double heart,

But walk in righteousness, my sons.
And it shall guide you on good paths,
And righteousness shall be your companion.

⁵ For I know that violence must increase on the earth,
And a great chastisement be executed on the earth,
Yea, it shall be cut off from its roots,
And its whole structure be destroyed.

⁶ And unrighteousness shall again be consummated on the earth,
And all the deeds of unrighteousness and of violence
And transgression shall prevail in a twofold degree.

⁷ And when sin and unrighteousness and blasphemy
And violence in all kinds of deeds increase,
And apostasy and transgression and uncleanness increase,

A great chastisement shall come from heaven upon all these,
And the holy Lord will come forth with wrath and chastisement
To execute judgement on earth.

⁸ In those days violence shall be cut off from its roots,
And the roots of unrighteousness together with deceit,
And they shall be destroyed from under heaven.

⁹ And all the idols of the heathen shall be abandoned,
And the temples burned with fire,
And they shall remove them from the whole earth,

And they (i.e. the heathen) shall be cast into the judgement of fire,
And shall perish in wrath and in grievous judgement for ever.

¹⁰ And the righteous shall arise from their sleep,
And wisdom shall arise and be given unto them.

[And after that the roots of unrighteousness shall be cut off, and the sinners shall be destroyed by the sword . . . shall be cut off from the blasphemers in every place, and those who plan violence and those who commit blasphemy shall perish by the sword.]

18 And now I tell you, my sons, and show you
The paths of righteousness and the paths of violence.
Yea, I will show them to you again
That ye may know what will come to pass.
19 And now, hearken unto me, my sons,
And walk in the paths of righteousness,
And walk not in the paths of violence;
For all who walk in the paths of unrighteousness shall perish for ever.'

[Chapter 93]

1,2 And after that Enoch both gave and began to recount from the books. And Enoch said:

' Concerning the children of righteousness and concerning the elect of the world,
And concerning the plant of uprightness, I will speak these things,
Yea, I Enoch will declare (them) unto you, my sons:

According to that which appeared to me in the heavenly vision,
And which I have known through the word of the holy angels,
And have learnt from the heavenly tablets.'

3 And Enoch began to recount from the books and said:
' I was born the seventh in the first week,
While judgement and righteousness still endured.

4 And after me there shall arise in the second week great wickedness,
And deceit shall have sprung up;
And in it there shall be the first end.

And in it a man shall be saved;
And after it is ended unrighteousness shall grow up,
And a law shall be made for the sinners.

And after that in the third week at its close
A man shall be elected as the plant of righteous judgement,
And his posterity shall become the plant of righteousness for evermore.

6 And after that in the fourth week, at its close,
Visions of the holy and righteous shall be seen,
And a law for all generations and an enclosure shall be made for them.

7 And after that in the fifth week, at its close,
The house of glory and dominion shall be built

for ever.

8 And after that in the sixth week all who live in it shall be blinded,
And the hearts of all of them shall godlessly forsake wisdom.
And in it a man shall ascend;
And at its close the house of dominion shall be burnt with fire,
And the whole race of the chosen root shall be dispersed.

9 And after that in the seventh week shall an apostate generation arise,
And many shall be its deeds,
And all its deeds shall be apostate.

10 And at its close shall be elected
The elect righteous of the eternal plant of righteousness,
To receive sevenfold instruction concerning all His creation.

11 [For who is there of all the children of men that is able to hear the voice of the Holy One without being troubled ? And who can think His thoughts ? and who is there that can behold all the works 12 of heaven ? And how should there be one who could behold the heaven, and who is there that could understand the things of heaven and see a soul or a spirit and could tell thereof, or ascend and see 13 all their ends and think them or do like them ? And who is there of all men that could know what is the breadth and the length of the earth, and to whom has been shown the measure of all of them ? 14 Or is there any one who could discern the length of the heaven and how great is its height, and upon what it is founded, and how great is the number of the stars, and where all the luminaries rest ?]

[Chapter 91]

12 And after that there shall be another, the eighth week, that of righteousness,
And a sword shall be given to it that a righteous judgement may be executed on the oppressors,
And sinners shall be delivered into the hands of the righteous.

13 And at its close they shall acquire houses through their righteousness,
And a house shall be built for the Great King in glory for evermore,
14d And all mankind shall look to the path of uprightness.

14a And after that, in the ninth week, the righteous judgement shall be revealed to the whole world,
b And all the works of the godless shall vanish from all the earth,
c And the world shall be written down for destruction.

15 And after this, in the tenth week in the seventh part,
There shall be the great eternal judgement,
In which He will execute vengeance amongst the angels.

16 And the first heaven shall depart and pass away,
And a new heaven shall appear,
And all the powers of the heavens shall give sevenfold light.

17 And after that there will be many weeks without number for ever,
And all shall be in goodness and righteousness,
And sin shall no more be mentioned for ever.

[Chapter 94]

1 And now I say unto you, my sons, love righteousness and walk therein;
For the paths of righteousness are worthy of acceptation,
But the paths of unrighteousness shall suddenly be destroyed and vanish.

2 And to certain men of a generation shall the paths of violence and of death be revealed,
And they shall hold themselves afar from them,
And shall not follow them.

3 And now I say unto you the righteous:
Walk not in the paths of wickedness, nor in the paths of death,
And draw not nigh to them, lest ye be destroyed.

4 But seek and choose for yourselves righteousness and an elect life,
And walk in the paths of peace,
And ye shall live and prosper.

5 And hold fast my words in the thoughts of your hearts,
And suffer them not to be effaced from your hearts;

For I know that sinners will tempt men to evilly-entreat wisdom,
So that no place may be found for her,
And no manner of temptation may minish.

6 Woe to those who build unrighteousness and oppression

And lay deceit as a foundation;

For they shall be suddenly overthrown,

And they shall have no peace.

7 Woe to those who build their houses with sin;
For from all their foundations shall they be overthrown,
And by the sword shall they fall.
[And those who acquire gold and silver in judgement suddenly shall perish.]

8 Woe to you, ye rich, for ye have trusted in your riches,
And from your riches shall ye depart,
Because ye have not remembered the Most High in the days of your riches.

9 Ye have committed blasphemy and unrighteousness,
And have become ready for the day of slaughter,
And the day of darkness and the day of the great judgement.

10 Thus I speak and declare unto you:

He who hath created you will overthrow you,

And for your fall there shall be no compassion,
And your Creator will rejoice at your destruction.

11 And your righteous ones in those days shall be
A reproach to the sinners and the godless.

[Chapter 95]

1 Oh that mine eyes were [a cloud of] waters
That I might weep over you,
And pour down my tears as a cloud of waters:
That so I might rest from my trouble of heart!

2 who has permitted you to practice reproaches and wickedness ?
And so judgement shall overtake you, sinners.

3 Fear not the sinners, ye righteous;
For again will the Lord deliver them into your hands,
That ye may execute judgement upon them according to your desires.

4 Woe to you who fulminate anathemas which cannot be reversed:
Healing shall therefore be far from you because of your sins.

5 Woe to you who requite your neighbour with evil;
For ye shall be requited according to your works.

6 Woe to you, lying witnesses,
And to those who weigh out injustice,
For suddenly shall ye perish.

7 Woe to you, sinners, for ye persecute the
righteous;
For ye shall be delivered up and persecuted
because of injustice,
And heavy shall its yoke be upon you.

[Chapter 96]

1 Be hopeful, ye righteous; for suddenly shall
the sinners perish before you,
And ye shall have lordship over them according
to your desires.
2 [And in the day of the tribulation of the
sinners,
Your children shall mount and rise as eagles,
And higher than the vultures will be your nest,
And ye shall ascend and enter the crevices of
the earth,
And the clefts of the rock for ever as coneys
before the unrighteous,
And the sirens shall sigh because of you-and
weep.]

3 Wherefore fear not, ye that have suffered;
For healing shall be your portion,
And a bright light shall enlighten you,
And the voice of rest ye shall hear from
heaven.

4 Woe unto you, ye sinners, for your riches
make you appear like the righteous,
But your hearts convict you of being sinners,
And this fact shall be a testimony against you
for a memorial of (your) evil deeds.

5 Woe to you who devour the finest of the
wheat,
And drink wine in large bowls,
And tread under foot the lowly with your
might.

6 Woe to you who drink water from every
fountain,
For suddenly shall ye be consumed and wither
away,
Because ye have forsaken the fountain of life.

7 Woe to you who work unrighteousness
And deceit and blasphemy:
It shall be a memorial against you for evil.

8 Woe to you, ye mighty,
Who with might oppress the righteous;
For the day of your destruction is coming.

In those days many and good days shall come
to the righteous-in the day of your judgement.

[Chapter 97]

1 Believe, ye righteous, that the sinners will
become a shame
And perish in the day of unrighteousness.
2 Be it known unto you (ye sinners) that the
Most High is mindful of your destruction,
And the angels of heaven rejoice over your
destruction.

3 What will ye do, ye sinners,
And whither will ye flee on that day of
judgement,
When ye hear the voice of the prayer of the
righteous ?

4 Yea, ye shall fare like unto them,
Against whom this word shall be a testimony:
" Ye have been companions of sinners."

5 And in those days the prayer of the righteous
shall reach unto the Lord,
And for you the days of your judgement shall
come.

6 And all the words of your unrighteousness
shall be read out before the Great Holy One,
And your faces shall be covered with shame,
And He will reject every work which is
grounded on unrighteousness.

7 Woe to you, ye sinners, who live on the mid
ocean and on the dry land,
Whose remembrance is evil against you.

8 Woe to you who acquire silver and gold in
unrighteousness and say:
" We have become rich with riches and have
possessions;
And have acquired everything we have desired.

9 And now let us do what we purposed:
For we have gathered silver,
9c And many are the husbandmen in our
houses."
9d And our granaries are (brim) full as with
water,
10 Yea and like water your lies shall flow away;
For your riches shall not abide
But speedily ascend from you;

For ye have acquired it all in unrighteousness,
And ye shall be given over to a great curse.

[Chapter 98]

1 And now I swear unto you, to the wise and to
the foolish,
For ye shall have manifold experiences on the
earth.

2 For ye men shall put on more adornments
than a woman,
And coloured garments more than a virgin:
In royalty and in grandeur and in power,
And in silver and in gold and in purple,
And in splendour and in food they shall be
poured out as water.

3 Therefore they shall be wanting in doctrine
and wisdom,
And they shall perish thereby together with
their possessions;
And with all their glory and their splendour,
And in shame and in slaughter and in great
destitution,
Their spirits shall be cast into the furnace of
fire.

4 I have sworn unto you, ye sinners, as a
mountain has not become a slave,
And a hill does not become the handmaid of a
woman,
Even so sin has not been sent upon the earth,
But man of himself has created it,
And under a great curse shall they fall who
commit it.

5 And barrenness has not been given to the
woman,
But on account of the deeds of her own hands
she dies without children.

6 I have sworn unto you, ye sinners, by the
Holy Great One,
That all your evil deeds are revealed in the
heavens,
And that none of your deeds of oppression are
covered and hidden.

7 And do not think in your spirit nor say in your heart that
ye do not know and that ye do not see 8 that every sin is
every day recorded in heaven in the presence of the Most
High. From henceforth ye know that all your oppression
wherewith ye oppress is written down every day till the day
of your judgement. 9 Woe to you, ye fools, for through your
folly shall ye perish: and ye transgress against the
wise, 10 and so good hap shall not be your portion. And
now, know ye that ye are prepared for the day of
destruction: wherefore do not hope to live, ye sinners, but
ye shall depart and die; for ye know no ransom; for ye are
prepared for the day of the great judgement, for the day of
tribulation and great shame for your spirits. 11 Woe to you,
ye obstinate of heart, who work wickedness and eat blood:
Whence have ye good things to eat and to drink and to be
filled ? From all the good things which the Lord the Most
High has placed in abundance on the earth; therefore ye
shall have no peace. 12 Woe to you who love the deeds of
unrighteousness: wherefore do ye hope for good hap unto

yourselves? know that ye shall be delivered into the hands
of the righteous, and they shall cut 13 off your necks and
slay you, and have no mercy upon you. Woe to you who
rejoice in the tribulation of the righteous; for no grave shall
be dug for you. Woe to you who set at nought the words
of 15 the righteous; for ye shall have no hope of life. Woe to
you who write down lying and godless words; for they write
down their lies that men may hear them and act godlessly
towards (their) 16 neighbour. Therefore they shall have no
peace but die a sudden death.

[Chapter 99]

1 Woe to you who work godlessness,
And glory in lying and extol them:
Ye shall perish, and no happy life shall be
yours.

2 Woe to them who pervert the words of
uprightness,
And transgress the eternal law,
And transform themselves into what they were
not [into sinners]:
They shall be trodden under foot upon the
earth.

3 In those days make ready, ye righteous, to
raise your prayers as a memorial,
And place them as a testimony before the
angels,
That they may place the sin of the sinners for a
memorial before the Most High.

4 In those days the nations shall be stirred up,
And the families of the nations shall arise on
the day of destruction.

5 And in those days the destitute shall go forth
and carry off their children,
And they shall abandon them, so that their
children shall perish through them:
Yea, they shall abandon their children (that are
still) sucklings, and not return to them,
And shall have no pity on their beloved ones.

6, 7 And again I swear to you, ye sinners, that sin is prepared
for a day of unceasing bloodshed. And they who worship
stones, and grave images of gold and silver and wood (and
stone) and clay, and those who worship impure spirits and
demons, and all kinds of idols not according to knowledge,
shall get no manner of help from them.

8 And they shall become godless by reason of
the folly of their hearts,
And their eyes shall be blinded through the fear
of their hearts
And through visions in their dreams.

9 Through these they shall become godless and
fearful;
For they shall have wrought all their work in a

lie,
And shall have worshiped a stone:
Therefore in an instant shall they perish.

10 But in those days blessed are all they who
accept the words of wisdom, and understand
them,
And observe the paths of the Most High, and
walk in the path of His righteousness,
And become not godless with the godless;
For they shall be saved.

11 Woe to you who spread evil to your
neighbours;
For you shall be slain in Sheol.

12 Woe to you who make deceitful and false
measures,
And (to them) who cause bitterness on the
earth;
For they shall thereby be utterly consumed.

13 Woe to you who build your houses through
the grievous toil of others,
And all their building materials are the bricks
and stones of sin;
I tell you ye shall have no peace.

14 Woe to them who reject the measure and
eternal heritage of their fathers
And whose souls follow after idols;
For they shall have no rest.

15 Woe to them who work unrighteousness and
help oppression,
And slay their neighbours until the day of the
great judgement.

16 For He shall cast down your glory,
And bring affliction on your hearts,
And shall arouse His fierce indignation
And destroy you all with the sword;
And all the holy and righteous shall remember
your sins.

[Chapter 100]

1 And in those days in one place the fathers
together with their sons shall be smitten
And brothers one with another shall fall in
death
Till the streams flow with their blood.

2 For a man shall not withhold his hand from
slaying his sons and his sons' sons,
And the sinner shall not withhold his hand
from his honoured brother:
From dawn till sunset they shall slay one
another.

3 And the horse shall walk up to the breast in
the blood of sinners,
And the chariot shall be submerged to its
height.

4 In those days the angels shall descend into the
secret places
And gather together into one place all those
who brought down sin
And the Most High will arise on that day of
judgement
To execute great judgement amongst sinners.

5 And over all the righteous and holy He will
appoint guardians from amongst the holy
angels
To guard them as the apple of an eye,
Until He makes an end of all wickedness and all
sin,
And though the righteous sleep a long sleep,
they have nought to fear.

6 And (then) the children of the earth shall see
the wise in security,
And shall understand all the words of this
book,
And recognize that their riches shall not be able
to save them
In the overthrow of their sins.

7 Woe to you, Sinners, on the day of strong
anguish,
Ye who afflict the righteous and burn them
with fire:
Ye shall be requited according to your works.

8 Woe to you, ye obstinate of heart,
Who watch in order to devise wickedness:
Therefore shall fear come upon you
And there shall be none to help you.

9 Woe to you, ye sinners, on account of the
words of your mouth,
And on account of the deeds of your hands
which your godlessness as wrought,
In blazing flames burning worse than fire shall
ye burn.

10 And now, know ye that from the angels He will inquire
as to your deeds in heaven, from the sun and from the
moon and from the stars in reference to your sins because
upon the earth ye execute 11 judgement on the righteous.
And He will summon to testify against you every cloud and
mist and dew and rain; for they shall all be withheld
because of you from descending upon you, and they 12 shall
be mindful of your sins. And now give presents to the rain
that it be not withheld from descending upon you, nor yet
the dew, when it has received gold and silver from you that
it may descend. When the hoar-frost and snow with their
chilliness, and all the snow-storms with all their plagues fall
upon you, in those days ye shall not be able to stand before
them.

[Chapter 101]

[1] Observe the heaven, ye children of heaven, and every work of the Most High, and fear ye Him [2] and work no evil in His presence. If He closes the windows of heaven, and withholds the rain and [3] the dew from descending on the earth on your account, what will ye do then? And if He sends His anger upon you because of your deeds, ye cannot petition Him; for ye spake proud and insolent [4] words against His righteousness: therefore ye shall have no peace. And see ye not the sailors of the ships, how their ships are tossed to and fro by the waves, and are shaken by the winds, and are [5] in sore trouble ? And therefore do they fear because all their goodly possessions go upon the sea with them, and they have evil forebodings of heart that the sea will swallow them and they will [6] perish therein. Are not the entire sea and all its waters, and all its movements, the work of the Most [7] High, and has He not set limits to its doings, and confined it throughout by the sand ? And at His reproof it is afraid and dries up, and all its fish die and all that is in it; But ye sinners that are [8] on the earth fear Him not. Has He not made the heaven and the earth, and all that is therein ? Who has given understanding and wisdom to everything that moves on the earth and in the sea. [9] Do not the sailors of the ships fear the sea ? Yet sinners fear not the Most High.

[Chapter 102]

[1] In those days when He hath brought a grievous fire upon you,
Whither will ye flee, and where will ye find deliverance ?
And when He launches forth His Word against you Will you not be affrighted and fear ?

[2] And all the luminaries shall be affrighted with great fear,
And all the earth shall be affrighted and tremble and be alarmed.

[3] And all the angels shall execute their commandst
And shall seek to hide themselves from the presence of the Great Glory,
And the children of earth shall tremble and quake;
And ye sinners shall be cursed for ever,
And ye shall have no peace.

[4] Fear ye not, ye souls of the righteous,
And be hopeful ye that have died in righteousness.

[5] And grieve not if your soul into Sheol has descended in grief,
And that in your life your body fared not according to your goodness,
But wait for the day of the judgement of sinners
And for the day of cursing and chastisement.

[6] And yet when ye die the sinners speak over you:
" As we die, so die the righteous,
And what benefit do they reap for their deeds ?

[7] Behold, even as we, so do they die in grief and darkness,
And what have they more than we ?
From henceforth we are equal.

[8] And what will they receive and what will they see for ever ?
Behold, they too have died,
And henceforth for ever shall they see no light."

[9] I tell you, ye sinners, ye are content to eat and drink, and rob and sin, and strip men naked, and [10] acquire wealth and see good days. Have ye seen the righteous how their end falls out, that no manner [11] of violence is found in them till their death ? " Nevertheless they perished and became as though they had not been, and their spirits descended into Sheol in tribulation."

[Chapter 103]

[1] Now, therefore, I swear to you, the righteous, by the glory of the Great and Honoured and [2] Mighty One in dominion, and by His greatness I swear to you.

I know a mystery
And have read the heavenly tablets,
And have seen the holy books,
And have found written therein and inscribed regarding them:

[3] That all goodness and joy and glory are prepared for them,
And written down for the spirits of those who have died in righteousness,
And that manifold good shall be given to you in recompense for your labours,
And that your lot is abundantly beyond the lot of the living.

[4] And the spirits of you who have died in righteousness shall live and rejoice,
And their spirits shall not perish, nor their memorial from before the face of the Great One
Unto all the generations of the world: wherefore no longer fear their contumely.

5 Woe to you, ye sinners, when ye have died,
If ye die in the wealth of your sins,
And those who are like you say regarding you:
' Blessed are the sinners: they have seen all their days.

[6] And how they have died in prosperity and in wealth,
And have not seen tribulation or murder in

their life;
And they have died in honour,
And judgement has not been executed on them during their life."

7 Know ye, that their souls will be made to descend into Sheol
And they shall be wretched in their great tribulation.

8 And into darkness and chains and a burning flame where there is grievous judgement shall your spirits enter;
And the great judgement shall be for all the generations of the world.
Woe to you, for ye shall have no peace.

9 Say not in regard to the righteous and good who are in life:
" In our troubled days we have toiled laboriously and experienced every trouble,
And met with much evil and been consumed,
And have become few and our spirit small.

10 And we have been destroyed and have not found any to help us even with a word:
We have been tortured [and destroyed], and not hoped to see life from day to day.

11 We hoped to be the head and have become the tail:
We have toiled laboriously and had no satisfaction in our toil;
And we have become the food of the sinners and the unrighteous,
And they have laid their yoke heavily upon us.

12 They have had dominion over us that hated us and smote us;
And to those that hated us we have bowed our necks
But they pitied us not.

13 We desired to get away from them that we might escape and be at rest,
But found no place whereunto we should flee and be safe from them.

14 And are complained to the rulers in our tribulation,
And cried out against those who devoured us,
But they did not attend to our cries

And would not hearken to our voice.

15 And they helped those who robbed us and devoured us and those who made us few; and they concealed their oppression, and they did not remove from us the yoke of those that devoured us and dispersed us and murdered us, and they concealed their murder, and remembered not that they had lifted up their hands against us.

[Chapter 104]

1 I swear unto you, that in heaven the angels remember you for good before the glory of the Great 2 One: and your names are written before the glory of the Great One. Be hopeful; for aforetime ye were put to shame through ill and affliction; but now ye shall shine as the lights of heaven, 3 ye shall shine and ye shall be seen, and the portals of heaven shall be opened to you. And in your cry, cry for judgement, and it shall appear to you; for all your tribulation shall be visited on the 4 rulers, and on all who helped those who plundered you. Be hopeful, and cast not away your hopes for ye shall have great joy as the angels of heaven. What shall ye be obliged to do? Ye shall not have to hide on the day of the great judgement and ye shall not be found as sinners, and the eternal 6 judgement shall be far from you for all the generations of the world. And now fear not, ye righteous, when ye see the sinners growing strong and prospering in their ways: be not companions with them, 7 but keep afar from their violence; for ye shall become companions of the hosts of heaven. And, although ye sinners say: " All our sins shall not be searched out and be written down," nevertheless 8 they shall write down all your sins every day. And now I show unto you that light and darkness, 9 day and night, see all your sins. Be not godless in your hearts, and lie not and alter not the words of uprightness, nor charge with lying the words of the Holy Great One, nor take account of your 10 idols; for all your lying and all your godlessness issue not in righteousness but in great sin. And now I know this mystery, that sinners will alter and pervert the words of righteousness in many ways, and will speak wicked words, and lie, and practice great deceits, and write books concerning 11 their words. But when they write down truthfully all my words in their languages, and do not change or minish ought from my words but write them all down truthfully -all that I first testified 12 concerning them. Then, I know another mystery, that books will be given to the righteous and the 13 wise to become a cause of joy and uprightness and much wisdom. And to them shall the books be given, and they shall believe in them and rejoice over them, and then shall all the righteous who have learnt therefrom all the paths of uprightness be recompensed.'

[Chapter 105]

1 In those days the Lord bade (them) to summon and testify to the children of earth concerning their wisdom: Show (it) unto them; for ye are their guides, and a recompense over the whole earth. 2 For I and My son will be united with them for ever in the paths of uprightness in their lives; and ye shall have peace: rejoice, ye children of uprightness. Amen.

Fragment of the Book of Noah

[Chapter 106]

1 And after some days my son Methuselah took a wife for his son Lamech, and she became 2 pregnant by him and bore a son. And his body was white as snow and red as the blooming of a rose, and the hair of his head and his long locks were white as wool, and his eyes beautiful. And when he opened his eyes, he lighted up the whole house like the sun, and the whole house 3 was very bright. And thereupon

he arose in the hands of the midwife, opened his mouth, and conversed with the Lord of righteousness. 4 And his father Lamech was afraid of him and 5 fled, and came to his father Methuselah. And he said unto him: ' I have begotten a strange son, diverse from and unlike man, and resembling the sons of the God of heaven; and his nature is different and he is not like us, and his eyes are as the rays of the sun, and his 6 countenance is glorious. And it seems to me that he is not sprung from me but from the angels, and I fear that in his days a wonder may be 7 wrought on the earth. And now, my father, I am here to petition thee and implore thee that thou mayest go to Enoch, our father, and learn from him the truth, for his dwelling-place is 8 amongst the angels.' And when Methuselah heard the words of his son, he came to me to the ends of the earth; for he had heard that 1 was there, and he cried aloud, and I heard his voice and I came to him. And 1 said unto him: ' Behold, here am I, my son, wherefore hast 9 thou come to me ? ' And he answered and said: ' Because of a great cause of anxiety have I come to thee, and because of a disturbing vision 10 have I approached. And now, my father, hear me: unto Lamech my son there hath been born a son, the like of whom there is none, and his nature is not like man's nature, and the colour of his body is whiter than snow and redder than the bloom of a rose, and the hair of his head is whiter than white wool, and his eyes are like the rays of the sun, and he opened his eyes and 11 thereupon lighted up the whole house. And he arose in the hands of the midwife, and opened 12 his mouth and blessed the Lord of heaven. And his father Lamech became afraid and fled to me, and did not believe that he was sprung from him, but that he was in the likeness of the angels of heaven; and behold I have come to thee that thou mayest make known to me the truth.' And I, Enoch, answered and said unto him: 'The Lord will do a new thing on the earth, and this I have already seen in a vision, and make known to thee that in the generation of my father Jared some of the angels of heaven transgressed the word of the Lord. And behold they commit sin and transgress the law, and have united themselves with women and commit sin with them, and have married some of them, and have begot children by them. And they shall produce on the earth giants not according to the spirit, but according to the flesh, and there shall be a great punishment on the earth, and the earth shall be cleansed from all impurity. Yea, there shall come a great destruction over the whole earth, and there shall be a deluge and 16 a great destruction for one year. And this son who has been born unto you shall be left on the earth, and his three children shall be saved with him: when all mankind that are on the earth 18 shall die [he and his sons shall be saved]. And now make known to thy son Lamech that he who has been born is in truth his son, and call his name Noah; for he shall be left to you, and he and his sons shall be saved from the destruction, which shall come upon the earth on account of all the sin and all the unrighteousness, which shall be consummated on the earth in his days. And after that there shall be still more unrighteousness than that which was first consummated on the earth; for I know the mysteries of the holy ones; for He, the Lord, has showed me and informed me, and I have read (them) in the heavenly tablets.

[Chapter 107]

1 And I saw written on them that generation upon generation shall transgress, till a generation of righteousness arises, and transgression is destroyed and sin passes away from the earth, and all 2 manner of good comes upon it. And now, my son, go and make known to thy son Lamech that this 3 son, which has been born, is in truth his son, and that (this) is no lie.' And when Methuselah had heard the words of his father Enoch-for he had shown to him everything in secret-he returned and showed (them) to him and called the name of that son Noah; for he will comfort the earth after all the destruction.

[Chapter 108]

1 Another book which Enoch wrote for his son Methuselah and for those who will come after him, 2 and keep the law in the last days. Ye who have done good shall wait for those days till an end is made of those who work evil; and an end of the might of the transgressors. And wait ye indeed till sin has passed away, for their names shall be blotted out of the book of life and out of the holy books, and their seed shall be destroyed for ever, and their spirits shall be slain, and they shall cry and make lamentation in a place that is a chaotic wilderness, and in the fire shall they burn; for there is no earth there. And I saw there something like an invisible cloud; for by reason of its depth I could not look over, and I saw a flame of fire blazing brightly, and things like shining 5 mountains circling and sweeping to and fro. And I asked one of the holy angels who was with me and said unto him: ' What is this shining thing? for it is not a heaven but only the flame of a blazing 6 fire, and the voice of weeping and crying and lamentation and strong pain.' And he said unto me: ' This place which thou seest-here are cast the spirits of sinners and blasphemers, and of those who work wickedness, and of those who pervert everything that the Lord hath spoken through the mouth 7 of the prophets-(even) the things that shall be. For some of them are written and inscribed above in the heaven, in order that the angels may read them and know that which shall befall the sinners, and the spirits of the humble, and of those who have afflicted their bodies, and been recompensed 8 by God; and of those who have been put to shame by wicked men: Who love God and loved neither gold nor silver nor any of the good things which are in the world, but gave over their bodies to torture. Who, since they came into being, longed not after earthly food, but regarded everything as a passing breath, and lived accordingly, and the Lord tried them much, and their spirits were 10 found pure so that they should bless His name. And all the blessings destined for them I have recounted in the books. And he hath assigned them their recompense, because they have been found to be such as loved heaven more than their life in the world, and though they were trodden under foot of wicked men, and experienced abuse and reviling from them and were put to shame, 11 yet they blessed Me. And now I will summon the spirits of the good who belong to the generation of light, and I will transform those who were born in darkness, who in the flesh were not recompensed 12 with such honour as their faithfulness deserved. And I will bring forth in shining light those who 13 have loved My holy name, and I will seat each on the throne of his honour. And they shall be resplendent for times without number; for righteousness is the judgement of God; for to the faithful 14 He will give faithfulness in the habitation of upright paths. And they shall see those who were , 15 born in darkness led into darkness, while the righteous shall be resplendent. And the sinners shall cry aloud and see them resplendent, and they indeed will go where days and seasons are prescribed for them.'

THE BOOK OF JUBILEES

Moses receives the tables of the law and instruction on past and future history which he is to inscribe in a book, 1-4. Apostasy of Israel, 5-9. Captivity of Israel and Judah, 10-13. Return of Judah and rebuilding of the temple, 15-18. Moses' prayer for Israel, 19-21. God's promise to redeem and dwell with them, 22-5, 28. Moses bidden to write down the future history of the world (the Book of Jubilees?), 26. And an angel to write down the law, 27. This angel takes the heavenly chronological tablets to dictate therefrom to Moses, 29.

THIS is the history of the division of the days of the law and of the testimony, of the events of the years, of their (year) weeks, of their Jubilees throughout all the years of the world, as the Lord spake to Moses on Mount Sinai when he went up to receive the tables of the law and of the commandment, according to the voice of God as he said unto him, 'Go up to the top of the Mount.'

[Chapter 1]

1. And it came to pass in the first year of the exodus of the children of Israel out of Egypt, in the third month, on the sixteenth day of the month, [2450 Anno Mundi] that God spake to Moses, saying: 'Come up to Me on the Mount, and I will give thee two tables of stone of the law and of the commandment, which I have written, that thou mayst teach them.'

2. And Moses went up into the mount of God, and the glory of the Lord abode on Mount Sinai, and a cloud overshadowed it six days.

3. And He called to Moses on the seventh day out of the midst of the cloud, and the appearance of the glory of the Lord was like a flaming fire on the top of the mount.

4. And Moses was on the Mount forty days and forty nights, and God taught him the earlier and the later history of the division of all the days of the law and of the testimony.

5. And He said: 'Incline thine heart to every word which I shall speak to thee on this mount, and write them in a book in order that their generations may see how I have not forsaken them for all the evil which they have wrought in transgressing the covenant which I establish between Me and thee for their generations this day on Mount Sinai.

6. And thus it will come to pass when all these things come upon them, that they will recognise that I am more righteous than they in all their judgments and in all their actions, and they will recognise that I have been truly with them.

7. And do thou write for thyself all these words which I declare unto, thee this day, for I know their rebellion and their stiff neck, before I bring them into the land of which I sware to their fathers, to Abraham and to Isaac and to Jacob, saying: ' Unto your seed will I give a land flowing with milk and honey.

8. And they will eat and be satisfied, and they will turn to strange gods, to (gods) which cannot deliver them from aught of their tribulation: and this witness shall be heard for a witness against them. For they will forget all My commandments, (even) all that I command them, and they will walk after the Gentiles, and after their uncleanness, and after their shame, and will serve their gods, and these will prove unto them an offence and a tribulation and an affliction and a snare.

9. And many will perish and they will be taken captive, and will fall into the hands of the enemy, because they have forsaken My ordinances and My commandments, and the festivals of My covenant, and My sabbaths, and My holy place which I have hallowed for Myself in their midst, and My tabernacle, and My sanctuary, which I have hallowed for Myself in the midst of the land, that I should set my name upon it, and that it should dwell (there).

10. And they will make to themselves high places and groves and graven images, and they will worship, each his own (graven image), so as to go astray, and they will sacrifice their children to demons, and to all the works of the error of their hearts.

11. And I will send witnesses unto them, that I may witness against them, but they will not hear, and will slay the witnesses also, and they will persecute those who seek the law, and they will abrogate and change everything so as to work evil before My eyes.

12. And I will hide My face from them, and I will deliver them into the hand of the Gentiles for captivity, and for a prey, and for devouring, and I will remove them from the midst of the land, and I will scatter them amongst the Gentiles.

13. And they will forget all My law and all My commandments and all My judgments, and will go astray as to new moons, and sabbaths, and festivals, and jubilees, and ordinances.

14. And after this they will turn to Me from amongst the Gentiles with all their heart and with all their soul and with all their strength, and I will gather them from amongst all the Gentiles, and they will seek me, so that I shall be found of them, when they seek me with all their heart and with all their soul.

15. And I will disclose to them abounding peace with righteousness, and I will remove them the plant of uprightness, with all My heart and with all My soul, and they shall be for a blessing and not for a curse, and they shall be the head and not the tail.

16. And I will build My sanctuary in their midst, and I will dwell with them, and I will be their God and they shall be My people in truth and righteousness.

17. And I will not forsake them nor fail them; for I am the Lord their God.'

18. And Moses fell on his face and prayed and said, 'O Lord my God, do not forsake Thy people and Thy inheritance, so that they should wander in the error of their hearts, and do not deliver them into the hands of their enemies, the Gentiles, lest they should rule over them and cause them to sin against Thee.

19. Let thy mercy, O Lord, be lifted up upon Thy people, and create in them an upright spirit, and let not the spirit of Beliar rule over them to accuse them before Thee, and to ensnare them from all the paths of righteousness, so that they may perish from before Thy face.

20. But they are Thy people and Thy inheritance, which thou hast delivered with thy great power

from the hands of the Egyptians: create in them a clean heart and a holy spirit, and let them not be ensnared in their sins from henceforth until eternity.'

21. And the Lord said unto Moses: 'I know their contrariness and their thoughts and their stiffneckedness, and they will not be obedient till they confess their own sin and the sin of their fathers.

22. And after this they will turn to Me in all uprightness and with all (their) heart and with all (their) soul, and I will circumcise the foreskin of their heart and the foreskin of the heart of their seed, and I will create in them a holy spirit, and I will cleanse them so that they shall not turn away from Me from that day unto eternity.

23. And their souls will cleave to Me and to all My commandments, and they will fulfil My commandments, and I will be their Father and they shall be My children.

24. And they all shall be called children of the living God, and every angel and every spirit shall know, yea, they shall know that these are My children, and that I am their Father in uprightness and righteousness, and that I love them.

25. And do thou write down for thyself all these words which I declare unto thee on this mountain, the first and the last, which shall come to pass in all the divisions of the days in the law and in the testimony and in the weeks and the jubilees unto eternity, until I descend and dwell with them throughout eternity.'

26. And He said to the angel of the presence: Write for Moses from the beginning of creation till My sanctuary has been built among them for all eternity.

27. And the Lord will appear to the eyes of all, and all shall know that I am the God of Israel and the Father of all the children of Jacob, and King on Mount Zion for all eternity. And Zion and Jerusalem shall be holy.'

28. And the angel of the presence who went before the camp of Israel took the tables of the divisions of the years -from the time of the creation- of the law and of the testimony of the weeks of the jubilees, according to the individual years, according to all the number of the jubilees [according, to the individual years], from the day of the [new] creation when the heavens and the earth shall be renewed and all their creation according to the powers of the heaven, and according to all the creation of the earth, until the sanctuary of the Lord shall be made in Jerusalem on Mount Zion, and all the luminaries be renewed for healing and for peace and for blessing for all the elect of Israel, and that thus it may be from that day and unto all the days of the earth.

[Chapter 2]

1 And the angel of the presence spake to Moses according to the word of the Lord, saying: Write the complete history of the creation, how in six days the Lord God finished all His works and all that He created, and kept Sabbath on the seventh day and hallowed it for all ages, and appointed it as a sign for all His works.

2 For on the first day He created the heavens which are above and the earth and the waters and all the spirits which serve before him -the angels of the presence, and the angels of sanctification, and the angels [of the spirit of fire and the angels] of the spirit of the winds, and the angels of the spirit of the clouds, and of darkness, and of snow and of hail and of hoar frost, and the angels of the voices and of the thunder and of the lightning, and the angels of the spirits of cold and of heat, and of winter and of spring and of autumn and of summer and of all the spirits of his creatures which are in the heavens and on the earth, (He created) the abysses and the darkness, eventide <and night>, and the light, dawn and day, which He hath prepared in the knowledge of his heart.

3 And thereupon we saw His works, and praised Him, and lauded before Him on account of all His works; for seven great works did He create on the first day.

4 And on the second day He created the firmament in the midst of the waters, and the waters were divided on that day -half of them went up above and half of them went down below the firmament (that was) in the midst over the face of the whole earth. And this was the only work (God) created on the second day.

5 And on the third day He commanded the waters to pass from off the face of the whole earth into one place, and the dry land to appear.

6 And the waters did so as He commanded them, and they retired from off the face of the earth into one place outside of this firmament, and the dry land appeared.

7 And on that day He created for them all the seas according to their separate gathering-places, and all the rivers, and the gatherings of the waters in the mountains and on all the earth, and all the lakes, and all the dew of the earth, and the seed which is sown, and all sprouting things, and fruit-bearing trees, and trees of the wood, and the garden of Eden, in Eden and all *plants after their kind.*

8 These four great works God created on the third day. And on the fourth day He created the sun and the moon and the stars, and set them in the firmament of the heaven, to give light upon all the earth, and to rule over the day and the night, and divide the light from the darkness.

9 And God appointed the sun to be a great sign on the earth for days and for sabbaths and for months and for feasts and for years and for sabbaths of years and for jubilees and for all seasons of the years.

10 And it divideth the light from the darkness [and] for prosperity, that all things may prosper which shoot and grow on the earth.

11 These three kinds He made on the fourth day. And on the fifth day He created great sea monsters in the depths of the waters, for these were the first things of flesh that were created by his hands, the fish and everything that moves in the waters, and everything that flies, the birds and all their kind.

12 And the sun rose above them to prosper (them), and above everything that was on the earth,

everything that shoots out of the earth, and all fruit-bearing trees, and all flesh.

13 These three kinds He created on the fifth day. And on the sixth day He created all the animals of the earth, and all cattle, and everything that moves on the earth.

14 And after all this He created man, a man and a woman created He them, and gave him dominion over all that is upon the earth, and in the seas, and over everything that flies, and over beasts and over cattle, and over everything that moves on the earth, and over the whole earth, and over all this He gave him dominion.

15 And these four kinds He created on the sixth day. And there were altogether two and twenty kinds.

16 And He finished all his work on the sixth day -all that is in the heavens and on the earth, and in the seas and in the abysses, and in the light and in the darkness, and in everything.

17 And He gave us a great sign, the Sabbath day, that we should work six days, but keep Sabbath on the seventh day from all work.

18 And all the angels of the presence, and all the angels of sanctification, these two great classes -He hath bidden us to keep the Sabbath with Him in heaven and on earth.

19 And He said unto us: 'Behold, I will separate unto Myself a people from among all the peoples, and these shall keep the Sabbath day, and I will sanctify them unto Myself as My people, and will bless them; as I have sanctified the Sabbath day and do sanctify (it) unto Myself, even so will I bless them, and they shall be My people and I will be their God.

20 And I have chosen the seed of Jacob from amongst all that I have seen, and have written him down as My first-born son,and have sanctified him unto Myself for ever and ever; and I will teach them the Sabbath day, that they may keep Sabbath thereon from all work.'

21 And thus He created therein a sign in accordance with which they should keep Sabbath with us on the seventh day, to eat and to drink, and to bless Him who has created all things as He has blessed and sanctified unto Himself a peculiar people above all peoples, and that they should keep Sabbath together with us.

22 And He caused His commands to ascend as a sweet savour acceptable before Him all the days . . .

23 There (were) two and twenty heads of mankind from Adam to Jacob, and two and twenty kinds of work were made until the seventh day; this is blessed and holy; and the former also is blessed and holy; and this one serves with that one for sanctification and blessing.

24 And to this (Jacob and his seed) it was granted that they should always be the blessed and holy ones of the first testimony and law, even as He had sanctified and blessed the Sabbath day on the seventh day.

25 He created heaven and earth and everything that He created in six days, and God made the seventh day holy, for all His works; therefore He commanded on its behalf that, whoever does any work thereon shall die, and that he who defiles it

shall surely die.

26 Wherefore do thou command the children of Israel to observe this day that they may keep it holy and not do thereon any work, and not to defile it, as it is holier than all other days.

27 And whoever profanes it shall surely die, and whoever does thereon any work shall surely die eternally, that the children of Israel may observe this day throughout their generations, and not be rooted out of the land; for it is a holy day and a blessed day.

28 And every one who observes it and keeps Sabbath thereon from all his work, will be holy and blessed throughout all days like unto us.

29 Declare and say to the children of Israel the law of this day both that they should keep Sabbath thereon, and that they should not forsake it in the error of their hearts; (and) that it is not lawful to do any work thereon which is unseemly, to do thereon their own pleasure, and that they should not prepare thereon anything to be eaten or drunk, and (that it is not lawful) to draw water, or bring in or take out thereon through their gates any burden, which they had not prepared for themselves on the sixth day in their dwellings.

30 And they shall not bring in nor take out from house to house on that day; for that day is more holy and blessed than any jubilee day of the jubilees; on this we kept Sabbath in the heavens before it was made known to any flesh to keep Sabbath thereon on the earth.

31 And the Creator of all things blessed it, but he did not sanctify all peoples and nations to keep Sabbath thereon, but Israel alone: them alone he permitted to eat and drink and to keep Sabbath thereon on the earth.

32 And the Creator of all things blessed this day which He had created for blessing and holiness and glory above all days.

33 This law and testimony was given to the children of Israel as a law for ever unto their generations.

[Chapter 3]

1 And on the six days of the second week we brought, according to the word of God, unto Adam all the beasts, and all the cattle, and all the birds, and everything that moves on the earth, and everything that moves in the water, according to their kinds, and according to their types: the beasts on the first day; the cattle on the second day; the birds on the third day; and all that which moves on the earth on the fourth day; and that which moves in the water on the fifth day.

2 And Adam named them all by their respective names, and as he called them, so was their name.

3 And on these five days Adam saw all these, male and female, according to every kind that was on the earth, but he was alone and found no helpmeet for him.

4 And the Lord said unto us: 'It is not good that the man should be alone: let us make a helpmeet for him.'

5 And the Lord our God caused a deep sleep to fall upon him, and he slept, and He took for the woman one rib from amongst his ribs, and this rib

was the origin of the woman from amongst his ribs, and He built up the flesh in its stead, and built the woman.

6   And He awaked Adam out of his sleep and on awaking he rose on the sixth day, and He brought her to him, and he knew her, and said unto her: "This is now bone of my bones and flesh of my flesh; she shall be called [my] wife; because she was taken from her husband.'

7   Therefore shall man and wife be one and therefore shall a man leave his father and his mother, and cleave unto his wife, and they shall be one flesh.

8   In the first week was Adam created, and the rib - his wife: in the second week He showed her unto him: and for this reason the commandment was given to keep in their defilement, for a male seven days, and for a female twice seven days.

9   And after Adam had completed forty days in the land where he had been created, we brought him into the garden of Eden to till and keep it, but his wife they brought in on the eightieth day, and after this she entered into the garden of Eden.

10 And for this reason the commandment is written on the heavenly tablets in regard to her that gives birth: 'if she bears a male, she shall remain in her uncleanness seven days according to the first week of days, and thirty and three days shall she remain in the blood of her purifying, and she shall not touch any hallowed thing, nor enter into the sanctuary, until she accomplishes these days which (are enjoined) in the case of a male child.

11 But in the case of a female child she shall remain in her uncleanness two weeks of days, according to the first two weeks, and sixty-six days in the blood of her purification, and they will be in all eighty days.'

12 And when she had completed these eighty days we brought her into the garden of Eden, for it is holier than all the earth besides and every tree that is planted in it is holy.

13 Therefore, there was ordained regarding her who bears a male or a female child the statute of those days that she should touch no hallowed thing, nor enter into the sanctuary until these days for the male or female child are accomplished.

14 This is the law and testimony which was written down for Israel, in order that they should observe (it) all the days.

15 And in the first week of the first jubilee, [1-7 A.M.] Adam and his wife were in the garden of Eden for seven years tilling and keeping it, and we gave him work and we instructed him to do everything that is suitable for tillage.

16 And he tilled (the garden), and was naked and knew it not, and was not ashamed, and he protected the garden from the birds and beasts and cattle, and gathered its fruit, and eat, and put aside the residue for himself and for his wife [and put aside that which was being kept].

17 And after the completion of the seven years, which he had completed there, seven years exactly, [8 A.M.] and in the second month, on the seventeenth day (of the month), the serpent came and approached the woman, and the serpent said to the woman, 'Hath God commanded you, saying, Ye shall not eat of every tree of the garden?'

18 And she said to it, 'Of all the fruit of the trees of the garden God hath said unto us, Eat; but of the fruit of the tree which is in the midst of the garden God hath said unto us, Ye shall not eat thereof, neither shall ye touch it, lest ye die.'

19 And the serpent said unto the woman, 'Ye shall not surely die: for God doth know that on the day ye shall eat thereof, your eyes will be opened, and ye will be as gods, and ye will know good and evil.

20 And the woman saw the tree that it was agreeable and pleasant to the eye, and that its fruit was good for food, and she took thereof and eat.

21 And when she had first covered her shame with figleaves, she gave thereof to Adam and he eat, and his eyes were opened, and he saw that he was naked.

22 And he took figleaves and sewed (them) together, and made an apron for himself, and ,covered his shame.

23 And God cursed the serpent, and was wroth with it for ever . . .

24 And He was wroth with the woman, because she harkened to the voice of the serpent, and did eat; and He said unto her: 'I will greatly multiply thy sorrow and thy pains: in sorrow thou shalt bring forth children, and thy return shall be unto thy husband, and he will rule over thee.'

25 And to Adam also he said, ' Because thou hast harkened unto the voice of thy wife, and hast eaten of the tree of which I commanded thee that thou shouldst not eat thereof, cursed be the ground for thy sake: thorns and thistles shall it bring forth to thee, and thou shalt eat thy bread in the sweat of thy face, till thou returnest to the earth from whence thou wast taken; for earth thou art, and unto earth shalt thou return.'

26 And He made for them coats of skin, and clothed them, and sent them forth from the Garden of Eden.

27 And on that day on which Adam went forth from the Garden, he offered as a sweet savour an offering, frankincense, galbanum, and stacte, and spices in the morning with the rising of the sun from the day when he covered his shame.

28 And on that day was closed the mouth of all beasts, and of cattle, and of birds, and of whatever walks, and of whatever moves, so that they could no longer speak: for they had all spoken one with another with one lip and with one tongue.

29 And He sent out of the Garden of Eden all flesh that was in the Garden of Eden, and all flesh was scattered according to its kinds, and according to its types unto the places which had been created for them.

30 And to Adam alone did He give (the wherewithal) to cover his shame, of all the beasts and cattle.

31 On this account, it is prescribed on the heavenly tablets as touching all those who know the judgment of the law, that they should cover their shame, and should not uncover themselves as the Gentiles uncover themselves.

32 And on the new moon of the fourth month, Adam and his wife went forth from the Garden of Eden, and they dwelt in the land of Elda in the land of their creation.

33 And Adam called the name of his wife Eve.

34 And they had no son till the first jubilee, [8 A.M.] and after this he knew her.

35 Now he tilled the land as he had been instructed in the Garden of Eden.

[Chapter 4]

1 And in the third week in the second jubilee [64-70 A.M.] she gave birth to Cain, and in the fourth [71-77 A.M.] she gave birth to Abel, and in the fifth [78-84 A.M.] she gave birth to her daughter Âwân.

2 And in the first (year) of the third jubilee [99-105 A.M.], Cain slew Abel because (God) accepted the sacrifice of Abel, and did not accept the offering of Cain.

3 And he slew him in the field: and his blood cried from the ground to heaven, complaining because he had slain him.

4 And the Lord reproved Cain because of Abel, because he had slain him, and he made him a fugitive on the earth because of the blood of his brother, and he cursed him upon the earth.

5 And on this account it is written on the heavenly tables, 'Cursed is ,he who smites his neighbour treacherously, and let all who have seen and heard say, So be it; and the man who has seen and not declared (it), let him be accursed as the other.'

6 And for this reason we announce when we come before the Lord our God all the sin which is committed in heaven and on earth, and in light and in darkness, and everywhere.

7 And Adam and his wife mourned for Abel four weeks of years, [99-127 A.M] and in the fourth year of the fifth week [130 A.M.] they became joyful, and Adam knew his wife again, and she bare him a son, and he called his name Seth; for he said 'GOD has raised up a second seed unto us on the earth instead of Abel; for Cain slew him.'

8 And in the sixth week [134-40 A.M.] he begat his daughter Azûrâ.

9 And Cain took Âwân his sister to be his wife and she bare him Enoch at the close of the fourth jubilee. [190-196 A.M.] And in the first year of the first week of the fifth jubilee, [197 A.M.] houses were built on the earth, and Cain built a city, and called its name after the name of his son Enoch.

10 And Adam knew Eve his wife and she bare yet nine sons.

11 And in the fifth week of the fifth jubilee [225-31 A.M.] Seth took Azûrâ his sister to be his wife, and in the fourth (year of the sixth week) [235 A.M.] she bare him Enos.

12 He began to call on the name of the Lord on the earth.

13 And in the seventh jubilee in the third week [309-15 A.M.] Enos took Nôâm his sister to be his wife, and she bare him a son in the third year of the fifth week, and he called his name Kenan.

14 And at the close of the eighth jubilee [325, 386-3992 A.M.] Kenan took Mûalêlêth his sister to be his wife, and she bare him a son in the ninth jubilee, in the first week in the third year of this week, [395 A.M] and he called his name Mahalalel.

15 And in the second week of the tenth jubilee [449-55 A.M.] Mahalalel took unto him to wife DinaH, the daughter of Barakiel the daughter of his father's brother, and she bare him a son in the third week in the sixth year, [461 A.M.] and he called his name Jared, for in his days the angels of the Lord descended on the earth, those who are named the Watchers, that they should instruct the children of men, and that they should do judgment and uprightness on the earth.

16 And in the eleventh jubilee [512-18 A.M.] Jared took to himself a wife, and her name was Baraka, the daughter of Râsûjâl, a daughter of his father's brother, in the fourth week of this jubilee, [522 A.M.] and she bare him a son in the fifth week, in the fourth year of the jubilee, and he called his name Enoch.

17 And he was the first among men that are born on earth who learnt writing and knowledge and wisdom and who wrote down the signs of heaven according to the order of their months in a book, that men might know the seasons of the years according to the order of their separate months.

18 And he was the first to write a testimony and he testified to the sons of men among the generations of the earth, and recounted the weeks of the jubilees, and made known to them the days of the years, and set in order the months and recounted the Sabbaths of the years as we made (them), known to him.

19 And what was and what will be he saw in a vision of his sleep, as it will happen to the children of men throughout their generations until the day of judgment; he saw and understood everything, and wrote his testimony, and placed the testimony on earth for all the children of men and for their generations.

20 And in the twelfth jubilee, [582-88] in the seventh week thereof, he took to himself a wife, and her name was Edna, the daughter of Danel, the daughter of his father's brother, and in the sixth year in this week [587 A.M.] she bare him a son and he called his name Methuselah.

21 And he was moreover with the angels of God these six jubilees of years, and they showed him everything which is on earth and in the heavens, the rule of the sun, and he wrote down everything.

22 And he testified to the Watchers, who had sinned with the daughters of men; for these had begun to unite themselves, so as to be defiled, with the daughters of men, and Enoch testified against (them) all.

23 And he was taken from amongst the children of men, and we conducted him into the Garden of Eden in majesty and honour, and behold there he writes down the condemnation and judgment of the world, and all the wickedness of the children of men.

24 And on account of it (God) brought the waters of the flood upon all the land of Eden; for there he was set as a sign and that he should testify against all the children of men, that he should recount all the deeds of the generations until the day of condemnation.

25 And he burnt the incense of the sanctuary, (even) sweet spices acceptable before the Lord on the Mount.

26 For the Lord has four places on the earth, the Garden of Eden, and the Mount of the East, and this mountain on which thou art this day, Mount Sinai, and Mount Zion (which) will be sanctified in the new creation for a sanctification of the earth; through it will the earth be sanctified from all (its) guilt and its uncleanness through- out the generations of the world.

27 And in the fourteenth jubilee [652 A.M.] Methuselah took unto himself a wife, Edna the daughter of Azrial, the daughter of his father's brother, in the third week, in the first year of this week, [701-7 A.M.] and he begat a son and called his name Lamech.

28 And in the fifteenth jubilee in the third week Lamech took to himself a wife, and her name was Betenos the daughter of Baraki'il, the daughter of his father's brother, and in this week she bare him a son and he called his name Noah, saying, "This one will comfort me for my trouble and all my work, and for the ground which the Lord hath cursed.'

29 And at the close of the nineteenth jubilee, in the seventh week in the sixth year [930 A.M.] thereof, Adam died, and all his sons buried him in the land of his creation, and he was the first to be buried in the earth.

30 And he lacked seventy years of one thousand years; for one thousand years are as one day in the testimony of the heavens and therefore was it written concerning the tree of knowledge: 'On the day that ye eat thereof ye shall die.' For this reason he did not complete the years of this day; for he died during it.

31 At the close of this jubilee Cain was killed after him in the same year; for his house fell upon him and he died in the midst of his house, and he was killed by its stones; for with a stone he had killed Abel, and by a stone was he killed in righteous judgment.

32 For this reason it was ordained on the heavenly tablets: With the instrument with which a man kills his neighbour with the same shall he be killed; after the manner that he wounded him, in like manner shall they deal with him.'

33 And in the twenty-fifth [1205 A.M.] jubilee Noah took to himself a wife, and her name was `Emzârâ, the daughter of Râkê'êl, the daughter of his father's brother, in the first year in the fifth week [1207 A.M.]: and in the third year thereof she bare him Shem, in the fifth year thereof [1209 A.M.] she bare him Ham, and in the first year in the sixth week [1212 A.M.] she bare him Japheth.

[Chapter 5]

1 And it came to pass when the children of men began to multiply on the face of the earth and daughters were born unto them, that the angels of God saw them on a certain year of this jubilee, that they were beautiful to look upon; and they took themselves wives of all whom they chose, and they bare unto them sons and they were giants.

2 And lawlessness increased on the earth and all flesh corrupted its way, alike men and cattle and beasts and birds and everything that walks on the earth -all of them corrupted their ways and their orders, and they began to devour each other, and lawlessness increased on the earth and every imagination of the thoughts of all men (was) thus evil continually.

3 And God looked upon the earth, and behold it was corrupt, and all flesh had corrupted its orders, and all that were upon the earth had wrought all manner of evil before His eyes.

4 And He said that He would destroy man and all flesh upon the face of the earth which He had created.

5 But Noah found grace before the eyes of the Lord.

6 And against the angels whom He had sent upon the earth, He was exceedingly wroth, and He gave commandment to root them out of all their dominion, and He bade us to bind them in the depths of the earth, and behold they are bound in the midst of them, and are (kept) separate.

7 And against their sons went forth a command from before His face that they should be smitten with the sword, and be removed from under heaven.

8 And He said 'My spirit shall not always abide on man; for they also are flesh and their days shall be one hundred and twenty years'.

9 And He sent His sword into their midst that each should slay his neighbour, and they began to slay each other till they all fell by the sword and were destroyed from the earth.

10 And their fathers were witnesses (of their destruction), and after this they were bound in the depths of the earth for ever, until the day of the great condemnation, when judgment is executed on all those who have corrupted their ways and their works before the Lord.

11 And He destroyed all from their places, and there was not left one of them whom He judged not according to all their wickedness.

12 And he made for all his works a new and righteous nature, so that they should not sin in their whole nature for ever, but should be all righteous each in his kind alway.

13 And the judgment of all is ordained and written on the heavenly tablets in righteousness -even (the judgment of) all who depart from the path which is ordained for them to walk in; and if they walk not therein, judgment is written down for every creature and for every kind.

14 And there is nothing in heaven or on earth, or in light or in darkness, or in Sheol or in the depth, or in the place of darkness (which is not judged); and all their judgments are ordained and written and engraved.

15 In regard to all He will judge,the great according to his greatness, and the small according to his smallness, and each according to his way.

16 And He is not one who will regard the person (of any), nor is He one who will receive gifts, if He says that He will execute judgment on each: if one gave everything that is on the earth, He will not regard the gifts or the person (of any), nor accept anything at his hands, for He is a righteous judge.

17 [And of the children of Israel it has been written and ordained: If they turn to him in righteousness

He will forgive all their transgressions and pardon all their sins.

18 It is written and ordained that He will show mercy to all who turn from all their guilt once each year.]

19 And as for all those who corrupted their ways and their thoughts before the flood, no man's person was accepted save that of Noah alone; for his person was accepted in behalf of his sons, whom (God) saved from the waters of the flood on his account; for his heart was righteous in all his ways, according as it was commanded regarding him, and he had not departed from aught that was ordained for him.

20 And the Lord said that he would destroy everything which was upon the earth, both men and cattle, and

21 beasts, and fowls of the air, and that which moveth on the earth. And He commanded Noah to make him an ark, that he might save himself from the waters of the flood.

22 And Noah made the ark in all respects as He commanded him, in the twenty-seventh jubilee of years, in the fifth week in the fifth year (on the new moon of the first month). [1307 A.M.]

23 And he entered in the sixth (year) thereof, [1308 A.M.] in the second month, on the new moon of the second month, till the sixteenth; and he entered, and all that we brought to him, into the ark, and the Lord closed it from without on the seventeenth evening.

24 And the Lord opened seven flood-gates of heaven, And the mouths of the fountains of the great deep, seven mouths in number.

25 And the flood-gates began to pour down water from the heaven forty days and forty nights, And the fountains of the deep also sent up waters, until the whole world was full of water.

26 And the waters increased upon the earth: Fifteen cubits did the waters rise above all the high mountains, And the ark was lift up above the earth, And it moved upon the face of the waters.

27 And the water prevailed on the face of the earth five months -one hundred and fifty days.

28 And the ark went and rested on the top of Lubar, one of the mountains of Ararat.

29 And (on the new moon) in the fourth month the fountains of the great deep were closed and the flood-gates of heaven were restrained; and on the new moon of the seventh month all the mouths of the abysses of the earth were opened, and the water began to descend into the deep below.

30 And on the new moon of the tenth month the tops of the mountains were seen, and on the new moon of the first month the earth became visible.

31 And the waters disappeared from above the earth in the fifth week in the seventh year [1309 A.M.] thereof, and on the seventeenth day in the second month the earth was dry.

32 And on the twenty-seventh thereof he opened the ark, and sent forth from it beasts, and cattle, and birds, and every moving thing.

[Chapter 6]

1 And on the new moon of the third month he went forth from the ark, and built an altar on that mountain.

2 And he made atonement for the earth, and took a kid and made atonement by its blood for all the guilt of the earth; for everything that had been on it had been destroyed, save those that were in the ark with Noah.

3 And he placed the fat thereof on the altar, and he took an ox, and a goat, and a sheep and kids, and salt, and a turtle-dove, and the young of a dove, and placed a burnt sacrifice on the altar, and poured thereon an offering mingled with oil, and sprinkled wine and strewed frankincense over everything, and caused a goodly savour to arise, acceptable before the Lord.

4 And the Lord smelt the goodly savour, and He made a covenant with him that there should not be any more a flood to destroy the earth; that all the days of the earth seed-time and harvest should never cease; cold and heat, and summer and winter, and day and night should not change their order, nor cease for ever.

5 'And you, increase ye and multiply upon the earth, and become many upon it, and be a blessing upon it. The fear of you and the dread of you I will inspire in everything that is on earth and in the sea.

6 And behold I have given unto you all beasts, and all winged things, and everything that moves on the earth, and the fish in the waters, and all things for food; as the green herbs, I have given you all things to eat.

7 But flesh, with the life thereof, with the blood, ye shall not eat; for the life of all flesh is in the blood, lest your blood of your lives be required. At the hand of every man, at the hand of every (beast) will I require the blood of man.

8 Whoso sheddeth man's blood by man shall his blood be shed, for in the image of God made He man.

9 And you, increase ye, and multiply on the earth.'

10 And Noah and his sons swore that they would not eat any blood that was in any flesh, and he made a covenant before the Lord God for ever throughout all the generations of the earth in this month.

11 On this account He spake to thee that thou shouldst make a covenant with the children of Israel in this month upon the mountain with an oath, and that thou shouldst sprinkle blood upon them because of all the words of the covenant, which the Lord made with them for ever.

12 And this testimony is written concerning you that you should observe it continually, so that you should not eat on any day any blood of beasts or birds or cattle during all the days of the earth, and the man who eats the blood of beast or of cattle or of birds during all the days of the earth, he and his seed shall be rooted out of the land.

13 And do thou command the children of Israel to eat no blood, so that their names and their seed may be before the Lord our God continually.

14 And for this law there is no limit of days, for it is for ever. They shall observe it throughout their generations, so that they may continue supplicating on your behalf with blood before the altar; every day and at the time of morning and

evening they shall seek forgiveness on your behalf perpetually before the Lord that they may keep it and not be rooted out.

15 And He gave to Noah and his sons a sign that there should not again be a flood on the earth.

16 He set His bow in the cloud for a sign of the eternal covenant that there should not again be a flood on the earth to destroy it all the days of the earth.

17 For this reason it is ordained and written on the heavenly tablets, that they should celebrate the feast of weeks in this month once a year, to renew the covenant every year.

18 And this whole festival was celebrated in heaven from the day of creation till the days of Noah - twenty-six jubilees and five weeks of years [1309-1659 A.M.]: and Noah and his sons observed it for seven jubilees and one week of years, till the day of Noah's death, and from the day of Noah's death his sons did away with (it) until the days of Abraham, and they eat blood.

19 But Abraham observed it, and Isaac and Jacob and his children observed it up to thy days, and in thy days the children of Israel forgot it until ye celebrated it anew on this mountain.

20 And do thou command the children of Israel to observe this festival in all their generations for a commandment unto them: one day in the year in this month they shall celebrate the festival.

21 For it is the feast of weeks and the feast of first fruits: this feast is twofold and of a double nature: according to what is written and engraven concerning it, celebrate it.

22 For I have written in the book of the first law, in that which I have written for thee, that thou shouldst celebrate it in its season, one day in the year, and I explained to thee its sacrifices that the children of Israel should remember and should celebrate it throughout their generations in this month, one day in every year.

23 And on the new moon of the first month, and on the new moon of the fourth month, and on the new moon of the seventh month, and on the new moon of the tenth month are the days of remembrance, and the days of the seasons in the four divisions of the year. These are written and ordained as a testimony for ever.

24 And Noah ordained them for himself as feasts for the generations for ever, so that they have become thereby a memorial unto him.

25 And on the new moon of the first month he was bidden to make for himself an ark, and on that (day) the earth became dry and he opened (the ark) and saw the earth.

26 And on the new moon of the fourth month the mouths of the depths of the abyss beneath were closed. And on the new moon of the seventh month all the mouths of the abysses of the earth were opened, and the waters began to descend into them.

27 And on the new moon of the tenth month the tops of the mountains were seen, and Noah was glad.

28 And on this account he ordained them for himself as feasts for a memorial for ever, and thus are they ordained.

29 And they placed them on the heavenly tablets, each had thirteen weeks; from one to another (passed) their memorial, from the first to the second, and from the second to the third, and from the third to the fourth.

30 And all the days of the commandment will be two and fifty weeks of days, and (these will make) the entire year complete. Thus it is engraven and ordained on the heavenly tablets.

31 And there is no neglecting (this commandment) for a single year or from year to year.

32 And command thou the children of Israel that they observe the years according to this reckoning-three hundred and sixty-four days, and (these) will constitute a complete year, and they will not disturb its time from its days and from its feasts; for everything will fall out in them according to their testimony, and they will not leave out any day nor disturb any feasts.

33 But if they do neglect and do not observe them according to His commandment, then they will disturb all their seasons and the years will be dislodged from this (order), [and they will disturb the seasons and the years will be dislodged] and they will neglect their ordinances.

34 And all the children of Israel will forget and will not find the path of the years, and will forget the new moons, and seasons, and sabbaths and they will go wrong as to all the order of the years.

35 For I know and from henceforth will I declare it unto thee, and it is not of my own devising; for the book (lies) written before me, and on the heavenly tablets the division of days is ordained, lest they forget the feasts of the covenant and walk according to the feasts of the Gentiles after their error and after their ignorance.

36 For there will be those who will assuredly make observations of the moon -how (it) disturbs the seasons and comes in from year to year ten days too soon.

37 For this reason the years will come upon them when they will disturb (the order), and make an abominable (day) the day of testimony, and an unclean day a feast day, and they will confound all the days, the holy with the unclean, and the unclean day with the holy; for they will go wrong as to the months and sabbaths and feasts and jubilees.

38 For this reason I command and testify to thee that thou mayst testify to them; for after thy death thy children will disturb (them), so that they will not make the year three hundred and sixty-four days only, and for this reason they will go wrong as to the new moons and seasons and sabbaths and festivals, and they will eat all kinds of blood with all kinds of flesh.

[Chapter 7]

1 And in the seventh week in the first year [1317 A.M.] thereof, in this jubilee, Noah planted vines on the mountain on which the ark had rested, named Lubar, one of the Ararat Mountains, and they produced fruit in the fourth year, [1320 A.M.] and he guarded their fruit, and gathered it in this year in the seventh month.

2   And he made wine therefrom and put it into a vessel, and kept it until the fifth year, [1321 A.M.] until the first day, on the new moon of the first month.

3   And he celebrated with joy the day of this feast, and he made a burnt sacrifice unto the Lord, one young ox and one ram, and seven sheep, each a year old, and a kid of the goats, that he might make atonement thereby for himself and his sons.

4   And he prepared the kid first, and placed some of its blood on the flesh that was on the altar which he had made, and all the fat he laid on the altar where he made the burnt sacrifice, and the ox and the ram and the sheep, and he laid all their flesh upon the altar.

5   And he placed all their offerings mingled with oil upon it, and afterwards he sprinkled wine on the fire which he had previously made on the altar, and he placed incense on the altar and caused a sweet savour to ascend acceptable before the Lord his God.

6   And he rejoiced and drank of this wine, he and his children with joy.

7   And it was evening, and he went into his tent, and being drunken he lay down and slept, and was uncovered in his tent as he slept.

8   And Ham saw Noah his father naked, and went forth and told his two brethren without.

9   And Shem took his garment and arose, he and Japheth, and they placed the garment on their shoulders and went backward and covered the shame of their father, and their faces were backward.

10 And Noah awoke from his sleep and knew all that his younger son had done unto him, and he cursed his son and said: 'Cursed be Canaan; an enslaved servant shall he be unto his brethren.'

11 And he blessed Shem, and said: 'Blessed be the Lord God of Shem, and Canaan shall be his servant.

12 God shall enlarge Japheth, and God shall dwell in the dwelling of Shem, and Canaan shall be his servant.'

13 And Ham knew that his father had cursed his younger son, and he was displeased that he had cursed his son. and he parted from his father, he and his sons with him, Cush and Mizraim and Put and Canaan.

14 And he built for himself a city and called its name after the name of his wife Ne'elatama'uk.

15 And Japheth saw it, and became envious of his brother, and he too built for himself a city, and he called its name after the name of his wife 'Adataneses.

16 And Shem dwelt with his father Noah, and he built a city close to his father on the mountain, and he too called its name after the name of his wife Sedeqetelebab.

17 And behold these three cities are near Mount Lubar; Sedeqetelebab fronting the mountain on its east; and Na'eltama'uk on the south; 'Adatan'eses towards the west.

18 And these are the sons of Shem: Elam, and Asshur, and Arpachshad -this (son) was born two years after the flood- and Lud, and Aram.

19 The sons of Japheth: Gomer and Magog and Madai and Javan, Tubal and Meshech and Tiras: these are the sons of Noah.

20 And in the twenty-eighth jubilee [1324-1372 A.M.] Noah began to enjoin upon his sons' sons the ordinances and commandments, and all the judgments that he knew, and he exhorted his sons to observe righteousness, and to cover the shame of their flesh, and to bless their Creator, and honour father and mother, and love their neighbour, and guard their souls from fornication and uncleanness and all iniquity.

21 For owing to these three things came the flood upon the earth, namely, owing to the fornication wherein the Watchers against the law of their ordinances went a whoring after the daughters of men, and took themselves wives of all which they chose: and they made the beginning of uncleanness.

22 And they begat sons the Naphidim, and they were all unlike, and they devoured one another: and the Giants slew the Naphil, and the Naphil slew the Eljo, and the Eljo mankind, and one man another.

23 And every one sold himself to work iniquity and to shed much blood, and the earth was filled with iniquity.

24 And after this they sinned against the beasts and birds, and all that moves and walks on the earth: and much blood was shed on the earth, and every imagination and desire of men imagined vanity and evil continually.

25 And the Lord destroyed everything from off the face of the earth; because of the wickedness of their deeds, and because of the blood which they had shed in the midst of the earth He destroyed everything.

26 'And we were left, I and you, my sons, and everything that entered with us into the ark, and behold I see your works before me that ye do not walk in righteousness: for in the path of destruction ye have begun to walk, and ye are parting one from another, and are envious one of another, and (so it comes) that ye are not in harmony, my sons, each with his brother.

27 For I see, and behold the demons have begun (their) seductions against you and against your children and now I fear on your behalf, that after my death ye will shed the blood of men upon the earth, and that ye, too, will be destroyed from the face of the earth.

28 For whoso sheddeth man's blood, and whoso eateth the blood of any flesh, shall all be destroyed from the earth.

29 And there shall not be left any man that eateth blood, or that sheddeth the blood of man on the earth, Nor shall there be left to him any seed or descendants living under heaven; For into Sheol shall they go, And into the place of condemnation shall they descend, And into the darkness of the deep shall they all be removed by a violent death.

30 There shall be no blood seen upon you of all the blood there shall be all the days in which ye have killed any beasts or cattle or whatever flies upon the earth, and work ye a good work to your souls by covering that which has been shed on the face of the earth.

31 And ye shall not be like him who eats with blood,

but guard yourselves that none may eat blood before you: cover the blood, for thus have I been commanded to testify to you and your children, together with all flesh.

32 And suffer not the soul to be eaten with the flesh, that your blood, which is your life, may not be required at the hand of any flesh that sheds (it) on the earth.

33 For the earth will not be clean from the blood which has been shed upon it; for (only) through the blood of him that shed it will the earth be purified throughout all its generations.

34 And now, my children, harken: work judgment and righteousness that ye maybe planted in righteousness over the face of the whole earth, and your glory lifted up before my God, who saved me from the waters of the flood.

35 And behold, ye will go and build for yourselves cities, and plant in them all the plants that are upon the earth, and moreover all fruit-bearing trees.

36 For three years the fruit of everything that is eaten will not be gathered: and in the fourth year its fruit will be accounted holy [and they will offer the first-fruits], acceptable before the Most High God, who created heaven and earth and all things. Let them offer in abundance the first of the wine and oil (as) first-fruits on the altar of the Lord, who receives it, and what is left let the servants of the house of the Lord eat before the altar which receives (it).

37 And in the fifth year make ye the release so that ye release it in righteousness and uprightness, and ye shall be righteous, and all that you plant shall prosper.

38 For thus did Enoch, the father of your father command Methuselah, his son, and Methuselah his son Lamech, and Lamech commanded me all the things which his fathers commanded him.

39 And I also will give you commandment, my sons, as Enoch commanded his son in the first jubilees: whilst still living, the seventh in his generation, he commanded and testified to his son and to his son's sons until the day of his death.'

[Chapter 8]

1 In the twenty-ninth jubilee, in the first week, [1373 A.M.] in the beginning thereof Arpachshad took to himself a wife and her name was Rasu'eja, the daughter of Susan, the daughter of Elam, and she bare him a son in the third year in this week, [1375 A.M.] and he called his name Kainam.

2 And the son grew, and his father taught him writing, and he went to seek for himself a place where he might seize for himself a city.

3 And he found a writing which former (generations) had carved on the rock, and he read what was thereon, and he transcribed it and sinned owing to it; for it contained the teaching of the Watchers in accordance with which they used to observe the omens of the sun and moon and stars in all the signs of heaven.

4 And he wrote it down and said nothing regarding it; for he was afraid to speak to Noah about it lest he should be angry with him on account of it.

5 And in the thirtieth jubilee, [1429 A.M.] in the second week, in the first year thereof, he took to himself a wife, and her name was Melka, the daughter of Madai, the son of Japheth, and in the fourth year [1432 A.M.] he begat a son, and called his name Shelah; for he said: "Truly I have been sent.'

6 [And in the fourth year he was born], and Shelah grew up and took to himself a wife, and her name was Mu'ak, the daughter of Kesed, his father's brother, in the one and thirtieth jubilee, in the fifth week, in the first year [1499 A.M.] thereof.

7 And she bare him a son in the fifth year [1503 A.M.] thereof, and he called his name Eber: and he took unto himself a wife, and her name was 'Azûrâd, the daughter of Nebrod, in the thirty-second jubilee, in the seventh week, in the third year thereof. [1564 A.M.]

8 And in the sixth year [1567 A.M.] thereof, she bare him son, and he called his name Peleg; for in the days when he was born the children of Noah began to divide the earth amongst themselves: for this reason he called his name Peleg.

9 And they divided (it) secretly amongst themselves, and told it to Noah.

10 And it came to pass in the beginning of the thirty-third jubilee [1569 A.M.] that they divided the earth into three parts, for Shem and Ham and Japheth, according to the inheritance of each, in the first year in the first week, when one of us who had been sent, was with them.

11 And he called his sons, and they drew nigh to him, they and their children, and he divided the earth into the lots, which his three sons were to take in possession, and they reached forth their hands, and took the writing out of the bosom of Noah, their father.

12 And there came forth on the writing as Shem's lot the middle of the earth which he should take as an inheritance for himself and for his sons for the generations of eternity, from the middle of the mountain range of Rafa, from the mouth of the water from the river Tina, and his portion goes towards the west through the midst of this river, and it extends till it reaches the water of the abysses, out of which this river goes forth and pours its waters into the sea Me'at, and this river flows into the great sea. And all that is towards the north is Japheth's, and all that is towards the south belongs to Shem.

13 And it extends till it reaches Karaso: this is in the bosom of the tongue which looks towards the south.

14 And his portion extends along the great sea, and it extends in a straight line till it reaches the west of the tongue which looks towards the south: for this sea is named the tongue of the Egyptian Sea.

15 And it turns from here towards the south towards the mouth of the great sea on the shore of (its) waters, and it extends to the west to 'Afra, and it extends till it reaches the waters of the river Gihon, and to the south of the waters of Gihon, to the banks of this river.

16 And it extends towards the east, till it reaches the Garden of Eden, to the south thereof, [to the south] and from the east of the whole land of

Eden and of the whole east, it turns to the east and proceeds till it reaches the east of the mountain named Rafa, and it descends to the bank of the mouth of the river Tina.

17 This portion came forth by lot for Shem and his sons, that they should possess it for ever unto his generations for evermore.

18 And Noah rejoiced that this portion came forth for Shem and for his sons, and he remembered all that he had spoken with his mouth in prophecy; for he had said: 'Blessed be the Lord God of Shem And may the Lord dwell in the dwelling of Shem.'

19 And he knew that the Garden of Eden is the holy of holies, and the dwelling of the Lord, and Mount Sinai the centre of the desert, and Mount Zion - the centre of the navel of the earth: these three were created as holy places facing each other.

20 And he blessed the God of gods, who had put the word of the Lord into his mouth, and the Lord for evermore.

21 And he knew that a blessed portion and a blessing had come to Shem and his sons unto the generations for ever -the whole land of Eden and the whole land of the Red Sea, and the whole land of the east and India, and on the Red Sea and the mountains thereof, and all the land of Bashan, and all the land of Lebanon and the islands of Kaftur, and all the mountains of Sanir and 'Amana, and the mountains of Asshur in the north, and all the land of Elam, Asshur, and Babel, and Susan and Ma'edai, and all the mountains of Ararat, and all the region beyond the sea, which is beyond the mountains of Asshur towards the north, a blessed and spacious land, and all that is in it is very good.

22 And for Ham came forth the second portion, beyond the Gihon towards the south to the right of the Garden, and it extends towards the south and it extends to all the mountains of fire, and it extends towards the west to the sea of 'Atel and it extends towards the west till it reaches the sea of Ma'uk -that (sea) into which everything which is not destroyed descends.

23 And it goes forth towards the north to the limits of Gadir, and it goes forth to the coast of the waters of the sea to the waters of the great sea till it draws near to the river Gihon, and goes along the river Gihon till it reaches the right of the Garden of Eden.

24 And this is the land which came forth for Ham as the portion which he was to occupy for ever for himself and his sons unto their generations for ever.

25 And for Japheth came forth the third portion beyond the river Tina to the north of the outflow of its waters, and it extends north- easterly to the whole region of Gog, and to all the country east thereof.

26 And it extends northerly to the north, and it extends to the mountains of Qelt towards the north, and towards the sea of Ma'uk, and it goes forth to the east of Gadir as far as the region of the waters of the sea.

27 And it extends until it approaches the west of Fara and it returns towards 'Aferag, and it extends easterly to the waters of the sea of Me'at.

28 And it extends to the region of the river Tina in a north-easterly direction until it approaches the boundary of its waters towards the mountain Rafa, and it turns round towards the north.

29 This is the land which came forth for Japheth and his sons as the portion of his inheritance which he should possess for himself and his sons, for their generations for ever; five great islands, and a great land in the north.

30 But it is cold, and the land of Ham is hot, and the land of Shem is neither hot nor cold, but it is of blended cold and heat.

[Chapter 9]

1 And Ham divided amongst his sons, and the first portion came forth for Cush towards the east, and to the west of him for Mizraim, and to the west of him for Put, and to the west of him [and to the west thereof] on the sea for Canaan.

2 And Shem also divided amongst his sons, and the first portion came forth for Ham and his sons, to the east of the river Tigris till it approaches the east, the whole land of India, and on the Red Sea on its coast, and the waters of Dedan, and all the mountains of Mebri and Ela, and all the land of Susan and all that is on the side of Pharnak to the Red Sea and the river Tina.

3 And for Asshur came forth the second Portion, all the land of Asshur and Nineveh and Shinar and to the border of India, and it ascends and skirts the river.

4 And for Arpachshad came forth the third portion, all the land of the region of the Chaldees to the east of the Euphrates, bordering on the Red Sea, and all the waters of the desert close to the tongue of the sea which looks towards Egypt, all the land of Lebanon and Sanir and 'Amana to the border of the Euphrates.

5 And for Aram there came forth the fourth portion, all the land of Mesopotamia between the Tigris and the Euphrates to the north of the Chaldees to the border of the mountains of Asshur and the land of 'Arara.

6 And there came forth for Lud the fifth portion, the mountains of Asshur and all appertaining to them till it reaches the Great Sea, and till it reaches the east of Asshur his brother.

7 And Japheth also divided the land of his inheritance amongst his sons.

8 And the first portion came forth for Gomer to the east from the north side to the river Tina; and in the north there came forth for Magog all the inner portions of the north until it reaches to the sea of Me'at.

9 And for Madai came forth as his portion that he should posses from the west of his two brothers to the islands, and to the coasts of the islands.

10 And for Javan came forth the fourth portion every island and the islands which are towards the border of Lud.

11 And for Tubal there came forth the fifth portion in the midst of the tongue which approaches towards the border of the portion of Lud to the second tongue, to the region beyond the second tongue unto the third tongue.

12 And for Meshech came forth the sixth portion, all

the region beyond the third tongue till it approaches the east of Gadir.

13 And for Tiras there came forth the seventh portion, four great islands in the midst of the sea, which reach to the portion of Ham [and the islands of Kamaturi came out by lot for the sons of Arpachshad as his inheritance].

14 And thus the sons of Noah divided unto their sons in the presence of Noah their father, and he bound them all by an oath, imprecating a curse on every one that sought to seize the portion which had not fallen (to him) by his lot.

15 And they all said, 'So be it; so be it ' for themselves and their sons for ever throughout their generations till the day of judgment, on which the Lord God shall judge them with a sword and with fire for all the unclean wickedness of their errors, wherewith they have filled the earth with transgression and uncleanness and fornication and sin.

[Chapter 10]

1 And in the third week of this jubilee the unclean demons began to lead astray the children of the sons of Noah, and to make to err and destroy them.

2 And the sons of Noah came to Noah their father, and they told him concerning the demons which were leading astray and blinding and slaying his sons' sons.

3 And he prayed before the Lord his God, and said:'God of the spirits of all flesh, who hast shown mercy unto me And hast saved me and my sons from the waters of the flood, And hast not caused me to perish as Thou didst the sons of perdition; For Thy grace has been great towards me, And great has been Thy mercy to my soul; Let Thy grace be lift up upon my sons, And let not wicked spirits rule over them Lest they should destroy them from the earth.

4 But do Thou bless me and my sons, that we may increase and Multiply and replenish the earth.

5 And Thou knowest how Thy Watchers, the fathers of these spirits, acted in my day: and as for these spirits which are living, imprison them and hold them fast in the place of condemnation, and let them not bring destruction on the sons of thy servant, my God; for these are malignant, and created in order to destroy.

6 And let them not rule over the spirits of the living; for Thou alone canst exercise dominion over them. And let them not have power over the sons of the righteous from henceforth and for evermore.'

7 And the Lord our God bade us to bind all.

8 And the chief of the spirits, Mastêmâ, came and said: 'Lord, Creator, let some of them remain before me, and let them harken to my voice, and do all that I shall say unto them; for if some of them are not left to me, I shall not be able to execute the power of my will on the sons of men; for these are for corruption and leading astray before my judgment, for great is the wickedness of the sons of men.'

9 And He said: Let the tenth part of them remain before him, and let nine parts descend into the place of condemnation.'

10 And one of us He commanded that we should teach Noah all their medicines; for He knew that they would not walk in uprightness, nor strive in righteousness.

11 And we did according to all His words: all the malignant evil ones we bound in the place of condemnation and a tenth part of them we left that they might be subject before Satan on the earth.

12 And we explained to Noah all the medicines of their diseases, together with their seductions, how he might heal them with herbs of the earth.

13 And Noah wrote down all things in a book as we instructed him concerning every kind of medicine. Thus the evil spirits were precluded from (hurting) the sons of Noah.

14 And he gave all that he had written to Shem, his eldest son; for he loved him exceedingly above all his sons.

15 And Noah slept with his fathers, and was buried on Mount Lubar in the land of Ararat.

16 Nine hundred and fifty years he completed in his life, nineteen jubilees and two weeks and five years. [1659 A.M.]

17 And in his life on earth he excelled the children of men save Enoch because of the righteousness, wherein he was perfect. For Enoch's office was ordained for a testimony to the generations of the world, so that he should recount all the deeds of generation unto generation, till the day of judgment.

18 And in the three and thirtieth jubilee, in the first year in the second week, Peleg took to himself a wife, whose name was Lomna the daughter of Sina'ar, and she bare him a son in the fourth year of this week, and he called his name Reu; for he said: 'Behold the children of men have become evil through the wicked purpose of building for themselves a city and a tower in the land of Shinar.'

19 For they departed from the land of Ararat eastward to Shinar; for in his days they built the city and the tower, saying, 'Go to, let us ascend thereby into heaven.'

20 And they began to build, and in the fourth week they made brick with fire, and the bricks served them for stone, and the clay with which they cemented them together was asphalt which comes out of the sea, and out of the fountains of water in the land of Shinar.

21 And they built it: forty and three years [1645-1688 A.M.] were they building it; its breadth was 203 bricks, and the height (of a brick) was the third of one; its height amounted to 5433 cubits and 2 palms, and (the extent of one wall was) thirteen stades (and of the other thirty stades).

22 And the Lord our God said unto us: Behold, they are one people, and (this) they begin to do, and now nothing will be withholden from them. Go to, let us go down and confound their language, that they may not understand one another's speech, and they may be dispersed into cities and nations, and one purpose will no longer abide with

23 And the Lord descended, and we descended with him to see the city and the tower which the children of men had built.

24 And he confounded their language, and they no longer understood one another's speech, and they ceased then to build the city and the tower.

25 For this reason the whole land of Shinar is called Babel, because the Lord did there confound all the language of the children of men, and from thence they were dispersed into their cities, each according to his language and his nation.

26 And the Lord sent a mighty wind against the tower and overthrew it upon the earth, and behold it was between Asshur and Babylon in the land of Shinar, and they called its name 'Overthrow'.

27 In the fourth week in the first year [1688 A.M.] in the beginning thereof in the four and thirtieth jubilee, were they dispersed from the land of Shinar.

28 And Ham and his sons went into the land which he was to occupy, which he acquired as his portion in the land of the south.

29 And Canaan saw the land of Lebanon to the river of Egypt, that it was very good, and he went not into the land of his inheritance to the west (that is to) the sea, and he dwelt in the land of Lebanon, eastward and westward from the border of Jordan and from the border of the sea.

30 And Ham, his father, and Cush and Mizraim his brothers said unto him: 'Thou hast settled in a land which is not thine, and which did not fall to us by lot: do not do so; for if thou dost do so, thou and thy sons will fall in the land and (be) accursed through sedition; for by sedition ye have settled, and by sedition will thy children fall, and thou shalt be rooted out for ever.

31 Dwell not in the dwelling of Shem; for to Shem and to his sons did it come by their lot.

32 Cursed art thou, and cursed shalt thou be beyond all the sons of Noah, by the curse by which we bound ourselves by an oath in the presence of the holy judge, and in the presence of Noah our father.'

33 But he did not harken unto them, and dwelt in the land of Lebanon from Hamath to the entering of Egypt, he and his sons until this day.

34 And for this reason that land is named Canaan.

35 And Japheth and his sons went towards the sea and dwelt in the land of their portion, and Madai saw the land of the sea and it did not please him, and he begged a (portion) from Ham and Asshur and Arpachshad, his wife's brother, and he dwelt in the land of Media, near to his wife's brother until this day.

36 And he called his dwelling-place, and the dwelling-place of his sons, Media, after the name of their father Madai.

[Chapter 11]

1 And in the thirty-fifth jubilee, in the third week, in the first year [1681 A.M.] thereof, Reu took to himself a wife, and her name was 'Ôrâ, the daughter of 'Ûr, the son of Kesed, and she bare him a son, and he called his name Sêrôh, in the seventh year of this week in this jubilee. [1687 A.M.]

2 And the sons of Noah began to war on each other, to take captive and to slay each other, and to shed the blood of men on the earth, and to eat blood, and to build strong cities, and walls, and towers, and individuals (began) to exalt themselves above the nation, and to found the beginnings of kingdoms, and to go to war people against people, and nation against nation, and city against city, and all (began) to do evil, and to acquire arms, and to teach their sons war, and they began to capture cities, and to sell male and female slaves.

3 And 'Ûr, the son of Kesed, built the city of 'Ara of the Chaldees, and called its name after his own name and the name of his father. And they made for themselves molten images, and they worshipped each the idol, the molten image which they had made for themselves, and they began to make graven images and unclean simulacra, and malignant spirits assisted and seduced (them) into committing transgression and uncleanness.

4 And the prince Mastêmâ exerted himself to do all this, and he sent forth other spirits, those which were put under his hand, to do all manner of wrong and sin, and all manner of transgression, to corrupt and destroy, and to shed blood upon the earth.

5 For this reason he called the name of Sêrôh, Serug, for every one turned to do all manner of sin and transgression.

6 And he grew up, and dwelt in Ur of the Chaldees, near to the father of his wife's mother, and he worshipped idols, and he took to himself a wife in the thirty-sixth jubilee, in the fifth week, in the first year thereof, [1744 A.M.] and her name was Melka, the daughter of Kaber, the daughter of his father's brother.

7 And she bare him Nahor, in the first year of this week, and he grew and dwelt in Ur of the Chaldees, and his father taught him the researches of the Chaldees to divine and augur, according to the signs of heaven.

8 And in the thirty-seventh jubilee in the sixth week, in the first year thereof, [1800 A.M.] he took to himself a wife, and her name was 'Ijaska, the daughter of Nestag of the Chaldees.

9 And she bare him Terah in the seventh year of this week. [1806 A.M.]

10 And the prince Mastêmâ sent ravens and birds to devour the seed which was sown in the land, in order to destroy the land, and rob the children of men of their labours. Before they could plough in the seed, the ravens picked (it) from the surface of the ground.

11 And for this reason he called his name Terah because the ravens and the birds reduced them to destitution and devoured their seed.

12 And the years began to be barren, owing to the birds, and they devoured all the fruit of the trees from the trees: it was only with great effort that they could save a little of all the fruit of the earth in their days.

13 And in this thirty-ninth jubilee, in the second week in the first year, [1870 A.M.] Terah took to himself a wife, and her name was 'Edna, the daughter of

'Abram, the daughter of his father's sister. And in the seventh year of this week [1876 A.M.] she bare him a son, and he called his name Abram, by the name of the father of his mother;

14 for he had died before his daughter had conceived a son.

15 And the child began to understand the errors of the earth that all went astray after graven images and after uncleanness, and his father taught him writing, and he was two weeks of years old, [1890 A.M.] and he separated himself from his father, that he might not worship idols with him.

16 And he began to pray to the Creator of all things that He might save him from the errors of the children of men, and that his portion should not fall into error after uncleanness and vileness.

17 And the seed time came for the sowing of seed upon the land, and they all went forth together to protect their seed against the ravens, and Abram went forth with those that went, and the child was a lad of fourteen years.

18 And a cloud of ravens came to devour the seed, and Abram ran to meet them before they settled on the ground, and cried to them before they settled on the ground to devour the seed, and said, ' Descend not: return to the place whence ye came,' and they proceeded to turn back.

19 And he caused the clouds of ravens to turn back that day seventy times, and of all the ravens throughout all the land where Abram was there settled there not so much as one.

20 And all who were with him throughout all the land saw him cry out, and all the ravens turn back, and his name became great in all the land of the Chaldees.

21 And there came to him this year all those that wished to sow, and he went with them until the time of sowing ceased: and they sowed their land, and that year they brought enough grain home and eat and were satisfied.

22 And in the first year of the fifth week [1891 A.M.] Abram taught those who made implements for oxen, the artificers in wood, and they made a vessel above the ground, facing the frame of the plough, in order to put the seed thereon, and the seed fell down therefrom upon the share of the plough, and was hidden in the earth, and they no longer feared the ravens.

23 And after this manner they made (vessels) above the ground on all the frames of the ploughs, and they sowed and tilled all the land, according as Abram commanded them, and they no longer feared the birds.

[Chapter 12]

1 And it came to pass in the sixth week, in the seventh year thereof, [1904 A.M.] that Abram said to Terah his father, saying, 'Father!'

2 And he said, 'Behold, here am I, my son.' And he said,'What help and profit have we from those idols which thou dost worship, And before which thou dost bow thyself?

3 For there is no spirit in them, For they are dumb forms, and a misleading of the heart. Worship them not:

4 Worship the God of heaven, Who causes the rain and the dew to descend on the earth And does everything upon the earth,And has created everything by His word, And all life is from before His face.

5 Why do ye worship things that have no spirit in them? For they are the work of (men's) hands,And on your shoulders do ye bear them, And ye have no help from them, But they are a great cause of shame to those who make them, And a misleading of the heart to those who worship them: Worship them not.'

6 And his father said unto him, I also know it, my son, but what shall I do with a people who have made me to serve before them?

7 And if I tell them the truth, they will slay me; for their soul cleaves to them to worship them and honour them.

8 Keep silent, my son, lest they slay thee.' And these words he spake to his two brothers, and they were angry with him and he kept silent.

9 And in the fortieth jubilee, in the second week, in the seventh year thereof, [1925 A.M.] Abram took to himself a wife, and her name was Sarai, the daughter of his father, and she became his wife.

10 And Haran, his brother, took to himself a wife in the third year of the third week, [1928 A.M.] and she bare him a son in the seventh year of this week, [1932 A.M.] and he called his name Lot.

11 And Nahor, his brother, took to himself a wife.

12 And in the sixtieth year of the life of Abram, that is, in the fourth week, in the fourth year thereof, [1936 A.M.] Abram arose by night, and burned the house of the idols, and he burned all that was in the house and no man knew it.

13 And they arose in the night and sought to save their gods from the midst of the fire.

14 And Haran hasted to save them, but the fire flamed over him, and he was burnt in the fire, and he died in Ur of the Chaldees before Terah his father, and they buried him in Ur of the Chaldees.

15 And Terah went forth from Ur of the Chaldees, he and his sons, to go into the land of Lebanon and into the land of Canaan, and he dwelt in the land of Haran, and Abram dwelt with Terah his father in Haran two weeks of years.

16 And in the sixth week, in the fifth year thereof, [1951 A.M.] Abram sat up throughout the night on the new moon of the seventh month to observe the stars from the evening to the morning, in order to see what would be the character of the year with regard to the rains, and he was alone as he sat and observed.

17 And a word came into his heart and he said: All the signs of the stars, and the signs of the moon and of the sun are all in the hand of the Lord. Why do I search (them) out?

18 If He desires, He causes it to rain, morning and evening; And if He desires, He withholds it, And all things are in his hand.'

19 And he prayed that night and said, 'My God, God Most High, Thou alone art my God, And Thee and Thy dominion have I chosen. And Thou hast

created all things, And all things that are the work of thy hands.

20 Deliver me from the hands of evil spirits who have dominion over the thoughts of men's hearts, And let them not lead me astray from Thee, my God.And stablish Thou me and my seed for ever That we go not astray from henceforth and for evermore.'

21 And he said, 'Shall I return unto Ur of the Chaldees who seek my face that I may return to them, am I to remain here in this place? The right path before Thee prosper it in the hands of Thy servant that he may fulfil (it) and that I may not walk in the deceitfulness of my heart, O my God.'

22 And he made an end of speaking and praying, and behold the word of the Lord was sent to him through me, saying: 'Get thee up from thy country, and from thy kindred and from the house of thy father unto a land which I will show thee, and I shall make thee a great and numerous nation.

23 And I will bless thee And I will make thy name great, And thou shalt be blessed in the earth, And in Thee shall all families of the earth be blessed, And I will bless them that bless thee, And curse them that curse thee.

24 And I will be a God to thee and thy son, and to thy son's son, and to all thy seed: fear not, from henceforth and unto all generations of the earth I am thy God.'

25 And the Lord God said: 'Open his mouth and his ears, that he may hear and speak with his mouth, with the language which has been revealed'; for it had ceased from the mouths of all the children of men from the day of the overthrow (of Babel).

26 And I opened his mouth, and his ears and his lips, and I began to speak with him in Hebrew in the tongue of the creation.

27 And he took the books of his fathers, and these were written in Hebrew, and he transcribed them, and he began from henceforth to study them, and I made known to him that which he could not (understand), and he studied them during the six rainy months.

28 And it came to pass in the seventh year of the sixth week [1953 A.M.] that he spoke to his father and informed him, that he would leave Haran to go into the land of Canaan to see it and return to him.

29 And Terah his father said unto him; Go in peace:May the eternal God make thy path straight. And the Lord [(be) with thee, and] protect thee from all evil, And grant unto thee grace, mercy and favour before those who see thee, And may none of the children of men have power over thee to harm thee; Go in peace.

30 And if thou seest a land pleasant to thy eyes to dwell in, then arise and take me to thee and take Lot with thee, the son of Haran thy brother as thine own son: the Lord be with thee.

31 And Nahor thy brother leave with me till thou returnest in peace, and we go with thee all together.'

[Chapter 13]

1 And Abram journeyed from Haran, and he took Sarai, his wife, and Lot, his brother Haran's son, to the land of Canaan, and he came into Asshur, and proceeded to Shechem, and dwelt near a lofty oak.

2 And he saw, and, behold, the land was very pleasant from the entering of Hamath to the lofty oak.

3 And the Lord said to him: "To thee and to thy seed will I give this land.'

4 And he built an altar there, and he offered thereon a burnt sacrifice to the Lord, who had appeared to him.

5 And he removed from thence unto the mountain . . . Bethel on the west and Ai on the east, and pitched his tent there.

6 And he saw and behold, the land was very wide and good, and everything grew thereon -vines and figs and pomegranates, oaks and ilexes, and terebinths and oil trees, and cedars and cypresses and date trees, and all trees of the field, and there was water on the mountains.

7 And he blessed the Lord who had led him out of Ur of the Chaldees, and had brought him to this land.

8 And it came to pass in the first year, in the seventh week, on the new moon of the first month, 1954 A.M.] that he built an altar on this mountain, and called on the name of the Lord: "Thou, the eternal God, art my God.'

9 And he offered on the altar a burnt sacrifice unto the Lord that He should be with him and not forsake him all the days of his life.

10 And he removed from thence and went towards the south, and he came to Hebron and Hebron was built at that time, and he dwelt there two years, and he went (thence) into the land of the south, to Bealoth, and there was a famine in the land.

11 And Abram went into Egypt in the third year of the week, and he dwelt in Egypt five years before his wife was torn away from him.

12 Now Tanais in Egypt was at that time built- seven years after Hebron.

13 And it came to pass when Pharaoh seized Sarai, the wife of Abram that the Lord plagued Pharaoh and his house with great plagues because of Sarai, Abram's wife.

14 And Abram was very glorious by reason of possessions in sheep, and cattle, and asses, and horses, and camels, and menservants, and maidservants, and in silver and gold exceedingly. And Lot also his brother's son, was wealthy.

15 And Pharaoh gave back Sarai, the wife of Abram, and he sent him out of the land of Egypt, and he journeyed to the place where he had pitched his tent at the beginning, to the place of the altar, with Ai on the east, and Bethel on the west, and he blessed the Lord his God who had brought him back in peace.

16 And it came to pass in the forty-first jubilee in the third year of the first week, [1963 A.M.] that he returned to this place and offered thereon a burnt sacrifice, and called on the name of the Lord, and said: "Thou, the most high God, art my God for ever and ever.'

17 And in the fourth year of this week [1964 A.M.] Lot parted from him, and Lot dwelt in Sodom, and the men of Sodom were sinners exceedingly.

18 And it grieved him in his heart that his brother's son had parted from him; for he had no children.

19 In that year when Lot was taken captive, the Lord said unto Abram, after that Lot had parted from him, in the fourth year of this week: 'Lift up thine eyes from the place where thou art dwelling, northward and southward, and westward and eastward.

20 For all the land which thou seest I will give to thee and to thy seed for ever, and I will make thy seed as the sand of the sea: though a man may number the dust of the earth, yet thy seed shall not be numbered.

21 Arise, walk (through the land) in the length of it and the breadth of it, and see it all; for to thy seed will I give it.' And Abram went to Hebron, and dwelt there.

22 And in this year came Chedorlaomer, king of Elam, and Amraphel, king of Shinar, and Arioch king of Sellasar, and Tergal, king of nations, and slew the king of Gomorrah, and the king of Sodom fled, and many fell through wounds in the vale of Siddim, by the Salt Sea.

23 And they took captive Sodom and Adam and Zeboim, and they took captive Lot also, the son of Abram's brother, and all his possessions, and they went to Dan.

24 And one who had escaped came and told Abram that his brother's son had been taken captive and (Abram) armed his household servants . . .

25 . . . . for Abram, and for his seed, a tenth of the first fruits to the Lord, and the Lord ordained it as an ordinance for ever that they should give it to the priests who served before Him, that they should possess it for ever.

26 And to this law there is no limit of days; for He hath ordained it for the generations for ever that they should give to the Lord the tenth of everything, of the seed and of the wine and of the oil and of the cattle and of the sheep.

27 And He gave (it) unto His priests to eat and to drink with joy before Him.

28 And the king of Sodom came to him and bowed himself before him, and said: 'Our Lord Abram, give unto us the souls which thou hast rescued, but let the booty be thine.'

29 And Abram said unto him: 'I lift up my hands to the Most High God, that from a thread to a shoe-latchet I shall not take aught that is thine lest thou shouldst say, I have made Abram rich; save only what the young men have eaten, and the portion of the men who went with me -Aner, Eschol, and Mamre. These shall take their portion.'

[Chapter 14]

1 After these things, in the fourth year of this week, on the new moon of the third month, the word of the Lord came to Abram in a dream, saying: 'Fear not, Abram; I am thy defender, and thy reward will be exceeding great.'

2 And he said: 'Lord, Lord, what wilt thou give me, seeing I go hence childless, and the son of Maseq,

the son of my handmaid, is the Dammasek Eliezer: he will be my heir, and to me thou hast given no seed.'

3 And he said unto him: 'This (man) will not be thy heir, but one that will come out of thine own bowels; he will be thine heir.'

4 And He brought him forth abroad, and said unto him: 'Look toward heaven and number the stars if thou art able to number them.'

5 And he looked toward heaven, and beheld the stars. And He said unto him: 'So shall thy seed be.'

6 And he believed in the Lord, and it was counted to him for righteousness.

7 And He said unto him: 'I am the Lord that brought thee out of Ur of the Chaldees, to give thee the land of the Canaanites to possess it for ever; and I will be God unto thee and to thy seed after thee.'

8 And he said: 'Lord, Lord, whereby shall I know that I shall inherit (it)?'

9 And He said unto him: 'Take Me an heifer of three years, and a goat of three years, and a sheep of three years, and a turtle-dove, and a pigeon.'

10 And he took all these in the middle of the month and he dwelt at the oak of Mamre, which is near Hebron.

11 And he built there an altar, and sacrificed all these; and he poured their blood upon the altar, and divided them in the midst, and laid them over against each other; but the birds divided he not.

12 And birds came down upon the pieces, and Abram drove them away, and did not suffer the birds to touch them.

13 And it came to pass, when the sun had set, that an ecstasy fell upon Abram, and lo ! an horror of great darkness fell upon him, and it was said unto Abram: 'Know of a surety that thy seed shall be a stranger in a land (that is) not theirs, and they shall bring them into bondage, and afflict them four hundred years.

14 And the nation also to whom they will be in bondage will I judge, and after that they shall come forth thence with much substance.

15 And thou shalt go to thy fathers in peace, and be buried in a good old age.

16 But in the fourth generation they shall return hither; for the iniquity of the Amorites is not yet full.'

17 And he awoke from his sleep, and he arose, and the sun had set; and there was a flame, and behold ! a furnace was smoking, and a flame of fire passed between the pieces.

18 And on that day the Lord made a covenant with Abram, saying: 'To thy seed will I give this land, from the river of Egypt unto the great river, the river Euphrates, the Kenites, the Kenizzites, the Kadmonites, the Perizzites, and the Rephaim, the Phakorites, and the Hivites, and the Amorites, and the Canaanites, and the Girgashites, and the Jebusites.

19 And the day passed, and Abram offered the pieces, and the birds, and their fruit offerings, and their drink offerings, and the fire devoured them.

20 And on that day we made a covenant with Abram, according as we had covenanted with Noah in this month; and Abram renewed the festival and

ordinance for himself for ever.

21 And Abram rejoiced, and made all these things known to Sarai his wife; and he believed that he would have seed, but she did not bear.

22 And Sarai advised her husband Abram, and said unto him: 'Go in unto Hagar, my Egyptian maid: it may be that I shall build up seed unto thee by her.'

23 And Abram harkened unto the voice of Sarai his wife, and said unto her, 'Do (so).' And Sarai took Hagar, her maid, the Egyptian, and gave her to Abram, her husband, to be his wife.

24 And he went in unto her, and she conceived and bare him a son, and he called his name Ishmael, in the fifth year of this week [1965 A.M.]; and this was the eighty-sixth year in the life of Abram.

[Chapter 15]

1 And in the fifth year of the fourth week of this jubilee, [1979 A.M.] in the third month, in the middle of the month, Abram celebrated the feast of the first-fruits of the grain harvest.

2 And he offered new offerings on the altar, the first-fruits of the produce, unto the Lord, an heifer and a goat and a sheep on the altar as a burnt sacrifice unto the Lord; their fruit offerings and their drink offerings he offered upon the altar with frankincense.

3 And the Lord appeared to Abram, and said unto him: 'I am God Almighty; approve thyself before me and be thou perfect.

4 And I will make My covenant between Me and thee, and I will multiply thee exceedingly.'

5 And Abram fell on his face, and God talked with him, and said:

6 'Behold my ordinance is with thee, And thou shalt be the father of many nations.

7 Neither shall thy name any more be called Abram, But thy name from henceforth, even for ever, shall be Abraham. For the father of many nations have I made thee.

8 And I will make thee very great, And I will make thee into nations, And kings shall come forth from thee.

9 And I shall establish My covenant between Me and thee, and thy seed after thee, throughout their generations, for an eternal covenant, so that I may be a God unto thee, and to thy seed after thee.

10 <And I will give to thee and to thy seed after thee> the land where thou hast been a sojourner, the land of Canaan, that thou mayst possess it for ever, and I will be their God.'

11 And the Lord said unto Abraham: 'And as for thee, do thou keep my covenant, thou and thy seed after thee: and circumcise ye every male among you, and circumcise your foreskins, and it shall be a token of an eternal covenant between Me and you.

12 And the child on the eighth day ye shall circumcise, every male throughout your generations, him that is born in the house, or whom ye have bought with money from any stranger, whom ye have acquired who is not of thy seed.

13 He that is born in thy house shall surely be circumcised, and those whom thou hast bought with money shall be circumcised, and My covenant shall be in your flesh for an eternal ordinance.

14 And the uncircumcised male who is not circumcised in the flesh of his foreskin on the eighth day, that soul shall be cut off from his people, for he has broken My covenant.'

15 And God said unto Abraham: 'As for Sarai thy wife, her name shall no more be called Sarai, but Sarah shall be her name.

16 And I will bless her, and give thee a son by her, and I will bless him, and he shall become a nation, and kings of nations shall proceed from him.'

17 And Abraham fell on his face, and rejoiced, and said in his heart: 'Shall a son be born to him that is a hundred years old, and shall Sarah, who is ninety years old, bring forth?'

18 And Abraham said unto God: 'O that Ishmael might live before thee!'

19 And God said: 'Yea, and Sarah also shall bear thee a son, and thou shalt call his name Isaac, and I will establish My covenant with him, an everlasting covenant, and for his seed after him.

20 And as for Ishmael also have I heard thee, and behold I will bless him, and make him great, and multiply him exceedingly, and he shall beget twelve princes, and I will make him a great nation.

21 But My covenant will I establish with Isaac, whom Sarah shall bear to thee, in these days, in the next year.'

22 And He left off speaking with him, and God went up from Abraham.

23 And Abraham did according as God had said unto him, and he took Ishmael his son, and all that were born in his house, and whom he had bought with his money, every male in his house, and circumcised the flesh of their foreskin.

24 And on the selfsame day was Abraham circumcised, and all the men of his house, <and those born in the house>, and all those, whom he had bought with money from the children of the stranger, were circumcised with him.

25 This law is for all the generations for ever, and there is no circumcision of the days, and no omission of one day out of the eight days; for it is an eternal ordinance, ordained and written on the heavenly tablets.

26 And every one that is born, the flesh of whose foreskin is not circumcised on the eighth day, belongs not to the children of the covenant which the Lord made with Abraham, but to the children of destruction; nor is there, moreover, any sign on him that he is the Lord's, but (he is destined) to be destroyed and slain from the earth, and to be rooted out of the earth, for he has broken the covenant of the Lord our God.

27 For all the angels of the presence and all the angels of sanctification have been so created from the day of their creation, and before the angels of the presence and the angels of sanctification He hath sanctified Israel, that they should be with Him and with His holy angels.

28 And do thou command the children of Israel and let them observe the sign of this covenant for their generations as an eternal ordinance, and they will not be rooted out of the land.

29 For the command is ordained for a covenant, that they should observe it for ever among all the children of Israel.

30 For Ishmael and his sons and his brothers and Esau, the Lord did not cause to approach Him, and he chose them not because they are the children of Abraham, because He knew them, but He chose Israel to be His people.

31 And He sanctified it, and gathered it from amongst all the children of men; for there are many nations and many peoples, and all are His, and over all hath He placed spirits in authority to lead them astray from Him.

32 But over Israel He did not appoint any angel or spirit, for He alone is their ruler, and He will preserve them and require them at the hand of His angels and His spirits, and at the hand of all His powers in order that He may preserve them and bless them, and that they may be His and He may be theirs from henceforth for ever.

33 And now I announce unto thee that the children of Israel will not keep true to this ordinance, and they will not circumcise their sons according to all this law; for in the flesh of their circumcision they will omit this circumcision of their sons, and all of them, sons of Beliar, will leave their sons uncircumcised as they were born.

34 And there will be great wrath from the Lord against the children of Israel. because they have forsaken His covenant and turned aside from His word, and provoked and blasphemed, inasmuch as they do not observe the ordinance of this law; for they have treated their members like the Gentiles, so that they may be removed and rooted out of the land. And there will no more be pardon or forgiveness unto them [so that there should be forgiveness and pardon] for all the sin of this eternal error.

[Chapter 16]

1 And on the new moon of the fourth month we appeared unto Abraham, at the oak of Mamre, and we talked with him, and we announced to him that a son would be given to him by Sarah his wife.

2 And Sarah laughed, for she heard that we had spoken these words with Abraham, and we admonished her, and she became afraid, and denied that she had laughed on account of the words.

3 And we told her the name of her son, as his name is ordained and written in the heavenly tablets (i.e.) Isaac,

4 And (that) when we returned to her at a set time, she would have conceived a son.

5 And in this month the Lord executed his judgments on Sodom, and Gomorrah, and Zeboim, and all the region of the Jordan, and He burned them with fire and brimstone, and destroyed them until this day, even as [lo] I have declared unto thee all their works, that they are wicked and sinners exceedingly, and that they defile themselves and commit fornication in their flesh, and work uncleanness on the earth.

6 And, in like manner, God will execute judgment on the places where they have done according to the uncleanness of the Sodomites, like unto the judgment of Sodom.

7 But Lot we saved; for God remembered Abraham, and sent him out from the midst of the overthrow.

8 And he and his daughters committed sin upon the earth, such as had not been on the earth since the days of Adam till his time; for the man lay with his daughters.

9 And, behold, it was commanded and engraven concerning all his seed, on the heavenly tablets, to remove them and root them out, and to execute judgment upon them like the judgment of Sodom, and to leave no seed of the man on earth on the day of condemnation.

10 And in this month Abraham moved from Hebron, and departed and dwelt between Kadesh and Shur in the mountains of Gerar.

11 And in the middle of the fifth month he moved from thence, and dwelt at the Well of the Oath.

12 And in the middle of the sixth month the Lord visited Sarah and did unto her as He had spoken and she conceived.

13 And she bare a son in the third month, and in the middle of the month, at the time of which the Lord had spoken to Abraham, on the festival of the first fruits of the harvest, Isaac was born.

14 And Abraham circumcised his son on the eighth day: he was the first that was circumcised according to the covenant which is ordained for ever.

15 And in the sixth year of the fourth week we came to Abraham, to the Well of the Oath, and we appeared unto him [as we had told Sarah that we should return to her, and she would have conceived a son.

16 And we returned in the seventh month, and found Sarah with child before us] and we blessed him, and we announced to him all the things which had been decreed concerning him, that he should not die till he should beget six sons more, and should see (them) before he died; but (that) in Isaac should his name and seed be called:

17 And (that) all the seed of his sons should be Gentiles, and be reckoned with the Gentiles; but from the sons of Isaac one should become a holy seed, and should not be reckoned among the Gentiles.

18 For he should become the portion of the Most High, and all his seed had fallen into the possession of God, that it should be unto the Lord a people for (His) possession above all nations and that it should become a kingdom and priests and a holy nation.

19 And we went our way, and we announced to Sarah all that we had told him, and they both rejoiced with exceeding great joy.

20 And he built there an altar to the Lord who had delivered him, and who was making him rejoice in the land of his sojourning, and he celebrated a festival of joy in this month seven days, near the altar which he had built at the Well of the Oath.

21 And he built booths for himself and for his servants on this festival, and he was the first to celebrate the feast of tabernacles on the earth.

22 And during these seven days he brought each day to the altar a burnt offering to the Lord, two oxen,

two rams, seven sheep, one he-goat, for a sin offering, that he might atone thereby for himself and for his seed.

23 And, as a thank-offering, seven rams, seven kids, seven sheep, and seven he-goats, and their fruit offerings and their drink offerings; and he burnt all the fat thereof on the altar, a chosen offering unto the Lord for a sweet smelling savour.

24 And morning and evening he burnt fragrant substances, frankincense and galbanum, and stackte, and nard, and myrrh, and spice, and costum; all these seven he offered, crushed, mixed together in equal parts (and) pure.

25 And he celebrated this feast during seven days, rejoicing with all his heart and with all his soul, he and all those who were in his house, and there was no stranger with him, nor any that was uncircumcised.

26 And he blessed his Creator who had created him in his generation, for He had created him according to His good pleasure; for He knew and perceived that from him would arise the plant of righteousness for the eternal generations, and from him a holy seed, so that it should become like Him who had made all things.

27 And he blessed and rejoiced, and he called the name of this festival the festival of the Lord, a joy acceptable to the Most High God.

28 And we blessed him for ever, and all his seed after him throughout all the generations of the earth, because he celebrated this festival in its season, according to the testimony of the heavenly tablets.

29 For this reason it is ordained on the heavenly tablets concerning Israel, that they shall celebrate the feast of tabernacles seven days with joy, in the seventh month, acceptable before the Lord -a statute for ever throughout their generations every year.

30 And to this there is no limit of days; for it is ordained for ever regarding Israel that they should celebrate it and dwell in booths, and set wreaths upon their heads, and take leafy boughs, and willows from the brook.

31 And Abraham took branches of palm trees, and the fruit of goodly trees, and every day going round the altar with the branches seven times [a day] in the morning, he praised and gave thanks to his God for all things in joy.

[Chapter 17]

1 And in the first year of the fifth week Isaac was weaned in this jubilee, [1982 A.M.] and Abraham made a great banquet in the third month, on the day his son Isaac was weaned.

2 And Ishmael, the son of Hagar, the Egyptian, was before the face of Abraham, his father, in his place, and Abraham rejoiced and blessed God because he had seen his sons and had not died childless.

3 And he remembered the words which He had spoken to him on the day on which Lot had parted from him, and he rejoiced because the Lord had given him seed upon the earth to inherit the earth, and he blessed with all his mouth the Creator of all things.

4 And Sarah saw Ishmael playing and dancing, and Abraham rejoicing with great joy, and she became jealous of Ishmael and said to Abraham, 'Cast out this bondwoman and her son; for the son of this bondwoman will not be heir with my son, Isaac.'

5 And the thing was grievous in Abraham's sight, because of his maidservant and because of his son, that he should drive them from him.

6 And God said to Abraham 'Let it not be grievous in thy sight, because of the child and because of the bondwoman; in all that Sarah hath said unto thee, harken to her words and do (them); for in Isaac shall thy name and seed be called.

7 But as for the son of this bondwoman I will make him a great nation, because he is of thy seed.'

8 And Abraham rose up early in the morning, and took bread and a bottle of water, and placed them on the shoulders of Hagar and the child, and sent her away.

9 And she departed and wandered in the wilderness of Beersheba, and the water in the bottle was spent, and the child thirsted, and was not able to go on, and fell down.

10 And his mother took him and cast him under an olive tree, and went and sat her down over against him, at the distance of a bow-shot; for she said, 'Let me not see the death of my child,' and as she sat she wept.

11 And an angel of God, one of the holy ones, said unto her, 'Why weepest thou, Hagar? Arise take the child, and hold him in thine hand; for God hath heard thy voice, and hath seen the child.'

12 And she opened her eyes, and she saw a well of water, and she went and filled her bottle with water, and she gave her child to drink, and she arose and went towards the wilderness of Paran.

13 And the child grew and became an archer, and God was with him, and his mother took him a wife from among the daughters of Egypt.

14 And she bare him a son, and he called his name Nebaioth; for she said, 'The Lord was nigh to me when I called upon him.'

15 And it came to pass in the seventh week, in the first year thereof, [2003 A.M.] in the first month in this jubilee, on the twelfth of this month, there were voices in heaven regarding Abraham, that he was faithful in all that He told him, and that he loved the Lord, and that in every affliction he was faithful.

16 And the prince Mastêmâ came and said before God, 'Behold, Abraham loves Isaac his son, and he delights in him above all things else; bid him offer him as a burnt-offering on the altar, and Thou wilt see if he will do this command, and Thou wilt know if he is faithful in everything wherein Thou dost try him.

17 And the Lord knew that Abraham was faithful in all his afflictions; for He had tried him through his country and with famine, and had tried him with the wealth of kings, and had tried him again through his wife, when she was torn (from him), and with circumcision; and had tried him through Ishmael and Hagar, his maid-servant, when he sent them away.

18 And in everything wherein He had tried him, he was found faithful, and his soul was not impatient,

and he was not slow to act; for he was faithful and a lover of the Lord.

[Chapter 18]

1   And God said to him, 'Abraham, Abraham'; and he said, Behold, (here) am I.'

2   And he said, Take thy beloved son whom thou lovest, (even) Isaac, and go unto the high country, and offer him on one of the mountains which I will point out unto thee.'

3   And he rose early in the morning and saddled his ass, and took his two young men with him, and Isaac his son, and clave the wood of the burnt offering, and he went to the place on the third day, and he saw the place afar off.

4   And he came to a well of water, and he said to his young men, 'Abide ye here with the ass, and I and the lad shall go (yonder), and when we have worshipped we shall come again to you.'

5   And he took the wood of the burnt-offering and laid it on Isaac his son, and he took in his hand the fire and the knife, and they went both of them together to that place.

6   And Isaac said to his father, 'Father;' and he said, 'Here am I, my son.' And he said unto him, 'Behold the fire, and the knife, and the wood; but where is the sheep for the burnt-offering, father?'

7   And he said, 'God will provide for himself a sheep for a burnt-offering, my son.' And he drew near to the place of the mount of God.

8   And he built an altar, and he placed the wood on the altar, and bound Isaac his son, and placed him on the wood which was upon the altar, and stretched forth his hand to take the knife to slay Isaac his son.

9   And I stood before him, and before the prince Mastêmâ, and the Lord said, 'Bid him not to lay his hand on the lad, nor to do anything to him, for I have shown that he fears the Lord.'

10 And I called to him from heaven, and said unto him: 'Abraham, Abraham;' and he was terrified and said: 'Behold, (here) am I.'

11 And I said unto him: 'Lay not thy hand upon the lad, neither do thou anything to him; for now I have shown that thou fearest the Lord, and hast not withheld thy son, thy first-born son, from me.'

12 And the prince Mastêmâ was put to shame; and Abraham lifted up his eyes and looked, and, behold a ram caught . . . by his horns, and Abraham went and took the ram and offered it for a burnt-offering in the stead of his son.

13 And Abraham called that place 'The Lord hath seen', so that it is said *in the mount* the Lord hath seen: that is Mount Sion.

14 And the Lord called Abraham by his name a second time from heaven, as he caused us to appear to speak to him in the name of the Lord.

15 And he said: 'By Myself have I sworn, saith the Lord,Because thou hast done this thing, And hast not withheld thy son, thy beloved son, from Me, That in blessing I will bless thee, And in multiplying I will multiply thy seed As the stars of heaven, And as the sand which is on the seashore.

    And thy seed shall inherit the cities of its enemies,

16 And in thy seed shall all nations of the earth be blessed;Because thou hast obeyed My voice, And I have shown to all that thou art faithful unto Me in all that I have said unto thee: Go in peace.'

17 And Abraham went to his young men, and they arose and went together to Beersheba, and Abraham [2010 A.M.] dwelt by the Well of the Oath.

18 And he celebrated this festival every year, seven days with joy, and he called it the festival of the Lord according to the seven days during which he went and returned in peace.

19 And accordingly has it been ordained and written on the heavenly tablets regarding Israel and its seed that they should observe this festival seven days with the joy of festival.

[Chapter 19]

1   And in the first year of the first week in the forty-second jubilee, Abraham returned and dwelt opposite Hebron, that is Kirjath Arba, two weeks of years.

2   And in the first year of the third week of this jubilee the days of the life of Sarah were accomplished, and she died in Hebron.

3   And Abraham went to mourn over her and bury her, and we tried him [to see] if his spirit were patient and he were not indignant in the words of his mouth; and he was found patient in this, and was not disturbed.

4   For in patience of spirit he conversed with the children of Heth, to the intent that they should give him a place in which to bury his dead.

5   And the Lord gave him grace before all who saw him, and he besought in gentleness the sons of Heth, and they gave him the land of the double cave over against Mamre, that is Hebron, for four hundred pieces of silver.

6   And they besought him saying, We shall give it to thee for nothing; but he would not take it from their hands for nothing, for he gave the price of the place, the money in full, and he bowed down before them twice, and after this he buried his dead in the double cave.

7   And all the days of the life of Sarah were one hundred and twenty-seven years, that is, two jubilees and four weeks and one year: these are the days of the years of the life of Sarah.

8   This is the tenth trial wherewith Abraham was tried, and he was found faithful, patient in spirit.

9   And he said not a single word regarding the rumour in the land how that God had said that He would give it to him and to his seed after him, and he begged a place there to bury his dead; for he was found faithful, and was recorded on the heavenly tablets as the friend of God.

10 And in the fourth year thereof he took a wife for his son Isaac and her name was Rebecca [2020 A.M.] [the daughter of Bethuel, the son of Nahor, the brother of Abraham] the sister of Laban and daughter of Bethuel; and Bethuel was the son of Melca, who was the wife of Nahor, the brother of Abraham.

11 And Abraham took to himself a third wife, and her name was Keturah, from among the daughters of his household servants, for Hagar had died before Sarah. And she bare him six sons, Zimram, and Jokshan, and Medan, and Midian, and Ishbak, and Shuah, in the two weeks of years.

12 And in the sixth week, in the second year thereof, Rebecca bare to Isaac two sons, Jacob and Esau,

13 and [2046 A.M.] Jacob was a smooth and upright man, and Esau was fierce, a man of the field, and hairy, and Jacob dwelt in tents.

14 And the youths grew, and Jacob learned to write; but Esau did not learn, for he was a man of the field and a hunter, and he learnt war, and all his deeds were fierce.

15 And Abraham loved Jacob, but Isaac loved Esau.

16 And Abraham saw the deeds of Esau, and he knew that in Jacob should his name and seed be called; and he called Rebecca and gave commandment regarding Jacob, for he knew that she (too) loved Jacob much more than Esau.

17 And he said unto her:My daughter, watch over my son Jacob, For he shall be in my stead on the earth, And for a blessing in the midst of the children of men, And for the glory of the whole seed of Shem.

18 For I know that the Lord will choose him to be a people for possession unto Himself, above all peoples that are upon the face of the earth.

19 And behold, Isaac my son loves Esau more than Jacob, but I see that thou truly lovest Jacob.

20 Add still further to thy kindness to him, And let thine eyes be upon him in love; For he shall be a blessing unto us on the earth from henceforth unto all generations of the earth.

21 Let thy hands be strong And let thy heart rejoice in thy son Jacob; For I have loved him far beyond all my sons.He shall be blessed for ever, And his seed shall fill the whole earth.

22 If a man can number the sand of the earth, His seed also shall be numbered.

23 And all the blessings wherewith the Lord hath blessed me and my seed shall belong to Jacob and his seed alway.

24 And in his seed shall my name be blessed, and the name of my fathers, Shem, and Noab, and Enoch, and Mahalalel, and Enos, and Seth, and Adam.

25 And these shall serveTo lay the foundations of the heaven, And to strengthen the earth, And to renew all the luminaries which are in the firmament.

26 And he called Jacob before the eyes of Rebecca his mother, and kissed him, and blessed him, and said:

27 'Jacob, my beloved son, whom my soul loveth, may God bless thee from above the firmament, and may He give thee all the blessings wherewith He blessed Adam, and Enoch, and Noah, and Shem; and all the things of which He told me, and all the things which He promised to give me, may he cause to cleave to thee and to thy seed for ever, according to the days of heaven above the earth.

28 And the Spirits of Mastêmâ shall not rule over thee or over thy seed to turn thee from the Lord, who is thy God from henceforth for ever.

29 And may the Lord God be a father to thee and thou the first-born son, and to the people alway.

30 Go in peace, my son.' And they both went forth together from Abraham.

31 And Rebecca loved Jacob, with all her heart and with all her soul, very much more than Esau; but Isaac loved Esau much more than Jacob.

[Chapter 20]

1 And in the forty-second jubilee, in the first year of the seventh week, Abraham called Ishmael, [2052 (2045?) A.M.] and his twelve sons, and Isaac and his two sons, and the six sons of Keturah, and their sons.

2 And he commanded them that they should observe the way of the Lord; that they should work righteousness, and love each his neighbour, and act on this manner amongst all men; that they should each so walk with regard to them as to do judgment and righteousness on the earth.

3 That they should circumcise their sons, according to the covenant which He had made with them, and not deviate to the right hand or the left of all the paths which the Lord had commanded us; and that we should keep ourselves from all fornication and uncleanness, [and renounce from amongst us all fornication and uncleanness].

4 And if any woman or maid commit fornication amongst you, burn her with fire and let them not commit fornication with her after their eyes and their heart; and let them not take to themselves wives from the daughters of Canaan; for the seed of Canaan will be rooted out of the land.

5 And he told them of the judgment of the giants, and the judgment of the Sodomites, how they had been judged on account of their wickedness, and had died on account of their fornication, and uncleanness, and mutual corruption through fornication.

6 'And guard yourselves from all fornication and uncleanness, And from all pollution of sin,Lest ye make our name a curse, And your whole life a hissing, And all your sons to be destroyed by the sword, And ye become accursed like Sodom, And all your remnant as the sons of Gomorrah.

7 I implore you, my sons, love the God of heaven And cleave ye to all His commandments.And walk not after their idols, and after their uncleannesses,

8 And make not for yourselves molten or graven gods;For they are vanity, And there is no spirit in them; For they are work of (men's) hands, And all who trust in them, trust in nothing.

9 Serve them not, nor worship them, But serve ye the most high God, and worship Him continually: And hope for His countenance always, And work uprightness and righteousness before Him,That He may have pleasure in you and grant you His mercy, And send rain upon you morning and evening, And bless all your works which ye have wrought upon the earth, And bless thy bread and thy water, And bless the fruit of thy womb

and the fruit of thy land, And the herds of thy cattle, and the flocks of thy sheep.

10 And ye will be for a blessing on the earth, And all nations of the earth will desire you,And bless your sons in my name, That they may be blessed as I am.

11 And he gave to Ishmael and to his sons, and to the sons of Keturah, gifts, and sent them away from Isaac his son, and he gave everything to Isaac his son.

12 And Ishmael and his sons, and the sons of Keturah and their sons, went together and dwelt from Paran to the entering in of Babylon in all the land which is towards the East facing the desert.

13 And these mingled with each other, and their name was called Arabs, and Ishmaelites.

[Chapter 21]

1. And in the sixth year of the seventh week of this jubilee Abraham called Isaac his son, and [2057 (2050?) A.M.] commanded him: saying, 'I am become old, and know not the day of my death, and am full of my days.

2. And behold, I am one hundred and seventy-five years old, and throughout all the days of my life I have remembered the Lord, and sought with all my heart to do His will, and to walk uprightly in all His ways.

3. My soul has hated idols, <and I have despised those that served them, and I have given my heart and spirit> that I might observe to do the will of Him who created me.

4. For He is the living God, and He is holy and faithful, and He is righteous beyond all, and there is with Him no accepting of (men's) persons and no accepting of gifts; for God is righteous, and executeth judgment on all those who transgress His commandments and despise His covenant.

5. And do thou, my son, observe His commandments and His ordinances and His judgments, and walk not after the abominations and after the graven images and after the molten images.

6. And eat no blood at all of animals or cattle, or of any bird which flies in the heaven.

7. And if thou dost slay a victim as an acceptable peace offering, slay ye it, and pour out its blood upon the altar, and all the fat of the offering offer on the altar with fine flour and the meat offering mingled with oil, with its drink offering -offer them all together on the altar of burnt offering; it is a sweet savour before the Lord.

8. And thou wilt offer the fat of the sacrifice of thank offerings on the fire which is upon the altar, and the fat which is on the belly, and all the fat on the inwards and the two kidneys, and all the fat that is upon them, and upon the loins and liver thou shalt remove, together with the kidneys.

9. And offer all these for a sweet savour acceptable before the Lord, with its meat-offering and with its drink- offering, for a sweet savour, the bread of the offering unto the Lord.

10. And eat its meat on that day and on the second day, and let not the sun on the second day go down upon it till it is eaten, and let nothing be left over for the third day; for it is not acceptable [for it is not approved] and let it no longer be eaten, and all who eat thereof will bring sin upon themselves; for thus I have found it written in the books of my forefathers, and in the words of Enoch, and in the words of Noah.

11. And on all thy oblations thou shalt strew salt, and let not the salt of the covenant be lacking in all thy oblations before the Lord.

12. And as regards the wood of the sacrifices, beware lest thou bring (other) wood for the altar in addition to these: cypress, bay, almond, fir, pine, cedar, savin, fig, olive, myrrh, laurel, aspalathus.

13. And of these kinds of wood lay upon the altar under the sacrifice, such as have been tested as to their appearance, and do not lay (thereon) any split or dark wood, (but) hard and clean, without fault, a sound and new growth; and do not lay (thereon) old wood, [for its fragrance is gone] for there is no longer fragrance in it as before.

14. Besides these kinds of wood there is none other that thou shalt place (on the altar), for the fragrance is dispersed, and the smell of its fragrance goes not up to heaven.

15. Observe this commandment and do it, my son, that thou mayst be upright in all thy deeds.

16. And at all times be clean in thy body, and wash thyself with water before thou approachest to offer on the altar, and wash thy hands and thy feet before thou drawest near to the altar; and when thou art done sacrificing, wash again thy hands and thy feet.

17. And let no blood appear upon you nor upon your clothes; be on thy guard, my son, against blood, be on thy guard exceedingly; cover it with dust.

18. And do not eat any blood for it is the soul; eat no blood whatever.

19. And take no gifts for the blood of man, lest it be shed with impunity, without judgment; for it is the blood that is shed that causes the earth to sin, and the earth cannot be cleansed from the blood of man save by the blood of him who shed it.

20. And take no present or gift for the blood of man: blood for blood, that thou mayest be accepted before the Lord, the Most High God; for He is the defence of the good: and that thou mayest be preserved from all evil, and that He may save thee from every kind of death.

21. I see, my son,
That all the works of the children of men are sin and wickedness,
And all their deeds are uncleanness and an abomination and a pollution,
And there is no righteousness with them.

22. Beware, lest thou shouldest walk in their ways
And tread in their paths,
And sin a sin unto death before the Most High God.
Else He will [hide His face from thee
And] give thee back into the hands of thy transgression,
And root thee out of the land, and thy seed likewise from under heaven,
And thy name and thy seed shall perish from the whole earth.

23. Turn away from all their deeds and all their uncleanness,
    And observe the ordinance of the Most High God,
    And do His will and be upright in all things.
24. And He will bless thee in all thy deeds,
    And will raise up from thee a plant of righteousness through all the earth, throughout all generations of the earth,
    And my name and thy name shall not be forgotten under heaven for ever.
25. Go, my son in peace.
    May the Most High God, my God and thy God, strengthen thee to do His will,
    And may He bless all thy seed and the residue of thy seed for the generations for ever, with all righteous blessings,
    That thou mayest be a blessing on all the earth.'
26. And he went out from him rejoicing.

[Chapter 22]

1. And it came to pass in the first week in the forty-fourth jubilee, in the second year, that is, the year in which Abraham died, that Isaac and Ishmael came from the Well of the Oath to celebrate the feast of weeks -that is, the feast of the first fruits of the harvest-to Abraham, their father, and Abraham rejoiced because his two sons had come.
2. For Isaac had many possessions in Beersheba, and Isaac was wont to go and see his possessions and to return to his father.
3. And in those days Ishmael came to see his father, and they both came together, and Isaac offered a sacrifice for a burnt offering, and presented it on the altar of his father which he had made in Hebron.
4. And he offered a thank offering and made a feast of joy before Ishmael, his brother: and Rebecca made new cakes from the new grain, and gave them to Jacob, her son, to take them to Abraham, his father, from the first fruits of the land, that he might eat and bless the Creator of all things before he died.
5. And Isaac, too, sent by the hand of Jacob to Abraham a best thank offering, that he might eat and drink.
6. And he eat and drank, and blessed the Most High God,
    Who hath created heaven and earth,
    Who hath made all the fat things of the earth,
    And given them to the children of men
    That they might eat and drink and bless their Creator.
7. 'And now I give thanks unto Thee, my God, because thou hast caused me to see this day: behold, I am one hundred three score and fifteen years, an old man and full of days, and all my days have been unto me peace.
8. The sword of the adversary has not overcome me in all that Thou hast given me and my children all the days of my life until this day.
9. My God, may Thy mercy and Thy peace be upon Thy servant, and upon the seed of his sons, that they may be to Thee a chosen nation and an inheritance from amongst all the nations of the earth from henceforth unto all the days of the generations of the earth, unto all the ages.'
10. And he called Jacob and said: 'My son Jacob, may the God of all bless thee and strengthen thee to do righteousness, and His will before Him, and may He choose thee and thy seed that ye may become a people for His inheritance according to His will alway.
11. And do thou, my son, Jacob, draw near and kiss me.' And he drew near and kissed him, and he said:
    'Blessed be my son Jacob
    And all the sons of God Most High, unto all the ages:
    May God give unto thee a seed of righteousness;
    And some of thy sons may He sanctify in the midst of the whole earth;
    May nations serve thee,
    And all the nations bow themselves before thy seed.
12. Be strong in the presence of men,
    And exercise authority over all the seed of Seth.
    Then thy ways and the ways of thy sons will be justified,
    So that they shall become a holy nation.
13. May the Most High God give thee all the blessings
    Wherewith He has blessed me
    And wherewith He blessed Noah and Adam;
    May they rest on the sacred head of thy seed from generation to generation for ever.
14. And may He cleanse thee from all unrighteousness and impurity,
    That thou mayest be forgiven all the transgressions; which thou hast committed ignorantly.
    And may He strengthen thee,
    And bless thee.
    And mayest thou inherit the whole earth,
15. And may He renew His covenant with thee.
    That thou mayest be to Him a nation for His inheritance for all the ages,
    And that He may be to thee and to thy seed a God in truth and righteousness throughout all the days of the earth.
16. And do thou, my son Jacob, remember my words,
    And observe the commandments of Abraham, thy father:
    Separate thyself from the nations,
    And eat not with them:
    And do not according to their works,
    And become not their associate;
    For their works are unclean,
    And all their ways are a Pollution and an abomination and uncleanness.
17. They offer their sacrifices to the dead
    And they worship evil spirits,
    And they eat over the graves,
    And all their works are vanity and nothingness.
18. They have no heart to understand
    And their eyes do not see what their works are,
    And how they err in saying to a piece of wood:
    'Thou art my God,'
    And to a stone: 'Thou art my Lord and thou art my deliverer.'
    [And they have no heart.]
19. And as for thee, my son Jacob,
    May the Most High God help thee

And the God of heaven bless thee
And remove thee from their uncleanness and from
all their error.

20. Be thou ware, my son Jacob, of taking a wife from
    any seed of the daughters of Canaan;
    For all his seed is to be rooted out of the earth.

21. For, owing to the transgression of Ham, Canaan
    erred,
    And all his seed shall be destroyed from off the
    earth and all the residue thereof,
    And none springing from him shall be saved on
    the day of judgment.

22. And as for all the worshippers of idols and the
    profane
    (b) There shall be no hope for them in the land of
    the living;
    (c) And there shall be no remembrance of them on
    the earth;
    (c) For they shall descend into Sheol,
    (d) And into the place of condemnation shall they
    go,
    As the children of Sodom were taken away from
    the earth
    So will all those who worship idols be taken away.

23. Fear not, my son Jacob,
    And be not dismayed, O son of Abraham:
    May the Most High God preserve thee from
    destruction,
    And from all the paths of error may he deliver
    thee.

24. This house have I built for myself that I might put
    my name upon it in the earth: [it is given to thee
    and to thy seed for ever], and it will be named the
    house of Abraham; it is given to thee and to thy
    seed for ever; for thou wilt build my house and
    establish my name before God for ever: thy seed
    and thy name will stand throughout all generations
    of the earth.'

25. And he ceased commanding him and blessing him.

26. And the two lay together on one bed, and Jacob
    slept in the bosom of Abraham, his father's father
    and he kissed him seven times, and his affection
    and his heart rejoiced over him.

27. And he blessed him with all his heart and said:
    'The Most High God, the God of all, and Creator
    of all, who brought me forth from Ur of the
    Chaldees that he might give me this land to inherit
    it for ever, and that I might establish a holy seed-
    blessed be the Most High for ever.'

28. And he blessed Jacob and said: 'My son, over
    whom with all my heart and my affection I rejoice,
    may Thy grace and Thy mercy be lift up upon him
    and upon his seed alway.

29. And do not forsake him, nor set him at nought
    from henceforth unto the days of eternity, and
    may Thine eyes be opened upon him and upon his
    seed, that Thou mayst preserve him, and bless
    him, and mayest sanctify him as a nation for Thine
    inheritance;

30. And bless him with all Thy blessings from
    henceforth unto all the days of eternity, and renew
    Thy covenant and Thy grace with him and with his
    seed according to all Thy good pleasure unto all
    the generations of the earth.'

[Chapter 23]

1. And he placed two fingers of Jacob on his eyes,
   and he blessed the God of gods, and he covered
   his face and stretched out his feet and slept the
   sleep of eternity, and was gathered to his fathers.

2. And notwithstanding all this Jacob was lying in his
   bosom, and knew not that Abraham, his father's
   father, was dead.

3. And Jacob awoke from his sleep, and behold
   Abraham was cold as ice, and he said 'Father,
   father'; but there was none that spake, and he
   knew that he was dead.

4. And he arose from his bosom and ran and told
   Rebecca, his mother; and Rebecca went to Isaac in
   the night, and told him; and they went together,
   and Jacob with them, and a lamp was in his hand,
   and when they had gone in they found Abraham
   lying dead.

5. And Isaac fell on the face of his father and wept
   and kissed him.

6. And the voices were heard in the house of
   Abraham, and Ishmael his son arose, and went to
   Abraham his father, and wept over Abraham his
   father, he and all the house of Abraham, and they
   wept with a great weeping.

7. And his sons Isaac and Ishmael buried him in the
   double cave, near Sarah his wife, and they wept for
   him forty days, all the men of his house, and Isaac
   and Ishmael, and all their sons, and all the sons of
   Keturah in their places; and the days of weeping
   for Abraham were ended.

8. And he lived three jubilees and four weeks of
   years, one hundred and seventy-five years, and
   completed the days of his life, being old and full of
   days.

9. For the days of the forefathers, of their life, were
   nineteen jubilees; and after the Flood they began
   to grow less than nineteen jubilees, and to decrease
   in jubilees, and to grow old quickly, and to be full
   of their days by reason of manifold tribulation and
   the wickedness of their ways, with the exception
   of Abraham.

10. For Abraham was perfect in all his deeds with the
    Lord, and well-pleasing in righteousness all the
    days of his life; and behold, he did not complete
    four jubilees in his life, when he had grown old by
    reason of the wickedness, and was full of his days.

11. And all the generations which shall arise from this
    time until the day of the great judgment shall grow
    old quickly, before they complete two jubilees, and
    their knowledge shall forsake them by reason of
    their old age Land all their know- ledge shall
    vanish away].

12. And in those days, if a man live a jubilee and a-half
    of years, they shall say regarding him: 'He has lived
    long, and the greater part of his days are pain and
    sorrow and tribulation, and there is no peace:

13. For calamity follows on calamity, and wound on
    wound, and tribulation on tribulation, and evil
    tidings on evil tidings, and illness on illness, and all
    evil judgments such as these, one with another,
    illness and overthrow, and snow and frost and ice,
    and fever, and chills, and torpor, and famine, and
    death, and sword, and captivity, and all kinds of
    calamities and pains.'

14. And all these shall come on an evil generation,

which transgresses on the earth: their works are uncleanness and fornication, and pollution and abominations.

15. Then they shall say: 'The days of the forefathers were many (even), unto a thousand years, and were good; but behold, the days of our life, if a man has lived many, are three score years and ten, and, if he is strong, four score years, and those evil, and there is no peace in the days of this evil generation.'

16. And in that generation the sons shall convict their fathers and their elders of sin and unrighteousness, and of the words of their mouth and the great wickednesses which they perpetrate, and concerning their forsaking the covenant which the Lord made between them and Him, that they should observe and do all His commandments and His ordinances and all His laws, without departing either to the right hand or the left.

17. For all have done evil, and every mouth speaks iniquity and all their works are an uncleanness and an abomination, and all their ways are pollution, uncleanness and destruction.

18. Behold the earth shall be destroyed on account of all their works, and there shall be no seed of the vine, and no oil; for their works are altogether faithless, and they shall all perish together, beasts and cattle and birds, and all the fish of the sea, on account of the children of men.

19. And they shall strive one with another, the young with the old, and the old with the young, the poor with the rich, the lowly with the great, and the beggar with the prince, on account of the law and the covenant; for they have forgotten commandment, and covenant, and feasts, and months, and Sabbaths, and jubilees, and all judgments.

20. And they shall stand <with bows and> swords and war to turn them back into the way; but they shall not return until much blood has been shed on the earth, one by another.

21. And those who have escaped shall not return from their wickedness to the way of righteousness, but they shall all exalt themselves to deceit and wealth, that they may each take all that is his neighbour's, and they shall name the great name, but not in truth and not in righteousness, and they shall defile the holy of holies with their uncleanness and the corruption of their pollution.

22. And a great punishment shall befall the deeds of this generation from the Lord, and He will give them over to the sword and to judgment and to captivity, and to be plundered and devoured.

23. And He will wake up against them the sinners of the Gentiles, who have neither mercy nor compassion, and who shall respect the person of none, neither old nor young, nor any one, for they are more wicked and strong to do evil than all the children of men.
And they shall use violence against Israel and transgression against Jacob,
And much blood shall be shed upon the earth,
And there shall be none to gather and none to bury.

24. In those days they shall cry aloud,
And call and pray that they may be saved from the hand of the sinners, the Gentiles;
But none shall be saved.

25. And the heads of the children shall be white with grey hair,
And a child of three weeks shall appear old like a man of one hundred years,
And their stature shall be destroyed by tribulation and oppression.

26. And in those days the children shall begin to study the laws,
And to seek the commandments,
And to return to the path of righteousness.

27. And the days shall begin to grow many and increase amongst those children of men
Till their days draw nigh to one thousand years.
And to a greater number of years than (before) was the number of the days.

28. And there shall be no old man
Nor one who is <not> satisfied with his days,
For all shall be (as) children and youths.

29. And all their days they shall complete and live in peace and in joy,
And there shall be no Satan nor any evil destroyer;
For all their days shall be days of blessing and healing.

30. And at that time the Lord will heal His servants,
And they shall rise up and see great peace,
And drive out their adversaries.
And the righteous shall see and be thankful,
And rejoice with joy for ever and ever,
And shall see all their judgments and all their curses on their enemies.

31. And their bones shall rest in the earth,
And their spirits shall have much joy,
And they shall know that it is the Lord who executes judgment,
And shows mercy to hundreds and thousands and to all that love Him

32. And do thou, Moses, write down these words; for thus are they written, and they record (them) on the heavenly tablets for a testimony for the generations for ever.

[Chapter 24]

1. And it came to pass after the death of Abraham, that the Lord blessed Isaac his son, and he arose from Hebron and went and dwelt at the Well of the Vision in the first year of the third week [2073 A.M.] of this jubilee, seven years.

2. And in the first year of the fourth week a famine began in the land, [2080 A.M.] besides the first famine, which had been in the days of Abraham.

3. And Jacob sod lentil pottage, and Esau came from the field hungry. And he said to Jacob his brother: 'Give me of this red pottage.' And Jacob said to him: 'Sell to me thy [primogeniture, this] birthright and I will give thee bread, and also some of this lentil pottage.'

4. And Esau said in his heart: 'I shall die; of what profit to me is this birthright?

5. 'And he said to Jacob: 'I give it to thee.' And Jacob said: 'Swear to me, this day,' and he sware unto him.

6. And Jacob gave his brother Esau bread and pottage, and he eat till he was satisfied, and Esau

despised his birthright; for this reason was Esau's name called Edom, on account of the red pottage which Jacob gave him for his birthright.

7. And Jacob became the elder, and Esau was brought down from his dignity.

8. And the famine was over the land, and Isaac departed to go down into Egypt in the second year of this week, and went to the king of the Philistines to Gerar, unto Abimelech.

9. And the Lord appeared unto him and said unto him: 'Go not down into Egypt; dwell in the land that I shall tell thee of, and sojourn in this land, and I will be with thee and bless thee.

10. For to thee and to thy seed will I give all this land, and I will establish My oath which I sware unto Abraham thy father, and I will multiply thy seed as the stars of heaven, and will give unto thy seed all this land.

11. And in thy seed shall all the nations of the earth be blessed, because thy father obeyed My voice, and kept My charge and My commandments, and My laws, and My ordinances, and My covenant; and now obey My voice and dwell in this land.'

12. And he dwelt in Gelar three weeks of years.

13. And Abimelech charged concerning him, [2080-2101 A.M.] and concerning all that was his, saying: 'Any man that shall touch him or aught that is his shall surely die.'

14. And Isaac waxed strong among the Philistines, and he got many possessions, oxen and sheep and camels and asses and a great household.

15. And he sowed in the land of the Philistines and brought in a hundred-fold, and Isaac became exceedingly great, and the Philistines envied him.

16. Now all the wells which the servants of Abraham had dug during the life of Abraham, the Philistines had stopped them after the death of Abraham, and filled them with earth.

17. And Abimelech said unto Isaac: 'Go from us, for thou art much mightier than we', and Isaac departed thence in the first year of the seventh week, and sojourned in the valleys of Gerar.

18. And they digged again the wells of water which the servants of Abraham, his father, had digged, and which the Philistines had closed after the death of Abraham his father, and he called their names as Abraham his father had named them.

19. And the servants of Isaac dug a well in the valley, and found living water, and the shepherds of Gerar strove with the shepherds of Isaac, saying: 'The water is ours'; and Isaac called the name of the well 'Perversity', because they had been perverse with us.

20. And they dug a second well, and they strove for that also, and he called its name 'Enmity'. And he arose from thence and they digged another well, and for that they strove not, and he called the name of it 'Room', and Isaac said: 'Now the Lord hath made room for us, and we have increased in the land.'

21. And he went up from thence to the Well of the Oath in the first year of the first week in the [2108 A.M.] forty-fourth jubilee.

22. And the Lord appeared to him that night, on the new moon of the first month, and said unto him: 'I am the God of Abraham thy father; fear not, for I am with thee, and shall bless thee and shall surely multiply thy seed as the sand of the earth, for the sake of Abraham my servant.'

23. And he built an altar there, which Abraham his father had first built, and he called upon the name of the Lord, and he offered sacrifice to the God of Abraham his father.

24. And they digged a well and they found living water.

25. And the servants of Isaac digged another well and did not find water, and they went and told Isaac that they had not found water, and Isaac said: 'I have sworn this day to the Philistines and this thing has been announced to us.'

26. And he called the name of that place the Well of the Oath; for there he had sworn to Abimelech and Ahuzzath his friend and Phicol the prefect Or his host.

27. And Isaac knew that day that under constraint he had sworn to them to make peace with them.

28. And Isaac on that day cursed the Philistines and said: 'Cursed be the Philistines unto the day of wrath and indignation from the midst of all nations; may God make them a derision and a curse and an object of wrath and indignation in the hands of the sinners the Gentiles and in the hands of the Kittim.

29. And whoever escapes the sword of the enemy and the Kittim, may the righteous nation root out in judgment from under heaven; for they shall be the enemies and foes of my children throughout their generations upon the earth.

30. And no remnant shall be left to them,
Nor one that shall be saved on the day of the wrath of judgment;
For destruction and rooting out and expulsion from the earth is the whole seed of the Philistines (reserved),
And there shall no longer be left for these Caphtorim a name or a seed on the earth.

31. For though he ascend unto heaven,
Thence shall he be brought down,
And though he make himself strong on earth,
Thence shall he be dragged forth,
And though he hide himself amongst the nations,
Even from thence shall he be rooted out;
And though he descend into Sheol,
There also shall his condemnation be great,
And there also he shall have no peace.

32. And if he go into captivity,
By the hands of those that seek his life shall they slay him on the way,
And neither name nor seed shall be left to him on all the earth;
For into eternal malediction shall he depart.'

33. And thus is it written and engraved concerning him on the heavenly tablets, to do unto him on the day of judgment, so that he may be rooted out of the earth.

[Chapter 25]

1. And in the second year of this week in this jubilee, Rebecca called Jacob her son, and spake unto [2109 A.M.] him, saying: 'My son, do not take thee a wife of the daughters of Canaan, as Esau, thy

brother, who took him two wives of the daughters of Canaan, and they have embittered my soul with all their unclean deeds: for all their deeds are fornication and lust, and there is no righteousness with them, for (their deeds) are evil.

2. And I, my son, love thee exceedingly, and my heart and my affection bless thee every hour of the day and watch of the night.

3. And now, my son, hearken to my voice, and do the will of thy mother, and do not take thee a wife of the daughters of this land, but only of the house of my father, and of my father's kindred. Thou shalt take thee a wife of the house of my father, and the Most High God will bless thee, and thy children shall be a righteous generation and a holy seed.'

4. And then spake Jacob to Rebecca, his mother, and said unto her: 'Behold, mother, I am nine weeks of years old, and I neither know nor have I touched any woman, nor have I betrothed myself to any, nor even think of taking me a wife of the daughters of Canaan.

5. For I remember, mother, the words of Abraham, our father, for he commanded me not to take a wife of the daughters of Canaan, but to take me a wife from the seed of my father's house and from my kindred.

6. I have heard before that daughters have been born to Laban, thy brother, and I have set my heart on them to take a wife from amongst them.

7. And for this reason I have guarded myself in my spirit against sinning or being corrupted in all my ways throughout all the days of my life; for with regard to lust and fornication, Abraham, my father, gave me many commands.

8. And, despite all that he has commanded me, these two and twenty years my brother has striven with me, and spoken frequently to me and said: 'My brother, take to wife a sister of my two wives'; but I refuse to do as he has done.

9. I swear before thee, mother, that all the days of my life I will not take me a wife from the daughters of the seed of Canaan, and I will not act wickedly as my brother has done.

10. Fear not, mother; be assured that I shall do thy will and walk in uprightness, and not corrupt my ways for ever.'

11. And thereupon she lifted up her face to heaven and extended the fingers of her hands, and opened her mouth and blessed the Most High God, who had created the heaven and the earth, and she gave Him thanks and praise.

12. And she said: 'Blessed be the Lord God, and may His holy name be blessed for ever and ever, who has given me Jacob as a pure son and a holy seed; for he is Thine, and Thine shall his seed be continually and throughout all the generations for evermore.

13. Bless him, O Lord, and place in my mouth the blessing of righteousness, that I may bless him.'

14. And at that hour, when the spirit of righteousness descended into her mouth, she placed both her hands on the head of Jacob, and said:

15. Blessed art thou, Lord of righteousness and God of the ages
And may He bless thee beyond all the generations of men.
May He give thee, my Son, the path of righteousness,
And reveal righteousness to thy seed.

16. And may He make thy sons many during thy life,
And may they arise according to the number of the months of the year.
And may their sons become many and great beyond the stars of heaven,
And their numbers be more than the sand of the sea.

17. And may He give them this goodly land -as He said He would give it to Abraham and to his seed after him alway-
And may they hold it as a possession for ever.

18. And may I see (born) unto thee, my son, blessed children during my life,
And a blessed and holy seed may all thy seed be.

19. And as thou hast refreshed thy mother's spirit during her life,
The womb of her that bare thee blesses thee thus,
[My affection] and my breasts bless thee
And my mouth and my tongue praise thee greatly.

20. Increase and spread over the earth,
And may thy seed be perfect in the joy of heaven and earth for ever;
And may thy seed rejoice,
And on the great day of peace may it have peace.

21. And may thy name and thy seed endure to all the ages,
And may the Most High God be their God,
And may the God of righteousness dwell with them,
And by them may His sanctuary be built unto all the ages.

22. Blessed be he that blesseth thee,
And all flesh that curseth thee falsely, may it be cursed.'

23. And she kissed him, and said to him;
'May the Lord of the world love thee
As the heart of thy mother and her affection rejoice in thee and bless thee.'
And she ceased from blessing.

[Chapter 26]

1. And in the seventh year of this week Isaac called Esau, his elder Son, and said unto him: ' I am [2114 A.M.] old, my son, and behold my eyes are dim in seeing, and I know not the day of my death.

2. And now take thy hunting weapons thy quiver and thy bow, and go out to the field, and hunt and catch me (venison), my son, and make me savoury meat, such as my soul loveth, and bring it to me that I may eat, and that my soul may bless thee before I die.'

3. But Rebecca heard Isaac speaking to Esau.

4. And Esau went forth early to the field to hunt and catch and bring home to his father.

5. And Rebecca called Jacob, her son, and said unto him: 'Behold, I heard Isaac, thy father, speak unto Esau, thy brother, saying: "Hunt for me, and make me savoury meat, and bring (it) to me that

6. I may eat and bless thee before the Lord before I die." And now, my son, obey my voice in that which I command thee: Go to thy flock and fetch

me two good kids of the goats, and I will make them savoury meat for thy father, such as he loves, and thou shalt bring (it) to thy father that he may eat and bless thee before the Lord before he die, and that thou mayst be blessed.'

7. And Jacob said to Rebecca his mother: 'Mother, I shall not withhold anything which my father would eat, and which would please him: only I fear, my mother, that he will recognise my voice and wish to touch me.

8. And thou knowest that I am smooth, and Esau, my brother, is hairy, and I shall appear before his eyes as an evildoer, and shall do a deed which he had not commanded me, and he will be wroth with me, and I shall bring upon myself a curse, and not a blessing.'

9. And Rebecca, his mother, said unto him: 'Upon me be thy curse, my son, only obey my voice.'

10. And Jacob obeyed the voice of Rebecca, his mother, and went and fetched two good and fat kids of the goats, and brought them to his mother, and his mother made them ~savoury meat~ such as he loved.

11. And Rebecca took the goodly rainment of Esau, her elder son, which was with her in the house, and she clothed Jacob, her younger son, (with them), and she put the skins of the kids upon his hands and on the exposed parts of his neck.

12. And she gave the meat and the bread which she had prepared into the hand of her son Jacob.

13. And Jacob went in to his father and said: 'I am thy son: I have done according as thou badest me: arise and sit and eat of that which I have caught, father, that thy soul may bless me.'

14. And Isaac said to his son: 'How hast thou found so quickly, my son?

15. 'And Jacob said: 'Because <the Lord> thy God caused me to find.'

16. And Isaac said unto him: Come near, that I may feel thee, my son, if thou art my son Esau or not.'

17. And Jacob went near to Isaac, his father, and he felt him and said: 'The voice is Jacob's voice, but the hands are the hands of Esau,'

18. and he discerned him not, because it was a dispensation from heaven to remove his power of perception and Isaac discerned not, for his hands were hairy as his brother Esau's, so that he blessed him.

19. And he said: 'Art thou my son Esau? ' and he said: 'I am thy son': and he said, 'Bring near to me that I may eat of that which thou hast caught, my son, that my soul may bless thee.'

20. And he brought near to him, and he did eat, and he brought him wine and he drank.

21. And Isaac, his father, said unto him: 'Come near and kiss me, my son.

22. And he came near and kissed him. And he smelled the smell of his raiment, and he blessed him and said: 'Behold, the smell of my son is as the smell of a <full> field which the Lord hath blessed.

23. And may the Lord give thee of the dew of heaven And of the dew of the earth, and plenty of corn and oil: Let nations serve thee, And peoples bow down to thee.

24. Be lord over thy brethren,

And let thy mother's sons bow down to thee; And may all the blessings wherewith the Lord hath blessed me and blessed Abraham, my father; Be imparted to thee and to thy seed for ever: Cursed be he that curseth thee, And blessed be he that blesseth thee.'

25. And it came to pass as soon as Isaac had made an end of blessing his son Jacob, and Jacob had gone forth from Isaac his father he hid himself and Esau, his brother, came in from his hunting.

26. And he also made savoury meat, and brought (it) to his father, and said unto his father: 'Let my father arise, and eat of my venison that thy soul may bless me.'

27. And Isaac, his father, said unto him: 'Who art thou? 'And he said unto him: 'I am thy first born, thy son Esau: I have done as thou hast commanded me.'

28. And Isaac was very greatly astonished, and said: 'Who is he that hath hunted and caught and brought (it) to me, and I have eaten of all before thou camest, and have blessed him: (and) he shall be blessed, and all his seed for ever.'

29. And it came to pass when Esau heard the words of his father Isaac that he cried with an exceeding great and bitter cry, and said unto his father: 'Bless me, (even) me also, father.'

30. And he said unto him: 'Thy brother came with guile, and hath taken away thy blessing.' And he said: 'Now I know why his name is named Jacob: behold, he hath supplanted me these two times: he took away my birth-right, and now he hath taken away my blessing.'

31. And he said: 'Hast thou not reserved a blessing for me, father?' and Isaac answered and said unto Esau: 'Behold, I have made him thy lord, And all his brethren have I given to him for servants, And with plenty of corn and wine and oil have I strengthened him: And what now shall I do for thee, my son?'

32. And Esau said to Isaac, his father: 'Hast thou but one blessing, O father? Bless me, (even) me also, father: '

33. And Esau lifted up his voice and wept. And Isaac answered and said unto him: 'Behold, far from the dew of the earth shall be thy dwelling, And far from the dew of heaven from above.

34. And by thy sword wilt thou live, And thou wilt serve thy brother. And it shall come to pass when thou becomest great, And dost shake his yoke from off thy neck, Thou shalt sin a complete sin unto death, And thy seed shall be rooted out from under heaven.'

35. And Esau kept threatening Jacob because of the blessing wherewith his father blessed him, and he said in his heart: 'May the days of mourning for my father now come, so that I may slay my brother Jacob.'

[Chapter 27]

1. And the words of Esau, her elder son, were told to Rebecca in a dream, and Rebecca sent and called Jacob her younger son,

2. and said unto him: 'Behold Esau thy brother will take vengeance on thee so as to kill thee.

3. Now, therefore, my son, obey my voice, and arise and flee thou to Laban, my brother, to Haran, and tarry with him a few days until thy brother's anger turns away, and he remove his anger from thee, and forget all that thou hast done; then I will send and fetch thee from thence.'

4. And Jacob said: 'I am not afraid; if he wishes to kill me, I will kill him.'

5. But she said unto him: 'Let me not be bereft of both my sons on one day.'

6. And Jacob said to Rebecca his mother: 'Behold, thou knowest that my father has become old, and does not see because his eyes are dull, and if I leave him it will be evil in his eyes, because I leave him and go away from you, and my father will be angry, and will curse me. I will not go; when he sends me, then only will I go.'

7. And Rebecca said to Jacob: 'I will go in and speak to him, and he will send thee away.'

8. And Rebecca went in and said to Isaac: 'I loathe my life because of the two daughters of Heth, whom Esau has taken him as wives; and if Jacob take a wife from among the daughters of the land such as these, for what purpose do I further live, for the daughters of Canaan are evil.'

9. And Isaac called Jacob and blessed him, and admonished him and said unto him: 'Do not take thee a wife of any of the daughters of Canaan;

10. arise and go to Mesopotamia, to the house of Bethuel, thy mother's father, and take thee a wife from thence of the daughters of Laban, thy mother's brother.

11. And God Almighty bless thee and increase and multiply thee that thou mayest become a company of nations, and give thee the blessings of my father Abraham, to thee and to thy seed after thee, that thou mayest inherit the land of thy sojournings and all the land which God gave to Abraham: go, my son, in peace.'

12. And Isaac sent Jacob away, and he went to Mesopotamia, to Laban the son of Bethuel the Syrian, the brother of Rebecca, Jacob's mother.

13. And it came to pass after Jacob had arisen to go to Mesopotamia that the spirit of Rebecca was grieved after her son, and she wept.

14. And Isaac said to Rebecca: 'My sister, weep not on account of Jacob, my son; for he goeth in peace, and in peace will he return.

15. The Most High God will preserve him from all evil, and will be with him; for He will not forsake him all his days;

16. For I know that his ways will be prospered in all things wherever he goes, until he return in peace to us, and we see him in peace.

17. Fear not on his account, my sister, for he is on the upright path and he is a perfect man: and he is faithful and will not perish. Weep not.'

18. And Isaac comforted Rebecca on account of her son Jacob, and blessed him.

19. And Jacob went from the Well of the Oath to go to Haran on the first year of the second week in the forty-fourth jubilee, and he came to Luz on the mountains, that is, Bethel, on the new moon of the first month of this week, [2115 A.M.] and he came to the place at even and turned from the way to the west of the road that night: and he slept there; for the sun had set.

20. And he took one of the stones of that place and laid <it at his head> under the tree, and he was journeying alone, and he slept.

21. And he dreamt that night, and behold a ladder set up on the earth, and the top of it reached to heaven, and behold, the angels of the Lord ascended and descended on it: and behold, the Lord stood upon it.

22. And he spake to Jacob and said: 'I am the Lord God of Abraham, thy father, and the God of Isaac; the land whereon thou art sleeping, to thee will I give it, and to thy seed after thee.

23. And thy seed shall be as the dust of the earth, and thou shalt increase to the west and to the east, to the north and the south, and in thee and in thy seed shall all the families of the nations be blessed.

24. And behold, I will be with thee, and will keep thee whithersoever thou goest, and I will bring thee again into this land in peace; for I will not leave thee until I do everything that I told thee of.'

25. And Jacob awoke from his sleep, and said, 'Truly this place is the house of the Lord, and I knew it not.' And he was afraid and said: 'Dreadful is this place which is none other than the house of God, and this is the gate of heaven.'

26. And Jacob arose early in the morning, and took the stone which he had put under his head and set it up as a pillar for a sign, and he poured oil upon the top of it. And he called the name of that place Bethel; but the name of the place was Luz at the first.

27. And Jacob vowed a vow unto the Lord, saying: 'If the Lord will be with me, and will keep me in this way that I go, and give me bread to eat and raiment to put on, so that I come again to my father's house in peace, then shall the Lord be my God, and this stone which I have set up as a pillar for a sign in this place, shall be the Lord's house, and of all that thou givest me, I shall give the tenth to thee, my God.'

[Chapter 28]

1. And he went on his journey, and came to the land of the east, to Laban, the brother of Rebecca, and he was with him, and served him for Rachel his daughter one week.

2. And in the first year of the third week [2122 A.M.] he said unto him: 'Give me my wife, for whom I have served thee seven years'; and Laban said unto Jacob: 'I will give thee thy wife.'

3. And Laban made a feast, and took Leah his elder daughter, and gave (her) to Jacob as a wife, and gave her Zilpah his handmaid for an hand-maid; and Jacob did not know, for he thought that she was Rachel.

4. And he went in unto her, and behold, she was Leah; and Jacob was angry with Laban, and said unto him: 'Why hast thou dealt thus with me? Did not I serve thee for Rachel and not for Leah? Why

hast thou wronged me?

5. Take thy daughter, and I will go; for thou hast done evil to me.' For Jacob loved Rachel more than Leah; for Leah's eyes were weak, but her form was very handsome; but Rachel had beautiful eyes and a beautiful and very handsome form.

6. And Laban said to Jacob: 'It is not so done in our country, to give the younger before the elder.' And it is not right to do this; for thus it is ordained and written in the heavenly tablets, that no one should give his younger daughter before the elder; but the elder, one gives first and after her the younger - and the man who does so, they set down guilt against him in heaven, and none is righteous that does this thing, for this deed is evil before the Lord.

7. And command thou the children of Israel that they do not this thing; let them neither take nor give the younger before they have given the elder, for it is very wicked.

8. And Laban said to Jacob: 'Let the seven days of the feast of this one pass by, and I shall give thee Rachel, that thou mayst serve me another seven years, that thou mayst pasture my sheep as thou didst in the former week.'

9. And on the day when the seven days of the feast of Leah had passed, Laban gave Rachel to Jacob, that he might serve him another seven years, and he gave to Rachel Bilhah, the sister of Zilpah, as a handmaid.

10. And he served yet other seven years for Rachel, for Leah had been given to him for nothing.

11. And the Lord opened the womb of Leah, and she conceived and bare Jacob a son, and he called his name Reuben, on the fourteenth day of the ninth month, in the first year of the third week. [2122 A.M.]

12. But the womb of Rachel was closed, for the Lord saw that Leah was hated and Rachel loved.

13. And again Jacob went in unto Leah, and she conceived, and bare Jacob a second son, and he called his name Simeon, on the twenty-first of the tenth month, and in the third year of this week. [2124 A.M.]

14. And again Jacob went in unto Leah, and she conceived, and bare him a third son, and he called his name Levi, in the new moon of the first month in the sixth year of this week. [2127 A.M.]

15. And again Jacob went in unto her, and she conceived, and bare him a fourth son, and he called his name Judah, on the fifteenth of the third month, in the first year of the fourth week. [2129 A.M.]

16. And on account of all this Rachel envied Leah, for she did not bear, and she said to Jacob: 'Give me children'; and Jacob said: 'Have I withheld from thee the fruits of thy womb? Have I forsaken thee?'

17. And when Rachel saw that Leah had borne four sons to Jacob, Reuben and Simeon and Levi and Judah, she said unto him: 'Go in unto Bilhah my handmaid, and she will conceive, and bear a son unto me.' (And she gave (him) Bilhah her handmaid to wife).

18. And he went in unto her, and she conceived, and bare him a son, and he called his name Dan, on the ninth of the sixth month, in the sixth year of the third week. [2127 A.M.]

19. And Jacob went in again unto Bilhah a second time, and she conceived, and bare Jacob another son, and Rachel called his name Napthali, on the fifth of the seventh month, in the second year of the fourth week. [2130 A.M.]

20. And when Leah saw that she had become sterile and did not bear, she envied Rachel, and she also gave her handmaid Zilpah to Jacob to wife, and she conceived, and bare a son, and Leah called his name Gad, on the twelfth of the eighth month, in the third year of the fourth week. [2131 A.M.]

21. And he went in again unto her, and she conceived, and bare him a second son, and Leah called his name Asher, on the second of the eleventh month, in the fifth year of the fourth week. [2133 A.M.]

22. And Jacob went in unto Leah, and she conceived, and bare a son, and she called his name Issachar, on the fourth of the fifth month, in the fourth year of the fourth week,[2132 A.M.] and she gave him to a nurse.

23. And Jacob went in again unto her, and she conceived, and bare two (children), a son and a daughter, and she called the name of the son Zabulon, and the name of the daughter Dinah, in the seventh of the seventh month, in the sixth year of the fourth week. [2134 A.M.]

24. And the Lord was gracious to Rachel, and opened her womb, and she conceived, and bare a son, and she called his name Joseph, on the new moon of the fourth month, in the sixth year in this fourth week. [2134 A.M.]

25. And in the days when Joseph was born, Jacob said to Laban: 'Give me my wives and sons, and let me go to my father Isaac, and let me make me an house; for I have completed the years in which I have served thee for thy two daughters, and I will go to the house of my father.'

26. And Laban said to Jacob: 'Tarry with me for thy wages, and pasture my flock for me again, and take thy wages.'

27. And they agreed with one another that he should give him as his wages those of the lambs and kids which were born black and spotted and white, (these) were to be his wages.

28. And all the sheep brought forth spotted and speckled and black, variously marked, and they brought forth again lambs like themselves, and all that were spotted were Jacob's and those which were not were Laban's.

29. And Jacob's possessions multiplied exceedingly, and he possessed oxen and sheep and asses and camels, and menservants and maid-servants.

30. And Laban and his sons envied Jacob, and Laban took back his sheep from him, and he observed him with evil intent.

[Chapter 29]

1. And it came to pass when Rachel had borne Joseph, that Laban went to shear his sheep; for they were distant from him a three days' journey.

2. And Jacob saw that Laban was going to shear his sheep, and Jacob called Leah and Rachel, and spake kindly unto them that they should come

with him to the land of Canaan.

3. For he told them how he had seen everything in a dream, even all that He had spoken unto him that he should return to his father's house, and they said: "To every place whither thou goest we will go with thee.'

4. And Jacob blessed the God of Isaac his father, and the God of Abraham his father's father, and he arose and mounted his wives and his children, and took all his possessions and crossed the river, and came to the land of Gilead, and Jacob hid his intention from Laban and told him not.

5. And in the seventh year of the fourth week Jacob turned (his face) toward Gilead in the first month, on the twenty-first thereof. [2135 A.M.] And Laban pursued after him and overtook Jacob in the mountain of Gilead in the third month, on the thirteenth thereof.

6. And the Lord did not suffer him to injure Jacob; for he appeared to him in a dream by night. And Laban spake to Jacob.

7. And on the fifteenth of those days Jacob made a feast for Laban, and for all who came with him, and Jacob sware to Laban that day, and Laban also to Jacob, that neither should cross the mountain of Gilead to the other with evil purpose.

8. And he made there a heap for a witness; wherefore the name of that place is called: 'The Heap of Witness,' after this heap.

9. But before they used to call the land of Gilead the land of the Rephaim; for it was the land of the Rephaim, and the Rephaim were born (there), giants whose height was ten, nine, eight down to seven cubits.

10. And their habitation was from the land of the children of Ammon to Mount Hermon, and the seats of their kingdom were Karnaim and Ashtaroth, and Edrei, and Misur, and Beon.

11. And the Lord destroyed them because of the evil of their deeds; for they were very malignant, and the Amorites dwelt in their stead, wicked and sinful, and there is no people to-day which has wrought to the full all their sins, and they have no longer length of life on the earth.

12. And Jacob sent away Laban, and he departed into Mesopotamia, the land of the East, and Jacob returned to the land of Gilead.

13. And he passed over the Jabbok in the ninth month, on the eleventh thereof. And on that day Esau, his brother, came to him, and he was reconciled to him, and departed from him unto the land of Seir, but Jacob dwelt in tents.

14. And in the first year of the fifth week in this jubilee [2136 A.M.] he crossed the Jordan, and dwelt beyond the Jordan, and he pastured his sheep from the sea of the heap unto Bethshan, and unto Dothan and unto the forest of Akrabbim.

15. And he sent to his father Isaac of all his substance, clothing, and food, and meat, and drink, and milk, and butter, and cheese, and some dates of the valley.

16. And to his mother Rebecca also four times a year, between the times of the months, between ploughing and reaping, and between autumn and the rain (season) and between winter and spring,

to the tower of Abraham.

17. For Isaac had returned from the Well of the Oath and gone up to the tower of his father Abraham, and he dwelt there apart from his son Esau.

18. For in the days when Jacob went to Mesopotamia, Esau took to himself a wife Mahalath, the daughter of Ishmael, and he gathered together all the flocks of his father and his wives, and went Up and dwelt on Mount Seir, and left Isaac his father at the Well of the Oath alone.

19. And Isaac went up from the Well of the Oath and dwelt in the tower of Abraham his father on the mountains of Hebron,

20. And thither Jacob sent all that he did send to his father and his mother from time to time, all they needed, and they blessed Jacob with all their heart and with all their soul.

[Chapter 30]

1. And in the first year of the sixth week [2143 A.M.] he went up to Salem, to the east of Shechem, in peace, in the fourth month.

2. And there they carried off Dinah, the daughter of Jacob, into the house of Shechem, the son of Hamor, the Hivite, the prince of the land, and he lay with her and defiled her, and she was a little girl, a child of twelve years.

3. And he besought his father and her brothers that she might be given to him to wife. And Jacob and his sons were wroth because of the men of Shechem; for they had defiled Dinah, their sister, and they spake to them with evil intent and dealt deceitfully with them and beguiled them.

4. And Simeon and Levi came unexpectedly to Shechem and executed judgment on all the men of Shechem, and slew all the men whom they found in it, and left not a single one remaining in it: they slew all in torments because they had dishonoured their sister Dinah.

5. And thus let it not again be done from henceforth that a daughter of Israel be defiled; for judgment is ordained in heaven against them that they should destroy with the sword all the men of the Shechemites because they had wrought shame in Israel.

6. And the Lord delivered them into the hands of the sons of Jacob that they might exterminate them with the sword and execute judgment upon them, and that it might not thus again be done in Israel that a virgin of Israel should be defiled.

7. And if there is any man who wishes in Israel to give his daughter or his sister to any man who is of the seed of the Gentiles he shall surely die, and they shall stone him with stones; for he hath wrought shame in Israel; and they shall burn the woman with fire, because she has dishonoured the name of the house of her father, and she shall be rooted out of Israel.

8. And let not an adulteress and no uncleanness be found in Israel throughout all the days of the generations of the earth; for Israel is holy unto the Lord, and every man who has defiled (it) shall surely die: they shall stone him with stones.

9. For thus has it been ordained and written in the heavenly tablets regarding all the seed of Israel: he

who defileth (it) shall surely die, and he shall be stoned with stones.

10. And to this law there is no limit of days, and no remission, nor any atonement: but the man who has defiled his daughter shall be rooted out in the midst of all Israel, because he has given of his seed to Moloch, and wrought impiously so as to defile it.

11. And do thou, Moses, command the children of Israel and exhort them not to give their daughters to the Gentiles, and not to take for their sons any of the daughters of the Gentiles, for this is abominable before the Lord.

12. For this reason I have written for thee in the words of the Law all the deeds of the Shechemites, which they wrought against Dinah, and how the sons of Jacob spake, saying: 'We will not give our daughter to a man who is uncircumcised; for that were a reproach unto us.'

13. And it is a reproach to Israel, to those who live, and to those that take the daughters of the Gentiles; for this is unclean and abominable to Israel.

14. And Israel will not be free from this uncleanness if it has a wife of the daughters of the Gentiles, or has given any of its daughters to a man who is of any of the Gentiles.

15. For there will be plague upon plague, and curse upon curse, and every judgment and plague and curse will come *upon him*: if he do this thing, or hide his eyes from those who commit uncleanness, or those who defile the sanctuary of the Lord, or those who profane His holy name, (then) will the whole nation together be judged for all the uncleanness and profanation of this man.

16. And there will be no respect of persons [and no consideration of persons] and no receiving at his hands of fruits and offerings and burnt-offerings and fat, nor the fragrance of sweet savour, so as to accept it: and so fare every man or woman in Israel who defiles the sanctuary.

17. For this reason I have commanded thee, saying: 'Testify this testimony to Israel: see how the Shechemites fared and their sons: how they were delivered into the hands of two sons of Jacob, and they slew them under tortures, and it was (reckoned) unto them for righteousness, and it is written down to them for righteousness.

18. And the seed of Levi was chosen for the priesthood, and to be Levites, that they might minister before the Lord, as we, continually, and that Levi and his sons may be blessed for ever; for he was zealous to execute righteousness and judgment and vengeance on all those who arose against Israel.

19. And so they inscribe as a testimony in his favour on the heavenly tablets blessing and righteousness before the God of all:

20. And we remember the righteousness which the man fulfilled during his life, at all periods of the year; until a thousand generations they will record it, and it will come to him and to his descendants after him, and he has been recorded on the heavenly tablets as a friend and a righteous man.

21. All this account I have written for thee, and have commanded thee to say to the children of Israel, that they should not commit sin nor transgress the ordinances nor break the covenant which has been ordained for them, (but) that they should fulfil it and be recorded as friends.

22. But if they transgress and work uncleanness in every way, they will be recorded on the heavenly tablets as adversaries, and they will be destroyed out of the book of life, and they will be recorded in the book of those who will be destroyed and with those who will be rooted out of the earth.

23. And on the day when the sons of Jacob slew Shechem a writing was recorded in their favour in heaven that they had executed righteousness and uprightness and vengeance on the sinners, and it was written for a blessing.

24. And they brought Dinah, their sister, out of the house of Shechem, and they took captive everything that was in Shechem, their sheep and their oxen and their asses, and all their wealth, and all their flocks, and brought them all to Jacob their father.

25. And he reproached them because they had put the city to the sword for he feared those who dwelt in the land, the Canaanites and the Perizzites.

26. And the dread of the Lord was upon all the cities which are around about Shechem, and they did not rise to pursue after the sons of Jacob; for terror had fallen upon them.

[Chapter 31]

1. And on the new moon of the month Jacob spake to all the people of his house. saying: 'Purify yourselves and change your garments, and let us arise and go up to Bethel, where I vowed a vow to Him on the day when I fled from the face of Esau my brother, because he has been with me and brought me into this land in peace, and put ye away the strange gods that are among you.'

2. And they gave up the strange gods and that which was in their ears and which was on their necks and the idols which Rachel stole from Laban her father she gave wholly to Jacob. And he burnt and brake them to pieces and destroyed them, and hid them under an oak which is in the land of Shechem.

3. And he went up on the new moon of the seventh month to Bethel. And he built an altar at the place where he had slept, and he set up a pillar there, and he sent word to his father Isaac to come to him to his sacrifice, and to his mother Rebecca.

4. And Isaac said: 'Let my son Jacob come, and let me see him before I die.'

5. And Jacob went to his father Isaac and to his mother Rebecca, to the house of his father Abraham, and he took two of his sons with him, Levi and Judah, and he came to his father Isaac and to his mother Rebecca.

6. And Rebecca came forth from the tower to the front of it to kiss Jacob and embrace him; for her spirit had revived when she heard: 'Behold Jacob thy son has come'; and she kissed him.

7. And she saw his two sons, and she recognised them, and said unto him: 'Are these thy sons, my son?' and she embraced them and kissed them, and blessed them, saying: 'In you shall the seed of Abraham become illustrious, and ye shall prove a

blessing on the earth.'

8. And Jacob went in to Isaac his father, to the chamber where he lay, and his two sons were with him, and he took the hand of his father, and stooping down he kissed him, and Isaac clung to the neck of Jacob his son, and wept upon his neck.

9. And the darkness left the eyes of Isaac, and he saw the two sons of Jacob, Levi, and Judah, and he said: 'Are these thy sons, my son? for they are like thee.'

10. And he said unto him that they were truly his sons: 'And thou hast truly seen that they are truly my sons'.

11. And they came near to him, and he turned and kissed them and embraced them both together.

12. And the spirit of prophecy came down into his mouth, and he took Levi by his right hand and Judah by his left.

13. And he turned to Levi first, and began to bless him first, and said unto him: May the God of all, the very Lord of all the ages, bless thee and thy children throughout all the ages.

14. And may the Lord give to thee and to thy seed greatness and great glory, and cause thee and thy seed, from among all flesh, to approach Him to serve in His sanctuary as the angels of the presence and as the holy ones. (Even) as they, shall the seed of thy sons be for glory and greatness and holiness, and may He make them great unto all the ages.

15. And they shall be judges and princes, and chiefs of all the seed of the sons of Jacob;
They shall speak the word of the Lord in righteousness,
And they shall judge all His judgments in righteousness.
And they shall declare My ways to Jacob
And My paths to Israel.
The blessing of the Lord shall be given in their mouths
To bless all the seed of the beloved.

16. Thy mother has called thy name Levi,
And justly has she called thy name;
Thou shalt be joined to the Lord
And be the companion of all the sons of Jacob;
Let His table be thine,
And do thou and thy sons eat thereof;
And may thy table be full unto all generations,
And thy food fail not unto all the ages.

17. And let all who hate thee fall down before thee,
And let all thy adversaries be rooted out and perish;
And blessed be he that blesses thee,
And cursed be every nation that curses thee.'

18. And to Judah he said:
'May the Lord give thee strength and power
To tread down all that hate thee;
A prince shalt thou be, thou and one of thy sons, over the sons of Jacob;
May thy name and the name of thy sons go forth and traverse every land and region.
Then shall the Gentiles fear before thy face,
And all the nations shall quake
[And all the peoples shall quake].

19. In thee shall be the help of Jacob,
And in thee be found the salvation of Israel.

20. And when thou sittest on the throne of honour of thy righteousness
There shall be great peace for all the seed of the sons of the beloved;
Blessed be he that blesseth thee,
And all that hate thee and afflict thee and curse thee
Shall be rooted out and destroyed from the earth and be accursed.'

21. And turning he kissed him again and embraced him, and rejoiced greatly; for he had seen the sons of Jacob his son in very truth.

22. And he went forth from between his feet and fell down and bowed down to him, and he blessed them and rested there with Isaac his father that night, and they eat and drank with joy.

23. And he made the two sons of Jacob sleep, the one on his right hand and the other on his left, and it was counted to him for righteousness.

24. And Jacob told his father everything during the night, how the Lord had shown him great mercy, and how he had prospered (him in) all his ways, and protected him from all evil.

25. And Isaac blessed the God of his father Abraham, who had not withdrawn his mercy and his righteousness from the sons of his servant Isaac.

26. And in the morning Jacob told his father Isaac the vow which he had vowed to the Lord, and the vision which he had seen, and that he had built an altar, and that everything was ready for the sacrifice to be made before the Lord as he had vowed, and that he had come to set him on an ass.

27. And Isaac said unto Jacob his son: 'I am not able to go with thee; for I am old and not able to bear the way: go, my son, in peace; for I am one hundred and sixty-five years this day; I am no longer able to journey; set thy mother (on an ass) and let her go with thee.

28. And I know, my son, that thou hast come on my account, and may this day be blessed on which thou hast seen me alive, and I also have seen thee, my son.

29. Mayest thou prosper and fulfil the vow which thou hast vowed; and put not off thy vow; for thou shalt be called to account as touching the vow; now therefore make haste to perform it, and may He be pleased who has made all things, to whom thou hast vowed the vow.'

30. And he said to Rebecca: 'Go with Jacob thy son'; and Rebecca went with Jacob her son, and Deborah with her, and they came to Bethel.

31. And Jacob remembered the prayer with which his father had blessed him and his two sons, Levi and Judah, and he rejoiced and blessed the God of his fathers, Abraham and Isaac.

32. And he said: 'Now I know that I have an eternal hope, and my sons also, before the God of all'; and thus is it ordained concerning the two; and they record it as an eternal testimony unto them on the heavenly tablets how Isaac blessed them.

[Chapter 32]

1. And he abode that night at Bethel, and Levi dreamed that they had ordained and made him the priest of the Most High God, him and his sons for

ever; and he awoke from his sleep and blessed the Lord.

2. And Jacob rose early in the morning, on the fourteenth of this month, and he gave a tithe of all that came with him, both of men and cattle, both of gold and every vessel and garment, yea, he gave tithes of all.

3. And in those days Rachel became pregnant with her son Benjamin. And Jacob counted his sons from him upwards and Levi fell to the portion of the Lord, and his father clothed him in the garments of the priesthood and filled his hands.

4. And on the fifteenth of this month, he brought to the altar fourteen oxen from amongst the cattle, and twenty-eight rams, and forty-nine sheep, and seven lambs, and twenty-one kids of the goats as a burnt-offering on the altar of sacrifice, well pleasing for a sweet savour before God.

5. This was his offering, in consequence of the vow which he had vowed that he would give a tenth, with their fruit-offerings and their drink- offerings.

6. And when the fire had consumed it, he burnt incense on the fire over the fire, and for a thank-offering two oxen and four rams and four sheep, four he-goats, and two sheep of a year old, and two kids of the goats; and thus he did daily for seven days.

7. And he and all his sons and his men were eating (this) with joy there during seven days and blessing and thanking the Lord, who had delivered him out of all his tribulation and had given him his vow.

8. And he tithed all the clean animals, and made a burnt sacrifice, but the unclean animals he gave (not) to Levi his son, and he gave him all the souls of the men.

9. And Levi discharged the priestly office at Bethel before Jacob his father in preference to his ten brothers, and he was a priest there, and Jacob gave his vow: thus he tithed again the tithe to the Lord and sanctified it, and it became holy unto Him.

10. And for this reason it is ordained on the heavenly tablets as a law for the tithing again the tithe to eat before the Lord from year to year, in the place where it is chosen that His name should dwell, and to this law there is no limit of days for ever.

11. This ordinance is written that it may be fulfilled from year to year in eating the second tithe before the Lord in the place where it has been chosen, and nothing shall remain over from it from this year to the year following.

12. For in its year shall the seed be eaten till the days of the gathering of the seed of the year, and the wine till the days of the wine, and the oil till the days of its season.

13. And all that is left thereof and becomes old, let it be regarded as polluted: let it be burnt with fire, for it is unclean.

14. And thus let them eat it together in the sanctuary, and let them not suffer it to become old.

15. And all the tithes of the oxen and sheep shall be holy unto the Lord, and shall belong to his priests, which they will eat before Him from year to year; for thus is it ordained and engraven regarding the tithe on the heavenly tablets.

16. And on the following night, on the twenty-second day of this month, Jacob resolved to build that place, and to surround the court with a wall, and to sanctify it and make it holy for ever, for himself and his children after him.

17. And the Lord appeared to him by night and blessed him and said unto him: "Thy name shall not be called Jacob, but Israel shall they name thy name.'

18. And He said unto him again: 'I am the Lord who created the heaven and the earth, and I will increase thee and multiply thee exceedingly, and kings shall come forth from thee, and they shall judge everywhere wherever the foot of the sons of men has trodden.

19. And I will give to thy seed all the earth which is under heaven, and they shall judge all the nations according to their desires, and after that they shall get possession of the whole earth and inherit it for ever.'

20. And He finished speaking with him, and He went up from him. and Jacob looked till He had ascended into heaven.

21. And he saw in a vision of the night, and behold an angel descended from heaven with seven tablets in his hands, and he gave them to Jacob, and he read them and knew all that was written therein which would befall him and his sons throughout all the ages.

22. And he showed him all that was written on the tablets, and said unto him: 'Do not build this place, and do not make it an eternal sanctuary, and do not dwell here; for this is not the place. Go to the house of Abraham thy father and dwell with Isaac thy father until the day of the death of thy father.

23. For in Egypt thou shalt die in peace, and in this land thou shalt be buried with honour in the sepulchre of thy fathers, with Abraham and Isaac.

24. Fear not, for as thou hast seen and read it, thus shall it all be; and do thou write down everything as thou hast seen and read.'

25. And Jacob said: 'Lord, how can I remember all that I have read and seen? 'And he said unto him: 'I will bring all things to thy remembrance.'

26. And he went up from him, and he awoke from his sleep, and he remembered everything which he had read and seen, and he wrote down all the words which he had read and seen.

27. And he celebrated there yet another day, and he sacrificed thereon according to all that he sacrificed on the former days, and called its name 'Addition,' for this day was added and the former days he called 'The Feast '.

28. And thus it was manifested that it should be, and it is written on the heavenly tablets: wherefore it was revealed to him that he should celebrate it, and add it to the seven days of the feast.

29. And its name was called 'Addition,' because that it was recorded amongst the days of the feast days, according to the number of the days of the year.

30. And in the night, on the twenty-third of this month, Deborah Rebecca's nurse died, and they buried her beneath the city under the oak of the river, and he called the name of this place, 'The river of Deborah,' and the oak, 'The oak of the mourning of Deborah.'

31. And Rebecca went and returned to her house to his father Isaac, and Jacob sent by her hand rams

and sheep and he-goats that she should prepare a meal for his father such as he desired.

32. And he went after his mother till he came to the land of Kabratan, and he dwelt there.

33. And Rachel bare a son in the night, and called his name 'Son of my sorrow '; for she suffered in giving him birth: but his father called his name Benjamin, on the eleventh of the eighth month in the first of the sixth week of this jubilee. [2143 A.M.]

34. And Rachel died there and she was buried in the land of Ephrath, the same is Bethlehem, and Jacob built a pillar on the grave of Rachel, on the road above her grave.

[Chapter 33]

1. And Jacob went and dwelt to the south of Magdaladra'ef. And he went to his father Isaac, he and Leah his wife, on the new moon of the tenth month.

2. And Reuben saw Bilhah, Rachel's maid, the concubine of his father, bathing in water in a secret place, and he loved her.

3. And he hid himself at night, and he entered the house of Bilhah [at night], and he found her sleeping alone on a bed in her house.

4. And he lay with her, and she awoke and saw, and behold Reuben was lying with her in the bed, and she uncovered the border of her covering and seized him, and cried out, and discovered that it was Reuben.

5. And she was ashamed because of him, and released her hand from him, and he fled.

6. And she lamented because of this thing exceedingly, and did not tell it to any one.

7. And when Jacob returned and sought her, she said unto him: 'I am not clean for thee, for I have been defiled as regards thee; for Reuben has defiled me, and has lain with me in the night, and I was asleep, and did not discover until he uncovered my skirt and slept with me.'

8. And Jacob was exceedingly wroth with Reuben because he had lain with Bilhah, because he had uncovered his father's skirt.

9. And Jacob did not approach her again because Reuben had defiled her. And as for any man who uncovers his father's skirt his deed is wicked exceedingly, for he is abominable before the Lord.

10. For this reason it is written and ordained on the heavenly tablets that a man should not lie with his father's wife, and should not uncover his father's skirt, for this is unclean: they shall surely die together, the man who lies with his father's wife and the woman also, for they have wrought uncleanness on the earth.

11. And there shall be nothing unclean before our God in the nation which He has chosen for Himself as a possession.

12. And again, it is written a second time: 'Cursed be he who lieth with the wife of his father, for he hath uncovered his father's shame'; and all the holy ones of the Lord said 'So be it; so be it.'

13. And do thou, Moses, command the children of Israel that they observe this word; for it (entails) a punishment of death; and it is unclean, and there is

no atonement for ever to atone for the man who has committed this, but he is to be put to death and slain, and stoned with stones, and rooted out from the midst of the people of our God.

14. For to no man who does so in Israel is it permitted to remain alive a single day on the earth, for he is abominable and unclean.

15. And let them not say: to Reuben was granted life and forgiveness after he had lain with his father's concubine, and to her also though she had a husband, and her husband Jacob, his father, was still alive.

16. For until that time there had not been revealed the ordinance and judgment and law in its completeness for all, but in thy days (it has been revealed) as a law of seasons and of days, and an everlasting law for the everlasting generations.

17. And for this law there is no consummation of days, and no atonement for it, but they must both be rooted out in the midst of the nation: on the day whereon they committed it they shall slay them.

18. And do thou, Moses, write (it) down for Israel that they may observe it, and do according to these words, and not commit a sin unto death; for the Lord our God is judge, who respects not persons and accepts not gifts.

19. And tell them these words of the covenant, that they may hear and observe, and be on their guard with respect to them, and not be destroyed and rooted out of the land; for an uncleanness, and an abomination, and a contamination, and a pollution are all they who commit it on the earth before our God.

20. And there is no greater sin than the fornication which they commit on earth; for Israel is a holy nation unto the Lord its God, and a nation of inheritance, and a priestly and royal nation and for (His own) possession; and there shall no such uncleanness appear in the midst of the holy nation.

21. And in the third year of this sixth week [2145 A.M.] Jacob and all his sons went and dwelt in the house of Abraham, near Isaac his father and Rebecca his mother.

22. And these were the names of the sons of Jacob: the first-born Reuben, Simeon, Levi, Judah, Issachar, Zebulon, the sons of Leah; and the sons of Rachel, Joseph and Benjamin; and the sons of Bilhah, Dan and Naphtali; and the sons of Zilpah, Gad and Asher; and Dinah, the daughter of Leah, the only daughter of Jacob.

23. And they came and bowed themselves to Isaac and Rebecca, and when they saw them they blessed Jacob and all his sons, and Isaac rejoiced exceedingly, for he saw the sons of Jacob, his younger son and he blessed them.

[Chapter 34]

1. And in the sixth year of this week of this forty-fourth jubilee [2148 A.M.] Jacob sent his sons to pasture their sheep, and his servants with them to the pastures of Shechem.

2. And the seven kings of the Amorites assembled themselves together against them, to slay them, hiding themselves under the trees, and to take

their cattle as a prey.

3. And Jacob and Levi and Judah and Joseph were in the house with Isaac their father; for his spirit was sorrowful, and they could not leave him: and Benjamin was the youngest, and for this reason remained with his father.

4. And there came the king[s] of Taphu and the king[s] of 'Aresa, and the king[s] of Seragan, and the king[s] of Selo, and the king[s] of Ga'as, and the king of Bethoron, and the king of Ma'anisakir, and all those who dwell in these mountains (and) who dwell in the woods in the land of Canaan.

5. And they announced this to Jacob saying: 'Behold, the kings of the Amorites have surrounded thy sons, and plundered their herds.'

6. And he arose from his house, he and his three sons and all the servants of his father, and his own servants, and he went against them with six thousand men, who carried swords.

7. And he slew them in the pastures of Shechem, and pursued those who fled, and he slew them with the edge of the sword, and he slew 'Aresa and Taphu and Saregan and Selo and 'Amani- sakir and Ga[ga]'as, and he recovered his herds.

8. And he prevailed over them, and imposed tribute on them that they should pay him tribute, five fruit products of their land, and he built Robel and Tamnatares.

9. And he returned in peace, and made peace with them, and they became his servants, until the day that he and his sons went down into Egypt.

10. And in the seventh year of this week [2149 A.M.] he sent Joseph to learn about the welfare of his brothers from his house to the land of Shechem, and he found them in the land of Dothan.

11. And they dealt treacherously with him, and formed a plot against him to slay him, but changing their minds, they sold him to Ishmaelite merchants, and they brought him down into Egypt, and they sold him to Potiphar, the eunuch of Pharaoh, the chief of the cooks, priest of the city of 'Elew.

12. And the sons of Jacob slaughtered a kid, and dipped the coat of Joseph in the blood, and sent (it) to Jacob their father on the tenth of the seventh month.

13. And he mourned all that night, for they had brought it to him in the evening, and he became feverish with mourning for his death, and he said: 'An evil beast hath devoured Joseph'; and all the members of his house [mourned with him that day, and they] were grieving and mourning with him all that day.

14. And his sons and his daughter rose up to comfort him, but he refused to be comforted for his son.

15. And on that day Bilhah heard that Joseph had perished, and she died mourning him, and she was living in Qafratef, and Dinah also, his daughter, died after Joseph had perished.

16. And there came these three mournings upon Israel in one month. And they buried Bilhah over against the tomb of Rachel, and Dinah also. his daughter, they buried there.

17. And he mourned for Joseph one year, and did not cease, for he said 'Let me go down to the grave mourning for my son'.

18. For this reason it is ordained for the children of Israel that they should afflict themselves on the tenth of the seventh month -on the day that the news which made him weep for Joseph came to Jacob his father- that they should make atonement for themselves thereon with a young goat on the tenth of the seventh month, once a year, for their sins; for they had grieved the affection of their father regarding Joseph his son.

19. And this day has been ordained that they should grieve thereon for their sins, and for all their transgressions and for all their errors, so that they might cleanse themselves on that day once a year.

20. And after Joseph perished, the sons of Jacob took unto themselves wives. The name of Reuben's wife is 'Ada; and the name of Simeon's wife is 'Adlba'a, a Canaanite; and the name of Levi's wife is Melka, of the daughters of Aram, of the seed of the sons of Terah; and the name of Judah's wife, Betasu'el, a Canaanite; and the name of Issachar's wife, Hezaqa: and the name of Zabulon's wife, Ni'iman; and the name of Dan's wife, 'Egla; and the name of Naphtali's wife, Rasu'u, of Mesopotamia; and the name of Gad's wife, Maka; and the name of Asher's wife, 'Ijona; and the name of Joseph's wife, Asenath, the Egyptian; and the name of Benjamin's wife, 'Ijasaka.

21. And Simeon repented, and took a second wife from Mesopotamia as his brothers.

[Chapter 35]

1. And in the first year of the first week of the forty-fifth jubilee [2157 A.M.] Rebecca called Jacob, her son, and commanded him regarding his father and regarding his brother, that he should honour them all the days of his life.

2. And Jacob said: 'I will do everything as thou hast commanded me; for this thing will be honour and greatness to me, and righteousness before the Lord, that I should honour them.

3. And thou too, mother, knowest from the time I was born until this day, all my deeds and all that is in my heart, that I always think good concerning all.

4. And how should I not do this thing which thou hast commanded me, that I should honour my father and my brother!

5. Tell me, mother, what perversity hast thou seen in me and I shall turn away from it, and mercy will be upon me.'

6. And she said unto him: 'My son, I have not seen in thee all my days any perverse but (only) upright deeds. And yet I will tell thee the truth, my son: I shall die this year, and I shall not survive this year in my life; for I have seen in a dream the day of my death, that I should not live beyond a hundred and fifty-five years: and behold I have completed all the days of my life which I am to live.'

7. And Jacob laughed at the words of his mother. because his mother had said unto him that she should die; and she was sitting opposite to him in possession of her strength, and she was not infirm in her strength; for she went in and out and saw, and her teeth were strong, and no ailment had touched her all the days of her life.

8. And Jacob said unto her: 'Blessed am I, mother, if

my days approach the days of thy life, and my strength remain with me thus as thy strength: and thou wilt not die, for thou art jesting idly with me regarding thy death.'

9. And she went in to Isaac and said unto him: 'One petition I make unto thee: make Esau swear that he will not injure Jacob, nor pursue him with enmity; for thou knowest Esau's thoughts that they are perverse from his youth, and there is no goodness in him; for he desires after thy death to kill him.

10. And thou knowest all that he has done since the day Jacob his brother went to Haran until this day: how he has forsaken us with his whole heart, and has done evil to us; thy flocks he has taken to himself, and carried off all thy possessions from before thy face.

11. And when we implored and besought him for what was our own, he did as a man who was taking pity on us.

12. And he is bitter against thee because thou didst bless Jacob thy perfect and upright son; for there is no evil but only goodness in him, and since he came from Haran unto this day he has not robbed us of aught, for he brings us everything in its season always, and rejoices with all his heart when we take at his hands and he blesses us, and has not parted from us since he came from Haran until this day, and he remains with us continually at home honouring us.'

13. And Isaac said unto her: 'I, too, know and see the deeds of Jacob who is with us, how that with all his heart he honours us; but I loved Esau formerly more than Jacob, because he was the firstborn; but now I love Jacob more than Esau, for he has done manifold evil deeds, and there is no righteousness in him, for all his ways are unrighteousness and violence, [and there is no righteousness around him.]

14. And now my heart is troubled because of all his deeds, and neither he nor his seed is to be saved, for they are those who will be destroyed from the earth and who will be rooted out from under heaven, for he has forsaken the God of Abraham and gone after his wives and after their uncleanness and after their error, he and his children.

15. And thou dost bid me make him swear that he will not slay Jacob his brother; even if he swear he will not abide by his oath, and he will not do good but evil only.

16. But if he desires to slay Jacob, his brother, into Jacob's hands will he be given, and he will not escape from his hands, [for he will descend into his hands.]

17. And fear thou not on account of Jacob; for the guardian of Jacob is great and powerful and honoured, and praised more than the guardian of Esau.'

18. And Rebecca sent and called Esau and he came to her, and she said unto him: 'I have a petition, my son, to make unto thee, and do thou promise to do it, my son.'

19. And he said: 'I will do everything that thou sayest unto me, and I will not refuse thy petition.'

20. And she said unto him: 'I ask you that the day I die, thou wilt take me in and bury me near Sarah, thy father's mother, and that thou and Jacob will love each other and that neither will desire evil against the other, but mutual love only, and (so) ye will prosper, my sons, and be honoured in the midst of the land, and no enemy will rejoice over you, and ye will be a blessing and a mercy in the eyes of all those that love you.'

21. And he said: 'I will do all that thou hast told me, and I shall bury thee on the day thou diest near Sarah, my father's mother, as thou hast desired that her bones may be near thy bones.

22. And Jacob, my brother, also, I shall love above all flesh; for I have not a brother in all the earth but him only: and this is no great merit for me if I love him; for he is my brother, and we were sown together in thy body, and together came we forth from thy womb, and if I do not love my brother, whom shall I love?

23. And I, myself, beg thee to exhort Jacob concerning me and concerning my sons, for I know that he will assuredly be king over me and my sons, for on the day my father blessed him he made him the higher and me the lower.

24. And I swear unto thee that I shall love him, and not desire evil against him all the days of my life but good only.'

25. And he sware unto her regarding all this matter. And she called Jacob before the eyes of Esau, and gave him commandment according to the words which she had spoken to Esau.

26. And he said: 'I shall do thy pleasure; believe me that no evil will proceed from me or from my sons against Esau, and I shall be first in naught save in love only.'

27. And they eat and drank, she and her sons that night, and she died, three jubilees and one week and one year old, on that night, and her two sons, Esau and Jacob, buried her in the double cave near Sarah, their father's mother.

[Chapter 36]

1. And in the sixth year of this week [2162 A.M.] Isaac called his two sons Esau and Jacob, and they came to him, and he said unto them: 'My sons, I am going the way of my fathers, to the eternal house where my fathers are.

2. Wherefore bury me near Abraham my father, in the double cave in the field of Ephron the Hittite, where Abraham purchased a sepulchre to bury in; in the sepulchre which I digged for myself, there bury me.

3. And this I command you, my sons, that ye practise righteousness and uprightness on the earth, so that the Lord may bring upon you all that the Lord said that he would do to Abraham and to his seed.

4. And love one another, my sons, your brothers as a man who loves his own soul, and let each seek in what he may benefit his brother, and act together on the earth; and let them love each other as their own souls.

5. And concerning the question of idols, I command and admonish you to reject them and hate them, and love them not, for they are full of deception for those that worship them and for those that

bow down to them.

6. Remember ye, my sons, the Lord God of Abraham your father, and how I too worshipped Him and served Him in righteousness and in joy, that He might multiply you and increase your seed as the stars of heaven in multitude, and establish you on the earth as the plant of righteousness which will not be rooted out unto all the generations for ever.

7. And now I shall make you swear a great oath -for there is no oath which is greater than it by the name glorious and honoured and great and splendid and wonderful and mighty, which created the heavens and the earth and all things together- that ye will fear Him and worship Him.

8. And that each will love his brother with affection and righteousness, and that neither will desire evil against his brother from henceforth for ever all the days of your life so that ye may prosper in all your deeds and not be destroyed.

9. And if either of you devises evil against his brother, know that from henceforth everyone that devises evil against his brother shall fall into his hand, and shall be rooted out of the land of the living, and his seed shall be destroyed from under heaven.

10. But on the day of turbulence and execration and indignation and anger, with flaming devouring fire as He burnt Sodom, so likewise will He burn his land and his city and all that is his, and he shall be blotted out of the book of the discipline of the children of men, and not be recorded in the book of life, but in that which is appointed to destruction, and he shall depart into eternal execration; so that their condemnation may be always renewed in hate and in execration and in wrath and in torment and in indignation and in plagues and in disease for ever.

11. I say and testify to you, my sons, according to the judgment which shall come upon the man who wishes to injure his brother.

12. And he divided all his possessions between the two on that day and he gave the larger portion to him that was the first-born, and the tower and all that was about it, and all that Abraham possessed at the Well of the Oath.

13. And he said: 'This larger portion I will give to the firstborn.'

14. And Esau said, 'I have sold to Jacob and given my birthright to Jacob; to him let it be given, and I have not a single word to say regarding it, for it is his.'

15. And Isaac said, May a blessing rest upon you, my sons, and upon your seed this day, for ye have given me rest, and my heart is not pained concerning the birthright, lest thou shouldest work wickedness on account of it.

16. May the Most High God bless the man that worketh righteousness, him and his seed for ever.'

17. And he ended commanding them and blessing them, and they eat and drank together before him, and he rejoiced because there was one mind between them, and they went forth from him and rested that day and slept.

18. And Isaac slept on his bed that day rejoicing; and he slept the eternal sleep, and died one hundred and eighty years old. He completed twenty-five weeks and five years; and his two sons Esau and Jacob buried him.

19. And Esau went to the land of Edom, to the mountains of Seir, and dwelt there.

20. And Jacob dwelt in the mountains of Hebron, in the tower of the land of the sojournings of his father Abraham, and he worshipped the Lord with all his heart and according to the visible commands according as He had divided the days of his generations.

21. And Leah his wife died in the fourth year of the second week of the forty-fifth jubilee, [2167 A.M.] and he buried her in the double cave near Rebecca his mother to the left of the grave of Sarah, his father's mother

22. and all her sons and his sons came to mourn over Leah his wife with him and to comfort him regarding her, for he was lamenting her for he loved her exceedingly after Rachel her sister died;

23. for she was perfect and upright in all her ways and honoured Jacob,and all the days that she lived with him he did not hear from her mouth a harsh word, for she was gentle and peaceable and upright and honourable.

24. And he remembered all her deeds which she had done during her life and he lamented her exceedingly; for he loved her with all his heart and with all his soul.

[Chapter 37]

1. And on the day that Isaac the father of Jacob and Esau died, [2162 A.M.] the sons of Esau heard that Isaac had given the portion of the elder to his younger son Jacob and they were very angry.

2. And they strove with their father, saying 'Why has thy father given Jacob the portion of the elder and passed over thee, although thou art the elder and Jacob the younger?'

3. And he said unto them 'Because I sold my birthright to Jacob for a small mess of lentils, and on the day my father sent me to hunt and catch and bring him something that he should eat and bless me, he came with guile and brought my father food and drink, and my father blessed him and put me under his hand.

4. And now our father has caused us to swear, me and him, that we shall not mutually devise evil, either against his brother, and that we shall continue in love and in peace each with his brother and not make our ways corrupt.'

5. And they said unto him, 'We shall not hearken unto thee to make peace with him; for our strength is greater than his strength, and we are more powerful than he; we shall go against him and slay him, and destroy him and his sons. And if thou wilt not go with us, we shall do hurt to thee also.

6. And now hearken unto us: Let us send to Aram and Philistia and Moab and Ammon, and let us choose for ourselves chosen men who are ardent for battle, and let us go against him and do battle with him, and let us exterminate him from the earth before he grows strong.'

7. And their father said unto them, 'Do not go and

do not make war with him lest ye fall before him.'

8. And they said unto him, 'This too, is exactly thy mode of action from thy youth until this day, and thou art putting thy neck under his yoke.

9. We shall not hearken to these words.' And they sent to Aram, and to 'Aduram to the friend of their father, and they hired along with them one thousand fighting men, chosen men of war.

10. And there came to them from Moab and from the children of Ammon, those who were hired, one thousand chosen men, and from Philistia, one thousand chosen men of war, and from Edom and from the Horites one thousand chosen fighting men, and from the Kittim mighty men of war.

11. And they said unto their father: Go forth with them and lead them, else we shall slay thee.'

12. And he was filled with wrath and indignation on seeing that his sons were forcing him to go before (them) to lead them against Jacob his brother.

13. But afterward he remembered all the evil which lay hidden in his heart against Jacob his brother; and he remembered not the oath which he had sworn to his father and to his mother that he would devise no evil all his days against Jacob his brother.

14. And notwithstanding all this, Jacob knew not that they were coming against him to battle, and he was mourning for Leah, his wife, until they approached very near to the tower with four thousand warriors and chosen men of war.

15. And the men of Hebron sent to him saying, 'Behold thy brother has come against thee, to fight thee, with four thousand girt with the sword, and they carry shields and weapons'; for they loved Jacob more than Esau. So they told him; for Jacob was a more liberal and merciful man than Esau.

16. But Jacob would not believe until they came very near to the tower.

17. And he closed the gates of the tower; and he stood on the battlements and spake to his brother Esau and said, 'Noble is the comfort wherewith thou hast come to comfort me for my wife who has died. Is this the oath that thou didst swear to thy father and again to thy mother before they died? Thou hast broken the oath, and on the moment that thou didst swear to thy father wast thou condemned.'

18. And then Esau answered and said unto him, 'Neither the children of men nor the beasts of the earth have any oath of righteousness which in swearing they have sworn (an oath valid) for ever; but every day they devise evil one against another, and how each may slay his adversary and foe.

19. And thou dost hate me and my children for ever. And there is no observing the tie of brotherhood with thee.

20. Hear these words which I declare unto thee, If the boar can change its skin and make its bristles as soft as wool, Or if it can cause horns to sprout forth on its head like the horns of a stag or of a sheep, Then will I observe the tie of brotherhood with thee And if the breasts separated themselves from their mother, for thou hast not been a brother to me.

21. And if the wolves make peace with the lambs so as not to devour or do them violence,

And if their hearts are towards them for good, Then there shall be peace in my heart towards thee

22. And if the lion becomes the friend of the ox and makes peace with him And if he is bound under one yoke with him and ploughs with him, Then will I make peace with thee.

23. And when the raven becomes white as the raza, Then know that I have loved thee And shall make peace with thee Thou shalt be rooted out, And thy sons shall be rooted out, And there shall be no peace for thee'

24. And when Jacob saw that he was (so) evilly disposed towards him with his heart, and with all his soul as to slay him, and that he had come springing like the wild boar which comes upon the spear that pierces and kills it, and recoils not from it;

25. then he spake to his own and to his servants that they should attack him and all his companions.

[Chapter 38]

1. And after that Judah spake to Jacob, his father, and said unto him: 'Bend thy bow, father, and send forth thy arrows and cast down the adversary and slay the enemy; and mayst thou have the power, for we shall not slay thy brother, for he is such as thou, and he is like thee let us give him (this) honour.'

2. Then Jacob bent his bow and sent forth the arrow and struck Esau, his brother (on his right breast) and slew him.

3. And again he sent forth an arrow and struck 'Adoran the Aramaean, on the left breast, and drove him backward and slew him.

4. And then went forth the sons of Jacob, they and their servants, dividing themselves into companies on the four sides of the tower.

5. And Judah went forth in front, and Naphtali and Gad with him and fifty servants with him on the south side of the tower, and they slew all they found before them, and not one individual of them escaped.

6. And Levi and Dan and Asher went forth on the east side of the tower, and fifty (men) with them, and they slew the fighting men of Moab and Ammon.

7. And Reuben and Issachar and Zebulon went forth on the north side of the tower, and fifty men with them, and they slew the fighting men of the Philistines.

8. And Simeon and Benjamin and Enoch, Reuben's son, went forth on the west side of the tower, and fifty (men) with them, and they slew of Edom and of the Horites four hundred men, stout warriors; and six hundred fled, and four of the sons of Esau fled with them, and left their father lying slain, as he had fallen on the hill which is in 'Aduram.

9. And the sons of Jacob pursued after them to the mountains of Seir. And Jacob buried his brother on the hill which is in 'Aduram, and he returned to his house.

10. And the sons of Jacob pressed hard upon the sons of Esau in the mountains of Seir, and bowed their

necks so that they became servants of the sons of Jacob.

11. And they sent to their father (to inquire) whether they should make peace with them or slay them.

12. And Jacob sent word to his sons that they should make peace, and they made peace with them, and placed the yoke of servitude upon them, so that they paid tribute to Jacob and to his sons always.

13. And they continued to pay tribute to Jacob until the day that he went down into Egypt.

14. And the sons of Edom have not got quit of the yoke of servitude which the twelve sons of Jacob had imposed on them until this day.

15. And these are the kings that reigned in Edom before there reigned any king over the children of Israel [until this day] in the land of Edom.

16. And Balaq, the son of Beor, reigned in Edom, and the name of his city was Danaba.

17. And Balaq died, and Jobab, the son of Zara of Boser, reigned in his stead.

18. And Jobab died, and 'Asam, of the land of Teman, reigned in his stead.

19. And 'Asam died, and 'Adath, the son of Barad, who slew Midian in the field of Moab, reigned in his stead, and the name of his city was Avith.

20. And 'Adath died, and Salman, from 'Amaseqa, reigned in his stead.

21. And Salman died,and Saul of Ra'aboth (by the) river, reigned in his stead.

22. And Saul died, and Ba'elunan, the son of Achbor, reigned in his stead.

23. And Ba'elunan, the son of Achbor died, and 'Adath reigned in his stead, and the name of his wife was Maitabith, the daughter of Matarat, the daughter of Metabedza'ab.

24. These are the kings who reigned in the land of Edom.

[Chapter 39]

1. And Jacob dwelt in the land of his father's sojournings in the land of Canaan. These are the generations of Jacob.

2. And Joseph was seventeen years old when they took him down into the land of Egypt, and Potiphar, an eunuch of Pharaoh, the chief cook bought him.

3. And he set Joseph over all his house and the blessing of the Lord came upon the house of the Egyptian on account of Joseph, and the Lord prospered him in all that he did.

4. And the Egyptian committed everything into the hands of Joseph; for he saw that the Lord was with him, and that the Lord prospered him in all that he did.

5. And Joseph's appearance was comely [and very beautiful was his appearance], and his master's wife lifted up her eyes and saw Joseph, and she loved him and besought him to lie with her.

6. But he did not surrender his soul, and he remembered the Lord and the words which Jacob, his father, used to read from amongst the words of Abraham, that no man should commit fornication with a woman who has a husband; that for him the punishment of death has been ordained in the heavens before the Most High God, and the sin

will be recorded against him in the eternal books continually before the Lord.

7. And Joseph remembered these words and refused to lie with her.

8. And she besought him for a year, but he refused and would not listen.

9. But she embraced him and held him fast in the house in order to force him to lie with her, and closed the doors of the house and held him fast; but he left his garment in her hands and broke through the door and fled without from her presence.

10. And the woman saw that he would not lie with her, and she calumniated him in the presence of his lord, saying 'Thy Hebrew servant, whom thou lovest, sought to force me so that he might lie with me; and it came to pass when I lifted up my voice that he fled and left his garment in my hands when I held him, and he brake through the door.'

11. And the Egyptian saw the garment of Joseph and the broken door, and heard the words of his wife, and cast Joseph into prison into the place where the prisoners were kept whom the king imprisoned.

12. And he was there in the prison; and the Lord gave Joseph favour in the sight of the chief of the prison guards and compassion before him, for he saw that the Lord was with him, and that the Lord made all that he did to prosper.

13. And he committed all things into his hands, and the chief of the prison guards knew of nothing that was with him, for Joseph did every thing, and the Lord perfected it.

14. And he remained there two years. And in those days Pharaoh, king of Egypt was wroth against his two eunuchs, against the chief butler, and against the chief baker, and he put them in ward in the house of the chief cook, in the prison where Joseph was kept.

15. And the chief of the prison guards appointed Joseph to serve them; and he served before them.

16. And they both dreamed a dream, the chief butler and the chief baker, and they told it to Joseph.

17. And as he interpreted to them so it befell them, and Pharaoh restored the chief butler to his office and the (chief) baker he slew, as Joseph had interpreted to them.

18. But the chief butler forgot Joseph in the prison, although he had informed him what would befall him, and did not remember to inform Pharaoh how Joseph had told him, for he forgot.

[Chapter 40]

1. And in those days Pharaoh dreamed two dreams in one night concerning a famine which was to be in all the land, and he awoke from his sleep and called all the interpreters of dreams that were in Egypt, and magicians, and told them his two dreams, and they were not able to declare (them).

2. And then the chief butler remembered Joseph and spake of him to the king, and he brought him forth from the prison, and he to]d his two dreams before him.

3. And he said before Pharaoh that his two dreams were one, and he said unto him: 'Seven years shall

come (in which there shall be) plenty over all the land of Egypt, and after that seven years of famine, such a famine as has not been in all the land.

4. And now let Pharaoh appoint overseers in all the land of Egypt, and let them store up food in every city throughout the days of the years of plenty, and there will be food for the seven years of famine, and the land will not perish through the famine, for it will be very severe.'

5. And the Lord gave Joseph favour and mercy in the eyes of Pharaoh, and Pharaoh said unto his servants. We shall not find such a wise and discreet man as this man, for the spirit of the Lord is with him.'

6. And he appointed him the second in all his kingdom and gave him authority over all Egypt, and caused him to ride in the second chariot of Pharaoh.

7. And he clothed him with byssus garments, and he put a gold chain upon his neck, and (a herald) proclaimed before him ' 'El 'El wa 'Abirer,' and placed a ring on his hand and made him ruler over all his house, and magnified him, and said unto him. 'Only on the throne shall I be greater than thou.'

8. And Joseph ruled over all the land of Egypt, and all the princes of Pharaoh, and all his servants, and all who did the king's business loved him, for he walked in uprightness, for he was without pride and arrogance, and he had no respect of persons, and did not accept gifts, but he judged in uprightness all the people of the land.

9. And the land of Egypt was at peace before Pharaoh because of Joseph, for the Lord was with him, and gave him favour and mercy for all his generations before all those who knew him and those who heard concerning him, and Pharaoh's kingdom was well ordered, and there was no Satan and no evil person (therein).

10. And the king called Joseph's name Sephantiphans, and gave Joseph to wife the daughter of Potiphar, the daughter of the priest of Heliopolis, the chief cook.

11. And on the day that Joseph stood before Pharaoh he was thirty years old [when he stood before Pharaoh].

12. And in that year Isaac died. And it came to pass as Joseph had said in the interpretation of his two dreams, according as he had said it, there were seven years of plenty over all the land of Egypt, and the land of Egypt abundantly produced, one measure (producing) eighteen hundred measures.

13. And Joseph gathered food into every city until they were full of corn until they could no longer count and measure it for its multitude.

[Chapter 41]

1. And in the forty-fifth jubilee, in the second week, (and) in the second year, [2165 A.M.] Judah took for his first-born Er, a wife from the daughters of Aram, named Tamar.

2. But he hated, and did not lie with her, because his mother was of the daughters of Canaan, and he wished to take him a wife of the kinsfolk of his mother, but Judah, his father, would not permit him.

3. And this Er, the first-born of Judah, was wicked, and the Lord slew him.

4. And Judah said unto Onan, his brother 'Go in unto thy brother's wife and perform the duty of a husband's brother unto her, and raise up seed unto thy brother.'

5. And Onan knew that the seed would not be his, (but) his brother's only, and he went into the house of his brother's wife, and spilt the seed on the ground, and he was wicked in the eyes of the Lord, and He slew him.

6. And Judah said unto Tamar, his daughter-in-law: 'Remain in thy father's house as a widow till Shelah my son be grown up, and I shall give thee to him to wife.'

7. And he grew up; but Bedsu'el, the wife of Judah, did not permit her son Shelah to marry. And Bedsu'el, the wife of Judah, died [2168 A.M.] in the fifth year of this week.

8. And in the sixth year Judah went up to shear his sheep at Timnah. [2169 A.M.] And they told Tamar: 'Behold thy father-in-law goeth up to Timnah to shear his sheep.'

9. And she put off her widow's clothes, and put on a veil, and adorned herself, and sat in the gate adjoining the way to Timnah.

10. And as Judah was going along he found her, and thought her to be an harlot, and he said unto her: 'Let me come in unto thee'; and she said unto him Come in,' and he went in.

11. And she said unto him: 'Give me my hire'; and he said unto her: 'I have nothing in my hand save my ring that is on my finger, and my necklace, and my staff which is in my hand.'

12. And she said unto him 'Give them to me until thou dost send me my hire', and he said unto her: 'I will send unto thee a kid of the goats'; and he gave them to her, *and he went in unto her*, and she conceived by him.

13. And Judah went unto his sheep, and she went to her father's house.

14. And Judah sent a kid of the goats by the hand of his shepherd, an Adullamite, and he found her not; and he asked the people of the place, saying: 'Where is the harlot who was here?' And they said unto him; 'There is no harlot here with us.'

15. And he returned and informed him, and said unto him that he had not found her: 'I asked the people of the place, and they said unto me: "There is no harlot here." '

16. And he said: 'Let her keep (them) lest we become a cause of derision.' And when she had completed three months, it was manifest that she was with child, and they told Judah, saying: 'Behold Tamar, thy daughter-in-law, is with child by whoredom.'

17. And Judah went to the house of her father, and said unto her father and her brothers: 'Bring her forth, and let them burn her, for she hath wrought uncleanness in Israel.'

18. And it came to pass when they brought her forth to burn her that she sent to her father-in-law the ring and the necklace, and the staff, saying: 'Discern whose are these, for by him am I with child.'

19. And Judah acknowledged, and said: 'Tamar is more righteous than I am.

20. And therefore let them burn her not' And for that reason she was not given to Shelah, and he did not again approach her.

21. And after that she bare two sons, Perez [2170 A.M.] and Zerah, in the seventh year of this second week.

22. And thereupon the seven years of fruitfulness were accomplished, of which Joseph spake to Pharaoh.

23. And Judah acknowledged that the deed which he had done was evil, for he had lain with his daughter-in-law, and he esteemed it hateful in his eyes, and he acknowledged that he had transgressed and gone astray, for he had uncovered the skirt of his son, and he began to lament and to supplicate before the Lord because of his transgression.

24. And we told him in a dream that it was forgiven him because he supplicated earnestly, and lamented, and did not again commit it.

25. And he received forgiveness because he turned from his sin and from his ignorance, for he transgressed greatly before our God; and every one that acts thus, every one who lies with his mother-in-law, let them burn him with fire that he may burn therein, for there is uncleanness and pollution upon them, with fire let them burn them.

26. And do thou command the children of Israel that there be no uncleanness amongst them, for every one who lies with his daughter-in-law or with his mother-in-law hath wrought uncleanness; with fire let them burn the man who has lain with her, and likewise the woman, and He will turn away wrath and punishment from Israel.

27. And unto Judah we said that his two sons had not lain with her, and for this reason his seed was stablished for a second generation, and would not be rooted out.

28. For in singleness of eye he had gone and sought for punishment, namely, according to the judgment of Abraham, which he had commanded his sons, Judah had sought to burn her with fire.

[Chapter 42]

1. And in the first year of the third week of the forty-fifth jubilee the famine began to come into the [2171 A.M.] land, and the rain refused to be given to the earth, for none whatever fell.

2. And the earth grew barren, but in the land of Egypt there was food, for Joseph had gathered the seed of the land in the seven years of plenty and had preserved it.

3. And the Egyptians came to Joseph that he might give them food, and he opened the store-houses where was the grain of the first year, and he sold it to the people of the land for gold.

4. <Now the famine was very sore in the land of Canaan>, and Jacob heard that there was food in Egypt, and he sent his ten sons that they should procure food for him in Egypt; but Benjamin he did not send, and <the ten sons of Jacob> arrived <in Egypt> among those that went (there).

5. And Joseph recognised them, but they did not recognise him, and he spake unto them and questioned them, and he said unto them; 'Are ye not spies and have ye not come to explore the approaches of the land? 'And he put them in ward.

6. And after that he set them free again, and detained Simeon alone and sent off his nine brothers.

7. And he filled their sacks with corn, and he put their gold in their sacks, and they did not know.

8. And he commanded them to bring their younger brother, for they had told him their father was living and their younger brother.

9. And they went up from the land of Egypt and they came to the land of Canaan; and they told their father all that had befallen them, and how the lord of the country had spoken roughly to them, and had seized Simeon till they should bring Benjamin.

10. And Jacob said: 'Me have ye bereaved of my children! Joseph is not and Simeon also is not, and ye will take Benjamin away. On me has your wickedness come.

11. 'And he said: 'My son will not go down with you lest perchance he fall sick; for their mother gave birth to two sons, and one has perished, and this one also ye will take from me. If perchance he took a fever on the road, ye would bring down my old age with sorrow unto death.'

12. For he saw that their money had been returned to every man in his sack, and for this reason he feared to send him.

13. And the famine increased and became sore in the land of Canaan, and in all lands save in the land of Egypt, for many of the children of the Egyptians had stored up their seed for food from the time when they saw Joseph gathering seed together and putting it in storehouses and preserving it for the years of famine.

14. And the people of Egypt fed themselves thereon during the first year of their famine.

15. But when Israel saw that the famine was very sore in the land, and that there was no deliverance, he said unto his sons: 'Go again, and procure food for us that we die not.'

16. And they said: 'We shall not go; unless our youngest brother go with us, we shall not go.'

17. And Israel saw that if he did not send him with them, they should all perish by reason of the famine

18. And Reuben said: 'Give him into my hand, and if I do not bring him back to thee, slay my two sons instead of his soul.'

19. And he said unto him: 'He shall not go with thee.' And Judah came near and said: 'Send him with me, and if I do not bring him back to thee, let me bear the blame before thee all the days of my life.'

20. And he sent him with them in the second year of this week on the [2172 A.m.] first day of the month, and they came to the land of Egypt with all those who went, and (they had) presents in their hands, stacte and almonds and terebinth nuts and pure honey.

21. And they went and stood before Joseph, and he saw Benjamin his brother, and he knew him, and said unto them: Is this your youngest brother?' And they said unto him: 'It is he.' And he said The Lord be gracious to thee, my son!'

22. And he sent him into his house and he brought

forth Simeon unto them and he made a feast for them, and they presented to him the gift which they had brought in their hands.

23. And they eat before him and he gave them all a portion, but the portion of Benjamin was seven times larger than that of any of theirs.

24. And they eat and drank and arose and remained with their asses.

25. And Joseph devised a plan whereby he might learn their thoughts as to whether thoughts of peace prevailed amongst them, and he said to the steward who was over his house: 'Fill all their sacks with food, and return their money unto them into their vessels, and my cup, the silver cup out of which I drink, put it in the sack of the youngest, and send them away.'

[Chapter 43]

1. And he did as Joseph had told him, and filled all their sacks for them with food and put their money in their sacks, and put the cup in Benjamin's sack.

2. And early in the morning they departed, and it came to pass that, when they had gone from thence, Joseph said unto the steward of his house: 'Pursue them, run and seize them, saying, "For good ye have requited me with evil; you have stolen from me the silver cup out of which my lord drinks." And bring back to me their youngest brother, and fetch (him) quickly before I go forth to my seat of judgment.'

3. And he ran after them and said unto them according to these words.

4. And they said unto him: 'God forbid that thy servants should do this thing, and steal from the house of thy lord any utensil, and the money also which we found in our sacks the first time, we thy servants brought back from the land of Canaan.

5. How then should we steal any utensil? Behold here are we and our sacks search, and wherever thou findest the cup in the sack of any man amongst us, let him be slain, and we and our asses will serve thy lord.'

6. And he said unto them: 'Not so, the man with whom I find, him only shall I take as a servant, and ye shall return in peace unto your house.'

7. And as he was searching in their vessels, beginning with the eldest and ending with the youngest, it was found in Benjamin's sack.

8. And they rent their garments, and laded their asses, and returned to the city and came to the house of Joseph, and they all bowed themselves on their faces to the ground before him.

9. And Joseph said unto them: 'Ye have done evil.' And they said: 'What shall we say and how shall we defend ourselves? Our lord hath discovered the transgression of his servants; behold we are the servants of our lord, and our asses also.

10. 'And Joseph said unto them: 'I too fear the Lord; as for you, go ye to your homes and let your brother be my servant, for ye have done evil. Know ye not that a man delights in his cup as I with this cup? And yet ye have stolen it from me.'

11. And Judah said: 'O my lord, let thy servant, I pray thee, speak a word in my lord's ear two brothers

did thy servant's mother bear to our father: one went away and was lost, and hath not been found, and he alone is left of his mother, and thy servant our father loves him, and his life also is bound up with the life of this (lad).

12. And it will come to pass, when we go to thy servant our father, and the lad is not with us, that he will die, and we shall bring down our father with sorrow unto death.

13. Now rather let me, thy servant, abide instead of the boy as a bondsman unto my lord, and let the lad go with his brethren, for I became surety for him at the hand of thy servant our father, and if I do not bring him back, thy servant will hear the blame to our father for ever.'

14. And Joseph saw that they were all accordant in goodness one with another, and he could not refrain himself, and he told them that he was Joseph.

15. And he conversed with them in the Hebrew tongue and fell on their neck and wept.

16. But they knew him not and they began to weep. And he said unto them: 'Weep not over me, but hasten and bring my father to me; and ye see that it is my mouth that speaketh and the eyes of my brother Benjamin see.

17. For behold this is the second year of the famine, and there are still five years without harvest or fruit of trees or ploughing.

18. Come down quickly ye and your households, so that ye perish not through the famine, and do not be grieved for your possessions, for the Lord sent me before you to set things in order that many people might live.

19. And tell my father that I am still alive, and ye, behold, ye see that the Lord has made me as a father to Pharaoh, and ruler over his house and over all the land of Egypt.

20. And tell my father of all my glory, and all the riches and glory that the Lord hath given me.'

21. And by the command of the mouth of Pharaoh he gave them chariots and provisions for the way, and he gave them all many-coloured raiment and silver.

22. And to their father he sent raiment and silver and ten asses which carried corn, and he sent them away.

23. And they went up and told their father that Joseph was alive, and was measuring out corn to all the nations of the earth, and that he was ruler over all the land of Egypt.

24. And their father did not believe it, for he was beside himself in his mind; but when he saw the wagons which Joseph had sent, the life of his spirit revived, and he said: 'It is enough for me if Joseph lives; I will go down and see him before I die.'

[Chapter 44]

1. And Israel took his journey from Haran from his house on the new moon of the third month, and he went on the way of the Well of the Oath, and he offered a sacrifice to the God of his father Isaac on the seventh of this month.

2. And Jacob remembered the dream that he had seen at Bethel, and he feared to go down into Egypt.

3. And while he was thinking of sending word to Joseph to come to him, and that he would not go down, he remained there seven days, if perchance he could see a vision as to whether he should remain or go down.

4. And he celebrated the harvest festival of the first-fruits with old grain, for in all the land of Canaan there was not a handful of seed [in the land], for the famine was over all the beasts and cattle and birds, and also over man.

5. And on the sixteenth the Lord appeared unto him, and said unto him, 'Jacob, Jacob'; and he said, 'Here am I.' And He said unto him: 'I am the God of thy fathers, the God of Abraham and Isaac; fear not to go down into Egypt, for I will there make of thee a great nation I will go down with thee, and I will bring thee up (again), and in this land shalt thou be buried, and Joseph shall put his hands upon thy eyes.

6. Fear not; go into Egypt.'

7. And his sons rose up, and his sons' sons, and they placed their father and their possessions upon wagons.

8. And Israel rose up from the Well of the Oath on the sixteenth of this third month, and he went to the land of Egypt.

9. And Israel sent Judah before him to his son Joseph to examine the Land of Goshen, for Joseph had told his brothers that they should come and dwell there that they might be near him.

10. And this was the goodliest (land) in the land of Egypt, and near to him, for all (of them) and also for the cattle.

11. And these are the names of the sons of Jacob who went into Egypt with Jacob their father.

12. Reuben, the First-born of Israel; and these are the names of his sons Enoch, and Pallu, and Hezron and Carmi-five.

13. Simeon and his sons; and these are the names of his sons: Jemuel, and Jamin, and Ohad, and Jachin, and Zohar, and Shaul, the son of the Zephathite woman-seven.

14. Levi and his sons; and these are the names of his sons: Gershon, and Kohath, and Merari-four.

15. Judah and his sons; and these are the names of his sons: Shela, and Perez, and Zerah-four.

16. Issachar and his sons; and these are the names of his sons: Tola, and Phua, and Jasub, and Shimron-five.

17. Zebulon and his sons; and these are the names of his sons: Sered, and Elon, and Jahleel-four.

18. And these are the sons of Jacob and their sons whom Leah bore to Jacob in Mesopotamia, six, and their one sister, Dinah and all the souls of the sons of Leah, and their sons, who went with Jacob their father into Egypt, were twenty-nine, and Jacob their father being with them, they were thirty.

19. And the sons of Zilpah, Leah's handmaid, the wife of Jacob, who bore unto Jacob Gad and Ashur.

20. And these are the names of their sons who went with him into Egypt. The sons of Gad: Ziphion, and Haggi, and Shuni, and Ezbon, <and Eri>, and Areli, and Arodi-eight.

21. And the sons of Asher: Imnah, and Ishvah, <and Ishvi>, and Beriah, and Serah, their one sister-six.

22. All the souls were fourteen, and all those of Leah were forty-four.

23. And the sons of Rachel, the wife of Jacob: Joseph and Benjamin.

24. And there were born to Joseph in Egypt before his father came into Egypt, those whom Asenath, daughter of Potiphar priest of Heliopolis bare unto him, Manasseh, and Ephraim-three.

25. And the sons of Benjamin: Bela and Becher and Ashbel, Gera, and Naaman, and Ehi, and Rosh, and Muppim, and Huppim, and Ard-eleven.

26. And all the souls of Rachel were fourteen.

27. And the sons of Bilhah, the handmaid of Rachel, the wife of Jacob, whom she bare to Jacob, were Dan and Naphtali.

28. And these are the names of their sons who went with them into Egypt. And the sons of Dan were Hushim, and Samon, and Asudi. and 'Ijaka, and Salomon-six.

29. And they died the year in which they entered into Egypt, and there was left to Dan Hushim alone.

30. And these are the names of the sons of Naphtali Jahziel, and Guni and Jezer, and Shallum, and 'Iv.

31. And 'Iv, who was born after the years of famine, died in Egypt.

32. And all the souls of Rachel were twenty-six.

33. And all the souls of Jacob which went into Egypt were seventy souls. These are his children and his children's children, in all seventy, but five died in Egypt before Joseph, and had no children.

34. And in the land of Canaan two sons of Judah died, Er and Onan, and they had no children, and the children of Israel buried those who perished, and they were reckoned among the seventy Gentile nations.

[Chapter 45]

1. And Israel went into the country of Egypt, into the land of Goshen, on the new moon of the fourth [2172 A.M]. month, in the second year of the third week of the forty-fifth jubilee.

2. And Joseph went to meet his father Jacob, to the land of Goshen, and he fell on his father's neck and wept.

3. And Israel said unto Joseph: 'Now let me die since I have seen thee, and now may the Lord God of Israel be blessed the God of Abraham and the God of Isaac who hath not withheld His mercy and His grace from His servant Jacob.

4. It is enough for me that I have seen thy face whilst I am yet alive; yea, true is the vision which I saw at Bethel. Blessed be the Lord my God for ever and ever, and blessed be His name.'

5. And Joseph and his brothers eat bread before their father and drank wine, and Jacob rejoiced with exceeding great joy because he saw Joseph eating with his brothers and drinking before him, and he blessed the Creator of all things who had preserved him, and had preserved for him his twelve sons.

6. And Joseph had given to his father and to his brothers as a gift the right of dwelling in the land of Goshen and in Rameses and all the region round about, which he ruled over before Pharaoh. And Israel and his sons dwelt in the land of

Goshen, the best part of the land of Egypt and Israel was one hundred and thirty years old when he came into Egypt.

7. And Joseph nourished his father and his brethren and also their possessions with bread as much as sufficed them for the seven years of the famine.

8. And the land of Egypt suffered by reason of the famine, and Joseph acquired all the land of Egypt for Pharaoh in return for food, and he got possession of the people and their cattle and everything for Pharaoh.

9. And the years of the famine were accomplished, and Joseph gave to the people in the land seed and food that they might sow (the land) in the eighth year, for the river had overflowed all the land of Egypt.

10. For in the seven years of the famine it had (not) overflowed and had irrigated only a few places on the banks of the river, but now it overflowed and the Egyptians sowed the land, and it bore much corn that year.

11. And this was the first year of [2178 A.M.] the fourth week of the forty-fifth jubilee.

12. And Joseph took of the corn of the harvest the fifth part for the king and left four parts for them for food and for seed, and Joseph made it an ordinance for the land of Egypt until this day.

13. And Israel lived in the land of Egypt seventeen years, and all the days which he lived were three jubilees, one hundred and forty-seven years, and he died in the fourth [2188 A.M.] year of the fifth week of the forty-fifth jubilee.

14. And Israel blessed his sons before he died and told them everything that would befall them in the land of Egypt; and he made known to them what would come upon them in the last days, and blessed them and gave to Joseph two portions in the land.

15. And he slept with his fathers, and he was buried in the double cave in the land of Canaan, near Abraham his father in the grave which he dug for himself in the double cave in the land of Hebron.

16. And he gave all his books and the books of his fathers to Levi his son that he might preserve them and renew them for his children until this day.

[Chapter 46]

1. And it came to pass that after Jacob died the children of Israel multiplied in the land of Egypt, and they became a great nation, and they were of one accord in heart, so that brother loved brother and every man helped his brother, and they increased abundantly and multiplied exceedingly, ten [2242 A.M.] weeks of years, all the days of the life of Joseph.

2. And there was no Satan nor any evil all the days of the life of Joseph which he lived after his father Jacob, for all the Egyptians honoured the children of Israel all the days of the life of Joseph.

3. And Joseph died being a hundred and ten years old; seventeen years he lived in the land of Canaan, and ten years he was a servant, and three years in prison, and eighty years he was under the king, ruling all the land of Egypt.

4. And he died and all his brethren and all that generation.

5. And he commanded the children of Israel before he died that they should carry his bones with them when they went forth from the land of Egypt.

6. And he made them swear regarding his bones, for he knew that the Egyptians would not again bring forth and bury him in the land of Canaan, for Makamaron, king of Canaan, while dwelling in the land of Assyria, fought in the valley with the king of Egypt and slew him there, and pursued after the Egyptians to the gates of 'Ermon.

7. But he was not able to enter, for another, a new king, had become king of Egypt, and he was stronger than he, and he returned to the land of Canaan, and the gates of Egypt were closed, and none went out and none came into Egypt.

8. And Joseph died in the forty-sixth jubilee, in the sixth week, in the second year, and they buried him in the land of Egypt, and [2242 A.M.] all his brethren died after him.

9. And the king of Egypt went forth to war with the king of Canaan [2263 A.M.] in the forty-seventh jubilee, in the second week in the second year, and the children of Israel brought forth all the bones of the children of Jacob save the bones of Joseph, and they buried them in the field in the double cave in the mountain.

10. And the most (of them) returned to Egypt, but a few of them remained in the mountains of Hebron, and Amram thy father remained with them.

11. And the king of Canaan was victorious over the king of Egypt, and he closed the gates of Egypt.

12. And he devised an evil device against the children of Israel of afflicting them and he said unto the people of Egypt: 'Behold the people of the children of Israel have increased and multiplied more than we.

13. Come and let us deal wisely with them before they become too many, and let us afflict them with slavery before war come upon us and before they too fight against us; else they will join themselves unto our enemies and get them up out of our land, for their hearts and faces are towards the land of Canaan.'

14. And he set over them taskmasters to afflict them with slavery; and they built strong cities for Pharaoh, Pithom, and Raamses and they built all the walls and all the fortifications which had fallen in the cities of Egypt.

15. And they made them serve with rigour, and the more they dealt evilly with them, the more they increased and multiplied.

16. And the people of Egypt abominated the children of Israel

[Chapter 47]

1. And in the seventh week, in the seventh year, in the forty-seventh jubilee, thy father went forth [2303 A.M.] from the land of Canaan, and thou wast born in the fourth week, in the sixth year thereof, in the [2330 A.M.] forty-eighth jubilee; this was the time of tribulation on the children of Israel.

2. And Pharaoh, king of Egypt, issued a command regarding them that they should cast all their male children which were born into the river.

3. And they cast them in for seven months until the day that thou wast born

4. And thy mother hid thee for three months, and they told regarding her. And she made an ark for thee, and covered it with pitch and asphalt, and placed it in the flags on the bank of the river, and she placed thee in it seven days, and thy mother came by night and suckled thee, and by day Miriam, thy sister, guarded thee from the birds.

5. And in those days Tharmuth, the daughter of Pharaoh, came to bathe in the river, and she heard thy voice crying, and she told her maidens to bring thee forth, and they brought thee unto her.

6. And she took thee out of the ark, and she had compassion on thee.

7. And thy sister said unto her: 'Shall I go and call unto thee one of the Hebrew women to nurse and suckle this babe for thee?'

8. And she said <unto her>: 'Go.' And she went and called thy mother Jochebed, and she gave her wages, and she nursed thee.

9. And afterwards, when thou wast grown up, they brought thee unto the daughter of Pharaoh, and thou didst become her son, and Amram thy father taught thee writing, and after thou hadst completed three weeks they brought thee into the royal court.

10. And thou wast three weeks of years at court until the time [2351-] when thou didst go forth from the royal court and didst see an Egyptian smiting thy friend who was [2372 A.M.] of the children of Israel, and thou didst slay him and hide him in the sand.

11. And on the second day thou didst and two of the children of Israel striving together, and thou didst say to him who was doing the wrong: 'Why dost thou smite thy brother?'

12. And he was angry and indignant, and said: 'Who made thee a prince and a judge over us? Thinkest thou to kill me as thou killedst the Egyptian yesterday?' And thou didst fear and flee on account of these words.

[Chapter 48]

1. And in the sixth year of the third week of the forty-ninth jubilee thou didst depart and dwell <in [2372 A.M.] the land of Midian>, five weeks and one year. And thou didst return into Egypt in the second week in the second year in the fiftieth jubilee.

2. And thou thyself knowest what He spake unto thee on [2410 A.M.] Mount Sinai, and what prince Mastêmâ desired to do with thee when thou wast returning into Egypt <on the way when thou didst meet him at the lodging-place>.

3. Did he not with all his power seek to slay thee and deliver the Egyptians out of thy hand when he saw that thou wast sent to execute judgment and vengeance on the Egyptians?

4. And I delivered thee out of his hand, and thou didst perform the signs and wonders which thou wast sent to perform in Egypt against Pharaoh, and against all his house, and against his servants and his people.

5. And the Lord executed a great vengeance on them for Israel's sake, and smote them through (the plagues of) blood and frogs, lice and dog-flies, and malignant boils breaking forth in blains; and their cattle by death; and by hail-stones, thereby He destroyed everything that grew for them; and by locusts which devoured the residue which had been left by the hail, and by darkness; and <by the death> of the first-born of men and animals, and on all their idols the Lord took vengeance and burned them with fire.

6. And everything was sent through thy hand, that thou shouldst declare (these things) before they were done, and thou didst speak with the king of Egypt before all his servants and before his people.

7. And everything took place according to thy words; ten great and terrible judgments came on the land of Egypt that thou mightest execute vengeance on it for Israel.

8. And the Lord did everything for Israel's sake, and according to His covenant, which he had ordained with Abraham that He would take vengeance on them as they had brought them by force into bondage.

9. And the prince Mastêmâ stood up against thee, and sought to cast thee into the hands of Pharaoh, and he helped the Egyptian sorcerers,

10. and they stood up and wrought before thee the evils indeed we permitted them to work, but the remedies we did not allow to be wrought by their hands.

11. And the Lord smote them with malignant ulcers, and they were not able to stand, for we destroyed them so that they could not perform a single sign.

12. And notwithstanding all (these) signs and wonders the prince Mastêmâ was not put to shame because he took courage and cried to the Egyptians to pursue after thee with all the powers of the Egyptians, with their chariots, and with their horses, and with all the hosts of the peoples of Egypt.

13. And I stood between the Egyptians and Israel, and we delivered Israel out of his hand, and out of the hand of his people, and the Lord brought them through the midst of the sea as if it were dry land.

14. And all the peoples whom he brought to pursue after Israel, the Lord our God cast them into the midst of the sea, into the depths of the abyss beneath the children of Israel, even as the people of Egypt had cast their children into the river He took vengeance on 1,000,000 of them, and one thousand strong and energetic men were destroyed on account of one suckling of the children of thy people which they had thrown into the river.

15. And on the fourteenth day and on the fifteenth and on the sixteenth and on the seventeenth and on the eighteenth the prince Mastêmâ was bound and imprisoned behind the children of Israel that he might not accuse them.

16. And on the nineteenth we let them loose that they might help the Egyptians and pursue the children of Israel.

17. And he hardened their hearts and made them

stubborn, and the device was devised by the Lord our God that He might smite the Egyptians and cast them into the sea.

18. And on the fourteenth we bound him that he might not accuse the children of Israel on the day when they asked the Egyptians for vessels and garments, vessels of silver, and vessels of gold, and vessels of bronze, in order to despoil the Egyptians in return for the bondage in which they had forced them to serve.

19. And we did not lead forth the children of Israel from Egypt empty handed.

[Chapter 49]

1. Remember the commandment which the Lord commanded thee concerning the passover, that thou shouldst celebrate it in its season on the fourteenth of the first month, that thou shouldst kill it before it is evening, and that they should eat it by night on the evening of the fifteenth from the time of the setting of the sun.

2. For on this night -the beginning of the festival and the beginning of the joy- ye were eating the passover in Egypt, when all the powers of Mastêmâ had been let loose to slay all the first-born in the land of Egypt, from the first-born of Pharaoh to the first-born of the captive maid-servant in the mill, and to the cattle.

3. And this is the sign which the Lord gave them: Into every house on the lintels of which they saw the blood of a lamb of the first year, into (that) house they should not enter to slay, but should pass by (it), that all those should be saved that were in the house because the sign of the blood was on its lintels.

4. And the powers of the Lord did everything according as the Lord commanded them, and they passed by all the children of Israel, and the plague came not upon them to destroy from amongst them any soul either of cattle, or man, or dog.

5. And the plague was very grievous in Egypt, and there was no house in Egypt where there was not one dead, and weeping and lamentation.

6. And all Israel was eating the flesh of the paschal lamb, and drinking the wine, and was lauding, and blessing, and giving thanks to the Lord God of their fathers, and was ready to go forth from under the yoke of Egypt, and from the evil bondage.

7. And remember thou this day all the days of thy life, and observe it from year to year all the days of thy life, once a year, on its day, according to all the law thereof, and do not adjourn (it) from day to day, or from month to month.

8. For it is an eternal ordinance, and engraven on the heavenly tablets regarding all the children of Israel that they should observe it every year on its day once a year, throughout all their generations; and there is no limit of days, for this is ordained for ever.

9. And the man who is free from uncleanness, and does not come to observe it on occasion of its day, so as to bring an acceptable offering before the Lord, and to eat and to drink before the Lord on the day of its festival, that man who is clean and close at hand shall be cut off: because he offered not the oblation of the Lord in its appointed season, he shall take the guilt upon himself.

10. Let the children of Israel come and observe the passover on the day of its fixed time, on the fourteenth day of the first month, between the evenings, from the third part of the day to the third part of the night, for two portions of the day are given to the light, and a third part to the evening.

11. This is that which the Lord commanded thee that thou shouldst observe it between the evenings.

12. And it is not permissible to slay it during any period of the light, but during the period bordering on the evening, and let them eat it at the time of the evening, until the third part of the night, and whatever is left over of all its flesh from the third part of the night and onwards, let them burn it with fire.

13. And they shall not cook it with water, nor shall they eat it raw, but roast on the fire: they shall eat it with diligence, its head with the inwards thereof and its feet they shall roast with fire, and not break any bone thereof; for of the children of Israel no bone shall be crushed.

14. For this reason the Lord commanded the children of Israel to observe the passover on the day of its fixed time, and they shall not break a bone thereof; for it is a festival day, and a day commanded, and there may be no passing over from day to day, and month to month, but on the day of its festival let it be observed.

15. And do thou command the children of Israel to observe the passover throughout their days, every year, once a year on the day of its fixed time, and it shall come for a memorial well pleasing before the Lord, and no plague shall come upon them to slay or to smite in that year in which they celebrate the passover in its season in every respect according to His command.

16. And they shall not eat it outside the sanctuary of the Lord, but before the sanctuary of the Lord, and all the people of the congregation of Israel shall celebrate it in its appointed season.

17. And every man who has come upon its day shall eat it in the sanctuary of your God before the Lord from twenty years old and upward; for thus is it written and ordained that they should eat it in the sanctuary of the Lord.

18. And when the children of Israel come into the land which they are to possess, into the land of Canaan, and set up the tabernacle of the Lord in the midst of the land in one of their tribes until the sanctuary of the Lord has been built in the land, let them come and celebrate the passover in the midst of the tabernacle of the Lord, and let them slay it before the Lord from year to year.

19. And in the days when the house has been built in the name of the Lord in the land of their inheritance, they shall go there and slay the passover in the evening, at sunset, at the third part of the day.

20. And they shall offer its blood on the threshold of the altar, and shall place its fat on the fire which is upon the altar, and they shall eat its flesh roasted with fire in the court of the house which has been sanctified in the name of the Lord.

21. And they may not celebrate the passover in their cities, nor in any place save before the tabernacle of the Lord, or before His house where His name hath dwelt; and they shall not go astray from the Lord.

22. And do thou, Moses, command the children of Israel to observe the ordinances of the passover, as it was commanded unto thee; declare thou unto them every year and the day of its days, and the festival of unleavened bread, that they should eat unleavened bread seven days, (and) that they should observe its festival, and that they bring an oblation every day during those seven days of joy before the Lord on the altar of your God.

23. For ye celebrated this festival with haste when ye went forth from Egypt till ye entered into the wilderness of Shur; for on the shore of the sea ye completed it.

[Chapter 50]

1. And after this law I made known to thee the days of the Sabbaths in the desert of Sin[ai], which is between Elim and Sinai.

2. And I told thee of the Sabbaths of the land on Mount Sinai, and I told thee of the jubilee years in the sabbaths of years: but the year thereof have I not told thee till ye enter the land which ye are to possess.

3. And the land also shall keep its sabbaths while they dwell upon it, and they shall know the jubilee year.

4. Wherefore I have ordained for thee the year-weeks and the years and the jubilees: there are forty-nine jubilees from the days of Adam until this day, [2410 A.M.] and one week and two years: and there are yet forty years to come (lit. 'distant') for learning the [2450 A.M.] commandments of the Lord, until they pass over into the land of Canaan, crossing the Jordan to the west.

5. And the jubilees shall pass by, until Israel is cleansed from all guilt of fornication, and uncleanness, and pollution, and sin, and error, and dwells with confidence in all the land, and there shall be no more a Satan or any evil one, and the land shall be clean from that time for evermore.

6. And behold the commandment regarding the Sabbaths -I have written (them) down for thee- and all the judgments of its laws.

7. Six days shalt thou labour, but on the seventh day is the Sabbath of the Lord your God. In it ye shall do no manner of work, ye and your sons, and your men- servants and your maid-servants, and all your cattle and the sojourner also who is with you.

8. And the man that does any work on it shall die: whoever desecrates that day, whoever lies with (his) wife, or whoever says he will do something on it, that he will set out on a journey thereon in regard to any buying or selling: and whoever draws water thereon which he had not prepared for himself on the sixth day, and whoever takes up any burden to carry it out of his tent or out of his house shall die.

9. Ye shall do no work whatever on the Sabbath day save what ye have prepared for yourselves on the sixth day, so as to eat, and drink, and rest, and keep Sabbath from all work on that day, and to bless the Lord your God, who has given you a day of festival and a holy day: and a day of the holy kingdom for all Israel is this day among their days for ever.

10. For great is the honour which the Lord has given to Israel that they should eat and drink and be satisfied on this festival day, and rest thereon from all labour which belongs to the labour of the children of men save burning frankincense and bringing oblations and sacrifices before the Lord for days and for Sabbaths.

11. This work alone shall be done on the Sabbath-days in the sanctuary of the Lord your God; that they may atone for Israel with sacrifice continually from day to day for a memorial well-pleasing before the Lord, and that He may receive them always from day to day according as thou hast been commanded.

12. And every man who does any work thereon, or goes a journey, or tills (his) farm, whether in his house or any other place, and whoever lights a fire, or rides on any beast, or travels by ship on the sea, and whoever strikes or kills anything, or slaughters a beast or a bird, or whoever catches an animal or a bird or a fish, or whoever fasts or makes war on the Sabbaths:

13. The man who does any of these things on the Sabbath shall die, so that the children of Israel shall observe the Sabbaths according to the commandments regarding the Sabbaths of the land, as it is written in the tablets, which He gave into my hands that I should write out for thee the laws of the seasons, and the seasons according to the division of their days.

Herewith is completed the account of the division of the days.

VITA ADAE ET EVAE

i 1 When they were driven out from paradise, they made themselves a booth, and spent seven days mourning and lamenting in great grief.

ii 1 But after seven days, they began to be hungry and started to look for victual to eat, and they

2 found it not. Then Eve said to Adam: 'My lord, I am hungry. Go, look for (something) for us to eat. Perchance the Lord God will look back and pity us and recall us to the place in which we were before.

iii 1 And Adam arose and walked seven days over all that land, and found no victual such as they

2 used to have in paradise. And Eve said to Adam: 'Wilt thou slay me? that I may die, and perchance God the Lord will bring thee into paradise, for on my account hast thou been driven thence.'

3 Adam answered: 'Forbear, Eve, from such words, that peradventure God bring not some other curse upon us. How is it possible that I should stretch forth my hand against my own flesh? Nay, let us arise and look for something for us to live on, that we fail not.'

iv 1 And they walked about and searched for nine days, and they found none such as they were used to have in paradise, but found only animals'

2 food. And Adam said to Eve: 'This hath the Lord provided for animals and brutes to eat;

3 but we used to have angels' food. But it is just and right that we lament before the sight of God who made us. Let us repent with a great penitence: perchance the Lord will be gracious to us and will pity us and give us a share of something for our living.'

v 1 And Eve said to Adam: 'What is penitence? Tell me, what sort of penitence am I to do? Let us not put too great a labour on ourselves, which we cannot endure, so that the Lord will not hearken to our prayers: and will turn away His countenance from us, because we have not

3 fulfilled what we promised. My lord, how much penitence hast thou thought (to do) for I have brought trouble and anguish upon thee?'

vi 1 And Adam said to Eve: 'Thou canst not do so much as I, but do only so much as thou hast strength for. For I will spend forty days fasting, but do thou arise and go to the river Tigris and lift up a stone and stand on it in the water up to thy neck in the deep of the river. And let no speech proceed out of thy mouth, since we are unworthy to address the Lord, for our lips are unclean from the unlawful and forbidden tree.

2 And do thou stand in the water of the river thirty-seven days. But I will spend forty days in the water of Jordan, perchance the Lord God will take pity upon us.'

vii 1 And Eve walked to the river Tigris and did

2 as Adam had told her. Likewise, Adam walked to the river Jordan and stood on a stone up to his neck in water.

viii 1 And Adam said: 'I tell thee, water of Jordan, grieve with me, and assemble to me all swimming (creatures), which are in thee, and let them surround me and mourn in company with me. Not for themselves let them lament, but for me; for it is not they that have sinned, but I.'

3 Forthwith, all living things came and surrounded him, and, from that hour, the water of Jordan stood (still) and its current was stayed.'

ix 1 And eighteen days passed by; then Satan was wroth and transformed himself into the brightness of angels, and went away to the river

2 Tigris to Eve, and found her weeping, and the devil himself pretended to grieve with her, and he began to weep and said to her: 'Come out of the river and lament no more. Cease now from sorrow and moans. Why art thou anxious

3 and thy husband Adam? The Lord God hath heard your groaning and hath accepted your penitence, and all we angels have entreated on your behalf, and made supplication to the Lord;

4 and he hath sent me to bring you out of the water and give you the nourishment which you had in paradise, and for which you are crying

5 out. Now come out of the water and I will conduct you to the place where your victual hath been made ready.'

x 1 But Eve heard and believed and went out of the water of the river, and her flesh was (trembling)

2 like grass, from the chill of the water. And when she had gone out, she fell on the earth and the devil raised her up and led her to Adam.

3 But when Adam had seen her and the devil with her, he wept and cried aloud and said: 'O Eve, Eve, where is the labour of thy penitence?

4 How hast thou been again ensnared by our adversary, by whose means we have been estranged from our abode in paradise and spiritual joy?'

xi 1 And when she heard this, Eve understood that (it was) the devil (who) had persuaded her to go out of the river; and she fell on her face on the earth and her sorrow and groaning and wailing

2 was redoubled. And she cried out and said: 'Woe unto thee, thou devil. Why dost thou attack us for no cause? What hast thou to do with us? What have we done to thee? for thou pursuest us with craft? Or why doth thy malice

3 assail us? Have we taken away thy glory and caused thee to be without honour? Why dost thou harry us, thou enemy (and persecute us) to the death in wickedness and envy?'

xii 1 And with a heavy sigh, the devil spake: 'O Adam! all my hostility, envy, and sorrow is for thee, since it is for thee that I have been expelled from my glory, which I possessed in the heavens

2 in the midst of the angels and for thee was I cast out in the earth.' Adam answered, 'What dost

3 thou tell me? What have I done to thee or what is my fault against thee? Seeing that thou hast received no harm or injury from us, why dost thou pursue us?'

xiii 1 The devil replied, 'Adam, what dost thou tell me? It is for thy sake that I have been hurled

2 from that place. When thou wast formed. I was hurled out of the presence of God and banished from the company of the angels. When God blew into thee the breath of life and thy face and likeness was made in the image of God, Michael also brought thee and made (us) worship thee in the sight of God; and God the Lord spake: Here is Adam. I have made thee in our image and likeness.'

xiv 1 And Michael went out and called all the angels saying: 'Worship the image of God as the Lord God hath commanded.'

And Michael himself worshipped first; then he called me and said: 'Worship the image of God

3 the Lord.' And I answered, 'I have no (need) to worship Adam.' And since Michael kept urging me to worship, I said to him, 'Why dost thou urge me? I will not worship an inferior and younger being (than I). I am his senior in the Creation, before he was made was I already made. It is his duty to worship me.'

xv 1,2 When the angels, who were under me, heard this, they refused to worship him. And Michael saith, 'Worship the image of God, but if thou wilt not worship him, the

Lord God will be wrath

3 with thee.' And I said, 'If He be wrath with me, I will set my seat above the stars of heaven and will be like the Highest.'

xvi 1 And God the Lord was wrath with me and banished me and my angels from our glory; and on

2 thy account were we expelled from our abodes into this world and hurled on the earth. And

3 straightway we were overcome with grief, since we had been spoiled of so great glory. And we

4 were grieved when we saw thee in such joy and luxury. And with guile I cheated thy wife and caused thee to be expelled through her (doing) from thy joy and luxury, as I have been driven out of my glory.

xvii 1 When Adam heard the devil say this, he cried out and wept and spake: 'O Lord my God, my life is in thy hands. Banish this Adversary far from me, who seeketh to destroy my soul, and give

2,3 me his glory which he himself hath lost.' And at that moment, the devil vanished before him. But Adam endured in his penance, standing for forty days (on end) in the water of Jordan.

xviii 1 And Eve said to Adam: 'Live thou, my Lord, to thee life is granted, since thou hast committed neither the first nor the second error. But I have erred and been led astray for I have not kept the commandment of God; and now banish me from the light of thy life and I will go to the sunsetting,

2 and there will I be, until I die.' And she began to walk towards the western parts and to mourn

3 and to weep bitterly and groan aloud. And she made there a booth, while she had in her womb offspring of three months old.

xix 1 And when the time of her bearing approached, she began to be distressed with pains, and she

2 cried aloud to the Lord and said: 'Pity me, O Lord, assist me.' And she was not heard and the

3 mercy of God did not encircle her. And she said to herself: 'Who shall tell my lord Adam? I implore you, ye luminaries of heaven, what time ye return to the east, bear a message to my lord Adam.'

xx 1 But in that hour, Adam said: 'The complaint of Eve hath come to me. Perchance, once more hath the serpent fought with her.'

2 And he went and found her in great distress. And Eve said: 'From the moment I saw thee, my lord, my grief-laden soul was refreshed. And now entreat the Lord God on my behalf to

3 hearken unto thee and look upon me and free me from my awful pains.' And Adam entreated the Lord for Eve.

xxi 1 And behold, there came twelve angels and two 'virtues', standing on the right and on the left

2 of Eve; and Michael was standing on the right; and he stroked her on the face as far as to the breast and said to Eve: 'Blessed art thou, Eve, for Adam's sake. Since his prayers and intercessions are great, I have been sent that thou mayst receive our help. Rise up now, and

3 prepare thee to bear. And she bore a son and he was shining; and at once the babe rose up and ran and bore a blade of grass in his hands, and gave it to his mother, and his name was called Cain.

xxii 1 And Adam carried Eve and the boy and led

2 them to the East. And the Lord God sent divers seeds by Michael the archangel and gave to Adam and showed him how to work and till the ground, that they might have fruit by which they and all their generations might live.

3 For thereafter Eve conceived and bare a son, whose name was Abel; and Cain and Abel used to stay together.

4 And Eve said to Adam: 'My lord, while I slept, I saw a vision, as it were the blood of our son Abel in the hand of Cain, who was gulping it down in his mouth. Therefore I have sorrow.'

5 And Adam said, 'Alas if Cain slew Abel. Yet let us separate them from each other mutually, and let us make for each of them separate dwellings.'

xxiii 1 And they made Cain an husbandman, (but) Abel they made a shepherd; in order that in this wise they might be mutually separated.

2 And thereafter, Cain slew Abel, but Adam was then one hundred and thirty years old, but Abel was slain when he was one hundred and twenty-two years. And thereafter Adam knew his wife and he begat a son and called his name Seth.

xxiv 1 And Adam said to Eve, 'Behold, I have begotten a son, in place of Abel, whom Cain slew.'

2 And after Adam had begotten Seth, he lived eight hundred years and begat thirty sons and thirty daughters; in all sixty-three children. And they were increased over the face of the earth in their nations.

xxv 1 And Adam said to Seth, 'Hear, my son Seth, that I may relate to thee what I heard and

2 saw after your mother and I had been driven out of paradise. When we were at prayer, there

3 came to me Michael the archangel, a messenger of God. And I saw a chariot like the wind and its wheels were fiery and I was caught up into the Paradise of righteousness, and I saw the Lord sitting and his face was flaming fire that could not be endured. And many thousands of angels were on the right and the left of that chariot.

xxvi 1 When I saw this, I was confounded, and terror seized me and I bowed myself down before

2 God with my face to the earth. And God said to me, 'Behold thou diest, since thou hast transgressed the commandment of God, for thou didst hearken rather to the voice of thy wife, whom I gave into thy power, that thou mightst hold her to thy will. Yet thou didst listen to her and didst pass by My words.'

xxvii 1 And when I heard these words of God, I fell prone on the earth and worshipped the Lord and said, 'My Lord, All powerful and merciful God, Holy and Righteous One, let not the name that is mindful of Thy majesty be blotted out, but convert my soul, for I die and my

2 breath will go out of my mouth. Cast me not out from Thy presence, (me) whom Thou didst form of the clay of the earth. Do not banish from Thy favour him whom Thou didst nourish.'

3 And lo! a word concerning thee came upon me and the Lord said to me, 'Since thy days were fashioned, thou hast been created with a love of knowledge; therefore there shall not be taken from thy seed for ever the (right) to serve Me.'

xxviii 1 And when I heard these words. I threw myself on the earth and adored the Lord God and said, 'Thou art the eternal and supreme God; and all creatures give thee honour and praise.

2 'Thou art the true Light gleaming above all light(s), the Living Life, infinite mighty Power. To Thee, the spiritual powers give honour and praise. Thou workest on the race of men the abundance of Thy mercy.'

3 After I had worshipped the Lord, straightway Michael, God's archangel, seized my hand and

4 cast me out of the paradise of 'vision' and of God's command. And Michael held a rod in his hand, and he

touched the waters, which were round about paradise, and they froze hard.

xxix 1 And I went across, and Michael the archangel went across with me, and he led me back to

2 the place whence he had caught me up. Hearken, my son Seth, even to the rest of the secrets [and sacraments] that shall be, which were revealed to me, when I had eaten of the tree of the

3 knowledge, and knew and perceived what will come to pass in this age; [what God intends to do

4 to his creation of the race of men. The Lord will appear in a flame of fire (and) from the mouth of His majesty He will give commandments and statutes [from His mouth will proceed a two-edged sword] and they will sanctify Him in the house of the habitation of His majesty.

5 And He will show them the marvellous place of His majesty. And then they will build a house to the Lord their God in the land which He shall prepare for them and there they will transgress His statutes and their sanctuary will be burnt up and their land will be deserted and they

6 themselves will be dispersed; because they have kindled the wrath of God. And once more He will cause them to come back from their dispersion; and again they will build the house of God;

7 and in the last time the house of God will be exalted greater than of old. And once more iniquity will exceed righteousness. And thereafter God will dwell with men on earth [in visible form]; and then, righteousness will begin to shine. And the house of God will be honoured in the age and their enemies will no more be able to hurt the men, who are believing in God; and God will stir up for Himself a faithful people, whom He shall save for eternity, and the impious shall be punished

8 by God their king, the men who refused to love His law. Heaven and earth, nights and days, and all creatures shall obey Him, and not overstep His commandment. Men shall not change their

9 works, but they shall be changed from forsaking the law of the Lord. Therefore the Lord shall repel from Himself the wicked, and the just shall shine like the sun, in the sight of God. And

10 in that time, shall men be purified by water from their sins. But those who are unwilling to be purified by water shall be condemned. And happy shall the man be, who hath ruled his soul, when the Judgement shall come to pass and the greatness of God be seen among men and their deeds be inquired into by God the just judge.

xxx 1 After Adam was nine hundred and thirty years old, since he knew that his days were coming to an end, he said: 'Let all my sons assemble themselves to me, that I may bless them before I die, and speak with them.'

2 And they were assembled in three parts, before his sight, in the house of prayer, where they used

3 to worship the Lord God. And they asked him (saying): 'What concerns thee, Father, that thou shouldst assemble us, and why dost thou lie on

4 thy bed?' Then Adam answered and said: 'My sons, I am sick and in pain.' And all his sons said to him: 'What does it mean, father, this illness and pain?'

xxxi 1 Then said Seth his son: 'O (my) lord, perchance thou hast longed after the fruit of paradise, which thou wast wont to eat, and therefore thou liest in sadness? Tell me and I will go to the nearest gates of paradise and put dust on my head and throw myself down on the earth before the gates of paradise and lament and make entreaty to God with loud lamentation; perchance he will hearken to me and

send his angel to bring me the fruit, for which thou hast longed.'

2 Adam answered and said: 'No, my son, I do not long (for this), but I feel weakness and great

3 pain in my body.' Seth answered, 'What is pain, my lord father? I am ignorant; but hide it not from us, but tell us (about it).'

And Adam answered and said: 'Hear me, my sons. When God made us, me and your mother, and placed us in paradise and gave us every tree bearing fruit to eat, he laid a prohibition on us concerning the tree of knowledge of good and evil, which is in the midst of paradise; (saying)

2 'Do not eat of it.' But God gave a part of paradise to me and (a part) to your mother: the trees of the eastern part and the north, which is over against Aquilo he gave to me, and to your mother he gave the part of the south and the western part.

xxxiii 1 (Moreover) God the Lord gave us two angels

2 to guard us. The hour came when the angels had ascended to worship in the sight of God; forthwith the adversary [the devil] found an opportunity while the angels were absent and the devil led your mother astray to eat of the

3 unlawful and forbidden tree. And she did eat and gave to me.

xxxiv 1 And immediately, the Lord God was wrath with us, and the Lord said to me: 'In that thou hast left behind my commandment and hast not kept my word, which I confirmed to thee; behold, I will bring upon thy body, seventy blows; with divers griefs, shalt thou be tormented, beginning at thy head and thine eyes and thine ears down to thy nails on thy toes, and in every

2 separate limb. These hath God appointed for chastisement. All these things hath the Lord sent to me and to all our race.'

xxxv 1 Thus spake Adam to his sons, and he was seized with violent pains, and he cried out with a loud voice, 'What shall I do? I am in distress. So cruel are the pains with which I am beset.' And when Eve had seen him weeping, she also began to weep herself, and said: 'O Lord my God, hand over to me his pain, for it is I who sinned.'

3 And Eve said to Adam: 'My lord, give me a part of thy pains, for this hath come to thee from fault of mine.'

xxxvi 1 And Adam said to Eve: 'Rise up and go with my son Seth to the neighbourhood of paradise, and put dust on your heads and throw yourselves on the ground and lament in the sight of

2 God. Perchance He will have pity (upon you) and send His angel across to the tree of His mercy, whence floweth the oil of life, and will give you a drop of it, to anoint me with it, that I may have rest from these pains, by which I am being consumed.'

Then Seth and his mother went off towards the gates of paradise. And while they were walking, lo! suddenly there came a beast

2 [a serpent] and attacked and bit Seth. And as soon as Eve saw it, she wept and said: 'Alas, wretched woman that I am. I am accursed since I have not kept the commandment of God.'

3 And Eve said to the serpent in a loud voice: 'Accursed beast! how (is it that) thou hast not feared to let thyself loose against the image of God, but hast dared to fight with it?'

xxxviii 1 The beast answered in the language of men: 'Is it not against you, Eve, that our malice (is directed)? Are not ye the objects of our rage?

2 Tell me, Eve, how was thy mouth opened to eat of the fruit? But now if I shall begin to reprove thee thou canst not bear it.'

xxxix 1 Then said Seth to the beast: 'God the Lord revile thee. Be silent, be dumb, shut thy mouth, accursed enemy of Truth, confounder and destroyer. Avaunt from the image of God till the day when the Lord God shall order thee to be brought to the ordeal.' And the beast said to Seth: 'See, I leave the presence of the image of God, as thou hast said.' Forthwith he left Seth, wounded by his teeth.

xl 1 But Seth and his mother walked to the regions of paradise for the oil of mercy to anoint the sick Adam: and they arrived at the gates of paradise, (and) they took dust from the earth and placed it on their heads, and bowed themselves with their faces to the earth and began to lament and

2 make loud moaning, imploring the Lord God to pity Adam in his pains and to send His angel to give them the oil from the 'tree of His mercy'.

xli 1 But when they had been praying and imploring for many hours, behold, the angel Michael ap-

2 peared to them and said: 'I have been sent to you from the Lord -I am set by God over the

3 bodies of men- I tell thee, Seth, (thou) man of God, weep not nor pray and entreat on account of the oil of the tree of mercy to anoint thy father Adam for the pains of his body.

xlii 1 'For I tell thee that in no wise wilt thou be able to receive thereof save in the last days.'

2 [When five thousand five hundred years have been fulfilled, then will come upon earth the most beloved king Christ, the son of God, to revive the body of Adam and with him to revive

3 the bodies of the dead. He Himself, the Son of God, when He comes will be baptized in the river of Jordan, and when He hath come out of the water of Jordan, then He will anoint from the

4 oil of mercy all that believe in Him. And the oil of mercy shall be for generation to generation for those who are ready to be born again of

5 water and the Holy Spirit to life eternal. Then the most beloved Son of God, Christ, descending on earth shall lead thy father Adam to Paradise to the tree of mercy.]

xliii 1 'But do thou, Seth, go to thy father Adam, since the time of his life is fulfilled. Six days hence, his soul shall go off his body and when it shall have gone out, thou shalt see great marvels in the heaven and in the earth and the

2 luminaries of heaven. With these words, straightway Michael departed from Seth.

3 And Eve and Seth returned bearing with them herbs of fragrance, i.e. nard and crocus and calamus and cinnamon.

xliv 1 And when Seth and his mother had reached Adam, they told him, how the beast [the serpent]

2 bit Seth. And Adam said to Eve: 'What hast thou done? A great plague hast thou brought upon us, transgression and sin for all our generations: and this which thou hast done, tell thy

3 children after my death, [for those who arise from us shall toil and fail but they shall be

4 wanting and curse us (and) say, All evils have our parents brought upon us, who were at the

5 beginning].' When Eve heard these words, she began to weep and moan.

xlv 1 And just as Michael the archangel had fore-

2 told, after six days came Adam's death. When Adam perceived that the hour of his death was at hand, he said to all his sons: 'Behold, I am nine hundred and thirty years old, and if I die,

3 bury me towards the sunrising in the field of yonder dwelling.' And it came to pass that when he had finished all his discourse, he gave up the ghost. (Then) was the sun darkened and the moon

xlvi 1 and the stars for seven days, and Seth in his mourning embraced from above the body of his father, and Eve was looking on the ground with hands folded over her head, and all her children wept most bitterly. And behold, there appeared

2 Michael the angel and stood at the head of Adam and said to Seth: 'Rise up from the body of thy

3 father and come to me and see what is the doom of the Lord God concerning him. His creature is he, and God hath pitied him.'

And all angels blew their trumpets, and cried:

xlvii 1 'Blessed art thou, O Lord, for thou hast had pity on Thy creature.'

xlviii 1 Then Seth saw the hand of God stretched out holding Adam and he handed him over to

2 Michael, saying: 'Let him be in thy charge till the day of Judgement in punishment, till the last years when I will convert his sorrow into joy.

3 Then shall he sit on the throne of him who hath been his supplanter.'

4 And the Lord said again to the angels Michael and Uriel: 'Bring me three linen clothes of byssus and spread them out over Adam and other linen clothes over Abel his son and bury Adam and Abel his son.'

5 And all the 'powers' of angels marched before Adam, and the sleep of the dead was

6 consecrated. And the angels Michael and Uriel buried Adam and Abel in the parts of Paradise, before the eyes of Seth and his mother

7 [and no one else], and Michael and Uriel said: 'Just as ye have seen, in like manner, bury your dead.'

xlix 1 Six days after, Adam died; and Eve perceived that she would die, (so) she assembled all her sons

2 and daughters, Seth with thirty brothers and thirty sisters, and Eve said to all, 'Hear me, my children, and I will tell you what the archangel Michael said to us when I and your father transgressed the command of God

3 On account of your transgression, Our Lord will bring upon your race the anger of his judgement, first by water, the second time by fire; by these two, will the Lord judge the whole human race

l 1 But hearken unto me, my children. Make ye then tables of stone and others of clay, and write

2 on them, all my life and your father's (all) that ye have heard and seen from us. If by water the Lord judge our race, the tables of clay will be dissolved and the tables of stone will remain; but if by fire, the tables of stone will be broken up and the tables of clay will be baked (hard).'

3 When Eve had said all this to her children, she spread out her hands to heaven in prayer, and bent her knees to the earth, and while she worshipped the Lord and gave him thanks, she gave up the ghost. Thereafter, all her children buried her with loud lamentation.

li 1 When they had been mourning four days, (then) Michael the archangel appeared and said

2 to Seth: 'Man of God, mourn not for thy dead more than six days, for on the seventh day is the sign of the resurrection and the rest of the age to come; on the seventh day the Lord rested from all His works.'

3 Thereupon Seth made the tables.

SLAVONIC VITA ADAE ET EVAE

xxviii 1 And we sat together before the gate of paradise, Adam weeping with his face bent down to the earth, lay on the ground lamenting. And seven days passed by and we had nothing
2 to eat and were consumed with great hunger, and I Eve cried with a loud voice: 'Pity me, O Lord, My Creator; for my sake Adam suffereth thus!'
xxxix 1 And I said to Adam: 'Rise up! my lord, that we may seek us food; for now my spirit faileth me and my heart within me is brought low.' Then Adam spake to me: 'I have thoughts of
2 killing thee, but I fear since God created thine image and thou showest penitence and criest to God; hence my heart hath not departed from thee.'
xxx 1 And Adam arose and we roamed through all lands and found nothing to eat save nettles (and) grass of the field. And we returned again to the gates of paradise and cried aloud and entreated: 'Have compassion on thy creature.
2 O Lord Creator, allow us food.'
xxxi 1 And for fifteen days continuously we entreated. Then we heard Michael the archangel and Joel
2 praying for us, and Joel the archangel was commanded by the Lord, and he took a seventh part of paradise and gave it to us. Then the
3 Lord said: 'Thorns and thistles shall spring up from under thy hands; and from thy sweat shalt thou eat (bread), and thy wife shall tremble when she looketh upon thee.'
xxxii 1 The archangel Joel said to Adam: 'Thus saith the Lord; I did not create thy wife to command thee, but to obey; why art thou obedient to thy wife?' Again Joel the archangel bade Adam separate the cattle and all kinds of flying and creeping things and animals, both wild and tame; and to give names to all things. Then indeed
3 he took the oxen and began to plough.
xxxiii 1 Then the devil approached and stood before the oxen, and hindered Adam in tilling the field and said to Adam: 'Mine are the things of
2 earth, the things of Heaven are God's; but if thou wilt be mine, thou shalt labour on the earth; but if thou wilt be God's, (pray) go away to paradise.' Adam said: 'The things
3 of Heaven are the Lord's, and the things of earth and Paradise and the whole Universe.'
xxxiv 1 The devil said: 'I do not suffer thee to till the field, except thou write the bond that thou art mine.' Adam replied: 'Whosoever is lord of
2 the earth, to the same do I (belong) and my children.' Then the devil was overcome with joy. (But Adam was not ignorant that the Lord
3 would descend on earth and tread the devil under foot.) The devil said: 'Write me thy
4 bond.' And Adam wrote: 'Who is lord of the earth, to the same do I belong and my children.'
xxxv 1 Eve said to Adam, 'Rise up, my lord, let us pray to God in this cause that He set us free from that devil, for thou art in this strait on my account.'
But Adam said: 'Eve, since thou repentest of
2 thy misdeed, my heart will hearken to thee, for the Lord created thee out of my ribs. Let us fast forty days perchance the Lord will have pity on us and will leave us
understanding and life.' I, for my part, said: 'Do thou, (my) lord,
3 fast forty days, but I will fast forty-four.'
xxxvi 1 And Adam said to me: 'Haste thee to the river,
named Tigris, and take a great stone and place it under thy feet, and enter into the stream and clothe thyself with water, as with a cloak, up to the neck, and pray to God in thy heart and let no word proceed out of thy mouth.' And
2 I said: 'O (my) lord, with my whole heart will I call upon God.' And Adam said to me:
3 'Take great care of thyself. Except thou seest me and all my tokens, depart not out of the water, nor trust in the words, which are said to thee, lest thou fall again into the snare.' And
4 Adam came to Jordan and he entered into the water and he plunged himself altogether into the flood, even (to) the hairs of his head, while he made supplication to God and sent (up) prayers to Him.
xxxvii 1 And there, the angels came together and all living creatures, wild and tame, and all birds that fly, (and) they surrounded Adam, like a wall, praying to God for Adam.
xxxviii 1 The devil came to me, wearing the form and brightness of an angel, and shedding big teardrops, (and) said to me: 'Come out of the water,
2 Eve, God hath heard thy prayers and (heard) us angels. God hath fulfilled the prayers of those who intercede on thy behalf. God hath sent me to thee, that thou mayst come out of the water.'
xxxix 1 But I (Eve) perceived that he was the devil and answered him nothing. But Adam (when) he returned from Jordan, saw the devil's footprints, and feared lest perchance he had deceived me; but when he had remarked me standing in the water he was overcome with joy (and) he took
2 me and led me out of the water.
xl 1 Then Adam cried out with a loud voice: 'Be silent, Eve, for already is my spirit straitened in my body; arise, go forth, utter prayers to God, till I deliver up my spirit to God.'
(Passage follows exactly parallel to Apocalypsis Mosis xxxii. seq., but in abbreviated form.)

APOCALYPSIS MOSIS

i 1 This is the story of Adam and Eve after they had gone out of Paradise. And Adam knew his wife
2 Eve and went upwards to the sun-rising and abode there eighteen years and two months. And
3 Eve conceived and bare two sons; Adiaphotos, who is called Cain and Amilabes who is called Abel.
ii 1 And after this, Adam and Eve were with one another and while they were sleeping, Eve said to Adam her lord: 'My lord, Adam, behold,
2 I have seen in a dream this night the blood of my son Amilabes who is styled Abel being poured into the mouth of Cain his brother and he went on drinking it without pity. But he begged him to leave him a little of it. Yet he hearkened
3 not to him, but gulped down the whole; nor did it stay in his stomach, but came out of his mouth. And Adam said, 'Let us arise and go
4 and see what has happened to them. (I fear) lest the adversary may be assailing them somewhere.'
iii 1 And they both went and found Abel murdered. I by the hand of Cain his brother. And God
2 saith to Michael the archangel: 'Say to Adam: " Reveal not the secret that thou knowest to Cain thy son, for he is a son of wrath. But grieve not, for I will give thee another son in his stead; he shall show (to thee) all that thou shalt do. Do thou tell him nothing."' Thus spake the archangel
3 to Adam. But he kept the word in his heart, and with him also Eve, though they grieved concerning Abel their son.
iv 1 And after this, Adam knew Eve his wife, and she conceived and bare Seth.
And Adam said to Eve: 'See! we have
2 begotten a son in place of Abel, whom Cain slew, let us give glory and sacrifice to God.'
v 1 And Adam begat thirty sons and thirty daughters and Adam lived nine hundred and thirty years; and he fell sick and cried with a loud
2 voice and said, 'Let all my sons come to me that I may see them before I die.'
3 And all assembled, for the earth was divided into three parts. And Seth his son said to him:
4 'Father Adam, what is thy complaint?'
5 And he saith, 'MY children, I am crushed by the burden of trouble.' And they say to him, 'What is trouble?'
vi 1 And Seth answered and said to him: 'Hast thou called to mind, father, the fruit of paradise of which thou usedst to eat, and hast been grieved in yearning for it?'
'If this be so, tell me, (and) I will go and
2 bring thee fruit from paradise. For I will set dung upon my head and will weep and pray that the Lord will hearken to me and send his angel (and bring me a plant from paradise), and I will bring it thee that thy trouble may cease from thee.'
Adam saith to him: 'Nay, my son Seth, but
3 I have (much) sickness and trouble!' Seth saith to him: 'And how hath this come upon thee?'
vii 1 And Adam said to him: 'When God made us, me and your mother, through whom also I die, He gave us power to eat of every tree which is in paradise, but, concerning that one only, He charged us not to eat of it, and through this one we are to die. And the hour drew nigh for the angels
2 who were guarding your mother to go up and worship the Lord, and I was far from her, and the enemy knew that she was alone and gave to her, and she ate of the tree of which she had been told not to eat.
3 Then she gave also to me to eat.
viii 1 'And God was wroth with us, and the Lord came into paradise and called me in a terrible voice and said: "Adam, where art thou? And why hidest thou from my face? Shall the house be able to hide itself from its builder?" And he saith to me: "Since thou hast abandoned my covenant, I have brought upon thy body seventy-two strokes; the trouble of the first stroke is a pain of the eyes, the second stroke an affection of the hearing, and likewise in turn all the strokes shall befall thee."'
ix 1 As he said this to his sons, Adam groaned sore and said: 'What shall I do? I am in great distress.'
And Eve wept and said: 'My lord
2 Adam, rise up and give me half of thy trouble and I will endure it; for it is on my account that this hath happened to thee, on my account thou art beset with toils and troubles.' But Adam
3 said to Eve, 'Arise and go with my son Seth near to paradise, and put earth upon your heads and weep and pray God to have mercy upon me and send his angel to paradise, and give me of the tree out of which the oil floweth, and bring it me, and I shall anoint myself and shall have rest from my complaint.'
x 1 Then Seth and Eve went towards paradise, and Eve saw her son, and a wild beast assailing him, and Eve wept and said: 'Woe is me; if
2 I come to the day of the Resurrection, all those who have sinned will curse me saying: Eve hath not kept the commandment of God.' And she
3 spake to the beast: 'Thou wicked beast, fearest thou not to fight with the image of God? How was thy mouth opened? How were thy teeth made strong? How didst thou not call to mind thy subjection? For long ago wast thou made subject to the image of God.' Then the beast
4 cried out and said:
xi 1 'It is not our concern, Eve, thy greed and thy wailing, but thine own; for (it is) from thee that the rule of the beasts hath arisen. How was thy
2 mouth opened to eat of the tree concerning which God enjoined thee not to eat of it? On this account, our nature also hath been transformed. Now therefore thou canst not endure it,
3 if I begin to reprove thee.'
xii 1 Then Seth speaketh to the beast, 'Close thy mouth and be silent and stand off from the image of God until the day of Judgment.' Then saith
2 the beast to Seth: 'Behold, I stand off from the image of God.' And he went to his lair.
xiii 1 And Seth went with Eve near paradise, and I they wept there, and prayed God to send his angel and give them the oil of mercy.
And God
2 sent the archangel Michael and he spake to Seth: 'Seth, man of God, weary not thyself with prayers and entreaties concerning the tree which floweth with oil to anoint thy father Adam. For it shall not be thine now, but in the end of the times.
3 Then shall all flesh be raised up from Adam till that great day,-all that shall be of the holy people. Then shall the delights of paradise be given to them and God shall be in their midst. And they shall no longer sin before his face, for the evil heart shall be taken from them and there shall be given them a heart understanding the good and to serve God only.
But do thou go back to thy father. For the

6 term of his life hath been fulfilled and he will live three days from to-day and will die. But when his soul is departing, thou shalt behold the awful (scene of) his passing.'

xiv 1 Thus spake the angel and departed from them. And Seth and Eve came to the hut where Adam was laid. And Adam saith to Eve: 'Eve, what

2 hast thou wrought in us? Thou hast brought upon us great wrath which is death, [lording it over all our race].' And he saith to her, 'Call all

3 our children and our children's children and tell them the manner of our transgression.'

xv 1 Then saith Eve to them: 'Hear all my children and children's children and I will relate to you

2 how the enemy deceived us. It befell that we were guarding paradise, each of us the portion

3 allotted to us from God. Now I guarded in my lot, the west and the south. But the devil went to Adam's lot, where the male creatures were. [For God divided the creatures; all the males he gave to your father and all the females he gave to me.]

xvi 1 And the devil spake to the serpent saying, Rise up, come to me and I will tell thee a word

2 whereby thou mayst have profit." And he arose and came to him. And the devil saith to him:

3 "I hear that thou art wiser than all the beasts, and I have come to counsel thee. Why dost thou eat of Adam's tares and not of paradise? Rise up and we will cause him to be cast out of paradise, even

4 as we were cast out through him." The serpent saith to him, "I fear lest the Lord be wroth with

5 me." The devil saith to him: "Fear not, only be my vessel and I will speak through thy mouth words to deceive him."

xvii 1 And instantly he hung himself from the wall of paradise, and when the angels ascended to

2 worship God, then Satan appeared in the form of an angel and sang hymns like the angels. And I bent over the wall and saw him, like an angel. But he saith to me: "Art thou Eve?" And I said

3 to him, "I am." 'What art thou doing in paradise?' And I said to him, "God set us to guard and

4 to eat of it." The devil answered through the mouth of the serpent: 'Ye do well but ye do not eat

5 of every plant." And I said: "Yea, we eat of all. save one only, which is in the midst of paradise, concerning which, God charged us not to eat of it: for, He said to us, on the day on which ye eat of it, ye shall die the death."

xviii 1 Then the serpent saith to me, "May God live! but I am grieved on your account, for I would not have you ignorant. But arise, (come) hither, hearken to me and eat and mind the value of that tree."

2,3 But I said to him, " I fear lest God be wroth with me as he told us." And he saith to me: "Fear not, for as soon as thou eatest of it, ye too shall be as God, in that ye shall know good and evil.

4 But God perceived this that ye would be like Him, so he envied you and said, Ye shall not eat of

5,6 it. Nay, do thou give heed to the plant and thou wilt see its great glory." Yet I feared to take of the fruit. And he saith to me: "Come hither, and I will give it thee. Follow me."

xix 1 And I opened to him and he walked a little way, then turned and said to me: "I have changed my

2 mind and I will not give thee to eat until thou swear to me to give also to thy husband." (And) I said. "What sort of oath shall I swear to thee? Yet what I know, I say to thee:

By the throne of the

3 Master, and by the Cherubim and the Tree of Life! I will give also to my husband to eat." And when he had received the oath from me, he went and poured upon the fruit the poison of his wickedness, which is lust, the root and beginning of every sin, and he bent the branch on the earth and I took of the fruit and I ate.

xx 1 And in that very hour my eyes were opened, and forthwith I knew that I was bare of the righteousness

2 with which I had been clothed (upon), and I wept and said to him: "Why hast thou

3 done this to me in that thou hast deprived me of the glory with which I was clothed?" But I wept also about the oath, which I had sworn. But he descended from the tree and vanished.

4 And I began to seek, in my nakedness, in my part for leaves to hide my shame, but I found none, for, as soon as I had eaten, the leaves showered down from all the trees in my part, except the fig tree

5 only. But I took leaves from it and made for myself a girdle and it was from the very same plant of which I had eaten.

xxi 1 And I cried out in that very hour, 'Adam, Adam, where art thou? Rise up, come to me and

2 I will show thee a great secret." But when your father came, I spake to him words of transgression

3 [which have brought us down from our great glory]. For, when he came, I opened my mouth and the devil was speaking, and I began to exhort him and said, "Come hither, my lord Adam, hearken to me and eat of the fruit of the tree of which God told us not to eat of it, and thou shalt be as

4 a God." And your father answered and said, "I fear lest God be wroth with me." And I said to

5 him, "Fear not, for as soon as thou hast eaten thou shalt know good and evil." And speedily I persuaded him, and he ate and straightway his eyes were opened and he too knew his nakedness.

6 And to me he saith, "O wicked woman! what have I done to thee that thou hast deprived me of the glory of God?"

xxii 1 And in that same hour, we heard the archangel Michael blowing with his trumpet and calling to

2 the angels and saying: "Thus saith the Lord, Come with me to Paradise and hear the judgement with which I shall judge Adam."

3 And when God appeared in paradise, mounted on the chariot of his cherubim with the angels proceeding before him and singing hymns of praises, all the plants of paradise, both of your father's lot

4 and mine, broke out into flowers. And the throne of God was fixed where the Tree of Life was.

xxiii 1 And God called Adam saying, "Adam, where art thou? Can the house be hidden from the presence

2 of its builder? "Then your father answered; "It is not because we think not to be found by thee, Lord, that we hide, but I was afraid, because I am naked, and I was ashamed before thy might,

3 (my) Master." God saith to him, "Who showed thee that thou art naked, unless thou hast forsaken my

4 commandment, which I delivered thee to keep (it)." Then Adam called to mind the word which I spake to him, (saying) "I will make thee secure before God"; and he turned and said to me: "Why hast thou done this?" And I said, "The serpent deceived me."

xxiv 1 God saith to Adam: 'Since thou hast disregarded my commandment and hast hearkened to thy wife, cursed is the earth in thy labours. Thou shalt work it and it shall not give its strength: thorns and thistles shall spring up for thee, and in the sweat of thy face shalt thou eat thy bread. [Thou shalt be in manifold toils; thou shalt be crushed by bitterness, but of sweetness shalt thou not taste.]

3 Weary shalt thou be and shalt not rest; by heat shalt thou be tired, by cold shalt thou be straitened: abundantly shalt thou busy thyself, but thou shalt not be rich; and thou shalt grow fat, but come to no end.

4 The beasts, over whom thou didst rule, shall rise up in rebellion against thee, for thou hast not kept my commandment."

xxv 1 And the Lord turned to me and said: "Since thou hast hearkened to the serpent, and turned

2 a deaf ear to my commandment, thou shalt be in throes of travail and intolerable agonies; thou shalt bear children in much trembling and in one hour thou shalt come to the birth, and lose thy

3 life, from thy sore trouble and anguish. But thou shalt confess and say: 'Lord, Lord, save me, and

4 I will turn no more to the sin of the flesh.' And on this account, from thine own words I will judge thee, by reason of the enmity which the enemy has planted in thee."

xxvi 1 But he turned to the serpent [in great wrath] and said: "Since thou hast done this, and become a thankless vessel until thou hast deceived the innocent hearts, accursed art thou among all beasts.

2 Thou shalt be deprived of the victual of which thou didst eat and shalt feed on dust all the days of

3 thy life: on thy breast and thy belly shalt thou walk and be robbed of hands and feet. There shall not be left thee ear nor wing, nor one limb of all that with which thou didst ensnare them in

4 thy malice and causedst them to be cast out of paradise; and I will put enmity between thee and his seed: he shall bruise thy head and thou shalt bruise his heel until the day of Judgement." xxvii 1,2 Thus he spake and bade the angels have us cast out of paradise: and as we were being driven out amid our loud lamentations, your father Adam besought the angels and said: "Leave me a little (space) that I may entreat the Lord that he have compassion on me and pity me, for I only

3 have sinned." And they left off driving him and Adam cried aloud and wept saying: "Pardon me O Lord, my deed." Then the Lord saith to the angels, "Why have ye ceased from driving Adam from paradise? Why do ye not cast him out? Is it I who have done wrong? Or is my judgement

5 badly judged?" Then the angels fell down on the ground and worshipped the Lord saying, "Thou art just, O Lord, and thou judgest righteous judgement."

xxviii 1 But the Lord turned to Adam and said: 'I will not suffer thee henceforward to be in paradise."

2 And Adam answered and said, " Grant me, O Lord, of the Tree of Life that I may eat of it, before

3 I be cast out." Then the Lord spake to Adam, "Thou shalt not take of it now, for I have commanded the cherubim with the flaming sword that turneth (every way) to guard it from thee that

4 thou taste not of it; but thou hast the war which the adversary hath put into thee, yet when thou art gone out of paradise, if thou shouldst keep thyself from all evil, as one about to die, when again the Resurrection hath come to pass, I will raise thee up and then there shall be given to thee the Tree of Life."

xxix 1,2 Thus spake the Lord and ordered us to be cast out

of paradise. But your father Adam wept before the angels opposite paradise and the angels say to him: "What wouldst thou have us to do,

3 Adam? "And your father saith to them, "Behold, ye cast me out. I pray you, allow me to take away fragrant herbs from paradise, so that I may offer an offering to God after I have gone out of paradise that he hear me." And the angels approached God and said: "JA'EL, Eternal King, command, my Lord, that there be given to Adam incense of sweet odour from paradise and seeds

5 for his food." And God bade Adam go in and take sweet spices and fragrant herbs from paradise

6 and seeds for his food. And the angels let him go and he took four kinds: crocus and nard and calamus and cinnamon and the other seeds for his food: and, after taking these, he went out of

7 paradise. And we were on the earth.

xxx 1 Now then, my children, I have shown you the way in which we were deceived; and do ye guard yourselves from transgressing against the good.'

xxxi 1 And when Eve had said this in the midst of her sons, while Adam was lying ill and bound to die

2 after a single day from the sickness which had fastened upon him, she saith to him: 'How is it that

3 thou diest and I live or how long have I to live after thou art dead? Tell me.' And Adam saith to her: 'Reck not of this, for thou tarriest not after me, but even both of us are to die together. And she shall lie in my place. But when I die, anoint me and let no man touch me till the

4 angel of the Lord shall speak somewhat concerning me. For God will not forget me, but will seek His own creature; and now arise rather and pray to God till I give up my spirit into His hands who gave it me. For we know not how we are to meet our Maker, whether He be wroth with us, or be merciful and intend to pity and receive us.'

xxxii 1,2 And Eve rose up and went outside and fell on the ground and began to say: I have sinned, O God, I have sinned, O God of All, I have sinned against Thee. I have sinned against the elect angels. I have sinned against the Cherubim. I have sinned against Thy fearful and unshakable Throne. I have sinned before Thee and all sin hath begun through my doing in the creation.'

3 Even thus prayed Eve on her knees; (and) behold, the angel of humanity came to her, and raised

4 her up and said: 'Rise up, Eve, (from thy penitence), for behold, Adam thy husband hath gone out of his body. Rise up and behold his spirit borne aloft to his Maker.'

xxxiii 1 And Eve rose up and wiped off her tears with her hand, and the angel saith to her, ' Lift Up thyself

2 from the earth.' And she gazed steadfastly into heaven, and beheld a chariot of light, borne by four bright eagles, (and) it were impossible for any man born of woman to tell the glory of them or

3 behold their face -and angels going before the chariot- and when they came to the place where your father Adam was, the chariot halted and the Seraphim. And I beheld golden censers, between your father and the chariot, and all the angels with censers and frankincense came in haste to the

5 incense-offering and blew upon it and the smoke of the incense veiled the firmaments. And the angels fell down and worshipped God, crying aloud and saying, JA'EL, Holy One, have pardon, for he is Thy image, and the work of Thy holy hands.'

xxxiv 1 And I Eve beheld two great and fearful wonders standing in the presence of God and I wept for

2 fear, and I cried aloud to my son Seth and said, 'Rise up, Seth, from the body of thy father Adam and come to me, and thou shalt see a spectacle which no man's eye hath yet beheld.'

xxxv 1 Then Seth arose and came to his mother and to her he saith: 'What is thy trouble? Why weepest thou?' (And) she saith to him: 'Look

2 up and see with thine eyes the seven heavens opened, and see how the soul of thy father lies on its face and all the holy angels are praying on his behalf and saying: 'Pardon him, Father of All, for he is Thine image." 'Pray, my child

3 Seth, what shall this mean? And will he one day be delivered into the hands of the Invisible Father, even our God? But who are the two

4 negroes who stand by at the prayers for thy father Adam?'

xxxvi 1 And Seth telleth his mother, that they are the sun and moon and themselves fall down and pray on behalf of my father Adam. Eve saith

2 to him: 'And where is their light and why have they taken on such a black appearance?' And

3 Seth answereth her, 'The light hath not left them, but they cannot shine before the Light of the Universe, the Father of Light; and on this account their light hath been hidden from them.

xxxvii 1 Now while Seth was saying this to his mother, lo, an angel blew the trumpet, and there stood up all the angels (and they were) lying on their faces, and they cried aloud in an awful voice and said: 'Blessed (be) the glory of the Lord from

2 the works of His making, for He hath pitied Adam the creature of His hands.' But when the

3 angels had said these words, lo, there came one of the seraphim with six wings and snatched up Adam and carried him off to the Acherusian lake, and washed him thrice, in the presence of God.

xxxix 1 And God saith to him: 'Adam, what hast thou done? If thou hadst kept my commandment, there would now be no rejoicing among those who are bringing thee down to this place. Yet, I tell thee that I will turn their joy to grief

2 and thy grief will I turn to joy, and I will transform thee to thy former glory? and set thee on the throne of thy deceiver. But he shall be cast

3 into this place to see thee sitting above him, then he shall be condemned and they that heard him, and he shall be grieved sore when he seeth thee sitting on his honourable throne.'

xxxvii

4 And he stayed there three hours, lying down, and thereafter the Father of all, sitting on his holy throne stretched out his hand, and took Adam and handed him over to the archangel Michael saying: 'Lift him up into Paradise unto the third Heaven, and leave him there until that fearful day of my reckoning, which I will make in the world.' Then Michael took Adam and left

6 him where God told him.

xxxviii 1 But after all this, the archangel asked concerning the laying out of the remains. And God

2 commanded that all the angels should assemble in His presence, each in his order, and all the angels assembled, some having censers in their hands, and others trumpets. And lo ! the 'Lord

3 of Hosts' came on and four winds drew Him and cherubim mounted on the winds and the angels from heaven escorting Him and they came on the earth, where was the body of Adam. And

4 they came to paradise and all the leaves of paradise were stirred so that all men begotten of Adam slept from the fragrance save Seth alone, because he was born 'according to the appointment of God '. Then Adam's body lay there in

5 paradise on the earth and Seth grieved exceedingly over him.

xl 1 Then God spake to the archangel(s) Michael, (Gabriel, Uriel, and Raphael): 'Go away

2 to Paradise in the third heaven, and strew linen clothes and cover the body of Adam and bring oil of the 'oil of fragrance' and pour it over him. And they acted thus did the three great angels and they prepared him for burial. And God said: 'Let the body of Abel also be

3 brought.' And they brought other linen clothes and prepared his (body) also. For he was unburied since the day when Cain his brother slew him; for wicked Cain took great pains to conceal (him) but could not, for the earth would not receive him for the body sprang up from the earth and a voice went out of the earth saying: 'I will not

5 receive a companion body, till the earth which was taken and fashioned in me cometh to me.' At that time, the angels took it and placed it on a rock, till Adam his father was buried. And

6 both were buried, according to the commandment of God, in the spot where God found the dust, and He caused the place to be dug for two. And God sent seven angels to paradise and they

7 brought many fragrant spices and placed them in the earth, and they took the two bodies and placed them in the spot which they had digged and builded.

xli 1 And God called and said, 'Adam, Adam.' And the body answered from the earth and said: 'Here am I, Lord.' And God saith to him: 'I told

2 thee (that) earth thou art and to earth shalt thou return. Again I promise to thee the Resurrection; I will raise thee up in the Resurrection with every man who is of thy seed.'

xlii 1 After these words, God made a seal and sealed the tomb, that no one might do anything to him for six days till his rib should return to him. Then the Lord and his angels went to their place.

2 And Eve also, when the six days were fulfilled,

3 fell asleep. But while she was living, she wept bitterly about Adam's falling on sleep, for she knew not where he was laid. For when the Lord came to paradise to bury Adam she was asleep, and her sons too, except Seth, till He bade Adam be prepared for burial; and no man knew on earth, except her son Seth. And Eve prayed (in

4 the hour of her death) that she might be buried in the place where her husband Adam was. And after she had finished her prayer, she saith: 'Lord,

5 Master, God of all rule, estrange not me thy handmaid from the body of Adam, for from his members didst thou make me. But deem me

6 worthy, even me unworthy that I am and a sinner, to enter into his tabernacle, even as I was with him in paradise, both without separation from each other; just as in our transgression, we were

7 (both) led astray and transgressed thy command, but were not separated. Even so, Lord, do not

8 separate us now.' But after she had prayed, she gazed heavenwards and groaned aloud and smote her breast and said: 'God of All, receive my spirit,' and straightway she delivered up her spirit to God.

xliii 1 And Michael came and taught Seth how to prepare Eve for burial. And there came three angels and they buried

her (body) where Adam's body was and Abel's. And
thereafter Michael

2 spake to Seth and saith: 'Lay out in this wise every man
that dieth till the day of the Resurrection.' And after giving
him this rule; he

3 saith to him: 'Mourn not beyond six days, but on the
seventh day, rest and rejoice on it, because on that very day,
God rejoiceth (yea) and we angels (too) with the righteous
soul, who hath passed away from the earth.' Even thus
spake

4 the angel, and ascended into heaven, glorifying (God) and
saying: 'Allelujah.'

[Holy, holy, holy is the Lord, in the glory of

5 God the Father, for to Him it is meet to give glory,
honour and worship, with the eternal life-giving spirit now
and always and for ever. Amen.]

[Holy, holy, holy is the Lord of Hosts. To whom be glory
and power for ever and for ever Amen.]

[Then the archangel Joel glorified God; saying, 'Holy, Holy,
Holy Lord, heaven and earth are full of thy glory.']

THE ASCENSION OF ISAIAH

CHAPTER 1

AND it came to pass in the twenty-sixth year of the reign of Hezediah king of Judah that he called Manasseh his son. Now he was his only one.

2. And he called him into the presence of Isaiah the son of Amoz the prophet, and into the presence of Josab the son of Isaiah, in order to deliver unto him the words of righteousness which the king himself had seen:

3. And of the eternal judgments and torments of Gehenna, and of the prince of this world, and of his angels, and his authorities and his powers.

4. And the words of the faith of the Beloved which he himself had seen in the fifteenth year of his reign during his illness.

5. And he delivered unto him the written words which Samnas the scribe had written, and also those which Isaiah, the son of Amoz, had given to him, and also to the prophets, that they might write and store up with him what he himself had seen in the king's house regarding the judgment of the angels, and the destruction of this world, and regarding the garments of the saints and their going forth, and regarding their transformation and the persecution and ascension of the Beloved.

6. In the twentieth year of the reign of Hezekiah, Isaiah had seen the words of this prophecy and had delivered them to Josab his son. And whilst he (Hezekiah) gave commands, Josab the son of Isaiah standing by.

7. Isaiah said to Hezekiah the king, but not in the presence of Manasseh only did he say unto him: `As the Lord liveth, and th3e Spirit which speaketh in me liveth, all these commands and these words will be made of none effect by Manasseh thy son, and through the agency of his hands I shall depart mid the torture of my body.

8. And Sammael Malchira will serve Manasseh, and execute all his desire, and he will become a follower of Beliar rather than of me:

9. And many in Jerusalem and in Judea he will cause to abandon the true faith, and Beliar will dwell in Manasseh, and by his hands I shall be sawn asunder.'

10. And when Hezekiah heard these words he wept very bitterly, and rent his garments, and placed earth upon his head, and fell on his face.

11. And Isaiah said unto him: `The counsel of Sammael against Manasseh is consummated: nought will avail thee."

12. And on that day Hezekiah resolved in his heart to slay Manasseh his son.

13. And Isaiah said to Hezekiah: `The Beloved hath made of none effect thy design, and the purpose of thy heart will not be accomplished, for with this calling have I been called and I shall inherit the heritage of the Beloved.'

CHAPTER 2

AND it came to pass after that Hezekiah died and Manasseh became king, that he did not remember the commands of Hezekiah his father, but forgat them, and Sammael abode in Manasseh and clung fast to him.

2. And Manasseh forsook the service of the God of his father, and he served Satan and his angels and his powers.

3. And he turned aside the house of his father, which had been before the face of Hezekiah (from) the words of wisdom and from the service of God.

4. And Manasseh turned aside his heart to serve Beliar; for

the angel of lawlessness, who is the ruler of this world, is Beliar, whose name is Mantanbuchus. and he delighted in Jerusalem because of Manasseh, and he made him strong in apostatizing (Israel) and in the lawlessness which were spread abroad in Jerusalem.

5. And witchcraft and magic increased and divination and auguration, and fornication, a [and adultery], and the persecution of the righteous by Manasseh and [Belachira, and] Tobia the Canaanite, and John of Anathoth, an by (Zadok) the chief of the works.

6. And the rest of the acts, behold they are written in the book of the Kings of Judah and Israel.

7. And, when Isaiah, the son of Amoz, saw the lawlessness which was being perpetrated in Jerusalem and the worship of Satan and his wantonness, he withdrew from Jerusalem and settled in Bethlehem of Judah.

8. And there also there was much lawlessness, and withdrawing from Bethlehem he settled on a mountain in a desert place.

9. And Micaiah the prophet, and the aged Ananias, and Joel and Habakkuk, and his son Josab, and many of the faithful who believed in the ascension into heaven, withdrew and settled on the mountain.

10. They were all clothed with garments of hair, and they were all prophets. And they had nothing with them but were naked, and they all lamented with a great lamentation because of the going astray of Israel.

11. And these eat nothing save wild herbs which they gathered on the mountains, and having cooked them, they lived thereon together with Isaiah the prophet. And they spent two years of days on the mountains and hills.

12. And after this, whilst they were in the desert, there was a certain man in Samaria named Belchira, of the family of Zedekiah, the son of Chenaan, a false prophet, whose dwelling was in Bethlehem. Now Hezekiah the son of Chanani, who was the brother of his father, and in the days of Ahab, king of Israel, had been the teacher of the 400. prophets of Baal, had himself smitten and reproved Micaiah the son of Amada the prophet.

13. And he, Micaiah, had been reproved by Ahab and cast into prison. (And he was) with Zedekiah the prophet: they were with Ahaziah the son of Ahab, king in Samaria.

14. And Elijah the prophet of Tebon of Gilead was reproving Ahaziah and Samaria, and prophesied regarding Ahaziah that he should die on his bed of sickness, and that Samaria should be delivered into the had of Leba Nasr because he had slain the prophets of God.

15. And when the false prophets, who were with Ahaziah the son of Ahab and their teacher Jalerjas of Mount Joel, had heard-

16. Now he was a brother of Zedekiah - when they persuaded Ahaziah the king of Aguaron and (slew) Micaiah.

CHAPTER 3

AND Belchira recognized and saw the place of Isaiah and the prophets who were with him; for he dwelt in the region of Bethlehem, and was an adherent of Manasseh. And he prophesied falsely in Jerusalem, and many belonging to Jerusalem were confederate with him, and he was a Samaritan.

2. And it came to pass when Alagar Zagar, king of Assyria, had come and captive, and led them away to the mountains of the medes and the rivers of Tazon;

3. This (Belchira), whilst still a youth, had escaped and come to Jerusalem in the days of Hezekiah king of Judah,

but he walked not in the ways of his father of Samaria; for he feared Hezekiah.

4. And he was found in the days of Hezekiah speaking words of lawlessness in Jerusalem.

5. And the servants of Hezekiah accused him, and he made his escape to the region of Bethlehem. And they persuaded...

6. And Belchira accused Isaiah and the prophets who were with him, saying: `Isaiah and those who are with him prophesy against Jerusalem and against the cities of Judah that they shall be laid waste and (against the children of Judah and) Benjamin also that they shall go into captivity, and also against thee, O lord the king, that thou shalt go (bound) with hooks and iron chains':

7. But they prophesy falsely against Israel and Judah.

8. And Isaiah himself hath said: `I see more than Moses the prophet.'

9. But Moses said: `No man can see God and live'; and Isaiah hath said: `I have seen God and behold I live.'

10. Know, therefore, O king, that he is lying. And Jerusalem also he hath called Sodom, and the princes of Judah and Jerusalem he hath declared to be the people of Gomorrah. And he brought many accusations against Isaiah and the prophets before Manasseh.

11. But Beliar dwelt in the heart of Manasseh and in the heart of the princes of Judah and Benjamin and of the eunuchs and of the councillors of the king.

12. And the words of Belchira pleased him [exceedingly], and he sent and seized Isaiah.

13. For Beliar was in great wrath against Isaiah by reason of the vision, and because of the exposure wherewith he had exposed Sammael, and because through him the going forth of the Beloved from the seventh heaven had been made known, and His transformation and His descent and the likeness into which He should be transformed (that is) the likeness of man, and the persecution wherewith he should be persecuted, and the torturers wherewith the children of Israel should torture Him, and the coming of His twelve disciples, and the teaching, and that He should before the sabbath be crucified upon the tree, and should be crucified together with wicked men, and that He should be buried in the sepulchre,

14. And the twelve who were with Him should be offended because of Him: and the watch of those who watched the sepulchre:

15. And the descent of the angel of the Christian Church, which is in the heavens, whom He will summon in the last days.

16. And that (Gabriel) the angel of the Holy Spirit, and Michael, the chief of the holy angels, on the third day will open the sepulchre:

17. And the Beloved sitting on their shoulders will come forth and send out His twelve disciples;

18. And they will teach all the nations and every tongue of the resurrection of the Beloved, and those who believe in His cross will be saved, and in His ascension into the seventh heaven whence He came:

19. And that many who believe in Him will speak through the Holy Spirit:

20. And many signs and wonders will be wrought in those days.

21. And afterwards, on the eve of His approach, His disciples will forsake the teachings of the Twelve Apostles, and their faith, and their love and their purity.

22. And there will be much contention on the eve of [His advent and] His approach.

23. And in those days many will love office, though devoid of wisdom.

24. And there will be many lawless elders, and shepherds dealing wrongly by their own sheep, and they will ravage (them) owing to their not having holy shepherds.

25. And many will change the honour of the garments of the saints for the garments of the covetous, and there will be much respect of persons in those days and lovers of the honour of this world.

26. And there will be much slander and vainglory at the approach of the Lord, and the Holy Spirit will withdraw from many.

27. And there will not be in those days many prophets, nor those who speak trustworthy words, save one here and there in divers places,

28. On account of the spirit of error and fornication and of vainglory, and of covetousness, which shall be in those, who will be called servants of that One and in those who will receive that One.

29. And there will be great hatred in the shepherds and elders towards each other.

30. For there will be great jealousy in the last days; for every one will say what is pleasing in his own eyes.

31. And they will make of none effect the prophecy of the prophets which were before me, and these my visions also will they make of none effect, in order to speak after the impulse of their own hearts.

CHAPTER 4

AND now Hezekiah and Josab my son, these are the days of the completion of the world.

2. After it is consummated, Beliar the great ruler, the king of this world, will descend, who hath ruled it since it came into being; yea, he will descent from his firmament in the likeness of a man, a lawless king, the slayer of his mother: who himself (even) this king.

3. Will persecute the plant which the Twelve Apostles of the Beloved have planted. Of the Twelve one will be delivered into his hands.

4. This ruler in the form of that king will come and there will come and there will come with him all the powers of this world, and they will hearken unto him in all that he desires.

5. And at his word the sun will rise at night and he will make the moon to appear at the sixth hour.

6. And all that he hath desired he will do in the world: he will do and speak like the Beloved and he will say: "I am God and before me there has been none."

7. And all the people in the world will believe in him. 8. And they will sacrifice to him and they will serve him saying: "This is God and beside him there is no other."

9. And they greater number of those who shall have been associated together in order to receive the Beloved, he will turn aside after him.

10. And there will be the power of his miracles in every city and region.

11. And he will set up his image before him in every city.

12. And he shall bear sway three years and seven months and twenty-seven days.

13. And many believers and saints having seen Him for whom they were hoping, who was crucified, Jesus the Lord Christ, [after that I, Isaiah, had seen Him who was crucified and ascended] and those also who were believers in Him - of these few in those days will be left as His servants, while they flee from desert to desert, awaiting the coming of the

Beloved.

14. And after (one thousand) three hundred and thirty-two days the Lord will come with His angels and with the armies of the holy ones from the seventh heaven with the glory of the seventh heaven, and He will drag Beliar into Gehenna and also his armies.

15. And He will give rest of the godly whom He shall find in the body in this world, [and the sun wil be ashamed]:

16. And to all who because of (their) faith in Him have execrated Beliar and his kings. But the saints will come with the Lord with their garments which are (now) stored up on high in the seventh heaven: with the Lord they will come, whose spirits are clothed, they will descend and be present in the world, and He will strengthen those, who have been found in the body, together with the saints, in the garments of the saints, and the Lord will minister to those who have kept watch in this world.

17. And afterwards they will turn themselves upward in their garments, and their body will be left in the world.

18. Then the voice of the Beloved will in wrath rebuke the things of heaven and the things of earth and the things of earth and the mountains and the hills and the cities and the desert and the forests and the angel of the sun and that of the moon, and all things wherein Beliar manifested himself and acted openly in this world, and there will be [a resurrection and] a judgment in their midst in those days, and the Beloved will cause fire to go forth from Him, and it will consume all the godless, and they will be as though they had not been created.

19. And the rest of the words of the vision is written in the vision of Babylon.

20. And the rest of the vision regarding the Lord, behold, it is written in three parables according to my words which are written in the book which I publicly prophesied.

21. And the descent of the Beloved into Sheol, behold, it is written in the section, where the Lord says: "Behold my Son will understand." And all these things, behold they are written [in the Psalms] in the parables of David, the son of Jesse, and in the Proverbs of Solomon his son, and in the words of Korah, and Ethan the Israelite, and in the words of Asaph, and in the rest of the Psalms also which the angel of the Spirit inspired.

22. (Namely) in those which have not the name written, and in the words of my father Amos, and of Hosea the prophet, and of Micah and Joel and Nahum and Jonah and Obadiah and Habakkuk and Haggai and Malachi, and in the words of Joseph the Just and in the words of Daniel.

CHAPTER 5

ON account of these visions, therefore, Beliar was wroth with Isaiah, and he dwelt in the heart of Manasseh and he sawed him in sunder with a wooden saw.

2. And when Isaiah was being sawn in sunder, Belchira stood up, accusing him, and all the false prophets stood up, laughing and rejoicing because of Isaiah.

3. And Belchira, with the aid of Mechembechus, stood up before Isaiah, [laughing] deriding;

4. And Belchira said to Isaiah: 'Say, "I have lied in all that I have spoken, and likewise the ways of Manasseh are good and right.

5. And the ways also of Belchira and of his associates are good."

6. And this he said to him when he began to be sawn in sunder.

7. But Isaiah was (absorbed) in a vision of the Lord, and though his eyes were open, he saw them (not).

8. And Belchira spake thus to Isaiah: "Say what I say unto thee and I will turn their hearts, and I will compel Manasseh and the princes of Judah and the people and all Jerusalem to reverence thee.

9. And Isaiah answered and said: "So far as I have utterance (I say): Damned and accused be thou and all they powers and all thy house.

10. For thou canst not take (from me) aught save the skin of my body."

11. And they seized and sawed in sunder Isaiah, the son of Amoz, with a wooden saw.

12. And Manasseh and Belchira and the false prophets and the princes and the people [and] all stood looking on.

13. And to the prophets who were with him he said before he had been sawn in sunder: "Go ye to the region of Tyre and Sidon; for for me only hath God mingled the cup."

14. And when Isaiah was being sawn in sunder, he neither cried aloud nor wept, but his lips spake with the Holy Spirit until he was sawn in twain.

15. This, Beliar did to Isaiah through Belchira and Manasseh; for Sammael was very wrathful against Isaiah from the days of Hezekiah, king of Judah, on account of the things which he had seen regarding the Beloved.

16. And on account of the destruction of Sammael, which he had seen through the Lord, while Hezekiah his father was still king. And he did according to the will of Satan.

CHAPTER 6

The Vision Which Isaiah the Son of Amoz Saw:
In the twentieth year of the reign of Hezekiah, king of Judah, came Isaiah the son of Amoz, and Josab the son of Isaiah to Hezekiah to Jerusalem from Galgala.

2. And (having entered) he sat down on the couch of the king, and they brought him a seat, but he would not sit (thereon).

3. And when Isaiah began to speak the words of faith and truth with King Hezekiah, all the princes of Israel were seated and the eunuchs and the councillors of the king. And there were there forty prophets and sons of the prophets: they had come from the villages and from the mountains and the plains when they had heard that Isaiah was coming from Galgala to Hezekiah.

4. And they had come to salute him and to hear his words.

5. And that he might place his hands upon them, and that they might prophesy and that he might hear their prophecy: and they were all before Isaiah.

6. And when Isaiah was speaking to Hezekiah the words of truth and faith, they all heard a door which one had opened and the voice of the Holy Spirit.

7. And the king summoned all the prophets and all the people who were found there, and they came. and Macaiah and the aged Ananias and Joel and Josab sat on his right hand (and on the left).

8. And it came to pass when they had all heard the voice of the Holy Spirit, they all worshipped on their knees, and glorified the God of truth, the Most High who is in the upper world and who sits on High the Holy One and who rest among His holy ones.

9. And they gave glory to Him who had thus bestowed a door in an alien world had bestowed (it) on a man.

10. And as he was speaking in the Holy Spirit in the hearing of all, he became silent and his mind was taken up from him and he saw not the men that stood before him.

11. Though his eyes indeed were open. Moreover his lips

were silent and the mind in his body was taken up from him.

12. But his breath was in him; for he was seeing a vision.

13. And the angel who was sent to make him see was not of this firmament, nor was he of the angels of glory of this world, but he had come from the seventh heaven.

14. And the people who stood near did (not) think, but the circle of the prophets (did), that the holy Isaiah had been taken up.

15. And the vision which the holy Isaiah saw was not from this world but from the world which is hidden from the flesh.

16. And after Isaiah had seen this vision, he narrated it to Hezekiah, and to Josab his son and to the other prophets who had come.

17. But the leaders and the eunuchs and the people did not hear, but only Samna the scribe, and Ijoaqem, and Asaph the recorder; for these also were doers of righteousness, and the sweet smell of the Spirit was upon them. But the people had not heard; for Micaiah and Josab his son had caused them to go forth, when the wisdom of this world had been taken form him and he became as one dead.

CHAPTER 7

AND the vision which Isaiah saw, he told to Hezekiah and Josab his son and Micaiah and the rest of the prophets, (and) said:

2. At this moment, when I prophesied according to the (words) heard which ye heard, I saw a glorious angel not like unto the glory of the angels which I used always to see, but possessing such glory ad position that I cannot describe the glory of that angel.

3. And having seized me by my hand he raised me on high, and I said unto him: "Who art thou, and what is thy name, and whither art thou raising me on high? for strength was given me to speak with him."

4. And he said unto me: "When I have raised thee on high [though the (various) degrees] and made thee see the vision, on account of which I have been sent, then thou wilt understand who I am: but my name thou dost not know.

5. Because thou wilt return into this thy body, but whither I am raising thee on high, thou wilt see; for for this purpose have I been sent."

6. And I rejoiced because he spake courteously to me.

7. And he said unto me: "Hast thou rejoiced because I have spoken courteously to thee?" And he said: "And thou wilt see how a grater also that I am will speak courteously and peaceably with thee."

8. And His Father also who is greater thou wilt see; for for this purpose have I been sent from the seventh heaven in order to explain all these things unto thee."

9. And we ascended to the firmament, I and he, and there I saw Sammael and his hosts, and there was great fighting therein and the angels of Satan were envying one another.

10. And as above so on the earth also; for the likeness of that which is in the firmament is here ont he earth.

11. And I said unto the angel (who was with me): "(What is this war and) what is this envying?"

12. And he said unto me: "So has it been since this world was made until now, and this war (will continue) till He, whom thou shalt see will come and destroy him."

13. And afterwards he caused me to ascend (to that which is) above the firmament: which is the (first) heaven.

14. And there I saw a throne in the midst, and on his right and on his left were angels.

15. And (the angels on the left were) not like unto the angels who stood on the right, but those who stood on the right had the greater glory, and they all praised with one voice, and there was a throne in the midst, and those who were out he left gave praise after them; but their voice was not such as the voice of those on the right, nor their praise like the praise of those.

16. And I asked the angel who conducted me, and I said unto him: "To whom is this praise sent?"

17. And he said unto me: "(it is sent) to the praise of (Him who sitteth in) the seventh heaven: to Him who rests in the holy world, and to His Beloved, whence I have been sent to thee. [Thither is it sent.]"

18. And again, he made me to ascend to the second heaven. now the height of that heaven is the same as from the haven to the earth [and to the firmament].

19. And (I saw there, as) in the first heaven, angels on the right and on the left, and a throne in the midst, and the praise of the angels in the second heaven; and he who sat on the throne in the second heaven was more glorious than all (the rest).

20. And there was great glory in the second heaven, and the praise also was not like the praise of those who were in the first heaven.

21. And I fell on my face to worship him, but he angel who conducted me did not permit me, but said unto me: "Worship neither throne nor angel which belongs to the six heavens - for for this cause I was sent to conduct thee j- until I tell thee in the seventh heaven.

22. For above all the heavens and their angels has thy throne been placed, and thy garments and thy crown which thou shalt see."

23. And I rejoiced with great joy, that those who love the Most High and His Beloved will afterwards ascend thither by the angel of the Holy Spirit.

24. And he raise me to the third heaven, and in like manner I saw those upon the right and upon the left, and there was a throne there in the midst; but the memorial of this world is there unheard of.

25. And I said to the angel who was with me; for the glory of my appearance was undergoing transformation as I ascended to each heaven in turn: "Nothing of the vanity of that world is here named."

26. And he answered me, and said unto me: "Nothing is named on account of its weakness, and nothing is hidden there of what is done."

27. And I wished to learn how it is know, and he answered me saying: "When I have raised thee to the seventh heaven whence I was sent, to that which is above these, then thou shalt know that there is nothing hidden from the thrones and from those who dwell in the heavens and from the angels. And the praise wherewith they praised and glory of him who sat on the throne was great, and the glory of the angels on the right hand and on the left was beyond that of the heaven which was below them.

28. And again he raised me to the fourth heaven, and the height from the third to the height from the third to the forth heaven was greater than from the earth to the firmament.

29. And there again I saw those who were on the right hand and those who were on the left, and him who sat on the throne was in the midst, and there also they were praising.

30. And the praise and glory of the angels on the right was greater than that of those on the left.

31. And again the glory of him who sat on the throne was

greater than that of the angels on the right, and their glory was beyond that of those who were below.

32. And he raised me to the fifth heaven.

33. And again I saw those upon the right hand and on the left, and him who sat on the throne possessing greater glory that those of the forth heaven.

34. And the glory of those on the right hand was greater than that of those on the left [from the third to the fourth].

35. And the glory of him who was on the throne was greater than that of the angels on the right hand.

36. And their praise was more glorious than that of the fourth heaven.

37. And I praised Him, who is not named and the Only-begotten who dwelleth in the heavens, whose name is not known to any flesh, who has bestowed such glory on the several heaves, and who makes great the glory of the angels, and more excellent the glory of Him who sitteth on the throne.

CHAPTER 8

AND again he raised me into the air of the sixth heaven, and I saw such glory as I had not seen in the five heavens.

2. For I saw angels possessing great glory.

3. And the praise there was holy and wonderful.

4. And I said to the angel who conducted me: "What is this which I see, my Lord?"

5. And he said: "I am not thy lord, but thy fellow servant."

6. And again I asked him, and I said unto him: "Why are there not angelic fellow servants (on the left)?"

7. And he said: "From the sixth heaven there are no longer angels on the left, nor a throne set in the midst, but (they are directed) by the power of the seventh heaven, where dwelleth He that is not named and the Elect One, whose name has not been made known, and none of the heavens can learn His name.

8. For it is He alone to whose voice all the heavens and thrones give answer. I have therefore been empowered and sent to raise thee here that thou mayest see this glory.

9. And that thou mayest see the Lord of all those heavens and these thrones.

10. Undergoing (successive) transformation until He resembles your form and likeness.

11. I indeed say unto thee, Isaiah; No man about to return into a body of that world has ascended or seen what thou seest or perceived what thou hast perceived and what thou wilt see.

12. For it has been permitted to thee in the lot of the Lord to come hither. [And from thence comes the power of the sixth heaven and of the air]."

13. And I magnified my Lord with praise, in that through His lot I should come hither.

14. And he said: "Hear, furthermore, therefore, this also from thy fellow servant: when from the body by the will of God thou hast ascended hither, then thou wilt receive the garment which thou seest, and likewise other numbered garments laid up (there) thou wilt see.

15. And then thou wilt become equal to the angels of the seventh heaven.

16. And he raised me up into the sixth heaven, and there were no (angels) on the left, nor a throne in the midst, but all had one appearance and their (power of) praise was equal.

17. And (power) was given to me also, and I also praised along with them and that angel also, and our praise was like theirs. 18. And there they all named the primal Father and His Beloved, the Christ, and the Holy Spirit, all with one voice.

19. And (their voice) was not like the voice of the angels in the five heavens.

20. [Nor like their discourse] but the voice was different there, and there was much light there.

21. And then, when I was in the sixth heaven I thought the light which I had seen in the five heavens to be but darkness.

22. And I rejoiced and praised Him who hath bestowed such lights on those who wait for His promise.

23. And I besought the angel who conducted me that I should not henceforth return to the carnal world.

24. I say indeed unto you, Hezekiah and Josab my son and Micaiah, that there is much darkness here.

25. And the angel who conducted me discovered what I thought and said: "If in this light thou dost rejoice, how much more wilt thou rejoice, when in the seventh heaven thou seest the light where is the Lord and His Beloved [whence I have been sent, who is to be called "Son" in this world.

26. Not (yet) hath been manifested he shall be in the corruptible world] and the garments, and the thrones, and the crowns which are laid up for the righteous, for those who trust in that Lord who will descend in your form. For the light which is there is great and wonderful.

27. And as concerning thy not returning into the body thy days are not yet fulfilled for coming here."

28. And when I heard (that) I was troubled, and he said: "Do not be troubled."

CHAPTER 9

AND he took me into the air of the seventh heaven, and moreover I heard a voice saying: "How far will he ascend that dwelleth in the flesh?" And I feared and trembled.

2. And when I trembled, behold, I heard from hence another voice being sent forth, and saying: "It is permitted to the holy Isaiah to ascend hither; for here is his garment."

3. And I asked the angel who was with me and said: "Who is he who forbade me and who is he who permitted me to ascend?"

4. And he said unto me: "He who forbade thee, is he who is over the praise-giving of the sixth heaven.

5. And He who permitted thee, this is thy Lord God, the Lord Christ, who will be called "Jesus" in the world, but His name thou canst not hear till thou hast ascended out of thy body."

6. And he raised me up into the seventh heaven, and I saw there a wonderful light and angels innumerable.

7. And there I saw the holy Abel and all the righteous.

8. And there I saw Enoch and all who were with him, stript of the garments of the flesh, and I saw them in their garments of the upper world, and they were like angels, standing there in great glory.

9. And there I saw Enoch and all who were with him, stript of the garments of the flesh, and I saw them in their garments of the upper world, and they were like angels, standing there in great glory.

10. But they sat not on their thrones, nor were their crowns of glory on them.

11. And I asked the angel who was with me: "How is it that they have received the garments, but have not the thrones and the crowns?"

12. And he said unto me: "Crowns and thrones of glory they do not receive, till the Beloved will descent in the form

in which you will see Him descent [will descent, I say] into the world in the last days the Lord, who will be called Christ.

13. Nevertheless they see and know whose will be thrones, and whose the crowns when He has descended and been made in your form, and they will think that He is flesh and is a man.

14. And the god of that world will stretch forth his hand against the Son, and they will crucify Him on a tree, and will slay Him not knowing who He is.

15. And thus His descent, as you will see, will be hidden even from the heavens, so that it will not be known who He is.

16. And when He hath plundered the angel of death, He will ascend on the third day, [and he will remain in that world five hundred and forty-five days].

17. And then many of the righteous will ascend with Him, whose spirits do not receive their garments till the Lord Christ ascend and they ascend with Him.

18. Then indeed they will receive their [garments and] thrones and crowns, when He has ascended into the seventh heaven."

19. And I said unto him that which I had asked him in the third heaven:

20. "Show me how everything which is done in that world is here made known."

21. And whilst I was still speaking with him, behold one of the angels who stood nigh, more glorious than the glory of that angel, who had raised me up from the world.

22. Showed me a book, [but not as a book of this world] and he opened it, and the book was written, but not as a book of this world. And he gave (it) to me and I read it, and lo! the deeds of the children of Israel were written therein, and the deeds of those whom I know (not), my son Josab.

23. And I said: "In truth, there is nothing hidden in the seventh heaven, which is done in this world."

24. And I saw there many garments laid up, and many thrones and many crowns.

25. And I said to the angel: "Whose are these garments and thrones and crowns?"

26. And he said unto me: "These garments many from that world will receive, believing in the words of That One, who shall be named as I told thee, and they will observe those things, and believe in them, and believe in His cross: for them are these laid up."

27. And I saw a certain One standing, whose glory surpassed that of all, and His glory was great and wonderful.

28. And after I had seen Him, all the righteous whom I had seen and also the angels whom I had seen came to Him. And Adam and Abel and Seth and all the righteous first drew near and worshipped Him, and they all praised Him with one voice, and I myself also gave praise with them, and my giving of praise was as theirs.

29. And then all the angels drew nigh and worshipped and gave praise.

30. And I was (again) transformed and became like an angel.

31. And thereupon the angel who conducted me said to me: "Worship this One," and I worshipped and praised.

32. And the angel said unto me: "This is the Lord of all the praise-givings which thou hast seen."

33. And whilst he was still speaking, I saw another Glorious One who was like Him, and the righteous drew nigh and worshipped and praised, and I praised together with them.

But my glory was not transformed into accordance with their form.

34. And thereupon the angels drew near and worshipped Him.

35. And I saw the Lord and the second angel, and they were standing.

36. And the second whom I saw was on he left of my Lord. And I asked: "Who is this?" and he said unto me: "Worship Him, for He is the angel of the Holy Spirit, who speaketh in thee and the rest of the righteous."

37. And I saw the great glory, the eyes of my spirit being open, and I could not thereupon see, nor yet could the angel who was with me, nor all the angels whom I had seen worshipping my Lord.

38. But I saw the righteous beholding with great power the glory of that One.

39. And my Lord drew nigh to me and the angel of the Spirit and He said: "See how it is given to thee to see God, and on thy account power is given to the angel who is with thee."

40. And I saw how my Lord and the angel of the Spirit worshipped, and they both together praised God.

41. And thereupon all the righteous drew near and worshipped.

42. And the angels drew near and worshipped and all the angels praised.

CHAPTER 10

AND thereupon I heard the voices and the giving of praise, which I had heard in each of the six heavens, ascending and being heard there:

2. And all were being sent up to that Glorious One whose glory I could not behold.

3. And I myself was hearing and beholding the praise (which was given) to Him.

4. And the Lord and the angel of the Spirit were beholding all and hearing all.

5. And all the praises which are sent up from the six heavens are not only heard, but seen.

6. And I heard the angel who conducted me and he said: "This is the Most High of the high ones, dwelling in the holy world, and resting in His holy ones, who will be called by the Holy Spirit through the lips of the righteous the Father of the Lord."

7. And I heard the voice of the Most High, the Father of my Lord, saying to my Lord Christ who will be called Jesus:

8. "Go forth and descent through all the heavens, and thou wilt descent to the firmament and that world: to the angel in Sheol thou wilt descend, but to Haguel thou wilt not go.

9. And thou wilt become like unto the likeness of all who are in the five heavens.

10. And thou wilt be careful to become like the form of the angels of the firmament [and the angels also who are in Sheol].

11. And none of the angels of that world shall know that Thou art with Me of the seven heavens and of their angels.

12. And they shall not know that Thou art with Me, till with a loud voice I have called (to) the heavens, and their angels and their lights, (even) unto the sixth heaven, in order that you mayest judge and destroy the princes and angels and gods of that world, and the world that is dominated by them:

13. For they have denied Me and said: "We alone are and there is none beside us."

14. And afterwards from the angels of death Thou wilt

ascend to Thy place. And Thou wilt not be transformed in each heaven, but in glory wilt Thou ascend and sit on My right hand.

15. And thereupon the princes and powers of that world will worship Thee."

16. These commands I heard the Great Glory giving to my Lord.

17. And so I saw my Lord go forth from the seventh heaven into the sixth heaven.

18. And the angel who conducted me [from this world was with me and] said unto me: "Understand, Isaiah, and see the transformation and descent of the Lord will appear."

19. And I saw, and when the angels saw Him, thereupon those in the sixth heaven praised and lauded Him; for He had not been transformed after the shape of the angels there, and they praised Him and I also praised with them.

20. And I saw when He descended into the fifth heaven, that in the fifth heaven He made Himself like unto the form of the angels there, and they did not praise Him (nor worship Him); for His form was like unto theirs.

21. And then He descended into the forth heaven, and made Himself like unto the form of the angels there.

22. And when they saw Him, they did not praise or laud Him; for His form was like unto their form.

23. And again I saw when He descended into the third heaven, and He made Himself like unto the form of the angels in the third heaven.

24. And those who kept the gate of the (third) heaven demanded the password, and the Lord gave (it) to them in order that He should not be recognized. And when they saw Him, they did not praise or laud Him; for His form was like unto their form.

25. And again I saw when He descended into the second heaven, and again He gave the password there; those who kept the gate proceeded to demand and the Lord to give.

26. And I saw when He made Himself like unto the form of the angels in the second heaven, and they saw Him and they did not praise Him; for His form was like unto their form.

27. And again I saw when He descended into the first heaven, and there also He gave the password to those who kept the gate, and He made Himself like unto the form of the angels who were on the left of that throne, and they neither praised nor lauded Him; for His form was like unto their form.

28. But as for me no one asked me on account of the angel who conducted me.

29. And again He descended into the firmament where dwelleth the ruler of this world, and He gave the password to those on the left, and His form was like theirs, and they did not praise Him there; but they were envying one another and fighting; for here there is a power of evil and envying about trifles.

30. And I saw when He descended and made Himself like unto the angels of the air, and He was like one of them.

31. And He gave no password; for one was plundering and doing violence to another.

CHAPTER 11

AFTER this I saw, and the angel who spoke with me, who conducted me, said unto me: "Understand, Isaiah son of Amoz; for for this purpose have I been sent from God."

2. And I indeed saw a woman of the family of David the prophet, named Mary, and Virgin, and she was espoused to a man named Joseph, a carpenter, and he also was of the seed and family of the righteous David of Bethlehem Judah.

3. And he came into his lot. And when she was espoused, she was found with child, and Joseph the carpenter was desirous to put her away.

4. But the angel of the Spirit appeared in this world, and after that Joseph did not put her away, but kept Mary and did not reveal this matter to any one.

5. And he did not approach May, but kept her as a holy virgin, though with child.

6. And he did not live with her for two months.

7. And after two months of days while Joseph was in his house, and Mary his wife, but both alone.

8. It came to pass that when they were alone that Mary straight-way looked with her eyes and saw a small babe, and she was astonished.

9. And after she had been astonished, her womb was found as formerly before she had conceived.

10. And when her husband Joseph said unto her: "What has astonished thee?" his eyes were opened and he saw the infant and praised God, because into his portion God had come.

11. And a voice came to them: "Tell this vision to no one."

12. And the story regarding the infant was noised broad in Bethlehem.

13. Some said: "The Virgin Mary hath borne a child, before she was married two months."

14. And many said: "She has not borne a child, nor has a midwife gone up (to her), nor have we heard the cries of (labour) pains." And they were all blinded respecting Him and they all knew regarding Him, though they knew not whence He was.

15. And they took Him, and went to Nazareth in Galilee.

16. And I saw, O Hezekiah and Josab my son, and I declare to the other prophets also who are standing by, that (this) hath escaped all the heavens and all the princes and all the gods of this world.

17. And I saw: In Nazareth He sucked the breast as a babe and as is customary in order that He might not be recognized.

18. And when He had grown up he worked great signs and wonders in the land of Israel and of Jerusalem.

19. And after this the adversary envied Him and roused the children of Israel against Him, not knowing who He was, and they delivered Him to the king, and crucified Him, and He descended to the angel (of Sheol).

20. In Jerusalem indeed I was Him being crucified on a tree:

21. And likewise after the third day rise again and remain days.

22. And the angel who conducted me said: "Understand, Isaiah": and I saw when He sent out the Twelve Apostles and ascended.

23. And I saw Him, and He was in the firmament, but He had not changed Himself into their form, and all the angels of the firmament and the Satans saw Him and they worshipped.

24. And there was much sorrow there, while they said: "How did our Lord descend in our midst, and we perceived not the glory [which has been upon Him], which we see has been upon Him from the sixth heaven?"

25. And He ascended into the second heaven, and He did not transform Himself, but all the angels who were on the right and on the left and the throne in the midst.

26. Both worshipped Him and praised Him and said: "How did our Lord escape us whilst descending, and we perceived

not?"

27. And in like manner He ascended into the third heaven, and they praised and said in like manner.

28. And in the fourth heaven and in the fifth also they said precisely after the same manner.

29. But there was one glory, and from it He did not change Himself.

30. And I saw when He ascended into the sixth heaven, and they worshipped and glorified Him.

31. But in all the heavens the praise increased (in volume).

32. And I saw how He ascended into the seventh heaven, and all the righteous and all the angels praised Him. And then I saw Him sit down on the right hand of that Great Glory whose glory I told you that I could not behold.

33. And also the angel of the Holy Spirit I saw sitting on the left hand.

34. And this angel said unto me: "Isaiah, son of Amoz, it is enough for thee;... for thou hast seen what no child of flesh has seen.

35. And thou wilt return into thy garment (of the flesh) until thy days are completed. Then thou wilt come hither."

36. These things Isaiah saw and told unto all that stood before him, and they praised. And he spake to Hezekiah the King and said: "I have spoken these things."

37. Both the end of this world;

38. And all this vision will be consummated in the last generations.

39. And Isaiah made him swear that he would not tell (it) to the people of Israel, nor give these words to any man to transcribe.

40. ...such things ye will read. and watch ye in the Holy Spirit in order they ye may receive your garments and thrones and crowns of glory which are laid up in the seventh heaven.

41. On account of these visions and prophecies Sammael Satan sawed in sunder Isaiah the son of Amoz, the prophet, by the hand of Manasseh.

42. And all these things Hezekiah delivered to Manasseh in the twenty-sixth year.

43. But Manasseh did not remember them nor place these things in his heart, but becoming the servant of Satan he was destroyed. Here endeth the vision of Isaiah the prophet with his ascension.

THE MARTYRDOM OF POLYCARP

THE MARTYRDOM OF SAINT POLYCARP, BISHOP OF SMYRNA

CHAPTER 0

1 The church of God which sojourneth in Smyrna, to the church of God that sojourneth in Philomelia, and to all the settlements of the holy and Catholic Church in every place, mercy, peace, and love from God the Father and our Lord Jesus Christ be multiplied unto you.

CHAPTER 1

1:1 We have written unto you, brethren, the things respecting those who were martyred, and concerning the blessed Polycarp, who made the persecution to cease, having as it were set his seal to it by his testimony. For almost all the things that went before happened in order that the Lord might show us from above the testimony that is according to the gospel;
1:2 for he endured to be betrayed, even as did the Lord, that we might become imitators of him, not as considering the things that concern ourselves only, but also the things that concern our neighbours; for it belongeth to true and firm love not only to desire to be saved itself, but also that all the brethren should be saved.

CHAPTER 2

2:1 Blessed, therefore, and noble are all the testimonies that happened according to the will of God, for it is right that we should be the more careful, and should ascribe unto God the authority over all things.
2:2 For who would not admire their nobility and endurance and obedience? who, though they were torn with stripes so that the internal arrangement of their flesh became evident even as far as the veins and arteries within, endured it, so that even the bystanders compassionated them and bemoaned them; and that others even arrived at such a pitch of nobility that none of them would either sob or groan, showing all of us that in that hour the martyrs of Christ departed being tortured in the flesh, or rather that the Lord, standing by, associated himself with them.
2:3 And applying themselves to the grace of Christ, they despised the torture of this world, purchasing by the endurance of a single hour remission from eternal punishment; and the fire of their harsh tormentors was cold to them, for they had before their eyes to escape the eternal and never-quenched fire; and with the eyes of their heart they looked up to the good things that are reserved for those that endure, which neither hath ear heard, nor eye seen, nor hath it entered into the heart of man; but which were shown by the Lord unto them, who were no longer men, but already angels.
2:4 And in like manner they who had been condemned to the wild beasts endured dreadful punishments, lying upon beds of prickles, and punished with various other tortures, in order that, if it were possible, the tyrant might turn them by assiduous punishment to a denial of the faith.

CHAPTER 3

3:1 For the devil contrived many things against them, but thanks be unto God, for he prevailed not against all. For the most noble Germanicus strengthened their cowardice through the patience that was in him, who also in a notable way fought against wild beasts. For when the proconsul would have persuaded him, charging him to have compassion on his youth, he drew upon himself the wild beast by force, wishing to be the sooner freed from their unjust and lawless life.
3:2 From this, therefore, all the multitude, wondering at the nobleness of the God-loving and God-fearing race of Christians, called out, Away with the Atheists; let Polycarp be sought for.

CHAPTER 4

4:1 But a certain man named Quintus, a Phrygian, who had newly come from Phrygia, when he saw the wild beasts, became afraid. This was he who constrained himself and others to come in of their own accord. This man, the proconsul, with much importunity, persuaded to swear and to sacrifice. On this account, brethren, we praise not them that give themselves up, since the gospel doth not so teach.

CHAPTER 5

5:1 But the most admirable Polycarp at the first, when he heard these things, was not disturbed, but desired to remain in the city. But the majority persuaded him to withdraw secretly; and he departed secretly to a villa not far from the city, and remained there with a few men, doing no other thing either by night or day but pray concerning all men, and for the churches that are in the world, as was his custom;
5:2 and as he prayed he fell into a trance three days before he was taken, and saw his pillow burning with fire, and he turned and said prophetically to those who were with him, I must be burned alive.

CHAPTER 6

6:1 And when those who sought him continued in the pursuit, he departed unto another villa, and straightway they who sought him came up. And when they found him not, they apprehended two lads, of whom the one, when put to the torture, confessed.
6:2 For it was impossible for him to escape their notice, since they who betrayed him were of his own household. For the Eirenarchus, which is the same office as Cleronomus, Herodes by name, hasted to bring him into the arena, that he indeed might fulfil his proper lot, by becoming a partaker of Christ, and that they who betrayed him might undergo the same punishment as Judas.

CHAPTER 7

7:1 Having, therefore, with them the lad, on the day of

the preparation, at the hour of dinner, there came out pursuers and horsemen, with their accustomed arms, as though going out against a thief. And having departed together late in the evening, they found him lying in a certain house, in an upper chamber. And he might have departed from thence unto another place, but was unwilling, saying, The will of the Lord be done.

7:2 And when he heard that they were present, he descended and talked with them. And they who were present wondered at the vigour of his age and his soundness of body, and that they had had to use so much trouble to capture so old a man. He straightway commanded that meat and drink should be set before them at that hour, as much as they wished, and asked them to grant him an hour to pray without molestation.

7:3 And when they suffered him, he stood and prayed, being full of the grace of God, so that he could not be silent for two hours, and they that heard him were astonished, and many repented that they had come against so divine an old man.

CHAPTER 8

8:1 And when he had finished his prayer, having made mention of all who had at any time come into contact with him, both small and great, noble and ignoble, and of the whole Catholic Church throughout the world, when the hour of his departure had come, having seated him on an ass, they led him into the city, it being the great Sabbath.

8:2 And the Eirenarch Herodes and his father Nicetes met him in a chariot, who, having transferred him into their car, seating themselves beside him, would have persuaded him, saying, What is the harm to say, Caesar, Caesar, and to sacrifice, and to do such like things, and thus to be saved? But he at the first did not answer them; but when they persisted, he said, I will not do that which ye advise me.

8:3 But they, when they had failed to persuade him, said unto him dreadful words, and thrust him with such haste from the chariot that in descending from the car he grazed his shin. And paying no attention to it, as though he had suffered nothing, he proceeded zealously and with eagerness, being led to the arena, there being such a noise in the arena that no one could even be heard.

CHAPTER 9

9:1 But to Polycarp, as he entered the arena, there came a voice from heaven, saying, Be strong, and play the man, O Polycarp. And the speaker no man saw; but the voice those of our people who were present heard. And when he was brought in there was a great tumult, when men heard that Polycarp was apprehended.

9:2 Then, when he had been brought in, the proconsul asked him if he was Polycarp. And when he confessed, he would have persuaded him to deny, saying, Have respect unto thine age, and other things like these, as is their custom to say: Swear by the fortunes of Caesar; Repent; Say, Away with the Atheists. But Polycarp, when he had looked with a grave face at all the multitude of lawless heathen in the arena, having beckoned unto them with his hand, sighed, and looking up unto heaven, said,

Away with the Atheists!

9:3 And when the proconsul pressed him, and said, Swear, and I will release thee, revile Christ; Polycarp said, Eighty and six years have I served him, and in nothing hath he wronged me; and how, then, can I blaspheme my King, who saved me?

CHAPTER 10

10:1 But when he again persisted, and said, Swear by the fortune of Caesar, he answered, If thou art vainly confident that I shall swear by the fortune of Caesar, as thou suggestest, and pretendest to be ignorant of me who I am, hear distinctly, I am a Christian. But if thou desirest to learn the scheme of Christianity, give me a day to speak, and hearken unto me.

10:2 The proconsul said, Persuade the people. But Polycarp said, I have thought thee indeed worthy to receive explanation, for we have been taught to render such honour as is fitting, and as does not injure us, to the powers and authorities ordained by God; but those I consider not worthy that I should make my defence before them.

CHAPTER 11

11:1 But the proconsul said unto him, I have wild beasts; I will deliver thee unto them, unless thou repentest. But he said, Call them, for repentance from the better to the worse is impossible for us; but it is a good thing to change from evil deeds to just ones.

11:2 But he said again unto him, I will cause thee to be consumed by fire if thou despisest the wild beasts, unless thou repentest. But Polycarp said, Thou threatenest me with fire that burneth but for a season, and is soon quenched. For thou art ignorant of the fire of the judgment to come, and of the eternal punishment reserved for the wicked. But why delayest thou? Bring whatever thou wishest.

CHAPTER 12

12:1 While he was saying these and more things, he was filled with courage and joy, and his face was filled with grace; so that he not only was not troubled and confused by the things said unto him, but, on the contrary, the proconsul was astonished, and sent his herald into the midst of the arena to proclaim a third time: Polycarp has confessed himself to be a Christian.

12:2 When this had been said by the herald, the whole multitude, both of Gentiles and Jews, that inhabit Smyrna, with irrestrainable anger and a loud voice, called out, This is the teacher of impiety, the father of the Christians, the destroyer of your gods, who teacheth many neither to sacrifice nor to worship the gods. Saying these things, they shouted out, and asked the Asiarch Philip to let loose a lion at Polycarp. But Philip replied that it was not lawful for him to do so, since he had finished the exhibition of wild beasts.

12:3 Then it seemed good unto them to shout with one voice that Polycarp should be burnt alive; for it was necessary that the vision that appeared unto him on his pillow should be fulfilled, when seeing it burning, he prayed, and said prophetically, turning to the faithful who were with him, I must be burnt alive.

CHAPTER 13

13:1 These things, therefore, happened with so great rapidity, that they took less time than the narration, the multitude quickly collecting logs and brushwood from the workshops and baths, the Jews especially lending their services zealously for this purpose, as is their custom.

13:2 But when the pyre was ready, having put off all his garments, and having loosed his girdle, he essayed to take off his shoes; not being in the habit of doing this previously, because each of the faithful used to strive which should be the first to touch his body, for, on account of his good conversation, he was, even before his martyrdom, adorned with every good gift.

13:3 Straightway, therefore, there were put around him the implements prepared for the pyre. And when they were about besides to nail him to it, he said, Suffer me thus, for he who gave me to abide the fire will also allow me, without the security of your nails, to remain on the pyre without moving.

CHAPTER 14

14:1 They, therefore, did not nail him, but bound him. But he, having placed his hands behind him, and being bound, like a notable ram appointed for offering out of a great flock, prepared as a whole burnt-offering acceptable unto God, having looked up unto heaven, said, O Lord God Almighty, Father of thy beloved and blessed Son Jesus Christ, through whom we have received our knowledge concerning thee, the God of angels and powers, and of the whole creation, and of all the race of the just who lived before thee,

14:2 I thank thee that thou hast deemed me worthy of this day and hour, that I should have my portion in the number of the martyrs, in the cup of thy Christ, unto the resurrection of eternal life, both of the soul and body, in the incorruptibility of the Holy Spirit. Among these may I be received before thee this day as a rich and acceptable sacrifice, even as thou hast prepared and made manifest beforehand, and hast fulfilled, thou who art the unerring and true God.

14:3 On this account, and concerning all things, I praise thee, I bless thee, I glorify thee, together with the eternal and heavenly Jesus Christ thy beloved Son, with whom to thee and the Holy Spirit be glory both now and for ever. Amen.

CHAPTER 15

15:1 And when he had uttered the Amen, and had finished his prayer, the men who superintended the fire kindled it. And a great flame breaking out, we, to whom it was given to see, saw a great wonder; for to this end also were we preserved, that we might announce what happened to the rest of mankind.

15:2 For the fire, assuming the form of a vault, like the sail of a vessel filled with the wind, defended the body of the martyr roundabout; and it was in the midst of the flame not like flesh burning, but like bread being baked, or like gold and silver glowing in the furnace. And we perceived such a sweet-smelling savour, as though from the breath of incense, or some other precious perfume.

CHAPTER 16

16:1 At last these wicked men, perceiving that his body could not be consumed by the fire, commanded the slaughterer to come near and plunge in a sword. And when he had done this, there came out a dove and an abundance of blood, so that it quenched the fire, and all the multitude wondered that there was such a difference between the unbelievers and the elect.

16:2 Of whom this most admirable martyr Polycarp was one, having been in our time an apostolic and prophetic teacher, and bishop of the Catholic church which is in Smyrna. For every word which he uttered from his mouth both hath been fulfilled, and shall be fulfilled.

CHAPTER 17

17:1 But the evil one, who is the opponent and envier, who is the enemy to the race of men, beholding both the greatness of his testimony and his conversation blameless from the beginning, how he was crowned with a crown of immortality, and how he carried off a prize that could not be spoken against, contrived that not even a relic of him should be taken by us, though many desired to do this, and to communicate with his holy flesh.

17:2 He suborned, therefore, Nicetes, the father of Herodes, and the brother of Alce, to make interest with the governor so as not to give his body to the tomb, Lest, said he, they abandon the crucified and begin to worship this man. And these things they said at the suggestion and instance of the Jews, who also kept watch when we were about to take the body from the fire, not knowing that we shall never be able to abandon Christ, who suffered for the salvation of the whole world of those who are saved, the blameless on behalf of sinners, nor to worship any one else.

17:3 Him we adore as the Son of God; but the martyrs, as the disciples and imitators of the Lord, we love according to their deserts, on account of their incomparable love for their King and Teacher, with whom may it be our lot to be partners and fellow-disciples.

CHAPTER 18

18:1 Therefore, the centurion, seeing the strife that had risen among the Jews, placed the body in the midst of the fire and burned it.

18:2 Thus we, having afterwards taken up his bones, more valuable than precious stones, laid them where it was suitable.

18:3 There, so far as is allowed us, when we are gathered together in exultation and joy, the Lord will enable us to celebrate the birthday of the martyrs, both for the memory of those who have contended, and for the exercise and preparation of those to come.

CHAPTER 19

19:1 Such were the things that happened to the blessed Polycarp, who together with those from Philadelphia was the twelfth who suffered martyrdom in Smyrna; but he alone is held in memory by all, so that he is spoken of in every place even by the Gentiles; not only being a distinguished teacher, but also an eminent martyr, whose testimony we desire to imitate, since it happened according to the Gospel of Christ.
19:2 For having overcome by patience the unjust governor, and so having received the crown of immortality, rejoicing together with the apostles and all the just, he glorifieth God and the Father, and blesseth our Lord Jesus Christ the Saviour of our souls, and the pilot of our bodies, and the shepherd of the Catholic Church throughout the world.

CHAPTER 20

20:1 Ye therefore desired that the things that had happened should be shown unto you more at length; but we for the present have related them unto you briefly by means of our brother Marcus. Now do ye, when ye have read these things, send on the letter to the brethren who are further off, that they also may glorify the Lord, who is making a selection from among his own servants.
20:2 To him who is able to bring us all in, by his grace and gift, into his eternal kingdom, through his only-begotten Son Jesus Christ; to him be the glory, honour, strength, majesty for ever. Amen. Salute all the saints. They who are with us salute you, and Evarestus who wrote these things, and all his house.

CHAPTER 21

21:1 Now the blessed Polycarp was martyred on the second day of the month Xanthicus, on the twenty-fifth of April, on the great Sabbath, at the eighth hour. But he was apprehended by Herodes, when Philip of Tralles was high priest, Statius Quadratus being proconsul, and Jesus Christ king for ever, to whom be glory, honour, majesty, and eternal throne, from generation to generation. Amen.

CHAPTER 22

22:1 We pray, brethren, that you may fare well, walking by the word of the gospel of Jesus Christ, with whom be glory to God and the Father, and the Holy Spirit, for the salvation of the holy elect, even as the blessed Polycarp hath born witness, in whose steps may we be found in the kingdom of Jesus Christ.
22:2 These things have been transcribed by Gaius, from the manuscripts of Irenaeus, the disciple of Polycarp, who also was a fellow-citizen to Irenaeus. But I, Socrates, made a copy in Corinth from the copies of Gaius. Grace be with you all.
22:3 But I, Pionius, afterwards copied them from the above written, having sought them out, after that the blessed Polycarp had made them manifest to me by a revelation, as I will show in what follows; having gathered them together, when they had already become almost obliterated by time, in order that the Lord Jesus Christ may gather me also together with his elect, unto his heavenly kingdom, to whom be glory with the Father and the Holy Spirit, world without end. Amen.

ACTS OF PERPETUA AND FELICITAS

CHAPTER I
WHEN THE SAINTS WERE APPREHENDED, ST. PERPETUA SUCCESSFULLY RESISTED HER FATHER'S PLEADING, WAS BAPTIZED WITH THE OTHERS, WAS THRUST INTO A FILTHY DUNGEON. ANXIOUS ABOUT HER INFANT, BY A VISION GRANTED TO HER, SHE UNDERSTOOD THAT HER MARTYRDOM WOULD TAKE PLACE VERY SHORTLY.

1. The young catechumens, Revocatus and his fellow-servant Felicitas, Saturninus and Secundulus, were apprehended. And among them also was Vivia Perpetua, respectably born, liberally educated, a married matron, having a father and mother and two brothers, one of whom, like herself, was a catechumen, and a son an infant at the breast. She herself was about twenty-two years of age. From this point onward she shall herself narrate the whole course of her martyrdom, as she left it described by her own hand and with her own mind.

2. "While" says she, "we were still with the persecutors, and my father, for the sake of his affection for me, was persisting in seeking to turn me away, and to cast me down from the faith — 'Father,' said I, 'do you see, let us say, this vessel lying here to be a little pitcher, or something else?' And he said, 'I see it to be so.' And I replied to him, 'Can it be called by any other name than what it is?' And he said, 'No.' 'Neither can I call myself anything else than what I am, a Christian.' Then my father, provoked at this saying, threw himself upon me, as if he would tear my eyes out. But he only distressed me, and went away overcome by the devil's arguments. Then, in a few days after I had been without my father, I gave thanks to the Lord; and his absence became a source of consolation to me. In that same interval of a few days we were baptized, and to me the Spirit prescribed that in the water baptism nothing else was to be sought for bodily endurance. After a few days we are taken into the dungeon, and I was very much afraid, because I had never felt such darkness. O terrible day! O the fierce heat of the shock of the soldiery, because of the crowds! I was very unusually distressed by my anxiety for my infant. There were present there Tertius and Pomponius, the blessed deacons who ministered to us, and had arranged by means of a gratuity that we might be refreshed by being sent out for a few hours into a pleasanter part of the prison. Then going out of the dungeon, all attended to their own wants. I suckled my child, which was now enfeebled with hunger. In my anxiety for it, I addressed my mother and comforted my brother, and commended to their care my son. I was languishing because I had seen them languishing on my account. Such solicitude I suffered for many days, and I obtained for my infant to remain in the dungeon with me; and forthwith I grew strong and was relieved from distress and anxiety about my infant; and the dungeon became to me as it were a palace, so that I preferred being there to being elsewhere.

3. "Then my brother said to me, 'My dear sister, you are already in a position of great dignity, and are such that you may ask for a vision, and that it may be made known to you whether this is to result in a passion or an escape.' And I, who knew that I was privileged to converse with the Lord, whose kindnesses I had found to be so great, boldly promised him, and said, 'Tomorrow I will tell you.' And I asked, and this was what was shown me. I saw a golden ladder of marvellous height, reaching up even to heaven, and very narrow, so that persons could only ascend it one by one; and on the sides of the ladder was fixed every kind of iron weapon. There were there swords, lances, hooks, daggers; so that if any one went up carelessly, or not looking upwards, he would be torn to pieces and his flesh would cleave to the iron weapons. And under the ladder itself was crouching a dragon of wonderful size, who lay in wait for those who ascended, and frightened them from the ascent. And Saturus went up first, who had subsequently delivered himself up freely on our account, not having been present at the time that we were taken prisoners. And he attained the top of the ladder, and turned towards me, and said to me, Perpetua, I am waiting for you; but be careful that the dragon do not bite you.' And I said, 'In the name of the Lord Jesus Christ, he shall not hurt me.' And from under the ladder itself, as if in fear of me, he slowly lifted up his head; and as I trod upon the first step, I trod upon his head. And I went up, and I saw an immense extent of garden, and in the midst of the garden a white-haired man sitting in the dress of a shepherd, of a large stature, milking sheep; and standing around were many thousand white-robed ones. And he raised his head, and looked upon me, and said to me, 'Thou are welcome, daughter.' And he called me, and from the cheese as he was milking he gave me as it were a little cake, and I received it with folded hands; and I ate it, and all who stood around said *Amen*. And at the sound of their voices I was awakened, still tasting a sweetness which I cannot describe. And I immediately related this to my brother, and we understood that it was to be a passion, and we ceased henceforth to have any hope in this world.

CHAPTER II
PERPETUA, WHEN BESIEGED BY HER FATHER, COMFORTS HIM. WHEN LED WITH OTHERS TO THE TRIBUNAL, SHE AVOWS HERSELF A CHRISTIAN, AND IS CONDEMNED WITH THE REST TO THE WILD BEASTS. SHE PRAYS FOR HER BROTHER DINOCRATES, WHO WAS DEAD.

I. "After a few days there prevailed a report that we should be heard. And then my father came to me from the city, worn out with anxiety. He came up to me, that he might cast me down, saying, 'Have pity my daughter, on my grey hairs. Have pity on your father, if I am worthy to be called a father by you. If with these hands I have brought you up to this flower of your age, if I have preferred you to all your brothers, do not deliver me up to the scorn of men. Have regard to your brothers, have regard to your mother and your aunt, have regard to your son, who will not be able to live after you.

Lay aside your courage, and do not bring us all to destruction; for none of us will speak in freedom if you should suffer anything.' These things said my father in his affection, kissing my hands, and throwing himself at my feet; and with tears he called me not Daughter, but Lady. And I grieved over the grey hairs of my father, that he alone of all my family would not rejoice over my passion. And I comforted him, saying, 'On that scaffold whatever God wills shall happen. For know that we are not placed in our own power, but in that of God.' And he departed from me in sorrow.

2. "Another day, while we were at dinner, we were suddenly taken away to be heard, and we arrived at the town-hall. At once the rumour spread through the neighbourhood of the public place, and an immense number of people were gathered together. We mount the platform. The rest were interrogated, and confessed. Then they came to me, and my father immediately appeared with my boy, and withdrew me from the step, and said in a supplicating tone, 'Have pity on your babe.' And Hilarianus the procurator, who had just received the power of life and death in the place of the proconsul Minucius Timinianus, who was deceased, said, 'Spare the grey hairs of your father, spare the infancy of your boy, offer sacrifice for the well-being of the emperors.' And I replied, 'I will not do so.' Hilarianus said, 'Are you a Christian?' And I replied, 'I am a Christian.'

And as my father stood there to cast me down from the faith, he was ordered by Hilarianus to be thrown down, and was beaten with rods. And my father's misfortune grieved me as if I myself had been beaten, I so grieved for his wretched old age. The procurator then delivers judgment on all of us, and condemns us to the wild beasts, and we went down cheerfully to the dungeon. Then, because my child had been used to receive suck from me, and to stay with me in the prison, I send Pomponius the deacon to my father to ask for the infant, but my father would not give it him. And even as God willed it, the child no long desired the breast, nor did my breast cause me uneasiness, lest I should be tormented by care for my babe and by the pain of my breasts at once.

3. "After a few days, whilst we were all praying, on a sudden, in the middle of our prayer, there came to me a word, and I named Dinocrates; and I was amazed that that name had never come into my mind until then, and I was grieved as I remembered his misfortune. And I felt myself immediately to be worthy, and to be called on to ask on his behalf. And for him I began earnestly to make supplication, and to cry with groaning to the Lord. Without delay, on that very night, this was shown to me in a vision. I saw Dinocrates going out from a gloomy place, where also there were several others, and he was parched and very thirsty, with a filthy countenance and pallid colour, and the wound on his face which he had when he died. This Dinocrates had been my brother after the flesh, seven years of age? who died miserably with disease — his face being so eaten out with cancer, that his death caused repugnance to all men. For him I

had made my prayer, and between him and me there was a large interval, so that neither of us could approach to the other. And moreover, in the same place where Dinocrates was, there was a pool full of water, having its brink higher than was the stature of the boy; and Dinocrates raised himself up as if to drink. And I was grieved that, although that pool held water, still, on account of the height to its brink, he could not drink. And I was aroused, and knew that my brother was in suffering. But I trusted that my prayer would bring help to his suffering; and I prayed for him every day until we passed over into the prison of the camp, for we were to fight in the camp-show. Then was the birthday of Geta Caesar, and I made my prayer for my brother day and night, groaning and weeping that he might be granted to me.

4. "Then, on the day on which we remained in fetters, this was shown to me. I saw that that place which I had formerly observed to be in gloom was now bright; and Dinocrates, with a clean body well clad, was finding refreshment. And where there had been a wound, I saw a scar; and that pool which I had before seen, I saw now with its margin lowered even to the boy's navel. And one drew water from the pool incessantly, and upon its brink was a goblet filled with water; and Dinocrates drew near and began to drink from it, and the goblet did not fail. And when he was satisfied, he went away from the water to play joyously, after the manner of children, and I awoke. Then I understood that he was translated from the place of punishment.

CHAPTER III
PERPETUA IS AGAIN TEMPTED BY HER FATHER. HER THIRD VISION, WHEREIN SHE IS LED AWAY TO STRUGGLE AGAINST AN EGYPTIAN. SHE FIGHTS, CONQUERS, AND RECEIVES THE REWARD.

1. "Again, after a few days, Pudens, a soldier, an assistant overseer of the prison, who began to regard us in great esteem, perceiving that the great power of God was in us, admitted many brethren to see us, that both we and they might be mutually refreshed. And when the day of the exhibition drew near my father, worn with suffering, came in to me, and began to tear out his beard, and to throw himself on the earth, and to cast himself down on his face, and to reproach his years, and to utter such words as might move all creation. I grieved for his unhappy old age.

2. "The day before that on which we were to fight, I saw in a vision that Pomponius the deacon came hither to the gate of the prison, and knocked vehemently. I went out to him, and opened the gate for him; and he was clothed in a richly ornamented white robe, and he had on manifold calliculae. And he said to me, 'Perpetua, we are waiting for you; come!' And he held his hand to me, and we began to go through rough and winding places. Scarcely at length had we arrived breathless at the amphitheatre, when he led me into the middle of the arena, and said to me, 'Do not fear, I am here with you,

and I am labouring with you;' and he departed. And I gazed upon an immense assembly in astonishment. And because I knew that I was given to the wild beasts, I marvelled that the wild beasts were not let loose upon me. Then there came forth against me a certain Egyptian, horrible in appearance, with his backers, to fight with me. And there came to me, as my helpers and encouragers, handsome youths; and I was stripped, and became a man? Then my helpers began to rub me with oil, as is the custom for contest; and I beheld that Egyptian on the other hand rolling in the dust. And a certain man came forth, of wondrous height, so that he even over-topped the top of the amphitheatre; and he wore a loose tunic and a purple robe between two bands over the middle of the breast; and he had on calliculae of varied form, made of gold and silver; and he carried a rod, as if he were a trainer of gladiators, and a green branch upon which were apples of gold. And he called for silence, and said, 'This Egyptian, if he should overcome this woman, shall kill her with the sword; and if she shall conquer him, she shall receive this branch.' Then he departed. And we drew near to one another, and began to deal out blows. He sought to lay hold of my feet, while I struck at his face with my heels; and I was lifted up in the air, and began thus to thrust at him as if spurning the earth. But when I saw that there was some delay I joined my hands so as to twine my fingers with one another; and I took hold upon his head, and he fell on his face, and I trod upon his head? And the people began to shout, and my backers to exult. And I drew near to the trainer and took the branch; and he kissed me, and said to me, 'Daughter, peace be with you:' and I began to go gloriously to the Sanavivarian gate. Then I awoke, and perceived that I was not to fight with beasts, but against the devil. Still I knew that the victory was awaiting me. This, so far, I have completed several days before the exhibition; but what passed at the exhibition itself let who will write."

CHAPTER IV
SATURUS, IN A VISION, AND PERPETUA BEING CARRIED BY ANGELS INTO THE GREAT LIGHT, BEHOLD THE MARTYRS. BEING BROUGHT TO THE THRONE OF GOD, ARE RECEIVED WITH A KISS. THEY RECONCILE OPTATUS THE BISHOP AND ASPASIUS THE PRESBYTER.

1. Moreover, also, the blessed Saturus related this his vision, which he himself committed to writing: — " We had suffered," says he, "and we were gone forth from the flesh, and we were beginning to be borne by four angels into the east; and their hands touched us not. And we floated not supine, looking upwards, but as if ascending a gentle slope. And being set free, we at length saw the first boundless light; and I said, 'Perpetua' (for she was at my side), 'this is what the Lord promised to us; we have received the promise.' And while we are borne by those same four angels, there appears to us a vast space which was like a pleasure-garden, having rose-trees and every kind of flower. And the height of the trees was after the measure of a cypress, and their leaves were falling incessantly. Moreover, there in the pleasure-garden four other angels appeared, brighter than the previous ones, who, when they saw us, gave us honour, and said to the rest of the angels, 'Here they are! Here they are!' with admiration. And those four angels who bore us, being greatly afraid, put us down; and we passed over on foot the space of a furlong in a broad path. There we found Jocundus and Saturninus and Artaxius, who having suffered the same persecution were burnt alive; and Quintus, who also himself a martyr had departed in the prison. And we asked of them where the rest were. And the angels said to us, 'Come first, enter and greet your Lord.'

2. "And we came near to place, the walls of which were such as if they were built of light; and before the gate of that place stood four angels, who clothed those who entered with white robes. And being clothed, we entered and saw the boundless light, and heard the united voice of some who said without ceasing, Holy! Holy! Holy!' And in the midst of that place we saw as it were a hoary man sitting, having snow-white hair, and with a youthful countenance; and his feet we saw not. And on his right hand and on his left were four-and-twenty elders, and behind them a great many others were standing. We entered with great wonder, and stood before the throne; and the four angels raised us up, and we kissed Him, and He passed His hand over our face. And the rest of the elders said to us, 'Let us stand;' and we stood and made peace. And the elders said to us, and enjoy.' And I said, 'Perpetua, you have what you wish.' And she said to me, 'Thanks be to God, that joyous as I was in the flesh, I am now more joyous here.'

3. "And we went forth, and saw before the entrance Optatus the bishop at the right hand, and Aspasius the presbyter, a teacher, at the left hand, separate and sad; and they cast themselves at our feet, and said to us, 'Restore peace between us, because you have gone forth and have left us thus.' And we said to them, 'Art not thou our father, and thou our presbyter, that you should cast yourselves at our feet?" And we prostrated ourselves, and we embraced them; and Perpetua began to speak with them, and we drew them apart in the pleasure-garden under a rose-tree. And while we were speaking with them, the angels said unto them, 'Let them alone, that they may refresh themselves; and if you have any dissensions between you, forgive one another.' And they drove them away. And they said to Optatus, 'Rebuke thy people, because they assemble to you as if returning from the circus, and contending about factious matters.' And then it seemed to us as if they would shut the doors. And in that place we began to recognise many brethren, and moreover martyrs. We were all nourished with an indescribable odour, which satisfied us. Then, I joyously awoke."

CHAPTER V
SECUNDULUS DIES IN THE PRISON. FELICITAS IS PREGNANT, BUT WITH MANY PRAYERS SHE BRINGS FORTH IN THE EIGHTH MONTH WITHOUT SUFFERING, THE COURAGE OF PERPETUA AND OF SATURUS UNBROKEN.

1. The above were the more eminent visions of the blessed martyrs Saturus and Perpetua themselves, which they themselves committed to writing. But God called Secundulus, while he has yet in the prison, by an earlier exit from the world, not without favour, so as to give a respite to the beasts. Nevertheless, even if his soul did not acknowledge cause for thankfulness, assuredly his flesh did.

2. But respecting Felicitas (for to her also the Lord's favour approached in the same way), when she had already gone eight months with child (for she had been pregnant when she was apprehended), as the day of the exhibition was drawing near, she was in great grief lest on account of her pregnancy she should be delayed — because pregnant women are not allowed to be publicly punished — and lest she should shed her sacred and guiltless blood among some who had been wicked subsequently. Moreover, also, her fellow-martyrs were painfully saddened lest they should leave so excellent a friend, and as it were companion, alone in the path of the same hope. Therefore, joining together their united cry, they poured forth their prayer to the Lord three days before the exhibition. Immediately after their prayer her pains came upon her, and when, with the difficulty natural to an eight months' delivery, in the labour of bringing forth she was sorrowing, some one of the servants of the Cataractarii said to her, "You who are in such suffering now, what will you do when you are thrown to the beasts, which you despised when you refused to sacrifice?" And she replied, "Now it is I that suffer what I suffer; but then there will be another in me, who will suffer for me, because I also am about to suffer for Him." Thus she brought forth a little girl, which a certain sister brought up as her daughter.

3. Since then the Holy Spirit permitted, and by permitting willed, that the proceedings of that exhibition should be committed to writing, although we are unworthy to complete the description of so great a glory; yet we obey as it were the command of the most blessed Perpetua, nay her sacred trust, and add one more testimony concerning her constancy and her loftiness of mind. While they were treated with more severity by the tribune, because, from the intimations of certain deceitful men, he feared lest thay should be withdrawn from the prison by some sort of magic incantations, Perpetua answered to his face, and said, "Why do you not at least permit us to be refreshed, being as we are objectionable to the most noble Caesar, and having to fight on his birthday? Or is it not your glory if we are brought forward fatter on that occasion?" The tribune shuddered and blushed, and commanded that they should be kept with more humanity, so that permission was given to their brethren and others to go in and be refreshed with them; even the keeper of the prison trusting them now himself.

4. Moreover, on the day before, when in that last meal, which they call the free meal, they were partaking as far as they could, not of a free supper, but of an agape; with the same firmness they were uttering such words as

these to the people, denouncing against them the judgment of the Lord, bearing witness to the felicity of their passion, laughing at the curiosity of the people who came together; while Saturus said, "Tomorrow is not enough for you, for you to behold with pleasure that which you hate. Friends today, enemies tomorrow. Yet note our faces diligently, that you may recognise them on that day of judgment." Thus all departed thence astonished, and from these things many believed.

CHAPTER VI
FROM THE PRISON THEY ARE LED FORTH WITH JOY INTO THE AMPHITHEATRE, ESPECIALLY PERPETUA AND FELICITAS. ALL REFUSE TO PUT ON PROFANE GARMENTS. THEY ARE SCOURGED, THEY ARE THROWN TO THE WILD BEASTS. SATURUS TWICE IS UNHURT. PERPETUA AND FELICITAS ARE THROWN DOWN; THEY ARE CALLED BACK TO THE SANAVIVARIAN GATE. SATURUS WOUNDED BY A LEOPARD, EXHORTS THE SOLDIER. THEY KISS ONE ANOTHER, AND ARE SLAIN WITH THE SWORD.

1. The day of their victory shone forth, and they proceeded from the prison into the amphitheatre, as if to an assembly, joyous and of brilliant countenances; if prechance shrinking, it was with joy, and not with fear. Perpetua followed with placid look, and with step and gait as a matron of Christ, beloved of God; casting down the luster of her eyes from the gaze of all. Moreover, Felicitas, rejoicing that she had safely brought forth, so that she might fight with the wild beasts; from the blood and from the midwife to the gladiator, to wash after childbirth with a second baptism. And when they were brought to the gate, and were constrained to put on the clothing — the men, that of the priests of Saturn, and the women, that of those who were consecrated to Ceres — that noble-minded woman resisted even to the end with constancy. For she said, "We have come thus far of our own accord, for this reason, that our liberty might not be restrained. For this reason we have yielded our minds, that we might not do any such thing as this: we have agreed on this with you." Injustice acknowledged the justice; the tribune yielded to their being brought as simply as they were. Perpetua sang psalms, already treading under foot the head of the Egyptian; Revocatus, and Saturninus, and Saturus uttered threatenings against the gazing people about this martyrdom. When they came within sight of Hilarianus, by gesture and nod, they began to say to Hilarianus, "Thou judgest us," say they, "but God will judge thee." At this the people, exasperated, demanded that they should be tormented with scourges as they passed along the rank of the venatores. And they indeed rejoiced that they should have incurred any one of their Lord's passions.

2. But He who had said, "Ask, and ye shall receive," gave to them when they asked, that death which each one had wished for. For when at any time they had been discoursing among themselves about their wish in respect of their martyrdom, Saturninus indeed had

professed that he wished that he might be thrown to all the beasts; doubtless that he might wear a more glorious crown. Therefore in the beginning of the exhibition he and Revocatus made trial of the leopard, and moreover upon the scaffold they were harassed by the bear. Saturus, however, held nothing in greater abomination than a bear; but he imagined that he would be put an end to with one bite of a leopard. Therefore, when a wild boar was supplied, it was the huntsman rather who had supplied that boar who was gored by that same beast, and died the day after the shows. Saturus only was drawn out; and when he had been bound on the floor near to a bear, the bear would not come forth from his den. And so Saturus for the second time is recalled unhurt.

3. Moreover, for the young women the devil prepared a very fierce cow, provided especially for that purpose contrary to custom, rivalling their sex also in that of the beasts. And so, stripped and clothed with nets, they were led forth. The populace shuddered as they saw one young woman of delicate frame, and another with breasts still dropping from her recent childbirth. So, being recalled, they are unbound. Perpetua is first led in. She was tossed, and fell on her loins; and when she saw her tunic torn from her side, she drew it over her as a veil for her middle, rather mindful of her modesty than her suffering. Then she was called for again, and bound up her dishevelled hair; for it was not becoming for a martyr to suffer with dishevelled hair, lest she should appear to be mourning in her glory. So she rose up; and when she saw Felicitas crushed, she approached and gave her her hand, and lifted her up. And both of them stood together; and the brutality of the populace being appeased, they were recalled to the Sanavivarian gate. Then Perpetua was received by a certain one who was still a catechumen, Rusticus by name, who kept close to her; and she, as if aroused from sleep, so deeply had she been in the Spirit and in an ecstasy, began to look round her, and to say to the amazement of all, "I cannot tell when we are to be led out to that cow." And when she had heard what had already happened, she did not believe it until she had perceived certain signs of injury in her body and in her dress, and had recognised the catechumen. Afterwards causing that catechumen and the brother to approach, she addressed them, saying, "Stand fast in the faith, and love one another, all of you, and be not offended at my sufferings."

4. The same Saturus at the other entrance exhorted the soldier Pudens, saying, "Assuredly here I am, as I have promised and foretold, for up to this moment I have felt no beast. And now believe with your whole heart. Lo, I am going forth to that beast, and I shall be destroyed with one bite of the leopard." And immediately at the conclusion of the exhibition he was thrown to the leopard; and with one bite of his he was bathed with such a quantity of blood, that the people shouted out to him as he was returning, the testimony of his second baptism, "Saved and washed, saved and washed." Manifestly he was assuredly saved who had been glorified in such a spectacle. Then to the soldier Pudens he said, "Farewell, and be mindful of my faith; and let not these things disturb, but confirm you." And at the

same time he asked for a little ring from his finger, and returned it to him bathed in his wound, leaving to him an inherited token and the memory of his blood. And then lifeless he is cast down with the rest, to be slaughtered in the usual place.

And when the populace called for them into the midst, that as the sword penetrated into their body they might make their eyes partners in the murder, they rose up of their own accord, and transferred themselves whither the people wished; but they first kissed one another, that they might consummate their martyrdom with the kiss of peace. The rest indeed, immoveable and in silence, received the sword-thrust; much more Saturus, who also had first ascended the ladder, and first gave up his spirit, for he also was waiting for Perpetua. But Perpetua, that she might taste some pain, being pierced between the ribs, cried out loudly, and she herself placed the wavering right hand of the youthful gladiator to her throat. Possibly such a woman could not have been slain unless she herself had willed it, because she was feared by the impure spirit.

O most brave and blessed martyrs! O truly called and chosen unto the glory of our Lord Jesus Christ! whom whoever magnifies, and honours, and adores, assuredly ought to read these examples for the edification of the Church, not less than the ancient ones, so that new virtues also may testify that one and the same Holy Spirit is always operating even until now, and God the Father Omnipotent, and His Son Jesus Christ our Lord, whose is the glory and infinite power for ever and ever. Amen.

THE PASSION OF THE SCILLITAN MARTYRS

When Præsens, for the second time, and Claudianus were the consuls, on the seventeenth day of July, at Carthage, there were set in the judgment-hall Speratus, Nartzalus, Cittinus, Donata, Secunda and Vestia.

Saturninus the proconsul said: Ye can win the indulgence of our lord the Emperor, if ye return to a sound mind.

Speratus said: We have never done ill, we have not lent ourselves to wrong, we have never spoken ill, but when ill-treated we have given thanks; because we pay heed to our Emperor.

Saturninus the proconsul said: We too are religious, and our religion is simple, and we swear by the genius of our lord the Emperor, and pray for his welfare, as ye also ought to do.

Speratus said: If thou wilt peaceably lend me thine ears, I can tell thee the mystery of simplicity.

Saturninus said: I will not lend mine ears to thee, when thou beginnest to speak evil things of our sacred rites; but rather swear thou by the genius of our lord the Emperor.

Speratus said: The empire of this world I know not; but rather I serve that God, *whom no man hath seen, nor with these eyes can see*. I have committed no theft; but if I have bought anything I pay the tax; because I know my Lord, the King of kings and Emperor of all nations.

Saturninus the proconsul said to the rest: Cease to be of this persuasion.

Speratus said: It is an ill persuasion to do murder, to speak false witness.

Saturninus the proconsul said: Be not partakers of this folly.

Cittinus said: We have none other to fear, save only our Lord God, who is in heaven.

Donata said: Honour to Cæsar as Cæsar: but fear to God.

Vestia said: I am a Christian.

Secunda said: What I am, that I wish to be.

Saturninus the proconsul said to Speratus: Dost thou persist in being a Christian?

Speratus said: I am a Christian. And with him they all agreed.

Saturninus the proconsul said: Will ye have a space to consider?

Speratus said: In a matter so straightforward there is no considering.

Saturninus the proconsul said: What are the things in your chest?

Speratus said: Books and epistles of Paul, a just man.

Saturninus the proconsul said: Have a delay of thirty days and bethink yourselves.

Speratus said a second time: I am a Christian. And with him they all agreed.

Saturninus the proconsul read out the decree from the tablet: Speratus, Nartzalus, Cittinus, Donata, Vestia, Secunda and the rest having confessed that they live according to the Christian rite, since after opportunity offered them of returning to the custom of the Romans they have obstinately persisted, it is determined that they be put to the sword.

Speratus said: We give thanks to God.

Nartzalus said: To-day we are martyrs in heaven; thanks be to God.

Saturninus the proconsul ordered it to be declared by the herald: Speratus, Nartzalus, Cittinus, Veturius, Felix, Aquilinus, Lætantius, Januaria, Generosa, Vestia, Donata and Secunda, I have ordered to be executed.

They all said: Thanks be to God.

And so they all together were crowned with martyrdom; and they reign with the Father and the Son and the Holy Ghost, for ever and ever. Amen.

THE DIDACHE

or Teaching of the Twelve Apostles

CHAPTER 1

1:1 There are two paths, one of life and one of death, and the difference is great between the two paths.

1:2 Now the path of life is this -- first, thou shalt love the God who made thee, thy neighbour as thyself, and all things that thou wouldest not should be done unto thee, do not thou unto another.

1:3 And the doctrine of these maxims is as follows. Bless them that curse you, and pray for your enemies. Fast on behalf of those that persecute you; for what thank is there if ye love them that love you? Do not even the Gentiles do the same? But do ye love them that hate you, and ye will not have an enemy.

1:4 Abstain from fleshly and worldly lusts. If any one give thee a blow on thy right cheek, turn unto him the other also, and thou shalt be perfect; if any one compel thee to go a mile, go with him two; if a man take away thy cloak, give him thy coat also; if a man take from thee what is thine, ask not for it again, for neither art thou able to do so.

1:5 Give to every one that asketh of thee, and ask not again; for the Father wishes that from his own gifts there should be given to all. Blessed is he who giveth according to the commandment, for he is free from guilt; but woe unto him that receiveth. For if a man receive being in need, he shall be free from guilt; but he who receiveth when not in need, shall pay a penalty as to why he received and for what purpose; and when he is in tribulation he shall be examined concerning the things that he has done, and shall not depart thence until he has paid the last farthing.

1:6 For of a truth it has been said on these matters, let thy almsgiving abide in thy hands until thou knowest to whom thou hast given.

CHAPTER 2

2:1 But the second commandment of the teaching is this.

2:2 Thou shalt not kill; thou shalt not commit adultery; thou shalt not corrupt youth; thou shalt not commit fornication; thou shalt not steal; thou shalt not use soothsaying; thou shalt not practise sorcery; thou shalt not kill a child by abortion, neither shalt thou slay it when born; thou shalt not covet the goods of thy neighbour;

2:3 thou shalt not commit perjury; thou shalt not bear false witness; thou shalt not speak evil; thou shalt not bear malice;

2:4 thou shalt not be double-minded or double-tongued, for to be double tongued is the snare of death.

2:5 Thy speech shall not be false or empty, but concerned with action.

2:6 Thou shalt not be covetous, or rapacious, or hypocritical, or malicious, or proud; thou shalt not take up an evil design against thy neighbour;

2:7 thou shalt not hate any man, but some thou shalt confute, concerning some thou shalt pray, and some thou shalt love beyond thine own soul.

CHAPTER 3

3:1 My child, fly from everything that is evil, and from everything that is like to it.

3:2 Be not wrathful, for wrath leadeth unto slaughter; be not jealous, or contentious, or quarrelsome, for from all these things slaughter ensues.

3:3 My child, be not lustful, for lust leadeth unto fornication; be not a filthy talker; be not a lifter up of the eye, for from all these things come adulteries.

3:4 My child, be not an observer of omens, since it leadeth to idolatry, nor a user of spells, nor an astrologer, nor a travelling purifier, nor wish to see these things, for from all these things idolatry ariseth.

3:5 My child, be not a liar, for lying leadeth unto theft; be not covetous or conceited, for from all these things thefts arise.

3:6 My child, be not a murmurer, since it leadeth unto blasphemy; be not self-willed or evil-minded, for from all these things blasphemies are produced;

3:7 but be thou meek, for the meek shall inherit the earth;

3:8 be thou longsuffering, and compassionate, and harmless, and peaceable, and good, and fearing alway the words that thou hast heard.

3:9 Thou shalt not exalt thyself, neither shalt thou put boldness into thy soul. Thy soul shall not be joined unto the lofty, but thou shalt walk with the just and humble.

3:10 Accept the things that happen to thee as good, knowing that without God nothing happens.

CHAPTER 4

4:1 My child, thou shalt remember both night and day him that speaketh unto thee the Word of God; thou shalt honour him as thou dost the Lord, for where the teaching of the Lord is given, there is the Lord;

4:2 thou shalt seek out day by day the favour of the saints, that thou mayest rest in their words;

4:3 thou shalt not desire schism, but shalt set at peace them that contend; thou shalt judge righteously; thou shalt not accept the person of any one to convict him of transgression;

4:4 thou shalt not doubt whether a thing shall be or not.

4:5 Be not a stretcher out of thy hand to receive, and a drawer of it back in giving.

4:6 If thou hast, give by means of thy hands a redemption for thy sins.

4:7 Thou shalt not doubt to give, neither shalt thou murmur when giving; for thou shouldest know who is the fair recompenser of the reward.

4:8 Thou shalt not turn away from him that is in need, but shalt share with thy brother in all things, and shalt not say that things are thine own; for if ye are partners in what is immortal, how much more in what is mortal?

4:9 Thou shalt not remove thine heart from thy son or from thy daughter, but from their youth shalt teach them the fear of God.

4:10 Thou shalt not command with bitterness thy servant or thy handmaid, who hope in the same God as thyself, lest they fear not in consequence the God who is over both; for he cometh not to call with respect of persons, but those whom the Spirit hath prepared.

4:11 And do ye servants submit yourselves to your masters with reverence and fear, as being the type of God.

4:12 Thou shalt hate all hypocrisy and everything that is not pleasing to God;

4:13 thou shalt not abandon the commandments of the Lord, but shalt guard that which thou hast received, neither adding thereto nor taking therefrom;

4:14 thou shalt confess thy transgressions in the Church, and shalt not come unto prayer with an evil conscience. This is the path of life.

CHAPTER 5

5:1 But the path of death is this. First of all, it is evil, and full of cursing; there are found murders, adulteries, lusts, fornication, thefts, idolatries, soothsaying, sorceries, robberies, false witnessings, hypocrisies, double-mindedness, craft, pride, malice, self-will, covetousness, filthy talking, jealousy, audacity, pride, arrogance;

5:2 there are they who persecute the good -- lovers of a lie, not knowing the reward of righteousness, not cleaving to the good nor to righteous judgment, watching not for the good but for the bad, from whom meekness and patience are afar off, loving things that are vain, following after recompense, having no compassion on the needy, nor labouring for him that is in trouble, not knowing him that made them, murderers of children, corrupters of the image of God, who turn away from him that is in need, who oppress him that is in trouble, unjust judges of the poor, erring in all things. From all these, children, may ye be delivered.

CHAPTER 6

6:1 See that no one make thee to err from this path of doctrine, since he who doeth so teacheth thee apart from God.

6:2 If thou art able to bear the whole yoke of the Lord, thou wilt be perfect; but if thou art not able, what thou art able, that do.

6:3 But concerning meat, bear that which thou art able to do. But keep with care from things sacrificed to idols, for it is the worship of the infernal deities.

CHAPTER 7

7:1 But concerning baptism, thus baptize ye: having first recited all these precepts, baptize in the name of the Father, and of the Son, and of the Holy Spirit, in running water;

7:2 but if thou hast not running water, baptize in some other water, and if thou canst not baptize in cold, in warm water;

7:3 but if thou hast neither, pour water three times on the head, in the name of the Father, and of the Son, and of the Holy Spirit.

7:4 But before the baptism, let him who baptizeth and him who is baptized fast previously, and any others who may be able. And thou shalt command him who is baptized to fast one or two days before.

CHAPTER 8

8:1 But as for your fasts, let them not be with the hypocrites, for they fast on the second and fifth days of the week, but do ye fast on the fourth and sixth days.

8:2 Neither pray ye as the hypocrites, but as the Lord hath commanded in his gospel so pray ye: Our Father in heaven, hallowed be thy name. Thy kingdom come. Thy will be done as in heaven so on earth. Give us this day our daily bread. And forgive us our debt, as we also forgive our debtors. And lead us not into temptation, but deliver us from the evil: for thine is the power, and the glory, for ever.

8:3 Thrice a day pray ye in this fashion.

CHAPTER 9

9:1 But concerning the Eucharist, after this fashion give ye thanks.

9:2 First, concerning the cup. We thank thee, our Father, for the holy vine, David thy Son, which thou hast made known unto us through Jesus Christ thy Son; to thee be the glory for ever.

9:3 And concerning the broken bread. We thank thee, our Father, for the life and knowledge which thou hast made known unto us through Jesus thy Son; to thee be the glory for ever.

9:4 As this broken bread was once scattered on the mountains, and after it had been brought together became one, so may thy Church be gathered together from the ends of the earth unto thy kingdom; for thine is the glory, and the power, through Jesus Christ, for ever.

9:5 And let none eat or drink of your Eucharist but such as have been baptized into the name of the Lord, for of a truth the Lord hath said concerning this, Give not that which is holy unto dogs.

CHAPTER 10

10:1 But after it has been completed, so pray ye.

10:2 We thank thee, holy Father, for thy holy name, which thou hast caused to dwell in our hearts, and for the knowledge and faith and immortality which thou hast made known unto us through Jesus thy Son; to thee be the glory for ever.

10:3 Thou, Almighty Master, didst create all things for the sake of thy name, and hast given both meat and drink, for men to enjoy, that we might give thanks unto thee, but to us thou hast given spiritual meat and drink, and life everlasting, through thy Son.

10:4 Above all, we thank thee that thou art able to save; to thee be the glory for ever.

10:5 Remember, Lord, thy Church, to redeem it from every evil, and to perfect it in thy love, and gather it together from the four winds, even that which has been sanctified for thy kingdom which thou hast prepared for it; for thine is the kingdom and the glory for ever.

10:6 Let grace come, and let this world pass away. Hosanna to the Son of David. If any one is holy let him come (to the Eucharist); if any one is not, let him repent. Maranatha. Amen.

10:7 But charge the prophets to give thanks, so far as they are willing to do so.

CHAPTER 11

11:1 Whosoever, therefore, shall come and teach you all these things aforesaid, him do ye receive;

11:2 but if the teacher himself turn and teach another doctrine with a view to subvert you, hearken not to him; but if he come to add to your righteousness, and the knowledge of the Lord, receive him as the Lord.

11:3 But concerning the apostles and prophets, thus do ye according to the doctrine of the Gospel.

11:4 Let every apostle who cometh unto you be received as the Lord.

11:5 He will remain one day, and if it be necessary, a second; but if he remain three days, he is a false prophet.

11:6 And let the apostle when departing take nothing but bread until he arrive at his resting-place; but if he ask for money, he is a false prophet.

11:7 And ye shall not tempt or dispute with any prophet who speaketh in the spirit; for every sin shall be forgiven, but this sin shall not be forgiven.

11:8 But not every one who speaketh in the spirit is a prophet, but he is so who hath the disposition of the Lord; by their dispositions they therefore shall be known, the false prophet and the prophet.

11:9 And every prophet who ordereth in the spirit that a table shall be laid, shall not eat of it himself, but if he do otherwise, he is a false prophet;

11:10 and every prophet who teacheth the truth, if he do not what he teacheth is a false prophet;

11:11 and every prophet who is approved and true, and ministering in the visible mystery of the Church, but who teacheth not others to do the things that he doth himself, shall not be judged of you, for with God lieth his judgment, for in this manner also did the ancient prophets.

11:12 But whoever shall say in the spirit, Give me money, or things of that kind, listen not to him; but if he tell you concerning others that are in need that ye should give unto them, let no one judge him.

CHAPTER 12

12:1 Let every one that cometh in the name of the Lord be received, but afterwards ye shall examine him and know his character, for ye have knowledge both of good and evil.

12:2 If the person who cometh be a wayfarer, assist him so far as ye are able; but he will not remain with you more than two or three days, unless there be a necessity.

12:3 But if he wish to settle with you, being a craftsman, let him work, and so eat;

12:4 but if he know not any craft, provide ye according to you own discretion, that a Christian may not live idle among you;

12:5 but if he be not willing to do so, he is a trafficker in Christ. From such keep aloof.

CHAPTER 13

13:1 But every true prophet who is willing to dwell among you is worthy of his meat,

13:2 likewise a true teacher is himself worthy of his meat, even as is a labourer.

13:3 Thou shalt, therefore, take the firstfruits of every produce of the wine-press and threshing-floor, of oxen and sheep, and shalt give it to the prophets, for they are your chief priests;

13:4 but if ye have not a prophet, give it unto the poor.

13:5 If thou makest a feast, take and give the firstfruits according to the commandment;

13:6 in like manner when thou openest a jar of wine or of oil, take the firstfruits and give it to the prophets;

13:7 take also the firstfruits of money, of clothes, and of every possession, as it shall seem good unto thee, and give it according to the commandment.

CHAPTER 14

14:1 But on the Lord's day, after that ye have assembled together, break bread and give thanks, having in addition confessed your sins, that your sacrifice may be pure.

14:2 But let not any one who hath a quarrel with his companion join with you, until they be reconciled, that your sacrifice may not be polluted,

14:3 for it is that which is spoken of by the Lord. In every place and time offer unto me a pure sacrifice, for I am a great King, saith the Lord, and my name is wonderful among the Gentiles.

CHAPTER 15

15:1 Elect, therefore, for yourselves bishops and deacons worthy of the Lord, men who are meek and not covetous, and true and approved, for they perform for you the service of prophets and teachers.

15:2 Do not, therefore, despise them, for they are those who are honoured among you, together with the prophets and teachers.

15:3 Rebuke one another, not in wrath but peaceably, as ye have commandment in the Gospel; and, but let no one speak to any one who walketh disorderly with regard to his neighbour, neither let him be heard by you until he repent.

15:4 But your prayers and your almsgivings and all your deeds so do, as ye have commandment in the Gospel of our Lord.

CHAPTER 16

16:1 Watch concerning your life; let not your lamps be quenched or your loins be loosed, but be ye ready, for ye know not the hour at which our Lord cometh.

16:2 But be ye gathered together frequently, seeking what is suitable for your souls; for the whole time of your faith shall profit you not, unless ye be found perfect in the last time.

16:3 For in the last days false prophets and seducers shall be multiplied, and the sheep shall be turned into wolves, and love shall be turned into hate;

16:4 and because iniquity aboundeth they shall hate each other, and persecute each other, and deliver each other up; and then shall the Deceiver of the world appear as the Son of God, and shall do signs and wonders, and the earth shall be delivered into his hands; and he shall do unlawful things, such as have never happened since the beginning of the world.

16:5 Then shall the creation of man come to the fiery trial of proof, and many shall be offended and shall perish; but they who remain in their faith shall be saved by the rock of offence itself.

16:6 And then shall appear the signs of the truth; first the sign of the appearance in heaven, then the sign of the sound of the trumpet, and thirdly the resurrection of the dead

16:7 -- not of all, but as it has been said, The Lord shall come and all his saints with him;

16:8 then shall the world behold the Lord coming on the clouds of heaven.

{The End of the Didache}

THE TESTAMENTS OF THE TWELVE PATRIARCHS

I.-The Testament of Reuben Concerning Thoughts

----

1. The copy of the Testament of Reuben, what things he charged his sons before he died in the hundred and twenty-fifth year of his life. When he was sick two years after the death of Joseph, his sons and his sons' sons were gathered together to visit him. And he said to them, My children, I am dying, and go the way of my fathers. And when he saw there Judah and Gad and Asher, his brethren, he said to them, Raise me up, my brethren, that I may tell to my brethren and to my children what things I have hidden in my heart, for from henceforth my strength faileth me. And he arose and kissed them, and said, weeping: Hear, my brethren, give ear to Reuben your father, what things I command you. And, behold, I call to witness against you this day the God of heaven, that ye walk not in the ignorance of youth and fornication wherein I ran greedily, and I defiled the bed of Jacob my father. For I tell you that He smote me with a sore plague in my loins for seven months; and had not Jacob our father prayed for me to the Lord, surely the Lord would have destroyed me. For I was thirty years old when I did this evil in the sight of the Lord, and for seven months I was sick even unto death; and I repented for seven years in the set purpose of my soul before the Lord. Wine and strong drink I drank not, and flesh entered not into my mouth, and I tasted not pleasant food, mourning over my sin, for it was great. And it shall not so be done in Israel.

2. And now hear me, my children, what things I saw in my repentance concerning the seven spirits of error. Seven spirits are given against man from Beliar, and they are chief of the works of youth; and seven spirits are given to him at his creation, that in them should be done every work of man. The first (1) spirit is of life, with which man's whole being is created. The second (2) spirit is of sight, with which ariseth desire. The third (3) spirit is of hearing, with which cometh teaching. The fourth (4) spirit is of smelling, with which taste is given to draw air and breath. The fifth (5) spirit is of speech, with which cometh knowledge. The sixth (6) spirit is of taste, with which cometh the eating of meats and drinks; and by them strength is produced, for in food is the foundation of strength. The seventh (7) spirit is of begetting and sexual intercourse, with which through love of pleasure sin also entereth in: wherefore it is the last in order of creation, and the first of youth, because it is filled with ignorance, which leadeth the young as a blind man to a pit, and as cattle to a precipice.

3. Besides all these, there is an eighth (8) spirit of sleep, with which is created entrancement of man's nature, and the image of death. With these spirits are mingled the spirits of error. The first (1), the spirit of fornication, dwelleth in the nature and in the senses; the second (2) spirit of insatiateness in the belly; the third (3) spirit of fighting in the liver and the gall. The fourth (4) is the spirit of fawning and trickery, that through over-officiousness a man may be fair in seeming. The fifth (5) is the spirit of arrogance, that a man may be stirred up and become high-minded. The sixth (6) is the spirit of lying, in perdition and in jealousy to feign words, and to conceal words from kindred and friends. The seventh (7) is the spirit of injustice, with which are theft and pilferings, that a man may work the desire of his heart; for injustice worketh together with the other spirits by means of craft. Besides all these, the spirit of sleep, the eighth (8) spirit, is conjoined with error and fantasy. And so perisheth every young man, darkening his mind from the truth, and not understanding the law of God, nor obeying the admonitions of his fathers, as befell me also in my youth.

And now, children, love the truth, and it shall preserve you. I counsel you, hear ye Reuben your father. Pay no heed to the sight of a woman, nor yet associate privately with a female under the authority of a husband, nor meddle with affairs of womankind. For had I not seen Bilhah bathing in a covered place, I had not fallen into this great iniquity. For my mind, dwelling on the woman's nakedness, suffered me not to sleep until I had done the abominable deed. For while Jacob our father was absent with Isaac his father, when we were in Gader, near to Ephratha in Bethlehem, Bilhah was drunk, and lay asleep uncovered in her chamber; and when I went in and beheld her nakedness, I wrought that impiety, and leaving her sleeping I departed. And forthwith an angel of God revealed to my father Jacob concerning my impiety, and he came and mourned over me, and touched her no more.

4. Pay no heed, therefore, to the beauty of women, and muse not upon their doings; but walk in singleness of heart in the fear of the Lord, and be labouring in works, and roaming in study and among your flocks, until the Lord give to you a wife whom He will, that ye suffer not as I did. Until my father's death I had not boldness to look stedfastly into the face of Jacob, or to speak to any of my brethren, because of my reproach; and even until now my conscience afflicteth me by reason of my sin. And my father comforted me; for he prayed for me unto the Lord, that the anger of the Lord might pass away from me, even as the Lord showed me. From henceforth, then, I was protected, and I sinned not. Therefore, my children, observe all things whatsoever I command you, and ye shall not sin. For fornication is the destruction of the soul, separating it from God, and bringing it near to idols, because it deceiveth the mind and understanding, and bringeth down young men into hell before their time. For many hath fornication destroyed; because, though a man be old or noble, it maketh him a reproach and a laughing-stock with Beliar and the sons of men. For in that Joseph kept himself from every woman, and purged his thoughts from all fornication, he found favour before the Lord and men. For the Egyptian woman did many things unto him, and called for magicians, and offered him love potions, and the purpose of his soul admitted no evil desire. Therefore the God of my fathers delivered him from every visible and hidden death. For if fornication overcome not the mind, neither shall Beliar overcome you.

5. Hurtful are women, my children; because, since they have no power or strength over the man, they act subtilly through outward guise how they may draw him to themselves; and whom they cannot overcome by strength, him they overcome by craft. For moreover the angel of God told me concerning them, and taught me that women

are overcome by the spirit of fornication more than men, and they devise in their heart against men; and by means of their adornment they deceive first their minds, and instil the poison by the glance of their eye, and then they take them captive by their doings, for a woman cannot overcome a man by force.

Therefore flee fornication, my children, and command your wives and your daughters that they adorn not their heads and their faces; because every woman who acteth deceitfully in these things hath been reserved to everlasting punishment. For thus they allured the Watchers before the flood; and as these continually beheld them, they fell into desire each of the other, and they conceived the act in their mind, and changed themselves into the shape of men, and appeared to them in their congress with their husbands; and the women, having in their minds desire toward their apparitions, gave birth to giants, for the Watchers appeared to them as reaching even unto heaven.

6. Beware, therefore, of fornication; and if you wish to be pure in your mind, guard your senses against every woman. And command them likewise not to company with men, that they also be pure in their mind. For constant meetings, even though the ungodly deed be not wrought, are to them an irremediable disease, and to us an everlasting reproach of Beliar; for fornication hath neither understanding nor godliness in itself, and all jealousy dwelleth in the desire thereof. Therefore ye will be jealous against the sons of Levi, and will seek to be exalted over them; but ye shall not be able, for God will work their avenging, and ye shall die by an evil death. For to Levi the Lord gave the sovereignty, and to Judah, and to me also with them, and to Dan and Joseph, that we should be for rulers. Therefore I command you to hearken to Levi, because he shall know the law of the Lord, and shall give ordinances for judgment and sacrifice for all Israel until the completion of the times of Christ, the High Priest whom the Lord hath declared. I adjure you by the God of heaven to work truth each one with his neighbour; and draw ye near to Levi in humbleness of heart, that ye may receive a blessing from his mouth. For he shall bless Israel; and *specially* Judah, because him hath the Lord chosen to rule over all the peoples. And worship we his Seed, because He shall die for us in wars visible and invisible, and shall be among you an everlasting king.

7. And Reuben died after that he had given command to his sons; and they placed him in a coffin until they bore him up from Egypt, and buried him in Hebron in the double cave where his fathers were.

II.-The Testament of Simeon Concerning Envy

----

1. The copy of the words of Simeon, what things he spake to his sons before he died, in the hundred and twentieth year of his life, in the year in which Joseph died. For they came to visit him when he was sick, and he strengthened himself and sat up and kissed them, and said to them:-

2. Hear, O my children, hear Simeon your father, what things I have in my heart. I was born of Jacob my father, his second son; and my mother Leah called me Simeon, because the Lord heard her prayer. I became strong exceedingly; I shrank from no deed, nor was I afraid of anything. For my heart was hard, and my mind was unmoveable, and my bowels unfeeling: because valour also has been given from the Most High to men in soul and in body. And at that time I was jealous of Joseph because our father loved him; and I set my mind against him to destroy him, because the prince of deceit sent forth the spirit of jealousy and blinded my mind, that I regarded him not as a brother, and spared not Jacob my father. But his God and the God of his fathers sent forth His angel, and delivered him out of my hands. For when I went into Shechem to bring ointment for the flocks, and Reuben to Dotham, where were our necessaries and all our stores, Judah our brother sold him to the Ishmaelites. And when Reuben came he was grieved, for he wished to have restored him safe to his father. But I was wroth against Judah in that he let him go away alive, and for five months I continued wrathful against him; but God restrained me, and withheld from me all working of my hands, for my right hand was half withered for seven days. And I knew, my children, that because of Joseph this happened to me, and I repented and wept; and I besought the Lord that He would restore my hand unto me, and that I might be kept from all pollution and envy, and from all folly. For I knew that I had devised an evil deed before the Lord and Jacob my father, on account of Joseph my brother, in that I envied him.

3. And now, children, take heed of the spirit of deceit and of envy. For envy ruleth over the whole mind of a man, and suffereth him neither to eat, nor to drink, nor to do any good thing: it ever suggesteth to him to destroy him that he envieth; and he that is envied ever flourisheth, but he that envieth fades away. Two years of days I afflicted my soul with fasting in the fear of the Lord, and I learnt that deliverance from envy cometh by the fear of God. If a man flee to the Lord, the evil spirit runneth away from him, and his mind becometh easy. And henceforward he sympathizeth with him whom he envied, and condemneth not those who love him, and so ceaseth from his envy.

4. And my father asked concerning me, because he saw that I was sad; and I said, I am pained in my liver. For I mourned more than they all, because I was guilty of the selling of Joseph. And when we went down into Egypt, and he bound the as a spy, I knew that I was suffering justly, and I grieved not. Now Joseph was a good man, and had the Spirit of God within him: compassionate and pitiful, he bore not malice against me; nay, he loved me even as the rest of his brothers. Take heed, therefore, my children, of all jealousy and envy, and walk in singleness of soul and with good heart, keeping in mind the brother of your father, that God may give to you also grace and glory, and blessing upon your heads, even as ye saw in him. All his days he reproached us not concerning this thing, but loved us as his own soul, and beyond his own sons; and he glorified us, and gave riches, and cattle, and fruits freely to us all. Do ye then also, my beloved children, love each one his brother with a good heart, and remove from you the spirit of envy, for this maketh savage the soul and destroyeth the body; it turneth his purposes into anger and war, and stirreth up unto blood, and leadeth the mind into frenzy, and suffereth not prudence to act in men: moreover, it taketh away sleep, and causeth tumult to the soul and trembling to the body. For even in sleep some malicious jealousy, deluding him, gnaweth at his soul, and with wicked spirits disturbeth it, and causeth the body to be

troubled, and the mind to awake from sleep in confusion; and as though having a wicked and poisonous spirit, so appeareth it to men.

5. Therefore was Joseph fair in appearance, and goodly to look upon, because there dwelt not in him any wickedness; for in trouble of the spirit the face declareth it. And now, my children, make your hearts good before the Lord, and your ways straight before men, and ye shall find grace before God and men. And take heed not to commit fornication, for fornication is mother of all evils, separating from God, and bringing near to Beliar. For I have seen it inscribed in the writing of Enoch that your sons shall with you be corrupted in fornication, and shall do wrong against Levi with the sword. But they shall not prevail against Levi, for he shall wage the war of the Lord, and shall conquer all your hosts; and there shall be a few divided in Levi and Judah, and there shall be none of you for sovereignty, even as also my father Jacob prophesied in his blessings.

6. Behold, I have foretold you all things, that I may be clear from the sin of your souls. Now, if ye remove from you your envy, and all your stiffneckedness, as a rose shall my bones flourish in Israel, and as a lily my flesh in Jacob, and my odour shall be as the odour of Libanus; and as cedars shall holy ones be multiplied from me for ever, and their branches shall stretch afar off. Then shall perish the seed of Canaan, and a remnant shall not be to Amalek, and all the Cappadocians shall perish, and all the Hittites shall be utterly destroyed. Then shall fail the land of Ham, and every people shall perish. Then shall all the earth rest from trouble, and all the world under heaven from war. Then shall Shem be glorified, because the Lord God, the Mighty One of Israel, shall appear upon earth as man, and saved by Him Adam. Then shall all the spirits of deceit be given to be trampled under foot, and men shall rule over the wicked spirits. Then will I arise in joy, and will bless the Most High because of His marvellous works, because God hath taken a body and eaten with men and saved men.

7. And now, my children, obey Levi, and in Judah shall ye be redeemed: and be not lifted up against these two tribes, for from them shall arise to you the salvation of God. For the Lord shall raise up from Levi as it were a Priest, and from Judah as it were a King, God and man. So shall He save all the Gentiles and the race of Israel. Therefore I command you all things, in order that ye also may command your children, that they may observe them throughout their generations.

8. And Simeon made an end of commanding his sons, and slept with his fathers, being an hundred and twenty years old. And they laid him in a coffin of incorruptible wood, to take up his bones to Hebron. And they carried them up in a war of the Egyptians secretly: for the bones of Joseph the Egyptians guarded in the treasure-house of the palace; for the sorcerers told them that at the departure of the bones of Joseph there should be throughout the whole of Egypt darkness and gloom, and an exceeding great plague to the Egyptians, so that even with a lamp a man should not recognise his brother.

9. And the sons of Simeon bewailed their father according to the law of mourning, and they were in Egypt until the day of their departure from Egypt by the hand of Moses.

III.-The Testament of Levi Concerning the Priesthood and Arrogance.

1. The copy of the words of Levi, what things he appointed to his sons, according to all that they should do, and what things should befall them until the day of judgment. He was in sound health when he called them to him, for it had been shown to him that he should die. And when they were gathered together be said to them :-

2. I Levi was conceived in Haran and born there, and after that I came with my father to Shechem. And I was young, about twenty years of age, when with Simeon I wrought the vengeance on Hamor for our sister Dinah. And when we were feeding our flocks in Abel-Maul, a spirit of understanding of the Lord came upon me, and I saw all men corrupting their way, and that unrighteousness had built to itself walls, and iniquity sat upon towers; and I grieved for the race of men, and I prayed to the Lord that I might be saved. Then there fell upon me a sleep, and I beheld a high mountain: this is the mountain of Aspis in Abel-Maul. And behold, the heavens were opened, and an angel of God said to me, Levi, enter. And I entered from the first heaven into the second, and I saw there water hanging between the one and the other. And I saw a third heaven far brighter than those two, for there was in it a height without bounds. And I said to the angel, Wherefore is this? And the angel said to me, Marvel not at these, for thou shall see four other heavens brighter than these, and without comparison, when thou shall have ascended thither: because thou shalt stand near the Lord, and shalt be His minister, and shall declare His mysteries to men, and shalt proclaim concerning Him who shall redeem Israel; and by thee and Judah shall the Lord appear among men, saving in them every race of men; and of the portion of the Lord shall be thy life, and He shall be thy field and vineyard, fruits, gold, silver.

3. Hear, then, concerning the seven heavens. The lowest is for this cause more gloomy, in that it is near all the iniquities of men. The second hath fire, snow, ice, ready for the day of the ordinance of the Lord, in the righteous judgment of God: in it are all the spirits of the retributions for vengeance on the wicked. In the third are the hosts of the armies which are ordained for the day of judgment, to work vengeance on the spirits of deceit and of Beliar. And the heavens up to the fourth above these are holy, for in the highest of all dwelleth the Great Glory, in the holy of holies, far above all holiness. In the heaven next to it are the angels of the presence of the Lord, who minister and make propitiation to the Lord for all the ignorances of the righteous; and they offer to the Lord a reasonable sweet-smelling savour, and a bloodless offering. And in the heaven below this are the angels who bear the answers to the angels of the presence of the Lord. And in the heaven next to this are thrones, dominions, in which hymns are ever offered to God. Therefore, whenever the Lord looketh upon us, all of us are shaken; yea, the heavens, and the earth, and the abysses, are shaken at the presence of His majesty; but the sons of men, regarding not these things, sin, and provoke the Most High.

4. Now, therefore, know that the Lord will execute judgment upon the sons of men; because when the rocks are rent, and the sun quenched, and the waters dried up,

and the fire trembling, and all creation troubled, and the invisible spirits melting away, and the grave spoiled in the suffering of the Most High, men unbelieving will abide in their iniquity, therefore with punishment shall they be judged. Therefore the Most High hath heard thy prayer, to separate thee from iniquity, and that thou shouldest become to Him a son, and a servant, and a minister of His presence. A shining light of knowledge shalt thou shine in Jacob, and as the sun shalt thou be to all the seed of Israel. And a blessing shall be given to thee, and to all thy seed, until the Lord shall visit all the heathen in the tender mercies of His Son, even for ever. Nevertheless thy sons shall lay hands upon Him to crucify Him; and therefore have counsel and understanding been given thee, that thou mightest instruct thy sons concerning Him, because he that blesseth Him shall be blessed, but they that curse Him shall perish.

5. And the angel opened to me the gates of heaven, and I saw the holy temple, and the Most High upon a throne of glory. And He said to me, Levi, I have given thee the blessings of the priesthood until that I shall come and sojourn in the midst of Israel. Then the angel brought me to the earth, and gave me a shield and a sword, and said, Work vengeance on Shechem because of Dinah, and I will be with thee, because the Lord hath sent me. And I destroyed at that time the sons of Hamor, as it is written in the heavenly tablets. And I said to Him, I pray Thee, O Lord, tell me Thy name, that I may call upon Thee in a day of tribulation. And He said, I am the angel who intercedeth for the race of Israel, that He smite them not utterly, because every evil spirit attacketh it. And after these things I was as it were awaked, and blessed the Most High, and the angel that intercedeth for the race of Israel, and for all the righteous.

6. And when I came to my father I found a brazen shield; wherefore also the name of the mountain is Aspis, which is near Gebal, on the right side of Abila; and I kept these words in my heart. I took counsel with my father, and with Reuben my brother, that he should bid the sons of Hamor that they should be circumcised; for I was jealous because of the abomination which they had wrought in Israel. And I slew Shechem at the first, and Simeon slew Hamor. And after this our brethren came and smote the city with the edge of the sword; and our father heard it and was wroth, and he was grieved in that they had received the circumcision, and after that had been put to death, and in his blessings he dealt otherwise *with us*. For we sinned because we had done this thing against his will, and he was sick upon that day. But I knew that the sentence of God was for evil upon Shechem; for they sought to do to Sarah as they did to Dinah our sister, and the Lord hindered them. And so they persecuted Abraham our father when he was a stranger, and they harried his flocks when they were multiplied upon him; and Jeblae his servant, born in his house, they shamefully handled. And thus they did to all strangers, taking away their wives by force, and the men themselves driving into exile. But the wrath of the Lord came suddenly upon them to the uttermost.

7. And I said to my father, Be not angry, sir, because by thee will the Lord bring to nought the Canaanites, and will give their land to thee, and to thy seed after thee. For from this day forward shall Shechem be called a city of them that

are without understanding; for as a man mocketh at a fool, so did we mock them, because they wrought folly in Israel to defile our sister. And we took our sister from thence, and departed, and came to Bethel.

8. And there I saw a thing again even as the former, after we had passed seventy days. And I saw seven men in white raiment saying to me, Arise, put on the robe of the priesthood, and the crown of righteousness, and the breastplate of understanding, and the garment of truth, and the diadem of faith, and the tiara of miracle, and the ephod of prophecy. And each one of them bearing each of these things put them on me, and said, From henceforth become a priest of the Lord, thou and thy seed for ever. And the first anointed me with holy oil, and gave to me the rod of judgment. The second washed me with pure water, and fed me with bread and wine, the most holy things, and clad me with a holy and glorious robe. The third clothed me with a linen vestment like to an ephod. The fourth put round me a girdle like unto purple. The fifth gave to me a branch of rich olive. The sixth placed a crown on my head. The seventh placed on my head a diadem of priesthood, and filled my hands with incense, so that I served as a priest to the Lord. And they said to me, Levi, thy seed shall be divided into three branches, for a sign of the glory of the Lord who is to come; and first shall he be that hath been faithful; no portion shall be greater than his. The second shall be in the priesthood. The third-a new name shall be called over Him, because He shall arise as King from Judah, and shall establish a new priesthood, after the fashion of the Gentiles, to all the Gentiles. And His appearing shall be unutterable, as of an exalted prophet of the seed of Abraham our father. Every desirable thing in Israel shall be for thee and for thy seed, and everything fair to look upon shall ye eat, and the table of the Lord shall thy seed apportion, and some of them shall be high priests, and judges, and scribes; for by their mouth shall the holy place be guarded. And when I awoke, I understood that this thing was like unto the former. And I hid this also in my heart, and told it not to any man upon the earth.

9. And after two days I and Judah went up to Isaac after our father; and the father of my father blessed me according to all the words of the visions which I had seen: and he would not come with us to Bethel. And when we came to Bethel, my father Jacob saw in a vision concerning me, that I should be to them for a priest unto the Lord; and he rose up early in the morning, and paid tithes of all to the Lord through me. And we came to Hebron to dwell there, and Isaac called me continually to put me in remembrance of the law of the Lord, even as the angel of God showed to me. And he taught me the law of the priesthood, of sacrifices, whole burnt-offerings, first-fruits, free-will offerings, thank-offerings. And each day he was instructing me, and was busied for me before the Lord. And he said to me, Take heed, my child, of the spirit of fornication; for this shall continue, and shall by thy seed pollute the holy things. Take therefore to thyself, while yet thou art young, a wife, not having blemish, nor yet polluted, nor of the race of the Philistines or Gentiles. And before entering into the holy place, bathe; and when thou offerest the sacrifice, wash; and again when thou finishest the sacrifice, wash. Of twelve trees ever having leaves, offer up *the fruits* to the Lord, as also Abraham taught me; and of every clean beast and clean bird offer a sacrifice to the Lord, and of every

firstling and of wine offer first-fruits; and every sacrifice thou shalt salt with salt.

10. Now, therefore, observe whatsoever I command you, children; for whatsoever things I have heard from my fathers I have made known to you. I am clear from all your ungodliness and transgression which ye will do in the end of the ages against the Saviour of the world, acting ungodly, deceiving Israel, and raising up against it great evils from the Lord. And ye will deal lawlessly with Israel, so that Jerusalem shall not endure your wickedness; but the veil of the temple shall be rent, so as not to cover your shame. And ye shall be scattered as captives among the heathen, and shall be for a reproach and for a curse, and for a trampling under foot. For the house which the Lord shall choose shall be called Jerusalem, as is contained in the book of Enoch the righteous.

11. Therefore, when I took a wife I was twenty-eight years old, and her name was Melcha. And she conceived and bare a son, and she called his name Gersham, for we were sojourners in our land: for Gersham is interpreted sojourning. And I saw concerning him that he would not be in the first rank. And Kohath was born in my thirty-fifth year, towards the east. And I saw in a vision that he was standing on high in the midst of all the congregation. Therefore I called his name Kohath, which meaneth, beginning of majesty and instruction. And thirdly, she bare to me Merari, in the fortieth year of my life; and since his mother bare him with difficulty, she called him Merari, which meaneth my bitterness, because he also died. And Jochebed was born in my sixty-fourth year, in Egypt, for I was renowned then in the midst of my brethren.

12. And Gersham took a wife, and she bare to him Lomni and Semei. And the sons of Kohath, Ambram, Isaar, Chebro, and Ozel. And the sons of Merari, Mooli and Homusi. And in my ninety-fourth year Ambram took Jochebed my daughter to him to wife, for they were born in one day, he and my daughter. Eight years old was I when I went into the land of Canaan, and eighteen years when I slew Shechem, and at nineteen years I became priest, and at twenty-eight years I took a wife, and at forty years I went into Egypt. And behold, ye are my children, my children even *of a* third generation. In my hundred and eighteenth year Joseph died.

13. And now, my children, I command you that ye fear our Lord with your whole heart, and walk in simplicity according to all His law. And do ye also teach your children learning, that they may have understanding in all their life, reading unceasingly the law of God; for every one who shall know the law of God shall be honoured, and shall not be a stranger wheresoever he goeth. Yea, many friends shall he gain more than his forefathers; and many men shall desire to serve him, and to hear the law from his mouth. Work righteousness, my children, upon the earth, that ye may find *treasure* in the heavens, and sow good things in your souls, that ye may find them in your life. For if ye sow evil things, ye shall reap all trouble and affliction. Get wisdom in the fear of God with diligence; for though there shall be a leading into captivity, and cities be destroyed, and lands and gold and silver and every possession shall perish, the wisdom of the wise none can take away, save the blindness of ungodliness and the palsy of sin: for even

among his enemies shall it be to him glorious, and in a strange country a home, and in the midst of foes shall it be found a friend. If a man teach these things and do them, he shall be enthroned with kings, as was also Joseph our brother.

14. And now, my children, I have learnt from the writing of Enoch that at the last ye will deal ungodly, laying your hands upon the Lord in all malice; and your brethren shall be ashamed because of you, and to all the Gentiles shall it become a mocking. For our father Israel shall be pure from the ungodliness of the chief priests who shall lay their hands upon the Saviour of the world. Pure is the heaven above the earth, and ye are the lights of the heaven as the sun and the moon. What shall all the Gentiles do if ye be darkened in ungodliness? So shall ye bring a curse upon our race for whom came the light of the world, which was given among you for the lighting up of every man. Him will ye desire to slay, teaching commandments contrary to the ordinances of God. The offerings of the Lord will ye rob, and from His portion will ye steal; and before ye sacrifice to the Lord, ye will take the choicest parts, in despitefulness eating them with harlots. Amid excesses will ye teach the commandments of the Lord, the women that have husbands will ye pollute, and the virgins of Jerusalem will ye defile; and with harlots and adulteresses will ye be joined. The daughters of the Gentiles will ye take for wives, purifying them with an unlawful purification; and your union shall be like unto Sodom and Gomorrah in ungodliness. And ye will be puffed up because of the priesthood lifting yourselves up against men. And not only so, but being puffed up also against the commands of God, ye will scoff at the holy things, mocking in despitefulness.

15. Therefore the temple which the Lord shall choose shall be desolate in uncleanness, and ye shall be captives throughout all nations, and ye shall be an abomination among them, and ye shall receive reproach and everlasting shame from the righteous judgment of God; and all who see you shall flee from you. And were it not for Abraham, Isaac, and Jacob our fathers, not one from my seed should be left upon the earth.

16. And now I have learnt in the book of Enoch that for seventy weeks will ye go astray, and will profane the priesthood, and pollute the sacrifices, and corrupt the law, and set at nought the words of the prophets. In perverseness ye will persecute righteous men, and hate the godly; the words of the faithful will ye abhor, and the man who reneweth the law in the power of the Most High will ye call a deceiver; and at last, as ye suppose, ye will slay Him, not understanding His resurrection, wickedly taking upon your own heads the innocent blood. Because of Him shall your holy places be desolate, polluted even to the ground, and ye shall have no place that is clean; but ye shall be among the Gentiles a curse and a dispersion, until He shall again look upon you, and in pity shall take you to Himself through faith and water.

17. And because ye have heard concerning the seventy weeks, hear also concerning the priesthood; for in each jubilee there shall be a priesthood. In the first jubilee, the first who is anointed into the priesthood shall be great, and shall speak to God as to a Father; and his priesthood shall be filled with the fear of the Lord, and in the day of his

gladness shall he arise for the salvation of the world. In the second jubilee, he that is anointed shall be conceived in the sorrow of beloved ones; and his priesthood shall be honoured, and shall be glorified among all. And the third priest shall be held fast in sorrow; and the fourth shall be in grief, because unrighteousness shall be laid upon him exceedingly, and all Israel shall hate each one his neighbour. The fifth shall be held fast in darkness, likewise also the sixth and the seventh. And in the seventh there shall be such pollution as I am not able to express, before the Lord and men, for they shall know it who do these things. Therefore shall they be in captivity and for a prey, and their land and their substance shall be destroyed. And in the fifth week they shall return into their desolate country, and shall renew the house of the Lord. And in the seventh week shall come the priests, worshippers of idols, contentious, lovers of money, proud, lawless, lascivious, abusers of children and beasts.

18. And after their punishment shall have come from the Lord, then will the Lord raise up to the priesthood a new Priest, to whom all the words of the Lord shall be revealed; and He shall execute a judgment of truth upon the earth, in the fulness of days. And His star shall arise in heaven, as a king shedding forth the light of knowledge in the sunshine of day, and He shall be magnified in the world until His ascension. He shall shine forth as the sun in the earth, and shall drive away all darkness from the world under heaven, and there shall be peace in all the earth. The heavens shall rejoice in His days, and the earth shall be glad, and the clouds shall be joyful, and the knowledge of the Lord shall be poured forth upon the earth, as the water of seas; and the angels of the glory of the presence of the Lord shall be glad in Him. The heavens shall be opened, and from the temple of glory shall the sanctification come upon Him with the Father's voice, as from Abraham the father of Isaac. And the glory of the Most High shall be uttered over Him, and the spirit of understanding and of sanctification shall rest upon Him in the water. He shall give the majesty of the Lord to His sons in truth for evermore; and there shall none succeed Him for all generations, even for ever. And in His priesthood shall all sin come to an end, and the lawless shall rest from evil, and the just shall rest in Him. And He shall open the gates of paradise, and shall remove the threatening sword against Adam; and He shall give to His saints to eat from the tree of life, and the spirit of holiness shall be on them. And Beliar shall be bound by Him, and He shall give power to His children to tread upon the evil spirits. And the Lord shall rejoice in His children, and the Lord shall be well pleased in His beloved for ever. Then shall Abraham and Isaac and Jacob be joyful, and I will be glad, and all the saints shall put on gladness.

19. And now, my children, ye have heard all; choose therefore for yourselves either the darkness or the light, either the law of the Lord or the works of Beliar. And we answered our father, saying, Before the Lord will we walk according to His law. And our father said, The Lord is witness, and His angels are witnesses, and I am witness, and ye are witnesses, concerning the word of your mouth. And we said, We are witnesses. And thus Levi ceased giving charge to his sons; and he stretched out his feet, and was gathered to his fathers, after he had lived a hundred and thirty-seven years. And they laid him in a coffin, and afterwards they buried him in Hebron, by the side of Abraham, and Isaac, and Jacob.

IV.-The Testament of Judah Concerning Fortitude, and Love of Money, and Fornication.

1. The copy of the words of Judah, what things he spake to his sons before he died. They gathered themselves together, and came to him, and he said to them: I was the fourth son born to my father, and my mother called me Judah, saying, I give thanks to the Lord, because He hath given to me even a fourth son. I was swift and active in my youth, and obedient to my father in everything. And I honoured my mother and my mother's sister. And it came to pass, when I became a man, that my father Jacob prayed over me, saying, Thou shall be a king, and prosperous in all things.

2. And the Lord showed me favour in all my works both in the field and at home. When I saw that I could run with the hind, then I caught it, and prepared meat for my father. I seized upon the roes in the chase, and all that was in the plains I outran. A wild mare I outran, and I caught it and tamed it; and I slew a lion, and plucked a kid out of its mouth. I took a bear by its paw, and rolled it over a cliff; and if any beast turned upon me, I rent it like a dog. I encountered the wild boar, and overtaking it in the chase, I tore it. A leopard in Hebron leaped upon the dog, and I caught it by the tail, and flung it from me, and it was dashed to pieces in the coasts of Gaza. A wild ox feeding in the field I seized by the horns; and whirling it round and stunning it, I cast it from me, and slew it.

3. And when the two kings of the Canaanites came in warlike array against our flocks, and much people with them, I by myself rustled upon King Sur and seized him; and I beat him upon the legs, and dragged him down, and so I slew him. And the other king, Taphue, I slew as he sat upon his horse, and so I scattered all the people. Achor the king, a man of giant stature, hurling darts before and behind as he sat on horseback, I slew; for I hurled a stone of sixty pounds weight, and cast it upon his horse, and killed him. And I fought with Achor for two hours, and I killed him; and I clave his shield into two parts, and I chopped off his feet. And as I stripped off his breastplate, behold, eight men his companions began to fight with me. I wound round therefore my garment in my hand; and I slang stones at them, and killed four of them, and the rest fled. And Jacob my father slew Beelisa, king of all the kings, a giant in strength, twelve cubits high; and fear fell upon them, and they ceased from making war with us. Therefore my father had no care in the wars when I was among my brethren. For he saw in a vision concerning me, that an angel of might followed me everywhere, that I should not be overcome.

4. And in the south there befell us a greater war than that in Shechem; and I joined in battle array with my brethren, and pursued a thousand men, and slew of them two hundred men and four kings. And I went up against them upon the wall, and two other kings I slew; and so we freed Hebron, and took all the captives of the kings.

5. On the next day we departed to Areta, a city strong and walled and inaccessible, threatening us with death. Therefore I and Gad approached on the east side of the city, and Reuben and Levi on the west and south. And they that were upon the wall, thinking that we were alone, charged down upon us; and so our brethren secretly

climbed up the wall on both sides by ladders, and entered into the city, while the men knew it not. And we took it with the edge of the sword; and those who had taken refuge in the tower,-we set fire to the tower, and took both it and them. And as we were departing the men of Thaffu set upon our captives, and we took it with our sons, and fought with them even to Thaffu; and we slew them, and burnt their city, and spoiled all the things that were therein.

6. And when I was at the waters of Chuzeba, the men of Jobel came against us to battle, and we fought with them; and their allies from Selom we slew, and we allowed them no means of escaping, and of coming against us. And the men of Machir came upon us on the fifth day, to carry away our captives; and we attacked them, and overcame them in fierce battle: for they were a host and mighty in themselves, and we slew them before they had gone up the ascent of the hill. And when we came to their city, their women rolled upon us stones from the brow of the hill on which the city stood. And I and Simeon hid ourselves behind the town, and seized upon the heights, and utterly destroyed the whole city.

7. And the next day it was told us that the cities of the two kings with a great host were coming against us. I therefore and Dan reigned ourselves to be Amorites, and went as allies into their city. And in the depth of night our brethren came, and we opened to them the gates; and we destroyed all the men and their substance, and we took for a prey all that was theirs, and their three walls we cast down. And we drew near to Thamna, where was all the refuge of the hostile kings. Then having received hurt I was wroth, and charged upon them to the brow of the hill; and they slang at me with stones and darts; and had not Dan my brother aided me, they would have been able to slay me. We came upon them therefore with wrath, and they all fled; and passing by another way, they besought my father, and he made peace with them, and we did to them no hurt, but made a truce with them, and restored to them all the captives. And I built Thamna, and my father built Rhambael. I was twenty years old when this war befell, and the Canaanites feared me and my brethren.

8. Moreover, I had much cattle, and I had for the chief of my herdsmen Iran the Adullamite. And when I went to him I saw Barsan, king of Adullam, and he made us a feast; and he entreated me, and gave me his daughter Bathshua to wife. She bare me Er, and Onan, and Shelah; and the two of them the Lord smote that they died childless: for Shelah lived, and his children are ye.

9. Eighteen years we abode at peace, our father and we, with his brother Esau, and his sons with us, after that we came from Mesopotamia, from Laban. And when eighteen years were fulfilled, in the fortieth year of my life, Esau, the brother of my father, came upon us with much people and strong; and he fell by the bow of Jacob, and was taken up dead in Mount Seir: even as he went above Iramna was he slain. And we pursued after the sons of Esau. Now they had a city with walls of iron and gates of brass; and we could not enter into it, and we encamped around, and besieged them. And when they opened not to us after twenty days, I set up a ladder in the sight of all, and with my shield upon my head I climbed up, assailed with stones of three talents' weight; and I climbed up, and slew four

who were mighty among them. And the next day Reuben and Gad entered in and slew sixty others. Then they asked from us terms of peace; and being aware of our father's purpose, we received them as tributaries. And they gave us two hundred cors of wheat, five hundred baths of oil, fifteen hundred measures of wine, until we went down into Egypt.

10. After these things, my son Er took to wife Tamar, from Mesopotamia, a daughter of Aram. Now Er was wicked, and he doubted concerning Tamar, because she was not of the land of Canaan. And on the third day an angel of the Lord smote him in the night, and he had not known her, according to the evil craftiness of his mother, for he did not wish to have children from her. In the days of the wedding-feast I espoused Onan to her; and he also in wickedness knew her not, though he lived with her a year. And when I threatened him, he lay with her, ...according to the command of his mother, and he also died in his wickedness. And I wished to give Shelah also to her, but my wife Bathshua suffered it not; for she bore a spite against Tamar, because she was not of the daughters of Canaan, as she herself was.

11. And I knew that the race of Canaan was wicked, but the thoughts of youth blinded my heart. And when I saw her pouring out wine, in the drunkenness of wine was I deceived, and I fell before her. And while I was away, she went and took for Shelah a wife from the land of Caanan. And when I knew what she had done, I cursed her in the anguish of my soul, and she also died in the wickedness of her sons.

12. And after these things, while Tamar was a widow, she heard after two years that I was going up to shear my sheep; then she decked herself in bridal array, and sat over against the city by the gate. For it is a law of the Amorites, that she who is about to marry sit in fornication seven days by the gate. I therefore, being drunk at the waters of Chozeb, recognised her not by reason of wine; and her beauty deceived me, through the fashion of her adorning. And I turned aside to her, and said, I would enter in to thee. And she said to me, What wilt thou give me? And I gave her my staff, and my girdle, and my royal crown; and I lay with her, and she conceived. I then, not knowing what she had done, wished to slay her; but she privily sent my pledges, and put me to shame. And when I called her, I heard also the secret words which I spoke when lying with her in my drunkenness; and I could not slay her, because it was from the Lord. For I said, Lest haply she did it in subtlety, and received the pledge from another woman: but I came near her no more till my death, because I had done this abomination in all Israel. Moreover, they who were in the city said that there was no bride in the city, because she came from another place, and sat for awhile in the gate, and she thought that no one knew that I had gone in to her. And after this we came into Egypt to Joseph, because of the famine. Forty and six years old was I, and seventy and three years lived I there.

13. And now, my children, in what things so ever I command you hearken to your father, and keep all my sayings to perform the ordinances of the Lord, and to obey the command of the Lord God. And walk not after your lusts, nor in the thoughts of your imaginations in the

haughtiness of your heart; and glory not in the works of the strength of youth, for this also is evil in the eyes of the Lord. For since I also gloried that in wars the face of no woman of goodly form ever deceived me, and upbraided Reuben my brother concerning Bilhah, the wife of my father, the spirits of jealousy and of fornication arrayed themselves within me, until I fell before Bathshua the Canaanite, and Tamar who was espoused to my sons, And I said to my father-in-law, I will counsel with my father, and so will I take thy daughter. And he showed me a boundless store of gold in his daughter's behalf, for he was a king. And he decked her with gold and pearls, and caused her to pour out wine for us at the feast in womanly beauty. And the wine led my eyes astray, and pleasure blinded my heart; and I loved her, and I fell, and transgressed the commandment of the Lord and the commandment of my fathers, and I took her to wife. And the Lord rewarded me according to the thought of my heart, insomuch that I had no joy in her children.

14. And now, my children, be not drunk with wine; for wine turneth the mind away from the truth, and kindleth in it the passion of lust, and leadeth the eyes into error. For the spirit of fornication hath wine as a minister to give pleasures to the mind; for these two take away the power from a man. For if a man drink wine to drunkenness, he disturbeth his mind with filthy thoughts to fornication, and exciteth his body to carnal union; and if the cause of the desire be present, he worketh the sin, and is not ashamed. Such is wine, my children; for he who is drunken reverenceth no man. For, lo, it made me also to err, so that I was not ashamed of the multitude in the city, because before the eyes of all I turned aside unto Tamar, and I worked a great sin, and I uncovered the covering of the shame of my sons. After that I drank wine I reverenced not the commandment of God, and I took a woman of Canaan to wife. Wherefore, my children, he who drinketh wine needeth discretion; and herein is discretion in drinking wine, that a man should drink as long as he keepeth decency; but if he go beyond this bound, the spirit of deceit attacketh his mind and worketh his will; and it maketh the drunkard to talk filthily, and to transgress and not to be ashamed, but even to exult in his dishonour, accounting himself to do well.

15. He that committeth fornication, and uncovereth his nakedness, hath become the servant of fornication, and escapeth not from the power thereof, even as I also was uncovered. For I gave my staff, that is, the stay of my tribe; and my girdle, that is, my power; and my diadem, that is, the glory of my kingdom. Then I repented for these things, and took no wine or flesh until my old age, nor did I behold any joy. And the angel of God showed me that for ever do women bear rule over king and beggar alike; and from the king they take away his glory, and from the valiant man his strength, and from the beggar even that little which is the stay of his poverty.

16. Observe therefore, my children, moderation in wine; for there are in it four evil spirits-of (1) lust, of (2) wrath, of (3) riot, of (4) filthy lucre. If ye drink wine in gladness, with shamefacedness, with the fear of God, ye shall live. For if ye drink not with shamefacedness, and the fear of God departeth from you, then cometh drunkenness, and shamelessness stealeth in. But *even* if ye drink not at all, take heed lest ye sin in words of outrage, and fighting, and slander, and transgression of the commandments of God; so shall ye perish before your time. Moreover, wine revealeth the mysteries of God and men to aliens, even as I also revealed the commandments of God and the mysteries of Jacob my father to the Canaanitish Bathshua, to whom God forbade to declare them. And wine also is a cause of war and confusion.

17. I charge you, therefore, my children, not to love money, nor to gaze upon the beauty of women; because for the sake of money and beauty I was led astray to Bathshua the Canaanite. For I know that because of these two things shall ye who are my race fall into wickedness; for even wise men among my sons shall they mar, and shall cause the kingdom of Judah to be diminished, which the Lord gave me because of my obedience to my father. For I never disobeyed a word of Jacob my father, for all things whatsoever he commanded I did. And Abraham, the father of my father, blessed me that I should be king in Israel, and Isaac further blessed me in like manner. And I know that from me shall the kingdom be established.

18. For I have read also in the books of Enoch the righteous what evils ye shall do in the last days. Take heed, therefore, my children, of fornication and the love of money; hearken to Judah your father, for these things do withdraw you from the law of God, and blind the understanding of the soul, and teach arrogance, and suffer not a man to have compassion upon his neighbour: they rob his soul of all goodness, and bind him in toils and troubles, and take away his sleep and devour his flesh, and hinder the sacrifices of God; and he remembereth not blessing, and he hearkeneth not to a prophet when he speaketh, and is vexed at the word of godliness. For one who serveth two passions contrary to the commandments of God cannot obey God, because they have blinded his soul, and he walketh in the day-time as in the night.

19. My children, the love of money leadeth to idols; because, when led astray through money, men make mention of those who are no gods, and it causeth him who hath it to fall into madness. For the sake of money I lost my children, and but for the repentance of my flesh, and the humbling of my soul, and the prayers of Jacob my father, I should have died childless. But the God of my fathers, who is pitiful and merciful, pardoned me, because I did it in ignorance. For the prince of deceit blinded me, and I was ignorant as a man and as flesh, being corrupted in sins; and I learnt my own weakness while thinking myself unconquerable.

20. Learn therefore, my children, that two spirits wait upon man-the spirit of truth and the spirit of error; and in the midst is the spirit of the understanding of the mind, to which it belongeth to turn whithersoever it will. And the works of truth and the works of error are written upon the breast of men, and each one of them the Lord knoweth. And there is no time at which the works of men can be hid from Him; for on the bones of his breast hath he been written down before the Lord. And the spirit of truth testifieth all things, and accuseth all; and he who sinneth is burnt up by his own heart, and cannot raise his face unto the Judge.

21. And now, my children, love Levi, that ye may abide, and exalt not yourselves against him, lest ye be utterly destroyed. For to me the Lord gave the kingdom, and to him the priesthood, and He set the kingdom beneath the priesthood. To me He gave the things upon the earth; to him the things in the heavens. As the heaven is higher than the earth, so is the priesthood of God higher than the kingdom upon the earth. For the Lord chose him above thee, to draw near to Him, and to eat of His table and first-fruits, even the choice things of the sons of Israel, and thou shall be to them as a sea. For as, on the sea, just and unjust are tossed about, some taken into captivity while others are enriched, so also shall every race of men be in thee, some are in jeopardy and taken captive, and others shall grow rich by means of plunder. For they who rule will be as great sea-monsters, swallowing up men like fishes: free sons and daughters do they enslave; houses, lands, flocks, money, will they plunder; and with the flesh of many will they wrongfully feed the ravens and the cranes; and they will go on further in evil, advancing on still in covetousness. And there shall be false prophets like tempests, and they shall persecute all righteous men.

22. And the Lord shall bring upon them divisions one against another, and there shall be continual wars in Israel; and among men of other race shall my kingdom be brought to an end, until the salvation of Israel shall come, until the appearing of the God of righteousness, that Jacob and all the Gentiles may rest in peace. And he shall guard the might of my kingdom for ever: for the Lord sware to me with an oath that the kingdom should never fail from me, and from my seed for all days, even for ever.

23. Now I have much grief, my children, because of your lewdness, and witchcrafts, and idolatries, which ye will work against the kingdom, following them that have familiar spirits ye will make your daughters singing girls and harlots for divinations and demons of error, and ye will be mingled in the pollutions of the Gentiles: for which things' sake the Lord shall bring upon you famine and pestilence, death and the sword, avenging siege, and dogs for the rending in pieces of enemies, and revilings of friends, destruction and blighting of eyes, children slaughtered, wives carried off, possessions plundered, temple of God in flames, your land desolated, your own selves enslaved among the Gentiles, and they shall make some of you eunuchs for their wives; and whenever ye will return to the Lord with humility of heart, repenting and walking in all the commandments of God, then will the Lord visit you in mercy and in love, bringing you from out of the bondage of your enemies.

24. And after these things shall a Star arise to you from Jacob in peace, and a Man shall rise from my seed, like the Sun of righteousness, walking with the sons of men in meekness and righteousness, and no sin shall be found in Him. And the heavens shall be opened above Him, to shed forth the blessing of the Spirit from the Holy Father; and He shall shed forth a spirit of grace upon you, and ye shall be unto Him sons in truth, and ye shall walk in His commandments, the first and the last. This is the Branch of God Most High, and this the Well-spring unto life for all flesh. Then shall the sceptre of my kingdom shine forth, and from your root shall arise a stem; and in it shall arise a rod of righteousness to the Gentiles, to judge and to save all that call upon the Lord.

25. And after these things shall Abraham and Isaac and Jacob arise unto life, and I and my brethren will be chiefs, even your sceptre in Israel: Levi first, I the second, Joseph third, Benjamin fourth, Simeon fifth, Issachar sixth, and so all in order. And the Lord blessed Levi; the Angel of the Presence, me; the powers of glory, Simeon; the heaven, Reuben; the earth, Issachar; the sea, Zebulun; the mountains, Joseph; the tabernacle, Benjamin; the lights of heaven, Dan; the fatness of earth, Naphtali; the sun, Gad; the olive, Asher: and there shall be one people of the Lord, and one tongue; and there shall no more be a spirit of deceit of Beliar, for he shall be cast into the fire for ever. And they who have died in grief shall arise in joy, and they who have lived in poverty for the Lord's sake shall be made rich, and they who have been in want shall be filled, and they who have been weak shall be made strong, and they who have been put to death for the Lord's sake shall awake in life. And the harts of Jacob shall run in joyfulness, and the eagles of Israel shall fly in gladness; but the ungodly shall lament, and sinners all weep, and all the people shall glorify the Lord for ever.

26. Observe, therefore, my children, all the law of the Lord, for there is hope for all them who follow His way aright. And he said to them: I die before your eyes this day, a hundred and nineteen years old. Let no one bury me in costly apparel, nor tear open my bowels, for this shall they who are kings do: and carry me up to Hebron with you. And Judah, when he had said these things, fell asleep; and his sons did according to all whatsoever he commanded them, and they buried him in Hebron with his fathers.

V.-The Testament of Issachar Concerning Simplicity.

1. The record of the words of Issachar. He called his sons, and said to them: Hearken, my children, to Issachar your father; give ear to my words, ye who are beloved of the Lord. I was the fifth son born to Jacob, even the hire of the mandrakes. For Reuben brought in mandrakes from the field, and Rachel met him and took them. And Reuben wept, and at his voice Leah my mother came forth. Now these mandrakes were sweet-smelling apples which the land of Aram produced on high ground below a ravine of water. And Rachel said, I will not give them to thee, for they shall be to me instead of children. Now there were two apples; and Leaf said, Let it suffice thee that thou hast taken the husband of my virginity: wilt thou also take these? And she said, Behold, let Jacob be to thee this night instead of the mandrakes of thy son. And Leah said to her, Boast not, and vaunt not thyself; for Jacob is mine, and I am the wife of his youth. But Rachel said, How so? for to me was he first espoused, and for my sake he served our father fourteen years. What shall I do to thee, because the craft and the subtlety of men are increased, and craft prospereth upon the earth? And were it not so, thou wouldest not now see the face of Jacob. For thou art not his wife, but in craft wert taken to him in my stead. And my father deceived me, and removed me on that night, and suffered me not to see him; for had I been there, it had not happened thus. And Rachel said, Take one mandrake, and for the other thou shalt hire him from me for one night. And Jacob knew

Leah, and she conceived and bare me, and on account of the hire I was called Issachar.

2. Then appeared to Jacob an angel of the Lord, saying, Two children shall Rachel bear; for she hath refused company with her husband, and hath chosen continency. And had not Leah my mother given up the two apples for the sake of his company, she would have borne eight sons; and for this thing she bare six, and Rachel two: because on account of the mandrakes the Lord visited her. For He knew that for the sake of children she wished to company with Jacob, and not for lust of pleasure. For she went further, and on the morrow too gave up Jacob that she might receive also the other mandrake. Therefore the Lord hearkened to Rachel because of the mandrakes: for though she desired them, she ate them not, but brought them to the priest of the Most High who was at that time, and offered them up in the house of the Lord.

3. When, therefore, I grew up, my children, I walked in uprightness of heart, and I became a husbandman for my parents and my brethren, and I brought in fruits from the field according to their season; and my father blessed me, for he saw that I walked in simplicity. And I was not a busybody in my doings, nor malicious and slanderous against my neighbour. I never spoke against any one, nor did I censure the life of any man, but walked in the simplicity of my eyes. Therefore when I was thirty years old I took to myself a wife, for my labour wore away my strength, and I never thought upon pleasure with women; but through my labour my sleep sufficed me, and my father always rejoiced in my simplicity. For on whatever I laboured I offered first to the Lord, by the hands of the priests, of all my produce and all first-fruits; then to my father, and then took for myself. And the Lord increased twofold His benefits in my hands; and Jacob also knew that God aided my simplicity, for on every poor man and every one in distress I bestowed the good things of the earth in simplicity of heart.

4. And now hearken to me, my children, and walk in simplicity of heart, for I have seen in it all that is well-pleasing to the Lord. The simple coveteth not gold, defraudeth not his neighbour, longeth not after manifold dainties, delighteth not in varied apparel, doth not picture to himself to live a long life, but only waiteth for the will of God, and the spirits of error have no power against him. For he cannot allow within his mind a thought of female beauty, that he should not pollute his mind in corruption. No envy can enter into his thoughts, no jealousy melteth away his soul, nor doth he brood over gain with insatiate desire; for he walketh in uprightness of life, and beholdeth all things in simplicity, not admitting in his eyes malice from the error of the world, lest he should see the perversion of any of the commandments of the Lord.

5. Keep therefore the law of God, my children, and get simplicity, and walk in guilelessness, not prying over-curiously into the commands of God and the business of your neighbour; but love the Lord and your neighbour, have compassion on the poor and weak. Bow down your back unto husbandry, and labour in tillage of the ground in all manner of husbandry, offering gifts unto the Lord with thanksgiving; for with the first-fruits of the earth did the Lord bless me, even as He blessed all the saints from Abel even until now. For no other portion is given to thee than of the fatness of the earth, whose fruits are raised by toil; for our father Jacob blessed me with blessings of the earth and of first-fruits. And Levi and Judah were glorified by the Lord among the sons of Jacob; for the Lord made choice of them, and to the one He gave the priesthood, to the other the kingdom. Them therefore obey, and walk in the simplicity of your father; for unto Gad hath it been given to destroy the temptations that are coming upon Israel.

6. I know, my children, that in the last times your sons will forsake simplicity, and will cleave unto avarice, and leaving guilelessness will draw near to malice, and forsaking the commandments of the Lord will cleave unto Beliar, and leaving husbandry will follow after their wicked devices, and shall be dispersed among the Gentiles, and shall serve their enemies. And do you therefore command these things to your children, that if they sin they may the more quickly return to the Lord; for He is merciful, and will deliver them even to bring them back into their land.

7. I am a hundred and twenty-two years old, and I know not against myself a sin unto death. Except my wife, I have not known any woman. I never committed fornication in the haughtiness of my eyes; I drank not wine, to be led astray thereby; I coveted not any desirable thing that was my neighbour's; guile never entered in my heart; a lie never passed through my lips; if any man grieved, I wept with him, and I shared my bread with the poor. I never ate alone; I moved no landmark; in all my days I wrought godliness and truth. I loved the Lord with all my strength; likewise also did I love every man even as my own children. So ye also do these things, my children, and every spirit of Beliar shall flee from you, and no deed of malicious men shall rule over you; and every wild beast shall ye subdue, having with yourselves the God of heaven walking with men in simplicity of heart.

And he commanded them that they should carry him up to Hebron, and bury him there in the cave with his fathers. And he stretched out his feet and died, the fifth son of Jacob, in a good old age; and with every limb sound, and with strength unabated, he slept the eternal sleep.

VI.-The Testament of Zebulun Concerning Compassion and Mercy.

1. The record of Zebulun, which he enjoined his children in the hundred and fourteenth year of his life, thirty-two years after the death of Joseph. And he said to them: Hearken to me sons of Zebulun, attend to the words of your father. I am Zebulun, a good gift to my parents. For when I was born our father was increased very exceedingly, both in flocks and herds, when with the streaked rods he had his portion. I know not, my children, that in all my days I have sinned, save only in thought. Nor do I remember that I have done any iniquity, except the sin of ignorance which I committed against Joseph; for I screened my brethren, not telling to my father what had been done. And I wept sore in secret, for I feared my brethren, because they had all agreed together, that if any one should declare the secret, he should be slain with the sword. But when they wished to kill him, I adjured them much with tears not to be guilty of this iniquity.

2. For Simeon and Gad came against Joseph to kill him. And Joseph fell upon his face, and said unto them, Pity me, my brethren, have compassion upon the bowels of Jacob our father lay not upon me your hands to shed innocent blood, for I have not sinned against you; yea, if I have sinned, with chastening chastise me, but lay not upon me your hand, for the sake of Jacob our father. And as he spoke these words, I pitied him and began to weep, and my heart melted within me, and all the substance of my bowels was loosened within my soul. And Joseph also wept, and I too wept with him; and my heart throbbed fast, and the joints of my body trembled, and I was not able to stand. And when he saw me weeping with him, and them coming against him to slay him, he fled behind me, beseeching them. And Reuben rose and said, My brethren, let us not slay him, but let us cast him into one of these dry pits which our fathers digged and found no water. For for this cause the Lord forbade that water should rise up in them, in order that Joseph might be preserved; and the Lord appointed it so, until they sold him to the Ishmaelites.

3. For in the price of Joseph, my children, I had no share; but Simeon and Gad and six other of our brethren took the price of Joseph, and bought sandals for themselves, their wives, and their children, saying, We will not eat of it, for it is the price of our brother's blood, but will tread it down under foot, because he said that he was king over us, and so let us see what his dreams mean. Therefore is it written in the writing of the law of Enoch, that whosoever will not raise up seed to his brother, his sandal shall be unloosed, and they shall spit into his face. And the brethren of Joseph wished not that their brother should live, and the Lord loosed unto them the sandal of Joseph. For when they came into Egypt they were unloosed by the servants of Joseph before the gate, and so made obeisance to Joseph after the fashion of Pharaoh. And not only did they make obeisance to him, but were spit upon also, falling down before him forthwith, and so they were put to shame before the Egyptians; for after this the Egyptians heard all the evils which we had done to Joseph.

4. After these things they brought forth food; for I through two days and two nights tasted nothing, through pity for Joseph. And Judah ate not with them, but watched the pit; for he feared lest Simeon and Gad should run back and slay him. And when they saw that I also ate not, they set me to watch him until he was sold. And he remained in the pit three days and three nights, and so was sold famishing. And when Reuben heard that while he was away Joseph had been sold, he rent his clothes about him, and mourned, saying, How shall I look in the face of Jacob my father? And he took the money, and ran after the merchants, and found no one; for they had left the main road, and journeyed hastily through rugged byways. And Reuben ate no food on that day, Dan therefore came to him, and said, Weep not, neither grieve for I have found what we can say to our father Jacob. Let us slay a kid of the goats, and dip in it the coat of Joseph; and we will say, Look, if this is the coat of thy son: for they stripped off from Joseph the coat of our father when they were about to sell him, and put upon him an old garment of a slave. Now Simeon had the coat, and would not give it up, wishing to rend it with his sword; for he was angry that Joseph lived, and that he had not slain him. Them we all rose up together against him, and said, If thou give it not up, we will say that thou alone

didst this wickedness in Israel; and so he gave it up, and they did even as Dan had said.

5. And now, my children, I bid you to keep the commands of the Lord, and to show mercy upon your neighbour, and to have compassion towards all, not towards men only, but also towards beasts. For for this thing's sake the Lord blessed me; and when all my brethren were sick I escaped without sickness, for the Lord knoweth the purposes of each. Have therefore compassion in your hearts, my children, because even as a man doeth to his neighbour, even so also will the Lord do to him. For the sons of my brethren were sickening, were dying on account of Joseph, because they showed not mercy in their hearts; but my sons were preserved without sickness, as ye know. And when I was in Canaan, by the sea-coast, I caught spoil of fish for Jacob my father; and when many were choked in the sea, I abode unhurt.

6. I was the first who made a boat to sail upon the sea, for the Lord gave me understanding and wisdom therein; and I let down a rudder behind it, and I stretched a sail on an upright mast in the midst; and sailing therein along the shores, I caught fish for the house of my father until we went into Egypt; and through compassion, I gave of my fish to every stranger. And if any man were a stranger, or sick, or aged, I boiled the fish and dressed them well, and offered them to all men as every man had need, bringing them together and having compassion upon them. Wherefore also the Lord granted me to take much fish: for he that imparteth unto his neighbour, receiveth manifold more from the Lord. For five years I caught fish, and gave thereof to every man whom I saw, and brought sufficient for all the house of my father. In the summer I caught fish, and in the winter I kept sheep with my brethren.

7. Now I will declare unto you what I did, I saw a man in distress and nakedness in wintertime, and had compassion upon him, and stole away a garment secretly from my house, and gave it to him who was in distress. Do you therefore, my children, from that which God bestoweth upon you, show compassion and mercy impartially to all men, and give to every man with a good heart. And if ye have not at the time wherewith to give to him that asketh you, have compassion for him in bowels of mercy. I know that my hand found not at the time wherewith to give to him that asked me, and I walked with him weeping for more than seven furlongs, and my bowels yearned towards him unto compassion.

8. Have therefore yourselves also, my children, compassion towards every man with mercy, that the Lord also may have compassion upon you, and have mercy upon you; because also in the last days God sendeth His compassion on the earth, and wheresoever He findeth bowels of mercy, He dwelleth in him. For how much compassion a man hath upon his neighbours, so much also hath the Lord upon him. For when we went down into Egypt, Joseph bore no malice against us, and when he saw me he was filled with compassion. And looking towards him, do ye also, my children, approve yourselves without malice, and love one another; and reckon not each one the evil of his brother, for this breaketh unity, and divideth all kindred, and troubleth the soul: for he who beareth malice hath not bowels of mercy.

9. Mark the waters, that they flow together, and sweep along stones, trees, sand; but if they are divided into many streams, the earth sucketh them up, and they become of no account. So also shall ye be if ye be divided. Divide not yourselves into two heads, for everything which the Lord made hath but one head; He gave two shoulders, hands, feet, but all the members are subject unto the one head. I have learnt by the writing of my fathers, that in the last days ye will depart from the Lord, and be divided in Israel, and ye will follow two kings, and will work every abomination, and every idol will ye worship, and your enemies shall lead you captive, and ye shall dwell among the nations with all infirmities and tribulations and anguish of soul. And after these things ye will remember the Lord, and will repent, and He will lead you back; for He is merciful and full of compassion, not imputing evil to the sons of men, because they are flesh, and the spirits of error deceive them in all their doings, And after these things shall the Lord Himself arise to you, the Light of righteousness, and healing and compassion shall be upon His wings. He shall redeem all captivity of the sons of men from Beliar, and every spirit of error shall be trodden down. And He shall bring back all the nations to zeal for Him, and ye shall see God in the fashion of a man whom the Lord shall choose, Jerusalem is His name. And again with the wickedness of your words will ye provoke Him to anger, and ye shall be cast away, even unto the time of consummation.

10. And now, my children, grieve not that I am dying, nor be troubled in that I am passing away from you. For I shall arise once more in the midst of you, as a ruler in the midst of his sons; and I will rejoice in the midst of my tribe, as many as have kept the law of the Lord, and the commandments of Zebulun their father. But upon the ungodly shall the Lord bring everlasting fire, and will destroy them throughout all generations. I am hastening away unto my rest, as did my fathers; but do ye fear the Lord your God with all your strength all the days of your life. And when he had said these things he fell calmly asleep, and his sons laid him in a coffin; and afterwards they carried him up to Hebron, and buried him with his fathers.

VII.-The Testament of Dan Concerning Anger and Lying.

1. The record of the words of Dan, which he spake to his sons in his last days. In the hundred and twenty-fifth year of his life he called together his family, and said: Hearken to my words, ye sons of Dan; give heed to the words of the mouth of your father. I have proved in my heart, and in my whole life, that truth with just dealing is good and well-pleasing to God, and that lying and anger are evil, because they teach man all wickedness. I confess this day to you, my children, that in my heart I rejoiced concerning the death of Joseph, a true and good man; and I rejoiced at the selling of Joseph, because his father loved him more than us. For the spirit of jealousy and of vainglory said to me, Thou also art his son. And one of the spirits of Beliar wrought with me, saying, Take this sword, and with it slay Joseph; so shall thy father love thee when he is slain. This is the spirit of anger that counselled me, that even as a leopard devoureth a kid, so should I devour Joseph. But the God of Jacob our father gave him not over into my hands that I should find him alone, nor suffered me to work this iniquity, that two tribes should be destroyed in Israel.

2. And now, my children, I am dying, and I tell you of a truth, that unless ye keep yourselves from the spirit of lying and of anger, and love truth and long-suffering, ye shall perish. There is blindness in anger, my children, and no wrathful man regardeth any, person with truth: for though it be a father or a mother, he behaveth towards them as enemies; though it be a brother, he knoweth him not; though it be a prophet of the Lord, he disobeyeth him; though a righteous man, he regardeth him not; a friend he doth not acknowledge. For the spirit of anger encompasseth him with the nets of deceit, and blindeth his natural eyes, and through lying darkeneth his mind, and giveth him a sight of his own making. And wherewith encompasseth he his eyes? In hatred of heart; and he giveth him a heart of his own against his brother unto envy.

3. My children, mischievous is anger, for it becometh as a soul to the soul itself; and the body of the angry man it maketh its own, and over his soul it getteth the mastery, and it bestoweth upon the body its own power, that it may work all iniquity; and whenever the soul doeth aught, it justifieth what has been done, since it seeth not. Therefore he who is wrathful, if he be a mighty man, hath a treble might in his anger; one by the might and aid of his servants, and a second by his wrath, whereby he persuadeth and overcometh in injustice: and having a third of the nature of his own body, and of his own self working the evil. And though the wrathful man be weak, yet hath he a might twofold of that which is by nature; for wrath ever aideth such in mischief. This spirit goeth always with lying at the right hand of Satan, that his works may be wrought with cruelty and lying.

4. Understand ye therefore the might of wrath, that it is vain. For it first of all stingeth him in word: then by deeds it strengtheneth him who is angry, and with bitter punishments disturbeth his mind, and so stirreth up with great wrath his soul. Therefore, when any one speaketh against you, be not ye moved unto anger, And if any man praiseth you as good, be not lifted up nor elated, either to the feeling or showing of pleasure. For first it pleaseth the hearing, and so stirreth up the understanding to understand the grounds for anger; and then, being wrathful, he thinketh that he is justly angry. If ye fall into any loss or ruin, my children, be hot troubled; for this very spirit maketh men desire that which hath perished, in order that they may he inflamed by the desire. If ye suffer loss willingly, be not vexed, for from vexation he raiseth up wrath with lying. And wrath with lying is a twofold mischief; and they speak one with another that they may disturb the mind; and when the soul is continually, disturbed, the Lord departeth from it, and Beliar ruleth over it.

5. Observe, therefore, my children, the commandments of the Lord, and keep His law; and depart from wrath, and hate lying, that the Lord may dwell among you, and Beliar may flee from you. Speak truth each one with his neighbour, so shall ye not fall into lust and confusion; but ye shall be in peace, having the God of peace, so shall no war prevail over yon. Love the Lord through all your life, unit one another with a true heart. For I know that in the last days ye will depart from the Lord, and will provoke Levi unto anger, and will fight against Judah; but ye shall not prevail against them. For an angel of the Lord shall

guide them both; for by them shall Israel stand. And whensoever ye depart from the Lord, ye will walk in all evil, working the abominations of the Gentiles, going astray with women of them that are ungodly; and the spirits of error shall work in you with all malice. For I have read in the book of Enoch the righteous, that your prince is Satan, and that all the spirits of fornication and pride shall be subject unto Levi, to lay a snare for the sons of Levi, to came them to sin before the Lord. And my sons will draw near unto Levi, and sin with them in all things; and the sons of Judah will be covetous, plundering other men's goods like lions. Therefore shall ye be led away with them in captivity, and there shall ye receive all the plagues of Egypt, and all the malice of the Gentiles: and so, when ye return to the Lord, ye shall obtain mercy, and He shall bring you into His sanctuary, calling peace upon you; and there shall arise unto you from the tribe of Judah and of Levi the salvation of the Lord; and He shall make war against Beliar, and He shall give the vengeance of victory to our coasts. And the captivity shall He take from Beliar, even the souls of the saints, and shall turn disobedient hearts unto the Lord, and shall give to them who call upon Him everlasting peace; and the saints shall rest in Eden, and the righteous shall rejoice in the new Jerusalem, which shall be unto the glory of God for ever and ever. And no longer shall Jerusalem endure desolation, nor Israel be led captive; for the Lord shall be in the midst of her, dwelling among men, even the Holy One of Israel reigning over them in humility and in poverty; and he who believeth on Him shall reign in truth in the heavens.

6. And now, my children, fear the Lord, and take heed unto yourselves of Satan and his spirits; and draw near unto God, and to the Angel that intercedeth for you, for He is a Mediator between God and man for the peace of Israel. He shall stand up against the kingdom of the enemy; therefore is the enemy eager to destroy all that call upon the Lord. For he knoweth that in the day on which Israel shall believe, the kingdom of the enemy shall be brought to an end; and the very angel of peace shall strengthen Israel, that it fall not into the extremity of evil. And it shall be in the time of the iniquity of Israel, that the Lord will depart from them, and will go after him that doeth His will, for unto none of His angels shall it be as unto him. And His name shall be in every place of Israel, and among the Gentiles-Saviour. Keep therefore yourselves, my children, from every evil work, and cast away wrath and all lying, and love truth and long-suffering; and the things which ye have heard from your father, do ye also impart to your children, that the Father of the Gentiles may receive you: for He is true and long-suffering, meek and lowly, and teacheth by His works the law of God. Depart, therefore, from all unrighteousness, and cleave unto, the righteousness of the law of the Lord: and bury me near my fathers.

7. And when he had said these things he kissed them, and slept the long sleep. And his sons buried him, and after that they carried up his bones to the side of Abraham, and Isaac, and Jacob. Nevertheless, as Dan had prophesied unto them that they should forget the law of their God, and should be alienated from the land of their inheritance, and from the race of Israel, and from their kindred, so also it came to pass.

VIII.-The Testament of Naphtali Concerning Natural Goodness.

1. The record of the testament of Naphtali, what things he ordained at the time of his death in the hundred and thirty-second year of his life. When his sons were gathered together in the seventh month, the fourth day of the month, he, being yet in good health, made them a feast and good cheer. And after he was awake in the morning, he said to them, I am dying; and they believed him not. And he blessed the Lord; and affirmed that after yesterday's feast he should die. He began then to say to his sons: Hear, my children; ye sons of Naphtali, hear the words of your father. I was born from Bilhah; and because Rachel dealt craftily, and gave Bilhah in place of herself to Jacob, and she bore me upon Rachel's lap, therefore was I called Naphtali. And Rachel loved me because I was born upon her lap; and when I was of young and tender form, she was wont to kiss me, and say, Would that I might see a brother of thine from my own womb, like unto thee: whence also Joseph was like unto me in all things, according to the prayers of Rachel. Now my mother was Bilhah, daughter of Rotheus the brother of Deborah, Rebecca's nurse, and she was born on one and the self-same day with Rachel. And Rotheus was of the family of Abraham, a Chaldean, fearing God, free-born and noble; and he was taken captive, and was bought by Laban; and he gave him Aena his handmaid to wife, and she bore a daughter, and called her Zilpah, after the name of the village in which he had been taken captive. And next she bore Bilhah, saying, My daughter is eager after what is new, for immediately that she was born she was eager for the breast.

2. And since I was swift on my feet like a deer, my father Jacob appointed me for all errands and messages, and as a deer did he give me his blessing. For as the potter knoweth the vessel, what it containeth, and bringeth clay thereto, so also doth the Lord make the body in accordance with the spirit, and according to the capacity of the body doth He implant the spirit, and the one is not deficient from the other by a third part of a hair; for by weight, and measure, and rule is every creature of the Most High. And as the potter knoweth the use of each vessel, whereto it sufficeth, so also doth the Lord know the body, how far it is capable for goodness, and when it beginneth in evil; for there is no created thing and no thought which the Lord knoweth not, for He created every man after His own image. As man's strength, so also is his work; and as his mind, so also is his work; and as his purpose, so also is his doing; as his heart, so also is his mouth; as his eye, so also is his sleep; as his soul, so also is his word, either in the law of the Lord or in the law of Beliar. And as there is a division between light and darkness, between seeing and hearing, so also is there a division between man and man, and between woman and woman; neither is it to be said that there is any superiority in anything, either of the face or of other like things. For God made all things good in their order, the five senses in the head, and He joineth on the neck to the head, the hair also for comeliness, the heart moreover for understanding, the belly for the dividing of the stomach, the calamus for health, the liver for wrath, the gall for bitterness. the spleen for laughter, the reins for craftiness, the loins for power, the ribs for containing, the back for strength, and so forth. So then, my children, be ye orderly unto good things in the fear of God, and do nothing disorderly in scorn or out of

its due season. For if thou bid the eye to hear, it cannot; so neither in darkness can ye do the works of light.

3. Be ye not therefore eager to corrupt your doings through excess, or with empty words to deceive your souls; because if ye keep silence in purity of heart, ye shall be able to hold fast the will of God, and to cast away the will of the devil. Sun and moon and stars change not their order; so also ye shall not change the law of God in the disorderliness of your doings. Nations went astray, and forsook the Lord, and changed their order, and followed stones and stocks, following after spirits of error. But ye shall not be so, my children, recognising in the firmament, in the earth, and in the sea, and in all created things, the Lord who made them all, that ye become not as Sodom, which changed the order of its nature. in like manner also the Watchers changed the order of their nature, whom also the Lord cursed at the flood, and for their sakes made desolate the earth, that it should be uninhabited and fruitless.

4. These things I say, my children, for I have read in the holy writing of Enoch that ye yourselves also will depart from the Lord, walking according to all wickedness of the Gentiles, and ye will do according to all the iniquity of Sodom. And the Lord will bring captivity upon you, and there shall ye serve your enemies, and ye shall be covered with all affliction and tribulation, until the Lord shall have consumed you all. And after that ye shall have been diminished and made few, ye will return and acknowledge the Lord your God; and He will bring you back into your own land, according to His abundant mercy. And it shall be, after that they shall come into the land of their fathers, they will again forget the Lord and deal wickedly; and the Lord shall scatter them upon the face of all the earth, until the compassion of the Lord shall come, a Man working righteousness and showing mercy unto all them that are afar off, and them that are near.

5. For in the fortieth year of my life, I saw *in a vision* that the sun and the moon were standing still on the Mount of Olives, at the east of Jerusalem. And behold Isaac, the father of my father, saith to us, Run and lay hold of them, each one according to his strength; and he that seizeth them, his shall be the sun and the moon. And we all of us ran together, and Levi laid hold of the sun, and Judah outstripped the others and seized the moon, and they were both of them lifted up with them. And when Levi became as a sun, a certain young man gave to him twelve branches of palm; and Judah was bright as the moon, and under his feet were twelve rays. And Levi and Judah ran, and laid hold each of the other. And, lo, a bull upon the earth, having two great horns, and an eagle's wings upon his back; and we wished to seize him, but could not. For Joseph outstripped us, and took him, and ascended up with him on high. And I saw, for I was there, and behold a holy writing appeared to us saying: Assyrians, Medes, Persians, Elamites, Gelachaeans, Chaldeans, Syrians, shall possess in captivity the twelve tribes of Israel.

6. And again, after seven months, I saw our father Jacob standing by the sea of Jamnia, and we his sons were with him. And, behold, there came a ship sailing by, full of dried flesh, without sailors or pilot: and there was written upon the ship, Jacob. And our father saith to us, Let us embark on our ship. And when we had gone on board, there arose a vehement storm, and a tempest of mighty wind; and our father, who was holding the helm, flew away from us. And we, being tost with the tempest, were borne along over the: sea; and the ship was filled with water and beaten about with a mighty wave, so that it was well-nigh broken in pieces. And Joseph fled away upon a little boat, and we all were divided upon twelve boards, and Levi and Judah were together. We therefore all were scattered even unto afar off. Then Levi, girt about with sackcloth, prayed for us all unto the Lord. And when the storm ceased, immediately the ship reached the land, as though in peace. And, lo, Jacob our father came, and we rejoiced with one accord.

7. These two dreams I told to my father; and he said to me, These things must be fulfilled in their season, after that Israel hath endured many things. Then my father saith unto me, I believe that Joseph liveth, for I see always that the Lord numbereth him with you. And he said, weeping, Thou livest, Joseph, my child, and I behold thee not, and thou seest not Jacob that begat thee. And he caused us also to weep at these words of his, and I burned in my heart to declare that he had been sold, but I feared my brethren.

8. Behold, my children, I have shown unto you the last times, that all shall come to pass in Israel. Do ye also therefore charge your children that they be united to Levi and to Judah. For through Judah shall salvation arise unto Israel, and in Him shall Jacob be blessed. For through his tribe shall God be seen dwelling among men on the earth, to save the race of Israel, and He shall gather together the righteous from the Gentiles. If ye work that which is good, my children, both men and angels will bless you; and God will be glorified through you among the Gentiles, and the devil will flee from you, and the wild beasts will fear you, and the angels will cleave to you. For as if a man rear up a child well, he hath a kindly remembrance thereof; so also for a good work there is a good remembrance with God. But him who doeth not that which is good, men and angels shall curse and God will be dishonoured among the heathen through him, and the devil maketh him his own as his peculiar instrument, and every wild beast shall master him, and the Lord will hate him. For the commandments of the law are twofold, and through prudence must they be fulfilled. For there is a season for a man to embrace his wife, and a season to abstain therefrom for his prayer. So then there are two commandments; and unless they be done in due order, they bring about sin. So also is it with the other commandments. Be ye therefore wise in God, and prudent, understanding the order of the commandments. and the laws of every work, that the Lord may love you.

9. And when he had charged them with many such words, he exhorted them that they should remove his bones to Hebron, and should bury him with his fathers. And when he had eaten and drunken with a merry heart, he covered his face and died. And his sons did according to all things whatsoever Napthtali their father had charged them.

IX.-The Testament of Gad Concerning Hatred.

1. The record of the testament of Gad, what things he spake unto his sons, in the hundred and twenty-seventh year of his life, saying: I was the seventh son born to Jacob, and I was valiant in keeping the flocks. I guarded at night

the flock; and whenever the lion came, or wolf, or leopard, or bear, or any wild beast against the fold, I pursued it, and with my hand seizing its foot, and whirling it round, I stunned it, and hurled it over two furlongs, and so killed it. Now Joseph was feeding the flock with us for about thirty days, and being tender, he fell sick by reason of the heat. And he returned to Hebron to his father, who made him lie down near him, because he loved him. And Joseph told our father that the sons of Zilpah and Bilhah were slaying the best of the beasts, and devouring them without the knowledge of Judah and Reuben. For he saw that I delivered a lamb out of the mouth of the bear, and I put the bear to death; and the lamb I slew, being grieved concerning it that it could not live, and we ate it, and he told our father. And I was wroth with Joseph for that thing until the day that he was sold into Egypt. And the spirit of hatred was in me, and I wished not either to see Joseph or to hear him. And he rebuked us to our faces for having eaten of the flock without Judah. And whatsoever things he told our father, he believed him.

2. I confess now my sin, my children, that oftentimes I wished to kill him, because I hated him to the death, and there were in no wise in me bowels of mercy towards him. Moreover, I hated him yet more because of his dreams; and I would have devoured him out of the land of the living, even as a calf devoureth the grass from the earth. Therefore I and Judah sold him to the Ishmaelites for thirty pieces of gold, and ten of them we hid, and showed the twenty to our brethren: and so through my covetousness I was fully bent on his destruction. And the God of my fathers delivered him from my hands, that I should not work iniquity in Israel.

3. And now, my children, hearken to the words of truth to work righteousness, and all the law of the Most High, and not go astray through the spirit of hatred, for it is evil in all the doings of men. Whatsoever a man doeth, that doth the hater abhor: though he worketh the law of the Lord, he praiseth him not; though he feareth the Lord, and taketh pleasure in that which is righteous, he loveth him not: he dispraiseth the truth, he envieth him that ordereth his way aright, he delighteth in evil-speaking, he loveth arrogance, for hatred hath blinded his soul; even as I also looked on Joseph.

4. Take heed therefore, my children, of hatred; for it worketh iniquity against the Lord Himself: for it will not hear the words of His commandments concerning the loving of one's neighbour, and it sinneth against God. For if a brother stumble, immediately it wisheth to proclaim it to all men, and is urgent that he should be judged for it, and be punished and slain. And if it be a servant, it accuseth him to his master, and with all affliction it deviseth against him, if it be possible to slay him. For hatred worketh in envy, and it ever sickeneth with envy against them that prosper in well-doing, when it seeth or heareth thereof. For as love would even restore to life the dead, and would call back them that are condemned to die, so hatred would slay the living, and those that have offended in a small matter it would not suffer to live. For the spirit of hatred worketh together with Satan through hastiness of spirit in all things unto men's death; but the spirit of love worketh together with the law of God in long-suffering unto the salvation of men.

5. Hatred is evil, because it continually abideth with lying, speaking against the truth; and it maketh small things to be great, and giveth heed to darkness as to light, and calleth the sweet bitter, and teacheth slander, and war, and violence, and every excess of evil; and it filleth the heart with devilish poison. And these things I say to you from experience, my children, that ye may flee hatred, and cleave to the love of the Lord. Righteousness casteth out hatred, humility destroyeth hatred. For he that is just and humble is ashamed to do wrong, being reproved not of another, but of his own heart, because the Lord vieweth his intent: he speaketh not against any man, because the fear of the Most High overcometh hatred. For, fearing lest he should offend the Lord, he will not do any wrong to any man, no, not even in thought. These things I learnt at last, after that I had repented concerning Joseph. For true repentance after a godly sort destroyeth unbelief, and driveth away the darkness, and enlighteneth the eyes, and giveth knowledge to the soul, and guideth the mind to salvation; and those things which it hath not learnt from man, it knoweth through repentance. For God brought upon me a disease of the heart; and had not the prayers of Jacob my father intervened, it had hardly failed that my spirit had departed. For by what things a man transgresseth, by the same also is he punished. For in that my heart was set mercilessly against Joseph, in my heart too I suffered mercilessly, and was judged for eleven months, for so long a time as I had been envious against Joseph until he was sold.

6. And now, my children, love ye each one his brother, and put away hatred from your hearts, loving one another in deed, and in word, and in thought of the soul. For in the presence of our father I spake peaceably with Joseph; and when I had gone out, the spirit of hatred darkened my mind, and moved my soul to slay him. Love ye therefore one another from your hearts; and if a man sin against thee, tell him of it gently, and drive out the poison of hatred, and foster not guile in thy soul. And if he confess and repent, forgive him; and if he deny it, strive not with him, lest he swear, and thou sin doubly. Let not a stranger hear your secrets amid your striving, lest he hate and become thy enemy, and work great sin against thee; for ofttimes he will talk guilefully with thee, or evilly overreach thee, taking his poison from himself. Therefore, if he deny it, and is convicted and put to shame, and is silenced, do not tempt him on. For he who denieth repenteth, so that he no more doeth wrong against thee; yea also, he will honour thee, and fear thee, and be at peace with thee. But if he be shameless, and abideth in his wrongdoing, even then forgive him from the heart, and give the vengeance to God.

7. If a man prospereth more than you, be not grieved, but pray also for him, that he may have perfect prosperity. For perchance it is expedient for you thus; and if he be further exalted, be not envious, remembering that all flesh shall die: and offer praise to God, who giveth things good and profitable to all men. Seek out the judgments of the Lord, and so shall thy mind rest and be at peace. And though a man become rich by evil means, even as Esau the brother of my father, be not jealous; but wait for the end of the Lord. For either He taketh His benefits away from the wicked, or leaveth them still to the repentant, or to the unrepentant reserveth punishment for ever. For the poor man who is free from envy, giving thanks to the Lord in all things, is rich among all men, because he hath not evil

jealousy of men. Put away, therefore, hatred from your souls, and love one another with uprightness of heart.

8. And do ye also tell these things to your children, that they honour Judah and Levi, for from them shall the Lord raise up a Saviour to Israel. For I know that at the last your children shall depart from them, and shall walk in all wickedness, and mischief, and corruption before the Lord. And when he had rested for a little while, he said again to them, My children, obey your father, and bury me near to my fathers. And he drew up his feet, and fell asleep in peace. And after five years they carried him up, and laid him in Hebron with his fathers.

X.-The Testament of Asher Concerning Two Faces of Vice and Virtue.

1. The record of the testament of Asher, what things he spake to his sons in the hundred and twentieth year of his life. While he was still in health, he said to them: Hearken, ye children of Asher, to your father, and I will declare to you all that is right in the sight of God. Two ways hath God given to the sons of men, and two minds, and two doings, and two places, and two ends. Therefore all things are by twos, one corresponding to the other. There are two ways of good and evil, with which are the two minds in our breasts distinguishing them. Therefore if the soul take pleasure in good, all its actions are in righteousness; and though it sin, it straightway repenteth. For, having his mind set upon righteousness, and casting away maliciousness, he straightway overthroweth the evil, and uprooteth the sin. But if his mind turn aside in evil, all his doings are in maliciousness, and he driveth away the good, and taketh unto him the evil, and is ruled by Beliar; and even though he work what is good, he perverteth it in evil. For whenever he beginneth as though to do good, he bringeth the end of his doing to work evil, seeing that the treasure of the devil is filled with the poison of an evil spirit.

2. There is then, he saith, a soul which speaketh the good for the sake of the evil, and the end of the doing leadeth to mischief. There is a man who showeth no compassion upon him who serveth his turn in evil; and this thing hath two aspects, but the whole is evil, And there is a man that loveth him that worketh evil; he likewise dwelleth in evil, because he chooseth even to die in an evil cause for his sake: and concerning this it is clear that it hath two aspects, but the whole is an evil work. And though there is love, it is but wickedness concealing the evil, even as it beareth a name that seemeth good, but the end of the doing tendeth unto evil. Another stealeth, worketh unjustly, plundereth, defraudeth, and withal pitieth the poor: this, too, hath a twofold aspect, but the whole is evil. Defrauding his neighbour he provoketh God, and sweareth falsely against the Most High, and yet pitieth the poor: the Lord who commandeth the law he setteth at nought and provoketh, and refresheth the poor; he defileth the soul, and maketh gay the body; he killeth many, and he pitieth a few: and this, too, hath a twofold aspect. Another committeth adultery and fornication, and abstaineth from meats; yet in his fasting he worketh evil, and by his power and his wealth perverteth many, and out of his excessive wickedness worketh the commandments: this, too, hath a twofold aspect, but the whole is evil. Such men are as swine or

hares; for they are half clean, but in very deed are unclean. For God in the Heavenly Tablets hath thus declared.

3. Do not ye therefore, my children, wear two faces like unto them, of goodness and of wickedness; but cleave unto goodness only, for in goodness doth God rest, and men desire it. From wickedness flee away, destroying the devil by your good works; for they that are double-faced serve not God, but their own lusts, so that they may please Beliar and men like unto themselves.

4. For good men, even they that are single of face, though they be thought by them that are double-faced to err, arc just before God. For many in killing the wicked do two works, an evil by a good; but the whole is good, because he hath uprooted and destroyed that which is evil. One man hateth him that showeth mercy, and doeth wrong to the adulterer and the thief: this, too, is double-faced, but the whole work is good, because he followeth the Lord's example, in that he receiveth not that which seemeth good with that which is really bad. Another desireth not to see good days with them that riot, lest he defile his mouth and pollute his soul: this, too, is double-faced, but the whole is good, for such men are like to stags and to hinds, because in a wild condition they seem to be unclean, but they are altogether clean; because they walk in a zeal for God, and abstain from what God also hateth and forbiddeth by His commandments, and they ward off the evil from the good.

5. Ye see therefore, my children, how that there are two in all things, one against the other, and the one is hidden by the other. Death succeedeth to life, dishonour to glory, night to day, and darkness to light; and all things are under the day, and just things trader life: wherefore also everlasting life awaiteth death. Nor may it be said that truth is a lie, nor right wrong; for all truth is under the light, even as all things are under God. All these things I proved in my life, and I wandered not from the truth of the Lord, and I searched out the commandments of the Most High, walking with singleness of face according to all my strength unto that which is good.

6. Take heed therefore ye also, my children, to the commandments of the Lord, following the truth with singleness of face, for they that are double-faced receive twofold punishment. Hate the spirits of error, which strive against men. Keep the law of the Lord, and give not heed unto evil as unto good; but look unto the thing that is good indeed, and keep it in all commandments of the Lord, having your conversation unto Him, and resting in Him: for the ends at which men aim do show their righteousness, and know the angels of the Lord from the angels of Satan. For if the soul depart troubled, it is tormented by the evil spirit which also it served in lusts and evil works; but if quietly and with joy it hath known the angel of peace, it shall comfort him in life.

7. Become not, my children, as Sodom, which knew not the angels of the Lord, and perished for ever, For I know that ye will sin, and ye shall be delivered into the hands of your enemies, and your land shall be made desolate, and ye shall be scattered unto the four corners of the earth. And ye shall be set at nought in the Dispersion as useless water, until the Most High shall visit the earth; and He shall come as man, with men eating and drinking, and in peace breaking the

head of the dragon through water. He shall save Israel and all nations, God speaking in the person of man. Therefore tell ye these things to your children, that they disobey Him not. For I have read in the Heavenly Tablets that in very deed ye will disobey Him, and act ungodly against Him, not giving heed to the law of God, but to the commandments of men. Therefore shall ye be scattered as Gad and as Dan my brethren, who shall know not their own lands, tribe, and tongue. But the Lord will gather you together in faith through the hope of His tender mercy, for the sake of Abraham, and Isaac, and Jacob.

8. And when he had said these things unto them, he charged them, saying: Bury me in Hebron. And he fell into a peaceful sleep, and died; and after this his sons did as he had charged them, and they carried him up and buried him with his fathers.

XI.-The Testament of Joseph Concerning Sobriety.

1. The record of the testament of Joseph. When he was about to die he called his sons and his brethren together, and said to them: My children and brethren, hearken to Joseph the beloved of Israel; give ear, my sons, unto your father. I have seen in my life envy and death, and I wandered not in the truth of the Lord. These my brethren hated me, and the Lord loved me: they wished to slay me, and the God of my fathers guarded me: they let me down into a pit, and the Most High brought me up again: I was sold for a slave, and the Lord made me free: I was taken into captivity, and His strong hand succoured me: I was kept in hunger, and the Lord Himself nourished me: I was alone, and God comforted me: I was sick, and the Most High visited me: I was in prison, and the Saviour showed favour unto me; in bonds, and He released me; amid slanders, and He pleaded my cause; amid bitter words of the Egyptians, and He rescued me; amid envy and guile, and He exalted me.

2. And thus Potipha the chief cook of Pharaoh entrusted to me his house, and I struggled against a shameless woman, urging me to transgress with her; but the God of Israel my father guarded me from the burning flame. I was cast into prison, I was beaten, I was mocked; and the Lord granted me to find pity in the sight of the keeper of the prison. For He will in no wise forsake them that fear Him, neither in darkness, nor in bonds, nor in tribulations, nor in necessities. For not as man is God ashamed, nor as the son of man is He afraid, nor as one that is earth-born is He weak, or can He be thrust aside; but in all places is He at hand, and in divers ways doth He comfort, departing for a little to try the purpose of the soul. In ten temptations He showed me approved, and in all of them I endured; for endurance is a mighty charm, and patience giveth many good things.

3. How often did the Egyptian threaten me with death! How often did she give me over to punishment, and then call me back, and threaten me when I would not company with her! And she said to me, Thou shalt be lord of me, and all that is mine, if thou wilt give thyself unto me, and thou shall be as our master. Therefore I remembered the words of the fathers of my father Jacob, and I entered into my chamber and prayed unto the Lord; and I fasted in those seven years, and I appeared to my master as one living delicately, for they that fast for God's sake receive beauty of face. And if one gave me wine, I drank it not; and I fasted for three days, and took my food and gave it to the poor and sick. And I sought the Lord early, and wept for the Egyptian woman of Memphis, for very unceasingly did she trouble me, and at night she came to me under the pretence of visiting me; and at first, because she had no male child, she feigned to count me as a son. And I prayed unto the Lord, and she bare a male child; therefore for a thee she embraced me as a son, and I knew it not. Last of all, she sought to draw me into fornication. And when I perceived it, I sorrowed even unto death; and when she had gone out I came to myself, and I lamented for her many days, because I saw her guile and her deceit. And I declared unto her the words of the Most High, if haply she would turn from her evil lust.

4. How often has she fawned upon me with words as a holy man, with guile in her talk, praising my chastity before her husband, while desiring to destroy me when we were alone. She lauded me openly as chaste, and in secret she said unto me, Fear not my husband; for he is persuaded concerning thy chastity, so that even should one tell him concerning us he would in no wise believe. For all these things I lay upon the ground in sackcloth, and I besought God that the Lord would deliver me from the Egyptian. And when she prevailed nothing, she came again to me under the plea of instruction, that she might know the word of the Lord. And she said unto me, If thou wiliest that I should leave my idols, be persuaded by me, and I will persuade my husband to depart from his idols, and we will walk in the law of thy Lord. And I said unto her, The Lord willeth not that those who reverence Him should be in uncleanness, nor doth He take pleasure in them that commit adultery. And she held her peace, longing to accomplish her evil desire. And I gave myself yet more to fasting and prayer, that the Lord should deliver me from her.

5. And again at another time she said unto me, If thou wilt not commit adultery, I will kill my husband, and so will I lawfully take thee to be my husband. I therefore, when I heard this, rent my garment, and said, Woman, reverence the Lord, and do not this evil deed, lest thou be utterly destroyed; for I will declare thy ungodly thought unto all men. She therefore, being afraid, besought that I would declare to no one her wickedness. And she departed, soothing me with gifts, and sending to me every delight of the sons of men.

6. And she sendeth to me food sprinkled with enchantments. And when the eunuch who brought it came, I looked up and beheld a terrible man giving me with the dish a sword, and I perceived that her scheme was for the deception of my soul. And when he had gone out I wept, nor did I taste that or any other of her food. So then after one day she came to me and observed the food, and said unto me, What is this; that thou hast not eaten of the food? And I said unto her, It is because thou filledst it with death; and how saidst thou, I come not near to idols but to the Lord alone? Now therefore know that the God of my father hath revealed unto me by an angel thy wickedness, and I have kept it to convict thee, if haply thou mayest see it and repent. But that thou mayest learn that the wickedness of the ungodly hath no power over them that

reverence God in chastity, I took it and ate it before her, saying, The God of my fathers and the Angel of Abraham shall be with me. And she fell upon her face at my feet, and wept; and I raised her up and admonished her, and she promised to do this iniquity no more.

7. But because her heart was set upon me to commit lewdness, she sighed, and her countenance fell. And when her husband saw her, he said unto her, Why is thy countenance fallen? And she said, I have a pain at my heart, and the groanings of my spirit do oppress me; and so he comforted her who was not sick. Then she rushed in to me while her husband was yet without, and said unto me, I will hang myself, or cast myself into a well or over a cliff, if thou wilt not consent unto me. And when I saw the spirit of Beliar was troubling her, I prayed unto the Lord, and said unto her, Why art thou troubled and disturbed, blinded in sins? Remember that if thou killest thyself, Sethon, the concubine of thy husband, thy rival, will beat thy children, and will destroy thy memorial from off the earth. And she said unto me, Lo then thou lovest me; this alone is sufficient for me, that thou carest for my life and my children: I have expectation that I shall enjoy my desire. And she knew not that because of my God I spake thus, and not because of her. For if a man hath fallen before the passion of a wicked desire, then by that hath he become enslaved, even as also was she. And if he hear any good thing with regard to the passion whereby he is vanquished, he receiveth it unto his wicked desire.

8. I declare unto you, my children, that it was about the sixth hour when she departed from me; and I knelt before the Lord all that day, and continued all the night; and about dawn I rose up weeping, and praying for a release from the Egyptian. At last, then, she laid hold of my garments, forcibly dragging me to have connection with her. When, therefore, I saw that in her madness she was forcibly holding my garments, I fled away naked. And she falsely accused me to her husband, and the Egyptian cast me into the prison in his house; and on the morrow, having scourged me, the Egyptian sent me into the prison in his house. When, therefore, I was in fetters, the Egyptian woman fell sick from her vexation, and listened to me how I sang praises unto the Lord while I was in the abode of darkness, and with glad voice rejoiced and glorified my God only because by a pretext I had been rid of the Egyptian woman.

9. How often hath she sent unto me, saying, Consent to fulfil my desire, and I will release thee from thy bonds, and I will free time from the darkness! And not even in thoughts did I incline unto her. For God loveth him who in a den of darkness fasteth with chastity, rather than him who in secret chambers liveth delicately without restraint. And whosoever liveth in chastity, and desireth also glory, and if the Most High knoweth that it is expedient for him, He bestoweth this also upon him, even as upon me. How often, though she were sick, did she come down to me at unlooked-for times, and listened to my voice as I prayed! And when I heard her groanings I held my peace. For when I was in her house she was wont to bare her arms, and breasts, and legs, that I might fall before her; for she was very beautiful, splendidly adorned for my deception. And the Lord guarded me from her devices.

10. Ye see therefore, my children, how great things patience worketh, and prayer with fasting. And if ye therefore follow after sobriety and purity in patience and humility of heart, the Lord will dwell among you, because He loveth sobriety. And wheresoever the Most High dwelleth, even though a man fall into envy, or slavery, or slander, the Lord who dwelleth in him, for his sobriety's sake not only delivereth him from evil, but also exalteth and glorifieth him, even as me. For in every way the man is guarded, whether in deed, or in word, or in thought. My brethren know how my father loved me, and I was not exalted in my heart; although I was a child, I had the fear of God in my thoughts. For I knew that all things should pass away, and I kept myself within bounds, and I honoured my brethren; and through fear of them I held my peace when I was sold, and revealed not my family to the Ishmaelites, that I was the son of Jacob, a great man and a mighty.

11. Do ye also, therefore, have the fear of God in your works, and honour your brethren. For every one who worketh the law of the Lord shall be loved by Him. And when I came to the Indocolpitae with the Ishmaelites, they asked me, and I said that I was a slave from their house, that I might not put my brethren to shame. And the eldest of them said unto me, Thou art not a slave, for even thy appearance doth make it manifest concerning thee. And he threatened me even unto death. But I said that I was their slave. Now when we came into Egypt, they strove concerning me. which of them should buy me and take me. Therefore it secured good to all that I should remain in Egypt with a merchant of their trade, until they should return bringing merchandise. And the Lord gave me favour in the eyes of the merchant, and he entrusted unto me his house. And the Lord blessed him by my means, and increased him in silver and gold, and I was with him three months and five days.

12. About that time the Memphian wife of Potiphar passed by with great pomp, and cast her eyes upon me, because her eunuchs told her concerning me. And she told her husband concerning the merchant, that he had become rich by means of a young Hebrew, saying, And they say that men have indeed stolen him out of the land of Canaan. Now therefore execute judgment with him, and take away the youth to be thy steward; so shall the God of the Hebrews bless thee, for grace from heaven is upon him.

13. And Potiphar was persuaded by her words, and commanded the merchant to be brought, and said unto him, What is this that I hear, that thou stealest souls out of the land of the Hebrews, and sellest them for slaves? The merchant therefore fell upon his face, and besought him, saying, I beseech thee, my lord, I know not what thou sayest. And he said, Whence then is thy Hebrew servant? And he said, The Ishmaelites entrusted him to me until they should return. And he believed him not, but commanded him to be stripped and beaten. And when he persisted, Potiphar said, Let the youth be brought. And when I was brought in, I did obeisance to the chief of the eunuchs-for he was third in rank with Pharaoh, being chief of all the eunuchs, and having wives and children and concubines. And he took me apart from him, and said unto me, Art thou a slave or free? And I said, A slave. And he said unto me, Whose slave art thou? And I said unto him, The Ishmaelites' And again he said unto me, How becamest

thou their slave? And I said, They bought me out of the land of Canaan. And he believed me not, and said, Thou liest: and he commanded me to be stripped and beaten.

14. Now the Memphian woman was looking through a window while I was being beaten, and she sent unto her husband, saying, Thy judgment is unjust; for thou dost even punish a free man who hath been stolen, as though he were a transgressor. And when I gave no other answer though I was beaten, he commanded that we should be kept in guard, until, said he, the owners of the boy shall come. And his wife said unto him, Wherefore dost thou detain in captivity this noble child, who ought rather to be set at liberty, and wait upon thee? For she wished to see me in desire of sin, and I was ignorant concerning all these things. Then said he to his wife, It is not the custom of the Egyptians to take away that which belongeth to others before proof is given. This he said concerning the merchant, and concerning me, that I must be imprisoned.

15. Now, after four and twenty days came the Ishmaelites; and having heard that Jacob my father was mourning because of me, they said unto me, How is it that thou saidst that thou wept a slave? and lo, we have learnt that thou art the son of a mighty man in the land of Canaan, and thy father grieveth for thee in sackcloth. And again I would have wept, but I restrained myself, that I should not put my brethren to shame. And I said, I know not, I am a slave. Then they take counsel to sell me, that I should not be found in their hands. For they feared Jacob, lest he should work upon them a deadly vengeance. For it had been heard that he was mighty with the Lord and with men. Then said the merchant unto them, Release me from the judgment of Potiphar. They therefore came and asked for me, saying, He was bought by us with money, And he sent us away.

16. Now the Memphian woman pointed me out to her husband, that he should buy me; for I hear, said she, that they are selling him. And she sent a eunuch to the Ishmaelites, and asked them to sell me; and since he was not willing to traffic with them, he returned. So when the eunuch had made trial of them, he made known to his mistress that they asked a large price for their slave. And she sent another eunuch, saying, Even though they demand two minae of gold, take heed not to spare the gold; only buy the boy, and bring him hither. And he gave them eighty pieces of gold for me, and told his mistress that a hundred had been given for me. And when I saw it I held my peace, that the eunuch should not be punished.

17. Ye see, my children, what great things I endured that I should not put my brethren to shame. Do ye also love one another, and with long-suffering hide ye one another's faults. For God delighteth in the unity of brethren, and in the purpose of a heart approved unto love. And when my brethren came into Egypt, and learnt that I returned their money unto them, and upbraided them not, yea, that I even comforted them, and after the death of Jacob I loved them more abundantly, and all things whatsoever he commanded I did very abundantly, then they marvelled. For I suffered them not to be afflicted even unto the smallest matter; and all that was in my hand I gave unto them. Their children were my children, and my children were as their servants; their life was my life, and all their suffering was my suffering, and all their sickness was my infirmity. My land was their land, my counsel their counsel, and I exalted not myself among them in arrogance because of my worldly glory, but I was among them as one of the least.

18. If ye also therefore walk in the commandments of the Lord, my children, He will exalt you there, and will bless you with good things for ever and ever. And if any one seeketh to do evil unto you, do ye by well-doing pray for him, and ye shall be redeemed of the Lord from all evil. For, behold, ye see that through long-suffering I took unto wife even the daughter of my master. And a hundred talents of gold were given me with her; for the Lord made them to serve me. And He gave me also beauty as a flower above the beautiful ones of Israel; and He preserved me unto old age in strength and in beauty, because I was like in all things to Jacob.

19. Hear ye also, my children, the visions which I saw. There were twelve deer feeding, and the nine were divided and scattered in the land, likewise also the three. And I saw that from Judah was born a virgin wearing a linen garment, and from her went forth a Lamb, without spot, and on His left hand there was as it were a lion; and all the beasts rushed against Him, and the lamb overcame them, and destroyed them, and trod them under foot. And because of Him the angels rejoiced, and men, and all the earth. And these things shall take place in their season, in the last days. Do ye therefore, my children, observe the commandments of the Lord, and honour Judah and Levi; for from them shall arise unto you the Lamb of God, by grace saving all the Gentiles and Israel. For His kingdom is an everlasting kingdom, which shall not be shaken; but my kingdom among yogi shall come to an end as a watcher's hammock, which after the summer will not appear.

20. I know that after my death the Egyptians will afflict you, but God will undertake your cause, and will bring you into that which He promised to your fathers. But carry ye up my bones with you; for when my bones are taken up, the Lord will be with you in light, and Beliar shall be in darkness with the Egyptians. And carry ye up Zilpah your mother, and lay her near Bilhah, by the hippodrome, by the side of Rachel. And when he had said these things, he stretched out his feet, and slept the long sleep. And all Israel bewailed him, and all Egypt, with a great lamentation. For he felt even for the Egyptians even as his own members, and showed them kindness, aiding them in every work, and counsel, and matter.

XII.-The Testament of Benjamin Concerning a Pure Mind.

1. The record of the words of Benjamin, which he set forth to his sons, after he had lived a hundred and twenty years. And he kissed them, and said: As Isaac was born to Abraham in his hundredth year, so also was I to Jacob. Now since Rachel died in giving me birth, I had no milk; therefore I was suckled by Bilhah her handmaid. For Rachel remained barren for twelve years after that she had borne Joseph: and she prayed the Lord with fasting twelve days, and she conceived and bare me. For our father loved Rachel dearly, and prayed that he might see two sons born from her: therefore was I called the son of days, which is Benjamin.

2. When therefore I went into Egypt, and Joseph my brother recognised me, he said unto me, What did they tell my father in that they sold me? And I said unto him, They dabbled thy coat with blood and sent it, and said, Look if this is the coat of thy son. And he said to me, Even so, brother; for when the Ishmaelites took me, one of them stripped off my coat, and gave me a girdle, and scourged me, and bade me run. And as he went away to hide my garment, a lion met him, and slew him; and so his fellows were afraid, and sold me to their companions.

3. Do ye also therefore, my children, love the Lord God of heaven, and keep His commandments, and be followers of the good and holy man Joseph; and let your mind be unto good, even as ye know me. He that hath his mind good seeth all things rightly. Fear ye the Lord, and love your neighbour; and even though the spirits of Beliar allure you into all troublous wickedness, yet shall no troublous wickedness have dominion over you, even as it bad not over Joseph my brother. How many men wished to slay him, and God shielded him! For he that feareth God and loveth his neighbour cannot be smitten by Beliar's spirit of the air, being shielded by the fear of God; nor can he be ruled over by the device of men or of beasts, for he is aided by the love of the Lord which he hath towards his neighbour. For he even besought our father Jacob that he would pray for our brethren, that the Lord would not impute to them the evil that they devised concerning Joseph. And thus Jacob cried out, My child Joseph, thou hast prevailed over the bowels of thy father Jacob. And he embraced him, and kissed him for two hours, saying, In thee shall be fulfilled the prophecy of heaven concerning the Lamb of God, even the Saviour of the world, that spotless shall He be delivered up for transgressors, and sinless shall He be put to death for ungodly men in the blood of the covenant, for the salvation of the Gentiles and of Israel, and shall destroy Beliar, and them that serve him.

4. Know ye, my children, the end of the good man? Be followers of his compassion in a good mind, that ye also may wear crowns of glory. The good man hath not a dark eye; for he showeth mercy to all men, even though they be sinners, even though they devise evil concerning him. So he that doeth good overcometh the evil, being shielded by Him that is good; and he loveth the righteous as his own soul. If any one is glorified, he envieth him not; if any one is enriched, he is not jealous; if any one is valiant, he praiseth him; he trusteth and laudeth him that is sober-minded; he showeth mercy to the poor; he is kindly disposed toward the weak; he singeth the praises of God; as for him who hath the fear of God, he protecteth him as with a shield; him that loveth God he aideth; him that rejecteth the Most High he admonisheth and turneth back; and him that hath the grace of a good spirit, he loveth even as his own soul.

5. If ye have a good mind, my children, then will both wicked men be at peace with you, and the profligate will reverence you and turn unto good; and the covetous shall not only cease from their inordinate desire, but shall even give the fruits of their covetousness to them that are afflicted. If ye do well, even the unclean spirits shall flee from you; yea, the very beasts shall flee from you in dread. For where the reverence for good works is present unto the mind, darkness fleeth away from him. For if any one is

injurious to a holy man, he repenteth; for the holy man showeth pity on his reviler, and holdeth his peace. And if any one betray a righteous soul, and the righteous man, though praying, be humbled for a little while, yet not long after he appeareth far more glorious, even as was Joseph my brother.

6. The mind of the good man is not in the power of the deceit of the spirit of Beliar, for the angel of peace guideth his soul. He gazeth not passionately on corruptible things, nor gathereth together riches unto desire of pleasure; he delighteth not in pleasure, he hurteth not his neighbour, be pampereth not himself with food, he erreth not in the pride of his eyes, for the Lord is his portion. The good mind admitted not the glory and dishonour of men, neither knoweth it any guile or lie, fighting or reviling; for the Lord dwelleth in him and lighteth up his soul, and he rejoiceth towards all men at every time. The good mind hath not two tongues, of blessing and of cursing, of insult and of honour, of sorrow and of joy, of quietness and of trouble, of hypocrisy and of truth, of poverty and of wealth; but it hath one disposition, pure and un-corrupt, concerning all men. It hath no double sight, nor double hearing; for in everything which he doeth, or speaketh, or seeth, he knoweth that the Lord watcheth his soul, and he cleanseth his mind that he be not condemned by God and men. But of Beliar every work is twofold, and hath no singleness.

7. Flee ye therefore, my children, the evil-doing of Beliar; for it giveth a sword to them that obeyeth, and the sword is the mother of seven evils. First the mind conceiveth through Beliar, and first there is envy; secondly, desperation; thirdly, tribulation; fourthly, captivity; fifthly, neediness; sixthly, trouble; seventhly, desolation. Therefore also Cain is delivered over to seven vengeances by God, for in every hundred years the Lord brought one plague upon him. Two hundred years he suffered, and in the nine hundredth year he was brought to desolation at the flood, for Abel his righteous brother's sake. In seven hundred years was Cain judged, and Lamech in seventy times seven; because for ever those who are likened unto Cain in envy unto hatred of brethren shall be judged with the same punishment.

8. Do ye also therefore, my children, flee ill-doing, envy, and hatred of brethren, and cleave to goodness and love. He that hath a pure mind in love, looketh not after a woman unto fornication; for he hath no defilement in his heart, because the Spirit of God resteth in him. For as the sun is not defiled by shining over dung and mire, but rather drieth up both and driveth away the ill smell: so also the pure mind, constrained among the defilements of the earth, rather edifieth, and itself suffereth no defilement.

9. Now I suppose, from the words of the righteous Enoch, that there will be also evil-doings among you: for ye will commit fornication with the fornication of Sodom, and shall perish all save a few, and will multiply inordinate lusts with women; and the kingdom of the Lord shall not be among you, for forthwith He will take it away. Nevertheless the temple of God shall be built in your portion, and shall be glorious among you. For He shall take it, and the twelve tribes shall be gathered together there, and all the Gentiles, until the Most High shall send forth His salvation in the visitation of His only-begotten one. And He shall enter into

the front of the temple, and there shall the Lord be treated with outrage, and He shall be lifted up upon a tree. And the veil of the temple shall be rent, and the Spirit of God shall descend upon the Gentiles as fire poured forth. And He shall arise from the grave, and shall ascend from earth into heaven: and I know how lowly He all be upon the earth, and how glorious in the heaven.

10. Now when Joseph was in Egypt, I longed to see his visage and the form of his countenance; and through the prayers of Jacob my father I saw him, while awake in the daytime, in his full and perfect shape. Know ye therefore, my children, that I am dying. Work therefore truth and righteousness each one with his neighbour, and judgment unto faithful doing, and keep the law of the Lord and His commandments; for these things do I teach you instead of all inheritance. Do ye also therefore give them to your children for an everlasting possession; for so did both Abraham, and Isaac, and Jacob. All these things they gave us for an inheritance, saying, Keep the commandments of God until the Lord shall reveal His salvation to all nations. Then shall ye see Enoch, Noah, and Shem, and Abraham, and Isaac, and Jacob, arising on the right hand in gladness. Then shall we also arise, each one over our tribe, worshipping the King of heaven, who appeared upon the earth in the form of a man of humility. And as many as believed on Him on the earth shall rejoice with Him; and then shall all men arise, some unto glory and some unto shame. And the Lord shall judge Israel first, even for the wrong they did unto Him; for when He appeared as a deliverer, God in the flesh, they believed Him not. And then shall He judge all the Gentiles, as many as believed Him not when He appeared upon earth. And He shall reprove Israel among the chosen ones of the Gentiles, even as He reproved Esau among the Midianites, who deceived their brethren, so that they fell into fornication and idolatry; and they were alienated from God, and became as they that were no children in the portion of them that fear the Lord. But if ye walk in holiness in the presence of the Lord, ye shall dwell in hope again in me, and all Israel shall be gathered unto the Lord.

11. And I shall no longer be called a ravening wolf on account of your ravages, but a worker of the Lord, distributing food to them that work what is good. And one shall rise up from my seed in the latter times, beloved of the Lord, hearing upon the earth His voice, enlightening with new knowledge all the Gentiles, bursting in upon Israel for salvation with the light of knowledge, and tearing it away from it like a wolf, and giving it to the synagogue of the Gentiles. And until the consummation of the ages shall he be in the synagogues of the Gentiles, and among their rulers, as a strain of music in the mouth of all; and he shall be inscribed in the holy books, both his work and his word, and he shall be a chosen one of God for ever; and because of him my father Jacob instructed me, saying, He shall fill up that which lacketh of thy tribe.

12. And when he finished his words, he said: I charge you, my children, carry up my bones out of Egypt, and bury me at Hebron, near my fathers. So Benjamin died a hundred and twenty-five years old, in a good old age, and they placed him in a coffin. And in the ninety-first year of the departure of the children of Israel from Egypt, they and their brethren brought up the bones of their fathers secretly in a place which is called Canaan; and they buried them in Hebron, by the feet of their fathers. And they returned from the land of Canaan, and dwelt in Egypt until the day of their departing from the land of Egypt.

CONSUMMATION OF THOMAS THE APOSTLE

At the command of King Misdeus the blessed Apostle Thomas was cast into prison; and he said: I glorify God, and I shall preach the word to the prisoners, so that all rejoiced at his presence. When, therefore, Juzanes the king's son, and Tertia his mother, and Mygdonia, and Markia, had become believers, but were not yet thought worthy of baptism, they took it exceedingly ill that the blessed one had been shut up. And having come to the prison, and given much money to the jailor, they went in to him. And he, seeing them, was glad, and glorified the Lord, and blessed them. And they entreated and begged the seal in the Lord, a beautiful young man having appeared to them in a dream, and ordered the apostle into the house of Juzanes.

And again the beautiful young man coming to them and Thomas, bade them do this on the coming night. And he ran before them, and gave them light on the way, and without noise opened the doors that had been secured, until all the mystery was completed. And having made them communicate in the Eucharist, and having talked much with them, and confirmed them in the faith, and commended them to the Lord, he went forth thence, leaving the women, and again went to be shut up. And they grieved and wept because Misdeus the king was to kill him.

And Thomas went and found the jailors fighting, and saying: What wrong have we done to that sorcerer, that, availing himself of his magic art, he has opened the doors of the prison, and wishes to set all the prisoners free? But let us go and let the king know about his wife and his son. And when he came they stripped him, and girded him with a girdle; and thus they stood before the king.

And Misdeus said to him: Art thou a slave, or a freeman? And Thomas answered and said to him: I am not a slave, and thou hast no power against me at all. And how, said Misdeus, hast thou run away and come to this country? And Thomas said: I came here that I might save many, and that I might by thy hands depart from this body. Misdeus says to him: Who is thy master? and what is his name? and of what country, and of whom is he? My Lord, says Thomas, is my Master and thine, being the Lord of heaven and earth. And Misdeus said: What is he called? And Thomas said: Thou canst not know His true name at this time; but I tell thee the name that has been given Him for a season—Jesus the Christ. And Misdeus said: I have not been in a hurry to destroy thee, but have restrained myself; but thou hast made a display of works, so that thy sorceries have been heard of in all the country. But now this will I do, that thy sorceries may also perish with thee, that our nation may be purified from them. And Thomas said: Dost thou call these things which will follow me sorceries? They shall never be removed from the people here.

And while these things were saying, Misdeus was considering in what manner he should put him to death; for he was afraid of the multitude standing round, many, even some of the chief men, having believed in

him. And he arose, and took Thomas outside of the city; and a few soldiers accompanied him with their arms. And the rest of the multitude thought that the king was wishing to learn something from him; and they stood and observed him closely. And when they had gone forth three stadia, he delivered him to four soldiers, and to one of the chief officers, and ordered them to take him up into the mountain and spear him; but he himself returned to the city.

And those present ran to Thomas, eager to rescue him; but he was led away by the soldiers who were with him. For there were two on each side having hold of him, because of sorcery. And the chief officer held him by the hand, and led him with honour. And at the same time the blessed apostle said: O the hidden mysteries of Thee, O Lord! for even to the close of life is fulfilled in us the riches of Thy grace, which does not allow us to be without feeling as to the body. For, behold, four have laid hold of me, and one leads me, since I belong to One, to whom I am going always invisibly. But now I learn that my Lord also, since He was a stranger, to whom I am going, who also is always present with me invisibly, was struck by one; but I am struck by four. And when they came to that place where they were to spear him, Thomas spoke thus to those spearing him: Hear me now, at least, when I am departing from my body; and let not your eyes be darkened in understanding, nor your ears shut up so as not to hear those things in which you have believed the God whom I preach, after being delivered in your souls from rashness; and behave in a manner becoming those who are free, being void of human glory, and live the life towards God. And he said to Juzanes: Son of an earthly king, but servant of Jesus Christ, give what is due to those who are to fulfil the command of Misdeus, in order that I may go apart from them and pray. And Juzanes having paid the soldiers, the apostle betook himself to prayer; and it was as follows:—

My Lord, and my God, and hope, and leader, and guide in all countries, I follow Thee along with all that serve Thee, and do Thou guide me this day on my way to Thee. Let no one take my soul, which Thou hast given to me. Let not publicans and beggars look upon me, nor let serpents slander me, and let not the children of the dragon hiss at me. Behold, I have fulfilled Thy work, and accomplished what Thou gavest me to do. I have become a slave, that I might receive freedom from Thee; do then give it to me, and make me perfect. And this I say not wavering, but that they may hear who need to hear. I glorify Thee in all, Lord and Master; for to Thee is due glory for ever. Amen.

And when he had prayed, he said to the soldiers: Come and finish the work of him that sent you. And the four struck him at once, and killed him. And all the brethren wept, and wrapped him up in beautiful shawls, and many linen cloths, and laid him in the tomb in which of old the kings used to be buried.

And Syphor and Juzanes did not go to the city, but spent the whole day there, and waited during the night. And Thomas appeared to them, and said: I am not there; why do you sit watching? for I have gone up, and received the things I hoped for; but rise up and walk, and after no long time you shall be brought beside me. And Misdeus and Charisius greatly afflicted Tertia and Mygdonia, but did not persuade them to abandon their opinions. And Thomas appeared, and said to them: Forget not the former things, for the holy and sanctifying Jesus Himself will aid you. And Misdeus and Charisius, when they could not persuade them not to be of this opinion, granted them their own will. And all the brethren assembled together, for the blessed one had made Syphorus a presbyter in the mountain, and Juzanius a deacon, when he was led away to die. And the Lord helped them, and increased the faith by means of them.

And after a long time, it happened that one of the sons of Misdeus was a demoniac; and the demon being stubborn, no one was able to heal him. And Misdeus considered, and said: I shall go and open the tomb, and take a bone of the apostle's body, and touch my son with it, and I know that he will be healed. And he went to do what he had thought of. And the blessed apostle appeared to him, and said: Thou didst not believe in me when alive; how wilt thou believe in me when I am dead? Fear not. Jesus Christ is kindly disposed to thee, through His great clemency. And Misdeus, when he did not find the bones (for one of the brethren had taken them, and carried them into the regions of the West), took some dust from where the bones had lain, and touched his son with it, and said: I believe in Thee, Jesus, now when he has left me who always afflicts men, that they may not look to Thy light which giveth understanding, O Lord, kind to men. And his son being healed in this manner, he met with the rest of the brethren who were under the rule of Syphorus, and entreated the brethren to pray for him, that he might obtain mercy from our Lord Jesus Christ; to whom be glory for ever and ever. Amen.

THE BOOK OF GIANTS

4Q203, 1Q23, 2Q26, 4Q530-532, 6Q8

Introduction and Commentary

The patriarch Enoch was as well-known to the ancients as he is obscure to contemporary Bible readers. Besides noting his age (365 years), the book of Genesis mentions only that he "walked with God," and subsequently "he was not, because God took him" (Gen. 5:24). This exalted manner of life and mysterious departure made Enoch a figure of considerable fascination, and a cycle of legends grew around him.

Many of these legends about Enoch were compiled in ancient times into several lengthy anthologies. The most significant and oldest of these is known simply as The Book of Enoch, comprising over one hundred chapters. This text survives in its entirety (although only in the Ethiopic language) and forms an important source for the religious thought of Judaism in the last few centuries B.C.E. Notably, remnants of several nearly complete copies of The Book of Enoch in Aramaic were found among the Dead Sea Scrolls, indicating that the collectors of these scrolls considered it a text of vital importance. All but one of the five major components of the Ethiopic anthology have been found among the scrolls. Even more intriguing is the fact that additional, previously unknown or little-known texts about Enoch were discovered at Qumran. The most significant of these is The Book of Giants.

Enoch lived before the Flood, during a time when the world, in ancient imagination, was very different. Human beings lived much longer; for instance, Enoch's son Methuselah reached the age of 969 years. Another difference was that angels and humans interacted freely—so freely, in fact, that some angels fathered children with human females. This fact is reported neutrally in Genesis (6:1-4), but other narratives view this episode as the source of the corruption that necessitated the punitive Flood. According to The Book of Enoch, the mingling of angel and human was actually the idea of Shernihaza, the leader of the evil angels, who lured 200 others to cohabit with women. The offspring of these unnatural unions were giants 450 feet tall. The wicked angels and the giants began to oppress the human population and teach them to do evil. For this reason, God decided to imprison the angels until the final judgment and to destroy the earth with a flood. Enoch's efforts to intercede with heaven on behalf of the fallen angels were unsuccessful (1 Enoch 6-16).

The Book of Giants retells part of this story and elaborates on the exploits of the giants, particularly the two children of Shemihaza, Ohya and Hahya. Since no complete manuscript of Giants exists, its exact contents and their order remain speculative. Most of the extant fragments concern the giants' ominous dreams and Enoch's efforts to interpret them and to intercede with God on their behalf. Unfortunately, little remains of the independent adventures of the giants, but it is likely that these tales were at least partially derived from ancient Near Eastern mythology. For instance, the name of one of the giants is Gilgamesh, the Babylonian hero and subject of a great epic written in the third millennium B.C.E.

BOOK OF GIANTS
RECONSTRUCTED TEXTS

A summary statement of the descent of the wicked angels, bringing both knowledge and havoc. Compare Genesis 6:1-2, 4.

1Q23 Frag. 9 + 14 + 15

2[. . .] they knew the secrets of [. . .] 3[. . . si]n was great in the earth [. . .] 4[. . .] and they killed manY [. .] 5[. . . they begat] giants [. . .]

The angels exploit the fruitfulness of the earth.

4Q531 Frag. 3

2[. . . everything that the] earth produced [. . .] [. . .] the great fish [. . .] 14[. . .] the sky with all that grew [. . .] 15[. . . fruit of] the earth and all kinds of grain and al1 the trees [. . .] 16[. . .] beasts and reptiles . . . [al]l creeping things of the earth and they observed all [. . .] |8[. . . eve]ry harsh deed and [. . .] utterance [. . .] l9[. . .] male and female, and among humans [. . .]

The two hundred angels choose animals on which to perform unnatural acts, including, presumably, humans.

1Q23 Frag. 1 + 6

[. . . two hundred] 2donkeys, two hundred asses, two hundred . . . rams of the] 3flock, two hundred goats, two hundred [. . . beast of the] 4field from every animal, from every [bird . . .] 5[. . .] for miscegenation [. . .]

The outcome of the demonic corruption was violence, perversion, and a brood of monstrous beings. Compare Genesis 6:4.

4Q531 Frag. 2

[. . .] they defiled [. . .] 2[. . . they begot] giants and monsters [. . .] 3[. . .] they begot, and, behold, all [the earth was corrupted . . .] 4[. . .] with its blood and by the hand of [. . .] 5[giant's] which did not suffice for them and [. . .] 6[. . .] and they were seeking to devour many [. . .] 7[. . .] 8[. . .] the monsters attacked it.

4Q532 Col. 2 Frags. 1 - 6

2[. . .] flesh [. . .] 3al[1 . . .] monsters [. . .] will be [. . .] 4[. . .] they would arise [. . .] lacking in true knowledge [. . .] because [. . .] 5[. . .] the earth [grew corrupt . . .] mighty [. . .] 6[. . .] they were considering [. . .] 7[. . .] from the angels upon [. . .] 8[. . .] in the end it will perish and die [. . .] 9[. . .] they caused great corruption in the [earth . . .] [. . . this did not] suffice to [. . .] "they will be [. . .]

The giants begin to be troubled by a series of dreams and visions. Mahway, the titan son of the angel Barakel, reports the first of these dreams to his fellow giants. He sees a tablet being immersed in water. When it emerges, all but three names have been washed away. The dream evidently symbolizes the destruction of all but Noah and his sons by the Flood.

2Q26

[. . .] they drenched the tablet in the wa[ter . . .] 2[. . .] the waters went up over the [tablet . . .] 3[. . .] they lifted out the tablet from the water of [. . .]

The giant goes to the others and they discuss the dream.

4Q530 Frag.7

[. . . this vision] is for cursing and sorrow. I am the one who confessed 2[. . .] the whole group of the castaways that I shall go to [. . .] 3[. . . the spirits of the sl]ain complaining about their killers and crying out 4[. . .] that we shall die together and be made an end of [. . .] much and I will be sleeping, and bread 6[. . .] for my dwelling; the vision and also [. . .] entered into the gathering of the giants 8[. . .]

6Q8

[. . .] Ohya and he said to Mahway [. . .] 2[. . .] without trembling. Who showed you all this vision, [my] brother? 3[. . .] Barakel, my father, was with me. 4[. . .] Before Mahway had finished telling what [he had seen . . .] 5[. . . said] to him, Now I have heard wonders! If a barren woman gives birth [. . .]

4Q530 Frag. 4

3[There]upon Ohya said to Ha[hya . . .] 4[. . . to be destroyed] from upon the earth and [. . .] 5[. . . the ea]rth. When 6[. . .] they wept before [the giants . . .]

4Q530 Frag. 7

3[. . .] your strength [. . .] 4[. . .] 5Thereupon Ohya [said] to Hahya [. . .] Then he answered, It is not for 6us, but for Azaiel, for he did [. . . the children of] angels 7are the giants, and they would not let all their poved ones] be neglected [. . . we have] not been cast down; you have strength [. . .]

The giants realize the futility of fighting against the forces of heaven. The first speaker may be Gilgamesh.

4Q531 Frag. 1

3[. . . I am a] giant, and by the mighty strength of my arm and my own great strength 4[. . . any]one mortal, and I have made war against them; but I am not [. . .] able to stand against them, for my opponents 6[. . .] reside in [Heav]en, and they dwell in the holy places. And not 7[. . . they] are stronger than I. 8[. . .] of the wild beast has come, and the wild man they call [me].
9[. . .] Then Ohya said to him, I have been forced to have a dream [. . .] the sleep of my eyes [vanished], to let me see a vision. Now I know that on [. . .] 11-12[. . .] Gilgamesh [. . .]

Ohya's dream vision is of a tree that is uprooted except for three of its roots; the vision's import is the same as that of the first dream.

6Q8 Frag. 2

1three of its roots [. . .] [while] I was [watching,] there came [. . . they moved the roots into] 3this garden, all of them, and not [. . .]

Ohya tries to avoid the implications of the visions. Above he stated that it referred only to the demon Azazel; here he suggests that the destruction is for the earthly rulers alone.

4Q530 Col. 2 1concerns the death of our souls [. . .] and all his comrades, [and Oh]ya told them what Gilgamesh said to him 2[. . .] and it was said [. . .] "concerning [. . .] the leader has cursed the potentates" 3and the giants were glad at his words. Then he turned and left [. . .]

More dreams afflict the giants. The details of this vision are obscure, but it bodes ill for the giants. The dreamers speak first to the monsters, then to the giants.

Thereupon two of them had dreams 4and the sleep of their eye, fled from them, and they arose and came to [. . . and told] their dreams, and said in the assembly of [their comrades] the monsters 6[. . . In] my dream I was watching this very night 7[and there was a garden . . .] gardeners and they were watering 8[. . . two hundred trees and] large shoots came out of their root 9[. . .] all the water, and the fire burned all 10[the garden . . .] They found the giants to tell them 11[the dream . . .]

Someone suggests that Enoch be found to interpret the vision.

[. . . to Enoch] the noted scribe, and he will interpret for us 12the dream. Thereupon his fellow Ohya declared and said to the giants, 13I too had a dream this night, O giants, and, behold, the Ruler of Heaven came down to earth 14[. . .] and such is the end of the dream. [Thereupon] all th e giants [and monsters! grew afraid 15and called Mahway. He came to them and the giants pleaded with him and sent him to Enoch 16[the noted scribe]. They said to him, Go [. . .] to you that 17[. . .] you have heard his voice. And he said to him, He wil1 [. . . and] interpret the dreams [. . .] **Col. 3** 3[. . .] how long the giants have to live. [. . .]

After a cosmic journey Mahway comes to Enoch and makes his request.

[. . . he mounted up in the air] 41ike strong winds, and flew with his hands like ea[gles . . . he left behind] 5the inhabited world and passed over Desolation, the great desert [. . .] 6and Enoch saw him and hailed him, and Mahway said to him [. . .] 7hither and thither a second time to Mahway [. . . The giants awaig 8your words, and all the monsters of the earth. If [. . .] has been carried [. . .] 9from the days of [. . .] their [. . .] and they will be added [. . .] 10[. . .] we would know from you their meaning [. . .] 11[. . . two hundred tr]ees that from heaven [came down . . .]

Enoch sends back a tablet with its grim message of judgment, but with hope for repentance.

4Q530 Frag. 2

The scribe [Enoch . . .] 2[. . .] 3a copy of the second tablet that [Epoch] se[nt . . .] 4in the very handwriting of Enoch the noted scribe [. . . In the name of God the great] 5and holy one, to Shemihaza and all [his companions . . .] 61et it be known to you that not [. . .] 7and the things you have done, and that your wives [. . .] 8they and their sons and the wives of [their sons . . .] 9by your licentiousness on the earth, and there has been upon you [. . . and the land is crying out] 10and complaining about you and the deeds of your children [. . .] 11the harm that you have done to it. [. . .] 12until Raphael arrives, behold, destruction [is coming, a great flood, and it will destroy all living things] 13and whatever is in the deserts and the seas. And the meaning of the matter [. . .] 14upon you for evil. But now, loosen the bonds bi[nding you to evil . . .] l5and pray.

A fragment apparently detailing a vision that Enoch saw.

4Q531 Frag. 7

3[. . . great fear] seized me and I fell on my face; I heard his voice [. . .] 4[. . .] he dwelt among human beings but he did not learn from them [. . .]

THE BOOK OF JASHER

Chapter 1

1 And God said, Let us make man in our image, after our likeness, and God created man in his own image.

2 And God formed man from the ground, and he blew into his nostrils the breath of life, and man became a living soul endowed with speech.

3 And the Lord said, It is not good for man to be alone; I will make unto him a helpmeet.

4 And the Lord caused a deep sleep to fall upon Adam, and he slept, and he took away one of his ribs, and he built flesh upon it, and formed it and brought it to Adam, and Adam awoke from his sleep, and behold a woman was standing before him.

5 And he said, This is a bone of my bones and it shall be called woman, for this has been taken from man; and Adam called her name Eve, for she was the mother of all living.

6 And God blessed them and called their names Adam and Eve in the day that he created them, and the Lord God said, Be fruitful and multiply and fill the earth.

7 And the Lord God took Adam and his wife, and he placed them in the garden of Eden to dress it and to keep it; and he commanded them and said unto them, From every tree of the garden you may eat, but from the tree of the knowledge of good and evil you shall not eat, for in the day that you eat thereof you shall surely die.

8 And when God had blessed and commanded them, he went from them, and Adam and his wife dwelt in the garden according to the command which the Lord had commanded them.

9 And the serpent, which God had created with them in the earth, came to them to incite them to transgress the command of God which he had commanded them.

10 And the serpent enticed and persuaded the woman to eat from the tree of knowledge, and the woman hearkened to the voice of the serpent, and she transgressed the word of God, and took from the tree of the knowledge of good and evil, and she ate, and she took from it and gave also to her husband and he ate.

11 And Adam and his wife transgressed the command of God which he commanded them, and God knew it, and his anger was kindled against them and he cursed them.

12 And the Lord God drove them that day from the garden of Eden, to till the ground from which they were taken, and they went and dwelt at the east of the garden of Eden; and Adam knew his wife Eve and she bore two sons and three daughters.

13 And she called the name of the first born Cain, saying, I have obtained a man from the Lord, and the name of the other she called Abel, for she said, In vanity we came into the earth, and in vanity we shall be taken from it.

14 And the boys grew up and their father gave them a possession in the land; and Cain was a tiller of the ground, and Abel a keeper of sheep.

15 And it was at the expiration of a few years, that they brought an approximating offering to the Lord, and Cain brought from the fruit of the ground, and Abel brought from the firstlings of his flock from the fat thereof, and God turned and inclined to Abel and his offering, and a fire came down from the Lord from heaven and consumed it.

16 And unto Cain and his offering the Lord did not turn, and he did not incline to it, for he had brought from the inferior fruit of the ground before the Lord, and Cain was jealous against his brother Abel on account of this, and he

sought a pretext to slay him.

17 And in some time after, Cain and Abel his brother, went one day into the field to do their work; and they were both in the field, Cain tilling and ploughing his ground, and Abel feeding his flock; and the flock passed that part which Cain had ploughed in the ground, and it sorely grieved Cain on this account.

18 And Cain approached his brother Abel in anger, and he said unto him, What is there between me and thee, that thou comest to dwell and bring thy flock to feed in my land?

19 And Abel answered his brother Cain and said unto him, What is there between me and thee, that thou shalt eat the flesh of my flock and clothe thyself with their wool?

20 And now therefore, put off the wool of my sheep with which thou hast clothed thyself, and recompense me for their fruit and flesh which thou hast eaten, and when thou shalt have done this, I will then go from thy land as thou hast said?

21 And Cain said to his brother Abel, Surely if I slay thee this day, who will require thy blood from me?

22 And Abel answered Cain, saying, Surely God who has made us in the earth, he will avenge my cause, and he will require my blood from thee shouldst thou slay me, for the Lord is the judge and arbiter, and it is he who will requite man according to his evil, and the wicked man according to the wickedness that he may do upon earth.

23 And now, if thou shouldst slay me here, surely God knoweth thy secret views, and will judge thee for the evil which thou didst declare to do unto me this day.

24 And when Cain heard the words which Abel his brother had spoken, behold the anger of Cain was kindled against his brother Abel for declaring this thing.

25 And Cain hastened and rose up, and took the iron part of his ploughing instrument, with which he suddenly smote his brother and he slew him, and Cain spilt the blood of his brother Abel upon the earth, and the blood of Abel streamed upon the earth before the flock.

26 And after this Cain repented having slain his brother, and he was sadly grieved, and he wept over him and it vexed him exceedingly.

27 And Cain rose up and dug a hole in the field, wherein he put his brother's body, and he turned the dust over it.

28 And the Lord knew what Cain had done to his brother, and the Lord appeared to Cain and said unto him, Where is Abel thy brother that was with thee?

29 And Cain dissembled, and said, I do not know, am I my brother's keeper? And the Lord said unto him, What hast thou done? The voice of thy brother's blood crieth unto me from the ground where thou hast slain him.

30 For thou hast slain thy brother and hast dissembled before me, and didst imagine in thy heart that I saw thee not, nor knew all thy actions.

31 But thou didst this thing and didst slay thy brother for naught and because he spoke rightly to thee, and now, therefore, cursed be thou from the ground which opened its mouth to receive thy brother's blood from thy hand, and wherein thou didst bury him.

32 And it shall be when thou shalt till it, it shall no more give thee its strength as in the beginning, for thorns and thistles shall the ground produce, and thou shalt be moving and wandering in the earth until the day of thy death.

33 And at that time Cain went out from the presence of the Lord, from the place where he was, and he went moving and wandering in the land toward the east of Eden, he and all belonging to him.

34 And Cain knew his wife in those days, and she conceived and bare a son, and he called his name Enoch, saying, In that time the Lord began to give him rest and quiet in the earth.

35 And at that time Cain also began to build a city: and he built the city and he called the name of the city Enoch, according to the name of his son; for in those days the Lord had given him rest upon the earth, and he did not move about and wander as in the beginning.

36 And Irad was born to Enoch, and Irad begat Mechuyael and Mechuyael begat Methusael.

Chapter 2

1 And it was in the hundred and thirtieth year of the life of Adam upon the earth, that he again knew Eve his wife, and she conceived and bare a son in his likeness and in his image, and she called his name Seth, saying, Because God has appointed me another seed in the place of Abel, for Cain has slain him.

2 And Seth lived one hundred and five years, and he begat a son; and Seth called the name of his son Enosh, saying, Because in that time the sons of men began to multiply, and to afflict their souls and hearts by transgressing and rebelling against God.

3 And it was in the days of Enosh that the sons of men continued to rebel and transgress against God, to increase the anger of the Lord against the sons of men.

4 And the sons of men went and they served other gods, and they forgot the Lord who had created them in the earth: and in those days the sons of men made images of brass and iron, wood and stone, and they bowed down and served them.

5 And every man made his god and they bowed down to them, and the sons of men forsook the Lord all the days of Enosh and his children; and the anger of the Lord was kindled on account of their works and abominations which they did in the earth.

6 And the Lord caused the waters of the river Gihon to overwhelm them, and he destroyed and consumed them, and he destroyed the third part of the earth, and notwithstanding this, the sons of men did not turn from their evil ways, and their hands were yet extended to do evil in the sight of the Lord.

7 And in those days there was neither sowing nor reaping in the earth; and there was no food for the sons of men and the famine was very great in those days.

8 And the seed which they sowed in those days in the ground became thorns, thistles and briers; for from the days of Adam was this declaration concerning the earth, of the curse of God, which he cursed the earth, on account of the sin which Adam sinned before the Lord.

9 And it was when men continued to rebel and transgress against God, and to corrupt their ways, that the earth also became corrupt.

10 And Enosh lived ninety years and he begat Cainan;

11 And Cainan grew up and he was forty years old, and he became wise and had knowledge and skill in all wisdom, and he reigned over all the sons of men, and he led the sons of men to wisdom and knowledge; for Cainan was a very wise man and had understanding in all wisdom, and with his wisdom he ruled over spirits and demons;

12 And Cainan knew by his wisdom that God would destroy the sons of men for having sinned upon earth, and that the Lord would in the latter days bring upon them the waters of the flood.

13 And in those days Cainan wrote upon tablets of stone, what was to take place in time to come, and he put them in his treasures.

14 And Cainan reigned over the whole earth, and he turned some of the sons of men to the service of God.

15 And when Cainan was seventy years old, he begat three sons and two daughters.

16 And these are the names of the children of Cainan; the name of the first born Mahlallel, the second Enan, and the third Mered, and their sisters were Adah and Zillah; these are the five children of Cainan that were born to him.

17 And Lamech, the son of Methusael, became related to Cainan by marriage, and he took his two daughters for his wives, and Adah conceived and bare a son to Lamech, and she called his name Jabal.

18 And she again conceived and bare a son, and called his name Jubal; and Zillah, her sister, was barren in those days and had no offspring.

19 For in those days the sons of men began to trespass against God, and to transgress the commandments which he had commanded to Adam, to be fruitful and multiply in the earth.

20 And some of the sons of men caused their wives to drink a draught that would render them barren, in order that they might retain their figures and whereby their beautiful appearance might not fade.

21 And when the sons of men caused some of their wives to drink, Zillah drank with them.

22 And the child-bearing women appeared abominable in the sight of their husbands as widows, whilst their husbands lived, for to the barren ones only they were attached.

23 And in the end of days and years, when Zillah became old, the Lord opened her womb.

24 And she conceived and bare a son and she called his name Tubal Cain, saying, After I had withered away have I obtained him from the Almighty God.

25 And she conceived again and bare a daughter, and she called her name Naamah, for she said, After I had withered away have I obtained pleasure and delight.

26 And Lamech was old and advanced in years, and his eyes were dim that he could not see, and Tubal Cain, his son, was leading him and it was one day that Lamech went into the field and Tubal Cain his son was with him, and whilst they were walking in the field, Cain the son of Adam advanced towards them; for Lamech was very old and could not see much, and Tubal Cain his son was very young.

27 And Tubal Cain told his father to draw his bow, and with the arrows he smote Cain, who was yet far off, and he slew him, for he appeared to them to be an animal.

28 And the arrows entered Cain's body although he was distant from them, and he fell to the ground and died.

29 And the Lord requited Cain's evil according to his wickedness, which he had done to his brother Abel, according to the word of the Lord which he had spoken.

30 And it came to pass when Cain had died, that Lamech and Tubal went to see the animal which they had slain, and they saw, and behold Cain their grandfather was fallen dead upon the earth.

31 And Lamech was very much grieved at having done this, and in clapping his hands together he struck his son and caused his death.

32 And the wives of Lamech heard what Lamech had done, and they sought to kill him.

33 And the wives of Lamech hated him from that day,

because he slew Cain and Tubal Cain, and the wives of Lamech separated from him, and would not hearken to him in those days.

34 And Lamech came to his wives, and he pressed them to listen to him about this matter.

35 And he said to his wives Adah and Zillah, Hear my voice O wives of Lamech, attend to my words, for now you have imagined and said that I slew a man with my wounds, and a child with my stripes for their having done no violence, but surely know that I am old and grey-headed, and that my eyes are heavy through age, and I did this thing unknowingly.

36 And the wives of Lamech listened to him in this matter, and they returned to him with the advice of their father Adam, but they bore no children to him from that time, knowing that God's anger was increasing in those days against the sons of men, to destroy them with the waters of the flood for their evil doings.

37 And Mahlallel the son of Cainan lived sixty-five years and he begat Jared; and Jared lived sixty-two years and he begat Enoch.

Chapter 3

1 And Enoch lived sixty-five years and he begat Methuselah; and Enoch walked with God after having begot Methuselah, and he served the Lord, and despised the evil ways of men.

2 And the soul of Enoch was wrapped up in the instruction of the Lord, in knowledge and in understanding; and he wisely retired from the sons of men, and secreted himself from them for many days.

3 And it was at the expiration of many years, whilst he was serving the Lord, and praying before him in his house, that an angel of the Lord called to him from Heaven, and he said, Here am I.

4 And he said, Rise, go forth from thy house and from the place where thou dost hide thyself, and appear to the sons of men, in order that thou mayest teach them the way in which they should go and the work which they must accomplish to enter in the ways of God.

5 And Enoch rose up according to the word of the Lord, and went forth from his house, from his place and from the chamber in which he was concealed; and he went to the sons of men and taught them the ways of the Lord, and at that time assembled the sons of men and acquainted them with the instruction of the Lord.

6 And he ordered it to be proclaimed in all places where the sons of men dwelt, saying, Where is the man who wishes to know the ways of the Lord and good works? let him come to Enoch.

7 And all the sons of men then assembled to him, for all who desired this thing went to Enoch, and Enoch reigned over the sons of men according to the word of the Lord, and they came and bowed to him and they heard his word.

8 And the spirit of God was upon Enoch, and he taught all his men the wisdom of God and his ways, and the sons of men served the Lord all the days of Enoch, and they came to hear his wisdom.

9 And all the kings of the sons of men, both first and last, together with their princes and judges, came to Enoch when they heard of his wisdom, and they bowed down to him, and they also required of Enoch to reign over them, to which he consented.

10 And they assembled in all, one hundred and thirty kings and princes, and they made Enoch king over them and they

were all under his power and command.

11 And Enoch taught them wisdom, knowledge, and the ways of the Lord; and he made peace amongst them, and peace was throughout the earth during the life of Enoch.

12 And Enoch reigned over the sons of men two hundred and forty-three years, and he did justice and righteousness with all his people, and he led them in the ways of the Lord.

13 And these are the generations of Enoch, Methuselah, Elisha, and Elimelech, three sons; and their sisters were Melca and Nahmah, and Methuselah lived eighty-seven years and he begat Lamech.

14 And it was in the fifty-sixth year of the life of Lamech when Adam died; nine hundred and thirty years old was he at his death, and his two sons, with Enoch and Methuselah his son, buried him with great pomp, as at the burial of kings, in the cave which God had told him.

15 And in that place all the sons of men made a great mourning and weeping on account of Adam; it has therefore become a custom among the sons of men to this day.

16 And Adam died because he ate of the tree of knowledge; he and his children after him, as the Lord God had spoken.

17 And it was in the year of Adam's death which was the two hundred and forty-third year of the reign of Enoch, in that time Enoch resolved to separate himself from the sons of men and to secret himself as at first in order to serve the Lord.

18 And Enoch did so, but did not entirely secret himself from them, but kept away from the sons of men three days and then went to them for one day.

19 And during the three days that he was in his chamber, he prayed to, and praised the Lord his God, and the day on which he went and appeared to his subjects he taught them the ways of the Lord, and all they asked him about the Lord he told them.

20 And he did in this manner for many years, and he afterward concealed himself for six days, and appeared to his people one day in seven; and after that once in a month, and then once in a year, until all the kings, princes and sons of men sought for him, and desired again to see the face of Enoch, and to hear his word; but they could not, as all the sons of men were greatly afraid of Enoch, and they feared to approach him on account of the Godlike awe that was seated upon his countenance; therefore no man could look at him, fearing he might be punished and die.

21 And all the kings and princes resolved to assemble the sons of men, and to come to Enoch, thinking that they might all speak to him at the time when he should come forth amongst them, and they did so.

22 And the day came when Enoch went forth and they all assembled and came to him, and Enoch spoke to them the words of the Lord and he taught them wisdom and knowledge, and they bowed down before him and they said, May the king live! May the king live!

23 And in some time after, when the kings and princes and the sons of men were speaking to Enoch, and Enoch was teaching them the ways of God, behold an angel of the Lord then called unto Enoch from heaven, and wished to bring him up to heaven to make him reign there over the sons of God, as he had reigned over the sons of men upon earth.

24 When at that time Enoch heard this he went and assembled all the inhabitants of the earth, and taught them wisdom and knowledge and gave them divine instructions, and he said to them, I have been required to ascend into

heaven, I therefore do not know the day of my going.

25 And now therefore I will teach you wisdom and knowledge and will give you instruction before I leave you, how to act upon earth whereby you may live; and he did so.

26 And he taught them wisdom and knowledge, and gave them instruction, and he reproved them, and he placed before them statutes and judgments to do upon earth, and he made peace amongst them, and he taught them everlasting life, and dwelt with them some time teaching them all these things.

27 And at that time the sons of men were with Enoch, and Enoch was speaking to them, and they lifted up their eyes and the likeness of a great horse descended from heaven, and the horse paced in the air;

28 And they told Enoch what they had seen, and Enoch said to them, On my account does this horse descend upon earth; the time is come when I must go from you and I shall no more be seen by you.

29 And the horse descended at that time and stood before Enoch, and all the sons of men that were with Enoch saw him.

30 And Enoch then again ordered a voice to be proclaimed, saying, Where is the man who delighteth to know the ways of the Lord his God, let him come this day to Enoch before he is taken from us.

31 And all the sons of men assembled and came to Enoch that day; and all the kings of the earth with their princes and counsellors remained with him that day; and Enoch then taught the sons of men wisdom and knowledge, and gave them divine instruction; and he bade them serve the Lord and walk in his ways all the days of their lives, and he continued to make peace amongst them.

32 And it was after this that he rose up and rode upon the horse; and he went forth and all the sons of men went after him, about eight hundred thousand men; and they went with him one day's journey.

33 And the second day he said to them, Return home to your tents, why will you go? perhaps you may die; and some of them went from him, and those that remained went with him six day's journey; and Enoch said to them every day, Return to your tents, lest you may die; but they were not willing to return, and they went with him.

34 And on the sixth day some of the men remained and clung to him, and they said to him, We will go with thee to the place where thou goest; as the Lord liveth, death only shall separate us.

35 And they urged so much to go with him, that he ceased speaking to them; and they went after him and would not return;

36 And when the kings returned they caused a census to be taken, in order to know the number of remaining men that went with Enoch; and it was upon the seventh day that Enoch ascended into heaven in a whirlwind, with horses and chariots of fire.

37 And on the eighth day all the kings that had been with Enoch sent to bring back the number of men that were with Enoch, in that place from which he ascended into heaven.

38 And all those kings went to the place and they found the earth there filled with snow, and upon the snow were large stones of snow, and one said to the other, Come, let us break through the snow and see, perhaps the men that remained with Enoch are dead, and are now under the stones of snow, and they searched but could not find him, for he had ascended into heaven.

Chapter 4

1 And all the days that Enoch lived upon earth, were three hundred and sixty-five years.

2 And when Enoch had ascended into heaven, all the kings of the earth rose and took Methuselah his son and anointed him, and they caused him to reign over them in the place of his father.

3 And Methuselah acted uprightly in the sight of God, as his father Enoch had taught him, and he likewise during the whole of his life taught the sons of men wisdom, knowledge and the fear of God, and he did not turn from the good way either to the right or to the left.

4 But in the latter days of Methuselah, the sons of men turned from the Lord, they corrupted the earth, they robbed and plundered each other, and they rebelled against God and they transgressed, and they corrupted their ways, and would not hearken to the voice of Methuselah, but rebelled against him.

5 And the Lord was exceedingly wroth against them, and the Lord continued to destroy the seed in those days, so that there was neither sowing nor reaping in the earth.

6 For when they sowed the ground in order that they might obtain food for their support, behold, thorns and thistles were produced which they did not sow.

7 And still the sons of men did not turn from their evil ways, and their hands were still extended to do evil in the sight of God, and they provoked the Lord with their evil ways, and the Lord was very wroth, and repented that he had made man.

8 And he thought to destroy and annihilate them and he did so.

9 In those days when Lamech the son of Methuselah was one hundred and sixty years old, Seth the son of Adam died.

10 And all the days that Seth lived, were nine hundred and twelve years, and he died.

11 And Lamech was one hundred and eighty years old when he took Ashmua, the daughter of Elishaa the son of Enoch his uncle, and she conceived.

12 And at that time the sons of men sowed the ground, and a little food was produced, yet the sons of men did not turn from their evil ways, and they trespassed and rebelled against God.

13 And the wife of Lamech conceived and bare him a son at that time, at the revolution of the year.

14 And Methuselah called his name Noah, saying, The earth was in his days at rest and free from corruption, and Lamech his father called his name Menachem, saying, This one shall comfort us in our works and miserable toil in the earth, which God had cursed.

15 And the child grew up and was weaned, and he went in the ways of his father Methuselah, perfect and upright with God.

16 And all the sons of men departed from the ways of the Lord in those days as they multiplied upon the face of the earth with sons and daughters, and they taught one another their evil practices and they continued sinning against the Lord.

17 And every man made unto himself a god, and they robbed and plundered every man his neighbor as well as his relative, and they corrupted the earth, and the earth was filled with violence.

18 And their judges and rulers went to the daughters of men and took their wives by force from their husbands according to their choice, and the sons of men in those

days took from the cattle of the earth, the beasts of the field and the fowls of the air, and taught the mixture of animals of one species with the other, in order therewith to provoke the Lord; and God saw the whole earth and it was corrupt, for all flesh had corrupted its ways upon earth, all men and all animals.

19 And the Lord said, I will blot out man that I created from the face of the earth, yea from man to the birds of the air, together with cattle and beasts that are in the field for I repent that I made them.

20 And all men who walked in the ways of the Lord, died in those days, before the Lord brought the evil upon man which he had declared, for this was from the Lord, that they should not see the evil which the Lord spoke of concerning the sons of men.

21 And Noah found grace in the sight of the Lord, and the Lord chose him and his children to raise up seed from them upon the face of the whole earth.

Chapter 5

1 And it was in the eighty-fourth year of the life of Noah, that Enoch the son of Seth died, he was nine hundred and five years old at his death.

2 And in the one hundred and seventy ninth year of the life of Noah, Cainan the son of Enosh died, and all the days of Cainan were nine hundred and ten years, and he died.

3 And in the two hundred and thirty fourth year of the life of Noah, Mahlallel the son of Cainan died, and the days of Mahlallel were eight hundred and ninety-five years, and he died.

4 And Jared the son of Mahlallel died in those days, in the three hundred and thirty-sixth year of the life of Noah; and all the days of Jared were nine hundred and sixty-two years, and he died.

5 And all who followed the Lord died in those days, before they saw the evil which God declared to do upon earth.

6 And after the lapse of many years, in the four hundred and eightieth year of the life of Noah, when all those men, who followed the Lord had died away from amongst the sons of men, and only Methuselah was then left, God said unto Noah and Methuselah, saying,

7 Speak ye, and proclaim to the sons of men, saying, Thus saith the Lord, return from your evil ways and forsake your works, and the Lord will repent of the evil that he declared to do to you, so that it shall not come to pass.

8 For thus saith the Lord, Behold I give you a period of one hundred and twenty years; if you will turn to me and forsake your evil ways, then will I also turn away from the evil which I told you, and it shall not exist, saith the Lord.

9 And Noah and Methuselah spoke all the words of the Lord to the sons of men, day after day, constantly speaking to them.

10 But the sons of men would not hearken to them, nor incline their ears to their words, and they were stiffnecked.

11 And the Lord granted them a period of one hundred and twenty years, saying, If they will return, then will God repent of the evil, so as not to destroy the earth.

12 Noah the son of Lamech refrained from taking a wife in those days, to beget children, for he said, Surely now God will destroy the earth, wherefore then shall I beget children?

13 And Noah was a just man, he was perfect in his generation, and the Lord chose him to raise up seed from his seed upon the face of the earth.

14 And the Lord said unto Noah, Take unto thee a wife, and beget children, for I have seen thee righteous before me in this generation.

15 And thou shalt raise up seed, and thy children with thee, in the midst of the earth; and Noah went and took a wife, and he chose Naamah the daughter of Enoch, and she was five hundred and eighty years old.

16 And Noah was four hundred and ninety-eight years old, when he took Naamah for a wife.

17 And Naamah conceived and bare a son, and he called his name Japheth, saying, God has enlarged me in the earth; and she conceived again and bare a son, and he called his name Shem, saying, God has made me a remnant, to raise up seed in the midst of the earth.

18 And Noah was five hundred and two years old when Naamah bare Shem, and the boys grew up and went in the ways of the Lord, in all that Methuselah and Noah their father taught them.

19 And Lamech the father of Noah, died in those days; yet verily he did not go with all his heart in the ways of his father, and he died in the hundred and ninety-fifth year of the life of Noah.

20 And all the days of Lamech were seven hundred and seventy years, and he died.

21 And all the sons of men who knew the Lord, died in that year before the Lord brought evil upon them; for the Lord willed them to die, so as not to behold the evil that God would bring upon their brothers and relatives, as he had so declared to do.

22 In that time, the Lord said to Noah and Methuselah, Stand forth and proclaim to the sons of men all the words that I spoke to you in those days, peradventure they may turn from their evil ways, and I will then repent of the evil and will not bring it.

23 And Noah and Methuselah stood forth, and said in the ears of the sons of men, all that God had spoken concerning them.

24 But the sons of men would not hearken, neither would they incline their ears to all their declarations.

25 And it was after this that the Lord said to Noah, The end of all flesh is come before me, on account of their evil deeds, and behold I will destroy the earth.

26 And do thou take unto thee gopher wood, and go to a certain place and make a large ark, and place it in that spot.

27 And thus shalt thou make it; three hundred cubits its length, fifty cubits broad and thirty cubits high.

28 And thou shalt make unto thee a door, open at its side, and to a cubit thou shalt finish above, and cover it within and without with pitch.

29 And behold I will bring the flood of waters upon the earth, and all flesh be destroyed, from under the heavens all that is upon earth shall perish.

30 And thou and thy household shall go and gather two couple of all living things, male and female, and shall bring them to the ark, to raise up seed from them upon earth.

31 And gather unto thee all food that is eaten by all the animals, that there may be food for thee and for them.

32 And thou shalt choose for thy sons three maidens, from the daughters of men, and they shall be wives to thy sons.

33 And Noah rose up, and he made the ark, in the place where God had commanded him, and Noah did as God had ordered him.

34 In his five hundred and ninety-fifth year Noah commenced to make the ark, and he made the ark in five years, as the Lord had commanded.

35 Then Noah took the three daughters of Eliakim, son of Methuselah, for wives for his sons, as the Lord had commanded Noah.

36 And it was at that time Methuselah the son of Enoch

died, nine hundred and sixty years old was he, at his death.

Chapter 6

1 At that time, after the death of Methuselah, the Lord said to Noah, Go thou with thy household into the ark; behold I will gather to thee all the animals of the earth, the beasts of the field and the fowls of the air, and they shall all come and surround the ark.

2 And thou shalt go and seat thyself by the doors of the ark, and all the beasts, the animals, and the fowls, shall assemble and place themselves before thee, and such of them as shall come and crouch before thee, shalt thou take and deliver into the hands of thy sons, who shall bring them to the ark, and all that will stand before thee thou shalt leave.

3 And the Lord brought this about on the next day, and animals, beasts and fowls came in great multitudes and surrounded the ark.

4 And Noah went and seated himself by the door of the ark, and of all flesh that crouched before him, he brought into the ark, and all that stood before him he left upon earth.

5 And a lioness came, with her two whelps, male and female, and the three crouched before Noah, and the two whelps rose up against the lioness and smote her, and made her flee from her place, and she went away, and they returned to their places, and crouched upon the earth before Noah.

6 And the lioness ran away, and stood in the place of the lions.

7 And Noah saw this, and wondered greatly, and he rose and took the two whelps, and brought them into the ark.

8 And Noah brought into the ark from all living creatures that were upon earth, so that there was none left but which Noah brought into the ark.

9 Two and two came to Noah into the ark, but from the clean animals, and clean fowls, he brought seven couples, as God had commanded him.

10 And all the animals, and beasts, and fowls, were still there, and they surrounded the ark at every place, and the rain had not descended till seven days after.

11 And on that day, the Lord caused the whole earth to shake, and the sun darkened, and the foundations of the world raged, and the whole earth was moved violently, and the lightning flashed, and the thunder roared, and all the fountains in the earth were broken up, such as was not known to the inhabitants before; and God did this mighty act, in order to terrify the sons of men, that there might be no more evil upon earth.

12 And still the sons of men would not return from their evil ways, and they increased the anger of the Lord at that time, and did not even direct their hearts to all this.

13 And at the end of seven days, in the six hundredth year of the life of Noah, the waters of the flood were upon the earth.

14 And all the fountains of the deep were broken up, and the windows of heaven were opened, and the rain was upon the earth forty days and forty nights.

15 And Noah and his household, and all the living creatures that were with him, came into the ark on account of the waters of the flood, and the Lord shut him in.

16 And all the sons of men that were left upon the earth, became exhausted through evil on account of the rain, for the waters were coming more violently upon the earth, and the animals and beasts were still surrounding the ark.

17 And the sons of men assembled together, about seven hundred thousand men and women, and they came unto Noah to the ark.

18 And they called to Noah, saying, Open for us that we may come to thee in the ark--and wherefore shall we die?

19 And Noah, with a loud voice, answered them from the ark, saying, Have you not all rebelled against the Lord, and said that he does not exist? and therefore the Lord brought upon you this evil, to destroy and cut you off from the face of the earth.

20 Is not this the thing that I spoke to you of one hundred and twenty years back, and you would not hearken to the voice of the Lord, and now do you desire to live upon earth?

21 And they said to Noah, We are ready to return to the Lord; only open for us that we may live and not die.

22 And Noah answered them, saying, Behold now that you see the trouble of your souls, you wish to return to the Lord; why did you not return during these hundred and twenty years, which the Lord granted you as the determined period?

23 But now you come and tell me this on account of the troubles of your souls, now also the Lord will not listen to you, neither will he give ear to you on this day, so that you will not now succeed in your wishes.

24 And the sons of men approached in order to break into the ark, to come in on account of the rain, for they could not bear the rain upon them.

25 And the Lord sent all the beasts and animals that stood round the ark. And the beasts overpowered them and drove them from that place, and every man went his way and they again scattered themselves upon the face of the earth.

26 And the rain was still descending upon the earth, and it descended forty days and forty nights, and the waters prevailed greatly upon the earth; and all flesh that was upon the earth or in the waters died, whether men, animals, beasts, creeping things or birds of the air, and there only remained Noah and those that were with him in the ark.

27 And the waters prevailed and they greatly increased upon the earth, and they lifted up the ark and it was raised from the earth.

28 And the ark floated upon the face of the waters, and it was tossed upon the waters so that all the living creatures within were turned about like pottage in a cauldron.

29 And great anxiety seized all the living creatures that were in the ark, and the ark was like to be broken.

30 And all the living creatures that were in the ark were terrified, and the lions roared, and the oxen lowed, and the wolves howled, and every living creature in the ark spoke and lamented in its own language, so that their voices reached to a great distance, and Noah and his sons cried and wept in their troubles; they were greatly afraid that they had reached the gates of death.

31 And Noah prayed unto the Lord, and cried unto him on account of this, and he said, O Lord help us, for we have no strength to bear this evil that has encompassed us, for the waves of the waters have surrounded us, mischievous torrents have terrified us, the snares of death have come before us; answer us, O Lord, answer us, light up thy countenance toward us and be gracious to us, redeem us and deliver us.

32 And the Lord hearkened to the voice of Noah, and the Lord remembered him.

33 And a wind passed over the earth, and the waters were still and the ark rested.

34 And the fountains of the deep and the windows of heaven were stopped, and the rain from heaven was restrained.

35 And the waters decreased in those days, and the ark rested upon the mountains of Ararat.

36 And Noah then opened the windows of the ark, and Noah still called out to the Lord at that time and he said, O Lord, who didst form the earth and the heavens and all that are therein, bring forth our souls from this confinement, and from the prison wherein thou hast placed us, for I am much wearied with sighing.

37 And the Lord hearkened to the voice of Noah, and said to him, When though shalt have completed a full year thou shalt then go forth.

38 And at the revolution of the year, when a full year was completed to Noah's dwelling in the ark, the waters were dried from off the earth, and Noah put off the covering of the ark.

39 At that time, on the twenty-seventh day of the second month, the earth was dry, but Noah and his sons, and those that were with him, did not go out from the ark until the Lord told them.

40 And the day came that the Lord told them to go out, and they all went out from the ark.

41 And they went and returned every one to his way and to his place, and Noah and his sons dwelt in the land that God had told them, and they served the Lord all their days, and the Lord blessed Noah and his sons on their going out from the ark.

42 And he said to them, Be fruitful and fill all the earth; become strong and increase abundantly in the earth and multiply therein.

Chapter 7

1 And these are the names of the sons of Noah: Japheth, Ham and Shem; and children were born to them after the flood, for they had taken wives before the flood.

2 These are the sons of Japheth; Gomer, Magog, Madai, Javan, Tubal, Meshech, and Tiras, seven sons.

3 And the sons of Gomer were Askinaz, Rephath and Tegarmah.

4 And the sons of Magog were Elichanaf and Lubal.

5 And the children of Madai were Achon, Zeelo, Chazoni and Lot.

6 And the sons of Javan were Elisha, Tarshish, Chittim and Dudonim.

7 And the sons of Tubal were Ariphi, Kesed and Taari.

8 And the sons of Meshech were Dedon, Zaron and Shebashni.

9 And the sons of Tiras were Benib, Gera, Lupirion and Gilak; these are the sons of Japheth according to their families, and their numbers in those days were about four hundred and sixty men.

10 And these are the sons of Ham; Cush, Mitzraim, Phut and Canaan, four sons; and the sons of Cush were Seba, Havilah, Sabta, Raama and Satecha, and the sons of Raama were Sheba and Dedan.

11 And the sons of Mitzraim were Lud, Anom and Pathros, Chasloth and Chaphtor.

12 And the sons of Phut were Gebul, Hadan, Benah and Adan.

13 And the sons of Canaan were Zidon, Heth, Amori, Gergashi, Hivi, Arkee, Seni, Arodi, Zimodi and Chamothi.

14 These are the sons of Ham, according to their families, and their numbers in those days were about seven hundred and thirty men.

15 And these are the sons of Shem; Elam, Ashur, Arpachshad, Lud and Aram, five sons; and the sons of Elam were Shushan, Machul and Harmon.

16 And the sons of Ashar were Mirus and Mokil, and the sons of Arpachshad were Shelach, Anar and Ashcol.

17 And the sons of Lud were Pethor and Bizayon, and the sons of Aram were Uz, Chul, Gather and Mash.

18 These are the sons of Shem, according to their families; and their numbers in those days were about three hundred men.

15

19 These are the generations of Shem; Shem begat Arpachshad and Arpachshad begat Shelach, and Shelach begat Eber and to Eber were born two children, the name of one was Peleg, for in his days the sons of men were divided, and in the latter days, the earth was divided.

20 And the name of the second was Yoktan, meaning that in his day the lives of the sons of men were diminished and lessened.

21 These are the sons of Yoktan; Almodad, Shelaf, Chazarmoveth, Yerach, Hadurom, Ozel, Diklah, Obal, Abimael, Sheba, Ophir, Havilah and Jobab; all these are the sons of Yoktan.

22 And Peleg his brother begat Yen, and Yen begat Serug, and Serug begat Nahor and Nahor begat Terah, and Terah was thirty-eight years old, and he begat Haran and Nahor.

23 And Cush the son of Ham, the son of Noah, took a wife in those days in his old age, and she bare a son, and they called his name Nimrod, saying, At that time the sons of men again began to rebel and transgress against God, and the child grew up, and his father loved him exceedingly, for he was the son of his old age.

24 And the garments of skin which God made for Adam and his wife, when they went out of the garden, were given to Cush.

25 For after the death of Adam and his wife, the garments were given to Enoch, the son of Jared, and when Enoch was taken up to God, he gave them to Methuselah, his son.

26 And at the death of Methuselah, Noah took them and brought them to the ark, and they were with him until he went out of the ark.

27 And in their going out, Ham stole those garments from Noah his father, and he took them and hid them from his brothers.

28 And when Ham begat his first born Cush, he gave him the garments in secret, and they were with Cush many days.

29 And Cush also concealed them from his sons and brothers, and when Cush had begotten Nimrod, he gave him those garments through his love for him, and Nimrod grew up, and when he was twenty years old he put on those garments.

30 And Nimrod became strong when he put on the garments, and God gave him might and strength, and he was a mighty hunter in the earth, yea, he was a mighty hunter in the field, and he hunted the animals and he built altars, and he offered upon them the animals before the Lord.

31 And Nimrod strengthened himself, and he rose up from amongst his brethren, and he fought the battles of his brethren against all their enemies round about.

32 And the Lord delivered all the enemies of his brethren in his hands, and God prospered him from time to time in his battles, and he reigned upon earth.

33 Therefore it became current in those days, when a man ushered forth those that he had trained up for battle, he

would say to them, Like God did to Nimrod, who was a mighty hunter in the earth, and who succeeded in the battles that prevailed against his brethren, that he delivered them from the hands of their enemies, so may God strengthen us and deliver us this day.

34 And when Nimrod was forty years old, at that time there was a war between his brethren and the children of Japheth, so that they were in the power of their enemies.

35 And Nimrod went forth at that time, and he assembled all the sons of Cush and their families, about four hundred and sixty men, and he hired also from some of his friends and acquaintances about eighty men, and be gave them their hire, and he went with them to battle, and when he was on the road, Nimrod strengthened the hearts of the people that went with him.

36 And he said to them, Do not fear, neither be alarmed, for all our enemies will be delivered into our hands, and you may do with them as you please.

37 And all the men that went were about five hundred, and they fought against their enemies, and they destroyed them, and subdued them, and Nimrod placed standing officers over them in their respective places.

38 And he took some of their children as security, and they were all servants to Nimrod and to his brethren, and Nimrod and all the people that were with him turned homeward.

39 And when Nimrod had joyfully returned from battle, after having conquered his enemies, all his brethren, together with those who knew him before, assembled to make him king over them, and they placed the regal crown upon his head.

40 And he set over his subjects and people, princes, judges, and rulers, as is the custom amongst kings.

41 And he placed Terah the son of Nahor the prince of his host, and he dignified him and elevated him above all his princes.

42 And whilst he was reigning according to his heart's desire, after having conquered all his enemies around, he advised with his counselors to build a city for his palace, and they did so.

43 And they found a large valley opposite to the east, and they built him a large and extensive city, and Nimrod called the name of the city that he built Shinar, for the Lord had vehemently shaken his enemies and destroyed them.

44 And Nimrod dwelt in Shinar, and he reigned securely, and he fought with his enemies and he subdued them, and he prospered in all his battles, and his kingdom became very great.

45 And all nations and tongues heard of his fame, and they gathered themselves to him, and they bowed down to the earth, and they brought him offerings, and he became their lord and king, and they all dwelt with him in the city at Shinar, and Nimrod reigned in the earth over all the sons of Noah, and they were all under his power and counsel.

46 And all the earth was of one tongue and words of union, but Nimrod did not go in the ways of the Lord, and he was more wicked than all the men that were before him, from the days of the flood until those days.

47 And he made gods of wood and stone, and he bowed down to them, and he rebelled against the Lord, and taught all his subjects and the people of the earth his wicked ways; and Mardon his son was more wicked than his father.

48 And every one that heard of the acts of Mardon the son of Nimrod would say, concerning him, From the wicked goeth forth wickedness; therefore it became a proverb in the whole earth, saying, From the wicked goeth forth

wickedness, and it was current in the words of men from that time to this.

49 And Terah the son of Nahor, prince of Nimrod's host, was in those days very great in the sight of the king and his subjects, and the king and princes loved him, and they elevated him very high.

50 And Terah took a wife and her name was Amthelo the daughter of Cornebo; and the wife of Terah conceived and bare him a son in those days.

51 Terah was seventy years old when he begat him, and Terah called the name of his son that was born to him Abram, because the king had raised him in those days, and dignified him above all his princes that were with him.

Chapter 8

1 And it was in the night that Abram was born, that all the servants of Terah, and all the wise men of Nimrod, and his conjurors came and ate and drank in the house of Terah, and they rejoiced with him on that night.

2 And when all the wise men and conjurors went out from the house of Terah, they lifted up their eyes toward heaven that night to look at the stars, and they saw, and behold one very large star came from the east and ran in the heavens, and he swallowed up the four stars from the four sides of the heavens.

3 And all the wise men of the king and his conjurors were astonished at the sight, and the sages understood this matter, and they knew its import.

4 And they said to each other, This only betokens the child that has been born to Terah this night, who will grow up and be fruitful, and multiply, and possess all the earth, he and his children for ever, and he and his seed will slay great kings, and inherit their lands.

5 And the wise men and conjurors went home that night, and in the morning all these wise men and conjurors rose up early, and assembled in an appointed house.

6 And they spoke and said to each other, Behold the sight that we saw last night is hidden from the king, it has not been made known to him.

7 And should this thing get known to the king in the latter days, he will say to us, Why have you concealed this matter from me, and then we shall all suffer death; therefore, now let us go and tell the king the sight which we saw, and the interpretation thereof, and we shall then remain clear.

8 And they did so, and they all went to the king and bowed down to him to the ground, and they said, May the king live, may the king live.

9 We heard that a son was born to Terah the son of Nahor, the prince of thy host, and we yesternight came to his house, and we ate and drank and rejoiced with him that night.

10 And when thy servants went out from the house of Terah, to go to our respective homes to abide there for the night, we lifted up our eyes to heaven, and we saw a great star coming from the east, and the same star ran with great speed, and swallowed up four great stars, from the four sides of the heavens.

11 And thy servants were astonished at the sight which we saw, and were greatly terrified, and we made our judgment upon the sight, and knew by our wisdom the proper interpretation thereof, that this thing applies to the child that is born to Terah, who will grow up and multiply greatly, and become powerful, and kill all the kings of the earth, and inherit all their lands, he and his seed forever.

12 And now our lord and king, behold we have truly

acquainted thee with what we have seen concerning this child.

13 If it seemeth good to the king to give his father value for this child, we will slay him before he shall grow up and increase in the land, and his evil increase against us, that we and our children perish through his evil.

14 And the king heard their words and they seemed good in his sight, and he sent and called for Terah, and Terah came before the king.

15 And the king said to Terah, I have been told that a son was yesternight born to thee, and after this manner was observed in the heavens at his birth.

16 And now therefore give me the child, that we may slay him before his evil springs up against us, and I will give thee for his value, thy house full of silver and gold.

17 And Terah answered the king and said to him: My Lord and king, I have heard thy words, and thy servant shall do all that his king desireth.

18 But my lord and king, I will tell thee what happened to me yesternight, that I may see what advice the king will give his servant, and then I will answer the king upon what he has just spoken; and the king said, Speak.

19 And Terah said to the king, Ayon, son of Mored, came to me yesternight, saying,

20 Give unto me the great and beautiful horse that the king gave thee, and I will give thee silver and gold, and straw and provender for its value; and I said to him, Wait till I see the king concerning thy words, and behold whatever the king saith, that will I do.

21 And now my lord and king, behold I have made this thing known to thee, and the advice which my king will give unto his servant, that will I follow.

22 And the king heard the words of Terah, and his anger was kindled and he considered him in the light of a fool.

23 And the king answered Terah, and he said to him, Art thou so silly, ignorant, or deficient in understanding, to do this thing, to give thy beautiful horse for silver and gold or even for straw and provender?

24 Art thou so short of silver and gold, that thou shouldst do this thing, because thou canst not obtain straw and provender to feed thy horse? and what is silver and gold to thee, or straw and provender, that thou shouldst give away that fine horse which I gave thee, like which there is none to be had on the whole earth?

25 And the king left off speaking, and Terah answered the king, saying, Like unto this has the king spoken to his servant;

26 I beseech thee, my lord and king, what is this which thou didst say unto me, saying, Give thy son that we may slay him, and I will give thee silver and gold for his value; what shall I do with silver and gold after the death of my son? who shall inherit me? surely then at my death, the silver and gold will return to my king who gave it.

27 And when the king heard the words of Terah, and the parable which he brought concerning the king, it grieved him greatly and he was vexed at this thing, and his anger burned within him.

28 And Terah saw that the anger of the king was kindled against him, and he answered the king, saying, All that I have is in the king's power; whatever the king desireth to do to his servant, that let him do, yea, even my son, he is in the king's power, without value in exchange, he and his two brothers that are older than he.

29 And the king said to Terah, No, but I will purchase thy younger son for a price.

30 And Terah answered the king, saying, I beseech thee my

lord and king to let thy servant speak a word before thee, and let the king hear the word of his servant, and Terah said, Let my king give me three days' time till I consider this matter within myself, and consult with my family concerning the words of my king; and he pressed the king greatly to agree to this.

31 And the king hearkened to Terah, and he did so and he gave him three days' time, and Terah went out from the king's presence, and he came home to his family and spoke to them all the words of the king; and the people were greatly afraid.

32 And it was in the third day that the king sent to Terah, saying, Send me thy son for a price as I spoke to thee; and shouldst thou not do this, I will send and slay all thou hast in thy house, so that thou shalt not even have a dog remaining.

33 And Terah hastened, (as the thing was urgent from the king), and he took a child from one of his servants, which his handmaid had born to him that day, and Terah brought the child to the king and received value for him.

34 And the Lord was with Terah in this matter, that Nimrod might not cause Abram's death, and the king took the child from Terah and with all his might dashed his head to the ground, for he thought it had been Abram; and this was concealed from him from that day, and it was forgotten by the king, as it was the will of Providence not to suffer Abram's death.

35 And Terah took Abram his son secretly, together with his mother and nurse, and he concealed them in a cave, and he brought them their provisions monthly.

36 And the Lord was with Abram in the cave and he grew up, and Abram was in the cave ten years, and the king and his princes, soothsayers and sages, thought that the king had killed Abram.

Chapter 9

1 And Haran, the son of Terah, Abram's oldest brother, took a wife in those days.

2 Haran was thirty-nine years old when he took her; and the wife of Haran conceived and bare a son, and he called his name Lot.

3 And she conceived again and bare a daughter, and she called her name Milca; and she again conceived and bare a daughter, and she called her name Sarai.

4 Haran was forty-two years old when he begat Sarai, which was in the tenth year of the life of Abram; and in those days Abram and his mother and nurse went out from the cave, as the king and his subjects had forgotten the affair of Abram.

5 And when Abram came out from the cave, he went to Noah and his son Shem, and he remained with them to learn the instruction of the Lord and his ways, and no man knew where Abram was, and Abram served Noah and Shem his son for a long time.

6 And Abram was in Noah's house thirty-nine years, and Abram knew the Lord from three years old, and he went in the ways of the Lord until the day of his death, as Noah and his son Shem had taught him; and all the sons of the earth in those days greatly transgressed against the Lord, and they rebelled against him and they served other gods, and they forgot the Lord who had created them in the earth; and the inhabitants of the earth made unto themselves, at that time, every man his god; gods of wood and stone which could neither speak, hear, nor deliver, and the sons of men served them and they became their gods.

7 And the king and all his servants, and Terah with all his household were then the first of those that served gods of wood and stone.

20

8 And Terah had twelve gods of large size, made of wood and stone, after the twelve months of the year, and he served each one monthly, and every month Terah would bring his meat offering and drink offering to his gods; thus did Terah all the days.

9 And all that generation were wicked in the sight of the Lord, and they thus made every man his god, but they forsook the Lord who had created them.

10 And there was not a man found in those days in the whole earth, who knew the Lord (for they served each man his own God) except Noah and his household, and all those who were under his counsel knew the Lord in those days.

11 And Abram the son of Terah was waxing great in those days in the house of Noah, and no man knew it, and the Lord was with him.

12 And the Lord gave Abram an understanding heart, and he knew all the works of that generation were vain, and that all their gods were vain and were of no avail.

13 And Abram saw the sun shining upon the earth, and Abram said unto himself Surely now this sun that shines upon the earth is God, and him will I serve.

14 And Abram served the sun in that day and he prayed to him, and when evening came the sun set as usual, and Abram said within himself, Surely this cannot be God?

15 And Abram still continued to speak within himself, Who is he who made the heavens and the earth? who created upon earth? where is he?

16 And night darkened over him, and he lifted up his eyes toward the west, north, south, and east, and he saw that the sun had vanished from the earth, and the day became dark.

17 And Abram saw the stars and moon before him, and he said, Surely this is the God who created the whole earth as well as man, and behold these his servants are gods around him: and Abram served the moon and prayed to it all that night.

18 And in the morning when it was light and the sun shone upon the earth as usual, Abram saw all the things that the Lord God had made upon earth.

19 And Abram said unto himself Surely these are not gods that made the earth and all mankind, but these are the servants of God, and Abram remained in the house of Noah and there knew the Lord and his ways' and he served the Lord all the days of his life, and all that generation forgot the Lord, and served other gods of wood and stone, and rebelled all their days.

20 And king Nimrod reigned securely, and all the earth was under his control, and all the earth was of one tongue and words of union.

21 And all the princes of Nimrod and his great men took counsel together; Phut, Mitzraim, Cush and Canaan with their families, and they said to each other, Come let us build ourselves a city and in it a strong tower, and its top reaching heaven, and we will make ourselves famed, so that we may reign upon the whole world, in order that the evil of our enemies may cease from us, that we may reign mightily over them, and that we may not become scattered over the earth on account of their wars.

22 And they all went before the king, and they told the king these words, and the king agreed with them in this affair, and he did so.

23 And all the families assembled consisting of about six

hundred thousand men, and they went to seek an extensive piece of ground to build the city and the tower, and they sought in the whole earth and they found none like one valley at the east of the land of Shinar, about two days' walk, and they journeyed there and they dwelt there.

24 And they began to make bricks and burn fires to build the city and the tower that they had imagined to complete.

25 And the building of the tower was unto them a transgression and a sin, and they began to build it, and whilst they were building against the Lord God of heaven, they imagined in their hearts to war against him and to ascend into heaven.

26 And all these people and all the families divided themselves in three parts; the first said We will ascend into heaven and fight against him; the second said, We will ascend to heaven and place our own gods there and serve them; and the third part said, We will ascend to heaven and smite him with bows and spears; and God knew all their works and all their evil thoughts, and he saw the city and the tower which they were building.

27 And when they were building they built themselves a great city and a very high and strong tower; and on account of its height the mortar and bricks did not reach the builders in their ascent to it, until those who went up had completed a full year, and after that, they reached to the builders and gave them the mortar and the bricks; thus was it done daily.

28 And behold these ascended and others descended the whole day; and if a brick should fall from their hands and get broken, they would all weep over it, and if a man fell and died, none of them would look at him.

29 And the Lord knew their thoughts, and it came to pass when they were building they cast the arrows toward the heavens, and all the arrows fell upon them filled with blood, and when they saw them they said to each other, Surely we have slain all those that are in heaven.

30 For this was from the Lord in order to cause them to err, and in order; to destroy them from off the face of the ground.

31 And they built the tower and the city, and they did this thing daily until many days and years were elapsed.

32 And God said to the seventy angels who stood foremost before him, to those who were near to him, saying, Come let us descend and confuse their tongues, that one man shall not understand the language of his neighbor, and they did so unto them.

33 And from that day following, they forgot each man his neighbor's tongue, and they could not understand to speak in one tongue, and when the builder took from the hands of his neighbor lime or stone which he did not order, the builder would cast it away and throw it upon his neighbor, that he would die.

34 And they did so many days, and they killed many of them in this manner.

35 And the Lord smote the three divisions that were there, and he punished them according to their works and designs; those who said, We will ascend to heaven and serve our gods, became like apes and elephants; and those who said, We will smite the heaven with arrows, the Lord killed them, one man through the hand of his neighbor; and the third division of those who said, We will ascend to heaven and fight against him, the Lord scattered them throughout the earth.

36 And those who were left amongst them, when they knew and understood the evil which was coming upon them, they forsook the building, and they also became

scattered upon the face of the whole earth.

37 And they ceased building the city and the tower; therefore he called that place Babel, for there the Lord confounded the Language of the whole earth; behold it was at the east of the land of Shinar.

38 And as to the tower which the sons of men built, the earth opened its mouth and swallowed up one third part thereof, and a fire also descended from heaven and burned another third, and the other third is left to this day, and it is of that part which was aloft, and its circumference is three days' walk.

39 And many of the sons of men died in that tower, a people without number.

Chapter 10

1 And Peleg the son of Eber died in those days, in the forty-eighth year of the life of Abram son of Terah, and all the days of Peleg were two hundred and thirty-nine years.

2 And when the Lord had scattered the sons of men on account of their sin at the tower, behold they spread forth into many divisions, and all the sons of men were dispersed into the four corners of the earth.

3 And all the families became each according to its language, its land, or its city.

4 And the sons of men built many cities according to their families, in all the places where they went, and throughout the earth where the Lord had scattered them.

5 And some of them built cities in places from which they were afterward extirpated, and they called these cities after their own names, or the names of their children, or after their particular occurrences.

6 And the sons of Japheth the son of Noah went and built themselves cities in the places where they were scattered, and they called all their cities after their names, and the sons of Japheth were divided upon the face of the earth into many divisions and languages.

7 And these are the sons of Japheth according to their families, Gomer, Magog, Medai, Javan, Tubal, Meshech and Tiras; these are the children of Japheth according to their generations.

8 And the children of Gomer, according to their cities, were the Francum, who dwell in the land of Franza, by the river Franza, by the river Senah.

9 And the children of Rephath are the Bartonim, who dwell in the land of Bartonia by the river Ledah, which empties its waters in the great sea Gihon, that is, oceanus.

10 And the children of Tugarma are ten families, and these are their names: Buzar, Parzunac, Balgar, Elicanum, Ragbib, Tarki, Bid, Zebuc, Ongal and Tilmaz; all these spread and rested in the north and built themselves cities.

11 And they called their cities after their own names, those are they who abide by the rivers Hithlah and Italac unto this day.

12 But the families of Angoli, Balgar and Parzunac, they dwell by the great river Dubnee; and the names of their cities are also according to their own names.

13 And the children of Javan are the Javanim who dwell in the land of Makdonia, and the children of Medaiare are the Orelum that dwell in the land of Curson, and the children of Tubal are those that dwell in the land of Tuskanah by the river Pashiah.

14 And the children of Meshech are the Shibashni and the children of Tiras are Rushash, Cushni, and Ongolis; all these went and built themselves cities; those are the cities that are situate by the sea Jabus by the river Cura, which

empties itself in the river Tragan.

15 And the children of Elishah are the Almanim, and they also went and built themselves cities; those are the cities situate between the mountains of Job and Shibathmo; and of them were the people of Lumbardi who dwell opposite the mountains of Job and Shibathmo, and they conquered the land of Italia and remained there unto this day.

16 And the children of Chittim are the Romim who dwell in the valley of Canopia by the river Tibreu.

17 And the children of Dudonim are those who dwell in the cities of the sea Gihon, in the land of Bordna.

18 These are the families of the children of Japheth according to their cities and languages, when they were scattered after the tower, and they called their cities after their names and occurrences; and these are the names of all their cities according to their families, which they built in those days after the tower.

19 And the children of Ham were Cush, Mitzraim, Phut and Canaan according to their generation and cities.

20 All these went and built themselves cities as they found fit places for them, and they called their cities after the names of their fathers Cush, Mitzraim, Phut and Canaan.

21 And the children of Mitzraim are the Ludim, Anamim, Lehabim, Naphtuchim, Pathrusim, Casluchim and Caphturim, seven families.

22 All these dwell by the river Sihor, that is the brook of Egypt, and they built themselves cities and called them after their own names.

23 And the children of Pathros and Casloch intermarried together, and from them went forth the Pelishtim, the Azathim, and the Gerarim, the Githim and the Ekronim, in all five families; these also built themselves cities, and they called their cities after the names of their fathers unto this day.

24 And the children of Canaan also built themselves cities, and they called their cities after their names, eleven cities and others without number.

25 And four men from the family of Ham went to the land of the plain; these are the names of the four men, Sodom, Gomorrah, Admah and Zeboyim.

26 And these men built themselves four cities in the land of the plain, and they called the names of their cities after their own names.

27 And they and their children and all belonging to them dwelt in those cities, and they were fruitful and multiplied greatly and dwelt peaceably.

28 And Seir the son of Hur, son of Hivi, son of Canaan, went and found a valley opposite to Mount Paran, and he built a city there, and he and his seven sons and his household dwelt there, and he called the city which he built Seir, according to his name; that is the land of Seir unto this day.

29 These are the families of the children of Ham, according to their languages and cities, when they were scattered to their countries after the tower.

30 And some of the children of Shem son of Noah, father of all the children of Eber, also went and built themselves cities in the places wherein they were scattered, and they called their cities after their names.

31 And the sons of Shem were Elam, Ashur, Arpachshad, Lud and Aram, and they built themselves cities and called the names of all their cities after their names.

32 And Ashur son of Shem and his children and household went forth at that time, a very large body of them, and they went to a distant land that they found, and they met with a very extensive valley in the land that they went to, and they

built themselves four cities, and they called them after their own names and occurrences.

33 And these are the names of the cities which the children of Ashur built, Ninevah, Resen, Calach and Rehobother; and the children of Ashur dwell there unto this day.

34 And the children of Aram also went and built themselves a city, and they called the name of the city Uz after their eldest brother, and they dwell therein; that is the land of Uz to this day.

35 And in the second year after the tower a man from the house of Ashur, whose name was Bela, went from the land of Ninevah to sojourn with his household wherever he could find a place; and they came until opposite the cities of the plain against Sodom, and they dwelt there.

36 And the man rose up and built there a small city, and called its name Bela, after his name; that is the land of Zoar unto this day.

37 And these are the families of the children of Shem according to their language and cities, after they were scattered upon the earth after the tower.

38 And every kingdom, city, and family of the families of the children of Noah built themselves many cities after this.

39 And they established governments in all their cities, in order to be regulated by their orders; so did all the families of the children of Noah forever.

Chapter 11

1 And Nimrod son of Cush was still in the land of Shinar, and he reigned over it and dwelt there, and he built cities in the land of Shinar.

2 And these are the names of the four cities which he built, and he called their names after the occurrences that happened to them in the building of the tower.

3 And he called the first Babel, saying, Because the Lord there confounded the language of the whole earth; and the name of the second he called Erech, because from there God dispersed them.

4 And the third he called Eched, saying there was a great battle at that place; and the fourth he called Calnah, because his princes and mighty men were consumed there, and they vexed the Lord, they rebelled and transgressed against him.

5 And when Nimrod had built these cities in the land of Shinar, he placed in them the remainder of his people, his princes and his mighty men that were left in his kingdom.

6 And Nimrod dwelt in Babel, and he there renewed his reign over the rest of his subjects, and he reigned securely, and the subjects and princes of Nimrod called his name Amraphel, saying that at the tower his princes and men fell through his means.

7 And notwithstanding this, Nimrod did not return to the Lord, and he continued in wickedness and teaching wickedness to the sons of men; and Mardon, his son, was worse than his father, and continued to add to the abominations of his father.

8 And he caused the sons of men to sin, therefore it is said, From the wicked goeth forth wickedness.

9 At that time there was war between the families of the children of Ham, as they were dwelling in the cities which they had built.

10 And Chedorlaomer, king of Elam, went away from the families of the children of Ham, and he fought with them and he subdued them, and he went to the five cities of the plain and he fought against them and he subdued them, and they were under his control.

11 And they served him twelve years, and they gave him a yearly tax.

12 At that time died Nahor, son of Serug, in the forty-ninth year of the life of Abram son of Terah.

13 And in the fiftieth year of the life of Abram son of Terah, Abram came forth from the house of Noah, and went to his father's house.

14 And Abram knew the Lord, and he went in his ways and instructions, and the Lord his God was with him.

15 And Terah his father was in those days, still captain of the host of king Nimrod, and he still followed strange gods.

16 And Abram came to his father's house and saw twelve gods standing there in their temples, and the anger of Abram was kindled when he saw these images in his father's house.

17 And Abram said, As the Lord liveth these images shall not remain in my father's house; so shall the Lord who created me do unto me if in three days' time I do not break them all.

18 And Abram went from them, and his anger burned within him. And Abram hastened and went from the chamber to his father's outer court, and he found his father sitting in the court, and all his servants with him, and Abram came and sat before him.

19 And Abram asked his father, saying, Father, tell me where is God who created heaven and earth, and all the sons of men upon earth, and who created thee and me. And Terah answered his son Abram and said, Behold those who created us are all with us in the house.

20 And Abram said to his father, My lord, shew them to me I pray thee; and Terah brought Abram into the chamber of the inner court, and Abram saw, and behold the whole room was full of gods of wood and stone, twelve great images and others less than they without number.

21 And Terah said to his son, Behold these are they which made all thou seest upon earth, and which created me and thee, and all mankind.

22 And Terah bowed down to his gods, and he then went away from them, and Abram, his son, went away with him.

23 And when Abram had gone from them he went to his mother and sat before her, and he said to his mother, Behold, my father has shown me those who made heaven and earth, and all the sons of men.

24 Now, therefore, hasten and fetch a kid from the flock, and make of it savory meat, that I may bring it to my father's gods as an offering for them to eat; perhaps I may thereby become acceptable to them.

25 And his mother did so, and she fetched a kid, and made savory meat thereof, and brought it to Abram, and Abram took the savory meat from his mother and brought it before his father's gods, and he drew nigh to them that they might eat; and Terah his father, did not know of it.

26 And Abram saw on the day when he was sitting amongst them, that they had no voice, no hearing, no motion, and not one of them could stretch forth his hand to eat.

27 And Abram mocked them, and said, Surely the savory meat that I prepared has not pleased them, or perhaps it was too little for them, and for that reason they would not eat; therefore tomorrow I will prepare fresh savory meat, better and more plentiful than this, in order that I may see the result.

28 And it was on the next day that Abram directed his mother concerning the savory meat, and his mother rose and fetched three fine kids from the flock, and she made of them some excellent savory meat, such as her son was fond of, and she gave it to her son Abram; and Terah his father

did not know of it.

29 And Abram took the savory meat from his mother, and brought it before his father's gods into the chamber; and he came nigh unto them that they might eat, and he placed it before them, and Abram sat before them all day, thinking perhaps they might eat.

30 And Abram viewed them, and behold they had neither voice nor hearing, nor did one of them stretch forth his hand to the meat to eat.

31 And in the evening of that day in that house Abram was clothed with the spirit of God.

32 And he called out and said, Wo unto my father and this wicked generation, whose hearts are all inclined to vanity, who serve these idols of wood and stone which can neither eat, smell, hear nor speak, who have mouths without speech, eyes without sight, ears without hearing, hands without feeling, and legs which cannot move; like them are those that made them and that trust in them.

33 And when Abram saw all these things his anger was kindled against his father, and he hastened and took a hatchet in his hand, and came unto the chamber of the gods, and he broke all his father's gods.

34 And when he had done breaking the images, he placed the hatchet in the hand of the great god which was there before them, and he went out; and Terah his father came home, for he had heard at the door the sound of the striking of the hatchet; so Terah came into the house to know what this was about.

35 And Terah, having heard the noise of the hatchet in the room of images, ran to the room to the images, and he met Abram going out.

36 And Terah entered the room and found all the idols fallen down and broken, and the hatchet in the hand of the largest, which was not broken, and the savory meat which Abram his son had made was still before them.

37 And when Terah saw this his anger was greatly kindled, and he hastened and went from the room to Abram.

38 And he found Abram his son still sitting in the house; and he said to him, What is this work thou hast done to my gods?

39 And Abram answered Terah his father and he said, Not so my lord, for I brought savory meat before them, and when I came nigh to them with the meat that they might eat, they all at once stretched forth their hands to eat before the great one had put forth his hand to eat.

40 And the large one saw their works that they did before him, and his anger was violently kindled against them, and he went and took the hatchet that was in the house and came to them and broke them all, and behold the hatchet is yet in his hand as thou seest.

41 And Terah's anger was kindled against his son Abram, when he spoke this; and Terah said to Abram his son in his anger, What is this tale that thou hast told? Thou speakest lies to me.

42 Is there in these gods spirit, soul or power to do all thou hast told me? Are they not wood and stone, and have I not myself made them, and canst thou speak such lies, saying that the large god that was with them smote them? It is thou that didst place the hatchet in his hands, and then sayest he smote them all.

43 And Abram answered his father and said to him, And how canst thou then serve these idols in whom there is no power to do any thing? Can those idols in which thou trustest deliver thee? can they hear thy prayers when thou callest upon them? can they deliver thee from the hands of thy enemies, or will they fight thy battles for thee against

thy enemies, that thou shouldst serve wood and stone which can neither speak nor hear?

44 And now surely it is not good for thee nor for the sons of men that are connected with thee, to do these things; are you so silly, so foolish or so short of understanding that you will serve wood and stone, and do after this manner?

45 And forget the Lord God who made heaven and earth, and who created you in the earth, and thereby bring a great evil upon your souls in this matter by serving stone and wood?

46 Did not our fathers in days of old sin in this matter, and the Lord God of the universe brought the waters of the flood upon them and destroyed the whole earth?

47 And how can you continue to do this and serve gods of wood and stone, who cannot hear, or speak, or deliver you from oppression, thereby bringing down the anger of the God of the universe upon you?

48 Now therefore my father refrain from this, and bring not evil upon thy soul and the souls of thy household.

49 And Abram hastened and sprang from before his father, and took the hatchet from his father's largest idol, with which Abram broke it and ran away.

50 And Terah, seeing all that Abram had done, hastened to go from his house, and he went to the king and he came before Nimrod and stood before him, and he bowed down to the king; and the king said, What dost thou want?

51 And he said, I beseech thee my lord, to hear me--Now fifty years back a child was born to me, and thus has he done to my gods and thus has he spoken; and now therefore, my lord and king, send for him that he may come before thee, and judge him according to the law, that we may be delivered from his evil.

52 And the king sent three men of his servants, and they went and brought Abram before the king. And Nimrod and all his princes and servants were that day sitting before him, and Terah sat also before them.

53 And the king said to Abram, What is this that thou hast done to thy father and to his gods? And Abram answered the king in the words that he spoke to his father, and he said, The large god that was with them in the house did to them what thou hast heard.

54 And the king said to Abram, Had they power to speak and eat and do as thou hast said? And Abram answered the king, saying, And if there be no power in them why dost thou serve them and cause the sons of men to err through thy follies?

55 Dost thou imagine that they can deliver thee or do anything small or great, that thou shouldst serve them? And why wilt thou not sense the God of the whole universe, who created thee and in whose power it is to kill and keep alive?

56 0 foolish, simple, and ignorant king, woe unto thee forever.

57 I thought thou wouldst teach thy servants the upright way, but thou hast not done this, but hast filled the whole earth with thy sins and the sins of thy people who have followed thy ways.

58 Dost thou not know, or hast thou not heard, that this evil which thou doest, our ancestors sinned therein in days of old, and the eternal God brought the waters of the flood upon them and destroyed them all, and also destroyed the whole earth on their account? And wilt thou and thy people rise up now and do like unto this work, in order to bring down the anger of the Lord God of the universe, and to bring evil upon thee and the whole earth?

59 Now therefore put away this evil deed which thou doest,

and serve the God of the universe, as thy soul is in his hands, and then it will be well with thee.

60 And if thy wicked heart will not hearken to my words to cause thee to forsake thy evil ways, and to serve the eternal God, then wilt thou die in shame in the latter days, thou, thy people and all who are connected with thee, hearing thy words or walking in thy evil ways.

61 And when Abram had ceased speaking before the king and princes, Abram lifted up his eyes to the heavens, and he said, The Lord seeth all the wicked, and he will judge them.

Chapter 12

1 And when the king heard the words of Abram he ordered him to be put into prison; and Abram was ten days in prison.

2 And at the end of those days the king ordered that all the kings, princes and governors of different provinces and the sages should come before him, and they sat before him, and Abram was still in the house of confinement.

3 And the king said to the princes and sages, Have you heard what Abram, the son of Terah, has done to his father? Thus has he done to him, and I ordered him to be brought before me, and thus has he spoken; his heart did not misgive him, neither did he stir in my presence, and behold now he is confined in the prison.

4 And therefore decide what judgment is due to this man who reviled the king; who spoke and did all the things that you heard.

5 And they all answered the king saying, The man who revileth the king should be hanged upon a tree; but having done all the things that he said, and having despised our gods, he must therefore be burned to death, for this is the law in this matter.

6 If it pleaseth the king to do this, let him order his servants to kindle a fire both night and day in thy brick furnace, and then we will cast this man into it. And the king did so, and he commanded his servants that they should prepare a fire for three days and three nights in the king's furnace, that is in Casdim; and the king ordered them to take Abram from prison and bring him out to be burned.

7 And all the king's servants, princes, lords, governors, and judges, and all the inhabitants of the land, about nine hundred thousand men, stood opposite the furnace to see Abram.

8 And all the women and little ones crowded upon the roofs and towers to see what was doing with Abram, and they all stood together at a distance; and there was not a man left that did not come on that day to behold the scene.

9 And when Abram was come, the conjurors of the king and the sages saw Abram, and they cried out to the king, saying, Our sovereign lord, surely this is the man whom we know to have been the child at whose birth the great star swallowed the four stars, which we declared to the king now fifty years since.

10 And behold now his father has also transgressed thy commands, and mocked thee by bringing thee another child, which thou didst kill.

11 And when the king heard their words, he was exceedingly wroth, and he ordered Terah to be brought before him.

12 And the king said, Hast thou heard what the conjurors have spoken? Now tell me truly, how didst thou; and if thou shalt speak truth thou shalt be acquitted.

13 And seeing that the king's anger was so much kindled, Terah said to the king, My lord and king, thou hast heard the truth, and what the sages have spoken is right. And the king said, How couldst thou do this thing, to transgress my orders and to give me a child that thou didst not beget, and to take value for him?

14 And Terah answered the king, Because my tender feelings were excited for my son, at that time, and I took a son of my handmaid, and I brought him to the king.

15 And the king said Who advised thee to this? Tell me, do not hide aught from me, and then thou shalt not die.

16 And Terah was greatly terrified in the king's presence, and he said to the king, It was Haran my eldest son who advised me to this; and Haran was in those days that Abram was born, two and thirty years old.

17 But Haran did not advise his father to anything, for Terah said this to the king in order to deliver his soul from the king, for he feared greatly; and the king said to Terah, Haran thy son who advised thee to this shall die through fire with Abram; for the sentence of death is upon him for having rebelled against the king's desire in doing this thing.

18 And Haran at that time felt inclined to follow the ways of Abram, but he kept it within himself.

19 And Haran said in his heart, Behold now the king has seized Abram on account of these things which Abram did, and it shall come to pass, that if Abram prevail over the king I will follow him, but if the king prevail I will go after the king.

20 And when Terah had spoken this to the king concerning Haran his son, the king ordered Haran to be seized with Abram.

21 And they brought them both, Abram and Haran his brother, to cast them into the fire; and all the inhabitants of the land and the king's servants and princes and all the women and little ones were there, standing that day over them.

22 And the king's servants took Abram and his brother, and they stripped them of all their clothes excepting their lower garments which were upon them.

23 And they bound their hands and feet with linen cords, and the servants of the king lifted them up and cast them both into the furnace.

24 And the Lord loved Abram and he had compassion over him, and the Lord came down and delivered Abram from the fire and he was not burned.

25 But all the cords with which they bound him were burned, while Abram remained and walked about in the fire.

26 And Haran died when they had cast him into the fire, and he was burned to ashes, for his heart was not perfect with the Lord; and those men who cast him into the fire, the flame of the fire spread over them, and they were burned, and twelve men of them died.

27 And Abram walked in the midst of the fire three days and three nights, and all the servants of the king saw him walking in the fire, and they came and told the king, saying, Behold we have seen Abram walking about in the midst of the fire, and even the lower garments which are upon him are not burned, but the cord with which he was bound is burned.

28 And when the king heard their words his heart fainted and he would not believe them; so he sent other faithful princes to see this matter, and they went and saw it and told it to the king; and the king rose to go and see it, and he saw Abram walking to and fro in the midst of the fire, and he saw Haran's body burned, and the king wondered greatly.

29 And the king ordered Abram to be taken out from the fire; and his servants approached to take him out and they

could not, for the fire was round about and the flame ascending toward them from the furnace.

30 And the king's servants fled from it, and the king rebuked them, saying, Make haste and bring Abram out of the fire that you shall not die.

31 And the servants of the king again approached to bring Abram out, and the flames came upon them and burned their faces so that eight of them died.

32 And when the king saw that his servants could not approach the fire lest they should be burned, the king called to Abram, O servant of the God who is in heaven, go forth from amidst the fire and come hither before me; and Abram hearkened to the voice of the king, and he went forth from the fire and came and stood before the king.

33 And when Abram came out the king and all his servants saw Abram coming before the king, with his lower garments upon him, for they were not burned, but the cord with which he was bound was burned.

34 And the king said to Abram, How is it that thou wast not burned in the fire?

35 And Abram said to the king, The God of heaven and earth in whom I trust and who has all in his power, he delivered me from the fire into which thou didst cast me.

36 And Haran the brother of Abram was burned to ashes, and they sought for his body, and they found it consumed.

37 And Haran was eighty-two years old when he died in the fire of Casdim. And the king, princes, and inhabitants of the land, seeing that Abram was delivered from the fire, they came and bowed down to Abram.

38 And Abram said to them, Do not bow down to me, but bow down to the God of the world who made you, and serve him, and go in his ways for it is he who delivered me from out of this fire, and it is he who created the souls and spirits of all men, and formed man in his mother's womb, and brought him forth into the world, and it is he who will deliver those who trust in him from all pain.

39 And this thing seemed very wonderful in the eyes of the king and princes, that Abram was saved from the fire and that Haran was burned; and the king gave Abram many presents and he gave him his two head servants from the king's house; the name of one was Oni and the name of the other was Eliezer.

40 And all the kings, princes and servants gave Abram many gifts of silver and gold and pearl, and the king and his princes sent him away, and he went in peace.

41 And Abram went forth from the king in peace, and many of the king's servants followed him, and about three hundred men joined him.

42 And Abram returned on that day and went to his father's house, he and the men that followed him, and Abram served the Lord his God all the days of his life, and he walked in his ways and followed his law.

43 And from that day forward Abram inclined the hearts of the sons of men to serve the Lord.

44 And at that time Nahor and Abram took unto themselves wives, the daughters of their brother Haran; the wife of Nahor was Milca and the name of Abram's wife was Sarai. And Sarai, wife of Abram, was barren; she had no offspring in those days.

45 And at the expiration of two years from Abram's going out of the fire, that is in the fifty-second year of his life, behold king Nimrod sat in Babel upon the throne, and the king fell asleep and dreamed that he was standing with his troops and hosts in a valley opposite the king's furnace.

46 And he lifted up his eyes and saw a man in the likeness of Abram coming forth from the furnace, and that he came

and stood before the king with his drawn sword, and then sprang to the king with his sword, when the king fled from the man, for he was afraid; and while he was running, the man threw an egg upon the king's head, and the egg became a great river.

47 And the king dreamed that all his troops sank in that river and died, and the king took flight with three men who were before him and he escaped.

48 And the king looked at these men and they were clothed in princely dresses as the garments of kings, and had the appearance and majesty of kings.

49 And while they were running, the river again turned to an egg before the king, and there came forth from the egg a young bird which came before the king, and flew at his head and plucked out the king's eye.

50 And the king was grieved at the sight, and he awoke out of his sleep and his spirit was agitated; and he felt a great terror.

51 And in the morning the king rose from his couch in fear, and he ordered all the wise men and magicians to come before him, when the king related his dream to them.

52 And a wise servant of the king, whose name was Anuki, answered the king, saying, This is nothing else but the evil of Abram and his seed which will spring up against my Lord and king in the latter days.

53 And behold the day will come when Abram and his seed and the children of his household will war with my king, and they will smite all the king's hosts and his troops.

54 And as to what thou hast said concerning three men which thou didst see like unto thyself, and which did escape, this means that only thou wilt escape with three kings from the kings of the earth who will be with thee in battle.

55 And that which thou sawest of the river which turned to an egg as at first, and the young bird plucking out thine eye, this means nothing else but the seed of Abram which will slay the king in latter days.

56 This is my king's dream, and this is its interpretation, and the dream is true, and the interpretation which thy servant has given thee is right.

57 Now therefore my king, surely thou knowest that it is now fifty-two years since thy sages saw this at the birth of Abram, and if my king will suffer Abram to live in the earth it will be to the injury of my lord and king, for all the days that Abram liveth neither thou nor thy kingdom will be established, for this was known formerly at his birth; and why will not my king slay him, that his evil may be kept from thee in latter days?

58 And Nimrod hearkened to the voice of Anuki, and he sent some of his servants in secret to go and seize Abram, and bring him before the king to suffer death.

59 And Eliezer, Abram's servant whom the king had given him, was at that time in the presence of the king, and he heard what Anuki had advised the king, and what the king had said to cause Abram's death.

60 And Eliezer said to Abram, Hasten, rise up and save thy soul, that thou mayest not die through the hands of the king, for thus did he see in a dream concerning thee, and thus did Anuki interpret it, and thus also did Anuki advise the king concerning thee.

61 And Abram hearkened to the voice of Eliezer, and Abram hastened and ran for safety to the house of Noah and his son Shem, and he concealed himself there and found a place of safety; and the king's servants came to Abram's house to seek him, but they could not find him, and they searched through out the country and he was not

to be found, and they went and searched in every direction and he was not to be met with.

62 And when the king's servants could not find Abram they returned to the king, but the king's anger against Abram was stilled, as they did not find him, and the king drove from his mind this matter concerning Abram.

63 And Abram was concealed in Noah's house for one month, until the king had forgotten this matter, but Abram was still afraid of the king; and Terah came to see Abram his son secretly in the house of Noah, and Terah was very great in the eyes of the king.

64 And Abram said to his father, Dost thou not know that the king thinketh to slay me, and to annihilate my name from the earth by the advice of his wicked counsellors?

65 Now whom hast thou here and what hast thou in this land? Arise, let us go together to the land of Canaan, that we may be delivered from his hand, lest thou perish also through him in the latter days.

66 Dost thou not know or hast thou not heard, that it is not through love that Nimrod giveth thee all this honor, but it is only for his benefit that he bestoweth all this good upon thee?

67 And if he do unto thee greater good than this, surely these are only vanities of the world, for wealth and riches cannot avail in the day of wrath and anger.

68 Now therefore hearken to my voice, and let us arise and go to the land of Canaan, out of the reach of injury from Nimrod; and serve thou the Lord who created thee in the earth and it will be well with thee; and cast away all the vain things which thou pursuest.

69 And Abram ceased to speak, when Noah and his son Shem answered Terah, saying, True is the word which Abram hath said unto thee.

70 And Terah hearkened to the voice of his son Abram, and Terah did all that Abram said, for this was from the Lord, that the king should not cause Abram's death.

Chapter 13

1 And Terah took his son Abram and his grandson Lot, the son of Haran, and Sarai his daughter-in-law, the wife of his son Abram, and all the souls of his household and went with them from Ur Casdim to go to the land of Canaan. And when they came as far as the land of Haran they remained there, for it was exceedingly good land for pasture, and of sufficient extent for those who accompanied them.

2 And the people of the land of Haran saw that Abram was good and upright with God and men, and that the Lord his God was with him, and some of the people of the land of Haran came and joined Abram, and he taught them the instruction of the Lord and his ways; and these men remained with Abram in his house and they adhered to him.

3 And Abram remained in the land three years, and at the expiration of three years the Lord appeared to Abram and said to him; I am the Lord who brought thee forth from Ur Casdim, and delivered thee from the hands of all thine enemies.

4 And now therefore if thou wilt hearken to my voice and keep my commandments, my statutes and my laws, then will I cause thy enemies to fall before thee, and I will multiply thy seed like the stars of heaven, and I will send my blessing upon all the works of thy hands, and thou shalt lack nothing.

5 Arise now, take thy wife and all belonging to thee and go to the land of Canaan and remain there, and I will there be unto thee for a God, and I will bless thee. And Abram rose and took his wife and all belonging to him, and he went to the land of Canaan as the Lord had told him; and Abram was fifty years old when he went from Haran.

6 And Abram came to the land of Canaan and dwelt in the midst of the city, and he there pitched his tent amongst the children of Canaan, inhabitants of the land.

7 And the Lord appeared to Abram when he came to the land of Canaan, and said to him, This is the land which I gave unto thee and to thy seed after thee forever, and I will make thy seed like the stars of heaven, and I will give unto thy seed for an inheritance all the lands which thou seest.

8 And Abram built an altar in the place where God had spoken to him, and Abram there called upon the name of the Lord.

9 At that time, at the end of three years of Abram's dwelling in the land of Canaan, in that year Noah died, which was the fifty-eighth year of the life of Abram; and all the days that Noah lived were nine hundred and fifty years and he died.

10 And Abram dwelt in the land of Canaan, he, his wife, and all belonging to him, and all those that accompanied him, together with those that joined him from the people of the land; but Nahor, Abram's brother, and Terah his father, and Lot the son of Haran and all belonging to them dwelt in Haran.

11 In the fifth year of Abram's dwelling in the land of Canaan the people of Sodom and Gomorrah and all the cities of the plain revolted from the power of Chedorlaomer, king of Elam; for all the kings of the cities of the plain had served Chedorlaomer for twelve years, and given him a yearly tax, but in those days in the thirteenth year, they rebelled against him.

12 And in the tenth year of Abram's dwelling in the land of Canaan there was war between Nimrod king of Shinar and Chedorlaomer king of Elam, and Nimrod came to fight with Chedorlaomer and to subdue him.

13 For Chedorlaomer was at that time one of the princes of the hosts of Nimrod, and when all the people at the tower were dispersed and those that remained were also scattered upon the face of the earth, Chedorlaomer went to the land of Elam and reigned over it and rebelled against his lord.

14 And in those days when Nimrod saw that the cities of the plain had rebelled, he came with pride and anger to war with Chedorlaomer, and Nimrod assembled all his princes and subjects, about seven hundred thousand men, and went against Chedorlaomer, and Chedorlaomer went out to meet him with five thousand men, and they prepared for battle in the valley of Babel which is between Elam and Shinar.

15 And all those kings fought there, and Nimrod and his people were smitten before the people of Chedorlaomer, and there fell from Nimrod's men about six hundred thousand, and Mardon the king's son fell amongst them.

16 And Nimrod fled and returned in shame and disgrace to his land, and he was under subjection to Chedorlaomer for a long time, and Chedorlaomer returned to his land and sent princes of his host to the kings that dwelt around him, to Arioch king of Elasar, and to Tidal king of Goyim, and made a covenant with them, and they were all obedient to his commands.

17 And it was in the fifteenth year of Abram's dwelling in the land of Canaan, which is the seventieth year of the life of Abram, and the Lord appeared to Abram in that year and he said to him, I am the Lord who brought thee out from Ur Casdim to give thee this land for an inheritance.

18 Now therefore walk before me and be perfect and keep

my commands, for to thee and to thy seed I will give this land for an inheritance, from the river Mitzraim unto the great river Euphrates.

19 And thou shalt come to thy fathers in peace and in good age, and the fourth generation shall return here in this land and shall inherit it forever; and Abram built an altar, and he called upon the name of the Lord who appeared to him, and he brought up sacrifices upon the altar to the Lord.

20 At that time Abram returned and went to Haran to see his father and mother, and his father's household, and Abram and his wife and all belonging to him returned to Haran, and Abram dwelt in Haran five years.

21 And many of the people of Haran, about seventy-two men, followed Abram and Abram taught them the instruction of the Lord and his ways, and he taught them to know the Lord.

22 In those days the Lord appeared to Abram in Haran, and he said to him, Behold, I spoke unto thee these twenty years back saying,

23 Go forth from thy land, from thy birth-place and from thy father's house, to the land which I have shown thee to give it to thee and to thy children, for there in that land will I bless thee, and make thee a great nation, and make thy name great, and in thee shall the families of the earth be blessed.

24 Now therefore arise, go forth from this place, thou, thy wife, and all belonging to thee, also every one born in thy house and all the souls thou hast made in Haran, and bring them out with thee from here, and rise to return to the land of Canaan.

25 And Abram arose and took his wife Sarai and all belonging to him and all that were born to him in his house and the souls which they had made in Haran, and they came out to go to the land of Canaan.

26 And Abram went and returned to the land of Canaan, according to the word of the Lord. And Lot the son of his brother Haran went with him, and Abram was seventy-five years old when he went forth from Haran to return to the land of Canaan.

27 And he came to the land of Canaan according to the word of the Lord to Abram, and he pitched his tent and he dwelt in the plain of Mamre, and with him was Lot his brother's son, and all belonging to him.

28 And the Lord again appeared to Abram and said, To thy seed will I give this land; and he there built an altar to the Lord who appeared to him, which is still to this day in the plains of Mamre.

Chapter 14

1 In those days there was in the land of Shinar a wise man who had understanding in all wisdom, and of a beautiful appearance, but he was poor and indigent; his name was Rikayon and he was hard set to support himself.

2 And he resolved to go to Egypt, to Oswiris the son of Anom king of Egypt, to show the king his wisdom; for perhaps he might find grace in his sight, to raise him up and give him maintenance; and Rikayon did so.

3 And when Rikayon came to Egypt he asked the inhabitants of Egypt concerning the king, and the inhabitants of Egypt told him the custom of the king of Egypt, for it was then the custom of the king of Egypt that he went from his royal palace and was seen abroad only one day in the year, and after that the king would return to his palace to remain there.

4 And on the day when the king went forth he passed judgment in the land, and every one having a suit came before the king that day to obtain his request.

5 And when Rikayon heard of the custom in Egypt and that he could not come into the presence of the king, he grieved greatly and was very sorrowful.

6 And in the evening Rikayon went out and found a house in ruins, formerly a bake house in Egypt, and he abode there all night in bitterness of soul and pinched with hunger, and sleep was removed from his eyes.

7 And Rikayon considered within himself what he should do in the town until the king made his appearance, and how he might maintain himself there.

8 And he rose in the morning and walked about, and met in his way those who sold vegetables and various sorts of seed with which they supplied the inhabitants.

9 And Rikayon wished to do the same in order to get a maintenance in the city, but he was unacquainted with the custom of the people, and he was like a blind man among them.

10 And he went and obtained vegetables to sell them for his support, and the rabble assembled about him and ridiculed him, and took his vegetables from him and left him nothing.

11 And he rose up from there in bitterness of soul, and went sighing to the bake house in which he had remained all the night before, and he slept there the second night.

12 And on that night again he reasoned within himself how he could save himself from starvation, and he devised a scheme how to act.

13 And he rose up in the morning and acted ingeniously, and went and hired thirty strong men of the rabble, carrying their war instruments in their hands, and he led them to the top of the Egyptian sepulchre, and he placed them there.

14 And he commanded them, saying, Thus saith the king, Strengthen yourselves and be valiant men, and let no man be buried here until two hundred pieces of silver be given, and then he may be buried; and those men did according to the order of Rikayon to the people of Egypt the whole of that year.

15 And in eight months time Rikayon and his men gathered great riches of silver and gold, and Rikayon took a great quantity of horses and other animals, and he hired more men, and he gave them horses and they remained with him.

16 And when the year came round, at the time the king went forth into the town, all the inhabitants of Egypt assembled together to speak to him concerning the work of Rikayon and his men.

17 And the king went forth on the appointed day, and all the Egyptians came before him and cried unto him, saying,

18 May the king live forever. What is this thing thou doest in the town to thy servants, not to suffer a dead body to be buried until so much silver and gold be given? Was there ever the like unto this done in the whole earth, from the days of former kings yea even from the days of Adam, unto this day, that the dead should not be buried only for a set price?

19 We know it to be the custom of kings to take a yearly tax from the living, but thou dost not only do this, but from the dead also thou exactest a tax day by day.

20 Now, O king, we can no more bear this, for the whole city is ruined on this account, and dost thou not know it?

21 And when the king heard all that they had spoken he was very wroth, and his anger burned within him at this affair, for he had known nothing of it.

22 And the king said, Who and where is he that dares to do this wicked thing in my land without my command? Surely

you will tell me.

23 And they told him all the works of Rikayon and his men, and the king's anger was aroused, and he ordered Rikayon and his men to be brought before him.

24 And Rikayon took about a thousand children, sons and daughters, and clothed them in silk and embroidery, and he set them upon horses and sent them to the king by means of his men, and he also took a great quantity of silver and gold and precious stones, and a strong and beautiful horse, as a present for the king, with which he came before the king and bowed down to the earth before him; and the king, his servants and all the inhabitants of Egypt wondered at the work of Rikayon, and they saw his riches and the present that he had brought to the king.

25 And it greatly pleased the king and he wondered at it; and when Rikayon sat before him the king asked him concerning all his works, and Rikayon spoke all his words wisely before the king, his servants and all the inhabitants of Egypt.

26 And when the king heard the words of Rikayon and his wisdom, Rikayon found grace in his sight, and he met with grace and kindness from all the servants of the king and from all the inhabitants of Egypt, on account of his wisdom and excellent speeches, and from that time they loved him exceedingly.

27 And the king answered and said to Rikayon, Thy name shall no more be called Rikayon but Pharaoh shall be thy name, since thou didst exact a tax from the dead; and he called his name Pharaoh.

28 And the king and his subjects loved Rikayon for his wisdom, and they consulted with all the inhabitants of Egypt to make him prefect under the king.

29 And all the inhabitants of Egypt and its wise men did so, and it was made a law in Egypt.

30 And they made Rikayon Pharaoh prefect under Oswiris king of Egypt, and Rikayon Pharaoh governed over Egypt, daily administering justice to the whole city, but Oswiris the king would judge the people of the land one day in the year, when he went out to make his appearance.

31 And Rikayon Pharaoh cunningly usurped the government of Egypt, and he exacted a tax from all the inhabitants of Egypt.

32 And all the inhabitants of Egypt greatly loved Rikayon Pharaoh, and they made a decree to call every king that should reign over them and their seed in Egypt, Pharaoh.

33 Therefore all the kings that reigned in Egypt from that time forward were called Pharaoh unto this day.

Chapter 15

1 And in that year there was a heavy famine throughout the land of Canaan, and the inhabitants of the land could not remain on account of the famine for it was very grievous.

2 And Abram and all belonging to him rose and went down to Egypt on account of the famine, and when they were at the brook Mitzraim they remained there some time to rest from the fatigue of the road.

3 And Abram and Sarai were walking at the border of the brook Mitzraim, and Abram beheld his wife Sarai that she was very beautiful.

4 And Abram said to his wife Sarai, Since God has created thee with such a beautiful countenance, I am afraid of the Egyptians lest they should slay me and take thee away, for the fear of God is not in these places.

5 Surely then thou shalt do this, Say thou art my sister to all that may ask thee, in order that it may be well with me, and that we may live and not be put to death.

6 And Abram commanded the same to all those that came with him to Egypt on account of the famine; also his nephew Lot he commanded, saying, If the Egyptians ask thee concerning Sarai say she is the sister of Abram.

7 And yet with all these orders Abram did not put confidence in them, but he took Sarai and placed her in a chest and concealed it amongst their vessels, for Abram was greatly concerned about Sarai on account of the wickedness of the Egyptians.

8 And Abram and all belonging to him rose up from the brook Mitzraim and came to Egypt; and they had scarcely entered the gates of the city when the guards stood up to them saying, Give tithe to the king from what you have, and then you may come into the town; and Abram and those that were with him did so.

9 And Abram with the people that were with him came to Egypt, and when they came they brought the chest in which Sarai was concealed and the Egyptians saw the chest.

10 And the king's servants approached Abram, saying, What hast thou here in this chest which we have not seen? Now open thou the chest and give tithe to the king of all that it contains.

11 And Abram said, This chest I will not open, but all you demand upon it I will give. And Pharaoh's officers answered Abram, saying, It is a chest of precious stones, give us the tenth thereof.

12 Abram said, All that you desire I will give, but you must not open the chest.

13 And the king's officers pressed Abram, and they reached the chest and opened it with force, and they saw, and behold a beautiful woman was in the chest.

14 And when the officers of the king beheld Sarai they were struck with admiration at her beauty, and all the princes and servants of Pharaoh assembled to see Sarai, for she was very beautiful. And the king's officers ran and told Pharaoh all that they had seen, and they praised Sarai to the king; and Pharaoh ordered her to be brought, and the woman came before the king.

15 And Pharaoh beheld Sarai and she pleased him exceedingly, and he was struck with her beauty, and the king rejoiced greatly on her account, and made presents to those who brought him the tidings concerning her.

16 And the woman was then brought to Pharaoh's house, and Abram grieved on account of his wife, and he prayed to the Lord to deliver her from the hands of Pharaoh.

17 And Sarai also prayed at that time and said, O Lord God thou didst tell my Lord Abram to go from his land and from his father's house to the land of Canaan, and thou didst promise to do well with him if he would perform thy commands; now behold we have done that which thou didst command us, and we left our land and our families, and we went to a strange land and to a people whom we have not known before.

18 And we came to this land to avoid the famine, and this evil accident has befallen me; now therefore, O Lord God, deliver us and save us from the hand of this oppressor, and do well with me for the sake of thy mercy.

19 And the Lord hearkened to the voice of Sarai, and the Lord sent an angel to deliver Sarai from the power of Pharaoh.

20 And the king came and sat before Sarai and behold an angel of the Lord was standing over them, and he appeared to Sarai and said to her, Do not fear, for the Lord has heard thy prayer.

21 And the king approached Sarai and said to her, What is that man to thee who brought thee hither? and she said, He

is my brother.

22 And the king said, It is incumbent upon us to make him great, to elevate him and to do unto him all the good which thou shalt command us; and at that time the king sent to Abram silver and gold and precious stones in abundance, together with cattle, men servants and maid servants; and the king ordered Abram to be brought, and he sat in the court of the king's house, and the king greatly exalted Abram on that night.

23 And the king approached to speak to Sarai, and he reached out his hand to touch her, when the angel smote him heavily, and he was terrified and he refrained from reaching to her.

24 And when the king came near to Sarai, the angel smote him to the ground, and acted thus to him the whole night, and the king was terrified.

25 And the angel on that night smote heavily all the servants of the king, and his whole household, on account of Sarai, and there was a great lamentation that night amongst the people of Pharaoh's house.

26 And Pharaoh, seeing the evil that befell him, said, Surely on account of this woman has this thing happened to me, and he removed himself at some distance from her and spoke pleasing words to her.

27 And the king said to Sarai, Tell me I pray thee concerning the man with whom thou camest here; and Sarai said, This man is my husband, and I said to thee that he was my brother for I was afraid, lest thou shouldst put him to death through wickedness.

28 And the king kept away from Sarai, and the plagues of the angel of the Lord ceased from him and his household; and Pharaoh knew that he was smitten on account of Sarai, and the king was greatly astonished at this.

29 And in the morning the king called for Abram and said to him, What is this thou hast done to me? Why didst thou say, She is my sister, owing to which I took her unto me for a wife, and this heavy plague has therefore come upon me and my household.

30 Now therefore here is thy wife, take her and go from our land lest we all die on her account. And Pharaoh took more cattle, men servants and maid servants, and silver and gold, to give to Abram, and he returned unto him Sarai his wife.

31 And the king took a maiden whom he begat by his concubines, and he gave her to Sarai for a handmaid.

32 And the king said to his daughter, It is better for thee my daughter to be a handmaid in this man's house than to be mistress in my house, after we have beheld the evil that befell us on account of this woman.

33 And Abram arose, and he and all belonging to him went away from Egypt; and Pharaoh ordered some of his men to accompany him and all that went with him.

34 And Abram returned to the land of Canaan, to the place where he had made the altar, where he at first had pitched his tent.

35 And Lot the son of Haran, Abram's brother, had a heavy stock of cattle, flocks and herds and tents, for the Lord was bountiful to them on account of Abram.

36 And when Abram was dwelling in the land the herdsmen of Lot quarrelled with the herdsmen of Abram, for their property was too great for them to remain together in the land, and the land could not bear them on account of their cattle.

37 And when Abram's herdsmen went to feed their flock they would not go into the fields of the people of the land, but the cattle of Lot's herdsmen did otherwise, for they were suffered to feed in the fields of the people of the land.

38 And the people of the land saw this occurrence daily, and they came to Abram and quarrelled with him on account of Lot's herdsmen.

39 And Abram said to Lot, What is this thou art doing to me, to make me despicable to the inhabitants of the land, that thou orderest thy herdsman to feed thy cattle in the fields of other people? Dost thou not know that I am a stranger in this land amongst the children of Canaan, and why wilt thou do this unto me?

40 And Abram quarrelled daily with Lot on account of this, but Lot would not listen to Abram, and he continued to do the same and the inhabitants of the land came and told Abram.

41 And Abram said unto Lot, How long wilt thou be to me for a stumbling block with the inhabitants of the land? Now I beseech thee let there be no more quarrelling between us, for we are kinsmen.

42 But I pray thee separate from me, go and choose a place where thou mayest dwell with thy cattle and all belonging to thee, but Keep thyself at a distance from me, thou and thy household.

43 And be not afraid in going from me, for if any one do an injury to thee, let me know and I will avenge thy cause from him, only remove from me.

44 And when Abram had spoken all these words to Lot, then Lot arose and lifted up his eyes toward the plain of Jordan.

45 And he saw that the whole of this place was well watered, and good for man as well as affording pasture for the cattle.

46 And Lot went from Abram to that place, and he there pitched his tent and he dwelt in Sodom, and they were separated from each other.

47 And Abram dwelt in the plain of Mamre, which is in Hebron, and he pitched his tent there, and Abram remained in that place many years.

Chapter 16

1 At that time Chedorlaomer king of Elam sent to all the neighboring kings, to Nimrod, king of Shinar who was then under his power, and to Tidal, king of Goyim, and to Arioch, king of Elasar, with whom he made a covenant, saying, Come up to me and assist me, that we may smite all the towns of Sodom and its inhabitants, for they have rebelled against me these thirteen years.

2 And these four kings went up with all their camps, about eight hundred thousand men, and they went as they were, and smote every man they found in their road.

3 And the five kings of Sodom and Gomorrah, Shinab king of Admah, Shemeber king of Zeboyim, Bera king of Sodom, Bersha king of Gomorrah, and Bela king of Zoar, went out to meet them, and they all joined together in the valley of Siddim.

4 And these nine kings made war in the valley of Siddim; and the kings of Sodom and Gomorrah were smitten before the kings of Elam.

5 And the valley of Siddim was full of lime pits and the kings of Elam pursued the kings of Sodom, and the kings of Sodom with their camps fled and fell into the lime pits, and all that remained went to the mountain for safety, and the five kings of Elam came after them and pursued them to the gates of Sodom, and they took all that there was in Sodom.

6 And they plundered all the cities of Sodom and Gomorrah, and they also took Lot, Abram's brother's son,

and his property, and they seized all the goods of the cities of Sodom, and they went away; and Unic, Abram's servant, who was in the battle, saw this, and told Abram all that the kings had done to the cities of Sodom, and that Lot was taken captive by them.

7 And Abram heard this, and he rose up with about three hundred and eighteen men that were with him, and he that night pursued these kings and smote them, and they all fell before Abram and his men, and there was none remaining but the four kings who fled, and they went each his own road.

8 And Abram recovered all the property of Sodom, and he also recovered Lot and his property, his wives and little ones and all belonging to him, so that Lot lacked nothing.

9 And when he returned from smiting these kings, he and his men passed the valley of Siddim where the kings had made war together.

10 And Bera king of Sodom, and the rest of his men that were with him, went out from the lime pits into which they had fallen, to meet Abram and his men.

11 And Adonizedek king of Jerusalem, the same was Shem, went out with his men to meet Abram and his people, with bread and wine, and they remained together in the valley of Melech.

12 And Adonizedek blessed Abram, and Abram gave him a tenth from all that he had brought from the spoil of his enemies, for Adonizedek was a priest before God.

13 And all the kings of Sodom and Gomorrah who were there, with their servants, approached Abram and begged of him to return them their servants whom he had made captive, and to take unto himself all the property.

14 And Abram answered the kings of Sodom, saying, As the Lord liveth who created heaven and earth, and who redeemed my soul from all affliction, and who delivered me this day from my enemies, and gave them into my hand, I will not take anything belonging to you, that you may not boast tomorrow, saying, Abram became rich from our property that he saved.

15 For the Lord my God in whom I trust said unto me, Thou shalt lack nothing, for I will bless thee in all the works of thy hands.

16 And now therefore behold, here is all belonging to you, take it and go; as the Lord liveth I will not take from you from a living soul down to a shoetie or thread, excepting the expense of the food of those who went out with me to battle, as also the portions of the men who went with me, Anar, Ashcol, and Mamre, they and their men, as well as those also who had remained to watch the baggage, they shall take their portion of the spoil.

17 And the kings of Sodom gave Abram according to all that he had said, and they pressed him to take of whatever he chose, but he would not.

18 And he sent away the kings of Sodom and the remainder of their men, and he gave them orders about Lot, and they went to their respective places.

19 And Lot, his brother's son, he also sent away with his property, and he went with them, and Lot returned to his home, to Sodom, and Abram and his people returned to their home to the plains of Mamre, which is in Hebron.

20 At that time the Lord again appeared to Abram in Hebron, and he said to him, Do not fear, thy reward is very great before me, for I will not leave thee, until I shall have multiplied thee, and blessed thee and made thy seed like the stars in heaven, which cannot be measured nor numbered.

21 And I will give unto thy seed all these lands that thou seest with thine eyes, to them will I give them for an inheritance forever, only be strong and do not fear, walk before me and be perfect.

22 And in the seventy-eighth year of the life of Abram, in that year died Reu, the son of Peleg, and all the days of Reu were two hundred and thirty-nine years, and he died.

23 And Sarai, the daughter of Haran, Abram's wife, was still barren in those days; she did not bear to Abram either son or daughter.

24 And when she saw that she bare no children she took her handmaid Hagar, whom Pharaoh had given her, and she gave her to Abram her husband for a wife.

25 For Hagar learned all the ways of Sarai as Sarai taught her, she was not in any way deficient in following her good ways.

26 And Sarai said to Abram, Behold here is my handmaid Hagar, go to her that she may bring forth upon my knees, that I may also obtain children through her.

27 And at the end of ten years of Abram's dwelling in the land of Canaan, which is the eighty-fifth year of Abram's life, Sarai gave Hagar unto him.

28 And Abram hearkened to the voice of his wife Sarai, and he took his handmaid Hagar and Abram came to her and she conceived.

29 And when Hagar saw that she had conceived she rejoiced greatly, and her mistress was despised in her eyes, and she said within herself, This can only be that I am better before God than Sarai my mistress, for all the days that my mistress has been with my lord, she did not conceive, but me the Lord has caused in so short a time to conceive by him.

30 And when Sarai saw that Hagar had conceived by Abram, Sarai was jealous of her handmaid, and Sarai said within herself, This is surely nothing else but that she must be better than I am.

31 And Sarai said unto Abram, My wrong be upon thee, for at the time when thou didst pray before the Lord for children why didst thou not pray on my account, that the Lord should give me seed from thee?

32 And when I speak to Hagar in thy presence, she despiseth my words, because she has conceived, and thou wilt say nothing to her; may the Lord judge between me and thee for what thou hast done to me.

33 And Abram said to Sarai, Behold thy handmaid is in thy hand, do unto her as it may seem good in thy eyes; and Sarai afflicted her, and Hagar fled from her to the wilderness.

34 And an angel of the Lord found her in the place where she had fled, by a well, and he said to her, Do not fear, for I will multiply thy seed, for thou shalt bear a son and thou shalt call his name Ishmael; now then return to Sarai thy mistress, and submit thyself under her hands.

35 And Hagar called the place of that well Beer-lahai-roi, it is between Kadesh and the wilderness of Bered.

36 And Hagar at that time returned to her master's house, and at the end of days Hagar bare a son to Abram, and Abram called his name Ishmael; and Abram was eighty-six years old when he begat him.

Chapter 17

1 And in those days, in the ninety-first year of the life of Abram, the children of Chittim made war with the children of Tubal, for when the Lord had scattered the sons of men upon the face of the earth, the children of Chittim went and embodied themselves in the plain of Canopia, and they built themselves cities there and dwelt by the river Tibreu.

2 And the children of Tubal dwelt in Tuscanah, and their

boundaries reached the river Tibreu, and the children of Tubal built a city in Tuscanan, and they called the name Sabinah, after the name of Sabinah son of Tubal their father, and they dwelt there unto this day.

3 And it was at that time the children of Chittim made war with the children of Tubal, and the children of Tubal were smitten before the children of Chittim, and the children of Chittim caused three hundred and seventy men to fall from the children of Tubal.

4 And at that time the children of Tubal swore to the children of Chittim, saying, You shall not intermarry amongst us, and no man shall give his daughter to any of the sons of Chittim.

5 For all the daughters of Tubal were in those days fair, for no women were then found in the whole earth so fair as the daughters of Tubal.

6 And all who delighted in the beauty of women went to the daughters of Tubal and took wives from them, and the sons of men, kings and princes, who greatly delighted in the beauty of women, took wives in those days from the daughters of Tubal.

7 And at the end of three years after the children of Tubal had sworn to the children of Chittim not to give them their daughters for wives, about twenty men of the children of Chittim went to take some of the daughters of Tubal, but they found none.

8 For the children of Tubal kept their oaths not to intermarry with them, and they would not break their oaths.

9 And in the days of harvest the children of Tubal went into their fields to get in their harvest, when the young men of Chittim assembled and went to the city of Sabinah, and each man took a young woman from the daughters of Tubal, and they came to their cities.

10 And the children of Tubal heard of it and they went to make war with them, and they could not prevail over them, for the mountain was exceedingly high from them, and when they saw they could not prevail over them they returned to their land.

11 And at the revolution of the year the children of Tubal went and hired about ten thousand men from those cities that were near them, and they went to war with the children of Chittim.

12 And the children of Tubal went to war with the children of Chittim, to destroy their land and to distress them, and in this engagement the children of Tubal prevailed over the children of Chittim, and the children of Chittim, seeing that they were greatly distressed, lifted up the children which they had had by the daughters of Tubal, upon the wall which had been built, to be before the eyes of the children of Tubal.

13 And the children of Chittim said to them, Have you come to make war with your own sons and daughters, and have we not been considered your flesh and bones from that time till now?

14 And when the children of Tubal heard this they ceased to make war with the children of Chittim, and they went away.

15 And they returned to their cities, and the children of Chittim at that time assembled and built two cities by the sea, and they called one Purtu and the other Ariza.

16 And Abram the son of Terah was then ninety-nine years old.

17 At that time the Lord appeared to him and he said to him, I will make my covenant between me and thee, and I will greatly multiply thy seed, and this is the covenant which I make between me and thee, that every male child be circumcised, thou and thy seed after thee.

18 At eight days old shall it be circumcised, and this covenant shall be in your flesh for an everlasting covenant.

19 And now therefore thy name shall no more be called Abram but Abraham, and thy wife shall no more be called Sarai but Sarah.

20 For I will bless you both, and I will multiply your seed after you that you shall become a great nation, and kings shall come forth from you.

Chapter 18

1 And Abraham rose and did all that God had ordered him, and he took the men of his household and those bought with his money, and he circumcised them as the Lord had commanded him.

2 And there was not one left whom he did not circumcise, and Abraham and his son Ishmael were circumcised in the flesh of their foreskin; thirteen years old was Ishmael when he was circumcised in the flesh of his foreskin.

3 And in the third day Abraham went out of his tent and sat at the door to enjoy the heat of the sun, during the pain of his flesh.

4 And the Lord appeared to him in the plain of Mamre, and sent three of his ministering angels to visit him, and he was sitting at the door of the tent, and he lifted his eyes and saw, and lo three men were coming from a distance, and he rose up and ran to meet them, and he bowed down to them and brought them into his house.

5 And he said to them, If now I have found favor in your sight, turn in and eat a morsel of bread; and he pressed them, and they turned in and he gave them water and they washed their feet, and he placed them under a tree at the door of the tent.

6 And Abraham ran and took a calf, tender and good, and he hastened to kill it, and gave it to his servant Eliezer to dress.

7 And Abraham came to Sarah into the tent, and he said to her, Make ready quickly three measures of fine meal, knead it and make cakes to cover the pot containing the meat, and she did so.

8 And Abraham hastened and brought before them butter and milk, beef and mutton, and gave it before them to eat before the flesh of the calf was sufficiently done, and they did eat.

9 And when they had done eating one of them said to him, I will return to thee according to the time of life, and Sarah thy wife shall have a son.

10 And the men afterward departed and went their ways, to the places to which they were sent.

11 In those days all the people of Sodom and Gomorrah, and of the whole five cities, were exceedingly wicked and sinful against the Lord and they provoked the Lord with their abominations, and they strengthened in aging abominably and scornfully before the Lord, and their wickedness and crimes were in those days great before the Lord.

12 And they had in their land a very extensive valley, about half a day's walk, and in it there were fountains of water and a great deal of herbage surrounding the water.

13 And all the people of Sodom and Gomorrah went there four times in the year, with their wives and children and all belonging to them, and they rejoiced there with timbrels and dances.

14 And in the time of rejoicing they would all rise and lay hold of their neighbor's wives, and some, the virgin daughters of their neighbors, and they enjoyed them, and

each man saw his wife and daughter in the hands of his neighbor and did not say a word.

15 And they did so from morning to night, and they afterward returned home each man to his house and each woman to her tent; so they always did four times in the year.

16 Also when a stranger came into their cities and brought goods which he had purchased with a view to dispose of there, the people of these cities would assemble, men, women and children, young and old, and go to the man and take his goods by force, giving a little to each man until there was an end to all the goods of the owner which he had brought into the land.

17 And if the owner of the goods quarreled with them, saying, What is this work which you have done to me, then they would approach to him one by one, and each would show him the little which he took and taunt him, saying, I only took that little which thou didst give me; and when he heard this from them all, he would arise and go from them in sorrow and bitterness of soul, when they would all arise and go after him, and drive him out of the city with great noise and tumult.

18 And there was a man from the country of Elam who was leisurely going on the road, seated upon his ass, which carried a fine mantle of divers colors, and the mantle was bound with a cord upon the ass.

19 And the man was on his journey passing through the street of Sodom when the sun set in the evening, and he remained there in order to abide during the night, but no one would let him into his house; and at that time there was in Sodom a wicked and mischievous man, one skillful to do evil, and his name was Hedad.

20 And he lifted up his eyes and saw the traveler in the street of the city, and he came to him and said, Whence comest thou and whither dost thou go?

21 And the man said to him, I am traveling from Hebron to Elam where I belong, and as I passed the sun set and no one would suffer me to enter his house, though I had bread and water and also straw and provender for my ass, and am short of nothing.

22 And Hedad answered and said to him, All that thou shalt want shall be supplied by me, but in the street thou shalt not abide all night.

23 And Hedad brought him to his house, and he took off the mantle from the ass with the cord, and brought them to his house, and he gave the ass straw and provender whilst the traveler ate and drank in Hedad's house, and he abode there that night.

24 And in the morning the traveler rose up early to continue his journey, when Hedad said to him, Wait, comfort thy heart with a morsel of bread and then go, and the man did so; and he remained with him, and they both ate and drank together during the day, when the man rose up to go.

25 And Hedad said to him, Behold now the day is declining, thou hadst better remain all night that thy heart may be comforted; and he pressed him so that he tarried there all night, and on the second day he rose up early to go away, when Hedad pressed him, saying, Comfort thy heart with a morsel of bread and then go, and he remained and ate with him also the second day, and then the man rose up to continue his journey.

26 And Hedad said to him, Behold now the day is declining, remain with me to comfort thy heart and in the morning rise up early and go thy way.

27 And the man would not remain, but rose and saddled

his ass, and whilst he was saddling his ass the wife of Hedad said to her husband, Behold this man has remained with us for two days eating and drinking and he has given us nothing, and now shall he go away from us without giving anything? and Hedad said to her, Be silent.

28 And the man saddled his ass to go, and he asked Hedad to give him the cord and mantle to tie it upon the ass.

29 And Hedad said to him, What sayest thou? And he said to him, That thou my lord shalt give me the cord and the mantle made with divers colors which thou didst conceal with thee in thy house to take care of it.

30 And Hedad answered the man, saying, This is the interpretation of thy dream, the cord which thou didst see, means that thy life will be lengthened out like a cord, and having seen the mantle colored with all sorts of colors, means that thou shalt have a vineyard in which thou wilt plant trees of all fruits.

31 And the traveler answered, saying, Not so my lord, for I was awake when I gave thee the cord and also a mantle woven with different colors, which thou didst take off the ass to put them by for me; and Hedad answered and said, Surely I have told thee the interpretation of thy dream and it is a good dream, and this is the interpretation thereof.

32 Now the sons of men give me four pieces of silver, which is my charge for interpreting dreams, and of thee only I require three pieces of silver.

33 And the man was provoked at the words of Hedad, and he cried bitterly, and he brought Hedad to Serak judge of Sodom.

34 And the man laid his cause before Serak the judge, when Hedad replied, saying, It is not so, but thus the matter stands; and the judge said to the traveler, This man Hedad telleth thee truth, for he is famed in the cities for the accurate interpretation of dreams.

35 And the man cried at the word of the judge, and he said, Not so my Lord, for it was in the day that I gave him the cord and mantle which was upon the ass, in order to put them by in his house; and they both disputed before the judge, the one saying, Thus the matter was, and the other declaring otherwise.

36 And Hedad said to the man, Give me four pieces of silver that I charge for my interpretations of dreams; I will not make any allowance; and give me the expense of the four meals that thou didst eat in my house.

37 And the man said to Hedad, Truly I will pay thee for what I ate in thy house, only give me the cord and mantle which thou didst conceal in thy house.

38 And Hedad replied before the judge and said to the man, Did I not tell thee the interpretation of thy dream? the cord means that thy days shall be prolonged like a cord, and the mantle, that thou wilt have a vineyard in which thou wilt plant all kinds of fruit trees.

39 This is the proper interpretation of thy dream, now give me the four pieces of silver that I require as a compensation, for I will make thee no allowance.

40 And the man cried at the words of Hedad and they both quarreled before the judge, and the judge gave orders to his servants, who drove them rashly from the house.

41 And they went away quarreling from the judge, when the people of Sodom heard them, and they gathered about them and they exclaimed against the stranger, and they drove him rashly from the city.

42 And the man continued his journey upon his ass with bitterness of soul, lamenting and weeping.

43 And whilst he was going along he wept at what had happened to him in the corrupt city of Sodom.

Chapter 19

1 And the cities of Sodom had four judges to four cities, and these were their names, Serak in the city of Sodom, Sharkad in Gomorrah, Zabnac in Admah, and Menon in Zeboyim.

2 And Eliezer Abraham's servant applied to them different names, and he converted Serak to Shakra, Sharkad to Shakrura, Zebnac to Kezobim, and Menon to Matzlodin.

3 And by desire of their four judges the people of Sodom and Gomorrah had beds erected in the streets of the cities, and if a man came to these places they laid hold of him and brought him to one of their beds, and by force made him to lie in them.

4 And as he lay down, three men would stand at his head and three at his feet, and measure him by the length of the bed, and if the man was less than the bed these six men would stretch him at each end, and when he cried out to them they would not answer him.

5 And if he was longer than the bed they would draw together the two sides of the bed at each end, until the man had reached the gates of death.

6 And if he continued to cry out to them, they would answer him, saying, Thus shall it be done to a man that cometh into our land.

7 And when men heard all these things that the people of the cities of Sodom did, they refrained from coming there.

8 And when a poor man came to their land they would give him silver and gold, and cause a proclamation in the whole city not to give him a morsel of bread to eat, and if the stranger should remain there some days, and die from hunger, not having been able to obtain a morsel of bread, then at his death all the people of the city would come and take their silver and gold which they had given to him.

9 And those that could recognize the silver or gold which they had given him took it back, and at his death they also stripped him of his garments, and they would fight about them, and he that prevailed over his neighbor took them.

10 They would after that carry him and bury him under some of the shrubs in the deserts; so they did all the days to any one that came to them and died in their land.

11 And in the course of time Sarah sent Eliezer to Sodom, to see Lot and inquire after his welfare.

12 And Eliezer went to Sodom, and he met a man of Sodom fighting with a stranger, and the man of Sodom stripped the poor man of all his clothes and went away.

13 And this poor man cried to Eliezer and supplicated his favor on account of what the man of Sodom had done to him.

14 And he said to him, Why dost thou act thus to the poor man who came to thy land?

15 And the man of Sodom answered Eliezer, saying, Is this man thy brother, or have the people of Sodom made thee a judge this day, that thou speakest about this man?

16 And Eliezer strove with the man of Sodom on account of the poor man, and when Eliezer approached to recover the poor man's clothes from the man of Sodom, he hastened and with a stone smote Eliezer in the forehead.

17 And the blood flowed copiously from Eliezer's forehead, and when the man saw the blood he caught hold of Eliezer, saying, Give me my hire for having rid thee of this bad blood that was in thy forehead, for such is the custom and the law in our land.

18 And Eliezer said to him, Thou hast wounded me and requirest me to pay thee thy hire; and Eliezer would not hearken to the words of the man of Sodom.

19 And the man laid hold of Eliezer and brought him to Shakra the judge of Sodom for judgment.

20 And the man spoke to the judge, saying, I beseech thee my lord, thus has this man done, for I smote him with a stone that the blood flowed from his forehead, and he is unwilling to give me my hire.

21 And the judge said to Eliezer, This man speaketh truth to thee, give him his hire, for this is the custom in our land; and Eliezer heard the words of the judge, and he lifted up a stone and smote the judge, and the stone struck on his forehead, and the blood flowed copiously from the forehead of the judge, and Eliezer said, If this then is the custom in your land give thou unto this man what I should have given him, for this has been thy decision, thou didst decree it.

22 And Eliezer left the man of Sodom with the judge, and he went away.

23 And when the kings of Elam had made war with the kings of Sodom, the kings of Elam captured all the property of Sodom, and they took Lot captive, with his property, and when it was told to Abraham he went and made war with the kings of Elam, and he recovered from their hands all the property of Lot as well as the property of Sodom.

24 At that time the wife of Lot bare him a daughter, and he called her name Paltith, saying, Because God had delivered him and his whole household from the kings of Elam; and Paltith daughter of Lot grew up, and one of the men of Sodom took her for a wife.

25 And a poor man came into the city to seek a maintenance, and he remained in the city some days, and all the people of Sodom caused a proclamation of their custom not to give this man a morsel of bread to eat, until he dropped dead upon the earth, and they did so.

26 And Paltith the daughter of Lot saw this man lying in the streets starved with hunger, and no one would give him any thing to keep him alive, and he was just upon the point of death.

27 And her soul was filled with pity on account of the man, and she fed him secretly with bread for many days, and the soul of this man was revived.

28 For when she went forth to fetch water she would put the bread in the water pitcher, and when she came to the place where the poor man was, she took the bread from the pitcher and gave it him to eat; so she did many days.

29 And all the people of Sodom and Gomorrah wondered how this man could bear starvation for so many days.

30 And they said to each other, This can only be that he eats and drinks, for no man can bear starvation for so many days or live as this man has, without even his countenance changing; and three men concealed themselves in a place where the poor man was stationed, to know who it was that brought him bread to eat.

31 And Paltith daughter of Lot went forth that day to fetch water, and she put bread into her pitcher of water, and she went to draw water by the poor man's place, and she took out the bread from the pitcher and gave it to the poor man and he ate it.

32 And the three men saw what Paltith did to the poor man, and they said to her, It is thou then who hast supported him, and therefore has he not starved, nor changed in appearance nor died like the rest.

33 And the three men went out of the place in which they were concealed, and they seized Paltith and the bread which was in the poor man's hand.

34 And they took Paltith and brought her before their

judges, and they said to them, Thus did she do, and it is she who supplied the poor man with bread, therefore did he not die all this time; now therefore declare to us the punishment due to this woman for having transgressed our law.

35 And the people of Sodom and Gomorrah assembled and kindled a fire in the street of the city, and they took the woman and cast her into the fire and she was burned to ashes.

36 And in the city of Admah there was a woman to whom they did the like.

37 For a traveler came into the city of Admah to abide there all night, with the intention of going home in the morning, and he sat opposite the door of the house of the young woman's father, to remain there, as the sun had set when be had reached that place; and the young woman saw him sitting by the door of the house.

38 And he asked her for a drink of water and she said to him, Who art thou? and he said to her, I was this day going on the road, and reached here when the sun set, so I will abide here all night, and in the morning I will arise early and continue my journey.

39 And the young woman went into the house and fetched the man bread and water to eat and drink.

40 And this affair became known to the people of Admah, and they assembled and brought the young woman before the judges, that they should judge her for this act.

41 And the judge said, The judgment of death must pass upon this woman because she transgressed our law, and this therefore is the decision concerning her.

42 And the people of those cities assembled and brought out the young woman, and anointed her with honey from head to foot, as the judge had decreed, and they placed her before a swarm of bees which were then in their hives, and the bees flew upon her and stung her that her whole body was swelled.

43 And the young woman cried out on account of the bees, but no one took notice of her or pitied her, and her cries ascended to heaven.

44 And the Lord was provoked at this and at all the works of the cities of Sodom, for they had abundance of food, and had tranquility amongst them, and still would not sustain the poor and the needy, and in those days their evil doings and sins became great before the Lord.

45 And the Lord sent for two of the angels that had come to Abraham's house, to destroy Sodom and its cities.

46 And the angels rose up from the door of Abraham's tent, after they had eaten and drunk, and they reached Sodom in the evening, and Lot was then sitting in the gate of Sodom, and when he saw them he rose to meet them, and he bowed down to the ground.

47 And he pressed them greatly and brought them into his house, and he gave them victuals which they ate, and they abode all night in his house.

48 And the angels said to Lot, Arise, go forth from this place, thou and all belonging to thee, lest thou be consumed in the iniquity of this city, for the Lord will destroy this place.

49 And the angels laid hold upon the hand of Lot and upon the hand of his wife, and upon the hands of his children, and all belonging to him, and they brought him forth and set him without the cities.

50 And they said to Lot, Escape for thy life, and he fled and all belonging to him.

51 Then the Lord rained upon Sodom and upon Gomorrah and upon all these cities brimstone and fire from the Lord

out of heaven.

52 And he overthrew these cities, all the plain and all the inhabitants of the cities, and that which grew upon the ground; and Ado the wife of Lot looked back to see the destruction of the cities, for her compassion was moved on account of her daughters who remained in Sodom, for they did not go with her.

53 And when she looked back she became a pillar of salt, and it is yet in that place unto this day.

54 And the oxen which stood in that place daily licked up the salt to the extremities of their feet, and in the morning it would spring forth afresh, and they again licked it up unto this day.

55 And Lot and two of his daughters that remained with him fled and escaped to the cave of Adullam, and they remained there for some time.

56 And Abraham rose up early in the morning to see what had been done to the cities of Sodom; and he looked and beheld the smoke of the cities going up like the smoke of a furnace.

57 And Lot and his two daughters remained in the cave, and they made their father drink wine, and they lay with him, for they said there was no man upon earth that could raise up seed from them, for they thought that the whole earth was destroyed.

58 And they both lay with their father, and they conceived and bare sons, and the first born called the name of her son Moab, saying, From my father did I conceive him; he is the father of the Moabites unto this day.

59 And the younger also called her son Benami; he is the father of the children of Ammon unto this day.

60 And after this Lot and his two daughters went away from there, and he dwelt on the other side of the Jordan with his two daughters and their sons, and the sons of Lot grew up, and they went and took themselves wives from the land of Canaan, and they begat children and they were fruitful and multiplied.

Chapter 20

1 And at that time Abraham journeyed from the plain of Mamre, and he went to the land of the Philistines, and he dwelt in Gerar; it was in the twenty-fifth year of Abraham's being in the land of Canaan, and the hundredth year of the life of Abraham, that he came to Gerar in the land of the Philistines.

2 And when they entered the land he said to Sarah his wife, Say thou art my sister, to any one that shall ask thee, in order that we may escape the evil of the inhabitants of the land.

3 And as Abraham was dwelling in the land of the Philistines, the servants of Abimelech, king of the Philistines, saw that Sarah was exceedingly beautiful, and they asked Abraham concerning her, and he said, She is my sister.

4 And the servants of Abimelech went to Abimelech, saying, A man from the land of Canaan is come to dwell in the land, and he has a sister that is exceeding fair.

5 And Abimelech heard the words of his servants who praised Sarah to him, and Abimelech sent his officers, and they brought Sarah to the king.

6 And Sarah came to the house of Abimelech, and the king saw that Sarah was beautiful, and she pleased him exceedingly.

7 And he approached her and said to her, What is that man to thee with whom thou didst come to our land? and Sarah answered and said He is my brother, and we came from the

land of Canaan to dwell wherever we could find a place.

8 And Abimelech said to Sarah, Behold my land is before thee, place thy brother in any part of this land that pleases thee, and it will be our duty to exalt and elevate him above all the people of the land since he is thy brother.

9 And Abimelech sent for Abraham, and Abraham came to Abimelech.

10 And Abimelech said to Abraham, Behold I have given orders that thou shalt be honored as thou desirest on account of thy sister Sarah.

11 And Abraham went forth from the king, and the king's present followed him.

12 As at evening time, before men lie down to rest, the king was sitting upon his throne, and a deep sleep fell upon him, and he lay upon the throne and slept till morning.

13 And he dreamed that an angel of the Lord came to him with a drawn sword in his hand, and the angel stood over Abimelech, and wished to slay him with the sword, and the king was terrified in his dream, and said to the angel, In what have I sinned against thee that thou comest to slay me with thy sword?

52

14 And the angel answered and said to Abimelech, Behold thou diest on account of the woman which thou didst yesternight bring to thy house, for she is a married woman, the wife of Abraham who came to thy house; now therefore return that man his wife, for she is his wife; and shouldst thou not return her, know that thou wilt surely die, thou and all belonging to thee.

15 And on that night there was a great outcry in the land of the Philistines, and the inhabitants of the land saw the figure of a man standing with a drawn sword in his hand, and he smote the inhabitants of the land with the sword, yea he continued to smite them.

16 And the angel of the Lord smote the whole land of the Philistines on that night, and there was a great confusion on that night and on the following morning.

17 And every womb was closed, and all their issues, and the hand of the Lord was upon them on account of Sarah, wife of Abraham, whom Abimelech had taken.

18 And in the morning Abimelech rose with terror and confusion and with a great dread, and he sent and had his servants called in, and he related his dream to them, and the people were greatly afraid.

19 And one man standing amongst the servants of the king answered the king, saying, O sovereign king, restore this woman to her husband, for he is her husband, for the like happened to the king of Egypt when this man came to Egypt.

20 And he said concerning his wife, She is my sister, for such is his manner of doing when he cometh to dwell in the land in which he is a stranger.

21 And Pharaoh sent and took this woman for a wife and the Lord brought upon him grievous plagues until he returned the woman to her husband.

22 Now therefore, O sovereign king, know what happened yesternight to the whole land, for there was a very great consternation and great pain and lamentation, and we know that it was on account of the woman which thou didst take.

23 Now, therefore, restore this woman to her husband, lest it should befall us as it did to Pharaoh king of Egypt and his subjects, and that we may not die; and Abimelech hastened and called and had Sarah called for, and she came before him, and he had Abraham called for, and he came before him.

24 And Abimelech said to them, What is this work you have been doing in saying you are brother and sister, and I took this woman for a wife?

25 And Abraham said, Because I thought I should suffer death on account of my wife; and Abimelech took flocks and herds, and men servants and maid servants, and a thousand pieces of silver, and he gave them to Abraham, and he returned Sarah to him.

26 And Abimelech said to Abraham, Behold the whole land is before thee, dwell in it wherever thou shalt choose.

27 And Abraham and Sarah, his wife, went forth from the king's presence with honor and respect, and they dwelt in the land, even in Gerar.

28 And all the inhabitants of the land of the Philistines and the king's servants were still in pain, through the plague which the angel had inflicted upon them the whole night on account of Sarah.

29 And Abimelech sent for Abraham, saying, Pray now for thy servants to the Lord thy God, that he may put away this mortality from amongst us.

30 And Abraham prayed on account of Abimelech and his subjects, and the Lord heard the prayer of Abraham, and he healed Abimelech and all his subjects.

Chapter 21

1 And it was at that time at the end of a year and four months of Abraham's dwelling in the land of the Philistines in Gerar, that God visited Sarah, and the Lord remembered her, and she conceived and bare a son to Abraham.

2 And Abraham called the name of the son which was born to him, which Sarah bare to him, Isaac.

3 And Abraham circumcised his son Isaac at eight days old, as God had commanded Abraham to do unto his seed after him; and Abraham was one hundred, and Sarah ninety years old, when Isaac was born to them.

4 And the child grew up and he was weaned, and Abraham made a great feast upon the day that Isaac was weaned.

5 And Shem and Eber and all the great people of the land, and Abimelech king of the Philistines, and his servants, and Phicol, the captain of his host, came to eat and drink and rejoice at the feast which Abraham made upon the day of his son Isaac's being weaned.

6 Also Terah, the father of Abraham, and Nahor his brother, came from Haran, they and all belonging to them, for they greatly rejoiced on hearing that a son had been born to Sarah.

7 And they came to Abraham, and they ate and drank at the feast which Abraham made upon the day of Isaac's being weaned.

8 And Terah and Nahor rejoiced with Abraham, and they remained with him many days in the land of the Philistines.

9 At that time Serug the son of Reu died, in the first year of the birth of Isaac son of Abraham.

10 And all the days of Serug were two hundred and thirty-nine years, and he died.

11 And Ishmael the son of Abraham was grown up in those days; he was fourteen years old when Sarah bare Isaac to Abraham.

12 And God was with Ishmael the son of Abraham, and he grew up, and he learned to use the bow and became an archer.

13 And when Isaac was five years old he was sitting with Ishmael at the door of the tent.

14 And Ishmael came to Isaac and seated himself opposite to him, and he took the bow and drew it and put the arrow in it, and intended to slay Isaac.

15 And Sarah saw the act which Ishmael desired to do to

her son Isaac, and it grieved her exceedingly on account of her son, and she sent for Abraham, and said to him, Cast out this bondwoman and her son, for her son shall not be heir with my son, for thus did he seek to do unto him this day.

16 And Abraham hearkened to the voice of Sarah, and he rose up early in the morning, and he took twelve loaves and a bottle of water which he gave to Hagar, and sent her away with her son, and Hagar went with her son to the wilderness, and they dwelt in the wilderness of Paran with the inhabitants of the wilderness, and Ishmael was an archer, and he dwelt in the wilderness a long time.

17 And he and his mother afterward went to the land of Egypt, and they dwelt there, and Hagar took a wife for her son from Egypt, and her name was Meribah.

18 And the wife of Ishmael conceived and bare four sons and two daughters, and Ishmael and his mother and his wife and children afterward went and returned to the wilderness.

19 And they made themselves tents in the wilderness, in which they dwelt, and they continued to travel and then to rest monthly and yearly.

20 And God gave Ishmael flocks and herds and tents on account of Abraham his father, and the man increased in cattle.

21 And Ishmael dwelt in deserts and in tents, traveling and resting for a long time, and he did not see the face of his father.

22 And in some time after, Abraham said to Sarah his wife, I will go and see my son Ishmael, for I have a desire to see him, for I have not seen him for a long time.

23 And Abraham rode upon one of his camels to the wilderness to seek his son Ishmael, for he heard that he was dwelling in a tent in the wilderness with all belonging to him.

24 And Abraham went to the wilderness, and he reached the tent of Ishmael about noon, and he asked after Ishmael, and he found the wife of Ishmael sitting in the tent with her children, and Ishmael her husband and his mother were not with them.

25 And Abraham asked the wife of Ishmael, saying, Where has Ishmael gone? and she said, He has gone to the field to hunt, and Abraham was still mounted upon the camel, for he would not get off to the ground as he had sworn to his wife Sarah that he would not get off from the camel.

26 And Abraham said to Ishmael's wife, My daughter, give me a little water that I may drink, for I am fatigued from the journey.

27 And Ishmael's wife answered and said to Abraham, We have neither water nor bread, and she continued sitting in the tent and did not notice Abraham, neither did she ask him who he was.

28 But she was beating her children in the tent, and she was cursing them, and she also cursed her husband Ishmael and reproached him, and Abraham heard the words of Ishmael's wife to her children, and he was very angry and displeased.

29 And Abraham called to the woman to come out to him from the tent, and the woman came and stood opposite to Abraham, for Abraham was still mounted upon the camel.

30 And Abraham said to Ishmael's wife, When thy husband Ishmael returneth home say these words to him,

31 A very old man from the land of the Philistines came hither to seek thee, and thus was his appearance and figure; I did not ask him who he was, and seeing thou wast not here he spoke unto me and said, When Ishmael thy

husband returneth tell him thus did this man say, When thou comest home put away this nail of the tent which thou hast placed here, and place another nail in its stead.

32 And Abraham finished his instructions to the woman, and he turned and went off on the camel homeward.

33 And after that Ishmael came from the chase he and his mother, and returned to the tent, and his wife spoke these words to him,

34 A very old man from the land of the Philistines came to seek thee, and thus was his appearance and figure; I did not ask him who he was, and seeing thou wast not at home he said to me, When thy husband cometh home tell him, thus saith the old man, Put away the nail of the tent which thou hast placed here and place another nail in its stead.

35 And Ishmael heard the words of his wife, and he knew that it was his father, and that his wife did not honor him.

36 And Ishmael understood his father's words that he had spoken to his wife, and Ishmael hearkened to the voice of his father, and Ishmael cast off that woman and she went away.

37 And Ishmael afterward went to the land of Canaan, and he took another wife and he brought her to his tent to the place where he then dwelt.

38 And at the end of three years Abraham said, I will go again and see Ishmael my son, for I have not seen him for a long time.

39 And he rode upon his camel and went to the wilderness, and he reached the tent of Ishmael about noon.

40 And he asked after Ishmael, and his wife came out of the tent and she said, He is not here my lord, for he has gone to hunt in the fields, and to feed the camels, and the woman said to Abraham, Turn in my lord into the tent, and eat a morsel of bread, for thy soul must be wearied on account of the journey.

41 And Abraham said to her, I will not stop for I am in haste to continue my journey, but give me a little water to drink, for I have thirst; and the woman hastened and ran into the tent and she brought out water and bread to Abraham, which she placed before him and she urged him to eat, and he ate and drank and his heart was comforted and he blessed his son Ishmael.

42 And he finished his meal and he blessed the Lord, and he said to Ishmael's wife, When Ishmael cometh home say these words to him,

43 A very old man from the land of the Philistines came hither and asked after thee, and thou wast not here; and I brought him out bread and water and he ate and drank and his heart was comforted.

44 And he spoke these words to me: When Ishmael thy husband cometh home, say unto him, The nail of the tent which thou hast is very good, do not put it away from the tent.

45 And Abraham finished commanding the woman, and he rode off to his home to the land of the Philistines; and when Ishmael came to his tent his wife went forth to meet him with joy and a cheerful heart.

46 And she said to him, An old man came here from the land of the Philistines and thus was his appearance, and he asked after thee and thou wast not here, so I brought out bread and water, and he ate and drank and his heart was comforted.

47 And he spoke these words to me, When Ishmael thy husband cometh home say to him, The nail of the tent which thou hast is very good, do not put it away from the tent.

48 And Ishmael knew that it was his father, and that his

wife had honored him, and the Lord blessed Ishmael.

Chapter 22

1 And Ishmael then rose up and took his wife and his children and his cattle and all belonging to him, and he journeyed from there and he went to his father in the land of the Philistines.

2 And Abraham related to Ishmael his son the transaction with the first wife that Ishmael took, according to what she did.

3 And Ishmael and his children dwelt with Abraham many days in that land, and Abraham dwelt in the land of the Philistines a long time.

4 And the days increased and reached twenty six years, and after that Abraham with his servants and all belonging to him went from the land of the Philistines and removed to a great distance, and they came near to Hebron, and they remained there, and the servants of Abraham dug wells of water, and Abraham and all belonging to him dwelt by the water, and the servants of Abimelech king of the Philistines heard the report that Abraham's servants had dug wells of water in the borders of the land.

5 And they came and quarreled with the servants of Abraham, and they robbed them of the great well which they had dug.

6 And Abimelech king of the Philistines heard of this affair, and he with Phicol the captain of his host and twenty of his men came to Abraham, and Abimelech spoke to Abraham concerning his servants, and Abraham rebuked Abimelech concerning the well of which his servants had robbed him.

7 And Abimelech said to Abraham, As the Lord liveth who created the whole earth, I did not hear of the act which my servants did unto thy servants until this day.

8 And Abraham took seven ewe lambs and gave them to Abimelech, saying, Take these, I pray thee, from my hands that it may be a testimony for me that I dug this well.

9 And Abimelech took the seven ewe lambs which Abraham had given to him, for he had also given him cattle and herds in abundance, and Abimelech swore to Abraham concerning the well, therefore he called that well Beersheba, for there they both swore concerning it.

10 And they both made a covenant in Beersheba, and Abimelech rose up with Phicol the captain of his host and all his men, and they returned to the land of the Philistines, and Abraham and all belonging to him dwelt in Beersheba and he was in that land a long time.

11 And Abraham planted a large grove in Beersheba, and he made to it four gates facing the four sides of the earth, and he planted a vineyard in it, so that if a traveler came to Abraham he entered any gate which was in his road, and remained there and ate and drank and satisfied himself and then departed.

12 For the house of Abraham was always open to the sons of men that passed and repassed, who came daily to eat and drink in the house of Abraham.

13 And any man who had hunger and came to Abraham's house, Abraham would give him bread that he might eat and drink and be satisfied, and any one that came naked to his house he would clothe with garments as he might choose, and give him silver and gold and make known to him the Lord who had created him in the earth; this did Abraham all his life.

14 And Abraham and his children and all belonging to him dwelt in Beersheba, and he pitched his tent as far as Hebron.

15 And Abraham's brother Nahor and his father and all belonging to them dwelt in Haran, for they did not come with Abraham to the land of Canaan.

16 And children were born to Nahor which Milca the daughter of Haran, and sister to Sarah, Abraham's wife, bare to him.

17 And these are the names of those that were born to him, Uz, Buz, Kemuel, Kesed, Chazo, Pildash, Tidlaf, and Bethuel, being eight sons, these are the children of Milca which she bare to Nahor, Abraham's brother.

18 And Nahor had a concubine and her name was Reumah, and she also bare to Nahor, Zebach, Gachash, Tachash and Maacha, being four sons.

19 And the children that were born to Nahor were twelve sons besides his daughters, and they also had children born to them in Haran.

20 And the children of Uz the first born of Nahor were Abi, Cheref, Gadin, Melus, and Deborah their sister.

21 And the sons of Buz were Berachel, Naamath, Sheva, and Madonu.

22 And the sons of Kemuel were Aram and Rechob.

23 And the sons of Kesed were Anamlech, Meshai, Benon and Yifi; and the sons of Chazo were Pildash, Mechi and Opher.

24 And the sons of Pildash were Arud, Chamum, Mered and Moloch.

25 And the sons of Tidlaf were Mushan, Cushan and Mutzi.

26 And the children of Bethuel were Sechar, Laban and their sister Rebecca.

27 These are the families of the children of Nahor, that were born to them in Haran; and Aram the son of Kemuel and Rechob his brother went away from Haran, and they found a valley in the land by the river Euphrates.

28 And they built a city there, and they called the name of the city after the name of Pethor the son of Aram, that is Aram Naherayim unto this day.

29 And the children of Kesed also went to dwell where they could find a place, and they went and they found a valley opposite to the land of Shinar, and they dwelt there.

30 And they there built themselves a city, and they called the name at the city Kesed after the name of their father, that is the land Kasdim unto this day, and the Kasdim dwelt in that land and they were fruitful and multiplied exceedingly.

31 And Terah, father of Nahor and Abraham, went and took another wife in his old age, and her name was Pelilah, and she conceived and bare him a son and he called his name Zoba.

32 And Terah lived twenty-five years after he begat Zoba.

33 And Terah died in that year, that is in the thirty-fifth year of the birth of Isaac son of Abraham.

34 And the days of Terah were two hundred and five years, and he was buried in Haran.

35 And Zoba the son of Terah lived thirty years and he begat Aram, Achlis and Merik.

36 And Aram son of Zoba son of Terah, had three wives and he begat twelve sons and three daughters; and the Lord gave to Aram the son of Zoba, riches and possessions, and abundance of cattle, and flocks and herds, and the man increased greatly.

37 And Aram the son of Zoba and his brother and all his household journeyed from Haran, and they went to dwell where they should find a place, for their property was too great to remain in Haran; for they could not stop in Haran together with their brethren the children of Nahor.

38 And Aram the son of Zoba went with his brethren, and

they found a valley at a distance toward the eastern country and they dwelt there.

39 And they also built a city there, and they called the name thereof Aram, after the name of their eldest brother; that is Aram Zoba to this day.

40 And Isaac the son of Abraham was growing up in those days, and Abraham his father taught him the way of the Lord to know the Lord, and the Lord was with him.

41 And when Isaac was thirty-seven years old, Ishmael his brother was going about with him in the tent.

42 And Ishmael boasted of himself to Isaac, saying, I was thirteen years old when the Lord spoke to my father to circumcise us, and I did according to the word of the Lord which he spoke to my father, and I gave my soul unto the Lord, and I did not transgress his word which he commanded my father.

43 And Isaac answered Ishmael, saying, Why dost thou boast to me about this, about a little bit of thy flesh which thou didst take from thy body, concerning which the Lord commanded thee?

44 As the Lord liveth, the God of my father Abraham, if the Lord should say unto my father, Take now thy son Isaac and bring him up an offering before me, I would not refrain but I would joyfully accede to it.

45 And the Lord heard the word that Isaac spoke to Ishmael, and it seemed good in the sight of the Lord, and he thought to try Abraham in this matter.

46 And the day arrived when the sons of God came and placed themselves before the Lord, and Satan also came with the sons of God before the Lord.

47 And the Lord said unto Satan, Whence comest thou? and Satan answered the Lord and said, From going to and fro in the earth, and from walking up and down in it.

48 And the Lord said to Satan, What is thy word to me concerning all the children of the earth? and Satan answered the Lord and said, I have seen all the children of the earth who serve thee and remember thee when they require anything from thee.

49 And when thou givest them the thing which they require from thee, they sit at their ease, and forsake thee and they remember thee no more.

50 Hast thou seen Abraham the son of Terah, who at first had no children, and he served thee and erected altars to thee wherever he came, and he brought up offerings upon them, and he proclaimed thy name continually to all the children of the earth.

51 And now that his son Isaac is born to him, he has forsaken thee, he has made a great feast for all the inhabitants of the land, and the Lord he has forgotten.

52 For amidst all that he has done he brought thee no offering; neither burnt offering nor peace offering, neither ox, lamb nor goat of all that he killed on the day that his son was weaned.

53 Even from the time of his son's birth till now, being thirty-seven years, he built no altar before thee, nor brought any offering to thee, for he saw that thou didst give what he requested before thee, and he therefore forsook thee.

54 And the Lord said to Satan, Hast thou thus considered my servant Abraham? for there is none like him upon earth, a perfect and an upright man before me, one that feareth God and avoideth evil; as I live, were I to say unto him, Bring up Isaac thy son before me, he would not withhold him from me, much more if I told him to bring up a burnt offering before me from his flock or herds.

55 And Satan answered the Lord and said, Speak then now unto Abraham as thou hast said, and thou wilt see whether he will not this day transgress and cast aside thy words.

Chapter 23

1 At that time the word of the Lord came to Abraham, and he said unto him, Abraham, and he said, Here I am.

2 And he said to him, Take now thy son, thine only son whom thou lovest, even Isaac, and go to the land of Moriah, and offer him there for a burnt offering upon one of the mountains which shall be shown to thee, for there wilt thou see a cloud and the glory of the Lord.

3 And Abraham said within himself, How shall I separate my son Isaac from Sarah his mother, in order to bring him up for a burnt offering before the Lord?

4 And Abraham came into the tent, and he sat before Sarah his wife, and he spoke these words to her,

5 My son Isaac is grown up and he has not for some time studied the service of his God, now tomorrow I will go and bring him to Shem, and Eber his son, and there he will learn the ways of the Lord, for they will teach him to know the Lord as well as to know that when he prayeth continually before the Lord, he will answer him, therefore there he will know the way of serving the Lord his God.

6 And Sarah said, Thou hast spoken well, go my lord and do unto him as thou hast said, but remove him not at a great distance from me, neither let him remain there too long, for my soul is bound within his soul.

7 And Abraham said unto Sarah, My daughter, let us pray to the Lord our God that he may do good with us.

8 And Sarah took her son Isaac and he abode all that night with her, and she kissed and embraced him, and gave him instructions till morning.

9 And she said to him, O my son, how can my soul separate itself from thee? And she still kissed him and embraced him, and she gave Abraham instructions concerning him.

10 And Sarah said to Abraham, O my lord, I pray thee take heed of thy son, and place thine eyes over him, for I have no other son nor daughter but him.

11 O forsake him not. If he be hungry give him bread, and if he be thirsty give him water to drink; do not let him go on foot, neither let him sit in the sun.

12 Neither let him go by himself in the road, neither force him from whatever he may desire, but do unto him as he may say to thee.

13 And Sarah wept bitterly the whole night on account of Isaac, and she gave him instructions till morning.

14 And in the morning Sarah selected a very fine and beautiful garment from those garments which she had in the house, that Abimelech had given to her.

15 And she dressed Isaac her son therewith, and she put a turban upon his head, and she enclosed a precious stone in the top of the turban, and she gave them provision for the road, and they went forth, and Isaac went with his father Abraham, and some of their servants accompanied them to see them off the road.

16 And Sarah went out with them, and she accompanied them upon the road to see them off, and they said to her, Return to the tent.

17 And when Sarah heard the words of her son Isaac she wept bitterly, and Abraham her husband wept with her, and their son wept with them a great weeping; also those who went with them wept greatly.

18 And Sarah caught hold of her son Isaac, and she held him in her arms, and she embraced him and continued to weep with him, and Sarah said, Who knoweth if after this day I shall ever see thee again?

19 And they still wept together, Abraham, Sarah and Isaac, and all those that accompanied them on the road wept with them, and Sarah afterward turned away from her son, weeping bitterly, and all her men servants and maid servants returned with her to the tent.

20 And Abraham went with Isaac his son to bring him up as an offering before the Lord, as He had commanded him.

21 And Abraham took two of his young men with him, Ishmael the son of Hagar and Eliezer his servant, and they went together with them, and whilst they were walking in the road the young men spoke these words to themselves,

22 And Ishmael said to Eliezer, Now my father Abraham is going with Isaac to bring him up for a burnt offering to the Lord, as He commanded him.

23 Now when he returneth he will give unto me all that he possesses, to inherit after him, for I am his first born.

24 And Eliezer answered Ishmael and said, Surely Abraham did cast thee away with thy mother, and swear that thou shouldst not inherit any thing of all he possesses, and to whom will he give all that he has, with all his treasures, but unto me his servant, who has been faithful in his house, who has served him night and day, and has done all that he desired me? to me will he bequeath at his death all that he possesses.

25 And whilst Abraham was proceeding with his son Isaac along the road, Satan came and appeared to Abraham in the figure of a very aged man, humble and of contrite spirit, and he approached Abraham and said to him, Art thou silly or brutish, that thou goest to do this thing this day to thine only son?

26 For God gave thee a son in thy latter days, in thy old age, and wilt thou go and slaughter him this day because he committed no violence, and wilt thou cause the soul of thine only son to perish from the earth?

27 Dost thou not know and understand that this thing cannot be from the Lord? for the Lord cannot do unto man such evil upon earth to say to him, Go slaughter thy child.

28 And Abraham heard this and knew that it was the word of Satan who endeavored to draw him aside from the way of the Lord, but Abraham would not hearken to the voice of Satan, and Abraham rebuked him so that he went away.

29 And Satan returned and came to Isaac; and he appeared unto Isaac in the figure of a young man comely and well favored.

30 And he approached Isaac and said unto him, Dost thou not know and understand that thy old silly father bringeth thee to the slaughter this day for naught?

31 Now therefore, my son, do not listen nor attend to him, for he is a silly old man, and let not thy precious soul and beautiful figure be lost from the earth.

32 And Isaac heard this, and said unto Abraham, Hast thou heard, my father, that which this man has spoken? even thus has he spoken.

33 And Abraham answered his son Isaac and said to him, Take heed of him and do not listen to his words, nor attend to him, for he is Satan, endeavoring to draw us aside this day from the commands of God.

34 And Abraham still rebuked Satan, and Satan went from them, and seeing he could not prevail over them he hid himself from them, and he went and passed before them in the road; and he transformed himself to a large brook of water in the road, and Abraham and Isaac and his two young men reached that place, and they saw a brook large and powerful as the mighty waters.

35 And they entered the brook and passed through it, and the waters at first reached their legs.

36 And they went deeper in the brook and the waters reached up to their necks, and they were all terrified on account of the water; and whilst they were going over the brook Abraham recognized that place, and he knew that there was no water there before.

37 And Abraham said to his son Isaac, I know this place in which there was no brook nor water, now therefore it is this Satan who does all this to us, to draw us aside this day from the commands of God.

38 And Abraham rebuked him and said unto him, The Lord rebuke thee, O Satan, begone from us for we go by the commands of God.

39 And Satan was terrified at the voice of Abraham, and he went away from them, and the place again became dry land as it was at first.

40 And Abraham went with Isaac toward the place that God had told him.

41 And on the third day Abraham lifted up his eyes and saw the place at a distance which God had told him of.

42 And a pillar of fire appeared to him that reached from the earth to heaven, and a cloud of glory upon the mountain, and the glory of the Lord was seen in the cloud.

43 And Abraham said to Isaac, My son, dost thou see in that mountain, which we perceive at a distance, that which I see upon it?

44 And Isaac answered and said unto his father, I see and lo a pillar of fire and a cloud, and the glory of the Lord is seen upon the cloud.

45 And Abraham knew that his son Isaac was accepted before the Lord for a burnt offering.

46 And Abraham said unto Eliezer and unto Ishmael his son, Do you also see that which we see upon the mountain which is at a distance?

47 And they answered and said, We see nothing more than like the other mountains of the earth. And Abraham knew that they were not accepted before the Lord to go with them, and Abraham said to them, Abide ye here with the ass whilst I and Isaac my son will go to yonder mount and worship there before the Lord and then return to you.

48 And Eliezer and Ishmael remained in that place, as Abraham had commanded.

49 And Abraham took wood for a burnt offering and placed it upon his son Isaac, and he took the fire and the knife, and they both went to that place.

50 And when they were going along Isaac said to his father, Behold, I see here the fire and wood, and where then is the lamb that is to be the burnt offering before the Lord?

51 And Abraham answered his son Isaac, saying, The Lord has made choice of thee my son, to be a perfect burnt offering instead of the lamb.

52 And Isaac said unto his father, I will do all that the Lord spoke to thee with joy and cheerfulness of heart.

53 And Abraham again said unto Isaac his son, Is there in thy heart any thought or counsel concerning this, which is not proper? tell me my son, I pray thee, O my son conceal it not from me.

54 And Isaac answered his father Abraham and said unto him, O my father, as the Lord liveth and as thy soul liveth, there is nothing in my heart to cause me to deviate either to the right or to the left from the word that he has spoken to thee.

55 Neither limb nor muscle has moved or stirred at this, nor is there in my heart any thought or evil counsel concerning this.

56 But I am of joyful and cheerful heart in this matter, and

I say, Blessed is the Lord who has this day chosen me to be a burnt offering before Him.

57 And Abraham greatly rejoiced at the words of Isaac, and they went on and came together to that place that the Lord had spoken of.

58 And Abraham approached to build the altar in that place, and Abraham was weeping, and Isaac took stones and mortar until they had finished building the altar.

59 And Abraham took the wood and placed it in order upon the altar which he had built.

60 And he took his son Isaac and bound him in order to place him upon the wood which was upon the altar, to slay him for a burnt offering before the Lord.

61 And Isaac said to his father, Bind me securely and then place me upon the altar lest I should turn and move, and break loose from the force of the knife upon my flesh and thereof profane the burnt offering; and Abraham did so.

62 And Isaac still said to his father, O my father, when thou shalt have slain me and burnt me for an offering, take with thee that which shall remain of my ashes to bring to Sarah my mother, and say to her, This is the sweet smelling savor of Isaac; but do not tell her this if she should sit near a well or upon any high place, lest she should cast her soul after me and die.

63 And Abraham heard the words of Isaac, and he lifted up his voice and wept when Isaac spake these words; and Abraham's tears gushed down upon Isaac his son, and Isaac wept bitterly, and he said to his father, Hasten thou, O my father, and do with me the will of the Lord our God as He has commanded thee.

64 And the hearts of Abraham and Isaac rejoiced at this thing which the Lord had commanded them; but the eye wept bitterly whilst the heart rejoiced.

65 And Abraham bound his son Isaac, and placed him on the altar upon the wood, and Isaac stretched forth his neck upon the altar before his father, and Abraham stretched forth his hand to take the knife to slay his son as a burnt offering before the Lord.

66 At that time the angels of mercy came before the Lord and spake to him concerning Isaac, saying,

67 0 Lord, thou art a merciful and compassionate King over all that thou hast created in heaven and in earth, and thou supportest them all; give therefore ransom and redemption instead of thy servant Isaac, and pity and have compassion upon Abraham and Isaac his son, who are this day performing thy commands.

68 Hast thou seen, O Lord, how Isaac the son of Abraham thy servant is bound down to the slaughter like an animal? now therefore let thy pity be roused for them, O Lord.

69 At that time the Lord appeared unto Abraham, and called to him, from heaven, and said unto him, Lay not thine hand upon the lad, neither do thou any thing unto him, for now I know that thou fearest God in performing this act, and in not withholding thy son, thine only son, from me.

70 And Abraham lifted up his eyes and saw, and behold, a ram was caught in a thicket by his horns; that was the ram which the Lord God had created in the earth in the day that he made earth and heaven.

71 For the Lord had prepared this ram from that day, to be a burnt offering instead of Isaac.

72 And this ram was advancing to Abraham when Satan caught hold of him and entangled his horns in the thicket, that he might not advance to Abraham, in order that Abraham might slay his son.

73 And Abraham, seeing the ram advancing to him and Satan withholding him, fetched him and brought him before the altar, and he loosened his son Isaac from his binding, and he put the ram in his stead, and Abraham killed the ram upon the altar, and brought it up as an offering in the place of his son Isaac.

74 And Abraham sprinkled some of the blood of the ram upon the altar, and he exclaimed and said, This is in the place of my son, and may this be considered this day as the blood of my son before the Lord.

75 And all that Abraham did on this occasion by the altar, he would exclaim and say, This is in the room of my son, and may it this day be considered before the Lord in the place of my son; and Abraham finished the whole of the service by the altar, and the service was accepted before the Lord, and was accounted as if it had been Isaac; and the Lord blessed Abraham and his seed on that day.

76 And Satan went to Sarah, and he appeared to her in the figure of an old man very humble and meek, and Abraham was yet engaged in the burnt offering before the Lord.

77 And he said unto her, Dost thou not know all the work that Abraham has made with thine only son this day? for he took Isaac and built an altar, and killed him, and brought him up as a sacrifice upon the altar, and Isaac cried and wept before his father, but he looked not at him, neither did he have compassion over him.

78 And Satan repeated these words, and he went away from her, and Sarah heard all the words of Satan, and she imagined him to be an old man from amongst the sons of men who had been with her son, and had come and told her these things.

79 And Sarah lifted up her voice and wept and cried out bitterly on account of her son; and she threw herself upon the ground and she cast dust upon her head, and she said, O my son, Isaac my son, O that I had this day died instead of thee. And she continued to weep and said, It grieves me for thee, O my son, my son Isaac, O that I had died this day in thy stead.

80 And she still continued to weep, and said, It grieves me for thee after that I have reared thee and have brought thee up; now my joy is turned into mourning over thee, I that had a longing for thee, and cried and prayed to God till I bare thee at ninety years old; and now hast thou served this day for the knife and the fire, to be made an offering.

81 But I console myself with thee, my son, in its being the word of the Lord, for thou didst perform the command of thy God; for who can transgress the word of our God, in whose hands is the soul of every living creature?

82 Thou art just, O Lord our God, for all thy works are good and righteous; for I also am rejoiced with thy word which thou didst command, and whilst mine eye weepeth bitterly my heart rejoiceth.

83 And Sarah laid her head upon the bosom of one of her handmaids, and she became as still as a stone.

84 She afterward rose up and went about making inquiries till she came to Hebron, and she inquired of all those whom she met walking in the road, and no one could tell her what had happened to her son.

85 And she came with her maid servants and men servants to Kireath-arba, which is Hebron, and she asked concerning her Son, and she remained there while she sent some of her servants to seek where Abraham had gone with Isaac; they went to seek him in the house of Shem and Eber, and they could not find him, and they sought throughout the land and he was not there.

86 And behold, Satan came to Sarah in the shape of an old man, and he came and stood before her, and he said unto

her, I spoke falsely unto thee, for Abraham did not kill his son and he is not dead; and when she heard the word her joy was so exceedingly violent on account of her son, that her soul went out through joy; she died and was gathered to her people.

87 And when Abraham had finished his service he returned with his son Isaac to his young men, and they rose up and went together to Beersheba, and they came home.

88 And Abraham sought for Sarah, and could not find her, and he made inquiries concerning her, and they said unto him, She went as far as Hebron to seek you both where you had gone, for thus was she informed.

89 And Abraham and Isaac went to her to Hebron, and when they found that she was dead they lifted up their voices and wept bitterly over her; and Isaac fell upon his mother's face and wept over her, and he said, O my mother, my mother, how hast thou left me, and where hast thou gone? O how, how hast thou left me!

90 And Abraham and Isaac wept greatly and all their servants wept with them on account of Sarah, and they mourned over her a great and heavy mourning.

Chapter 24

1 And the life of Sarah was one hundred and twenty-seven years, and Sarah died; and Abraham rose up from before his dead to seek a burial place to bury his wife Sarah; and he went and spoke to the children of Heth, the inhabitants of the land, saying,

2 I am a stranger and a sojourner with you in your land; give me a possession of a burial place in your land, that I may bury my dead from before me.

3 And the children of Heth said unto Abraham, behold the land is before thee, in the choice of our sepulchers bury thy dead, for no man shall withhold thee from burying thy dead.

4 And Abraham said unto them, If you are agreeable to this go and entreat for me to Ephron, the son of Zochar, requesting that he may give me the cave of Machpelah, which is in the end of his field, and I will purchase it of him for whatever he desire for it.

5 And Ephron dwelt among the children of Heth, and they went and called for him, and he came before Abraham, and Ephron said unto Abraham, Behold all thou requirest thy servant will do; and Abraham said, No, but I will buy the cave and the field which thou hast for value, In order that it may be for a possession of a burial place for ever.

6 And Ephron answered and said, Behold the field and the cave are before thee, give whatever thou desirest; and Abraham said, Only at full value will I buy it from thy hand, and from the hands of those that go in at the gate of thy city, and from the hand of thy seed for ever.

7 And Ephron and all his brethren heard this, and Abraham weighed to Ephron four hundred shekels of silver in the hands of Ephron and in the hands of all his brethren; and Abraham wrote this transaction, and he wrote it and testified it with four witnesses.

8 And these are the names of the witnesses, Amigal son of Abishna the Hittite, Adichorom son of Ashunach the Hivite, Abdon son of Achiram the Gomerite, Bakdil the son of Abudish the Zidonite.

9 And Abraham took the book of the purchase, and placed it in his treasures, and these are the words that Abraham wrote in the book, namely:

10 That the cave and the field Abraham bought from Ephron the Hittite, and from his seed, and from those that go out of his city, and from their seed for ever, are to be a

purchase to Abraham and to his seed and to those that go forth from his loins, for a possession of a burial place for ever; and he put a signet to it and testified it with witnesses.

11 And the field and the cave that was in it and all that place were made sure unto Abraham and unto his seed after him, from the children of Heth; behold it is before Mamre in Hebron, which is in the land of Canaan.

12 And after this Abraham buried his wife Sarah there, and that place and all its boundary became to Abraham and unto his seed for a possession of a burial place.

13 And Abraham buried Sarah with pomp as observed at the interment of kings, and she was buried in very fine and beautiful garments.

14 And at her bier was Shem, his sons Eber and Abimelech, together with Anar, Ashcol and Mamre, and all the grandees of the land followed her bier.

15 And the days of Sarah were one hundred and twenty-seven years and she died, and Abraham made a great and heavy mourning, and he performed the rites of mourning for seven days.

16 And all the inhabitants of the land comforted Abraham and Isaac his son on account of Sarah.

17 And when the days of their mourning passed by Abraham sent away his son Isaac, and he went to the house of Shem and Eber, to learn the ways of the Lord and his instructions, and Abraham remained there three years.

18 At that time Abraham rose up with all his servants, and they went and returned homeward to Beersheba, and Abraham and all his servants remained in Beersheba.

19 And at the revolution of the year Abimelech king of the Philistines died in that year; he was one hundred and ninety-three years old at his death; and Abraham went with his people to the land of the Philistines, and they comforted the whole household and all his servants, and he then turned and went home.

20 And it was after the death of Abimelech that the people of Gerar took Benmalich his son, and he was only twelve years old, and they made him lying in the place of his father.

21 And they called his name Abimelech after the name of his father, for thus was it their custom to do in Gerar, and Abimelech reigned instead of Abimelech his father, and he sat upon his throne.

22 And Lot the son of Haran also died in those days, in the thirty-ninth year of the life of Isaac, and all the days that Lot lived were one hundred and forty years and he died.

23 And these are the children of Lot, that were born to him by his daughters, the name of the first born was Moab, and the name of the second was Benami.

24 And the two sons of Lot went and took themselves wives from the land of Canaan, and they bare children to them, and the children of Moab were Ed, Mayon, Tarsus, and Kanvil, four sons, these are fathers to the children of Moab unto this day.

25 And all the families of the children of Lot went to dwell wherever they should light upon, for they were fruitful and increased abundantly.

26 And they went and built themselves cities in the land where they dwelt, and they called the names of the cities which they built after their own names.

27 And Nahor the son of Terah, brother to Abraham, died in those days in the fortieth year of the life of Isaac, and all the days of Nahor were one hundred and seventy-two years and he died and was buried in Haran.

28 And when Abraham heard that his brother was dead he grieved sadly, and he mourned over his brother many days.

29 And Abraham called for Eliezer his head servant, to give him orders concerning his house, and he came and stood before him.

30 And Abraham said to him, Behold I am old, I do not know the day of my death; for I am advanced in days; now therefore rise up, go forth and do not take a wife for my son from this place and from this land, from the daughters of the Canaanites amongst whom we dwell.

31 But go to my land and to my birthplace, and take from thence a wife for my son, and the Lord God of Heaven and earth who took me from my father's house and brought me to this place, and said unto me, To thy seed will I give this land for an inheritance for ever, he will send his angel before thee and prosper thy way, that thou mayest obtain a wife for my son from my family and from my father's house.

32 And the servant answered his master Abraham and said, Behold I go to thy birthplace and to thy father's house, and take a wife for thy son from there; but if the woman be not willing to follow me to this land, shall I take thy son back to the land of thy birthplace?

33 And Abraham said unto him, Take heed that thou bring not my son hither again, for the Lord before whom I have walked he will send his angel before thee and prosper thy way.

34 And Eliezer did as Abraham ordered him, and Eliezer swore unto Abraham his master upon this matter; and Eliezer rose up and took ten camels of the camels of his master, and ten men from his master's servants with him, and they rose up and went to Haran, the city of Abraham and Nahor, in order to fetch a wife for Isaac the son of Abraham; and whilst they were gone Abraham sent to the house of Shem and Eber, and they brought from thence his son Isaac.

35 And Isaac came home to his father's house to Beersheba, whilst Eliezer and his men came to Haran; and they stopped in the city by the watering place, and he made his camels to kneel down by the water and they remained there.

36 And Eliezer, Abraham's servant, prayed and said, O God of Abraham my master; send me I pray thee good speed this day and show kindness unto my master, that thou shalt appoint this day a wife for my master's son from his family.

37 And the Lord hearkened to the voice of Eliezer, for the sake of his servant Abraham, and he happened to meet with the daughter of Bethuel, the son of Milcah, the wife of Nahor, brother to Abraham, and Eliezer came to her house.

38 And Eliezer related to them all his concerns, and that he was Abraham's servant, and they greatly rejoiced at him.

39 And they all blessed the Lord who brought this thing about, and they gave him Rebecca, the daughter of Bethuel, for a wife for Isaac.

40 And the young woman was of very comely appearance, she was a virgin, and Rebecca was ten years old in those days.

41 And Bethuel and Laban and his children made a feast on that night, and Eliezer and his men came and ate and drank and rejoiced there on that night.

42 And Eliezer rose up in the morning, he and the men that were with him, and he called to the whole household of Bethuel, saying, Send me away that I may go to my master; and they rose up and sent away Rebecca and her nurse Deborah, the daughter of Uz, and they gave her silver and gold, men servants and maid servants, and they blessed her.

43 And they sent Eliezer away with his men; and the servants took Rebecca, and he went and returned to his master to the land of Canaan.

44 And Isaac took Rebecca and she became his wife, and he brought her into the tent.

45 And Isaac was forty years old when he took Rebecca, the daughter of his uncle Bethuel, for a wife.

Chapter 25

1 And it was at that time that Abraham again took a wife in his old age, and her name was Keturah, from the land of Canaan.

2 And she bare unto him Zimran, Jokshan, Medan, Midian, Ishbak and Shuach, being six sons. And the children of Zimran were Abihen, Molich and Narim.

3 And the sons of Jokshan were Sheba and Dedan, and the sons of Medan were Amida, Joab, Gochi, Elisha and Nothach; and the sons of Midian were Ephah, Epher, Chanoch, Abida and Eldaah.

4 And the sons of Ishbak were Makiro, Beyodua and Tator.

5 And the sons of Shuach were Bildad, Mamdad, Munan and Meban; all these are the families of the children of Keturah the Canaanitish woman which she bare unto Abraham the Hebrew.

6 And Abraham sent all these away, and he gave them gifts, and they went away from his son Isaac to dwell wherever they should find a place.

7 And all these went to the mountain at the east, and they built themselves six cities in which they dwelt unto this day.

8 But the children of Sheba and Dedan, children of Jokshan, with their children, did not dwell with their brethren in their cities, and they journeyed and encamped in the countries and wildernesses unto this day.

9 And the children of Midian, son of Abraham, went to the east of the land of Cush, and they there found a large valley in the eastern country, and they remained there and built a city, and they dwelt therein, that is the land of Midian unto this day.

10 And Midian dwelt in the city which he built, he and his five sons and all belonging to him.

11 And these are the names of the sons of Midian according to their names in their cities, Ephah, Epher, Chanoch, Abida and Eldaah.

12 And the sons of Ephah were Methach, Meshar, Avi and Tzanua, and the sons of Epher were Ephron, Zur, Alirun and Medin, and the sons of Chanoch were Reuel, Rekem, Azi, Alyoshub and Alad.

13 And the sons of Abida were Chur, Melud, Kerury, Molchi; and the sons of Eldaah were Miker, and Reba, and Malchiyah and Gabol; these are the names of the Midianites according to their families; and afterward the families of Midian spread throughout the land of Midian.

14 And these are the generations of Ishmael the son Abraham, whom Hagar, Sarah's handmaid, bare unto Abraham.

15 And Ishmael took a wife from the land of Egypt, and her name was Ribah, the same is Meribah.

16 And Ribah bare unto Ishmael Nebayoth, Kedar, Adbeel, Mibsam and their sister Bosmath.

17 And Ishmael cast away his wife Ribah, and she went from him and returned to Egypt to the house of her father, and she dwelt there, for she had been very bad in the sight of Ishmael, and in the sight of his father Abraham.

18 And Ishmael afterward took a wife from the land of Canaan, and her name was Malchuth, and she bare unto

him Nishma, Dumah, Masa, Chadad, Tema, Yetur, Naphish and Kedma.

19 These are the sons of Ishmael, and these are their names, being twelve princes according to their nations; and the families of Ishmael afterward spread forth, and Ishmael took his children and all the property that he had gained, together with the souls of his household and all belonging to him, and they went to dwell where they should find a place.

20 And they went and dwelt near the wilderness of Paran, and their dwelling was from Havilah unto Shur, that is before Egypt as thou comest toward Assyria.

21 And Ishmael and his sons dwelt in the land, and they had children born to them, and they were fruitful and increased abundantly.

22 And these are the names of the sons of Nebayoth the first born of Ishmael; Mend, Send, Mayon; and the sons of Kedar were Alyon, Kezem, Chamad and Eli.

23 And the sons of Adbeel were Chamad and Jabin; and the sons of Mibsam were Obadiah, Ebedmelech and Yeush; these are the families of the children of Ribah the wife of Ishmael.

24 And the sons of Mishma the son of Ishmael were Shamua, Zecaryon and Obed; and the sons of Dumah were Kezed, Eli, Machmad and Amed.

25 And the sons of Masa were Melon, Mula and Ebidadon; and the sons of Chadad were Azur, Minzar and Ebedmelech; and the sons of Tema were Seir, Sadon and Yakol.

26 And the sons of Yetur were Merith, Yaish, Alyo, and Pachoth; and the sons of Naphish were Ebed-Tamed, Abiyasaph and Mir; and the sons of Kedma were Calip, Tachti, and Omir; these were the children of Malchuth the wife of Ishmael according to their families.

27 All these are the families of Ishmael according to their generations, and they dwelt in those lands wherein they had built themselves cities unto this day.

28 And Rebecca the daughter of Bethuel, the wife of Abraham's son Isaac, was barren in those days, she had no offspring; and Isaac dwelt with his father in the land of Canaan; and the Lord was with Isaac; and Arpachshad the son of Shem the son of Noah died in those days, in the forty-eighth year of the life of Isaac, and all the days that Arpachshad lived were four hundred and thirty-eight years, and he died.

Chapter 26

1 And in the fifty-ninth year of the life of Isaac the son of Abraham, Rebecca his wife was still barren in those days.

2 And Rebecca said unto Isaac, Truly I have heard, my lord, that thy mother Sarah was barren in her days until my Lord Abraham, thy father, prayed for her and she conceived by him.

3 Now therefore stand up, pray thou also to God and he will hear thy prayer and remember us through his mercies.

4 And Isaac answered his wife Rebecca, saying, Abraham has already prayed for me to God to multiply his seed, now therefore this barrenness must proceed to us from thee.

5 And Rebecca said unto him, But arise now thou also and pray, that the Lord may hear thy prayer and grant me children, and Isaac hearkened to the words of his wife, and Isaac and his wife rose up and went to the land of Moriah to pray there and to seek the Lord, and when they had reached that place Isaac stood up and prayed to the Lord on account of his wife because she was barren.

6 And Isaac said, O Lord God of heaven and earth, whose goodness and mercies fill the earth, thou who didst take my father from his father's house and from his birthplace, and didst bring him unto this land, and didst say unto him, To thy seed will I give the land, and thou didst promise him and didst declare unto him, I will multiply thy seed as the stars of heaven and as the sand of the sea, now may thy words be verified which thou didst speak unto my father.

7 For thou art the Lord our God, our eyes are toward thee to give us seed of men, as thou didst promise us, for thou art the Lord our God and our eyes are directed toward thee only.

8 And the Lord heard the prayer of Isaac the son of Abraham, and the Lord was entreated of him and Rebecca his wife conceived.

9 And in about seven months after the children struggled together within her, and it pained her greatly that she was wearied on account of them, and she said to all the women who were then in the land, Did such a thing happen to you as it has to me? and they said unto her, No.

10 And she said unto them, Why am I alone in this amongst all the women that were upon earth? and she went to the land of Moriah to seek the Lord on account of this; and she went to Shem and Eber his son to make inquiries of them in this matter, and that they should seek the Lord in this thing respecting her.

11 And she also asked Abraham to seek and inquire of the Lord about all that had befallen her.

12 And they all inquired of the Lord concerning this matter, and they brought her word from the Lord and told her, Two children are in thy womb, and two nations shall rise from them; and one nation shall be stronger than the other, and the greater shall serve the younger.

13 And when her days to be delivered were completed, she knelt down, and behold there were twins in her womb, as the Lord had spoken to her.

14 And the first came out red all over like a hairy garment, and all the people of the land called his name Esau, saying, That this one was made complete from the womb.

15 And after that came his brother, and his hand took hold of Esau's heel, therefore they called his name Jacob.

16 And Isaac, the son of Abraham, was sixty years old when he begat them.

17 And the boys grew up to their fifteenth year, and they came amongst the society of men. Esau was a designing and deceitful man, and an expert hunter in the field, and Jacob was a man perfect and wise, dwelling in tents, feeding flocks and learning the instructions of the Lord and the commands of his father and mother.

18 And Isaac and the children of his household dwelt with his father Abraham in the land of Canaan, as God had commanded them.

19 And Ishmael the son of Abraham went with his children and all belonging to them, and they returned there to the land of Havilah, and they dwelt there.

20 And all the children of Abraham's concubines went to dwell in the land of the east, for Abraham had sent them away from his son, and had given them presents, and they went away.

21 And Abraham gave all that he had to his son Isaac, and he also gave him all his treasures.

22 And he commanded him saying, Dost thou not know and understand the Lord is God in heaven and in earth, and there is no other beside him?

23 And it was he who took me from my father's house, and from my birth place, and gave me all the delights upon earth; who delivered me from the counsel of the wicked,

for in him did I trust.

24 And he brought me to this place, and he delivered me from Ur Casdim; and he said unto me, To thy seed will I give all these lands, and they shall inherit them when they keep my commandments, my statutes and my judgments that I have commanded thee, and which I shall command them.

25 Now therefore my son, hearken to my voice, and keep the commandments of the Lord thy God, which I commanded thee, do not turn from the right way either to the right or to the left, in order that it may be well with thee and thy children after thee forever.

26 And remember the wonderful works of the Lord, and his kindness that he has shown toward us, in having delivered us from the hands of our enemies, and the Lord our God caused them to fall into our hands; and now therefore keep all that I have commanded thee, and turn not away from the commandments of thy God, and serve none beside him, in order that it may be well with thee and thy seed after thee.

27 And teach thou thy children and thy seed the instructions of the Lord and his commandments, and teach them the upright way in which they should go, in order that it may be well with them forever.

28 And Isaac answered his father and said unto him, That which my Lord has commanded that will I do, and I will not depart from the commands of the Lord my God, I will keep all that he commanded me; and Abraham blessed his son Isaac, and also his children; and Abraham taught Jacob the instruction of the Lord and his ways.

29 And it was at that time that Abraham died, in the fifteenth year of the life of Jacob and Esau, the sons of Isaac, and all the days of Abraham were one hundred and seventy-five years, and he died and was gathered to his people in good old age, old and satisfied with days, and Isaac and Ishmael his sons buried him.

30 And when the inhabitants of Canaan heard that Abraham was dead, they all came with their kings and princes and all their men to bury Abraham.

31 And all the inhabitants of the land of Haran, and all the families of the house of Abraham, and all the princes and grandees, and the sons of Abraham by the concubines, all came when they heard of Abraham's death, and they requited Abraham's kindness, and comforted Isaac his son, and they buried Abraham in the cave which he bought from Ephron the Hittite and his children, for the possession of a burial place.

32 And all the inhabitants of Canaan, and all those who had known Abraham, wept for Abraham a whole year, and men and women mourned over him.

33 And all the little children, and all the inhabitants of the land wept on account of Abraham, for Abraham had been good to them all, and because he had been upright with God and men.

34 And there arose not a man who feared God like unto Abraham, for he had feared his God from his youth, and had served the Lord, and had gone in all his ways during his life, from his childhood to the day of his death.

35 And the Lord was with him and delivered him from the counsel of Nimrod and his people, and when he made war with the four kings of Elam he conquered them.

36 And he brought all the children of the earth to the service of God, and he taught them the ways of the Lord, and caused them to know the Lord.

37 And he formed a grove and he planted a vineyard therein, and he had always prepared in his tent meat and drink to those that passed through the land, that they might satisfy themselves in his house.

38 And the Lord God delivered the whole earth on account of Abraham.

39 And it was after the death of Abraham that God blessed his son Isaac and his children, and the Lord was with Isaac as he had been with his father Abraham, for Isaac kept all the commandments of the Lord as Abraham his father had commanded him; he did not turn to the right or to the left from the right path which his father had commanded him.

Chapter 27

1 And Esau at that time, after the death of Abraham, frequently went in the field to hunt.

2 And Nimrod king of Babel, the same was Amraphel, also frequently went with his mighty men to hunt in the field, and to walk about with his men in the cool of the day.

3 And Nimrod was observing Esau all the days, for a jealousy was formed in the heart of Nimrod against Esau all the days.

4 And on a certain day Esau went in the field to hunt, and he found Nimrod walking in the wilderness with his two men.

5 And all his mighty men and his people were with him in the wilderness, but they removed at a distance from him, and they went from him in different directions to hunt, and Esau concealed himself for Nimrod, and he lurked for him in the wilderness.

6 And Nimrod and his men that were with him did not know him, and Nimrod and his men frequently walked about in the field at the cool of the day, and to know where his men were hunting in the field.

7 And Nimrod and two of his men that were with him came to the place where they were, when Esau started suddenly from his lurking place, and drew his sword, and hastened and ran to Nimrod and cut off his head.

8 And Esau fought a desperate fight with the two men that were with Nimrod, and when they called out to him, Esau turned to them and smote them to death with his sword.

9 And all the mighty men of Nimrod, who had left him to go to the wilderness, heard the cry at a distance, and they knew the voices of those two men, and they ran to know the cause of it, when they found their king and the two men that were with him lying dead in the wilderness.

10 And when Esau saw the mighty men of Nimrod coming at a distance, he fled, and thereby escaped; and Esau took the valuable garments of Nimrod, which Nimrod's father had bequeathed to Nimrod, and with which Nimrod prevailed over the whole land, and he ran and concealed them in his house.

11 And Esau took those garments and ran into the city on account of Nimrod's men, and he came unto his father's house wearied and exhausted from fight, and he was ready to die through grief when he approached his brother Jacob and sat before him.

12 And he said unto his brother Jacob, Behold I shall die this day, and wherefore then do I want the birthright? And Jacob acted wisely with Esau in this matter, and Esau sold his birthright to Jacob, for it was so brought about by the Lord.

13 And Esau's portion in the cave of the field of Machpelah, which Abraham had bought from the children of Heth for the possession of a burial ground, Esau also sold to Jacob, and Jacob bought all this from his brother Esau for value given.

14 And Jacob wrote the whole of this in a book, and he

testified the same with witnesses, and he sealed it, and the book remained in the hands of Jacob.

15 And when Nimrod the son of Cush died, his men lifted him up and brought him in consternation, and buried him in his city, and all the days that Nimrod lived were two hundred and fifteen years and he died.

16 And the days that Nimrod reigned upon the people of the land were one hundred and eighty-five years; and Nimrod died by the sword of Esau in shame and contempt, and the seed of Abraham caused his death as he had seen in his dream.

17 And at the death of Nimrod his kingdom became divided into many divisions, and all those parts that Nimrod reigned over were restored to the respective kings of the land, who recovered them after the death of Nimrod, and all the people of the house of Nimrod were for a long time enslaved to all the other kings of the land.

Chapter 28

1 And in those days, after the death of Abraham, in that year the Lord brought a heavy famine in the land, and whilst the famine was raging in the land of Canaan, Isaac rose up to go down to Egypt on account of the famine, as his father Abraham had done.

2 And the Lord appeared that night to Isaac and he said to him, Do not go down to Egypt but rise and go to Gerar, to Abimelech king of the Philistines, and remain there till the famine shall cease.

3 And Isaac rose up and went to Gerar, as the Lord commanded him, and he remained there a full year.

4 And when Isaac came to Gerar, the people of the land saw that Rebecca his wife was of a beautiful appearance, and the people of Gerar asked Isaac concerning his wife, and he said, She is my sister, for he was afraid to say she was his wife lest the people of the land should slay him on account of her.

5 And the princes of Abimelech went and praised the woman to the king, but he answered them not, neither did he attend to their words.

6 But he heard them say that Isaac declared her to be his sister, so the king reserved this within himself.

7 And when Isaac had remained three months in the land, Abimelech looked out at the window, and he saw, and behold Isaac was sporting with Rebecca his wife, for Isaac dwelt in the outer house belonging to the king, so that the house of Isaac was opposite the house of the king.

8 And the king said unto Isaac, What is this thou hast done to us in saying of thy wife, She is my sister? how easily might one of the great men of the people have lain with her, and thou wouldst then have brought guilt upon us.

9 And Isaac said unto Abimelech, Because I was afraid lest I die on account of my wife, therefore I said, She is my sister.

10 At that time Abimelech gave orders to all his princes and great men, and they took Isaac and Rebecca his wife and brought them before the king.

11 And the king commanded that they should dress them in princely garments, and make them ride through the streets of the city, and proclaim before them throughout the land, saying, This is the man and this is his wife; whoever toucheth this man or his wife shall surely die. And Isaac returned with his wife to the king's house, and the Lord was with Isaac and he continued to wax great and lacked nothing.

12 And the Lord caused Isaac to find favor in the sight of Abimelech, and in the sight of all his subjects, and Abimelech acted well with Isaac, for Abimelech remembered the oath and the covenant that existed between his father and Abraham.

13 And Abimelech said unto Isaac, Behold the whole earth is before thee; dwell wherever it may seem good in thy sight until thou shalt return to thy land; and Abimelech gave Isaac fields and vineyards and the best part of the land of Gerar, to sow and reap and eat the fruits of the ground until the days of the famine should have passed by.

14 And Isaac sowed in that land, and received a hundred-fold in the same year, and the Lord blessed him.

15 And the man waxed great, and he had possession of flocks and possession of herds and great store of servants.

16 And when the days of the famine had passed away the Lord appeared to Isaac and said unto him, Rise up, go forth from this place and return to thy land, to the land of Canaan; and Isaac rose up and returned to Hebron which is in the land of Canaan, he and all belonging to him as the Lord commanded him.

17 And after this Shelach the son at Arpachshad died in that year, which is the eighteenth year of the lives of Jacob and Esau; and all the days that Shelach lived were four hundred and thirty-three years and he died.

18 At that time Isaac sent his younger son Jacob to the house of Shem and Eber, and he learned the instructions of the Lord, and Jacob remained in the house of Shem and Eber for thirty-two years, and Esau his brother did not go, for he was not willing to go, and he remained in his father's house in the land of Canaan.

19 And Esau was continually hunting in the fields to bring home what he could get, so did Esau all the days.

20 And Esau was a designing and deceitful man, one who hunted after the hearts of men and inveigled them, and Esau was a valiant man in the field, and in the course of time went as usual to hunt; and he came as far as the field of Seir, the same is Edom.

21 And he remained in the land of Seir hunting in the field a year and four months.

22 And Esau there saw in the land of Seir the daughter of a man of Canaan, and her name was Jehudith, the daughter of Beeri, son of Epher, from the families of Heth the son of Canaan.

23 And Esau took her for a wife, and he came unto her; forty years old was Esau when he took her, and he brought her to Hebron, the land of his father's dwelling place, and he dwelt there.

24 And it came to pass in those days, in the hundred and tenth year of the life of Isaac, that is in the fiftieth year of the life of Jacob, in that year died Shem the son of Noah; Shem was six hundred years old at his death.

25 And when Shem died Jacob returned to his father to Hebron which is in the land of Canaan.

26 And in the fifty-sixth year of the life of Jacob, people came from Haran, and Rebecca was told concerning her brother Laban the son of Bethuel.

27 For the wife of Laban was barren in those days, and bare no children, and also all his handmaids bare none to him.

28 And the Lord afterward remembered Adinah the wife of Laban, and she conceived and bare twin daughters, and Laban called the names of his daughters, the name of the elder Leah, and the name of the younger Rachel.

29 And those people came and told these things to Rebecca, and Rebecca rejoiced greatly that the Lord had visited her brother and that he had got children.

Chapter 29

1 And Isaac the son of Abraham became old and advanced in days, and his eyes became heavy through age; they were dim and could not see.

2 At that time Isaac called unto Esau his son, saying, Get I pray thee thy weapons, thy quiver and thy bow, rise up and go forth into the field and get me some venison, and make me savory meat and bring it to me, that I may eat in order that I may bless thee before my death, as I have now become old and gray-headed.

3 And Esau did so; and he took his weapon and went forth into the field to hunt for venison, as usual, to bring to his father as he had ordered him, so that he might bless him.

4 And Rebecca heard all the words that Isaac had spoken unto Esau, and she hastened and called her son Jacob, saying, Thus did thy father speak unto thy brother Esau, and thus did I hear, now therefore hasten thou and make that which I shall tell thee.

5 Rise up and go, I pray thee, to the flock and fetch me two fine kids of the goats, and I will get the savory meat for thy father, and thou shalt bring the savory meat that he may eat before thy brother shall have come from the chase, in order that thy father may bless thee.

6 And Jacob hastened and did as his mother had commanded him, and he made the savory meat and brought it before his father before Esau had come from his chase.

7 And Isaac said unto Jacob, Who art thou, my son? And he said, I am thy first born Esau, I have done as thou didst order me, now therefore rise up I pray thee, and eat of my hunt, in order that thy soul may bless me as thou didst speak unto me.

8 And Isaac rose up and he ate and he drank, and his heart was comforted, and he blessed Jacob and Jacob went away from his father; and as soon as Isaac had blessed Jacob and he had gone away from him, behold Esau came from his hunt from the field, and he also made savory meat and brought it to his father to eat thereof and to bless him.

9 And Isaac said unto Esau, And who was he that has taken venison and brought it me before thou camest and whom I did bless? And Esau knew that his brother Jacob had done this, and the anger of Esau was kindled against his brother Jacob that he had acted thus toward him.

10 And Esau said, Is he not rightly called Jacob? for he has supplanted me twice, he took away my birthright and now he has taken away my blessing; and Esau wept greatly; and when Isaac heard the voice of his son Esau weeping, Isaac said unto Esau, What can I do, my son, thy brother came with subtlety and took away thy blessing; and Esau hated his brother Jacob on account of the blessing that his father had given him, and his anger was greatly roused against him.

11 And Jacob was very much afraid of his brother Esau, and he rose up and fled to the house of Eber the son of Shem, and he concealed himself there on account of his brother, and Jacob was sixty-three years old when he went forth from the land of Canaan from Hebron, and Jacob was concealed in Eber's house fourteen years on account of his brother Esau, and he there continued to learn the ways of the Lord and his commandments.

12 And when Esau saw that Jacob had fled and escaped from him, and that Jacob had cunningly obtained the blessing, then Esau grieved exceedingly, and he was also vexed at his father and mother; and he also rose up and took his wife and went away from his father and mother to the land of Seir, and he dwelt there; and Esau saw there a woman from amongst the daughters of Heth whose name was Bosmath, the daughter of Elon the Hittite, and he took her for a wife in addition to his first wife, and Esau called her name Adah, saying the blessing had in that time passed from him.

13 And Esau dwelt in the land of Seir six months without seeing his father and mother, and afterward Esau took his wives and rose up and returned to the land of Canaan, and Esau placed his two wives in his father's house in Hebron.

14 And the wives of Esau vexed and provoked Isaac and Rebecca with their works, for they walked not in the ways of the Lord, but served their father's gods of wood and stone as their father had taught them, and they were more wicked than their father.

15 And they went according to the evil desires of their hearts, and they sacrificed and burnt incense to the Baalim, and Isaac and Rebecca became weary of them.

16 And Rebecca said, I am weary of my life because of the daughters of Heth; if Jacob take a wife of the daughters of Heth, such as these which are of the daughters of the land, what good then is life unto me?

17 And in those days Adah the wife of Esau conceived and bare him a son, and Esau called the name of the son that was born unto him Eliphaz, and Esau was sixty-five years old when she bare him.

18 And Ishmael the son of Abraham died in those days, in the sixty-forth year of the life of Jacob, and all the days that Ishmael lived were one hundred and thirty-seven years and he died.

19 And when Isaac heard that Ishmael was dead he mourned for him, and Isaac lamented over him many days.

20 And at the end of fourteen years of Jacob's residing in the house of Eber, Jacob desired to see his father and mother, and Jacob came to the house of his father and mother to Hebron, and Esau had in those days forgotten what Jacob had done to him in having taken the blessing from him in those days.

21 And when Esau saw Jacob coming to his father and mother he remembered what Jacob had done to him, and he was greatly incensed against him and he sought to slay him.

22 And Isaac the son of Abraham was old and advanced in days, and Esau said, Now my father's time is drawing nigh that he must die, and when he shall die I will slay my brother Jacob.

23 And this was told to Rebecca, and she hastened and sent and called for Jacob her son, and she said unto him, Arise, go and flee to Haran to my brother Laban, and remain there for some time, until thy brother's anger be turned from thee and then shalt thou come back.

24 And Isaac called unto Jacob and said unto him, Take not a wife from the daughters of Canaan, for thus did our father Abraham command us according to the word of the Lord which he had commanded him, saying, Unto thy seed will I give this land; if thy children keep my covenant that I have made with thee, then will I also perform to thy children that which I have spoken unto thee and I will not forsake them.

25 Now therefore my son hearken to my voice, to all that I shall command thee, and refrain from taking a wife from amongst the daughters of Canaan; arise, go to Haran to the house of Bethuel thy mother's father, and take unto thee a wife from there from the daughters of Laban thy mother's brother.

26 Therefore take heed lest thou shouldst forget the Lord thy God and all his ways in the land to which thou goest,

and shouldst get connected with the people of the land and pursue vanity and forsake the Lord thy God.

27 But when thou comest to the land serve there the Lord, do not turn to the right or to the left from the way which I commanded thee and which thou didst learn.

28 And may the Almighty God grant thee favor in the sight of the people of the earth, that thou mayest take there a wife according to thy choice; one who is good and upright in the ways of the Lord.

29 And may God give unto thee and thy seed the blessing of thy father Abraham, and make thee fruitful and multiply thee, and mayest thou become a multitude of people in the land whither thou goest, and may God cause thee to return to this land, the land of thy father's dwelling, with children and with great riches, with joy and with pleasure.

30 And Isaac finished commanding Jacob and blessing him, and he gave him many gifts, together with silver and gold, and he sent him away; and Jacob hearkened to his father and mother; he kissed them and arose and went to Padan-aram; and Jacob was seventy-seven years old when he went out from the land of Canaan from Beersheba.

31 And when Jacob went away to go to Haran Esau called unto his son Eliphaz, and secretly spoke unto him, saying, Now hasten, take thy sword in thy hand and pursue Jacob and pass before him in the road, and lurk for him, and slay him with thy sword in one of the mountains, and take all belonging to him and come back.

32 And Eliphaz the son of Esau was an active man and expert with the bow as his father had taught him, and he was a noted hunter in the field and a valiant man.

33 And Eliphaz did as his father had commanded him, and Eliphaz was at that time thirteen years old, and Eliphaz rose up and went and took ten of his mother's brothers with him and pursued Jacob.

34 And he closely followed Jacob, and he lurked for him in the border of the land of Canaan opposite to the city of Shechem.

35 And Jacob saw Eliphaz and his men pursuing him, and Jacob stood still in the place in which he was going, in order to know what this was, for he did not know the thing; and Eliphaz drew his sword and he went on advancing, he and his men, toward Jacob; and Jacob said unto them, What is to do with you that you have come hither, and what meaneth it that you pursue with your swords.

36 And Eliphaz came near to Jacob and he answered and said unto him, Thus did my father command me, and now therefore I will not deviate from the orders which my father gave me; and when Jacob saw that Esau had spoken to Eliphaz to employ force, Jacob then approached and supplicated Eliphaz and his men, saying to him,

37 Behold all that I have and which my father and mother gave unto me, that take unto thee and go from me, and do not slay me, and may this thing be accounted unto thee a righteousness.

38 And the Lord caused Jacob to find favor in the sight of Eliphaz the son of Esau, and his men, and they hearkened to the voice of Jacob, and they did not put him to death, and Eliphaz and his men took all belonging to Jacob together with the silver and gold that he had brought with him from Beersheba; they left him nothing.

39 And Eliphaz and his men went away from him and they returned to Esau to Beersheba, and they told him all that had occurred to them with Jacob, and they gave him all that they had taken from Jacob.

40 And Esau was indignant at Eliphaz his son, and at his men that were with him, because they had not put Jacob to death.

41 And they answered and said unto Esau, Because Jacob supplicated us in this matter not to slay him, our pity was excited toward him, and we took all belonging to him and brought it unto thee; and Esau took all the silver and gold which Eliphaz had taken from Jacob and he put them by in his house.

42 At that time when Esau saw that Isaac had blessed Jacob, and had commanded him, saying, Thou shalt not take a wife from amongst the daughters of Canaan, and that the daughters of Canaan were bad in the sight of Isaac and Rebecca,

43 Then he went to the house of Ishmael his uncle, and in addition to his older wives he took Machlath the daughter of Ishmael, the sister of Nebayoth, for a wife.

Chapter 30

1 And Jacob went forth continuing his road to Haran, and he came as far as mount Moriah, and he tarried there all night near the city of Luz; and the Lord appeared there unto Jacob on that night, and he said unto him, I am the Lord God of Abraham and the God of Isaac thy father; the land upon which thou liest I will give unto thee and thy seed.

2 And behold I am with thee and will keep thee wherever thou goest, and I will multiply thy seed as the stars of Heaven, and I will cause all thine enemies to fall before thee; and when they shall make war with thee they shall not prevail over thee, and I will bring thee again unto this land with joy, with children, and with great riches.

3 And Jacob awoke from his sleep and he rejoiced greatly at the vision which he had seen; and he called the name of that place Bethel.

4 And Jacob rose up from that place quite rejoiced, and when he walked his feet felt light to him for joy, and he went from there to the land of the children of the East, and he returned to Haran and he set by the shepherd's well.

5 And he there found some men; going from Haran to feed their flocks, and Jacob made inquiries of them, and they said, We are from Haran.

6 And he said unto them, Do you know Laban, the son of Nahor? and they said, We know him, and behold his daughter Rachel is coming along to feed her father's flock.

7 Whilst he was yet speaking with them, Rachel the daughter of Laban came to feed her father's sheep, for she was a shepherdess.

8 And when Jacob saw Rachel, the daughter of Laban, his mother's brother, he ran and kissed her, and lifted up his voice and wept.

9 And Jacob told Rachel that he was the son of Rebecca, her father's sister, and Rachel ran and told her father, and Jacob continued to cry because he had nothing with him to bring to the house of Laban.

10 And when Laban heard that his sister's son Jacob had come, he ran and kissed him and embraced him and brought him into the house and gave him bread, and he ate.

11 And Jacob related to Laban what his brother Esau had done to him, and what his son Eliphaz had done to him in the road.

12 And Jacob resided in Laban's house for one month, and Jacob ate and drank in the house of Laban, and afterward Laban said unto Jacob, Tell me what shall be thy wages, for how canst thou serve me for nought?

13 And Laban had no sons but only daughters, and his other wives and handmaids were still barren in those days;

and these are the names of Laban's daughters which his wife Adinah had borne unto him; the name of the elder was Leah and the name of the younger was Rachel; and Leah was tender-eyed, but Rachel was beautiful and well favored, and Jacob loved her.

14 And Jacob said unto Laban, I will serve thee seven years for Rachel thy younger daughter; and Laban consented to this and Jacob served Laban seven years for his daughter Rachel.

15 And in the second year of Jacob's dwelling in Haran, that is in the seventy ninth year of the life of Jacob, in that year died Eber the son of Shem, he was four hundred and sixty-four years old at his death.

16 And when Jacob heard that Eber was dead he grieved exceedingly, and he lamented and mourned over him many days.

17 And in the third year of Jacob's dwelling in Haran, Bosmath, the daughter of Ishmael, the wife of Esau, bare unto him a son, and Esau called his name Reuel.

18 And in the fourth year of Jacob's residence in the house of Laban, the Lord visited Laban and remembered him on account of Jacob, and sons were born unto him, and his first born was Beor, his second was Alib, and the third was Chorash.

19 And the Lord gave Laban riches and honor, sons and daughters, and the man increased greatly on account of Jacob.

20 And Jacob in those days served Laban in all manner of work, in the house and in the field, and the blessing of the Lord was in all that belonged to Laban in the house and in the field.

21 And in the fifth year died Jehudith, the daughter of Beeri, the wife of Esau, in the land of Canaan, and she had no sons but daughters only.

22 And these are the names of her daughters which she bare to Esau, the name of the elder was Marzith, and the name of the younger was Puith.

23 And when Jehudith died, Esau rose up and went to Seir to hunt in the field, as usual, and Esau dwelt in the land of Seir for a long time.

24 And in the sixth year Esau took for a wife, in addition to his other wives, Ahlibamah, the daughter of Zebeon the Hivite, and Esau brought her to the land of Canaan.

25 And Ahlibamah conceived and bare unto Esau three sons, Yeush, Yaalan, and Korah.

26 And in those days, in the land of Canaan, there was a quarrel between the herdsmen of Esau and the herdsmen of the inhabitants of the land of Canaan, for Esau's cattle and goods were too abundant for him to remain in the land of Canaan, in his father's house, and the land of Canaan could not bear him on account of his cattle.

27 And when Esau saw that his quarreling increased with the inhabitants of the land of Canaan, he rose up and took his wives and his sons and his daughters, and all belonging to him, and the cattle which he possessed, and all his property that he had acquired in the land of Canaan, and he went away from the inhabitants of the land to the land of Seir, and Esau and all belonging to him dwelt in the land of Seir.

28 But from time to time Esau would go and see his father and mother in the land of Canaan, and Esau intermarried with the Horites, and he gave his daughters to the sons of Seir, the Horite.

29 And he gave his elder daughter Marzith to Anah, the son of Zebeon, his wife's brother, and Puith he gave to Azar, the son of Bilhan the Horite; and Esau dwelt in the mountain, he and his children, and they were fruitful and multiplied.

Chapter 31

1 And in the seventh year, Jacob's service which he served Laban was completed, and Jacob said unto Laban, Give me my wife, for the days of my service are fulfilled; and Laban did so, and Laban and Jacob assembled all the people of that place and they made a feast.

2 And in the evening Laban came to the house, and afterward Jacob came there with the people of the feast, and Laban extinguished all the lights that were there in the house.

3 And Jacob said unto Laban, Wherefore dost thou do this thing unto us? and Laban answered, Such is our custom to act in this land.

4 And afterward Laban took his daughter Leah, and he brought her to Jacob, and he came to her and Jacob did not know that she was Leah.

5 And Laban gave his daughter Leah his maid Zilpah for a handmaid.

6 And all the people at the feast knew what Laban had done to Jacob, but they did not tell the thing to Jacob.

7 And all the neighbors came that night to Jacob's house, and they ate and drank and rejoiced, and played before Leah upon timbrels, and with dances, and they responded before Jacob, Heleah, Heleah.

8 And Jacob heard their words but did not understand their meaning, but he thought such might be their custom in this land.

9 And the neighbors spoke these words before Jacob during the night, and all the lights that were in the house Laban had that night extinguished.

10 And in the morning, when daylight appeared, Jacob turned to his wife and he saw, and behold it was Leah that had been lying in his bosom, and Jacob said, Behold now I know what the neighbors said last night, Heleah, they said, and I knew it not.

11 And Jacob called unto Laban, and said unto him, What is this that thou didst unto me? Surely I served thee for Rachel, and why didst thou deceive me and didst give me Leah?

12 And Laban answered Jacob, saying, Not so is it done in our place to give the younger before the elder now therefore if thou desirest to take her sister likewise, take her unto thee for the service which thou wilt serve me for another seven years.

13 And Jacob did so, and he also took Rachel for a wife, and he served Laban seven years more, and Jacob also came to Rachel, and he loved Rachel more than Leah, and Laban gave her his maid Bilhah for a handmaid.

14 And when the Lord saw that Leah was hated, the Lord opened her womb, and she conceived and bare Jacob four sons in those days.

15 And these are their names, Reuben Simeon, Levi, and Judah, and she afterward left bearing.

16 And at that time Rachel was barren, and she had no offspring, and Rachel envied her sister Leah, and when Rachel saw that she bare no children to Jacob, she took her handmaid Bilhah, and she bare Jacob two sons, Dan and Naphtali.

17 And when Leah saw that she had left bearing, she also took her handmaid Zilpah, and she gave her to Jacob for a wife, and Jacob also came to Zilpah, and she also bare Jacob two sons, Gad and Asher.

18 And Leah again conceived and bare Jacob in those days

two sons and one daughter, and these are their names, Issachar, Zebulon, and their sister Dinah.

19 And Rachel was still barren in those days, and Rachel prayed unto the Lord at that time, and she said, O Lord God remember me and visit me, I beseech thee, for now my husband will cast me off, for I have borne him no children.

20 Now O Lord God, hear my supplication before thee, and see my affliction, and give me children like one of the handmaids, that I may no more bear my reproach.

21 And God heard her and opened her womb, and Rachel conceived and bare a son, and she said, The Lord has taken away my reproach, and she called his name Joseph, saying, May the Lord add to me another son; and Jacob was ninety-one years old when she bare him.

22 At that time Jacob's mother, Rebecca, sent her nurse Deborah the daughter of Uz, and two of Isaac's servants unto Jacob.

23 And they came to Jacob to Haran and they said unto him, Rebecca has sent us to thee that thou shalt return to thy father's house to the land of Canaan; and Jacob hearkened unto them in this which his mother had spoken.

24 At that time, the other seven years which Jacob served Laban for Rachel were completed, and it was at the end of fourteen years that he had dwelt in Haran that Jacob said unto Laban, give me my wives and send me away, that I may go to my land, for behold my mother did send unto me from the land at Canaan that I should return to my father's house.

25 And Laban said unto him, Not so I pray thee; if I have found favor in thy sight do not leave me; appoint me thy wages and I will give them, and remain with me.

26 And Jacob said unto him, This is what thou shalt give me for wages, that I shall this day pass through all thy flock and take away from them every lamb that is speckled and spotted and such as are brown amongst the sheep, and amongst the goats, and if thou wilt do this thing for me I will return and feed thy flock and keep them as at first.

27 And Laban did so, and Laban removed from his flock all that Jacob had said and gave them to him.

28 And Jacob placed all that he had removed from Laban's flock in the hands of his sons, and Jacob was feeding the remainder of Laban's flock.

29 And when the servants of Isaac which he had sent unto Jacob saw that Jacob would not then return with them to the land of Canaan to his father, they then went away from him, and they returned home to the land of Canaan.

30 And Deborah remained with Jacob in Haran, and she did not return with the servants of Isaac to the land of Canaan, and Deborah resided with Jacob's wives and children in Haran.

31 And Jacob served Laban six years longer, and when the sheep brought forth, Jacob removed from them such as were speckled and spotted, as he had determined with Laban, and Jacob did so at Laban's for six years, and the man increased abundantly and he had cattle and maid servants and men servants, camels, and asses.

32 And Jacob had two hundred drove of cattle, and his cattle were of large size and of beautiful appearance and were very productive, and all the families of the sons of men desired to get some of the cattle of Jacob, for they were exceedingly prosperous.

33 And many of the sons of men came to procure some of Jacob's flock, and Jacob gave them a sheep for a man servant or a maid servant or for an ass or a camel, or whatever Jacob desired from them they gave him.

34 And Jacob obtained riches and honor and possessions by means of these transactions with the sons of men, and the children of Laban envied him of this honor.

35 And in the course of time he heard the words of Laban's sons, saying, Jacob has taken away all that was our father's, and of that which was our father's has he acquired all this glory.

36 And Jacob beheld the countenance of Laban and of his children, and behold it was not toward him in those days as it had been before.

37 And the Lord appeared to Jacob at the expiration of the six years, and said unto him, Arise, go forth out of this land, and return to the land of thy birthplace and I will be with thee.

38 And Jacob rose up at that time and he mounted his children and wives and all belonging to him upon camels, and he went forth to go to the land of Canaan to his father Isaac.

39 And Laban did not know that Jacob had gone from him, for Laban had been that day sheep-shearing.

40 And Rachel stole her father's images, and she took them and she concealed them upon the camel upon which she sat, and she went on.

41 And this is the manner of the images; in taking a man who is the first born and slaying him and taking the hair off his head, and taking salt and salting the head and anointing it in oil, then taking a small tablet of copper or a tablet of gold and writing the name upon it, and placing the tablet under his tongue, and taking the head with the tablet under the tongue and putting it in the house, and lighting up lights before it and bowing down to it.

42 And at the time when they bow down to it, it speaketh to them in all matters that they ask of it, through the power of the name which is written in it.

43 And some make them in the figures of men, of gold and silver, and go to them in times known to them, and the figures receive the influence of the stars, and tell them future things, and in this manner were the images which Rachel stole from her father.

44 And Rachel stole these images which were her father's, in order that Laban might not know through them where Jacob had gone.

45 And Laban came home and he asked concerning Jacob and his household, and he was not to be found, and Laban sought his images to know where Jacob had gone, and could not find them, and he went to some other images, and he inquired of them and they told him that Jacob had fled from him to his father's, to the land of Canaan.

46 And Laban then rose up and he took his brothers and all his servants, and he went forth and pursued Jacob, and he overtook him in mount Gilead.

47 And Laban said unto Jacob, What is this thou hast done to me to flee and deceive me, and lead my daughters and their children as captives taken by the sword?

48 And thou didst not suffer me to kiss them and send them away with joy, and thou didst steal my gods and didst go away.

49 And Jacob answered Laban, saying, Because I was afraid lest thou wouldst take thy daughters by force from me; and now with whomsoever thou findest thy gods he shall die.

50 And Laban searched for the images and he examined in all Jacob's tents and furniture, but could not find them.

51 And Laban said unto Jacob, We will make a covenant together and it shall be a testimony between me and thee; if thou shalt afflict my daughters, or shalt take other wives besides my daughters, even God shall be a witness between

me and thee in this matter.

52 And they took stones and made a heap, and Laban said, This heap is a witness between me and thee, therefore he called the name thereof Gilead.

53 And Jacob and Laban offered sacrifice upon the mount, and they ate there by the heap, and they tarried in the mount all night, and Laban rose up early in the morning, and he wept with his daughters and he kissed them, and he returned unto his place.

54 And he hastened and sent off his son Beor, who was seventeen years old, with Abichorof the son of Uz, the son of Nahor, and with them were ten men.

55 And they hastened and went and passed on the road before Jacob, and they came by another road to the land of Seir.

56 And they came unto Esau and said unto him, Thus saith thy brother and relative, thy mother's brother Laban, the son of Bethuel, saying,

57 Hast thou heard what Jacob thy brother has done unto me, who first came to me naked and bare, and I went to meet him, and brought him to my house with honor, and I made him great, and I gave him my two daughters for wives and also two of my maids.

58 And God blessed him on my account, and he increased abundantly, and had sons, daughters and maid servants.

59 He has also an immense stock of flocks and herds, camels and asses, also silver and gold in abundance; and when he saw that his wealth increased, he left me whilst I went to shear my sheep, and he rose up and fled in secrecy.

60 And he lifted his wives and children upon camels, and he led away all his cattle and property which he acquired in my land, and he lifted up his countenance to go to his father Isaac, to the land of Canaan.

61 And he did not suffer me to kiss my daughters and their children, and he led my daughters as captives taken by the sword, and he also stole my gods and he fled.

62 And now I have left him in the mountain of the brook of Jabuk, him and all belonging to him; he lacketh nothing.

63 If it be thy wish to go to him, go then and there wilt thou find him, and thou canst do unto him as thy soul desireth; and Laban's messengers came and told Esau all these things.

64 And Esau heard all the words of Laban's messengers, and his anger was greatly kindled against Jacob, and he remembered his hatred, and his anger burned within him.

65 And Esau hastened and took his children and servants and the souls of his household, being sixty men, and he went and assembled all the children of Seir the Horite and their people, being three hundred and forty men, and took all this number of four hundred men with drawn swords, and he went unto Jacob to smite him.

66 And Esau divided this number into several parts, and he took the sixty men of his children and servants and the souls of his household as one head, and gave them in care of Eliphaz his eldest son.

67 And the remaining heads he gave to the care of the six sons of Seir the Horite, and he placed every man over his generations and children.

68 And the whole of this camp went as it was, and Esau went amongst them toward Jacob, and he conducted them with speed.

69 And Laban's messengers departed from Esau and went to the land of Canaan, and they came to the house of Rebecca the mother of Jacob and Esau.

70 And they told her saying, Behold thy son Esau has gone against his brother Jacob with four hundred men, for he

heard that he was coming, and he is gone to make war with him, and to smite him and to take all that he has.

71 And Rebecca hastened and sent seventy two men from the servants of Isaac to meet Jacob on the road; for she said, Peradventure, Esau may make war in the road when he meets him.

72 And these messengers went on the road to meet Jacob, and they met him in the road of the brook on the opposite side of the brook Jabuk, and Jacob said when he saw them, This camp is destined to me from God, and Jacob called the name of that place Machnayim.

73 And Jacob knew all his father's people, and he kissed them and embraced them and came with them, and Jacob asked them concerning his father and mother, and they said, They were well.

74 And these messengers said unto Jacob, Rebecca thy mother has sent us to thee, saying, I have heard, my son, that thy brother Esau has gone forth against thee on the road with men from the children of Seir the Horite.

75 And therefore, my son, hearken to my voice and see with thy counsel what thou wilt do, and when he cometh up to thee, supplicate him, and do not speak rashly to him, and give him a present from what thou possessest, and from what God has favored thee with.

76 And when he asketh thee concerning thy affairs, conceal nothing from him, perhaps he may turn from his anger against thee and thou wilt thereby save thy soul, thou and all belonging to thee, for it is thy duty to honor him, for he is thy elder brother.

77 And when Jacob heard the words of his mother which the messengers had spoken to him, Jacob lifted up his voice and wept bitterly, and did as his mother then commanded him.

Chapter 32

1 And at that time Jacob sent messengers to his brother Esau toward the land of Seir, and he spoke to him words of supplication.

2 And he commanded them, saying, Thus shall ye say to my lord, to Esau, Thus saith thy servant Jacob, Let not my lord imagine that my father's blessing with which he did bless me has proved beneficial to me.

3 For I have been these twenty years with Laban, and he deceived me and changed my wages ten times, as it has all been already told unto my lord.

4 And I served him in his house very laboriously, and God afterward saw my affliction, my labor and the work of my hands, and he caused me to find grace and favor in his sight.

5 And I afterward through God's great mercy and kindness acquired oxen and asses and cattle, and men servants and maid servants.

6 And now I am coming to my land and my home to my father and mother, who are in the land of Canaan; and I have sent to let my lord know all this in order to find favor in the sight of my lord, so that he may not imagine that I have of myself obtained wealth, or that the blessing with which my father blessed me has benefited me.

7 And those messengers went to Esau, and found him on the borders of the land of Edom going toward Jacob, and four hundred men of the children of Seir the Horite were standing with drawn swords.

8 And the messengers of Jacob told Esau all the words that Jacob had spoken to them concerning Esau.

9 And Esau answered them with pride and contempt, and said unto them, Surely I have heard and truly it has been

told unto me what Jacob has done to Laban, who exalted him in his house and gave him his daughters for wives, and he begat sons and daughters, and abundantly increased in wealth and riches in Laban's house through his means.

10 And when he saw that his wealth was abundant and his riches great he fled with all belonging to him, from Laban's house, and he led Laban's daughters away from the face of their father, as captives taken by the sword without telling him of it.

11 And not only to Laban has Jacob done thus but also unto me has he done so and has twice supplanted me, and shall I be silent?

12 Now therefore I have this day come with my camps to meet him, and I will do unto him according to the desire of my heart.

13 And the messengers returned and came to Jacob and said unto him, We came to thy brother, to Esau, and we told him all thy words, and thus has he answered us, and behold he cometh to meet thee with four hundred men.

14 Now then know and see what thou shalt do, and pray before God to deliver thee from him.

15 And when he heard the words of his brother which he had spoken to the messengers of Jacob, Jacob was greatly afraid and he was distressed.

16 And Jacob prayed to the Lord his God, and he said, O Lord God of my fathers, Abraham and Isaac, thou didst say unto me when I went away from my father's house, saying,

17 I am the Lord God of thy father Abraham and the God of Isaac, unto thee do I give this land and thy seed after thee, and I will make thy seed as the stars of heaven, and thou shalt spread forth to the four sides of heaven, and in thee and in thy seed shall all the families of the earth be blessed.

18 And thou didst establish thy words, and didst give unto me riches and children and cattle, as the utmost wishes of my heart didst thou give unto thy servant; thou didst give unto me all that I asked from thee, so that I lacked nothing.

19 And thou didst afterward say unto me, Return to thy parents and to thy birth place and I will still do well with thee.

20 And now that I have come, and thou didst deliver me from Laban, I shall fall in the hands of Esau who will slay me, yea, together with the mothers of my children.

21 Now therefore, O Lord God, deliver me, I pray thee, also from the hands of my brother Esau, for I am greatly afraid of him.

22 And if there is no righteousness in me, do it for the sake of Abraham and my father Isaac.

23 For I know that through kindness and mercy have I acquired this wealth; now therefore I beseech thee to deliver me this day with thy kindness and to answer me.

24 And Jacob ceased praying to the Lord, and he divided the people that were with him with the flocks and cattle into two camps, and he gave the half to the care of Damesek, the son of Eliezer, Abraham's servant, for a camp, with his children, and the other half he gave to the care of his brother Elianus the son of Eliezer, to be for a camp with his children.

25 And he commanded them, saying, Keep yourselves at a distance with your camps, and do not come too near each other, and if Esau come to one camp and slay it, the other camp at a distance from it will escape him.

26 And Jacob tarried there that night, and during the whole night he gave his servants instructions concerning the forces and his children.

27 And the Lord heard the prayer of Jacob on that day, and

the Lord then delivered Jacob from the hands of his brother Esau.

28 And the Lord sent three angels of the angels of heaven, and they went before Esau and came to him.

29 And these angels appeared unto Esau and his people as two thousand men, riding upon horses furnished with all sorts of war instruments, and they appeared in the sight of Esau and all his men to be divided into four camps, with four chiefs to them.

30 And one camp went on and they found Esau coming with four hundred men toward his brother Jacob, and this camp ran toward Esau and his people and terrified them, and Esau fell off the horse in alarm, and all his men separated from him in that place, for they were greatly afraid.

31 And the whole of the camp shouted after them when they fled from Esau, and all the warlike men answered, saying,

32 Surely we are the servants of Jacob, who is the servant of God, and who then can stand against us? And Esau said unto them, O then, my lord and brother Jacob is your lord, whom I have not seen for these twenty years, and now that I have this day come to see him, do you treat me in this manner?

33 And the angels answered him saying, As the Lord liveth, were not Jacob of whom thou speaketh thy brother, we had not let one remaining from thee and thy people, but only on account of Jacob we will do nothing to them.

34 And this camp passed from Esau and his men and it went away, and Esau and his men had gone from them about a league when the second camp came toward him with all sorts of weapons, and they also did unto Esau and his men as the first camp had done to them.

35 And when they had left it to go on, behold the third camp came toward him and they were all terrified, and Esau fell off the horse, and the whole camp cried out, and said, Surely we are the servants of Jacob, who is the servant of God, and who can stand against us?

36 And Esau again answered them saying, O then, Jacob my lord and your lord is my brother, and for twenty years I have not seen his countenance and hearing this day that he was coming, I went this day to meet him, and do you treat me in this manner?

37 And they answered him, and said unto him, As the Lord liveth, were not Jacob thy brother as thou didst say, we had not left a remnant from thee and thy men, but on account of Jacob of whom thou speakest being thy brother, we will not meddle with thee or thy men.

38 And the third camp also passed from them, and he still continued his road with his men toward Jacob, when the fourth camp came toward him, and they also did unto him and his men as the others had done.

39 And when Esau beheld the evil which the four angels had done to him and to his men, he became greatly afraid of his brother Jacob, and he went to meet him in peace.

40 And Esau concealed his hatred against Jacob, because he was afraid of his life on account of his brother Jacob, and because he imagined that the four camps that he had lighted upon were Jacob's servants.

41 And Jacob tarried that night with his servants in their camps, and he resolved with his servants to give unto Esau a present from all that he had with him, and from all his property; and Jacob rose up in the morning, he and his men, and they chose from amongst the cattle a present for Esau.

42 And this is the amount of the present which Jacob chose

from his flock to give unto his brother Esau: and he selected two hundred and forty head from the flocks, and he selected from the camels and asses thirty each, and of the herds he chose fifty kine.

43 And he put them all in ten droves, and he placed each sort by itself, and he delivered them into the hands of ten of his servants, each drove by itself.

44 And he commanded them, and said unto them, Keep yourselves at a distance from each other, and put a space between the droves, and when Esau and those who are with him shall meet you and ask you, saying, Whose are you, and whither do you go, and to whom belongeth all this before you, you shall say unto them, We are the servants of Jacob, and we come to meet Esau in peace, and behold Jacob cometh behind us.

45 And that which is before us is a present sent from Jacob to his brother Esau.

46 And if they shall say unto you, Why doth he delay behind you, from coming to meet his brother and to see his face, then you shall say unto them, Surely he cometh joyfully behind us to meet his brother, for he said, I will appease him with the present that goeth to him, and after this I will see his face, peradventure he will accept of me.

47 So the whole present passed on in the hands of his servants, and went before him on that day, and he lodged that night with his camps by the border of the brook of Jabuk, and he rose up in the midst of the night, and he took his wives and his maid servants, and all belonging to him, and he that night passed them over the ford Jabuk.

48 And when he passed all belonging to him over the brook, Jacob was left by himself, and a man met him, and he wrestled with him that night until the breaking of the day, and the hollow of Jacob's thigh was out of joint through wrestling with him.

49 And at the break of day the man left Jacob there, and he blessed him and went away, and Jacob passed the brook at the break of day, and he halted upon his thigh.

50 And the sun rose upon him when he had passed the brook, and he came up to the place of his cattle and children.

51 And they went on till midday, and whilst they were going the present was passing on before them.

52 And Jacob lifted up his eyes and looked, and behold Esau was at a distance, coming along with many men, about four hundred, and Jacob was greatly afraid of his brother.

53 And Jacob hastened and divided his children unto his wives and his handmaids, and his daughter Dinah he put in a chest, and delivered her into the hands of his servants.

54 And he passed before his children and wives to meet his brother, and he bowed down to the ground, yea he bowed down seven times until he approached his brother, and God caused Jacob to find grace and favor in the sight of Esau and his men, for God had heard the prayer of Jacob.

55 And the fear of Jacob and his terror fell upon his brother Esau, for Esau was greatly afraid of Jacob for what the angels of God had done to Esau, and Esau's anger against Jacob was turned into kindness.

56 And when Esau saw Jacob running toward him, he also ran toward him and he embraced him, and he fell upon his neck, and they kissed and they wept.

57 And God put fear and kindness toward Jacob in the hearts of the men that came with Esau, and they also kissed Jacob and embraced him.

58 And also Eliphaz, the son of Esau, with his four brothers, sons of Esau, wept with Jacob, and they kissed him and embraced him, for the fear of Jacob had fallen upon them all.

59 And Esau lifted up his eyes and saw the women with their offspring, the children of Jacob, walking behind Jacob and bowing along the road to Esau.

60 And Esau said unto Jacob, Who are these with thee, my brother? are they thy children or thy servants? and Jacob answered Esau and said, They are my children which God hath graciously given to thy servant.

61 And whilst Jacob was speaking to Esau and his men, Esau beheld the whole camp, and he said unto Jacob, Whence didst thou get the whole of the camp that I met yesternight? and Jacob said, To find favor in the sight of my lord, it is that which God graciously gave to thy servant.

62 And the present came before Esau, and Jacob pressed Esau, saying, Take I pray thee the present that I have brought to my lord, and Esau said, Wherefore is this my purpose? keep that which thou hast unto thyself.

63 And Jacob said, It is incumbent upon me to give all this, since I have seen thy face, that thou still livest in peace.

64 And Esau refused to take the present, and Jacob said unto him, I beseech thee my lord, if now I have found favor in thy sight, then receive my present at my hand, for I have therefore seen thy face, as though I had seen a god-like face, because thou wast pleased with me.

65 And Esau took the present, and Jacob also gave unto Esau silver and gold and bdellium, for he pressed him so much that he took them.

66 And Esau divided the cattle that were in the camp, and he gave the half to the men who had come with him, for they had come on hire, and the other half he delivered unto the hands of his children.

67 And the silver and gold and bdellium he gave in the hands of Eliphaz his eldest son, and Esau said unto Jacob, Let us remain with thee, and we will go slowly along with thee until thou comest to my place with me, that we may dwell there together.

68 And Jacob answered his brother and said, I would do as my lord speaketh unto me, but my lord knoweth that the children are tender, and the flocks and herds with their young who are with me, go but slowly, for if they went swiftly they would all die, for thou knowest their burdens and their fatigue.

69 Therefore let my lord pass on before his servant, and I will go on slowly for the sake of the children and the flock, until I come to my lord's place to Seir.

70 And Esau said unto Jacob, I will place with thee some of the people that are with me to take care of thee in the road, and to bear thy fatigue and burden, and he said, What needeth it my lord, if I may find grace in thy sight?

71 Behold I will come unto thee to Seir to dwell there together as thou hast spoken, go thou then with thy people for I will follow thee.

72 And Jacob said this to Esau in order to remove Esau and his men from him, so that Jacob might afterward go to his father's house to the land of Canaan.

73 And Esau hearkened to the voice of Jacob, and Esau returned with the four hundred men that were with him on their road to Seir, and Jacob and all belonging to him went that day as far as the extremity of the land of Canaan in its borders, and he remained there some time.

Chapter 33

1 And in some time after Jacob went away from the borders of the land, and he came to the land of Shalem, that is the city of Shechem, which is in the land of Canaan,

and he rested in front of the city.

2 And he bought a parcel of the field which was there, from the children of Hamor the people of the land, for five shekels.

3 And Jacob there built himself a house, and he pitched his tent there, and he made booths for his cattle, therefore he called the name of that place Succoth.

4 And Jacob remained in Succoth a year and six months.

5 At that time some of the women of the inhabitants of the land went to the city of Shechem to dance and rejoice with the daughters of the people of the city, and when they went forth then Rachel and Leah the wives of Jacob with their families also went to behold the rejoicing of the daughters of the city.

6 And Dinah the daughter of Jacob also went along with them and saw the daughters of the city, and they remained there before these daughters whilst all the people of the city were standing by them to behold their rejoicings, and all the great people of the city were there.

7 And Shechem the son of Hamor, the prince of the land was also standing there to see them.

8 And Shechem beheld Dinah the daughter of Jacob sitting with her mother before the daughters of the city, and the damsel pleased him greatly, and he there asked his friends and his people, saying, Whose daughter is that sitting amongst the women, whom I do not know in this city?

9 And they said unto him, Surely this is the daughter of Jacob the son of Isaac the Hebrew, who has dwelt in this city for some time, and when it was reported that the daughters of the land were going forth to rejoice she went with her mother and maid servants to sit amongst them as thou seest.

10 And Shechem beheld Dinah the daughter of Jacob, and when he looked at her his soul became fixed upon Dinah.

11 And he sent and had her taken by force, and Dinah came to the house of Shechem and he seized her forcibly and lay with her and humbled her, and he loved her exceedingly and placed her in his house.

12 And they came and told the thing unto Jacob, and when Jacob heard that Shechem had defiled his daughter Dinah, Jacob sent twelve of his servants to fetch Dinah from the house of Shechem, and they went and came to the house of Shechem to take away Dinah from there.

13 And when they came Shechem went out to them with his men and drove them from his house, and he would not suffer them to come before Dinah, but Shechem was sitting with Dinah kissing and embracing her before their eyes.

14 And the servants of Jacob came back and told him, saying, When we came, he and his men drove us away, and thus did Shechem do unto Dinah before our eyes.

15 And Jacob knew moreover that Shechem had defiled his daughter, but he said nothing, and his sons were feeding his cattle in the field, and Jacob remained silent till their return.

16 And before his sons came home Jacob sent two maidens from his servants' daughters to take care of Dinah in the house of Shechem, and to remain with her, and Shechem sent three of his friends to his father Hamor the son of Chiddekem, the son of Pered, saying, Get me this damsel for a wife.

17 And Hamor the son of Chiddekem the Hivite came to the house of Shechem his son, and he sat before him, and Hamor said unto his son, Shechem, Is there then no woman amongst the daughters of thy people that thou wilt take an Hebrew woman who is not of thy people?

18 And Shechem said to him, Her only must thou get for me, for she is delightful in my sight; and Hamor did

according to the word of his son, for he was greatly beloved by him.

19 And Hamor went forth to Jacob to commune with him concerning this matter, and when he had gone from the house of his son Shechem, before he came to Jacob to speak unto him, behold the sons of Jacob had come from the field, as soon as they heard the thing that Shechem the son of Hamor had done.

20 And the men were very much grieved concerning their sister, and they all came home fired with anger, before the time of gathering in their cattle.

21 And they came and sat before their father and they spoke unto him kindled with wrath, saying, Surely death is due to this man and to his household, because the Lord God of the whole earth commanded Noah and his children that man shall never rob, nor commit adultery; now behold Shechem has both ravaged and committed fornication with our sister, and not one of all the people of the city spoke a word to him.

22 Surely thou knowest and understandest that the judgment of death is due to Shechem, and to his father, and to the whole city on account of the thing which he has done.

23 And whilst they were speaking before their father in this matter, behold Hamor the father of Shechem came to speak to Jacob the words of his son concerning Dinah, and he sat before Jacob and before his sons.

24 And Hamor spoke unto them, saying, The soul of my son Shechem longeth for your daughter; I pray you give her unto him for a wife and intermarry with us; give us your daughters and we will give you our daughters, and you shall dwell with us in our land and we will be as one people in the land.

25 For our land is very extensive, so dwell ye and trade therein and get possessions in it, and do therein as you desire, and no one shall prevent you by saying a word to you.

26 And Hamor ceased speaking unto Jacob and his sons, and behold Shechem his son had come after him, and he sat before them.

27 And Shechem spoke before Jacob and his sons, saying, May I find favor in your sight that you will give me your daughter, and whatever you say unto me that will I do for her.

28 Ask me for abundance of dowry and gift, and I will give it, and whatever you shall say unto me that will I do, and whoever he be that will rebel against your orders, he shall die; only give me the damsel for a wife.

29 And Simeon and Levi answered Hamor and Shechem his son deceitfully, saying, All you have spoken unto us we will do for you.

30 And behold our sister is in your house, but keep away from her until we send to our father Isaac concerning this matter, for we can do nothing without his consent.

31 For he knoweth the ways of our father Abraham, and whatever he sayeth unto us we will tell you, we will conceal nothing from you.

32 And Simeon and Levi spoke this unto Shechem and his father in order to find a pretext, and to seek counsel what was to be done to Shechem and to his city in this matter.

33 And when Shechem and his father heard the words of Simeon and Levi, it seemed good in their sight, and Shechem and his father came forth to go home.

34 And when they had gone, the sons of Jacob said unto their father, saying, Behold, we know that death is due to these wicked ones and to their city, because they

transgressed that which God had commanded unto Noah and his children and his seed after them.

35 And also because Shechem did this thing to our sister Dinah in defiling her, for such vileness shall never be done amongst us.

36 Now therefore know and see what you will do, and seek counsel and pretext what is to be done to them, in order to kill all the inhabitants of this city.

37 And Simeon said to them, Here is a proper advice for you: tell them to circumcise every male amongst them as we are circumcised, and if they do not wish to do this, we shall take our daughter from them and go away.

38 And if they consent to do this and will do it, then when they are sunk down with pain, we will attack them with our swords, as upon one who is quiet and peaceable, and we will slay every male person amongst them.

39 And Simeon's advice pleased them, and Simeon and Levi resolved to do unto them as it was proposed.

40 And on the next morning Shechem and Hamor his father came again unto Jacob and his sons, to speak concerning Dinah, and to hear what answer the sons of Jacob would give to their words.

41 And the sons of Jacob spoke deceitfully to them, saying, We told our father Isaac all your words, and your words pleased him.

42 But he spoke unto us, saying, Thus did Abraham his father command him from God the Lord of the whole earth, that any man who is not of his descendants that should wish to take one of his daughters, shall cause every male belonging to him to be circumcised, as we are circumcised, and then we may give him our daughter for a wife.

43 Now we have made known to you all our ways that our father spoke unto us, for we cannot do this of which you spoke unto us, to give our daughter to an uncircumcised man, for it is a disgrace to us.

44 But herein will we consent to you, to give you our daughter, and we will also take unto ourselves your daughters, and will dwell amongst you and be one people as you have spoken, if you will hearken to us, and consent to be like us, to circumcise every male belonging to you, as we are circumcised.

45 And if you will not hearken unto us, to have every male circumcised as we are circumcised, as we have commanded, then we will come to you, and take our daughter from you and go away.

46 And Shechem and his father Hamor heard the words of the sons of Jacob, and the thing pleased them exceedingly, and Shechem and his father Hamor hastened to do the wishes of the sons of Jacob, for Shechem was very fond of Dinah, and his soul was riveted to her.

47 And Shechem and his father Hamor hastened to the gate of the city, and they assembled all the men of their city and spoke unto them the words of the sons of Jacob, saying,

48 We came to these men, the sons of Jacob, and we spoke unto them concerning their daughter, and these men will consent to do according to our wishes, and behold our land is of great extent for them, and they will dwell in it, and trade in it, and we shall be one people; we will take their daughters, and our daughters we will give unto them for wives.

49 But only on this condition will these men consent to do this thing, that every male amongst us be circumcised as they are circumcised, as their God commanded them, and when we shall have done according to their instructions to

be circumcised, then will they dwell amongst us, together with their cattle and possessions, and we shall be as one people with them.

50 And when all the men of the city heard the words of Shechem and his father Hamor, then all the men of their city were agreeable to this proposal, and they obeyed to be circumcised, for Shechem and his father Hamor were greatly esteemed by them, being the princes of the land.

51 And on the next day, Shechem and Hamor his father rose up early in the morning, and they assembled all the men of their city into the middle of the city, and they called for the sons of Jacob, who circumcised every male belonging to them on that day and the next.

52 And they circumcised Shechem and Hamor his father, and the five brothers of Shechem, and then every one rose up and went home, for this thing was from the Lord against the city of Shechem, and from the Lord was Simeon's counsel in this matter, in order that the Lord might deliver the city of Shechem into the hands of Jacob's two sons.

Chapter 34

1 And the number of all the males that were circumcised, were six hundred and forty-five men, and two hundred and forty-six children.

2 But Chiddekem, son of Pered, the father of Hamor, and his six brothers, would not listen unto Shechem and his father Hamor, and they would not be circumcised, for the proposal of the sons of Jacob was loathsome in their sight, and their anger was greatly roused at this, that the people of the city had not hearkened to them.

3 And in the evening of the second day, they found eight small children who had not been circumcised, for their mothers had concealed them from Shechem and his father Hamor, and from the men of the city.

4 And Shechem and his father Hamor sent to have them brought before them to be circumcised, when Chiddekem and his six brothers sprang at them with their swords, and sought to slay them.

5 And they sought to slay also Shechem and his father Hamor and they sought to slay Dinah with them on account of this matter.

6 And they said unto them, What is this thing that you have done? are there no women amongst the daughters of your brethren the Canaanites, that you wish to take unto yourselves daughters of the Hebrews, whom ye knew not before, and will do this act which your fathers never commanded you?

7 Do you imagine that you will succeed through this act which you have done? and what will you answer in this affair to your brethren the Canaanites, who will come tomorrow and ask you concerning this thing?

8 And if your act shall not appear just and good in their sight, what will you do for your lives, and me for our lives, in your not having hearkened to our voices?

9 And if the inhabitants of the land and all your brethren the children of Ham, shall hear of your act, saying,

10 On account of a Hebrew woman did Shechem and Hamor his father, and all the inhabitants of their city, do that with which they had been unacquainted and which their ancestors never commanded them, where then will you fly or where conceal your shame, all your days before your brethren, the inhabitants of the land of Canaan?

11 Now therefore we cannot bear up against this thing which you have done, neither can we be burdened with this yoke upon us, which our ancestors did not command us.

12 Behold tomorrow we will go and assemble all our brethren, the Canaanitish brethren who dwell in the land, and we will all come and smite you and all those who trust in you, that there shall not be a remnant left from you or them.

13 And when Hamor and his son Shechem and all the people of the city heard the words of Chiddekem and his brothers, they were terribly afraid of their lives at their words, and they repented of what they had done.

14 And Shechem and his father Hamor answered their father Chiddekem and his brethren, and they said unto them, All the words which you spoke unto us are true.

15 Now do not say, nor imagine in your hearts that on account of the love of the Hebrews we did this thing that our ancestors did not command us.

16 But because we saw that it was not their intention and desire to accede to our wishes concerning their daughter as to our taking her, except on this condition, so we hearkened to their voices and did this act which you saw, in order to obtain our desire from them.

17 And when we shall have obtained our request from them, we will then return to them and do unto them that which you say unto us.

18 We beseech you then to wait and tarry until our flesh shall be healed and we again become strong, and we will then go together against them, and do unto them that which is in your hearts and in ours.

19 And Dinah the daughter of Jacob heard all these words which Chiddekem and his brothers had spoken, and what Hamor and his son Shechem and the people of their city had answered them.

20 And she hastened and sent one of her maidens, that her father had sent to take care of her in the house of Shechem, to Jacob her father and to her brethren, saying:

21 Thus did Chiddekem and his brothers advise concerning you, and thus did Hamor and Shechem and the people of the city answer them.

22 And when Jacob heard these words he was filled with wrath, and he was indignant at them, and his anger was kindled against them.

23 And Simeon and Levi swore and said, As the Lord liveth, the God of the whole earth, by this time tomorrow, there shall not be a remnant left in the whole city.

24 And twenty young men had concealed themselves who were not circumcised, and these young men fought against Simeon and Levi, and Simeon and Levi killed eighteen of them, and two fled from them and escaped to some lime pits that were in the city, and Simeon and Levi sought for them, but could not find them.

25 And Simeon and Levi continued to go about in the city, and they killed all the people of the city at the edge of the sword, and they left none remaining.

26 And there was a great consternation in the midst of the city, and the cry of the people of the city ascended to heaven, and all the women and children cried aloud.

27 And Simeon and Levi slew all the city; they left not a male remaining in the whole city.

28 And they slew Hamor and Shechem his son at the edge of the sword, and they brought away Dinah from the house of Shechem and they went from there.

29 And the sons of Jacob went and returned, and came upon the slain, and spoiled all their property which was in the city and the field.

30 And whilst they were taking the spoil, three hundred men stood up and threw dust at them and struck them with stones, when Simeon turned to them and he slew them all

with the edge of the sword, and Simeon turned before Levi, and came into the city.

31 And they took away their sheep and their oxen and their cattle, and also the remainder of the women and little ones, and they led all these away, and they opened a gate and went out and came unto their father Jacob with vigor.

32 And when Jacob saw all that they had done to the city, and saw the spoil that they took from them, Jacob was very angry at them, and Jacob said unto them, What is this that you have done to me? behold I obtained rest amongst the Canaanitish inhabitants of the land, and none of them meddled with me.

33 And now you have done to make me obnoxious to the inhabitants of the land, amongst the Canaanites and the Perizzites, and I am but of a small number, and they will all assemble against me and slay me when they hear of your work with their brethren, and I and my household will be destroyed.

34 And Simeon and Levi and all their brothers with them answered their father Jacob and said unto him, Behold we live in the land, and shall Shechem do this to our sister? why art thou silent at all that Shechem has done? and shall he deal with our sister as with a harlot in the streets?

35 And the number of women whom Simeon and Levi took captives from the city of Shechem, whom they did not slay, was eighty-five who had not known man.

36 And amongst them was a young damsel of beautiful appearance and well favored, whose name was Bunah, and Simeon took her for a wife, and the number of the males which they took captives and did not slay, was forty-seven men, and the rest they slew.

37 And all the young men and women that Simeon and Levi had taken captives from the city of Shechem, were servants to the sons of Jacob and to their children after them, until the day of the sons of Jacob going forth from the land of Egypt.

38 And when Simeon and Levi had gone forth from the city, the two young men that were left, who had concealed themselves in the city, and did not die amongst the people of the city, rose up, and these young men went into the city and walked about in it, and found the city desolate without man, and only women weeping, and these young men cried out and said, Behold, this is the evil which the sons of Jacob the Hebrew did to this city in their having this day destroyed one of the Canaanitish cities, and were not afraid of their lives of all the land of Canaan.

39 And these men left the city and went to the city of Tapnach, and they came there and told the inhabitants of Tapnach all that had befallen them, and all that the sons of Jacob had done to the city of Shechem.

40 And the information reached Jashub king of Tapnach, and he sent men to the city of Shechem to see those young men, for the king did not believe them in this account, saying, How could two men lay waste such a large town as Shechem?

41 And the messengers of Jashub came back and told him, saying, We came unto the city, and it is destroyed, there is not a man there; only weeping women; neither is any flock or cattle there, for all that was in the city the sons of Jacob took away.

42 And Jashub wondered at this, saying, How could two men do this thing, to destroy so large a city, and not one man able to stand against them?

43 For the like has not been from the days of Nimrod, and not even from the remotest time, has the like taken place; and Jashub, king of Tapnach, said to his people, Be

courageous and we will go and fight against these Hebrews, and do unto them as they did unto the city, and we will avenge the cause of the people of the city.

44 And Jashub, king of Tapnach, consulted with his counsellors about this matter, and his advisers said unto him, Alone thou wilt not prevail over the Hebrews, for they must be powerful to do this work to the whole city.

45 If two of them laid waste the whole city, and no one stood against them, surely if thou wilt go against them, they will all rise against us and destroy us likewise.

46 But if thou wilt send to all the kings that surround us, and let them come together, then we will go with them and fight against the sons of Jacob; then wilt thou prevail against them.

47 And Jashub heard the words of his counsellors, and their words pleased him and his people, and he did so; and Jashub king of Tapnach sent to all the kings of the Amorites that surrounded Shechem and Tapnach, saying,

48 Go up with me and assist me, and we will smite Jacob the Hebrew and all his sons, and destroy them from the earth, for thus did he do to the city of Shechem, and do you not know of it?

49 And all the kings of the Amorites heard the evil that the sons of Jacob had done to the city of Shechem, and they were greatly astonished at them.

50 And the seven kings of the Amorites assembled with all their armies, about ten thousand men with drawn swords, and they came to fight against the sons of Jacob; and Jacob heard that the kings of the Amorites had assembled to fight against his sons, and Jacob was greatly afraid, and it distressed him.

51 And Jacob exclaimed against Simeon and Levi, saying, What is this act that you did? why have you injured me, to bring against me all the children of Canaan to destroy me and my household? for I was at rest, even I and my household, and you have done this thing to me, and provoked the inhabitants of the land against me by your proceedings.

52 And Judah answered his father, saying, Was it for naught my brothers Simeon and Levi killed all the inhabitants of Shechem? Surely it was because Shechem had humbled our sister, and transgressed the command of our God to Noah and his children, for Shechem took our sister away by force, and committed adultery with her.

53 And Shechem did all this evil and not one of the inhabitants of his city interfered with him, to say, Why wilt thou do this? surely for this my brothers went and smote the city, and the Lord delivered it into their hands, because its inhabitants had transgressed the commands of our God. Is it then for naught that they have done all this?

54 And now why art thou afraid or distressed, and why art thou displeased at my brothers, and why is thine anger kindled against them?

55 Surely our God who delivered into their hand the city of Shechem and its people, he will also deliver into our hands all the Canaanitish kings who are coming against us, and we will do unto them as my brothers did unto Shechem.

56 Now be tranquil about them and cast away thy fears, but trust in the Lord our God, and pray unto him to assist us and deliver us, and deliver our enemies into our hands.

57 And Judah called to one of his father's servants, Go now and see where those kings, who are coming against us, are situated with their armies.

58 And the servant went and looked far off, and went up opposite Mount Sihon, and saw all the camps of the kings standing in the fields, and he returned to Judah and said,

Behold the kings are situated in the field with all their camps, a people exceedingly numerous, like unto the sand upon the sea shore.

59 And Judah said unto Simeon and Levi, and unto all his brothers, Strengthen yourselves and be sons of valor, for the Lord our God is with us, do not fear them.

60 Stand forth each man, girt with his weapons of war, his bow and his sword, and we will go and fight against these uncircumcised men; the Lord is our God, He will save us.

61 And they rose up, and each girt on his weapons of war, great and small, eleven sons of Jacob, and all the servants of Jacob with them.

62 And all the servants of Isaac who were with Isaac in Hebron, all came to them equipped in all sorts of war instruments, and the sons of Jacob and their servants, being one hundred and twelve men, went towards these kings, and Jacob also went with them.

63 And the sons of Jacob sent unto their father Isaac the son of Abraham to Hebron, the same is Kireath-arba, saying,

64 Pray we beseech thee for us unto the Lord our God, to protect us from the hands of the Canaanites who are coming against us, and to deliver them into our hands.

65 And Isaac the son of Abraham prayed unto the Lord for his sons, and he said, O Lord God, thou didst promise my father, saying, I will multiply thy seed as the stars of heaven, and thou didst also promise me, and establish thou thy word, now that the kings of Canaan are coming together, to make war with my children because they committed no violence.

66 Now therefore, O Lord God, God of the whole earth, pervert, I pray thee, the counsel of these kings that they may not fight against my sons.

67 And impress the hearts of these kings and their people with the terror of my sons and bring down their pride, and that they may turn away from my sons.

68 And with thy strong hand and outstretched arm deliver my sons and their servants from them, for power and might are in thy hands to do all this.

69 And the sons of Jacob and their servants went toward these kings, and they trusted in the Lord their God, and whilst they were going, Jacob their father also prayed unto the Lord and said, O Lord God, powerful and exalted God, who has reigned from days of old, from thence till now and forever;

70 Thou art He who stirreth up wars and causeth them to cease, in thy hand are power and might to exalt and to bring down; O may my prayer be acceptable before thee that thou mayest turn to me with thy mercies, to impress the hearts of these kings and their people with the terror of my sons, and terrify them and their camps, and with thy great kindness deliver all those that trust in thee, for it is thou who canst bring people under us and reduce nations under our power.

Chapter 35

1 And all the kings of the Amorites came and took their stand in the field to consult with their counsellors what was to be done with the sons of Jacob, for they were still afraid of them, saying, Behold, two of them slew the whole of the city of Shechem.

2 And the Lord heard the prayers of Isaac and Jacob, and he filled the hearts of all these kings' advisers with great fear and terror that they unanimously exclaimed,

3 Are you silly this day, or is there no understanding in you, that you will fight with the Hebrews, and why will you take

a delight in your own destruction this day?

4 Behold two of them came to the city of Shechem without fear or terror, and they killed all the inhabitants of the city, that no man stood up against them, and how will you be able to fight with them all?

5 Surely you know that their God is exceedingly fond of them, and has done mighty things for them, such as have not been done from days of old, and amongst all the gods of nations, there is none can do like unto his mighty deeds.

6 Surely he delivered their father Abraham, the Hebrew, from the hand of Nimrod, and from the hand of all his people who had many times sought to slay him.

7 He delivered him also from the fire in which king Nimrod had cast him, and his God delivered him from it.

8 And who else can do the like? surely it was Abraham who slew the five kings of Elam, when they had touched his brother's son who in those days dwelt in Sodom.

9 And took his servant that was faithful in his house and a few of his men, and they pursued the kings of Elam in one night and killed them, and restored to his brother's son all his property which they had taken from him.

10 And surely you know the God of these Hebrews is much delighted with them, and they are also delighted with him, for they know that he delivered them from all their enemies.

11 And behold through his love toward his God, Abraham took his only and precious son and intended to bring him up as a burnt offering to his God, and had it not been for God who prevented him from doing this, he would then have done it through his love to his God.

12 And God saw all his works, and swore unto him, and promised him that he would deliver his sons and all his seed from every trouble that would befall them, because he had done this thing, and through his love to his God stifled his compassion for his child.

13 And have you not heard what their God did to Pharaoh king of Egypt, and to Abimelech king of Gerar, through taking Abraham's wife, who said of her, She is my sister, lest they might slay him on account of her, and think of taking her for a wife? and God did unto them and their people all that you heard of.

14 And behold, we ourselves saw with our eyes that Esau, the brother of Jacob, came to him with four hundred men, with the intention of slaying him, for he called to mind that he had taken away from him his father's blessing.

15 And he went to meet him when he came from Syria, to smite the mother with the children, and who delivered him from his hands but his God in whom he trusted? he delivered him from the hand of his brother and also from the hands of his enemies, and surely he again will protect them.

16 Who does not know that it was their God who inspired them with strength to do to the town of Shechem the evil which you heard of?

17 Could it then be with their own strength that two men could destroy such a large city as Shechem had it not been for their God in whom they trusted? he said and did unto them all this to slay the inhabitants of the city in their city.

18 And can you then prevail over them who have come forth together from your city to fight with the whole of them, even if a thousand times as many more should come to your assistance?

19 Surely you know and understand that you do not come to fight with them, but you come to war with their God who made choice of them, and you have therefore all come this day to be destroyed.

20 Now therefore refrain from this evil which you are endeavoring to bring upon yourselves, and it will be better for you not to go to battle with them, although they are but few in numbers, because their God is with them.

21 And when the kings of the Amorites heard all the words of their advisers, their hearts were filled with terror, and they were afraid of the sons of Jacob and would not fight against them.

22 And they inclined their ears to the words of their advisers, and they listened to all their words, and the words of the counsellors greatly pleased the kings, and they did so.

23 And the kings turned and refrained from the sons of Jacob, for they durst not approach them to make war with them, for they were greatly afraid of them, and their hearts melted within them from their fear of them.

24 For this proceeded from the Lord to them, for he heard the prayers of his servants Isaac and Jacob, for they trusted in him; and all these kings returned with their camps on that day, each to his own city, and they did not at that time fight with the sons of Jacob.

25 And the sons of Jacob kept their station that day till evening opposite mount Sihon, and seeing that these kings did not come to fight against them, the sons of Jacob returned home.

Chapter 36

1 At that time the Lord appeared unto Jacob saying, Arise, go to Bethel and remain there, and make there an altar to the Lord who appeareth unto thee, who delivered thee and thy sons from affliction.

2 And Jacob rose up with his sons and all belonging to him, and they went and came to Bethel according to the word of the Lord.

3 And Jacob was ninety-nine years old when he went up to Bethel, and Jacob and his sons and all the people that were with him, remained in Bethel in Luz, and he there built an altar to the Lord who appeared unto him, and Jacob and his sons remained in Bethel six months.

4 At that time died Deborah the daughter of Uz, the nurse of Rebecca, who had been with Jacob; and Jacob buried her beneath Bethel under an oak that was there.

5 And Rebecca the daughter of Bethuel, the mother of Jacob, also died at that time in Hebron, the same is Kireath-arba, and she was buried in the cave of Machpelah which Abraham had bought from the children of Heth.

6 And the life of Rebecca was one hundred and thirty-three years, and she died and when Jacob heard that his mother Rebecca was dead he wept bitterly for his mother, and made a great mourning for her, and for Deborah her nurse beneath the oak, and he called the name of that place Allon-bachuth.

7 And Laban the Syrian died in those days, for God smote him because he transgressed the covenant that existed between him and Jacob.

8 And Jacob was a hundred years old when the Lord appeared unto him, and blessed him and called his name Israel, and Rachel the wife of Jacob conceived in those days.

9 And at that time Jacob and all belonging to him journeyed from Bethel to go to his father's house, to Hebron.

10 And whilst they were going on the road, and there was yet but a little way to come to Ephrath, Rachel bare a son and she had hard labor and she died.

11 And Jacob buried her in the way to Ephrath, which is Bethlehem, and he set a pillar upon her grave, which is

there unto this day; and the days of Rachel were forty-five years and she died.

12 And Jacob called the name of his son that was born to him, which Rachel bare unto him, Benjamin, for he was born to him in the land on the right hand.

13 And it was after the death of Rachel, that Jacob pitched his tent in the tent of her handmaid Bilhah.

14 And Reuben was jealous for his mother Leah on account of this, and he was filled with anger, and he rose up in his anger and went and entered the tent of Bilhah and he thence removed his father's bed.

15 At that time the portion of birthright, together with the kingly and priestly offices, was removed from the sons of Reuben, for he had profaned his father's bed, and the birthright was given unto Joseph, the kingly office to Judah, and the priesthood unto Levi, because Reuben had defiled his father's bed.

16 And these are the generations of Jacob who were born to him in Padan-aram, and the sons of Jacob were twelve.

17 The sons of Leah were Reuben the first born, and Simeon, Levi, Judah, Issachar, Zebulun, and their sister Dinah; and the sons of Rachel were Joseph and Benjamin.

18 The sons of Zilpah, Leah's handmaid, were Gad and Asher, and the sons of Bilhah, Rachel's handmaid, were Dan and Naphtali; these are the sons of Jacob which were born to him in Padan-aram.

19 And Jacob and his sons and all belonging to him journeyed and came to Mamre, which is Kireath-arba, that is in Hebron, where Abraham and Isaac sojourned, and Jacob with his sons and all belonging to him, dwelt with his father in Hebron.

20 And his brother Esau and his sons, and all belonging to him went to the land of Seir and dwelt there, and had possessions in the land of Seir, and the children of Esau were fruitful and multiplied exceedingly in the land of Seir.

21 And these are the generations of Esau that were born to him in the land of Canaan, and the sons of Esau were five.

22 And Adah bare to Esau his first born Eliphaz, and she also bare to him Reuel, and Ahlibamah bare to him Jeush, Yaalam and Korah.

23 These are the children of Esau who were born to him in the land of Canaan; and the sons of Eliphaz the son of Esau were Teman, Omar, Zepho, Gatam, Kenaz and Amalex, and the sons of Reuel were Nachath, Zerach, Shamah and Mizzah.

24 And the sons of Jeush were Timnah, Alvah, Jetheth; and the sons of Yaalam were Alah, Phinor and Kenaz.

25 And the sons of Korah were Teman, Mibzar, Magdiel and Eram; these are the families of the sons of Esau according to their dukedoms in the land of Seir.

26 And these are the names of the sons of Seir the Horite, inhabitants of the land of Seir, Lotan, Shobal, Zibeon, Anah, Dishan, Ezer and Dishon, being seven sons.

27 And the children of Lotan were Hori, Heman and their sister Timna, that is Timna who came to Jacob and his sons, and they would not give ear to her, and she went and became a concubine to Eliphaz the son of Esau, and she bare to him Amalek.

28 And the sons of Shobal were Alvan, Manahath, Ebal, Shepho, and Onam, and the sons of Zibeon were Ajah, and Anah, this was that Anah who found the Yemim in the wilderness when he fed the asses of Zibeon his father.

29 And whilst he was feeding his father's asses he led them to the wilderness at different times to feed them.

30 And there was a day that he brought them to one of the deserts on the sea shore, opposite the wilderness of the people, and whilst he was feeding them, behold a very heavy storm came from the other side of the sea and rested upon the asses that were feeding there, and they all stood still.

31 And afterward about one hundred and twenty great and terrible animals came out from the wilderness at the other side of the sea, and they all came to the place where the asses were, and they placed themselves there.

32 And those animals, from their middle downward, were in the shape of the children of men, and from their middle upward, some had the likeness of bears, and some the likeness of the keephas, with tails behind them from between their shoulders reaching down to the earth, like the tails of the ducheephath, and these animals came and mounted and rode upon these asses, and led them away, and they went away unto this day.

33 And one of these animals approached Anah and smote him with his tail, and then fled from that place.

34 And when he saw this work he was exceedingly afraid of his life, and he fled and escaped to the city.

35 And he related to his sons and brothers all that had happened to him, and many men went to seek the asses but could not find them, and Anah and his brothers went no more to that place from that day following, for they were greatly afraid of their lives.

36 And the children of Anah the son of Seir, were Dishon and his sister Ahlibamah, and the children of Dishon were Hemdan, Eshban, Ithran and Cheran, and the children of Ezer were Bilhan, Zaavan and Akan, and the children of Dishon were Uz and Aran.

37 These are the families of the children of Seir the Horite, according to their dukedoms in the land of Seir.

38 And Esau and his children dwelt in the land of Seir the Horite, the inhabitant of the land, and they had possessions in it and were fruitful and multiplied exceedingly, and Jacob and his children and all belonging to them, dwelt with their father Isaac in the land of Canaan, as the Lord had commanded Abraham their father.

Chapter 37

1 And in the one hundred and fifth year of the life of Jacob, that is the ninth year of Jacob's dwelling with his children in the land of Canaan, he came from Padan-aram.

2 And in those days Jacob journeyed with his children from Hebron, and they went and returned to the city of Shechem, they and all belonging to them, and they dwelt there, for the children of Jacob obtained good and fat pasture land for their cattle in the city of Shechem, the city of Shechem having then been rebuilt, and there were in it about three hundred men and women.

3 And Jacob and his children and all belonging to him dwelt in the part of the field which Jacob had bought from Hamor the father of Shechem, when he came from Padan-aram before Simeon and Levi had smitten the city.

4 And all those kings of the Canaanites and Amorites that surrounded the city of Shechem, heard that the sons of Jacob had again come to Shechem and dwelt there.

5 And they said, Shall the sons of Jacob the Hebrew again come to the city and dwell therein, after that they have smitten its inhabitants and driven them out? shall they now return and also drive out those who are dwelling in the city or slay them?

6 And all the kings of Canaan again assembled, and they came together to make war with Jacob and his sons.

7 And Jashub king of Tapnach sent also to all his neighboring kings, to Elan king of Gaash, and to Ihuri king

of Shiloh, and to Parathon king of Chazar, and to Susi king of Sarton, and to Laban king of Bethchoran, and to Shabir king of Othnay-mah, saying,

8 Come up to me and assist me, and let us smite Jacob the Hebrew and his sons, and all belonging to him, for they are again come to Shechem to possess it and to slay its inhabitants as before.

9 And all these kings assembled together and came with all their camps, a people exceedingly plentiful like the sand upon the sea shore, and they were all opposite to Tapnach.

10 And Jashub king of Tapnach went forth to them with all his army, and he encamped with them opposite to Tapnach without the city, and all these kings they divided into seven divisions, being seven camps against the sons of Jacob.

11 And they sent a declaration to Jacob and his son, saying, Come you all forth to us that we may have an interview together in the plain, and revenge the cause of the men of Shechem whom you slew in their city, and you will now again return to the city of Shechem and dwell therein, and slay its inhabitants as before.

12 And the sons of Jacob heard this and their anger was kindled exceedingly at the words of the kings of Canaan, and ten of the sons of Jacob hastened and rose up, and each of them girt on his weapons of war; and there were one hundred and two of their servants with them equipped in battle array.

13 And all these men, the sons of Jacob with their servants, went toward these kings, and Jacob their father was with them, and they all stood upon the heap of Shechem.

14 And Jacob prayed to the Lord for his sons, and he spread forth his hands to the Lord, and he said, O God, thou art an Almighty God, thou art our father, thou didst form us and we are the works of thine hands; I pray thee deliver my sons through thy mercy from the hand of their enemies, who are this day coming to fight with them and save them from their hand, for in thy hand is power and might, to save the few from the many.

15 And give unto my sons, thy servants, strength of heart and might to fight with their enemies, to subdue them, and make their enemies fall before them, and let not my sons and their servants die through the hands of the children of Canaan.

16 But if it seemeth good in thine eyes to take away the lives of my sons and their servants, take them in thy great mercy through the hands of thy ministers, that they may not perish this day by the hands of the kings of the Amorites.

17 And when Jacob ceased praying to the Lord the earth shook from its place, and the sun darkened, and all these kings were terrified and a great consternation seized them.

18 And the Lord hearkened to the prayer of Jacob, and the Lord impressed the hearts of all the kings and their hosts with the terror and awe of the sons of Jacob.

19 For the Lord caused them to hear the voice of chariots, and the voice of mighty horses from the sons of Jacob, and the voice of a great army accompanying them.

20 And these kings were seized with great terror at the sons of Jacob, and whilst they were standing in their quarters, behold the sons of Jacob advanced upon them, with one hundred and twelve men, with a great and tremendous shouting.

21 And when the kings saw the sons of Jacob advancing toward them, they were still more panic struck, and they were inclined to retreat from before the sons of Jacob as at first, and not to fight with them.

22 But they did not retreat, saying, It would be a disgrace to us thus twice to retreat from before the Hebrews.

23 And the sons of Jacob came near and advanced against all these kings and their armies, and they saw, and behold it was a very mighty people, numerous as the sand of the sea.

24 And the sons of Jacob called unto the Lord and said, Help us O Lord, help us and answer us, for we trust in thee, and let us not die by the hands of these uncircumcised men, who this day have come against us.

25 And the sons of Jacob girt on their weapons of war, and they took in their hands each man his shield and his javelin, and they approached to battle.

26 And Judah, the son of Jacob, ran first before his brethren, and ten of his servants with him, and he went toward these kings.

27 And Jashub, king of Tapnach, also came forth first with his army before Judah, and Judah saw Jashub and his army coming toward him, and Judah's wrath was kindled, and his anger burned within him, and he approached to battle in which Judah ventured his life.

28 And Jashub and all his army were advancing toward Judah, and he was riding upon a very strong and powerful horse, and Jashub was a very valiant man, and covered with iron and brass from head to foot.

29 And whilst he was upon the horse, he shot arrows with both hands from before and behind, as was his manner in all his battles, and he never missed the place to which he aimed his arrows.

30 And when Jashub came to fight with Judah, and was darting many arrows against Judah, the Lord bound the hand of Jashub, and all the arrows that he shot rebounded upon his own men.

31 And notwithstanding this, Jashub kept advancing toward Judah, to challenge him with the arrows, but the distance between them was about thirty cubits, and when Judah saw Jashub darting forth his arrows against him, he ran to him with his wrath-excited might.

32 And Judah took up a large stone from the ground, and its weight was sixty shekels, and Judah ran toward Jashub, and with the stone struck him on his shield, that Jashub was stunned with the blow, and fell off from his horse to the ground.

33 And the shield burst asunder out of the hand of Jashub, and through the force of the blow sprang to the distance of about fifteen cubits, and the shield fell before the second camp.

34 And the kings that came with Jashub saw at a distance the strength of Judah, the son of Jacob, and what he had done to Jashub, and they were terribly afraid of Judah.

35 And they assembled near Jashub's camp, seeing his confusion, and Judah drew his sword and smote forty-two men of the camp of Jashub, and the whole of Jashub's camp fled before Judah, and no man stood against him, and they left Jashub and fled from him, and Jashub was still prostrate upon the ground.

36 And Jashub seeing that all the men of his camp had fled from him, hastened and rose up with terror against Judah, and stood upon his legs opposite Judah.

37 And Jashub had a single combat with Judah, placing shield toward shield, and Jashub's men all fled, for they were greatly afraid of Judah.

38 And Jashub took his spear in his hand to strike Judah upon his head, but Judah had quickly placed his shield to his head against Jashub's spear, so that the shield of Judah received the blow from Jashub's spear, and the shield was split in too.

39 And when Judah saw that his shield was split, he hastily

drew his sword and smote Jashub at his ankles, and cut off his feet that Jashub fell upon the ground, and the spear fell from his hand.

40 And Judah hastily picked up Jashub's spear, with which he severed his head and cast it next to his feet.

41 And when the sons of Jacob saw what Judah had done to Jashub, they all ran into the ranks of the other kings, and the sons of Jacob fought with the army of Jashub, and the armies of all the kings that were there.

42 And the sons of Jacob caused fifteen thousand of their men to fall, and they smote them as if smiting at gourds, and the rest fled for their lives.

43 And Judah was still standing by the body of Jashub, and stripped Jashub of his coat of mail.

44 And Judah also took off the iron and brass that was about Jashub, and behold nine men of the captains of Jashub came along to fight against Judah.

45 And Judah hastened and took up a stone from the ground, and with it smote one of them upon the head, and his skull was fractured, and the body also fell from the horse to the ground.

46 And the eight captains that remained, seeing the strength of Judah, were greatly afraid and they fled, and Judah with his ten men pursued them, and they overtook them and slew them.

47 And the sons of Jacob were still smiting the armies of the kings, and they slew many of them, but those kings daringly kept their stand with their captains, and did not retreat from their places, and they exclaimed against those of their armies that fled from before the sons of Jacob, but none would listen to them, for they were afraid of their lives lest they should die.

48 And all the sons of Jacob, after having smitten the armies of the kings, returned and came before Judah, and Judah was still slaying the eight captains of Jashub, and stripping off their garments.

49 And Levi saw Elon, king of Gaash, advancing toward him, with his fourteen captains to smite him, but Levi did not know it for certain.

50 And Elon with his captains approached nearer, and Levi looked back and saw that battle was given him in the rear, and Levi ran with twelve of his servants, and they went and slew Elon and his captains with the edge of the sword.

Chapter 38

1 And Ihuri king of Shiloh came up to assist Elon, and he approached Jacob, when Jacob drew his bow that was in his hand and with an arrow struck Ihuri which caused his death.

2 And when Ihuri king of Shiloh was dead, the four remaining kings fled from their station with the rest of the captains, and they endeavored to retreat, saying, We have no more strength with the Hebrews after their having killed the three kings and their captains who were more powerful than we are.

3 And when the sons of Jacob saw that the remaining kings had removed from their station, they pursued them, and Jacob also came from the heap of Shechem from the place where he was standing, and they went after the kings and they approached them with their servants.

4 And the kings and the captains with the rest of their armies, seeing that the sons of Jacob approached them, were afraid of their lives and fled till they reached the city of Chazar.

5 And the sons of Jacob pursued them to the gate of the city of Chazar, and they smote a great smiting amongst the kings and their armies, about four thousand men, and whilst they were smiting the army of the kings, Jacob was occupied with his bow confining himself to smiting the kings, and he slew them all.

6 And he slew Parathon king of Chazar at the gate of the city of Chazar, and he afterward smote Susi king of Sarton, and Laban king of Bethchorin, and Shabir king of Machnaymah, and he slew them all with arrows, an arrow to each of them, and they died.

7 And the sons of Jacob seeing that all the kings were dead and that they were broken up and retreating, continued to carry on the battle with the armies of the kings opposite the gate of Chazar, and they still smote about four hundred of their men.

8 And three men of the servants of Jacob fell in that battle, and when Judah saw that three of his servants had died, it grieved him greatly, and his anger burned within him against the Amorites.

9 And all the men that remained of the armies of the kings were greatly afraid of their lives, and they ran and broke the gate of the walls of the city of Chazar, and they all entered the city for safety.

10 And they concealed themselves in the midst of the city of Chazar, for the city of Chazar was very large and extensive, and when all these armies had entered the city, the sons of Jacob ran after them to the city.

11 And four mighty men, experienced in battle, went forth from the city and stood against the entrance of the city, with drawn swords and spears in their hands, and they placed themselves opposite the sons of Jacob, and would not suffer them to enter the city.

12 And Naphtali ran and came between them and with his sword smote two of them, and cut off their heads at one stroke.

13 And he turned to the other two, and behold they had fled, and he pursued them, overtook them, smote them and slew them.

14 And the sons of Jacob came to the city and saw, and behold there was another wall to the city, and they sought for the gate of the wall and could not find it, and Judah sprang upon the top of the wall, and Simeon and Levi followed him, and they all three descended from the wall into the city.

15 And Simeon and Levi slew all the men who ran for safety into the city, and also the inhabitants of the city with their wives and little ones, they slew with the edge of the sword, and the cries of the city ascended up to heaven.

16 And Dan and Naphtali sprang upon the wall to see what caused the noise of lamentation, for the sons of Jacob felt anxious about their brothers, and they heard the inhabitants of the city speaking with weeping and supplications, saying, Take all that we possess in the city and go away, only do not put us to death.

17 And when Judah, Simeon, and Levi had ceased smiting the inhabitants of the city, they ascended the wall and called to Dan and Naphtali, who were upon the wall, and to the rest of their brothers, and Simeon and Levi informed them of the entrance into the city, and all the sons of Jacob came to fetch the spoil.

18 And the sons of Jacob took the spoil of the city of Chazar, the flocks and herds, and the property, and they took all that could be captured, and went away that day from the city.

19 And on the next day the sons of Jacob went to Sarton, for they heard that the men of Sarton who had remained in the city were assembling to fight with them for having slain

their king, and Sarton was a very high and fortified city, and it had a deep rampart surrounding the city.

20 And the pillar of the rampart was about fifty cubits and its breadth forty cubits, and there was no place for a man to enter the city on account of the rampart, and the sons of Jacob saw the rampart of the city, and they sought an entrance in it but could not find it.

21 For the entrance to the city was at the rear, and every man that wished to come into the city came by that road and went around the whole city, and he afterwards entered the city.

22 And the sons of Jacob seeing they could not find the way into the city, their anger was kindled greatly, and the inhabitants of the city seeing that the sons of Jacob were coming to them were greatly afraid of them, for they had heard of their strength and what they had done to Chazar.

23 And the inhabitants of the city of Sarton could not go out toward the sons of Jacob after having assembled in the city to fight against them, lest they might thereby get into the city, but when they saw that they were coming toward them, they were greatly afraid of them, for they had heard of their strength and what they had done to Chazar.

24 So the inhabitants of Sarton speedily took away the bridge of the road of the city, from its place, before the sons of Jacob came, and they brought it into the city.

25 And the sons of Jacob came and sought the way into the city, and could not find it and the inhabitants of the city went up to the top of the wall, and saw, and behold the sons of Jacob were seeking an entrance into the city.

26 And the inhabitants of the city reproached the sons of Jacob from the top of the wall, and they cursed them, and the sons of Jacob heard the reproaches, and they were greatly incensed, and their anger burned within them.

27 And the sons of Jacob were provoked at them, and they all rose and sprang over the rampart with the force of their strength, and through their might passed the forty cubits' breadth of the rampart.

28 And when they had passed the rampart they stood under the wall of the city, and they found all the gates of the city enclosed with iron doors.

29 And the sons of Jacob came near to break open the doors of the gates of the city, and the inhabitants did not let them, for from the top of the wall they were casting stones and arrows upon them.

30 And the number of the people that were upon the wall was about four hundred men, and when the sons of Jacob saw that the men of the city would not let them open the gates of the city, they sprang and ascended the top of the wall, and Judah went up first to the east part of the city.

31 And Gad and Asher went up after him to the west corner of the city, and Simeon and Levi to the north, and Dan and Reuben to the south.

32 And the men who were on the top of the wall, the inhabitants of the city, seeing that the sons of Jacob were coming up to them, they all fled from the wall, descended into the city, and concealed themselves in the midst of the city.

33 And Issachar and Naphtali that remained under the wall approached and broke the gates of the city, and kindled a fire at the gates of the city, that the iron melted, and all the sons of Jacob came into the city, they and all their men, and they fought with the inhabitants of the city of Sarton, and smote them with the edge of the sword, and no man stood up before them.

34 And about two hundred men fled from the city, and they all went and hid themselves in a certain tower in the city, and Judah pursued them to the tower and he broke down the tower, which fell upon the men, and they all died.

35 And the sons of Jacob went up the road of the roof of that tower, and they saw, and behold there was another strong and high tower at a distance in the city, and the top of it reached to heaven, and the sons of Jacob hastened and descended, and went with all their men to that tower, and found it filled with about three hundred men, women and little ones.

36 And the sons of Jacob smote a great smiting amongst those men in the tower and they ran away and fled from them.

37 And Simeon and Levi pursued them, when twelve mighty and valiant men came out to them from the place where they had concealed themselves.

38 And those twelve men maintained a strong battle against Simeon and Levi, and Simeon and Levi could not prevail over them, and those valiant men broke the shields of Simeon and Levi, and one of them struck at Levi's head with his sword, when Levi hastily placed his hand to his head, for he was afraid of the sword, and the sword struck Levi's hand, and it wanted but little to the hand of Levi being cut off.

39 And Levi seized the sword of the valiant man in his hand, and took it forcibly from the man, and with it he struck at the head of the powerful man, and he severed his head.

40 And eleven men approached to fight with Levi, for they saw that one of them was killed, and the sons of Jacob fought, but the sons of Jacob could not prevail over them, for those men were very powerful.

41 And the sons of Jacob seeing that they could not prevail over them, Simeon gave a loud and tremendous shriek, and the eleven powerful men were stunned at the voice of Simeon's shrieking.

42 And Judah at a distance knew the voice of Simeon's shouting, and Naphtali and Judah ran with their shields to Simeon and Levi, and found them fighting with those powerful men, unable to prevail over them as their shields were broken.

43 And Naphtali saw that the shields of Simeon and Levi were broken, and he took two shields from his servants and brought them to Simeon and Levi.

44 And Simeon, Levi and Judah on that day fought all three against the eleven mighty men until the time of sunset, but they could not prevail over them.

45 And this was told unto Jacob, and he was sorely grieved, and he prayed unto the Lord, and he and Naphtali his son went against these mighty men.

46 And Jacob approached and drew his bow, and came nigh unto the mighty men, and slew three of their men with the bow, and the remaining eight turned back, and behold, the war waged against them in the front and rear, and they were greatly afraid of their lives, and could not stand before the sons of Jacob, and they fled from before them.

47 And in their flight they met Dan and Asher coming toward them, and they suddenly fell upon them, and fought with them, and slew two of them, and Judah and his brothers pursued them, and smote the remainder of them, and slew them.

48 And all the sons of Jacob returned and walked about the city, searching if they could find any men, and they found about twenty young men in a cave in the city, and Gad and Asher smote them all, and Dan and Naphtali lighted upon the rest of the men who had fled and escaped from the second tower, and they smote them all.

49 And the sons of Jacob smote all the inhabitants of the city of Sarton, but the women and little ones they left in the city and did not slay them.

50 And all the inhabitants of the city of Sarton were powerful men, one of them would pursue a thousand, and two of them would not flee from ten thousand of the rest of men.

51 And the sons of Jacob slew all the inhabitants of the city of Sarton with the edge of the sword, that no man stood up against them, and they left the women in the city.

52 And the sons of Jacob took all the spoil of the city, and captured what they desired, and they took flocks and herds and property from the city, and the sons of Jacob did unto Sarton and its inhabitants as they had done to Chazar and its inhabitants, and they turned and went away.

Chapter 39

1 And when the sons of Jacob went from the city of Sarton, they had gone about two hundred cubits when they met the inhabitants of Tapnach coming toward them, for they went out to fight with them, because they had smitten the king of Tapnach and all his men.

2 So all that remained in the city of Tapnach came out to fight with the sons of Jacob, and they thought to retake from them the booty and the spoil which they had captured from Chazar and Sarton.

3 And the rest of the men of Tapnach fought with the sons of Jacob in that place, and the sons of Jacob smote them, and they fled before them, and they pursued them to the city of Arbelan, and they all fell before the sons of Jacob.

4 And the sons of Jacob returned and came to Tapnach, to take away the spoil of Tapnach, and when they came to Tapnach they heard that the people of Arbelan had gone out to meet them to save the spoil of their brethren, and the sons of Jacob left ten of their men in Tapnach to plunder the city, and they went out toward the people of Arbelan.

5 And the men of Arbelan went out with their wives to fight with the sons of Jacob, for their wives were experienced in battle, and they went out, about four hundred men and women.

6 And all the sons of Jacob shouted with a loud voice, and they all ran toward the inhabitants of Arbelan, and with a great and tremendous voice.

7 And the inhabitants of Arbelan heard the noise of the shouting of the sons of Jacob, and their roaring like the noise of lions and like the roaring of the sea and its waves.

8 And fear and terror possessed their hearts on account of the sons of Jacob, and they were terribly afraid of them, and they retreated and fled before them into the city, and the sons of Jacob pursued them to the gate of the city, and they came upon them in the city.

9 And the sons of Jacob fought with them in the city, and all their women were engaged in slinging against the sons of Jacob, and the combat was very severe amongst them the whole of that day till evening.

10 And the sons of Jacob could not prevail over them, and the sons of Jacob had almost perished in that battle, and the sons of Jacob cried unto the Lord and greatly gained strength toward evening, and the sons of Jacob smote all the inhabitants of Arbelan by the edge of the sword, men, women and little ones.

11 And also the remainder of the people who had fled from Sarton, the sons of Jacob smote them in Arbelan, and the sons of Jacob did unto Arbelan and Tapnach as they had done to Chazar and Sarton, and when the women saw that all the men were dead, they went upon the roofs of the city and smote the sons of Jacob by showering down stones like rain.

12 And the sons of Jacob hastened and came into the city and seized all the women and smote them with the edge of the sword, and the sons of Jacob captured all the spoil and booty, flocks and herds and cattle.

13 And the sons of Jacob did unto Machnaymah as they had done to Tapnach, to Chazar and to Shiloh, and they turned from there and went away.

14 And on the fifth day the sons of Jacob heard that the people of Gaash had gathered against them to battle, because they had slain their king and their captains, for there had been fourteen captains in the city of Gaash, and the sons of Jacob had slain them all in the first battle.

15 And the sons of Jacob that day girt on their weapons of war, and they marched to battle against the inhabitants of Gaash, and in Gaash there was a strong and mighty people of the people of the Amorites, and Gaash was the strongest and best fortified city of all the cities of the Amorites, and it had three walls.

16 And the sons of Jacob came to Gaash and they found the gates of the city locked, and about five hundred men standing at the top of the outer-most wall, and a people numerous as the sand upon the sea shore were in ambush for the sons of Jacob from without the city at the rear thereof.

17 And the sons of Jacob approached to open the gates of the city, and whilst they were drawing nigh, behold those who were in ambush at the rear of the city came forth from their places and surrounded the sons of Jacob.

18 And the sons of Jacob were enclosed between the people of Gaash, and the battle was both to their front and rear, and all the men that were upon the wall, were casting from the wall upon them, arrows and stones.

19 And Judah, seeing that the men of Gaash were getting too heavy for them, gave a most piercing and tremendous shriek and all the men of Gaash were terrified at the voice of Judah's cry, and men fell from the wall at his powerful shriek, and all those that were from without and within the city were greatly afraid of their lives.

20 And the sons of Jacob still came nigh to break the doors of the city, when the men of Gaash threw stones and arrows upon them from the top of the wall, and made them flee from the gate.

21 And the sons of Jacob returned against the men of Gaash who were with them from without the city, and they smote them terribly, as striking against gourds, and they could not stand against the sons of Jacob, for fright and terror had seized them at the shriek of Judah.

22 And the sons of Jacob slew all those men who were without the city, and the sons of Jacob still drew nigh to effect an entrance into the city, and to fight under the city walls, but they could not for all the inhabitants of Gaash who remained in the city had surrounded the walls of Gaash in every direction, so that the sons of Jacob were unable to approach the city to fight with them.

23 And the sons of Jacob came nigh to one corner to fight under the wall, the inhabitants of Gaash threw arrows and stones upon them like showers of rain, and they fled from under the wall.

24 And the people of Gaash who were upon the wall, seeing that the sons of Jacob could not prevail over them from under the wall, reproached the sons of Jacob in these words, saying,

25 What is the matter with you in the battle that you cannot

prevail? can you then do unto the mighty city of Gaash and its inhabitants as you did to the cities of the Amorites that were not so powerful? Surely to those weak ones amongst us you did those things, and slew them in the entrance of the city, for they had no strength when they were terrified at the sound of your shouting.

26 And will you now then be able to fight in this place? Surely here you will all die, and we will avenge the cause of those cities that you have laid waste.

27 And the inhabitants of Gaash greatly reproached the sons of Jacob and reviled them with their gods, and continued to cast arrows and stones upon them from the wall.

28 And Judah and his brothers heard the words of the inhabitants of Gaash and their anger was greatly roused, and Judah was jealous of his God in this matter, and he called out and said, O Lord, help, send help to us and our brothers.

29 And he ran at a distance with all his might, with his drawn sword in his hand, and he sprang from the earth and by dint of his strength, mounted the wall, and his sword fell from his hand.

30 And Judah shouted upon the wall, and all the men that were upon the wall were terrified, and some of them fell from the wall into the city and died, and those who were yet upon the wall, when they saw Judah's strength, they were greatly afraid and fled for their lives into the city for safety.

31 And some were emboldened to fight with Judah upon the wall, and they came nigh to slay him when they saw there was no sword in Judah's hand, and they thought of casting him from the wall to his brothers, and twenty men of the city came up to assist them, and they surrounded Judah and they all shouted over him, and approached him with drawn swords, and they terrified Judah, and Judah cried out to his brothers from the wall.

32 And Jacob and his sons drew the bow from under the wall, and smote three of the men that were upon the top of the wall, and Judah continued to cry and he exclaimed, O Lord help us, O Lord deliver us, and he cried out with a loud voice upon the wall, and the cry was heard at a great distance.

33 And after this cry he again repeated to shout, and all the men who surrounded Judah on the top of the wall were terrified, and they each threw his sword from his hand at the sound of Judah's shouting and his tremor, and fled.

34 And Judah took the swords which had fallen from their hands, and Judah fought with them and slew twenty of their men upon the wall.

35 And about eighty men and women still ascended the wall from the city and they all surrounded Judah, and the Lord impressed the fear of Judah in their hearts, that they were unable to approach him.

36 And Jacob and all who were with him drew the bow from under the wall, and they slew ten men upon the wall, and they fell below the wall, before Jacob and his sons.

37 And the people upon the wall seeing that twenty of their men had fallen, they still ran toward Judah with drawn swords, but they could not approach him for they were greatly terrified at Judah's strength.

38 And one of their mighty men whose name was Arud approached to strike Judah upon the head with his sword, when Judah hastily put his shield to his head, and the sword hit the shield, and it was split in two.

39 And this mighty man after he had struck Judah ran for his life, at the fear of Judah, and his feet slipped upon the

wall and he fell amongst the sons of Jacob who were below the wall, and the sons of Jacob smote him and slew him.

40 And Judah's head pained him from the blow of the powerful man, and Judah had nearly died from it.

41 And Judah cried out upon the wall owing to the pain produced by the blow, when Dan heard him, and his anger burned within him, and he also rose up and went at a distance and ran and sprang from the earth and mounted the wall with his wrath-excited strength.

42 And when Dan came upon the wall near unto Judah all the men upon the wall fled, who had stood against Judah, and they went up to the second wall, and they threw arrows and stones upon Dan and Judah from the second wall, and endeavored to drive them from the wall.

43 And the arrows and stones struck Dan and Judah, and they had nearly been killed upon the wall, and wherever Dan and Judah fled from the wall, they were attacked with arrows and stones from the second wall.

44 And Jacob and his sons were still at the entrance of the city below the first wall, and they were not able to draw their bow against the inhabitants of the city, as they could not be seen by them, being upon the second wall.

45 And Dan and Judah when they could no longer bear the stones and arrows that fell upon them from the second wall, they both sprang upon the second wall near the people of the city, and when the people of the city who were upon the second wall saw that Dan and Judah had come to them upon the second wall, they all cried out and descended below between the walls.

46 And Jacob and his sons heard the noise of the shouting from the people of the city, and they were still at the entrance of the city, and they were anxious about Dan and Judah who were not seen by them, they being upon the second wall.

47 And Naphtali went up with his wrath-excited might and sprang upon the first wall to see what caused the noise of shouting which they had heard in the city, and Issachar and Zebulun drew nigh to break the doors of the city, and they opened the gates of the city and came into the city.

48 And Naphtali leaped from the first wall to the second, and came to assist his brothers, and the inhabitants of Gaash who were upon the wall, seeing that Naphtali was the third who had come up to assist his brothers, they all fled and descended into the city, and Jacob and all his sons and all their young men came into the city to them.

49 And Judah and Dan and Naphtali descended from the wall into the city and pursued the inhabitants of the city, and Simeon and Levi were from without the city and knew not that the gate was opened, and they went up from there to the wall and came down to their brothers into the city.

50 And the inhabitants of the city had all descended into the city, and the sons of Jacob came to them in different directions, and the battle waged against them from the front and the rear, and the sons of Jacob smote them terribly, and slew about twenty thousand of them men and women, not one of them could stand up against the sons of Jacob.

51 And the blood flowed plentifully in the city, and it was like a brook of water, and the blood flowed like a brook to the outer part of the city, and reached the desert of Bethchorin.

52 And the people of Bethchorin saw at a distance the blood flowing from the city of Gaash, and about seventy men from amongst them ran to see the blood, and they came to the place where the blood was.

53 And they followed the track of the blood and came to

the wall of the city of Gaash, and they saw the blood issue from the city, and they heard the voice of crying from the inhabitants of Gaash, for it ascended unto heaven, and the blood was continuing to flow abundantly like a brook of water.

54 And all the sons of Jacob were still smiting the inhabitants of Gaash, and were engaged in slaying them till evening, about twenty thousand men and women, and the people of Chorin said, Surely this is the work of the Hebrews, for they are still carrying on war in all the cities of the Amorites.

55 And those people hastened and ran to Bethchorin, and each took his weapons of war, and they cried out to all the inhabitants of Bethchorin, who also girt on their weapons of war to go and fight with the sons of Jacob.

56 And when the sons of Jacob had done smiting the inhabitants of Gaash, they walked about the city to strip all the slain, and coming in the innermost part of the city and farther on they met three very powerful men, and there was no sword in their hand.

57 And the sons of Jacob came up to the place where they were, and the powerful men ran away, and one of them had taken Zebulun, who he saw was a young lad and of short stature, and with his might dashed him to the ground.

58 And Jacob ran to him with his sword and Jacob smote him below his loins with the sword, and cut him in two, and the body fell upon Zebulun.

59 And the second one approached and seized Jacob to fell him to the ground, and Jacob turned to him and shouted to him, whilst Simeon and Levi ran and smote him on the hips with the sword and felled him to the ground.

60 And the powerful man rose up from the ground with wrath-excited might, and Judah came to him before he had gained his footing, and struck him upon the head with the sword, and his head was split and he died.

61 And the third powerful man, seeing that his companions were killed, ran from before the sons of Jacob, and the sons of Jacob pursued him in the city; and whilst the powerful man was fleeing he found one of the swords of the inhabitants of the city, and he picked it up and turned to the sons of Jacob and fought them with that sword.

62 And the powerful man ran to Judah to strike him upon the head with the sword, and there was no shield in the hand of Judah; and whilst he was aiming to strike him, Naphtali hastily took his shield and put it to Judah's head, and the sword of the powerful man hit the shield of Naphtali and Judah escaped the sword.

63 And Simeon and Levi ran upon the powerful man with their swords and struck at him forcibly with their swords, and the two swords entered the body of the powerful man and divided it in two, length-wise.

64 And the sons of Jacob smote the three mighty men at that time, together with all the inhabitants of Gaash, and the day was about to decline.

65 And the sons of Jacob walked about Gaash and took all the spoil of the city, even the little ones and women they did not suffer to live, and the sons of Jacob did unto Gaash as they had done to Sarton and Shiloh.

Chapter 40

1 And the sons of Jacob led away all the spoil of Gaash, and went out of the city by night.

2 They were going out marching toward the castle of Bethchorin, and the inhabitants of Bethchorin were going to the castle to meet them, and on that night the sons of Jacob fought with the inhabitants of Bethchorin, in the castle of Bethchorin.

3 And all the inhabitants of Bethchorin were mighty men, one of them would not flee from before a thousand men, and they fought on that night upon the castle, and their shouts were heard on that night from afar, and the earth quaked at their shouting.

4 And all the sons of Jacob were afraid of those men, as they were not accustomed to fight in the dark, and they were greatly confounded, and the sons of Jacob cried unto the Lord, saying, Give help to us O Lord, deliver us that we may not die by the hands of these uncircumcised men.

5 And the Lord hearkened to the voice of the sons of Jacob, and the Lord caused great terror and confusion to seize the people of Bethchorin, and they fought amongst themselves the one with the other in the darkness of night, and smote each other in great numbers.

6 And the sons of Jacob, knowing that the Lord had brought a spirit of perverseness amongst those men, and that they fought each man with his neighbor, went forth from among the bands of the people of Bethchorin and went as far as the descent of the castle of Bethchorin, and farther, and they tarried there securely with their young men on that night.

7 And the people of Bethchorin fought the whole night, one man with his brother, and the other with his neighbor, and they cried out in every direction upon the castle, and their cry was heard at a distance, and the whole earth shook at their voice, for they were powerful above all the people of the earth.

8 And all the inhabitants of the cities of the Canaanites, the Hittites, the Amorites, the Hivites and all the kings of Canaan, and also those who were on the other side of the Jordan, heard the noise of the shouting on that night.

9 And they said, Surely these are the battles of the Hebrews who are fighting against the seven cities, who came nigh unto them; and who can stand against those Hebrews?

10 And all the inhabitants of the cities of the Canaanites, and all those who were on the other side of the Jordan, were greatly afraid of the sons of Jacob, for they said, Behold the same will be done to us as was done to those cities, for who can stand against their mighty strength?

11 And the cries of the Chorinites were very great on that night, and continued to increase; and they smote each other till morning, and numbers of them were killed.

12 And the morning appeared, and all the sons of Jacob rose up at daybreak and went up to the castle, and they smote those who remained of the Chorinites in a terrible manner, and they were all killed in the castle.

13 And the sixth day appeared, and all the inhabitants of Canaan saw at a distance all the people of Bethchorin lying dead in the castle of Bethchorin, and strewed about as the carcasses of lambs and goats.

14 And the sons of Jacob led all the spoil which they had captured from Gaash and went to Bethchorin, and they found the city full of people like the sand of the sea, and they fought with them, and the sons of Jacob smote them there till evening time.

15 And the sons of Jacob did unto Bethchorin as they had done to Gaash and Tapnach, and as they had done to Chazar, to Sarton and to Shiloh.

16 And the sons of Jacob took with them the spoil of Bethchorin and all the spoil of the cities, and on that day they went home to Shechem.

17 And the sons of Jacob came home to the city of Shechem, and they remained without the city, and they then rested there from the war, and tarried there all night.

18 And all their servants together with all the spoil that they had taken from the cities, they left without the city, and they did not enter the city, for they said, Peradventure there may be yet more fighting against us, and they may come to besiege us in Shechem.

19 And Jacob and his sons and their servants remained on that night and the next day in the portion of the field which Jacob had purchased from Hamor for five shekels, and all that they had captured was with them.

20 And all the booty which the sons of Jacob had captured, was in the portion of the field, immense as the sand upon the sea shore.

21 And the inhabitants of the land observed them from afar, and all the inhabitants of the land were afraid of the sons of Jacob who had done this thing, for no king from the days of old had ever done the like.

22 And the seven kings of the Canaanites resolved to make peace with the sons of Jacob, for they were greatly afraid of their lives, on account of the sons of Jacob.

23 And on that day, being the seventh day, Japhia king of Hebron sent secretly to the king of Ai, and to the king of Gibeon, and to the king of Shalem, and to the king of Adulam, and to the king of Lachish, and to the king of Chazar, and to all the Canaanitish kings who were under their subjection, saying,

24 Go up with me, and come to me that we may go to the sons of Jacob, and I will make peace with them, and form a treaty with them, lest all your lands be destroyed by the swords of the sons of Jacob, as they did to Shechem and the cities around it, as you have heard and seen.

25 And when you come to me, do not come with many men, but let every king bring his three head captains, and every captain bring three of his officers.

26 And come all of you to Hebron, and we will go together to the sons of Jacob, and supplicate them that they shall form a treaty of peace with us.

27 And all those kings did as the king of Hebron had sent to them, for they were all under his counsel and command, and all the kings of Canaan assembled to go to the sons of Jacob, to make peace with them; and the sons of Jacob returned and went to the portion of the field that was in Shechem, for they did not put confidence in the kings of the land.

28 And the sons of Jacob returned and remained in the portion of the field ten days, and no one came to make war with them.

29 And when the sons of Jacob saw that there was no appearance of war, they all assembled and went to the city of Shechem, and the sons of Jacob remained in Shechem.

30 And at the expiration of forty days, all the kings of the Amorites assembled from all their places and came to Hebron, to Japhia, king of Hebron.

31 And the number of kings that came to Hebron, to make peace with the sons of Jacob, was twenty-one kings, and the number of captains that came with them was sixty-nine, and their men were one hundred and eighty-nine, and all these kings and their men rested by Mount Hebron.

32 And the king of Hebron went out with his three captains and nine men, and these kings resolved to go to the sons of Jacob to make peace.

33 And they said unto the king of Hebron, Go thou before us with thy men, and speak for us unto the sons of Jacob, and we will come after thee and confirm thy words, and the king of Hebron did so.

34 And the sons of Jacob heard that all the kings of Canaan had gathered together and rested in Hebron, and the sons of Jacob sent four of their servants as spies, saying, Go and spy these kings, and search and examine their men whether they are few or many, and if they are but few in number, number them all and come back.

35 And the servants of Jacob went secretly to these kings, and did as the sons of Jacob had commanded them, and on that day they came back to the sons of Jacob, and said unto them, We came unto those kings, and they are but few in number, and we numbered them all, and behold, they were two hundred and eighty-eight, kings and men.

36 And the sons of Jacob said, They are but few in number, therefore we will not all go out to them; and in the morning the sons of Jacob rose up and chose sixty two of their men, and ten of the sons of Jacob went with them; and they girt on their weapons of war, for they said, They are coming to make war with us, for they knew not that they were coming to make peace with them.

37 And the sons of Jacob went with their servants to the gate of Shechem, toward those kings, and their father Jacob was with them.

38 And when they had come forth, behold, the king of Hebron and his three captains and nine men with him were coming along the road against the sons of Jacob, and the sons of Jacob lifted up their eyes, and saw at a distance Japhia, king of Hebron, with his captains, coming toward them, and the sons of Jacob took their stand at the place of the gate of Shechem, and did not proceed.

39 And the king of Hebron continued to advance, he and his captains, until he came nigh to the sons of Jacob, and he and his captains bowed down to them to the ground, and the king of Hebron sat with his captains before Jacob and his sons.

40 And the sons of Jacob said unto him, What has befallen thee, O king of Hebron? why hast thou come to us this day? what dost thou require from us? and the king of Hebron said unto Jacob, I beseech thee my lord, all the kings of the Canaanites have this day come to make peace with you.

41 And the sons of Jacob heard the words of the king of Hebron, and they would not consent to his proposals, for the sons of Jacob had no faith in him, for they imagined that the king of Hebron had spoken deceitfully to them.

42 And the king of Hebron knew from the words of the sons of Jacob, that they did not believe his words, and the king of Hebron approached nearer to Jacob, and said unto him, I beseech thee, my lord, to be assured that all these kings have come to you on peaceable terms, for they have not come with all their men, neither did they bring their weapons of war with them, for they have come to seek peace from my lord and his sons.

43 And the sons of Jacob answered the king of Hebron, saying, Send thou to all these kings, and if thou speakest truth unto us, let them each come singly before us, and if they come unto us unarmed, we shall then know that they seek peace from us.

44 And Japhia, king of Hebron, sent one of his men to the kings, and they all came before the sons of Jacob, and bowed down to them to the ground, and these kings sat before Jacob and his sons, and they spoke unto them, saying,

45 We have heard all that you did unto the kings of the Amorites with your sword and exceedingly mighty arm, so that no man could stand up before you, and we were afraid of you for the sake of our lives, lest it should befall us as it did to them.

46 So we have come unto you to form a treaty of peace

between us, and now therefore contract with us a covenant of peace and truth, that you will not meddle with us, inasmuch as we have not meddled with you.

47 And the sons of Jacob knew that they had really come to seek peace from them, and the sons of Jacob listened to them, and formed a covenant with them.

48 And the sons of Jacob swore unto them that they would not meddle with them, and all the kings of the Canaanites swore also to them, and the sons of Jacob made them tributary from that day forward.

49 And after this all the captains of these kings came with their men before Jacob, with presents in their hands for Jacob and his sons, and they bowed down to him to the ground.

50 And these kings then urged the sons of Jacob and begged of them to return all the spoil they had captured from the seven cities of the Amorites, and the sons of Jacob did so, and they returned all that they had captured, the women, the little ones, the cattle and all the spoil which they had taken, and they sent them off, and they went away each to his city.

51 And all these kings again bowed down to the sons of Jacob, and they sent or brought them many gifts in those days, and the sons of Jacob sent off these kings and their men, and they went peaceably away from them to their cities, and the sons of Jacob also returned to their home, to Shechem.

52 And there was peace from that day forward between the sons of Jacob and the kings of the Canaanites, until the children of Israel came to inherit the land of Canaan.

Chapter 41

1 And at the revolution of the year the sons of Jacob journeyed from Shechem, and they came to Hebron, to their father Isaac, and they dwelt there, but their flocks and herds they fed daily in Shechem, for there was there in those days good and fat pasture, and Jacob and his sons and all their household dwelt in the valley of Hebron.

2 And it was in those days, in that year, being the hundred and sixth year of the life of Jacob, in the tenth year of Jacob's coming from Padan-aram, that Leah the wife of Jacob died; she was fifty-one years old when she died in Hebron.

3 And Jacob and his sons buried her in the cave of the field of Machpelah, which is in Hebron, which Abraham had bought from the children of Heth, for the possession of a burial place.

4 And the sons of Jacob dwelt with their father in the valley of Hebron, and all the inhabitants of the land knew their strength and their fame went throughout the land.

5 And Joseph the son of Jacob, and his brother Benjamin, the sons of Rachel, the wife of Jacob, were yet young in those days, and did not go out with their brethren during their battles in all the cities of the Amorites.

6 And when Joseph saw the strength of his brethren, and their greatness, he praised them and extolled them, but he ranked himself greater than them, and extolled himself above them; and Jacob, his father, also loved him more than any of his sons, for he was a son of his old age, and through his love toward him, he made him a coat of many colors.

7 And when Joseph saw that his father loved him more than his brethren, he continued to exalt himself above his brethren, and he brought unto his father evil reports concerning them.

8 And the sons of Jacob seeing the whole of Joseph's conduct toward them, and that their father loved him more

than any of them, they hated him and could not speak peaceably to him all the days.

9 And Joseph was seventeen years old, and he was still magnifying himself above his brethren, and thought of raising himself above them.

10 At that time he dreamed a dream, and he came unto his brothers and told them his dream, and he said unto them, I dreamed a dream, and behold we were all binding sheaves in the field, and my sheaf rose and placed itself upon the ground and your sheaves surrounded it and bowed down to it.

11 And his brethren answered him and said unto him, What meaneth this dream that thou didst dream? dost thou imagine in thy heart to reign or rule over us?

12 And he still came, and told the thing to his father Jacob, and Jacob kissed Joseph when he heard these words from his mouth, and Jacob blessed Joseph.

13 And when the sons of Jacob saw that their father had blessed Joseph and had kissed him, and that he loved him exceedingly, they became jealous of him and hated him the more.

14 And after this Joseph dreamed another dream and related the dream to his father in the presence of his brethren, and Joseph said unto his father and brethren, Behold I have again dreamed a dream, and behold the sun and the moon and the eleven stars bowed down to me.

15 And his father heard the words of Joseph and his dream, and seeing that his brethren hated Joseph on account of this matter, Jacob therefore rebuked Joseph before his brethren on account of this thing, saying, What meaneth this dream which thou hast dreamed, and this magnifying thyself before thy brethren who are older than thou art?

16 Dost thou imagine in thy heart that I and thy mother and thy eleven brethren will come and bow down to thee, that thou speakest these things?

17 And his brethren were jealous of him on account of his words and dreams, and they continued to hate him, and Jacob reserved the dreams in his heart.

18 And the sons of Jacob went one day to feed their father's flock in Shechem, for they were still herdsmen in those days; and whilst the sons of Jacob were that day feeding in Shechem they delayed, and the time of gathering in the cattle was passed, and they had not arrived.

19 And Jacob saw that his sons were delayed in Shechem, and Jacob said within himself, Peradventure the people of Shechem have risen up to fight against them, therefore they have delayed coming this day.

20 And Jacob called Joseph his son and commanded him, saying, Behold thy brethren are feeding in Shechem this day, and behold they have not yet come back; go now therefore and see where they are, and bring me word back concerning the welfare of thy brethren and the welfare of the flock.

21 And Jacob sent his son Joseph to the valley of Hebron, and Joseph came for his brothers to Shechem, and could not find them, and Joseph went about the field which was near Shechem, to see where his brothers had turned, and he missed his road in the wilderness, and knew not which way he should go.

22 And an angel of the Lord found him wandering in the road toward the field, and Joseph said unto the angel of the Lord, I seek my brethren; hast thou not heard where they are feeding? and the angel of the Lord said unto Joseph, I saw thy brethren feeding here, and I heard them say they would go to feed in Dothan.

23 And Joseph hearkened to the voice of the angel of the

Lord, and he went to his brethren in Dothan and he found them in Dothan feeding the flock.

24 And Joseph advanced to his brethren, and before he had come nigh unto them, they had resolved to slay him.

25 And Simeon said to his brethren, Behold the man of dreams is coming unto us this day, and now therefore come and let us kill him and cast him in one of the pits that are in the wilderness, and when his father shall seek him from us, we will say an evil beast has devoured him.

26 And Reuben heard the words of his brethren concerning Joseph, and he said unto them, You should not do this thing, for how can we look up to our father Jacob? Cast him into this pit to die there, but stretch not forth a hand upon him to spill his blood; and Reuben said this in order to deliver him from their hand, to bring him back to his father.

27 And when Joseph came to his brethren he sat before them, and they rose upon him and seized him and smote him to the earth, and stripped the coat of many colors which he had on.

28 And they took him and cast him into a pit, and in the pit there was no water, but serpents and scorpions. And Joseph was afraid of the serpents and scorpions that were in the pit. And Joseph cried out with a loud voice, and the Lord hid the serpents and scorpions in the sides of the pit, and they did no harm unto Joseph.

29 And Joseph called out from the pit to his brethren, and said unto them, What have I done unto you, and in what have I sinned? why do you not fear the Lord concerning me? am I not of your bones and flesh, and is not Jacob your father, my father? why do you do this thing unto me this day, and how will you be able to look up to our father Jacob?

30 And he continued to cry out and call unto his brethren from the pit, and he said, O Judah, Simeon, and Levi, my brethren, lift me up from the place of darkness in which you have placed me, and come this day to have compassion on me, ye children of the Lord, and sons of Jacob my father. And if I have sinned unto you, are you not the sons of Abraham, Isaac, and Jacob? if they saw an orphan they had compassion over him, or one that was hungry, they gave him bread to eat, or one that was thirsty, they gave him water to drink, or one that was naked, they covered him with garments!

31 And how then will you withhold your pity from your brother, for I am of your flesh and bones, and if I have sinned unto you, surely you will do this on account of my father!

32 And Joseph spoke these words from the pit, and his brethren could not listen to him, nor incline their ears to the words of Joseph, and Joseph was crying and weeping in the pit.

33 And Joseph said, O that my father knew, this day, the act which my brothers have done unto me, and the words which they have this day spoken unto me.

34 And all his brethren heard his cries and weeping in the pit, and his brethren went and removed themselves from the pit, so that they might not hear the cries of Joseph and his weeping in the pit.

Chapter 42

1 And they went and sat on the opposite side, about the distance of a bow-shot, and they sat there to eat bread, and whilst they were eating, they held counsel together what was to be done with him, whether to slay him or to bring him back to his father.

2 They were holding the counsel, when they lifted up their eyes, and saw, and behold there was a company of Ishmaelites coming at a distance by the road of Gilead, going down to Egypt.

3 And Judah said unto them, What gain will it be to us if we slay our brother? peradventure God will require him from us; this then is the counsel proposed concerning him, which you shall do unto him: Behold this company of Ishmaelites going down to Egypt,

4 Now therefore, come let us dispose of him to them, and let not our hand be upon him, and they will lead him along with them, and he will be lost amongst the people of the land, and we will not put him to death with our own hands. And the proposal pleased his brethren and they did according to the word of Judah.

5 And whilst they were discoursing about this matter, and before the company of Ishmaelites had come up to them, seven trading men of Midian passed by them, and as they passed they were thirsty, and they lifted up their eyes and saw the pit in which Joseph was immured, and they looked, and behold every species of bird was upon him.

6 And these Midianites ran to the pit to drink water, for they thought that it contained water, and on coming before the pit they heard the voice of Joseph crying and weeping in the pit, and they looked down into the pit, and they saw and behold there was a youth of comely appearance and well favored.

7 And they called unto him and said, Who art thou and who brought thee hither, and who placed thee in this pit, in the wilderness? and they all assisted to raise up Joseph and they drew him out, and brought him up from the pit, and took him and went away on their journey and passed by his brethren.

8 And these said unto them, Why do you do this, to take our servant from us and to go away? surely we placed this youth in the pit because he rebelled against us, and you come and bring him up and lead him away; now then give us back our servant.

9 And the Midianites answered and said unto the sons of Jacob, Is this your servant, or does this man attend you? peradventure you are all his servants, for he is more comely and well favored than any of you, and why do you all speak falsely unto us?

10 Now therefore we will not listen to your words, nor attend to you, for we found the youth in the pit in the wilderness, and we took him; we will therefore go on.

11 And all the sons of Jacob approached them and rose up to them and said unto them, Give us back our servant, and why will you all die by the edge of the sword? And the Midianites cried out against them, and they drew their swords, and approached to fight with the sons of Jacob.

12 And behold Simeon rose up from his seat against them, and sprang upon the ground and drew his sword and approached the Midianites and he gave a terrible shout before them, so that his shouting was heard at a distance, and the earth shook at Simeon's shouting.

13 And the Midianites were terrified on account of Simeon and the noise of his shouting, and they fell upon their faces, and were excessively alarmed.

14 And Simeon said unto them, Verily I am Simeon, the son of Jacob the Hebrew, who have, only with my brother, destroyed the city of Shechem and the cities of the Amorites; so shall God moreover do unto me, that if all your brethren the people of Midian, and also the kings of Canaan, were to come with you, they could not fight against me.

15 Now therefore give us back the youth whom you have taken, lest I give your flesh to the birds of the skies and the beasts of the earth.

16 And the Midianites were more afraid of Simeon, and they approached the sons of Jacob with terror and fright, and with pathetic words, saying,

17 Surely you have said that the young man is your servant, and that he rebelled against you, and therefore you placed him in the pit; what then will you do with a servant who rebels against his master? Now therefore sell him unto us, and we will give you all that you require for him; and the Lord was pleased to do this in order that the sons of Jacob should not slay their brother.

18 And the Midianites saw that Joseph was of a comely appearance and well-favored; they desired him in their hearts and were urgent to purchase him from his brethren.

19 And the sons of Jacob hearkened to the Midianites and they sold their brother Joseph to them for twenty pieces of silver, and Reuben their brother was not with them, and the Midianites took Joseph and continued their journey to Gilead.

20 They were going along the road, and the Midianites repented of what they had done, in having purchased the young man, and one said to the other, What is this thing that we have done, in taking this youth from the Hebrews, who is of comely appearance and well favored.

21 Perhaps this youth is stolen from the land of the Hebrews, and why then have we done this thing? and if he should be sought for and found in our hands we shall die through him.

22 Now surely hardy and powerful men have sold him to us, the strength of one of whom you saw this day; perhaps they stole him from his land with their might and with their powerful arm, and have therefore sold him to us for the small value which we gave unto them.

23 And whilst they were thus discoursing together, they looked, and behold the company of Ishmaelites which was coming at first, and which the sons of Jacob saw, was advancing toward the Midianites, and the Midianites said to each other, Come let us sell this youth to the company of Ishmaelites who are coming toward us, and we will take for him the little that we gave for him, and we will be delivered from his evil.

24 And they did so, and they reached the Ishmaelites, and the Midianites sold Joseph to the Ishmaelites for twenty pieces of silver which they had given for him to his brethren.

25 And the Midianites went on their road to Gilead, and the Ishmaelites took Joseph and they let him ride upon one of the camels, and they were leading him to Egypt.

26 And Joseph heard that the Ishmaelites were proceeding to Egypt, and Joseph lamented and wept at this thing that he was to be so far removed from the land of Canaan, from his father, and he wept bitterly whilst he was riding upon the camel, and one of their men observed him, and made him go down from the camel and walk on foot, and notwithstanding this Joseph continued to cry and weep, and he said, O my father, my father.

27 And one of the Ishmaelites rose up and smote Joseph upon the cheek, and still he continued to weep; and Joseph was fatigued in the road, and was unable to proceed on account of the bitterness of his soul, and they all smote him and afflicted him in the road, and they terrified him in order that he might cease from weeping.

28 And the Lord saw the ambition of Joseph and his trouble, and the Lord brought down upon those men

darkness and confusion, and the hand of every one that smote him became withered.

29 And they said to each other, What is this thing that God has done to us in the road? and they knew not that this befell them on account of Joseph. And the men proceeded on the road, and they passed along the road of Ephrath where Rachel was buried.

30 And Joseph reached his mother's grave, and Joseph hastened and ran to his mother's grave, and fell upon the grave and wept.

31 And Joseph cried aloud upon his mother's grave, and he said, O my mother, my mother, O thou who didst give me birth, awake now, and rise and see thy son, how he has been sold for a slave, and no one to pity him.

32 O rise and see thy son, weep with me on account of my troubles, and see the heart of my brethren.

33 Arouse my mother, arouse, awake from thy sleep for me, and direct thy battles against my brethren. O how have they stripped me of my coat, and sold me already twice for a slave, and separated me from my father, and there is no one to pity me.

34 Arouse and lay thy cause against them before God, and see whom God will justify in the judgment, and whom he will condemn.

35 Rise, O my mother, rise, awake from thy sleep and see my father how his soul is with me this day, and comfort him and ease his heart.

36 And Joseph continued to speak these words, and Joseph cried aloud and wept bitterly upon his mother's grave; and he ceased speaking, and from bitterness of heart he became still as a stone upon the grave.

37 And Joseph heard a voice speaking to him from beneath the ground, which answered him with bitterness of heart, and with a voice of weeping and praying in these words:

38 My son, my son Joseph, I have heard the voice of thy weeping and the voice of thy lamentation; I have seen thy tears; I know thy troubles, my son, and it grieves me for thy sake, and abundant grief is added to my grief.

39 Now therefore my son, Joseph my son, hope to the Lord, and wait for him and do not fear, for the Lord is with thee, he will deliver thee from all trouble.

40 Rise my son, go down unto Egypt with thy masters, and do not fear, for the Lord is with thee, my son. And she continued to speak like unto these words unto Joseph, and she was still.

41 And Joseph heard this, and he wondered greatly at this, and he continued to weep; and after this one of the Ishmaelites observed him crying and weeping upon the grave, and his anger was kindled against him, and he drove him from there, and he smote him and cursed him.

42 And Joseph said unto the men, May I find grace in your sight to take me back to my father's house, and he will give you abundance of riches.

43 And they answered him, saying, Art thou not a slave, and where is thy father? and if thou hadst a father thou wouldst not already twice have been sold for a slave for so little value; and their anger was still roused against him, and they continued to smite him and to chastise him, and Joseph wept bitterly.

44 And the Lord saw Joseph's affliction, and Lord again smote these men, and chastised them, and the Lord caused darkness to envelope them upon the earth, and the lightning flashed and the thunder roared, and the earth shook at the voice of the thunder and of the mighty wind, and the men were terrified and knew not where they should go.

45 And the beasts and camels stood still, and they led them, but they would not go, they smote them, and they crouched upon the ground; and the men said to each other, What is this that God has done to us? what are our transgressions, and what are our sins that this thing has thus befallen us?

46 And one of them answered and said unto them, Perhaps on account of the sin of afflicting this slave has this thing happened this day to us; now therefore implore him strongly to forgive us, and then we shall know on whose account this evil befalleth us, and if God shall have compassion over us, then we shall know that all this cometh to us on account of the sin of afflicting this slave.

47 And the men did so, and they supplicated Joseph and pressed him to forgive them; and they said, We have sinned to the Lord and to thee, now therefore vouchsafe to request of thy God that he shall put away this death from amongst us, for we have sinned to him.

48 And Joseph did according to their words, and the Lord hearkened to Joseph, and the Lord put away the plague which he had inflicted upon those men on account of Joseph, and the beasts rose up from the ground and they conducted them, and they went on, and the raging storm abated and the earth became tranquilized, and the men proceeded on their journey to go down to Egypt, and the men knew that this evil had befallen them on account of Joseph.

49 And they said to each other, Behold we know that it was on account of his affliction that this evil befell us; now therefore why shall we bring this death upon our souls? Let us hold counsel what to do to this slave.

50 And one answered and said, Surely he told us to bring him back to his father; now therefore come, let us take him back and we will go to the place that he will tell us, and take from his family the price that we gave for him and we will then go away.

51 And one answered again and said, Behold this counsel is very good, but we cannot do so for the way is very far from us, and we cannot go out of our road.

52 And one more answered and said unto them, This is the counsel to be adopted, we will not swerve from it; behold we are this day going to Egypt, and when we shall have come to Egypt, we will sell him there at a high price, and we will be delivered from his evil.

53 And this thing pleased the men and they did so, and they continued their journey to Egypt with Joseph.

Chapter 43

1 And when the sons of Jacob had sold their brother Joseph to the Midianites, their hearts were smitten on account of him, and they repented of their acts, and they sought for him to bring him back, but could not find him.

2 And Reuben returned to the pit in which Joseph had been put, in order to lift him out, and restore him to his father, and Reuben stood by the pit, and he heard not a word, and he called out Joseph! Joseph! and no one answered or uttered a word.

3 And Reuben said, Joseph has died through fright, or some serpent has caused his death; and Reuben descended into the pit, and he searched for Joseph and could not find him in the pit, and he came out again.

4 And Reuben tore his garments and he said, The child is not there, and how shall I reconcile my father about him if he be dead? and he went to his brethren and found them grieving on account of Joseph, and counseling together how to reconcile their father about him, and Reuben said unto his brethren, I came to the pit and behold Joseph was not there, what then shall we say unto our father, for my father will only seek the lad from me.

5 And his brethren answered him saying, Thus and thus we did, and our hearts afterward smote us on account of this act, and we now sit to seek a pretext how we shall reconcile our father to it.

6 And Reuben said unto them, What is this you have done to bring down the grey hairs of our father in sorrow to the grave? the thing is not good, that you have done.

7 And Reuben sat with them, and they all rose up and swore to each other not to tell this thing unto Jacob, and they all said, The man who will tell this to our father or his household, or who will report this to any of the children of the land, we will all rise up against him and slay him with the sword.

8 And the sons of Jacob feared each other in this matter, from the youngest to the oldest, and no one spoke a word, and they concealed the thing in their hearts.

9 And they afterward sat down to determine and invent something to say unto their father Jacob concerning all these things.

10 And Issachar said unto them, Here is an advice for you if it seem good in your eyes to do this thing, take the coat which belongeth to Joseph and tear it, and kill a kid of the goats and dip it in its blood.

11 And send it to our father and when he seeth it he will say an evil beast has devoured him, therefore tear ye his coat and behold his blood will be upon his coat, and by your doing this we shall be free of our father's murmurings.

12 And Issachar's advice pleased them, and they hearkened unto him and they did according to the word of Issachar which he had counselled them.

13 And they hastened and took Joseph's coat and tore it, and they killed a kid of the goats and dipped the coat in the blood of the kid, and then trampled it in the dust, and they sent the coat to their father Jacob by the hand of Naphtali, and they commanded him to say these words:

14 We had gathered in the cattle and had come as far as the road to Shechem and farther, when we found this coat upon the road in the wilderness dipped in blood and in dust; now therefore know whether it be thy son's coat or not.

15 And Naphtali went and he came unto his father and he gave him the coat, and he spoke unto him all the words which his brethren had commanded him.

16 And Jacob saw Joseph's coat and he knew it and he fell upon his face to the ground, and became as still as a stone, and he afterward rose up and cried out with a loud and weeping voice and he said, It is the coat of my son Joseph!

17 And Jacob hastened and sent one of his servants to his sons, who went to them and found them coming along the road with the flock.

18 And the sons of Jacob came to their father about evening, and behold their garments were torn and dust was upon their heads, and they found their father crying out and weeping with a loud voice.

19 And Jacob said unto his sons, Tell me truly what evil have you this day suddenly brought upon me? and they answered their father Jacob, saying, We were coming along this day after the flock had been gathered in, and we came as far as the city of Shechem by the road in the wilderness, and we found this coat filled with blood upon the ground, and we knew it and we sent unto thee if thou couldst know it.

20 And Jacob heard the words of his sons and he cried out with a loud voice, and he said, It is the coat of my son, an

evil beast has devoured him; Joseph is rent in pieces, for I sent him this day to see whether it was well with you and well with the flocks and to bring me word again from you, and he went as I commanded him, and this has happened to him this day whilst I thought my son was with you.

21 And the sons of Jacob answered and said, He did not come to us, neither have we seen him from the time of our going out from thee until now.

22 And when Jacob heard their words he again cried out aloud, and he rose up and tore his garments, and he put sackcloth upon his loins, and he wept bitterly and he mourned and lifted up his voice in weeping and exclaimed and said these words,

23 Joseph my son, O my son Joseph, I sent thee this day after the welfare of thy brethren, and behold thou hast been torn in pieces; through my hand has this happened to my son.

24 It grieves me for thee Joseph my son, it grieves me for thee; how sweet wast thou to me during life, and now how exceedingly bitter is thy death to me.

25 0 that I had died in thy stead Joseph my son, for it grieves me sadly for thee my son, O my son, my son. Joseph my son, where art thou, and where hast thou been drawn? arouse, arouse from thy place, and come and see my grief for thee, O my son Joseph.

26 Come now and number the tears gushing from my eyes down my cheeks, and bring them up before the Lord, that his anger may turn from me.

27 0 Joseph my son, how didst thou fall, by the hand of one by whom no one had fallen from the beginning of the world unto this day; for thou hast been put to death by the smiting of an enemy, inflicted with cruelty, but surely I know that this has happened to thee, on account of the multitude of my sins.

28 Arouse now and see how bitter is my trouble for thee my son, although I did not rear thee, nor fashion thee, nor give thee breath and soul, but it was God who formed thee and built thy bones and covered them with flesh, and breathed in thy nostrils the breath of life, and then he gave thee unto me.

29 Now truly God who gave thee unto me, he has taken thee from me, and such then has befallen thee

30 And Jacob continued to speak like unto these words concerning Joseph, and he wept bitterly; he fell to the ground and became still.

31 And all the sons of Jacob seeing their father's trouble, they repented of what they had done, and they also wept bitterly.

32 And Judah rose up and lifted his father's head from the ground, and placed it upon his lap, and he wiped his father's tears from his cheeks, and Judah wept an exceeding great weeping, whilst his father's head was reclining upon his lap, still as a stone.

33 And the sons of Jacob saw their father's trouble, and they lifted up their voices and continued to weep, and Jacob was yet lying upon the ground still as a stone.

34 And all his sons and his servants and his servant's children rose up and stood round him to comfort him, and he refused to be comforted.

35 And the whole household of Jacob rose up and mourned a great mourning on account of Joseph and their father's trouble, and the intelligence reached Isaac, the son of Abraham, the father of Jacob, and he wept bitterly on account of Joseph, he and all his household, and he went from the place where he dwelt in Hebron, and his men with him, and he comforted Jacob his son, and he refused to be comforted.

36 And after this, Jacob rose up from the ground, and his tears were running down his cheeks, and he said unto his sons, Rise up and take your swords and your bows, and go forth into the field, and seek whether you can find my son's body and bring it unto me that I may bury it.

37 Seek also, I pray you, among the beasts and hunt them, and that which shall come the first before you seize and bring it unto me, perhaps the Lord will this day pity my affliction, and prepare before you that which did tear my son in pieces, and bring it unto me, and I will avenge the cause of my son.

38 And his sons did as their father had commanded them, and they rose up early in the morning, and each took his sword and his bow in his hand, and they went forth into the field to hunt the beasts.

39 And Jacob was still crying aloud and weeping and walking to and fro in the house, and smiting his hands together, saying, Joseph my son, Joseph my son.

40 And the sons of Jacob went into the wilderness to seize the beasts, and behold a wolf came toward them, and they seized him, and brought him unto their father, and they said unto him, This is the first we have found, and we have brought him unto thee as thou didst command us, and thy son's body we could not find.

41 And Jacob took the beast from the hands of his sons, and he cried out with a loud and weeping voice, holding the beast in his hand, and he spoke with a bitter heart unto the beast, Why didst thou devour my son Joseph, and how didst thou have no fear of the God of the earth, or of my trouble for my son Joseph?

42 And thou didst devour my son for naught, because he committed no violence, and didst thereby render me culpable on his account, therefore God will require him that is persecuted.

43 And the Lord opened the mouth of the beast in order to comfort Jacob with its words, and it answered Jacob and spoke these words unto him,

44 As God liveth who created us in the earth, and as thy soul liveth, my lord, I did not see thy son, neither did I tear him to pieces, but from a distant land I also came to seek my son who went from me this day, and I know not whether he be living or dead.

45 And I came this day into the field to seek my son, and your sons found me, and seized me and increased my grief, and have this day brought me before thee, and I have now spoken all my words to thee.

46 And now therefore, O son of man, I am in thy hands, and do unto me this day as it may seem good in thy sight, but by the life of God who created me, I did not see thy son, nor did I tear him to pieces, neither has the flesh of man entered my mouth all the days of my life.

47 And when Jacob heard the words of the beast he was greatly astonished, and sent forth the beast from his hand, and she went her way.

48 And Jacob was still crying aloud and weeping for Joseph day after day, and he mourned for his son many days.

Chapter 44

1 And the sons of Ishmael who had bought Joseph from the Midianites, who had bought him from his brethren, went to Egypt with Joseph, and they came upon the borders of Egypt, and when they came near unto Egypt, they met four men of the sons of Medan the son of Abraham, who had gone forth from the land of Egypt on their journey.

2 And the Ishmaelites said unto them, Do you desire to purchase this slave from us? and they said, Deliver him over to us, and they delivered Joseph over to them, and they beheld him, that he was a very comely youth and they purchased him for twenty shekels.

3 And the Ishmaelites continued their journey to Egypt and the Medanim also returned that day to Egypt, and the Medanim said to each other, Behold we have heard that Potiphar, an officer of Pharaoh, captain of the guard, seeketh a good servant who shall stand before him to attend him, and to make him overseer over his house and all belonging to him.

4 Now therefore come let us sell him to him for what we may desire, if he be able to give unto us that which we shall require for him.

5 And these Medanim went and came to the house of Potiphar, and said unto him, We have heard that thou seekest a good servant to attend thee, behold we have a servant that will please thee, if thou canst give unto us that which we may desire, and we will sell him unto thee.

6 And Potiphar said, Bring him before me, and I will see him, and if he please me I will give unto you that which you may require for him.

7 And the Medanim went and brought Joseph and placed him before Potiphar, and he saw him, and he pleased him exceedingly, and Potiphar said unto them, Tell me what you require for this youth?

8 And they said, Four hundred pieces of silver we desire for him, and Potiphar said, I will give it you if you bring me the record of his sale to you, and will tell me his history, for perhaps he may be stolen, for this youth is neither a slave, nor the son of a slave, but I observe in him the appearance of a goodly and handsome person.

9 And the Medanim went and brought unto him the Ishmaelites who had sold him to them, and they told him, saying, He is a slave and we sold him to them.

10 And Potiphar heard the words of the Ishmaelites in his giving the silver unto the Medanim, and the Medanim took the silver and went on their journey, and the Ishmaelites also returned home.

11 And Potiphar took Joseph and brought him to his house that he might serve him, and Joseph found favor in the sight of Potiphar, and he placed confidence in him, and made him overseer over his house, and all that belonged to him he delivered over into his hand.

12 And the Lord was with Joseph and he became a prosperous man, and the Lord blessed the house of Potiphar for the sake of Joseph.

13 And Potiphar left all that he had in the hand of Joseph, and Joseph was one that caused things to come in and go out, and everything was regulated by his wish in the house of Potiphar.

14 And Joseph was eighteen years old, a youth with beautiful eyes and of comely appearance, and like unto him was not in the whole land of Egypt.

15 At that time whilst he was in his master's house, going in and out of the house and attending his master, Zelicah, his master's wife, lifted up her eyes toward Joseph and she looked at him, and behold he was a youth comely and well favored.

16 And she coveted his beauty in her heart, and her soul was fixed upon Joseph, and she enticed him day after day, and Zelicah persuaded Joseph daily, but Joseph did not lift up his eyes to behold his master's wife.

17 And Zelicah said unto him, How goodly are thy appearance and form, truly I have looked at all the slaves, and have not seen so beautiful a slave as thou art; and Joseph said unto her, Surely he who created me in my mother's womb created all mankind.

18 And she said unto him, How beautiful are thine eyes, with which thou hast dazzled all the inhabitants of Egypt, men and women; and he said unto her, How beautiful they are whilst we are alive, but shouldst thou behold them in the grave, surely thou wouldst move away from them.

19 And she said unto him, How beautiful and pleasing are all thy words; take now, I pray thee, the harp which is in the house, and play with thy hands and let us hear thy words.

20 And he said unto her, How beautiful and pleasing are my words when I speak the praise of my God and his glory; and she said unto him, How very beautiful is the hair of thy head, behold the golden comb which is in the house, take it I pray thee, and curl the hair of thy head.

21 And he said unto her, How long wilt thou speak these words? cease to utter these words to me, and rise and attend to thy domestic affairs.

22 And she said unto him, There is no one in my house, and there is nothing to attend to but to thy words and to thy wish; yet notwithstanding all this, she could not bring Joseph unto her, neither did he place his eye upon her, but directed his eyes below to the ground.

23 And Zelicah desired Joseph in her heart, that he should lie with her, and at the time that Joseph was sitting in the house doing his work, Zelicah came and sat before him, and she enticed him daily with her discourse to lie with her, or ever to look at her, but Joseph would not hearken to her.

24 And she said unto him, If thou wilt not do according to my words, I will chastise thee with the punishment of death, and put an iron yoke upon thee.

25 And Joseph said unto her, Surely God who created man looseth the fetters of prisoners, and it is he who will deliver me from thy prison and from thy judgment.

26 And when she could not prevail over him, to persuade him, and her soul being still fixed upon him, her desire threw her into a grievous sickness.

27 And all the women of Egypt came to visit her, and they said unto her, Why art thou in this declining state? thou that lackest nothing; surely thy husband is a great and esteemed prince in the sight of the king, shouldst thou lack anything of what thy heart desireth?

28 And Zelicah answered them, saying, This day it shall be made known to you, whence this disorder springs in which you see me, and she commanded her maid servants to prepare food for all the women, and she made a banquet for them, and all the women ate in the house of Zelicah.

29 And she gave them knives to peel the citrons to eat them, and she commanded that they should dress Joseph in costly garments, and that he should appear before them, and Joseph came before their eyes and all the women looked on Joseph, and could not take their eyes from off him, and they all cut their hands with the knives that they had in their hands, and all the citrons that were in their hands were filled with blood.

30 And they knew not what they had done but they continued to look at the beauty of Joseph, and did not turn their eyelids from him.

31 And Zelicah saw what they had done, and she said unto them, What is this work that you have done? behold I gave you citrons to eat and you have all cut your hands.

32 And all the women saw their hands, and behold they were full of blood, and their blood flowed down upon their garments, and they said unto her, this slave in your house has overcome us, and we could not turn our eyelids from

him on account of his beauty.

33 And she said unto them, Surely this happened to you in the moment that you looked at him, and you could not contain yourselves from him; how then can I refrain when he is constantly in my house, and I see him day after day going in and out of my house? how then can I keep from declining or even from perishing on account of this?

34 And they said unto her, the words are true, for who can see this beautiful form in the house and refrain from him, and is he not thy slave and attendant in thy house, and why dost thou not tell him that which is in thy heart, and sufferest thy soul to perish through this matter?

35 And she said unto them, I am daily endeavoring to persuade him, and he will not consent to my wishes, and I promised him everything that is good, and yet I could meet with no return from him; I am therefore in a declining state as you see.

36 And Zelicah became very ill on account of her desire toward Joseph, and she was desperately lovesick on account of him, and all the people of the house of Zelicah and her husband knew nothing of this matter, that Zelicah was ill on account of her love to Joseph.

37 And all the people of her house asked her, saying, Why art thou ill and declining, and lackest nothing? and she said unto them, I know not this thing which is daily increasing upon me.

38 And all the women and her friends came daily to see her, and they spoke with her, and she said unto them, This can only be through the love of Joseph; and they said unto her, Entice him and seize him secretly, perhaps he may hearken to thee, and put off this death from thee.

39 And Zelicah became worse from her love to Joseph, and she continued to decline, till she had scarce strength to stand.

40 And on a certain day Joseph was doing his master's work in the house, and Zelicah came secretly and fell suddenly upon him, and Joseph rose up against her, and he was more powerful than she, and he brought her down to the ground.

41 And Zelicah wept on account of the desire of her heart toward him, and she supplicated him with weeping, and her tears flowed down her cheeks, and she spoke unto him in a voice of supplication and in bitterness of soul, saying,

42 Hast thou ever heard, seen or known of so beautiful a woman as I am, or better than myself, who speak daily unto thee, fall into a decline through love for thee, confer all this honor upon thee, and still thou wilt not hearken to my voice?

43 And if it be through fear of thy master lest he punish thee, as the king liveth no harm shall come to thee from thy master through this thing; now, therefore pray listen to me, and consent for the sake of the honor which I have conferred upon thee, and put off this death from me, and why should I die for thy sake? and she ceased to speak.

44 And Joseph answered her, saying, Refrain from me, and leave this matter to my master; behold my master knoweth not what there is with me in the house, for all that belongeth to him he has delivered into my hand, and how shall I do these things in my master's house?

45 For he hath also greatly honored me in his house, and he hath also made me overseer over his house, and he hath exalted me, and there is no one greater in this house than I am, and my master hath refrained nothing from me, excepting thee who art his wife, how then canst thou speak these words unto me, and how can I do this great evil and sin to God and to thy husband?

46 Now therefore refrain from me, and speak no more such words as these, for I will not hearken to thy words. But Zelicah would not hearken to Joseph when he spoke these words unto her, but she daily enticed him to listen to her.

47 And it was after this that the brook of Egypt was filled above all its sides, and all the inhabitants of Egypt went forth, and also the king and princes went forth with timbrels and dances, for it was a great rejoicing in Egypt, and a holiday at the time of the inundation of the sea Sihor, and they went there to rejoice all the day.

48 And when the Egyptians went out to the river to rejoice, as was their custom, all the people of the house of Potiphar went with them, but Zelicah would not go with them, for she said, I am indisposed, and she remained alone in the house, and no other person was with her in the house.

49 And she rose up and ascended to her temple in the house, and dressed herself in princely garments, and she placed upon her head precious stones of onyx stones, inlaid with silver and gold, and she beautified her face and skin with all sorts of women's purifying liquids, and she perfumed the temple and the house with cassia and frankincense, and she spread myrrh and aloes, and she afterward sat in the entrance of the temple, in the passage of the house, through which Joseph passed to do his work, and behold Joseph came from the field, and entered the house to do his master's work.

50 And he came to the place through which he had to pass, and he saw all the work of Zelicah, and he turned back.

51 And Zelicah saw Joseph turning back from her, and she called out to him, saying What aileth thee Joseph? come to thy work, and behold I will make room for thee until thou shalt have passed to thy seat.

52 And Joseph returned and came to the house, and passed from thence to the place of his seat, and he sat down to do his master's work as usual and behold Zelicah came to him and stood before him in princely garments, and the scent from her clothes was spread to a distance.

53 And she hastened and caught hold of Joseph and his garments, and she said unto him, As the king liveth if thou wilt not perform my request thou shalt die this day, and she hastened and stretched forth her other hand and drew a sword from beneath her garments, and she placed it upon Joseph's neck, and she said, Rise and perform my request, and if not thou diest this day.

54 And Joseph was afraid of her at her doing this thing, and he rose up to flee from her, and she seized the front of his garments, and in the terror of his flight the garment which Zelicah seized was torn, and Joseph left the garment in the hand of Zelicah, and he fled and got out, for he was in fear.

55 And when Zelicah saw that Joseph's garment was torn, and that he had left it in her hand, and had fled, she was afraid of her life, lest the report should spread concerning her, and she rose up and acted with cunning, and put off the garments in which she was dressed, and she put on her other garments.

56 And she took Joseph's garment, and she laid it beside her, and she went and seated herself in the place where she had sat in her illness, before the people of her house had gone out to the river, and she called a young lad who was then in the house, and she ordered him to call the people of the house to her.

57 And when she saw them she said unto them with a loud voice and lamentation, See what a Hebrew your master has brought to me in the house, for he came this day to lie with me.

58 For when you had gone out he came to the house, and seeing that there was no person in the house, he came unto me, and caught hold of me, with intent to lie with me.

59 And I seized his garments and tore them and called out against him with a loud voice, and when I had lifted up my voice he was afraid of his life and left his garment before me, and fled.

60 And the people of her house spoke nothing, but their wrath was very much kindled against Joseph, and they went to his master and told him the words of his wife.

61 And Potiphar came home enraged, and his wife cried out to him, saying, What is this thing that thou hast done unto me in bringing a He. brew servant into my house, for he came unto me this day to sport with me; thus did he do unto me this day.

62 And Potiphar heard the words of his wife, and he ordered Joseph to be punished with severe stripes, and they did so to him.

63 And whilst they were smiting him, Joseph called out with a loud voice, and he lifted up his eyes to heaven, and he said, O Lord God, thou knowest that I am innocent of all these things, and why shall I die this day through falsehood, by the hand of these uncircumcised wicked men, whom thou knowest?

64 And whilst Potiphar's men were beating Joseph, he continued to cry out and weep, and there was a child there eleven months old, and the Lord opened the mouth of the child, and he spake these words before Potiphar's men, who were smiting Joseph, saying,

65 What do you want of this man, and why do you do this evil unto him? my mother speaketh falsely and uttereth lies; thus was the transaction.

66 And the child told them accurately all that happened, and all the words of Zelicah to Joseph day after day did he declare unto them.

67 And all the men heard the words of the child and they wondered greatly at the child's words, and the child ceased to speak and became still.

68 And Potiphar was very much ashamed at the words of his son, and he commanded his men not to beat Joseph any more, and the men ceased beating Joseph.

69 And Potiphar took Joseph and ordered him to be brought to justice before the priests, who were judges belonging to the king, in order to judge him concerning this affair.

70 And Potiphar and Joseph came before the priests who were the king's judges, and he said unto them, Decide I pray you, what judgment is due to a servant, for thus has he done.

71 And the priests said unto Joseph, Why didst thou do this thing to thy master? and Joseph answered them, saying, Not so my lords, thus was the matter; and Potiphar said unto Joseph, Surely I entrusted in thy hands all that belonged to me, and I withheld nothing from thee but my wife, and how couldst thou do this evil?

72 And Joseph answered saying, Not so my lord, as the Lord liveth, and as thy soul liveth, my lord, the word which thou didst hear from thy wife is untrue, for thus was the affair this day.

73 A year has elapsed to me since I have been in thy house; hast thou seen any iniquity in me, or any thing which might cause thee to demand my life?

74 And the priests said unto Potiphar, Send, we pray thee, and let them bring before us Joseph's torn garment, and let us see the tear in it, and if it shall be that the tear is in front of the garment, then his face must have been opposite to her and she must have caught hold of him, to come to her, and with deceit did thy wife do all that she has spoken.

75 And they brought Joseph's garment before the priests who were judges, and they saw and behold the tear was in front of Joseph, and all the judging priests knew that she had pressed him, and they said, The judgment of death is not due to this slave for he has done nothing, but his judgment is, that he be placed in the prison house on account of the report, which through him has gone forth against thy wife.

76 And Potiphar heard their words, and he placed him in the prison house, the place where the king's prisoners are confined, and Joseph was in the house of confinement twelve years.

77 And notwithstanding this, his master's wife did not turn from him, and she did not cease from speaking to him day after day to hearken to her, and at the end of three months Zelicah continued going to Joseph to the house of confinement day by day, and she enticed him to hearken to her, and Zelicah said unto Joseph, How long wilt thou remain in this house? but hearken now to my voice, and I will bring thee out of this house.

78 And Joseph answered her, saying, It is better for me to remain in this house than to hearken to thy words, to sin against God; and she said unto him, If thou wilt not perform my wish, I will pluck out thine eyes, add fetters to thy feet, and will deliver thee into the hands of them whom thou didst not know before.

79 And Joseph answered her and said, Behold the God of the whole earth is able to deliver me from all that thou canst do unto me, for he openeth the eyes of the blind, and looseth those that are bound, and preserveth all strangers who are unacquainted with the land.

80 And when Zelicah was unable to persuade Joseph to hearken to her, she left off going to entice him; and Joseph was still confined in the house of confinement. And Jacob the father of Joseph, and all his brethren who were in the land of Canaan still mourned and wept in those days on account of Joseph, for Jacob refused to be comforted for his son Joseph, and Jacob cried aloud, and wept and mourned all those days.

Chapter 45

1 And it was at that time in that year, which is the year of Joseph's going down to Egypt after his brothers had sold him, that Reuben the son of Jacob went to Timnah and took unto him for a wife Eliuram, the daughter of Avi the Canaanite, and he came to her.

2 And Eliuram the wife of Reuben conceived and bare him Hanoch, Palu, Chetzron and Carmi, four sons; and Simeon his brother took his sister Dinah for a wife, and she bare unto him Memuel, Yamin, Ohad, Jachin and Zochar, five sons.

3 And he afterward came to Bunah the Canaanitish woman, the same is Bunah whom Simeon took captive from the city of Shechem, and Bunah was before Dinah and attended upon her, and Simeon came to her, and she bare unto him Saul.

4 And Judah went at that time to Adulam, and he came to a man of Adulam, and his name was Hirah, and Judah saw there the daughter of a man from Canaan, and her name was Aliyath, the daughter of Shua, and he took her, and came to her, and Aliyath bare unto Judah, Er, Onan and Shiloh; three sons.

5 And Levi and Issachar went to the land of the east, and they took unto themselves for wives the daughters of Jobab the son of Yoktan, the son of Eber; and Jobab the son of

Yoktan had two daughters; the name of the elder was Adinah, and the name of the younger was Aridah.

6 And Levi took Adinah, and Issachar took Aridah, and they came to the land of Canaan, to their father's house, and Adinah bare unto Levi, Gershon, Kehath and Merari; three sons.

7 And Aridah bare unto Issachar Tola, Puvah, Job and Shomron, four sons; and Dan went to the land of Moab and took for a wife Aphlaleth, the daughter of Chamudan the Moabite, and he brought her to the land of Canaan.

8 And Aphlaleth was barren, she had no offspring, and God afterward remembered Aphlaleth the wife of Dan, and she conceived and bare a son, and she called his name Chushim.

9 And Gad and Naphtali went to Haran and took from thence the daughters of Amuram the son of Uz, the son of Nahor, for wives.

10 And these are the names of the daughters of Amuram; the name of the elder was Merimah, and the name of the younger Uzith; and Naphtali took Merimah, and Gad took Uzith; and brought them to the land of Canaan, to their father's house.

11 And Merimah bare unto Naphtali Yachzeel, Guni, Jazer and Shalem, four sons; and Uzith bare unto Gad Zephion, Chagi, Shuni, Ezbon, Eri, Arodi and Arali, seven sons.

12 And Asher went forth and took Adon the daughter of Aphlal, the son of Hadad, the son of Ishmael, for a wife, and he brought her to the land of Canaan.

13 And Adon the wife of Asher died in those days: she had no offspring; and it was after the death of Adon that Asher went to the other side of the river and took for a wife Hadurah the daughter of Abimael, the son of Eber, the son of Shem.

14 And the young woman was of a comely appearance, and a woman of sense, and she had been the wife of Malkiel the son of Elam, the son of Shem.

15 And Hadurah bare a daughter unto Malkiel, and he called her name Serach, and Malkiel died after this, and Hadurah went and remained in her father's house.

16 And after the death of the wife at Asher he went and took Hadurah for a wife, and brought her to the land of Canaan, and Serach her daughter he also brought with them, and she was three years old, and the damsel was brought up in Jacob's house.

17 And the damsel was of a comely appearance, and she went in the sanctified ways of the children of Jacob; she lacked nothing, and the Lord gave her wisdom and understanding.

18 And Hadurah the wife of Asher conceived and bare unto him Yimnah, Yishvah, Yishvi and Beriah; four sons.

19 And Zebulun went to Midian, and took for a wife Merishah the daughter of Molad, the son of Abida, the son of Midian, and brought her to the land of Canaan.

20 And Merushah bare unto Zebulun Sered, Elon and Yachleel; three sons.

21 And Jacob sent to Aram, the son of Zoba, the son of Terah, and he took for his son Benjamin Mechalia the daughter of Aram, and she came to the land of Canaan to the house of Jacob; and Benjamin was ten years old when he took Mechalia the daughter of Aram for a wife.

22 And Mechalia conceived and bare unto Benjamin Bela, Becher, Ashbel, Gera and Naaman, five sons; and Benjamin went afterward and took for a wife Aribath, the daughter of Shomron, the son of Abraham, in addition to his first wife, and he was eighteen years old; and Aribath bare unto Benjamin Achi, Vosh, Mupim, Chupim, and Ord; five sons.

23 And in those days Judah went to the house of Shem and took Tamar the daughter of Elam, the son of Shem, for a wife for his first born Er.

24 And Er came to his wife Tamar, and she became his wife, and when he came to her he outwardly destroyed his seed, and his work was evil in the sight of the Lord, and the Lord slew him.

25 And it was after the death of Er, Judah's first born, that Judah said unto Onan, go to thy brother's wife and marry her as the next of kin, and raise up seed to thy brother.

26 And Onan took Tamar for a wife and he came to her, and Onan also did like unto the work of his brother, and his work was evil in the sight of the Lord, and he slew him also.

27 And when Onan died, Judah said unto Tamar, Remain in thy father's house until my son Shiloh shall have grown up, and Judah did no more delight in Tamar, to give her unto Shiloh, for he said, Peradventure he will also die like his brothers.

28 And Tamar rose up and went and remained in her father's house, and Tamar was in her father's house for some time.

29 And at the revolution of the year, Aliyath the wife of Judah died; and Judah was comforted for his wife, and after the death of Aliyath, Judah went up with his friend Hirah to Timnah to shear their sheep.

30 And Tamar heard that Judah had gone up to Timnah to shear the sheep, and that Shiloh was grown up, and Judah did not delight in her.

31 And Tamar rose up and put off the garments of her widowhood, and she put a vail upon her, and she entirely covered herself, and she went and sat in the public thoroughfare, which is upon the road to Timnah.

32 And Judah passed and saw her and took her and he came to her, and she conceived by him, and at the time of being delivered, behold, there were twins in her womb, and he called the name of the first Perez, and the name of the second Zarah.

Chapter 46

1 In those days Joseph was still confined in the prison house in the land of Egypt.

2 At that time the attendants of Pharaoh were standing before him, the chief of the butlers and the chief of the bakers which belonged to the king of Egypt.

3 And the butler took wine and placed it before the king to drink, and the baker placed bread before the king to eat, and the king drank of the wine and ate of the bread, he and his servants and ministers that ate at the king's table.

4 And whilst they were eating and drinking, the butler and the baker remained there, and Pharaoh's ministers found many flies in the wine, which the butler had brought, and stones of nitre were found in the baker's bread.

5 And the captain of the guard placed Joseph as an attendant on Pharaoh's officers, and Pharaoh's officers were in confinement one year.

6 And at the end of the year, they both dreamed dreams in one night, in the place of confinement where they were, and in the morning Joseph came to them to attend upon them as usual, and he saw them, and behold their countenances were dejected and sad.

7 And Joseph asked them, Why are your countenances sad and dejected this day? and they said unto him, We dreamed a dream, and there is no one to interpret it; and Joseph said unto them, Relate, I pray you, your dream unto me, and

God shall give you an answer of peace as you desire.

8 And the butler related his dream unto Joseph, and he said, I saw in my dream, and behold a large vine was before me, and upon that vine I saw three branches, and the vine speedily blossomed and reached a great height, and its clusters were ripened and became grapes.

9 And I took the grapes and pressed them in a cup, and placed it in Pharaoh's hand and he drank; and Joseph said unto him, The three branches that were upon the vine are three days.

10 Yet within three days, the king will order thee to be brought out and he will restore thee to thy office, and thou shalt give the king his wine to drink as at first when thou wast his butler; but let me find favor in thy sight, that thou shalt remember me to Pharaoh when it will be well with thee, and do kindness unto me, and get me brought forth from this prison, for I was stolen away from the land of Canaan and was sold for a slave in this place.

11 And also that which was told thee concerning my master's wife is false, for they placed me in this dungeon for naught; and the butler answered Joseph, saying, If the king deal well with me as at first, as thou last interpreted to me, I will do all that thou desirest, and get thee brought out of this dungeon.

12 And the baker, seeing that Joseph had accurately interpreted the butler's dream, also approached, and related the whole of his dream to Joseph.

13 And he said unto him, In my dream I saw and behold three white baskets upon my head, and I looked, and behold there were in the upper-most basket all manner of baked meats for Pharaoh, and behold the birds were eating them from off my head.

14 And Joseph said unto him, The three baskets which thou didst see are three days, yet within three days Pharaoh will take off thy head, and hang thee upon a tree, and the birds will eat thy flesh from off thee, as thou sawest in thy dream.

15 In those days the queen was about to be delivered, and upon that day she bare a son unto the king of Egypt, and they proclaimed that the king had gotten his first born son and all the people of Egypt together with the officers and servants of Pharaoh rejoiced greatly.

16 And upon the third day of his birth Pharaoh made a feast for his officers and servants, for the hosts of the land of Zoar and of the land of Egypt.

17 And all the people of Egypt and the servants of Pharaoh came to eat and drink with the king at the feast of his son, and to rejoice at the king's rejoicing.

18 And all the officers of the king and his servants were rejoicing at that time for eight days at the feast, and they made merry with all sorts of musical instruments, with timbrels and with dances in the king's house for eight days.

19 And the butler, to whom Joseph had interpreted his dream, forgot Joseph, and he did not mention him to the king as he had promised, for this thing was from the Lord in order to punish Joseph because he had trusted in man.

20 And Joseph remained after this in the prison house two years, until he had completed twelve years.

Chapter 47

1 And Isaac the son of Abraham was still living in those days in the land of Canaan; he was very aged, one hundred and eighty years old, and Esau his son, the brother of Jacob, was in the land of Edom, and he and his sons had possessions in it amongst the children of Seir.

2 And Esau heard that his father's time was drawing nigh to die, and he and his sons and household came unto the land of Canaan, unto his father's house, and Jacob and his sons went forth from the place where they dwelt in Hebron, and they all came to their father Isaac, and they found Esau and his sons in the tent.

3 And Jacob and his sons sat before his father Isaac, and Jacob was still mourning for his son Joseph.

4 And Isaac said unto Jacob, Bring me hither thy sons and I will bless them; and Jacob brought his eleven children before his father Isaac.

5 And Isaac placed his hands upon all the sons of Jacob, and he took hold of them and embraced them, and kissed them one by one, and Isaac blessed them on that day, and he said unto them, May the God of your fathers bless you and increase your seed like the stars of heaven for number.

6 And Isaac also blessed the sons of Esau, saying, May God cause you to be a dread and a terror to all that will behold you, and to all your enemies.

7 And Isaac called Jacob and his sons, and they all came and sat before Isaac, and Isaac said unto Jacob, The Lord God of the whole earth said unto me, Unto thy seed will I give this land for an inheritance if thy children keep my statutes and my ways, and I will perform unto them the oath which I swore unto thy father Abraham.

8 Now therefore my son, teach thy children and thy children's children to fear the Lord, and to go in the good way which will please the Lord thy God, for if you keep the ways of the Lord and his statutes the Lord will also keep unto you his covenant with Abraham, and will do well with you and your seed all the days.

9 And when Isaac had finished commanding Jacob and his children, he gave up the ghost and died, and was gathered unto his people.

10 And Jacob and Esau fell upon the face of their father Isaac, and they wept, and Isaac was one hundred and eighty years old when he died in the land of Canaan, in Hebron, and his sons carried him to the cave of Machpelah, which Abraham had bought from the children of Heth for a possession of a burial place.

11 And all the kings of the land of Canaan went with Jacob and Esau to bury Isaac, and all the kings of Canaan showed Isaac great honor at his death.

12 And the sons of Jacob and the sons of Esau went barefooted round about, walking and lamenting until they reached Kireath-arba.

13 And Jacob and Esau buried their father Isaac in the cave of Machpelah, which is in Kireath-arba in Hebron, and they buried him with very great honor, as at the funeral of kings.

14 And Jacob and his sons, and Esau and his sons, and all the kings of Canaan made a great and heavy mourning, and they buried him and mourned for him many days.

15 And at the death of Isaac, he left his cattle and his possessions and all belonging to him to his sons; and Esau said unto Jacob, Behold I pray thee, all that our father has left we will divide it in two parts, and I will have the choice, and Jacob said, We will do so.

16 And Jacob took all that Isaac had left in the land of Canaan, the cattle and the property, and he placed them in two parts before Esau and his sons, and he said unto Esau, Behold all this is before thee, choose thou unto thyself the half which thou wilt take.

17 And Jacob said unto Esau, Hear thou I pray thee what I will speak unto thee, saying, The Lord God of heaven and earth spoke unto our fathers Abraham and Isaac, saying, Unto thy seed will I give this land for an inheritance forever.

18 Now therefore all that our father has left is before thee, and behold all the land is before thee; choose thou from them what thou desirest.

19 If thou desirest the whole land take it for thee and thy children forever, and I will take this riches, and it thou desirest the riches take it unto thee, and I will take this land for me and for my children to inherit it forever.

20 And Nebayoth, the son of Ishmael, was then in the land with his children, and Esau went on that day and consulted with him, saying.

21 Thus has Jacob spoken unto me, and thus has he answered me, now give thy advice and we will hear.

22 And Nebayoth said, What is this that Jacob hath spoken unto thee? behold all the children of Canaan are dwelling securely in their land, and Jacob sayeth he will inherit it with his seed all the days.

23 Go now therefore and take all thy father's riches and leave Jacob thy brother in the land, as he has spoken.

24 And Esau rose up and returned to Jacob, and did all that Nebayoth the son of Ishmael had advised; and Esau took all the riches that Isaac had left, the souls, the beasts, the cattle and the property, and all the riches; he gave nothing to his brother Jacob; and Jacob took all the land of Canaan, from the brook of Egypt unto the river Euphrates, and he took it for an everlasting possession, and for his children and for his seed after him forever.

25 Jacob also took from his brother Esau the cave of Machpelah, which is in Hebron, which Abraham had bought from Ephron for a possession of a burial place for him and his seed forever.

26 And Jacob wrote all these things in the book of purchase, and he signed it, and he testified all this with four faithful witnesses.

27 And these are the words which Jacob wrote in the book, saying: The land of Canaan and all the cities of the Hittites, the Hivites, the Jebusites, the Amorites, the Perizzites, and the Gergashites, all the seven nations from the river of Egypt unto the river Euphrates.

28 And the city of Hebron Kireath-arba, and the cave which is in it, the whole did Jacob buy from his brother Esau for value, for a possession and for an inheritance for his seed after him forever.

29 And Jacob took the book of purchase and the signature, the command and the statutes and the revealed book, and he placed them in an earthen vessel in order that they should remain for a long time, and he delivered them into the hands of his children.

30 Esau took all that his father had left him after his death from his brother Jacob, and he took all the property, from man and beast, camel and ass, ox and lamb, silver and gold, stones and bdellium, and all the riches which had belonged to Isaac the son of Abraham; there was nothing left which Esau did not take unto himself, from all that Isaac had left after his death.

31 And Esau took all this, and he and his children went home to the land of Seir the Horite, away from his brother Jacob and his children.

32 And Esau had possessions amongst the children of Seir, and Esau returned not to the land of Canaan from that day forward.

33 And the whole land of Canaan became an inheritance to the children of Israel for an everlasting inheritance, and Esau with all his children inherited the mountain of Seir.

Chapter 48

1 In those days, after the death of Isaac, the Lord commanded and caused a famine upon the whole earth.

2 At that time Pharaoh king of Egypt was sitting upon his throne in the land of Egypt, and lay in his bed and dreamed dreams, and Pharaoh saw in his dream that he was standing by the side of the river of Egypt.

3 And whilst he was standing he saw and behold seven fat fleshed and well favored kine came up out of the river.

4 And seven other kine, lean fleshed and ill favored, came up after them, and the seven ill favored ones swallowed up the well favored ones, and still their appearance was ill as at first.

5 And he awoke, and he slept again and he dreamed a second time, and he saw and behold seven ears of corn came up upon one stalk, rank and good, and seven thin ears blasted with the east wind sprang, up after them, and the thin ears swallowed up the full ones, and Pharaoh awoke out of his dream.

6 And in the morning the king remembered his dreams, and his spirit was sadly troubled on account of his dreams, and the king hastened and sent and called for all the magicians of Egypt, and the wise men, and they came and stood before Pharaoh.

7 And the king said unto them, I have dreamed dreams, and there is none to interpret them; and they said unto the king, relate thy dreams to thy servants and let us hear them.

8 And the king related his dreams to them, and they all answered and said with one voice to the king, may the king live forever; and this is the interpretation of thy dreams.

9 The seven good kine which thou didst see denote seven daughters that will be born unto thee in the latter days, and the seven kine which thou sawest come up after them, and swallowed them up, are for a sign that the daughters which will be born unto thee will all die in the life-time of the king.

10 And that which thou didst see in the second dream of seven full good ears of corn coming up upon one stalk, this is their interpretation, that thou wilt build unto thyself in the latter days seven cities throughout the land of Egypt; and that which thou sawest of the seven blasted ears of corn springing up after them and swallowing them up whilst thou didst behold them with thine eyes, is for a sign that the cities which thou wilt build will all be destroyed in the latter days, in the life-time of the king.

11 And when they spoke these words the king did not incline his ear to their words, neither did he fix his heart upon them, for the king knew in his wisdom that they did not give a proper interpretation of the dreams; and when they had finished speaking before the king, the king answered them, saying, What is this thing that you have spoken unto me? surely you have uttered falsehood and spoken lies; therefore now give the proper interpretation of my dreams, that you may not die.

12 And the king commanded after this, and he sent and called again for other wise men, and they came and stood before the king, and the king related his dreams to them, and they all answered him according to the first interpretation, and the king's anger was kindled and he was very wroth, and the king said unto them, Surely you speak lies and utter falsehood in what you have said.

13 And the king commanded that a proclamation should be issued throughout the land of Egypt, saying, It is resolved by the king and his great men, that any wise man who knoweth and understandeth the interpretation of dreams, and will not come this day before the king, shall die.

14 And the man that will declare unto the king the proper interpretation of his dreams, there shall be given unto him

all that he will require from the king. And all the wise men of the land of Egypt came before the king, together with all the magicians and sorcerers that were in Egypt and in Goshen, in Rameses, in Tachpanches, in Zoar, and in all the places on the borders of Egypt, and they all stood before the king.

15 And all the nobles and the princes, and the attendants belonging to the king, came together from all the cities of Egypt, and they all sat before the king, and the king related his dreams before the wise men, and the princes, and all that sat before the king were astonished at the vision.

16 And all the wise men who were before the king were greatly divided in their interpretation of his dreams; some of them interpreted them to the king, saying, The seven good kine are seven kings, who from the king's issue will be raised over Egypt.

17 And the seven bad kine are seven princes, who will stand up against them in the latter days and destroy them; and the seven ears of corn are the seven great princes belonging to Egypt, who will fall in the hands of the seven less powerful princes of their enemies, in the wars of our lord the king.

18 And some of them interpreted to the king in this manner, saying, The seven good kine are the strong cities of Egypt, and the seven bad kine are the seven nations of the land of Canaan, who will come against the seven cities of Egypt in the latter days and destroy them.

19 And that which thou sawest in the second dream, of seven good and bad ears of corn, is a sign that the government of Egypt will again return to thy seed as at first.

20 And in his reign the people of the cities of Egypt will turn against the seven cities of Canaan who are stronger than they are, and will destroy them, and the government of Egypt will return to thy seed.

21 And some of them said unto the king, This is the interpretation of thy dreams; the seven good kine are seven queens, whom thou wilt take for wives in the latter days, and the seven bad kine denote that those women will all die in the lifetime of the king.

22 And the seven good and bad ears of corn which thou didst see in the second dream are fourteen children, and it will be in the latter days that they will stand up and fight amongst themselves, and seven of them will smite the seven that are more powerful.

23 And some of them said these words unto the king, saying, The seven good kine denote that seven children will be born to thee, and they will slay seven of thy children's children in the latter days; and the seven good ears of corn which thou didst see in the second dream, are those princes against whom seven other less powerful princes will fight and destroy them in the latter days, and avenge thy children's cause, and the government will again return to thy seed.

24 And the king heard all the words of the wise men of Egypt and their interpretation of his dreams, and none of them pleased the king.

25 And the king knew in his wisdom that they did not altogether speak correctly in all these words, for this was from the Lord to frustrate the words of the wise men of Egypt, in order that Joseph might go forth from the house of confinement, and in order that he should become great in Egypt.

26 And the king saw that none amongst all the wise men and magicians of Egypt spoke correctly to him, and the king's wrath was kindled, and his anger burned within him.

27 And the king commanded that all the wise men and magicians should go out from before him, and they all went out from before the king with shame and disgrace.

28 And the king commanded that a proclamation be sent throughout Egypt to slay all the magicians that were in Egypt, and not one of them should be suffered to live.

29 And the captains of the guards belonging to the king rose up, and each man drew his sword, and they began to smite the magicians of Egypt, and the wise men.

30 And after this Merod, chief butler to the king, came and bowed down before the king and sat before him.

31 And the butler said unto the king, May the king live forever, and his government be exalted in the land.

32 Thou wast angry with thy servant in those days, now two years past, and didst place me in the ward, and I was for some time in the ward, I and the chief of the bakers.

33 And there was with us a Hebrew servant belonging to the captain of the guard, his name was Joseph, for his master had been angry with him and placed him in the house of confinement, and he attended us there.

34 And in some time after when we were in the ward, we dreamed dreams in one night, I and the chief of the bakers; we dreamed, each man according to the interpretation of his dream.

35 And we came in the morning and told them to that servant, and he interpreted to us our dreams, to each man according to his dream, did he correctly interpret.

36 And it came to pass as he interpreted to us, so was the event; there fell not to the ground any of his words.

37 And now therefore my lord and king do not slay the people of Egypt for naught; behold that slave is still confined in the house by the captain of the guard his master, in the house of confinement.

38 If it pleaseth the king let him send for him that he may come before thee and he will make known to thee, the correct interpretation of the dream which thou didst dream.

39 And the king heard the words of the chief butler, and the king ordered that the wise men of Egypt should not be slain.

40 And the king ordered his servants to bring Joseph before him, and the king said unto them, Go to him and do not terrify him lest he be confused and will not know to speak properly.

41 And the servants of the king went to Joseph, and they brought him hastily out of the dungeon, and the king's servants shaved him, and he changed his prison garment and he came before the king.

42 And the king was sitting upon his royal throne in a princely dress girt around with a golden ephod, and the fine gold which was upon it sparkled, and the carbuncle and the ruby and the emerald, together with all the precious stones that were upon the king's head, dazzled the eye, and Joseph wondered greatly at the king.

43 And the throne upon which the king sat was covered with gold and silver, and with onyx stones, and it had seventy steps.

44 And it was their custom throughout the land of Egypt, that every man who came to speak to the king, if he was a prince or one that was estimable in the sight of the king, he ascended to the king's throne as far as the thirty-first step, and the king would descend to the thirty-sixth step, and speak with him.

45 If he was one of the common people, he ascended to the third step, and the king would descend to the fourth and speak to him, and their custom was, moreover, that any man who understood to speak in all the seventy languages,

he ascended the seventy steps, and went up and spoke till he reached the king.

46 And any man who could not complete the seventy, he ascended as many steps as the languages which he knew to speak in.

47 And it was customary in those days in Egypt that no one should reign over them, but who understood to speak in the seventy languages.

48 And when Joseph came before the king he bowed down to the ground before the king, and he ascended to the third step, and the king sat upon the fourth step and spoke with Joseph.

49 And the king said unto Joseph, I dreamed a dream, and there is no interpreter to interpret it properly, and I commanded this day that all the magicians of Egypt and the wise men thereof, should come before me, and I related my dreams to them, and no one has properly interpreted them to me.

50 And after this I this day heard concerning thee, that thou art a wise man, and canst correctly interpret every dream that thou hearest.

51 And Joseph answered Pharaoh, saying, Let Pharaoh relate his dreams that he dreamed; surely the interpretations belong to God; and Pharaoh related his dreams to Joseph, the dream of the kine, and the dream of the ears of corn, and the king left off speaking.

52 And Joseph was then clothed with the spirit of God before the king, and he knew all the things that would befall the king from that day forward, and he knew the proper interpretation of the king's dream, and he spoke before the king.

53 And Joseph found favor in the sight of the king, and the king inclined his ears and his heart, and he heard all the words of Joseph. And Joseph said unto the king, Do not imagine that they are two dreams, for it is only one dream, for that which God has chosen to do throughout the land he has shown to the king in his dream, and this is the proper interpretation of thy dream:

54 The seven good kine and ears of corn are seven years, and the seven bad kine and ears of corn are also seven years; it is one dream.

55 Behold the seven years that are coming there will be a great plenty throughout the land, and after that the seven years of famine will follow them, a very grievous famine; and all the plenty will be forgotten from the land, and the famine will consume the inhabitants of the land.

56 The king dreamed one dream, and the dream was therefore repeated unto Pharaoh because the thing is established by God, and God will shortly bring it to pass.

57 Now therefore I will give thee counsel and deliver thy soul and the souls of the inhabitants of the land from the evil of the famine, that thou seek throughout thy kingdom for a man very discreet and wise, who knoweth all the affairs of government, and appoint him to superintend over the land of Egypt.

58 And let the man whom thou placest over Egypt appoint officers under him, that they gather in all the food of the good years that are coming, and let them lay up corn and deposit it in thy appointed stores.

59 And let them keep that food for the seven years of famine, that it may be found for thee and thy people and thy whole land, and that thou and thy land be not cut off by the famine.

60 Let all the inhabitants of the land be also ordered that they gather in, every man the produce of his field, of all sorts of food, during the seven good years, and that they place it in their stores, that it may be found for them in the days of the famine and that they may live upon it.

61 This is the proper interpretation of thy dream, and this is the counsel given to save thy soul and the souls of all thy subjects.

62 And the king answered and said unto Joseph, Who sayeth and who knoweth that thy words are correct? And he said unto the king, This shall be a sign for thee respecting all my words, that they are true and that my advice is good for thee.

63 Behold thy wife sitteth this day upon the stool of delivery, and she will bear thee a son and thou wilt rejoice with him; when thy child shall have gone forth from his mother's womb, thy first born son that has been born these two years back shall die, and thou wilt be comforted in the child that will be born unto thee this day.

64 And Joseph finished speaking these words to the king, and he bowed down to the king and he went out, and when Joseph had gone out from the king's presence, those signs which Joseph had spoken unto the king came to pass on that day.

65 And the queen bare a son on that day and the king heard the glad tidings about his son, and he rejoiced, and when the reporter had gone forth from the king's presence, the king's servants found the first born son of the king fallen dead upon the ground.

66 And there was great lamentation and noise in the king's house, and the king heard it, and he said, What is the noise and lamentation that I have heard in the house? and they told the king that his first born son had died; then the king knew that all Joseph's words that he had spoken were correct, and the king was consoled for his son by the child that was born to him on that day as Joseph had spoken.

Chapter 49

1 After these things the king sent and assembled all his officers and servants, and all the princes and nobles belonging to the king, and they all came before the king.

2 And the king said unto them, Behold you have seen and heard all the words of this Hebrew man, and all the signs which he declared would come to pass, and not any of his words have fallen to the ground.

3 You know that he has given a proper interpretation of the dream, and it will surely come to pass, now therefore take counsel, and know what you will do and how the land will be delivered from the famine.

4 Seek now and see whether the like can be found, in whose heart there is wisdom and knowledge, and I will appoint him over the land.

5 For you have heard what the Hebrew man has advised concerning this to save the land therewith from the famine, and I know that the land will not be delivered from the famine but with the advice of the Hebrew man, him that advised me.

6 And they all answered the king and said, The counsel which the Hebrew has given concerning this is good; now therefore, our lord and king, behold the whole land is in thy hand, do that which seemeth good in thy sight.

7 Him whom thou chooses, and whom thou in thy wisdom knowest to be wise and capable of delivering the land with his wisdom, him shall the king appoint to be under him over the land.

8 And the king said to all the officers: I have thought that since God has made known to the Hebrew man all that he has spoken, there is none so discreet and wise in the whole land as he is; if it seem good in your sight I will place him

over the land, for he will save the land with his wisdom.

9 And all the officers answered the king and said, But surely it is written in the laws of Egypt, and it should not be violated, that no man shall reign over Egypt, nor be the second to the king, but one who has knowledge in all the languages of the sons of men.

10 Now therefore our lord and king, behold this Hebrew man can only speak the Hebrew language, and how then can he be over us the second under government, a man who not even knoweth our language?

11 Now we pray thee send for him, and let him come before thee, and prove him in all things, and do as thou see fit.

12 And the king said, It shall be done tomorrow, and the thing that you have spoken is good; and all the officers came on that day before the king.

13 And on that night the Lord sent one of his ministering angels, and he came into the land of Egypt unto Joseph, and the angel of the Lord stood over Joseph, and behold Joseph was lying in the bed at night in his master's house in the dungeon, for his master had put him back into the dungeon on account of his wife.

14 And the angel roused him from his sleep, and Joseph rose up and stood upon his legs, and behold the angel of the Lord was standing opposite to him; and the angel of the Lord spoke with Joseph, and he taught him all the languages of man in that night, and he called his name Jehoseph.

15 And the angel of the Lord went from him, and Joseph returned and lay upon his bed, and Joseph was astonished at the vision which he saw.

16 And it came to pass in the morning that the king sent for all his officers and servants, and they all came and sat before the king, and the king ordered Joseph to be brought, and the king's servants went and brought Joseph before Pharaoh.

17 And the king came forth and ascended the steps of the throne, and Joseph spoke unto the king in all languages, and Joseph went up to him and spoke unto the king until he arrived before the king in the seventieth step, and he sat before the king.

18 And the king greatly rejoiced on account of Joseph, and all the king's officers rejoiced greatly with the king when they heard all the words of Joseph.

19 And the thing seemed good in the sight of the king and the officers, to appoint Joseph to be second to the king over the whole land of Egypt, and the king spoke to Joseph, saying,

20 Now thou didst give me counsel to appoint a wise man over the land of Egypt, in order with his wisdom to save the land from the famine; now therefore, since God has made all this known to thee, and all the words which thou hast spoken, there is not throughout the land a discreet and wise man like unto thee.

21 And thy name no more shall be called Joseph, but Zaphnath Paaneah shall be thy name; thou shalt be second to me, and according to thy word shall be all the affairs of my government, and at thy word shall my people go out and come in.

22 Also from under thy hand shall my servants and officers receive their salary which is given to them monthly, and to thee shall all the people of the land bow down; only in my throne will I be greater than thou.

23 And the king took off his ring from his hand and put it upon the hand of Joseph, and the king dressed Joseph in a princely garment, and he put a golden crown upon his head, and he put a golden chain upon his neck.

24 And the king commanded his servants, and they made him ride in the second chariot belonging to the king, that went opposite to the king's chariot, and he caused him to ride upon a great and strong horse from the king's horses, and to be conducted through the streets of the land of Egypt.

25 And the king commanded that all those that played upon timbrels, harps and other musical instruments should go forth with Joseph; one thousand timbrels, one thousand mecholoth, and one thousand nebalim went after him.

26 And five thousand men, with drawn swords glittering in their hands, and they went marching and playing before Joseph, and twenty thousand of the great men of the king girt with girdles of skin covered with gold, marched at the right hand of Joseph, and twenty thousand at his left, and all the women and damsels went upon the roofs or stood in the streets playing and rejoicing at Joseph, and gazed at the appearance of Joseph and at his beauty.

27 And the king's people went before him and behind him, perfuming the road with frankincense and with cassia, and with all sorts of fine perfume, and scattered myrrh and aloes along the road, and twenty men proclaimed these words before him throughout the land in a loud voice:

28 Do you see this man whom the king has chosen to be his second? all the affairs of government shall be regulated by him, and he that transgresses his orders, or that does not bow down before him to the ground, shall die, for he rebels against the king and his second.

29 And when the heralds had ceased proclaiming, all the people of Egypt bowed down to the ground before Joseph and said, May the king live, also may his second live; and all the inhabitants of Egypt bowed down along the road, and when the heralds approached them, they bowed down, and they rejoiced with all sorts of timbrels, mechol and nebal before Joseph.

30 And Joseph upon his horse lifted up his eyes to heaven, and called out and said, He raiseth the poor man from the dust, He lifteth up the needy from the dunghill. O Lord of Hosts, happy is the man who trusteth in thee.

31 And Joseph passed throughout the land of Egypt with Pharaoh's servants and officers, and they showed him the whole land of Egypt and all the king's treasures.

32 And Joseph returned and came on that day before Pharaoh, and the king gave unto Joseph a possession in the land of Egypt, a possession of fields and vineyards, and the king gave unto Joseph three thousand talents of silver and one thousand talents of gold, and onyx stones and bdellium and many gifts.

33 And on the next day the king commanded all the people of Egypt to bring unto Joseph offerings and gifts, and that he that violated the command of the king should die; and they made a high place in the street of the city, and they spread out garments there, and whoever brought anything to Joseph put it into the high place.

34 And all the people of Egypt cast something into the high place, one man a golden ear-ring, and the other rings and ear-rings, and different vessels of gold and silver work, and onyx stones and bdellium did he cast upon the high place; every one gave something of what he possessed.

35 And Joseph took all these and placed them in his treasuries, and all the officers and nobles belonging to the king exalted Joseph, and they gave him many gifts, seeing that the king had chosen him to be his second.

36 And the king sent to Potiphera, the son of Ahiram priest of On, and he took his young daughter Osnath and gave

her unto Joseph for a wife.

37 And the damsel was very comely, a virgin, one whom man had not known, and Joseph took her for a wife; and the king said unto Joseph, I am Pharaoh, and beside thee none shall dare to lift up his hand or his foot to regulate my people throughout the land of Egypt.

38 And Joseph was thirty years old when he stood before Pharaoh, and Joseph went out from before the king, and he became the king's second in Egypt.

39 And the king gave Joseph a hundred servants to attend him in his house, and Joseph also sent and purchased many servants and they remained in the house of Joseph.

40 Joseph then built for himself a very magnificent house like unto the houses of kings, before the court of the king's palace, and he made in the house a large temple, very elegant in appearance and convenient for his residence; three years was Joseph in erecting his house.

41 And Joseph made unto himself a very elegant throne of abundance of gold and silver, and he covered it with onyx stones and bdellium, and he made upon it the likeness of the whole land of Egypt, and the likeness of the river of Egypt that watereth the whole land of Egypt; and Joseph sat securely upon his throne in his house and the Lord increased Joseph's wisdom.

42 And all the inhabitants of Egypt and Pharaoh's servants and his princes loved Joseph exceedingly, for this thing was from the Lord to Joseph.

43 And Joseph had an army that made war, going out in hosts and troops to the number of forty thousand six hundred men, capable of bearing arms to assist the king and Joseph against the enemy, besides the king's officers and his servants and inhabitants of Egypt without number.

44 And Joseph gave unto his mighty men, and to all his host, shields and javelins, and caps and coats of mail and stones for slinging.

Chapter 50

1 At that time the children of Tarshish came against the sons of Ishmael, and made war with them, and the children of Tarshish spoiled the Ishmaelites for a long time.

2 And the children of Ishmael were small in number in those days, and they could not prevail over the children of Tarshish, and they were sorely oppressed.

3 And the old men of the Ishmaelites sent a record to the king of Egypt, saying, Send I pray thee unto thy servants officers and hosts to help us to fight against the children of Tarshish, for we have been consuming away for a long time.

4 And Pharaoh sent Joseph with the mighty men and host which were with him, and also his mighty men from the king's house.

5 And they went to the land of Havilah to the children of Ishmael, to assist them against the children of Tarshish, and the children of Ishmael fought with the children of Tarshish, and Joseph smote the Tarshishites and he subdued all their land, and the children of Ishmael dwell therein unto this day.

6 And when the land of Tarshish was subdued, all the Tarshishites ran away, and came on the border of their brethren the children of Javan, and Joseph with all his mighty men and host returned to Egypt, not one man of them missing.

7 And at the revolution of the year, in the second year of Joseph's reigning over Egypt, the Lord gave great plenty throughout the land for seven years as Joseph had spoken, for the Lord blessed all the produce of the earth in those

days for seven years, and they ate and were greatly satisfied.

8 And Joseph at that time had officers under him, and they collected all the food of the good years, and heaped corn year by year, and they placed it in the treasuries of Joseph.

9 And at any time when they gathered the food Joseph commanded that they should bring the corn in the ears, and also bring with it some of the soil of the field, that it should not spoil.

10 And Joseph did according to this year by year, and he heaped up corn like the sand of the sea for abundance, for his stores were immense and could not be numbered for abundance.

11 And also all the inhabitants of Egypt gathered all sorts of food in their stores in great abundance during the seven good years, but they did not do unto it as Joseph did.

12 And all the food which Joseph and the Egyptians had gathered during the seven years of plenty, was secured for the land in stores for the seven years of famine, for the support of the whole land.

13 And the inhabitants of Egypt filled each man his store and his concealed place with corn, to be for support during the famine.

14 And Joseph placed all the food that he had gathered in all the cities of Egypt, and he closed all the stores and placed sentinels over them.

15 And Joseph's wife Osnath the daughter of Potiphera bare him two sons, Manasseh and Ephraim, and Joseph was thirty-four years old when he begat them.

16 And the lads grew up and they went in his ways and in his instructions, they did not deviate from the way which their father taught them, either to the right or left.

17 And the Lord was with the lads, and they grew up and had understanding and skill in all wisdom and in all the affairs of government, and all the king's officers and his great men of the inhabitants of Egypt exalted the lads, and they were brought up amongst the king's children.

18 And the seven years of plenty that were throughout the land were at an end, and the seven years of famine came after them as Joseph had spoken, and the famine was throughout the land.

19 And all the people of Egypt saw that the famine had commenced in the land of Egypt, and all the people of Egypt opened their stores of corn for the famine prevailed over them.

20 And they found all the food that was in their stores, full of vermin and not fit to eat, and the famine prevailed throughout the land, and all the inhabitants of Egypt came and cried before Pharaoh, for the famine was heavy upon them.

21 And they said unto Pharaoh, Give food unto thy servants, and wherefore shall we die through hunger before thy eyes, even we and our little ones?

22 And Pharaoh answered them, saying, And wherefore do you cry unto me? did not Joseph command that the corn should be laid up during the seven years of plenty for the years of famine? and wherefore did you not hearken to his voice?

23 And the people of Egypt answered the king, saying, As thy soul liveth, our lord, thy servants have done all that Joseph ordered, for thy servants also gathered in all the produce of their fields during the seven years of plenty and laid it in the stores unto this day.

24 And when the famine prevailed over thy servants we opened our stores, and behold all our produce was filled with vermin and was not fit for food.

25 And when the king heard all that had befallen the

inhabitants of Egypt, the king was greatly afraid on account of the famine, and he was much terrified; and the king answered the people of Egypt, saying, Since all this has happened unto you, go unto Joseph, do whatever he shall say unto you, transgress not his commands.

26 And all the people of Egypt went forth and came unto Joseph, and said unto him, Give unto us food, and wherefore shall we die before thee through hunger? for we gathered in our produce during the seven years as thou didst command, and we put it in store, and thus has it befallen us.

27 And when Joseph heard all the words of the people of Egypt and what had befallen them, Joseph opened all his stores of the produce and he sold it unto the people of Egypt.

28 And the famine prevailed throughout the land, and the famine was in all countries, but in the land of Egypt there was produce for sale.

29 And all the inhabitants of Egypt came unto Joseph to buy corn, for the famine prevailed over them, and all their corn was spoiled, and Joseph daily sold it to all the people of Egypt.

30 And all the inhabitants of the land of Canaan and the Philistines, and those beyond the Jordan, and the children of the east and all the cities of the lands far and nigh heard that there was corn in Egypt, and they all came to Egypt to buy corn, for the famine prevailed over them.

31 And Joseph opened the stores of corn and placed officers over them, and they daily stood and sold to all that came.

32 And Joseph knew that his brethren also would come to Egypt to buy corn, for the famine prevailed throughout the earth. And Joseph commanded all his people that they should cause it to be proclaimed throughout the land of Egypt, saying,

33 It is the pleasure of the king, of his second and of their great men, that any person who wishes to buy corn in Egypt shall not send his servants to Egypt to purchase, but his sons, and also any Egyptian or Canaanite, who shall come from any of the stores from buying corn in Egypt, and shall go and sell it throughout the land, he shall die, for no one shall buy but for the support of his household.

34 And any man leading two or three beasts shall die, for a man shall only lead his own beast.

35 And Joseph placed sentinels at the gates of Egypt, and commanded them, saying, Any person who may come to buy corn, suffer him not to enter until his name, and the name of his father, and the name of his father's father be written down, and whatever is written by day, send their names unto me in the evening that I may know their names.

36 And Joseph placed officers throughout the land of Egypt, and he commanded them to do all these things.

37 And Joseph did all these things, and made these statutes, in order that he might know when his brethren should come to Egypt to buy corn; and Joseph's people caused it daily to be proclaimed in Egypt according to these words and statutes which Joseph had commanded.

38 And all the inhabitants of the east and west country, and of all the earth, heard of the statutes and regulations which Joseph had enacted in Egypt, and the inhabitants of the extreme parts of the earth came and they bought corn in Egypt day after day, and then went away.

39 And all the officers of Egypt did as Joseph had commanded, and all that came to Egypt to buy corn, the gate keepers would write their names, and their fathers' names, and daily bring them in the evening before Joseph.

Chapter 51

1 And Jacob afterward heard that there was corn in Egypt, and he called unto his sons to go to Egypt to buy corn, for upon them also did the famine prevail, and he called unto his sons, saying,

2 Behold I hear that there is corn in Egypt, and all the people of the earth go there to purchase, now therefore why will you show yourselves satisfied before the whole earth? go you also down to Egypt and buy us a little corn amongst those that come there, that we may not die.

3 And the sons of Jacob hearkened to the voice of their father, and they rose up to go down to Egypt in order to buy corn amongst the rest that came there.

4 And Jacob their father commanded them, saying, When you come into the city do not enter together in one gate, on account of the inhabitants of the land.

5 And the sons of Jacob went forth and they went to Egypt, and the sons of Jacob did all as their father had commanded them, and Jacob did not send Benjamin, for he said, Lest an accident might befall him on the road like his brother; and ten of Jacob's sons went forth.

6 And whilst the sons of Jacob were going on the road, they repented of what they had done to Joseph, and they spoke to each other, saying, We know that our brother Joseph went down to Egypt, and now we will seek him where we go, and if we find him we will take him from his master for a ransom, and if not, by force, and we will die for him.

7 And the sons of Jacob agreed to this thing and strengthened themselves on account of Joseph, to deliver him from the hand of his master, and the sons of Jacob went to Egypt; and when they came near to Egypt they separated from each other, and they came through ten gates of Egypt, and the gate keepers wrote their names on that day, and brought them to Joseph in the evening.

8 And Joseph read the names from the hand of the gate-keepers of the city, and he found that his brethren had entered at the ten gates of the city, and Joseph at that time commanded that it should be proclaimed throughout the land of Egypt, saying,

9 Go forth all ye store guards, close all the corn stores and let only one remain open, that those who come may purchase from it.

10 And all the officers of Joseph did so at that time, and they closed all the stores and left only one open.

11 And Joseph gave the written names of his brethren to him that was set over the open store, and he said unto him, Whosoever shall come to thee to buy corn, ask his name, and when men of these names shall come before thee, seize them and send them, and they did so.

12 And when the sons of Jacob came into the city, they joined together in the city to seek Joseph before they bought themselves corn.

13 And they went to the walls of the harlots, and they sought Joseph in the walls of the harlots for three days, for they thought that Joseph would come in the walls of the harlots, for Joseph was very comely and well favored, and the sons of Jacob sought Joseph for three days, and they could not find him.

14 And the man who was set over the open store sought for those names which Joseph had given him, and he did not find them.

15 And he sent to Joseph, saying, These three days have passed, and those men whose names thou didst give unto

me have not come; and Joseph sent servants to seek the men in all Egypt, and to bring them before Joseph.

16 And Joseph's servants went and came into Egypt and could not find them, and went to Goshen and they were not there, and then went to the city of Rameses and could not find them.

17 And Joseph continued to send sixteen servants to seek his brothers, and they went and spread themselves in the four corners of the city, and four of the servants went into the house of the harlots, and they found the ten men there seeking their brother.

18 And those four men took them and brought them before him, and they bowed down to him to the ground, and Joseph was sitting upon his throne in his temple, clothed with princely garments, and upon his head was a large crown of gold, and all the mighty men were sitting around him.

19 And the sons of Jacob saw Joseph, and his figure and comeliness and dignity of countenance seemed wonderful in their eyes, and they again bowed down to him to the ground.

20 And Joseph saw his brethren, and he knew them, but they knew him not, for Joseph was very great in their eyes, therefore they knew him not.

21 And Joseph spoke to them, saying, From whence come ye? and they all answered and said, Thy servants have come from the land of Canaan to buy corn, for the famine prevails throughout the earth, and thy servants heard that there was corn in Egypt, so they have come amongst the other comers to buy corn for their support.

22 And Joseph answered them, saying, If you have come to purchase as you say, why do you come through ten gates of the city? it can only be that you have come to spy through the land.

23 And they all together answered Joseph, and said, Not so my lord, we are right, thy servants are not spies, but we have come to buy corn, for thy servants are all brothers, the sons of one man in the land of Canaan, and our father commanded us, saying, When you come to the city do not enter together at one gate on account of the inhabitants of the land.

24 And Joseph again answered them and said, That is the thing which I spoke unto you, you have come to spy through the land, therefore you all came through ten gates of the city; you have come to see the nakedness of the land.

25 Surely every one that cometh to buy corn goeth his way, and you are already three days in the land, and what do you do in the walls of harlots in which you have been for these three days? surely spies do like unto these things.

26 And they said unto Joseph, Far be it from our lord to speak thus, for we are twelve brothers, the sons of our father Jacob, in the land of Canaan, the son of Isaac, the son of Abraham, the Hebrew, and behold the youngest is with our father this day in the land of Canaan, and one is not, for he was lost from us, and we thought perhaps he might be in this land, so we are seeking him throughout the land, and have come even to the houses of harlots to seek him there.

27 And Joseph said unto them, And have you then sought him throughout the earth, that there only remained Egypt for you to seek him in? And what also should your brother do in the houses of harlots, although he were in Egypt? have you not said, That you are from the sons of Isaac, the son of Abraham, and what shall the sons of Jacob do then in the houses of harlots?

28 And they said unto him, Because we heard that Ishmaelites stole him from us, and it was told unto us that they sold him in Egypt, and thy servant, our brother, is very comely and well favored, so we thought he would surely be in the houses of harlots, therefore thy servants went there to seek him and give ransom for him.

29 And Joseph still answered them, saying, Surely you speak falsely and utter lies, to say of yourselves that you are the sons of Abraham; as Pharaoh liveth you are spies, therefore have you come to the houses of harlots that you should not be known.

30 And Joseph said unto them, And now if you find him, and his master requireth of you a great price, will you give it for him? and they said, It shall be given.

31 And he said unto them, And if his master will not consent to part with him for a great price, what will you do unto him on his account? and they answered him, saying, If he will not give him unto us we will slay him, and take our brother and go away.

32 And Joseph said unto them, That is the thing which I have spoken to you; you are spies, for you are come to slay the inhabitants of the land, for we heard that two of your brethren smote all the inhabitants of Shechem, in the land of Canaan, on account of your sister, and you now come to do the like in Egypt on account of your brother.

33 Only hereby shall I know that you are true men; if you will send home one from amongst you to fetch your youngest brother from your father, and to bring him here unto me, and by doing this thing I will know that you are right.

34 And Joseph called to seventy of his mighty men, and he said unto them, Take these men and bring them into the ward.

35 And the mighty men took the ten men, they laid hold of them and put them into the ward, and they were in the ward three days.

36 And on the third day Joseph had them brought out of the ward, and he said unto them, Do this for yourselves if you be true men, so that you may live, one of your brethren shall be confined in the ward whilst you go and take home the corn for your household to the land of Canaan, and fetch your youngest brother, and bring him here unto me, that I may know that you are true men when you do this thing.

37 And Joseph went out from them and came into the chamber, and wept a great weeping, for his pity was excited for them, and he washed his face, and returned to them again, and he took Simeon from them and ordered him to be bound, but Simeon was not willing to be done so, for he was a very powerful man and they could not bind him.

38 And Joseph called unto his mighty men and seventy valiant men came before him with drawn swords in their hands, and the sons of Jacob were terrified at them.

39 And Joseph said unto them, Seize this man and confine him in prison until his brethren come to him, and Joseph's valiant men hastened and they all laid hold of Simeon to bind him, and Simeon gave a loud and terrible shriek and the cry was heard at a distance.

40 And all the valiant men of Joseph were terrified at the sound of the shriek, that they fell upon their faces, and they were greatly afraid and fled.

41 And all the men that were with Joseph fled, for they were greatly afraid of their lives, and only Joseph and Manasseh his son remained there, and Manassah the son of Joseph saw the strength of Simeon, and he was exceedingly wroth.

42 And Manassah the son of Joseph rose up to Simeon,

and Manassah smote Simeon a heavy blow with his fist against the back of his neck, and Simeon was stilled of his rage.

43 And Manassah laid hold of Simeon and he seized him violently and he bound him and brought him into the house of confinement, and all the sons of Jacob were astonished at the act of the youth.

44 And Simeon said unto his brethren, None of you must say that this is the smiting of an Egyptian, but it is the smiting of the house of my father.

45 And after this Joseph ordered him to be called who was set over the storehouse, to fill their sacks with corn as much as they could carry, and to restore every man's money into his sack, and to give them provision for the road, and thus did he unto them.

46 And Joseph commanded them, saying, Take heed lest you transgress my orders to bring your brother as I have told you, and it shall be when you bring your brother hither unto me, then will I know that you are true men, and you shall traffic in the land, and I will restore unto you your brother, and you shall return in peace to your father.

47 And they all answered and said, According as our lord speaketh so will we do, and they bowed down to him to the ground.

48 And every man lifted his corn upon his ass, and they went out to go to the land of Canaan to their father; and they came to the inn and Levi spread his sack to give provender to his ass, when he saw and behold his money in full weight was still in his sack.

49 And the man was greatly afraid, and he said unto his brethren, My money is restored, and lo, it is even in my sack, and the men were greatly afraid, and they said, What is this that God hath done unto us?

50 And they all said, And where is the Lord's kindness with our fathers, with Abraham, Isaac, end Jacob, that the Lord has this day delivered us into the hands of the king of Egypt to contrive against us?

51 And Judah said unto them, Surely we are guilty sinners before the Lord our God in having sold our brother, our own flesh, and wherefore do you say, Where is the Lord's kindness with our fathers?

52 And Reuben said unto them, Said I not unto you, do not sin against the lad, and you would not listen to me? now God requireth him from us, and how dare you say, Where is the Lord's kindness with our fathers, whilst you have sinned unto the Lord?

53 And they tarried over night in that place, and they rose up early in the morning and laded their asses with their corn, and they led them and went on and came to their father's house in the land of Canaan.

54 And Jacob and his household went out to meet his sons, and Jacob saw and behold their brother Simeon was not with them, and Jacob said unto his sons, Where is your brother Simeon, whom I do not see? and his sons told him all that had befallen them in Egypt.

Chapter 52

1 And they entered their house, and every man opened his sack and they saw and behold every man's bundle of money was there, at which they and their father were greatly terrified.

2 And Jacob said unto them, What is this that you have done to me? I sent your brother Joseph to inquire after your welfare and you said unto me, A wild beast did devour him.

3 And Simeon went with you to buy food and you say the king of Egypt hath confined him in prison, and you wish to take Benjamin to cause his death also, and bring down my grey hairs with sorrow to the grave on account of Benjamin and his brother Joseph.

4 Now therefore my son shall not go down with you, for his brother is dead and he is left alone, and mischief may befall him by the way in which you go, as it befell his brother.

5 And Reuben said unto his father, Thou shalt slay my two sons if I do not bring thy son and place him before thee; and Jacob said unto his sons, Abide ye here and do not go down to Egypt, for my son shall not go down with you to Egypt, nor die like his brother.

6 And Judah said unto them, refrain ye from him until the corn is finished, and he will then say, Take down your brother, when he will find his own life and the life of his household in danger from the famine.

7 And in those days the famine was sore throughout the land, and all the people of the earth went and came to Egypt to buy food, for the famine prevailed greatly amongst them, and the sons of Jacob remained in Canaan a year and two months until their corn was finished.

8 And it came to pass after their corn was finished, the whole household of Jacob was pinched with hunger, and all the infants of the sons of Jacob came together and they approached Jacob, and they all surrounded him, and they said unto him, Give unto us bread, and wherefore shall we all perish through hunger in thy presence?

9 Jacob heard the words of his son's children, and he wept a great weeping, and his pity was roused for them, and Jacob called unto his sons and they all came and sat before him.

10 And Jacob said unto them, And have you not seen how your children have been weeping over me this day, saying, Give unto us bread, and there is none? now therefore return and buy for us a little food.

11 And Judah answered and said unto his father, If thou wilt send our brother with us we will go down and buy corn for thee, and if thou wilt not send him then we will not go down, for surely the king of Egypt particularly enjoined us, saying, You shall not see my face unless your brother be with you, for the king of Egypt is a strong and mighty king, and behold if we shall go to him without our brother we shall all be put to death.

12 Dost thou not know and hast thou not heard that this king is very powerful and wise, and there is not like unto him in all the earth? behold we have seen all the kings of the earth and we have not seen one like that king, the king of Egypt; surely amongst all the kings of the earth there is none greater than Abimelech king of the Philistines, yet the king of Egypt is greater and mightier than he, and Abimelech can only be compared to one of his officers.

13 Father, thou hast not seen his palace and his throne, and all his servants standing before him; thou hast not seen that king upon his throne in his pomp and royal appearance, dressed in his kingly robes with a large golden crown upon his head; thou hast not seen the honor and glory which God has given unto him, for there is not like unto him in all the earth.

14 Father, thou hast not seen the wisdom, the understanding and the knowledge which God has given in his heart, nor heard his sweet voice when he spake unto us.

15 We know not, father, who made him acquainted with our names and all that befell us, yet he asked also after thee, saying, Is your father still living, and is it well with him?

16 Thou hast not seen the affairs of the government of

Egypt regulated by him, without inquiring of Pharaoh his lord; thou hast not seen the awe and fear which he impressed upon all the Egyptians.

17 And also when we went from him, we threatened to do unto Egypt like unto the rest of the cities of the Amorites, and we were exceedingly wroth against all his words which he spoke concerning us as spies, and now when we shall again come before him his terror will fall upon us all, and not one of us will be able to speak to him either a little or a great thing.

18 Now therefore father, send we pray thee the lad with us, and we will go down and buy thee food for our support, and not die through hunger. And Jacob said, Why have you dealt so ill with me to tell the king you had a brother? what is this thing that you have done unto me?

19 And Judah said unto Jacob his father, Give the lad into my care and we will rise up and go down to Egypt and buy corn, and then return, and it shall be when we return if the lad be not with us, then let me bear thy blame forever.

20 Hast thou seen all our infants weeping over thee through hunger and there is no power in thy hand to satisfy them? now let thy pity be roused for them and send our brother with us and we will go.

21 For how will the Lord's kindness to our ancestors be manifested to thee when thou sayest that the king of Egypt will take away thy son? as the Lord liveth I will not leave him until I bring him and place him before thee; but pray for us unto the Lord, that he may deal kindly with us, to cause us to be received favorably and kindly before the king of Egypt and his men, for had we not delayed surely now we had returned a second time with thy son.

22 And Jacob said unto his sons, I trust in the Lord God that he may deliver you and give you favor in the sight of the king of Egypt, and in the sight of all his men.

23 Now therefore rise up and go to the man, and take for him in your hands a present from what can be obtained in the land and bring it before him, and may the Almighty God give you mercy before him that he may send Benjamin and Simeon your brethren with you.

24 And all the men rose up, and they took their brother Benjamin, and they took in their hands a large present of the best of the land, and they also took a double portion of silver.

25 And Jacob strictly commanded his sons concerning Benjamin, Saying, Take heed of him in the way in which you are going, and do not separate yourselves from him in the road, neither in Egypt.

26 And Jacob rose up from his sons and spread forth his hands and he prayed unto the Lord on account of his sons, saying, O Lord God of heaven and earth, remember thy covenant with our father Abraham, remember it with my father Isaac and deal kindly with my sons and deliver them not into the hands of the king of Egypt; do it I pray thee O God for the sake of thy mercies and redeem all my children and rescue them from Egyptian power, and send them their two brothers.

27 And all the wives of the sons of Jacob and their children lifted up their eyes to heaven and they all wept before the Lord, and cried unto him to deliver their fathers from the hand of the king of Egypt.

28 And Jacob wrote a record to the king of Egypt and gave it into the hand of Judah and into the hands of his sons for the king of Egypt, saying,

29 From thy servant Jacob, son of Isaac, son of Abraham the Hebrew, the prince of God, to the powerful and wise king, the revealer of secrets, king of Egypt, greeting.

30 Be it known to my lord the king of Egypt, the famine was sore upon us in the land of Canaan, and I sent my sons to thee to buy us a little food from thee for our support.

31 For my sons surrounded me and I being very old cannot see with my eyes, for my eyes have become very heavy through age, as well as with daily weeping for my son, for Joseph who was lost from before me, and I commanded my sons that they should not enter the gates of the city when they came to Egypt, on account of the inhabitants of the land.

32 And I also commanded them to go about Egypt to seek for my son Joseph, perhaps they might find him there, and they did so, and thou didst consider them as spies of the land.

33 Have we not heard concerning thee that thou didst interpret Pharaoh's dream and didst speak truly unto him? how then dost thou not know in thy wisdom whether my sons are spies or not?

34 Now therefore, my lord and king, behold I have sent my son before thee, as thou didst speak unto my sons; I beseech thee to put thy eyes upon him until he is returned to me in peace with his brethren.

35 For dost thou not know, or hast thou not heard that which our God did unto Pharaoh when he took my mother Sarah, and what he did unto Abimelech king of the Philistines on account of her, and also what our father Abraham did unto the nine kings of Elam, how he smote them all with a few men that were with him?

36 And also what my two sons Simeon and Levi did unto the eight cities of the Amorites, how they destroyed them on account of their sister Dinah?

37 And also on account of their brother Benjamin they consoled themselves for the loss of his brother Joseph; what will they then do for him when they see the hand of any people prevailing over them, for his sake?

38 Dost thou not know, O king of Egypt, that the power of God is with us, and that also God ever heareth our prayers and forsaketh us not all the days?

39 And when my sons told me of thy dealings with them, I called not unto the Lord on account of thee, for then thou wouldst have perished with thy men before my son Benjamin came before thee, but I thought that as Simeon my son was in thy house, perhaps thou mightest deal kindly with him, therefore I did not this thing unto thee.

40 Now therefore behold Benjamin my son cometh unto thee with my sons, take heed of him and put thy eyes upon him, and then will God place his eyes over thee and throughout thy kingdom.

41 Now I have told thee all that is in my heart, and behold my sons are coming to thee with their brother, examine the face of the whole earth for their sake and send them back in peace with their brethren.

42 And Jacob gave the record to his sons into the care of Judah to give it unto the king of Egypt.

Chapter 53

1 And the sons of Jacob rose up and took Benjamin and the whole of the presents, and they went and came to Egypt and they stood before Joseph.

2 And Joseph beheld his brother Benjamin with them and he saluted them, and these men came to Joseph's house.

3 And Joseph commanded the superintendent of his house to give to his brethren to eat, and he did so unto them.

4 And at noon time Joseph sent for the men to come before him with Benjamin, and the men told the superintendent of Joseph's house concerning the silver that

was returned in their sacks, and he said unto them, It will be well with you, fear not, and he brought their brother Simeon unto them.

5 And Simeon said unto his brethren, The lord of the Egyptians has acted very kindly unto me, he did not keep me bound, as you saw with your eyes, for when you went out from the city he let me free and dealt kindly with me in his house.

6 And Judah took Benjamin by the hand, and they came before Joseph, and they bowed down to him to the ground.

7 And the men gave the present unto Joseph and they all sat before him, and Joseph said unto them, Is it well with you, is it well with your children, is it well with your aged father? and they said, It is well, and Judah took the record which Jacob had sent and gave it into the hand of Joseph.

8 And Joseph read the letter and knew his father's writing, and he wished to weep and he went into an inner room and he wept a great weeping; and he went out.

9 And he lifted up his eyes and beheld his brother Benjamin, and he said, Is this your brother of whom you spoke unto me? And Benjamin approached Joseph, and Joseph placed his hand upon his head and he said unto him, May God be gracious unto thee my son.

10 And when Joseph saw his brother, the son of his mother, he again wished to weep, and he entered the chamber, and he wept there, and he washed his face, and went out and refrained from weeping, and he said, Prepare food.

11 And Joseph had a cup from which he drank, and it was of silver beautifully inlaid with onyx stones and bdellium, and Joseph struck the cup in the sight of his brethren whilst they were sitting to eat with him.

12 And Joseph said unto the men, I know by this cup that Reuben the first born, Simeon and Levi and Judah, Issachar and Zebulun are children from one mother, seat yourselves to eat according to your births.

13 And he also placed the others according to their births, and he said, I know that this your youngest brother has no brother, and I, like him, have no brother, he shall therefore sit down to eat with me.

14 And Benjamin went up before Joseph and sat upon the throne, and the men beheld the acts of Joseph, and they were astonished at them; and the men ate and drank at that time with Joseph, and he then gave presents unto them, and Joseph gave one gift unto Benjamin, and Manasseh and Ephraim saw the acts of their father, and they also gave presents unto him, and Osnath gave him one present, and they were five presents in the hand of Benjamin.

15 And Joseph brought them out wine to drink, and they would not drink, and they said, From the day on which Joseph was lost we have not drunk wine, nor eaten any delicacies.

16 And Joseph swore unto them, and he pressed them hard, and they drank plentifully with him on that day, and Joseph afterward turned to his brother Benjamin to speak with him, and Benjamin was still sitting upon the throne before Joseph.

17 And Joseph said unto him, Hast thou begotten any children? and he said, Thy servant has ten sons, and these are their names, Bela, Becher, Ashbal, Gera, Naaman, Achi, Rosh, Mupim, Chupim, and Ord, and I called their names after my brother whom I have not seen.

18 And he ordered them to bring before him his map of the stars, whereby Joseph knew all the times, and Joseph said unto Benjamin, I have heard that the Hebrews are acquainted with all wisdom, dost thou know anything of this?

19 And Benjamin said, Thy servant is knowing also in all the wisdom which my father taught me, and Joseph said unto Benjamin, Look now at this instrument and understand where thy brother Joseph is in Egypt, who you said went down to Egypt.

20 And Benjamin beheld that instrument with the map of the stars of heaven, and he was wise and looked therein to know where his brother was, and Benjamin divided the whole land of Egypt into four divisions, and he found that he who was sitting upon the throne before him was his brother Joseph, and Benjamin wondered greatly, and when Joseph saw that his brother Benjamin was so much astonished, he said unto Benjamin, What hast thou seen, and why art thou astonished?

21 And Benjamin said unto Joseph, I can see by this that Joseph my brother sitteth here with me upon the throne, and Joseph said unto him, I am Joseph thy brother, reveal not this thing unto thy brethren; behold I will send thee with them when they go away, and I will command them to be brought back again into the city, and I will take thee away from them.

22 And if they dare their lives and fight for thee, then shall I know that they have repented of what they did unto me, and I will make myself known to them, and if they forsake thee when I take thee, then shalt thou remain with me, and I will wrangle with them, and they shall go away, and I will not become known to them.

23 At that time Joseph commanded his officer to fill their sacks with food, and to put each man's money into his sack, and to put the cup in the sack of Benjamin, and to give them provision for the road, and they did so unto them.

24 And on the next day the men rose up early in the morning, and they loaded their asses with their corn, and they went forth with Benjamin, and they went to the land of Canaan with their brother Benjamin.

25 They had not gone far from Egypt when Joseph commanded him that was set over his house, saying, Rise, pursue these men before they get too far from Egypt, and say unto them, Why have you stolen my master's cup?

26 And Joseph's officer rose up and he reached them, and he spoke unto them all the words of Joseph; and when they heard this thing they became exceedingly wroth, and they said, He with whom thy master's cup shall be found shall die, and we will also become slaves.

27 And they hastened and each man brought down his sack from his ass, and they looked in their bags and the cup was found in Benjamin's bag, and they all tore their garments and they returned to the city, and they smote Benjamin in the road, continually smiting him until he came into the city, and they stood before Joseph.

28 And Judah's anger was kindled, and he said, This man has only brought me back to destroy Egypt this day.

29 And the men came to Joseph's house, and they found Joseph sitting upon his throne, and all the mighty men standing at his right and left.

30 And Joseph said unto them, What is this act that you have done, that you took away my silver cup and went away? but I know that you took my cup in order to know thereby in what part of the land your brother was.

31 And Judah said, What shall we say to our lord, what shall we speak and how shall we justify ourselves, God has this day found the iniquity of all thy servants, therefore has he done this thing to us this day.

32 And Joseph rose up and caught hold of Benjamin and took him from his brethren with violence, and he came to

the house and locked the door at them, and Joseph commanded him that was set over his house that he should say unto them, Thus saith the king, Go in peace to your father, behold I have taken the man in whose hand my cup was found.

Chapter 54

1 And when Judah saw the dealings of Joseph with them, Judah approached him and broke open the door, and came with his brethren before Joseph.

2 And Judah said unto Joseph, Let it not seem grievous in the sight of my lord, may thy servant I pray thee speak a word before thee? and Joseph said unto him, Speak.

3 And Judah spoke before Joseph, and his brethren were there standing before them; and Judah said unto Joseph, Surely when we first came to our lord to buy food, thou didst consider us as spies of the land, and we brought Benjamin before thee, and thou still makest sport of us this day.

4 Now therefore let the king hear my words, and send I pray thee our brother that he may go along with us to our father, lest thy soul perish this day with all the souls of the inhabitants of Egypt.

5 Dost thou not know what two of my brethren, Simeon and Levi, did unto the city of Shechem, and unto seven cities of the Amorites, on account of our sister Dinah, and also what they would do for the sake of their brother Benjamin?

6 And I with my strength, who am greater and mightier than both of them, come this day upon thee and thy land if thou art unwilling to send our brother.

7 Hast thou not heard what our God who made choice of us did unto Pharaoh on account of Sarah our mother, whom he took away from our father, that he smote him and his household with heavy plagues, that even unto this day the Egyptians relate this wonder to each other? so will our God do unto thee on account of Benjamin whom thou hast this day taken from his father, and on account of the evils which thou this day heapest over us in thy land; for our God will remember his covenant with our father Abraham and bring evil upon thee, because thou hast grieved the soul of our father this day.

8 Now therefore hear my words that I have this day spoken unto thee, and send our brother that he may go away lest thou and the people of thy land die by the sword, for you cannot all prevail over me.

9 And Joseph answered Judah, saying, Why hast thou opened wide thy mouth and why dost thou boast over us, saying, Strength is with thee? as Pharaoh liveth, if I command all my valiant men to fight with you, surely thou and these thy brethren would sink in the mire.

10 And Judah said unto Joseph, Surely it becometh thee and thy people to fear me; as the Lord liveth if I once draw my sword I shall not sheathe it again until I shall this day have slain all Egypt, and I will commence with thee and finish with Pharaoh thy master.

11 And Joseph answered and said unto him, Surely strength belongeth not alone to thee; I am stronger and mightier than thou, surely if thou drawest thy sword I will put it to thy neck and the necks of all thy brethren.

12 And Judah said unto him, Surely if I this day open my mouth against thee I would swallow thee up that thou be destroyed from off the earth and perish this day from thy kingdom. And Joseph said, Surely if thou openest mouth I have power and might to close thy mouth with a stone until thou shalt not be able to utter a word; see how

many stones are before us, truly I can take a stone, and force it into thy mouth and break thy jaws.

13 And Judah said, God is witness between us, that we have not hitherto desired to battle with thee, only give us our brother and we will go from thee; and Joseph answered and said, As Pharaoh liveth, if all the kings of Canaan came together with you, you should not take him from my hand.

14 Now therefore go your way to your father, and your brother shall be unto me for a slave, for he has robbed the king's house. And Judah said, What is it to thee or to the character of the king, surely the king sendeth forth from his house, throughout the land, silver and gold either in gifts or expenses, and thou still talkest about thy cup which thou didst place in our brother's bag and sayest that he has stolen it from thee?

15 God forbid that our brother Benjamin or any of the seed of Abraham should do this thing to steal from thee, or from any one else, whether king, prince, or any man.

16 Now therefore cease this accusation lest the whole earth hear thy words, saying, For a little silver the king of Egypt wrangled with the men, and he accused them and took their brother for a slave.

17 And Joseph answered and said, Take unto you this cup and go from me and leave your brother for a slave, for it is the judgment of a thief to be a slave.

18 And Judah said, Why art thou not ashamed of thy words, to leave our brother and to take thy cup? Surely if thou givest us thy cup, or a thousand times as much, we will not leave our brother for the silver which is found in the hand of any man, that we will not die over him.

19 And Joseph answered, And why did you forsake your brother and sell him for twenty pieces of silver unto this day, and why then will you not do the same to this your brother?

20 And Judah said, the Lord is witness between me and thee that we desire not thy battles; now therefore give us our brother and we will go from thee without quarreling.

21 And Joseph answered and said, If all the kings of the land should assemble they will not be able to take your brother from my hand; and Judah said, What shall we say unto our father, when he seeth that our brother cometh not with us, and will grieve over him?

22 And Joseph answered and said, This is the thing which you shall tell unto your father, saying, The rope has gone after the bucket.

23 And Judah said, Surely thou art a king, and why speakest thou these things, giving a false judgment? woe unto the king who is like unto thee.

24 And Joseph answered and said, There is no false judgment in the word that I spoke on account of your brother Joseph, for all of you sold him to the Midianites for twenty pieces of silver, and you all denied it to your father and said unto him, An evil beast has devoured him, Joseph has been torn to pieces.

25 And Judah said, Behold the fire of Shem burneth in my heart, now I will burn all your land with fire; and Joseph answered and said, Surely thy sister-in-law Tamar, who killed your sons, extinguished the fire of Shechem.

26 And Judah said, If I pluck out a single hair from my flesh, I will fill all Egypt with its blood.

27 And Joseph answered and said, Such is your custom to do as you did to your brother whom you sold, and you dipped his coat in blood and brought it to your father in order that he might say an evil beast devoured him and here is his blood.

28 And when Judah heard this thing he was exceedingly

wroth and his anger burned within him, and there was before him in that place a stone, the weight of which was about four hundred shekels, and Judah's anger was kindled and he took the stone in one hand and cast it to the heavens and caught it with his left hand.

29 And he placed it afterward under his legs, and he sat upon it with all his strength and the stone was turned into dust from the force of Judah.

30 And Joseph saw the act of Judah and he was very much afraid, but he commanded Manassah his son and he also did with another stone like unto the act of Judah, and Judah said unto his brethren, Let not any of you say, this man is an Egyptian, but by his doing this thing he is of our father's family.

31 And Joseph said, Not to you only is strength given, for we are also powerful men, and why will you boast over us all? and Judah said unto Joseph, Send I pray thee our brother and ruin not thy country this day.

32 And Joseph answered and said unto them, Go and tell your father, an evil beast hath devoured him as you said concerning your brother Joseph.

33 And Judah spoke to his brother Naphtali, and he said unto him, Make haste, go now and number all the streets of Egypt and come and tell me; and Simeon said unto him, Let not this thing be a trouble to thee; now I will go to the mount and take up one large stone from the mount and level it at every one in Egypt, and kill all that are in it.

34 And Joseph heard all these words that his brethren spoke before him, and they did not know that Joseph understood them, for they imagined that he knew not to speak Hebrew.

35 And Joseph was greatly afraid at the words of his brethren lest they should destroy Egypt, and he commanded his son Manasseh, saying, Go now make haste and gather unto me all the inhabitants of Egypt, and all the valiant men together, and let them come to me now upon horseback and on foot and with all sorts of musical instruments, and Manasseh went and did so.

36 And Naphtali went as Judah had commanded him, for Naphtali was lightfooted as one of the swift stags, and he would go upon the ears of corn and they would not break under him.

37 And he went and numbered all the streets of Egypt, and found them to be twelve, and he came hastily and told Judah, and Judah said unto his brethren, Hasten you and put on every man his sword upon his loins and we will come over Egypt, and smite them all, and let not a remnant remain.

38 And Judah said, Behold, I will destroy three of the streets with my strength, and you shall each destroy one street; and when Judah was speaking this thing, behold the inhabitants of Egypt and all the mighty men came toward them with all sorts of musical instruments and with loud shouting.

39 And their number was five hundred cavalry and ten thousand infantry, and four hundred men who could fight without sword or spear, only with their hands and strength.

40 And all the mighty men came with great storming and shouting, and they all surrounded the sons of Jacob and terrified them, and the ground quaked at the sound of their shouting.

41 And when the sons of Jacob saw these troops they were greatly afraid of their lives, and Joseph did so in order to terrify the sons of Jacob to become tranquilized.

42 And Judah, seeing some of his brethren terrified, said unto them, Why are you afraid whilst the grace of God is

with us? and when Judah saw all the people of Egypt surrounding them at the command of Joseph to terrify them, only Joseph commanded them, saying, Do not touch any of them.

43 Then Judah hastened and drew his sword, and uttered a loud and bitter scream, and he smote with his sword, and he sprang upon the ground and he still continued to shout against all the people.

44 And when he did this thing the Lord caused the terror of Judah and his brethren to fall upon the valiant men and all the people that surrounded them.

45 And they all fled at the sound of the shouting, and they were terrified and fell one upon the other, and many of them died as they fell, and they all fled from before Judah and his brethren and from before Joseph.

46 And whilst they were fleeing, Judah and his brethren pursued them unto the house of Pharaoh, and they all escaped, and Judah again sat before Joseph and roared at him like a lion, and gave a great and tremendous shriek at him.

47 And the shriek was heard at a distance, and all the inhabitants of Succoth heard it, and all Egypt quaked at the sound of the shriek, and also the walls of Egypt and of the land of Goshen fell in from the shaking of the earth, and Pharaoh also fell from his throne upon the ground, and also all the pregnant women of Egypt and Goshen miscarried when they heard the noise of the shaking, for they were terribly afraid.

48 And Pharaoh sent word, saying, What is this thing that has this day happened in the land of Egypt? and they came and told him all the things from beginning to end, and Pharaoh was alarmed and he wondered and was greatly afraid.

49 And his fright increased when he heard all these things, and he sent unto Joseph, saying, Thou hast brought unto me the Hebrews to destroy all Egypt; what wilt thou do with that thievish slave? send him away and let him go with his brethren, and let us not perish through their evil, even we, you and all Egypt.

50 And if thou desirest not to do this thing, cast off from thee all my valuable things, and go with them to their land, if thou delightest in it, for they will this day destroy my whole country and slay all my people; even all the women of Egypt have miscarried through their screams; see what they have done merely by their shouting and speaking, moreover if they fight with the sword, they will destroy the land; now therefore choose that which thou desirest, whether me or the Hebrews, whether Egypt or the land of the Hebrews.

51 And they came and told Joseph all the words of Pharaoh that he had said concerning him, and Joseph was greatly afraid at the words of Pharaoh and Judah and his brethren were still standing before Joseph indignant and enraged, and all the sons of Jacob roared at Joseph, like the roaring of the sea and its waves.

52 And Joseph was greatly afraid of his brethren and on account of Pharaoh, and Joseph sought a pretext to make himself known unto his brethren, lest they should destroy all Egypt.

53 And Joseph commanded his son Manasseh, and Manasseh went and approached Judah, and placed his hand upon his shoulder, and the anger of Judah was stilled.

54 And Judah said unto his brethren, Let no one of you say that this is the act of an Egyptian youth for this is the work of my father's house.

55 And Joseph seeing and knowing that Judah's anger was

stilled, he approached to speak unto Judah in the language of mildness.

56 And Joseph said unto Judah, Surely you speak truth and have this day verified your assertions concerning your strength, and may your God who delighteth in you, increase your welfare; but tell me truly why from amongst all thy brethren dost thou wrangle with me on account of the lad, as none of them have spoken one word to me concerning him.

57 And Judah answered Joseph, saying, Surely thou must know that I was security for the lad to his father, saying, If I brought him not unto him I should bear his blame forever.

58 Therefore have I approached thee from amongst all my brethren, for I saw that thou wast unwilling to suffer him to go from thee; now therefore may I find grace in thy sight that thou shalt send him to go with us, and behold I will remain as a substitute for him, to serve thee in whatever thou desirest, for wheresoever thou shalt send me I will go to serve thee with great energy.

59 Send me now to a mighty king who has rebelled against thee, and thou shalt know what I will do unto him and unto his land; although he may have cavalry and infantry or an exceeding mighty people, I will slay them all and bring the king's head before thee.

60 Dost thou not know or hast thou not heard that our father Abraham with his servant Eliezer smote all the kings of Elam with their hosts in one night, they left not one remaining? and ever since that day our father's strength was given unto us for an inheritance, for us and our seed forever.

61 And Joseph answered and said, You speak truth, and falsehood is not in your mouth, for it was also told unto us that the Hebrews have power and that the Lord their God delighteth much in them, and who then can stand before them?

62 However, on this condition will I send your brother, if you will bring before me his brother the son of his mother, of whom you said that he had gone from you down to Egypt; and it shall come to pass when you bring unto me his brother I will take him in his stead, because not one of you was security for him to your father, and when he shall come unto me, I will then send with you his brother for whom you have been security.

63 And Judah's anger was kindled against Joseph when he spoke this thing, and his eyes dropped blood with anger, and he said unto his brethren, How doth this man this day seek his own destruction and that of all Egypt!

64 And Simeon answered Joseph, saying, Did we not tell thee at first that we knew not the particular spot to which he went, and whether he be dead or alive, and wherefore speaketh my lord like unto these things?

65 And Joseph observing the countenance of Judah discerned that his anger began to kindle when he spoke unto him, saying, Bring unto me your other brother instead of this brother.

66 And Joseph said unto his brethren, Surely you said that your brother was either dead or lost, now if I should call him this day and he should come before you, would you give him unto me instead of his brother?

67 And Joseph began to speak and call out, Joseph, Joseph, come this day before me, and appear to thy brethren and sit before them.

68 And when Joseph spoke this thing before them, they looked each a different way to see from whence Joseph would come before them.

69 And Joseph observed all their acts, and said unto them, Why do you look here and there? I am Joseph whom you sold to Egypt, now therefore let it not grieve you that you sold me, for as a support during the famine did God send me before you.

70 And his brethren were terrified at him when they heard the words of Joseph, and Judah was exceedingly terrified at him.

71 And when Benjamin heard the words of Joseph he was before them in the inner part of the house, and Benjamin ran unto Joseph his brother, and embraced him and fell upon his neck, and they wept.

72 And when Joseph's brethren saw that Benjamin had fallen upon his brother's neck and wept with him, they also fell upon Joseph and embraced him, and they wept a great weeping with Joseph.

73 And the voice was heard in the house of Joseph that they were Joseph's brethren, and it pleased Pharaoh exceedingly, for he was afraid of them lest they should destroy Egypt.

74 And Pharaoh sent his servants unto Joseph to congratulate him concerning his brethren who had come to him, and all the captains of the armies and troops that were in Egypt came to rejoice with Joseph, and all Egypt rejoiced greatly about Joseph's brethren.

75 And Pharaoh sent his servants to Joseph, saying, Tell thy brethren to fetch all belonging to them and let them come unto me, and I will place them in the best part of the land of Egypt, and they did so.

76 And Joseph commanded him that was set over his house to bring out to his brethren gifts and garments, and he brought out to them many garments being robes of royalty and many gifts, and Joseph divided them amongst his brethren.

77 And he gave unto each of his brethren a change of garments of gold and silver, and three hundred pieces of silver, and Joseph commanded them all to be dressed in these garments, and to be brought before Pharaoh.

78 And Pharaoh seeing that all Joseph's brethren were valiant men, and of beautiful appearance, he greatly rejoiced.

79 And they afterward went out from the presence of Pharaoh to go to the land of Canaan, to their father, and their brother Benjamin was with them.

80 And Joseph rose up and gave unto them eleven chariots from Pharaoh, and Joseph gave unto them his chariot, upon which he rode on the day of his being crowned in Egypt, to fetch his father to Egypt; and Joseph sent to all his brothers' children, garments according to their numbers, and a hundred pieces of silver to each of them, and he also sent garments to the wives of his brethren from the garments of the king's wives, and he sent them.

81 And he gave unto each of his brethren ten men to go with them to the land of Canaan to serve them, to serve their children and all belonging to them in coming to Egypt.

82 And Joseph sent by the hand of his brother Benjamin ten suits of garments for his ten sons, a portion above the rest of the children of the sons of Jacob.

83 And he sent to each fifty pieces of silver, and ten chariots on the account of Pharaoh, and he sent to his father ten asses laden with all the luxuries of Egypt, and ten she asses laden with corn and bread and nourishment for his father, and to all that were with him as provisions for the road.

84 And he sent to his sister Dinah garments of silver and

gold, and frankincense and myrrh, and aloes and women's ornaments in great plenty, and he sent the same from the wives of Pharaoh to the wives of Benjamin.

85 And he gave unto all his brethren, also to their wives, all sorts of onyx stones and bdellium, and from all the valuable things amongst the great people of Egypt, nothing of all the costly things was left but what Joseph sent of to his father's household.

86 And he sent his brethren away, and they went, and he sent his brother Benjamin with them.

87 And Joseph went out with them to accompany them on the road unto the borders of Egypt, and he commanded them concerning his father and his household, to come to Egypt.

88 And he said unto them, Do not quarrel on the road, for this thing was from the Lord to keep a great people from starvation, for there will be yet five years of famine in the land.

89 And he commanded them, saying, When you come unto the land of Canaan, do not come suddenly before my father in this affair, but act in your wisdom.

90 And Joseph ceased to command them, and he turned and went back to Egypt, and the sons of Jacob went to the land of Canaan with joy and cheerfulness to their father Jacob.

91 And they came unto the borders of the land, and they said to each other, What shall we do in this matter before our father, for if we come suddenly to him and tell him the matter, he will be greatly alarmed at our words and will not believe us.

92 And they went along until they came nigh unto their houses, and they found Serach, the daughter of Asher, going forth to meet them, and the damsel was very good and subtle, and knew how to play upon the harp.

93 And they called unto her and she came before them, and she kissed them, and they took her and gave unto her a harp, saying, Go now before our father, and sit before him, and strike upon the harp, and speak these words.

94 And they commanded her to go to their house, and she took the harp and hastened before them, and she came and sat near Jacob.

95 And she played well and sang, and uttered in the sweetness of her words, Joseph my uncle is living, and he ruleth throughout the land of Egypt, and is not dead.

96 And she continued to repeat and utter these words, and Jacob heard her words and they were agreeable to him.

97 He listened whilst she repeated them twice and thrice, and joy entered the heart of Jacob at the sweetness of her words, and the spirit of God was upon him, and he knew all her words to be true.

98 And Jacob blessed Serach when she spoke these words before him, and he said unto her, My daughter, may death never prevail over thee, for thou hast revived my spirit; only speak yet before me as thou hast spoken, for thou hast gladdened me with all thy words.

99 And she continued to sing these words, and Jacob listened and it pleased him, and he rejoiced, and the spirit of God was upon him.

100 Whilst he was yet speaking with her, behold his sons came to him with horses and chariots and royal garments and servants running before them.

101 And Jacob rose up to meet them, and saw his sons dressed in royal garments and he saw all the treasures that Joseph had sent to them.

102 And they said unto him, Be informed that our brother Joseph is living, and it is he who ruleth throughout the land of Egypt, and it is he who spoke unto us as we told thee.

103 And Jacob heard all the words of his sons, and his heart palpitated at their words, for he could not believe them until he saw all that Joseph had given them and what he had sent him, and all the signs which Joseph had spoken unto them.

104 And they opened out before him, and showed him all that Joseph had sent, they gave unto each what Joseph had sent him, and he knew that they had spoken the truth, and he rejoiced exceedingly an account of his son.

105 And Jacob said, It is enough for me that my son Joseph is still living, I will go and see him before I die.

106 And his sons told him all that had befallen them, and Jacob said, I will go down to Egypt to see my son and his offspring.

107 And Jacob rose up and put on the garments which Joseph had sent him, and after he had washed, and shaved his hair, he put upon his head the turban which Joseph had sent him.

108 And all the people of Jacob's house and their wives put on the garments which Joseph had sent to them, and they greatly rejoiced at Joseph that he was still living and that he was ruling in Egypt,

109 And all the inhabitants of Canaan heard of this thing, and they came and rejoiced much with Jacob that he was still living.

110 And Jacob made a feast for them for three days, and all the kings of Canaan and nobles of the land ate and drank and rejoiced in the house of Jacob.

Chapter 55

1 And it came to pass after this that Jacob said, I will go and see my son in Egypt and will then come back to the land of Canaan of which God had spoken unto Abraham, for I cannot leave the land of my birth-place.

2 Behold the word of the Lord came unto him, saying, Go down to Egypt with all thy household and remain there, fear not to go down to Egypt for I will there make thee a great nation.

3 And Jacob said within himself, I will go and see my son whether the fear of his God is yet in his heart amidst all the inhabitants of Egypt.

4 And the Lord said unto Jacob, Fear not about Joseph, for he still retaineth his integrity to serve me, as will seem good in thy sight, and Jacob rejoiced exceedingly concerning his son.

5 At that time Jacob commanded his sons and household to go to Egypt according to the word of the Lord unto him, and Jacob rose up with his sons and all his household, and he went out from the land of Canaan from Beersheba, with joy and gladness of heart, and they went to the land of Egypt.

6 And it came to pass when they came near Egypt, Jacob sent Judah before him to Joseph that he might show him a situation in Egypt, and Judah did according to the word of his father, and he hastened and ran and came to Joseph, and they assigned for them a place in the land of Goshen for all his household, and Judah returned and came along the road to his father.

7 And Joseph harnessed the chariot, and he assembled all his mighty men and his servants and all the officers of Egypt in order to go and meet his father Jacob, and Joseph's mandate was proclaimed in Egypt, saying, All that do not go to meet Jacob shall die.

8 And on the next day Joseph went forth with all Egypt a great and mighty host, all dressed in garments of fine linen

and purple and with instruments of silver and gold and with their instruments of war with them.

9 And they all went to meet Jacob with all sorts of musical instruments, with drums and timbrels, strewing myrrh and aloes all along the road, and they all went after this fashion, and the earth shook at their shouting.

10 And all the women of Egypt went upon the roofs of Egypt and upon the walls to meet Jacob, and upon the head of Joseph was Pharaoh's regal crown, for Pharaoh had sent it unto him to put on at the time of his going to meet his father.

11 And when Joseph came within fifty cubits of his father, he alighted from the chariot and he walked toward his father, and when all the officers of Egypt and her nobles saw that Joseph had gone on foot toward his father, they also alighted and walked on foot toward Jacob.

12 And when Jacob approached the camp of Joseph, Jacob observed the camp that was coming toward him with Joseph, and it gratified him and Jacob was astonished at it.

13 And Jacob said unto Judah, Who is that man whom I see in the camp of Egypt dressed in kingly robes with a very red garment upon him and a royal crown upon his head, who has alighted from his chariot and is coming toward us? and Judah answered his father, saying, He is thy son Joseph the king; and Jacob rejoiced in seeing the glory of his son.

14 And Joseph came nigh unto his father and he bowed to his father, and all the men of the camp bowed to the ground with him before Jacob.

15 And behold Jacob ran and hastened to his son Joseph and fell upon his neck and kissed him, and they wept, and Joseph also embraced his father and kissed him, and they wept and all the people of Egypt wept with them.

16 And Jacob said unto Joseph, Now I will die cheerfully after I have seen thy face, that thou art still living and with glory.

17 And the sons of Jacob and their wives and their children and their servants, and all the household of Jacob wept exceedingly with Joseph, and they kissed him and wept greatly with him.

18 And Joseph and all his people returned afterward home to Egypt, and Jacob and his sons and all the children of his household came with Joseph to Egypt, and Joseph placed them in the best part of Egypt, in the land of Goshen.

19 And Joseph said unto his father and unto his brethren, I will go up and tell Pharaoh, saying, My brethren and my father's household and all belonging to them have come unto me, and behold they are in the land of Goshen.

20 And Joseph did so and took from his brethren Reuben, Issachar Zebulun and his brother Benjamin and he placed them before Pharaoh.

21 And Joseph spoke unto Pharaoh, saying, My brethren and my father's household and all belonging to them, together with their flocks and cattle have come unto me from the land of Canaan, to sojourn in Egypt; for the famine was sore upon them.

22 And Pharaoh said unto Joseph, Place thy father and brethren in the best part of the land, withhold not from them all that is good, and cause them to eat of the fat of the land.

23 And Joseph answered, saying, Behold I have stationed them in the land of Goshen, for they are shepherds, therefore let them remain in Goshen to feed their flocks apart from the Egyptians.

24 And Pharaoh said unto Joseph, Do with thy brethren all that they shall say unto thee; and the sons of Jacob bowed down to Pharaoh, and they went forth from him in peace, and Joseph afterward brought his father before Pharaoh.

25 And Jacob came and bowed down to Pharaoh, and Jacob blessed Pharaoh, and he then went out; and Jacob and all his sons, and all his household dwelt in the land of Goshen.

26 In the second year, that is in the hundred and thirtieth year of the life of Jacob, Joseph maintained his father and his brethren, and all his father's household, with bread according to their little ones, all the days of the famine; they lacked nothing.

27 And Joseph gave unto them the best part of the whole land; the best of Egypt had they all the days of Joseph; and Joseph also gave unto them and unto the whole of his father's household, clothes and garments year by year; and the sons of Jacob remained securely in Egypt all the days of their brother.

28 And Jacob always ate at Joseph's table, Jacob and his sons did not leave Joseph's table day or night, besides what Jacob's children consumed in their houses.

29 And all Egypt ate bread during the days of the famine from the house of Joseph, for all the Egyptians sold all belonging to them on account of the famine.

30 And Joseph purchased all the lands and fields of Egypt for bread on the account of Pharaoh, and Joseph supplied all Egypt with bread all the days of the famine, and Joseph collected all the silver and gold that came unto him for the corn which they bought throughout the land, and he accumulated much gold and silver, besides an immense quantity of onyx stones, bdellium and valuable garments which they brought unto Joseph from every part of the land when their money was spent.

31 And Joseph took all the silver and gold that came into his hand, about seventy two talents of gold and silver, and also onyx stones and bdellium in great abundance, and Joseph went and concealed them in four parts, and he concealed one part in the wilderness near the Red sea, and one part by the river Perath, and the third and fourth part he concealed in the desert opposite to the wilderness of Persia and Media.

32 And he took part of the gold and silver that was left, and gave it unto all his brothers and unto all his father's household, and unto all the women of his father's household, and the rest he brought to the house of Pharaoh, about twenty talents of gold and silver.

33 And Joseph gave all the gold and silver that was left unto Pharaoh, and Pharaoh placed it in the treasury, and the days of the famine ceased after that in the land, and they sowed and reaped in the whole land, and they obtained their usual quantity year by year; they lacked nothing.

34 And Joseph dwelt securely in Egypt, and the whole land was under his advice, and his father and all his brethren dwelt in the land of Goshen and took possession of it.

35 And Joseph was very aged, advanced in days, and his two sons, Ephraim and Manasseh, remained constantly in the house of Jacob, together with the children of the sons of Jacob their brethren, to learn the ways of the Lord and his law.

36 And Jacob and his sons dwelt in the land of Egypt in the land of Goshen, and they took possession in it, and they were fruitful and multiplied in it.

Chapter 56

1 And Jacob lived in the land of Egypt seventeen years, and the days of Jacob, and the years of his life were a hundred and forty seven years.

2 At that time Jacob was attacked with that illness of which he died and he sent and called for his son Joseph from Egypt, and Joseph his son came from Egypt and Joseph came unto his father.

3 And Jacob said unto Joseph and unto his sons, Behold I die, and the God of your ancestors will visit you, and bring you back to the land, which the Lord sware to give unto you and unto your children after you, now therefore when I am dead, bury me in the cave which is in Machpelah in Hebron in the land of Canaan, near my ancestors.

4 And Jacob made his sons swear to bury him in Machpelah, in Hebron, and his sons swore unto him concerning this thing.

5 And he commanded them, saying, Serve the Lord your God, for he who delivered your fathers will also deliver you from all trouble.

6 And Jacob said, Call all your children unto me, and all the children of Jacob's sons came and sat before him, and Jacob blessed them, and he said unto them, The Lord God of your fathers shall grant you a thousand times as much and bless you, and may he give you the blessing of your father Abraham; and all the children of Jacob's sons went forth on that day after he had blessed them.

7 And on the next day Jacob again called for his sons, and they all assembled and came to him and sat before him, and Jacob on that day blessed his sons before his death, each man did he bless according to his blessing; behold it is written in the book of the law of the Lord appertaining to Israel.

8 And Jacob said unto Judah, I know my son that thou art a mighty man for thy brethren; reign over them, and thy sons shall reign over their sons forever.

9 Only teach thy sons the bow and all the weapons of war, in order that they may fight the battles of their brother who will rule over his enemies.

10 And Jacob again commanded his sons on that day, saying, Behold I shall be this day gathered unto my people; carry me up from Egypt, and bury me in the cave of Machpelah as I have commanded you.

11 Howbeit take heed I pray you that none of your sons carry me, only yourselves, and this is the manner you shall do unto me, when you carry my body to go with it to the land of Canaan to bury me,

12 Judah, Issachar and Zebulun shall carry my bier at the eastern side; Reuben, Simeon and Gad at the south, Ephraim, Manasseh and Benjamin at the west, Dan, Asher and Naphtali at the north.

13 Let not Levi carry with you, for he and his sons will carry the ark of the covenant of the Lord with the Israelites in the camp, neither let Joseph my son carry, for as a king so let his glory be; howbeit, Ephraim and Manasseh shall be in their stead.

14 Thus shall you do unto me when you carry me away; do not neglect any thing of all that I command you; and it shall come to pass when you do this unto me, that the Lord will remember you favorably and your children after you forever.

15 And you my sons, honor each his brother and his relative, and command your children and your children's children after you to serve the Lord God of your ancestors all the days.

16 In order that you may prolong your days in the land, you and your children and your children's children for ever, when you do what is good and upright in the sight of the Lord your God, to go in all his ways.

17 And thou, Joseph my son, forgive I pray thee the prongs of thy brethren and all their misdeeds in the injury that they heaped upon thee, for God intended it for thine and thy children's benefit.

18 And O my son leave not thy brethren to the inhabitants of Egypt, neither hurt their feelings, for behold I consign them to the hand of God and in thy hand to guard them from the Egyptians; and the sons of Jacob answered their father saying, O, our father, all that thou hast commanded us, so will we do; may God only be with us.

19 And Jacob said unto his sons, So may God be with you when you keep all his ways; turn not from his ways either to the right or the left in performing what is good and upright in his sight.

20 For I know that many and grievous troubles will befall you in the latter days in the land, yea your children and children's children, only serve the Lord and he will save you from all trouble.

21 And it shall come to pass when you shall go after God to serve him and will teach your children after you, and your children's children, to know the Lord, then will the Lord raise up unto you and your children a servant from amongst your children, and the Lord will deliver you through his hand from all affliction, and bring you out of Egypt and bring you back to the land of your fathers to inherit it securely.

22 And Jacob ceased commanding his sons, and he drew his feet into the bed, he died and was gathered to his people.

23 And Joseph fell upon his father and he cried out and wept over him and he kissed him, and he called out in a bitter voice, and he said, O my father, my father.

24 And his son's wives and all his household came and fell upon Jacob, and they wept over him, and cried in a very loud voice concerning Jacob.

25 And all the sons of Jacob rose up together, and they tore their garments, and they all put sackcloth upon their loins, and they fell upon their faces, and they cast dust upon their heads toward the heavens.

26 And the thing was told unto Osnath Joseph's wife, and she rose up and put on a sack and she with all the Egyptian women with her came and mourned and wept for Jacob.

27 And also all the people of Egypt who knew Jacob came all on that day when they heard this thing, and all Egypt wept for many days.

28 And also from the land of Canaan did the women come unto Egypt when they heard that Jacob was dead, and they wept for him in Egypt for seventy days.

29 And it came to pass after this that Joseph commanded his servants the doctors to embalm his father with myrrh and frankincense and all manner of incense and perfume, and the doctors embalmed Jacob as Joseph had commanded them.

30 And all the people of Egypt and the elders and all the inhabitants of the land of Goshen wept and mourned over Jacob, and all his sons and the children of his household lamented and mourned over their father Jacob many days.

31 And after the days of his weeping had passed away, at the end of seventy days, Joseph said unto Pharaoh, I will go up and bury my father in the land of Canaan as he made me swear, and then I will return.

32 And Pharaoh sent Joseph, saying, Go up and bury thy father as he said, and as he made thee swear; and Joseph rose up with all his brethren to go to the land of Canaan to bury their father Jacob as he had commanded them.

33 And Pharaoh commanded that it should be proclaimed throughout Egypt, saying, Whoever goeth not up with

Joseph and his brethren to the land of Canaan to bury Jacob, shall die.

34 And all Egypt heard of Pharaoh's proclamation, and they all rose up together, and all the servants of Pharaoh, and the elders of his house, and all the elders of the land of Egypt went up with Joseph, and all the officers and nobles of Pharaoh went up as the servants of Joseph, and they went to bury Jacob in the land of Canaan.

35 And the sons of Jacob carried the bier upon which he lay; according to all that their father commanded them, so did his sons unto him.

36 And the bier was of pure gold, and it was inlaid round about with onyx stones and bdellium; and the covering of the bier was gold woven work, joined with threads, and over them were hooks of onyx stones and bdellium.

37 And Joseph placed upon the head of his father Jacob a large golden crown, and he put a golden scepter in his hand, and they surrounded the bier as was the custom of kings during their lives.

38 And all the troops of Egypt went before him in this array, at first all the mighty men of Pharaoh, and the mighty men of Joseph, and after them the rest of the inhabitants of Egypt, and they were all girded with swords and equipped with coats of mail, and the trappings of war were upon them.

39 And all the weepers and mourners went at a distance opposite to the bier, going and weeping and lamenting, and the rest of the people went after the bier.

40 And Joseph and his household went together near the bier barefooted and weeping, and the rest of Joseph's servants went around him; each man had his ornaments upon him, and they were all armed with their weapons of war.

41 And fifty of Jacob's servants went in front of the bier, and they strewed along the road myrrh and aloes, and all manner of perfume, and all the sons of Jacob that carried the bier walked upon the perfumery, and the servants of Jacob went before them strewing the perfume along the road.

42 And Joseph went up with a heavy camp, and they did after this manner every day until they reached the land of Canaan, and they came to the threshing floor of Atad, which was on the other side of Jordan, and they mourned an exceeding great and heavy mourning in that place.

43 And all the kings of Canaan heard of this thing and they all went forth, each man from his house, thirty-one kings of Canaan, and they all came with their men to mourn and weep over Jacob.

44 And all these kings beheld Jacob's bier, and behold Joseph's crown was upon it, and they also put their crowns upon the bier, and encircled it with crowns.

45 And all these kings made in that place a great and heavy mourning with the sons of Jacob and Egypt over Jacob, for all the kings of Canaan knew the valor of Jacob and his sons.

46 And the report reached Esau, saying, Jacob died in Egypt, and his sons and all Egypt are conveying him to the land of Canaan to bury him.

47 And Esau heard this thing, and he was dwelling in mount Seir, and he rose up with his sons and all his people and all his household, a people exceedingly great, and they came to mourn and weep over Jacob.

48 And it came to pass, when Esau came he mourned for his brother Jacob, and all Egypt and all Canaan again rose up and mourned a great mourning with Esau over Jacob in that place

49 And Joseph and his brethren brought their father Jacob from that place, and they went to Hebron to bury Jacob in the cave by his fathers.

50 And they came unto Kireath-arba, to the cave, and as they came Esau stood with his sons against Joseph and his brethren as a hindrance in the cave, saying, Jacob shall not be buried therein, for it belongeth to us and to our father.

51 And Joseph and his brethren heard the words of Esau's sons, and they were exceedingly wroth, and Joseph approached unto Esau, saying, What is this thing which they have spoken? surely my father Jacob bought it from thee for great riches after the death of Isaac, now five and twenty years ago, and also all the land of Canaan he bought from thee and from thy sons, and thy seed after thee.

52 And Jacob bought it for his sons and his seed after him for an inheritance for ever, and why speakest thou these things this day?

53 And Esau answered, saying, Thou speakest falsely and utterest lies, for I sold not anything belonging to me in all this land, as thou sayest, neither did my brother Jacob buy aught belonging to me in this land.

54 And Esau spoke these things in order to deceive Joseph with his words, for Esau knew that Joseph was not present in those days when Esau sold all belonging to him in the land of Canaan to Jacob.

55 And Joseph said unto Esau, Surely my father inserted these things with thee in the record of purchase, and testified the record with witnesses, and behold it is with us in Egypt.

56 And Esau answered, saying unto him, Bring the record, all that thou wilt find in the record, so will we do.

57 And Joseph called unto Naphtali his brother, and he said, Hasten quickly, stay not, and run I pray thee to Egypt and bring all the records; the record of the purchase, the sealed record and the open record, and also all the first records in which all the transactions of the birth-right are written, fetch thou.

58 And thou shalt bring them unto us hither, that we may know from them all the words of Esau and his sons which they spoke this day.

59 And Naphtali hearkened to the voice of Joseph and he hastened and ran to go down to Egypt, and Naphtali was lighter on foot than any of the stags that were upon the wilderness, for he would go upon ears of corn without crushing them.

60 And when Esau saw that Naphtali had gone to fetch the records, he and his sons increased their resistance against the cave, and Esau and all his people rose up against Joseph and his brethren to battle.

61 And all the sons of Jacob and the people of Egypt fought with Esau and his men, and the sons of Esau and his people were smitten before the sons of Jacob, and the sons of Jacob slew of Esau's people forty men.

62 And Chushim the son of Dan, the son of Jacob, was at that time with Jacob's sons, but he was about a hundred cubits distant from the place of battle, for he remained with the children of Jacob's sons by Jacob's bier to guard it.

63 And Chushim was dumb and deaf, still he understood the voice of consternation amongst men.

64 And he asked, saying, Why do you not bury the dead, and what is this great consternation? and they answered him the words of Esau and his sons; and he ran to Esau in the midst of the battle, and he slew Esau with a sword, and he cut off his head, and it sprang to a distance, and Esau fell amongst the people of the battle.

65 And when Chushim did this thing the sons of Jacob

prevailed over the sons of Esau, and the sons of Jacob buried their father Jacob by force in the cave, and the sons of Esau beheld it.

66 And Jacob was buried in Hebron, in the cave of Machpelah which Abraham had bought from the sons of Heth for the possession of a burial place, and he was buried in very costly garments.

67 And no king had such honor paid him as Joseph paid unto his father at his death, for he buried him with great honor like unto the burial of kings.

68 And Joseph and his brethren made a mourning of seven days for their father.

Chapter 57

1 And it was after this that the sons of Esau waged war with the sons of Jacob, and the sons of Esau fought with the sons of Jacob in Hebron, and Esau was still lying dead, and not buried.

2 And the battle was heavy between them, and the sons of Esau were smitten before the sons of Jacob, and the sons of Jacob slew of the sons of Esau eighty men, and not one died of the people of the sons of Jacob; and the hand of Joseph prevailed over all the people of the sons of Esau, and he took Zepho, the son of Eliphaz, the son of Esau, and fifty of his men captive, and he bound them with chains of iron, and gave them into the hand of his servants to bring them to Egypt.

3 And it came to pass when the sons of Jacob had taken Zepho and his people captive, all those that remained were greatly afraid of their lives from the house of Esau, lest they should also be taken captive, and they all fled with Eliphaz the son of Esau and his people, with Esau's body, and they went on their road to Mount Seir.

4 And they came unto Mount Seir and they buried Esau in Seir, but they had not brought his head with them to Seir, for it was buried in that place where the battle had been in Hebron.

5 And it came to pass when the sons of Esau had fled from before the sons of Jacob, the sons of Jacob pursued them unto the borders of Seir, but they did not slay a single man from amongst them when they pursued them, for Esau's body which they carried with them excited their confusion, so they fled and the sons of Jacob turned back from them and came up to the place where their brethren were in Hebron, and they remained there on that day, and on the next day until they rested from the battle.

6 And it came to pass on the third day they assembled all the sons of Seir the Horite, and they assembled all the children of the east, a multitude of people like the sand of the sea, and they went and came down to Egypt to fight with Joseph and his brethren, in order to deliver their brethren.

7 And Joseph and all the sons of Jacob heard that the sons of Esau and the children of the east had come upon them to battle in order to deliver their brethren.

8 And Joseph and his brethren and the strong men of Egypt went forth and fought in the city of Rameses, and Joseph and his brethren dealt out a tremendous blow amongst the sons of Esau and the children of the east.

9 And they slew of them six hundred thousand men, and they slew amongst them all the mighty men of the children of Seir the Horite; there were only a few of them left, and they slew also a great many of the children of the east, and of the children of Esau; and Eliphaz the son of Esau, and the children of the east all fled before Joseph and his brethren.

10 And Joseph and his brethren pursued them until they came unto Succoth, and they yet slew of them in Succoth thirty men, and the rest escaped and they fled each to his city.

11 And Joseph and his brethren and the mighty men of Egypt turned back from them with joy and cheerfulness of heart, for they had smitten all their enemies.

12 And Zepho the son of Eliphaz and his men were still slaves in Egypt to the sons of Jacob, and their pains increased.

13 And when the sons of Esau and the sons of Seir returned to their land, the sons of Seir saw that they had all fallen into the hands of the sons of Jacob, and the people of Egypt, on account of the battle of the sons of Esau.

14 And the sons of Seir said unto the sons of Esau, You have seen andtherefore you know that this camp was on your account, and not one mighty man or an adept in war remaineth.

15 Now therefore go forth from our land, go from us to the land of Canaan to the land of the dwelling of your fathers; wherefore shall your children inherit the effects of our children in latter days?

16 And the children of Esau would not listen to the children of Seir, and the children of Seir considered to make war with them.

17 And the children of Esau sent secretly to Angeas king of Africa, the same is Dinhabah, saying,

18 Send unto us some of thy men and let them come unto us, and we will fight together with the children of Seir the Horite, for they have resolved to fight with us to drive us away from the land.

19 And Angeas king of Dinhabah did so, for he was in those days friendly to the children of Esau, and Angeas sent five hundred valiant infantry to the children of Esau, and eight hundred cavalry.

20 And the children of Seir sent unto the children of the east and unto the children of Midian, saying, You have seen what the children of Esau have done unto us, upon whose account we are almost all destroyed, in their battle with the sons of Jacob.

21 Now therefore come unto us and assist us, and we will fight them together, and we will drive them from the land and be avenged of the cause of our brethren who died for their sakes in their battle with their brethren the sons of Jacob.

22 And all the children of the east listened to the children of Seir, and they came unto them about eight hundred men with drawn swords, and the children of Esau fought with the children of Seir at that time in the wilderness of Paran.

23 And the children of Seir prevailed then over the sons of Esau, and the children of Seir slew on that day of the children of Esau in that battle about two hundred men of the people of Angeas king of Dinhabah.

24 And on the second day the children of Esau came again to fight a second time with the children of Seir, and the battle was sore upon the children of Esau this second time, and it troubled them greatly on account of the children of Seir.

25 And when the children of Esau saw that the children of Seir were more powerful than they were, some men of the children of Esau turned and assisted the children of Seir their enemies.

26 And there fell yet of the people of the children of Esau in the second battle fifty-eight men of the people at Angeas king of Dinhabah.

27 And on the third day the children of Esau heard that

some of their brethren had turned from them to fight against them in the second battle; and the children of Esau mourned when they heard this thing.

28 And they said, What shall we do unto our brethren who turned from us to assist the children of Seir our enemies? and the children of Esau again sent to Angeas king of Dinhabah, saying,

29 Send unto us again other men that with them we may fight with the children of Seir, for they have already twice been heavier than we were.

30 And Angeas again sent to the children of Esau about six hundred valiant men, and they came to assist the children of Esau.

31 And in ten days' time the children of Esau again waged war with the children of Seir in the wilderness of Paran, and the battle was very severe upon the children of Seir, and the children of Esau prevailed at this time over the children of Seir, and the children of Seir were smitten before the children of Esau, and the children of Esau slew from them about two thousand men.

32 And all the mighty men of the children of Seir died in this battle, and there only remained their young children that were left in their cities.

33 And all Midian and the children of the east betook themselves to flight from the battle, and they left the children of Seir and fled when they saw that the battle was severe upon them, and the children of Esau pursued all the children of the east until they reached their land.

34 And the children of Esau slew yet of them about two hundred and fifty men and from the people of the children of Esau there fell in that battle about thirty men, but this evil came upon them through their brethren turning from them to assist the children of Seir the Horite, and the children of Esau again heard of the evil doings of their brethren, and they again mourned on account of this thing.

35 And it came to pass after the battle, the children of Esau turned back and came home unto Seir, and the children of Esau slew those who had remained in the land of the children of Seir; they slew also their wives and little ones, they left not a soul alive except fifty young lads and damsels whom they suffered to live, and the children of Esau did not put them to death, and the lads became their slaves, and the damsels they took for wives.

36 And the children of Esau dwelt in Seir in the place of the children of Seir, and they inherited their land and took possession of it.

37 And the children of Esau took all belonging in the land to the children of Seir, also their flocks, their bullocks and their goods, and all belonging to the children of Seir, did the children of Esau take, and the children of Esau dwelt in Seir in the place of the children of Seir unto this day, and the children of Esau divided the land into divisions to the five sons of Esau, according to their families.

38 And it came to pass in those days, that the children of Esau resolved to crown a king over them in the land of which they became possessed. And they said to each other, Not so, for he shall reign over us in our land, and we shall be under his counsel and he shall fight our battles, against our enemies, and they did so.

39 And all the children of Esau swore, saying, That none of their brethren should ever reign over them, but a strange man who is not of their brethren, for the souls of all the children of Esau were embittered every man against his son, brother and friend, on account of the evil they sustained from their brethren when they fought with the children of Seir.

40 Therefore the sons of Esau swore, saying, From that day forward they would not choose a king from their brethren, but one from a strange land unto this day.

41 And there was a man there from the people of Angeas king of Dinhabah; his name was Bela the son of Beor, who was a very valiant man, beautiful and comely and wise in all wisdom, and a man of sense and counsel; and there was none of the people of Angeas like unto him.

42 And all the children of Esau took him and anointed him and they crowned him for a king, and they bowed down to him, and they said unto him, May the king live, may the king live.

43 And they spread out the sheet, and they brought him each man earrings of gold and silver or rings or bracelets, and they made him very rich in silver and in gold, in onyx stones and bdellium, and they made him a royal throne, and they placed a regal crown upon his head, and they built a palace for him and he dwelt therein, and he became king over all the children of Esau.

44 And the people of Angeas took their hire for their battle from the children of Esau, and they went and returned at that time to their master in Dinhabah.

45 And Bela reigned over the children of Esau thirty years, and the children of Esau dwelt in the land instead of the children of Seir, and they dwelt securely in their stead unto this day.

Chapter 58

1 And it came to pass in the thirty-second year of the Israelites going down to Egypt, that is in the seventy-first year of the life of Joseph, in that year died Pharaoh king of Egypt, and Magron his son reigned in his stead.

2 And Pharaoh commanded Joseph before his death to be a father to his son, Magron, and that Magron should be under the care of Joseph and under his counsel.

3 And all Egypt consented to this thing that Joseph should be king over them, for all the Egyptians loved Joseph as of heretofore, only Magron the son of Pharaoh sat upon, his father's throne, and he became king in those days in his father's stead.

4 Magron was forty-one years old when he began to reign, and forty years he reigned in Egypt, and all Egypt called his name Pharaoh after the name of his father, as it was their custom to do in Egypt to every king that reigned over them.

5 And it came to pass when Pharaoh reigned in his father's stead, he placed the laws of Egypt and all the affairs of government in the hand of Joseph, as his father had commanded him.

6 And Joseph became king over Egypt, for he superintended over all Egypt, and all Egypt was under his care and under his counsel, for all Egypt inclined to Joseph after the death of Pharaoh, and they loved him exceedingly to reign over them.

7 But there were some people amongst them, who did not like him, saying, No stranger shall reign over us; still the whole government of Egypt devolved in those days upon Joseph, after the death of Pharaoh, he being the regulator, doing as he liked throughout the land without any one interfering.

8 And all Egypt was under the care of Joseph, and Joseph made war with all his surrounding enemies, and he subdued them; also all the land and all the Philistines, unto the borders of Canaan, did Joseph subdue, and they were all under his power and they gave a yearly tax unto Joseph.

9 And Pharaoh king of Egypt sat upon his throne in his

father's stead, but he was under the control and counsel of Joseph, as he was at first under the control of his father.

10 Neither did he reign but in the land of Egypt only, under the counsel of Joseph, but Joseph reigned over the whole country at that time, from Egypt unto the great river Perath.

11 And Joseph was successful in all his ways, and the Lord was with him, and the Lord gave Joseph additional wisdom, and honor, and glory, and love toward him in the hearts of the Egyptians and throughout the land, and Joseph reigned over the whole country forty years.

12 And all the countries of the Philistines and Canaan and Zidon, and on the other side of Jordan, brought presents unto Joseph all his days, and the whole country was in the hand of Joseph, and they brought unto him a yearly tribute as it was regulated, for Joseph had fought against all his surrounding enemies and subdued them, and the whole country was in the hand of Joseph, and Joseph sat securely upon his throne in Egypt.

13 And also all his brethren the sons of Jacob dwelt securely in the land, all the days of Joseph, and they were fruitful and multiplied exceedingly in the land, and they served the Lord all their days, as their father Jacob had commanded them.

14 And it came to pass at the end of many days and years, when the children of Esau were dwelling quietly in their land with Bela their king, that the children of Esau were fruitful and multiplied in the land, and they resolved to go and fight with the sons of Jacob and all Egypt, and to deliver their brother Zepho, the son of Eliphaz, and his men, for they were yet in those days slaves to Joseph.

15 And the children of Esau sent unto all the children of the east, and they made peace with them, and all the children of the east came unto them to go with the children of Esau to Egypt to battle.

16 And there came also unto them of the people of Angeas, king of Dinhabah, and they also sent unto the children of Ishmael and they also came unto them.

17 And all this people assembled and came unto Seir to assist the children of Esau in their battle, and this camp was very large and heavy with people, numerous as the sand of the sea, about eight hundred thousand men, infantry and cavalry, and all these troops went down to Egypt to fight with the sons of Jacob, and they encamped by Rameses.

18 And Joseph went forth with his brethren with the mighty men of Egypt, about six hundred men, and they fought with them in the land of Rameses; and the sons of Jacob at that time again fought with the children of Esau, in the fiftieth year of the sons of Jacob going down to Egypt, that is the thirtieth year of the reign of Bela over the children of Esau in Seir.

19 And the Lord gave all the mighty men of Esau and the children of the east into the hand of Joseph and his brethren, and the people of the children of Esau and the children of the east were smitten before Joseph.

20 And of the people of Esau and the children of the east that were slain, there fell before the sons of Jacob about two hundred thousand men, and their king Bela the son of Beor fell with them in the battle, and when the children of Esau saw that their king had fallen in battle and was dead, their hands became weak in the combat.

21 And Joseph and his brethren and all Egypt were still smiting the people of the house of Esau, and all Esau's people were afraid of the sons of Jacob and fled from before them.

22 And Joseph and his brethren and all Egypt pursued them a day's journey, and they slew yet from them about three hundred men, continuing to smite them in the road; and they afterward turned back from them.

23 And Joseph and all his brethren returned to Egypt, not one man was missing from them, but of the Egyptians there fell twelve men.

24 And when Joseph returned to Egypt he ordered Zepho and his men to be additionally bound, and they bound them in irons and they increased their grief.

25 And all the people of the children of Esau, and the children of the east, returned in shame each unto his city, for all the mighty men that were with them had fallen in battle.

26 And when the children of Esau saw that their king had died in battle they hastened and took a man from the people of the children of the east; his name was Jobab the son of Zarach, from the land of Botzrah, and they caused him to reign over them instead of Bela their king.

27 And Jobab sat upon the throne of Bela as king in his stead, and Jobab reigned in Edom over all the children of Esau ten years, and the children of Esau went no more to fight with the sons of Jacob from that day forward, for the sons of Esau knew the valor of the sons of Jacob, and they were greatly afraid of them.

28 But from that day forward the children of Esau hated the sons of Jacob, and the hatred and enmity were very strong between them all the days, unto this day.

29 And it came to pass after this, at the end of ten years, Jobab, the son of Zarach, from Botzrah, died, and the children of Esau took a man whose name was Chusham, from the land of Teman, and they made him king over them instead of Jobab, and Chusham reigned in Edom over all the children of Esau for twenty years.

30 And Joseph, king of Egypt, and his brethren, and all the children of Israel dwelt securely in Egypt in those days, together with all the children of Joseph and his brethren, having no hindrance or evil accident and the land of Egypt was at that time at rest from war in the days of Joseph and his brethren.

Chapter 59

1 And these are the names of the sons of Israel who dwelt in Egypt, who had come with Jacob, all the sons of Jacob came unto Egypt, every man with his household.

2 The children of Leah were Reuben, Simeon, Levi, Judah, Issachar and Zebulun, and their sister Dinah.

3 And the sons of Rachel were Joseph and Benjamin.

4 And the sons of Zilpah, the handmaid of Leah, were Gad and Asher.

5 And the sons of Bilhah, the handmaid of Rachel, were Dan and Naphtali.

6 And these were their offspring that were born unto them in the land of Canaan, before they came unto Egypt with their father Jacob.

7 The sons of Reuben were Chanoch, Pallu, Chetzron and Carmi.

8 And the sons of Simeon were Jemuel, Jamin, Ohad, Jachin, Zochar and Saul, the son of the Canaanitish woman.

9 And the children of Levi were Gershon, Kehath and Merari, and their sister Jochebed, who was born unto them in their going down to Egypt.

10 And the sons of Judah were Er, Onan, Shelah, Perez and Zarach.

11 And Er and Onan died in the land of Canaan; and the sons of Perez were Chezron and Chamul.

12 And the sons of Issachar were Tola, Puvah, Job and

Shomron.

13 And the sons of Zebulun were Sered, Elon and Jachleel, and the son of Dan was Chushim.

14 And the sons of Naphtali were Jachzeel, Guni, Jetzer and Shilam.

15 And the sons of Gad were Ziphion, Chaggi, Shuni, Ezbon, Eri, Arodi and Areli.

16 And the children of Asher were Jimnah, Jishvah, Jishvi, Beriah and their sister Serach; and the sons of Beriah were Cheber and Malchiel.

17 And the sons of Benjamin were Bela, Becher, Ashbel, Gera, Naaman, Achi, Rosh, Mupim, Chupim and Ord.

18 And the sons of Joseph, that were born unto him in Egypt, were Manasseh and Ephraim.

19 And all the souls that went forth from the loins of Jacob, were seventy souls; these are they who came with Jacob their father unto Egypt to dwell there: and Joseph and all his brethren dwelt securely in Egypt, and they ate of the best of Egypt all the days of the life of Joseph.

20 And Joseph lived in the land of Egypt ninety-three years, and Joseph reigned over all Egypt eighty years.

21 And when the days of Joseph drew nigh that he should die, he sent and called for his brethren and all his father's household, and they all came together and sat before him.

22 And Joseph said unto his brethren and unto the whole of his father's household, Behold I die, and God will surely visit you and bring you up from this land to the land which he swore to your fathers to give unto them.

23 And it shall be when God shall visit you to bring you up from here to the land of your fathers, then bring up my bones with you from here.

24 And Joseph made the sons of Israel to swear for their seed after them, saying, God will surely visit you and you shall bring up my bones with you from here.

25 And it came to pass after this that Joseph died in that year, the seventy-first year of the Israelites going down to Egypt.

26 And Joseph was one hundred and ten years old when he died in the land of Egypt, and all his brethren and all his servants rose up and they embalmed Joseph, as was their custom, and his brethren and all Egypt mourned over him for seventy days.

27 And they put Joseph in a coffin filled with spices and all sorts of perfume, and they buried him by the side of the river, that is Sihor, and his sons and all his brethren, and the whole of his father's household made a seven day's mourning for him.

28 And it came to pass after the death of Joseph, all the Egyptians began in those days to rule over the children of Israel, and Pharaoh, king of Egypt, who reigned in his father's stead, took all the laws of Egypt and conducted the whole government of Egypt under his counsel, and he reigned securely over his people.

Chapter 60

1 And when the year came round, being the seventy-second year from the Israelites going down to Egypt, after the death of Joseph, Zepho, the son of Eliphaz, the son of Esau, fled from Egypt, he and his men, and they went away.

2 And he came to Africa, which is Dinhabah, to Angeas king of Africa, and Angeas received them with great honor, and he made Zepho the captain of his host.

3 And Zepho found favor in the sight of Angeas and in the sight of his people, and Zepho was captain of the host to Angeas king of Africa for many days.

4 And Zepho enticed Angeas king of Africa to collect all his army to go and fight with the Egyptians, and with the sons of Jacob, and to avenge of them the cause of his brethren.

5 But Angeas would not listen to Zepho to do this thing, for Angeas knew the strength of the sons of Jacob, and what they had done to his army in their warfare with the children of Esau.

6 And Zepho was in those days very great in the sight of Angeas and in the sight of all his people, and he continually enticed them to make war against Egypt, but they would not.

7 And it came to pass in those days there was in the land of Chittim a man in the city of Puzimna, whose name was Uzu, and he became degenerately deified by the children of Chittim, and the man died and had no son, only one daughter whose name was Jania.

8 And the damsel was exceedingly beautiful, comely and intelligent, there was none seen like unto her for beauty and wisdom throughout the land.

9 And the people of Angeas king of Africa saw her and they came and praised her unto him, and Angeas sent to the children of Chittim, and he requested to take her unto himself for a wife, and the people of Chittim consented to give her unto him for a wife.

10 And when the messengers of Angeas were going forth from the land of Chittim to take their journey, behold the messengers of Turnus king of Bibentu came unto Chittim, for Turnus king of Bibentu also sent his messengers to request Jania for him, to take unto himself for a wife, for all his men had also praised her to him, therefore he sent all his servants unto her.

11 And the servants of Turnus came to Chittim, and they asked for Jania, to be taken unto Turnus their king for a wife.

12 And the people of Chittim said unto them, We cannot give her, because Angeas king of Africa desired her to take her unto him for a wife before you came, and that we should give her unto him, and now therefore we cannot do this thing to deprive Angeas of the damsel in order to give her unto Turnus.

13 For we are greatly afraid of Angeas lest he come in battle against us and destroy us, and Turnus your master will not be able to deliver us from his hand.

14 And when the messengers of Turnus heard all the words of the children of Chittim, they turned back to their master and told him all the words of the children of Chittim.

15 And the children of Chittim sent a memorial to Angeas, saying, Behold Turnus has sent for Jania to take her unto him for a wife, and thus have we answered him; and we heard that he has collected his whole army to go to war against thee, and he intends to pass by the road of Sardunia to fight against thy brother Lucus, and after that he will come to fight against thee.

16 And Angeas heard the words of the children of Chittim which they sent to him in the record, and his anger was kindled and he rose up and assembled his whole army and came through the islands of the sea, the road to Sardunia, unto his brother Lucus king of Sardunia.

17 And Niblos, the son of Lucus, heard that his uncle Angeas was coming, and he went out to meet him with a heavy army, and he kissed him and embraced him, and Niblos said unto Angeas, When thou askest my father after his welfare, when I shall go with thee to fight with Turnus, ask of him to make me captain of his host, and Angeas did so, and he came unto his brother and his brother came to

meet him, and he asked him after his welfare.

18 And Angeas asked his brother Lucus after his welfare, and to make his son Niblos captain of his host, and Lucus did so, and Angeas and his brother Lucus rose up and they went toward Turnus to battle, and there was with them a great army and a heavy people.

19 And he came in ships, and they came into the province of Ashtorash, and behold Turnus came toward them, for he went forth to Sardunia, and intended to destroy it and afterward to pass on from there to Angeas to fight with him.

20 And Angeas and Lucus his brother met Turnus in the valley of Canopia, and the battle was strong and mighty between them in that place.

21 And the battle was severe upon Lucus king of Sardunia, and all his army fell, and Niblos his son fell also in that battle.

22 And his uncle Angeas commanded his servants and they made a golden coffin for Niblos and they put him into it, and Angeas again waged battle toward Turnus, and Angeas was stronger than he, and he slew him, and he smote all his people with the edge of the sword, and Angeas avenged the cause of Niblos his brother's son and the cause of the army of his brother Lucus.

23 And when Turnus died, the hands of those that survived the battle became weak, and they fled from before Angeas and Lucus his brother.

24 And Angeas and his brother Lucus pursued them unto the highroad, which is between Alphanu and Romah, and they slew the whole army of Turnus with the edge of the sword.

25 And Lucus king of Sardunia commanded his servants that they should make a coffin of brass, and that they should place therein the body of his son Niblos, and they buried him in that place.

26 And they built upon it a high tower there upon the highroad, and they called its name after the name of Niblos unto this day, and they also buried Turnus king of Bibentu there in that place with Niblos.

27 And behold upon the highroad between Alphanu and Romah the grave of Niblos is on one side and the grave of Turnus on the other, and a pavement between them unto this day.

28 And when Niblos was buried, Lucus his father returned with his army to his land Sardunia, and Angeas his brother king of Africa went with his people unto the city of Bibentu, that is the city of Turnus.

29 And the inhabitants of Bibentu heard of his fame and they were greatly afraid of him, and they went forth to meet him with weeping and supplication, and the inhabitants of Bibentu entreated of Angeas not to slay them nor destroy their city; and he did so, for Bibentu was in those days reckoned as one of the cities of the children of Chittim; therefore he did not destroy the city.

30 But from that day forward the troops of the king of Africa would go to Chittim to spoil and plunder it, and whenever they went, Zepho the captain of the host of Angeas would go with them.

31 And it was after this that Angeas turned with his army and they came to the city of Puzimna, and Angeas took thence Jania the daughter of Uzu for a wife and brought her unto his city unto Africa.

Chapter 61

1 And it came to pass at that time Pharaoh king of Egypt commanded all his people to make for him a strong palace in Egypt.

2 And he also commanded the sons of Jacob to assist the Egyptians in the building, and the Egyptians made a beautiful and elegant palace for a royal habitation, and he dwelt therein and he renewed his government and he reigned securely.

3 And Zebulun the son of Jacob died in that year, that is the seventy-second year of the going down of the Israelites to Egypt, and Zebulun died a hundred and fourteen years old, and was put into a coffin and given into the hands of his children.

4 And in the seventy-fifth year died his brother Simeon, he was a hundred and twenty years old at his death, and he was also put into a coffin and given into the hands of his children.

5 And Zepho the son of Eliphaz the son of Esau, captain of the host to Angeas king of Dinhabah, was still daily enticing Angeas to prepare for battle to fight with the sons of Jacob in Egypt, and Angeas was unwilling to do this thing, for his servants had related to him all the might of the sons of Jacob, what they had done unto them in their battle with the children of Esau.

6 And Zepho was in those days daily enticing Angeas to fight with the sons of Jacob in those days.

7 And after some time Angeas hearkened to the words of Zepho and consented to him to fight with the sons of Jacob in Egypt, and Angeas got all his people in order, a people numerous as the sand which is upon the sea shore, and he formed his resolution to go to Egypt to battle.

8 And amongst the servants of Angeas was a youth fifteen years old, Balaam the son of Beor was his name and the youth was very wise and understood the art of witchcraft.

9 And Angeas said unto Balaam, Conjure for us, I pray thee, with the witchcraft, that we may know who will prevail in this battle to which we are now proceeding.

10 And Balaam ordered that they should bring him wax, and he made thereof the likeness of chariots and horsemen representing the army of Angeas and the army of Egypt, and he put them in the cunningly prepared waters that he had for that purpose, and he took in his hand the boughs of myrtle trees, and he exercised his cunning, and he joined them over the water, and there appeared unto him in the water the resembling images of the hosts of Angeas falling before the resembling images of the Egyptians and the sons of Jacob.

11 And Balaam told this thing to Angeas, and Angeas despaired and did not arm himself to go down to Egypt to battle, and he remained in his city.

12 And when Zepho the son of Eliphaz saw that Angeas despaired of going forth to battle with the Egyptians, Zepho fled from Angeas from Africa, and he went and came unto Chittim.

13 And all the people of Chittim received him with great honor, and they hired him to fight their battles all the days, and Zepho became exceedingly rich in those days, and the troops of the king of Africa still spread themselves in those days, and the children of Chittim assembled and went to Mount Cuptizia on account of the troops of Angeas king of Africa, who were advancing upon them.

14 And it was one day that Zepho lost a young heifer, and he went to seek it, and he heard it lowing round about the mountain.

15 And Zepho went and he saw and behold there was a large cave at the bottom of the mountain, and there was a great stone there at the entrance of the cave, and Zepho split the stone and he came into the cave and he looked and

behold, a large animal was devouring the ox; from the middle upward it resembled a man, and from the middle downward it resembled an animal, and Zepho rose up against the animal and slew it with his swords.

16 And the inhabitants of Chittim heard of this thing, and they rejoiced exceedingly, and they said, What shall we do unto this man who has slain this animal that devoured our cattle?

17 And they all assembled to consecrate one day in the year to him, and they called the name thereof Zepho after his name, and they brought unto him drink offerings year after year on that day, and they brought unto him gifts.

18 At that time Jania the daughter of Uzu wife of king Angeas became ill, and her illness was heavily felt by Angeas and his officers, and Angeas said unto his wise men, What shall I do to Jania and how shall I heal her from her illness? And his wise men said unto him, Because the air of our country is not like the air of the land of Chittim, and our water is not like their water, therefore from this has the queen become ill.

19 For through the change of air and water she became ill, and also because in her country she drank only the water which came from Purmah, which her ancestors had brought up with bridges.

20 And Angeas commanded his servants, and they brought unto him in vessels of the waters of Purmah belonging to Chittim, and they weighed those waters with all the waters of the land of Africa, and they found those waters lighter than the waters of Africa.

21 And Angeas saw this thing, and he commanded all his officers to assemble the hewers of stone in thousands and tens of thousands, and they hewed stone without number, and the builders came and they built an exceedingly strong bridge, and they conveyed the spring of water from the land of Chittim unto Africa, and those waters were for Jania the queen and for all her concerns, to drink from and to bake, wash and bathe therewith, and also to water therewith all seed from which food can be obtained, and all fruit of the ground.

22 And the king commanded that they should bring of the soil of Chittim in large ships, and they also brought stones to build therewith, and the builders built palaces for Jania the queen, and the queen became healed of her illness.

23 And at the revolution of the year the troops of Africa continued coming to the land of Chittim to plunder as usual, and Zepho son of Eliphaz heard their report, and he gave orders concerning them and he fought with them, and they fled before him, and he delivered the land of Chittim from them.

24 And the children of Chittim saw the valor of Zepho, and the children of Chittim resolved and they made Zepho king over them, and he became king over them, and whilst he reigned they went to subdue the children of Tubal, and all the surrounding islands.

25 And their king Zepho went at their head and they made war with Tubal and the islands, and they subdued them, and when they returned from the battle they renewed his government for him, and they built for him a very large palace for his royal habitation and seat, and they made a large throne for him, and Zepho reigned over the whole land of Chittim and over the land of Italia fifty years.

Chapter 62

1 In that year, being the seventy-ninth year of the Israelites going down to Egypt, died Reuben the son of Jacob, in the land of Egypt; Reuben was a hundred and twenty-five years old when he died, and they put him into a coffin, and he was given into the hands of his children.

2 And in the eightieth year died his brother Dan; he was a hundred and twenty years at his death, and he was also put into a coffin and given into the hands of his children.

3 And in that year died Chusham king of Edom, and after him reigned Hadad the son of Bedad, for thirty-five years; and in the eighty-first year died Issachar the son of Jacob, in Egypt, and Issachar was a hundred and twenty-two years old at his death, and he was put into a coffin in Egypt, and given into the hands of his children.

4 And in the eighty-second year died Asher his brother, he was a hundred and twenty-three years old at his death, and he was placed in a coffin in Egypt, and given into the hands of his children.

5 And in the eighty-third year died Gad, he was a hundred and twenty-five years old at his death, and he was put into a coffin in Egypt, and given into the hands of his children.

6 And it came to pass in the eighty-fourth year, that is the fiftieth year of the reign of Hadad, son of Bedad, king of Edom, that Hadad assembled all the children of Esau, and he got his whole army in readiness, about four hundred thousand men, and he directed his way to the land of Moab, and he went to fight with Moab and to make them tributary to him.

7 And the children of Moab heard this thing, and they were very much afraid, and they sent to the children of Midian to assist them in fighting with Hadad, son of Bedad, king of Edom.

8 And Hadad came unto the land of Moab, and Moab and the children of Midian went out to meet him, and they placed themselves in battle array against him in the field of Moab.

9 And Hadad fought with Moab, and there fell of the children of Moab and the children of Midian many slain ones, about two hundred thousand men.

10 And the battle was very severe upon Moab, and when the children of Moab saw that the battle was sore upon them, they weakened their hands and turned their backs, and left the children of Midian to carry on the battle.

11 And the children of Midian knew not the intentions of Moab, but they strengthened themselves in battle and fought with Hadad and all his host, and all Midian fell before him.

12 And Hadad smote all Midian with a heavy smiting, and he slew them with the edge of the sword, he left none remaining of those who came to assist Moab.

13 And when all the children of Midian had perished in battle, and the children at Moab had escaped, Hadad made all Moab at that time tributary to him, and they became under his hand, and they gave a yearly tax as it was ordered, and Hadad turned and went back to his land.

14 And at the revolution of the year, when the rest of the people of Midian that were in the land heard that all their brethren had fallen in battle with Hadad for the sake of Moab, because the children of Moab had turned their backs in battle and left Midian to fight, then five of the princes of Midian resolved with the rest of their brethren who remained in their land, to fight with Moab to avenge the cause of their brethren.

15 And the children of Midian sent to all their brethren the children of the east, and all their brethren, all the children of Keturah came to assist Midian to fight with Moab.

16 And the children of Moab heard this thing, and they were greatly afraid that all the children of the east had assembled together against them for battle, and they the

children of Moab sent a memorial to the land of Edom to Hadad the son of Bedad, saying,

17 Come now unto us and assist us and we will smite Midian, for they all assembled together and have come against us with all their brethren the children of the east to battle, to avenge the cause of Midian that fell in battle.

18 And Hadad, son of Bedad, king of Edom, went forth with his whole army and went to the land of Moab to fight with Midian, and Midian and the children of the east fought with Moab in the field of Moab, and the battle was very fierce between them.

19 And Hadad smote all the children of Midian and the children of the east with the edge of the sword, and Hadad at that time delivered Moab from the hand of Midian, and those that remained of Midian and of the children of the east fled before Hadad and his army, and Hadad pursued them to their land, and smote them with a very heavy slaughter, and the slain fell in the road.

20 And Hadad delivered Moab from the hand of Midian, for all the children of Midian had fallen by the edge of the sword, and Hadad turned and went back to his land.

21 And from that day forth, the children of Midian hated the children of Moab, because they had fallen in battle for their sake, and there was a great and mighty enmity between them all the days.

22 And all that were found of Midian in the road of the land of Moab perished by the sword of Moab, and all that were found of Moab in the road of the land of Midian, perished by the sword of Midian; thus did Midian unto Moab and Moab unto Midian for many days.

23 And it came to pass at that time that Judah the son of Jacob died in Egypt, in the eighty-sixth year of Jacob's going down to Egypt, and Judah was a hundred and twenty-nine years old at his death, and they embalmed him and put him into a coffin, and he was given into the hands of his children.

24 And in the eighty-ninth year died Naphtali, he was a hundred and thirty-two years old, and he was put into a coffin and given into the hands of his children.

25 And it came to pass in the ninety-first year of the Israelites going down to Egypt, that is in the thirtieth year of the reign of Zepho the son of Eliphaz, the son of Esau, over the children of Chittim, the children of Africa came upon the children of Chittim to plunder them as usual, but they had not come upon them for these thirteen years.

26 And they came to them in that year, and Zepho the son of Eliphaz went out to them with some of his men and smote them desperately, and the troops of Africa fled from before Zepho and the slain fell before him, and Zepho and his men pursued them, going on and smiting them until they were near unto Africa.

27 And Angeas king of Africa heard the thing which Zepho had done, and it vexed him exceedingly, and Angeas was afraid of Zepho all the days.

Chapter 63

1 And in the ninety-third year died Levi, the son of Jacob, in Egypt, and Levi was a hundred and thirty-seven years old when he died, and they put him into a coffin and he was given into the hands of his children.

2 And it came to pass after the death of Levi, when all Egypt saw that the sons of Jacob the brethren of Joseph were dead, all the Egyptians began to afflict the children of Jacob, and to embitter their lives from that day unto the day of their going forth from Egypt, and they took from their hands all the vineyards and fields which Joseph had given unto them, and all the elegant houses in which the people of Israel lived, and all the fat of Egypt, the Egyptians took all from the sons of Jacob in those days.

3 And the hand of all Egypt became more grievous in those days against the children of Israel, and the Egyptians injured the Israelites until the children of Israel were wearied of their lives on account of the Egyptians.

4 And it came to pass in those days, in the hundred and second year of Israel's going down to Egypt, that Pharaoh king of Egypt died, and Melol his son reigned in his stead, and all the mighty men of Egypt and all that generation which knew Joseph and his brethren died in those days.

5 And another generation rose up in their stead, which had not known the sons of Jacob and all the good which they had done to them, and all their might in Egypt.

6 Therefore all Egypt began from that day forth to embitter the lives of the sons of Jacob, and to afflict them with all manner of hard labor, because they had not known their ancestors who had delivered them in the days of the famine.

7 And this was also from the Lord, for the children of Israel, to benefit them in their latter days, in order that all the children of Israel might know the Lord their God.

8 And in order to know the signs and mighty wonders which the Lord would do in Egypt on account of his people Israel, in order that the children of Israel might fear the Lord God of their ancestors, and walk in all his ways, they and their seed after them all the days.

9 Melol was twenty years old when he began to reign, and he reigned ninety-four years, and all Egypt called his name Pharaoh after the name of his father, as it was their custom to do to every king who reigned over them in Egypt.

10 At that time all the troops of Angeas king of Africa went forth to spread along the land of Chittim as usual for plunder.

11 And Zepho the son of Eliphaz the son of Esau heard their report, and he went forth to meet them with his army, and he fought them there in the road.

12 And Zepho smote the troops of the king of Africa with the edge of the sword, and left none remaining of them, and not even one returned to his master in Africa.

13 And Angeas heard of this which Zepho the son of Eliphaz had done to all his troops, that he had destroyed them, and Angeas assembled all his troops, all the men of the land of Africa, a people numerous like the sand by the sea shore.

14 And Angeas sent to Lucus his brother, saying, Come to me with all thy men and help me to smite Zepho and all the children of Chittim who have destroyed my men, and Lucus came with his whole army, a very great force, to assist Angeas his brother to fight with Zepho and the children of Chittim.

15 And Zepho and the children of Chittim heard this thing, and they were greatly afraid and a great terror fell upon their hearts.

16 And Zepho also sent a letter to the land of Edom to Hadad the son of Bedad king of Edom and to all the children of Esau, saying,

17 I have heard that Angeas king of Africa is coming to us with his brother for battle against us, and we are greatly afraid of him, for his army is very great, particularly as he comes against us with his brother and his army likewise.

18 Now therefore come you also up with me and help me, and we will fight together against Angeas and his brother Lucus, and you will save us out of their hands, but if not, know ye that we shall all die.

19 And the children of Esau sent a letter to the children of Chittim and to Zepho their king, saying, We cannot fight against Angeas and his people for a covenant of peace has been between us these many years, from the days of Bela the first king, and from the days of Joseph the son of Jacob king of Egypt, with whom we fought on the other side of Jordan when he buried his father.

20 And when Zepho heard the words of his brethren the children of Esau he refrained from them, and Zepho was greatly afraid of Angeas.

21 And Angeas and Lucus his brother arrayed all their forces, about eight hundred thousand men, against the children of Chittim.

22 And all the children of Chittim said unto Zepho, Pray for us to the God of thy ancestors, peradventure he may deliver us from the hand of Angeas and his army, for we have heard that he is a great God and that he delivers all who trust in him.

23 And Zepho heard their words, and Zepho sought the Lord and he said,

24 0 Lord God of Abraham and Isaac my ancestors, this day I know that thou art a true God, and all the gods of the nations are vain and useless.

25 Remember now this day unto me thy covenant with Abraham our father, which our ancestors related unto us, and do graciously with me this day for the sake of Abraham and Isaac our fathers, and save me and the children of Chittim from the hand of the king of Africa who comes against us for battle.

26 And the Lord hearkened to the voice of Zepho, and he had regard for him on account of Abraham and Isaac, and the Lord delivered Zepho and the children of Chittim from the hand of Angeas and his people.

27 And Zepho fought Angeas king of Africa and all his people on that day, and the Lord gave all the people of Angeas into the hands of the children of Chittim.

28 And the battle was severe upon Angeas, and Zepho smote all the men of Angeas and Lucus his brother, with the edge of the sword, and there fell from them unto the evening of that day about four hundred thousand men.

29 And when Angeas saw that all his men perished, he sent a letter to all the inhabitants of Africa to come to him, to assist him in the battle, and he wrote in the letter, saying, All who are found in Africa let them come unto me from ten years old and upward; let them all come unto me, and behold if he comes not he shall die, and all that he has, with his whole household, the king will take.

30 And all the rest of the inhabitants of Africa were terrified at the words of Angeas, and there went out of the city about three hundred thousand men and boys, from ten years upward, and they came to Angeas.

31 And at the end of ten days Angeas renewed the battle against Zepho and the children of Chittim, and the battle was very great and strong between them.

32 And from the army of Angeas and Lucus, Zepho sent many of the wounded unto his hand, about two thousand men, and Sosiphtar the captain of the host of Angeas fell in that battle.

33 And when Sosiphtar had fallen, the African troops turned their backs to flee, and they fled, and Angeas and Lucus his brother were with them.

34 And Zepho and the children of Chittim pursued them, and they smote them still heavily on the road, about two hundred men, and they pursued Azdrubal the son of Angeas who had fled with his father, and they smote twenty of his men in the road, and Azdrubal escaped from

the children of Chittim, and they did not slay him.

35 And Angeas and Lucus his brother fled with the rest of their men, and they escaped and came into Africa with terror and consternation, and Angeas feared all the days lest Zepho the son of Eliphaz should go to war with him.

Chapter 64

1 And Balaam the son of Beor was at that time with Angeas in the battle, and when he saw that Zepho prevailed over Angeas, he fled from there and came to Chittim.

2 And Zepho and the children of Chittim received him with great honor, for Zepho knew Balaam's wisdom, and Zepho gave unto Balaam many gifts and he remained with him.

3 And when Zepho had returned from the war, he commanded all the children of Chittim to be numbered who had gone into battle with him, and behold not one was missed.

4 And Zepho rejoiced at this thing, and he renewed his kingdom, and he made a feast to all his subjects.

5 But Zepho remembered not the Lord and considered not that the Lord had helped him in battle, and that he had delivered him and his people from the hand of the king of Africa, but still walked in the ways of the children of Chittim and the wicked children of Esau, to serve other gods which his brethren the children of Esau had taught him; it is therefore said, From the wicked goes forth wickedness.

6 And Zepho reigned over all the children of Chittim securely, but knew not the Lord who had delivered him and all his people from the hand of the king of Africa; and the troops of Africa came no more to Chittim to plunder as usual, for they knew of the power of Zepho who had smitten them all at the edge of the sword, so Angeas was afraid of Zepho the son of Eliphaz, and of the children of Chittim all the days.

7 At that time when Zepho had returned from the war, and when Zepho had seen how he prevailed over all the people of Africa and had smitten them in battle at the edge of the sword, then Zepho advised with the children of Chittim, to go to Egypt to fight with the sons of Jacob and with Pharaoh king of Egypt.

8 For Zepho heard that the mighty men of Egypt were dead and that Joseph and his brethren the sons at Jacob were dead, and that all their children the children of Israel remained in Egypt.

9 And Zepho considered to go to fight against them and all Egypt, to avenge the cause of his brethren the children of Esau, whom Joseph with his brethren and all Egypt had smitten in the land of Canaan, when they went up to bury Jacob in Hebron.

10 And Zepho sent messengers to Hadad, son of Bedad, king of Edom, and to all his brethren the children of Esau, saying,

11 Did you not say that you would not fight against the king of Africa for he is a member of your covenant? behold I fought with him and smote him and all his people.

12 Now therefore I have resolved to fight against Egypt and the children of Jacob who are there, and I will be revenged of them for what Joseph, his brethren and ancestors did to us in the land of Canaan when they went up to bury their father in Hebron.

13 Now then if you are willing to come to me to assist me in fighting against them and Egypt, then shall we avenge the cause of our brethren.

14 And the children of Esau hearkened to the words of

Zepho, and the children of Esau gathered themselves together, a very great people, and they went to assist Zepho and the children of Chittim in battle.

15 And Zepho sent to all the children of the east and to all the children of Ishmael with words like unto these, and they gathered themselves and came to the assistance of Zepho and the children of Chittim in the war upon Egypt.

16 And all these kings, the king of Edom and the children of the east, and all the children of Ishmael, and Zepho the king of Chittim went forth and arrayed all their hosts in Hebron.

17 And the camp was very heavy, extending in length a distance of three days' journey, a people numerous as the sand upon the sea shore which can not be counted.

18 And all these kings and their hosts went down and came against all Egypt in battle, and encamped together in the valley of Pathros.

19 And all Egypt heard their report, and they also gathered themselves together, all the people of the land of Egypt, and of all the cities belonging to Egypt, about three hundred thousand men.

20 And the men of Egypt sent also to the children of Israel who were in those days in the land of Goshen, to come to them in order to go and fight with these kings.

21 And the men of Israel assembled and were about one hundred and fifty men, and they went into battle to assist the Egyptians.

22 And the men of Israel and of Egypt went forth, about three hundred thousand men and one hundred and fifty men, and they went toward these kings to battle, and they placed themselves from without the land of Goshen opposite Pathros.

23 And the Egyptians believed not in Israel to go with them in their camps together for battle, for all the Egyptians said, Perhaps the children of Israel will deliver us into the hand of the children of Esau and Ishmael, for they are their brethren.

24 And all the Egyptians said unto the children of Israel, Remain you here together in your stand and we will go and fight against the children of Esau and Ishmael, and if these kings should prevail over us, then come you altogether upon them and assist us, and the children of Israel did so.

25 And Zepho the son of Eliphaz the son of Esau king of Chittim, and Hadad the son of Bedad king of Edom, and all their camps, and all the children of the east, and children of Ishmael, a people numerous as sand, encamped together in the valley of Pathros opposite Tachpanches.

26 And Balaam the son of Beor the Syrian was there in the camp of Zepho, for he came with the children of Chittim to the battle, and Balaam was a man highly honored in the eyes of Zepho and his men.

27 And Zepho said unto Balaam, Try by divination for us that we may know who will prevail in the battle, we or the Egyptians.

28 And Balaam rose up and tried the art of divination, and he was skillful in the knowledge of it, but he was confused and the work was destroyed in his hand.

29 And he tried it again but it did not succeed, and Balaam despaired of it and left it and did not complete it, for this was from the Lord, in order to cause Zepho and his people to fall into the hand of the children of Israel, who had trusted in the Lord, the God of their ancestors, in their war.

30 And Zepho and Hadad put their forces in battle array, and all the Egyptians went alone against them, about three hundred thousand men, and not one man of Israel was with them.

31 And all the Egyptians fought with these kings opposite Pathros and Tachpanches, and the battle was severe against the Egyptians.

32 And the kings were stronger than the Egyptians in that battle, and about one hundred and eighty men of Egypt fell on that day, and about thirty men of the forces of the kings, and all the men of Egypt fled from before the kings, so the children of Esau and Ishmael pursued the Egyptians, continuing to smite them unto the place where was the camp of the children of Israel.

33 And all the Egyptians cried unto the children of Israel, saying, Hasten to us and assist us and save us from the hand of Esau, Ishmael and the children of Chittim.

34 And the hundred and fifty men of the children of Israel ran from their station to the camps of these kings, and the children of Israel cried unto the Lord their God to deliver them.

35 And the Lord hearkened to Israel, and the Lord gave all the men of the kings into their hand, and the children of Israel fought against these kings, and the children of Israel smote about four thousand of the kings' men.

36 And the Lord threw a great consternation in the camp of the kings, so that the fear of the children of Israel fell upon them.

37 And all the hosts of the kings fled from before the children of Israel and the children of Israel pursued them continuing to smite them unto the borders of the land of Cush.

38 And the children of Israel slew of them in the road yet two thousand men, and of the children of Israel not one fell.

39 And when the Egyptians saw that the children of Israel had fought with such few men with the kings, and that the battle was so very severe against them,

40 All the Egyptians were greatly afraid of their lives on account of the strong battle, and all Egypt fled, every man hiding himself from the arrayed forces, and they hid themselves in the road, and they left the Israelites to fight.

41 And the children of Israel inflicted a terrible blow upon the kings' men, and they returned from them after they had driven them to the border of the land of Cush.

42 And all Israel knew the thing which the men of Egypt had done to them, that they had fled from them in battle, and had left them to fight alone.

43 So the children of Israel also acted with cunning, and as the children of Israel returned from battle, they found some of the Egyptians in the road and smote them there.

44 And whilst they slew them, they said unto them these words:

45 Wherefore did you go from us and leave us, being a few people, to fight against these kings who had a great people to smite us, that you might thereby deliver your own souls?

46 And of some which the Israelites met on the road, they the children of Israel spoke to each other, saying, Smite, smite, for he is an Ishmaelite, or an Edomite, or from the children of Chittim, and they stood over him and slew him, and they knew that he was an Egyptian.

47 And the children of Israel did these things cunningly against the Egyptians, because they had deserted them in battle and had fled from them.

48 And the children of Israel slew of the men of Egypt in the road in this manner, about two hundred men.

49 And all the men of Egypt saw the evil which the children of Israel had done to them, so all Egypt feared greatly the children of Israel, for they had seen their great power, and that not one man of them had fallen.

50 So all the children of Israel returned with joy on their road to Goshen, and the rest of Egypt returned each man to his place.

Chapter 65

1 And it came to pass after these things, that all the counsellors of Pharaoh, king of Egypt, and all the elders of Egypt assembled and came before the king and bowed down to the ground, and they sat before him.

2 And the counsellors and elders of Egypt spoke unto the king, saying,

3 Behold the people of the children of Israel is greater and mightier than we are, and thou knowest all the evil which they did to us in the road when we returned from battle.

4 And thou hast also seen their strong power, for this power is unto them from their fathers, for but a few men stood up against a people numerous as the sand, and smote them at the edge of the sword, and of themselves not one has fallen, so that if they had been numerous they would then have utterly destroyed them.

5 Now therefore give us counsel what to do with them, until we gradually destroy them from amongst us, lest they become too numerous for us in the land.

6 For if the children of Israel should increase in the land, they will become an obstacle to us, and if any war should happen to take place, they with their great strength will join our enemy against us, and fight against us, destroy us from the land and go away from it.

7 So the king answered the elders of Egypt and said unto them, This is the plan advised against Israel, from which we will not depart,

8 Behold in the land are Pithom and Rameses, cities unfortified against battle, it behooves you and us to build them, and to fortify them.

9 Now therefore go you also and act cunningly toward them, and proclaim a voice in Egypt and in Goshen at the command of the king, saying,

10 All ye men of Egypt, Goshen, Pathros and all their inhabitants! the king has commanded us to build Pithom and Rameses, and to fortify them for battle; who amongst you of all Egypt, of the children of Israel and of all the inhabitants of the cities, are willing to build with us, shall each have his wages given to him daily at the king's order; so go you first and do cunningly, and gather yourselves and come to Pithom and Rameses to build.

11 And whilst you are building, cause a proclamation of this kind to be made throughout Egypt every day at the command of the king.

12 And when some of the children of Israel shall come to build with you, you shall give them their wages daily for a few days.

13 And after they shall have built with you for their daily hire, drag yourselves away from them daily one by one in secret, and then you shall rise up and become their task-masters and officers, and you shall leave them afterward to build without wages, and should they refuse, then force them with all your might to build.

14 And if you do this it will be well with us to strengthen our land against the children of Israel, for on account of the fatigue of the building and the work, the children of Israel will decrease, because you will deprive them from their wives day by day.

15 And all the elders of Egypt heard the counsel of the king, and the counsel seemed good in their eyes and in the eyes of the servants of Pharaoh, and in the eyes of all Egypt, and they did according to the word of the king.

16 And all the servants went away from the king, and they caused a proclamation to be made in all Egypt, in Tachpanches and in Goshen, and in all the cities which surrounded Egypt, saying,

17 You have seen what the children of Esau and Ishmael did to us, who came to war against us and wished to destroy us.

18 Now therefore the king commanded us to fortify the land, to build the cities Pithom and Rameses, and to fortify them for battle, if they should again come against us.

19 Whosoever of you from all Egypt and from the children of Israel will come to build with us, he shall have his daily wages given by the king, as his command is unto us.

20 And when Egypt and all the children of Israel heard all that the servants of Pharaoh had spoken, there came from the Egyptians, and the children of Israel to build with the servants of Pharaoh, Pithom and Rameses, but none of the children of Levi came with their brethren to build.

21 And all the servants of Pharaoh and his princes came at first with deceit to build with all Israel as daily hired laborers, and they gave to Israel their daily hire at the beginning.

22 And the servants of Pharaoh built with all Israel, and were employed in that work with Israel for a month.

23 And at the end of the month, all the servants of Pharaoh began to withdraw secretly from the people of Israel daily.

24 And Israel went on with the work at that time, but they then received their daily hire, because some of the men of Egypt were yet carrying on the work with Israel at that time; therefore the Egyptians gave Israel their hire in those days, in order that they, the Egyptians their fellow-workmen, might also take the pay for their labor.

25 And at the end of a year and four months all the Egyptians had withdrawn from the children of Israel, so that the children of Israel were left alone engaged in the work.

26 And after all the Egyptians had withdrawn from the children of Israel they returned and became oppressors and officers over them, and some of them stood over the children of Israel as task masters, to receive from them all that they gave them for the pay of their labor.

27 And the Egyptians did in this manner to the children of Israel day by day, in order to afflict in their work.

28 And all the children of Israel were alone engaged in the labor, and the Egyptians refrained from giving any pay to the children of Israel from that time forward.

29 And when some of the men of Israel refused to work on account of the wages not being given to them, then the exactors and the servants of Pharaoh oppressed them and smote them with heavy blows, and made them return by force, to labor with their brethren; thus did all the Egyptians unto the children of Israel all the days.

30 And all the children of Israel were greatly afraid of the Egyptians in this matter, and all the children of Israel returned and worked alone without pay.

31 And the children of Israel built Pithom and Rameses, and all the children of Israel did the work, some making bricks, and some building, and the children of Israel built and fortified all the land of Egypt and its walls, and the children of Israel were engaged in work for many years, until the time came when the Lord remembered them and brought them out of Egypt.

32 But the children of Levi were not employed in the work with their brethren of Israel, from the beginning unto the day of their going forth from Egypt.

33 For all the children of Levi knew that the Egyptians had

spoken all these words with deceit to the Israelites, therefore the children of Levi refrained from approaching to the work with their brethren.

34 And the Egyptians did not direct their attention to make the children of Levi work afterward, since they had not been with their brethren at the beginning, therefore the Egyptians left them alone.

35 And the hands of the men of Egypt were directed with continued severity against the children of Israel in that work, and the Egyptians made the children of Israel work with rigor.

36 And the Egyptians embittered the lives of the children of Israel with hard work, in mortar and bricks, and also in all manner of work in the field.

37 And the children of Israel called Melol the king of Egypt "Meror, king of Egypt," because in his days the Egyptians had embittered their lives with all manner of work.

38 And all the work wherein the Egyptians made the children of Israel labor, they exacted with rigor, in order to afflict the children of Israel, but the more they afflicted them, the more they increased and grew, and the Egyptians were grieved because of the children of Israel.

Chapter 66

1 At that time died Hadad the son of Bedad king of Edom, and Samlah from Mesrekah, from the country of the children of the east, reigned in his place.

2 In the thirteenth year of the reign of Pharaoh king of Egypt, which was the hundred and twenty-fifth year of the Israelites going down into Egypt, Samlah had reigned over Edom eighteen years.

3 And when he reigned, he drew forth his hosts to go and fight against Zepho the son of Eliphaz and the children of Chittim, because they had made war against Angeas king of Africa, and they destroyed his whole army.

4 But he did not engage with him, for the children of Esau prevented him, saying, He was their brother, so Samlah listened to the voice of the children of Esau, and turned back with all his forces to the land of Edom, and did not proceed to fight against Zepho the son of Eliphaz.

5 And Pharaoh king of Egypt heard this thing, saying, Samlah king of Edom has resolved to fight the children of Chittim, and afterward he will come to fight against Egypt.

6 And when the Egyptians heard this matter, they increased the labor upon the children of Israel, lest the Israelites should do unto them as they did unto them in their war with the children of Esau in the days of Hadad.

7 So the Egyptians said unto the children of Israel, Hasten and do your work, and finish your task, and strengthen the land, lest the children of Esau your brethren should come to fight against us, for on your account will they come against us.

8 And the children of Israel did the work of the men of Egypt day by day, and the Egyptians afflicted the children of Israel in order to lessen them in the land.

9 But as the Egyptians increased the labor upon the children of Israel, so did the children of Israel increase and multiply, and all Egypt was filled with the children of Israel.

10 And in the hundred and twenty-fifth year of Israel's going down into Egypt, all the Egyptians saw that their counsel did not succeed against Israel, but that they increased and grew, and the land of Egypt and the land of Goshen were filled with the children of Israel.

11 So all the elders of Egypt and its wise men came before the king and bowed down to him and sat before him.

12 And all the elders of Egypt and the wise men thereof said unto the king, May the king live forever; thou didst counsel us the counsel against the children of Israel, and we did unto them according to the word of the king.

13 But in proportion to the increase of the labor so do they increase and grow in the land, and behold the whole country is filled with them.

14 Now therefore our lord and king, the eyes of all Egypt are upon thee to give them advice with thy wisdom, by which they may prevail over Israel to destroy them, or to diminish them from the land; and the king answered them saying, Give you counsel in this matter that we may know what to do unto them.

15 And an officer, one of the king's counsellors, whose name was Job, from Mesopotamia, in the land of Uz, answered the king, saying,

16 If it please the king, let him hear the counsel of his servant; and the king said unto him, Speak.

17 And Job spoke before the king, the princes, and before all the elders of Egypt, saying,

18 Behold the counsel of the king which he advised formerly respecting the labor of the children of Israel is very good, and you must not remove from them that labor forever.

19 But this is the advice counselled by which you may lessen them, if it seems good to the king to afflict them.

20 Behold we have feared war for a long time, and we said, When Israel becomes fruitful in the land, they will drive us from the land if a war should take place.

21 If it please the king, let a royal decree go forth, and let it be written in the laws of Egypt which shall not be revoked, that every male child born to the Israelites, his blood shall be spilled upon the ground.

22 And by your doing this, when all the male children of Israel shall have died, the evil of their wars will cease; let the king do so and send for all the Hebrew midwives and order them in this matter to execute it; so the thing pleased the king and the princes, and the king did according to the word of Job.

23 And the king sent for the Hebrew midwives to be called, of which the name of one was Shephrah, and the name of the other Puah.

24 And the midwives came before the king, and stood in his presence.

25 And the king said unto them, When you do the office of a midwife to the Hebrew women, and see them upon the stools, if it be a son, then you shall kill him, but if it be a daughter, then she shall live.

26 But if you will not do this thing, then will I burn you up and all your houses with fire.

27 But the midwives feared God and did not hearken to the king of Egypt nor to his words, and when the Hebrew women brought forth to the midwife son or daughter, then did the midwife do all that was necessary to the child and let it live; thus did the midwives all the days.

28 And this thing was told to the king, and he sent and called for the midwives and he said to them, Why have you done this thing and have saved the children alive?

29 And the midwives answered and spoke together before the king, saying,

30 Let not the king think that the Hebrew women are as the Egyptian women, for all the children of Israel are hale, and before the midwife comes to them they are delivered, and as for us thy handmaids, for many days no Hebrew woman has brought forth upon us, for all the Hebrew women are their own midwives, because they are hale.

31 And Pharaoh heard their words and believed them in

this matter, and the midwives went away from the king, and God dealt well with them, and the people multiplied and waxed exceedingly.

Chapter 67

1 There was a man in the land of Egypt of the seed of Levi, whose name was Amram, the son of Kehath, the son of Levi, the son of Israel.

2 And this man went and took a wife, namely Jochebed the daughter of Levi his father's sister, and she was one hundred and twenty-six years old, and he came unto her.

3 And the woman conceived and bare a daughter, and she called her name Miriam, because in those days the Egyptians had embittered the lives of the children of Israel.

4 And she conceived again and bare a son and she called his name Aaron, for in the days of her conception, Pharaoh began to spill the blood of the male children of Israel.

5 In those days died Zepho the son of Eliphaz, son of Esau, king of Chittim, and Janeas reigned in his stead.

6 And the time that Zepho reigned over the children of Chittim was fifty years, and he died and was buried in the city of Nabna in the land of Chittim.

7 And Janeas, one of the mighty men of the children of Chittim, reigned after him and he reigned fifty years.

8 And it was after the death of the king of Chittim that Balaam the son of Beor fled from the land of Chittim, and he went and came to Egypt to Pharaoh king of Egypt.

9 And Pharaoh received him with great honor, for he had heard of his wisdom, and he gave him presents and made him for a counsellor, and aggrandized him.

10 And Balaam dwelt in Egypt, in honor with all the nobles of the king, and the nobles exalted him, because they all coveted to learn his wisdom.

11 And in the hundred and thirtieth year of Israel's going down to Egypt, Pharaoh dreamed that he was sitting upon his kingly throne, and lifted up his eyes and saw an old man standing before him, and there were scales in the hands of the old man, such scales as are used by merchants.

12 And the old man took the scales and hung them before Pharaoh.

13 And the old man took all the elders of Egypt and all its nobles and great men, and he tied them together and put them in one scale.

14 And he took a milk kid and put it into the other scale, and the kid preponderated over all.

15 And Pharaoh was astonished at this dreadful vision, why the kid should preponderate over all, and Pharaoh awoke and behold it was a dream.

16 And Pharaoh rose up early in the morning and called all his servants and related to them the dream, and the men were greatly afraid.

17 And the king said to all his wise men, Interpret I pray you the dream which I dreamed, that I may know it.

18 And Balaam the son of Beor answered the king and said unto him, This means nothing else but a great evil that will spring up against Egypt in the latter days.

19 For a son will be born to Israel who will destroy all Egypt and its inhabitants, and bring forth the Israelites from Egypt with a mighty hand.

20 Now therefore, O king, take counsel upon this matter, that you may destroy the hope of the children of Israel and their expectation, before this evil arise against Egypt.

21 And the king said unto Balaam, And what shall we do unto Israel? surely after a certain manner did we at first counsel against them and could not prevail over them.

22 Now therefore give you also advice against them by which we may prevail over them.

23 And Balaam answered the king, saying, Send now and call thy two counsellors, and we will see what their advice is upon this matter and afterward thy servant will speak.

24 And the king sent and called his two counsellors Reuel the Midianite and Job the Uzite, and they came and sat before the king.

25 And the king said to them, Behold you have both heard the dream which I have dreamed, and the interpretation thereof; now therefore give counsel and know and see what is to be done to the children of Israel, whereby we may prevail over them, before their evil shall spring up against us.

26 And Reuel the Midianite answered the king and said, May the king live, may the king live forever.

27 If it seem good to the king, let him desist from the Hebrews and leave them, and let him not stretch forth his hand against them.

28 For these are they whom the Lord chose in days of old, and took as the lot of his inheritance from amongst all the nations of the earth and the kings of the earth; and who is there that stretched his hand against them with impunity, of whom their God was not avenged?

29 Surely thou knowest that when Abraham went down to Egypt, Pharaoh, the former king of Egypt, saw Sarah his wife, and took her for a wife, because Abraham said, She is my sister, for he was afraid, lest the men of Egypt should slay him on account of his wife.

30 And when the king of Egypt had taken Sarah then God smote him and his household with heavy plagues, until he restored unto Abraham his wife Sarah, then was he healed.

31 And Abimelech the Gerarite, king of the Philistines, God punished on account of Sarah wife of Abraham, in stopping up every womb from man to beast.

32 When their God came to Abimelech in the dream of night and terrified him in order that he might restore to Abraham Sarah whom he had taken, and afterward all the people of Gerar were punished on account of Sarah, and Abraham prayed to his God for them, and he was entreated of him, and he healed them.

33 And Abimelech feared all this evil that came upon him and his people, and he returned to Abraham his wife Sarah, and gave him with her many gifts.

34 He did so also to Isaac when he had driven him from Gerar, and God had done wonderful things to him, that all the water courses of Gerar were dried up, and their productive trees did not bring forth.

35 Until Abimelech of Gerar, and Ahuzzath one of his friends, and Pichol the captain of his host, went to him and they bent and bowed down before him to the ground.

36 And they requested of him to supplicate for them, and he prayed to the Lord for them, and the Lord was entreated of him and he healed them.

37 Jacob also, the plain man, was delivered through his integrity from the hand of his brother Esau, and the hand of Laban the Syrian his mother's brother, who had sought his life; likewise from the hand of all the kings of Canaan who had come together against him and his children to destroy them, and the Lord delivered them out of their hands, that they turned upon them and smote them, for who had ever stretched forth his hand against them with impunity?

38 Surely Pharaoh the former, thy father's father, raised Joseph the son of Jacob above all the princes of the land of Egypt, when he saw his wisdom, for through his wisdom he rescued all the inhabitants of the land from the famine.

39 After which he ordered Jacob and his children to come down to Egypt, in order that through their virtue, the land of Egypt and the land of Goshen might be delivered from the famine.

40 Now therefore if it seem good in thine eyes, cease from destroying the children of Israel, but if it be not thy will that they shall dwell in Egypt, send them forth from here, that they may go to the land of Canaan, the land where their ancestors sojourned.

41 And when Pharaoh heard the words of Jethro he was very angry with him, so that he rose with shame from the king's presence, and went to Midian, his land, and took Joseph's stick with him.

42 And the king said to Job the Uzite, What sayest thou Job, and what is thy advice respecting the Hebrews?

43 So Job said to the king, Behold all the inhabitants of the land are in thy power, let the king do as it seems good in his eyes.

44 And the king said unto Balaam, What dost thou say, Balaam, speak thy word that we may hear it.

45 And Balaam said to the king, Of all that the king has counselled against the Hebrews will they be delivered, and the king will not be able to prevail over them with any counsel.

46 For if thou thinkest to lessen them by the flaming fire, thou canst not prevail over them, for surely their God delivered Abraham their father from Ur of the Chaldeans; and if thou thinkest to destroy them with a sword, surely Isaac their father was delivered from it, and a ram was placed in his stead.

47 And if with hard and rigorous labor thou thinkest to lessen them, thou wilt not prevail even in this, for their father Jacob served Laban in all manner of hard work, and prospered.

48 Now therefore, O King, hear my words, for this is the counsel which is counselled against them, by which thou wilt prevail over them, and from which thou shouldst not depart.

49 If it please the king let him order all their children which shall be born from this day forward, to be thrown into the water, for by this canst thou wipe away their name, for none of them, nor of their fathers, were tried in this manner.

50 And the king heard the words of Balaam, and the thing pleased the king and the princes, and the king did according to the word of Balaam.

51 And the king ordered a proclamation to be issued and a law to be made throughout the land of Egypt, saying, Every male child born to the Hebrews from this day forward shall be thrown into the water.

52 And Pharaoh called unto all his servants, saying, Go now and seek throughout the land of Goshen where the children of Israel are, and see that every son born to the Hebrews shall be cast into the river, but every daughter you shall let live.

53 And when the children of Israel heard this thing which Pharaoh had commanded, to cast their male children into the river, some of the people separated from their wives and others adhered to them.

54 And from that day forward, when the time of delivery arrived to those women of Israel who had remained with their husbands, they went to the field to bring forth there, and they brought forth in the field, and left their children upon the field and returned home.

55 And the Lord who had sworn to their ancestors to multiply them, sent one of his ministering angels which are in heaven to wash each child in water, to anoint and swathe it and to put into its hands two smooth stones from one of which it sucked milk and from the other honey, and he caused its hair to grow to its knees, by which it might cover itself; to comfort it and to cleave to it, through his compassion for it.

56 And when God had compassion over them and had desired to multiply them upon the face of the land, he ordered his earth to receive them to be preserved therein till the time of their growing up, after which the earth opened its mouth and vomited them forth and they sprouted forth from the city like the herb of the earth, and the grass of the forest, and they returned each to his family and to his father's house, and they remained with them.

57 And the babes of the children of Israel were upon the earth like the herb of the field, through God's grace to them.

58 And when all the Egyptians saw this thing, they went forth, each to his field with his yoke of oxen and his ploughshare, and they ploughed it up as one ploughs the earth at seed time.

59 And when they ploughed they were unable to hurt the infants of the children of Israel, so the people increased and waxed exceedingly.

60 And Pharaoh ordered his officers daily to go to Goshen to seek for the babes of the children of Israel.

61 And when they had sought and found one, they took it from its mother's bosom by force, and threw it into the river, but the female child they left with its mother; thus did the Egyptians do to the Israelites all the days.

Chapter 68

1 And it was at that time the spirit of God was upon Miriam the daughter of Amram the sister of Aaron, and she went forth and prophesied about the house, saying, Behold a son will be born unto us from my father and mother this time, and he will save Israel from the hands of Egypt.

2 And when Amram heard the words of his daughter, he went and took his wife back to the house, after he had driven her away at the time when Pharaoh ordered every male child of the house of Jacob to be thrown into the water.

3 So Amram took Jochebed his wife, three years after he had driven her away, and he came to her and she conceived.

4 And at the end of seven months from her conception she brought forth a son, and the whole house was filled with great light as of the light of the sun and moon at the time of their shining.

5 And when the woman saw the child that it was good and pleasing to the sight, she hid it for three months in an inner room.

6 In those days the Egyptians conspired to destroy all the Hebrews there.

7 And the Egyptian women went to Goshen where the children of Israel were, and they carried their young ones upon their shoulders, their babes who could not yet speak.

8 And in those days, when the women of the children of Israel brought forth, each woman had hidden her son from before the Egyptians, that the Egyptians might not know of their bringing forth, and might not destroy them from the land.

9 And the Egyptian women came to Goshen and their children who could not speak were upon their shoulders, and when an Egyptian woman came into the house of a Hebrew woman her babe began to cry.

10 And when it cried the child that was in the inner room answered it, so the Egyptian women went and told it at the house of Pharaoh.

11 And Pharaoh sent his officers to take the children and slay them; thus did the Egyptians to the Hebrew women all the days.

12 And it was at that time, about three months from Jochebed's concealment of her son, that the thing was known in Pharaoh's house.

13 And the woman hastened to take away her son before the officers came, and she took for him an ark of bulrushes, and daubed it with slime and with pitch, and put the child therein, and she laid it in the flags by the river's brink.

14 And his sister Miriam stood afar off to know what would be done to him, and what would become of her words.

15 And God sent forth at that time a terrible heat in the land of Egypt, which burned up the flesh of man like the sun in his circuit, and it greatly oppressed the Egyptians.

16 And all the Egyptians went down to bathe in the river, on account of the consuming heat which burned up their flesh.

17 And Bathia, the daughter of Pharaoh, went also to bathe in the river, owing to the consuming heat, and her maidens walked at the river side, and all the women of Egypt as well.

18 And Bathia lifted up her eyes to the river, and she saw the ark upon the water, and sent her maid to fetch it.

19 And she opened it and saw the child, and behold the babe wept, and she had compassion on him, and she said, This is one of the Hebrew children.

20 And all the women of Egypt walking on the river side desired to give him suck, but he would not suck, for this thing was from the Lord, in order to restore him to his mother's breast.

21 And Miriam his sister was at that time amongst the Egyptian women at the river side, and she saw this thing and she said to Pharaoh's daughter, Shall I go and fetch a nurse of the Hebrew women, that she may nurse the child for thee?

22 And Pharaoh's daughter said to her, Go, and the young woman went and called the child's mother.

23 And Pharaoh's daughter said to Jochebed, Take this child away and suckle it for me, and I will pay thee thy wages, two bits of silver daily; and the woman took the child and nursed it.

24 And at the end of two years, when the child grew up, she brought him to the daughter of Pharaoh, and he was unto her as a son, and she called his name Moses, for she said, Because I drew him out of the water.

25 And Amram his father called his name Chabar, for he said, It was for him that he associated with his wife whom he had turned away.

26 And Jochebed his mother called his name Jekuthiel, Because, she said, I have hoped for him to the Almighty, and God restored him unto me.

27 And Miriam his sister called him Jered, for she descended after him to the river to know what his end would be.

28 And Aaron his brother called his name Abi Zanuch, saying, My father left my mother and returned to her on his account.

29 And Kehath the father of Amram called his name Abigdor, because on his account did God repair the breach of the house of Jacob, that they could no longer throw their male children into the water.

30 And their nurse called him Abi Socho, saying, In his

tabernacle was he hidden for three months, on account of the children of Ham.

31 And all Israel called his name Shemaiah, son of Nethanel, for they said, In his days has God heard their cries and rescued them from their oppressors.

32 And Moses was in Pharaoh's house, and was unto Bathia, Pharaoh's daughter, as a son, and Moses grew up amongst the king's children.

Chapter 69

1 And the king of Edom died in those days, in the eighteenth year of his reign, and was buried in his temple which he had built for himself as his royal residence in the land of Edom.

2 And the children of Esau sent to Pethor, which is upon the river, and they fetched from there a young man of beautiful eyes and comely aspect, whose name was Saul, and they made him king over them in the place of Samlah.

3 And Saul reigned over all the children of Esau in the land of Edom for forty years.

4 And when Pharaoh king of Egypt saw that the counsel which Balaam had advised respecting the children of Israel did not succeed, but that still they were fruitful, multiplied and increased throughout the land of Egypt,

5 Then Pharaoh commanded in those days that a proclamation should be issued throughout Egypt to the children of Israel, saying, No man shall diminish any thing of his daily labor.

6 And the man who shall be found deficient in his labor which he performs daily, whether in mortar or in bricks, then his youngest son shall be put in their place.

7 And the labor of Egypt strengthened upon the children of Israel in those days, and behold if one brick was deficient in any man's daily labor, the Egyptians took his youngest boy by force from his mother, and put him into the building in the place of the brick which his father had left wanting.

8 And the men of Egypt did so to all the children of Israel day by day, all the days for a long period.

9 But the tribe of Levi did not at that time work with the Israelites their brethren, from the beginning, for the children of Levi knew the cunning of the Egyptians which they exercised at first toward the Israelites.

Chapter 70

1 And in the third year from the birth of Moses, Pharaoh was sitting at a banquet, when Alparanith the queen was sitting at his right and Bathia at his left, and the lad Moses was lying upon her bosom, and Balaam the son of Beor with his two sons, and all the princes of the kingdom were sitting at table in the king's presence.

2 And the lad stretched forth his hand upon the king's head, and took the crown from the king's head and placed it on his own head.

3 And when the king and princes saw the work which the boy had done, the king and princes were terrified, and one man to his neighbor expressed astonishment.

4 And the king said unto the princes who were before him at table, What speak you and what say you, O ye princes, in this matter, and what is to be the judgment against the boy on account of this act?

5 And Balaam the son of Beor the magician answered before the king and princes, and he said, Remember now, O my lord and king, the dream which thou didst dream many days since, and that which thy servant interpreted unto thee.

6 Now therefore this is a child from the Hebrew children, in whom is the spirit of God, and let not my lord the king imagine that this youngster did this thing without knowledge.

7 For he is a Hebrew boy, and wisdom and understanding are with him, although he is yet a child, and with wisdom has he done this and chosen unto himself the kingdom of Egypt.

8 For this is the manner of all the Hebrews to deceive kings and their nobles, to do all these things cunningly, in order to make the kings of the earth and their men tremble.

9 Surely thou knowest that Abraham their father acted thus, who deceived the army of Nimrod king of Babel, and Abimelech king of Gerar, and that he possessed himself of the land of the children of Heth and all the kingdoms of Canaan.

10 And that he descended into Egypt and said of Sarah his wife, she is my sister, in order to mislead Egypt and her king.

11 His son Isaac also did so when he went to Gerar and dwelt there, and his strength prevailed over the army of Abimelech king of the Philistines.

12 He also thought of making the kingdom of the Philistines stumble, in saying that Rebecca his wife was his sister.

13 Jacob also dealt treacherously with his brother, and took from his hand his birthright and his blessing.

14 He went then to Padan-aram to the house of Laban his mother's brother, and cunningly obtained from him his daughter, his cattle, and all belonging to him, and fled away and returned to the land of Canaan to his father.

15 His sons sold their brother Joseph, who went down into Egypt and became a slave, and was placed in the prison house for twelve years.

16 Until the former Pharaoh dreamed dreams, and withdrew him from the prison house, and magnified him above all the princes in Egypt on account of his interpreting his dreams to him.

17 And when God caused a famine throughout the land he sent for and brought his father and all his brothers, and the whole of his father's household, and supported them without price or reward, and bought the Egyptians for slaves.

18 Now therefore my lord king behold this child has risen up in their stead in Egypt, to do according to their deeds and to trifle with every king, prince and judge.

19 If it please the king, let us now spill his blood upon the ground, lest he grow up and take away the government from thy hand, and the hope of Egypt perish after he shall have reigned.

20 And Balaam said to the king, Let us moreover call for all the judges of Egypt and the wise men thereof, and let us know if the judgment of death is due to this boy as thou didst say, and then we will slay him.

21 And Pharaoh sent and called for all the wise men of Egypt and they came before the king, and an angel of the Lord came amongst them, and he was like one of the wise men of Egypt.

22 And the king said to the wise men, Surely you have heard what this Hebrew boy who is in the house has done, and thus has Balaam judged in the matter.

23 Now judge you also and see what is due to the boy for the act he has committed.

24 And the angel, who seemed like one of the wise men of Pharaoh, answered and said as follows, before all the wise men of Egypt and before the king and the princes:

25 If it please the king let the king send for men who shall bring before him an onyx stone and a coal of fire, and place them before the child, and if the child shall stretch forth his hand and take the onyx stone, then shall we know that with wisdom has the youth done all that he has done, and we must slay him.

26 But if he stretch forth his hand upon the coal, then shall we know that it was not with knowledge that he did this thing, and he shall live.

27 And the thing seemed good in the eyes of the king and the princes, so the king did according to the word of the angel of the Lord.

28 And the king ordered the onyx stone and coal to be brought and placed before Moses.

29 And they placed the boy before them, and the lad endeavored to stretch forth his hand to the onyx stone, but the angel of the Lord took his hand and placed it upon the coal, and the coal became extinguished in his hand, and he lifted it up and put it into his mouth, and burned part of his lips and part of his tongue, and he became heavy in mouth and tongue.

30 And when the king and princes saw this, they knew that Moses had not acted with wisdom in taking off the crown from the king's head.

31 So the king and princes refrained from slaying the child, so Moses remained in Pharaoh's house, growing up, and the Lord was with him.

32 And whilst the boy was in the king's house, he was robed in purple and he grew amongst the children of the king.

33 And when Moses grew up in the king's house, Bathia the daughter of Pharaoh considered him as a son, and all the household of Pharaoh honored him, and all the men of Egypt were afraid of him.

34 And he daily went forth and came into the land of Goshen, where his brethren the children of Israel were, and Moses saw them daily in shortness of breath and hard labor.

35 And Moses asked them, saying, Wherefore is this labor meted out unto you day by day?

36 And they told him all that had befallen them, and all the injunctions which Pharaoh had put upon them before his birth.

37 And they told him all the counsels which Balaam the son of Beor had counselled against them, and what he had also counselled against him in order to slay him when he had taken the king's crown from off his head.

38 And when Moses heard these things his anger was kindled against Balaam, and he sought to kill him, and he was in ambush for him day by day.

39 And Balaam was afraid of Moses, and he and his two sons rose up and went forth from Egypt, and they fled and delivered their souls and betook themselves to the land of Cush to Kikianus, king of Cush.

40 And Moses was in the king's house going out and coming in, the Lord gave him favor in the eyes of Pharaoh, and in the eyes of all his servants, and in the eyes of all the people of Egypt, and they loved Moses exceedingly.

41 And the day arrived when Moses went to Goshen to see his brethren, that he saw the children of Israel in their burdens and hard labor, and Moses was grieved on their account.

42 And Moses returned to Egypt and came to the house of Pharaoh, and came before the king, and Moses bowed down before the king.

43 And Moses said unto Pharaoh, I pray thee my lord, I

have come to seek a small request from thee, turn not away my face empty; and Pharaoh said unto him, Speak.

44 And Moses said unto Pharaoh, Let there be given unto thy servants the children of Israel who are in Goshen, one day to rest therein from their labor.

45 And the king answered Moses and said, Behold I have lifted up thy face in this thing to grant thy request.

46 And Pharaoh ordered a proclamation to be issued throughout Egypt and Goshen, saying,

47 To you, all the children of Israel, thus says the king, for six days you shall do your work and labor, but on the seventh day you shall rest, and shall not preform any work, thus shall you do all the days, as the king and Moses the son of Bathia have commanded.

48 And Moses rejoiced at this thing which the king had granted to him, and all the children of Israel did as Moses ordered them.

49 For this thing was from the Lord to the children of Israel, for the Lord had begun to remember the children of Israel to save them for the sake of their fathers.

50 And the Lord was with Moses and his fame went throughout Egypt.

51 And Moses became great in the eyes of all the Egyptians, and in the eyes of all the children of Israel, seeking good for his people Israel and speaking words of peace regarding them to the king.

Chapter 71

1 And when Moses was eighteen years old, he desired to see his father and mother and he went to them to Goshen, and when Moses had come near Goshen, he came to the place where the children of Israel were engaged in work, and he observed their burdens, and he saw an Egyptian smiting one of his Hebrew brethren.

2 And when the man who was beaten saw Moses he ran to him for help, for the man Moses was greatly respected in the house of Pharaoh, and he said to him, My lord attend to me, this Egyptian came to my house in the night, bound me, and came to my wife in my presence, and now he seeks to take my life away.

3 And when Moses heard this wicked thing, his anger was kindled against the Egyptian, and he turned this way and the other, and when he saw there was no man there he smote the Egyptian and hid him in the sand, and delivered the Hebrew from the hand of him that smote him.

4 And the Hebrew went to his house, and Moses returned to his home, and went forth and came back to the king's house.

5 And when the man had returned home, he thought of repudiating his wife, for it was not right in the house of Jacob, for any man to come to his wife after she had been defiled.

6 And the woman went and told her brothers, and the woman's brothers sought to slay him, and he fled to his house and escaped.

7 And on the second day Moses went forth to his brethren, and saw, and behold two men were quarreling, and he said to the wicked one, Why dost thou smite thy neighbor?

8 And he answered him and said to him, Who has set thee for a prince and judge over us? dost thou think to slay me as thou didst slay the Egyptian? and Moses was afraid and he said, Surely the thing is known?

9 And Pharaoh heard of this affair, and he ordered Moses to be slain, so God sent his angel, and he appeared unto Pharaoh in the likeness of a captain of the guard.

10 And the angel of the Lord took the sword from the hand of the captain of the guard, and took his head off with it, for the likeness of the captain of the guard was turned into the likeness of Moses.

11 And the angel of the Lord took hold of the right hand of Moses, and brought him forth from Egypt, and placed him from without the borders of Egypt, a distance of forty days' journey.

12 And Aaron his brother alone remained in the land of Egypt, and he prophesied to the children of Israel, saying,

13 Thus says the Lord God of your ancestors, Throw away, each man, the abominations of his eyes, and do not defile yourselves with the idols of Egypt.

14 And the children of Israel rebelled and would not hearken to Aaron at that time.

15 And the Lord thought to destroy them, were it not that the Lord remembered the covenant which he had made with Abraham, Isaac and Jacob.

16 In those days the hand of Pharaoh continued to be severe against the children of Israel, and he crushed and oppressed them until the time when God sent forth his word and took notice of them.

Chapter 72

1 And it was in those days that there was a great war between the children of Cush and the children of the east and Aram, and they rebelled against the king of Cush in whose hands they were.

2 So Kikianus king of Cush went forth with all the children of Cush, a people numerous as the sand, and he went to fight against Aram and the children of the east, to bring them under subjection.

3 And when Kikianus went out, he left Balaam the magician, with his two sons, to guard the city, and the lowest sort of the people of the land.

4 So Kikianus went forth to Aram and the children of the east, and he fought against them and smote them, and they all fell down wounded before Kikianus and his people.

5 And he took many of them captives and he brought them under subjection as at first, and he encamped upon their land to take tribute from them as usual.

6 And Balaam the son of Beor, when the king of Cush had left him to guard the city and the poor of the city, he rose up and advised with the people of the land to rebel against king Kikianus, not to let him enter the city when he should come home.

7 And the people of the land hearkened to him, and they swore to him and made him king over them, and his two sons for captains of the army.

8 So they rose up and raised the walls of the city at the two corners, and they built an exceeding strong building.

9 And at the third corner they dug ditches without number, between the city and the river which surrounded the whole land of Cush, and they made the waters of the river burst forth there.

10 At the fourth corner they collected numerous serpents by their incantations and enchantments, and they fortified the city and dwelt therein, and no one went out or in before them.

11 And Kikianus fought against Aram and the children of the east and he subdued them as before, and they gave him their usual tribute, and he went and returned to his land.

12 And when Kikianus the king of Cush approached his city and all the captains of the forces with him, they lifted up their eyes and saw that the walls of the city were built up and greatly elevated, so the men were astonished at this.

13 And they said one to the other, It is because they saw

that we were delayed, in battle, and were greatly afraid of us, therefore have they done this thing and raised the city walls and fortified them so that the kings of Canaan might not come in battle against them.

14 So the king and the troops approached the city door and they looked up and behold, all the gates of the city were closed, and they called out to the sentinels, saying, Open unto us, that we may enter the city.

15 But the sentinels refused to open to them by the order of Balaam the magician, their king, they suffered them not to enter their city.

16 So they raised a battle with them opposite the city gate, and one hundred and thirty men of the army at Kikianus fell on that day.

17 And on the next day they continued to fight and they fought at the side of the river; they endeavored to pass but were not able, so some of them sank in the pits and died.

18 So the king ordered them to cut down trees to make rafts, upon which they might pass to them, and they did so.

19 And when they came to the place of the ditches, the waters revolved by mills, and two hundred men upon ten rafts were drowned.

20 And on the third day they came to fight at the side where the serpents were, but they could not approach there, for the serpents slew of them one hundred and seventy men, and they ceased fighting against Cush, and they besieged Cush for nine years, no person came out or in.

21 At that time that the war and the siege were against Cush, Moses fled from Egypt from Pharaoh who sought to kill him for having slain the Egyptian.

22 And Moses was eighteen years old when he fled from Egypt from the presence of Pharaoh, and he fled and escaped to the camp of Kikianus, which at that time was besieging Cush.

23 And Moses was nine years in the camp of Kikianus king of Cush, all the time that they were besieging Cush, and Moses went out and came in with them.

24 And the king and princes and all the fighting men loved Moses, for he was great and worthy, his stature was like a noble lion, his face was like the sun, and his strength was like that of a lion, and he was counsellor to the king.

25 And at the end of nine years, Kikianus was seized with a mortal disease, and his illness prevailed over him, and he died on the seventh day.

26 So his servants embalmed him and carried him and buried him opposite the city gate to the north of the land of Egypt.

27 And they built over him an elegant strong and high building, and they placed great stones below.

28 And the king's scribes engraved upon those stones all the might of their king Kikianus, and all his battles which he had fought, behold they are written there at this day.

29 Now after the death of Kikianus king of Cush it grieved his men and troops greatly on account of the war.

30 So they said one to the other, Give us counsel what we are to do at this time, as we have resided in the wilderness nine years away from our homes.

31 If we say we will fight against the city many of us will fall wounded or killed, and if we remain here in the siege we shall also die.

32 For now all the kings of Aram and of the children of the east will hear that our king is dead, and they will attack us suddenly in a hostile manner, and they will fight against us and leave no remnant of us.

33 Now therefore let us go and make a king over us, and let us remain in the siege until the city is delivered up to us.

34 And they wished to choose on that day a man for king from the army of Kikianus, and they found no object of their choice like Moses to reign over them.

35 And they hastened and stripped off each man his garments and cast them upon the ground, and they made a great heap and placed Moses thereon.

36 And they rose up and blew with trumpets and called out before him, and said, May the king live, may the king live!

37 And all the people and nobles swore unto him to give him for a wife Adoniah the queen, the Cushite, wife of Kikianus, and they made Moses king over them on that day.

38 And all the people of Cush issued a proclamation on that day, saying, Every man must give something to Moses of what is in his possession.

39 And they spread out a sheet upon the heap, and every man cast into it something of what he had, one a gold earring and the other a coin.

40 Also of onyx stones, bdellium, pearls and marble did the children of Cush cast unto Moses upon the heap, also silver and gold in great abundance.

41 And Moses took all the silver and gold, all the vessels, and the bdellium and onyx stones, which all the children of Cush had given to him, and he placed them amongst his treasures.

42 And Moses reigned over the children of Cush on that day, in the place of Kikianus king of Cush.

Chapter 73

1 In the fifty-fifth year of the reign of Pharaoh king of Egypt, that is in the hundred and fifty-seventh year of the Israelites going down into Egypt, reigned Moses in Cush.

2 Moses was twenty-seven years old when he began to reign over Cush, and forty years did he reign.

3 And the Lord granted Moses favor and grace in the eyes of all the children of Cush, and the children of Cush loved him exceedingly, so Moses was favored by the Lord and by men.

4 And in the seventh day of his reign, all the children of Cush assembled and came before Moses and bowed down to him to the ground.

5 And all the children spoke together in the presence of the king, saying, Give us counsel that we may see what is to be done to this city.

6 For it is now nine years that we have been besieging round about the city, and have not seen our children and our wives.

7 So the king answered them, saying, If you will hearken to my voice in all that I shall command you, then will the Lord give the city into our hands and we shall subdue it.

8 For if we fight with them as in the former battle which we had with them before the death of Kikianus, many of us will fall down wounded as before.

9 Now therefore behold here is counsel for you in this matter; if you will hearken to my voice, then will the city be delivered into our hands.

10 So all the forces answered the king, saying, All that our lord shall command that will we do.

11 And Moses said unto them, Pass through and proclaim a voice in the whole camp unto all the people, saying,

12 Thus says the king, Go into the forest and bring with you of the young ones of the stork, each man a young one in his hand.

13 And any person transgressing the word of the king, who shall not bring his young one, he shall die, and the king will

take all belonging to him.

14 And when you shall bring them they shall be in your keeping, you shall rear them until they grow up, and you shall teach them to dart upon, as is the way of the young ones of the hawk.

15 So all the children of Cush heard the words of Moses, and they rose up and caused a proclamation to be issued throughout the camp, saying,

16 Unto you, all the children of Cush, the king's order is, that you go all together to the forest, and catch there the young storks each man his young one in his hand, and you shall bring them home.

17 And any person violating the order of the king shall die, and the king will take all that belongs to him.

18 And all the people did so, and they went out to the wood and they climbed the fir trees and caught, each man a young one in his hand, all the young of the storks, and they brought them into the desert and reared them by order of the king, and they taught them to dart upon, similar to the young hawks.

19 And after the young storks were reared, the king ordered them to be hungered for three days, and all the people did so.

20 And on the third day, the king said unto them, strengthen yourselves and become valiant men, and put on each man his armor and gird on his sword upon him, and ride each man his horse and take each his young stork in his hand.

21 And we will rise up and fight against the city at the place where the serpents are; and all the people did as the king had ordered.

22 And they took each man his young one in his hand, and they went away, and when they came to the place of the serpents the king said to them, Send forth each man his young stork upon the serpents.

23 And they sent forth each man his young stork at the king's order, and the young storks ran upon the serpents and they devoured them all and destroyed them out of that place.

24 And when the king and people had seen that all the serpents were destroyed in that place, all the people set up a great shout.

25 And they approached and fought against the city and took it and subdued it, and they entered the city.

26 And there died on that day one thousand and one hundred men of the people of the city, all that inhabited the city, but of the people besieging not one died.

27 So all the children of Cush went each to his home, to his wife and children and to all belonging to him.

28 And Balaam the magician, when he saw that the city was taken, he opened the gate and he and his two sons and eight brothers fled and returned to Egypt to Pharaoh king of Egypt.

29 They are the sorcerers and magicians who are mentioned in the book of the law, standing against Moses when the Lord brought the plagues upon Egypt.

30 So Moses took the city by his wisdom, and the children of Cush placed him on the throne instead of Kikianus king of Cush.

31 And they placed the royal crown upon his head, and they gave him for a wife Adoniah the Cushite queen, wife of Kikianus.

32 And Moses feared the Lord God of his fathers, so that he came not to her, nor did he turn his eyes to her.

33 For Moses remembered how Abraham had made his servant Eliezer swear, saying unto him, Thou shalt not take a woman from the daughters of Canaan for my son Isaac.

34 Also what Isaac did when Jacob had fled from his brother, when he commanded him, saying, Thou shalt not take a wife from the daughters of Canaan, nor make alliance with any of the children of Ham.

35 For the Lord our God gave Ham the son of Noah, and his children and all his seed, as slaves to the children of Shem and to the children of Japheth, and unto their seed after them for slaves, forever.

36 Therefore Moses turned not his heart nor his eyes to the wife of Kikianus all the days that he reigned over Cush.

37 And Moses feared the Lord his God all his life, and Moses walked before the Lord in truth, with all his heart and soul, he turned not from the right way all the days of his life; he declined not from the way either to the right or to the left, in which Abraham, Isaac and Jacob had walked.

38 And Moses strengthened himself in the kingdom of the children of Cush, and he guided the children of Cush with his usual wisdom, and Moses prospered in his kingdom.

39 And at that time Aram and the children of the east heard that Kikianus king of Cush had died, so Aram and the children of the east rebelled against Cush in those days.

40 And Moses gathered all the children of Cush, a people very mighty, about thirty thousand men, and he went forth to fight with Aram and the children of the east.

41 And they went at first to the children of the east, and when the children of the east heard their report, they went to meet them, and engaged in battle with them.

42 And the war was severe against the children of the east, so the Lord gave all the children of the east into the hand of Moses, and about three hundred men fell down slain.

43 And all the children of the east turned back and retreated, so Moses and the children of Cush followed them and subdued them, and put a tax upon them, as was their custom.

44 So Moses and all the people with him passed from there to the land of Aram for battle.

45 And the people of Aram also went to meet them, and they fought against them, and the Lord delivered them into the hand of Moses, and many of the men of Aram fell down wounded.

46 And Aram also were subdued by Moses and the people of Cush, and also gave their usual tax.

47 And Moses brought Aram and the children of the east under subjection to the children of Cush, and Moses and all the people who were with him, turned to the land of Cush.

48 And Moses strengthened himself in the kingdom of the children of Cush, and the Lord was with him, and all the children of Cush were afraid of him.

Chapter 74

1 In the end of years died Saul king of Edom, and Baal Chanan the son of Achbor reigned in his place.

2 In the sixteenth year of the reign of Moses over Cush, Baal Chanan the son of Achbor reigned in the land of Edom over all the children of Edom for thirty-eight years.

3 In his days Moab rebelled against the power of Edom, having been under Edom since the days of Hadad the son of Bedad, who smote them and Midian, and brought Moab under subjection to Edom.

4 And when Baal Chanan the son of Achbor reigned over Edom, all the children of Moab withdrew their allegiance from Edom.

5 And Angeas king of Africa died in those days, and Azdrubal his son reigned in his stead.

6 And in those days died Janeas king of the children of

Chittim, and they buried him in his temple which he had built for himself in the plain of Canopia for a residence, and Latinus reigned in his stead.

7 In the twenty-second year of the reign of Moses over the children of Cush, Latinus reigned over the children of Chittim forty-five years.

8 And he also built for himself a great and mighty tower, and he built therein an elegant temple for his residence, to conduct his government, as was the custom.

9 In the third year of his reign he caused a proclamation to be made to all his skilful men, who made many ships for him.

10 And Latinus assembled all his forces, and they came in ships, and went therein to fight with Azrubal son of Angeas king of Africa, and they came to Africa and engaged in battle with Azrubal and his army.

11 And Latinus prevailed over Azrubal, and Latinus took from Azrubal the aqueduct which his father had brought from the children of Chittim, when he took Janiah the daughter of Uzi for a wife, so Latinus overthrew the bridge of the aqueduct, and smote the whole army of Azrubal a severe blow.

12 And the remaining strong men of Azrubal strengthened themselves, and their hearts were filled with envy, and they courted death, and again engaged in battle with Latinus king of Chittim.

13 And the battle was severe upon all the men of Africa, and they all fell wounded before Latinus and his people, and Azrubal the king also fell in that battle.

14 And the king Azrubal had a very beautiful daughter, whose name was Ushpezena, and all the men of Africa embroidered her likeness on their garments, on account of her great beauty and comely appearance.

15 And the men of Latinus saw Ushpezena, the daughter of Azrubal, and praised her unto Latinus their king.

16 And Latinus ordered her to be brought to him, and Latinus took Ushpezena for a wife, and he turned back on his way to Chittim.

17 And it was after the death of Azrubal son of Angeas, when Latinus had turned back to his land from the battle, that all the inhabitants of Africa rose up and took Anibal the son of Angeas, the younger brother of Azrubal, and made him king instead at his brother over the whole land at Africa.

18 And when he reigned, he resolved to go to Chittim to fight with the children of Chittim, to avenge the cause of Azrubal his brother, and the cause of the inhabitants of Africa, and he did so.

19 And he made many ships, and he came therein with his whole army, and he went to Chittim.

20 So Anibal fought with the children of Chittim, and the children of Chittim fell wounded before Anibal and his army, and Anibal avenged his brother's cause.

21 And Anibal continued the war for eighteen years with the children of Chittim, and Anibal dwelt in the land of Chittim and encamped there for a long time.

22 And Anibal smote the children of Chittim very severely, and he slew their great men and princes, and of the rest of the people he smote about eighty thousand men.

23 And at the end of days and years, Anibal returned to his land of Africa, and he reigned securely in the place of Azrubal his brother.

Chapter 75

1 At that time, in the hundred and eightieth year of the Israelites going down into Egypt, there went forth from Egypt valiant men, thirty thousand on foot, from the children of Israel, who were all of the tribe of Joseph, of the children of Ephraim the son of Joseph.

2 For they said the period was completed which the Lord had appointed to the children of Israel in the times of old, which he had spoken to Abraham.

3 And these men girded themselves, and they put each man his sword at his side, and every man his armor upon him, and they trusted to their strength, and they went out together from Egypt with a mighty hand.

4 But they brought no provision for the road, only silver and gold, not even bread for that day did they bring in their hands, for they thought of getting their provision for pay from the Philistines, and if not they would take it by force.

5 And these men were very mighty and valiant men, one man could pursue a thousand and two could rout ten thousand, so they trusted to their strength and went together as they were.

6 And they directed their course toward the land of Gath, and they went down and found the shepherds of Gath feeding the cattle of the children of Gath.

7 And they said to the shepherds, Give us some of the sheep for pay, that we may eat, for we are hungry, for we have eaten no bread this day.

8 And the shepherds said, Are they our sheep or cattle that we should give them to you even for pay? so the children of Ephraim approached to take them by force.

9 And the shepherds of Gath shouted over them that their cry was heard at a distance, so all the children of Gath went out to them.

10 And when the children of Gath saw the evil doings of the children of Ephraim, they returned and assembled the men of Gath, and they put on each man his armor, and came forth to the children of Ephraim for battle.

11 And they engaged with them in the valley of Gath, and the battle was severe, and they smote from each other a great many on that day.

12 And on the second day the children of Gath sent to all the cities of the Philistines that they should come to their help, saying,

13 Come up unto us and help us, that we may smite the children of Ephraim who have come forth from Egypt to take our cattle, and to fight against us without cause.

14 Now the souls of the children of Ephraim were exhausted with hunger and thirst, for they had eaten no bread for three days. And forty thousand men went forth from the cities of the Philistines to the assistance of the men of Gath.

15 And these men were engaged in battle with the children of Ephraim, and the Lord delivered the children of Ephraim into the hands of the Philistines.

16 And they smote all the children of Ephraim, all who had gone forth from Egypt, none were remaining but ten men who had run away from the engagement.

17 For this evil was from the Lord against the children of Ephraim, for they transgressed the word of the Lord in going forth from Egypt, before the period had arrived which the Lord in the days of old had appointed to Israel.

18 And of the Philistines also there fell a great many, about twenty thousand men, and their brethren carried them and buried them in their cities.

19 And the slain of the children of Ephraim remained forsaken in the valley of Gath for many days and years, and were not brought to burial, and the valley was filled with men's bones.

20 And the men who had escaped from the battle came to

Egypt, and told all the children of Israel all that had befallen them.

21 And their father Ephraim mourned over them for many days, and his brethren came to console him.

22 And he came unto his wife and she bare a son, and he called his name Beriah, for she was unfortunate in his house.

Chapter 76

1 And Moses the son of Amram was still king in the land of Cush in those days, and he prospered in his kingdom, and he conducted the government of the children of Cush in justice, in righteousness, and integrity.

2 And all the children of Cush loved Moses all the days that he reigned over them, and all the inhabitants of the land of Cush were greatly afraid of him.

3 And in the fortieth year of the reign of Moses over Cush, Moses was sitting on the royal throne whilst Adoniah the queen was before him, and all the nobles were sitting around him.

4 And Adoniah the queen said before the king and the princes, What is this thing which you, the children of Cush, have done for this long time?

5 Surely you know that for forty years that this man has reigned over Cush he has not approached me, nor has he served the gods of the children of Cush.

6 Now therefore hear, O ye children of Cush, and let this man no more reign over you as he is not of our flesh.

7 Behold Menacrus my son is grown up, let him reign over you, for it is better for you to serve the son of your lord, than to serve a stranger, slave of the king of Egypt.

8 And all the people and nobles of the children of Cush heard the words which Adoniah the queen had spoken in their ears.

9 And all the people were preparing until the evening, and in the morning they rose up early and made Menacrus, son of Kikianus, king over them.

10 And all the children of Cush were afraid to stretch forth their hand against Moses, for the Lord was with Moses, and the children of Cush remembered the oath which they swore unto Moses, therefore they did no harm to him.

11 But the children of Cush gave many presents to Moses, and sent him from them with great honor.

12 So Moses went forth from the land of Cush, and went home and ceased to reign over Cush, and Moses was sixty-six years old when he went out of the land of Cush, for the thing was from the Lord, for the period had arrived which he had appointed in the days of old, to bring forth Israel from the affliction of the children of Ham.

13 So Moses went to Midian, for he was afraid to return to Egypt on account of Pharaoh, and he went and sat at a well of water in Midian.

14 And the seven daughters of Reuel the Midianite went out to feed their father's flock.

15 And they came to the well and drew water to water their father's flock.

16 So the shepherds of Midian came and drove them away, and Moses rose up and helped them and watered the flock.

17 And they came home to their father Reuel, and told him what Moses did for them.

18 And they said, An Egyptian man has delivered us from the hands of the shepherds, he drew up water for us and watered the flock.

19 And Reuel said to his daughters, And where is he? wherefore have you left the man?

20 And Reuel sent for him and fetched him and brought him home, and he ate bread with him.

21 And Moses related to Reuel that he had fled from Egypt and that he reigned forty years over Cush, and that they afterward had taken the government from him, and had sent him away in peace with honor and with presents.

22 And when Reuel had heard the words of Moses, Reuel said within himself, I will put this man into the prison house, whereby I shall conciliate the children of Cush, for he has fled from them.

23 And they took and put him into the prison house, and Moses was in prison ten years, and whilst Moses was in the prison house, Zipporah the daughter of Reuel took pity over him, and supported him with bread and water all the time.

24 And all the children of Israel were yet in the land of Egypt serving the Egyptians in all manner of hard work, and the hand of Egypt continued in severity over the children of Israel in those days.

25 At that time the Lord smote Pharaoh king of Egypt, and he afflicted with the plague of leprosy from the sole of his foot to the crown of his head; owing to the cruel treatment of the children of Israel was this plague at that time from the Lord upon Pharaoh king of Egypt.

26 For the Lord had hearkened to the prayer of his people the children of Israel, and their cry reached him on account of their hard work.

27 Still his anger did not turn from them, and the hand of Pharaoh was still stretched out against the children of Israel, and Pharaoh hardened his neck before the Lord, and he increased his yoke over the children of Israel, and embittered their lives with all manner of hard work.

28 And when the Lord had inflicted the plague upon Pharaoh king of Egypt, he asked his wise men and sorcerers to cure him.

29 And his wise men and sorcerers said unto him, That if the blood of little children were put into the wounds he would be healed.

30 And Pharaoh hearkened to them, and sent his ministers to Goshen to the children of Israel to take their little children.

31 And Pharaoh's ministers went and took the infants of the children of Israel from the bosoms of their mothers by force, and they brought them to Pharaoh daily, a child each day, and the physicians killed them and applied them to the plague; thus did they all the days.

32 And the number of the children which Pharaoh slew was three hundred and seventy-five.

33 But the Lord hearkened not to the physicians of the king of Egypt, and the plague went on increasing mightily.

34 And Pharaoh was ten years afflicted with that plague, still the heart of Pharaoh was more hardened against the children of Israel.

35 And at the end of ten years the Lord continued to afflict Pharaoh with destructive plagues.

36 And the Lord smote him with a bad tumor and sickness at the stomach, and that plague turned to a severe boil.

37 At that time the two ministers of Pharaoh came from the land of Goshen where all the children of Israel were, and went to the house of Pharaoh and said to him, We have seen the children of Israel slacken in their work and negligent in their labor.

38 And when Pharaoh heard the words of his ministers, his anger was kindled against the children of Israel exceedingly, for he was greatly grieved at his bodily pain.

39 And he answered and said, Now that the children of Israel know that I am ill, they turn and scoff at us, now

therefore harness my chariot for me, and I will betake myself to Goshen and will see the scoff of the children of Israel with which they are deriding me; so his servants harnessed the chariot for him.

40 And they took and made him ride upon a horse, for he was not able to ride of himself;

41 And he took with him ten horsemen and ten footmen, and went to the children of Israel to Goshen.

42 And when they had come to the border of Egypt, the king's horse passed into a narrow place, elevated in the hollow part of the vineyard, fenced on both sides, the low, plain country being on the other side.

43 And the horses ran rapidly in that place and pressed each other, and the other horses pressed the king's horse.

44 And the king's horse fell into the low plain whilst the king was riding upon it, and when he fell the chariot turned over the king's face and the horse lay upon the king, and the king cried out, for his flesh was very sore.

45 And the flesh of the king was torn from him, and his bones were broken and he could not ride, for this thing was from the Lord to him, for the Lord had heard the cries of his people the children of Israel and their affliction.

46 And his servants carried him upon their shoulders, a little at a time, and they brought him back to Egypt, and the horsemen who were with him came also back to Egypt.

47 And they placed him in his bed, and the king knew that his end was come to die, so Aparanith the queen his wife came and cried before the king, and the king wept a great weeping with her.

48 And all his nobles and servants came on that day and saw the king in that affliction, and wept a great weeping with him.

49 And the princes of the king and all his counselors advised the king to cause one to reign in his stead in the land, whomsoever he should choose from his sons.

50 And the king had three sons and two daughters which Aparanith the queen his wife had borne to him, besides the king's children of concubines.

51 And these were their names, the firstborn Othri, the second Adikam, and the third Morion, and their sisters, the name of the elder Bathia and of the other Acuzi.

52 And Othri the first born of the king was an idiot, precipitate and hurried in his words.

53 But Adikam was a cunning and wise man and knowing in all the wisdom of Egypt, but of unseemly aspect, thick in flesh, and very short in stature; his height was one cubit.

54 And when the king saw Adikam his son intelligent and wise in all things, the king resolved that he should be king in his stead after his death.

55 And he took for him a wife Gedudah daughter of Abilot, and he was ten years old, and she bare unto him four sons.

56 And he afterward went and took three wives and begat eight sons and three daughters.

57 And the disorder greatly prevailed over the king, and his flesh stank like the flesh of a carcass cast upon the field in summer time, during the heat of the sun.

58 And when the king saw that his sickness had greatly strengthened itself over him, he ordered his son Adikam to be brought to him, and they made him king over the land in his place.

59 And at the end of three years, the king died, in shame, disgrace, and disgust, and his servants carried him and buried him in the sepulcher of the kings of Egypt in Zoan Mizraim.

60 But they embalmed him not as was usual with kings, for his flesh was putrid, and they could not approach to embalm him on account of the stench, so they buried him in haste.

61 For this evil was from the Lord to him, for the Lord had requited him evil for the evil which in his days he had done to Israel.

62 And he died with terror and with shame, and his son Adikam reigned in his place.

Chapter 77

1 Adikam was twenty years old when he reigned over Egypt, he reigned four years.

2 In the two hundred and sixth year of Israel's going down to Egypt did Adikam reign over Egypt, but he continued not so long in his reign over Egypt as his fathers had continued their reigns.

3 For Melol his father reigned ninety-four years in Egypt, but he was ten years sick and died, for he had been wicked before the Lord.

4 And all the Egyptians called the name of Adikam Pharaoh like the name of his fathers, as was their custom to do in Egypt.

5 And all the wise men of Pharaoh called the name of Adikam Ahuz, for short is called Ahuz in the Egyptian language.

6 And Adikam was exceedingly ugly, and he was a cubit and a span and he had a great beard which reached to the soles of his feet.

7 And Pharaoh sat upon his father's throne to reign over Egypt, and he conducted the government of Egypt in his wisdom.

8 And whilst he reigned he exceeded his father and all the preceding kings in wickedness, and he increased his yoke over the children of Israel.

9 And he went with his servants to Goshen to the children of Israel, and he strengthened the labor over them and he said unto them, Complete your work, each day's task, and let not your hands slacken from our work from this day forward as you did in the days of my father.

10 And he placed officers over them from amongst the children of Israel, and over these officers he placed taskmasters from amongst his servants.

11 And he placed over them a measure of bricks for them to do according to that number, day by day, and he turned back and went to Egypt.

12 At that time the task-masters of Pharaoh ordered the officers of the children of Israel according to the command of Pharaoh, saying,

13 Thus says Pharaoh, Do your work each day, and finish your task, and observe the daily measure of bricks; diminish not anything.

14 And it shall come to pass that if you are deficient in your daily bricks, I will put your young children in their stead.

15 And the task-masters of Egypt did so in those days as Pharaoh had ordered them.

16 And whenever any deficiency was found in the children of Israel's measure of their daily bricks, the task-masters of Pharaoh would go to the wives of the children of Israel and take infants of the children of Israel to the number of bricks deficient, they would take them by force from their mother's laps, and put them in the building instead of the bricks;

17 Whilst their fathers and mothers were crying over them and weeping when they heard the weeping voices of their infants in the wall of the building.

18 And the task-masters prevailed over Israel, that the

Israelites should place their children in the building, so that a man placed his son in the wall and put mortar over him, whilst his eyes wept over him, and his tears ran down upon his child.

19 And the task-masters of Egypt did so to the babes of Israel for many days, and no one pitied or had compassion over the babes of the children of Israel.

20 And the number of all the children killed in the building was two hundred and seventy, some whom they had built upon instead of the bricks which had been left deficient by their fathers, and some whom they had drawn out dead from the building.

21 And the labor imposed upon the children of Israel in the days of Adikam exceeded in hardship that which they performed in the days of his father.

22 And the children of Israel sighed every day on account of their heavy work, for they had said to themselves, Behold when Pharaoh shall die, his son will rise up and lighten our work!

23 But they increased the latter work more than the former, and the children of Israel sighed at this and their cry ascended to God on account of their labor.

24 And God heard the voice of the children of Israel and their cry, in those days, and God remembered to them his covenant which he had made with Abraham, Isaac and Jacob.

25 And God saw the burden of the children of Israel, and their heavy work in those days, and he determined to deliver them.

26 And Moses the son of Amram was still confined in the dungeon in those days, in the house of Reuel the Midianite, and Zipporah the daughter of Reuel did support him with food secretly day by day.

27 And Moses was confined in the dungeon in the house of Reuel for ten years.

28 And at the end of ten years which was the first year of the reign of Pharaoh over Egypt, in the place of his father,

29 Zipporah said to her father Reuel, No person inquires or seeks after the Hebrew man, whom thou didst bind in prison now ten years.

30 Now therefore, if it seem good in thy sight, let us send and see whether he is living or dead, but her father knew not that she had supported him.

31 And Reuel her father answered and said to her, Has ever such a thing happened that a man should be shut up in a prison without food for ten years, and that he should live?

32 And Zipporah answered her father, saying, Surely thou hast heard that the God of the Hebrews is great and awful, and does wonders for them at all times.

33 He it was who delivered Abraham from Ur of the Chaldeans, and Isaac from the sword of his father, and Jacob from the angel of the Lord who wrestled with him at the ford of Jabbuk.

34 Also with this man has he done many things, he delivered him from the river in Egypt and from the sword of Pharaoh, and from the children of Cush, so also can he deliver him from famine and make him live.

35 And the thing seemed good in the sight of Reuel, and he did according to the word of his daughter, and sent to the dungeon to ascertain what became of Moses.

36 And he saw, and behold the man Moses was living in the dungeon, standing upon his feet, praising and praying to the God of his ancestors.

37 And Reuel commanded Moses to be brought out of the dungeon, so they shaved him and he changed his prison garments and ate bread.

38 And afterward Moses went into the garden of Reuel which was behind the house, and he there prayed to the Lord his God, who had done mighty wonders for him.

39 And it was that whilst he prayed he looked opposite to him, and behold a sapphire stick was placed in the ground, which was planted in the midst of the garden.

40 And he approached the stick and he looked, and behold the name of the Lord God of hosts was engraved thereon, written and developed upon the stick.

41 And he read it and stretched forth his hand and he plucked it like a forest tree from the thicket, and the stick was in his hand.

42 And this is the stick with which all the works of our God were performed, after he had created heaven and earth, and all the host of them, seas, rivers and all their fishes.

43 And when God had driven Adam from the garden of Eden, he took the stick in his hand and went and tilled the ground from which he was taken.

44 And the stick came down to Noah and was given to Shem and his descendants, until it came into the hand of Abraham the Hebrew.

45 And when Abraham had given all he had to his son Isaac, he also gave to him this stick.

46 And when Jacob had fled to Padan-aram, he took it into his hand, and when he returned to his father he had not left it behind him.

47 Also when he went down to Egypt he took it into his hand and gave it to Joseph, one portion above his brethren, for Jacob had taken it by force from his brother Esau.

48 And after the death of Joseph, the nobles of Egypt came into the house of Joseph, and the stick came into the hand of Reuel the Midianite, and when he went out of Egypt, he took it in his hand and planted it in his garden.

49 And all the mighty men of the Kinites tried to pluck it when they endeavored to get Zipporah his daughter, but they were unsuccessful.

50 So that stick remained planted in the garden of Reuel, until he came who had a right to it and took it.

51 And when Reuel saw the stick in the hand of Moses, he wondered at it, and he gave him his daughter Zipporah for a wife.

Chapter 78

1 At that time died Baal Channan son of Achbor, king of Edom, and was buried in his house in the land of Edom.

2 And after his death the children of Esau sent to the land of Edom, and took from there a man who was in Edom, whose name was Hadad, and they made him king over them in the place of Baal Channan, their king.

3 And Hadad reigned over the children of Edom forty-eight years.

4 And when he reigned he resolved to fight against the children of Moab, to bring them under the power of the children of Esau as they were before, but he was not able, because the children of Moab heard this thing, and they rose up and hastened to elect a king over them from amongst their brethren.

5 And they afterward gathered together a great people, and sent to the children of Ammon their brethren for help to fight against Hadad king of Edom.

6 And Hadad heard the thing which the children of Moab had done, and was greatly afraid of them, and refrained from fighting against them.

7 In those days Moses, the son of Amram, in Midian, took Zipporah, the daughter of Reuel the Midianite, for a wife.

8 And Zipporah walked in the ways of the daughters of Jacob, she was nothing short of the righteousness of Sarah, Rebecca, Rachel and Leah.

9 And Zipporah conceived and bare a son and he called his name Gershom, for he said, I was a stranger in a foreign land; but he circumcised not his foreskin, at the command of Reuel his father-in-law.

10 And she conceived again and bare a son, but circumcised his foreskin, and called his name Eliezer, for Moses said, Because the God of my fathers was my help, and delivered me from the sword of Pharaoh.

11 And Pharaoh king of Egypt greatly increased the labor of the children of Israel in those days, and continued to make his yoke heavier upon the children of Israel.

12 And he ordered a proclamation to be made in Egypt, saying, Give no more straw to the people to make bricks with, let them go and gather themselves straw as they can find it.

13 Also the tale of bricks which they shall make let them give each day, and diminish nothing from them, for they are idle in their work.

14 And the children of Israel heard this, and they mourned and sighed, and they cried unto the Lord on account of the bitterness of their souls.

15 And the Lord heard the cries of the children of Israel, and saw the oppression with which the Egyptians oppressed them.

16 And the Lord was jealous of his people and his inheritance, and heard their voice, and he resolved to take them out of the affliction of Egypt, to give them the land of Canaan for a possession.

Chapter 79

1 And in those days Moses was feeding the flock of Reuel the Midianite his father-in-law, beyond the wilderness of Sin, and the stick which he took from his father-in-law was in his hand.

2 And it came to pass one day that a kid of goats strayed from the flock, and Moses pursued it and it came to the mountain of God to Horeb.

3 And when he came to Horeb, the Lord appeared there unto him in the bush, and he found the bush burning with fire, but the fire had no power over the bush to consume it.

4 And Moses was greatly astonished at this sight, wherefore the bush was not consumed, and he approached to see this mighty thing, and the Lord called unto Moses out of the fire and commanded him to go down to Egypt, to Pharaoh king of Egypt, to send the children of Israel from his service.

5 And the Lord said unto Moses, Go, return to Egypt, for all those men who sought thy life are dead, and thou shalt speak unto Pharaoh to send forth the children of Israel from his land.

6 And the Lord showed him to do signs and wonders in Egypt before the eyes of Pharaoh and the eyes of his subjects, in order that they might believe that the Lord had sent him.

7 And Moses hearkened to all that the Lord had commanded him, and he returned to his father-in-law and told him the thing, and Reuel said to him, Go in peace.

8 And Moses rose up to go to Egypt, and he took his wife and sons with him, and he was at an inn in the road, and an angel of God came down, and sought an occasion against him.

9 And he wished to kill him on account of his first born son, because he had not circumcised him, and had transgressed the covenant which the Lord had made with Abraham.

10 For Moses had hearkened to the words of his father-in-law which he had spoken to him, not to circumcise his first born son, therefore he circumcised him not.

11 And Zipporah saw the angel of the Lord seeking an occasion against Moses, and she knew that this thing was owing to his not having circumcised her son Gershom.

12 And Zipporah hastened and took of the sharp rock stones that were there, and she circumcised her son, and delivered her husband and her son from the hand of the angel of the Lord.

13 And Aaron the son of Amram, the brother of Moses, was in Egypt walking at the river side on that day.

14 And the Lord appeared to him in that place, and he said to him, Go now toward Moses in the wilderness, and he went and met him in the mountain of God, and he kissed him.

15 And Aaron lifted up his eyes, and saw Zipporah the wife of Moses and her children, and he said unto Moses, Who are these unto thee?

16 And Moses said unto him, They are my wife and sons, which God gave to me in Midian; and the thing grieved Aaron on account of the woman and her children.

17 And Aaron said to Moses, Send away the woman and her children that they may go to her father's house, and Moses hearkened to the words of Aaron, and did so.

18 And Zipporah returned with her children, and they went to the house of Reuel, and remained there until the time arrived when the Lord had visited his people, and brought them forth from Egypt from the hand at Pharaoh.

19 And Moses and Aaron came to Egypt to the community of the children of Israel, and they spoke to them all the words of the Lord, and the people rejoiced an exceeding great rejoicing.

20 And Moses and Aaron rose up early on the next day, and they went to the house of Pharaoh, and they took in their hands the stick of God.

21 And when they came to the king's gate, two young lions were confined there with iron instruments, and no person went out or came in from before them, unless those whom the king ordered to come, when the conjurors came and withdrew the lions by their incantations, and this brought them to the king.

22 And Moses hastened and lifted up the stick upon the lions, and he loosed them, and Moses and Aaron came into the king's house.

23 The lions also came with them in joy, and they followed them and rejoiced as a dog rejoices over his master when he comes from the field.

24 And when Pharaoh saw this thing he was astonished at it, and he was greatly terrified at the report, for their appearance was like the appearance of the children of God.

25 And Pharaoh said to Moses, What do you require? and they answered him, saying, The Lord God of the Hebrews has sent us to thee, to say, Send forth my people that they may serve me.

26 And when Pharaoh heard their words he was greatly terrified before them, and he said to them, Go today and come back to me tomorrow, and they did according to the word of the king.

27 And when they had gone Pharaoh sent for Balaam the magician and to Jannes and Jambres his sons, and to all the magicians and conjurors and counsellors which belonged to the king, and they all came and sat before the king.

28 And the king told them all the words which Moses and

his brother Aaron had spoken to him, and the magicians said to the king, But how came the men to thee, on account of the lions which were confined at the gate?

29 And the king said, Because they lifted up their rod against the lions and loosed them, and came to me, and the lions also rejoiced at them as a dog rejoices to meet his master.

30 And Balaam the son of Beor the magician answered the king, saying, These are none else than magicians like ourselves.

31 Now therefore send for them, and let them come and we will try them, and the king did so.

32 And in the morning Pharaoh sent for Moses and Aaron to come before the king, and they took the rod of God, and came to the king and spoke to him, saying,

33 Thus said the Lord God of the Hebrews, Send my people that they may serve me.

34 And the king said to them, But who will believe you that you are the messengers of God and that you come to me by his order?

35 Now therefore give a wonder or sign in this matter, and then the words which you speak will be believed.

36 And Aaron hastened and threw the rod out of his hand before Pharaoh and before his servants, and the rod turned into a serpent.

37 And the sorcerers saw this and they cast each man his rod upon the ground and they became serpents.

38 And the serpent of Aaron's rod lifted up its head and opened its mouth to swallow the rods of the magicians.

39 And Balaam the magician answered and said, This thing has been from the days of old, that a serpent should swallow its fellow, and that living things devour each other.

40 Now therefore restore it to a rod as it was at first, and we will also restore our rods as they were at first, and if thy rod shall swallow our rods, then shall we know that the spirit of God is in thee, and if not, thou art only an artificer like unto ourselves.

41 And Aaron hastened and stretched forth his hand and caught hold of the serpent's tail and it became a rod in his hand, and the sorcerers did the like with their rods, and they got hold, each man of the tail of his serpent, and they became rods as at first.

42 And when they were restored to rods, the rod of Aaron swallowed up their rods.

43 And when the king saw this thing, he ordered the book of records that related to the kings of Egypt, to be brought, and they brought the book of records, the chronicles of the kings of Egypt, in which all the idols of Egypt were inscribed, for they thought of finding therein the name of Jehovah, but they found it not.

44 And Pharaoh said to Moses and Aaron, Behold I have not found the name of your God written in this book, and his name I know not.

45 And the counsellors and wise men answered the king, We have heard that the God of the Hebrews is a son of the wise, the son of ancient kings.

46 And Pharaoh turned to Moses and Aaron and said to them, I know not the Lord whom you have declared, neither will I send his people.

47 And they answered and said to the king, The Lord God of Gods is his name, and he proclaimed his name over us from the days of our ancestors, and sent us, saying, Go to Pharaoh and say unto him, Send my people that they may serve me.

48 Now therefore send us, that we may take a journey for three days in the wilderness, and there may sacrifice to him,

for from the days of our going down to Egypt, he has not taken from our hands either burnt offering, oblation or sacrifice, and if thou wilt not send us, his anger will be kindled against thee, and he will smite Egypt either with the plague or with the sword.

49 And Pharaoh said to them, Tell me now his power and his might; and they said to him, He created the heaven and the earth, the seas and all their fishes, he formed the light, created the darkness, caused rain upon the earth and watered it, and made the herbage and grass to sprout, he created man and beast and the animals of the forest, the birds of the air and the fish of the sea, and by his mouth they live and die.

50 Surely he created thee in thy mother's womb, and put into thee the breath of life, and reared thee and placed thee upon the royal throne of Egypt, and he will take thy breath and soul from thee, and return thee to the ground whence thou wast taken.

51 And the anger of the king was kindled at their words, and he said to them, But who amongst all the Gods of nations can do this? my river is mine own, and I have made it for myself.

52 And he drove them from him, and he ordered the labor upon Israel to be more severe than it was yesterday and before.

53 And Moses and Aaron went out from the king's presence, and they saw the children of Israel in an evil condition for the task-masters had made their labor exceedingly heavy.

54 And Moses returned to the Lord and said, Why hast thou ill treated thy people? for since I came to speak to Pharaoh what thou didst send me for, he has exceedingly ill used the children of Israel.

55 And the Lord said to Moses, Behold thou wilt see that with an outstretched hand and heavy plagues, Pharaoh will send the children of Israel from his land.

56 And Moses and Aaron dwelt amongst their brethren the children of Israel in Egypt.

57 And as for the children of Israel the Egyptians embittered their lives, with the heavy work which they imposed upon them.

Chapter 80

1 And at the end of two years, the Lord again sent Moses to Pharaoh to bring forth the children of Israel, and to send them out of the land of Egypt.

2 And Moses went and came to the house of Pharaoh, and he spoke to him the words of the Lord who had sent him, but Pharaoh would not hearken to the voice of the Lord, and God roused his might in Egypt upon Pharaoh and his subjects, and God smote Pharaoh and his people with very great and sore plagues.

3 And the Lord sent by the hand of Aaron and turned all the waters of Egypt into blood, with all their streams and rivers.

4 And when an Egyptian came to drink and draw water, he looked into his pitcher, and behold all the water was turned into blood; and when he came to drink from his cup the water in the cup became blood.

5 And when a woman kneaded her dough and cooked her victuals, their appearance was turned to that of blood.

6 And the Lord sent again and caused all their waters to bring forth frogs, and all the frogs came into the houses of the Egyptians.

7 And when the Egyptians drank, their bellies were filled with frogs and they danced in their bellies as they dance

when in the river.

8 And all their drinking water and cooking water turned to frogs, also when they lay in their beds their perspiration bred frogs.

9 Notwithstanding all this the anger of the Lord did not turn from them, and his hand was stretched out against all the Egyptians to smite them with every heavy plague.

10 And he sent and smote their dust to lice, and the lice became in Egypt to the height of two cubits upon the earth.

11 The lice were also very numerous, in the flesh of man and beast, in all the inhabitants of Egypt, also upon the king and queen the Lord sent the lice, and it grieved Egypt exceedingly on account of the lice.

12 Notwithstanding this, the anger of the Lord did not turn away, and his hand was still stretched out over Egypt.

13 And the Lord sent all kinds of beasts of the field into Egypt, and they came and destroyed all Egypt, man and beast, and trees, and all things that were in Egypt.

14 And the Lord sent fiery serpents, scorpions, mice, weasels, toads, together with others creeping in dust.

15 Flies, hornets, fleas, bugs and gnats, each swarm according to its kind.

16 And all reptiles and winged animals according to their kind came to Egypt and grieved the Egyptians exceedingly.

17 And the fleas and flies came into the eyes and ears of the Egyptians.

18 And the hornet came upon them and drove them away, and they removed from it into their inner rooms, and it pursued them.

19 And when the Egyptians hid themselves on account of the swarm of animals, they locked their doors after them, and God ordered the Sulanuth which was in the sea, to come up and go into Egypt.

20 And she had long arms, ten cubits in length of the cubit of a man.

21 And she went upon the roofs and uncovered the raftering and flooring and cut them, and stretched forth her arm into the house and removed the lock and the bolt, and opened the houses of Egypt.

22 Afterward came the swarm of animals into the houses of Egypt, and the swarm of animals destroyed the Egyptians, and it grieved them exceedingly.

23 Notwithstanding this the anger of the Lord did not turn away from the Egyptians, and his hand was yet stretched forth against them.

24 And God sent the pestilence, and the pestilence pervaded Egypt, in the horses and asses, and in the camels, in herds of oxen and sheep and in man.

25 And when the Egyptians rose up early in the morning to take their cattle to pasture they found all their cattle dead.

26 And there remained of the cattle of the Egyptians only one in ten, and of the cattle belonging to Israel in Goshen not one died.

27 And God sent a burning inflammation in the flesh of the Egyptians, which burst their skins, and it became a severe itch in all the Egyptians from the soles of their feet to the crowns of their heads.

28 And many boils were in their flesh, that their flesh wasted away until they became rotten and putrid.

29 Notwithstanding this the anger of the Lord did not turn away, and his hand was still stretched out over all Egypt.

30 And the Lord sent a very heavy hail, which smote their vines and broke their fruit trees and dried them up that they fell upon them.

31 Also every green herb became dry and perished, for a mingling fire descended amidst the hail, therefore the hail and the fire consumed all things.

32 Also men and beasts that were found abroad perished of the flames of fire and of the hail, and all the young lions were exhausted.

33 And the Lord sent and brought numerous locusts into Egypt, the Chasel, Salom, Chargol, and Chagole, locusts each of its kind, which devoured all that the hail had left remaining.

34 Then the Egyptians rejoiced at the locusts, although they consumed the produce of the field, and they caught them in abundance and salted them for food.

35 And the Lord turned a mighty wind of the sea which took away all the locusts, even those that were salted, and thrust them into the Red Sea; not one locust remained within the boundaries of Egypt.

36 And God sent darkness upon Egypt, that the whole land of Egypt and Pathros became dark for three days, so that a man could not see his hand when he lifted it to his mouth.

37 At that time died many of the people of Israel who had rebelled against the Lord and who would not hearken to Moses and Aaron, and believed not in them that God had sent them.

38 And who had said, We will not go forth from Egypt lest we perish with hunger in a desolate wilderness, and who would not hearken to the voice of Moses.

39 And the Lord plagued them in the three days of darkness, and the Israelites buried them in those days, without the Egyptians knowing of them or rejoicing over them.

40 And the darkness was very great in Egypt for three days, and any person who was standing when the darkness came, remained standing in his place, and he that was sitting remained sitting, and he that was lying continued lying in the same state, and he that was walking remained sitting upon the ground in the same spot; and this thing happened to all the Egyptians, until the darkness had passed away.

41 And the days of darkness passed away, and the Lord sent Moses and Aaron to the children of Israel, saying, Celebrate your feast and make your Passover, for behold I come in the midst of the night amongst all the Egyptians, and I will smite all their first born, from the first born of a man to the first born of a beast, and when I see your Passover, I will pass over you.

42 And the children of Israel did according to all that the Lord had commanded Moses and Aaron, thus did they in that night.

43 And it came to pass in the middle of the night, that the Lord went forth in the midst of Egypt, and smote all the first born of the Egyptians, from the first born of man to the first born of beast.

44 And Pharaoh rose up in the night, he and all his servants and all the Egyptians, and there was a great cry throughout Egypt in that night, for there was not a house in which there was not a corpse.

45 Also the likenesses of the first born of Egypt, which were carved in the walls at their houses, were destroyed and fell to the ground.

46 Even the bones of their first born who had died before this and whom they had buried in their houses, were raked up by the dogs of Egypt on that night and dragged before the Egyptians and cast before them.

47 And all the Egyptians saw this evil which had suddenly come upon them, and all the Egyptians cried out with a loud voice.

48 And all the families of Egypt wept upon that night, each

man for his son and each man for his daughter, being the first born, and the tumult of Egypt was heard at a distance on that night.

49 And Bathia the daughter of Pharoah went forth with the king on that night to seek Moses and Aaron in their houses, and they found them in their houses, eating and drinking and rejoicing with all Israel.

50 And Bathia said to Moses, Is this the reward for the good which I have done to thee, who have reared thee and stretched thee out, and thou hast brought this evil upon me and my father's house?

51 And Moses said to her, Surely ten plagues did the Lord bring upon Egypt; did any evil accrue to thee from any of them? did one of them affect thee? and she said, No.

52 And Moses said to her, Although thou art the first born to thy mother, thou shalt not die, and no evil shall reach thee in the midst of Egypt.

53 And she said, What advantage is it to me, when I see the king, my brother, and all his household and subjects in this evil, whose first born perish with all the first born of Egypt?

54 And Moses said to her, Surely thy brother and his household, and subjects, the families of Egypt, would not hearken to the words of the Lord, therefore did this evil come upon them.

55 And Pharoah king of Egypt approached Moses and Aaron, and some of the children of Israel who were with them in that place, and he prayed to them, saying,

56 Rise up and take your brethren, all the children of Israel who are in the land, with their sheep and oxen, and all belonging to them, they shall leave nothing remaining, only pray for me to the Lord your God.

57 And Moses said to Pharoah, Behold though thou art thy mother's first born, yet fear not, for thou wilt not die, for the Lord has commanded that thou shalt live, in order to show thee his great might and strong stretched out arm.

58 And Pharoah ordered the children of Israel to be sent away, and all the Egyptians strengthened themselves to send them, for they said, We are all perishing.

59 And all the Egyptians sent the Israelites forth, with great riches, sheep and oxen and precious things, according to the oath of the Lord between him and our Father Abraham.

60 And the children of Israel delayed going forth at night, and when the Egyptians came to them to bring them out, they said to them, Are we thieves, that we should go forth at night?

61 And the children of Israel asked of the Egyptians, vessels of silver, and vessels of gold, and garments, and the children of Israel stripped the Egyptians.

62 And Moses hastened and rose up and went to the river of Egypt, and brought up from thence the coffin of Joseph and took it with him.

63 The children of Israel also brought up, each man his father's coffin with him, and each man the coffins of his tribe.

Chapter 81

1 And the children of Israel journeyed from Rameses to Succoth, about six hundred thousand men on foot, besides the little ones and their wives.

2 Also a mixed multitude went up with them, and flocks and herds, even much cattle.

3 And the sojourning of the children of Israel, who dwelt in the land of Egypt in hard labor, was two hundred and ten years.

4 And at the end of two hundred and ten years, the Lord brought forth the children of Israel from Egypt with a strong hand.

5 And the children of Israel traveled from Egypt and from Goshen and from Rameses, and encamped in Succoth on the fifteenth day of the first month.

6 And the Egyptians buried all their first born whom the Lord had smitten, and all the Egyptians buried their slain for three days.

7 And the children of Israel traveled from Succoth and encamped in Ethom, at the end of the wilderness.

8 And on the third day after the Egyptians had buried their first born, many men rose up from Egypt and went after Israel to make them return to Egypt, for they repented that they had sent the Israelites away from their servitude.

9 And one man said to his neighbor, Surely Moses and Aaron spoke to Pharaoh, saying, We will go a three days' journey in the wilderness and sacrifice to the Lord our God.

10 Now therefore let us rise up early in the morning and cause them to return, and it shall be that if they return with us to Egypt to their masters, then shall we know that there is faith in them, but if they will not return, then will we fight with them, and make them come back with great power and a strong hand.

11 And all the nobles of Pharaoh rose up in the morning, and with them about seven hundred thousand men, and they went forth from Egypt on that day, and came to the place where the children of Israel were.

12 And all the Egyptians saw and behold Moses and Aaron and all the children of Israel were sitting before Pi-hahiroth, eating and drinking and celebrating the feast of the Lord.

13 And all the Egyptians said to the children of Israel, Surely you said, We will go a journey for three days in the wilderness and sacrifice to our God and return.

14 Now therefore this day makes five days since you went, why do you not return to your masters?

15 And Moses and Aaron answered them, saying, Because the Lord our God has testified in us, saying, You shall no more return to Egypt, but we will betake ourselves to a land flowing with milk and honey, as the Lord our God had sworn to our ancestors to give to us.

16 And when the nobles of Egypt saw that the children of Israel did not hearken to them, to return to Egypt, they girded themselves to fight with Israel.

17 And the Lord strengthened the hearts of the children of Israel over the Egyptians, that they gave them a severe beating, and the battle was sore upon the Egyptians, and all the Egyptians fled from before the children of Israel, for many of them perished by the hand of Israel.

18 And the nobles of Pharaoh went to Egypt and told Pharaoh, saying, The children of Israel have fled, and will no more return to Egypt, and in this manner did Moses and Aaron speak to us.

19 And Pharoah heard this thing, and his heart and the hearts of all his subjects were turned against Israel, and they repented that they had sent Israel; and all the Egyptians advised Pharaoh to pursue the children of Israel to make them come back to their burdens.

20 And they said each man to his brother, What is this which we have done, that we have sent Israel from our servitude?

21 And the Lord strengthened the hearts of all the Egyptians to pursue the Israelites, for the Lord desired to overthrow the Egyptians in the Red Sea.

22 And Pharaoh rose up and harnessed his chariot, and he

ordered all the Egyptians to assemble, not one man was left excepting the little ones and the women.

23 And all the Egyptians went forth with Pharaoh to pursue the children of Israel, and the camp of Egypt was an exceedingly large and heavy camp, about ten hundred thousand men.

24 And the whole of this camp went and pursued the children of Israel to bring them back to Egypt, and they reached them encamping by the Red Sea.

25 And the children of Israel lifted up their eyes, and beheld all the Egyptians pursuing them, and the children of Israel were greatly terrified at them, and the children of Israel cried to the Lord.

26 And on account of the Egyptians, the children of Israel divided themselves into four divisions, and they were divided in their opinions, for they were afraid of the Egyptians, and Moses spoke to each of them.

27 The first division was of the children of Reuben, Simeon, and Issachar, and they resolved to cast themselves into the sea, for they were exceedingly afraid of the Egyptians.

28 And Moses said to them, Fear not, stand still and see the salvation of the Lord which He will effect this day for you.

29 The second division was of the children of Zebulun, Benjamin and Naphtali, and they resolved to go back to Egypt with the Egyptians.

30 And Moses said to them, Fear not, for as you have seen the Egyptians this day, so shall you see them no more for ever.

31 The third division was of the children of Judah and Joseph, and they resolved to go to meet the Egyptians to fight with them.

32 And Moses said to them, Stand in your places, for the Lord will fight for you, and you shall remain silent.

33 And the fourth division was of the children of Levi, Gad, and Asher, and they resolved to go into the midst of the Egyptians to confound them, and Moses said to them, Remain in your stations and fear not, only call unto the Lord that he may save you out of their hands.

34 After this Moses rose up from amidst the people, and he prayed to the Lord and said,

35 O Lord God of the whole earth, save now thy people whom thou didst bring forth from Egypt, and let not the Egyptians boast that power and might are theirs.

36 So the Lord said to Moses, Why dost thou cry unto me? speak to the children of Israel that they shall proceed, and do thou stretch out thy rod upon the sea and divide it, and the children of Israel shall pass through it.

37 And Moses did so, and he lifted up his rod upon the sea and divided it.

38 And the waters of the sea were divided into twelve parts, and the children of Israel passed through on foot, with shoes, as a man would pass through a prepared road.

39 And the Lord manifested to the children of Israel his wonders in Egypt and in the sea by the hand of Moses and Aaron.

40 And when the children of Israel had entered the sea, the Egyptians came after them, and the waters of the sea resumed upon them, and they all sank in the water, and not one man was left excepting Pharaoh, who gave thanks to the Lord and believed in him, therefore the Lord did not cause him to perish at that time with the Egyptians.

41 And the Lord ordered an angel to take him from amongst the Egyptians, who cast him upon the land of Ninevah and he reigned over it for a long time.

42 And on that day the Lord saved Israel from the hand of Egypt, and all the children of Israel saw that the Egyptians had perished, and they beheld the great hand of the Lord, in what he had performed in Egypt and in the sea.

43 Then sang Moses and the children of Israel this song unto the Lord, on the day when the Lord caused the Egyptians to fall before them.

44 And all Israel sang in concert, saying, I will sing to the Lord for He is greatly exalted, the horse and his rider has he cast into the sea; behold it is written in the book of the law of God.

45 After this the children of Israel proceeded on their journey, and encamped in Marah, and the Lord gave to the children of Israel statutes and judgments in that place in Marah, and the Lord commanded the children of Israel to walk in all his ways and to serve him.

46 And they journeyed from Marah and came to Elim, and in Elim were twelve springs of water and seventy date trees, and the children encamped there by the waters.

47 And they journeyed from Elim and came to the wilderness of Sin, on the fifteenth day of the second month after their departure from Egypt.

48 At that time the Lord gave the manna to the children of Israel to eat, and the Lord caused food to rain from heaven for the children of Israel day by day.

49 And the children of Israel ate the manna for forty years, all the days that they were in the wilderness, until they came to the land of Canaan to possess it.

50 And they proceeded from the wilderness of Sin and encamped in Alush.

51 And they proceeded from Alush and encamped in Rephidim.

52 And when the children of Israel were in Rephidim, Amalek the son of Eliphaz, the son of Esau, the brother of Zepho, came to fight with Israel.

53 And he brought with him eight hundred and one thousand men, magicians and conjurers, and he prepared for battle with Israel in Rephidim.

54 And they carried on a great and severe battle against Israel, and the Lord delivered Amalek and his people into the hands of Moses and the children of Israel, and into the hand of Joshua, the son of Nun, the Ephrathite, the servant of Moses.

55 And the children of Israel smote Amalek and his people at the edge of the sword, but the battle was very sore upon the children of Israel.

56 And the Lord said to Moses, Write this thing as a memorial for thee in a book, and place it in the hand of Joshua, the son of Nun, thy servant, and thou shalt command the children of Israel, saying, When thou shalt come to the land of Canaan, thou shalt utterly efface the remembrance of Amalek from under heaven.

57 And Moses did so, and he took the book and wrote upon it these words, saying,

58 Remember what Amalek has done to thee in the road when thou wentest forth from Egypt.

59 Who met thee in the road and smote thy rear, even those that were feeble behind thee when thou wast faint and weary.

60 Therefore it shall be when the Lord thy God shall have given thee rest from all thine enemies round about in the land which the Lord thy God giveth thee for an inheritance, to possess it, that thou shalt blot out the remembrance of Amalek from under heaven, thou shalt not forget it.

61 And the king who shall have pity on Amalek, or upon his memory or upon his seed, behold I will require it of him, and I will cut him off from amongst his people.

62 And Moses wrote all these things in a book, and he enjoined the children of Israel respecting all these matters.

Chapter 82

1 And the children of Israel proceeded from Rephidim and they encamped in the wilderness of Sinai, in the third month from their going forth from Egypt.

2 At that time came Reuel the Midianite, the father-in-law of Moses, with Zipporah his daughter and her two sons, for he had heard of the wonders of the Lord which he had done to Israel, that he had delivered them from the hand of Egypt.

3 And Reuel came to Moses to the wilderness where he was encamped, where was the mountain of God.

4 And Moses went forth to meet his father-in-law with great honor, and all Israel was with him.

5 And Reuel and his children remained amongst the Israelites for many days, and Reuel knew the Lord from that day forward.

6 And in the third month from the children of Israel's departure from Egypt, on the sixth day thereof, the Lord gave to Israel the ten commandments on Mount Sinai.

7 And all Israel heard all these commandments, and all Israel rejoiced exceedingly in the Lord on that day.

8 And the glory of the Lord rested upon Mount Sinai, and he called to Moses, and Moses came in the midst of a cloud and ascended the mountain.

9 And Moses was upon the mount forty days and forty nights; he ate no bread and drank no water, and the Lord instructed him in the statutes and judgments in order to teach the children of Israel.

10 And the Lord wrote the ten commandments which he had commanded the children of Israel upon two tablets of stone, which he gave to Moses to command the children of Israel.

11 And at the end of forty days and forty nights, when the Lord had finished speaking to Moses on Mount Sinai, then the Lord gave to Moses the tablets of stone, written with the finger of God.

12 And when the children of Israel saw that Moses tarried to come down from the mount, they gathered round Aaron, and said, As for this man Moses we know not what has become of him.

13 Now therefore rise up, make unto us a god who shall go before us, so that thou shalt not die.

14 And Aaron was greatly afraid of the people, and he ordered them to bring him gold and he made it into a molten calf for the people.

15 And the Lord said to Moses, before he had come down from the mount, Get thee down, for thy people whom thou didst bring forth from Egypt have corrupted themselves.

16 They have made to themselves a molten calf, and have bowed down to it, now therefore leave me, that I may consume them from off the earth, for they are a stiffnecked people.

17 And Moses besought the countenance of the Lord, and he prayed to the Lord for the people on account of the calf which they had made, and he afterward descended from the mount and in his hands were the two tablets of stone, which God had given him to command the Israelites.

18 And when Moses approached the camp and saw the calf which the people had made, the anger of Moses was kindled and he broke the tablets under the mount.

19 And Moses came to the camp and he took the calf and burned it with fire, and ground it till it became fine dust, and strewed it upon the water and gave it to the Israelites to drink.

20 And there died of the people by the swords of each other about three thousand men who had made the calf.

21 And on the morrow Moses said to the people, I will go up to the Lord, peradventure I may make atonement for your sins which you have sinned to the Lord.

22 And Moses again went up to the Lord, and he remained with the Lord forty days and forty nights.

23 And during the forty days did Moses entreat the Lord in behalf of the children of Israel, and the Lord hearkened to the prayer of Moses, and the Lord was entreated of him in behalf of Israel.

24 Then spake the Lord to Moses to hew two stone tablets and to bring them up to the Lord, who would write upon them the ten commandments.

25 Now Moses did so, and he came down and hewed the two tablets and went up to Mount Sinai to the Lord, and the Lord wrote the ten commandments upon the tablets.

26 And Moses remained yet with the Lord forty days and forty nights, and the Lord instructed him in statutes and judgments to impart to Israel.

27 And the Lord commanded him respecting the children of Israel that they should make a sanctuary for the Lord, that his name might rest therein, and the Lord showed him the likeness of the sanctuary and the likeness of all its vessels.

28 And at the end of the forty days, Moses came down from the mount and the two tablets were in his hand.

29 And Moses came to the children of Israel and spoke to them all the words of the Lord, and he taught them laws, statutes and judgments which the Lord had taught him.

30 And Moses told the children of Israel the word of the Lord, that a sanctuary should be made for him, to dwell amongst the children of Israel.

31 And the people rejoiced greatly at all the good which the Lord had spoken to them, through Moses, and they said, We will do all that the Lord has spoken to thee.

32 And the people rose up like one man and they made generous offerings to the sanctuary of the Lord, and each man brought the offering of the Lord for the work of the sanctuary, and for all its service.

33 And all the children of Israel brought each man of all that was found in his possession for the work of the sanctuary of the Lord, gold, silver and brass, and every thing that was serviceable for the sanctuary.

34 And all the wise men who were practiced in work came and made the sanctuary of the Lord, according to all that the Lord had commanded, every man in the work in which he had been practiced; and all the wise men in heart made the sanctuary, and its furniture and all the vessels for the holy service, as the Lord had commanded Moses.

35 And the work of the sanctuary of the tabernacle was completed at the end of five months, and the children of Israel did all that the Lord had commanded Moses.

36 And they brought the sanctuary and all its furniture to Moses; like unto the representation which the Lord had shown to Moses, so did the children of Israel.

37 And Moses saw the work, and behold they did it as the Lord had commanded him, so Moses blessed them.

Chapter 83

1 And in the twelfth month, in the twenty-third day of the month, Moses took Aaron and his sons, and he dressed them in their garments, and anointed them and did unto them as the Lord had commanded him, and Moses brought

up all the offerings which the Lord had on that day commanded him.

2 Moses afterward took Aaron and his sons and said to them, For seven days shall you remain at the door of the tabernacle, for thus am I commanded.

3 And Aaron and his sons did all that the Lord had commanded them through Moses, and they remained for seven days at the door of the tabernacle.

4 And on the eighth day, being the first day of the first month, in the second year from the Israelites' departure from Egypt, Moses erected the sanctuary, and Moses put up all the furniture of the tabernacle and all the furniture of the sanctuary, and he did all that the Lord had commanded him.

5 And Moses called to Aaron and his sons, and they brought the burnt offering and the sin offering for themselves and the children of Israel, as the Lord had commanded Moses.

6 On that day the two sons of Aaron, Nadab and Abihu, took strange fire and brought it before the Lord who had not commanded them, and a fire went forth from before the Lord, and consumed them, and they died before the Lord on that day.

7 Then on the day when Moses had completed to erect the sanctuary, the princes of the children of Israel began to bring their offerings before the Lord for the dedication of the altar.

8 And they brought up their offerings each prince for one day, a prince each day for twelve days.

9 And all the offerings which they brought, each man in his day, one silver charger weighing one hundred and thirty shekels, one silver bowl of seventy shekels after the shekel of the sanctuary, both of them full of fine flour, mingled with oil for a meat offering.

10 One spoon, weighing ten shekels of gold, full of incense.

11 One young bullock, one ram, one lamb of the first year for a burnt offering.

12 And one kid of the goats for a sin offering.

13 And for a sacrifice of peace offering, two oxen, five rams, five he-goats, five lambs of a year old.

14 Thus did the twelve princes of Israel day by day, each man in his day.

15 And it was after this, in the thirteenth day of the month, that Moses commanded the children of Israel to observe the Passover.

16 And the children of Israel kept the Passover in its season in the fourteenth day of the month, as the Lord had commanded Moses, so did the children of Israel.

17 And in the second month, on the first day thereof, the Lord spoke unto Moses, saying,

18 Number the heads of all the males of the children of Israel from twenty years old and upward, thou and thy brother Aaron and the twelve princes of Israel.

19 And Moses did so, and Aaron came with the twelve princes of Israel, and they numbered the children of Israel in the wilderness of Sinai.

20 And the numbers of the children of Israel by the houses of their fathers, from twenty years old and upward, were six hundred and three thousand, five hundred and fifty.

21 But the children of Levi were not numbered amongst their brethren the children of Israel.

22 And the number of all the males of the children of Israel from one month old and upward, was twenty-two thousand, two hundred and seventy-three.

23 And the number of the children of Levi from one month old and above, was twenty-two thousand.

24 And Moses placed the priests and the Levites each man to his service and to his burden to serve the sanctuary of the tabernacle, as the Lord had commanded Moses.

25 And on the twentieth day of the month, the cloud was taken away from the tabernacle of testimony.

26 At that time the children of Israel continued their journey from the wilderness of Sinai, and they took a journey of three days, and the cloud rested upon the wilderness of Paran; there the anger of the Lord was kindled against Israel, for they had provoked the Lord in asking him for meat, that they might eat.

27 And the Lord hearkened to their voice, and gave them meat which they ate for one month.

28 But after this the anger of the Lord was kindled against them, and he smote them with a great slaughter, and they were buried there in that place.

29 And the children of Israel called that place Kebroth Hattaavah, because there they buried the people that lusted flesh.

30 And they departed from Kebroth Hattaavah and pitched in Hazeroth, which is in the wilderness of Paran.

31 And whilst the children of Israel were in Hazeroth, the anger of the Lord was kindled against Miriam on account of Moses, and she became leprous, white as snow.

32 And she was confined without the camp for seven days, until she had been received again after her leprosy.

33 The children of Israel afterward departed from Hazeroth, and pitched in the end of the wilderness of Paran.

34 At that time, the Lord spoke to Moses to send twelve men from the children of Israel, one man to a tribe, to go and explore the land of Canaan.

35 And Moses sent the twelve men, and they came to the land of Canaan to search and examine it, and they explored the whole land from the wilderness of Sin to Rechob as thou comest to Chamoth.

36 And at the end of forty days they came to Moses and Aaron, and they brought him word as it was in their hearts, and ten of the men brought up an evil report to the children of Israel, of the land which they had explored, saying, It is better for us to return to Egypt than to go to this land, a land that consumes its inhabitants.

37 But Joshua the son of Nun, and Caleb the son of Jephuneh, who were of those that explored the land, said, The land is exceedingly good.

38 If the Lord delight in us, then he will bring us to this land and give it to us, for it is a land flowing with milk and honey.

39 But the children of Israel would not hearken to them, and they hearkened to the words of the ten men who had brought up an evil report of the land.

40 And the Lord heard the murmurings of the children of Israel and he was angry and swore, saying,

41 Surely not one man of this wicked generation shall see the land from twenty years old and upward excepting Caleb the son of Jephuneh and Joshua the son of Nun.

42 But surely this wicked generation shall perish in this wilderness, and their children shall come to the land and they shall possess it; so the anger of the Lord was kindled against Israel, and he made them wander in the wilderness for forty years until the end of that wicked generation, because they did not follow the Lord.

43 And the people dwelt in the wilderness of Paran a long time, and they afterward proceeded to the wilderness by the way of the Red Sea.

Chapter 84

1 At that time Korah the son of Jetzer the son of Kehath the son of Levi, took many men of the children of Israel, and they rose up and quarreled with Moses and Aaron and the whole congregation.

2 And the Lord was angry with them, and the earth opened its mouth, and swallowed them up, with their houses and all belonging to them, and all the men belonging to Korah.

3 And after this God made the people go round by the way of Mount Seir for a long time.

4 At that time the Lord said unto Moses, Provoke not a war against the children of Esau, for I will not give to you of any thing belonging to them, as much as the sole of the foot could tread upon, for I have given Mount Seir for an inheritance to Esau.

5 Therefore did the children of Esau fight against the children of Seir in former times, and the Lord had delivered the children of Seir into the hands of the children of Esau, and destroyed them from before them, and the children of Esau dwelt in their stead unto this day.

6 Therefore the Lord said to the children of Israel, Fight not against the children of Esau your brethren, for nothing in their land belongs to you, but you may buy food of them for money and eat it, and you may buy water of them for money and drink it.

7 And the children of Israel did according to the word of the Lord.

8 And the children of Israel went about the wilderness, going round by the way of Mount Sinai for a long time, and touched not the children of Esau, and they continued in that district for nineteen years.

9 At that time died Latinus king of the children of Chittim, in the forty-fifth year of his reign, which is the fourteenth year of the children of Israel's departure from Egypt.

10 And they buried him in his place which he had built for himself in the land of Chittim, and Abimnas reigned in his place for thirty-eight years.

11 And the children of Israel passed the boundary of the children of Esau in those days, at the end of nineteen years, and they came and passed the road of the wilderness of Moab.

12 And the Lord said to Moses, besiege not Moab, and do not fight against them, for I will give you nothing of their land.

13 And the children of Israel passed the road of the wilderness of Moab for nineteen years, and they did not fight against them.

14 And in the thirty-sixth year of the children of Israel's departing from Egypt the Lord smote the heart of Sihon, king of the Amorites, and he waged war, and went forth to fight against the children of Moab.

15 And Sihon sent messengers to Beor the son of Janeas, the son of Balaam, counsellor to the king of Egypt, and to Balaam his son, to curse Moab, in order that it might be delivered into the hand of Sihon.

16 And the messengers went and brought Beor the son of Janeas, and Balaam his son, from Pethor in Mesopotamia, so Beor and Balaam his son came to the city of Sihon and they cursed Moab and their king in the presence of Sihon king of the Amorites.

17 So Sihon went out with his whole army, and he went to Moab and fought against them, and he subdued them, and the Lord delivered them into his hands, and Sihon slew the king of Moab.

18 And Sihon took all the cities of Moab in the battle; he also took Heshbon from them, for Heshbon was one of the cities of Moab, and Sihon placed his princes and his nobles in Heshbon, and Heshbon belonged to Sihon in those days.

19 Therefore the parable speakers Beor and Balaam his son uttered these words, saying, Come unto Heshbon, the city of Sihon will be built and established.

20 Woe unto thee Moab! thou art lost, O people of Kemosh! behold it is written upon the book of the law of God.

21 And when Sihon had conquered Moab, he placed guards in the cities which he had taken from Moab, and a considerable number of the children of Moab fell in battle into the hand of Sihon, and he made a great capture of them, sons and daughters, and he slew their king; so Sihon turned back to his own land.

22 And Sihon gave numerous presents of silver and gold to Beor and Balaam his son, and he dismissed them, and they went to Mesopotamia to their home and country.

23 At that time all the children of Israel passed from the road of the wilderness of Moab, and returned and surrounded the wilderness of Edom.

24 So the whole congregation came to the wilderness of Sin in the first month of the fortieth year from their departure from Egypt, and the children of Israel dwelt there in Kadesh, of the wilderness of Sin, and Miriam died there and she was buried there.

25 At that time Moses sent messengers to Hadad king of Edom, saying, Thus says thy brother Israel, Let me pass I pray thee through thy land, we will not pass through field or vineyard, we will not drink the water of the well; we will walk in the king's road.

26 And Edom said to him, Thou shalt not pass through my country, and Edom went forth to meet the children of Israel with a mighty people.

27 And the children of Esau refused to let the children of Israel pass through their land, so the Israelites removed from them and fought not against them.

28 For before this the Lord had commanded the children of Israel, saying, You shall not fight against the children of Esau, therefore the Israelites removed from them and did not fight against them.

29 So the children of Israel departed from Kadesh, and all the people came to Mount Hor.

30 At that time the Lord said to Moses, Tell thy brother Aaron that he shall die there, for he shall not come to the land which I have given to the children of Israel.

31 And Aaron went up, at the command of the Lord, to Mount Hor, in the fortieth year, in the fifth month, in the first day of the month.

32 And Aaron was one hundred and twenty-three years old when he died in Mount Hor.

Chapter 85

1 And king Arad the Canaanite, who dwelt in the south, heard that the Israelites had come by the way of the spies, and he arranged his forces to fight against the Israelites.

2 And the children of Israel were greatly afraid of him, for he had a great and heavy army, so the children of Israel resolved to return to Egypt.

3 And the children of Israel turned back about the distance of three days' journey unto Maserath Beni Jaakon, for they were greatly afraid on account of the king Arad.

4 And the children of Israel would not get back to their places, so they remained in Beni Jaakon for thirty days.

5 And when the children of Levi saw that the children of Israel would not turn back, they were jealous for the sake

of the Lord, and they rose up and fought against the Israelites their brethren, and slew of them a great body, and forced them to turn back to their place, Mount Hor.

6 And when they returned, king Arad was still arranging his host for battle against the Israelites.

7 And Israel vowed a vow, saying, If thou wilt deliver this people into my hand, then I will utterly destroy their cities.

8 And the Lord hearkened to the voice of Israel, and he delivered the Canaanites into their hand, and he utterly destroyed them and their cities, and he called the name of the place Hormah.

9 And the children of Israel journeyed from Mount Hor and pitched in Oboth, and they journeyed from Oboth and they pitched at Ije-abarim, in the border of Moab.

10 And the children of Israel sent to Moab, saying, Let us pass now through thy land into our place, but the children of Moab would not suffer the children of Israel to pass through their land, for the children of Moab were greatly afraid lest the children of Israel should do unto them as Sihon king of the Amorites had done to them, who had taken their land and had slain many of them.

11 Therefore Moab would not suffer the Israelites to pass through his land, and the Lord commanded the children of Israel, saying, That they should not fight against Moab, so the Israelites removed from Moab.

12 And the children of Israel journeyed from the border of Moab, and they came to the other side of Arnon, the border of Moab, between Moab and the Amorites, and they pitched in the border of Sihon, king of the Amorites, in the wilderness of Kedemoth.

13 And the children of Israel sent messengers to Sihon, king of the Amorites, saying,

14 Let us pass through thy land, we will not turn into the fields or into the vineyards, we will go along by the king's highway until we shall have passed thy border, but Sihon would not suffer the Israelites to pass.

15 So Sihon collected all the people of the Amorites and went forth into the wilderness to meet the children of Israel, and he fought against Israel in Jahaz.

16 And the Lord delivered Sihon king of the Amorites into the hand of the children of Israel, and Israel smote all the people of Sihon with the edge of the sword and avenged the cause of Moab.

17 And the children of Israel took possession of the land of Sihon from Aram unto Jabuk, unto the children of Ammon, and they took all the spoil of the cities.

18 And Israel took all these cities, and Israel dwelt in all the cities of the Amorites.

19 And all the children of Israel resolved to fight against the children of Ammon, to take their land also.

20 So the Lord said to the children of Israel, Do not besiege the children of Ammon, neither stir up battle against them, for I will give nothing to you of their land, and the children of Israel hearkened to the word of the Lord, and did not fight against the children of Ammon.

21 And the children of Israel turned and went up by the way of Bashan to the land of Og, king of Bashan, and Og the king of Bashan went out to meet the Israelites in battle, and he had with him many valiant men, and a very strong force from the people of the Amorites.

22 And Og king of Bashan was a very powerful man, but Naaron his son was exceedingly powerful, even stronger than he was.

23 And Og said in his heart, Behold now the whole camp of Israel takes up a space of three parsa, now will I smite them at once without sword or spear.

24 And Og went up Mount Jahaz, and took therefrom one large stone, the length of which was three parsa, and he placed it on his head, and resolved to throw it upon the camp of the children of Israel, to smite all the Israelites with that stone.

25 And the angel of the Lord came and pierced the stone upon the head of Og, and the stone fell upon the neck of Og that Og fell to the earth on account of the weight of the stone upon his neck.

26 At that time the Lord said to the children of Israel, Be not afraid of him, for I have given him and all his people and all his land into your hand, and you shall do to him as you did to Sihon.

27 And Moses went down to him with a small number of the children of Israel, and Moses smote Og with a stick at the ankles of his feet and slew him.

28 The children of Israel afterward pursued the children of Og and all his people, and they beat and destroyed them till there was no remnant left of them.

29 Moses afterward sent some of the children of Israel to spy out Jaazer, for Jaazer was a very famous city.

30 And the spies went to Jaazer and explored it, and the spies trusted in the Lord, and they fought against the men of Jaazer.

31 And these men took Jaazer and its villages, and the Lord delivered them into their hand, and they drove out the Amorites who had been there.

32 And the children of Israel took the land of the two kings of the Amorites, sixty cities which were on the other side of Jordan, from the brook of Arnon unto Mount Herman.

33 And the children of Israel journeyed and came into the plain of Moab which is on this side of Jordan, by Jericho.

34 And the children of Moab heard all the evil which the children of Israel had done to the two kings of the Amorites, to Sihon and Og, so all the men of Moab were greatly afraid of the Israelites.

35 And the elders of Moab said, Behold the two kings of the Amorites, Sihon and Og, who were more powerful than all the kings of the earth, could not stand against the children of Israel, how then can we stand before them?

36 Surely they sent us a message before now to pass through our land on their way, and we would not suffer them, now they will turn upon us with their heavy swords and destroy us; and Moab was distressed on account of the children of Israel, and they were greatly afraid of them, and they counselled together what was to be done to the children of Israel.

37 And the elders of Moab resolved and took one of their men, Balak the son of Zippor the Moabite, and made him king over them at that time, and Balak was a very wise man.

38 And the elders of Moab rose up and sent to the children of Midian to make peace with them, for a great battle and enmity had been in those days between Moab and Midian, from the days of Hadad the son of Bedad king of Edom, who smote Midian in the field of Moab, unto these days.

39 And the children of Moab sent to the children of Midian, and they made peace with them, and the elders of Midian came to the land of Moab to make peace in behalf of the children of Midian.

40 And the elders of Moab counselled with the elders of Midian what to do in order to save their lives from Israel.

41 And all the children of Moab said to the elders of Midian, Now therefore the children of Israel lick up all that are round about us, as the ox licks up the grass of the field, for thus did they do to the two kings of the Amorites who are stronger than we are.

42 And the elders of Midian said to Moab, We have heard that at the time when Sihon king of the Amorites fought against you, when he prevailed over you and took your land, he had sent to Beor the son of Janeas and to Balaam his son from Mesopotamia, and they came and cursed you; therefore did the hand of Sihon prevail over you, that he took your land.

43 Now therefore send you also to Balaam his son, for he still remains in his land, and give him his hire, that he may come and curse all the people of whom you are afraid; so the elders of Moab heard this thing, and it pleased them to send to Balaam the son of Beor.

44 So Balak the son of Zippor king of Moab sent messengers to Balaam, saying,

45 Behold there is a people come out from Egypt, behold they cover the face of the earth, and they abide over against me.

46 Now therefore come and curse this people for me, for they are too mighty for me, peradventure I shall prevail to fight against them, and drive them out, for I heard that he whom thou blessest is blessed, and whom thou cursest is cursed.

47 So the messengers of Balak went to Balaam and brought Balaam to curse the people to fight against Moab.

48 And Balaam came to Balak to curse Israel, and the Lord said to Balaam, Curse not this people for it is blessed.

49 And Balak urged Balaam day by day to curse Israel, but Balaam hearkened not to Balak on account of the word of the Lord which he had spoken to Balaam.

50 And when Balak saw that Balaam would not accede to his wish, he rose up and went home, and Balaam also returned to his land and he went from there to Midian.

51 And the children of Israel journeyed from the plain of Moab, and pitched by Jordan from Beth-jesimoth even unto Abel-shittim, at the end of the plains of Moab.

52 And when the children of Israel abode in the plain of Shittim, they began to commit whoredom with the daughters of Moab.

53 And the children of Israel approached Moab, and the children of Moab pitched their tents opposite to the camp of the children of Israel.

54 And the children of Moab were afraid of the children of Israel, and the children of Moab took all their daughters and their wives of beautiful aspect and comely appearance, and dressed them in gold and silver and costly garments.

55 And the children of Moab seated those women at the door of their tents, in order that the children of Israel might see them and turn to them, and not fight against Moab.

56 And all the children of Moab did this thing to the children of Israel, and every man placed his wife and daughter at the door of his tent, and all the children of Israel saw the act of the children of Moab, and the children of Israel turned to the daughters of Moab and coveted them, and they went to them.

57 And it came to pass that when a Hebrew came to the door of the tent of Moab, and saw a daughter of Moab and desired her in his heart, and spoke with her at the door of the tent that which he desired, whilst they were speaking together the men of the tent would come out and speak to the Hebrew like unto these words:

58 Surely you know that we are brethren, we are all the descendants of Lot and the descendants of Abraham his brother, wherefore then will you not remain with us, and wherefore will you not eat our bread and our sacrifice?

59 And when the children of Moab had thus overwhelmed him with their speeches, and enticed him by their flattering words, they seated him in the tent and cooked and sacrificed for him, and he ate of their sacrifice and of their bread.

60 They then gave him wine and he drank and became intoxicated, and they placed before him a beautiful damsel, and he did with her as he liked, for he knew not what he was doing, as he had drunk plentifully of wine.

61 Thus did the children of Moab to Israel in that place, in the plain of Shittim, and the anger of the Lord was kindled against Israel on account of this matter, and he sent a pestilence amongst them, and there died of the Israelites twenty-four thousand men.

62 Now there was a man of the children of Simeon whose name was Zimri, the son of Salu, who connected himself with the Midianite Cosbi, the daughter of Zur, king of Midian, in the sight of all the children of Israel.

63 And Phineas the son of Elazer, the son of Aaron the priest, saw this wicked thing which Zimri had done, and he took a spear and rose up and went after them, and pierced them both and slew them, and the pestilence ceased from the children of Israel.

Chapter 86

1 At that time after the pestilence, the Lord said to Moses, and to Elazer the son of Aaron the priest, saying,

2 Number the heads of the whole community of the children of Israel, from twenty years old and upward, all that went forth in the army.

3 And Moses and Elazer numbered the children of Israel after their families, and the number of all Israel was seven hundred thousand, seven hundred and thirty.

4 And the number of the children of Levi, from one month old and upward, was twenty-three thousand, and amongst these there was not a man of those numbered by Moses and Aaron in the wilderness of Sinai.

5 For the Lord had told them that they would die in the wilderness, so they all died, and not one had been left of them excepting Caleb the son of Jephuneh, and Joshua the son of Nun.

6 And it was after this that the Lord said to Moses, Say unto the children of Israel to avenge upon Midian the cause of their brethren the children of Israel.

7 And Moses did so, and the children of Israel chose from amongst them twelve thousand men, being one thousand to a tribe, and they went to Midian.

8 And the children of Israel warred against Midian, and they slew every male, also the five princes of Midian, and Balaam the son of Beor did they slay with the sword.

9 And the children of Israel took the wives of Midian captive, with their little ones and their cattle, and all belonging to them.

10 And they took all the spoil and all the prey, and they brought it to Moses and to Elazer to the plains of Moab.

11 And Moses and Elazer and all the princes of the congregation went forth to meet them with joy.

12 And they divided all the spoil of Midian, and the children of Israel had been revenged upon Midian for the cause of their brethren the children of Israel.

Chapter 87

1 At that time the Lord said to Moses, Behold thy days are approaching to an end, take now Joshua the son of Nun thy servant and place him in the tabernacle, and I will command him, and Moses did so.

2 And the Lord appeared in the tabernacle in a pillar of

cloud, and the pillar of cloud stood at the entrance of the tabernacle.

3 And the Lord commanded Joshua the son of Nun and said unto him, Be strong and courageous, for thou shalt bring the children of Israel to the land which I swore to give them, and I will be with thee.

4 And Moses said to Joshua, Be strong and courageous, for thou wilt make the children of Israel inherit the land, and the Lord will be with thee, he will not leave thee nor forsake thee, be not afraid nor disheartened.

5 And Moses called to all the children of Israel and said to them, You have seen all the good which the Lord your God has done for you in the wilderness.

6 Now therefore observe all the words of this law, and walk in the way of the Lord your God, turn not from the way which the Lord has commanded you, either to the right or to the left.

7 And Moses taught the children of Israel statutes and judgments and laws to do in the land as the Lord had commanded him.

8 And he taught them the way of the Lord and his laws; behold they are written upon the book of the law of God which he gave to the children of Israel by the hand of Moses.

9 And Moses finished commanding the children of Israel, and the Lord said to him, saying, Go up to the Mount Abarim and die there, and be gathered unto thy people as Aaron thy brother was gathered.

10 And Moses went up as the Lord had commanded him, and he died there in the land of Moab by the order of the Lord, in the fortieth year from the Israelites going forth from the land of Egypt.

11 And the children of Israel wept for Moses in the plains of Moab for thirty days, and the days of weeping and mourning for Moses were completed.

Chapter 88

1 And it was after the death of Moses that the Lord said to Joshua the son of Nun, saying,

2 Rise up and pass the Jordan to the land which I have given to the children of Israel, and thou shalt make the children of Israel inherit the land.

3 Every place upon which the sole of your feet shall tread shall belong to you, from the wilderness of Lebanon unto the great river the river of Perath shall be your boundary.

4 No man shall stand up against thee all the days of thy life; as I was with Moses, so will I be with thee, only be strong and of good courage to observe all the law which Moses commanded thee, turn not from the way either to the right or to the left, in order that thou mayest prosper in all that thou doest.

5 And Joshua commanded the officers of Israel, saying, Pass through the camp and command the people, saying, Prepare for yourselves provisions, for in three days more you will pass the Jordan to possess the land.

6 And the officers of the children of Israel did so, and they commanded the people and they did all that Joshua had commanded.

7 And Joshua sent two men to spy out the land of Jericho, and the men went and spied out Jericho.

8 And at the end of seven days they came to Joshua in the camp and said to him, The Lord has delivered the whole land into our hand, and the inhabitants thereof are melted with fear because of us.

9 And it came to pass after that, that Joshua rose up in the morning and all Israel with him, and they journeyed from Shittim, and Joshua and all Israel with him passed the Jordan; and Joshua was eighty-two years old when he passed the Jordan with Israel.

10 And the people went up from Jordan on the tenth day of the first month, and they encamped in Gilgal at the eastern corner of Jericho.

11 And the children of Israel kept the Passover in Gilgal, in the plains of Jericho, on the fourteenth day at the month, as it is written in the law of Moses.

12 And the manna ceased at that time on the morrow of the Passover, and there was no more manna for the children of Israel, and they ate of the produce of the land of Canaan.

13 And Jericho was entirely closed against the children of Israel, no one came out or went in.

14 And it was in the second month, on the first day of the month, that the Lord said to Joshua, Rise up, behold I have given Jericho into thy hand with all the people thereof; and all your fighting men shall go round the city, once each day, thus shall you do for six days.

15 And the priests shall blow upon trumpets, and when you shall hear the sound of the trumpet, all the people shall give a great shouting, that the walls of the city shall fall down; all the people shall go up every man against his opponent.

16 And Joshua did so according to all that the Lord had commanded him.

17 And on the seventh day they went round the city seven times, and the priests blew upon trumpets.

18 And at the seventh round, Joshua said to the people, Shout, for the Lord has delivered the whole city into our hands.

19 Only the city and all that it contains shall be accursed to the Lord, and keep yourselves from the accursed thing, lest you make the camp of Israel accursed and trouble it.

20 But all the silver and gold and brass and iron shall be consecrated to the Lord, they shall come into the treasury of the Lord.

21 And the people blew upon trumpets and made a great shouting, and the walls of Jericho fell down, and all the people went up, every man straight before him, and they took the city and utterly destroyed all that was in it, both man and woman, young and old, ox and sheep and ass, with the edge of the sword.

22 And they burned the whole city with fire; only the vessels of silver and gold, and brass and iron, they put into the treasury of the Lord.

23 And Joshua swore at that time, saying, Cursed be the man who builds Jericho; he shall lay the foundation thereof in his first-born, and in his youngest son shall he set up the gates thereof.

24 And Achan the son of Carmi, the son of Zabdi, the son of Zerah, son of Judah, dealt treacherously in the accursed thing, and he took of the accursed thing and hid it in the tent, and the anger of the Lord was kindled against Israel.

25 And it was after this when the children of Israel had returned from burning Jericho, Joshua sent men to spy out also Ai, and to fight against it.

26 And the men went up and spied out Ai, and they returned and said, Let not all the people go up with thee to Ai, only let about three thousand men go up and smite the city, for the men thereof are but few.

27 And Joshua did so, and there went up with him of the children of Israel about three thousand men, and they fought against the men of Ai.

28 And the battle was severe against Israel, and the men of Ai smote thirty-six men of Israel, and the children of Israel

fled from before the men of Ai.

29 And when Joshua saw this thing, he tore his garments and fell upon his face to the ground before the Lord, he, with the elders of Israel, and they put dust upon their heads.

30 And Joshua said, Why O Lord didst thou bring this people over the Jordan? what shall I say after the Israelites have turned their backs against their enemies?

31 Now therefore all the Canaanites, inhabitants of the land, will hear this thing, and surround us and cut off our name.

32 And the Lord said to Joshua, Why dost thou fall upon thy face? rise, get thee off, for the Israelites have sinned, and taken of the accursed thing; I will no more be with them unless they destroy the accursed thing from amongst them.

33 And Joshua rose up and assembled the people, and brought the Urim by the order of the Lord, and the tribe of Judah was taken, and Achan the son of Carmi was taken.

34 And Joshua said to Achan, Tell me my son, what hast thou done, and Achan said, I saw amongst the spoil a goodly garment of Shinar and two hundred shekels of silver, and a wedge of gold of fifty shekels weight; I coveted them and took them, and behold they are all hid in the earth in the midst of the tent.

35 And Joshua sent men who went and took them from the tent of Achan, and they brought them to Joshua.

36 And Joshua took Achan and these utensils, and his sons and daughters and all belonging to him, and they brought them into the valley of Achor.

37 And Joshua burned them there with fire, and all the Israelites stoned Achan with stones, and they raised over him a heap of stones, therefore did he call that place the valley of Achor, so the Lord's anger was appeased, and Joshua afterward came to the city and fought against it.

38 And the Lord said to Joshua, Fear not, neither be thou dismayed, behold I have given into thy hand Ai, her king and her people, and thou shalt do unto them as thou didst to Jericho and her king, only the spoil thereof and the cattle thereof shall you take for a prey for yourselves; lay an ambush for the city behind it.

39 So Joshua did according to the word of the Lord, and he chose from amongst the sons of war thirty thousand valiant men, and he sent them, and they lay in ambush for the city.

40 And he commanded them, saying, When you shall see us we will flee before them with cunning, and they will pursue us, you shall then rise out of the ambush and take the city, and they did so.

41 And Joshua fought, and the men of the city went out toward Israel, not knowing that they were lying in ambush for them behind the city.

42 And Joshua and all the Israelites feigned themselves wearied out before them, and they fled by the way of the wilderness with cunning.

43 And the men of Ai gathered all the people who were in the city to pursue the Israelites, and they went out and were drawn away from the city, not one remained, and they left the city open and pursued the Israelites.

44 And those who were lying in ambush rose up out of their places, and hastened to come to the city and took it and set it on fire, and the men of Ai turned back, and behold the smoke of the city ascended to the skies, and they had no means of retreating either one way or the other.

45 And all the men of Ai were in the midst of Israel, some on this side and some on that side, and they smote them so

that not one of them remained.

46 And the children of Israel took Melosh king of Ai alive, and they brought him to Joshua, and Joshua hanged him on a tree and he died.

47 And the children of Israel returned to the city after having burned it, and they smote all those that were in it with the edge of the sword.

48 And the number of those that had fallen of the men of Ai, both man and woman, was twelve thousand; only the cattle and the spoil of the city they took to themselves, according to the word of the Lord to Joshua.

49 And all the kings on this side Jordan, all the kings of Canaan, heard of the evil which the children of Israel had done to Jericho and to Ai, and they gathered themselves together to fight against Israel.

50 Only the inhabitants of Gibeon were greatly afraid of fighting against the Israelites lest they should perish, so they acted cunningly, and they came to Joshua and to all Israel, and said unto them, We have come from a distant land, now therefore make a covenant with us.

51 And the inhabitants of Gibeon over-reached the children of Israel, and the children of Israel made a covenant with them, and they made peace with them, and the princes of the congregation swore unto them, but afterward the children of Israel knew that they were neighbors to them and were dwelling amongst them.

52 But the children of Israel slew them not; for they had sworn to them by the Lord, and they became hewers of wood and drawers of water.

53 And Joshua said to them, Why did you deceive me, to do this thing to us? and they answered him, saying, Because it was told to thy servants all that you had done to all the kings of the Amorites, and we were greatly afraid of our lives, and we did this thing.

54 And Joshua appointed them on that day to hew wood and to draw water, and he divided them for slaves to all the tribes of Israel.

55 And when Adonizedek king of Jerusalem heard all that the children of Israel had done to Jericho and to Ai, he sent to Hoham king of Hebron and to Piram king at Jarmuth, and to Japhia king of Lachish and to Deber king of Eglon, saying,

56 Come up to me and help me, that we may smite the children of Israel and the inhabitants of Gibeon who have made peace with the children of Israel.

57 And they gathered themselves together and the five kings of the Amorites went up with all their camps, a mighty people numerous as the sand of the sea shore.

58 And all these kings came and encamped before Gibeon, and they began to fight against the inhabitants of Gibeon, and all the men of Gibeon sent to Joshua, saying, Come up quickly to us and help us, for all the kings of the Amorites have gathered together to fight against us.

59 And Joshua and all the fighting people went up from Gilgal, and Joshua came suddenly to them, and smote these five kings with a great slaughter.

60 And the Lord confounded them before the children at Israel, who smote them with a terrible slaughter in Gibeon, and pursued them along the way that goes up to Beth Horon unto Makkedah, and they fled from before the children of Israel.

61 And whilst they were fleeing, the Lord sent upon them hailstones from heaven, and more of them died by the hailstones, than by the slaughter of the children of Israel.

62 And the children of Israel pursued them, and they still smote them in the road, going on and smiting them.

63 And when they were smiting, the day was declining toward evening, and Joshua said in the sight of all the people, Sun, stand thou still upon Gibeon, and thou moon in the valley of Ajalon, until the nation shall have revenged itself upon its enemies.

64 And the Lord hearkened to the voice of Joshua, and the sun stood still in the midst of the heavens, and it stood still six and thirty moments, and the moon also stood still and hastened not to go down a whole day.

65 And there was no day like that, before it or after it, that the Lord hearkened to the voice of a man, for the Lord fought for Israel.

Chapter 89

1 Then spoke Joshua this song, on the day that the Lord had given the Amorites into the hand of Joshua and the children of Israel, and he said in the sight of all Israel,

2 Thou hast done mighty things, O Lord, thou hast performed great deeds; who is like unto thee? my lips shall sing to thy name.

3 My goodness and my fortress, my high tower, I will sing a new song unto thee, with thanksgiving will I sing to thee, thou art the strength of my salvation.

4 All the kings of the earth shall praise thee, the princes of the world shall sing to thee, the children of Israel shall rejoice in thy salvation, they shall sing and praise thy power.

5 To thee, O Lord, did we confide; we said thou art our God, for thou wast our shelter and strong tower against our enemies.

6 To thee we cried and were not ashamed, in thee we trusted and were delivered; when we cried unto thee, thou didst hear our voice, thou didst deliver our souls from the sword, thou didst show unto us thy grace, thou didst give unto us thy salvation, thou didst rejoice our hearts with thy strength.

7 Thou didst go forth for our salvation, with thine arm thou didst redeem thy people; thou didst answer us from the heavens of thy holiness, thou didst save us from ten thousands of people.

8 The sun and moon stood still in heaven, and thou didst stand in thy wrath against our oppressors and didst command thy judgments over them.

9 All the princes of the earth stood up, the kings of the nations had gathered themselves together, they were not moved at thy presence, they desired thy battles.

10 Thou didst rise against them in thine anger, and didst bring down thy wrath upon them; thou didst destroy them in thine anger, and cut them off in thine heart.

11 Nations have been consumed with thy fury, kingdoms have declined because of thy wrath, thou didst wound kings in the day of thine anger.

12 Thou didst pour out thy fury upon them, thy wrathful anger took hold of them; thou didst turn their iniquity upon them, and didst cut them off in their wickedness.

13 They did spread a trap, they fell therein, in the net they hid, their foot was caught.

14 Thine hand was ready for all thine enemies who said, Through their sword they possessed the land, through their arm they dwelt in the city; thou didst fill their faces with shame, thou didst bring their horns down to the ground, thou didst terrify them in thy wrath, and didst destroy them in thine anger.

15 The earth trembled and shook at the sound of thy storm over them, thou didst not withhold their souls from death, and didst bring down their lives to the grave.

16 Thou didst pursue them in thy storm, thou didst consume them in thy whirlwind, thou didst turn their rain into hail, they fell in deep pits so that they could not rise.

17 Their carcasses were like rubbish cast out in the middle of the streets.

18 They were consumed and destroyed in thine anger, thou didst save thy people with thy might.

19 Therefore our hearts rejoice in thee, our souls exalt in thy salvation.

20 Our tongues shall relate thy might, we will sing and praise thy wondrous works.

21 For thou didst save us from our enemies, thou didst deliver us from those who rose up against us, thou didst destroy them from before us and depress them beneath our feet.

22 Thus shall all thine enemies perish O Lord, and the wicked shall be like chaff driven by the wind, and thy beloved shall be like trees planted by the waters.

23 So Joshua and all Israel with him returned to the camp in Gilgal, after having smitten all the kings, so that not a remnant was left of them.

24 And the five kings fled alone on foot from battle, and hid themselves in a cave, and Joshua sought for them in the field of battle, and did not find them.

25 And it was afterward told to Joshua, saying, The kings are found and behold they are hidden in a cave.

26 And Joshua said, Appoint men to be at the mouth of the cave, to guard them, lest they take themselves away; and the children of Israel did so.

27 And Joshua called to all Israel and said to the officers of battle, Place your feet upon the necks of these kings, and Joshua said, So shall the Lord do to all your enemies.

28 And Joshua commanded afterward that they should slay the kings and cast them into the cave, and to put great stones at the mouth of the cave.

29 And Joshua went afterward with all the people that were with him on that day to Makkedah, and he smote it with the edge of the sword.

30 And he utterly destroyed the souls and all belonging to the city, and he did to the king and people thereof as he had done to Jericho.

31 And he passed from there to Libnah and he fought against it, and the Lord delivered it into his hand, and Joshua smote it with the edge of the sword, and all the souls thereof, and he did to it and to the king thereof as he had done to Jericho.

32 And from there he passed on to Lachish to fight against it, and Horam king of Gaza went up to assist the men of Lachish, and Joshua smote him and his people until there was none left to him.

33 And Joshua took Lachish and all the people thereof, and he did to it as he had done to Libnah.

34 And Joshua passed from there to Eglon, and he took that also, and he smote it and all the people thereof with the edge of the sword.

35 And from there he passed to Hebron and fought against it and took it and utterly destroyed it, and he returned from there with all Israel to Debir and fought against it and smote it with the edge of the sword.

36 And he destroyed every soul in it, he left none remaining, and he did to it and the king thereof as he had done to Jericho.

37 And Joshua smote all the kings of the Amorites from Kadesh-barnea to Azah, and he took their country at once, for the Lord had fought for Israel.

38 And Joshua with all Israel came to the camp to Gilgal.

39 When at that time Jabin king of Chazor heard all that

Joshua had done to the kings of the Amorites, Jabin sent to Jobat king of Midian, and to Laban king of Shimron, to Jephal king of Achshaph, and to all the kings of the Amorites, saying,

40 Come quickly to us and help us, that we may smite the children of Israel, before they come upon us and do unto us as they have done to the other kings of the Amorites.

41 And all these kings hearkened to the words of Jabin, king of Chazor, and they went forth with all their camps, seventeen kings, and their people were as numerous as the sand on the sea shore, together with horses and chariots innumerable, and they came and pitched together at the waters of Merom, and they were met together to fight against Israel.

42 And the Lord said to Joshua, Fear them not, for tomorrow about this time I will deliver them up all slain before you, thou shalt hough their horses and burn their chariots with fire.

43 And Joshua with all the men of war came suddenly upon them and smote them, and they fell into their hands, for the Lord had delivered them into the hands of the children of Israel.

44 So the children of Israel pursued all these kings with their camps, and smote them until there was none left of them, and Joshua did to them as the Lord had spoken to him.

45 And Joshua returned at that time to Chazor and smote it with the sword and destroyed every soul in it and burned it with fire, and from Chazor, Joshua passed to Shimron and smote it and utterly destroyed it.

46 From there he passed to Achshaph and he did to it as he had done to Shimron.

47 From there he passed to Adulam and he smote all the people in it, and he did to Adulam as he had done to Achshaph and to Shimron.

48 And he passed from them to all the cities of the kings which he had smitten, and he smote all the people that were left of them and he utterly destroyed them.

49 Only their booty and cattle the Israelites took to themselves as a prey, but every human being they smote, they suffered not a soul to live.

50 As the Lord had commanded Moses so did Joshua and all Israel, they failed not in anything.

51 So Joshua and all the children of Israel smote the whole land of Canaan as the Lord had commanded them, and smote all their kings, being thirty and one kings, and the children of Israel took their whole country.

52 Besides the kingdoms of Sihon and Og which are on the other side Jordan, of which Moses had smitten many cities, and Moses gave them to the Reubenites and the Gadites and to half the tribe of Manasseh.

53 And Joshua smote all the kings that were on this side Jordan to the west, and gave them for an inheritance to the nine tribes and to the half tribe of Israel.

54 For five years did Joshua carry on the war with these kings, and he gave their cities to the Israelites, and the land became tranquil from battle throughout the cities of the Amorites and the Canaanites.

Chapter 90

1 At that time in the fifth year after the children of Israel had passed over Jordan, after the children of Israel had rested from their war with the Canaanites, at that time great and severe battles arose between Edom and the children of Chittim, and the children of Chittim fought against Edom.

2 And Abianus king of Chittim went forth in that year, that is in the thirty-first year of his reign, and a great force with him of the mighty men of the children of Chittim, and he went to Seir to fight against the children of Esau.

3 And Hadad the king of Edom heard of his report, and he went forth to meet him with a heavy people and strong force, and engaged in battle with him in the field of Edom.

4 And the hand of Chittim prevailed over the children of Esau, and the children of Chittim slew of the children of Esau, two and twenty thousand men, and all the children of Esau fled from before them.

5 And the children of Chittim pursued them and they reached Hadad king of Edom, who was running before them and they caught him alive, and brought him to Abianus king of Chittim.

6 And Abianus ordered him to be slain, and Hadad king of Edom died in the forty-eighth year of his reign.

7 And the children of Chittim continued their pursuit of Edom, and they smote them with a great slaughter and Edom became subject to the children of Chittim.

8 And the children of Chittim ruled over Edom, and Edom became under the hand of the children of Chittim and became one kingdom from that day.

9 And from that time they could no more lift up their heads, and their kingdom became one with the children of Chittim.

10 And Abianus placed officers in Edom and all the children of Edom became subject and tributary to Abianus, and Abianus turned back to his own land, Chittim.

11 And when he returned he renewed his government and built for himself a spacious and fortified palace for a royal residence, and reigned securely over the children of Chittim and over Edom.

12 In those days, after the children of Israel had driven away all the Canaanites and the Amorites, Joshua was old and advanced in years.

13 And the Lord said to Joshua, Thou art old, advanced in life, and a great part of the land remains to be possessed.

14 Now therefore divide this land for an inheritance to the nine tribes and to the half tribe of Manasseh, and Joshua rose up and did as the Lord had spoken to him.

15 And he divided the whole land to the tribes of Israel as an inheritance according to their divisions.

16 But to the tribe at Levi he gave no inheritance, the offerings of the Lord are their inheritance as the Lord had spoken of them by the hand of Moses.

17 And Joshua gave Mount Hebron to Caleb the son of Jephuneh, one portion above his brethren, as the Lord had spoken through Moses.

18 Therefore Hebron became an inheritance to Caleb and his children unto this day.

19 And Joshua divided the whole land by lots to all Israel for an inheritance, as the Lord had commanded him.

20 And the children of Israel gave cities to the Levites from their own inheritance, and suburbs for their cattle, and property, as the Lord had commanded Moses so did the children of Israel, and they divided the land by lot whether great or small.

21 And they went to inherit the land according to their boundaries, and the children of Israel gave to Joshua the son of Nun an inheritance amongst them.

22 By the word of the Lord did they give to him the city which he required, Timnath-serach in Mount Ephraim, and he built the city and dwelt therein.

23 These are the inheritances which Elazer the priest and Joshua the son of Nun and the heads of the fathers of the tribes portioned out to the children of Israel by lot in

Shiloh, before the Lord, at the door of the tabernacle, and they left off dividing the land.

24 And the Lord gave the land to the Israelites, and they possessed it as the Lord had spoken to them, and as the Lord had sworn to their ancestors.

25 And the Lord gave to the Israelites rest from all their enemies around them, and no man stood up against them, and the Lord delivered all their enemies into their hands, and not one thing failed of all the good which the Lord had spoken to the children of Israel, yea the Lord performed every thing.

26 And Joshua called to all the children of Israel and he blessed them, and commanded them to serve the Lord, and he afterward sent them away, and they went each man to his city, and each man to his inheritance.

27 And the children of Israel served the Lord all the days of Joshua, and the Lord gave them rest from all around them, and they dwelt securely in their cities.

28 And it came to pass in those days, that Abianus king of Chittim died, in the thirty-eighth year of his reign, that is the seventh year of his reign over Edom, and they buried him in his place which he had built for himself, and Latinus reigned in his stead fifty years.

29 And during his reign he brought forth an army, and he went and fought against the inhabitants of Britannia and Kernania, the children of Elisha son of Javan, and he prevailed over them and made them tributary.

30 He then heard that Edom had revolted from under the hand of Chittim, and Latinus went to them and smote them and subdued them, and placed them under the hand of the children of Chittim, and Edom became one kingdom with the children of Chittim all the days.

31 And for many years there was no king in Edom, and their government was with the children of Chittim and their king.

32 And it was in the twenty-sixth year after the children of Israel had passed the Jordan, that is the sixty-sixth year after the children of Israel had departed from Egypt, that Joshua was old, advanced in years, being one hundred and eight years old in those days.

33 And Joshua called to all Israel, to their elders, their judges and officers, after the Lord had given to all the Israelites rest from all their enemies round about, and Joshua said to the elders of Israel, and to their judges, Behold I am old, advanced in years, and you have seen what the Lord has done to all the nations whom he has driven away from before you, for it is the Lord who has fought for you.

34 Now therefore strengthen yourselves to keep and to do all the words of the law of Moses, not to deviate from it to the right or to the left, and not to come amongst those nations who are left in the land; neither shall you make mention of the name of their gods, but you shall cleave to the Lord your God, as you have done to this day.

35 And Joshua greatly exhorted the children of Israel to serve the Lord all their days.

36 And all the Israelites said, We will serve the Lord our God all our days, we and our children, and our children's children, and our seed for ever.

37 And Joshua made a covenant with the people on that day, and he sent away the children of Israel, and they went each man to his inheritance and to his city.

38 And it was in those days, when the children of Israel were dwelling securely in their cities, that they buried the coffins of the tribes of their ancestors, which they had brought up from Egypt, each man in the inheritance of his children, the twelve sons of Jacob did the children of Israel bury, each man in the possession of his children.

39 And these are the names of the cities wherein they buried the twelve sons of Jacob, whom the children of Israel had brought up from Egypt.

40 And they buried Reuben and Gad on this side Jordan, in Romia, which Moses had given to their children.

41 And Simeon and Levi they buried in the city Mauda, which he had given to the children of Simeon, and the suburb of the city was for the children of Levi.

42 And Judah they buried in the city of Benjamin opposite Bethlehem.

43 And the bones of Issachar and Zebulun they buried in Zidon, in the portion which fell to their children.

44 And Dan was buried in the city of his children in Eshtael, and Naphtali and Asher they buried in Kadesh-naphtali, each man in his place which he had given to his children.

45 And the bones of Joseph they buried in Shechem, in the part of the field which Jacob had purchased from Hamor, and which became to Joseph for an inheritance.

46 And they buried Benjamin in Jerusalem opposite the Jebusite, which was given to the children of Benjamin; the children of Israel buried their fathers each man in the city of his children.

47 And at the end of two years, Joshua the son of Nun died, one hundred and ten years old, and the time which Joshua judged Israel was twenty-eight years, and Israel served the Lord all the days of his life.

48 And the other affairs of Joshua and his battles and his reproofs with which he reproved Israel, and all which he had commanded them, and the names of the cities which the children of Israel possessed in his days, behold they are written in the book of the words of Joshua to the children of Israel, and in the book of the wars of the Lord, which Moses and Joshua and the children of Israel had written.

49 And the children of Israel buried Joshua in the border of his inheritance, in Timnath-serach, which was given to him in Mount Ephraim.

50 And Elazer the son of Aaron died in those days, and they buried him in a hill belonging to Phineas his son, which was given him in Mount Ephraim.

Chapter 91

1 At that time, after the death of Joshua, the children of the Canaanites were still in the land, and the Israelites resolved to drive them out.

2 And the children of Israel asked of the Lord, saying, Who shall first go up for us to the Canaanites to fight against them? and the Lord said, Judah shall go up.

3 And the children of Judah said to Simeon, Go up with us into our lot, and we will fight against the Canaanites and we likewise will go up with you, in your lot, so the children of Simeon went with the children of Judah.

4 And the children of Judah went up and fought against the Canaanites, so the Lord delivered the Canaanites into the hands of the children of Judah, and they smote them in Bezek, ten thousand men.

5 And they fought with Adonibezek in Bezek, and he fled from before them, and they pursued him and caught him, and they took hold of him and cut off his thumbs and great toes.

6 And Adonibezek said, Three score and ten kings having their thumbs and great toes cut off, gathered their meat under my table, as I have done, so God has requited me, and they brought him to Jerusalem and he died there.

7 And the children of Simeon went with the children of Judah, and they smote the Canaanites with the edge of the sword.

8 And the Lord was with the children of Judah, and they possessed the mountain, and the children of Joseph went up to Bethel, the same is Luz, and the Lord was with them.

9 And the children of Joseph spied out Bethel, and the watchmen saw a man going forth from the city, and they caught him and said unto him, Show us now the entrance of the city and we will show kindness to thee.

10 And that man showed them the entrance of the city, and the children of Joseph came and smote the City with the edge of the sword.

11 And the man with his family they sent away, and he went to the Hittites and he built a city, and he called the name thereof Luz, so all the Israelites dwelt in their cities, and the children at Israel dwelt in their cities, and the children of Israel served the Lord all the days of Joshua, and all the days of the elders, who had lengthened their days after Joshua, and saw the great work of the Lord, which he had performed for Israel.

12 And the elders judged Israel after the death of Joshua for seventeen years.

13 And all the elders also fought the battles of Israel against the Canaanites and the Lord drove the Canaanites from before the children of Israel, in order to place the Israelites in their land.

14 And he accomplished all the words which he had spoken to Abraham, Isaac, and Jacob, and the oath which he had sworn, to give to them and to their children, the land of the Canaanites.

15 And the Lord gave to the children of Israel the whole land of Canaan, as he had sworn to their ancestors, and the Lord gave them rest from those around them, and the children of Israel dwelt securely in their cities.

16 Blessed be the Lord for ever, amen, and amen.

17 Strengthen yourselves, and let the hearts of all you that trust in the Lord be of good courage.

THE END

GOSPELS

The Burial of Christ.

Gustave Doré (1891)

THE GOSPEL OF THOMAS

Prologue
These are the hidden sayings that the living Jesus spoke and Didymos Judas Thomas wrote down.

Saying 1: True Meaning
And he said, "Whoever discovers the meaning of these sayings won't taste death."

Saying 2: Seek and Find
Jesus said, "Whoever seeks shouldn't stop until they find. When they find, they'll be disturbed. When they're disturbed, they'll be […] amazed, and reign over the All."

Saying 3: Seeking Within
Jesus said, "If your leaders tell you, 'Look, the kingdom is in heaven,' then the birds of heaven will precede you. If they tell you, 'It's in the sea,' then the fish will precede you. Rather, the kingdom is within you and outside of you. "When you know yourselves, then you'll be known, and you'll realize that you're the children of the living Father. But if you don't know yourselves, then you live in poverty, and you are the poverty."

Saying 4: First and Last
Jesus said, "The older person won't hesitate to ask a little seven-day-old child about the place of life, and they'll live, because many who are first will be last, and they'll become one."

Saying 5: Hidden and Revealed
Jesus said, "Know what's in front of your face, and what's hidden from you will be revealed to you, because there's nothing hidden that won't be revealed."

Saying 6: Public Ritual
His disciples said to him, "Do you want us to fast? And how should we pray? Should we make donations? And what food should we avoid?"
Jesus said, "Don't lie, and don't do what you hate, because everything is revealed in the sight of heaven; for there's nothing hidden that won't be revealed, and nothing covered up that will stay secret."

Saying 7: The Lion and the Human
Jesus said, "Blessed is the lion that's eaten by a human and then becomes human, but how awful for the human who's eaten by a lion, and the lion becomes human."

Saying 8: The Parable of the Fish
He said, "The human being is like a wise fisher who cast a net into the sea and drew it up from the sea full of little fish. Among them the wise fisher found a fine large fish and cast all the little fish back down into the sea, easily choosing the large fish. Anyone who has ears to hear should hear!"

Saying 9: The Parable of the Sower
Jesus said, "Look, a sower went out, took a handful of seeds, and scattered them. Some fell on the roadside; the birds came and gathered them. Others fell on the rock; they didn't take root in the soil and ears of grain didn't rise toward heaven. Yet others fell on thorns; they choked the seeds and worms ate them. Finally, others fell on good soil; it produced fruit up toward heaven, some sixty times as much and some a hundred and twenty."

Saying 10: Jesus and Fire (1)
Jesus said, "I've cast fire on the world, and look, I'm watching over it until it blazes."

Saying 11: Those Who Are Living Won't Die (1)
Jesus said, "This heaven will disappear, and the one above it will disappear too. Those who are dead aren't alive, and those who are living won't die. In the days when you ate what was dead, you made it alive. When you're in the light, what will you do? On the day when you were one, you became divided. But when you become divided, what will you do?"

Saying 12: James the Just
The disciples said to Jesus, "We know you're going to leave us. Who will lead us then?"
Jesus said to them, "Wherever you are, you'll go to James the Just, for whom heaven and earth came into being."

Saying 13: Thomas' Confession
Jesus said to his disciples, "If you were to compare me to someone, who would you say I'm like?"
Simon Peter said to him, "You're like a just angel."
Matthew said to him, "You're like a wise philosopher."
Thomas said to him, "Teacher, I'm completely unable to say whom you're like."
Jesus said, "I'm not your teacher. Because you've drunk, you've become intoxicated by the bubbling spring I've measured out."
He took him aside and told him three things. When Thomas returned to his companions, they asked, "What did Jesus say to you?"
Thomas said to them, "If I tell you one of the things he said to me, you'll pick up stones and cast them at me, and fire will come out of the stones and burn you up."

Saying 14: Public Ministry
Jesus said to them, "If you fast, you'll bring guilt upon yourselves; and if you pray, you'll be condemned; and if you make donations, you'll harm your spirits.
"If they welcome you when you enter any land and go around in the countryside, heal those who are sick among them and eat whatever they give you, because it's not what goes into your mouth that will defile you. What comes out of your mouth is what will defile you."

Saying 15: Worship
Jesus said, "When you see the one who wasn't born of a woman, fall down on your face and worship that person. That's your Father."

Saying 16: Not Peace, but War
Jesus said, "Maybe people think that I've come to cast peace on the world, and they don't know that I've come to cast divisions on the earth: fire, sword, and war. Where there are five in a house, there'll be three against two and two against three, father against and son and son against father. They'll stand up and be one."

Saying 17: Divine Gift
Jesus said, "I'll give you what no eye has ever seen, no ear has ever heard, no hand has ever touched, and no human mind has ever thought."

Saying 18: Beginning and End
The disciples said to Jesus, "Tell us about our end. How will it come?"
Jesus said, "Have you discovered the beginning so that you can look for the end? Because the end will be where the beginning is. Blessed is the one who will stand up in the beginning. They'll know the end, and won't taste death."

Saying 19: Five Trees in Paradise
Jesus said, "Blessed is the one who came into being before coming into being. If you become my disciples and listen to my message, these stones will become your servants; because there are five trees in paradise which don't change in summer or winter, and their leaves don't fall. Whoever knows them won't taste death."

Saying 20: The Parable of the Mustard Seed
The disciples asked Jesus, "Tell us, what can the kingdom of heaven be compared to?"
He said to them, "It can be compared to a mustard seed. Though it's the smallest of all the seeds, when it falls on tilled soil it makes a plant so large that it shelters the birds of heaven."

Saying 21: The Parables of the Field, the Bandits, and the Reaper
Mary said to Jesus, "Whom are your disciples like?"
He said, "They're like little children living in a field which isn't theirs. When the owners of the field come, they'll say, 'Give our field back to us.' They'll strip naked in front of them to let them have it and give them their field.
"So I say that if the owner of the house realizes the bandit is coming, they'll watch out beforehand and won't let the bandit break into the house of their domain and steal their possessions. You, then, watch out for the world! Prepare to defend yourself so that the bandits don't attack you, because what you're expecting will come. May there be a wise person among you!
"When the fruit ripened, the reaper came quickly, sickle in hand, and harvested it. Anyone who has ears to hear should hear!"

Saying 22: Making the Two into One
Jesus saw some little children nursing. He said to his disciples, "These nursing children can be compared to those who enter the kingdom."
They said to him, "Then we'll enter the kingdom as little children?"
Jesus said to them, "When you make the two into one, and make the inner like the outer and the outer like the inner, and the upper like the lower, and so make the male and the female a single one so that the male won't be male nor the female female; when you make eyes in the place of an eye, a hand in the place of a hand, a foot in the place of a foot, and an image in the place of an image; then you'll enter [the kingdom]."

Saying 23: Those Who are Chosen (1)
Jesus said, "I'll choose you, one out of a thousand and two out of ten thousand, and they'll stand as a single one."

Saying 24: Light
His disciples said, "Show us the place where you are, because we need to look for it."
He said to them, "Anyone who has ears to hear should hear! Light exists within a person of light, and they light up the whole world. If they don't shine, there's darkness."

Saying 25: Love and Protect
Jesus said, "Love your brother as your own soul. Protect them like the pupil of your eye."

Saying 26: Speck and Beam
Jesus said, "You see the speck that's in your brother's eye, but you don't see the beam in your own eye. When you get the beam out of your own eye, then you'll be able to see clearly to get the speck out of your brother's eye."

Saying 27: Fasting and Sabbath
"If you don't fast from the world, you won't find the kingdom. If you don't make the Sabbath into a Sabbath, you won't see the Father."

Saying 28: The World is Drunk
Jesus said, "I stood in the middle of the world and appeared to them in the flesh. I found them all drunk; I didn't find any of them thirsty. My soul ached for the children of humanity, because they were blind in their hearts and couldn't see. They came into the world empty and plan on leaving the world empty. Meanwhile, they're drunk. When they shake off their wine, then they'll change."

Saying 29: Spirit and Body
Jesus said, "If the flesh came into existence because of spirit, that's amazing. If spirit came into existence because of the body, that's really amazing! But I'm amazed at how [such] great wealth has been placed in this poverty."

Saying 30: Divine Presence
Jesus said, "Where there are three deities, they're divine. Where there are two or one, I'm with them."

Saying 31: Prophet and Doctor
Jesus said, "No prophet is welcome in their own village. No doctor heals those who know them."

Saying 32: The Parable of the Fortified City
Jesus said, "A city built and fortified on a high mountain can't fall, nor can it be hidden."

Saying 33: The Parable of the Lamp
Jesus said, "What you hear with one ear, listen to with both, then proclaim from your rooftops. No one lights a lamp and puts it under a basket or in a hidden place. Rather, they put it on the stand so that everyone who comes and goes can see its light."

Saying 34: The Parable of Those Who Can't See
Jesus said, "If someone who's blind leads someone else who's blind, both of them fall into a pit."

Saying 35: The Parable of Binding the Strong
Jesus said, "No one can break into the house of the strong and take it by force without tying the hands of the strong. Then they can loot the house."

Saying 36: Anxiety
Jesus said, "Don't be anxious from morning to evening or from evening to morning about what you'll wear."

Saying 37: Seeing Jesus
His disciples said, "When will you appear to us? When will

we see you?"
Jesus said, "When you strip naked without being ashamed, and throw your clothes on the ground and stomp on them as little children would, then [you'll] see the Son of the Living One and won't be afraid."

Saying 38: Finding Jesus
Jesus said, "Often you've wanted to hear this message that I'm telling you, and you don't have anyone else from whom to hear it. There will be days when you'll look for me, but you won't be able to find me."

Saying 39: The Keys of Knowledge
Jesus said, "The Pharisees and the scholars have taken the keys of knowledge and hidden them. They haven't entered, and haven't let others enter who wanted to. So be wise as serpents and innocent as doves."

Saying 40: A Grapevine
Jesus said, "A grapevine has been planted outside of the Father. Since it's malnourished, it'll be pulled up by its root and destroyed."

Saying 41: More and Less
Jesus said, "Whoever has something in hand will be given more, but whoever doesn't have anything will lose even what little they do have."

Saying 42: Passing By
Jesus said, "Become passersby."

Saying 43: The Tree and the Fruit
His disciples said to him, "Who are you to say these things to us?"
"You don't realize who I am from what I say to you, but you've become like those Judeans who either love the tree but hate its fruit, or love the fruit but hate the tree."

Saying 44: Blasphemy
Jesus said, "Whoever blasphemes the Father will be forgiven, and whoever blasphemes the Son will be forgiven, but whoever blasphemes the Holy Spirit will not be forgiven, neither on earth nor in heaven."

Saying 45: Good and Evil
Jesus said, "Grapes aren't harvested from thorns, nor are figs gathered from thistles, because they don't produce fruit. [A person who's good] brings good things out of their treasure, and a person who's [evil] brings evil things out of their evil treasure. They say evil things because their heart is full of evil."

Saying 46: Greater than John the Baptizer
Jesus said, "From Adam to John the Baptizer, no one's been born who's so much greater than John the Baptizer that they shouldn't avert their eyes. But I say that whoever among you will become a little child will know the kingdom and become greater than John."

Saying 47: The Parables of Divided Loyalties, New Wine in Old Wineskins, and New Patch on Old Cloth
Jesus said, "It's not possible for anyone to mount two horses or stretch two bows, and it's not possible for a servant to follow two leaders, because they'll respect one and despise the other.

"No one drinks old wine and immediately wants to drink new wine. And new wine isn't put in old wineskins, because they'd burst. Nor is old wine put in new wineskins, because it'd spoil.
"A new patch of cloth isn't sewn onto an old coat, because it'd tear apart."

Saying 48: Unity (1)
Jesus said, "If two make peace with each other in a single house, they'll say to the mountain, 'Go away,' and it will."

Saying 49: Those Who Are Chosen (2)
Jesus said, "Blessed are those who are one – those who are chosen, because you'll find the kingdom. You've come from there and will return there."

Saying 50: Our Origin and Identity
Jesus said, "If they ask you, 'Where do you come from?' tell them, 'We've come from the light, the place where light came into being by itself, [established] itself, and appeared in their image.'
"If they ask you, 'Is it you?' then say, 'We are its children, and we're chosen by our living Father.'
"If they ask you, 'What's the sign of your Father in you?' then say, 'It's movement and rest.'"

Saying 51: The New World
His disciples said to him, "When will the dead have rest, and when will the new world come?"
He said to them, "What you're looking for has already come, but you don't know it."

Saying 52: Twenty-Four Prophets
His disciples said to him, "Twenty-four prophets have spoken in Israel, and they all spoke of you."
He said to them, "You've ignored the Living One right in front of you, and you've talked about those who are dead."

Saying 53: True Circumcision
His disciples said to him, "Is circumcision useful, or not?"
He said to them, "If it were useful, parents would have children who are born circumcised. But the true circumcision in spirit has become profitable in every way."

Saying 54: Those Who Are Poor
Jesus said, "Blessed are those who are poor, for yours is the kingdom of heaven."

Saying 55: Discipleship (1)
Jesus said, "Whoever doesn't hate their father and mother can't become my disciple, and whoever doesn't hate their brothers and sisters and take up their cross like I do isn't worthy of me."

Saying 56: The World is a Corpse
Jesus said, "Whoever has known the world has found a corpse. Whoever has found a corpse, of them the world isn't worthy."

Saying 57: The Parable of the Weeds
Jesus said, "My Fathers' kingdom can be compared to someone who had [good] seed. Their enemy came by night and sowed weeds among the good seed. The person didn't let anyone pull out the weeds, 'so that you don't pull out the wheat along with the weeds,' they said to them. 'On the day of the harvest, the weeds will be obvious. Then they'll be

pulled out and burned.'"

Saying 58: Finding Life
Jesus said, "Blessed is the person who's gone to a lot of trouble. They've found life."

Saying 59: The Living One
Jesus said, "Look for the Living One while you're still alive. If you die and then try to look for him, you won't be able to."

Saying 60: Don't Become a Corpse
They saw a Samaritan carrying a lamb to Judea. He said to his disciples, "What do you think he's going to do with that lamb?"
They said to him, "He's going to kill it and eat it."
He said to them, "While it's living, he won't eat it, but only after he kills it and it becomes a corpse."
They said, "He can't do it any other way."
He said to them, "You, too, look for a resting place, so that you won't become a corpse and be eaten."

Saying 61: Jesus and Salome
Jesus said, "Two will rest on a couch. One will die, the other will live."
Salome said, "Who are you, Sir, to climb onto my couch and eat off my table as if you're from someone?"
Jesus said to her, "I'm the one who exists in equality. Some of what belongs to my Father was given to me."
"I'm your disciple."
"So I'm telling you, if someone is /equal\, they'll be full of light; but if they're divided, they'll be full of darkness."

Saying 62: Mysteries
Jesus said, "I tell my mysteries to [those who are worthy of my] mysteries. Don't let your left hand know what your right hand is doing."

Saying 63: The Parable of the Rich Fool
Jesus said, "There was a rich man who had much money. He said, 'I'll use my money to sow, reap, plant, and fill my barns with fruit, so that I won't need anything.' That's what he was thinking to himself, but he died that very night. Anyone who has ears to hear should hear!"

Saying 64: The Parable of the Dinner Party
Jesus said, "Someone was planning on having guests. When dinner was ready, they sent their servant to call the visitors.
"The servant went to the first and said, 'My master invites you.'
"They said, 'Some merchants owe me money. They're coming tonight. I need to go and give them instructions. Excuse me from the dinner.'
"The servant went to another one and said, 'My master invites you.'
"They said, "I've just bought a house and am needed for the day. I won't have time.'
"The servant went to another one and said, 'My master invites you.'
"They said, 'My friend is getting married and I'm going to make dinner. I can't come. Excuse me from the dinner.'
"The servant went to another one and said, 'My master invites you.'
"They said, 'I've just bought a farm and am going to collect the rent. I can't come. Excuse me.'
"The servant went back and told the master, 'The ones you've invited to the dinner have excused themselves.'
"The master said to their servant, 'Go out to the roads and bring whomever you find so that they can have dinner.'
"Buyers and merchants won't [enter] the places of my Father."

Saying 65: The Parable of the Sharecroppers
He said, "A [creditor] owned a vineyard. He leased it out to some sharecroppers to work it so he could collect its fruit.
"He sent his servant so that the sharecroppers could give him the fruit of the vineyard. They seized his servant, beat him, and nearly killed him.
"The servant went back and told his master. His master said, 'Maybe he just didn't know them.' He sent another servant, but the tenants beat that one too.
"Then the master sent his son, thinking, 'Maybe they'll show some respect to my son.'
"Because they knew that he was the heir of the vineyard, the sharecroppers seized and killed him. Anyone who has ears to hear should hear!"

Saying 66: The Rejected Cornerstone
Jesus said, "Show me the stone the builders rejected; that's the cornerstone."

Saying 67: Knowing Isn't Everything
Jesus said, "Whoever knows everything, but is personally lacking, lacks everything."

Saying 68: Persecution
Jesus said, "Blessed are you when you're hated and persecuted, and no place will be found where you've been persecuted."

Saying 69: Those Who Are Persecuted
Jesus said, "Blessed are those who've been persecuted in their own hearts. They've truly known the Father. Blessed are those who are hungry, so that their stomachs may be filled."

Saying 70: Salvation is Within
Jesus said, "If you give birth to what's within you, what you have within you will save you. If you don't have that within [you], what you don't have within you [will] kill you."

Saying 71: Destroying the Temple
Jesus said, "I'll destroy [this] house, and no one will be able to build it [...]"

Saying 72: Not a Divider
[Someone said to him], "Tell my brothers to divide our inheritance with me."
He said to him, "Who made me a divider?"
He turned to his disciples and said to them, "Am I really a divider?"

Saying 73: Workers for the Harvest
Jesus said, "The harvest really is plentiful, but the workers are few. So pray that the Lord will send workers to the harvest."

Saying 74: The Empty Well
He said, "Lord, many are gathered around the well, but there's nothing to drink."

Saying 75: The Bridal Chamber

Jesus said, "Many are waiting at the door, but those who are one will enter the bridal chamber."

Saying 76: The Parable of the Pearl

Jesus said, "The Father's kingdom can be compared to a merchant with merchandise who found a pearl. The merchant was wise; they sold their merchandise and bought that single pearl for themselves.

"You, too, look for the treasure that doesn't perish but endures, where no moths come to eat and no worms destroy."

Saying 77: Jesus is the All

Jesus said, "I'm the light that's over all. I am the All. The All has come from me and unfolds toward me.

"Split a log; I'm there. Lift the stone, and you'll find me there."

Saying 78: Into the Desert

Jesus said, "What did you go out into the desert to see? A reed shaken by the wind? A [person] wearing fancy clothes, [like your] rulers and powerful people? They (wear) fancy [clothes], but can't know the truth."

Saying 79: Listening to the Message

A woman in the crowd said to him, "Blessed is the womb that bore you, and the breasts that nourished you."

He said to [her], "Blessed are those who have listened to the message of the Father and kept it, because there will be days when you'll say, 'Blessed is the womb that didn't conceive and the breasts that haven't given milk.'"

Saying 80: The World is a Body

Jesus said, "Whoever has known the world has found the body; but whoever has found the body, of them the world isn't worthy."

Saying 81: Riches and Renunciation (1)

Jesus said, "Whoever has become rich should become a ruler, and whoever has power should renounce it."

Saying 82: Jesus and Fire (2)

Jesus said, "Whoever is near me is near the fire, and whoever is far from me is far from the kingdom."

Saying 83: Light and Images

Jesus said, "Images are revealed to people, but the light within them is hidden in the image of the Father's light. He'll be revealed, but his image will be hidden by his light."

Saying 84: Our Previous Images

Jesus said, "When you see your likeness, you rejoice. But when you see your images that came into being before you did – which don't die, and aren't revealed – how much you'll have to bear!"

Saying 85: Adam Wasn't Worthy

Jesus said, "Adam came into being from a great power and great wealth, but he didn't become worthy of you. If he had been worthy, [he wouldn't have tasted] death."

Saying 86: Foxes and Birds

Jesus said, "[The foxes have dens] and the birds have nests, but the Son of Humanity has nowhere to lay his head and rest."

Saying 87: Body and Soul

Jesus said, "How miserable is the body that depends on a body, and how miserable is the soul that depends on both."

Saying 88: Angels and Prophets

Jesus said, "The angels and the prophets will come to you and give you what belongs to you. You'll give them what you have and ask yourselves, 'When will they come and take what is theirs?'"

Saying 89: Inside and Outside

Jesus said, "Why do you wash the outside of the cup? Don't you know that whoever created the inside created the outside too?"

Saying 90: Jesus' Yoke is Easy

Jesus said, "Come to me, because my yoke is easy and my requirements are light. You'll be refreshed."

Saying 91: Reading the Signs

They said to him, "Tell us who you are so that we may trust you."

He said to them, "You read the face of the sky and the earth, but you don't know the one right in front of you, and you don't know how to read the present moment."

Saying 92: Look and Find

Jesus said, "Look and you'll find. I didn't answer your questions before. Now I want to give you answers, but you aren't looking for them."

Saying 93: Don't Throw Pearls to Pigs

"Don't give what's holy to the dogs, or else it might be thrown on the manure pile. Don't throw pearls to the pigs, or else they might […]"

Saying 94: Knock and It Will Be Opened

Jesus [said], "Whoever looks will find, [and whoever knocks], it will be opened for them."

Saying 95: Giving Money

[Jesus said], "If you have money, don't lend it at interest. Instead, give [it to] someone from whom you won't get it back."

Saying 96: The Parable of the Yeast

Jesus [said], "The Father's kingdom can be compared to a woman who took a little yeast and [hid] it in flour. She made it into large loaves of bread. Anyone who has ears to hear should hear!"

Saying 97: The Parable of the Jar of Flour

Jesus said, "The Father's kingdom can be compared to a woman carrying a jar of flour. While she was walking down [a] long road, the jar's handle broke and the flour spilled out behind her on the road. She didn't know it, and didn't realize there was a problem until she got home, put down the jar, and found it empty."

Saying 98: The Parable of the Assassin

Jesus said, "The Father's kingdom can be compared to a man who wanted to kill someone powerful. He drew his sword in his house and drove it into the wall to figure out whether his hand was strong enough. Then he killed the powerful one."

Saying 99: Jesus' True Family

The disciples said to him, "Your brothers and mother are standing outside."

He said to them, "The people here who do the will of my Father are my brothers and mother; they're the ones who will enter my Father's kingdom."

Saying 100: Give to Caesar What Belongs to Caesar

They showed Jesus a gold coin and said to him, "Those who belong to Caesar demand tribute from us."

He said to them, "Give to Caesar what belongs to Caesar, give to God what belongs to God, and give to me what belongs to me."

Saying 101: Discipleship (2)

"Whoever doesn't hate their [father] and mother as I do can't become my [disciple], and whoever [doesn't] love their [father] and mother as I do can't become my [disciple]. For my mother […], but [my] true [Mother] gave me Life."

Saying 102: The Dog in the Feeding Trough

Jesus said, "How awful for the Pharisees who are like a dog sleeping in a feeding trough for cattle, because the dog doesn't eat, and [doesn't let] the cattle eat either."

Saying 103: The Parable of the Bandits

Jesus said, "Blessed is the one who knows where the bandits are going to enter. [They can] get up to assemble their defenses and be prepared to defend themselves before they arrive."

Saying 104: Prayer and Fasting

They said to [Jesus], "Come, let's pray and fast today."

Jesus said, "What have I done wrong? Have I failed?

"Rather, when the groom leaves the bridal chamber, then people should fast and pray."

Saying 105: Knowing Father and Mother

Jesus said, "Whoever knows their father and mother will be called a bastard."

Saying 106: Unity (2)

Jesus said, "When you make the two into one, you'll become Children of Humanity, and if you say 'Mountain, go away!', it'll go."

Saying 107: The Parable of the Lost Sheep

Jesus said, "The kingdom can be compared to a shepherd who had a hundred sheep. The largest one strayed. He left the ninety-nine and looked for that one until he found it. Having gone through the trouble, he said to the sheep: 'I love you more than the ninety-nine.'"

Saying 108: Becoming Like Jesus

Jesus said, "Whoever drinks from my mouth will become like me, and I myself will become like them; then, what's hidden will be revealed to them."

Saying 109: The Parable of the Hidden Treasure

Jesus said, "The kingdom can be compared to someone who had a treasure [hidden] in their field. [They] didn't know about it. After they died, they left it to their son. The son didn't know it either. He took the field and sold it. "The buyer plowed the field, [found] the treasure, and began to loan money at interest to whomever they wanted."

Saying 110: Riches and Renunciation (2)

Jesus said, "Whoever has found the world and become rich should renounce the world."

Saying 111: Those Who are Living Won't Die (2)

Jesus said, "The heavens and the earth will roll up in front of you, and whoever lives from the Living One won't see death."

Doesn't Jesus say, "Whoever finds themselves, of them the world isn't worthy"?

Saying 112: Flesh and Soul

Jesus said, "How awful for the flesh that depends on the soul. How awful for the soul that depends on the flesh."

Saying 113: The Kingdom is Already Present

His disciples said to him, "When will the kingdom come?"

"It won't come by looking for it. They won't say, 'Look over here!' or 'Look over there!' Rather, the Father's kingdom is already spread out over the earth, and people don't see it."

Saying 114: Peter and Mary

Simon Peter said to them, "Mary should leave us, because women aren't worthy of life."

Jesus said, "Look, am I to make her a man? So that she may become a living spirit too, she's equal to you men, because every woman who makes herself manly will enter the kingdom of heaven."

THE UNKNOWN GOSPEL:

EGERTON PAPYRUS 2

Fragment 1, verso (↓)

[...] to the lawyers ["...all] the wrongdoers [...] and not me [...] how does he do it?"

[Then he turned] to [the] rulers of the people and made this statement: "Search [the] scriptures; [you think] you have life in them. They [testify] about me. Don't [think] I've come to accuse [you] before my Father. [The one who accuses] you is Moses, in whom [you] hope."

But they [said,] "We know [well] God [spoke] to Moses, but you -- we don't know [where you're from."]

Jesus [told them] in reply, "Now [you] stand accused because [you don't believe those who've been approved] by him; because if [you believed Moses,] you'd believe [me, for] he [wrote] about me to your ancestors [...]"

Fragment 1, recto (→)

[...] stones together [so they could stone him.] And the [rulers] laid their [hands] on him [so that] they might seize him and [deliver him] to the crowd. But they [could] not seize him, because the hour of his arrest [had] not yet [come.] So the Lord escaped [from their hands] and withdrew from [them.]

And look, someone with leprosy approached [him] and said, "Teacher Jesus, while I was [traveling] with [others] who had [leprosy] and eating at the inn [with them,] I [contracted leprosy] myself. But if [you want to,] you can cure me."

Now the Lord [told him, "I want to:] be cured." [And immediately] the leprosy left him.

Then Jesus [told] him, ["Go] and show [yourself] to the [priests] and offer [what Moses ordered for] your cure, and don't sin anymore [...]"

Fragment 2, recto (→)

[...] to him, examining him to test him: "Teacher Jesus, we know that you've come [from God,] because the things you do [testify] above and beyond all the prophets. [So tell] us: is it right [to give] kings what belongs to them? [Should we pay] them, or [not?"]

But since Jesus knew what [they] were thinking, [he scolded them] and asked [them,] "Why do you pay me lip service as a Teacher but [don't do] what [I say? Isaiah] accurately prophesied [about] you when he said:

[These people honor] me with their [lips,]
[but] their [heart] is [far] from [me.]
[They worship me pointlessly,]
[... rules ...]

Fragment 2, verso (↓)

[...] enclosed in the [place ...] being subjected uncertainly [... its] weight unweighed [...] but [while] they were puzzled [as] to [his] strange question, Jesus walked and stood [on the] bank of the Jordan [river.] And reaching out with [his] right hand [...] and he sowed [on] the [...] and then [...] water [...] the [...] and [...] he produced [...] fruit [...]

GOSPEL OF PETER

THE GOSPEL ACCORDING TO PETER

1 But of the Jews none washed his hands, neither Herod nor any one of his judges. And when they had refused to wash them, Pilate rose up. And then Herod the king commandeth that the Lord be taken, saying to them, What things soever I commanded you to do unto him, do.

2 And there was standing there Joseph the friend of Pilate and of the Lord; and, knowing that they were about to crucify him, he came to Pilate and asked the body of the Lord for burial. And Pilate sent to Herod and asked his body. And Herod said, Brother Pilate, even if no one had asked for him, we purposed to bury him, especially as the sabbath draweth on: for it is written in the law, that the sun set not upon one that hath been put to death.

3 And he delivered him to the people on the day before the unleavened bread, their feast. And they took the Lord and pushed him as they ran, and said, Let us drag away the Son of God, having obtained power over him. And they clothed him with purple, and set him on the seat of judgement, saying, Judge righteously, O king of Israel. And one of them brought a crown of thorns and put it on the head of the Lord. And others stood and spat in his eyes, and others smote his cheeks: others pricked him with a reed; and some scourged him, saying, With this honour let us honour the Son of God.

4 And they brought two malefactors, and they crucified the Lord between them. But he held his peace, as though having no pain. And when they had raised the cross, they wrote the title: This is the king of Israel. And having set his garments before him they parted them among them, and cast lots for them. And one of those malefactors reproached them, saying, We for the evils that we have done have suffered thus, but this man, who hath become the Saviour of men, what wrong hath he done to you? And they, being angered at him, commanded that his legs should not be broken, that he might die in torment.

5 And it was noon, and darkness came over all Judaea: and they were troubled and distressed, lest the sun had set, whilst he was yet alive: [for] it is written for them, that the sun set not on him that hath been put to death. And one of them said, Give him to drink gall with vinegar. And they mixed and gave him to drink, and fulfilled all things, and accomplished their sins against their own head. And many went about with lamps, supposing that it was night, and fell down. And the Lord cried out, saying, My power, my power, thou hast forsaken me. And when he had said it he was taken up. And in that hour the vail of the temple of Jerusalem was rent in twain.

6 And then they drew out the nails from the hands of the Lord, and laid him upon the earth, and the whole earth quaked, and great fear arose. Then the sun shone, and it was found the ninth hour: and the Jews rejoiced, and gave his body to Joseph that he might bury it, since he had seen what good things he had done. And he took the Lord, and washed him, and rolled him in a linen cloth, and brought him into his own tomb, which was called the Garden of Joseph.

7 Then the Jews and the elders and the priests, perceiving what evil they had done to themselves, began to lament and to say, Woe for our sins: the judgement hath drawn nigh, and the end of Jerusalem. And I with my companions was grieved; and being wounded in mind we hid ourselves: for we were being sought for by them as malefactors, and as wishing to set fire to the temple. And upon all these things we fasted and sat mourning and weeping night and day until the sabbath.

8 But the scribes and Pharisees and elders being gathered together one with another, when they heard that all the people murmured and beat their breasts saying, If by his death these most mighty signs have come to pass, see how righteous he is,--the eiders were afraid and came to Pilate, beseeching him and saying, Give us soldiers, that we may guard his sepulchre for three days, lest his disciples come and steal him away, and the people suppose that he is risen from the dead and do us evil. And Pilate gave them Petronius the centurion with soldiers to guard the tomb. And with them came elders and scribes to the sepulchre, and having rolled a great stone together with the centurion and the soldiers, they all together who were there set it at the door of the sepulchre; and they affixed seven seals, and they pitched a tent there and guarded it. And early in the morning as the sabbath. was drawing on, there came a multitude from Jerusalem and the region round about, that they might see the sepulchre that was sealed.

9 And in the night in which the Lord's day was drawing on, as the soldiers kept guard two by two in a watch, there was a great voice in the heaven; and they saw the heavens opened, and two men descend from thence with great light and approach the tomb. And that stone which was put at the door rolled of itself and made way in part; and the tomb was opened, and both the young men entered in.

10 When therefore those soldiers saw it, they awakened the centurion and the elders; for they too were hard by keeping guard. And, as they declared what things they had seen, again they see three men come forth from the tomb, and two of them supporting one, and a cross following them: and of the two the head reached unto the heaven, but the head of him that was led by them overpassed the heavens. And they heard a voice from the heavens, saying, Thou hast preached to them that sleep. And a response was heard from the cross, Yea.

11 They therefore considered one with another whether to go away and shew these things to Pilate. And while they yet thought thereon, the heavens again are seen to open, and a certain man to descend and enter into the sepulchre. When the centurion and they that were with him saw these things, they hastened in the night to Pilate, leaving the tomb which they were watching, and declared all things which they had seen, being greatly distressed and saying, Truly he was the Son of God. Pilate answered and said, I am pure from the blood of the Son of God: but it was ye who determined this. Then they all drew near and besought him and entreated him to command the centurion and the soldiers to say nothing of the things which they had seen: For it is better, say they, for us to be guilty of the greatest sin before

God, and not to fall into the hands of the people of the Jews and to be stoned. Pilate therefore commanded the centurion and the soldiers to say nothing.

12 And at dawn upon the Lord's day Mary Magdalen, a disciple of the Lord, fearing because of the Jews, since they were burning with wrath, had not done at the Lord's sepulchre the things which women are wont to do for those that die and for those that are beloved by them--she took her friends with her and came to the sepulchre where he was laid. And they feared lest the Jews should see them, and they said, Although on that day on which he was crucified we could not weep and lament, yet now let us do these things at his sepulchre. But who shall roll away for us the stone that was laid at the door of the sepulchre, that we may enter in and sit by him and do the things that are due? For the stone was great, and we fear lest some one see us. And if we cannot, yet if we but set at the door the things which we bring for a memorial of him, we will weep and lament, until we come unto our home.

13 And they went and found the tomb opened, and coming near they looked in there; and they see there a certain young man sitting in the midst of the tomb, beautiful and clothed in a robe exceeding bright: who said to them, Wherefore are ye come? Whom seek ye? Him that was crucified? He is risen and gone. But if ye believe not, look in and see the place where he lay, that he is not [here]; for he is risen and gone thither, whence he was sent. Then the women feared and fled.

14 Now it was the last day of the unleavened bread, and many were going forth, returning to their homes, as the feast was ended. But we, the twelve disciples of the Lord, wept and were grieved: and each one, being grieved for that which was come to pass, departed to his home. But I Simon Peter and Andrew my brother took our nets and went to the sea; and there was with us Levi the son of Alphaeus, whom the Lord . . .

MATTHEW XXVII.

24 When Pilate saw that he could prevail nothing, but that rather a tumult was made, he took water, and washed his hands before the multitude, saying, I am innocent of the blood of this just person: see ye to it.

25 Then answered all the people, and said, His blood be on us, and on our children.

[cf. v. 57.]

26. Then released he Barabbas unto them: and when he had scourged Jesus, he delivered him to be crucified.

27 Then the soldiers of the governor took Jesus into the common hall, and gathered unto him the whole band of soldiers.

28 And they stripped him, and put on him a scarlet robe.

29 And when they had platted a crown of thorns, they put it upon his head, and a reed in his right hand: and they bowed the knee before him, and mocked him, saying, Hail, King of the Jews!

30 And they spit upon

MARK XV.

[cf. v. 43.]

[cf. v. 42.]

15 And so Pilate, willing to content the people, released Barabbas unto them, and delivered Jesus, when he had scourged him, to be crucified.

16 And the soldiers led him away into the hall, called Praetorium; and they call together the whole band.

17 And they clothed him with purple, and platted a crown of thorns, and put it about his head, 18 And began to salute him, Hail, King of the Jews!

19 And they smote him on the head with a reed, and did spit upon him, and bowing their knees worshipped him.

LUKE XXIII.

[2 cf. Lk. xxiii. 7.]

[3 cf. Lk. xxii. 66; Acts iv 27.]

[cf. v. 50.]

[4 cf. Lk. xxiii. 12.]

24 And Pilate gave sentence that it should be as they required.

25 And he released unto them him that for sedition and murder was cast into prison, whom they had desired; but he delivered Jesus to their will.

JOHN XIX.

[1 cf. John passim.]

[cf. v. 38.]

[cf. xix. 31.]

16 Then delivered he him therefore unto them to be crucified. And they took Jesus, and led him away.

PETER.

1 But of the Jews none washed his hands, neither Herod nor any one of his judges.

2 And when they had refused to wash them, Pilate rose up. And then Herod the king commandeth that the Lord be taken, saying to them, What things soever I commanded you to do unto him, do.

3 And there was come there Joseph the friend of Pilate and of the Lord; and, knowing that they were about to crucify him, he came to Pilate and asked the body of the Lord for burial.

4 And Pilate sent to Herod and asked his body.

5 And Herod said, Brother Pilate, even if no one had asked for him, we purposed to bury him, especially as the sabbath draweth on: for it is written in the law, that the sun set not upon one that hath been put to death. And he delivered him to the people on the day before the unleavened bread, their feast.

6 And they took the Lord and pushed him as they ran, and said, Let us drag away the Son of God, having obtained power over him.

7 And they clothed him with purple, and set him on the seat of judgement, saying, Judge righteously, O King of Israel. And one of them brought a crown of thorns and put it on the head of the Lord. And others stood and spat in his eyes, and others smote his cheeks: others pricked him with a reed; and some scourged him, saying, With this honour let us honour the Son of God.

MATTHEW. him, and took the reed, and smote him on the head.

31 And after that they had mocked him, they took the robe off from him, and put his own raiment on him, and led him away to crucify him.

32 And as they came out, they found a man of Cyrene, Simon by name: him they compelled to bear his cross.

33 And when they were come unto a place called Golgotha, that MARK.

20 And when they had mocked him, they took off the purple from him, and put his own clothes on him, and led him out to crucify him.

21 And they compel one Simon a Cyrenian, who passed by, coming out of the country, the father of Alexander and Rufus, to bear his cross.

22 And they bring him unto the place Golgotha, which is, LUKE.

26 And as they led him away, they laid hold upon one Simon, a Cyrenian, coming out of the country, and on him they laid the cross, that he might bear it after Jesus.

27 And there followed him a great company of people, and of women, which also bewailed and lamented him.

28 But Jesus turning unto them said, Daughters of Jerusalem, weep not for me, but weep for yourselves, and for your children.

29 For, behold, the days are coming, in the which they shall say, Blessed are the barren, and the wombs that never bare, and the paps which never gave suck.

30 Then shall they begin to say to the mountains, Fall on us; and to the hills, Cover us.

31 For if they do these things in a green tree, what shall be done in the dry?

32 And there were also two other, malefactors, led with him to be put to death.

33 And when they were come to the place, which is called Calvary, JOHN.

17 And he bearing his cross went forth into a place called the place of a skull, which is called in the Hebrew Golgotha:

PETER.

MATTHEW. is to say, a place of a skull, 34 They gave him vinegar to drink mingled with gall: and when he had tasted thereof, he would not drink.

35 And they crucified him; and parted his garments, casting lots: that it might be fulfilled which was spoken by the prophet, They parted my garments among them, and upon my vesture did they cast lots.

36 And sitting down they watched him there; 37 And set up over his head his accusation written, THIS IS JESUS THE KING OF THE JEWS.

38 Then were there two thieves crucified with him, one on the right hand, and another on the left.

39 And they that MARK. being interpreted, The place of a skull.

23 And they gave him to drink wine mingled with myrrh: but he received it not.

24 And when they had crucified him, they parted his garments, casting lots upon them, what every man should take.

25 And it was the third hour, and they crucified him.

26 And the superscription of his accusation was written over, THE KING OF THE JEWS.

27 And with him they crucify two thieves; the one on his right hand, and the other on his left.

28 And the scripture LUKE. there they crucified him, and the malefactors, one on the right hand, and the other on the left.

34 Then said Jesus, Father, forgive them; for they know not what they do. And they parted his raiment, and cast lots.

35 And the people stood beholding. And the rulers also with them derided him, saying, He saved others; let him save himself, if he be Christ, the chosen of God.

36 And the soldiers also mocked him, coming to him, and offering him vinegar, 37 And saying, If thou be the King of the Jews, save thyself.

38 And a superscription also was written over him in letters of Greek, and Latin, and Hebrew, THIS IS THE KING OF THE jews.

JOHN.

18 Where they crucified him, and two other with him, on either side one, and Jesus in the midst.

[cf. vv. 23, 24.]

19 And Pilate wrote a title, and put it on the cross. And the writing was, JESUS OF NAZARETH THE KING OF THE JEWS.

20 This title then read many of the Jews: for the place where Jesus was crucified was nigh to the city: and it was

PETER.

10 And they brought two malefactors, and they crucified the Lord between them.

But he held his peace, as though having no pain.

11 And when they had raised the cross, they wrote upon it, This is the King of Israel.

12 And having set his garments before him, they parted them among them, and cast lots for them.

MATTHEW. passed by reviled him, wagging their heads, 40 And saying, Thou that destroyest the temple, and buildest it in three days, save thyself. If thou be the Son of God, come down from the cross.

41 Likewise also the chief priests mocking him, with the scribes and elders, said, 42 He saved others; himself he cannot save. If he be the King of Israel, let him now come down from the cross, and we will believe him.

43 He trusted in God; let him deliver him now, if he will have him: for he said, I am the Son of God.

[cf. v. 35.]

44 The thieves also, which were crucified with him, cast the same in his teeth.

MARK. was fulfilled, which saith, And he was numbered with the transgressors.

29 And they that passed by railed on him, wagging their heads and saying, Ah, thou that destroyest the temple, and

buildest it in three days, 30 Save thyself, and come down from the cross.

31 Likewise also the chief priests mocking said among themselves with the scribes, He saved others; himself he cannot save.

32 Let Christ the King of Israel descend now from the cross, that we may see and believe.

[cf. v. 24.]

And they that were crucified with him reviled him.

LUKE.

39 And one of the malefactors which were hanged railed on him, saying, If thou be Christ, save thyself and, us.

40 But the other answering rebuked him, saying, Dost not thou fear God, seeing thou JOHN. written in Hebrew, and Greek, and Latin.

21 Then said the chief priests of the Jews to Pilate, Write not, The King of the Jews; but that he said, I am King of the Jews.

22 Pilate answered, What I have written I have written.

23 Then the soldiers, when they had crucified Jesus, took his garments, and made four parts, to every soldier a part; and also his coat: now the coat was without seam, woven from the top throughout.

24 They said therefore among themselves, Let us not rend it, but cast lots for it, whose it shall be: that the scripture might be fulfilled, which saith, They parted my raiment among them, and for my vesture they did cast lots. These things therefore the soldiers did.

PETER.

[cf.V. 12.]

13 And one of those malefactors reproached them, saying, We for the evils that we have done have suffered thus, but this man, who hath become the Saviour of men, what wrong hath he done to you?

MATTHEW.

45 Now from the sixth hour there was darkness over all the land unto the ninth hour.

46 And about the ninth hour Jesus cried with a loud voice, saying, Eli, Eli, lama sabachthani? that is to say, My God, my God, why hast thou forsaken me?

MARK.

33 And when the sixth hour was come, there was darkness over the whole land until the ninth hour.

34 And at the ninth hour Jesus cried with a loud voice, saying, Eloi, Eloi, lama sabachthani? which is, being interpreted, My God, my God, why hast thou forsaken me?

LUKE. art in the same condemnation?

41 And we indeed justly; for we receive the due reward of our deeds: but this man hath done nothing amiss.

42 And he said unto Jesus, Lord, remember me when thou comest into thy kingdom.

43 And Jesus said unto him, Verily I say unto thee, To day shalt thou be with me in paradise.

44 And it was about the sixth hour, and there was a darkness over all the earth until the ninth hour.

45 And the sun was darkened, and the veil of the temple was rent in the midst.

JOHN.

25 Now there stood by the cross of Jesus his mother, and his mother's sister, Mary the wife of Cleophas, and Mary Magdalene.

26 When Jesus therefore saw his mother, and the disciple standing by, whom he loved, he saith unto his mother, Woman, behold thy son!

27 Then saith he to the disciple, Behold thy mother! And from that hour that disciple took her unto his own home.

PETER.

14 And they, being angered at him, commanded that his legs should not be broken, that he might die in torment.

15 And it was noon, and darkness came over all Judaea: and they were troubled and distressed, lest the sun had set, whilst he was yet alive: [for] it is written for them, that the sun set not on him that hath been put to death.

MATTHEW.

47 Some of them that stood there, when they heard that, said, This man calleth for Elias.

48 And straightway one of them ran, and took a spunge, and filled it with vinegar, and put it on a reed, and gave him to drink.

49 The rest said, Let be, let us see whether Elias will come to save him.

50 Jesus, when he had cried again with a loud voice, yielded up the ghost.

51 And, behold, the veil of the temple was rent in twain from the top to the bottom; and the earth did quake, and the rocks rent; 52 And the graves were opened; and many

bodies of the saints which slept arose, 53 And came out of the graves after his resurrection, and went into the holy city, and appeared unto many.

MARK.

35 And some of them that stood by, when they heard it, said, Behold, he calleth Elias.

36 And one ran and filled a spunge full of vinegar, and put it on a reed, and gave him to drink, saying, Let alone; let us see whether Elias will come to take him down.

37 And Jesus cried with a loud voice, and gave up the ghost.

38 And the veil of the temple was rent in twain from the top to the bottom.

LUKE.

46 And when Jesus had cried with a loud voice, he said, Father, into thy hands I commend my spirit: and having said thus, he gave up the ghost.

JOHN.

28 After this, Jesus knowing that all things were now accomplished, that the scripture might be fulfilled, saith, I thirst.

29 Now there was set a vessel full of vinegar: and they filled a spunge with vinegar, and put it upon hyssop, and put it to his mouth.

30 When Jesus therefore had received the vinegar, he said, It is finished: and he bowed his head, and gave up the ghost.

31 The Jews therefore, because it was the preparation, that the bodies should not remain upon the cross on the sabbath day, (for that sabbath day was an high day,) besought Pilate that their legs might be broken, and that they might be taken away.

32 Then came the soldiers, and brake the legs of the first, and of the other which was crucified with him.

33 But when they came to Jesus, and saw that he was dead already, they brake not his legs:

PETER.

16 And one of them said, Give him to drink gall with vinegar. And they mixed and gave him to drink, 17 and fulfilled all things, and accomplished their sins against their own head.

18 And many went about with lamps, supposing that it was night, and fell down. 19 And the Lord cried out, saying, My power, my power, thou hast forsaken me.

And when he had said it he was taken up.

20 And in that hour the vail of the temple of Jerusalem was rent in twain.

MATTHEW.

54 Now when the centurion, and they that were with him, watching Jesus, saw the earthquake, and those things that were done, they feared greatly, saying, Truly this was the Son of God.

55 And many women were there beholding afar off, which followed Jesus from Galilee, ministering unto him:

56 Among which was Mary Magdalene, and Mary the mother of James and Joses, and the mother of Zebedee's children.

57 When the even was come, there came a rich man of Arimathaea, named Joseph,who also himself was Jesus' disciple:

MARK.

39 And when the centurion, which stood over against him, saw that he so cried out, and gave up the ghost, he said, Truly this man was the Son of God.

40 There were also women looking on afar off: among whom was Mary Magdalene, and Mary the mother of James the less and of Joses, and Salome; 41 (Who also, when he was in Galilee, followed him, and ministered unto him;) and many other women which came up with him unto Jerusalem.

42 And now when the even was come, because it was the preparation, that is, the day before the sabbath, 43 Joseph of Arimathaea, an honourable counsellor, which also waited for the kingdom of God, came, and went in boldly unto Pilate LUKE.

47 Now when the centurion saw what was done, he glorified God, saying, Certainly this was a righteous man.

48 And all the people that came together to that sight, beholding the things which were done, smote their breasts, and returned.

49 And all his acquaintance, and the women that followed him from Galilee, stood afar off, beholding these things.

50 And, behold, there was a man named Joseph, a counsellor; and he was a good man, and a just:

51 (The same had not JOHN.

34 But one of the soldiers with a spear pierced his side, and forthwith came there out blood and water.

35 And he that saw it bare record, and his record is true: and he knoweth that he saith true, that ye might believe.

36 For these things were done, that the scripture should be fulfilled, A bone of him shall not be broken.

37 And again another scripture saith, They shall look on him whom they pierced.

38 And after this Joseph of Arimathaea, being a disciple of Jesus, but secretly for fear of the Jews, besought Pilate that he might

PETER.

21 And then they drew out the nails from the hands of the Lord, and laid him upon the earth, and the whole earth quaked, and great fear arose.

22 Then the sun shone, and it was found the ninth hour:

23 and the Jews rejoiced, and

MATTHEW.

58 He went to Pilate, and begged the body of Jesus. Then Pilate commanded the body to be delivered.

59 And when Joseph had taken the body, he wrapped it in a clean linen cloth, 60 And laid it in his own new tomb, which he had hewn out in the rock: and he rolled a great stone to the door of the sepulchre, and departed.

61 And there was Mary Magdalene, and the other Mary, sitting over against the sepulchre.

MARK. and craved the body of Jesus.

44 And Pilate marvelled if he were already dead: and calling unto him the centurion, he asked him whether he had been any while dead.

45 And when he knew it of the centurion, he gave the body to Joseph.

46 And he bought fine linen, and took him down, and wrapped him in the linen, and laid him in a sepulchre which was hewn out of a rock, and rolled a stone unto the door of the sepulchre.

47 And Mary Magdalene and Mary the mother of Joses beheld where he was laid.

LUKE. consented to the counsel and deed of them;) he was of Arimathaea, a city of the Jews: who also himself waited for the kingdom of God.

52 This man went unto Pilate, and begged the body of Jesus.

53 And he took it down, and wrapped it in linen, and laid it in a sepulchre that was hewn in stone, wherein never man before was laid.

54 And that day was the preparation, and the sabbath drew on.

55 And the women also,which came with him from Galilee, followed after, and beheld the sepulchre, and how his body was laid.

56 And they returned, and prepared spices and ointments; and rested the sabbath day according to the commandment.

JOHN. take away the body of Jesus: and Pilate gave him leave. He came therefore, and took the body of Jesus.

39 And there came also Nicodemus, which at the first came to Jesus by night, and brought a mixture of myrrh and aloes, about an hundred pound weight.

40 Then took they the body of Jesus, and wound it in linen clothes with the spices, as the manner of the Jews is to bury.

41 Now in the place where he was crucified there was a garden; and in the garden a new sepulchre, wherein was never man yet laid.

42 There laid they Jesus therefore because of the Jews' preparation day; for the sepulchre was nigh at hand.

PETER. gave his body to Joseph that he might bury it, since he had seen what good things he had done.

24 And he took the Lord, and washed him, and wrapped him in a linen cloth, and brought him into his own tomb, which was called the Garden of Joseph.

25 Then the Jews and the elders and the priests, perceiving what evil they had done to themselves, began to lament and to say, Woe for our sins: the judgement hath drawn nigh, and the end of Jerusalem.

26 And I with my companions was grieved; and being wounded in mind we hid ourselves: for we were being sought for by them as malefactors, and as wishing to set fire to the temple.

MATTHEW.

[1 cf. Mt. ix. 15.]

62 NOW the next day, that followed the day of the preparation, the chief priests and Pharisees came together unto Pilate, 63 Saying, Sir, we remember that that deceiver said, while he was yet alive, After three days I will rise again.

64 Command therefore that the sepulchre be made sure until the third day, lest his disciples come by night, and steal him away, and say unto the people, He is risen from the dead: so the last error shall be worse than the first.

65 Pilate said unto them, Ye have a watch: go your way, make it as sure as ye can.

66 So they went, and made the sepulchre sure, sealing the stone, and setting a watch.

MARK.

[1 cf. Mk. ii. 20.]

[2 cf. Mk. xvi. 10.]

LUKE.

JOHN.

PETER.

27 And upon all these things we fasted 1 and sat mourning 2 and weeping 2 night and day until the sabbath.

28 But the scribes and Pharisees and elders being gathered together one with another, when they heard that all the people murmured and beat their breasts, saying, If by his death these most mighty signs have come to pass, see how just he is,--29 the elders were afraid and came to Pilate, beseeching him and saying, 30 Give us soldiers, that we may guard his sepulchre for three days, lest his disciples come and steal him away, and the people suppose that he is risen from the dead and do us evil.

31 And Pilate gave them Petronius the centurion with soldiers to guard the tomb. And with them came the elders and scribes to the sepulchre, 32 And having rolled a great stone together with the centurion and the soldiers, they all together who were there set it at the door of the sepulchre; 33 And they affixed seven seals, and they pitched a tent there and guarded it.

34 And early in the morning as the sabbath was drawing on, there came a multitude from Jerusalem and the region round about, that they might see the sepulchre that was sealed.

35 And in the night in which the Lord's day was drawing on, as the soldiers kept guard two by two in a watch, there was a great voice in the heaven; 36 and they saw the heavens opened, and two men descend from thence with great light and approach the tomb. 37 And that stone which was put at the door rolled of itself and made way in part; and the tomb was opened, and both the young men entered in.

38 When therefore those soldiers saw it, they awakened the centurion and the elders,--for they too were hard by keeping guard; 39 and, as they declared what things they had seen, again they see three men coming forth from the tomb, and two of them supporting one, and a cross following them. 40 And of the two the head reached unto the heaven, but the head of him that was led by them overpassed the heavens. 41 And they heard a voice from the heavens, saying, Hast thou preached to them that sleep? 42 And a response was heard from the cross, Yea.

43 They therefore considered one with another whether to go away and shew these things to Pilate. 44 And while they yet thought thereon, the heavens again are seen to open, and a certain man to descend and enter into the sepulchre. 45 When the centurion and they that were with him saw

these things, they hastened in the night to Pilate, leaving the tomb which they were

MATTHEW.

[cf. Mt. xxvii. 24.]

CHAPTER XXVIII.

1 In the end of the sabbath, as it began to dawn toward the first day of the week, came Mary Magdalene and the other Mary to see the sepulchre.

2 And, behold, there was a great earthquake: for the angel of the Lord descended from heaven, and came and rolled back the stone from the door, and sat upon it.

3 His countenance was like lightning, and his raiment white as snow:

MARK.

CHAPTER XVI.

1 And when the sabbath was past, Mary Magdalene, and Mary the mother of James, and Salome, had bought sweet spices, that they might come and anoint him.

2 And very early in the morning the first day of the week, they came unto the sepulchre at the rising of the sun.

3 And they said among themselves, Who shall roll us away the stone from the door of the sepulchre?

4 And when they looked, they saw that the stone was rolled away: for it was very great.

5 And entering into the sepulchre, they saw a young man sitting on the right side, clothed in a long white garment; and they were affrighted.

LUKE.

CHAPTER XXIV.

1 Now upon the first day of the week, very early in the morning, they came unto the sepulchre, bringing the spices which they had prepared, and certain others with them.

2 And they found the stone rolled away from the sepulchre.

3 And they entered in, and found not the body of the Lord Jesus.

4 And it came to pass, as they were much perplexed thereabout, behold, two men stood by them in shining garments:

5 And as they were afraid, and bowed down their faces to the earth, JOHN.

CHAPTER XX.

1 The first day of the week cometh Mary Magdalene early, when it was yet dark, unto the sepulchre, and seeth the stone taken away from the sepulchre.

PETER. watching, and declared all things which they had seen, being greatly distressed and saying, Truly he was the Son of God. 46 Pilate answered and said, I am pure from the blood of the Son of God: but ye determined this.

47 Then they all drew near and besought him and entreated him to command the centurion and the soldiers to say nothing of the things which they had seen: 48 For it is better, say they, for us to incur the greatest sin before God, and not to fall into the hands of the people of the Jews and to be stoned. 49 Pilate therefore commanded the centurion and the soldiers to say nothing.

50 And at dawn upon the Lord's day, Mary Magdalen, a disciple of the Lord, fearing because of the Jews, since they were burning with wrath, had not done at the Lord's sepulchre the things which the women are wont to do for those that die and for those that are beloved by them--51 she took her friends with her and came to the sepulchre where he was laid.

52 And they feared lest the Jews should see them, and they said, Although on the day on which he was crucified we could not weep and lament, yet now let us do these things at his sepulchre.

53 But who shall roll away for us the stone that was laid at the door of the sepulchre, that we may enter in and sit by him and do the things that are due? 54 For the stone was great, and we fear lest some one see us. And if we cannot, yet if we but set at the door the things which we bring for a memorial of him, we will weep and lament, until we come unto our home.

55 And they went away and found the tomb opened, and coming near they looked in there; and they see there a certain young man sitting in the midst of the tomb, beautiful and clothed in a robe exceeding bright;

MATTHEW.

4 And for fear of him the keepers did shake, and became as dead 5 And the angel answered and said unto the women, Fear not ye: for I know that ye seek Jesus, which was crucified.

6 He is not here: for he is risen, as he said. Come, see the place where the Lord lay.

7 And go quickly, and tell his disciples that he is risen from the dead; and, behold, he goeth before you into Galilee; there shall ye see him: lo, I have told you.

8 And they departed quickly from the sepulchre with fear and great joy; and did run to bring his disciples word.

MARK.

6 And he saith unto them, Be not affrighted: ye seek Jesus of Nazareth, which was crucified: he is risen; he is not here: behold the place where they laid him.

7 But go your way, tell his disciples and Peter that he goeth before you into Galilee: there shall ye see him, as he said unto you.

8 And they went out quickly, and fled from the sepulchre; for they trembled and were amazed: neither said they any thing to any man; for they were afraid.

[Levi, etc.; cf. Mk. ii.

LUKE. they said unto them, Why seek ye the living among the dead?

6 He is not here, but is risen: remember how he spake unto you when he was yet in Galilee, 7 Saying, The Son of man must be delivered into the hands of sinful men, and be crucified, and the third day rise again.

8 And they remembered his words, 9 And returned from the sepulchre, and told all these things unto the eleven, and to all the rest.

JOHN.

PETER. who said to them, 56 Wherefore are ye come? Whom seek ye? Him that was crucified? He is risen and gone. But if ye believe not, look in and see the place where he lay, that he is not [here]; for he is risen and gone away thither, whence he was sent.

57 Then the women feared and fled.

58 Now it was the last day of the unleavened bread, and many were going forth, returning to their homes, as the feast was ended. 59 But we, the twelve disciples of the Lord, mourned and were grieved: and each one, being grieved for that which was come to pass, departed to his home. 60 But I, Simon Peter and Andrew my brother, took our nets and went to the sea; and there was with us Levi the son of Alphaeus, whom the Lord . . .

GOSPEL OF MARY

Pages 1 through 6 are missing.

An Eternal Perspective

7 "Then will [matter] be [destroyed], or not?"
The Savior said, "Every nature, every form, every creature exists in and with each other, but they'll dissolve again into their own roots, because the nature of matter dissolves into its nature alone. Anyone who has ears to hear should hear!"
Peter said to him, "Since you've explained everything to us, tell us one more thing. What's the sin of the world?"
The Savior said, "Sin doesn't exist, but you're the ones who make sin when you act in accordance with the nature of adultery, which is called 'sin.' That's why the Good came among you, up to the things of every nature in order to restore it within its root."
Then he continued and said, "That's why you get sick and die, because [you love **8** what tricks you. Anyone who] can understand should understand!
"Matter [gave birth to] a passion that has no image because it comes from what's contrary to nature. Then confusion arises in the whole body. That's why I told you to be content at heart. If you're discontented, find contentment in the presence of the various images of nature. Anyone who has ears to hear should hear!"

The Gospel

When the Blessed One said these things, he greeted them all and said, "Peace be with you! Acquire my peace. Be careful not to let anyone mislead you by saying, 'Look over here!' or 'Look over there!' Because the Son of Humanity exists within you. Follow him! Those who seek him will find him.
"Go then and preach the gospel about the kingdom. Don't **9** lay down any rules beyond what I've given you, nor make a law like the lawgiver, lest you be bound by it." When he said these things, he left. But they grieved and wept bitterly. They said, "How can we go up to the Gentiles to preach the gospel about the kingdom of the Son of Humanity? If they didn't spare him, why would they spare us?"

Mary and Jesus

Then Mary arose and greeted them all. She said to her brothers (and sisters), "Don't weep and grieve or let your hearts be divided, because his grace will be with you all and will protect you. Rather we should praise his greatness because he's prepared us and made us Humans."

When Mary said these things, she turned their hearts [toward] the Good and they [started] to debate the words of [the Savior].
10 Peter said to Mary, "Sister, we know the Savior loved you more than all other women. Tell us the words of the Savior that you remember – the things which you know that we don't, and which we haven't heard."
In response Mary said, "I'll tell you what's hidden from you." So she started to tell them these words:
"I," she said, "I saw the Lord in a vision and I said to him, 'Lord, I saw you in a vision today.'
"In response he said to me, 'You're blessed because you didn't waver at the sight of me. For where the mind is, there is the treasure.'
"I said to him, 'Lord, now does the one who sees the vision see it /in\ the soul /or\ in the spirit?'
"In response the Savior said, 'They don't see in the soul or in the spirit, but the mind which [exists] between the two is [what] sees the vision [and] it [that …]

Pages 11 through 14 are missing.

Overcoming the Powers

15 "And Desire said, 'I didn't see you going down, but now I see you're going up. So why are you lying, since you belong to me?'
"In response the soul said, 'I saw you, but you didn't see me or know me. I was to you just a garment, and you didn't recognize me.' When it said these things, it left, rejoicing greatly.
"Again, it came to the third power, which is called 'Ignorance.' [It] interrogated the soul and [said], 'Where are you going? In wickedness you're bound. Since you're bound, don't judge!'
"[And] the soul said, 'Why do you judge me, since I haven't judged? I was bound, even though I haven't bound. They didn't recognize me, but I've recognized that everything will dissolve – both the things of the [earth] **16** and the things of [heaven].'
"When the soul had overcome the third power, it went up and saw the fourth power, which took seven forms:
The first form is Darkness;
The second, Desire;
The third, Ignorance;
The fourth, Zeal for Death;
The fifth, the Kingdom of the Flesh;
The sixth, the Foolish 'Wisdom' of Flesh;
The seventh, the 'Wisdom' of Anger.
"These are the seven powers of Wrath.
"They ask the soul, 'Where do you come from, you murderer, and where are you going, conqueror of space?'
"In response the soul said, 'What binds me has been killed, what surrounds me has been overcome, my

desire is gone, and ignorance has died. In a [world] I
was released **17** from a world, [and] in a type from a
type which is above, and from the chain of
forgetfulness which exists only for a time. From
now on I'll receive the rest of the time of the season
of the age in silence.'"
When Mary said these things, she fell silent because
the Savior had spoken with her up to this point.

Conflict over Authority

In response Andrew said to the brothers (and
sisters), 'Say what you will about what she's said, I
myself don't believe that the Savior said these
things, because these teachings seem like different
ideas."
In response Peter spoke out with the same
concerns. He asked them concerning the Savior:
"He didn't speak with a woman without our
knowledge and not publicly with us, did he? Will we
turn around and all listen to her? Did he prefer her
to us?"

18 Then Mary wept and said to Peter, "My brother
Peter, what are you thinking? Do you really think
that I thought this up by myself in my heart, or that
I'm lying about the Savior?"
In response Levi said to Peter, "Peter, you've always
been angry. Now I see you debating with this
woman like the adversaries. But if the Savior made
her worthy, who are you then to reject her? Surely
the Savior knows her very well. That's why he loved
her more than us.
"Rather we should be ashamed, clothe ourselves
with perfect Humanity, acquire it for ourselves as he
instructed us, and preach the gospel, not laying
down any other rule or other law beyond what the
Savior said."
When **19** [Levi said these things], they started to go
out to teach and to preach.

GOSPEL OF NICODEMUS

Part I.-The Acts of Pilate

First Greek Form.

Memorials of Our Lord Jesus Christ, Done in the Time of Pontius Pilate.

Prologue.-I Ananias, of the propraetor's body-guard, being learned in the law, knowing our Lord Jesus Christ from the Holy Scriptures, coming to Him by faith, and counted worthy of the holy baptism, searching also the memorials written at that time of what was done in the case of our Lord Jesus Christ, which the Jews had laid up in the time of Pontius Pilate, found these memorials written in Hebrew, and by the favour of God have translated them into Greek for the information of all who call upon the name of our Master Jesus Christ, in the seventeenth year of the reign of our Lord Flavius Theodosius, and the sixth of Flavius Valentinianus, in the ninth indiction.

All ye, therefore, who read and transfer into other books, remember me, and pray for me, that God may be merciful to me, and pardon my sins which I have sinned against Him.

Peace be to those who read, and to those who hear and to their households. Amen.

In the fifteenth year of the government of Tiberius Caesar, emperor of the Romans, and Herod being king of Galilee, in the nineteenth year of his rule, on the eighth day before the Kalends of April, which is the twenty-fifth of March, in the consulship of Rufus and Rubellio, in the fourth year of the two hundred and second Olympiad, Joseph Caiaphas being high priest of the Jews.

The account that Nicodemus wrote in Hebrew, after the cross and passion of our Lord Jesus Christ, the Saviour God, and left to those that came after him, is as follows:-

Chapter 1.

Having called a council, the high priests and scribes Annas and Caiaphas and Seines and Dathaes, and Gamaliel, Judas, Levi and Nephthalim, Alexander and Jairus, and the rest of the Jews, came to Pilate accusing Jesus about many things, saying: We know this man to be the son of Joseph the carpenter, born of Mary; and he says that he is the Son of God, and a king; moreover, he profanes the Sabbath, and wishes to do away with the law of our fathers. Pilate says: And what are the things which he does, to show that he wishes to do away with it? The Jews say: We have a law not to cure any one on the Sabbath; but this man has on the Sabbath cured the lame and the crooked, the withered and the blind and the paralytic, the dumb and the demoniac, by evil practices. Pilate says to them: What evil practices? They say to him: He is a magician, and by Beelzebul prince of the demons be casts out the demons, and all are subject to him. Pilate says to them: This is not casting out the demons by an unclean spirit, but by the god Aesculapius.

The Jews say to Pilate: we entreat your highness that he stand at thy tribunal, and be heard. And Pilate having called them, says: Tell me how I, being a procurator, can try a king? They say to him: W do not say that he is a king, but he himself says that he is. And Pilate having called the runner, says to him: Let Jesus be brought in with respect. And the runner going out, and recognising Him, adored Him, and took his cloak into his hand, and spread it on the ground, and says to him: My lord, walk on this, and come in, for the procurator calls thee. And the Jews seeing what the runner had done, cried out against Pilate, saying: Why hast thou ordered him to come in by a runner, and not by a crier? for assuredly the runner, when he saw him, adored him, and spread his doublet on the ground, and made him walk like a king.

And Pilate having called the runner, says to him: Why hast thou done this, and spread out thy cloak upon the earth, and made Jesus walk upon it? The runner says to him: My lord procurator, when thou didst send me to Jerusalem to Alexander, I saw him sitting upon an ass, and the sons of the Hebrews held branches in their hands, and shouted; and other spread their clothes under him saying, Save now, thou who art in the highest: blessed is he that cometh in the name of the Lord.

The Jews cry out, and say, to the runner: The soils of the Hebrews shouted in Hebrew; whence then hast thou the Greek? The runner says to them: I asked one of the Jews, and said, What is it they are shouting in Hebrew? And he interpreted it for me. Pilate says to them: And what did they shout in Hebrew? The Jews say to him: Hosanna Membrome Baruchamma Adonai. Pilate says to them: And this hosanna, etc., how is it interpreted? The Jews say to him: Save now in the highest; blessed is he; that cometh in the name of the Lord. Pilate says to them: If you bear witness to the words spoken by the children, in what has the runner done wrong? And they were silent. And the procurator says to the runner: Go out, and bring him in what way thou wilt. And the runner going out, did in the same manner as before, and says to Jesus: My lord, come in; the procurator calleth thee.

And Jesus going in, and the standard-bearers holding their standards, the tops of the standards were bent down, and adored Jesus. And the Jews seeing the bearing of the standards, how they were bent down and adored Jesus, cried out vehemently against the standard-bearers. And Pilate says to the Jews: Do you not wonder how the tops of the standards were bent down, and adored Jesus? The Jews say to Pilate: We saw how the standard-bearers bent them down, and adored him. And the procurator having called the standard-bearers, says to them: Why have you done this? They say to Pilate: We are Greeks and temple-slaves, and how could we adore him? and assuredly, as we were holding them up, the tops bent down of their own accord, and adored him.

Pilate says to the rulers of the synagogue and the elders of the people: Do you choose for yourselves men strong and powerful, and let them hold up the standards, and let us see whether they will bend down with them. And the elders of the Jews picked out twelve men powerful and strong, and made them hold up the standards six by six; and they were placed in front of the procurator's tribunal. And Pilate says to the runner: Take him outside of the praetorium, and bring him in again in whatever way may please thee. And Jesus and the runner went out of the praetorium. And Pilate, summoning those who had formerly held up the standards, says to them: I have sworn by tile health of Caesar, that if the standards do not bend down when Jesus comes in, I will cut off your heads. And the procurator ordered Jesus to come in the second time. And the runner did in the same manner as before, and made many entreaties to Jesus to walk on his cloak. And He walked on it, and went ill. And as He went in, the standards were again bent down, and adored Jesus.

Chapter 2.

And Pilate seeing this, was afraid, and sought to go away from the tribunal; but when he was still thinking of going away, his wife sent to him, saying: Have nothing to do with this just man, for many things have I suffered on his account this night. And Pilate, summoning the Jews, says to them: You know that my wife is a worshipper of God, and prefers to adhere to the Jewish religion along with you. They say to him: Yes; we know. Pilate says to them: Behold, my wife has sent to me, saying, Have nothing to do with this just man, for many things have I suffered on account of him this night. And the Jews answering, say unto Pilate: Did we not tell thee that he was a sorcerer? behold, he has sent a dream to thy wife.

And Pilate, having summoned Jesus, says to Him: What do these witness against thee? Sayest thou nothing? And Jesus said: Unless they had the power, they would say nothing; for every one has the power of his own mouth to speak both good and evil. They shall see to it.

And the eiders of the Jews answered, and said to Jesus: What shall we see? first, that thou wast born of fornication; secondly, that thy birth in Bethlehem was the cause of the murder of the infants; thirdly, that thy father Joseph and thy mother Mary fled into Egypt because they had no confidence in the people.

Some of the bystanders, pious men of the Jews, say: we deny that he was born of fornication; for we know that Joseph espoused Mary, and he was not born of fornication. Pilate says to the Jews who said that he was of fornication: This story of yours is not true, because they were betrothed, as also these fellow-countrymen of yours say. Annas and Caiaphas say to Pilate: All the multitude of us cry out that he was born of fornication,

and are not believed; these are proselytes, and his disciples. And Pilate, calling Annas and Caiaphas, says to them: What are proselytes? They say to him: They are by birth children of the Greeks, and have now become Jews. And those that said that He was not born of fornication, viz.-Lazarus, Asterius, Antonius, James, Atones, Zeras, Samuel, Isaac, Phinees, Crispus, Agrippas, and Judas -say: We are not proselytes, but are children of the Jews, and speak of the truth; for we were present at the betrothal of Joseph and Mary.

And Pilate, calling these twelve men who said that He was not born of fornication, says to them: I adjure you by the health of Caesar, to tell me whether it be true that you say, that he was not born of fornication. They say to Pilate: We have a law against taking oaths, because it is a sin; but they will swear by the health of Caesar, that it is not as we have said, and we are liable to death. Pilate says to Annas and Caiaphas: Have you nothing to answer to this? Annas and Caiaphas say to Pilate: These twelve are believed when they say that he was not born of fornication; all the multitude of us cry out that he was born of fornication, and that he is a sorcerer, and he says that he is the Son of God and a king, and we are not believed.

And Pilate orders all the multitude to go out, except the twelve men who said that He was not born of fornication, and he ordered Jesus to be separated from them. And Pilate says to them: For what reason do they wish to put him to death? They say to him: They are angry because he cures on the Sabbath. Pilate says: For a good work do they wish to put him to death? They say to him: Yes.

Chapter 3.

And Pilate, filled with rage, went outside of the praetorium, and said to them: I take the sun to witness that I find no fault in this man. The Jews answered and said to the procurator: Unless this man were an evil-doer, we should not have delivered him to thee. And Pilate said, Do you take him, and judge him according to your law. The Jews said to Pilate: It is not lawful for us to put any one to death. Pilate said: Has God said that you are not to put to death, but that I am?

And Pilate went again into the praetorium, and spoke to Jesus privately, and said to Him: Art thou the king of the Jews? Jesus answered Pilate: Dost thou say this of thyself, or have others said it to thee of me? Pilate answered Jesus: Am I also a Jew? Thy nation and the chief priests have given thee up to me. What hast thou done? Jesus answered: My kingdom is not of this world; for if my kingdom were of this world, my servants would fight in order that I should not be given up to the Jews: but now my kingdom is not from thence. Pilate said to Him: Art thou then a king? Jesus answered him: Thou sayest that I am a king. Because for this have I been born, and have I come, in order that every one who is of the truth might hear my voice. Pilate says to him: What is truth? Jesus says to him: Truth is from heaven. Pilate says: Is truth not upon earth? Jesus says to Pilate: Thou seest how those who speak the truth are judged by those that have the power upon earth.

Chapter 4.

And leaving Jesus within the praetorium, Pilate went out to the Jews, and said to them: I find no fault in him. The Jews say to him: He said, I can destroy this temple, and in three days build it. Pilate says: What temple? The Jews say: The one that Solomon built in forty-six years, and this man speaks of pulling it down and building it in three days. Pilate says to them: I am innocent of the blood of this just man. See you to it. The Jews say: His blood be upon us, and upon our children.

And Pilate having summoned the eiders and priests and Levites, said to them privately: Do not act thus, because no charge that you bring against him is worthy of death; for your charge is about curing and Sabbath profanation. The elders and the priests and the Levites say: If any one speak evil against Caesar, is he worthy of death or not? Pilate says: He is worthy of death The Jews say to Pilate: If any one speak evil against Caesar, he is worthy of death; but this man has spoken evil against God.

And the procurator ordered the Jews to go outside of the praetorium; and summoning Jesus, he says to Him: What shall I do to thee? Jesus says to Pilate: As it has been given to thee. Pilate says: How given? Jesus says: Moses and the prophets have proclaimed beforehand of my death and resurrection. And the Jews noticing this, and hearing it, say to Pilate: What more wilt thou hear of this blasphemy? Pilate says to the Jews: If these words be blasphemous, do you take him for the blasphemy, and lead him away to your synagogue, and judge him according to your law. The Jews say to Pilate: Our law bears that a man who wrongs his fellow-men is worthy to receive forty save one; but he that blasphemeth God is to be stoned with stones.

Pilate says to them: Do you take him, and punish him in whatever way you please. The Jews say to Pilate: we wish that he be crucified. Pilate says: He is not deserving of crucifixion.

And the procurator, looking round upon the crowds of the Jews standing by, sees many of the Jews weeping, and says: All the multitude do not wish him to die. The elders of the Jews say: For this reason all the multitude of us have come, that he should die. Pilate says to the Jews: Why should he die? The Jews say: Because he called himself Son of God, and King.

Chapter 5.

And one Nicodemus, a Jew, stood before the procurator, and said: I beseech your honour, let me say a few words. Pilate says: Say on. Nicodemus says: I said to the elders and the priests and Levites, and to all the multitude of the Jews in the synagogue, What do you seek to do with this man? This man many miracles and strange things,

which no one has done or will do. Let him go, and do not wish any evil against him. If the miracles which he does are of God, they will stand; but if man, they will come to nothing. For assuredly Moses, being sent by God into Egypt, did many miracles, which the Lord commanded him to do before Pharaoh king of Egypt. And there were there Jannes and Jambres, servants of Pharaoh, and they also did not a few of the miracles which Moses did; and the Egyptians took them to be gods-this Jannes and this Jambres. But, since the miracles which they did were not of God, both they and those who believed in them were destroyed. And now release this man, for he is not deserving of death.

The Jews say to Nicodemus: Thou hast become his disciple, and therefore thou defendest him. Nicodemus says to them: Perhaps, too, the procurator has become his disciple, because he defends him. Has the emperor not appointed him to this place of dignity? And the Jews were vehemently enraged, and gnashed their teeth against Nicodemus. Pilate says to I them: Why do you gnash your teeth against him when you hear the truth? The Jews say to Nicodemus: Mayst thou receive his truth and his portion. Nicodemus says: Amen, amen; may I receive it, as you have said.

Chapter 6.

One of the Jews, stepping up, asked leave of the procurator to say a word. The procurator says: If thou wishest to say any thing, say on And the Jew said: Thirty-eight years I lay in my bed in great agony. And when Jesus came, many demoniacs, and many lying ill of various diseases, were cured by him. And some young men, taking pity on me, carried me, bed and all, and took me to him. And when Jesus saw me, bed had compassion on me, and said to me: Take up thy couch and walk. And I took up my couch, and walked. The Jews say to pilate: Ask him on what day it was that he was cured. He that had been cured says: On a Sabbath. The Jews say: Is not this the very thing that we said, that on a Sabbath he cures and casts out demons?

And another Jew stepped up and said: I was born blind; I heard sounds, but saw not a face. And as Jesus passed by, I cried out with a loud voice, Pity me, O son of David. And he pitied me, and put his hands upon my eyes, and I instantly received my sight. And another Jew stepped up and said: I was crooked, and he straightened me with a word. And another said: I was a leper, and he cured me with a word.

Chapter 7.

And a woman cried out from a distance, and said: I had an issue of blood, and I touched the hem of his garment, and the issue of blood which I had had for twelve years was stopped. The Jews say: we have a law, that a woman's evidence is not to be received.

Chapter 8.

And others, a multitude both of men and women, cried out, saying: This man is a prophet, and the demons are subject to him. Pilate says to them who said that the demons were subject to Him: Why, then, were not your teachers also subject to him? They say to Pilate: We do not know. And others said: He raised Lazarus from the tomb after he had been dead four days. And the procurator trembled, and said to all the multitude of the Jews: Why do you wish to pour out innocent blood?

Chapter 9.

And having summoned Nicodemus and the twelve men that said He was not born of fornication, he says to them: What shall I do, because there is an insurrection among the people? They say to him: We know not; let them see to it. Again Pilate, having summoned all the multitude of the Jews, says: You know that it is customary, at the feast of unleavened bread, to release one prisoner to you. I have one condemned prisoner in the prison, a murderer named Barabbas, and this man standing in your presence, Jesus, in whom I find no fault. Which of them do you wish me to release to you? And they cry out: Barabbas. Pilate says: What, then, shall we do to Jesus who is called Christ? The Jews say: Let him be crucified. And others said: Thou art no friend of Caesar's if thou release this man, because he called himself Son of God and king. You wish, then, this man to be king, and not Caesar?

And Pilate, in a rage, says to the Jews: Always has your nation been rebellious, and you always speak against your benefactors. The Jews say: What benefactors? He says to them: Your God led you out of the land of Egypt from bitter slavery, and brought you safe through the sea as through dry land, and in the desert fed you with manna, and gave you quails, and quenched your thirst with water from a rock, and gave you a law; and in all these things you provoked your God to anger, and sought a molten calf. And you exasperated your God, and He sought to slay you. And Moses prayed for you, and you were not put to death. And now you charge me with hating the emperor.

And rising up from the tribunal, he sought to go out. And the Jews cry out, and say: We know that Caesar is king, and not Jesus. For assuredly the magi brought gifts to him as to a king. And when Herod heard from the magi that a king had been born, he sought to slay him; and his father Joseph, knowing this, took him and his mother, and they fled into Egypt. And Herod hearing of it, destroyed the children of the Hebrews that had been born in Bethlehem.

And when Pilate heard these words, he was afraid; and ordering the crowd to keep silence, because they were crying out, he said to them: So this is he whom Herod sought? The Jews say: Yes, it is he. And, taking water, Pilate washed his hands in the face of the sun, saying: I am innocent of the blood of this just man; see you to it. Again the Jews cry out: His blood be upon us, and upon our children.

Then Pilate ordered the curtain of the tribunal where he was sitting to be drawn, and says to Jesus: Thy nation has charged thee with being a king. On this account I sentence thee, first to be scourged, according to the enactment of venerable kings, and then to be fastened on the cross in the garden where thou wast seized. And let Dysmas and Gestas, the two malefactors, be crucified with thee.

Chapter 10.

And Jesus went forth out of the praetorium, and the two malefactors with Him. And when they came to the place, they stripped Him of his clothes, and girded Him with a towel, and put a crown of thorns on Him round His head. And they crucified Him; and at the same time also they hung up the two malefactors along with Him. And Jesus said: Father, forgive them, for they know not what they do. And the soldiers parted His clothes among them; and the people stood looking at Him. And the chief priests, and the rulers with them, mocked Him, saying: He saved others; let him save himself. If he be the Son of God, let him come down from the cross. And the soldiers made sport of Him, coming near and offering Him vinegar mixed with gall, and said: Thou art the king of the Jews; save thyself.

And Pilate, after the sentence, ordered the charge made against Him to be inscribed as a superscription in Greek, and Latin, and Hebrew, according to what the Jews had said: He is king of the Jews.

And one of the malefactors hanging up spoke to Him, saying: If thou be the Christ, save thyself and us. And Dysmas answering, reproved him, saying: Dost thou not fear God, because thou art in the same condemnation? And we indeed justly, for we receive the fit punishment of our deeds; but this man has done no evil. And he said to Jesus: Remember me, Lord, in Thy kingdom. And Jesus said to him: Amen, amen; I say to thee, To-day shalt thou be with me in Paradise.

Chapter 11.

And it was about the sixth hour, and there was darkness over the earth until the ninth hour, the sun being darkened; and the curtain of the temple was split in the middle. And crying out with a loud voice, Jesus said: Father, Baddach Ephkid Ruel, which is, interpreted: Into Thy hands I commit my spirit. And having said this, He gave up the ghost. And the centurion, seeing what had happened, glorified God, and said: This was a just man. And all the crowds that were present at this spectacle, when they saw what had happened, beat their breasts and went away.

And the centurion reported what had happened to the procurator. And when the procurator and his wife heard it, they were exceedingly grieved, and neither ate nor drank that day. And Pilate sent for the Jews, and said to them: Have you seen what has happened? And they say: There has been an eclipse of the sun in the usual way.

And His acquaintances were standing at a distance, and the women who came with Him from Galilee, seeing these things. And a man named Joseph, a councillor from the city of Arimathaea, who also waited for the kingdom of God, went to Pilate, and begged the body of Jesus. And he took it down, and wrapped it in clean linen, and placed it in a tomb hewn out of the rock, in which no one had ever lain.

Chapter 12.

And the Jews, hearing that Joseph had begged the booty of Jesus, sought him and the twelve who said that Jesus was not born of fornication, and Nicodemus, and many others who had stepped up before Pilate and declared His good works. And of all these that were hid, Nicodemus alone was seen by them, because he was a ruler of the Jews. And Nicodemus says to them: How have you come into the synagogue? The Jews say to him: How hast thou come into the synagogue? for thou art a confederate of his, and his portion is with thee in the world to come. Nicodemus says: Amen, amen. And likewise Joseph also stepped out and said to them: Why are you angry against me because I begged the body of Jesus? Behold, I have put him in my new tomb, wrapping him in clean linen; and I have rolled a stone to the door of the tomb. And you have acted not well against the just man, because you have not repented of crucifying him, but also have pierced him with a spear. And the Jews seized Joseph, and ordered him to be secured until the first day of the week, and said to him: Know that the time does not allow us to do anything against thee, because the Sabbath is dawning; and know that thou shall not be deemed worthy of burial, but we shall give thy flesh to the birds of the air. Joseph says to them: These are the words of the arrogant Goliath, who reproached the living God and holy David. For God has said by the prophet, Vengeance is mine, and I will repay, saith the Lord. And now he that is uncircumcised in flesh, but circumcised in heart, has taken water, and washed his hands in the face of the sun, saying, I am innocent of the blood of this just man; see ye to it. And you answered and said to Pilate, His blood be upon us, and upon our children. And now I am afraid lest the wrath of God come upon you, and upon your children, as you have said. And the Jews, hearing these words, were embittered in their souls, and seized Joseph, and locked him into a room where there was no window; and guards were stationed at the door, and they sealed the door where Joseph was locked in.

And on the Sabbath, the rulers of the synagogue, and the priests and the Levites, made a decree that all should be found in the synagogue on the first day of the week. And rising up early, all the multitude in the synagogue consulted by what death they should slay him. And when the Sanhedrin was sitting, they ordered him to be brought with much indignity. And having opened the door, they found him not. And all the people were surprised, and struck with dismay, because they found the seals unbroken. and because Caiaphas had the key.

And they no longer dared to lay hands upon those who had spoken before Pilate in Jesus' behalf.

Chapter 13.

And while they were still sitting in the synagogue, and wondering about Joseph, there come some of the guard whom the Jews had begged of Pilate to guard the tomb of Jesus, that His disciples might not come and steal Him. And they reported to the rulers of the synagogue, and the priests and the Levites, what had happened: how there had been a great earthquake; and we saw an angel coming down from heaven, and he rolled away the stone from the mouth of the tomb, and sat upon it; and he shone like snow, and like lightning. And we were very much afraid, and lay like dead men; and we heard the voice of the angel saying to the women who remained beside the tomb, Be not afraid, for I know that you seek Jesus who was crucified. He is not here: He is risen, as He said. Come, see the place where the Lord lay: and go quickly, and tell His disciples that He is risen from the dead, and is in Galilee.

The Jews say: To what women did he speak? The men of the guard say: We do not know who they were. The Jews say: At what time was this? The men of the guard say: At midnight. The Jews say: And wherefore did you not lay hold of them? The men of the guard say: We were like dead men from fear, not expecting to see the light of day, and how could we lay hold of them? The Jews say: As the Lord liveth, we do not believe you. The men of the guard say to the Jews: You have seen so great miracles in the case of this man, and have not believed; and how can you believe us? And assuredly you have done well to swear that the Lord liveth, for indeed He does live. Again the men of the guard say: We have heard that you have locked up the man that begged the body of Jesus, and put a seal on the door; and that you have opened it, and not found him. Do you then give us the man whom you were guarding, and we shall give you Jesus. The Jews say: Joseph has gone away to his own city. The men of the guard say to the Jews: And Jesus has risen, as we heard from the angel, and is in Galilee.

And when the Jews heard these words, they were very much afraid, and said: We must take care lest this story be heard, and all incline to Jesus. And the Jews called a council, and paid down a considerable sum of money, and gave it to the soldiers, saying: Say, while we slept, his disciples came by night and stole him; and if this come to the ears of the procurator, we shall persuade him, and keep you out of trouble. And they took it, and said as the had been instructed.

Chapter 14.

And Phinees a priest, and Adas a teacher, and Haggai a Levite, came down from Galilee to Jerusalem, and said to the rulers of the synagogue, and the priests and the Levites: We saw Jesus and his disciples sitting on the mountain called Mamilch; and he said to his disciples, Go into all the world, and preach to every creature: he that believeth and is baptized shall be saved, and he that believeth not shall be condemned. And these signs shall attend those who have believed: in my name they shall cast out demons, speak new tongues, take up serpents; and if they drink any deadly thing, it shall by no means hurt them; they shall lay hands on the sick, and they shall be well. And while Jesus was speaking to his disciples, we saw him taken up to heaven.

The elders and the priests and Levites say: Give glory to the God of Israel, and confess to Him whether you have heard and seen those things of which you have given us an account. And those who had given the account said: As the Lord liveth, the God of our fathers Abraham, Isaac, and Jacob, we heard these things, and saw him taken up into heaven. The ciders and the priests and the Levites say to them: Have you come to give us this announcement, or to offer prayer to God? And they say: To offer prayer to God. The elders and the chief priests and the Levites say to them: If you have come to offer prayer to God, why then have you told these idle tales in the presence of all the people? Says Phinees the priest, and Atlas the teacher, and Haggai the Levite to the rulers of the synagogues. and the priests and the Levites: If what we have said and seen be sinful, behold, we are before you; do to us as seems good in your eyes. And they took the law, and made them swear upon it, not to give any more an account of these matters to any one. And they gave them to cat and drink, and sent them out of the city, having given them also money, and three men with them; and they sent them away to Galilee. And these men having gone into Galilee, the chief priests, and the rulers of the synagogue, and the elders, came together into the synagogue, and locked the door, and lamented with a great lamentation, saying: Is this a miracle that has happened in Israel? And Annas and Caiaphas said: Why are you so much moved? Why do you weep? Do you not know that his disciples have given a sum of gold to the guards of the tomb, and have instructed them to say that an angel came down and rolled away the stone from the door of the tomb? And the priests and the elders sand: Be it that his disciples have stolen his body; how is it that the life has come into his body, and that he is going, about in Galilee? And they being unable to give an answer to these things, said, after great hesitation: It is not lawful for us to believe the uncircumcised.

Chapter 15.

And Nicodemus stood up, and stood before the Sanhedrin, saying: You say well; you are not ignorant, you people of the Lord, of these men that come down from Galilee, that they fear God, and are men of substance, haters of covetousness, men of peace; and they have declared with an oath. We saw Jesus upon the mountain Mamilch with his disciples, and he taught what we heard from him, and we saw him taken up into heaven. And no one asked them in what form he went up. For assuredly, as the book of the Holy Scriptures

taught us, Helias also was taken up into heaven, and Elissaeus cried out with a loud voice, and Helias threw his sheepskin upon Elissaeus, and Elissaeus threw his sheepskin upon the Jordan, and crossed, and came into Jericho. And the children of the prophets met him, and said, O Elissaeus, where is thy master Helias? And he said, He has been taken up into heaven. And they said to Elissaeus, Has not a spirit seized him, arid thrown him upon one of the mountains? But let us take our servants with us, and seek him. And they persuaded Elissaeus, and he went away with them. And they sought him three days, and did not find him; and they knew he had been taken up. And now listen to me, and let us send into every district of Israel, and see lest perchance Christ has been taken up by a spirit, and thrown upon one of the mountains? And this proposal pleased all. And they sent into every district of Israel, and sought Jesus, and did not find Him; but they found Joseph in Arimathaea, and no one dared to lay hands on him.

And they reported to the elders, and the priests, and the Levites: We have gone round to every district of Israel, and have not found Jesus; but Joseph we have found in Arimathaea. And hearing about Joseph, they were glad, and gave glory to the God of Israel. And the rulers of the synagogue, and the priests and the Levites, having held a council as to the manner in which they should meet with Joseph, took a piece of paper, and wrote to Joseph as follows:-

Peace to thee! We know that we have sinned against God, and against thee; and we have prayed to the God of Israel, that thou shouldst deign to come to thy fathers, and to thy children, because we have all been grieved. For having opened the door, we did not find thee. And we know that we have counselled evil counsel against thee; but the Lord has defended thee, and the Lord Himself has scattered to the winds our counsel against thee, O honourable father Joseph.

And they chose from all Israel seven men, friends of Joseph, whom also Joseph himself was acquainted with; and the rulers of the synagogue, and the priests and the Levites, say to them: Take notice: if, after receiving our letter, he read it, know that he will come with you to us; but if he do not read it, know that he is ill-disposed towards us. And having saluted him in peace, return to us. And having blessed the men, they dismissed them. And the men came to Joseph, and did reverence to him, and said to him: Peace to thee! And he said: Peace to you, and to all the people of Israel! And they gave him the roll of the letter. And Joseph having received it, read the letter and rolled it up, and blessed God, and said: Blessed be the Lord God, who has delivered Israel, that they should not shed innocent blood; and blessed be the Lord, who sent out His angel, and covered me under his wings. And he set a table for them; and they ate and drank, and slept there. And they rose up early, and prayed. And Joseph saddled his ass, and set out with the men; and they came to the holy city Jerusalem. And all the people met Joseph, and cried out: Peace to thee in thy coming in! And he said to all the people: Peace to you! and he kissed them. And the people prayed with Joseph, and they were astonished at the sight of him. And Nicodemus received him into his house, and made a great feast, and called Annas and Caiaphas, and the elders, and the priests, and the Levites to his house. And they rejoiced, eating and drinking with Joseph; and after singing hymns, each proceeded to his own house. But Joseph remained in the house of Nicodemus.

And on the following day, which was the preparation, the rulers of the synagogue and the priests and the Levites went early to the house of Nicodemus; and Nicodemus met them, and said: Peace to you! And they said: Peace to thee, and to Joseph, and to all thy house, and to all the house of Joseph! And he brought them into his house. And all the Sanhedrin sat down, and Joseph sat down between Annas and Caiaphas: and no one dared to say a word to him. And Joseph said: Why have you called me? And they signalled to Nicodemus to speak to Joseph. And Nicodemus, opening his mouth, said to Joseph: Father, thou knowest that the honourable teachers, and the priests and the Levites, see to learn a word from thee. And Joseph said: Ask. And Annas and Caiaphas having taken the law, made Joseph swear, saying: Give glory to the God of Israel, and give Him confession; for Achar being made to swear by the prophet Jesus, did not forswear himself, but declared unto him all, and did not hide a word from him. Do thou also accordingly not hide from us to the extent of a word. And Joseph said: I shall not hide from you one word. And they said to him: With grief were we grieved because thou didst beg the body of Jesus, and wrap it in clean linen, and lay it in a tomb. And on account of this we secured thee in a room where there was no windows: and we put locks and seals upon the doors and guards kept watching where thou wast locked in And on the first day of the week we opened, and found thee not, and were grieved exceedingly; and astonishment fell upon all the people of the Lord until yesterday. And now relate to us what has happened to thee.

And Joseph said: On the preparation, about the tenth hour, you locked me up, and I remained all the Sabbath. And at midnight, as I was standing and praying, the room where you locked me in was hung up by the four corners, and I saw a light like lightning into my eyes. And I was afraid, and fell to the ground. And some one took me by the hand, and removed me from the place where I had fallen; and moisture of water was poured from my head even to my feet, and a smell of perfumes came about my nostrils. And he wiped my face, and kissed me, and said to me, Fear not, Joseph; open thine eyes, and see who it is that speaks to thee. And looking up, I saw Jesus. And I trembled and thought it was a phantom; and I said the commandments, and he said them with me. Even so you are not ignorant that a phantom, if it meet anybody, and hear the commandments, takes to flight. And seeing that he said them with the, I said to him, Rabbi Helias. And he said to me, I am not Helias. And I said to him, Who art thou, my lord? And he said to me, I am Jesus, whose body thou didst beg from Pilate; and thou didst clothe me with clean, linen. and didst put a napkin on my face, and

didst lay me in thy new tomb, and didst roll a great stone to the door of the tomb. And I said to him that was speaking to me, Show me the place where I laid thee. And he carried me away, and showed me the place where I laid him; and the linen cloth was lying in it, and the napkin for his face. And I knew that it was Jesus. And he took me by the hand, and placed me, though the doors were locked, in the middle of my house, and led me away to my bed, and said to me, Peace to thee! And he kissed me, and said to me, For forty days go not forth out of thy house; for, behold, I go to my brethren into Galilee.

Chapter 16.

And the rulers of the synagogue, and the priests and the Levites, when they heard these words from Joseph, became as dead, and fell to the ground, and fasted until the ninth hour. And Nicodemus, along with Joseph, exhorted Annas and Caiaphas, the priests and the Levites, saying: Rise up and stand upon your feet, and taste bread, and strengthen your souls, because to-morrow is the Sabbath of the Lord. And they rose up, and prayed to God, and ate and drank, and departed every man to his own house.

And on the Sabbath our teachers and the priests and Levites sat questioning each other, and saying: What is this wrath that has come upon us? for we know his father and mother. Levi, a teacher, says: I know that his parents fear God, and do not withdraw themselves from the prayers, and give the tithes thrice a year. And when Jesus was born, his parents brought him to this place, and gave sacrifices and burnt-offerings to God. And when the great teacher Symeon took him into his arms, he said, Now Thou sendest away Thy servant, Lord, according to Thy word, in peace; for mine eyes have seen Thy salvation, which Thou hast prepared before the face of all the peoples: a light for the revelation of the Gentiles, and the glory of Thy people Israel. And Symeon blessed them, and said to Mary his mother, I give thee good news about this child. And Mary said, It is well, my lord. And Symeon said to her, It is well; behold, he lies for the fall and rising again of many in Israel, and for a sign spoken against; and of thee thyself a sword shall go through the soul, in order that the reasoning of many hearts may be revealed.

They say to the teacher Levi: How knowest thou these things? Levi says to them: Do you not know that from him I learned the law? The Sanhedrin say to him: We wish to see thy father. And they sent for his father. And they asked him; and he said to them: Why have you not believed my son? The blessed and just Symeon himself taught him the law. The Sanhedrin says to Rabbi Levi: Is the word that you have said true? And he said: It is true. And the rulers of the synagogue, and the priests and the Levites, said to themselves: Come, let us send into Galilee to the three men that came and told about his teaching and his taking up, and let them tell us how they saw him taken up. And this saying pleased all. And they sent away the three men who had already gone away into

Galilee with them; and they say to them: Say to Rabbi Adas, and Rabbi Phinees, and Rabbi Haggai: Peace to you, and all who are with you! A great inquiry having taken place in tile Sanhedrin, we have been sent to you to call you to this holy place, Jerusalem.

And the men set out into Galilee, and found them sitting and considering the law; and they saluted them in peace. And the men who were in Galilee said to those who had come to them: Peace upon all Israel! And they said: Peace to you! And they again said to them: Why have you come? And those who had been sent said: The Sanhedrin call you to the holy city Jerusalem. And when the men heard that they were sought by the Sanhedrin, they prayed to God, and reclined with the men, and ate and drank, and rose up, and set out in peace to Jerusalem.

And on the following day the Sanhedrin sat in the synagogue, and asked them, saying: Did you really see Jesus sitting on the mountain Mamilch teaching his eleven disciples, and did you see him taken up? And the men answered them, and said: As we saw him taken up, so also we said.

Annas says: Take them away from one another, and let us see whether their account agrees. And they took them away from one another. And first they call Adas, and say to him: How didst thou see Jesus taken up? Adas says: While he was yet sitting on the mountain Mamilch, and teaching his disciples, we saw a cloud overshadowing both him and his disciples. And the cloud took him up into heaven, and his disciples lay upon their face upon the earth. And they call Phinees the priest, and ask him also, saying: How didst thou see Jesus taken up? And he spoke in like manner. And they again asked Haggai, and he spoke in like manner. And the Sanhedrin said: The law of Moses holds: At the mouth of two or three every word shall be established. Buthem, a teacher, says: It is written in the law, And Enoch walked with God, and is not, because God took him. Jairus, a readier, said: And the death of holy Moses we have heard of, and have not seen it; for it is written in the law of the Lord, And Moses died from the mouth of the Lord, and no man knoweth of his sepulchre unto this day. And Rabbi Levi said: Why did Rabbi Symeon say, when he saw Jesus, "Behold, he lies for the fall and rising again of many in Israel, and for a sign spoken against?" And Rabbi Isaac said: It is written in the law, Behold, I send my messenger before thy face, who shall go before thee to keep thee in every good way, because my name has been called upon him.

Then Annas and Caiaphas said: Rightly have you said what is written in the law of Moses, that no one saw the death of Enoch, and no one has named the death of Moses; hut Jesus was tried before Pilate, and we saw him receiving blows and spittings on his face, and the soldiers put about him a crown of thorns, and he was scourged, and received sentence from Pilate, and was crucified upon the Cranium, and two robbers with him; and they gave him to drink vinegar with gall, and

Longinus the soldier pierced his side with a spear; and Joseph our honourable father begged his body, and, as he says, he is risen; and as the three teachers say, We saw him taken up into heaven; and Rabbi Levi has given evidence of what was said by Rabbi Symeon, and that he said, Behold, he lies for the fall and rising again of many in Israel, and for a sign spoken against. And all the teachers said to all the people of the Lord: If this was from the Lord, and is wonderful in your eyes, knowing you shall know, O house of Jacob, that it is written, Cursed is every one that hangeth upon a tree. And another Scripture teaches: The gods which have not made the heaven and the earth shall be destroyed. And the priests and the Levites said to each other: If his memorial be until the year that is called Jobel, know that it shall it endure for ever, and he hath raised for himself a new people. Then the rulers of the synagogue, and the priests and the Levites, announced to all Israel, saying: Cursed is that man who shall worship the work of man's hand, and cursed is the man who shall worship the creatures more than the Creator. And all the people said, Amen, amen.

And all the people praised the Lord, and said: Blessed is the Lord, who hath given rest to His people Israel, according to all that He hath spoken; there hath not fallen one word of every good word of His that He spoke to Moses His servant. May the Lord our God be with us, as He was with our fathers: let Him not destroy us. And let Him not destroy us, that we may incline our hearts to Him, that we may walk in all His ways, that we may keep His commandments and His judgments which He commanded to our fathers. And the Lord shall be for a king over all the earth in that day; and there shall he one Lord, and His name one. The Lord is our king: He shall save us. There is none like Thee, O Lord. Great art Thou, O Lord, and great is Thy name. By Thy power heal us. O Lord, and we shall be healed: save us, O Lord, and we shall be saved; because we are Thy lot and heritage. And the Lord will not leave His people, for His great name's sake; for the Lord has begun to make us into His people.

And all, having sung praises, went away each man to his own house, glorifying God; for His is the glory for ever and ever. Amen.

GOSPEL OF NICODEMUS

Part II.-The Descent of Christ into Hell

Greek Form.

Chapter I (17).

Joseph says: And why do you wonder that Jesus has risen? But it is wonderful that He has not risen alone, but that He has also raised many others of the dead who have appeared in Jerusalem to many. And if you do not know the others, Symeon at least, who received Jesus, and his two sons whom He has raised up-them at least you know. For we buried them not long ago; but now their tombs are seen open *and* empty, and they are alive, and dwelling in Arimathaea. They therefore sent men, and they found their tombs open and empty. Joseph says: Let us go to Arimathaea and find them.

Then rose up the chief priests Annas and Caiaphas, and Joseph, and Nicodemus, and Gamaliel, and others with them, and went away to Arimathaea, and found those whom Joseph spoke of. They made prayer, therefore, and saluted each other. Then they came with them to Jerusalem, and brought them into the synagogue, and secured the doors, and placed in the midst the old *covenant* of the Jews; and the chief priests said to them: We wish you to swear by the God of Israel and Adonai, and so that you tell the truth, how you have risen, and who has raised you from the dead.

The men who had risen having heard this, made upon their faces the sign of the cross, and said to the chief priests: Give us paper and ink and pen. These therefore they brought. And sitting down, they wrote thus:-

Chapter 2 (18).

O Lord Jesus Christ, the resurrection and the life of the world, grant us grace that we may give an account of Thy resurrection, and Thy miracles which Thou didst in Hades. We then were in Hades, with all who had fallen asleep since the beginning of the world. And at the hour of midnight there rose a light as if of the sun, and shone into these dark *regions;* and we were all lighted up, and saw each other. And straightway our father Abraham was united with the patriarchs and the prophets, and at the same time they were filled with joy, and said to each other: This light is from a great source of light. The prophet Hesaias, who was there present, said: This light is from the Father, and from the Son, and from the Holy Spirit; about whom I prophesied when yet alive, saying, The land of Zabulon, and the land of Nephthalim, the people that sat in darkness, have seen a great light.

Then there came into the midst another, an ascetic from the desert; and the patriarchs said to him: Who art thou? And he said: I am John, the last of the prophets, who made the paths of the Son of God straight, and proclaimed to the people repentance for the remission of sins. And the Son of God came to me; and I, seeing Him a long way off, said to the people: Behold the Lamb of God, who taketh away the sin of the world. And with my hand I baptized Him in the river Jordan, and I saw like a dove also the Holy Spirit coming upon Him; and I heard also the voice of God, even the Father, thus saying: This is my beloved Son, in whom I am well pleased. And on this account He sent me also to you, to proclaim how the only begotten Son of God is coming here, that whosoever shall believe in Him shall be saved, and whosoever shall not believe in Him shall be condemned. On this account I say to you all, in order that when you see Him you all may adore Him, that now only is for you the time of repentance for having adored idols in the vain upper world, and for the sins you have committed, and that this is impossible at any other time.

Chapter 3 (19).

While John, therefore, was thus teaching those in Hades, the first created and forefather Adam heard, and said to his son Seth: My son, I wish thee to tell the forefathers of the race of men and the prophets where I sent thee, when it fell to my lot to die. And Seth said: Prophets and patriarchs, hear. When my father Adam, the first created, was about to fall once upon a time into death, he sent me to make entreaty to God very close by the gate of paradise, that He would guide me by an angel to the tree of compassion and that I might take oil and anoint my father, and that he might rise up from his sickness: which thing, therefore, I also did. And after the prayer an angel of the Lord came, and said to me: What, Seth, dost thou ask? Dost thou ask oil which raiseth up the sick, or the tree from which this oil flows, on account of the sickness of thy father? This is not to be found now. Go, therefore, and tell thy father, that after the accomplishing of five thousand five hundred years from the creation of the world, thou shall come into the earth the only begotten Son of God, being made man; and He shall anoint him with this oil, and shall raise him up; and shall wash clean, with water and with the Holy Spirit, both him and those out of him, and then shall he be healed of every disease; but now this is impossible.

When the patriarchs and the prophets heard these words, they rejoiced greatly.

Chapter 4 (20).

And when all were in such joy, came Satan the heir of darkness, and said to Hades: O all-devouring and insatiable, hear my words. There is of the race of the Jews one named Jesus, calling himself the Son of God; and being a man, by our working with them the Jews have crucified him: and now when he is dead, be ready that we may secure him here. For I know that he is a man, and I heard him also saying, My soul is exceeding sorrowful, even unto death. He has also done me many evils when living with mortals in the upper world. For wherever he found my servants, he persecuted them; and whatever men I made crooked, blind, lame, lepers, or any such thing, by a single word he healed them; and many whom I had got ready to be buried, even these through a single word he brought to life again.

Hades says: And is this *man* so powerful as to do such things by a single word? or if he be so, canst thou withstand him? It seems to me that, if he be so, no one will be able to withstand him. And if thou sayest that thou didst hear him dreading death, he said this mocking thee, and laughing, wishing to seize thee with the strong hand; and woe, woe to thee, to all eternity!

Satan says: O all-devouring and insatiable Hades, art thou so afraid at hearing of our common enemy? I was not afraid of him, but worked in the Jews, and they crucified him, and gave him also to drink gall with vinegar. Make ready, then, in order that you may lay fast hold of him when he comes.

Hades answered: Heir of darkness, son of destruction, devil, thou hast just now told me that many whom thou hadst made ready to be buried, be brought to life again by a single word. And if he has delivered others from the tomb, how and with what power shall he be laid hold of by us? For I not long ago swallowed down one dead, Lazarus by name; and not long after, one of the living by a single word dragged him up by force out of my bowels: and I think that it was he of whom thou speakest. If, therefore, we receive him here, I am afraid lest perchance we be in danger even about the rest. For, lo, all those that I have swallowed from eternity I perceive to be in commotion, and I am pained in my belly. And the snatching away of Lazarus beforehand seems to me to be no good sign: for not like a dead body, but like an eagle, he flew out of me; for so suddenly did the earth throw him out. Wherefore also I adjure even thee, for thy benefit and for mine, not to bring him here; for I think that he is coming here to raise all the dead. And this I tell thee: by the darkness in which we live, if thou bring him here, not one of the dead will be left behind in it to me.

Chapter 5 (21).

While Satan and Hades were thus speaking to each other, there was a great voice like thunder, saying: Lift up your gates, O ye rulers; and be ye lifted up, ye everlasting gates; and the King of glory shall come in. When Hades heard, he said to Satan: Go forth, if thou art able, and withstand him. Satan therefore went forth to the outside. Then Hades says to his demons: Secure well and strongly the gates of brass and the bars of iron, and attend to my bolts, and stand in order, and see to everything; for if he come in here, woe will seize us.

The forefathers having heard this, began all to revile him, saying: O all-devouring and insatiable! open, that the King of glory may come in. David the prophet says: Dost thou not know, O blind, that I when living in the world prophesied this saying: Lift up your gates, O ye rulers? Hesaias said: I, foreseeing this by the Holy Spirit,

wrote: The dead shall rise up, and those in their tombs shall be raised, and those in the earth shall rejoice. And where, O death, is thy sting? where, O Hades, is thy victory?

There came, then, again a voice saying: Lift up the gates. Hades, hearing the voice the second time, answered as if forsooth he did not know, and says: Who is this King of glory? The angels of the Lord say: The Lord strong and mighty, the Lord mighty in battle. And immediately with these words the brazen gates were shattered, and the iron bars broken, and all the dead who had been bound came out of the prisons, and we with the n And the King of glory came in in the form of a man, and all the dark places of Hades were lighted up.

Chapter 6 (22).

Immediately Hades cried out: We have been conquered: woe to us! But who art thou, that hast such power and might? and what art thou, who comest here without sin who art seen to be small and yet of great power, lowly and exalted, the slave and the master, the soldier and the king, who hast power over the dead and the living? Thou wast nailed on the cross, and placed in the tomb; and now thou art free, and hast destroyed all our power. Art thou then the Jesus about whom the chief satrap Satan told us, that through cross and death thou art to inherit the whole world?

Then the King of glory seized the chief satrap Satan by the head, and delivered him to His angels, and said: With iron chains bind his hands and his feet, and his neck, and his mouth. Then He delivered him to Hades, and said: Take him, and keep him secure till my second appearing.

Chapter 7 (23).

And Hades receiving Satan, said to him: Beelzebul, heir of fire and punishment, enemy of the saints, through what necessity didst thou bring about that the King of glory should be crucified, so that he should come here and deprive us *of our power?* Turn and see that not one of the dead has been left in me, but all that thou hast gained through the tree of knowledge, all hast thou lost through the tree of the cross: and all thy joy has been turned into grief; and wishing to put to death the King of glory, thou hast put thyself to death. For, since I have received thee to keep thee safe, by experience shalt thou learn how many evils I shall do unto thee. O arch-devil, the beginning of death, root of sin, end of all evil, what evil didst thou find in Jesus, that thou shouldst compass his destruction? how hast thou dared to do such evil? how hast thou busied thyself to bring down such a man into this darkness, through whom thou hast been deprived of all who have died from eternity?

Chapter 8 (24).

While Hades was thus discoursing to Satan, the King of glory stretched out His right hand, and took hold of our forefather Adam, and raised him. Then turning also to the rest, He said: Come all with me, as many as have died through the tree which he touched: for, behold, I again raise you all up through the tree of the cross. Thereupon He brought them all out, and our forefather Adam seemed to be filled with joy, and said: I thank Thy majesty, O Lord, that Thou hast brought me up out of the lowest Hades. Likewise also all the prophets and the saints said: We thank Thee, O Christ, Saviour of the world, that Thou hast brought our life up out of destruction.

And after they had thus spoken, the Saviour blessed Adam with the sign of the cross on his forehead, and did this also to tire patriarchs, and prophets, and martyrs, and forefathers; and He took them, and sprang up out of Hades. And while He was going, the holy fathers accompanying Him sang praises, saying: Blessed is He that cometh in the name of the Lord: Alleluia; to Him be the glory of oil the saints.

Chapter 9 (25).

And setting out to paradise, He took hold of our forefather Adam by the hand, and delivered him, and all the just, to the archangel Michael. And as they were going into the door of paradise, there met them two old men, to whom the holy fathers said: Who are you, who have not seen death, and have not come down into Hades, but who dwell in paradise in your bodies and your souls? One of them answered, and said: I am Enoch, who was well-pleasing to God, and who was translated hither by Him; and this is Helias the Thesbite; and we are also to live until the end of the world; and then we are to be sent by God to withstand Antichrist, and to be slain by him, and after three days to rise again, and to be snatched up in clouds to meet the Lord.

Chapter 10 (26).

While they were thus speaking, there came another lowly man, carrying also upon his shoulders a cross, to whom the holy fathers said: Who art thou, who hast the look of a robber; and what is the cross which thou bearest upon thy shoulders? He answered: I, as you say, was a robber and a thief in the world, and for these things the Jews laid hold of me, and delivered me to the death of the cross, along with our Lord Jesus Christ. While, then, He was hanging upon the cross, I, seeing the miracles that were done, believed in Him, and entreated Him, and said, Lord, when Thou shall be King, do not forget me. And immediately He said to me, Amen, amen: to-day, I say unto thee, shalt thou be with me in paradise. Therefore I came to paradise carrying my cross; and finding the archangel Michael, I said to him, Our Lord Jesus, who has been crucified, has sent me here; bring me, therefore, to the gate of Eden. And the flaming sword, seeing the sign of the cross, opened to me, and I went in. Then the archangel says to me, Wait a little, for there cometh also the forefather of the race of men, Adam, with the just, that they too may come in. And now, seeing you, I came to meet you.

The saints hearing these things, all cried out with a loud voice: Great is our Lord, and great is His strength.

Chapter 11 (27).

All these things we saw and heard; we, the two brothers, who also have been sent by Michael the archangel, and have been ordered to proclaim the resurrection of the Lord, but first to go away to the Jordan and to be baptized. Thither also we have gone, and have been baptized with the rest of the dead who have risen. Thereafter also we came to Jerusalem, and celebrated the passover of the resurrection. But now we are going away, being unable to stay here. And the love of God, even the Father, and the grace of our Lord Jesus Christ, and the communion of the Holy Spirit, be with you all.

Having written these things, and secured the rolls, they gave the half to the chief priests, and the half to Joseph and Nicodemus. And they immediately disappeared: to the glory of our Lord Jesus Christ. Amen.

DIATESSARON

THE TEXT OF THE DIATESSARON

SECTION I.

In the beginning was the Word, and the Word was with God, and God is the 3 Word. This was in the beginning with God. Everything was by his hand, and 4 without him not even one existing thing was made. In him was life, and the life 5 is the light of men. And the light shineth in the darkness, and the darkness apprehended it not.

6 There was in the days of Herod the king a priest whose name was Zacharias, of the family of Abijah; and his wife was of the daughters of Aaron, and her name 7 was Elizabeth. And they were both righteous before God, walking in all his com- 8 mands, and in the uprightness of God without reproach. And they had no son, for 9 Elizabeth was barren, and they had both advanced in age. And while he discharged Arabic. the duties of priest in the order of his service before God, according to the custom of the priesthood it was his turn to burn incense; so he entered the temple of the Lord. And the whole gathering of the people were praying without at the time of the incense. And there appeared unto Zacharias the angel of the Lord, standing at the right of the altar of incense; and Zacharias was troubled when he saw him, and fear fell upon him. But the angel said unto him, Be not agitated, Zacharias, for thy prayer is heard, and thy wife Elizabeth shall bear thee a son, and thou shall call his name John; and thou shalt have joy and gladness, and many shall rejoice at his birth. And he shall be great before the Lord, and shall not drink wine nor strong drink, and he shall be filled with the Holy Spirit while he is in his mother's womb. And he shall turn back many of the children of Israel to the Lord their God. And he shall go before him in the spirit, and in the power of Elijah the prophet, to turn back the heart of the fathers to the sons, and those that obey not to the knowledge of the righteous; and to prepare for the Lord a perfect people. And Zacharias said unto the angel, How shall I know this, since I am an old man and my wife is advanced in years? And the angel answered and said unto him, I am Gabriel, that standeth before God; and I was sent to speak unto thee, and give thee tidings of this. Henceforth thou shall be speechless, and shalt not be able to speak until the day in which this shall come to pass, because thou didst not trust this my word, which shall be accomplished in its time. And the people were stand- Arabic, ing awaiting Zacharias, and they were perplexed at his delaying in the temple. And when Zacharias went out, he was not able to speak unto them: so they knew that he had seen in the temple a vision; and he made signs unto them, and continued dumb. And when the days of his service were completed, he departed to his dwelling.

25 And after those days Elizabeth his wife conceived; and she hid herself five months, and said, This hath the Lord done unto me in the days when he looked upon me, to remove my reproach from among men.

27 And in the sixth month Gabriel the angel was sent from God to Galilee to a city called Nazareth, to a virgin given in marriage to a man named Joseph, of the house of David; and the virgin's name was Mary. And the angel entered unto her and said unto her, Peace be unto thee, thou who art filled with grace. Our Lord is with thee, thou blessed amongst women. And she, when she beheld, was agitated at his word, and pondered what this salutation could be. And the angel said unto her, Fear not, Mary, for thou hast found favour with God. Thou shall now con- ceive, and bear a son, and call his name Jesus. This shall be great, and shall be called the Son of the Most High; and the Lord God will give him the throne of David his father: and he shall rule over the house of Jacob for ever; and to his kingdom there shall be no end. Mary said unto the angel, How shall this be to me when no man hath known me? The angel answered and said unto her, The Arabic. Holy Spirit will come, and the power of the Most High shall rest upon thee, and therefore shall he that is born of thee be pure, and shall be called the Son of God. And lo, Elizabeth thy kinswoman, she also hath conceived a son in her old age; and this is the sixth month with her, her that is called barren. For nothing is difficult for God. Mary said, Lo, I am the handmaid of the Lord; let it be unto me according unto thy word. And the angel departed from her.

40 And then Mary arose in those days and went in haste into the hill country, to a city of Judah; and entered into the house of Zacharias, and asked for the health of Elizabeth. And when Elizabeth heard the salutation of Mary, the babe leaped in her womb. And Elizabeth was filled with the Holy Spirit; and cried with a loud voice and said unto Mary, Blessed art thou amongst women, and blessed is the fruit that is in thy womb. Whence have I this privilege, that the mother of my Lord should come unto me? When the sound of thy salutation reached my ears, with great joy rejoiced the babe in my womb. And blessed is she who believed that what was spoken to her from the Lord would be fulfilled. And Mary said, My soul doth magnify the Lord, And my spirit hath rejoiced in God my Saviour, Who hath looked upon the low estate of his handmaiden:

Lo, henceforth, all generations shall pronounce blessing on me.
For he hath done great things for me, who is mighty,
And holy is his name.
And his mercy embraceth them who fear him,
Throughout the ages and the times.
He wrought the victory with his arm,
And scattered them that prided themselves in their opinions.
He overthrew them that acted haughtily from their thrones,
And raised the lowly.
He satisfied with good things the hungry,
And left the rich without anything.
He helped Israel his servant,
And remembered his mercy
(According as he spake with our fathers)
Unto Abraham and unto his seed for ever.

And Mary abode with Elizabeth about three months, and returned unto her house.

And Elizabeth's time of delivery was come; and she brought forth a son. And her neighbours and kinsfolk heard that God had multiplied his mercy towards her; and they rejoiced with her. And when it was the eighth day, they came to circumcise the child, and called him Zacharias, calling him by the name of his father. And his mother answered and said unto them, Not so; but he shall be called John. And they said unto her, There is no man of thy kindred that is called by this name. 63, And they made signs to his father, saying, How dost thou wish to name him? And he asked for a tablet, and wrote and said, His name is John. And every one wondered. And immediately his mouth was opened, and his tongue, and he spake and praised God. And fear fell on all their neighbours: and this was spoken of in all the mountains of Judah. And all who heard pondered in their hearts and said, What shall this child be? And the hand of the Lord was with him.

68 And Zacharias his father was filled with the Holy Spirit, and prophesied and said, Blessed is the Lord, the God of Israel, Who hath cared for his people, and wrought for it salvation; And hath raised for us the horn of salvation Arabic, In the house of David his servant (As he spake by the mouth of his holy prophets from eternity), That he might save us from our enemies, And from the hand of all them that hate us.

73 And he hath performed his mercy towards our fathers, And remembered his holy covenants, And the oath which he sware unto Abraham our father, That he would give us deliverance from the hand of our enemies, And without fear we shall serve before him All our days with equity and righteousness.

77 And as for thee, O child, prophet of the Most High shalt thou be called.

Thou shalt go forth before the face of the Lord to prepare his way, To give the knowledge of salvation unto his people, For the forgiveness of their sins, Through the mercy of the compassion of our God, With which he careth for us, to appear from on high To give light to them that sit in darkness and under the shadow of death, And to set straight our feet in the way of peace.

81 And the child grew and became strong in the spirit, and abode in the desert until the time of his appearing unto the children of Israel.

SECTION II.

2 1 Arabic, Now the birth of Jesus the Messiah was on this wise: In the time when his mother was given in marriage to Joseph, before they came together, 2 she was found with child of the Holy Spirit. And Joseph her husband was a just man and did not wish to expose her, and he purposed to put her away secretly. 3 But when he thought of this, the angel of the Lord appeared unto him in a dream, and said unto him, Joseph, son of David, fear not to take Mary thy wife, for that 4 which is begotten in her is of the Holy Spirit. She shall bear a son, and thou shalt 5 call his name Jesus, and he shall save s his people from their sins.And all this was that the saying from the Lord by the prophet might be fulfilled:

6 Behold, the virgin shall conceive, and bear a son, And they shall call his name Immanuel, 7 which is, being interpreted, With us is our God. And when Joseph arose from his 8 sleep, he did as the angel of the Lord

commanded him, and took his wife; and knew her not until she brought forth her firstborn son.

9 And in those days there went forth a decree from Augustus Caesar that all the people of his dominion should be enrolled. This first enrolment was while Quirinius was governor of Syria. And every man went to be enrolled in his city. And Joseph went up also from Nazareth, a city of Galilee, to Judaea, to the city of David which is called Bethlehem (for he was of the house of David and of his tribe), with Arabic. Mary his betrothed, she being with child, to be enrolled there. And while she was there the days for her being delivered were accomplished. And she brought forth her firstborn son; and she wrapped him in swaddling cloths and laid him in a manger, because there was no place for them where they were staying.

16 And there were in that region shepherds abiding, keeping their flock in the watch of the night. And behold, the angel of God came unto them, and the glory of the Lord shone upon them; and they were greatly terrified. And the angel said unto them, Be not terrified; for I bring you tidings of great joy which shall be to the whole world; there is born to you this day a Saviour, which is the Lord the Mes- siah, in the city of David. And this is a sign for you: ye shall find a babe wrapped in swaddling cloths and laid in a manger. And there appeared with the angels suddenly many heavenly forces praising God and saying, Praise be to God in the highest, And on the earth peace, and good hope to men.

23 And when the angels departed from them to heaven, the shepherds spake to one another and said, We will go to Bethlehem and see this word which hath been, as the Lord made known unto us. And they came with haste, and found Mary and Joseph, and the babe laid in a manger. And when they saw, they reported the word which was spoken to them about the child. And all that heard wondered at the description which the shepherds described to them. But Mary kept these sayings and discriminated them in her heart. And those shepherds returned, magnifying and praising God for all that they had seen and heard, according as it was described unto them.

29 Arabic. And when eight days were fulfilled that the child should be circumcised, his name was called Jesus, being that by which he was called by the angel before his conception in the womb.

30 And when the days of their purification according to the law of Moses were completed, they took him up to Jerusalem to present him before the Lord (as it is written in the law of the Lord, Every male opening the womb shall be called the holy thing of the Lord), and to give a sacrificial victim as it is said in the law of 33 the Lord, A pair of doves or two young pigeons. And there was in Jerusalem a man whose name was Simeon; and this man was upright and pious, and expecting the consolation of Israel; and the Holy Spirit was upon him. And it had been said unto him by the Holy Spirit, that he should not see death till he had seen with his eyes the Messiah of the Lord. And this man came by the Spirit to the temple; and at the time when his parents brought in the child Jesus, that they might present for him a sacrifice, as it is written in the law, he bare him in his arms and praised God and said, Now loosest thou the bonds of

thy servant, O Lord, in peace, According to thy saying; For mine eye hath witnessed thy mercy, Which thou hast made ready because of the whole world; A light for the unveiling of the nations, And a glory to thy people Israel.

41 And Joseph and his mother were marvelling at the things which were being said concerning him. And Simeon blessed them and said to Mary his mother, Behold, he is set for the overthrow and rising of many in Israel; and for a sign of contention; and a spear shall pierce through thine own soul; that the thoughts of the hearts of many may be revealed. And Anna the prophetess, the daughter of Phanuel, of the tribe of Asher, was also advanced in years (and she dwelt with her husband seven years from her virginity, and she remained a widow about eighty-four years); and she left not the temple, and served night and day with 46 fasting and prayer. And she also rose in that hour and thanked the Lord, and she spake of him with every one who was expecting the deliverance of Jerusalem. And when they had accomplished everything according to what is in the law of the Lord, they returned to Galilee, to Nazareth their city.

SECTION III.

3 2 And after that, the Magi came from the east to Jerusalem, and said, Where is the King of the Jews which was born? We have seen his star in the east, and have 3 come to worship him. And Herod the king heard, and he was troubled, and all 4 Jerusalem with him. And he gathered all the chief priests and the scribes of the 5 people, and asked them in what place the Messiah should be born. They said, In Bethlehem of Judaea: thus it is written in the prophet, 6 Thou also, Bethlehem of Judah, Art not contemptible among the kings of Judah: From thee shall go forth a king, And he shall be a shepherd to my people Israel.

7 Then Herod called the Magi secretly, and inquired of them the time at which 8 the star appeared to them. And he sent them to Bethlehem, and said unto them, Go and search about the child diligently; and when ye have found him, come and 9 make known to me, that I also may go and worship him. And they, when they Arabic, heard the king, departed; and lo, the star which they had seen in the east went before them, until it came and stood above the place where the child 10, was. And when they beheld the star, they rejoiced with very great joy. And they entered the house and beheld the child with Mary his mother, and fell down worshipping him, and opened their saddle-bags and offered to him offerings, gold and myrrh and frankincense. And they saw in a dream a that they should not return to Herod, and they travelled by another way in going to their country.

13 And when they had departed, the angel of the Lord appeared in a dream to Joseph, and said unto him, Rise, take the child and his mother, and flee into Egypt, and be thou there until I speak to thee; for Herod is determined to seek the child to slay him. And Joseph arose and took the child and his mother in the night, and fled into Egypt, and remained in it until the time of the death of Herod: that that might be fulfilled which was said by the Lord in the prophet, which said, From Egypt did I call my son. And Herod then, when he saw that he was mocked of the Magi,

was very angry, and sent and killed all the male children which were in Bethlehem and all its borders, from two years old and under, according to the time which he had inquired from the Magi. Then was fulfilled the saying in Jeremiah the prophet, which said, A voice was heard in Ramah, Weeping and much lamentation; Rachel weeping for her children, And not willing to be consoled for their loss.

19 But when Herod the king died, the angel of the Lord appeared in a dream to Joseph in Egypt, and said unto him, Rise and take the child and his mother, and Arabic. go into the land of Israel; for they have died who sought the child's life. And Joseph rose and took the child and his mother, and came to the land of Israel. But when he heard that Archelaus had become king over Judaea instead of Herod his father, he feared to go thither; and he saw in a dream that he should go into the land of Galilee, and that he should abide in a city called Nazareth: that the saying in the prophet might be fulfilled, that he should be called a Nazarene.

24 And the child grew, and became strong in spirit, becoming filled with wisdom; and the grace of God was upon him.

25 And his kinsfolk used to go every year to Jerusalem at the feast of the pass- over. And when he was twelve years old, they went up according to their custom, to the feast. And when the days were accomplished, they returned; and the child Jesus remained in Jerusalem, and Joseph and his mother knew not: and they supposed that he was with the children of their company. And when they had gone one day's journey, they sought him beside their people and those who knew them, and they found him not; so they returned to Jerusalem and sought him again. And after three days they found him in the temple, sitting in the midst of the teach- ers, hearing them and asking them questions; and all who heard him wondered at his wisdom and his words. And when they saw him they wondered, and his mother said unto him, My son, why hast thou dealt with us thus? behold, I and thy father have been seeking for thee with much anxiety. And he said unto them, Why were ye seeking me? know ye not that I must be in the house of my Father? And they understood not the word which he spake unto them. And he went down with them, and came to Nazareth; and he was obedient to them: and his mother used to keep all these sayings in her heart.

36 Arabic. And Jesus grew in his stature and wisdom, and in grace with God and men.

37 And in the fifteenth year of the reign of Tiberius Caesar, when Pontius Pilate was governor in Judaea, and one of the four rulers, Herod, in Galilee; and Philip his brother, one of the four rulers, in Ituraea and in the district of Trachonitis; and Lysanias, one of the four rulers, in Abilene; in the chief-priesthood of Annas and Caiaphas, the command of God went forth to John the son of Zacharias in the desert. And he came into all the region which is about Jordan, proclaiming the baptism of repentance unto the forgiveness of sins. And he was preaching in the wilderness of Judaea, and saying, Repent ye; the kingdom of heaven is come near. This is he that was spoken of in Isaiah the prophet, The

voice which crieth in the desert, Prepare ye the way of the Lord, And make straight in the plain, paths for our God.

44 All the valleys shall become filled, And all the mountains and hills shall become low; And the rough shall become plain, And the difficult place, easy; And all flesh shall see the salvation of God.

46 This man came to bear witness, that he might bear witness to the light, that every man might believe through his mediation. He was not the light, bat that he might bear witness to the light, which was the light of truth, that giveth light to every man coming into the world. He was in the world, and the world was made 50 by him, and the world knew him not. He came unto his own, and his own received him not. And those who received him, to them gave he the power that they might be sons of God,--those which believe in his name: which were born, not of blood, nor of the will of the flesh, nor of the will of a man, but of God. And the Word became flesh, and took up his abode among us; and we saw his glory as the glory of the only Son from the Father, which is full of grace and equity. John bare wit- Arabic, ness of him, and cried, and said, This is he that I said cometh after me and was before me, because he was before me. And of his fulness received we all grace for grace. For the law was given through the mediation of Moses, but truth and grace were through Jesus Christ.

SECTION IV.

4 1 No man hath seen God at any time; the only Son, God, which is in the bosom of his Father, he hath told of him.

2 And this is the witness of John when the Jews sent to him from Jerusalem priests 3 and Levites to ask him, Who art thou? And he acknowledged, and denied not; 4 and he confessed that he was not the Messiah. And they asked him again, What then? Art thou Elijah? And he said, I am not he. Art thou a prophet? He 5 said, No. They said unto him, Then who art thou? that we may answer them that 6 sent us. What sayest thou of thyself? And he said, I am the voice that crieth in 7 the desert, Repair ye the way of the Lord, as said Isaiah the prophet. And they 8 that were sent were from the Pharisees. And they asked him and said unto him, Why baptizest thou now, when thou art not the Messiah, nor Elijah, nor a prophet? 9 John answered and said unto them, I baptize with water: among you is standing one whom ye know not: this is he who I said cometh after me and was before me, the latchets of whose shoes I am not worthy to unloose. And that was in Bethany beyond Jordan, where John was baptizing.

12 Now John's raiment was camel's hair, and he was girded with skins, and his food Arabic, was of locusts and honey of the wilderness. Then went out unto him the people of Jerusalem, and all Judaea, and all the region which is about the Jordan; and they were baptized of him in the river Jordan, confessing their sins. But when he saw many of the Pharisees and Sadducees coming to be baptized, he said unto them, Ye children of vipers, who hath led you to flee from the wrath to come? 16, Do now the fruits which are worthy of repentance; and think and say not within yourselves, We have a father, even Abraham; for I say unto you, that God is able to raise up of these stones children unto Abraham. Behold, the axe hath been laid at the roots

of the trees, and so every tree that beareth not good fruit shall be taken and cast into the fire. And the multitudes were asking him and saying, What shall we do? He answered and said unto them, He that hath two tunics shall give to him that hath not; and he that hath food shall do likewise. And the publicans also came to be baptized, and they said unto him, Teacher, what shall we do? He said unto them, Seek not more than what ye are commanded to seek. And the servants of the guard asked him and said, And we also, what shall we do? He said unto them, Do not violence to any man, nor wrong him; and let your allowances satisfy you.

24 And when the people were conjecturing about John, and all of them thinking in their hearts whether he were haply the Messiah, John answered and said unto them, I baptize you with water; there cometh one after me who is stronger than I, the latchets of whose shoes I am not worthy to loosen; he will baptize you with the Holy Spirit and fire: who taketh the fan in his hand to cleanse his threshing-floors, Arabic, and the wheat he gathereth into his garners, while the straw he shall burn in fire which can not be put out.

27 And other things he taught and preached among the people.

28 Then came Jesus from Galilee to the Jordan to John, to be baptized of him. And Jesus was about thirty years old, and it was supposed that he was the son of Joseph. And John saw Jesus coming unto him, and said, This is the Lamb of God, that taketh on itself the burden of the sins of the world! This is he concerning whom I said, There cometh after me a man who was before me, because he was before me. And I knew him not; but that he should be made manifest to Israel, for this cause came I to baptize with water. And John was hindering him and saying, I have need of being baptized by thee, and comest thou to me? Jesus answered him and said, Suffer this now: thus it is our duty to fulfil all righteous- 35 ness. Then he suffered him. And when all the people were baptized, Jesus also was baptized. And immediately he went up out of the water, and heaven opened Arabic, to him, and the Holy Spirit descended upon him in the similitude of the body of a dove; and lo, a voice from heaven, saying, This is my beloved Son, in whom I am well pleased. And John bare witness and said, I beheld the Spirit descend from heaven like a dove; and it abode upon him. But I knew him not; but he that sent me to baptize with water, he said unto me, Upon whomsoever thou shalt behold the Spirit descending and lighting upon him, the same is he that baptizeth with the Holy Spirit. And I have seen and borne witness that this is the Son of God.

42, And Jesus returned from the Jordan, filled with the Holy Spirit. And immediately the Spirit took him out into the wilderness, to be tried of the devil; and he was with the beasts. And he fasted forty days and forty nights. And he ate noth- ing in those days, and at the end of them he hungered. And the tempter came and said unto him, If thou art the Son of God, speak, and these stones shah become bread. He answered and said, It is written, Not by bread alone shall man live, but by every word that proceedeth out of the mouth of God. Then the devil brought him to the holy city, and set him on the pinnacle of the temple, and said unto him, If thou art the Son of God, cast thyself down: for it is written, He shall give his angels charge concerning thee: And they shall take thee on their arms, So that thy foot shall not stumble against a stone.

49 Jesus said unto him, And it is written also, Thou shalt not tempt the Lord thy God. And the devil took him up to a high mountain, and shewed him all the king- Arabic, doms of the earth, and their glory, in the least time; and the devil said unto him, To thee will I give all this dominion, and its glory, which is delivered to me that I may give it to whomsoever I will. If then thou wilt worship before me, all of it shall be thine.

SECTION V.

51 Jesus answered and said unto him, Get thee hence, Satan: for it is written, Thou 2 shalt worship the Lord thy God, and him alone shalt thou serve. And when the 3 devil had completed all his temptations, he departed from him for a season. And behold, the angels drew near and ministered unto him.

4,5 And next day John was standing, and two of his disciples; and he saw Jesus as 6 he was walking, and said, Behold, the Lamb of God! And his two disciples heard 7 him saying this, and they followed Jesus. And Jesus turned and saw them coming after him, and said unto them, What seek ye? They said unto him, Our master, 8 where art thou staying? And he said unto them, Come and see. And they came and saw his place, and abode with him that day: and it was about the tenth hour. 9 One of the two which heard from John, and followed Jesus, was Andrew the brother of Simon. And he saw first Simon his brother, and said unto him, We have found the Messiah. And he brought him unto Jesus. And Jesus looked upon him and said, Thou art Simon, son of Jonah: thou shalt be called Cephas.

12 And on the next day Jesus desired to go forth to Galilee, and he found Philip, Arabic, and said unto him, Follow me. Now Philip was of Bethsaida, of the city of Andrew and Simon. And Philip found Nathanael, and said unto him, He of whom Moses did write in the law and in the prophets, we have found that he is Jesus the son of Joseph of Nazareth. Nathanael said unto him, Is it possible that there can be any good thing from Nazareth? Philip said unto him, Come and see. And Jesus saw Nathanael coming to him, and said of him, This is indeed a son of Israel in whom is no guile. And Nathanael said unto him, Whence knowest thou me? Jesus said unto him, Before Philip called thee, while thou wast under the 18 fig tree, I saw thee. Nathanael answered and said unto him, My Master, thou art the Son of God; thou art the King of Israel. Jesus said unto him, Because I said unto thee, I saw thee under the fig tree, hast thou believed? thou shalt see what is greater than this. And he said unto him, Verily, verily, I say unto you, Henceforth ye shall see the heavens opened, and the angels of God ascending and descending upon the Son of man.

21 And Jesus returned in the power of the Spirit to Galilee.

22 And on the third day there was a feast in Cana, a city of Galilee; and the mother of Jesus was there: and Jesus also and his disciples were invited to the feast. And they lacked wine: and his mother said unto Jesus, They have no wine.

And Jesus said unto her, What have I to do with thee, woman? hath not mine hour come? And his mother said unto the servants, What he saith unto you, do. And there were there six vessels of stone, placed for the Jews' purification, such as Arabic, would contain two or three jars. And Jesus said unto them, Fill the vessels with water. And they filled them to the top. He said unto them, Draw out now, and present to the ruler of the feast. And they did so. And when the ruler of the company tasted that water which had become wine, and knew not whence it was (but the servants knew, because they filled up the water), the ruler of the company called the bridegroom, and said unto him, Every man presenteth first the good wine, and on intoxication he bringeth what is poor; but thou hast kept the good wine until now. And this is the first sign which Jesus did in Cans of Galilee, and manifested his glory; and his disciples believed on him. And his fame spread in all the coun- try which was around them. And he taught in their synagogues, and was glorified by every man. And he came to Nazareth, where he had been brought up, and entered, according to his custom, into the synagogue on the sabbath day, and stood up to read. And he was given the book of Isaiah the prophet. And Jesus opened the book and found the place where it was written, The Spirit of the Lord is upon me, And for this anointed he me, to preach good tidings to the poor; And he hath sent me to heal the broken-hearted, And to proclaim forgiveness to the evil-doers, and sight to the blind, And to bring the broken into forgiveness,

38 And to proclaim an acceptable year of the Lord.

39 And he rolled up the book and gave it to the servant, and went and sat down: and the eyes of all that were in the synagogue were observing him. And he began to say unto them, To-day hath this scripture been fulfilled which ye have heard with your ears. And they all bare him witness, and wondered at the words of grace which were proceeding from his mouth.

42 Arabic, And from that time began Jesus to proclaim the gospel of the kingdom of God, and to say, Repent ye, and believe in the gospel. The time is fulfilled, and the kingdom of heaven hath come near.

44 And while he was walking on the shore of the sea of Galilee, he saw two brethren, Simon who was called Cephas, and Andrew his brother, casting their nets into the sea; for they were fishers. And Jesus said unto them, Follow me, and I will make you fishers of men. And they immediately left their nets there and followed him. And when he went on from thence, he saw other two brothers, James the son of Zebedee, and John his brother, in the ship with Zebedee their father, mending their nets; and Jesus called them. And they immediately forsook the ship and their father Zebedee, and followed him.

And when the multitude gathered unto him to hear the word of God, while he was standing on the shore of the sea of Gennesaret, he saw two boats standing beside the sea, while the two fishers which were gone out of them were washing their nets. And one of them belonged to Simon Cephas. And Jesus went up and sat down in it, and commanded that they should move away a little from the land into 52 the water. And he sat down and taught the multitudes from the boat. And when he had left off his speaking, he said unto Simon, Put out into the deep, and cast your net for a draught. And Simon answered and said unto him, My Master, we toiled all night and caught nothing; now at thy word I will cast the net. And when they did this, there were enclosed a great many fishes; and their net was on the point of breaking. And they beckoned to their comrades that were in the other boat, to come and help them. And when they came, they filled both boats, so that they were on the point of sinking.

SECTION VI.

61 Arabic, But when Simon Cephas saw this he fell before the feet of Jesus, and said unto him, My Lord, I beseech of thee to depart from me, for I am 2 a sinful man. And amazement took possession of him, and of all who were with him, 3 because of the draught of the fishes which they had taken. And thus also were James and John the sons of Zebedee overtaken, who were Simon's partners. And Jesus said 4 unto Simon, Fear not; henceforth thou shalt be a fisher of men unto life. And they brought the boats to the land; and they left everything, and followed him.

5 And after that came Jesus and his disciples into the land of Judaea; and he went 6 about there with them, and baptized. And John also was baptizing in AEnon, which is beside Salim, because there was much water there: and they came, and were bap- 8 tized. And John was not yet come into prison. And there was an inquiry between 9 one of John's disciples and one of the Jews about purifying. And they came unto John, and said unto him, Our master, he that was with thee beyond Jordan, to whom thou hast borne witness, behold, he also baptizeth, and many come to him. John answered and said unto them, A man can receive nothing of himself, except it be given him from heaven. Ye are they that bear witness unto me that I said, I am not the Messiah, but I am one sent before him. And he that hath a bride is a bridegroom: and the friend of the bridegroom is he that standeth and listeneth to him, and rejoiceth greatly because of the bridegroom's voice. Lo now, behold, my 13, Arabic, joy becometh complete. And he must increase and I decrease. For he that is come from above is higher than everything; and he that is of the earth, of the earth he is, and of the earth he speaketh; and he that came down from heaven is higher than all. And he beareth witness of what he hath seen and heard: and no man receiveth his witness. And he that hath received his witness hath asserted that he is truly God. And he whom God hath sent speaketh the words of God: God gave not the Spirit by measure. The Father loveth the Son, and hath put everything in his hands. Whosoever believeth in the Son hath eternal life; but whosoever obeyeth not the Son shall not see life, but the wrath of God cometh upon him.

20 And Jesus learned that the Pharisees had heard that he had received many disciples, and that he was baptizing more than John (not that Jesus was himself bap- tizing, but his disciples); and so he left Judaea.

23 And Herod the governor, because he used to be rebuked by John because of Herodias the wife of Philip his brother, and for all the sins which he was commit- ting, added to all that also this, that he shut up John in prison.

25 And when Jesus heard that John was delivered up, he went away to Galilee. And he entered again into Cana, where he had made the water wine. And there was at Capernaum a king's servant, whose son was sick. And this man heard that Jesus was come from Judaea to Galilee; and he went to him, and besought of him that he would come down and heal his son; for he had come near unto death. 28, Jesus said unto him, Except ye see signs and wonders, ye do not believe. The Arabic, king's servant said unto him, My Lord, come down, that the child die not. Jesus said unto him, Go; for thy son is alive. And that man believed the word which Jesus spake, and went. And when he went down, his servants met him and told him, and said unto him, Thy son is alive. And he asked them at what time he recovered. They said unto him, Yesterday at the seventh hour the fever left him. And his father knew that that was at that hour in which Jesus said unto him, Thy son is alive. And he believed, he and the whole people of his house. And this is the second sign which Jesus did when he returned from Judaea to Galilee. And he was preaching in the synagogues of Galilee.

36 And he left Nazareth, and came and dwelt in Capernaum by the sea shore, in the borders of Zebulun and Naphtali: that it might be fulfilled which was said in Isaiah the prophet, who said, The land of Zebulun, the land of Naphtali, The way of the sea, the passage of the Jordan, Galilee of the nations:

39 The people sitting in darkness Saw a great light, And those sitting in the region and in the shadow of death, There appeared to them a light.

40 And he taught them on the sabbaths. And they wondered because of his doctrine: for his word was as if it were authoritative. And there was in the synagogue a man with an unclean devil, and he cried out with a loud voice, and said, Let me alone; what have I to do with thee, thou Jesus of Nazareth? art thou come for our destruction? I know thee who thou art, thou Holy One of God. And Jesus rebuked him, and said, Stop up thy mouth, and come out of him. And the demon threw him in the midst and came out of him, having done him no harm. And great amaze- Arabic, ment took hold upon every man. And they talked one with another, and said, What is this word that orders the unclean spirits with power and authority, and they come out? And the news of him spread abroad in all the region which was around them.

46 And when Jesus went out of the synagogue, he saw a man sitting among the publicans, named Matthew: and he said unto him, Come after me. And he rose, and followed him.

47, And Jesus came to the house of Simon and Andrew with James and John. And Simon's wife's mother was oppressed with a great fever, and they besought him for her. And he stood over her and rebuked her fever, and it left her, and immediately she rose and ministered to them. And at even they brought to him many that had demons: and he cast out their devils with the word. And all that had sick, their diseases being divers and malignant, brought them unto him. And he laid his hand on them one by one and healed them: that that might be fulfilled which was said in the prophet Isaiah, who said, He taketh our pains and beareth our diseases. And all the city was gathered together unto the door of Jesus. And he cast out devils also from many, as they were crying out and saying, Thou art the Messiah, the Son of God; and he rebuked them. And he suffered not the demons to speak, because they knew him that he was the Lord the Messiah.

SECTION VII.

7 Arabic, And in the morning of that day he went out very early, and went to a desert place, and was there praying. And Simon and those that were with him sought him. And when they found him, they said unto him, All the people seek for thee. He said unto them, Let us go into the adjacent villages and towns, that I may preach there also; for to this end did I come. And the multitudes were seeking him, and came till they reached him; and they took hold of him, that he should not go away from them. But Jesus said unto them, I must preach of the kingdom of God in other cities also: for because of this gospel was I sent. And Jesus was going about all the cities and the villages, and teaching in their synagogues, and preaching the gospel of the kingdom, and healing all the diseases and all the sicknesses, 8 and casting out the devils.

And his fame became known that he was teaching in 9 every place and being glorified by every man. And when he passed by, he saw Levi the son of Alphaeus sitting among the tax-gatherers; and he said unto him, Follow me: and he rose and followed him. And the news of him was heard of in all the land of Syria: and they brought unto him all those whom grievous ills had befallen through divers diseases, and those that were enduring torment, and those that were possessed, and lunatics, and paralytics; and he healed them.

11, And after some days Jesus entered into Capernaum again. And when they heard that he was in the house, many gathered, so that it could not hold them, even about Arabic, the door; and he made known to them the word of God. And there were there some of the Pharisees and the teachers of the law, sitting, come from all the villages of Galilee, and Judaea, and Jerusalem; and the power of the Lord was present to heal them. And some men brought a bed with a man on it who was paralytic. And they sought to bring him in and lay him before him. And when they found no way to bring him in because of the multitude of people, they went up to the roof, and let him down with his bed from the roofing, into the midst before Jesus. And when Jesus saw their faith, he said unto the paralytic, My son, thy sins are for- given thee. And the scribes and Pharisees began to think within their hearts, Why doth this man blaspheme? Who is it that is able to forgive sins, but God alone? 18 And Jesus knew by the spirit that they were thinking this within themselves, and he said unto them, Why do ye think this within your heart? Which is better, that it should be said to the paralytic, Thy sins are forgiven thee, or that it should be said to him, Arise, and take thy bed, and walk? That ye may know that the Son of man is empowered on earth to forgive sins (and he said to the paralytic), I say unto thee, Arise, take thy bed, and go to thine house. And he rose forthwith, and took his bed, and went out in the presence of all. And he went to his house praising God. And when those multitudes saw, they feared; and amazement took possession of them, and they praised God, who had given such power to men. And they said,

We have seen marvellous things to-day, of which we have never before seen the like.

25 Arabic, And after that, Jesus went out, and saw a publican, named Levi, sitting among the publicans: and he said unto him, Follow me. And he left everything, and rose, and followed him. And Levi made him a great feast in his house. And there was a great multitude of the publicans and others sitting with him. And the scribes and Pharisees murmured, and said unto his disciples, Why do ye eat and drink with the publicans and sinners? Jesus answered and said unto them, The physician seeketh not those who are well, but those that are afflicted with grievous 30, sickness. I came not to call the righteous, but the sinners, to repentance. And they said unto him, Why do the disciples of John fast always, and pray, and the Pharisees also, but thy disciples eat and drink? He said unto them, Ye cannot make the sons of the marriage feast fast, while the bridegroom is with them. Days will come, when the bridegroom is taken away from them; then will they fast in those days. And he spake unto them a parable: No man inserteth a new patch and seweth it in a worn garment, lest the newness of the new take from the worn, and there occur a great rent. And no man putteth fresh wine into old skins, lest the wine burst the skins, and the skins be destroyed, and the wine spilled; but they put the fresh wine in the new skins, and both are preserved. And no man drinketh old wine and straightway desireth fresh; for he saith, The old is better.

37 And while Jesus was walking on the sabbath day among the sown fields, his disciples hungered. And they were rubbing the ears with their hands, and eating. But some of the Pharisees, when they saw them, said unto him, See, why do thy disciples on the sabbath day that which is not lawful? But Jesus said unto them, Have ye not read in olden time what David did, when he had need and hungered, he and those that were with him? how he entered the house of God, when Abiathar was high priest, and ate the bread of the table of the Lord, which it was not lawful that any should eat, save the priests, and gave to them that were with him also? And he said unto them, The sabbath was created because of man, and man was not created because of the sabbath. Or have ye not read in the law, that the priests in the temple profane the sabbath, and yet they are blameless? I say unto you now, that here is what is greater than the temple. If ye had known this. I love mercy, not sacrifice, ye would not have condemned those on whom is no blame. The Lord of the sabbath is the Son of man. And his relatives heard, and went out to take him, and said, He hath gone out of his mind.

47 And on the next sabbath day he entered into the synagogue and was teach- ing. And there was there a man whose right hand was withered. And the scribes and the Pharisees were watching him, whether he would heal on the sabbath day, that they might find the means of accusing him. But he knew their thoughts, and said unto the man whose hand was withered, Rise and come near into the midst of the synagogue. And when he came and stood, Jesus said unto them, I ask you, which is lawful to be done on the sabbath day, good or evil? shall lives be saved or Arabic, destroyed? But they were silent. Regarding them with anger, being grieved because of the hardness of their hearts. And he said unto the man, Stretch out thy hand.

And he stretched it out: and his hand became straight. Then he said unto them, What man of you shall have one sheep, and if it fall into a well on the sabbath day, will not take it and lift it out? And how much is man better than a sheep! Wherefore it is lawful on the sabbath to do good.

SECTION VIII.

8 1 And the Pharisees went out, and consulted together concerning him, that they 2 might destroy him. And Jesus perceived, and removed thence: and great multitudes 3 followed him; and he healed all of them: and he forbade them that they should 4 not make him known: that the saying in Isaiah the prophet might be fulfilled, which said, 5 Behold, my servant with whom I am pleased; My beloved in whom my soul hath delighted:

My spirit have I put upon him, And he shall proclaim to the nations judgement.

6 He shall not dispute, nor cry out; And no man shall hear his voice in the marketplace.

7 And a bruised reed shall he not break, And a smoking lamp shall he not extinguish, until he shall bring forth judgement unto victory.

8 And the nations shall rejoice in his name.

9 And in those days Jesus went out to the mountain that he might pray, and he spent the night there in prayer to God. And when the morning was come, he called the disciples. And he went towards the sea: and there followed him much people from Galilee that he might pray, and from Judaea, and from Jerusalem, and from Idumaea, and from beyond Jordan, and from Tyre, and from Sidon, and from De- 12 capolis; and great multitudes came unto him, which had heard what he did. And he spake to his disciples to bring him the boat because of the multitudes, that they might not throng him. And he healed many, so that they were almost falling on Arabic, him on account of their seeking to get near him. And those that had plagues and unclean spirits, as soon as they beheld him, would fall, and cry out, and say, Thou art the Son of God. And he rebuked them much, that they should not make him known. And those that were under the constraint of un- clean spirits were healed. And all of the crowd were seeking to come near him; because power went out from him, and he healed them all.

18, And when Jesus saw the multitudes, he went up to the mountain. And he called his disciples, and chose from them twelve; and they are those whom he named apostles: Simon, whom he named Cephas, and Andrew his brother, and James and John, and Philip and Bartholomew, and Matthew and Thomas, and James the son of Alphaeus, and Simon which was called the Zealot, and Judas the son of James, and Judas the Iscariot, being he that had betrayed him. And Jesus went down with them and stood in the plain, and the company of his disciples, and the great multitude of people. And these twelve he chose to be with him, and that he might send them to preach, and to have power to heal the sick and to cast out devils.

26 Then he lifted up his eyes unto them, and opened his mouth, and taught them, and said, Blessed are the poor in spirit: for the kingdom of heaven is theirs.

28 Blessed are the sorrowful: for they shall be comforted.

29 Blessed are the humble: for they shall inherit the earth.

30 Blessed are they that hunger and thirst after righteousness: for they shall be satisfied.

31 Blessed are the merciful: for on them shall be mercy.

32 Arabic, Blessed are the pure in their hearts: for they shall see God.

33 Blessed are the peacemakers: for they shall be called the sons of God.

34 Blessed are they that were persecuted for righteousness' sake: for the kingdom of heaven is theirs.

35 Blessed are ye when men shall hate you, and separate you from them, and persecute you, and reproach you, and shall speak against you with all evil talk, for my sake, falsely. Then rejoice and be glad, for your reward is great in heaven: for so persecuted they the prophets before you.

37 But woe unto you rich! for ye hive received your consolation.

38 Woe unto you that are satisfied! ye shall hunger.

Woe unto you that laugh now! ye shall weep and be sad.

39 Woe unto you when men praise you! for so did their fathers use to do to the false prophets.

40 Unto you do I say, ye which hear, Ye are the salt of the earth: if then the salt become tasteless, wherewith shall it be salted? For any purpose it is of no use, but is thrown outside, and men tread upon it. Ye are the light of the world. It is impossible that a city built on a mountain should be hid. Neither do they light a lamp and place it under a bushel, but on the lamp-stand, and it giveth light to all who are in the house. So shall your light shine before men, that they may see your good works, and glorify your Father which is in heaven. There is nothing secret that shall not be revealed, or hidden that shall not be known. Whoever hath ears that hear, let him hear.

46 Think not that I came to destroy the law or the prophets; I came not to destroy, but to complete. Verily I say unto you, Until heaven and earth shall pass, there Arabic, shall not pass one point or one letter of the law, until all of it shall be accomplished. Every one who shall violate now one of these small commandments, and shall teach men so, shall be called lacking in the kingdom of heaven: every one that shall do and teach shall be called great in the kingdom of heaven. I say unto you now, unless your righteousness abound more than that of the scribes and Pharisees, ye shall not enter the kingdom of heaven.

50 Ye have heard that it was said to the ancients, Do not kill; and every one that killeth is worthy of the judgement. But I say unto you that every one who is angry with his brother without a cause is worthy of the judgement; and every one that saith to his brother, Thou foul one, is condemned by the synagogue; and whoso- 52 ever saith to him, Thou fool, is worthy of the fire of Gehenna. If thou art now offering thy gift at the altar, and rememberest there that thy brother hath conceived against thee any grudge, leave thy gift at the altar, and go first and satisfy thy brother, and then return and offer thy gift. Join thine adversary quickly, and while thou art still with him in the way, give a ransom and free thyself from him; test thine adversary deliver thee to the judge, and the judge deliver thee to the tax- collector, and thou fall into prison. And verily I say unto thee, Thou shall not go out thence until thou payest the last farthing.

57, Ye have heard that it was said, Do not commit adultery: but I now say unto you, that every one that looketh at a woman lusting after her hath forthwith already Arabic, committed adultery with her in his heart. If thy right eye injure thee, put p. 34 it out and cast it from thee; for it is preferable for thee that one of thy members should perish, and not thy whole body go into the fire of hell. And if thy right hand injure thee, cut it off and cast it from thee; and it is better for thee that one of thy members should perish, and not thy whole body fall into Gehenna. It was said that he that putteth away his wife should give her a writing of divorcement: but I say unto you, that every one that putteth away his wife, except for the cause of adultery, hath made it lawful for her to commit adultery: and whosoever taketh one that is put away committeth adultery.

SECTION IX.

9 1 Ye have heard also that it was said unto the ancients, Lie not, but perform unto 2 God in thy oaths: but I say unto you, Swear not at all; neither by heaven, for it 3 is God's throne; nor by the earth, for it is a footstool under his feet; nor yet by 4 Jerusalem, for it is the city of the great King. Neither shalt thou swear by thy 5 head, for thou canst not make in it one lock of hair black or white. But your word shall be either Yea or Nay, and what is in excess of this is of the evil one.

6, 7 Ye have heard that it was said, Eye for eye, and tooth for tooth: but I say unto you, Stand not in opposition to the evil; but whosoever smiteth thee on thy right 8 cheek, turn to him also the other. And he that would sue thee, and take thy tunic, 9 leave to him also thy wrapper. And whosoever compelleth thee one mite, go with Arabic, him twain. And he that asketh thee, give unto him: and he that would borrow of thee, prevent him not. And prosecute not him that taketh thy substance. And as ye desire that men should do to you, so do ye also to them.

12, Ye have heard that it was said, Love thy neighbour and hate thine enemy: but I say unto you, Love your enemies, and pray for those that curse you, and deal well with those that hate you, and pray for those who take you with violence and persecute you; that ye may be sons of your heavenly Father, who maketh his sun to rise on the good and the evil, and sendeth down his rain on the righteous and the unrighteous. If ye love them that love you, what reward shall ye have? for the pub- licans and sinners also love those that love them. And if ye do a kindness to those who treat you well, where is your superiority? for sinners also do likewise. And if ye lend to him of whom ye hope for a reward, where is your superiority? for the sinners also lend to sinners, seeking recompense from them. But love your enemies, and do good to them, and lend, and cut not off the hope of any man; that your reward may be great, and ye may be the children of the Highest: for he is lenient towards the wicked and the ungrateful. Be ye merciful, even as your Father also is merciful. And if ye inquire for the good of your brethren only, what more have ye done than others? is not this the conduct of the publicans also? Be ye now perfect, even as your Father which is in heaven is perfect.

22 Consider your alms; do them not before men to let them see you: and if it be not so, ye have no reward before your Father which is in the heavens. When then thou givest an alms now, do not sound a trumpet before thee, as do the people of hypocrisy, Arabic, in the synagogues and the marketplaces, that men may praise them. And verily say I unto you, They have received their reward. But thou, when thou doest alms, let thy left hand not know what thy right hand doeth; that thine alms may be concealed: and thy Father which seeth in secret shall reward thee openly.

26 And whenever thou prayest, be not as the hypocrites, who love to stand in the synagogues and in the corners of the marketplaces for prayers, that men may be- hold them. And verily say I unto you, They have received their reward. But thou, when thou prayest, enter into thy closet, and fasten thy door, and pray to thy Father in secret, and thy Father which seeth in secret shall reward thee openly. And whenever ye pray, be not babblers, as the heathen; for they think that by the abundance of their words they shall be heard. Then be not ye now like unto them: for your Father knoweth your request before ye ask him. One of his disciples said unto him, Our Lord, teach us to pray, as John taught his disciples. Jesus said unto them, Thus now pray ye now: Our Father which art in heaven, Hallowed be thy 33, name. Thy kingdom come. Thy will be done, as in heaven, so on earth. Give us the food of to-day. And forgive, us our trespasses, as we forgave those that trespassed against us. And bring us not into temptations, but deliver us from the evil one. For thine is the kingdom, and the power, and the glory, for ever and ever. If ye forgive Arabic, men their wrong-doing, your Father which is in heaven will forgive you. p. 37 But if ye forgive not men, neither will your Father pardon your wrong-doing.

39 When ye fast, do not frown, as the hypocrites; for they make their faces austere, that they may be seen of men that they are fasting. Verily I say unto you, They have received their reward. But when thou fastest, wash thy face and anoint thy head; that thou make not an appearance to men of fasting, but to thy Father which is in secret: and thy Father which seeth in secret shall reward thee.

42 Be not agitated, little flock; for your Father hath delighted to give you the king- dom. Sell your possessions, and give in alms; take to yourselves purses that wax not old. Lay not up treasure on earth, where moth and worm corrupt, and where thieves break through and steal: but lay up for yourselves treasure in heaven, where moth and

worm do not corrupt, nor thieves break through nor steal: for where your treasure is, there also will your heart be. The lamp of the body is the eye: if then thine eye now be sound, thy whole body also shall be light. But if thine eye be evil, all thy body shall be dark. And if the light which is in thee is darkness, how great is thy darkness! Be watchful that the light which is in thee be not darkness. Because that, if thy whole body is light, and have no part dark, it shall all be light, as the lamp giveth light to thee with its flame.

SECTION X.

10 1 Arabic, NO man can serve two masters; and that because it is necessary that he hate one of them and love the other, and honour one of them and despise the 2 other. Ye cannot serve God and possessions. And because of this I say unto you, Be not anxious for yourselves, what ye shall eat and what ye shall drink; neither for your bodies, what ye shall put on. Is not the life better than the food, and the body 3 than the raiment? Consider the birds of the heaven, which sow not, nor reap, nor store in barns; and yet your Father which is in heaven feedeth them. Are not ye 4 better than they? Who of you when he trieth is able to add to his stature one 5 cubit? If then ye are not able for a small thing, why are ye anxious about the 7 rest? Consider the wild lily, how it grows, although it toils not, nor spins; and I say unto you that Solomon in the greatness of his glory was not clothed like one of 8 them. And if God so clothe the grass of the field, which to-day is, and to-morrow 9 is cast into the oven, how much more shall be unto you, O ye of little faith! Be not anxious, so as to say, What shall we eat? or, What shall we drink? or, With what shall we be clothed? Neither let your minds be perplexed in this: all these things the nations of the world seek; and your Father which is in heaven knoweth your need of all these things. Seek ye first the kingdom of God, and his righteous- Arabic. ness; and all these shall come to you as something additional for you. Be not anxious for the morrow; for the morrow shall be anxious for what belongs to it. Sufficient unto the day is its evil.

13 Judge not, that ye be not judged: condemn not, that ye be not condemned: forgive, and it shall be forgiven you: release, and ye shall be released: give, that ye may be given unto; with good measure, abundant, full, they shall thrust into your bosoms. With what measure ye measure it shall be measured to you. See to it what ye hear: with what measure ye measure it shall be measured to you; and ye shall be given more. I say unto those that hear, He that hath shall be given unto; and he that hath not, that which he regards as his shall be taken from him. And he spake unto them a parable, Can a blind man haply guide a blind man? shall they not both fall into a hollow? A disciple is not better than his master; 19 every perfect man shall be as his master. Why lookest thou at the mote which is in the eye of thy brother, but considerest not the column that is in thine own eye? Or how canst thou say to thy brother, Brother, I will take out the mote from thine eye; and the column which is in thine eye thou seest not? Thou hypocrite, take out first the column from thine eye; and then shalt thou see to take out the mote from the eye of thy brother.

21 Give not that which is holy unto the dogs, neither cast your pearls before the swine, lest they trample them with their feet, and return and wound you. And he said unto them, Who of you, that hath a friend, goeth to him at midnight, and saith unto him, My friend, lend me three loaves; for a friend hath come to me from a journey, and I have nothing to offer to him: and that friend shall Arabic, answer him from within, and say unto him, Trouble me not; for the door is shut, and my children are with me in bed, and I cannot rise and give thee? And verily I say unto you, If he will not give him because of friendship, yet because of his importunity he will rise and give him what he seeketh. And I also say unto you, Ask, and ye shall be given unto; seek, and ye shall find; knock, and it shall be opened unto you. Every one that asketh receiveth, and he that seeketh findeth, and he that knocketh, it shall be opened to him. What father of you, shall his son ask for bread--will he, think you, give him a stone? and if he ask of him a fish, will he, think you, instead of the fish give him a serpent? and if he ask him for an egg, will he, think you, extend to him a scorpion? If ye then, although being evil, know the gifts which are good, and give them to your children, how much more shall your Father which is in heaven give the Holy Spirit to them that ask him? Whatsoever ye would that men should do to you, do ye even so to them: this is the law and the prophets.

32 Enter ye by the narrow gate; for the wide gate and the broad way lead to de- struction, and many they be which go therein. How narrow is the gate and straitened the way leading to life! and few be they that find it.

34 Beware of false prophets, which come to you in sheep's clothing, while within they are ravening wolves. But by their fruits ye shall know them. For every tree is known by its fruit. For figs are not gathered of thorns, neither are grapes plucked of briers. Even so every good tree bringeth forth good fruit, but the evil tree bringeth Arabic, forth evil fruit. The good tree cannot bring forth evil fruit, neither can the evil tree bring forth good fruit. The good man from the good treasures that are in his heart bringeth forth good things; and the evil man from the evil treasures that are in his heart bringeth forth evil things: and from the overflowings of the heart the lips speak. Every tree that beareth not good fruit is cut down and cast 40, into the fire. Therefore by their fruits ye shall know them. Not all that say unto me, My Lord, my Lord, shall enter the kingdom of the heavens; but he that doeth the will of my Father which is in heaven. Many shall say unto me in that day, My Lord, my Lord, did we not prophesy in thy name, and in thy name cast out devils, and in thy name do many powers? Then shall I say unto them, I never knew you: depart from me, ye servants of iniquity. Every man that cometh unto me, and heareth my sayings, and doeth them, I will shew you to what he is like: he is like the wise man which built a house, and digged and went deep, and laid the foundations on a rock: and the rain came down, and the rivers overflowed, and the winds blew, and shook that house, and it fell not: for its foundation was laid on rocks. And every one that heareth these my words, and doeth them not, is like 48 the foolish man which built his house on sand, without foundation: and the rain descended, and the rivers overflowed, and the winds blew, and smote upon that house, and it fell: and the fall of it was great.

SECTION XI.

11 1 Arabic, And when Jesus finished these sayings, the multitudes were astonished 2 at his teaching; and that because he was teaching them as one having authority, not as their scribes and the Pharisees.

3 And when he descended from the mountain, great multitudes followed him.

4 And when Jesus entered Capernaum, the servant of one of the chiefs was in an 5 evil case, and he was precious to him, and he was at the point of death. And he 6 heard of Jesus, and came to him with the elders of the Jews; and he besought him, and said, My Lord, my boy is laid in the house paralysed, and he is suffering griev- 7 ous torment. And the elders urgently requested of him, and said, He is worthy that 8 this should be done unto him: for he loveth our people, and he also built the syna- gogue for us. Jesus said unto him, I will come and heal him. That chief answered and said, My Lord, I am not worthy that my roof should shade thee; but it sufficeth that thou speak a word, and my lad shall be healed. And I also am a man in obedience to authority, having under my hand soldiers: and I say to this one, Go, and he goeth; and to another, Come, and he cometh; and to my servant that he do this, and he doeth it. And when Jesus heard that, he marvelled at him, and turned and said unto the multitude that were coming with him, Verily I say unto you, I have not found in Israel the like of this faith. I say unto you, that many shall come from Arabic, the east and the west, and shall recline with Abraham and Isaac and Jacob p. in the kingdom of heaven: but the children of the kingdom shall be cast forth into the outer darkness: and there shall be weeping and gnashing of teeth. And Jesus said to that chief, Go thy way; as thou hast believed, so shall it be unto thee. And his lad was healed in that hour. And that chief returned to the house and found that sick servant healed.

17 And the day after, he was going to a city called Nain, and his disciples with him, and a great multitude. And when he was come near the gate of the city, he saw a crowd accompanying one that was dead, the only son of his mother; and his mother was a widow: and there was with her a great multitude of the people of the city. And when Jesus saw her, he had compassion on her, and said unto her, Weep not. And he went and advanced to the bier, and the bearers of it stood still; and he said, Young man, I say unto thee, Arise. And that dead man sat up and began to speak; and he gave him to his mother. And fear came on all the people: and they praised God, and said, There hath risen among us a great prophet: and, God 23 hath had regard to his people. And this news concerning him spread in all Judaea, and in all the region which was about them.

24 And when Jesus saw great multitudes surrounding him, he commanded them to depart to the other side. And while they were going in the way, there came one of the scribes and said unto him, My Master, I will follow thee whithersoever thou goest. Jesus said unto him, The foxes have holes, and the birds of the heaven have nests; but the Son of man hath not a place in which to lay his head. And he said unto another, Follow me. And he said unto him, My Lord, suffer me first to go and bury my father. Jesus said unto him, Leave the dead to bury their dead; but thou, follow me and preach the kingdom of God. And another said unto him, I will fol- Arabic, low thee, my Lord; but

first suffer me to go and salute my household and come. Jesus said unto him, There is no one who putteth his hand to the plough and looketh behind him, and yet is fit for the kingdom of God.

31 And he said to them on that day in the evening, Let us go over to the other side of the lake; and he left the multitudes. And Jesus went up and sat in the ship, he and his disciples, and there were with them other ships. And there occurred on the sea a great tempest of whirlwind and wind, and the ship was on the point of sinking from the greatness of the waves. But Jesus was sleeping on a cushion in the stern of the ship; and his disciples came and awoke him, and said unto him, Our Lord, save us; lo, we perish. And he rose, and rebuked the winds and the turbulence of the water, and said to the sea, Be still, for thou art rebuked; and the wind was still, and there was a great calm. And he said unto them, Why are ye thus afraid? and why have ye no faith? And they feared greatly. And they marvelled, and said one to another, Who, think you, is this, who commandeth also the wind and the waves and the sea, and they obey him?

38 And they departed and came to the country of the Gadarenes, which is on the other side, opposite the land of Galilee. And when he went out of the ship to the land, there met him from among the tombs a man who had a devil for a long time, and wore no clothes, neither dwelt in a house, but among the tombs. And no man was Arabic, able to bind him with chains, because an y time that he was bound with chains and fetters he cut the chains and loosened the fetters; and he was snatched away of the devil into the desert, and no man was able to quiet him; and at all times, in the night and in the day, he would be among the tombs and in the mountains; and no man was able to pass by that way; and he would cry out and wound himself with stones. And when he saw Jesus at a distance, he hastened and worshipped him, and cried with a loud voice and said, What have we to do with thee, Jesus, Son of the most high God? I adjure thee by God, torment me not. And Jesus commanded the unclean spirit to come out of the man: and he had suffered a long time since the time when he came into captivity to it.

And Jesus asked him, What is thy name? He said unto him, Legion; for there had entered into him many devils. And they besought him that he would not command them to depart into the depths. And there was there a herd of many swine, feeding in the mountain, and those devils besought him to give them leave to enter the swine; and he gave them leave. And the devils went out of the man and entered into the swine. And that herd hastened to the summit and fell down into the midst of the sea, about two thousand, and they were choked in the water. And when the keepers saw what happened, they fled, and told those in the cities and villages. And the people went out to see what had happened; and they came to Jesus, and found the man whose Arabic, devils had gone out, clothed, modest, seated at the feet of Jesus; and they feared. And they reported what they saw, and how the man was healed who had a devil, and concerning those swine also.

SECTION XII.

12 1 And all the multitude of the Gadarenes entreated him to depart from them, because that great fear took hold upon them.

2, 3 But Jesus went up into the ship, and crossed, and came to his city. And that man from whom the devils went out entreated that he might stay with him; but 4 Jesus sent him away, and said unto him, Return to thy house, and make known what 5 God hath done for thee. And he went, and began to publish in Decapolis what Jesus had done for him; and they all marvelled.

6 And when Jesus had crossed in the ship to that side, a great multitude received 7 him; and they were all looking for him. And a man named Jairus, the chief of the 8 synagogue, fell before the feet of Jesus, and besought him much, and said unto him, I have an only daughter, and she is come nigh unto death; but come and lay thy 9 hand upon her, and she shall live. And Jesus rose, and his disciples, and they fol- lowed him. And there joined him a great multitude, and they pressed him.

11, And a woman, which had a flow of blood for twelve years, had suffered much of many physicians, and spent all that she had, and was not benefited at all, but her trouble increased further. And when she heard of Jesus, she came in the thronging of Arabic, the crowd behind him, and touched a his garments; and she thought within herself, If I could reach to touch his garments, I should live. And immediately the fountain of her blood was dried; and she felt in her body that she was healed of her plague. And Jesus straightway knew within himself that power had gone out of him; and he turned to the crowd, and said, Who approached unto my garments? And on their denying, all of them, Simon Cephas and those with him said unto him, Our Master, the multitudes throng thee and press thee, and sayest thou, Who ap- proached unto me? And he said, Some one approached unto me; and I knew that power went forth from me. And that woman, when she saw that she was not hid from him, came fearing and agitated (for she knew what had happened to her), and fell down and worshipped him, and told, in the presence of all the people, for what reason she touched him, and how she was healed immediately. And Jesus said unto her, Be of good courage, daughter; thy faith hath made thee alive; depart in peace, and be whole from thy plague.

22 And while he was yet speaking, there came a man from the house of the chief of the synagogue, and said unto him, Thy daughter hath died; so trouble not the teacher. But Jesus heard, and said unto the father of the maid, Fear not: but be- lieve only, and she shall live. And he suffered no man to go with him, except Simon Cephas, and James, and John the brother of James. And they reached the house of the chief of the synagogue; and he saw them agitated, weeping and wail- ing. And he entered, and said unto them, Why are ye agitated and weeping? the Arabic, maid hath not died, but she is sleeping. And they laughed at him, for they knew that she had died. And he put every man forth without, and took the father of the maid, and her mother, and Simon, and James, and John, and entered into the place where the maid was laid. And he took hold of the hand of the maid, and said unto her, Maid, arise. And her spirit returned, and straightway she arose and walked: and she was about twelve years of age. And he commanded that

there should be given to her something to eat. And her father wondered greatly: and he warned them that they should tell no man what had happened. And this report spread in all that land.

33 And when Jesus crossed over from there, there joined him two blind men, crying out, and saying, Have mercy on us, thou son of David. And when he came to the house, those two blind men came to him: and Jesus said unto them, Believe ye that I am able to do this? They said unto him, Yea, our Lord.

Then he touched their eyes, and said, As ye have believed, it shall be unto you. And immediately their eyes were opened. And Jesus forbade them, and said, See that no man know. But they went out and published the news in all that land.

38 And when Jesus went out, they brought to him a dumb man having a devil. And on the going out of the devil that dumb man spake. And the multitudes marvelled, and said, It was never so seen in Israel And Jesus was going about in all the cities and in the villages, and teaching in their synagogues, and proclaiming the good news of the kingdom, and healing every disease Arabic, and sickness; and many followed him. And when Jesus saw the multitudes, p. he had compassion on them, for they were wearied and scattered, as sheep that have no shepherd. And he called his twelve disciples, and gave them power and much authority over all devils and diseases; and sent them two and two, that they might proclaim the kingdom of God, and to heal the sick. And he charged them, and said, Walk not in the way of the heathen, nor enter into the cities of the Sa- 45, maritans. Go especially unto the sheep that are lost of the sons of Israel. And when ye go, proclaim and say, The kingdom of heaven is come near. And heal the sick, and cleanse the lepers, and cast out the devils: freely ye have received, freely 48, give. Get you not gold, nor silver, nor brass in your purses; and take nothing for the way, except a staff only; nor bag, nor bread; neither shall ye have two tunics, nor shoes, nor staff, but be shod with sandals; for the labourer is worthy of his food. And whatever city or village ye enter, inquire who is worthy in it, and there be until 52, ye go out. And when ye enter into the house, ask for the peace of the house: and if the house is worthy, your peace shall come upon it; but if it is not worthy, your peace shall return unto you. And whosoever shall not receive you, nor hear your sayings, when ye go out from that house, or from that village, shake off the dust Arabic, that is under your feet against them for a testimony. And verily I say p. 50 unto you, To the land of Sodom and Gomorrah there shall be rest in the day of judgement, rather than to that city.

SECTION XIII.

13 1 I am sending you as lambs among wolves: be ye now wise as serpents, and harmless as doves. Beware of men: they shall deliver you to the councils of the magistrates, and scourge you in their synagogues; and shall bring you before governors and kings for my sake, for a testimony against them and against the nations. And when they deliver you up, be not s anxious, nor consider beforehand, what ye shall say; but ye shall be given in that hour what ye ought to speak. Ye do not speak, but the Spirit of your Father

speaketh in you. The brother shall deliver up his brother to death, and the father his son; and the sons shall rise against their parents, and put them to death. And ye shall be hated of every man because of my name; but he that endureth unto the end of the matter shall be saved. When they expel you from this city, flee to another. Verily I say unto you, Ye shall not finish all the cities of the people of Israel, until the Son of man come.

9, A disciple is not superior to his lord, nor a servant to his master. For it is enough then for the disciple that he be as his lord, and the servant as his master. If they have called the master of the house Beelzebul, how much more the people of his house! Fear them not therefore: for there is nothing covered, that shall Arabic, not be revealed; nor hid, that shall not be disclosed and published. What I say unto you in the darkness, speak ye in the light; and what ye have told secretly in the ears in closets, let it be proclaimed on the housetops. I say unto you now, my beloved, Be not agitated at those who kill the body, but have no power to kill the soul. I will inform you whom ye shall fear: him which is able to destroy soul and body in hell. Yea, I say unto you, Be afraid of him especially. Are not two sparrows sold for a farthing in a bond? and one of them shall not fall on the ground without your Father. But what concerns you: even the hair of your heads 17, also is numbered. Fear not therefore; ye are better than many sparrows. Every man who confesseth me now before men, I also will confess him before my Father which is in heaven; but whosoever denieth me before men, I also will deny him before my Father which is in heaven.

20 Think ye that I am come to cast peace into the earth? I came not to cast peace, but to cast dissension. Henceforth there shall be five in one house, three of them disagreeing with two, and the two with the three. The father shall become hostile to his son, and the son to his father; and the mother to her daughter, and the daughter to her mother; and the mother in law to her daughter in law, and the daughter in law to her mother in law: and a man's enemies shall be the people of his house. Whosoever loveth father or mother better than me is not worthy of me; and whoso-Arabic, ever loveth son or daughter more than his love of me is not worthy of me. And every one that doth not take his cross and follow me is not worthy of me. Whosoever findeth his life shall lose it; and whosoever loseth his life for my sake shah find it.

27 And whosoever receiveth you receiveth me; and whosoever receiveth me re- ceiveth him that sent me. And whosoever receiveth a prophet in the name of a prophet shall take a prophet's reward; and whosoever shall receive a righteous man in the name of a righteous man shall take a righteous man's reward. And every one that shall give to drink to one of these least ones a drink of water only, in the name of a disciple, verily I say unto you, he shall not lose his reward.

30 And when Jesus finished charging his twelve disciples, he removed thence to teach and preach in their cities. And while they were going in the way they entered into a certain village; and a woman named Martha entertained him in her house. And she had a sister named Mary, and she came and sat at the feet of our Lord, and heard his sayings. But Martha was disquieted by much serving; and she came and said unto him, My Lord, givest thou no heed that my sister left me alone to serve? speak to her that she help me. Jesus answered and said unto her, Martha, Martha, thou art solicitous and impatient on account of many things: but what is sought is one thing. But Mary hath chosen for herself a good portion, and that which shall not be taken from her.

36 And the apostles went forth, and preached to the people that they might repent. And they cast out many devils, and anointed many sick with oil, and healed them. 38, And the disciples of John told him s of all these things. And when John heard in Arabic, the prison of the doings of the Messiah, he called two of his disciples, and sent them to Jesus, and said, Art thou he that cometh, or look we for another? And they came to Jesus, and said unto him, John the Baptist hath sent us unto thee, and said. Art thou he that cometh, or look we for another? And in that hour he cured many of diseases, and of plagues of an evil spirit; and he gave sight to many blind. Jesus answered and said unto them, Go and tell John everything ye have seen and heard: the blind see, and the lame walk, and the lepers are cleansed, and the blind hear, and the dead rise, and the poor have the gospel preached to them. And blessed is he who doubteth not in me.

And when John's disciples departed, Jesus began to say to the multitudes concerning John, What went ye out into the wilderness to see? a reed shaken with the winds? And if not, then what went ye out to see? a man clothed in soft raiment? Behold, they that are in magnificent garments and in voluptuousness are in the abode of kings. And if not, then what went ye out to see? a prophet? Yea, I say unto you, and more than a prophet. This is he of whom it is written, I am sending my messenger before thy face To prepare the way before thee.

SECTION XIV.

14 1 Verily I say unto you, There hath not arisen among those whom women have borne a greater than John the Baptist; but he that is little now in the kingdom of heaven is greater than he.

2 Arabic, And all the people which heard, and the publicans, justified: God, for 3 they had been baptized with the baptism of John. But the Pharisees and the scribes wronged the purpose of God in themselves, in that they were not baptized of 4 him. And from the days of John the Baptist until now the kingdom of heaven is 5 snatched away by violence. The law and the prophets were until John; and after that, the kingdom of God is preached, and all press to enter it: and they that exert them- 7 selves snatch it away. All the prophets and the law until John prophesied. And if ye 8 will, then receive it, that he is Elijah, which is to come. Whosoever hath ears that hear 9 let him hear. Easier is the perishing of heaven and earth, than the passing away of one point of the law. To whom then shall I liken the people of this generation, and to whom are they like? They are like the children sitting in the market, which call to their companions, and say, We sang to you, and ye danced not; we wailed to you, and ye wept not. John the Baptist came neither eating bread nor drinking wine; and ye said, He hath demons: and the Son of man came eating and drinking; and ye said, Behold, a

gluttonous man, and a drinker of wine, and an associate of pub- 14, 15 licans and sinners! And wisdom was justified of all her children. And when he said that, they came to the house. And there gathered unto him again multitudes, so that they found not bread to eat. And while he was casting out a devil which was dumb, when he cast out that devil, that dumb man spake. And the multitudes Arabic. marvelled. And the Pharisees, when they heard, said, This man doth not cast out the devils, except by Beelzebul the chief of the demons, which is in him. 18, And others requested of him a sign from heaven, to tempt him. And Jesus knew their thoughts, and said unto them in parables, Every kingdom that withstandeth itself shall become desolate; and every house or city that disagreeth with itself shall not stand: and if a devil cast out a devil, he withstandeth himself; neither shall he be able to stand, but his end shall be. Then how now shall his kingdom stand? for ye said that I cast out devils by Beelzebul. And if I by Beelzebul cast out the devils, then your children, by what do they cast them out? And for this cause they shall be judges against you. But if I by the Spirit of God cast out devils, then the king- dom of God is come near unto you. Or how can a man enter into the house of a valiant man, and seize his garments, if he do not beforehand secure himself from that valiant man? and then will he cut off his house. But when the valiant man is armed, guarding his house, his possessions are in peace. But if one come who is more valiant than he, he overcometh him, and taketh his whole armour, on which he relieth, and divideth his spoil. Whosoever is not with me is against me; and whosoever gathereth not with me scattereth abroad. For this reason I say unto you, Arabic. that all sins and blasphemies with which men blaspheme shall be forgiven them: but whosoever shall blaspheme against the Holy Spirit, there is no forgiveness for him for ever, but he is deserving of eternal punishment: because they said that he had an unclean spirit. And he said also, Every one that speaketh a word against the Son of man, it shall be forgiven him; but whosoever speaketh against the Holy Spirit, it shall not be forgiven him, neither in this world, nor in the world to come. Either ye must make a good tree and its fruit good; or ye must make an evil tree and its fruit evil: for the tree is known by its fruit. Ye children of vipers, how can ye, being evil, speak good things? from the overflowings of the heart the mouth speaketh. The good man from the good treasures which are in his heart bringeth forth good things; and the wicked man from the evil treasures which are in his heart bringeth forth evils. I say unto you, that every idle word which men shall speak, they shall give an answer for in the day of judgement: for by thy sayings thou shalt be justified, and by thy sayings thou shalt be judged.

37 And he said to the multitudes, When ye see the clouds appear from the west, straightway ye say that there cometh rain; and so it cometh to pass. And when the south wind bloweth, ye say that there will be heat; and it cometh to pass. And when the evening is come, ye say, It will be fair weather, for the heaven has become red. And in the morning ye say, To-day there will be severe weather, for the redness Arabic. Of the heaven is paling. Ye hypocrites, ye know to examine the face of the P. heaven and the earth; but the signs of this time ye know not to discern. Then they brought to him one possessed of a demon, dumb and blind; and he healed him, so that the dumb and blind began to speak and see. And all the multitudes wondered, and said, Is this, think you, the son of David?

43 And the apostles returned unto Jesus, and told him everything that they had done and wrought. And he said unto them, Come, let us go into the desert alone, and rest yea little. And many were going and returning, and they had not leisure, not even to eat bread.

45 And after that, there came to him one of the Pharisees, and besought him that he would eat bread with him. And he entered into the house of that Pharisee, and reclined. And there was in that city a woman that was a sinner; and when she knew that he was sitting in the house of that Pharisee, she took a box of sweet oint- 47 ment, and stood behind him, towards his feet, weeping, and began to wet his feet with her tears, and to wipe them with the hair of her head, and to kiss his feet, and anoint them with the sweet ointment. And when that s Pharisee saw it, who invited him, he thought within himself, and said, This man, if he were a prophet, would know who she is and what is her history: for the woman which touched him was a sinner.

SECTION XV.

15 1 Jesus answered and said unto him, Simon, I have something to say unto thee. And 2 he said unto him, Say on, my Master. Jesus said unto him, There were two debtors Arabic. to one creditor; and one of them owed five hundred pence, and the other 3 owed fifty pence. And because they had not wherewith to pay, he forgave 4 them both. Which of them ought to love him more? Simon answered and said, I suppose, he to whom he forgave most. Jesus said unto him, Thou hast judged rightly. 5 And he turned to that woman, and said to Simon, Dost thou see this woman? I entered into thy dwelling, and thou gavest me not water to wash my feet: but this 6 woman hath bathed my feet with her tears, and dried them with her hair. And thou kissedst me not: but this woman, since she entered, hath not ceased to kiss my 7 feet. And thou anointedst not my head with oil: but this woman hath anointed 8 my feet with sweet ointment. And for this, I say unto thee, Her many sins are forgiven her, because she loved much; for he to whom little is forgiven loveth little. And he said unto that woman, Thy sins are forgiven thee. And those that were in- vited began to say within themselves, Who is this that forgiveth sins also? And Jesus said to that woman, Thy faith hath saved thee; go in peace. And many believed in him when they saw the signs which he was doing. But Jesus did not trust himself to them, for he knew every man, and he needed not any man to testify to him concerning every man; for he knew what was in man.

15 And after that, Jesus set apart from his disciples other seventy, and sent them two and two before his face to every region and city whither he was purposing to go. And he said unto them, The harvest is abundant, and the labourers are few: entreat now the Lord of the harvest, that he send forth labourers into his harvest. Go Arabic, ye: and lo, I am sending you as lambs among wolves. Take not with you purses, nor a wallet, nor shoes; neither salute any man in the way. And whatsoever house ye enter, first salute that house: and if there be there a son of peace, let your peace rest upon him; but if there be not, your peace shall return to you. And be ye in that house eating and drinking what they have: for the labourer is worthy of his hire. And remove not from house to house. And into whatsoever city

ye enter, and they receive you, eat what is presented to you: and heal the sick that are therein, and say unto them, The kingdom of God is come near unto you. But whatsoever city ye enter, and they receive you not, go out into the market, and say, Even the dust that clave to our feet from your city, we shake off against you; but know this, that the kingdom of God is come near unto you. I say unto you, that for Sodom there shall be quiet in the day of judgement, but there shall not be for that city. Then began Jesus to rebuke the cities in which there had been many mighty works, and they repented not. And he said, Woe unto thee, Chorazin! woe unto thee, Bethsaida! if there had been in Tyre and Sidon the signs which were in thee, it may be that they would have repented in sackcloth and ashes. Howbeit I say unto you, that for Tyre and Sidon there shall be rest in the day of judgement, more than for you. And thou, Capernaum, which art exalted unto heaven, shalt sink down unto Hades; for if there had been in Sodom the wonders which were in thee, it would have remained until this day. And now I say unto thee, that for the land of Sodom there shall be quiet in the day of judgement, more than for thee.

32 Arabic. And he said again unto his apostles, Whosoever heareth you heareth me; and whosoever heareth me heareth him that sent me: and whosoever wrongeth you wrongeth me; and whosoever wrongeth me wrongeth him that sent me.

33 And those seventy returned with great joy, and said unto him, Our Lord, even the devils also are subject unto us in thy name. He said unto them, I beheld Satan fallen like lightning from heaven. Behold, I am giving you authority to tread upon serpents and scorpions, and the whole race of the enemy; and nothing shall hurt you. Only ye must not rejoice that the devils are subject unto you; but be glad that your names are written in heaven.

37 And in that hour Jesus rejoiced in the Holy Spirit, and said, I acknowledge thee, my Father, Lord of heaven and earth, that thou didst hide these things from the wise and understanding, and didst reveal them unto children: yea, my Father; so was thy will. And he turned to his disciples, and said unto them, Everything hath been delivered to me of my Father: and no man knoweth who the Son is, save the Father; and who the Father is, save the Son, and to whomsoever the Son willeth to reveal him. Come unto me, all of you, ye that are wearied and bearers of bur- dens, and I will give you rest. Bear my yoke upon you, and learn of me; for I am gentle and lowly in my heart: and ye shall find rest unto your souls. For my yoke is pleasant, and my burden is light.

42 And while great multitudes were going with him, he turned, and said unto them, Whosoever cometh unto me, and hateth not his father, and his mother, and his brethren, and his sisters, and his wife, and his children, and himself also, cannot Arabic, be a disciple to me. And whosoever doth not take his cross, and follow p. me, cannot be a disciple to me. Which of you desireth to build a tower, and doth not sit down first and reckon his expenses and whether he hath enough to complete it? lest when he hath laid the foundations, and is not able to finish, all that behold him laugh at him, and say, This man began to build, and was not able to 48 finish. Or what king goeth to the battle to fight with another king, and doth not consider first

whether he is able with ten thousand to meet him that cometh to him with twenty thousand? And if he is not able, he sendeth unto him while he is afar off, and seeketh peace. So shall every man of you consider, that desireth to be a disciple to me; for if he renounceth not all that he hath, he cannot be a disciple to me.

SECTION XVI.

16 1 Then answered certain of the scribes and Pharisees, that they might tempt him, 2 and said, Teacher, we desire to see a sign from thee. He answered and said, This evil and adulterous generation seeketh a sign; and it shall not be given a sign, 3 except the sign of Jonah the prophet. And as Jonah was a sign to the inhabitants 4 of Nineveh, so shall the Son of man also be to this generation. And as Jonah was in the belly of the great fish three days and three nights, so shall the Son of man 5 be in the heart of the earth three days and three nights. The queen of the south shall rise in the judgement with the people of this generation, and condemn them: for she came from the ends of the earth that she might hear the wisdom of Solomon; 6 Arabic, and behold, here is a better than Solomon. The men of Nineveh shall stand in the judgement with this generation, and condemn it: for they repented at 7 the preaching of Jonah; and behold, here is a greater than Jonah. The unclean spirit, when he goeth out of the man, departeth, and goeth about through places wherein are no waters, that he may find rest for himself; and when he findeth it not, he 8 saith, I will return to my house whence I came out. And if he come and find it 9 adorned and set in order, then he goeth, and associateth with himself seven other spirits worse than himself; and they enter and dwell in it: and the end of that man shall be worse than his beginning. Thus shall it be unto this evil generation.

11 And while he was saying that, a woman from the multitude lifted up her voice, and said unto him, Blessed is the womb that bare thee, and the breasts that nursed thee. But he said unto her, Blessed is he that heareth the word of God, and keepeth it.

13 And while he was speaking unto the multitude, there came unto him his mother and his brethren, and sought to speak with him; and they were not able, because of the multitude; and they stood without and sent, calling him unto them. A man said unto him, Behold, thy mother and thy brethren are standing without, and seek to speak with thee. But he answered unto him that spake unto him, Who is my mother? and who are my brethren? And he beckoned with his hand, stretching it out towards his disciples, and said, Behold, my mother! and behold, my brethren! And every man that shall do the will of my Father which is in heaven is my brother, and my sister, and my mother.

19 And after that, Jesus was going about in the cities and in the villages, and pro- Arabic, claiming and preaching the kingdom of God, and his; twelve with him, and the women which had been healed of diseases and of evil spirits, Mary that was called Magdalene, from whom he had cast out seven devils, and Joanna the wife of Chuza Herod's steward, and Susanna, and many others, who were ministering to them of their substance.

22 And after that, Jesus went out of the house, and sat on the sea shore. And there gathered unto him great multitudes. And when the press of the people was great upon him, he went up and sat in the boat; and all the multitude was standing on the shore of the sea. And he spake to them much in parables, and said, The sower went forth to sow: and when he sowed, some fell on the beaten highway; and it was trodden upon, and the birds ate it.

And other fell on the rocks: and some, where there was not much earth; and straightway it sprang up, because it had no depth in the earth: and when the sun rose, it withered; and because it had no root, it dried up. And some fell among thorns; and the thorns sprang up with it, and choked it; and it yielded no fruit. And other fell into excellent and good ground; and it came up, and grew, and brought forth fruit, some thirty, and some sixty, and some a hundred. And when he said that, he cried, He that hath ears that hear, let him hear. And when they were alone, his disciples came, and asked him, and said unto him, What is this parable? and why spakest thou unto them in parables? He Arabic, answered and said unto them, Unto you is given the knowledge of the secrets of the kingdom of God; but it is not given unto them that are without. He that hath shall be given unto, and there shall be added; and he that hath not, that which he hath shah be taken from him also. For this cause therefore I speak unto them in parables; because they see, and see not; and hear, and hear not, nor understand. And in them is being fulfilled the prophecy of Isaiah, who said, Hearing they shall hear, and shall not understand; And seeing they shall see, and shall not perceive:

36 The heart of this people is waxed gross, And their hearing with their ears is become heavy, And they have closed their eyes; Lest they should see with their eyes, And hear with their ears, And understand with their hearts, And should return, And I should heal them.

37, But ye, blessed are your eyes, which see; and your ears, which hear. Blessed are the eyes which see what ye see. Verily I say unto you, Many of the prophets and the righteous longed to see what ye see, and saw not; and to hear what ye hear, and heard not. When ye know not this parable, how shall ye know all para- 41, 42 bles? Hear ye the parable of the sower. The sower which sowed, sowed the word of God. Every one who heareth the word of the kingdom, and understandeth it not, the evil one cometh and snatcheth away the word that hath been sown in his heart: and this is that which was sown on the middle of the highway. But that which was sown on the rocks is he that heareth the word, and straightway receiveth 45, Arabic, it with joy; only, it hath no root in his soul, but his belief in it is for a time; and whenever there is distress or persecution because of a word, he stumbleth quickly. And that which was sown among the thorns is he that heareth the word; and the care of this world, and the error of riches, and the rest of the other lusts enter, and choke the word, and it becometh without fruit. And that which was sown in good ground is he that heareth my word in a pure and good heart, and understandeth it, and holdeth to it, and bringeth forth fruit with patience, and produceth either a hundredfold or sixtyfold or thirty.

49 And he said, So is the kingdom of God, like a man who casteth seed into the earth, and sleepeth and riseth by night and day, and the seed groweth and cometh up, whence he knoweth not. And the earth bringeth it to the fruit; and first it will be blade, and after it ear, and at last perfect wheat in the ear: and whenever the fruit ripeneth, he bringeth immediately the sickle, for the harvest hath come.

SECTION XVII.

17 1 And he set forth to them another parable, and said, The kingdom of heaven is like a man who sowed good seed in his field; but when men slept, his enemy came and sowed tares among the wheat, and went away. And when the blade sprang up and brought forth fruit, there were noticed the tares also. And the servants of the master of the house came, and said unto him, Our lord, didst thou not sow good seed in thy field? whence are there tares in it? He said unto them, An enemy hath done this. His servants said unto him, Wilt thou that we go 6 and separate it? He said unto them, Perhaps, when ye separate the tares, ye would 7 root up with them wheat also. Leave them to grow both together until the harvest: and in the time of the harvest I will say unto the reapers, Separate the tares first, and bind them in bundles to be burned with fire; and gather the wheat into my barns.

8, 9 And he set forth to them another parable, and said, To what is the kingdom of God like? and to what shall I liken it? and in what parable shall I set it forth? It is like a grain of mustard seed, which a man took, and planted in his field: and of the number of the things that are sown in the earth it is smaller than all of the things which are sown, which are upon the earth; but when it is grown, it is greater than all the herbs, and produceth large branches, so that the birds of heaven make their nests in its branches.

13, And he set forth to them another parable: To what shall I liken the kingdom of God? It is like the leaven which a woman took, and kneaded into three measures of flour, until the whole of it was leavened.

16 And Jesus spake all that to the multitudes by way of parables, according as they were able to hear. And without parables spake he not unto them; that the saying of the Lord through the prophet might be fulfilled:

I will open my mouth in parables; And I will utter secrets which were before the foundations of the world.

18 But he explained to his disciples privately everything.

19 Then Jesus left the multitudes, and came to the house. And his disciples came Arabic. unto him, and said unto him, Explain unto us that parable about the tares and the field. He answered and said unto them, He that sowed good seed is the Son of man; and the field is the world; and the good seed are the children of the kingdom; and the tares are the children of the evil one; and the enemy that sowed them is Satan; and the harvest is the end of the world; and the reapers are the angels. And as the tares are separated and burned in the fire, so shall it be in the end of this world. The Son of man shall send his angels, and separate from his kingdom all things that injure, and all the doers of iniquity, and they shall cast them into the furnace of fire: and there shall be weeping and gnashing of teeth.

Then the righteous shall shine as the sun in the kingdom of their Father. Whosoever hath ears that hear, let him hear.

27 And again the kingdom of heaven is like treasure hid in a field: that which a man found and hid; and, for his pleasure in it, went and sold all that he had, and bought that field.

28 And again the kingdom of heaven is like a man that is a merchant seeking ex- cellent pearls; and when he found one pearl of great price, he went and sold everything that he had, and bought it.

30 And again the kingdom of heaven is like a net that was cast into the sea, and gathered of every kind: and when it was filled, they drew it up on to the shore of the sea, and sat down to select; and the good of them they threw into the vessels, and the bad they threw outside. Thus shall it be in the end of the world: the angels shall go forth, and separate the wicked from among the good, and shall cast them into the furnace of fire: there shall be weeping and gnashing of teeth.

34 Jesus said unto them, Have ye understood all these things? They said unto Arabic, him, Yea, our Lord. He said unto them, Therefore every scribe that be- cometh a disciple of the kingdom of heaven is like a man that is a householder, who bringeth out of his treasures the new and the old.

36, And when Jesus had finished all these parables, he removed thence, and came to his city; and he taught them in their synagogues, so that they were perplexed. And when the sabbath came, Jesus began to teach in the synagogue; and many of those that heard marvelled, and said, Whence came these things to this man? And many envied him and gave no heed to him, but said, What is this wisdom that is given to this man, that there should happen at his hands such as these mighty works? Is not this a carpenter, son of a carpenter? and is not his mother called Mary? and his brethren, James, and Joses, and Simon, and Judas? And his sisters, all of them, lo, are they not all with us? Whence hath this man all these things? And they were in doubt concerning him. And Jesus knew their opinion, and said unto them, Will ye haply" say unto me this proverb, Physician, heal first thyself: and all that we have heard that thou didst in Capernaum, do here also in thine own city? And he said, Verily I say unto you, A prophet is not received in his own city, nor among his brethren: for a prophet is not despised, save in his own city, and among his own kin, and in his own house. Verily I say unto you, In the days of Elijah the prophet, there were many widows among the children of Israel, when the heaven held back three years and six months, and there was a great famine in all the land; and Elijah Arabic, was not sent to one of them, save to Zarephath of Sidon, to a woman that was a widow. And many lepers were among the children of Israel in the days of Elisha the prophet; but not one of them was cleansed, save Naaman the Nabathaean. And he was not able to do there many mighty works, because of their unbelief; except that he laid his hand upon a few of the sick, and healed them. And he mar- velled at their lack of faith. And when those who were in the synagogue heard, 51 they were all filled with wrath; and they rose up, and brought him forth outside the city, and brought him to the brow of the hill

upon which their city was built, that they might cast him from its summit: but he passed through among them and went away.

53 And he went about in the villages which were around Nazareth, and taught in their synagogues.

SECTION XVIII.

18 1 At that time Herod the tetrarch heard of the fame of Jesus, and all the things which came to pass at his hand; and he marvelled, for he had obtained excellent 2 information concerning him. And same men said that John the Baptist was risen 3 from among the dead; and others said that Elijah had appeared; and others, Jere- 4 miah; and others, that a prophet of the old prophets was risen; and others said that he 5 was a prophet like one of the prophets. Herod said to his servants, This is John the Baptist, he whom I beheaded; he is risen from among the dead: therefore mighty 6 Arabic. works result from him. For Herod himself had sent and taken John, and cast him into prison, for the sake of Herodias his brother Philip's wife, whom he 7 had taken. And John said to Herod, Thou hast no authority to take the wife of thy 8 brother. And Herodias avoided him and wished to kill him; and she could not.

9 But Herod feared John, for he knew that he was a righteous man and a holy; and he guarded him, and heard him much, and did, and obeyed him with gladness. And he wished to kill him; but he feared the people, for they adhered to him as the prophet. And there was a celebrated day, and Herod had made a feast for his great men on the day of his anniversary, and for the officers and for the chief men of Galilee. And the daughter of Herodias came in and danced in the midst of the company, and pleased Herod and those that sat with him. And the king said to the damsel, Ask of me what thou wilt, and I will give it thee. And he sware unto her, Whatsoever thou shalt ask, I will give it thee, to the half of my kingdom. And she went out, and said unto her mother, What shall I ask him? She said unto her, The head of John the Baptist. And immediately she came in hastily to the king, and said unto him, I desire in this hour that thou give me on a dish the head of John the Baptist. And the king was exceeding sorry; but because of the oath and the guests he did not wish to refuse her. But immediately the king sent an executioner, and commanded that he should bring the head of John: and he went and cut off the head of John in the prison, and brought it on a dish, and delivered it to the damsel; and the damsel gave it to her mother. And his disciples heard, and came Arabic, and took his body, and buffed it. And they came and told Jesus what had happened. And for this cause Herod said, I beheaded John: who is this, of whom I hear these things. And he desired to see him. And Jesus, when he heard, removed thence in a boat to a waste place alone, to the other side of the sea of the Galilee of Tiberias.

22 And many saw them going, and knew them, and hastened by land from all the cities, and came thither beforehand; for they saw the signs which he was doing on the 23, sick. And Jesus went up into the mountain, and sat there with his disciples. And the feast of the passover of the Jews was near. And Jesus lifted up his eyes, and saw great multitudes coming to him. And he was moved with

compassion for them, for they were like sheep that were without a shepherd. And he received them, and spake to them concerning the kingdom of God, and healed those who had need of healing. And when the evening approached, his disciples came to him, and said unto him, The place is desert, and the time is past; send away the multitudes of the people, that they may go to the towns and villages which are around us, and buy for themselves bread; for they have nothing to eat. But he said unto them, They have no need to go away; give ye them what may be eaten. They said unto him, We have not here enough. He said unto Philip, Whence shall we buy bread that these may eat? 31, And he said that proving him; and he knew what he was resolved to do. Philip said Arabic. unto him, Two hundred pennyworth of bread would not suffice them after p. 72 every one of them hath taken a small amount. One of his disciples said unto him (namely, Andrew the brother of Simon Cephas), Here is a lad having five loaves of barley and two fishes: but this amount, what is it for all these? But wilt thou that we go and buy for all the people what may be eaten? for we have no more than these five loaves and the two fishes. And the grass was plentiful in that place. Jesus said unto them, Arrange all the people that they may sit down on the grass, fifty people in a company. And the disciples did so. And all the people sat down by companies, by hundreds and fifties. Then Jesus said unto them, Bring hither those five loaves and the two fishes. And when they brought him that, Jesus took the bread and the fish, and looked to heaven, and blessed, and divided, and gave to his disciples to set before them; and the disciples set for the multitudes the bread and the fish; and they ate, all of them, and were satisfied. And when they were satisfied, he said unto his disciples, Gather the fragments that remain over, that noth- ing be lost. And they gathered, and filled twelve baskets with fragments, being those that remained over from those which ate of the five barley loaves and the two fishes. And those people who ate were five thousand, besides the women and children. Arabic, And straightway he pressed his disciples to go up into the ship, and that they should go before him unto the other side to Bethsaida, while he himself should send away the multitudes. And those people who saw the sign which Jesus did, said, Of a truth this is a prophet who hath come into the world. And Jesus knew their purpose to come and take him, and make him a king; and he left them, and went up into the mountain alone for prayer.

47, And when the nightfall was near, his disciples went down unto the sea, and sat in a boat, and came to the side of Capernaum. And the darkness came on, and Jesus had not come to them. And the sea was stirred up against them by reason of a violent wind that blew. And the boat was distant from the land many furlongs, and they were much damaged by the waves, and the wind was against them.

SECTION XIX.

19 1 And in the fourth watch of the night Jesus came unto them, walking upon the 2 water, after they had rowed with difficulty about twenty-five or thirty furlongs.

19 And when he drew near unto their boat, his disciples saw him walking on the water; and they were troubled, and supposed that it was a false appearance; and they cried out from their fear. But Jesus straightway spoke unto them, and said, Take courage, for it is I; fear not. Then Cephas answered and said unto him, My Lord, if it be thou, bid me to come unto thee on the water. And Jesus said unto him, Come. And Cephas went down out of the boat, and walked on the water to come unto Jesus. But Arabic, when he saw the wind strong, he feared, and was on the point of sink- ing; and he lifted up his voice, and said, My Lord, save me. And immediately our Lord stretched out his hand and took hold of him, and said unto him, 9 Thou of little faith, why didst thou doubt? And when Jesus came near, he went up unto them into the boat, he and Simon, and immediately the wind ceased. And those that were in the ship came and worshipped him, and said, Truly thou art the Son of God. And straightway that ship arrived at the land which they made for. And when they came out of the ship to the land, they marvelled greatly and were perplexed in themselves: and they had not understood by means of that bread, because their heart was gross.

14 And when the people of that region knew of the arrival of Jesus, they made haste in all that land, and began to bring those that were diseased, borne in their beds to the place where they heard that he was. And wheresoever the place might be which he entered, of the villages or the cities, they laid the sick in the markets, and sought of him that they might touch were it only the edge of his garment: and all that touched him were healed and lived.

16 And on the day after that, the multitude which was standing on the shore of the sea saw that there was there no other ship save that into which the disciples had gone up, and that Jesus went not up into the ship with his disciples (but there were other ships from Tiberias near the place where they ate the bread when Jesus blessed it): and when that multitude saw that Jesus was not there, nor yet his disciples, they Arabic, went up into those ships, and came to Capernaum, and sought Jesus. And when they found him on the other side of the sea, they said unto him, Our Master, when camest thou hither? Jesus answered and said unto them, Verily, verily, I say unto you, Ye have not sought me because of your seeing the signs, but because of your eating the bread and being satisfied. Serve not the food which perisheth, but the food which abideth in eternal life, which the Son of man will give unto you: him hath God the Father sealed. They said unto him, What shall we do that we may work the work of God? Jesus answered and said unto them, This is the work of God, that ye believe in him whom he hath sent. They said unto him, What sign hast thou done, that we may see, and believe in thee? what hast thou wrought? Our fathers ate the manna in the wilderness; as it was written, Bread from heaven gave he them to eat. Jesus said unto them, Verily, verily, I say unto you, Moses gave you not bread from heaven; but my Father gave you the bread of truth n from heaven. The bread of God is that which came down from heaven and gave the 28, world life. They said unto him, Our Lord, give us at all times this bread. Jesus said unto them, I am the bread of life: whosoever cometh unto me shall not hun- ger, and whosoever believeth in me shall not thirst for ever. But I said unto you, Ye have seen me, and have not believed. And all that my Father hath given to me cometh unto me; and whosoever cometh unto me I shall not cast him forth with- out. I came down from heaven, not to do my own will, but to do the will of him that sent me; and this is the will of him that sent me, that I should lose nothing of Arabic, that which he gave me, but raise it up in the last

day. This is the will of my Father, that every one that seeth the Son, and believeth in him, should have eternal life; and I will raise him up in the last day.

35 The Jews therefore murmured against him because of his saying, I am the bread which came down from heaven. And they said, Is not this Jesus, the son of Joseph, whose father and mother we know? then how saith this man, I came down from 37, heaven? Jesus answered and said unto them, Murmur not one with another. No man is able to come unto me, except the Father which sent me draw him; and I will raise him up in the last day. It is written in the prophet, They shall all be the taught of God. Every one who heareth from the Father now, and learneth of him, cometh unto me. No man now seeth the Father; but he that is from God, he it is that seeth the Father. Verily, verily, I say unto you, Whosoever believeth in me hath eternal 42, life. I am the bread of life. Your fathers ate the manna in the wilderness, and they died. This is the bread which came down from heaven, that a man may eat of it, and not die. I am the bread of life which came down from heaven: and if a man eat of this bread he shall live for ever: and the bread which I shall give is my body, which I give for the life of the world.

46 The Jews therefore quarrelled one with another, and said, How can he give us Arabic, his body that we may eat it? Jesus said unto them, Verily, verily, I say unto you, If ye do not eat the body of the Son of man and drink his blood, ye shall not have life in yourselves. Whosoever eateth of my body and drinketh of my blood hath eternal life; and I will raise him up in the last day. My body truly is meat, and my blood truly is drink. Whosoever eateth my body and drinketh my blood abideth in me, and I in him--as the living Father sent me, and I am alive because of the Father; and whosoever eateth me, he also shall live because of me. This is the bread which came down from heaven: and not according as your fathers ate the manna, and died: whosoever eateth of this bread shall live for ever. This he said in the synagogue, when he was teaching in Capernaum. And many of his disciples, when they heard, said, This word is hard; who is he that can hear it?

SECTION XX.

20 1 And Jesus knew within himself that his disciples were murmuring because of a that, and he said unto them, Doth this trouble you? What if ye should see the Son 3 of man then ascend to the place where he was of old? It is the spirit that quickeneth, and the body profiteth nothing: the words that I speak unto you are spirit 4 and life. But there are some of you that do not believe. And Jesus knew beforehand who they were who should not believe, and who it was that should betray 5 him. And he said unto them, Therefore I said unto you, No man can come unto me, if that hath not been given him by the Father.

6 Arabic, And because of this word many of his disciples turned back and walked 7 not with him. And Jesus said unto the twelve, Do ye haply also wish to 8 go away? Simon Cephas answered and said, My Lord, to whom shall we go? thou 9 hast the words of eternal life. And we have believed and known that thou art the Messiah, the Son of the living God. Jesus said unto them, Did not I choose you, ye company of the twelve, and of you one is a devil? He said

that because of Judas the son of Simon Iscariot; for he, being of the twelve, was purposed to betray him.

12 And while he was speaking, one of the Pharisees came asking of him that he would eat with him: and he went in, and reclined to meat. And that Pharisee, when he saw it, marvelled that he had not first cleansed himself before his eating. Jesus said unto him, Now do ye Pharisees wash the outside of the cup and the dish, and ye think that ye are cleansed; but your inside is full of injustice and wickedness.

15, Ye of little mind, did not he that made the outside make the inside? Now give what ye have in alms, and everything shall be clean unto you.

17, And there came to him Pharisees and scribes, come from Jerusalem. And when they saw some of his disciples eating bread while they had not washed their hands, they found fault. For all of the Jews and the Pharisees, if they wash not their hands thoroughly, eat not; for they held to the ordinance of the elders. And they ate not what was bought from the market, except they washed it; and many other things did they keep of what they had received, such as the washing of cups, and measures, and vessels of brass, and couches. And scribes and Pharisees asked him, Why do thy disciples not walk according to the ordinances of the elders, but eat bread without washing their hands? Jesus answered and said unto them, Why do ye also overstep the command of God by reason of your ordinance? God said, Honour thy father and thy mother; and, Whosoever revileth his father and his mother shall surely die. But ye say, If a man say to his father or to his mother, What thou receivest from me is an offering,--and ye suffer him not to do any- thing for his father or his mother; and ye make void and reject the word of God by reason of the ordinance that ye have ordained and commanded, such as the wash- ing of cups and measures, and what resembles that ye do much. And ye forsook the command of God, and held to the ordinance of men. Do ye well to wrong the command of God in order that ye may establish your ordinance? Ye hypocrites, well did Isaiah the prophet prophesy concerning you, and say, This people honoureth me with its lips; But their heart is very far from me.

31 But in vain do they fear me, In that they teach the commands of men.

32 And Jesus called all the multitude, and said unto them. Hear me, all of you, and understand: nothing without the man, which then enters him, is able to defile him; but what goeth out of him, that it is which defileth the man. He that hath ears that hear, let him hear. Then his disciples drew near, and said unto him, Knowest thou that the Pharisees which heard this word were angry? He answered and said unto them, Every plant which my Father which is in heaven planted not shall be Arabic, uprooted. Let them alone; for they are blind leading blind. And if the blind lead the blind, both of them shall fall into a hollow.

38 And when Jesus entered the house from the multitude, Simon Cephas asked him, and said unto him, My Lord, explain to us that parable. He said unto them, Do ye also thus not understand? Know ye not that everything that entereth into the man from without cannot defile him; because it entereth not into his heart; it entereth into his

stomach only, and thence is cast forth in the cleansing which maketh clean all the food? The thing which goeth forth from the mouth of the man pro- ceedeth from his heart, and it is that which defileth the man. From within the heart of men proceed evil thoughts, fornication, adultery, theft, false witness, murder, injustice, wickedness, deceit, stupidity, evil eye, calumny, pride, foolishness: these evils all of them from within proceed from the heart, and they are the things which defile the man: but if a man eat while he washeth not his hands, he is not defiled.

46 And Jesus went out thence, and came to the borders of Tyre and Sidon. And he entered into a certain house, and desired that no man should know it; and he could not be hid. But straightway a Canaanitish woman, whose daughter had an 48, unclean spirit, heard of him. And that woman was a Gentile of Emesa of Syria. And she came out after him, crying out, and saying, Have mercy upon me, my Lord, thou son of David; for my daughter is seized in an evil way by Satan. And he answered Arabic. her not a word. And his disciples came and besought him, and said, Send her away: for she crieth after us. He answered and said unto them, I was not sent except to the sheep that are gone astray of the house of Israel. But she came and worshipped him, and said, My Lord, help me, have mercy upon me.

53 Jesus said unto her, It is not seemly that the children's bread should be taken and thrown to the dogs. But she said, Yea, my Lord: the dogs also eat of the crumbs that fall from their masters' tables, and live. Then said Jesus unto her, O woman, great is thy faith: it shall be unto thee as thou hast desired. Go then thy way; and because of this word, the devil is gone out of thy daughter. And her daughter was healed in that hour. And that woman went away to her house, and found her daughter laid upon the bed, and the devil gone out of her.

SECTION XXI.

21 1 And Jesus went out again from the borders of Tyre and Sidon, and came to the 2 sea of Galilee, towards the borders of Decapolis. And they brought unto him one dumb and deaf, and entreated him that he would lay his hand upon him and heal 3 him. And he drew him away from the multitude, and went away alone, and spat 4 upon his fingers, and thrust them into his ears, and touched his tongue; and looked 5 to heaven, and sighed, and said unto him, Be opened. And in that hour his ears 6 were opened, and the bond of his tongue was loosed, and he spake with ease. And Jesus charged them much that they should not tell this to any man: but the more 7 he charged them, the mare they increased in publishing, and marvelled much, and Arabic. said, This man doeth everything well: he made the deaf to hear, and those that lacked speech to speak.

8, 9 And while he was passing through the land of Samaria, he came to one of the cities of the Samaritans, called Sychar, beside the field which Jacob gave to Joseph to his son. And there was there a spring of water of Jacob's. And Jesus was fatigued from the exertion of the way, and sat at the spring. And the time was about the sixth hour. And a woman of Samaria came to draw water; and Jesus said unto her, Give me water, that I may drink. And Iris disciples had entered into the city to buy for themselves food. And that Samaritan woman said unto him, How dost thou, being a Jew, ask me to give thee to drink, while I am a Samaritan woman? (And the Jews mingle not with the Samaritans. Jesus answered and said unto her, If thou knewest the gift of God, and who this is that said unto thee, Give me to drink; thou wouldest ask him, and he would give thee the water of life. That woman said unto him, My Lord, thou hast no bucket, and the well is deep: from whence hast thou the water of life? Can it be that thou art greater than our father Jacob, who gave us this well, and drank from it, and his children, and his sheep? Jesus answered and said unto her, Every one that drinketh of this water shall thirst again: but whosoever drinketh of the water which I shall give him shall not thirst for ever: but the water which I shall give him shall be in him a spring of water springing up unto eternal life. That woman said unto him, My Lord, give me of this water, that I may not thirst again, neither come and draw water from here. Jesus said unto her, Arabic. Go and call thy husband, and come hither. She said unto him, I have no 22 husband. Jesus said unto her, Thou saidst well, I have no husband: five husbands hast thou had, and this man whom thou hast now is not thy husband; and in this thou saidst truly. That woman said unto him, My Lord, I perceive thee to be a prophet. Our fathers worshipped in this mountain; and ye say that in Jeru- salem is the place in which worship must be. Jesus said unto her, Woman, believe me, an hour cometh, when neither in this mountain, nor yet in Jerusalem, shall ye wor- ship the Father. Ye worship that which ye know not: but we worship that which we know: for salvation is of the Jews. But an hour cometh, and now is, when the true worshippers shall worship the Father in spirit and truth: and the Father also seeketh such as these worshippers. For God is a Spirit: and they that worship him must worship him in spirit and in truth. That woman said unto him, I know that the Messiah cometh: and when he is come, he will teach us everything. Jesus said unto her, I that speak unto thee am he.

31 And while he was speaking, his disciples came; and they wondered how he would speak with a woman; but not one of them said unto him, What seekest thou? or, What speakest thou with her? And the woman left her waterpot, and went to the city, and said to the people, Come, and see a man who told me all that ever I did: 34 perhaps then he is the Messiah. And people went out from the city, and came to him. And in the mean while his disciples besought him, and said unto him, Our 36, master, eat. And he said unto them, I have food to eat that ye know not. And the disciples said amongst themselves, Can any one have brought him aught to eat?

Jesus said unto them, My food is to do the will of him that sent me, and to accomplish his work. Said ye not that after four months cometh the harvest? behold, I therefore say unto you, Lift up your eyes, and behold the lands, that they have become white, and the harvest is already come. And he that reapeth receiveth his wages, and gathereth the fruit of eternal life; and the sower and the reaper rejoice together. For in this is found the word of truth, One soweth, and another reapeth. And I sent you to reap that in which ye have not laboured: others laboured, and ye have entered on their labour.

43 And from that city many of the Samaritans believed in him because of the words of that woman, who testified and said, He told me all that ever I did. And when those

Samaritans came unto him, they besought him to abide with them; and he 45, abode with them two days. And many believed in him because of his word; and they said to that woman, Now not because of thy saying have we believed in him: we have heard and known that this truly is the Messiah, the Saviour of the world.

47, And after two days Jesus went out thence and departed to Galilee. And Jesus testified that a prophet is not honoured in his own city.And when he came to Galilee, the Galilaeans received him.

SECTION XXII.

22 1 And when Jesus came to a certain village, there drew near to him a leper, and fell at his feet, and besought him, and said unto him, If thou wilt, thou art able to cleanse me. And Jesus had mercy upon him, and stretched forth his hand, and touched him, and said, I will cleanse thee. And immediately his leprosy departed from him, and he was cleansed. And he sternly charged him, and sent him out, Arabic, and said unto him, See that thou tell not any man: but go and shew thyself to the priests, and offer an offering for thy cleansing as Moses com- 6 manded for their testimony. But he, when he went out, began to publish much, and spread abroad the news, so that Jesus could not enter into any of the cities openly, for the extent to which the report of him spread, but he remained without in a des- 7 ert place. And much people came unto him from one place and another, to hear 8 his word, and that they might be healed of their pains. And he used to withdraw from them into the desert, and pray.

9 And after that, was the feast of the Jews; and Jesus went up to Jerusalem. And there was in Jerusalem a place prepared for bathing, which was called in Hebrew the House of Mercy, having five porches. And there were laid in them much people of the sick, and blind, and lame, and paralysed, waiting for the moving of the water. And the angel from time to time went down into the place of bathing, and moved the water; and the first that went down after the moving of the water, every pain that he had was healed. And a man was there who had a disease for thirty-eight years. And Jesus saw this man laid, and knew that he had been thus a long time; and he said unto him, Wouldest thou be made whole? That diseased one answered and said, Yea, my Lord, I have no man, when the water moveth, to put me into the bathing-place; but when I come, another goeth down before 16, me. Jesus said unto him, Rise, take thy bed, and walk. And immediately that man was healed; and he rose, and carried his bed, and walked.

18 And that day was a sabbath. And when the Jews saw that healed one, they said unto him, It is a sabbath: thou hast no authority to carry thy bed. And he answered and said unto them, He that made me whole, the same said unto me, Take thy bed, Arabic, and walk. They asked him therefore, Who is this man that said unto thee, p. 86 Take thy bed, and walk? But he that was healed knew not who it was; for Jesus had removed from that place to another, because of the press of the great mul- titude which was in that place. And after two days Jesus happened upon him in the temple, and said unto him, Behold, thou art whole: sin not again, lest there come upon thee what is worse than the first. And that man went, and said to the Jews that it was

Jesus that had healed him. And because of that the Jews persecuted Jesus and sought to kill him, because he was doing this on the sabbath. And Jesus said unto them, My Father worketh until now, and I also work. And because of this especially the Jews sought to kill him, not because he profaned the sabbath only; but for his saying also that God was his Father, and his making himself equal with God. Jesus answered and said unto them, Verily, verily, I say unto you, The Son cannot do anything of himself, but what he seeth the Father do; what the Father doeth, that the Son also doeth like him. The Father loveth his Son, and everything that he doeth he sheweth him: and more than these works will he shew him, that ye may marvel. And as the Father raiseth the dead and giveth them life, so the Son also giveth life to whomsoever he will. And the Father judgeth no man, but hath given all judgement unto the Son; that every man may honour the Son, as he honoureth the Father. And he that honoureth not the Son honoureth not the Father which sent him. Verily, verily, I say unto you, Whosoever heareth my word, and believeth in him that sent me, hath eternal. life, and cometh not into judgement, but passeth from Arabic. death unto life. Verily, verily, I say unto you, An hour shall come, and now is also, when the dead shall hear the voice of the Son of God; and those which hear shall live. And as the Father hath life in himself, likewise he gave to the Son also that he might have life in himself, and authority to do judgement also, because he is the Son of man. Marvel not then at that: I mean the coming of the hour when all that are in the tombs shall hear his voice, and shall come forth: those that have done good, to the resurrection of life; and those that have done evil deeds, to the resurrection of judgement.

38 I am not able of myself to do anything; but as I hear, I judge: and my judge- ment is just; I seek not my own will, but the will of him that sent me. I bear wit- ness of myself, and so a my witness is not true. It is another that beareth witness of me; and I know that the witness which he beareth of me is true. Ye have sent unto John, and he hath borne witness of the truth. But not from man do I seek witness; but I say that ye may live. That was a lamp which shineth and giveth light: and ye were pleased to glory now in his light. But I have witness greater than that of John: the works which my Father hath given me to accomplish, those works which I do, bear witness of me, that the Father hath sent me. And the Father which sent me, he hath borne witness of me. Ye have neither heard his voice at any time, nor seen his appearance. And his word abideth not in you; because in him whom he hath sent ye do not believe. Search the scriptures, in which ye rejoice that ye have eternal life; and they bear witness of me; and ye do not wish to come to 49. Arabic. me, that ye may have eternal life. I seek not praise of men. But I know you, that the love of God is not in you. I am come in the name of my Father, and ye received me not; but if another come in his own name, that one will 52 ye receive. And how can ye believe, while ye receive praise one from another, and praise from God, the One, ye seek not? Can it be that ye think that I will accuse you before the Father? Ye have one that accuseth you, Moses, in whom ye have rejoiced. If ye believed Moses, ye would believe me also; Moses wrote of me. And if ye believed not his writings, how shall ye believe my words?

SECTION XXIII.

23 1 And Jesus departed thence, and came to the side of the sea of Galilee, and went up into the mountain, and sat there. And there came unto him great multitudes, having with them lame, and blind, and dumb, and maimed, and many others, and they cast them at the feet of Jesus: for they had seen all the signs which he did in Jerusalem, when they were gathered at the feast. And he healed them all. And those multitudes marvelled when they saw dumb men speak, and maimed men healed, and lame men walk, and blind men see; and they praised the God of Israel.

5 And Jesus called his disciples, and said unto them, I have compassion on this multitude, because of their continuing with me three days, having nothing to eat; and to send them away fasting I am not willing, lest they faint in the way, some of them having come from far. His disciples said unto him, Whence have we in the desert bread wherewith to satisfy all this multitude? Jesus said unto them, How 8 many loaves have ye? They said unto him, Seven, and a few small fishes. And he 9 commanded the multitudes to sit down upon the ground; and he took those seven loaves and the fish, and blessed, and brake, and gave to his disciples to set before them; and the disciples set before the multitudes. And they all ate, and were satisfied: and they took that which remained over of the fragments, seven basketfuls. And the people that ate were four thousand men, besides the women and children. And when the multitudes departed, he went up into the boat, and came to the borders of Magada.

13 And the Pharisees and Sadducees came to him, and began to seek a discussion with him. And they asked him to shew them a sign from heaven, tempting him. And Jesus sighed within himself, and said, What sign seeketh this evil and adulterous generation? It seeketh a sign, and it shall not be given a sign, except the sign of Jonah the prophet. Verily I say unto you, This generation shall not be given a sign. And he left them, and went up into the boat, and went away to that side.

17 And his disciples forgot to take with them bread, and there was not with them in the boat, not even one loaf. And Jesus charged them, and said, Take heed, and guard yourselves from the leaven of the Pharisees and Sadducees, and from the leaven of Herod. And they reflected within themselves that they had taken with them no bread. And Jesus knew, and said unto them, Why think ye within yourselves, O ye of little faith, and are anxious, because ye have no bread? until now do ye not per- ceive, neither understand? is your heart yet hard? And have ye eyes, and yet see not? Arabic, and have ye ears, and yet hear not? and do ye not remember when I brake those five loaves for five thousand? and how many baskets full of broken pieces took ye up? They said, Twelve. He said unto them, And the seven also for four thousand: how many baskets full of broken pieces took ye up? They said, Seven. He said unto them, How have ye not understood thaI I spake not to you because of the bread, but that ye should beware of the leaven of the Pharisees and Sadducees? Then they understood that he spake, not that they should beware of the leaven of the bread, but of the doctrine of the Pharisees and Sadducees, which he called leaven.

26 And after that, he came to Bethsaida. And they brought to him a certain blind man, and besought him that he would touch him. And he took the hand of that blind man, and led him out without the village, and spat in his eyes, and laid his hand on him, and asked him, What seest thou? And that blind man looked in- tently, and said unto him, I see men as trees walking. And he placed his hand again on his eyes; and they were restored, and he saw everything clearly. And he sent him to his house, and said, Do not enter even into the village, nor tell any man in the village.

31 And Jesus went forth, and his disciples, to the villages of Caesarea Philippi. And while he was going in the way, and his disciples alone, he asked his disciples, and said, What do men say of me that I am, the Son of man? They said unto him, Some say, John the Baptist; and others, Elijah; and others, Jeremiah, or one of the 34, prophets. He said unto them, And ye, what say ye that I am? Simon Cephas an- Arabic. swered and said, Thou art the Messiah, the Son of the living God. Jesus an- swered and said unto him, Blessed art thou, Simon son of Jonah: flesh and blood hath not revealed it unto thee, but my Father which is in heaven. And I say unto thee also, that thou art Cephas, and on this rock will I build my church; and the gates of Hades shall not prevail against it. To thee will I give the keys of the kingdom of heaven: and whatsoever thou shalt bind on earth shall be bound in heaven; and whatsoever thou shalt loose on earth shall be loosed in heaven. And he sternly charged his disciples, and warned them that they should not tell any man concern- ing him, that he was the Messiah. And henceforth began Jesus to shew to his dis- ciples that he was determined to go to Jerusalem, and suffer much, and be rejected of the elders, and of the chief priests, and of the scribes, and be killed, and on the third day rise. And he was speaking plainly. And Simon Cephas, as one grieved for him, said, Far be thou, my Lord, from that. And he turned, and looked upon his disciples, and rebuked Simon, and said, Get thee behind me, Satan: for thou art a stumblingblock unto me: for thou thinkest not of what pertains to God, but of what pertains to men.

45 And Jesus called the multitudes with his disciples, and said unto them, Whosoever would come after me, let him deny himself, and take his cross every day, and come after me. And whosoever would save his life shall lose it; and whosoever loseth his life for my sake, and for the sake of my gospel, shall save it. What shall a man profit, if he gain all the world, and destroy his own life, or lose it? or what Arabic, will a man give in ransom for his life? Whosoever shall deny me and my sayings in this sinful and adulterous generation, the Son of man also will deny him, when he cometh in the glory of his Father with his holy angels. For the Son of man is about to come in the glory of his Father with his holy angels; and then shall he reward each man according to his works.

SECTION XXIV.

24 1 And he said unto them, Verily I say unto you, There be here now some standing that shall not taste death, until they see the kingdom of God come with strength, and the Son of man who cometh in his kingdom.

2 And after six days Jesus took Simon Cephas, and James, and John his brother, 3 and brought them up into a high

mountain, the three of them only. And while they 4 were praying, Jesus changed, and became after the fashion of another person; and his face shone like the sun, and his raiment was very white like the snow, and as 5 the light of lightning, so that nothing on earth can whiten like it. And there ap- 6 peared unto him Moses and Elijah talking to Jesus. And they thought that the time 7 of his decease which was to be accomplished at Jerusalem was come. And Simon and those that were with him were heavy in the drowsiness of steep; and with effort they roused themselves, and saw his glory, and those two men that were standing with him. 8 Arabic. And when they began to depart from him, Simon said unto Jesus, My 9 Master, it is good for us to be here: and if thou wilt, we will make here three tabernacles; one for thee, and one for Moses, and one for Elijah; not know- ing what he said, because of the fear which took possession of them. And while he was yet saying that, a bright cloud overshadowed them. And when they saw Moses and Elijah that they had entered into that cloud, they feared again. And a voice was heard out of the cloud, saying, This is my beloved Son, whom I have chosen; hear ye therefore him. And when this voice was heard, Jesus was found alone. And the disciples, when they heard the voice, fell on their faces from the fear which took hold of them. And Jesus came and touched them and said, Arise, be not afraid. And they lifted up their eyes, and saw Jesus as he was.

17 And when they went down from the mountain, Jesus charged them, and said unto them, Tell not what ye have seen to any man, until the Son of man rise from among the dead. And they kept the word within themselves, and told no man in those days what they had seen. And they reflected among themselves, What is this word which he spake unto us, I, when I am risen from among the dead? And his disciples asked him, and said, What is that which the scribes say, then, that Elijah must first come? He said unto them, Elijah cometh first to set in order everything, Arabic, and as it was written of the Son of man, that he should suffer many things, and be rejected. But I say unto you, that Elijah is come, and they knew him not, and have done unto him whatsoever they desired, as it was written of him. 23, In like manner the Son of man is to suffer of them. Then understood the disciples that he spake unto them concerning John the Baptist.

25 And on that day whereon they came down from the mountain, there met him a multitude of many people standing with his disciples, and the scribes were discuss- ing with them. And the people, when they saw Jesus, were perplexed, and in the midst of their joy hastened and saluted him. And on that day came certain of the Pharisees, and said unto him, Get thee out, and go hence; for Herod seeketh to kill thee. Jesus said unto them, Go ye and say to this fox, Behold, I am casting out demons, and I heal to- day and to-morrow, and on the third day I am perfected. Nevertheless I must be watchful a to-day and to-morrow, and on the last day I shall depart; for it cannot be that a prophet perish outside of Jerusalem.

30 And after that, there came to him a man from that multitude, and fell upon his knees, and said unto him, I beseech thee, my Lord, look upon my son; he is my only child: and the spirit cometh upon him suddenly. A lunacy hath come upon him, and he meeteth with evils. And when

it cometh upon him, it beateth him about; and he foameth, and gnasheth his teeth, and wasteth; and many times it hath thrown him into the water and into the fire to destroy him, and it hardly leaveth him after Arabic. bruising him. And I brought him near to thy disciples, and they could P. not heal him. Jesus answered and said, O faithless and perverse generation, till when shall I be with you? and till when shall I bear with you? bring thy son hither. And he brought him unto him: and when the spirit saw him, immediately it beat him about; and he fell upon the ground, and was raging and foaming. And Jesus asked his father, How long is the time during which he hath been thus? He said unto him, From his youth until now. But, my Lord, help me wherein thou canst, and have mercy upon me. Jesus said unto him, If thou canst believe! All things are possible to him that believeth. And immediately the father of the child cried out, weeping, and said, I believe, my Lord; help my lack of faith. And when Jesus saw the hastening of the people, and their coming at the sound, he rebuked that unclean spirit, and said to it, Thou dumb spirit that speakest not, I command thee, come out of him, and enter not again into him. And that spirit, devil, cried out much, and bruised him, and came out; and that child fell as one dead, and many thought that he had died. But Jesus took him by his hand, and raised him up, and gave him to his father; and that child was healed from that hour. And the people all marvelled at the greatness of God.

45 And when Jesus entered into the house, his disciples came, and asked him privately, and said unto him, Why were we not able to heal him? Jesus said unto Arabic. them, Because of your unbelief. Verily I say unto you, If ye have faith as a grain of mustard seed, ye shall say to this mountain, Remove hence; and it shall remove; and nothing shall overcome you. But it is impossible to cast out this kind by anything except by fasting and prayer.

48 And when he went forth thence, they passed through Galilee: and he would not that any man should know it. And he taught his disciples, and said unto them, Keep ye these sayings in your ears and your hearts: for the Son of man is to be delivered into the hands of men, and they shall kill him; and when he is killed, he shall rise on the third day. But they knew not the word which he spake unto them, for it was concealed from them, that they should not perceive it; and they feared to ask him about this word. And they were exceeding sorrowful.

SECTION XXV.

25 1 And in that day this thought presented itself to his disciples, and they said, which 2 haply should be the greatest among them. And when they came to Capernaum, and entered into the house, Jesus said unto them, What were ye considering in the 3 way among yourselves? And they were silent because they had considered that matter.

4 And when Simon went forth without, those that received two dirhams for the tribute came to Cephas, and said unto him, Doth your master not give his two 5 dirhams? He said unto them, Yea. And when Cephas entered the house, Jesus anticipated him, and said unto him, What thinkest thou, Simon? the kings of the earth, from whom do they receive custom and tribute? from their sons, or from 6 Arabic. strangers? Simon said unto him, From strangers. Jesus said

unto him, p. Children then are free. Simon said unto him, Yea. Jesus said unto him, 7 Give thou also unto them, like the stranger. But, lest it trouble them, go thou to the sea, and cast a hook; and the first fish that cometh up, open its mouth, and thou shall find a stater: take therefore that, and give for me and thee.

8 And in that hour came the disciples to Jesus, and said unto him, Who, thinkest 9 thou, is greater in the kingdom of heaven? And Jesus knew the thought of their heart, and called a child, and set him in the midst, and took him in his arms, and said unto them, Verily I say unto you, If ye do not return, and become as children, 11 ye shall not enter the kingdom of heaven. Every one that shall receive in my name such as this child hath received me: and whosoever receiveth me receiveth not me, but him that sent me. And he who is little in your company, the same shall be great. But whosoever shall injure one of these little ones that believe in me, it were better for him that a great millstone should be hanged about his neck, and he should be drowned in the depths of the sea.

14 John answered and said, Our Master, we saw one casting out devils in thy name; and we prevented him, because he followed not thee with us. Jesus said unto them, Prevent him not; for no man doeth powers in my name, and can hasten to speak evil 16, of me. Every one who is not in opposition to you is with you. Woe unto the world Arabic. because of trials! but woe unto that man by whose hand the trials come If thy hand or thy foot injure thee, cut it off, and cast it from thee; for it is better for thee to enter into life being halt or maimed, and not that thou shouldest have two hands or two feet, and fall into the hell of fire that burneth for ever; 19, where their worm dieth not, and their fire is not quenched. And if thine eye seduce thee, pluck it out, and cast it from thee; for it is better for thee to enter the kingdom of God with one eye, than that thou shouldest have two eyes, and fall into the 22, fire of Gehenna; where their worm dieth not, and their fire is not quenched. Every one shall be salted with fire, and every sacrifice shall be salted with salt. How good is salt! but if the salt also be tasteless, wherewith shall it be salted? It is fit neither for the land nor for dung, but they cast it out. He that hath ears to hear, let him hear. Have ye salt in yourselves. and be in peace one with another.

27 And he arose from thence, and came to the borders of Judaea beyond Jordan: and there went unto him thither great multitudes, and he healed them; and he taught them also, according to his custom. And the Pharisees came unto him, tempting him, and asking him, Is it lawful for a man to put away his wife? He said, What did Moses command you? They said, Moses made it allowable for us, saying, Who- 31 soever will, let him write a writing of divorcement, and put away his wife. Jesus answered and said unto them, Have ye not read, He that made them from the beginning made them male and female, and said, For this reason shall the man leave his father Arabic, and his mother, and cleave to his wife; and they both shall be one body? So then they are not twain, but one body; the thing, then, which God hath joined together, let no man put asunder. And those Pharisees said unto him, Why did Moses consent that a man should give a writing of divorcement and put her away? Jesus said unto them, Moses because of the hardness of your hearts gave you leave to divorce your wives; but in

the beginning it was not so. I say unto you, Whosoever putteth away his wife without fornication, and marrieth another, hath exposed her to adultery. And his disciples, when he entered the house, asked him again about that. And he said unto them, Every one who putteth away his wife, and marrieth another, hath exposed her to adultery. And any woman that leaveth her husband, and becometh another's, hath committed adultery. And whosoever marrieth her that is divorced hath committed adultery. And his disciples said unto him, If there be between the man and the woman such a case as this, it is not good for a man to marry. He said unto them, Not every man can endure this saying, except him to whom it is given. There are eunuchs which from their mother's womb were born so; and there are eunuchs which through men became eunuchs; and there are eunuchs which made themselves eunuchs for the sake of the kingdom of heaven. He that is able to be content, let him be content.

43 Then they brought to him children, that he should lay his hand upon them, and pray: and his disciples were rebuking those that were bringing them. And Jesus saw, and it was distressing to him; and he said unto them, Suffer the children to Arabic. come unto me, and prevent them not; for those that are like these have the kingdom of God. Verily I say unto you, Whosoever receiveth not the kingdom of God as this child, shall not enter it. And he took them in his arms, and laid his hand upon them, and blessed them.

SECTION XXVI.

26 2 And there came unto him publicans and sinners to hear his word. And the scribes and the Pharisees murmured, and said, This man receiveth sinners, and 3 eateth with them. And Jesus, when he beheld their murmuring, spake unto them 4 this parable: What man of you, having an hundred sheep, if one of them were lost, would not leave the ninety-nine in the wilderness, and go and seek the straying one 5 till he found it? Verily I say unto you, When he findeth it, he will rejoice over it 6 more than over the ninety-nine that went not astray; and bear it on his shoulders, and bring it to his house, and call his friends and neighbours, and say unto them, 7 Rejoice with me, since I have found my straying sheep. So your Father which is in heaven willeth not that one of these little ones that have strayed should perish, 8 and he seeketh for them repentance. I say unto you, Thus there shall be rejoicing in heaven over one sinner that repenteth, more than over ninety-nine righteous persons that do not need repentance.

9 And what woman having ten drachmas would lose one of them, and not light a lamp, and sweep the house, and seek it with care till she found it; and when she found it, call her friends and neighbours, and say unto them, Rejoice with me, as I have found my drachma that was lost? I say unto you, Thus there shall be joy Arabic. before the angels of God over the one sinner that repenteth, more than over the ninety-nine righteous persons that do not need repentance.

12, And Jesus spoke unto them also another parable: A man had two sons: and the younger son said unto him, My father, give me my portion that belongeth to me of thy goods. And he divided between them his property. And after a few days the younger son gathered everything that belonged to him, and went into a far country, and there squandered his property by living prodigally. And when he had exhausted everything he had, there occurred a great dearth in that country. And when he was in want, he went and joined himself to one of the people of a city of that country; and that man sent him into the field to feed the swine. And he used to long to fill his belly with the carob that those swine were eating: and no man gave him. And when he returned unto himself, he said, How many hired servants now in my father's house have bread enough and to spare, while I here perish with hunger! I will arise and go to my father's house, and say unto him, My father, I have sinned in heaven and before thee, and am not worthy now to be called thy son: make me as one of thy hired servants. And he arose, and came to his father. But his father saw him while he was at a distance, and was moved with compassion for him, and ran, and fell on his breast, and kissed him. And his son said unto him, My father, I have sinned in heaven and before thee, and am not worthy to be called thy son. His father said unto his servants, Bring forth a stately robe, and put it on him; and put a ring on his hand, and put on him shoes on his feet: and bring and slay a fatted ox, that we may eat and make merry: for this my son was dead, and is Arabic. alive; and was lost, and is found. And they began to be merry. Now his eider son was in the field; and when he came and drew near to the house, he heard the sound of many singing. And he called one of the lads, and asked him what this was. He said unto him, Thy brother hath arrived; and thy father hath slain a fatted ox, since he hath received him safe and sound. And he was angry, and would not enter; so his father went out, and besought him to enter. And he said to his father, How many years do I serve thee in bondage, and I never transgressed a commandment of thine; and thou hast never given me a kid, that I might make merry with my friends? but this thy son, when he had squandered thy 32 property with harlots, and come, thou hast slain for him a fatted ox. His father said unto him, My son, thou art at all times with me, and everything I have is thine. It behoveth thee to rejoice and make merry, since this thy brother was dead, and is alive; and was lost, and is found.

34 And he spake a parable unto his disciples: There was a rich man, and he had a steward; and he was accused to him that he had squandered his property. So his lord called him, and said unto him, What is this that I hear regarding thee? Give me the account of thy stewardship; for it is now impossible that thou shouldest be a steward for me. The steward said within himself, What shall I do, seeing that my lord taketh from me the stewardship?

To dig I am not able; and to beg I am ashamed. I know what I will do, that, when I go out of the stewardship, they may receive me into their houses. And he called one after another of his lord's 39 debtors, and said to the first, How much owest thou my lord? He said unto him, An hundred portions of oil. He said unto him, Take thy writing, and sit down, and write quickly fifty portions. And he said to the next, And thou, how much owest thou my lord? He said unto him, An hundred cors of wheat. He said unto him, Take Arabic, thy writing, and sit down, and write eighty cors. And our lord com- mended the sinful steward because he had done a wise deed; for the chil- dren of this world are wiser than the children of the light in this their age. And I also say unto you, Make unto yourselves friends with the wealth of this unrighteousness; so that, when it is

exhausted, they may receive you into their tents for ever. He who is faithful in a little is faithful also in much: and he who is unrighteous in a little is unrighteous also in much. If then in the wealth of unrighteousness ye were not trustworthy, who will intrust you with the truth? If ye are not found faithful in what does not belong to you, who will give you what belongeth to you?

SECTION XXVII.

27 Therefore the kingdom of heaven is like a certain king, who would make a reckoning with his servants. And when he began to make it, they brought to him one who owed him ten talents. And because he had not wherewith to pay, his lord ordered that he should be sold, he, and his wife, and children, and all that he 4 had, and payment be made. So that servant fell down and worshipped him, and said unto him, My lord, have patience with me, and I shall pay thee everything. 5 And the lord of that servant had compassion, and released him, and forgave him his 6 debt. And that servant went out, and found one of his fellow-servants, who owed him Arabic. a hundred pence; and he took him, and dealt severely with him, and said 7 unto him, Give me what thou owest. Sothe fellow-servant fell down at his 8 feet, and besought him, and said, Grant me respite, and I will pay thee. And he would not; but took him, and cast him into prison, till he should give him his debt. 9 And when their fellow-servants saw what happened, it distressed them much; and they came and told their lord of all that had taken place. Then his lord called him, and said unto him, Thou wicked servant, all that debt I forgave thee, because thou besoughtest me: was it not then incumbent on thee also to have mercy on thy fellow-servant, as I had mercy on thee? And his lord became wroth, and delivered him to the scourgers, till he should pay all that he owed. So shall my Father which is in heaven do unto you, if one forgive not his brother his wrong conduct from his heart. Take heed within yourselves: if thy brother sin, rebuke him; and if he repent, forgive him. And if he act wrongly towards thee seven times in a day, and on that day return seven times unto thee, and say, I repent towards thee; forgive him. And if thy brother act wrongly towards thee, go and reprove him between thee and him alone: if he hear thee, thou hast gained thy brother. But if he hear thee not, take with thee one or two, and so at the mouth of two or three every saying shall be established. And if he listen not to these also, tell the congregation; and if he listen not even to the congregation, let him be unto thee as a publican and a Gen- tile. Verily I say unto you, All that ye bind on earth shall be bound in heaven: and what ye loose on earth shall be loosed in heaven. I say unto you also, If two of you agree on earth to ask, everything shall be granted them from my Father Arabic, which is in heaven. For where two or three are gathered in my name, there am l amongst them. Then Cephas drew near to him, and said unto him, My Lord, how many times, if my brother act wrongly towards me, should I forgive him? until seven times? Jesus said unto him, I say not unto thee, Until seven; but, Until sev-24 enty times seven, seven. And the servant that knoweth his lord's will, and maketh not ready for him according to his will, shall meet with much punishment; but he that knoweth not, and doeth something for which he meriteth punishment, shall meet with slight punishment. Every one to whom much hath been given, much shall be asked of him; and he that hath had much committed to him, much shall be required at his hand. I came to cast fire upon the

earth; and I would that it had been kindled already. And I have a baptism to be baptized with, and greatly am I straitened till it be accomplished. See that ye despise not one of these little ones that believe in me. Verily I say unto you, Their angels at all times see the face of my Father which is in heaven. The Son of man came to save the thing which was lost.

30 And after that, Jesus walked in Galilee; and he did not like to walk in Judaea, because the Jews sought to kill him. And there came people who told him of the Galilaeans, those whose blood Pilate had mingled with their sacrifices. Jesus answered and said unto them, Do ye imagine that those Galilaeans were sinners more than all the Galilaeans, so that this thing has come upon them? Nay. Verily I say unto you now, that ye shall all also, if ye repent not, likewise perish. Or perchance those eighteen on whom the palace fell in Siloam, and slew them, do ye imagine that they were to be condemned more than all the people that dwell Arabic, in Jerusalem? Nay. Verily I say unto you, If ye do not all repent, ye p. 106 shall perish like them.

36 And he spake unto them this parable: A man had a fig tree planted in his vineyard; and he came and sought fruit thereon, and found none. So he said to the husbandman, Lo, three years do I come and seek fruit on this fig tree, and find none: cut it down; why doth it render the ground unoccupied? The husbandman said unto him, My lord, leave it this year also, that I may dig about it, and dung it; then if it bear fruit--! and if not, then cut it down in the coming year.

40 And when Jesus was teaching on the sabbath day in one of the synagogues, there was there a woman that had a spirit of disease eighteen years; and she was bowed down, and could not straighten herself at all. And Jesus saw her, and called her, and said unto her, Woman, be loosed from thy disease. And he put his hand upon her; and immediately she was straightened, and praised God. And the chief of the synagogue answered with anger, because Jesus had healed on a sabbath, and said unto the multitudes, There are six days in which work ought to be done; come in them and be healed, and not on the sabbath day. But Jesus answered and said unto him, Ye hypocrites, doth not each of you on the sabbath day loose his ox or his ass from the manger, and go and water it? Ought not this woman, who is a daughter of Abraham, and whom the devil hath bound eighteen years, to be loosed from this bond on the sabbath day? And when he said this, they were all put to shame, those standing, who were opposing him: and all the people were pleased with all the wonders that proceeded from his hand.

SECTION XXVIII.

28 2 Arabic. And at that time the feast of tabernacles of the Jews drew near. So the brethren of Jesus said unto him, Remove now hence, and go to Judaea, that 3 thy disciples may see the deeds that thou doest. For no man doeth a thing secretly 4 and wisheth to be apparent. If thou doest this, shew thyself to the world. For 5 up to this time not even the brethren of Jesus believed on him. Jesus said unto them, My time till now has not arrived; but as for you, your time is alway ready. 6 It is not possible for the world to hate you; but me it hateth, for I bear witness 7 against it, that its

deeds are evil. As for you, go ye up unto this feast: but I go 8 not up now to this feast; for my time has not yet been completed. He said this, and remained behind in Galilee.

9 But when his brethren went up unto the feast, he journeyed from Galilee, and to came to the borders of Judaea, to the country beyond Jordan; and there came after him great multitudes, and he healed them all there. And he went out, and proceeded to the feast, not openly, but as one that conceals himself. And the Jews sought him at the feast, and said, In what place is this man? And there occurred much murmuring there in the great multitude that came to the feast, on his account. For some said, He is good: and others said, Nay, but he leadeth the people astray. But no man spake of him openly for fear of the Jews.

15 Arabic. But when the days of the feast of tabernacles were half over, Jesus went up to the temple, and taught. And the Jews wondered, and said, How doth this man know writing, seeing he hath not learned? Jesus answered and said, My doc- trine is not mine, but his that sent me.

Whoever wisheth to do his will understandeth my doctrine? whether it be from God, or whether I speak of mine own accord. Whosoever speaketh of his own accord seeketh praise for himself; but whosoever seeketh praise for him that sent him, he is true, and unrighteousness in his heart there is none. Did not Moses give you the law, and no man of you keepeth the law? Why seek ye to kill me? The multitude answered and said unto him, Thou hast demons: who seeketh to kill thee? Jesus answered and said unto them, I did one deed, and ye all marvel because of this. Moses hath given you circumcision (not because it is from Moses, but it is from the fathers); and ye on the sabbath circumcise a man. And if a man is circumcised on the sabbath day, that the law of Moses may not be broken; are ye angry at me, because I healed on the sabbath day the whole man? Judge not with hypocrisy, but judge righteous judgement.

26 And some people from Jerusalem said, Is not this he whom they seek to slay? And lo, he discourseth with them openly, and they say nothing unto him. Think you that our elders have learned that this is the Messiah indeed? But this man is known whence he is; and the Messiah, when he cometh, no man knoweth whence he is. So Jesus lifted up his voice as he taught in the temple, and said, Ye both know me, and know whence I am; and of my own accord am I not come, but he Arabic. that sent me is true, he whom ye know not: but I know him; for I am from him, and he sent me. And they sought to seize him: and no man laid a hand on him, because his hour had not yet come. But many of the multitude believed on him; and they said, The Messiah, when he cometh, can it be that he will do more than these signs that this man doeth?

33 And a man of that multitude said unto our Lord, Teacher, say to my brother that he divide with me the inheritance. Jesus said unto him, Man, who is it that appointed me over you as a judge and divider? And he said unto his disciples, Take heed within yourselves of all inordinate desire; for it is not in abundance of 36 possessions that life shall be. And he gave them this parable: The ground of a rich man brought forth abundant

produce: and he pondered within himself, and said, What shall I do, since I have no place to store my produce? And he said, I will do this: I will pull down the buildings of my barns, and build them, and make them greater; and store there all my wheat and my goods. And I will say to my soul, Soul, thou hast much goods laid by for many years; take thine ease, eat, drink, enjoy thyself. God said unto him, O than of little intelligence, this night shall thy soul be taken from thee; and this that thou hast prepared, whose shall it be? So is he that layeth up treasures for himself, and is not rich in God.

42 And while Jesus was going in the way, there came near to him a young man of the rulers, and fell on his knees, and asked him, and said, Good Teacher, what is it that I must do that I may have eternal life? Jesus said unto him, Why callest thou me good, while there is none good but the one, even God? Thou knowest the com- mandments. If thou wouldest enter into life, keep the commandments. The young Arabic. man said unto him, Which of the commandments? Jesus said unto him, Thou shalt not commit adultery, Thou shalt not steal, Thou shalt not kill, Thou shalt not bear false witness, Thou shall not do injury, Honour thy father and thy mother: and, Love thy neighbour as thyself. That young man said unto him, All these have I kept from my youth: what then is it that I lack? And Jesus looked intently at him, and loved him, and said unto him, If thou wouldest be perfect, what thou lackest is one thing: go away and sell everything that thou hast, and give to the poor, and thou shalt have treasure in heaven: and take thy cross, and follow me. And that young man frowned at this word, and went away feeling sad; for he was very rich. And when Jesus saw his sadness, he looked towards his disciples, and said unto them, How hard it is for them that have possessions to enter the kingdom of God!

SECTION XXIX.

29 1 Verily I say unto you, It is difficult for a rich man to enter the kingdom of 2 heaven. And I say unto you also, that it is easier for a camel to enter the eye of 3 a needle, than for a rich man to enter the kingdom of God. And the disciples were wondering at these sayings. And Jesus answered and said unto them again, My children, how hard it is for those that rely on their possessions to enter the 4 kingdom of God! And those that were listening wondered more, and said amongst 5 themselves, being agitated, Who, thinkest thou, can be saved? And Jesus looked at them intently, and said unto them, With men this is not possible, but with God it is. 6 Arabic, it is possible for God to do everything. Simon Cephas said unto him, Lo, we have left everything, and followed thee; what is it, thinkest thou, that we 7 shall have? Jesus said unto them, Verily I say unto you, Ye that have followed me, in the new world, when the Son of man shall sit on the throne of his glory, ye also 8 shall sit on twelve thrones, and shall judge the twelve tribes of Israel. Verily I say unto you, No man leaveth houses, or brothers, or sisters, or father, or mother, or wife, or children, or kinsfolk, or lands, because of the kingdom of God, or for my 9 sake, and the sake of my gospel, who shall not obtain many times as much in this time, and in the world to come inherit eternal life: and now in this time, houses, and brothers, and sisters, and mothers, and children, and lands, with persecution; 11 and in the world to come everlasting life. Many that are first shall be last, and that are last shall be first.

12 And when the Pharisees heard all this, because of their love for wealth they scoffed at him. And Jesus knew what was in their hearts, and said unto them, Ye are they that justify yourselves before men; while God knows your hearts: the thing that is lofty with men is base before God.

14 And he began to say, A certain man was rich, and wore silk and purple, and en- joyed himself every day in splendour: and there was a poor man named Lazarus, and he was cast down at the door of the rich man, afflicted with sores, and he longed to fill Arabic, his belly with the crumbs that fell from the table of that rich man; yea, even the dogs used to come and lick his sores. And it happened that that poor man died, and the angels conveyed him into the bosom of Abraham: and the rich man also died, and was buried. And while he was being tormented in Hades, he lifted up his eyes from afar, and saw Abraham with Lazarus in his bosom. And he called with a loud voice, and said, My father Abraham, have mercy upon me, and send Lazarus to wet the tip of his finger with water, and moisten my tongue for me; for, behold, I am burned in this flame. Abraham said unto him, My son, remember that thou receivedst thy good things in thy life, and Lazarus his afflictions: but now, behold, he is at rest here, and thou art tormented. And in addition to all this, there is between us and you a great abyss placed, so that they that would cross unto you from hence cannot, nor yet from thence do they cross unto us. He said unto him, Then I beseech thee, my father, to send him to my father's house; for I have five brethren; let him go, that they also sin not, and come to the abode of this torment. Abraham said unto him, They have Moses and the prophets; let them hear them. He said unto him, Nay, my father Abraham: but let a man from the dead go unto them, and they will repent. Abraham said unto him, If they listen neither to Moses nor to the prophets, neither if a man from the dead rose would they believe him.

27 The kingdom of heaven is like a man that is a householder, which went out early in the morning to hire labourers for his vineyard. And he agreed with the labourers on one penny a day for each labourer, and he sent them into his vineyard. And he went Arabic, out in three hours, and saw others standing in the market idle. He said unto them, Go ye also into my vineyard, and what is right I will pay you. And they went. And he went out also at the sixth and the ninth hour, and did like- wise, and sent them. And about the eleventh hour he went out, and found others standing idle. He said unto them, Why are ye standing the whole day idle? They said unto him, Because no one hath hired us. He said unto them, Go ye also into the vineyard, and what is right ye shall receive. So when evening came, the lord of the vineyard said unto his steward, Call the labourers, and pay them their wages; and begin with the later ones, and end with the former ones. And those of eleven hours came, and received each a penny. When therefore the first came, they supposed that they should receive something more; and they also received each a penny. And when they received it, they spake angrily against the householder, and said, These last worked one hour, and thou hast made them equal with us, who have suffered the heat of the day, and its burden. He answered and said unto one of them, My friend, I do thee no wrong:

was it not for a penny that thou didst bargain with me? Take what is thine, and go thy way; for I wish to give this last as I have given thee. Or am I not entitled to do with what is mine what I choose? Or is thine eye perchance evil, because I am good? Thus shall the last ones be first, and the first last. The called are many, and the chosen are few.

43 And when Jesus entered into the house of one of the chiefs of the Pharisees to eat bread on the sabbath day, and they were watching him to see what he would 44,45 do, and there was before him a man which had the dropsy, Jesus answered and said unto the scribes and the Pharisees, Is it lawful on the sabbath to heal? But Arabic, they were silent. So he took him, and healed him, and sent him away. And he said unto them, Which of you shall have his son or his ox fall on the sabbath day into a well, and not lift him up straightway, and draw water for him? And they were not able to answer him a word to that.

SECTION XXX.

30 1 And he spake a parable unto those which were bidden there, because he saw 2 them choose the places that were in the highest part of the sitting room: When a man invites thee to a feast, do not go and sit at the head of the room; lest there 3 be there a man more honourable than thou, and he that invited you come and say unto thee, Give the place to this man: and thou be ashamed when thou risest and 4 takest another place. But when thou art invited, go and sit last; so that when he that invited thee cometh, he may say unto thee, My friend, go up higher: and 5 thou shalt have praise before all that were invited with thee. For every one that exalteth himself shall be abased; and every one that abaseth himself shall be exalted.

6 And he said also to him that had invited him, When thou makest a feast a or a banquet, do not invite thy friends, nor even thy brethren, nor thy kinsmen, nor thy 7 rich neighbours; lest haply they also invite thee, and thou have this reward. But when thou makest a feast, invite the poor, and those with withered hand, and the 8 lame, and the blind: and blessed art thou, since they have not the means to reward 9 thee; that thy reward may be at the rising of the righteous. And when one of them that were invited heard that, he said unto him, Blessed is he that shall eat bread in the kingdom of God.

10, Jesus answered again in parables, and said, The kingdom of heaven hath been lik- Arabic, ened to a certain king, which made a feast for his son, and prepared a great banquet, and invited many: and he sent his servants at the time of the feast to inform them that were invited, Everything is made ready for you; come. And they would not come, but began all of them with one voice to make excuse. And the first said unto them, Say to him, I have bought a field, and I must needs go out to see it: I pray thee to release me, for I ask to be excused. And another said, I have bought five yoke of oxen, and I am going to examine them: I pray thee to release me, for I ask to be excused. And another said, I have married a wife, and therefore I cannot come. And the king sent also other servants, and said, Say to those that were invited, that my feast is ready, and my oxen and my fatlings are slain, and everything is ready: come to the feast. But they made light of it, and went, one to his field, and another to his merchandise: and

the rest took his servants, and entreated them shamefully, and killed them. And one of the servants came, and informed his lord of what had happened. And when the king heard, he became angry, and sent his armies; and they destroyed those murderers, and burned their cities. Then he said to his servants, The feast is prepared, but those that were invited were not worthy. Go out quickly into the markets and into the partings of the ways of the city, and bring in hither the poor, and those with pains, and the lame, and the blind. And the servants did as the king commanded them. And they came, and said unto him, Our lord, we have done all that thou com- mandedst us, and there is here still room. So the lord said unto his servants, Go out into the roads, and the ways, and the paths, and every one that ye find, invite Arabic, to the feast, and constrain them to enter, till my house is filled. I say unto you, that no one of those people that were invited shall taste of my feast. And those servants went out into the roads, and gathered all that they found, good and bad: and the banquet-house was filled with guests. And the king entered to see those who were seated, and he saw there a man not wearing a festive garment: and he said unto him, My friend, how didst thou come in here not having on festive gar- ments? And he was silent. Then the king said to the servants, Bind his hands and his feet, and put him forth into the outer darkness; there shall be weeping and gnashing of teeth. The called are many; and the chosen, few.

31 And after that, the time of the feast of unleavened bread of the Jews arrived, and Jesus went out to go to Jerusalem. And as he went in the way, there met him ten persons who were lepers, and stood afar off: and they lifted up their voice, and said, Our Master, Jesus, have mercy upon us. And when he saw them, he said unto them, Go and shew yourselves unto the priests. And when they went, they were cleansed. And one of them, when he saw himself cleansed, returned, and was praising God with a loud voice; and he fell on his face before the feet of Jesus, giving him thanks: and this man was a Samaritan. Jesus answered and said, Were not those that were cleansed ten? where then are the nine? Not one of them turned aside to come and praise God, but this man who is of a strange people. He said unto him, Arise, and go thy way; for thy faith hath given thee life.

40 And while they were going up in the way to Jerusalem, Jesus went in front of them; and they wondered, and followed him fearing. And he took his twelve disciples apart, and began to tell them privately what was about to befall him. And he said unto Arabic, them, We are going up to Jerusalem, and all the things shall be fulfilled that are written in the prophets concerning the Son of man. He shall be delivered to the chief priests and the scribes; and they shall condemn him to death, and deliver him to the peoples; and they shall treat him shamefully, and scourge him, and spit in his face, and humble him, and crucify him, and slay him: and on the third day he shall rise. But they understood not one thing of this; but this word was hidden from them, and they did not perceive these things that were addressed to them.

46 Then came near to him the mother of the (two) sons of Zebedee, she and her (two) sons, and worshipped him, and asked of him a certain thing. And he said unto her, What

wouldest thou? And James and John, her two sons, came forward, and said unto him, Teacher, we would that all that we ask thou wouldest do unto us. He said unto them, What would ye that I should do unto you? They said unto him, Grant us that we may sit, the one on thy right, and the other So on thy left, in thy kingdom and thy glory. And Jesus said unto them, Ye know not what ye ask. Are ye able to drink the cup that I am to drink? and with the baptism that I am to be baptized with, will ye be baptized? And they said unto him, We are able. Jesus said unto them, The cup that I drink ye shall drink; and with the baptism wherewith I am baptized ye shall be baptized: but that ye should sit on my right and on my left is not mine to give; but it is for him for whom my Father hath prepared it.

SECTION XXXI.

31 1 And when the ten heard, they were moved with anger against James and John. 2 And Jesus called them, and said unto them, Ye know that the rulers of the nations are their lords; and their great men are set in authority over them. Not thus shall it Arabic, be amongst you: but he amongst you that would be great, let him be to you a 4 servant; and whoever of you would be first, let him be to every man a 5 bond-servant: even as the Son of man also came not to be served, but to serve, and 6 to give himself a ransom in place of the many. He said this, and was going about 7 the villages and the cities, and teaching; and he went to Jerusalem. And a man asked him, Are those that shall be saved few? Jesus answered and said unto 8 them, Strive ye to enter at the narrow door: I say unto you now, that many shall 9 seek to enter, and shall not be able --from the time when the master of the house riseth, and closeth the door, and ye shall be standing without, and shall knock at the door, and shall begin to say, Our lord, open unto us; and he shall answer and say, I say unto you, I know you not whence ye are: and ye shall begin to say,

Before thee we did eat and drink, and in our markets didst thou teach; and he shall say unto you, I know you not whence ye are; depart from me, ye servants of untruth. There shall be weeping and gnashing of teeth, when ye see Abraham, and Isaac, and Jacob, and all the prophets, in the kingdom of God, while ye are put forth without. And they shall come from the east and the west, and from the north and the south, and shah sit down in the kingdom of God. And there shall then be last that have become first, and first that have become last.

15, And when Jesus entered and passed through Jericho, there was a man named Zac- chaeus, rich, and chief of the publicans. And he desired to see Jesus who he was; and he was not able for the pressure of the crowd, because Zacchaeus was little of stature. Arabic, And he hastened, and went before Jesus, and went up into an unripe fig tree to see Jesus: for he was to pass thus. And when Jesus came to that place, he saw him, and said unto him, Make haste, and come down, Zacchaeus: to-day I must be in thy house. And he hastened, and came down, and received him joyfully. And when they all saw, they murmured, and said, He hath gone in and lodged with a man that is a sinner. So Zacchaeus stood, and said unto Jesus, My Lord, now half of my possessions I give to the poor, and what I have unjustly taken from every man I give him fourfold. Jesus said unto him, To-day is salva- tion come to this house,

because this man also is a son of Abraham. For the Son of man came to seek and save the thing that was lost.

25 And when Jesus went out of Jericho, he and his disciples, there came after him a great multitude. And there was a blind man sitting by the way side begging. And his name was Timaeus, the son of Timaeus. And he heard the sound of the multitude passing, and asked, Who is this? They said unto him, Jesus the Naza- rene passeth by. And when he heard that it was Jesus, he called out with a loud voice, and said, Jesus, son of David, have mercy on me. And those that went before Jesus were rebuking him, that he should hold his peace: but he cried the more, and said, Son of David, have mercy on me. And Jesus stood, and commanded that they should call him. And they called the blind man, and said unto him, Be of good courage, and rise; for, behold, he calleth thee. And the blind 33 man threw away his garment, and rose, and came to Jesus. Jesus said unto him, What dost thou wish that I should do unto thee? And that blind man said unto him, My Lord and Master, that my eyes may be opened, so that I may see thee. Arabic, And Jesus had compassion on him, and touched his eyes, and said unto him, See; for thy faith hath saved thee. And immediately he received his sight, and came after him, and praised God; and all the people that saw praised God.

36 And he spake a parable because he was nearing Jerusalem, and they supposed that at that time the kingdom of God was about to appear. He said unto them, A man, a son of a great race, went into a far country, to receive a kingdom, and return. And he called his ten servants, and gave them ten shares, and said unto them, Trade till the time of my coming. But the people of his city hated him, and sent messengers after him, and said, We will not that this man reign over us. And when he had received a kingdom, and returned, he said that the servants to whom he had given the money should be called unto him, that he might know what each of them had traded. And the first came, and said, My lord, thy share hath gained ten shares. The king said unto him, Thou good and faithful servant, who hast been found faithful in a little, be thou set over ten districts. And the second came, and said, My lord, thy portion hath gained five portions. And he said unto him also, And thou shall be set over five districts. And another came, and said, My lord, here is thy portion, which was with me laid by in a napkin: I feared thee, because thou art a hard man, and takest what thou didst not leave, and seekest what thou didst not give, and reapest what thou didst not sow. His lord said unto him, From thy mouth shall I judge thee, thou wicked and idle servant, who wast untrustworthy. Thou knewest that I am a hard man, and take what I did not leave, and reap what I did not sow: why didst thou not put my money at usury, and so I might come and seek it, with its gains? And he said unto those that were standing in front of him, Take from him the share, and give it to him that hath 50, Arabic, ten shares. They said unto him, Our lord, he hath ten shares. He said unto them, I say unto you, Every one that hath shall be given unto; and he that hath not, that which he hath also shall be taken from him. And those mine enemies who would not that I should reign over them, bring them, and slay them before me.

SECTION XXXII.

32 1 And when Jesus entered Jerusalem, he went up to the temple of God, and found 2 there oxen and sheep and doves. And when he beheld those that sold and those that bought, and the money-changers sitting, he made for himself a scourge of rope, and drove them all out of the temple, and the sheep and the oxen, and the money-changers; and he threw down their money, and upset their tables, and the seats of them that sold the doves; and he was teaching, and saying unto them, Is it not written, My house is a house of prayer for all peoples? and ye have made it a den for robbers. And he said unto those that sold the doves, Take this hence, and make not my Father's house a house of merchandise. And he suffered not any one to carry vessels inside the temple.

And his disciples remembered the scripture, The zeal of thy house hath eaten me up. The Jews answered and said unto him, What sign hast thou shewn us, that thou doest this? Jesus answered and said unto them, Destroy this temple, and I shall raise it in three days. The Jews said unto him, This temple was built in forty-six years, and wilt thou raise it in three days? 10 But he spake unto them of the temple of his body, that when they destroyed it, he Arabic, would raise it in three days. When therefore he rose from among the dead, his disciples remembered that he said this; and they believed the scriptures, and the word that Jesus spake.

12 And when Jesus sat down over against the treasury, he observed how the multitudes were casting their offerings into the treasury: and many rich men were 13, throwing in much. And there came a poor widow, and cast in two mites. And Jesus called his disciples, and said unto them, Verily I say unto you, This poor widow cast into the treasury more than all the people: and all of these cast into the place of the offering of God of the superfluity of their wealth; while this woman of her want threw in all that she possessed. And he spake unto them this parable, concerning people who trusted in them- selves that they are righteous, and despised every man: Two men went up to the temple to pray; one of them a Pharisee, and the other a publican. And the Pharisee stood apart, and prayed thus, O Lord, I thank thee, since I am not like the rest of men, the unjust, the profligate, the extortioners, or even like this publican; but I fast two days a week, and tithe all my possessions. And the publican was standing at a distance, and he would not even lift up his eyes to heaven, but was beating upon his breast, and saying, O Lord, have mercy on me, me the sinner. I say unto you, that this man went down justified to his house more than the Pharisee. Every one that exalteth himself shall be abased; and every one that abaseth himself shall be exalted.

22 Arabic, And when eventide was come, he left all the people, and went outside the city to Bethany, he and his twelve, and he remained there. And all the people, because they knew the place, came to him, and he received them; and them that had need of healing he healed. And on the morning of the next day, when he returned to the city from Bethany, he hungered. And he saw a fig tree at a distance on the beaten highway, having on it leaves. And he came unto it, expecting to find something on it; and when he came, he found nothing on it but the leaves--it was not the season of figs--and he said unto it, Henceforward for ever let no man eat fruit of thee. And his disciples heard.

27 And they came to Jerusalem. And there was there a man of the Pharisees, named Nicodemus, ruler of the Jews. This man came unto Jesus by night, and said unto him, My Master, we know that thou hast been sent from God as a teacher; and no man can do these signs that thou doest, except him whom God is with. Jesus answered and said unto him, Verily, verily, I say unto thee, If a man be not born a second time, he cannot see the kingdom of God. Nicodemus said unto him, How can a man who is old be born? can he, think you, return again to his mother's womb a second time, to enter and be born? Jesus answered and said unto him, Verily, verily, I say unto thee, If a man be not born of water and the Spirit, he cannot enter the kingdom of God. For he that is born of flesh is flesh; and he that 33 is born of Spirit is spirit.

Wonder not that I said unto thee that ye must be born a Arabic, second time. The wind bloweth where it listeth, and thou hearest its voice, but thou knowest not from what place it cometh, nor whither it goeth: so is every man that is born of the Spirit. Nicodemus answered and said unto him, How can that be? Jesus answered and said unto him, Art thou teaching Israel, and yet knowest not these things? Verily, verily, I say unto thee, What we know we say, and what we have seen we witness: and ye receive not our witness. If I said unto you what is on earth, and ye believed not, how then, if I say unto you what is in heaven, will ye believe? And no man hath ascended up into heaven, except him that descended from heaven, the Son of man, which is in heaven. And as Moses lifted up the serpent in the wilderness, so is the Son of man to be lifted up; so that every man who may believe in him may not perish, but have eternal life. God so loved the world, that he should give his only Son; and so every one that believeth on him should not perish, but should have eternal life. God sent not his Son into the world to judge the world; but that the world might be saved by his hand. He that believeth in him shall not be judged: but he that believeth not is condemned beforehand, because he hath not believed in the name of the only Son, the Son of God. This is the judgement, that the light came into the world, and men loved the darkness more than the light; because their deeds were evil. Whosoever doeth evil deeds hateth the light, and cometh not to the 47 light, lest his deeds be reproved. But he that doeth the truth cometh to the light, that his deeds may be known, that they have been done in God.

xxxxxx

that fig tree which thou didst curse hath dried up. And Jesus answered and said 6 unto them, Let there be in you the faith of God. Verily I say unto you, if ye believe, and doubt not in your hearts, and assure yourselves that that will be which 7 ye say, ye shall have what ye say. And if ye say to this mountain, Remove, and 8 fall into the sea, it shall be. And all that ye ask God in prayer, and believe, he will give you. And the apostles said unto our Lord, Increase our faith. He said unto them, If there be in you faith like a grain of mustard, ye shall say to this fig tree, Be thou torn up, and be thou planted in the sea; and it will obey you. Who of you hath a servant driving a yoke of oxen or tending sheep, and if he come from the field, will say unto him straightway, Go and sit down? Nay, he will say unto him, Make ready for me wherewith I may sup, and gird thy waist, and serve me, till I eat and drink; and afterwards thou shalt eat and drink also. Doth that servant haply, who did what he was bid, receive his praise? I think not. So ye also, when ye have done all that ye were bid, say, We are idle servants; what it was our duty to do, we have done.

15 For this reason I say unto you, Whatever ye pray and ask, believe that ye Arabic, receive, and ye shall have. And when ye stand to pray, forgive what is in your heart against any man; and your Father which is in heaven will forgive you also your wrong-doings. But if ye forgive not men their wrong-doings, neither will your Father forgive you also your wrong-doings.

18 And he spake unto them a parable also, that they should pray at all times, and not be slothful: There was a judge in a city, who feared not God, nor was ashamed for men: and there was a widow in that city; and she came unto him, and said, Avenge me of mine adversary. And he would not for a long time: but afterwards he said within himself, If of God I have no fear, and before men I have no shame; yet because this widow vexeth me, I will avenge her, that she come not at all times 23, and annoy me. And our Lord said, Hear ye what the judge of injustice said. And shall not God still more do vengeance for his elect, who call upon him in the night and in the day, and grant them respite? I say unto you, He will do vengeance for them speedily. Thinkest thou the Son of man will come and find faith on the earth?

26, And they came again to Jerusalem. And it came to pass, on one of the days, as Jesus was walking in the temple, and teaching the people, and preaching the gospel, that the chief priests and the scribes with the elders came upon him, and said unto him, Tell us: By what power doest thou this? and who gave thee this power to do that? And Jesus said unto them, I also will ask you one word, and if ye tell me, I also shall tell you by what power I do that. The baptism of John, from what place is it? from heaven or of men? Tell me. And they reflected within them- Arabic, selves, and said, If we shall say unto him, From heaven; he will say unto p. 127 us, For what reason did ye not believe him? But if we shall say, Of men; we fear that the people will stone us, all of them. And all of them were holding to John, that he was a true prophet. They answered and said unto him, We know not. Jesus said unto them, Neither tell I you also by what power I work. What think ye? A man had two sons; and he went to the first, and said unto him, My son, go to-day, and till in the vineyard. And he answered and said, I do not wish to: but finally he repented, and went. And he went to the other, and said unto him likewise. And he answered and said, Yea, my lord: and went not. Which of these two did the will of his father? They said unto him, The first. Jesus said unto them, Verily I say unto you, The publicans and harlots go before you into the kingdom of God. John came unto you in the way of righteousness, and ye believed him not; but the publicans and harlots believed him; and ye, not even when ye saw, did ye repent at last, that ye might believe in him.

40 Hear another parable: A man was a householder, and planted a vineyard, and surrounded it with a hedge, and digged in it a winepress, and built in it a tower, 41, and gave it to husbandmen, and went to a distance for a long time.

So when the time of the fruits came, he sent his servants unto the husbandmen, that they might send him of the produce of his vineyard. And those husbandmen beat him, and sent him away empty. And he sent unto them another servant also; and they stoned him, and wounded him, and sent him away with shameful handling. And he sent again another; and they slew him. And he sent many other servants unto them. And the husbandmen took his servants, and one they beat, and another they stoned, and another they slew. So he sent again other servants more than the first; and Arabic, they did likewise with them. So the owner of the vineyard said, What shall I do? I will send my beloved son: it may be they will see him and be 49, ashamed. So at last he sent unto them his beloved son that he had. But the husbandmen, when they saw the son, said amongst themselves, This is the heir. 51, And they said, We will slay him, and so the inheritance will be ours. So they took him, and put him forth without the vineyard, and slew him. When then the lord of the vineyard shall come, what will he do with those husbandmen? They said unto him, He will destroy them in the worst of ways, and give the vineyard to other husbandmen, who will give him fruit in its season. Jesus said unto them, Have ye never read in the scripture, The stone which the builders declared to be base, The same came to be at the head of the corner:

56 From God was this, And it is wonderful in our eyes?

57 Therefore I say unto you, The kingdom of God shall be taken from you, and given to a people that will produce fruit. And whosoever falleth on this stone shall be broken in pieces: but on whomsoever it falleth, it will grind him to powder. And when the chief priests and the Pharisees heard his parables, they perceived that it was concerning them he spake. And they sought to seize him; and they feared the multitude, because they were holding to him as the prophet.

SECTION XXXIV.

34 1 Then went the Pharisees and considered how they might ensnare him in a word, 2 and deliver him into the power of the judge, and into the power of the ruler. And they sent unto him their disciples, with the kinsfolk of Herod; and they said unto him, Arabic, Teacher, we know that thou speakest the truth, and teachest the way of God with equity, and art not lifted up by any man: for thou actest not so as to 3 be seen of any man. Tell us now, What is thy opinion? Is it lawful that we should 4 pay the tribute to Caesar, or not? shall we give, or shall we not give? But Jesus knew 5 their deceit, and said unto them, Why tempt ye me, ye hypocrites? Shew me the 6 penny of the tribute. So they brought unto him a penny. Jesus said unto them, To whom belongeth this image and inscription? They said unto him, To Caesar. 8 He said unto them, Give what is Caesar's to Caesar, and what is God's to God. And they could not make him slip in a single word before the people; and they marvelled at his word, and refrained.

9 And on that day came the Sadducees, and said unto him, There is no life for the dead. And they asked him, and said unto him, Teacher, Moses said unto us, If a man die, not having children, let his brother take his wife, and raise up seed for his brother. Now there were with us seven brethren: and the first took a wife, and died without

children; and the second took his wife, and died without children; and the third also took her; and in like manner the seven of them also, and they 14, died without leaving children. And last of them all the woman died also. At the resurrection, then, which of these seven shall have this woman? for all of them took her. Jesus answered and said unto them, Is it not for this that ye have erred, because ye know not the scriptures, nor the power of God? And the sons of this world take wives, and the women become the men's; but those that have become worthy of that world, and the resurrection from among the dead, do not take wives, and the women also do not become the men's. Nor is it possible that they should die; but they are like the angels, and are the children of God, because they have become the children of the resurrection. For in the resurrection of the dead, have ye not read in the book of Moses, how from the bush God said unto him, I am the God of Abraham, and the God of Isaac, and the God of Jacob? And God is not the God of the dead, but of the living: for all of them are alive with him. And ye have erred greatly.

22, And when the multitudes heard, they were wondering at his teaching. And some of the scribes answered and said unto him, Teacher, thou hast well said. But the rest of the Pharisees, when they saw his silencing the Sadducees on this point, gathered against him to contend with him.

And one of the scribes, of those that knew the law, when he saw the excellence of his answer to them, desired to try him, and said unto him, What shall I do to inherit eternal life? and, Which of the commandments is greater, and has precedence in the law? Jesus said unto him, The first of all the commandments is, Hear, O 28 Israel; The Lord our God, the Lord is one: and thou shalt love the Lord thy God with all thy heart, and with all thy soul, and with all thy thought, and with all thy 29, strength. This is the great and preeminent commandment. And the second, which is like it, is, Thou shall love thy neighbour as thyself. And another commandment greater than these two there is not. On these two commandments, then, are hung the Arabic, law and the prophets. That scribe said unto him, Excellent! my Master; thou hast said truly that he is one, and there is no other outside of him: and that a man should love him with all his heart, and with all his thought, and with all his soul, and with all his strength, and that he should love his neighbour as himself, is better than all savours and sacrifices. And Jesus saw him that he had answered wisely; and he answered and said unto him, Thou art not far from the 35, kingdom of God. Thou hast: spoken rightly: do this, and thou shalt live. And he, as his desire was to justify himself, said unto him, And who is my neighbour? Jesus said unto him, A man went down from Jerusalem to Jericho; and the robbers fell upon him, and stripped him, and beat him, his life remaining in him but little, and went away. And it happened that there came down a certain priest that way; and he saw him, and passed by. And likewise a Levite also came and reached that place, and saw him, and passed by. And a certain Samaritan, as he journeyed, came to the place where he was, and saw him, and had compassion on him, and came near, and bound up his strokes, and poured on them wine and oil; and he set him on the ass, and brought him to the inn, and expended his care upon him. And on the morrow of that day he took out two pence, and gave them to the innkeeper, and said unto him, Care for him; and if thou spendest upon him

more, when I return, I shall give thee. Who of these three now, thinkest thou, is nearest to him that fell among the robbers? And he said unto him, He that had compas-Arabic, sion on him. Jesus said unto him, Go, and do thou also likewise. And p. 132 no man dared afterwards to ask him anything.

46 And he was teaching every day in the temple. But the chief priests and scribes and the eiders of the people sought to destroy him: and they could not find what they should do with him; and all the people were hanging upon him to hear him. And many of the multitude believed on him, and said, The Messiah, when he cometh, can it be that he will do more than these signs that this man doeth? And the Pharisees heard the multitudes say that of him; and the chief priests sent officers to seize him. And Jesus said unto them, I am with you but a short time yet, and I go to him that sent me. And ye shall seek me, and shall not find me: and where I shall be, ye shall not be able to come. The Jews said within themselves, Whither hath this man determined to go that we shall not be able to find him? can it be that he is determined to go to the regions of the nations, and teach the heathen? What is this word that he said, Ye shall seek me, and shall not find me: and where I am, ye cannot come?

SECTION XXXV.

35 1 And on the great day, which is the last of the feast, Jesus stood, crying out and 2 saying, If any man is thirsty, let him come unto me, and drink. Every one that believeth in me, as the scriptures said, there shall flow from his belly rivers of pure water. He said that referring to the Spirit, which those who believed in him were to receive: for the Spirit was not yet granted; and because Jesus had not yet been Arabic, glorified. And many of the multitude that heard his words said, This is in truth the prophet. And others said, This is the Messiah. But others said, Can it be that the Messiah will come from Galilee? Hath not the scripture said that from the seed of David, and from Bethlehem, the village of David, the 7 Messiah cometh? And there occurred a dissension in the multitude because of him. 8 And some of them were wishing to seize him; but no man laid a hand upon him.

9 And those officers came to the chief priests and Pharisees: and the priests said unto them, Why did ye not bring him? The officers said, Never spake man thus as speaketh this man. The Pharisees said unto them, Perhaps ye also have gone 12, astray? Hath any of the rulers or the Pharisees haply believed in him? except this people which knows not the law; they are accursed. Nicodemus, one of them, he that had come to Jesus by night, said unto them, Doth our law haply condemn a man, except it hear him first and know what he hath done? They answered and said unto him, Art thou also haply from Galilee? Search, and see that a prophet riseth not from Galilee.

17, And when the Pharisees assembled, Jesus asked them, and said, What say ye of the Messiah? whose son is he? They said unto him, The son of David. He said unto them, And how doth David in the Holy Spirit call him Lord? for he said, The Lord said unto my Lord, Sit on my right hand, That I may put thine enemies under thy feet.

21, If then David calleth him Lord, how is he his son? And no one was able to answer him; and no man dared from that day again to ask him of anything.

23 And Jesus addressed them again, and said, I am the light of the world; and he that followeth me shall not walk in darkness, but shall find the light of life. The Pharisees Arabic, said unto him, Thou bearest witness to thyself; thy witness is not true. Jesus 25 answered and said unto them, If I bear witness to myself, my witness is true; for I know whence I came, and whither I go; but ye know not whence I came, or 26, whither I go. And ye judge after the flesh; and I judge no man. And even if I judge, my judgement is true; because I am not alone, but I and my Father which 28, sent me. And in your law it is written, that the witness of two men is true. I am he that beareth witness to myself, and my Father which sent me beareth witness to me. They said unto him, Where is thy Father? Jesus answered and said unto them, Ye know not me, nor my Father: for did ye know me, ye would know my Father. He said these sayings in the treasury, where he was teaching in the 32 temple: and no man seized him; because his hour had not yet come. Jesus said unto them again, I go truly, and ye shall seek me and not find me, and ye shall die in your sins: and where I go, ye cannot come. The Jews said, Will he haply kill himself, that he saith, Where I go, ye cannot come? He said unto them, Ye are from below; and I am from above: ye are of this world; and I am not of this world. I said unto you, that ye shall die in your sins: if ye believe not that I am he, ye shall die in your sins. The Jews said, And thou, who art thou? Jesus said unto them, If I should begin to speak unto you, I have concerning you many words and judgement: but he that sent me is true; and I, what I heard from him is what 38, I say in the world. And they knew not that he meant by that the Father. Jesus Arabic, said unto them again, When ye have lifted up the Son of man, then ye shall know that I am he: and I do nothing of myself, but as my Father taught me, so I speak. And he that sent me is with me; and my Father hath not left me alone; because I do what is pleasing to him at all times. And while he was saying that, many believed in him.

42 And Jesus said to those Jews that believed in him, If ye abide in my words, truly ye are my disciples: and ye shall know the truth, and the truth shall make you free. They said unto him, We are the seed of Abraham, and have never served any man in the way of slavery: how then sayest thou, Ye shall be free children? Jesus said unto them, Verily, verily, I say unto you, Every one that doeth a sin is a slave of sin. And the slave doth not remain for ever in the house; but the son remaineth 47, for ever. And if the Son set you free, truly ye shall be free children. I know that ye are the seed of Abraham; but ye seek to slay me, because ye are unable for my word.

And what I saw with my Father, I say: and what ye saw with your father, ye do. They answered and said unto him, Our father is Abraham. Jesus said unto them, If ye were the children of Abraham, ye would do the deeds of Abraham. Now, behold, ye seek to kill me, a man that speak with you the truth, that I heard from God: this did Abraham not do. And ye do the deeds of your father. They said unto him, We were not born of fornication; we have one Father, who is God. Jesus said unto them, If God were your Father, ye would love me: I proceeded and came from God; and it

was not of my own self that I came, but he sent Arabic, me. Why then do ye not know my word? Because ye cannot hear my word. Ye are from the father, the devil, and the lust of your father do ye desire to do, who from the beginning is a slayer of men, and in the truth standeth not, because the truth is not in him. And when he speaketh untruth, he speaketh from himself: for he is a liar, and the father of untruth. And I who speak the truth, ye believe me not. Who of you rebuketh me for a sin? And if I speak the truth, ye do not believe me. Whosoever is of God heareth the words of God: therefore do ye not hear, because ye are not of God. The Jews answered and said unto him, Did we not say well that thou art a Samaritan, and hast demons? Jesus said unto them, As for me, I have not a devil; but my Father do I honour, and ye dishonour me. I seek not my glory: here is one who seeketh and judgeth.

SECTION XXXVI.

36 1 Verily, verily, I say unto you, Whosoever keepeth my word shall not see death 2 for ever. The Jews said unto him, Now we know that thou hast demons. Abraham is dead, and the prophets; and thou sayest, Whosoever keepeth my word shall not 3 taste death for ever. Art thou haply greater than our father Abraham, who is 4 dead, and than the prophets, which are dead? whom makest thou thyself? Jesus said unto them, If I glorify myself, my glory is nothing: my Father is he that 5 glorifieth me; of whom ye say, that he is our God; and yet ye have not known him: but I know him; and if I should say that I know him not, I should become 6 Arabic, a liar like you: but I know him, and keep his word. Abraham your father 7 longed to see my day; and he saw, and rejoiced. The Jews said unto him, 8 Thou art now not fifty years old, and hast thou seen Abraham? Jesus said unto 9 them, Verily, verily, I say unto you, Before Abraham was, I am. And they take stones to stone him: but Jesus concealed himself, and went out of the temple. And he passed through them, and went his way.

And as he passed, he saw a man blind from his mother's womb. And his disciples asked him, and said, Our Master, who sinned, this man, or his parents, so that he was born blind? Jesus said unto them, Neither did he sin, nor his parents: but that the works of God may be seen in him. It is incumbent on me to do the deeds of him that sent me, while it is day: a night will come, and no man will be able to busy himself. As long as I am in the world, I am the light of the world. And when he said that, he spat upon the ground, and made clay of his spittle, and smeared it on the eyes of the blind man, and said unto him, Go and wash thyself in the pool of Siloam. And he went and washed, and came seeing. And his neighbours, which saw him of old begging, said, Is not this he that was sitting begging? And some said, It is he; and others said, Nay, but he resembles him much. He 19, said, I am he. They said unto him, How then were thine eyes opened? He answered and said unto them, A man named Jesus made clay, and smeared it on my eyes, and said unto me, Go and wash in the water of Siloam: and I went and washed, and received sight. They said unto him, Where is he? He said, I know not. 22, Arabic, And they brought him that was previously blind to the Pharisees. And the day in which Jesus made clay and opened with it his eyes was a sabbath day. And again the Pharisees asked him, How didst thou receive sight? And he said unto them, He put clay on mine eyes, and I washed, and received sight.

The people of the Pharisees said, This man is not from God, for he keepeth not the sabbath. And others said, How can a man that is a sinner do these signs? And there came 26 to be a division amongst them. And again they said to that blind man, Thou, then, what sayest thou of him that opened for thee thine eyes? He said unto them, I say that he is a prophet. And the Jews did not believe concerning him, that he was blind, and received sight, until they summoned the parents of him who received sight, and asked them, Is this your son, of whom ye said that he was born blind? how then, behold, doth he now see? His parents answered and said, We know that this is our son, and that he was born blind: but how he has come to see now, or who it is that opened his eyes, we know not: and he also has reached his prime; ask him, and he will speak for himself. This said his parents, because they were fearing the Jews: and the Jews decided, that if any man should confess of him that he was the Messiah, they would put him out of the synagogue. For this reason said his parents, He hath reached his prime; ask him. And they called the man a second time, him that was blind, and said unto him, Praise God: we know that this man is a sinner. He answered and said unto them, Whether he be a sinner, I know not: I know one thing, that I was blind, and I now see. They said unto him again, Arabic, What did he unto thee? how opened he for thee thine eyes? He said unto them, I said unto you, and ye did not hear: what wish ye further to hear? ye also, do ye wish to become disciples to him? And they reviled him, and said unto him, Thou art the disciple of that man; but as for us, we are the disciples of Moses. And we know that God spake unto Moses: but this man, we know not whence he is. The man answered and said unto them, From this is the wonder, because ye know not whence he is, and mine eyes hath he opened. And we know that God heareth not the voice of sinners: but whosoever feareth him, and doeth his will, him he heareth. From eternity hath it not been heard of, that a man opened the eyes of a blind man, who had been born in blindness. If then this man were not from God, he could not do that. They answered and said unto him, Thou wast all of thee born in sins, and dost thou teach us? And they put him forth without.

44 And Jesus heard of his being put forth without, and found him, and said unto him, Dost thou believe in the Son of God? He that was made whole answered and said, Who is he, my Lord, that I may believe in him? Jesus said unto him, Thou hast seen him, and he that speaketh to thee is he. And he said, I believe, my Lord. And he fell down worshipping him.

SECTION XXXVII.

37 1 And Jesus said, To judge the world am I come, so that they that see not may 2 see, and they that see may become blind. And some of the Pharisees which were 3 with him heard that, and they said unto him, Can it be that we are blind? Jesus said unto them, If ye were blind, ye should not have sin: but now ye say, We see: and because of this your sin remaineth. 4 Arabic, Verily, verily, I say unto you, Whosoever entereth not into the fold of the sheep by the door, but goeth up from another place, that man is a thief and a 6 stealer. But he that entereth by the door is the shepherd of the sheep. And therefore the keeper of the door openeth for him the door; and the sheep hear his

voice: and 7 he calleth his sheep by their names, and they go forth unto him. And when he putteth forth his sheep, he goeth before them, and his sheep follow him: because 8 they know his voice. And after a stranger will the sheep not go, but they flee from 9 him: because they hear not the voice of a stranger. This parable spake Jesus unto them: but they knew not what he was saying unto them. Jesus said unto them again, Verily, verily, I say unto you, I am the door of the sheep. And all that came are thieves and stealers: but the sheep heard them not. I am the door: and if a man enter by me, he shall live, and shall go in and go out, and shall find pasture. And the stealer cometh not, save that he may steal, and kill, and destroy: but I came that they might have life, and that they might have the thing that is better. I am the good shepherd; and the good shepherd giveth himself for his sheep. But the hireling, who is not a shepherd, and whose the sheep are not, when he seeth the wolf as it cometh, leaveth the sheep, and fleeth, and the wolf cometh, and snatcheth away the sheep, and scattereth them: and the hireling fleeth because he is an hireling, and hath no care for the sheep. I am the 18 good shepherd; and I know what is mine, and what is mine knoweth me, as my Father knoweth me, and I know my Father; and I give myself for the sheep. And I have other sheep also, that are not of this flock: them also I must invite, and they shall hear my voice; and all the sheep shall be one, and the shepherd one. Arabic, And therefore doth my Father love me, because I give my life, that I may 21 take it again. No man taketh it from me, but I leave it of my own choice. And I have the right to leave it, and have the right also to take it. And this commandment did I receive of my Father.

22 And there occurred a disagreement among the Jews because of these sayings. And many of them said, He hath a devil, and is afflicted with madness; why listen ye to him? And others said, These sayings are not those of men possessed with demons. Can a demon haply open the eyes of a blind man?

25, And the feast of the dedication came on at Jerusalem: and it was winter. And Jesus was walking in the temple in the porch of Solomon. The Jews therefore surrounded him, and said unto him, Until when dost thou make our hearts anxious? If thou art the Messiah, tell us plainly. He answered and said unto them, I told you, and ye believe not: and the deeds that I do in my Father's name bear witness 29, to me. But ye believe not, because ye are not of my sheep, as I said unto you. And my sheep hear my voice, and I know them, and they come after me: and I give them eternal life; and they shall not perish for ever, nor shall any man snatch them out of my hands. For the Father, who hath given them unto me, is greater than all; and no man is able to take them from the hand of my Father. I and 34, my Father are one. And the Jews took stones to stone him. Jesus said unto them, Many good deeds from my Father have I shewed you; because of which of them, then, do ye stone me? The Jews said unto him, Not for the good deeds do we stone thee, but because thou blasphemest; and, whilst thou art a man, makest thy self God. Jesus said unto them, Is it not thus written in your law, I said, Ye are gods? Arabic, And if he called those gods--for to them came the word of God (and it is not possible in the scripture that anything should be undone)--he then, whom the Father hath sanctified and sent into the world, do ye say that he blasphemeth; because I said unto you, I am the Son of God? If then I do not the deeds of my Father, ye believe me not. But if I do, even if ye believe not me, believe the deeds: that ye may know and believe that my Father is in me, and I in my Father. And they sought again to take him: and he went forth out of their hands.

43 And he went beyond Jordan to the place where John was baptizing formerly; and abode there. And many people came unto him; and they said, John did not work even one sign: but all that John said of this man is truth. And many believed in him. And there was a sick man, named Lazarus, of the village of Bethany, the brother of Mary and Martha. And Mary was she that anointed with sweet ointment the feet of Jesus, and wiped them with her hair; and Lazarus, who was sick, was the brother of this woman. And his sisters sent unto Jesus, and said unto him, Our Lord, behold, he whom thou lovest is sick. But Jesus said, This sickness is not unto death, but for the glorifying of God, that the Son of God may be glorified 50, because of it. And Jesus loved Martha, and Mary, and Lazarus. And when he heard that he was sick, he abode in the place where he was two days. And after that, he said unto his disciples, Come, let us go into Judaea. His disciples said unto him, Our Arabic, Master, now the Jews desire to stone thee; and goest thou again thither? 54, Jesus said unto them, Is not the day of twelve hours? If then a man walk in the day, he stumbleth not, because he seeth the light of the world. But if a man walk in the night, he stumbleth, because there is no lamp in him. This said Jesus: and after that, he said unto them, Lazarus our friend hath fallen asleep; but I am going to awaken him. His disciples said unto him, Our Lord, if he hath fallen asleep, he will recover. But Jesus said that concerning his death: while they supposed that he spake of lying down to sleep. Then Jesus said unto them plainly, Lazarus is dead. And I am glad that I was not there for your sakes, that ye may believe; but let us go thither. Thomas, who is called Thama, said to the disciples, his companions, Let us also go, and die with him.

SECTION XXXVIII.

38 2 And Jesus came to Bethany, and found him already four days in the grave. And Bethany was beside Jerusalem, and its distance from it was a sum of fifteen fur- 3 longs; and many of the Jews came unto Mary and Martha, to comfort their heart 4 because of their brother. And Martha, when she heard that Jesus had come, went 5 out to meet him: but Mary was sitting in the house. Martha then said unto Jesus, 6 My Lord, if thou hadst been here, my brother had not died. But I know now that, 7 whatever thou shalt ask of God, he will give thee. Jesus said unto her, Thy brother shall 8 rise. Martha said unto him, I know that he shall rise in the resurrection at the last day.

Jesus said unto her, I am the resurrection, and the life: whosoever believeth in Arabic, me, even though he die, he shall live: and every living one that believeth in me shall never die. Believest thou this? She said unto him, Yea, my Lord: I believe that thou art the Messiah, the Son of God, that cometh into the world. And when she had said that, she went and called Mary her sister secretly, and said unto her, Our Master hath come, and summoneth thee. And Mary, when she heard, rose in haste, and came unto him. (And Jesus then had not come into the village, but was in the place where Martha met him.) And the Jews also that were with her in the house, to comfort her, when they saw

that Mary rose up and went out in haste, went after her, because they supposed that she was going to the tomb to weep. And Mary, when she came to where Jesus was, and saw him, fell at his feet, and said unto him, If thou hadst been here, my Lord, my brother had not died. And Jesus came; and when he saw her weeping, and the Jews that were with her weeping, he was troubled in himself, and sighed; and he said, In what place have ye laid him? And they said unto him, Our Lord, come and see. And the tears of Jesus came. The Jews therefore said, See the greatness of his love for him! But some of them said, Could not this man, who opened the eyes of that blind man, have caused that this man also should not die? And Jesus came to the place of burial, being troubled within himself. And the place of burial was a cave, and a stone was placed at its door. Jesus therefore said, Take these stones away.

Martha, the sister of him that was dead, said unto him, My Lord, he hath come to stink for some time: he hath been four days dead. Jesus said unto her, Did not I say Arabic, unto thee, If thou believest, thou shall see the glory of God? And they re- moved those stones. And Jesus lifted his eyes on high,and said, My Father, I thank thee Since thou didst hear me. And I know that thou at all times hearest me: but I say this unto thee because of this multitude that is standing, that they may believe that thou didst send me. And when he had said that, he cried with a loud voice, Lazarus, come forth. And that dead man came out, having his hands and feet bound with bandages, and his face wrapped in a scarf. Jesus said unto them, Loose him, and let him go.

29 And many of the Jews which came unto Mary, when they saw the deed of Jesus, believed in him. But some of them went to the Pharisees, and informed them of all that Jesus did.

31 And the chief priests and the Pharisees gathered, and said, What shall we do? for lo, this man doeth many signs. And if we leave him thus, all men will believe in him: and the Romans will come and take our country and people. And one of them, who was called Caiaphas, the chief priest he was in that year, said unto them, Ye know not anything, nor consider that it is more advantageous for us that one man should die instead of the people, and not that the whole people perish. And this he said not of himself: but because he was the chief priest of that year, he prophesied that Jesus was to die instead of the people; and not instead of the people alone, but that he might gather the scattered children of God together. And from that day they considered how to kill him. Arabic, And Jesus did not walk openly amongst the Jews, but departed thence to a place near the wilderness, to a town called Ephraim; and he was there, going about with his disciples. And the passover of the Jews was near: and many went up from the villages unto Jerusalem before the feast, to purify themselves. And they sought for Jesus, and said one to another in the temple, What think ye of his holding back from the feast? And the chief priests and the Pharisees had given commandment, that, if any man knew in what place he was, he should reveal it to them, that they might take him.

42 And when the days of his going up were accomplished, he prepared himself that he might go to Jerusalem. And he sent messengers before him, and departed, and entered into

a village of Samaria, that they might make ready for him. And they received him not, because he was prepared for going to Jerusalem. And when James and John his disciples saw it, they said unto him, Our Lord, wilt thou that we speak, and fire come down from heaven, to extirpate them, as did Elijah also? And Jesus turned, and rebuked them, and said, Ye know not of what spirit ye are. Verily the Son of man did not come to destroy lives, but to give life. And they went to another village.

SECTION XXXIX.

39 1 And Jesus six days before the passover came to Bethany, where was Lazarus, 2 whom Jesus raised from among the dead. And they made a feast for him there: 3 and Martha was serving; while Lazarus was one of them that sat with him. And 4 at the time of Jesus' being at Bethany in the house of Simon the leper, great multitudes of the Jews heard that Jesus was there: and they came, not because of Jesus alone, but Arabic, that they might look also on Lazarus, whom he raised from among the dead. 6 And the chief priests considered how they might kill Lazarus also; because 7 many of the Jews were going on his account, and believing in Jesus And Mary took a case of the ointment of fine nard, of great price, and opened it, and poured 8 it out on the head of Jesus as he was reclining; and she anointed his feet, and wiped them with her hair: and the house was filled with the odour of the ointment.

9, But Judas Iscariot, one of the disciples, he that was to betray him, said, Why was not this ointment sold for three hundred pence, and given unto the poor? This he said, not because of his care for the poor, but because he was a thief, and the chest was with him, and what was put into it he used to bear. And that displeased the rest of the disciples also within themselves, and they said, Why went this ointment to waste? It was possible that it should be sold for much, and the poor be given it. And they were angry with Mary. And Jesus perceived it, and said unto them, Leave her; why molest ye her? a good work hath she accomplished on me: for the day of my burial kept she it. At all times the poor are with you, and when ye wish ye can do them a kindness: but I am not at all times with you. And for this cause, when she poured this ointment on my body, it is as if she did it for my bur- ial, and anointed my body beforehand. And verily I say unto you, In every place where this my gospel shall be proclaimed in all the world, what she did shall be told for a memorial of her. 18, Arabic, And when Jesus said that, he went out leisurely to go to Jerusalem, And p. 148 when he arrived at Bethphage and at Bethany, beside the mount which is called the mount of Olives, Jesus sent two of his disciples, and he said unto them, Go into this village that is opposite you: and when ye enter it, ye shall find an ass tied, and 22 a colt with him, which no man ever yet mounted: loose him, and bring them unto me. And if any man say unto you, Why loose ye them? say unto him thus, We seek them for our Lord; and straightway send them hither. All this was, that what was said in the prophet might be fulfilled, which said, Say ye unto the daughter of Zion, Behold, thy King cometh unto thee, Meek, and riding upon an ass, And upon a colt the foal of an ass.

25 And the disciples did not know this at that time: but after that Jesus was glorified, his disciples remembered that these things were written of him, and that this they had done unto him. And when the two disciples went, they found as he had said unto them, and they did as Jesus charged them. And when they loosed them, their owners said unto them, Why loose ye them? They said unto them, We seek them for our Lord. And they let them go. And they brought the ass and the colt, and they placed on the colt their garments; and Jesus mounted it. And most of the multitudes spread their garments on the ground before him: and others cut branches from the trees, and threw them in the way. And when he neared his descent from Arabic, the mount of Olives, all the disciples began to rejoice and to praise God with a loud voice for all the powers which they had seen; and they said, Praise in the highest; Praise to the Son of David: Blessed is he that cometh in the name of the Lord; and blessed is the kingdom that cometh, that of our father David: Peace in heaven, and praise in the highest. And a great multitude, that which came to the feast, when they heard that Jesus was coming to Jerusalem, took young palm branches, and went forth to meet him, and cried and said, Praise: Blessed is he that cometh in the name of the Lord, the King of Israel. Certain therefore of the Pharisees from among the multitudes 37 said unto him, Our Master, rebuke thy disciples. He said unto them, Verily I say unto you, If these were silent, the stones would cry out.

38, And when he drew near, and saw the city, he wept over it, and said, Would that thou hadst known the things that are for thy peace, in this thy day! now that is hidden from thine eyes. There shall come unto thee days when thine enemies shall encompass thee, and straiten thee from every quarter, and shall get possession of thee, and thy children within thee; and they shall not leave in thee a stone upon another; because thou knewest not the time of thy visitation.

42 And when he entered into Jerusalem, the whole city was agitated, and they said, Who is this? And the multitudes said, This is Jesus, the prophet that is from Naza- reth of Galilee. And the multitude which was with him bare witness that he called Lazarus from the grave, and raised him from among the dead. And for this cause great multitudes went out to meet him, because they heard the sign which he did.

SECTION XL.

40 1 Arabic, And when Jesus entered the temple, they brought unto him blind and 2 lame: and he healed them. But when the chief priests and the Pharisees saw the wonders that he did, and the children that were crying in the temple and 3 saying, Praise be to the Son of David: it distressed them, and they said, Hearest thou not what these say? Jesus said unto them, Yea: did ye not read long ago, From 4 the mouths of children and infants thou hast chosen my praise? And the Pharisees said one to another, Behold, do ye not see that nothing availeth us? for lo, the whole world hath followed him.

5 And there were among them certain Gentiles also, which had come up to wor- 6 ship at the feast: these therefore came to Philip, who was of Bethsaida of Galilee, 7 and asked him, and said unto him, My lord, we wish to see Jesus. And Philip 8 came and told Andrew: and Andrew

and Philip told Jesus. And Jesus answered and said unto them, The hour is come nigh, in which the Son of man is to be glori- 9 fied. Verily, verily, I say unto you, A grain of wheat, if it fall not and die in the earth, remaineth alone; but if it die, it beareth much fruit. He that loveth his life destroyeth it; and he that hateth his life in this world shall keep it unto the life eter- nal. If a man serve me, he will follow me; and where I am, there shall my servant be also: and whosoever serveth me, the Father will honour him. Now is my soul trou-Arabic, bled: and what shall I say? My Father, deliver me from this hour. But for this cause came I unto this hour. My Father, glorify thy name. And a 14 voice was heard from heaven, I have glorified it, and shall glorify it. And the multitude that were standing heard, and said, This is thunder: and others said, An angel speaketh to him. Jesus answered and said unto them, Not because of me was this voice, but because of you. Now is the judgement of this world; and the prince of this world shall now be cast forth. And I, when I am lifted up from the earth, shall draw every man unto me. This he said, that he might shew by what manner of death he should die. The multitudes said unto him, We have heard out of the law that the Messiah abideth for ever: how then sayest thou, that the Son of man is to be lifted up? who is this, the Son of man? Jesus said unto them, Another little while is the light with you. Walk so long as ye have light, test the darkness overtake you; for he that walketh in the darkness knoweth not whither he goeth. So long as ye have light, believe the light, that ye may be the children of the light.

22 And when certain of the Pharisees asked of Jesus, when the kingdom of God should come, he answered and said unto them, The kingdom of God cometh not with expectation: neither shall they say, Lo, it is here! nor, Lo, it is there! for the kingdom of God is within you.

24 And in the daytime he was teaching in the temple; and at night he used to go out, and pass the night in the mount called the mount of Olives.And all the people came to him in the morning in the temple, to hear his word.

26, Then spoke Jesus unto the multitudes and his disciples, and said unto them, On Arabic, the seat of Moses are seated the scribes and Pharisees: everything that they say unto you now to keep, keep and do: but according to their deeds do ye not; for they say, and do not. And they bind heavy burdens, and lay them on the shoulders of the people; while they with one of their fingers will not come 30, near them. But all their deeds they do to make a shew before men. And all the multitude were hearing that with pleasure.

32 And in the course of his teaching he said unto them, Guard yourselves from the scribes, who desire to walk in robes, and love salutation in the marketplaces, and sitting in the highest places of the synagogues, and at feasts in the highest parts of the rooms: and they broaden their amulets, and lengthen the cords of their cloaks, and love that they should be called by men, My master, and devour widows' houses, because a of their prolonging' their prayers; these then shall receive greater judge- ment. But ye, be ye not called masters: for your master is one; all ye are brethren. Call not then to yourselves any one father on earth: for your Father is one, who is in heaven. And be not called directors: for your director is one, even the Messiah. 39, He

that is great among you shall be unto you a minister. Whosoever shall exalt himself shall be abased; and whosoever shall abase himself shall be exalted.

41 Woe unto you, Pharisees! because ye love the highest places in the synagogues, and salutation in the marketplaces.

42 Woe unto you, scribes and Pharisees, hypocrites! because ye devour widows' houses, because of your prolonging your prayers: for this reason then ye shall receive greater judgement.

43 Woe unto you, scribes and Pharisees, hypocrites! because ye have shut the kingdom of God before men.

44 Arabic Woe unto you that know the law! for ye concealed the keys of knowledge: ye enter not, and those that are entering ye suffer not to enter.

45 Woe unto you, scribes and Pharisees, hypocrites! because ye compass land and sea to draw s one proselyte; and when he is become so, ye make him a son of hell twice as much as yourselves.

46 Woe unto you, ye blind! guides! because ye say, Whosoever sweareth by the temple, it is nothing; but whosoever sweareth by the gold that is in the temple, shall be condemned. Ye blind foolish ones: which is greater, the gold, or the temple which sanctifieth the gold? And, Whosoever sweareth by the altar, it is nothing; but whosoever sweareth by the offering that is upon it, shall be condemned. Ye blind foolish ones: which is greater, the offering, or the altar which sanctifieth the offering? Whosoever then sweareth by the altar, hath sworn by it, and by all that is upon it. And whosoever sweareth by the temple, hath sworn by it, and by him that is dwelling in it. And whosoever sweareth by heaven, hath sworn by the throne of God, and by him that sitteth upon it.

53 Woe unto you, scribes and Pharisees, hypocrites! because ye tithe mint and rue and dill and cummin and all herbs, and ye leave the important matters of the law, judgement, and mercy, and faith, and the love of God: this ought ye to do, and not to leave that undone. Ye blind guides, which strain out a gnat, and swallow n camels.

55 Woe unto you, scribes and Pharisees, hypocrites! because ye cleanse the outside of the cup and of the platter, while the inside of them is full of injustice and wrong. Ye blind Pharisees, cleanse first the inside of the cup and of the platter, then shall the outside of them be cleansed.

57 Arabic, Woe unto you, scribes and Pharisees, hypocrites! because ye resem- ble whited sepulchres, which appear from the outside beautiful, but within full of the bones of the dead, and all uncleanness. So ye also from without appear unto men like the righteous, but within ye are full of wrong and hypocrisy.

59 One of the scribes answered and said unto him, Teacher, in this saying of thine thou art casting a slur on us. He said, And to you also, ye scribes, woe! for ye lade men

with heavy burdens, and ye with one of your fingers come not near those burdens.

61 Woe unto you, scribes and Pharisees, hypocrites! for ye build the tombs of the prophets, which your fathers killed, and adorn the burying-places of the righteous, and say, If we had been in the days of our fathers, we should not have been partakers with them in the blood of the prophets. Wherefore, behold, ye witness against 64 yourselves, that ye are the children of those that slew the prophets. And ye also, ye fill up the measure of your fathers. Ye serpents, ye children of vipers, where shall ye flee from the judgement of Gehenna?

SECTION XLI.

41 1 Therefore, behold, I, the wisdom of God, am sending unto you prophets, and apostles, and wise men, and scribes: and some of them ye shall slay and crucify; and some of them ye shall beat in your synagogues, and persecute from city to 2 city: that there may come on you all the blood of the righteous that hath been poured upon the ground from the blood of Abel the pure to the blood of Zachariah the son of Barachiah, whom ye slew between the temple and the altar. 3 Verily I say unto you, All these things shall come upon this generation,

4 Arabic, O Jerusalem, Jerusalem, slayer of the prophets, and stoner of them that are sent unto her! how many times did I wish to gather thy children, as 5 a hen gathereth her chickens under her wings, and ye would not! Your house shall 6 be left over you desolate. Verily I say unto you, Ye shall not see me henceforth, till ye shall say Blessed is he that cometh in the name of the Lord. 7 And many of the rulers also believed on him; but because of the Pharisees they 8 were not confessing him, lest they be put s out of the synagogue: and they loved 9 the praise of men more than the praising of God. And Jesus cried and said, Whosoever believeth in me, believeth not in me, but in him that sent me. And whosoever seeth me hath seen him that sent me. I am come a light into the world, and so every one that believeth in me abideth not in the darkness. And whosoever heareth my sayings, and keepeth them not, I judge him not: for I came not to judge the world, but to give the world life. Whosoever wrongeth me, and receiveth not my sayings, there is one that judgeth him: the word that I spake, it shall judge him at the last day. I from myself did not speak: but the Father which sent me, he hath given me commandment, what I should say, and what I should speak; and I know that his commandment is eternal life. The things that I say now, as my Father hath said unto me, even so I say.

16 And when he said that unto them, the scribes and Pharisees began their evil-doing, being angry with him, and finding fault with his sayings, and harassing him in many things; seeking to catch something from his mouth, that they might be able to calumniate him.

18 And when there gathered together myriads of great multitudes, which almost trode one upon another, Jesus began to say unto his disciples, Preserve yourselves from the leaven of the Pharisees, which is hypocrisy. For there is nothing concealed, that shall not be revealed: nor hid, that shall not be known. Everything that ye have said in the darkness shall be heard in the light; and what ye have spoken secretly in the ears in the inner chambers shall be proclaimed on the roofs.

21, This said Jesus, and he went and hid himself from them. But notwithstanding his having done all these signs before them, they believed not in him: that the word of Isaiah the prophet might be fulfilled, who said, My Lord, who is he that hath believed to hear us?

And the arm of the Lord, to whom hath it appeared?

24 And for this reason it is not possible for them to believe, because Isaiah also said, They have blinded their eyes, and made dark their heart; That they may not see with their eyes, and understand with their heart, And turn, So that I should heal them.

26 This said Isaiah when he saw his glory, and spake of him.

27 And when Jesus went out of the temple, certain of his disciples came forward to shew him the buildings of the temple, and its beauty and greatness, and the strength of the stones that were laid in it, and the elegance of its building, and that it was adorned with noble stones and beautiful colours. Jesus answered and said unto them, See ye these great buildings? verily I say unto you, Days will come, when there shall not be left here a stone upon another, that shall not be cast down.

31 And two days before the passover of unleavened bread, the chief priests and the scribes sought how they might take him by deceit, and kill him: and they said, It shall not be at the feast, lest the people be agitated.

33 And when Jesus sat on the mount of Olives opposite the temple, his disciples, Simon Cephas and James and John and Andrew, came forward unto him, and said unto him between themselves and him, Teacher, tell us when that shall be, and what is the sign Arabic, of thy coming and the end of the world. Jesus answered and said unto them, Days will come, when ye shall long to see one of the days of the Son of 36, man, and shall not behold. Take heed lest any man lead you astray. Many shall come in my name, and say, I am the Messiah; and they shall say, The time is come near, and shall lead many astray: go not therefore after them. And when ye hear of wars and tidings of insurrections, see to it, be not agitated: for these things must first be; only the end is not yet come. Nation shall rise against nation, and king- dom against kingdom: and great earthquakes shall be in one place and another, and there shall be famines and deaths and agitations: and there shall be fear and terror and great signs that shall appear from heaven, and there shall be great 42, storms. All these things are the beginning of travail. But before all of that, they shall lay hands upon you, and persecute you, and deliver you unto the synagogues and into prisons, and bring you before kings and judges for my name's sake. And that shall be unto you for a witness. But first must my gospel be preached unto all nations. And when they bring you into the synagogues before the rulers and the authorities, be not anxious beforehand how ye shall answer for yourselves, or what ye 47, shall say: because it is not ye that speak, but the Holy Spirit. Lay it to your heart, not Arabic, to be anxious

before the time what ye shah say: and I shall give you under- standing and wisdom,s which all your adversaries shall not be able to gainsay. And then shall they deliver you unto constraint, and shall kill you: and ye shall be hated of all nations because of my name. And then shall many go astray, and they 52 shall hate one another, and deliver one another unto death. And your parents, and your brethren, and your kinsfolk, and your friends shall deliver you up, and shall 53, slay some of you. But a lock of hair from your heads shall not perish. And by your patience ye shall gain your souls. And many men, false prophets, shall arise, 56 and lead many astray. And because of the abounding of iniquity, the love of many shall wax cold. But he that endureth to the end, the same shall be saved. And this, the gospel of the kingdom, shall be preached in all the world for a testimony to all nations; and then shall come the end of all.

SECTION XLII.

42 1 But when ye see Jerusalem with the army compassing it about, then know that 2 its desolation is come near. Those then that are in Judaea at that time shall flee to the mountain; and those that are within her shall flee; and those that are in the 3 villages shall not enter her. For these days are the days of vengeance, that all that 4 is written may be fulfilled. And when ye see the unclean sign of desolation, spoken of in Daniel the prophet, standing in the pure place, he that readeth shall understand, 5,6 and then he that is in Judaea shall flee in to the mountain: and let him that is on the 7 roof not go down, nor enter in to take anything from his house: and let him that is in 8 Arabic, the field not turn behind him to take his garment. Woe to them that are with child and to them that give suck in those days! there shall be great 9 distress in the land, and wrath against this nation. And they shall fall on the edge of the sword, and shall be taken captive to every land: and Jerusalem shall be trodden down of the nations, until the times of the nations be ended.

10 Then if any man say unto you, The Messiah is here; or, Lo, he is there; believe him not: there shall rise then false Messiahs and prophets of lying, and shall do signs and wonders, in order that they may lead astray even the elect also, if they be able. But as for you, beware: for I have acquainted you with everything beforehand. If then they say unto you, Lo, he is in the desert; go not out, lest ye be taken: and if they say unto you, Lo, he is in the chamber; believe not. And as the lightning appeareth from the east, and is seen unto the west; so shall be the coming of the Son of man. But first he must suffer much and be rejected by this generation. Pray therefore that your flight be not in winter, nor on a sabbath: there shall be then great tribulation, the like of which there hath not been from the beginning of the world till now, nor shall be. And except the Lord had shortened those days, no flesh would have lived: but because of the elect, whom he elected, 19 he shortened those days. And there shall be signs in the sun and the moon and the stars; and upon the earth affliction of the nations, and rubbing of hands for the con- Arabic. fusion of the noise of the sea, and an earthquake: the souls of men shall go forth from fear of that which is to come upon the earth. And in those days, straightway after the distress of those days, the sun shall become dark, and the moon shall not shew its light, and the stars shall fall from

heaven, and the powers of heaven shall be convulsed: and then shall appear the sign of the Son of man in heaven: and at that time all the tribes of the earth shall wail, and look unto the Son of man coming on the clouds of heaven with power and much glory. And he shall send his angels with the great trumpet, and they shall gather his elect from the four winds, from one end of heaven to the other. But when these things begin to be, be of good cheer, and lift up your heads; for your salvation is come near.

25 Learn the example of the fig tree: when it letteth down its branches, and put- teth forth its leaves, ye know that the summer is come; so ye also, when ye see these things begun to be, know ye that the kingdom of God hath arrived at the door. Verily I say unto you, This generation shall not pass away, until all these 28 things shall be. Heaven and earth shall pass away, but my sayings shall not pass away.

29 Take heed to yourselves, that your hearts become not heavy with inordinate desire, and drunkenness, and the care of the world at any time, and that day come upon you suddenly: for it is as a shock that shocks all the inhabitants that are on the face of the whole earth. Watch at all times, and pray, that ye may be worthy to escape Arabic. from all the things that are to be, and that ye may stand before the Son of 32 man. Of that day and of that hour hath no man learned, not even the angels of heaven, neither the Son, but the Father. See ye, and watch and pray: for ye know not when that time will be. It is as a man, who journeyed, and left his house, and gave his authority to his servants, and appointed every man to his work, and 35 charged the porter to be wakeful. Be wakeful then: since ye know not when the lord of the house cometh, in the evening, or in the middle of the night, or when the cock croweth, or in the morning; lest he come unexpectedly, and find you sleeping. The thing that I say unto you, unto all of you do I say it, Be ye watchful.

38 For as it was in the days of Noah, so shall the coming of the Son of man be. As they were before the flood eating and drinking, and taking wives, and giving wives to men, until the day in which Noah entered into the ark, and they perceived not till the flood came, and took them all; so shall the coming of the Son of man be. And as it was in the days of Lot; they were eating and drinking, and selling and buying, and planting and building, on the day in which Lot went out from Sodom, and the Lord rained fire and brimstone from heaven, and destroyed them 43, all: so shall it be in the day in which the Son of man is revealed. And in that day, whosoever is on the roof, and his garments in the house, let him not go down to take them: and he that is in the field shall not turn behind him. Remember Lot's wife. Whosoever shall desire to save his life shall destroy it: but whosoever shall destroy his life shall save it. Verily I say unto you, In that night there shall be two on Arabic, one bed; one shall be taken, and another left. And two women shall be grind- p. 162 ing at one mill; one shall be taken, and another left. And two shall be in the field; one shall be taken, and another left. They answered and said unto him, To what place, our Lord? He said unto them, Where the body is, there will the eagles 51, gather. Be attentive now: for ye know not at what hour your Lord cometh. Know this: if the master of the house had known in what watch the thief would come, he would have been attentive, and would not make it possible that his house should be broken

through. Therefore be ye also ready: for in the hour that ye think not the Son of man cometh.

SECTION XLIII.

43 1 Simon Cephas said unto him, Our Lord, is it to us that thou hast spoken this 2 parable, or also to every man? Jesus said unto him, Who, thinkest thou, is the servant, the master of the house, trusted with control, whom his lord set over his 3 household, to give them their food in its season? Blessed is that servant, whom his 4 lord shall come and find having done so. Verily I say unto you, He will set him 5 over all that he hath. But if that evil servant say in his heart, My lord delayeth his 6 coming; and shall begin to beat his servants and the maidservants of his lord, and 7 shall begin to eat and to drink with the drunken; the lord of that servant shall come 8 in the day that he thinketh not, and in the hour that he knoweth not, and shall Arabic, judge him, and appoint his portion with the hypocrites, and with those that are not faithful: there shall be weeping and gnashing of teeth.

9 Then shall the kingdom of heaven be like unto ten virgins, those that took their lamps, and went forth to meet the bridegroom and the bride. Five of them were wise, and five foolish. And those foolish ones took their lamps, and took not with 12, them oil: but those wise ones took oil in vessels along with their lamps. When then the bridegroom delayed, they all slumbered and slept. But in the middle of the night there occurred a cry, Behold, the bridegroom cometh! Go forth therefore to meet him. Then all those virgins arose, and made ready their lamps. The foolish said unto the wise, Give us of your oil; for our lamps are gone out. But those wise answered and said, Perhaps there will not be enough for us and you: but go ye to the sellers, and buy for yourselves. And when they went away to buy, the bridegroom came; and those that were ready went in with him to the marriage feast: and the door was shut. And at last those other virgins also came and said, Our Lord, our Lord, open unto us. He answered and said unto them, Verily I say unto you, 21 I know you not. Watch then, for ye know not that day nor that hour.

22 It is as a man, who went on a journey, and called his servants, and delivered unto them his possessions. And unto one he gave five talents, and another two, and another one; every one according to his strength; and went on his journey forthwith. He Arabic, then that received the five talents went and traded with them, and gained 25, other five. And so also he of the two gained other two. But he that re- ceived the one went and digged in the earth, and hid the money of his lord. And after a long time the lord of those servants came, and took from them the account. And he that received five talents came near and brought other five, and said, My lord, thou gavest me five talents: lo, I have gained other five in addition to them. His lord said unto him, Well done, thou good and faithful servant: over a little hast thou been faithful, over much will I set thee: enter into the joy of thy lord. And he that had the two came near and said, My lord, thou gavest me two talents: lo, other two have I gained in addition to them. His lord said unto him, Good, thou faithful servant: over a little hast thou been faithful, over much will I set thee: enter into the joy of thy lord. And he also that received the one talent came forward and said, My lord, I knew thee that thou an a

severe man, who reapest where thou sowest not, and gatherest where thou didst not scatter: and so I was afraid, and went away and hid thy talent in the earth: lo, thou hast what is thine. His lord answered and said unto him, Thou wicked and slothful servant, thou knewest me 35 that I reap where I sowed not, and gather where I did not scatter; it was incumbent on thee to put my money to the bank, and then I should come and seek it with its gains. Take now from him the talent, and give it to him that hath ten talents. Whosoever hath shall be given, and he shall have more: but he that hath not, even Arabic, what he hath shall be taken from him. And the unprofitable servant, put him forth into the outer darkness: there shall be the weeping and gnashing of teeth.

39, Your loins shall be girded, and your lamps lit; and ye shall be like the people that are looking for their lord, when he shall return from the feast; so that, when he cometh and knocketh, they may at once open unto him. Blessed are those servants, whom their lord shall come and find attentive: verily I say unto you, that he will gird his waist, and make them sit down, and pass through them and serve them. And if he come in the second watch, or the third, and find thus, blessed are those servants.

43 But when the Son of man cometh in his glory, and all his pure angels with him, then shall he sit on the throne of his glory: and he will gather before him all the nations, and separate them the one from the other, like the shepherd who separateth the sheep from the goats; and will set the sheep on his right, and the goats on his left. Then shall the King say to those that are at his right, Come, ye blessed of my Father, inherit the kingdom prepared for you from the foundations of the world: I hungered, and ye gave me to eat; and I thirsted, and ye gave me to drink; and I was a stranger, and ye took me in; and I was naked, and ye clothed me; and I was sick, and ye visited me; and I was in prison, and ye cared for me. Then shall those righteous say unto him, Our Lord, when saw we thee hungry, and fed thee? or thirsty, and gave thee to drink? And when saw we thee a stranger, and took thee in? or naked, and clothed thee? And when saw we thee sick, or imprisoned, and cared for thee? The King shall answer an d say unto them, Verily I say unto you, What Arabic, ye did to one of these my brethren, the little ones, ye did unto me. Then shall he say unto those that are on his left also, Depart from me, ye cursed, 54 into the eternal fire prepared for the devil and his hosts: I hungered, and ye fed me not; and I thirsted, and ye did not give me to drink; and I was a stranger, and ye took me not in; and I was naked, and ye clothed me not; and I was sick, and im- prisoned, and ye visited me not. Then shall those also answer and say, Our Lord, when saw we thee an hungred, or athirst, or naked, or a stranger, or sick, or im- prisoned, and did not minister unto thee? Then shall he answer and say unto them, Verily I say unto you, When ye did it not unto one of these little ones, ye did it not unto me also. And these shall go away into eternal punishment: but the righteous into eternal life.

SECTION XLIV.

41 2 And when Jesus finished all these sayings, he said unto his disciples, Ye know that after two days will be the passover, and the Son of man is delivered up to be 3 crucified. Then gathered together the chief priests, and the

scribes, and the elders 4 of the people, unto the court of the chief priest, who was called Caiaphas; and they took counsel together concerning Jesus, that they might seize him by subtilty, and 5 kill him. But they said, Not during the feast, lest there take place a disturbance among the people; for they feared the people.

6 And Satan entered into Judas who was called Iscariot, who was of the number 7 of the twelve. And he went away, and communed with the chief priests, and the scribes, and those that held command in the temple, and said unto them, What 8 Arabic, would ye pay me, and I will deliver him unto you? And they, when they heard it, were pleased, and made ready for him thirty pieces of money. 9 And he promised them, and from that time he sought an opportunity that he might deliver unto them Jesus without the multitude. And on the first day of unleavened bread the disciples came to Jesus, and said unto him, Where wilt thou that we go and make ready for thee that thou mayest eat the passover?

11 And before the feast of the passover, Jesus knew that the hour was arrived for his departure from this world unto his Father; and he loved his own in this world, and to the last he loved them. And at the time of the feast, Satan put into the heart of Judas, the son of Simon Iscariot, to deliver him up. And Jesus, because he knew that the Father had delivered into his hands everything, and that he came forth from the Father, and goeth unto God, rose from supper, and laid aside his garments; and took a towel, and girded his waist, and poured water into a bason, and began to wash the feet of his disciples, and to wipe them with the towel where- with his waist was girded. And when he came to Simon Cephas, Simon said unto 17 him, Dost thou, my Lord, wash for me my feet? Jesus answered and said unto him, What I do, now thou knowest not; but afterwards thou shall learn. Simon said unto him, Thou shalt never wash for me my feet. Jesus said unto him, If I wash thee not, thou hast no part with me. Simon Cephas said unto him, Then, my Lord, wash not for me my feet alone, but my hands also and my head. Jesus said unto him, He that batheth needeth not to wash save his feet, whereas his whole body is clean: and ye also are clean, but not all of you. For Jesus knew him that should betray him; therefore said he, Ye are not all clean.

22 Arabic. So when he had washed their feet, he took his garments, and sat down, and said unto them, Know ye what I have done unto you? Ye call me, Master, and, Lord: and ye say well; so I am. If then I, now, who am your Lord and Master, have washed for you your feet, how needful is it that ye should wash one another's feet! This have I given you as an example, that as I have done to you so ye should do also. Verily, verily, I say unto you, No servant is greater than his lord; nor an apostle greater than he that sent him. If ye know that, ye are happy if ye do it. My saying this is not for all of you: for I know whom I have chosen: but that the scripture might be fulfilled, He that eateth with me bread lifted against me his heel. Henceforth I say unto you before it come to pass, that, when it cometh to pass, ye may believe that I am he. Verily, verily, I say unto you, Whosoever receiveth whomsoever I send receiveth me; and whosoever receiveth me receiveth him that sent me.

31 Who is the great one, he that sitteth, or he that serveth? is it not he that sitteth? I am among you as he that serveth. But ye are they that have continued with me in my temptations; I promise you, as my Father promised me, the kingdom, that ye may eat and drink at the table of my kingdom.

34 And the first day came, the feast of unleavened bread, on which the Jews were wont to sacrifice the passover. And Jesus sent two of his disciples, Cephas and John, and said unto them, Go and make ready for us the passover, that we may eat. 36, And they said unto him, Where wilt thou that we make ready for thee? He said unto them, Go, enter the city; and at the time of your entering, there shall meet you a man bearing a pitcher of water; follow him, and the place where he entereth, say to such an one, the master of the house, Our Master saith, My time is come, and Arabic, at thy house I keep the passover. Where then is the lodging-place where p. 169 I shall eat with my disciples? And he will shew you a large upper room spread and made ready: there then make ready for us. And his two disciples went out, and came to the city, and found as he had said unto them: and they made ready the passover as he had said unto them.

41 And when the evening was come, and the time arrived, Jesus came and reclined, and the twelve apostles with him. And he said unto them, With desire I have desired to eat this passover with you before I suffer: I say unto you, that henceforth I shall not eat it, until it is fulfilled in the kingdom of God.

44 Jesus said that, and was agitated s in his spirit, and testified, and said, Verily, verily, I say unto you, One of you, he that eateth with me, shall betray me. And they were very sorrowful; and they began to say unto him, one after another of them, Can it be Lord? He answered and said unto them, One of the twelve, he that dippeth his hand with me in the dish, will betray me. And Io, the hand of him that betrayeth me is on the table. And the Son of man goeth, as it is written of him: woe then to that man by whose hand the Son of man is betrayed! for it would have been better for that man had he not been born. And the disciples looked one on another, for they knew not to whom he referred; and they began to search among themselves, who that might be who was to do this.

SECTION XLV.

45 2 Arabic,And one of his disciples was sitting in his bosom, he whom Jesus loved. To him Simon Cephas beckoned, that he should ask him who this was, con- 3 cerning whom he spake. And that disciple leaned on Jesus' breast, and said unto him, 4 My Lord, who is this? Jesus answered and said, He to whom I shall dip bread, and give it. And Jesus dipped bread, and gave to Judas, the son of Simon Iscariot. 5 And after the bread, Satan entered him. And Jesus said unto him, What thou 6 desirest to do, hasten the doing of it. And no man of them that sat knew why he 7 said this unto him. And some of them thought, because Judas had the box, that he was bidding him buy what would be needed for the feast; or, that he might pay 8 something to the poor. Judas the betrayer answered and said, Can it be I, my 9 Master? Jesus said unto him, Thou hast said. And Judas took the bread straightway, and went forth without: and it was still night.

10 And Jesus said, Now is the Son of man being glorified, and God is being glorified in him; and if God is glorified in him, God also will glorify him in him, and straightway will glorify him. 12 And while they were eating, Jesus took bread, and blessed, and divided; and he gave to his disciples, and said unto them, Take and eat; this is my body. And he Arabic, took a cup, and gave thanks, and blessed, and gave them, and said, Take 14, and drink of it, all of you. And they drank of it, all of them. And he said unto them, This is my blood, the new covenant, that is shed for many for the forgiveness of sins. I say unto you, I shall not drink henceforth of this, the juice of the vine, until the day in which I drink with you new wine in the kingdom of God. And thus do ye in remembrance of me. And Jesus said unto Simon, Simon, behold, Satan asketh that he may sift you like wheat: but I entreat for thee, that thou lose not thy faith: and do thou, at some time, turn and strengthen thy brethren. My children, another little while am I with you. And ye shall seek me: and as I said unto the Jews, Whither I go, ye cannot come; I say unto you now also. A new commandment I give you, that ye may love one another; and as I have loved you, so shall ye also love one another. By this shall every man know that ye are my disciples. if ye have love one to another. Simon Cephas said unto him, Our Lord, whither goest thou? Jesus answered and said unto him, Whither I go, thou canst not now follow me; but later thou shall come.

23 Then said Jesus unto them, Ye all shall desert me this night: it is written, I will smite the shepherd, and the sheep of the flock shall be scattered. But after my rising, I shall go before you into Galilee. Simon Cephas answered and said unto him, My Lord, if every man desert thee, I shall at no time desert thee. I am with thee ready for imprisonment and for death. And my life will I give up for thee. Arabic, Jesus said unto him, Wilt thou give up thy life for me? Verily, verily, I say unto thee, Thou shall to-day, during this night, before the cock crow twice, three times deny me, that thou knowest me not. But Cephas said the more, Even if it lead to death with thee, I shall not deny thee, my Lord. And in like manner said all the disciples also.

Then Jesus said unto them, Let not your hearts be troubled: believe in God, and believe in me. The stations in my Father's house are many, else I should have told you. I go to prepare for you a place. And if I go to prepare for you a place, I shall return again, and take you unto me: and so where I am, there ye 32, 33 shall be also. And the place that I go ye know, and the way ye know. Thomas said unto him, Our Lord, we know not whither thou goest; and how is the way for us to the knowledge of that? Jesus said unto him, I am the way, and the truth, and the life: and no man cometh unto my Father, but through me. And if ye had known me, ye should have known my Father: and from henceforth ye know him, and have seen him. Philip said unto him, Our Lord, shew us the Father, and it suf- ficeth us. Jesus said unto him, Have I been all this time with you, and dost thou not know me, Philip? whosoever hath seen me hath seen the Father; how then sayest thou, Shew us the Father? Believest thou not that I am in my Father, and my Father in me? and the saying that I say, I say not of myself: but my Father who dwelleth in me, he doeth these deeds. Believe that I am in my Father, and my Father in me: Arabic, or else believe for the sake of the deeds. Verily, verily, I say unto you, Whosoever believeth in me, the deeds that I do shall he do also; and more than that shall he do: I go unto

the Father. And what ye shall ask in my name, I shall do unto you, that the Father may be glorified in his Son. And if ye 43, ask me is in my name, I will do it. If ye love me, keep my commandments.

And I will entreat of my Father, and he will send unto you another Paraclete, that he may be with you for ever, even the Spirit of truth: whom the world cannot receive; for it hath not seen him, nor known him: but ye know him; for he hath dwelt with you, and is in you. I will not leave you orphans: I will come unto you. Another little while, and the world seeth me not; but ye see me that I live, and ye shall live also. And in that day ye shall know that I am in my Father, and ye in me, and I in you.

SECTION XLVI.

46 1 Whosoever hath my commandments, and keepeth them, he it is that loveth me: and he that loveth me shall be loved of my Father, and I will love him, and will 2 shew myself unto him. Judas (not Iscariot) said unto him, My Lord, what is the 3 purpose of thy intention to shew thyself to us, and not to the world? Jesus answered and said unto him, Whosoever loveth me will keep my word: and my Father will love him, and to him will we come, and make our abode with him. 4 But he that loveth me not keepeth not my word: and this word that ye hear is not my word, but the Father's which sent me.

5, 6 This have I spoken unto you, while I was yet with you. But the Paraclete, the Holy Spirit, whom my Father will send in my name, he will teach you everything, and 7 Arabic, he will bring to your remembrance all that I say unto you. Peace I leave you; my peace I give unto you: and not as this world giveth, give I unto you. 8 Let your heart not be troubled, nor fearful. Ye heard that I said unto you, that I go away, and come unto you. If ye loved me, ye would rejoice, that I go away to my 9 Father: for my Father is greater than I. And now I say unto you before it come to pass, that, when it cometh to pass, ye may believe me. Now I will not speak with you much: the Archon of the world will come, and he will have nothing in me: but that the world may know that I love my Father, and as my Father charged me, so I do.

12 And he said unto them, When I sent you without purses, or wallets, and shoes, lacked ye perchance anything? They said unto him, Nothing. He said unto them, Henceforth, whosoever hath a purse, let him take it, and likewise the wallet also: and whosoever hath not a sword, shall sell his garment, and buy for himself a sword. I say unto you, that this scripture also must be fulfilled in me, that I should be reckoned with the transgressors: for all that is said of me is fulfilled in me. His disciples said unto him, Our Lord, lo, here are two swords. He said unto them, They are sufficient. Arise, let us go hence. And they arose, and praised, and went forth, and went, according to their custom, to the mount of Olives, he and his disciples.

17 And he said unto them, I am the true vine, and my Father is the husbandman. Every branch that produceth not fruit in me, he taketh it: and that which giveth fruit, he cleanseth it, that it may give much fruit. Ye are already clean because of the word that I have spoken unto you. Abide in me, and I in you. And as the branch of the Arabic,

vine cannot produce fruit of itself, if it be not abiding in the vine; so too ye also, if ye abide not in me. I am the vine, and ye are the branches: He then that abideth in me, and I in him, he giveth much fruit: for without me ye can- not do anything. And if a man abide not in me, he is cast without, like a withered branch; and it is gathered, and cast into the fire, that it may be burned. If ye abide in me, and my word abide in you, everything that ye desire to ask shall be done unto you. And herein is the Father glorified, that ye may give much fruit; and ye shall be my disciples. And as my Father loved me, I loved you also: abide in my love. If ye keep my commands, ye shall abide in my love; as I have kept my Father's commands, and abode in his love. I have spoken that unto you, that my joy may be in you, and your joy be fulfilled. This is my commandment, that ye love one another, as I loved you. And no love is greater than this, namely, that a man should give his life for his friends. Ye are my friends, if ye do all that I command you. I call you not now servants; for the servant knoweth not what his lord doeth: my friends have I now called you; for everything that I heard from my Father I have made known unto you. Ye did not choose me, but I chose I you, and appointed you, that ye also should go and bear fruit, and that your fruit should 33 abide; and that all that ye shall ask my Father in my name, he may give you. This I command you, that ye love one another. And if the world hate you, know that before you it hated me. If then ye were of the world, the world would love its own: but ye are not of the world: I chose you out of the world: therefore the world Arabic, hateth you. Remember the word that I said unto you, that no servant is greater than his lord. And if they persecuted me, you also will they persecute; and if they kept my word, your word also will they keep. But all these things will they do unto you for my name's sake, for they have not known him that sent me. And if I had not come and spoken unto them, they had not had sin: but now they have no excuse for their sins. Whosoever hateth me, also hateth my Father. And if I had not done the deeds before them that no other man did, they would not have had sin: but now they have seen and hated me and my Father also: that the word may be fulfilled that is written in their law, They hated me for nothing. But when the Paraclete is come, whom I will send unto you from my Father, even the Spirit of truth, which goeth forth from my Father, he shall bear witness of me: and ye also bear witness, because from the beginning ye have been with me.

44, I have said that unto you, that ye may not stumble. And they shall put you out of their synagogues: and there cometh an hour when every one that killeth you shall think that he hath offered unto God an offering. And they will do that, because they do not know me, nor my Father. I have said that unto you, so that when its time is come, ye may remember it, that I told you. And this hitherto I said not unto you, because I was with you. But now I go unto him that sent me; and no man of you asketh me whither I go. I have said that unto you now, and grief hath come and taken possession of your hems. But I say the truth unto you; It is better for you that I go away: for if I go not away, the Paraclete will not come unto you; Arabic, but if I go away, I will send him unto you. And when he cometh, he will reprove the world for sin, and for righteousness, and for judgement: 52, for sin, because they have not believed in me; and for righteousness, because I go to my Father; and for judgement, because the Archon of this world hath been judged. And further have I many things to speak unto you, but ye cannot tarry now. Howbeit when the Spirit of truth is come, he will remind you of all the truth: he will say nothing from himself; but everything that he heareth, that shall he say: and he shall make known unto you the things that are to be. And he shall glorify me; for from me shall he take and shew you. All that my Father hath is mine: therefore said I unto you, that he taketh of mine, and shall shew you.

SECTION XLVII.

47 1 A little while, and ye shall not behold me; and a little while again, and ye shall 2 behold me; because I go to the Father. His disciples therefore said one to another, What is this that he hath said unto us, A little while, and ye shall not behold me; and a little while again, and ye shall behold me: and, I go to my Father? And they said, What is this little while that he hath said? We know not what he speaketh. And Jesus perceived that they were seeking to ask him, and said unto them, Do ye inquire among yourselves concerning this, that I said unto you, A little while, and ye behold me not, and a little while again, and ye shall behold me? Verily, verily, I say unto you, that ye shall weep and grieve, but the world shall rejoice: and ye shall be sorrowful, but your grief shall turn to joy.

For, a woman when the time is come for her that she should bring forth, the arrival of the day of her bringing forth distresseth her: but whenever she hath brought forth a son, she remembereth not her distress, for joy at the birth of a man into the 7 world. And ye now also grieve: but I shall see you, and your hearts shall rejoice, 8 Arabic, and your joy no man taketh from you. And in that day ye shall ask me nothing. And verily, verily, I say unto you, All that ye ask my Father 9 in my name, he will give you. Hitherto ye have asked nothing in my name: ask, and ye shall receive, that your joy may be complete.

10 I have spoken unto you now in aenigmas: but there will come an hour when a I shall not speak to you in aenigmas, but shall reveal unto you the Father plainly, in that day when ye shall ask in my name: and I say not unto you, that I shall entreat the Father for you; for the Father loveth you, because ye have loved me, 13 and have believed that I came forth from my Father. I came forth from my Father, and came into the world: and I leave the world, and go unto my Father. His disciples said unto him, Lo, thy speech is now plain, and thou hast not said one thing in an aenigma. Now, lo, we know that thou knowest everything, and needest not that any man should ask thee: and by this we believe that thou camest forth 16, from God. Jesus said unto them, Believe that an hour cometh, and lo, it hath come, and ye shall be scattered, every one of you to his place, and shall leave me alone: and yet I am not alone, because the Father is with me. This have I said unto you, that in me ye may have peace. And in the world trouble shall overtake you: but be of good courage; for I have overcome the world.

19 This said Jesus, and lifted up his eyes unto heaven, and said, My Father, the hour is come; glorify thy Son, that thy Son may glorify thee: as thou gavest him authority over all flesh, that all that thou hast given him, he might give them eternal life. And this is eternal life, that they should know that thou alone art true God, and that he Arabic, whom thou didst send is Jesus the Messiah. I glorified thee in the

earth, P. 179 and the work which thou gavest me to do I have accomplished. And now glorify thou me, O Father, beside thee, with that glory which I had with thee before the world was. I made known thy name to the men whom thou gavest me out of the world: thine they were, and thou gavest them to me; and they have kept 25, thy word. Now they know that all that thou hast given me is from thee: and the sayings which thou gavest me I have given unto them; and they received them, and knew of a truth that I came forth from thee, and believed that thou didst send me. And I ask for their sake: and my asking is not for the world, but for those whom thou hast given me; for they are thine: and all that is mine is thine, and all that is thine is mine: and I am glorified in them. And now I am not in the world, and they are in the world, and I come to thee. My holy Father, keep them in thy name which thou hast given unto me, that they may be one, as we are. When I was with them in the world, I kept them in thy name: and I kept those whom thou gavest unto me: and no man of them hath perished, but the son of perdition; that the scripture might be fulfilled. Now I come to thee: and this I say in the world, that my joy may be complete in them. I have given them thy word; and the world hated them, because they were not of the world, as I was not of the world. And I ask not this, that thou take them from the world, but that thou keep them from the 34, evil one. They were not of the world, as I was not of the world. O Father, sanctify them in thy truth: for thy word is truth. And as thou didst send me into the world, I Arabic, also send them into the world. And for their sake I sanctify myself, that they P. 180 also may be sanctified in the truth. Neither for these alone do I ask, but for 39 the sake of them that believe in me through their word; that they may be all one; as thou art in me, and I in thee, and so they also shall be one in us: that the world may believe that thou didst send me. And the glory which thou hast given unto me I have given unto them; that they may be one, as we are one; I in them, and thou in me, that they may be perfect into one; and that the world may know that thou didst send me, and that I loved them, as thou lovedst me. Father, and those whom thou hast given me, I wish that, where I am, they may be with me also; that they may behold my glory, which thou hast given me: for thou lovedst me before the foundation of the world. My righteous Father, and the world knew thee not, but I know thee; and they knew that thou didst send me; and I made known unto them thy name, and will make it known to them; that the love wherewith thou lovedst me may be in them, and I shall be in them.

SECTION XLVIII.

48 1 This said Jesus, and went forth with his disciples to a place which was called Gethsemane, on the side that is in the plain of Kidron, the mountain, the place 2 in which was a garden; and he entered thither, he and his disciples. And Judas the 3 betrayer knew that place: for Jesus oft-times met with his disciples there. And when Jesus came to the place, he said to his disciples, Sit ye here, so that I may go and pray; 5 Arabic, and pray ye, that ye enter not into temptations. And he took with him Cephas and the sons of Zebedee together, James and John; and he began to 6 look sorrowful, and to be anxious. And he said unto them, My soul is distressed unto 7 death: abide ye here, and watch with me. And he withdrew from them a little, 8 the space of a stone's throw; and he kneeled, and fell on his face, and prayed, so 9 that, if it were possible, this hour might pass

him. And he said, Father, thou art able for all things; if thou wilt, let this cup pass me: but let not my will be done, but let thy will be done. And he came to his disciples, and found them sleeping; and he said unto Cephas, Simon, didst thou sleep? Could ye thus not for one hour watch with me? Watch and pray, that ye enter not into temptations: the spirit is willing and ready, but the body is weak. And he went again a second time, and prayed, and said, My Father, if it is not possible with regard to this cup that it pass, except I drink it, thy will be done. And he returned again, and found his disciples sleeping, for their eyes were heavy from their grief and anxiety; and they knew not what to say to him. And he left them, and went away again, and prayed a third time, and said the very same word. And there appeared unto him an angel from heaven, encouraging him. And being afraid he prayed continuously: and his sweat Arabic, became like a stream of blood, and fell on the ground. Then he rose from his prayer, and came to his disciples, and found them sleeping. And he said unto them, Sleep now, and rest: the end hath arrived, and the hour hath come; and behold, the Son of man is betrayed into the hands of sinners. Arise, let us go: for he hath come that betrayeth me.

22 And while he was still speaking, came Judas the betrayer, one of the twelve, and with him a great multitude carrying lanterns and torches and swords and staves, from the chief priests and scribes and eiders of the people, and with him the foot- soldiers of the Romans. And Judas the betrayer gave them a sign, and said, He whom I shall kiss, he is he: take him with care, and lead him away.

And Jesus, because he knew everything that should come upon him, went forth unto them. And immediately Judas the betrayer came to Jesus, and said, Peace, my Master; and kissed him. And Jesus said unto him, Judas, with a kiss betrayest thou the Son of man? Was it for that thou camest, my friend? And Jesus said to those that came unto him, Whom seek ye? They said unto him, Jesus the Nazarene. Jesus said unto them, I am he. And Judas the betrayer also was standing with them. And when Jesus said unto them, I am he, they retreated backward, and fell to the ground. And Jesus asked them again, Whom seek ye? They answered, Jesus the Nazarene. Jesus said unto them, I told you that I am he: and if ye seek me, let these go away: that the word might be fulfilled which he spake, Of those Arabic whom thou hast given me I lost not even one. Then came those that were with Judas, and seized Jesus, and took him.

34 And when his disciples saw what happened, they said, Our Lord, shall we smite them with swords? And Simon Cephas had a sword, and he drew it, and struck the servant of the chief priest, and cut off his right ear. And the name of that ser- vant was Malchus. Jesus said unto Cephas, The cup which my Father hath given me, shall I not drink it? Put the sword into its sheath: for all that take with the sword shall die by the sword. Thinkest thou that I am not able to ask of my Father, and he shall now raise up for me more than twelve tribes of angels? Then how should the scriptures which were spoken be fulfilled, that thus it must be? Your leave in this. And he touched the ear of him that was struck, and healed it. And in that hour Jesus said to the multitudes, As they come out against a thief are ye come out against me with swords and staves to take me? Daily was I with you in the temple sitting teaching, and ye took

me not: but this is your hour, and the power of darkness.
And that was, that the scriptures of the prophets might be
fulfilled. Then the disciples all left him, and fled. And the
footsoldiers and the officers and the soldiers of the Jews
seized Jesus, and came. And a certain young man followed
him, and he was wrapped in a towel, naked: and they seized
him; so he Arabic, left the towel, and fled naked. Then they
took Jesus, and bound him, and brought him to Annas first;
because he was the father in law of Caiaphas, who was
chief priest that year. And Caiaphas was he that counselled
the Jews, that it was necessary that one man should die
instead of the people.

49 And Simon Cephas and one of the other disciples
followed Jesus. And the chief priest knew that disciple, and
he entered with Jesus into the court; but Simon was
standing without at the door. And that other disciple,
whom the chief priest knew, went out and spake unto her
that kept the door, and she brought Simon in. And when
the maid that kept the door saw Simon, she looked
stedfastly at him, and said unto him, Art not thou also one
of the disciples of this man, I mean Jesus the Nazarene?
But he denied, and said, Woman, I know him not, neither
know I even what thou sayest. And the servants and the
soldiers rose, and made a fire in the middle of the court,
that they might warm themselves; for it was cold. And
when the fire burned up, they sat down around it. And
Simon also came, and sat down with them to warm himself,
that he might see the end of what should happen.

SECTION XLIX.

49 2 And the chief priest asked Jesus about his disciples,
and about his doctrine. And Jesus said unto him, I was
speaking openly to the people; and I ever taught in the
synagogue, and in the temple, where all the Jews gather;
and I have spoken nothing in 3 Arabic, secret. Why askest
thou me? ask those that have heard, what I spake unto 4
them: for they know all that I said. And when he had said
that, one of the soldiers which were standing there struck
the cheek of Jesus, and said unto him, Dost thou thus
answer the chief priest? Jesus answered and said unto him,
If I 6 have spoken evil, bear witness of evil: but if well, why
didst thou smite me? And Annas sent Jesus bound unto
Caiaphas the chief priest.

7 And when Jesus went out, Simon Cephas was standing in
the outer court warm- 8 ing himself. And that maid saw
him again, and began to say to those that stood 9 by, This
man also was there with Jesus the Nazarene. And those that
stood by came forward and said to Cephas, Truly thou art
one of his disciples. And he denied again with an oath, I
know not the man. And after a little one of the servants of
the chief priest, the kinsman of him whose ear Simon cut
off, saw him; and he disputed and said, Truly this matt was
with him: and he also is a Galilaean; and his speech
resembles. And he said unto Simon, Did not I see thee with
him in the garden? Then began Simon to curse, and to
swear, I know not this man whom ye have mentioned. And
immediately, while he was speaking, the cock crew twice.
And in that hour Jesus turned, he being without, and
looked stedfastly at Cephas. And Simon remembered the
word of our Lord, which he said unto him, 17, Before the
cock crow twice, thou shalt deny me thrice. And Simon
went forth without, and wept bitterly.

19 Arabic, And when the morning approached, the servants
of all the chief priests and the scribes and the elders of the
people and all the multitude assembled, 20, and made a
plot; and they took counsel against Jesus to put him to
death. And they sought false witnesses who should witness
against him, that they might put him to 22, death, and they
found not; but many false witnesses came, but their witness
did not 24, agree. But at last there came two lying
witnesses, and said, We heard him say, I will destroy this
temple of God that is made with hands, and will build
another not 26, made with hands after three days. And not
even so did their witness agree. But Jesus was silent. And
the chief priest rose in the midst, and asked Jesus, and said,
Answerest thou not a word concerning anything? what do
these witness against 29, thee? But Jesus was silent, and
answered him nothing. And they took him up into their
assembly, and said unto him, If thou art the Messiah, tell
us. He said unto them, If I tell you, ye will not believe me:
and if I ask you, ye will not answer me a word, nor let me
go. And the chief priest answered and said unto him, I
adjure thee by the living God, that thou tell us whether
thou art the Messiah, the 34, Son of the living God. Jesus
said unto him, Thou hast said that I am he. They all said
unto him, Then thou art now the Son of God? Jesus said,
Ye have said that I am he. I say unto you, that henceforth
ye shall see the Son of man sitting Arabic, at the right hand
of power, and coming on the clouds of heaven. Then the
chief priest rent his tunic, and said, He hath blasphemed.
And they all said, Why should we seek now witnesses? we
have heard now the blasphemy from his mouth. 39, What
then think ye? They all answered and said, He is worthy of
death. Then some of them drew near, and spat in his face,
and struck him, and scoffed at him. And the soldiers struck
him on his cheeks, and said, Prophesy unto us, thou Messiah: who is he that struck thee? And many other things
spake they falsely, and said against him.

43 And all of their assembly arose, and took Jesus, and
brought him bound to the praetorium, and delivered him
up to Pilate the judge; but they entered not into the
praetorium, that they might not be defiled when they
should eat the passover. And Jesus stood before the judge.
And Pilate went forth unto them without, and said unto
them, What accusation have ye against this man? They
answered and said unto him, If he had not been doing evils,
neither should we have delivered him up unto thee. We
found this man leading our people astray, and restraining
from giving tribute to Caesar, and saying of himself that he
is the King, the Messiah. Pilate said unto them, Then take
ye him, and judge him according to your law.

The Jews said unto him, We have no authority to put a man
to death: that the word might be fulfilled, which Jesus
spake, when he made known by what manner of death he
was to die. And Pilate entered into the praetorium, and
called Jesus, and said unto him, Art St thou the King of the
Jews? Jesus said unto him, Of thyself saidst thou this, or
did others tell it thee concerning me? Pilate said unto him,
Am I, forsooth, a Jew? The sons of thy nation and the chief
priests delivered thee unto me: what hast thou done? Jesus
said unto him, My kingdom is not of this world: if my
kingdom were of this world, then would my servants fight,
that I should not be delivered to the Jews: now my
kingdom is not from hence. Pilate said unto him, Then
thou art a king? Jesus said unto him, Thou hast said that I
am a king. And for this was I born, and for this came I into

the world, that I should bear witness 55 of the truth. And every one that is of the truth heareth my voice. Pilate said unto him, And what is the truth? And when he said that, he went out again unto the Jews.

SECTION L.

50 1 And Pilate said unto the chief priests and the multitude, I have not found 2 against this man anything. But they cried out and said, He hath disquieted our people with his teaching in all Judaea, and he began from Galilee and unto this 3 place. And Pilate, when he heard the name of Galilee, asked, Is this man a Gali- 4 laean? And when he learned that he was under the jurisdiction of Herod, he sent him to Herod: for he was in Jerusalem in those days.

5 And Herod, when he saw Jesus, rejoiced exceedingly: for he had desired to see him for a long time, because he had heard regarding him many things; and he counted on 6 Arabic, seeing some sign from him. And he questioned him with many words; but 7 Jesus answered him not a word. And the scribes and chief priests were 8 standing by, and they accused him vehemently. And Herod scoffed at him, he and his servants; and when he had scoffed at him, he clothed him in robes of scarlet, 9 and sent him to Pilate. And on that day Pilate and Herod became friends, there having been enmity between them before that.

10, And Pilate called the chief priests and the rulers of the people, and said unto them, Ye brought unto me this man, as the perverter of your people: and I have tried him before you, and have not found in this man any cause of all that ye seek against him: nor yet Herod: for I sent him unto him; and he hath done nothing for which he should deserve death. So now I will chastise him, and let 14, him go. The multitude all cried out and said, Take him from us, take him. And the chief priests and the elders accused him of many things. And during their accusation he answered not a word. Then Pilate said unto him, Hearest thou not how many things they witness against thee? And he answered him not, not even one word: and Pilate marvelled at that. And when the judge sat on his tribune, his wife sent unto him, and said unto him, See that thou have nothing to do with that righteous man: for I have suffered much in my dream to-day because of him.

20 And at every feast the custom of the judge was to release to the people one prisoner, him whom they would. And there was in their prison a well-known pris- 22, oner, called Barabbas. And when they assembled, Pilate said unto them, Ye have a custom, that I should release unto you a prisoner at the passover: will ye that I 24 release unto you the King of the Jews? And they all cried out and said, Release not Arabic, unto us this man, but release unto us Barabbas. And this Barabbas was a robber, who for sedition and murder, which was in the city, was cast into the prison. And all the people cried out and began to ask him to do as the custom was that he should do with them. And Pilate answered and said unto them, Whom will ye that I release unto you? Barabbas, or Jesus which is called the Messiah, the King of the Jews? For Pilate knew that envy had moved them to deliver him up. And the chief priests and the elders asked the multitudes to deliver Barabbas, and to destroy Jesus. The judge answered and said unto them, Whom of the two will ye that I release unto

you? They said, Barabbas. Pilate said unto them, And Jesus which is called the Messiah, what shall I do with him? They all cried out and said, Crucify him. And Pilate spake to them again, for he desired to release Jesus; but they cried out and said, Crucify him, crucify him, and release unto us Barabbas. And Pilate said unto them a third time, What evil hath this man done? I have not found in him any cause to necessitate death: I will chastise him and let him go. But they increased in importunity with a loud voice, and asked him to crucify him. And their voice, and the voice of the chief priests, prevailed. Then Pilate released unto them that one who was cast into prison for sedition and murder, Barabbas, whom they asked for: and he scourged Jesus with whips. Then the footsoldiers of the judge took Jesus, and went into the praetorium, and Arabic, gathered unto him all of the footsoldiers. And they stripped him, and put on him a scarlet cloak. And they clothed him in garments of purple, and plaited a crown of thorns, and placed it on his head, and a reed in his right hand; and while they mocked at him and laughed, they fell down on their knees before him, and bowed down to him, and said, Hail, King of the Jews! And they spat in his face, and took the reed from his hand, and struck him on his head, and smote his cheeks. And Pilate went forth without again, and said unto the Jews, I bring him forth to you, that ye may know that I do not find, in examining him, even one crime. And Jesus went forth without, wearing the crown of thorns and the purple garments. Pilate said unto them, Behold, the man! And when the chief priests and the soldiers saw him, they cried out and said, Crucify him, crucify him. Pilate said unto them, Take him yourselves, and crucify him: for I find not a cause against him. The Jews said unto him, We have a law, and according to our law he deserves death, because he made himself the Son of God. And when Pilate heard this word, his fear increased; and he entered again into the porch, and said to Jesus, Whence art thou? But Jesus answered him not a word. Pilate said unto him, Speakest thou not unto me? knowest thou not that I have authority to release thee, and have authority to crucify thee? Jesus said unto him, Thou hast not any authority over me, if thou wert not given it from above: therefore the sin of him that delivered me up unto thee is greater than thy sin. And for this word Pilate wished to release him: but the Jews cried out, If thou let him go, thou art not a friend of Caesar: for every one that maketh himself a king is against Caesar.

SECTION LI.

51 1 Arabic, And when Pilate heard this saying, he took Jesus out, and sat on the tribune in the place which was called the pavement of stones, but in the He- 2 brew called Gabbatha. And that day was the Friday of the passover: and it had reached 3 about the sixth hour. And he said to the Jews, Behold, your King! And they cried out, Take him, take him, crucify him, crucify him. Pilate said unto them, Shall I crucify your King? The chief priests said unto him, We have no king except 4 Caesar. And Pilate, when he saw it, and he was gaining nothing, but the tumult was increasing, took water, and washed his hands before the multitude, and said, I 5 am innocent of the blood of this innocent man: ye shall know. And all the people 6 answered and said, His blood be on us, and on our children. Then Pilate commanded to grant them their request; and delivered up Jesus to be crucified, according to their wish.

7 Then Judas the betrayer, when he saw Jesus wronged, went and returned the 8 thirty pieces of money to the chief priests and the eiders, and said, I have sinned in my betraying innocent blood. And they said unto him, And we, what must we do? 9 know thou. And he threw down the money in the temple, and departed; and he went away and hanged himself. And the chief priests took the money, and said, We have not authority to cast it into the place of the offering, for it is the price of blood. And they took counsel, and bought with it the plain of the potter, for the burial of strangers. Therefore that plain was called, The field of blood, unto 13 Arabic, this day. Therein was fulfilled the saying in the prophet which said, I took thirty pieces of money, the price of the precious one, which was fixed by the children of Israel; and I paid them for the plain of the potter, as the Lord commanded me.

15 And the Jews took Jesus, and went away to crucify him. And when he bare his cross and went out, they stripped him of those purple and scarlet garments which he had on, and put on him his own garments. And while they were going with him, they found a man, a Cyrenian, coming from the country, named Simon, the father of Alexander and Rufus: and they compelled this man to bear the cross of Jesus. And they took the cross and laid it upon him, that he might bear it, and come after Jesus; and Jesus went, and his cross behind him.

19 And there followed him much people, and women which were lamenting and raving. But Jesus turned unto them and said, Daughters of Jerusalem, weep not for me: weep for yourselves, and for your children. Days are coming, when they shall say, Blessed are the barren, and the womb's that bare not, and the breasts that gave not suck. Then shall they begin to say to the mountains, Fall on us; and to the hills, Cover us. For if they do so in the green tree, what shall be in the dry?

24 And they brought with Jesus two others of the malefactors, to be put to death.

25 And when they came unto a certain place called The skull, and called in the Hebrew Golgotha, they crucified him there: they crucified with him these two malefactors, one on his right, and the other on his left. And the scripture was Arabic, fulfilled, which saith, He was numbered with the transgressors. And they gave him to drink wine and myrrh, and vinegar which had been mixed with the myrrh; and he tasted, and would not drink; and he received it not.

28 And the soldiers, when they had crucified Jesus, took his garments, and cast lots for them in four parts, to every party of the soldiers a part; and his tunic was without sewing, from the top woven throughout. And they said one to another, Let us not rend it, but cast lots for it, whose it shall be: and the scripture was fulfilled, which saith, They divided my garments among them, And cast the lot for my vesture.

30, This the soldiers did. And they sat and guarded him there. And Pilate wrote on a tablet the cause of his death, and put it on the wood of the cross above his head. And there was written upon it thus: THIS IS JESUS THE NAZARENE THE NAZARENE, THE KING OF THE Jews. And this tablet read many of the Jews: for the place where Jesus was crucified was near the city: and it was written in Hebrew and Greek and Latin. And the chief priests said unto Pilate, Write not, The King of the Jews; but, He it is that said, I am the King of the Jews. Pilate said unto them, What hath been written hath been written. And the people were standing beholding; and they that passed by were reviling him, and shaking their heads, and saying, Thou that destroyest the temple, and buildest it in three days, save thyself if thou art the Son of God, and come down from the cross. And in like manner the chief priests and the Arabic, scribes and the elders and the Pharisees derided him, and laughed one with 38, another, and said, The saviour of others cannot save himself. If he is the Messiah, the chosen of God, and the King of Israel, let him come down now from the cross, that we may see, and believe in him. He that relieth on God--let him deliver him now, if he is pleased with him: for he said, I am the Son of God. And the soldiers also scoffed at him in that they came near unto him, and brought him vinegar, and said unto him, If thou art the King of the Jews, save thyself. And likewise the two robbers also that were crucified with him reproached him. And one of those two malefactors who were crucified with him reviled him, and said, If thou art the Messiah, save thyself, and save us also. But his comrade rebuked him, and said, Dost thou not even fear God, being thyself also in this condemnation? And we with justice, and as we deserved, and according to our deed, have we been rewarded: but this man hath not done anything unlawful. And he said unto Jesus, Remember me, my Lord, when thou comest in thy kingdom. Jesus said unto him, Verily I say unto thee, To-day shalt thou be with me in Paradise. And there stood by the cross of Jesus his mother, and his mother's sister, Mary that was related to Clopas, and Mary Magdalene. And Jesus saw his mother, and that disciple whom he loved standing by; and he said to his mother, 51 Woman, behold, thy son! And he said to that disciple, Behold, thy mother! And from that hour that disciple took her unto himself.

52 Arabic, And from the sixth hour darkness was on all the land unto the ninth hour, and the sun became dark. And at the ninth hour Jesus cried out with a loud voice, and said, Yail, Yaili, why hast thou forsaken me? which is, My God, my God, why hast thou forsaken me? And some of those that stood there, when they heard, said, This man called Elijah.

SECTION LII.

52 1 And after that, Jesus knew that all things were finished; and that the scripture 2 might be accomplished, he said, I thirst. And there was set a vessel full of vinegar: and in that hour one of them hasted, and took a sponge, and filled it with that 3 vinegar, and fastened it on a reed, and brought it near his mouth to give him a 4 drink. And when Jesus had taken that vinegar, he said, Everything is finished. 5 But the rest said, Let be, that we may see whether Elijah cometh to save him. 7 And Jesus said, My Father, forgive them; for they know not what they do. And Jesus cried again with a loud voice, and said, My Father, into thy hands I commend my spirit. He said that, and bowed his head, and gave up his spirit. 8 And immediately the face of the door of the temple was rent into two parts from 9 top to bottom; and the earth was shaken; and the stones were split to pieces; and the Arabic, tombs were opened; and the

bodies of many saints which slept, arose and p. 197 came forth; and after his resurrection they entered into the holy city and appeared unto many. And the officer of the footsoldiers, and they that were with him who were guarding Jesus, when they saw the earthquake, and the things which came to pass, feared greatly, and praised God, and said, This man was righteous; and, Truly he was the Son of God. And all the multitudes that were come together to the sight, when they saw what came to pass, returned and smote upon their breasts.

And the Jews, because of the Friday, said, Let these bodies not remain on their crosses, because it is the morning of the sabbath (for that sabbath was a great day); and they asked of Pilate that they might break the legs of those that were crucified, and take them down. And the soldiers came, and brake the legs of the first, and that other which was crucified with him: but when they came to Jesus, they saw that he had died before, so they brake not his legs: but one of the soldiers pierced him in his side with a spear, and immediately there came forth blood and water. And he that hath seen hath borne witness, and his witness is true: and he 19 knoweth that he hath said the truth, that ye also may believe. This he did, that the scripture might be fulfiled, which saith, A bone shall not be broken in him; and the scripture also which saith, Let them look upon him whom they pierced.

21 And there were in the distance all the acquaintance of Jesus standing, and the women that came with him from Galilee, those that followed him and ministered. One of them was Mary Magdalene; and Mary the mother of James the little and Arabic Joses, and the mother of the sons of Zebedee, and Salome, and many others which came up with him unto Jerusalem; and they saw that.

24 And when the evening of the Friday was come, because of the entering of the sabbath, there came a rich man, a noble of Ramah, a city of Judah, named Joseph, and he was a good man and upright; and he was a disciple of Jesus, but was concealing himself for fear of the Jews. And he did not agree with the accusers 27 in their desire and their deeds: and he was looking for the kingdom of God. And this man went boldly, and entered in unto Pilate, and asked of him the body of Jesus. And Pilate wondered how he had died already: and he called the officer of the footsoldiers, and asked him concerning his death before the time. And when he knew, he commanded him to deliver up his body unto Joseph. And Joseph bought for him a winding cloth of pure linen, and took down the body of Jesus, and wound it in they came and took it. And there came unto him Nicodemus also, who of old came unto Jesus by night; and he brought with him perfume of myrrh and aloes, about a hundred pounds. And they took the body of Jesus, and wound it in the linen and the perfume, as was the custom of the Jews to bury.

33 And there was in the place where Jesus was crucified a garden; and in that garden a new tomb cut out in a rock? wherein was never man yet laid. And they left Jesus there because the sabbath had come in, and because the tomb was near. And they pushed a great stone, and thrust n it against the door of the sepulchre, and went away. And Mary Magdalene and Mary that was related to Joses came to Arabic the sepulchre after them, and sat opposite the sepulchre, and saw the body, how they took it in and laid it there. And they returned, and ointment and perfume, and prepared it, that they might come and anoint him. And on the day which was the sabbath day they desisted according to the command.

40, And the chief priests and the Pharisees gathered unto Pilate, and said unto him, Our lord, we remember that that misleader said, while he was alive, After three days I rise. And now send beforehand and guard the tomb until the third day, lest his disciples come and steal him by night, and they will say unto the people that he is risen from the dead: and the last error shall be worse than the first. He said unto them, And have ye not guards? go, and take precautions as ye know how. And they went, and set guards at the tomb, and sealed that stone, with the guards.

45 And in the evening of the sabbath, which is the morning of the first day, and in the dawning while the darkness yet remained, came Mary Magdalene and the other Mary and other women to see the tomb. They brought with them the perfume which they had prepared, and said among themselves, Who is it that will remove for us the stone from the door of the tomb? for it was very great. And when they said thus, there occurred a great earthquake; and an angel came down from heaven, and came and removed the stone from the door. And they came and found the stone removed from the sepulchre, and the angel sitting upon the stone. And his appearance was as the lightning, and his raiment white as the snow: and for fear of him the guards were troubled, and became as dead men. And when he went away, the women entered into the sepulchre; and they found Arabic not the body of Jesus. And they saw there a young man sitting on the right, strayed in a white garment; and they were amazed. And the angel answered and said unto the women, Fear ye not: for I know that ye seek Jesus the Nazarene, who hath been crucified. He is not here; but he is risen, as he said. Come and see the place where our Lord lay.

SECTION LIII.

53 1 And while they marvelled at that, behold, two men standing above them, their 2 raiment shining: and they were seized with fright, and bowed down their face to 3 the earth: and they said unto them, Why seek ye the living one with the dead? He is not here; he is risen: remember what he was speaking unto you while he was in 4 Galilee, and saying, The Son of man is to be delivered up into the hands of sinners, 5 and to be crucified, and on the third day to rise. But go in haste, and say to his disciples and to Cephas, He is risen from among the dead; and lo, he goeth before 6 you into Galilee; and there ye shall see him, where he said unto you: lo, I have 7 told you. And they remembered his sayings; and they departed in haste from the 8 tomb with joy and great fear, and hastened and went; and perplexity and fear 9 encompassed them; and they told no man anything, for they were afraid. And Mary hastened, and came to Simon Cephas, and to that other disciple whom Jesus loved, and said unto them, They have taken our Lord from the sepulchre, and I know not where they have laid him. And Simon went out, and that other disciple, and came to the sepulchre. And they hastened both together: and that disciple outran Simon, and came first to the sepulchre; and he looked down, and saw the linen laid; but

he went not in. And Simon came after him, and entered into the Arabic, sepulchre, and saw the linen laid; and the scarf with which his head was bound was not with the linen, but wrapped and laid aside in a certain place. Then entered that disciple which came first to the sepulchre, and saw, and believed. And they knew not yet from the scriptures that the Messiah was to rise from among the dead. And those two disciples went to their place.

18 But Mary remained at the tomb weeping: and while she wept, she looked down into the tomb; and she saw two angels sitting in white raiment, one of them toward his pillow, and the other toward his feet, where the body of Jesus had been laid. And they said unto her, Woman, why weepest thou? She said unto them, They have taken my Lord, and I know not where they have left him. She said that, and turned behind her, and saw Jesus standing, and knew not that it was Jesus. Jesus said unto her, Woman, why weepest thou? whom seekest thou? And she supposed him to be the gardener, and said, My lord, if thou hast taken him, tell me where thou hast laid him, that I may go and take him Jesus said unto her, Mary. She turned, and said unto him in Hebrew, Rabboni; which is, being interpreted, Teacher. Jesus said unto her, Touch me not; for I have not ascended yet unto my Father: go to my brethren, and say unto them, I ascend unto my Father and your Father, and my God and your God.

25 And on the First-day on which he rose, he appeared first unto Mary Magdalene, from whom he had cast out seven demons. And some of those guards came to the city, and informed the chief priests of Arabic, all that had happened. And they assembled with the elders, and took counsel; and they gave money, not a little, to the guards, and said unto them, Say ye, His disciples came and stole him by night, while we were sleeping.

29 And if the judge hear that, we will make a plea with him, and free you of blame. And they, when they took the money, did according to what they taught them. And this word spread among the Jews unto this day.

31 And then came Mary Magdalene, and announced to the disciples that she had seen our Lord, and that he had said that unto her.

32 And while the first women were going in the way to inform his disciples, Jesus met them, and said unto them, Peace unto you. And they came and took hold of his feet, and worshipped him. Then said Jesus unto them, Fear not: but go and say to my brethren that they depart into Galilee, and there they shall see me. And those women returned, and told all that to the eleven, and to the rest of the disciples; and to those that had been with him, for they were saddened and weeping. And those were Mary Magdalene, and Joanna, and Mary the mother of James, and the rest who were with them: and they were those that told the apostles. And they, when they heard them say that he was alive and had appeared unto them, did not believe them: and these sayings were before their eyes as the sayings of madness. Arabic, And after that, he appeared to two of them, on that day, and while they were going to the village which was named Emmaus, and whose distance from Jerusalem was sixty furlongs. And they were talking the one of them with the 41 other of all the things which

had happened. And during the time of their talking and inquiring with one another, Jesus came and reached them, and walked with them. But their eyes were veiled that they should not know him. And he said unto them, What are these sayings which ye address the one of you to the other, as ye walk and are sad? One of them, whose name was Cleopas, answered and said unto him, Art thou perchance alone a stranger to Jerusalem, since thou knowest not what was in it in these days? He said unto them, What was? They said unto him, Concerning Jesus, he who was from Nazareth, a man who was a prophet, and powerful in speech and deeds before God and before all the people: and the chief priests and the elders delivered him up to the sentence of death, and crucified him. But we supposed that he was the one who was to deliver Israel. And since all these things happened there have passed three days. But certain women of us also informed us that they had come to the sepulchre; and when they found not his body, they came and told us that they had seen there the angels, and they said concerning him that he was alive. And some of us also went to the sepulchre, and found the matter as the women had said: only they saw him not. Then said Jesus unto them, Ye lacking in discernment, and heavy in heart to believe! Was it not in all the sayings of the prophets that the Messiah was to suffer these things, and to Arabic, enter into his glory? And he began from Moses and from all the prophets, and interpreted to them concerning himself from all the scriptures. And they drew near unto the village, whither they were going: and he was leading them to imagine that he was as if going to a distant region. And they pressed him, and said unto him, Abide with us: for the day hath declined now to the darkness. And he went in to abide with them. And when he sat with them, he took bread, and blessed, and brake, and gave to them. And straightway their eyes were opened, and they knew him; and he was taken away from them. And they said the one to the other, Was not our heart heavy within us, while he was speaking to us in the way, and interpreting to us the scriptures?

59 And they rose in that hour, and returned to Jerusalem, and found the eleven gathered, and those that were with them, saying, Truly our Lord is risen, and hath appeared to Simon. And they related what happened in the way, and how they knew him when he brake the bread. Neither believed they that also.

SECTION LIV.

54 1 And while they talked together, the evening of that day arrived which was the First-day; and the doors were shut where the disciples were, because of the fear of the 2 Jews; and Jesus came and stood among them, and said unto them, Peace be with you: I am he; fear not. But they were agitated, and became afraid, and supposed that they 3 saw a spirit. Jesus said unto them, Why are ye agitated? and why do thoughts rise 4 Arabic, in your hearts? See my hands and my feet, that I am he: feel me, and know that a spirit hath not flesh and bones, as ye see me having that. 5 And when he had said this, he shewed them his hands and his feet and his side. 6 And they were until this time unbelieving, from their joy and their wonder. He 7 said unto them, Have ye anything here to eat? And they gave him a portion of broiled fish and of honey. And he took it, and ate before them. 8 And he said unto them, These are the sayings which I spake unto you, while I was with you, that

everything must be fulfilled, which is written in the law of 9 Moses, and the prophets, and the psalms, concerning me. Then opened he their heart, that they might understand the scriptures; and he said unto them, Thus it is written, and thus it is necessary that the Messiah suffer, and rise from among the dead on the third day; and that repentance unto the forgiveness of sins be preached in his name among all the peoples; and the beginning shall be from Jerusalem. And ye shall be witnesses of that. And I send unto you the promise of my Father. And when the disciples heard that, they were glad. And Jesus said unto them again, Peace be with you: as my Father hath sent me, I also send you. And when he had said this, he breathed on them, and said unto them, Receive ye the Holy Spirit: 16 and if ye forgive sins to any man, they shall be forgiven him; and if ye retain them against any man, they shall be retained.

17 But Thomas, one of the twelve, called Thama, was not there with the disciples when Jesus came. The disciples therefore said unto him, We have seen our Lord. But he said unto them, If I do not see in his hands the places of the nails, and put on them my fingers, and pass my hand over his side, I will not believe.

19 And after eight days, on the next First-day, the disciples were assembled again within, and Thomas with them. And Jesus came, the doors being shut, and stood Arabic, in the midst, and said unto them, Peace be with you. And he said to Thomas, Bring hither thy finger, and behold my hands; and bring hither thy hand, and spread it on my side: and be not unbelieving, but believing. Thomas answered and said unto him, My Lord and my God. Jesus said unto him, Now since thou hast seen me, thou hast believed: blessed are they that have not seen me, and have believed.

23 And many other signs did Jesus before his disciples, and they are they which are not written in this book: but these that are written also are that ye may believe in Jesus the Messiah, the Son of God; and that when ye have believed, ye may have in his name eternal life. And after that, Jesus shewed himself again to his disciples at the sea of Tiberias; and he shewed himself unto them thus. And there were together Simon Cephas, and Thomas which was called Twin, and Nathanael who was of Cana of Galilee, and the sons of Zebedee, and two other of the disciples. Simon Cephas said unto them, I go to catch fish. They said unto him, And we also come with thee. And they went forth, and went up into the boat; and in that night they caught nothing. And when the morning arrived, Jesus stood on the shore of the sea: but the disciples knew not that it was Jesus. And Jesus said unto them, Children, have ye anything to eat? They said unto him, No. He said unto them, Cast your net from the right side of the boat, and ye shall find. And they threw, and they were not able to draw the net for the abundance of the fish that were come into it. And that disciple whom Jesus loved said to Cephas, This is our Lord. And Simon, when he heard that it was our Lord, took his tunic, and girded it on his waist (for he was naked), and cast himself into the sea to come to Jesus. But some others of the disciples came in the boat (and they were not far from the land, but about two Arabic, hundred cubits), and drew that net of fish. And when they went up on the land, they saw live coals laid, and fish laid thereon, and bread. And Jesus said unto them, Bring of this fish which ye have now caught. Simon Cephas therefore went up, and dragged the net to the land, full of great fish, a hundred and fifty-three fishes: and with all this weight that net was not rent. And Jesus said unto them,. Come and sit down. And no man of the disciples dared to ask him who he was, for they knew that it was our Lord. But he did not appear to them in his own 37, form. And Jesus came, and took bread and fish, and gave unto them. This is the third time that Jesus appeared to his disciples, when he had risen from among the dead.

39 And when they had breakfasted, Jesus said to Simon Cephas, Simon, son of Jonah, lovest thou me more than these? He said unto him, Yea, my Lord; thou knowest that I love thee. Jesus said unto him, Feed for me my lambs. He said unto him again a second time, Simon, son of Jonah, lovest thou me? He said unto him, Yea, my Lord; thou knowest that I love thee. He said unto him, Feed for me my sheep. He said unto him again the third time, Simon, son of Jonah, lovest thou me? And it grieved Cephas that he said unto him three times, Lovest thou me? He said unto him, My Lord, thou knowest everything; thou knowest that I love thee. Jesus said unto him, Feed for me my sheep. Verily, verily, I say unto thee, When thou wast a child, thou didst gird thy waist for thyself, and go whither Arabic, thou wouldest: but when thou shall be old, thou shalt stretch out thy hands, and another shall gird thy waist, and take thee whither thou wouldest not. He said that to him to explain by what death he was to glorify God. And when he had said that, he said unto him, Come after me. And Simon Cephas turned, and saw that disciple whom Jesus loved following him; he which at the supper leaned on Jesus' breast, and said, My Lord, who is it that betrayeth thee? When therefore Cephas saw him, he said to Jesus, My Lord, and this man, what shall be in his case? Jesus said unto him, If I will that this man remain until I come, what is 47 that to thee? follow thou me. And this word spread among the brethren, that that disciple should not die: but Jesus said not that he should not die; but, If I will that this man remain until I come, what is that to thee?

48 This is the disciple which bare witness of that, and wrote it: and we know that his witness is true.

SECTION LV.

55 1 But the eleven disciples went into Galilee, to the mountain s where Jesus had 2 appointed them. And when they saw him, they worshipped him: but there were of 3 them who doubted. And while they sat there he appeared to them again, and upbraided them for their lack of faith and the hardness of their hearts, those that saw him when he was risen, and believed not. 4 Arabic, Then said Jesus unto them, I have been given all authority in heaven 5 and earth; and as my Father hath sent me, so I also send you. Go now into 6 all the world, and preach my gospel in all the creation; and teach all the peoples, and 7 baptize them in the name of the Father and the Son and the Holy Spirit; and teach them to keep all whatsoever I commanded you: and lo, I am with you all the days, unto 8 the end of the world. For whosoever believeth and is baptized shall be saved; but 9 whosoever believeth not shall be rejected. And the signs which shall attend those that believe in me are these: that they shall cast out devils in my name; and they shall speak with new tongues; and they shall take up serpents, and if they drink deadly poison, it shall not injure

them; and they shall lay their hands on the diseased, and
they shall be healed. But ye, abide in the city of Jerusalem,
until ye be clothed with power from on high.

12 And our Lord Jesus, after speaking to them, took them
out to Bethany: and he lifted up his hands, and blessed
them. And while he blessed them, he was separated from
them, and ascended into heaven, and sat down at the right
hand of God. And they worshipped him, and returned to
Jerusalem with great joy: and at all times they were in the
temple, praising and blessing God. Amen.

16 And from thence they went forth, and preached in every
place; and our Lord helped them, and confirmed their
sayings by the signs which they did.

17 And here are also many other things which Jesus did,
which if they were written every one of them, not even the
world, according to my opinion, would contain the books
which should be written.

SUBSCRIPTIONS

I. IN BORGIAN MS

Here endeth the Gospel which Tatianus compiled and
named Diatessaron, i.e., The Fourfold, a compilation from
the four Gospels of the holy Apostles, the excellent
Evangelists (peace be upon them). It was translated by the
excellent and learned priest, Abu'l Faraj 'Abdulla ibn-at-
Tayyib (may God grant him favour), from Syriac into
Arabic, from an exemplar written by 'Isa ibn-'Ali al-
Motatabbib, pupil of Honain ibn-Ishak (God have mercy
on them both). Amen.

2. IN VATICAN MS.

Here endeth, by the help of God, the holy Gospel that
Titianus compiled from the four Gospels, which is known
as Diatessaron. And praise be to God, as he is entitled to it
and lord of it! And to him be the glory for ever.

OXYRHYNCHUS PAPYRUS 5575

Sayings of Jesus

recto (→)

[…] (the rich man) died. [I tell you, don't] be anxious about [your life], what you'll eat, [nor the] body, what [you'll wear], because I tell you, [unless] you fast from [the world], you'll never find [the kingdom], and unless you […] the world, [you'll never …] the Father [… the] birds, how […] and [your] heavenly Father [feeds them …] so you […] much […]

verso (↓)

[…] how [they grow …] Solomon […] in [his] glory […] the Father [clothes] grass which [dries up] and is thrown into the oven, [he'll clothe] you […] so you […] also […] because [your] Father [knows] your need, [but] look for [the kingdom and all these things will be given …]

Notes

recto (→)

(the rich man) died. Cp. Thomas 63: "a rich man … died." See also Luke 12:16-21.

[don't] be anxious. Cp. Matthew 6:25; Luke 12:22; Thomas 36.

[unless] you fast from [the world]. Cp. Thomas 27.

[the] birds. Cp. Matthew 6:26; Luke 12:24.

verso (↓)

how [they grow]. Cp. Matthew 6:28-30; Luke 12:27,28; Thomas 36.

so you. Cp. Matthew 6:32,33; Luke 12:30,31.

THE STRANGER'S BOOK

59 The [Stranger's Book]

Introduction

"My [son, let's pray to God …] to the Father of all the ages, to send us a spirit of knowledge to reveal the mysteries, so that we may know ourselves; specifically, where [we've] come from, where we're going, and what we need to do to live."

And they left and went up on a mountain called 'Tabor.' And they knelt down and prayed, "O Lord God, the One above all the great realms, the One who has no beginning and no end, give us a spirit of knowledge to reveal your mysteries, so that we may know ourselves; specifically, where we've come from, where we're going, and what we need to do to live."

The Temptation of Stranger

After Stranger had said these words, [Satan] appeared **60** [on] the earth, since he [binds the world]. He said, "[…] while you're walking up on this mountain, because although you seek, you won't find anything. But come to me, and [take for] yourself what's in my [world]. Eat my good things. Take for yourself silver, gold, and clothes." In response Stranger said, "Depart from me, Satan, because I don't seek you but my Father, who is above all the great realms; because I've been called 'Stranger,' since I'm from another race. I'm not from your race." Then the one who binds the [world] told him, "We **61** ourselves […] in my [world]."

[Then] Stranger said to him, "Depart from [me], Satan! Go away, because I don't [belong to] you."

Then Satan [departed] from him, after having angered him many times; and he wasn't able to deceive [him]. And when he had been defeated, he went away to his place in great shame.

The Transfiguration of Stranger

Then Stranger cried out in a loud voice, "O God, you who are in the great realms, hear my voice, have mercy on me, and save me from every evil! Look on me and hear me in this deserted place. Now [let your] indescribable [light] shine on me **62** […] your light. Yes, Lord, help me, because [I] don't know […] forever and ever."

And while I said these things, look! A bright cloud surrounded me. Because of the way it was shining, I couldn't gaze into the light around it. And I heard something from the cloud and the light. It shone on me and said, "O Stranger, the sound of your prayer has been heard, and I've been sent here to tell you the gospel before you leave [this place], so that **63** you may [know …] reveal [… body] dissolve […] the [spirit…]

The Ascent of Stranger

"[… above. But] when you go, [you'll] come to the first Power, which is the power of Desire. And it will bind you and [ask] you, 'Where are [you] going, O Stranger?' But say, 'What bound me has been killed, and I've been released. I'll go up to my Father, the One above all the great realms.' And it will release you.

"Then you'll come to the second Power, which is the power of Darkness. [And it] will bind [you and] **64** [ask you], 'Where [are you going, O Stranger?' But say, 'What bound me has been killed, and I've been released. I'll go up to my Father, the One above all the great realms.' Then it will release you.]

"[And you'll] come to the [third] Power, which is called 'Ignorance.' It will bind you and say to you, 'Where [are you going, O] Stranger?' But say to it, 'What bound me has been killed, and I've been released. I'll go up to my Father, the One above all the great realms.' Then it will release you.

"And you'll come to the fourth Power, which [… Death. It will say to you, 'Where are you going, O Stranger?'] **65** [But say, 'What bound me has been killed, and I've been released. I'll go up to my Father, the One above all the great realms.' And it will release you.]

"[And you'll come to the fifth] Power, [which is the] Kingdom [of the] Flesh. [And it will] say to you, '[Where are] you [going, O Stranger?' But say, 'What bound] me has been [killed], and I've [been] released. [Now] then, I'll go up to my Father, [the One] above [all the great realms.' And it will] release you.

"[And you'll come to the sixth Power, which is the Foolish] 'Wisdom' [of Flesh. And] it will say to you, 'Where [are you going,] O [Stranger]?' But say to [it, 'What] bound me [has been killed, and I've been released. I'll go up to my Father], **66** [the One above all the great realms.' And it will release you.]

"[…] in […] and you'll [go up] over [these] angels […] myriads of [holy] angels [… myriads of] angels […] Don't be faint of heart […] Be strong [… O Stranger], because you […] Don't be afraid […] which was said […]"

An unknown number of pages are missing.

Conclusion

Last Page Stranger […] he sent […] so that they might [… the] judgment. [Peace to the one] who wrote them down [and to those who will] preserve them.

GOSPEL OF THE EGYPTIANS

Clem. Alex. *Strom.* iii. 9. 64.

Whence it is with reason that after the Word had told about the End, Salome saith: Until when shall men *continue to* die? (Now, the Scripture speaks of man in two senses, the one that is seen, and the soul: and again, of him that is in a state of salvation, and him that is not: and sin is called the death of the soul) and it is advisedly that the Lord makes an answer: So long as women bear *children*.

66. And why do not they who walk by anything rather than the true rule of the Gospel go on to quote the rest of that which was said to Salome: for when she had said, 'I have done well, then, in not bearing *children*?' (as if childbearing were not the right thing to accept) the Lord answers and says: Every plant eat thou, but that which hath bitterness eat not.

iii. 13. 92. When Salome inquired when the things concerning which she asked should be known, the Lord said: When ye have trampled on the garment of shame, and when the two become one and the male with the female *is* neither male nor female. In the first place, then, we have not this saying in the four Gospels that have been delivered to us, but in that according to the Egyptians.

(The so-called Second Epistle of Clement has this, in a slightly different form, c. xii. 2: For the Lord himself being asked by some one when his kingdom should come, said: When the two shall be one, and the outside (that which is without) as the inside (that which is within), and the male with the female neither male nor female.)

There are allusions to the saying in the Apocryphal Acts, see pp. 335, 429, 450.

iii. 6. 45. The Lord said to Salome when she inquired: How long shall death prevail? 'As long as ye women bera *children*', not because life is an ill, and the creation evil: but as showing the sequence of nature: for in all cases birth is followed by decay.

Excerpts from Theodotus, 67. And when the Saviour says to Salome that there shall be death as long as women bear *children*, he did not say it as abusing birth, for that is necessary for the salvation of believers.

Strom. iii. 9. 63. But those who set themselves against God's creation because of continence, which has a fair-sounding name, quote also those words which were spoken to Salome, of which I made mention before. They are contained, I think (*or* I take it) in the Gospel according to the Egyptians. For they say that 'the Savior himself said: I came to destroy the works of the female'. By *female* he means lust: by *works*, birth and decay.

Hippolytus *against Heresies*, v. 7. (The Naassenes) say that the soul is very hard to find and to perceive; for it does not continue in the same fashion or shape or in one emotion so that one can either describe it or comprehend its essence. And they have these various changes *of the soul*, set forth in the Gospel entitled according to the Egyptians.

Epiphanius, *Heresy* lxii. 2 (Sabellians). Their whole deceit (error) and the strength of it they draw from some apocryphal books, especially from what is called the Egyptian Gospel, to which some have given that name. For in it many suchlike things are recorded (*or* attributed) as from the person of the Saviour, *said* in a corner, purporting that he showed his disciples that the same person was Father, Son, and Holy Spirit.

GOSPEL OF THE HEBREWS

1.   It is written in the Gospel of the Hebrews:

When Christ chose to come to earth among men, the benevolent Father called upon a great power in heaven, named Michael, and entrusted Christ to its care. This power then entered the world and was called Mary, and Christ resided in her womb for seven months.

(Cyril of Jerusalem, *Discourse on Mary Theotokos* 12a)

2.   According to the Gospel written in the Hebrew language, which the Nazarenes read, the entire fount of the Holy Spirit will descend upon him. Additionally, in the Gospel we have just referred to, the following is written:

And it happened when the Lord emerged from the water, the entire fount of the Holy Spirit descended upon Him, rested on Him, and spoke to Him: My son, in all the prophets I awaited you so that you might come and I could rest in you. For you are my rest; you are my firstborn Son who reigns forever.

(Jerome, *Commentary on Isaiah* 4 [on Isaiah 11:2])

3.   And if anyone accept the Gospel of the Hebrews - here the Savior says:

In the same way, my mother, the Holy Spirit, took me by a single hair and transported me to the great mountain Tabor.

(Origen, *Commentary on John* 2.12.87 [on John 1:3])

4.   As also it stands written in the Gospel of the Hebrews:

He who marvels shall reign, and he who has reigned shall find rest.

(Clement, *Stromateis* 2.9.45.5)

To those words (from Plato, *Timaeus* 90) this is equivalent:

He who seeks will not rest until he finds; and he who has found shall marvel; and he who has marveled shall reign; and he who has reigned shall rest.

(Ibid., 5.14.96.3)

5.   As we have read in the Hebrew Gospel, the Lord says to His disciples:

And never be joyful, except when you behold your brother with love.

(Jerome, *Commentary on Ephesians* 3 [on Ephesians 5:4])

6.   In the Gospel according to the Hebrews, which the Nazarenes customarily read, one of the most grievous offenses is listed as:

He who has grieved the spirit of his brother.

(Jerome, *Commentary on Ezekiel* 6 [on Ezekiel 18:7])

7.   The Gospel called according to the Hebrews, which I recently translated into Greek and Latin and which Origen frequently uses, records after the resurrection of the Savior:

And when the Lord had given the linen cloth to the servant of the priest, He went to James and appeared to him. For James had sworn that he would not eat bread from the moment he had drunk the cup of the Lord until he should see Him risen from the dead. Shortly thereafter, the Lord said: Bring a table and bread! And immediately it added: He took the bread, blessed it, broke it, and gave it to James the Just, saying: My brother, eat your bread, for the Son of Man is risen from the dead.

(Jerome, *De viris inlustribus* 2)

GOSPEL OF THE EBIONITES

All our knowledge of this is derived from Epiphanius, and he uses very confusing language about it (as about many other things). The passages are as follows:

And they (the Ebionites) receive the Gospel according to Matthew. For this they too, like the followers of Cerinthus and Merinthus, use to the exclusion of others. And they call it according to the Hebrews, as the truth is, that Matthew alone of New Testament writers made his exposition and preaching of the Gospel in Hebrew and in Hebrew letters.

Epiphanius goes on to say that he had heard of Hebrew versions of John and Acts kept privately in the treasuries (Geniza?) at Tiberias, and continues:

In the Gospel they have, called according to Matthew, but not wholly complete, but falsified and mutilated (they call it the Hebrew *Gospel*), it is contained that 'There was a certain man named Jesus, and he was about thirty years old, who chose us. And coming unto Capernaum he entered into the house of Simon who was surnamed Peter, and opened his mouth and said: As I passed by the lake of Tiberias, I chose John and James the sons of Zebedee, and Simon and Andrew and <Philip and Bartholomew, James *the son* of Alphaeus and Thomas> Thaddaeus and Simon the Zealot and Judas the Iscariot: and thee, Matthew, as thou satest as the receipt of custom I called, and thou followedst me. You therefore I will to be twelve apostles for a testimony unto (of) Israel.

And:

John was baptizing, and there went out unto him Pharisees and were baptized, and all Jerusalem. And John had raiment of camel's hair and a leathern girdle about his loins: and his meat (it saith) was wild honey, whereof the taste is the *taste* of manna, as a cake *dipped* in oil. That, forsooth, they may pervert the word of truth into a lie and for locusts put a cake *dipped* in honey (sic).

These Ebionites were vegetarians and objected to the idea of eating locusts. A locust in Greek is akris, and the word they used for cake is enkris, so the change is slight. We shall meet with this tendency again.

And the beginning of their Gospel says that: It came to pass in the days of Herod the king of Judaea <when Caiaphas was high priest> that there came <a certain man> John <by name>, baptizing with the baptism of repentance in the river Jordan, who was said to be of the lineage of Aaron the priest, child of Zecharias and Elisabeth, and all went out unto him.

The borrowing from St. Luke is very evident here. He goes on:

And after a good deal more it continues that:

After the people were baptized, Jesus also came and was baptized by John; and as he came up from the water, the heavens were opened, and he saw the Holy Ghost in the likeness of a dove that descended and entered into him: and a voice from heaven saying: Thou art my beloved Son, in thee I am well pleased: and again: This day have I begotten thee. And straightway there shone about the place a great light. Which when John saw (it saith) he saith unto him: Who art thou, Lord? and again *there was* a voice from heaven saying unto him: This is my beloved Son in whom I am well pleased. And then (it saith) John fell down before him and said: I beseech thee, Lord, baptize thou me. But he prevented him saying: Suffer it (*or* let it go): for thus it behoveth that all things should be fulfilled.

And on this account they say that Jesus was begotten of the seed of a man, and was chosen; and so by the choice *of God* he was called the Son of God from the Christ that came into him from above in the likeness of a dove. And they deny that he was begotten of God the Father, but say that he was created as one of the archangels, yet greater, and that he is Lord of the angels and of all things made by the Almighty, and that he came and taught, as the Gospel (so called) current among them contains, that, 'I came to destroy the sacrifices, and if ye cease not from sacrificing, the wrath *of God* will not cease from you'.

(With reference to the Passover and the evasion of the idea that Jesus partook of flesh:)

They have changed the saying, as is plain to all from the combination of phrases, and have made the disciples say: Where wilt thou that we make ready for thee to eat the Passover? and him, forsooth, say Have I desired with desire to eat this flesh *of* the Passover with you?

These fragments show clearly that the Gospel was designed to support a particular set of views. They enable us also to distinguish it from the Gospel according to the Hebrews, for, among other things, the accounts of the Baptism in the two are quite different. Epiphanius is only confusing the issue when he talks of it as the Hebrew Gospel - or rather, the Ebionites may be guilty of the confusion, for he attributes the name to them.

The Gospel according to the Twelve, or 'of the Twelve', mentioned by Origen (Ambrose and Jerome) is identified by Zahn with the Ebionite Gospel. He makes a good case for the identification. If the two are not identical, it can only be said that we know nothing of the Gospel according to the Twelve.

Revillout, indeed, claims the title for certain Coptic fragments of narratives of the Passion which are described in their propery place in this collection: but no one has been found to follow his lead.

FAYYUM FRAGMENT

The Fayyum Fragment (Papyrus Vindobonensis Greek 2325 [P. Vienna G. 2325]) is a papyrus fragment that may contain a portion of the New Testament, consisting of only about 100 Greek letters. This fragment was originally discovered in Al-Fayyum, Egypt, and was translated in 1885 by Gustav Bickell after being found in the papyrus collection of Archduke Rainer Joseph of Austria in Vienna.

The surviving manuscript is severely damaged, with fewer than a hundred Greek letters preserved. Based on the style of handwriting, it is believed to have been copied around the end of the third century. The text appears to parallel Mark 14:26–31, presenting a more concise account. It remains uncertain whether the fragment is an abbreviated version of the synoptic gospels or a source text upon which they were based, possibly the apocryphal Gospel of Peter.

Papyrus Vindobonensis 2325

...l]ead out, when he s[a]i[d]: A[ll]
of you [on this] night will be scandaliz[ed]
[according to] what is written: I shall strike the [shep-]
herd and the] sheep shall be scatter[ed. When]
[said] Pet{er}: Even if all, n[ot I....]
[...J{esu}s: Befor]e a cock twice cr[ows, thrice]
[you will d]en[y me].

As he led them out, he said, "You will all fall away tonight according to the scripture: 'I will strike the shepherd and the sheep will be scattered.'"

Then Peter said, "Even if everyone else denies you, I won't."

Jesus said, "Before the cock crows twice, you will deny me three times today."

It is not certain that this is a fragment of a Gospel: it may be, and is by many held to be, a somewhat abridged quotation made by a preacher or commentator. It omits, for instance, the clause: After I am risen I will go before you into Galilee. If the preacher or expositor wished to emphasize Peter's denial, he might easily pass over these words. On the other hand the first editor of it, and others, have thought that the omission was a mark of early date.

The word for *crow* is literally *cry cuckoo*.

THE GOSPEL OF THE BIRTH OF MARY

In the primitive ages there was a Gospel extant bearing this name, attributed to St. Matthew, and received as genuine and authentic by several of the ancient Christian sects. It is to be found in the works of Jerome, a Father of the Church, who flourished in the fourth century, from whence the present translation is made. His contemporaries, Epiphanius, Bishop of Salamis, and Austin, also mention a Gospel under this title. The ancient copies differed from Jerome's, for from one of them the learned Faustus, a native of Britain, who became Bishop of Riez, in Provence, endeavoured to prove that Christ was not the Son of God till after his baptism; and that he was not of the house of David and tribe of Judah, because, according to the Gospel he cited, the Virgin herself was not of this tribe, but of the tribe of Levi; her father being a priest of the name of Joachim. It was likewise from this Gospel that the sect of the Collyridians, established the worship and offering of manchet bread and cracknels, or fine wafers, as sacrifices to Mary, whom they imagined to have been born of a Virgin, as Christ is related in the Canonical Gospel to have been born of her. Epiphanius likewise cites a passage concerning the death of Zacharias, which is not in Jerome's copy, viz. "That it was the occasion of the death of Zacharias in the temple, that when he had seen a vision, he, through surprise, was willing to disclose it, and his mouth was stopped. That which he saw was at the time of his offering incense, and it was a man standing in the form of an ass. When he was gone out, and had a mind to speak thus to the people, *Woe unto you, whom do ye worship?* he who had appeared to him in the temple took away the use of his speech. Afterwards when he recovered it, and was able to speak, he declared this to the Jews, and they slew him. They add (viz. the Gnostics in this book), that on this very account the high-priest was appointed by their lawgiver (by God to Moses), to carry little bells, that whensoever he went into the temple to sacrifice, he, whom they worshipped, hearing the noise of the bells, might have time enough to hide himself; and not be caught in that ugly shape and figure."—The principal part of this Gospel is contained in the Protevangelion of James, which follows next in order.

CHAP. I.

1 *The parentage of Mary.* 7 *Joachim her father, and Anna her mother, go to Jerusalem to the feast of the dedication.* 9 *Issachar the high priest reproaches Joachim for being childless.*

THE blessed and ever glorious Virgin Mary, sprung from the royal race and family of David, was born in the city of Nazareth, and educated at Jerusalem, in the temple of the Lord.

2 Her father's name was Joachim, and her mother's Anna. The family of her father was of Galilee and the city of Nazareth. The family of her mother was of Bethlehem.

3 Their lives were plain and right in the sight of the Lord, pious and faultless before men. For they divided all their substance into three parts:

4 One of which they devoted to the temple and officers of the temple; another they distributed among strangers, and persons in poor circumstances; and the third they reserved for themselves and the uses of their own family.

5 In this manner they lived for about twenty years chastely, in the favour of God, and the esteem of men, without any children.

6 But they vowed, if God should favour them with any issue, they would devote it to the service of the Lord; on which account they went at every feast in the year to the temple of the Lord

7 And it came to pass, that when the feast of the dedication drew near, Joachim, with some others of his tribe, went up to Jerusalem, and at that time, Issachar was high-priest;

8 Who, when he saw Joachim along with the rest of his neighbours, bringing his offering, despised both him and his offerings, and asked him,

9 Why he, who had no children, would presume to appear among those who had? Adding, that his offerings could never be acceptable to God, who was judged by him unworthy to have children; the Scripture having said, Cursed is every one who shall not beget a male in Israel.

10. He further said, that he ought first to be free from that curse by begetting some issue, and then come with his offerings into the presence of God.

11 But Joachim being much confounded with the shame of such reproach, retired to the shepherds, who were with the cattle in their pastures;

12 For he was not inclined to return home, lest his neighbours, who were present and heard all this from the high-priest, should publicly reproach him in the same manner.

CHAP. II.

1 *An angel appears to Joachim,* 9 *and informs him that Anna shall conceive and bring forth a daughter, who shall be called Mary,* 11 *be brought up in the temple,* 12 *and while yet a virgin, in a way unparalleled, bring forth the Son of God:* 13 *gives him a sign,* 14 *and departs.*

BUT when he had been there for some time, on a certain day when he was alone, the angel of the Lord stood by him with a prodigious light.

2 To whom, being troubled at the appearance, the angel who had appeared to him, endeavouring to compose him said:

3 Be not afraid, Joachim, nor troubled at the sight of me, for I am an angel of the Lord sent by him to you, that I might inform you, that your prayers are heard, and your alms ascended in the sight of God.

4 For he hath surely seen your shame, and heard you unjustly reproached for not having children: for God is the avenger of sin, and not of nature;

5 And so when he shuts the womb of any person, he does it for this reason, that he may in a more wonderful manner again open it, and that which is born appear to be not the product of lust, but the gift of God.

6 For the first mother of your nation Sarah, was she not

barren even till her eightieth year: And yet even in the end of her old age brought forth Isaac, in whom the promise was made a blessing to all nations.

7 Rachel also, so much in favour with God, and beloved so much by holy Jacob, continued barren for a long time, yet afterwards was the mot her of Joseph, who was not only governor of Egypt, but delivered many nations from perishing with hunger.

8 Who among the judges was more valiant than Samson, or more holy than Samuel? And yet both their mothers were barren.

9 But if reason will not convince you of the truth of my words, that there are frequent conceptions in advanced years, and that those who were barren have brought forth to their great surprise; therefore Anna your wife shall bring you a daughter, and you shall call her name Mary;

10 She shall, according to your vow, be devoted to the Lord from her infancy, and be filled with the Holy Ghost from her mother's womb;

11 She shall neither eat nor drink anything which is unclean, nor shall her conversation be without among the common people, but in the temple of the Lord; that so she may not fall under any slander or suspicion of what is bad.

12 So in the process of her years, as she shall be in a miraculous manner born of one that was barren, so she shall, while yet a virgin, in a way unparalleled, bring forth the Son of the most High God, who shall, be called Jesus, and, according to the signification of his name, be the Saviour of all nations.

13 And this shall be a sign to you of the things which I declare, namely, when you come to the golden gate of Jerusalem, you shall there meet your wife Anna, who being very much troubled that you returned no sooner, shall then rejoice to see you.

14 When the angel had said this he departed from him.

CHAP. III.

1 *The angel appears to Anna; 2 tells her a daughter shall be born unto her, 3 devoted to the service of the Lord in the temple, 5, who, being a virgin and not knowing man, shall bring forth the Lord, 6 and gives her a sign therefore. 8 Joachim and Anna meet and rejoice, 10 and praise the Lord. 11 Anna conceives, and brings forth a daughter called Mary.*

AFTERWARDS the angel appeared to Anna his wife saying: Fear not, neither think that which you see is a spirit.

2 For I am that angel who hath offered up your prayers and alms before God, and am now sent to you, that I may inform you, that a daughter will be born unto you, who shall be called Mary, and shall be blessed above all women.

3 She shall be, immediately upon her birth, full of the grace of the Lord, and shall continue during the three years of her weaning in her father's house, and afterwards, being devoted to the service of the Lord, shall not depart from the temple, till she arrives to years of discretion.

4 In a word, she shall there serve the Lord night and day in fasting and prayer, shall abstain from every unclean

thing, and never know any man;

5 But, being an unparalleled instance without any pollution or defilement, and a virgin not knowing any man, shall bring forth a son, and a maid shall bring forth the Lord, who both by his grace and name and works, shall be the Saviour of the world.

6 Arise therefore, and go up to Jerusalem, and when you shall come to that which is called the golden gate (because it is gilt with gold), as a sign of what I have told you, you shall meet your husband, for whose safety you have been so much concerned.

7 When therefore you find these things thus accomplished, believe that all the rest which I have told you, shall also undoubtedly be accomplished.

8 According therefore to the command of the angel, both of them left the places where they were, and when they came to the place specified in the angel's prediction, they met each other.

9 Then, rejoicing at each other's vision, and being fully satisfied in the promise of a child, they gave due thanks to the Lord, who exalts the humble.

10 After having praised the Lord, they returned home, and lived in a cheerful and assured expectation of the promise of God.

11 So Anna conceived, and brought forth a daughter, and, according to the angel's command, the parents did call her name Mary.

CHAP. IV.

1 *Mary brought to the temple at three years old. 6 Ascends the stairs of the temple by miracle. 8 Her parents sacrificed and returned home.*

AND when three years were expired, and the time of her weaning complete, they brought the Virgin to the temple of the Lord with offerings.

2 And there were about the temple, according to the fifteen Psalms of degrees, fifteen stairs to ascend.

3 For the temple being built in a mountain, the altar of burnt-offering, which was without, could not be come near but by stairs;

4 The parents of the blessed Virgin and infant Mary put her upon one of these stairs;

5 But while they were putting off their clothes, in which they had travelled, and according to custom putting on some that were more neat and clean,

6 In the mean time the Virgin of the Lord in such a manner went up all the stairs one after another, without the help of any to lead or lift her, that any one would have judged from hence that she was of perfect age.

7 Thus the Lord did, in the infancy of his Virgin, work this extraordinary work, and evidence by this miracle how great she was like to be hereafter.

8 But the parents having offered up their sacrifice, according to the custom of the law, and perfected their vow, left the Virgin with other virgins in the apartments of the temple, who were to be brought up there, and they returned home.

CHAP. V.

2 *Mary ministered unto by angels. 4 The high-priest orders all*

virgins of fourteen years old to quit the temple and endeavour to be married. 5 Mary refuses, 6 having vowed her virginity to the Lord. 7 The high-priest commands a meeting of the chief persons of Jerusalem, 11 who seek the Lord for counsel in the matter. 13 A voice from the mercy-seat. 15 The high priest obeys it by ordering all the unmarried men of the house of David to bring their rods to the altar, 17 that his rod which should flower, and on which the Spirit of God should sit, should betroth the Virgin.

BUT the Virgin of the Lord, as she advanced in fears, increased also in perfections, and according to the saying of the Psalmist, her father and mother forsook her, but the Lord took care of her.

2 For she every day had the conversation of angels, and every day received visitors from God, which preserved her from all sorts of evil, and caused her to abound with all good things;

3 So that when at length she arrived to her fourteenth year, as the wicked could not lay anything to her charge worthy of reproof, so all good persons, who were acquainted with her, admired her life and conversation.

4 At that time the high-priest made a public order, That all the virgins who had public settlements in the temple, and were come to this age, should return home, and, as they were now of a proper maturity, should, according to the custom of their country, endeavour to be married.

5 To which command, though all the other virgins readily yielded obedience, Mary the Virgin of the Lord alone answered, that she could not comply with it.

6 Assigning these reasons, that both she and her parents had devoted her to the service of the Lord; and besides, that she had vowed virginity to the Lord, which vow she was resolved never to break through by lying with a man.

7 The high priest being hereby brought into a difficulty,

8 Seeing he durst neither on the one hand dissolve the vow, and disobey the Scripture, which says, Vow and pay,

9 Nor on the other hand introduce a custom, to which the people were strangers, commanded,

10 That at the approaching feast all the principal persons both of Jerusalem and the neighbouring places should meet together, that he might have their advice, how he had best proceed in so difficult a case.

11 When they were accordingly met, they unanimously agreed to seek the Lord, and ask counsel from him on this matter.

12 And when they were all engaged in prayer, the high-priest, according to the usual way, went to consult God.

13 And immediately there was a voice from the ark, and the mercy seat, which all present heard, that it must be inquired or sought out by a prophecy of Isaiah to whom the Virgin should be given and be betrothed;

14 For Isaiah saith, there shall come forth a rod out of the stem of Jesse, and a flower shall spring out of its root,

15 And the Spirit of the Lord shall rest upon him, the Spirit of Wisdom and Understanding, the Spirit of Counsel and Might, the Spirit of Knowledge and Piety, and the Spirit of the fear of the Lord shall fill him.

16 Then, according to this prophecy, he appointed, that all the men of the house and family of David, who were marriageable, and not married, should bring their several rods to the altar,

17 And out of whatsoever person's rod after it was brought, a flower should bud forth, and on the top of it the Spirit of the Lord should sit in the appearance of a dove, he should be the man to whom the Virgin should be given and be betrothed.

CHAP. VI.

1 *Joseph draws back his rod. 5 The dove pitches on it. He betroths Mary and returns to Bethlehem. 7 Mary returns to her parents' house at Galilee.*

AMONG the rest there was a man named Joseph, of the house and family of David, and a person very far advanced in years, who drew back his rod, when every one besides presented his.

2 So that when nothing appeared agreeable to the heavenly voice, the high-priest judged it proper to consult God again,

3 Who answered that he to whom the Virgin was to be betrothed was the only person of those who were brought together, who had not brought his rod.

4 Joseph therefore was betrayed.

5 For, when he did bring his rod, and a dove coming from Heaven pitched upon the top of it, every one plainly saw, that the Virgin was to be betrothed to him:

6 Accordingly, the usual ceremonies of betrothing being over, he returned to his own city of Bethlehem, to set his house in order, and make the needful for the marriage.

7 But the Virgin of the Lord, Mary, with seven other virgins of the same age, who had been weaned at the same time, and who had been appointed to attend her by the priest, returned to her parents' house in Galilee.

CHAP. VII.

7 *The salutation of the Virgin by Gabriel, who explains to her that she shall conceive, without lying with a man, while a Virgin, 19 by the Holy Ghost coming upon her without the heats of lust. 21 She submits.*

NOW at this time of her first coming into Galilee, the angel Gabriel was sent to her from God, to declare to her the conception of our Saviour, and the manner and way of her conceiving him.

2 Accordingly going into her, he filled the chamber where she was with a prodigious light, and in a most courteous manner saluting her, he said,

3 Hail, Mary! Virgin of the Lord most acceptable! O Virgin full of Grace! The Lord is with you, you are blessed above all women, you are blessed above all men, that have been hitherto born.

4 But the Virgin, who had before been well acquainted with the countenances of angels, and to whom such light from heaven was no uncommon thing,

5 Was neither terrified with the vision of the angel, nor astonished at the greatness of the light, but only troubled about the angel's words:

6 And began to consider what so extraordinary a salutation should mean, what it did portend, or what sort of end it would have.

7 To this thought the angel, divinely inspired, replies;

8 Fear not, Mary, as though I intended anything

inconsistent with your chastity in this salutation:

9 For you have found favour with the Lord, because you made virginity your choice.

10 Therefore while you are a Virgin, you shall conceive without sin, and bring forth a son.

11 He shall be great, because he shall reign from sea to sea, and from the rivers to the ends of the earth.

12 And he shall be called the Son of the Highest; for he who is born in a mean state on earth reigns in an exalted one in heaven.

13 And the Lord shall give him the throne of his father David, and he shall reign over the house of Jacob for ever, and of his kingdom there shall be no end.

14 For he is the King of Kings, and Lord of Lords, and his throne is for ever and ever.

15 To this discourse of the angel the Virgin replied not, as though she were unbelieving, but willing to know the manner of it.

16 She said, How can that be? For seeing, according to my vow, I have never known any man, how can I bear a child without the addition of a man's seed?

17 To this the angel replied and said, Think not, Mary, that you shall conceive in the ordinary way.

18 For, without lying with a man, while a Virgin, you shall conceive; while a Virgin, you shall bring forth; and while a Virgin shall give suck.

19 For the Holy Ghost shall come upon you, and the power of the Most High shall overshadow you, without any of the heats of lust.

20 So that which shall be born of you shall be only holy, be. cause it only is conceived without sin, and being born, shall be called the Son of God.

21 Then Mary stretching forth her hands, and lifting her eyes to heaven, said, Behold the handmaid of the Lord! Let it be unto me according to thy word.

CHAP. VIII.

1 *Joseph returns to Galilee to marry the Virgin he had betrothed.* 4 *perceives she is with child,* 5 *is uneasy,* 7 *purposes to put her away privily,* 8 *is told by the angel of the Lord it is not the work of man but the Holy Ghost,* 12 *Marries her, but keeps chaste,* 13 *removes with her to Bethlehem,* 15 *where she brings forth Christ.*

JOSEPH therefore went from Judæa to Galilee, with intention to marry the Virgin who was betrothed to him:

2 For it was now near three months since she was betrothed to him.

3 At length it plainly appeared she was with child, and it could not be hid from Joseph:

4 For going to the Virgin in a free manner, as one espoused, and talking familiarly with her, he perceived her to be with child.

5 And thereupon began to be uneasy and doubtful, not knowing what course it would be best to take;

6 For being a just man, he was not willing to expose her, nor defame her by the suspicion of being a whore, since he was a pious man.

7 He purposed therefore privately to put an end to their agreement, and as privately to put her away.

8 But while he was meditating these things, behold the angel of the Lord appeared to him in his sleep, and said

Joseph, son of David, fear not;

9 Be not willing to entertain any suspicion of the Virgin's being guilty of fornication, or to think any thing amiss of her, neither be afraid to take her to wife;

10 For that which is begotten In her and now distresses your mind, is not the work of man, but the Holy Ghost.

11 For she of all women is that only Virgin who shall bring forth the Son of God, and you shall call his name Jesus, that is, Saviour: for he will save his people from their sins.

12 Joseph thereupon, according to the command of the angel, married the Virgin, and did not know her, but kept her in chastity.

13 And now the ninth month from her conception drew near, when Joseph took his wife and what other things were necessary to Bethlehem, the city from whence he came.

14 And it came to pass, while they were there, the days were fulfilled for her bringing forth.

15 And she brought forth her first-born son, as the holy Evangelists have taught, even our Lord Jesus Christ, who with the Father, Son, and Holy Ghost, lives and reigns to everlasting ages.

THE PROTEVANGELION

or, an historical account of the birth of christ, and the perpetual virgin mary, his mother, by james the lesser, cousin and brother of the lord jesus, chief apostle and first bishop of the christians in Jerusalem.

This Gospel is ascribed to James. The allusions to it in the ancient Fathers are frequent, and their expressions indicate that it had obtained a very general credit in the Christian world. The controversies founded upon it chiefly relate to the age of Joseph at the birth of Christ, and to his being a widower with children, before his marriage with the Virgin. It seems material to remark, that the legends of the latter ages affirm the virginity of Joseph, notwithstanding Epiphanius, Hilary, Chrysostom, Cyril, Euthymius, Thephylact, Occumenius, and indeed all the Latin Fathers till Ambrose, and the Greek Fathers afterwards, maintain the opinions of Joseph's age and family, founded upon their belief in the authenticity of this book. It is supposed to have been originally composed in Hebrew. Postellus brought the MS. of this Gospel from the Levant, translated it into Latin, and sent it to Oporimus, a printer at Basil, where Bibliander, a Protestant Divine, and the Professor of Divinity at Zurich, caused it to be printed in 1552. Postellus asserts that it was publicly read as canonical in the eastern churches, they making no doubt that James was the author of it. It is, nevertheless, considered apocryphal by some of the most learned divines in the Protestant and Catholic churches.

CHAP. I.

1 *Joachim, a rich man,* 2 *offers to the Lord,* 3 *is opposed by Reuben the high-priest, because he has not begotten issue in Israel,* 6 *retires into the wilderness and fasts forty days and forty nights.*

IN the history of the twelve tribes of Israel we read there was a certain person called Joachim, who being very rich, made double offerings to the Lord God, having made this resolution:

my substance shall be for the benefit of the whole people, and that I may find mercy from the Lord God for the forgiveness of my sins.

2 But at a certain great feast of the Lord, when the children of Israel offered their gifts, and Joachim also offered his, Reuben the high-priest opposed him, saying it is not lawful for thee to offer thy gifts, seeing thou hast not begot any issue in Israel.

3 At this Joachim being concerned very much, went away to consult the registries of the twelve tribes, to see whether he was the only person who had begot no issue.

4 But upon inquiry he found that all the righteous had raised up seed in Israel:

5 Then he called to mind the patriarch Abraham, How that God in the end of his life had given him his son Isaac; upon which he was exceedingly distressed, and would not be seen by his wife:

6 But retired into the wilderness, and fixed his tent there, and fasted forty days and forty nights, saying to himself,

7 I will not go down either to eat or drink, till the Lord my God shall look down upon me, but prayer shall be my meat and drink.

CHAP. II.

1 *Anna, the wife of Joachim, mourns her barrenness,* 6 *is reproached with it by Judith her maid,* 9 *sits under a laurel tree and prays to the Lord.*

IN the meantime his wife Anna was distressed and perplexed on a double account, and said I will mourn both for my widowhood and my barrenness.

2 Then drew near a great feast of the Lord, and Judith her maid said, How long will you thus afflict your soul? The feast of the Lord is now come, when it is unlawful for any one to mourn.

3 Take therefore this hood which was given by one who makes such things, for it is not fit that I, who am a servant, should wear it, but it well suits a person of your greater character.

4 But Anna replied, Depart from me, I am not used to such things; besides, the Lord hath greatly humbled me.

5 I fear some ill-designing person hath given thee this, and thou art come to pollute me with my sin.

6 Then Judith her maid answered, What evil shall I wish you when you will not hearken to me?

7 I cannot wish you a greater curse than you are under, in that God hath shut up your womb, that you should not be a mother in Israel.

8 At this Anna was exceedingly troubled, and having on her wedding garment, went about three o'clock in the afternoon to walk in her garden.

9 And she saw a laurel-tree, and sat under it, and prayed unto the Lord, saying,

10 O God of my fathers, bless me and regard my prayer as thou didst bless the womb of Sarah, and gavest her a son Isaac.

CHAP. III.

1 *Anna perceiving a sparrow's nest in the laurels bemoans her barrenness.*

AND as she was looking towards heaven she perceived a sparrow's nest in the laurel,

2 And mourning within herself, she said, Wo is me, who begat me? and what womb did bear me, that I should be thus accursed before the children of Israel, and that they should reproach and deride me in the temple of my God: Wo is me, to what can I be compared?

3 I am not comparable to the very beasts of the earth, for even the beasts of the earth are fruitful before thee, O Lord! Wo is me, to what can I be compared?

4 I am not comparable to the brute animals, for even the brute animals are fruitful before thee, O Lord! Wo is me, to what am I comparable?

5 I cannot be compared to these waters, for even the waters are fruitful before thee, O Lord! Wo is me, to what can I be compared?

6 I am not comparable to the waves of the sea; for these, whether they are calm, or in motion, with the fishes which are in them, praise thee, O Lord! Wo is me, to what can I be compared?

7 I am not comparable to the very earth, for the earth produces its fruits, and praises thee, O Lord!

CHAP. IV.

1 *An Angel appears to Anna and tells her she shall conceive; two angels appear to her on the same errand.* 5 *Joachim sacrifices.* 8 *Anna*

goes to meet him, 9 *rejoicing that she shall conceive.*

THEN an angel of the Lord stood by her and said, Anna, Anna, the Lord hath heard thy prayer; thou shalt conceive and bring forth, and thy progeny shall be spoken of in all the world.

2 And Anna answered, As the Lord my God liveth, whatever I bring forth, whether it be male or female, I will devote it to the Lord my God, and it shall minister to him in holy things, during its whole life.

3 And behold there appeared two angels, saying unto her, Behold Joachim thy husband is coming with his shepherds.

4 For an angel of the Lord hath also come down to him, and said, The Lord God hath heard thy prayer, make haste and go hence, for behold Anna thy wife shall conceive.

5 And Joachim went down and called his shepherds, saying Bring me hither ten she-lambs without spot or blemish, and they shall be for the Lord my God.

6 And bring me twelve calves without blemish, and the twelve calves shall be for the priests and the elders.

7 Bring me also a hundred goats, and the hundred goats shall be for the whole people.

8 And Joachim went down with the shepherds, and Anna stood by the gate and saw Joachim coming with the shepherds.

9 And she ran, and hanging about his neck, said, Now I know that the Lord hath greatly blessed me:

10 For behold, I who was a widow am no longer a widow, and I who was barren shall conceive.

CHAP. V.

1 *Joachim abides the first day in his house, but sacrifices on the morrow.* 2 *consults the plate on the priest's forehead.* 3 *And is without sin.* 6 *Anna brings forth a daughter,* 9 *whom she calls Mary.*

AND Joachim abode the first day in his house, but on the morrow he brought his offerings and said,

2 If the Lord be propitious to me let the plate which is on the priest's forehead 1 make it manifest.

3 And he consulted the plate which the priest wore, and saw it, and behold sin was not found in him.

4 And Joachim said, Now I know that the Lord is propitious to me, and hath taken away all my sins.

5 And he went down from the temple of the Lord justified, and he went to his own house.

6 And when nine months were fulfilled to Anna, she brought forth, and said to the midwife, What have I brought forth?

7 And she told her, a girl.

8 Then Anna said, the Lord hath this day magnified my soul; and she laid her in bed.

9 And when the days of her purification were accomplished, she gave suck to the child, and called her name Mary.

CHAP. VI.

1 *Mary at nine months old, walks nine steps,* 3 *Anna keeps her holy,* 4 *When she is a year old, Joachim makes a great feast.* 7 *Anna gives her the breast, and sings a song to the Lord.*

AND the child increased in strength every day, so that when she was nine months old, her mother put her upon the ground to try if she could stand; and when she had walked nine steps, she came again to her mother's lap.

2 Then her mother caught her up, and said, As the Lord my God liveth, thou shalt not walk again on this earth till I bring thee into the temple of the Lord.

3 Accordingly she made her chamber a holy place, and suffered nothing uncommon or unclean to come near her, but invited certain undefiled daughters of Israel, and they drew her aside.

4 But when the child was a year old, Joachim made a great feast, and invited the priests, scribes, elders, and all the people of Israel;

5 And Joachim then made an offering of the girl to the chief priests, and they blessed her, saying, The God of our fathers bless this girl, and give her a name famous and lasting through all generations. And all the people replied, So be it, Amen.

6 Then Joachim a second time offered her to the priests, and they blessed her, saying, O most high God, regard this girl, and bless her with an everlasting blessing.

7 Upon this her mother took her up, and gave her the breast, and sung the following song to the Lord.

8 I will sing a new song unto the Lord my God, for he hath visited me, and taken away from me the reproach of mine enemies, and hath given me the fruit of his righteousness, that it may now be told the sons of Reuben, that Anna gives suck.

9 Then she put the child to rest in the room which she had consecrated, and she went out and ministered unto them.

10 And when the feast was ended, they went away rejoicing and praising the God of Israel.

CHAP. VII.

3 *Mary being three years old, Joachim causes certain virgins to light each a lamp, and goes with her to the temple.* 5 *The high-priest places her on the third step of the altar, and she dances with her feet.*

BUT the girl grew, and when she was two years old, Joachim said to Anna, Let us lead her to the temple of the Lord, that we may perform our vow, which we have vowed unto the Lord God, lest he should be angry with us, and our offering be unacceptable.

2 But Anna said, Let us wait the third year, lest she should be at a loss to know her father. And Joachim said, Let us then wait.

3 And when the child was three years old, Joachim said, Let us invite the daughters of the Hebrews, who are undefiled, and let them take each a lamp, and let them be lighted, that the child may not turn back again, and her mind be set against the temple of the Lord.

4 And they did thus till they ascended into the temple of the Lord. And the high-priest received her, and blessed her, and said, Mary, the Lord God hath magnified thy name to all generations, and to the very end of time by thee will the Lord shew his redemption to the children of Israel,

5 And he placed her upon the third step of the altar, and the Lord gave unto her grace, and she danced with her feet, and all the house of Israel loved her.

CHAP. VIII.

2 *Mary fed in the temple by angels,* 3 *when twelve years old the priests consult what to do with her.* 6 *The angel of the Lord warns Zacharias to call together all the widowers, each bringing a rod.* 7 *The people meet by sound of trumpet.* 8 *Joseph throws away his hatchet, and goes to the meeting,* 11 *a dove comes forth from his rod, and alights on his head.* 12 *He is chosen to betroth the Virgin.* 13 *refuses because he is*

an old man, 15 *is compelled,* 16 *takes her home, and goes to mind his trade of building.*

AND her parents went away filled with wonder, and praising God, because the girl did not return back to them.

2 But Mary continued in the temple as a dove educated there, and received her food from the hand of an angel.

3 And when she was twelve years of age, the priests met in a council, and said, Behold, Mary is twelve years of age; what shall we do with her, for fear lest the holy place of the Lord our God should be defiled?

4 Then replied the priests to Zacharias the high-priest, Do you stand at the altar of the Lord, and enter into the holy place, and make petitions concerning her, and whatsoever the Lord shall manifest unto you, that do.

5 Then the high-priest entered into the Holy of Holies, and taking away with him the breastplate of judgment made prayers concerning her;

6 And behold the angel of the Lord came to him, and said, Zacharias, Zacharias, Go forth and call together all the widowers among the people, and let every one of them bring his rod, and he by whom the Lord shall shew a sign shall be the husband of Mary.

7 And the criers went out through all Judæa, and the trumpet of the Lord sounded, and all the people ran and met together.

8 Joseph also, throwing away the hatchet, went out to meet them; and when they were met, they went to the high-priest, taking every man his rod.

9 After the high-priest had received their rods, he went into the temple to pray;

10 And when he had finished his prayer, he took the rods, And went forth and distributed them, and there was no miracle attended them.

11 The last rod was taken by Joseph, and behold a dove proceeded out of the rod, and flew upon the head of Joseph.

12 And the high-priest said, Joseph, Thou art the person chosen to take the Virgin of the Lord, to keep her for him:

13 But Joseph refused, saying, I am an old man, and have children, but she is young, and I fear lest I should appear ridiculous in Israel.

14 Then the high-priest replied, Joseph, fear the Lord thy God, and remember how God dealt with Dathan, Korah, and Abiram, how the earth opened and swallowed them up, because of their contradiction.

15 Now therefore, Joseph, fear God, lest the like things should happen in your family.

16 Joseph then being afraid, took her unto his house, and Joseph said unto Mary, Behold, I have taken thee from the temple of the Lord, and now I will leave thee in my house; I must go to mind my trade of building. he Lord be with thee.

CHAP. IX.

1 *The priests desire a new veil for the temple,* 3 *seven virgins cast lots for making different parts of it,* 4 *the lot to spin the true purple falls to Mary.* 5 *Zacharias, the high priest, becomes dumb.* 7 *Mary takes a pot to draw water, and hears a voice,* 8 *trembles and begins to work,* 9 *an angel appears, and salutes her, and tells her she shall conceive by the Holy Ghost,* 17 *she submits,* 19 *visits her cousin Elizabeth, whose child in her womb leaps.*

AND it came to pass, in a council of the priests, it was said, Let us make a new veil for the temple.

2 And the high-priest said, Call together to me seven undefiled virgins of the tribe of David.

3 And the servants went and brought them into the temple of the Lord, and the high-priest said unto them Cast lots before me now, who of you shall spin the golden thread, who the blue, who the scarlet, who the fine linen, and who the true purple.

4 Then the high-priest knew Mary, that she was of the tribe of David; and he called her, and the true purple fell to her lot to spin, and she went away to her own house.

5 But from that time Zacharias the high-priest became dumb, and Samuel was placed in his room till Zacharias spoke again.

6 But Mary took the true purple, and did spin it.

7 And she took a pot, and went out to draw water, and heard a voice saying unto her, Hail thou who art full of grace, the Lord is with thee; thou art blessed among women.

8 And she looked round to the right and to the left (to see) whence that voice came, and then trembling went into her house, and laying down the water-pot she took the purple, and sat down in her seat to work it.

9 And behold the angel of the Lord stood by her, and said, Fear not, Mary, for thou hast found favour in the sight of God;

10 Which when she heard, she reasoned with herself what that sort of salutation meant.

11 And the angel said unto her, The Lord is with thee, and thou shalt conceive:

12 To which she replied, What! shall I conceive by the living God, and bring forth as all other women do?

13 But the angel returned answer, Not so, O Mary, but the Holy Ghost shall come upon thee, and the power of the Most High shall overshadow thee;

14 Wherefore that which shall be born of thee shall be holy, and shall be called the Son of the Living God, and thou shalt call his name Jesus; for he shall save his people from their sins.

15 And behold thy cousin Elizabeth, she also hath conceived a son in her old age.

16 And this now is the sixth month with her, who was called barren; for nothing is impossible with God.

17 And Mary said, Behold the handmaid of the Lord; let it be unto me according to thy word.

18 And when she had wrought her purple, she carried it to the high-priest, and the high-priest blessed her, saying, Mary, the Lord God hath magnified thy name, and thou shalt be blessed in all the ages of the world.

19 Then Mary, filled with joy, went away to her cousin Elizabeth, and knocked at the door.

20 Which when Elizabeth heard, she ran and opened to her, and blessed her, and said, Whence is this to me, that the mother of my Lord should come unto me?

21 For lo! as soon as the voice of thy salutation reached my ears, that which is in me leaped and blessed thee.

22 But Mary, being ignorant of all those mysterious things which the archangel Gabriel had spoken to her, lifted up her eyes to heaven, and said, Lord! What am I, that all the generations of the earth should call me blessed?

23 But perceiving herself daily to grow big, and being afraid, she went home, and hid herself from the children of Israel; and was fourteen years old when all these things happened.

CHAP. X.

1 *Joseph returns from building houses, finds the Virgin grown big,*

*being six months' gone with child, 2 is jealous and
troubled, 8 reproaches her, 10 she affirms her innocence, 13 he leaves
her, 16 determines to dismiss her privately, 17 is warned in a dream
that Mary is with child by the Holy Ghost, 20 and glorifies God who
hath shewn him such favour.*

AND when her sixth month was come, Joseph returned
from his building houses abroad, which was his trade, and
entering into the house, found the Virgin grown big:

2 Then smiting upon his face, he said, With what face can I
look up to the Lord my God? or, what shall I say
concerning this young woman?

3 For I received her a Virgin out of the temple of the Lord
my God, and have not preserved her such!

4 Who has thus deceived me? Who has committed this evil
in my house, and seducing the Virgin from me, hath defiled
her?

5 Is not the history of Adam exactly accomplished in me?

6 For in the very instant of his glory, the serpent came and
found Eve alone, and seduced her.

7 Just after the same manner it has happened to me.

8 Then Joseph arising from the ground, called her, and said,
O thou who hast been so much favoured by God, why hast
thou done this?

9 Why hast thou thus debased thy soul, who wast educated
in the Holy of Holies, and received thy food from the hand
of angels?

10 But she, with a flood of tears, replied, I am innocent,
and have known no man.

11 Then said Joseph, How comes it to pass you are with
child?

12 Mary answered, As the Lord my God liveth, I know not
by what means.

13 Then Joseph was exceedingly afraid, and went away
from her, considering what he should do with her; and he
thus reasoned with himself:

14 If I conceal her crime, I shall be found guilty by the law
of the Lord;

15 And if I discover her to the children of Israel, I fear, lest
she being with child by an angel, I shall be found to betray
the life of an innocent person:

16 What therefore shall I do? I will privately dismiss her.

17 Then the night was come upon him, when behold an
angel of the Lord appeared to him in a dream, and said,

18 Be not afraid to take that young woman, for that which
is within her is of the Holy Ghost; .

19 And she shall bring forth a son, and thou shalt call his
name Jesus, for he shall save his people from their sins.

20 Then Joseph arose from his sleep, and glorified the God
of Israel, who had shown him such favour, and preserved
the Virgin.

CHAP. XI.

*3 Annas visits Joseph, perceives the Virgin big with child, 4 informs
the high priest that Joseph had privately married her. 8 Joseph and
Mary brought to trial on the charge. 17 Joseph drinks the water of the
Lord as an ordeal, and receiving no harm, returns home.*

THEN came Annas the scribe, and said to Joseph,
Wherefore have we not seen you since your return?

2 And Joseph replied, Because I was weary after my
journey, and rested the first day.

3 But Annas turning about perceived the Virgin big with
child.

4 And went away to the priest, and told him, Joseph in
whom you placed so much confidence, is guilty of a

notorious crime, in that he hath defiled the Virgin whom he
received out of the temple of the Lord, and hath privately
married her, not discovering it to the children of Israel.

5 Then said the priest, Hath Joseph done this?

6 Annas replied, If you send any of your servants, you will
find that she is with child.

7 And the servants went, and found it as he said.

8 Upon this both she and Joseph were brought to their
trial, and the priest said unto her, Mary, what hast thou
done?

9 Why hast thou debased thy soul, and forgot thy God,
seeing thou wast brought up in the Holy of Holies, and
didst receive thy food from the hands of angels, and
heardest their songs?

10 Why hast thou done this?

11 To which with a flood of tears she answered, As the
Lord my God liveth, I am innocent in his sight, seeing I
know no man.

12 Then the priest said to Joseph, Why hast thou done this?

13 And Joseph answered, As the Lord my God liveth, I
have not been concerned with her.

14 But the priest said, Lie not, but declare the truth; thou
hast privately married her, and not discovered it to the
children of Israel, and humbled thyself under the mighty
hand (of God), that thy seed might be blessed.

15 And Joseph was silent.

16 Then said the priest (to Joseph), You must restore to the
temple of the Lord the Virgin which you took thence.

17 But he wept bitterly, and the priest added, I will cause
you both to drink the water of the Lord, 1 which is for trial,
and so your iniquity shall be laid open before you.

18 Then the priest took the water, and made Joseph drink,
and sent him to a mountainous place.

19 And he returned perfectly well, and all the people
wondered that his guilt was not discovered.

20 So the priest said, Since the Lord hath not made your
sins evident, neither do I condemn you.

21 So he sent them away.

22 Then Joseph took Mary, and went to his house, rejoicing
and praising the God of Israel.

CHAP. XII.

*1 A decree from Augustus for taxing the Jews. 5 Joseph puts Mary
on an ass, to return to Bethlehem, 6 she looks sorrowful, 7 she
laughs, 8 Joseph inquires the cause of each, 9 she tells him she sees two
persons, one mourning and the other rejoicing, 10 the delivery being
near, he takes her from the ass, and places her in a cave.*

AND it came to pass, that there went forth a decree from
the Emperor Augustus, that all the Jews should be taxed,
who were of Bethlehem in Judæa:

2 And Joseph said, I will take care that my children be
taxed: but what shall I do with this young woman?

3 To have her taxed as my wife I am ashamed; and if I tax
her as my daughter, all Israel knows she is not my daughter.

4 When the time of the Lord's appointment shall come, let
him do as seems good to him.

5 And he saddled the ass, and put her upon it, and Joseph
and Simon followed after her, and arrived at Bethlehem
within three miles.

6 Then Joseph turning about saw Mary sorrowful, and said
within himself, Perhaps she is in pain through that which is
within her.

7 But when he turned about again he saw her laughing, and
said to her,

8 Mary, how happens it, that I sometimes see sorrow, and sometimes laughter and joy in thy countenance?

9 And Mary replied to him, I see two people with mine eyes, the one weeping and mourning, the other laughing and rejoicing.

10 And he went again across the way, and Mary said to Joseph, Take me down from the ass, for that which is in me presses to come forth.

11 But Joseph replied, Whither shall I take thee? for the place is desert.

12 Then said Mary again to Joseph, take me down, for that which is within me mightily presses me.

13 And Joseph took her down.

14 And he found there a cave, and let her into it.

CHAP. XIII.

1 *Joseph seeks a Hebrew midwife,* 2 *perceives the fowls stopping in their flight,* 3 *the working people at their food not moving,* 8 *the sheep standing still,* 9 *the shepherd fixed and immoveable,* 10 *and kids with their mouths touching the water but not drinking.*

AND leaving her and his sons in the cave, Joseph went forth to seek a Hebrew midwife in the village of Bethlehem.

2 But as I was going (said Joseph) I looked up into the air, and I saw the clouds astonished, and the fowls of the air stopping in the midst of their flight.

3 And I looked down towards the earth, and saw a table spread, and working people sitting around it, but their hands were upon the table, and they did not move to eat.

4 They who had meat in their mouths did not eat.

5 They who lifted their hands up to their heads did not draw them back:

6 And they who lifted them up to their mouths did not put anything in;

7 But all their faces were fixed upwards.

8 And I beheld the sheep dispersed, and yet the sheep stood still.

9 And the shepherd lifted up his hand to smite them, and his hand continued up.

10. And I looked unto a river, and saw the kids with their mouths close to the water, and touching it, but they did not drink.

CHAP. XIV.

1 *Joseph finds a midwife.* 10 *A bright cloud overshadows the care.* 11 *A great light in the cave, gradually increases until the infant is born.* 13 *The midwife goes out, and tells Salome that she has seen a virgin bring forth.* 17 *Salome doubts it.* 20 *her hand withers,* 22 *she supplicates the Lord,* 28 *is cured,* 30 *but warned not to declare what she had seen.*

THEN I beheld a woman coming down from the mountains, and she said to me, Where art thou going, O man?

2 And I said to her, I go to inquire for a Hebrew midwife.

3 She replied to me, Where is the woman that is to be delivered?

4 And I answered, In the cave, and she is betrothed to me.

5 Then said the midwife, Is she not thy wife?

6 Joseph answered, It is Mary, who was educated in the Holy of Holies, in the house of the Lord, and she fell to my lot, and is not my wife, but has conceived by the Holy Ghost.

7 The midwife said, Is this true?

8 He answered, Come and see.

9 And the midwife went along with him, and stood in the cave.

10 Then a bright cloud overshadowed the cave, and the midwife said, This day my soul is magnified, for mine eyes have seen surprising things, and salvation is brought forth to Israel.

11 But on a sudden the cloud became a great light in the cave, so that their eyes could not bear it.

12 But the light gradually decreased, until the infant appeared, and sucked the breast of his mother Mary.

13 Then the midwife cried out, and said, How glorious a day is this, wherein mine eyes have seen this extraordinary sight!

14 And the midwife went out from the cave, and Salome met her.

15 And the midwife said to her, Salome, Salome, I will tell you a most surprising thing which I saw,

16 A virgin hath brought forth, which is a thing contrary to nature.

17 To which Salome replied, As the Lord my God liveth, unless I receive particular proof of this matter, I will not believe that a virgin hath brought forth.

18 Then Salome went in, and the midwife said, Mary, shew thyself, for a great controversy is risen concerning thee.

19 And Salome received satisfaction.

20 But her hand was withered, and she groaned bitterly.

21 And said, Woe to me, because of mine iniquity; for I have tempted the living God, and my hand is ready to drop off.

22 Then Salome made her supplication to the Lord, and said, O God of my fathers, remember me, for I am of the seed of Abraham, and Isaac, and Jacob.

23 Make me not a reproach among the children of Israel, but restore me sound to my parents.

24 For thou well knowest, O Lord, that I have performed many offices of charity in thy name, and have received my reward from thee.

25 Upon this an angel of the Lord stood by Salome, and said, The Lord God hath heard thy prayer, reach forth thy hand to the child, and carry him, and by that means thou shalt be restored.

26 Salome, filled with exceeding joy, went to the child, and said, I will touch him:

27 And she purposed to worship him, for she said, This is a great king which is born in Israel.

28 And straightway Salome was cured.

29 Then the midwife went out of the cave, being approved by God.

30 And lo! a voice came to Salome, Declare not the strange things which thou hast seen, till the child shall come to Jerusalem.

31 So Salome also departed, approved by God.

CHAP. XV.

1 *Wise men come from the east.* 3. *Herod alarmed;* 8 *desires them if they find the child, to bring him word.* 10 *They visit the cave, and offer the child their treasure,* 11 *and being warned in a dream, do not return to Herod, but go home another way.*

THEN Joseph was preparing to go away, because there arose a great disorder in Bethlehem by the coming of some wise men from the east,

2 Who said, Where is the king of the Jews born? For we

have seen his star in the east, and are come to worship him.

3 When Herod heard this, he was exceedingly troubled, and sent messengers to the wise men, and to the priests, and inquired of them in the town-hall,

4 And said unto them, Where have you it written concerning Christ the king, or where should he be born?

5 Then they say unto him, In Bethlehem of Judæa; for thus it is written: And thou Bethlehem in the land of Judah, art not the least among the princes of Judah, for out of thee shall come a ruler, who shall rule my people Israel.

6 And having sent away the chief priests, he inquired of the men in the town-hall, and said unto them, What sign was it ye saw concerning the king that is born?

7 They answered him, We saw an extraordinary large star shining among the stars of heaven, and so out-shined all the other stars, as that they became not visible, and we knew thereby that a great king was born in Israel, and therefore we are come to worship him.

8 Then said Herod to them, Go and make diligent inquiry; and if ye find the child, bring me word again, that I may come and worship him also.

9 So the wise men went forth, and behold, the star which they saw in the east went before them, till it came and stood over the cave where the young child was with Mary his mother

10 Then they brought forth oat of their treasures, and offered unto him gold and frankincense, and myrrh.

11 And being warned in a dream by an angel, that they should not return to Herod through Judæa, they departed into their own country by another way.

CHAP. XVI.

1 *Herod enraged, orders the infants in Bethlehem to be slain.* 2 *Mary puts her infant in an ox manger.* 3 *Elizabeth flees with her son John to the mountains.* 6 *A mountain miraculously divides and receives them.* 9 *Herod incensed at the escape of John, causes Zacharias to be murdered at the altar,* 23 *the roofs of the temple rent, the body miraculously conveyed, and the blood petrified.* 25 *Israel mourns for him.* 27 *Simeon chosen his successor by lot.*

THEN Herod perceiving that e he was mocked by the wise men, and being very angry, commanded certain men to go and to kill all the children that were in Bethlehem, from two years old and under.

2 But Mary hearing that the children were to be killed, being under much fear, took the child, and wrapped him up in swaddling clothes, and laid him in an ox-manger, because there was no room for them in the inn.

3 Elizabeth also, hearing that her son John was about to be searched for, took him and went up unto the mountains, and looked around for a place to hide him;

4 And there was no secret place to be found.

5 Then she groaned within herself, and said, O mountain of the Lord, receive the mother with the child.

6 For Elizabeth could not climb up.

7 And instantly the mountain was divided and received them.

8 And there appeared to them an angel of the Lord, to preserve them.

9 But Herod made search after John, and sent servants to Zacharias, when he was (ministering) at the altar, and said unto him, Where hast thou hid thy son?

10 He replied to them, I am a minister of God, and a servant at the altar; how should I know where my son is?

11 So the servants went back, and told Herod the whole; at which he was incensed, and said, Is not this son of his like to be king in Israel?

12 He sent therefore again his servants to Zacharias, saying, Tell us the truth, where is thy son, for you know that your life is in my hand.

13 So the servants went and told him all this:

14 But Zacharias replied to them, I am a martyr for God, and if he shed my blood, the Lord will receive my soul.

15 Besides know that ye shed innocent blood.

16 However Zacharias was murdered in the entrance of the temple and altar, and about the partition;

17 But the children of Israel knew not when he was killed.

18 Then at the hour of salutation the priests went into the temple, but Zacharias did not according to custom meet them and bless them;

19 Yet they still continued waiting for him to salute them;

20 And when they found he did not in a long time come, one of them ventured into the holy place where the altar was, and he saw blood lying upon the ground congealed;

21 When, behold, a voice from heaven said, Zacharias is murdered, and his blood shall not be wiped away, until the revenger of his blood come.

22 But when he heard this, he was afraid, and went forth and told the priests what he had seen and heard; and they all went in, and saw the fact.

23 Then the roofs of the temple howled, and were rent from the top to the bottom:

24 And they could not find the body, but only blood made hard like stone.

25 And they went awry, and told the people, that Zacharias was murdered, and all the tribes of Israel heard thereof, and mourned for him, and lamented three days.

26 Then the priests took counsel together concerning a person to succeed him.

27 And Simeon and the other priests cast lots, and the lot fell upon Simeon.

28 For he had been assured by the Holy Spirit, that he should not die, till he had seen Christ come in the flesh..

I James wrote this History in Jerusalem: and when the disturbance was I retired into a desert place, until the death of Herod. And the disturbance ceased at Jerusalem. That which remains is, that I glorify God that he hall; given me such wisdom to write unto you who are spiritual, and who love God: to whom (be ascribed) glory and dominion for ever and ever, Amen.

THE FIRST GOSPEL OF THE INFANCY OF JESUS CHRIST

CHAP. I.

1 *Caiaphas relates, that Jesus when in his cradle, informed his mother, that he was the Son. of God. 5 Joseph and Mary going to Bethlehem to be taxed, Mary's time of bringing forth arrives, and she goes into a cave. 8 Joseph fetches in a Hebrew woman, the cave filled with great lights. 11 The infant born, 17 cures the woman, 19 arrival of the shepherds.*

THE following accounts we found in the book of Joseph the high-priest, called by some Caiaphas

2 He relates, that Jesus spake even when he was in the cradle, and said to his mother:

3 Mary, I am Jesus the Son of God, that word which thou didst bring forth according to the declaration of the angel Gabriel to thee, and my father hath sent me for the salvation of the world.

4 In the three hundred and ninth year of the æra of Alexander, Augustus published a decree that all persons should go to be taxed in their own country.

5 Joseph therefore arose, and with Mary his spouse he went to Jerusalem, and then came to Bethlehem, that he and his family might be taxed in the city of his fathers.

6 And when they came by the cave, Mary confessed to Joseph that her time of bringing forth was come, and she could not go on to the city, and said, Let us go into this cave.

7 At that time the sun was very near going down.

8 But Joseph hastened away, that he might fetch her a midwife; and when he saw an old Hebrew woman who was of Jerusalem, he said to her, Pray come hither, good woman, and go into that cave, and you will there see a woman just ready to bring forth.

9 It was after sunset, when the old woman and Joseph with her reached the cave, and they both went into it.

10 And behold, it was all filled with lights, greater than the light of lamps and candles, and greater than the light of the sun itself.

11 The infant was then wrapped up in swaddling clothes, and sucking the breasts of his mother St. Mary.

12 When they both saw this light, they were surprised; the old woman asked St. Mary, Art thou the mother of this child?

13 St. Mary replied, She was.

14 On which the old woman said, Thou art very different from all other women.

15 St. Mary answered, As there is not any child like to my son, so neither is there any woman like to his mother.

16 The old woman answered, and said, O my Lady, I am come hither that I may obtain an everlasting reward.

17 Then our Lady, St. Mary, said to her, Lay thine hands upon the infant; which, when she had done, she became whole.

18 And as she was going forth, she said, From henceforth, all the days of my life, I will attend upon and be a servant of this infant.

19 After this, when the shepherds came, and had made a fire, and they were exceedingly rejoicing, the heavenly host appeared to them, praising and adoring the supreme God.

20 And as the shepherds were engaged in the same employment, the cave at that time seemed like a glorious temple, because both the tongues of angels and men united to adore and magnify God, on account of the birth of the Lord Christ.

21 But when the old Hebrew woman saw all these evident miracles, she gave praises to God, and said, I thank thee, O God, thou God of Israel, for that mine eyes have seen the birth of the Saviour of the world.

CHAP II.

1 *The child circumcised in the cave, 2 and the old woman preserving his foreskin or navel-string in a box of spikenard, Mary afterwards anoints Christ with it. 5 Christ brought to the temple, 6 shines, 7 angels stand around him adoring. 8 Simeon praises Christ.*

AND when the time of his circumcision was come, namely, the eighth day, on which the law commanded the child to be circumcised, they circumcised him in the cave.

2 And the old Hebrew woman took the foreskin (others say she took the navel-string), and preserved it in an alabaster-box of old oil of spikenard.

3 And she had a son who was a druggist, to whom she said, Take heed thou sell not this alabaster box of spikenard-ointment, although thou shouldst be offered three hundred pence for it.

4 Now this is that alabaster-box which Mary the sinner procured, and poured forth the ointment out of it upon the head and the feet of our Lord Jesus Christ, and wiped it off with the I hairs of her head.

5 Then after ten days they brought him to Jerusalem, and on the fortieth day from his birth they presented him in the temple before the Lord, making the proper offerings for him, according to the requirement of the law of Moses: namely, that every male which opens the womb shall be called holy unto God.

6 At that time old Simeon saw him shining as a pillar of light, when St. Mary the Virgin, his mother, carried him in her arms, and was filled with the greatest pleasure at the sight.

7 And the angels stood around him, adoring him, as a king's guards stand around him.

8 Then Simeon going near to St. Mary, and stretching forth his hands towards her, said to the Lord Christ, Now, O my Lord, thy servant shall depart in peace, according to thy word;

9 For mine eyes have seen thy mercy, which thou hast prepared for the salvation of all nations; a light to all people, and the glory of thy people Israel.

10 Hannah the prophetess was also present, and drawing near, she gave praises to God, and celebrated the happiness of Mary.

CHAP. III.

1 *The wise men visit Christ. Mary gives them one of his swaddling clothes. 3 An angel appears to them in the form of a star. They return and make a fire, and worship the swaddling cloth, and put it in the fire, where it remains unconsumed.*

AND it came to pass, when the Lord Jesus was born at Bethlehem, a city of Judæa, in the time of Herod the King; the wise men came from the East to Jerusalem, according to the prophecy of Zoradascht, 1 and brought with them offerings: namely, gold, frankincense, and myrrh, and worshipped him, and offered to him their gifts.

2 Then the Lady Mary took one of his swaddling clothes in

which the infant was wrapped, and gave it to them instead of a blessing, which they received from her as a most noble present.

3 And at the same time there appeared to them an angel in the form of that star which had before been their guide in their journey; the light of which they followed till they returned into their own country.

4 On their return their kings and princes came to them inquiring, What they had seen and done? What sort of journey and return they had? What company they had on the road?

5 But they produced the swaddling cloth which St. Mary had given to them, on account whereof they kept a feast.

6 And having, according to the custom of their country, made a fire, they worshipped it.

7 And casting the swaddling cloth into it, the fire took it, and kept it.

8 And when the fire was put out, they took forth the swaddling cloth unhurt, as much as if the fire had not touched it.

9 Then they began to kiss it, and put it upon their heads and their eyes, saying, This is certainly an undoubted truth, and it is really surprising that the fire could not burn it, and consume it.

10 Then they took it, and with the greatest respect laid it up among their treasures.

CHAP. IV.

1 *Herod intends to put Christ to death.* 3 *An angel warns Joseph to take the child and its mother into Egypt.* 6 *Consternation on their arrival.* 13

The idols fall down. 15 *Mary washes Christ's swaddling clothes, and hangs them to dry on a post.* 16 *A son of the chief priest puts one on his head, and being possessed of devils, they leave him.*

NOW Herod, perceiving that the wise men did delay, and not return to him, called together the priests and wise men and said, Tell me in what place the Christ should be born?

2 And when they replied, in Bethlehem, a city of Judaea, he began to contrive in his own mind the death of the Lord Jesus Christ.

3 But an angel of the Lord appeared to Joseph in his sleep, and said, Arise, take the child and his mother, and go into Egypt as soon as the cock crows. So he arose, and went.

4 And as he was considering with himself about his journey, the morning came upon him.

5 In the length of the journey the girts of the saddle broke.

6 And now he drew near to a great city, in which there was an idol, to which the other idols and gods of Egypt brought their offerings and vows.

7 And there was by this idol a priest ministering to it, who, as often as Satan spoke out of that idol, related the things he said to the inhabitants of Egypt, and those countries.

8 This priest had a son three years old, who was possessed with a great multitude of devils, who uttered many strange things, and when the devils seized him, walked about naked with his clothes torn, throwing stones at those whom he saw.

9 Near to that idol was the inn of the city, into which when Joseph and St. Mary were come, and had turned into that inn, all the inhabitants of the city were astonished.

10 And all the magistrates and priests of the idols assembled before that idol, and made inquiry there, saying, What means all this consternation, and dread, which has fallen upon all our country?

11 The idol answered them, The unknown God is come hither, who is truly God; nor is there any one besides him, who is worthy of divine worship; for he is truly the Son of God.

12 At the fame of him this country trembled, and at his coming it is under the present commotion and consternation; and we ourselves are affrighted by the greatness of his power.

13 And at the same instant this idol fell down, and at his fall all the inhabitants of Egypt, besides others, ran together.

14 But the son of the priest, when his usual disorder came upon him, going into the inn, found there Joseph and St. Mary, whom all the rest had left behind and forsook.

15 And when the Lady St. Mary had washed the swaddling clothes of the Lord Christ, and hanged them out to dry upon a post, the boy possessed with the devil took down one of them, and put it upon his head.

16 And presently the devils began to come out of his mouth, and fly away in the shape of crows and serpents.

17 From that time the boy was healed by the power of the Lord Christ, and he began to sing praises, and give thanks to the Lord who had healed him.

18 When his father saw him restored to his former state of health, he said, My son, what has happened to thee, and by what means wert thou cured?

19 The son answered, When the devils seized me, I went into the inn, and there found a very handsome woman with a boy, whose swaddling clothes she had just before washed, and hanged out upon a post.

20 One of these I took, and put it upon my head, and immediately the devils left me, and fled away.

21 At this the father exceedingly rejoiced, and said, My son, perhaps this boy is the son of the living God, who made the heavens and the earth.

22 For as soon as he came amongst us, the idol was broken, and all the gods fell down, and were destroyed by a greater power.

23 Then was fulfilled the prophecy which saith, Out of Egypt I have called my son.

CHAP. V.

1 *Joseph and Mary leave Egypt.* 3 *Go to the haunts of robbers,* 4 *Who, hearing a mighty noise as of a great army, flee away.*

NOW Joseph and Mary, when they heard that the idol was fallen down and destroyed, were seized with fear and trembling, and said, When we were in the land of Israel, Herod, intending to kill Jesus, slew for that purpose all the infants at Bethlehem, and that neighbourhood.

2 And there is no doubt but the Egyptians if they come to hear that this idol is broken and fallen down, will burn us with fire.

3 They went therefore hence to the secret places of robbers, who robbed travellers as they pass by, of their carriages and their clothes, and carried them away bound.

4 These thieves upon their coming heard a great noise, such as the noise of a king with a great army and many horses, and the trumpets sounding at his Overture from his own city, at which they were so affrighted as to leave all their booty behind them, and fly away in haste.

5 Upon this the prisoners arose, and loosed each other's bonds, and taking each man his bags, they went away, and saw Joseph and Mary coming towards them, and inquired,

Where is that king, the noise of whose approach the robbers heard, and left us, so that we are now come off safe?

6 Joseph answered, He will come after us.

CHAP. VI.

1 Mary looks on a woman in whom Satan had taken up his abode, and she becomes dispossessed. 5 Christ kissed by a bride made dumb by sorcerers, cures her, 11 miraculously cures a gentlewoman in whom Satan had taken up his abode. 16 A leprous girl cured by the water in which he was washed, and becomes the servant of Mary and Joseph. 20 The leprous son of a prince's wife cured in like manner. 37 His mother offers large gifts to Mary, and dismisses her.

THEN they went into another where there was a woman possessed with a devil, and in whom Satan, that cursed rebel, had taken up his abode.

2 One night, when she went to fetch water, she could neither endure her clothes on, nor to be in any house; but as often as they tied her with chains or cords, she brake them, and went out into desert places, and sometimes standing where roads crossed, and in churchyards, would throw stones at men.

3 When St. Mary saw this w man, she pitied her; whereupon Satan presently left her, and fled away in the form of a young man, saying, Wo to me, because of thee, Mary, and thy son.

4 So the woman was delivered from her torment; but considering herself naked, she blushed, and avoided seeing any man, and having put on her clothes, went home, and gave au account of her case to her father and relations, who, as they were the best of the city, entertained St. Mary and Joseph with the greatest respect.

5 The next morning having received a sufficient supply of provisions for the road, they went from them, and about the evening of the day arrived at another town, where a marriage was then about to be solemnized; but by the arts of Satan and the practices of some sorcerers, the bride was become so dumb, that she could not so much as open her mouth.

6 But when this dumb bride saw the Lady St. Mary entering into the town, and carrying the Lord Christ in her arms, she stretched out her hands to the Lord Christ, and took him in her arms, and closely hugging him, very often kissed him, continually moving him and pressing him to her body.

7 Straightway the string of her tongue was loosed, and her ears were opened, and she began to sing praises unto God, who had restored her.

8 So there was great joy among the inhabitants of the town that night, who thought that God and his angels were come down among them.

9 In this place they abode three days, meeting with the greatest respect and most splendid entertainment.

10 And being then furnished by the people with provisions for the road, they departed and went to another city, in which they were inclined to lodge, because it was a famous place.

11 There was in this city a gentlewoman, who, as she went down one day to the river to bathe, behold cursed Satan leaped upon her in the form of a serpent,

12 And folded himself about her belly, and every night lay upon her.

13 This woman seeing the Lady St. Mary, and the Lord Christ the infant in her bosom, asked the Lady St. Mary, that she would give her the child to kiss, and carry in her arms.

14 When she had consented, and as soon as the woman had moved the child, Satan left her, and fled away, nor did the woman ever afterwards see him.

15 Hereupon all the neighbours praised the Supreme God, and the woman rewarded them with ample beneficence.

16 On the morrow the same woman brought perfumed water to wash the Lord Jesus; and when she had washed him, she preserved the water.

17 And there was a girl there, whose body was white with a leprosy, who being sprinkled with this water, and washed, was instantly cleansed from her leprosy.

18 The people therefore said Without doubt Joseph and Mary, and that boy are Gods, for they do not look like mortals.

19 And when they were making ready to go away, the girl, who had been troubled with the leprosy, came and desired they would permit her to go along with them; so they consented, and the girl went with them till. they came to a city, in which was the palace of a great king, and whose house was not far from the inn.

20 Here they staid, and when the girl went one day to the prince's wife, and found her in a sorrowful and mournful condition, she asked her the reason of her tears.

21 She replied, Wonder not at my groans, for I am under a great misfortune, of which I dare not tell any one.

22 But, says the girl, if you will entrust me with your private grievance, perhaps I may find you a remedy for it.

23 Thou, therefore, says the prince's wife, shalt keep the secret, and not discover it to any one alive!

24 I have been married to this prince, who rules as king over large dominions, and lived long with him, before he had any child by me.

25 At length I conceived by him, but alas! I brought forth a leprous son; which, when he saw, he would not own to be his, but said to me,

26 Either do thou kill him, or send him to some nurse in such a place, that he may be never heard of; and now take care of yourself; I will never see you more.

27 So here I pine, lamenting my wretched and miserable circumstances. Alas, my son! alas, my husband! Have I disclosed it to you?

28 The girl replied, I have found a remedy for your disease, which I promise you, for I also was leprous, but God hath cleansed me, even he who is called Jesus, the son of the Lady Mary.

29 The woman inquiring where that God was, whom she spake of, the girl answered He lodges with you here in the same house.

30 But how can this be? says she; where is he? Behold, replied the girl, Joseph and Mary; and the infant who is with them is called Jesus: and it is he who delivered me from my disease and torment.

31 But by what means, says she, were you cleansed from your leprosy? Will you not tell me that?

32 Why not? says the girl; I took the water with which his body had been washed, and poured it upon me, and my leprosy vanished.

33 The prince's wife then arose and entertained them, providing a great feast for Joseph among a large company of men.

34 And the next day took perfumed water to wash the Lord Jesus, and afterwards poured the same water upon her son, whom she had brought with her, and her son was instantly cleansed from his leprosy.

35 Then she sang thanks and praises unto God, and said,

Blessed is the mother that bare thee, O Jesus!

36 Dost thou thus cure men of the same nature with thyself, with the water with which thy body is washed?

37 She then offered very large gifts to the Lady Mary, and sent her away with all imaginable respect.

CHAP. VII.

1 A man who could not enjoy his wife, freed from his disorder. 5 A young man who had been bewitched, and turned into a mule, miraculously cured by Christ being put on his back. 28 and is married to the girl who had been cured of leprosy.

THEY came afterwards to another city, and had a mind to lodge there.

2 Accordingly they went to a man's house, who was newly married, but by the influence of sorcerers could not enjoy his wife:

3 But they lodging at his house that night, the man was freed of his disorder:

4 And when they were pre paring early in the morning to go forward on their journey, the new married person hindered them, and provided a noble entertainment for them?

5 But going forward on the morrow, they came to another city, and saw three women going from a certain grave with great weeping.

6 When St. Mary saw them, she spake to the girl who was their companion, saying, Go and inquire of them, what is the matter with them, and what misfortune has befallen them?

7 When the girl asked them, they made her no answer, but asked her again, Who are ye, and where are ye going? For the day is far spent, and the night is at hand.

8 We are travellers, saith the girl, and are seeking for an inn to lodge at.

9 They replied, Go along with us, and lodge with us.

10 They then followed them, and were introduced into a new house, well furnished with all sorts of furniture.

11 It was now winter-time, and the girl went into the parlour where these women were, and found them weeping and lamenting, as before.

12 By them stood a mule, covered over with silk, and an ebony collar hanging down from his neck, whom they kissed, and were feeding.

13 But when the girl said, How handsome, ladies, that mule is! they replied with tears, and said, This mule, which you see, was our brother, born of this same mother as we:

14 For when our father died, and left us a very large estate, and we had only this brother, and we endeavoured to procure him a suitable match, and thought he should be married as other men, some giddy and jealous woman bewitched him without our knowledge.

15 And we, one night, a little before day, while the doors of the house were all fast shut, saw this our brother was changed into a mule, such as you now see him to be:

16 And we, in the melancholy condition in which you see us, having no father to comfort us, have applied to all the wise men, magicians, and diviners in the world, but they have been of no service to us.

17 As often therefore as we find ourselves oppressed with grief, we rise and go with this our mother to our father's tomb, where, when we have cried sufficiently we return home.

18 When the girl had heard this, she said, Take courage, and cease your fears, for you have a remedy for your afflictions near at hand, even among you and in the midst of your house,

19 For I was also leprous; but when I saw this woman, and this little infant with her, whose name is Jesus, I sprinkled my body with the water with which his mother had washed him, and I was presently made well.

20 And I am certain that he is also capable of relieving you under your distress. Wherefore, arise, go to my mistress, Mary, and when you have brought her into your own parlour, disclose to her the secret, at the same time, earnestly beseeching her to compassionate your case.

21 As soon as the women had heard the girl's discourse, they hastened away to the Lady St. Mary, introduced themselves to her, and sitting down before her, they wept.

22 And said, O our Lady St. Mary, pity your handmaids, for we have no head of our family, no one older than us; no father, or brother to go in and out before us.

23 But this mule, which you see, was our brother, which some woman by witchcraft have brought into this condition which you see: we therefore entreat you to compassionate us.

24 Hereupon St. Mary was grieved at their case, and taking the Lord Jesus, put him upon the back of the mule.

25 And said to her son, O Jesus Christ, restore (or heal) according to thy extraordinary power this mule, and grant him to have again the shape of a man and a rational creature, as he had formerly.

26 This was scarce said by the Lady St. Mary, but the mule immediately passed into a human form, and became a young man without any deformity.

27 Then he and his mother and the sisters worshipped the Lady St. Mary, and lifting the child upon their heads, they kissed him, and said, Blessed is thy mother, O Jesus, O Saviour of the world! Blessed are the eyes which are so happy as to see thee.

28 Then both the sisters told their mother, saying, Of a truth our brother is restored to his former shape by the help of the Lord Jesus Christ, and the kindness of that girl, who told us of Mary and her son.

29 And inasmuch as our brother is unmarried, it is fit that we marry him to this girl their servant.

30 When they had consulted Mary in this matter, and she had given her consent, they made a splendid wedding for this girl.

31 And so their sorrow being turned into gladness, and their mourning into mirth, they began to rejoice. and to make merry, and sing, being dressed in their richest attire, with bracelets.

32 Afterwards they glorified and praised God, saying, O Jesus son of David who changest sorrow into gladness, and mourning into mirth!

33 After this Joseph and Mary tarried there ten days, then went away, having received great respect from those people;

34 Who, when they took their leave of them, and returned home, cried,

35 But especially the girl.

CHAP. VIII.

1 Joseph and Mary pass through a country infested by robbers, 3 Titus, a humane thief, offers Dumachus, his comrade, forty groats to let Joseph and Mary pass unmolested. 6 Jesus prophesies that the thieves, Dumachus and Titus, shall be crucified with him, and that Titus shall go before him into Paradise. 10 Christ causes a well to spring from a sycamore tree, and Mary washes his coat in it. 11 A balsam grows there from his sweat: They go to Memphis, where Christ works more miracles. Return to Judæa. 15 being warned, depart for Nazareth.

IN their journey from hence they came into a desert country, and were told it was infested with robbers; so Joseph and St. Mary prepared to pass through it in the night.

2 And as they were going along, behold they saw two robbers asleep in the road, and with them a great number of robbers, who were their confederates, also asleep.

3 The names of these two were Titus and Dumachus; and Titus said to Dumachus, I beseech thee let those persons go along quietly, that our company may not perceive anything of them:

4 But Dumachus refusing, Titus again said, I will give thee forty groats, and as a pledge take my girdle, which he gave him he had done speaking, that he might not open his mouth, or make a noise.

5 When the Lady St. Mary saw the kindness which this robber did shew them, she said to him, The Lord God will receive thee to his right hand, and grant thee pardon of thy sins.

6 Then the Lord Jesus answered, and said to his mother, When thirty years are expired, O mother, the Jews will crucify me at Jerusalem;

7 And these two thieves shall be with me at the same time upon the cross, Titus on my right hand, and Dumachus on my left, and from that time Titus shall go before me into paradise:

8 And when she had said, God forbid this should be thy lot, O my son, they went on to a city in which were several idols; which, as soon as they came near to it, was turned into hills of sand.

9 Hence they went to that sycamore tree, which is now called Matarea;

10 And in Matarea the Lord Jesus caused a well to spring forth, in which St. Mary washed his coat;

11 And a balsam is produced, or grows, in that country from the sweat which ran down there from the Lord Jesus.

12 Thence they proceeded to Memphis, and saw Pharaoh, and abode three years in Egypt.

13 And the Lord Jesus did very many miracles in Egypt, which are neither to be found in the Gospel of the Infancy nor in the Gospel of Perfection.

14 At the end of three years he returned out of Egypt, and when he came near to Judas, Joseph was afraid to enter;

15 For hearing that Herod was dead, and that Archelaus his son reigned in his stead, he was afraid;

16 And when he went to Judæa, an angel of God appeared to him, and said, O Joseph, go into the city Nazareth, and abide there.

17 It is strange indeed that he, who is the Lord of all countries, should be thus carried backward and forward through so many countries.

CHAP. IX.

2 Two sick children cured by water wherein Christ was washed.
WHEN they came afterwards into the city Bethlehem, they found there several very desperate distempers, which became so troublesome to children by seeing them, that most of them died.

2 There was there a woman who had a sick son, whom she brought, when he was at the point of death, to the Lady St. Mary, who saw her when she was washing Jesus Christ.

3 Then said the woman, O my Lady Mary, look down upon this my son, who is afflicted with most dreadful pains.

4. St. Mary hearing her, said, Take a little of that water with which I have washed my son, and sprinkle it upon him.

5 Then she took a little of that water, as St. Mary had commanded, and sprinkled it upon her son, who being wearied with his violent pains, had fallen asleep; and after he had slept a little, awaked perfectly well and recovered.

6 The mother being abundantly glad of this success, went again to St. Mary, and St. Mary said to her, Give praise to God, who hath cured this thy son.

7 There was in the same place another woman, a neighbour of her, whose son was now cured.

8 This woman's son was afflicted with the same disease, and his eyes were now almost quite shut, and she was lamenting for him day and night.

9 The mother of the child which was cured, said to her, Why do you not bring your son to St. Mary, as I brought my son to her, when he was in the agonies of death; and he was cured by that water, with which the body of her son Jesus was washed?

10 When the woman heard her say this, she also went, and having procured the same water, washed her son with it, whereupon his body and his eyes were instantly restored to their former state.

11 And when she brought her son to St. Mary, and opened his case to her, she commanded her to give thanks to God for the recovery of her son's health, and tell no one what had happened.

CHAP. X.

1 Two wives of one man, each have a son sick. 2 One of them, named Mary, and whose son's name was Caleb, presents the Virgin with a handsome carpet, and Caleb is cured; but the son of the other wife dies, 4 which occasions a difference between the women. 5 The other wife puts Caleb into a hot oven, and he is miraculously preserved; 9 she afterwards throws him into a well, and he is again preserved; 11 his mother appeals to the Virgin against the other wife, 12, whose downfall the Virgin prophesies, 13 and who accordingly falls into the well, 14 therein fulfilling a saying of old.

THERE were in the same city two wives of one man, who had each a son sick. One of them was called Mary and her son's name was Caleb.

2 She arose, and taking her son, went to the Lady St. Mary, the mother of Jesus, and offered her a very handsome carpet, saying, O my Lady Mary accept this carpet of me, and instead of it give me a small swaddling cloth.

3 To this Mary agreed, and when the mother of Caleb was gone, she made a coat for her son of the swaddling cloth, put it on him, and his disease was cured; but the son of the other wife died.

4 Hereupon there arose between them, a difference in doing the business of the family by turns, each her week.

5 And when the turn of Mary the mother of Caleb came, and she was heating the oven to bake bread, and went away to fetch the meal, she left her son Caleb by the oven;

6 Whom, the other wife, her rival, seeing to be by himself, took and cast him into the oven, which was very hot, and then went away.

7 Mary on her return saw her son Caleb lying in the middle of the oven laughing, and the oven quite as cold as though it had not been before heated, and knew that her rival the other wife had thrown him into the fire.

8 When she took him out, she brought him to the Lady St.

Mary, and told her the story, to whom she replied, Be quiet, I am concerned lest thou shouldest make this matter known.

9 After this her rival, the other wife, as she was drawing water at the well, and saw Caleb playing by the well, and that no one was near, took him, and threw him into the well.

10 And when some men came to fetch water from the well, they saw the boy sitting on the superficies of the water, and drew him out with ropes, and were exceedingly surprised at the child, and praised God.

11 Then came the mother and took him and carried him to the Lady St. Mary, lamenting and saying, O my Lady, see what my rival hath done to my son, and how she hath cast him into the well, and I do not question but one time or other she will be the occasion of his death.

12 St. Mary replied to her, God will vindicate your injured cause.

13 Accordingly a few days after, when the other wife came to the well to draw water, her foot was entangled in the rope, so that she fell headlong into the well, and they who ran to her assistance, found her skull broken, and bones bruised.

14 So she came to a bad end, and in her was fulfilled that saying of the author, They digged a well, and made it deep, but fell themselves into the pit which they prepared.

CHAP. XI.

1 *Bartholomew, when a child and sick, miraculously restored by being laid on Christ's bed.*

ANOTHER woman in that city had likewise two sons sick.

2 And when one was dead, the other, who lay at the point of death, she took in her arms to the Lady St. Mary, and in a flood of tears addressed herself to her, saying,

3 O my Lady, help and relieve me; for I had two sons, the one I have just now buried, the other I see is just at the point of death, behold how I (earnestly) seek favour from God, and pray to him.

4 Then she said, O Lord, thou art gracious, and merciful, and kind; thou hast given me two sons; one of them thou hast taken to thyself, O spare me this other.

5 St. Mary then perceiving the greatness of her sorrow, pitied her and said, Do thou place thy son in my son's bed, and cover him with his clothes.

6 And when she had placed him in the bed wherein Christ lay, at the moment when his eyes were just closed by death; as soon as ever the smell of the garments of the Lord Jesus Christ reached the boy, his eyes were opened, and calling with a loud voice to his mother, he asked for bread, and when he had received it, he sucked it.

7 Then his mother said, O Lady Mary, now I am assured that the powers of God do dwell in you, so that thy son can cure children who are of the same sort as himself, as soon as they touch his garments.

8 This boy who was thus cured, is the same who in the Gospel is called Bartholomew.

CHAP. XII.

1 *A leprous woman healed by Christ's washing water.* 7 *A princess healed by it and restored to her husband.*

AGAIN there was a leprous woman who went to the Lady St. Mary, the mother of Jesus, and said, O my Lady, help me.

2 St. Mary replied, what help dost thou desire? Is it gold or silver, or that thy body be cured of its leprosy?

3 Who, says the woman, can grant me this?

4 St. Mary replied to her, Wait a little till I have washed my son Jesus, and put him to bed.

5 The woman waited, as she was commanded; and Mary when she had put Jesus in bed, giving her the water with which she had washed his body, said, Take some of the water, and pour it upon thy body;

6 Which when she had done, she instantly became clean, and praised God, and gave thanks to him.

7 Then she went away, after she had abode with her three days:

8 And going into the city, she saw a certain prince, who had married another prince's daughter;

9 But when he came to see her, he perceived between her eyes the signs of leprosy like a star, and thereupon declared the marriage dissolved and void.

10 When the woman saw these persons in this condition, exceedingly sorrowful, and shedding abundance of tears, she inquired of them the reason of their crying.

11 They replied, Inquire not into our circumstances; for we are net able to declare our misfortunes to any person whatsoever.

12 But still she pressed and desired them to communicate their case to her, intimating, that perhaps she might be able to direct them to a remedy.

13 So when they shewed the young woman to her, and the signs of the leprosy, which appeared between her eyes,

14 She said, I also, whom ye see in this place, was afflicted with the same distemper, and going on some business to Bethlehem, I went into a certain cave, and saw a woman named Mary, who had a son called Jesus.

15 She seeing me to be leprous, was concerned for me, and gave me some water with which she had washed her son's body; with that I sprinkled my body, and became clean.

16 Then said these women, Will you, Mistress, go along with us, and shew the Lady St. Mary to us?

17 To which she consenting, they arose and went to the Lady St. Mary, taking with them very noble presents.

18 And when they came in and offered their presents to her, they showed the leprous young woman what they brought with them to her.

19 Then said St. Mary, The mercy of the Lord Jesus Christ rest upon you;

20 And giving them a little of that water with which she had washed the body of Jesus Christ, she bade them wash the diseased person with it; which when they had done, she was presently cured;

21 So they, and all who were present, praised God; and being filled with joy, they went back to their own city, and gave praise to God on that account.

22 Then the prince hearing that his wife was cured, took her home and made a second marriage, giving thanks unto God for the recovery of his wife's health.

CHAP. XIII.

1 *A girl, whose blood Satan sucked, receives one of Christ's swaddling clothes from the Virgin.* 14 *Satan comes like a dragon, and she shews it to him; flames and burning coals proceed from it and fall upon him;* 19 *he is miraculously discomfited, and leaves the girl.*

THERE was also a girl, who was afflicted by Satan;

2 For that cursed spirit did frequently appear to her in the

shape of a dragon, and was inclined to swallow her up, and had so sucked out all her blood, that she looked like a dead carcase.

3 As often as she came to herself, with her hands wringed about her head she would cry out, and say, Wo, Wo is me, that there is no one to be found who can deliver me from that impious dragon!

4 Her father and mother, and all who were about her and saw her, mourned and wept over her;

5 And all who were present would especially be under sorrow and in tears, when they heard her bewailing, and saying, My brethren and friends, is there no one who can deliver me from this murderer?

6 Then the prince's daughter, who had been cured of her leprosy, hearing the complaint of that girl, went upon the top of her castle, and saw her with her hands twisted about her head, pouring out a flood of tears, and all the people that were about her in sorrow.

7 Then she asked the husband of the possessed person, Whether his wife's mother was alive? He told her, That her father and mother were both alive.

8 Then she ordered her mother to be sent to her: to whom, when she saw her coming, she said, Is this possessed girl thy daughter? She moaning and bewailing said, Yes, madam, I bore her.

9 The prince's daughter answered, Disclose the secret of her case to me, for I confess to you that I was leprous, but the Lady Mary, the mother of Jesus Christ, healed me.

10 And if you desire your daughter to be restored to her former state, take her to Bethlehem, and inquire for Mary the mother of Jesus, and doubt not but your daughter will be cured; for I do not question but you will come home with great joy at your daughter's recovery.

11 As soon as ever she had done speaking, she arose and went with her daughter to the place appointed, and to Mary, and told her the case of her daughter.

12 When St. Mary had heard her story, she gave her a little of the water with which she had washed the body of her son Jesus, and bade her pour it upon the body of her daughter.

13 Likewise she gave her one of the swaddling cloths of the Lord Jesus, and said, Take this swaddling cloth and shew it to thine enemy as often as thou seest him; and she sent them away in peace.

14 After they had left that city and returned home, and the time was come in which Satan was wont to seize her, in the same moment this cursed spirit appeared to her in the shape of a huge dragon, and the girl seeing him was afraid.

15 The mother said to her, Be not afraid daughter; let him alone till he come nearer to thee! then shew him the swaddling cloth, which the Lady Mary gave us, and we shall see the event.

16 Satan then coming like a dreadful dragon, the body of the girl trembled for fear.

17 But as soon as she had put the swaddling cloth upon her head, and about her eyes, and shewed it to him, presently there issued forth from the swaddling cloth flames and burning coals, and fell upon the dragon.

18 Oh! how great a miracle was this, which was done: as soon as the dragon saw the swaddling cloth of the Lord Jesus, fire went forth and was scattered upon his head and eyes; so that he cried out with a loud voice, What have I to do with thee, Jesus, thou son of Mary, Whither shall I flee from thee?

19 So he drew back much affrighted, and left the girl.

20 And she was delivered from this trouble, and sang praises and thanks to God, and with her all who were present at the working of the miracle.

CHAP. XIV.

1 *Judas when a boy possessed by Satan, and brought by his parents to Jesus to be cured, whom he tries to bite, 7 but failing, strikes Jesus and makes him cry out. Whereupon Satan goes from Jesus in the shape of a dog.*

ANOTHER woman likewise lived there, whose son was possessed by Satan.

2 This boy, named Judas, as often as Satan seized him, was inclined to bite all that were present; and if he found no one else near him, he would bite his own hands and other parts.

3 But the mother of this miserable boy, hearing of St. Mary and her son Jesus, arose presently, and taking her son in her arms, brought him to the Lady Mary.

4 In the meantime, James and Joses had taken away the infant, the Lord Jesus, to play at a proper season with other children; and when they went forth, they sat down and the Lord Jesus with them.

5 Then Judas, who was possessed, came and sat down at the right hand of Jesus.

6 When Satan was acting upon him as usual, he went about to bite the Lord Jesus.

7 And because he could not do it, he struck Jesus on the right side, so that he cried out.

8 And in the same moment Satan went out of the boy, and ran away like a mad dog.

9 This same boy who struck Jesus, and out of whom Satan went in the form of a dog, was Judas Iscariot, who betrayed him to the Jews.

10 And that same side, on which Judas struck him, the Jews pierced with a spear.

CHAP. XV.

1 *Jesus and other boys play together, and make day figures of animals. 4 Jesus causes them to walk, 6 also makes day birds, which he causes to fly, and eat and drink. 7 The children's parents alarmed, and take Jesus for a sorcerer. 8 He goes to a dyer's shop, and throws all the cloths into the furnace, and works a miracle therewith. 15 Whereupon the Jews praise God.*

AND when the Lord Jesus was seven years of age, he was on a certain day with other boys his companions about the same age.

2 Who when they were at play, made clay into several shapes, namely, asses, oxen, birds, and other figures,

3 Each boasting of his work, and endeavouring to exceed the rest.

4 Then the Lord Jesus said to the boys, I will command these figures which I have made to walk.

5 And immediately they moved, and when he commanded them to return, they returned.

6 He had also made the figures of birds and sparrows, which, when he commanded to fly, did fly, and when he commanded to stand still, did stand still; and if he gave them meat and drink, they did eat and drink.

7 When at length the boys went away, and related these things to their parents, their fathers said to them, Take heed, children, for the future, of his company, for he is a sorcerer; shun and avoid him, and from henceforth never play with him.

8 On a certain day also, when the Lord Jesus was playing with the boys, and running about, he passed by a dyer's shop, whose name was Salem.

9 And there were in his shop many pieces of cloth belonging to the people of that city, which they designed to dye of several colours.

10 Then the Lord Jesus going into the dyer's shop, took all the cloths, and threw them into the furnace.

11 When Salem came home, and saw the cloths spoiled, he began to make a great noise, and to chide the Lord Jesus, saying,

12 What hast thou done to me, O thou Son of Mary? Thou hast injured both me and my neighbours; they all desired their cloths of a proper colour; but .thou hast come, and spoiled them all.

13 The Lord Jesus replied, I will change the colour of every cloth to what colour thou desirest;

14 And then he presently began to take the cloths out of the furnace, and they were all dyed of those same colours which the dyer desired.

15 And when the Jews saw this surprising miracle, they praised God

CHAP. XVI.

1 *Christ miraculously widens or contracts the gates, milk-pails, sieves, or bones, not properly made by Joseph,* 4 *he not being skilful at his carpenter's trade.* 5 *The King of Jerusalem gives Joseph an order for a throne.* 6 *Joseph works on it for two years in the king's palace, and makes it two spans too short. The king being angry with. him,* 10 *Jesus comforts him,* 13 *commands him to pull one side of the throne, while he pulls the other, and brings it to its proper dimensions.* 14 *Whereupon the bystanders praise God.*

AND Joseph, wheresoever he went in the city, took the Lord Jesus with him, where he was sent for to work to make gates, or milk-pails, or sieves, or boxes; the Lord Jesus was with him wheresoever he went.

2 And as often as Joseph had anything in his work, to make longer or shorter, or wider, or narrower, the Lord Jesus would stretch his hand towards it.

3 And presently it became as Joseph would have it.

4 So that he had no need to finish anything with his own hands, for he was not very skilful at his carpenter's trade.

5 On a certain time the King of Jerusalem sent for him, and said, I would have thee make me a throne of the same dimensions

p. 54

with that place in which I commonly sit.

6 Joseph obeyed, and forthwith began the work, and continued two years in the king's palace before he finished it.

7 And when he came to fix it in its place, he found it wanted two spans on each side of the appointed measure.

8 Which, when the king saw, he was very angry with Joseph;

9 And Joseph afraid of the king's anger, went to bed without his supper, taking not any thing to eat.

10 Then the Lord Jesus asked him, What he was afraid of?

11 Joseph replied, Because I have lost my labour in the work which I have been about these two years.

12 Jesus said to him, Fear not, neither be cast down;

13 Do thou lay hold on one side of the throne, and I will the other, and we will bring it to its just dimensions.

14 And when Joseph had done as the Lord Jesus said, and each of them had with strength drawn his side, the throne obeyed, and was brought to the proper dimensions of the place:

15 Which miracle when they who stood by saw, they were astonished, and praised God.

16 The throne was made of the same wood, which was in being in Solomon's time, namely, wood adorned with various shapes and figures.

CHAP. XVII.

1 *Jesus plays with boys at hide and seek.* 3 *Some women put his playfellows in a furnace,* 7 *where they are transformed by Jesus into kids.* 10 *Jesus calls them to go and play, and they me restored to their former shape.*

ON another day the Lord Jesus going out into the street, and seeing some boys who were met to play, joined himself to their company:

2 But when they saw him, they hid themselves, and left him to seek for them:

3 The Lord Jesus came to the gate of a certain house, and asked some women who were standing there, Where the boys were gone?

4 And when they answered, That there was no one there; the Lord Jesus said, Who are those whom ye see in the furnace?

5 They answered, They were kids of three years old.

6 Then Jesus cried out aloud, and said, Come out hither, O ye kids, to your shepherd;

7 And presently the boys came forth like kids, and leaped about him; which when the women saw, they were exceedingly amazed, and trembled.

8 Then they immediately worshipped the Lord Jesus, and beseeched him, saying, O our Lord Jesus, son of Mary, thou art truly that good shepherd of Israel! have mercy on thy handmaids, who stand before thee, who do not doubt, but that thou, O Lord, art come to save, and not to destroy.

9 After that, when the Lord Jesus said, the children of Israel are like Ethiopians among the people; the women said, Thou, Lord, knowest all things, nor is any thing concealed from thee; but now we entreat thee, and beseech of thy mercy that thou wouldst restore those boys to their former state.

10 Then Jesus said, Come hither O boys, that we may go and play; and immediately, in the presence of these women, the kids were changed and returned into the shape of boys.

CHAP. XVIII.

1 *Jesus becomes the king of his playfellows, and they crown him with flowers,* 4 *miraculously causes a serpent who had bitten Simon the Cananite, then a boy, to suck our all the poison again;* 16 *the serpent bursts, and Christ restores the boy to health.*

IN the month Adar Jesus gathered together the boys, and ranked them as though he had been a king.

2 For they spread their garments on the ground for him to sit on; and having made a crown of flowers, put it upon his head, and stood on his right and left as the guards of a king.

3 And if any one happened to pass by, they took him by force, and said, Come hither, and worship the king, that you may have a prosperous journey.

4 In the mean time, while these things were doing, there came certain men, carrying a boy upon a couch;

5 For this boy having gone with his companions to the mountain to gather wood, and having found there a

partridge's nest, and put his hand in to take out the eggs, was stung by a poisonous serpent, which leaped out of the nest; so that he was forced to cry out for the help of his companions: who, when they came, found him lying upon the earth like a dead person.

6 After which his neighbours came and carried him back into the city.

7 But when they came to the place where the Lord Jesus was sitting like a king, and the other boys stood around him like his ministers, the boys made haste to meet him, who was bitten by the serpent, and said to his neighbours, Come and pay your respects to the king;

8 But when, by reason of their sorrow, they refused to come, the boys drew them, and forced them against their wills to come.

9 And when they came to the Lord Jesus, he inquired, On what account they carried that boy?

10 And when they answered, that a serpent had bitten him, the Lord Jesus said to the boys, Let us go and kill that serpent.

11 But when the parents of the boy desired to be excused, because their son lay at the point of death; the boys made answer, and said, Did not ye hear what the king said? Let us go and kill the serpent; and will not ye obey him?

12 So they brought the couch back again, whether they would or not.

13 And when they were come to the nest, the Lord Jesus said to the boys, Is this the serpent's lurking place? They said, It was.

14 Then the Lord Jesus calling the serpent, it presently came forth and submitted to him; to whom he said, Go and suck out all the poison which thou hast infused into that boy;

15 So the serpent crept to the boy, and took away all its poison again.

16 Then the Lord Jesus cursed the serpent so that it immediately burst asunder, and died.

17 And he touched the boy with his hand to restore him to his former health;

18 And when he began to cry, the Lord Jesus said, Cease crying, for hereafter thou shalt be my disciple;

19 And this is that Simon the Canaanite, who is mentioned in the Gospel.

CHAP. XIX.

1 *James being bitten by a viper, Jesus blows on the wound and cures him.* 4. *Jesus charged with throwing a boy from the roof of a house,* 10 *miraculously causes the dead boy to acquit Mm,* 12 *fetches water for his mother, breaks the pitcher and miraculously gathers the water in his mantle and brings it home,* 16 *makes fish-pools on the Sabbath,* 20 *causes a boy to die who broke them down,* 22 *another boy run against him, whom he also causes to die.*

ON another day Joseph sent his son James to gather wood and the Lord Jesus went with him;

2 And when they came to the place where the wood was, and James began to gather it, behold, a venomous viper bit him, so that he began to cry, and make a noise.

3 The Lord Jesus seeing him in this condition, came to him, and blowed upon the place where the viper had bit him, and it was instantly well.

4 On a certain day the Lord Jesus was with some boys, who were playing on the housetop, and one of the boys fell down, and presently died.

5 Upon which the other boys all running away, the Lord Jesus was left alone on the house-top.

6 And the boy's relations came to him and said to the Lord Jesus, Thou didst throw our son down from the housetop.

7 But he denying it, they cried out, Our son is dead, and this is he who killed him.

8 The Lord Jesus replied to them, Do not charge me with a crime, of which you are not able to convict me, but let us go ask the boy himself, who will bring the truth to light.

9 Then the Lord Jesus going down stood over the head of the dead boy, and said with a loud voice, Zeinunus, Zeinunus, who threw thee down from the housetop?

10 Then the dead boy answered, thou didst not throw me down, but such a one did.

11 And when the Lord Jesus bade those who stood by to take notice of his words, all who were present praised God on account of that miracle.

12 On a certain time the Lady St. Mary had commanded the Lord Jesus to fetch her some water out of the well;

13 And when he had gone to fetch the water, the pitcher, when it was brought up full, brake.

14 But Jesus spreading his mantle gathered up the water again, and brought it in that to his mother.

15 Who, being astonished at this wonderful thing, laid up this, and all the other things which she had seen, in her memory.

16 Again on another day the Lord Jesus was with some boys by a river and they drew water out of the river by little channels, and made little fish-pools.

17 But the Lord Jesus had made twelve sparrows, and placed them about his pool on each side, three on a side.

18 But it was the Sabbath day, and the son of Hanani a Jew came by, and saw them making these things, and said, Do ye thus make figures of clay on the Sabbath? And he ran to them, and broke down their fish-pools.

19 But when the Lord Jesus clapped his hands over the sparrows which he had made, they fled away chirping.

20 At length the son of Hanani coming to the fish-pool of Jesus to destroy it, the water vanished away, and the Lord Jesus said to him,

21 In like manner as this water has vanished, so shall thy life vanish; and presently the boy died.

22 Another time, when the Lord Jesus was coming home in the evening with Joseph, he met a boy, who ran so hard against him, that he threw him down;

23 To whom the Lord Jesus said, As thou hast thrown me down, so shalt thou fall, nor ever rise.

24 And that moment the boy fell down and died.

CHAP. XX.

1 *Sent to school to Zaccheus to learn his letters, and teaches Zaccheus.* 13 *Sent to another schoolmaster.* 14 *refuses to tell his letters, and the schoolmaster going to whip him his hand withers and he dies.*

THERE was also at Jerusalem one named Zaccheus, who was a schoolmaster.

2 And he said to Joseph, Joseph, why dost thou not send Jesus to me, that he may learn his letters?

3 Joseph agreed, and told St. Mary;

4 So they brought him to that master; who, as soon as he saw him, wrote out an alphabet for him.

5 And he bade him say Aleph; and when he had said Aleph, the master bade him pronounce Beth.

6 Then the Lord Jesus said to him, Tell me first the meaning of the letter Aleph, and then I will pronounce

Beth.

7 And when the master threatened to whip him, the Lord Jesus explained to him the meaning of the letters Aleph and Beth;

8 Also which were the straight figures of the letters, which the oblique, and what letters had double figures; which had points, and which had none; why one letter went before another; and many other things he began to tell him, and explain, of which the master himself had never heard, nor read in any book.

9 The Lord Jesus farther said to the master, Take notice how I say to thee; then he began clearly and distinctly to say Aleph, Beth, Gimel, Daleth, and so on to the end of the alphabet.

10 At this the master was so surprised, that he said, I believe this boy was born before Noah;

11 And turning to Joseph, he said, Thou hast brought a boy to me to be taught, who is more learned than any master.

12 He said also unto St. Mary, This your son has no need of any learning.

13 They brought him then to a more learned master, who, when he saw him, said, say Aleph.

14 And when he had said Aleph, the master bade him pronounce Beth; to which the Lord Jesus replied, Tell me first the meaning of the letter Aleph, and then I will pronounce Beth.

15 But this master, when he lift up his hand to whip him, had his hand presently withered, and he died.

16 Then said Joseph to St. Mary, henceforth we will not allow him to go out of the house; for every one who displeases him is killed.

CHAP. XXI.

1 *Disputes miraculously with the doctors in the temple,* 7 *on law,* 9 *on astronomy,* 12 *on physics and metaphysics,* 21 *is worshipped by a philosopher,* 28 *and fetched home by his mother.*

AND when he was twelve years old, they brought him to Jerusalem to the feast; and when the feast was over, they returned.

2 But the Lord Jesus continued behind in the temple among the doctors and elders, and learned men of Israel; to whom he proposed several questions of learning, and also gave them answers:

3 For he said to them, Whose son is the Messiah? They answered, the son of David:

4 Why then, said he, does he in the spirit call him Lord? when he saith, The Lord said to my Lord, sit thou at my right hand, till I have made thine enemies thy footstool.

5 Then a certain principal Rabbi asked him, Hast thou read books?

6 Jesus answered, he had read both books, and the things which were contained in books.

7 And he explained to them the books of the law, and precepts, and statutes: and the mysteries which are contained in the books of the prophets; things which the mind of no creature could reach.

8 Then said that Rabbi, I never yet have seen or heard of such knowledge! What do you think that boy will be!

9 When a certain astronomer, who was present, asked the Lord Jesus, Whether he had studied astronomy?

10 The Lord Jesus replied, and told him the number of the spheres and heavenly bodies, as also their triangular, square, and sextile aspect; their progressive and retrograde motion; their size and several prognostications; and other things

which the reason of man had never discovered.

11 There was also among them a philosopher well skilled in physic and natural philosophy, who asked the Lord Jesus, Whether he had studied physic?

12 He replied, and explained to him physics and metaphysics.

13 Also those things which were above and below the power of nature;

14 The powers also of the body, its humours, and their effects.

15 Also the number of its members, and bones, veins, arteries, and nerves;

16 The several constitutions of body, hot and dry, cold and moist, and the tendencies of them;

17 How the soul operated upon the body;

18 What its various sensations and faculties were;

19 The faculty of speaking, anger, desire;

20 And lastly the manner of its composition and dissolution; and other things, which the understanding of no creature had ever reached.

21 Then that philosopher arose, and worshipped the Lord Jesus, and said, O Lord Jesus, from henceforth I will be thy disciple and servant.

22 While they were discoursing on these and such like things, the Lady St. Mary came in, having been three days walking about with Joseph, seeking for him.

23 And when she saw him sitting among the doctors, and in his turn proposing questions to them, and giving answers, she said to him, My son, why hast thou done thus by us? Behold I and thy father have been at much pains in seeking thee.

24 He replied, Why did ye seek me? Did ye not know that I ought to be employed in my father's house?

25 But they understood not the words which he said to them.

26 Then the doctors asked Mary, Whether this was her son? And when she said, He was, they said, O happy Mary, who hast borne such a son.

27 Then he returned with them to Nazareth, and obeyed them in all things.

28 And his mother kept all these things in her mind;

29 And the Lord Jesus grew in stature and wisdom, and favour with God and man.

CHAP. XXII.

1 *Conceals his miracles,* 2 *studies the law and is baptised.*

NOW from this time Jesus began to conceal his miracles and secret works,

2 And he gave himself to the study of the law, till he arrived to the end of his thirtieth year;

3 At which time the Father publicly owned him at Jordan, sending down this voice from heaven, This is my beloved son, in whom I am well pleased;

4 The Holy Ghost being also present in the form of a dove.

5 This is he whom we worship with all reverence, because he gave us our life and being, and brought us from our mother's womb.

6 Who, for our sakes, took a human body, and hath redeemed us, so that he might so embrace us with everlasting mercy, and shew his free, large, bountiful grace and goodness to us.

7 To him be glory and praise, and power, and dominion, from henceforth and for evermore, Amen.

INFANCY GOSPEL OF JAMES

The Protoevangelium of James
The Birth of Mary the Holy Mother of God,
and Very Glorious Mother of Jesus Christ

IN THE RECORDS OF THE TWELVE TRIBES OF ISRAEL was Joachim, a man rich exceedingly; and he brought his offerings double, saying: There shall be of my superabundance to all the people, and there shall be the offering for my forgiveness to the Lord for a propitiation for me. For the great day of the Lord was at hand, and the sons of Israel were bringing their offerings. And there stood over against him Rubim, saying: It is not meet for thee first to bring thine offerings, because thou hast not made seed in Israel. And Joachim was exceedingly grieved, and went away to the registers of the twelve tribes of the people, saying: I shall see the registers of the twelve tribes of Israel, as to whether I alone have not made seed in Israel. And he searched, and found that all the righteous had raised up seed in Israel. And he called to mind the patriarch Abraham, that in the last day God gave him a son Isaac. And Joachim was exceedingly grieved, and did not come into the presence of his wife; but he retired to the desert, and there pitched his tent, and fasted forty days and forty nights, saying in himself: I will not go down either for food or for drink until the Lord my God shall look upon me, and prayer shall be my food and drink.

2. And his wife Anna mourned in two mournings, and lamented in two lamentations, saying: I shall bewail my widowhood; I shall bewail my childlessness. And the great day of the Lord was at hand; and Judith her maid-servant said: How long dost thou humiliate thy soul? Behold, the great day of the Lord is at hand, and it is unlawful for thee to mourn. But take this head-band, which the woman that made it gave to me; for it is not proper that I should wear it, because I am a maid-servant, and it has a royal appearance. And Anna said: Depart from me; for I have not done such things, and the Lord has brought me very low. I fear that some wicked person has given it to thee, and thou hast come to make me a sharer in thy sin. And Judith said: Why should I curse thee, seeing that the Lord hath shut thy womb, so as not to give thee fruit in Israel? And Anna was grieved exceedingly, and put off her garments of mourning, and cleaned her head, and put on her wedding garments, and about the ninth hour went down to the garden to walk. And she saw a laurel, and sat under it, and prayed to the Lord, saying: O God of our fathers, bless me and hear my prayer, as Thou didst bless the womb of Sarah, and didst give her a son Isaac.

3. And gazing towards the heaven, she saw a sparrow's nest in the laurel, and made a lamentation in herself, saying: Alas! who begot me? and what womb produced me? because I have become a curse in the presence of the sons of Israel, and I have been reproached, and they have driven me in derision out of the temple of the Lord. Alas! to what have I been likened? I am not like the fowls of the heaven, because even the fowls of the heaven are productive before Thee, O Lord. Alas! to what have I been likened? I am not like the beasts of the earth, because even the beasts of the earth are productive before Thee, O Lord. Alas! to what have I been likened? I am not like these waters, because even these waters are productive before Thee, O Lord. Alas! to what have I been likened? I am not like this earth, because even the earth bringeth forth its fruits in season, and blesseth Thee, O Lord.

4. And, behold, an angel of the Lord stood by, saying: Anna, Anna, the Lord hath heard thy prayer, and thou shalt conceive, and shall bring forth; and thy seed shall be spoken of in all the world. And Anna said: As the Lord my God liveth, if I beget either male or female, I will bring it as a gift to the Lord my God; and it shall minister to Him in holy things all the days of its life. And, behold, two angels came, saying to her: Behold, Joachim thy husband is coming with his flocks. For an angel of the Lord went down to him, saying: Joachim, Joachim, the Lord God hath heard thy prayer Go down hence; for, behold, thy wife Anna shall conceive. And Joachim went down and called his shepherds, saying: Bring me hither ten she-lambs without spot or blemish, and they shall be for the Lord my God; and bring me twelve tender calves, and they shall be for the priests and the elders; and a hundred goats for all the people. And, behold, Joachim came with his flocks; and Anna stood by the gate, and saw Joachim coming, and she ran anti hung upon his neck, saying: Now I know that the Lord God hath blessed me exceedingly; for, behold the widow no longer a widow, and I the childless shall conceive. And Joachim rested the first day in his house.

5. And on the following day he brought his offerings, saying in himself: If the Lord God has been rendered gracious to me, the plate on the priest's forehead will make it manifest to me. And Joachim brought his offerings, and observed attentively the priest's plate when he went up to the altar of the Lord, and he saw no sin in himself. And Joachim said: Now I know that the Lord has been gracious unto me, and has remitted all my sins. And he went down from the temple of the Lord justified, and departed to his own house. And her months were fulfilled, and in the ninth month Anna brought forth. And she said to the midwife: What have I brought forth? and she said: A girl. And said Anna: My soul has been magnified this day. And she laid her down. And the days having been fulfilled, Anna was purified, and gave the breast to the child, and called her name Mary.

6. And the child grew strong day by day; and when she was six months old, her mother set her on the ground to try whether she could stand, and she walked seven steps and came into her bosom; and she snatched her up, saying: As the Lord my God liveth, thou shall not walk on this earth until I bring thee into the temple of the Lord. And she made a sanctuary in her bed-chamber, and allowed nothing common or unclean to pass through her. And she called the undefiled daughters of the Hebrews, and they led her astray. And when she was

a year old, Joachim made a great feast, and invited the priests, and the scribes, and the elders, and all the people of Israel. And Joachim brought the child to the priests; and they blessed her, saying: O God of our fathers, bless this child, and give her an everlasting name to be named in all generations. And all the people said: So be it, so be it, amen. And he brought her to the chief priests; and they blessed her, saying: O God most high, look upon this child, and bless her with the utmost blessing, which shall be for ever. And her mother snatched her up, and took her into the sanctuary of her bed-chamber, and gave her the breast. And Anna made a song to the Lord God, saying: I will sing a song to the Lord my God, for He hath looked upon me, and hath taken away the reproach of mine enemies; and the Lord hath given the the fruit of His righteousness, singular in its kind, and richly endowed before Him. Who will tell the sons of Rubim that Anna gives suck? Hear, hear, ye twelve tribes of Israel, that Anna gives suck. And she laid her to rest in the bed-chamber of her sanctuary, and went out and ministered unto them. And when the supper was ended, they went down rejoicing, and glorifying the God of Israel.

7. And her months were added to the child. And the child was two years old, and Joachim said: Let us take her up to the temple of the Lord, that we may pay the vow that we have vowed, lest perchance the Lord send to us, and our offering be not received. And Anna said: Let us wait for the third year, in order that the child may not seek for father or mother. And Joachim said: So let us wait. And the child was three years old, and Joachim said: Invite the daughters of the Hebrews that are undefiled, and let them take each a lamp, and let them stand with the lamps burning, that the child may not turn back, and her heart be captivated from the temple of the Lord. And they did so until they went up into the temple of the Lord. And the priest received her, and kissed her, and blessed her, saying: The Lord has magnified thy name in all generations. In thee, on the last of the days, the Lord will manifest His redemption to the sons of Israel. And he set her down upon the third step of the altar, and the Lord God sent grace upon her; and she danced with her feet, and all the house of Israel loved her.

8. And her parents went down marvelling, and praising the Lord God, because the child had not turned back. And Mary was in the temple of the Lord as if she were a dove that dwelt there, and she received food from the hand of an angel. And when she was twelve years old there was held a council of the priests, saying: Behold, Mary has reached the age of twelve years in the temple of the Lord. What then shall we do with her, test perchance she defile the sanctuary of the Lord? And they said to the high priest: Thou standest by the altar of the Lord; go in, and pray concerning her; and whatever the Lord shall manifest unto thee, that also will we do. And the high priest went in, taking the robe with the twelve bells into the holy of holies; and he prayed concerning her. And behold an angel of the Lord stood by him, saying unto him: Zacharias, Zacharias, go out and assemble the widowers of the people, and let them bring

each his rod; and to whomsoever the Lord shall show a sign, his wife shall she be. And the heralds went out through all the circuit of Judaea, and the trumpet of the Lord sounded, and all ran.

9. And Joseph, throwing away his axe, went out to meet them; and when they had assembled, they went away to the high priest, taking with them their rods. And he, taking the rods of all of them, entered into the temple, and prayed; and having ended his prayer, he took the rods and came out, and gave them to them: but there was no sign in them, and Joseph took his rod last; and, behold, a dove came out of the rod, and flew upon Joseph's head. And the priest said to Joseph, Thou hast been chosen by lot to take into thy keeping the virgin of the Lord. But Joseph refused, saying: I have children, and I am an old man, and she is a young girl. I am afraid lest I become a laughing-stock to the sons of Israel. And the priest said to Joseph: Fear the Lord thy God, and remember what the Lord did to Dathan, and Abiram, and Korah; how the earth opened, and they were swallowed up on account of their contradiction. And now fear, O Joseph, lest the same things happen in thy house. And Joseph was afraid, and took her into his keeping. And Joseph said to Mary: Behold, I have received thee from the temple of the Lord; and now I leave thee in my house, and go away to build my buildings, and I shall come to thee. The Lord will protect thee.

10. And there was a council of the priests, saying: Let us make a veil for the temple of the Lord. And the priest said: Call to me the undefiled virgins of the family of David. And the officers went away, and sought, and found seven virgins. And the priest remembered the child Mary, that she was of the family of David, and undefiled before God. And the officers went away and brought her. And they brought them into the temple of the Lord. And the priest said: Choose for me by lot who shall spin the gold, and the white, and the fine linen, and the silk, and the blue, and the scarlet, and the true purple. And the true purple and the scarlet fell to the lot of Mary, and she took them, and went away to her house. And at that time Zacharias was dumb, and Samuel was in his place until the time that Zacharias spake. And Mary took the scarlet, and span it.

11. And she took the pitcher, and went out to fill it with water. And, behold, a voice saying: Hail, thou who hast received grace; the Lord is with thee; blessed art thou among women! And she looked round, on the right hand and on the left, to see whence this voice came. And she went away, trembling, to her house, and put down the pitcher; and taking the purple, she sat down on her seat, and drew it out. And, behold, an angel of the Lord stood before her, saying: Fear not, Mary; for thou hast found grace before the Lord of all, and thou shalt conceive, according to His word. And she hearing, reasoned with herself, saying: Shall I conceive by the Lord, the living God? and shall I bring forth as every woman brings forth? And the angel of the Lord said: Not so, Mary; for the power of the Lord shall

overshadow thee: wherefore also that holy thing which shall be born of thee shall be called the Son of the Most High. And thou shalt call His name Jesus, for He shall save His people from their sins. And Mary said: Behold, the servant of the Lord before His face: let it be unto me according to thy word.

12. And she made the purple and the scarlet, and took them to the priest. And the priest blessed her, and said: Mary, the Lord God hath magnified thy name, and thou shall be blessed in all the generations of the earth. And Mary, with great joy, went away to Elizabeth her kinswoman, and knocked at the door. And when Elizabeth heard her, she threw away the scarlet, and ran to the door, and opened it; and seeing Mary, she blessed her, and said: Whence is this to me, that the mother of my Lord should come to me? for, behold, that which is in me leaped and blessed thee. But Mary had forgotten the mysteries of which the archangel Gabriel had spoken, and gazed up into heaven, and said: Who am I, O Lord, that all the generations of the earth should bless me? And she remained three months with Elizabeth; and day by day she grew bigger. And Mary being afraid, went away to her own house, and hid herself from the sons of Israel. And she was sixteen years old when these mysteries happened.

13. And she was in her sixth month; and, behold, Joseph came back from his building, and, entering into his house, he discovered that she was big with child. And he smote his face, and threw himself on the ground upon the sackcloth, and wept bitterly, saying: With what face shall I look upon the Lord my God? and what prayer shall I make about this maiden? because I received her a virgin out of the temple of the Lord, and I have not watched over her. Who is it that has hunted me down? Who has done this evil thing in my house, and defiled the virgin? Has not the history of Adam been repeated in me? For just as Adam was in the hour of his singing praise, and the serpent came, and found Eve alone, and completely deceived her, so it has happened to me also. And Joseph stood up from the sackcloth, and called Mary, and said to her: O thou who hast been cared for by God, why hast thou done this and forgotten the Lord thy God? Why hast thou brought low thy soul, thou that wast brought up in the holy of holies, and that didst receive food from the hand of an angel? And she wept bitterly, saying: I am innocent, and have known no man. And Joseph said to her: Whence then is that which is in thy womb? And she said: As the Lord my God liveth, I do not know whence it is to me.

14. And Joseph was greatly afraid, and retired from her, and considered what he should do in regard to her. And Joseph said: If I conceal her sin, I find myself fighting against the law of the Lord; and if I expose her to the sons of Israel, I am afraid lest that which is in her be from an angel, and I shall be found giving up innocent blood to the doom of death. What then shall I do with her? I will put her away from me secretly. And night came upon him; and, behold, an angel of the Lord appears to him in a dream, saying: Be not afraid for this maiden, for that which is in her is of the Holy Spirit; and she will bring forth a Son, and thou shall call His name Jesus, for He will save His people from their sins. And Joseph arose from sleep, and glorified the God of Israel, who had given him this grace; and he kept her.

15. And Annas the scribe came to him, and said: Why hast thou not appeared in our assembly? And Joseph said to him: Because I was weary from my journey, and rested the first day. And he turned, and saw that Mary was with child. And he ran away to the priest? and said to him: Joseph, whom thou didst vouch for, has committed a grievous crime. And the priest said: How so? And he said: He has defiled the virgin whom he received out of the temple of the Lord, and has married her by stealth, and has not revealed it to the sons of Israel. And the priest answering, said: Has Joseph done this? Then said Annas the scribe: Send officers, and thou wilt find the virgin with child. And the officers went away, and found it as he had said; and they brought her along with Joseph to the tribunal. And the priest said: Mary, why hast thou done this? and why hast thou brought thy soul low, and forgotten the Lord thy God? Thou that wast reared in the holy of holies, and that didst receive food from the hand of an angel, and didst hear the hymns, and didst dance before Him, why hast thou done this? And she wept bitterly, saying: As the Lord my God liveth, I am pure before Him, and know not a man. And the priest said to Joseph: Why hast thou done this? And Joseph said: As the Lord liveth, I am pure concerning her. Then said the priest: Bear not false witness, but speak the truth. Thou hast married her by stealth, and hast not revealed it to the sons of Israel, and hast not bowed thy head under the strong hand, that thy seed might be blessed. And Joseph was silent.

16. And the priest said: Give up the virgin whom thou didst receive out of the temple of the Lord. And Joseph burst into tears. And the priest said: I will give you to drink of the water of the ordeal of the Lord, and He shall make manifest your sins in your eyes. And the priest took the water, and gave Joseph to drink and sent him away to the hill-country; and he returned unhurt. And he gave to Mary also to drink, and sent her away to the hill-country; and she returned unhurt. And all the people wondered that sin did not appear in them. And the priest said: If the Lord God has not made manifest your sins, neither do I judge you. And he sent them away. And Joseph took Mary, and went away to his own house, rejoicing and glorifying the God of Israel.

17. And there was an order from the Emperor Augustus, that all in Bethlehem of Judaea should be enrolled. And Joseph said: I shall enrol my sons, but what shall I do with this maiden? How shall I enrol her? As my wife? I am ashamed. As my daughter then? But all the sons of Israel know that she is not my daughter. The day of the Lord shall itself bring it to pass as the Lord will. And he saddled the ass, and set her upon it; and his son led it, and Joseph followed. And when they had come within three miles, Joseph turned and saw her sorrowful; and he said to himself: Likely that which is in her distresses her.

And again Joseph turned and saw her laughing. And he said to her: Mary, how is it that I see in thy face at one time laughter, at another sorrow? And Mary said to Joseph: Because I see two peoples with my eyes; the one weeping and lamenting, and the other rejoicing and exulting. And they came into the middle of the road, and Mary said to him: Take me down from off the ass, for that which is in me presses to come forth. And he took her down from off the ass, and said to her: Whither shall I lead thee, and cover thy disgrace? for the place is desert.

18. And he found a cave there, and led her into it; and leaving his two sons beside her, he went out to seek a widwife in the district of Bethlehem. And I Joseph was walking, and was not walking; and I looked up into the sky, and saw the sky astonished; and I looked up to the pole of the heavens, and saw it standing, and the birds of the air keeping still. And I looked down upon the earth, and saw a trough lying, and work-people reclining: and their hands were in the trough. And those that were eating did not eat, and those that were rising did not carry it up, and those that were conveying anything to their mouths did not convey it; but the faces of all were looking upwards. And I saw the sheep walking, and the sheep stood still; and the shepherd raised his hand to strike them, and his hand remained up. And I looked upon the current of the river, and I saw the mouths of the kids resting on the water and not drinking, and all things in a moment were driven from their course.

19. And I saw a woman coming down from the hill-country, and she said to me: O man, whither art thou going? And I said: I am seeking an Hebrew midwife. And she answered and said unto me: Art thou of Israel? And I said to her: Yes. And she said: And who is it that is bringing forth in the cave? And I said: A woman betrothed to me. And she said to me: Is she not thy wife? And I said to her: It is Mary that was reared in the temple of the Lord, and I obtained her by lot as my wife. And yet she is not my wife, but has conceived of the Holy Spirit. And the widwife said to him: Is this true? And Joseph said to her: Come and see. And the midwife went away with him. And they stood in the place of the cave, and behold a luminous cloud overshadowed the cave. And the midwife said: My soul has been magnified this day, because mine eyes have seen strange things -- because salvation has been brought forth to Israel. And immediately the cloud disappeared out of the cave, and a great light shone in the cave, so that the eyes could not bear it. And in a little that light gradually decreased, until the infant appeared, and went and took the breast from His mother Mary. And the midwife cried out, and said: This is a great day to me, because I have seen this strange sight. And the midwife went forth out of the cave, and Salome met her. And she said to her: Salome, Salome, I have a strange sight to relate to thee: a virgin has brought forth -- a thing which her nature admits not of. Then said Salome: As the Lord my God liveth, unless I thrust in my finger, and search the parts, I will not believe that a virgin has brought forth.

20. And the midwife went in, and said to Mary: Show thyself; for no small controversy has arisen about thee. And Salome put in her finger, and cried out, and said: Woe is me for mine iniquity and mine unbelief, because I have tempted the living God; and, behold, my hand is dropping off as if burned with fire. And she bent her knees before the Lord, saying: O God of my fathers, remember that I am the seed of Abraham, and Isaac, and Jacob; do not make a show of me to the sons of Israel, but restore me to the poor; for Thou knowest, O Lord, that in Thy name I have performed my services, and that I have received my reward at Thy hand. And, behold, an angel of the Lord stood by her, saying to her: Salome, Salome, the Lord hath heard thee. Put thy hand to the infant, and carry it, and thou wilt have safety and joy. And Salome went and carried it, saying: I will worship Him, because a great King has been born to Israel. And, behold, Salome was immediately cured, and she went forth out of the cave justified. And behold a voice saying: Salome, Salome, tell not the strange things thou hast seen, until the child has come into Jerusalem.

21. And, behold, Joseph was ready to go into Judaea. And there was a great commotion in Bethlehem of Judaea, for Magi came, saying: Where is he that is born king of the Jews? for we have seen his star in the east, and have come to worship him. And when Herod heard, he was much disturbed, and sent officers to the Magi. And he sent for the priests, and examined them, saying: How is it written about the Christ? where is He to be born? And they said: In Bethlehem of Judaea, for so it is written. And he sent them away. And he examined the Magi, saying to them: What sign have you seen in reference to the king that has been born? And the Magi said: We have seen a star of great size shining among these stars, and obscuring their light, so that the stars did not appear; and we thus knew that a king has been born to Israel, and we have come to worship him. And Herod said: Go and seek him; and if you find him, let me know, in order that I also may go and worship him. And the Magi went out. And, behold, the star which they had seen in the east went before them until they came to the cave, and it stood over the top of the cave. And the Magi saw the infant with His mother Mary; and they brought forth from their bag gold, and frankincense, and myrrh. And having been warned by the angel not to go into Judaea, they went into their own country by another road.

22. And when Herod knew that he had been mocked by the Magi, in a rage he sent murderers, saying to them: Slay the children from two years old and under. And Mary, having heard that the children were being killed, was afraid, and took the infant and swaddled Him, and put Him into an ox-stall. And Elizabeth, having heard that they were searching for John, took him and went up into the hill-country, and kept looking where to conceal him. And there was no place of concealment. And Elizabeth, groaning with a loud voice, says: O mountain of God, receive mother and child. And immediately the mountain was cleft, and received her. And a light shone about them, for an angel of the Lord was with them, watching over them.

23. And Herod searched for John, and sent officers to Zacharias, saying: Where hast thou hid thy son? And he, answering, said to them: I am the servant of God in holy things, and I sit constantly in the temple of the Lord: I do not know where my son is. And the officers went away, and reported all these things to Herod. And Herod was enraged, and said: His son is destined to be king over Israel. And he sent to him again, saying: Tell the truth; where is thy son? for thou knowest that thy life is in my hand. And Zacharias said: I am God's martyr, if thou sheddest my blood; for the Lord will receive my spirit, because thou sheddest innocent blood at the vestibule of the temple of the Lord. And Zacharias was murdered about daybreak. And the sons of Israel did not know that he had been murdered.

24. But at the hour of the salutation the priests went away, and Zacharias did not come forth to meet them with a blessing, according to his custom. And the priests stood waiting for Zacharias to salute him at the prayer, and to glorify the Most High. And he still delaying, they were all afraid. But one of them ventured to go in, and he saw clotted blood beside the altar; and he heard a voice saying: Zacharias has been murdered, and his blood shall not be wiped up until his avenger come. And hearing this saying, he was afraid, and went out and told it to the priests. And they ventured in, and saw what had happened; and the fretwork of the temple made a wailing noise, and they rent their clothes from the top even to the bottom. And they found not his body, but they found his blood turned into stone. And they were afraid, and went out and reported to the people that Zacharias had been murdered. And all the tribes of the people heard, and mourned, and lamented for him three days and three nights. And after the three days, the priests consulted as to whom they should put in his place; and the lot fell upon Simeon. For it was he who had been warned by the Holy Spirit that he should not see death until he should see the Christ in the flesh.

And I James that wrote this history in Jerusalem, a commotion having arisen when Herod died, withdrew myself to the wilderness until the commotion in Jerusalem ceased, glorifying the Lord God, who had given me the gift and the wisdom to write this history. And grace shall be with them that fear our Lord Jesus Christ, to whom be glory to ages of ages. Amen.

INFANCY GOSPEL OF THOMAS

First Greek Form

Thomas the Israelite Philosopher's Account of the Infancy of the Lord.

1. I Thomas, an Israelite, write you this account, that all the brethren from among the heathen may know the miracles of our Lord Jesus Christ in His infancy, which He did after His birth in our country. The beginning of it is as follows:-

2. This child Jesus, when five years old, was playing in the ford of a mountain stream; and He collected the flowing waters into pools, and made them clear immediately, and by a word alone He made them obey Him. And having made some soft clay, He fashioned out of it twelve sparrows. And it was the Sabbath when He did these things. And there were also many other children playing with Him. And a certain Jew, seeing what Jesus was doing, playing on the Sabbath, went off immediately, and said to his father Joseph: Behold, thy son is at the stream, and has taken clay, and made of it twelve birds, and has profaned the Sabbath. And Joseph, coming to the place and seeing, cried out to Him, saying: Wherefore doest thou on the Sabbath what it is not lawful to do? And Jesus clapped His hands, and cried out to the sparrows, and said to them: Off you go! And the sparrows flew, and went off crying. And the Jews seeing this were amazed, and went away and reported to their chief men what they had seen Jesus doing.

3. And the son of Annas the scribe was standing there with Joseph; and he took a willow branch, and let out the waters which Jesus had collected. And Jesus, seeing what was done, was angry, and said to him: O wicked, impious, and foolish! what harm did the pools and the waters do to thee? Behold, even now thou shalt be dried up like a tree, and thou shalt not bring forth either leaves, or root, or fruit. And straightway that boy was quite dried up. And Jesus departed, and went to Joseph's house. But the parents of the boy that had been dried up took him up, bewailing his youth, and brought him to Joseph, and reproached him because, *said they*, thou hast such a child doing such things.

4. After that He was again passing through the village; and a boy ran up against Him, and struck His shoulder. And Jesus was angry, and said to him: Thou shalt not go back the way thou camest. And immediately he fell down dead. And some who saw what had taken place, said: Whence was this child begotten, that every word of his is certainly accomplished? And the parents of the dead boy went away to Joseph, and blamed him, saying: Since thou hast such a child, it is impossible for thee to live with us in the village; or else teach him to bless, and not to curse: for he is killing our children.

5. And Joseph called the child apart, and admonished Him, saying: Why doest thou such things, and these people suffer, and hate us, and persecute us? And Jesus said: I know that these words of thine are not thine own; nevertheless for thy sake I will be silent; but they shall bear their punishment. And straightway those that accused Him were struck blind. And those who saw it were much afraid and in great perplexity, and said about Him: Every word which he spoke, whether good or bad, was an act, and became a wonder. And when they saw that Jesus had done such a thing, Joseph rose and took hold of His ear, and pulled it hard. And the child was very angry, and said to him: It is enough for thee to seek, and not to find; and most certainly thou hast not done wisely. Knowest thou not that I am thine? Do not trouble me.

6. And a certain teacher, Zacchaeus by name, was standing in a certain place, and heard Jesus thus speaking to his father; and he wondered exceedingly, that, being a child, he should speak in such a way. And a few days thereafter he came to Joseph, and said to him: Thou hast a sensible child, and he has some mind. Give him to me, then, that he may learn letters; and I shall teach him along with the letters all knowledge, both how to address all the elders, and to honour them as forefathers and fathers, and how to love those of his own age. And He said to him all the letters from the Alpha even to the Omega, clearly and with great exactness. And He looked upon the teacher Zacchaeus, and said to him: Thou who art ignorant of the nature of the Alpha, how canst thou teach others the Beta? Thou hypocrite! first, if thou knowest. teach the A, and then we shall believe thee about the B. Then He began to question the teacher about the first letter, and he was not able to answer Him. And in the hearing of many, the child says to Zacchaeus: Hear, O teacher, the order of the first letter, and notice here how it has lines, and a middle stroke crossing those which thou seest common; (lines) brought together; the highest part supporting them, and again bringing them under one head; with three points *of intersection*; of the same kind; principal and subordinate; of equal length. Thou hast the lines of the A.

7. And when the teacher Zacchaeus heard the child speaking such and so great allegories of the first letter, he was at a great loss about such a narrative, and about His teaching. And He said to those that were present: Alas! I, wretch that I am, am at a loss, bringing shame upon myself by having dragged this child hither. Take him away, then, I beseech thee, brother Joseph. I cannot endure the sternness of his look; I cannot make out his meaning at all. That child does not belong to this earth; he can tame even fire. Assuredly he was born before the creation of the world. What sort of a belly bore him, what sort of a womb nourished him, I do not know. Alas! my friend, he has carried me away; I cannot get at his meaning: thrice wretched that I am, I have deceived myself. I made a struggle to have a scholar, and I was found to have a teacher. My mind is filled with shame, my friends, because I, an old man, have been conquered by a child. There is nothing for me but despondency and death on account of this boy, for I am not able at this

hour to look him in the face; and when everybody says that I have been beaten by a little child, what can I say? And how can I give an account of the lines of the first letter that he spoke about? I know not, O my friends; for I can make neither beginning nor end of him. Therefore, I beseech thee, brother Joseph, take him home. What great thing he is, either god or angel, or what I am to say, I know not.

8. And when the Jews were encouraging Zacchaeus, the child laughed aloud, and said: Now let thy learning bring forth fruit, and let the blind in heart see. I am here from above, that I may curse them, and call them to the things that are above, as He that sent me on your account has commanded me. And when the child ceased speaking, immediately all were made whole who had fallen under His curse. And no one after that dared to make Him angry, lest He should curse him, and he should be maimed.

9. And some days after, Jesus was playing in an upper room of a certain house, and one of the children that were playing with Him fell down from the house, and was killed. And, when the other children saw this, they ran away, and Jesus alone stood still. And the parents of the dead child coming, reproached...and they threatened Him. And Jesus leaped down from the roof, and stood beside the body of the child, and cried with a loud voice, and said: Zeno-for that was his name-stand up, and tell me; did I throw thee down? And he stood up immediately, and said: Certainly not, my lord; thou didst not throw me down, but hast raised me up. And those that saw this were struck with astonishment. And the child's parents glorified God on account of the miracle that had happened, and adored Jesus.

10. A few days after, a young man was splitting wood in the corner, and the axe came down and cut the sole of his foot in two, and he died from loss of blood. And there was a great commotion, and people ran together, and the child Jesus ran there too. And He pressed through the crowd, and laid hold of the young man's wounded foot, and he was cured immediately. And He said to the young man: Rise up now, split the wood, and remember me. And the crowd seeing what had happened, adored the child, saying: Truly the Spirit of God dwells in this child.

11. And when He was six years old, His mother gave Him a pitcher, and sent Him to draw water, and bring it into the house. But He struck against some one in the crowd, and the pitcher was broken. And Jesus unfolded the cloak which He had on, and filled it with water, and carried it to His mother. And His mother, seeing the miracle that had happened, kissed Him, and kept within herself the mysteries which she had seen Him doing.

12. And again in seed-time the child went out with His father to sow corn in their land. And while His father was sowing, the child Jesus also sowed one gain of corn. And when He had reaped it, and threshed it, He made a hundred kors; and calling all the poor of the village to the threshing-floor, He gave them the corn, and Joseph took away what was left of the corn. And He was eight years old when He did this miracle.

13. And His father was a carpenter, and at that time made ploughs and yokes. And a certain rich man ordered him to make him a couch. And one of what is called the cross pieces being too short, they did not know what to do. The child Jesus said to His father Joseph: Put down the two pieces of wood, and make them even in the middle. And Joseph did as the child said to him. And Jesus stood at the other end, and took hold of the shorter piece of wood, and stretched it, and made it equal to the other. And His father Joseph saw it, and wondered, and embraced the child, and blessed Him, saying: Blessed am I, because God has given me this child.

14. And Joseph, seeing that the child was vigorous in mind and body, again resolved that He should not remain ignorant of the letters, and took Him away, and handed Him over to another teacher. And the teacher said to Joseph: I shall first teach him the Greek letters, and then the Hebrew. For the teacher was aware of the trial that had been made of the child, and was afraid of Him. Nevertheless he wrote out the alphabet, and gave Him all his attention for a long time, and He made him no answer. And Jesus said to him: If thou art really a teacher, and art well acquainted with the letters, tell me the power of the Alpha, and I will tell thee the power of the Beta. And the teacher was enraged at this, and struck Him on the head. And the child, being in pain, cursed him; and immediately he swooned away, and fell to the ground on his face. And the child returned to Joseph's house; and Joseph was grieved, and gave orders to His mother, saying: Do not let him go outside of the door, because those that make him angry die.

15. And after some time, another master again, a genuine friend of Joseph, said to him: Bring the child to my school; perhaps I shall be able to flatter him into learning his letters. And Joseph said: If thou hast the courage, brother, take him with thee. And he took Him with him in fear and great agony; but the child went along pleasantly. And going boldly into the school, He found a book lying on the reading-desk; and taking it, He read not the letters that were in it, but opening His mouth, He spoke by the Holy Spirit, and taught the law to those that were standing round. And a great crowd having come together, stood by and heard Him, and wondered at the ripeness of His teaching, and the readiness of His words, and that He, child as He was, spoke in such a way. And Joseph hearing of it, was afraid, and ran to the school, in doubt lest his master too should be without experience. And the master said to Joseph: Know, brother, that I have taken the child as a scholar, and he is full of much grace and wisdom; but I beseech thee, brother, take him home. And when the child heard this, He laughed at him directly, and said: Since thou hast spoken aright, and witnessed aright, for thy sake he also that was struck down shall be cured. And immediately

the other master was cured. And Joseph took the child, and went away home.

16. And Joseph sent his son James to tie up wood and bring it home, and the child Jesus also followed him. And when James was gathering the fagots, a viper bit James' hand. And when he was racked *with pain*, and at the point of death, Jesus came near and blew upon the bite; and the pain ceased directly, and the beast burst, and instantly James remained safe and sound.

17. And after this the infant of one of Joseph's neighbours fell sick and died, and its mother wept sore. And Jesus heard that there was great lamentation and commotion, and ran in haste, and found the child dead, and touched his breast, and said: I say to thee, child, be not dead, but live, and be with thy mother. And directly it looked up and laughed. And He said to the woman: Take it, and give it milk, and remember me. And seeing this, the crowd that was standing by wondered, and said: Truly this child was either God or an angel of God, for every word of his is a certain fact. And Jesus went out thence, playing with the other children.

18. And some time after there occurred a great commotion while a house was building, and Jesus stood up and went away to the place. And seeing a man lying dead, He took him by the hand, and said: Man, I say to thee, arise, and go on with thy work. And directly he rose up, and adored Him. And seeing this, the crowd wondered, and said: This child is from heaven, for he has saved many souls from death, and he continues to save during all his life.

19. And when He was twelve years old His parents went as usual to Jerusalem to the feast of the passover with their fellow-travellers. And after the passover they were coming home again. And while they were coming home, the child Jesus went back to Jerusalem. And His parents thought that He was in the company. And having gone one day's journey, they sought for Him among their relations; and not finding Him, they were in great grief, and turned back to the city seeking for Him. And after the third day they found Him in the temple, sitting in the midst of the teachers, both hearing the law and asking them questions. And they were all attending to Him, and wondering that He, being a child, was shutting the mouths of the elders and teachers of the people, explaining the main points of the law and the parables of the prophets. And His mother Mary coming up, said to Him: Why hast thou done this to us, child? Behold, we have been seeking for thee in great trouble. And Jesus said to them: Why do you seek me? Do you not know that I must be about my Father's business? And the scribes and the Pharisees said: Art thou the mother of this child? And she said: I am. And they said to her: Blessed art thou among women, for God hath blessed the fruit of thy womb; for such glory, and such virtue and wisdom, we have neither seen nor heard ever. And Jesus rose up, and followed His mother, and was subject to His parents. And His mother observed all these things that had happened. And Jesus advanced in wisdom, and stature, and grace. To whom be glory for ever and ever. Amen.

THE GOSPEL OF JUDAS

Introduction

33 This is the secret message of judgment Jesus spoke with Judas Iscariot over a period of eight days, three days before he celebrated Passover.

When he appeared on earth, he did signs and great wonders for the salvation of humanity. Some [walked] in the way of righteousness, but others walked in their transgression, so the twelve disciples were called. He started to tell them about the mysteries beyond the world and what would happen at the end. Often he didn't reveal himself to his disciples, but you'd find him in their midst as a child.

Jesus Criticizes the Disciples

One day he was with his disciples in Judea. He found them sitting together practicing their piety. When he [came up to] his disciples 34 sitting together praying over the bread, [he] laughed.

The disciples said to him, "Master, why are you laughing at [our] prayer? What have we done? [This] is what's right."

He answered and said to them, "I'm not laughing at you. You're not doing this because you want to, but because through this your God [will be] praised."

They said, "Master, you […] are the Son of our God!"

Jesus said to them, "How do [you] know me? Truly [I] say to you, no generation of the people among you will know me."

When his disciples heard this, [they] started to get angry and furious and started to curse him in their hearts.

But when Jesus noticed their ignorance, [he said] to them, "Why are you letting your anger trouble you? Has your God within you and [his stars] 35 become angry with your souls? If any of you is [strong enough] among humans to bring out the perfect Humanity, stand up and face me."

All of them said, "We're strong enough." But their spirits weren't brave enough to stand before [him] – except Judas Iscariot. He was able to stand before him, but he couldn't look him in the eye, so he looked away.

Judas [said] to him, "I know who you are and where you've come from. You've come from the immortal realm of Barbelo, and I'm not worthy to utter the name of the one who's sent you."

Then Jesus, knowing that he was thinking about what's exalted, said to him, "Come away from the others and I'll tell you the mysteries of the kingdom. Not so that you'll go there, but you'll grieve much 36 because someone else will replace you to complete the twelve [elements] before their God."

Judas said to him, "When will you tell me these things, and when will the great day of light dawn for the generation […]?"

But when he said these things, Jesus left him.

Another Generation

The next morning, he appeared to his disciples. [And] they said to him, "Master, where did [you] go and what did you do when you left us?"

Jesus said to them, "I went to another great and holy generation."

His disciples said to him, "Lord, what great generation is better and holier than us, that's not in these realms?"

Now when Jesus heard this, he laughed. He said to them, "Why are you wondering in your hearts about the strong and holy generation? 37 Truly I say to you, no one born [of] this realm will see that [generation], no army of angels from the stars will rule over it, and no person of mortal birth will be able to join it, because that generation doesn't come from […] that has become […] the generation of the people among [them] is from the generation of the great people […] the powerful authorities who […] nor the powers […] those by which you rule."

When his disciples heard these things, they were each troubled in their spirit. They couldn't say a thing.

The Disciples' Vision

Another day Jesus came up to them. They said to him, "Master, we've seen you in a dream, because we had great [dreams last] night."

But Jesus said, "Why […] hidden yourselves?"

38 And they [said, "We saw] a great [house, with a great] altar [in it, and] twelve people – we'd say they were priests – and a name. And a crowd of people was waiting at the altar [until] the priests [finished receiving] the offerings. We kept waiting too."

[Jesus said], "What were they like?"

And they said, "[Some] fast [for] two weeks. Others sacrifice their own children; others their wives, praising and humbling themselves among each other. Others sleep with men; others murder; yet others commit many sins and do criminal things. [And] the people standing [before] the altar invoke your [name]! 39 And in all their sacrificing, they fill the [altar] with their offerings." When they said this, [they] fell silent because they were troubled.

Jesus said to them, "Why are you troubled? Truly I say to you, all the priests standing before that altar invoke my name. And [again], I say to you, my name has been written on this [house] of the generations of the stars by the human generations. [And they] have shamefully planted fruitless trees in my name." Jesus said to them, "You're the ones receiving the offerings on the altar you've seen. That's the God you serve, and you're the twelve people you've seen. And the animals you saw brought in to be sacrificed are the crowd you lead astray 40 before that altar. [Your minister] will stand up and use my name like that, and [the] generations of the pious will be loyal to him. After him, another person will present [those who sleep around], and another those who murder children, and another those who sleep with men, and those who fast, and the rest of impurity, crime, and error. And those who say, 'We're equal to the angels' – they're the stars that finish everything. It's been said to the human generations, 'Look, God has accepted your sacrifice from the hands of priests,' that is, the minister of error. But the Lord who commands is the Lord over everything. On the last day, they'll be found guilty."

41 Jesus said [to them], "Stop [sacrificing animals]. You've [offered them] over the altar, over your stars with your angels where they've already been completed. So let them become […] with you and let them [become] clear."

His disciples [said to him], "Cleanse us from our [sins] that we've committed through the deceit of the angels."

Jesus said to them, "It's not possible […], nor [can] a fountain quench the fire of the entire inhabited world. Nor can a [city's] well satisfy all the generations, except the great, stable one. A single lamp won't illuminate all the realms, except the second generation, nor can a baker feed all creation 42 under [heaven]."

And [when the disciples heard] these [things], they said to [him], "Master, help us and save us!"

Jesus said to them, "Stop struggling against me. Each one of you has his own star, [and …] of the stars will […] what belongs to it […] I wasn't sent to the corruptible generation, but to the strong and incorruptible generation, because no enemy has ruled [over] that generation, nor any of the stars. Truly I say to you, the pillar of fire will fall quickly and that generation won't be moved by the stars."

Jesus and Judas

And when Jesus [said] these things, he left, [taking] Judas Iscariot with him. He said to him, "The water on the exalted mountain is [from] 43 […] it didn't come to [water … the well] of the tree of [the fruit …] of this realm […] after a time […], but came to water God's paradise and the enduring [fruit], because [it] won't corrupt that generation's [walk of life], but [it will exist] for all eternity."

Judas said to [him, "Tell] me, what kind of fruit does this generation have?"

Jesus said, "The souls of every human generation will die; however, when these people have completed the time in the kingdom and the spirit leaves them, their bodies will die but their souls will live, and they'll be taken up."

Judas said, "What will the rest of the human generations do?"

Jesus said, "It's not possible 44 to sow on [rock] and harvest its fruit. In the same way, it's [not possible to sow on] the [defiled] race along with the perishable wisdom [and] the hand which created mortal humans so that their souls may go up to the realms above. [Truly] I say to you, [no ruler], angel, [or] power will be able to see the [places] that [this great], holy generation [will see]." When Jesus said this, he left.

Judas said, "Master, just as you've listened to all of them, now listen to me too, because I've seen a great vision."

But Jesus laughed when he heard this. He said to him, "Why are you all worked up, you thirteenth demon? But speak up, and I'll bear with you."

Judas said to him, "In the vision, I saw myself. The twelve disciples are stoning me and 45 chasing [me rapidly]. And I also came to the place where [I had followed] you. I saw [a house in this place], and my eyes couldn't [measure] its size. Great people surrounded it, and that house had a roof of greenery. In the middle of the house was [a crowd …]. Master, take me in with these people!"

[Jesus] answered and said, "Your star has led you astray, Judas," and that "no person of mortal birth is worthy to enter the house you've seen, because that place is reserved for those who are holy. Neither the sun nor the moon will rule there, nor the day, but those who are holy will always stand in the realm with the holy angels. Look, I've told you the mysteries of the kingdom 46 and I've taught you about the error of the stars and […] sent [on high] over the twelve realms."

Judas said, "Master, surely my seed doesn't dominate the rulers, does it?"

Jesus answered and said to him, "Come, let me [tell] you [about the holy generation. Not so that you'll go there], but you'll grieve much when you see the kingdom and all its generation."

When Judas heard this, he said to him, "What good has it done me that you've separated me from that generation?"

Jesus answered and said, "You'll become the thirteenth, and will be cursed by the other generations and will rule over them. In the last days they'll […] to you and you won't go up 47 to the holy generation."

Jesus Reveals Everything to Judas

Jesus said, "[Come] and I'll teach you about the [mysteries that no] human [will] see, because there exists a great and boundless realm whose horizons no angelic generation has seen, [in] which is a [great] invisible Spirit, which no [angelic] eye has ever seen, no heart has ever comprehended, and it's never been called by any name.

"And a luminous cloud appeared there. And he (the Spirit) said, 'Let an angel come into being to attend me.' And a great angel, the Self-Begotten, the God of the Light, emerged from the cloud. And because of him, another four angels came into being from another cloud, and they attended the angelic Self-Begotten. And said 48 the [Self-Begotten], 'Let [a realm] come into being,' and it came into being [just as he said]. And he [created] the first luminary to rule over it. And he said, 'Let angels come into being to serve [it,' and myriads] without number came into being. And he said, '[Let a] luminous realm come into being,' and it came into being. He created the second luminary to rule over it, along with myriads of angels without number to offer service. And that's how he created the rest of the realms of light. And he made them to be ruled, and created for them myriads of angels without number to assist them.

"And Adamas was in the first cloud of light that no angel could ever see among all those called 'God.' 49 And [Adamas begat Seth in] that [place after the] image [of …] and after the likeness of [this] angel. He made the incorruptible [generation] of Seth appear to the twelve androgynous [luminaries. And then] he made seventy-two luminaries appear in the incorruptible generation according to the Spirit's will. Then the seventy-two luminaries themselves made three hundred sixty luminaries appear in the incorruptible generation according to the Spirit's will so that there'd be five for each. And the twelve realms of the twelve luminaries make up their father, with six heavens for each realm so there are seventy-two heavens for the seventy-two luminaries, and for each one 50 [of them five] firmaments [for a total of] three hundred sixty [firmaments. They] were given authority and a [great] army of angels without number for honor and service,

along with virgin spirits [too] for the honor and [service] of all the realms and the heavens with their firmaments.

"Now the crowd of those immortals is called 'cosmos' – that is, 'perishable' – by the father and the seventy-two luminaries with the Self-Begotten and his seventy-two realms. That's where the first human appeared with his incorruptible powers. In the realm that appeared with his generation is the cloud of knowledge and the angel who's called 51 [Eleleth …] After these things [Eleleth] said, 'Let twelve angels come into being [to] rule over Chaos and [Hades]. And look, from the cloud there appeared an [angel] whose face flashed with [fire] and whose likeness was [defiled] by blood. His name was Nebro, which means 'Rebel.' Others call him Yaldabaoth. And another angel, Saklas, came from the cloud too. So Nebro created six angels – and Saklas (did too) – to be assistants. They brought out twelve angels in the heavens, with each of them receiving a portion in the heavens.

"And the twelve rulers spoke with the twelve angels: 'Let each of you 52 […] and let them […] generation […five] angels:

The first [is Yaoth], who's called 'the Good One.'
The second is Harmathoth, [the eye of fire].
The [third] is Galila.
The fourth [is] Yobel.
The fifth is Adonaios.

"These are the five who ruled over Hades and are the first over Chaos.

"Then Saklas said to his angels, 'Let's create a human being after the likeness and the image.' And they fashioned Adam and his wife Eve, who in the cloud is called 'Life,' because by this name all the generations seek him, and each of them calls her by their names. Now Saklas didn't 53 [command …] give birth, except […] among the generations […] which this […] and the [angel] said to him, 'Your life will last for a limited time, with your children.'"

Then Judas said to Jesus, "[How] long can a person live?"

Jesus said, "Why are you amazed that the lifespans of Adam and his generation are limited in the place he's received his kingdom with his ruler?"

Judas said to Jesus, "Does the human spirit die?"

Jesus said, "This is how it is. God commanded Michael to loan spirits to people so that they might serve. Then the Great One commanded Gabriel to give spirits to the great generation with no king – the spirit along with the soul. So the [rest] of the souls 54 […] light [… the] Chaos […] seek [the] spirit within you which you've made to live in this flesh from the angelic generations. Then God caused knowledge to be brought to Adam and those with him, so that the kings of Chaos and Hades might not rule over them."

[Then] Judas said to Jesus, "So what will those generations do?"

Jesus said, "Truly I say to you, the stars complete all these things. When Saklas completes the time span that's been determined for him, their first star will appear with the generations, and they'll finish what's been said. Then they'll sleep around in my name, murder their children, 55 and [they'll ...] evil and [...] the realms, bringing the generations and presenting them to Saklas. [And] after that [...] will bring the twelve tribes of [Israel] from [...], and the [generations] will all serve Saklas, sinning in my name. And your star will [rule] over the thirteenth realm." Then Jesus [laughed].

[Judas] said, "Master, why [are you laughing at me?"

Jesus] answered [and said], "I'm not laughing [at you but] at the error of the stars, because these six stars go astray with these five warriors, and they'll all be destroyed along with their creations."

Then Judas said to Jesus, "What will those do who've been baptized in your name?"

The Betrayal

Jesus said, "Truly I say [to you], this baptism 56 [which they've received in] my name [...] will destroy the whole generation of the earthly Adam. Tomorrow they'll torture the one who bears me. Truly I [say] to you, no hand of a mortal human [will fall] upon me. Truly [I say] to you, Judas, those who offer sacrifices to Saklas [...] everything that's evil. But you'll do more than all of them, because you'll sacrifice the human who bears me. Your horn has already been raised, your anger has been kindled, your star has ascended, and your heart has [strayed]. 57 Truly [I say to you], your last [... and] the [... the thrones] of the realm have [been defeated], the kings have grown weak, the angelic generations have grieved, and the evil [they sowed ...] is destroyed, [and] the [ruler] is wiped out. [And] then the [fruit] of the great generation of Adam will be exalted, because before heaven, earth, and the angels, that generation from the realms exists. Look, you've been told everything. Lift up your eyes and see the cloud with the light in it and the stars around it. And the star that leads the way is your star."

Then Judas looked up and saw the luminous cloud, and he entered it. Those standing on the ground heard a voice from the cloud saying, 58 "[. . . the] great [generation . . .] and [. . .]." And Judas didn't see Jesus anymore.

Immediately there was a disturbance among [the] Jews, more than [...] Their high priests grumbled because he'd gone into the guest room to pray. But some scribes were there watching closely so they could arrest him during his prayer, because they were afraid of the people, since they all regarded him as a prophet.

And they approached Judas and said to him, "What are you doing here? Aren't you Jesus' disciple?"

Then he answered them as they wished. Then Judas received some money and handed him over to them.

The Gospel of Judas.

GOSPEL OF TRUTH

Prologue

16 The Gospel of Truth is a joy for those who've received grace from the Father of Truth, that they might know him through the power of the Word that came from the fullness – the one who's in the thought and mind of the Father. They call him "Savior." That's the name of the work he'll do to redeem those who had become **17** ignorant of the Father. And the term "the Gospel" is the revelation of hope, the discovery of those who search for him.

Error and Forgetfulness

Since all searched for the one from whom they had come – all were within him, the uncontainable, inconceivable one who's beyond every thought – (and) since ignorance of the Father caused anguish and terror, and the anguish grew thick like a fog, so that no one could see – Error was strengthened. It worked on its own matter in vain, not knowing the Truth.

It happened in a deluding way, as it (Error) prepared with power, in beauty, a substitute for the Truth. Now this wasn't humiliating for the uncontainable, inconceivable one, because the anguish and forgetfulness and delusion of deceit were like nothing, whereas the Truth is established, unchangeable, unperturbed, beyond beauty. Because of this, disregard Error, since it has no root.

It happened in a fog concerning the Father. It happens (now) since it (Error) prepares works in forgetfulness and terror, so that with them it (Error) might attract those in the middle and imprison them.

The forgetfulness of Error wasn't revealed; it wasn't a **18** [thought] from the Father. Forgetfulness didn't come into being from the Father, though it did come into being because of him. What comes into being within him is the knowledge, which was revealed so that forgetfulness might be dissolved, and the Father might be known. Forgetfulness came into being because the Father was unknown, so when the Father comes to be known, forgetfulness won't exist anymore.

The Gospel

This is the Gospel of the one they search for, revealed to those who are complete through the mercies of the Father, the hidden mystery. Through it (the Gospel), Jesus Christ enlightened those who were in darkness through forgetfulness. He enlightened them; he showed them a Way, and the Way is the Truth which he taught them.

As a result, Error was angry. It pursued him. It was threatened by him and brought to nothing. They nailed him (Jesus) to a tree, and he became the fruit of the Father's knowledge. However, it (the fruit) didn't cause destruction when it was eaten, but those who ate it were given joy in the discovery. He discovered them in himself and they discovered him in themselves.

As for the uncontainable, inconceivable one – the Father, the complete one who made all – all are within him, and all need him. Although he kept their completion within himself which he didn't give to all, the Father wasn't jealous. Indeed, what jealousy is there between him and his members? **19** For if, like this, the generation [received the completion,] they couldn't have come [...] the Father. He keeps their completion within himself, giving it to them to return to him with a unitary knowledge in completion. He's the one who made all, and all are within him, and all need him.

Like someone who's unknown, he wants to be known and loved – because what did all need if not the knowledge of the Father?

He became a guide, peaceful and leisurely. He came and spoke the Word as a teacher in places of learning. Those who were wise in their own estimation came up to him to test him, but he confounded them because they were vain. They hated him because they weren't wise in Truth. After all of them, all the little children came too; theirs is the knowledge of the Father. When they were strengthened, they received teaching about the Father's expressions. They knew and they were known; they received glory and they gave glory. In their hearts the living Book of the Living was revealed, which was written in the thought and mind **20** [of the] Father, and before the [foundation] of all within his incomprehensibility. This (book) is impossible to take, since it permits the one who takes it to be killed. No one could've been revealed among those who'd been entrusted with salvation unless the book had appeared. Because of this, the merciful and faithful Jesus patiently suffered until he took that book, since he knows that his death is life for many.

When a will hasn't yet been opened, the wealth of the deceased master of the house is hidden; so too all were hidden while the Father of all was invisible. They were from him, from whom every realm comes. Because of this:

Jesus was revealed,
put on that book,
was nailed to a tree,
and published the Father's edict on the cross.
Oh, what a great teaching!
Drawing himself down to death,
he clothed himself in eternal life,
stripped himself of the perishable rags,
and clothed himself in incorruptibility,
which no one can take from him.

When he entered the empty realms of terror, he passed through those who were stripped by forgetfulness, being knowledge and completion, proclaiming the things that are in the heart **21** [...] teach those who will [receive teaching].

The Book of the Living

Now those who will receive teaching [are] the living who are written in the Book of the Living. They receive teaching about themselves, and they receive it from the Father, returning to him again.

Since the completion of all is in the Father, it's necessary for all to go up to him. Then, if someone has knowledge, they receive what are their own, and he draws them to himself, because the one who's ignorant is in need. And it's a great need, since they need what will complete them. Since the completion of all is in the Father, it's necessary for all to go up to him, and for each one to receive what are their own. He inscribed these things beforehand, having prepared them to give to those who came out from him.

Those whose names he knew beforehand were called at the end, so that the one who has knowledge is the one whose name the Father has called, because those whose name hasn't been spoken are ignorant. Indeed, how can someone hear if their name hasn't been called? For the one who's ignorant until the end is a delusion of forgetfulness, and they'll dissolve with it. Otherwise, why do these miserable ones have no **22** name? Why do they have no voice?

So if someone has knowledge, they're from above. If they're called, they hear, they reply, and they turn to the one who calls them. And they go up to him, and they know how they are called. Having knowledge, they do the will of the one who called them, they want to please him, and they receive rest. Each one's name becomes their own. The one who has knowledge like this knows where they come from and where they're going. They know like one who, having been drunk, turns from their drunkenness, and having returned to themselves, restores what are their own.

He's returned many from Error. He went before them to the realms from which they had moved away. They had received Error because of the depth of the one who surrounds every realm, though nothing surrounds him. It's a great wonder that they were in the Father, not knowing him, and that they were able to come out by themselves, since they weren't able to grasp and know the one in whom they were. He revealed his will as knowledge in harmony with all that emanated from him. This is the knowledge of the living book which he revealed to the **23** generations at the end, letters from him revealing how they're not vowels or consonants, so that one might read them and think they're meaningless, but they're letters of the Truth – they speak and know themselves. Each letter is a complete thought, like a book that's complete, since they're letters written by the Unity, the Father having written them so that the generations, by means of his letters, might know the Father.

The Return to Unity

His Wisdom meditates on the Word,
his teaching speaks it,
his knowledge has revealed it,
his patience is a crown upon it,
his joy is in harmony with it,
his glory has exalted it,
his image has revealed it,
his rest has received it,
his love made a body around it,
his faith embraced it.
In this way, the Word of the Father goes out in all, as the fruit **24** [of] his heart and an expression of his will. But it supports all. It chooses them and also takes the expression of all, purifying them, returning them to the Father and to the Mother, Jesus of infinite sweetness. The Father reveals his bosom, and his bosom is the Holy Spirit. He reveals what's hidden of himself; what's hidden of himself is his Son – so that through the mercies of the Father, the generations may know him and cease their work in searching for the Father, resting in him and knowing that this is the rest. He's filled the need and dissolved its appearance – its appearance is the world in which it served, because where there's envy and strife there's need, but where there's Unity there's completion. Since need came into being because the Father wasn't known, when the Father is known, from then on, need will no longer exist. As someone's ignorance dissolves when they gain knowledge, and as darkness dissolves when the light appears, **25** so also need dissolves in completion. So the appearance is revealed from then on, but it'll dissolve in the harmony of Unity.

For now, their works lie scattered. In time, Unity will complete the realms. Within Unity each one will receive themselves, and within knowledge they'll purify themselves from multiplicity into Unity, consuming matter within themselves like fire, and darkness by light, death by life. If indeed these things have happened to each one of us, then it's right for us to think about all, so that this house will be holy and silent for the Unity.

The Parable of the Jars

It's like some who've left their home, having jars that weren't any good in places. They broke them, but the master of the house doesn't suffer any loss. Instead he rejoices, because in place of the bad jars are ones that are full and complete. For this is **26** the judgment that's come from above; it's judged everyone. It's a drawn, two-edged sword which cuts both ways. The Word, which is in the hearts of those who speak it, appeared. It isn't just a sound, but it was incarnated (embodied). A great disturbance arose among the jars, because some were empty, others filled; some provided for, others poured out; some purified, others broken. All the realms were shaken and disturbed, because they didn't have order or stability. Error was anxious. It didn't know what to do; it grieved, mourned, and hurt itself, because it knew nothing. The knowledge, which is its (Error's) destruction, approached it (Error) and all that emanated from it. Error is empty, with nothing inside it.

Truth came into their midst, and all that emanated knew it. They welcomed the Father in Truth with a complete power that joins them with the Father. Truth is the Father's mouth; the Holy Spirit is his tongue. Everyone who loves the Truth and are joined to the **27** Truth are joined to the Father's mouth. By his tongue they'll receive the Holy Spirit. This is the revelation of the Father and his manifestation to his generations. He revealed what was hidden of himself; he explained it, because who has anything, if not the Father alone?

Coming into Being

Every realm emanates from him. They know they've come out from him like children who are from someone who's completely mature. They knew they hadn't yet received form or a name. The Father gives birth to each one. Then, when they receive form from his knowledge, although they're really within him, they don't know him. But the Father is complete, knowing every realm that's within him. If he wants to, he reveals whomever he wants, giving them a form and a name. He gives a name to them, and causes those to come into being who, before they come into being, are ignorant of the one who made them.

I'm not saying, then, that those who haven't yet come into being are nothing, but they exist **28** in the one who will want them to come into being when he wants, like a later time. Before everything is revealed, he knows what he'll produce. But the fruit which he hasn't yet revealed doesn't yet know anything, nor does it do anything. In addition, every realm which is itself in the Father is from the one who exists, who establishes them from what doesn't exist. For those who have no root have no fruit either. They think to themselves, "I've come into being," but they'll dissolve by themselves. Because of this, those who didn't exist at all won't exist.

The Parable of the Nightmares

What, then, did he want them to think of themselves? He wanted to them to think, "I've come into being like the shadows and phantoms of the night." When the light shines on the terror which they received, they know that it's nothing. In this way, they were ignorant of the Father, whom **29** they didn't see. Since it was terror and disturbance and instability and doubt and division, many illusions were at work among them, and vain ignorance, like they were deep in sleep and found themselves in nightmares. Either they're running somewhere, or unable to run away from someone; or they're fighting, or being beaten; or they've fallen from heights, or fly through the air without wings. Sometimes, too, it's like someone is killing them, even though no one's chasing them; or they themselves are killing those around them, covered in their blood. Until those who are going through all these nightmares can wake up, they see nothing, because these things are nothing.

That's the way it is with those who've cast off ignorance like sleep. They don't regard it as anything, nor do they regard its **30** other works as real, but they abandon them like a dream in the night. They value the knowledge of the Father like they value the light. The ignorant have acted like they're asleep; those who've come to knowledge have acted like they've awakened. Good for the one who returns and awakens! Blessed is the one who's opened the eyes of those who can't see! The Holy Spirit hurried after them to revive them. Having given a hand to the one who lay on the ground, it set them up on their feet, because they hadn't yet arisen. It gave them the knowledge of the Father and the revelation of the Son, because when they saw him and heard him, he granted them to taste him and to grasp the beloved Son.

The Revelation of the Son

When he was revealed, he taught them about the Father, the uncontainable one, and breathed into them what's in the thought, doing his will. When many had received the light, they turned **31** to him. For the material ones were strangers, who didn't see his form or know him. For he came by means of fleshly form, and nothing could block his path, because incorruptibility can't be grasped. Moreover, he said new things while he spoke about what's in the Father's heart and brought out the complete Word. When the light spoke through his mouth, and by his voice gave birth to life, he gave them thought, wisdom, mercy, salvation, and the Spirit of power from the infinity and sweetness of the Father. He caused punishments and torments to cease, because they led astray into Error and bondage those who needed mercy. He dissolved and confounded them with knowledge. He became:
a Way for those who were led astray,
knowledge for those who were ignorant,
a discovery for those who were searching,
strength for those who were wavering, and
purity for those who were impure.

The Parable of the Sheep

He's the shepherd who left behind the ninety- **32** nine sheep which weren't lost. He went and searched for the one which was lost. He rejoiced when he found it, because ninety-nine is a number expressed with the left hand. However, when the one is found, the numerical sum moves to the right hand. In this way, what needs the one – that is, the whole right hand – draws what it needs, takes it from the left hand, and moves it to the right, so the number becomes one hundred. This is a symbol of the sound of these numbers; this is the Father. Even on the Sabbath, he worked for the sheep which he found fallen in the pit. He saved the life of the sheep, having brought it up from the pit, so that you may know in your hearts – you're children of the knowledge of the heart – what is the Sabbath, on which it isn't right for salvation to be idle, so that you may speak of the day which is above, which has no night, and of the light that doesn't set, because it's complete. Speak then from the heart, because you're the completed day, and the light that doesn't cease dwells within you. Speak of the Truth with those who search for it, and of knowledge with those who've sinned in their Error.

Doing the Father's Will

33 Strengthen the feet of those who stumble, and reach out to those who are sick. Feed those who are hungry, and give rest to those who are weary. Raise up those who want to arise, and awaken those who sleep, because you're the understanding that's unsheathed. If strength is like this, it becomes stronger.

Be concerned about yourselves. Don't be concerned about other things which you've rejected from yourselves. Don't return to eat your vomit. Don't be eaten by worms, because you've already shaken it off. Don't become a dwelling-place for the devil, because you've already brought him to naught. Don't strengthen your obstacles which are collapsing, as though you're a support. For the lawless one is nothing, to be treated more harshly than the just, doing his works among others.

Do then the Father's will, because you're from him. For the Father is sweet, and goodness is in his will. He knows what's yours, that you may find rest in them. For by the fruits they know what's yours, because the children of the Father **34** are his fragrance, since they're from the grace of his expression. Because of this, the Father loves his fragrance, and reveals it in every place. And when it mixes with matter, it gives his fragrance to the light, and in tranquility he causes it to rise above every form and every sound. For it's not the ears that smell the fragrance, but it's the Spirit that smells, and draws the fragrance to itself, and sinks down into the Father's fragrance. He shelters it, then, and takes it to the place from which it came, from the first fragrance which has grown cold. It's something in a soul-endowed delusion, like cold water sunk into loose earth. Those who see it think that it's just earth. Afterwards, it dissolves again. If a breath draws it, it becomes warm. So the fragrances which are cold are from the division. Because of this, faith came. It dissolved the division, and it brought the fullness that's warm with love, so that the cold may not return, but rather the unitary thought of completion.

Restoring what was Needed

This is the Word of the Gospel of the discovery of the fullness, which comes for those who are awaiting **35** the salvation which is coming from above. The hope for which they're waiting is waiting for those whose image is light with no shadow in it. If at that time the fullness comes, the need of matter doesn't come through the infinity of the Father, who comes to give time to the need – although no one can say that the incorruptible one will come like this. But the depth of the Father multiplied, and the thought of Error didn't exist with him. It's something that's fallen, which is easily set upright in the discovery of the one who's to come to what he'll return, because the return is called "repentance."

Because of this, incorruptibility breathed out. It followed after the one who sinned, so that they might rest, because forgiveness is what remains for the light in need, the Word of fullness. For the doctor hurries to the place where there's sickness, because that's what he (or she) wants to do. The one in need, then, doesn't hide it, because one (the doctor) has what they need. In this way the fullness, which has no need but fills the need, is what he **36** provided from himself to fill up what's needed, so that they might receive grace; because when they were in need, they didn't have grace. Because of this, a diminishing took place where there is no grace. When what was diminished was restored, what they needed was revealed as fullness. This is the discovery of the light of Truth which enlightened them, because it doesn't change.

Because of this, they spoke of Christ in their midst: "Seek, and those who were disturbed will receive a return – and he'll anoint them with ointment." The ointment is the mercy of the Father, who will have mercy on them. But those whom he anointed are those who have been completed, because full jars are the ones that are anointed. But when the anointing of one

dissolves, it empties, and the cause of the need is the place where the ointment leaks, because a breath and its power draws it. But from the one who has no need, no seal is removed, nor is anything emptied, but what it needs is filled again by the Father, who's complete.

The Father's Paradise

He's good. He knows his plants, because he planted them in his paradise. Now his paradise is a place of rest. This **37** is the completion in the Father's thought, and these are the words of his meditation. Each of his words is the work of his one will in the revelation of his Word. When they were still in the depths of his thought, the Word – which was the first to come out – revealed them along with a mind that speaks the one Word in a silent grace. He was called "the Thought," since they were in it before being revealed. It happened, then, that he was the first to come out at the time when it pleased the one who wanted it. Now the Father rests in his will, and is pleased with it.

Nothing happens without him, nor does anything happen without the will of the Father, but his will is incomprehensible. His trace is the will, and no one can know him, nor does he exist for people to scrutinize so that they might grasp him, but when he wills, what he wills is this – even if the sight doesn't please them in any way before God – the will of the Father, because he knows the beginning of all of them, and their end, for in the end he'll greet them directly. Now the end is receiving knowledge of the one who's hidden; this is the Father, **38** from whom the beginning has come, and to whom all who've come out from him will return. They were revealed for the glory and the joy of his name.

The Father's Name

Now the name of the Father is the Son. He's the one who first gave a name to the one who comes out from him, who was himself, and he gave birth to him as a Son. He gave him his name which belonged to him. He's the one to whom everything around the Father belongs. The name and the Son are his. It's possible for him to be seen; the name, however, is invisible, because it alone is the mystery of the invisible which comes to ears that are filled completely with it by him. For indeed, the Father's name isn't spoken, but it's revealed through a Son.

In this way, then, the name is great. Who, then, will be able to utter a name for him, the great name, except him alone to whom the name belongs, and the children of the name, those in whom the Father's name rests, and who themselves, in turn, rest in his name? Since the Father is unbegotten, it's he alone who gave birth to him for himself as a name, before he had made the generations, so that the Father's name might be over their head as Lord, which is the **39** true name, confirmed in his command in complete power. For the name isn't from words and naming; the name, rather, is invisible. He gave a name to him alone. He alone sees him, he alone having the power to give him a name, because whoever doesn't exist has no name. For what name will they give one who doesn't exist? But the one who exists, exists also with his name, and he alone knows it, and he's given a name to him alone. This is the Father; his name is the Son. He didn't hide it within, then, but it existed. The Son alone gave a name. The name, then, belongs to the Father, as the name of the Father is the beloved Son. Where, indeed, would he find a name, except from the Father?

But doubtless one will ask their neighbor, "Who is it who'll give a name to the one who existed before them, as if **40** offspring didn't receive a name from those who gave them birth?" First, then, it's right for us to consider what the name is. It's the true name, the name from the Father, because it's the proper name. So he didn't receive the name on loan, the way others do, according to the form in which each one will be produced. This, then, is the proper name. There's no one else who gave it to him. But he's unnameable, indescribable, until the time when he who's complete spoke of him alone. And it's he who has the power to speak his name and to see him. So when it pleased him that his beloved name should be his Son, and he gave the name to him who came out from the depth, he disclosed his secrets, knowing that the Father is without evil. Because of this, he brought him out so that he might speak about the place, and his resting place from which he had come, **41** and to glorify the fullness, the greatness of his name, and the Father's sweetness.

The Place of Rest

Each one will speak about the place from which they came, and they'll hurry to return again to the place where they received their restoration to receive from the place where they were, receiving a taste from that place and receiving nourishment, receiving growth.

And their place of rest is their fullness. All that have emanated from the Father, then, are fullnesses, and the roots of all that have emanated from him are within the one who caused them all to grow. He gave them their destinies. Then each one was revealed, so that through their own thought […] for the place to which they send their thought is their root, which takes them up through all the heights, up to the Father. They embrace his head, which is rest for them, and they're grasped, approaching him, as though to say that they receive his expression by means of kisses. But they're not revealed **42** in this way, because they neither exalted themselves, nor wanted the Father's glory, nor did they think of him as trivial or harsh or wrathful; but he's without evil, unperturbed, and sweet. He knows every realm before they've come into existence, and he has no need to be instructed. This is the way of those who possess something of the immeasurable greatness from above, as they wait for the complete one alone, who's a Mother for them. And they don't go down to Hades, nor do they have envy or groaning, nor death within them, but they rest in the one who rests, not striving nor twisting around in the search for Truth. But they themselves are the Truth, and the Father is within them, and they're in the Father, being complete. They're undivided from the truly good one. They don't need anything, but they rest, refreshed in the Spirit. And they'll listen to their root. They'll devote themselves to those things that they'll find in their root and not suffer loss to their soul. This is the place of the blessed; this is their place.

Conclusion

As for the others, then, may they know, where they're at, that it's not right **43** for me, having come to the place of rest, to say anything else, but I'll come to be in it, and will devote myself continually to the Father of all and the true brothers (and sisters), those upon whom the Father's love is emptied and in whose midst there is no need. They're the ones who are revealed in Truth; they exist in the true eternal life, and they speak of the light that's complete and that's filled with the Father's seed, and that's in his heart and in the fullness. His Spirit rejoices in it, and glorifies the one in whom it existed, because he's good. And his children are complete, and worthy of his name, because he's the Father. It's children like this that he loves.

GOSPEL OF PHILIP

Gentiles, Hebrews, and Christians

51 A Hebrew creates a Hebrew, and [those] of this kind are called "a proselyte." But a [proselyte] doesn't create (another) proselyte. They're like […] and they create others […] **52** it's good enough for them that they come into being.

The slave seeks only freedom; they don't seek their master's property. But the son isn't just a son; he claims his father's inheritance for himself. Those who inherit the dead are themselves dead, and they inherit the dead. Those who inherit the living are themselves alive, and they inherit (both) the living and the dead. The dead can't inherit anything, because how can the dead inherit? If the dead inherits the living they won't die, but the dead will live even more! A gentile doesn't die, because they've never lived in order that they may die. Whoever has believed in the Truth has lived, and is at risk of dying, because they're alive since the day Christ came. The world is created, the cities gentrified, and the dead carried out.

When we were Hebrews, we were fatherless – we had (only) our mother. But when we became Christians, we gained both father and mother.

Life, Death, Light, and Darkness

Those who sow in the winter reap in the summer. The winter is the world, the summer the other age. Let's sow in the world so that we may reap in the summer. Because of this, it's not right for us to pray in the winter. The summer follows the winter. But if someone reaps in the winter they won't reap, but uproot, as this kind won't produce fruit […] it doesn't just come out […] but in the other Sabbath […] it's fruitless.

Christ came **53** to buy some, but to save others, and to redeem yet others. He bought those who were strangers, made them his own, and set them apart as a pledge as he wanted to. It wasn't just when he appeared that he laid down his life when he wanted to, but since the day the world came into being he laid down his life when he wanted to. Then he came first to take it, since it had been pledged. It was dominated by the robbers that had captured it, but he saved it; and those who are good in the world he redeemed, as well as those who are bad.

The light and the darkness, the right and the left, are brothers of each other. They're inseparable. So, those who are good aren't good, those who are bad aren't bad, nor is life (really) life, nor is death (really) death. Because of this, each one will be dissolved into its origin from the beginning. But those who are exalted above the world are indissoluble and eternal.

Names

The names that are given to those who are worldly are very deceptive, because they turn the heart away from what's right to what's not right, and someone who hears "God" doesn't think of what's right but thinks of what's not right.

So also with "the Father," "the Son," "the Holy Spirit," "the life," "the light," "the resurrection," "the church," and all the others – they don't think of [what's right] but think of what's [not] right, [unless] they've learned what's right. The [names that were heard] exist in the world […] **54** [deceive. If they existed] in the (eternal) age they wouldn't have been used as names in the world, nor would they have been placed among worldly things. They have an end in the (eternal) age.

There's one name that isn't uttered in the world: the name which the Father gave to the Son. It's exalted over ·everything; it's the Father's name, because the Son wouldn't have become father unless he had taken the name of the Father. Those who have this name know it, but don't say it; and those who don't have it, don't know it. But Truth brought names into the world for us, because it's impossible for us to learn it (Truth) without these names. There's only one Truth, but it's many things for us, to teach this one thing in love through many things.

The Rulers

The rulers wanted to deceive humanity, because they (the rulers) saw that they (humanity) had a kinship with those that are truly good. They took the name of those that are good and gave it to those that aren't good, to deceive them (humanity) by the names and bind them to those that aren't good; and then, what a favor they do for them! They take them from those that aren't good and place them among those that are good. They knew what they were doing, because they wanted to take those who were free and place them in slavery forever. There are powers that exist […] humanity, not wanting them to be [saved], so that they may be […] because if humanity [was saved], sacrifices [wouldn't] happen […] and animals offered **55** up to the powers, because those to whom offerings were made were animals. They were offered up alive, but when they were offered up they died. A human was offered up to God dead, and he lived.

Before Christ came, there wasn't any bread in the world – just as Paradise, where Adam was, had many trees to feed the animals but no wheat to feed humanity. Humanity used to eat like the animals, but when Christ, the perfect human, came, he brought bread from heaven so that humanity would be fed with the food of humanity.

The rulers thought they did what they did by their own power and will, but the Holy Spirit was secretly accomplishing everything it wanted to through them. Truth, which has existed from the beginning, is sown everywhere; and many see it being sown, but few see it being reaped.

The Virgin Birth

Some say that "Mary conceived by the Holy Spirit." They're wrong; they don't know what they're saying. When did a woman ever conceive by a woman? "Mary is the virgin whom no power defiled" is the great testimony of those Hebrews who became (the first) apostles and (the) apostolic (successors). The virgin whom no power defiled […] the powers defiled themselves.

And the Lord [wouldn't] have said, "my [Father who is in] heaven" unless [he] had another father. Instead, he would simply have said ["my Father."] The Lord said to the [disciples, "…] **56** [from] every [house] and bring into the Father's house, but don't steal (anything) from the Father's house or carry it away."

Jesus, Christ, Messiah, Nazarene

"Jesus" is a hidden name; "Christ" is a revealed name. So "Jesus" is not translated, but he's called by his name "Jesus." But the name "Christ" in Syriac is "Messiah," in Greek "Christ," and all the others have it according to their own language. "The Nazarene" reveals what's hidden. Christ has everything within himself, whether human or angel or mystery, and the Father.

The Resurrection

Those who say that the Lord died first and then arose are wrong, because he arose first and (then) he died. Anyone who doesn't first acquire the resurrection won't die. As God lives, that one would /die\!

No one will hide something great and valuable in a great thing, but often someone has put countless thousands into something worth (only) a penny. It's the same with the soul; a valuable thing came to be in a contemptible body.

Some are afraid that they'll arise naked. So they want to arise in the flesh, and [they] don't know that those who wear the [flesh] are naked. Those […] to strip themselves naked [are] not naked. "Flesh [and blood won't] inherit [God's] kingdom." What is it that **57** won't inherit? That which is on us. But what is it, too, that will inherit? It is Jesus' (flesh) and blood. Because of this, he said, "Whoever doesn't eat my flesh and drink my blood doesn't have life in them." What's his flesh? It's the Word, and his blood is the Holy Spirit. Whoever has received these have food, drink, and clothing.

(So) I myself disagree with the others who say, "It won't arise." Both (sides) are wrong. You who say, "the flesh won't arise," tell me what will arise, so that we may honor you. You say, "the spirit in the flesh and this other light in the flesh." (But) this saying is in the flesh too, because whatever you say, you can't say apart from the flesh. It's necessary to arise in this flesh, since everything exists in it. In this world, people are better than the clothes they wear. In the kingdom of heaven, the clothes are better than the people who wear them.

Everything is purified by water and fire – the visible by the visible, the hidden by the hidden. Some things are hidden by things that are visible. There's water in water, and fire in chrism.

Seeing Jesus

Jesus took all of them by stealth, because he didn't appear as he was, but he appeared as [they'd] be able to see him. He appeared to them (in) [all these] (ways): he [appeared] to [the] great as great. He [appeared] to the small as small. He [appeared] **58** [to the] angels as an angel, and to humans as a human. So his Word hid itself from everyone. Some did see him, thinking they were seeing themselves. But when he appeared to his disciples in glory on the mountain, he wasn't small. He became great, but he made the disciples great (too) so that they would be able to see him as great.

He said on that day in the Eucharist, "You who've united the perfect light with the Holy Spirit, unite the angels with us too, with the images!"

Don't despise the lamb, because without him it's impossible to see the door. No one will be able to approach the king naked.

Father, Son, and Holy Spirit

The children of the heavenly human are more numerous than those of the earthly human. If Adam has so many children, even though they die, how many children does the perfect human have – those who don't die, but are begotten all the time?

The father makes a son, but it's impossible for a son to make a son, because it's impossible for someone who's been born to beget (sons); the son begets brothers, not sons. All who are begotten in the world are begotten physically, and the others in […] are begotten by him […] out there to the human […] in the […] heavenly place […] it from the mouth […] the Word came out from there **59** they would be nourished from the mouth [and] become perfect. The perfect are conceived and begotten through a kiss. Because of this we kiss each other too, conceiving from the grace within each other.

There were three who traveled with the Lord all the time: His mother Mary, her sister, and Magdalene, who is called his companion; because Mary is his sister, his mother, and his partner.

"The Father" and "The Son" are single names; "the Holy Spirit" is a double name, because they're everywhere. They're in heaven, they're below, they're hidden, and they're revealed. The Holy Spirit is revealed below and hidden in heaven.

Those who are holy are served through the evil powers, because the Holy Spirit has blinded them so that they think they're serving a (regular) human when they're (really) working for the holy ones. So a disciple asked the Lord one day about a worldly thing. He told him, "Ask your Mother, and she'll give you from someone else."

The apostles said to the disciples, "May our entire offering acquire salt." They called […] "salt." Without it, the offering doesn't [become] acceptable. But Wisdom [is] childless; because of this [she's] called […], this of salt, the place they'll […] in their own way. The Holy Spirit […] **60** […] many children.

What belongs to the father belongs to the son, and he himself – the son – as long as he's little, is not entrusted with what's his. When he becomes a man, his father gives him everything that belongs to him.

Those who've been begotten by the Spirit and go astray, go astray through it too. Because of this, through this one Spirit it blazes, that is, the fire, and it's extinguished.

Echamoth is one thing and Echmoth another. Echamoth is simply Wisdom, but Echmoth is the Wisdom of Death, which knows death. This is called "the little Wisdom."

Humans and Animals

There are animals that submit to humans, like the calf, the donkey, and others of this kind. Others are not submissive, and live alone in the wilderness. Humanity ploughs the field with the submissive animals, and consequently nourishes itself and the animals, whether submissive or not. That's what it's like with the perfect human: they plough with the submissive powers, preparing for everyone that will exist. So because of this the whole place stands, whether the good or the evil, and the right and the left. The Holy Spirit shepherds everyone and rules all the powers – those that are submissive, those that [aren't], and those that are alone – because truly it […] confines them [so that …] want to, they won't be able to [leave].

[The one who's been] formed [is beautiful, but] you'd find his children being **61** noble forms. If he weren't formed but begotten, you'd find that his seed was noble. But now he was formed, and he begot. What nobility is this? First there was adultery, and then murder; and he (Cain) was begotten in adultery, because he was the son of the serpent. Because of this he became a murderer like his father too, and he killed his brother (Abel). Every partnership between those who are dissimilar is adultery.

Becoming Christians

God is a dyer. Like the good dyes – they're called true – die with what's been dyed in them, so it is with those who were dyed by God. Because his dyes are immortal, they become immortal by means of his colors. But God baptizes in water.

It's impossible for anyone to see anything that really exists unless they become like them. It's not like the person in the world who sees the sun without becoming a sun, and who sees heaven and earth and everything else without becoming them. That's the way it is. But you've seen something of that place, and have become them. You saw the Spirit, you became spirit; you saw Christ, you became Christ; you saw [the Father, you] will become father. Because of this, [here] you see everything and don't [see yourself], but you see yourself [there], because you'll [become] what you see.

Faith receives; love gives. [No one will be able to] **62** [receive] without faith, and no one will be able to give without love. So we believe in order that we may receive, but we give in order that we may love, since anyone who doesn't give with love doesn't get anything out of it. Whoever hasn't received the Lord is still a Hebrew.

The apostles before us called (him) "Jesus the Nazarene Messiah," that is, "Jesus the Nazarene Christ." The last name is "Christ," the first is "Jesus," the middle one is "the

Nazarene." "Messiah" has two meanings: both "Christ" and "the measured." "Jesus" in Hebrew is "the redemption." "Nazara" is "the truth." So "the Nazarene" is "the truth." "Christ" is the one who was measured. "The Nazarene" and "Jesus" are the ones who were measured.

A pearl doesn't become less valuable if it's cast down into the mud, nor will it become more valuable if it's anointed with balsam; but it's valuable to its owner all the time. That's what it's like with God's children: no matter where they are, they're still valuable to their Father.

If you say, "I'm a Jew," no one will be moved. If you say, "I'm a Roman," no one will be disturbed. If you say, "I'm a Greek," "a Barbarian," "a slave," ["a free person,"] no one will be troubled. [If] you [say,] "I'm a Christian," the […] will tremble. If only [… of] this kind, this one [who …] won't be able to endure [hearing] his name.

God is a human-eater. **63** Because of this, the human is [sacrificed] to him. Before the human was sacrificed, animals were sacrificed, because those to whom they were sacrificed weren't gods.

Vessels of glass and pottery come into being by means of fire. But if glass vessels break they're remade, because they came into being by means of a breath, but if pottery vessels break they're destroyed, because they came into being without breath.

A donkey turning a millstone traveled a hundred miles. When it was released, it still found itself in the same place. Many people travel, but don't get anywhere. When evening came, they saw neither city nor village, nor anything created or natural, nor power nor angel. The wretches worked in vain.

The Eucharist is Jesus, because in Syriac he's called "Pharisatha," that is, "the one who's spread out," because Jesus came to crucify the world.

The Lord went into Levi's place of dyeing. He took seventy-two colors and threw them into the vat. He brought all of them out white and said, "That's the way the Son of Humanity has come [as] a dyer."

The Wisdom who is called "the barren" is the Mother [of the angels] and [the] companion of the [… Mary] Magdalene [… loved her] more than the disciples [… he] kissed her on her [… many] times. The rest of […] **64** […] they said to him, "Why do you love her more than all of us?" The Savior said to them in reply, "Why don't I love you like her? When a person who's blind and one who sees are both in the dark, they're no different from one another. When the light comes, the one who sees will see the light, and the one who's blind will remain in the dark."

The Lord said, "Blessed is the one who exists before existing, because they who exist did exist, and will exist."

The superiority of humanity isn't revealed, but exists in what's hidden. So it (humanity) masters animals that are stronger, that are greater in terms of that which is revealed and that which is hidden. This allows them to survive; but if humanity separates from them (the animals), they kill, bite, and eat each other, because they didn't find food. But now they've found food because humanity has worked the earth.

If someone goes down into the water and comes up without having received anything, and says, "I'm a Christian," they've borrowed the name at interest. But if they receive the Holy Spirit, they have the gift of the name. Whoever has received a gift doesn't have it taken away, but whoever has borrowed it at interest has to give it back. That's what it's like when someone comes into being in a mystery.

The Mystery of Marriage

[The] mystery of marriage [is] great, because [without] it the world would [not exist]; because [the] structure of [the world …], but the structure [… the marriage]. Think about the [intimate …] defiled, because it has […] power. Its image **65** exists in a [defilement].

The impure spirits take male and female [forms]. The males are those that are intimate with the souls which dwell in a female form, and the females are those that mingle with those in a male form through disobedience. No one will be able to escape being bound by them without receiving a male power and a female one – the groom and the bride – in the image of the bridal chamber. When the foolish females see a male sitting alone, they jump on him, play with him, and defile him. In the same way, when the foolish males see a beautiful female sitting alone, they seduce and coerce her, wanting to defile her. But if they see the husband and his wife sitting together, the females can't go inside the husband, nor the males inside the wife. That's what it's like when the image unites with the angel; no one will be able to dare to go inside the [male] or the female.

Overcoming the World

Whoever comes out of the world can no longer be bound because they were in the world. They're revealed to be above the desire of the [… and] fear. They're master over […] they're better than envy. If […] come, they (the powers) bind and choke [them]. How will [they] be able to escape the [great powers …]? How will they be able to […]? There are some who [say], "We're faithful," in order that […] **66** [impure spirit] and demon, because if they had the Holy Spirit, no impure spirit would cling to them. Don't fear the flesh, nor love it. If you fear it, it'll master you; if you love it, it'll swallow and choke you.

Someone exists either in this world, or in the resurrection, or in the middle places. May I never be found there! There's both good and evil in this world. Its good things aren't good, and its evil things aren't evil. But there's an evil after this world which is truly evil: that which is called "the middle." It's death. While we're in this world, it's right for us to acquire the resurrection for ourselves, so that when we're stripped of the flesh we'll be found in the rest and not travel in the middle, because many stray on the way.

It's good to come out of the world before one sins. There are some who neither want to nor can, but others who, if they wanted to, (still) wouldn't benefit, because they didn't act. The wanting makes them sinners. But (even) if they don't want, justice will (still) be hidden from them. It's not the will, and it's not the act.

An apostle saw [in a] vision some people confined in a burning house, and bound with burning […], thrown […] of the burning […] them in […] and they said to them [… able] to be saved […] they didn't want to, and they received […] punishment, which is called **67** "the [outer] darkness," because it […].

The soul and the spirit came into being from water and fire. The offspring of the bridal chamber was from water and fire and light. The fire is the chrism, the light is the fire. I'm not talking about that formless fire, but of the other one whose form is white, which is bright and beautiful, and which gives beauty.

Truth didn't come into the world naked, but it came in types and images. It (the world) won't receive it in any other way. There's a rebirth, and an image of rebirth. It's truly necessary to be begotten again through the image. What's the resurrection and the image? Through the image it's necessary for it to arise. The bridal chamber and the image? Through the image it's necessary for them to enter the truth, which is the restoration. It's not only necessary for those who acquire the name of the Father and the Son and the Holy Spirit, but they too have been acquired for you. If someone doesn't acquire them, the name will also be taken from them. But they're received in the chrism of the […] of the power of the cross. The apostles called this "[the] right and the left," because this person is no longer a [Christian], but a Christ.

The Lord [did] everything in a mystery: a baptism, a chrism, a Eucharist, a redemption, a bridal chamber […] he [said], "I came to make [the below] like the [above and the outside] like the [inside, and to unite] them in the place." […] here through [types …] Those who say, "[…] there's one above […," they're wrong, because] what's revealed **68** is that […], that [which] is called "what's below," and what's hidden is to it what's above it, because it's good, and they say "inside and what's outside and what's outside the outside." So the Lord called destruction "the outer darkness." There's nothing outside it.

He said, "My Father who's hidden." He said, "Enter your closet, shut the door behind you, and pray to your Father who's hidden," that is, the one who's within all of them. But the one who's within all of them is the fullness. Beyond that, there's nothing else within. This is what's called "that which is above them."

Before Christ, some came from where they were no longer able to enter, and they went where they were no longer able to come out. Then Christ came. He brought out those who entered, and brought in those who went out.

Adam, Eve, and the Bridal Chamber

When Eve was [in] Adam, death didn't exist. When she separated from him, death came into being. If he [enters] again and receives it for himself, there will be no death.

"[My] God, my God, why, Lord, [have] you forsaken me?" He said this on the cross, because he was divided in that place. [...] that he was begotten through that which [...] from God. The [...] from the dead [...] exists, but [...] he's perfect [...] of flesh, but this [...] is true flesh [...] isn't true, [but ...] image of the true.

69 A bridal chamber isn't for the animals, nor for the slaves, nor for the impure, but it's for free people and virgins.

We're begotten again through the Holy Spirit, but we're begotten through Christ by two things. We're anointed through the Spirit. When we were begotten, we were united.

Without light, no one can see themselves in water or in a mirror; nor again will you be able to see in light without water or mirror. Because of this, it's necessary to baptize in both: in the light and in the water, but the light is the chrism.

There were three houses of offering in Jerusalem. The one which opens to the west is called "the Holy." The other one, which opens to the south, is called "the Holy of the Holy." The third, which opens to the east, is called "the Holy of the Holies," the place where the high priest enters alone. Baptism is "the Holy" house. [Redemption] is "the Holy of the Holy." "The [Holy] of the Holies" is the bridal chamber. The [baptism] includes the resurrection [with] the redemption. The redemption is in the bridal chamber. But [the] bridal chamber is better than [...] You won't find its [...] those who pray [...] Jerusalem. [...] Jerusalem who [... Jerusalem], being seen [...] these that are called "[the Holies] of the Holies" [... the] veil torn [...] bridal chamber except the image [... which] **70** [is above. So] its veil was torn from top to bottom, because it was necessary for some from below to go up above.

The powers can't see those who have put on the perfect light, and they can't bind them. But one will put on that light in the mystery of the union.

If the female wouldn't have been separated from the male, she wouldn't have died with the male. His separation was the beginning of death. Because of this, Christ came to repair the separation that existed since the beginning by uniting the two again. He'll give life to those who died as a result of the separation by uniting them. Now, the wife unites with her husband in the bridal chamber, and those who have united in the bridal chamber won't be separated any longer. Because of this, Eve separated from Adam, because she didn't unite with him in the bridal chamber.

It was through a breath that Adam's soul came into being. Its partner was the spirit. That which was given to him was his mother. His soul was [taken] and he was given [life] (Eve) in its place. When he was united [...] words that were better than the powers, and they envied him [...] spiritual partner [...] hidden [...] that is, the [...] themselves [...] bridal chamber so that [...] Jesus appeared [... the] Jordan, the [fullness of the kingdom] of heaven. He who [was begotten] before everything **71** was begotten again. He [who was anointed] first was anointed again. He who was redeemed, redeemed again.

If it's necessary to speak of a mystery: the Father of everything united with the virgin who came down, and a fire enlightened him on that day. He revealed the great bridal chamber, so his body came into being on that day. He came out of the bridal chamber like the one who came into being from the groom and the bride. That's the way Jesus established everything within himself. It's also necessary for each of the disciples to enter into his rest through these things.

Adam came into being from two virgins: from the Spirit and from the virgin earth. So Christ was begotten from a virgin, to rectify the fall that occurred in the beginning.

There are two trees growing in Paradise. One begets [animals], the other begets humans. Adam [ate] from the tree that begot animals, [and he] became an animal, and he begot [animals]. So Adam's children worship the [animals]. The tree [...] is fruit [...] this they [...] ate the [...] fruit of the [...] beget humans [...] of the human of [...] God makes the human, [... humans] make [God]. **72** That's what it's like in the world: humans make gods and worship their creation. It would be better for the gods to worship humans!

The truth is that the work of humankind comes from their power, so they're called "the powers." Their works are their children, who come into being through rest; so their power exists in their works, but the rest is revealed in their children. And you'll find that this extends to the image. And this is the person in the image: they do their works through their power, but they beget their children through rest.

In this world, the slaves work for the free. In the kingdom of heaven, the free will serve the slaves. The children of the bridal chamber will serve the children of the [marriage. The] children of the bridal chamber have a [single] name: "Rest." [Being] together they don't need to take form, [because they have] contemplation [...] they're many [...] with those who are in the [...] the glories of the [...] not [...] them [...] go down to the [water ...] they'll redeem themselves [...] that is, those who have [...] in his name, because he said: "[That's the way] we'll fulfill **73** all righteousness."

Baptism, Chrism, Eucharist, Bridal Chamber

Those who say that they'll die first and (then) they'll rise are wrong. If they don't first receive the resurrection while they're living, they won't receive anything when they die. It's the same when they talk about baptism and they say "Baptism is a great thing," because those who receive it will live.

Philip the apostle said, "Joseph the carpenter planted a garden because he needed wood for his trade. It was he who made the cross from the trees he planted, and his offspring hung from what he planted. His offspring was Jesus, and the plant was the cross." But the Tree of Life is in the middle of Paradise, and from the olive tree came the chrism, and from that the resurrection.

This world eats corpses. All that are eaten in it die also. Truth eats life, so no one nourished by [Truth] will die. Jesus came from that place, he brought food from there, and to those who wanted, he gave them [to eat, so that] they won't die.

[God …] a Paradise, [human …] Paradise, there are […] and […] of God […] those in [it …] I wish that [Paradise …] they'll say to me, "[… eat] this," or "don't eat [that …] **74** wish." The tree of knowledge is the place where I'll eat everything. It killed Adam, but here it makes humanity live. The Law was the tree. It has the power to give the knowledge of good and evil. It neither kept them from evil nor placed them in the good, but it created death for those who ate from it; because when it said, "Eat this, don't eat that," it became the beginning of death.

The chrism is better than baptism, since we're called "Christians" because of the chrism, not because of baptism. And it was because of the chrism that Christ was named, because the Father anointed the Son, and the Son anointed the apostles, and the apostles anointed us. Whoever is anointed has everything: the resurrection, the light, the cross, the Holy Spirit. The Father gave this to him in the bridal chamber, and he received it. The Father was in the Son and the Son in the Father. This is [the kingdom] of heaven.

The Lord said [it] well: "Some went to the kingdom of heaven laughing and they came out […] a Christian […] and as soon as [… went down] into the water and he […] everything about […] it's [a] game, [but … disregard] this […] to the kingdom of [heaven …] if they disregard […] and if they scorn it as a game, [… out] laughing. It's the same way **75** with the bread and the cup and the oil, though there's one better than these.

The world came into being through a transgression, because the one who created it wanted to create it imperishable and immortal. He fell away and didn't get what he wanted, because the world wasn't imperishable, and the one who created it wasn't imperishable; because things aren't imperishable, but rather children. Nothing will be able to receive imperishability without becoming a child. But whoever can't receive, how much more will they be unable to give?

The cup of prayer has wine and water, since it's laid down as the type of the blood over which they give thanks. It fills with the Holy Spirit, and it belongs to the completely perfect human. Whenever we drink this, we'll receive the perfect human. The living water is a body. It's necessary for us to put on the living human. So coming down to the water, they strip themselves so that they'll put on that one.

A horse begets a horse, a human begets a human, and a god begets god. It's the same way with [the groom] and [brides too]. They [come into being] from the […] No Jew […] from […] exists and […] from the Jews […] the Christians […] called these […] "the chosen race of […]" **76** and "the true human" and "the Son of the Human" and "the seed of the Son of the Human." This true race is known in the world. These are the places where the children of the bridal chamber exist.

In this world, union is between male and female, the place of power and weakness; in the (eternal) age, the union is like something else, but we refer to them by the same names. There are other names, however, that are above every name that's named, and they're better than the strong, because where there's force, there are those who are even more powerful. They're not (two) different things, but they're both the same thing. This is what won't be able to come down upon the fleshly heart.

Isn't it necessary for everyone who has everything to know themselves completely? Some who don't know themselves won't be able to enjoy what they have, but those who've come to understand themselves will enjoy them.

Not only won't they be able to bind the perfect human, they won't be able to see them (the perfect human), because if they see them they'll bind them. There's no other way for someone to acquire this grace for themselves [except by] putting on the perfect light [and] becoming the perfect [light. Whoever has put it on] themselves will go […] this is the perfect […] for us to become […] before we came to […] whoever receives everything […] these places, they'll be able to […] that place, but they'll [… the middle] as incomplete. **77** Only Jesus knows the end of this one.

The holy man (priest) is completely holy, down to his (very) body, because if he receives the bread he'll make it holy, or the cup, or anything else that he takes and purifies. Why won't he purify the body too?

As Jesus perfected the water of baptism, that's the way he poured out death. So we go down into the water, but we don't go down into death, so that we won't be poured out into the spirit of the world. When it blows, the winter comes. When the Holy Spirit breathes, the summer comes.

Whoever knows the truth is a free person, and the free person doesn't sin, because "whoever sins is the slave of sin." Truth is the Mother, but knowledge is the joining. Those who aren't given to sin are called "free" by the world. These who aren't given to sin are made proud by the knowledge of the truth. That's what makes them free and exalts them over everything. But "love builds up," and whoever has been made free through knowledge is a slave because of love for those who aren't yet able to attain [the] freedom of knowledge, [but] knowledge makes them able [to] become free. Love […] anything its own […] it […] its own. It never [says "…"] or "this is mine," [but "…"] are yours." Spiritual love is wine with fragrance. **78** All those who will anoint themselves with it enjoy it. While those who are anointed stay around, those who are nearby also enjoy it. If those who are anointed with ointment leave them and go, those who aren't anointed but are only nearby remain in their stench. The Samaritan didn't give anything to the wounded man except wine with oil. It wasn't anything but the ointment, and it healed the wounds, because "love covers a multitude of sins."

The children to whom a woman gives birth will look like the man she loves. If it's her husband, they look like her husband; if it's an adulterer, they look like the adulterer. Often, if a woman sleeps with her husband because she has to, but her heart is with the adulterer with whom she is intimate and she bears a child, the child she bears looks like the adulterer. But you who exist with the Son of God, don't love the world; rather, love the Lord, so that those you'll beget may not come to look like the world, but will come to look like the Lord.

The human unites with the human, the horse unites with the horse, the donkey unites with the donkey. Species unite [with] similar species. That's what it's like when spirit unites with spirit, the [Word] is intimate with the Word, [and light is] intimate [with light. If you] become human, [it's the human who will] love you. If you become [spirit], it's the Spirit who will unite with you. [If] you become Word, it's the Word that **79** will unite with you. If [you] become light, it's the light which will be intimate with you. If you become one of those from above, those from above will rest upon you. If you become horse or donkey or calf or dog or sheep or any other of the animals which are outside or below, neither human nor spirit nor Word nor light nor those from above nor those inside will be able to love you. They won't be able to rest within you, and you'll have no part in them.

Whoever is an unwilling slave will be able to be made free. Whoever has become free by the grace of their master and has sold themselves (back) into slavery won't be able to be made free any longer.

Spiritual Growth

The world is farmed through four things. They gather into barns through water, earth, wind, and light. And in the same way, God farms through four things too: through faith, hope, love, and knowledge. Our earth is the faith in which we're rooted. [And] the [water] is the hope through which [we're] nourished. The wind is the love through which we grow. And the light [is] the knowledge through which we [ripen]. Grace exists in [four kinds. It's] earthly, it's [heavenly, …] the heaven of the heaven […] through [….] Blessed is the one who hasn't […] **80** a soul. This one is Jesus Christ. He went all over the place and didn't burden anyone. So, blessed is someone like this; they're a perfect person, because the Word tells us about how hard it is to keep up. How will we be able to achieve such a great thing? How will he give rest to everyone? First and foremost, it's not right to cause anyone grief – whether great or small, or faithless or faithful – and then give rest to those who are (already) at rest among those who are well off. There are some who benefit from giving rest to the one who's well off. Whoever does good can't give rest to them because they can't just do whatever they want; they can't cause grief because they can't cause distress, but sometimes the one who's well off causes them grief. They're not like that, but it's their (own) evil that causes them grief. Whoever has the nature (of the perfect person) gives joy to the one who's good, but some grieve terribly at this.

A householder acquired everything, whether child or slave or cattle or dog or pig or wheat [or] barley or straw or hay or […] or meat and acorn. [But they're] wise and understand what to feed each [one]. To the children they served bread […] but [… the] slaves they served […], and to the cattle [they threw barley] and straw and hay. To [the] dogs they threw bones [and] to [the pigs] they threw acorns **81** and slops. That's what it's like with the disciple of God. If they're wise, they understand what it means to be a

disciple. The bodily forms won't deceive them, but they'll look at the condition of the soul of each one and speak with them. There are many animals in the world that are made in human form. They (the disciple) recognizes them. To the pigs they'll throw acorns, but to the cattle they'll throw barley with straw and hay. To the dogs they'll throw bones, to the slaves they'll give the appetizer, and to the children they'll give the perfect (food).

There's the Son of Humanity, and there's the son of the Son of Humanity. The Lord is the Son of Humanity, and the son of the Son of Humanity is the one who creates through the Son of Humanity. The Son of Humanity received from God the ability to create. He (also) has the ability to beget. The one who received the ability to create is a creature; the one who received the ability to beget is begotten. The one who creates can't beget; the one who begets can create. They say, "The one who creates, begets." But what they beget is a creature. [So] their begotten aren't their children, but they're […]. The one who creates works [publicly], and are themselves [revealed]. The one who begets, begets [secretly], and they're hidden […] the image. [Again], the one who [creates, creates] publicly, but the one who begets, [begets] children secretly.

No [one will be able to] know [when the husband] **82** and the wife are intimate with each other, except they themselves, because the marriage of the world is a mystery for those who have married. If the defiled marriage is hidden, how much more is the undefiled marriage a true mystery! It's not fleshly, but pure. It isn't of desire, but of the will. It isn't of the darkness or the night, but it's of the day and the light. If a marriage is stripped naked, it becomes pornography – not only if the bride receives the seed of another man, but even if she leaves the chamber and is seen, she commits adultery. Let her reveal herself to her father, her mother, the best man, and the groom's children. They're allowed to enter the bridal chamber every day. But let the others yearn just to hear her voice and enjoy her perfume, and, like dogs, let them eat the crumbs that fall from the table. Grooms and brides belong to the bridal chamber. No one will be able to see the groom and the bride unless [they become] such.

Uprooting Evil

When Abraham […] to see what he was going to see, [he] circumcised the flesh of the foreskin, [telling] us that it's necessary to destroy the flesh.

[Most (things)] of [the] world can stand up and live as long as their [insides are hidden. If they're revealed], they die, as [illustrated] by the visible human. [As long as] the human's guts are hidden, **83** the human is alive. If their guts are exposed and come out of them, the human will die. It's the same way with the tree. While its root is hidden, it blossoms and grows. If its root is exposed, the tree dries up. That's what it's like with everything that's born in the world, not only the revealed, but also the hidden; because as long as the root of evil is hidden, it's strong. But if it's recognized, it dissolves, and if it's revealed, it dies. So the Word says, "Already the axe is laid at the root of the trees." It won't (just) cut, (because) that which will be cut blossoms again. Rather, the axe digs down into the ground until it brings up the root. Jesus plucked out the root completely, but others did so partially. As for us, let every one of us dig down to the root of the evil within and pluck it out from its root in us. It'll be uprooted if we recognize it. But if we don't recognize it, it takes root within us and bears its fruit in us. It masters us, and we're forced to serve it. It captures us so that we do what we do [not] want to; and we do [not] do what we want to. [It's] powerful because we haven't recognized it. It's active as long as [it exists]. [Ignorance] is the mother of [all evil]. Ignorance will cause [death, because] what exists from [ignorance] neither did exist nor [does exist], nor will they come into being [...] **84** they'll be perfected when the whole truth is revealed, because the truth is like ignorance. When it's hidden, it rests within itself, but if it's revealed and recognized, it's glorified inasmuch as it's stronger than ignorance and error. It gives freedom. The Word says, "If you'll know the truth, the truth will make you free." Ignorance is slavery; knowledge is freedom. If we know the truth, we'll find the fruits of truth within us. If we unite with it, it'll receive our fullness.

Now we have what's revealed of creation. We say, "Those who are strong are honorable, but those who are hidden are weak and scorned." That's what it's like with those who are revealed of the truth; they're weak and scorned, but the hidden are strong and honorable. But the mysteries of the truth are revealed in types and images.

The chamber is hidden, however; it's the Holy in the Holy. At first, the veil concealed how God managed the creation, but when the veil is torn and what's inside is revealed, then this house will be left behind [like] a desert, or rather, will be [destroyed]. And all divinity will flee [from] these places, not into the Holies [of the] Holies, because it won't be able to unite with the pure [light] and the [flawless] fullness, [but] it'll come to be under the wings of the cross [and under] its arms. This ark will [become their] salvation when the flood **85** of water surges over them. If some belong to the priesthood, they'll be able to enter inside the veil with the high priest. So the veil wasn't torn only at the top, since it would've been open only to those at the top; nor was it torn only at the bottom, since it would've been revealed only to those at the bottom; but it was torn from the top to the bottom. Those at the top opened to us the bottom, so that we'll enter the secret of the truth. This truly is what's honorable, what's strong, but we'll enter there through scorned types and weaknesses. They're humbled in the presence of the perfect glory. There's glory that's better than glory; there's power that's better than power. So the perfect was opened to us with the secrets of the truth, and the Holies of the Holies were revealed, and the chamber invited us in.

As long as it's hidden, evil is inactive, but it hasn't been removed from among the Holy Spirit's seed. They're slaves of evil. But whenever it's revealed, then the perfect light will flow out upon everyone, and all of them who are in it will [receive the chrism]. Then the slaves will be made free and the captives will be redeemed. "[Every] plant [which] my Father who's in heaven [hasn't] planted [will be] uprooted." Those who are separated will unite [...] will be filled.

Conclusion

Everyone who will [enter] the chamber will kindle their [lamp], because [it's] like the marriages which are [...] happen at night, the fire [...] **86** at night and is put out. But the mysteries of this marriage are fulfilled in the day and the light. Neither that day nor its light ever sets.

If anyone becomes a child of the bridal chamber, they'll receive the light. If anyone doesn't receive it while they're here, they won't be able to receive it in the other place. Whoever will receive that light won't be seen or bound, and no one will be able to trouble someone like this even while they dwell in the world. Moreover, when they leave the world, they've already received the Truth in the images. The world has become the (eternal) ages, because the (eternal) age is the fullness for them, and it's like this: it's revealed to them alone. It's not hidden in the darkness and the night, but it's hidden in a perfect day and a holy light.

THE GOSPEL OF Q

Q is the designation given to a hypothetical sayings source that many scholars believe was incorporated into the Gospels of Luke and Matthew. Though some notable scholars have questioned the theory, others have proposed reconstructions of Q based on a careful comparison of New Testament Gospels. Since no manuscripts of Q have survived from antiquity, the translation is based on the Greek text printed in The Critical Edition of Q. The versification follows that of Luke and Matthew.

(QLk 3:2) John [. . .] (3) [. . .] the entire region around the Jordan [. . .]

(7) He told the crowds who went out to be baptized, "You offspring of vipers, who warned you to flee from the fury to come? (8) So bear fruit worthy of change! Don't start to say to yourselves, 'We have Abraham for our ancestor,' because I tell you that God is able to raise up children for Abraham from these stones.

(9) "Even now the axe lies at the root of the trees! So every tree that doesn't bear good fruit is cut down and thrown into the fire.

(16) "I baptize you in water, but one who's greater than I will come, the thong of whose sandals I'm not worthy to loosen. He'll baptize you in holy Spirit and fire. (17) His pitchfork is in his hand to clean out his threshing floor, and to gather the wheat into his barn; but he'll burn up the chaff with a fire that can't be put out."

(21) [...] Jesus [...] baptized [...] heaven opened (22) and [...] the Spirit [...] on him [...] Son [...]

(4:1) Jesus was led by the Spirit into the desert (2) to be tested by the devil. He didn't eat anything for forty days [...] he was hungry.

(3) And the devil told him, "If you're God's Son, tell these stones to turn into bread."

(4) And Jesus replied, "It's written, 'A person shouldn't live on bread alone.'"

(9) The devil led him to Jerusalem, set him on the pinnacle of the temple, and said, "If you're God's Son, throw yourself down, (10) because it's written, 'God will put God's angels in charge of you,' (11) and 'On their hands they'll bear you up, so that you don't dash your foot against a stone.'"

(12) And in reply Jesus told him, "It's been said, 'Don't test the Lord, your God.'"

(5) Then the devil took him to a very high mountain and showed him all the empires of the world and their glory and told him, (6) "I'll give you all these, (7) if you'll bow to me."

(8) And in reply Jesus told him, "It's written: 'Bow to the Lord your God, and serve God only.'"

(13) And the devil left him.

(16) [...] Nazareth [...]

(6:20) He looked up at his disciples and said:
Blessed are you who are poor,
because yours is God's reign.
(21) Blessed are you who are hungry,
because you'll be full.
Blessed are you who mourn,
because you'll be comforted.
(22) "Blessed are you when they criticize you, persecute you, and spread lies about you because of the Son of Humanity. (23) Rejoice and be glad, because your heavenly reward is great; for that's how they persecuted the prophets before you.

(27) "Love your enemies, (28) and pray for those who persecute you. (35) You'll become children of your Father, who makes the sun rise on those who are evil and those who are good, and sends rain on those who are just and those who are unjust.

(29) "When someone slaps you on the cheek, offer the other one too. When someone sues you for your shirt, give them your coat too. (QMt 5:41) When someone makes you go one mile, go an extra mile. (QLk 6:30) Give to everyone who asks you, and when someone borrows your things, don't ask for them back.

(31) "Treat people how you want them to treat you. (32) If you love those who love you, why should you be rewarded? Don't even toll collectors do that? (34) And if you lend to those from whom you expect repayment, why should you be rewarded? Don't even gentiles do that? (36) Be merciful, just like your Father.

(37) "Don't judge, and you won't be judged; (QMt 7:2) because you'll be judged the way that you judge. (QLk 6:38) And you'll be measured the way that you measure.

(39) "Can someone who can't see guide another person who can't see? Won't they both fall into a pit? (40) A disciple isn't greater than their teacher. It's enough for the disciple to become like their teacher.

(41) "Why do you see the speck that's in your brother's eye, but don't consider the beam that's in your own eye? (42) How can you tell your brother, 'Let me get that speck out of your eye,' when you don't see the beam that's in your own eye? You hypocrite! First get the beam out of your own eye, and then you'll see clearly to get the speck out of your brother's eye.

(43) "No good tree bears rotten fruit, nor does a rotten tree bear good fruit. (44) Every tree is known by its own fruit. Are figs gathered from thorns, or grapes from thistles? (45) The person who's good brings good things out of their good treasure, and the person who's evil brings evil things out of evil treasure, because one's mouth speaks from the overflow of the heart.

(46) "Why do you call me, 'Master, Master,' and don't do what I say? (47) Everyone who hears my words and acts on them (48) can be compared to someone building a house on bedrock. When the rain poured, and the floods came, and the winds blew and pounded that house, it didn't collapse, because it was founded on bedrock. (49) But everyone who hears my words and doesn't act on them is like someone who built a house on the sand. When the rain poured, and the floods came, and the winds blew and pounded that house, it collapsed immediately. How great was its fall!"

(7:1) And so when it happened that he had finished saying these things, he went to Capernaum. (3) A centurion approached and begged him and said, "My boy is sick." And Jesus told him, "I'll go heal him."

(6) And the centurion replied, "Master, I'm not worthy for you to come under my roof. (7) Just say the word, and my boy will be healed. (8) I'm also in a chain of command, with soldiers under me. I tell one, 'Go,' and they go; I tell another, 'Come,' and they come; I tell my servant, 'Do this,' and they do it."

(9) Jesus was amazed when he heard this. He told his followers, "I'm telling you the truth: I haven't found such trust even in Israel."

(18) When John heard all these things, he sent his disciples (19) to ask him, "Are you the coming one, or should we

look for someone else?"

(22) And he replied to them, "Go and tell John what you've heard and seen. Those who:
are blind, regain their sight;
have challenges of mobility, walk;
have leprosy, are cured;
are deaf, hear;
are dead, are raised up;
are poor, have good news announced to them.
(23) "Blessed is the one who isn't scandalized by me."
(24) And when they had left, he started to talk to the crowds about John. "What did you go out into the desert to see? A reed shaken by the wind? (25) Then what did you go out to see? A man wearing fancy clothes? Look, those who wear fancy clothes live in palaces. (26) Then what did you go out to see? A prophet? Yes, I'm telling you, and much more than a prophet, (27) because it's written about him:
Look, I'm sending my messenger ahead of you,
who'll prepare your path for you.
(28) "I'm telling you that John is greater than anyone who's been born, but whoever is least in God's reign is still greater than he, (29) because John came to you […] the toll collectors and […] (30) but […] him.
(31) "To what, then, can I compare this generation? What's it like? (32) It's like children sitting in the marketplaces calling to each other:
We played the flute for you,
but you didn't dance.
We mourned,
But you didn't weep.
(33) "John didn't come eating or drinking, and you say, 'He's demonized!' (34) The Son of Humanity has come eating and drinking, and you say, 'Look, a glutton and a drunk, a friend of toll collectors and outsiders!' (35) But Wisdom is vindicated by her children."

(9:57) And someone told him, "I'll follow you wherever you go."
(58) And Jesus told him, "Foxes have holes and birds of the sky have nests, but the Son of Humanity has nowhere to rest his head."
(59) But someone else told him, "Master, let me go and bury my father first."
(60) But he told him, "Follow me, and let the dead bury their own dead."

(10:2) He told his disciples, "The harvest is plentiful, but the workers are few. So ask the Lord of the harvest to send workers into the fields. (3) Go! Look, I send you out like lambs among wolves. (4) Don't carry a purse, bag, sandals, or staff. Don't greet anyone on the road. (5) Whenever you enter a house, first say, 'Peace to this house.' (6) If a peaceful person is there, let your blessing rest on them; but if not, take back your blessing. (7) Stay in the same house, eating and drinking whatever they give you, because the worker is worthy of their wages. Don't move around from house to house. (8) If they welcome you in whatever town you enter, eat whatever is set before you. (9) Heal those who are sick there and tell them, 'God's reign is at hand!' (10) But if they don't welcome you in whatever town you enter, when you're leaving that town, (11) shake the dust from your feet. (12) I'm telling you that on that day, it'll be better for Sodom than for that town!
(13) "Woe to you, Chorazin! Woe to you, Bethsaida! If the great deeds done in your midst had been done in Tyre and Sidon, they would have changed a long time ago in

sackcloth and ashes. (14) But it will be better for Tyre and Sidon than for you in the judgment! (15) And you, Capernaum, you don't think you'll be exalted to heaven, do you? You'll fall down to Hades!
(16) "Whoever welcomes you welcomes me, and whoever welcomes me welcomes the one who sent me."
(21) Then he said, "Thank you, Father, Lord of heaven and earth, for hiding these things from the wise and learned and revealing them to children. Yes, Father, this was what you wanted. (22) My Father has given me everything. No one knows who the son is except the Father, or who the Father is except the son, and the one to whom the son wants to reveal him.
(23) "Blessed are the eyes that see what you see. (24) I'm telling you that many prophets and rulers wanted to see what you see, but didn't see it; and to hear what you hear, but didn't hear it.

(11:2) "When you pray, say:
Father,
We honor your holy name.
Let your reign come.
(3) Give us our daily bread today.
(4) Forgive us our debts,
because we too forgive everyone who's indebted to us.
Don't put us in harm's way.
(9) "I'm telling you, ask and you'll receive. Look and you'll find. Knock and it'll be opened for you, (10) because everyone who asks receives. The one who looks finds. To one who knocks it'll be opened. (11) Which of you would give your child a stone if they ask for bread? (12) Or who would give them a snake if they ask for fish? (13) So if you, evil as you are, know how to give good gifts to your children, how much more will the heavenly Father give good things to those who ask!"
(14) He was casting out a demon that couldn't speak. And when the demon came out, the person who couldn't speak started talking. And the crowds were amazed. (15) But some said, "He casts out demons with the power of Beelzebul, the ruler of the demons!"
(17) Knowing what they were thinking, he told them, "Every divided empire is devastated, and a divided house will fall. (18) If the Enemy is divided, how will its empire endure? (19) But if Beelzebul gives me power to cast out demons, who gives your people power to cast them out? So they prove you wrong. (20) But if I cast out demons by the finger of God, then God's reign has come to you!
(23) "Whoever isn't with me is against me, and whoever doesn't gather with me, scatters. (24) When the impure spirit leaves someone, it journeys through arid places looking for rest, but doesn't find it. Then it says, 'I'll return to the home I left'; (25) and when it comes back, it finds it swept and organized. (26) Then it goes out and brings seven other spirits that are even more evil, and they move in and live there. That person ends up even worse off than before."
(16) Some demanded him to show a sign. (29) But he said, "This is an evil generation. It demands a sign, but no sign will be provided except the sign of Jonah! (30) As Jonah became a sign to the Ninevites, so the Son of Humanity will be a sign to this generation. (31) The queen of the South will rise up in the judgment with this generation and will condemn it, because she came from the ends of the earth to hear Solomon's wisdom; and look, something greater than Solomon is here. (32) The people of Nineveh will rise up in the judgment with this generation and will

condemn it, because they changed in response to Jonah's announcement, and look, something greater than Jonah is here.

(33) "No one lights a lamp and hides it, but puts it on a lampstand, and it enlightens everyone in the house. (34) Your eye is the body's lamp. If your eye is single, your whole body is full of light. If your eye is evil, your whole body is dark. (35) So if the light within you is dark, how dark it is!

(42) "Woe to you, Pharisees! You tithe your mint, dill, and cumin, but you ignore justice, mercy, and trust. You should've done these without ignoring the others.

(39) "Woe to you, Pharisees! You clean the outside of the cup and dish, but inside they're full of greed and decadence. (41) Clean the inside of the cup, and its outside will be clean too.

(43) "Woe to you, Pharisees! You love the place of honor at banquets, the front seat in the synagogues, and accolades in the marketplaces. (44) Woe to you, because you're like unmarked graves that people walk on without knowing it.

(46) "And woe to you, lawyers! You load people with burdens that are hard to bear, but you yourselves won't even lift a finger to help them.

(52) "Woe to you, lawyers! You shut people out of God's reign. You didn't enter, and didn't let those enter who are trying to do so.

(47) "Woe to you, because you build the tombs of the prophets whom your ancestors killed. (48) You prove that you're the descendants of your ancestors. (49) So Wisdom said, 'I'll send prophets and sages. Some of them they'll kill and persecute.' (50) So this generation will be guilty of the blood of all the prophets shed from the beginning of the world, (51) from the blood of Abel to the blood of Zechariah, who died between the altar and the sanctuary. Yes, I'm telling you that this generation will be held responsible.

(12:2) "Nothing is concealed that won't be revealed, nor hidden that won't be made known. (3) Whatever I tell you in the dark, say in the light; and whatever you hear whispered in your ear, announce from the housetops.

(4) "Don't be afraid of those who kill the body but can't kill the soul. (5) Instead, fear the one who can kill both the soul and the body in Gehenna.

(6) "Don't five sparrows cost two pennies? Yet not one of them will fall to the ground without your Father's permission. (7) Even the hairs of your head are all numbered. Don't be afraid, because you're more valuable than many sparrows.

(8) "Everyone who publicly acknowledges me, the Son of Humanity will acknowledge in front of the angels. (9) But whoever publicly denies me will be denied in front of the angels. (10) Whoever speaks out against the Son of Humanity will be forgiven, but whoever speaks out against the holy Spirit won't be forgiven. (11) When they bring you before the synagogues, don't worry about how or what you should say, (12) because the holy Spirit will teach you at that time what you should say.

(33) "Don't store treasures for yourselves here on earth, where moth and rust destroy and robbers break in and steal. Instead, store treasures for yourselves in heaven, where neither moth nor rust destroy and where robbers don't break in or steal. (34) Because where your treasure is, there your heart will be too.

(22) "So I'm telling you not to worry about your life, about what you'll eat; or about your body, what you'll wear. (23)

Isn't life more than food, and the body more than clothes? (24) Think about how the ravens don't sow, reap, or gather into barns, yet God feeds them. Aren't you more valuable than the birds?

(25) "Which of you can grow any taller by worrying? (26) And why worry about clothes? (27) Look at how the lilies grow. They don't work or spin, yet I'm telling you that even Solomon in all his glory wasn't dressed like one of these. (28) But if God clothes the grass of the field, which is here today and is thrown into the oven tomorrow, won't God clothe you even more, you who have little trust? (29) So don't worry. Don't ask, 'What are we going to eat?' or 'What are going to drink?' or 'What are we going to wear?' (30) The gentiles look for all these things, but your Father knows that you need all of them. (31) Instead, look for God's reign, and all these things will be given to you too.

(39) "But know this: If the master of the house had known at what time the robber was coming, he wouldn't have let his house be broken into. (40) You too should be ready, because the Son of Humanity is coming when you don't expect it.

(42) "Then who is the trustworthy and wise servant who was entrusted by their master to hand out rations to the household at the right time? (43) Blessed is that servant whose master finds them doing so when he comes. (44) I'm telling you the truth: he'll put them in charge of all that he owns. (45) But if that servant says in their heart, 'My master is late,' and starts to beat the other servants and to eat and drink with those who are addicted to alcohol, (46) the master of that servant will come when they don't expect it, at a time that they don't know, and will rip them to shreds and throw them out with those who are untrustworthy.

(49) "I came to cast fire on the earth, and how I wish it were already kindled! (51) Do you think that I came to bring peace on earth? I didn't come to bring peace, but a sword! (53) Because I've come:

To pit son against father,
daughter against her mother,
daughter-in-law against her mother-in-law."

(54) He told them, "When it's evening, you say, 'There'll be good weather, because the sky is red.' (55) In the morning, 'There'll be wintry weather today, because the sky is red and threatening.' (56) You know how to interpret the appearance of the sky. Why don't you know how to interpret the time?

(58) "When you're going with your adversary, do your best to settle the case on the way there, or else your adversary may hand you over to the judge, and the judge to the officer, and the officer may throw you into prison. (59) I'm telling you that you won't get out of there until you've paid the very last penny!

(13:18) "What is God's reign like, and to what should I compare it? (19) It can be compared to a mustard seed which someone sowed in their garden. It grew and became a tree, and the birds of the sky nested in its branches."

(20) "And again: To what should I compare God's reign? (21) It can be compared to yeast which a woman hid in fifty pounds of flour until it was all fermented.

(24) "Enter through the narrow door, because many will try to enter, though only a few will succeed. (25) When the master of the house gets up and locks the door, you'll be standing outside and knocking on it, saying, 'Master, open up for us!'

"But he'll reply, 'I don't know you.'

(26) "Then you'll start saying, 'We ate and drank with you,

and you taught in our streets.'

(27) "But he'll tell you, 'I don't know you. Get away from me, you criminals!'

(29) "Many will come from east and west and dine (28) with Abraham, Isaac, and Jacob in God's reign, but you'll be thrown out into the outer darkness, where there'll be weeping and grinding of teeth. (30) Those who are last will be first, and those who are first will be last.

(34) "Jerusalem, Jerusalem, who kills the prophets and stones those who are sent to her! How often I would've gathered your children together, like a hen gathers her chicks under her wings, but you wouldn't let me! (35) Look, your house is left abandoned. I'm telling you that you won't see me until the time comes when you say, 'Blessed is the one who comes in the name of the Lord!'

(14:11) "Whoever exalts themselves will be humbled, and whoever humbles themselves will be exalted.

(16) "Someone planning a great dinner invited many guests. (17) When dinner was ready, they sent their servant to tell the invited guests, 'Come, because it's ready now!' (18) "One excused himself because of his farm. (19) Another excused himself because of his business. (21) The servant went back and told their master all this. Then the master of the house became angry and told the servant, (23) 'Go out to the highways and urge people to come in so that my house may be filled.'

(26) "Whoever doesn't hate father and mother can't be my disciple, and whoever doesn't hate son and daughter can't be my disciple. (27) Whoever doesn't carry their own cross and follow me can't be my disciple.

(17:33) "Whoever tries to find their life will lose it, but whoever loses their life for my sake will find it.

(14:34) "Salt is good, but if it's lost its flavor, how can you get it back? (35) It's no good for the soil or the manure pile. It's thrown away.

(16:13) "No one can follow two masters, because they'll either hate one and love the other, or they'll be devoted to one and despise the other. You can't serve both God and Mammon.

(16) "The Torah and the prophets were announced until John. Since then, God's reign has been violated, and the violent plunder it. (17) But it's easier for heaven and earth to disappear than for one smallest letter or one tiny pen stroke to drop out of the Torah.

(18) "Everyone who divorces his wife and remarries is unfaithful to her, and whoever marries someone who's divorced is unfaithful too.

(17:1) "There's no way that people won't be tripped up, but woe to the one who causes it! (2) It'd be better for them if a millstone were hung around their neck and they were thrown into the sea, than for them to trip up one of these little ones.

(15:4) "Which of you, if you had a hundred sheep and lost one of them, wouldn't leave the ninety-nine in the hills and go after the one that got lost? (5) When they find it, (7) I'm telling you that they'll rejoice over it more than over the ninety-nine that didn't wander off.

(8) "Or what woman with ten silver coins, if she loses one, wouldn't light a lamp, sweep the house, and look everywhere until she found it? (9) When she finds it, she calls together her friends and neighbors and says, 'Rejoice with me, because I've found the coin that I'd lost!' (10) In the same way, I'm telling you, the angels rejoice over one wrongdoer who changes.

(17:3) "If your brother offends you, correct him. If he changes, forgive him. (4) Even if he offends you seven times a day, then forgive him seven times.

(5) "If you had trust as big as a mustard seed, you could tell this mulberry tree, 'Be uprooted and be planted in the sea,' and it would obey you."

(20) When he was asked when God's reign would come, he replied to them, "The coming of God's reign can't be observed. (21) Nor will they say, 'Look over here!' or 'Look over there!' Because look, God's reign is among you.

(23) "If they tell you, 'Look, he's in the desert!' don't go out; or 'Look, he's inside,' don't follow, (24) because as the lightning flashes in the east and is seen in the west, so will the Son of Humanity be in his day. (37) Where there's a corpse, there the vultures will gather.

(26) "As it was in the days of Noah, so it will be in the day of the Son of Humanity. (27) In those days they were eating and drinking, marrying and giving in marriage, until the day that Noah entered the ark, and the flood came and swept all of them away. (30) That's what it will be like on the day the Son of Humanity is revealed.

(34) "I'm telling you, there'll be two men in the field; one will be taken and the other will be left. (35) There'll be two women grinding at the mill; one will be taken and the other will be left.

(19:12) "A certain person went on a trip. (13) He called ten of his servants, gave them ten minas, and told them, 'Do business with this until I return.'

(15) "After a long time the master of those servants returned to settle accounts with them. (16) The first one came and said, 'Master, your mina has made ten more minas.'

(17) "He told him, 'Well done, good servant! Since you've been trustworthy with a little, I'll put you in charge of much.'

(18) "The second came and said, 'Master, Your mina has made five minas.'

(19) "He told him, 'Well done, good servant! Since you've been trustworthy with a little, I'll put you in charge of much.'

(20) "The other came and said, 'Master, (21) I know you're a strict man, reaping where you didn't sow and gathering where you didn't scatter. I went out and hid your mina in the ground. Look, here's what belongs to you!'

(22) "He told him, 'You evil servant! You knew that I reap what I didn't sow and gather where I didn't scatter? (23) So why didn't you invest my money with the bankers? Then when I returned, I would've gotten it back, with interest. (24) So take the mina away from him and give it to the one who has ten minas, (26) because everyone who has will be given more, but whoever doesn't have will lose even what little they do have.'

(22:28) "You who've followed me (30) will sit on thrones, judging the twelve tribes of Israel."

The Triumph Of Christianity Over Paganism.

Gustave Doré (1868?)

ACTS

THE ACTS OF PETER

Written, probably by a resident in Asia Minor (he does not know much about Rome), not later than A. D. 200, in Greek. The author has read the Acts of John very carefully, and modelled his language upon them. However, he was not so unorthodox as Leucius, though his language about the Person of our Lord (ch. xx) has rather suspicious resemblances to that of the Acts of John.

The length of the book as given by the Stichometry of Nicephorus was 2,750 lines-fifty lines less than the canonical Acts. The portions we have may be about the length of St. Mark's Gospel; and about 1,000 lines may be wanting. Such is Zaha's estimate.

We have:

1. A short episode in Coptic.

2. A large portion in Latin preserved in a single manuscript of the seventh century at Vercelli: often called the Vercelli Acts. It includes the martyrdom.

3. The martyrdom, preserved separately, in two good Greek copies, in Latin, and in many versions-Coptic, Slavonic, Syriac, Armenian, Arabic, Ethiopic.

Also:

One or two important quotations from lost portions; a small fragment of the original in a papyrus; certain passages-speeches of Peter- transferred by an unscrupulous writer to the Life of St. Abercius of Hierapolis.

A Latin paraphrase of the martyrdom, attributed to Linus, Peter's successor in the bishopric of Rome, was made from the Greek, and is occasionally useful.

I

THE COPTIC FRAGMENT

This is preserved separately in an early papyrus manuscript (fourth-fifth century) now at Berlin; the other contents of it are Gnostic writings which have not yet been published. I follow C. Schmidt's rendering of it. It has a title at the end: The Act of Peter On the first day of the week, that is, on the Lord's day, a multitude gathered together, and they brought unto Peter many sick that he might heal them. And one of the multitude adventured to say unto Peter: Lo, Peter, in our presence thou hast made many blind to see and the deaf to hear and the lame to walk, and hast succoured the weak and given them strength: but wherefore hast thou not succoured thy daughter, the virgin, which grew up beautiful and hath believed in the name of God? For behold, her one side is wholly palsied, and she lieth there stretched out in the corner helpless. We see them that have been healed by thee: thine own daughter thou hast neglected.

But Peter smiled and said unto him: My son, it is manifest unto God alone wherefore her body is not whole. Know

then that God is not weak nor powerless to grant his gift unto my daughter: but that thy soul may be convinced, and they that are here present may the more believe -then he looked unto his daughter and said to her: Raise thyself up from thy place, without any helping thee save Jesus only, and walk whole before all these, and come unto me. And she arose and came to him; and the multitude rejoiced at that which was come to pass. Then said Peter unto them: Behold, your heart is convinced that God is not without strength concerning all things that we ask of him. Then they rejoiced yet more and praised God. And Peter said to his daughter: Go unto thy place, and lay thee down and be again in thine infirmity, for this is expedient for me and for thee. And the maiden went back and lay down in her place and was as beforetime: and the whole multitude wept, and entreated Peter to make her whole.

But Peter said unto them: As the Lord liveth, this is expedient for her and for me. For on the day when she was born unto me I saw a vision, and the Lord said unto me: Peter, this day is a great temptation born unto thee, for this daughter will bring hurt unto many souls if her body continue whole. But I thought that the vision did mock me.

Now when the maiden was ten years old, a stumbling-block was prepared for many by reason of her. And an exceeding rich man, by name Ptolemaeus, when he had seen the maiden with her mother bathing, sent unto her to take her to wife; but her mother consented not. And he sent oft-times to her, and could not wait.

[Here a leaf is lost: the sense, however, is not hard to supply. Augustine speaks (quoting Apocryphal Acts) of a daughter of Peter struck with palsy at the prayer of her father.

Ptolemaeus, unable to win the maiden by fair means, comes and carries her off. Peter hears of it and prays God to protect her. His prayer is heard. She is struck with palsy on one side of her body. Then the text resumes.]

The servants of Ptolemaeus brought the maiden and laid her down before the door of the house and departed.

But when I perceived it, I and her mother, we went down and found the maiden, that one whole side of her body from her toes even to her head was palsied and withered: and we bore her away, praising the Lord which had preserved his handmaid from defilement and shame and (corruption?). This is the cause of the matter, why the maiden continueth so unto this day.

Now, then, it is fitting for you to know the end of Ptolemaeus. He went home and sorrowed night and day over that which had befallen him, and by reason of the many tears which he shed, he became blind. And when he had resolved to rise up and hang himself, lo, about the ninth hour of the day, he saw a great light which enlightened the whole house, and heard a voice saying unto him: Ptolemaeus, God hath not given thee the vessels for corruption and shame, and yet more doth it not become thee which hast believed in me to defile my virgin, whom thou shalt know as thy sister, even as if I were unto you both one spirit (sic). But rise up and go quickly unto the house of the apostle Peter, and thou shalt see my glory; he shall make known unto thee what thou must do.

But Ptolemaeus was not negligent, and bade his servants show him the way and bring him unto me. And when they were come to me, he told me all that had befallen him by the power of our Lord Jesus Christ. Then did he see with the eyes of his flesh, and with the eyes of his soul, and much people believed (hoped) in Christ: and he did them good and gave them the gift of God.

Thereafter Ptolemaeus died, departing out of this life, and went unto his Lord: and when he made his will he bequeathed a piece of land in the name of my daughter, because through her he had believed in God and was made whole. But I unto whom the disposition thereof fell, exercised it with great carefulness: I sold the land, and God alone knoweth neither I nor my daughter (received the price). I sold the land and kept nought back of the price, but gave all the money unto the poor.

Know therefore, thou servant of Jesus Christ, that God directeth (?) them that are his, and prepareth good for every one of them, although we think that God hath forgotten us. Therefore now, brethren, let us be sorrowful and watch and pray, and so shall the goodness of God look upon us, whereon we wait.

And yet further discourse did Peter hold before them all, and glorified the name of Christ the Lord and gave them all of the bread: and when he had distributed it, he rose up and went unto his house.

The scene of this episode is probably Jerusalem. The subject of it was often used by later writers, most notably, perhaps, by the author of the late Acts of SS. Nereus and Achilleus (fifth or sixth century), who gives the daughter a name, Petronilla, which has passed into Kalendars, and as Perronelle, Pernel, or Parnell has become familiar.

A few critics have questioned whether this piece really belongs to the Acts of Peter: but the weight of probability and of opinion is against them. Nothing can be plainer than that it is an extract from a larger book, and that it is ancient (the manuscript may be of the fourth century). Moreover, Augustine, in dealing with apocryphal Acts, alludes to the story contained in it. What other large book of ancient date dealing with Peter's doings can we imagine save the Acts?

II

THE GARDENER'S DAUGHTER

Augustine (Against Adimantus, xvii. 5), says to his Manichaean opponent: the story of Peter killing Ananias and Sapphira by a word is very stupidly blamed by those who in the apocryphal Acts read and admire both the incident I mentioned about the apostle Thomas (the death of the cup-bearer at the feast in his Acts) 'and that the daughter of Peter himself was stricken with palsy at the prayer of her father, and that the daughter of a gardener died at the prayer of Peter. Their answer is that it was expedient for them, that the one should be disabled by

palsy and the other should die: but they do not deny that it happened at the prayer of the apostle'.

This allusion to the gardener's daughter remained a puzzle until lately. But a passage in the Epistle of Titus (already quoted) tells us the substance of the story.

A certain gardener had a daughter, a virgin, her father's only child: he begged Peter to pray for her. Upon his request, the apostle answered him that the Lord would give her that which was useful for her soul. Immediately the girl fell dead.

O worthy gain and suitable to God, to escape the insolence of the flesh and mortify the boastfulness of the blood! But that old man, faithless, and not knowing the greatness of the heavenly favour, ignorant of the divine benefit, entreated Peter that his only daughter might be raised again. And when she was raised, not many days after, as it might be to-day, the slave of a believer who lodged in the house ran upon her and ruined the girl, and both of them disappeared.

This was evidently a contrast to the story of Peter's daughter, and probably followed immediately upon it in the Acts. There is another sentence appropriate to the situation, which Dom de Bruyne found in a Cambrai MS. of the thirteenth century -a collection of apophthegms- and printed with the extracts from the Epistle of Titus.

That the dead are not to be mourned overmuch, Peter, speaking to one who lamented without patience the loss of his daughter, said: So many assaults of the devil, so many warrings of the body, so many disasters of the world hath she escaped, and thou sheddest tears as if thou knewest not what thou sufferest in thyself (what good hath befallen thee).

This might very well be part of Peter's address to the bereaved gardener.

III

THE VERCELLI ACTS

I. At the time when Paul was sojourning in Rome and confirming many in the faith, it came also to pass that one by name Candida, the wife of Quartus that was over the prisons, heard Paul and paid heed to his words and believed. And when she had instructed her husband also and he believed, Quartus suffered Paul to go whither he would away from the city: to whom Paul said: If it be the will of God, he will reveal it unto me. And after Paul had fasted three days and asked of the Lord that which should be profitable for him, he saw a vision, even the Lord saying unto him: Arise, Paul, and become a physician in thy body (i.e. by going thither in person) to them that are in Spain.

He therefore, having related to the brethren what God had commanded, nothing doubting, prepared himself to set forth from the city. But when Paul was about to depart, there was great weeping throughout all the brotherhood, because they thought that they should see Paul no more, so that they even rent their clothes. For they had in mind also how that Paul had oftentimes contended with the doctors of the Jews and confuted them, saying: Christ, upon whom your fathers laid hands, abolished their sabbaths and fasts and holy-days and circumcision, and the doctrines of men and the rest of the traditions he did abolish. But the brethren lamented (and adjured) Paul by the coming of our Lord Jesus Christ, that he should not be absent above a year, saying: We know thy love for thy brethren; forget not us when thou art come thither, neither begin to forsake us, as little children without a mother. And when they besought him long with tears, there came a sound from heaven, and a great voice saying: Paul the servant of God is chosen to minister all the days of his life: by the hands of Nero the ungodly and wicked man shall he be perfected before your eyes. And a very great fear fell upon the brethren because of the voice which came from heaven: and they were confirmed yet more in the faith.

II. Now they brought unto Paul bread and water for the sacrifice, that he might make prayer and distribute it to every one. Among whom it befell that a woman named Rufina desired, she also, to receive the Eucharist at the hands of Paul: to whom Paul, filled with the spirit of God, said as she drew near: Rufina, thou comest not worthily unto the altar of God, arising from beside one that is not thine husband but an adulterer, and assayest to receive the Eucharist of God. For behold Satan shall trouble thine heart and cast thee down in the sight of all them that believe in the Lord, that they which see and believe may know that they have believed in the living God, the searcher of hearts. But if thou repent of thine act, he is faithful that is able to blot out thy sin and set thee free from this sin: but if thou repent not, while thou art yet in the body, devouring fire and outer darkness shall receive thee for ever. And immediately Rufina fell down, being stricken with palsy (?) from her head unto the nails of her feet, and she had no power to speak (given her) for her tongue was bound. And when both they that believed (in the faith) and the neophytes saw it, they beat their breasts, remembering their old sins, and mourned and said: We know not if God will forgive the former sins which we have committed. Then Paul called for silence and said: Men and brethren which now have begun to believe on Christ, if ye continue not in your former works of the tradition of your fathers, and keep yourselves from all guile and wrath and fierceness and adultery and defilement, and from pride and envy and contempt and enmity, Jesus the living God will forgive you that ye did in ignorance. Wherefore, ye servants of God, arm yourselves every one in your inner man with peace, patience, gentleness, faith, charity, knowledge, wisdom, love of the brethren, hospitality, mercy, abstinence, chastity, kindness, justice: then shall ye have for your guide everlastingly the first-begotten of all creation, and shall have strength in peace with our Lord. And when they had heard these things of Paul, they besought him to pray for them. And Paul lifted up his voice and said: O eternal God, God of the heavens, God of unspeakable majesty (divinity), who hast stablished all things by thy word, who hast bound upon all the world the chain of thy grace, Father of thine holy Son Jesus Christ, we together pray thee through thy Son Jesus Christ, strengthen the souls which were before unbelieving but now are faithful. Once I was a blasphemer, now I am blasphemed; once I was a persecutor, now do I suffer persecution of others; once I was the enemy of Christ, now I pray that I may be his friend: for I trust in his promise and in his mercy; I account myself faithful and that I have received forgiveness of my former sins. Wherefore I exhort you also, brethren, to believe in the Lord the Father Almighty, and to put all your trust in our Lord Jesus Christ his Son, believing in him, and no man shall be able to uproot you from his promise. Bow your knees therefore together and commend me unto the Lord, who am about to set forth unto another nation, that his grace may go before me and dispose my journey aright, that he may receive his vessels holy and believing, that they, giving thanks for my preaching of the word of the Lord, may be well grounded in the faith. But the brethren wept long and prayed unto the Lord with Paul, saying: Be thou, Lord Jesus Christ, with Paul and restore him unto us whole: for we know our weakness which is in us even to this day.

III. And a great multitude of women were kneeling and praying and beseeching Paul; and they kissed his feet and accompanied him unto the harbour. But Dionysius and Balbus, of Asia, knights of Rome, and illustrious men, and a senator by name Demetrius abode by Paul on his right hand and said: Paul, I would desire to leave the city if I were not a magistrate, that I might not depart from thee. Also from Caesar's house Cleobius and Iphitus and Lysimachus and Aristaeus and two matrons Berenice and Philostrate, with Narcissus the presbyter [after they had] accompanied him to the harbour: but whereas a storm of the sea came on, he (Narcissus?) sent the brethren back to Rome, that if any would, he might come down and hear Paul until he set sail: and hearing that, the brethren went up unto the city. And when they told the brethren that had remained in the city, and the report was spread abroad, some on beasts, and some on foot, and others by way of the Tiber came down to the harbour, and were confirmed in the faith for three days, and on the fourth day until the fifth hour, praying together with Paul, and making the offering: and they put all that was needful on the ship and delivered him two young men, believers, to sail with him, and bade him farewell in the Lord and returned to Rome.

There has been great dispute about these three chapters, whether they are not an excerpt from the Acts of Paul, or whether they are an addition made by the writer of the Greek original of the Vercelli Acts.

If they are from the Acts of Paul, it means that in those Acts Paul was represented as visiting Rome twice, and going to Spain between the visits. Evidently, if this was so, he did not return straight from Spain to Rome: at least the Coptic gives no indication that the prophecies of Cleobius and Myrte were uttered in Spain.

The question is a difficult one. All allow that the writer of the Acts of Peter knew and used the Acts of Paul: but there is strong opposition to the idea that Paul related two visits to Rome.

The writer of Paul obviously knew the canonical Acts very well and obviously took great liberties with them. Did he go so far, one wonders, as to suppress and ignore the whole story of the trial before Felix and the shipwreck? If he told of but one visit to Rome -the final one- it appears that he did: for the conditions described in the Martyrdom -Paul quite free and martyred very shortly after his arrival- are totally irreconcilable with Luke (Paul arriving in custody and living two years at least in the city).

IV. Now after a few days there was a great commotion in the midst of the church, for some said that they had seen wonderful works done by a certain man whose name was Simon, and that he was at Aricia, and they added further that he said he was a great power of God and without God he did nothing. Is not this the Christ? but we believe in him whom Paul preached unto us; for by him have we seen the dead raised, and men Delivered from divers infirmities: but this man seeketh contention, we know it (or, but what this contention is, we know not) for there is no small stir made among us. Perchance also he will now enter into Rome; for yesterday they besought him with great acclamations, saying unto him: Thou art God in Italy, thou art the saviour of the Romans: haste quickly unto Rome. But he spake to the people with a shrill voice, saying: Tomorrow about the seventh hour ye shall see me fly over the gate of the city in the form (habit) wherein ye now see me speaking unto you. Therefore, brethren, if it seem good unto you, let us go and await carefully the issue of the matter. They all therefore ran together and came unto the gate. And when it was the seventh hour, behold suddenly a dust was seen in the sky afar off, like a smoke shining with rays stretching far from it. And when he drew near to the gate, suddenly he was not seen: and thereafter he appeared, standing in the midst of the people; whom they all worshipped, and took knowledge that he was the same that was seen of them the day before.

And the brethren were not a little offended among themselves, seeing, moreover, that Paul was not at Rome, neither Timotheus nor Barnabas, for they had been sent into Macedonia by Paul, and that there was no man to comfort us, to speak nothing of them that had but just become catechumens. And as Simon exalted himself yet more by the works which he did, and many of them daily called Paul a sorcerer, and others a deceiver, of so great a multitude that had been stablished in the faith all fell away save Narcissus the presbyter and two women in the lodging of the Bithynians, and four that could no longer go out of their house, but were shut up (day and night): these gave themselves unto prayer (by day and night), beseeching the Lord that Paul might return quickly, or some other that should visit his servants, because the devil had made them fall by his wickedness.

V. And as they prayed and fasted, God was already teaching Peter at Jerusalem of that which should come to pass. For whereas the twelve years which the Lord Christ had enjoined upon him were fulfilled, he showed him a vision after this manner, saying unto him: Peter, that Simon the sorcerer whom thou didst cast out of Judaea, convicting him, hath again come before thee (prevented thee) at Rome. And that shalt thou know shortly (or, and that thou mayest know in few words): for all that did believe in me hath Satan made to fall by his craft and working: whose Power Simon approveth himself to be. But delay thee not: set forth on the morrow, and there shalt thou find a ship ready, setting sail for Italy, and within few days I will show thee my grace which hath in it no grudging. Peter then, admonished by the vision, related it unto the brethren without delay, saying: It is necessary for me to go up unto Rome to fight with the enemy and adversary of the Lord and of our brethren.

And he went down to Caesarea and embarked quickly in the ship, whereof the ladder was already drawn up, not taking any provision with him. But the governor of the ship whose name was Theon looked on Peter and said: Whatsoever we have, all is thine. For what thank have we, if we take in a man like unto ourselves who is in uncertain case (difficulty) and share not all that we have with thee? but only let us have a prosperous voyage. But Peter, giving him thanks for that which he offered, himself fasted while he was in the ship, sorrowful in mind and again consoling himself because God accounted him worthy to be a minister in his service.

And after a few days the governor of the ship rose up at the hour of his dinner and asked Peter to eat with him, and said to him: O thou, whoever thou art, I know thee not, but as I reckon, I take thee for a servant of God. For as I was steering my ship at midnight I perceived the voice of a man from heaven saying to me: Theon, Theon! And twice it called me by my name and said to me: Among them that sail with thee let Peter be greatly honoured by thee, for by him shalt thou and the rest be preserved safe without any hurt after such a course as thou hopest not for. And Peter believed that God would vouchsafe to show his providence upon the sea unto them that were in the ship, and thenceforth began Peter to declare unto Theon the mighty works of God, and how the Lord had chosen him from among the apostles, and for what business he sailed unto Italy: and daily he communicated unto him the word of God. And considering him he perceived by his walk that he was of one mind in the faith and a worthy minister (deacon).

Now when there was a calm upon the ship in Hadria (the Adriatic), Theon showed it to Peter, saying unto him: If thou wilt account me worthy, whom thou mayest baptize with the seal of the Lord thou hast an opportunity. For all that were in the ship had fallen asleep, being drunken. And Peter went down by a rope and baptized Theon in the name of the Father and the Son and the Holy Ghost: and he came up out of the water rejoicing with great joy, and Peter also was glad because God had accounted Theon worthy of his name. Arid it came to pass when Theon was baptized, there appeared in the same place a youth shining and beautiful, saying unto them: Peace be unto you. And immediately Peter and Theon went up and entered into the cabin; and Peter took bread and gave thanks unto the Lord which had accounted him worthy of his holy ministry, and for that the youth had appeared unto them, saying: Peace be unto you. And he said: Thou best and alone holy one, it is thou that hast appeared unto us, O God Jesu Christ, and in thy name hath this man now been washed and sealed with thy holy seal. Therefore in thy name do I impart unto him thine eucharist, that he may be thy perfect servant without blame for ever.

And as they feasted and rejoiced in the Lord, suddenly there came a wind, not vehement but moderate, at the ship's prow, and ceased not for six days and as many nights, until they came unto Puteoli.

VI. And when they had touched at Puteoli, Theon leapt out of the ship and went unto the inn where he was wont to lodge, to prepare to receive Peter. Now he with whom he lodged was one by name Ariston, which alway feared the

Lord, and because of the Name Theon entrusted himself with him (had dealings with him). And when he was come to the inn and saw Ariston, Theon said unto him: God who hath accounted thee worthy to serve him hath communicated his grace unto me also by his holy servant Peter, who hath now sailed with me from Judaea, being commanded by our Lord to come unto Italy. And when he heard that, Ariston fell upon Theon's neck and embraced him and besought him to bring him to the ship and show him Peter. For Ariston said that since Paul set forth unto Spain there was no man of the brethren with whom he could refresh himself, and, moreover, a certain Jew had broken into the city, named Simon, and with his charms of sorcery and his wickedness hath he made all the brotherhood fall away this way and that, so that I also fled from Rome, expecting the coming of Peter: for Paul had told us of him, and I also have seen many things in a vision. Now, therefore, I believe in my Lord that he will build up again his ministry, for all this deceit shall be rooted out from among his servants. For our Lord Jesus Christ is faithful, who is able to restore our minds. And when Theon heard these things from Ariston, who wept, his spirit was raised (increased) yet more and he was the more strengthened, because he perceived that he had believed on the living God.

But when they came together unto the ship, Peter looked upon them and smiled, being filled with the Spirit; so that Ariston falling on his face at Peter's feet, said thus: Brother and lord, that hast part in the holy mysteries and showest the right way which is in the Lord Jesus Christ our God, who by thee hath shown unto us his coming: we have lost all them whom Paul had delivered unto us, by the working of Satan; but now I trust in the Lord who hath commanded thee to come unto us, sending thee as his messenger, that he hath accounted us worthy to see his great and wonderful works by thy means. I pray thee therefore, make haste unto the city: for I left the brethren which have stumbled, whom I saw fall into the temptation of the devil, and fled hither, saying unto them: Brethren, stand fast in the faith, for it is of necessity that within these two months the mercy of our Lord bring his servant unto you. For I had seen a vision, even Paul, saying unto me: Ariston, flee thou out of the city. And when I heard it, I believed without delay and went forth in the Lord, although I had an infirmity in my flesh, and came hither; and day by day I stood upon the sea-shore asking the sailors: Hath Peter sailed with you? But now through the abundance of the grace of God I entreat thee, let us go up unto Rome without delay, lest the teaching of this wicked man prevail yet further. And as Ariston said this with tears, Peter gave him his hand and raised him up from the earth, and Peter also groaning, said with tears: He hath prevented us which tempteth all the world by his angels; but he that hath power to save his servants from all temptations shall quench his deceits and put him beneath the feet of them that have believed in Christ whom we preach.

And, as they entered in at the gate, Theon entreated Peter, saying: Thou didst not refresh thyself on any day in so great a voyage (sea): and now after (before) so hard a journey wilt thou set out forthwith from the ship? tarry and refresh thyself, and so shalt thou set forth: for from hence to Rome upon a pavement of flint I fear lest thou be hurt by the shaking. But Peter answered and said to them: What if it come to pass that a millstone were hung upon me, and

likewise upon the enemy of our Lord, even as my Lord said unto us of any that offended one of the brethren, and I were drowned in the sea? but it might be not only a millstone, but that which is far worse, even that I which am the enemy of this persecutor of his servants should die afar off from them that have believed on the Lord Jesus Christ (so Ficker: the sentence is corrupt; the sense is that Peter must at all costs be with his fellow-Christians, or he will incur even worse punishment than that threatened by our Lord's words). And by no exhortation could Theon prevail to persuade him to tarry there even one day.

But Theon himself delivered all that was in the ship to be sold for the price which he thought good, and followed Peter unto Rome; whom Ariston brought unto the abode of Narcissus the presbyter.

VII. Now the report was noised through the city unto the brethren that were dispersed, because of Simon, that he might show him to be a deceiver and a persecutor of good men. All the multitude therefore ran together to see the apostle of the Lord stay (himself, or the brethren) on Christ. And on the first day of the week when the multitude was assembled to see Peter, Peter began to say with a loud voice: Ye men here present that trust in Christ, ye that for a little space have suffered temptation, learn for what cause God sent his Son into the world, and wherefore he made him to be born of the Virgin Mary; for would he so have done if not to procure us some grace or dispensation? even because he would take away all offence and all ignorance and all the contrivance of the devil, his attempts (beginnings) and his strength wherewith he prevailed aforetime, before our God shined forth in the world. And whereas men through ignorance fell into death by many and divers infirmities, Almighty God, moved with compassion, sent his Son into the world. With whom I was; and he (or I) walked upon the water, whereof I myself remain a witness, and do testify that he then worked in the world by signs and wonders, all of which he did.

I do confess, dearly-beloved brethren, that I was with him: yet I denied him, even our Lord Jesus Christ, and that not once only, but thrice; for there were evil dogs that were come about me as they did unto the Lord's prophets. And the Lord imputed it not unto me, but turned unto me and had compassion on the infirmity of my flesh, when (or so that) afterward I bitterly bewailed myself, and lamented the weakness of my faith, because I was befooled by the devil and kept not in mind the word of my Lord. And now I say unto you, O men and brethren, which are gathered together in the name of Jesus Christ: against you also hath the deceiver Satan aimed his arrows, that ye might depart out of the way. But faint not, brethren, neither let your spirit fall, but be strong and persevere and doubt not: for if Satan caused me to stumble, whom the Lord had in great honour, so that I denied the light of mine hope, and if he overthrew me and persuaded me to flee as if I had put my trust in a man, what think ye will he do unto you which are but young in the faith? Did ye suppose that he would not turn you away to make you enemies of the kingdom of God, and cast you down into perdition by a new (or the last) deceit? For whomsoever he casteth out from the hope of our Lord Jesus Christ, he is a son of perdition for ever. Turn yourselves, therefore, brethren, chosen of the Lord, and be strong in God Almighty, the Father of our Lord

Jesus Christ, whom no man hath seen at any time, neither can see, save he who hath believed in him. And be ye aware whence this temptation hath come upon you. For it is not only by words that I would convince you that this is Christ whom I preach, but also by deeds and exceeding great works of power do I exhort you by the faith that is in Christ Jesus, that none of you look for any other save him that was despised and mocked of the Jews, even this Nazarene which was crucified and died and the third day rose again.

VIII. And the brethren repented and entreated Peter to fight against Simon: (who said that he was the power of God, and lodged in the house of Marcellus a senator, whom he had convinced by his charms) saying: Believe us, brother Peter: there was no man among men so wise as this Marcellus. All the widows that trusted in Christ had recourse unto him; all the fatherless were fed by him; and what more, brother? all the poor called Marcellus their patron, and his house was called the house of the strangers and of the poor, and the emperor said unto him: I will keep thee out of every office, lest thou despoil the provinces to give gifts unto the Christians. And Marcellus answered: All my goods are also thine. And Caesar said to him: Mine they would be if thou keptest them for me; but now they are not mine, for thou givest them to whom thou wilt, and I know not to what vile persons. Having this, then, before our eyes, brother Peter, we report it to thee, how the great mercy of this man is turned unto blasphemy; for if he had not turned, neither should we have departed from the holy faith of God our Lord. And now doth this Marcellus in anger repent him of his good deeds, saying: All this substance have I spent in all this time, vainly believing that I gave it for the knowledge of God! So that if any stranger cometh to the door of his house, he smiteth him with a staff and biddeth him be beaten, saying: Would God I had not spent so much money upon these impostors: and yet more doth he say, blaspheming. But if there abide in thee any mercy of our Lord and aught of the goodness of his commandments, do thou succour the error of this man who hath done so many alms-deeds unto the servants of God.

And Peter, when he perceived this, was smitten with sharp affliction and said: O the divers arts and temptations of the devil! O the contrivances and devices of the wicked! he that nourisheth up for himself a mighty fire in the day of wrath, the destruction of simple men, the ravening wolf, the devourer and scatterer of eternal life! Thou didst enmesh the first man in concupiscence and bind him with thine old iniquity and with the chain of the flesh: thou art wholly the exceeding bitter fruit of the tree of bitterness, who sendest divers lusts upon men. Thou didst compel Judas my fellow-disciple and fellow-apostle to do wickedly and deliver up our Lord Jesus Christ, who shall punish thee therefor. Thou didst harden the heart of Herod and didst inflame Pharaoh and compel him to fight against Moses the holy servant of God; thou didst give boldness unto Caiaphas, that he should deliver our Lord Jesus Christ unto the unrighteous multitude; and even until now thou shootest at innocent souls with thy poisonous arrows. Thou wicked one, enemy of all men, be thou accursed from the Church of him the Son of the holy God omnpotent and as a brand cast out of the fire shalt thou be quenched by the servants of our Lord Jesus Christ. Upon thee let thy blackness be turned and upon thy children, an evil seed; upon thee be turned thy wickedness and thy threatenings; upon thee and

thine angels be thy temptations, thou beginning of malice and bottomless pit of darkness! Let thy darkness that thou hast be with thee and with thy vessels which thou ownest! Depart from them that shall believe in God, depart from the servants of Christ and from them that desire to be his soldiers. Keep thou to thyself thy garments of darkness! Without cause knockest thou at other men's doors, which are not thine but of Christ Jesus that keepeth them. For thou, ravening wolf, wouldest carry off the sheep that are not thine but of Christ Jesus, who keepeth them with all care and diligence.

IX. As Peter spake thus with great sorrow of mind, many were added unto them that believed on the Lord. But the brethren besought Peter to join battle with Simon and not suffer him any longer to vex the people. And without delay Peter went quickly out of the synagogue (assembly) and went unto the house of Marcellus, where Simon lodged: and much people followed him. And when he came to the door, he called the porter and said to him: Go, say unto Simon: Peter because of whom thou fleddest out of Judaea waiteth for thee at the door. The porter answered and said to Peter: Sir, whether thou be Peter, I know not: but I have a command; for he had knowledge that yesterday thou didst enter into the city, and said unto me: Whether it be by day or by night, at whatsoever hour he cometh, say that I am not within. And Peter said to the young man: Thou hast well said in reporting that which he compelled thee to say. And Peter turned unto the people that followed him and said: Ye shall now see a great and marvellous wonder. And Peter seeing a great dog bound with a strong chain, went to him and loosed him, and when he was loosed the dog received a man's voice and said unto Peter: What dost thou bid me to do, thou servant of the unspeakable and living God? Peter said unto him: Go in and say unto Simon in the midst of his company: Peter saith unto thee, Come forth abroad, for thy sake am I come to Rome, thou wicked one and deceiver of simple souls. And immediately the dog ran and entered in, and rushed into the midst of them that were with Simon, and lifted up his forefeet and in a loud voice said: Thou Simon, Peter the servant of Christ who standeth at the door saith unto thee: Come forth abroad, for thy sake am I come to Rome, thou most wicked one and deceiver of simple souls. And when Simon heard it, and beheld the incredible sight, he lost the words wherewith he was deceiving them that stood by, and all of them were amazed.

X. But when Marcellus saw it he went out to the door and cast himself at Peter's feet and said: Peter, I embrace thy feet, thou holy servant of the holy God; I have sinned greatly: but exact thou not my sins, if there be in thee the true faith of Christ, whom thou preachest, if thou remember his commandments, to hate no man, to be unkind to no man, as I learned from thy fellow apostle Paul; keep not in mind my faults, but pray for me unto the Lord, the holy Son of God whom I have provoked to wrath -for I have persecuted his servants- that I be not delivered with the sins of Simon unto eternal fire; who so persuaded me, that I set up a statue to him with this inscription: 'To Simon the new (young) God.' If I knew, O Peter, that thou couldest be won with money, I would give thee all my substance, yea I would give it and despise it, that I might gain my soul. If I had sons, I would account them as nothing, if only I might believe in the living God. But I confess that he would not have deceived me save that he said that he was the power of God; yet will I tell thee, O most gentle (sweet) Peter: I was not worthy to hear thee, thou servant of God, neither was I stablished in the faith of God which is in Christ; therefore was I made to stumble. I beseech thee, therefore, take not ill that which I am about to say, that Christ our Lord whom thou preachest in truth said unto thy fellow-apostles in thy presence: If ye have faith as a grain of mustard seed, ye shall say unto this mountain: Remove thyself: and straightway it shall remove itself. But this Simon said that thou, Peter, wast without faith when thou didst doubt, in the waters. And I have heard that Christ said this also: They that are with me have not understood me. If, then, ye upon whom he laid his hands, whom also he chose, did doubt, I, therefore, having this witness, repent me, and take refuge in thy prayers. Receive my soul, who have fallen away from our Lord and from his promise. But I believe that he will have mercy upon me that repent. For the Almighty is faithful to forgive me my sins.

But Peter said with a loud voice: Unto thee, our Lord, be glory and splendour, O God Almighty, Father of our Lord Jesus Christ. Unto thee be praise and glory and honour, world without end. Amen. Because thou hast now fully strengthened and stablished us in thee in the sight of all, holy Lord, confirm thou Marcellus, and send thy peace upon him and upon his house this day: and whatsoever is lost or out of the way, thou alone canst turn them all again; we beseech thee, Lord, shepherd of the sheep that once were scattered, but now shall be gathered in one by thee. So also receive thou Marcellus as one of thy lambs and suffer him no longer to go astray (revel) in error or ignorance. Yea, Lord, receive him that with anguish and tears entreateth thee.

XI. And as Peter spake thus and embraced Marcellus, Peter turned himself unto the multitude that stood by him and saw there one that laughed (smiled), in whom was a very evil spirit. And Peter said unto him: Whosoever thou art that didst laugh, show thyself openly unto all that are present. And hearing this the young man ran into the court of the house and cried out with a loud voice and dashed himself against the wall and said: Peter, there is a great contention between Simon and the dog whom thou sentest; for Simon saith to the dog: Say that I am not here. Unto whom the dog saith more than thou didst charge him; and when he hath accomplished the mystery which thou didst command him, he shall die at thy feet. But Peter said: And thou also, devil, whosoever thou art, in the name of our Lord Jesus Christ, go out of that young man and hurt him not at all: show thyself unto all that stand here. When the young man heard it, he ran forth and caught hold on a great statue of marble which was set in the court of the house, and brake it in pieces with his feet. Now it was a statue of Caesar. Which Marcellus beholding smote his forehead and said unto Peter: A great crime hath been committed; for if this be made known unto Caesar by some busybody, he will afflict us with sore punishments. And Peter said to him: I see thee not the same that thou wast a little while ago, for thou saidst that thou wast ready to spend all thy substance to save thy soul. But if thou indeed repentest, believing in Christ with thy whole heart, take in thine hands of the water that runneth down, and pray to the Lord, and in his name sprinkle it upon the broken pieces of the statue and it shall be whole as it was before. And Marcellus, nothing doubting, but believing with his whole heart, before he

took the water lifted up his hands and said: I believe in thee, O Lord Jesu Christ: for I am now proved by thine apostle Peter, whether I believe aright in thine holy name. Therefore I take water in mine hands, and in thy name do I sprinkle these stones that the statue may become whole as it was before. If, therefore, Lord, it be thy will that I continue in the body and suffer nothing at Caesar's hand, let this stone be whole as it was before. And he sprinkled the water upon the stones, and the statue became whole, whereat Peter exulted that Marcellus had not doubted in asking of the Lord, and Marcellus was exalted in spirit for that such a sign was first wrought by his hands; and he therefore believed with his whole heart in the name of Jesus Christ the Son of God, by whom all things impossible are made possible.

XII. But Simon within the house said thus to the dog: Tell Peter that I am not within. Whom the dog answered in the presence of Marcellus: Thou exceeding wicked and shameless one, enemy of all that live and believe on Christ Jesus, here is a dumb animal sent unto thee which hath received a human voice to confound thee and show thee to be a deceiver and a liar. Hast thou taken thought so long, to say at last: 'Tell him that I am not within?' Art thou not ashamed to utter thy feeble and useless words against Peter the minister and apostle of Christ, as if thou couldst hide thee from him that hath commanded me to speak against thee to thy face: and that not for thy sake but for theirs whom thou wast deceiving and sending unto destruction? Cursed therefore shalt thou be, thou enemy and corrupter of the way of the truth of Christ, who shall prove by fire that dieth not and in outer darkness, thine iniquities that thou hast committed. And having thus said, the dog went forth and the people followed him, leaving Simon alone. And the dog came unto Peter as he sat with the multitude that was come to see Peter's face, and the dog related what he had done unto Simon. And thus spake the dog unto the angel and apostle of the true God: Peter, thou wilt have a great contest with the enemy of Christ and his servants, and many that have been deceived by him shalt thou turn unto the faith; wherefore thou shalt receive from God the reward of thy work. And when the dog had said this he fell down at the apostle Peter's feet and gave up the ghost. And when the great multitude saw with amazement the dog speaking, they began then, some to throw themselves down at Peter's feet, and some said: Show us another sign, that we may believe in thee as the minister of the living God, for Simon also did many signs in our presence and therefore did we follow him.

XIII. And Peter turned and saw a herring (sardine) hung in a window, and took it and said to the people: If ye now see this swimming in the water like a fish, will ye be able to believe in him whom I preach? And they said with one voice: Verily we will believe thee. Then he said -now there was a bath for swimming at hand: In thy name, O Jesu Christ, forasmuch as hitherto it is not believed in, in the sight of all these live and swim like a fish. And he cast the herring into the bath, and it lived and began to swim. And all the people saw the fish swimming, and it did not so at that hour only, lest it should be said that it was a delusion (phantasm), but he made it to swim for a long time, so that they brought much people from all quarters and showed them the herring that was made a living fish, so that certain of the people even cast bread to it; and they saw that it was whole. And seeing this, many followed Peter and believed in the Lord.

And they assembled themselves day and night unto the house of Narcissus the presbyter. And Peter discoursed unto them of the scriptures of the prophets and of those things which our Lord Jesus Christ had wrought both in word and in deeds.

XIV. But Marcellus was confirmed daily by the signs which he saw wrought by Peter through the grace of Jesus Christ which he granted unto him. And Mareellus ran upon Simon as he sat in his house in the dining chamber, and cursed him and said unto him: Thou most adverse and pestilent of men, corrupter of my soul and my house, who wouldest have made me fall away from my Lord and Saviour Christ! and laying hands on him he commanded him to be thrust out of his house. And the servants having received such licence, covered him with reproaches; some buffeted his face, others beat him with sticks, others cast stones, others emptied out vessels full of filth upon his head, even those who on his account had fled from their master and been a long time fettered; and other their fellowservants of whom he had spoken evil to their master reproached him. saying to him: Now by the will of God who hath had mercy on us and on our master, do we recompense thee with a fit reward. And Simon, shrewdly beaten and cast out of the house, ran unto the house where Peter lodged, even the house of Narcissus, and standing at the gate cried out: Lo, here am I, Simon: come thou down, Peter, and I will convict thee that thou hast believed on a man which is a Jew and a carpenter's son.

XV. And when it was told Peter that Simon had said this, Peter sent unto him a woman which had a sucking child, saying to her: Go down quickly, and thou wilt find one that seeketh me. For thee there is no need that thou answer him at all, but keep silence and hear what the child whom thou holdest shall say unto him. The woman therefore went down. Now the child whom she suckled was seven months old; and it received a man's voice and said unto Simon: O thou abhorred of God and men, and destruction of truth, and evil seed of all corruption, O fruit by nature unprofitable! but only for a short and little season shalt thou be seen, and thereafter eternal punishment is laid up for thee. Thou son of a shameless father, that never puttest forth thy roots for good but for poison, faithless generation void of all hope! thou wast not confounded when a dog reproved thee; I a child am compelled of God to speak, and not even now art thou ashamed. But even against thy will, on the sabbath day that cometh, another shall bring thee into the forum of Julius that it may be shown what manner of man thou art. Depart therefore from the gate wherein walk the feet of the holy; for thou shalt no more corrupt the innocent souls whom thou didst turn out of the way and make sad; in Christ, therefore, shall be shown thine evil nature, and thy devices shall be cut in pieces. And now speak I this last word unto thee: Jesus Christ saith to thee: Be thou stricken dumb in my name, and depart out of Rome until the sabbath that cometh. And forthwith he became dumb and his speech was bound; and he went out of Rome until the sabbath and abode in a stable. But the woman returned with the child unto Peter and told him and the rest of the brethren what the child had said unto Simon:

and they magnified the Lord which had shown these things unto men.

XVI. Now when the night fell, Peter, while yet waking, beheld Jesus clad in a vesture of brightness, smiling and saying unto him: Already is much people of the brotherhood returned through me and through the signs which thou hast wrought in my name. But thou shalt have a contest of the faith upon the sabbath that cometh, and many more of the Gentiles and of the Jews shall be converted in my name unto me who was reproached and mocked and spat upon. For I will be present with thee when thou askest for signs and wonders, and thou shalt convert many: but thou shalt have Simon opposing thee by the works of his father; yet all his works shall be shown to be charms and contrivances of sorcery. But now slack thou not, and whomsoever I shall send unto thee thou shalt establish in my name. And when it was light, he told the brethren how the Lord had appeared unto him and what he had commanded him:

XVII. [This episode, inserted most abruptly, is believed by Vouaux to have been inserted here by the compiler of the Greek original of the Vercelli Acts: but it was not composed by him, but transferred with very slight additions from the earlier part of the Acts-now lost- of which the scene was laid in Judaea. I incline to favour this view.)

But believe ye me, men and brethren, I drove this Simon out of Judaea where he did many evils with his magical charms, lodging in Judaea with a certain woman Eubula, who was of honourable estate in this world, having store of gold and pearls of no small price. Here did Simon enter in by stealth with two others like unto himself, and none of the household saw them two, but Simon only, and by means of a spell they took away all the woman's gold, and disappeared. But Eubula, when she found what was done, began to torture her household, saying: Ye have taken occasion by this man of God and spoiled me, when ye saw him entering in to me to honour a mere woman; but his name is as the name of the Lord.

As I fasted for three days and prayed that this matter should be made plain, I saw in a vision Italicus and Antulus (Antyllus?) whom I had instructed in the name of the Lord, and a boy naked and chained giving me a wheaten loaf and saying unto me: Peter, endure yet two days and thou shalt see the mighty works of God. As for all that is lost out of the house of Eubula, Simon hath used art magic and hath caused a delusion, and with two others hath stolen it away: whom thou shalt see on the third day at the ninth hour, at the gate which leadeth unto Neapolis, selling unto a goldsmith by name Agrippinus a young satyr of gold of two pound weight, having in it a precious stone. But for thee there is no need that thou touch it, lest thou be defiled; but let there be with thee some of the matron's servants, and thou shalt show them the shop of the goldsmith and depart from them. For by reason of this matter shall many believe on the name of the Lord, and all that which these men by their devices and wickedness have oft-times stolen shall be openly showed. When I heard that, I went unto Eubula and found her sitting with her clothes rent and her hair disordered, mourning; unto whom I said: Eubula, rise up from thy mourning and compose thy face and order thy hair and put on raiment befitting thee, and pray unto the

Lord Jesus Christ that judgeth every soul: for he is the invisible Son of God, by whom thou must be saved, if only thou repent with thine whole heart of thy former sins: and receive thou power from him; for behold, by me the Lord saith to thee: Thou shalt find all whatsoever thou hast lost. And after thou hast received them, take thou care that he find thee, that thou mayest renounce this present world and seek for everlasting refreshment. Hearken therefore unto this: Let certain of thy people keep watch at the gate that leadeth to Neapolis on the day after to-morrow at about the ninth hour, and they shall see two young men having a young satyr of gold, of two pound weight, set with gems, as a vision hath shown me: which thing they will offer for sale to one Agrippinus of the household of godliness and of the faith which is in the Lord Jesus Christ: by whom it shall be showed thee that thou shouldest believe in the living God and not on Simon the magician, the unstable devil, who hath desired that thou shouldest remain in sorrow, and thine innocent household be tormented; who by fair words and speech only hath deceived thee, and with his mouth only spake of godliness, whereas he is wholly possessed of ungodliness. For when thou didst think to keep holy-day, and settedst up thine idol and didst veil it and set out all thine ornaments upon a table (round three-legged table), he brought in two young men whom no man of yours saw, by a magic charm, and they stole away thine ornaments and were no more seen. But his device hath had no success (place); for my God hath manifested it unto me, to the end thou shouldest not be deceived, neither perish in hell, for those sins which thou hast committed ungodly and contrary to God, who is full of all truth, and the righteous judge of quick and dead; and there is none other hope of life unto men save through him, by whom those things which thou hast lost are recovered unto thee: and now do thou gain thine own soul.

But she cast herself down before my feet, saying: O man, who thou art I know not; but him I received as a servant of God, and whatsoever he asked of me to give it unto the poor, I gave much by his hands, and beside that I did give much unto him. What hurt did I do him, that he should contrive all this against mine house? Unto whom Peter said: There is no faith to be put in words, but in acts and deeds: but we must go on with that we have begun. So I left her and went with two stewards of Eubula and came to Agrippinus and said to him: See that thou take note of these men; for to-morrow two young men will come to thee, desiring to sell thee a young satyr of gold set with jewels, which belongeth to the mistress of these: and thou shalt take it as it were to look upon it, and praise the work of the craftsman, and then when these come in, God will bring the rest to the proof. And on the next day the stewards of the matron came about the ninth hour, and also those young men, willing to sell unto Agrippinus the young satyr of gold. And they being forthwith taken, it was reported unto the matron, and she in distress of mind came to the deputy, and with a loud voice declared all that had befallen her. And when Pompeius the deputy beheld her in distress of mind, who never had come forth abroad, he forthwith rose up from the judgement seat and went unto the praetorium, and bade those men to be brought and tortured; and while they were being tormented they confessed that they did it in the service of Simon, which, said they, persuaded us thereto with money. And being tortured a long time, they confessed that all that Eubula had lost was laid up under the earth in a cave on the other

side of the gate, and many other things besides. And when Pompeius heard this, he rose up to go unto the gate, with those two men, each of them bound with two chains. And lo, Simon came in at the gate, seeking them because they tarried long. And he seeth a great multitude coming, and those two bound with chains; and he understood and betook him to flight, and appeared no more in Judaea unto this day. But Eubula, when she had recovered all her goods, gave them for the service of the poor, and believed on the Lord Jesus Christ and was comforted; and despised and renounced this world, and gave unto the widows and fatherless, and clothed the poor. And after a long time she received her rest (sleep). Now these things, dearly beloved brethren, were done in Judaea, whereby he that is called the angel of Satan was driven out thence.

XVIII. Brethren, dearest and most beloved, let us fast together and pray unto the Lord. For he that drove him out thence is able also to root him out of this place: and let him grant unto us power to withstand him and his magical charms, and to prove that he is the angel of Satan. For on the sabbath our Lord shall bring him, though he would not, unto the forum of Julius. Let us therefore bow our knees unto Christ, which heareth us, though we cry not; it is he that seeth us, though he be not seen with these eyes, yet is he in us: if we will, he will not forsake us. Let us therefore purify our souls of every evil temptation, and God will not depart from us. Yea, if we but wink with our eyes, he is present with us.

XIX. Now after these things were spoken by Peter, Marcellus also came in, and said: Peter, I have for thee cleansed mine whole house from the footsteps (traces) of Simon, and wholly done away even his wicked dust. For I took water and called upon the holy name of Jesus Christ, together with mine other servants which belong unto him, and sprinkled all my house and all the dining chambers and all the porticoes, even unto the outer gate, and said: I know that thou, Lord Jesu Christ, art pure and untouched of any uncleanness: so let mine enemy and adversary be driven out from before thy face. And now, thou blessed one, have I bidden the widows and old women to assemble unto thee in my house which is purified (MS. common), that they may pray with us. And they shall receive every one a piece of gold in the name of the ministry (service), that they may be called indeed servants of Christ. And all else is now prepared for the service. I entreat thee, therefore, O blessed Peter, consent unto their request, so that thou also pay honour unto (ornament) their prayers in my stead; let us then go and take Narcissus also, and whosoever of the brethren are here. So then Peter consented unto his simplicity, to fulfil his desire, and went forth with him and the rest of the brethren.

XX. But Peter entered in, and beheld one of the aged women, a widow, that was blind, and her daughter giving her her hand and leading her into Marcellus' house; and Peter said unto her: Come hither, mother: from this day forward Jesus giveth thee his right hand, by whom we have light unapproachable which no darkness hideth; who saith unto thee by me: Open thine eyes and see, and walk by thyself. And forthwith the widow saw Peter laying his hand upon her.

And Peter entered into the dining-hall and saw that the Gospel was being read, and he rolled up the book and said: Ye men that believe and hope in Christ, learn in what manner the holy Scripture of our Lord ought to be declared: whereof we by his grace wrote that which we could receive, though yet it appear unto you feeble, yet according to our power, even that which can be endured to be borne by (or instilled into) human flesh. We ought therefore first to know the will and the goodness of God, how that when error was everywhere spread abroad, and many thousands of men were being cast down into perdition, God was moved by his mercy to show himself in another form and in the likeness of man, concerning which neither the Jews nor we were able worthily to be enlightened. For every one of us according as he could contain the sight, saw, as he was able. Now will I expound unto you that which was newly read unto you. Our Lord, willing that I should behold his majesty in the holy mount - I, when I with the sons of Zebedee saw the brightness of his light, fell as one dead and shut mine eyes, and heard such a voice from him as I am not able to describe, and thought myself to be blinded by his brightness. And when I recovered (breathed again) a little I said within myself: Peradventure my Lord hath brought me hither that he might blind me. And I said: If this also be thy will, Lord, I resist not. And he gave me his hand and raised me up; and when I arose I saw him again in such a form as I was able to take in. As, therefore, the merciful God, dearly beloved brethren, carried our infirmities and bare our sins (as the prophet saith: He beareth our sins and suffereth for us; but we did esteem him to be in affliction and smitten with plagues), for he is in the Father and the Father in him -he also is himself the fulness of all majesty, who hath shown unto us all his good things: he did eat and drink for our sakes, himself being neither an-hungered nor athirst; he carried and bare reproaches for our sakes, he died and rose again because of us; who both defended me when I sinned and comforted me by his greatness, and will comfort you also that ye may love him: this God who is great and small, fair and foul, young and old, seen in time and unto eternity invisible; whom the hand of man hath not held, yet is he held by his servants; whom no flesh hath seen, yet now seeth; who is the word proclaimed by the prophets and now appearing (so Gk.: Lat. not heard of but now known); not subject to suffering, but having now made trial of suffering for our sake (or like unto us); never chastised, yet now chastised; who was before the world and hath been comprehended in time; the great beginning of all principality, yet delivered over unto princes; beautiful, but among us lowly; seen of all yet foreseeing all (MS. foul of view, yet foreseeing). This Jesus ye have, brethren, the door, the light, the way, the bread, the water, the life, the resurrection, the refreshment, the pearl, the treasure, the seed, the abundance (harvest), the mustard seed, the vine, the plough, the grace, the faith, the word: he is all things and there is none other greater than he. Unto him be praise, world without end. Amen.

XXI. And when the ninth hour was fully come, they rose up to make prayer. And behold certain widows, of the aged, unknown to Peter, which sat there, being blind and not believing, cried out, saying unto Peter: We sit together here, O Peter, hoping and believing in Christ Jesus: as therefore thou hast made one of us to see, we entreat thee, lord Peter, grant unto us also his mercy and pity. But Peter said to them: If there be in you the faith that is in Christ, if it be firm in you, then perceive in your mind that which ye see not with your eyes, and though your ears are closed, yet let them be open in your mind within you. These eyes shall again be shut, seeing nought but men and oxen and dumb beasts and stones and sticks; but not every eye seeth Jesus Christ. Yet now, Lord, let thy sweet and holy name succour these persons; do thou touch their eyes; for thou art able - that these may see with their eyes.

And when all had prayed, the hall wherein they were shone as when it lighteneth, even with such a light as cometh in the clouds, yet not such a light as that of the daytime, but unspeakable, invisible, such as no man can describe, even such that we were beside ourselves with bewilderment, calling on the Lord and saying: Have mercy, Lord, upon us thy servants: what we are able to bear, that, Lord, give thou us; for this we can neither see nor endure. And as we lay there, only those widows stood up which were blind; and the bright light which appeared unto us entered into their eyes and made them to see. Unto whom Peter said: Tell us what ye saw. And they said: We saw an old man of such comeliness as we are not able to declare to thee; but others said: We saw a young man; and others: We saw a boy touching our eyes delicately, and so were our eyes opened. Peter therefore magnified the Lord, saying: Thou only art the Lord God, and of what lips have we need to give thee due praise? and how can we give thee thanks according to thy mercy? Therefore, brethren, as I told you but a little while since, God that is constant is greater than our thoughts, even as we have learned of these aged widows, how that they beheld the Lord in divers forms.

XXII. And having exhorted them all to think upon (understand) the Lord with their whole heart, he began together with Marcellus and the rest of the brethren to minister unto the virgins of the Lord, and to rest until the morning.

Unto whom Marcellus said: Ye holy and inviolate virgins of the Lord, hearken: Ye have a place to abide in, for these things that are called mine, whose are they save yours? depart not hence, but refresh yourselves: for upon the sabbath which cometh, even to-morrow, Simon hath a controversy with Peter the holy one of God: for as the Lord hath ever been with him, lo will Christ the Lord now stand for him as his apostle. For Peter hath continued tasting nothing, but fasting yet a day, that he may overcome the wicked adversary and persecutor of the Lord's truth. For lo, my young men are come announcing that they have seen scaffolds being set up in the forum, and much people saying: To-morrow at daybreak two Jews are to contend here concerning the teaching (?) of God. Now therefore let us watch until the morning, praying and beseeching our Lord Jesus Christ to hear our prayers on behalf of Peter.

And Marcellus turned to sleep for a short space, and awoke and said unto Peter: O Peter, thou apostle of Christ, let us go boldly unto that which lieth before us. For just now when I turned myself to sleep for a little, I beheld thee sitting in a high place and before thee a great multitude, and a woman exceeding foul, in sight like an Ethiopian, not an Egyptian, but altogether black and filthy, clothed in rags, and with an iron collar about her neck and chains upon her hands and feet, dancing. And when thou sawest me thou saidst to me with a loud voice: Marcellus the whole power of Simon and of his God is this woman that danceth; do thou behead her. And I said to thee: Brother Peter, I am a senator of a high race, and I have never defiled my hands, neither killed so much as a sparrow at any time. And thou hearing it didst begin to cry out yet more: Come thou, our true sword, Jesu Christ. and cut not off only the head of this devil, but hew all her limbs in pieces in the sight of all these Whom I have approved in thy service. And immediately one like unto thee, O Peter, having a sword, hewed her in pieces: so that I looked earnestly upon you both, both on thee and on him that cut in pieces that devil, and marvelled greatly to see how alike ye were. And I awaked, and have told unto thee these signs of Christ. And when Peter heard it he was the more filled with courage, for that Marcellus had seen these things, knowing that the Lord alway careth for his own. And being joyful and refreshed by these words, he rose up to go unto the forum.

XXIII. Now the brethren were gathered together, and all that were in Rome, and took places every one for a piece of gold: there came together also the senators and the prefects and those in authority. And Peter came and stood in the midst, and all cried out: Show us, O Peter, who is thy God and what is his greatness which hath given thee confidence. Begrudge not the Romans; they are lovers of the gods. We have had proof of Simon, let us have it of thee; convince us, both of you, whom we ought truly to believe. And as they said these things, Simon also came in, and standing in trouble of mind at Peter's side, at first he looked at him.

And after long silence Peter said: Ye men of Rome, be ye true judges unto us, for I say that I have believed on the living and true God; and I promise to give you proofs of him, which are known unto me, as many among you also can bear witness. For ye see that this man is now rebuked and silent, knowing that I drove him out of Judaea because of the deceits which he practised upon Eubula, an honourable and simple woman, by his art magic; and being driven out from thence, he is come hither, thinking to escape notice among you; and lo, he standeth face to face with me. Say now, Simon, didst thou not at Jerusalem fall at my feet and Paul's, when thou sawest the healings that were wrought by our hands, and say: I pray you take of me a payment as much as ye will, that I may be able to lay hands on men and do such mighty works? And we when we heard it cursed thee, saying: Dost thou think to tempt us as if we desired to possess money? And now, fearest thou not at all? My name is Peter, because the Lord Christ vouchsafed to call me 'prepared for all things': for I trust in the living God by whom I shall put down thy sorceries. Now let him do in your presence the wonders which he did aforetime: and what I have now said of him, will ye not believe it?

But Simon said: Thou presumest to speak of Jesus of Nazareth, the son of a carpenter, and a carpenter himself, whose birth is recorded (or whose race dwelleth) in Judaea. Hear thou, Peter: the Romans have understanding: they are no fools. And he turned to the people and said: Ye men of Rome, is God born? is he crucified? he that hath a master is no God. And when he so spake, many said: Thou sayest well, Simon.

XXIV. But Peter said: Anathema upon thy words against (or in) Christ! Presumest thou to speak thus, whereas the prophet saith of him: Who shall declare his generation?

And another prophet saith: And we saw him and he had no beauty nor comeliness. And: In the last times shall a child be born of the Holy Ghost: his mother knoweth not a man, neither doth any man say that he is his father. And again he saith: She hath brought forth and not brought forth.[From the apocryphal Ezekiel (lost)] And again: Is it a small thing for you to weary men (lit. Is it a small thing that ye make a contest for men)? Behold, a virgin shall conceive in the womb. And another prophet saith, honouring the Father: Neither did we hear her voice, neither did a midwife come in.[From the Ascension of Isaiah, xi. 14] Another prophet saith: Born not of the womb of a woman, but from a heavenly place came he down. And: A stone was cut out without hands, and smote all the kingdoms. And: The stone which the builders rejected, the same is become the head of the corner; and he calleth him a stone elect, precious. And again a prophet saith concerning him: And behold, I saw one like the Son of man coming upon a cloud. And what more? O ye men of Rome, if ye knew the Scriptures of the prophets, I would expound all unto you: by which Scriptures it was necessary that this should be spoken in a mystery, and that the kingdom of God should be perfected. But these things shall be opened unto you hereafter. Now turn I unto thee, Simon: do thou some one thing of those wherewith thou didst before deceive them, and I will bring it to nought through my Lord Jesus Christ. And Simon plucked up his boldness and said: If the prefect allow it (prepare yourselves and delay not for my sake).

XXV. But the prefect desired to show patience unto both, that he might not appear to do aught unjustly. And the prefect put forward one of his servants and said thus unto Simon: Take this man and deliver him to death. And to Peter he said: And do thou revive him. And unto the people the prefect said: It is now for you to judge whether of these two is acceptable unto God, he that killeth or he that maketh alive. And straightway Simon spake in the ear of the lad and made him speechless, and he died.

And as there began to be a murmuring among the people, one of the widows who were nourished (refreshed) in Marcellus' house, standing behind the multitude, cried out: O Peter, servant of God, my son is dead, the only one that I had. And the people made place for her and led her unto Peter: and she cast herself down at his feet, saying: I had one only son, which with his hands (shoulders) furnished me with nourishment: he raised me up, he carried me: now that he is dead, who shall reach me a hand? Unto whom Peter said: Go, with these for witness, and bring hither thy son, that they may see and be able to believe that by the power of God he is raised, and that this man (Simon) may behold it and fail (or, and she when she saw him, fell down). And Peter said to the young men: We have need of some young men, and, moreover, of such as will believe. And forthwith thirty young men arose, which were prepared to carry her or to bring thither her son that was dead. And whereas the widow was hardly returned to herself, the young men took her up; and she was crying out and saying: Lo, my son, the servant of Christ hath sent unto thee: tearing her hair and her face. Now the young men which were come examined (Gk. apparently, held) the lad's nostrils to see whether he were indeed dead; and seeing that he was dead of a truth, they had compassion on the old woman and said: If thou so will, mother, and hast confidence in the God of Peter, we will take him up and carry him thither that he may raise him up and restore him unto thee.

XXVI. And as they said these things, the prefect (in the forum, Lat.), looking earnestly upon Peter (said: What sayest thou Peter?) Behold my lad is dead, who also is dear unto the emperor, and I spared him not, though I had with me other young men; but I desired rather to make trial (tempt) of thee and of the God whom thou (preachest), whether ye be true, and therefore I would have this lad die. And Peter said: God is not tempted nor proved, O Agrippa, but if he be loved and entreated he heareth them that are worthy. But since now my God and Lord Jesus Christ is tempted among you, who hath done so great signs and wonders by my hands to turn you from your sins -now also in the sight of all do thou, Lord, at my word, by thy power raise up him whom Simon hath slain by touching him. And Peter said unto the master of the lad: Go, take hold on his right hand, and thou shalt have him alive and walking with thee. And Agrippa the prefect ran and went to the lad and took his hand and raised him up. And all the multitude seeing it cried: One is the God, one is the God of Peter.

XXVII. In the meanwhile the widow's son also was brought upon a bed by the young men, and the people made way for them and brought them unto Peter. And Peter lifted up his eyes unto heaven and stretched forth his hands and said: O holy Father of thy Son Jesus Christ. who hast granted us thy power, that we may through thee ask and obtain, and despise all that is in the world, and follow thee only, who art seen of few and wouldest be known of many: shine thou about us, Lord, enlighten us, appear thou, raise up the son of this aged widow, which cannot help herself without her son. And I, repeating the word of Christ my Lord, say unto thee: Young man, arise and walk with thy mother so long as thou canst do her good; and thereafter shalt thou serve me after a higher sort, ministering in the lot of a deacon of the bishop (or, and of a bishop). And immediately the dead man rose up, and the multitudes saw it and marvelled, and the people cried out: Thou art God the Saviour, thou, the God of Peter, the invisible God, the Saviour. And they spake among themselves, marvelling indeed at the power of a man that called upon his Lord with a word; and they received it unto sanctification.

XXVIII. The fame of it therefore being spread throughout the city, there came the mother of a certain senator, and cast herself into the midst of the people, and fell at Peter's feet, saying: I have learned from my people that thou art a servant of the merciful God, and dost impart his grace unto all them that desire this light. Impart therefore the light unto my son, for I know that thou begrudgest none; turn not away from a matron that entreateth thee. Unto whom Peter said: Wilt thou believe on my God, by whom thy son shall be raised? And the mother said with a loud voice, weeping: I believe, O Peter, I believe! and all the people cried out: Grant the mother her son. But Peter said: Let him be brought hither before all these. And Peter turned himself to the people and said: Ye men of Rome, I also am one of yourselves, and bear a man's body and am a sinner, but have obtained mercy: look not therefore upon me as though I did by mine own power that which I do, but by the power of my Lord Jesus Christ, who is the judge of quick and dead. In him do I believe and by him am I sent, and have confidence when I call upon him to raise the dead. Go thou therefore also, O woman, and cause thy son to be brought hither and to rise again. And the woman passed through the midst of the people and went into the street, running, with great joy, and believing in her mind she came unto her house, and by means of her young men she took him up and came unto the forum. Now she bade the young men put caps [pilei, a sign that they were now freed.] on their heads, and to walk before the bier, and all that she had determined to burn upon the body of her son to be borne before his bier; and when Peter saw it he had compassion upon the dead body and upon her. And she came unto the multitude, while all bewailed her; and a great crowd of senators and matrons followed after, to behold the wonderful works of God: for this Nicostratus which was dead was exceeding noble and beloved of the senate. And they brought him and set him down before Peter. And Peter called for silence, and with a loud voice said: Ye men of Rome, let there now be a just judgement betwixt me and Simon; and judge ye whether of us two believeth in the living God, he or I. Let him raise up the body that lieth here, and believe in him as the angel of God. But if he be not able, and I call upon my God and restore the son alive unto his mother, then believe ye that this man is a sorcerer and a deceiver, which is entertained among you. And when all they heard these things, they thought that it was right which Peter had spoken, and they encouraged Simon, saying: Now, if there be aught in thee, show it openly! either overcome, or thou shall be overcome! (or, convince us, or thou shalt be convicted). Why standest thou still? Come, begin! But Simon, when he saw them all instant with him, stood silent; and thereafter, when he saw the people silent and looking upon him, Simon cried out, saying: Ye men of Rome, if ye behold the dead man arise, will ye cast Peter out of the city? And all the people said: We will not only cast him out, but on the very instant will we burn him with fire.

Then Simon went to the head of the dead man and stooped down and thrice raised himself up (or, and said thrice: Raise thyself), and showed the people that he (the dead) lifted his head and moved it, and opened his eyes and bowed himself a little unto Simon. And straightway they began to ask for wood and torches, wherewith to burn Peter. But Peter receiving strength of Christ, lifted up his voice and said unto them that cried out against him: Now see I, ye people of Rome, that ye are -I must not say fools and vain, so long as your eyes and your ears and your hearts are blinded. How long shall your understanding be darkened? see ye not that ye are bewitched, supposing that a dead man is raised, who hath not lifted himself up? It would have sufficed me, ye men of Rome, to hold my peace and die without speaking, and to leave you among the deceits of this world; but I have the chastisement of fire unquenchable before mine eyes. If therefore it seem good unto you, let the dead man speak, let him arise if he liveth, let him loose his jaw that is bound, with his hands, let him call upon his mother, let him say unto you that cry out: Wherefore cry ye? let him beckon unto us with his hand. If now ye would see that he is dead, and yourselves bewitched, let this man depart from the bier, who hath persuaded you to depart from Christ, and ye shall see that the dead man is such as ye saw him brought hither.

But Agrippa the prefect had no longer patience, but thrust away Simon with his own hands, and again the dead man lay as he was before. And the people were enraged, and turned away from the sorcery of Simon and began to cry out: Hearken, O Caesar! if now the dead riseth not, let Simon burn instead of Peter, for verily he hath blinded us. But Peter stretched forth his hand and said: O men of Rome, have patience! I say not unto you that if the lad be raised Simon shall burn; for if I say it, ye will do it. The people cried out: Against thy will, Peter, we will do it. Unto whom Peter said: If ye continue in this mind the lad shall not arise: for we know not to render evil for evil, but we have learned to love our enemies and pray for our persecutors. For if even this man can repent, it were better; for God will not remember evil. Let him come, therefore, into the light of Christ; but if he cannot, let him possess the part of his father the devil, but let not your hands be defiled. And when he had thus spoken unto the people, he went unto the lad, and before he raised him, he said to his mother: These young men whom thou hast set free in the honour of thy son, can yet serve their God when he liveth, being free; for I know that the soul of some is hurt if they shall see thy son arise and know that these shall yet be in bondage: but let them all continue free and receive their sustenance as they did before, for thy son is about to rise again; and let them be with him. And Peter looked long upon her, to see her thoughts. And the mother of the lad said: What other can I do? therefore before the prefect I say: whatsoever I was minded to burn upon the body of my son, let them possess it. And Peter said: Let the residue be distributed unto the widows. Then Peter rejoiced in soul and said in the spirit: O Lord that art merciful, Jesu Christ, show thyself unto thy Peter that calleth upon thee like as thou hast always shown him mercy and loving-kindness: and in the presence of all these which have obtained freedom, that these may become thy servants, let Nicostratus now arise. And Peter touched the lad's side and said: Arise. And the lad arose and put off his grave clothes and sat up and loosed his jaw, and asked for other raiment; and he came down from the bier and said unto Peter: I pray thee, O man of God, let us go unto our Lord Christ whom I saw speaking with me; who also showed me unto thee and said to thee: Bring him hither unto me, for he is mine. And when Peter heard this of the lad, he was strengthened yet more in soul by the help of the Lord; and Peter said unto the people: Ye men of Rome, it is thus that the dead are raised up, thus do they converse, thus do they arise and walk, and live so long time as God willeth. Now therefore, ye that have come together unto the sight, if ye turn not from these your evil ways, and from all your gods that are made with hands, and from all uncleanness and concupiscence, receive fellowship with Christ, believing, that ye may obtain everlasting life.

XXIX. And in the same hour they worshipped him as a God, falling down at his feet, and the sick whom they had at home, that he might heal them.

But the prefect seeing that so great a multitude waited upon Peter, signified to Peter that he should withdraw himself: and Peter told the people to come unto Marcellus' house. But the mother of the lad besought Peter to set foot in her house. But Peter had appointed to be with Marcellus on the Lord's day, to see the widows even as Marcellus had promised, to minister unto them with his own hands. The lad therefore that was risen again said: I depart not from

Peter. And his mother, glad and rejoicing, went unto her own house. And on the next day after the sabbath she came to Marcellus' house bringing unto Peter two thousand pieces of gold, and saying unto Peter: Divide these among the virgins of Christ which serve him. But the lad that was risen from the dead, when he saw that he had given nothing to any man, went home and opened the press and himself offered four thousand pieces of gold, saying unto Peter: Lo, I also which was raised, offer a double offering, and myself also from this day forward as a speaking sacrifice unto God.

Here begins the original Greek text as preserved in one of our two manuscripts (that at Mt. Athos). The second (Patmos) manuscript begins, as do the versions, at ch. xxxiii. The Greek and not the Latin is followed in the translation.

XXX. Now on the Lord's day as Peter discoursed unto the brethren and exhorted them unto the faith of Christ, there being present many of the senate and many knights and rich women and matrons, and being confirmed in the faith, one woman that was there, exceeding rich, which was surnamed Chryse because every vessel of hers was of gold - for from her birth she never used a vessel of silver or glass, but golden ones only- said unto Peter: Peter, thou servant of God, he whom thou callest God appeared unto me in a dream and said: Chryse, carry thou unto Peter my minister ten thousand pieces of gold; for thou owest them to him. I have therefore brought them, fearing lest some harm should be done me by him that appeared unto me, which also departed unto heaven. And so saying, she laid down the money and departed. And Peter seeing it glorified the Lord, for that they that were in need should be refreshed. Certain, therefore, of them that were there said unto him: Peter, hast thou not done ill to receive the money of her? for she is ill spoken of throughout all Rome for fornication, and because she keepeth not to one husband, yea, she even hath to do with the young men of her house. Be not therefore a partner with the table of Chryse, but let that which came from her be returned unto her. But Peter hearing it laughed and said to the brethren: What this woman is in the rest of her way of life, I know not, but in that I have received this money, I did it not foolishly; for she did pay it as a debtor unto Christ, and giveth it unto the servants of Christ: for he himself hath provided for them.

XXXI. And they brought unto him also the sick on the sabbath, beseeching that they might recover of their diseases. And many were healed that were sick of the palsy, and the gout, and fevers tertian and quartan, and of every disease of the body were they healed, believing in the name of Jesus Christ, and very many were added every day unto the grace of the Lord.

But Simon the magician, after a few days were past, promised the multitude to convict Peter that he believed not in the true God but was deceived. And when he did many lying wonders, they that were firm in the faith derided him. For in diningchambers he made certain spirits enter in, which were only an appearance, and not existing in truth. And what should I more say? though he had oft-times been convicted of sorcory, he made lame men seem whole for a little space, and blind likewise, and once he appeared to make many dead to live and move, as he did with Nicostratus (Gk. Stratonicus). But Peter followed him throughout and convicted him always unto the beholders: and when he now made a sorry figure and was derided by the people of Rome and disbelieved for that he never succeeded m the things which he promised to perform, being in such a plight at last he said to them: Men of Rome, ye think now that Peter hath prevailed over me, as more powerful, and ye pay more heed to him: ye are deceived. For to-morrow I shall forsake you, godless and impious that ye are, and fly up unto God whose Power I am, though I am become weak. Whereas, then, ye have fallen, I am He that standeth, and I shall go up to my Father and say unto him: Me also, even thy son that standeth, have they desired to pull down; but I consented not unto them, and am returned back unto myself.

XXXII. And already on the morrow a great multitude assembled at the Sacred Way to see him flying. And Peter came unto the place, having seen a vision (or, to see the sight), that he might convict him in this also; for when Simon entered into Rome, he amazed the multitudes by flying: but Peter that convicted him was then not yet living at Rome: which city he thus deceived by illusion, so that some were carried away by him (amazed at him).

So then this man standing on an high place beheld Peter and began to say: Peter, at this time when I am going up before all this people that behold me, I say unto thee: If thy God is able, whom the Jews put to death, and stoned you that were chosen of him, let him show that faith in him is faith in God, and let it appear at this time, if it be worthy of God. For I, ascending up, will show myself unto all this multitude, who I am. And behold when he was lifted up on high, and all beheld him raised up above all Rome and the temples thereof and the mountains, the faithful looked toward Peter. And Peter seeing the strangeness of the sight cried unto the Lord Jesus Christ: If thou suffer this man to accomplish that which he hath set about, now will all they that have believed on thee be offended, and the signs and wonders which thou hast given them through me will not be believed: hasten thy grace, O Lord, and let him fall from the height and be disabled; and let him not die but be brought to nought, and break his leg in three places. And he fell from the height and brake his leg in three places. Then every man cast stones at him and went away home, and thenceforth believed Peter.

But one of the friends of Simon came quickly out of the way (or arrived from a journey), Gemellus by name, of whom Simon had received much money, having a Greek woman to wife, and saw him that he had broken his leg, and said: O Simon, if the Power of God is broken to pieces, shall not that God whose Power thou art, himself be blinded? Gemellus therefore also ran and followed Peter, saying unto him: I also would be of them that believe on Christ. And Peter said: Is there any that grudgeth it, my brother? come thou and sit with us.

But Simon in his affliction found some to carry him by night on a bed from Rome unto Aricia; and he abode there a space, and was brought thence unto Terracina to one Castor that was banished from Rome upon an accusation of sorcery. And there he was sorely cut (Lat. by two physicians), and so Simon the angel of Satan came to his end.

[Here the Martyrdom proper begins in the Patmos MS. and the versions.]

XXXIII. Now Peter was in Rome rejoicing in the Lord with the brethren, and giving thanks night and day for the multitude which was brought daily unto the holy name by the grace of the Lord. And there were gathered also unto Peter the concubines of Agrippa the prefect, being four, Agrippina and Nicaria and Euphemia and Doris; and they, hearing the word concerning chastity and all the oracles of the Lord, were smitten in their souls, and agreeing together to remain pure from the bed of Agrippa they were vexed by him.

Now as Agrippa was perplexed and grieved concerning them -and he loved them greatly- he observed and sent men privily to see whither they went, and found that they went unto Peter. He said therefore unto them when they returned: That Christian hath taught you to have no dealings with me: know ye that I will both destroy you, and burn him alive. They, then, endured to suffer all manner of evil at Agrippa's hand, if only they might not suffer the passion of love, being strengthened by the might of Jesus.

XXXIV. And a certain woman which was exceeding beautiful, the wife of Albinus, Caesar's friend, by name Xanthippe, came, she also, unto Peter, with the rest of the matrons, and withdrew herself, she also, from Albinus. He therefore being mad, and loving Xanthippe, and marvelling that she would not sleep even upon the same bed with him, raged like a wild beast and would have dispatched Peter; for he knew that he was the cause of her separating from his bed. Many other women also, loving the word of chastity, separated themselves from their husbands, because they desired them to worship God in sobriety and cleanness. And whereas there was great trouble in Rome, Albinus made known his state unto Agrippa, saying to him: Either do thou avenge me of Peter that hath withdrawn my wife, or I will avenge myself. And Agrippa said: I have suffered the same at his hand, for he hath withdrawn my concubines. And Albinus said unto him: Why then tarriest thou, Agrippa? let us find him and put him to death for a dealer in curious arts, that we may have our wives again, and avenge them also which are not able to put him to death, whose wives also he hath parted from them.

XXXV. And as they considered these things, Xanthippe took knowledge of the counsel of her husband with Agrippa, and sent and showed Peter, that he might depart from Rome. And the rest of the brethren, together with Marcellus, besought him to depart. But Peter said unto them: Shall we be runaways, brethren? and they said to him: Nay, but that thou mayest yet be able to serve the Lord. And he obeyed the brethren's voice and went forth alone, saying: Let none of you come forth with me, but I will go forth alone, having changed the fashion of mine apparel. And as he went forth of the city, he saw the Lord entering into Rome. And when he saw him, he said: Lord, whither goest thou thus (or here)? And the Lord said unto him: I go into Rome to be crucified. And Peter said unto him: Lord, art thou (being) crucified again? He said unto him: Yea, Peter, I am (being) crucified again. And Peter came to himself: and having beheld the Lord ascending up into heaven, he returned to Rome, rejoicing, and glorifying the

Lord, for that he said: I am being crucified: the which was about to befall Peter.

XXXVI. He went up therefore again unto the brethren, and told them that which had been seen by him: and they lamented in soul, weeping and saying: We beseech thee, Peter, take thought for us that are young. And Peter said unto them: If it be the Lord's will, it cometh to pass, even if we will it not; but for you, the Lord is able to stablish you in his faith, and will found you therein and make you spread abroad, whom he himself hath planted, that ye also may plant others through him. But I, so long as the Lord will that I be in the flesh, resist not; and again if he take me to him I rejoice and am glad.

And while Peter thus spake, and all the brethren wept, behold four soldiers took him and led him unto Agrippa. And he in his madness (disease) commanded him to be crucified on an accusation of godlessness.

The whole multitude of the brethren therefore ran together, both of rich and poor, orphans and widows, weak and strong, desiring to see and to rescue Peter, while the people shouted with one voice, and would not be silenced: What wrong hath Peter done, O Agrippa? Wherein hath he hurt thee? tell the Romans! And others said: We fear lest if this man die, his Lord destroy us all.

And Peter when he came unto the place stilled the people and said: Ye men that are soldiers of Christ! ye men that hope in Christ! remember the signs and wonders which ye have seen wrought through me, remember the compassion of God, how many cures he hath wrought for you. Wait for him that cometh and shall reward every man according to his doings. And now be ye not bitter against Agrippa; for he is the minister of his father's working. And this cometh to pass at all events, for the Lord hath manifested unto me that which befalleth. But why delay I and draw not near unto the cross?

XXXVII. And having approached and standing by the cross he began to say: O name of the cross, thou hidden mystery! O grace ineffable that is pronounced in the name of the cross! O nature of man, that cannot be separated from God! O love (friendship) unspeakable and inseparable, that cannot be shown forth by unclean lips! I seize thee now, I that am at the end of my delivery hence (or, of my coming hither). I will declare thee, what thou art: I will not keep silence of the mystery of the cross which of old was shut and hidden from my soul. Let not the cross be unto you which hope in Christ, this which appeareth: for it is another thing, different from that which appeareth, even this passion which is according to that of Christ. And now above all, because ye that can hear are able to hear it of me, that am at the last and final hour of my life, hearken: Separate your souls from every thing that is of the senses, from every thing that appeareth, and does not exist in truth. Blind these eyes of yours, close these ears of yours, put away your doings that are seen; and ye shall perceive that which concerneth Christ, and the whole mystery of your salvation: and let thus much be said unto you that hear, as if it had not been spoken. But now it is time for thee, Peter, to deliver up thy body unto them that take it. Receive it then, ye unto whom it belongeth. I beseech you the executioners, crucify me thus, with the head downward and

not otherwise: and the reason wherefore, I will tell unto them that hear.

XXXVIII. And when they had hanged him up after the manner he desired, he began again to say: Ye men unto whom it belongeth to hear, hearken to that which I shall declare unto you at this especial time as I hang here. Learn ye the mystery of all nature, and the beginning of all things, what it was. For the first man, whose race I bear in mine appearance (or, of the race of whom I bear the likeness), fell (was borne) head downwards, and showed forth a manner of birth such as was not heretofore: for it was dead, having no motion. He, then, being pulled down -who also cast his first state down upon the earth- established this whole disposition of all things, being hanged up an image of the creation (Gk. vocation) wherein he made the things of the right hand into left hand and the left hand into right hand, and changed about all the marks of their nature, so that he thought those things that were not fair to be fair, and those that were in truth evil, to be good. Concerning which the Lord saith in a mystery: Unless ye make the things of the right hand as those of the left, and those of the left as those of the right, and those that are above as those below, and those that are behind as those that are before, ye shall not have knowedge of the kingdom.

This thought, therefore, have I declared unto you; and the figure wherein ye now see me hanging is the representation of that man that first came unto birth. Ye therefore, my beloved, and ye that hear me and that shall hear, ought to cease from your former error and return back again. For it is right to mount upon the cross of Christ, who is the word stretched out, the one and only, of whom the spirit saith: For what else is Christ, but the word, the sound of God? So that the word is the upright beam whereon I am crucified. And the sound is that which crosseth it, the nature of man. And the nail which holdeth the cross-tree unto the upright in the midst thereof is the conversion and repentance of man.

XXXIX. Now whereas thou hast made known and revealed these things unto me, O word of life, called now by me wood (or, word called now by me the tree of life), I give thee thanks, not with these lips that are nailed unto the cross, nor with this tongue by which truth and falsehood issue forth, nor with this word which cometh forth by means of art whose nature is material, but with that voice do I give thee thanks, O King, which is perceived (understood) in silence, which is not heard openly, which proceedeth not forth by organs of the body, which goeth not into ears of flesh, which is not heard of corruptible substance, which existeth not in the world, neither is sent forth upon earth, nor written in books, which is owned by one and not by another: but with this, O Jesu Christ, do I give thee thanks, with the silence of a voice, wherewith the spirit that is in me loveth thee, speaketh unto thee, seeth thee, and beseecheth thee. Thou art perceived of the spirit only, thou art unto me father, thou my mother, thou my brother, thou my friend, thou my bondsman, thou my steward: thou art the All and the All is in thee: and thou Art, and there is nought else that is save thee only.

Unto him therefore do ye also, brethren, flee, and if ye learn that in him alone ye exist, ye shall obtain those things whereof he saith unto you: 'which neither eye hath seen nor ear heard, neither have they entered into the heart of man.' We ask, therefore, for that which thou hast promised to give unto us, O thou undefiled Jesu. We praise thee, we give thee thanks, and confess to thee, glorifying thee, even we men that are yet without strength, for thou art God alone, and none other: to whom be glory now and unto all ages. Amen.

XL. And when the multitude that stood by pronounced the Amen with a great sound, together with the Amen Peter gave up his spirit unto the Lord.

And Marcellus not asking leave of any, for it was not possible, when he saw that Peter had given up the ghost, took him down from the cross with his own hands and washed him in milk and wine: and cut fine seven minae of mastic, and of myrrh and aloes and indian leaf other fifty, and perfumed (embalmed) his body and filled a coffin of marble of great price with Attic honey and laid it in his own tomb.

But Peter by night appeared unto Marcellus and said: Marcellus, hast thou heard that the Lord saith: Let the dead be buried of their own dead? And when Marcellus said: Yea, Peter said to him: That, then, which thou hast spent on the dead, thou hast lost: for thou being alive hast like a dead man cared for the dead. And Marcellus awoke and told the brethren of the appearing of Peter: and he was with them that had been stablished in the faith of Christ by Peter, himself also being stablished yet more until the coming of Paul unto Rome.

XLI. [This last chapter, and the last sentence of XL, are thought by Vouaux to be an addition by the author of i-iii, in other words by the compiler of the Greek original of the Vercelli Acts.]

But Nero, learning thereafter that Peter was departed out of this life, blamed the prefect Agrippa, because he had been put to death without his knowledge; for he desired to punish him more sorely and with greater torment, because Peter had made disciples of certain of them that served him, and had caused them to depart from him: so that he was very wrathful and for a long season spake not unto Agrippa: for he sought to destroy all them that had been made disciples by Peter. And he beheld by night one that scourged him and said unto him: Nero, thou canst not now persecute nor destroy the servants of Christ: refrain therefore thine hands from them. And so Nero, being greatly affrighted by such a vision, abstained from harming the disciples at that time when Peter also departed this life.

And thenceforth the brethren were rejoicing with one mind and exulting in the Lord, glorifying the God and Saviour (Father?) of our Lord Jesus Christ with the Holy Ghost, unto whom be glory, world without end. Amen.

THE ACTS OF JOHN

Introduction

The length of this book is given in the Stichometry of Nicephorus as 2,500 lines: the same number as for St. Matthew's Gospel. We have large portions of it in the original, and a Latin version (purged, it is important to note, of all traces of unorthodoxy) of some lost episodes, besides a few scattered fragments. These will be fitted together in what seems the most probable order.

The best edition of the Greek remains is in Bonnet, Acta Apost. Apocr. 11.1, 1898: the Latin is in Book V of the Historia Apostolica of Abdias (Fabricius, Cod. Apoer. N. T.: there is no modern edition).

The beginning of the book is lost. It probably related in some form a trial, and banishment of John to Patmos. A distinctly late Greek text printed by Bonnet (in two forms) as cc. 1-17 of his work tells how Domitian, on his accession, persecuted the Jews. They accused the Christians in a letter to him: he accordingly persecuted the Christians. He heard of John's teaching in Ephesus and sent for him: his ascetic habits on the voyage impressed his captors. He was brought before Domitian, and made to drink poison, which did not hurt him: the dregs of it killed a criminal on whom it was tried: and John revived him; he also raised a girl who was slain by an unclean spirit. Domitian, who was much impressed, banished him to Patmos. Nerva recalled him. The second text tells how he escaped shipwreck on leaving Patmos, swimming on a cork; landed at Miletus, where a chapel was built in his honour, and went to Ephesus. All this is late: but an old story, known to Tertullian and to other Latin writers, but to no Greek, said that either Domitian at Rome or the Proconsul at Ephesus cast John into a caldron of boiling oil which did him no hurt. The scene of this was eventually fixed at the Latin Gate in Rome (hence the St. John Port Latin of our calendar, May 6th). We have no detailed account of this, but it is conjectured to have been told in the early part of the Leucian Acts. If so, it is odd that no Greek writer mentions it.

Leaving for the time certain small fragments which may perhaps have preceded the extant episodes, I proceed to the first long episode (Bonnet, c. 18).

[John is going from Miletus to Ephesus.)

Text

18 Now John was hastening to Ephesus, moved thereto by a vision. Damonicus therefore, and Aristodemus his kinsman, and a certain very rich man Cleobius, and the wife of Marcellus, hardly prevailed to keep him for one day in Miletus, reposing themselves with him. And when very early in the morning they had set forth, and already about four miles of the journey were accomplished, a voice came from heaven in the hearing of all of us, saying: John, thou art about to give glory to thy Lord in Ephesus, whereof thou shalt know, thou and all the brethren that are with thee, and certain of them that are there, which shall believe by thy means. John therefore pondered, rejoicing in himself, what it should be that should befall (meet) him at Ephesus, and said: Lord, behold I go according to thy will: let that be done which thou desirest.

19 And as we drew near to the city, Lycomedes the praetor of the Ephesians, a man of large substance, met us, and falling at John's feet besought him, saying: Is thy name John? the God whom thou preachest hath sent thee to do good unto my wife, who hath been smitten with palsy now these seven days and lieth incurable. But glorify thou thy God by healing her, and have compassion on us. For as I was considering with myself what resolve to take in this matter, one stood by me and said: Lycomedes, cease from this thought which warreth against thee, for it is evil (hard): submit not thyself unto it. For I have compassion upon mine handmaid Cleopatra, and have sent from Miletus a man named John who shall raise her up and restore her to thee whole. Tarry not, therefore, thou servant of the God who hath manifested himself unto me, but hasten unto my wife who hath no more than breath. And straightway John went from the gate, with the brethren that were with him and Lycomedes, unto his house. But Cleobius said to his young men: Go ye to my kinsman Callippus and receive of him comfortable entertainment -for I am come hither with his son- that we may find all things decent.

20 Now when Lycomedes came with John into the house wherein his wife lay, he caught hold again of his feet and said: See, lord, the withering of the beauty, see the youth, see the renowned flower of my poor wife, whereat all Ephesus was wont to marvel: wretched me, I have suffered envy, I have been humbled, the eye of mine enemies hath smitten me: I have never wronged any, though I might have injured many, for I looked before to this very thing, and took care, lest I should see any evil or any such ill fortune as this. What profit, then, hath Cleopatra from my anxiety? what have I gained by being known for a pious man until this day? nay, I suffer more than the impious, in that I see thee, Cleopatra, lying in such plight. The sun in his course shall no more see me conversing with thee: I will go before thee, Cleopatra, and rid myself of life: I will not spare mine own safety though it be yet young. I will defend myself before Justice, that I have rightly deserted, for I may indict her as judging unrighteously. I will be avenged on her when I come before her as a ghost of life. I will say to her: Thou didst force me to leave the light when thou didst rob me of Cleopatra: thou didst cause me to become a corpse when thou sentest me this ill fortune: thou didst compel me to insult Providence, by cutting off my joy in life (my confidence).

21 And with yet more words Lycomedes addressing Cleopatra came near to the bed and cried aloud and lamented: but John pulled him away, and said: Cease from these lamentations and from thine unfitting words: thou must not disobey him that (?) appeared unto thee: for know that thou shalt receive thy consort again. Stand, therefore, with us that have come hither on her account and pray to the God whom thou sawest manifesting himself unto thee in dreams. What, then, is it, Lycomedes? Awake, thou also, and open thy soul. Cast off the heavy sleep from thee: beseech the Lord, entreat him for thy wife, and he will raise her up. But he fell upon the floor and lamented, fainting. [It

is evident from what follows that Lycomedes died: but the text does not say so; some words may have fallen out.]

John therefore said with tears: Alas for the fresh (new) betraying of my vision! for the new temptation that is prepared for me! for the new device of him that contriveth against me! the voice from heaven that was borne unto me in the way, hath it devised this for me? was it this that it foreshowed me should come to pass here, betraying me to this great multitude of the citizens because of Lycomedes? the man lieth without breath, and I know well that they will not suffer me to go out of the house alive. Why tarriest thou, Lord (or, what wilt thou do)? why hast thou shut off from us thy good promise? Do not, I beseech thee, Lord, do not give him cause to exult who rejoiceth in the suffering of others; give him not cause to dance who alway derideth us; but let thy holy name and thy mercy make haste. Raise up these two dead whose death is against me.

22 And even as John thus cried out, the city of the Ephesians ran together to the house of Lycomedes, hearing that he was dead. And John, beholding the great multitude that was come, said unto the Lord: Now is the time of refreshment and of confidence toward thee, O Christ; now is the time for us who are sick to have the help that is of thee, O physician who healest freely; keep thou mine entering in hither safe from derision. I beseech thee, Jesu, succour this great multitude that it may come to thee who art Lord of all things: behold the affliction, behold them that lie here. Do thou prepare, even from them that are assembled for that end, holy vessels for thy service, when they behold thy gift. For thyself hast said, O Christ, 'Ask, and it shall be given you'. We ask therefore of thee, O king, not gold, not silver, not substance, not possessions, nor aught of what is on earth and perisheth, but two souls, by whom thou shalt convert them that are here unto thy way, unto thy teaching, unto thy liberty (confidence), unto thy most excellent (or unfailing) promise: for when they perceive thy power in that those that have died are raised, they will be saved, some of them. Do thou thyself, therefore, give them hope in thee: and so go I unto Cleopatra and say: Arise in the name of Jesus Christ.

23 And he came to her and touched her face and said: Cleopatra, He saith, whom every ruler feareth, and every creature and every power, the abyss and all darkness, and unsmiling death, and the height of heaven, and the circles of hell [and the resurrection of the dead, and the sight of the blind], and the whole power of the prince of this world, and the pride of the ruler: Arise, and be not an occasion unto many that desire not to believe, or an affliction unto souls that are able to hope and to be saved. And Cleopatra straightway cried with a loud voice: I arise, master: save thou thine handmaid.

Now when she had arisen seven days, the city of the Ephesians was moved at the unlooked-for sight. And Cleopatra asked concerning her husband Lycomedes, but John said to her: Cleopatra, if thou keep thy soul unmoved and steadfast, thou shalt forthwith have Lycomedes thine husband standing here beside thee, if at least thou be not disturbed nor moved at that which hath befallen, having believed on my God, who by my means shall grant him unto thee alive. Come therefore with me into thine other bedchamber, and thou shalt behold him, a dead corpse indeed, but raised again by the power of my God.

24 And Cleopatra going with John into her bedchamber, and seeing Lycomedes dead for her sake, had no power to speak (suffered in her voice), and ground her teeth and bit her tongue, and closed her eyes, raining down tears: and with calmness gave heed to the apostle. But John had compassion on Cleopatra when he saw that she neither raged nor was beside herself, and called upon the perfect and condescending mercy, saying: Lord Jesus Christ, thou seest the pressure of sorrow, thou seest the need; thou seest Cleopatra shrieking her soul out in silence, for she constraineth within her the frenzy that cannot be borne; and I know that for Lycomedes' sake she also will die upon his body. And she said quietly to John: That have I in mind, master, and nought else.

And the apostle went to the couch whereon Lycomedes lay, and taking Cleopatra's hand he said: Cleopatra, because of the multitude that is present, and thy kinsfolk that have come in, with strong crying, say thou to thine husband: Arise and glorify the name of God, for he giveth back the dead to the dead. And she went to her husband and said to him according as she was taught, and forthwith raised him up. And he, when he arose, fell on the floor and kissed John's feet, but he raised him, saying: O man, kiss not my feet but the feet of God by whose power ye are both arisen.

25 But Lycomedes said to John: I entreat and adjure thee by the God in whose name thou hast raised us, to abide with us, together with all them that are with thee. Likewise Cleopatra also caught his feet and said the same. And John said to them: For tomorrow I will be with you. And they said to him again: We shall have no hope in thy God, but shall have been raised to no purpose, if thou abide not with us. And Cleobius with Aristodemus and Damonicus were touched in the soul and said to John: Let us abide with them, that they continue without offence towards the Lord. So he continued there with the brethren.

26 There came together therefore a gathering of a great multitude on John's account; and as he discoursed to them that were there, Lycomedes, who had a friend who was a skilful painter, went hastily to him and said to him: You see me in a great hurry to come to you: come quickly to my house and paint the man whom I show you without his knowing it. And the painter, giving some one the necessary implements and colours, said to Lycomedes: Show him to me, and for the rest have no anxiety. And Lycomedes pointed out John to the painter, and brought him near him, and shut him up in a room from which the apostle of Christ could be seen. And Lycomedes was with the blessed man, feasting on the faith and the knowledge of our God, and rejoiced yet more in the thought that he should possess him in a portrait.

27 The painter, then, on the first day made an outline of him and went away. And on the next he painted him in with his colours, and so delivered the portrait to Lycomedes to his great joy. And lie took it and set it up in his own bedchamber and hung it with garlands: so that later John, when he perceived it, said to him: My beloved child, what is it that thou always doest when thou comest in from the bath into thy bedchamber alone? do not I pray with

thee and the rest of the brethren? or is there something thou art hiding from us? And as he said this and talked jestingly with him, he went into the bedchamber, and saw the portrait of an old man crowned with garlands, and lamps and altars set before it. And he called him and said: Lycomedes, what meanest thou by this matter of the portrait? can it be one of thy gods that is painted here? for I see that thou art still living in heathen fashion. And Lycomedes answered him: My only God is he who raised me up from death with my wife: but if, next to that God, it be right that the men who have benefited us should be called gods -it is thou, father, whom I have had painted in that portrait, whom I crown and love and reverence as having become my good guide.

28 And John who had never at any time seen his own face said to him: Thou mockest me, child: am I like that in form, thy Lord? how canst thou persuade me that the portrait is like me? And Lycomedes brought him a mirror. And when he had seen himself in the mirror and looked earnestly at the portrait, he said: As the Lord Jesus Christ liveth, the portrait is like me: yet not like me, child, but like my fleshly image; for if this painter, who hath imitated this my face, desireth to draw me in a portrait, he will be at a loss, the colours that are now given to thee, and boards and plaster (?) and glue (?), and the position of my shape, and old age and youth and all things that are seen with the eye.

29 But do thou become for me a good painter, Lycomedes. Thou hast colours which he giveth thee through me, who painteth all of us for himself, even Jesus, who knoweth the shapes and appearances and postures and dispositions and types of our souls. And the colours wherewith I bid thee paint are these: faith in God, knowledge, godly fear, friendship, communion, meekness, kindness, brotherly love, purity, simplicity, tranquillity, fearlessness, griefiessness, sobriety, and the whole band of colours that painteth the likeness of thy soul, and even now raiseth up thy members that were cast down, and levelleth them that were lifted up, and tendeth thy bruises, and healeth thy wounds, and ordereth thine hair that was disarranged, and washeth thy face, and chasteneth thine eyes, and purgeth thy bowels, and emptieth thy belly, and cutteth off that which is beneath it; and in a word, when the whole company and mingling of such colours is come together, into thy soul, it shall present it to our Lord Jesus Christ undaunted, whole (unsmoothed), and firm of shape. But this that thou hast now done is childish and imperfect: thou hast drawn a dead likeness of the dead.

There need be no portion of text lost at this point: but possibly some few sentences have been omitted. The transition is abrupt and the new episode has not, as elsewhere, a title of its own.

30 And he commanded Verus (Berus), the brother that ministered to him, to gather the aged women that were in all Ephesus, and made ready, he and Cleopatra and Lycomedes, all things for the care of them. Verus, then, came to John, saying: Of the aged women that are here over threescore years old I have found four only sound in body, and of the rest some . . . . (a word gone) and some palsied and others sick. And when he heard that, John kept silence for a long time, and rubbed his face and said: O the slackness (weakness) of them that dwell in Ephesus! O the state of dissolution, and the weakness toward God! O devil, that hast so long mocked the faithful in Ephesus! Jesus, who giveth me grace and the gift to have my confidence in him, saith to me in silence: Send after the old women that are sick and come (be) with them into the theatre, and through me heal them: for there are some of them that will come unto this spectacle whom by these healings I will convert and make them useful for some end.

31 Now when all the multitude was come together to Lycomedes, he dismissed them on John's behalf, saying: Tomorrow come ye to the theatre, as many as desire to see the power of God. And the multitude, on the morrow, while it was yet night, came to the theatre: so that the proconsul also heard of it and hasted and took his sent with all the people. And a certain praetor, Andromeus, who was the first of the Ephesians at that time, put it about that John had promised things impossible and incredible: But if, said he, he is able to do any such thing as I hear, let him come into the public theatre, when it is open, naked, and holding nothing in his hands, neither let him name that magical name which I have heard him utter.

32 John therefore, having heard this and being moved by. these words, commanded the aged women to be brought into the theatre: and when they were all brought into the midst, some of them upon beds and others lying in a deep sleep, and all the city had run together, and a great silence was made, John opened his mouth and began to say:

33 Ye men of Ephesus, learn first of all wherefore I am visiting in your city, or what is this great confidence which I have towards you, so that it may become manifest to this general assembly and to all of you (or, so that I manifest myself to). I have been sent, then, upon a mission which is not of man's ordering, and not upon any vain journey; neither am I a merchant that make bargains or exchanges; but Jesus Christ whom I preach, being compassionate and kind, desireth by my means to convert all of you who are held in unbelief and sold unto evil lusts, and to deliver you from error; and by his power will I confound even the unbelief of your praetor, by raising up them that lie before you, whom ye all behold, in what plight and in what sicknesses they are. And to do this (to confound Andronicus) is not possible for me if they perish: therefore shall they be healed.

34 But this first I have desired to sow in your ears, even that ye should take care for your souls -on which account I am come unto you- and not expect that this time will be for ever, for it is but a moment, and not lay up treasures upon the earth where all things do fade. Neither think that when ye have gotten children ye can rest upon them (?), and try not for their sakes to defraud and overreach. Neither, ye poor, be vexed if ye have not wherewith to minister unto pleasures; for men of substance when they are diseased call you happy. Neither, ye rich, rejoice that ye have much money, for by possessing these things ye provide for yourselves grief that ye cannot be rid of when ye lose them; and besides, while it is with you, ye are afraid lest some one attack you on account of it.

35 Thou also that art puffed up because of the shapeliness of thy body, and art of an high look, shalt see the end of the promise thereof in the grave; and thou that rejoicest in

adultery, know that both law and nature avenge it upon thee, and before these, conscience; and thou, adulteress, that art an adversary of the law, knowest not whither thou shalt come in the end. And thou that sharest not with the needy, but hast monies laid up, when thou departest out of this body and hast need of some mercy when thou burnest in fire, shalt have none to pity thee; and thou the wrathful and passionate, know that thy conversation is like the brute beasts; and thou, drunkard and quarreller, learn that thou losest thy senses by being enslaved to a shameful and dirty desire.

36 Thou that rejoicest in gold and delightest thyself with ivory and jewels, when night falleth, canst thou behold what thou lovest? thou that art vanquished by soft raiment, and then leavest life, will those things profit thee in the place whither thou goest? And let the murderer know that the condign punishment is laid up for him twofold after his departure hence. Likewise also thou poisoner, sorcerer, robber, defrauder, sodomite, thief, and as many as are of that band, ye shall come at last, as your works do lead you, unto unquenchable fire, and utter darkness, and the pit of punishment, and eternal threatenings. Wherefore, ye men of Ephesus, turn yourselves, knowing this also, that kings, rulers, tyrants, boasters, and they that have conquered in wars, stripped of all things when they depart hence, do suffer pain, lodged in eternal misery.

37 And having thus said, John by the power of God healed all the diseases.

This sentence must be an abridgement of a much longer narration. The manuscript indicates no break at this point: but we must suppose a not inconsiderable loss of text. For one thing, Andronicus, who is here an unbeliever, appears as a convert in the next few lines. Now he is, as we shall see later, the husband of an eminent believer, Drusiana; and his and her conversion will have been told at some length; and I do not doubt that among other things there was a discourse of John persuading them to live in continence.

37 (continued.) Now the brethren from Miletus said unto John: We have continued a long time at Ephesus; if it seem good to thee, let us go also to Smyrna; for we hear already that the mighty works of God have reached it also. And Andronicus said to them: Whensoever the teacher willeth, then let us go. But John said: Let us first go unto the temple of Artemis, for perchance there also, if we show ourselves, the servants of the Lord will be found.

38 After two days, then, was the birthday of the idol temple. John therefore, when all were clad in white, alone put on black raiment and went up into the temple. And they took him and essayed to kill him. But John said: Ye are mad to set upon me, a man that is the servant of the only God. And he gat him up upon an high pedestal and said unto them:

39 Ye run hazard, men of Ephesus, of being like in character to the sea: every river that floweth in and every spring that runneth down, and the rains, and waves that press upon each other, and torrents full of rocks are made salt together by the bitter telementt (MS. promise!) that is therein. So ye also remaining unchanged unto this day toward true godliness are become corrupted by your

ancient rites of worship. How many wonders and healings of diseases have ye seen wrought through me? And yet are ye blinded in your hearts and cannot recover sight. What is it, then, O men of Ephesus? I have adventured now and come up even into this your idol temple. I will convict you of being most godless, and dead from the understanding of mankind. Behold, I stand here: ye all say that ye have a goddess, even Artemis: pray then unto her that I alone may die; or else I only, if ye are not able to do this, will call upon mine own god, and for your unbelief I will cause every one of you to die.

40 But they who had beforetime made trial of him and had seen dead men raised up, cried out: Slay us not so, we beseech thee, John. We know that thou canst do it. And John said to them: If then ye desire not to die, let that which ye worship be confounded, and wherefore it is confounded, that ye also may depart from your ancient error. For now is it time that either ye be converted by my God, or I myself die by your goddess; for I will pray in your presence and entreat my God that mercy be shown unto you.

41 And having so said he prayed thus: O God that art God above all that are called gods, that until this day hast been set at nought in the city of the Ephesians; that didst put into my mind to come into this place, whereof I never thought; that dost convict every manner of worship by turning men unto thee; at whose name every idol fleeth and every evil spirit and every unclean power; now also by the flight of the evil spirit here at thy name, even of him that deceiveth this great multitude, show thou thy mercy in this place, for they have been made to err.

42 And as John spake these things, immediately the altar of Artemis was parted into many pieces, and all the things that were dedicated in the temple fell, and [MS. that which seemed good to him] was rent asunder, and likewise of the images of the gods more than seven. And the half of the temple fell down, so that the priest was slain at one blow by the falling of the (?roof, ? beam). The multitude of the Ephesians therefore cried out: One is the God of John, one is the God that hath pity on us, for thou only art God: now are we turned to thee, beholding thy marvellous works! have mercy on us, O God, according to thy will, and save us from our great error! And some of them, lying on their faces, made supplication, and some kneeled and besought, and some rent their clothes and wept, and others tried to escape.

43 But John spread forth his hands, and being uplifted in soul, said unto the Lord: Glory be to thee, my Jesus, the only God of truth, for that thou dost gain (receive) thy servants by divers devices. And having so said, he said to the people: Rise up from the floor, ye men of Ephesus, and pray to my God, and recognize the invisible power that cometh to manifestation, and the wonderful works which are wrought before your eyes. Artemis ought to have succoured herself: her servant ought to have been helped of her and not to have died. Where is the power of the evil spirit? where are her sacrifices? where her birthdays? where her festivals? where are the garlands? where is all that sorcery and the poisoning (witchcraft) that is sister thereto?

44 But the people rising up from off the floor went hastily and cast down the rest of the idol temple, crying: The God of John only do we know, and him hereafter do we worship, since he hath had mercy upon us! And as John came down from thence, much people took hold of him, saying: Help us, O John! Assist us that do perish in vain! Thou seest our purpose: thou seest the multitude following thee and hanging upon thee in hope toward thy God. We have seen the way wherein we went astray when we lost him: we have seen our gods that were set up in vain: we have seen the great and shameful derision that is come to them: but suffer us, we pray thee, to come unto thine house and to be succoured without hindrance. Receive us that are in bewilderment.

45 And John said to them: Men (of Ephesus), believe that for your sakes I have continued in Ephesus, and have put off my journey unto Smyrna and to the rest of the cities, that there also the servants of Christ may turn to him. But since I am not yet perfectly assured concerning you, I have continued praying to my God and beseeching him that I should then depart from Ephesus when I have confirmed you in the faith: and whereas I see that this is come to pass and yet more is being fulfilled, I will not leave you until I have weaned you like children from the nurse's milk, and have set you upon a firm rock.

46 John therefore continued with them, receiving them in the house of Andromeus. And one of them that were gathered laid down the dead body of the priest of Artemis before the door [of the temple], for he was his kinsman, and came in quickly with the rest, saying nothing of it. John, therefore, after the discourse to the brethren, and the prayer and the thanksgiving (eucharist) and the laying of hands upon every one of the congregation, said by the spirit: There is one here who moved by faith in God hath laid down the priest of Artemis before the gate and is come in, and in the yearning of his soul, taking care first for himself, hath thought thus in himself: It is better for me to take thought for the living than for my kinsman that is dead: for I know that if I turn to the Lord and save mine own soul, John will not deny to raise up the dead also. And John arising from his place went to that into which that kinsman of the priest who had so thought was entered, and took him by the hand and said: Hadst thou this thought when thou camest unto me, my child? And he, taken with trembling and affright, said: Yes, lord, and cast himself at his feet. And John said: Our Lord is Jesus Christ, who will show his power in thy dead kinsman by raising him up.

47 And he made the young man rise, and took his hand and said: It is no great matter for a man that is master of great mysteries to continue wearying himself over small things: or what great thing is it to rid men of diseases of the body? And yet holding the young man by the hand he said: I say unto thee, child, go and raise the dead thyself, saying nothing but this only: John the servant of God saith to thee, Arise. And the young man went to his kinsman and said this only -and much people was with him- and entered in unto John, bringing him alive. And John, when he saw him that was raised, said: Now that thou art raised, thou dost not truly live, neither art partaker or heir of the true life: wilt thou belong unto him by whose name and power thou wast raised? And now believe, and thou shall live unto

all ages. And he forthwith believed upon the Lord Jesus and thereafter clave unto John.

[Another manuscript (Q. Paris Gr. 1468, of the eleventh century) has another form of this story. John destroys the temple of Artemis, and then 'we' go to Smyrna and all the idols are broken: Bucolus, Polycarp, and Andronicus are left to preside over the district. There were there two priests of Artemis, brothers, and one died. The raising is told much as in the older text, but more shortly.

'We' remained four years in the region, which was wholly converted, and then returned to Ephesus.]

48 Now on the next day John, having seen in a dream that he must walk three miles outside the gates, neglected it not, but rose up early and set out upon the way, together with the brethren.

And a certain countryman who was admonished by his father not to take to himself the wife of a fellow labourer of his who threatened to kill him -this young man would not endure the admonition of his father, but kicked him and left him without speech (sc. dead). And John, seeing what had befallen, said unto the Lord: Lord, was it on this account that thou didst bid me come out hither to-day?

49 But the young man, beholding the violence (sharpness) of death, and looking to be taken, drew out the sickle that was in his girdle and started to run to his own abode; and John met him and said: Stand still, thou most shameless devil, and tell me whither thou runnest bearing a sickle that thirsteth for blood. And the young man was troubled and cast the iron on the ground, and said to him: I have done a wretched and barbarous deed and I know it, and so I determined to do an evil yet worse and more cruel, even to die myself at once. For because my father was alway curbing me to sobriety, that I should live without adultery, and chastely, I could not endure him to reprove me, and I kicked him and slew him, and when I saw what was done, I was hasting to the woman for whose sake I became my father's murderer, with intent to kill her and her husband, and myself last of all: for I could not bear to be seen of the husband of the woman, and undergo the judgement of death.

50 And John said to him: That I may not by going away and leaving you in danger give place to him that desireth to laugh and sport with thee, come thou with me and show me thy father, where he lieth. And if I raise him up for thee, wilt thou hereafter abstain from the woman that is become a snare to thee. And the young man said: If thou raisest up my father himself for me alive, and if I see him whole and continuing in life, I will hereafter abstain from her.

51 And while he was speaking, they came to the place where the old man lay dead, and many passers-by were standing near thereto. And John said to the youth: Thou wretched man, didst thou not spare even the old age of thy father? And he, weeping and tearing his hair, said that he repented thereof; and John the servant of the Lord said: Thou didst show me I was to set forth for this place, thou knewest that this would come to pass, from whom nothing can be hid of things done in life, that givest me power to

work every cure and healing by thy will: now also give me this old man alive, for thou seest that his murderer is become his own judge: and spare him, thou only Lord, that spared not his father (because he) counselled him for the best.

52 And with these words he came near to the old man and said: My Lord will not be weak to spread out his kind pity and his condescending mercy even unto thee: rise up therefore and give glory to God for the work that is come to pass at this moment. And the old man said: I arise, Lord. And he rose and sat up and said: I was released from a terrible life and had to bear the insults of my son, dreadful and many, and his want of natural affection, and to what end hast thou called me back, O man of the living God? (And John answered him: If) thou art raised only for the same end, it were better for thee to die; but raise thyself unto better things. And he took him and led him into the city, preaching unto him the grace of God, so that before he entered the gate the old man believed.

53 But the young man, when he beheld the unlooked-for raising of his father, and the saving of himself, took a sickle and mutilated himself, and ran to the house wherein he had his adulteress, and reproached her, saying: For thy sake I became the murderer of my father and of you two and of myself: there thou hast that which is alike guilty of all. For on me God hath had mercy, that I should know his power.

54 And he came back and told John in presence of the brethren what he had done. But John said to him: He that put it into thine heart, young man, to kill thy father and become the adulterer of another man's wife, the same made thee think it a right deed to take away also the unruly members. But thou shouldest have done away, not with the place of sin, but the thought which through those members showed itself harmful: for it is not the instruments that are injurious, but the unseen springs by which every shameful emotion is stirred and cometh to light. Repent therefore, my child, of this fault, and having learnt the wiles of Satan thou shalt have God to help thee in all the necessities of thy soul. And the young man kept silence and attended, having repented of his former sins, that he should obtain pardon from the goodness of God: and he did not separate from John.

55 When, then, these things had been done by him in the city of the Ephesians, they of Smyrna sent unto him saying: We hear that the God whom thou preachest is not envious, and hath charged thee not to show partiality by abiding in one place. Since, then, thou art a preacher of such a God, come unto Smyrna and unto the other cities, that we may come to know thy God, and having known him may have our hope in him.

[Q has the above story also, and continues with an incident which is also quoted in a different form (and not as from these Acts) by John Cassian. Q has it thus:

Now one day as John was seated, a partridge flew by and came and played in the dust before him; and John looked on it and wondered. And a certain priest came, who was one of his hearers, and came to John and saw the partridge playing in the dust before him, and was offended in himself and said: Can such and so great a man take pleasure in a partridge playing in the dust? But John perceiving in the spirit the thought of him, said to him: It were better for thee also, my child, to look at a partridge playing in the dust and not to defile thyself with shameful and profane practices: for he who awaiteth the conversion and repentance of all men hath brought thee here on this account: for I have no need of a partridge playing in the dust. For the partridge is thine own soul.

Then the elder, hearing this and seeing that he was not bidden, but that the apostle of Christ had told him all that was in his heart, fell on his face on the earth and cried aloud, saying: Now know I that God dwelleth in thee, O blessed John! for he that tempteth thee tempteth him that cannot be tempted. And he entreated him to pray for him. And he instructed him and delivered him the rules (canons) and let him go to his house, glorifying God that is over all.

Cassian, Collation XXIV. 21, has it thus:

It is told that the most blessed Evangelist John, when he was gently stroking a partridge with his hands, suddenly saw one in the habit of a hunter coming to him. He wondered that a man of such repute and fame should demean himself to such small and humble amusements, and said: Art thou that John whose eminent and widespread fame hath enticed me also with great desire to know thee? Why then art thou taken up with such mean amusements? The blessed John said to him: What is that which thou carriest in thy hands? A bow, said he. And why, said he, dost thou not bear it about always stretched? He answered him: I must not, lest by constant bending the strength of its vigour be wrung and grow soft and perish, and when there is need that the arrows be shot with much strength at some beast, the strength being lost by excess of continual tension, a forcible blow cannot be dealt. Just so, said the blessed John, let not this little and brief relaxation of my mind offend thee, young man, for unless it doth sometimes ease and relax by some remission the force of its tension, it will grow slack through unbroken rigour and will not be able to obey the power of the Spirit.

The only common point of the two stories is that St. John amuses himself with a partridge, and a spectator thinks it unworthy of him. The two morals differ wholly. The amount of text lost here is of quite uncertain length. It must have told of the doings at Smyrna, and also, it appears, at Laodicca (see the title of the next section). One of the episodes must have been the conversion of a woman of evil life (see below, 'the harlot that was chaste ')-]

Our best manuscript prefixes a title to the next section:

From Laodicca to Ephesus the second time.

58 Now when some long time had passed, and none of the brethren had been at any time grieved by John, they were then grieved because he had said: Brethren, it is now time for me to go to Ephesus (for so have I agreed with them that dwell there) lest they become slack, now for a long time having no man to confirm them. But all of you must have your minds steadfast towards God, who never forsaketh us.

But when they heard this from him, the brethren lamented because they were to be parted from him. And John said: Even if I be parted from you, yet Christ is always with you: whom if ye love purely ye will have his fellowship without reproach, for if he be loved, he preventeth (anticipateth) them that love him.

59 And having so said, and bidden farewell to them, and left much money with the brethren for distribution, he went forth unto Ephesus, while all the brethren lamented and groaned. And there accompanied him, of Ephesus, both Andronicus and Drusiana and Lycomedes and Cleobius and their families. And there followed him Aristobula also, who had heard that her husband Tertullus had died on the way, and Aristippus with Xenophon, and the harlot that was chaste, and many others, whom he exhorted at all times to cleave to the Lord, and they would no more be parted from him.

60 Now on the first day we arrived at a deserted inn, and when we were at a loss for a bed for John, we saw a droll matter. There was one bedstead lying somewhere there without coverings, whereon we spread the cloaks which we were wearing, and we prayed him to lie down upon it and rest, while the rest of us all slept upon the floor. But he when he lay down was troubled by the bugs, and as they continued to become yet more troublesome to him, when it was now about the middle of the night, in the hearing of us all he said to them: I say unto you, O bugs, behave yourselves, one and all, and leave your abode for this night and remain quiet in one place, and keep your distance from the servants of God. And as we laughed, and went on talking for some time, John addressed himself to sleep; and we, talking low, gave him no disturbance (or, thanks to him we were not disturbed).

61 But when the day was now dawning I arose first, and with me Verus and Andronicus, and we saw at the door of the house which we had taken a great number of bugs standing, and while we wondered at the great sight of them, and all the brethren were roused up because of them, John continued sleeping. And when he was awaked we declared to him what we had seen. And he sat up on the bed and looked at them and said: Since ye have well behaved yourselves in hearkening to my rebuke, come unto your place. And when he had said this, and risen from the bed, the bugs running from the door hasted to the bed and climbed up by the legs thereof and disappeared into the joints. And John said again: This creature hearkened unto the voice of a man, and abode by itself and was quiet and trespassed not; but we which hear the voice and commandments of God disobey and are light-minded: and for how long?

62 After these things we came to Ephesus: and the brethren there, who had for a long time known that John was coming, ran together to the house of Andronicus (where also he came to lodge), handling his feet and laying his hands upon their own faces and kissing them (and many rejoiced even to touch his vesture, and were healed by touching the clothes of the holy apostle. [So the Latin, which has this section; the Greek has: so that they even touched his garments).]

63 And whereas there was great love and joy unsurpassed among the brethren, a certain one, a messenger of Satan, became enamoured of Drusiana, though he saw and knew that she was the wife of Andronicus. To whom many said: It is not possible for thee to obtain that woman, seeing that for a long time she has even separated herself from her husband for godliness' sake. Art thou only ignorant that Andronicus, not being aforetime that which now he is, a God-fearing man, shut her up in a tomb, saying: Either I must have thee as the wife whom I had before, or thou shalt die. And she chose rather to die than to do that foulness. If, then, she would not consent, for godliness' sake, to cohabit with her lord and husband, but even persuaded him to be of the same mind as herself, will she consent to thee desiring to be her seducer? depart from this madness which hath no rest in thee: give up this deed which thou canst not bring to accomplishment.

64 But his familiar friends saying these things to him did not convince him, but with shamelessness he courted her with messages; and when he learnt the insults and disgraces which she returned, he spent his life in melancholy (or better, she, when she learnt of this disgrace and insult at his hand, spent her life in heaviness). And after two days Drusiana took to her bed from heaviness, and was in a fever and said: Would that I had not now come home to my native place, I that have become an offence to a man ignorant of godliness! for if it were one who was filled with the word of God, he would not have gone to such a pitch of madness. But now (therefore) Lord, since I am become the occasion of a blow unto a soul devoid of knowledge, set me free from this chain and remove me unto thee quickly. And in the presence of John, who knew nothing at all of such a matter, Drusiana departed out of life not wholly happy, yea, even troubled because of the spiritual hurt of the man.

65 But Andronicus, grieved with a secret grief, mourned in his soul, and wept openly, so that John checked him often and said to him: Upon a better hope hath Drusiana removed out of this unrighteous life. And Andronicus answered him: Yea, I am persuaded of it, O John, and I doubt not at all in regard of trust in my God: but this very thing do I hold fast, that she departed out of life pure.

66 And when she was carried forth, John took hold on Andronicus, and now that he knew the cause, he mourned more than Andronicus. And he kept silence, considering the provocation of the adversary, and for a space sat still. Then, the brethren being gathered there to hear what word he would speak of her that was departed, he began to say:

67 When the pilot that voyageth, together with them that sail with him, and the ship herself, arriveth in a calm and stormless harbour, then let him say that he is safe. And the husbandman that hath committed the seed to the earth, and toiled much in the care and protection of it, let him then take rest from his labours, when he layeth up the seed with manifold increase in his barns. Let him that enterpriseth to run in the course, then exult when he beareth home the prize. Let him that inscribeth his name for the boxing, then boast himself when he receiveth the crowns: and so in succession is it with all contests and crafts, when they do not fail in the end, but show themselves to be like that which they promised (corrupt).

68 And thus also I think is it with the faith which each one of us practiseth, that it is then discerned whether it be indeed true, when it continueth like itself even until the end of life. For many obstacles fall into the way, and prepare disturbance for the minds of men: care, children, parents, glory, poverty, flattery, prime of life, beauty, conceit, lust, wealth, anger, uplifting, slackness, envy, jealousy, neglect, fear, insolence, love, deceit, money, pretence, and other such obstacles, as many as there are in this life: as also the pilot sailing a prosperous course is opposed by the onset of contrary winds and a great storm and mighty waves out of calm, and the husbandman by untimely winter and blight and creeping things rising out of the earth, and they that strive in the games 'just do not win', and they that exercise crafts are hindered by the divers difficulties of them.

69 But before all things it is needful that the believer should look before at his ending and understand it in what manner it will come upon him, whether it will be vigorous and sober and without any obstacle, or disturbed and clinging to the things that are here, and bound down by desires. So is it right that a body should be praised as comely when it is wholly stripped, and a general as great when he hath accomplished every promise of the war, and a physician as excellent when he hath succeeded in every cure, and a soul as full of faith and worthy (or receptive) of God when it hath paid its promise in full: not that soul which began well and was dissolved into all the things of this life and fell away, nor that which is numb, having made an effort to attain to better things, and then is borne down to temporal things, nor that which hath longed after the things of time more than those of eternity, nor that which exchangeth those that endure not, nor that which hath honoured the works of dishonour that deserve shame, nor that which taketh pledges of Satan, nor that which hath received the serpent into its own house, nor that which suffereth reproach for God's sake and then is [not] ashamed, nor that which with the mouth saith yea, but indeed approveth not itself: but that which hath prevailed not to be made weak by foul pleasure, not to be overcome by light-mindedness, not to be caught by the bait of love of money, not to be betrayed by vigour of body or wrath.

70 And as John was discoursing yet further unto the brethren that they should despise temporal things in respect of the eternal, he that was enamoured of Drusiana, being inflamed with an horrible lust and possession of the many-shaped Satan, bribed the steward of Andronicus who was a lover of money with a great sum: and he opened the tomb and gave him opportunity to wreak the forbidden thing upon the dead body. Not having succeeded with her when alive, he was still importunate after her death to her body, and said: If thou wouldst not have to do with me while thou livedst, I will outrage thy corpse now thou art dead. With this design, and having managed for himself the wicked act by means of the abominable steward, he rushed with him to the sepulchre; they opened the door and began to strip the grave-clothes from the corpse, saying: What art thou profited, poor Drusiana? couldest thou not have done this in life, which perchance would not have grieved thee, hadst thou done it willingly?

71 And as these men were speaking thus, and only the accustomed shift now remained on her body, a strange spectacle was seen, such as they deserve to suffer who do such deeds. A serpent appeared from some quarter and dealt the steward a single bite and slew him: but the young man it did not strike; but coiled about his feet, hissing terribly, and when he fell mounted on his body and sat upon him.

72 Now on the next day John came, accompanied by Andronicus and the brethren, to the sepulchre at dawn, it being now the third day from Drusiana's death, that we might break bread there. And first, when they set out, the keys were sought for and could not be found; but John said to Andronicus: It is quite right that they should be lost, for Drusiana is not in the sepulchre; nevertheless, let us go, that thou mayest not be neglectful, and the doors shall be opened of themselves, even as the Lord hath done for us many such things.

73 And when we were at the place, at the commandment of the master, the doors were opened, and we saw by the tomb of Drusiana a beautiful youth, smiling: and John, when he saw him, cried out and said: Art thou come before us hither too, beautiful one? and for what cause? And we heard a voice saying to him: For Drusiana's sake, whom thou art to raise up-for I was within a little of finding her - and for his sake that lieth dead beside her tomb. And when the beautiful one had said this unto John he went up into the heavens in the sight of us all. And John, turning to the other side of the sepulchre, saw a young man-even Callimachus, one of the chief of the Ephesians-and a huge serpent sleeping upon him, and the steward of Andronicus, Fortunatus by name, lying dead. And at the sight of the two he stood perplexed, saying to the brethren: What meaneth such a sight? or wherefore hath not the Lord declared unto me what was done here, he who hath never neglected me?

74 And Andronicus seeing those corpses, leapt up and went to Drusiana's tomb, and seeing her lying in her shift only, said to John: I understand what has happened, thou blessed servant of God, John. This Callimachus was enamoured of my sister; and because he never won her, though he often assayed it, he hath bribed this mine accursed steward with a great sum, perchance designing, as now we may see, to fulfil by his means the tragedy of his conspiracy, for indeed Callimachus avowed this to many, saying: If she will not consent to me when living, she shall be outraged when dead. And it may be, master, that the beautiful one knew it and suffered not her body to be insulted, and therefore have these died who made that attempt. And can it be that the voice that said unto thee, 'Raise up Drusiana', foreshowed this? because she departed out of this life in sorrow of mind. But I believe him that said that this is one of the men that have gone astray; for thou wast bidden to raise him up: for as to the other, I know that he is unworthy of salvation. But this one thing I beg of thee: raise up Callimachus first, and he will confess to us what is come about.

75 And John, looking upon the body, said to the venomous beast: Get thee away from him that is to be a servant of Jesus Christ; and stood up and prayed over him thus: O God whose name is glorified by us, as of right: O God who subduest every injurious force: O God whose will is accomplished, who alway hearest us: now also let thy gift be accomplished in this young man; and if there be any dispensation to be wrought through him, manifest it unto

us when he is raised up. And straightway the young man rose up, and for a whole hour kept silence.

76 But when he came to his right senses, John asked of him about his entry into the sepulchre, what it meant, and learning from him that which Andronicus had told him, namely, that he was enamoured of Drusiana, John inquired of him again if he had fulfilled his foul intent, to insult a body full of holiness. And he answered him: How could I accomplish it when this fearful beast struck down Fortunatus at a blow in my sight: and rightly, since he encouraged my frenzy, when I was already cured of that unreasonable and horrible madness: but me it stopped with affright, and brought me to that plight in which ye saw me before I arose. And another thing yet more wondrous I will tell thee, which yet went nigh to slay and was within a little of making me a corpse. When my soul was stirred up with folly and the uncontrollable malady was troubling me, and I had now torn away the grave-clothes in which she was clad, and I had then come out of the grave and laid them as thou seest, I went again to my unholy work: and I saw a beautiful youth covering her with his mantle, and from his eyes sparks of light came forth unto her eyes; and he uttered words to me, saying: Callimachus, die that thou mayest live. Now who he was I knew not, O servant of God; but that now thou hast appeared here, I recognize that he was an angel of God, that I know well; and this I know of a truth that it is a true God that is proclaimed by thee, and of it I am persuaded. But I beseech thee, be not slack to deliver me from this calamity and this fearful crime, and to present me unto thy God as a man deceived with a shameful and foul deceit. Beseeching help therefore of thee, I take hold on thy feet. I would become one of them that hope in Christ, that the voice may prove true which said to me, 'Die that thou mayest live': and that voice hath also fulfilled its effect, for he is dead, that faithless, disorderly, godless one, and I have been raised by thee, I who will be faithful, God-fearing, knowing the truth, which I entreat thee may be shown me by thee.

77 And John, filled with great gladness and perceiving the whole spectacle of the salvation of man, said: What thy power is, Lord Jesu Christ, I know not, bewildered as I am at thy much compassion and boundless long-suffering. O what a greatness that came down into bondage! O unspeakable liberty brought into slavery by us! O incomprehensible glory that is come unto us! thou that hast kept the dead tabernacle safe from insult; that hast redeemed the man that stained himself with blood and chastened the soul of him that would defile the corruptible body; Father that hast had pity and compassion on the man that cared not for thee; We glorify thee, and praise and bless and thank thy great goodness and long-suffering, O holy Jesu, for thou only art God, and none else: whose is the might that cannot be conspired against, now and world without end. Amen.

78 And when he had said this John took Callimachus and saluted (kissed) him, saying: Glory be to our God, my child, who hath had mercy on thee, and made me worthy to glorify his power, and thee also by a good course to depart from that thine abominable madness and drunkenness, and hath called thee unto his own rest and unto renewing of life.

79 But Andronicus, beholding the dead Callimachus raised, besought John, with the brethren, to raise up Drusiana also, saying: O John, let Drusiana arise and spend happily that short space (of life) which she gave up through grief about Callimachus, when she thought she had become a stumbling block to him: and when the Lord will, he shall take her again to himself. And John without delay went unto her tomb and took her hand and said: Upon thee that art the only God do I call, the more than great, the unutterable, the incomprehensible: unto whom every power of principalities is subjected: unto whom all authority boweth: before whom all pride falleth down and keepeth silence: whom devils hearing of tremble: whom all creation perceiving keepeth its bounds. Let thy name be glorified by us, and raise up Drusiana, that Callimachus may yet more be confirmed unto thee who dispensest that which unto men is without a way and impossible, but to thee only possible, even salvation and resurrection: and that Drusiana may now come forth in peace, having about her not any the least hindrance -now that the young man is turned unto thee- in her course toward thee.

80 And after these words John said unto Drusiana: Drusiana, arise. And she arose and came out of the tomb; and when she saw herself in her shift only, she was perplexed at the thing, and learned the whole accurately from Andronicus, the while John lay upon his face, and Callimachus with voice and tears glorified God, and she also rejoiced, glorifying him in like manner.

81 And when she had clothed herself, she turned and saw Fortunatus lying, and said unto John: Father, let this man also rise, even if he did assay to become my betrayer. But Callimachus, when he heard her say that, said: Do not, I beseech thee, Drusiana, for the voice which I heard took no thought of him, but declared concerning thee only, and I saw and believed: for if he had been good, perchance God would have had mercy on him also and would have raised him by means of the blessed John: he knew therefore that the man was come to a bad end [Lat. he judged him worthy to die whom he did not declare worthy to rise again]. And John said to him: We have not learned, my child, to render evil for evil: for God, though we have done much ill and no good toward him, hath not given retribution unto us, but repentance, and though we were ignorant of his name he did not neglect us but had mercy on us, and when we blasphemed him, he did not punish but pitied us, and when we disbelieved him he bore us no grudge, and when we persecuted his brethren he did not recompense us evil but put into our minds repentance and abstinence from evil, and exhorted us to come unto him, as he hath thee also, my son Callimachus, and not remembering thy former evil hath made thee his servant, waiting upon his mercy. Wherefore if thou allowest not me to raise up Fortunatus, it is for Drusiana so to do.

82 And she, delaying not, went with rejoicing of spirit and soul unto the body of Fortunatus and said: Jesu Christ, God of the ages, God of truth, that hast granted me to see wonders and signs, and given to me to become partaker of thy name; that didst breathe thyself into me with thy many-shaped countenance, and hadst mercy on me in many ways; that didst protect me by thy great goodness when I was oppressed by Andronicus that was of old my husband; that didst give me thy servant Andronicus to be my brother;

that hast kept me thine handmaid pure unto this day; that didst raise me up by thy servant John, and when I was raised didst show me him that was made to stumble free from stumbling; that hast given me perfect rest in thee, and lightened me of the secret madness; whom I have loved and affectioned: I pray thee, O Christ, refuse not thy Drusiana that asketh thee to raise up Fortunatus, even though he assayed to become my betrayer.

83 And taking the hand of the dead man she said: Rise up, Fortunatus, in the name of our Lord Jesus Christ. And Fortunatus arose, and when he saw John in the sepulchre, and Andronicus, and Drusiana raised from the dead, and Callimachus a believer, and the rest of the brethren glorifying God, he said: O, to what have the powers of these clever men attained! I did not want to be raised, but would rather die, so as not to see them. And with these words he fled and went out of the sepulchre.

84 And John, when he saw the unchanged mind (soul) of Fortunatus, said: O nature that is not changed for the better! O fountain of the soul that abideth in foulness! O essence of corruption full of darkness! O death exulting in them that are thine! O fruitless tree full of fire! O tree that bearest coals for fruit! O matter that dwellest with the madness of matter (al. O wood of trees full of unwholesome shoots) and neighbour of unbelief! Thou hast proved who thou art, and thou art always convicted, with thy children. And thou knowest not how to praise the better things: for thou hast them not. Therefore, such as is thy way (?fruit), such also is thy root and thy nature. Be thou destroyed from among them that trust in the Lord: from their thoughts, from their mind, from their souls, from their bodies, from their acts) their life, their conversation, from their business, their occupations, their counsel, from the resurrection unto (or rest in) God, from their sweet savour wherein thou wilt share, from their faith, their prayers, from the holy bath, from the eucharist, from the food of the flesh, from drink, from clothing, from love, from care, from abstinence, from righteousness: from all these, thou most unholy Satan, enemy of God, shall Jesus Christ our God and of all that are like thee and have thy character, make thee to perish.

85 And having thus said, John prayed, and took bread and bare it into the sepulchre to break it; and said: We glorify thy name, which converteth us from error and ruthless deceit: we glorify thee who hast shown before our eyes that which we have seen: we bear witness to thy loving-kindness which appeareth in divers ways: we praise thy merciful name, O Lord (we thank thee), who hast convicted them that are convicted of thee: we give thanks to thee, O Lord Jesu Christ, that we are persuaded of thy which is unchanging: we give thanks to thee who hadst need of our nature that should be saved: we give thanks to thee that hast given us this sure , for thou art alone, both now and ever. We thy servants give thee thanks, O holy one, who are assembled with intent and are gathered out of the world (or risen from death).

86 And having so prayed and given glory to God, he went out of the sepulchre after imparting unto all the brethren of the eucharist of the Lord. And when he was come unto Andronicus' house he said to the brethren: Brethren, a spirit within me hath divined that Fortunatus is about to die

of blackness (poisoning of the blood) from the bite of the serpent; but let some one go quickly and learn if it is so indeed. And one of the young men ran and found him dead and the blackness spreading over him, and it had reached his heart: and came and told John that he had been dead three hours. And John said: Thou hast thy child, O devil.

'John therefore was with the brethren rejoicing in the Lord.' This sentence is in the best manuscript. In Bonnet's edition It introduces the last section of the Acts, which follows immediately in the manuscript. It may belong to either episode. The Latin has: And that day he spent joyfully with the brethren.

There cannot be much of a gap between this and the next section, which is perhaps the most interesting in the Acts.

The greater part of this episode is preserved only in one very corrupt fourteenth-century manuscript at Vienna. Two important passages (93-5 (part) and 97-8 (part)) were read at the Second Nicene Council and are preserved in the Acts thereof: a few lines of the Hymn are also cited in Latin by Augustine (Ep. 237 (253) to Ceretius): he found it current separately among the Priscillianists. The whole discourse is the best popular exposition we have of the Docetic view of our Lord's person.

87 Those that were present inquired the cause, and were especially perplexed, because Drusiana had said: The Lord appeared unto me in the tomb in the likeness of John, and in that of a youth. Forasmuch, therefore, as they were perplexed and were, in a manner, not yet stablished in the faith, so as to endure it steadfastly, John said (or John bearing it patiently, said):

88 Men and brethren, ye have suffered nothing strange or incredible as concerning your perception of the , inasmuch as we also, whom he chose for himself to be apostles, were tried in many ways: I, indeed, am neither able to set forth unto you nor to write the things which I both saw and heard: and now is it needful that I should fit them for your hearing; and according as each of you is able to contain it I will impart unto you those things whereof ye are able to become hearers, that ye may see the glory that is about him, which was and is, both now and for ever.

For when he had chosen Peter and Andrew, which were brethren, he cometh unto me and James my brother, saying: I have need of you, come unto me. And my brother hearing that, said: John, what would this child have that is upon the sea-shore and called us? And I said: What child? And he said to me again: That which beckoneth to us. And I answered: Because of our long watch we have kept at sea, thou seest not aright, my brother James; but seest thou not the man that standeth there, comely and fair and of a cheerful countenance? But he said to me: Him I see not, brother; but let us go forth and we shall see what he would have.

89 And so when we had brought the ship to land, we saw him also helping along with us to settle the ship: and when we departed from that place, being minded to follow him, again he was seen of me as having rather bald, but the beard thick and flowing, but of James as a youth whose beard was newly come. We were therefore perplexed, both

of us, as to what that which we had seen should mean. And after that, as we followed him, both of us were by little and little perplexed as we considered the matter. Yet unto me there then appeared this yet more wonderful thing: for I would try to see him privily, and I never at any time saw his eyes closing (winking), but only open. And oft-times he would appear to me as a small man and uncomely, and then again as one reaching unto heaven. Also there was in him another marvel: when I sat at meat he would take me upon his own breast; and sometimes his breast was felt of me to be smooth and tender, and sometimes hard like unto stones, so that I was perplexed in myself and said: Wherefore is this so unto me? And as I considered this, he .
.

90 And at another time he taketh with him me and James and Peter unto the mountain where he was wont to pray, and we saw in him a light such as it is not possible for a man that useth corruptible (mortal) speech to describe what it was like. Again in like manner he bringeth us three up into the mountain, saying: Come ye with me. And we went again: and we saw him at a distance praying. I, therefore, because he loved me, drew nigh unto him softly, as though he could not see me, and stood looking upon his hinder parts: and I saw that he was not in any wise clad with garments, but was seen of us naked, and not in any wise as a man, and that his feet were whiter than any snow, so that the earth there was lighted up by his feet, and that his head touched the heaven: so that I was afraid and cried out, and he, turning about, appeared as a man of small stature, and caught hold on my beard and pulled it and said to me: John, be not faithless but believing, and not curious. And I said unto him: But what have I done, Lord? And I say unto you, brethren, I suffered so great pain in that place where he took hold on my beard for thirty days, that I said to him: Lord, if thy twitch when thou wast in sport hath given me so great pain, what were it if thou hadst given me a buffet? And he said unto me: Let it be thine henceforth not to tempt him that cannot be tempted.

91 But Peter and James were wroth because I spake with the Lord, and beckoned unto me that I should come unto them and leave the Lord alone. And I went, and they both said unto me: He (the old man) that was speaking with the Lord upon the top of the mount, who was he? for we heard both of them speaking. And I, having in mind his great grace, and his unity which hath many faces, and his wisdom which without ceasing looketh upon us, said: That shall ye learn if ye inquire of him.

92 Again, once when all we his disciples were at Gennesaret sleeping in one house, I alone having wrapped myself in my mantle, watched (or watched from beneath my mantle) what he should do: and first I heard him say: John, go thou to sleep. And I thereon feigning to sleep saw another like unto him [sleeping], whom also I heard say unto my Lord: Jesus, they whom thou hast chosen believe not yet on thee (or do they not yet, &c.?). And my Lord said unto him: Thou sayest well: for they are men.

93 Another glory also will I tell you, brethren: Sometimes when I would lay hold on him, I met with a material and solid body, and at other times, again, when I felt him, the substance was immaterial and as if it existed not at all. And if at any time he were bidden by some one of the Pharisees

and went to the bidding, we went with him, and there was set before each one of us a loaf by them that had bidden us, and with us he also received one; and his own he would bless and part it among us: and of that little every one was filled, and our own loaves were saved whole, so that they which bade him were amazed. And oftentimes when I walked with him, I desired to see the print of his foot, whether it appeared on the earth; for I saw him as it were lifting himself up from the earth: and I never saw it. And these things I speak unto you, brethren, for the encouragement of your faith toward him; for we must at the present keep silence concerning his mighty and wonderful works, inasmuch as they are unspeakable and, it may be, cannot at all be either uttered or heard.

94 Now before he was taken by the lawless Jews, who also were governed by (had their law from) the lawless serpent, he gathered all of us together and said: Before I am delivered up unto them let us sing an hymn to the Father, and so go forth to that which lieth before us. He bade us therefore make as it were a ring, holding one another's hands, and himself standing in the midst he said: Answer Amen unto me. He began, then, to sing an hymn and to say:

Glory be to thee, Father.

And we, going about in a ring, answered him: Amen.

Glory be to thee, Word: Glory be to thee, Grace. Amen.

Glory be to thee, Spirit: Glory be to thee, Holy One:

Glory be to thy glory. Amen.

We praise thee, O Father; we give thanks to thee, O Light, wherein darkness

dwelleth not. Amen.

95 Now whereas (or wherefore) we give thanks, I say:

I would be saved, and I would save. Amen.

I would be loosed, and I would loose. Amen.

I would be wounded, and I would wound. Amen.

I would be born, and I would bear. Amen.

I would eat, and I would be eaten. Amen.

I would hear, and I would be heard. Amen.

I would be thought, being wholly thought. Amen.

I would be washed, and I would wash. Amen.

Grace danceth. I would pipe; dance ye all. Amen.

I would mourn: lament ye all. Amen.

The number Eight (lit. one ogdoad) singeth praise with us. Amen.

The number Twelve danceth on high. Amen.

The Whole on high hath part in our dancing. Amen.

Whoso danceth not, knoweth not what cometh to pass. Amen.

I would flee, and I would stay. Amen.

I would adorn, and I would be adorned. Amen.

I would be united, and I would unite. Amen.

A house I have not, and I have houses. Amen.

A place I have not, and I have places. Amen.

A temple I have not, and I have temples. Amen.

A lamp am I to thee that beholdest me. Amen.

A mirror am I to thee that perceivest me. Amen.

A door am I to thee that knockest at me. Amen.

A way am I to thee a wayfarer. .

96 Now answer thou (or as thou respondest) unto my dancing. Behold thyself in me who speak, and seeing what I do, keep silence about my mysteries.

Thou that dancest, perceive what I do, for thine is this passion of the manhood, which I am about to suffer. For thou couldest not at all have understood what thou sufferest if I had not been sent unto thee, as the word of the Father. Thou that sawest what I suffer sawest me as suffering, and seeing it thou didst not abide but wert wholly moved, moved to make wise. Thou hast me as a bed, rest upon me. Who I am, thou shalt know when I depart. What now I am seen to be, that I am not. Thou shalt see when thou comest. If thou hadst known how to suffer, thou wouldest have been able not to suffer. Learn thou to suffer, and thou shalt be able not to suffer. What thou knowest not, I myself will teach thee. Thy God am I, not the God of the traitor. I would keep tune with holy souls. In me know thou the word of wisdom. Again with me say thou: Glory be to thee, Father; glory to thee, Word; glory to thee, Holy Ghost. And if thou wouldst know concerning me, what I was, know that with a word did I deceive all things and I was no whit deceived. I have leaped: but do thou understand the whole, and having understood it, say: Glory be to thee, Father. Amen.

97 Thus, my beloved, having danced with us the Lord went forth. And we as men gone astray or dazed with sleep fled this way and that. I, then, when I saw him suffer, did not even abide by his suffering, but fled unto the Mount of Olives, weeping at that which had befallen. And when he was crucified on the Friday, at the sixth hour of the day, darkness came upon all the earth. And my Lord standing in the midst of the cave and enlightening it, said: John, unto the multitude below in Jerusalem I am being crucified and pierced with lances and reeds, and gall and vinegar is given me to drink. But unto thee I speak, and what I speak hear thou. I put it into thy mind to come up into this mountain, that thou mightest hear those things which it behoveth a disciple to learn from his teacher and a man from his God.

98 And having thus spoken, he showed me a cross of light fixed (set up), and about the cross a great multitude, not having one form: and in it (the cross) was one form and one likenesst [so the MS.; I would read: and therein was one form and one likeness: and in the cross another multitude, not having one form]. And the Lord himself I beheld above the cross, not having any shape, but only a voice: and a voice not such as was familiar to us, but one sweet and kind and truly of God, saying unto me: John, it is needful that one should hear these things from me, for I have need of one that will hear. This cross of light is sometimes called the (or a) word by me for your sakes, sometimes mind, sometimes Jesus, sometimes Christ, sometimes door, sometimes a way, sometimes bread, sometimes seed, sometimes resurrection, sometimes Son, sometimes Father, sometimes Spirit, sometimes life, sometimes truth, sometimes faith, sometimes grace. And by these names it is called as toward men: but that which it is in truth, as conceived of in itself and as spoken of unto you (MS. us), it is the marking-off of all things, and the firm uplifting of things fixed out of things unstable, and the harmony of wisdom, and indeed wisdom in harmony [this last clause in the MS. is joined to the next: 'and being wisdom in harmony']. There are of the right hand and the left, powers also, authorities, lordships and demons, workings, threatenings, wraths, devils, Satan, and the lower root whence the nature of the things that come into being proceeded.

99 This cross, then, is that which fixed all things apart (al. joined all things unto itself) by the (or a) word, and separate off the things that are from those that are below (lit. the things from birth and below it), and then also, being one, streamed forth into all things (or, made all flow forth. I suggested: compacted all into). But this is not the cross of wood which thou wilt see when thou goest down hence: neither am I he that is on the cross, whom now thou seest not, but only hearest his (or a) voice. I was reckoned to be that which I am not, not being what I was unto many others: but they will call me (say of me) something else which is vile and not worthy of me. As, then, the place of rest is neither seen nor spoken of, much more shall I, the Lord thereof, be neither seen .

100 Now the multitude of one aspect (al. of one aspect) that is about the cross is the lower nature: and they whom thou seest in the cross, if they have not one form, it is because not yet hath every member of him that came down been comprehended. But when the human nature (or the upper nature) is taken up, and the race which draweth near unto me and obeyeth my voice, he that now heareth me shall be united therewith, and shall no more be that which now he is, but above them, as I also now am. For so long as thou callest not thyself mine, I am not that which I am (or was): but if thou hear me, thou, hearing, shalt be as I am, and I shall be that which I was, when I thee as I am with myself. For from me thou art that (which I am). Care

not therefore for the many, and them that are outside the mystery despise; for know thou that I am wholly with the Father, and the Father with me.

101 Nothing, therefore, of the things which they will say of me have I suffered: nay, that suffering also which I showed unto thee and the rest in the dance, I will that it be called a mystery. For what thou art, thou seest, for I showed it thee; but what I am I alone know, and no man else. Suffer me then to keep that which is mine, and that which is thine behold thou through me, and behold me in truth, that I am, not what I said, but what thou art able to know, because thou art akin thereto. Thou hearest that I suffered, yet did I not suffer; that I suffered not, yet did I suffer; that I was pierced, yet I was not smitten; hanged, and I was not hanged; that blood flowed from me, and it flowed not; and, in a word, what they say of me, that befell me not, but what they say not, that did I suffer. Now what those things are I signify unto thee, for I know that thou wilt understand. Perceive thou therefore in me the praising (al. slaying al. rest) of the (or a) Word (Logos), the piercing of the Word, the blood of the Word, the wound of the Word, the hanging up of the Word, the suffering of the Word, the nailing (fixing) of the Word, the death of the Word. And so speak I, separating off the manhood. Perceive thou therefore in the first place of the Word; then shalt thou perceive the Lord, and in the third place the man, and what he hath suffered.

102 When he had spoken unto me these things, and others which I know not how to say as he would have me, he was taken up, no one of the multitudes having beheld him. And when I went down I laughed them all to scorn, inasmuch as he had told me the things which they have said concerning him; holding fast this one thing in myself, that the Lord contrived all things symbolically and by a dispensation toward men, for their conversion and salvation.

103 Having therefore beheld, brethren, the grace of the Lord and his kindly affection toward us, let us worship him as those unto whom he hath shown mercy, not with our fingers, nor our mouth, nor our tongue, nor with any part whatsoever of our body, but with the disposition of our soul -even him who became a man apart from this body: and let us watch because (or we shall find that) now also he keepeth ward over prisons for our sake, and over tombs, in bonds and dungeons, in reproaches and insults, by sea and on dry land, in scourgings, condemnations, conspiracies, frauds, punishments, and in a word, he is with all of us, and himself suffereth with us when we suffer, brethren. When he is called upon by each one of us, he endureth not to shut his ears to us, but as being everywhere he hearkeneth to all of us; and now both to me and to Drusiana, -forasmuch as he is the God of them that are shut up-bringing us help by his own compassion.

104 Be ye also persuaded, therefore, beloved, that it is not a man whom I preach unto you to worship, but God unchangeable, God invincible, God higher than all authority and all power, and elder and mightier than all angels and creatures that are named, and all aeons. If then ye abide in him, and are builded up in him, ye shall possess your soul indestructible.

105 And when he had delivered these things unto the brethren, John departed, with Andronicus, to walk. And Drusiana also followed afar off with all the brethren, that they might behold the acts that were done by him, and hear his speech at all times in the Lord.

The remaining episode which is extant in the Greek is the conclusion of the book, the Death or Assumption of John. Before it must be placed the stories which we have only in the Latin (of 'Abdias' and another text by 'Mellitus', i.e. Melito), and the two or three isolated fragments.

(Lat. XIV.) Now on the next (or another) day Craton, a philosopher, had proclaimed in the market-place that he would give an example of the contempt of riches: and the spectacle was after this manner. He had persuaded two young men, the richest of the city, who were brothers, to spend their whole inheritance and buy each of them a jewel, and these they brake in pieces publicly in the sight of the people. And while they were doing this, it happened by chance that the apostle passed by. And calling Craton the philosopher to him, he said: That is a foolish despising of the world which is praised by the mouths of men, but long ago condemned by the judgement of God. For as that is a vain medicine whereby the disease is not extirpated, so is it a vain teaching by which the faults of souls and of conduct are not cured. But indeed my master taught a youth who desired to attain to eternal life, in these words; saying that if he would be perfect, he should sell all his goods and give to the poor, and so doing he would gain treasure in heaven and find the life that has no ending. And Craton said to him: Here the fruit of covetousness is set forth in the midst of men, and hath been broken to pieces. But if God is indeed thy master and willeth this to be, that the sum of the price of these jewels should be given to the poor, cause thou the gems to be restored whole, that what I have done for the praise of men, thou mayest do for the glory of him whom thou callest thy master. Then the blessed John gathered together the fragments of the gems, and holding them in his hands, lifted up his eyes to heaven and said: Lord Jesu Christ, unto whom nothing is impossible: who when the world was broken by the tree of concupiscence, didst restore it again in thy faithfulness by the tree of the cross: who didst give to one born blind the eyes which nature had denied him, who didst recall Lazarus, dead and buried, after the fourth day unto the light; and has subjected all diseases and all sicknesses unto the word of thy power: so also now do with these precious stones which these, not knowing the fruits of almsgiving, have broken in pieces for the praise of men: recover thou them, Lord, now by the hands of thine angels, that by their value the work of mercy may be fulfilled, and make these men believe in thee the unbegotten Father through thine only-begotten Son Jesus Christ our Lord, with the Holy Ghost the illuminator and sanctifier of the whole Church,

world without end. And when the faithful who were with the apostle had answered and said Amen, the fragments of the gems were forthwith so joined in one that no mark at all that they had been broken remained in them. And Craton the philosopher, with his disciples, seeing this, fell at the feet of the apostle and believed thenceforth (or immediately) and was baptized, with them all, and began himself publicly to preach the faith of our Lord Jesus Christ.

XV. Those two brothers, therefore, of whom we spake, sold the gems which they had bought by the sale of their inheritance and gave the price to the poor; and thereafter a very great multitude of believers began to be joined to the apostle.

And when all this was done, it happened that after the same example, two honourable men of the city of the Ephesian sold all their goods and distributed them to the needy, and followed the apostle as he went through the cities preaching the word of God. But it came to pass, when they entered the city of Pergamum, that they saw their servants walking abroad arrayed in silken raiment and shining with the glory of this world: whence it happened that they were pierced with the arrow of the devil and became sad, seeing themselves poor and clad with a single cloak while their own servants were powerful and prosperous. But the apostle of Christ, perceiving these wiles of the devil, said: I see that ye have changed your minds and your countenances on this account, that, obeying the teaching of my Lord Jesus Christ, ye have given all ye had to the poor. Now, if ye desire to recover that which ye formerly possessed of gold, silver, and precious stones, bring me some straight rods, each of you a bundle. And when they had done so, he called upon the name of the Lord Jesus Christ, and they were turned into gold. And the apostle said to them: Bring me small stones from the seashore. And when they had done this also, he called upon the majesty of the Lord, and all the pebbles were turned into gems. Then the blessed John turned to those men and said to them: Go about to the goldsmiths and jewellers for seven days, and when ye have proved that these are true gold and true jewels, tell me. And they went, both of them, and after seven days returned to the apostle, saying: Lord, we have gone about the shops of all the goldsmiths, and they have all said that they never saw such pure gold. Likewise the jewellers have said the same, that they never saw such excellent and precious gems.

XVI. Then the holy John said unto them: Go, and redeem to you the lands which ye have sold, for ye have lost the estates of heaven. Buy yourselves silken raiment, that for a time ye may shine like the rose which showeth its fragrance and redness and suddenly fadeth away. For ye sighed at beholding your servants and groaned that ye were become poor. Flourish, therefore, that ye may fade: be rich for the time, that ye may be beggars for ever. Is not the Lord's hand able to make riches overflowing and unsurpassably glorious? but he hath appointed a conflict for souls, that they may believe that they shall have eternal riches, who for his name's sake have refused temporal wealth. Indeed, our master told us concerning a certain rich man who feasted every day and shone with gold and purple, at whose door lay a beggar, Lazarus, who desired to receive even the crumbs that fell from his table, and no man gave unto him. And it came to pass that on one day they died, both of them, and that beggar was taken into the rest which is in Abraham's bosom, but the rich man was cast into flaming fire: out of which he lifted up his eyes and saw Lazarus, and prayed him to dip his finger in water and cool his mouth for he was tormented in the flames. And Abraham answered him and said: Remember, son, that thou receivedst good things in thy life, but this Lazarus likewise evil things. Wherefore rightly is he now comforted while thou art tormented, and besides all this, a great gulf is fixed between you and us, so that neither can they come thence

hither, nor hither thence. But he answered: I have five brethren: I pray that some one may go to warn them, that they come not into this flame. And Abraham said to him: They have Moses and the prophets, let them hear them. To that he answered: Lord, unless one rise up again, they will not believe. Abraham said to him: If they believe not Moses and the prophets, neither will they believe, if one rise again. And these words our Lord and Master confirmed by examples of mighty works: for when they said to him: Who hath come hither from thence, that we may believe him? he answered: Bring hither the dead whom ye have. And when they had brought unto him a young man which was dead (Ps.-Mellitus: three dead corpses), he was waked up by him as one that sleepeth, and confirmed all his words.

But wherefore should I speak of my Lord, when at this present there are those whom in his name and in your presence and sight I have raised from the dead: in whose name ye have seen palsied men healed, lepers cleansed, blind men enlightened, and many delivered from evil spirits ? But the riches of these mighty works they cannot have who have desired to have earthly wealth. Finally, when ye yourselves went unto the sick and called upon the name of Jesus Christ, they were healed: ye did drive out devils and restore light to the blind. Behold, this grace is taken from you, and ye are become wretched, who were mighty and great. And where as there was such fear of you upon the devils that at your bidding they left the men whom they possessed, now ye will be in fear of the devils. For he that loveth money is the servant of Mammon: and Mammon is the name of a devil who is set over carnal gains, and is the master of them that love the world. But even the lovers of the world do not possess riches, but are possessed of them. For it is out of reason that for one belly there should be laid up so much food as would suffice a thousand, and for one body so many garments as would furnish clothing for a thousand men. In vain, therefore, is that stored up which cometh not into use, and for whom it is kept, no man knoweth, as the Holy Ghost saith by the prophet: In vain is every man troubled who heapeth up riches and knoweth not for whom he gathereth them. Naked did our birth from women bring us into this light, destitute of food and drink: naked will the earth receive us which brought us forth. We possess in common the riches of the heaven, the brightness of the sun is equal for the rich and the poor, and likewise the light of the moon and the stars, the softness of the air and the drops of rain, and the gate of the church and the fount of sanctification and the forgiveness of sins, and the sharing in the altar, and the eating of the body and drinking of the blood of Christ, and the anointing of the chrism, and the grace of the giver, and the visitation of the Lord, and the pardon of sin: in all these the dispensing of the Creator is equal, without respect of persons. Neither doth the rich man use these gifts after one manner and the poor after another.

But wretched and unhappy is the man who would have something more than sufficeth him: for of this come heats of fevers rigours of cold, divers pains in all the members of the body, and he can neither be fed with food nor sated with drink, that covetousness may learn that money will not profit it, which being laid up bringeth to the keepers thereof anxiety by day and night, and suffereth them not even for an hour to be quiet and secure. For while they guard their houses against thieves, till their estate, ply the plough, pay taxes, build storehouses, strive for gain, try to baffle the attacks of the strong, and to strip the weak, exercise their wrath on whom they can, and hardly bear it from others, shrink not from playing at tables and from public shows, fear not to defile or to be defiled, suddenly do they depart out of this world, naked, bearing only their own sins with them, for which they shall suffer eternal punishment.

XVII. While the apostle was thus speaking, behold there was brought to him by his mother, who was a widow, a young man who thirty days before had first married a vvife. And the people which were waiting upon the burial came with the widowed mother and cast themselves at the apostle's feet all together with groans, weeping, and mourning, and besought him that in the name of his God, as he had done with Drusiana, so he would raise up this young man also. And there was so great weeping of them all that the apostle himself could hardly refrain from crying and tears. He cast himself down, therefore, in prayer, and wept a long time: and rising from prayer spread out his hands to heaven, and for a long space prayed within himself. And when he had so done thrice, he commanded the body which was swathed to be loosed, and said: Thou youth Stacteus, who for love of thy flesh hast quickly lost thy soul: thou youth which knewest not thy creator nor perceivedst the Saviour of men, and wast ignorant of thy true friend, and therefore didst fall into the snare of the worst enemy: behold, I have poured out tears and prayers unto my Lord for thine ignorance, that thou mayest rise from the dead, the bands of death being loosed, and declare unto these two, to Atticus and Eugenius, how great glory they have lost, and how great punishment they have incurred. Then Stacteus arose and worshipped the apostle, and began to reproach his disciples, saying: I beheld your angels vveeping, and the angels of Satan rejoicing at your overthrow. For now in a little time ye have lost the kingdom that was prepared for you, and the dwellingplaces builded of shining stones, full of joy, of feasting and delights, full of everlasting life and eternal light: and have gotten yourselves places of darkness, full of dragons, of roaring flames, of torments, and punishments unsurpassable, of pains and anguish, fear and horrible trembling. Ye have lost the places full of unfading flowers, shining, full of the sounds of instruments of music (organs), and have gotten on the other hand places wherein roaring and howling and mourning ceaseth not day nor night. Nothing else remaineth for you save to ask the apostle of the Lord that like as he hath raised me to life, he would raise you also from death unto salvation and bring back your souls which now are blotted out of the book of life.

XVIII. Then both he that had been raised and all the people together with Atticus and Eugenius, cast themselves at the apostle's feet and besought him to intercede for them with the Lord. Unto whom the holy apostle gave this answer: that for thirty days they should offer penitence to God, and in that space pray especially that the rods of gold might return to their nature and likewise the stones return to the meanness wherein they were made. And it came to pass that after thirty days were accomplished, and neither the rods were turncd into wood nor the gems into pebbles, Atticus and Eugenius came and said to the apostle: Thou hast always taught mercy, and preached forgiveness, and bidden that one man should spare another. And if God willeth that a man should forgive a man, how much more

shall he, as he is God, both forgive and spare men. We are confounded for our sin: and whereas we have cried with our eyes which lusted after the world, we do now repent with eyes that weep. We pray thee, Lord, we pray thee, apostle of God, show in deed that mercy which in word thou hast always promised. Then the holy John said unto them as they wept and repented, and all interceded for them likewise: Our Lord God used these words when he spake concerning sinners: I will not the death of a sinner, but I will rather that he be converted and live. For when the Lord Jesus Christ taught us concerning the penitent, he said: Verily I say unto you, there is great joy in heaven over one sinner that repenteth and turneth himself from his sins: and there is more joy over him than over ninety and nine which have not sinned. Wherefore I would have you know that the Lord accepteth the repentance of these men. And he turned unto Atticus and Eugenius and said: Go, carry back the rods unto the wood whence ye took them, for now are they returned to their own nature, and the stones unto the sea-shore, for they are become common stones as they were before. And when this was accomplished, they received again the grace which they had lost, so that again they cast out devils as before time and healed the sick and enlightened the blind, and daily the Lord did many mighty works by their means.

XIX tells shortly the destruction oi the temple of Ephesus and the conversion of 12,000 people.

Then follows the episode of the poison-cup in a form which probably represents the story in the Leucian Acts. (We have seen that the late Greek texts place it at the beginning, in the presence of Domitian.)

XX. Now when Aristodemus, who was chief priest of all those idols, saw this, filled with a wicked spirit, he stirred up sedition among the people, so that one people prepared themselves to fight against the other. And John turned to him and said: Tell me, Aristodemus, what can I do to take away the anger from thy soul? And Aristodemus said: If thou wilt have me believe in thy God, I will give thee poison to drink, and if thou drink it, and die not, it will appear that thy God is true. The apostle answered: If thou give me poison to drink, when I call on the name of my Lord, it will not be able to harm me. Aristodemus said again: I will that thou first see others drink it and die straightway that so thy heart may recoil from that cup. And the blessed John said: I have told thee already that I am prepared to drink it that thou mayest believe on the Lord Jesus Christ when thou seest me whole after the cup of poison. Aristodemus therefore went to the proconsul and asked of him two men who were to undergo the sentence of death. And when he had set them in the midst of the market-place before all the people, in the sight of the apostle he made them drink the poison: and as soon as they had drunk it, they gave up the ghost. Then Aristodemus turned to John and said: Hearken to me and depart from thy teaching wherewith thou callest away the people from the worship of the gods; or take and drink this, that thou mayest show that thy God is almighty, if after thou hast drunk, thou canst remain whole. Then the blessed Jolm, as they lay dead which had drunk the poison, like a fearless and brave man took the cup, and making the sign of the cross, spake thus: My God, and the Father of our Lord Jesus Christ, by whose word the heavens were established, unto whom all things are subject, whom all creation serveth, whom all power obeyeth, feareth, and trembleth, when we call on thee for succour: whose name the serpent hearing is still, the dragon fleeth, the viper is quiet, the toad (which is called a frog) is still and strengthless, the scorpion is quenched, the basilisk vanquished, and the phalangia (spider) doth no hurt -in a word, all venomous things, and the fiercest reptiles and noisome beasts, are pierced (or covered with darkness). [Ps.- Mellitus adds: and all roots hurtful to the health of men dry up.] Do thou, I say, quench the venom of this poison, put out the deadly workings thereof, and void it of the strength which it hath in it: and grant in thy sight unto all these whom thou hast created, eyes that they may see, and ears that they may hear and a heart that they may understand thy greatness. And when he had thus said, he armed his mouth and all his body with the sign of the cross and drank all that was in the cup. And after be had drunk, he said: I ask that they for whose sake I have drunk, be turned unto thee, O Lord, and by thine enlightening receive the salvation which is in thee. And when for the space of three hours the people saw that John was of a cheerful countenance, and that there was no sign at all of paleness or fear in him, they began to cry out with a loud voice: He is the one true God whom John worshippeth.

XXI. But Aristodemus even so believed not, though the people reproached him: but turned unto John and said: This one thing I lack -if thou in the name of thy God raise up these that have died by this poison, my mind will be cleansed of all doubt. When he said that, the people rose against Aristodemus saying: We will burn thee and thine house if thou goest on to trouble the apostle further with thy words. John, therefore, seeing that there was a fierce sedition, asked for silence, and said in the hearing of all: The first of the virtues of God which we ought to imitate is patience, by which we are able to bear with the foolishness of unbelievers. Wherefore if Aristodemus is still held by unbelief, let us loose the knots of his unbelief. He shall be compelled, even though late, to acknowledge his creator - for I will not cease from this work until a remedy shall bring help to his wounds, and like physicians which have in their hands a sick man needing medicine, so also, if Aristodemus be not yet cured by that which hath now been done, he shall be cured by that which I will now do. And he called Aristodemus to him, and gave him his coat, and he himself stood clad only in his mantle. And Aristodemus said to him: Wherefore hast thou given me thy coat? John said to him: That thou mayest even so be put to shame and depart from thine unbelief. And Aristodemus said: And how shall thy coat make me to depart from unbelief? The apostle answered: Go and cast it upon the bodies of the dead, and thou shalt say thus: The apostle of our Lord Jesus Christ hath sent me that in his name ye may rise again, that all may know that life and death are servants of my Lord Jesus Christ. Which when Aristodemus had done, and had seen them rise, he worshipped John, and ran quickly to the proconsul and began to say with a loud voice: Hear me, hear me, thou proconsul; I think thou rememberest that I have often stirred up thy wrath against John and devised many things against him daily, wherefore I fear lest I feel his wrath: for he is a god hidden in the form of a man and hath drunk poison, and not only continueth whole, but them also which had died by the poison he hath recalled to life by my means, by the touch of his coat, and they have no mark of death upon them.

Which when the proconsul heard he said: And what wilt thou have me to do? Aristodemus answered: Let us go and fall at his feet and ask pardon, and whatever he commandeth us let us do. Then they came together and cast themselves down and besought forgiveness: and he received them and offered prayer and thanksgiving to God, and he ordained them a fast of a week, and when it was fulfilled he baptized them in the name of the Lord Jesus Christ and his Almighty Father and the Holy Ghost the illuminator. [And when thev were baptized, with all their house and their servants and their kindred, they brake all their idols and built a church in the name of Saint John: wherein he himself was taken up, in manner following :]

This bracketed sentence, of late complexion, serves to introduce the last episode of the book.

[James gives two additional fragments that do not fit in any other place. These fragments are very broken and are not of much use for this present project. However, if there is intrest in them, they can be found on pages 264-6 of the text.]

The last episode of these Acts (as is the case with several others of the Apocryphal Acts) was preservcd separately for reading in church on the Saint's day. We have it in at least nine Greek manuscripts, and in many versions: Latin, Syriac, Armenian, Coptic, Ethiopic, Slavonic.

106 John therefore continued with the brethren, rejoicing in the Lord. And on the morrow, being the Lord's day, and all the brethren being gathered together, he began to say unto them: Brethren and fellow-servants and coheirs and partakers with me in the kingdom of the Lord, ye know the Lord, hovv many mighty works he hath granted you by my means, how many wonders, healings, signs, how great spiral gifts, teachings, governings, refreshings, ministries, knowledges, glories, graces, gifts, beliefs, communions, all which ye have seen given you by him in your sight, yet not seen by these eyes nor heard by these ears. Be ye therefore stablished in him, remembering him in your every deed, knowing the mystery of the dispensation which hath come to pass towards men, for what cause the Lord hath l accomplished it. He beseecheth you by me, brethren, and entreateth you, desiring to remain without grief, without insult, not conspired against, not chastened: for he knoweth even the insult that cometh of you, he knoweth even dishonour, he knoweth even conspiracy, he knoweth even chastisement, from them that hearken not to his commandments.

107 Let not then our good God be grieved, the compassionate, the merciful, the holy, the pure, the undefiled, the immaterial, the only, the one, the unchangeable, the simple, the guileless, the unwrathful, even our God Jesus Christ, who is above every name that we can utter or conceive, and more exalted. Let him rejoice with us because we walk aright, let him be glad because we live purely, let him be refreshed because our conversation is sober. Let him be without care because we live continently, let him be pleased because we communicate one with another, let him smile because we are chaste, let him be merry because we love him. These things I now speak unto you, brethren, because I am hasting unto the work set before me, and already being perfected by the Lord. For

what else could I have to say unto you? Ye have the pledge of our God, ye have the earnest of his goodness, ye have his presence that cannot be shunned. If, then, ye sin no more, he forgiveth you that ye did in ignorance: but if after that ye have known him and he hath had mercy on you, ye walk again in the like deeds, both the former will be laid to your charge, and also ye will not have a part nor mercy before him.

108 And when he had spoken this unto them, he prayed thus: O Jesu who hast woven this crown with thy weaving, who hast joined together these many blossoms into the unfading flower of thy cormtenance, who hast sown in them these words: thou only tender of thy servants, and physician who healest freely: only doer of good and despiser of none, only merciful and lover of men, only saviour and righteous, only seer of all, who art in all and everywhere present and containing all things and filling all things: Christ Jesu, God, Lord, that with thy gifts and thy mercy shelterest them that trust in thee, that knowest clearly the wiles and the assaults of him that is everywhere our adversary, which he deviseth against us: do thou only, O Lord, succour thy servants by thy visitation. Even so, Lord.

109 And he asked for bread, and gave thanks thus: What praise or what offering or what thanksgiving shall we, breaking this bread, name save thee only, O Lord Jesu? We glorify thy name that was said by the Father: we glorify thy name that was said through the Son (or we glorify the name of Father that was said by thee . . . the name of Son that was said by thee): we glorify thine entering of the Door. We glorify the resurrection shown unto us by thee. We glorify thy way, we glorify of thee the seed, the word, the grace, the faith, the salt, the unspeakable (al. chosen) pearl, the treasure, the plough, the net, the greatness, the diadem, him that for us was called Son of man, that gave unto us truth, rest, knowledge, power, the commandment, the confidence, hope, love, liberty, refuge in thee. For thou, Lord, art alone the root of immortality, and the fount of incorruption, and the seat of the ages: called by all these names for us now that calling on thee by them we may make known thy greatness which at the present is invisible unto us, but visible only unto the pure, being portrayed in thy manhood only.

110 And he brake the bread and gave unto all of us, praying over each of the brethren that he might be worthy of the grace of the Lord and of the most holy eucharist. And he partook also himself likewise, and said: Unto me also be there a part with you, and: Peace be with you, my beloved.

111 After that he said unto Verus: Take with thee some two men, with baskets and shovels, and follow me. And Verus without delay did as he was bidden by John the servant of God. The blessed John therefore went out of the house and walked forth of the gates, having told the more part to depart from him. And when he was come to the tomb of a certain brother of ours he said to the young men: Dig, my children. And they dug and he was instant with them yet more, saying: Let the trench be deeper. And as they dug he spoke unto them the word of God and exhorted them that were come with him out of the house, edifying and perfecting them unto the greatness of God, and praying over each one of us. And when the young men

had finished the trench as he desired, we knowing nothing of it, he took off his garments wherein he was clad and laid them as it were for a pallet in the bottom of the trench: and standing in his shift only he stretched his hands upward and prayed thus:

112 O thou that didst choose us out for the apostleship of the Gentiles: O God that sentest us into the world: that didst reveal thyself by the law and the prophets: that didst never rest, but alway from the foundation of the world savedst them that were able to be saved: that madest thyself known through all nature: that proclaimedst thyself even among beasts: that didst make the desolate and savage soul tame and quiet: that gavest thyself to it when it was athirst for thy words: that didst appear to it in haste when it was dying: that didst show thyself to it as a law when it was sinking into lawlessness: that didst manifest thyself to it when it had been vanquished by Satan: that didst overcome its adversary when it fled unto thee: that avest it thine hand and didst raise it up from the things of Hades: that didst not leave it to walk after a bodily sort (in the body): that didst show to it its own enemy: that hast made for it a clear knowledge toward thee: O God, Jesu, the Father of them that are above the heavens, the Lord of them that are in the heavens, the law of them that are in the other, the course of them that are in the air, the keeper of them that are on the earth, the fear of them that are under the earth, the grace of them that are thine own: receive also the soul of thy John, which it may be is accounted worthy by thee.

113 O thou who hast kept me until this hour for thyself and untouched by union with a woman: who when in my youth I desired to marry didst appear unto me and say to me: John I have need of thee: who didst prepare for me also a sickness of the body: who when for the third time I would marry didst forthwith prevent me, and then at the third hour of the day saidst unto me on the sea: John, if thou hadst not been mine, I would have suffered thee to marry: who for two years didst blind me (or afflict mine eyes), and grant me to mourn and entreat thee: who in the third year didst open the eyes of my mind and also grant me my visible eyes: who when I saw clearly didst ordain that it should be grievous to me to look upon a woman: who didst save me from the temporal fantasy and lead me unto that which endureth always: who didst rid me of the foul madness that is in the flesh: who didst take me from the bitter death and establish me on thee alone: who didst muzzle the secret disease of my soul and cut off the open deed: who didst afflict and banish him that raised tumult in me: who didst make my love of thee spotless: who didst make my joining unto thee perfect and unbroken: who didst give me undoubting faith in thee, who didst order and make clear my inclination toward thee: thou who givest unto every man the due reward of his works, who didst put into my soul that I should have no possession save thee only: for what is more precious than thee? Now therefore Lord, whereas I have accomplished the dispensation wherewith I was entrusted, account thou me worthy of thy rest, and grant me that end in thee which is salvation unspeakable and unutterable.

114 And as I come unto thee, let the fire go backward, let the darkness be overcome, let the gulf be without strength, let the furnace die out, let Gehenna be quenched. Let angels follow, let devils fear, let rulers be broken, let

powers fall; let the places of the right hand stand fast, let them of the left hand not remain. Let the devil be muzzled, let Satan be derided, let his wrath be burned out, Iet his madness be stilled, let his vengeance be ashamed, let his assault be in pain, let his children be smitten and all his roots plucked up. And grant me to accomplish the journey unto thee without suffering insolence or provocation, and to receive that which thou hast promised unto them that live purely and have loved thee only.

115 And having sealed himself in every part, he stood and said: Thou art with me, O Lord Jesu Christ: and laid himself down in the trench where he had strown his garments: and having said unto us: Peace be with you, brethren, he gave up his spirit rejoicing.

The less good Greek manuscripts and some versions are not content with this simple ending. The Latin says that after the prayer a great light appeared over the apostle for the space of an hour, so bright that no one could look at it. (Then he laid himself down and gave up the ghost.) We who were there rejoiced, some of us, and some mourned. . . . And forthwith manna issuing from the tomb was seen of all, which manna that place produceth even unto this day, &c. But perhaps the best conclusion is that of one Greek manuscript:

We brought a linen cloth and spread it upon him, and went into the city. And on the day following we went forth and found not his body, for it was translated by the power of our Lord Jesus Christ, unto whom be glory, &c.

Another says: On the morrow we dug in the place, and him we found not, but only his sandals, and the earth moving (lit. springing up like a well), and after that we remembered that which was spoken by the Lord unto Peter, &c.

Augustine (on John xxi) reports the belief that in his time the earth over the grave was seen to move as if stirred by John's breathing.

THE ACTS OF PAUL

Introduction

This book, Tertullian tells us, was composed shortly before his time in honour of Paul by a presbyter of Asia, who was convicted of the imposture and degraded from his office. The date of it may therefore be about A.D. 160. The author was an orthodox Christian.

Our authorities for it are:

1. The sadly mutilated Coptic MS. at Heidelberg, of the sixth century at latest.

2. The Acts of Paul and Thecla, a single episode which has been preserved complete in Greek and many versions: parts of it exist in the Coptic.

3. The correspondence with the Corinthians, partly preserved in the Coptic, and current separately in Armenian and Latin.

4. The Martyrdom, the concluding episode of the Acts, preserved separately (as in the case of John and others) in Greek and other versions.

5.Detached fragments or quotations.

The length of the whole book is given as 8,600 lines (Stichometry of Nicephorus), or 8,560 (Stichometry of the Codex Claromontanus): the Canonical Acts are given by the same two authorities respectively as 2,800 and 2,600. We have, perhaps, 1,800 lines of the Acts of Paul. The text of the Coptic MS. is miserably defective, and the restoration of it, in the episodes which are preserved in it alone, is a most difficult process: Professor Carl Schmidt has done practically all that can be expected, with infinite labour and great acuteness. In treating the defective episodes I shall follow him closely, but shall not attempt to represent all the broken lines.

I

The first extant page of the Coptie MS. seems to be p.9.

p.9. Paul went into (the house) at the place where the (dead) was. But Phila the wife of Panchares (Anchares, MS., see below) was very wroth and said to her husband in (great anger): Husband, thou hast gone . . . . the wild beasts, thou hast not begotten . . . . thy son . . . . where is mine?

p.10 (he hath not) desired food . . . to bury him. But (Panchares) stood in the sight of all and made his prayer at the ninth hour, until the people of the city came to bear the boy out. When he had prayed, Paul (came) and saw . . . and of Jesus Christ . . . . the boy . . . the prayer.

p.11 (a small piece only) . . . multitude . . . eight days . . . they thought that he raised up the (boy). But when Paul had remained

p.12. They asked? him? . . . the men listened to him . . . they sent for Panchares . . . and cried out, saying: We believe, Panchares, . . . but save the city from . . many things, which they said. Panchares said unto them: Judge ye whether your good deeds (?)

p.13 is not possible . . . but to (testify) . . . God who hath . . . his Son according to . . . salvation, and I also believe that, my brethren, there is no other God, save Jesus Christ the son of the Blessed, unto whom is glory for ever, Amen. But when they saw that he would not turn to them, they pursued Paul, and caught him, and brought him back into the city, ill-using (?) him, and cast stones at him and thrust him out of their city and out of their country. But Panchares would not return evil for evil: he shut the door of his house and went in with his wife . . . fasting . . . But when it was evening Paul came to him and said:

p.14. God hath . . . Jesus Christ.

These are the last words of the episode. The situation is a little cleared by a sentence in the Greek Acts of Titus ascribed to Zenas (not earlier than the fifth century?): "They arrived at Antioch and found Barnabas the son of Panchares, whom Paul raised up.' Barnabas may be a mistake, but Panchares is, I doubt not, right: for the Coptic definite article is p prefixed to the word, and the Coptic translator finding Panchares in his text has confused the initial of it with his own definite article, and cut it out.

We have, then, a husband Panchares and wife Phila at Antioch (in Pisidia perhaps: this is disputed), and their son (possibly named Barnabas) is dead. Phila reproaches Panchares with want of parental affection. I take it that he is a believer, and has not mourned over his son, perhaps knowing that Paul was at hand and hoping for his help. Panchares prays till his fellow-townsmen come to carry out the body for burial. Paul arrives: at some point he raises the dead: but the people are irritated and some catastrophe threatens them at Paul's hands.

Panchares makes a profession of faith, the result of which is Paul's ill-treatment and banishment. But Paul returns secretly and reassures Panchares.

II

The next episode is that of Paul and Thecla, in which the Greek text exists, and will be followed. In the Coptic it has a title:

After the flight from Antioch, when he would go to Iconium.

It is possible that in this episode the author of the Acts may have used a local legend, current in his time, of a real Christian martyr Thecla. It is otherwise difficult to account for the very great popularity of the cult of St. Thecla, which spread over East and West, and made her the most famous of virgin martyrs. Moreover, one historical personage is introduced into the story, namely, Queen Tryphaena, who was the widow, it seems, of Cotys, King of Thrace, and the mother of Polemo II, King of Pontus. She was a great-

niece of the Emperor Claudius. Professor W. M. Ramsay
has contended that there was a written story of Thecla
which was adapted by the author of the Acts: but his view
is not generally accepted.

1 When Paul went up unto Iconium after he fled from
Antioch, there journeyed with him Demas and
Hermogenes the coppersmith, which were full of
hypocrisy, and flattered Paul as though they loved him. But
Paul, looking only unto the goodness of Christ, did them
no evil, but loved them well, so that he assayed to make
sweet unto them all the oracles of the Lord, and of the
teaching and the interpretation (of the Gospel) and of the
birth and resurrection of the Beloved, and related unto
them word by word all the great works of Christ, how they
were revealed unto him (Copt. adds: how that Christ was
born of Mary the virgin, and of the seed of David).

2 And a certain man named Onesiphorus, when he heard
that Paul was come to Iconium, went out with his children
Simmias and Zeno and his wife Lectra to meet him, that he
might receive him into his house: for Titus had told him
what manner of man Paul was in appearance; for he had
not seen him in the flesh, but only in the spirit.

3 And he went by the king's highway that leadeth unto
Lystra and stood expecting him, and looked upon them
that came, according to the description of Titus. And he
saw Paul coming, a man little of stature, thin-haired upon
the head, crooked in the legs, of good state of body, with
eyebrows joining, and nose somewhat hooked, full of grace:
for sometimes he appeared like a man, and sometimes he
had the face of an angel.

4 And when Paul saw Onesiphorus he smiled, and
Onesiphorus said: Hail, thou servant of the blessed God.
And he said: Grace be with thee and with thine house. But
Demas and Hermogenes were envious, and stirred up their
hypocrisy yet more, so that Demas said: Are we not
servants of the Blessed, that thou didst not salute us so?
And Onesiphorus said: I see not in you any fruit of
righteousness, but if ye be such, come ye also into my
house and refresh yourselves.

5 And when Paul entered into the house of Onesiphorus,
there was great joy, and bowing of knees and breaking of
bread, and the word of God concerning abstinence (or
continence) and the resurrection; for Paul said:

Blessed are the pure in heart, for they shall see God.

Blessed are they that keep the flesh chaste, for they shall
become the temple of God.

Blessed are they that abstain (or the continent), for unto
them shall God speak.

Blessed are they that have renounced this world, for they
shall be well-pleasing unto God.

Blessed are they that possess their wives as though they had
them not, for they shall inherit God.

Blessed are they that have the fear of God, for they shall
become angels of God.

6 Blessed are they that tremble at the oracles of God, for
they shall be comforted.

Blessed are they that receive the wisdom of Jesus Christ,
for they shall be called sons of the Most High.

Blessed are they that have kept their baptism pure, for they
shall rest with the Father and with the Son.

Blessed are they that have compassed the understanding of
Jesus Christ, for they shall be in light.

Blessed are they that for love of God have departed from
the fashion of this world, for they shall judge angels, and
shall be blessed at the right hand of the Father.

Blessed are the merciful, for they shall obtain mercy and
shall not see the bitter day of judgement. Blessed are the
bodies of the virgins, for they shall be well- pleasing unto
God and shall not lose the reward of their continence
(chastity), for the word of the Father shall be unto them a
work of salvation in the day of his Son, and they shall have
rest world Without end.

7 And as Paul was saying these things in the midst of the
assembly (church) in the house of Onesiphorus, a certain
virgin, Thecla, whose mother was Theocleia, which was
betrothed to an husband, Thamyris, sat at the window hard
by, and hearkened night and day unto the word concerning
chastity which was spoken by Paul: and she stirred not
from the window, but was led onward (or pressed onward)
by faith, rejoicing exceedingly: and further, when she saw
many women and virgins entering in to Paul, she also
desired earnestly to be accounted worthy to stand before
Paul's face and to hear the word of Christ; for she had not
yet seen the appearance of Paul, but only heard his speech.

8 Now as she removed not from the window, her mother
sent unto Thamyris, and he came with great joy as if he
were already to take her to wife. Thamyris therefore said to
Theocleia: Where is my Thecla? And Theocicia said: I have
a new tale to tell thee, Thamyris: for for three days and
three nights Thecla ariseth not from the window, neither to
eat nor to drink, but looking earnestly as it were upon a
joyful spectacle, she so attendeth to a stranger who
teacheth deceitful and various words, that I marvel how the
great modesty of the maiden is so hardly beset.

9 O Thamyris, this man upsetteth the whole city of the
Iconians, and thy Thecla also, for all the women and the
young men go in to him and are taught by him. Ye must,
saith he, fear one only God and live chastely. And my
daughter, too, like a spider at the window, bound by his
words, is held by a new desire and a fearful passion: for she
hangeth upon the things that he speaketh, and the maiden
is captured. But go thou to her and speak to her; for she is
betrothed unto thee.

10 And Thamyris went to her, alike loving her and fearing
because of her disturbance (ecstasy), and said: Thecla, my
betrothed, why sittest thou thus? and what passion is it that

holdeth thee in amaze; turn unto thy Thamyris and be ashamed. And her mother also said the same: Thecla, why sittest thou thus, looking downward, and answering nothing, but as one stricken? And they wept sore, Thamyris because he failed of a wife, and Theocleia of a child, and the maidservants of a mistress; there was, therefore, great confusion of mourning in the house. And while all this was so, Thecla turned not away, but paid heed to the speech of Paul.

11 But Thamyris leapt up and went forth into the street and watched them that went in to Paul and came out. And he saw two men striving bitterly with one another, and said to them: Ye men, tell me who ye are, and who is he that is within with you, that maketh the souls of young men and maidens to err, deceiving them that there may be no marriages but they should live as they are. I promise therefore to give you much money if ye will tell me of him: for I am a chief man of the city.

12 And Demas and Hermogenes said unto him: Who this man is, we know not; but he defraudeth the young men of wives and the maidens of husbands, saying: Ye have no resurrection otherwise, except ye continue chaste, and defile not the flesh but keep it pure.

13 And Thamyris said to them: Come, ye men, into mine house and refresh yourselves with me. And they went to a costly banquet and much wine and great wealth and a brilliant table. And Thamyris made them drink, for he loved Thecla and desired to take her to wife: and at the dinner Thamyris said: Tell me, ye men, what is his teaching, that I also may know it: for I am not a little afflicted concerning Thecla because she so loveth the stranger, and I am defrauded of my marriage.

14 And Demas and Hermogenes said: Bring him before Castelius the governor as one that persuadeth the multitudes with the new doctrine of the Christians; and so will he destroy him and thou shalt have thy wife Thecla. And we will teach thee of that resurrection which he asserteth, that it is already come to pass in the children which we have, and we rise again when we have come to the knowledge of the true God.

15 But when Thamyris heard this of them, he was filled with envy and wrath, and rose up early and went to the house of Onesiphorus with the rulers and officers and a great crowd with staves, saying unto Paul: Thou hast destroyed the city of the Iconians and her that was espoused unto me, so that she will not have me: let us go unto Castelius the governor. And all the multitude said: Away with the wizard, for he hath corrupted all our wives. And the multitude rose up together against him.

16 And Thamyris, standing before the judgement seat, cried aloud and said: 0 proconsul, this is the man-we know not whence he is-who alloweth not maidens to marry: let him declare before thee wherefore he teacheth such things. And Demas and Hermogenes said to Thamyris: Say thou that he is a Christian, and so wilt thou destroy him. But the governor kept his mind steadfast and called Paul, saying unto him: Who art thou, and what teachest thou? for it is no light accusation that these bring against thee.

17 And Paul lifted up his voice and said: If I am this day examined what I teach, hearken, 0 proconsul. The living God, the God of vengeance, the jealous God, the God that hath need of nothing, but desireth the salvation of men, hath sent me, that I may sever them from corruption and uncleanness and all pleasure and death, that they may sin no more. Wherefore God hath sent his own Child, whom I preach and teach that men should have hope in him who alone hath had compassion upon the world that was in error; that men may no more be under judgement but have faith and the fear of God and the knowledge of sobriety and the love of truth. If then I teach the things that have been revealed unto me of God, what wrong do I O proconsul? And the governor having heard that, commanded Paul to be bound and taken away to prison until he should have leisure to hear him more carefully.

18 But Thecla at night took off her bracelets and gave them to the doorkeeper, and when the door was opened for her she went into the prison, and gave the jailer a mirror of silver and so went in to Paul and sat by his feet and heard the wonderful works of God. And Paul feared not at all, but walked in the confidence of God: and her faith also was increased as she kissed his chains.

19 Now when Thecla was sought by her own people and by Thamyris, she was looked for through the streets as one lost; and one of the fellow-servants of the doorkeeper told that she went out by night. And they examined the doorkeeper and he told them that she was gone to the stranger unto the prison; and they went as he told them and found her as it were bound with him, in affection. And they went forth thence and gathered the multitude to them and showed it to the governor.

20 And he commanded Paul to be brought to the judgement seat; but Thecla rolled herself upon the place where Paul taught when he sat in the prison. And the governor commanded her also to be brought to the judgement seat, and she went exulting with joy. And when Paul was brought the second time the people cried out more vehemently: He is a sorcerer, away with him! But the governor heard Paul gladly concerning the holy works of Christ: and he took counsel, and called Thecla and said: Why wilt thou not marry Thamyris, according to the law of the Iconians? but she stood looking earnestly upon Paul, and when she answered not, her mother Theocleia cried out, saying: Burn the lawless one, burn her that is no bride in the midst of the theatre, that all the women which have been taught by this man may be affrighted.

21 And the governor was greatly moved: and he scourged Paul and sent him out of the city, but Thecla he condemned to be burned. And straightway the governor arose and went to the theatre: and all the multitude went forth unto the dreadful spectacle. But Thecla, as the lamb in the wilderness looketh about for the shepherd, so sought for Paul: and she looked upon the multitude and saw the Lord sitting, like unto Paul, and said: As if I were not able to endure, Paul is come to look upon me. And she earnestly paid heed to him: but he departed into the heavens.

22 Now the boys and the maidens brought wood and hay to burn Thecla: and when she was brought in naked, the governor wept and marvelled at the power that was in her.

And they laid the wood, and the executioner bade her mount upon the pyre: and she, making the sign of the cross, went up upon the wood. And they lighted it, and though a great fire blazed forth, the fire took no hold on her; for God had compassion on her, and caused a sound under the earth, and a cloud overshadowed her above, full of rain and hail, and all the vessel of it was poured out so that many were in peril of death, and the fire was quenched, and Thecla was preserved.

23 Now Paul was fasting with Onesiphorus and his wife and their children in an open sepulchre on the way whereby they go from Iconium to Daphne. And when many days were past, as they fasted, the boys said unto Paul: We are anhungered. And they had not wherewith to buy bread, for Onesiphorus had left the goods of this world, and followed Paul with all his house. But Paul took off his upper garment and said: Go, child, buy several loaves and bring them. And as the boy was buying, he saw his neighbour Thecla, and was astonished, and said: Thecla, whither goest thou? And she said: I seek Paul, for I was preserved from the fire. And the boy said: Come, I will bring thee unto him, for he mourneth for thee and prayeth and fasteth now these six days.

24 And when she came to the sepulchre unto Paul, who had bowed his knees and was praying and saying: O Father of Christ, let not the fire take hold on Thecla, but spare her, for she is thine: she standing behind him cried out: O Father that madest heaven and earth, the Father of thy beloved child Jesus Christ, I bless thee for that thou hast preserved me from the fire, that I might see Paul. And Paul arose and saw her and said: O God the knower of hearts, the Father of our Lord Jesus Christ, I bless thee that thou hast speedily accomplished that which I asked of thee, and hast hearkened unto me.

25 And there was much love within the sepulchre, for Paul rejoiced, and Onesiphorus, and all of them. And they had five loaves, and herbs, and water (and salt), and they rejoiced for the holy works of Christ. And Thecla said unto Paul: I will cut my hair round about and follow thee whithersoever thou goest. But he said: The time is ill-favoured and thou art comely: beware lest another temptation take thee, worse than the first, and thou endure it not but play the coward. And Thecla said: Only give me the seal in Christ, and temptation shall not touch me. And Paul said: Have patience, Thecla, and thou shalt receive the water.

26 And Paul sent away Onesiphorus with all his house unto Iconium, and so took Thecla and entered into Antioch: and as they entered in, a certain Syriarch, Alexander by name, saw Thecla and was enamoured of her, and would have bribed (flattered) Paul with money and gifts. But Paul said: I know not the woman of whom thou speakest, neither is she mine. But as he was of great power, he himself embraced her in the highway; and she endured it not, but sought after Paul and cried out bitterly, saying: Force not the stranger, force not the handmaid of God. I am of the first of the Iconians, and because I would not marry Thamyris, I am cast out of the city. And she caught at Alexander and rent his cloak and took the wreath from his head and made him a mocking-stock.

27 But he alike loving her and being ashamed of what had befallen him, brought her before the governor; and when she confessed that she had done this, he condemned her to the beasts; But the women were greatly amazed, and cried out at the judgement seat: An evil judgement, an impious judgement! And Thecla asked of the governor that she might remain a virgin until she should fight the beasts; and a certain rich queen, Tryphaena by name, whose daughter had died, took her into her keeping, and had her for a consolation.

28 Now when the beasts were led in procession, they bound her to a fierce lioness, and the queen Tryphaena followed after her: but the lioness, when Thecla was set upon her, licked her feet, and all the people marvelled. Now the writing (title) of her accusation was: Guilty of sacrilege. And the women with their children cried out from above: O God, an impious judgement cometh to pass in this city. And after the procession Tryphaena took her again. For her daughter Falconilla, which was dead, had said to her in a dream: Mother, thou shalt take in my stead Thecla the stranger that is desolate, that she may pray for me and I be translated into the place of the righteous.

29 When therefore Tryphaena received her after the procession, she alike bewailed her because she was to fight the beasts on the morrow, and also, loving her closely as her own daughter Falconilla; and said: Thecla, my second child, come, pray thou for my child that she may live for ever; for this have I seen in a dream. And she without delay lifted up her voice and said: O my God, Son of the Most High that art in heaven, grant unto her according to her desire, that her daughter Faleonilla may live for ever. And after she had said this, Tryphaena bewailed her, considering that so great beauty was to be cast unto the beasts.

30 And when it was dawn, Alexander came to take her-for it was he that was giving the games-saying: The governor is set and the people troubleth us: give me her that is to fight the beasts, that I may take her away. But Tryphaena cried aloud so that he fled away, saying: A second mourning for my Falconilla cometh about in mine house, and there is none to help, neither child, for she is dead, nor kinsman, for I am a widow. O God of Thecla my child, help thou Thecla.

31 And the governor sent soldiers to fetch Thecla: and Tryphaena left her not, but herself took her hand and led her up, saying: I did bring my daughter Falconilla unto the sepulchre; but thee, Thecla, do I bring to fight the beasts. And Thecla wept bitterly and groaned unto the Lord, saying: Lord God in whom I believe, with whom I have taken refuge, that savedst me from the fire, reward thou Tryphaena who hath had pity on thine handmaid, and hath kept me pure.

32 There was therefore a tumult, and a voice of the beasts, and shouting of the people, and of the women which sat together, some saying: Bring in the sacrilegious one! and the women saying: Away with the city for this unlawful deed! away with all us, thou proconsul! it is a bitter sight, an evil judgement!

38 But Thecla, being taken out of the hand of Tryphaena, was stripped and a girdle put upon her, and was cast into

the stadium: and lions and bears were set against her. And a fierce lioness running to her lay down at her feet, and the press of women cried aloud. And a bear ran upon her; but the lioness ran and met him, and tore the bear in sunder. And again a lion, trained against men, which was Alexander's, ran upon her, and the lioness wrestled with him and was slain along with him. And the women bewailed yet more, seeing that the lioness also that succoured her was dead.

34 Then did they put in many beasts, while she stood and stretched out her hands and prayed. And when she had ended her prayer, she turned and saw a great tank full of water, and said: Now is it time that I should wash myself. And she cast herself in, saying: In the name of Jesus Christ do I baptize myself on the last day. And all the women seeing it and all the people wept, saying: Cast not thyself into the water: so that even the governor wept that so great beauty should be devoured by seals. So, then, she cast herself into the water in the name of Jesus Christ; and the seals, seeing the light of a flash of fire, floated dead on the top of the water. And there was about her a cloud of fire, so that neither did the beasts touch her, nor was she seen to be naked.

35 Now the women, when other more fearful beasts were put in, shrieked aloud, and some cast leaves, and others nard, others cassia, and some balsam, so that there was a multitude of odours; and all the beasts that were struck thereby were held as it were in sleep and touched her not; so that Alexander said to the governor: I have some bulls exceeding fearful, let us bind the criminal to them. And the governor frowning, allowed it, saying: Do that thou wilt. And they bound her by the feet between the bulls, and put hot irons under their bellies that they might be the more enraged and kill her. They then leaped forward; but the flame that burned about her, burned through the ropes, and she was as one not bound.

36 But Tryphaena, standing by the arena, fainted at the entry, so that her handmaids said: The queen Tryphaena is dead! And the governor stopped the games and all the city was frightened, and Alexander falling at the governor's feet said: Have mercy on me and on the city, and let the condemned go, lest the city perish with her; for if Caesar hear this, perchance he will destroy us and the city, because his kinswoman the queen Tryphaena hath died at the entry.

37 And the governor called Thecla from among the beasts, and said to her: Who art thou? and what hast thou about thee that not one of the beasts hath touched thee? But she said: I am the handmaid of the living God; and what I have about me-it is that I have believed on that his Son in whom God is well pleased; for whose sake not one of the beasts hath touched me. For he alone is the goal (or way) of salvation and the substance of life immortal; for unto them that are tossed about he is a refuge, unto the oppressed relief, unto the despairing shelter, and in a word, whosoever believeth not on him, shall not live, but die everlastingly.

38 And when the governor heard this, he commanded garments to be brought and said: Put on these garments. And she said: He that clad me when I was naked among the beasts, the same in the day of judgement will clothe me with salvation. And she took the garments and put them

on. And the governor forthwith issued out an act, saying: I release unto you Thecla the godly, the servant of God. And all the women cried out with a loud voice and as with one mouth gave praise to God, saying: One is the God who hath preserved Thecla: so that with their voice all the city shook.

39 And Tryphaena, when she was told the good tidings, met her with much people and embraced Thecla and said: Now do I believe that the dead are raised up: now do I believe that my child liveth: come within, and I will make thee heir of all my substance. Thecla therefore went in with her and rested in her house eight days, teaching her the word of God, so that the more part of the maid-servants also believed, and there was great joy in the house.

40 But Thecla yearned after Paul and sought him, sending about in all places; and it was told her that he was at Myra. And she took young men and maids, and girded herself, and sewed her mantle into a cloak after the fashion of a man, and departed into Myra, and found Paul speaking the word of God, and went to him. But he when he saw her and the people that were with her was amazed, thinking in himself: Hath some other temptation come upon her? But she perceived it, and said to him: I have received the washing, 0 Paul; for he that hath worked together with thee in the Gospel hath worked with me also unto my baptizing.

41 And Paul took her by the hand and brought her into the house of Hermias, and heard all things from her; so that Paul marvelled much, and they that heard were confirmed, and prayed for Tryphaena. And Thecla arose and said to Paul: I go unto Iconium. And Paul said: Go, and teach the word of God. Now Tryphaena had sent her much apparel and gold, so that she left of it with Paul for the ministry of the poor.

42 But she herself departed unto Iconium. And she entered into the house of Onesiphorus, and fell down upon the floor where Paul had sat and taught the oracles of God, and wept, saying: O God of me and of this house, where the light shone upon me, Jesu Christ the Son of God, my helper in prison, my helper before the governors, my helper in the fire, my helper among the beasts, thou art God, and unto thee be the glory for ever. Amen.

43 And she found Thamyris dead, but her mother living. And she saw her mother and said unto her: Theocleia my mother, canst thou believe that the Lord liveth in the heavens? for whether thou desirest money, the Lord will give it thee through me: or thy child, lo, I am here before thee. And when she had so testified, she departed unto Seleucia, and after she had enlightened many with the word of God, she slept a good sleep.

A good many manuscripts add that Theoeleia was not converted, but the Coptic does not support them: it ends the episode as above.

A long appendix is given by other Greek copies, telling how in Thecla's old age (she was ninety) she was living on Mount Calamon or Calameon, and some evil-disposed young men went up to ill-treat her: and she prayed, and the rock opened and she entered it, and it closed after her.

Some add that she went underground to Rome: this, to account for the presence of her body there.

Copt., p.38 of the MS.

III

When he was departed from Antioch and taught in Myra (Myrrha).

When Paul was teaching the word of God in Myra, there was there a man, Hermoerates by name, who had the dropsy, and he put himself forward in the sight of all, and said to Paul: Nothing is impossible with God, but especially with him whom thou preachest; for when he came he healed many, even that God whose servant thou art. Lo, I and my wife and my children, we cast ourselves at thy feet: have pity on me that I also may believe as thou hast believed on the living God.

Paul said unto him: I will restore thee (thine health) not for reward, but through the name of Jesus Christ thou shalt become whole in the presence of all these. (And he touched his body) drawing his hand downwards: and his belly opened and much water ran from him and . . . he fell down like a dead man, so that some said: It is better for him to die than to continue in pain. But when Paul had quieted the people, he took his hand and raised him up and asked him, saying: Hermocrates, ask for what thou desirest. And he said: I would eat. And he took a loaf and gave him to eat. And in that hour he was whole, and received the grace of the seal in the Lord, he and his wife.

But Hermippus his son was angry with Paul, and sought for a set time wherein to rise up with them of his own age and destroy him. For he wished that his father should not be healed but should die, that he might soon be master of his goods. But Dion, his younger son, heard Paul gladly.

Now all they that were with Hermippus took counsel to fight against Paul so that Hermippus . . . and sought to kill him

Dion fell down and died: but Hermippus watered Dion with his tears.

But Hermocrates mourned sore, for he loved Dion more than his other son. (Yet) he sat at Paul's feet, and forgat that Dion was dead. But when Dion was dead, his mother Nympha rent her clothes and went unto Paul and set herself before the face of Hermocrates her husband and of Paul. And when Paul saw her, he was affrighted and said: Wherefore art thou thus, Nympha? But she said to him: Dion is dead; and the whole multitude wept when they beheld her. And Paul looked upon the people that mourned and sent young men, saying to them: Go and bring me him hither. And they went: but Hermippus caught hold of the body (of Dion) in the street and cried out

A leaf lost.

the word in him (them?). But an angel of the Lord had said unto him in the night: Paul, thou hast to-day a great conflict

against thy body, but God, the Father of his Son Jesus Christ, will protect thee.

When Paul had arisen, he went unto his brethren, and remained (sorrowful?) saying: What meaneth this vision? And while Paul thought upon this, he saw Hermippus coming, having a sword drawn in his hand, and with him many other young men with staves. And Paul said unto them: I am not a robber, neither a murderer. The God of all things, the Father of Christ, will turn your hands backward, and your sword into its sheath, and your strength into weakness: for I am a servant of God, though I be alone and a stranger, and small and of no reputation (?) among the Gentiles. But do thou, 0 God, look down upon their counsel and suffer me not to be brought to nought by them.

And when Hermippus ran upon Paul with his sword drawn, straightway he ceased to see, so that he cried out aloud, saying: My dear comrades, forget not your friend Hermippus. For I have sinned, 0 Paul, I have pursued after innocent blood. Learn, ye foolish and ye of understanding, that this world is nought, gold is nought, all money is nought: I that glutted myself with all manner of goods am now a beggar and entreat of you all: Hearken to me all ye my companions, and every one that dwelleth in Myra. I have mocked at a man who hath saved my father: I have mocked at a man who hath raised up my brother Dion . . . I have mocked at a man who . . . without doing me any evil. But entreat ye of him: behold, he hath saved my father and raised up my brother; he is able therefore to save me also. But Paul stood there weeping alike before God, for that he heard him quickly, and before man, for that the proud was brought low. And he turned himself and went up . . . But the young men took the feet and bore Hermippus and brought him to the place where Paul was teaching and laid him down before the door and went unto their house. And when they were gone a great multitude came to the house of Hermocrates; and another great multitude entered in, to see whether Hermippus were shut up there. And Hermippus besought every one that went in, that they would entreat Paul, with him. But they that went in saw Hermocrates and Nympha, how they rejoiced greatly at the raising up of Dion, and distributed victuals and money unto the widows for his recovery. And they beheld Hermippus their son in the state of this second affliction, and how he took hold on the feet of every one, and on the feet of his parents also, and prayed them, as one of the strangers, that he might be healed. And his parents were troubled, and lamented to every one that came in, so that some said: Wherefore do these weep? for Dion is arisen. But Hermocrates possessed goods . . . and brought the value of the goods and took it and distributed it. And Hermocrates, troubled in mind and desiring that they might be satisfied, said: Brethren, let us leave the food . . . . and occupy ourselves . . . Hermocrates. And immediately Nympha cried out in great affliction unto Paul . . they said: Nympha, Hermocrates calleth upon God that your son Hermippus may see and cease to grieve, for he hath resisted Christ and his minister. But they and Paul prayed to God. And when Hermippus recovered his sight, he turned himself to his mother Nympha, and said to her: Paul came unto me and laid his hand upon me while I wept, and in that hour I saw all things clearly. And she took his hand and led him unto the widows and Paul. But while Paul wept bitterly,

Hermippus gave thanks, saying unto them: Every one that believeth, shall . . .

A leaf gone

. . . concord and peace . . . Amen.

And when Paul had confirmed the brethren that were in Myra, he departed unto Sidon.

IV

When he was departed from Myra .

Now when Paul was departed from Myra and would go unto Sidon there was great sadness of the brethren that were in Pisidia and Pamphylia, because they yearned after his word and his holy appearance in Christ; so that some from Perga followed Paul, namely Thrasymachus and Cleon with their wives Aline (?) and Chrysa, Cleon's wife. And on the way they nourished Paul: and they were eating their bread under a tree (?). And as he was about to say Amen, there came (five lines broken: the words 'the brethren' and 'idol' occur) . . . . table of devils . . . he dieth therefor, but every one that believeth on Jesus Christ who hath saved us from all defilement and all uncleanness and all evil thoughts, he shall be manifest. And they drew near unto the table (three lines broken. 'Idol' occurs) . . . . stood . . . a mighty idol. And an old man . . . . stood up among them, saying unto them: Ye men, (wait a little and see) what befalleth the priests which would draw near unto our gods: for verily when our fellow-citizen Charinus hearkened and would . . . . against the gods, there died he and his (father). And thereupon died Xanthus also, Chrysa (?), and (Hermocrates?) died, sick of the dropsy, and his wife Nympha.

Two leaves at least gone.

(Paul is speaking)

after the manner of strange men. Wherefore presume ye to do that which is not seemly (?)? Or have ye not heard of that which came to pass, which God brought upon Sodom and Gomorrha, because they robbed . . . . after the manner of strangers and of women? God did not . . . . them but cast them down into hell. Now therefore we are not men of this fashion that ye say, nor such as ye think, but we are preachers of the living God and his Beloved. But that ye may not marvel, understand . . . the miracles (?) which bear witness for us. But they hearkened not unto him, but took the men and put them into the temple of Apollo, to keep them until the morrow, whereon they assembled the whole city. And many and costly were the victuals which they gave them.

But Paul, who was fasting now the third day, testified all the night long, being troubled, and smote his face and said: O God, look down upon their threatenings and suffer us not to slide, and let not our adversaries cast us down, but save us and bring down quickly thy righteousness upon us. And as Paul cast himself down, with the brethren, Thrasymachus and Cleon, then the temple fell . . . . so that they that belonged to the temple and the magistrates that

were set over it . . . . others of them in the . . . . for (the one part) fell down . . . . fell down . . . . round about, in the midst of the two parts. And they went in and beheld what had happened, and marvelled that . . . . in their . . . . and that the . . . . rejoiced over the falling of the temple (?). And they cried out, saying: Verily these are the works of the men of a mighty God! And they departed and proclaimed in the city: Apollo the god of the Sidonians is fallen, and the half of his temple. And all the dwellers in the city ran to the temple and saw Paul and them that were with him, how they wept at this temptation, that they were made a spectacle for all men. But the multitude cried out: Bring them into the theatre. And the magistrates came to fetch them; and they groaned bitterly with one soul.

About two leaves gone.

(Paul speaking) through me. Consider . . . . (nine lines much broken, 'the way of life (conversation) of Christ', 'not in the faith', occur) . . . . Egyptians . . . . and they . . . But the multitude . . . . and followed after Paul, crying: Praised be the God . . . . who hath sent Paul . . . that we should not . . . . of death. But Theudes . . . . and prayed at Paul's feet and embraced his feet, that he should give him the seal in the Lord. But he commanded them to go to Tyre . . . . in health (or farewell), and they put Paul (in a ship?) and went with him.

The purpose of confining Paul and his companions in the temple appears to have been connected with the sins of the cities of the plain of which Paul speaks.

The Acts of Titus, quoted before, have a sentence referring to this and the next episode: 'And Paul healed Aphphia the wife of Chrysippus who was possessed with a devil: and fasting for seven days he overthrew the idol of Apollo.' The Acts place this immediately after the conversion and preaching at Damascus, and put the Panehares episode later. They are not to be trusted, therefore, as a guide to the order of our book.

V

When he was departed out of Sidon and would go unto Tyre.

Now when Paul was entered unto Tyre there came a multitude of Jews . . . . in to him. These . . . . and they heard the mighty works . . . They marvelled . . . . Amphion (= Aphphia of the Acts of Titus) . . . . saying . . . . in . . . . Chrysippus . . . . devil with him . . . . many . . . . When Paul came . . . . he said: He . . . . God and will not be an evil spirit (?) . . . . in (?) Amphion . . . . through the evil spirit . . . . without any one's having . . . . she said to him: Save me that I die not. And while the multitude . . . . then arose the other (?) evil spirit . . . . And forthwith the devils fled away. And when the multitude saw this, by the power of God, they praised him who had (given such power) unto Paul. And there was there one by name... rimus, who had a son born to him which was dumb.

On the next page is a proper name, Lix (or perhaps Kilix, a Cilician), and later the words, 'I preach the good tidings of the Saviour . . . . SonofGod'.

On the next page. Lix perhaps occurs again, and 'Moses'.

The next begins: for that which we say cometh to pass forthwith. Behold we will bring him hither unto thee that he may . . . . thee, to hear the truth of thy . . . .

Next page. On God whose desire is come to pass in him, this is the wise man . . . . . . the Father and he hath sent Jesus Christ.

Next page, turned toward the East. Moses . . .

. . . in Syria in Cyrene

Again I say unto you . . . I, that do the works . . .

that a man is not justifed by the Law, but that he is justified by the works of righteousness, and he . . .

Next page has the words 'liberty', 'and the yoke', 'all flesh'; and, 'and every one confess that Jesus Christ is the glory of the Father'.

Next page, lower part: is not water in him, but . . . being water, I am not hungry but I am thirsty; I am not but not to . . . . to suffer them, to be (devoured) by wild beasts, not to be able . . . . from the earth, but not to suffer them to be burnt by the fire, are these things of the present age testified, he which was a persecutor . . .

Next page, lower part, (Cle)anthes. the law of God which is called . . . . who walketh here before them, hath he not followed us throughout all the cities . . . And when . . . . he turned himself toward the East after this (after two lines) such words, neither preacheth he as thou preachest them, 0 Paul, that thou mayest not . . . .

Next page begins: Thou art in the presence (sight, face) of Jerusalem, but I trust in the Lord that thou wilt . . .

The name 'Saul' is almost certain some lines later.

Next page begins: whom they crucified.

And at the end: raised up our flesh.

Next page, 7th line, For since the day when . . . . persecuted the apostles which were (with me? se. Peter) out of Jerusalem, I hid myself that I might have comfort, and we nourish them which stand, through the word according to the promise (?) of his grace. I have fallen into many troubles and have subjected myself to the law, as for your sakes. But thought by night and by day in my trouble on Jesus Christ, waiting for him as a lamb . . . . when they crucified him he did not . . . did not resist . . . . was not troubled.

The above may be a speech of Peter. We have seen some indication that Paul is now at Jerusalem, and the conjecture is that a dialogue between him and Peter occurred in this place.

The next page undoubtedly mentions Peter.

Line 1 has 'Paul', line 3, 'twelve (?) shepherds'.

Line 5, through Paul. But . . . . was troubled because of the questioning (examination) that (was come) upon Peter and he cried out, saying: Verily, God is one, and there is no God beside him: one also is Jesus Christ his Son, whom we . . . this, whom thou preachest, did we crucify, whom expect in great glory, but ye say that he is God and Judge of the living and the dead, the King of the ages, for the in the form of man.

VI

Paul is condemned to the mines in an unknown place. Longinus and Firmilla have a daughter, Frontina, who is to be thrown down from a rock, and Paul with her. It is my distinct opinion that Fontina is already dead: her body is to be thus contumeliously treated because she has become a Christian.

The upper part of the page has Longinus twice in lines 1, 2; 'Paul' in 1.7. Then:

For since . . . . the mine, there hath not . . . nothing good hath befallen mine house. And he advised that the men which were to throw Frontina down, should throw down Paul also with her, alive. Now Paul knew these things, but he worked fasting, in great cheerfulness, for two days with the prisoners. They commanded that on the third day the men . . . . should bring forth Frontina: and the whole city followed after her. And Firmilla and Longinus lamented and the soldiers . . . But the prisoners carried the bed (bier). And when Paul saw the great mourning with the daughter and eight . . .

Next page, line 8. Paul alive with the daughter. But when Paul had taken the daughter in his arms, he groaned unto the Lord Jesus Christ because of the sorrow of Firmilla, and cast himself on his knees in the mire . . . . praying for Frontina with her in one (a) prayer. In that hour Frontina rose up. And the whole multitude was afraid, and fled. Paul took the hand of the daughter and led her through the city unto the house of Longinus, and the whole multitude said with one voice: God is one, who hath made heaven and earth, who hath granted the life of the daughter in the presence of Paul . . . a loaf. and he gave thanks to him.

Some lines later.

to Philippi (?).

VII

When he was departed from . . . and would go .

Now when Paul was come to Philippi . . . he entered into the house of . . . . and there was great joy (among the brethren) and to every one.

On the following page begins the episode of the correspondence with the Corinthians, which was circulated separately in Syriac, Latin, and Armenian, and found a place in the Syriac collection of Pauline epistles (and is commented on with the rest by Ephraem the Syrian), and in the Armenian Bible. We have it in (a) many Armenian MSS., (b) in Ephraem s commentary-only extant in Armenian, (c) in three Latin MSS., at Milan, Laon, and Paris: as well as in the Coptic MS., which is here less fragmentary than in the preceding pages.

We begin with a short narrative, introducing the letter of the Corinthians to Paul; then follows another short piece of narrative, extant in Armenian only; then Paul's reply, commonly called the 'Third Epistle to the Corinthians'.

There are various phrases and whole sentences, especially in the Armenian and the Milan MS. of the Latin, which are absent from the Coptic and the Laon MS. and are regarded, rightly, as interpolations.

These will be distinguished by small capitals.

The page of the Coptic MS. on which the correspondence begins is fragmentary at the beginning.

1.1. the lawless one

1.2. the reward. They . . . . in

1.3. a prayer . . . . every

1.4. one, and every one (?)

1.6. Paul . . . . again (or together).

1.7. prayed that a messenger be sent to Philippi. For the Corinthians were in great trouble concerning Paul, that he would depart out of the world, before it was time. For there were certain men come to Corinth, Simon and Cleobius, saying: There is no resurrection of the flesh, but that of the spirit only: and that the body of man is not the creation of God; and also concerning the world, that God did not create it, and that God knoweth not the world, and that Jesus Christ was not crucified, but it was an appearance (i.e. but only in appearance), and that lie was not born of Mary, nor of the seed of David. And in a word, there were many things which they had taught in Corinth, deceiving many other men, (and deceiving also) themselves. When therefore the Corinthians heard that Paul was at Philippi, they sent a letter unto Paul to Macedonia by Threptus and Eutychus the deacons. And the letter was after this manner.

I. 1 Stephanus and the elders (presbyters) that are with him, even Daphnus and Eubulus and Theophilus and Zenon, unto Paul THEIR BROTHER ETERNAL greeting in the Lord.

2 There have come unto Corinth two men, Simon and Cleobius, which are overthrowing the faith of many with evil (CORRUPT) words, 3 which do thou prove AND EXAMINE: 4 for we have never heard such words from thee nor from the other apostles: 5 but all that we have received from thee or from them, that do we hold fast. 6 Since therefore the Lord hath had mercy on us, that while thou art still in the flesh we may hear these things again from thee, 7 if it be possible, either come unto us or write unto us. 8 For we believe, according as it hath been

revealed unto Theonoe, that the Lord hath delivered thee out of the hand of the lawless one (enemy, Laon).

9 Now the things which these men say and teach are these: 10 They say that we must not use the prophets, 11 and that God is not Almighty, 12 and that there shall be no resurrection of the flesh, 13 and that man was not made by God, 14 and that Christ came not down (is not come, Copt.) in the flesh, neither was born of Mary, 15 and that the world is not of God, but of the angels.

16 Wherefore, brother, WE PRAY THEE use all diligence to come unto us, that the church of the Corinthians may remain without offence, and the madness of these men may be made plain. Farewell ALWAYS in the Lord.

II. 1 The deacons Threptus and Eutyches brought the letter unto Philippi, 2 so that Paul received it, being in bonds because of Stratonice the wife of Apollophanes, AND HE FORGAT HIS BONDS, and was sore afflicted, 3 and cried out, saying: It were better for me to die and to be with the Lord, than to continue in the flesh and to hear such things AND THE CALAMITIES OF FALSE DOCTRINE, so that trouble cometh upon trouble. 4 And over and above this so great affliction I am in bonds and behold these evils whereby the devices of Satan are accomplished. (4 Harnack: may not the priests (intrigues) of Satan anticipate me while (or after) I suffer (have suffered) fetters for the sake (?) of men.) 5 Paul therefore, in great affliction, wrote a letter, answering thus:

III.1 Paul, a prisoner of Jesus Christ, unto the brethren which are in Corinth, greeting.

2 Being in the midst of many tribulations, I marvel not if the teachings of the evil one run abroad apace. 3 For my Lord Jesus Christ will hasten his coming, and will set at nought (no longer endure the insolence of) them that falsify his words.

4 For I delivered unto you in the beginning the things which I received of the HOLY apostles which were before me, who were at all times with Jesus Christ: 5 namely, that our Lord Jesus Christ was born of Mary WHICH IS of the seed of David ACCORDING TO THE FLESH, the Holy Ghost being sent forth from heaven from the Father unto her BY THE ANGEL GABRIEL, 6 that he (JESUS) might come down into this world and redeem all flesh by his flesh, and raise us up from the dead in the flesh, like as he hath shown to us in himself for an ensample. 7 And because man was formed by his Father, 8 therefore was he sought when he was lost, that he might be quickened by adoption. 9 For to this end did God Almighty who made heaven and earth first send the prophets unto the Jews, that they might be drawn away from their sins. 10 For he designed to save the house of Israel: therefore he conferred a portion of the spirit of Christ upon the prophets and sent them unto the Jews first (or unto the first Jews), and they proclaimed the true worship of God for a long space of time. 11 But the prince of iniquity, desiring to be God, laid hands on them and slew them (banished them from God, Laon MS.), and bound all flesh by evil lusts (AND THE END OF THE WORLD BY JUDGEMENT DREW NEAR).

12 But God Almighty, who is righteous, would not cast away his own creation, BUT HAD COMPASSION ON THEM FROM HEAVEN, 13 and sent his spirit into Mary IN GALILEE, [14 Milan MS. and Arm.: WHO BELIEVED WITH ALL HER HEART AND RECEIVED THE HOLY GHOST IN HER WOMB, THAT JESUS MIGHT COME INTO THE WORLD,] 15 that by that flesh whereby that wicked one had brought in death (had triumphed), by the same he should be shown to be overcome. 16 For by his own body Jesus Christ saved all flesh [AND RESTORED IT UNTO LIFE], 17 that he might show forth the temple of righteousness in his body. 18 In whom (or whereby) we are saved (Milan, Paris: in whom if we believe we are set free).

19 They therefore (Paris MS.; Arm. has: Know therefore that. Laon has: They therefore who agree with them) are not children of righteousness but children of wrath who reject the wisdom (providence?) of God, saying that the heaven and the earth and all that are in them are not the work of God. 20 THEY THEREFORE ARE CHILDREN OF WRATH, for cursed are they, following the teaching of the serpent, 21 whom do ye drive out from you and flee from their doctrine. [Arm., Milan, Paris: 22 FOR YE ARE NOT CHILDREN OF DISOBEDIENCE, BUT OF THE WELL-BELOVED CHURCH. 23 THEREFORE IS THE TIME OF THE RESURRECTION PROCLAIMED UNTO ALL.]

24 And as for that which they say, that there is no resurrection of the flesh, they indeed shall have no resurrection UNTO LIFE, BUT UNTO JUDGEMENT, 25 because they believe not in him that is risen from the dead, NOT BELIEVING NOR UNDERSTANDING, 26 for they know not, O Corinthians, the seeds of wheat or of other seeds (grain), how they are cast bare into the earth and are corrupted and rise again by the will of God with bodies, and clothed. 27 And not only that [body] which is cast in riseth again, but manifold more blessing itself [i.e. fertile and prospering]. 28 And if we must not take an example from seeds ONLY, BUT FROM MORE NOBLE BODIES, 29 ye know how Jonas the son of Amathi, when he would not preach to them of Nineve, BUT FLED, was swallowed by the sea-monster; 30 and after three days and three nights God heard the prayer of Jonas out of the lowest hell, and no part of him was consumed, not even an hair nor an eyelash. 31 How much more, O YE OF LITTLE FAITH, shall he raise up you that have believed in Christ Jesus, like as he himself arose. 32 Likewise also a dead man was cast upon the bones of the prophet Helisaetis by the children of Israel, and he arose, both body and soul and bones and spirit (Laon: arose in his body); how much more shall ye which have been cast upon the body and bones and spirit of the Lord [Milan, Paris: how much more, O ye of little faith, shall ye which have been cast on him] arise again in that day having your flesh whole, EVEN AS HE AROSE? [33 Arm., Milan, Paris: LIKEWISE ALSO CONCERNING THE PROPHET HELIAS: HE RAISED UP THE WIDOW'S SON FROM DEATH: HOW MUCH MORE SHALL THE LORD JESUS RAISE YOU UP FROM DEATH AT THE SOUND OF THE TRUMPET, IN THE TWINKLING OF AN EYE? FOR HE HATH SHOWED US AN ENSAMPLE IN HIS OWN BODY.]

34 If, then, ye receive any other doctrine, GOD SHALL BE WITNESS AGAINST YOU; AND let no man trouble me, 35 for I bear these bonds that I may win Christ, and I therefore bear his marks in my body that I may attain unto the resurrection of the dead. 86 And whoso receiveth (abideth in) the rule which he hath received by the blessed prophets and the holy gospel, shall receive a recompense from the Lord, AND WHEN HE RISETH FROM THE DEAD SHALL OBTAIN ETERNAL LIFE. 37 But whoso trans- gresseth these things, with him is the fire, and with them that walk in like manner (Milan, Paris: with them that go before in the same way, WHO ARE MEN WITHOUT GOD), 38 which are a generation of vipers, 39 whom do ye reject in the power of the Lord, 40 and peace, GRACE, AND LOVE shall be with you.

[Laon adds: This I found in an old book, entitled the third to the Corinthians, though it is not in the Canon.]

VIII

AT EPHESUS

This episode is not traceable in the Coptic MS. but it undoubtedly formed part of the Acts, though its place is uncertain. It is preserved in an allusion by Hippolytus (early third century) and in an abstract by Nicephorus Callisti (fourteenth century) in his Ecclesiastical history (ii. 25). There is also a sentence in the Acts of Titus:

'They departed from Crete and came to Asia: and at Ephesus twelve thousand believed at the teaching of the holy Paul: there also he fought with beasts, being thrown to a lion.'

HIPPOLYTUS in his Commentary on Daniel, iii. 29, says:

For if we believe that when Paul was condemned to the beasts the lion that was set upon him lay down at his feet and licked him, how shall we not believe that which happened in the case of Daniel?

NICEPHORUS:

Now they who drew up the travels of Paul have related that he did many other things, and among them this, which befell when he was at Ephesus. Hieronymus being governor, Paul used liberty of speech, and he (Hieronymus) said that he (Paul) was able to speak well, but that this was not the time for such words. But the people of the city, fiercely enraged, put Paul's feet into irons, and shut him up in the prison, till he should be exposed as a prey to the lions. But Eubula and Artemilla, wives of eminent men among the Ephesians, being his attached disciples, and visiting him by night, desired the grace of the divine washing. And by God's power, with angels to escort them and enlighten the gloom of night with the excess of the brightness that was in them, Paul, loosed from his iron fetters, went to the sea-shore and initiated them into holy baptism, and returning to his bonds without any of those in care of the prison perceiving it, was reserved as a prey for the lions.

A lion, then, of huge size and unmatched strength was let loose upon him, and it ran to him in the stadium and lay down at his feet. And when many other savage beasts, too, were let loose, it was permitted to none of them to touch the holy body, standing like a statue in prayer. At this juncture a violent and vast hailstorm poured down all at once with a great rush, and shattered the heads of many men and beasts as well, and shore off the ear of Hieronymus himself. And thereafter, with his followers, he came to the God of Paul and received the baptism of salvation. But the lion escaped to the mountains.

And thence Paul sailed to Macedonia and Greece, and thereafter through Macedonia came to Troas and to Miletus, and from there set out for Jerusalem.

Now it is not surprising that Luke has not narrated this fight with the beasts along with the other Acts: for it is not permitted to entertain doubt because (or seeing that) John alone of the evangelists has told of the raising of Lazarus: for we know that not every one writes, believes, or knows everything, but according as the Lord has imparted to each, as the spirit divides to each, so does he perceive and believe and write spiritually the things of the spirit.

Hippolytus is a voucher for the early date of the story, and Nicephorus for its source. It will be recognized, moreover, at once as being quite in the manner of our author. The anger of the Ephesians, it cannot be doubted, was roused by Paul's preaching of continence, to which Eubula and Artemilla had become converts. The episode is really little more than a repetition of Thecla, with Paul for the principal figure.

IX

FRAGMENTS: SCENES OF FAREWELL

(Paul speaking) . . . thanksgiving (?)

The grace of the Lord will walk with me until I have fulfilled all the dispensations which shall come upon me with patience. But they were sorrowful, and fasted. And Cleobius was in the Spirit and said unto them: Brethren, (the Lord) will suffer Paul to fulfil every dispensation and thereafter will suffer him to go up (to Jerusalem). But thereafter shall be . . . . in much instruction and knowledge and sowing of the word, so that men shall envy him, and so he shall depart out of this world. But when Paul and the brethren heard this, they lifted up their voices, saying:

Next page, first extant line, 'beheld'. Second, 'shall say'. Third, But the Spirit came upon Myrte so that she said unto them: Brethren . . . and look upon this sign, that ye . . . For Paul the servant of the Lord shall save many in Rome, so that of them shall be no number, and he will manifest himself more than all the faithful. Thereafter shall . . . . of the Lord Jesus Christ come . . . . a great grace is . . . .at Rome. And this is the manner wherein the Spirit spake unto Myrte. And every one took the bread, and they were in joy, according to the custom of the fast, through . . . . and the psalms of David and . . . . he rejoiced.

On the next page the only significant words are 'to Rome'; 'the brethren'; 'grieved'; 'took the bread'; 'praised the Lord'; 'were very sorrowful'.

The next has ends of lines: 'the Lord'; 'risen'; 'Jesus'; 'Paul said to him'. The last is 'he (or they) greeted'.

Two more pages have nothing of moment. The next is concerned with the Martyrdom.

X

THE MARTYRDOM

This, preserved separately to be read on the day of Commemoration, exists in two Greek copies, an incomplete Latin version, and versions in Syriac, Coptic, Ethiopic, Slavonic, besides fragments in our Coptic MS.

I. Now there were awaiting Paul at Rome Luke from Galatia (Gaul, Gk.) and Titus from Dalmatia: whom when Paul saw he was glad: and hired a grange outside Rome, wherein with the brethren he taught the word of truth, and he became noised abroad and many souls were added unto the Lord, so that there was a rumour throughout all Rome, and much people came unto him from the household of Caesar, believing, and there was great joy.

And a certain Patroclus, a cup-bearer of Caesar, came at even unto the grange, and not being able because of the press to enter in to Paul, he sat in a high window and listened to him teaching the word of God. But whereas the evil devil envied the love of the brethren, Patroclus fell down from the window and died, and forthwith it was told unto Nero.

But Paul perceiving it by the spirit said: Men and brethren, the evil one hath gained occasion to tempt you: go out of the house and ye shall find a lad fallen from the height and now ready to give up the ghost; take him up and bring him hither to me. And they went and brought him; and when the people saw it they were troubled. But Paul said: Now, brethren, let your faith appear; come all of you and let us weep unto our Lord Jesus Christ, that this lad may live and we continue in quietness. And when all had lamented, the lad received his spirit again, and they set him on a beast and sent him back alive, together with the rest that were of Caesar's household.

II. But Nero, when he heard of the death of Patroclus, was sore grieved, and when he came in from the bath he commanded another to be set over the wine. But his servants told him, saying: Caesar, Patroclus liveth and standeth at the table. And Caesar, hearing that Patroclus lived, was affrighted and would not go in. But when he went in, he saw Patroclus, and was beside himself, and said: Patroclus, livest thou? And he said: I live, Caesar. And he said: Who is he that made thee to live? And the lad, full of the mind of faith, said: Christ Jesus, the king of the ages. And Caesar was troubled and said: Shall he, then, be king of the ages and overthrow all kingdoms? Patroclus saith unto him: Yea, he overthroweth all kingdoms and he alone shall be for ever, and there shall be no kingdom that shall escape him. And he smote him on the face and said:

Patroclus, art thou also a soldier of that king? And he said: Yea, Lord Caesar, for he raised me when I was dead. And Barsabas Justus of the broad feet, and Urion the Cappadocian, and Festus the Galatian, Caesar's chief men, said: We also are soldiers of the king of the ages. And he shut them up in prison, having grievously tormented them, whom he loved much, and commanded the soldiers of the great king to be sought out, and set forth a decree to this effect, that all that were found to be Christians and soldiers of Christ should be slain.

III. And among many others Paul also was brought, bound: unto whom all his fellow-prisoners gave heed; so that Caesar perceived that he was over the camp. And he said to him: Thou that art the great king's man, but my prisoner, how thoughtest thou well to come by stealth into the government of the Romans and levy soldiers out of my province? But Paul, filled with the Holy Ghost, said before them all: 0 Caesar, not only out of thy province do we levy soldiers, but out of the whole world. For so hath it been ordained unto us, that no man should be refused who wisheth to serve my king. And if it like thee also to serve him (Lat. thou wilt not repent thereof: but think not that the wealth, &c., which seems better), it is not wealth nor the splendour that is now in this life that shall save thee; but if thou submit and entreat him, thou shalt be saved; for in one day (or one day) he shall fight against the world with fire. And when Caesar heard that, he commanded all the prisoners to be burned with fire, but Paul to be beheaded after the law of the Romans.

But Paul kept not silence concerning the word, but communicated with Longus the prefect and Cestus the centurion.

Nero therefore went on (was) (perhaps add 'raging') in Rome, slaying many Christians without a hearing, by the working of the evil one; so that the Romans stood before the palace and cried It sufficeth, Caesar! for the men are our own! thou destroyest the strength of the Romans! Then at that he was persuaded and ceased, and commanded that no man should touch any Christian, until he should learn throughly concerning them.

IV. Then was Paul brought unto him after the decree; and he abode by his word that he should be beheaded. And Paul said: Caesar, it is not for a little space that I live unto my king; and if thou behead me, this will I do: I will arise and show myself unto thee that I am not dead but live unto my Lord Jesus Christ, who cometh to judge the world.

But Longus and Cestus said unto Paul: Whence have ye this king, that ye believe in him and will not change your mind, even unto death? And Paul communicated unto them the word and said: Ye men that are in this ignorance and error, change your mind and be saved from the fire that cometh upon all the world: for we serve not, as ye suppose, a king that cometh from the earth, but from heaven, even the living God, who because of the iniquities that are done in this world, cometh as a judge; and blessed is that man who shall believe in him and shall live for ever when he cometh to burn the world and purge it throughly. Then they beseeching him said: We entreat thee, help us, and we will let thee go. But he answered and said: I am not a deserter of Christ, but a lawful soldier of the living God: if I had

known that I should die, O Longus and Cestus, I would have done it, but seeing that I live unto God and love myself, I go unto the Lord, to come with him in the glory of his Father. They say unto him: How then shall we live when thou art beheaded?

V. And while they yet spake thus, Nero sent one Parthenius and Pheres to see if Paul were already beheaded; and they found him yet alive. And he called them to him and said: Believe on the living God, which raiseth me and all them that believe on him from the dead. And they said: We go now unto Nero; but when thou diest and risest again, then will we believe on thy God. And as Longus and Cestus entreated him yet more concerning salvation, he saith to them: Come quickly unto my grave in the morning and ye shall find two men praying, Titus and Luke. They shall give you the seal in the Lord.

Then Paul stood with his face to the east and lifted up his hands unto heaven and prayed a long time, and in his prayer he conversed in the Hebrew tongue with the fathers, and then stretched forth his neck without speaking. And when the executioner (speculator) struck off his head, milk spurted upon the cloak of the soldier. And the soldier and all that were there present when they saw it marvelled and glorified God which had given such glory unto Paul: and they went and told Caesar what was done.

VI. And when he heard it, while he marvelled long and was in perplexity, Paul came about the niuth hour, when many philosophers and the centurion were standing with Caesar, and stood before them all and said: Caesar, behold, I, Paul, the soldier of God, am not dead, but live in my God. But unto thee shall many evils befall and great punishment, thou wretched man, because thou hast shed unjustly the blood of the righteous, not many days hence. And having so said Paul departed from him. But Nero hearing it and being greatly troubled commanded the prisoners to be loosed, and Patroclus also and Barsabas and them that were with him.

VII. And as Paul charged them, Longus and Cestus the centurion went early in the morning and approached with fear unto the grave of Paul. And when they were come thither they saw two men praying, and Paul betwixt them, so that they beholding the wondrous marvel were amazed, but Titus and Luke being stricken with the fear of man when they saw Longus and Cestus coming toward them, turned to flight. But they pursued after them, saying: We pursue you not for death but for life, that ye may give it unto us, as Paul promised us, whom we saw just now standing betwixt you and praying. And when they heard that, Titus and Luke rejoiced and gave them the seal in the Lord, glorifying the God and Father of our Lord Jesus Christ (Copt. and glorified the Lord Jesus Christ and all the saints).

Unto whom be glory world without end. Amen.

The Coptic MS. has a colophon: The Acts of Paul according to the Apostle.

ACTS OF ANDREW

Introduction

We have no ancient record of the length of this book, as we had in the cases of John, Paul, and Peter (but I suspect it was the most prolix of all the five), and we have fewer relics of the original text than for those. We have, however, a kind of abstract of the whole, written in Latin by Gregory of Tours: and there are Greek Encomia of the apostle which also help to the reconstruction of the story. The Martyrdom (as in other cases) exists separately, in many texts. Max Bonnet has established the relations of these to each other: and J. Flamion has made a most careful study of all the fragments.

The best specimen of the original text which we have is a fragment preserved in a Vatican MS., tenth-eleventh centuries, containing discourses of Andrew shortly before his passion. There are also a few ancient quotations.

These Acts may be the latest of the five leading apostolic romances. They belong to the third century: C. A. D. 260?

It was formerly thought that the Acts of Andrew and Matthias (Matthew) were an episode of the original romance: but this view has ceased to be held. That legend is akin to the later Egyptian romances about the apostles of which an immense number were produced in the fifth and later centuries. An abstract of them will be given in due course.

The epitome by Gregory of Tours is considered by Flamion to give on the whole the best idea of the contents of the original Acts. The latest edition of it is that by M. Bonnet in the Monumenta Germaniac Historica (Greg. Turon. II. 821-47). The greater part appears as Lib. III of the Historia Apostolica of (Pseudo-)Abdias, in a text much altered, it seems, in the sixteenth century by Wolfgang Lazius: reprinted in Fabricius' Cod. Apocr. N. T.

Gregory's prologue is as follows:

The famous triumphs of the apostles are, I believe, not unknown to any of the faithful, for some of them are taught us in the pages of the gospel, others are related in the Acts of the Apostles, and about some of them books exist in which the actions of each apostle are recorded; yet of the more part we have nothing but their Passions in writing.

Now I have come upon a book on the miracles (virtues, great deeds) of St. Andrew the apostle, which, because of its excessive verbosity, was called by some apocryphal. And of this I thought good to extract and set out the 'virtues' only, omitting all that bred weariness, and so include the wonderful miracles within the compass of one small volume, which might both please the reader and ward off the spite of the adverse critic: for it is not the multitude of words, but the soundness of reason and the purity of mind that produce unblemished faith.

[What follows is a full abstract, not a version, of Gregory's text.]

Text

1 After the Ascension the apostles dispersed to preach in various countries. Andrew began in the province of Achaia, but Matthew went to the city of Mermidona. (The rest of 1 and the whole of 2 give a short abstract of the Acts of Andrew and Matthew which Gregory either found prefixed to his copy of the Acts of Andrew, or thought himself obliged to notice, because of the popularity of the story.)

2 Andrew left Mermidona and came back to his own allotted district. Walking with his disciples he met a blind man who said: 'Andrew, apostle of Christ, I know you can restore my sight, but I do not wish for that: only bid those with you to give me enough money to clothe and feed myself decently.' Andrew said: 'This is the devil's voice, who will not allow the man to recover his sight.' He touched his eyes and healed him. Then, as be had but a vile rough garment, Andrew said: 'Take the filthy garment off him and clothe him afresh.' All were ready to strip themselves, and Andrew said: 'Let him have what will suffice him.' He returned home thankful.

3 Demetrius of Amasea had an Egyptian boy of whom he was very fond, who died of a fever. Demetrius hearing of Andrew's miracles, came, fell at his feet, and besought help. Andrew pitied him, came to the house, held a very long discourse, turned to the bier, raised the boy, and restored him to his master. All believed and were baptized.

4 A Christian lad named Sostratus came to Andrew privately and told him: 'My mother cherishes a guilty passion for me: I have repulsed her, and she has gone to the proconsul to throw the guilt on me. I would rather die than expose her.' The officers came to fetch the boy, and Andrew prayed and went with him. The mother accused him. The proconsul bade him defend himself. He was silent, and so continued, until the proconsul retired to take counsel. The mother began to weep. Andrew said: 'Unhappy woman, that dost not fear to cast thine own guilt on thy son.' She said to the proconsul: 'Ever since my son entertained his wicked wish he has been in constant company with this man.' The proconsul was enraged, ordered the lad to be sewn into the leather bag of parricides and drowned in the river, and Andrew to be imprisoned till his punishment should be devised. Andrew prayed, there was an earthquake, the proconsul fell from his seat, every one was prostrated, and the mother withered up and died. The proconsul fell at Andrew's feet praying for mercy. The earthquake and thunder ceased, and he healed those who had been hurt. The proconsul and his house were baptized.

5 The son of Cratinus (Gratinus) of Sinope bathed in the women's bath and was seized by a demon. Cratinus wrote to Andrew for help: he himself had a fever and his wife dropsy. Andrew went there in a vehicle. The boy tormented by the evil spirit fell at his feet. He bade it depart and so it did, with outcries. He then went to Cratinus' bed and told him he well deserved to suffer because of his loose life, and bade him rise and sin no more. He was healed. The wife was rebuked for her infidelity. 'If she is to return to her former sin, let her not now be healed: if she can keep from

it, let her be healed.' The water broke out of her body and she was cured. The apostle brake bread and gave it her. She thanked God, believed with all her house, and relapsed no more into sin. Cratinus afterwards sent Andrew great gifts by his servants, and then, with his wife, asked him in person to accept them, but he refused saying: 'It is rather for you to give them to the needy.'

6 After this he went to Nicaea where were seven devils living among the tombs by the wayside, who at noon stoned passersby and had killed many. And all the city came out to meet Andrew with olive branches, crying: 'Our salvation is in thee, O man of God.' When they had told him all, he said: 'If you believe in Christ you shall be freed.' They cried: 'We will.' He thanked God and commanded the demons to appear; they came in the form of dogs. Said he: "These are your enemies: if you profess your belief that I can drive them out in Jesus' name, I will do so.' They cried out: 'We believe that Jesus Christ whom thou preachest is the Son of God.' Then he bade the demons go into dry and barren places and hurt no man till the last day. They roared and vanished. The apostle baptized the people and made Callistus bishop.

7 At the gate of Nicomedia he met a dead man borne on a bier, and his old father supported by slaves, hardly able to walk, and his old mother with hair torn, bewailing. 'How has it happened ?' he asked. 'He was alone in his chamber and seven dogs rushed on him and killed him.' Andrew sighed and said: "This is an ambush of the demons I banished from Nicaea. What will you do, father, if I restore your son ?' 'I have nothing more precious than him, I will give him.' He prayed: 'Let the spirit of this lad return.' The faithful responded, 'Amen'. Andrew bade the lad rise, and he rose, and all cried: 'Great is the God of Andrew.' The parents offered great gifts which he refused, but took the lad to Macedonia, instructing him.

8 Embarking in a ship he sailed into the Hellespont, on the way to Byzantium. There was a great storm. Andrew prayed and there was calm. They reached Byzantium.

9 Thence proceeding through Thrace they met a troop of armed men who made as if to fall on them. Andrew made the sign of the cross against them, and prayed that they might be made powerless. A bright angel touched their swords and they all fell down, and Andrew and his company passed by while they worshipped him. And the angel departed in a great light.

10 At Perinthus he found a ship going to Macedonia, and an angel told him to go on board. As he preached the captain and the rest heard and were converted, and Andrew glorified God for making himself known on the sea.

11 At Philippi were two brothers, one of whom had two sons, the other two daughters. They were rich and noble, and said: "There is no family as good as ours in the place: let us marry our sons to our daughters.' It was agreed and the earnest paid by the father of the sons. On the wedding-day a word from God came to them: 'Wait till my servant Andrew comes: he will tell you what you should do.' All preparations had been made, and guests bidden, but they waited. On the third day Andrew came: they went out to meet him with wreaths and told him how they had been

charged to wait for him, and how things stood. His face was shining so that they marvelled at him. He said: 'Do not, my children, be deceived: rather repent, for you have sinned in thinking to join together those who are near of kin. We do not forbid or shun marriage [this cannot be the author's original sentiment: it is contradicted by all that we know of the Acts]. It is a divine institution: but we condemn incestuous unions.' The parents were troubled and prayed for pardon. The young people saw Andrew's face like that of an angel, and said: 'We are sure that your teaching is true.' The apostle blessed them and departed.

12 At Thessalonica was a rich noble youth, Exoos, who came without his parents' knowledge and asked to be shown the way of truth. He was taught, and believed, and followed Andrew taking no care of his worldly estate. The parents heard that he was at Philippi and tried to bribe him with gifts to leave Andrew. He said: 'Would that you had not these riches, then would you know the true God, and escape his wrath.' Andrew, too, came down from the third storey and preached to them, but in vain: he retired and shut the doors of the house. They gathered a band and came to burn the house, saying: 'Death to the son who has forsaken his parents': and brought torches, reeds, and faggots, and set the house on fire. It blazed up. Exoos took a bottle of water and prayed: 'Lord Jesu Christ, in whose hand is the nature of all the elements, who moistenest the dry and driest the moist, coolest the hot and kindlest the quenched, put out this fire that thy servants may not grow evil, but be more enkindled unto faith.' He sprinkled the flames and they died. 'He is become a sorcerer,' said the parents, and got ladders, to climb up and kill them, but God blinded them. They remained obstinate, but one Lysimachus, a citizen, said: 'Why persevere? God is fighting for these. Desist, lest heavenly fire consume you.' They were touched, and said: "This is the true God.' It was now night, but a light shone out, and they received sight. They went up and fell before Andrew and asked pardon, and their repentance made Lysimachus say: "Truly Christ whom Andrew preaches is the Son of God.' All were converted except the youth's parents, who cursed him and went home again, leaving all their money to public uses. Fifty days after they suddenly died, and the citizens, who loved the youth, returned the property to him. He did not leave Andrew, but spent his income on the poor.

13 The youth asked Andrew to go with him to Thessalonica. All assembled in the theatre, glad to see their favourite. The youth preached to them, Andrew remaining silent, and all wondered at his wisdom. The people cried out: 'Save the son of Carpianus who is ill, and we will believe.' Carpianus went to his house and said to the boy: 'You shall be cured to-day, Adimantus.' He said: 'Then my dream is come true: I saw this man in a vision healing me.' He rose up, dressed, and ran to the theatre, outstripping his father, and fell at Andrew's feet. The people seeing him walk after twenty-three years, cried: "There is none like the God of Andrew.'

14 A citizen had a son possessed by an unclean spirit and asked for his cure. The demon, foreseeing that he would be cast out, took the son aside into a chamber and made him hang himself. The father said: 'Bring him to the theatre: I believe this stranger is able to raise him.' He said the same to Andrew. Andrew said to the people: 'What will it profit

you if you see this accomplished and do not believe?' They said: 'Fear not, we will believe.' The lad was raised and they said: 'It is enough, we do believe.' And they escorted Andrew to the house with torches and lamps, for it was night, and he taught them for three days.

15 Medias of Philippi came and prayed for his sick son. Andrew wiped his cheeks and stroked his head, saying: 'Be comforted, only believe,' and went with him to Philippi. As they entered the city an old man met them and entreated for his sons, whom for an unspeakable crime Medias had imprisoned, and they were putrefied with sores. Andrew said: 'How can you ask help for your son when you keep these men bound? Loose their chains first, for your unkindness obstructs my prayers.' Medias, penitent, said: 'I will loose these two and seven others of whom you have not been told.' They were brought, tended for three days, cured, and freed. Then the apostle healed the son, Philomedes, who had been ill twenty-two years. The people cried: 'Heal our sick as well.' Andrew told Philomedes to visit them in their houses and bid them rise in the name of Jesus Christ, by which he had himself been healed. This was done, and all believed and offered gifts, which Andrew did not accept.

16 A citizen, Nicolaus, offered a gilt chariot and four white mules and four white horses as his most precious possession for the cure of his daughter. Andrew smiled. 'I accept your gifts, but not these visible ones: if you offer this for your daughter, what will you for your soul? That is what I desire of you, that the inner man may recognize the true God, reject earthly things and desire eternal . . .' He persuaded all to forsake their idols, and healed the girl. His fame went through all Macedonia.

17 Next day as he taught, a youth cried out: 'What hast thou to do with us. Art thou come to turn us out of our own place?' Andrew summoned him: 'What is your work?' 'I have dwelt in this boy from his youth and thought never to leave him: but three days since I heard his father say, "I shall go to Andrew": and now I fear the torments thou bringest us and I shall depart.' The spirit left the boy. And many came and asked: 'In whose name dost thou cure our sick?'

Philosophers also came and disputed with him, and no one could resist his teaching.

18 At this time, one who opposed him went to the proconsul Virinus and said: 'A man is arisen in Thessalonica who says the temples should be destroyed and ceremonies done away, and all the ancient law abolished, and one God worshipped, whose servant he says he is.' The proconsul sent soldiers and knights to fetch Andrew. They found his dwelling: when they entered, his face so shone that they fell down in fear. Andrew told those present the proconsul's purpose. The people armed themselves against the soldiers, but Andrew stopped them. The proconsul arrived; not finding Andrew in the appointed place, he raged like a lion and sent twenty more men. They, on arrival, were confounded and said nothing. The proconsul sent a large troop to bring him by force. Andrew said: 'Have you come for me?' 'Yes, if you are the sorcerer who says the gods ought not to be worshipped.' 'I am no sorcerer, but the apostle of Jesus Christ whom I preach.' At

this, one of the soldiers drew his sword and cried: 'What have I to do with thee, Virinus, that thou sendest me to one who can not only cast me out of this vessel, but burn me by his power? Would that you would come yourself! you would do him no harm.' And the devil went out of the soldier and he fell dead. On this came the proconsul and stood before Andrew but could not see him. 'I am he whom thou seekest.' His eyes were opened, and he said in anger: 'What is this madness, that thou despisest us and our officers? Thou art certainly a sorcerer. Now will I throw thee to the beasts for contempt of our gods and us, and we shall see if the crucified whom thou preachest will help thee.' Andrew: 'Thou must believe, proconsul, in the true God and his Son whom he hath sent, specially now that one of thy men is dead.' And after long prayer he touched the soldier: 'Rise up: my God Jesus Christ raiseth thee.' He arose and stood whole. The people cried: 'Glory be to our God.' The proconsul: 'Believe not, O people, believe not the sorcerer.' They said: 'This is no sorcery but sound and true teaching.' The proconsul: 'I shall throw this man to the beasts and write about you to Caesar, that ye may perish for contemning his laws.' They would have stoned him, and said: 'Write to Caesar that the Macedonians have received the word of God, and forsaking their idols, worship the true God.'

Then the proconsul in wrath retired to the praetorium, and in the morning brought beasts to the stadium and had the Apostle dragged thither by the hair and beaten with clubs. First they sent in a fierce boar who went about him thrice and touched him not. The people praised God. A bull led by thirty soldiers and incited by two hunters, did not touch Andrew but tore the hunters to pieces, roared, and fell dead. 'Christ is the true God,' said the people. An angel was seen to descend and strengthen the apostle. The proconsul in rage sent in a fierce leopard, which left every one alone but seized and strangled the proconsul's son; but Virinus was so angry that he said nothing of it nor cared. Andrew said to the people: 'Recognize now that this is the true God, whose power subdues the beasts, though Virinus knows him not. But that ye may believe the more, I will raise the dead son, and confound the foolish father.' After long prayer, he raised him. The people would have slain Virinus, but Andrew restrained them, and Virinus went to the praetorium, confounded.

19 After this a youth who followed the apostle sent for his mother to meet Andrew. She came, and after being instructed, begged him to come to their house, which was devastated by a great serpent. As Andrew approached, it hissed loudly and with raised head came to meet him; it was fifty cubits long: every one fell down in fear. Andrew said: 'Hide thy head, foul one, which thou didst raise in the beginning for the hurt of mankind, and obey the servants of God, and die.' The serpent roared, and coiled about a great oak near by and vomited poison and blood and died.

Andrew went to the woman's farm, where a child killed by the serpent lay dead. He said to the parents: 'Our God who would have you saved hath sent me here that you may believe on him. Go and see the slayer slain.' They said: 'We care not so much for the child's death, if we be avenged.' They went, and Andrew said to the proconsul's wife (her conversion has been omitted by Gregory): 'Go and raise the boy.' She went, nothing doubting, and said: 'In the name of my God Jesus Christ, rise up whole.' The parents returned and found their child alive, and fell at Andrew's feet.

20 On the next night he saw a vision which he related. 'Hearken, beloved, to my vision. I beheld, and lo, a great mountain raised up on high, which had on it nothing earthly, but only shone with such light, that it seemed to enlighten all the world. And lo, there stood by me my beloved brethren the apostles Peter and John; and John reached his hand to Peter and raised him to the top of the mount, and turned to me and asked me to go up after Peter, saying: "Andrew, thou art to drink Peter's cup." And he stretched out his hands and said: "Draw near to me and stretch out thy hands so as to join them unto mine, and put thy head by my head." When I did so I found myself shorter than John. After that he said to me: "Wouldst thou know the image of that which thou seest, and who it is that speaketh to thee?" and I said: "I desire to know it." And he said to me: "I am the word of the cross whereon thou shalt hang shortly, for his name's sake whom thou preachest." And many other things said he unto me, of which I must now say nothing, but they shall be declared when I come unto the sacrifice. But now let all assemble that have received the word of God, and let me commend them unto the Lord Jesus Christ, that he may vouchsafe to keep them unblemished in his teaching. For I am now being loosed from the body, and go unto that promise which he hath vouchsafed to promise me, who is the Lord of heaven and earth, the Son of God Almighty, very God with the Holy Ghost, continuing for everlasting ages.'

(I feel sure that John in the latter part of this vision has been substituted by Gregory for Jesus. The echoes of the Acts of John and of Peter are very evident here.)

All the brethren wept and smote their faces. When all were gathered, Andrew said: 'Know, beloved, that I am about to leave you, but I trust in Jesus whose word I preach, that he will keep you from evil, that this harvest which I have sown among you may not be plucked up by the enemy, that is, the knowledge and teaching of my Lord Jesus Christ. But do ye pray always and stand firm in the faith, that the Lord may root out all tares of offence and vouchsafe to gather you into his heavenly garner as pure wheat.' So for five days he taught and confirmed them: then he spread his hands and prayed: 'Keep, I beseech thee, O Lord, this flock which hath now known thy salvation, that the wicked one may not prevail against it, but that what by thy command and my means it hath received, it may be able to preserve inviolate for ever.' And all responded 'Amen'. He took bread, brake it with thanksgiving, gave it to all, saying: 'Receive the grace which Christ our Lord God giveth you by me his servant.' He kissed every one and commended them to the Lord, and departed to Thessalonica, and after teaching there two days, he left them.

21 Many faithful from Macedonia accompanied him in two ships. And all were desirous of being on Andrew's ship, to hear him. He said: 'I know your wish, but this ship is too small. Let the servants and baggage go in the larger ship, and you with me in this.' He gave them Anthimus to comfort them, and bade them go into another ship which he ordered to keep always near . . . that they might see him and hear the word of God. (This is a little confused.) And as he slept a little, one fell overboard. Anthimus roused

him, saying: 'Help us, good master; one of thy servants perisheth.' He rebuked the wind, there was a calm, and the man was borne by the waves to the ship. Anthimus helped him on board and all marvelled. On the twelfth day they reached Patrae in Achaia, disembarked, and went to an inn.

22 Many asked him to lodge with them, but he said he could only go where God bade him. That night he had no revelation, and the next night, being distressed at this, he heard a voice saying: 'Andrew, I am alway with thee and forsake thee not,' and was glad.

Lesbius the proconsul was told in a vision to take him in, and sent a messenger for him. He came, and entering the proconsul's chamber found him lying as dead with closed eyes; he struck him on the side and said: 'Rise and tell us what hath befallen thee.' Lesbius said: 'I abominated the way which you teach and sent soldiers in ships to the proconsul of Macedonia to send you bound to me, but they were wrecked and could not reach their destination. As I continued in my purpose of destroying your Way, two black men (Ethiopes) appeared and scourged me, saying: "We can no longer prevail here, for the man is coming whom you mean to persecute. So to-night, while we still have the power, we will avenge ourselves on you." And they beat me sorely and left me. But now do you pray that I may be pardoned and healed.' Andrew preached the word and all believed, and the proconsul was healed and confirmed in the faith.

23 Now Trophima, once the proconsul's mistress, and now married to another, left her husband and clave to Andrew. Her husband came to her lady (Lesbius' wife) and said she was renewing her liaison with the proconsul. The wife, enraged, said: 'This is why my husband has left me these six months.' She called her steward (procurator) and had Trophima sentenced as a prostitute and sent to the brothel. Lesbius knew nothing, and was deceived by his wife, when he asked about her. Trophima in the brothel prayed continually, and had the Gospel on her bosom, and no one could approach her. One day one offered her violence, and the Gospel fell to the ground. She cried to God for help and an angel came, and the youth fell dead. After that, she raised him, and all the city ran to the sight.

Lesbius' wife went to the bath with the steward, and as they bathed an ugly demon came and killed them both. Andrew heard and said: 'It is the judgement of God for their usage of Trophima.' The lady's nurse, decrepit from age, was carried to the spot, and supplicated for her. Andrew said to Lesbius: 'Will you have her raised?' 'No, after all the ill she has done.' 'We ought not to be unmerciful.' Lesbius went to the praetorium; Andrew raised his wife, who remained shamefaced: he bade her go home and pray. 'First', she said, 'reconcile me to Trophima whom I have injured.' 'She bears you no malice.' He called her and they were reconciled. Callisto was the wife.

Lesbius, growing in faith, came one day to Andrew and confessed all his sins. Andrew said: 'I thank God, my son, that thou fearest the judgement to come. Be strong in the Lord in whom thou believest.' And he took his hand and walked with him on the shore.

24 They sat down, with others, on the sand, and he taught. A corpse was thrown up by the sea near them. 'We must learn', said Andrew, 'what the enemy has done to him.' So he raised him, gave him a garment, and bade him tell his story. He said: 'I am the son of Sostratus, of Macedonia, lately come from Italy. On returning home I heard of a new teaching, and set forth to find out about it. On the way here we were wrecked and all drowned.' And after some thought, he realized that Andrew was the man he sought, and fell at his feet and said: 'I know that thou art the servant of the true God. I beseech thee for my companions, that they also may be raised and know him.' Then Andrew instructed him, and thereafter prayed God to show the bodies of the other drowned men: thirty-nine were washed ashore, and all there prayed for them to be raised. Philopator, the youth, said: 'My father sent me here with a great sum. Now he is blaspheming God and his teaching. Let it not be so.' Andrew ordered the bodies to be collected, and said: 'Whom will you have raised first?' He said: 'Warus my foster-brother.' So he was first raised and then the other thirty-eight. Andrew prayed over each, and then told the brethren each to take the hand of one and say: 'Jesus Christ the son of the living God raiseth thee.'

Lesbius gave much money to Philopator to replace what he had lost, and he abode with Andrew.

25 A woman, Calliopa, married to a murderer, had an illegitimate child and suffered in travail. She told her sister to call on Diana for help; when she did so the devil appeared to her at night and said: 'Why do you trouble me with vain prayers? Go to Andrew in Achaia.' She came, and he accompanied her to Corinth, Lesbius with him. Andrew said to Calliopa: 'You deserve to suffer for your evil life: but believe in Christ, and you will be relieved, but the child will be born dead.' And so it was.

26 Andrew did many signs in Corinth. Sostratus the father of Philopator, warned in a vision to visit Andrew, came first to Achaia and then to Corinth. He met Andrew walking with Lesbius, recognized him by his vision, and fell at his feet. Philopator said: 'This is my father, who seeks to know what he must do.' Andrew: 'I know that he is come to learn the truth; we thank God who reveals himself to believers.' Leontius the servant of Sostratus, said to him: 'Seest thou, sir, how this man's face shineth?' 'I see, my beloved,' said Sostratus; 'let us never leave him, but live with him and hear the words of eternal life.' Next day they offered Andrew many gifts, but he said: 'It is not for me to take aught of you but your own selves. Had I desired money, Lesbius is richer.'

27 After some days he bade them prepare him a bath; and going there saw an old man with a devil, trembling exceedingly. As he wondered at him, another, a youth, came out of the bath and fell at his feet, saying: 'What have we to do with thee, Andrew? Hast thou come here to turn us out of our abodes?' Andrew said to the people: 'Fear not,' and drove out both the devils. Then, as he bathed, he told them: 'The enemy of mankind lies in wait everywhere, in baths and in rivers; therefore we ought always to invoke the Lord's name, that he may have w power over us.'

They brought their sick to him to be healed, and so they did from other cities.

28 An old man, Nicolaus, came with clothes rent and said: 'I am seventy-four years old and have always been a libertine. Three days ago I heard of your miracles and teaching. I thought I would turn over a new leaf, and then again that I would not. in this doubt, I took a Gospel and prayed God to make me forget my old devices. A few days after, I forgot the Gospel I had about me, and went to the brothel. The woman said: "Depart, old man, depart: thou art an angel of God, touch me not nor approach me, for I see in thee a great mystery." Then I remembered the Gospel, and am come to you for help and pardon.' Andrew discoursed long against incontinence, and prayed from the sixth to the ninth hour. He rose and washed his face and said: 'I will not eat till I know if God will have mercy on this man.' A second day he fasted, but had no revelation until the fifth day, when he wept vehemently and said: 'Lord, we obtain mercy for the dead, and now this man that desireth to know thy greatness, wherefore should he not return and thou heal him?' A voice from heaven said: 'Thou hast prevailed for the old man; but like as thou art worn with fasting, let him also fast, that he may be saved.' And he called him and preached abstinence. On the sixth day he asked the brethren all to pray for Nicolaus, and they did. Andrew then took food and permitted the rest to eat. Nicolaus went home, gave away all his goods, and lived for six months on dry bread and water. Then he died. Andrew was not there, but in the place where he was he heard a voice: 'Andrew, Nicolaus for whom thou didst intercede, is become mine.' And he told the brethren that Nicolaus was dead, and prayed that he might rest in peace.

29 And while he abode in that place (probably Lacedaemon) Antiphanes of Megara came and said: 'If there be in thee any kindness, according to the command of the Saviour whom thou preachest, show it now.' Asked what his story was, he told it. Returning from a journey, I heard the porter of my house crying out. They told me that he and his wife and son were tormented of a devil. I went upstairs and found other servants gnashing their teeth, running at me, and laughing madly. I went further up and found they had beaten my wife: she lay with her hair over her face unable to recognize me. Cure her, and I care nothing for the others.' Andrew said: 'There is no respect of persons with God. Let us go there.' They went from Lacedaemon to Megara, and when they entered the house, all the devils cried out: 'What dost thou here, Andrew? Go where thou art permitted: this house is ours.' He healed the wife and all the possessed persons, and Antiphanes and his wife became firm adherents.

30 He returned to Patrae where Egeas was now proconsul, and one Iphidamia, who had been converted by a disciple, Sosias, came and embraced his feet and said: 'My lady Maximilla who is in a fever has sent for you. The proconsul is standing by her bed with his sword drawn, meaning to kill himself when she expires.' He went to her, and said to Egeas: 'Do thyself no harm, but put up thy sword into his place. There will be a time when thou wilt draw it on me.' Egeas did not understand, but made way. Andrew took Maximilla's hand, she broke into a sweat, and was well: he bade them give her food. The proconsul sent him 100 pieces of silver, but he would not look at them.

31 Going thence he saw a sick man lying in the dirt begging, and healed him.

32 Elsewhere he saw a blind man with wife and son, and said: 'This is indeed the devil's work: he has blinded them in soul and body.' He opened their eyes and they believed.

33 One who saw this said: 'I beg thee come to the harbour; there is a man, the son of a sailor, sick fifty years, cast out of the house, lying on the shore, incurable, full of ulcers and worms.' They went to him. The sick man said: 'Perhaps you are the disciple of that God who alone can save.' Andrew said: 'I am he who in the name of my God can restore thee to health,' and added: 'In the name of Jesus Christ, rise and follow me.' He left his filthy rags and followed, the pus and worms flowing from him. They went into the sea, and the apostle washed him in the name of the Trinity and he was whole, and ran naked through the city proclaiming the true God.

34 At this time the proconsul's brother Stratocles arrived from Italy. One of his slaves, Alcman, whom he loved, was taken by a devil and lay foaming in the court. Stratocles hearing of it said: 'Would the sea had swallowed me before I saw this.' Maximilla and Iphidamia said: 'Be comforted: there is here a man of God, let us send for him.' When he came he took the boy's hand and raised him whole. Stratocles believed and clave to Andrew.

35 Maximilla went daily to the praetorium and sent for Andrew to teach there. Egeas was away in Macedonia, angry because Maximilla had left him since her conversion. As they were all assembled one day, he returned, to their great terror. Andrew prayed that he might not be suffered to enter the place till all had dispersed. And Egeas was at once seized with indisposition, and in the interval the apostle signed them all and sent them away, himself last. But Maximilla on the first opportunity came to Andrew and received the word of God and went home. [At about this point we must place the episodes quoted by Evodius of Uzala: see below.]

36 After this Andrew was taken and imprisoned by Egeans, and all came to the prison to be taught. After a few days he was scourged and crucified; he hung for three days, preaching, and expired, as is fully set forth in his Passion. Maximilla embalmed and buried his body.

37 From the tomb comes manna like flour, and oil: the amount shows the barrenness or fertility of the coming season -as I have told in my first book of Miracles. I have not set out his Passion at length, because I find it well done by some one else.

38 This much have I presumed to write, unworthy, unlettered, &c. The author's prayer for himself ends the book. May Andrew, on whose death-day he was born, intercede to save him.

(The Passion to which Gregory alludes is that which begins Conversante et docente'.)

Of the detached fragments and quotations which precede the Passion there are three:

(a) One is in the Epistle of Titus.

When, finally, Andrew also [John has been cited shortly before] had come to a wedding, he too, to manifest the glory of God, disjoined certain who were intended to marry each other, men and women, and instructed them to continue holy in the single state.

No doubt this refers to the story in Gregory, ch. 11. Gregory, it may be noted, has altered the story (or has used an altered text), for the marriage of cousins was not forbidden till Theodosius' time (so Flamion). He or his source has imagined the relationship between the couples; in the original Acts none need have existed: the mere fact of the marriage was enough.

(b) The next are in a tract by Evodius, bishop of Uzala, against the Manichees:

Observe, in the Acts of Leucius which he wrote under the name of the apostles, what manner of things you accept about Maximilla the wife of Egetes: who, refusing to pay her due to her husband (though the apostle has said: Let the husband pay the due to the wife and likewise the wife to the husband: 1 Cor. vii. 3), imposed her maid Euclia upon her husband, decking her out, as is there written, with wicked (lit. hostile) enticements and paintings, and substituted her as deputy for herself at night, so that he in ignorance used her as his wife.

There also is it written, that when this same Maximilla and Iphidamia were gone together to hear the apostle Andrew, a beautiful child, who, Leucius would have us understand, was either God or at least an angel, escorted them to the apostle Andrew and went to the praetorium of Egetes, and entering their chamber feigned a woman's voice, as of Maximilla, complaining of the sufferings of womankind, and of Iphidamia replying. When Egetes heard this dialogue, he went away. [These incidents must have intervened between cc. 35 and 36 of Gregory of Tours.]

(c) Evodius quotes another sentence, not certainly from the Acts of Andrew, but more in their manner than in that of John or Peter:

In the Acts written by Leucius, which the Manichees receive, it is thus written:

For the deceitful figments and pretended shows and collection (force, compelling) of visible things do not even proceed from their own nature, but from that man who of his own will has become worse through seduction.

It is obscure enough, in original and version: but is the kind of thing that would appeal to those who thought of material things and phenomena as evil.

We do not wonder that such narratives as that which Evodius quotes have been expunged, either by Gregory or his source, from the text.

The next passage is a fragment of some pages in length found by M. Bonnet in a Vatican MS. (Gr. 808) of tenth to eleventh century. There is no doubt that it is a piece of the original Acts. It is highly tedious in parts. Andrew in prison discourses to the brethren.

1 . . . is there in you altogether slackness? are ye not yet convinced of yourselves that ye do not yet bear his goodness? let us be reverent, let us rejoice with ourselves in the bountiful (ungrudging) fellowship which cometh of him. Let us say unto ourselves: Blessed is our race! by whom hath it been loved? blessed is our state! of whom hath it obtained mercy? we are not cast on the ground, we that have been recognized by so great highness: we are not the offspring of time, afterward to be dissolved by time; we are not a contrivance (product) of motion, made to be again destroyed by itself, nor things of earthly birth. ending again therein. We belong, then, to a greatness, unto which we aspire, of which we are the property, and peradventure to a greatness that hath mercy upon us. We belong to the better; therefore we flee from the worse: we belong to the beautiful, for whose sake we reject the foul; to the righteous, by whom we cast away the unrighteous, to the merciful, by whom we reject the unmerciful; to the Saviour, by whom we recognize the destroyer; to the light, by whom we have cast away the darkness; to the One, by whom we have turned away from the many; to the heavenly, by whom we have learned to know the earthly; to the abiding, by whom we have seen the transitory. If we desire to offer unto God that hath had mercy on us a worthy thanksgiving or confidence or hymn or boasting, what better cause (theme) have we than that we have been recognized by him?

2 And having discoursed thus to the brethren, he sent them away every one to his house, saying to them: Neither are ye ever forsaken of me, ye that are servants of Christ, because of the love that is in him: neither again shall I be forsaken of you because of his intercession (mediation). And every one departed unto his house: and there was among them rejoicing after this sort for many days, while Aegeates took not thought to prosecute the accusation against the Apostle. Every one of them then was confirmed at that time in hope toward the Lord, and they assembled without fear in the prison, with Maximilla, Iphidamia, and the rest, continually, being sheltered by the protection and grace of the Lord.

3 But one day Aegeates, as he was hearing causes, remembered the matter concerning Andrew: and as one seized with madness, he left the cause which he had in hand, and rose up from the judgement seat and ran quickly to the praetorium, inflamed with love of Maximilla and desiring to persuade her with flatteries. And Maximilla was beforehand with him, coming from the prison and entering the house. And he went in and said to her:

4 Maximilla, thy parents counted me worthy of being thy consort, and gave me thine hand in marriage, not looking to wealth or descent or renown, but it may be to my good disposition of soul: and, that I may pass over much that I might utter in reproach of thee, both of that which I have enjoyed at thy parents' hands and thou from me during all our life, I am come, leaving the court, to learn of thee this one thing: answer me then reasonably, if thou wert as the wife of former days, living with me in the way we know, sleeping, conversing, bearing offspring with me, I would deal well with thee in all points; nay more, I would set free the stranger whom I hold in prison: but if thou wilt not to thee I would do nothing harsh, for indeed I cannot; but him, whom thou affectionest more than me, I will afflict

yet more. Consider, then, Maximilla, to whether of the two thou inclinest, and answer me to-morrow; for I am wholly armed for this emergency.

5 And with these words he went out; but Maximilla again at the accustomed hour, with Iphidamia, went to Andrew: and putting his hands before her own eyes, and then putting them to her mouth, she began to declare to him the whole rmatter of the demand of Aegeates. And Andrew answered her: I know, Maximilla my child, that thou thyself art moved to resist the whole attraction (promise) of nuptial union, desiring to be quit of a foul and polluted way of life: and this hath long been firmly held in thine (MS. mine) intention; but now thou wishest for the further testimony of mine opinion. I testify, O Maximilla: do it not; be not vanquished by the threat of Aegeates: be not overcome by his discourse: fear not his shameful counsels: fall not to his artful flatteries: consent not to surrender thyself to his impure spells, but endure all his torments looking unto us for a little space, and thou shalt see him whoily numbed and withering away from thee and from all that are akin to thee. But (For) that which I most needed to say to thee -for I rest not till I fulfil the business which is seen, and which cometh to pass in thy person- hath escaped me: and rightly in thee do I behold Eve repenting, and in myself Adam returning; for that which she suffered in ignorance, thou now (for whose soul I strive) settest right by returning: and that which the spirit suffered which was overthrown with her and slipped away from itself, is set right in me, with thee who seest thyself being brought back. For her defect thou hast remedied by not suffering like her; and his imperfection I have perfected by taking refuge with God, that which she disobeyed thou hast obeyed: that whereto he consented I flee from: and that which they both transgressed we have been aware of, for it is ordained that every one should correct (and raise up again) his own fall.

6 I, then, having said this as I have said it, would go on to speak as followeth: Well done, O nature that art being saved for thou hast been strong and hast not hidden thyself (from God like Adam)! Well done, O soul that criest out of what thou hast surfered, and returnest unto thyself ! Well done, O man that understandest what is thine and dost press on to what is thine! Well done, thou that hearest what is spoken, for I see thee to be greater than things that are thought or spoken! I recognize thee as more powerful than the things which seemed to overpower thee; as more beautiful than those which cast thee down into foulness, which brought thee down into captivity. Perceiving then, O man, all this in thyself, that thou art immaterial, holy light, akin to him that is unborn, that thou art intellectual, heavenly, translucent, pure, above the flesh, above the world, above rulers, above principalities, over whom thou art in truth, then comprehend thyself in thy condition and receive full knowledge and understand wherein thou excellest: and beholding thine own face in thine essence, break asunder all bonds -I say not only those that are of thy birth, but those that are above birth, whereof we have set forth to thee the names which are excceding great -desire earnestly to see him that is revealed unto thee, him who doth not come into being, whom perchance thou alone shalt recognize with confidence.

7 These things have I spoken of thee, Maximilla, for in their meaning the things I have spoken reach unto thee.

Like as Adam died in Eve because he consented unto her confession, so do I now live in thee that keepest the Lord's commandment and stablishest thyself in the rank (dignity) of thy being. But the threats of Aegeates do thou trample down, Maximilla, knowing that we have God that hath mercy on us. And let not his noise move thee, but continue chaste- and let him punish me not only with such torments as bonds, but let him cast me to the beasts or burn me with fire, and throw me from a precipice. And what need I say? there is but this one body; let him abuse that as he will, for it is akin to himself.

8 And yet again unto thee is my speech, Maximilla: I say unto thee, give not thyself over unto Aegeates: withstand his ambushes- for indeed, Maximilla, I have seen my Lord saying unto me: Andrew, Aegeates' father the devil will loose thee from this prison. Thine, therefore, let it be henceforth to keep thyself chaste and pure, holy, unspotted, sincere, free from adultery, not reconciled to the discourses of our enemy, unbent, unbroken, tearless, unwounded, not storm-tossed, undivided, not stumbling without fellow-feeling for the works of Cain. For if thou give not up thyself, Maximilla, to what is contrary to these, I also shall rest, though I be thus forced to leave this life for thy sake that is, for mine own. But if I were thrust out hence, even I, who, it may be, might avail through thee to profit others that are akin to me, and if thou wert persuaded by the discourse of Aegeates and the flatteries of his father the serpent, so that thou didst turn unto thy former works, know thou that on thine account I should be tormented until thou thyself sawest that I had contemned life for the sake of a soul which was not worthy.

9 I entreat, therefore, the wise man that is in thee that thy mind continue clear seeing. I entreat thy mind that is not seen, that it be preserved whole: I beseech thee, love thy Jesus, and yield not unto the worse. Assist me, thou whom I entreat as a man, that I may become perfect: help me also, that thou mayest recognize thine own true nature: feel with me in my suffering, that thou mayest take knowledge of what I suffer, and escape suffering see that which I see, and thou shalt be blind to what thou seest: see that which thou shouldst, and thou shalt not see that thou shouldst not: hearken to what I say, and cast away that which thou hast heard.

10 These things have I spoken unto thee and unto every one that heareth, if he will hear. But thou, O Stratocles, said he, looking toward him, Why art thou so oppressed, with many tears and groanings to be heard afar off? what is the lowness of spirit that is on thee? why thy much pain and thy great anguish? dost thou take note of what is said, and wherefore I pray thee to be disposed in mind as my child? (or, my child, to be composed in mind): dost thou perceive unto whom my words are spoken? hath each of them taken hold on thine understanding? have they whetted (MS. touched) thine intellectual part? have I thee as one that hath hearkened to me? do I find myself in thee? is there in thee one that speaketh whom I see to be mine own? doth he love him that speaketh in me and desire to have fellowship with him? doth he wish to be made one with him? doth lie hasten to become his friend? doth he yearn to be joined with him? doth he find in him any rest? hath he where to lay his head? doth nought oppose him there? nought that is wroth with him, resisteth him, hateth him, fleeth from him,

is savage, avoideth, turneth away, starteth off, is burdened, maketh war, talketh with others, is flattered by others, agreeth with others? Doth nothing else disturb him? Is there one within that is strange to me? an adversary, a breaker of peace, an enemy, a cheat, a sorcerer, a crooked dealer, unsound, guileful, a hater of men, a hater of the word, one like a tyrant, boastful, puffed up, mad, akin to the serpent, a weapon of the devil, a friend of the fire, belonging to darkness? Is there in thee any one, Stratocles, that cannot endure my saying these things? Who is it? Answer: do I talk in vain? have I spoken in vain? Nay, saith the man in thee, Stratocles, who now again weepeth.

11 And Andrew took the band of Stratocles and said: I have him whom I loved; I shall rest on him whom I look for; for thy yet groaning, and weeping without restraint, is a sign unto me that I have already found rest, that I have not spoken to thee these words which are akin to me, in vain.

12 And Stratocles answered him: Think not, most blessed Andrew, that there is aught else that afflicteth me but thee; for the words that come forth of thee are like arrows of fire shot against me, and every one of them reacheth me and verily burneth me up. That part of my soul which inclineth to what I hear is tormented, divining the affliction that is to follow, for thou thyself departest, and, I know, nobly: but hereafter when I seek thy care and affection, where shall I find it, or in whom? I have received the seeds of the words of salvation, and thou wast the sower: but that they should sprout up and grow needs none other but thee, most blessed Andrew. And what else have I say to thee but this? I need much mercy and help from thee, to become worthy of the seed I have from thee, which will not otherwise increase perpetually or grow up into the light except thou willest it, and prayest for them and for the whole of me.

13 And Andrew answered him: This, my child, was what I beheld in thee myself. And I glorify my Lord that my thought of thee walked not on the void, but knew what it said. But that ye may know the truth, to-morrow doth Aegeates deliver me up to be crucified: for Maximilla the servant of the Lord will enrage the enemy that is in him, unto whom he belongeth, by not consenting to that which is hateful to her; and by turning against me he will think to console himself.

14 Now while the apostle spake these things, Maximilla was not there, for she having heard throughout the words wherewith he answered her, and being in part composed by them, and of such a mind as the words pointed out, set forth not inadvisedly nor without purpose and went to the praetorium. And she bade farewell to all the life of the flesh, and when Aegeates brought to her the same demand which he had told her to consider, whether she would lie with him, she rejected it- and thenceforth he bent himself to putting Andrew to death, and thought to what death he should expose him. And when of all deaths crucifixion alone prevailed with him, he went away with his like and dined; and Maximilla, the Lord going before her in the likeness of Andrew, with Iphidamia came back to the prison- and there being therein a great gathering of the brethren, she found Andrew discoursing thus:

15 I, brethren, was sent forth by the Lord as an apostle unto these regions whereof my Lord thought me worthy,

not to teach any man, but to remind every man that is akin to such words that they live in evils which are temporal, delighting in their injurious delusions: wherefrom I have always exhorted you also to depart, and encouraged you to press toward things that endure, and to take flight from all that is transitory (flowing)- for ye see that none of you standeth, but that all things, even to the customs of men, are easily changeable. And this befalleth because the soul is untrained and erreth toward nature and holdeth pledges toft its error. I therefore account them blessed who have become obedient unto the word preached, and thereby see the mysteries of their own nature; for whose sake all things have been builded up.

16 I enjoin you therefore, beloved children, build yourselves firmly upon the foundation that hath been laid for you, which is unshaken, and against which no evil-willer can conspire. Be then, rooted upon this foundation: be established, remembering what ye have seen (or heard) and all that hath come to pass while I walked with you all. Ye have seen works wrought through me which ye have no power to disbelieve, and such signs come to pass as perchance even dumb nature will proclaim aloud; I have delivered you words which I pray may so be received by you as the words themselves would have it. Be established then, beloved upon all that ye have seen, and heard, and partaken of. And God on whom ye have believed shall have mercy on you and present you lmto himself, giving you rest unto all ages.

17 Now as for that which is to befall me, let it not really trouble you as some strange spectacle, that the servant of God unto whom God himself hath granted much in deeds and words, should by an evil man be driven out of this temporal life: for not only unto me will this come to pass, but unto all them that have loved and believed on him and confess him. The devil that is wholly shameless will arm his own children against them, that they may consent unto him; and he will not have his desire. And wherefore he essayeth this I will tell you. From the beginning of all things, and if I may so say, since he that hath no beginning came down to be under his rule, the enemy that is a foe to peace driveth away from (God) such a one as doth not belong indeed to him, but is some one of the weaker sort and not fully enlightened (?), nor yet able to recognize himself. And because he knoweth him not, therefore must he be fought against by him (the devil). For he, thinking that he possesseth him and is his master for ever, opposeth him so much, that he maketh their enmity to be a kind of friendship: for suggesting to him his own thoughts, he often portrayeth them as pleasurable and specious (MS. deceitful), by which he thinketh to prevail over him. He was not, then, openly shown to be an enemy, for he feigned a friendship that was worthy of him.

18 And this his work he carried on so long that he (man) forgat to recognize it, but he (the devil) knew it himself: that is, he, because of his gifts . But when the mystery of grace was lighted up, and the counsel of rest manifested, and the light of the word shown, and the race of them that were saved was proved, warring against many pleasures, the enemy himself despised, and himself, through the goodness of him that had mercy on us, derided because of his own gifts, by which he had thought to triumph over man- he began to plot against us with hatred and enmity and

assaults; and this hath he dctcrmined, not to cease from us till he thinketh to separate us (from God).

For before, our enemy was without care, and offered us a feigned friendship which was worthy of him, and was able not to fear that we, deceived by him, should depart from him. But when the light of dispensation was kindled, it made , I say not stronger, . For it exposed that part of his nature which was hidden and which thought to escape notice, and made it confess what it is.

Knowing therefore, brethren, that which shall be, let us be vigilant, not discontented, not making a proud figure, not carrying upon our souls marks of him which are not our own: but wholly lifted upward by the whole word, let us all gladly await the end, and take our flight away from him, that he may be henceforth shown as he is, who our nature unto (or against) our . . .

THE MARTYRDOM

The original text of this, as Flamion shows, has to be picked out of several Greek and Latin authorities.

Bonnet prints the Martyrdom in several forms (Act. Apost. Apocr. ii. 1): on pp. 1-37 we have the Passion in three texts.

The uppermost is the Latin letter of the presbyters and deacons of Achaia. This, as Bonnet has proved, is the original of the two Greek versions printed below it. The first editors of this Letter thought it might be a genuine document. But it is really an artificial thing. The greater part of it consists of a dialogue between Andrew and Aegeates: the narrative of the actual Passion is rather brief.

Of the two Greek versions, the first, which begins "ha tois ophthalmois"(greek) is a faithful version of the Latin.

The other, which begins "haper tois ophthalmois"(greek) has a number of insertions taken from the original Acts, ultimately, perhaps through the medium of a 'Passion', circulated separately, such as we have had in the cases of John, Paul, and Peter. This text is called by Flamion the Epitre grecque. Ep. gr.

On pp. 38-45 follows the fragment of discourses which has just been translated. Very likely this is a relic of a separate Passion cut off from the end of the original Acts.

On pp. 46-57 is the 'Martyrium prius'. This tells (after speaking of the dispersion of the apostles) of the cure and conversion of Lesbius, destruction of temples, dismissal of Lesbius by Caesar, vision of Andrew that Aegeates is to put him to death, arrest of Andrew, and martyrdom. It contains many speeches. This is Mart. 1.

On pp. 58-64 is the 'Martyrium alterum' in two texts, which begins at once with the arrest of the apostle by Aegeates-after he has spent the night in discoursing to the brethren.

Mart. II, A, B are the two texts of this. Besides these Bonnet has published in the Analecta Bollandiana and separately (as Supplementum Codicis Apocryphi, ii, 1895) thc following documents:

1 Acts of Andrew with Encomium: called for short Laudatio, which recounts the journeys at considerable length, and some of the miracles which we have seen in Gregory, and then the Passion (cc. 44-9) and the Translation to Constantinople.

2. A Greek Martyrdom, of which cc. 1-8 recount the journeys, and from 9 onwards the Passion, with a good deal of matter from the original Acts. This is called Narratio.

3. A Latin Passion- that known to Gregory, which begins Conversante et docente: it forms the end of Book III of Abdias' Historia Apostolica, and is there tacked on to Gregory's book of Miracles.

Using all these sources, Flamion has with great pains indicated which portions he assigns to the original Acts, and I shall follow him here. The resultant text is a kind of mosaic, of which the sources shall be indicated in the margin.

And after he had thus discoursed throughout the night to the brethren, and praved with them and committed them unto the Lord, early in the morning Aegeates the proconsul sent for the apostle Andrew out of the prison and said to him: The end of thy judgement is at hand, thou stranger, enemy of this present life and foe of all mine house. Wherefore hast thou thought good to intrude into places that are not thine, and to corrupt my wife who was of old obedient unto me? why hast thou done this against me and against all Achaia ? Therefore shalt thou receive from me a gift in recompense of that thou hast wrought against me.

And he commanded him to be scourged by seven men and afterward to be crucified: and charged the executioners that his legs should be left unpierced, and so he should be hanged up: thinking by this means to torment him the more.

Now the report was noised throughout all Patrae that the stranger, the righteous man, the servant of Christ whom Aegeates held prisoner, was being crucified, having done nothing amiss: and they ran together with one accord unto the sight, being wroth with the proconsul because of his impious judgement.

And as the executioners led him unto the place to fulfil that which was commanded them, Stratocles heard what was come to pass, and ran hastily and overtook them, and beheld the blessed Andrew violently haled by the executioners like a malefactor. And he spared them not, but beating every one of them soundly and tearing their coats from top to bottom, he caught Andrew away from them, saying: Ye may thank the blessed man who hath instructed me and taught me to refrain from extremity of wrath: for else I would have showed you what Stratocles is able to do, and what is the power of the foul Aegeates. For we have learnt to endure that which others inflict upon us. And he took the hand of the apostle and went with him to the place by the sea-shore where he was to be crucified.

But the soldiers who had received him from the proconsul left him with Stratocles, and returned and told Aegeates, saying: As we went with Andrew Stratocles prevented us,

and rent our coats and pulled him away from us and took him with him, and lo, here we are as thou seest. And Aegeates answered them: Put on other raiment and go and fulfil that which I commanded you, upon the condemned man: but be not seen of Stratocles, neither answer him again if he ask aught of you; for I know the rashness of his soul, what it is, and if he were provoked he would not even spare me. And they did as Aegeates said unto them.

But as Stratocles went with the apostle unto the place appointed, Andrew perceived that he was wroth with Aegeates and was reviling him in a low voice, and said unto him: My child Stratocles, I would have thee henceforth possess thy soul unmoved, and remove from thyself this temper, and neither be inwardly disposed thus toward the things that seem hard to thee, nor be inflamed outwardly: for it becometh the servant of Jesus to be worthy of Jesus. And another thing will I say unto thee and to the brethren that walk with me: that the man that is against us, when he dareth aught against us and findeth not one to consent unto him, is smitten and beaten and wholly deadened because he hath not accomplished that which he undertook; let us therefore, little children, have him alway before our eyes, lest if we fall asleep he slaughter us (you) like an adversary.

And as he spake this and yet more unto Stratocles and them that were with him, they came to the place where he was to be crucified: and (seeing the cross set up at the edge of the sand by the sea-shore) he left them all and went to the cross and spake unto it (as unto a living creature, with a loud voice):

Hail, O cross, yea be glad indeed! Well know I that thou shalt henceforth be at rest, thou that hast for a long time been wearied, being set up and awaiting me. I come unto thee whom I know to belong to me. I come unto thee that hast yearned after me. I know thy mystery, for the which thou art set up: for thou art planted in the world to establish the things that are unstable: and the one part of thee stretcheth up toward heaven that thou mayest signify the heavenly word (or, the word that is above) (the head of all things): and another part of thee is spread out to the right hand and the left that it may put to flight the envious and adverse power of the evil one, and gather into one the things that are scattered abroad (or, the world): And another part of thee is planted in the earth, and securely set in the depth, that thou mayest join the things that are in the earth and that are under the earth unto the heavenly things (Laud. that thou mayest draw up them that be under the earth and them that are held in the places beneath the earth, and join, &c.).

O cross, device (contrivance) of the salvation of the Most High! O cross, trophy of the victory [of Christ] over the enemies! O cross, planted upon the earth and having thy fruit in the heavens! O name of the cross, filled with all things (lit. a thing filled with all).

Well done, O cross, that hast bound down the mobility of the world (or, the circumference)! Well done, O shape of understanding that hast shaped the shapeless (earth?)! Well done, O unseen chastisement that sorely chastisest the substance of the knowledge that hath many gods, and drivest out from among mankind him that devised it! Well done, thou that didst clothe thyself with the Lord, and didst bear the thief as a fruit, and didst call the apostle to repentance, and didst not refuse to accept us!

But how long delay I, speaking thus, and embrace not the cross, that by the cross I may be made alive, and by the cross (win) the common death of all and depart out of life?

Come hither ye ministers of joy unto me, ye servants of Aegeates: accomplish the desire of us both, and bind the lamb unto the wood of suffering, the man unto the maker, the soul unto the Saviour.

And the blessed Andrew having thus spoken, standing upon the earth, looked earnestly upon the cross, and bade the brethren that the executioners should come and do that which was commanded them; for they stood afar off.

And they came and bound his hands and his feet and nailed them not; for such a charge had they from Aegeates; for he wished to afflict him by hanging him up, and that in the night he might be devoured alive by dogs (Laud. that he might be wearied out and permit Maximilla to live with him). And they left him hanging and departed from him.

And when the multitudes that stood by of them that had been made disciples in Christ by him saw that they had done unto him none of the things accustomed with them that are crucified, they hoped to hear something again from him. For as he hung, he moved his head and smiled. And Stratocles asked him, saying: Wherefore smilest thou, servant of God? thy laughter maketh us to mourn and weep because we are bereaved of thee. And the blessed Andrew answered him: Shall I not laugh, my son Stratocles, at the vain assault (ambush) of Aegeates, whereby he thinketh to punish us? we are strangers unto him and his conspiracies. He hath not to hear; for if he had, he would have heard that the man of Jesus cannot be punished, because he is henceforth known of him.

And thereafter he spake unto them all in common, for the heathen also were come together, being wroth at the unjust judgement of Aegeates.

Ye men that are here present, and women and children, old and young, bond and free, and all that will hear, take ye no heed of the vain deceit of this present life, but heed us rather who hang here for the Lord's sake and are about to depart out of this body: and renounce all the lusts of the world and contemn (spit upon) the worship of the abominable idols, and run unto the true worshipping of our God that lieth not, and make yourselves a temple pure and ready to receive the word. (Narr. then becomes obviously late: Ep. Gr., which is far shorter, ends: And hasten to overtake my soul as it hasteneth toward heavenly things, and in a word despise all temporal things, and establish your minds as men believing in Christ.)

And the multitudes hearing the things which he spake departed not from the place; and Andrew continued speaking yet more unto them, for a day and a night. And on the day following, beholding his endurance and constancy of soul and wisdom of spirit and strength of mind, they were wroth, and hastened with one accord unto Aegeates, to the judgement-seat where he sat, and cried out against

him, saying: What is this judgement of thine, O proconsul? thou hast ill judged! thou hast condemned unjustly: thy court is against law! What evil hath this man done? wherein hath he offended? The city is troubled: thou injurest us all! destroy not Caesar's city! give us the righteous man! restore us the holy man! slay not a man dear to God! destroy not a man gentle and pious! lo, two days is he hanged up and yet liveth, and hath tasted nothing, and yet refresheth all us with his words, and lo, we believe in the God whom he preacheth. Take down the righteous man and we will all turn philosophers; loose the chaste man and all Patrae will be at peace, set free the wise man and all Achaia shall be set free by him! (or, obtain mercy.)

But when at the first Aegeates would not hear them, but beckoned with the hand to the people that they should depart, they were filled with rage and were at the point to do him violence, being in number about two thousand (Narr., Ep. Gr., Mart. II: 20,000).

And when the proconsul saw them to be after a sort mad, he feared lest there should be a rising against him, and rose up from the judgement-seat and went with them, promising to release Andrew. And some went before and signified to the apostle and to the rest of the people that were there, wherefore the proconsul was coming. And all the multitude of the disciples rejoiced together with Maximilla and Iphidamia and Stratocles.

But when Andrew heard it, he began to say: O the dullness and disobedience and simplicity of them whom I have taught! how much have I spoken, and even to this day I have not persuaded them to flee from the love of earthly things! but they are yet bound unto them and continue in them, and will not depart from them. What meaneth this affection and love and sympathy with the flesh? how long heed ye worldly and temporal things? how long understand ye not the things that be above us, and press not to overtake them? leave me henceforth to be put to death in the manner which ye behold, and let no man by any means loose me from these bonds, for so is it appointed unto me to depart out of the body and be present with the Lord, with whom also I am crucified. And this shall be accomplished.

And he turned unto Aegeates and said with a loud voice: Wherefore art thou come, Aegeates, that art an alien unto me? what wilt thou dare afresh, what contrive, or what fetch? tell us that thou hast repented and art come to loose us? nay, not if thou repentest, indeed, Aegeates, will I now consent unto thee, not if thou promise me all thy substance will I depart from myself, not if thou say that thou art mine will I trust thee. And dost thou, proconsul, loose him that is bound? him that hath been set free? that hath been recognized by his kinsman? that hath obtained mercy and is beloved of him? dost thou loose him that is alien to thee? the stranger? that only appeareth to thee? I have one with whom I shall be for ever, with whom I shall converse for unnumbered ages. Unto him do I go, unto him do I hasten, who made thee also known unto me, who said to me: Understand thou Aegeates and his gifts let not that fearful one afright thee, nor think that he holdeth thee who art mine. He is thine enemy: he is pestilent, a deceiver, a corrupter, a madman, a sorcerer, a cheat, a murderer, wrathful, without compassion. Depart therefore from me, thou worker of all iniquity. (Ep. Gr. He is thine enemy. Therefore I know thee, through him that permitted me to know. I depart from thee. For I and they that are akin to me hasten toward that which is ours, and leave thee to be what thou wast, and what thou knowest not thyself to be.)

And the Proconsul hearing this stood speechless and as it were beside himself; but as all the city made an e uproar that he should loose Andrew, he drew near to the cross to loose him and take him down. But the blessed Andrew cried out with a loud voice: Suffer not Lord, thine Andrew that hath been bound upon thy cross, to be loosed again; give not me that am upon thy mystery to the shameless devil; O Jesu Christ, let not thine adversary loose him that is hung upon thy grace; O Father, let not this mean (little) one humble any more him that hath known thy greatness. But do thou, Jesu Christ, whom I have seen, whom I hold, whom I love, in whom I am and shall be, receive me in peace into thine everlasting tabernacles, that by my going out there may be an entering in unto thee of many that are akin to me, and that they may rest in thy majesty. And having so said, and yet more glorified the Lord, he gave up the ghost, while we all wept and lamented at our parting from him.

And after the decease of the blessed Andrew, Maximilla together with Stratocles, caring nought for them that stood by, drew near and herself loosed his body: and when it was evening she paid it the accustomed care and buried it (hard by the sea-shore). And she continued separate from Aegeates because of his brutal soul and his wicked manner of life: and she led a reverend and quiet life, filled with the love of Christ, among the brethren. Whom Aegeates solicited much, and promised that she should have the rule over his affairs; but being unable to persuade her, he arose in the dead of night and unknown to them of his house cast himself down from a great height and perished.

But Stratocles, which was his brother after the flesh, would not touch aught of the things that were left of his substance; for the wretched man died without offspring: but said: Let thy goods go with thee, Aegeates.

For of these things we have no need, for they are polluted; but for me, let Christ be my friend and I his servant, and all my substance do I offer unto him in whom I have believed, and I pray that by worthy hearing of the blessed teaching of the apostle I may appear a partaker with him in the ageless and unending kingdom. And so the uproar of the people ceased, and all were glad at the amazing and untimely and sudden fall of the impious and lawless Aegeates.

[Not much of this last paragraph from Narr. can be original. All the texts end with a statement that the apostle suffered on the 30th of November.]

THE ACTS OF PAUL AND THECLA

CHAP. I.

1 Demas and Hermogenes become Paul's companions. 4 Paul visits Onesiphorus. 8 Invited by Demas and Hermogenes. 11 Preaches to the household of Onesiphorus. 12 His sermon.

WHEN Paul went up to Iconium, after his flight from Antioch, Demas and Hermogenes became his companions, who were then full of hypocrisy.

2 But Paul looking only at the goodness of God, did them no harm, but loved them greatly.

3 Accordingly he endeavoured to make agreeable to them, all

p. 100

the oracles and doctrines of Christ, and the design of the Gospel of God's well-beloved Son, instructing them in the knowledge of Christ, as it was revealed to him.

4 And a certain man named Onesiphorus, hearing that Paul was come to Iconium, went out speedily to meet him, together with his wife Lectra, and his sons Simmia and Zeno, to invite him to their house.

5 For Titus had given them a description of Paul's personage, they as yet not knowing him in person, but only being acquainted with his character.

6 They went in the king's highway to Lystra, and stood there waiting for him, comparing all who passed by, with that description which Titus had given them.

7 At length they saw a man coming (namely Paul), of a low stature, bald (or shaved) on the head, crooked thighs, handsome legs, hollow-eyed; had a crooked nose; full of grace; for sometimes he appeared as a man, sometimes he had the countenance of an angel. And Paul saw Onesiphorus, and was glad.

8 And Onesiphorus said: Hail, thou servant of the blessed God. Paul replied, The grace of God be with thee and thy family.

9 But Demos and Hermogenes were moved with envy, and, under a show of great religion, Demas said, And are not we also servants of the blessed God? Why didst thou not salute us?

10 Onesiphorus replied, Because I have not perceived in, you the fruits of righteousness; nevertheless, if ye are of that sort, ye shall be welcome to my house also.

11 Then Paul went into the house of Onesiphorus, and there was great joy among the family on that account: and they employed themselves in prayer, breaking of bread, and hearing Paul preach the word of God concerning temperance and the resurrection, in the following manner:

12 Blessed are the pure in heart; for they shall see God.

13 Blessed are they who keep their flesh undefiled (or pure); for they shall be the temple of God.

14 Blessed are the temperate (or chaste); for God will reveal himself to them.

15 Blessed are they who abandon their secular enjoyments; for they shall be accepted of God.

16 Blessed are they who have wives, as though they had them not; for they shall be made angels of God.

17 Blessed are they who tremble at the word of God; for they shall be comforted.

18 Blessed are they who keep their baptism pure; for they shall find peace with the Father, Son, and Holy Ghost.

19 Blessed are they who pursue the wisdom (or doctrine) of Jesus Christ; for they shall be called the sons of the Most High.

20 Blessed are they who observe the instructions of Jesus Christ; for they shall dwell in eternal light.

21 Blessed are they, who for the love of Christ abandon the glories of the world; for they shall judge angels, and be placed at the right hand of Christ, and shall not suffer the bitterness of the last judgment.

22 Blessed are the bodies and souls of virgins; for they are acceptable to God, and shall not lose the reward of their virginity; for the word of their (heavenly) Father shall prove effectual to their salvation in the day of his Son, and they shall enjoy rest for evermore.

CHAP. II.

1 Thecla listens anxiously to Paul's preaching. 5 Thamyris, her admirer, concerts with Theoclia her mother to dissuade her, 12 in vain. 14 Demos and Hermogenes viler Paul to Thamyria.

WHILE Paul was preach this sermon in the church which was in the house of Onesiphorus, a certain virgin, named Thecla (whose mother's name was Theoclia, and who was betrothed to a man named Thamyris) sat at a certain window in her house.

2 From whence, by the advantage of a window in the house where Paul was, she both night and day heard Paul's sermons concerning God, concerning charity, concerning faith in Christ, and concerning prayer;

3 Nor would she depart from the window, till with exceeding joy she was subdued to the doctrines of faith.

4 At length, when she saw many women and virgins going in to Paul, she earnestly desired that she might be thought worthy to appear in his presence, and hear the word of Christ; for she had not yet seen Paul's person, but only heard his sermons, and that alone.

5 But when she would not be prevailed upon to depart from the window, her mother sent to Thamyris, who came with the greatest pleasure, as hoping now to marry her. Accordingly he said to Theoclia, Where is my Thecla?

6 Theoclia replied, Thamyris, I have something very strange to tell you; for Thecla, for the space of three days, will not move from the window not so much as to eat or drink, but is so intent in hearing the artful and delusive discourses of a certain foreigner, that I perfectly admire, Thamyris, that a young woman of her known modesty, will suffer herself to be so prevailed upon.

7 For that man has disturbed the whole city of Iconium, and even your Thecla, among others, All the women and young men flock to him to receive his doctrine; who, besides all the rest, tells them that there is but one God, who alone is to be worshipped, and that we ought to live in chastity.

8 Notwithstanding this, my daughter Thecla, like a spider's web fastened to the window, is captivated by the discourses of Paul, and attends upon them with prodigious eagerness, and vast delight; and thus, by attending on what he says, the young woman is seduced. Now then do you go, and speak to her, for she is betrothed to you.

9 Accordingly Thamyris went, and having saluted her, and taking care not to surprise her, he said, Thecla, my spouse, why sittest thou in this melancholy posture? What strange impressions are made upon thee? Turn to Thamyris, and blush.

10 Her mother also spake to her after the same manner, and said, Child, why dost thou sit so melancholy, and, like one astonished, makest no reply?

11 Then they wept exceedingly, Thamyria, that he had lost

his spouse; Theoclia, that she had lost her daughter; and the maids, that they had lost their mistress; and there was an universal mourning in the family.

12 But all these things made no impression upon Thecla, so as to incline her so much as to turn to them, and take notice of them; for she still regarded the discourses of Paul.

13 Then Thamyris ran forth into the street to observe who they were who went into Paul, and came out from him; and he saw two men engaged in a very warm dispute, and said to them;

14 Sirs, what business have you here? and who is that man within, belonging to you, who deludes the minds of men, both young men and virgins, persuading them, that they ought not to marry, but continue as they are?

15 I promise to give you a considerable sum, if you will give me a just account of him; for I am the chief person of this city.

16 Demas and Hermogenes replied, We cannot so exactly tell who he is; but this we know, that he deprives young men of their (intended) wives, and virgins of their (intended) husbands, by teaching, There can be no future resurrection, unless ye continue in chastity, and do not defile your flesh.

CHAP. III.

1 *They betray Paul.* 7 *Thamyris arrests him with officers.*

THEN said Thamyris, Come along with me to my house, and refresh yourselves. So they went to a very splendid entertainment, where there was wine in abundance, and very rich provision.

2 They were brought to a table richly spread, and made to drink plentifully by Thamyris, on account of the love he had for Thecla and his desire to marry her.

3 Then Thamyris said, I desire ye would inform me what the doctrines of this Paul are, that I may understand them; for I am under no small concern about Thecla, seeing she so delights in that stranger's discourses, that I am in danger of losing my intended wife.

4 Then Demas and Hermogenes answered both together, and said, Let him be brought before the governor Castellius, as one who endeavours to persuade the people into the new religion of the Christians, and he, according to the order of Cæsar, will put him to death, by which means you will obtain your wife;

5 While we at the same time will teach her, that the resurrection which he speaks of is already come, and consists in our having children; and that we then arose again, when we came to the knowledge of God.

6 Thamyris having this account from them, was filled with hot resentment:

7 And rising early in the morning he went to the house of Onesiphorus, attended by the magistrates, the jailor, and a great multitude of people with staves, and said to Paul;

8 Thou hast perverted the city of Iconium, and among the rest, Thecla, who is betrothed to me, so that now she will not marry me. Thou shalt therefore go with us to the governor Castellius.

9 And all the multitude cried out, Away with this impostor (magician), for he has perverted the minds of our wives, and all the people hearken to him.

CHAP. IV.

1 *Paul accused before the governor by Thamyris.* 5 *Defends*

himself. 9 *Is committed to Prison,* 10 *and visited by Thecla.*

THEN Thamyris standing before the governor's judgment-seat, spake with a loud voice in the following manner.

2 O governor, I know not whence this man cometh; but he is one who teaches that matrimony is unlawful. Command him therefore to declare before you for what reason he publishes such doctrines.

3 While he was saying thus, Demas and Hermogenes (whispered to Thamyris, and) said; Say that he is a Christian, and he will presently be put to death.

4 But the governor was more deliberate, and calling to Paul, he said, Who art thou? What dost thou teach? They seem to lay gross crimes to thy charge.

5 Paul then spake with a loud voice, saying, As I am now called to give an account, O governor, of my doctrines, I desire your audience.

6 That God, who is a God of vengeance, and who stands in need of nothing but the salvation of his creatures, has sent me to reclaim them from their wickedness and corruptions, from all (sinful) pleasures, and from death; and to persuade them to sin no more.

7 On this account, God sent his Son Jesus Christ, whom I preach, and in whom I instruct men to place their hopes as that l person who only had such compassion on the deluded world, that it might not, O governor, be condemned, but have faith, the fear of God, the knowledge of religion, and the love of truth.

8 So that if I only teach those things which I have received by revelation from God, where is my crime?

9 When the governor heard this, he ordered Paul to be bound, and to be put in prison, till he should be more at leisure to hear him more fully.

10 But in the night, Thecla taking off her ear-rings, gave them to the turnkey of the prison, who then opened the doors to her, and let her in;

11 And when she made a present of a silver looking-glass to the jailor, was allowed to go into the room where Paul was; then she sat down at his feet, and heard from him the great things of God.

12 And as she perceived Paul not to be afraid of suffering, but that by divine assistance he behaved himself with courage, her faith so far increased that she kissed his chains.

CHAP. V.

1 *Thecla sought and found by her relations.* 4 *Brought with Paul before the governor.* 9 *Ordered to be burnt, and Paul to be whipt.* 15 *Thecla miraculously saved.*

AT length Thecla was missed, and sought for by the family and by Thamyris in every street, as though she had been lost, but one of the porter's fellow-servants told them, that she had gone out in the night-time.

2 Then they examined the porter, and he told them, that she was gone to the prison to the strange man.

3 They went therefore according to his direction, and there found her; and when they came out, they got a mob together, and went and told the governor all that happened.

4 Upon which he ordered Paul to be brought before his judgment seat.

5 Thecla in the mean time lay wallowing on the ground in the prison, in that same place where Paul had sat to teach her; upon which the governor also ordered her to be brought before his judgment-seat; which summons she received with joy, and went.

6 When Paul was brought thither, the mob with more vehemence cried out, He is a magician, let him die.

7 Nevertheless the governor attended with pleasure upon Paul's discourses of the holy works of Christ; and, after a council called, he summoned Thecla, and said to her, Why do you not, according to the law of the Iconians, marry Thamyris?

8 She stood still, with her eyes fixed upon Paul; and finding she made no reply, Theoclia, her mother, cried out, saying, Let the unjust creature be burnt; let her be burnt in the midst of the theatre, for refusing Thamyris, that all women may learn from her to avoid such practices.

9 Then the governor was exceedingly concerned, and ordered Paul to be whipt out of the city, and Thecla to be burnt.

10 So the governor arose, and went immediately into the theatre; and all the people went forth to see the dismal sight.

11 But Thecla, just as a lamb in the wilderness looks every way to see his shepherd, looked around for Paul;

12 And as she was looking upon the multitude, she saw the Lord Jesus in the likeness of Paul, and said to herself, Paul is come to see me in my distressed circumstances. And she fixed her eyes upon him; but he instantly ascended up to heaven, while she looked on him.

13 Then the young men and women brought wood and straw for the burning of Thecla; who, being brought naked to the stake, extorted tears from the governor, with surprise beholding the greatness of her beauty.

14 And when they had placed the wood in order, the people commanded her to go upon it; which she did, first making the sign of the cross.

15 Then the people set fire to the pile; though the flame was exceeding large, it did not touch her, for God took compassion on her, and caused a great eruption from the earth beneath, and a cloud from above to pour down great quantities of rain and hail;

16 Insomuch that by the rupture of the earth, very many were in great danger, and some were killed, the fire was extinguished, and Thecla preserved.

CHAP. VI.

1 *Paul with Onesiphorus in a cave.* 7 *Thecla discovers Paul;* 12 *proffers to follow him:* 13 *he exhorts her not for fear of fornication.*

IN the mean time Paul, together with Onesiphorus, his wife and children, was keeping a fast in a certain cave, which was in the road from Iconium to Daphne.

2 And when they had fasted for several days, the children said to Paul, Father, we are hungry, and have not wherewithal to buy bread; for Onesiphorus had left all his substance to follow Paul with his family.

KEY TO THE PLATE "HELL."

1. *Entrance to the confines of Hell.*
2. *Charon in his bark.*
3. *The Minotaur roaring at the approach of condemned souls.*
4. *Souls agitated by the impure breath of evil spirits.*
5. *Cerberus devouring the souls of gourmands.*
6. *The avaricious and prodigal condemned to carry burdens.*
7. *The envious and angry cast into the Styx.*
8. *Tower and wall of the evil city.*
9. *In this ditch are those who have sinned against their neighbors;*

Centaurs shoot arrows at them.
10. *Those who have sinned against themselves are here tormented by Harpies.*
11. *Rain of fire for those who have sinned against God.*
12. *Soul of the tyrant Gerion cast into the flames.*
13. *Debauchees and corruptors of youth flogged by devils.*
14. *Poisonous gulf into which flatterers are plunged.*
15. *Lake of fire in the caldrons into which Simonaics are cast.*
16. *Sorcerers and diviners, their faces turned backward.*
17. *Bog of boiling pitch for cheats, thieves, and deceivers.*
18. *Hypocrite crucified.*
19. *Perfidious advisers plunged into a flaming ditch.*
20. *For scandalous persons: one holds his head in his hand.*
21. *Robbers and other criminals tormented by a centaur armed with serpents.*
22. *Alchemists and quacks a prey to leprosy.*
23. *Well of ice, for traitors and the ungrateful.*
24. *Pluto in the midst of a glacier devouring the damned.*
25. *The holy city of Jerusalem.*

3 Then Paul, taking off his coat, said to the boy, Go, child, and buy bread, and bring it hither.

4 But while the boy was buying the bread, he saw his neighbour Thecla and was surprised, and said to her. Thecla, where are you going?

5 She replied, I am in pursuit of Paul, having been delivered from the flames.

6 The boy then said, I will bring you to him, for he is under great concern on your account, and has been in prayer and fasting these six days.

7 When Thecla came to the cave, she found Paul upon his knees praying and saying, O holy Father, O Lord Jesus Christ, grant that the fire may not touch Thecla; but be her helper, for she is thy servant.

8 Thecla then standing behind him, cried out in the following words: O sovereign Lord, Creator of heaven and earth, the Father of thy beloved and holy Son, I praise thee that thou hast preserved me from the fire, to see Paul again.

9 Paul then arose, and when he saw her, said, O God, who searchest the heart, Father of my Lord Jesus Christ, I praise thee that thou hast answered my prayer.

10 And there prevailed among them in the cave an entire affection to each other; Paul, Onesiphorus, and all that were with them being filled with joy.

11 They had five loaves, some herbs and water, and they solaced each other in reflections upon the holy works of Christ.

12 Then said Thecla to Paul, If you be pleased with it, I will follow you whithersoever you go.

13 He replied to her, Persons are now much given to fornication, and you being handsome, I am afraid lest you should meet with greater temptation than the former, and should not withstand, but be overcome by it.

14 Thecla replied, Grant me only the seal of Christ, and no temptation shall affect me.

15 Paul answered, Thecla, wait with patience, and you shall receive the gift of Christ.

CHAP. VII.

1 *Paul and Thecla go to Antioch.* 2 *Alexander, a magistrate, falls in love with Thecla: kisses her by force:* 5 *she resists him:* 6 *is carried before the governor, and condemned to be thrown to wild beasts.*

THEN Paul sent back Onesiphorus and his family to their own home, and taking Thecla along with him, went for

Antioch;

2 And as soon as they came into the city, a certain Syrian, named Alexander, a magistrate, in the city, who had done many considerable services for the city during his magistracy, saw Thecla and fell in love with her, and endeavoured by many rich presents to engage Paul m his interest.

3 But Paul told him, I know not the woman of whom you speak, nor does she belong to me.

4 But he being a person of great power in Antioch, seized her in the street and kissed her; which Thecla would not bear, but looking about for Paul, cried out in a distressed loud tone, Force me not, who am a stranger; force me not, who am a servant of God; I am one of the principal persons of Iconium, and was obliged to leave that city because I would not be married to Thamyris.

5 Then she laid hold on Alexander, tore his coat, and took his crown off his head, and made him appear ridiculous before all the people.

6 But Alexander, partly as he loved her, and partly being ashamed of what had been done, 1 led her to the governor, and upon her confession of what she had done,' he condemned her to be thrown among the beasts.

CHAP. VIII.

2 Thecla entertained by Trifina; 3 brought out to the wild beasts; a she-lion licks her feet. 5 Trifina upon a vision of her deceased daughter, adopts Thecla, 11 who is taken to the amphitheatre again.

WHICH when the people saw, they said: The judgments passed in this city are unjust. But Thecla desired the favour of the governor, that her chastity might not be attacked, but preserved till she should be cast to the beasts.

2 The governor then inquired, Who would entertain her; upon which a certain very rich widow, named Trifina, whose daughter was lately dead, desired that she might have the keeping of her; and she began to treat her in her house as her own daughter.

3 At length a day came, when the beasts were to be brought forth to be seen; and Thecla was brought to the amphitheatre, and put into a den in which was an exceeding fierce she-lion, in the presence of a multitude of spectators.

4 Trifina, without any surprise, accompanied Thecla, and the she-lion licked the feet of Thecla. The title written which denotes her crime, was, Sacrilege. Then the woman cried out, O God, the judgments of this city are unrighteous.

5 After the beasts had been shewn, Trifina took Thecla home with her, and they went to bed; and behold, the daughter of Trifina, who was dead, appeared to her mother, and said; Mother, let the young woman, Thecla, be reputed by you as your daughter in my stead; and desire her that she should pray for me, that I may be translated to a state of happiness.

6 Upon which Trifina, with a mournful air, said, My daughter Falconilla has appeared to me, and ordered me to receive you in her room; wherefore I desire, Thecla, that you would pray for my daughter, that she may be translated into a state of happiness, and to life eternal.

7 When Thecla heard this, she immediately prayed to the Lord, and said: O Lord God of heaven and earth, Jesus Christ, thou Son of the Most High, grant that her daughter Falconilla may live forever. Trifina hearing this groaned again, and said: O unrighteous judgments! O unreasonable wickedness! that such a creature should (again) be cast to

the beasts!

8 On the morrow, at break of day, Alexander came to Trifina's house, and said: The governor and the people are waiting; bring the criminal forth.

9 But Trifina ran in so violently upon him, that he was affrighted, and ran away. Trifina was one of the royal family; and she thus expressed her sorrow, and said; Alas! I have trouble in my house' nn two accounts, and there is no one who will relieve me, either under the loss of my daughter, or my being unable to save Thecla. But now, O Lord God, be thou the helper of Thecla thy servant.

10 While she was thus engaged, the governor sent one of his own officers to bring Thecla. Trifina took her by the hand, and, going with her, said: I went with Falconilla to her grave, and. now must go with Thecla to the beasts.

11 When Thecla heard this, she weeping prayed, and said: O Lord God, whom I have made my confidence and refuge, reward Trifina for her compassion to me, and preserving my chastity.

12 Upon this there was a great noise in the amphitheatre; the beasts roared, and the people cried out, Bring in the criminal.

13 But the woman cried out, and said: Let the whole city suffer for such crimes; and order all of us, O governor, to the same punishment. O unjust judgment! O cruel sight!

14 Others said, Let the whole city be destroyed for this vile action. Kill us all, O governor. O cruel sight! O unrighteous judgment.

CHAP. IX.

1 Thecla thrown naked to the wild beasts; 2 they all refuse to attack her; 8 throws herself into a pit of water. 10 other wild beasts refuse her. 11 Tied to wild bulls. 13 Miraculously saved. 15 Released. 24 Entertained by Trifina.

THEN Thecla was taken out of the hand of Trifina, stripped naked, had a girdle put on, and thrown into the place appointed for fighting with the beasts: and the lions and the bears were let loose upon her.

2 But a she-lion, which was of all the most fierce, ran to Thecla, and fell down at her feet. Upon which the multitude of women shouted aloud.

3 Then a she-bear ran fiercely towards her; but the she-lion met the bear, and tore it to pieces.

4 Again, a he-lion, who had been wont to devour men, and which belonged to Alexander, ran towards her; but the she-lion encountered the he-lion, and they killed each other.

5 Then the women were under a greater concern, because the she-lion, which had helped Thecla, was dead.

6 Afterwards they brought out many other wild beasts; but Thecla stood with her hands stretched towards heaven, and prayed; and when she had done praying, she turned about, and saw a pit of water, and said, Now it is a proper time for me to be baptized.

7 Accordingly she threw herself into the water, and said, In thy name, O my Lord Jesus Christ, I am this last day baptized. The women and the people seeing this, cried out, and said, Do not throw yourself into the water. And the governor himself cried out, to think that the fish (sea-calves) were like to devour so much beauty.

8 Notwithstanding all this, Thecla threw herself into the water, in the name of our Lord Jesus Christ.

9 But the fish (sea-calves,) when they saw the lighting and fire, were killed, and swam dead upon the surface of the water, and a cloud of fire surrounded Thecla, so that as the

beasts could not come near her, so the people could not see her nakedness.

10 Yet they turned other wild beasts upon her; upon which they made a very mournful outcry; and some of them scattered spikenard, others cassia, others amomus (a sort of spikenard, or the herb of Jerusalem, or ladies-rose) others ointment; so that the quantity of ointment was large, in proportion to the number of people; and upon this all the beasts lay as though they had been fast asleep, and did not touch Thecla.

11 Whereupon Alexander said to the Governor, I have some very terrible bulls; let us bind her to them. To which the governor, with concern, replied, You may do what you think fit.

12 Then they put a cord round Thecla's waist, which bound also her feet, and with it tied her to the bulls, to whose privy-parts they applied red-hot irons, that so they being the more tormented, might more violently drag Thecla about, till they had killed her.

13 The bulls accordingly tore about, making a most hideous noise; but the flame which was about Thecla, burnt off the cords which were fastened to the members of the bulls, and she stood in the middle of the stage, as unconcerned as if she had not been bound.

14 But in the mean time Trifina, who sat upon one of the benches, fainted away and died; upon which the whole city was under a very great concern.

15 And Alexander himself was afraid, and desired the governor, saying: I entreat you, take compassion on me and the city, and release this woman, who has fought with the beasts; lest, both you and I, and the whole city be destroyed

16 For if Cæsar should have any account of what has passed now, he will certainly immediately destroy the city, because Trifina, a person of royal extract, and a relation of his, is dead upon her seat.

17 Upon this the governor called Thecla from among the beasts to him, and said to her, Who art thou? and what are thy circumstances, that not one of the beasts will touch thee?

18 Thecla replied to him; I am a servant of the living God; and as to my state, I am a believer on Jesus Christ his Son, in whom God is well pleased; and for that reason none of the beasts could touch me.

19 He alone is the way to eternal salvation, and the foundation of eternal life. He is a refuge to those who are in distress; a support to the afflicted, hope and defence to those who are hopeless; and, in a word, all those who do not believe on him, shall not live, but suffer eternal death.

20 When the govern or heard these things, he ordered her clothes to be brought, and said to her put on your clothes.

21 Thecla replied: May that God who clothed me when I was naked among the beasts, in the day of judgment clothe your soul with the robe of salvation. Then she took her clothes, and put them on; and the governor immediately published an order in these words; I release to you Thecla the servant of God.

22 Upon which the women cried out together with a loud voice, and with one accord gave praise unto God, and said; There is but one God, who is the God of Thecla; the one God who delivered Thecla.

23 So loud were their voices that the whole city seemed to be shaken; and Trifina herself heard the glad tidings, and arose again, and ran with the multitude to meet Thecla; and embracing her, said: Now I believe there shall be a resurrection of the dead; now I am persuaded that my daughter is alive. Come therefore home with me, my

daughter Thecla, and I will make over all that I have to you.

24 So Thecla went with Trifina, and was entertained there a few days, teaching her the word of the Lord, whereby many young women were converted; and there was great joy in the family of Trifina.

25 But Thecla longed to see Paul, and inquired and sent everywhere to find him; and when at length she was informed that he was at Myra, in Lycia, she took with her many young men and women; and putting on a girdle, and dressing herself in the habit of a man, she went to him to Myra in Lycia, and there found Paul preaching the word of God; and she stood by him among the throng.

CHAP. X.

1 Thecla visits Paul. 8 Visits Onesiphorus. 8 Visits her mother. 9 Who repulses her. 12 Is tempted by the devil. Works miracles.

BUT it was no small surprise to Paul when he saw her and the people with her; for he imagined some fresh trial was coining upon them;

2 Which when Thecla perceived, she said to him: I have been baptized, O Paul; for he who assists you in preaching, has assisted me to baptize.

3 Then Paul took her, and led her to the house of Hermes; and Thecla related to Paul all that had befallen her in Antioch, insomuch that Paul exceedingly wondered, and all who heard were confirmed in the faith, and prayed for Trifina's happiness.

4 Then Thecla arose, and said to Paul, I am going to Iconium. Paul replied to her: Go, and teach the word of the Lord.

5 But Trifina had sent large sums of money to Paul, and also clothing by the hands of Thecla, for the relief of the poor.

6 So Thecla went to Iconium. And when she came to the house of Onesiphorus, she fell down upon the floor where Paul had sat and preached, and, mixing tears with her prayers, she praised and glorified God in the following words:

7 O Lord the God of this house, in which I was first enlightened by thee; O Jesus, son of the living God, who wast my helper before the governor, my helper in the fire, and my helper among the beasts; thou alone art God forever and ever. Amen.

8 Thecla now (on her return) found Thamyris dead, but her mother living. So calling her mother, she said to her: Theoclia, my mother, is it possible for you to be brought to a belief, that there is but one Lord God, who dwells in the heavens? If you desire great riches, God will give them to you by me; if you want your daughter again, here I am.

9 These and many other things she represented to her mother, (endeavouring) to persuade her (to her own opinion). But her mother Theoclia gave no credit to the things which were said by the martyr Thecla.

10 So that Thecla perceiving she discoursed to no purpose, signing her whole body with the sign (of the cross), left the house and went to Daphine; and when she came there, she went to the cave, where she had found Paul with Onesiphorus, and fell down on the ground; and wept before God.

11 When she departed thence, she went to Seleucia, and enlightened many in the knowledge of Christ.

12 And a bright cloud conducted her in her journey.

13 And after she had arrived at Seleucia she went to a place

out of the city, about the distance of a furlong, being afraid of the inhabitants, because they were worshippers of idols.

14 And she was led (by the cloud) into a mountain called Calamon, or Rodeon. There she abode many years, and underwent a great many grievous temptations of the devil, which she bore in a becoming manner, by the assistance which she had from Christ.

15 At length certain gentlewomen hearing of the virgin Thecla, went to her, and were instructed by her in the oracles of God, and many of them abandoned this world, and led a monastic life with her.

16 Hereby a good report was spread everywhere of Thecla, and she wrought several (miraculous) cures, so that all the city and adjacent countries brought their sick to that mountain, and before they came as far as the door of the cave, they were instantly cured of whatsoever distemper they had.

17 The unclean spirits were cast out, making a noise; all received their sick made whole, and glorified God, who had bestowed such power on the virgin Thecla;

18 Insomuch that the physicians of Seleucia were now of no more account, and lost all the profit of their trade, because no one regarded them; upon which they were filled with envy, and began to contrive what methods to take with this servant of Christ.

CHAP. XI.

1 *Is attempted to be ravished,* 12 *escapes by a rock opening,* 17 *and closing miraculously.*

THE devil then suggested bad advice to their minds; and being on a certain day met together to consult, they reasoned among each other thus: The virgin is a priestess of the great goddess Diana, and whatsoever she requests from her, is granted, because she is a virgin, and so is beloved by all the gods.

2 Now then let us procure some rakish fellows, and after we have made them sufficiently drunk, and given them a good sum of money, let us order them to go and debauch this virgin, promising them, if they do it, a larger reward.

3 (For they thus concluded among themselves, that if they be able to debauch her, the gods will no more regard her, nor Diana cure the sick for her.)

4 They proceeded according to this resolution, and the fellows went to the mountain, and as fierce as lions to the cave, knocking at the door.

5 The holy martyr Thecla, relying upon the God in whom she believed, opened the door, although she was before apprized of their design, and said to them, Young men, what is your business?

6 They replied, Is there any one within, whose name is Thecla? She answered, What would you have with her? They said, We have a mind to lie with her.

7 The blessed Thecla answered: Though I am a mean old woman, I am the servant of my Lord Jesus Christ; and though you have a vile design against me, ye shall not be able to accomplish it. They replied: It is impossible but we must be able to do with you what we have a mind.

8 And while they were saying this, they laid hold on her by main force, and would have ravished her. Then she with the (greatest) mildness said to them: Young men have patience, and see the glory of the Lord.

9 And while they held her, she looked up to heaven and said; O God most reverend, to whom none can be likened; who makest thyself glorious over thine enemies; who didst

deliver me from the fire, and didst not give me up to Thamyris, didst not give me up to Alexander; who deliveredst me from the wild beasts; who didst preserve me in the deep waters; who hast everywhere been my helper, and hast glorified thy name in me;

10 Now also deliver me from the hands of these wicked and unreasonable men, nor suffer them to debauch my chastity which I have hitherto preserved for thy honour; for I love thee and long for thee, and worship thee, O Father, Son, and Holy Ghost, for evermore. Amen.

11 Then came a voice from heaven, saying, Fear not, Thecla, my faithful servant, for I am with thee. Look and see the place which is opened for thee: there thy eternal abode shall be; there thou shalt receive the beatific vision.

12 The blessed Thecla observing, saw the rock opened to as large a degree as that a man might enter in; she did as she was commanded, bravely fled from the vile crew, and went into the rock, which instantly so closed, that there was not any crack visible where it had opened.

13 The men stood perfectly astonished at so prodigious a miracle, and had no power to detain the servant of God; but only, catching hold of her veil, or hood, they tore off a piece of it;

14 And even that was by the permission of God, for the confirmation of their faith who should come to see this venerable place, and to convey blessings to those in succeeding ages, who should believe on our Lord Jesus Christ from a pure heart.

15 Thus suffered that first martyr and apostle of God, and virgin, Thecla; who came from Iconium at eighteen years of age; afterwards, partly in journeys and travels, and partly in a monastic life in the cave, she lived seventy-two years; so that she was ninety years old when the Lord translated her.

16 Thus ends her life.

17 The day which is kept sacred to her memory, is the twenty-fourth of September, to the glory of the Father, and the Son, and the Holy Ghost, now and for evermore. Amen.

THE ACTS OF THOMAS

ACTS OF THE HOLY APOSTLE THOMAS

The First Act, when he went into India with Abbanes the merchant.

At that season all we the apostles were at Jerusalem, Simon which is called Peter and Andrew his brother, James the son of Zebedee and John his brother, Philip and Bartholomew, Thomas and Matthew the publican, James the son of Alphaeus and Simon the Canaanite, and Judas the brother of James: and we divided the regions of the world, that every one of us should go unto the region that fell to him and unto the nation whereunto the Lord sent him.

According to the lot, therefore, India fell unto Judas Thomas, which is also the twin: but he would not go, saying that by reason of the weakness of the flesh he could not travel, and 'I am an Hebrew man; how can I go amongst the Indians and preach the truth?' And as he thus reasoned and spake, the Saviour appeared unto him by night and saith to him: Fear not, Thomas, go thou unto India and preach the word there, for my grace is with thee. But he would not obey, saying: Whither thou wouldest send me, send me, but elsewhere, for unto the Indians I will not go.

2 And while he thus spake and thought, it chanced that there was there a certain merchant come from India whose name was Abbanes, sent from the King Gundaphorus [Gundaphorus is a historical personage who reigned over a part of India in the first century after Christ. His coins bear his name in Greek, as Hyndopheres], and having commandment from him to buy a carpenter and bring him unto him.

Now the Lord seeing him walking in the market-place at noon said unto him: Wouldest thou buy a carpenter? And he said to him: Yea. And the Lord said to him: I have a slave that is a carpenter and I desire to sell him. And so saying he showed him Thomas afar off, and agreed with him for three litrae of silver unstamped, and wrote a deed of sale, saying: I, Jesus, the son of Joseph the carpenter, acknowledge that I have sold my slave, Judas by name, unto thee Abbanes, a merchant of Gundaphorus, king of the Indians. And when the deed was finished, the Saviour took Judas Thomas and led him away to Abbanes the merchant, and when Abbanes saw him he said unto him: Is this thy master? And the apostle said: Yea, he is my Lord. And he said: I have bought thee of him. And thy apostle held his peace.

3 And on the day following the apostle arose early, and having prayed and besought the Lord he said: I will go whither thou wilt, Lord Jesus: thy will be done. And he departed unto Abbanes the merchant, taking with him nothing at all save only his price. For the Lord had given it unto him, saying: Let thy price also be with thee, together with my grace, wheresoever thou goest.

And the apostle found Abbanes carrying his baggage on board the ship; so he also began to carry it aboard with him. And when they were embarked in the ship and were set down Abbanes questioned the apostle, saying: What craftsmanship knowest thou? And he said: In wood I can make ploughs and yokes and augers (ox-goads, Syr.), and boats and oars for boats and masts and pulleys; and in stone, pillars and temples and court-houses for kings. And Abbanes the merchant said to him: Yea, it is of such a workman that we have need. They began then to sail homeward; and they had a favourable wind, and sailed prosperously till they reached Andrapolis, a royal city.

4 And they left the ship and entered into the city, and lo, there were noises of flutes and water-organs, and trumpets sounded about them; and the apostle inquired, saying: What is this festival that is in this city? And they that were there said to him: Thee also have the gods brought to make merry in this city. For the king hath an only daughter, and now he giveth her in marriage unto an husband: this rejoicing, therefore, and assembly of the wedding to-day is the festival which thou hast seen. And the king hath sent heralds to proclaim everywhere that all should come to the marriage, rich and poor, bond and free, strangers and citizens: and if any refuse and come not to the marriage he shall answer for it unto the king. And Abbanes hearing that, said to the apostle: Let us also go, lest we offend the king, especially seeing we are strangers. And he said: Let us go.

And after they had put up in the inn and rested a little space they went to the marriage; and the apostle seeing them all set down (reclining), laid himself, he also, in the midst, and all looked upon him, as upon a stranger and one come from a foreign land: but Abbanes the merchant, being his master, laid himself in another place.

5 And as they dined and drank, the apostle tasted nothing; so they that were about him said unto him: Wherefore art thou come here, neither eating nor drinking? but he answered them, saying: I am come here for somewhat greater than the food or the drink, and that I may fulfil the king's will. For the heralds proclaim the king's message, and whoso hearkeneth not to the heralds shall be subject to the king's judgement.

So when they had dined and drunken, and garlands and unguents were brought to them, every man took of the unguent, and one anointed his face and another his beard and another other parts of his body; but the apostle anointed the top of his head and smeared a little upon his nostrils, and dropped it into his ears and touched his teeth with it, and carefully anointed the parts about his heart: and the wreath that was brought to him, woven of myrtle and other flowers, he took, and set it on his head, and took a branch of calamus and held it in his hand.

Now the flute-girl, holding her flute in her hand, went about to them all and played, but when she came to the place where the apostle was, she stood over him and played at his head for a long space: now this flute-girl was by race an Hebrew.

6 And as the apostle continued looking on the ground, one of the cup-bearers stretched forth his hand and gave him a buffet; and the apostle lifted up his eyes and looked upon him that smote him and said: My God will forgive thee in the life to come this iniquity, but in this world thou shalt

show forth his wonders and even now shall I behold this hand that hath smitten me dragged by dogs. And having so said, he began to sing and to say this song:

The damsel is the daughter of light, in whom consisteth and dwelleth the proud brightness of kings, and the sight of her is delightful, she shineth with beauty and cheer. Her garments are like the flowers of spring, and from them a waft of fragrance is borne; and in the crown of her head the king is established which with his immortal food (ambrosia) nourisheth them that are founded upon him; and in her head is set truth, and with her feet she showeth forth joy. And her mouth is opened, and it becometh her well: thirty and two are they that sing praises to her. Her tongue is like the curtain of the door, which waveth to and fro for them that enter in: her neck is set in the fashion of steps which the first maker hath wrought, and her two hands signify and show, proclaiming the dance of the happy ages, and her fingers point out the gates of the city. Her chamber is bright with light and breatheth forth the odour of balsam and all spices, and giveth out a sweet smell of myrrh and Indian leaf, and within are myrtles strown on the floor, and of all manner of odorous flowers, and the door-posts(?) are adorned with freedst. 7 And surrounding her her groomsmen keep her, the number of whom is seven, whom she herself hath chosen. And her bridesmaids are seven, and they dance before her. And twelve in number are they that serve before her and are subject unto her, which have their aim and their look toward the bridegroom, that by the sight of him they may be enlightened; and for ever shall they be with her in that eternal joy, and shall be at that marriage whereto the princes are gathered together and shall attend at that banquet whereof the eternal ones are accounted worthy, and shall put on royal raiment and be clad in bright robes; and in joy and exultation shall they both be and shall glorify the Father of all, whose proud light they have received, and are enlightened by the sight of their lord; whose immortal food they have received, that hath no failing (excrementum, Syr.), and have drunk of the wine that giveth then neither thirst nor desire. And they have glorified and praised with the living spirit, the Father of truth and the mother of wisdom.

8 And when he had sung and ended this song, all that were there present gazed upon him; and he kept silence, and they saw that his likeness was changed, but that which was spoken by him they understood not, forasmuch as he was an Hebrew and that which he spake was said in the Hebrew tongue. But the flute-girl alone heard all of it, for she was by race an Hebrew and she went away from him and played to the rest, but for the most part she gazed and looked upon him, for she loved him well, as a man of her own nation; moreover he was comely to look upon beyond all that were there. And when the flute-girl had played to them all and ended, she sat down over against him, gazing and looking earnestly upon him. But he looked upon no man at all, neither took heed of any but only kept his eyes looking toward the ground, waiting the time when he might depart thence.

But the cup-bearer that had buffeted him went down to the well to draw water; and there chanced to be a lion there, and it slew him and left him lying in that place, having torn his lirmbs in pieces, and forthwith dogs seized his

members, and among them one black dog holding his right hand in his mouth bare it into the place of the banquet.

9 And all when they saw it were amazed and inquired which of them it was that was missing. And when it became manifest that it was the hand of the cup-bearer which had smitten the apostle, the flute-girl brake her flute and cast it away and went and sat down at the apostle's feet, saying: This is either a god or an apostle of God, for I heard him say in the Hebrew tongue: ' I shall now see the hand that hath smitten me dragged by dogs', which thing ye also have now beheld; for as he said, so hath it come about. And some believed her, and some not.

But when the king heard of it, he came and said to the apostle: Rise up and come with me, and pray for my daughter: for she is mine only-begotten, and to-day I give her in marriage. But the apostle was not willing to go with him, for the Lord was not yet revealed unto him in that place. But the king led him away against his will unto the bride-chamber that he might pray for them.

10 And the apostle stood, and began to pray and to speak thus: My Lord and mv God, that travellest with thy servants, that guidest and correctest them that believe in thee, the refuge and rest of the oppressed, the hope of the poor and ransomer of captives, the physician of the souls that lie sick and saviour of all creation, that givest life unto the world and strengthenest souls; thou knowest things to come, and by our means accomplishest them: thou Lord art he that revealeth hidden mysteries and maketh manifest words that are secret: thou Lord art the planter of the good tree, and of thine hands are all good works engendered: thou Lord art he that art in all things and passest through all, and art set in all thy works and manifested in the working of them all. Jesus Christ, Son of compassion and perfect saviour, Christ, Son of the living God, the undaunted power that hast overthrown the enemy, and the voice that was heard of the rulers, and made all their powers to quake, the ambassador that wast sent from the height and camest down even unto hell, who didst open the doors and bring up thence them that for many ages were shut up in the treasury of darkness, and showedst them the way that leadeth up unto the height: l beseech thee, Lord Jesu, and offer unto thce supplication for these young persons, that thou wouldest do for them the things that shall help them and be expedient and profitable for them. And he laid his hands on them and said: The Lord shall be with you, and left them in that place and departed.

11 And the king desired the groomsmen to depart out of the bride-chamber; and when all were gone out and the doors were shut, the bridegrroom lifted up the curtain of the bride-chamber to fetch the bride unto him. And he saw the Lord Jesus bearing the likeness of Judas Thomas and speaking with the bride; even of him that but now had blessed them and gone out from them, the apostle; and he saith unto him: Wentest thou not out in the sight of all? how then art thou found here? But the Lord said to him: I am not Judas which is also called Thomas but I am his brother. And the Lord sat down upon the bed and bade them also sit upon chairs, and began to say unto them:

12 Remember, my children, what my brother spake unto you and what he delivered before you: and know this, that

if ye abstain from this foul intercourse, ye become holy temples, pure, being quit of impulses and pains, seen and unseen, and ye will acquire no cares of life or of children, whose end is destruction: and if indeed ye get many children, for their sakes ye become grasping and covetous, stripping orphans and overreaching widows, and by so doing subject yourselves to grievous punishments. For the more part of children become useless oppressed of devils, some openly and some invisibly, for they become either lunatic or half withered or blind or deaf or dumb or paralytic or foolish; and if they be sound, again they will be vain, doing useless or abominable acts, for they will be caught either in adultery or murder or theft or fornication, and by all these vvill ye be afflicted.

But if ye be persuaded and keep your souls chaste before God, there will come unto you living children whom these blemishes touch not, and ye shall be without care, leading a tranquil life without grief or anxiety, looking to receive that incorruptible and true marriage, and ye shall be therein groomsmen entering into that bride-chamber which is full of immortality and light.

13 And when the young people heard these things, they believed the Lord and gave themselves up unto him, and abstained from foul desire and continued so, passing the night in that place. And the Lord departed from before them, saying thus: The grace of the Lord shall be with you.

And when the morning was come the king came to meet them and furnished a table and brought it in before the bridegroom and the bride. And he found them sitting over against each other and the face of the bride he found unveiled, and the bridegroom was right joyful.

And the mother came unto the bride and said: Why sittest thou so, child, and art not ashamed, but art as if thou hadst lived with thine husband a long season? And her father said: Because of thy great love toward thine husband dost thou not even veil thyself?

14 And the bride answered and said: Verily, father, I am in great love, and I pray my Lord that the love which I have perceived this night may abide with me, and I will ask for that husband of whom I have learned to-day: and therefore I will no more veil myself, because the mirror (veil) of shame is removed from me; and therefore am I no more ashamed or abashed, because the deed of shame and confusion is departed far from me; and that I am not confounded, it is because my astonishment hath not continued with me; and that I am in cheerfulness and joy, it is because the day of my joy hath not been troubled; and that I have set at nought this husband and this marriage that passeth away from before mine eyes, it is because I am joined in another marriage; and that I have had no intercourse with a husband that is temporal, whereof the end is with lasciviousness and bitterness of soul, it is because I am yoked unto a true husband.

15 And while the bride was saying yet more than this, the bridegroom answered and said: I give thee thanks, O Lord, that hast been proclaimed by the stranger, and found in us; who hast removed me far from corruption and sown life in me; who hast rid me of this disease that is hard to be healed and cured and abideth for ever, and hast implanted sober

health in me; who hast shown me thyself and revealed unto me all my state wherein I am; who hast redeemed me from falling and led me to that which is better, and set me free from temporal things and made me worthy of those that are immortal and everlasting; that hast made thyself lowly even down to me and my littleness, that thou mayest present me unto thy greatness and unite me unto thyself; who hast not withheld thine own bowels from me that was ready to perish, but hast shown me how to seek myself and know who I was, and who and in what manner I now am, that I may again become that which I was: whom I knew not, but thyself didst seek me out: of whom I was not aware, but thyself hast taken me to thee: whom I have perceived, and now am not able to be unmindful of him: whose love burneth within me, and I cannot speak it as is fit, but that which I am able to say of it is little and scanty, and not fitly proportioned unto his glory: yet he blameth me not that presume to say unto him even that which I know not: for it is because of his love that I say even this much.

16 Now when the king heard these things from the bridegroom and the bride, he rent his clothes and said unto them that stood by him: Go forth quickly and go about the whole city, and take and bring me that man that is a sorcerer who by ill fortune came unto this city; for with mine own hands I brought him into this house, and I told him to pray over this mine ill-starred daugllter; and whoso findeth and bringeth him to me, I will give him whatsoever he asketh of me. They went, therefore and went about seeking him, and found him not; for he had set sail. They went also unto the inn where he had lodged and found there the flute-girl weeping and afflicted because he had not taken her with him. And when they told her the matter that had befallen with the young people she was exceeding glad at hearing it, and put away her grief and said: Now have I also found rest here. And she rose up and went unto them, and was with them a long time, until they had instructed the king also. And many of the brethren also gathered there until they heard the report of the apostle, that he was come unto the cities of India and was teaching there: and they departed and joined themselves unto him.

The Second Act: concerning his coming unto the king Gundaphorus.

17 Now when the apostle was come into the cities of India with Abbanes the merchant, Abbanes went to salute the king Gundaphorus, and reported to him of the carpenter whom he had brought with him. And the king was glad, and commanded him to come in to him. So when he was come in the king said unto him: What craft understandest thou? The apostle said unto him: The craft of carpentering and of building. The king saith unto him: What craftsmanship, then, knowest thou in wood, and what in stone? The apostle saith: In wood: ploughs, yokes, goads, pulleys, and boats and oars and masts; and in stone: plllars, temples, and court-houses for kings. And the king said: Canst thou build me a palace? And he answered: Yea, I can both build and furnish it; for to this end am I come, to build and to do the work of a carpenter.

18 And the king took him and went out of the city gates and began to speak with him on the way concerning the building of the court-house, and of the foundations, how

they should be laid, until they came to the place wherein he desired that the building should be; and he said: Here will I that the building should be. And the apostle said: Yea, for this place is suitable for the building. But the place was woody and there was much water there. So the king said: Begin to build. But he said: I cannot begin to build now at this season. And the king said: When canst thou begin? And he said: I will begin in the month Dius and finish in Xanthicus. But the king marvelled and said: Every building is builded in summer, and canst thou in this very winter build and make ready a palace? And the apostle said: Thus it must be, and no otherwise is it possible. And the king said: If, then, this seem good to thee, draw me a plan, how the work shall be, because I shall return hither after some long time. And the apostle took a reed and drew, measuring the place; and the doors he set toward the sunrising to look toward the light, and the windows toward the west to the breezes, and the bakehouse he appointed to be toward the south and the aqueduct for the service toward the north. And the king saw it and said to the apostle: Verily thou art a craftsman and it belitteth thee to be a servant of kings. And he left much money with him and departed from him.

19 And from time to time he sent money and provision, and victual for him and the rest of the workmen. But Thomas receiving it all dispensed it, going about the cities and the villages round about, distributing and giving alms to the poor and afflicted, and relieving them, saying: The king knoweth how to obtain recompense fit for kings, but at this time it is needful that the poor should have refreshment.

After these things the king sent an ambassador unto the apostle, and wrote thus: Signify unto me what thou hast done or what I shall send thee, or of what thou hast need. And the apostle sent unto him, saying: The palace (praetorium) is builded and only the roof remaineth. And the king hearing it sent him again gold and silver (lit. unstamped), and wrote unto him: Let the palace be roofed, if it is done. And the apostle said unto the Lord: I thank thee O Lord in all things, that thou didst die for a little space that I might live for ever in thee, and that thou hast sold me that by me thou mightest set free many. And he ceased not to teach and to refresh the afflicted, saying: This hath the Lord dispensed unto you, and he giveth unto every man his food: for he is the nourisher of orphans and steward of the widows, and unto all that are afflicted he is relief and rest.

20 Now when the king came to the city he inquired of his friends concerning the palace which Judas that is called Thomas was building for him. And they told him: Neither hath he built a palace nor done aught else of that he promised to perform, but he goeth about the cities and countries, and whatsoever he hath he giveth unto the poor, and teacheth of a new God, and healeth the sick, and driveth out devils, and doeth many other wonderful things; and we think him to be a sorcerer. Yet his compassions and his cures which are done of him freely, and moreover the simplicity and kindness of him and his faith, do declare that he is a righteous man or an apostle of the new God whom he preacheth; for he fasteth continually and prayeth, and eateth bread only, with salt, and his drink is water, and he weareth but one garment alike in fair weather and in winter, and receiveth nought of any man, and that he hath he

giveth unto others. And when the king heard that, he rubbed his face with his hands, and shook his head for a long space.

21 And he sent for the merchant which had brought him, and for the apostle, and said unto him: Hast thou built me the palace? And he said: Yea. And the king said: When, then, shall we go and see it? but he answered him and said: Thou canst not see it now, but when thou departest this life, then thou shalt see it. And the king was exceeding wroth, and commanded both the merchant and Judas which is called Thomas to be put in bonds and cast into prison until he should inquire and learn unto whom the king's money had been given, and so destroy both him and the merchant.

And the apostle went unto the prison rejoicing, and said to the merchant: Fear thou nothing, only believe in the God that is preached by me, and thou shalt indeed be set free from this world, but from the world to come thou shalt receive life. And the king took thought with what death he should destroy them. And when he had determined to flay them alive and burn them with fire, in the same night Gad the king's brother fell sick, and by reason of his vexation and the deceit which the king had suffered he was greatly oppressed; and sent for the king and said unto him: O king my brother, I commit unto thee mine house and my children; for I am vexed by reason of the provocation that hath befallen thee, and lo, I die; and if thou visit not with vengeance upon the head of that sorcerer, thou wilt give my soul no rest in hell. And the king said to his brother: All this night have I considered how I should put him to death and this hath seemed good to me, to flay him and burn him with fire, both him and the merchant which brought him (Syr. Then the brother of the king said to him: And if there be anything else that is worse than this, do it to him; and I give thee charge of my house and my children).

22 And as they talked together, the soul of his brother Gad departed. And the king mourned sore for Gad, for he loved him much, and commanded that he should be buried in royal and precious apparel (Syr. sepulchre). Now after this angels took the soul of Gad the king's brother and bore it up into heaven, showing unto him the places and dwellings that were there, and inquired of him: In which place wouldest thou dwell? And when they drew near unto the building of Thomas the apostle which he had built for the king, Gad saw it and said unto the angels: I beseech you, my lords, suffer me to dwell in one of the lowest rooms of these. And they said to him: Thou canst not dwell in this building. And he said: Wherefore ? And they say unto him: This is that palace which that Christian builded for thy brother. And he said: I beseech you, my lords, suffer me to go to my brother, that I may buy this palace of him, for my brother knoweth not of what sort it is, and he will sell it unto me.

23 Then the angels let the soul of Gad go. And as they were putting his grave clothes upon him, his soul entered into him and he said to them that stood about him: Call my brother unto me, that I may ask one petition of him. Straightway therefore they told the king, saying: Thy brother is revived. And the king ran forth with a great company and came unto his brother and entered in and stood by his bed as one amazed, not being able to speak to

him. And his brother said: I know and am persuaded, my brother, that if any man had asked of thee the half of thy kingdom, thou wouldest have given it him for my sake; therefore I beg of thee to grant me one favour which I ask of thee, that thou wouldest sell me that which I ask of thee. And the king answered and said: And what is it which thou askest me to sell thee? And he said: Convince me by an oath that thou wilt grant it me. And the king sware unto him: One of my possessions, whatsoever thou shalt ask, I will give thee. And he saith to him: Sell me that palace which thou hast in the heavens? And the king said: Whence should I have a palace in the heavens? And he said: Even that which that Christian built for thee which is now in the prison, whom the merchant brought unto thee, having purchased him of one Jesus: I mean that Hebrew slave whom thou desiredst to punish as having suffered deceit at his hand: whereat I was grieved and died, and am now revived.

24 Then the king considering the matter, understood it of those eternal benefits which should come to him and which concerned him, and said: That palace I cannot sell thee, but I pray to enter into it and dwell therein and to be accounted worthy of the inhabiters of it, but if thou indeed desirest to buy such a palace, lo, the man liveth and shall build thee one better than it. And forthwith he sent and brought out of prison the apostle and the merchant that was shut up with him, saying: I entreat thee, as a man that entreateth the minister of God, that thou wouldest pray for me and beseech him whose minister thou art to forgive me and overlook that which I have done unto thee or thought to do, and that I may become a worthy inhabiter of that dwelling for the which I took no pains, but thou hast builded it for me, labouring alone, the grace of thy God working with thee, and that I also may become a servant and serve this God whom thou preachest. And his brother also fell down before the apostle and said: I entreat and supplicate thee before thy God that I may become worthy of his ministry and service, and that it may fall to me to be worthy of the things that were shown unto me by his angels.

25 And the apostle, filled with joy, said: I praise thee, O Lord Jesu, that thou hast revealed thy truth in these men; for thou only art the God of truth, and none other, and thou art he that knoweth all things that are unknown to the most; thou, Lord, art he that in all things showest compassion and sparest men. For men by reason of the error that is in them have overlooked thee but thou hast not overlooked them. And now at mv supplication and request do thou receive the king and his brother and join them unto thy fold, cleansing them with thy washing and anointing them with thine oil from the error that encompasseth them: and keep them also from the wolves, bearing them into thy meadows. And give them drink out of thine immortal fountain which is neither fouled nor drieth up; for they entreat and supplicate thee and desire to become thy servants and ministers, and for this they are content even to be persecuted of thine enemies, and for thy sake to be hated of them and to be mocked and to die, like as thou for our sake didst suffer all these things, that thou mightest preserve us, thou that art Lord and verily the good shepherd. And do thou grant them to have confidence in thee alone, and the succour that cometh of thee and the hope of their salvation which they look for from thee alone; and that they may be grounded in thy mysteries and

receive the perfect good of thy graces and gifts, and flourish in thy ministry and come to perfection in thy Father.

26 Being therefore wholly set upon the apostle, both the king Gundaphorus and Gad his brother followed him and departed not from him at all, and they also relieved them that had need giving unto all and refreshing all. And they besought him that they also might henceforth receive the seal of the word, saying unto him: Seeing that our souls are at leisure and eager toward God, give thou us the seal; for we have heard thee say that the God whom thou preachest knoweth his own sheep by his seal. And the apostle said unto them: I also rejoice and entreat you to receive this seal, and to partake with me in this eucharist and blessing of the Lord, and to be made perfect therein. For this is the Lord and God of all, even Jesus Christ whom I preach, and he is the father of truth, in whom I have taught you to believe. And he commanded them to bring oil, that they might receive the seal by the oil. They brought the oil therefore, and lighted many lamps; for it was night (Syr. whom I preach: and the king gave orders that the bath should be closed for seven days, and that no man should bathe in it: and when the seven days were done, on the eighth day they three entered into the bath by night that Judas might baptize them. And many lamps were lighted in the bath).

27 And the apostle arose and sealed them. And the Lord was revealed unto them by a voice, saying: Peace be unto you brethren. And they heard his voice only, but his likeness they saw not, for they had not yet received the added sealing of the seal (Syr. had not been baptized). And the apostle took the oil and poured it upon their heads and anointed and chrismed them, and began to say (Syr. And Judas went up and stood upon the edge of the cistern and poured oil upon their heads and said):

Come, thou holy name of the Christ that is above every name.

Come, thou power of the Most High, and the compassion that is perfect.

Come, gift (charism) of the Most High.

Come, compassionate mother.

Come, communion of the male.

Come, she that revealeth the hidden mysteries.

Come, mother of the seven houses, that thy rest may be in the eighth house.

Come, elder of the five members, mind, thought, reflection, consideration, reason; communicate with these young men.

Come, holy spirit, and cleanse their reins and their heart, and give them the added seal, in the name of the Father and Son and Holy Ghost.

And when they were sealed, there appeared unto them a youth holding a lighted torch, so that their lamps became dim at the approach of the light thereof. And he went forth and was no more seen of them. And the apostle said unto the Lord: Thy light, O Lord, is not to be contained by us, and we are not able to bear it, for it is too great for our sight.

And when the dawn came and it was morning, he brake bread and made them partakers of the eucharist of the Christ. And they were glad and rejoiced.

And many others also, believing, were added to them, and came into the refuge of the Saviour.

28 And the apostle ceased not to preach and to say unto them: Ye men and women, boys and girls, young men and maidens, strong men and aged, whether bond or free, abstain from fornication and covetousness and the service of the belly: for under these three heads all iniquity cometh about. For fornication blindeth the mind and darkeneth the eyes of the soul, and is an impediment to the life (conversation) of the body, turning the whole man unto weakness and casting the whole body into sickness. And greed putteth the soul into fear and shame; being within the body it seizeth upon the goods of others, and is under fear lest if it restore other men's goods to their owner it be put to shame. And the service of the belly casteth the soul into thoughts and cares and vexations, taking thought lest it come to be in want, and have need of those things that are far from it. If, then, ye be rid of these ye become free of care and grief and fear, and that abideth with you which was said by the Saviour: Take no thought for the morrow, for the morrow shall take thought for the things of itself. Remember also that word of him of whom I spake: Look at the ravens and see the fowls of the heaven, that they neither sow nor reap nor gather into barns, and God dispenseth unto them; how much more unto you, O ye of little faith? But look ye for his coming and have your hope in him and believe on his name. For he is the judge of quick and dead, and he giveth to every one according to their deeds, and at his coming and his latter appearing no man hath any word of excuse when he is to be judged by him, as though he had not heard. For his heralds do proclaim in the four quarters (climates) of the world. Repent ye, therefore, and believe the promise and receive the yoke of meekness and the light burden, that ye may live and not die. These things get, these keep. Come forth of the darkness that the light may receive you! Come unto him that is indeed good, that ye may receive grace of him and implant his sign in your souls.

29 And when he had thus spoken, some of them that stood by said: It is time for the creditor to receive the debt. And he said unto them: He that is lord of the debt desireth alway to receive more; but let us give him that which is due. And he blessed them, and took bread and oil and herbs and salt and blessed and gave unto them; but he himself continued his fast, for the Lord's day was coming on (Syr. And he himself ate, because the Sunday was dawning).

And when night fell and he slept, the Lord came and stood at his head, saying: Thomas, rise early, and having blessed them all, after the prayer and the ministry go by the eastern road two miles and there will I show thee my glory: for by thy going shall many take refuge with me, and thou shalt bring to light the nature and power of the enemy. And he

rose up from sleep and said unto the brethren that were with him: Children, the Lord would accomplish somewhat by me to-day, but let us pray, and entreat of him that we may have no impediment toward him, but that as at all times, so now also it may be done according to his desire and will by us. And having so said, he laid his hands on them and blessed them, and brake the bread of the eucharist and gave it them, saying: This eucharist shall be unto you for compassion and mercy, and not unto judgement and retribution. And they said Amen.

Note by Professor F. C. Burliitt, D.D.

In the Acts of Thomas, 27, the apostle, being about to baptize Gundaphorus the king of India with his brother Gad, invokes the holy name of the Christ, and among other invocations says (according to the best Greek text):

'Come, O elder of the five members, mind, idea, thoughtfulness, consideration, reasoning, communicate with these youths.'

What is the essential distinction of these five words for 'mind', and what is ment by the 'elder' (presbuteros, greek)? We turn to the Syriac, as the original language in which our tale was composed though our present text, which rests here on two manuscripts, has now and then been bowdlerized in the direction of more conventional phraseology, a process that the Greek has often escaped. Here in the Syriac we find (Wright, p.193, l.13; E.Tr., p.166, last line but one):

' Come, Messenger of reconciliation, and communicate with the minds of these youths.'

The word for 'Come' is fem., while 'Messenger' (Izgadda) is masc. This is because the whole prayer is an invocation of the Holy Spirit, which in old Syriac is invariably treated as feminine. The word for Messenger is that used in the Manichaean cosmogony for a heavenly Spirit sent from the Divine Light: this Spirit appeared as androgynous, so that the use of the word here with the feminine verb is not inappropriate. It further leads us to look out for other indications of Manichaean phraseology in the passage. But first it suggests to us that [presbuteros] in our passage is a corruption of, or is used for, [presbeutes], 'an ambassador'.

As for the five words for 'mind', they are clearly the equivalents of [hauna, mad'a, re'yana, mahshebhatha, tar'itha], named by Theodore bar Khoni as the Five Shekhinas, or Dwellings, or Manifestations, of the Father of Greatness, the title by which the Manichaeans spoke of the ultimate Source of Light. There is a good discussion of these five words by M. A. Kugener in F. Cumont's [Recherches sur le Manicheisme] i, p. 10, note 3. In English we may say:

hauna means 'sanity'

mad'a means 'reason'

re'yana means 'mind'

mahshabhetha means 'imagination'

tar'itha means 'intention'

The Greek terms, used here and also in Acta Archelai, 9, are in my opinion merely equivalents for the Syriac terms.

Act the Third: concerning the servent

30 And the apostle went forth to go where the Lord had bidden him; and when he was near to the second mile (stone) and had turned a little out of the way, he saw the body of a comely youth lying, and said: Lord, is it for this that thou hast brought me forth, to come hither that I might see this (trial) temptation? thy will therefore be done as thou desirest. And he began to pray and to say: O Lord, the judge of quick and dead, of the quick that stand by and the dead that lie here, and master and father of all things; and father not only of the souls that are in bodies but of them that have gone forth of them, for of the souls also that are in pollutions (al. bodies) thou art lord and judge; come thou at this hour wherein I call upon thee and show forth thy glory upon him that lieth here. And he turned himself unto them that followed him and said: This thing is not come to pass without cause, but the enemy hath effected it and brought it about that he may assault (?) us thereby; and see ye that he hath not made use of another sort, nor wrought through any other creature save that which is his subjcct.

31 And when he had so said, a great (Syr. black) serpent (dragon) came out of a hole, beating with his head and shaking his tail upon the ground, and with (using) a loud voice said unto the apostle: I will tell before thee the cause wherefor I slew this man, since thou art come hither for that end, to reprove my works. And the apostle said: Yea, say on. And the serpent: There is a certain beautiful woman in this village over against us; and as she passed by me (or my place) I saw her and was enamoured of her, and I followed her and kept watch upon her; and I found this youth kissing her, and he had intercourse with her and did other shameful acts with her: and for me it was easy to declare them before thee, for I know that thou art the twin brother of the Christ and alway abolishest our nature (Syr. easy for me to say, but to thee I do not dare to utter them because I know that the ocean-flood of the Messiah will destroy our nature): but because I would not affright her, I slew him not at that time, but waited for him till he passed by in the evening and smote and slew him, and especially because he adventured to do this upon the Lord's day.

And the apostlc inquired of him, saying: Tell me of what seed and of what race thou art. 32 And he said unto him: I am a reptile of the reptile nature and noxious son of the noxious father: of him that hurt and smote the four brethren which stood upright (om. Syr.: the elerments or four cardinal points may be meant) I am son to him that sitteth on a throne over all the earth that receiveth back his own from them that borrow: I am son to him that girdeth about the sphere: and I am kin to him that is outside the ocean, whose tail is set in his own mouth: I am he that entered through the barrier (fence) into paradise and spake with Eve the things which my father bade me speak unto her: I am he that kindled and inflamed Cain to kill his own brother, and on mine account did thorns and thistles grow up in the earth: I am he that cast down the angels from above and bound them in lusts after women, that children born of earth might come of them and I might work my will in them: I am he that hardened Pharaoh's heart that he should slay the children of Israel and enslave them with the yoke of cruelty: I am he that caused the multitude to err in the wilderness when they made the calf: I am he that inflamed Herod and enkindled Caiaphas unto false accusation of a lie before Pilate; for this was fitting to me: I am he that stirred up Judas and bribed him to deliver up the Christ: I am he that inhabiteth and holdeth the deep of hell (Tartarus), but the Son of God hath wronged rne, against my will, and taken (chosen) them that were his own from me: I am kin to him that is to come from the east, unto whom also power is given to do what he will upon the earth.

33 And wllen that serpent had spoken these things in the hearing of all the people, the apostle lifted up his voice on high and said: Cease thou henceforth, O most shameless one, and be put to confusion and die wholly, for the end of thy destruction is come, and dare not to tell of what thou hast done by them that have become subject unto thee. And I charge thee in the name of that Jesus who until now contendeth with you for the men that are his own, that thou suck out thy venom which thou hast put into this man, and draw it forth and take it from him. But the serpent said: Not yet is the end of our time come as thou hast said. Wherefore compellest thou me to take back that which I have put into this man, and to die before my time? for mine own father, when he shall draw forth and suck out that which he hath cast into the creation, then shall his end come. And the apostle said unto him: Show, then, now the nature of thy father. And the serpent came near and set his mouth upon the wound of the young man and sucked forth the gall out of it. And by little and little the colour of the young man which was as purple, became white, but the serpent swelled up. And when the serpent had drawn up all the gall into himself, the young man leapt up and stood, and ran and fell at the apostle's feet: but the serpent being swelled up, burst and died, and his venom and gall were shed forth; and in the place where his venom was shed there came a great gulf, and that serpent was swallowed up therein. And the apostle said unto the king and his brother: Take workmen and fill up that place, and lay foundations and build houses upon them, that it may be a dwelling-place for strangers.

34 But the youth said unto the apostle with many tears: Wherein have I sinned against thee? for thou art a man that hast two forms, and wheresoever thou wilt, there thou art found, and art restrained of no man, as I behold. For I saw that man that stood by thee and said unto thee: I have many wonders to show forth by thy means and I have great works to accomplish by thee, for which thou shalt receive a reward; and thou shalt make many to live, and they shall be in rest in light eternal as children of God. Do thou then, saith he, speaking unto thee of me, quicken this youth that hath been stricken of the enemy and be at all times his overseer. Well, therefore, art thou come hither, and well shalt thou depart again unto him, and yet he never shall leave thee at any time. But I am become without care or reproach: and he hath enlightened me from the care of the night and I am at rest from the toil of the day: and I am set free from him that provoked me to do thus, sinning against him that taught me to do contrary thereto: and I have lost him that is the kinsman of the night that compelled me to sin by his own deeds, and have found him that is of the

light, and is my kinsman. I have lost him that darkeneth and blindeth his own subjects that they may not know what they do and, being ashamed at their own works, may depart from him, and their works come to an end; and have found him whose works are light and his deeds truth, which if a man doeth he repenteth not of them. And I have left him with whom lying abideth, and before whom darkness goeth as a veil, and behind him followeth shame, shameless in indolence; and I have found him that showeth me fair things that I may take hold on them, even the son of the truth that is akin unto concord, who scattereth away the mist and enlighteneth his own creation, and healeth the wounds thereof and overthroweth the enemies thereof. But I beseech thee, O man of God, cause me to behold him again, and to see him that is now become hidden from me, that I may also hear his voice whereof I am not able to express the wonder, for it belongeth not to the nature of this bodily organ.

[Before this speech Syr. (Wright) inserts one of equal length, chiefly about man's free will and fall. But the fifth-century palimpsest edited by Mrs. Lewis agrees with the Greek.]

35 And the apostle answered him, saying: If thou depart from these things whereof thou hast received knowledge, as thou hast said, and if thou know who it is that hath wrought this in thee, and learn and become a hearer of him whom now in thy fervent love thou seekest; thou shalt both see him and be with him for ever, and in his rest shalt thou rest, and shalt be in his joy. But if thou be slackly disposed toward him and turn again unto thy former deeds, and leave that beauty and that bright countenance which now was showed thee, and forget the shining of his light which now thou desirest, not only wilt thou be bereaved of this life but also of that which is to come and thou wilt depart unto him whom thou saidst thou hadst lost, and will no more behold him whom thou saidst thou hadst found.

36 And when the apostle had said this, he went into the city holding the hand of that youth, and saying unto him: These things which thou hast seen, my child, are but a few of the many which God hath, for he doth not give us good tidings concerning these things that are seen, but greater things than these doth he promise us; but so long as we are in the body we are not able to speak and show forth those which he shall give unto our souls. If we say that he giveth us light, it is this which is seen, and we have it: and if we say it of wealth, which is and appeareth in the world, we name it (we speak of something which is in the world, Syr.), and we need it not, for it hath been said: Hardly shall a rich man enter into the kingdom of heaven: and if we speak of apparel of raiment wherewith they that are luxurious in this life are clad, it is named (we mention something that nobles wear, Syr.), and it hath been said: They that wear soft raiment are in the houses of kings. And if of costly banquets, concerning these we have received a commandment to beware of them, not to be weighed down With revelling and drunkenness and cares of this life - speaking of things that are- and it hath been said: Take no thought for your life (soul), what ye shall eat or what ye shall drink, neither for your body, what ye shall put on, for the soul is more than the meat and the body than the raiment. And of rest, if we speak of this temporal rest, a judgement is appointed for this also. But we speak of the world which is above, of God and angels, of watchers and holy ones of the immortal (ambrosial) food and the drink of the true vine, of raiment that endureth and groweth not old, of things which eye hath not seen nor ear heard, neither have they entered into the heart of sinful men, the things which God hath prepared for them that love him. Of these things do we converse and of these do we bring good tidings. Do thou therefore also believe on him that thou mayest live, and put thy trust in him, and thou shalt not die. For he is not persuaded with gifts, that thou shouldest offer them to him, neither is he in need of sacrifices, that thou shouldest sacrifice unto him. But look thou unto him, and he will not overlook thee; and turn unto him, and he will not forsake thee. For his comeliness and his beauty will make thee wholly desirous to love him: and indeed he permitteth thee not to turn thyself away.

37 And when the apostle had said these things unto that youth, a great multitude joined themselves unto them. And the apostle looked and saw them raising themselves on high that they might see him, and they were going up into high places; and the apostle said unto them: Ye men that are come unto the assembly of Christ, and would believe on Jesus, take example hereby, and see that if ye be not lifted up, ye cannot see me who am little, and are not able to spy me out who am like unto you. If, then, ye cannot see me who am like you unless ye lift yourselves up a little from the earth, how can ye see him that dwelleth in the height and now is found in the depth, unless ye first lift yourselves up out of your former conversation, and your unprofitable deeds, and your desires that abide not, and the wealth that is left here, and the possession of earth that groweth old, and the raiment that corrupteth, and the beauty that waxeth old and vanisheth away, and yet more out of the whole body wherein all these things are stored up, and which groweth old and becometh dust, returning unto its own nature? For it is the body which maintaineth all these things. But rather believe on our Lord Jesus Christ, vvhom we preach, that your hope may be in him and in him ye may have life world without end, that he may become your fellow traveller in this land of error, and may be to you an harbour in this troublous sea. And he shall be to you a fountain springing up in this thirsty land and a chamber fill of food in this place of them that hunger, and a rest unto your souls, yea, and a physician for your bodies.

38 Then the multitude of them that were gathered together hearing these things wept, and said unto the apostle: O man of God, the God whom thou preachest, we dare not say that we are his, for the works which we have done are alien unto him and not pleasing to him; but if he will have compassion on us and pity us and save us, overlooking our former deeds, and will set us free from the evils which we committed being in error, and not impute them unto us nor make remembrance of our former sins, we will become his servants and will accomplish his will unto the end. And the apostle answered them and said: He reckoneth not against you, neither taketh account of the sins which ye committed being in error, but overlooketh your transgressions which ye have done in ignorance.

The Fourth Act: concerning the colt

39 And while the apostle yet stood in the highway and spake with the multitude, A she ass's colt came and stood

before him (Syr. adds, And Judas said: It is not without the direction of God that this colt has come hither. But to thee I say, O colt that by the grace of our Lord there shall be given to thee speech before these multitudes who are standing here; and do thou say whatsoever thou wilt, that they may believe in the God of truth whom we preach. And the mouth of the colt was opened, and it spake by the power of our Lord and said to him) and opened its mouth and said: Thou twin of Christ, apostle of the Most High and initiate in the hidden word of Christ who receivest his secret oracles, fellow worker with the Son of God, who being free hast become a bondman, and being sold hast brought many into liberty. Thou kinsman of the great race that hath condemned the enemy and redeemed his own, that hast become an occasion of life unto man in the land of the Indians; for thou hast come (against thy will, Syr.) unto men that were in error, and by thy appearing and thy divine words they are now turning unto the God of truth which sent thee: mount and sit upon me and repose thyself until thou enter into the city. And the apostle answered and said: O Jesu Christ (Son) that understandest the perfect mercy! O tranquillity and quiet that now art spoken of (speakest, Syr.) by (among) brute beasts! O hidden rest, that art manifested by thy working, Saviour of us and nourisher, keeping us and resting in alien bodies! O Saviour of our souls! spring that is sweet and unfailing; fountain secure and clear and never polluted; defender and helper in the fight of thine own servants, turning away and scaring the enemy from us, that fightest in many battles for us and makest us conquerors in all; our true and undefeated champion (athlete); our holy and victorious captain: glorious and giving unto thine own a joy that never passeth away, and a relief wherein is none affliction; good shepherd that givest thyself for thine own sheep, and hast vanquished the wolf and redeemed thine own lambs and led them into a good pasture: we glorify and praise thee and thine invisible Father and thine holy sipirit [and] the mother of all creation.

40 And when the apostle had said these things, all the multitude that were there looked upon him, expecting to hear what he would answer to the colt. And the apostle stood a long time as it were astonied, and looked up into heaven and said to the colt: Of whom art thou and to whom belongest thou? for marvellous are the things that are shown forth by thy mouth, and amazing and such as are hidden frorn the many. And the colt answered and said: I am of that stock that served Balaam, and thy lord also and teacher sat upon one that appertained unto me by race. And I also have now been sent to give thee rest by thy sitting upon me: and (that) I may receive (Syr. these may be confirmed in) faith, and unto me may be added that portion which now I shall receive by thy service wherewith I serve thee; and when I have ministered unto thee, it shall be taken from me. And the apostle said unto him: He is able who granted thee this gift, to cause it to be fulfilled unto the end in thee and in them that belong unto thee by race: for as to this mystery I am weak and powerless. And he would not sit upon him. But the colt besought and entreated him that he might be blessed of him by ministering unto him. Then the apostic mounted him and sat upon him; and they followed him, some going before and some following after, and all of them ran, desiring to see the end, and how he would dismiss the colt.

41 But when he came near to the city gates he dismounted from him, saying: Depart, and be thou kept safe where thou wert. And straightway the colt fell to the ground at the apostle's feet and died. And all they that were present were sorry and said to the apostle: Bring him to life and raise him up. But he answered and said unto them: I indeed am able to raise him by the name of Jesus Christ: but this is by all means expedient (or, this is by any means expedient). For he that gave him speech that he might talk was able to cause that he should not die; and I raise him not, not as being unable, but because this is that which is expedient and profitable for him. And he bade them that were present to dig a trench and bury his body and they did as they were commanded.

The Fifth Act: concerning the devil that took up his abode in the woman

42 And the apostle entered into the city and all the multitude followed him. And he thought to go unto the parents of the young man whom he had made alive when he was slain by the serpent: for they earnestly besought him to come unto them and enter into their house. But a very beautiful woman on a sudden uttered an exceeding loud cry, saying: O Apostle of the new God that art come into India, and servant of that holy and only good God; for by thee is he preached, the Saviour of the souls that come unto him, and by thee are healed the bodies of them that are tormented by the enemy, and thou art he that is become an occasion of life unto all that turn unto him: command me to be brought before thee that I may tell thee what hath befallen me, and peradventure of thee I may have hope, and these that stand by thee may be more confident in the God whom thou preachest. For I am not a little tormented by the adversary now this five years' space [one Greek MS. And the apostle bade her come unto him, and the woman stood before him and said: I, O servant of him that is indeed God am a woman: the rest have, As a woman] I was sitting at the first in quiet, and peace encompassed me on every side and I had no care for anything, for I took no thought for any other. 43 And it fell out one day that as I came out from the bath there met me a man troubled and disturbed, and his voice and speech seemed to me exceeding faint and dim; and he stood before me and said: I and thou will be in one love and we will have intercourse together as a man with his wife; And I answered and said to him: I never had to do with my betrothed, for I refused to marry, and how shall I yield myself to thee that wouldest have intercourse with me in adulterous wise? And having so said, I passed on, and I said to rny handmaid that was with me: Sawest thou that youth and his shamelessness, how boldly he spake with me, and had no shame? but she said to me: I saw an old man speaking to thee. And when I was in mine house and had dined my soul suggested unto me some suspicion and especially because he was seen of me in two forms; and having this in my mind I fell asleep. He came, therefore, in that night and was joined unto me in his foul intercourse. And when it was day I saw him and fled from him, and on the night following that he came and abused me; and now as thou seest me I have spent five years being troubled by him, and he hath not departed from me. But I know and am persuaded that both devils and spirits and destroyers are subject unto thee and are filled with trembling at thy prayers: pray thou therefore for me and drive away from me the devil that ever troubleth me, that I also may be set free and be gathered unto the nature

that is mine from the beginning, and receive the grace that hath been given unto my kindred.

44 And the apostle said: O evil that cannot be restrained! O shamelessness of the enemy! O envious one that art never at rest! O hideous one that subduest the comely! O thou of many forms! As he will he appeareth, but his essence cannot be changed. O the crafty and faithless one! O the bitter tree whose fruits are like unto him! O the devil that overcometh them that are alien to him! O the deceit that useth impudence! O the wickedness that creepeth like a serpent, and that is of his kindred! (Syr. wrongly adds a clause bidding the devil show himself.) And when the apostle said this, the malicious one came and stood before him, no man seeing him save the woman and the apostle, and with an exceeding loud voice said in the hearing of all: 45 What have we to do with thee, thou apostle of the Most High! What have we to do with thee, thou servant of Jesus Christ? What have we to do with thee, thou counsellor of the holy Son of God? Wherefore wilt thou destroy us, whereas our time is not yet come? Wherefore wilt thou take away our power? for unto this hour we had hope and time remaining to us. What have we to do with thee? Thou hast power over thine own, and we over ours. Wherefore wilt thou act tyrannously against us, when thou thyself teachest others not to act tyrannously? Wherefore dost thou crave other men's goods and not suffice thyself with thine own? Wherefore art thou made like unto the Son of God which hath done us wrong? for thou resemblest him altogether as if thou wert born of him. For we thought to have brought him under the yoke like as we have the rest, but he turned and made us subject unto him: for we knew him not; but he deceived us with his form of all uncomeliness and his poverty and his neediness: for seeing him to be such, we thought that he was a man wearing flesh, and knew not that it is he that giveth life unto men. And he gave us power over our own, and that we should not in this present time leave them but have our walk in them: but thou wouldest get more than thy due and that which was given thee, and afflict us altogether.

46 And having said this the devil wept, saying: I leave thee, my fairest consort, whom long since I found and rested in thee; I forsake thee, my sure sister, my beloved in whom I was well pleased. What I shall do I know not, or on whom I shall call that he may hear me and help me. I know what I will do: I will depart unto some place where the report of this man hath not been heard, and peradventure I shall call thee, my beloved by another name (Syr. for thee my beloved I shall find a substitute). And he lifted up his voice and said: Abide in peace for thou hast taken refuge with one greater than I, but I will depart and seek for one like thee, and if I find her not, I will return unto thee again: for I know that whilst thou art near unto this man thou hast a refuge in him, but when he departeth thou wilt be such as thou wast before he appeared, and him thou wilt forget, and I shall have opportunity and confidence: but now I fear the name of him that hath saved thee. And having so said the devil vanished out of sight: only when he departed fire and smoke were seen there: and all that stood there were astonied.

47 And the apostle seeing it, said unto them: This devil hath shown nought that is alien or strange to him, but his own nature, wherein also he shall be consumed, for verily the fire shall destroy him utterly and the smoke of it shall be scattered abroad. And he began to say:

Jesu, the hidden mystery that hath been revealed unto us, thou art he that hast shown unto us many mysteries; thou that didst call me apart from all my fellows and spakest unto me three (one, Syr.) words wherewith I am inflamed, and am not able to speak them unto others. Jesu, man that wast slain, dead buried! Jesu, God of God, Saviour that quickenest the dead, and healest the sick! Jesu, that wert in need like and savest as one that hath no need, that didst catch the fish for the breakfast and the dinner and madest all satisfied with a little bread. Jesu, that didst rest from the weariness of wayfaring like a man, and walkedst on the waves like a God. 48 Jesu most high, voice arising from perfect mercy, Saviour of all, the right hand of the light, overthrowing the evil one in his own nature, and gathering all his nature into one place; thou of many forms, that art only begotten, first-born of many brethren God of the Most High God, man despised until now (Syr. and humble). Jesu Christ that neglectest us not when we call upon thee, that art become an occasion of life unto all mankind, that for us wast judged and shut up in prison, and loosest all that are in bonds, that wast called a deceiver and redeemest thine own from error: I beseech thee for these that stand here and believe on thee, for they entreat to obtain thy gifts, having good hope in thy help, and having their refuge in thy greatness; they hold their hearing ready to listen unto the words that are spoken by us. Let thy peace come and tabernacle in them and renew them from their former deeds, and let them put off the old man with his deeds, and put on the new that now is proclaimed unto them by me.

49 And he laid his hands on them and blessed them, saying: The grace of our Lord Jesus Christ shall be upon you for ever. And they said, Amen. And the woman besought him, saying: O apostle of the Most High, give me the seal, that that enemy return not again unto me. Then he caused her to come near unto him (Syr. went to a river which was close by there), and laid his hands upon her and sealed her in the name of the Father and the Son and the Holy Ghost; and many others also were sealed with her. And the apostle bade his minister (deacon) to set forth a table; and he set forth a stool which they found there, and spread a linen cloth upon it and set on the bread of blessing; and the apostle stood by it and said: Jesu, that hast accounted us worthy to partake of the eucharist of thine holy body and blood, lo, we are bold to draw near unto thine eucharist and to call upon thine holy name: come thou and communicate unto us (Syr. adds more).

50 And he began to say: Come, O perfect compassion, Come O communion of the male, Come, she that knoweth the mysteries of him that is chosen, Come, she that hath part in all the combats of the noble champion (athlete), Come, the silence that revealeth the great things of the whole greatness, Come, she that manifesteth the hidden things and maketh the unspeakable things plain, the holy dove that beareth the twin young, Come, the hidden mother, Come, she that is manifest in her deeds and giveth joy and rest unto them that are joined unto her: Come and communicate with us in this eucharist which we celebrate in thy name and in the love-feast wherein we are gathered together at thy calling. (Syr. has other clauses and not few

variants.) And having so said he marked out the cross upon the bread, and brake it, and began to distribute it. And first he gave unto the woman, saying: This shall be unto thee for remission of sins and eternal transgressions (Syr. and for the everlasting resurrection). And after her he gave unto all the others also which had received the seal (Syr. and said to them: Let this eucharist be unto you for life and rest, and not for judgement and vengeance. And they said, Amen. Cf. 29 fin.).

The Sixth Act: of the youth that murdered the Woman.

51 Now there was a certain youth who had wrought an abominable deed, and he came near and received of the eucharist with his mouth: but his two hands withered up, so that he could no more put them unto his own mouth. And they that were there saw him and told the apostle what had befallen; and the apostle called him and said unto him: Tell me, my child, and be not ashamed, what was it that thou didst and camest hither? for the eucharist of the Lord hath convicted thee. For this gift which passeth among many doth rather heal them that with faith and love draw near thereto, but thee it hath withered away; and that which is come to pass hath not befallen without some effectual cause. And the Youth, being convicted by the eucharist of the Lord, came and tell at the apostle's feet and besought him, saying: I have done an evil deed, yet I thought to do somewhat good. I was enamoured of a woman that dwelleth at an inn without the city, and she also loved me; and when I heard of thee and believed, that thou proclaimest a living God, I came and received of thee the seal with the rest; for thou saidst: Whosoever shall partake in the polluted union, and especially in adultery, he shall not have life with the God whom I preach. Whereas therefore I loved her much, I entreated her and would have persuaded her to become my consort in chastity and pure conversation, which thou also teachest: but she would not. When, therefore, she consented not, I took a sword and slew her: for I could not endure to see her commit adultery with another man.

52 When the apostle heard this he said: O insane union how ruinest thou unto shamelessness! O unrestrained lust, how hast thou stirred up this man to do this! O work of the serpent, how art thou enraged against thine own! And the apostle bade water to be brought to him in a bason; and when the water was brought, he said: Come, ye waters from the living waters, that were sent unto us, the true from the true, the rest that was sent unto us from the rest, the power of salvation that cometh from that power which conquereth all things and subdueth them unto its own will: come and dwell in these waters, that the gift of the Holy Ghost may be perfcctly consummated in them. And he said unto the youth: Go, wash thy hands in these waters. And when he had washed they were restored; and the apostle said unto him: Believest thou in our Lord Jesus Christ that he is able to do all things? And he said: Though I be the least, yet I believe. But I committed this deed thinking that I was doing somewhat good: for I besought her as I told thee, but she would not obey me, to keep herself chaste.

53 And the apostle said to him: Come, let us go unto the inn where thou didst commit this deed. And the youth went before the apostle in the way, and when they came to the inn they found her Iying dead. And the apostle when he saw her was sorry, for she was a comely girl. And he commanded her to be brought into the midst of the inn: and they laid her on a bed and brought her forth and set her down in the midst of the court of the inn. And the apostle laid his hand upon her and began to say: Jesu, who alway showest thyself unto us; for this is thy will, that we should at all times seek thee, and thyself hast given us this power, to ask and to receive, and hast not only permitted this, but hast taught us to pray: who art not seen of our bodily eyes, but art never hidden from the eyes of our soul, and in thine aspect art concealed, but in thy works art manifested unto us: and in thy many acts we have known thee so far as we are able, and thyself hast given us thy gifts without measure, saying: Ask and it shall be given unto you, seek and ye shall find, knock and it shall be opened unto you: we beseech thee, therefore, having the fear (suspicion) of our sins; and we ask of thee, not riches, not gold, not silver, not possessions, not aught else of the things which come of the earth and return again unto the earth; but this we ask of thee and entreat, that in thine holy name thou wouldest raise up the woman that lieth here, by thy power, to the glory and faith of them that stand by.

54 And he said unto the youth (Syr. ' Stretch thy mind towards our Lord,' and he signed him with the cross), having signed (sealed) him: Go and take hold on her hand and say unto her: I with my hands slew thee with iron, and with my hands in the faith of Jesus I raise thee up. So the youth went to her and stood by her, saying: I have believed in thee, Christ Jesu. And he looked unto Judas Thomas the apostle and said to him: Pray for me that my Lord may come to my help, whom I also call upon. And he laid his hand upon her hand and said: Come, Lord Jesu Christ: unto her grant thou life and unto me the earnest of faith in thee. And straightway as he drew her hand she sprang up and sat up, looking upon the great company that stood by. And she saw the apostle also standing over against her, and leaving the bed she leapt forth and fell at his feet and caught hold on his raiment, saying: I beseech thee, my lord where is that other that was with thee, who left me not to remain in that fearful and cruel place, but delivered me unto thee, saying: Take thou this woman, that she may be made perfect, and hereafter be gathered into her place?

55 And the apostle said unto her: Relate unto us where thou hast been. And she answered: Dost thou who wast with me and unto whom I was delivered desire to hear? And she began to say: [This desciption of hell-tourments is largely derived from the Apocalypse of Peter] A man took me who was hateful to look upon altogether black, and his raiment exceedingly foul, and took me away to a place wherein were many pits (chasms), and a great stench and hateful odour issued thence. And he caused me to look into every pit, and I saw in the (first) pit flaming fire, and wheels of fire ran round there, and souls were hanged upon those wheels, and were dashed (broken) against each other; and very great crying and howling was there, and there was none to deliver. And that man said to me: These souls are of thy tribe, and when the number of their days is accomplishcd (lit. in the days of the number) they are (were) delivered unto torment and affliction, and then are others brought in in their stead, and likewise these into another place. These are they that have reversed the intercourse of male and female. And I looked and saw infants heaped one upon another and struggling with each other as they lay on them. And he answered and said to me:

These are the children of those others, and therefore are they set here for a testimony against them. (Syr. omits this clause of the children, and lengthens and dilutes the preceding speech.)

56 And he took me unto another pit, and I stooped and looked and saw mire and worms welling up, and souls wallowing there, and a great gnashing of teeth was heard thence from them. And that man said unto me: These are the souls of women which forsook their husbands and committed adultery with others, and are brought into this torment. Another pit he showed me whereinto I stooped and looked and saw souls hanging, some by the tongue, some by the hair, some by the hands, and some head downward by the feet, and tormented (smoked) with smoke and brimstone; concerning whom that man that was with me answered me: The souls which are hanged by the tongue are slanderers, that uttered lying and shameful words, and were not ashamed, and they that are hanged by the hair are unblushing ones which had no modesty and went about in the world bareheaded; and they that are hanged by the hands, these are they that took away and stole other men's goods, and never gave aught to the needy nor helped the afflicted, but did so, desiring to take all, and had no thought at all of justice or of the law; and they that hang upside down by the feet, these are they that lightly and readily ran in evil ways and disorderly paths, not visiting the sick nor escorting them that depart this life, and therefore each and every soul receiveth that which was done by it. (Syr. omits almost the whole section.)

57 Again he took me and showed me a cave exceeding dark, breathing out a great stench, and many souls were looking out desiring to get somewhat of the air, but their keepers suffered them not to look forth. And he that was with me said: This is the prison of those souls which thou sawest: for when they have fulfilled their torments for that which each did, thereafter do others succeed them: and there be some that are wholly consumed and (some, Syr.) that are delivered over unto other torments. And they that kept the souls which were in the dark cave said unto the man that had taken me: Give her unto us that we may bring her in unto the rest until the time cometh for her to be delivered unto torment. But he answered them: I give her not unto you, for I fear him that delivered her to me: for I was not charged to leave her here, but I take her back with me until I shall receive order concerning her. And he took me and brought me unto another place wherein were men being sharply tormented (Syr. where men were). And he that was like unto thee took me and delivered me to thee, saying thus to thee: Take her, for she is one of the sheep that have gone astray. And I was taken by thee, and now am I before thee. I beseech thee, therefore, and supplicate that I may not depart unto those places of punishment which I have seen.

58 And the apostle said: Ye have heard what this woman hath related: and there are not these torments only, but others also, worse than these; and ye, if ye turn not unto this God whom I preach, and abstain from your former works and the deeds which ye committed without knowledge, shall have your end in those torments. Believe therefore on Christ Jesus, and he will forgive you the sins ye have committed hitherto, and will cleanse you from all your bodily lusts that abide on the earth, and will heal you of all your trespasses which follow you and depart with you and are found upon (before) you. Put off therefore every one of you the old man, and put on the new, and forsake your former walk and conversation; and let them that stole steal no more, but live by labouring and working; and let the adulterous no more fornicate, lest they deliver themselves unto eternal torment; for adultery is before God exceeding evil beyond other sins. And put away from you covetousness and lying and drunkenness and slandering, and render not evil for evil: for all these things are strange and alien unto the God who is preached by me: but rather walk ye in faith and meekness and holiness and hope, wherein God delighteth, that ye may become his own, expecting of him the gifts which some few only do receive.

59 All the people therefore believed and gave their souls obediently unto the living God and Christ Jesus, rejoicing in the blessed works of the Most High and in his holy service. And they brought much money for the service of the widows: for the apostle had them gathered together in the cities, and unto all of them he sent provision by his own ministers (deacons), both clothes and nourishment. And he himself ceased not preaching and speaking to them and showing that this is Jesus Christ whom the scriptures proclaimed, who is come and was crucified, and raised the third day from the dead. And next he showed them plainly, beginning from the prophets, the things concerning the Christ, that it was necessary that he should come, and that in him should be accomplished all things that were foretold of him. And the fame of him went forth into all the cities and countries, and all that had sick or them that were oppressed by unclean spirits brought them, and some they laid in the way whereby he should pass, and he healed them all by the power of the Lord. Then all that were healed by him said with one accord: Glory be to thee, Jesu, who hast granted us all alike healing through thy servant and apostle Thomas. And now being whole and rejoicing, we beseech thee that we may be of thy flock, and be numbered among thy sheep; receive us therefore, Lord, and impute not unto us our transgressions and our former faults which we committed being in ignorance.

60 And the apostle said: Glory be to the only-begotten of the Father! Glory be to the first-born of many brethren! Glory be to thee, the defender and helper of them that come unto thy refuge! that sleepest not, and awakest them that are asleep that livest and givest life to them that lie in death! O God Jesu Christ, Son of the living God, redeemer and helper, refuge and rest of all that are weary (labour) in thy work, giver of healing to them that for thy name s sake bear the burden and heat of the day: we give thanks for (to) the gifts that are given us of thee and granted us by thy help and thy dispensation that cometh unto us from thee.

61 Perfect thou therefore these things in us unto the end that we may have the boldness that is in thee: look upon us for for thy sake have we forsaken our homes and our parents, and for thy sake have we gladly and willingly become strangers: look upon us, Lord, for we have forsaken our own possessions for thy sake, that we might gain thee the possession that cannot be taken away: look upon us, Lord, for we have forsaken them that belong unto us by race, that we might be joined unto thy kinship: look upon us, Lord, that have forsaken our fathers and mothers and fosters, that we might behold thy Father, and be

satisfied with his divine food: look upon us, Lord, for for thy sake have we forsaken our bodily consorts and our earthly fruits, that we might be partakers in that enduring and true fellowship, and bring forth true fruits, whose nature is from above, which no man can take from us, with whom we shall abide and who shall abide with us.

The Seventh Act: of the Captain.

62 Now while the apostle Thomas was proclaiming throughout all India the word of God, a certain captain of the king Misdaeus (Mazdai, Syr.) came to him and said unto him: I have heard of thee that thou takest no reward of any man, but even that thou hast thou givest to them that need. For if thou didst receive rewards, I would have sent thee a great sum, and would not have come myself, for the king doeth nought without me: for I have much substance and am rich, even one of the rich men of India. And I have never done wrong to any; but the contrary hath befallen me. I have a wife, and of her I had a daughter and I am well affectioned toward her, as also nature requireth and have never made trial of another wife. Now it chanced that there was a wedding in our city, and they that made the marriage feast were well beloved of me: they came in therefore and bade me to it, bidding also my mife and her daughter. Forasmuch then as they were my good friends I could not refuse: I sent her therefore, though she desired not to go, and with them I sent also many servants: so they departed, both she and her daughter, decked with many ornaments.

63 And when it was evening and the time was come to depart from the wedding I sent lamps and torches to meet them: and I stood in the street to espy when she should come and I should see her with my daughter. And as I stood I heard a sound of lamentation. Woe for her! vvas heard out of every mouth. And my servants with their clothes rent came to me and told me what was done. We saw, said they, a man and a boy with him. And the man laid his hand upon thy wife, and the boy upon thy daughter: and they fled from them: and we smote (wounded) them with our swords, but our swords fell to the ground. And the same hour the womem fell down, gnashing their teeth and beating their heads upon the earth and seeing this we came to tell it thee. And when I heard this of my servants I rent my clothes and smote my face with my hands, and becoming like one mad I ran along the street, and came and found them cast in the market-place; and I took them and brought them to my house, and after a long space they awaked and stood up, and sat down.

64 I began therefore to inquire of my wife: What is it that hath befallen thee? And she said to me: Knowest thou not what thou hast done unto me? for I prayed thee that I might not go to the wedding, because I was not of even health in my body; and as I went on the way and came near to the aqueduct wherein the water floweth, I saw a black man standing over against me nodding at me with his head, and a boy like unto him standing by him; and I said to my daughter: Look at those two hideous men, whose teeth are like milk and their lips like soot. And we left them and went towards the aqueduct; and when it was sunset and we departed from the wedding, as we passed by with the young men and drew near the aqueduct, my daughter saw them first, and was affrighted and fled towards me; and after her I also beheld them coming against us: and the servants that

were with us fled from them (Syr.) and they struck us, and cast down both me and my daughter. And when she had told me these things, the devils came upon them again and threw them down: and from that hour they are not able to come forth, but are shut up in one room or a second (Syr. in a room within another): and on their account I suffer much, and am distressed: for the devils throw them down wheresoever they find them, and strip them naked. I beseech and supplicate thee before God, help me and have pity on me, for it is now three years that a table hath not been set in my house, and my wife and my daughter have not sat at a table: and especially for mine unhappy daughter, which hath not seen any good at all in this world.

65 And the apostle, hearing these things from the captain, was greatly grieved for him, and said unto him: Believest thou that Jesus will heal them? And the captain said: Yea. And the apostle said: Commit thyself then unto Jesus, and he will heal them and procure them succour. And the captain said: Show me him, that I may entreat him and believe in him. And the apostle said: He appeareth not unto these bodily eyes, but is found by the eyes of the mind. The captain therefore lifted up his voice and said: I believe thee, Jesu, and entreat and supplicate thee, help my little faith which I have in thee. And the apostle commanded Xenophon (Syr. Xanthippus) the deacon to assemble all the brethren; and when the whole multitude was gathered, the apostle stood in the midst and said:

66 Children and brethren that have believed on the Lord, abide in this faith, preaching Jesus who was proclaimed unto you by me, to bring you hope in him; and forsake not (be not forsaken of) him, and he will not forsake you. While ye sleep in this slumber that weigheth down the sleepers, he, sleeping not, keepeth watch over you; and when ye sail and are in peril and none can help, he walking upon the waters supporteth and aideth. For I am now departing from you, and it appeareth not if I shall again see you according to the flesh. Be ye not therefore like unto the people of Israel, who losing sight of their pastors for an hour, stumbled. But I leave unto you Xenophon the deacon in my stead; for he also like myself proclaimeth Jesus: for neither am I aught, nor he, but Jesus only; for I also am a man clothed with a body, a son of man like one of you; for neither have I riches as it is found with some, which also convict them that possess them, being wholly useless, and left behind upon the earth, whence also they came, and they bear away with them the transgressions and blemishes of sins which befall men by their means. And scantly are rich men found in almsgivillg: but the merciful and lowly in heart, these shall inherit the kingdom of God: for it is not beauty that endureth with men, for they that trust in it, when age cometh upon them, shall suddenly be put to shame: all things therefore have their time; in their season are they loved and hated. Let your hope then be in Jesus Christ the Son of God, which is always loved, and always desired: and be mindful of us, as we of you: for we too, if we fulfil not the burden of the commandments are not worthy to be preachers of this name, and hereafter shall we pay the price (punishment) of our own head.

67 And he prayed with them and continued with them a long time in prayer and supplication, and committing them unto the Lord, he said: O Lord that rulest over every soul that is in the body; Lord, Father of the souls that have their

hope in thee and expect thy mercies: that redeemest from error the men that are thine own and settest free from bondage and corruption thy subjects that come unto thy refuge: be thou in the flock of Xenophon and anoint it with holy oil, and heal it of sores, and preserve it from the ravening wolves. And he laid his hand on them and said: The peace of the Lord shall be upon you and shall journey with us.

The Eighth Act: of the wild asses.

68 The apostle therefore went forth to depart on the way: and they all escorted him, weeping and adjuring him to make remembrance of them in his prayers and not to forget them. He went up then and sat upon the chariot, leaving all the brethren, and the captain came and awaked the driver, saying: I entreat and pray that I may become worthy to sit beneath his feet, and I will be his driver upon this way, that he also may become my guide in that way whereby few go.

69 And when they had journeyed about two miles, the apostle begged of the captain and made him arise and caused him to sit by him, suffering the driver to sit in his own place. And as they went along the road, it came to pass that the beasts were wearied with the great heat and could not be stirred at all. And the captain was greatly vexed and wholly cast down, and thought to run on his own feet and bring other beasts for the use of the chariot; but the apostle said: Let not thine heart be troubled nor affrighted, but believe on Jesus Christ whom I have proclaimed unto thee, and thou shalt see great wonders. And he looked and saw a herd of wild asses feeding by the wayside, and said to the captain: If thou hast believed on Christ Jesus, go unto that herd of wild asses and say: Judas Thomas the apostle of Christ the new God saith unto you: Let four of you come, of whom we have need (or, of whom we may have use).

70 And the captain went in fear, for they were many; and as he went, they came to meet him; and when they were near, he said unto them: Judas Thomas the apostle of the new God commandeth you: Let four of you come, of whom I have need. And when the wild asses heard it, they ran with one accord and came to him, and when they came they did him reverence. [Syr. has a long prayer: And Judas Thomas the apostle of our Lord lifted up his voice in praise and said: Glorious art thou, God of truth and Lord of all natures, for thou didst will with thy will, and make all thy works and finish all thy creatures, and bring them to the rule of their nature, and lay upon them all thy fear that they might be subject to thy command. And thy will trod the path from thy secrecy to manifestation, and was caring for every soul that thou didst make, and was spoken of by the mouth of all the prophets, in all visions and sounds and voices; but Israel did not obey because of their evil inclination. And thou, because thou art Lord of all, hast a care for the creatures, so that thou spreadest over us thy mercy in him who came by thy will and put on the body, thy creature, which thou didst will and form according to thy glorious wisdom. He whom thou didst appoint in thy secrecy and establish in thy manifestation, to him thou hast given the name of Son, he who was thy will, the power of thy thought; so that ye are by various names, the Father and the Son and the Spirit, for the sake of the government of thy creatures, for the nourishing of all natures, and ye are one in glory and power and will; and ye are divided without

being separated, and are one though divided, and all subsists in thee and is subject to thee, because all is thine. And I rely upon thee, Lord, and by thy command have subjected these dumb beasts, that thou mightest show thy ministering power upon us and upon them because it is needful, and that thy name might be glorified in us and in the beasts that cannot speak.] And the apostle said unto them: Peace be unto you. Yoke ye four of you in the stead of these beasts that have come to a stand. And every one of them came and pressed to be yoked: there were then four stronger than the rest, which also were yoked. And the rest, some went before and some followed. And when they had journeyed a little way he dismissed the colts, saying: I say unto you the inhabiters of the desert, depart unto your pastures, for if I had had need of all, ye would all have gone with me; but now go unto your place wherein ye dwell. And they departed quietly until they were no more seen.

71 Now as the apostle and the captain and the driver went on, the wild asses drew the chariot quietly and evenly, lest they should disturb the apostle of God. And when they came near to the city gate they turned aside and stood still before the doors of the captain's house. And the captain said: It is not possible for me to relate what hath happened, but when I see the end I will tell it. The whole city therefore came to see the wild asses under the yoke; and they had heard also the report of the apostle that he was to come and visit them. And the apostle asked the captain: Where is thy dwelling, and whither dost thou bring us? And he said to him: Thou thyself knowest that we stand before the doors, and these which by thy commandment are come with thee know it better than I.

72 And having so said he came down from the chariot. The apostle therefore began to say: Jesu Christ, that art blasphemed by the ignorance of thee in this country; Jesu, the report of whom is strange in this city; Jesu, that receivest all (Syr. sendest on before the apostles in every country and in every city, and all thine that are worthy are glorified in thee; Jesu, that didst take a form and become as a man, and wert seen of all us that thou mightest not separate us from thine own love: thou, Lord, art he that gavest thyself for us, and with thy blood hast purchased us and gained us as a possession of great price: and what have we to give thee, Lord, in exchange for thy life which thou gavest for us? for that which we would give, thou gavest us: and this is, that we should entreat of thee and live.

73 And when he had so said, many assembled from every quarter to see the apostle of the new God. And again the apostle said: Why stand we idle? Jesu, Lord, the hour is come: what wilt thou have done? command therefore that that be fulfilled which needeth to be done. Now the captain's wife and her daughter were sore borne down by the devils, so that they of the house thought they would rise up no more: for they suffered them not to partake of aught, but cast them down upon their beds recognizing no man until that day when the apostle came thither. And the apostle said unto one of the wild asses that were yoked on the right hand: Enter thou within the gate, and stand there and call the devils and say to them: Judas Thomas the apostle and disciple of Jesus Christ saith unto you: Come forth hither: for on your account am I sent and unto them that pertain to you by race, to destroy you and chase you

unto your place, until the time of the end come and ye go down into your own deep of darkness.

74 And that wild ass went in, a great multitude being with him, and said: Unto you I speak, the enemies of Jesus that is called Christ: unto you I speak that shut your eyes lest ye see the light: unto you I speak, children of Gehenna and of destruction, of him that ceaseth not from evil until now, that alway reneweth his workings and the things that befit his being: unto you I speak, most shameless, that shall perish by your own hands. And what I shall say of your destruction and end, and what I shall tell, I know not. For there are many things and innumerable to the hearing: and greater are your doings than the torment that is reserved for you (Syr. however great your bodies, they are too small for your retributions). But unto thee I speak, devil, and to thy son that followeth with thee: for now am I sent against you. And wherefore should I make many words concerning your nature and root, which yourselves know and are not ashamed? but Judas Thomas the apostle of Christ Jesus saith unto you, he that by much love and affection is sent hither: Before all this multitude that standeth here, come forth and tell me of what race ye are.

75 And straightway the woman came forth with her daughter, both like dead persons and dishonoured in aspect: and the apostle beholding them was grieved. especially for the girl, and saith unto the devils: God forbid that for you there should be sparing or propitiation, for ye know not to spare nor to have pity: but in the name of Jesus, depart from them and stand by their side. And when the apostle had so said, the women fell down and became as dead; for they neither had breath nor uttered speech: but the devil answered with a loud voice and said: Art thou come hither again, thou that deridest our nature and race? art thou come again, that blottest out our devices? and as I take it, thou wouldest not suffer us to be upon the earth at all: but this at this time thou canst not accomplish. And the apostle guessed that this devil was he that had been driven out from that other woman.

76 And the devil said: I beseech thee, give me leave to depart even whither thou wilt, and dwell there and take commandment from thee, and I will not fear the ruler that hath authority over me. For like as thou art come to preach good tidings, so I also am come to destroy; and like as, if thou fulfil not the will of him that sent thee, he will bring punishment upon thy head, so I also if I do not the will of him that sent me, before the season and time appointed, shall be sent unto mine own nature; and like as thy Christ helpeth thee in that thou doest, so also my father helpeth me in that I do; and like as for thee he prepareth vessels worthy of thine inhabiting, so also for me he seeketh out vessels whereby I may accomplish his deeds; and like as he nourisheth and provideth for his subjects, so also for me he prepareth chastisements and torments, with them that become my dwellingplaces (Syr. those in whom I dwell); and like as for a recompense of thy working he giveth thee eternal life, so also unto me he giveth for a reward of my works eternal destruction; and like as thou art refreshed by thy prayer and thy good works and spiritual thanksgivings, so I also am refreshed by murders and adulteries and sacrifices made with wine upon altars (Syr. sacrifices and libations of wine), and like as thou convertest men unto eternal life, so I also pervert them that obey me unto

eternal destruction and torment: and thou receivest thine own and I mine.

77 And when the devil had said these things and yet more the apostle said: Jesus commandeth thee and thy son by me to enter no more into the habitation of man: but go ye forth and depart and dwell wholly apart from the habitation of men. And the devils said unto him: Thou hast laid on us a harsh commandment: but what wilt thou do unto them that now are concealed from thee? for they that have wrought all the images rejoice in them more than thee: and many of them do the more part worship, and perform their will, sacrificing to them and bringing them food, by libations and by wine and water and offering with oblations. And the apostle said: They also shall now be abolished, · with their works. And suddenly the devils vanished away: but the women lay cast upon the earth as if were dead, and without speech.

78 And the wild asses stood together and parted not one from another; but he to whom speech was given by the power of the Lord -while all men kept silence, and looked to see what they would do- the wild ass said unto the apostle: Why standest thou idle, O apostle of Christ the Most High, who looketh that thou shouldest ask of him the best of learning? Wherefore then tarriest thou? (Syr. that thou shouldest ask him, and he would give thee? Why delayest thou, good disciple?) for lo, thy teacher desireth to show by thy hands his mighty works. Why standest thou still, O herald of the hidden one? for thy (Lord) willeth to manifest through thee his unspeakable things, which he reserveth for them that are worthy of him, to hear them. Why restest thou, O doer of mighty works in the name of the Lord? for thy Lord encourageth thee and engendereth boldness in thee. Fear not, therefore; for he will not forsake the soul that belongeth unto thee by birth. Begin therefore to call upon him and he will readily hearken to thee. Why standest thou marvelling at all his acts and his workings? for these are small things which he hath shown by thy means. And what wilt thou tell concerning his great gifts? for thou wilt not be sufficient to declare them. And why marvellest thou at his cures of the body which he worketh? (Syr. which come to an end) especially when thou knowest that healing of his which is secure and lasting, which he bringeth forth by his own nature? And why lookest thou unto this temporal life, and hast no thought of that which is eternal (Syr. when thou canst every day think on that which is eternal)?

79 But unto you the multitudes that stand by and look to see these that are cast down raised up, I say, believe in the apostle of Jesus Christ: believe the teacher of truth, believe him that showeth you the truth, believe Jesus, believe on the Christ that was born, that the born may live by his life: who also was raised up through infancy, that perfection might appear by his manhood (man). He did teach his own disciples: for he is the teacher of the truth and maketh wise men wise (Syr. who went to school that through him perfect wisdom might be known: he taught his teacher because he was the teacher of verity and the master of the wise). Who also offered the gift in the temple that he might show that all the (every) offering was sanctified. This is his apostle, the shewer-forth of truth: this is he that performeth the will of him that sent him. But there shall come false apostles and prophets of lawlessness, whose end

shall be according to their deeds; preaching indeed and ordaining to flee from ungodliness, but themselves at all times detected in sins, clad indeed with sheep's clothing, but within, ravening wolves. Who suffice not themselves with one wife but corrupt many women; who, saying that they despise children, destroy many children (boys), for whom they vvill pay the penalty; that content not themselves wiih their own possessions, but desire that all useless things should minister unto them only; professing to be his disciples; and with their mouth they utter one thing, but in their heart they think another; charging other men to beware of evil, but they themselves perform nought that is good; who are accounted temperate, and charge other men to abstain from fornication theft, and covetousness, but in all these things do they themselves walk secretly, teaching other men not to do them.

80 And when the wild ass had declared all these things, all men gazed upon him. And when he ceased the apostle said: What I shall think concerning thy beauty, O Jesu, and what I shall tell of thee, I know not, or rather I am not able, for I have no power to declare it, O Christ that art in rest, and only wise that only knowest the inward of the heart and understandest the thought. Glory be to thee, merciful and tranquil. Glory to thee, wise word. Glory to thy compassion that was born unto us. Glory to thy mercy that was spread out over us. Glory to thy greatness that was made small for us. Glory to thy most high kingship that was humbled for us. Glory to thy might which was enfeebled for us. Glory to thy Godhead that for us was seen in likeness of men. Glory to thy manhood that died for us that it might make us live. Glory to thy resurrection from the dead; for thereby rising and rest cometh unto our souls. Glory and praise (good report) to thine ascending into the heavens; for thereby thou hast shewed us the path of the height, and promised that we shall sit with thee on thy right hand and with thee judge the twelve tribes of Israel. Thou art the heavenly word of the Father: thou art the hidden light of the understanding, shewer of the way of truth, driver away of darkness, and blotter-out of error.

81 Having thus spoken, the apostle stood over the women, saying: My Lord and my God, I am not divided from thee (or doubt not concerning thee), nor as one unbelieving do I call upon thee, who art always our helper and succourer and raiser-up; who breathest thine own power into us and encouragest us and givest confidence in love unto thine own servants. I beseech thee, let these souls be healed and rise up and become such as they were before they were smitten of the devils. And when he thus spake the women turned and sat up. And the apostle bade the captain that his servants should take them and bring them within (Syr. and give them food, for they had not eaten for many days). And when they were gone in, the apostle said unto the wild asses, Follow me. And they went after him until he had brought them without the gate. And when they had gone out, he said to them: Depart in peace unto your pastures. The wild asses therefore went away willingly; and the apostle stood and took heed to them lest they should be hurt of any, until they had gone afar off and were no more seen. And the apostle returned with the multitude into the house of the captain.

The Ninth Act: of the Wife of Charisius.

82 Now it chanced that a certain woman, the wife of Charisius, that was next unto the king, whose name was Mygdonia, came to see and behold the new name and the new God who was being proclaimed, and the new apostle who had come to visit their country: and she was carried by her own servants; and because of the great crowd and the narrow way they were not able to bring her near unto him. And she sent unto her husband to send her more to minister to her; and they came and approached her, pressing upon the people and beating them. And the apostle saw it and said to them: Wherefore overthrow ye them that come to hear the word, and are eager for it? and ye desire to be near me but are far off, as it was said of the multitude that came unto the Lord: Having eyes ye see not, and having ears ye hear not; and he said to the multitudes: He that hath ears to hear, let him hear; and: Come unto me, all ye that labour and are heavy laden, and I will give you rest.

83 And looking upon them that carried her, he said unto them: This blessing and this admonition [Here and elsewhere there is a marked divergence between the texts of U and P, the Roman and Paris MSS.: Bonnet prints them separately. P is on the whole much shorter. Syr. differs from both. I follow U, but it is very corrupt.] which was promised unto them is for you that are heavily burdened now. Ye are they that carry burdens grievous to be borne, and are borne about by her command. And though ye are men, they lay on you loads as on brute beasts, for they that have authority over you think that ye are not men such as themselves, whether bond or free. For neither shall possessions profit the rich, nor poverty save the poor from judgement; nor have we received a commandment which we are not able to perform, nor hath he laid on us burdens grievous to be borne nhich we are not able to carry; nor building which men build; nor to hew stones and prepare houses, as your craftsmen do by their own knowledge. But this commandment have we received of the Lord, that that which pleaseth not us when it is done by another this we should not do to any other man.

84 Abstain therefore first from adultery, for this is the beginning of all evils, and next from theft, which enticed Judas Iscariot, and brought him unto hanging; (and from covetousness,) for as many as yield unto covetousness see not that which they do; and from vainglory and from all foul deeds, especially them of the body, whereby cometh eternal condemnation. For this is the chief city of all evils; and likewise it bringeth them that hold their heads (necks) high unto tyranny, and draweth them down unto the deep, and subdueth them under its hands that they see not what they do; wherefore the things done of them are hidden from them.

85 But do ye become well-pleasing unto God in all good things, in meekness and quietness: for these doth God spare, and granteth eternal life and setteth death at nought. And in gentleness which followeth on all good things, and overcometh all enemies and alone receiveth the crown of victory: with gentleness (Syr.), and stretching out of the hand to the poor, and supplying the want of the needy, and distributing to them that are in necessity, especially them that walk in holiness. For this is chosen before God and leadeth unto eternal life: for this is before God the chief city of all good: for they that strive not in the course

(stadium) of Christ shall not obtain holiness. And holiness did appear from God, doing away fornication, overthrowing the enemy, well-pleasing unto God: for she is an invincible champion (athlete), having honour from God, glorified of many: she is an ambassador of peace, announcing peace: if any gain her he abideth without care, pleasing the Lord, expecting the time of redemption: for she doeth nothing amiss, but giveth life and rest and joy unto all that gain her. [P has nothing of this, and Syr. makes better sense, but is not very interesting.]

86 But meekness hath overcome death and brought him under authority, meekness hath enslaved the enemy (U and P and Syr. now present the same text), meekness is the good yoke: meekness feareth not and opposeth not the many: meekness is peace and joy and exaltation of rest. Abide ye therefore in holiness and receive freedom from me, and be near unto meekness for in these three heads is portrayed the Christ whom I proclaim unto you. Holiness is the temple of Christ, and he that dwelleth in her getteth her for an habitation , because for forty days and forty nights he fasted, tasting nothing: and he that keepeth her shall dwell in her as on a mountain. And meekness is his boast: for he said unto Peter our fellow apostle: Turn back thy sword and put it again into the sheath thereof: for if I had willed so to do, could I not have brought more than twelve legions of angels from my Father?

87 And when the apostle had said these things in the hearing of all the multitude, they trode and pressed upon one another: and the wife of Charisius the king's kinsman leapt out of her chair and cast herself on the earth before the apostle, and caught his feet and besought and said: O disciple of the living God, thou art come into a desert country, for we live in the desert; being like to brute beasts in our conversation, but now shall we be saved by thy hands; I beseech thee, therefore, take thought of me, and pray for me, that the compassion of the God whom thou preachest may come upon me, and I may become his dwelling place and be joined in prayer and hope and faith in him, and I also may receive the seal and become an holy temple and he may dwell in me.

88 And the apostle said: I do pray and entreat for you all, brethren, that believe on the Lord, and for you, sisters, that hope in Christ, that in all of you the word of God may tabernacle and have his tabernacle therein: for we have no power over them (Syr. because ye are given power over your own souls). And he began to say unto the woman Mygdonia: Rise up from the earth and compose thyself (take off thine ornaments, P; be mindful of thyself, Syr.). For this attire that is put on shall not profit thee nor the beauty of thy body, nor thine apparel, neither yet the fame of thy rank, nor the authority of this world, nor the polluted intercourse with thine husband shall avail thee if thou be bereaved of the true fellowship: for the appearance (fantasy) of ornamenting cometh to nought, and the body waxeth old and changeth, and raiment weareth out, and authority and lordship pass away (U corrupt; P abridges; Syr. has: passeth away accompanied with punishment, according as each person hath conducted himself in it), and the fellowship of procreation also passeth away, and is as it were condemnation. Jesus only abideth ever, and they that hope in him. Thus he spake, and said unto the woman: Depart in peace, and the Lord shall make thee worthy of

his own mysteries. But she said: I fear to go away, lest thou forsake me and depart unto another nation. But the apostle said to her: Even if I go, I shall not leave thee alone, but Jesus of his compassion will be with thee. And she fell down and did him reverence and departed unto her house.

89 Now Charisius, the kinsman of Misdaeus the king, bathed himself and returned and laid him down to dine. And he inquired concerning his wife, where she was; for she had not come out of her own chamber to meet him as she was wont. And her handmaids said to him: She is not well. And he entered quickly into the chamber and found her lying on the bed and veiled: and he unveiled her and kissed her, saying: Wherefore art thou sorrowful to-day? And she said: I am not well. And he said unto her: Wherefore then didst thou not keep the guise of thy freedom (Syr. pay proper respect to thy position as a free woman) and remain in thy house, but didst go and listen unto vain speeches and look upon works of sorcery? but rise up and dine with me, for I cannot dine without thee. But she said to him: To-day I decline it, for I am greatly afeared.

90 And when Charisius heard this of Mygdonia, he would not go forth to dinner, but bade his servants bring her to dine with him (Syr. bring food to him that he might sup in her presence): when then they brought it in, he desired her to dine with him, but she excused herself; since then she would not, he dined alone, saying unto her: On thine account I refused to dine with Misdaeus the king, and thou, wast thou not willing to dine with me? but she said: It is because I am not well. Charisius therefore rose up as he was wont and would sleep with her, but she said: Did I not tell thee that for today I refused it?

91 When he heard that he went to another bed and slept; and awaking out of sleep he said: My lady Mygdonia, hearken to the dream which I have seen. I saw myself lie at meat near to Misdaeus the king, and a dish of all sorts was set before us: and I saw an eagle come down from heaven and carry off from before me and the king two partridges, which he set against his heart; and again he came over us and flew about above us, and the king bade a bow to be brought to him; and the eagle again caught away from before us a pigeon and a dove, and the king shot an arrow at him, and it passed through him from one side to the other and hurt him not; and he being unscathed rose up into his own nest. And I awoke, and I am full of fear and sore vexed, because I had tasted of the partridge, and he suffered me not to put it to my mouth again. And Mygdonia said unto him: Thy dream is good: for thou every day eatest partridges, but this eagle had not tasted of a partridge until now.

92 And when it was morning Charisius went and dressed himself and shod his right foot with his left shoe; and he stopped, and said to Mygdonia: What then is this matter? for look, the dream and this action of mine! But Mygdonia said to him: And this also is not evil, but seemeth to me very good; for from an unlucky act there will be a change unto the better. And he washed his hands and went to salute Misdaeus the king.

93 And likewise Mygdonia rose up early and went to salute Judas Thomas the apostle, and she found him discoursing

with the captain and all the multitude, and he was advising them and speaking of the woman which had received the Lord in her soul, whose wife she was; and the captain said: She is the wife of Charisius the kinsman of Misdaeus the king. And: Her husband is a hard man, and in every thing that he saith to the king he obeyeth him: and he will not suffer her to continue in this mind which she hath promised; for often-times hath he praised her before the king, saying that there is none other like her in love: all things therefore that thou speakest unto her are strange unto her. And the apostle said: If verily and surely the Lord hath risen upon her soul and she hath received the seed that was cast on her, she will have no care of this temporal life, nor fear death, neither will Charisius be able to harm her at all: for greater is he whom she hath received into her soul, if she have received him indeed.

94 And Mygdonia hearing this said unto the apostle: In truth, my lord, I have received the seed of thy words, and I will bear fruit like unto such seed. The apostle saith: Our souls give praise and thanks unto thee, O Lord, for they are thine: our bodies give thanks unto thee, which thou hast accounted worthy to become the dwelling-place of thy heavenly gift. And he said also to them that stood by: Blessed are the holy, whose souls have never condemned them, for they have gained them and are not divided against themselves: blessed are the spirits of the pure, and they that have received the heavenly crown whole from the world (age) which hath been appointed them: blessed are the bodies of the holy, for they have been made worthy to become temples of God, that Christ may dwell in them: blessed are ye, for ye have power to forgive sins: blessed are ye if ye lose not that which is committed unto you, but rejoicing and departing bear it away with you: blessed are ye the holy, for unto you it is given to ask and receive: blessed are ye meek for you hath God counted worthy to become heirs of the heavenly kingdom. Blessed are ye meek, for ye are they that have overcome the enemy: blessed are ye meek, for ye shall see the face of the Lord. Blessed are ye that hunger for the Lord's sake for for you is rest laid up, and your souls rejoice from henceforth. Blessed are ye that are quiet, (for ye have been counted worthy) to be set free from sin [and from the exchange of clean and unclean beasts]. And when the apostle had said these things in the hearing of all the multitude, Mygdonia was the more confirmed in the faith and glory and greatness of Christ.

95 But Charisius the kinsman and friend of Misdaeus the king came to his breakfast and found not his wife in the house; and he inquired of all that were in his house: Whither is your mistress oone? And one of them answered and said: She is gone unto that stranger. And when he heard this of his servant, he was wroth with the other servants because they had not straightway told him what was done: and he sat down and waited for her. And when it was evening and she was come into the house he said to her: Where wast thou? And she answered and said: With the physician. And he said: Is that stranger a physician? And she said: Yea, he is a physician of souls: for most physicians do heal bodies that are dissolved, but he souls that are not destroyed. Charisius, hearing this, was very angry in his mind with Mygdonia because of the apostle, but he answered her nothing, for he was afraid; for she was above him both in wealth and birth: but he departed to dinner, and she went into her chamber. And he said to the servants: Call her to dinner. But she would not come.

96 And when he heard that she would not come out of her chamber, he went in and said unto her: Wherefore wilt thou not dine with me and perchance not sleep with me as the wont is? yea, concerning this I have the greater suspicion, for I have heard that that sorcerer and deceiver teacheth that a man should not live with his wife, and that which nature requireth and the godhead hath ordained he overthroweth. When Charisius said these things, Mygdonia kept silence. He saith to her again: My lady and consort Mygdonia, be not led astray by deceitful and vain words, nor by the works of sorcery which I have heard that this man performeth in the name of Father, Son, and Holy Ghost; for it was never yet heard in the world that any raised the dead, and, as I hear, it is reported of this man that he raiseth dead men. And for that he neither eateth nor drinketh, think not that for righteousness sake he neither eateth nor drinketh but this he doth because he possesseth nought, for what should he do which hath not even his daily bread? And he hath one garment because he is poor, and as for his not receiving aught of any (he doth so, to be sure, because he knoweth in himself that he doth not verily heal any man, Syr.).

97 And when Charisius so said, Mygdonia was silent as any stone, but she prayed, asking when it should be day, that she might go to the apostle of Christ. And he withdrew from her and went to dinner heavy in mind, for he thought to sleep with her according to the wont. And when he was gone out, she bowed her knees and prayed, saying: Lord God and Master, merciful Father, Saviour Christ, do thou give me strength to overcome the shamelessness of Charisius, and grant me to keep the holiness wherein thou delightest, that I also may by it find eternal life. And when she had so prayed she laid herself on her bed and veiled herself.

98 But Charisius having dined came upon her, and she cried out, saying: Thou hast no more any room by me: for my Lord Jesus is greater than thou, who is with me and resteth in me. And he laughed and said: Well dost thou mock, saying this of that sorcerer, and well dost thou deride him, who saith: Ye have no life with God unless ye purify yourselves. And when he had so said he essayed to sleep with her, but she endured it not and cried out bitterly and said: I call upon thee, Lord Jesu, forsake me not! for with thee have I made my refuge; for when I learned that thou art he that seekest out them that are veiled in ignorance and savest them that are held in error And now I entreat thee whose report I have heard and believed, come thou to my help and save me from the shamelessness of Charisius, that his foulness may not get the upper hand of me. And she smote her hands together (tied his hands, Syr.) and fled from him naked, and as she went forth she pulled down the curtain of the bed-chamber and wrapped it about her; and went to her nurse, and slept there with her.

99 But Charisius was in heaviness all night, and smote his face with his hands, and he was minded to go that very hour and tell the king concerning the violence that was done him, but he considered with himself, saying: If the great heaviness which is upon me compelleth me to go now unto the king, who will bring me in to him? for I know that my abuse hath overthrown me from my high looks and my vainglory and majesty, and hath cast me down into this vileness and separated my sister Mygonia from me. Yea, if

the king himself stood before the dools at this hour, I could not have gone out and answered him. But I will wait until dawn, and I know that whatsoever I ask of the king, he granteth it me: and I will tell him of the madness of this stranger, how that it tyrannously casteth down the great and illustrious into the depth. For it is not this that grieveth me, that I am deprived of her companying, but for her am I grieved, because her greatness of soul is humbled: being an honourable lady in whom none of her house ever found fault (condemned), she hath fled away naked, running out of her own bedchamber, and I know not whither she is gone; and it may be that she is gone mad by the means of that sorcerer, and in her madness hath gone forth into the market-place to seek him; for there is nothing that appealeth unto her lovable except him and the things that are spoken by him.

100 And so saving he began to lament and say: Woe to me, O my consort, and to thee besides! for I am too quickly bereaved of thee. Woe is me, my most dear one, for thou excellest all my race: neither son nor daughter have I had of thee that I might find rest in them; neither hast thou yet dwelt with me a full year, and an evil eye hath caught thee from me. Would that the violence of death had taken thee, and I should yet have reckoned myself among kings and nobles: but that I should suffer this at the hands of a stranger, and belike he is a slave that hath run away, to mine ill fortune and the sorrow of mine unhappy soul! Let there be no impediment for me until I destroy him and avenge this night, and may I not be well-pleasing before Misdaeus the king if he avenge me not with the head of this stranger; (and I will also tell him) of Siphor the captain vvho hath been the occasion of this. For by his means did fhe stranger appear here, and lodgeth at his house: and many there be that go in and come out whom he teacheth a new doctrine; saying that none can live if he quit not all his substance and become a renouncer like himself: and he striveth to make many partakers with him.

101 And as Charisius thought on these things, the day dawned: and after the night (?) he put on a mean habit, and shod himself, and went downcast and in heaviness to salute the king. And when the king saw him he said: Wherefore art thou sorrowful, and comest in such garb? and I see that thy countenance is changed. And Charisius said unto the king: I have a new thing to tell thee and a new desolation which Siphor hath brought into India, even a certain Hebrew, a sorcerer, whom he hath sitting in his house and who departeth not from him: and many are there that go in to him: whom also he teacheth of a new God, and layeth on them new laws such as never yet were heard, saving: It is impossible for you to enter into that eternal life which I proclaim unto you, unless ye rid you of your wives, and likewise the wives of their husbands. And it chanced that mine unlucky wife also went to him and became a hearer of his words, and she believed them, and in the night she forsook me and ran unto the stranger. But send thou for both Siphor and that sorcerer that is hid with (in) him, and visit it (?) on their head, lest all that are of our nation perish.

102 And when Misdaeus his friend heard this he saith to him: Be not grieved nor heavy, for I will send for him and avenge thee, and thou shalt have thy wife again, and the others that cannot I will avenge. And the king went forth and sat on the judgement seat, and when he was set he commanded Siphor the captain to be called. They went therefore unto his house and found him sitting on the right hand of the apostle and Mygdonia at his feet, hearkening to him with all the multitude. And they that were sent from the king said unto Siphor: Sittest thou here listening to vain words, and Misdaeus the king in his wrath thinketh to destroy thee because of this sorcerer and deceiver whom thou hast brought into thine house? And Siphor hearing it was cast down, not because of the king's threat against him, but for the apostle, because the king was disposed contrary to him. And he said to the apostle: I am grieved concerning thee: for I told thee at the first that that woman is the wife of Charisius the king's friend and kinsman, and he will not suf'fer her to perform that she hath promised, and all that he asketh of the king he granteth him. But the apostle said unto Siphor: Fear nothing, but believe in Jesus that pleadeth for us all, for unto his refuge are we gathered together. And Siphor, hearing that, put his garment about him and went unto Misdaeus the king,

103 And the apostle inquired of Mygdonia: What was the cause that thy husband was wroth with thee and devised this against us? And she said: Because I gave not myself up unto his corruption (destruction): for he desired last night to subdue me and subject me unto that passion which he serveth: and he to whom I have committed my soul delivered me out of his hands; and I fled away from him naked, and slept with my nurse: but that which befell him I know not, wherefore he hath contrived this. The apostle saith: These things will not hurt us; but believe thou on Jesus, and he shall overthrow the wrath of Charisius and his madness and his impulse; and he shall be a companion unto thee in the fearful way, and he shall guide thee into his kingdom, and shall bring thee unto eternal life giving thee that confidence which passeth not away nor changeth.

104 Now Siphor stood before the king, and he inquired of him: Who is that sorcerer and whence, and what teacheth he whom thou hast lurking in thine house? And Siphor answered the king: Thou art not ignorant, O king, what trouble and grief I, with my friends had concerning my wife, whom thou knowest and many others remember, and concerning my daughter, whom I value more than all my possessions, what a time and trial I suffered; for I became a laughing-stock and a curse in all our country. And I heard the report of this man and went to him and entreated him, and took him and brought him hither. And as I came by the way I saw wonderful and amazing things: and here also many did hear the wild ass and concerning that devil whom he drove out, and healed my wife and daughter, and now are they whole; and he asked no reward but requireth faith and holiness, that men should become partakers with him in that which he doeth: and this he teacheth to worship and fear one God, the ruler of all things, and Jesus Christ his Son, that they may have eternal life. And that which he eateth is bread and salt, and his drink is water from evening unto evening, and he maketh many prayers; and whatsoever he asketh of his God, he giveth him. And he teacheth that this God is holy and mighty, and that Christ is living and maketh alive, wherefore also he chargeth them that are there present to come unto him in holiness and purity and love and faith.

105 And when Misdaeus the king heard these things of Siphor he sent many soldiers unto the house of Siphor the

captain, to bring Thomas the apostle and all that were found there. And they that were sent entered in and found him teaching much people; and Mygdonia sat at his feet. And when they beheld the great multitude that were about him, they feared, and departed to their king and said: We durst not say aught unto him, for there was a great multitude about him, and Mygdonia sitting at his feet was listening to the things that were spoken by him. And when Misdaeus the king and Charisius heard these things, Charisius leaped out from before the king and drew much people with him and said: I will bring him, O king, and Mygdonia whose understanding he hath taken away. And he came to the house of Siphor the captain, greatly disturbed, and found him (Thomas) teaching: but Mygdonia he found not, for she had withdrawn herself unto her house, having learnt that it had been told her husband that she was there.

106 And Charisius said unto the apostle: Up, thou wicked one and destroyer and enemy of mine house: for me thy sorcery harmeth not, for I will visit thy sorcery on thine head. And when he so said, the apostle looked upon him and said unto him: Thy threatenings shall return upon thee, for me thou wilt not harm any whit: for greater than thee and thy king and all your army is the Lord Jesus Christ in whom I have my trust. And Chalisius took a kerchief (turban, Syr.) of one of his slaves and cast it about the neck of the apostle, saying: Hale him and bring him away; let me see if his God is able to deliver him out of my hands. And they haled him and led him away to Misdaeus the king. And the apostle stood before the king, and the king said to him: Tell me who thou art and by what power thou doest these things. But the apostle kept silence. And the king commanded his officers (subjects) that he should be scourged with an hundred and twenty-eight (hundred and fifty, Syr.) blows, and bound, and be cast into the prison; and they bound him and led him away. And the king and Charisius considered how they should put him to death, for the multitude worshipped him as God. And they had it in mind to say: The stranger hath reviled the king and is a deceiver.

107 But the apostle went unto the prison rejoicing and exulting, and said: I praise thee, Jesu, for that thou hast not only made me worthy of faith in thee, but also to endure much for thy sake. I give thee thanks therefore, Lord, that thou hast taken thought for me and given me patience: I thank thee Lord, that for thy sake I am called a sorcerer and a wizard. Receive thou me therefore with the blessing (Syr. Iet me receive of the blessing) of the poor, and of the rest of the weary, and of the blessings of them whom men hate and persecute and revile, and speak evil words of them. For lo, for thy sake I am hated: lo for thy sake I am cut off from the many, and for thy sake they call me such an one as I am not.

108 And as he prayed, all the prisoners looked on him, and besought him to pray for them: and when he had prayed and was set down, he began to utter a psalm in this wise:

[Here follows the Hymn of the Soul: a most remarkable composition, originally Syriac, and certainly older than the Acts, with which it has no real connexion. We have it in Greek in one manuscript, the Vallicellian, and in a paraphrase by Nicetas of Thessalonica, found and edited by Bonnet.]

1 When I was an infant child

in the palace of my Father

2 and resting in the wealth and luxury of my nurturers,

out of the East, our native country, my parents provisioned me and sent me.

4 And of the wealth of those their treasures they put together a load

5 both great and light, that I might carry it alone.

6 Gold is the load, of them that are above (or of the land of the Ellaeans or Gilaeans),

and silver of the great treasures (or of Gazzak the great)

7 and stones, chalcedonies from the Indians

and pearls from the Kosani (Kushan).

8 And they armed me with adamant

9 and they took off from me (Gr. put on me) the garment set with gems, spangled with gold, which they had made for me because they loved me

10 and the robe that was yellow in hue, made for my stature.

11 And they made a covenant with me, and inscribed it on mine understanding, that I should forget it, and said:

12 If thou go down into Egypt, and bring back thence the one pearl

13 which is there girt about by the devouring serpent

14 thou shalt put on the garment set with gems, and that robe whereupon it resteth (or which is thereon)

15 and become with thy brother that is next unto us (Gr. of the well-remembered) an heir (Gr. herald) in our kingdom.

109. 16 And I came out of the East by a road difficult and fearful, with two guides

17 and I was untried in travelling by it.

18 And I passed by the borders of the Mosani (Maishan) where is the resort of the merchants of the East,

19 and reached the land of the Babylonians .

20 But when I entered into Egypt, the guides left me which had journeyed with me.

21 And I set forth by the quickest way to the serpent, and by his hole I abode

22 watching for him to slumber and sleep, that I might take my pearl from him.

23 And forasmuch as I was alone I made mine aspect strange, and appeared as an alien to my people.

24 And there I saw my kinsman from the East, the freeborn

25 a lad of grace and beauty, a son of princes (or an anointed one).

26 He came unto me and dwelt with me,

27 and I had him for a companion, and made him my friend and partaker in my journey (or merchandise).

28 And I charged him to beware of the Egyptians, and of partaking of those unclean things (or consorting with those unclean men).

29 And I put on their raiment, lest I should seem strange, as one that had come from without

30 to recover the pearl; and lest the Egyptians should awake the serpent against me.

31 But, I know not by what occasion, they learned that I was not of their country.

32 And with guile they mingled for me a deceit, and I tasted of their food.

33 And I knew no more that I was a king's son, and I became a servant unto their king.

34 And I forgat also the pearl for which my fathers had sent me,

35 and by means of the heaviness of their food I fell into a deep sleep.

110. 36 But when this befell me, my fathers also were ware of it, and grieved for me

37 and a proclamation was published in our kingdom, that all should meet at our doors.

38 And then the kings of Parthia and they that bare office and the great ones of the East

39 made a resolve concerning me, that I should not be left in Egypt,

40 and the princes wrote unto me signifying thus (and every noble signed his name to it, Syr.):

41 From the (thy) Father the King of kings, and thy mother that ruleth the East,

42 and thy brother that is second unto us; unto our son that is in Egypt, peace.

43 Rise up and awake out of sleep, and hearken unto the words of the letter

44 and remember that thou art a son of kings; lo, thou hast come under the yoke of bondage.

45 Remember the pearl for the which thou wast sent into Egypt (Gr. puts this after 46).

46 Remember thy garment spangled with gold,

47 Thy name is named in the book of life,

48 and with thy brother whom thou hast received in our kingdom.

111. 49 and the King [as ambassador] sealed it

50 because of the evil ones, even the children of the Babylonians and the tyrannous demons of Labyrinthus (Sarbug, Syr.).

51

52 It flew and lighted down by me, and became all speech.>

53 And I at the voice of it and the feeling of it started up out of sleep

54 and I took it up and kissed it and read it.

55 And it was written concerning that which was recorded in mine heart.

56 And I remembered forthwith that I was a son of kings, and my freedom yearned (sought) after its kind.

57 I remembered also the pearl for the which I was sent down into Egypt

58 and I began (or came) with charms against the terrible serpent,

59 and I overcame him (or put him to sleep) by naming the name of my Father upon him,

60 .

61 And I caught away the pearl and turned back to bear it unto my fathers.

62 And I stripped off the filthy garment and left it in their land,

63 and directed my way forthwith to the light of my fatherland in the East.

64 And on the way I found my letter that had awakened me,

65 and it, like as it had taken a voice and raised me when I slept, so also guided me with the light that came from it.

66 For at times the royal garment of silk before mine eyes,

67

68 and with love leading me and drawing me onward,

69 I passed by Labyrinthus (Sarbug), and I left Babylon upon my left hand

70 and I came unto Meson (Mesene; Maishan) the great,

71 that lieth on the shore of the sea,

72

73 from the heights of Warkan (Hyrcania?) had my parents sent thither

74 by the hand of their treasurers, unto whom they committed it because of their faithfulness>.

112. 75 But I remembered not the brightness of it; for I was yet a child and very young when I had left it in the palace ot my Father,

76 but suddenly, [when] I saw the garment made like unto me as it had been in a mirror.

77 And I beheld upon it all myself (or saw it wholly in myself) and I knew and saw myself through it,

78 that we were divided asunder, being of one; and again were one in one shape.

79 Yea, the treasurers also which brought me the garment

80 I beheld, that they were two, yet one shape was upon both, one royal sign was set upon both of them.

81 The money and the wealth had they in their hands, and paid me the due price,

82 and the lovely garment, which was variegated with bright colours

83 with gold and precious stones and pearls of comely hue

84 they were fastened above (or in the height)

85 .

86 And the likeness of the King of kings was all in all of it.

87 Sapphire stones were fitly set in it above (or, like the sapphire stone also were its manifold hues).

113. 88 And again I saw that throughout it motions of knowledge were being sent forth,

89 and it was ready to utter speech.

90 And I heard it speak :

91 I am of him that is more valiant than all men, for whose sake I was reared up with the Father himself.

92 And I also perceived his stature (so Gr.- Syr. I perceived in myself that my stature grew in accordance with his working).

93 And all its royal motions rested upon me as it grew toward the impulse of it (And with its kingly motions it was spreading itself toward me).

94 And it hastened, reaching out from the hand of unto him that would receive it

95 and me also did yearning arouse to start forth and meet it and receive it.

96 And I stretched forth and received it, and adorned myself with the beauty of the colours thereof (mostly Syr.; Gr. corrupt)

97 and in my royal robe excelling in beauty I arrayed myself wholly.

98 And when I had put it on, I was lifted up unto the place of peace (sahltation) and homage

99 and I bowed my head and worshipped the brightness of the Father which had sent it unto me.

100 for I had performed his commandments, and he likewise that which he had promised,

101 and at the doors of his palace which was from the beginning I mingled among ,

102 and he rejoiced over me and received me with him into his palace,

103 and all his servants do praise him vvith sweet voices.

104 And he promised me that with him I shall be sent unto the gates of the king,

105 that with my gifts and my pearl we may appear together before the king.

[Immediately on this, in the Syriac, follows a Song of Praise of Thomas the apostle consisting of forty-two ascriptions of praise and four final clauses (Wright, pp. 245-51). It has no bearing on the Acts, and is not in itself so remarkable as to need to be inserted here.]

114 And Charisius went home glad, thinking that his wife would be with him, and that she had become such as she

was before, even before she heard the divine word and believed on Jesus. And he went, and found her with her hair dishevelled and her clothes rent, and when he saw it he said unto her: My lady Mygdonia, why doth this cruel disease keep hold on thee? and wherefore hast thou done this? I am thine husband from thy virginity, and both the gods and the law grant me to have rule over thee, what is this great madness of thine, that thou art become a derision in all our nation? but put thou away the care that cometh of that sorcerer; and I will remove his face from among us, that thou mayest see him no more.

115 But Mygdonia when she heard that gave herself up unto grief, groaning and lamenting and Charisius said again; Have I then so much wronged the gods that they have afflicted me with such a disease? what is my great offence that they have cast me into such humiliation? I beseech thee. Mygdonia trangle my soul no more with the pitiful sight of thee and thy mean appearance and afflict not mine heart with care for thee I am Charisius thine husband, whom all the nation honoureth and feareth. What must I do? I know not whither to turn. What am I to think? shall I keep silence and endure? yet who can be patient when men take his treasure? and who can endure to lose thy sweet ways? and what is there for me? (Syr. thy beauties which are ever before me) the fragrance of thee is in my nostrils, and thy bright face is fixed in mine eyes. They are taking away my soul, and the fair body which I rejoiced to see they are destroying, and that sharpest of eyes they are blinding and cutting off my right hand: my joy is turning to grief and my life to death, and the light of it is being dyed (?) with darkness. Let no man of you my kindred henceforth look on me; from you no help hath come to me, nor will I hereafter worship the gods of the east that have enwrapped me in such calamities, nor pray to them any more nor sacrifice to them, for I am bereaved of my spouse. And what else should I ask of them? for all my glory is taken away, yet am I a prince and next unto the king in power; but Mygdonia hath set me at nought, and taken away all these things. (Would that some one would blind one of my eyes, and that thine eyes would look upon me as they were wont, Syr. which has more clauses, to the same effect.)

116 And while Charisius spake thus with tears, Mygdonia sat silent and looking upon the ground; and again he came unto her and said: My lady Mygdonia, most desired of me, remember that out of all the women that are in India I chose and took thee as the most beautiful, though I might have joined to myself in marriage many more beautiful: but yet I lie, Mygdonia, for by the gods it would not have been possible to find another like thee in the land of India; but woe is me alway, for thou wilt not even answer me a word: but if thou wilt, revile me, so that I may only be vouchsafed a word from thee. Look at me, for I am more comely than that sorcerer: but thou art my wealth and honour: and all men know that there is none like me: and thou art my race and kindred; and lo, he taketh thee away from me.

117 And when Charisius had so said, Mygdonia saith unto him: He whom I love is better than thee and thy substance: for thy substance is of earth and returneth unto the earth; but he whom I love is of heaven and will take me with him unto heaven. Thy wealth shall pass away, and thy beauty shall vanish, and thy robes, and thy many works: and thou shalt be alone, naked, with thy transgressions. Call not to

my remembrance thy deeds (unto me), for I pray the Lord that I may forget thee, so as to remember no more those former pleasures and the custom of the body; which shall pass away as a shadow, but Jesus only endureth for ever, and the souls which hope in him. Jesus himself shall quit me of the shameful deeds which I did with thee. And when Charisius heard this, he turned him to sleep, vexed (dissolved) in soul, saying to her: Consider it by thyself all this night: and if thou wilt be with me such as thou wast before, and not see that sorcerer, I will do all according to thy mind, and if thou wilt remove thine affection from him I will take him out of the prison and let him go and remove into another country, and I will not vex thee, for I know that thou makest much of the stranger. And not with thee first did this matter come about, for many other women also hath he deceived with thee; and they have awaked sober and returned to themselves: do not thou then make nought of my words and cause me to be a reproach among the Indians.

118 And Charisius having thus spoken went to sleep: but she took ten denarii (20 zuze, Syr.), and went secretly to give them to the gaolers that she might enter in to the apostle. But on the way Judus Thomas came and met her, and she saw him and was afraid, for she thought that he was one of the rulers: for a great light went before him. And she said to herself as she fled: have lost thee, O my unhappy soul! for thou wilt not again see Judas the apostle of the living , and not yet hast thou received the holy seal. And she fled and ran into a narrow place and there hid herself, saying: I would rather choose to be killed (taken) by the poorer, whom it is possible to persuade, than to fall into the hand of this mighty ruler, who will despise gifts.

The Tenth Act: wherein Mygdonia receiveth baptism.

119 And while Mygdonia thought thus with herself, Judas came and stood over her, and she saw him and was afraid, and fell down and became lifeless with terror. But he stood by her and took her by the hand and said unto her: Fear not, Mygdonia: Jesus will not leave thee, neither will the Lord unto whom thou hast committed thy soul overlook thee. His compassionate rest will not forsake thee: he that is kind will not forsake thee, for his kindness' sake, nor he that is good for his goodness' sake. Rise up then from the earth, thou that art become wholly above it: look on the light, for the Lord leaveth not them that love him to walk in darkness: behold him that travelleth with his servants, that he is unto them a defender in perils. And Mygdonia arose and looked on him and said: Whither wentest thou, my lord? and who is he that brought thee out of prison to behold the sun? Judas Thomas saith unto her: My Lord Jesus is mightier than all powers and all kings and rulers.

120 And Mygdonia said: Give me the seal of Jesus Christ and I shall (let me) receive the gift at thy hands before thou departest out of life. And she took him with her and entered into the court and awaked her nurse, saying unto her: Narcia (Gr. Marcia), my mother and nurse, all thy service and refreshment thou hast done for me from my childhood until my present age are vain, and for them I owe thee thanks which are temporal; do for me now also a ravour, that thou mayest for ever receive a recompense from him that giveth great gifts. And Narcia in answer saith: What wilt thou, my daughter Mygdonia, and what is

to be done for thy pleasure? for the honours which thou didst promise me before, the stranger hath not suffered thee to accomplish, and thou hast made me a reproach among all the nation. And now what is this new thing that thou commandest me? And Mygdonia saith: Become thou partaker with me in eternal life, that I may receive of thee perfect nurture: take bread and bring it me, and wine mingled with water, and spare my freedom (take pity on me a free-born woman, Syr.). And the nurse said: I will bring thee many loaves, and for water flagons of wine, and fulfil thy desire. But she saith to the nurse: Flagons I desire not, nor the many loaves: but this only, bring wine mingled with water and one loaf, and oil .

121 And when Narcia had brought these things, Mygdonia stood before the apostle with her head bare; and he took the oil and poured it on her head, saying: Thou holy oil given unto us for sanctification, sccret mystery whereby the cross was shown unto us, thou art the straightener of the crooked limbs, thou art the humbler (softener) of hard things (works), thou art it that showeth the hidden treasures, thou art the sprout of goodness; let thy power come, let it be established upon thy servant Mygdonia, and heal thou her by this freedom. And when the oil was poured upon her he bade her nurse unclothe her and gird a linen cloth about her; and there was there a fountain of water upon which the apostle went up, and baptized Mygdonia in the name of the Father and the Son and the Holy Ghost. And when she was baptized and clad, he brake bread and took a cup of water and made her a partaker in the body of Christ and the cup of the Son of God, and said: Thou hast received thy seal, get for thyself eternal life. And immediately there was heard from above a voice saying: Yea, amen. And when Narcia heard that voice, she was amazed, and besought the apostle that she also might receive the seal; and the apostle gave it her and said: Let the care of the Lord be about thee as about the rest.

122 And having done these things the apostle returned unto the prison, and found the doors open and the guards still sleeping. And Thomas said: Who is like thee, O God? who withholdest not thy loving affection and care from any who is like thee, the merciful, who hast delivered thy creatures out of evil. Life that hath subdued death, rest that hath ended toil. Glory be to the only-begotten of the Father. Glory to the compassionate that was sent forth of his heart. And when he had said thus, the guards waked and beheld all the doors open, and the prisoners <+ asleep, Syr.>, and said in themselves: Did not we fasten the doors? and how are they now open, and the prisoners within?

123 But at the dawn Charisius went unto Mygdonia , and found them praying and saying: O new God that by the stranger hast come hither unto us, hidden God of the dwellers in India (Syr. who art hidden from); God that hast shown thy glory by thine apostle Thomas, God whose report we have heard and believed on thee; God, unto whom we are come to be saved; God, who for love of man and for pity didst come down unto our littleness; God who didst seek us out when we knew him (thee) not; God that dwellest in the heights and from whom the depths are not hid: turn thou away from us the madness of Charisius. And Charisius hearing that said to Mygdonia: Rightly callest thou me evil and mad and foul I for if I had not borne with thy disobedience, and given thee liberty, thou wouldest not

have called on God against me and made mention of my name before God. But believe me, Mygdonia that in that sorcerer there is no profit, and what he promiseth to perform he cannot: but I will perform before thy sight all that I promise, that thou mayest believe, and bear with my words and be to me as thou wast beforetime.

124 And he came near and besought her again, saying: If thou wilt be persuaded of me, I shall henceforth have no grief; remember that day when thou didst meet me first; tell the truth: was I more beautiful unto thee at that time, or Jesus at this? And Mygdonia said: That time required its own, and this time also; that was the time of the beginning, but this of the end; that was the time of temporal life, this of eternal; that of pleasure that passeth away, but this of pleasure that abideth for ever; that, of day and night, this of day without night. Thou sawest that marriage that was passing, and here, and single but this marriage continueth for ever; that was a partnership of corruption, but this of eternal life; those groomsmen (and maids) were men and women of time, but these abide unto the end. That marriage upon earth setteth up dropping dew of the love of men (Syr. That union was founded upon the earth where there is an unceasing press: this is founded upon the bridge of fire upon which is sprinkled grace: both corrupt); that bride-chamber is taken down again, but this remaineth always; that bed was strown with coverlets (that grow old), but this with love and faith. Thou art a bridegroom that passest away and art dissolved (changed), but Jesus is a true bridegroom, enduring for ever immortal, that dowry was of money and robes that grow old, but this is of living words which never pass away.

125 And when Charisius heard these things he went unto the king and told him all: and the king commanded Judas to be brought, that he might judge him and destroy him. But Charisius said: Have patience a little, O king, and first persuade the man making him afraid, that he may persuade Mygdonia to be unto me as formerly. And Misdaeus sent and fetched the apostle of Christ, and all the prisoners were grieved because the apostle departed from them, for they yearned after him, saying: Even the comfort which we had have they taken away from us.

126 And Misdaeus said unto Judas: Wherefore teachest thou this new doctrine, which both gods and men hate, and which hath nought of profit? And Judas said: What evil do I teach? And Misdaeus said: Thou teachest, saying that men with the God whom thou preachest. Judas saith: Thou sayest true, O king: thus do I teach. For tell me, art thou not wroth with thy soldiers if they wait on thee in filthy garments? if then thou, being a king of earth and returning unto earth, request thy subjects to be reverend in their doings, are ye wroth and said ye that I teach ill when I say that they who serve my king must be reverend and pure and free from all grief and care of children and unprofitable riches and vain trouble? For indeed thou wouldest have thy subjects follow thy conversation and thy manners, and thou punishest them if they despise thy commandments: how much more must they that believe on him serve my God with much reverence and cleanness and security, and be quit of all pleasures of the body, adultery and prodigality and theft and drunkenness and belly-service and foul deeds?

127 And Misdaeus hearing these things said: Lo, I let thee go: go then and persuade Mygdonia, the wife of Charisius, not to desire to depart from him. Judas saith unto him: Delay not if thou hast aught to do: for her, if she hath rightly received what she hath learned, neither iron nor fire nor aught else stronger than these will avail to hurt or to root out him that is held in her soul. Misdaeus saith unto Judas: Some poisons do dissolve other poisons, and a theriac cureth the bites of the viper; and thou if thou wilt canst give a solvent of those diseases, and make peace and concord betwixt this couple: for by so doing thou wilt spare thyself, for not yet art thou sated with life; and know thou that if thou do not persuade her, I will catch thee away out of this life which is desirable unto all men. And Judas said: This life hath been given as a loan, and this time is one that changeth, but that life whereof I teach is incorruptible; and beauty and youth that are seen shall in a little cease to be. The king saith to him: I have counselled thee for the best, but thou knowest thine own affairs.

128 And as the apostle went forth from before the king, Charisius came to him and entreated him and said: I beseech thee, O man: I have not sinned against thee or any other at any time, nor against the gods; wherefore hast thou stirred up this great calamity against me? and for what cause hast thou brought such disturbance upon mine house? and what profit hast thou of it? but if thou thinkest to gain somewhat, tell me the gain, what it is, and I will procure it for thee without labour. To what end dost thou make me mad, and cast thyself into destruction? for if thou persuade her not, I will both dispatch thee and finally take myself out of life. But if, as thou sayest, after our departing hence there is there life and death, and also condemnation and victory and a place of judgement, then will I also go in thither to be judged with thee: and if that God whom thou preachest is just and awardeth punishment justly, I know that I shall gain my cause against thee; for thou hast injured me, having suffered no wrong at my hands: for indeed even here I am able to avenge myself on thee and bring upon thee all that thou hast done unto me. Therefore be thou persuaded, and come home with me and persuade Mygdonia to be with me as she was at first, before she beheld thee. And Judas saith to him: Believe me, my child that if men loved God as much as they love one another, they would ask of him all things and receive them, and none would do them violence (there would be nothing which would not obey them, Syr.).

129 And as Thomas said this, they came unto the house of Charisius and found Mygdonia sitting and Narcia standing by her, and her hand supporting her cheek; and she was saying: Let the remainder of the days of my life, O mother, be cut off from me, and all the hours become as one hour, and let me depart out of life that I may go the sooner and behold that beautiful one, whose report I have heard, even that living one and giver of life unto them that believe on him, where is not day and night, nor light and darkness, nor good and evil, nor poor and rich, nor male and female, nor free and bond, nor proud that subjecteth the humble. And as she spake the apostle stood by her, and forthwith she rose up and did him reverence. Then Charisius said unto him: Seest thou how she feareth and honoureth thee and all that thou shalt bid her she will do willingly?

130 And as he so spake, Judas saith unto Mygdonia: My daughter Mygdonia, obey that which thy brother Charisius saith. And Mygdonia saith: If thou wast not able the deed in word wilt thou compel me to endure the act? for I have heard of thee that this life is of no profit, and this relief is for a time, and these possessions are transitory. And again thou saidst that whoso renounceth this life shall receive the life eternal, and whoso hateth the light of day and night shall behold a light that is not overtaken, that whoso despiseth this money shall find other and eternal money. But now because thou art in fear. Who that hath done somewhat and is praised for the work changeth it? straightway overthroweth it from the foundation? who diggeth a spring water in a thirsty land and straightway filleth it in? who findeth a treasure and useth it not? And Charisius heard it and said: I will not imitate you, neither will I hasten to destroy you; nor though I may so do, will I put bonds about thee (but thee I will bind, Syr.); and I will not suffer thee to speak with this sorcerer; and if thou obey me, well, but if not, I know what I must do.

131 And Judas went out of Charisius' house and departed unto the house of Siphor and lodged there with him. And Siphor said: I will prepare for Judas a hall (triclinium) wherein he may teach (Syr. Siphor said to Judas: Prepare thyself an apartment, &c.). And he did so; and Siphor said : I and my wife and daughter will dwell henceforth in holiness, and in chastity, and in one affection. I beseech thee that we may receive of thee the seal, and become worshippers of the true God and numbered among his sheep and lambs. And Judas said: I am afraid to speak that which I think: yet I know somewhat, and what I know it is not possible for me to utter.

132 And he began to say concerning baptism: This baptism is remission of sins (the Greek MSS. U and P have divergent texts, both obscure): this bringeth forth again light that is shed about us: this bringeth to new birth the new man (this is the restorer of understandings Syr.): this mingleth the spirit (with the body), raiseth up in threefoldwise a new man and partaker of the remission of sins. Glory be to thee, hidden one, that art communicated in baptism. Glory to thee the unseen power that is in baptism. Glory to thee, renewal, whereby are renewed they that are baptized and with affection take hold upon thee.

And having thus said, he poured oil over their heads and said: Glory be to thee the love of compassion (bowels). Glory to thee name of Christ. Glory to thee, power established in Christ. And he commanded a vessel to be brought, and baptized them in the name of the Father and the Son and the Holy Ghost.

133 And when they were baptized and clad, he set bread on the table and blessed it, and said: Bread of life, the which who eat abide incorruptible: Bread that filleth the hungry souls with the blessing thereof: thou art he that vouchsafest to receive a gift, that thou mayest become unto us remission of sins, and that they who eat thee may become immortal: we invoke upon thee the name of the mother, of the unspeakable mystery of the hidden powers and authorities (? we name the name of the unspeakable mystery, that is hidden from all &c.): we invoke upon thee the name of [thy?] Jesus. And he said: Let the powers of blessing come, and be established in this bread, that all the

souls which partake of it may be washed from their sins. And he brake and gave unto Siphor and his wife and daughter.

The Eleventh Act: concerning the wife of Misdaeus.

134 Now Misdaeus the king, when he had let Judas go, dined and went home, and told his wife what had befallen Charisius their kinsman, saying: See what hath come to pass to that unhappy man, and thou thyself knowest, my sister Tertia, that a man hath nought better than his own wife on whom he resteth; but it chanced that his wife went unto that sorcerer of whom thou hast heard that he is come to the land of the Indians, and fell into his charms and is parted from her own husband; and he knoweth not what he should do. And when I would have destroyed the malefactor, he would not have it. But do thou go and counsel her to incline unto her husband, and forsake the vain words of the sorcerer.

135 And as soon as she arose Tertia went to the house of Charisius her husband's, and found Mygdonia lying upon the earth in humiliation, and ashes and sackcloth were spread under her, and she was praying that the Lord would forgive her her former sins and she might soon depart out of life. And Tertia said unto her: Mygdonia, my dear sister and companion what is this hand (Syr. this folly)? what is the disease that hath overtaken thee? and why doest thou the deeds of madmen? Know thyself and come back unto thine own way, come near unto thy many kinsfolk, and spare thy true husband Charisius, and do not things unbefitting a free-woman. Mygdonia saith unto her: O Tertia, thou hast not yet heard the preacher of life: not yet hath he touched thine ears, not yet hast thou tasted the medicine of life nor art freed from corruptible mourning. Thou standest in the life of time, and the everlasting life and salvation thou knowest not, and perceivest not the incorruptible fellowship. Thou standest clad in robes that grow old and desirest not those that are eternal, and art proud of this beauty which vanisheth and hast no thought of the holiness of thy soul; and art rich in a multitude of servants, (and hast not freed thine own soul from servitude, Syr.) and pridest thyself in the glory that cometh of many, but redeemest not thyself from the condemnation of death.

136 And when Tertia heard this of Mygdonia she said: I pray thee, sister, bring me unto that stranger that teacheth these great things, that I also may go and hear him, and be taught to worship the God whom he preacheth, and become partaker of his prayers, and a sharer in all that thou hast told me of. And Mygdonia saith to her: He is in the house of Siphor the captain; for he is become the occasion of life unto all them that are being saved in India. And hearing that, Tertia went quickly to Siphor's house, that she might see the new apostle that was come thither. And when she entered in, Judas said unto her: What art thou come to see? a man that is a stranger and poor and contemptible and needy, having neither riches nor substance; yet one thing I possess which neither kings nor rulers can take away, that neither perisheth nor ceaseth, which is Jesus the Saviour of all mankind, the Son of the living God, who hath given life unto all that believe on him and take refuge with him and are known to be of the number of his servants (sheep, Syr.). Unto whom saith Tertia: May I become a partaker of this life which thou promisest that all

they shall receive who come together unto the assembly of God. And the apostle said: The treasury of the holy king is opened wide, and they which worthily partake of the good things that are therein do rest, and resting do reign: but first, no man cometh unto him that is unclean and vile: for he knoweth our inmost hearts and the depths of our thought, and it is not possible for any to escape him. Thou, then, if verily thou believest in him, shalt be made worthy of his mysteries; and he will magnify thee and enrich thee, and make thee to be an heir of his hingdom.

137 And Tertia having heard this returned home rejoicing, and found her husband awaiting her, not having dined, and when Misdaeus saw her he said: Whence is it that thine entering in to-day is more beautiful? and wherefore art thou come walking, which beseemeth not free-born women like thee? And Tertia saith unto him: I owe thee the greatest of thanks for that thou didst send me unto Mygdonia, for I went and heard of a new life, and I saw the new apostle of the God that giveth life unto them that believe on him and fulfil his commandments; I ought therefore myself to recompense thee for this favour and admonition with good advice; for thou shalt be a great king in heaven if thou obey me and fear the God that is preached by the strangrer, and keep thyself holy unto the living God. For this kingdom passeth away, and thy comfort will be turned into affliction: but go thou to that man, and believe him, and thou shalt live unto the end. And when Misdaeus heard these things of his wife, he smote his face with his hands and rent his clothes and said: May the soul of Charisius find no rest, for he hath hurt me to the soul; and may he have no hope, for he hath taken away my hope. And he went out greatly vexed.

138 And he found Charisius his friend in the market-place, and said unto him: Why hast thou cast me into hell to be another companion to thyself? why hast thou emptied and defrauded me to gain nought? why hast thou hurt me and profited thyself not at all? why hast thou slain me and thyself not lived? Why hast thou wronged me and thyself not got justice? why didst thou not suffer me to destroy that sorcerer before he corrupted my house with his wickedness? And he kept hold upon (was upbraiding, Syr.) Charisius. And Charisius saith: Why, what hath befallen thee? Misdaeus said: He hath bewitched Tertia. And they went both of them unto the house of Siphor the captain, and found Judas sitting and teaching. And all they that were there rose up before the king, but he arose not. And Misdaeus perceived that it was he, and took hold of the seat and overset it, and took up the seat with both his hands and smote his head so that he wounded it, and delivered him to his soldiers, saying: Take him away, and hale him with violence and not gently, that his shame may be manifest unto all men. And they haled him and took him to the place where Misdaeus judged, and he stood there, held of the soldiers of Misdaeus.

The Twelfth Act: concerning Ouazanes (Iuzanes) the son of Misdaeus.

139 And Ouazanes (Iuzanes, P; Vizan, Syr.) the son of Misdaeus came unto the soldiers and said: Give me him that I may speak with him until the king cometh. And they gave him up, and he brought him in where the king gave judgement. And Iuzanes saith: Knowest thou not that I am

the son of Misdaeus the king, and I have power to say unto the king what I will, and he will sufier thee to live? tell me then, who is thy God, and what power dost thou claim and glory in it? for if it be some power or art of magic, tell it me and teach me, and I will let thee go. Judas saith unto him: Thou art the son of Misdacus the king who is king for a time, but I am the servant of Jesus Christ the eternal king, and thou hast power to say to thy father to save whom thou wilt in the temporal life wherein men continue not, which thou and thy father grant, but I beseech my Lord and intercede for men, and he giveth them a new life which is altogether enduring. And thou boastest thyself of possessions and servants and robes and luxury and unclean chamberings, but I boast myself of povertv and philosophy and humility and lasting and prayer and the fellowship of the Holy Ghost and of my brethren that are worthy of God: and I boast myself of eternal life. And thou reliest on (hast taken refuge with) a man like unto thyself and not able to save his own soul from judgement and death, but I rely upon the living God, upon the saviour of kings and princes, who is the judge of all men. And ye indeed to-day perchance are, and to-morrow are no more, but I have taken refuge with him that abideth for ever and knoweth all our seasons and times. And if thou wilt become the servant of this God thou shalt soon do so; but show that thou wilt be a servant worthy of him hereby: first by holiness (puritv), which is the head of all good things, and then by fellowship with this God whom I preach, and philosophy and simplicity and love and faith and in him, and unity of pure food (simplicity of pure i e, Syr.).

140 And the young man was persuaded by the Lord and sought occasion how he might let Judas escape: but while he thought thereon, the king came, and the soldiers took Judas and led him forth. And Iuzanes went forth with him and stood beside him. And when the king was set he bade Judas be brought in, with his hands bound behind him; and he was brought into the midst and stood there. And the king saith: Tell me who thou art and by what power thou doest these things. And Judas saith to him: I am a man like thee, and by the power of Jesus Christ I do these things. And Misdaeus saith: Tell me the truth before I destroy thee. And Judas saith: Thou hast no power against me, as thou supposest, and thou wilt not hurt me at all. And the king was wroth at his words, and commanded to heat iron plates and set him upon them barefoot; and as the soldiers took off his shoes he said: The wisdom of God is better than the wisdom of men. Thou Lord and King (do thou take counsel against them, Syr.) and let thy goodness resist his wrath. And they brought the plates which were like fire, and set the apostle upon them, and straightway water sprang up abundantly from the earth, so that the plates were swallowed up in it, and they that held him let him go and withdrew themselves.

141 And the king seeing the abundance of water said to Judas: Ask thy God that he deliver me from this death, that I perish not in the flood. And the apostle prayed and said: Thou that didst bind this element (nature) and gather it into one place and send it forth into divers lands; that didst bring disorder into order, that grantest mighty works and great wonders by the hands of Judas thy servant; that hast mercy on my soul, that I may alway receive thy brightness; that givest wages unto them that have laboured; thou saviour of my soul, restoring it unto its own nature that it may have no fellowship with hurtful things; that hast alway

been the occasion of life: do thou restrain this element that it lift not up itself to destroy; for there are some of them that stand here who shall believe on thee and live. And when he had prayed, the water was swallowed up by little and little, and the place became dry. And when Misdaeus saw it he commanded him to be taken to the prison: Until I shall consider how he must be used.

142 And as Judas was led away to the prison they all followed him, and Iuzanes the king's son walked at his right hand, and Siphor at the left. And he entered into the prison and sat down, and Iuzanes and Siphor, and he persuaded his wife and his daughter to sit down, for they also were come in to hear the word ot life. For they knew that Misdaeus would slay him because of the excess of his anger. And Judas began to say: O liberator of my soul from the bondage of the many, because I gave myself to be sold ; behold, I rejoice and exult, knowing that the times are fulfilled for me to enter in and receive . Lo, I am to be set free from the cares that are on the earth; lo, I fulfil mine hope and reccive truth; lo, I am set free from sorrow and put on joy alone; lo, I become careless and griefless and dwell in rest; lo, I am set free from bondage and am called unto liberty; lo, I have served times and seasons, and I am lifted up above times and seasons; lo, I receive my wages from my recompenser, who giveth without reckoning (number) because his wealth sufficeth for the gift; and I shall not put it on again; lo, I sleep and awake, and I shall no more go to sleep; lo, I die and live again, and I shall no more taste of death; lo, they rejoice and expect me, that I may come and be with their kindred and be set as a flower in their crown; Io, I reign in the kingdom whereon I set my hope, even frorm hence; lo, the rebellious fall before me, for I have escaped them; lo, (unto me) the peace hath come, whereunto all are gathered.

143 And as the apostle spake thus, all that were there hearkened, supposing that in that hour he would depart out of life. And again he said: Believe on the physician of all , both seen and unseen, and on the saviour of the souls that need help from him. This is the free-born of kings, this the physician of his creatures; this is he that was reproached of his own slaves; this is the Father of the height and the Lord of nature and the Judge (? Father of nature and Lord of the height and supreme Judge, Syr.): he came of the greatest, the only-begotten son of the deep; and he was called the son of (became visible through, Syr.) Mary the virgin, and was termed the son of Joseph the carpenter: he whose littleness (we beheld) with the eyes of our body, but his greatness we received by faith, and saw it in his works whose human body we felt also with our hands, and his aspect we saw transfigured (changed) with our eyes, but his heavenly semblance on the mount we were not able to see: he that made the rulers stumble and did violence unto death: he, the truth that lieth not, that at the last paid the tribute for himself and his disciplcs: whom the prince beholding feared and the powers that were with him were troubled; and the prince bare witness (asked him, Syr.) who he was and from whence, and knew not the truth, because he is alien from truth: he that having authority over the world, and the pleasures therein, and the possessions and the comfort, all these things and turneth away his subjects, that they should not use them.

144 Alld having fulfilled these sayings, he arose and prayed thus: our Father, which art in heaven: hallowed be thy name: Thy kingdom come: Thy will be done, as in heaven so upon earth: and forgive us our debts as we also have forgiven our debtors. And lead us not into temptation, but deliver us from the evil one.

My Lord and God, hope and confidence and teacher, thou hast taught me to pray thus, behold, I pray this prayer and fulfil thy commandment: be thou with me unto the end; thou art he that from childhood hast sown life in me and kept me from corruption; thou art he that hast brought me unto the poverty of this world, and exhorted me unto the true riches; thou art he that hast made me known unto myself and showed me that I am thine; and I have kept myself pure from woman, that that which thou requirest be not found in defilement.

[At the words 'My Lord and God' begins the double text, represented on the one hand by the MS. U and on the other by the Paris MS. P, and three (partly four) others. These insert the prayer after ch. 167. Their text, I believe, may be the original Greek. I follow it here, repeating the first paragraph.]

(144) My Lord and God, my hope and my confidence and my teacher, that hast implanted courage in me, thou didst teach me to pray thus; behold, I pray thy prayer and bring thy will to fulfilment: be thou with me unto the end. Thou art he that from my youth up didst give me patience in temptation and me life and preserve me from corruption; thou art he that didst bring me into the poverty of this world and fill me with the true riches; thou art he that didst show me that I was thine: wherefore I was never joined unto a wife, that the temple worthy of thee might not be found in pollution.

145 My mouth sufficeth not to praise thee, neither am I able to conceive the care and providence (carefulness) which hath been about me from thee which thou hast had for me). For I desired to gain riches, but thou by a vision didst show me that they are full of loss and iniury to them that gain them and I believed thy showing, and continued in the poverty of the world until thou, the true riches wert revealed unto me, who didst fill both me and the rest that were worthy of thee with thine own riches and set free thine own from care and anxiety. I have therefore fulfilled thy commandments, O Lord, and accomplished thy will, and become poor and needy and a stranger and a bondman and set at nought and a prisoner and hungry and thirsty and nalied and unshod, and I have toiled for thy sake, that my confidence might not perish and my hope that is in thee might not be confounded and my much labour might not be in vain and my weariness not be counted for nought: let not my prayers and rmy continual fastings perish, and my great zeal toward thee; let not my seed of wheat be changed for tares out of thy land, Iet not the enemy carry it away and mingle his own tares therewith; for thy land verily receiveth not his tares, neither indeed can they be laid up in thine houses.

146 I have planted thy vine in the earth, it hath sent down its roots into the depth and its growth is spread out in the height, and the fruits of it are stretched forth upon the earth, and they that are worthy of thee are made glad by

them, whom also thou hast gained. The money which thou hast from me I laid down upon the table (bank); this, when thou requirest it, restore unto me with usury, as thou hast promised. With thy one mind have I traded and have made ten, thou hast added rnore to me beside that I had, as thou didst covenant. I have forgiven my debtor the mine, require thou it not at my hands. I was bidden to the supper and I came: and I refused the land and the yoke of oxen and the wife, that I might not for their sake be rejected; I was bidden to the wedding, and I put on white raiment, that I might be worthy of it and not be bound hand and foot and cast into the outer darkness. My lamp with its bright light expecteth the master coming from the marriage, that it may receive him, and I may not (? he may not) see it dimmed because the oil is spent. Mine eyes, O Christ, look upon thee, and mine heart exulteth with joy because I have fulfilled thy will and perfected thy commandments; that I may be likened unto that watchful and careful servant who in his eagerness neglecteth not to keep vigil (other MSS.: I have not slumbered idly in keeping thy commandments: in the first sleep and at midnight and at cockcrow, that mine eyes may behold thee, &c.). All the night have I laboured to keep mine house from robbers, lest it be broken through.

147 My loins have I girt close with truth and bound my shoes on my feet, that I may never see them gaping: mine hands have I put unto the yoked plough and have not turned away backward, lest my furrows go crooked. The plough-land is become white and the harvest is come, that I may receive my wages. My garment that groweth old I have worn out, and the labour that hath brought me unto rest have I accomplished. I have kept the first watch and the second and the third, that I may behold thy face and adore thine holy brightness. I have rooted out the worst (pulled down my barns, Syr.) and left thern desolate upon earth, that I may be filled full from thy treasures (Gr. MSS. add: all my substance have I sold, that I may gain thee the pearl). The moist spring that was in me have I dried up, that I may live and rest beside thine inexhaustible spring (al. and Syr.: rest beside thy living spring). The captive whom thou didst commit to me I have slain, that he which is set free in me may not fall from his confidence. Him that was inward have I made outward and the outward , and all thy fullness hath been fulfilled in me. I have not returned unto the things that are behind, but have gone forward unto the things that are before, that I become not a reproach. The dead man have I quickened, and the living one have I overcome, and that which was lacking have I filled up (Syr. Wright, not the older one, inserts negatives, ' not quickened ', &c.), that I may receive the crown of victory, and the power of Christ may be accomplished in me. I have received reproach upon earth, but give thou me the return and the recompense in the heavens. (U omits practically all this chapter.)

148 Let not the powers and the officers perceive me, and let them not have any thought concerning me; let not the publicans and exactors ply their calling upon me; let not the weak and the evil cry out against me that am valiant and humble, and when I am borne upward let them not rise up to stand before me, by thy power, O Jesu, which surroundeth me as a crown: for they do flee and hide themselves, they cannot look on thee: but (for) suddenly do they fall upon them that are subject to them, and the portion of tile sons of the evil one doth itself cry out and convict them; and it is not hid from them, nor their nature

is made known: the children of the evil one are separated off. Do thou then grant me, Lord, that I may pass by in quietness and joy and peace, and pass over and stand before the judge, and let not the devil (or slanderer) look upon me; let his eyes be blinded by thy light which thou hast made to dwell in me, close thou up (muzzle) his mouth: for he hath found nought against me.

[We revert to U.]

149 And he said again unto them that were about him: believe in the Saviour of them that have laboured in his service: for my soul already flourisheth because my time is near to receive him; for he being beautiful draweth me on always to speak concerning his beauty, what it is though I be not able and suffice not to speak it worthily: thou that art the light (feeder, Syr.) of my poverty and the supplier of my defects and nurturer of my need: be thou with me until I come and receive thee for evermore.

The Thirteenth Act: wherein Iuzanes receiveth baptism with the rest.

150 And Iuzanes the youth besought the apostle, saying: I pray thee, O man, apostle of God, suffer me to go, and I will persuade the gaoler to permit thee to come home with me, that by thee I may receive the seal, and become thy minister and a keeper of the commandments of the God whom thou preachest. For indeed, formerly I walked in those things which thou teachest, until my father compelled me and joined me unto a wife by name Mnesara; for I am in my one-and-twentieth year, and have now been seven years married, and before I was joined in marriage I knew no other woman, wherefore also I was accounted useless of my father, nor have I ever had son or daughter of this wife and also my wife herself hath lived with me in chastity all this time, and to-day, if she had been in health, and had listened to thee, I know well that both I should have been at rest and she would have received eternal life; but she is in peril and afflicted with much illness; I will therefore persuade the keeper that he promise to come with me, for I live by myself: and thou shalt also heal that unhappy one. And Judas the apostle of the Most High, hearing this, said to Iuzanes: If thou believest, thou shalt see the marvels of God, and how he saveth his servants.

151 And as they spake thus together, Tertia and Mvgdonia and Narcia stood at the door of the prison, and they gave the gaoler 363 staters of silver and entered in to Judas; and found Iuzanes and Siphor and his wife and daughter, and all the prisoners sitting and hearing the word. And when they stood by him he said to them: Who hath suffered you to come unto us? and who opened unto you the sealed door that ye came forth? Tertia saith unto him: Didst not thou open the door for us and tell us to come into the prison that we might take our brethren that were there, and then should the Lord show forth his glory in us? And when we came near the door, I know not how, thou wast parted from us and hid thyself and camest hither before us where also we heard the noise of the door, when thou didst shut us out. We gave money therefore to the keepers and came in and lo, we are here praying thee that we may persuade thee and let thee escape until the king's wrath against thee shall cease. Unto whom Judas said: Tell us first of all how ye were shut up.

152 And she saith to him: Thou wast with us, and didst never leave us for one hour, and askest thou how we were shut up? but if thou desirest to hear, hear. The king Misdaeus sent for me and said unto me: Not yet hath that sorcercr prevailed over thee, for, as I hear, he bewitcheth men with oil and water and bread, and hath not yet bewitched thee; but obey thou me, for if not, I will imprison thee and wear thee out, and him I will destroy; for I know that if he hath not yet given thee oil and water and bread, he hath not prevailed to get power over thee. And I said unto him: Over my body thou hast authority, and do thou all that thou wilt; but my soul I will not let perish with thee. And hearing that he shut me up in a chamber (beneath his dining-hall, Syr.): and Charisius brought Mygdonia and shut her up with me: and thou broughtest us out and didst bring us even hither; but give thou us the seal quickly, that the hope of Misdacus who counselleth thus may be cut off.

153 And when the apostle heard this, he said: Glory be to thee, O Jesu of many forms, glory to thee that appearest in the guise of our poor manhood: glory to thee that encouragest us and makest us strong and givest grace and consolest and standest by us in all perils, and strengthenest our weakness. And as he thus spake, the gaoler came and said: Put out the lamps, lest any accuse you unto the king. And then they extinguished the lamps, and turned to sleep; but the apostle spake unto the Lord: It is the time now, O Jesu, for thee to make haste; for, lo the children of darkness sit (make us to sit, Syr.) in their own darkness, do thou therefore enlighten us with the light of thy nature. And on a sudden the whole prison was light as the day: and while all they that were in the prison slept a deep sleep, they only that had believed in the Lord continued waking.

154 Judas therefore saith to Iuzanes: Go thou before and make ready the things for our need. Iuzanes thererore saith: And who will open me the doors of the prison? for the gaolers shut them and are gone to sleep. And Judas saith: Believe in Jesus, and thou shalt find the doors open. And when he went forth and departed from them, all the rest followed after him. And as Iuzanes was gone on before, Mnesara his wife met him coming unto the prison. And she knew him and said: My brother Iuzanes, is it thou? and he saith, Yea, and art thou Mnesara? and she saith Yea. Iuzanes said unto her; Whither walkest thou, especialiy at so untimely an hour? and how wast thou able to rise up? And she said: This youth laid his hand on me and raised me up, and in a dream I say that I should go where the stranger sitteth, and become perfectly whole. Iuzanes saith to her: What youth is with thee? And she said: Seest thou not him that is on my right hand, leading me by the hand?

155 And while they spake together thus, Judas, with Siphor and his wife and daughter and Tertia and Mygdonia and Narcia came unto Iuzanes' house. And Mnesara the wife of Iuzanes seeing him did reverence and said: Art thou come that savedst us from the sore disease? thou art he whom I saw in the night delivering unto me this youth to bring me to the prison. But thy goodness suffered me not to grow weary, but thou thyself art come unto me. And so saying she turned about and saw the youth no more; and finding him not, she saith to the apostle: I am not able to walk alone: for the youth whom thou gavest me is not here. And Judas said: Jesus will henceforth lead thee. And thereafter

she came running unto him. And when they entered into the house of Iuzanes the son of Misdaeus the king though it was yet night, a great light shined and was shed about them.

156 And then Judas began to pray and to speak thus: O companion and defender (ally) and hope of the weak and confidence of the poor: refuge and lodging of the weary: voice that came forth of the height (sleep, Gr.): comforter dwelling in the midst: port and harbour of them that pass through the regions of the rulers: physician that healest without payment: who among men wast crucified for many: who didst go down into hell with great might: the sight of whom the princes of death endured not; and thou camest up with great glory, and gathering all them that fled unto thee didst prepare a way, and in thy footsteps all they journeyed whom thou didst redeem; and thou broughtest them into thine own fold and didst join them with thy sheep: son of mercy, the son that for love of man wast sent unto us from the perfect country (fatherland) that is above, the Lord of all possessions (undefiled possessions, Syr.): that servest thy servants that they may live: that fillest creation with thine own riches: the poor, that wast in need and didst hunger forty days: that satisfiest thirsty souls with thine own good things; be thou with Iuzanes the son of Misdaeus and with Tertia and Mnesara, and gather them into thy fold and mingle them with thy number; Be unto them a guide in the land of error: be unto them a physician in the land of sickness: be unto them a rest in the land of the weary: sanctify them in a polluted land: be their physician both of bodies and souls: make them holy temples of thee, and let thine holy spirit dwell in them.

157 Having thus prayed over them, the apostle said unto Mygdonia: Unclothe thy sisters. And she took off their clothes and girded them with girdles and brought them: but Iuzanes had first gone before, and they came after him; and the apostle took oil in a cup of silver and spake thus over it: Fruit more beautifull than all other fruits, unto which none other whatsoever may be compared: altogether merciful: fervent with the force of the word: power of the tree which men putting upon them overcome their adversaries: crowner of the conquerors: help (symbol) and joy of the sick: that didst announce unto men their salvation that showest light to them that are in darkness; whose leaf is bitter, but in thy most sweet fruit thou art fair, that art rough to the sight but soft to the taste; seeming to be weak, but in the greatness of thy strength able to bear the power that beholdeth all things. Having thus said [a corrupt word follows]: Jesu: let his victorious might come and be established in this oil, like as it was established in the tree (wood) that was its kin, even his might at that time, whereof they that crucified thee could not endure the word: let the gift also come whereby breathing upon his (thine) enemies thou didst cause them to go backward and fall headlong and let it rest on this oil, whereupon we invoke thine holy name. And having thus said, he poured it first upon the head of Iuzanes and then upon the women's heads, saying: In thy name, O Jesu Christ, let it be unto these souls for remission of sins and for turning back of the adversary and for salvation of their souls. And he commanded Mygdonia to anoint them but he himself anointed Iuzanes. And having anointed them he led them down into the water in the name of the Father and the Son and the Holy Ghost.

158 And when they were come up, he took bread and a cup, and blessed it and said: Thine holy body w}lich was crucified for us do we eat, and thy blood that was shed for us unto salvation do we drink; let therefore thy body be unto us salvation and thy blood for remission of sins. And for the gall which thou didst drink for our sakes let the gall of the devil be removed from us: and for the vinegar which thou hast drunk for us, let our weakness be made strong: and for the spitting which thou didst receive for us, let us receive the dew of thy goodness: and by (or for) the reed wherewith they smote thee for us, let us receive the perfect house: and whereas thou receivedst a crown of thorns for our sake, let us that have loved thee put on a crown that fadeth not away; and for the linen cloth wherein thou wast Wrapped, let us also be girt about with thy power that is not vanquished and for the new tomb and the burial let us receive renewing of soul and body: and for that thou didst rise up and revive, let us revive and live and stand before thee in righteous judgement. And he brake and gave the eucharist unto Iuzanes and Tertia and Mnesara and the wife and daughter of Siphor and said: Let this eucharist be unto you for salvation and joy and health of your souls. And they said: Amen. And a voice was heard, saying: Amen: fear ye not, but only believe.

[THE MARTYRDOM]

Here we revert to the text of P and its companions.

159 And after these things Judas departed to be imprisoned.

And Tertia with Mygdonia and Narcia also went to be imprisoned. And the apostle Thomas said unto them -the multitude of them that had believed being present: Daughters and sisters and fellow-servants which have believed in my Lord and God, ministers of my Jesus, hearken to me this day: for I do deliver my word unto you, and I shall no more speak with you in this flesh nor in this world; for I go up unto my Lord and God Jesus Christ, unto him that sold me, unto that Lord that humbled himself even unto me the little, and brought me up unto eternal greatness, that vouchsafed to me to become his servant in truth and steadfastness: unto him do I depart, knowing that the time is fulfilled, and the day appointed hath drawn near for me to go and receive my recompense from my Lord and God: for my recompenser is righteous, who knoweth me, how I ought to receive my reward; for he is not grudging nor envious, but is rich in his gifts, he is not a lover of craft (OT sparing) in that he giveth, for he hath confidence in his possessions which cannot fail.

160 I am not Jesus, but I am his servant: I am not Christ, but I am his minister; I am not the Son of God, but I pray to become worthy of God. Continue ye in the faith of Christ: continue in the hope of the Son of God: faint not at affliction, neither be divided in mind if ye see me mocked or that I am shut up in prison ; for I do accomplish his will. For if I had willed not to die, I know in Christ that I am able thereto: but this which is called death, is not death, but a setting free from the body; wherefore I receive gladly this setting free from the body, that I may depart and see him that is beautiful and full of mercy, him that is to be loved: for I have endured much toil in his service, and have laboured for his grace that is come upon me, which

departeth not from me. Let not Satan, then, enter you by stealth and catch away your thoughts: let there be in you no place for him: for he is mighty whom ye have received. Look for the coming of Christ, for he shall come and receive you, and this is he whom ye shall see when he cometh.

161 When the apostle had ended these sayings, they went into the house, and the apostle Thomas said: Saviour that didst suffer many things for us, let these doors be as they were and let seals be set on them. And he left them and went to be imprisoned: and they wept and were in heaviness, for they knew that Misdaeus would slay him (not knowing that, M. would release him, P.).

162 And the apostle found the keepers wrangling and saying: Wherein have we sinned against this wizard? for by his art magic he hath opened the doors and would have had all the prisoners escape: but let us go and report it unto the king, and tell him concerning his wife and his son. And as they disputed thus, Thomas held his peace. They rose up early, therefore, and went unto the king and said unto him: Our lord and king, do thou take away that sorcerer and cause him to be shut up elsewhere, for we are not able to keep him; for except thy good fortune had kept the prison, all the condemned persons would have escaped for now this second time have we found the doors open: and also thy wife, O king, and thy son and the rest depart not from him. And the king, hearing that, went, and found the seals that were set on the doors whole; and he took note of the doors also, and said to the keepers: Wherefore lie ye? for the seals are whole. How said ye that Tertia and Mygdonia come unto him into the prison? And the keepers said: We have told thee the truth.

163 And Misdaeus went to the prison and took his seat, and sent for the apostle Thomas and stripped him (and girded him with a girdle) and set him before him and saith unto him: Art thou bond or free? Thomas said: I am the bondsman of one only, over whom thou hast no authority. And Misdaeus saith to him: How didst thou run away and come into this country? And Thomas said: I was sold hither by my master, that I might save many, and by thy hands depart out of this world. And Misdaeus said: Who is thy lord? and what is his name? and of what country is he? And Thomas said: My Lord is thy master and he is Lord of heaven and earth. And Misdaeus saith: What is his name? Thomas saith: Thou canst not hear his true name at this time: but the name that was given unto him is Jesus Christ. And Misdaeus saith unto him: I have not made haste to destroy thee, but have had long patience with thee: but thou hast added unto thine evil deeds, and thy sorceries are dispersed abroad and heard of throughout all the country: but this I do that thy sorceries may depart with thee, and our land be cleansed from them. Thomas saith unto him; These sorceries depart with me when I set forth hence, and know thou this that I shall never forsake them that are here.

164 When the apostle had said these things, Misdaeus considered how he should put him to death; for he was afraid because of the much people that were subject unto him, for many also of the nobles and of them that were in authority believed on him. He took him therefore and went forth out of the city; and armed soldiers also went with

him. And the people supposed that the king desired to learn somewhat of him, and they stood still and gave heed. And when they had walked one mile, he delivered him unto four soldiers and an officer, and commanded them to take him into the mountain and there pierce him with spears and put an end to him, and return again to the city. And saying thus unto the soldiers, he himself also returned unto the city.

165 But the men ran after Thomas, desiring to deliver him from death. And two soldiers went at the right hand of the apostle and two on his left, holding spears, and the officer held his hand and supported him. And the apostle Thomas said: O the hidden mysteries which even until our departure are accomplished in us! O riches of his glory, who will not suffer us to be swallowed up in this passion of the body! Four are they that cast me down, for of four am I made; and one is he that draweth me, for of one I am, and unto him I go. And this I now understand, that my Lord and God Jesus Christ being of one was pierced by one, but I, which am of four, am pierced by four.

166 And being come up into the mountain unto the place where he was to be slain, he said unto them that held him, and to the rest: Brethren, hearken unto me now at the last; for I am come to my departure out of the body. Let not then the eyes of your heart be blinded, nor your ears be made deaf. Believe on the God whom I preach, and be not guides unto yourselves in the hardness of your heart, but walk in all your liberty, and in the glory that is toward men, and the life that is toward God.

167 And he said unto Iuzanes: Thou son (to the son, P) of the (earthly) king Misdaeus and minister (to the minister) of our Lord Jesus Christ: give unto the servants of Misdaeus their price that they may suffer me to go and pray. And Iuzanes persuaded the soldiers to let him pray. And the blessed Thomas went to pray, and kneeled down, and rose up and stretched forth his hands unto heaven, and spake thus:

[Here P and the rest give -rightly- the prayer of cc. 144-8. U and its companions give the foilowing: He turned to his prayer; and it was this: My Lord and my God, and hope and redeemer and leader and guide in all countries, be thou with all them that serve thee, and guide me this day as I come unto thee. Let not any take my soul which I have committed unto thee: let not the publicans see me, and let not the exactors accuse me falsely (play the sycophant with me). Let not the serpent see me, and let not the children of the dragon hiss at me. Behold, Lord, I have accomplished thy work and perfected thy commandment. I have become a bondman; therefore to-day do I receive freedom. Do thou therefore give me this and perfect me: and this I sav, not for that I doubt, but that they may hear for whom it is needful to hear.]

168 And when he had thus prayed he said unto the soldiers: Come hither and accomplish the commandments of him that sent you. And the four came and pierced him with their spears, and he fell down and died.

And all the brethren wept; and they brought beautiful robes and much and fair linen, and buried him in a royal sepulchre wherein the former (first) kings were laid.

169 But Siphor and Iuzanes would not go down to the city, but continued sitting by him all the day. And the apostle Thomas appeared unto them and said: Why sit ye here and keep watch over me? I am not here, but I have gone up and received all that I was promised. But rise up and go down hence; for after a little time ye also shall be gathered unto me.

But Misdaeus and Charisius took away Mygdonia and Tertia and afflicted them sorely: howbeit they consented not unto their will. And the apostle appeared unto them and said: Be not deceived: Jesus the holy, the living one, shall quickly send help unto you. And Misdaeus and Charisius, when they perceived that Mygdonia and Tertia obeyed them not, suffered them to live according to their own desire.

And the brethren gathered together and rejoiced in the grace of the Holy Ghost: now the apostle Thomas when he departed out of the world made Siphor a presbyter and Iuzanes a deacon, when he went up into the mountain to die. And the Lord wrought with them, and many were added unto the faith.

170 Now it came to pass after a long time that one of the children of Misdaeus the king was smitten by a devil, and no man could cure him, for the devil was exceeding fierce. And Misdaeus the king took thought and sad: I will go and open the sepulchre, and take a bone of the apostle of God and hang it upon my son and he shall be healed. But while Misdaeus thought upon this, the apostle Thomas appeared to him and said unto him: Thou believedst not on a living man, and wilt thou believe on the dead? yet fear not, for my Lord Jesus Christ hath compassion on thee and pitieth thee of his goodness.

And he went and opened the sepulchre, but found not the apostle there, for one of the brethren had stolen him away and taken him unto Mesopotamia; but from that place where the bones of the apostle had lain Misdaeus took dust and put it about his son's neck, saying: I believe on thee, Jesu Christ, now that he hath left me which troubleth men and opposeth them lest they should see thee. And when he had hung it upon his son, the lad became whole.

Misdaeus the king therefore was also gathered among the brethren, and bowed his head under the hands of Siphor the priest; and Siphor said unto the brethren: Pray ye for Misdaeus the king, that he may obtain mercy of Jesus Christ, and that he may no more remember evil against him. They all therefore, with one accord rejoicing, rmade prayer for him; and the Lord that loveth men, the King of Kings and Lord of lords, granted Misdaeus also to have hope in him; and he was gathered with the multitude of them that had believed in Christ, glorifying the Father and the Son and the Holy Ghost, whose is power and adoration, now and for ever and world without end. Amen.

THE ACTS OF PHILIP

CHAPTER 1

Of the Journeyings of Philip the Apostle.

From the Fifteenth Acts Until the End, and Among Them the Martyrdom.

About the time when the Emperor Trajan received the government of the Romans, after Simon the son of Clopas, who was bishop of Jerusalem, had suffered martyrdom in the eighth year of his reign, being the second bishop of the church there after James who bore the name of brother of the Lord, Philip the apostle, going through the cities and regions of Lydia and Asia, preached to all the Gospel of Christ.

And having come to the city of Ophioryma, which is called Hierapolis of Asia, he was entertained by a certain believer, Stachys by name. And there was with him also Bartholomew, one of the seventy disciples of the Lord, and his sister Mariamme, and his disciples that followed him. All the men of the city therefore, having left their work, ran to the house of Stachys, hearing about the works which Philip did. And many men and women having assembled in the house of Stachys, Philip along with Bartholomew taught them the things of Jesus.

And Philip's sister Mariamme, sitting in the entry of the house of Stachys, addressed herself to those coming, persuading them to listen to the apostles, saying to them: Our brethren, and sons of my Father in heaven, ye are the excellent riches, and the substance of the city above, the delight of the habitation which God has prepared for those that love Him. Trample under foot the snares of the enemy, the writing serpent. For his path is crooked, since he is the son of the wicked one, and the poison of wickedness is in him; and his father is the devil, the author of death, and his mother corruption; rage in his eyes and destruction in his mouth, and his path is Hades. Wherefore flee from him that has no substance, the shapeless one that has no shape in all the creation, whether in the heaven or in the earth, whether in the flying creatures or the beasts. For everything is taken away from his shape; for among the beasts of the earth and the fowls of the heaven is the knowledge of him, that the serpent trails his belly and his breast; and Tartarus is his dwelling-place, and he goes in the darkness, since he has confidence in nothing. Flee therefore from him, that his poison may not be poured out into your mouth. But be rather believing, holy, of good works, having no deceit. Take away from yourselves the wicked disposition, that is, the evil desires through which the serpent, the wicked dragon, the prince of evil, has produced the pasture of destruction and death for the soul, since all the desire of the wicked has proceeded from him. And this is the root of iniquity, the maintenance of evils, the death of souls: for the desire of the enemy is armed against the believers, and comes forth from the darkness, and walks in the darkness, taking in hand to war with those who are in the light. For this is the beginning of concupiscence. Wherefore you who wish to come to us, and the rather that God has come through us to you as a father to his own children, wishing to have mercy upon you, and to deliver you from the wicked snare of the enemy, flee from the evil lusts of the enemy, and cast them completely out of your mind, hating openly the father of evils, and loving Jesus,

who is light, and life, and truth, and the Saviour of all who desire Him. Having run, therefore, to Him, take hold of Him in love, that He may bring you up out of the pit of the wicked, and having cleansed you, set you blameless, living in truth, in the presence of His Father.

And all these things Philip said to the multitudes that had come together to worship as in old times the serpents and the viper, of which also they set up images and worshipped them. Wherefore also they called Hierapolis Ophioryma. And these things having been said by Philip, Bartholomew and Mariamme and his disciples, and Stachys being along with him, all the people gave ear, and a great multitude of them fleeing from the enemy were turned to Jesus, and were added to Philip and those about him. And the faithful were the more confirmed in the love of Christ.

And Nicanora, the wife of the proconsul, lying in bed under various diseases, especially of the eyes, having heard about the Apostle Philip and his teaching, believed in the Lord. For she had even before this heard about Him; and having called upon His name, she was released from the troubles that afflicted her. And rising up, she went forth out of her house through the side door, carried by her own slaves in a silver litter, and went into the house of Stachys, where the apostles were.

And when she came before the gate of the house, Mariamme, the sister of Philip the apostle, seeing her, spoke to her in the Hebrew tongue before Philip and Bartholomew, and all the multitude of those who had believed, saying: Alemakan, ikasame, marmare, nachaman, mastranan, achaman; which is, Daughter of the father, thou art my mistress, thou hast been given as a pledge to the serpent; but Jesus our Redeemer has come to deliver thee through us, to break thy bands, and cut them, and to remove them from thee from their root, because thou art my sister, one mother brought us forth twins. Thou hast forsaken thy father, thou hast forsaken the path leading thee to the dwelling-place of thy mother, being in error; thou hast left the temple of that deception, and of the temporary glory, and hast come to us, fleeing from the enemy, because he is the dwelling-place of death. Behold, now thy Redeemer has come to redeem thee; Christ the Sun of righteousness has risen upon thee, to enlighten thee.

And when Nicanora, standing before the door, heard these things, she took courage before all, crying out, and saying: I am a Hebrew, and a daughter of the Hebrews; speak with me in the language of my fathers. For, having heard the preaching of my fathers, I was straightway cured of the disease and the troubles that encompassed me. I therefore adore the goodness of God who has caused you to be spoiled even to this city, on account of His true stone held in honour, in order that through you we may receive the knowledge of Him, and may live with you, having believed in Him.

Nicanora having thus spoken, the Apostle Philip, along with Bartholomew and Mariamme and those with them, prayed for her to God, saying: Thou who bringest the dead to life, Christ Jesus the Lord, who hast freed us through baptism from the slavery of death, completely deliver also this woman from the error, the enemy; make her alive in Thy life, and perfect her in Thy perfection, in order that she may be found in the country of her fathers in freedom, having a portion in Thy goodness, O Lord Jesus.

And all having sent up the amen along with the Apostle Philip, behold, there came the tyrant, the husband of Nicanora, raging like an unbroken horse; and having laid hold of his wife's garments, he cried out, saying: O

Nicanora, did not I leave thee in bed? how hadst thou so much strength as to come to these magicians? And how hast thou been cured of the inflammation of thine eyes? Now, therefore, unless thou tell me who thy physician is, and what is his name, I shall punish thee with various punishments, and shall not have compassion upon thee. And she answering, says to him: O tyrant, cast out from thee this tyranny of thine, forsake this wickedness of thine; abandon this life lasting only for a season; run away from the brutality of thy worthless disposition; flee from the wicked dragon and his lusts; throw from thee the works and the dart of the man-slaying serpent; renounce the abominable and wicked sacrifices of the idols, which are the husbandry of the enemy, the hedge of darkness; make for thyself a life chaste and pure, that being in holiness thou mayst be able to know my Physician, and to get His name. If therefore thou wishest me to be beside thee, prepare thyself to live in chastity and self-restraint, and in fear of the true God, and I shall live with thee all my life; only cleanse thyself from the idols, and from all their filth. And when the gloomy tyrant her husband heard these words of hers, he seized her by the hair of her head, and dragged her along, kicking her, and saying: It will be a fine thing for thee to be cut off by the sword, or to see thee from beside me committing fornication with these foreign magicians; for I see that thou hast fallen into the madness of these deceivers. Thee first of them, therefore, I shall cut off by an evil death; and then, not sparing them, I shall cut their sinews, and put them to a most cruel death. And having turned, he said to those about him: Bring out for me those impostors of magicians. And the public executioners having run into the house of Stachys, and laid hold of the Apostle Philip, and Bartholomew and Mariamme, dragged them along, leading them to where the proconsul was. And the most faithful Stachys followed, and all the faithful.

And the proconsul seeing them, gnashed his teeth, saying: Torture these deceivers that have deceived many women, and young men and girls, saying that they are worshippers of God, while they are an abomination. And he ordered thongs of raw hide to be brought, and Philip and Bartholomew and Mariamme to be beaten; and after they had been scourged with the thongs, he ordered their feet to be tied, and them to be dragged through the streets of the city as far as the gate of their temple. And a great crowd was assembled, so that scarcely any one stayed at home; and they all wondered at their patience, as they were being violently and inhumanly dragged along.

And the proconsul, having tortured the Apostle Philip and the saints who were with him, ordered them to be brought, and secured in the temple of the idol of the viper by its priests, until he should decide by what death he should destroy each of them. And many of the crowd believed in the grace of Christ, and were added to the Apostle Philip, and those with him, having renounced the idol of the viper, and were confirmed in the faith, being magnified by the endurance of the saints; and all together with their voice glorified God, saying the amen.

And when they were shut up in the temple of the viper— both Philip the Apostle, and Bartholomew and Mariamme—the priests of the viper assembled in the same place, and a great crowd, about seven thousand men; and having run to the proconsul, they cried out, saying: Avenge us of the foreigners, and magicians, and corrupters and seducers of men. For ever since they came to us, our city has been filled with every evil deed; and they have also

killed the serpents, the sons of our goddess; and they have also shut the temple, and the altar has been desolated; and we have not found the wine which had been brought in order that the viper, having drunk of it, might go to sleep. But if thou wishest to know that they are really magicians, look and see how they wish to bewitch us, saying, Live in chastity and piety, after believing in God; and how also they have come into the city; and how also the dragons have not struck them blind, or even killed them; and how also they have not drunk their blood; but even they who keep our city from every foreigner have been cast down by these men.

And the proconsul, having heard these things, was the more inflamed with rage, and filled with wrath and threatening; and he was exceedingly enraged, and said to the priests: Why *need you speak*, when they have bewitched my own wife? And from that time she has spoken to me with strange words; and praying all the night through, she speaks in a strange tongue with a light shining round her; and groaning aloud, she says, Jesus the true light has come to me. And I, having gone forth from my chamber, wished to look down through the window and see Jesus, the light which she spoke of; and like lightning it came upon me, so that I was within a little of being blinded; and from that time forth I am afraid of my wife, on account of her luminous Jesus. Tell me, ye priests, what I am to do. And they said to him: O proconsul, assuredly we are no longer priests; for ever since thou didst shut them up, in consequence of them praying, not only has the temple been shaken from the foundations, but it is also assuredly falling down.

Then the proconsul ordered to bring Philip and those with him forth out of the temple, and to bring them up to the tribunal, saying to the public executioner: Strip Philip and Bartholomew and Mariamme, and search thoroughly to try to find their enchantments. Having therefore first stripped Philip, then Bartholomew, they came also to Mariamme; and dragging her along, they said: Let us strip her naked, that all may see her, how she follows men; for she especially deceives all the women. And the tyrant says to the priests: Proclaim throughout the whole city round about that all should come, men and women, that they may see her indecency, that she travels about with these magicians, and no doubt commits adultery with them. And he ordered Philip to be hanged, and his ankles to be pierced, and to bring also iron hooks, and his heels also to be driven through, and to be hanged head downwards, opposite the temple on a certain tree; and stretch out Bartholomew opposite Philip, having nailed his hands on the wall of the gate of the temple.

And both of them smiled, seeing each other, both Philip and Bartholomew; for they were as if they were not tortured: for their punishments were prizes and crowns. And when also they had stripped Mariamme, behold, straightway the semblance of her body was changed in the presence of all, and straightway there was about her a cloud of fire before all; and they could not longer look at all on the place in which the holy Mariamme was, but they all fled from her.

And Philip spoke with Bartholomew in the Hebrew tongue saying: Where is our brother John? for, behold, I am being released from the body; and who is he that has prayed for us? Because they have also laid hands on our sister Mariamme, contrary to what is meet; and, behold, they have set fire to the house of Stachys, saying, Let us burn it, since he entertained them. Dost thou wish then,

Bartholomew, fire to come from heaven, and that we should burn them up?

And as Philip was thus speaking, behold, also John entered into the city like one of their fellow-citizens; and moving about in the street, he asked: Who are these men, and why are they punished? And they say to him: It cannot be that thou art of our city, and askest about these men, who have wronged many: for they have shut up our gods, and by their magic have cut off both the serpents and the dragons; and they have also raised many of the dead, who have struck us with amazement, detailing many punishments *against us*, and they wish also, these strangers who are hanging, to pray for fire out of heaven, and to burn up us and our city.

Then says John: Let us go, and do you show me them. They led John, therefore, as their fellow-citizen, to where Philip was; and there was there a great crowd, and the proconsul, and the priests. And Philip, seeing John, said to Bartholomew in Hebrew: Brother, John has come, who was in Barek, where the living water is. And John saw Philip hanging head downwards both by the ankles and the heels; and he also saw Bartholomew stretched out on the wall of the temple; and he said to them: The mystery of him that was hanged between the heaven and the earth shall be with you.

And he said also to the men of that city: Ye men who dwell in Ophioryma Hierapolis, great is the ignorance which is among you, for you have erred in the path of error. The dragon breathing has breathed upon you, and blinded you in three ways; that is, he has made you blind in body, and blind in soul, and blind in spirit: and you have been struck by the destroyer. Look upon the whole creation, whether in the earth, or in the heaven, or in the waters, that the serpent has no resemblance to anything above; but he is of the stock of corruption, and has been brought to nothing by God; and on this account he is twisted and crooked, and there is no life in him; and anger, and rage, and darkness, and fire, and smoke are in all his members. And now, therefore, why do you punish these men because they have told you that the serpent is your enemy?

And when they heard these words from John, they raised their hands against him, saying: We thought thee to be a fellow-citizen, but now thou hast shown thyself that thou art their companion. Like them, so also thou shalt be put to death; for the priests have intended to squeeze out your blood, and having mixed it with wine, to bring it to the viper to drink it. When, therefore, the priests attempted to lay hold of John, their hands were paralyzed. And John said to Philip: Let us not at all render evil for evil. And Philip said to John: Behold now, where is my Lord Jesus, who told me not to avenge myself? But for my part, I shall not endure it longer; but I will accomplish upon them my threat, and will destroy them all.

And John and Bartholomew and Mariamme restrained him, saying: Our Master was beaten, was scourged, was extended *on the cross*, was made to drink gall and vinegar, and said, Father, forgive them, for they know not what they do. And this He taught, saying: Learn of me, for I am meek and lowly in heart. Let us also therefore be patient. Philip says: Go away, and do not mollify me; for I will not bear that they have hanged me head down, and pierced my ankles and my heels with irons. And thou, John, beloved of God, how much hast thou reasoned with them, and thou hast not been listened to! Wherefore go away from me, and I will curse them, and they shall be

destroyed utterly to a man. And he began to curse them, invoking, and crying out in Hebrew: Abalo, aremun, iduthael, tharseleon, nachoth, aidunaph, teletoloi: that is, O Father of Christ, the only and Almighty God; O God, whom all ages dread, powerful and impartial Judge, whose name is in Thy dynasty Sabaoth, blessed art Thou for everlasting: before Thee tremble dominions and powers of the celestials, and the fire-breathing threats of the cherubic living ones; the King, holy in majesty, whose name came upon the wild beasts of the desert, and they were tamed, and praised Thee with a rational voice; who lookest upon us, and readily grantest our requests; who knewest us before we were fashioned; the Overseer of all: now, I pray, let the great Hades open its mouth; let the great abyss swallow up these the ungodly, who have not been willing to receive the word of truth in this city. So let it be, Sabaoth. And, behold, suddenly the abyss was opened, and the whole of the place in which the proconsul was sitting was swallowed up, and the whole of the temple, and the viper which they worshipped, and great crowds, and the priests of the viper, about seven thousand men, besides women and children, except where the apostles were: they remained unshaken. And the proconsul was swallowed up into the abyss; and their voices came up from beneath, saying, with weeping: Have mercy upon us, O God of Thy glorious apostles, because we now see the judgments of those who have not confessed the crucified One: behold, the cross illumines us. O Jesus Christ, manifest Thyself to us, because we are all coming down alive into Hades, and are being scourged because we have unjustly crucified Thine apostles. And a voice was heard of one, saying: I shall be merciful to you in the cross of light.

And there remained both Stachys and all his house, and the wife of the proconsul, and fifty other women who had believed with her upon the Lord, and a multitude besides, both of men and women, and a hundred virgins who had not been swallowed up because of their chastity, having been sealed with the seal of Christ.

Then the Lord, having appeared unto Philip, said: O Philip, didst thou not hear: Thou shalt not render evil for evil? and why hast thou inflicted such destruction? O Philip, whosoever putteth his hand to the plough, and looketh backwards; is his furrow well set? or who gives up his own lamp to another, and himself sits in darkness? or who forsakes his own dwelling-place, and dwells on a dunghill himself? And who, giving away his own garment in winter, goes naked? or what enemy rejoices in the joy of the man that hates him? and what soldier goes to war without a full suit of armour? and what slave who has fulfilled his master's order will not be commended? and who in the race-course, having nobly run, does not receive the prize? and who that has washed his garments willingly defiles them? Behold, my bride chamber is ready; but blessed is he who has been found in it wearing the shining garment: he it is who receives the crown upon his head. Behold, the supper is ready; and blessed is he who is invited, and is ready to go to Him that has invited him. The harvest of the field is much, and blessed is the good labourer. Behold the lilies and all the flowers, and it is the good husbandman who is the first to get a share of them. And how hast thou become, O Philip, unmerciful, having cursed thine enemies in wrath?

Philip says: Why art Thou angry with me, Lord, because I have cursed mine enemies? for why dost Thou not tread them under foot, because they are yet alive in the abyss? And knowest Thou, Lord, that because of Thee I came into this city, and in Thy name I have persecuted all the error of the idols, and all the demons? The dragons have withered away, and the serpents. And since these men have not received Thy light, therefore have I cursed them, and they have gone down to Hades alive.

And the Saviour says to Philip: But since thou hast disobeyed me, and hast requited evil for evil, and hast not kept my commandment, on this account thou shalt finish thy course gloriously indeed, and shalt be led by the hand by my holy angels, and shalt come with them even to the paradise of delight; and they indeed shall come beside me into paradise, but thee will I order to be shut outside of paradise for forty days, in terror under the flaming and turning sword, and thou shalt groan because thou hast done evil to those who have done evil to thee. And after forty days I shall send my archangel Michael; and he, having taken hold of the sword guarding paradise, shall bring thee into it, and thou shalt see all the righteous who have walked in their innocence, and then thou shalt worship the glory of my Father in the heavens. Nevertheless the sign of thy departure shall be glorified in my cross. And Bartholomew having gone away into Lycaonia, shall there also be himself crucified; and Mariamme shall lay her body in the river Jordan. But I, O Philip, will not endure thee, because thou hast swallowed up the men into the abyss; but, behold, my Spirit is in them, and I shall bring them up from the dead; and thus they, seeing thee, shall believe in the glory of Him that sent thee. And the Saviour having turned, stretched up His hand, and marked a cross in the air coming down from above even to the abyss, and it was full of light, and had its form after the likeness of a ladder. And all the multitude that had gone down from the city into the abyss came up on the ladder of the luminous cross; but there remained below the proconsul, and the viper which they worshipped. And when the multitude had come up, having looked upon Philip hanging head downwards, they lamented with a great lamentation at the lawless action which they had done. And they also saw Bartholomew, and Mariamme having her former appearance. And, behold, the Lord went up into the heavens in the sight of Philip, and Bartholomew and Mariamme, and Stachys, and all the unbelieving people, and silently they glorified God in fear and trembling. And all the multitudes cried out, saying: He alone is God, whom these men proclaim in truth; He alone is God, who sent these men for our salvation. Let us therefore truly repent for our great error, because we are by no means worthy of everlasting life. Now we believe, because we have seen great wonders, because the Saviour has brought us up from the abyss. And they all fell upon their face, and adored Philip, and entreated him, ready to flee: Do not do another miracle, and again send us away into the abyss. And they prayed that they might become worthy of the appearing of Christ.

And Philip, yet hanging, addressed them, and said: Hear and learn how great are the powers of my God, remembering what you have seen below, and how your city has been overturned, with the exception of the house which received me; and now the sweetness of my God has brought you up out of the abyss, and I am obliged to walk round paradise for forty days on your account, because I was enraged against you into requiting you. And this commandment alone I have not kept, in that I did not give you good in return for evil. But I say unto you, From this time forth, in the goodness of God, reject the evil, that you may become worthy of the thanksgiving of the Lord.

And some of the faithful ran up to take down Philip, and take off him the iron grapnels, and the hooks out of his ankles. But Philip said: Do not, my children, do not come near me on account of this, for thus shall be my end. Listen to me, ye who have been enlightened in the Lord, that I came to this city, not to make any merchandise, or do any other thing; but I have been destined to go out of my body in this city in the case in which you see me. Grieve not, then, that I am hanging thus; for I bear the stamp of the first man, who was brought to the earth head downwards, and again, through the wood of the cross brought to life out of the death of the transgression. And now I accomplish that which hath been enjoined upon me; for the Lord said to me, Unless you shall make that of you which is down to be up, and that which is on the left to be on the right, you shall not enter into my kingdom. Be ye not therefore likened to the unchanged type, for all the world has been changed, and every soul dwelling in a body is in forgetfulness of heavenly things; but let not us possessing the glory of the heavenly seek that which is without, which is the body and the house of slavery. Be not unbelieving, but believing, and forgive each other's faults. Behold, I hang six days, and I have blame from the true Judge, because I altogether requited you evil, and put a stumbling-block in the way of my rectitude. And now I am going up on high; be not sorrowful, but rather rejoice, because I am leaving this dwelling-place, my body, having escaped from the corruption of the dragon, who punishes every soul that is in sins.

And Philip, having looked round upon the multitudes, said: O ye who have come up out of the dead from Hades, and the swallowing up of the abyss,—and the luminous cross led you up on high, through the goodness of the Father, and the Son, and the Holy Ghost,—He being God became man, having been made flesh out of the Virgin Mary, immortal, abiding in flesh; and having died, He raised the dead, having had pity on mankind, having taken away the sting of sin. He was great, and became small for our sake, until He should enlarge the small, and bring them into His greatness. And He it is who has sweetness; and they spat upon Him, giving Him gall to drink, in order that He might make those who were bitter against Him to taste of His sweetness. Cleave then to Him, and do not forsake Him, for He is our life to everlasting.

And when Philip had finished this announcement, he says to them, Loose Bartholomew; and having gone up, they loosed him. And after loosing him, Philip says to him: Bartholomew, my brother in the Lord, thou knowest that the Lord has sent thee with me to this city, and thou hast shared with me in all the dangers with our sister Mariamme; but I know that the going forth from thy body has been appointed in Lycaonia, and it has been decreed to Mariamme to go forth from the body in the river Jordan. Now therefore I command you, that when I have gone forth from my body, you shall build a church in this place; and let the leopard and the kid of the goats come into the church, for a sign to those that believe; and let Nicanora provide for them until they shall go forth from the body; and when they shall have gone forth, bury them by the gate of the church. And lay your peace upon the house of Stachys, as Christ laid His peace on this city. And let all the virgins who believe stand in that house each day, watching over the sick, walking two and two; but let them have no communication with young men, that Satan may not tempt them: for he is a creeping serpent, and he caused Adam by means of Eve to slip into death. Let it not be so again in this time as in the case of Eve. But do thou, O Bartholomew, look to them well: and thou shalt give these injunctions to Stachys, and appoint him bishop. Do not entrust the place of the bishopric to a young man, that the Gospel of Christ may not be brought to shame; and let every one that teacheth have his works equal to his words. But I am going to the Lord, and take my body and prepare it for burial with Syriac sheets of paper; and do not put round me flaxen cloth, because the body of my Lord was wrapped in linen. And having prepared my body for burial in the sheets of paper, bind it tight with papyrus reeds, and bury it in the church; and pray for me forty days, in order that the Lord may forgive me the transgression wherein I transgressed, in requiting those who did evil to me. See, O Bartholomew, where my blood shall drop upon the earth, a plant shall spring up from my blood, and shall become a vine, and shall produce fruit of a bunch of grapes; and having taken the cluster, press it into the cup; and having partaken of it on the third day, send up on high the Amen, in order that the offering may be complete. And Philip, having said these things, prayed thus: O Lord Jesus Christ, Father of the ages, King of the light, who hast made us wise in Thy wisdom, and hast given us Thine understanding, and hast bestowed upon us the counsel of Thy goodness, who hast never at any time left us, Thou art He who taketh away the disease of those who flee to Thee for refuge; Thou art the Son of the living God, who hast given us Thy presence of wisdom, who hast given us signs and wonders, and hast turned those who have gone astray; who crownest those who overcome the adversary, Thou excellent Judge. Come now, Jesus, and give me the everlasting crown of victory against every adverse dominion and power, and do not let their dark air hide me when I shall cross the waters of fire and all the abyss. O my Lord Jesus Christ, let not the enemy have ground to accuse me at Thy tribunal: but put on me Thy glorious robe, Thy seal of light that ever shines, until I shall pass by all the powers of the world, and the wicked dragon that lieth in wait for us. Now therefore, my Lord Jesus Christ, make me to meet Thee in the air, having forgiven me the recompense which I recompensed to my enemies; and transform the form of my body into angelic glory, and give me rest in Thy blessedness; and let me receive the promise from Thee which Thou hast promised to Thy saints to everlasting. And having thus spoken, Philip gave up the ghost, while all the multitudes were looking upon him, and weeping, and saying: The life of this spirit has been accomplished in peace. And they said the Amen.

And Bartholomew and Mariamme took down his body, and did as Philip had commanded them, and buried it in that place. And there was straightway a voice out of the heavens: Philip the apostle has been crowned with an incorruptible crown by Jesus Christ, the Judge of the contest. And all shouted out the Amen.

And after the three days the plant of the vine sprouted up where the blood of the holy Philip had dropped. And they did all that had been commanded them by him, offering an offering for forty days, praying without ceasing. And they built the church in that place, having appointed Stachys bishop in the church. And Nicanora and all the faithful assembled, and did not cease, all of them, glorifying God on account of the wonders that had happened among them. And all the city believed in the name of Jesus. And Bartholomew commanded Stachys to baptize those who believed into the name of the Father, and the Son, and the Holy Ghost.

And after the forty days, the Saviour, having appeared in the form of Philip, said to Bartholomew and Mariamme: My beloved brethren, do you wish to rest in the rest of God? Paradise has been opened to me, and I have entered into the glory of Jesus. Go away to the place appointed for you; for the plant that has been set apart and planted in this city shall bear excellent fruit. Having therefore saluted the brethren, and prayed for each of them, they departed from the city of Ophioryma, the Hierapolis of Asia; and Bartholomew departed into Lycaonia, and Mariamme proceeded to the Jordan; and Stachys and those with him remained, maintaining the church in Christ Jesus our Lord, to whom be glory and strength for ever and ever. Amen.

CHAPTER 2

Acts of Saint Philip the Apostle When He Went to Upper Hellas.

And it came to pass in those days, when Philip entered into the city of Athens called Hellas, there assembled to him three hundred philosophers, saying: Let us go and see what his wisdom is; for they say about the wise men of Asia, that their wisdom is great. For they thought that Philip was a philosopher, since he was travelling in the dress of a recluse; and they did not know that he was an apostle of Christ. For the dress which Jesus gave to His disciples was a mantle only, and a linen cloth. Thus, then, Philip was going about. On this account, therefore, when the philosophers of Hellas saw him, they were afraid. They assembled therefore into one place, and said to each other: Come, let us look into our books, lest somehow this stranger overcome us, and put us to shame.

And having done so, they came together to the same place, and say to Philip: We have doctrines of our fathers in which we are pleased, seeking after knowledge; but if thou hast anything new, O stranger, show it to us without envy boldly: for we have need of nothing else, but only to hear something new.

And Philip answering, said to them: O philosophers of Hellas, if you wish to hear some new thing, and are desirous of something new, you ought to throw away from you the disposition of the old man; as my Lord said, It is impossible to put new wine into old bottles, since the bottle is burst, and the wine spilled, and the bottle destroyed. But they put new wine into fresh bottles, so that both may be preserved. And these things the Lord said in parables, teaching us in His holy wisdom, that many will love the new wine, not having a bottle fresh and new. And I love you, O men of Hellas, and I congratulate you for having said, We love something new. For instruction really new and fresh my Lord has brought into the world, in order that He might sweep away all worldly instruction.

The philosophers say: Who is it that thou callest thy Lord? Philip says: My Lord is Jesus in heaven. And they said to him: Show him to our comprehension without envy, that we also may believe in him. And Philip said: He with whom I am about to make you acquainted as Lord, is above every name; there is no other. And this only I say: As you have said, Do not refuse us through envy, let it not be that I should refuse you; but rather in great exultation and in great joy I have to reveal to you that name, for I have no other work in this world than this proclamation. For when my Lord came into this world, He chose us, being twelve in number, having filled us with the Holy Spirit; from His light He made us know who He was, and commanded us to preach all salvation through Him, because there is no other name named out of heaven than this. On this account I have come to you, to make you fully assured, not in word only, but also in the showing forth of wonderful works in the name of our Lord Jesus Christ. And when the philosophers heard this, they say to Philip: This name that has been heard of by us from thee we have never found in the books of our fathers; now, therefore, how can we know about thy words? And moreover, in addition, they say to him: Allow us three days, that we may consult with each other about this name; for we lay no little stress upon this—to apostatize from our fathers' religion. Philip therefore says to them: Consult as you wish; for there is no deceit in the matter.

And the three hundred philosophers having assembled, spoke with each other, saying: You know that this man has brought a strange philosophy, and the words spoken by him bring us to distraction. What, then, shall we do about him, or about the name of him who is called Jesus, the king of the ages, whom he speaks of? And moreover they say to each other: Assuredly we cannot reason with him, but the high priest of the Jews can. If therefore it seem good, let us send to him, in order that he may stand up to this stranger, and that we may learn accurately the name that is preached. They wrote therefore to Jerusalem after this manner:—The philosophers of Hellas to Ananias, the great high priest of the Jews in Jerusalem. There being between thee and us at all times great…as thou knowest that we Athenians are searchers after truth. A certain foreigner has come to Hellas, Philip by name; and, in a word, he has disturbed us exceedingly, both by words and by extraordinary miracles, and he introduces a glorious name, Jesus, professing himself to be his disciple. And he does also wonders of which we write to you, in that he has cast out demons that have been long in men, and makes the deaf hear, the blind see; and what is more wonderful—which also we should have first mentioned—he has raised up men after they were dead, that have fairly completed the number of their days. And the fame of him has gone abroad into all Hellas and Macedonia; and there are many coming to him from the cities round about, bringing those who are ill with various diseases, and he heals them all through the name of Jesus. On this account, therefore, come to us without any reluctance, that thou thyself mayst announce to us what Jesus, this name which he teaches, means. For on this account also we have sent this letter to thee, O high priest. And when he had read, he was filled with great wrath, and rent his clothes, and said: Has that deceiver gone even to Athens, among the philosophers, to lead them astray? And the Mansemat—that is, Satan—entered into Ananias unawares, and filled him with anger and rage; and he said: If I allow that Philip himself, and those with him, to live, the law will be entirely destroyed, and their teaching will likely fill the whole earth. And the high priest went into his own house, and the teachers of the law, and the Pharisees; and they consulted with each other, saying: What shall we do about these things? And they say to the high priest Ananias: Stand up and arm thyself, and five hundred able men out of the people, and go away to Athens, and by all means kill Philip, and thus thou shalt overturn his teaching.

And having put on the high priest's robe, he came to Hellas in great pomp, with the five hundred men. And Philip was in the house of a certain chief man of the city, with the brethren who had believed. And the high priest and those with him, and the three hundred philosophers, went up to the gateway of the house where Philip was; and it was told Philip that they were outside. And he rose up and went out. And when the high priest saw him, he says to him: O Philip, sorcerer and magician, for I know thee, that in Jerusalem thy master the deceiver called thee Son of Thunder. Was not the whole of Judæa sufficient for you, but you have come here also to deceive men who are searchers after wisdom? And Philip said: Would that, O Ananias, thy covering of unbelief were taken away from thy heart, that thou mightst know my words, and from them learn whether I am a deceiver, or thou!

Ananias having heard this, said to Philip: I shall give answer to all. And Philip said: Speak. The high priest says: O men of Hellas, this Philip believes in a man called Jesus, who was born among us, who also taught this heresy, and destroyed the law and the temple, and brought to nought the purification through Moses, and the new moons, because he says, These have not been commanded by God. And when we saw that he thus destroyed the law, we stood up against him, and crucified him, that his teaching might not be fulfilled. For many changes were brought in by him; and he gave an evil testimony, for he ate all things in common, and mixed with blood, after the manner of the Gentiles. And having given him up, we put him to death, and buried him in a tomb; and these disciples of his having stolen him, have proclaimed everywhere that he has risen from the dead, and have led astray a great multitude by professing that he is at the right hand of God in heaven. But now these men, themselves having the circumcision as we also have, have not followed it, since they began to do many deeds of power in Jerusalem through the name of Jesus; and having been cast out of Jerusalem, they go about the world, and deceive all men by the magic of that Jesus, as also now this Philip has come to you to deceive you by the same means. But I shall carry him away with myself to Jerusalem, because Archelaus the king is also searching for him to kill him.

And when the multitude standing round heard this, those indeed who had been confirmed in the faith were not shaken nor made to waver; for they knew that Philip would conquer in the glory of Jesus. Philip therefore stated his case in the power of Christ with great boldness, exulting and saying: I, O men of Athens, and those of you who are philosophers, have come to you, not to teach you with words, but by the showing forth of miracles; and in part you have quickly seen the things that have come to pass through me, in that name by which the high priest himself is cast off. For, behold, I shall cry to my God, and teach you, and you will prove the words of both.

The high priest having heard this, ran to Philip, wishing to scourge him, and that same hour his whole hand was dried up, and his eyes were blinded; and in like manner also the five hundred who were with him were also themselves blinded. And they reviled and cursed the high priest, saying: Coming out of Jerusalem we said to thee, Refrain; for, being men, we cannot fight against God. But we entreat thee, O Philip, apostle of the God Jesus, give us the light that is through him, that we also may truly be his slaves.

And Philip, having seen what had come to pass, said: O weak nature! which has thrown itself upon us, but straightway has been brought down low into itself; O bitter sea! which rouses its waves against us, and thinks to cast us out, but which by itself lulls its waves to rest. Now therefore, O our good steward Jesus, the holy light, Thou hast not overlooked us who are all together crying up to Thee in all good works, but hast come to finish them through us. Now therefore come, Lord Jesus; reprove the folly of these men.

The high priest says to Philip: Dost thou then think to turn us away from the traditions of our fathers, and the God of the desert, and Moses; and dost thou imagine that thou wilt make us followers of Jesus the Nazarene? Then Philip says to him: Behold, I shall pray to my God to come and manifest Himself before thee and the five hundred, and before all here; for perhaps thou wilt change thy mind, and believe. But if even to the end thou remain in unbelief, there is coming upon thee an extraordinary thing, which shall be spoken of to generations of generations—that also thou shalt go down alive, down into Hades, before the face of all seeing thee, because thou yet abidest in unbelief, because also thou seekest to turn away this multitude from the true life. And Philip prayed, saying: O holy Father of the holy Son Jesus Christ, who hast granted to me to believe in Him, send Thy beloved Son Jesus Christ to reprove the unbelieving high priest, that Thy name may be glorified in Christ the Beloved.

And while Philip was yet crying out this, suddenly the heavens were opened, and Jesus appeared coming down in most excellent glory, and in lightning; and His face was shining sevenfold more than the sun, and His garments were whiter than snow, so that also all the idols of Athens fell suddenly to the ground. And the people fled in anguish; and the demons dwelling among them cried out: Behold, we also flee because of Him who has appeared to the city, Jesus the Son of God. Then Philip says to the high priest: Hearest thou the demons crying out because of Him who has been seen, and believest thou not in Him who is present that He is Lord of all? The high priest says: I have no other God than the one in the desert. And as Jesus was going up into heaven there happened a very great earthquake, so that the place on which they stood was cleft; and the crowds ran and fell at the feet of the apostle, crying out: Have mercy upon us, O man of God! In like manner also the five hundred men cried out themselves also again: Have mercy upon us, O Philip, that we may know thee, and through thee Jesus the light of life: for we said to this unbelieving high priest, Being sinful men, we cannot fight against God.

Then Philip says: There is no hatred in us, but the grace of Christ will make you receive your sight; but I will make the high priest receive his sight before you, that at this you may the more believe. And a voice out of heaven was brought to Philip: O Philip, son once of thunder, but now of meekness, whatever thou mayst ask of my Father, He shall do for thee. And all the crowd was terror-struck at the voice, for the sound of it was greater than that of thunder. Then Philip says to the high priest: In the name of the power of the voice of my Lord, receive thy sight, Ananias. And immediately he received his sight, and looked round, and said: What is there in the magic of Jesus, that this Philip within a short time has made me blind, and again within a short time has made me receive my sight? Dost thou then, said Philip, believe in Jesus? The high priest says: You do not think, do you, that you can bewitch me, and persuade me? And the five hundred who were with him, having heard that their high priest, having received his sight, was yet unbelieving, said to the bystanders to pray Philip that he should make them receive their sight, that, *said they*, we may cut off this

unbelieving high priest.

And Philip said: Do not avenge yourselves upon the wicked. And he says to the high priest: There will be a certain great sign upon thee. He says to Philip: I know that thou art a sorcerer and a disciple of Jesus: thou dost not bewitch me. And the apostle said to Jesus: Sabarthan, sabathabt, bramanuch, come quickly. And immediately the earth was cleft in the place where Ananias was, and swallowed him up as far as the knees. And Ananias cried out: O great *is the* power of the true witchcraft, because it has cleft the earth, when Philip threatened it in Hebrew, and adjured it; and it holds me even to the knees, and by the heels some hooks as it were drag me downwards, that I may believe in Philip; but he cannot persuade me, for from Jerusalem I know his magic tricks.

And Philip, enraged, said: O earth, lay fast hold of him, even to the navel. And immediately it dragged him down. And he said: The one of my feet underneath is turned into ice, and the other is frightfully hot; but by thy magic, Philip, I will not be overcome. Except, therefore, that I am sore tortured underneath, I do not believe at all. And the crowds wished to stone him. And Philip says: Not so; for this has in the meantime happened, that he has been swallowed up as far as the navel, that the salvation of your souls may be effected, because he would almost have drawn you by his wicked words into unbelief. But if even he repented, I should bring him up out of the earth to the salvation of his soul; but assuredly he is not worthy of salvation. If, then, he remain in unbelief, you shall see him sunk down into the abyss, unless the Lord intends to raise those who are in Hades, that they may confess that Jesus is Lord. For in that day every tongue shall confess that Jesus is Lord, and that there is one glory of the Father, and the Son, with the Holy Spirit for evermore.

And Philip, having said this, extended his right hand, stretching it through the air over the five hundred men in the name of Jesus. And their eyes were opened, and they all praised God with one mouth, saying: We bless Thee, O Christ Jesus, the God of Philip, that thou hast driven the blindness away from us, and hast given us Thy light, the Gospel. And Philip rejoiced exceedingly at their words, because they were thus confirmed in the faith. And after this, Philip, having turned to the high priest, said: Confess thou also in a pure heart that Jesus is Lord, that thou mayst be saved, like those with thee. But the high priest laughed at Philip, and remained in unbelief.

Philip then, seeing that he remained in unbelief, having looked at him, says to the earth: Open thy mouth, and swallow him up as far as his neck in the presence of those who have believed in Christ Jesus. And in the same hour the earth, having opened its mouth, received him as far as the neck. And the multitude communed with each other on account of the wonders that had happened.

A certain chief man of the city came crying out, and saying: O blessed apostle, a certain demon has assailed my son, and cried out, saying to me, Since thou hast allowed a foreigner to come into your city, thou who hast been the first to do away with our worship and our sacrifices, what shall I do for thee, except to kill this thine only begotten son? And after he said this, he strangled my son. Now therefore, I beseech thee, O apostle of Christ, do not allow my joy to be turned into sorrow, because I also have believed thy words.

And the apostle, having heard this, said: I wonder at the activity of the demons, that it is active in every place, and dares to assail those to whose help I have not been able to come, as now they have tried you, wishing to cause you to offend. And he says to the man: Bring me thy son, and I will give him to thee alive, through my Christ. And rejoicing, he ran to bring his son. And when he came near his house, he cried out, saying: My son, I have come to thee to carry thee to the apostle, so that he may present thee to me living. And he ordered his slaves to carry the bed; and his son was twenty-three years old. And when Philip saw him, he was moved; and he turned to the high priest, and said: This has happened as a chance for thee: if, therefore, I shall raise him up, wilt thou henceforth believe? And he says: I know your magic arts, that thou wilt raise him up; but I will not believe thee. And Philip, enraged, said: A curse upon thee! then go down altogether into the abyss before the face of all these. And at the same hour he went down into Hades alive, except that the high priest's robe flew off from him; and because of this, from that day, no one knew what became of the priest's robe. And the apostle turned round and prayed for the boy; and having driven the demon away from him, he raised him up, and set him beside his father alive.

And the multitude having beheld this, cried out: The God of Philip is the only God, who has punished the unbelief of the high priest, and driven away the demon from the young man, and raised him up from the dead. And the five hundred having seen the high priest swallowed up into the abyss, and the other miracles, besought Philip, and he gave them the seal in Christ. And Philip abode in Athens two years; and having founded a church, appointed a bishop and a presbyter, and so went away to Parthia, preaching Christ. To whom be glory for ever. Amen.

CHAPTER 3

Addition to Acts of Philip.

(From a Paris ms.)

And he taught them thus: My brethren, sons of my Father—for you are of my family as to Christ, substance of my city, the Jerusalem above, the delight of my dwelling-place—why have you been taken captive by your enemy the serpent, twisted, crooked, and perverse, to whom God has given neither hands nor feet? And crooked is his going, since he is the son of the wicked one; for his father is death, and his mother corruption, and ruin is in his body. Do not go then into his destruction; for you are in bondage by the unbelief and deception of his son, who is without order, and has no substance; formless, and has no form in the whole creation, either in the heaven or in the earth, or among the fishes that are in the waters. But if you see him, flee from him, since he has no resemblance to men: his dwelling is the abyss, and he walks in darkness. Flee, then, from him, that his venom may not be poured out upon you: if his venom be poured out upon your body, you walk in his wickedness. But remain rather in the true worship, being faithful, reverent, and good, without guile. Flee from Satan the dragon, and remove from you his wicked seed, namely desire, by which he begets disease in the soul, which is the venom of the serpent. For desire is of the serpent from the beginning, and she it is who arms herself against the faithful; for she came forth out of the darkness, and returns to the darkness. You ought therefore, after coming to us, or

rather through us to God, to throw out the venom of the devil from your bodies.

And as the apostle was saying this, behold, Nicanora came forth from her house, and went with her slaves into the house of Stachys. And when she came near the door of the house, behold, Mariamme spoke to her in the Syriac language: Helikomaei, kosma, etaa, mariacha. And she explained her words, saying: O daughter of the Spirit, thou art my lady, who hast been given in pledge to the serpent; but I have come to deliver thee: I shall break thy bonds, and cut them from their root. Behold, the Deliverer that frees thee has come: behold, the Sun of righteousness has risen to enlighten thee.

And when she was thus speaking, the gloomy tyrant came running and panting. And Nicanora, who was before the door, heard this, and took courage before them all, crying out and saying: I am a Hebrew, a daughter of the Hebrews; speak with me in the language of my fathers, because I have heard your preaching, and have been cured of this my disease. I reverence and glorify the goodness of God, in that He hath made you to be utterly spoiled in this earth. And when she said this, the tyrant came, and took hold of her garments, and said: O Nicanora, did I not leave thee lying on the bed from thy disease? Whence, then, hast thou found this power and strength, so as to be able to come to these magicians? Unless, then, thou tell who is the healer, I shall punish thee most severely. And Nicanora answered, and said: O rearer of tyrants, cast away from thyself this tyranny, and forget thy wicked works, and abandon this temporary life, and put away vainglory, because it passes like a shadow: seek rather what is everlasting, and take away from thyself the beastly and impious work of base desire, and reject vain intercourse, which is the husbandry of death, the dark prison; and overturn the middle wall of corruption, and prepare for thyself a life chaste and spotless, that we may altogether live in sanctity. If, then, thou wishest me to remain with thee, I will live with thee in continence.

And when the tyrant heard these words, he seized her by the hair of the head, and dragged her along, kicking her, and saying: It would be better for thee to be put to death by my sword, than to be seen with these foreign magicians and deceivers. I will punish thee, therefore, and put to death those who have deceived thee. And he turned in a rage to the executioners who followed him, and said: Bring me these impostors. And the executioners ran to the house of Stachys, and laid hold of Philip, and Bartholomew, and Mariamme, with the leopard and the kid of the goats, and dragged them along, and brought them.

When the tyrant saw them, he gnashed his teeth against them, and said: Drag along these magicians and deceivers that have deceived many souls of women by saying, We are worshippers of God. And he caused thongs to be brought, and bound their feet. And he ordered them to be dragged along from the gate as far as the temple. And great multitudes came together to that place. And they wondered exceedingly at the leopard and the kid; for they were speaking like men, and some of the multitude believed the words of the apostles.

And the priests said to the tyrant: These men are magicians. And when he heard that, he burned with rage, and was filled with anger; and he ordered Philip, and Bartholomew, and Mariamne to be stripped, saying: Search them. Perhaps you will find their sorcery. And the executioners stripped them, and laid hold of Mariamne, and dragged her along, saying: Uncover her, that they may learn that it is a woman who follows them. And he ordered to bring clubs and strong cords; and after piercing Philip's ankles they brought hooks, and put the cords through his ankles, and hung him head downwards on a tree that was before the door of the temple; and they fixed pegs into the temple wall, and left him. And after binding Bartholomew hand and foot, they extended him naked on the wall; and when they had stripped Mariamne, the appearance of her body was changed, and became a glass chest filled with light, and they could not come near her.

And Philip spoke with Bartholomew in Hebrew: Where is John to-day, in the day of our need? for behold, we are being delivered from our bodies. And they have laid hands on Mariamne beyond what is seemly, and they have scourged the leopard and the kid of the goats, and have set fire to the house of Stachys, because he took us in. Let us therefore speak, that fire may come down from heaven and burn them up.

And as Philip was thus speaking, behold, John came into the city, and walked about the street, and asked those in the city: What is the commotion, and who are these men, and why are they punished? And they say to him: Art thou not of this city? And dost thou not know about these men, how they disturbed our houses, and the whole city? Moreover, they have even persuaded our wives to go away from us on the pretence of religion, proclaiming a foreign name, viz. Christ's; and they have also shut our temples by the sorcery they have, and they have put to death the serpents that are in the city by foreign names that we have never known. And they have fixed their abode in the house of Stachys the blind man, whom they made to recover his sight through the spittle of a woman who accompanies them; and it is perhaps she who has all the sorcery: and there accompany them a leopard and a kid, speaking like men. But if ever you have seen such doings, you will not be put about by them. And John answered, and said to them: Show me them. And they brought him to the temple where Philip was hanging. And when Philip saw John, he said to Bartholomew: O my brother, behold the son of Barega—that is the living water—has come. And John saw Philip hanging head down, tied by his ankles; and saw Bartholomew also bound to the temple wall.

And he said to the men of the city: O children of the serpent, how great is your folly! for the way of deceit has deceived you, the wicked dragon breathing has breathed upon you: why do you punish these men for saying the serpent is your enemy?

And when they heard these words from John, they laid their hands upon him, saying: We called thee our fellow-citizen, but now thy speech has made thee manifest that thou also art in communion with them. Thou also, therefore, shalt be put to the same death as they, for the priests have decided thus: Let us drain out their blood as they hang head downward, and mix it with wine, and offer it to the viper.

And when they were thus speaking, behold, Mariamne rose up from the place in which she was, and came back to her former appearance.

And the priests reached forth their hands towards John, wishing to lay hold of him, and they could not. Then Philip with Bartholomew said to John: Where is Jesus, who enjoins upon us not to take into our own hands vengeance on those that torture us? for after this I will not endure them. And Philip spoke in Hebrew, and said: My Father Uthael, i.e., O Christ, Father of majesty, whose name all the ages fear, who art powerful, and the power of the universe, whose name goes forth in lordship, Eloa: Blessed art Thou to the ages; Thou whom dominions and powers fear, trembling before Thy face; King of honour! Father of majesty! whose name has gone forth to the wild beasts of the desert, and they have become quiet because of Thee, and through Thee the serpents have departed from us: Hear us before we ask. Thou who seest us before we call, who knowest our thoughts, the All-surveyor of all, who sends forth from Himself unnumbered compassions; let the abyss open its mouth, and swallow up these godless persons who will not accept the word of Thy truth.

And in that very hour the abyss opened its mouth, and all that place was violently shaken, from the proconsul to all the multitude along with the priests; and they were all sunk down. And the places where the apostles and all who were with them were remained unshaken, and the house of Stachys, and Nicanora the tyrant's wife, and the twenty-four wives who fled from their husbands, and the forty virgins who had not known men. These alone did not go down into the abyss, because they had become servants, and had received the word of God, and His seal; but all the rest of the city were swallowed down into the abyss.

And the Saviour having appeared at that hour, said to Philip: Who is it that has put his hand to the plough, and has turned back from making the furrow straight? or who gives his light to others, and himself remains sitting in darkness? or who dwells in the dirt, and leaves his dwelling-place to strangers? or who lays down his garment, and goes out in the days of winter naked? or what slave that has done his master's service, shall not be called by him to supper? or who runs with zeal in the racecourse, and does not get the prize? Philip, behold my bridal chamber is ready, and blessed is he who has his own shining garment; for he it is who gets the crown of joy upon his head. Behold, the supper is ready, and blessed is he who is called by the bridegroom. Great is the harvest of the field; blessed is the able workman.

And when Philip heard these words from the Saviour, he answered and said to him: Thou didst give us leave, O Jesus of Nazareth, and dost Thou not enjoin us to smite those who do not wish Thee to reign over them? But this we know, that Thy name has not been proclaimed in all the world, and Thou hast sent us to this city. And I did not intend to come into this city, and Thou didst send me, after giving me Thy true commandment, that I should drive away all deceit, and bring to nothing every idol and demon, and all the power of the unclean one. And when I came here, the demons fled from our faces through Thy name, and the dragons and the serpents withered away, but these men did not take to themselves Thy true light; and for this reason I resolved to bring them low, according to their folly.

And the Saviour said: O Philip, since thou hast forsaken this commandment of mine, not to render evil for evil, for this reason thou shalt be debarred in the next world for forty years from being in the place of my promise: besides, this is the end of thy departure from the body in this place; and Bartholomew has his lot in Lycaonia, and shall be crucified there; and Mariamne shall lay down her body in the river Jordan.

And the Saviour turned and stretched out His hand, and made the sign of the cross in the air; and it was full of light, and had its form after the likeness of a ladder. And all the multitude of the men of the city who had gone down into the abyss came up upon the ladder of the cross of light and none of them remained in the abyss, but only the tyrant and the priests, and the viper which they worshipped. And when the multitudes came up from the abyss, they looked and saw Philip hanging head down, and Bartholomew upon the wall of the temple, and they also found Mariamne in her first shape. And the Saviour went up into heaven in the sight of Philip and Bartholomew and Mariamne, and the leopard and the kid of the goats, and Nicanora and Stachys; and they all with a loud voice glorified God with fear and trembling, crying out: There is one God who has sent us His salvation, whose name these men proclaim: we repent therefore of the error in which we were before yesterday, not being worthy of eternal life; and we believe, having seen the wonderful things that have come to pass through us. And some of them threw themselves on their faces, and worshipped the apostles; and others made ready to flee, saying: There may be another earthquake like the one that has just happened.

And stretching out his hands, the Apostle Philip, hanging head down, said: Men of the city, hear these words which I am going to say to you, hanging head down. Ye have learned how great are the powers of God, and the wonders which you saw when your city was destroyed by the earthquake which came upon it. And this was manifest to you, that the house of Stachys was not destroyed and that he did not go down into the abyss, because he believed on the true God, and received us His servants. And I, having fulfilled all the will of my God, am His debtor for what I requited to him that did evil to me.

And some of those who had been baptized ran to loose Philip hanging head down. And he answered and said to them: My brethren,... those who are virgins in the members of their flesh and commit fornication in their hearts, and the fornication of their eyes, shall abound like the deluge. And they grow immoderate from listening to persuasive pleasures, forgetting the God of the knowledge of the Gospel; and their hearts are full of arrogance, eating and drinking in their worship, forgetting the holy commandment, and despising it. That generation is turned aside; but blessed is he that retires into his retreat, for he shall obtain rest in his departure. Knowest thou not, Bartholomew, that the word of our Lord is true life and knowledge? for the Lord said to us in His teaching, Every one who shall look upon a woman, and lust after her in his heart, has completed adultery. And on this account our brother Peter fled from every place in which a woman was, and yet there was scandal on account of his own daughter; and he prayed to the Lord, and she had paralysis of her side, that she might not be deceived. Thou seest, brother, that the sight of the eyes brings gainsaying, and the beginning of sin, as it is written, She looked, and saw the tree, that it was pleasing to her eyes, and good for food, and she was deceived. Let the hearing, then, of the virgins be holy; and in their going out let them walk two and two, for many are the wiles of the enemy. Let their walk and conversation be well ordered, that they may be saved; but if not, let their fruit be common.

My brother Bartholomew, give these promises to Stachys, and appoint him ruler and bishop in the Church, that he may be like thee, teaching well. Do not entrust the office to a man too young: appoint not such a one to the chair of the teachers, lest thou profane the witness of Christ. For he that teaches should have his works corresponding to his words, that the word may be ready on every occasion in its own glory. But I am being released from my body, hanging head down. Take, then, my body, and prepare it for burial in Syrian paper, and do not put about it linen cloth, since they put it upon the body of our Lord, and wrap it close in paper and papyrus, and put it in the vestibule of the holy church. And pray over me for forty days, that God may forgive the transgression which I did, in that I requited evil to him that did evil to me, and there may not be for me in the world to come the forty years.

And after thus speaking, Philip prayed, saying: My Lord Jesus Christ, Father of the ages, King of all light, who makest us wise in Thy wisdom, who hast given us the exalted knowledge, who hast graciously conferred upon us the counsel of Thy goodness, who hast never departed from us; Thou who takest away disease from those who take refuge in Thee; Thou who hast given us the Word, to turn unto Thee those who have been led astray; Thou who hast given us signs and wonders on behalf of those of little faith; Thou who presentest the crown to those who have conquered; Thou who art the judge of the games, who hast given us the crown of joy, who speakest with us, that we may be able to withstand those that hurt us; Thou art He who sows and reaps, and completes, and increases, and vivifies all Thine own servants: reproaches and threats are to us help and power through those who turn to Thee through us, who are Thy servants. Come, Lord, and give me the crown of victory in the presence of men. Let not their dark air envelope me, nor their smoke burn the shape of my soul, that I may cross the waters of the abyss, and not sink in them. My Lord Jesus Christ, let not the enemy find anything that he can bring against me in the presence of Thee, the true Judge, but clothe me in Thy shining robe, and...(The rest is wanting.)

ACTS OF THADDÆUS

Lebbæus, who also is Thaddæus, was of the city of Edessa—and it is the metropolis of Osroene, in the interior of the Armenosyrians—an Hebrew by race, accomplished and most learned in the divine writings. He came to Jerusalem to worship in the days of John the Baptist; and having heard his preaching and seen his angelic life, he was baptized, and his name was called Thaddæus. And having seen the appearing of Christ, and His teaching, and His wonderful works, he followed Him, and became His disciple; and He chose him as one of the twelve, the tenth apostle according to the Evangelists Matthew and Mark.

In those times there was a governor of the city of Edessa, Abgarus by name. And there having gone abroad the fame of Christ, of the wonders which He did, and of His teaching, Abgarus having heard of it, was astonished, and desired to see Christ, and could not leave his city and government. And about the days of the Passion and the plots of the Jews, Abgarus, being seized by an incurable disease, sent a letter to Christ by Ananias the courier, to the following effect:—To Jesus called Christ, Abgarus the governor of the country of the Edessenes, an unworthy slave. The multitude of the wonders done by thee has been heard of by me, that thou healest the blind, the lame, and the paralytic, and curest all the demoniacs; and on this account I entreat thy goodness to come even to us, and escape from the plottings of the wicked Jews, which through envy they set in motion against thee. My city is small, but large enough for both. Abgarus enjoined Ananias to take accurate account of Christ, of what appearance He was, and His stature, and His hair, and in a word everything.

And Ananias, having gone and given the letter, was carefully looking at Christ, but was unable to fix Him in his mind. And He knew as knowing the heart, and asked to wash Himself; and a towel was given Him; and when He had washed Himself, He wiped His face with it. And His image having been imprinted upon the linen, He gave it to Ananias, saying: Give this, and take back this message, to him that sent thee: Peace to thee and thy city! For because of this I am come, to suffer for the world, and to rise again, and to raise up the forefathers. And after I have been taken up into the heavens I shall send thee my disciple Thaddæus, who shall enlighten thee, and guide thee into all the truth, both thee and thy city.

And having received Ananias, and fallen down and adored the likeness, Abgarus was cured of his disease before Thaddæus came.

And after the passion, and the resurrection, and the ascension, Thaddæus went to Abgarus; and having found him in health, he gave him an account of the incarnation of Christ, and baptized him, with all his house. And having instructed great multitudes, both of Hebrews and Greeks, Syrians and Armenians, he baptized them in the name of the Father, and Son, and Holy Spirit, having anointed them with the holy perfume; and he communicated to them of the undefiled mysteries of the sacred body and blood of our Lord Jesus Christ, and delivered to them to keep and observe the law of Moses, and to give close heed to the things that had been said by the apostles in Jerusalem. For year by year they came together to the passover, and again he imparted to them the Holy Spirit.

And Thaddæus along with Abgarus destroyed idol-temples and built churches; ordained as bishop one of his disciples, and presbyters, and deacons, and gave them the rule of the psalmody and the holy liturgy. And having left them, he went to the city of Amis, great metropolis of the Mesechaldeans and Syrians, that is, of Mesopotamia-Syria, beside the river Tigris. And he having gone into the synagogue of the Jews along with his disciples on the Sabbath-day, after the reading of the law the high priest said to Thaddæus and his disciples: Men, whence are you? and why are you here?

And Thaddæus said: No doubt you have heard of what has taken place in Jerusalem about Jesus Christ, and we are His disciples, and witnesses of the wonderful things which He did and taught, and how through hatred the chief priests delivered Him to Pilate the procurator of Judæa. And Pilate, having examined Him and found no case, wished to let Him go; but they cried out, If thou let him go, thou art not Cæsar's friend, because he proclaims himself king. And he being afraid, washed his hands in the sight of the multitude, and said, I am innocent of the blood of this man; see ye to it. And the chief priests answered and said, His blood be upon us and our children. And Pilate gave him up to them. And they took Him, and spit upon Him, with the soldiers, and made a great mock of Him, and crucified Him, and laid Him in the tomb, and secured it well, having also set guards upon Him. And on the third day before dawn He rose, leaving His burial-clothes in the tomb. And He was seen first by His mother and other women, and by Peter and John first of my fellow disciples, and thereafter to us the twelve, who ate and drank with Him after His resurrection for many days. And He sent us in His name to proclaim repentance and remission of sins to all the nations, that those who were baptized, having had the kingdom of the heavens preached to them, would rise up incorruptible at the end of this age; and He gave us power to expel demons, and heal every disease and every malady, and raise the dead.

And the multitudes having heard this, brought together their sick and demoniacs. And Thaddæus, having gone forth along with his disciples, laid his hand upon each one of them, and healed them all by calling upon the name of Christ. And the demoniacs were healed before Thaddæus came near them, the spirits going out of them. And for many days the people ran together from different places, and beheld what was done by Thaddæus. And hearing his teaching, many believed, and were baptized, confessing their sins.

Having therefore remained with them for five years, he built a church; and having appointed as bishop one of his disciples, and presbyters, and deacons, and prayed for them, he went away, going round the cities of Syria, and teaching, and healing all the sick; whence he brought many cities and countries to Christ through His teaching. Teaching, therefore, and evangelizing along with the disciples, and healing the sick, he went to Berytus, a city of Phœnicia by the sea; and there, having taught and enlightened many, he fell asleep on the twenty-first of the month of August. And the disciples having come together, buried him with great honour; and many sick were healed, and they gave glory to the Father, and the Son, and the Holy Spirit, for ever and ever. Amen.

THE HISTORY OF JOSEPH THE CARPENTER

In the name of God, of one essence and three persons. The History of the death of our father, the holy old man, Joseph the carpenter.

May his blessings and prayers preserve us all, O brethren! Amen.

His whole life was one hundred and eleven years, and his departure from this world happened on the twenty-sixth of the month Abib, which answers to the month Ab. May his prayer preserve us! Amen. And, indeed, it was our Lord Jesus Christ Himself who related this history to His holy disciples on the Mount of Olives, and all Joseph's labour, and the end of his days. And the holy apostles have preserved this conversation, and have left it written down in the library at Jerusalem. May their prayers preserve us! Amen.

1. It happened one day, when the Saviour, our Master, God, and Saviour Jesus Christ, was sitting along with His disciples, and they were all assembled on the Mount of Olives, that He said to them: O my brethren and friends, sons of the Father who has chosen you from all men, you know that I have often told you that I must be crucified, and must die for the salvation of Adam and his posterity, and that I shall rise from the dead. Now I shall commit to you the doctrine of the holy gospel formerly announced to you, that you may declare it throughout the whole world. And I shall endow you with power from on high, and fill you with the Holy Spirit. And you shall declare to all nations repentance and remission of sins. For a single cup of water, if a man shall find it in the world to come, is greater and better than all the wealth of this whole world. And as much ground as one foot can occupy in the house of my Father, is greater and more excellent than all the riches of the earth. Yea, a single hour in the joyful dwelling of the pious is more blessed and more precious than a thousand years among sinners: inasmuch as their weeping and lamentation shall not come to an end, and their tears shall not cease, nor shall they find for themselves consolation and repose at any time for ever. And now, O my honoured members, go declare to all nations, tell them, and say to them: Verily the Saviour diligently inquires into the inheritance which is due, and is the administrator of justice. And the angels will cast down their enemies, and will fight for them in the day of conflict. And He will examine every single foolish and idle word which men speak, and they shall give an account of it. For as no one shall escape death, so also the works of every man shall be laid open on the day of judgment, whether they have been good or evil. Tell them also this word which I have said to you to-day: Let not the strong man glory in his strength, nor the rich man in his riches; but let him who wishes to glory, glory in the Lord.

2. There was a man whose name was Joseph, sprung from a family of Bethlehem, a town of Judah, and the city of King David. This same man, being well furnished with wisdom and learning, was made a priest in the temple of the Lord. He was, besides, skilful in his trade, which was that of a carpenter; and after the manner of all men, he married a wife. Moreover, he begot for himself sons and daughters, four sons, namely, and two daughters. Now these are their names—Judas, Justus, James, and Simon. The names of the two daughters were Assia and Lydia. At length the wife of righteous Joseph, a woman intent on the divine glory in all her works, departed this life. But Joseph, that righteous man, my father after the flesh, and the spouse of my mother Mary, went away with his sons to his trade, practising the art of a carpenter.

3. Now when righteous Joseph became a widower, my mother Mary, blessed, holy, and pure, was already twelve years old. For her parents offered her in the temple when she was three years of age, and she remained in the temple of the Lord nine years. Then when the priests saw that the virgin, holy and God-fearing, was growing up, they spoke to each other, saying: Let us search out a man, righteous and pious, to whom Mary may be entrusted until the time of her marriage; lest, if she remain in the temple, it happen to her as is wont to happen to women, and lest on that account we sin, and God be angry with us.

4. Therefore they immediately sent out, and assembled twelve old men of the tribe of Judah. And they wrote down the names of the twelve tribes of Israel. And the lot fell upon the pious old man, righteous Joseph. Then the priests answered, and said to my blessed mother: Go with Joseph, and be with him till the time of your marriage. Righteous Joseph therefore received my mother, and led her away to his own house. And Mary found James the Less in his father's house, broken-hearted and sad on account of the loss of his mother, and she brought him up. Hence Mary was called the mother of James. Thereafter Joseph left her at home, and went away to the shop where he wrought at his trade of a carpenter. And after the holy virgin had spent two years in his house her age was exactly fourteen years, including the time at which he received her.

5. And I chose her of my own will, with the concurrence of my Father, and the counsel of the Holy Spirit. And I was made flesh of her, by a mystery which transcends the grasp of created reason. And three months after her conception the righteous man Joseph returned from the place where he worked at his trade; and when he found my virgin mother pregnant, he was greatly perplexed, and thought of sending her away secretly. But from fear, and sorrow, and the anguish of his heart, he could endure neither to eat nor drink that day.

6. But at mid-day there appeared to him in a dream the prince of the angels, the holy Gabriel, furnished with a command from my Father; and he said to him: Joseph, son of David, fear not to take Mary as thy wife: for she has conceived of the Holy Spirit; and she will bring forth a son, whose name shall be called Jesus. He it is who shall rule all nations with a rod of iron. Having thus spoken, the angel departed from him. And Joseph rose from his sleep, and did as the angel of the Lord had said to him; and Mary abode with him.

7. Some time after that, there came forth an order from Augustus Cæsar the king, that all the habitable world should be enrolled, each man in his own city. The old man therefore, righteous Joseph, rose up and took the

virgin Mary and came to Bethlehem, because the time of her bringing forth was at hand. Joseph then inscribed his name in the list; for Joseph the son of David, whose spouse Mary was, was of the tribe of Judah. And indeed Mary, my mother, brought me forth in Bethlehem, in a cave near the tomb of Rachel the wife of the patriarch Jacob, the mother of Joseph and Benjamin.

8. But Satan went and told this to Herod the Great, the father of Archelaus. And it was this same Herod who ordered my friend and relative John to be beheaded. Accordingly he searched for me diligently, thinking that my kingdom was to be of this world. But Joseph, that pious old man, was warned of this by a dream. Therefore he rose and took Mary my mother, and I lay in her bosom. Salome also was their fellow-traveller. Having therefore set out from home, he retired into Egypt, and remained there the space of one whole year, until the hatred of Herod passed away.

9. Now Herod died by the worst form of death, atoning for the shedding of the blood of the children whom he wickedly cut off, though there was no sin in them. And that impious tyrant Herod being dead, they returned into the land of Israel, and lived in a city of Galilee which is called Nazareth. And Joseph, going back to his trade of a carpenter, earned his living by the work of his hands; for, as the law of Moses had commanded, he never sought to live for nothing by another's labour.

10. At length, by increasing years, the old man arrived at a very advanced age. He did not, however, labour under any bodily weakness, nor had his sight failed, nor had any tooth perished from his mouth. In mind also, for the whole time of his life, he never wandered; but like a boy he always in his business displayed youthful vigour, and his limbs remained unimpaired, and free from all pain. His life, then, in all, amounted to one hundred and eleven years, his old age being prolonged to the utmost limit.

11. Now Justus and Simeon, the elder sons of Joseph, were married, and had families of their own. Both the daughters were likewise married, and lived in their own houses. So there remained in Joseph's house, Judas and James the Less, and my virgin mother. I moreover dwelt along with them, not otherwise than if I had been one of his sons. But I passed all my life without fault. Mary I called my mother, and Joseph father, and I obeyed them in all that they said; nor did I ever contend against them, but complied with their commands, as other men whom earth produces are wont to do; nor did I at any time arouse their anger, or give any word or answer in opposition to them. On the contrary, I cherished them with great love, like the pupil of my eye.

12. It came to pass, after these things, that the death of that old man, the pious Joseph, and his departure from this world, were approaching, as happens to other men who owe their origin to this earth. And as his body was verging on dissolution, an angel of the Lord informed him that his death was now close at hand. Therefore fear and great perplexity came upon him. So he rose up and went to Jerusalem; and going into the temple of the Lord, he poured out his prayers there before the sanctuary, and said:

13. O God! author of all consolation, God of all compassion, and Lord of the whole human race; God of

my soul, body, and spirit; with supplications I reverence thee, O Lord and my God. If now my days are ended, and the time draws near when I must leave this world, send me, I beseech Thee, the great Michael, the prince of Thy holy angels: let him remain with me, that my wretched soul may depart from this afflicted body without trouble, without terror and impatience. For great fear and intense sadness take hold of all bodies on the day of their death, whether it be man or woman, beast wild or tame, or whatever creeps on the ground or flies in the air. At the last all creatures under heaven in whom is the breath of life are struck with horror, and their souls depart from their bodies with strong fear and great depression. Now therefore, O Lord and my God, let Thy holy angel be present with his help to my soul and body, until they shall be disserved from each other. And let not the face of the angel, appointed my guardian from the day of my birth, be turned away from me; but may he be the companion of my journey even until he bring me to Thee: let his countenance be pleasant and gladsome to me, and let him accompany me in peace. And let not demons of frightful aspect come near me in the way in which I am to go, until I come to Thee in bliss. And let not the doorkeepers hinder my soul from entering paradise. And do not uncover my sins, and expose me to condemnation before Thy terrible tribunal. Let not the lions rush in upon me; nor let the waves of the sea of fire overwhelm my soul—for this must every soul pass through—before I have seen the glory of Thy Godhead. O God, most righteous Judge, who in justice and equity wilt judge mankind, and wilt render unto each one according to his works, O Lord and my God, I beseech Thee, be present to me in Thy compassion, and enlighten my path that I may come to Thee; for Thou art a fountain overflowing with all good things, and with glory for evermore. Amen.

14. It came to pass thereafter, when he returned to his own house in the city of Nazareth, that he was seized by disease, and had to keep his bed. And it was at this time that he died, according to the destiny of all mankind. For this disease was very heavy upon him, and he had never been ill, as he now was, from the day of his birth. And thus assuredly it pleased Christ to order the destiny of righteous Joseph. He lived forty years unmarried; thereafter his wife remained under his care forty-nine years, and then died. And a year after her death, my mother, the blessed Mary, was entrusted to him by the priests, that he should keep her until the time of her marriage. She spent two years in his house; and in the third year of her stay with Joseph, in the fifteenth year of her age, she brought me forth on earth by a mystery which no creature can penetrate or understand, except myself, and my Father and the Holy Spirit, constituting one essence with myself.

15. The whole age of my father, therefore, that righteous old man, was one hundred and eleven years, my Father in heaven having so decreed. And the day on which his soul left his body was the twenty-sixth of the month Abib. For now the fine gold began to lose its splendour, and the silver to be worn down by use—I mean his understanding and his wisdom. He also loathed food and drink, and lost all his skill in his trade of carpentry, nor did he any more pay attention to it. It

came to pass, then, in the early dawn of the twenty-sixth day of Abib, that Joseph, that righteous old man, lying in his bed, was giving up his unquiet soul. Wherefore he opened his mouth with many sighs, and struck his hands one against the other, and with a loud voice cried out, and spoke after the following manner:—

16. Woe to the day on which I was born into the world! Woe to the womb which bare me! Woe to the bowels which admitted me! Woe to the breasts which suckled me! Woe to the feet upon which I sat and rested! Woe to the hands which carried me and reared me until I grew up! For I was conceived in iniquity, and in sins did my mother desire me. Woe to my tongue and my lips, which have brought forth and spoken vanity, detraction, falsehood, ignorance, derision, idle tales, craft, and hypocrisy! Woe to mine eyes, which have looked upon scandalous things! Woe to mine ears, which have delighted in the words of slanderers! Woe to my hands, which have seized what did not of right belong to them! Woe to my belly and my bowels, which have lusted after food unlawful to be eaten! Woe to my throat, which like a fire has consumed all that it found! Woe to my feet, which have too often walked in ways displeasing to God! Woe to my body; and woe to my miserable soul, which has already turned aside from God its Maker! What shall I do when I arrive at that place where I must stand before the most righteous Judge, and when He shall call me to account for the works which I have heaped up in my youth? Woe to every man dying in his sins! Assuredly that same dreadful hour, which came upon my father Jacob, when his soul was flying forth from his body, is now, behold, near at hand for me. Oh! how wretched I am this day, and worthy of lamentation! But God alone is the disposer of my soul and body; He also will deal with them after His own good pleasure.

17. These are the words spoken by Joseph, that righteous old man. And I, going in beside him, found his soul exceedingly troubled, for he was placed in great perplexity. And I said to him: Hail! my father Joseph, thou righteous man; how is it with thee? And he answered me: All hail! my well-beloved son. Indeed, the agony and fear of death have already environed me; but as soon as I heard Thy voice, my soul was at rest. O Jesus of Nazareth! Jesus, my Saviour! Jesus, the deliverer of my soul! Jesus, my protector! Jesus! O sweetest name in my mouth, and in the mouth of all those that love it! O eye which seest, and ear which hearest, hear me! I am Thy servant; this day I most humbly reverence Thee, and before Thy face I pour out my tears. Thou art altogether my God; Thou art my Lord, as the angel has told me times without number, and especially on that day when my soul was driven about with perverse thoughts about the pure and blessed Mary, who was carrying Thee in her womb, and whom I was thinking of secretly sending away. And while I was thus meditating, behold, there appeared to me in my rest angels of the Lord, saying to me in a wonderful mystery: O Joseph, thou son of David, fear not to take Mary as thy wife; and do not grieve thy soul, nor speak unbecoming words of her conception, because she is with child of the Holy Spirit, and shall bring forth a son, whose name shall be called Jesus, for He shall save His

people from their sins. Do not for this cause wish me evil, O Lord! for I was ignorant of the mystery of Thy birth. I call to mind also, my Lord, that day when the boy died of the bite of the serpent. And his relations wished to deliver Thee to Herod, saying that Thou hadst killed him; but Thou didst raise him from the dead, and restore him to them. Then I went up to Thee, and took hold of Thy hand, saying: My son, take care of thyself. But Thou didst say to me in reply: Art thou not my father after the flesh? I shall teach thee who I am. Now therefore, O Lord and my God, do not be angry with me, or condemn me on account of that hour. I am Thy servant, and the son of Thine handmaiden; but Thou art my Lord, my God and Saviour, most surely the Son of God.

18. When my father Joseph had thus spoken, he was unable to weep more. And I saw that death now had dominion over him. And my mother, virgin undefiled, rose and came to me, saying: O my beloved son, this pious old man Joseph is now dying. And I answered: Oh my dearest mother, assuredly upon all creatures produced in this world the same necessity of death lies; for death holds sway over the whole human race. Even thou, O my virgin mother, must look for the same end of life as other mortals. And yet thy death, as also the death of this pious man, is not death, but life enduring to eternity. Nay more, even I must die, as concerns the body which I have received from thee. But rise, O my venerable mother, and go in to Joseph, that blessed old man, in order that thou mayst see what will happen as his soul ascends from his body.

19. My undefiled mother Mary, therefore, went and entered the place where Joseph was. And I was sitting at his feet looking at him, for the signs of death already appeared in his countenance. And that blessed old man raised his head, and kept his eyes fixed on my face; but he had no power of speaking to me, on account of the agonies of death, which held him in their grasp. But he kept fetching many sighs. And I held his hands for a whole hour; and he turned his face to me, and made signs for me not to leave him. Thereafter I put my hand upon his breast, and perceived his soul now near his throat, preparing to depart from its receptacle.

20. And when my virgin mother saw me touching his body, she also touched his feet. And finding them already dead and destitute of heat, she said to me: O my beloved son, assuredly his feet are already beginning to stiffen, and they are as cold as snow. Accordingly she summoned his sons and daughters, and said to them: Come, as many as there are of you, and go to your father; for assuredly he is now at the very point of death. And Assia, his daughter, answered and said: Woe's me, O my brothers, this is certainly the same disease that my beloved mother died of. And she lamented and shed tears; and all Joseph's other children mourned along with her. I also, and my mother Mary, wept along with them.

21. And turning my eyes towards the region of the south, I saw Death already approaching, and all Gehenna with him, closely attended by his army and his satellites; and their clothes, their faces, and their mouths poured forth flames. And when my father Joseph saw them coming straight to him, his eyes dissolved in tears, and at

the same time he groaned after a strange manner. Accordingly, when I saw the vehemence of his sighs, I drove back Death and all the host of servants which accompanied him. And I called upon my good Father, saying:—

22. O Father of all mercy, eye which seest, and ear which hearest, hearken to my prayers and supplications in behalf of the old man Joseph; and send Michael, the prince of Thine angels, and Gabriel, the herald of light, and all the light of Thine angels, and let their whole array walk with the soul of my father Joseph, until they shall have conducted it to Thee. This is the hour in which my father has need of compassion. And I say unto you, that all the saints, yea, as many men as are born in the world, whether they be just or whether they be perverse, must of necessity taste of death.

23. Therefore Michael and Gabriel came to the soul of my father Joseph, and took it, and wrapped it in a shining wrapper. Thus he committed his spirit into the hands of my good Father, and He bestowed upon him peace. But as yet none of his children knew that he had fallen asleep. And the angels preserved his soul from the demons of darkness which were in the way, and praised God even until they conducted it into the dwelling-place of the pious.

24. Now his body was lying prostrate and bloodless; wherefore I reached forth my hand, and put right his eyes and shut his mouth, and said to the virgin Mary: O my mother, where is the skill which he showed in all the time that he lived in this world? Lo! it has perished, as if it had never existed. And when his children heard me speaking with my mother, the pure virgin, they knew that he had already breathed his last, and they shed tears, and lamented. But I said to them: Assuredly the death of your father is not death, but life everlasting: for he has been freed from the troubles of this life, and has passed to perpetual and everlasting rest. When they heard these words, they rent their clothes, and wept.

25. And, indeed, the inhabitants of Nazareth and of Galilee, having heard of their lamentation, flocked to them, and wept from the third hour even to the ninth. And at the ninth hour they all went together to Joseph's bed. And they lifted his body, after they had anointed it with costly unguents. But I entreated my Father in the prayer of the celestials—that same prayer which with my own hand I made before I was carried in the womb of the virgin Mary, my mother. And as soon as I had finished it, and pronounced the amen, a great multitude of angels came up; and I ordered two of them to stretch out their shining garments, and to wrap in them the body of Joseph, the blessed old man.

26. And I spoke to Joseph, and said: The smell or corruption of death shall not have dominion over thee, nor shall a worm ever come forth from thy body. Not a single limb of it shall be broken, nor shall any hair on thy head be changed. Nothing of thy body shall perish, O my father Joseph, but it will remain entire and uncorrupted even until the banquet of the thousand years. And whosoever shall make an offering on the day of thy remembrance, him will I bless and recompense in the congregation of the virgins; and whosoever shall give food to the wretched, the poor, the widows, and orphans from the work of his hands, on the day on which thy

memory shall be celebrated, and in thy name, shall not be in want of good things all the days of his life. And whosoever shall have given a cup of water, or of wine, to drink to the widow or orphan in thy name, I will give him to thee, that thou mayst go in with him to the banquet of the thousand years. And every man who shall present an offering on the day of thy commemoration will I bless and recompense in the church of the virgins: for one I will render unto him thirty, sixty, and a hundred. And whosoever shall write the history of thy life, of thy labour, and thy departure from this world, and this narrative that has issued from my mouth, him shall I commit to thy keeping as long as he shall have to do with this life. And when his soul departs from the body, and when he must leave this world, I will burn the book of his sins, nor will I torment him with any punishment in the day of judgment; but he shall cross the sea of flames, and shall go through it without trouble or pain. And upon every poor man who can give none of those things which I have mentioned this is incumbent: viz., if a son is born to him, he shall call his name Joseph. So there shall not take place in that house either poverty or any sudden death for ever.

27. Thereafter the chief men of the city came together to the place where the body of the blessed old man Joseph had been laid, bringing with them burial-clothes; and they wished to wrap it up in them after the manner in which the Jews are wont to arrange their dead bodies. And they perceived that he kept his shroud fast; for it adhered to the body in such a way, that when they wished to take it off, it was found to be like iron— impossible to be moved or loosened. Nor could they find any ends in that piece of linen, which struck them with the greatest astonishment. At length they carried him out to a place where there was a cave, and opened the gate, that they might bury his body beside the bodies of his fathers. Then there came into my mind the day on which he walked with me into Egypt, and that extreme trouble which he endured on my account. Accordingly, I bewailed his death for a long time; and lying upon his body, I said:—

28. O Death! who makest all knowledge to vanish away, and raisest so many tears and lamentations, surely it is God my Father Himself who hath granted thee this power. For men die for the transgression of Adam and his wife Eve, and Death spares not so much as one. Nevertheless, nothing happens to any one, or is brought upon him, without the command of my Father. There have certainly been men who have prolonged their life even to nine hundred years; but they died. Yea, though some of them have lived longer, they have, notwithstanding, succumbed to the same fate; nor has any one of them ever said: I have not tasted death. For the Lord never sends the same punishment more than once, since it hath pleased my Father to bring it upon men. And at the very moment when it, going forth, beholds the command descending to it from heaven, it says: I will go forth against that man, and will greatly move him. Then, without delay, it makes an onset on the soul, and obtains the mastery of it, doing with it whatever it will. For, because Adam did not the will of my Father, but transgressed His commandment, the wrath of my Father was kindled against him, and He

doomed him to death; and thus it was that death came into the world. But if Adam had observed my Father's precepts, death would never have fallen to his lot. Think you that I can ask my good Father to send me a chariot of fire, which may take up the body of my father Joseph, and convey it to the place of rest, in order that it may dwell with the spirits? But on account of the transgression of Adam, that trouble and violence of death has descended upon all the human race. And it is for this cause that I must die according to the flesh, for my work which I have created, that they may obtain grace.

29. Having thus spoken, I embraced the body of my father Joseph, and wept over it; and they opened the door of the tomb, and placed his body in it, near the body of his father Jacob. And at the time when he fell asleep he had fulfilled a hundred and eleven years. Never did a tooth in his mouth hurt him, nor was his eyesight rendered less sharp, nor his body bent, nor his strength impaired; but he worked at his trade of a carpenter to the very last day of his life; and that was the six-and-twentieth of the month Abib.

30. And we apostles, when we heard these things from our Saviour, rose up joyfully, and prostrated ourselves in honour of Him, and said: O our Saviour, show us Thy grace. Now indeed we have heard the word of life: nevertheless we wonder, O our Saviour, at the fate of Enoch and Elias, inasmuch as they had not to undergo death. For truly they dwell in the habitation of the righteous even to the present day, nor have their bodies seen corruption. Yet that old man Joseph the carpenter was, nevertheless, Thy father after the flesh. And Thou hast ordered us to go into all the world and preach the holy Gospel; and Thou hast said: Relate to them the death of my father Joseph, and celebrate to him with annual solemnity a festival and sacred day. And whosoever shall take anything away from this narrative, or add anything to it, commits sin. We wonder especially that Joseph, even from that day on which Thou wast born in Bethlehem, called Thee his son after the flesh. Wherefore, then, didst Thou not make him immortal as well as them, and Thou sayest that he was righteous and chosen?

31. And our Saviour answered and said: Indeed, the prophecy of my Father upon Adam, for his disobedience, has now been fulfilled. And all things are arranged according to the will and pleasure of my Father. For if a man rejects the commandment of God, and follows the works of the devil by committing sin, his life is prolonged; for he is preserved in order that he may perhaps repent, and reflect that he must be delivered into the hands of death. But if any one has been zealous of good works, his life also is prolonged, that, as the fame of his old age increases, upright men may imitate him. But when you see a man whose mind is prone to anger, assuredly his days are shortened; for it is these that are taken away in the flower of their age. Every prophecy, therefore, which my Father has pronounced concerning the sons of men, must be fulfilled in every particular. But with reference to Enoch and Elias, and how they remain alive to this day, keeping the same bodies with which they were born; and as to what concerns my father Joseph, who has not been allowed as well as they to remain in the body: indeed, though a man live in the world many myriads of years, nevertheless at some time or other he is compelled to exchange life for death. And I say to you, O my brethren, that they also, Enoch and Elias, must towards the end of time return into the world and die—in the day, namely, of commotion, of terror, of perplexity, and affliction. For Antichrist will slay four bodies, and will pour out their blood like water, because of the reproach to which they shall expose him, and the ignominy with which they, in their lifetime, shall brand him when they reveal his impiety.

32. And we said: O our Lord, our God and Saviour, who are those four whom Thou hast said Antichrist will cut off from the reproach they bring upon him? The Lord answered: They are Enoch, Elias, Schila, and Tabitha. When we heard this from our Saviour, we rejoiced and exulted; and we offered all glory and thanksgiving to the Lord God, and our Saviour Jesus Christ. He it is to whom is due glory, honour, dignity, dominion, power, and praise, as well as to the good Father with Him, and to the Holy Spirit that giveth life, henceforth and in all time for evermore. Amen.

The Vision of Death.

Gustave Doré (1865)

APOCALYPSES

APOCALYPSE OF PETER

1 . . . . many of them will be false prophets, and will teach divers ways and doctrines of perdition: but these will become sons of perdition. 3. And then God will come unto my faithful ones who hunger and thirst and are afflicted and purify their souls in this life; and he will judge the sons of lawlessness.

4. And furthermore the Lord said: Let us go into the mountain: Let us pray.. And going with him, we, the twelve disciples, begged that he would show us one of our brethren, the righteous who are gone forth out of the world, in order that we might see of what manner of form they are, and having taken courage, might also encourage the men who hear us.

6. And as we prayed, suddenly there appeared two men standing before the Lord towards the East, on whom we were not able to look; 7, for there came forth from their countenance a ray as of the sun, and their raiment was shining, such as eye of man never saw; for no mouth is able to express or heart to conceive the glory with which they were endued, and the beauty of their appearance. 8. And as we looked upon them, we were astounded; for their bodies were whiter than any snow and ruddier than any rose; 9, and the red thereof was mingled with the white, and I am utterly unable to express their beauty; 10, for their hair was curly and bright and seemly both on their face and shoulders, as it were a wreath woven of spikenard and divers-coloured flowers, or like a rainbow in the sky, such was their seemliness.

11. Seeing therefore their beauty we became astounded at them, since they appeared suddenly. 12. And I approached the Lord and said: Who are these? 13. He saith to me: These are your brethren the righteous, whose forms ye desired to see. 14. And I said to him: And where are all the righteous ones and what is the aeon in which they are and have this glory?

15. And the Lord showed me a very great country outside of this world, exceeding bright with light, and the air there lighted with the rays of the sun, and the earth itself blooming with unfading flowers and full of spices and plants, fair-flowering and incorruptible and bearing blessed fruit. 16. And so great was the perfume that it was borne thence even unto us. 17. And the dwellers in that place were clad in the raiment of shining angels and their raiment was like unto their country; and angels hovered about them there. 18. And the glory of the dwellers there was equal, and with one voice they sang praises alternately to the Lord God, rejoicing in that place. 19. The Lord saith to us: This is the place of your high-priests, the righteous men.

20. And over against that place I saw another, squalid, and it was the place of punishment; and those who were punished there and the punishing angels had their raiment dark like the air of the place.

21. And there were certain there hanging by the tongue: and these were the blasphemers of the way of righteousness; and under them lay fire, burning and punishing them. 22. And there was a great lake, full of flaming mire, in which were certain men that pervert righteousness, and tormenting angels afflicted them.

23. And there were also others, women, hanged by their hair over that mire that bubbled up: and these were they who adorned themselves for adultery; and the men who mingled with them in the defilement of adultery, were hanging by the feet and their heads in that mire. And I said: I did not believe that I should come into this place.

24. And I saw the murderers and those who conspired with them, cast into a certain strait place, full of evil snakes, and smitten by those beasts, and thus turning to and fro in that punishment; and worms, as it were clouds of darkness, afflicted them. And the souls of the murdered stood and looked upon the punishment of those murderers and said: O God, thy judgment is just.

25. And near that place I saw another strait place into which the gore and the filth of those who were being punished ran down and became there as it were a lake: and there sat women having the gore up to their necks, and over against them sat many children who were born to them out of due time, crying; and there came forth from them sparks of fire and smote the women in the eyes: and these were the accursed who conceived and caused abortion.

26. And other men and women were burning up to the middle and were cast into a dark place and were beaten by evil spirits, and their inwards were eaten by restless worms: and these were they who persecuted the righteous and delivered them up.

27. And near those there were again women and men gnawing their own lips, and being punished and receiving a red-hot iron in their eyes: and these were they who blasphemed and slandered the way of righteousness.

28. And over against these again other men and women gnawing their tongues and having flaming fire in their mouths: and these were the false witnesses.

29. And in a certain other place there were pebbles sharper than swords or any spit, red-hot, and women and men in tattered and filthy raiment rolled about on them in punishment: and these were the rich who trusted in their riches and had no pity for orphans and widows, and despised the commandment of God.

30. And in another great lake, full of pitch and blood and mire bubbling up, there stood men and women up to their knees: and these were the usurers and those who take interest on interest.

31. And other men and women were being hurled down from a great cliff and reached the bottom, and again

were driven by those who were set over them to climb
up upon the cliff, and thence were hurled down again,
and had no rest from this punishment: and these were
they who defiled their bodies acting as women; and the
women who were with them were those who lay with
one another as a man with a woman.

32. And alongside of that cliff there was a place full of
much fire, and there stood men who with their own
hands had made for themselves carven images instead of
God. And alongside of these were other men and
women, having rods and striking each other and never
ceasing from such punishment.

33. And others again near them, women and men,
burning and turning themselves and roasting: and these
were they that leaving the way of God

FRAGMENTS OF THE APOCALYPSE OF PETER.

1. CLEMENS ALEXANDRINUS, Eclog. 48. For
instance, Peter in the Apocalypse says that the children
who are born out of due time shall be of the better part:
and that these are delivered over to a care-taking angel
that they may attain a share of knowledge and gain the
better abode [after suffering what they would have
suffered if they had been in the body: but the others
shall merely obtain salvation as injured beings to whom
mercy is shown, and remain without punishment,
receiving this as a reward].*

2. CLEM. ALEX. Eclog. 49. But the milk of the women
running down from their breasts and congealing shall
engender small flesh eating beasts: and these run up
upon them and devour them.

3. MACARIUS MAGNES, Apocritica iv., 6 cf. 16. The
earth, it (sc. the Apoc. of Peter) says, "shall present all
men before God at the day of judgment, being itself also
to be judged, with the heaven also which encompasses
it."

4. CLEM. ALEX. Eclog. 41. The scripture says that
infants that have been exposed are delivered to a care-
taking angel, by whom they are educated and so grow
up, and they will be, it says, as the faithful of a hundred
years old are here.

5. METHODIUS, Conviv. ii., 6. Whence also we have
received in divinely-inspired scriptures that untimely
births are delivered to care-taking angels, even if they are
the offspring of adultery.

THE APOCALYPSE OF THE VIRGIN

The Apocalypse of the Holy Mother of God Concerning the Chastisements.

I. The all-holy mother of God was about to proceed to the Mount of Olives to pray; and praying to the Lord our God she said: In the name of the Father and the Son and the Holy Spirit; let the archangel Gabriel descend, that he may tell me concerning the chastisements and concerning things in heaven and on the earth and under the earth. And as she said the word the archangel Michael descended with the angels of the East and the West and angels of the South and the North, and they saluted the highly favoured one and said to her: Hail, reflection of the Father, hail dwelling of the Son, hail command of the Holy Spirit, hail firmament of the seven heavens, hail firmament of the eleven strongholds, hail worship of the angels, hail loftier than the prophets unto the throne of God. And the holy mother of God said to the angel: Hail Michael, commander-in-chief, the minister of the invisible Father, hail Michael, commander-in-chief, associate of my Son, hail Michael, commander-in-chief, most dread of the six-winged, hail Michael, commander-in-chief, who rules through all things and art worthy to stand beside the throne of the Lord, hail Michael, commander-in-chief, who art about to sound the trumpet and awaken those who have been asleep for ages: hail Michael, commander-in-chief, first of all unto the throne of God.

II. And having greeted all the angels in like manner, the highly favoured one prayed the commander-in-chief regarding the chastisements, saying: Tell to me all things on the earth. And the commander-in-chief said to her: If thou askest me, highly favoured one, I will tell thee. And the highly favoured one said to him: How many are the chastisements with which the race of man is chastised? And the archangel said to her: The chastisements are innumerable. And the highly favoured one said to him: Tell me the things in heaven and on the earth.

III. Then the commander-in-chief, Michael, commanded the Western angels that revelation should be made, and Hades opened, and she saw those who were chastised in Hades: and there lay there a multitude of men and women, and there was a great lamentation. And the highly favoured one asked the commander-in-chief: Who are these and what is their sin? And the commander-in-chief said: These, all holy, are those who did not worship the Father and the Son and the Holy Spirit and for this cause they are thus chastised here.

IV. And she saw in another place a great darkness: and the all holy said: What is this darkness and who are they who are being chastised? And the commander-in-chief said: Many souls are lying in this darkness. And the all holy one said: Let this darkness be taken away in order that I may see this chastisement also. And the commander-in-chief said to the highly favoured one: It is not possible, all holy, that thou shouldst see this chastisement also. And the angels guarding them answered and said: We have a command from the invisible Father that they shall not see the light till thy blessed Son shall shine forth. And plunged in grief the all holy lifted up her eyes to the angels touching the undefiled word of the Father, and said: In the name of the Father and the Son and the Holy Spirit let the darkness be taken away, that I may see this chastisement also. And straightway that darkness was lifted up and covered the seven heavens: and there lay a great multitude of both men and women, and there arose a great lamentation and a great cry began. And seeing them the all holy wept and said to them: What are ye doing, wretched ones? Who are ye? And how are ye found there? and there was no voice or hearkening. And the angels guarding them said: Why do ye not speak to the highly favoured one? And those who were under chastisement said to her: O highly favoured one, from eternity we see not the light, and we are not able to keep off that up there. And splashing pitch flowed down upon them: and seeing them the all holy wept. And again those who were being chastised said to her: How dost thou ask concerning us, holy lady, Mother of God? Thy blessed Son came to The earth and did not make enquiry concerning us, neither Abraham the patriarch, nor John the Baptist, nor Moses the great prophet, nor the Apostle Paul, and unto us their light shone not: and now, all holy Mother of God, the armour of the Christians, the bringer of great comfort on account of the Christians, how dost thou ask concerning us? Then the all holy Mother of God said to Michael, the commander-in-chief: What is their sin? And Michael, the commander-in-chief, said: These are they who did not believe in the Father and the Son and the Holy Spirit, and did not confess thee to be the Mother of God, and that the Lord Jesus Christ was born of thee and took flesh, and for this cause they are chastised there. And again weeping, the all holy Mother of God said to them: Why did ye so greatly err, wretched ones? Did ye not hear that the whole creation names my name? And having said these words the darkness fell over them as it was from the beginning.

V. And the commander-in-chief said: Whither wouldst thou go, highly favoured one? to the West or to the South? And the highly favoured answered: Let us go to the South. And immediately there appeared the cherubim and the seraphim and four hundred angels, and led out the highly favoured one to the South, where came out the river of fire, and there there lay a multitude of men and women, some up to the girdle, others up to the neck, and others up to the crown of the head: and seeing them the all holy Mother of God cried out with a loud voice to the commander-in-chief and said: Who are these, and what is their sin who stand in the fire up to the girdle? And the commander-in-chief said: These, all holy one, are they who inherited the curse of father and mother, and for this cause they are thus chastised here as accursed.

VI. And the all holy one said: And who are these standing in the fire up to the breasts? And the commander-in-chief said: These are whosoever cast off their wives and defiled them in adultery, and for this cause they are thus chastised here.

VII. And the all holy one said to the commander-in-chief: Who are these standing up to the neck in the flame of the fire? And the commander-in-chief said: These, all holy one, are whosoever ate of the flesh of men. And the all holy one said: And how is it possible for one man to eat of the flesh of another? And the commander-in-chief said: Listen, all holy one, and I will tell thee: These are they whosoever brought down their own children out of their own wombs and cast them out as food for dogs, and whosoever gave up their brothers in the presence of kings and governors, these ate the flesh of man, and for this cause they are thus chastised.

VIII. And the all holy one said: Who are these set in the fire up to the crown? And the commander-in-chief said: These, all holy one, are whosoever lay hold of the precious cross and swear to a lie: by the power of the cross of the Lord. The angels tremble and worship with fear, and men lay hold of it and swear to a lie and do not know what they testify: and for this cause they are thus chastised here.

IX. And in another place the all holy one saw a man hung by the feet, and worms devoured him. And she asked the commander-in-chief: Who is this and what is his sin? And the commander-in-chief said: This is he who took usury for his gold, and for this cause he is thus chastised here.

X. And she saw a woman hanging by her two ears, and all the beasts came out of her mouth and gnawed her in pieces: and the highly favoured one asked the commander-in-chief: Who is she, and what is her sin? And the commander-in-chief said: She is she who turned aside into strange houses and those of her neighbours and spoke evil words to make strife, and for that cause she is thus chastised here.

XI. And seeing these things the all holy Mother of God wept and said to the commander-in-chief: It were well for man that he had not been born. And the commander-in-chief said: Verily, all holy one, thou hast not seen the great chastisements. And the all holy one said to the commander-in-chief: Come, Michael, great commander-in-chief, and lead me that I may see all the chastisements. And the commander-in-chief said: Where dost thou wish, all holy one, that we should go? And the highly favoured one answered: To the West: and straightway the cherubim appeared and led the highly favoured to the West.

XII. And she saw a cloud full of fire and in it there was a multitude of men and women. And the all holy one said: What was their sin? And the commander-in-chief said: These, all holy one, are they who on the morning of the Lord's day sleep like the dead, and for that reason they are thus chastised here. And the all holy one said: If anyone cannot rise, what shall he do? And the commander-in-chief said: Listen, all holy one: if anyone's house is fastened on the four (sides?) and surrounds him and he cannot come out, he has forgiveness.

XIII. And she saw in another place burning benches of fire and on them sat a multitude of men and women and burned on them. And the all holy one asked: Who are these and what is their sin? And the commander-in-chief said: These, all holy one, are they who do not rise up to the presbyter when they enter into the church of God, and for this cause they are thus chastised here.

XIV. And the all holy one saw in another place an iron tree and it had branches of iron, and on it there hung a multitude of men and women by their tongues. And seeing them the all holy one wept, and asked the commander-in-

chief saying: Who are these and what was their sin? And the commander-in-chief said: These are perjurers, blasphemers, slanderers, whosoever divided brothers from brothers. And the all holy one said: How is it possible to divide brothers from brothers? And the commander-in-chief said: Listen, all holy one, and I will tell thee about this: When some from among the nations desired to be baptised, he would say to them one word: Thou foul-feeding, unbelieving Gentile; because he thus blasphemed, he shall receive ceaseless retribution.

XV. And in another place the all holy one saw a man hanging from his four extremities, and from his nails blood gushed vehemently, and his tongue was tied in a flame of fire, and he was unable to groan and say the *Kyrie eleison me*. And when she had seen him the all holy one wept and herself said the *Kyrie eleison* thrice: and after the saying of the prayer, came the angel who had authority over the scourge and loosed the man's tongue: and the all holy one asked the commander-in-chief: Who is this wretched one who has this chastisement? And the commander-in-chief said: This, all holy one, is the steward who did not the will of God, but ate the things of the church and said: "He who ministers to the altar shall be nourished from the altar": and for this cause he is thus chastised here. And the all holy one said: Let it be unto him according to his faith. And again he tied his tongue.

XVI. And Michael, the commander-in-chief said: Come hither, all holy one, and I will show unto thee where the priests are chastised. And the all holy one came out and saw presbyters hanging by their twenty nails, and fire came out of their heads. And seeing them the all holy one asked the commander-in-chief: Who are these and what is their sin? And the commander-in-chief said: These, all holy one, are they who stand beside the throne of God, and when they sang of the body of our Lord Jesus Christ, the pearls fell out, and the awful throne of heaven shook and the footstool of our Lord Jesus Christ trembled, and they did not perceive it: and for this cause they are thus chastised here.

XVII. And the all holy one saw a man and a winged beast having three heads like flames of fire: the two heads were towards his eyes and the third head towards his mouth. And seeing him the all holy one asked the commander-in-chief: Who is this, that he cannot save himself from the mouth of the dragon? And the commander-in-chief said to her: This, all holy one, is the reader who does not practise in his own habits according to what is worthy of the holy Gospel: and for this cause he is thus chastised here.

XVIII. And the commander-in-chief said: Come hither, all holy one, and I will show thee where the angelic and archangelic form is chastised. She proceeded and saw them lying in the fire and the sleepless worm gnawed them: and the all holy one said: Who are these, and what is their sin? And the commander-in-chief said: These, all holy one, are they who possessed the archangelic and apostolic form: hearken, all holy one, concerning this: on earth they were called patriarchs and bishops, and they were not worthy of their name: on earth they heard 'Bless (the Lord) ye saints,' and in heaven they were not called saints, because they did not act as bearers of the archangelic form: and for this cause they are thus chastised here.

XIX. And she saw women hanging by their nails, and a flame of fire came out of their mouth and burned them: and all the beasts coming out of the fire gnawed them to pieces, and groaning they cried out: Have pity on us, have pity, for we are chastised worse than all those who are under chastisement. And seeing them the all holy one wept, and asked the commander-in-chief, Michael: Who are these and what is their sin? And the commander-in-chief said: These are the wives of presbyters who did not honour the presbyters, but after the death of the presbyter took husbands, and for this cause they are thus chastised here.

XX. And the all holy one saw after the same manner also a deaconess hanging from a crag and a beast with two heads devoured her breasts. And the all holy one asked: What is her sin? And the commander-in-chief said: She, all holy one, is an archdeaconess who defiled her body in fornication, and for this cause she is thus chastised here.

XXI. And she saw other women hanging over the fire, and all the beasts devoured them. And the all holy one asked the commander-in-chief: Who are these and what is their sin? And he said: These are they who did not do the will of God, lovers of money and those who took interest on accounts, and the immodest.

XXII. And when she had heard these things the all holy one wept and said: Woe unto sinners. And the commander-in-chief said: Why dost thou lament, all holy one? Now verily thou hast not seen the great chastisements. And the highly favoured one said: Come, Michael, the great commander-in-chief of the powers above, tell me how I may see all the chastisements. And the commander-in-chief said: Where dost thou wish that we should go, all holy one? to the East or towards the left parts of Paradise? And the all holy one said: To the left parts of Paradise.

XXIII. And immediately when she had spoken, the cherubim and seraphim stood beside her and led the highly favoured one out to the left parts of Paradise. And behold, there was a great river, and the appearance of the river was blacker than pitch, and in it there were a multitude of men and women: it boiled like a furnace of forges, and its waves were like a wild sea over the sinners: and when the waves rose, they sank the sinners ten thousand cubits and they were unable to keep it off and say: Have mercy on us, thou just judge: for the sleepless worm devoured them, and there was no reckoning of the number of those who devoured them. And seeing the all holy Mother of God the angels who chastised them cried out with one voice: Holy is God who has compassion on account of the Mother of God: we give thee thanks, O Son of God, that from eternity we did not see the light, and to-day through the Mother of God we have seen the light: and again they shouted with one voice, saying: Hail, highly favoured Mother of God: Hail, lamp of the inaccessible light: Hail to thee also, Michael, the commander-in-chief, thou that art ambassador from the whole creation: for we, seeing the chastisement of sinners are greatly grieved. And the all holy one, when she saw the angels humbled on account of

the sinners, lamented and said: Woe to sinners and their neighbours. And the all holy one said: Let us see the sinners. And the highly favoured one, coming with the archangel Michael and all the armies of the angels lifted up one voice saying: Lord have mercy. And after the making of the prayer earnestly, the wave of the river rested and the fiery waves grew calm, and the sinners appeared as a grain of mustard-seed: and seeing them the all holy one lamented and said: What is this river, and what are its waves? And the commander-in-chief said: This river is the outer fire, and those who are being tortured are the Jews who crucified our Lord Jesus Christ the Son of God, and who refused holy baptism; and those who commit fornication and sin against the sweet and passionless perfume of marriage, and he who debauches mother and daughter, and the poisoners and those who slay with the sword, and the women who strangle their offspring. And the all holy one said: According to their faith so be it unto them. And straightway the waves rose over the sinners and the darkness covered them. And the commander-in-chief said: Hearken, thou highly favoured one: if anyone shall be cast into this darkness, his remembrance shall never be in the sight of God. And the all holy Mother of God said: Woe to sinners, because the flame of the fire is everlasting.

XXIV. And the commander-in-chief said: Come hither, all holy one, and I will show unto thee the lake of fire: and see thou where the race of the Christians is chastised. And the all holy one proceeded and saw: and some she heard, but others she did not see: and she asked the commander-in-chief: Who are these, and what is their sin? And the commander-in-chief said: These, all holy one, are those who were baptised and arrayed under the oracle of Christ, but worked the works of the devil and wasted the time of their repentance: and for this cause they are thus chastised here.

XXV. And she said: I pray, one request will I make of thee, let me also be chastised with the Christians, because they are the children of my son. And the commander-in-chief said: Rest thou in Paradise, holy lady, Mother of God. And the all holy one said: I pray thee, move the fourteen firmaments and the seven heavens, and let us pray for the Christians that the Lord our God may hearken unto us and have mercy on them. And the commander-in-chief said: As the Lord God liveth, the great name, seven times a day and seven times a night, when we lead up the hymn of the Lord, we make remembrance for the sake of sinners, and the Lord accounts us as naught.

XXVI. And the all holy one said: I pray thee, commander-in-chief, command the armies of the angels and let them place me on the height of heaven and let me into the presence of the invisible Father. And immediately the commander-in-chief commanded, and the chariot of the cherubim and seraphim appeared, and they exalted the highly favoured one to the height of heaven and placed her in the presence of the invisible Father: And she stretched forth her hands to the undefiled throne of the Father and said: Have mercy, O Lord, on the Christian sinners, for I saw them being chastised and I cannot bear their complaint. Let me go forth and be chastised myself for the Christians. I do not pray, O Lord, for the unbelieving Jews, but for the Christians I entreat thy compassion. And there came a second voice from the invisible Father saying: How can I have mercy on them, when they did not have mercy on their own brothers? And the all holy one said: Lord, have mercy on the sinners: behold the chastisements, for every creature on the earth calls upon my name: and when the soul comes forth out of the body, it cries saying, "Holy Lady, Mother of God." Then the Lord said to her: Hearken, all holy Mother of God, if anyone names and calls upon thy name, I will not forsake him, either in heaven or on earth.

XXVII. And the all holy one said: Where is Moses? Where are all the prophets and fathers who never sinned? Where art thou, holy Paul of God? where is the holy Lord's Day, the boast of the Christians? where is the power of the precious and life-giving cross, which delivered Adam and Eve from the ancient curse? Then Michael and all the angels raised one voice saying: Lord, have mercy on the sinners. Then Moses also cried: Have mercy, Lord, on those to whom I gave thy law. Then John also called: Have mercy, Lord, on those to whom I gave thy Gospel. Then Paul cried: Have mercy, Lord, on those to whom I brought thy epistles in the Church. And the Lord God said: Hearken, all ye righteous: if according to the law which Moses gave, and according to the Gospel which John gave, and according to the epistles which Paul carried, they thus be judged. And they had nothing to say except, Have mercy, O just judge.

XXVIII. And the all holy Mother of God said: Have mercy, Lord, on the Christians, because they kept thy law and gave heed to thy gospel, but they were simple ones. Then the Lord said to her: Hearken, all holy one: if anyone did evil to them and they did not requite him the evil, thou sayest well that they attended to both my law and my gospel, but if he did not do them wrong and they requited him evil, how may I say that these are holy men? now they shall be rewarded according to their wrongdoing. Then all hearing the voice of the Lord had nothing to answer; and the all holy one, when she saw that the saints were at a loss, and their Lord did not hear, and his mercy was hidden from them, then the all holy one said: Where is Gabriel, who announced unto me the "Hail, thou that from eternity shalt conceive him who is without beginning like the Father," and now does not look upon sinners? Where is the great commander-in-chief? come hither, all ye saints whom God justified, and let us fall down in the presence of the invisible Father, in order that the Lord God may hear us, and have mercy on sinners. Then Michael, the commander-in-chief, and all the saints fell on their faces in the presence of the invisible Father, saying: Have mercy, Lord, on the Christian sinners.

XXIX. Then the Lord, seeing the prayer of the saints, had compassion and said: Go down, my beloved son, and because of the prayer of the saints let thy face shine on earth to sinners. Then the Lord came down from his undefiled throne: and when they saw Him, those who were under chastisement raised one voice saying: Have mercy on us, King of ages. Then the Lord of all things said: Hearken, all ye sinners and righteous men: I made paradise and made man after my image: but he transgressed, and for his own sins was delivered to death: but I did not suffer the works of my hands to be tyrannized over by the serpent: wherefore I bowed the heavens and came down and was born of Mary, the holy undefiled Mother of God, that I might set you free: I was baptised in Jordan in order that I might save the creature (nature) which had grown old under sin: I was nailed to the cross to free you from the ancient curse: I asked for water and ye gave me vinegar mingled with gall: I was laid in the grave: I trampled on the enemy: I raised up mine elect, and even thus ye would not hear me. But now, because of the prayer of my mother Mary, because she has wept much for your sake, and because of Michael my archangel, and because of the multitude of my saints, I grant you to have rest on the day of Pentecost to glorify the Father and the Son and the Holy Spirit.

XXX. Then all the angels and archangels, thrones, lordships, authorities, governments, powers, and the many-eyed cherubim and the six-winged seraphim and all the apostles and prophets and martyrs and all the saints raised one voice, saying: Glory to thee, O Lord: glory to thee, lover of men: glory to thee, King of ages: glory be to thy compassion: glory be to thy long suffering: glory be to thy unspeakable justice of judgment, because thou hast been long-suffering with sinners and impious men: Thine is it to pity and to save. To him be the glory and the power to the Father and to the Son and to the Holy Spirit for ever and ever. Amen.

THE APOCALYPSE OF SEDRACH

The Word of the holy and blessed Sedrach concerning love and concerning repentance and Orthodox Christians, and concerning the Second Coming of our Lord Jesus Christ. Lord give thy blessing.

I. Beloved, let us prefer nothing in honour except sincere love: for in many things we stumble every day and night and hour. And for this cause let us gain love, for it covereth a multitude of sins: for what is the profit, my children, if we have all things, and have not saving love…

O blessed love, supplier of all good things. Blessed is the man who has gained the true faith and sincere love, according as the Master said, there is no greater love than this that a man should lay down his life for his friend. Cf. John xv. 13.

II. And invisibly he received a voice in his ears: Come hither, Sedrach, since thou wishest and desirest to converse with God and ask of him that he may reveal unto thee whatever thou wishest to ask. And Sedrach said: What, Sir? And the voice said to him: I was sent to thee to raise thee here into heaven. And he said: I desired to speak mouth to mouth with God: I am not fit, Sir, to come into heaven. And stretching out his wings he took him up and he came into heaven to the very flame, and he set him as high as the third heaven, and in it stood the flame of the divinity.

III. And the Lord saith to him: Welcome, my beloved Sedrach: What suit hast thou against God who created thee, that thou saidst, I desired to speak face to face with God? Sedrach saith to him: Yea, verily, the son hath a suit with the Father: my Lord, why didst thou make the earth? The Lord saith to him: For man's sake. Sedrach saith: And why didst Thou make the sea? Why didst Thou scatter every good thing on the earth? The Lord saith to him: For man's sake. Sedrach saith to him: If thou didst these things, why wilt Thou destroy him? And the Lord said: Man is my work and the creature of my hands, and I discipline him as I find good.

IV. Sedrach saith to him: Chastisement and fire are thy discipline: they are bitter, my Lord: it were well for man if he had not been born: why then didst thou make him, my Lord? Why didst thou weary thine undefiled hands and create man, since thou didst not intend to have mercy on him? God saith to him: I made Adam the first creature and placed him in Paradise in the midst of the tree of life and said to him: Eat of all the fruits, but beware of the tree of life: for if thou eat of it, thou shalt die the death. But he transgressed my commandment, and being beguiled by the devil ate of the tree.

V. Sedrach saith to him: Of thy will Adam was beguiled, my Lord: Thou commandest thine angels to make approach to Adam, and the first of the angels himself transgressed thy commandment and did not make approach to him, and Thou didst banish him, because he transgressed thy commandment and did not make any approach to the work of thine hands: if thou lovedst man, why didst Thou not slay the devil, the worker of unrighteousness? Who is able to fight an invisible spirit? And he as a smoke enters into the hearts of men and teaches them every sin: he fights against thee, the immortal God, and what can wretched man then do to him? But have mercy, O Lord, and stop the chastisements: but if not, count me also with the sinners: if thou wilt have no mercy on the sinners, where are thy mercies, where is thy compassion, O Lord?

VI. God saith to him: Be it known unto thee that I ordered all things to be placable to him: I gave him understanding and made him the heir of heaven and earth, and I subjected all things to him, and every living thing flees from him and from before his face: but he, having received of mine, became alien, adulterous, and sinful: tell me, what father, having given his son his portion, when he takes his substance and leaves his father and goes away and becomes an alien and serves an alien, when the father sees that the son has deserted him, does not darken his heart, and does not the father go and take his substance and banish him from his glory because he deserted his father? And how have I, the wonderful and jealous God, given him everything, and he having received these things has become an adulterer and a sinner?

VII. Sedrach saith to him: Thou, O Lord, didst create man. Thou knewest of what sort of mind he was and of what sort of knowledge we are, and thou makest it a cause for chastisement: but cast him forth; for shall not I alone fill up the heavenly places? But if that is not to be so save man too, O Lord. He failed by thy will, wretched man. Why dost thou waste words on me, Sedrach? I created Adam and his wife and the sun and said: Behold each other how bright he is, and the wife of Adam is brighter in the beauty of the moon and he was the giver of her life. Sedrach saith: but of what profit are beauties if they die away into the earth? How didst thou say, O Lord, Thou shalt not return evil for evil? How is it, O Lord? the word of Thy divinity never lies, and why dost Thou retaliate on man? or dost thou not in so doing render evil for evil? I know that among the quadrupeds there is no other so wily and unreasonable as the mule. But we strike it with the bridle when we wish: and thou hast angels: send them forth to guard them, and when man inclines towards sin, to take hold of his foot and not let him go whither he would.

VIII. God saith to him: If I catch him by the foot, he will say, Thou hast given me no joy in the world. But I have left him to his own will because I loved him. Wherefore I sent forth my righteous angels to guard him night and day. Sedrach saith: I know, O Lord, that of all thy creatures Thou chiefly lovedst man, of the quadrupeds the sheep, of woods the olive, of fruits the vine, of flying things the bee, of rivers the Jordan, of cities Jerusalem. And all these man also loves, my Lord. God saith to Sedrach: I will ask thee one thing, Sedrach: if thou answerest me, then I may fitly help thee, even though thou hast tempted thy creator. Sedrach saith: Speak. The Lord God saith: Since I made all things, how many men were born and how many died, and how many are to die and how many hairs have they? Tell me, Sedrach, since the heaven was created and the earth, how many trees grew in the world, and how many fell, and how many are to fall, and how many are to arise, and how many leaves have they? Tell me, Sedrach, since I made the sea, how many waves arose and how many fell, and how many are to arise, and how many winds blow along the margin of the sea? Tell me, Sedrach, from the creation of the world of the æons, when the air rained, how many drops fell upon the world, and how many are to fall? And Sedrach said: Thou alone knowest all these things, O Lord; thou only understandest all these things: only, I pray thee, deliver man from chastisement, and I shall not be separated from our race.

IX. And God said to his only begotten Son: Go, take the soul of Sedrach my beloved, and place it in Paradise. The only begotten Son saith to Sedrach: Give me the trust which our Father deposited in the womb of thy mother in the holy tabernacle of thy body from a child. Sedrach saith: I will not give thee my soul. God saith to him: And wherefore was I sent to come hither, and thou pleadest against me? For I was commanded by my Father not to take thy soul with violence; but if not, (then) give me thy most greatly desired soul.

X. And Sedrach saith to God: And whence dost Thou intend to take my soul, and from which limb? And God saith to him: Dost thou not know that it is placed in the midst of thy lungs and thy heart and is dispersed into all thy limbs? It is brought up through the throat and gullet and the mouth and at whatever hour it is predestined to come forth, it is scattered, and brought together from the points of the nails and from all the limbs, and there is a great necessity that it should be separated from the body and parted from the heart. When Sedrach had heard all these things and had considered the memory of death he was greatly astounded, and Sedrach said to God: O Lord, give me a little respite that I may weep, for I have heard that tears are able to do much and much remedy comes to the lowly body of thy creature.

XI. And weeping and bewailing he began to say: O marvellous head of heavenly adornment: O radiant as the sun which shines on heaven and earth: thy hairs are known from Teman, thine eyes from Bosor, thine ears from thunder, thy tongue from a trumpet, and thy brain is a small creation, thy head the energy of the whole body: O friendly and most fair beloved by all, and now falling into the earth it must become forgotten. O hands, mild, fair-fingered, worn with toil by which the body is nourished: O hands, deftest of all, heaping up from all quarters ye made ready houses. O fingers adorned and decked with gold and silver (rings): and great worlds are led by the fingers: the three joints

enfold the palms, and heap up beautiful things: and now ye must become aliens to the world. O feet, skilfully walking about, self-running, most swift, unconquerable: O knees, fitted together, because without you the body does not move: the feet run along with the sun and the moon in the night and in the day, heaping up all things, foods and drinks, and nourishing the body: O feet, most swift and fair runners, moving on the face of the earth, getting ready the house with every good thing: O feet which bear up the whole body, that run up to the temples, making repentance and calling on the saints, and now ye are to remain motionless. O head and hands and feet, until now I have kept you. O soul, what sent thee into the humble and wretched body? and now being separated from it, thou art going up where the Lord calleth thee, and the wretched body goes away to judgment. O body well-adorned, hair clothed with stars, head of heavenly adornment and dress: O face well-anointed, light-bringing eyes, voice trumpet-like, tongue placable, chin fairly adorned, hairs like the stars, head high as heaven, body decked out, light-bringing eyes that know all things—and now you shall fall into the earth and under the earth your beauty shall disappear.

XII. Christ saith to him: Stay, Sedrach; how long dost thou weep and groan? Paradise is opened to thee, and, dying, thou shalt live. Sedrach saith to him: Once more I will speak unto thee, O Lord: How long shall I live before I die? and do not disregard my prayer. The Lord saith to him: Speak, O Sedrach. Sedrach saith: If a man shall live eighty or ninety or an hundred years, and live these years in sin, and again shall turn, and the man live in repentance, in how many days dost thou forgive him his sins? God saith to him: If he shall live an hundred or eighty years and shall turn and repent for three years and do the fruit of righteousness, and death shall overtake him, I will not remember all his sins.

XIII. Sedrach saith to him: The three years are a long time, my Lord, lest death overtake him and he fulfil not his repentance: have mercy, Lord, on thine image and have compassion, for the three years are many. God saith to him: If a man live an hundred years and remember his death and confess before men and I find him, after a time I will forgive all his sins. Sedrach saith again: I will again beseech thy compassion for thy creature. The time is long lest death overtake him and snatch him suddenly. The Saviour saith to him: I will ask thee one word, Sedrach, my beloved, then thou shalt ask me in turn: if the man shall repent for forty days I will not remember all his sins which he did.

XIV. And Sedrach saith to the archangel Michael: Hearken to me, O powerful chief, and help thou me and be my envoy that God may have mercy on the world. And falling on their faces, they besought the Lord and said: O Lord, teach us how and by what sort of repentance and by what labour man shall be saved. God saith: By repentances, by intercessions, by liturgies, by tears in streams, in hot groanings. Dost thou not know that my prophet David was saved by tears, and the rest were saved in one moment? Thou knowest, Sedrach, that there are nations which have not the law and which do the works of the law: for if they are unbaptized and my divine spirit come unto them and they turn to my baptism, I also receive them with my righteous ones into Abraham's bosom. And there are some who have been baptized with my baptism and who have shared in my divine part and become reprobate in complete reprobation and will not repent: and I suffer them with much compassion and much pity and wealth in order that they may repent, but they do the things which my divinity hates, and did not hearken to the wise man asking (them), saying, we by no means justify a sinner. Dost thou not most certainly know that it is written: And those who repent never see chastisement? And they did not hearken to the Apostles or to my word in the Gospels, and they grieve my angels, and verily they do not attend to my messenger in the assemblies (for communion) and in my services, and they do not stand in my holy churches, but they stand and do not fall down and worship in fear and trembling, but boast things which I do not accept, or my holy angels.

XV. Sedrach saith to God: O Lord, Thou alone art sinless and very compassionate, having compassion and pity for sinners, but thy divinity said: I am not come to call the righteous but sinners to repentance. And the Lord said to Sedrach: Dost thou not know, Sedrach, that the thief was saved in one moment to repent? Dost thou not know that my apostle and evangelist was saved in one moment? *"Peccatores enim non salvantur,"* for their hearts are like rotten stone: these are they who walk in impious ways and who shall be destroyed with Antichrist. Sedrach saith: O my Lord, Thou also saidst: My divine spirit entered into the nations which, not having the law, do the things of the law. So also the thief and the apostle and evangelist and the rest of those who have already got into thy Kingdom. O my Lord; so likewise do Thou pardon those who have sinned to the last: for life is very toilsome and there is no time for repentance.

XVI. The Lord saith to Sedrach: I made man in three stages: when he is young, I overlooked his stumblings as he was young: and again when he was a man I considered his purpose: and again when he grows old, I watch him till he repent. Sedrach saith: O Lord, Thou knowest and understandest all these things: but have sympathy for sinners. The Lord saith to him: Sedrach, my beloved, I promise to have sympathy and bring down the forty days to twenty: and whosoever shall remember thy name shall not see the place of chastisement, but shall be with the just in a place of refreshment and rest: and if anyone shall record this wonderful word his sins shall not be reckoned against him for ever and ever. And Sedrach saith: O Lord, and if anyone shall bring enlightenment to thy servant, save him, O Lord, from all evil. And Sedrach, the servant of the Lord, saith: Now take my soul, O Lord. And God took him and placed him in Paradise with all the saints. To whom be the glory and the power for ever and ever. Amen.

THE NARRATIVE OF ZOSIMUS

The Narrative of Zosimus Concerning the Life of the Blessed

I. About that time there was in the desert a certain man named Zosimus, who for forty years ate no bread, and drank no wine, and saw not the face of man. This man was entreating God that he might see the way of life of the blessed, and behold an angel of the Lord was sent saying to him, Zosimus, man of God, behold I am sent by the Most High, the God of all, to tell thee that thou shalt journey to the blessed, but shalt not dwell with them. But exalt not thy heart, saying, For forty years I have not eaten bread, for the word of God is more than bread, and the spirit of God is more than wine. And as for thy saying, I have not seen the face of man, behold the face of the great king is nigh thee. Zosimus said, I know that the Lord can do whatsoever he will. The angel said to him, Know this also, that thou art not worthy of one of their delights, but arise and set out.

II. And I, Zosimus, issuing from my cave with God leading me, set out not knowing which way I went, and after I had travelled forty days my spirit grew faint and my body failed, and being exhausted I sat down, and continued praying in that place for three days. And, behold, there came a beast from the desert, whose name is the camel, and placing its knees on the ground, it received me upon its neck and went into the desert and set me down. There there was much howling of wild beasts, and gnashing of teeth, and deadly poison. And becoming afraid, I prayed to the Lord, and there came in that place a great earthquake with noise, and a storm of wind blew and lifted me from the earth, and exalted me on its wing, and I was praying and journeying till it set me upon a place beside a river, and the name of the river is Eumeles. And behold when I desired to cross the river, some one cried as if from the water, saying, Zosimus, man of God, thou canst not pass through me, for no man can divide my waters: but look up from the waters to the heaven. And looking up I saw a wall of cloud stretching from the waters to the heaven, and the cloud said, Zosimus, man of God, through me no bird passes out of this world, nor breath of wind, nor the sun itself, nor can the tempter in this world pass through me.

III. And I was astonished at these words, and at the voice that spake these things to me. And as I prayed, behold two trees sprang up out of the earth, fair and beautiful, laden with fragrant fruits. And the tree on this side bent down and received me on its top, and was lifted up exceedingly above the middle of the river, and the other tree met me and received me in its branches and bending down set me on the ground; and both trees were lifted up and set me away from the river on the other side. In that place I rested three days, and arising again I went forward, whither I knew not, and that place was filled with much fragrance, and there was no mountain on either hand, but the place was level and flowery, all crowned with garlands, and all the land beautiful.

IV. And I saw there a naked man sitting, and said in myself, Surely this is not the tempter. And I remembered the voice of the cloud that it said to me, Not even the tempter in this world passes through me. And thus taking courage I said to him, Hail, brother. And he answering said to me, The grace of my God be with thee. Again I said to him, Tell me, man of God, who thou art? He answered

and said to me, Who art thou rather? And I answered and told him all concerning myself, and that I had prayed to God and he had brought me into that place. He answered and said to me, I also know that thou art a man of God, for if not, thou couldst not have passed through the cloud and the river and the air. For the breadth of the river is about thirty thousand paces, and the cloud reaches to heaven, and the depth of the river to the abyss.

V. And having ended this discourse the man spoke again, Hast thou come hither out of the vanity of the world? I said to him, Wherefore art thou naked? He said, How knowest thou that I am naked? Thou wearest skins of the cattle of the earth, that decay together with thy body, but look up to the height of heaven and behold of what nature my clothing is. And looking up into heaven I saw his face as the face of an angel, and his clothing as lightning, which passes from the east to the west, and I was greatly afraid, thinking that it was the son of God, and trembled, falling upon the ground. And giving me his hand he raised me up, saying, Arise, I also am one of the blessed. Come with me, that I may lead thee to the elders. And laying hold of my hand he walked about with me and led me toward a certain crowd, and there were in that crowd elders like sons of God, and young men were standing beside the elders. And as I came near to them, they said, This man has come hither out of the vanity of the world; come, let us beseech the Lord and he will reveal to us this mystery. Surely the end is not at hand, that the man of vanity is come hither? Then they arose and besought the Lord with one accord, and behold two angels came down from heaven and said, Fear not the man, for God has sent him, that he may remain seven days and learn your ways of life, and then he shall go forth and depart to his own place. The angels of God having said this ascended into heaven before our eyes.

VI. Then the elders of the blessed gave me over to one of the attendants, saying, Keep him for seven days. So the attendant receiving me led me to his cave, and we sat under a tree partaking of food. For from the sixth hour even to the sixth, then we ate, and the water came out from the root of the tree sweeter than honey, and we drank our fill, and again the water sank down into its place. And all the country of those there heard of me, that there had come thither a man out of the vanity of the world, and all the country was stirred up, and they came to see me because it seemed strange to them. Therefore they were asking me all things and I was answering them, and I became faint in spirit and in body, and besought the man of God that served me, and said, I beseech thee, brother, if any come to see me, tell them He is not here, so that I may rest a little. And the man of God cried out saying, Woe is me, that the story of Adam is summed up in me, for Satan deceived him through Eve, and this man by his flattery desires to make me a liar while he is here. Take me away from hence, for I shall flee from the place. For behold he wishes to sow in me seeds of the world of vanity. And all the multitude and the elders rose up against me, and said, Depart from us, man; we know not whence thou art come to us. But I lamented with great lamentation, and my senses left me, and I cried out to the elders, saying, Forgive me, my lords, and the elders stilled them and made quietness. Then I related to them all from the beginning till that time, and said, I besought the Lord to come to you, and he deemed me worthy. And the elders said, And now what wilt thou we should do to thee? I said to them, I desire to learn of you your way of life.

VII. And they rejoiced with great joy, and taking up tables of stone they wrote on them with their nails, thus, Hear, ye sons of men, hear ye us who are become blessed, that we also are of you; for when the prophet Jeremiah proclaimed that the city of Jerusalem should be delivered into the hands of the destroyers, he rent his garments, and put sackcloth upon his loins, and sprinkled dust upon his head, and took earth upon his bed, and told all the people to turn from their wicked way. And our father Rechab, the son of Aminadab, heard him and said to us, Ye sons and daughters of Rechab, hearken to your father, and put off your garments from your body, and drink no vessel of wine, and eat no bread from the fire, and drink not strong drink and honey until the Lord hear your entreaty. And we said, All that he has commanded us we shall do and hearken. So we cast away our clothing from our bodies, and we ate no bread from the fire, and drank no vessel of wine nor honey nor strong drink, and we lamented with a great lamentation and besought the Lord, and he heard our prayer and turned away his anger from the city of Jerusalem, and there came to the city of Jerusalem mercy from the Lord, and he pitied its people, and turned away his deadly anger.

VIII. And after these things the king of the city of Jerusalem died, and there arose another king. And all the people gathered to him and informed him concerning us, and said, There are certain of thy people, who have changed their way from us. Therefore the king summoned them, and asked them wherefore they had done this; and he sent for us and asked, Who are ye and of what worship and of what country? And we said to him, We are the sons of thy servant, and our father is Rechab the son of Jonadab, and when Jeremiah the prophet preached in the days of thy father the king, he proclaimed death to the city of Jerusalem, saying, Yet three days and all the city shall be put to death. And the king thy father hearing this repented of his sins, and issued a command to all to turn aside from their wicked way. And our father thy servant hearing it charged us, saying, Drink no vessel of wine, and eat no bread from the fire, until the Lord shall hear your entreaty. And we hearkened to the commandment of our father, and made naked our bodies, we drank no wine and ate no bread, and we prayed to the Lord for the city of Jerusalem, and the Lord pitied his people and turned away his anger, and we saw it and our soul was rejoiced, and we said, It is good for us to be so.

IX. And the king said to us, Ye have done well. Now therefore mingle with my people, and eat bread and drink wine, and glorify your Lord, and ye shall be serving God and the king. But we said, We will not disobey God. Then the king was enraged and set us in prison, and we passed that night there. And behold a light shone in the building, and an angel uncovered the prison and laid hold of the crowns of our heads, and took us out of the prison, and set us beside the water of the river, and said to us, Whithersoever the water goes, go ye also. And we travelled with the water and with the angel. When therefore he had brought us to this place, the river was dried up and the water was swallowed up by the abyss, and he made a wall round this country, and there came a wall of cloud, and shadowed above the water; and he did not scatter us over all the earth, but gave to us this country.

X. Hear, ye sons of men, hear the way of life of the blessed. For God placed us in this land, for we are holy but not immortal. For the earth produces most fragrant fruit, and out of the trunks of the trees comes water sweeter than honey, and these are our food and drink. We are also praying night and day, and this is all our occupation. Hear, ye sons of men; with us there is no vine, nor ploughed field, nor works of wood or iron, nor have we any house or building, nor fire nor sword, nor iron wrought or unwrought, nor silver nor gold, nor air too heavy or too keen. Neither do any of us take to themselves wives, except for so long as to beget two children, and after they have produced two children they withdraw from each other and continue in chastity, not knowing that they were ever in the intercourse of marriage, but being in virginity as from the beginning. And the one child remains for marriage, and the other for virginity.

XI. And there is no count of time, neither weeks nor months nor years, for all our day is one day. In our caves lie the leaves of trees, and this is our couch under the trees. But we are not naked of body, as ye wrongly imagine, for we have the garment of immortality and are not ashamed of each other. At the sixth hour of every day we eat, for the fruit of the tree falls of itself at the sixth hour, and we eat and drink our fill, and again the water sinks into its place. We also know you who are there in the world, and who are in sins, and your works, for every day the angels of the Lord come and tell them to us, and the number of your years. But we pray for you to the Lord, because we also are of you and of your race, except that God has chosen us, and has set us in this place without sin. And the angels of God dwell with us every day, and tell us all things concerning you, and we rejoice with the angels over the works of the just, but over the works of sinners we mourn and lament, praying to the Lord that he may cease from his anger and spare your offences.

XII. But when the time of the forty days comes, all the trees cease from their fruits, and the manna that he gave to our fathers rains down from heaven, and the manna is sweeter than honey. Thus we know that the season of the year is changed. But when the time of the holy passover comes, then again the trees put forth fragrant fruit, and thus we know that it is the beginning of the year. But the feast of the resurrection of the Lord is performed with much watching, for we continue watching for three days and three nights.

XIII. We know also the time of our end, for we have no torment nor disease nor pain in our bodies, nor exhaustion nor weakness, but peace and great patience and love. For our soul is not troubled by the angels to go forth, for the angels rejoice when they receive our souls, and the souls also rejoice with the angels when they behold them; as a bride receives the bridegroom, so our soul receives the announcement of the holy angels, saying nothing more than only this, The Lord calls thee. Then the soul quits the body and goes to the angels, and the angels seeing the soul coming forth spotless rejoice, and spreading out their robes receive it. Then the angels call it blessed, saying, Blessed art then, O soul, because the will of the Lord is fulfilled in thee.

XIV. The time of our life is this. If one quits the body in his youth, the days of his life here are three hundred and sixty years, and he that quits the body in old age, the days of his life here are six hundred and eighty-eight years. And the day of our completion is made known to us by the angels, and when the angels of God come to take us, we go with them, and the elders, seeing the angels, gather together all the people and we depart together with the angels, singing psalms, until the angels arrive at the place of our abode. And because we have no tools, the angels of God themselves make the grave for our body, and thus he that is called by God goes down, and all salute him from small to great, sending him on his way and bidding him farewell. Then the soul quits the body and the angels receive it, but we see the shape of the soul as a shape of light, perfect in all the body apart from the distinction of male and female.

XV. Then the angels taking it up sing a song and hymn, making melody to God, and again other troops of angels come in haste to meet them, saluting the soul that is coming and entering into the firmaments. And when it has come to the place where it is to worship God, the son of God himself, together with the angels, receives the soul of the blessed one and bears it to the undefiled father of the ages, and again, when the angels sing above, we being below listen to them, and again we sing and they listen in heaven above, and thus between us and the angels there arises a giving of praise in hymns. But when the soul of the blessed one, falling upon its face, worships the Lord, then we also falling down worship the Lord in that same hour, and when the Lord raises it up then we also arise; and when it goes to its appointed place, we also go into the church, fulfilling the eucharist of the Lord.

Having written these things, and all the life of the blessed, we gave them to our brother Zosimus, and escorted him as far as the place of trees beside the river Eumeles.

XVI. And I, Zosimus, besought again the blessed ones to make entreaty for me to the Lord that the trees might receive me to take me across. And they all cried to the Lord and said, O God that hast shown us thy marvels and hast made thy servant Zosimus to come to us out of the world of vanity, set him again in his own place with peace, and command these trees to bow down and take up thy servant and set him on the further side. And as they finished their prayer, the trees straightway bent down before them, and received me as on the second day before; and being set on the other side of the river I cried with a loud voice and said, Men of righteousness, who are brothers of the holy angels, grant me your prayer in peace, for behold I depart from you. And making prayer they all cried out, saying, Peace, peace be with you, brother.

XVII. Then I prayed to the Lord, and there came to me a storm of wind, and received me upon its wings, and carried me to the place where it found me sitting, and left me there in peace. And raising its voice the wind said to me, Blessed art thou, Zosimus, that thou hast been numbered with the blessed. And the beast from the desert, whose name is the camel, came and received me upon its neck and carried me eighty and five stations, and set me in the place where it found me praying, and left me in peace, crying and saying, Blessed art thou, Zosimus, that thou hast been numbered with the blessed.

XVIII. But seeing me thus praised, Satan desired to tempt me and throw his dart at me from his station, but an angel of God came and said to me, Zosimus, behold Satan is coming to tempt thee, but the Lord will fight for thee, for the glory of thy faith must bind Satan. And an angel of God appeared, crying and saying, Welcome, blessed one of Christ. Come and I shall lead thee to the cave that is the dwelling-place of thy body, for thy cave shall be a testimony of the desert, a healing of the sick that come to it, a place of trial and touch-stone of demons. And laying hold of my hand he strengthened me, and led me for forty days to the cave where I had dwelt. And there was there a table of righteousness, and I spent the night with the angels of God. And I placed the tablets that were given me by the holy blessed ones on the step of the altar in my cave.

XIX. And, behold, when the angels of God ascended, the Devil came, having a fierce shape, and possessed with anger and gall, and said to me, I knew that God would do with thee as with the blessed ones, and that they shall be free from sin and be above the angels, and therefore I brought in an evil design, and entered into the vessel of the serpent, an evil-doer added to evil-doer. And by this I made the first man Adam to transgress and taste of the tree of life, since God had commanded him not to eat of it, that he might remain equal in glory to God and the holy angels; and thou again hast gone and brought this commandment, but now that they may not be without sin, I shall show thee how I shall destroy thee and all those that receive this commandment, so that they may not be without sin, and the book that thou hast brought.

XX. Saying these things the Devil departed from me, and after eight days he brought with him one thousand three hundred and sixty demons, and dragged me from the cave as I prayed, and they beat me, tossing me about between them, for forty days. And after the forty days the devil lamented before me and said, Woe is me that through one man I have lost the world, for he has vanquished me by his prayer. And he began to run from me, but I laying hold of him stayed him and said, Thou shalt not run away and flee from me until thou swearest to me never again to tempt man. And lamenting with great and violent lamentation he swore to me by the firmament of heaven, So long as thy dwelling is here, and after thee, I will not come upon this place. Then I let him go, sending him and the demons with him into eternal fire. Then the angel came, who had companied with me at the table, and led me into my cave with great glory.

XXI. After this I lived thirty-six years, and communicated the way of life of the blessed to the fathers in the desert. But the Devil wept because of the tables of the life of the blessed, saying, If this get abroad in the world, I shall be mocked, and these will remain without sin and I alone in folly. And after the completion of the thirty-six years, the angels of God came to me as to the blessed.

And all the monks were gathered together and all who heard it, and this testament was read to all of them, and in such life he gave up his soul to God.

XXII. And I, Cryseos, being one of those in the desert, spread it abroad and gave it to all that were willing to learn it and profit by it. Therefore the angels of God helped to bury the body of Zosimus as a precious gift, and we saw the soul of the blessed one shining seven times brighter than the sun. And straightway upon that place there came up seven palm-trees and overshadowed the cave. There came up also a fountain of water in that place, holy water, and unto this day a healing and salvation to all the sick that come to it. Peace be to all that have heard the memorial of the holy Zosimus; the Lord is the advocate and helper of all to the endless ages of ages. Amen.

APOCALYPSE OF THOMAS

A. Verona fragment (eighth century) and Wilhelm's text (Munich Clm. 4585, ninth century).

Here beginneth the epistle of the Lord unto Thomas. Hear thou, Thomas, the things which must come to pass in the last times: there shall be famine and war and earthquakes in divers places, snow and ice and great drought shall there be and many dissensions among the peoples, blasphemy, iniquity, envy and villainy, indolence, pride and intemperance, so that every man shall speak that which pleaseth him. And my priests shall not have peace among themselves, but shall sacrifice unto me with deceitful mind: therefore will I not look upon them. Then shall the priests behold the people departing from the house of the Lord and turning unto the world (?) and setting up (or, transgressing) landmarks in the house of God. And they shall claim (vindicate) for themselves many [things and] places that were lost and that shall be subject unto Caesar (?) as also they were aforetime: giving poll-taxes of (for) the cities, even gold and silver and the chief men of the cities shall be condemned (here Verona ends: Munich continues) and their substance brought into the treasury of the kings, and they shall be filled.

For there shall be great disturbance throughout all the people, and death. The house of the Lord shall be desolate, and their altars shall be abhorred, so that spiders weave their webs therein. The place of holiness shall be corrupted, the priesthood polluted, distress (agony) shall increase, virtue shall be overcome, joy perish, and gladness depart. In those days evil shall abound: there shall be respecters of persons, hymns shall cease out of the house of the Lord, truth shall be no more, covetousness shall abound among the priests; an upright man (al. an upright priesthood) shall not be found.

On a sudden there shall arise near the last time a king, a lover of the law, who shall hold rule not for long: he shall leave two sons. The first is named of the first letter (A, Arcadius), the second of the eighth (H, Honorius). The first shall die before the second (Arcadius died in 408- Honorius in 423).

Thereafter shall arise two princes to oppress the nations under whose hands there shall be a very great famine in the right-hand part of the east, so that nation shall rise up against nation and be driven out from their own borders.

Again another king shall arise, a crafty man (?), and shall command a golden image of Caesar (?) to be made (al. to be worshipped in the house of God), wherefore (?) martyrdoms shall abound. Then shall faith return unto the servants of the Lord, and holiness shall be multiplied and distress (agony) increase. The mountains shall be comforted and shall drop down sweetness of fire from the facet, that the number of the saints may be accomplished.

After a little space there shall arise a king out of the east, a lover of the law, who shall cause all good things and necessary to abound in the house of the Lord: he shall show mercy unto the widows and to the needy, and command a royal gift to be given unto the priests: in his days shall be abundance of all things.

And after that again a king shall arise in the south part of the world, and shall hold rule a little space: in whose days the treasury shall fail because of the wages of the Roman soldiers so that the substance of all the aged shall be commanded (to be taken) and given to the king to distribute.

Thereafter shall be plenty of corn and wine and oil, but great dearness of money, so that the substance of gold and silver shall be given for corn, and there shall be great dearth.

At that time shall be very great rising (?) of the sea, so that no man shall tell news to any man. The kings of the earth and the princes and the captains shall be troubled, and no man shall speak freely (boldly). Grey hairs shall be seen upon boys, and the young (?) shall not give place unto the aged.

After that shall arise another king, a crafty man, who shall hold rule for a short space: in whose days there shall be all manner of evils, even the death of the race of men from the east even unto Babylon. And thereafter death and famine and sword in the land of Chanaan even unto (Rome?). Then shall all the fountains of waters and wells boil over (?) and be turned into blood (or, into dust and blood). The heaven shall be moved, the stars shall fall upon the earth, the sun shall be cut in half like the moon, and the moon shall not give her light. There shall be great signs and wonders in those days when Antichrist draweth near. These are the signs unto them that dwell in the earth. In those days the pains of great travail shall come upon them. (al. In those days, when Antichrist now draweth near, these are the signs. Woe unto them that dwell on the earth; in those days great pains of travail shall come upon them.) Woe unto them that build, for they shall not inhabit. Woe unto them that break up the fallow, for they shall labour without cause. Woe unto them that make marriages, for unto famine and need shall they beget sons. Woe unto them that join house to house or field to field, for all things shall be consumed with fire. Woe unto them that look not unto (?) themselves while time alloweth, for hereafter shall they be condemned for ever. Woe unto them that turn away from the poor when he asketh.

[Here is a break: the text goes on: For I am of the high and powerful: I am the Father of all. (al. And know ye: I am the Father most high: I am the Father of all spirits.) This, as we shall see, is the beginning of the older(?) and shorter text, and of the Vienna fragment: only, in the latter, some words now unintelligible precede it: not the words, however, which are in Wilhelm's text. I will continue with Wilhelm.]

These are the seven signs the ending of this world. There shall be in all the earth famine and great pestilences and much distress: then shall all men be led captive among all nations and shall fall by the edge of the sword.

On the first day of the judgement will be a great marvel (or, the beginning shall be). At the third hour of the day shall be a great and mighty voice in the firmament of the heaven, and a great cloud of blood coming down out of the north, and great thunderings and mighty lightnings shall follow that cloud, and there shall be a rain of blood upon all the earth. These are the signs of the first day (Monday in the Anglo-Saxon, and so for the other days).

And on the second day there shall be a great voice in the firmament of the heaven, and the earth shall be moved out of its place: and the gates of heaven shall be opened in the firmament of heaven toward the east, and a great power shall be sent belched) forth by the gates of heaven and shall cover all the heaven even until evening (al. and there shall be fears and tremblings in the world). These are the signs of the second day.

And on the third day, about the second hour, shall be a voice in heaven, and the abysses of the earth shall utter their voice from the four corners of the world. The first heaven shall be rolled up like a book and shall straightway vanish. And because of the smoke and stench of the brimstone of the abyss the days shall be darkened unto the tenth hour. Then shall all men say: I think that the end draweth near, that we shall perish. These are the signs of the third day.

And on the fourth day at the first hour, the earth of the east shall speak, the abyss shall roar: then shall all the earth be moved by the strength of an earthquake. In that day shall all the idols of the heathen fall, and all the buildings of the earth. These are the signs of the fourth day.

And on the fifth day, at the sixth hour, there shall be great thunderings suddenly in the heaven, and the powers of light and the wheel of the sun shall be caught away, and there shall be great darkness over the world until evening, and the stars shall be turned away from their ministry. In that day all nations shall hate the world and despise the life of this world. These are the signs of the fifth day.

And on the sixth day there shall be signs in heaven. At the fourth hour the firmament of heaven shall be cloven from the east unto the west. And the angels of the heavens shall be looking forth upon the earth the opening of the heavens. And all men shall see above the earth the host of the angels looking forth out of heaven. Then shall all men flee.

(Here Wilhelm's text ends abruptly.)
B. Bihlmeyer's text, from Munich Clm. 4563 (eleventh to twelfth century, from Benedictbeuren): and the Vienna fragment.

Hear thou, O Thomas, for I am the Son of God the Father and I am the father of all spirits. Hear thou of me the signs which shall come to pass at the end of this world, when the end of the world shall be fulfilled (Vienna: that it pass away) before mine elect depart out of the world. I will tell thee that which shall come to pass openly unto men (or, will tell thee openly, &c.): but when these things shall be the princes of the angels know not, seeing it is now hidden from before
Then shall there be in the world sharings (participations) between king and king, and in all the earth shall be great famine great pestilences, and many distresses, and the sons of men shall be led captive among all nations and shall fall by the edge of the sword (and there shall be great commotion in the world: Vienna omits). Then after that when the hour of the end draweth nigh there shall be for seven days great signs in heaven, and the powers of the heavens shall be moved.
Then shall there be on the first day the beginning: at the

third hour of the day a great and mighty voice in the firmament of heaven and a bloody cloud coming up (down, Vienna) out of the north, and great thunderings and mighty lightnings shall follow it, and it shall cover the whole heaven, and there shall be a rain of blood upon all the earth. These are the signs of the first day.

And on the second day there shall be a great voice in the firmament of heaven, and the earth shall be moved out of its place, and the gates of heaven shall be opened in the firmament of heaven toward the east, and the (smoke of a great fire shall break forth through the gates of heaven and shall cover all the heaven until evening. In that day there shall be fears and great terrors in the world. These are the signs of the second day. Vienna is defective here).

But on the third day about the third hour shall be a great voice in heaven, and the abysses of the earth (Vienna ends) shall roar from the four corners of the world; the pinnacles (so) of the firmament of heaven shall be opened, and all the air shall be filled with pillars of smoke. There shall be a stench of brimstone, very evil, until the tenth hour, and men shall say: We think the time draweth nigh that we perish. These are the signs of the third day.

And on the fourth day at the first hour, from the land of the east the abyss shall melt (so) and roar. Then shall all the earth be shaken by the might of an earthquake. In that day shall the ornaments of the heathen fall, and all the buildings of the earth, before the might of the earthquake. These are the signs of the fourth day.

But on the fifth day at the sixth hour, suddenly there shall be a great thunder in heaven, and the powers of light and the wheel of the sun shall be caught away (MS. opened), and there shall be great darkness in the world until evening, and the air shall be gloomy (sad) without sun or moon, and the stars shall cease from their ministry. In that day shall all nations behold as in a mirror (?) (or, behold it as sackcloth) and shall despise the life of this world. These are the signs of the fifth day.

And on the sixth day at the fourth hour there shall be a great voice in heaven, and the firmament of the heaven shall be cloven from the east unto the west, and the angels of the heavens shall be looking forth upon the earth by the openings of the heavens, and all these that are on the earth shall behold the host of the angels looking forth out of heaven. Then shall all men flee unto the monuments (mountains ?) and hide themselves from the face of the righteous angels, and say: Would that the earth would open and swallow us up! And such things shall come to pass as never were since this world was created.

Then shall they behold me coming from above in the light of my Father with the power and honour of the holy angels. Then at my coming shall the fence of fire of paradise be done away -because paradise is girt round about with fire. And this shall be that perpetual fire that shall consume the earth and all the elements of the world.

Then shall the spirits and souls of all men come forth from paradise and shall come upon all the earth: and every one of them shall go unto his own body, where it is laid up, and every one of them shall say: Here lieth my body. And when the great voice of those spirits shall be heard, then shall there be a great earthquake over all the world, and by the might thereof the mountains shall be cloven from above and the rocks from beneath. Then shall every spirit return into his own vessel and the bodies of the saints which have fallen asleep shall arise. Then shall their bodies be changed into the image and likeness and the honour of the holy angels, and into the power of the image of mine holy Father. Then shall they be clothed with the vesture of life eternal, out of the cloud of light which hath never been seen in this world; for that cloud cometh down out of the highest realm of the heaven from the power of my Father. And that cloud shall compass about with the beauty thereof all the spirits that have believed in me.

Then shall they be clothed, and shall be borne by the hand of the holy angels like as I have told you aforetime. Then also shall they be lifted up into the air upon a cloud of light, and shall go with me rejoicing unto heaven, and then shall they continue in the light and honour of my Father. Then shall there be unto them great gladness with my Father and before the holy angels These are the signs of the sixth day.

And on the seventh day at the eighth hour there shall be voices in the four corners of the heaven. And all the air shall be shaken, and filled with holy angels, and they shall make war among them all the day long. And in that day shall mine elect be sought out by the holy angels from the destruction of the world. Then shall all men see that the hour of their destruction draweth near. These are the signs of the seventh day.

And when the seven days are passed by, on the eighth day at the sixth hour there shall be a sweet and tender voice in heaven from the east. Then shall that angel be revealed which hath power over the holy angels: and all the angels shall go forth with him, sitting upon chariots of the clouds of mine holy Father (so) rejoicing and running upon the air beneath the heaven to deliver the elect that have believed in me. And they shall rejoice that the destruction of this world hath come.

The words of the Saviour unto Thomas are ended, concerning the end of this world.

THE REVELATION OF STEPHEN

The 'Revelation called of Stephen' is condemned, like that of Thomas, in the Gelasian Decree. Sixtus Senensis, Bibliotheca Sancta (1593), p. 115, says: 'The Apocalypse of Stephen the first martyr who was one of the seven deacons of the apostles was prized by the Manichaean heretics as Serapion witnesses.' Serapion of Thmuis he elsewhere says (p. 299),wrote a large and very notable work against the Manichaeans in Greek 'which I have lately read'. Our texts of Serapion contain no mention of the Apocalypse of Stephen. But no Manichaean would have cared about the book which I am going to speak of. [I must record one of the very rare errors of Fabricius here. He (Cod. Apocr. N.T.,i, p.965) cites Sixtus Senensis as saying (on the authority of Serapion) that the Manichaeans so prized the Revelation of Stephen as to carry it in the skin of their thighs! This long puzzled me, and I could not find it in Sixtus. But at last I noticed that at the end of the article just preceding Stephanus, Victor Vitensis is quoted to this effect: The Manichaeans so honoured their teacher that they used to have these words inscribed on the skin of their thighs. 'Manichaeus, disciple of Christ Jesus'. Perhaps some one has already explained this in print; if so, I have not seen it.]
It has been usually guessed that the writing so described was the account of the finding of St. Stephen's body, the whereabouts of which was revealed by Gamaliel in a vision to Lucian. With Stephen were found the bodies of Gamaliel and his son Abibas, and of Nicodemus. Lucian's narrative was known to Augustine: it purports to be of the year 415, and there is little in it, as compared with similar 'inventions' of relics, which justifies its being solemnly condemned as apocryphal .
So says I. Franko, who in 1906 (Zeitschr. f. Ntl. Wiss.) published a Slavonic romance which, he says, is the real beginning of Lucian's narrative.

The substance of it is this:
Two years after the Ascension there was a contest about Jesus. Many learned men had assembled at Jerusalem from Ethiopia, the Thebaid, Alexandria, Jerusalem, Asia, Mauretania and Babylon. There was a great clamour among them like thunder, lasting till the fourth hour. Stephen, a learned man of the tribe of Benjamin, stood on a high place and addressed the assembly. Why this tumult? said he. Blessed is he who has not doubted concerning Jesus. Born of a pure virgin he filled the world with light. By Satan's contrivances Herod slew 14,000 (144,000) children. He spoke of the miracles of Jesus. Woe to the unbelievers when he shall come as judge, with angels, a fiery chariot, a mighty wind: the stars shall fall, the heavens open, the books be brought forward. The twelve angels who are set over every soul shall unveil the deeds of men. The sea shall move and give up what is in it. The mountains fall, all the surface of the earth becomes smooth. Great winged thrones are set. The Lord, and Christ, and the Holy Spirit take their seats. The Father bids Jesus sit on his right hand.
At this point the crowd cried out: Blasphemy! and took Stephen before Pilate.
Pilate stood on the steps and reproached them: You compelled me to crucify the Innocent; why rage against

this man? Why gnash your teeth? Are ye yet foolish? They led Stephen away. Caiaphas ordered him to be beaten till the blood ran. And he prayed: Lay not this sin to their charge. We saw how angels ministered to him. In the morning Pilate called his wife and two children: they baptized themselves and praised God.
Three thousand men now assembled and disputed with Stephen for three days and three nights. On the fourth day they took counsel and sent to Caesarea of Palestine for Saul of Tarsus, who had a commission to seize upon Christians. He took his place on the judgement seat and said: I wonder that thou, a wise man, and my kinsman, believest all this. None of the Sanhedrin have given up the Law. I have been through all Judaea, Galilee, Peraea, Damascus, and the city of the Jesitites to seek out believers.
Stephen lifted up his hands and said: Silence, persecutor! Recognize the Son of God. Thou makest me doubt of my own descent. But I see that thou shalt ere long drink of the same cup as I. What thou doest, do quickly. Saul rent his clothes and beat Stephen. Gamaliel, Saul's teacher, sprang forth and gave Saul a buffet, saying: Did I teach thee such conduct? know that what this man saith is acceptable and good.
Saul was yet more enraged, and looked fiercely on him, saying: I spare thine old age, but thou shalt reap a due reward for this. Gamaliel answered: I ask nothing better than to suffer with Christ. The elders rent their clothes, cast dust on their heads, and cried: Crucify the blasphemers.
Saul said: Guard them until the morrow. Next day he sat on the judgement seat and had them brought before him, and they were led away to be crucified. An angel came and cast away the cross, and Stephen's wounds were healed. Seven men came and poured molten lead into his mouth and pitch into his ears. They drove nails into his breast and feet, and he prayed for their forgiveness. Again an angel came down and healed him, and a great multitude believed.
Next day all assembled and took him out of the city to judge him. He mounted upon a stone and addressed them: How long will ye harden your hearts? The Law and the Prophets spake of Christ. In the first Law, and the second, and the other books it is written: When the year of the covenant cometh I will send my beloved angel, the good spirit of sonship, from a pure maiden, the fruit of truth, without ploughshare and without seed, and an image of sowing (?), and the fruit shall grow after the . . . of planting for ever from the word of my covenant, and signs shall come to pass. And Isaiah saith: Unto us a child is born, &c. And again: Behold, a virgin shall conceive, &c. And the prophet Nathan said: I saw one, a maiden and without touch of man, and a man child in her arms, and that was the Lord of the earth unto the end of the earth. And again the prophet Baruch saith: Christ the eternal appeareth as a stone from the mountain and breaketh in pieces the idol temples of the . . . David also said: Arise, O Lord, unto thy resting place, &c. Understand then, O foolish ones, what the prophet saith: In this word shalt thou judge.
And he looked up to heaven and said: I see the heaven opened and the Son of man standing at the right hand of God.

Then they laid hands on him, saying: He blasphemeth! Gamaliel said: Wherein? This righteous man hath seen the Son saying to the Father: Lo, the Jews rage against me and cease not to ill-treat them that confess my name. And the Father said: Sit thou on my right hand until I make thine enemies thy footstool.

Then they bound Stephen and took him away to Alexander, the reader, who was a chief of the people, and of the troop in Tiberias.

In the fourth watch of the night, a light as of lightning shone round about him, and a voice said: Be strong. Thou art my first martyr, and thine hour is nigh. I will write the record of thee in the book of everlasting life. The Jews took counsel and decreed that he should be stoned. There were with him Abibas, Nicodemus, Gamaliel, Pilate, his wife and two children, and a multitude of believers. Saul stood forth and beckoned, and said: It would have been better that this man should not be slain, because of his great wisdom: but forasmuch as he is an apostate, I condemn Stephen to be stoned. The people said: He shall be stoned: but those who stood in the front rank with staves looked on each other and durst not lay hands on him: for he was renowned among the people.

Saul was wroth, and stripped those servants of their garments and laid them on the table; and commanded the men to stone Stephen.

Stephen looked round and said: Saul, Saul, that which thou doest unto me to-day, that same will the Jews do unto thee to-morrow. And when thou sufferest, thou shalt think on me.

The people cast stones upon him so thickly that the light of the sun was darkened. Nicodemus and Gamaliel put their arms about him and shielded him, and were slain, and gave up their souls to Christ.

Stephen prayed, saying: Forgive them that stone us, for by their means we trust to enter into thy kingdom. And at the tenth hour he gave up the ghost. Then beautiful youths appeared, and fell upon the bodies and wept aloud: and the people beheld the souls borne up by angels into heaven, and saw the heavens open and the hosts coming to meet the souls. And the people mourned for three days and three nights.

Pilate took the bodies and put each one into a silver coffin with his name upon it: but Stephen's coffin was gilt: and he laid them in his secret sepulchre. But Stephen prayed: Let my body be buried in my land of Serasima in Kapogemala (Caphargamala) until the revealing, when the martyrs that follow me shall be gathered together. And an angel came and removed the bodies thither. But Pilate rose early to burn incense before the bodies, and found them not; and rent his clothes, saying: Was I then not worthy to be thy servant? On the night following, Stephen appeared and said to him: Weep not. I prayed God to hide our bodies. In the time of our revealing one of thy seed shall find us after a vision, and thy desire shall be fulfilled. But build a house of prayer and celebrate our feast in the month of April. After seven months thou also shalt rest. And Pilate did so: and he died, and was buried at Kapartasala: and his wife also died in peace. But the holy martyrs appeared thrice to venerable and believing men, speaking to them, and revealing divine words: for after their death many

believed.

One of Franko's two manuscripts omits all mention of Pilate, who is indeed not necessary to the story. The statements about him are quite irreconcilable with other legends, even those of the Eastern Church which take the favourable view of him.

Franko is clearly right in saying that this romance implies a continuation, and most likely right in holding that the Lucian-narrative implies a previous story. But the extravagance of the Slavonic text is such that one cannot but think it has been improved by the translator: and if Pilate could be gratuitously inserted -as I think he has been- by one redactor, others may equally well have been at work.

THE VISION OF PAUL THE APOSTLE

Here beginneth the Vision of Saint Paul the Apostle.

But I will come to visions and revelations of the Lord. I knew a man in Christ fourteen years ago, whether in the body I know not, or whether out of the body I know not—God knoweth—that such an one was caught up unto the third heaven: and I knew such a man, whether in the body or out of the body I know not—God knoweth—that he was caught up into paradise and heard secret words which it is not lawful for men to utter. For such an one will I boast, but for myself I will boast nothing, save of mine infirmities.

1 At what time was it made manifest? In the consulate of Theodosius Augustus the younger and Cynegius, a certain honourable man then dwelling at Tarsus, in the house which had been the house of Saint Paul, an angel appeared unto him by night and gave him a revelation, saying that he should break up the foundation of the house and publish that which he found; but he thought this to be a lying vision.

2 But a third time the angel came, and scourged him and compelled him to break up the foundation. And he dug, and found a box of marble inscribed upon the sides : therein was the revelation of Saint Paul, and his shoes wherein he walked when he taught the word of God. But he feared to open that box, and brought it to the judge; and the judge took it, sealed as it was with lead, and sent it to the emperor Theodosius, fearing that it might be somewhat strange; and the emperor when he received it, opened it and found the revelation of Saint Paul. A copy thereof he sent to Jerusalem and the original he kept with him. (Gr. reverses this: he kept the copy and sent away the original. It adds: And there was written therein as followeth.)

3 Now while I was in the body, wherein I was caught up unto the third heaven, the word of the Lord came unto me, saying: Speak unto this people: How long will ye transgress, and add sin upon sin, and tempt the Lord that made you?[4] Saying that ye are Abraham's children but doing the works of Satan (so Gr. ; Lat. Ye are the sons of God, doing the work of the devil), walking in the confidence of God, boasting in your name only, but being poor because of the matter of sin. Remember therefore and know that the whole creation is subject unto God, but mankind only sinneth. It hath dominion over the whole creation, and sinneth more than the whole of nature.

4 For oftentimes hath the sun, the great light, appealed unto the Lord, saying: O Lord God Almighty, I look forth upon the ungodliness and unrighteousness of men. Suffer me, and I will do unto them according to my power, that they may know that thou art God alone. And there came a voice unto it, saying: All these things do I know, for mine eye seeth and mine ear heareth, but my long-suffering beareth with them until they turn and repent. But if they return not unto me, I will judge them all.

5 And sometimes the moon and the stars have appealed unto the Lord, saying: O Lord God Almighty, unto us hast thou given rule over the night; how long shall we look upon the ungodliness and fornications and murders which the children of men commit? suffer us to do unto them according unto our powers, that they may know that thou art God alone. And there came a voice unto them, saying: I know all these things, and mine eye looketh upon them and mine ear heareth, but my long-suffering beareth with them until they turn and repent. But if they return not unto me, I will judge them.

6 Oftentimes also the sea hath cried out, saying: O Lord God Almighty, men have polluted thine holy name in me: suffer me and I will arise and cover every wood and tree and all the world, till I blot out all the children of men from before thy face, that they may know that thou art God alone. And again a voice came, saying: I know all, for mine eye seeth all things, and mine ear heareth, but my long-suffering beareth with them until they turn and repent. But if they return not, I will judge them.
Sometimes also the waters have appealed against the children of men, saying: O Lord God Almighty, the children of men have all defiled thine holy name. And there came a voice, saying: I know all things before they come to pass, for mine eye seeth and mine ear heareth all things: but my long-suffering beareth with them until they turn. And if not, I will judge. Often also hath the earth cried out unto the Lord against the children of men, saying: O Lord God Almighty, I suffer hurt more than all thy creation, bearing the fornications, adulteries, murders, thefts, forswearings, sorceries, and witchcrafts of men, and all the evils that they do, so that the father riseth up against the son, and the son against the father, the stranger against the stranger, every one to defile his neighbour's wife. The father goeth up upon his son's bed, and the son likewise goeth up upon the couch of his father; and with all these evils have they that offer a sacrifice unto thy name polluted thine holy place. Therefore do I suffer hurt more than the whole creation, and I would not yield mine excellence and my fruits unto the children of men. Suffer me and I will destroy the excellence of my fruits. And there came a voice and said: I know all things, and there is none that can hide himself from his sin. And their ungodliness do I know; but my holiness suffereth them until they turn and repent. But if they return not unto me, I will judge them.

7 Behold *then* ye children of men. The creature is subject unto God; but mankind alone sinneth.
Therefore, ye children of men, bless ye the Lord God without ceasing at all hours and on all days; but especially when the sun setteth. For in that hour do all the angels go unto the Lord to worship him and to present the deeds of men which every man doeth from morning until evening, whether they be good or evil. And there is an angel that goeth forth rejoicing from the man in whom he dwelleth <and another goeth with a sad countenance, *Gr.*>.
When therefore the sun is set, at the first hour of the night, in the same hour *goeth* the angel of every people and of every man and woman, which protect and keep them, because man is the image of God: and likewise at the hour of morning, which is the twelfth hour of the night, do all the angels of men and women go to meet God and present all the work which every man hath wrought, whether good or evil. And every day and night do the angels present unto God the account of all the deeds of mankind. Unto you, therefore, I say, O children of men, bless ye the Lord God without ceasing all the days of your life.

8 At the hour appointed, therefore, all the angels, every one rejoicing, come forth before God together to meet him and worship him at the hour that is set; †and lo, suddenly at the *set* time there was a meeting,† and the angels came to worship in the presence of God, and the spirit came forth to meet them, and there was a voice, saying: Whence come ye, our angels, bringing burdens of news?

9 They answered and said: We are come from them that have renounced the world for thy holy name's sake, wandering as strangers and in the caves of the rocks, and weeping every hour that they dwell on the earth and hungering and thirsting for thy name's sake; with their loins girt, holding in their hands the incense of their heart, and praying and blessing at every hour, suffering anguish and subduing themselves, weeping and lamenting more than all that dwell on the earth. And we that are their angels do mourn with them; whither therefore it pleaseth thee, command us to go and minister †lest they do otherwise, but the poor† more than all that dwell on the earth. (The sense required as shown by *Gr.* is that the angels ask that these good men may continue in goodness.) And the voice of God came unto them, saying: Know ye that from henceforth my grace shall be established with you, and mine help, which is my dearly beloved Son, shall be with them, ruling them at all times; and he shall minister unto them and never forsake them, for their place is his habitation.

10 When, then, these angels departed, lo, there came other angels to worship in the presence of the majesty, to meet therewith, and they were weeping. And the spirit of God went forth to meet them, and the voice of God came, saying: Whence are ye come, our angels, bearing burdens, ministers of the news of the world? They answered and said in the presence of God: We are come from them which have called upon thy name; and the snares of the world have made them wretched, devising many excuses at all times, and not making so much as one pure prayer out of their whole heart all the time of their life. Wherefore then must we be with men that are sinners? And the voice of God came unto them: Ye must minister unto them until they turn and repent; but if they return not unto me, I will judge them.
Know therefore, O children of men, that whatsoever is wrought by you, the angels tell it unto God, whether it be good or evil.

11 [*Syr.* Again, after these things, I saw one of the spiritual ones coming unto me, and he caught me up in the spirit, and carried me to the third heaven.]
And the angel answered and said unto me: Follow me, and I will show thee the place of the righteous where they are taken when they are dead. And thereafter will I take thee to the bottomless pit and show thee the souls of the sinners, into what manner of place they are taken when they are dead.
And I went after the angel, and he took me into heaven, and I looked upon the firmament, and saw there the powers; and there was forgetfulness which deceiveth and draweth unto itself the hearts of men, and the spirit of slander and the spirit of fornication and the spirit of wrath and the spirit of insolence, and there were the princes of wickedness. These things saw I beneath the firmament of the heaven.
And again I looked and saw angels without mercy, having

no pity, whose countenances were full of fury, and their teeth sticking forth out of their mouth: their eyes shone like the morning star of the east, and out of the hairs of their head and out of their mouth went forth sparks of fire. And I asked the angel, saying: Who are these, Lord? And the angel answered and said unto me: These are they which are appointed unto the souls of sinners in the hour of necessity, even of them that have not believed that they had the Lord for their helper and have not trusted in him.

12 And I looked into the height and beheld other angels whose faces shone like the sun, and their loins were girt with golden girdles, holding palms in their hands, and the sign of God, clad in raiment whereon was written the name of the Son of God, full of all gentleness and mercy. And I asked the angel and said: Who are these, Lord, that are of so great beauty and compassion? And the angel answered and said unto me: These are the angels of righteousness that are sent to bring the souls of the righteous in the hour of necessity, even them that have believed that they had the Lord for their helper. And I said unto him: Do the righteous and the sinners of necessity meet [witnesses] when they are dead? And the angel answered and said unto me: The way whereby all pass unto God is one: but the righteous having an holy helper with them are not troubled when they go to appear in the presence of God.

13 And I said unto the angel: I would see the souls of the righteous and of the sinners as they depart out of the world. And the angel answered and said unto me: Look down upon the earth. And I looked down from heaven upon the earth and beheld the whole world, and it was as nothing in my sight; and I saw the children of men as though they were nought, and failing utterly; and I marvelled, and said unto the angel: Is this the greatness of men? And the angel answered and said unto me: This it is, and these are they that do hurt from morning until evening. And I looked, and saw a great cloud of fire spread over the whole world, and said unto the angel: What is this, Lord? And he said to me: This is the unrighteousness that is mingled +by the princes of sinners† (*Gr.* mingled with the destruction of sinners; *Syr.* mingled with the prayers of the sons of men).

14 And I when I heard that sighed and wept, and said unto the angel: I would wait for the souls of the righteous and of the sinners, and see in what fashion they depart out of the body. And the angel answered and said unto me: Look again upon the earth. And I looked and saw the whole world: and men were as nought, and failing utterly ; and I looked and saw a certain man about to die; and the angel said to me: He whom thou seest is righteous. And again I looked and saw all his works that he had done for the name of God, and all his desires which he remembered and which he remembered not, all of them stood before his face in the hour of necessity. And I saw that the righteous man had grown *in righteousness*, and found rest and confidence: and before he departed out of the world there stood by him holy angels, and also evil ones: and I saw them all; but the evil ones found no abode in him, but the holy ones had power over his soul and ruled it until it went out of the body. And they stirred up the soul, saying: O soul, take knowledge of thy body whence thou art come out; for thou must needs return into the same body at the day of resurrection, to receive that which is promised unto all the righteous. They received therefore the soul out of

the body, and straightway kissed it as one daily known of them, saying unto it: Be of good courage, for thou hast done the will of God while thou abodest on the earth. And there came to meet it the angel that watched it day by day, and he said unto it: Be of good courage, O soul: for I rejoice in thee because thou hast done the will of God on the earth; for I told unto God all thy works, how they stood. Likewise also the spirit came forth to meet it and said: O soul, fear not, neither be troubled, until thou come unto a place which thou never knewest; but I will be thine helper, for I have found in thee a place of refreshment in the time when I dwelt in thee, when I was (thou wast?) on the earth. And the spirit [thereof] strengthened it, and the angel thereof took it up and carried it into the heaven. †And the angel said† (*Syr.* And there went out to meet it wicked powers, those that are under heaven. And there reached it the spirit of error, and said): Whither runnest thou, O soul, and presumest to enter heaven? stay and let us see if there be aught of ours in thee. And lo! we have found nothing in thee. I behold also the help of God, and thine angel; and the spirit rejoiceth with thee because thou didst the will of God upon earth. (*Syr. has more here.* There is a conflict between the good and evil angels. The spirit of error first laments. Then the spirit of the tempter and of fornication meet it and it escapes, and they lament. All the principalities and evil spirits come to meet it and find nothing, and gnash their teeth. The guardian angel bids them go back, 'Ye tempted this soul and it would not listen to you'. And the voice of many angels is heard rejoicing over the soul. Probably this is original matter.) And they brought it until it did worship in the presence of God. And when they (it?) had ceased, forthwith Michael and all the host of the angels fell and worshipped the footstool of his feet and his gates, and said together unto the soul: This is the God of all, which made *thee* in his image and likeness. And the angel returned and declared, saying: Lord, remember his works; for this is the soul whereof I did report the works unto thee, Lord, doing according to thy judgement. And likewise the spirit said: I am the spirit of quickening that breathed upon it; for I had refreshment in it in the time when I dwelt therein, doing according to thy judgement. And the voice of God came, saying: Like as this *soul* hath not grieved me, neither will I grieve it, for like as it hath had mercy, I also will have mercy. Let it be delivered therefore unto Michael the angel of the covenant, and let him lead it into the paradise of rejoicing that it become fellow-heir with all the saints. And thereafter I heard the voices of thousands of thousands of angels and archangels and the cherubim and the four-and-twenty elders uttering hymns and glorifying the Lord and crying: Righteous art thou, O Lord, and just are thy judgements, and there is no respect of persons with thee, but thou rewardest every man according to thy judgement. And the angel answered and said unto me: Hast thou believed and known that whatsoever every one of you hath done, he beholdeth it at the hour of his necessity? And I said: Yea, Lord.

15 And he said unto me: Look down again upon the earth and wait for the soul of a wicked man going forth of the body, one that hath provoked the Lord day and night, saying: I know nought else in this world, I will eat and drink and enjoy the things that are in the world. For who is he that hath gone down into hell and come up and told us that there is a judgement there? And again I looked and saw all the despising of the sinner, and all that he did, and they

stood together before him in the hour of necessity: and it came to pass in that hour when he was led out of his body to the judgement, that he (*MS.* I) said: It were better for me (*MS.* him) that I (he) had not been born. And after that the holy angels and the evil and the soul of the sinner came together, and the holy angels found no place in it. But the evil angels threatened (had power over) it, and when they brought it forth out of the body, the angels admonished it thrice, saying: O wretched soul, look upon thy flesh whence thou art come out; for thou must needs return into thy flesh at the day of resurrection to receive the due reward for thy sins and for thy wickedness.

16 And when they had brought it forth, the accustomed (i. e. guardian) angel went before it and said unto it: O miserable soul, I am the angel that clave unto thee and day by day reported unto the Lord thine evil deeds, whatsoever thou wroughtest by night or day; and if it had been in my power I would not have ministered unto thee even one day; but of this I could do nothing, *for God* is merciful and a just judge, and he commanded us not to cease ministering unto *your* soul till ye should repent: but thou hast lost the time of repentance. I indeed am become a stranger unto thee and thou to me. Let us go then unto the just judge: I will not leave thee until I know that from this day I am become a stranger unto thee. (Here *Copt.* inserts a quite similar speech of the spirit to the soul, which may be original.) And the spirit confounded it, and the angel troubled it. When therefore they were come unto the principalities, and it would now go to enter into heaven, one burden (labour, suffering) was laid upon it after another: error and forgetfulness and whispering met it, and the spirit of fornication and the rest of the powers, and said unto it: Whither goest thou, wretched soul, and darest to run forward into heaven? Stay, that we may see whether we have property of ours in thee, for we see not with thee an holy helper. (*Syr.* adds: And the angel answered and said: Know ye that it is a soul of the Lord, and he will not cast it aside, neither will I surrender the image of God into the hand of the wicked one. The Lord supported me all the days of the life of the soul, and he can support and help me: and I will not cast it off until it go up before the throne of God on high. When he shall see it, he hath power over it, and will send it whither he pleases.) And after that I heard voices in the height of the heavens, saying: Present this miserable soul unto God, that it may know that there is a God, whom it hath despised. When therefore it was entered into the heaven, all the angels, even thousands of thousands, saw it, and all cried out with one voice, saying: Woe unto thee, miserable soul, for thy works which thou diddest upon the earth ; what answer wilt thou make unto God when thou drawest near to worship him? The angel which was with it answered and said: Weep with me, my dearly beloved, for I have found no rest in this soul. And the angels answered him and said: Let this soul be taken away out of our midst, for since it came in, the stench of it is passed upon us the angels. And thereafter it was presented, to worship in the presence of God; and the angel showed it the Lord God that made it after his own image and likeness. And its angel ran before it, saying: O Lord God Almighty, I am the angel of this soul, whose works I presented unto thee day and night, not doing according to thy judgement. And likewise the spirit said: I am the spirit which dwelt in it ever since it was made, and I know *it* in itself, and it followed not my will: judge it, Lord, according to thy judgement. And the voice of God came

unto it and said: Where is thy fruit that thou hast yielded, worthy of those good things which thou hast received? did I put a distance even of a day between thee and the righteous? did I not make the sun to rise upon thee even as upon the righteous? And it was silent, having nothing to answer; and again the voice came, saying: Just is the judgement of God, and there is no respect of persons with God, for whosoever hath done his mercy, he will have mercy on him, and whoso hath not had mercy, neither shall God have mercy on him.. Let him therefore be delivered unto the angel Tartaruchus (*Gr.* Temeluchus) that is set over the torments, and let him cast him into the outer darkness, where is weeping and gnashing of teeth, and let him be there until the great day of judgement. And after that I heard the voice of the angels and archangels saying: Righteous art thou, O Lord, and just is thy judgement.

17 And again I beheld, and lo, a soul which was brought by two angels, weeping and saying: Have mercy on me, thou righteous God, O God the judge; for to-day it is seven days since I went forth out of my body, and I was delivered unto these two angels, and they have brought me unto those places which I had never seen. And God the righteous judge said unto it: What hast thou done? for thou hast never wrought mercy; therefore wast thou delivered unto such angels, which have no mercy, and because thou hast not done right, therefore neither have they dealt pitifully with thee in the hour of thy necessity. Confess therefore thy sins which thou hast committed when thou wert in the world. And it answered and said: Lord, I have not sinned. And the righteous Lord God was wroth with indignation when it said: I have not sinned; for it lied. And God said: Thinkest thou that thou art yet in the world? If every one of you there when he sinneth, hideth and concealeth his sin from his neighbour, yet here no thing is hidden, for when the souls come to worship before the throne, both the good works and the sins of every one are made manifest. And when the soul heard that, it held its peace, having no answer. And I heard the Lord God, the righteous judge, saying again: Come, thou angel of this soul, and stand in the midst. And the angel of the sinful soul came, having a writing in his hands, and said: These, Lord, that are in mine hands, are all the sins of this soul from its youth up unto this day, even from ten years from its birth: and if thou bid me, Lord, I can tell the acts thereof since it began to be fifteen years old. And the Lord God the righteous judge said: I say unto thee, O angel, I desire not of thee the account since it began to be fifteen years old: but declare its sins of five years before that it died and came hither. And again God the righteous judge said: For by myself I swear, and by mine holy angels and by my power, that if it had repented five years before it died, *even* for the walk (conversation) of one year, there should be forgetfulness of all the evil which it committed before, and it should have pardon and remission of sins: but now let it perish. And the angel of the sinful soul answered and said: Command, Lord, that (such and such an) angel to bring forth those (such and such) souls.

18 And in that same hour the souls were brought forth into the midst, and the soul of the sinner knew them. And the Lord said unto the soul of the sinner: I say unto thee, O soul, confess thy deeds which thou didst upon these souls whom thou seest, when they were in the world. And it answered and said: Lord, it is not yet a full year since I slew this one and shed its blood upon the earth, and with

another I committed fornication; and not that only, but I did it much harm by taking away its substance. And the Lord God the righteous judge said: Knewest thou not that he that doth violence to another, if he that suffered violence die first, he is kept in this place until he that hurt him dieth, and then do both of them appear before the judge? and now hath every one received according as he did. And I heard a voice saying: Let that soul be delivered into the hands of Tartaruchus, and he must be taken down into hell. Let him take him into the lower prison and let him be cast into torments and be left there until the great day of judgement. And again I heard thousands of thousands of angels singing an hymn unto the Lord and saying: Righteous art thou, O Lord, and just are thy judgements.

19 The angel answered and said unto me: Hast thou perceived all these things? And I said: Yea, Lord. And he said unto me: Follow me again, and I will take thee and show thee the places of the righteous. And I followed the angel and he took me up unto the third heaven and set me before the door of a gate; and I looked on it and saw, and the gate was of gold, and there were two pillars of gold full of golden letters; and the angel turned again to me and said: Blessed art thou if thou enterest in by these gates, for it is not permitted to any to enter save only to those that have kept goodness and pureness of their bodies in all things. And I asked the angel and said: Lord, tell me for what cause are these letters set upon these tables? The angel answered and said unto me: These are the names of the righteous that minister unto God with their whole heart, which dwell on the earth. And again I said: Lord, then are their names <written while they are yet on the earth? And he said: Not only are their names written, but> also their countenance and the likeness of them that serve God is in heaven, and they are known unto the angels: for they know them that with their whole heart serve God before they depart out of the world.

20 And when I had entered within the gate of paradise there came to meet me an old man whose face shone like the sun, and he embraced me and said: Hail, Paul, dearly beloved of God. And he kissed me with a joyful countenance, *but* he wept, and I said unto him: Father (*Lat.* Brother), why weepest thou? And again sighing and weeping he said: Because we are vexed by men, and they grieve us sore; for many are the good things which the Lord hath prepared, and great are his promises, but many receive them not. And I asked the angel and said: Who is this, Lord? And he said unto me: This is Enoch the scribe of righteousness.
And I entered within that place and straightway I saw Elias, and he came and saluted me with gladness and joy. And when he had seen me, he turned himself away and wept and said unto me: Paul, mayest thou receive *the reward of* thy labour which thou hast done among mankind. As for me, I have seen great and manifold good things which God hath prepared for all the righteous, and great are the promises of God, but the more part receive them not; yea hardly through much toil doth one and another enter into these places.

21 And the angel answered and said unto me: What things soever I now show thee here, and whatsoever thou hearest, reveal them not unto any upon earth. And he led me and showed me: and I heard there words which it is not lawful

for a man to utter; and again he said: Yet again follow me and I will show thee that which thou must relate and tell openly.

And he brought me down from the third heaven, and led me into the second heaven, and again he led me to the firmament, and from the firmament he led me unto the gates of heaven. And the beginning of the foundation thereof was upon the river that watereth all the earth. And I asked the angel and said: Lord, what is this river of water? and he said unto me: This is the Ocean. And suddenly I came out of heaven, and perceived that it is the light of the heaven that shineth upon all the earth (*or*, all that land). And there the earth (*or*, land) was seven times brighter than silver. And I said: Lord, what is this place? and he said unto me: This is the land of promise. Hast thou not yet heard that which is written: Blessed are the meek, for they shall inherit the earth? The souls therefore of the righteous when they are gone forth of the body are sent for the time into this place. And I said unto the angel: Shall then this land be made manifest after (*Lat*. before) a time? The angel answered and said unto me: When Christ whom thou preachest cometh to reign, then by the decree of God the first earth shall be dissolved, and then shall this land of promise be shown and it shall be like dew or a cloud; and then shall the Lord Jesus Christ the eternal king be manifested and shall come with all his saints to dwell therein; and he shall reign over them a thousand years, and they shall eat of the good things which now I will show thee.

22 And I looked round about that land and saw a river flowing with milk and honey. And there were at the brink of the river trees planted, full of fruits: now every tree bare twelve fruits in the year, and they had various and divers fruits: and I saw the fashion (creation) of that place and all the work of God, and there I saw palm-trees of twenty cubits and others of ten cubits: and that land was seven times brighter than silver. And the trees were full of fruits from the root even to the upper branches. (*Lat*. is confused here. *Copt*. has: From the root of each tree up to its heart there were ten thousand branches with tens of thousands of clusters, [and there were ten thousand clusters on each branch,] and there were ten thousand dates in each cluster. And thus was it also with the vines. Every vine had ten thousand branches, and each branch had upon it ten thousand bunches of grapes, and every bunch had on it ten thousand grapes. And there were other trees there, myriads of myriads of them, and their fruit was in the same proportion.) And I said unto the angel: Wherefore doth every tree bring forth thousands of fruits? The angel answered and said unto me: Because the Lord God of his bounty giveth his gifts in abundance unto the worthy; for they also of their own will afflicted themselves when they were in the world, doing all things for his holy name's sake. And again I said unto the angel: Lord, are these the only promises which the most holy Lord God promiseth? and he answered and said unto me: No; for there are greater by seven times than these. But I say unto thee, that when the righteous are gone forth out of the body *and* shall see the promises and the good things which God hath prepared for them, yet again they shall sigh and cry, saying: Wherefore did we utter a word out of our mouth to provoke our neighbour even for a day? And I asked again and said: Be these the only promises of God? And the angel answered and said unto me: These which now thou seest are for them that are married and keep the purity of their marriage, being

continent. But unto the virgins, and unto them that hunger and thirst after righteousness and afflict themselves for the name of the Lord, God will give things sevenfold greater than these, which now I will show thee.

And after that he took me out of that place where I saw these things, and lo, a river, and the waters of it were white exceedingly, more than milk; and I said unto the angel: What is this? and he said to me: This is the lake Acherusa where is the city of Christ but not every man is suffered to enter into that city: for this is the way that leadeth unto God, and if any be a fornicator or ungodly, and turn and repent and bear fruits meet for repentance, first when he cometh out of the body he is brought and worshippeth God, and then by the commandment of the Lord he is delivered unto Michael the angel, and he washeth him in the lake Acherusa and so bringeth him in to the city of Christ with them that have done no sin. And I marvelled and blessed the Lord God for all the things which I saw.

23 And the angel answered and said unto me: Follow me, and I will bring thee into the city of Christ. And he stood by (upon) the lake Acherusa, and set me in a golden ship, and angels as it were three thousand sang an hymn before me until I came even unto the city of Christ. And they that dwelt in the city of Christ rejoiced greatly over me as I came unto them, and I entered in and saw the city of Christ. And it was all of gold, and twelve walls compassed it about, and there were twelve towers within (a tower on each wall, *Copt*.; 12,000 towers, *Syr*.), and every wall had a furlong between them (i. e. the walls were a furlong apart, so *Syr*.; *Copt*. the circumference of each was 100 furlongs) round about; and I said unto the angel: Lord, how much is one furlong? The angel answered and said unto me: It is as much as there is betwixt the Lord God and the men that are on the earth, for the great city of Christ is alone. And there were twelve gates in the circuit of the city, of great beauty, and four rivers that compassed it about. There was a river of honey, and a river of milk, and a river of wine, and a river of oil. And I said unto the angel: What are these rivers that compass this city about? And he saith to me: These are the four rivers which flow abundantly for them that are in this land of promise, whereof the names are *these*: the river of honey is called Phison, and the river of milk Euphrates, and the river of oil Geon, and the river of wine Tigris. Whereas therefore when *the righteous* were in the world they used not their power over these things, but hungered and afflicted themselves for the Lord God's sake, therefore when they enter into this city, the Lord will give them these things without number (?) and without all measure.

24 And I when I entered in by the gate saw before the doors of the city trees great and high, having no fruits, but leaves only. And I saw a few men scattered about in the midst of the trees, and they mourned sore when they saw any man enter into the city. And those trees did penance for them, humbling themselves and bowing down, and again raising themselves up.

And I beheld it and wept with them, and I asked the angel and said: Lord, who are these that are not permitted to enter into the city of Christ ? And he said unto me: These are they that did earnestly renounce *the world* day and night with fasting, but had an heart proud above other men, glorifying and praising themselves, and doing nought for their neighbours. For some they greeted friendly, but unto others they said not even 'Hail', and unto whom they would they opened, and if they did any small thing for their neighbour they were puffed up. And I said: What then, Lord? their pride hath prevented them from entering into the city of Christ? And the angel answered and said unto me: The root of all evils is pride. Are they better than the Son of God who came unto the Jews in great humility? And I asked him and said: Wherefore is it then that the trees humble themselves and are again raised up? And the angel answered and said unto me: All the time that these spent upon earth (Of old time they were on the earth, *Copt.*) serving God (they served God): *but* because of the shame and reproaches of men they were ashamed (did blush) for a time and humbled themselves; but they were not grieved, neither did repent, to cease from this pride that was in them (and one day they bowed themselves because of the disgrace of man, for they cannot endure the pride that is in him, *Copt.*). This is the cause why the trees humble themselves and again are raised up. And I asked and said: For what cause are they let in unto the gates of the city? The angel answered and said unto me: Because of the great goodness of God, and because this is the entry of all his saints which do enter into this city. Therefore are they left in this place, that when Christ the eternal king entereth in with his saints, when he cometh in, all the righteous shall entreat for them; and then shall they enter into the city with them: yet none of them is able to have confidence such as they have that have humbled themselves, serving the Lord God all their life long.

25 But I went forward and the angel led me and brought me unto the river of honey, and I saw there Esaias and Jeremias and Ezekiel and Amos and Micheas and Zacharias, even the prophets lesser and greater, and they greeted me in the city. I said unto the angel: What is this path? and he said unto me: This is the path of the prophets: every one that hath grieved his soul and not done his own will for God's sake, when he is departed out of the world and hath been brought unto the Lord God and worshipped him, then by the commandment of God he is delivered unto Michael, and he bringeth him into the city unto this place of the prophets, and they greet him as their friend and neighbour, because he hath performed the will of God.

26 Again he led me where was the river of milk, and I saw in that place all the children whom the king Herod slew for the name of Christ, and they greeted me, and the angel said unto me: All they that keep chastity in cleanness, when they are gone out of the body, after they worship the Lord God, are delivered unto Michael and brought unto the children: and they greet them, saying: They are our brothers and friends and members: among them shall they inherit the promises of God.

27 Again he took me and brought me to the north side of the city, and led me to where was the river of wine; and I saw there Abraham, Isaac, and Jacob, Lot and Job and other saints, and they greeted me. And I asked and said: What is this place, Lord? The angel answered and said unto me: All they that are entertainers of strangers, when they are departed out of the world, first worship the Lord God, and *then* are delivered unto Michael and brought by this path into the city, and all the righteous greet him as a son and brother, and say unto him: Because thou hast kept kindliness and the entertainment of strangers, come thou and have an inheritance in the city of our Lord God. Every one of the righteous shall receive the good things of God in the city according to his deeds.

28 And again he took me to the river of oil on the east side of the city. And I saw there men rejoicing and singing psalms, and said: Who are these, Lord? and the angel said unto me: These are they that have devoted themselves unto God with their whole heart, and had in them no pride. For all that rejoice in the Lord God and sing praises to the Lord. with their whole heart are brought here into this city.

29 And he took me into the midst of the city, by the twelve walls (to the twelfth wall, *Copt.*). Now there was in that place an higher wall; and I asked and said: Is there in the city of Christ a wall more excellent in honour than this place? And the angel answered and said unto me: The second is better than the first, and likewise the third than the second; for one excelleth the other even unto the twelfth wall. And I said: Wherefore, Lord, doth one excel another in glory? show me. And the angel answered and said unto me: All they that have in them even a little slandering or envy or pride, somewhat is taken away from a glory, even if he be in the city of Christ. Look thou behind thee.

And I turned myself and saw golden thrones set at the several gates, and upon them men having golden crowns and jewels: and I looked and saw within among the twelve men, thrones set in another order (row, fashion?), which appeared of much glory so that no man is able to declare the praise of them. And I asked the angel and said: Lord, who is upon the throne? And the angel answered and said unto me: These are the thrones of them that had goodness and understanding of heart and *yet* made themselves foolish for the Lord God's sake, knowing neither the Scriptures nor many psalms, but keeping in mind one chapter of the precepts of God they performed it with great diligence, and had a right intent before the Lord God; and for these great wonder shall take hold upon all the saints before the Lord God, who shall speak one with another, saying: Stay and behold the unlearned that know nothing [more], how they have earned such and so fair raiment and so great glory because of their innocency.

And I saw in the midst of the city an altar exceeding high. And there was one standing by the altar whose visage shone like the sun, and he held in his hands a psaltery and an harp and sang praises, saying: Alleluia. And his voice filled all the city. And when all that were upon the towers and the gates heard him, they answered: Alleluia, so that the foundations of the city were shaken. And I' asked the angel and said: Who is this, Lord, that is of so great might? And the angel said unto me: This is David. This is the city of Jerusalem; and when Christ the king of eternity shall come in the fullness (confidence, freedom) of his kingdom, he shall again go before him to sing praises, and all the righteous together shall sing praises, answering: Alleluia. And I said: Lord, how is it that David only above the rest of the saints maketh (made) the beginning of singing praises? And the angel answered and said unto me: When (*or*, because) Christ the Son of God sitteth on the right hand of his Father, this David shall sing praises before him in the seventh heaven: and as it is done in the heavens, so likewise is it below: for without David it is not lawful to offer a sacrifice unto God: but it must needs be that David sing praises at the hour of the offering of the body and blood of Christ: as it is performed in heaven, so also is it upon earth.

30 And I said unto the angel: Lord, what is Alleluia? And the angel answered and said unto me: Thou dost examine and inquire of all things. And he said unto me: Alleluia is spoken in the Hebrew, that is the speech of God and of the angels: now the interpretation of Alleluia is this: *tecel . cat . marith . macha* (*Gr.* thĕbel marēmatha). And I said: Lord, what is *tecel cat marith macha*? And the angel answered and said unto me: This is *tecel cat marith macha*: Let us bless him all together. I asked the angel and said: Lord, do all they that say Alleluia bless God? And the angel answered and said unto me: So it is: and again, if any sing Alleluia, and they that are present sing not with him, they commit sin in 'that they sing not with him. And I said: Lord, doth a man likewise sin if he be doting or very aged? The angel answered and said unto me: Not so: but he that is able, and singeth not with him, know ye that such a one is a despiser of the word, for it would be proud and unworthy that he should not bless the Lord God his creator.

31 And when he had ceased speaking unto me, he led me out without the city through the midst of the trees and back from the place of the land of good things (*or,* men) and set me at the river of milk and honey: and after that he led me unto the ocean that beareth the foundations of the heaven. The angel answered and said unto me: Perceivest thou that thou goest hence? And I said: Yea, Lord. And he said unto me: Come, follow me, and I will show thee the souls of the ungodly and the sinners, that thou mayest know what manner of place *they have.* And I went with the angel and he took me by the way of the sunsetting, and I saw the beginning of the heaven, founded upon a great river of water, and I asked: What is this river of water? And he said unto me: This is the ocean which compasseth the whole earth about. And when I was come beyond (to the outside of) the ocean, I looked and there was no light in that place, but darkness and sorrow and sadness: and I sighed. And I saw there a river of fire burning with heat, and in it was a multitude of men and women sunk up to the knees, and other men up to the navel; others also up to the lips and others up to the hair: and I asked the angel and said: Lord, who are these in the river of fire? And the angel answered and said unto me: They are neither hot nor cold, for they were not found either in the number of the righteous or in the number of the wicked; for they passed the time of their life upon the earth, spending some days in prayer, but other days in sins and fornications, until their death. And I asked and said: Who are these, Lord, that are sunk up to their knees in the fire? He answered and said unto me: These are they which when they are come out of the church occupy themselves in disputing with idle (alien) talk. But these that are sunk up to the navel are they who, when they have received the body and blood of Christ, go and commit fornication, and did not cease from their sins until they died; and they that are sunk up to their lips are they that slandered one another when they gathered in the church of God ; but they that are sunk up to the eyebrows are they that beckon one to another, and privily devise evil against their neighbours.

32 And I saw on the north side a place of sundry and diverse torments, full of men and women, and a river of fire flowed down upon them. And I beheld and saw pits exceeding deep, and in them many souls together, and the depth of that place was as it were three thousand cubits; and I saw them groaning and weeping and saying: Have mercy on us, Lord. And no man had mercy on them. And I asked the angel and said: Who are these, Lord? And the angel answered and said unto me: These are they that trusted not in the Lord that they could have him for their helper. And I inquired and said: Lord, if these souls continue thus, thirty or forty generations being cast one upon another, if (unless?) they be cast down yet deeper, I trow the pits would not contain them. And he said to me: The abyss hath no measure: for beneath it there followeth also that which is beneath: and so it is that if a strong man took a stone and cast it into an exceeding deep well and after many hours (long time) it reacheth the earth, so also is the abyss. For when the souls are cast therein, hardly after five hundred years do they come at the bottom.

33 And I when I heard it, mourned and lamented for the race of men. The angel answered and said unto me: Wherefore mournest thou? art thou more merciful than God? for inasmuch as God is good and knoweth that there are torments, he beareth patiently with mankind, leaving every one to do his own will for the time that he dwelleth on the earth.

34 Yet again I looked upon the river of fire, and I saw there a man caught *by the throat* (*Copt.* an old man who was being dragged along, and they immersed him up to the knees. And the angel Aftemeloukhos came with a great fork of fire, &c. *Syr.* similar. Some sentences are lost in *Lat.*) by angels, keepers of hell (Tartaruchi), having in their hands an iron of three hooks wherewith they pierced the entrails of that old man. And I asked the angel and said: Lord, who is this old man upon whom such torments are inflicted? And the angel answered and said unto me: He whom thou seest was a priest who fulfilled not well his ministry, for when he was eating and drinking and whoring he offered the sacrifice unto the Lord at his holy altar.

35 And I saw not far off another old man whom four evil angels brought, running quickly, and they sank him up to his knees in the river of fire, and smote him with stones and wounded his face like a tempest, and suffered him not to say: Have mercy on me. And I asked the angel and he said unto me: He whom thou seest was a bishop, and he fulfilled not well his bishopric: for he received indeed a great name, but entered not into (walked not in) the holiness of him that gave him that name all his life; for he gave not righteous judgement, and had not compassion on widows and orphans: but now it is recompensed unto him according to his iniquity and his doings.

36 And I saw another man in the river of fire sunk up to the knees: and his hands were stretched out and bloody, and worms issued out of his mouth and his nostrils, and he was groaning and lamenting and crying out, and said: Have mercy on me for I suffer hurt more than the rest that are in this torment. And I asked: Who is this, Lord? And he said unto me: This whom thou seest was a deacon, who devoured the offerings and committed fornication and did not right in the sight of God: therefore without ceasing he payeth the penalty. And I looked and saw beside him another man whom they brought with haste and cast him into the river of fire, and he was there up to the knees; and the angel that was over the torments came, having a great razor, red-hot, and therewith he cut the lips of that man and the tongue likewise. And I sighed and wept and asked: Who is this man, Lord? And he said unto me: This that thou seest was

a reader and read unto the people: but he kept not the commandments of God: now also he payeth his own penalty.

37 And I saw another multitude of pits in the same place, and in the midst thereof a river filled with a multitude of men and women, and worms devoured them. But I wept and sighed and asked the angel: Lord, who are these? And he said unto me: These are they that extorted usury on usury and trusted in their riches, not having hope in God, that he was their helper.

And after that I looked and saw a very strait place, and there was as it were a wall, and round about it fire. And I saw within it men and women gnawing their tongues, and asked: Who are these, Lord? And he said unto me: These are they that mocked at the word of God in the church, not attending thereto, but as it were making nought of God and of his angels: therefore now likewise do they pay the due penalty.

38 And I looked in and saw another pool (*Lat.* old man!) beneath in the pit, and the appearance of it was like blood: and I asked and said: Lord, what is this place? And he said unto me: Into this pit do all the torments flow. And I saw men and women sunk up to the lips, and asked: Who are these, Lord? And he said unto me: These are the sorcerers which gave unto men and women magical enchantments, and they found no rest (i. e. did not cease ?) until they died. And again I saw men and women of a very black countenance in a pit of fire, and I sighed and wept and asked: Who are these, Lord? And he said unto me: These are whoremongers and adulterers who, having wives of their own, committed adultery, and likewise the women after the same sort committed adultery, having their own husbands: therefore do they pay the penalty without ceasing.

39 And I saw there girls clad in black raiment, and four fearful angels holding in their hands red-hot chains, and they put them upon their necks (heads) and led them away into darkness. And again I wept and asked the angel: Who are these, Lord? And he said unto me: These are they which being virgins defiled their virginity, and their parents knew it not: wherefore without ceasing they pay the due penalty. And again I beheld there men and women with their hands and feet cut *off* and naked, in a place of ice and snow, and worms devoured them. And when I saw it I wept and asked: Who are these, Lord? and he said unto me: These are they that injured the fatherless and widows and the poor, and trusted not in the Lord: wherefore without ceasing they pay the due penalty.

And I looked and saw others hanging over a channel of water, and their tongues were exceeding dry, and many fruits were set in their sight, and they were not suffered to take of them. And I asked: Who are these, Lord? And he said unto me: These are they that brake the fast before the time appointed: therefore without ceasing do they pay this penalty.

And I saw other men and women hanged by their eyebrows and their hair, and a river of fire drew them, and I said: Who are these, Lord? And he said unto me: These are they that gave themselves not unto their own husbands and wives, but unto adulterers, and therefore without ceasing they pay the due penalty. (For this *Copt.* has: men and women hung head downwards, torches burning before their faces, serpents girt about them devouring them. These

are the women that beautified themselves with paints and unguents and went to church to ensnare men. *Syr.* and *Gr.* omit.)

And I saw other men and women covered with dust, and their appearance was as blood, and they were in a pit of pitch and brimstone and borne down in a river of fire. And I asked: Who are these, Lord? And he said unto me: These are they that committed the wickedness of Sodom and Gomorrah, men with men, wherefore they pay the penalty without ceasing. (*Copt., Syr., Gr.* omit this paragraph.)

40 And I looked and saw men and women clad in white (bright) apparel, and their eyes were blind, and they were set in a pit, and I asked: Who are these, Lord? And he said unto me: These are they of the heathen that gave alms and knew not the Lord God; wherefore without ceasing they pay the due penalty.

And I looked and saw other men and women upon a spit of fire, and beasts tearing them, and they were not suffered to say: Lord, have mercy on us. And I saw the angel of the torments (Aftemeloukhos, *Copt.*) laying most fierce torments upon them and saying: Acknowledge the Son of God. For it was told you before, *but* when the scriptures of God were read unto you, ye paid no heed: wherefore the judgement of God is just, for your evil doings have taken hold upon you, and brought you into these torments. But I sighed and wept; and I inquired and said: Who are these men and women that are strangled in the fire and pay the penalty? And he answered me: These are the women which defiled the creation of God when they brought forth children from the womb, and these are the men that lay with them. But their children appealed unto the Lord God and unto the angels that are over the torments, saying: Avenge us of our parents: for they have defiled the creation of God. Having the name of God, but not observing his commandments, they gave us for food unto dogs and to be trampled on by swine, and others they cast into the river (*Copt.* adds: and did not permit us to grow up into righteous men and to serve God). But those children were delivered unto the angels of Tartarus (*Gr.* unto an angel) that they should bring them into a spacious place of mercy: but their fathers and mothers were haled (strangled) into everlasting torment.

And thereafter I saw men and women clad in rags full of pitch and brimstone of fire, and there were dragons twined about their necks and shoulders and feet, and angels having horns of fire constrained them and smote them and closed up their nostrils, saying unto them: Wherefore knew ye not the time wherein it was right for you to repent and serve God, and ye did not? And I asked: Who are these, Lord? And he said unto me: These are they that seemed to renounce the world (*Lat.* God), wearing our garb, but the snares of the world made them to be miserable: they showed no charity and had no pity upon the widows and fatherless: the stranger and pilgrim they did not take in, neither offered one oblation nor had pity on their neighbour: and their prayer went not up even one day pure unto the Lord God; but the many snares of the world held them back, and they were not able to do right in the sight of God. And the angels carried (*Lat.* surrounded) them about into the place of torments: and they that were in torments saw them and said unto them: We indeed when we lived in the world neglected God, and ye did so likewise. And we when we were in the world knew that we were sinners, but of you it was said: These are righteous and servants of God: now we know that ye were *only* called by the name of the Lord. Wherefore also they pay the due penalty.

And I sighed and wept and said: Woe unto men! woe unto the sinners! to what end were they born? And the angel answered and said unto me: Wherefore weepest thou? Art thou more merciful than the Lord God which is blessed for ever, who hath established the judgement and left every man of his own will to choose good or evil and to do as pleaseth him? Yet again I wept very sore, and he said unto me: Weepest thou, when as yet thou hast not seen the greater torments? Follow me, and thou shalt see sevenfold greater than these.

41 And he took me from the north side (to the west, *Syr.*) and set me over a well, and I found it sealed with seven seals. And the angel that was with me answered and said unto the angel of that place: Open the mouth of the well, that Paul the dearly beloved of God may behold; for power hath been given unto him to see all the torments of hell. And the angel said unto me: Stand afar off, that thou mayest be able to endure the stench of this place. When therefore the well was opened, straightway there arose out of it a stench hard and evil exceedingly, which surpassed all the torments: and I looked into the well and saw masses (lumps) of fire burning on every side, and anguish, and there was straitness in the mouth of the pit so as to take but one man in. And the angel answered and said unto me: If any be cast into the well of the abyss, and it be sealed over him, there shall never be remembrance made of him in the presence of the Father and the Son and the Holy Ghost or of the holy angels. And I said: Who are they, Lord, that are cast into this well? And he said unto me: They are whosoever confesseth not that Christ is come in the flesh and that the Virgin Mary bare him, and whosoever *saith of* the bread and the cup of blessing of the Eucharist that it is not the body and blood of Christ.

42 And I looked from the north unto the west and saw there the worm that sleepeth not, and in that place was gnashing of teeth. And the worms were of the measure of one cubit, and on them were two heads; and I saw there men and women in cold and gnashing of teeth. And I asked and said: Lord, who are they that are in this place? And he said unto me: These are they which say that Christ rose not from the dead, and that this flesh riseth not again. And I inquired and said: Lord, is there no fire nor heat in this place? And he said unto me: In this place is nothing else but cold and snow. And again he said to me: Even if the sun (seven suns, *Copt.*) rose upon them, they would not be warmed, because of the excessive cold of this place, and the snow. And when I heard this I spread forth mine hands and wept and sighed, and again I said: It were better for us if we had not been born, all we that are sinners.

43 But when they that were in that place saw me weeping, with the angel, they also cried out and wept, saying: Lord God, have mercy upon us.

And after that I beheld the heaven open and Michael the archangel coming down out of heaven, and with him all the host of the angels; and they came even unto them that were set in torment. And they when they saw them wept again and cried out and said: Have mercy upon us, thou Michael, archangel, have mercy upon us and upon the race of men, for it is by thy prayers that the earth standeth. We have now seen the judgement and have known the Son of God. It was not possible for us to pray for this before we came into

this place: for we heard that there was a judgement, before we departed out of the world, but the snares and the life of the world suffered us not to repent. And Michael answered and said: Hearken when Michael speaketh: I am he that stands in the presence of God alway. As the Lord liveth, before whose face I stand, I cease not for one day nor one night to pray continually for the race of men; and I indeed pray for them that are upon earth: but they cease not from committing wickednesses and fornication. And they bring not *forth* aught of good while they are upon earth; and ye have wasted in vanity the time wherein ye ought to have repented. But I have prayed alway, and now do I entreat that God would send dew and that rain may be sent upon the earth, and still pray I until the earth yield her fruits: and I say that if any man doeth but a little good I will strive for him and protect him until he escape the judgement of torment. Where then be your prayers? where be your repentances? ye have lost the time despicably. Yet now weep ye, and I will weep with you, and the angels that are with me, together with the dearly beloved Paul, if peradventure the merciful God will have pity and grant you refreshment. And they when they heard these words cried out and wept sore, and all said with one voice: Have mercy upon us, O Son of God. And I, Paul, sighed and said: O Lord God, have mercy upon thy creature, have mercy on the children of men, have mercy upon thine image.

44 I beheld and saw the heaven shake like unto a tree that is moved by the wind: and suddenly they cast themselves down upon their faces before the throne: and I saw the four-and-twenty elders and the four beasts worshipping God: and I saw the altar and the veil and the throne, and all of them were rejoicing, and the smoke of a sweet odour rose up beside the altar of the throne of God; and I heard a. voice saying: For what cause do ye entreat me, our angels, and our ministers? And they cried out, saying: We entreat thee, beholding thy great goodness unto mankind. And thereafter I saw the Son of God coming down out of heaven, and on his head was a crown. And when they that were in torments saw him they all cried out with one voice, saying: Have mercy upon us, O exalted Son of God (*or*, Son of God Most High): thou art he that hast granted refreshment unto all that are in heaven and earth; have mercy upon us likewise: for since we beheld thee we have been refreshed. And there went forth a voice from the Son of God throughout all the torments, saying:

What *good* works have ye done that ye should ask of me refreshment? My blood was shed for you, and not even so did ye repent: for your sake I bare a crown of thorns on mine head, for you I received buffets upon my cheeks, and not even so did ye repent. I asked for water when I hanged upon the cross, and they gave me vinegar mingled with gall: with a spear did they open my right side: for my name's sake have they slain my servants the prophets, and the righteous: and for all these things did I give you a place of repentance, and ye would not. Yet now because of Michael the archangel of my covenant and the angels that are with him, and because of Paul my dearly beloved whom I would not grieve, and because of your brethren that are in the world and do offer oblations, and because of your sons, for in them are my commandments, and yet more because of mine own goodness: on that day whereon I rose from the dead I grant unto all you that are in torment refreshment for a day and a night for ever. And all they cried out and said: We bless thee, O Son of God, for that thou hast granted us rest for a day and a night: for better unto us is the refreshment of one day than the whole time of our life wherein we were upon earth: and if we had known clearly that this place was appointed for them that sin, we should have done none other work whatsoever, neither traded nor done any wickedness. For what profit was our pride in the world? (*Copt.* What profit was it to us to be born into the world?) For this our pride is taken captive, which came up out of our mouth against our neighbour (*Copt.* our life is like the breath of our mouth): *and this* pain and our sore anguish and tears and the worms which are under us, these are worse unto us than the torments which we †suffer†. (This is hardly sense, but *Copt.* agrees; should it not have been 'these are worse than not to have been born'?) And as they thus spake, the angels of torment and the evil angels were wroth with them and said: How long have ye wept and sighed? for ye have had no mercy. For this is the Judgement of God *on him* that hath not had mercy. Yet have ye received this great grace, even refreshment for the night and day of the Lord's day, because of Paul the dearly beloved of God who hath come down unto you.

45 And after these things the angel said unto me: Hast thou seen all these things? And I said: Yea, Lord. And he said unto me: Follow me, and I will bring thee into Paradise, that the righteous which are there may see thee: for, behold, they hope to see thee, and are ready to come and meet thee with joy and exultation. And I followed after the angel in the swiftness of the Holy Ghost, and he set me in Paradise and said unto me: This is Paradise, wherein Adam and his wife erred. And I entered into Paradise and saw the head of the waters, and the angel beckoned unto me and said to me: Behold, saith he, these waters: for this is the river Phison that compasseth about all the land of Evila, and this other is Geon that goeth about all the land of Egypt and Ethiopia, and this other is Tigris that is over against the Assyrians, and this other is Euphrates that watereth the land of Mesopotamia. And I entered in further and saw a tree planted, out of whose roots flowed waters, and out of it was the beginning of the four rivers, and the Spirit of God rested upon that tree, and when the spirit breathed the waters flowed forth: and I said: Lord, is this tree that which maketh the waters to flow? And he said unto me: Because in the beginning, before the heaven and the earth were made to appear, and all things were invisible, the Spirit of God moved (was borne) upon the waters; but since by the commandment of God the heaven and the earth appeared the spirit hath rested upon this tree; wherefore when the spirit breatheth, the waters flow out from the tree. And he took hold on mine hand and led me unto the tree of the knowledge of good and evil, and said: This is the tree whereby death entered into the world, and Adam taking of it from his wife did eat, and death entered into the world. And he showed me another tree in the midst of Paradise, and saith unto me: This is the tree of life.

46 And as I yet looked upon the tree, I saw a virgin coming from afar off, and two hundred angels before her singing hymns: and I inquired and said: Lord, who is this that cometh in such glory? and he said unto me: This is Mary the virgin, the mother of the Lord. And she came near and saluted me, and said: Hail, Paul, dearly beloved of God and angels and men. For all the saints have besought my son Jesus who is my Lord, that thou shouldest come here in the body that they might see thee before thou didst depart out of the world. And the Lord said to them: Wait and be ye patient: yet a little while, and ye shall see him, and he shall

be with you for ever. And again they all with one accord said unto him: Grieve us not, for we desire to see him while he is in the flesh, for by him hath thy name been greatly glorified in the world, and we have seen that he hath excelled (done away with) all the works whether of the lesser or the greater. For we inquire of them that come hither, saying: Who is he that guided you in the world? and they have told us: There is one in the world whose name is Paul; he declareth Christ, preaching him, and we believe that by the power and sweetness of his speech many have entered into the kingdom. Behold, all the righteous are behind me, coming to meet thee. But I say unto thee, Paul, that for this cause I come first to meet them that have performed the will of my son and my Lord Jesus Christ, even I come first to meet them and leave them not as strangers until they meet *with him* in peace.

47 While she was yet speaking I saw three men coming from afar, very beautiful, after the appearance of Christ, and their forms were shining, and their angels; and I asked: Who are these, Lord? And he answered: These are the fathers of the people, Abraham, Isaac, and Jacob. And they came near and greeted me, and said: Hail, Paul, dearly beloved of God and men: blessed is he that endureth violence for the Lord's sake. And Abraham answered me and said: This is my son Isaac, and Jacob my best beloved, and we knew the Lord and followed him. Blessed are all they that have believed thy word that they may inherit the kingdom of God by labour and self-sacrifice (renunciation) and sanctification and humility and charity and meekness and right faith in the Lord: and we also had devotion unto the Lord whom thou preachest, covenanting that we will come unto every soul of them that believe in him, and minister unto him as fathers minister unto their sons. While they yet spake I saw twelve men coming from afar with honour, and I asked: Who are these, Lord? And he said: These are the patriarchs. And they came and saluted me and said: Hail, Paul, dearly beloved of God and men. The Lord hath not grieved us, that we might see thee yet being in the body, before thou departedst out of the world. And every one of them signified his name unto me in order, from Ruben unto Benjamin; and Joseph said unto me: I am he that was sold; and I say unto thee, Paul, that *for* all that my brethren did unto me, in nothing did I deal evilly with them, not in all the labour which they laid upon me, nor did I hurt them in any thing (*Copt.* kept no evil thought against them) from morning until evening. Blessed is he that is hurt for the Lord's sake and hath endured, for the Lord will recompense him manifold more when he departeth out of the world.

48 While he yet spake I saw another coming from afar, beautiful, and his angels singing hymns, and I asked: Who is this, Lord, that is fair of countenance? And he said unto me: Dost thou not know him? And I said: No, Lord. And he said to me: This is Moses the lawgiver, unto whom God gave the law. And when he was nigh me, straightway he wept, and after that he greeted me; and I said unto him: Why weepest thou? for I have heard that thou excellest all men in meekness. And he answered, saying: I weep for them whom I planted with much labour, for they have borne no fruit, neither doth any of them do well. And I have seen all the sheep whom I fed that they are scattered and become as having no shepherd, and that all the labours which I have endured for the children of Israel are come to nought, and however great wonders I did in their midst

[and] they understood not: and I marvel how the strangers and uncircumcised and idolaters are converted and entered into the promises of God, but Israel hath not entered in: and now I say unto thee, O brother Paul, that in that hour when the people hanged up Jesus whom thou preachest, God the Father of all, which gave me the law, and Michael and all the angels and archangels, and Abraham and Isaac and Jacob and all the righteous wept over the Son of God that was hanged on the cross. And in that hour all the saints waited upon me, looking on me.and saying: Behold, Moses, what they of thy people have done unto the Son of God. Therefore blessed art thou, O Paul, and blessed is the generation and people that hath believed thy word.

49 While he yet spake there came other twelve and saw me and said: Art thou Paul that is glorified in heaven and upon earth? And I answered and said: Who are ye? The first answered and said: I am Esaias whose head Manasses cut with a saw of wood. And the second said likewise: I am Jeremias who was stoned by the children of Israel, and slain. And the third said: I am Ezechiel whom the children of Israel dragged by the feet over the stones in the mountain until they scattered my brains abroad: and all of us endured these labours, desiring to save the children of Israel: and I say unto thee that after the toils which they laid upon me I would cast myself down upon my face before the Lord, praying for them and bowing my knees unto the second hour of the Lord's day, even until Michael came and raised me up from the earth. Blessed art thou, Paul, and blessed is the people that hath believed through thee. And as they passed by, I saw another, fair of countenance, and asked: Who is this, Lord? [And when he saw me he was glad] and he said unto me: This is Lot, which was found righteous in Sodom. And he came near and greeted me and said: Blessed art thou, Paul, and blessed is the generation unto whom thou hast ministered. And I answered and said unto him: Art thou Lot, that wast found righteous in Sodom? And he said: I entertained angels in mine house as strangers, and when they of the city would have done them violence I offered them my two daughters, virgins, that had never known man, and gave them to them, saying: Use them as ye will, only do no ill unto these men, for therefore have they entered under the roof of mine house. Therefore ought we to have confidence, and know that whatsoever any man hath done, God recompenseth him manifold more when he cometh (they come) unto him. Blessed art thou, Paul, and blessed is the generation which hath believed thy word.
When therefore he had ceased speaking unto me, I saw another coming from afar off, very beautiful in the face, and smiling, and his angels singing hymns, and I said unto the angel that was with me: Hath, then, every one of the righteous an angel for his fellow? And he saith to me: Every one of the saints hath his own, that standeth by him and singeth hymns, and the one departeth not from the other. And I said: Who is this, Lord? And he said: This is Job. And he drew near and greeted me and said: Brother Paul, thou hast great praise with God and men. Now I am Job, which suffered much for the season of thirty years by the issue of a plague; and in the beginning the blains that came forth of my body were as grains of wheat; but on the third day they became like an ass's foot, and the worms that fell from them were four fingers long: and thrice the devil appeared unto me and saith to me: Speak a word against the Lord, and die. *But* I said unto him: If thus be the will of God that I continue in the plague all the time of my life

until I die, I will not rest from blessing the Lord God, and I shall receive the greater reward. For I know that the sufferings of this world are nought compared with the refreshment that is thereafter: wherefore blessed art thou, Paul, and blessed is the people which hath believed by thy means.

50 While he yet spake there came another crying out from afar off and saying: Blessed art thou, Paul, and blessed am I that have seen thee the beloved of the Lord. And I asked the angel: Who is this, Lord? and he answered and said unto me: This is Noe of the days of the flood. And straightway we greeted one another, and he, rejoicing greatly, said unto me: Thou art (*or*, Art thou) Paul the best beloved of God. And I asked him: Who art thou? And he said: I am Noe that was in the days of the flood: but I say unto thee, Paul, that I spent an hundred years making the ark, not putting off the coat (tunic) which I wore, and I shaved not the hair of mine head. Furthermore I kept continence, not coming near mine own wife, and in those hundred years the hair of mine head grew not in greatness, neither was my raiment soiled. And I besought men at that time, saying: Repent, for a flood of waters cometh upon you. But they mocked me and derided my words; and again they said unto me: This is the time of them that would play and sin as much as they will, that have leave to fornicate not a little (*Lat.* confused; other versions omit): for God looketh not on these things, neither knoweth what is done of us men, and moreover there is no flood of waters coming upon this world. And they ceased not from their sins until God blotted out all flesh that had the breath of life in it. But know thou that God loveth one righteous man more than all the world of the wicked. Therefore blessed art thou, O Paul, and blessed is the people that hath believed by thy means.

51 And I turned myself and saw other righteous ones coming from afar off, and I asked the angel: Who are these, Lord? and he answered me: These are Elias and Eliseus. And they greeted me, and I said unto them: Who are ye? And one of them answered and said: I am Elias the prophet of God. I am Elias that prayed, and because of my word the heaven rained not for three years and six months, because of the iniquities of men. Righteous and true is God, who doeth the will of his servants; for oftentimes the angels besought the Lord for rain, and he said: Be patient until my servant Elias pray and entreat for this, and I will send rain upon the earth.

The End of the Vision of Saint Paul.

REVELATION OF JOHN

Revelation of Saint John the Theologian

After the taking up of our Lord Jesus Christ, I John was alone upon Mount Tabor, where also He showed us His undefiled Godhead; and as I was not able to stand, I fell upon the ground, and prayed to the Lord, and said: O Lord my God, who hast deemed me worthy to be Thy servant, hear my voice, and teach me about Thy coming. When Thou shalt come to the earth, what will happen? The heaven and the earth, and the sun and the moon, what will happen to them in those times? Reveal to me all; for I am emboldened, because Thou listenest to Thy servant.

And I spent seven days praying; and after this a cloud of light caught me up from the mountain, and set me before the face of the heaven. And I heard a voice saying to me: Look up, John, servant of God, and know. And having looked up, I saw the heaven opened, and there came forth from within the heaven a smell of perfumes of much sweet odour; and I saw an exceeding great flood of light, more resplendent than the sun. And again I heard a voice saying to me: Behold, righteous John. And I directed my sight, and saw a book lying, of the thickness, methought, of seven mountains; and the length of it the mind of man cannot comprehend, having seven seals. And I said: O Lord my God, reveal to me what is written in this book. And I heard a voice saying to me: Hear, righteous John. In this book which thou seest there have been written the things in the heaven, and the things in the earth, and the things in the abyss, and the judgments and righteousness of all the human race. And I said: Lord, when shall these things come to pass? and what do those times bring? And I heard a voice saying to me: Hear, righteous John. There shall be in that time abundance of corn and wine, such as there hath never been upon the earth, nor shall ever be until those times come. Then the ear of corn shall produce a half chœnix, and the bend of the branch shall produce a thousand clusters, and the cluster shall produce a half jar of wine; and in the following year there shall not be found upon the face of all the earth a half chœnix of corn or a half jar of wine.

And again I said: Lord, thereafter what wilt Thou do? And I heard a voice saying to me: Hear, righteous John. Then shall appear the denier, and he who is set apart in the darkness, who is called Antichrist. And again I said: Lord, reveal to me what he is like. And I heard a voice saying to me: The appearance of his face is dusky; the hairs of his head are sharp, like darts; his eyebrows like a wild beast's; his right eye like the star which rises in the morning, and the other like a lion's; his mouth about one cubit; his teeth span long; his fingers like scythes; the print of his feet of two spans; and on his face an inscription, Antichrist; he shall be exalted even to heaven, and shall be cast down even to Hades, making false displays. And then will I make the heaven brazen, so that it shall not give moisture upon the earth; and I will hide the clouds in secret places, so that they shall not bring moisture upon the earth; and I will command the horns of the wind, so that the wind shall not blow upon the earth.

And again I said: Lord, and how many years will he do this upon the earth? And I heard a voice saying to me: Hear, righteous John. Three years shall those times be; and I will make the three years like three months, and the three months like three weeks, and the three weeks like three days, and the three days like three hours, and the three hours like three seconds, as said the prophet David, His throne hast Thou broken down to the ground; Thou hast shortened the days of his time; Thou hast poured shame upon him. And then I shall send forth Enoch and Elias to convict him; and they shall show him to be a liar and a deceiver; and he shall kill them at the altar, as said the prophet, Then shall they offer calves upon Thine altar. And again I said: Lord, and after that what will come to pass? And I heard a voice saying to me: Hear, righteous John. Then all the human race shall die, and there shall not be a living man upon all the earth. And again I said: Lord, after that what wilt Thou do? And I heard a voice saying to me: Hear, righteous John. Then will I send forth mine angels, and they shall take the ram's horns that lie upon the cloud; and Michael and Gabriel shall go forth out of the heaven and sound with those horns, as the prophet David foretold, With the voice of a trumpet of horn. And the voice of the trumpet shall be heard from the one quarter of the world to the other; and from the voice of that trumpet all the earth shall be shaken, as the prophet foretold, And at the voice of the bird every plant shall arise; that is, at the voice of the archangel all the human race shall arise. And again I said: Lord, those who are dead from Adam even to this day, and who dwell in Hades from the beginning of the world, and who die at the last ages, what like shall they arise? And I heard a voice saying to me: Hear, righteous John. All the human race shall arise thirty years old.

And again I said: Lord, they die male and female, and some old, and some young, and some infants. In the resurrection what like shall they arise? And I heard a voice saying to me: Hear, righteous John. Just as the bees are, and differ not one from another, but are all of one appearance and one size, so also shall every man be in the resurrection. There is neither fair, nor ruddy, nor black, neither Ethiopian nor different countenances; but they shall all arise of one appearance and one stature. All the human race shall arise without bodies, as I told you that in the resurrection they neither marry nor are given in marriage, but are as the angels of God.

And again I said: Lord, is it possible in that world to recognise each other, a brother his brother, or a friend his friend, or a father his own children, or the children their own parents? And I heard a voice saying to me: Hear, John. To the righteous there is recognition, but to the sinners not at all; they cannot in the resurrection recognise each other. And again I John said: Lord, is there there recollection of the things that are here, either fields or vineyards, or other things here? And I heard a voice saying to me: Hear, righteous John. The prophet David speaks, saying, I remembered that we are dust: as for man, his days are as grass; as a flower of the field, so he shall flourish: for a wind hath passed over it, and it shall be no more, and it shall not any longer know its place. And again the same said: His spirit shall go forth, and he returns to his earth; in that day all his thoughts shall perish.

And again I said: Lord, and after that what wilt Thou do? And I heard a voice saying to me: Hear, righteous John. Then will I send forth mine angels over the face of all the earth, and they shall lift off the earth everything honourable, and everything precious, and the venerable and holy images, and the glorious and precious crosses, and the sacred vessels of the churches, and the divine and sacred books; and all the precious and holy things shall be lifted up by clouds into the air. And then will I order to be lifted up the great and venerable sceptre, on which I stretched forth my hands, and all the orders of my angels shall do reverence to it. And then shall be lifted up all the race of men upon clouds, as the Apostle Paul foretold. Along with them we shall be snatched up in clouds to meet the Lord in the air. And then shall come forth every evil spirit, both in the earth and in the abyss, wherever they are on the face of all the earth, from the rising of the sun even to the setting, and they shall be united to him that is served by the devil, that is, Antichrist, and they shall be lifted up upon the clouds.

And again I said: Lord, and after that what wilt Thou do? And I heard a voice saying to me: Hear, righteous John. Then shall I send forth mine angels over the face of all the earth, and they shall burn up the earth eight thousand five hundred cubits, and the great mountains shall be burnt up, and all the rocks shall be melted and shall become as dust, and every tree shall be burnt up, and every beast, and every creeping thing creeping upon the earth, and every thing moving upon the face of the earth, and every flying thing flying in the air; and there shall no longer be upon the face of all the earth anything moving, and the earth shall be without motion.

And again I said: Lord, and after that what wilt Thou do? And I heard a voice saying to me: Hear, righteous John. Then shall I uncover the four parts of the east, and there shall come forth four great winds, and they shall sweep all the face of the earth from the one end of the earth to the other; and the Lord shall sweep sin from off the earth, and the earth shall be made white like snow, and it shall become as a leaf of paper, without cave, or mountain, or hill, or rock; but the face of the earth from the rising even to the setting of the sun shall be like a table, and white as snow; and the reins of the earth shall be consumed by fire, and it shall cry unto me, saying, I am a virgin before thee, O Lord, and there is no sin in me; as the prophet David said aforetime, Thou shalt sprinkle me with hyssop, and I shall be made pure; Thou shalt wash me, and I shall be made whiter than snow. And again he said: Every chasm shall be filled up, and every mountain and hill brought low, and the crooked places shall be made straight, and the rough ways into smooth; and all flesh shall see the salvation of God.

And again I said: Lord, and after that what wilt Thou do? And I heard a voice saying to me: Hear, righteous John. Then shall the earth be cleansed from sin, and all the earth shall be filled with a sweet smell, because I am about to come down upon the earth; and then shall come forth the great and venerable sceptre, with thousands of angels worshipping it, as I said before; and then shall appear the sign of the Son of man from the heaven with power and great glory. And then the worker of iniquity with his servants shall behold it, and gnash his teeth exceedingly, and all the unclean spirits shall be turned to flight. And then, seized by invisible power, having no means of flight, they shall gnash their teeth against him, saying to him: Where is thy power? How hast thou led us astray?

and we have fled away, and have fallen away from the glory which we had beside Him who is coming to judge us, and the whole human race. Woe to us! because He banishes us into outer darkness.

And again I said: Lord, and after that what wilt Thou do? And I heard a voice saying to me: Then will I send an angel out of heaven, and he shall cry with a loud voice, saying, Hear, O earth, and be strong, saith the Lord; for I am coming down to thee. And the voice of the angel shall be heard from the one end of the world even to the other, and even to the remotest part of the abyss. And then shall be shaken all the power of the angels and of the many-eyed ones, and there shall be a great noise in the heavens, and the nine regions of the heaven shall be shaken, and there shall be fear and astonishment upon all the angels. And then the heavens shall be rent from the rising of the sun even to the setting, and an innumerable multitude of angels shall come down to the earth; and then the treasures of the heavens shall be opened, and they shall bring down every precious thing, and the perfume of incense, and they shall bring down to the earth Jerusalem robed like a bride. And then there shall go before me myriads of angels and archangels, bearing my throne, crying out, Holy, holy, holy, Lord of Sabaoth; heaven and earth are full of Thy glory. And then will I come forth with power and great glory, and every eye in the clouds shall see me; and then every knee shall bend, of things in heaven, and things on earth, and things under the earth. And then the heaven shall remain empty; and I will come down upon the earth, and all that is in the air shall be brought down upon the earth, and all the human race and every evil spirit along with Antichrist, and they shall all be set before me naked, and chained by the neck.

And again I said: Lord, what will become of the heavens, and the sun, and the moon, along with the stars? And I heard a voice saying to me: Behold, righteous John. And I looked, and saw a Lamb having seven eyes and seven horns. And again I heard a voice saying to me: I will bid the Lamb come before me, and will say, Who will open this book? And all the multitudes of the angels will answer, Give this book to the Lamb to open it. And then will I order the book to be opened. And when He shall open the first seal, the stars of the heaven shall fall, from the one end of it to the other. And when He shall open the second seal, the moon shall be hidden, and there shall be no light in her. And when He shall open the third seal, the light of the sun shall be withheld, and there shall not be light upon the earth. And when He shall open the fourth seal, the heavens shall be dissolved, and the air shall be thrown into utter confusion, as saith the prophet: And the heavens are the works of Thy hands; they shall perish, but Thou endurest, and they shall all wax old as a garment. And when He shall open the fifth seal, the earth shall be rent, and all the tribunals upon the face of all the earth shall be revealed. And when He shall open the sixth seal, the half of the sea shall disappear. And when He shall open the seventh seal, Hades shall be uncovered.
And I said: Lord, who will be the first to be questioned, and to receive judgment? And I heard a voice saying to me, The unclean spirits, along with the adversary. I bid them go into outer darkness, where the depths are. And I said: Lord, and in what place does it lie? And I heard a voice saying to me: Hear, righteous John. As big a stone as a man of thirty years old can roll, and let go down into the

depth, even falling down for twenty years will not arrive at the bottom of Hades; as the prophet David said before, And He made darkness His secret place.

And I said: Lord, and after them what nation will be questioned? And I heard a voice saying to me: Hear, righteous John. There will be questioned of Adam's race those nations, both the Greek and those who have believed in idols, and in the sun, and in the stars, and those who have defiled the faith by heresy, and who have not believed the holy resurrection, and who have not confessed the Father, and the Son, and the Holy Ghost: then will I send them away into Hades, as the prophet David foretold, Let the sinners be turned into Hades, and all the nations that forget God. And again he said: They were put in Hades like sheep; death shall be their shepherd.

And again I said: Lord, and after them whom wilt Thou judge? And I heard a voice saying to me: Hear, righteous John. Then the race of the Hebrews shall be examined, who nailed me to the tree like a malefactor. And I said: And what punishment will these get, and in what place, seeing that they did such things to Thee? And I heard a voice saying to me: They shall go away into Tartarus, as the prophet David foretold, They cried out, and there was none to save; to the Lord, and He did not hearken to them. And again the Apostle Paul said: As many as have sinned without law shall also perish without law, and as many as have sinned in law shall be judged by means of law.

And again I said: Lord, and what of those who have received baptism? And I heard a voice saying to me: Then the race of the Christians shall be examined, who have received baptism; and then the righteous shall come at my command, and the angels shall go and collect them from among the sinners, as the prophet David foretold: The Lord will not suffer the rod of the sinners in the lot of the righteous; and all the righteous shall be placed on my right hand, and shall shine like the sun. As thou seest, John, the stars of heaven, that they were all made together, but differ in light, so shall it be with the righteous and the sinners; for the righteous shall shine as lights and as the sun, but the sinners shall stand in darkness.

And again I said: Lord, and do all the Christians go into one punishment?—kings, high priests, priests, patriarchs, rich and poor, bond and free? And I heard a voice saying to me: Hear, righteous John. As the prophet David foretold, The expectation of the poor shall not perish for ever. Now about kings: they shall be driven like slaves, and shall weep like infants; and about patriarchs, and priests, and Levites, of those that have sinned, they shall be separated in their punishments, according to the nature of the peculiar transgression of each,—some in the river of fire, and some to the worm that dieth not, and others in the seven-mouthed pit of punishment. To these punishments the sinners will be apportioned.

And again I said: Lord, and where will the righteous dwell? And I heard a voice saying to me: Then shall paradise be revealed; and the whole world and paradise shall be made one, and the righteous shall be on the face of all the earth with my angels, as the Holy Spirit foretold through the prophet David: The righteous shall inherit the earth, and dwell therein for ever and ever.

And again I said: Lord, how great is the multitude of the angels? and which is the greater, that of angels or of men? And I heard a voice saying to me: As great as is the multitude of the angels, so great is the race of men, as the prophet has said, He set bounds to the nations according to the number of the angels of God.

And again I said: Lord, and after that what wilt Thou do? and what is to become of the world? Reveal to me all. And I heard a voice saying to me: Hear, righteous John. After that there is no pain, there is no grief, there is no groaning; there is no recollection of evils, there are no tears, there is no envy, there is no hatred of brethren, there is no unrighteousness, there is no arrogance, there is no slander, there is no bitterness, there are none of the cares of life, there is no pain from parents or children, there is no pain from gold, there are no wicked thoughts, there is no devil, there is no death, there is no night, but all is day. As I said before, And other sheep I have, which are not of this fold, that is, men who have been made like the angels through their excellent course of life; them also must I bring, and they will hear my voice, and there shall be one fold, one shepherd.

And again I heard a voice saying to me: Behold, thou hast heard all these things, righteous John; deliver them to faithful men, that they also may teach others, and not think lightly of them, nor cast our pearls before swine, lest perchance they should trample them with their feet. And while I was still hearing this voice, the cloud brought me down, and put me on Mount Thabor. And there came a voice to me, saying: Blessed are those who keep judgment and do righteousness in all time. And blessed is the house where this description lies, as the Lord said, He that loveth me keepeth my sayings in Christ Jesus our Lord; to Him be glory for ever. Amen.

REVELATION OF PAUL

Revelation of the holy Apostle Paul: the things which were revealed to him when he went up even to the third heaven, and was caught up into paradise, and heard unspeakable words.

There dwelt a certain nobleman in the city of Tarsus, in the house of St. Paul the apostle, in the government of Theodosius the worshipful king, and of the most illustrious Gratianus; and there was revealed to him an angel of the Lord, saying: Upturn the foundation of this house, and lift up what thou shalt find. But he thought that he had had a dream. And the angel having persisted even to a third vision, the nobleman was compelled to upturn the foundation; and having dug, he found a marble box containing this revelation; and having taken it, he showed it to the ruler of the city. And the ruler, seeing it sealed up with lead, sent it to the King Theodosius, thinking that it was something else. And the king having received it, and transcribed it, sent the original writing to Jerusalem. And there was written in it thus:—

The word of the Lord came to me, saying: Say to this people, Till when do you sin, and add to your sin, and provoke to anger the God who made you, saying that you are children to Abraham, but doing the works of Satan, going on in speaking against God, boasting only in your addressing *of God*, but poor on account of the substance of sin? Know, ye sons of men, that the whole creation has been made subject to God; but the human race alone, by sinning, provokes God to anger. For often the great light, the sun, has come before God, saying against men: Lord God Almighty, how long dost Thou endure all the sin of men? Command me, and I will burn them up. And there came a voice to him: My long-suffering endures them all, that they may repent; but if not, they shall come to me, and I will judge them. And often also the moon and the stars have come before God, saying: Lord God Almighty, Thou hast given us the dominion of the night, and we no longer cover the thefts, and adulteries, and blood-sheddings of men; command us, and we shall do marvels against them. And there came a voice: My long-suffering bears with them, that they may turn to me; but if not, they shall come to me, and I will judge them. And in like manner also the sea cried out, saying: Lord God Almighty, the sons of men have profaned Thy holy name; command me, and I shall rise up and cover the earth, and wipe out from it the sons of men. And there came a voice, saying: My long-suffering bears with them, that they may repent; but if not, they shall come to me, and I will judge them. You see, ye sons of men, that the whole creation has been made subject to God, but the human race alone sins before God. On account of all these things, bless God without ceasing, and yet more when the sun is setting. For at this hour all the angels come to God to adore Him, and they bring before Him the works of men, of each what he has done from morning even to evening, whether good or evil. And one angel goes rejoicing on account of man when he

behaves well, and another goes with a sad countenance. All the angels at the appointed hour meet for the worship of God, to bring each day's works of men. But do ye men bless God without ceasing. Whenever, therefore, at the appointed hour the angels of pious men come, rejoicing and singing psalms, they meet for the worship of the Lord; and, behold, the Spirit of God *says* to them: Whence do ye come rejoicing? And they answered and said: We are here from the pious men, who in all piety spend their life, fearing the name of God. Command them, Lord, to abide even to the end in Thy righteousness. And there came to them a voice: I have both kept and will keep them void of offence in my kingdom. And when it came to pass that they went away, there came other angels with a cheerful countenance, shining like the sun. And behold a voice to them: Whence have ye come? And they answered and said: We have come from those who have held themselves aloof from the world and the things in the world for Thy holy name's sake, who in deserts, and mountains, and caves, and the dens of the earth, in beds on the ground, and in fastings, spend their life. Command us to be with them. And there came a voice: Go with them in peace, guarding them. Moreover, when they went away, behold, there came other angels to worship before God, mourning and weeping. And the Spirit went forth to meet them, and there came a voice to them: Whence have ye come? And they answered and said: We have come from those who have been called by Thy name, and are slaves to the matter of sin. Why, then, is it necessary to minister unto them? And there came a voice to them: Do not cease to minister unto them; perhaps they will turn; but if not, they shall come to me, and I will judge them. Know, sons of men, that all that is done by you day by day, the angels write in the heavens. Do you therefore cease not to bless God.

And I was in the Holy Spirit, and an angel says to me: Come, follow me, that I may show thee the place of the just, where they go after their end. And I went along with the angel, and he brought me up into the heavens under the firmament; and I perceived and saw powers great and dreadful, full of wrath, and through the mouth of them a flame of fire coming out, and clothed in garments of fire. And I asked the angel: Who are these? And he said to me: These are they who are sent away to the souls of the sinners in the hour of necessity; for they have not believed that there is judgment and retribution. And I looked up into the heaven, and saw angels, whose faces shone like the sun, girded with golden girdles, having in their hands prizes, on which the name of the Lord was inscribed, full of all meekness and compassion. And I asked the angel: Who are these? And he answered and said to me: These are they who are sent forth in the day of the resurrection to bring the souls of the righteous, who intrepidly walk according to God. And I said to the angel: I wish to see the souls of the righteous and of the sinners, how they go out of the world. And the angel said to me: Look to the earth. And I looked, and saw the whole world as nothing disappearing before me. And I said to the angel: Is this the greatness of men? And he said to me: Yes; for thus every unjust man disappears. And I looked, and saw a cloud of fire wrapped over all the world; and I said: What is this, my lord? And he said to me: This is the unrighteousness mingled with the destruction of the sinners. And I wept, and said to the angel: I wished to see the departures of the righteous and of the sinners, in what manner they go out of the world. And the angel says to me: Paul, look down, and see what thou hast asked. And I looked, and saw one of the sons of men falling near death. And the angel says to me: This is a righteous man, and, behold, all his works stand beside him in the hour of his necessity. And there were beside him good angels, and along with them also evil angels. And the evil angels indeed found no place in him, but the good took possession of the soul of the righteous man, and said to it: Take note of the body whence thou art coming out; for it is necessary for thee again to return to it in the day of the resurrection, that thou mayst receive what God hath promised to the righteous. And the good angels who had received the soul of the righteous man, saluted it, as being well known to them. And it went with them; and the Spirit came forth to meet them, saying: Come, soul, enter into the place of the resurrection, which God hath prepared for His righteous ones. And the angel said to me: Look down to the earth, and behold the soul of the impious, how it goes forth from its tabernacle, which has provoked God to anger, saying, Let us eat and drink; for who is it that has gone down to Hades, and come up and announced that there is judgment and retribution? And take heed, and see all his works which he has done standing before him. And the evil angels came and the good. The good therefore found no place of rest in it, but the evil took possession of it, saying: O wretched soul, pay heed to thy flesh; take note of that whence thou art coming forth, for thou must return into thy flesh in the day of the resurrection, that thou mayst receive the recompense of thy sins. And when it had gone forth from its tabernacle, the angel who had lived along with it ran up to it, saying to it: O wretched soul, whither goest thou? I am he who each day wrote down thy sins. Thou hast destroyed the time of repentance; be exceedingly ashamed. And when it came, all the angels saw it, and cried out with one voice, saying: Woe to thee, wretched soul! what excuse hast thou come to give to God? And the angel of that soul said: Weep for it, all of you, along with me. And the angel came up, and worshipped the Lord, saying: Lord, behold the soul which has dwelt in wickedness in its time, and in its temporary life; do to it according to Thy decision. And there came a voice to that soul, saying: Where is the fruit of thy righteousness? And it was silent, not being able to give an answer. And again there came a voice to it: He who has shown mercy will have mercy shown to him; he who has not shown mercy will not have mercy shown to him. Let this soul be delivered to the merciless angel Temeluch, and let it be cast into outer darkness, where there is weeping and gnashing of teeth. And there was a voice as of tens of thousands, saying: Righteous art Thou, O Lord, and righteous is Thy judgment. And moreover I saw, and, behold, another soul was led by an angel; and it wept, saying: Have mercy upon me, O righteous Judge, and deliver me from the hand of this angel, because he is dreadful and merciless. And a voice came to it, saying: Thou wast altogether merciless, and for this reason thou hast been delivered up to such an angel. Confess thy sins which thou hast done in the world. And that soul said: I have not sinned, O righteous Judge. And the Lord said to that soul: Verily thou seemest as if thou wert in the world, and wert hiding thy deeds from men. Knowest thou not that whensoever any one dies, his deeds run before him, whether they are good or evil? And when it heard this, it was silent. And I heard the Judge saying: Let the angel come, having in his hands the record of thy sins. And the Judge says to the angel: I say to thee the angel, Disclose all. Say what he has done five years before his death. By myself I swear to thee, that in the first period of his life there was forgetfulness of all his former sins. And the angel answered and said: Lord, command the souls to stand beside their angels; and that same hour they stood beside them. And the lord of that soul said: Take note of these souls, and whether thou hast in any way sinned against them. And it answered and said: Lord, a year has not been completed since I killed the one and lived with the other. And not only this, but I also wronged it. And the Lord said to it: Knowest thou not that he who wrongs any one in the world is kept, as soon as he dies, in the place until he whom he has wronged come, and both shall be judged before me, and each receive according to his works? And I heard a voice saying: Let this soul be delivered to the angel Tartaruch, and guarded till the great day of judgment. And I heard a voice as of tens of thousands saying: Righteous art Thou, O Lord, and righteous Thy judgment.

And the angel says to me: Hast thou seen all these things? And I answered: Yes my lord. And again he said to me: Come, follow me, and I shall show thee the place of the righteous. And I followed him, and he set me before the doors of the city. And I saw a golden gate, and two golden pillars before it, and two golden plates upon it full of inscriptions. And the angel said to me: Blessed is he who shall enter into these doors; because not every one goeth in, but only those who have single-mindedness, and guiltlessness, and a pure heart. And I asked the angel: For what purpose have the inscriptions been graven on these plates? And he said to me: These are the names of the righteous, and of those who serve God. And I said to him: Is it so that their names have been inscribed in heaven itself while they are yet alive? And the angel said to me:... of the angels, such as serve Him well are acknowledged by God. And straightway the gate was opened, and there came forth a hoary-headed man to meet us; and he said to me: Welcome, Paul, beloved of God! and, with a joyful countenance, he kissed me with tears. And I said to him: Father, why weepest thou? And he said to me: Because God hath prepared many good things for men, and they do not His will in order that they may enjoy them. And I asked the angel: My lord, who is this? And he said to me: This is Enoch, the witness of the last day. And the angel says to me: See that whatever I show thee in this place thou do not announce, except what I tell thee. And he set me upon the river whose source springs up in the circle of heaven; and it is this river which encircleth the whole earth. And he says to me: This river is Ocean. And there was then a great light. And I said: My lord, what is this? And he said to me: This is the land of the meek. Knowest thou not that it is written, Blessed are the meek, for they shall inherit the earth? The souls of the righteous, therefore, are kept in this place. And I said to the angel: When, then, will they be made manifest? And he said to me: When the Judge shall come in the day of the resurrection, and sit down. Then, accordingly, shall he command, and shall reveal the earth, and it shall be lighted up; and the saints shall appear in it, and shall delight themselves in the good that have been reserved from the foundation of the world. And there were by the bank of the river, trees planted, full of different fruits. And I looked towards the rising of the sun, and I saw there trees of great size full of fruits; and that land was more brilliant than silver and gold; and there were vines growing on those date-palms, and myriads of shoots, and myriads of clusters on each branch. And I said to the archangel: What is this, my lord? And he says to me: This is the Acherusian lake, and within it the city of God. All are not permitted to enter into it, except whosoever shall repent of his sins; and as soon as he shall repent, and alter his life, he is delivered to Michael, and they cast him into the Acherusian lake, and then he brings him in the city of God, near the righteous. And I wondered and blessed God at all that I saw. And the angel said to me: Follow me, that I may bring thee into the city of God, and into its light. And its light was greater than the light of the world, and greater than gold, and walls encircled it. And the length and the breadth of it were a hundred stadia. And I saw twelve gates, exceedingly ornamented, leading into the city; and four rivers encircled it, flowing with milk, and honey, and oil, and wine. And I said to the angel: My lord, what are these rivers? And he said to me: These are the righteous who, when in the world, did not make use of these things, but humbled themselves for the sake of God; and here they receive a recompense ten thousand fold.

And I, going into the city, saw a very lofty tree before the doors of the city, having no fruit, and a few men under it; and they wept exceedingly, and the trees bent down to them. And I, seeing them, wept, and asked the angel: Who are these, that they have not turned to go into the city? And he said to me: Yes, the root of all evils is vainglory. And I said: And these trees, why have they thus humbled themselves? And the angel answered and said to me: For this reason the trees are not fruit-bearing, because they have not withheld themselves from vaunting. And I asked the angel: My lord, for what reason have they been put aside before the doors of the city? And he answered and said to me: On account of the great goodness of God, since by this way Christ is going to come into the city, and that those who go along with Him may plead for these men, and that they may be brought in along with them. And I was going along, guided by the angel, and he set me upon the river. And I saw there all the prophets; and they came and saluted me, saying: Welcome, Paul, beloved of God. And I said to the angel: My lord, who are these? And he said to

me: These are all the prophets, and these are the songs of all the prophecies, and of whoever hath grieved his soul, not doing its will, for God's sake. Having departed, then, he comes here, and the prophets salute him. And the angel brought me to the south of the city, where the river of milk is. And I saw there all the infants that King Herod slew for the Lord's name's sake. And the angel took me again to the east of the city, and I saw there Abraham, Isaac, Jacob. And I asked the angel: My lord, what place is this? And he said to me: Every one who is hospitable to men comes hither when he comes out of the world, and they salute him as a friend of God on account of his love to strangers. And again he took me away to another place, and I saw there a river like oil on the north of the city, and I saw people there rejoicing and singing praises. And I asked: Who are these, my lord? And he said to me: These are they who have given themselves up to God; for they are brought into this city. And I looked, and saw in the midst of the city an altar, great and very lofty; and there was one standing near the altar, whose face shone like the sun, and he had in his hands a psaltery and a harp, and he sung the Alleluia delightfully, and his voice filled all the city. And all with one consent accompanied him, so that the city was shaken by their shouting. And I asked the angel: Who is this that singeth delightfully, whom all accompany? And he said to me: This is the prophet David; this is the heavenly Jerusalem. When, therefore, Christ shall come in His second appearing, David himself goes forth with all the saints. For as it is in the heavens, so also upon earth: for it is not permitted without David to offer sacrifice even in the day of the sacrifice of the precious body and blood of Christ; but it is necessary for David to sing the Alleluia. And I asked the angel: My lord, what is the meaning of Alleluia? It is called in Hebrew, thebel, marematha—speech to God who founded all things: let us glorify Him in the same. So that every one who sings the Alleluia glorifies God.

When these things, therefore, had been thus said to me by the angel, he led me outside of the city, and the Acherusian lake, and the good land, and set me upon the river of the ocean that supports the firmament of the heaven, and said to me: Knowest thou where I am going? And I said: No, my lord. And he said to me: Follow me, that I may show thee where the souls of the impious and the sinners are. And he took me to the setting of the sun, and *where* the beginning of the heaven had been founded upon the river of the ocean. And I saw beyond the river, and there was no light there, but darkness, and grief, and groaning; and I saw a bubbling river, and a great multitude both of men and women who had been cast into it, some up to the knees, others up to the navel, and many even up to the crown of the head. And I asked: Who are these? And he said to me: These are they who lived unrepenting in fornications and adulteries. And I saw at the south-west of the river another river, where there flowed a river of fire, and there was there a multitude of many souls. And I asked the angel: Who are these, my lord? And he said to me: These are the thieves, and slanderers, and flatterers, who did not set up God as their help, but hoped in the vanity of their riches. And I said to him: What is the depth of this river? And he said to me: Its depth has no measure, but it is immeasurable. And I groaned and wept because of mankind. And the angel said to me: Why weepest thou? Art thou more merciful than God? for, being holy, God, repenting over men, waits for their conversion and repentance; but they, deceived by their own will, come here, and are eternally punished. And I looked into the fiery river, and saw an old man dragged along by two, and they pulled him in up to the knee. And the angel Temeluch coming, laid hold of an iron with his hand, and with it drew up the entrails of that old man through his mouth. And I asked the angel: My lord, who is this that suffers this punishment? And he said to me: This old man whom thou seest was a presbyter; and when he had eaten and drunk, then he performed the service of God. And I saw there another old man carried in haste by four angels; and they threw him into the fiery river up to the girdle, and he was frightfully burnt by the lightnings. And I said to the angel: Who is this, my lord? And he said to me: This whom thou seest was a bishop, and that name indeed he was well pleased to have; but in the goodness of God he did not walk, righteous judgment he did not judge, the widow and the orphan he did not pity, he was neither affectionate nor hospitable; but now he has been recompensed according to his works. And I looked, and saw in the middle of the river another man up to the navel, having his hands all bloody, and worms were coming up through his mouth. And I asked the angel: Who is this, my lord? And he said to me: This whom thou seest was a deacon, who ate and drank, and ministered to God. And I looked to another place where there was a brazen wall in flames, and within it men and women eating up their own tongues, dreadfully judged. And I asked the angel: Who are these, my lord? And he said to me: These are they who in the church speak against their neighbours, and do not attend to the word of God. And I looked, and saw a bloody pit. And I said: What is this pit? And he said to me: This is the place where are cast the wizards, and sorcerers, and the whoremongers, and the adulterers, and those that oppress widows and orphans. And I saw in another place women wearing black, and led away into a dark place. And I asked: Who are these, my lord? And he said to me: These are they who did not listen to their parents, but before their marriage defiled their virginity. And I saw women wearing white robes, being blind, and standing upon obelisks of fire; and an angel was mercilessly beating them, saying: Now you know where you are; you did not attend when the Scriptures were read to you. And the angel said to me: These are they who corrupted themselves and killed their infants. Their infants therefore came crying out: Avenge us of our mothers. And they were given to an angel to be carried away into a spacious place, but their parents into everlasting fire.

And the angel took me up from these torments, and set me above a well, which had seven seals upon its mouth. And the angel who was with me said to the angel at the well of that place: Open the well, that Paul the beloved of God may see, because there has been given to him authority to see the torments. And the angel of the place said to me: Stand afar off, until I open the seals. And when he had opened them, there came forth a stench which it was impossible to bear. And having come near the place, I saw that well filled with darkness and gloom, and great narrowness of space in it. And the angel who was with me said to me: This place of the well which thou seest is cast off from the glory of God, and none of the angels is importunate in behalf of them; and as many as have professed that the holy Mary is not the mother of God, and that the Lord did not become man out of her, and that the bread of the thanksgiving and the cup of blessing are not His flesh and blood, are cast into this well: and as I said before no angel is importunate in their behalf. And I saw towards the setting of the sun, where there is weeping and gnashing of teeth, many men and women there tormented. And I said to the angel: Who are these, my lord? And he said to me: These are they who say that there is no resurrection of the dead; and to them mercy never comes.

Having heard this, I wept bitterly; and looking up into the firmament, I saw the heaven opened, and the archangel Gabriel coming down with hosts of angels, who were going round about all the torments. And they who were judged in the torments seeing them, all cried out with one loud voice: Have mercy upon us, Gabriel, who standest in the presence of God; for we heard that there was a judgment: behold, we know it. And the archangel Gabriel answered and said: As the Lord liveth, beside whom I stand, night and day without ceasing I plead in behalf of the race of men; but they did not do any good when in life, but spent the period of their life in vanity. And now I shall weep, even I, along with the beloved Paul; perhaps the good Lord may have compassion, and grant you remission. And they assented with one voice: Have mercy upon us, O Lord. And they fell down before God, and supplicated, saying: Have mercy, O Lord, upon the sons of men whom Thou hast made after Thine image. And the heaven was shaken like a leaf, and I saw the four and twenty elders lying on their face; and I saw the altar, and the throne, and the veil; and all of them entreated the glory of God; and I saw the Son of God with glory and great power coming down to the earth. And when the sound of the trumpet took place, all who were in the torments cried out, saying: Have mercy upon us Son of God; for to Thee has been given power over things in heaven, and things on earth, and things under the earth. And there came a voice saying: What good work have you done, that you are asking for rest? For you have done as you wished, and have not repented, but you have spent your life in profligacy. But now for the sake of Gabriel, the angel of my righteousness and for the sake of Paul my beloved, I give you a night and the day of the holy Lord's day, on which I rose from the dead, for rest. And all who were in the torments cried out, saying: We bless Thee, O Son of the living God; better for us is such rest than the life which we lived when spending our time in the world.

And after these things the angel says to me: Behold, thou hast seen all the torments: come, follow me, that I may lead thee away to paradise, and that thou mayst change thy soul by the sight of the righteous; for many desire to salute thee. And he took me by an impulse of the Spirit, and brought me into paradise. And he says to me: This is paradise, where Adam and Eve transgressed. And I saw there a beautiful tree of great size, on which the Holy Spirit rested; and from the root of it there came forth all manner of most sweet-smelling water, parting into four channels. And I said to the angel: My lord, what is this tree, that there comes forth from it a great abundance of this water, and where does it go? And he answered and said to me: Before the heaven and the earth existed, He divided them into four kingdoms and heads, of which the names are Phison, Gehon, Tigris, Euphrates. And having again taken hold of me by the hand, he led me near the tree of the knowledge of good and evil. And he says to me: This is the tree by means of which death came into the world, and Adam took of the fruit of it from his wife, and ate; and thereafter they were cast out hence. And he showed me another, the tree of life, and said to me: This the cherubim and the flaming sword guard. And when I was closely observing the tree, and wondering, I saw a woman coming from afar off, and a multitude of angels singing praises to her. And I asked the angel: Who is this, my lord, who is in so great honour and beauty? And the angel says to me: This is the holy Mary, the mother of the Lord. And she came and saluted me, saying: Welcome, Paul, beloved of God, and angels, and men; thou hast proclaimed the word of God in the world, and established churches, and all bear testimony to thee who have been saved by means of thee: for, having been delivered from the deception of idols through thy teaching, they come here.

While they were yet speaking to me, I gazed, and saw other three men coming. And I asked the angel: Who are these, my lord? And he said to me: These are Abraham, Isaac, and Jacob, the righteous forefathers. And they came and saluted me, saying: Welcome, Paul, beloved of God....God did not grieve us. But we know thee in the flesh, before thou camest forth out of the world. And in succession they told me their names from Abraham to Manasseh. And one of them, Joseph who was sold in Egypt, says to me: Hear me, Paul, friend of God: I did not requite my brethren who cursed me. For blessed is he who is able to endure trial, because the Lord will give him in requital sevenfold reward in the world to come. And while he was yet speaking with me, I saw another coming afar off, and the appearance of him was as the appearance of an angel. And I asked the angel, saying: My lord, who is this? And he said to me: This is Moses the lawgiver, by whom God led forth the children of Israel out of the slavery of Egypt. And when he came near me, he saluted me weeping. And I said to him: Father, why weepest thou, being righteous and meek? And he answered and said to me: I must weep for every man, because I brought trouble upon a people that does not understand, and they have not borne fruit; and I see the sheep of which I was shepherd scattered, and the toil which I toiled for the children of Israel has been counted for nothing; and they saw powers and hosts in the midst of them, and they did not understand; and I see the Gentiles worshipping, and believing through thy word, and being converted, and coming here, and out of my people that was so great not one has understood. For, when the Jews hanged the Son of God upon the cross, all the angels and archangels, and the righteous, and the whole creation of things in heaven, and things in earth, and things under the earth, lamented and mourned with a great lamentation, but the impious and insensate Jews did not understand; wherefore there has been prepared for them the fire everlasting, and the worm that dies not.

While he was yet speaking, there came other three, and saluted me, saying: Welcome, Paul, beloved of God, the boast of the churches, and model of angels. And I asked: Who are you? And the first said: I am Isaiah, whom Manasseh sawed with a wood saw. And the second said: I am Jeremiah, whom the Jews stoned, but they remained burnt up with everlasting fire. And the third said: I am Ezekiel, whom the slayers of the Messiah pierced; all these things have we endured, and we have not been able to turn the stony heart of the Jews. And I threw myself on my face, entreating the goodness of God, because He had had mercy upon me, and had delivered me from the race of the Hebrews. And there came a voice saying: Blessed art thou, Paul, beloved of God; and blessed are those who through thee have believed in the name of our Lord Jesus Christ, because for them has been prepared everlasting life.

While this voice was yet speaking, there came another, crying: Blessed art thou, Paul. And I asked the angel: Who is this, my lord? And he said to me: This is Noah, who lived in the time of the deluge. And when we had saluted each other, I asked him: Who art thou? And he said to me: I am Noah, who in a hundred years built the ark, and without putting off the coat which I wore, or shaving my head; moreover, I practised continence, and did not come near my wife; and in the hundred years my coat was not dirtied, and the hair of my head was not diminished. And I ceased not to proclaim to men, Repent, for, behold, a deluge is coming. And no one paid heed; but all derided me, not refraining from their lawless deeds, until the water of the deluge came and destroyed them all.

And looking away, I saw other two from afar off. And I asked the angel: Who are these, my lord? And he said to me: These are Enoch and Elias. And they came and saluted me, saying: Welcome, Paul, beloved of God! And I said to them: Who are you? And Elias the prophet answered and said to me: I am Elias the prophet, who prayed to God, and He caused that no rain should come down upon the earth for three years and six months, on account of the unrighteousness of the sons of men. For often, of a truth, even the angel besought God on account of the rain; and I heard, Be patient until Elias my beloved shall pray, and I send rain upon the earth.

REVELATION OF ESDRAS

Word and Revelation of Esdras, the Holy Prophet
and Beloved of God.

It came to pass in the thirtieth year, on the twenty-second of the month, I was in my house. And I cried out and said to the Most High: Lord, give the glory, in order that I may see Thy mysteries. And when it was night, there came an angel, Michael the archangel, and says to me: O Prophet Esdras, refrain from bread for seventy *weeks*. And I fasted as he told me. And there came Raphael the commander of the host, and gave me a storax rod. And I fasted twice sixty weeks. And I saw the mysteries of God and His angels. And I said to them: I wish to plead before God about the race of the Christians. It is good for a man not to be born rather than to come into the world. I was therefore taken up into heaven, and I saw in the first heaven a great army of angels; and they took me to the judgments. And I heard a voice saying to me: Have mercy on us, O thou chosen of God, Esdras. Then began I to say: Woe to sinners when they see one who is just more than the angels, and they themselves are in the Gehenna of fire! And Esdras said: Have mercy on the works of Thine hands, Thou who art compassionate, and of great mercy. Judge me rather than the souls of the sinners; for it is better that one soul should be punished, and that the whole world should not come to destruction. And God said: I will give rest in paradise to the righteous, and I have become merciful. And Esdras said: Lord, why dost Thou confer benefits on the righteous? for just as one who has been hired out, and has served out his time, goes and again works as a slave when he come to his masters, so also the righteous has received his reward in the heavens. But have mercy on the sinners, for we know that Thou art merciful. And God said: I do not see how I can have mercy upon them. And Esdras said: They cannot endure Thy wrath. And God said: This is *the fate* of such. And God said: I wish to have thee like Paul and John, as thou hast given me uncorrupted the treasure that cannot be stolen, the treasure of virginity, the bulwark of men. And Esdras said: It is good for a man not to be born. It is good not to be in life. The irrational *creatures* are better than man, because they have no punishment; but Thou hast taken us, and given us up to judgment. Woe to the sinners in the world to come! because their judgment is endless, and the flame unquenchable. And while I was thus speaking to him, there came Michael and Gabriel, and all the apostles; and they said: Rejoice, O faithful man of God! And Esdras said: Arise, and come hither with me, O Lord, to judgment. And the Lord said: Behold, I give thee my covenant between me and thee, that you may receive it. And Esdras said: Let us plead in Thy hearing. And God said: Ask Abraham your father how a son pleads with his father, and come plead with us. And Esdras said: As the Lord liveth, I will not cease pleading with Thee in behalf of the race of the Christians. Where are Thine ancient compassions, O Lord? Where is Thy long-suffering? And God said: As I have made night and day, I have made the righteous and the sinner; and

he should have lived like the righteous. And the prophet said: Who made Adam the first-formed? And God said: My undefiled hands. And I put him in paradise to guard the food of the tree of life; and thereafter he became disobedient, and did this in transgression. And the prophet said: Was he not protected by an angel? and was not his life guarded by the cherubim to endless ages? and how was he deceived who was guarded by angels? for Thou didst command all to be present, and to attend to what was said by Thee. But if Thou hadst not given him Eve, the serpent would not have deceived her; but whom Thou wilt Thou savest, and whom Thou wilt Thou destroyest. And the prophet said: Let us come, my Lord, to a second judgment. And God said: I cast fire upon Sodom and Gomorrah. And the prophet said: Lord, Thou dealest with us according to our deserts. And God said: Your sins transcend my clemency. And the prophet said: Call to mind the Scriptures, my Father, who hast measured out Jerusalem, and set her up again. Have mercy, O Lord, upon sinners; have mercy upon Thine own creatures; have pity upon Thy works. Then God remembered those whom He had made, and said to the prophet: How can I have mercy upon them? Vinegar and gall did they give me to drink, and not even then did they repent. And the prophet said: Reveal Thy cherubim, and let us go together to judgment; and show me the day of judgment, what like it is. And God said: Thou hast been deceived, Esdras; for such is the day of judgment as that in which there is no rain upon the earth; for it is a merciful tribunal as compared with that day. And the prophet said: I will not cease to plead with Thee, unless I see the day of the consummation. And God said: Number the stars and the sand of the sea; and if thou shalt be able to number this, thou art also able to plead with me. And the prophet said: Lord, Thou knowest that I wear human flesh; and how can I count the stars of the heaven, and the sand of the sea? And God said: My chosen prophet, no man will know that great day and the appearing that comes to judge the world. For thy sake, my prophet, I have told thee the day; but the hour have I not told thee. And the prophet said: Lord, tell me also the years. And God said: If I see the righteousness of the world, that it has abounded, I will have patience with them; but if not, I will stretch forth my hand, and lay hold of the world by the four quarters, and bring them all together into the valley of Jehoshaphat, and I will wipe out the race of men, so that the world shall be no more. And the prophet said: And how can Thy right hand be glorified? And God said: I shall be glorified by my angels. And the prophet said: Lord, if Thou hast resolved to do this, why didst Thou make man? Thou didst say to our father Abraham, Multiplying I will multiply thy seed as the stars of the heaven, and as the sand that is by the sea-shore; and where is Thy promise? And God said: First will I make an earthquake for the fall of four-footed beasts and of men; and when you see that brother gives up brother to death, and that children shall rise up against their parents, and that a woman forsakes her own husband, and when nation shall rise up against nation in war, then will you know that the end is near.

For then neither brother pities brother, nor man wife, nor children parents, nor friends friends, nor a slave his master; for he who is the adversary of men shall come up from Tartarus, and shall show men many things. What shall I make of thee, Esdras? and wilt thou yet plead with me? And the prophet said: Lord, I shall not cease to plead with Thee. And God said: Number the flowers of the earth. If thou shalt be able to number them, thou art able also to plead with me. And the prophet said: Lord, I cannot number *them*. I wear human flesh; but I shall not cease to plead with Thee. I wish, Lord, to see also the under parts of Tartarus. And God said: Come down and see. And He gave me Michael, and Gabriel, and other thirty-four angels; and I went down eighty-five steps, and they brought me down five hundred steps, and I saw a fiery throne, and an old man sitting upon it; and his judgment was merciless. And I said to the angels: Who is this? and what is his sin? And they said to me: This is Herod, who for a time was a king, and ordered to put to death the children from two years old and under. And I said: Woe to his soul! And again they took me down thirty steps, and I there saw boilings up of fire, and in them *there was* a multitude of sinners; and I heard their voice, but saw not their forms. And they took me down lower many steps, which I could not measure. And I there saw old men, and fiery pivots turning in their ears. And I said: Who are these? and what is their sin? And they said to me: These are they who would not listen. And they took me down again other five hundred steps, and I there saw the worm that sleeps not, and fire burning up the sinners. And they took me down to the lowest part of destruction, and I saw there the twelve plagues of the abyss. And they took me away to the south, and I saw there a man hanging by the eyelids; and the angels kept scourging him. And I asked: Who is this? and what is his sin? And Michael the commander said to me: This is one who lay with his mother; for having put into practice a small wish, he has been ordered to be hanged. And they took me away to the north, and I saw there a man bound with iron chains. And I asked: Who is this? And he said to me: This is he who said, I am the Son of God, that made stones bread, and water wine. And the prophet said: My lord, let me know what is his form, and I shall tell the race of men, that they may not believe in him. And he said to me: The form of his countenance is like that of a wild beast; his right eye like the star that rises in the morning, and the other without motion; his mouth one cubit; his teeth span long; his fingers like scythes; the track of his feet of two spans; and in his face an inscription, Antichrist. He has been exalted to heaven; he shall go down to Hades. At one time he shall become a child; at another, an old man. And the prophet said: Lord, and how dost Thou permit him, and he deceives the race of men? And God said: Listen, my prophet. He becomes both child and old man, and no one believes him that he is my beloved Son. And after this a trumpet, and the tombs shall be opened, and the dead shall be raised incorruptible. Then the adversary, hearing the dreadful threatening, shall be hidden in outer darkness. Then the heaven, and the earth, and the sea shall be destroyed. Then shall I burn the heaven eighty

cubits, and the earth eight hundred cubits. And the prophet said: And how has the heaven sinned? And God said: Since…there is evil. And the prophet said: Lord, and the earth, how has it sinned? And God said: Since the adversary, having heard the dreadful threatening, shall be hidden, even on account of this will I melt the earth, and with it the opponent of the race of men. And the prophet said: Have mercy, Lord, upon the race of the Christians. And I saw a woman hanging, and four wild beasts sucking her breasts. And the angels said to me: She grudged to give her milk, but even threw her infants into the rivers. And I saw a dreadful darkness, and a night that had no stars nor moon; nor is there there young or old, nor brother with brother, nor mother with child, nor wife with husband. And I wept, and said: O Lord God, have mercy upon the sinners. And as I said this, there came a cloud and snatched me up, and carried me away again into the heavens. And I saw there many judgments; and I wept bitterly, and said: It is good for a man not to have come out of his mother's womb. And those who were in torment cried out, saying: Since thou hast come hither, O holy one of God, we have found a little remission. And the prophet said: Blessed are they that weep for their sins. And God said: Hear, O beloved Esdras. As a husbandman casts the seed of the corn into the ground, so also the man casts his seed into the parts of the woman. The first *month* it is all together; the second it increases in size; the third it gets hair; the fourth it gets nails; the fifth it is turned into milk; and the sixth it is made ready, and receives life; the seventh it is completely furnished; the ninth the barriers of the gate of the woman are opened; and it is born safe and sound into the earth. And the prophet said: Lord, it is good for man not to have been born. Woe to the human race then, when Thou shalt come to judgment! And I said to the Lord: Lord, why hast Thou created man, and delivered him up to judgment? And God said, with a lofty proclamation: I will not by any means have mercy on those who transgress my covenant. And the prophet said: Lord, where is Thy goodness? And God said: I have prepared all things for man's sake, and man does not keep my commandments. And the prophet said: Lord, reveal to me the judgments and paradise. And the angels took me away towards the east, and I saw the tree of life. And I saw there Enoch, and Elias, and Moses, and Peter, and Paul, and Luke, and Matthias, and all the righteous, and the patriarchs. And I saw there the keeping of the air within bounds, and the blowing of the winds, and the storehouses of the ice, and the eternal judgments. And I saw there a man hanging by the skull. And they said to me: This man removed landmarks. And I saw there great judgments. And I said to the Lord: O Lord God, and what man, then, who has been born has not sinned? And they took me lower down into Tartarus, and I saw all the sinners lamenting and weeping and mourning bitterly. And I also wept, seeing the race of men thus tormented. Then God says to me: Knowest thou, Esdras, the names of the angels at the end of the world? Michael, Gabriel, Uriel, Raphael, Gabuthelon, Aker, Arphugitonos, Beburos, Zebuleon.

Then there came a voice to me: Come hither and die, Esdras, my beloved; give that which hath been entrusted to thee. And the prophet said: And whence can you bring forth my soul? And the angels said: We can put it forth through the mouth. And the prophet said: Mouth to mouth have I spoken with God, and it comes not forth thence. And the angels said: Let us bring it out through thy nostrils. And the prophet said: My nostrils have smelled the sweet savour of the glory of God. And the angels said: We can bring it out through thine eyes. And the prophet said: Mine eyes have seen the back parts of God. And the angels said: We can bring it out through the crown of thy head. And the prophet said: I walked about with Moses also on the mountain, and it comes not forth thence. And the angels said: We can put it forth through the points of thy nails. And the prophet said: My feet also have walked about on the altar. And the angels went away without having done anything, saying: Lord, we cannot get his soul. Then He says to His only begotten Son: Go down, my beloved Son, with a great host of angels, and take the soul of my beloved Esdras. For the Lord, having taken a great host of angels, says to the prophet: Give me the trust which I entrusted to thee; the crown has been prepared for thee. And the prophet said: Lord, if Thou take my soul from me, who will be left to plead with Thee for the race of men? And God said: As thou art mortal, and of the earth, do not plead with me. And the prophet said: I will not cease to plead. And God said: Give up just now the trust; the crown has been prepared for thee. Come and die, that thou mayst obtain it. Then the prophet began to say with tears: O Lord, what good have I done pleading with Thee, and I am going to fall down into the earth? Woe's me, woe's me, that I am going to be eaten up by worms! Weep, all ye saints and ye righteous, for me, who have pleaded much, and who am delivered up to death. Weep for me, all ye saints and ye righteous, because I have gone to the pit of Hades. And God said to him: Hear, Esdras, my beloved. I, who am immortal, endured a cross; I tasted vinegar and gall; I was laid in a tomb, and I raised up my chosen ones; I called Adam up out of Hades, that *I might save* the race of men. Do not therefore be afraid of death: for that which is from me—that is to say, the soul—goes to heaven; and that which is from the earth—that is to say, the body—goes to the earth, from which it was taken. And the prophet said: Woe's me! woe's me! what shall I set about? what shall I do? I know not. And then the blessed Esdras began to say: O eternal God, the Maker of the whole creation, who hast measured the heaven with a span, and who holdest the earth as a handful, who ridest upon the cherubim, who didst take the prophet Elias to the heavens in a chariot of fire, who givest food to all flesh, whom all things dread and tremble at from the face of Thy power,—listen to me, who have pleaded much, and give to all who transcribe this book, and have it, and remember my name, and honour my memory, give them a blessing from heaven; and bless him in all things, as Thou didst bless Joseph at last, and remember not his former wickedness in the day of his judgment. And as many as have not believed this book shall be burnt up like Sodom and Gomorrah. And there came to him a voice, saying: Esdras, my beloved, all things whatever thou hast asked will I give to each one. And immediately he gave up his precious soul with much honour, in the month of October, on the twenty-eighth. And they prepared him for burial with incense and psalms; and his precious and sacred body dispenses strength of soul and body perpetually to those who have recourse to him from a longing desire. To whom is due glory, strength, honour, and adoration,—to the Father, and to the Son, and to the Holy Spirit, now and ever, and to ages of ages. Amen.

REVELATION OF MOSES

Account and life of Adam and Eve, the first-created, revealed by God to His servant Moses, when he received from the hand of the Lord the tables of the law of the covenant, instructed by the archangel Michael.

This is the account of Adam and Eve. After they went forth out of paradise, Adam took Eve his wife, and went up into the east. And he remained there eighteen years and two months; and Eve conceived and brought forth two sons, Diaphotus called Cain, and Amilabes called Abel.

And after this, Adam and Eve were with one another; and when they lay down, Eve said to Adam her lord: My lord, I have seen in a dream this night the blood of my son Amilabes, who is called Abel, thrown into the mouth of Cain his brother, and he drank it without pity. And he entreated him to grant him a little of it, but he did not listen to him, but drank it all up; and it did not remain in his belly, but came forth out of his mouth. And Adam said to Eve: Let us arise, and go and see what has happened to them, lest perchance the enemy should be in any way warring against them.

And having both gone, they found Abel killed by the hand of Cain his brother. And God says to the archangel Michael: Say to Adam, Do not relate the mystery which thou knowest to thy son Cain, for he is a son of wrath. But grieve thyself not; for I will give thee instead of him another son, who shall show thee all things, as many as thou shalt do to him; but do thou tell him nothing. This God said to His angel; and Adam kept the word in his heart, and with him Eve also, having grief about Abel their son.

And after this, Adam knew his wife Eve, and she conceived and brought forth Seth. And Adam says to Eve: Behold, we have brought forth a son instead of Abel whom Cain slew; let us give glory and sacrifice to God.

And Adam had thirty sons and thirty daughters. And he fell into disease, and cried with a loud voice, and said: Let all my sons come to me, that I may see them before I die. And they were all brought together, for the earth was inhabited in three parts; and they all came to the door of the house into which he had entered to pray to God. And his son Seth said: Father Adam, what is thy disease? And he says: My children, great trouble has hold of me. And they say: What is the trouble and disease? And Seth answered and said to him: Is it that thou rememberest the *fruits* of paradise of which thou didst eat, and grievest thyself because of the desire of them? If it is so, tell me, and I will go and bring thee fruit from paradise. For I will put dung upon my head, and weep and pray, and the Lord will hearken to me, and send his angel; and I shall bring *it* to thee, that thy trouble may cease from thee. Adam says to him: No, my son Seth; but I have disease and trouble. Seth says to him: And how have they come upon thee? Adam said

to him: When God made us, me and your mother, for whose sake also I die, He gave us every plant in paradise; but about one he commanded us not to eat of it, because on account of it we should die. And the hour was at hand for the angels who guarded your mother to go up and worship the Lord; and the enemy gave to her, and she ate of the tree, knowing that I was not near her, nor the holy angels; then she gave me also to eat. And when we had both eaten, God was angry with us. And the Lord, coming into paradise, set His throne, and called with a dreadful voice, saying, Adam, where art thou? and why art thou hidden from my face? shall the house be hidden from him that built it? And He says, Since thou hast forsaken my covenant, I have brought upon thy body seventy strokes. The trouble of the first stroke is the injury of the eyes; the trouble of the second stroke, of the hearing; and so in succession, all the strokes shall overtake thee.

And Adam thus speaking to his sons, groaned out loud, and said: What shall I do? I am in great grief. And Eve also wept, saying: My lord Adam, arise, give me the half of thy disease, and let me bear it, because through me this has happened to thee; through me thou art in distresses and troubles. And Adam said to Eve: Arise, and go with our son Seth near paradise, and put earth upon your heads, and weep, beseeching the Lord that He may have compassion upon me, and send His angel to paradise, and give me of the tree in which flows the oil out of it, and that thou mayest bring it to me; and I shall anoint myself, and have rest, and show thee the manner in which we were deceived at first.

And Seth and Eve went into the regions of paradise. And as they were going along, Eve saw her son, and a wild beast fighting with him. And Eye wept, saying: Woe's me, woe's me; for if I come to the day of the resurrection, all who have sinned will curse me, saying, Eve did not keep the commandment of God. And Eve cried out to the wild beast, saying: O thou evil wild beast, wilt thou not be afraid to fight with the image of God? How has thy mouth been opened? how have thy teeth been strengthened? how hast thou not been mindful of thy subjection, that thou wast formerly subject to the image of God? Then the wild beast cried out, saying: O Eve, not against us thy upbraiding nor thy weeping, but against thyself, since the beginning of the wild beasts was from thee. How was thy mouth opened to eat of the tree about which God had commanded thee not to eat of it? For this reason also our nature has been changed. Now, therefore, thou shalt not be able to bear up, if I begin to reproach thee. And Seth says to the wild beast: Shut thy mouth and be silent, and stand off from the image of God till the day of judgment. Then the wild beast says to Seth: Behold, I stand off, Seth, from the image of God. Then the wild beast fled, and left him wounded, and went to his covert.

And Seth went with his mother Eve near paradise: and they wept there, beseeching God to send His angel, to give them the oil of compassion. And God sent to them the archangel Michael, and he said to them these words: Seth, man of God, do not weary thyself praying in this supplication about the tree in which flows the oil to anoint thy father Adam; for it will not happen to thee now, but at the last times. Then shall arise all flesh from Adam even to that great day, as many as shall be a holy people; then shall be given to them all the delight of paradise, and God shall be in the midst of them; and there shall not any more be sinners before Him, because the wicked heart shall be taken from them, and there shall be given to them a heart made to understand what is good, and to worship God only. Do thou again go to thy father, since the measure of his life has been fulfilled, equal to three days. And when his soul goes out, thou wilt behold its dreadful passage.

And the angel, having said this, went away from them. And Seth and Eve came to the tent where Adam was lying. And Adam says to Eve: Why didst thou work mischief against us, and bring upon us great wrath, which is death, holding sway over all our race? And he says to her: Call all our children, and our children's children, and relate to them the manner of our transgression.

Then Eve says to them: Listen, all my children, and my children's children, and I shall relate to you how our enemy deceived us. It came to pass, while we were keeping paradise, that we kept each the portion allotted to him by God. And I was keeping in my lot the south and west. And the devil went into the lot of Adam where were the male wild beasts; since God parted to us the wild beasts, and had given all the males to your father, and all the females He gave to me, and each of us watched his own. And the devil spoke to the serpent, saying, Arise, come to me, and I shall tell you a thing in which thou mayst be of service. Then the serpent came to him, and the devil says to him, I hear that thou art more sagacious than all the wild beasts, and I have come to make thy acquaintance; and I have found thee greater than all the wild beasts, and they associate with thee; notwithstanding, thou doest reverence to one far inferior. Why eatest thou of the tares of Adam and his wife, and not of the fruit of paradise? Arise and come hither, and we shall make him be cast out of paradise through his wife, as we also were cast out through him. The serpent says to him, I am afraid lest the Lord be angry with me. The devil says to him, Be not afraid; only become my instrument, and I will speak through thy mouth a word by which thou shalt be able to deceive him. Then straightway he hung by the walls of paradise about the hour when the angels of God went up to worship. Then Satan came in the form of an angel, and praised God as did the angels; and looking out from the wall, I saw him like an angel. And says he to me, Art thou Eve? And I said to him, I am. And says he to me, What doest thou in paradise? And I said to him, God has set us to keep it, and to eat of it. The devil answered me through the mouth of the serpent, Ye do well, but you do not eat of every plant. And I say to him, Yes, of every plant we eat, but one only which is in the midst of paradise, about which God has commanded us not to eat of it, since you will die the death. Then says the serpent to me, As God liveth, I am grieved for you, because you

are like cattle. For I do not wish you to be ignorant of this; but rise, come hither, listen to me, and eat, and perceive the value of the tree, as He told us. But I said to him, I am afraid lest God be angry with me. And he says to me, Be not afraid; for as soon as thou eatest, thine eyes shall be opened, and ye shall be as gods in knowing what is good and what is evil. And God, knowing this, that ye shall be like Him, has had a grudge against you, and said, Ye shall not eat of it. But do thou observe the plant, and thou shalt see great glory about it. And I observed the plant, and saw great glory about it. And I said to him, It is beautiful to the eyes to perceive; and I was afraid to take of the fruit. And he says to me, Come, I will give to thee: follow me. And I opened to him, and he came inside into paradise, and went through it before me. And having walked a little, he turned, and says to me, I have changed my mind, and will not give thee to eat. And this he said, wishing at last to entice and destroy me. And he says to me, Swear to me that thou wilt give also to thy husband. And I said to him, I know not by what oath I shall swear to thee; but what I know I say to thee, By the throne of the Lord, and the cherubim, and the tree of life, I will give also to my husband to eat. And when he had taken the oath from me, then he went and ascended upon it. And he put upon the fruit which he gave me to eat the poison of his wickedness, that is, of his desire; for desire is the head of all sin. And I bent down the branch to the ground, and took of the fruit, and ate. And in that very hour mine eyes were opened. and I knew that I was stripped of the righteousness with which I had been clothed; and I wept, saying, What is this thou hast done to me, because I have been deprived of the glory with which I was clothed? And I wept too about the oath. And he came down out of the tree, and went out of sight. And I sought leaves in my portion, that I might cover my shame; and I did not find them from the plants of paradise, since, at the time that I ate, the leaves of all the plants in my portion fell, except of the fig alone. And having taken leaves off it, I made myself a girdle, and it is from those plants of which I ate. And I cried out with a loud voice, saying, Adam, Adam, where art thou? Arise, come to me, and I shall show thee a great mystery. And when your father came, I said to him words of wickedness, which brought us down from great glory. For as soon as he came I opened my mouth, and the devil spoke; and I began to advise him, saying, Come hither, my lord Adam, listen to me, and eat of the fruit of the tree of which God said to us not to eat of it, and thou shalt be as God. And your father answered and said, I am afraid lest God be angry with me. And I said to him, Be not afraid, for as soon as thou shalt eat thou shalt know good and evil. And then I quickly persuaded him, and he ate; and his eyes were opened, and he was aware, he also, of his nakedness. And he says to me, O wicked woman, why hast thou wrought mischief in us? Thou hast alienated me from the glory of God. And that same hour we heard the archangel Michael sounding his trumpet, calling the angels, saying, Thus saith the Lord, Come with me to paradise, and hear the word in which I judge Adam. And when we heard the archangel sounding, we said, Behold, God is coming into paradise to judge us. And we were afraid, and hid ourselves. And

God came up into paradise, riding upon a chariot of cherubim, and the angels praising Him. When God came into paradise, the plants both of Adam's lot and of my lot bloomed, and all lifted themselves up; and the throne of God was made ready where the tree of life was. And God called Adam, saying, Adam, where art thou hidden, thinking that I shall not find thee? Shall the house be hidden from him that built it? Then your father answered and said, Not, Lord, did we hide ourselves as thinking that we should not be found by Thee; but I am afraid, because I am naked, and stand in awe of Thy power, O Lord. God says to him, Who hath shown thee that thou art naked, unless it be that thou hast forsaken my commandment which I gave thee to keep it? Then Adam remembered the word which I spake to him when I wished to deceive him, I will put thee out of danger from God. And he turned and said to me, Why hast thou done this? And I also remembered the word of the serpent, and said, The serpent deceived me. God says to Adam, Since thou hast disobeyed my commandment, and obeyed thy wife, cursed is the ground in thy labours. For whenever thou labourest it, and it will not give its strength, thorns and thistles shall it raise for thee; and in the sweat of thy face shalt thou eat thy bread. And thou shalt be in distresses of many kinds. Thou shalt weary thyself, and rest not; thou shalt be afflicted by bitterness, and shall not taste of sweetness; thou shalt be afflicted by heat, and oppressed by cold; and thou shalt toil much, and not grow rich; and thou shalt make haste, and not attain thine end; and the wild beasts, of which thou wast lord, shall rise up against thee in rebellion, because thou hast not kept my commandment. And having turned to me, the Lord says to me, Since thou hast obeyed the serpent, and disobeyed my commandment, thou shalt be in distresses and unbearable pains; thou shalt bring forth children with great tremblings; and in one hour shalt thou come *to bring them forth*, and lose thy life in consequence of thy great straits and pangs. And thou shalt confess, and say, Lord, Lord, save me; and I shall not return to the sin of the flesh. And on this account in thine own words I shall judge thee, on account of the enmity which the enemy hath put in thee; and thou shalt turn again to thy husband, and he shall be thy lord. And after speaking thus to me, He spoke to the serpent in great wrath, saying to him, Since thou hast done this, and hast become an ungracious instrument until thou shouldst deceive those that were remiss in heart, cursed art thou of all the beasts. Thou shalt be deprived of the food which thou eatest; and dust shalt thou eat all the days of thy life; upon thy breast and belly shalt thou go, and thou shalt be deprived both of thy hands and feet; there shall not be granted thee ear, nor wing, nor one limb of all which those have whom thou hast enticed by thy wickedness, and hast caused them to be cast out of paradise. And I shall put enmity between thee and between his seed. He shall lie in wait for thy head, and thou for his heel, until the day of judgment. And having thus said, He commands His angels that we be cast out of paradise. And as we were being driven along, and were lamenting, your father Adam entreated the angels, saying, Allow me a little, that I may entreat God, and that He may have compassion upon me, and pity me, for

I only have sinned. And they stopped driving him. And Adam cried out with weeping, saying, Pardon me, Lord, what I have done. Then says the Lord to His angels, Why have you stopped driving Adam out of paradise? It is not that the sin is mine, or that I have judged ill? Then the angels, falling to the ground, worshipped the Lord, saying, Just art Thou, Lord, and judgest what is right. And turning to Adam, the Lord said, I will not permit thee henceforth to be in paradise. And Adam answered and said, Lord, give me of the tree of life, that I may eat before I am cast out. Then the Lord said to Adam, Thou shalt not now take of it, for it has been assigned to the cherubim and the flaming sword, which turneth to guard it on account of thee, that thou mayst not taste of it and be free from death for ever, but that thou mayst have the war which the enemy has set in thee. But when thou art gone out of paradise, if thou shalt keep thyself from all evil, as being destined to die, I will again raise thee up when the resurrection comes, and then there shall be given thee of the tree of life, and thou shalt be free from death for ever. And having thus said, the Lord commanded us to be cast out of paradise. And your father wept before the angels over against paradise. And the angels say to him, What dost thou wish that we should do for thee, Adam? And your father answered and said to the angels, Behold, you cast me out. I beseech you, allow me to take sweet odours out of paradise, in order that, after I go out, I may offer sacrifice to God, that God may listen to me. And the angels, advancing, said to God, Jael, eternal King, order to be given to Adam sacrifices of sweet odour out of paradise. And God ordered Adam to go, that he might take perfumes of sweet odour out of paradise for his food. And the angels let him go, and he gathered both kinds—saffron and spikenard, and calamus and cinnamon, and other seeds for his food; and having taken them, he went forth out of paradise. And we came to the earth.

Now, then, my children, I have shown you the manner in which we were deceived. But do ye watch over yourselves, so as not to forsake what is good.

And when she had thus spoken in the midst of her sons, and Adam was lying in his disease, and he had one other day before going out of the body, Eve says to Adam: Why is it that thou diest, and I live? or how long time have I to spend after thou diest? tell me. Then says Adam to Eve: Do not trouble thyself about matters; for thou wilt not be long after me, but we shall both die alike, and thou wilt be laid into my place. And when I am dead you will leave me, and let no one touch me, until the angel of the Lord shall say something about me; for God will not forget me, but will seek His own vessel which He fashioned. Arise, rather, pray to God until I restore my spirit into the hands of Him who has given it; because we know not how we shall meet Him who made us, whether He shall be angry with us, or turn and have mercy upon us. Then arose Eve, and went outside; and falling to the ground, she said: I have sinned, O God; I have sinned, O Father of all; I have sinned to Thee, I have sinned against Thy chosen angels, I have sinned against the cherubim, I have sinned against Thine unshaken throne; I have sinned, O Lord, I have sinned much, I have sinned before Thee, and every sin through me has come upon the creation. And while Eve was still praying, being on her knees, behold, there came to her the angel of humanity, and raised her up, saying: Arise, Eve, from thy repentance; for, behold, Adam thy husband has gone forth from his body; arise and see his spirit carried up to Him that made it, to meet Him.

And Eve arose, and covered her face with her hand; and the angel says to her: Raise thyself from the things of earth. And Eve gazed up into heaven, and she saw a chariot of light going along under four shining eagles— and it was not possible for any one born of woman to tell the glory of them, or to see the face of them—and angels going before the chariot. And when they came to the place where your father Adam was lying, the chariot stood still, and the seraphim between your father and the chariot. And I saw golden censers, and three vials; and, behold, all the angels with incense, and the censers, and the vials, came to the altar, and blew them up, and the smoke of the incense covered the firmaments. And the angels fell down and worshipped God, crying out and saying: Holy Jael, forgive; for he is Thine image, and the work of Thine holy hands.

And again, I Eve saw two great and awful mysteries standing before God. And I wept for fear, and cried out to my son Seth, saying: Arise, Seth, from the body of thy father Adam, and come to me, that thou mayst see what the eye of no one hath ever seen; and they are praying for thy father Adam.

Then Seth arose and went to his mother, and said to her: What has befallen thee? and why weepest thou? She says to him: Look up with thine eyes, and see the seven firmaments opened, and see with thine eyes how the body of thy father lies upon its face, and all the holy angels with him, praying for him, and saying: Pardon him, O Father of the universe; for he is Thine image. What then, my child Seth, will this be? and when will he be delivered into the hands of our invisible Father and God? And who are the two dark-faced ones who stand by at the prayer of thy father? And Seth says to his mother: These are the sun and the moon, and they are falling down and praying for my father Adam. Eve says to him: And where is their light, and why have they become black-looking? And Seth says to her: They cannot shine in the presence of the Light of the universe, and for this reason the light from them has been hidden.

And while Seth was speaking to his mother, the angels lying upon their faces sounded their trumpets, and cried out with an awful voice, saying, Blessed be the glory of the Lord upon what He has made, for He has had compassion upon Adam, the work of His hands. When the angels had sounded this forth, there came one of the six-winged seraphim, and hurried Adam to the Acherusian lake, and washed him in presence of God. And he spent three hours lying, and thus the Lord of the universe, sitting upon His holy throne, stretched forth His hands, and raised Adam, and delivered him to the archangel Michael, saying to him: Raise him into paradise, even to the third heaven, and let him be there until that great and dreadful day which I am to bring upon the world. And the archangel Michael, having taken Adam, led him away, and anointed him, as God said to him at the pardoning of Adam.

After all these things, therefore, the archangel asked about the funeral rites of the remains; and God commanded that all the angels should come together into His presence, each according to his rank. And all the angels were assembled, some with censers, some with trumpets. And the Lord of Hosts went up, and the winds drew Him, and cherubim riding upon the winds, and the angels of heaven went before Him; and they came to where the body of Adam was, and took it. And they came to paradise, and all the trees of paradise were moved so that all begotten from Adam hung their heads in sleep at the sweet smell, except Seth, because he had been begotten according to the appointment of God.

The body of Adam, then, was lying on the ground in paradise, and Seth was grieved exceedingly about him. And the Lord God says: Adam, why hast thou done this? If thou hadst kept my commandment, those that brought thee down to this place would not have rejoiced. Nevertheless I say unto thee, that I will turn their joy into grief, but I will turn thy grief into joy; and having turned, I will set thee in thy kingdom, on the throne of him that deceived thee; and he shall be cast into this place, that thou mayst sit upon him. Then shall be condemned, he and those who hear him; and they shall be much grieved, and shall weep, seeing thee sitting upon his glorious throne.

And then He said to the archangel Michael: Go into paradise, into the third heaven, and bring me three cloths of fine linen and silk. And God said to Michael, Gabriel, Uriel, and Raphael: Cover Adam's body with the cloths, and bring olive oil of sweet odour, and pour upon him. And having thus done, they prepared his body for burial. And the Lord said: Let also the body of Abel be brought. And having brought other cloths, they prepared it also for burial, since it had not been prepared for burial since the day on which his brother Cain slew him. For the wicked Cain, having taken great pains to hide it, had not been able; for the earth did not receive it, saying: I will not receive a body into companionship until that dust which was taken up and fashioned upon me come to me. And then the angels took it up, and laid it on the rock until his father died. And both were buried, according to the commandment of God, in the regions of paradise, in the place in which God found the dust. And God sent seven angels into paradise, and they brought many sweet-smelling herbs, and laid them in the earth; and thus they took the two bodies, and buried them in the place which they had dug and built.

And God called Adam, and said: Adam, Adam. And the body answered out of the ground, and said: Here am I, Lord. And the Lord says to him: I said to thee, Dust thou art, and unto dust thou shalt return. Again I promise thee the resurrection. I will raise thee up in the

last day in the resurrection, with every man who is of thy
seed.

And after these words God made a three-cornered seal,
and sealed the tomb, that no one should do anything to
him in the six days, until his rib should return to
him. And the beneficent God and the holy angels
having laid him in his place, after the six days Eve also
died. And while she lived she wept about her falling
asleep, because she knew not where her body was to be
laid. For when the Lord was present in paradise when
they buried Adam, both she and her children fell asleep,
except Seth, as I said. And Eve, in the hour of her
death, besought that she might be buried where Adam
her husband was, saying thus: My Lord, Lord and God
of all virtue, do not separate me, Thy servant, from the
body of Adam, for of his members Thou madest me; but
grant to me, even me, the unworthy and the sinner, to be
buried by his body. And as I was along with him in
paradise, and not separated from him after the
transgression, so also let no one separate us. After
having prayed, therefore, she looked up into heaven, and
stood up, and said, beating her breast: God of all,
receive my spirit. And straightway she gave up her spirit
to God.

And when she was dead, the archangel Michael stood
beside her; and there came three angels, and took her
body, and buried it where the body of Abel was. And
the archangel Michael said to Seth: Thus bury every man
that dies, until the day of the resurrection. And after
having given this law, he said to him: Do not mourn
beyond six days. And on the seventh day, rest, and
rejoice in it, because in it God and we the angels rejoice
in the righteous soul that has departed from
earth. Having thus spoken, the archangel Michael went
up into heaven, glorifying, and saying the Alleluia: Holy,
holy, holy Lord, to the glory of God the Father, because
to Him is due glory, honour, and adoration, with His
unbeginning and life-giving Spirit, now and ever, and to
ages of ages. Amen.

LETTERS AND
TEACHINGS

THE EPISTULA APOSTOLORUM

EPISTLE OF THE APOSTLES

The authorities for the text are: (a) a Coptic MS. of the fourth or fifth century at Cairo, mutilated; (b) a complete version in Ethiopic; (c) a leaf of a fifth-century MS. in Latin, palimpsest, at Vienna. The only edition which makes use of all the authorities is C. Schmidt's, 1919. The Ethiopic was previously edited by Guerrier in *Patrologia orientalis* under the title of *Testament of our Lord in Galilee*. A notice of the text by Guerrier in the *Revue de l'Orient Chretien* (1907) enabled me to identify it with the Coptic text, of which Schmidt had given a account to the Berlin Academy. As to the date and character of the book, Sehmidt's verdict is that it was written in Asia Minor about A.D. 160 by an orthodox Catholic. The orthodoxy has been questioned (see a review by G. Bardy in *Revue Biblique*, 1921). No ancient writer mentions it, and very few traces of its use can be found: the (third ?)-century poet Commodian seems to use it in one place (see 11).

There has so far been no English rendering of the text; my version depends on Schmidt and Guerrier.

In the Ethiopic version another writing, a prophecy of our Lord concerning the signs of the end, is prefixed to the Epistle. Parts of the this recur in the Syriac *Testament of the Lord* and part is repeated in the Epistle itself. It is noteworthy that this prophecy ends with a passage which is identical with one quoted by Clement of Alexandria from a source he does not name he does not name - only calling it 'the Scripture'.

Testament 11 in Guerrier.	Clem. Alex. *Protrept*. ciii.
And the righteous, that have walked in the way of righteousness, shall inherit the glory of God; and the power shall be given to them which no eye hath seen and no ear heard; and they shall rejoice in my kingdom.	But the saints of the Lord shall inherit the glory of God, and his power. *Tell me what glory, O blessed one.* That which eye hath not seen nor ear heard, neither hath it come upon the heart of man; and they shall rejoice at the kingdom of their Lord for ever. Amen.

A similar passage is in the *Apostolic Constitutions*, vii. 22. On the possible derivation from the Apocalypse of Elias see my *Lost Apocrypha of O.T.*, p. 54.

The first four leaves of the Coptic MS. are lost, so we depend on the Ethiopic for the opening of the text.

1 The book which Jesus Christ revealed unto his disciples: and how that Jesus Christ revealed the book for the company (college) of the apostles, the disciples of Jesus Christ, even the book *which is* for all men. Simon and Cerinthus, the false apostles, concerning whom it is written that no man shall cleave unto them, for there is in them deceit wherewith they bring men to destruction. (The book hath been written) that ye may be not flinch nor be troubled, and depart not from the word of the Gospel which ye have heard. Like as we heard it, we keep it in remembrance and have written it for the whole world. We commend you our sons and our daughters in joy <in the grace of God (?)> in the name of God the Father the Lord of the world, and of Jesus Christ. Let grace be multiplied upon you.

2 *We*, John, Thomas, Peter, Andrew, James, Philip, Batholomew, Matthew, Nathanael, Judas Zelotes, and Cephas, write unto the churches of the east and the west, of the north and the south, the declaring and imparting unto you that which concerneth our Lord Jesus Christ: we do write according as we have seen and heard and touched him, after that he was risen from the dead: and how that he revealed unto us things mighty and wonderful and true.

3 This know we: that our Lord and Redeemer Jesus Christ is God the Son of God, who was sent of God the Lord of the whole world, the maker and creator *of it*, who is named by all names, and high above all powers, Lord of lords, King of kings, Ruler of rulers, the heavenly one, that sitteth above the cherubim and seraphim at the right hand of the throne of the Father: who by his word *made* the heavens, and formed the earth and that which is in it, and set bounds to the sea that it should not pass: the deeps also and fountains, that they should spring forth and flow over the earth: the day and the night, the sun and the moon, did he establish, and the stars in the heaven: that did separate the light from the darkness: that called forth hell, and in the twinkling of an eye ordained the rain of the winter, the snow (cloud), the hail, and the ice, and the days in their several seasons: that maketh the earth to quake and again establisheth it: that created man in his own image, after his likeness, and by the fathers of old and the prophets is it declared (*or*, and spake in parables with the fathers of old and the prophets in verity), of whom the apostles preached, and whom the disciples did touch. In God, the Lord, the Son of God, do we believe, that he is the word become flesh: that of Mary the holy virgin he took a body, begotten of the Holy Ghost, not of the will (lust) of the flesh, but by the will of God: that he was wrapped in swaddling clothes in Bethlehem and made manifest, and grew up and came to ripe age, when *also* we beheld *it*.

4 This did our Lord Jesus Christ, who was sent by Joseph and Mary his mother to be taught. [And] when he that taught him said unto him: Say Alpha: then answered he and said: Tell thou me first what is Beta (*probably*: Tell thou me first what is <Alpha and then will I tell thee what is> Beta. Cf. the Marcosian story quoted by Irenaeus (see above, Gospel of Thomas, p. 15). The story is in our texts of the Gospel of Thomas, and all the

Infancy Gospels). This thing which then came to pass is to true and of verity.

5 Thereafter was there a marriage in Cana of Galilee; and they bade him with his mother and his brethren, and he changed water into wine. He raised the dead, he caused the lame to walk: him whose hand was withered he caused to stretch it out, and the woman which had suffered an issue of blood twelve years touched the hem of his garment and was healed in the same hour. And when we marvelled at the miracle which was done, he said: Who touched me? Then said we: Lord, the press of men hath touched thee. But he answered and said unto us: I perceive that a virtue is gone out of me. Straightway that woman came before him, and answered and said unto him: Lord, I touched thee. And he answered and said unto her: Go, thy faith hath made thee whole. Thereafter he made the deaf to hear and the blind to see; out of them that were possessed he cast out the unclean spirits, and cleansed the lepers. The spirit which dwelt in a man, whereof the name was Legion, cried out against Jesus, saying: Before the time of our destruction is come, thou art come to drive us out. But the Lord Jesus rebuked him, saying: Go out of this man and do him no hurt. And he entered into the swine and drowned them in the water and they were choked.

Thereafter he did walk upon the sea, and the winds blew, and he cried out against them (rebuked them), and the waves of the sea were made calm. And when we his disciples had no money, we asked him: What shall we do because of the tax-gatherer? And he answered and told us: Let one of you cast an hook into the deep, and take out a fish, and he shall find therein a penny: that give unto the tax-gatherer for me and you. And thereafter when we had no bread, but only five loaves and two fishes, he commanded the people to sit them down, and the number of them was five thousand, besides children and women. We did set pieces of bread before them, and they ate and were filled, and there remained over, and we filled twelve baskets full of the fragments, asking one another and saying: What *mean* these five loaves? They are the symbol of our faith in the Lord of the Christians (in the great christendom), *even* in the Father, the Lord Almighty, and in Jesus Christ our redeemer, in the Holy Ghost the comforter, in the holy church, and in the remission of sins.

6 These things did our Lord and Saviour reveal unto us and teach us. And we do even as he, that ye may become partakers in the grace of our Lord and in our ministry and our giving of thanks (glory), and think upon life eternal. Be ye steadfast and waver not in the knowledge and confidence of our Lord Jesus Christ, and he will have mercy on you and save you everlastingly, world without end.

Here begins the Coptic text.

7 Cerinthus and Simon are come to go to and fro in the world, but they are enemies of our Lord Jesus Christ, for they do pervert the word and the true thing, even (faith in) Jesus Christ. Keep yourselves therefore far from them, for death is in them, and great pollution and corruption, even in these on whom shall come judgement and the end and everlasting destruction.

8 Therefore have we not shrunk from writing unto you concerning the testimony of Christ our Saviour, of what he did, when we followed with him, how he enlightened our understanding...

9 Concerning whom we testify that the Lord is he who was crucified by Pontius Pilate and Archelaus between the two thieves (and with them he was taken down from the tree of the cross, *Eth.*), and was buried in a place which is called the place of a skull (*Kranion*). And thither went three women, Mary, she that was kin to Martha, and Mary Magdalene (Sarrha, Martha, and Mary, *Eth.*), and took ointments to pour upon the body, weeping and mourning over that which was come to pass. And when they drew near to the sepulchre, they looked in and found not the body (*Eth.* they found the stone rolled away and opened the entrance).

10 And as they mourned and wept, the Lord showed himself unto them and said to them: For whom weep ye? weep no more. I am he whom ye seek. But let one of you go to your brethren and say: Come ye, the Master is risen from the dead. Martha (Mary, *Eth.*) came and told us. We said unto her: What haw we to do with thee, woman ? He that is dead and buried, is it possible that he should live? And we believed her not that the Saviour was risen from the dead. Then she returned unto the Lord and said unto him: None of them hath believed me, that thou livest. He said: Let another of you go unto them and tell them again. Mary (Sarrha, *Eth.*) came and told us again, and we believed her not; and she returned unto the Lord and she also told him.

11 Then said the Lord unto Mary and her sisters: Let us go unto them. And he came and found us within (sitting veiled or fishing, *Eth.*), and called us out; but we thought that it was a phantom and believed not that it was the Lord. Then said he unto us: Come, fear ye not. I am your master, even he, O Peter, whom thou didst deny thrice; and dost thou now deny again? And we came unto him, doubting in our hearts whether it were he. Then said he unto us: Wherefore doubt ye still, and are unbelieving? I am he that spake unto you of my flesh and my death and my resurrection. But that ye may know that I am he, do thou, Peter, put thy finger into the print of the nails in mine hands, and thou also, Thomas, put thy finger into the wound of the spear in my side; but thou, Andrew, look on my feet and see whether they press the earth; for it is written in the prophet: A phantom of a devil maketh no footprint on the earth.

12 And we touched him, that we might learn of a truth whether he were risen in the flesh; and we fell on our faces (and worshipped him) confessing our sin, that we had been unbelieving. Then said our Lord and Saviour unto us: Rise up, and I will reveal unto you that which is above the heaven and in the heaven, and your rest which

is in the kingdom of heaven. For my Father hath given me power (sent me, *Eth.*) to take you up thither, and them also that believe on me.

13 Now that which he revealed unto us is this, which he spake: It came to pass when I was about (minded) to come hither from the Father of all things, and passed through the heavens, then did I put on the wisdom of the Father, and I put on the power of his might. I was in heaven, and I passed by the archangels and the angels in their likeness, like as if I were one of them, among the princedoms and powers. I passed through them because I possessed the wisdom of him that had sent me. Now the chief captain of the angels, [is] Michael, and Gabriel and Uriel and Raphael followed me unto the fifth firmament (heaven), for they thought in their heart that I was one of them; such power was given me of my Father. And on that day did I adorn the archangels with a wonderful voice (so *Copt.*: *Eth.*, *Lat.*, I made them quake--amazed them), so that they should go unto the altar of the Father and serve and fulfil the ministry until I should return unto him. And so wrought I the likeness by my wisdom; for I became all things in all, that I might praise the dispensation of the Father and fulfil the glory of him that sent me (*the verbs might well be transposed*) and return unto him. (*Here the Latin omits a considerable portion of text without notice, to near the beginning of c.* 17.)

14 For ye know that the angel Gabriel brought the message unto Mary. And we answered: Yea, Lord. He answered and said unto us: Remember ye not, then, that I said unto you a little while ago: I became an angel among the angels, and I became all things in all? We said unto him: Yea, Lord. Then answered he and said unto us: On that day whereon I took the form of the angel Gabriel, I appeared unto Mary and spake with her. Her heart accepted me, and she believed (She believed and laughed, *Eth.*), and I formed myself and entered into her body. I became flesh, for I alone was a minister unto myself in that which concerned Mary (I was mine own messenger, *Eth.*) in the appearance of the shape of an angel. For so must I needs (or, was I wont to) do. Thereafter did I return to my Father (*Copt.* After my return to the Father, *and run on*).

15 But do ye commemorate my death. Now when the Passover (Easter, pascha) cometh, one of you shall be cast into prison for my name's sake; and he will be in grief and sorrow, because ye keep the Easter while he is in prison and separated from you, for he will be sorrowful because he keepeth not Easter with you. And I will send my power in the form of mine angel Gabriel, and the doors of the prison shall open. And he shall come forth and come unto you and keep the night-watch with you until the cock crow. And when ye have accomplished the memorial which is made of me, and the Agape (love-feast), he shall again be cast into prison for a testimony, until he shall come out thence and preach that which I have delivered unto you.

And we said unto him: Lord, is it then needful that we should again take the cup and drink? (Lord, didst not thou thyself fulfil the drinking of the Passover? is it then needful that we should accomplish it again? *Eth.*) He said unto us: Yea, it is needful, until the day when I come again, with them that have been put to death for my sake (come with my wounds, *Eth.*).

16 Then said we to him: Lord, that which thou hast revealed unto us (revealest, *Eth.*) is great. Wilt thou come in the power of any creature or in an appearance of any kind ? (In what power or form wilt thou come? *Eth.*) He answered and said unto us: Verily I say unto you, I shall come like the sun when it is risen, and my brightness will be seven times the brightness thereof! The wings of the clouds shall bear me in brightness, and the sign of the cross shall go before me, and I shall come upon earth to judge the quick and the dead.

17 We said unto him: Lord, after how many years shall this come to pass ? He said unto us: When the hundredth part and the twentieth part is fulfilled, between the Pentecost and the feast of unleavened bread, then shall the coming of my Father be (*so Copt.*: When an hundred and fifty years are past, in the days of the feast of Passover and Pentecost, &c., *Eth.*: . . . (*imperfect word*) year is fulfilled, between the unleavened bread and Pentecost shall be the coming of my Father, *Lat.*).

We said unto him: Now sayest thou unto us: I will come; and how sayest thou: He that sent me is he that shall come? Then said he to us: I am wholly in the Father and my Father is in me. Then said we to him: Wilt thou indeed forsake us until thy coming? Where can we find a master? But he answered and said unto us: Know ye not, then, that like as until now I have been here, so also was I there, with him that sent me? And we said to him: Lord, is it then possible that thou shouldest be both here and there? But he answered us: I am wholly in the Father and the Father in me, because of (in regard of) the likeness of the form and the power and the fullness and the light and the full measure and the voice. I am the word, I am become unto him a thing, that is to say (*word gone*) of the thought, fulfilled in the type (likeness); I have into the Ogdoad (eighth number), which is the Lord's day. (*In place of these sentences Eth. has*: I am of his resemblance and form, of his power and completeness, and of his light. I am his complete (fulfilled, entire) Word.

18 But it came to pass after he was crucified, and dead and arisen again, *when* the work *was fulfilled* which was accomplished in the flesh, and he was crucified and the ascension come to pass at the end of the days, then said he thus, &c. *It is an interpolation, in place of words which the translator did not understand, or found heretical.*) But the whole fulfilment of the fulfilment shall ye see after the redemption which hath come to pass by me, and ye shall see me, how I go up unto my Father which is in heaven. But behold, now, I give unto you a new commandment: Love one another and [*a leaf lost in Copt.*] obey one another, that peace may rule alway among you. Love

your enemies, and what ye would not that man do unto you, that do unto no man.

19 And this preach ye also and teach them that believe on me, and preach the kingdom of heaven of my Father, and how my Father hath given me the power, that ye may bring near the children of my heavenly Father. Preach ye, and they shall obtain faith, that ye may be they for whom it is ordained that they shall bring his children unto heaven.

And we said unto him: Lord, unto thee it is possible to accomplish that whereof thou tellest us; but how shall we be able to do it? He said to us: Verily I say unto you, preach and proclaim as I *command you*, for I will be with you, for it is my good pleasure to be with you, that ye may be heirs with me in the kingdom of heaven, *even the kingdom* of him that sent me. Verily I say unto you, ye shall be my brethren and my friends, for my Father hath found pleasure in you: and so also shall they be that believe on me by your means. Verily I say unto you, such and so great joy hath my Father prepared for you that the angels and the powers desired and do desire to see it and look upon it; but it is not given unto them to behold the glory of my Father. We said unto him: Lord, what is this whereof thou speakest to us?

Copt. begins again: words are missing.

He answered us: Ye shall behold a light, more excellent than that which shineth... (shineth more brightly than the light, and is more perfect than perfection. And the Son shall become perfect through the Father who is Light, for the Father is perfect which bringeth to pass death and resurrection, and ye shall see a perfection more perfect than the perfect. And I am wholly at the right hand of the Father, even in him that maketh perfect. *So Eth.: Copt. has gaps).*

And we said unto him: Lord, in all things art thou become salvation and life unto us, for that thou makest known such a hope unto us. And he said to us: Be of good courage and rest in me. Verily I say unto you, your rest shall be above (?), in the place where is neither eating nor drinking, nor care (*Copt.* joy) nor sorrow, nor passing away of them that are therein: for ye *shall* have no part in (the things of earth, *Eth.*) but ye shall be received in the everlastingness of my Father. Like as I am in him, so shall ye also be in me.

Again we said unto him: In what form? in the fashion of angels, or in flesh ? And he answered and said unto us: Lo, I have put on your flesh, wherein I was born and crucified, and am risen again through my Father which is in heaven, that the prophecy of David the prophet might be fulfilled, in regard of that which was declared concerning me and my death and resurrection, saying:

Lord, they are increased that fight with me, and many are they that are risen up against me.

Many there be that say to my soul: There is no help for him in his God.

But thou, O Lord, art my defender: thou art my worship, and the lifter up of my head.

I did call upon the Lord with my voice and he heard me (out of the high place of his temple, *Eth.*).

I laid me down and slept, and rose up again: for thou, O Lord, art my defender.

I will not be afraid for ten thousands of the people, that have set themselves against me round about.

Up, Lord, and help me, O my God: for thou hast smitten down all them that without cause are mine enemies: thou hast broken the teeth of the ungodly.

Salvation belongeth unto the Lord, and his good pleasure is upon his people (Ps. iii. 1-8).

If, therefore, all the words which were spoken by the prophets have been fulfilled in me (for I myself was in them), how much more shall that which I say unto you come to pass indeed, that he which sent me may be glorified by you and by them that believe on me?

20 And when he had said this unto us, we said to him: In all things hast thou had mercy on us and saved us, and hast revealed all things unto us; but yet would we ask of thee somewhat if thou give us leave. And he said unto us: I know that ye pay heed, and that your heart is well-pleased when ye hear me: now concerning that which ye desire, I will speak good words unto you. 21 For verily I say unto you: Like as my Father hath raised me from the dead, so shall ye also rise (in the flesh, *Eth.*) and be taken up into the highest heaven, unto the place whereof I have told you from the beginning, unto the place which he who sent me hath prepared for you. And so will I accomplish all dispensations (all grace, *Eth.*), even I who am unbegotten and yet begotten of mankind, who am without flesh and yet have borne flesh <and have grown up like unto you that were born in flesh, *Eth.*>: for to that end am I come, that (*gap in Copt.: Eth. continues*) ye might rise from the dead in your flesh, in the second birth, even a vesture that shall not decay, together with all them that hope and believe in him that sent me: for so is the will of my Father, that I should give unto you, and unto them whom it pleaseth me, the hope of the kingdom.

Then said we unto him: Great is that which thou sufferest us to hope, and tellest us. And he answered and said: Believe ye that everything that I tell you shall come to pass ? We answered and said: Yea, Lord. (*Copt. resumes for a few lines: then another gap. I follow Eth.*) He said unto us: Verily I say unto you, that I have obtained the whole power of my Father, that I may bring back into light them that dwell in darkness, them that are in corruption into incorruption, them that are in death into life, and that I may loose them that are in fetters. For that which is impossible with men, is possible with the Father. I am the hope of them that despair, the helper of them that have no saviour, the wealth of the poor, the health of the sick, and the resurrection of the dead.

22 When he had thus said, we said unto him: Lord, is it true that the flesh shall be judged together with the soul and the spirit, and that the one part shall rest in heaven and the other part be punished everlastingly yet living? And he said unto us: (*Copt. resumes*) How long will ye inquire and doubt?

23 Again we said unto him: Lord, there is necessity upon us to inquire of thee--because thou hast commanded us to preach--that we ourselves may learn assuredly of thee and be profitable preachers, and that they which are instructed by us may believe in thee. Therefore must we needs inquire of thee.

24 He answered us and said: Verily I say unto you, the resurrection of the flesh shall come to pass with the soul therein and the spirit. And we said unto him: Lord, is it then possible that that which is dissolved and brought to nought should become whole? and we ask thee not as unbelieving, neither as if it were impossible unto thee; but verily we believe that that which thou sayest shall come to pass. And he was wroth with us and said: O ye of little faith, how long will ye ask questions? But what ye will, tell it me, and I myself will tell you without grudging: only keep ye my commandments and do that which I bid you, and turn not away your face from any man, that I turn not my face away from you, but without shrinking and fear and without respect of persons, minister ye in the way that is direct and narrow and strait. So shall my Father himself rejoice over you.

25 Again we said unto him: Lord, already are we ashamed that we question thee oft-times and burden thee. And he answered and said unto us: I know that in faith and with your whole heart ye do question me; therefore do I rejoice over you, for verily I say unto you: I rejoice, and my Father that is in me, because ye question me; and your importunity (shamelessness) is unto me rejoicing and unto you it giveth life. And when he had so said unto us, we were glad that we had questioned him, and we said to him: Lord, in all things thou makest us alive and hast mercy on us. Wilt thou now declare unto us that which we shall ask thee? Then said he unto us: Is it the flesh that passeth away, or is it the spirit? We said unto him: The flesh is it that passeth away. Then said he unto us: That which hath fallen shall rise again, and that which was lost shall be found, and that which was weak shall recover, that in these things that are so created the glory of my Father may be revealed. As he hath done unto me, so will I do unto all that believe in me.

26 Verily I say unto you: the flesh shall arise, and the soul, alive, that their defence may come to pass on that day in regard of that that they have done, whether it be good or evil: that there may be a choosing-out of the faithful who have kept the commandments of my Father

that sent me; and so shall the judgement be accomplished with strictness. For my Father said unto me: My Son, in the day of judgement thou shalt have no respect for the rich, neither pity for the poor, but according to the sins of every man shalt thou deliver him unto everlasting torment. But unto my beloved that have done the commandments of my Father that sent me will I give the rest of life in the kingdom of my Father which is in heaven, and they shall behold that which he hath given me. And he hath given me authority to do that which I will, and to give that which I have promised and determined to give and grant unto them.

27 For to that end went I down unto the place of Lazarus, and preached unto the righteous and the prophets, that they might come out of the rest which is below and come up into that which is above; and I poured out upon them with my right hand the water (?) (baptism, *Eth.*) of life and forgiveness and salvation from all evil, as I have done unto you and unto them that believe on me. But if any man believe on me and do not my commandments, although he have confessed my name, he hath no profit therefrom but runneth a vain race: for such will find themselves in perdition and destruction, because they have despised my commandments.

28 But so much the more have I redeemed you, the children of light, from all evil and from the authority of the rulers (archons), and every one that believeth on me by your means. For that which I have promised unto you will I give unto them also, that they may come out of the prison-house and the fetters of the rulers. We answered and said: Lord, thou hast given unto us the rest of life and hast given us <joy?> by wonders, unto the confirmation of faith: wilt thou now preach the same unto us, seeing that thou hast preached it unto the <righteous> and the prophets? Then said he unto us: Verily I say unto you, all that have believed on me and that believe in him that sent me will I take up into the heaven, unto the place which my Father hath prepared for the elect, and I will give you the kingdom, the chosen kingdom, in rest, and everlasting life.

29 But all they that have offended against my commandments and have taught other doctrine, (perverting) the Scripture and adding thereto, striving after their own glory, and that teach with other words them that believe on me in uprightness, if they make them fall thereby, shall receive everlasting punishment. We said unto him: Lord, shall there then be teaching by others, diverse from that which thou hast spoken unto us ? He said unto us: It must needs be, that the evil and the good may be made manifest; and the judgement shall be manifest upon them that do these things, and according to their works shall they be judged and shall be delivered unto death.

Again we said unto him: Lord, blessed are we in that we see thee and hear thee declaring such things, for our eyes have beheld these great wonders that thou hast done. He answered and said unto us: Yea, rather blessed are they that have not seen and yet have believed, for they shall be called children of the kingdom, and they shall be perfect among the perfect, and I will be unto them life in the kingdom of my Father.

Again we said unto him: Lord, how shall men be able to believe that thou wilt depart and leave us; for thou sayest unto us: There shall come a day and an hour when I shall ascend unto my Father?

30 But he said unto us: Go ye and preach unto the twelve tribes, and preach also unto the heathen, and to all the land of Israel from the east to the west and from the south unto the north, and many shall believe on <me> the Son of God. But we said unto him: Lord, who will believe us, or hearken unto us, or (how shall we be able, *Eth.*) to teach the powers and signs and wonders which thou hast done ? Then answered he and said to us: Go ye and preach the mercifulness of my Father, and that which he hath done through me will I myself do through you, for I am in you, and I will give you my peace, and I will give you a power of my spirit, that ye may prophesy to them unto life eternal. And unto the others also will I give my power, that they may teach the residue of the peoples.

(*Six leaves lost in Copt.: Eth. continues.*)

31 And behold a man shall meet you, whose name is Saul, which being interpreted is Paul: he is a Jew, circumcised according to the law, and he shall receive my voice from heaven with fear and terror and trembling. And his eyes shall be blinded, and by your hands by the sign of the cross shall they be protected (healed: *other Eth. MSS.* with spittle by your hands shall his eyes, &c.). Do ye unto him all that I have done unto you. Deliver it (? the word of God) unto the other. And at the same time that man shall open his eyes and praise the Lord, even my Father which is in heaven. He shall obtain power among the people and shall preach and instruct; and many that hear him shall obtain glory and be redeemed. But thereafter shall men be wroth with him and deliver him into the hands of his enemies, and he shall bear witness before kings that are mortal, and his end shall be that he shall turn unto me, whereas he persecuted me *at the first.* He shall preach and teach and abide with the elect, as a chosen vessel and a wall that shall not be overthrown, *yea,* the last of the last shall become a preacher unto the Gentiles, made perfect by the will of my Father. Like as ye have learned from the Scripture that your fathers the prophets spake of me, and in me it is indeed fulfilled.

And he said unto us: Be ye also therefore guides unto them; and all things that I said unto you, and that ye write concerning me (tell ye them), that I am the word of the Father and that the Father is in me. Such also shall ye be unto that man, as becometh you. Instruct him and bring to his mind that which is spoken of me in the Scripture and is fulfilled, and thereafter shall he become the salvation of the Gentiles.

32 And we asked him: Lord, is there for us and for them the self-same expectation of the inheritance? He answered and said unto us: Are then the fingers of the hand like unto each other, or the ears of corn in the field, or do *all* fruit-trees bear the same fruit? Doth not every one bear fruit according to its nature? And we said unto him: Lord, wilt thou again speak unto us in parables? Then said he unto us: Lament not. Verily I say unto you, ye are my brethren, and my companions in the kingdom of heaven unto my Father, for so is his good pleasure. Verily I say unto you, unto them also whom ye teach and who believe on me will I give that expectation.

33 And we asked him again: When shall we meet with that man, and when wilt thou depart unto thy Father and our God and Lord? He answered and said unto us: That man will come out of the land of Cilicia unto Damascus of Syria, to root up the church which ye must found there. It is I that speak through you; and he shall come quickly: and he shall become strong in the faith, that the word of the prophet may be fulfilled, which saith: Behold, out of Syria will I begin to call together a new Jerusalem, and Sion will I subdue unto me, and it shall be taken, and the place which is childless shall be called the son and daughter of my Father, and my bride. For so hath it pleased him that sent me. But that man will I turn back, that he accomplish not his evil desire, and the praise of my Father shall be perfected in him, and after that I am gone home and abide with my Father, I will speak unto him from heaven, and all things shall be accomplished which I have told you before concerning him.

34 And we said unto him again: Lord, so many great things hast thou told us and revealed unto us as never yet were spoken, and in all hast thou given us rest and been gracious unto us. After thy resurrection thou didst reveal unto us all things that we might be saved indeed; but thou saidst unto us only: There shall be wonders and strange appearances in heaven and on earth before the end of the world come. Tell us now, how shall we perceive it? And he answered us: I will teach it you; and not that which shall befall you only, but them also whom ye shall teach and who shall believe, as well as them who shall hear that man and believe on me. In those years and days shall it come to pass.

And we said again unto him: Lord, what shall come to pass? And he said unto us: Then shall they that believe and they that believe not hear (see, *Eth.*) a trumpet in the heaven, a vision of great stars which shall be seen in the day, wonderful sights in heaven reaching down to the earth; stars which fall upon the earth like fire, and a great and mighty hail of fire (a star shining from the east unto this place, like unto fire, *Eth.* 2). The sun and the moon fighting one with the other, a continual rolling and noise of thunders and lightnings, thunder and earthquake; cities falling and men perishing in their overthrow, a continual dearth for lack of rain, a terrible pestilence and great mortality, mighty and untimely, so that they that die lack burial: and the bearing forth of brethren and sisters and kinsfolk shall be upon one bier. The kinsman shall show no favour to his kinsman, nor any man to his neighbour. And they that were overthrown shall rise up and behold them that overthrew them, that they lack burial, for the pestilence shall be full of hatred and pain and envy: and men shall take from one and give to another. And thereafter shall it wax yet worse than before. (Bewail ye them that have not hearkened unto my commandments, *Eth.* 2.)

85 Then shall my Father be wroth at the wickedness of men, for many are their transgressions, and the abomination of their uncleanness weigheth heavy upon them in the corruption of their life.

And we asked him: What of them that trust in thee? He answered and said unto us: Ye are yet slow of heart; and how long? Verily I say unto you, as the prophet David spake of me and of my people, so shall it be (?) for them also that believe on me. But they that are deceivers in the world and enemies of righteousness, upon them shall come the fulfilment of the prophecy of David, who said: Their feet are swift to shed blood, their tongue uttereth slander, adders' poison is under their lips. I behold thee companying with thieves, and partaking with adulterers, thou continuest speaking against thy brother and puttest stumbling-blocks before thine own mother's son. What thinkest thou, that I shall be like unto thee? Behold now how the prophet of God hath spoken of all, that all things may be fulfilled which he said aforetime.

36 And again we said unto him: Lord, will not then the nations say: Where is their God? And he answered and said unto us: Thereby shall the elect be known, that they, being plagued with such afflictions, come forth. We said: Will then their departure out of the world be by a pestilence which giveth them pain? He answered us: Nay, but if they suffer such affliction, it will be a proving of them, whether they have faith and remember these my sayings, and fulfil my commandments. These shall arise, and short will be their expectation, that he may be glorified that sent me, and I with him. For he hath sent me unto you to tell you these things; and that ye may impart them unto Israel and the Gentiles and they may hear, and they also be redeemed and believe on me and escape the woe of the destruction. But whoso escapeth from the destruction of death, him will they take and hold him fast in the prison-house in torments like the torments of a thief.

And we said unto him: Lord, will they *that believe* be *treated* like the unbelievers, and wilt thou punish them that have escaped from the pestilence? And he said unto us: If they that believe in my name deal like the sinners, then have they done as though they had not believed. And we said again to him: Lord, have they on whom this lot hath fallen no life? He answered and said unto us: Whoso hath accomplished the praise of my Father, he *shall abide in* the resting-place of my Father.

37 Then said we unto him: Lord, teach us what shall come to pass thereafter? And he answered us: In those years and days shall war be kindled upon war; the four

ends of the earth shall be in commotion and fight against each other. Thereafter shall be quakings of clouds (*or,* clouds of locusts), darkness, and dearth, and persecutions of them that believe on me and against the elect. Thereupon shall come doubt and strife and transgressions against one another. And there shall be many that believe on my name and yet follow after evil and spread vain doctrine. And men shall follow after them and their riches, and be subject unto their pride, and lust for drink, and bribery, and there shall be respect of persons among them.

38 But they that desire to behold the face of God and respect not the persons of the rich sinners, and are not ashamed before the people that lead them astray, but rebuke (?) them, they shall be crowned by the Father. And they also shall be saved that rebuke their neighbours, for they are sons of wisdom and of faith. But if they become not children of wisdom, whoso hateth his brother and persecuteth him and showeth him no favour, him will God despise and reject.

(Copt. resumes.)

But they that walk in truth and in the knowledge of the faith, and have love towards me--for they have endured insult--they shall be praised for that they walk in poverty and endure them that hate them and put them to shame. Men have stripped them naked, for they despised them because they continued in hunger and thirst, but after they have endured patiently, they shall have the blessedness of heaven, and they shall be with me for ever. But woe unto them that walk in pride and boasting, for their end is perdition.

39 And we said unto him: Lord, is this thy purpose, that thou leavest us, to come upon them? (Will all this come to pass, *Eth.*) He answered and said unto us: After what manner shall the judgement be? whether righteous or unrighteous? (In *Copt.* and *Eth.* the general sense is the same: but the answer of Jesus in the form of a question is odd, and there is probably a corruption.)

We said unto him: Lord, in that day they will say unto thee: Thou hast not distinguished between (*probably*: will they not say unto thee: Thou hast distinguished between) righteousness and unrighteousness, between the light and the darkness, and evil and good? Then said he: I will answer them and say: Unto Adam was power given to choose one of the two: he chose the light and laid his hand thereon, but the darkness he left behind him and cast away from him. Therefore have all men power to believe in the light which is life, and which is the Father that hath sent me. And every one that believeth and doeth the works of the light shall live in them; but if there be any that confesseth that he belongeth unto the light, and doeth the works of darkness, such an one hath no defence to utter, neither can he lift up his face to look upon the Son of God, which Son am I. For I will say unto him: As thou soughtest, so hast thou found, and as thou askedst, so hast thou received. Therefore condemnest thou me, O man? Wherefore hast thou departed from me and denied me? And wherefore hast thou confessed me and yet denied me? hath not every man power to live and to die? Whoso then hath kept my commandments shall be a son of the light, that is, of the Father that is in me. But because of them that corrupt my words am I come down from heaven. I am the word: I became flesh, and I wearied myself (or, suffered) and taught, saying: The heavy laden shall be saved, and they that are gone astray shall go astray for ever. They shall be chastised and tormented in their flesh and in their soul.

40 And we said unto him: O Lord, verily we are sorrowful for their sake. And he said unto us: Ye do rightly, for the righteous are sorry for the sinners, and pray for them, making prayer unto my Father. Again we said unto him: Lord, is there none that maketh intercession unto thee (so Eth.)? And he said unto us: Yea, and I will hearken unto the prayer of the righteous which they make for them.

When he had so said unto us, we said to him: Lord, in all things hast thou taught us and had mercy on us and saved us, that we might preach unto them that are worthy to be saved, and that we might obtain a recompense with thee. (Shall we be partakers of a recompense from thee? Eth.) 41 He answered and said unto us: Go and preach, and ye shall be labourers, and fathers, and ministers. We said unto him: Thou art he (or, Art thou he) that shalt preach by us. (Lord, thou art our father. Eth.) Then answered he us, saying: Be not (or, Are not ye) all fathers or all masters. (Are then all fathers, or all servants, or all masters? Eth.) We said unto him: Lord, thou art he that saidst unto us: Call no man your father upon earth, for one is your Father, which is in heaven, and your master. Wherefore sayest thou now unto us: Ye shall be fathers of many children, and servants and masters? He answered and said unto us: According as ye have said (Ye have rightly said, Eth.). For verily I say unto you: whosoever shall hear you and believe on me, shall receive of you the light of the seal through me, and baptism through me: ye shall be fathers and servants and masters.

42 But we said unto him: Lord, how may it be that every one of us should be these three? He said unto us: Verily I say unto you: Ye shall be called fathers, because with praiseworthy heart and in love ye have revealed unto them the things of the kingdom of heaven. And ye shall be called servants, because they shall receive the baptism of life and the remission of their sins at my hand through you. And ye shall be called masters, because ye have given them the word without grudging, and have admonished them, and when ye admonished them, they turned themselves (were converted). Ye were not afraid of their riches, nor ashamed before their face, but ye kept the commandments of my Father and fulfilled them. And ye shall have a great reward with my Father which is in heaven, and they shall have forgiveness of sins and everlasting life, and be partakers in the kingdom of heaven.

And we said unto him: Lord, even if every one of us had ten thousand tongues to speak withal, we could not thank thee, for that thou promisest such things unto us. Then answered he us, saying: Only do ye that which I say unto you, even as I myself also have done it. 43 And ye shall be like the wise virgins which watched and slept not, but went forth unto the lord into the bridechamber: but the foolish *virgins* were not able to watch, but slumbered. And we said unto him: Lord, who are the wise and who are the foolish? He said unto us: Five wise and five foolish; for these are they of whom the prophet hath spoken: Sons of God are they. Hear now their names.

But we wept and were troubled for them that slumbered. He said unto us: The five wise are Faith and Love and Grace and Peace and Hope. Now they of the faithful which possess this (these) shall be guides unto them that have believed on me and on him that sent me. For I am the Lord and I am the bridegroom whom they have received, and they have entered in to the house of the bridegroom and are laid down with me in the bridal chamber rejoicing. But the five foolish, when they had slept and had awaked, came unto the door of the bridal chamber and knocked, for the doors were shut. Then did they weep and lament that no man opened unto them.

We said unto him: Lord, and their wise sisters that were within in the bridegroom's house, did they continue without opening unto them, and did they not sorrow for their sakes nor entreat the bridegroom to open unto them? He answered us, saying: They were not yet able to obtain favour for them. We said unto him: Lord, on what day shall they enter in for their sisters' sake? Then said he unto us: He that is shut out, is shut out. And we said unto him: Lord, is this word (determined?). Who then are the foolish? He said unto us: Hear their names. They are Knowledge, Understanding (Perception), Obedience, Patience, and Compassion. These are they that slumbered in them that have believed and confessed me but have not fulfilled my commandments. 44 On account of them that have slumbered, they shall remain outside the kingdom and the fold of the shepherd and his sheep. But whoso shall abide outside the sheepfold, him will the wolves devour, and he shall be (condemned?) and die in much affliction: in him shall be no rest nor endurance, and (Eth.) although he be hardly punished, and rent in pieces and devoured in long and evil torment, yet shall he not be able to obtain death quickly.

45 And we said unto him: Lord, well hast thou revealed all this unto us. Then answered he us, saying: Understand ye not (or, Ye understand not) these words? We said unto him: Yea, Lord. By five shall men enter into thy kingdom <and by five shall men remain without>: notwithstanding, they that watched were with thee the Lord and bridegroom, even though they rejoiced not because of them that slumbered (yet will they have no pleasure, because of, Eth.). He said unto us: They will indeed rejoice that they have entered in with the bridegroom, the Lord; and they are sorrowful

because of them that slumbered, for they are their sisters. For all ten are daughters of God, even the Father. Then said we unto him: Lord, is it then for thee to show them favour on account of their sisters? (It becometh thy majesty to show them favour, *Eth.*) He said unto us: <It is not mine,> but his that sent me, and I am consenting with him (It is not yours, &c., *Eth.*).

46 But be ye upright and preach rightly and teach, and be not abashed by any man and fear not any man, and especially the rich, for they do not my commandments, but boast themselves (swell) in their riches. And we said unto him: Lord, tell us if it be the rich only. He answered, saying unto us: If any man who is not rich and possesseth a small livelihood giveth unto the poor and needy, men will call him a benefactor.

47 But if any man fall under the load <because> of sin that he hath committed, then shall his neighbour correct him because of the good that he hath done unto his neighbour. And if his neighbour correct him and he return, he shall be saved, and he that corrected him shall receive a reward and live for ever. For a needy man, if he see him that hath done him good sin, and correct him not, shall be judged with severe judgement. Now if a blind man lead a blind, they both fall into a ditch: and whoso respecteth persons for their sake, shall be as the two <blind>, as the prophet hath said: Woe unto them that respect persons and justify the ungodly for reward, even they whose God is their belly. Behold that judgement shall be their portion. For verily I say unto you: On that day will I neither have respect unto the rich nor pity for the poor.

48 If thou behold a sinner, admonish him betwixt him and thee: (if he hear thee, thou hast gained thy brother, *Eth.*) and if he hear thee not, then take to thee another, as many as three, and instruct thy brother: again, if he hear thee not, let him be unto thee

(*Copt. defective from this point.*)

as an heathen man or a publican.

49 If thou hear aught against thy brother, give it no credence; slander not, and delight not in hearing slander. For thus it is written: Suffer not thine ear to receive aught against thy brother: but if thou seest aught, correct him, rebuke him, and convert him.

And we said unto him: Lord, thou hast in all things taught us and warned us. But, Lord, concerning the believers, even them to whom it belongeth to believe in the preaching of thy name: is it determined that among them also there shall be doubt and division, jealousy, confusion, hatred, and envy? For thou sayest: They shall find fault with one another and respect the person of them that sin, and hate them that rebuke them. And he answered and said unto us: How then shall the judgement come about, that the corn should be gathered into the garner and the chaff thereof cast into the fire?

50 They that hate such things, and love me and rebuke them that fulfil not my commandments, shall be hated and persecuted and despised and mocked. Men will of purpose speak of them that which is not true, and will band themselves together against them that love me. But these will rebuke them, that they may be saved. But them that will rebuke and chasten and warn them, them will they (the others) hate, and thrust them aside, and despise them, and hold themselves far from them that wish them good. But they that endure such things shall be like unto the martyrs with the Father, because they have striven for righteousness, and have not striven for corruption.

And we asked him: Lord, shall such things be among us? And he answered us: Fear not; it shall not be in many, but in a few. We said unto him: Yet tell us, in what manner it shall come to pass. And he said unto us: There shall come forth another doctrine, and a confusion, and because they shall strive after their own advancement, they shall bring forth an unprofitable doctrine. And therein shall be a deadly corruption (of uncleanness), and they shall teach it, and shall turn away them that believe on me from my commandments and cut them off from eternal life. But woe unto them that falsify this my word and commandment, and draw away them that hearken to them from the life of the doctrine and separate themselves from the commandment of life: *for* together with them they shall come into everlasting judgement.

51 And when he had said this, and had finished his discourse with us, he said unto us again: Behold, on the third day and at the third hour shall he come which hath sent me, that I may depart with him. And as he so spake, there was thunder and lightning and an earthquake, and the heavens parted asunder, and there appeared a light (bright) cloud which bore him up. And *there came* voices of many angels, rejoicing and singing praises and saying: Gather us, O Priest, unto the light of the majesty. And when they drew nigh unto the firmament, we heard his voice *saying unto us*: Depart hence in peace.

THE EPISTLES OF JESUS CHRIST AND ABGARUS KING OF EDESSA

The first writer who makes any mention of the Epistles that passed between Jesus Christ and Abgarus, is Eusebius, Bishop of Caesarea, in Palestine, who flourished in the early part of the fourth century. For their genuineness, he appeals to the public registers and records of the City of Edessa in Mesopotamia, where Abgarus reigned, affirms that he found them written, in the Syriac language. He published a Greek translation of them, in his Ecclesiastical History.

The learned world have been much divided on this subject; but, notwithstanding that the erudite Grabe, with Archbishop Cave, Dr. Parker, and other divines, has strenuously contended for their admission into the canon of Scripture, they are deemed apocryphal. The Rev. Jeremiah Jones observes, that the common people in England have this Epistle in their houses, in many places, fixed in a frame, with the picture of Christ before it; and that they generally, with much honesty and devotion, regard it as the word of God, and the genuine Epistle of Christ.

CHAP. I.

A copy of a letter written by King Abgarus to Jesus, and sent to him by Ananias, his footman, to Jerusalem, 5 *inviting him to Edessa.*

ABGARUS, king of Edessa, to Jesus the good Saviour, who appears at Jerusalem, greeting.

2 I have been informed concerning you and your cures, which are performed without the use of medicines and herbs.

3 For it is reported, that you cause the blind to see, the lame to walk, do both cleanse lepers, and cast out unclean spirits and devils, and restore them to health

p. 63

who have been long diseased, and raisest up the dead;

4 All which when I heard, I was persuaded of one of these two, viz: either that you are God himself descended from heaven, who do these things, or the son of God.

5 On this account therefore I have wrote to you, earnestly to desire you would take the trouble of a journey hither, and cure a disease which I am under.

6 For I hear the Jews ridicule you, and intend you mischief.

7 My city is indeed small, but neat, and large enough for us both.

CHAP. II.

The answer of Jesus by Ananias the footman to Abgarus the king, 3 *declining to visit Edessa.*

ABGARUS, you are happy, forasmuch as you have believed on me, whom ye have not seen.

2 For it is written concerning me, that those who have seen me should not believe on me, that they who have not seen might believe and live.

3 As to that part of your letter, which relates to my giving you a visit, I must inform you, that I must fulfil all the ends of my mission in this country, and after that be received up again to him who sent me.

4 But after my ascension I will send one of my disciples, who will cure your disease, and give life to you, and all that are with you.

THE EPISTLE OF PAUL THE APOSTLE TO THE LAODICEANS

This Epistle has been highly esteemed by several learned men of the church of Rome and others. The Quakers have printed a translation and plead for it, as the reader may see, by consulting Poole's Annotations on Col. vi. 16. Sixtus Senensis mentions two MSS., the one in the Sorbonne Library at Paris, which is a very ancient copy, and the other in the Library of Joannes a Viridario, at Padua, which he transcribed and published, and which is the authority for the following translation. There is a very old translation of this Epistle in the British Museum, among the Harleian MSS., Cod. 1212.

1 *He salutes the brethren.* 3 *exhorts them to persevere in good works,* 4 *and not to be moved by vain speaking.* 6 *Rejoices in his bonds,* 10 *desires them to live in the fear of the Lord.*

PAUL an Apostle, not of men, neither by man, but by Jesus Christ, to the brethren which are at Laodicea.

2 Grace be to you, and Peace, from God the Father and our Lord Jesus Christ.

3 I thank Christ in every prayer of mine, that ye may continue and persevere in good works looking for that which is promised in the day of judgment.

4 Let not the vain speeches of any trouble you who pervert the truth, that they may draw you aside from the truth of the Gospel which I have preached.

5 And now may God grant, that my converts may attain to a perfect knowledge of the truth of the Gospel, be beneficent, and doing good works which accompany salvation.

6 And now my bonds, which I suffer in Christ, are manifest, in which I rejoice and am glad.

7 For I know that this shall turn to my salvation for ever, which shall be through your prayer, and the supply of the Holy Spirit.

8 Whether I live or die; (for) to me to live shall be a life to Christ, to die will be joy.

9 And our Lord will grant us his mercy, that ye may have the same love, and be like-minded.

10 Wherefore, my beloved, as ye have heard of the coming of the Lord, so think and act in fear, and it shall be to you life eternal;

11 For it is God who worketh in you;

12 And do all things without sin.

13 And what is best, my beloved, rejoice in the Lord Jesus Christ, and avoid all filthy lucre.

14 Let all your requests be made known to God, and be steady in the doctrine of Christ.

15 And whatsoever things are sound and true, and of good report, and chaste, and just, and lovely, these things do.

16 Those things which ye have heard, and received, think on these things, and peace shall be with you.

17 All the saints salute you.

18 The grace of our Lord Jesus Christ be with your spirit. Amen.

19. Cause this Epistle to be read to the Colossians, and the Epistle of the Colossians to be read among you.

THE LETTER OF PONTIUS PILATE

Which He Wrote to the Roman Emperor, Concerning Our Lord Jesus Christ.

Pontius Pilate to Tiberius Cæsar the emperor, greeting.

Upon Jesus Christ, whose case I had clearly set forth to thee in my last, at length by the will of the people a bitter punishment has been inflicted, myself being in a sort unwilling and rather afraid.

A man, by Hercules, so pious and strict, no age has ever had nor will have. But wonderful were the efforts of the people themselves, and the unanimity of all the scribes and chief men and elders, to crucify this ambassador of truth, notwithstanding that their own prophets, and after our manner the sibyls, warned them against it: and supernatural signs appeared while he was hanging, and, in the opinion of philosophers, threatened destruction to the whole world. His disciples are flourishing, in their work and the regulation of their lives not belying their master; yea, in his name most beneficent.

Had I not been afraid of the rising of a sedition among the people, who were just on the point of breaking out, perhaps this man would still have been alive to us; although, urged more by fidelity to thy dignity than induced by my own wishes, I did not according to my strength resist that innocent blood free from the whole charge *brought against it*, but unjustly, through the malignity of men, should be sold and suffer, yet, as the Scriptures signify, to their own destruction.

Farewell. 28th March.

THE EPISTLE OF IGNATIUS TO THE MAGNESIANS

CHAP. I.

4 Mentions the arrival of Damon, their bishop, and others, 6 whom he exhorts them to reverence, notwithstanding he was a young man.

IGNATIUS who is also called Theophorus; to the blessed (church) by the grace of God the Father in Jesus Christ our Saviour: in whom I salute the church which is at Magnesia near the Mæander: and wish it all joy in God the Father and in Jesus Christ.

2 When I heard of your well ordered love and charity in God, being full of joy, I desired much to speak unto you in the faith of Jesus Christ.

3 For having been thought worthy to obtain a most excellent name, in the bonds which I carry about, I salute the churches; wishing in them a union both of the body and spirit of Jesus Christ, our eternal life: as also of faith and charity, to which nothing is preferred: but especially of Jesus and the Father in whom if we undergo all the injuries of the prince of this pre sent world, and escape, we shall enjoy God.

4 Seeing then I have been judged worthy to see you, by Damas your most excellent bishop; and by your very worthy presbyters, Bassus and Apollonius; and by my fellow-servant Sotio, the deacon;

5 In whom I rejoice, forasmuch as he is the subject unto his bishop as to the grace of God, and to the presbytery as to the law of Jesus Christ; I determined to write unto you.

6 Wherefore it will become you also not to use your bishop too familiarly upon the account of his youth; but to yield all reverence to him according to the power of God the Father; as also I perceive that your holy presbyters do: not considering is age, which indeed to appearance is young; but as becomes those who are prudent in God, submitting to him, or rather not to him, but to the Father of our Lord Jesus Christ, the bishop of us all.

7 It will therefore behoove you with all sincerity, to obey your bishop; in honour him whose pleasure it is that ye should do so.

8 Because he that does not do so, deceives not the bishop whom he sees, but affronts him that is invisible. For whatsoever of this kind is done, it reflects not upon man, but upon God, who knows the secrets of our hearts.

9 It is therefore fitting, that we should not only be called Christians, but be so.

10 As some call indeed their governor, bishop; but yet do all things without him.

11 But I can never think that such as these have a good conscience, seeing that they are not gathered together thoroughly according to God's commandment.

CHAP. II.

1 That as all must die, 4 he exhorts them to live orderly and in unity.

SEEING then all things have an end, there are these two indifferently set before us, death and life: and every one shall depart unto his proper place.

2 For as there are two sorts of coins, the one of God, the other of the world; and each of these has its proper inscription engraven upon it; so also is it here.

3 The unbelievers are of this world; but the faithful, through charity, have the character of God the Father by Jesus Christ: by whom if we are not readily disposed to die after the likeness of his passion, his life is not in us.

4 Forasmuch, therefore, as I have in the persons before mentioned seen all of you in faith and charity; I exhort you that ye study to do all things in divine concord:

5 Your bishop presiding in the place of God; your presbyters in the place of the council of the Apostles; and your deacons most dear to me being entrusted with the ministry of Jesus Christ; who was the Father before all ages, and appeared in the end to us.

6 Wherefore taking the same holy course, see that ye all reverence one another: and let no one look upon his neighbour after the flesh; but do ye all mutually love each other in Jesus Christ.

7 Let there be nothing that may be able to make a division among you; but be ye united to your bishop, and those who preside over you, to be your pattern and direction in the way to immortality.

8 As therefore the Lord did nothing without the Father, being united to him; neither by himself nor yet by his Apostles, so neither do ye do anything without your bishop and presbyters:

9 Neither endeavour to let anything appear rational to yourselves apart;

10 But being come together into the same place have one common prayer; one supplication; one mind; one hope; one in charity, and in joy undefiled.

11 There is one Lord Jesus Christ, than whom nothing is better. Wherefore come ye all together as unto one temple of God; as to one altar, as to one Jesus Christ; who proceeded from one Father, and exists in one, and is returned to one.

CHAP. III.

1 He cautions them against false opinions. 4 Especially those of Ebion and the Judaizing Christians.

BE not deceived with strange doctrines; nor with old fables which are unprofitable. For if we still continue to live according to the Jewish law, we do confess ourselves not to have received grace. For even the most holy prophets lived according to Christ Jesus.

2 And for this cause were they persecuted, being inspired by his grace, to convince the unbelievers and disobedient that there is one God who has manifested himself by Jesus Christ his Son; who is his eternal word, not coming forth from silence, who in all things pleased him that sent him.

3 Wherefore if they who were brought up in these ancient laws came nevertheless to the newness of hope: no longer observing sabbaths, but keeping the Lord's day in which also our life is sprung up by him, and through his death, whom yet some deny:

4 (By which mystery we have been brought to believe and therefore wait that we may be found the disciples of Jesus Christ, our only master:)

5 How shall we be able to live different from him whose disciples the very prophets themselves being, did by the spirit expect him as their master.

6 And therefore he whom they justly waited for, being come, raised them up from the dead.

7 Let us not then be insensible of his goodness; for should he have dealt with us according to our works, we had not no had a being.

8 Wherefore being become his disciples, let us learn to live according to the rules of Christianity; for whosoever is called by any other name besides this, he is not of God.

9 Lay aside therefore the old and sour and evil leaven; and be ye changed into the new leaven, which is Jesus Christ.

10 Be ye salted in him, lest any one among you should be corrupted; for by your savour ye shall be judged.

11 It is absurd to name Jesus Christ, and to Judaize. For the Christian religion did not embrace the Jewish, but the Jewish the Christian; that so every tongue that believed might be gathered together unto God.

12 These things, my beloved, I write unto you; not that I know of any among you that lie under this error; but as one of the least among you, I am desirous to forewarn you, that ye fall not into the snares of false doctrine.

13 But that ye be fully instructed in the birth, and suffering, and resurrection of Jesus Christ, our hope; which was accomplished in the time of the government of Pontius Pilate, and that most truly and certainly and from which God forbid that any among you should be turned aside.

CHAP. IV.

1 *Commends their faith and piety; exhorts them to persevere;* 10 *desires their prayers for himself and the church at Antioch.*

MAY I therefore have joy of you in all things, if I shall be worthy of it. For though I am bound, yet I am not worthy to be compared to one of you that are at liberty.

2 I know that ye are not puffed up; for ye have Jesus Christ in your hearts.

3 And especially when I commend you, I know that ye are ashamed, as it is written, The just man condemneth himself.

4 Study therefore to be confirmed in the doctrine of our Lord, and of his Apostles; that so whatever ye do, ye may prosper both in body and spirit, in faith and charity, in the Son, and in the Father and in the Holy Spirit: in the beginning, and in the end.

5 Together with your most worthy bishop, and the well-wrought spiritual crown of your presbytery, and your deacons, which are according to God.

6 Be subject to your bishop, and to one another, as Jesus Christ to the Father, according to the flesh: and the Apostles both to Christ, and to the Father, and to the Holy Ghost: that so ye may be united both in body and spirit.

7 Knowing you to be full of God, I have the more briefly exhorted you.

8 Be mindful of me in your prayers, that I may attain unto God, and of the Church that is in Syria, from which I am not worthy to be called.

9 For I stand in need of your joint prayers in God, and of your charity, that the church which is in Syria may be thought worthy to be nourished by your church.

10 The Ephesians from Smyrna salute you, from which place I write unto you: (being present here to the glory of God, in like manner as you are,) who have in all things refreshed me, together with Polycarp, the bishop of the Smyrnæans.

11 The rest of the churches in the honour of Jesus Christ, salute you.

12 Farewell, and be ye strengthened in the concord of God: enjoying his inseparable spirit, which is Jesus Christ.

To the Magnesians.

THE EPISTLE OF IGNATIUS TO THE TRALLIANS

CHAP. I.

1 Acknowledges the coming of their bishop. 5 Commends them for their subjection to their bishop, priests, and deacons; and exhorts them to continue in it: 15 is afraid even of his over-great desire to suffer, lest it should be prejudicial to him.

IGNATIUS, who is also called Theophorus, to the holy church which is at Tralles in Asia: beloved of God the Father of Jesus Christ, elect and worthy of God, having peace through the flesh and blood, and passion of Jesus Christ our hope, in the resurrection which is by him: which also I salute in its fulness, continuing in the apostolical character, wishing all joy and happiness unto it.

2 I have heard of your blameless and constant disposition through patience, which not only appears in your outward conversation, but is naturally rooted and grounded in you.

3 In like manner as Polybius your bishop has declared unto me, who came to me to Smyrna, by the will of God and Jesus Christ, and so rejoiced together with me in my bonds for Jesus Christ, that in effect I saw your whole church in him.

4 Having therefore received testimony of your good will towards me for God's sake, by him; I seemed to find you, as also I knew that ye were the followers of God.

5 For whereas ye are subject to your bishop as to Jesus Christ, ye appear to me to live not after the manner of men, but according to Jesus Christ; who died for us, that so believing in his death, ye might escape death.

6 It is therefore necessary, that as ye do, so without your bishop, you should do nothing: also be ye subject to your presbyters, as to the Apostles of Jesus Christ our hope; in whom if we walk, we shall be found in him.

7 The deacons also, as being the ministers of the mysteries of Jesus Christ, must by all means please ye. For they are not the ministers of meat and drink, but of the church of God. Wherefore they must avoid all offences, as they would do fire.

8 In like manner let us reverence the deacons as Jesus Christ; and the bishop as the father; and the presbyters as the Sanhedrim of God, and college of the Apostles.

9 Without these there is no church. Concerning all which I am persuaded that ye think after the very same manner: for I have received, and even now have with me, the pattern of your love, in your bishop.

10 Whose very look is instructive; and whose mildness powerful: whom I am persuaded, the very Atheists themselves cannot but reverence.

11 But because I have a love towards you, I will not write any more sharply unto you about this matter, though I very well might; but now I have done so; lest being a condemned man, I should seem to prescribe to you as an Apostle.

12 I have great knowledge in God; but I refrain myself, lest I should perish in my boasting.

13 For now I ought the more to fear; and not to hearken to those that would puff me up.

14 For they that speak to me, in my praise, chasten me.

15 For I indeed desire to suffer, but I cannot tell whether I am worthy so to do.

16 And this desire, though to others it does not appear, yet to myself it is for that very reason the more violent. I have, therefore, need of moderation; by which the prince of this world is destroyed.

17 Am I not able to write to you of heavenly things?— But I fear lest I should harm you, who are yet but babes in Christ: (excuse me this care;) and lest per chance being not able to receive them, ye should be choken with them.

18 For even I myself, although I am in bonds, yet am not therefore able to understand heavenly things:

19 As the places of the angels, and the several companies of them, under their respective princes; things visible and invisible; but in these I am yet a learner.

20 For many things are wanting to us, that we come not short of God.

CHAP. II.

1 Warns them against heretics, 4 exhorts them to humility and unity, 10 briefly sets before them the true doctrine concerning Christ.

I EXHORT you therefore, or rather not I, but the love of Jesus Christ; that ye use none but Christian nourishment; abstaining from pasture which is of another kind, I mean heresy.

2 For they that are heretics, confound together the doctrine of Jesus Christ, with their own poison: whilst they seem worthy of belief:

3 As men give a deadly potion mixed with sweet wine; which he who drinks of, does with the treacherous pleasure sweetly drink in his own death.

4 Wherefore guard yourselves against such persons. And that you will do if you are not puffed up; but continue inseparable from Jesus Christ our God, and from your bishop, and from the commands of the Apostles.

5 He that is within the altar is pure; but he that is without, that is, that does anything without the bishop, the presbyters, and deacons, is not pure in his conscience.

6 Not that I know there is any thing of this nature among you; but I fore-arm you, as being greatly beloved by me, foreseeing the snares of the devil.

7 Wherefore putting on meekness, renew yourselves in faith, that is, the flesh of the Lord; and in charity, that is, the blood of Jesus Christ.

8 Let no man have any grudge against his neighbour. Give no occasion to the Gentiles; lest by means of a few foolish men, the whole congregation of God be evil spoken of.

9 For woe to that man through whose vanity my name is blasphemed by any.

10 Stop your ears therefore, as often as any one shall speak contrary to Jesus Christ; who was of the race of David, of the Virgin Mary.

11 Who was truly born and did eat and drink; was truly persecuted under Pontius Pilate; was truly crucified and dead; both those in heaven and on earth, being spectators of it.

12 Who was also truly raised from the dead by his Father. after the same manner as he will also raise up us who believe in him by Christ Jesus; without whom we have no true life.

13 But if, as some who are Atheists, that is to say infidels, pretend, that he only seemed to suffer: (they themselves only seeming to exist) why then am I bound?—Why do I desire to fight with beasts?—Therefore do I die in vain: therefore I will not speak falsely against the Lord.

14 Flee therefore these evil sprouts which bring forth deadly fruit; of which if any one taste, he shall presently die.

15 For these are not the plants of the Father; seeing if they were, they would appear to be the branches of the cross, and their fruit would be incorruptible; by which he invites you through his passion, who are members of him.

16 For the head cannot be without its members, God having promised a union, that is himself.

CHAP. III.

He again exhorts to unity: and desires their prayers for himself and for his church at Antioch.

I SALUTE you from Smyrna, together with the churches of God that are present with me; who have refreshed me in all things, both in the flesh and in the spirit.

2 My bonds, which I carry about me for the sake of Christ, beseeching him that I may attain unto God) exhort you, that you continue in concord among yourselves and in prayer with one another.

3 For it becomes every one of you, especially the presbyters, to refresh the bishop, to the honour of the Father of Jesus Christ and of the Apostles.

4 I beseech you, that you hearken to me in love; that I may not by those things which I write, rise up in witness against you.

5 Pray also for me; who through the mercy of God stand in need of your prayers, that I may be worthy of the portion which I am about to obtain that I be not found a reprobate.

6 The love of those who are at Smyrna and Ephesus salute you. Remember in your prayers the church of Syria, from which I am not worthy to be called, being one of the least of it.

7 Fare ye well in Jesus Christ; being subject to your bishop as to the command of God; and so likewise to the presbytery.

8 Love every one his brother with an unfeigned heart. My soul be your expiation, not only now, but when I shall have attained unto God; for I am yet under danger.

9 But the Father is faithful in Jesus Christ, to fulfil both mine and your petition; in whom may ye be found unblamable.

To the Trallians.

THE EPISTLE OF IGNATIUS TO THE ROMANS

CHAP. I.

He testifies his desire to see, and his hopes of suffering for Christ, 5 which he earnestly entreats them not to prevent, 10 but to pray for him, that God would strengthen him to the combat.

IGNATIUS, who is also called Theophorus, to the church which has obtained mercy from the majesty of the Most High Father, and his only begotten Son Jesus Christ; beloved, and illuminated through the will of who willeth all things which are according to the love of Jesus Christ our God which also presides in the place of the region of the Romans; and which I salute in the name of Jesus Christ (as being) united both in flesh and spirit to all his commands, and filled with the grace of God; (all joy) in Jesus Christ our God.

2 Forasmuch as I have at last obtained through my prayers to God, to see your faces, which I much desired to do; being bound in Jesus Christ, I hope ere long to salute you, if it shall be the will of God to grant me to attain unto the end I long for.

3 For the beginning is well disposed, if I shall but have grace, without hindrance, to receive what is appointed for me.

4 But I fear your love, lest it do me an injury. For it is easy for you to do what you please; but it will be hard for me to attain unto God, if you spare me.

5 But I would not that ye should please men, but God whom also ye do please. For neither shall I hereafter have such an opportunity of going unto God; nor will you if ye shall now be silent, ever be entitled to a better work. For if you shall be silent in my behalf, I shall be made partaker of God.

6 But if you shall love my body, I shall have my course again to run. Wherefore ye cannot do me a greater kindness, than to suffer me to be sacrificed unto God, now that the altar is already prepared:

7 That when ye shall be gathered together in love, ye may give thanks to the Father through Christ Jesus; that he has vouchsafed to bring a bishop of Syria unto you, being called from the east unto the west.

8 For it is good for me to set from the world, unto God; that I may rise again unto him.

9 Ye have never envied any one; ye have taught other. I would therefore that ye should now do those things yourselves, which in your instructions you have prescribed to others.

10 Only pray for me, that God would give me both inward and outward strength, that I may not only say, but will; nor be only called a Christian, but be found one.

11 For if I shall be found a Christian, I may then deservedly be called one; and be thought faithful, when I shall no longer appear to the world.

12 Nothing is good, that is seen.

13 For even our God, Jesus Christ, now that he is in the Father, does so much the more appear.

14 A Christian is not a work of opinion; but of greatness of mind, (especially when he is hated by the world.)

CHAP. II.

Expresses his great desire and determination to suffer martyrdom.

I WRITE to the churches, and signify to them all, that am willing to die for God, unless hinder me.

2 I beseech you that you shew not an unseasonable good will towards me. Suffer me to be food to the wild beasts; by whom I shall attain unto God.

3 For I am the wheat of God; and I shall be ground by the teeth of the wild beasts, that I may be found the pure bread of Christ.

4 Rather encourage the beasts, that they may become my sepulchre; and may leave nothing of my body; that being dead I mazy not be troublesome to any.

5 Then shall I be truly the disciple of Jesus Christ, when the world shall not see so much as my body, Pray therefore unto Christ for me, that by these instruments I may be made the sacrifice of God.

6 I do not, as Peter and Paul, command you. They were Apostles, I a condemned man; they were free, but I am even to this day a servant:

7 But if I shall suffer, I shall then become the freeman of Jesus Christ, and shall rise free. And now, being in bonds, I learn, not to desire anything.

8 From Syria even unto Rome, I fight with beasts both by sea and land; both night and day: being bound to ten leopards, that is to say, to such a band of soldiers; who, though treated with all manner of kindness, are the worse for it.

9 But I am the more instructed by their injuries; yet am I not therefore justified.

10 May I enjoy the wild beasts that are prepared for me; which also I wish may exercise all their fierceness upon me.

11 And whom for that end I will encourage, that they may be sure to devour me, and not serve me as they have done some, whom out of fear they have not touched. But, and if they will not do it willingly, I will provoke them to it.

12 Pardon me in this matter; I know what is profitable for me. Now I begin to be a disciple. Nor shall anything move me, whether visible or invisible, that I may attain to Jesus Christ.

13 Let fire, and the cross; let the companies of wild beasts; let breakings of bones and tearing of members; let the shattering in pieces of the whole body, and all the wicked torments of the devil come upon me; only let me enjoy Jesus Christ.

14 All the ends of the world, and the kingdoms of it, will profit me nothing: I would rather die for Jesus Christ, than rule to the utmost ends of the earth. Him I seek who died for us; him I desire, that rose again for us. This is the gain that is laid up for me.

15 Pardon me, my brethren, ye shall not hinder me from living. Nor seeing I desire to go to God, may you separate me from him, for the sake of this world; nor reduce me by any of the desires of it. Suffer me to enter into pure light: Where being come, I shall be indeed the servant of God.

16 Permit me to imitate the passion of my God. If any one has him within himself, let him consider what I desire; and let him have compassion on me, as knowing

how I am straightened.

CHAP. III.

Further expresses his desire to suffer.

THE prince of this world would fain carry me away, and corrupt my resolution towards my God. Let none of you therefore help him: Rather do ye join with me, that is, with God.

2 Do not speak with Jesus Christ, and yet covet the world. Let not any envy dwell with you; No not though I myself when I shall be come unto you, should exhort you to it, yet do not ye hearken to me; but rather believe what I now write to you.

3 For though I am alive, at the writing this, yet my desire is to die. My love is crucified; (and the fire that is within me does not desire any water; but being alive and springing within me, says,) Come to the Father.

4 I take no pleasure in the food of corruption, nor in the pleasures of this life.

5 I desire the bread of God which is the flesh of Jesus Christ, (of the seed of David; and the drink that I long for) is his blood, which is incorruptible love.

6 I have no desire to live any longer after the manner of men, neither shall I, if you consent. Be ye therefore willing, that ye yourselves also may be pleasing to God. I exhort you in a few words; I pray you believe me.

7 Jesus Christ will shew you that I speak truly. My mouth is without deceit, and the Father hath truly spoken by it. Pray therefore for me, that I may accomplish what I desire.

8 I have not written to you after the flesh, but according to the will of God. If I shall suffer, ye have loved me; but if I shall be rejected, ye have hated me.

9 Remember in your prayers the church of Syria, which now enjoys God for its shepherd instead of me: Let Jesus Christ only oversee it, and your charity.

10 But I am even ashamed to be reckoned as one of them: For neither am I worthy, being the least among them, and as one born out of due season. But through mercy I have obtained to be somebody, if I shall get unto God.

11 My spirit salutes you; and the charity of the churches that have received me in the name of Jesus Christ; not as a passenger. For even they that were not near to me in the way, have gone before me to the next city to meet me.

12 These things I write to you from Smyrna, by the most worthy of the church of Ephesus.

13 There is now with me, together with many others, Crocus, most beloved of me. As for those which are come from Syria, and are gone before me to Rome, to the glory of God, I suppose you are not ignorant of them.

14 Ye shall therefore signify to them, that I draw near, for they are all worthy both of God and of you: Whom it is fit that you refresh in all things.

15 This have I written to you, the day before the ninth of the calends of September. Be strong unto the end, in the patience of Jesus Christ.

To the Romans.

THE EPISTLE OF IGNATIUS TO THE PHILADELPHIANS

CHAP. I.

Commends their bishop whom they had sent unto him, 5 warns them against divisions and schism.

IGNATIUS, who is also called Theophorus, to the church of God the Father, and our Lord Jesus Christ, which is at Philadelphia in Asia; which has obtained mercy, being fixed in the concord of God, and rejoicing evermore in the passion of our Lord, and being fulfilled in all mercy through his resurrection: Which also I salute in the blood of Jesus Christ, which is our eternal and undefiled joy; especially if they are at unity with the bishop, and presbyters who are with him, and the deacons appointed according to the mind of Jesus Christ; whom he has settled according to his own will in all firmness by his Holy Spirit:

2 Which bishop I know obtained that great ministry among you, not of himself, neither by men, nor out of vain glory; but by the love of God the Father, and our Lord Jesus Christ.

3 Whose moderation I admire; who by his silence is able to do more than others with all their vain talk. For he is fitted to the commands, as the harp to its strings.

4 Wherefore my soul esteems his mind towards God most happy, knowing it to be fruitful in all virtue, and perfect; full of constancy, free from passion, and according to all the moderation of the living God.

5 Wherefore as becomes the children both of the light and of truth; flee divisions and false doctrines; but where your shepherd is, there do ye, as sheep, follow after.

6 For there are many wolves who seem worthy of belief with a false pleasure lead captive those that run in the course of God; but in the concord they shall find no place.

7 Abstain therefore from evil herbs which Jesus does not dress; because such are not the plantation of the Father. Not that I have found any division among you, but rather all manner of purity.

8 For as many as are of God, and of Jesus Christ, are also with their bishop. And as many as shall with repentance return into the unity of the church, even these shall also be the servants of God, that they may live according to Jesus.

9 Be not deceived, brethren; if any one follows him that makes a schism in the church, he shall not inherit the kingdom of God. If any one walks after any other opinion, he agrees not with the passion of Christ.

10 Wherefore let it be your endeavour to partake all of the same holy eucharist.

11 For there is but one flesh of our Lord Jesus Christ; and one cup in the unity of his blood; one altar;

12 As also there is one bishop, together with his presbytery, and the deacons my fellow-servants: that so whatsoever ye do, ye may do it according to the will of God.

CHAP. II.

Desires their prayers, and to be united but not to Judaize.

MY brethren, the love I have towards you makes me the more large; and having a great joy in you, I endeavour to secure you against danger; or rather not I, but Jesus Christ; in whom being bound I the more fear, as being yet only on the way to suffering.

2 But your prayer to God shall make me perfect, that I may attain to that portion, which by God's mercy is allotted to me: Fleeing to the Gospel as to the flesh of Christ; and to the Apostles as to the presbytery of the church.

3 Let us also love the prophets, forasmuch as they also have led us to the Gospel, and to hope in Christ, and to expect him.

4 In whom also believing they were saved in the unity of Jesus Christ; being holy men, worthy to be loved, and had in wonder;

5 Who have received testimony from Jesus Christ, and are numbered in the Gospel of our common hope.

6 But if any one shall preach the Jewish law unto you, hearken not unto him; for it is better to receive the doctrine of Christ from one that has been circumcised, than Judaism from one that has not.

7 But if either the one, or other, do not speak concerning Christ Jesus, they seem to me to be but as monuments and sepulchres of the dead, upon which are written only the names of men.

8 Flee therefore the wicked arts and snares of the prince of this world; lest at any time being oppressed by his cunning ye grow cold in your charity. But come all together into the same place with an undivided heart.

9 And I bless my God that I have a good conscience towards you, and that no one among you has whereof to boast either openly or privately, that I have been burthensome to him in much or little.

10 And I wish to all among whom I have conversed, that it may not turn to a witness against them.

11 For although some would have deceived me according to the flesh, yet the spirit, being from God, is not deceived; for it knows both whence it comes and whither it goes, and reproves the secrets of the heart.

12 I cried whilst I was among you; I spake with a loud voice: attend to the bishop, and to the presbytery, and to the deacons.

13 Now some supposed that I spake this as foreseeing the division that should come among you.

14 But he is my witness for whose sake I am in bonds that I knew nothing from any man. But the spirit spake, saying on this wise: Do nothing without the bishop:

15 Keep your bodies as the temples of God: Love unity; Flee divisions; Be the followers of Christ, as he was of his Father.

16 I therefore did as became me, as a man composed to unity. For where there is division, and wrath, God dwelleth not.

17 But the Lord forgives all that repent, if they return to the unity of God, and to the council of the bishop.

18 For I trust in the grace of Jesus Christ that he will free you from every bond.

19 Nevertheless I exhort you that you do nothing out of strife, but according to the instruction of Christ.

20 Because I have heard of some who say; unless I find

it written in the originals, I will not believe it to be
written in the Gospel. And when I said, It is written;
they answered what lay before them in their corrupted
copies.

21 But to me Jesus Christ is instead of all the
uncorrupted monuments in the world; together with
those undefiled monuments, his cross, and death, and
resurrection, and the faith which is by him; by which I
desire, through your prayers, to be justified.

22 The priests indeed are good; but much better is the
High Priest to whom the Holy of Holies has been
committed; and who alone has been entrusted with the
secrets of God.

23 He is the door of the Father; by which Abraham, and
Isaac, and Jacob, and all the prophets, enter in; as well as
the Apostles, and the church.

24 And all these things tend to the unity which is of
God. Howbeit the Gospel has some. what in it far above
all other dispensations; namely, the appearance of our
Saviour, the Lord Jesus Christ, his passion and
resurrection.

25 For the beloved prophets referred to him; but the
gospel is the perfection of incorruption. All therefore
together are good, if ye believe with charity.

CHAP. III.

*Informs them he had heard that the persecution was stopped at
Antioch, and directs them to send a messenger hitherto to
congratulate with the church.*

NOW as concerning the church of Antioch which is in
Syria, seeing I am told that through your prayers and the
bowels which ye have towards it in Jesus Christ, it is in
peace; it will become you, as the church of God, to
ordain some deacon to go to them thither as the
ambassador of God; that he may rejoice with them when
they meet together, and glorify God's name.

2 Blessed be that man in Jesus Christ, who shall be
found worthy of such a ministry; and ye yourselves also
shall be glorified.

3 Now if you be willing, it is not impossible for you to
do this for the grace of God; as also the other
neighbouring churches have sent them, some bishops,
some priests and deacons.

4 As concerning Philo the deacon of Cilicia, a most
worthy man, he still ministers unto me in the word of
God: together with Rheus of Agathopolis, a singular
good person, who has followed me even from Syria, not
regarding his life: These also bear witness unto you.

5 And I myself give thanks to God for you that you
receive them as the Lord shall receive you. But for those
that dishonoured them, may they be forgiven through
the grace of Jesus Christ.

6 The charity of the brethren that are at Troas salutes
you: from whence also I now write by Burrhus, who was
sent together with me by those of Ephesus and Smyrna,
for respect sake.

7 May our Lord Jesus Christ honour them; in whom they
hope, both in flesh, and soul, and spirit; in faith, in love,
in unity. Farewell in Christ Jesus our common hope.

To the Philadelphians.

THE EPISTLE OF IGNATIUS TO THE SMYRNÆANS

CHAP. I.

1 Declares his joy for their firmness in the Gospel. 4 Enlarges on the person of Christ, against such as pretend that Christ did not really suffer.

IGNATIUS, who is also called Theophorus, to the church of God the Father, and of the beloved Jesus Christ, which God hath mercifully blessed with every good gift; being filled with faith and charity, so that this is wanting in no gift; most worthy of God, and fruitful in saints: the church which is at Smyrna in Asia; all joy, through his immaculate spirit, and the word of God.

2 I glorify God, even Jesus Christ, who has given you such wisdom.

3 For I have observed that you are settled in an immovable faith, as if you were nailed to the cross of our Lord Jesus Christ, both in the flesh and in the spirit; and are confirmed in love through the blood of Christ; being fully persuaded of those things which relate unto our Lord.

4 Who truly was of the race of David according to the flesh, but the Son of God according to the will and power of God; truly born of the Virgin, and baptized of John; that so all righteousness might be fulfilled by him.

5 He was also truly crucified by Pontius Pilate, and Herod the Tetrarch, being nailed for us in the flesh; by the fruits of which we are, even by his most blessed passion.

6 That he might set up a token for all ages through his resurrection, to all his holy and faithful servants, whether they be Jews or Gentiles, in one body of his church.

7 Now all these things he suffered for us that we might be saved. And he suffered truly, as he also truly raised up himself: And not, as some unbelievers say, that he only seemed to suffer, they themselves only seeming to be.

8 And as they believe so shall it happen unto them; when being divested of the body they shall become mere spirits.

9 But I know that even after his resurrection he was in the flesh; and I believed that he is still so.

10 And when he came to those who were with Peter, he said unto them, Take, handle me, and see that I am not an incorporeal dæmon. And straightway they felt and believed; being convinced both by his flesh and spirit.

11 For this cause they despised death, and were found to be above it.

12 But after his resurrection he did eat and drink with them, as he was flesh; although as to his Spirit he was united to the Father.

CHAP. II.

1 Exhorts them against heretics. 8 The danger of their doctrine.

NOW these things, beloved, put you in mind of, not questioning but that you yourselves also believe that they are so.

2 But I arm you before-hand against certain beasts in the shape of men whom you must not only not receive, but if it be possible must not meet with.

3 Only you must pray for them, that if it be the will of God they may repent; which yet will be very hard. But of this our Lord Jesus Christ has the power, who is our true life.

4 For if all these things were done only in shew by our Lord, then do I also seem only to be bound.

5 And why have I given up myself to death, to the fire, to the sword, to wild beasts!

6 But now the nearer I am to the sword, the nearer I am to God: when I shall come among the wild beasts, I shall come to God.

7 Only in the name of Jesus Christ, I undergo all, to suffer together with him; he who was made a perfect man strengthening me.

8 Whom some not knowing, do deny; or rather have been denied by him, being the advocates of death, rather than of the truth. Whom neither the prophecies, nor the law of Moses have persuaded; nor the Gospel itself even to this day, nor the sufferings of every one of us.

9 For they think also the same things of us. For what does a man profit me, if he shall praise me, and blaspheme my Lord; not confessing that he was truly made man?

10 Now he that doth not say this, does in effect deny him, and is in death. But for the names of such as do this, they being unbelievers, I thought it not fitting to write them unto you.

11 Yea, God forbid that I should make any mention of them, till they shall repent to a true belief of Christ's passion, which is our resurrection.

12 Let no man deceive himself; both the things which are in heaven and the glorious angels, and princes, whether visible or invisible, if they believe not in the blood of Christ, it shall be to them to condemnation.

13 He that is able to receive this, let him receive it. Let no man's place or state in the world puff him up: that which is worth all his faith and charity, to which nothing is to be preferred.

14 But consider those who are of a different opinion from us, as to what concerns the grace of Jesus Christ which is come unto us, how contrary they are to the design of God.

15 They have no regard to charity, no care of the widow, the fatherless, and the oppressed; of the bond or free, of the hungry or thirsty.

16 They abstain from the eucharist, and from the public offices; because they confess not the eucharist to be the flesh of our Saviour Jesus Christ; which suffered for our sins, and which the Father of his goodness, raised again from the dead.

17 And for this cause contradicting the gift of God, they die in their disputes: but much better would it be for them to receive it, that they might one day rise through it.

18 It will therefore become you to abstain from such persons; and not to speak with them neither in private nor in public.

19 But to hearken to the prophets, and especially to the Gospel, in which both Christ's passion is manifested unto us, and his resurrection perfectly declared.

20 But flee all divisions, as the beginning of evils.

CHAP. III.

1 Exhorts them to follow their bishop and pastors; but especially their bishop. 6 Thanks them for their kindness, 11 and acquaints them with the ceasing of the persecution at Antioch.

SEE that ye all follow your bishop, as Jesus Christ, the Father; and the presbytery, as the Apostles. And reverence the deacons, as the command of God.

2 Let no man do anything of what belongs to the church separately from the bishop.

3 Let that eucharist be looked upon as well established, which is either offered by the bishop, or by him to whom the bishop has given his consent.

4 Wheresoever the bishop shall appear, there let the people also be: as where Jesus Christ is, there is the Catholic church.

5 It is not lawful without the bishop, neither to baptize, nor to celebrate the Holy Communion; but whatsoever he shall approve of, that is also pleasing unto God; that so whatever is done, may be sure and well done.

6 For what remains, it is very reasonable that we should repent whilst there is yet time to return unto God.

7 It is a good thing to have a due regard both to God, and to the bishop: he that honours the bishop, shall be honoured of God. But he that does anything without his knowledge, ministers unto the devil.

8 Let all things therefore abound to you in charity; seeing that ye are worthy.

9 Ye have refreshed me in all things; so shall Jesus Christ you. Ye have loved me both when I was present with you, and now being absent, ye cease not to do so.

10 May God be your reward, from whom whilst ye undergo all things, ye shall attain unto him.

11 Ye have done well in that ye have received Philo, and Rheus Agathopus, who followed me for the word of God, as the deacons of Christ our God.

12 Who also gave thanks unto the Lord for you, forasmuch as ye have refreshed them in all things. Nor shall any thing that you have done be lost to you.

13 My soul be for yours, and my bonds which ye have not despised, nor been ashamed of. Wherefore neither shall Jesus Christ, our perfect faith, be ashamed of you.

14 Your prayer is come to the church of Antioch which is in Syria. From whence being sent bound with chains becoming God, I salute the churches; being not worthy to be called from thence, as being the least among them.

15 Nevertheless by the will of God I have been thought worthy of this honour; not for that I think I have deserved it, but by the grace of God.

16 Which I wish may be perfectly given unto me, that through your prayers I may attain unto God.

17 And therefore that your work may be fully accomplished both upon earth and in heaven; it will be fitting, and for the honour of God, that your church appoint some worthy delegate, who being come as far as Syria, may rejoice together with them that they are in peace; and that they are again restored to their former state, and have again received their proper body.

18 Wherefore I should think it a worthy action, to send some one from you with an epistle, to congratulate with them their peace in God; and that through your prayers they have now gotten to their harbor.

19 For inasmuch as ye are perfect yourselves, you ought to think those things that are perfect. For when you are desirous to do well, God is ready to enable you thereunto.

20 The love of the brethren that are at Troas salute you; from whence I write to you by Burrhus whom you sent with me, together with the Ephesians your brethren; and who has in all things refreshed me.

21 And I would to God that all would imitate him, as being a pattern of the ministry of God. May his grace fully reward him.

22 I salute your very worthy bishop, and your venerable presbytery; and your deacons, my fellow-servants; and all of you in general, and every one in particular, in the name of Jesus Christ, and in his flesh and blood; in his passion and resurrection both fleshly and spiritually; and in the unity of God with you.

23 Grace be with you, and mercy, and peace, and patience, for evermore.

24 I salute the families of my brethren, with their wives and children; and the virgins that are called widows. Be strong in the power of the Holy Ghost. Philo, who is present with me salutes you.

25 I salute the house of Tavias, and pray that it may be strengthened in faith and charity, both of flesh and spirit.

26 I salute Alce my well-beloved, together with the incomparable Daphnus, and Eutechnus, and all by name.

27 Farewell in the grace of God.

To the Smyrnæans from Troas.

THE EPISTLE OF IGNATIUS TO POLYCARP

CHAP. I.

Blesses God for the firm establishment of Polycarp in the faith, and gives him particular directions for improving it.

IGNATIUS, who is also called Theophorus, to Polycarp, bishop of the church which is at Smyrna; their overseer, but rather himself overlooked by God the Father, and the Lord Jesus Christ: all happiness.

2 Having known that thy mind towards God, is fixed as it were upon an immovable rock; I exceedingly give thanks, that I have been thought worthy to behold thy blessed face, in which may I always rejoice in God.

3 Wherefore I beseech thee by the grace of God with which thou art clothed, to press forward in thy course, and to exhort all others that they may be saved.

4 Maintain thy place with all care both of flesh and spirit: Make it thy endeavour to preserve unity, than which nothing is better. Bear with all men, even as the Lord with thee.

5 Support all in love, as also thou dost. Pray without ceasing: ask more understanding than what thou already hast. Be watchful, having thy spirit always awake.

6 Speak to every one according as God shall enable thee. Bear the infirmities of all, as a perfect combatant; where the labour is great, the gain is the more.

7 If thou shalt love the good disciples, what thank is it? But rather do thou subject to thee those that are mischievous, in meekness.

8 Every wound is not healed with the same plaster: if the accessions of the disease be vehement, modify them with soft remedies: be in all things wise as a serpent, but harmless as a dove.

9 For this cause thou art composed of flesh and spirit; that thou mayest modify those things that appear before thy face.

10 And as for those that are not seen, pray to God that he would reveal them unto thee, that so thou mayest be wanting in nothing, but mayest abound in every gift.

11 The times demand thee, as the pilots the winds; and he that is tossed in a tempest, the haven where he would be; that thou mayst attain unto God.

12 Be sober as the combatant of God: the crown proposed to thee is immortality, and eternal life; concerning which thou art also fully persuaded. I will be thy surety in all things, and my bonds, which thou hast loved.

13 Let not those that seem worthy of credit, but teach other doctrines, disturb thee. Stand firm and immovable, as au anvil when it is beaten upon.

14 It is the part of a brave combatant to be wounded, and yet overcome. But especially we ought to endure all things for God's sake, that he may bear with us.

15 Be every day better than other: consider the times; and expect him, who is above all time, eternal, invisible, though for our sakes made visible: impalpable, and impassable, yet for us subjected to sufferings; enduring all manner of ways for our salvation.

CHAP. II.

1 Continues his advice, 6 and teaches him how to advise others. 12 Enforces unity and subjection to the bishop.

LET not the widows be neglected: be thou after God, their guardian.

2 Let nothing be done without thy knowledge and consent; neither do thou anything but according to the will of God; as also thou dost, with all constancy.

3 Let your assemblies be more full: inquire into all by name.

4 Overlook not the men and maid servants; neither let them be puffed up: but rather let them be the more subject to the glory of God, that they may obtain from him a better liberty.

5 Let them not desire to be set free at the public cost, that they be not slaves to their own lusts.

6 Flee evil arts; or rather, make not any mention of them.

7 Say to my sisters, that they love the Lord; and be satisfied with their own husbands, both in the flesh and spirit.

8 In like manner, exhort my brethren, in the name of Jesus Christ, that they love their wives, even as the Lord the Church.

9 If any man can remain in a virgin state, to the honour of the flesh of Christ, let him remain without boasting; but if he boast, he is undone. And if he desire to be more taken notice of than the bishop he is corrupted.

10 But it becomes all such as are married, whether men or women to come together with the consent of the bishop, that so their marriage may be according to godliness, and not in lust.

11 Let all things be done to the honour of God.

12 Hearken unto the bishop, that God also may hearken unto you. My soul be security for them that submit to their bishop, with their presbyters and deacons. And may my portion be together with theirs in God.

13 Labour with one another; contend together, run together, suffer together; sleep together, and rise together; as the stewards, and assessors, and ministers of God.

14 Please him under whom ye war, and from whom ye receive your wages. Let none of you be found a deserter; but let your baptism remain, as your arms; your faith, as your helmet; your charity, as your spear; your patience, as your whole armour.

15 Let your works be your charge, that so you may receive a suitable reward. Be longsuffering therefore towards each other in meekness: as God is towards you.

16 Let me have joy of you in all things.

CHAP. III.

1 Greets Polycarp on the peace of the church at Antioch: and desires him to write to that and other churches.

NOW forasmuch as the church of Antioch in Syria, is, as I am told, [one word illegible.—JBH] through your prayers; I also have been the more comforted and without care in God; if so be that by suffering, I shall attain unto God; that through your prayers I may be found a disciple of Christ.

2 It will be very fit, O most worthy Polycarp, to call a select council, and choose some one whom ye particularly love, and who is patient of labour; that he may be the messenger of God; and that going unto Syria, he may glorify your incessant love, to the praise of Christ.

3 A Christian has not the power of himself: but must be always at leisure for God's service. Now this work is both God's and your's: when ye shall have perfected it.

4 For I trust through the grace of God that ye are ready to every good work that is fitting for you in the Lord.

5 Knowing therefore your earnest affection for the truth, I have exhorted you by these short letters.

6 But forasmuch as I have not been able to write to all the churches, because I must suddenly sail from Troas to Neapolis; (for so is the command of those to whose pleasure I am subject;) do you write to the churches that are near you, as being instructed in the will of God, that they also may do in like manner.

7 Let those that are able send messengers; and let the rest send their letters by those who shall be sent by you: that you may be glorified to all eternity, of which you are worthy.

8 I salute all by name, particularly the wife of Epitropus, with all her house and children. I salute Attalus my well-beloved.

9 I salute him who shall be thought worthy to be sent by you into Syria. Let grace be ever with him, and with Polycarp who sends him.

10 I wish you all happiness in our God, Jesus Christ; in whom continue, in the unity and protection of God.

11 I salute Alce my well-beloved. Farewell in the Lord.

To Polycarp.

THE EPISTLE OF POLYCARP TO THE PHILIPPIANS

The genuineness of this Epistle is controverted, but implicitly believed by Archbishop Wake, whose translation is below. There is also a translation by Dr. Cave, attached to his life of Polycarp.

CHAP. I.

Commends the Philippians for their respect to those who suffered for the Gospel; and for their own faith.

POLYCARP, and the presbyters that are with him, to the church of God which is at Philippi: mercy unto you and peace from God Almighty; and the Lord Jesus Christ, our Saviour, be multiplied.

2 I rejoiced greatly with you in our Lord Jesus Christ, that ye received the images of a true love, and accompanied, as it is behooved you, those who were in bonds, becoming saints; which are the crowns of such as are truly chosen by God and our Lord:

3 As also that the root of the faith which was preached from ancient times, remains firm in you to this day; and brings forth fruit to our Lord Jesus Christ, who suffered himself to be brought even to the death for our sins.

4 Whom God hath raised up, having loosed the pains of death, whom having not seen, ye love; in whom though now ye see him not, yet believing ye rejoice with joy unspeakable and full of glory.

5 Into which many desire to enter; knowing that by grace ye are saved; not by works, but by the will of God through Jesus Christ.

6 Wherefore girding up the loins of your minds; serve the Lord with fear, and in truth: laying aside all empty and vain speech, and the error of many; believing in him that raised up our Lord Jesus Christ from the dead, and hath given him glory and a throne at his right hand.

7 To whom all things are made subject, both that are in heaven, and that are in earth; whom every living creature shall worship; who shall come to be the judge of the quick and dead.: whose blood God shall require of them that believe in him.

8 But he that raised up Christ from the dead, shall also raise up us in like manner, if we do his will and walk according to his commandments; and love those things which he loved:

9 Abstaining from all unrighteousness; inordinate affection, and love of money; from evil speaking; false witness; not rendering evil for evil, or railing for railing, or striking for striking, or cursing for cursing.

10 But remembering what the Lord has taught us saying, Judge not, and ye shall not be judged; forgive and ye shall be forgiven; be ye merciful, and ye shall obtain mercy; for with the same measure that ye mete withal, it shall be measured to you again.

11 And again, that blessed are the poor, and they that are persecuted for righteousness' sake; for theirs is the kingdom of God.

CHAP. II.

2 Exhorts to Faith, Hope, and Charity. 5 Against covetousness, and as to the duties of husbands, wives, widows, 6 deacons, young men, virgins, and presbyters.

THESE things, my brethren, I took not the liberty of myself to write unto you concerning righteousness, but you yourselves before encouraged me to it.

2 For neither can I, nor any other such as I am, come up to the wisdom of the blessed and renowned Paul: who being himself in person with those who then lived, did with all exactness and soundness teach the word of truth; and being gone from you wrote an epistle to you.

3 Into which if you look, you will be able to edify yourselves in the faith that has been delivered unto you; which is the mother of us all; being followed with hope, and led on by a general love, both towards God and towards Christ, and towards our neighbour.

4 For if any man has these things he has fulfilled the law of righteousness: for he that has charity is far from all sin.

5 But the love of money is the root of all evil. Knowing therefore that as we brought nothing into this world, so neither may we carry any thing out; let us arm ourselves with the armour of righteousness.

6 And teach ourselves first to walk according to the commandments of the Lord; and then your wives to walk likewise according to the faith that is given to them; in charity, and in purity; loving their own husbands with all sincerity, and all others alike with all temperance; and to bring up their children in the instruction and fear of the Lord.

7 The widows likewise teach that they be sober as to what concerns the faith of the Lord: praying always for all men; being far from all detraction, evil speaking, false witness; from covetousness, and from all evil.

8 Knowing that they are the altars of God, who sees all blemishes, and from whom nothing is hid; who searches out the very reasonings, and thoughts, and secrets of our hearts.

9 Knowing therefore that God is not mocked, we ought to walk worthy both of his command and of his glory.

10 Also the deacons must be blameless before him, as the ministers of God in Christ, and not of men. Not false accusers; not double tongued; not lovers of money; but moderate in all things; compassionate, careful; walking according to the truth of the Lord, who was the servant of all.

11 Whom if we please in this present world we shall also be made partakers of that which is to come, according as he has promised to us, that he will raise us from the dead; and that if we shall walk worthy of him, we shall also reign together with him, if we believe.

12 In like manner the younger men must be unblameable in all things; above all, taking care of their purity, and to restrain themselves from all evil. For it is good to be cut off from the lusts that are in the world; because every such lust warreth against the spirit: and neither fornicators, nor effeminate, nor abusers of themselves with mankind, shall inherit the kingdom of God; nor they who do such things as are foolish and unreasonable.

13 Wherefore ye must needs abstain from all these things, being subject to the priests and deacons, as unto God and Christ.

14 The virgins admonish to walk in a spotless and pure conscience.

15 And let the elders be compassionate and merciful towards all; turning them from their errors; seeking out those that are weak; not forgetting the widows, the fatherless, and the poor; but always providing what is good both in the sight of God and man.

16 Abstaining from all wrath, respect of persons, and unrighteous judgment: and especially being free from all covetousness.

17 Not easy to believe any thing against any; not severe in judgment; knowing that we are all debtors in point of sin.

18 If therefore we pray to the Lord that he would forgive us, we ought also to forgive others; for we are all in the sight of our Lord and God; and must all stand before the judgment seat of Christ; and shall every one give an account of himself.

19 Let us therefore serve him in fear, and with all reverence as both himself hath commanded; and as the Apostles who have preached the Gospel unto us, and the prophets who have foretold the coming of our Lord have taught us.

20 Being zealous of what is good; abstaining from all offence, and from false brethren; and from those who bear the name of Christ in hypocrisy; who deceive vain men.

CHAP. III.

1 *As to faith in our Saviour Christ: his nature and sufferings, the resurrection and judgment. 3 Exhorts to prayer 5 and steadfastness in the faith, from the examples of Christ, 7 and Apostles and saints, and exhorts to carefulness in all well-doing.*

FOR whosoever does not confess that Jesus Christ is come in the flesh, he is Antichrist: and whoever does not confess his suffering upon the cross, is from the devil.

2 And whosoever perverts the oracles of the Lord to his own lusts; and says that there shall neither be any resurrection, nor judgment, he is the first-born of Satan.

3 Wherefore leaving the vanity of many, and their false doctrines; let us return to the word that was delivered to us from the beginning; Watching unto prayer; and persevering in fasting.

4 With supplication beseeching the all seeing God not to lead us into temptation; as the Lord hath said, The spirit is truly willing, but the flesh is weak.

5 Let us therefore without ceasing hold steadfastly to him who is our hope, and the earnest of our righteousness, even Jesus Christ; Who his own self bare our sins in his own body on the tree: who did no sin, neither was guile found in his mouth. But suffered all for us that we might live through him.

6 Let us therefore imitate his patience; and if we suffer for his name, let us glorify him; for this example he has given us by himself, and so have we believed.

7 Wherefore I exhort all of you that ye obey the word of righteousness, and exercise all patience; which ye have seen set forth before our eyes, not only in the blessed Ignatius, and Zozimus, and Rufus; but in others among yourselves; and in Paul himself, and the rest of the Apostles:

8 Being confident of this, that all, these have not run in vain; but in faith and righteousness, and are gone to the place that was due to them from the Lord; with whom they also suffered.

9 For they loved not this present world; but him who died, and was raised again by God for us.

10 Stand therefore in these things, and follow the example of the Lord; being firm and immutable in the faith, lovers of the brotherhood, lovers of one another: companions together in the truth, being kind and gentle towards each other, despising none.

11 When it is in your power to do good, defer it not, for charity delivered from death.

12 Be all of you subject one to another, having your conversation honest among the Gentiles; that by your

The Epistle of Polycarp to the Philippians

good works, both ye yourselves may receive praise, and the Lord may not be blasphemed through you. But wo be to him by whom the name of the Lord is blasphemed.

13 Therefore teach all men sobriety; in which do ye also exercise yourselves.

CHAP. IV.

Valens, a presbyter, having fallen into the sin of covetousness, he exhorts them against it.

I AM greatly afflicted for Valens, who was once a presbyter among you; that he should so little understand the place that was given to him in the church. Wherefore I admonish you that ye abstain from covetousness; and that ye be chaste, and true of speech.

2 Keep yourselves from all evil. For he that in these things cannot govern himself how shall he be able to prescribe them to another?

3 If a man does not keep himself from covetousness, he shall be polluted with idolatry and be judged as if he were a Gentile.

4 But who of you are ignorant of the judgment of God? Do we not know that the saints shall judge the world, as Paul teaches?

5 But I have neither perceived nor heard any thing of this kind in you, among whom the blessed Paul laboured; and who are named in the beginning of his Epistle.

6 For he glories of you in all the churches who then only knew God; for we did not then know him. Wherefore, my brethren,

I am exceedingly sorry both for him, and for his wife; to whom God grant a true repentance.

7 And be ye also moderate upon this occasion; and look not upon such as enemies, but call them back as suffering, and erring members, that ye may save your whole body: for by so doing, ye shall edify your own selves.

8 For I trust that ye are well exercised in the Holy Scriptures, and that nothing is hid from you; but at present it is not granted unto me to practice that which is written, Be angry and sin not; and again, Let not the sun go down upon your wrath.

9 Blessed be he that believeth and remembereth these things; which also I trust you do.

10 Now the God and Father of our Lord Jesus Christ; and he himself who is our everlasting high-priest, the Son of God, even Jesus Christ, build you up in faith and in truth and in all meekness and lenity; in patience and long-suffering, in forbearance and chastity.

11 And grant unto you a lot and portion among his saints; and us with you, and to all that are under the heavens, who shall believe in our Lord Jesus Christ, and in his Father who raised him from the dead.

12 Pray for all the saints: pray also for kings, and all that are in authority; and for those who persecute you, and hate you, and for the enemies of the cross; that your fruit may be manifest in all; and that ye may be perfect in Christ.

13 Ye wrote to me, both ye, and also Ignatius, that if any one went from hence into Syria, he should bring your letters with him; which also I will take care of, as soon as I shall have a convenient opportunity; either by myself, or him whom I shall send upon your account.

14 The Epistles of Ignatius which he wrote unto us, together with what others of his have come to our hands, we have sent to you, according to your order; which are subjoined to this epistle.

15 By which we may be greatly profited; for they treat of faith and patience, and of all things that pertain to edification in the Lord Jesus.

161 What you know certainly of Ignatius, and those that are with him signify to us.

17 If These things have I written unto you by Crescens, whom by this present epistle I have recommended to you, and do now again commend.

18 For he has had his conversation without blame among us; and I suppose also with you.

19 Ye will also have regard unto his sister when she shall come unto you.

20 Be ye safe in the Lord Jesus Christ; and in favour with all yours. Amen.

LETTERS OF HEROD AND PILATE

Connecting Roman History with the Death of Christ at Jerusalem.

These letters occur in a Syriac MS., of the sixth or seventh century, in the British Museum. Dr. Tischendorf states in his Apocalypses Apocryphæ (Prolegg. p. 56) that he has a copy of the same in Greek from a Paris MS., of which he says "scripture satis differt, non item argumentum." The letters are followed by a few extracts which seem to have been added by some copyist, although they are followed by the subscription to Pilate's letter. We suppose that by Justinus, we are to understand Justus of Tiberias of whom Josephus speaks as a historian of his tine. We cannot venture an opinion favorable to the genuineness of this extract, because Photius says Justus did not mention Christ. By Theodorus, we understand the Emperor Tiberius. The question and answer agree in sense with what is read in the "Anaphora," or response of Pilate.

LETTER OF HEROD TO PILATE THE GOVERNOR.

Herod to Pontius Pilate the Governor of Jerusalem: Peace.

I AM in great anxiety. I write these things unto thee, that when thou hast heard them thou mayest be grieved for me. For as my daughter Herodias, who is dear to me, was playing upon a pool of water which had ice upon it, it broke under her, and all her body went down, and her head was cut off and remained on the surface of the ice. And behold, her mother is holding her head upon her knees in her lap, and my whole house is in great sorrow. For I, when I heard of the man Jesus, wished to come to thee, that I might see him alone, and hear his word, whether it was like that of the sons of men. And it is certain that because of the many evil things which were done by me to John the Baptist, and because I mocked the Christ, behold I receive the reward of righteousness, for I have shed much blood of others' children upon the earth. Therefore the judgments of God are righteous; for every man receives according to his thought. But since thou wast worthy to see that God-man, therefore it becometh you to pray for me.

My son Azbonius also is in the agony of the hour of death.

And I too am in affliction and great trial, because I have the dropsy; and am in great distress, because I persecuted the introducer of baptism by water, which was John. Therefore, my brother, the judgments of God are righteous.

And my wife, again, through all her grief for her daughter, is become blind in her left eye, because we desired to blind the Eye of righteousness. There is no peace to the doers of evil, saith the Lord. For already great affliction cometh upon the priests and upon the writers of the law; because they delivered unto thee the Just One. For this is the consummation of the world,

that they consented that the Gentiles should become heirs. For the children of light shall be cast out, for they have not observed the things which were preached concerning the Lord, and concerning his Son. Therefore gird up thy loins, and receive righteousness, thou with thy wife remembering Jesus night and day; and the kingdom shall belong to you Gentiles, for we the (chosen) people have mocked the Righteous One.

Now if there is place for our request, O Pilate, because we were at one time in power, bury my household carefully; for it is right that we should be buried by thee, rather than by the priests, whom, after a little time, as the Scriptures say, at the coming of Jesus Christ, vengeance shall overtake.

Fare thee well, with Procla thy wife.

I send thee the earrings of my daughter and my own ring, that they may be unto thee a memorial of my decease. For already do worms begin to issue from my body, and lo, I am receiving temporal judgment, and I am afraid of the judgment to come. For in both we stand before the works of the living God; but this judgment, which is temporal, is for a time, while that to come is judgment for ever.

End of the Letter to Pilate the Governor.

LETTER OF PILATE TO HEROD.

Pilate to Herod the Tetrarch: Peace.

KNOW and see, that in the day when thou didst deliver Jesus unto me, I took pity on myself, and testified by washing my hands (that I was innocent), concerning him who rose from the grave after three days, and had performed thy pleasure in him, for thou didst desire me to be associated with thee in his crucifixion. But I now learn from the executioners and from the soldiers who watched his sepulchre that he rose from the dead. And I have especially confirmed what was told me, that he appeared bodily in Galilee, to the same form, and with the same voice, and with the same doctrine, and with the sane disciples, not having changed in anything, but preaching with boldness his resurrection, and an everlasting kingdom.

And behold, heaven and earth rejoice; and behold, Procla my wife is believing in the visions which appeared unto her, when thou sentest that I should deliver Jesus to the people of Israel, because of the ill-will they had. Now when Procla, my wife, heard that Jesus was risen, and had appeared in Galilee, she took with her Longinus the centurion and twelve soldiers, the same that had watched at the sepulchre, and went to greet the face of Christ, as if to a great spectacle, and saw him with his disciples.

Now while they were standing, and wondering, and gazing at him, he looked at them, and said to them, What is it? Do ye believe in me? Procla, know that in the covenant which God gave to the fathers, it is said that every body which had perished should live by means of my death, which ye have seen. And now, ye see that I live, whom ye crucified. And I suffered many things, till that I was laid in the sepulchre. But now, hear me, and believe in my Father—God who is in me. For I loosed the cords of death, and brake the gates of Sheol; and my coming shall be hereafter.

And when Procla my wife and the Romans heard these things, they came and told me, weeping; for they also were against him, when they devised the evils which they had done unto him. So that, I also was on the couch of my bed in affliction, and put on a garment of mourning, and took unto me fifty Romans with my wife and went into Galilee.

And when I was going in the way I testified these things; that Herod did these things by me, that he took counsel with me, and constrained me to arm my hands against him, and to judge him that judgeth all, and to scourge the Just One, Lord of the just. And when we drew nigh to him, O Herod, a great voice was heard from heaven, and dreadful thunder, and the earth trembled, and gave forth a sweet smell, like unto which was never perceived even in the temple of Jerusalem. Now while I stood in the way, our Lord saw me as he stood and talked with his disciples. But I prayed in my heart, for I knew that it was he whom ye delivered unto me, that he was Lord of created things and Creator of all. But we, when we saw him, all of us fell upon our faces before his feet. And I said with a loud voice, I have sinned, O Lord, in that I sat and judged thee, who avengest all in truth. And lo, I know that thou art God, the Son of God, and I beheld thy humanity and not thy divinity. But Herod, with the children of Israel, constrained me to do evil unto thee. Have pity, therefore, upon me, O God of Israel!

And my wife, in great anguish, said, God of heaven and of earth, God of Israel, reward me not according to the deeds of Pontius Pilate, nor according to the will of the children of Israel, nor according to the thought of the sons of the priests; but remember my husband in thy glory!

Now our Lord drew near and raised up me and my wife, and the Romans; and I looked at him and saw there were on him the scars of his cross. And he said, That which all the righteous fathers hoped to receive, and saw not—in thy time the Lord of Time, the Son of Man, the Son of the Most High, who is for ever, arose from the dead, and is glorified on high by all that he created, and established for ever and ever.

1. Justinus, one of the writers that were in the days of Augustus and Tiberius and Gaius, wrote in his third discourse: Now Mary the Galilæan, who bare the Christ that was crucified in Jerusalem, had not been with a husband. And Joseph did not abandon her; but Joseph continued in sanctity without a wife, he and his five sons by a former wife; and Mary continued without a husband.

2. Theodorus wrote to Pilate the Governor: Who was the man, against whom there was a complaint before thee, that he was crucified by the men of Palestine? If the many demanded this righteously, why didst thou not consent to their righteousness? And if they demanded this unrighteously, how didst thou transgress the law and command what was far from righteousness?

Pilate sent to him:—Because he wrought signs I did not wish to crucify him: and since his accusers said, He calleth himself a king, I crucified him.

3. Josephus saith: Agrippa, the king, was clothed in a robe woven with silver, and saw the spectacle in the theatre of Cæsarea. When the people saw that his raiment flashed, they said to him, Hitherto we feared thee as a man: henceforth thou art exalted above the nature of mortals. And he saw an angel standing over him, and he smote him as unto death. 1

End of the Letter of Pilate to Herod.

THE EPISTLE OF PONTIUS PILATE,

Which he Wrote to the Roman Emperor Concerning our Lord Jesus Christ.

Pontius Pilate to Tiberius Cæsar—Greeting:

UPON Jesus Christ, whom I fully made known to thee in my last, a bitter punishment hath at length been inflicted by the will of the people, although I was unwilling and apprehensive. In good truth, no age ever had or will have a man so good and strict. But the people made a wonderful effort, and all their scribes, chiefs and elders agreed to crucify this ambassador of truth, their own prophets, like the Sibyls with us, advising the contrary; and when he was hanged supernatural signs appeared, and in the judgment of philosophers menaced the whole world with ruin. His disciples flourish, not belying their master by their behavior and continence of life; nay, in his name they are most beneficent. 1 Had I not feared a sedition might arise among the people, who were almost furious, perhaps this man would have yet been living with us. Although, being rather compelled by fidelity to thy dignity, than led by my own inclination, I did not strive with all my might to prevent the sale and suffering of righteous blood, guiltless of every accusation, unjustly, indeed, through the maliciousness of men, and yet, as the Scriptures interpret, to their own destruction.

Farewell. The 5th of the Calends of April.

THE REPORT OF PILATE THE GOVERNOR,

Concerning our Lord Jesus Christ; which was Sent to Augustus Cæsar, in Rome.

IN those days, when our Lord Jesus Christ was crucified under Pontius Pilate, the governor of Palestine and Phoenicia, the things here recorded came to pass in Jerusalem, and were done by the Jews against the Lord. Pilate therefore sent the same to Cæsar in Rome, along with his private report, writing thus:

To the most potent, august, divine and awful Augustus Cæsar, Pilate, the administrator of the Eastern Province: I have received information, most excellent one, in consequence of which I am seized with fear and trembling. For in this province which I administer, one of whose cities is called Jerusalem, the whole multitude of Jews delivered unto me a certain man called Jesus, and brought many accusations against him, which they were unable to establish by consistent evidence. But they charged him with one heresy in particular, namely, That Jesus said the Sabbath was not a rest, nor to be observed by them. For he performed many cures on that day, and made the blind see, and the lame walk, raised the dead, cleansed lepers, healed the paralytic who were wholly unable to move their body or brace their nerves, but could only speak and discourse, and he gave them power to walk and run, removing their infirmity by his word alone. There is another very mighty deed which is strange to the gods we have: he raised up a man who had been four days dead, summoning him by his word alone, when the dead man had begun to decay, and his body was corrupted by the worms which had been bred, and had the stench of a dog; but, seeing him lying in the tomb he commanded him to run, nor did the dead man at all delay, but as a bridegroom out of his chamber, so did he go forth from his tomb, filled with abundant perfume. Moreover, even such as were strangers, and clearly demoniacs, who had their dwelling in deserts, and devoured their own flesh, and wandered about like cattle and creeping things, he turned into inhabiters of cities, and by a word rendered them rational, and prepared them to become wise and powerful, and illustrious, taking their food with all the enemies of the unclean spirits which were destructive in them, and which he cast into the depth of the sea.

And, again, there was another who had a withered hand, and not only the hand but rather the half of the body of the man was like a stone, and he had neither the shape of a man nor the symmetry of a body: even him He healed with a word and rendered whole. And a woman also, who had an issue of blood for a long time, and whose veins and arteries were exhausted, and who did not bear a human body, being like one dead, and daily speechless, so that all the physicians of the district were unable to cure her, for there remained unto her not a hope of life; but as Jesus passed by she mysteriously received strength by his shadow falling on her, from behind she touched the hem of his garment, and immediately, in that very hour, strength filled her exhausted limbs, and as if she had never suffered anything, she began to run along towards Capernaum, her own city, so that she reached it in a six days' journey.

And I have made known these things which I have recently been informed of, and which Jesus did on the Sabbath. And he did other miracles greater than these, so that I have observed greater works of wonder done by him than by the gods whom we worship.

But Herod and Archelaus and Philip, Annas and Caiaphas, with all the people, delivered him to me, making a great tumult against me in order that I might try him. Therefore, I commanded him to be crucified, when I had first scourged him, though I found no cause in him for evil accusations or dealings.

Now when he was crucified, there was darkness over all the world, and the sun was obscured for half a day, and the stars appeared, but no lustre was seen in them; and the moon lost its brightness, as though tinged with blood; and the world of the departed was swallowed up; so that the very sanctuary of the temple, as they call it, did not appear to the Jews themselves at their fall, but they perceived a chasm in the earth, and the rolling of successive thunders. And amid this terror the dead appeared rising again, as the Jews themselves bore witness, and said that it was Abraham, and Isaac, and Jacob, and the twelve patriarchs, and Moses, and Job, who had died before, as they say, some three thousand five hundred years. And there were very many whom I myself saw appearing in the body, and they made lamentation over the Jews, because of the transgression which was committed by them, and because of the destruction of the Jews and of their law.

And the terror of the earthquake continued from the sixth hour of the preparation until the ninth hour; and when it was evening on the first day of the week, there came a sound from heaven, and the heaven became seven times more luminous than on all other days. And at the third hour of the night the sun appeared more luminous than it had ever shone, lighting up the whole hemisphere. And as lightning-flashes suddenly come forth in a storm, so there were seen men, lofty in stature, and surpassing in glory, a countless host, crying out, and their voice was heard as that of exceedingly loud thunder, Jesus that was crucified is risen again: come up from Hades ye that were enslaved in the subterraneous recesses of Hades. And the chasm in the earth was as if it had no bottom; but it was so that the very foundations of the earth appeared, with those that shouted in heaven, and walked in the body among the dead that were raised. And He that raised up all the dead and bound Hades said, Say to my disciples He goeth before you into Galilee, there shall ye see Him.

And all that night the light ceased not shining. And many of the Jews died in the chasm of the earth, being swallowed up, so that on the morrow most of those who had been against Jesus were not to be found. Others saw the apparition of men rising again whom none of us had ever seen. One synagogue of the Jews was alone left in Jerusalem itself, for they all disappeared in that ruin. Therefore being astounded by that terror, and being possessed with the most dreadful trembling, I have written what I saw at that time and sent it to thine excellency; and I have inserted what was done against Jesus by the Jews, and sent it to thy divinity, my lord.

THE REPORT OF PONTIUS PILATE,

Governor of Judea;

Which was sent to Tiberius Cæsar in Rome.

To the most potent, august, dreadful, and divine Augustus, Pontius Pilate, administrator of the Eastern Province.

I HAVE undertaken to communicate to thy goodness by this my writing, though possessed with much fear and trembling, most excellent king, the present state of affairs, as the result hath shown. For as I administered this province, my lord, according to the command of thy serenity, which is one of the eastern cities called Jerusalem, wherein the temple of the nation of the Jews is erected, all the multitude of the Jews, being assembled, delivered up to me a certain man called Jesus, bringing many and endless accusations against him; but they could not convict him in anything. But they had one heresy against him, that he said the sabbath was not their proper rest.

Now that man wrought many cures and good works: he caused the blind to see, he cleansed lepers, he raised the dead, he healed paralytics, who could not move at all, but had only voice, and all their bones in their places; and he gave them strength to walk and run, enjoining it by his word alone. And he did another yet more mighty work, which had been strange even among our gods, he raised from the dead one Lazarus, who had been dead four days, commanding by a word alone that the dead man should be raised, when his body was already corrupted by worms which bred in his wounds. And he commanded the fetid body, which lay in the grave, to run, and as bridegroom from his chamber so he went forth from his grave, full of sweet perfume. And some that were grievously afflicted by demons, and had their dwellings in desert places, and devoured the flesh of their own limbs, and went up and down among creeping things and wild beasts, he caused to dwell in cities in their own houses, and by a word made them reasonable, and caused to become wise and honorable those that were vexed by unclean spirits, and the demons that were in them he sent out into a herd of swine into the sea and drowned them. Again, another who had a withered hand, and lived in suffering, and had not even the half of his body sound, he made whole by a word alone. And a woman who had an issue of blood for a long time, so that because of the discharge all the joints of her bones were seen and shone through like glass, for all the physicians had dismissed her without hope, and had not cleansed her, for there was in her no hope of health at all; but once, as Jesus was passing by she touched from behind the hem of his garments, and in that very hour the strength of her body was restored, and she was made whole, as if she had no affliction, and began to run fast towards her own city of Paneas. And these things happened thus: but the Jews reported that Jesus did these things on the sabbath. And I saw that greater marvels had been wrought by him than by the gods whom we worship. Him then Herod and Archelaus and Philip, and Annas and Caiaphas, with all the people, delivered up to me, to put him on his trial. And because many raised a tumult against me, I commanded that he should be crucified.

Now when he was crucified darkness came over all the world; the sun was altogether hidden, and the sky appeared dark while it was yet day, so that the stars were seen, though still they had their lustre obscured, wherefore, I suppose your excellency is not unaware that in all the world they lighted their lamps from the sixth hour until evening. And the moon, which was like blood, did not shine all night long, although it was at the full, and the stars and Orion made lamentation over the Jews, because of the transgression committed by them. And on the first day of the week, about the third hour of the night, the sun appeared as it never shone before, and the whole heaven became bright. And as lightnings come in a storm, so certain men of lofty stature, in beautiful array, and of indescribable glory, appeared in the air, and a countless host of angels, crying out and saying, Glory to God in the highest, and on earth peace, good will

among men: Come up from Hades, ye who are in bondage in the depths of Hades. And at their voice all the mountains and hills were moved, and the rocks were rent, and great chasms were made in the earth, so that the very places of the abyss were visible.

And amid the terror dead men were seen rising again, so that the Jews who saw it said, We beheld Abraham and Isaac, and Jacob, and the twelve patriarchs, who died some two thousand five hundred years before, and we beheld Noah clearly in the body. And all the multitude walked about and sang hymns to God with a loud voice, saying, The Lord our God, who hath risen from the dead, hath made alive all the dead, and Hades he hath spoiled and slain.

Therefore, my lord king, all that night the light ceased not. But many of the Jews died, and were sunk and swallowed up in the chasms that night, so that not even their bodies were to be seen. Now I mean, that those of the Jews suffered who spake against Jesus. And but one synagogue remained in Jerusalem, for all the synagogues which had been against Jesus were overwhelmed. Through that terror, therefore, being amazed and being seized with great trembling, in that very hour, I ordered what had been done by them all to be written, and I have sent it to thy mightiness.

THE TRIAL AND CONDEMNATION OF PILATE.

NOW when the letters came to the city of the Romans, and were read to Cæsar with no few standing there, they were all terrified, because, through the transgression of Pilate, the darkness and the earthquake had happened to all the world. And Cæsar, being filled with anger, sent soldiers and commanded that Pilate should be brought as a prisoner.

And when he was brought to the city of the Romans, and Cæsar heard that he was come, he sat in the temple of the gods, above all the senate, and with all the army, and with all the multitude of his power, and commanded that Pilate should stand in the entrance. And Cæsar said to him, Most impious one, when thou sawest so great signs done by that man, why didst thou dare to do thus? By daring to do an evil deed thou hast ruined all the world.

And Pilate said, King and Autocrat, I am not guilty of these things, but it is the multitude of the Jews who are precipitate and guilty. And Cæsar said, And who are they? Pilate saith, Herod, Archelaus, Philip, Annas and Caiaphas, and all the multitude of the Jews. Cæsar saith, For what cause didst thou execute their purpose? And Pilate said, Their nation is seditious and insubordinate, and not submissive to thy power. And Cæsar said, When they delivered him to thee thou oughtest to have made him secure and sent him to me, and not consented to them to crucify such a man, who was just and wrought such great and good miracles, as thou saidst in thy report. For by such miracles Jesus was manifested to be the Christ, the King of the Jews.

And when Cæsar said this and himself named the name of Christ, all the multitude of the gods fell down together, and became like dust where Cæsar sat with the senate. And all the people that stood near Cæsar were filled with trembling because of the utterance of the word and the fall of their gods, and being seized with fear they all went away, every man to his house, wondering at what had happened. And Cæsar commanded Pilate to be safely kept, that he might know the truth about Jesus.

And on the morrow when Cæsar sat in the capitol with all the senate, he undertook to question Pilate again. And Cæsar said, Say the truth, most impious one, for through thy impious deed which thou didst commit against Jesus, even here the doing of thy evil works were manifested, in that the gods were brought to ruin. Say then, who is he that was crucified, for his name hath destroyed all the gods? Pilate said, And verily his records are true; for even I myself was convinced by his works that he was greater than all the gods whom we venerate. And Cæsar said, For what cause then didst thou perpetrate against him such daring and doing, not being ignorant of him, or assuredly designing some mischief to my government? And Pilate said, I did it because of the transgression and sedition of the lawless and ungodly Jews.

And Cæsar was filled with anger, and held a council with all his senate and officers, and ordered a decree to be written against the Jews thus:—

To Licianus who holdeth the first place in the East Country. Greeting:

I have been informed of the audacity perpetrated very recently by the Jews inhabiting Jerusalem and the cities round about, and their lawless doing, how they compelled Pilate to crucify a certain god called Jesus, through which great transgression of theirs the world was darkened and drawn into ruin. Determine therefore, with a body of soldiers, to go to them there at once and proclaim their subjection to bondage by this decree. By obeying and proceeding against them, and scattering them abroad in all nations, enslave them, and by driving their nation from all Judea as soon as possible show, wherever this hath not yet appeared, that they are full of evil.

And when this decree came into the East Country, Licianus obeyed, through fear of the decree, and laid waste all the nation of the Jews, and caused those that were left in Judea, to go into slavery with them that were scattered among the Gentiles, that it might be known by Cæsar that these things had been done by Licianus against the Jews in the East Country, and to please him. And again Cæsar resolved to have Pilate questioned, and commanded a captain, Albius by name, to cut off Pilate's head, saying, As he laid hands upon the just man, that is called Christ, he also shall fall in like manner, and find no deliverance.

And when Pilate came to the place he prayed in silence, saying, O Lord, destroy not me with the wicked Hebrews, for I should not have laid hands upon thee, but for the nation of lawless Jews, because they provoked sedition against mss but thou knowest that I did it in ignorance. Destroy me not, therefore, for this my sin, nor be mindful of the evil that is in me, O Lord, and in thy servant Procla who standeth with me in this the hour of my death, whom thou taughtest to prophecy that thou must be nailed to the cross. Do not punish her too in my sin, but forgive us, and number us in the

portion of thy just ones. And behold, when Pilate had finished his prayer, there came a voice from heaven, saying, All generations and the families of the Gentiles shall call thee blessed, because under thee were fulfilled all these things that were spoken by the prophets concerning me; and thou thyself must appear as my witness at my second coming, when I shall judge the twelve tribes of Israel, and them that have not confessed my name. And the Prefect cut off the head of Pilate, and behold an angel of the Lord received it. And when his wife Procla saw the angel coming and receiving his head, she also, being filled with joy, forthwith gave up the ghost, and was buried with her husband.

THE DEATH OF PILATE,

WHO CONDEMNED JESUS.

NOW whereas Tiberius Cæsar emperor of the Romans was suffering from a grievous sickness, and hearing that there was at Jerusalem a certain physician, Jesus by name, who healed all diseases by his word alone; not knowing that the Jews and Pilate had put him to death, he thus bade one of his attendants, Volusianus by name, saying, Go as quickly as thou canst across the sea, and tell Pilate, my servant and friend, to send me this physician to restore me to my original health. And Volusianus, having heard the order of the emperor, immediately departed, and came to Pilate, as it was commanded him. And he told the same Pilate what had been committed to him by Tiberius Cæsar, saying, Tiberius Cæsar, emperor of the Romans, thy Lord, having heard that in this city there is a physician who healeth diseases by his word alone, earnestly entreateth thee to send him to him to heal his disease. And Pilate was greatly terrified on hearing this, knowing that through envy he had caused him to be slain. Pilate answered the messenger, saying thus, This man was a malefactor, and a man who drew after himself all the people; so, after counsel taken of the wise men of the city, I caused him to be crucified. And as the messenger returned to his lodgings he met a certain woman named Veronica, who had been acquainted with Jesus, and he said, O woman, there was a certain physician in this city, who healed the sick by his word alone, why have the Jews slain him? And she began to weep, saying, Ah, me, my lord, it was my God and my Lord whom Pilate through envy delivered up, condemned, and commanded to be crucified. Then he, grieving greatly, said, I am exceedingly sorry that I cannot fulfil that for which my lord hath sent me.

Veronica said to him, When my Lord went about preaching, and I was very unwillingly deprived of his presence, I desired to have his picture painted for me, that while I was deprived of his presence, at least the figure of his likeness might give me consolation. And when I was taking the canvas to the painter to be painted, my Lord met me and asked whither I was going. And when I had made known to him the cause of my journey, He asked me for the canvas, and gave it back to me printed with the likeness of his venerable face. Therefore, if thy lord will devoutly look upon the sight of this, he will straightway enjoy the benefit of health.

Is a likeness of this kind to be procured with gold or silver? he asked. No, said she, but with a pious sentiment of devotion. Therefore, I will go with thee, and carry the likeness to Cæsar to look upon, and will return.

So Volusianus came with Veronica to Rome, and said to Tiberius the emperor, Jesus, whom thou hast long desired, Pilate and the Jews have surrendered to an unjust death, and through envy fastened to the wood of the cross. Therefore, a certain matron hath come with me bringing the likeness of the same Jesus, and if thou wilt devoutly gaze upon it, thou wilt presently obtain the benefit of thy health. So Cæsar caused the way to be spread with cloths of silk, and ordered the portrait to be presented to him; and as soon as he had looked upon it he regained his original health.

Then Pontius Pilate was apprehended by command of Cæsar and brought to Rome. Cæsar, hearing that Pilate had come to Rome, was filled with exceeding wrath against him, and caused him to be brought to him. Now Pilate brought with him the seamless coat of Jesus, and wore it when before the emperor. As soon as the emperor saw him he laid aside all his wrath, and forthwith rose to him, and was unable to speak harshly to him in anything: and he who in his absence seemed so terrible and fierce now in his presence is found comparatively gentle.

And when he had dismissed him, he soon became terribly inflamed against him, declaring himself wretched, because he had not expressed to him the anger of his bosom. And immediately he had him recalled, swearing and protesting that he was a child of death, and unfitted to live upon earth. And when he saw him he instantly greeted him, and laid aside all the fury of his mind.

All were astonished, and he was astonished himself, that he was so enraged against Pilate while absent, and could say nothing to him sharply while he was present. At length, by Divine suggestion, or perhaps by the persuasion of some Christian, he had him stripped of the coat, and soon resumed against him his original fury of mind. And when the emperor was wondering very much about this, they told him it had been the coat of the Lord Jesus. Then the emperor commanded him to be kept in prison till he should take counsel with the wise men what ought to be done with him. And after a few days sentence was given against Pilate that he should be condemned to the most ignominious death. When Pilate heard this he slew himself with his own dagger, and by such a death put an end to his life.

When Pilate's death was made known Cæsar said, Truly he has died a most ignominious death, whose own hand has not spared him. He was therefore fastened to a great block of stone and sunk in the river Tiber. But wicked and unclean spirits, rejoicing in his wicked and unclean body, all moved about in the water, and caused in the air dreadful lightning and tempests, thunder and hail, so that all were seized with horrible fear. On which account the Romans dragged him out of the river Tiber, bore him away in derision to Vienne, and sunk him in the river Rhone. For Vienne means, as it were, Way of Gehenna, because it was then a place of cursing. And evil spirits were there and did the same things.

Those men, therefore, not enduring to be so harassed by demons, removed the vessel of cursing from them and sent it to be buried in the territory of Losania. But when they were troubled exceedingly by the aforesaid vexations, they put it away from them and sunk it in a certain pool surrounded by mountains, where even yet, according to the account of some, sundry diabolical contrivances are said to issue forth.

THE TESTAMENT OF SOLOMON

1. Testament of Solomon, son of David, who was king in Jerusalem, and mastered and controlled all spirits of the air, on the earth and under the earth. By means of them also he wrought all the transcendent works of the Temple. Telling also of the authorities they wield against men, and by what angels these demons are brought to naught.

Of the sage Solomon.

Blessed art thou, Lord God, who didst give to Solomon such authority. Glory to thee and might unto the ages. Amen.

2. And behold, when the Temple of the city of Jerusalem was being builded, and the artificers were working thereat, *Ornias* the demon came among them toward sunset; and he took away the half of the pay of the chief-deviser's little boy, as well as half his food. He also continued to suck the thumb of his right hand every day. And the child grew thin although he was very much loved by the king.

3. So King Solomon called the boy one day, and questioned him, saying: "Do I not love thee more than all the artisans who are working in the Temple of God? Do I not give thee double wages and a double supply of food? How is it that day by day and hour by hour thou growest thinner?"

4. But the child said to the king: "I pray thee, O king. Listen to what has befallen all that thy child hath. After we are all released from our work on the Temple of God, after sunset, when I lie down to rest, one of the evil demons comes and takes away from me the half of my pay and half of my food. Then he also takes hold of my right hand and sucks my thumb. And lo, my soul is oppressed, and so my body waxes thinner every day."

5. Now when I Solomon heard this, I entered the Temple of God, and prayed with all my soul, night and day, that the demon might be delivered into my hands, and that I might gain authority over him. And it came about through my prayer that grace was given to me from the Lord *Sabaôth* by Michael his archangel. [He brought me] a little ring, having a seal consisting of an engraved stone, and said to me: "Take, O Solomon, king, son of David, the gift which the Lord God has sent thee, the highest Sabaôth. With it thou shalt lock up all the demons of the earth, male and female; and with their help thou shalt build up Jerusalem. [But] thou [must] wear this seal of God. And this engraving of the seal of the ring sent thee is a *Pentalpha*."

6. And I Solomon was overjoyed, and praised and glorified the God of heaven and earth. And on the morrow I called the boy, and gave him the ring, and said to him: "Take this, and at the hour in which the demon shall come unto thee, throw this ring at the chest of the demon, and say to him: 'In the name of God, King Solomon calls thee hither.' And then do thou come running to me, without having any misgivings or fear in respect of aught thou mayest hear on the part of the demon."

7. So the child took the ring, and went off; and behold, at the customary hour *Ornias*, the fierce demon, came like a burning fire to take the pay from the child. But the child, according to the instructions received from the king, threw the ring at the chest of the demon, and said: "King Solomon calls thee hither." And then he went off at a run to the king. But the demon cried out aloud, saying: "Child, why hast thou done this to me? Take the ring off me, and I will render to thee the gold of the earth. Only take this off me, and forbear to lead me away to Solomon."

8. But the child said to the demon: "As the Lord God of Israel liveth, I will not brook thee. So come hither." And the child came at a run, rejoicing, to the king, and said: "I have brought the demon, O king, as thou didst command me, O my master. And behold, he stands before the gates of the court of thy palace, crying out, and supplicating with a loud voice; offering me the silver and gold of the earth if I will only not bring him unto thee."

9. And when Solomon heard this, he rose up from his throne, and went outside into the vestibule of the court of his palace; and there he saw the demon, shuddering and trembling. And he said to him: "Who art thou?" And the demon answered: "I am called *Ornias*."

10. And Solomon said to him: "Tell me, O demon, to what zodiacal sign thou art subject." And he answered: "To the Water-pourer. And those who are consumed with desire for noble virgins upon earth . . . ., these I strangle. But in case there is no disposition to sleep, I am changed into three forms. Whenever men come to be enamoured of women, I metamorphose myself into a comely female; and I take hold of the men in their sleep, and play with them. And after a while I again take to my wings, and hie me to heavenly regions. I also appear as a lion, and I am commanded by all the demons. I am offspring of the archangel *Uriel*, the power of God."

11. I Solomon, having heard the name of the archangel, prayed and glorified God, the Lord of heaven and earth. And I sealed the demon and set him to work at stone-cutting, so that he might cut the stones in the Temple, which, lying along the shore, had been brought by the Sea of Arabia. But he, fearful of the iron, continued and said to me: "I pray thee, King Solomon, let me go free; and I will bring you all the demons." And as he was not willing to be subject to me, I prayed the archangel Uriel to come and succour me; and I forthwith beheld the archangel Uriel coming down to me from the heavens.

12. And the angel bade the whales of the sea come out of the abyss. And he cast his destiny upon the ground, and that [destiny] made subject [to him] the great demon. And he commanded the great demon and bold, *Ornias*, to cut stones at the Temple. And accordingly I Solomon glorified the God of heaven and Maker of the earth. And he bade *Ornias* come with his destiny, and I gave him the seal, saying: "Away with thee, and bring me hither the prince of all the demons."

13. So *Ornias* took the finger-ring, and went off to *Beelzeboul*, who has kingship over the demons. He said to him: "Hither! Solomon calls thee." But *Beelzeboul*, having heard, said to him: "Tell me, who is this Solomon of whom thou speakest to me?" Then *Ornias* threw the ring at the chest of *Beelzeboul*, saying: "Solomon the king calls thee." But *Beelzeboul* cried aloud with a mighty voice,

and shot out a great burning flame of fire; and he arose, and followed *Ornias*, and came to Solomon.

14. And when I saw the prince of demons, I glorified the Lord God, Maker of heaven and earth, and I said: "Blessed art thou, Lord God Almighty, who hast given to Solomon thy servant wisdom, the assessor of the wise, and hast subjected unto me all the power of the devil."

15. And I questioned him, and said: "Who art thou?" The demon replied: "I am *Beelzeboul*, the exarch of the demons. And all the demons have their chief seats close to me. And I it is who make manifest the apparition of each demon." And he promised to bring to me in bonds all the unclean spirits. And I again glorified the God of heaven and earth, as I do always give thanks to him.

16. I then asked of the demon if there were females among them. And when he told me that there were, I said that I desired to see them. So *Beelzeboul* went off at high speed, and brought unto me *Onoskelis*, that had a very pretty shape, and the skin of a fair-hued woman; and she tossed her head.

17. And when she was come, I said to her: "Tell me, who art thou?" But she said to me: "I am called *Onoskelis*, a spirit wrought …, lurking upon the earth. There is a golden cave where I lie. But I have a place that ever shifts. At one time I strangle men with a noose; at another, I creep up from the nature to the arms. But my most frequent dwelling-places are the precipices, caves, ravines. Oftentimes, however, do I consort with men in the semblance of a woman, and above all with those of a dark skin. For they share my star with me; since they it is who privily or openly worship my star, without knowing that they harm themselves, and but whet my appetite for further mischief. For they wish to provide money by means of memory, but I supply a little to those who worship me fairly."

18. And I Solomon questioned her about her birth, and she replied: "I was born of a voice untimely, the so-called echo of a man's ordure dropped in a wood."

19. And I said to her: "Under what star dost thou pass?" And she answered me: "Under the star of the full moon, for the reason that the moon travels over most things." Then I said to her: "And what angel is it that frustrates thee?" And she said to me: "He that in thee is reigning." And I thought that she mocked me, and bade a soldier strike her. But she cried aloud, and said: "I am [subjected] to thee, O king, by the wisdom of God given to thee, and by the angel *Joel*."

20. So I commanded her to spin the hemp for the ropes used in the building of the house of God; and accordingly, when I had sealed and bound her, she was so overcome and brought to naught as to stand night and day spinning the hemp.

21. And I at once bade another demon to be led unto me; and instantly there approached me the demon *Asmodeus*, bound, and I asked him: "Who art thou?" But he shot on me a glance of anger and rage, and said: "And who art thou?" And I said to him: "Thus punished as thou art, answerest thou me?" But he, with rage, said to me: "But how shall I answer thee, for thou art a son of man; whereas I was born an angel's seed by a daughter of man, so that no word of our heavenly kind addressed to the earthborn can be overweening. Wherefore also my star is bright in heaven, and men call

it, some the *Wain*, and some the dragon's-child. I keep near unto this star. So ask me not many things; for thy kingdom also after a little time is to be disrupted, and thy glory is but for a season. And short will be thy tyranny over us; and then we shall again have free range over mankind, so as that they shall revere us as if we were gods, not knowing, men that they are, the names of the angels set over us."

22. And I Solomon, on hearing this, bound him more carefully, and ordered him to be flogged with thongs of ox-hide, and to tell me humbly what was his name and what his business. And he answered me thus: "I am called *Asmodeus* among mortals, and my business is to plot against the newly wedded, so that they may not know one another. And I sever them utterly by many calamities, and I waste away the beauty of virgin women, and estrange their hearts."

23. And I said to him: "Is this thy only business?" And he answered me: "I transport men into fits of madness and desire, when they have wives of their own, so that they leave them, and go off by night and day to others that belong to other men; with the result that they commit sin, and fall into murderous deeds."

24. And I adjured him by the name of the Lord *Sabaóth*, saying: "Fear God, *Asmodeus*, and tell me by what angel thou art frustrated." But he said: "By *Raphael*, the archangel that stands before the throne of God. But the liver and gall of a fish put me to flight, when smoked over ashes of the tamarisk." I again asked him, and said: "Hide not aught from me. For I am Solomon, son of David, King of Israel. Tell me the name of the fish which thou reverest." And he answered: "It is the *Glanos* by name, and is found in the rivers of Assyria; wherefore it is that I roam about in those parts."

25. And I said to him: "Hast thou nothing else about thee, *Asmodeus*?" And he answered: "The power of God knoweth, which hath bound me with the indissoluble bonds of yonder one's seal, that whatever I have told thee is true. I pray thee, King Solomon, condemn me not to [go into] water." But I smiled, and said to him: "As the Lord God of my fathers liveth, I will lay iron on thee to wear. But thou shalt also make the clay for the entire construction of the Temple, treading it down with thy feet." And I ordered them to give him ten water-jars to carry water in. And the demon groaned terribly, and did the work I ordered him to do. And this I did, because that fierce demon *Asmodeus* knew even the future. And I Solomon glorified God, who gave wisdom to me, Solomon his servant. And the liver of the fish and its gall I hung on the spike of a reed, and burned it over *Asmodeus*, because of his being so strong, and his unbearable malice was thus frustrated.

26. And I summoned again to stand before me *Beelzeboul*, the prince of demons, and I sat him down on a raised seat of honour, and said to him: "Why art thou alone, prince of the demons?" And he said to me: "Because I alone am left of the angels of heaven that came down. For I was first angel in the first heaven, being entitled *Beelzeboul*. And now I control all those who are bound in *Tartarus*. But I too have a child, and he haunts the Red Sea. And on any suitable occasion he comes up to me again, being subject to me; and reveals to me what he has done, and I support him.

27. I Solomon said unto him: "*Beelzeboul*, what is thy employment?" And he answered me: "I destroy kings. I ally myself with foreign tyrants. And my own demons I set on to men, in order that the latter may believe in them and be lost. And the chosen servants of God, priests and faithful men, I excite unto desires for wicked sins, and evil heresies, and lawless deeds; and they obey me, and I bear them on to destruction. And I inspire men with envy, and [desire for] murder, and for wars and sodomy, and other evil things. And I will destroy the world."

28. So I said to him: "Bring to me thy child, who is, as thou sayest, in the Red Sea." But he said to me: "I will not bring him to thee. But there shall come to me another demon, called *Ephippas*. Him will I bind, and he will bring him up from the deep unto me." And I said to him: "How comes thy son to be in the depth of the sea, and what is his name?" And he answered me: "Ask me not, for thou canst not learn from me. However, he will come to thee by my command, and will tell thee openly."

29. I said to him: "Tell me by what angel thou art frustrated." And he answered: "By the holy and precious name of the Almighty God, called by the Hebrews by a row of numbers, of which the sum is 644, and among the Greeks it is *Emmanue1*. And if one of the Romans adjure me by the great name of the power *Eleêth*, I disappear at once."

30. I Solomon was astounded when I heard this; and I ordered him to saw up Theban marbles. And when he began to saw the marbles, the other demons cried out with a loud voice, howling because of their king *Beelzeboul*.

31. But I Solomon questioned him, saying: "If thou wouldst gain a respite, discourse to me about the things in heaven." And *Beelzeboul* said: "Hear, O king, if thou burn gum, and incense, and bulbs of the sea, with nard and saffron, and light seven lamps in an earthquake, thou wilt firmly fix thy house. And if, being pure, thou light them at dawn in the sun alight, then wilt thou see the heavenly dragons, how they wind themselves along and drag the chariot of the sun."

32. And I Solomon, having heard this, rebuked him, and said: "Silence for this present, and continue to saw the marbles as I commanded thee." And I Solomon praised God, and commanded another demon to present himself to me. And one came before me who carried his face high up in the air, but the rest of the spirit curled away like a snail. And it broke through the few soldiers, and raised also a terrible dust on the ground, and carried it upwards; and then again hurled it back to frighten us, and asked what questions I could ask as a rule. And I stood up, and spat on the ground in that spot, and sealed with the ring of God. And forthwith the dust-wind stopped. Then I asked him, saying: "Who art thou, wind?" Then he once more shook up a dust, and answered me: "What wouldst thou have, King Solomon?" I answered him: "Tell me what thou art called, and I would fain ask thee a question. But so far I give thanks to God who has made me wise to answer their evil plots."

33. But [the demon] answered me: "I am the spirit of the ashes (*Tephras*)." And I said to him: "What is thy pursuit?" And he said: "I bring darkness on men, and set

fire to fields; and I bring homesteads to naught. But most busy am I in summer. However, when I get an opportunity, I creep into corners of the wall, by night and day. For I am offspring of the great one, and nothing less." Accordingly I said to him: "Under what star dost thou lie?" And he answered: "In the very tip of the moon's horn, when it is found in the south. There is my star. For I have been bidden to restrain the convulsions of the hemitertian fever; and this is why many men pray to the hemitertian fever, using these three names: *Bultala*, *Thallal*, Melchal. And I heal them." And I said to him: "I am Solomon; when therefore thou wouldst do harm, by whose aid dost thou do it?" But he said to me: " By the angel's, by whom also the third day's fever is lulled to rest." So I questioned him, and said: " And by what name'?" And he answered: "That of the archangel Azael." And I summoned the archangel Azael, and set a seal on the demon, and commanded him to seize great stones, and toss them up to the workmen on the higher parts of the Temple. And, being compelled, the demon began to do what he was bidden to do.

34. And I glorified God afresh who gave me this authority, and ordered another demon to come before me. And there came seven spirits ^ females, bound and woven together, fair in appearance and comely. And I Solomon, seeing them, questioned them and said: "Who are ye?" But they, with one accord, said with one voice': "We are of the thirty-three elements of the cosmic ruler of the darkness*." And the first said: "I am Deception." The second: "I am Strife." The third: " I am Klothod, which is battle." The fourth: "I am Jealousy." The fifth: "I am Power." The sixth: "I am Error." The seventh: " I am the worst of all, and our stars are in heaven. Seven stars humble in sheen, and all together. And we are called as it were goddesses. We change our place all together, and together we live, sometimes in Lydia, sometimes in Olympus, sometimes in a great mountain."

35. So I Solomon questioned them one by one, beginning with the fii-st, and going down to the seventh. The first said: "I am Deception, I deceive and weave snares here and there. I whet and excite heresies. But I have an angel who frustrates me, LamechalaV

36. Likewise also the second said: " I am Strife, strife of strifes. I bring timbers, stones, hangers, my weapons on the spot. But I have an angel who frustrates me, Baruchiachel."

37. Likewise also the third said: " I am called Kloihod S which is battle, and I cause the well-behaved to scatter and fall foul one of the other. And why do I say so much? I have an angel that frustrates me, Marmarath."

38. Likewise also the fourth said: "I cause men to forget their sobriety and moderation. I part them and split them into parties; for Strife follows me hand in hand. I rend the husband from the sharer of his bed, and children from parents, and brothers from sisters. But why tell so much to my despite? I have an angel that frustrates me, the great Balthial."

39. Likewise also the fifth said: " I am Power. By power I raise up tyrants and tear down kings. To all rebels I furnish power. I have an angel that frustrates me, Asteradth."

40. Likewise also the sixth said: " I am Error King Solomon. And I will make thee to err, as I have before

made thee to err, when I caused thee to slay thy own brother '. I will lead you into error, so as to pry into graves *; and I teach them that dig, and I lead errant souls away from all piety, and many other evil traits are mine. But I have an angel that frustrates me, Uriel."

41. Likewise also the seventh said: "I am the worst, and I make thee worse off than thou wast; because I will impose the bonds of Artemis °. But the locust ° will set me free, for by means thereof is it fated that thou shalt achieve my desire For if one were wise, he would not turn his steps toward me."

42. So I Solomon, having heard and wondered, sealed them with my ring; and since they were so considerable, I bade them dig the foundations of the Temple of God. For the length of it was 250 cubits. And I bade them be industrious, and with one murmur of joint protest they began to perform the tasks enjoined.

43. But I Solomon glorified the Lord, and bade another demon come before me. And there was brought to me a demon having all the limbs of a man, but without a head. And I, seeing him, said to him: " Tell me, who art thou? " And he answered: " I am a demon." So I said to him: " Which? " And he answered me: " I am called Envy. For I delight to devour heads, being desirous to secure for myself a head; but I do not eat enough, but am anxious to have such a head as thou hast."

44. I Solomon, on hearing this, sealed him, stretching out my hand against his chest. Whereon the demon leapt up, and threw himself down, and gave a groan, saying: " Woe is me! where am I come to? O traitor Ornias, I cannot see! " So I said to him: " I am Solomon. Tell me then how thou dost manage to see." And he answered me: "By means of my feelings." I then, Solomon, having heard his voice come up to me, asked him how he managed to speak. And he answered me: " I, King Solomon, am wholly voice, for I have inherited the voices of many men. For in the case of all men who are called dumb, I it is who smashed their heads, when they were children and had reached their eighth day. Then when a child is crying in the night, I become a spirit, and glide by means of his voice. ... In the crossways^ also I have many services to render, and my encounter is fraught with harm. For I grasp in an instant a man's head, and with my hands, as with a sword, I cut it off, and put it on to myself. And in this way, by means of the fire which is in me, through my neck it is swallowed up. I it is that sends grave mutilations and incurable on men's feet, and inflict sores."

45. And I Solomon, on hearing this, said to him: " Tell me how thou dost discharge forth the fire? Out of what sources dost thou emit it?" And the spirit said to me: " From the Day-star^ For here hath not yet been found that Elburion, to whom men offer prayers and kindle lights. And his name is invoked by the seven demons before me. And he cherishes them."

46. But I said to him: " Tell me his name." But he answered: "I cannot tell thee. For if I tell his name, I render myself incurable. But he will come in response to his name." And on hearing this, I Solomon said to him: "Tell me then, by what angel thou art frustrated?" And he answered: "By the fiery flash of lightning." And I bowed myself before the Lord God of Israel, and bade bim remain in the keeping of Beelzehoul until lax'^

should come.

47. Then I ordered another demon to come before me, and there came into my presence a hound, having a very large shape, and it spoke vsrith a loud voice, and said, " Hail, Lord, King Solomon! " And I Solomon was astounded. I said to it: " Who art thou, hound? " And it answered: " I do indeed seem to thee to be a hound, but before thou wast, King Solomon, I was a man, that wrought many unholy deeds on earth. I was surpassingly learned in letters, and was so mighty that I could hold the stars of heaven back. And many divine works did I prepare. For I do harm to men who follow after our star, and turn them to .... '^ And I seize the frenzied men by the larynx, and so destroy them."

48. And I Solomon said to him: " What is thy name? " And he answered: "Staff*" (Rabdos). And I said to him: "What is thine employment? And what results canst thou achieve? " And he replied: " Give me thy man. and I will lead him away into a mountainous spot, and will show him a green * stone, tossed to and fro ', with which thou mayest adorn the Temple of the Lord God."

49. And I Solomon, on hearing this, ordered my servant to set off with him, and to take the finger-ring bearing the seal of God with him. And I said to him: "Whoever shall show thee the green stone, seal him with this finger-ring. And mark the spot with care, and bring me the demon hither. And the demon showed him the green stone, and he sealed it, and brought the demon to me. And I Solomon decided to confine with my seal on my right hand the two, the headless demon, likewise the hound, that was so huge ^; he should be bound as well. And I bade the hound keep safe the fiery spirit, so that lamps as it were might by day and night cast their light through its maw on the artisans at work.

50. And I Solomon took from the mine of that stone 200 shekels for the supports of the table of incense, which was similar in appearance. And I Solomon glorified the Lord God, and then closed round the treasure of that stone. And I ordered afresh the demons to cut marble for the construction of the house of God. And I Solomon prayed to the Lord, and asked the hound, saying: " By what angel art thou frustrated? " And the demon replied: " By the great Brieus ^"

51. And I praised the Lord God of heaven and earth, and bade another demon come forward to me; and there came before me one in the form of a lion roaring. And he stood and answered me, saying: "O king, in the form which I have, I am a spirit quite incapable of being perceived. Upon all men who lie prostrate with sickness I leap, coming stealthily along; and I render the man weak, so that his habit of body is enfeebled. But I have also another glory, O king. I cast out demons, and I have legions under my control. And I am capable of being received^ in my dwelling-places, along with all the demons belonging to the legions under me," But I Solomon, on hearing this, asked him: "What is thy name?" But he answered: "Lion-bearer, Rath" in kind." And I said to him: " How art thou to be frustrated along with thy legions? What angel is it that frustrates thee? " And he answered: " If I tell thee my name, I bind not myself alone, but also the legion of demons under me."

52. So I said to him: " I adjure thee in the name of the God SabaSth, to tell me by what name thou art

frustrated along with thy host. "And the spirit answered me: " The ' great among men,' who is to suffer many things at the hands of men, whose name is the figure 644, which is Emmanuel; he it is who has bound us, and who will then come and plunge us from the steep ° under water. He is noised abroad in the three letters which bring him down^."

53. And I Solomon, on hearing this, glorified God, and condemned his legion to carry wood from the thicket. And I condemned the lion-shaped one himself to saw up the wood small with his teeth, for burning in the unquenchable furnace for the Temple of God.

54. And I worshipped the Lord God of Israel, and bade another demon come forward. And there came before me a dragon, threeheaded, of fearful hue. And I questioned him: "Who art thou?" And he answered me: " I am a caltrop-like spirit ^, whose activity is in three lines. But I blind children in women's wombs, and twirl their ears round. And I make them deaf ^ and mute. And I have again in my third head means of slipping in'. And I smite men in the limbless * part of the body, and cause them to fall down, and foam, and grind their teeth. But I have my own way of being frustrated, Jerusalem being signified in writing, unto the place called ' of the head ' For there is fore-appointed the angel of the great counsel, and now he will openly dwell on the cross. He doth frastrate me, and to him am I subject."

55. " But in the place where thou sittest, King Solomon, standeth a column in the air, of purple. . . . ° The demon called EpMppas hath brought [it] up from the Red Sea, from inner Arabia. He it is that shall be shut up in a skin-bottle and brought before thee. But at the entrance of the Temple, which thou hast begun to build, King Solomon, lies stored much gold, which dig thou up and carry off." And I Solomon sent my servant, and found it to be as the demon told me. And I sealed him with my ring, and praised the Lord God.

56. So I said to him: " What art thou called? " And the demon said: " I am the crest ' of dragons." And I bade him make bricks in the Temple. He had human hands.

57. And I adored the Lord God of Israel, and bade another demon present himself. And there came before me a spirit in woman's form, that had a head without any limbs ', and her hair was dishevelled. And I said to her: "Who art thou?" But she answered: "Nay, who art thou? And why dost thou want to hear concerning me? But, as thou wouldst learn, here I stand bound before thj' face. Go then into thy royal storehouses and wash thy hands. Then sit down afresh before thy tribunal, and ask me questions; and thou shalt learn, king, who I am."

58. And I Solomon did as she enjoined me, and restrained myself because of the wisdom dwelling in me '; in order that I might hear of her deeds, and reprehend them, and manifest them to men. And I sat down, and said to the demon: " Who art thou? " And she said: " I am called among men Obizuth; and by night I sleep not, but go my rounds over all the world, and visit women in childbirth. And divining the hour I take my stand '; and if I am lucky, I strangle the child. But if not, I retire to another place. For I cannot for a single night retire unsuccessful. For I am a fierce ' spirit, of myriad names and many shapes. And now hither, now thither I roam. And to westering parts I go my rounds. But as it now is,

though thou hast sealed me round with the ring of God, thou hast done nothing. 1 am not standing before thee, and thou wilt not be able to command me. For I have no work other than the destruction of children, and the making their ears to be deaf, and the working of evil to their eyes, and the binding their mouths with a bond, and the ruin of their minds, and paining of their bodies."

59. When I Solomon heard this, I marvelled at her appearance, for I beheld all her body to be in darkness. But her glance was altogether bright and greeny, and her hair was tossed wildly like a dragon's; and the whole of her limbs were invisible. And her voice was very clear as it came to me. And I cunningly said: " Tell me by what angel thou art frustrated, evil spirit? " But she answered me: "By the angel of God called Afardf, which is interpreted Raphael, by whom I am frustrated now and for all time. His name, if any man know it, and write the same on a woman in childbirth, then I shall not be able to enter her. Of this name the number is 640 *." And I Solomon having heard this, and having glorified the Lord, ordered her hair to be bound, and that she should be hung up in front of the Temple of God; that all the children of Israel, as they passed, might see it, and glorify the Lord God of Israel, who had given me this authority, with wisdom and power from God, by means of this signet.

60. And I again ordered another demon to come before me. And there came, rolling itself along, one in appearance like to a dragon, but having the face and hands of a man. And all its limbs, except its feet, were those of a dragon; and it had wings on its back. And when I beheld it, I was astonied, and said: " Who art thou, demon, and what art thou called? And whence hast thou come? Tell me."

61. And the spirit answered and said: " This is the first time I have stood before thee, King Solomon. I am a spirit made into a god among men, but now brought to naught by the ring and wisdom vouchsafed to thee by God. Now I am the so-called winged dragon', and I chamber not with many women, but only with a few that are of fair shape, which possess the name of xull, of this star. And I pair with them in the guise of a spirit winged in form, coitnm hahens per nates. And she on whom I have leapt goes heavy with child, and that which is born of her becomes eros. But since such offspring cannot be carried by men, the woman in question breaks wind. Such is my role. Suppose then only that I am satisfied, and all the other demons molested and disturbed by thee will speak the whole truth. But those composed of fire ^ will cause to be burned up by fire the material of the logs which is to be collected by them for the building in the Temple."

62. And as the demon said this, I saw the spirit going forth from his mouth, and it consumed the wood of the frankincense-tree, and burned up all the logs which we had placed in the Temple of God. And I Solomon saw what the spirit had done, and I marvelled.

63. And, having glorified God, I asked the dragon-shaped demon, and said: " Tell me, by what angel art thou frustrated '? " And he answered: " By the great angel which has its seat in the second heaven, which is called in Hebrew Bazazath. And I Solomon, having heard this, and having invoked his angel, condemned

him to saw up marbles for the building of the Temple of God; and I praised God, and commanded another demon to come before me.

64. And there came before my face another spirit, as it were a woman in the form she had. But on her shoulders she had two other heads with hands. And I asked her, and said: " Tell me, who art thou? " And she said to me: " I am EnSpsigos, who also have a myriad names." And I said to her: " By what angel art thou frustrated? " But she said to me: "What seekest, what askest thou? I undergo changes, like the goddess I am called. And I change again, and pass into possession of another shape. And be not desirous therefore to know all that concerns me. But since thou art before me for this much, hearken. I have my abode in the moon, and for that reason I possess three forms. At times I am magically ' invoked by the wise as Kronos. At other times, in connexion with those who bring me down, I come down and appear in another shape. The measure of the element '^ is inexplicable and indefinable, and not to be frustrated. I then, changing into these three forms, come down and become such as thou seest me; but I am frustrated by the angel Bathanael, who sits in the third heaven. This then is why I speak to thee. Yonder temple cannot contain ' me."

65. I therefore Solomon prayed to my God, and I invoked the angel of whom Enepsigos spoke to me, and used my seal. And I sealed her with a triple chain, and (placed) beneath her the fastening of the chain. I used the seal of God, and the spirit prophesied to me, saying: "This is what thou, King Solomon, doest to us. But after a time thy kingdom shall be broken, and again in season this Temple shall be riven asunder*; and all Jerusalem shall be undone by the King of the Persians and Medes and Chaldaeans. And the vessels of this Temple, which thou makest, shall be put to servile uses of the gods; and along with them all the jars, in which thou dost shut us up, shall be broken by the hands of men. And then we shall go forth in great power hither and thither, and be disseminated all over the world. And we shall lead astray the inhabited world for a long season, until the Son of God is stretched upon the cross. For never before doth arise a king like unto him, one frustrating us all, whose mother shall not have contact with man. Who else can receive such authority over spirits, except he, whom the first devil will seek to tempt, but will not prevail over? The number of his name is 644 which is Emmanuel. Wherefore, King Solomon, thy time is evil, and thy years short and evil, and to thy servant shall thy kingdom be given *."

66. And I Solomon, having heard this, glorified God. And though I marvelled at the apology of the demons, I did not credit it until it came true. And I did not believe their words; but when they were realized, then I understood, and at my death I wrote this Testament to the children of Israel, and gave it to them, so that they might know the powers of the demons and their shapes, and the names of their angels, by which these angels are frustrated. And I glorified the Lord God of Israel, and commanded the spirit to be bound with bonds indissoluble.

67. And having praised God, I commanded another spirit to come before me; and there came before my face

another demon, having in front the shape of ahorse, but behind of a fish. And he had a mighty voice, and said to me: " King Solomon, I am a fierce spirit of the sea, and 1 am greedy of gold and silver. I am such a spirit as rounds itself and comes over the expanses of the water of the sea, and I trip up the men who sail thereon. For I round myself into a wave ', and transform myself, and then throw myself on ships and come right in on them. And that is my business, and my way of getting hold of money and men. For I take the men, and whirl them round with myself, and hurl the men out of the sea. For I am not covetous of men's bodies, but cast them up out of the sea so far. But since Beelzebotd, ruler of the spirits of air and of those under the earth, and lord of earthly ones, hath a joint kingship with us in respect of the deeds of each one of us, therefore I went up from the sea, to get a certain outlook ^ in his company.

68. "But I also have another character and rdle. I metamorphose myself into waves ^, and come up from the sea. And I show myself to men, so that those on earth call me Kunolsl-paston *, because I assume the human form. And my name is a true one. For by my passage up into men, I send forth a certain nausea. I came then to take counsel with the prince Beeleeboul; and he bound me and delivered me into thy hands. And I am here before thee because of this seal, and thou dost now torment me ^. Behold now, in two or three days the spirit that converseth with thee will fail, because I shall have no water."

69. And I said to him: " Tell me by what angel thou art frus trated." And he answered: " By lameth." And I glorified God. I commanded the spirit to be thrown into a phial along with ten jugs of sea- water of two measures each And I sealed them round above with marbles and asphalt and pitch in the mouth of the vesseP. And having sealed it with my ring, I ordered it to be deposited in the Temple of God. And 1 ordered another spirit to come before me.

70. And there came before my face another enslaved' spirit, having obscurely the form of a man, with gleaming eyes, and bearing in his hand a blade. And I asked: " Who art thou? " But he answered: "I am a lascivious* spirit, engendered of a giant man who died in the massacre in the time of the giants." I said to him: " Tell me what thou art employed on upon earth, and where thou hast thy dwelling."

71. Andhe said: "My dwelling is in fruitful places, but my procedure is this. I seat myself beside the men who pass along among the tombs, and in untimely season I assume the form of the dead; and if I catch any one, I at once destroy him with my sword. But if I cannot destroy him, I cause him to be possessed with a demon, and to devour his own flesh, and the hair to fall off his chin." But I said to him: " Do thou then be in fear of the God of heaven and of earth, and tell me by what angel thou art frustrated." And he answered: " He destroys me who is to become Saviour, a man whose number °, if any one shall write it on his forehead % he will defeat me, and in fear I shall quickly retreat. And, indeed, if any one write this sign on him, I shall be in fear." And I Solomon, on hearing this, and having glorified the Lord God, shut up this demon like the rest.

72. And I commanded another demon to come before

me. And there came before my face thirty-six spirits, their heads shapeless like dogs, but in themselves they were human in form; with faces of asses, faces of oxen, and faces of birds. And I Solomon, on hearing and seeing them, wondered, and I asked them and said: " Who are you?" But they, of one accord with one voice, said ': " We are the thirtysix elements, the world-rulers " of this darkness. But, King Solomon, thou wilt not wrong us nor imprison us, nor lay command on us; but since the Lord God has given thee authority over every spirit, in the air, and on the earth, and under the earth, therefore do we also present ourselves before thee like the other spirits, from ram and bull, from both twin and crab, lion and virgin, scales and scorpion, archer, goat-homed, water-pourer, and fish.

73. Then I Solomon invoked the name of the Lord Sahadth, and questioned each in turn as to what was its character. And I bade each one come forward and tell of its actions. Then the first one came foi-ward, and said: "I am the first decanus^ of the zodiacal circle, and I am called the ram, and with me are these two." So I put to them the question: "Who are ye called?" The first said: "1, Lord, am called Ruax, and I cause the heads of men to be idle, and I pillage their brows. But let me only hear the words, 'Michael, imprison Ruax,' and at once I retreat."

74. And the second said: " I am called Barsafael, and I cause those who are subject to my hour * to feel the pain of migrain '. If only I hear the words, ' Gabriel, imprison Barsafael,' at once I retreat."

75. The third said: " I am called ArStosael. I do harm to eyes, and grievously injure them. Only let me hear the words, ' Uriel, imprison AraiosaeV {sic), at once I retreat *"

76. The fifth said: " I am called Iitdal, and I bring about a block in the ears and deafness of hearing. If I hear, ' Uruel Ivdal,' I at once retreat."

77. The sixth said: "I am called Sphendonael. I cause tumours of the parotid gland, and inflammations of the tonsils, and tetanic recurvation °. If I hear, ' Sabrael, imprison SphendonaSl,' at once I retreat."

78. And the seventh said: " I am called SphandSr, and I weaken the strength of the shoulders, and cause them to tremble; and I paralyze the nerves of the hands, and I break and bruise the bones of the neck. And I, I suck out the marrow. But if I hear the words, 'Arail, imprison Sphanddr,' I at once retreat."

79. And the eighth said: " I am called Belhel. I distort the hearts and minds of men. If I hear the words, 'AraSl, imprison Belhel,' I at once retreat."

80. And the ninth said: " I am called Kurtael. I send colics in the bowels. I induce pains. If I hear the words, 'ladth, imprison Kurtail,' I at once retreat."

81. The tenth said: "I am called Metaihiax. I cause the reins to ache. If I hear the words, 'AddnaSl, imprison Metathiax,' I at once retreat."

82. The eleventh said: " I am called KatanikotaSl. I create strife and wrongs in men's homes, and send on them hard temper. If any one would be at peace in his home, let him write on seven leaves of laurel the names of the angel that frustrates me, along with these names: lae, led, sons of Sabadth, in the name of the great God let him shut up Katanikotall. Then let him wash the laurel-leaves

in water, and sprinkle his house with the water, from within to the outside. And at once I retreat."

83. The twelfth said: " I am called SaphathoraM, and I inspire partisanship in men, and delight in causing them to stumble. If any one will write on paper these names of angels, laed, leald, Idelet, Sabadth, Ithoih, Bae, and having folded it up, wear it round his neck or against his ear, I at once retreat and dissipate the drunken fit."

84. The thirteenth said: " I am called Bobil {sic), and I cause nervous illness by my assaults. If I hear the name of the great ' Adonael, imprison BoihoihM, *I at once retreat."*

85. The fourteenth said: "I am called KumeatSl, and I inflict shivering fits and torpor. If only I hear the words: 'ZdroSl, imprison Kumentael,' I at once retreat."

86. The fifteenth said: " I am called Roeled. I cause cold and frost and pain in the stomach. Let me only hear the words: '7a a;, bide not, be not warmed, for Solomon is fairer than eleven fathers,' I at retreat."

87. The sixteenth said: " I am called Atrax. I inflict upon men fevers, irremediable and harmful. If you would imprison me, chop up coriander' and smear it on the lips, reciting the following charm: ' The fever which is from dirt. I exorcise the e by the throne of the most high God, retreat from dirt and retreat from the creature fashioned by God.' And at once I retreat."

88. The seventeenth said: " I am called Ieropael. On the stomach of men I sit, and cause convulsions in the bath and in the road; and wherever I be found, or find a man, I throw him down. But if any one will say to the afflicted into their ear these names, three times over, into the right ear: ' ludarizi, Sabuni, DendS,^ I at once retreat."

89. The eighteenth said: " I am called Buldumich. I separate wife from husband and bring about a grudge between them. If any one write down the names of thy sires, Solomon, on paper and place it in the ante-chamber of his house, I retreat thence. And the legend written shall be as follows: ' The God of Abram, and the God of Isaac, and the God of Jacob commands thee— retire from this house in peace.' And I at once retire."

90. The nineteenth said: " I am called Na6th, and I take my seat on the knees of men. If any one write on paper: ' Phnunohoeol, depart Nathath, and touch thou not the neck,' I at once retreat."

91. The twentieth said: "I am called Marderd. I send on men incurable fever. If any one write on the leaf of a book: ' Sphener, Rafael, retire, drag me not about, flay me not, and tie it round his neck,' I at once retreat."

92. The twenty-first said: "I am called Alath, and I cause coughing and hard-breathing in children. If any one write on paper: ' Eorex, do thou pursue Alath,' and fasten it round his neck, 1 at once retire . . . ' "

93. The twenty-third said: " I am called Nefthada. 1 cause the reins to ache, and I bring about dysury. If any one write on a plate of tin the words: ' lathdth, TJruel, Nephthada, *and iasten it round the loins, I at once retreat."*

94. The twenty-fourth said: " I am called Akton. I cause ribs and lumbic muscles to ache. If one engrave on copper material, taken from a ship which has missed its anchorage, this: ' Marmaraoth, Sabadth, pursue Akton,' and fasten it round the loin, I at once retreat."

95. The twenty-fifth said: " I am called Anatreih, and I send burnings and fevers into the entrails. But if I hear: '

Arara, Charara,' instantly do I retreat."

96. The twenty-sixth said: " I am called Enenuth. I steal away men's minds, and change their hearts, and make a man toothless (?). If one write: ' Allazool, pursue Enenuth,^ and tie the paper round him, I at once retreat."

97. The twenty-seventh said: "I am called Pheth. I make men consumptive and cause hemorrhagia. If one exorcise me in wine, sweet-smelling and unmixed by the eleventh aeon'^, and say: ' I exorcise thee by the eleventh aeon to stop, I demand, Pheth (Axidpheth),' then give it to the patient to drink, and I at once retreat."

98. The twenty-eighth said: " I am called Harpax, and I send sleeplessness on men. If one vrrite ' Kokphnedismos,' and bind it round the temples, I at once retire."

99. The twenty-ninth said: " I am called Anoster. 1 engender uterine mania and pains in the bladder. If one powder into pure oil three seeds of laurel and smear it on, saying: ' I exorcise thee, Anoster. Stop by Marmarad,' at once I retreat."

100. The thirtieth said: " I am called AUeborifh. If in eating fish one has swallowed a bone, then he must take a bone from the fish and cough, and at once I retreat."

101. The thirty-first said: "I am called Hephesikirefh, and cause lingering disease. If you throw salt, rubbed in the hand, into oil and smear it on the patient, saying: ' Seraphim, Cherubim, help me! ' I at once retire."

102. The thirty-second said: " I am called Ichthion. I paralyze muscles and contuse them. If I hear: ' Adonaeth, help! ' I at once retire."

103. The thirty-third said: " I am called Agehonidn. I lie among swaddling-clothes and in the precipice. And if any one write on fig-leaves ' Li/curgos,' taking away one letter at a time, and write it, reversing the letters, I retire at once. ' Lycurgos, yeurgos, kurgos, yrgos, gos, os ^.' "

104. The thirty-fourth said: " I am called Autothith. I cause grudges and fighting. Therefore I am frustrated by Alpha and Omega, if written down."

105. The thirty-fifth said: " I am called Phthenoth. 1 cast evil eye on every man. Therefore, the eye much-suifering, if it be drawn, frustrates me."

106. The thirty-sixth said: " I am called Bianakith. I have a grudge against the body. I lay waste houses, I cause flesh to decay, and all else that is similar. If a man write on the front-door of his house: 'Meltd, Ardu, Anaath,' I flee from that place."

107. And I Solomon, when I heard this, glorified the God of heaven and earth. And I commanded them to fetch water in the Temple of God. And I furthermore prayed to the Lord God to cause the demons without, that hamper humanity, to be bound and made to approach the Temple of God. Some of these demons I condemned to do the heavy work of the construction of the Temple of God. Others I shut up in prisons. Others I ordered to wrestle with fire in (the making of) gold and silver, sitting down by lead and spoon. And to make readj' places for the other demons in which they should be confined.

108. And I Solomon had much quiet in all the earth, and spent my life in profound peace, honoured by all men and by all under heaven. And I built the entire Temple of the Lord God. And my kingdom was prosperous, and my army was with me. And for the rest the city of Jerusalem had repose, rejoicing and delighted. And all the kings of the earth came to me from the ends of the earth to behold the Temple which I builded to the Lord God. And having heard of the wisdom given to me, they did homage to me in the Temple, bringing gold and silver and precious stones, many and divers, and bronze, and iron, and lead, and cedar logs. And woods that decay not they brought me, for the equipment of the Temple of God.

109. And among them also the queen of the south, being a witch ', came in great concern and bowed low before me to the earth. And having heard my wisdom, she glorified the God of Israel, and she made formal trial of all my wisdom, of all the love in which I instructed her, according to the wisdom imparted to me. And all the sons of Israel glorified God.

110. And behold, in those days one of the workmen, of ripe old age, threw himself down before me, and said: " King Solomon, pity me, because I am old." So I bade him stand up, and said: " Tell me, old man, all you will." And he answered: " I beseech you, king, I have an only-bom son, and he insults and beats me openly, and plucks out the hair of my head, and threatens me with a painful death. Therefore I beseech you, avenge me."

111. And I Solomon, on hearing this, felt compunction as I looked at his old age; and I bade the child be brought to me. And when he was brought I questioned him whether it were true. And the youth said: "I was not so filled with madness as to strike my father with my hand. Be kind to me, king. For I have not dared to commit such impiety, poor wretch that I am." But I Solomon, on hearing this from the youth, exhorted the old man to reflect on the matter, and accept his son's apology. However, he would not, but said he would rather let him die. And as the old man would not yield, I was about to pronounce sentence on the youth, when I saw Ornias the demon laughing. I was very angry at the demon's laughing in my presence; and I ordered my men to remove the other parties, and bring forward Ornias before my tribunal. And when he was brought before me, I said to him: " Accursed one, why didst thou look at me and laugh? " And the demon answered: "Prithee, king, it was not because of thee I laughed, but because of this ill-starred old man and the wretched youth, his son. For after three days his son will die untimely; and lo, the old man desires to foully make away with him."

112. But I Solomon, having heard this, said to the demon: " Is that true that thou speakest?" And he answered: "It is true, king." And I, on hearing that, bade them remove the demon, and that they should again bring before me the old man with his son. I bade them make friends with one another again, and I supplied them with food. And then I told the old man after three days to bring his son again to me here; " and," said I, "I will. attend to him." And they saluted me, and went their way.

113. And when they were gone I ordered Omias to be brought forward, and said to him: " Tell me how you know this; " and he answered: " We demons ascend into the firmament of heaven, and fly about among the stars. And we hear the sentences which go forth upon the souls of men, and forthwith we come, and whether by

force of influence *, or by fire, or by sword, or by some accident, we veil our act of destruction; and if a man does not die by some untimely disaster or by violence, then we demons transform ourselves in such a way as to appear to men and be worshipped in our human nature." 114. I therefore, having heard this, glorified the Lord God, and again I questioned the demon, saying: " Tell me how ye can ascend into heaven, being demons, and amidst the stars and holy angels intermingle." And he answered: "Just as things are fulfilled in heaven, so also on earth (are fulfilled) the types * of all of them. For there are principalities, authorities, world -rulers', and we demons fly about in the air; and we hear the voices of the heavenly beings, and survey all the powers. And as having no ground (basis) on which to alight and rest, we lose strength and fall off like leaves from trees. And men seeing us imagine that the stars are falling from heaven. But it is not really so, king; but we fall because of our weakness, and because we have nowhere anything to lay hold of; and so we fall down like lightnings* in the depth of night and suddenly. And we set cities in flames and fire the fields. For the stars have firm foundations in the heaven, like the sun and the moon."
115. And I Solomon, having heard this, ordered the demon to be guarded for five days. And after the five days I recalled the old man, and was about to question him. But he came to me in grief and with black face. And I said to him: " Tell me, old man, where is thy son? And what means this garb? " And he answered: " Lo, I am become childless, and sit by my son's grave in despair. For it is already two days that he is dead." But I Solomon, on hearing that, and knowing that the demon Omias had told me the truth, glorified the God of Israel.
116. And the queen of the south saw all this, and marvelled, glorifying the God of Israel; and she beheld the Temple of the Lord being builded. And she gave a siklos * of gold and one hundred myriads of silver and choice bronze, and she went into the Temple. And (she beheld) the altar of incense and the brazen supports {a.va<f)6povs) of this altar, and the gems of the lamps flashing forth of different colours, and of the lamp-stand of stone, and of emerald, and hyacinth, and sapphire; and she beheld the vessels of gold, and silver, and bronze, and wood, and the folds of skins dyed red with madder. And she saw the bases of the pillars of the Temple of the Lord. All were of one gold . . . . ^ apart from the demons whom I condemned to labour. And there was peace in the circle of my kingdom and over all the earth.
117. And it came to pass, while I was in my kingdom, the King of the Arabians, Adares, sent me a letter, and the writing of the letter was written as follows: —
" To King Solomon, all hail! Lo, we have heard, and it hath been heard unto all the ends of the earth, concerning the wisdom vouchsafed in thee, and that thou art a man merciful from the Lord. And understanding hath been granted thee over all the spirits of the air, and on earth, and under the earth. Now, forasmuch as there is present in the land of Arabia a spirit of the following kind: at early dawn there begins to blow a certain wind until the third hour. And its blast is harsh and terrible, and it slays man and beast. And no spirit can live upon earth against this demon. I pray thee

then, forasmuch as the spirit is a wind, contrive something according to the wisdom given in thee by the Lord thy God, and deign to send a man able to capture it. And behold, King Solomon, I and my people and all my land will serve thee unto death. And all Arabia shall be at peace with thee, if thou wilt perform this act of righteousness for us. Wherefore we pray thee, contemn not our humble prayer, and suffer not to be utterly brought to naught the eparchy subordinated to thy authority. Because we are thy suppliants, both I and my people and all my land. Farewell to my Lord. All health! "
118. And I Solomon read this epistle; and I folded it up and gave it to my people, and said to them: " After seven days shalt thou remind me of this epistle. And Jerusalem was built, and the Temple was being completed. And there was a stone ', the end stone of the comer lying there, great, chosen out, one which I desired to lay in the head of the corner of the completion of the Temple. And all the workmen, and all the demons helping them, came to the same place to bring up the stone and lay it on the pinnacle ^ of the holy Temple, and were not strong enough to stir it, and lay it upon the corner allotted to it. For that stone was exceedingly great and useful for the comer of the Temple."
119. And after seven days, being reminded of the epistle oi Adares, King of Arabia, I called my servant and said to him: " Order thy camel and take for thyself a leather flask, and take also this seal. And go away into Arabia to the place in which the evil spirit blows; and there take the flask, and the signet-ring in front of the mouth of the flask, and (hold them) towards the blast of the spirit. And when the flask is blown out, thou wilt understand that the demon is (in it). Then hastily tie up the mouth of the flask, and seal it securely with the seal-ring, and lay it carefully on the camel and bring it me hither. And if on the way it offer thee gold or silver or treasure in return for letting it go, see that thou be not persuaded. But arrange without using oath to release it. And then if it point out to the places where are gold or silver, mark the places and seal them with this seal. And bring the demon to me. And now depart, and fare thee well."
120. Then the youth did as was bidden him. And he ordered his camel, and laid on it a flask, and set off into Arabia. And the men of that region would not believe that he would be able to catch the evil spirit. And when it was dawn, the servant stood before the spirit's blast, and laid the flask on the ground, and the finger-ring on the mouth of the flask. And the demon blew through the middle of the finger-ring into the mouth of the flask, and going in blew out the flask. But the man promptly stood up to it and drew tight with his hand the mouth of the flask, in the name of the Lord God of Sabadth. And the demon remained within the flask. And after that the youth remained in that land three days to make trial. And the spirit no longer blew against that city. And all the Arabs knew that he had safely shut in the spirit.
121. Then the youth fastened the flask on the camel, and the Arabs sent him forth on his way with much honour and precious gifts, praising and magnifying the God of Israel. But the youth brought in the bag and laid it in the middle of the Temple. And on the next day, I King Solomon, went into the Temple of God and sat in deep

distress about the stone of the end of the corner. And when I entered the Temple, the flask stood up and walked around some seven steps, and then fell on its mouth and did homage to me. And I marvelled that even along with the bottle the demon still had power and could walk about; and I commanded it to stand up. And the flask stood up, and stood on its feet all blown out. And I questioned him, saying: " Tell me, who art thou? " And the spirit within said: "I am the demon called Ephippas, that is in Arabia." And I said to him: " Is this thy name? " And he answered: " Yes; wheresoever I will, I alight and set fire and do to death."

122. And I said to him: " By what angel art thou frustrated?" And he answered: " By the only-ruling God, that hath authority over me even to be heard. He that is to be bom of a virgin and crucified by the Jews on a cross. Whom the angels and archangels worship. He doth frustrate me, and enfeeble me of my great strength, which has been given me by my father the devil." And I said to him: "What canst thou do? " And he answered: " I am able to remove * mountains, to overthrow the oaths of kings. I wither trees and make their leaves to fall o£f." And I said to him: " Canst thou raise this stone, and lay it for the beginning of this comer which exists in the fair plan of the Temple ^? " And he said: " Not only raise this, king; but also, with the help of the demon who presides over the Red Sea, I will bring up the pillar of air', and will stand it where thou wilt in Jerusalem.

123. Saying this, I laid stress on him, and the flask became as if depleted of air. And I placed it under the stone, and (the spirit) girded himself up, and lifted it up top of the flask. And the flask went up the steps, carrying the stone, and laid it down at the end of the entrance of the Temple. And I Solomon, beholding the stone raised aloft and placed on a foundation, said: " Truly the Scripture is fulfilled, which says: ' The stone which the builders rejected on trial, that same is become the head of the comer.' For this it is not mine to grant, but God's, that the demon should be strong enough to lift up so great a stone and deposit it in the place I wished."

124. And Ephippas led the demon of the Red Sea with the column. And they both took the column and raised it aloft from the earth. And I outwitted * these two spirits, so that they could not shake the entire earth in a moment of time. And then I sealed round with my ring on this side and that, and said: "Watch." And the spirits have remained upholding it until this day, for proof of the wisdom vouchsafed to me. And there the pillar was hanging, of enormous size, in mid air, supported by the winds. And thus the spirits appeared underneath, like air, supporting it. And if one looks fixedly, the pillar is a little oblique, being supported by the spirits; and it is so to this day.

125. And I Solomon questioned the other spirit, which came up with the pillar from the depth of the Red Sea. And I said to him: "Who art thou, and what calls thee? And what is thy business? For I hear many things about thee." And the demon answered: "I, O King Solomon, am called *Abezithibod*. I am a descendant of the archangel. Once as I sat in the first heaven, of which the name is *Ameleouth*—I then am a fierce spirit and winged, and with a single wing, plotting against every spirit under

heaven. I was present when Moses went in before Pharaoh, king of Egypt, and I hardened his heart. I am he whom *Iannes* and *Iambres* invoked homing with Moses in Egypt. I am he who fought against Moses with wonders with signs."

126. I said therefore to him: "How wast thou found in the Red Sea?" And he answered: "In the exodus of the sons of Israel I hardened the heart of Pharaoh. And I excited his heart and that of his ministers. And I caused them to pursue after the children of Israel. And Pharaoh followed with (me) and all the Egyptians. Then I was present there, and we followed together. And we all came up upon the Red Sea. And it came to pass when the children of Israel had crossed over, the water returned and hid all the host of the Egyptians and all their might. And I remained in the sea, being kept under this pillar. But when *Ephippas* came, being sent by thee, shut up in the vessel of a flask, he fetched me up to thee."

127. I, therefore, Solomon, having heard this, glorified God and adjured the demons not to disobey me, but to remain supporting the pillar. And they both sware, saying: "The Lord thy God liveth, we will not let go this pillar until the world's end. But on whatever day this stone fall, then shall be the end of the world."

128. And I Solomon glorified God, and adorned the Temple of the Lord with all fair-seeming. And I was glad in spirit in my kingdom, and there was peace in my days. And I took wives of my own from every land, who were numberless. And I marched against the *Jebusaeans*, and there I saw a Jebusaean, daughter of a man; and fell violently in love with her, and desired to take her to wife along with my other wives. And I said to their priests: "Give me the *Sonmanites* (i.e. Shunammite) to wife." But the priests of *Moloch* said to me: "If thou lovest this maiden, go in and worship our gods, the great god *Raphan* and the god called *Moloch*." I therefore was in fear of the glory of God, and did not follow to worship. And I said to them: "I will not worship a strange god. What is this proposal, that ye compel me to do so much?" But they said: "…by our fathers."

129. And when I answered that I would on no account worship strange gods, they told the maiden not to sleep with me until I complied and sacrificed to the gods. I then was moved, but crafty *Eros* brought and laid by her for me five grasshoppers, saying: "Take these grasshoppers, and crush them together in the name of the god *Moloch*; and then will I sleep with you." And this I actually did. And at once the Spirit of God departed from me, and I became weak as well as foolish in my words. And after that I was obliged by her to build a temple of idols to *Baal*, and to *Rapha*, and to *Moloch*, and to the other idols.

130. I then, wretch that I am, followed her advice, and the glory of God quite departed from me; and my spirit was darkened, and I became the sport of idols and demons. Wherefore I wrote out this *Testament*, that ye who get possession of it may pray, and attend to the last things, and not to the first. So that ye may find grace for ever and ever. Amen.

Judith shows the head of Holofernes. Judith 13:14

Gustave Doré (1866)

DEUTEROCANONICAL BOOKS

1 ESDRAS

1Esdr.1

[1] And Josias held the feast of the passover in Jerusalem unto his Lord, and offered the passover the fourteenth day of the first month; [2] Having set the priests according to their daily courses, being arrayed in long garments, in the temple of the Lord. [3] And he spake unto the Levites, the holy ministers of Israel, that they should hallow themselves unto the Lord, to set the holy ark of the Lord in the house that king Solomon the son of David had built: [4] And said, Ye shall no more bear the ark upon your shoulders: now therefore serve the Lord your God, and minister unto his people Israel, and prepare you after your families and kindreds, [5] According as David the king of Israel prescribed, and according to the magnificence of Solomon his son: and standing in the temple according to the several dignity of the families of you the Levites, who minister in the presence of your brethren the children of Israel, [6] Offer the passover in order, and make ready the sacrifices for your brethren, and keep the passover according to the commandment of the Lord, which was given unto Moses. [7] And unto the people that was found there Josias gave thirty thousand lambs and kids, and three thousand calves: these things were given of the king's allowance, according as he promised, to the people, to the priests, and to the Levites. [8] And Helkias, Zacharias, and Syelus, the governors of the temple, gave to the priests for the passover two thousand and six hundred sheep, and three hundred calves. [9] And Jeconias, and Samaias, and Nathanael his brother, and Assabias, and Ochiel, and Joram, captains over thousands, gave to the Levites for the passover five thousand sheep, and seven hundred calves. [10] And when these things were done, the priests and Levites, having the unleavened bread, stood in very comely order according to the kindreds, [11] And according to the several dignities of the fathers, before the people, to offer to the Lord, as it is written in the book of Moses: and thus did they in the morning. [12] And they roasted the passover with fire, as appertaineth: as for the sacrifices, they sod them in brass pots and pans with a good savour, [13] And set them before all the people: and afterward they prepared for themselves, and for the priests their brethren, the sons of Aaron. [14] For the priests offered the fat until night: and the Levites prepared for themselves, and the priests their brethren, the sons of Aaron. [15] The holy singers also, the sons of Asaph, were in their order, according to the appointment of David, to wit, Asaph, Zacharias, and Jeduthun, who was of the king's retinue. [16] Moreover the porters were at every gate; it was not lawful for any to go from his ordinary service: for their brethren the Levites prepared for them. [17] Thus were the things that belonged to the sacrifices of the Lord accomplished in that day, that they might hold the passover, [18] And offer sacrifices upon the altar of the Lord, according to the commandment of king Josias. [19] So the children of Israel which were present held the passover at that time, and the feast of sweet bread seven days. [20] And such a passover was not kept in Israel since the time of the prophet Samuel. [21] Yea, all the kings of Israel held not such a passover as Josias, and the priests, and the Levites, and the Jews, held with all Israel that were found dwelling at Jerusalem. [22] In the eighteenth year of the reign of Josias was this passover kept. [23] And the works or Josias were upright before his Lord with an heart full of godliness. [24] As for the things that came to pass in his time, they were written in former times, concerning those that sinned, and did wickedly against the Lord above all people and kingdoms, and how they grieved him exceedingly, so that the words of the Lord rose up against Israel. [25] Now after all these acts of Josias it came to pass, that Pharaoh the king of Egypt came to raise war at Carchamis upon Euphrates: and Josias went out against him. [26] But the king of Egypt sent to him, saying, What have I to do with thee, O king of Judea? [27] I am not sent out from the Lord God against thee; for my war is upon Euphrates: and now the Lord is with me, yea, the Lord is with me hasting me forward: depart from me, and be not against the Lord. [28] Howbeit Josias did not turn back his chariot from him, but undertook to fight with him, not regarding the words of the prophet Jeremy spoken by the mouth of the Lord: [29] But joined battle with him in the plain of Magiddo, and the princes came against king Josias. [30] Then said the king unto his servants, Carry me away out of the battle; for I am very weak. And immediately his servants took him away out of the battle. [31] Then gat he up upon his second chariot; and being brought back to Jerusalem died, and was buried in his father's sepulchre. [32] And in all Jewry they mourned for Josias, yea, Jeremy the prophet lamented for Josias, and the chief men with the women made lamentation for him unto this day: and this was given out for an ordinance to be done continually in all the nation of Israel. [33] These things are written in the book of the stories of the kings of Judah, and every one of the acts that Josias did, and his glory, and his understanding in the law of the Lord, and the things that he had done before, and the things now recited, are reported in the book of the kings of Israel and Judea. [34] And the people took Joachaz the son of Josias, and made him king instead of Josias his father, when he was twenty and three years old. [35] And he reigned in Judea and in Jerusalem three months: and then the king of Egypt deposed him from reigning in Jerusalem. [36] And he set a tax upon the land of an hundred talents of silver and one talent of gold. [37] The king of Egypt also made king Joacim his brother king of Judea and Jerusalem. [38] And he bound Joacim and the nobles: but Zaraces his brother he apprehended, and brought him out of Egypt. [39] Five and twenty years old was Joacim when he was made king in the land of Judea and Jerusalem; and he did evil before the Lord. [40] Wherefore against him Nabuchodonosor the king of Babylon came up, and bound him with a chain of brass, and carried him into Babylon. [41] Nabuchodonosor also took of the holy vessels of the Lord, and carried them away, and set them in his own temple at Babylon. [42] But those things that are recorded of him, and of his uncleaness and impiety, are written in the chronicles of the kings. [43] And Joacim his son reigned in his stead: he was made king being eighteen years old; [44] And reigned but three months and ten days in Jerusalem; and did evil before the Lord. [45] So after a year Nabuchodonosor sent and caused him to be brought into Babylon with the holy vessels of the Lord; [46] And made Zedechias king of

Judea and Jerusalem, when he was one and twenty years old; and he reigned eleven years: [47] And he did evil also in the sight of the Lord, and cared not for the words that were spoken unto him by the prophet Jeremy from the mouth of the Lord. [48] And after that king Nabuchodonosor had made him to swear by the name of the Lord, he forswore himself, and rebelled; and hardening his neck, his heart, he transgressed the laws of the Lord God of Israel. [49] The governors also of the people and of the priests did many things against the laws, and passed all the pollutions of all nations, and defiled the temple of the Lord, which was sanctified in Jerusalem. [50] Nevertheless the God of their fathers sent by his messenger to call them back, because he spared them and his tabernacle also. [51] But they had his messengers in derision; and, look, when the Lord spake unto them, they made a sport of his prophets: [52] So far forth, that he, being wroth with his people for their great ungodliness, commanded the kings of the Chaldees to come up against them; [53] Who slew their young men with the sword, yea, even within the compass of their holy temple, and spared neither young man nor maid, old man nor child, among them; for he delivered all into their hands. [54] And they took all the holy vessels of the Lord, both great and small, with the vessels of the ark of God, and the king's treasures, and carried them away into Babylon. [55] As for the house of the Lord, they burnt it, and brake down the walls of Jerusalem, and set fire upon her towers: [56] And as for her glorious things, they never ceased till they had consumed and brought them all to nought: and the people that were not slain with the sword he carried unto Babylon:

[57] Who became servants to him and his children, till the Persians reigned, to fulfil the word of the Lord spoken by the mouth of Jeremy: [58] Until the land had enjoyed her sabbaths, the whole time of her desolation shall she rest, until the full term of seventy years.

1Esdr.2

[1] In the first year of Cyrus king of the Persians, that the word of the Lord might be accomplished, that he had promised by the mouth of Jeremy; [2] The Lord raised up the spirit of Cyrus the king of the Persians, and he made proclamation through all his kingdom, and also by writing, [3] Saying, Thus saith Cyrus king of the Persians; The Lord of Israel, the most high Lord, hath made me king of the whole world, [4] And commanded me to build him an house at Jerusalem in Jewry. [5] If therefore there be any of you that are of his people, let the Lord, even his Lord, be with him, and let him go up to Jerusalem that is in Judea, and build the house of the Lord of Israel: for he is the Lord that dwelleth in Jerusalem. [6] Whosoever then dwell in the places about, let them help him, those, I say, that are his neighbours, with gold, and with silver, [7] With gifts, with horses, and with cattle, and other things, which have been set forth by vow, for the temple of the Lord at Jerusalem. [8] Then the chief of the families of Judea and of the tribe of Benjamin stood up; the priests also, and the Levites, and all they whose mind the Lord had moved to go up, and to build an house for the Lord at Jerusalem, [9] And they that dwelt round about them, and helped them in all things with silver and gold, with horses and cattle, and with very many free gifts of a great number whose minds were stirred up

thereto. [10] King Cyrus also brought forth the holy vessels, which Nabuchodonosor had carried away from Jerusalem, and had set up in his temple of idols. [11] Now when Cyrus king of the Persians had brought them forth, he delivered them to Mithridates his treasurer: [12] And by him they were delivered to Sanabassar the governor of Judea. [13] And this was the number of them; A thousand golden cups, and a thousand of silver, censers of silver twenty nine, vials of gold thirty, and of silver two thousand four hundred and ten, and a thousand other vessels. [14] So all the vessels of gold and of silver, which were carried away, were five thousand four hundred threescore and nine. [15] These were brought back by Sanabassar, together with them of the captivity, from Babylon to Jerusalem. [16] But in the time of Artexerxes king of the Persians Belemus, and Mithridates, and Tabellius, and Rathumus, and Beeltethmus, and Semellius the secretary, with others that were in commission with them, dwelling in Samaria and other places, wrote unto him against them that dwelt in Judea and Jerusalem these letters following; [17] To king Artexerxes our lord, Thy servants, Rathumus the storywriter, and Semellius the scribe, and the rest of their council, and the judges that are in Celosyria and Phenice. [18] Be it now known to the lord king, that the Jews that are up from you to us, being come into Jerusalem, that rebellious and wicked city, do build the marketplaces, and repair the walls of it and do lay the foundation of the temple. [19] Now if this city and the walls thereof be made up again, they will not only refuse to give tribute, but also rebel against kings. [20] And forasmuch as the things pertaining to the temple are now in hand, we think it meet not to neglect such a matter, [21] But to speak unto our lord the king, to the intent that, if it be thy pleasure it may be sought out in the books of thy fathers: [22] And thou shalt find in the chronicles what is written concerning these things, and shalt understand that that city was rebellious, troubling both kings and cities: [23] And that the Jews were rebellious, and raised always wars therein; for the which cause even this city was made desolate. [24] Wherefore now we do declare unto thee, O lord the king, that if this city be built again, and the walls thereof set up anew, thou shalt from henceforth have no passage into Celosyria and Phenice. [25] Then the king wrote back again to Rathumus the storywriter, to Beeltethmus, to Semellius the scribe, and to the rest that were in commission, and dwellers in Samaria and Syria and Phenice, after this manner; [26] I have read the epistle which ye have sent unto me: therefore I commanded to make diligent search, and it hath been found that that city was from the beginning 614racticing against kings; [27] And the men therein were given to rebellion and war: and that mighty kings and fierce were in Jerusalem, who reigned and exacted tributes in Celosyria and Phenice. [28] Now therefore I have commanded to hinder those men from building the city, and heed to be taken that there be no more done in it; [29] And that those wicked workers proceed no further to the annoyance of kings, [30] Then king Artexerxes his letters being read, Rathumus, and Semellius the scribe, and the rest that were in commission with them, removing in haste toward Jerusalem with a troop of horsemen and a multitude of people in battle array, began to hinder the builders; and the building of the temple in Jerusalem ceased until the second year of the reign of Darius king of the Persians.

1Esdr.3

[1] Now when Darius reigned, he made a great feast unto all his subjects, and unto all his household, and unto all the princes of Media and Persia, [2] And to all the governors and captains and lieutenants that were under him, from India unto Ethiopia, of an hundred twenty and seven provinces. [3] And when they had eaten and drunken, and being satisfied were gone home, then Darius the king went into his bedchamber, and slept, and soon after awaked. [4] Then three young men, that were of the guard that kept the king's body, spake one to another; [5] Let every one of us speak a sentence: he that shall overcome, and whose sentence shall seem wiser than the others, unto him shall the king Darius give great gifts, and great things in token of victory: [6] As, to be clothed in purple, to drink in gold, and to sleep upon gold, and a chariot with bridles of gold, and an headtire of fine linen, and a chain about his neck: [7] And he shall sit next to Darius because of his wisdom, and shall be called Darius his cousin. [8] And then every one wrote his sentence, sealed it, and laid it under king Darius his pillow; [9] And said that, when the king is risen, some will give him the writings; and of whose side the king and the three princes of Persia shall judge that his sentence is the wisest, to him shall the victory be given, as was appointed. [10] The first wrote, Wine is the strongest. [11] The second wrote, The king is strongest. [12] The third wrote, Women are strongest: but above all things Truth beareth away the victory. [13] Now when the king was risen up, they took their writings, and delivered them unto him, and so he read them: [14] And sending forth he called all the princes of Persia and Media, and the governors, and the captains, and the lieutenants, and the chief officers; [15] And sat him down in the royal seat of judgment; and the writings were read before them. [16] And he said, Call the young men, and they shall declare their own sentences. So they were called, and came in. [17] And he said unto them, Declare unto us your mind concerning the writings. Then began the first, who had spoken of the strength of wine; [18] And he said thus, O ye men, how exceeding strong is wine! it causeth all men to err that drink it: [19] It maketh the mind of the king and of the fatherless child to be all one; of the bondman and of the freeman, of the poor man and of the rich: [20] It turneth also every thought into jollity and mirth, so that a man remembereth neither sorrow nor debt: [21] And it maketh every heart rich, so that a man remembereth neither king nor governor; and it maketh to speak all things by talents: [22] And when they are in their cups, they forget their love both to friends and brethren, and a little after draw out swords: [23] But when they are from the wine, they remember not what they have done. [24] O ye men, is not wine the strongest, that enforceth to do thus? And when he had so spoken, he held his peace.

1Esdr.4

[1] Then the second, that had spoken of the strength of the king, began to say, [2] O ye men, do not men excel in strength that bear rule over sea and land and all things in them? [3] But yet the king is more mighty: for he is lord of all these things, and hath dominion over them; and whatsoever he commandeth them they do. [4] If he bid them make war the one against the other, they do it: if he send them out against the enemies, they go, and break down mountains walls and towers. [5] They slay and are slain, and transgress not the king's commandment: if they get the victory, they bring all to the king, as well the spoil, as all things else. [6] Likewise for those that are no soldiers, and have not to do with wars, but use 615lways615ry, when they have reaped again that which they had sown, they bring it to the king, and compel one another to pay tribute unto the king. [7] And yet he is but one man: if he command to kill, they kill; if he command to spare, they spare; [8] If he command to smite, they smite; if he command to make desolate, they make desolate; if he command to build, they build; [9] If he command to cut down, they cut down; if he command to plant, they plant. [10] So all his people and his armies obey him: furthermore he lieth down, he eateth and drinketh, and taketh his rest: [11] And these keep watch round about him, neither may any one depart, and do his own business, neither disobey they him in any thing. [12] O ye men, how should not the king be mightiest, when in such sort he is obeyed? And he held his tongue. [13] Then the third, who had spoken of women, and of the truth, (this was Zorobabel) began to speak. [14] O ye men, it is not the great king, nor the multitude of men, neither is it wine, that excelleth; who is it then that ruleth them, or hath the lordship over them? Are they not women? [15] Women have borne the king and all the people that bear rule by sea and land. [16] Even of them came they: and they nourished them up that planted the vineyards, from whence the wine cometh. [17] These also make garments for men; these bring glory unto men; and without women cannot men be. [18] Yea, and if men have gathered together gold and silver, or any other goodly thing, do they not love a woman which is comely in favour and beauty? [19] And letting all those things go, do they not gape, and even with open mouth fix their eyes fast on her; and have not all men more desire unto her than unto silver or gold, or any goodly thing whatsoever? [20] A man leaveth his own father that brought him up, and his own country, and cleaveth unto his wife. [21] He sticketh not to spend his life with his wife. And remembereth neither father, nor mother, nor country. [22] By this also ye must know that women have dominion over you: do ye not labour and toil, and give and bring all to the woman? [23] Yea, a man taketh his sword, and goeth his way to rob and to steal, to sail upon the sea and upon rivers; [24] And looketh upon a lion, and goeth in the darkness; and when he hath stolen, spoiled, and robbed, he bringeth it to his love. [25] Wherefore a man loveth his wife better than father or mother. [26] Yea, many there be that have run out of their wits for women, and become servants for their sakes. [27] Many also have perished, have erred, and sinned, for women. [28] And now do ye not believe me? Is not the king great in his power? Do not all regions fear to touch him? [29] Yet did I see him and Apame the king's concubine, the daughter of the admirable Bartacus, sitting at the right hand of the king, [30] And taking the crown from the king's head, and setting it upon her own head; she

also struck the king with her left hand. [31] And yet for all this the king gaped and gazed upon her with open mouth: if she laughed upon him, he laughed also: but if she took any displeasure at him, the king was fain to flatter, that she might be reconciled to him again. [32] O ye men, how can it be but women should be strong, seeing they do thus? [33] Then the king and the princes looked one upon another: so he began to speak of the truth. [34] O ye men, are not women strong? great is the earth, high is the heaven, swift is the sun in his course, for he compasseth the heavens round about, and fetcheth his course again to his own place in one day. [35] Is he not great that maketh these things? Therefore great is the truth, and stronger than all things. [36] All the earth crieth upon the truth, and the heaven blesseth it: all works shake and tremble at it, and with it is no unrighteous thing. [37] Wine is wicked, the king is wicked, women are wicked, all the children of men are wicked, and such are all their wicked works; and there is no truth in them; in their unrighteousness also they shall perish. [38] As for the truth, it endureth, and is 616lways strong; it liveth and conquereth for evermore. [39] With her there is no accepting of persons or rewards; but she doeth the things that are just, and refraineth from all unjust and wicked things; and all men do well like of her works. [40] Neither in her judgment is any unrighteousness; and she is the strength, kingdom, power, and majesty, of all ages. Blessed be the God of truth. [41] And with that he held his peace. And all the people then shouted, and said, Great is Truth, and mighty above all things. [42] Then said the king unto him, Ask what thou wilt more than is appointed in the writing, and we will give it thee, because thou art found wisest; and thou shalt sit next me, and shalt be called my cousin. [43] Then said he unto the king, Remember thy vow, which thou hast vowed to build Jerusalem, in the day when thou camest to thy kingdom, [44] And to send away all the vessels that were taken away out of Jerusalem, which Cyrus set apart, when he vowed to destroy Babylon, and to send them again thither. [45] Thou also hast vowed to build up the temple, which the Edomites burned when Judea was made desolate by the Chaldees. [46] And now, O lord the king, this is that which I require, and which I desire of thee, and this is the princely liberality proceeding from thyself: I desire therefore that thou make good the vow, the performance whereof with thine own mouth thou hast vowed to the King of heaven. [47] Then Darius the king stood up, and kissed him, and wrote letters for him unto all the treasurers and lieutenants and captains and governors, that they should safely convey on their way both him, and all those that go up with him to build Jerusalem. [48] He wrote letters also unto the lieutenants that were in Celosyria and Phenice, and unto them in Libanus, that they should bring cedar wood from Libanus unto Jerusalem, and that they should build the city with him. [49] Moreover he wrote for all the Jews that went out of his realm up into Jewry, concerning their freedom, that no officer, no ruler, no lieutenant, nor treasurer, should forcibly enter into their doors; [50] And that all the country which they hold should be free without tribute; and that the Edomites should give over the villages of the Jews which then they held: [51] Yea, that there should be yearly given twenty talents to the building of the temple, until the time that it were built; [52] And other ten talents yearly, to maintain the burnt offerings upon the altar every day, as they had a commandment to offer seventeen: [53] And that all they that went from Babylon to build the city should have free liberty, as well they as their posterity, and all the priests that went away. [54] He wrote also concerning. The charges, and the priests' vestments wherein they minister; [55] And likewise for the charges of the Levites, to be given them until the day that the house were finished, and Jerusalem builded up. [56] And he commanded to give to all that kept the city pensions and wages. [57] He sent away also all the vessels from Babylon, that Cyrus had set apart; and all that Cyrus had given in commandment, the same charged he also to be done, and sent unto Jerusalem. [58] Now when this young man was gone forth, he lifted up his face to heaven toward Jerusalem, and praised the King of heaven, [59] And said, From thee cometh victory, from thee cometh wisdom, and thine is the glory, and I am thy servant. [60] Blessed art thou, who hast given me wisdom: for to thee I give thanks, O Lord of our fathers. [61] And so he took the letters, and went out, and came unto Babylon, and told it all his brethren. [62] And they praised the God of their fathers, because he had given them freedom and liberty [63] To go up, and to build Jerusalem, and the temple which is called by his name: and they feasted with instruments of musick and gladness seven days.

1Esdr.5

[1] After this were the principal men of the families chosen according to their tribes, to go up with their wives and sons and daughters, with their menservants and maidservants, and their cattle. [2] And Darius sent with them a thousand horsemen, till they had brought them back to Jerusalem safely, and with musical [instruments] tabrets and flutes. [3] And all their brethren played, and he made them go up together with them. [4] And these are the names of the men which went up, according to their families among their tribes, after their several heads. [5] The priests, the sons of Phinees the son of Aaron: Jesus the son of Josedec, the son of Saraias, and Joacim the son of Zorobabel, the son of Salathiel, of the house of David, out of the kindred of Phares, of the tribe of Judah; [6] Who spake wise sentences before Darius the king of Persia in the second year of his reign, in the month Nisan, which is the first month. [7] And these are they of Jewry that came up from the captivity, where they dwelt as strangers, whom Nabuchodonosor the king of Babylon had carried away unto Babylon. [8] And they returned unto Jerusalem, and to the other parts of Jewry, every man to his own city, who came with Zorobabel, with Jesus, Nehemias, and Zacharias, and Reesaias, Enenius, Mardocheus. Beelsarus, Aspharasus, Reelius, Roimus, and Baana, their guides. [9] The number of them of the nation, and their governors, sons of Phoros, two thousand an hundred seventy and two; the sons of Saphat, four hundred seventy and two: [10] The sons of Ares, seven hundred fifty and six: [11] The sons of Phaath Moab, two thousand eight hundred and twelve: [12] The sons of Elam, a thousand two hundred fifty and four: the sons of Zathul, nine hundred forty and five: the sons of Corbe, seven hundred and five: the sons of Bani, six hundred forty and eight: [13] The sons of Bebai, six hundred twenty and three: the sons of Sadas, three

thousand two hundred twenty and two: [14] The sons of Adonikam, six hundred sixty and seven: the sons of Bagoi, two thousand sixty and six: the sons of Adin, four hundred fifty and four: [15] The sons of Aterezias, ninety and two: the sons of Ceilan and Azetas threescore and seven: the sons of Azuran, four hundred thirty and two: [16] The sons of Ananias, an hundred and one: the sons of Arom, thirty two: and the sons of Bassa, three hundred twenty and three: the sons of Azephurith, an hundred and two: [17] The sons of Meterus, three thousand and five: the sons of Bethlomon, an hundred twenty and three: [18] They of Netophah, fifty and five: they of Anathoth, an hundred fifty and eight: they of Bethsamos, forty and two: [19] They of Kiriathiarius, twenty and five: they of Caphira and Beroth, seven hundred forty and three: they of Pira, seven hundred: [20] They of Chadias and Ammidoi, four hundred twenty and two: they of Cirama and Gabdes, six hundred twenty and one: [21] They of Macalon, an hundred twenty and two: they of Betolius, fifty and two: the sons of Nephis, an hundred fifty and six: [22] The sons of Calamolalus and Onus, seven hundred twenty and five: the sons of Jerechus, two hundred forty and five: [23] The sons of Annas, three thousand three hundred and thirty. [24] The priests: the sons of Jeddu, the son of Jesus among the sons of Sanasib, nine hundred seventy and two: the sons of Meruth, a thousand fifty and two: [25] The sons of Phassaron, a thousand forty and seven: the sons of Carme, a thousand and seventeen. [26] The Levites: the sons of Jessue, and Cadmiel, and Banuas, and Sudias, seventy and four. [27] The holy singers: the sons of Asaph, an hundred twenty and eight. [28] The porters: the sons of Salum, the sons of Jatal, the sons of Talmon, the sons of Dacobi, the sons of Teta, the sons of Sami, in all an hundred thirty and nine. [29] The servants of the temple: the sons of Esau, the sons of Asipha, the sons of Tabaoth, the sons of Ceras, the sons of Sud, the sons of Phaleas, the sons of Labana, the sons of Graba, [30] The sons of Acua, the sons of Uta, the sons of Cetab, the sons of Agaba, the sons of Subai, the sons of Anan, the sons of Cathua, the sons of Geddur, [31] The sons of Airus, the sons of Daisan, the sons of Noeba, the sons of Chaseba, the sons of Gazera, the sons of Azia, the sons of Phinees, the sons of Azare, the sons of Bastai, the sons of Asana, the sons of Meani, the sons of Naphisi, the sons of Acub, the sons of Acipha, the sons of Assur, the sons of Pharacim, the sons of Basaloth, [32] The sons of Meeda, the sons of Coutha, the sons of Charea, the sons of Charcus, the sons of Aserer, the sons of Thomoi, the sons of Nasith, the sons of Atipha. [33] The sons of the servants of Solomon: the sons of Azaphion, the sons of Pharira, the sons of Jeeli, the sons of Lozon, the sons of Israel, the sons of Sapheth, [34] The sons of Hagia, the sons of Pharacareth, the sons of Sabi, the sons of Sarothie, the sons of Masias, the sons of Gar, the sons of Addus, the sons of Suba, the sons of Apherra, the sons of Barodis, the sons of Sabat, the sons of Allom. [35] All the ministers of the temple, and the sons of the servants of Solomon, were three hundred seventy and two. [36] These came up from Thermeleth and Thelersas, Charaathalar leading them, and Aalar; [37] Neither could they shew their families, nor their stock, how they were of Israel: the sons of Ladan, the son of Ban, the sons of Necodan, six hundred fifty and two. [38] And of the priests that usurped the office of the priesthood, and were not found: the sons of Obdia, the sons of Accoz, the sons of Addus, who married Augia one of the daughters of Barzelus, and was named after his name. [39] And when the description of the kindred of these men was sought in the register, and was not found, they were removed from executing the office of the priesthood: [40] For unto them said Nehemias and Atharias, that they should not be partakers of the holy things, till there arose up an high priest clothed with doctrine and truth. [41] So of Israel, from them of twelve years old and upward, they were all in number forty thousand, beside menservants and womenservants two thousand three hundred and sixty. [42] Their menservants and handmaids were seven thousand three hundred forty and seven: the singing men and singing women, two hundred forty and five: [43] Four hundred thirty and five camels, seven thousand thirty and six horses, two hundred forty and five mules, five thousand five hundred twenty and five beasts used to the yoke. [44] And certain of the chief of their families, when they came to the temple of God that is in Jerusalem, vowed to set up the house again in his own place according to their ability, [45] And to give into the holy treasury of the works a thousand pounds of gold, five thousand of silver, and an hundred priestly vestments. [46] And so dwelt the priests and the Levites and the people in Jerusalem, and in the country, the singers also and the porters; and all Israel in their villages. [47] But when the seventh month was at hand, and when the children of Israel were every man in his own place, they came all together with one consent into the open place of the first gate which is toward the east. [48] Then stood up Jesus the son of Josedec, and his brethren the priests and Zorobabel the son of Salathiel, and his brethren, and made ready the altar of the God of Israel, [49] To offer burnt sacrifices upon it, according as it is expressly commanded in the book of Moses the man of God. [50] And there were gathered unto them out of the other nations of the land, and they erected the altar upon his own place, because all the nations of the land were at enmity with them, and oppressed them; and they offered sacrifices according to the time, and burnt offerings to the Lord both morning and evening. [51] Also they held the feast of tabernacles, as it is commanded in the law, and offered sacrifices daily, as was meet: [52] And after that, the continual oblations, and the sacrifice of the sabbaths, and of the new moons, and of all holy feasts. [53] And all they that had made any vow to God began to offer sacrifices to God from the first day of the seventh month, although the temple of the Lord was not yet built. [54] And they gave unto the masons and carpenters money, meat, and drink, with cheerfulness. [55] Unto them of Zidon also and Tyre they gave carrs, that they should bring cedar trees from Libanus, which should be brought by floats to the haven of Joppa, according as it was commanded them by Cyrus king of the Persians. [56] And in the second year and second month after his coming to the temple of God at Jerusalem began Zorobabel the son of Salathiel, and Jesus the son of Josedec, and their brethren, and the priests, and the Levites, and all they that were come unto Jerusalem out of the captivity: [57] And they laid the foundation of the house of God in the first day of the second month, in the second year after they were come to Jewry and Jerusalem. [58] And they appointed the Levites from twenty years old over the works of the Lord.

Then stood up Jesus, and his sons and brethren, and Cadmiel his brother, and the sons of Madiabun, with the sons of Joda the son of Eliadun, with their sons and brethren, all Levites, with one accord setters forward of the business, labouring to advance the works in the house of God. So the workmen built the temple of the Lord. [59] And the priests stood arrayed in their vestments with musical instruments and trumpets; and the Levites the sons of Asaph had cymbals, [60] Singing songs of thanksgiving, and praising the Lord, according as David the king of Israel had ordained. [61] And they sung with loud voices songs to the praise of the Lord, because his mercy and glory is for ever in all Israel. [62] And all the people sounded trumpets, and shouted with a loud voice, singing songs of thanksgiving unto the Lord for the rearing up of the house of the Lord. [63] Also of the priests and Levites, and of the chief of their families, the ancients who had seen the former house came to the building of this with weeping and great crying. [64] But many with trumpets and joy shouted with loud voice, [65] Insomuch that the trumpets might not be heard for the weeping of the people: yet the multitude sounded marvellously, so that it was heard afar off. [66] Wherefore when the enemies of the tribe of Judah and Benjamin heard it, they came to know what that noise of trumpets should mean. [67] And they perceived that they that were of the captivity did build the temple unto the Lord God of Israel. [68] So they went to Zorobabel and Jesus, and to the chief of the families, and said unto them, We will build together with you. [69] For we likewise, as ye, do obey your Lord, and do sacrifice unto him from the days of Azbazareth the king of the Assyrians, who brought us hither. [70] Then Zorobabel and Jesus and the chief of the families of Israel said unto them, It is not for us and you to build together an house unto the Lord our God. [71] We ourselves alone will build unto the Lord of Israel, according as Cyrus the king of the Persians hath commanded us. [72] But the heathen of the land lying heavy upon the inhabitants of Judea, and holding them strait, hindered their building; [73] And by their secret plots, and popular persuasions and commotions, they hindered the finishing of the building all the time that king Cyrus lived: so they were hindered from building for the space of two years, until the reign of Darius.

1Esdr.6

[1] Now in the second year of the reign of Darius Aggeus and Zacharias the son of Addo, the prophets, prophesied unto the Jews in Jewry and Jerusalem in the name of the Lord God of Israel, which was upon them. [2] Then stood up Zorobabel the son of Salatiel, and Jesus the son of Josedec, and began to build the house of the Lord at Jerusalem, the prophets of the Lord being with them, and helping them. [3] At the same time came unto them Sisinnes the governor of Syria and Phenice, with Sathrabuzanes and his companions, and said unto them, [4] By whose appointment do ye build this house and this roof, and perform all the other things? And who are the workmen that perform these things? [5] Nevertheless the elders of the Jews obtained favour, because the Lord had visited the captivity; [6] And they were not hindered from building, until such time as signification was given unto Darius concerning them, and an answer received. [7] The

copy of the letters which Sisinnes, governor of Syria and Phenice, and Sathrabuzanes, with their companions, rulers in Syria and Phenice, wrote and sent unto Darius; To king Darius, greeting: [8] Let all things be known unto our lord the king, that being come into the country of Judea, and entered into the city of Jerusalem we found in the city of Jerusalem the ancients of the Jews that were of the captivity [9] Building an house unto the Lord, great and new, of hewn and costly stones, and the timber already laid upon the walls. [10] And those works are done with great speed, and the work goeth on prosperously in their hands, and with all glory and diligence is it made. [11] Then asked we these elders, saying, By whose commandment build ye this house, and lay the foundations of these works? [12] Therefore to the intent that we might give knowledge unto thee by writing, we demanded of them who were the chief doers, and we required of them the names in writing of their principal men. [13] So they gave us this answer, We are the servants of the Lord Ih made heaven and earth. [14] And as for this house, it was builded many years ago by a king of Israel great and strong, and was finished. [15] But when our fathers provoked God unto wrath, and sinned against the Lord of Israel which is in heaven, he gave them over into the power of Nabuchodonosor king of Babylon, of the Chaldees; [16] Who pulled down the house, and burned it, and carried away the people captives unto Babylon. [17] But in the first year that king Cyrus reigned over the country of Babylon Cyrus the king wrote to build up this house. [18] And the holy vessels of gold and of silver, that Nabuchodonosor had carried away out of the house at Jerusalem, and had set them in his own temple those Cyrus the king brought forth again out of the temple at Babylon, and they were delivered to Zorobabel and to Sanabassarus the ruler, [19] With commandment that he should carry away the same vessels, and put them in the temple at Jerusalem; and that the temple of the Lord should be built in his place. [20] Then the same Sanabassarus, being come hither, laid the foundations of the house of the Lord at Jerusalem; and from that time to this being still a building, it is not yet fully ended. [21] Now therefore, if it seem good unto the king, let search be made among the records of king Cyrus: [22] And if it be found that the building of the house of the Lord at Jerusalem hath been done with the consent of king Cyrus, and if our lord the king be so minded, let him signify unto us thereof. [23] Then commanded king Darius to seek among the records at Babylon: and so at Ecbatane the palace, which is in the country of Media, there was found a roll wherein these things were recorded. [24] In the first year of the reign of Cyrus king Cyrus commanded that the house of the Lord at Jerusalem should be built again, where they do sacrifice with continual fire: [25] Whose height shall be sixty cubits and the breadth sixty cubits, with three rows of hewn stones, and one row of new wood of that country; and the expences thereof to be given out of the house of king Cyrus: [26] And that the holy vessels of the house of the Lord, both of gold and silver, that Nabuchodonosor took out of the house at Jerusalem, and brought to Babylon, should be restored to the house at Jerusalem, and be set in the place where they were before. [27] And also he commanded that Sisinnes the governor of Syria and Phenice, and Sathrabuzanes, and their companions, and those which were appointed rulers in Syria and Phenice, should be careful not to meddle with the place, but suffer Zorobabel, the servant of the Lord, and governor of Judea, and the elders of the Jews, to build the house of the Lord in that place. [28] I have commanded also to have it built up whole again; and that they look diligently to help those that be of the captivity of the Jews, till the house of the Lord be finished: [29] And out of the tribute of Celosyria and Phenice a portion carefully to be given these men for the sacrifices of the Lord, that is, to Zorobabel the governor, for bullocks, and rams, and lambs; [30] And also corn, salt, wine, and oil, and that continually every year without further question, according as the priests that be in Jerusalem shall signify to be daily spent: [31] That offerings may be made to the most high God for the king and for his children, and that they may pray for their lives. [32] And he commanded that whosoever should transgress, yea, or make light of any thing afore spoken or written, out of his own house should a tree be taken, and he thereon be hanged, and all his goods seized for the king. [33] The Lord therefore, whose name is there called upon, utterly destroy every king and nation, that stretcheth out his hand to hinder or endamage that house of the Lord in Jerusalem.

[34] I Darius the king have ordained that according unto these things it be done with diligence.

1Esdr.7

[1] Then Sisinnes the governor of Celosyria and Phenice, and Sathrabuzanes, with their companions following the commandments of king Darius, [2] Did very carefully oversee the holy works, assisting the ancients of the Jews and governors of the temple. [3] And so the holy works prospered, when Aggeus and Zacharias the prophets prophesied. [4] And they finished these things by the commandment of the Lord God of Israel, and with the consent of Cyrus, Darius, and Artexerxes, kings of Persia. [5] And thus was the holy house finished in the three and twentieth day of the month Adar, in the sixth year of Darius king of the Persians [6] And the children of Israel, the priests, and the Levites, and others that were of the captivity, that were added unto them, did according to the things written in the book of Moses. [7] And to the dedication of the temple of the Lord they offered an hundred bullocks two hundred rams, four hundred lambs; [8] And twelve goats for the sin of all Israel, according to the number of the chief of the tribes of Israel. [9] The priests also and the Levites stood arrayed in their vestments, according to their kindreds, in the service of the Lord God of Israel, according to the book of Moses: and the porters at every gate. [10] And the children of Israel that were of the captivity held the passover the fourteenth day of the first month, after that the priests and the Levites were sanctified. [11] They that were of the captivity were not all sanctified together: but the Levites were all sanctified together. [12] And so they offered the passover for all them of the captivity, and for their brethren the priests, and for themselves. [13] And the children of Israel that came out of the captivity did eat, even all they that had separated themselves from the abominations of the people of the land, and sought the Lord. [14] And they kept the feast of unleavened bread seven days, making merry before the Lord, [15] For that he had turned the counsel of the king of Assyria toward them, to strengthen their hands in

the works of the Lord God of Israel.

1Esdr.8

[1] And after these things, when Artexerxes the king of the Persians reigned came Esdras the son of Saraias, the son of Ezerias, the son of Helchiah, the son of Salum, [2] The son of Sadduc, the son of Achitob, the son of Amarias, the son of Ezias, the son of Meremoth, the son of Zaraias, the son of Savias, the son of Boccas, the son of Abisum, the son of Phinees, the son of Eleazar, the son of Aaron the chief priest. [3] This Esdras went up from Babylon, as a scribe, being very ready in the law of Moses, that was given by the God of Israel. [4] And the king did him honour: for he found grace in his sight in all his requests. [5] There went up with him also certain of the children of Israel, of the priest of the Levites, of the holy singers, porters, and ministers of the temple, unto Jerusalem, [6] In the seventh year of the reign of Artexerxes, in the fifth month, this was the king's seventh year; for they went from Babylon in the first day of the first month, and came to Jerusalem, according to the prosperous journey which the Lord gave them. [7] For Esdras had very great skill, so that he omitted nothing of the law and commandments of the Lord, but taught all Israel the ordinances and judgments. [8] Now the copy of the commission, which was written from Artexerxes the king, and came to Esdras the priest and reader of the law of the Lord, is this that followeth; [9] King Artexerxes unto Esdras the priest and reader of the law of the Lord sendeth greeting: [10] Having determined to deal graciously, I have given order, that such of the nation of the Jews, and of the priests and Levites being within our realm, as are willing and desirous should go with thee unto Jerusalem. [11] As many therefore as have a mind thereunto, let them depart with thee, as it hath seemed good both to me and my seven friends the counsellors; [12] That they may look unto the affairs of Judea and Jerusalem, agreeably to that which is in the law of the Lord; [13] And carry the gifts unto the Lord of Israel to Jerusalem, which I and my friends have vowed, and all the gold and silver that in the country of Babylon can be found, to the Lord in Jerusalem, [14] With that also which is given of the people for the temple of the Lord their God at Jerusalem: and that silver and gold may be collected for bullocks, rams, and lambs, and things thereunto appertaining; [15] To the end that they may offer sacrifices unto the Lord upon the altar of the Lord their God, which is in Jerusalem. [16] And whatsoever thou and thy brethren will do with the silver and gold, that do, according to the will of thy God. [17] And the holy vessels of the Lord, which are given thee for the use of the temple of thy God, which is in Jerusalem, thou shalt set before thy God in Jerusalem. [18] And whatsoever thing else thou shalt remember for the use of the temple of thy God, thou shalt give it out of the king's treasury. [19] And I king Artexerxes have also commanded the keepers of the treasures in Syria and Phenice, that whatsoever Esdras the priest and the reader of the law of the most high God shall send for, they should give it him with speed, [20] To the sum of an hundred talents of silver, likewise also of wheat even to an hundred cors, and an hundred pieces of wine, and other things in abundance. [21] Let all things be

performed after the law of God diligently unto the most high God, that wrath come not upon the kingdom of the king and his sons. [22] I command you also, that ye require no tax, nor any other imposition, of any of the priests, or Levites, or holy singers, or porters, or ministers of the temple, or of any that have doings in this temple, and that no man have authority to impose any thing upon them. [23] And thou, Esdras, according to the wisdom of God ordain judges and justices, that they may judge in all Syria and Phenice all those that know the law of thy God; and those that know it not thou shalt teach. [24] And whosoever shall transgress the law of thy God, and of the king, shall be punished diligently, whether it be by death, or other punishment, by penalty of money, or by imprisonment. [25] Then said Esdras the scribe, Blessed be the only Lord God of my fathers, who hath put these things into the heart of the king, to glorify his house that is in Jerusalem: [26] And hath honoured me in the sight of the king, and his counsellors, and all his friends and nobles.

[27] Therefore was I encouraged by the help of the Lord my God, and gathered together men of Israel to go up with me. [28] And these are the chief according to their families and several dignities, that went up with me from Babylon in the reign of king Artexerxes: [29] Of the sons of Phinees, Gerson: of the sons of Ithamar, Gamael: of the sons of David, Lettus the son of Sechenias: [30] Of the sons of Pharez, Zacharias; and with him were counted an hundred and fifty men: [31] Of the sons of Pahath Moab, Eliaonias, the son of Zaraias, and with him two hundred men: [32] Of the sons of Zathoe, Sechenias the son of Jezelus, and with him three hundred men: of the sons of Adin, Obeth the son of Jonathan, and with him two hundred and fifty men: [33] Of the sons of Elam, Josias son of Gotholias, and with him seventy men: [34] Of the sons of Saphatias, Zaraias son of Michael, and with him threescore and ten men: [35] Of the sons of Joab, Abadias son of Jezelus, and with him two hundred and twelve men: [36] Of the sons of Banid, Assalimoth son of Josaphias, and with him an hundred and threescore men: [37] Of the sons of Babi, Zacharias son of Bebai, and with him twenty and eight men: [38] Of the sons of Astath, Johannes son of Acatan, and with him an hundred and ten men: [39] Of the sons of Adonikam the last, and these are the names of them, Eliphalet, Jewel, and Samaias, and with them seventy men: [40] Of the sons of Bago, Uthi the son of Istalcurus, and with him seventy men. [41] And these I gathered together to the river called Theras, where we pitched our tents three days: and then I surveyed them. [42] But when I had found there none of the priests and Levites, [43] Then sent I unto Eleazar, and Iduel, and Masman, [44] And Alnathan, and Mamaias, and Joribas, and Nathan, Eunatan, Zacharias, and Mosollamon, principal men and learned. [45] And I bade them that they should go unto Saddeus the captain, who was in the place of the treasury: [46] And commanded them that they should speak unto Daddeus, and to his brethren, and to the treasurers in that place, to send us such men as might execute the priests' office in the house of the Lord. [47] And by the mighty hand of our Lord they brought unto us skilful men of the sons of Moli the son of Levi, the son of Israel, Asebebia, and his sons, and his brethren, who were eighteen. [48] And Asebia, and Annus, and Osaias his brother, of the sons of Channuneus, and

their sons, were twenty men. [49] And of the servants of the temple whom David had ordained, and the principal men for the service of the Levites to wit, the servants of the temple two hundred and twenty, the catalogue of whose names were shewed. [50] And there I vowed a fast unto the young men before our lord, to desire of him a prosperous journey both for us and them that were with us, for our children, and for the cattle: [51] For I was ashamed to ask the king footmen, and horsemen, and conduct for safeguard against our adversaries. [52] For we had said unto the king, that the power of the Lord our God should be with them that seek him, to support them in all ways. [53] And again we besought our Lord as touching these things, and found him favourable unto us. [54] Then I separated twelve of the chief of the priests, Esebrias, and Assanias, and ten men of their brethren with them: [55] And I weighed them the gold, and the silver, and the holy vessels of the house of our Lord, which the king, and his council, and the princes, and all Israel, had given. [56] And when I had weighed it, I delivered unto them six hundred and fifty talents of silver, and silver vessels of an hundred talents, and an hundred talents of gold, [57] And twenty golden vessels, and twelve vessels of brass, even of fine brass, glittering like gold. [58] And I said unto them, Both ye are holy unto the Lord, and the vessels are holy, and the gold and the silver is a vow unto the Lord, the Lord of our fathers. [59] Watch ye, and keep them till ye deliver them to the chief of the priests and Levites, and to the principal men of the families of Israel, in Jerusalem, into the chambers of the house of our God. [60] So the priests and the Levites, who had received the silver and the gold and the vessels, brought them unto Jerusalem, into the temple of the Lord. [61] And from the river Theras we departed the twelfth day of the first month, and came to Jerusalem by the mighty hand of our Lord, which was with us: and from the beginning of our journey the Lord delivered us from every enemy, and so we came to Jerusalem. [62] And when we had been there three days, the gold and silver that was weighed was delivered in the house of our Lord on the fourth day unto Marmoth the priest the son of Iri. [63] And with him was Eleazar the son of Phinees, and with them were Josabad the son of Jesu and Moeth the son of Sabban, Levites: all was delivered them by number and weight. [64] And all the weight of them was written up the same hour. [65] Moreover they that were come out of the captivity offered sacrifice unto the Lord God of Israel, even twelve bullocks for all Israel, fourscore and sixteen rams, [66] Threescore and twelve lambs, goats for a peace offering, twelve; all of them a sacrifice to the Lord. [67] And they delivered the king's commandments unto the king's stewards' and to the governors of Celosyria and Phenice; and they honoured the people and the temple of God. [68] Now when these things were done, the rulers came unto me, and said, [69] The nation of Israel, the princes, the priests and Levites, have not put away from them the strange people of the land, nor the pollutions of the Gentiles to wit, of the Canaanites, Hittites, Pheresites, Jebusites, and the Moabites, Egyptians, and Edomites. [70] For both they and their sons have married with their daughters, and the holy seed is mixed with the strange people of the land; and from the beginning of this matter the rulers and the great men have been partakers of this iniquity. [71] And as soon as I had heard these things, I rent my clothes, and the holy garment, and pulled off the hair from off my head and beard, and sat me down sad and very heavy. [72] So all they that were then moved at the word of the Lord God of Israel assembled unto me, whilst I mourned for the iniquity: but I sat still full of heaviness until the evening sacrifice. [73] Then rising up from the fast with my clothes and the holy garment rent, and bowing my knees, and stretching forth my hands unto the Lord, [74] I said, O Lord, I am confounded and ashamed before thy face; [75] For our sins are multiplied above our heads, and our ignorances have reached up unto heaven. [76] For ever since the time of our fathers we have been and are in great sin, even unto this day. [77] And for our sins and our fathers' we with our brethren and our kings and our priests were given up unto the kings of the earth, to the sword, and to captivity, and for a prey with shame, unto this day. [78] And now in some measure hath mercy been shewed unto us from thee, O Lord, that there should be left us a root and a name in the place of thy sanctuary; [79] And to discover unto us a light in the house of the Lord our God, and to give us food in the time of our servitude. [80] Yea, when we were in bondage, we were not forsaken of our Lord; but he made us gracious before the kings of Persia, so that they gave us food; [81] Yea, and honoured the temple of our Lord, and raised up the desolate Sion, that they have given us a sure abiding in Jewry and Jerusalem. [82] And now, O Lord, what shall we say, having these things? For we have transgressed thy commandments, which thou gavest by the hand of thy servants the prophets, saying, [83] That the land, which ye enter into to possess as an heritage, is a land polluted with the pollutions of the strangers of the land, and they have filled it with their uncleanness. [84] Therefore now shall ye not join your daughters unto their sons, neither shall ye take their daughters unto your sons. [85] Moreover ye shall never seek to have peace with them, that ye may be strong, and eat the good things of the land, and that ye may leave the inheritance of the land unto your children for evermore. [86] And all that is befallen is done unto us for our wicked works and great sins; for thou, O Lord, didst make our sins light, [87] And didst give unto us such a root: but we have turned back again to transgress thy law, and to mingle ourselves with the uncleanness of the nations of the land. [88] Mightest not thou be angry with us to destroy us, till thou hadst left us neither root, seed, nor name? [89] O Lord of Israel, thou art true: for we are left a root this day. [90] Behold, now are we before thee in our iniquities, for we cannot stand any longer by reason of these things before thee. [91] And as Esdras in his prayer made his confession, weeping, and lying flat upon the ground before the temple, there gathered unto him from Jerusalem a very great multitude of men and women and children: for there was great weeping among the multitude. [92] Then Jechonias the son of Jeelus, one of the sons of Israel, called out, and said, O Esdras, we have sinned against the Lord God, we have married strange women of the nations of the land, and now is all Israel aloft. [93] Let us make an oath to the Lord, that we will put away all our wives, whichh we have taken of the heathen, with their children, [94] Like as thou hast decreed, and as many as do obey the law of the Lord. [95] Arise and put in execution: for to thee doth this

matter appertain, and we will be with thee: do valiantly. [96] So Esdras arose, and took an oath of the chief of the priests and Levites of all Israel to do after these things; and so they sware.

1Esdr.9

[1] Then Esdras rising from the court of the temple went to the chamber of Joanan the son of Eliasib, [2] And remained there, and did eat no meat nor drink water, mourning for the great iniquities of the multitude. [3] And there was a proclamation in all Jewry and Jerusalem to all them that were of the captivity, that they should be gathered together at Jerusalem: [4] And that whosoever met not there within two or three days according as the elders that bare rule appointed, their cattle should be seized to the use of the temple, and himself cast out from them that were of the captivity. [5] And in three days were all they of the tribe of Judah and Benjamin gathered together at Jerusalem the twentieth day of the ninth month. [6] And all the multitude sat trembling in the broad court of the temple because of the present foul weather. [7] So Esdras arose up, and said unto them, Ye have transgressed the law in marrying strange wives, thereby to increase the sins of Israel. [8] And now by confessing give glory unto the Lord God of our fathers, [9] And do his will, and separate yourselves from the heathen of the land, and from the strange women. [10] Then cried the whole multitude, and said with a loud voice, Like as thou hast spoken, so will we do. [11] But forasmuch as the people are many, and it is foul weather, so that we cannot stand without, and this is not a work of a day or two, seeing our sin in these things is spread far: [12] Therefore let the rulers of the multitude stay, and let all them of our habitations that have strange wives come at the time appointed, [13] And with them the rulers and judges of every place, till we turn away the wrath of the Lord from us for this matter. [14] Then Jonathan the son of Azael and Ezechias the son of Theocanus accordingly took this matter upon them: and Mosollam and Levis and Sabbatheus helped them. [15] And they that were of the captivity did according to all these things. [16] And Esdras the priest chose unto him the principal men of their families, all by name: and in the first day of the tenth month they sat together to examine the matter. [17] So their cause that held strange wives was brought to an end in the first day of the first month. [18] And of the priests that were come together, and had strange wives, there were found: [19] Of the sons of Jesus the son of Josedec, and his brethren; Matthelas and Eleazar, and Joribus and Joadanus. [20] And they gave their hands to put away their wives and to offer rams to make reconcilement for their errors. [21] And of the sons of Emmer; Ananias, and Zabdeus, and Eanes, and Sameius, and Hiereel, and Azarias. [22] And of the sons of Phaisur; Elionas, Massias Israel, and Nathanael, and Ocidelus and Talsas. [23] And of the Levites; Jozabad, and Semis, and Colius, who was called Calitas, and Patheus, and Judas, and Jonas. [24] Of the holy singers; Eleazurus, Bacchurus. [25] Of the porters; Sallumus, and Tolbanes. [26] Of them of Israel, of the sons of Phoros; Hiermas, and Eddias, and Melchias, and Maelus, and Eleazar, and Asibias, and Baanias. [27] Of the sons of Ela; Matthanias, Zacharias, and Hierielus, and Hieremoth,

and Aedias. [28] And of the sons of Zamoth; Eliadas, Elisimus, Othonias, Jarimoth, and Sabatus, and Sardeus. [29] Of the sons of Babai; Johannes, and Ananias and Josabad, and Amatheis. [30] Of the sons of Mani; Olamus, Mamuchus, Jedeus, Jasubus, Jasael, and Hieremoth. [31] And of the sons of Addi; Naathus, and Moosias, Lacunus, and Naidus, and Mathanias, and Sesthel, Balnuus, and Manasseas. [32] And of the sons of Annas; Elionas and Aseas, and Melchias, and Sabbeus, and Simon Chosameus. [33] And of the sons of Asom; Altaneus, and Matthias, and Baanaia, Eliphalet, and Manasses, and Semei. [34] And of the sons of Maani; Jeremias, Momdis, Omaerus, Juel, Mabdai, and Pelias, and Anos, Carabasion, and Enasibus, and Mamnitanaimus, Eliasis, Bannus, Eliali, Samis, Selemias, Nathanias: and of the sons of Ozora; Sesis, Esril, Azaelus, Samatus, Zambis, Josephus. [35] And of the sons of Ethma; Mazitias, Zabadaias, Edes, Juel, Banaias. [36] All these had taken strange wives, and they put them away with their children. [37] And the priests and Levites, and they that were of Israel, dwelt in Jerusalem, and in the country, in the first day of the seventh month: so the children of Israel were in their habitations. [38] And the whole multitude came together with one accord into the broad place of the holy porch toward the east: [39] And they spake unto Esdras the priest and reader, that he would bring the law of Moses, that was given of the Lord God of Israel. [40] So Esdras the chief priest brought the law unto the whole multitude from man to woman, and to all the priests, to hear law in the first day of the seventh month. [41] And he read in the broad court before the holy porch from morning unto midday, before both men and women; and the multitude gave heed unto the law. [42] And Esdras the priest and reader of the law stood up upon a pulpit of wood, which was made for that purpose. [43] And there stood up by him Mattathias, Sammus, Ananias, Azarias, Urias, Ezecias, Balasamus, upon the right hand: [44] And upon his left hand stood Phaldaius, Misael, Melchias, Lothasubus, and Nabarias. [45] Then took Esdras the book of the law before the multitude: for he sat honourably in the first place in the sight of them all. [46] And when he opened the law, they stood all straight up. So Esdras blessed the Lord God most High, the God of hosts, Almighty. [47] And all the people answered, Amen; and lifting up their hands they fell to the ground, and worshipped the Lord. [48] Also Jesus, Anus, Sarabias, Adinus, Jacubus, Sabateas, Auteas, Maianeas, and Calitas, Asrias, and Joazabdus, and Ananias, Biatas, the Levites, taught the law of the Lord, making them withal to understand it. [49] Then spake Attharates unto Esdras the chief priest. and reader, and to the Levites that taught the multitude, even to all, saying, [50] This day is holy unto the Lord; (for they all wept when they heard the law:) [51] Go then, and eat the fat, and drink the sweet, and send part to them that have nothing; [52] For this day is holy unto the Lord: and be not sorrowful; for the Lord will bring you to honour. [53] So the Levites published all things to the people, saying, This day is holy to the Lord; be not sorrowful. [54] Then went they their way, every one to eat and drink, and make merry, and to give part to them that had nothing, and to make great cheer; [55] Because they understood the words wherein they were instructed, and for the which they had been assembled.

2 ESDRAS

4Ezra.1

[1] The second book of the prophet Esdras, the son of Saraias, the son of Azarias, the son of Helchias, the son of Sadamias, the sou of Sadoc, the son of Achitob, [2] The son of Achias, the son of Phinees, the son of Heli, the son of Amarias, the son of Aziei, the son of Marimoth, the son of And he spake unto the of Borith, the son of Abisei, the son of Phinees, the son of Eleazar, [3] The son of Aaron, of the tribe of Levi; which was captive in the land of the Medes, in the reign of Artexerxes king of the Persians. [4] And the word of the Lord came unto me, saying, [5] Go thy way, and shew my people their sinful deeds, and their children their wickedness which they have done against me; that they may tell their children's children: [6] Because the sins of their fathers are increased in them: for they have forgotten me, and have offered unto strange gods. [7] Am not I even he that brought them out of the land of Egypt, from the house of bondage? But they have provoked me unto wrath, and despised my counsels. [8] Pull thou off then the hair of thy head, and cast all evil upon them, for they have not been obedient unto my law, but it is a rebellious people. [9] How long shall I forbear them, into whom I have done so much good? [10] Many kings have I destroyed for their sakes; Pharaoh with his servants and all his power have I smitten down. [11] All the nations have I destroyed before them, and in the east I have scattered the people of two provinces, even of Tyrus and Sidon, and have slain all their enemies. [12] Speak thou therefore unto them, saying, Thus saith the Lord, [13] I led you through the sea and in the beginning gave you a large and safe passage; I gave you Moses for a leader, and Aaron for a priest. [14] I gave you light in a pillar of fire, and great wonders have I done among you; yet have ye forgotten me, saith the Lord. [15] Thus saith the Almighty Lord, The quails were as a token to you; I gave you tents for your safeguard: nevertheless ye murmured there, [16] And triumphed not in my name for the destruction of your enemies, but ever to this day do ye yet murmur. [17] Where are the benefits that I have done for you? When ye were hungry and thirsty in the wilderness, did ye not cry unto me, [18] Saying, Why hast thou brought us into this wilderness to kill us? It had been better for us to have served the Egyptians, than to die in this wilderness. [19] Then had I pity upon your mournings, and gave you manna to eat; so ye did eat angels' bread. [20] When ye were thirsty, did I not cleave the rock, and waters flowed out to your fill? for the heat I covered you with the leaves of the trees. [21] I divided among you a fruitful land, I cast out the Canaanites, the Pherezites, and the Philistines, before you: what shall I yet do more for you? saith the Lord. [22] Thus saith the Almighty Lord, When ye were in the wilderness, in the river of the Amorites, being athirst, and blaspheming my name, [23] I gave you not fire for your blasphemies, but cast a tree in the water, and made the river sweet. [24] What shall I do unto thee, O Jacob? Thou, Juda, wouldest not obey me: I will turn me to other nations, and unto those will I give my name, that they may keep my statutes. [25] Seeing ye have forsaken me, I will forsake you

also; when ye desire me to be gracious unto you, I shall have no mercy upon you. [26] Whensoever ye shall call upon me, I will not hear you: for ye have defiled your hands with blood, and your feet are swift to commit manslaughter. [27] Ye have not as it were forsaken me, but your own selves, saith the Lord. [28] Thus saith the Almighty Lord, Have I not prayed you as a father his sons, as a mother her daughters, and a nurse her young babes, [29] That ye would be my people, and I should be your God; that ye would be my children, and I should be your father? [30] I gathered you together, as a hen gathereth her chickens under her wings: but now, what shall I do unto you? I will cast you out from my face. [31] When ye offer unto me, I will turn my face from you: for your solemn feastdays, your new moons, and your circumcisions, have I forsaken. [32] I sent unto you my servants the prophets, whom ye have taken and slain, and torn their bodies in pieces, whose blood I will require of your hands, saith the Lord. [33] Thus saith the Almighty Lord, Your house is desolate, I will cast you out as the wind doth stubble. [34] And your children shall not be fruitful; for they have despised my commandment, and done the thing that is an evil before me. [35] Your houses will I give to a people that shall come; which not having heard of me yet shall believe me; to whom I have shewed no signs, yet they shall do that I have commanded them. [36] They have seen no prophets, yet they shall call their sins to remembrance, and acknowledge them. [37] I take to witness the grace of the people to come, whose little ones rejoice in gladness: and though they have not seen me with bodily eyes, yet in spirit they believe the thing that I say. [38] And now, brother, behold what glory; and see the people that come from the east: [39] Unto whom I will give for leaders, Abraham, Isaac, and Jacob, Oseas, Amos, and Micheas, Joel, Abdias, and Jonas, [40] Nahum, and Abacuc, Sophonias, Aggeus, Zachary, and Malachy, which is called also an angel of the Lord.

4Ezra.2

[1] Thus saith the Lord, I brought this people out of bondage, and I gave them my commandments by menservants the prophets; whom they would not hear, but despised my counsels. [2] The mother that bare them saith unto them, Go your way, ye children; for I am a widow and forsaken. [3] I brought you up with gladness; but with sorrow and heaviness have I lost you: for ye have sinned before the Lord your God, and done that thing that is evil before him. [4] But what shall I now do unto you? I am a widow and forsaken: go your way, O my children, and ask mercy of the Lord. [5] As for me, O father, I call upon thee for a witness over the mother of these children, which would not keep my covenant, [6] That thou bring them to confusion, and their mother to a spoil, that there may be no offspring of them. [7] Let them be scattered abroad among the heathen, let their names be put out of the earth: for they have despised my covenant. [8] Woe be unto thee, Assur, thou that hidest the unrighteous in thee! O thou wicked people, remember what I did unto Sodom and Gomorrha; [9] Whose land lieth in clods of pitch and heaps of ashes: even so also will I do unto them that hear me not, saith the Almighty Lord. [10] Thus saith the Lord

unto Esdras, Tell my people that I will give them the kingdom of Jerusalem, which I would have given unto Israel. [11] Their glory also will I take unto me, and give these the everlasting tabernacles, which I had prepared for them. [12] They shall have the tree of life for an ointment of sweet savour; they shall neither labour, nor be weary. [13] Go, and ye shall receive: pray for few days unto you, that they may be shortened: the kingdom is already prepared for you: watch. [14] Take heaven and earth to witness; for I have broken the evil in pieces, and created the good: for I live, saith the Lord. [15] Mother, embrace thy children, and bring them up with gladness, make their feet as fast as a pillar: for I have chosen thee, saith the Lord. [16] And those that be dead will I raise up again from their places, and bring them out of the graves: for I have known my name in Israel. [17] Fear not, thou mother of the children: for I have chosen thee, saith the Lord. [18] For thy help will I send my servants Esau and Jeremy, after whose counsel I have sanctified and prepared for thee twelve trees laden with divers fruits, [19] And as many fountains flowing with milk and honey, and seven mighty mountains, whereupon there grow roses and lilies, whereby I will fill thy children with joy. [20] Do right to the widow, judge for the fatherless, give to the poor, defend the orphan, clothe the naked, [21] Heal the broken and the weak, laugh not a lame man to scorn, defend the maimed, and let the blind man come into the sight of my clearness. [22] Keep the old and young within thy walls. [23] Wheresoever thou findest the dead, take them and bury them, and I will give thee the first place in my resurrection. [24] Abide still, O my people, and take thy rest, for thy quietness still come. [25] Nourish thy children, O thou good nurse; stablish their feet. [26] As for the servants whom I have given thee, there shall not one of them perish; for I will require them from among thy number. [27] Be not weary: for when the day of trouble and heaviness cometh, others shall weep and be sorrowful, but thou shalt be merry and have abundance. [28] The heathen shall envy thee, but they shall be able to do nothing against thee, saith the Lord. [29] My hands shall cover thee, so that thy children shall not see hell. [30] Be joyful, O thou mother, with thy children; for I will deliver thee, saith the Lord. [31] Remember thy children that sleep, for I shall bring them out of the sides of the earth, and shew mercy unto them: for I am merciful, saith the Lord Almighty. [32] Embrace thy children until I come and shew mercy unto them: for my wells run over, and my grace shall not fail. [33] I Esdras received a charge of the Lord upon the mount Oreb, that I should go unto Israel; but when I came unto them, they set me at nought, and despised the commandment of the Lord. [34] And therefore I say unto you, O ye heathen, that hear and understand, look for your Shepherd, he shall give you everlasting rest; for he is nigh at hand, that shall come in the end of the world. [35] Be ready to the reward of the kingdom, for the everlasting light shall shine upon you for evermore. [36] Flee the shadow of this world, receive the joyfulness of your glory: I testify my Saviour openly. [37] O receive the gift that is given you, and be glad, giving thanks unto him that hath led you to the heavenly kingdom. [38] Arise up and stand, behold the number of those that be sealed in the feast of the Lord;

[39] Which are departed from the shadow of the world, and have received glorious garments of the Lord. [40] Take thy number, O Sion, and shut up those of thine that are clothed in white, which have fulfilled the law of the Lord. [41] The number of thy children, whom thou longedst for, is fulfilled: beseech the power of the Lord, that thy people, which have been called from the beginning, may be hallowed. [42] I Esdras saw upon the mount Sion a great people, whom I could not number, and they all praised the Lord with songs. [43] And in the midst of them there was a young man of a high stature, taller than all the rest, and upon every one of their heads he set crowns, and was more exalted; which I marvelled at greatly. [44] So I asked the angel, and said, Sir, what are these? [45] He answered and said unto me, These be they that have put off the mortal clothing, and put on the immortal, and have confessed the name of God: now are they crowned, and receive palms. [46] Then said I unto the angel, What young person is it that crowneth them, and giveth them palms in their hands? [47] So he answered and said unto me, It is the Son of God, whom they have confessed in the world. Then began I greatly to commend them that stood so stiffly for the name of the Lord. [48] Then the angel said unto me, Go thy way, and tell my people what manner of things, and how great wonders of the Lord thy God, thou hast seen.

4Ezra.3

[1] In the thirtieth year after the ruin of the city I was in Babylon, and lay troubled upon my bed, and my thoughts came up over my heart: [2] For I saw the desolation of Sion, and the wealth of them that dwelt at Babylon. [3] And my spirit was sore moved, so that I began to speak words full of fear to the most High, and said, [4] O Lord, who bearest rule, thou spakest at the beginning, when thou didst plant the earth, and that thyself alone, and commandedst the people, [5] And gavest a body unto Adam without soul, which was the workmanship of thine hands, and didst breathe into him the breath of life, and he was made living before thee. [6] And thou leadest him into paradise, which thy right hand had planted, before ever the earth came forward. [7] And unto him thou gavest commandment to love thy way: which he transgressed, and immediately thou appointedst death in him and in his generations, of whom came nations, tribes, people, and kindreds, out of number. [8] And every people walked after their own will, and did wonderful things before thee, and despised thy commandments. [9] And again in process of time thou broughtest the flood upon those that dwelt in the world, and destroyedst them. [10] And it came to pass in every of them, that as death was to Adam, so was the flood to these. [11] Nevertheless one of them thou 624ightie, namely, Noah with his household, of whom came all righteous men. [12] And it happened, that when they that dwelt upon the earth began to multiply, and had gotten them many children, and were a great people, they began again to be more ungodly than the first. [13] Now when they lived so wickedly before thee, thou didst choose thee a man from among them, whose name was Abraham. [14] Him thou lovedst, and unto him only thou shewedst thy will: [15] And madest an everlasting covenant with him, promising him that thou wouldest never forsake his

seed. [16] And unto him thou gavest Isaac, and unto Isaac also thou gavest Jacob and Esau. As for Jacob, thou didst choose him to thee, and put by Esau: and so Jacob became a great multitude. [17] And it came to pass, that when thou leadest his seed out of Egypt, thou broughtest them up to the mount Sinai. [18] And bowing the heavens, thou didst set fast the earth, movedst the whole world, and madest the depths to tremble, and troubledst the men of that age. [19] And thy glory went through four gates, of fire, and of earthquake, and of wind, and of cold; that thou 625ightiest give the law unto the seed of Jacob, and diligence unto the generation of Israel. [20] And yet tookest thou not away from them a wicked heart, that thy law might bring forth fruit in them. [21] For the first Adam bearing a wicked heart transgressed, and was overcome; and so be all they that are born of him. [22] Thus infirmity was made permanent; and the law (also) in the heart of the people with the malignity of the root; so that the good departed away, and the evil abode still. [23] So the times passed away, and the years were brought to an end: then didst thou raise thee up a servant, called David: [24] Whom thou commandedst to build a city unto thy name, and to offer incense and oblations unto thee therein. [25] When this was done many years, then they that inhabited the city forsook thee, [26] And in all things did even as Adam and all his generations had done: for they also had a wicked heart: [27] And so thou gavest thy city over into the hands of thine enemies. [28] Are their deeds then any better that inhabit Babylon, that they should therefore have the dominion over Sion? [29] For when I came thither, and had seen impieties without number, then my soul saw many evildoers in this thirtieth year, so that my heart failed me. [30] For I have seen how thou sufferest them sinning, and hast spared wicked doers: and hast destroyed thy people, and hast preserved thine enemies, and hast not signified it. [31] I do not remember how this way may be left: Are they then of Babylon better than they of Sion? [32] Or is there any other people that knoweth thee beside Israel? Or what generation hath so believed thy covenants as Jacob? [33] And yet their reward appeareth not, and their labour hath no fruit: for I have gone here and there through the heathen, and I see that they flow in wealth, and think not upon thy commandments. [34] Weigh thou therefore our wickedness now in the balance, and their's also that dwell the world; and so shall thy name no where be found but in Israel. [35] Or when was it that they which dwell upon the earth have not sinned in thy sight? Or what people have so kept thy commandments? [36] Thou shalt find that Israel by name hath kept thy precepts; but not the heathen.

4Ezra.4

[1] And the angel that was sent unto me, whose name was Uriel, gave me an answer, [2] And said, Thy heart hath gone to far in this world, and thinkest thou to comprehend the way of the most High? [3] Then said I, Yea, my lord. And he answered me, and said, I am sent to shew thee three ways, and to set forth three similitudes before thee: [4] Whereof if thou canst declare me one, I will shew thee also the way that thou desirest to see, and I shall shew thee from whence the wicked heart cometh. [5] And I said, Tell on, my lord. Then said he unto me, Go thy way, weigh me

the weight of the fire, or measure me the blast of the wind, or call me again the day that is past. [6] Then answered I and said, What man is able to do that, that thou shouldest ask such things of me? [7] And he said unto me, If I should ask thee how great dwellings are in the midst of the sea, or how many springs are in the beginning of the deep, or how many springs are above the firmament, or which are the outgoings of paradise: [8] Peradventure thou wouldest say unto me, I never went down into the deep, nor as yet into hell, neither did I ever climb up into heaven. [9] Nevertheless now have I asked thee but only of the fire and wind, and of the day wherethrough thou hast passed, and of things from which thou canst not be separated, and yet canst thou give me no answer of them. [10] He said moreover unto me, Thine own things, and such as are grown up with thee, canst thou not know; [11] How should thy vessel then be able to comprehend the way of the Highest, and, the world being now outwardly corrupted to understand the corruption that is evident in my sight? [12] Then said I unto him, It were better that we were not at all, than that we should live still in wickedness, and to suffer, and not to know wherefore. [13] He answered me, and said, I went into a forest into a plain, and the trees took counsel, [14] And said, Come, let us go and make war against the sea that it may depart away before us, and that we may make us more woods. [15] The floods of the sea also in like manner took counsel, and said, Come, let us go up and subdue the woods of the plain, that there also we may make us another country. [16] The thought of the wood was in vain, for the fire came and consumed it. [17] The thought of the floods of the sea came likewise to nought, for the sand stood up and stopped them. [18] If thou wert judge now betwixt these two, whom wouldest thou begin to justify? or whom wouldest thou condemn? [19] I answered and said, Verily it is a foolish thought that they both have devised, for the ground is given unto the wood, and the sea also hath his place to bear his floods. [20] Then answered he me, and said, Thou hast given a right judgment, but why judgest thou not thyself also? [21] For like as the ground is given unto the wood, and the sea to his floods: even so they that dwell upon the earth may understand nothing but that which is upon the earth: and he that dwelleth above the heavens may only understand the things that are above the height of the heavens. [22] Then answered I and said, I beseech thee, O Lord, let me have understanding: [23] For it was not my mind to be curious of the high things, but of such as pass by us daily, namely, wherefore Israel is given up as a reproach to the heathen, and for what cause the people whom thou hast loved is given over unto ungodly nations, and why the law of our forefathers is brought to nought, and the written covenants come to none effect, [24] And we pass away out of the world as grasshoppers, and our life is astonishment and fear, and we are not worthy to obtain mercy. [25] What will he then do unto his name whereby we are called? of these things have I asked. [26] Then answered he me, and said, The more thou searchest, the more thou shalt marvel; for the world hasteth fast to pass away, [27] And cannot comprehend the things that are promised to the righteous in time to come: for this world is full of unrighteousness and infirmities. [28] But as concerning the things whereof thou askest me, I will tell thee; for the evil is sown, but the destruction thereof is not yet come. [29] If therefore that which is sown be not turned upside down, and if the place where the evil is sown pass not away, then cannot it come that is sown with good. [30] For the grain of evil seed hath been sown in the heart of Adam from the beginning, and how much ungodliness hath it brought up unto this time? and how much shall it yet bring forth until the time of threshing come? [31] Ponder now by thyself, how great fruit of wickedness the grain of evil seed hath brought forth. [32] And when the ears shall be cut down, which are without number, how great a floor shall they fill?

[33] Then I answered and said, How, and when shall these things come to pass? wherefore are our years few and evil? [34] And he answered me, saying, Do not thou hasten above the most Highest: for thy haste is in vain to be above him, for thou hast much exceeded. [35] Did not the souls also of the righteous ask question of these things in their chambers, saying, How long shall I hope on this fashion? when cometh the fruit of the floor of our reward? [36] And unto these things Uriel the archangel gave them answer, and said, Even when the number of seeds is filled in you: for he hath weighed the world in the balance. [37] By measure hath he measured the times; and by number hath he numbered the times; and he doth not move nor stir them, until the said measure be fulfilled. [38] Then answered I and said, O Lord that bearest rule, even we all are full of impiety. [39] And for our sakes peradventure it is that the floors of the righteous are not filled, because of the sins of them that dwell upon the earth. [40] So he answered me, and said, Go thy way to a woman with child, and ask of her when she hath fulfilled her nine months, if her womb may keep the birth any longer within her. [41] Then said I, No, Lord, that can she not. And he said unto me, In the grave the chambers of souls are like the womb of a woman: [42] For like as a woman that travaileth maketh haste to escape the necessity of the travail: even so do these places haste to deliver those things that are committed unto them. [43] From the beginning, look, what thou desirest to see, it shall be shewed thee. [44] Then answered I and said, If I have found favour in thy sight, and if it be possible, and if I be meet therefore, [45] Shew me then whether there be more to come than is past, or more past than is to come. [46] What is past I know, but what is for to come I know not. [47] And he said unto me, Stand up upon the right side, and I shall expound the similitude unto thee. [48] So I stood, and saw, and, behold, an hot burning oven passed by before me: and it happened that when the flame was gone by I looked, and, behold, the smoke remained still. [49] After this there passed by before me a watery cloud, and sent down much rain with a storm; and when the stormy rain was past, the drops remained still. [50] Then said he unto me, Consider with thyself; as the rain is more than the drops, and as the fire is greater than the smoke; but the drops and the smoke remain behind: so the quantity which is past did more exceed. [51] Then I prayed, and said, May I live, thinkest thou, until that time? or what shall happen in those days? [52] He answered me, and said, As for the tokens whereof thou askest me, I may tell thee of them in part: but as touching thy life, I am not sent to shew thee; for I do not know it.

4Ezra.5

[1] Nevertheless as coming the tokens, behold, the days shall come, that they which dwell upon earth shall be taken in a great number, and the way of truth shall be hidden, and the land shall be barren of faith. [2] But iniquity shall be increased above that which now thou seest, or that thou hast heard long ago. [3] And the land, that thou seest now to have root, shalt thou see wasted suddenly. [4] But if the most High grant thee to live, thou shalt see after the third trumpet that the sun shall suddenly shine again in the night, and the moon thrice in the day: [5] And blood shall drop out of wood, and the stone shall give his voice, and the people shall be troubled: [6] And even he shall rule, whom they look not for that dwell upon the earth, and the fowls shall take their flight away together: [7] And the Sodomitish sea shall cast out fish, and make a noise in the night, which many have not known: but they shall all hear the voice thereof. [8] There shall be a confusion also in many places, and the fire shall be oft sent out again, and the wild beasts shall change their places, and menstruous women shall bring forth monsters: [9] And salt waters shall be found in the sweet, and all friends shall destroy one another; then shall wit hide itself, and understanding withdraw itself into his secret chamber, [10] And shall be sought of many, and yet not be found: then shall unrighteousness and incontinency be multiplied upon earth. [11] One land also shall ask another, and say, Is righteousness that maketh a man righteous gone through thee? And it shall say, No. [12] At the same time shall men hope, but nothing obtain: they shall labour, but their ways shall not prosper. [13] To shew thee such tokens I have leave; and if thou wilt pray again, and weep as now, and fast even days, thou shalt hear yet greater things. [14] Then I awaked, and an extreme fearfulness went through all my body, and my mind was troubled, so that it fainted. [15] So the angel that was come to talk with me held me, comforted me, and set me up upon my feet. [16] And in the second night it came to pass, that Salathiel the captain of the people came unto me, saying, Where hast thou been? And why is thy countenance so heavy? [17] Knowest thou not that Israel is committed unto thee in the land of their captivity? [18] Up then, and eat bread, and forsake us not, as the shepherd that leaveth his flock in the hands of cruel wolves. [19] Then said I unto him, Go thy ways from me, and come not nigh me. And he heard what I said, and went from me. [20] And so I fasted seven days, mourning and weeping, like as Uriel the angel commanded me. [21] And after seven days so it was, that the thoughts of my heart were very grievous unto me again, [22] And my soul recovered the spirit of understanding, and I began to talk with the most High again, [23] And said, O Lord that bearest rule, of every wood of the earth, and of all the trees thereof, thou hast chosen thee one only vine: [24] And of all lands of the whole world thou hast chosen thee one pit: and of all the flowers thereof one lily: [25] And of all the depths of the sea thou hast filled thee one river: and of all builded cities thou hast hallowed Sion unto thyself: [26] And of all the fowls that are created thou hast named thee one dove: and of all the cattle that are made thou hast provided thee one sheep: [27] And among all the

multitudes of people thou hast gotten thee one people: and unto this people, whom thou lovedst, thou gavest a law that is approved of all. [28] And now, O Lord, why hast thou given this one people over unto many? And upon the one root hast thou prepared others, and why hast thou scattered thy only one people among many? [29] And they which did gainsay thy promises, and believed not thy covenants, have trodden them down. [30] If thou didst so much hate thy people, yet shouldest thou punish them with thine own hands. [31] Now when I had spoken these words, the angel that came to me the night afore was sent unto me, [32] And said unto me, Hear me, and I will instruct thee; hearken to the thing that I say, and I shall tell thee more. [33] And I said, Speak on, my Lord. Then said he unto me, Thou art sore troubled in mind for Israel's sake: lovest thou that people better than he that made them? [34] And I said, No, Lord: but of very grief have I spoken: for my reins pain me every hour, while I labour to comprehend the way of the most High, and to seek out part of his judgment. [35] And he said unto me, Thou canst not. And I said, Wherefore, Lord? Whereunto was I born then? Or why was not my mother's womb then my grave, that I might not have seen the travail of Jacob, and the wearisome toil of the stock of Israel? [36] And he said unto me, Number me the things that are not yet come, gather me together the dross that are scattered abroad, make me the flowers green again that are withered, [37] Open me the places that are closed, and bring me forth the winds that in them are shut up, shew me the image of a voice: and then I will declare to thee the thing that thou labourest to know. [38] And I said, O Lord that bearest rule, who may know these things, but he that hath not his dwelling with men? [39] As for me, I am unwise: how may I then speak of these things whereof thou askest me? [40] Then said he unto me, Like as thou canst do none of these things that I have spoken of, even so canst thou not find out my judgment, or in the end the love that I have promised unto my people. [41] And I said, Behold, O Lord, yet art thou nigh unto them that be reserved till the end: and what shall they do that have been before me, or we that be now, or they that shall come after us? [42] And he said unto me, I will liken my judgment unto a ring: like as there is no slackness of the last, even so there is no swiftness of the first. [43] So I answered and said, Couldest thou not make those that have been made, and be now, and that are for to come, at once; that thou 627ightiest shew thy judgment the sooner? [44] Then answered he me, and said, The creature may not haste above the maker; neither may the world hold them at once that shall be created therein. [45] And I said, As thou hast said unto thy servant, that thou, which givest life to all, hast given life at once to the creature that thou hast created, and the creature bare it: even so it might now also bear them that now be present at once. [46] And he said unto me, Ask the womb of a woman, and say unto her, If thou bringest forth children, why dost thou it not together, but one after another? Pray her therefore to bring forth ten children at once. [47] And I said, She cannot: but must do it by distance of time. [48] Then said he unto me, Even so have I given the womb of the earth to those that be sown in it in their times. [49] For like as a young child may not bring forth the things that belong to the aged, even so have I disposed the world which I created. [50] And I asked,

and said, Seeing thou hast now given me the way, I will proceed to speak before thee: for our mother, of whom thou hast told me that she is young, draweth now nigh unto age. [51] He answered me, and said, Ask a woman that beareth children, and she shall tell thee. [52] Say unto her, Wherefore are unto they whom thou hast now brought forth like those that were before, but less of stature? [53] And she shall answer thee, They that be born in the the strength of youth are of one fashion, and they that are born in the time of age, when the womb faileth, are otherwise. [54] Consider thou therefore also, how that ye are less of stature than those that were before you. [55] And so are they that come after you less than ye, as the creatures which now begin to be old, and have passed over the strength of youth. [56] Then said I, Lord, I beseech thee, if I have found favour in thy sight, shew thy servant by whom thou visitest thy creature.

4Ezra.6

[1] And he said unto me, In the beginning, when the earth was made, before the borders of the world stood, or ever the winds blew, [2] Before it thundered and lightened, or ever the foundations of paradise were laid, [3] Before the fair flowers were seen, or ever the moveable powers were established, before the innumerable multitude of angels were gathered together, [4] Or ever the heights of the air were lifted up, before the measures of the firmament were named, or ever the chimneys in Sion were hot, [5] And ere the present years were sought out, and or ever the inventions of them that now sin were turned, before they were sealed that have gathered faith for a treasure: [6] Then did I consider these things, and they all were made through me alone, and through none other: by me also they shall be ended, and by none other. [7] Then answered I and said, What shall be the parting asunder of the times? or when shall be the end of the first, and the beginning of it that followeth? [8] And he said unto me, From Abraham unto Isaac, when Jacob and Esau were born of him, Jacob's hand held first the heel of Esau. [9] For Esau is the end of the world, and Jacob is the beginning of it that followeth. [10] The hand of man is betwixt the heel and the hand: other question, Esdras, ask thou not. [11] I answered then and said, O Lord that bearest rule, if I have found favour in thy sight, [12] I beseech thee, shew thy servant the end of thy tokens, whereof thou shewedst me part the last night. [13] So he answered and said unto me, Stand up upon thy feet, and hear a mighty sounding voice. [14] And it shall be as it were a great motion; but the place where thou standest shall not be moved. [15] And therefore when it speaketh be not afraid: for the word is of the end, and the foundation of the earth is understood. [16] And why? because the speech of these things trembleth and is moved: for it knoweth that the end of these things must be changed. [17] And it happened, that when I had heard it I stood up upon my feet, and hearkened, and, behold, there was a voice that spake, and the sound of it was like the sound of many waters. [18] And it said, Behold, the days come, that I will begin to draw nigh, and to visit them that dwell upon the earth, [19] And will begin to make inquisition of them, what they be that have hurt unjustly with their unrighteousness, and when the affliction of Sion

shall be fulfilled; [20] And when the world, that shall begin to vanish away, shall be finished, then will I shew these tokens: the books shall be opened before the firmament, and they shall see all together: [21] And the children of a year old shall speak with their voices, the women with child shall bring forth untimely children of three or four months old, and they shall live, and be raised up. [22] And suddenly shall the sown places appear unsown, the full storehouses shall suddenly be found empty: [23] And tha trumpet shall give a sound, which when every man heareth, they shall be suddenly afraid. [24] At that time shall friends fight one against another like enemies, and the earth shall stand in fear with those that dwell therein, the springs of the fountains shall stand still, and in three hours they shall not run. [25] Whosoever remaineth from all these that I have told thee shall escape, and see my salvation, and the end of your world. [26] And the men that are received shall see it, who have not tasted death from their birth: and the heart of the inhabitants shall be changed, and turned into another meaning. [27] For evil shall be put out, and deceit shall be quenched. [28] As for faith, it shall flourish, corruption shall be overcome, and the truth, which hath been so long without fruit, shall be declared. [29] And when he talked with me, behold, I looked by little and little upon him before whom I stood. [30] And these words said he unto me; I am come to shew thee the time of the night to come. [31] If thou wilt pray yet more, and fast seven days again, I shall tell thee greater things by day than I have heard. [32] For thy voice is heard before the most High: for the Mighty hath seen thy righteous dealing, he hath seen also thy chastity, which thou hast had ever since thy youth.

[33] And therefore hath he sent me to shew thee all these things, and to say unto thee, Be of good comfort and fear not [34] And hasten not with the times that are past, to think vain things, that thou mayest not hasten from the latter times. [35] And it came to pass after this, that I wept again, and fasted seven days in like manner, that I might fulfil the three weeks which he told me. [36] And in the eighth night was my heart vexed within me again, and I began to speak before the most High. [37] For my spirit was greatly set on fire, and my soul was in distress. [38] And I said, O Lord, thou spakest from the beginning of the creation, even the first day, and saidst thus; Let heaven and earth be made; and thy word was a perfect work. [39] And then was the spirit, and darkness and silence were on every side; the sound of man's voice was not yet formed. [40] Then commandedst thou a fair light to come forth of thy treasures, that thy work might appear. [41] Upon the second day thou madest the spirit of the firmament, and commandedst it to part asunder, and to make a division betwixt the waters, that the one part might go up, and the other remain beneath. [42] Upon the third day thou didst command that the waters should be gathered in the seventh part of the earth: six pats hast thou dried up, and kept them, to the intent that of these some being planted of God and tilled might serve thee. [43] For as soon as thy word went forth the work was made. [44] For immediately there was great and innumerable fruit, and many and divers pleasures for the taste, and flowers of unchangeable colour, and odours of wonderful smell: and this was done the third day. [45] Upon the fourth day thou commandedst that the sun should shine, and the moon give her light, and the stars

should be in order: [46] And gavest them a charge to do service unto man, that was to be made. [47] Upon the fifth day thou saidst unto the seventh part, where the waters were gathered that it should bring forth living creatures, fowls and fishes: and so it came to pass. [48] For the dumb water and without life brought forth living things at the commandment of God, that all people might praise thy wondrous works. [49] Then didst thou ordain two living creatures, the one thou calledst Enoch, and the other Leviathan; [50] And didst separate the one from the other: for the seventh part, namely, where the water was gathered together, might not hold them both. [51] Unto Enoch thou gavest one part, which was dried up the third day, that he should dwell in the same part, wherein are a thousand hills:

[52] But unto Leviathan thou gavest the seventh part, namely, the moist; and hast kept him to be devoured of whom thou wilt, and when. [53] Upon the sixth day thou gavest commandment unto the earth, that before thee it should bring forth beasts, cattle, and creeping things: [54] And after these, Adam also, whom thou madest lord of all thy creatures: of him come we all, and the people also whom thou hast chosen. [55] All this have I spoken before thee, O Lord, because thou madest the world for our sakes

[56] As for the other people, which also come of Adam, thou hast said that they are nothing, but be like unto spittle: and hast likened the abundance of them unto a drop that falleth from a vessel. [57] And now, O Lord, behold, these heathen, which have ever been reputed as nothing, have begun to be lords over us, and to devour us. [58] But we thy people, whom thou hast called thy firstborn, thy only begotten, and thy fervent lover, are given into their hands. [59] If the world now be made for our sakes, why do we not possess an inheritance with the world? how long shall this endure?

4Ezra.7

[1] And when I had made an end of speaking these words, there was sent unto me the angel which had been sent unto me the nights afore: [2] And he said unto me, Up, Esdras, and hear the words that I am come to tell thee. [3] And I said, Speak on, my God. Then said he unto me, The sea is set in a wide place, that it might be deep and great. [4] But put the case the entrance were narrow, and like a river; [5] Who then could go into the sea to look upon it, and to rule it? if he went not through the narrow, how could he come into the broad? [6] There is also another thing; A city is builded, and set upon a broad field, and is full of all good things: [7] The entrance thereof is narrow, and is set in a dangerous place to fall, like as if there were a fire on the right hand, and on the left a deep water: [8] And one only path between them both, even between the fire and the water, so small that there could but one man go there at once. [9] If this city now were given unto a man for an inheritance, if he never shall pass the danger set before it, how shall he receive this inheritance? [10] And I said, It is so, Lord. Then said he unto me, Even so also is Israel's portion. [11] Because for their sakes I made the world: and when Adam transgressed my statutes, then was decreed that now is done. [12] Then were the entrances of this world made narrow, full of sorrow and travail: they are but few and evil, full of perils,: and very painful. [13] For the

entrances of the elder world were wide and sure, and brought immortal fruit. [14] If then they that live labour not to enter these strait and vain things, they can never receive those that are laid up for them. [15] Now therefore why disquietest thou thyself, seeing thou art but a corruptible man? and why art thou moved, whereas thou art but mortal? [16] Why hast thou not considered in thy mind this thing that is to come, rather than that which is present? [17] Then answered I and said, O Lord that bearest rule, thou hast ordained in thy law, that the righteous should inherit these things, but that the ungodly should perish. [18] Nevertheless the righteous shall suffer strait things, and hope for wide: for they that have done wickedly have suffered the strait things, and yet shall not see the wide. [19] And he said unto me. There is no judge above God, and none that hath understanding above the Highest. [20] For there be many that perish in this life, because they despise the law of God that is set before them. [21] For God hath given strait commandment to such as came, what they should do to live, even as they came, and what they should observe to avoid punishment. [22] Nevertheless they were not obedient unto him; but spake against him, and imagined vain things; [23] And deceived themselves by their wicked deeds; and said of the most High, that he is not; and knew not his ways: [24] But his law have they despised, and denied his covenants; in his statutes have they not been faithful, and have not performed his works. [25] And therefore, Esdras, for the empty are empty things, and for the full are the full things. [26] Behold, the time shall come, that these tokens which I have told thee shall come to pass, and the bride shall appear, and she coming forth shall be seen, that now is withdrawn from the earth. [27] And whosoever is delivered from the foresaid evils shall see my wonders. [28] For my son Jesus shall be revealed with those that be with him, and they that remain shall rejoice within four hundred years. [29] After these years shall my son Christ die, and all men that have life. [30] And the world shall be turned into the old silence seven days, like as in the former judgments: so that no man shall remain. [31] And after seven days the world, that yet awaketh not, shall be raised up, and that shall die that is corrupt [32] And the earth shall restore those that are asleep in her, and so shall the dust those that dwell in silence, and the secret places shall deliver those souls that were committed unto them. [33] And the most High shall appear upon the seat of judgment, and misery shall pass away, and the long suffering shall have an end: [34] But judgment only shall remain, truth shall stand, and faith shall wax strong: [35] And the work shall follow, and the reward shall be shewed, and the good deeds shall be of force, and wicked deeds shall bear no rule. [36] Then said I, Abraham prayed first for the Sodomites, and Moses for the fathers that sinned in the wilderness: [37] And Jesus after him for Israel in the time of Achan: [38] And Samuel and David for the destruction: and Solomon for them that should come to the sanctuary: [39] And Helias for those that received rain; and for the dead, that he might live: [40] And Ezechias for the people in the time of Sennacherib: and many for many. [41] Even so now, seeing corruption is grown up, and wickedness increased, and the righteous have prayed for the ungodly: wherefore shall it not be so

now also? [42] He answered me, and said, This present life is not the end where much glory doth abide; therefore have they prayed for the weak. [43] But the day of doom shall be the end of this time, and the beginning of the immortality for to come, wherein corruption is past, [44] Intemperance is at an end, infidelity is cut off, righteousness is grown, and truth is sprung up. [45] Then shall no man be able to save him that is destroyed, nor to oppress him that hath gotten the victory. [46] I answered then and said, This is my first and last saying, that it had been better not to have given the earth unto Adam: or else, when it was given him, to have restrained him from sinning. [47] For what profit is it for men now in this present time to live in heaviness, and after death to look for punishment? [48] O thou Adam, what hast thou done? for though it was thou that sinned, thou art not fallen alone, but we all that come of thee. [49] For what profit is it unto us, if there be promised us an immortal time, whereas we have done the works that bring death? [50] And that there is promised us an everlasting hope, whereas ourselves being most wicked are made vain? [51] And that there are laid up for us dwellings of health and safety, whereas we have lived wickedly? [52] And that the glory of the most High is kept to defend them which have led a wary life, whereas we have walked in the most wicked ways of all? [53] And that there should be shewed a paradise, whose fruit endureth for ever, wherein is security and medicine, since we shall not enter into it? [54] (For we have walked in unpleasant places.) [55] And that the faces of them which have used abstinence shall shine above the stars, whereas our faces shall be blacker than darkness? [56] For while we lived and committed iniquity, we considered not that we should begin to suffer for it after death. [57] Then answered he me, and said, This is the condition of the battle, which man that is born upon the earth shall fight; [58] That, if he be overcome, he shall suffer as thou hast said: but if he get the victory, he shall receive the thing that I say. [59] For this is the life whereof Moses spake unto the people while he lived, saying, Choose thee life, that thou mayest live. [60] Nevertheless they believed not him, nor yet the prophets after him, no nor me which have spoken unto them, [61] That there should not be such heaviness in their destruction, as shall be joy over them that are persuaded to salvation. [62] I answered then, and said, I know, Lord, that the most High is called merciful, in that he hath mercy upon them which are not yet come into the world, [63] And upon those also that turn to his law; [64] And that he is patient, and long suffereth those that have sinned, as his creatures; [65] And that he is bountiful, for he is ready to give where it needeth; [66] And that he is of great mercy, for he multiplieth more and more mercies to them that are present, and that are past, and also to them which are to come. [67] For if he shall not multiply his mercies, the world would not continue with them that inherit therein. [68] And he pardoneth; for if he did not so of his goodness, that they which have committed iniquities might be eased of them, the ten thousandth part of men should not remain living. [69] And being judge, if he should not forgive them that are cured with his word, and put out the multitude of contentions, [70] There should be very few left peradventure in an innumerable multitude.

4Ezra.8

[1] And he answered me, saying, The most High hath made this world for many, but the world to come for few. [2] I will tell thee a similitude, Esdras; As when thou askest the earth, it shall say unto thee, that it giveth much mould whereof earthen vessels are made, but little dust that gold cometh of: even so is the course of this present world. [3] There be many created, but few shall be saved. [4] So answered I and said, Swallow then down, O my soul, understanding, and devour wisdom. [5] For thou hast agreed to give ear, and art willing to prophesy: for thou hast no longer space than only to live. [6] O Lord, if thou suffer not thy servant, that we may pray before thee, and thou give us seed unto our heart, and culture to our understanding, that there may come fruit of it; how shall each man live that is corrupt, who beareth the place of a man? [7] For thou art alone, and we all one workmanship of thine hands, like as thou hast said. [8] For when the body is fashioned now in the mother's womb, and thou givest it members, thy creature is preserved in fire and water, and nine months doth thy workmanship endure thy creature which is created in her. [9] But that which keepeth and is kept shall both be preserved: and when the time cometh, the womb preserved delivereth up the things that grew in it. [10] For thou hast commanded out of the parts of the body, that is to say, out of the breasts, milk to be given, which is the fruit of the breasts, [11] That the thing which is fashioned may be nourished for a time, till thou disposest it to thy mercy. [12] Thou broughtest it up with thy righteousness, and nurturedst it in thy law, and reformedst it with thy judgment. [13] And thou shalt mortify it as thy creature, and quicken it as thy work. [14] If therefore thou shalt destroy him which with so great labour was fashioned, it is an easy thing to be ordained by thy commandment, that the thing which was made might be preserved. [15] Now therefore, Lord, I will speak; touching man in general, thou knowest best; but touching thy people, for whose sake I am sorry; [16] And for thine inheritance, for whose cause I mourn; and for Israel, for whom I am heavy; and for Jacob, for whose sake I am troubled; [17] Therefore will I begin to pray before thee for myself and for them: for I see the falls of us that dwell in the land. [18] But I have heard the swiftness of the judge which is to come. [19] Therefore hear my voice, and understand my words, and I shall speak before thee. This is the beginning of the words of Esdras, before he was taken up: and I said, [20] O Lord, thou that dwellest in everlastingness which beholdest from above things in the heaven and in the air; [21] Whose throne is inestimable; whose glory may not be comprehended; before whom the hosts of angels stand with trembling, [22] Whose service is conversant in wind and fire; whose word is true, and sayings constant; whose commandment is strong, and ordinance fearful; [23] Whose look drieth up the depths, and indignation maketh the mountains to melt away; which the truth witnesseth: [24] O hear the prayer of thy servant, and give ear to the petition of thy creature. [25] For while I live I will speak, and so long as I have understanding I will answer. [26] O look not upon the sins of thy people; but on them which serve thee in truth. [27] Regard not the wicked inventions of the heathen, but the desire of those that keep thy testimonies in afflictions. [28] Think not upon those that have walked feignedly before thee: but remember them, which according to thy will have known thy fear. [29] Let it not be thy will to destroy them which have lived like beasts; but to look upon them that have clearly taught thy law. [30] Take thou no indignation at them which are deemed worse than beasts; but love them that always put their trust in thy righteousness and glory. [31] For we and our fathers do languish of such diseases: but because of us sinners thou shalt be called merciful. [32] For if thou hast a desire to have mercy upon us, thou shalt be called merciful, to us namely, that have no works of righteousness. [33] For the just, which have many good works laid up with thee, shall out of their own deeds receive reward. [34] For what is man, that thou shouldest take displeasure at him? Or what is a corruptible generation, that thou shouldest be so bitter toward it? [35] For in truth them is no man among them that be born, but he hath dealt wickedly; and among the faithful there is none which hath not done amiss. [36] For in this, O Lord, thy righteousness and thy goodness shall be declared, if thou be merciful unto them which have not the confidence of good works. [37] Then answered he me, and said, Some things hast thou spoken aright, and according unto thy words it shall be. [38] For indeed I will not think on the disposition of them which have sinned before death, before judgment, before destruction: [39] But I will rejoice over the disposition of the righteous, and I will remember also their pilgrimage, and the salvation, and the reward, that they shall have. [40] Like as I have spoken now, so shall it come to pass. [41] For as the husbandman soweth much seed upon the ground, and planteth many trees, and yet the thing that is sown good in his season cometh not up, neither doth all that is planted take root: even so is it of them that are sown in the world; they shall not all be saved. [42] I answered then and said, If I have found grace, let me speak. [43] Like as the husbandman's seed perisheth, if it come not up, and receive not thy rain in due season; or if there come too much rain, and corrupt it: [44] Even so perisheth man also, which is formed with thy hands, and is called thine own image, because thou art like unto him, for whose sake thou hast made all things, and likened him unto the husbandman's seed. [45] Be not wroth with us but spare thy people, and have mercy upon thine own inheritance: for thou art merciful unto thy creature. [46] Then answered he me, and said, Things present are for the present, and things to cometh for such as be to come. [47] For thou comest far short that thou shouldest be able to love my creature more than I: but I have ofttimes drawn nigh unto thee, and unto it, but never to the unrighteous. [48] In this also thou art marvellous before the most High: [49] In that thou hast humbled thyself, as it becometh thee, and hast not judged thyself worthy to be much glorified among the righteous. [50] For many great miseries shall be done to them that in the latter time shall dwell in the world, because they have walked in great pride. [51] But understand thou for thyself, and seek out the glory for such as be like thee. [52] For unto you is paradise opened, the tree of life is planted, the time to come is prepared, plenteousness is made ready, a city is builded, and rest is allowed, yea, perfect goodness and wisdom. [53] The root of evil is sealed up from you,

weakness and the moth is hid from you, and corruption is fled into hell to be forgotten: [54] Sorrows are passed, and in the end is shewed the treasure of immortality. [55] And therefore ask thou no more questions concerning the multitude of them that perish. [56] For when they had taken liberty, they despised the most High, thought scorn of his law, and forsook his ways. [57] Moreover they have trodden down his righteous, [58] And said in their heart, that there is no God; yea, and that knowing they must die. [59] For as the things aforesaid shalt receive you, so thirst and pain are prepared for them: for it was not his will that men should come to nought: [60] But they which be created have defiled the name of him that made them, and were unthankful unto him which prepared life for them. [61] And therefore is my judgment now at hand. [62] These things have I not shewed unto all men, but unto thee, and a few like thee. Then answered I and said, [63] Behold, O Lord, now hast thou shewed me the multitude of the wonders, which thou wilt begin to do in the last times: but at what time, thou hast not shewed me.

4Ezra.9

[1] He answered me then, and said, Measure thou the time diligently in itself: and when thou seest part of the signs past, which I have told thee before, [2] Then shalt thou understand, that it is the very same time, wherein the Highest will begin to visit the world which he made. [3] Therefore when there shall be seen earthquakes and uproars of the people in the world: [4] Then shalt thou well understand, that the most High spake of those things from the days that were before thee, even from the beginning. [5] For like as all that is made in the world hath a beginning and an end, and the end is manifest: [6] Even so the times also of the Highest have plain beginnings in wonder and powerful works, and endings in effects and signs. [7] And every one that shall be saved, and shall be able to escape by his works, and by faith, whereby ye have believed, [8] Shall be preserved from the said perils, and shall see my salvation in my land, and within my borders: for I have sanctified them for me from the beginning. [9] Then shall they be in pitiful case, which now have abused my ways: and they that have cast them away despitefully shall dwell in torments. [10] For such as in their life have received benefits, and have not known me; [11] And they that have loathed my law, while they had yet liberty, and, when as yet place of repentance was open unto them, understood not, but despised it; [12] The same must know it after death by pain. [13] And therefore be thou not curious how the ungodly shall be punished, and when: but enquire how the righteous shall be saved, whose the world is, and for whom the world is created. [14] Then answered I and said, [15] I have said before, and now do speak, and will speak it also hereafter, that there be many more of them which perish, than of them which shall be saved: [16] Like as a wave is greater than a drop. [17] And he answered me, saying, Like as the field is, so is also the seed; as the flowers be, such are the colours also; such as the workman is, such also is the work; and as the husbandman Is himself, so is his husbandry also: for it was the time of the world. [18] And now when I prepared the world, which was not yet made, even for them to dwell in that now live,

no man spake against me. [19] For then every one obeyed: but now the manners of them which are created in this world that is made are corrupted by a perpetual seed, and by a law which is unsearchable rid themselves. [20] So I considered the world, and, behold, there was peril because of the devices that were come into it. [21] And I saw, and spared it greatly, and have kept me a grape of the cluster, and a plant of a great people. [22] Let the multitude perish then, which was born in vain; and let my grape be kept, and my plant; for with great labour have I made it perfect. [23] Nevertheless, if thou wilt cease yet seven days more, (but thou shalt not fast in them, [24] But go into a field of flowers, where no house is builded, and eat only the flowers of the field; taste no flesh, drink no wine, but eat flowers only;) [25] And pray unto the Highest continually, then will I come and talk with thee. [26] So I went my way into the field which is called Ardath, like as he commanded me; and there I sat among the flowers, and did eat of the herbs of the field, and the meat of the same satisfied me. [27] After seven days I sat upon the grass, and my heart was vexed within me, like as before: [28] And I opened my mouth, and began to talk before the most High, and said, [29] O Lord, thou that shewest thyself unto us, thou wast shewed unto our fathers in the wilderness, in a place where no man treadeth, in a barren place, when they came out of Egypt. [30] And thou spakest saying, Hear me, O Israel; and mark my words, thou seed of Jacob. [31] For, behold, I sow my law in you, and it shall bring fruit in you, and ye shall be honoured in it for ever. [32] But our fathers, which received the law, kept it not, and observed not thy ordinances: and though the fruit of thy law did not perish, neither could it, for it was thine; [33] Yet they that received it perished, because they kept not the thing that was sown in them. [34] And, lo, it Is a custom, when the ground hath received seed, or the sea a ship, or any vessel meat or drink, that, that being perished wherein it was sown or cast into, [35] That thing also which was sown, or cast therein, or received, doth perish, and remaineth not with us: but with us it hath not happened so. [36] For we that have received the law perish by sin, and our heart also which received it [37] Notwithstanding the law perisheth not, but remaineth in his force. [38] And when I spake these things in my heart, I looked back with mine eyes, and upon the right side I saw a woman, and, behold, she mourned and wept with a loud voice, and was much grieved in heart, and her clothes were rent, and she had ashes upon her head. [39] Then let I my thoughts go that I was in, and turned me unto her, [40] And said unto her, Wherefore weepest thou? why art thou so grieved in thy mind? [41] And she said unto me, Sir, let me alone, that I may bewail myself, and add unto my sorrow, for I am sore vexed in my mind, and brought very low. [42] And I said unto her, What aileth thee? tell me. [43] She said unto me, I thy servant have been barren, and had no child, though I had an husband thirty years, [44] And those thirty years I did nothing else day and night, and every hour, but make my, prayer to the Highest. [45] After thirty years God heard me thine handmaid, looked upon my misery, considered my trouble, and gave me a son: and I was very glad of him, so was my husband also, and all my neighbours: and we gave great honour unto the Almighty. [46] And I nourished him with great travail. [47] So when he grew up, and came to the time that he should have a

wife, I made a feast.
4Ezra.10

[1] And it so came to pass, that when my son was entered into his wedding chamber, he fell down, and died. [2] Then we all overthrew the lights, and all my neighbours rose up to comfort me: so I took my rest unto the second day at night. [3] And it came to pass, when they had all left off to comfort me, to the end I might be quiet; then rose I up by night and fled, and came hither into this field, as thou seest.

[4] And I do now purpose not to return into the city, but here to stay, and neither to eat nor drink, but continually to mourn and to fast until I die. [5] Then left I the meditations wherein I was, and spake to her in anger, saying, [6] Thou foolish woman above all other, seest thou not our mourning, and what happeneth unto us? [7] How that Sion our mother is full of all heaviness, and much humbled, mourning very sore? [8] And now, seeing we all mourn and are sad, for we are all in heaviness, art thou grieved for one son? [9] For ask the earth, and she shall tell thee, that it is she which ought to mourn for the fall of so many that grow upon her. [10] For out of her came all at the first, and out of her shall all others come, and, behold, they walk almost all into destruction, and a multitude of them is utterly rooted out. [11] Who then should make more mourning than she, that hath lost so great a multitude; and not thou, which art sorry but for one? [12] But if thou sayest unto me, My lamentation is not like the earth's, because I have lost the fruit of my womb, which I brought forth with pains, and bare with sorrows; [13] But the earth not so: for the multitude present in it according to the course of the earth is gone, as it came: [14] Then say I unto thee, Like as thou hast brought forth with labour; even so the earth also hath given her fruit, namely, man, ever since the beginning unto him that made her. [15] Now therefore keep thy sorrow to thyself, and bear with a good courage that which hath befallen thee. [16] For if thou shalt acknowledge the determination of God to be just, thou shalt both receive thy son in time, and shalt be commended among women. [17] Go thy way then into the city to thine husband. [18] And she said unto me, That will I not do: I will not go into the city, but here will I die. [19] So I proceeded to speak further unto her, and said, [20] Do not so, but be counselled. By me: for how many are the adversities of Sion? Be comforted in regard of the sorrow of Jerusalem. [21] For thou seest that our sanctuary is laid waste, our altar broken down, our temple destroyed; [22] Our psaltery is laid on the ground, our song is put to silence, our rejoicing is at an end, the light of our candlestick is put out, the ark of our covenant is spoiled, our holy things are defiled, and the name that is called upon us is almost profaned: our children are put to shame, our priests are burnt, our Levites are gone into captivity, our virgins are defiled, and our wives ravished; our righteous men carried away, our little ones destroyed, our young men are brought in bondage, and our strong men are become weak; [23] And, which is the greatest of all, the seal of Sion hath now lost her honour; for she is delivered into the hands of them that hate us. [24] And therefore shake off thy great heaviness, and put away the multitude of sorrows, that the Mighty may be merciful unto thee again, and the Highest shall give thee rest and ease from thy labour. [25]

And it came to pass while I was talking with her, behold, her face upon a sudden shined exceedingly, and her countenance glistered, so that I was afraid of her, and mused what it might be. [26] And, behold, suddenly she made a great cry very fearful: so that the earth shook at the noise of the woman. [27] And I looked, and, behold, the woman appeared unto me no more, but there was a city builded, and a large place shewed itself from the foundations: then was I afraid, and cried with a loud voice, and said, [28] Where is Uriel the angel, who came unto me at the first? For he hath caused me to fall into many trances, and mine end is turned into corruption, and my prayer to rebuke. [29] And as I was speaking these words behold, he came unto me, and looked upon me. [30] And, lo, I lay as one that had been dead, and mine understanding was taken from me: and he took me by the right hand, and comforted me, and set me upon my feet, and said unto me, [31] What aileth thee? And why art thou so disquieted? And why is thine understanding troubled, and the thoughts of thine heart? [32] And I said, Because thou hast forsaken me, and yet I did according to thy words, and I went into the field, and, lo, I have seen, and yet see, that I am not able to express. [33] And he said unto me, Stand up manfully, and I will advise thee. [34] Then said I, Speak on, my lord, in me; only forsake me not, lest I die frustrate of my hope. [35] For I have seen that I knew not, and hear that I do not know. [36] Or is my sense deceived, or my soul in a dream? [37] Now therefore I beseech thee that thou wilt shew thy servant of this vision. [38] He answered me then, and said, Hear me, and I shall inform thee, and tell thee wherefore thou art afraid: for the Highest will reveal many secret things unto thee. [39] He hath seen that thy way is right: for that thou sorrowest continually for thy people, and makest great lamentation for Sion. [40] This therefore is the meaning of the vision which thou lately sawest: [41] Thou sawest a woman mourning, and thou begannest to comfort her: [42] But now seest thou the likeness of the woman no more, but there appeared unto thee a city builded. [43] And whereas she told thee of the death of her son, this is the solution: [44] This woman, whom thou sawest is Sion: and whereas she said unto thee, even she whom thou seest as a city builded, [45] Whereas, I say, she said unto thee, that she hath been thirty years barren: those are the thirty years wherein there was no offering made in her. [46] But after thirty years Solomon builded the city and offered offerings: and then bare the barren a son. [47] And whereas she told thee that she nourished him with labour: that was the dwelling in Jerusalem. [48] But whereas she said unto thee, That my son coming into his marriage chamber happened to have a fail, and died: this was the destruction that came to Jerusalem. [49] And, behold, thou sawest her likeness, and because she mourned for her son, thou begannest to comfort her: and of these things which have chanced, these are to be opened unto thee. [50] For now the most High seeth that thou art grieved unfeignedly, and sufferest from thy whole heart for her, so hath he shewed thee the brightness of her glory, and the comeliness of her beauty: [51] And therefore I bade thee remain in the field where no house was builded: [52] For I knew that the Highest would shew this unto thee. [53] Therefore I commanded thee to go into the field, where no foundation of any building was. [54] For in the place wherein the Highest beginneth to shew his city, there can no man's building be able to stand. [55] And therefore fear not, let not thine heart be affrighted, but go thy way in, and see the beauty and greatness of the building, as much as thine eyes be able to see: [56] And then shalt thou hear as much as thine ears may comprehend. [57] For thou art blessed above many other, and art called with the Highest; and so are but few. [58] But to morrow at night thou shalt remain here; [59] And so shall the Highest shew thee visions of the high things, which the most High will do unto them that dwell upon the earth in the last days. So I slept that night and another, like as he commanded me.

4Ezra.11

[1] Then saw I a dream, and, behold, there came up from the sea an eagle, which had twelve feathered wings, and three heads. [2] And I saw, and, behold, she spread her wings over all the earth, and all the winds of the air blew on her, and were gathered together. [3] And I beheld, and out of her feathers there grew other contrary feathers; and they became little feathers and small. [4] But her heads were at rest: the head in the midst was greater than the other, yet rested it with the residue. [5] Moreover I beheld, and, lo, the eagle flew with her feathers, and reigned upon earth, and over them that dwelt therein. [6] And I saw that all things under heaven were subject unto her, and no man spake against her, no, not one creature upon earth. [7] And I beheld, and, lo, the eagle rose upon her talons, and spake to her feathers, saying, [8] Watch not all at once: sleep every one in his own place, and watch by course: [9] But let the heads be preserved for the last. [10] And I beheld, and, lo, the voice went not out of her heads, but from the midst of her body. [11] And I numbered her contrary feathers, and, behold, there were eight of them. [12] And I looked, and, behold, on the right side there arose one feather, and reigned over all the earth; [13] And so it was, that when it reigned, the end of it came, and the place thereof appeared no more: so the next following stood up. and reigned, and had a great time; [14] And it happened, that when it reigned, the end of it came also, like as the first, so that it appeared no more. [15] Then came there a voice unto it, and said, [16] Hear thou that hast borne rule over the earth so long: this I say unto thee, before thou beginnest to appear no more, [17] There shall none after thee attain unto thy time, neither unto the half thereof. [18] Then arose the third, and reigned as the other before, and appeared no more also. [19] So went it with all the residue one after another, as that every one reigned, and then appeared no more. [20] Then I beheld, and, lo, in process of time the feathers that followed stood up upon the right side, that they might rule also; and some of them ruled, but within a while they appeared no more: [21] For some of them were set up, but ruled not. [22] After this I looked, and, behold, the twelve feathers appeared no more, nor the two little feathers: [23] And there was no more upon the eagle's body, but three heads that rested, and six little wings. [24] Then saw I also that two little feathers divided themselves from the six, and remained under the head that was upon the right side: for the four continued in their

place. [25] And I beheld, and, lo, the feathers that were under the wing thought to set up themselves and to have the rule. [26] And I beheld, and, lo, there was one set up, but shortly it appeared no more. [27] And the second was sooner away than the first. [28] And I beheld, and, lo, the two that remained thought also in themselves to reign: [29] And when they so thought, behold, there awaked one of the heads that were at rest, namely, it that was in the midst; for that was greater than the two other heads. [30] And then I saw that the two other heads were joined with it. [31] And, behold, the head was turned with them that were with it, and did eat up the two feathers under the wing that would have reigned. [32] But this head put the whole earth in fear, and bare rule in it over all those that dwelt upon the earth with much oppression; and it had the governance of the world more than all the wings that had been. [33] And after this I beheld, and, lo, the head that was in the midst suddenly appeared no more, like as the wings. [34] But there remained the two heads, which also in like sort ruled upon the earth, and over those that dwelt therein. [35] And I beheld, and, lo, the head upon the right side devoured it that was upon the left side. [36] Then I head a voice, which said unto me, Look before thee, and consider the thing that thou seest. [37] And I beheld, and lo, as it were a roaring lion chased out of the wood: and I saw that he sent out a man's voice unto the eagle, and said, [38] Hear thou, I will talk with thee, and the Highest shall say unto thee, [39] Art not thou it that remainest of the four beasts, whom I made to reign in my world, that the end of their times might come through them? [40] And the fourth came, and overcame all the beasts that were past, and had power over the world with great fearfulness, and over the whole compass of the earth with much wicked oppression; and so long time dwelt he upon the earth with deceit. [41] For the earth hast thou not judged with truth. [42] For thou hast afflicted the meek, thou hast hurt the peaceable, thou hast loved liars, and destroyed the dwellings of them that brought forth fruit, and hast cast down the walls of such as did thee no harm. [43] Therefore is thy wrongful dealing come up unto the Highest, and thy pride unto the Mighty. [44] The Highest also hath looked upon the proud times, and, behold, they are ended, and his abominations are fulfilled. [45] And therefore appear no more, thou eagle, nor thy horrible wings, nor thy wicked feathers nor thy malicious heads, nor thy hurtful claws, nor all thy vain body: [46] That all the earth may be refreshed, and may return, being delivered from thy violence, and that she may hope for the judgment and mercy of him that made her.

4Ezra.12

[1] And it came to pass, whiles the lion spake these words unto the eagle, I saw, [2] And, behold, the head that remained and the four wings appeared no more, and the two went unto it and set themselves up to reign, and their kingdom was small, and fill of uproar. [3] And I saw, and, behold, they appeared no more, and the whole body of the eagle was burnt so that the earth was in great fear: then awaked I out of the trouble and trance of my mind, and from great fear, and said unto my spirit, [4] Lo, this hast thou done unto me, in that thou searchest out the ways of the Highest. [5] Lo, yet am I weary in my mind, and very

weak in my spirit; and little strength is there in me, for the great fear wherewith I was afflicted this night. [6] Therefore will I now beseech the Highest, that he will comfort me unto the end. [7] And I said, Lord that bearest rule, if I have found grace before thy sight, and if I am justified with thee before many others, and if my prayer indeed be come up before thy face; [8] Comfort me then, and shew me thy servant the interpretation and plain difference of this fearful vision, that thou mayest perfectly comfort my soul. [9] For thou hast judged me worthy to shew me the last times. [10] And he said unto me, This is the interpretation of the vision: [11] The eagle, whom thou sawest come up from the sea, is the kingdom which was seen in the vision of thy brother Daniel. [12] But it was not expounded unto him, therefore now I declare it unto thee. [13] Behold, the days will come, that there shall rise up a kingdom upon earth, and it shall be feared above all the kingdoms that were before it. [14] In the same shall twelve kings reign, one after another: [15] Whereof the second shall begin to reign, and shall have more time than any of the twelve. [16] And this do the twelve wings signify, which thou sawest. [17] As for the voice which thou heardest speak, and that thou sawest not to go out from the heads but from the midst of the body thereof, this is the interpretation: [18] That after the time of that kingdom there shall arise great strivings, and it shall stand in peril of failing: nevertheless it shall not then fall, but shall be restored again to his beginning. [19] And whereas thou sawest the eight small under feathers sticking to her wings, this is the interpretation: [20] That in him there shall arise eight kings, whose times shall be but small, and their years swift. [21] And two of them shall perish, the middle time approaching: four shall be kept until their end begin to approach: but two shall be kept unto the end. [22] And whereas thou sawest three heads resting, this is the interpretation: [23] In his last days shall the most High raise up three kingdoms, and renew many things therein, and they shall have the dominion of the earth, [24] And of those that dwell therein, with much oppression, above all those that were before them: therefore are they called the heads of the eagle. [25] For these are they that shall accomplish his wickedness, and that shall finish his last end.

[26] And whereas thou sawest that the great head appeared no more, it signifieth that one of them shall die upon his bed, and yet with pain. [27] For the two that remain shall be slain with the sword. [28] For the sword of the one shall devour the other: but at the last shall he fall through the sword himself. [29] And whereas thou sawest two feathers under the wings passing over the head that is on the right side; [30] It signifieth that these are they, whom the Highest hath kept unto their end: this is the small kingdom and full of trouble, as thou sawest. [31] And the lion, whom thou sawest rising up out of the wood, and roaring, and speaking to the eagle, and rebuking her for her unrighteousness with all the words which thou hast heard; [32] This is the anointed, which the Highest hath kept for them and for their wickedness unto the end: he shall reprove them, and shall upbraid them with their cruelty. [33] For he shall set them before him alive in judgment, and shall rebuke them, and correct them. [34] For the rest of my people shall he deliver with mercy, those that have been

pressed upon my borders, and he shall make them joyful until the coming of the day of judgment, whereof I have spoken unto thee from the the the beginning. [35] This is the dream that thou sawest, and these are the interpretations. [36] Thou only hast been meet to know this secret of the Highest. [37] Therefore write all these things that thou hast seen in a book, and hide them: [38] And teach them to the wise of the people, whose hearts thou knowest may comprehend and keep these secrets. [39] But wait thou here thyself yet seven days more, that it may be shewed thee, whatsoever it pleaseth the Highest to declare unto thee. And with that he went his way. [40] And it came to pass, when all the people saw that the seven days were past, and I not come again into the city, they gathered them all together, from the least unto the greatest, and came unto me, and said, [41] What have we offended thee? And what evil have we done against thee, that thou 634orsakes us, and sittest here in this place? [42] For of all the prophets thou only art left us, as a cluster of the vintage, and as a candle in a dark place, and as a haven or ship preserved from the tempest. [43] Are not the evils which are come to us sufficient? [44] If thou shalt forsake us, how much better had it been for us, if we also had been burned in the midst of Sion? [45] For we are not better than they that died there. And they wept with a loud voice. Then answered I them, and said, [46] Be of good comfort, O Israel; and be not heavy, thou house of Jacob: [47] For the Highest hath you in remembrance, and the Mighty hath not forgotten you in temptation. [48] As for me, I have not forsaken you, neither am I departed from you: but am come into this place, to pray for the desolation of Sion, and that I might seek mercy for the low estate of your sanctuary. [49] And now go your way home every man, and after these days will I come unto you. [50] So the people went their way into the city, like as I commanded them: [51] But I remained still in the field seven days, as the angel commanded me; and did eat only in those days of the flowers of the field, and had my meat of the herbs

4Ezra.13

[1] And it came to pass after seven days, I dreamed a dream by night: [2] And, lo, there arose a wind from the sea, that it moved all the waves thereof. [3] And I beheld, and, lo, that man waxed strong with the thousands of heaven: and when he turned his countenance to look, all the things trembled that were seen under him. [4] And whensoever the voice went out of his mouth, all they burned that heard his voice, like as the earth faileth when it feeleth the fire. [5] And after this I beheld, and, lo, there was gathered together a multitude of men, out of number, from the four winds of the heaven, to subdue the man that came out of the sea [6] But I beheld, and, lo, he had graved himself a great mountain, and flew up upon it. [7] But I would have seen the region or place whereout the hill was graven, and I could not. [8] And after this I beheld, and, lo, all they which were gathered together to subdue him were sore afraid, and yet durst fight. [9] And, lo, as he saw the violence of the multitude that came, he neither lifted up his hand, nor held sword, nor any instrument of war: [10] But only I saw that he sent out of his mouth as it had been a blast of fire, and out of his lips a flaming breath, and out of

his tongue he cast out sparks and tempests. [11] And they were all mixed together; the blast of fire, the flaming breath, and the great tempest; and fell with violence upon the multitude which was prepared to fight, and burned them up every one, so that upon a sudden of an innumerable multitude nothing was to be perceived, but only dust and smell of smoke: when I saw this I was afraid.

[12] Afterward saw I the same man come down from the mountain, and call unto him another peaceable Multitude. [13] And there came much people unto him, whereof some were glad, some were sorry, and some of them were bound, and other some brought of them that were offered: then was I sick through great fear, and I awaked, and said, [14] Thou hast shewed thy servant these wonders from the beginning, and hast counted me worthy that thou shouldest receive my prayer: [15] Shew me now yet the interpretation of this dream. [16] For as I conceive in mine understanding, woe unto them that shall be left in those days and much more woe unto them that are not left behind! [17] For they that were not left were in heaviness. [18] Now understand I the things that are laid up in the latter days, which shall happen unto them, and to those that are left behind. [19] Therefore are they come into great perils and many necessities, like as these dreams declare. [20] Yet is it easier for him that is in danger to come into these things, than to pass away as a cloud out of the world, and not to see the things that happen in the last days. And he answered unto me, and said, [21] The interpretation of the vision shall I shew thee, and I will open unto thee the thing that thou hast required. [22] Whereas thou hast spoken of them that are left behind, this is the interpretation: [23] He that shall endure the peril in that time hath kept himself: they that be fallen into danger are such as have works, and faith toward the Almighty. [24] Know this therefore, that they which be left behind are more blessed than they that be dead. [25] This is the meaning of the vision: Whereas thou sawest a man coming up from the midst of the sea: [26] The same is he whom God the Highest hath kept a great season, which by his own self shall deliver his creature: and he shall order them that are left behind. [27] And whereas thou sawest, that out of his mouth there came as a blast of wind, and fire, and storm; [28] And that he held neither sword, nor any instrument of war, but that the rushing in of him destroyed the whole multitude that came to subdue him; this is the interpretation: [29] Behold, the days come, when the most High will begin to deliver them that are upon the earth. [30] And he shall come to the astonishment of them that dwell on the earth. [31] And one shall undertake to fight against another, one city against another, one place against another, one people against another, and one realm against another. [32] And the time shall be when these things shall come to pass, and the signs shall happen which I shewed thee before, and then shall my Son be declared, whom thou sawest as a man ascending. [33] And when all the people hear his voice, every man shall in their own land leave the battle they have one against another. [34] And an innumerable multitude shall be gathered together, as thou sawest them, willing to come, and to overcome him by fighting. [35] But he shall stand upon the top of the mount Sion. [36] And Sion shall come, and shall be shewed to all men, being prepared and builded, like as thou sawest the hill graven without hands. [37] And this my Son shall rebuke the wicked inventions of those nations, which for their wicked life are fallen into the tempest; [38] And shall lay before them their evil thoughts, and the torments wherewith they shall begin to be tormented, which are like unto a flame: and he shall destroy them without labour by the law which is like unto me. [39] And whereas thou sawest that he gathered another peaceable multitude unto him; [40] Those are the ten tribes, which were carried away prisoners out of their own land in the time of Osea the king, whom Salmanasar the king of Assyria led away captive, and he carried them over the waters, and so came they into another land. [41] But they took this counsel among themselves, that they would leave the multitude of the heathen, and go forth into a further country, where never mankind dwelt, [42] That they might there keep their statutes, which they never kept in their own land. [43] And they entered into Euphrates by the narrow places of the river. [44] For the most High then shewed signs for them, and held still the flood, till they were passed over. [45] For through that country there was a great way to go, namely, of a year and a half: and the same region is called Arsareth.

[46] Then dwelt they there until the latter time; and now when they shall begin to come, [47] The Highest shall stay the springs of the stream again, that they may go through: therefore sawest thou the multitude with peace. [48] But those that be left behind of thy people are they that are found within my borders. [49] Now when he destroyeth the multitude of the nations that are gathered together, he shall defend his people that remain. [50] And then shall he shew them great wonders. [51] Then said I, O Lord that bearest rule, shew me this: Wherefore have I seen the man coming up from the midst of the sea? [52] And he said unto me, Like as thou canst neither seek out nor know the things that are in the deep of the sea: even so can no man upon earth see my Son, or those that be with him, but in the day time. [53] This is the interpretation of the dream which thou sawest, and whereby thou only art here lightened. [54] For thou hast forsaken thine own way, and applied thy diligence unto my law, and sought it. [55] Thy life hast thou ordered in wisdom, and hast called understanding thy mother. [56] And therefore have I shewed thee the treasures of the Highest: after other three days I will speak other things unto thee, and declare unto thee mighty and wondrous things. [57] Then went I forth into the field, giving praise and thanks greatly unto the most High because of his wonders which he did in time; [58] And because he governeth the same, and such things as fall in their seasons: and there I sat three days.

4Ezra.14

[1] And it came to pass upon the third day, I sat under an oak, and, behold, there came a voice out of a bush over against me, and said, Esdras, Esdras. [2] And I said, Here am I, Lord And I stood up upon my feet. [3] Then said he unto me, In the bush I did manifestly reveal myself unto Moses, and talked with him, when my people served in Egypt: [4] And I sent him and led my people out of Egypt, and brought him up to the mount of where I held him by me a long season, [5] And told him many wondrous things, and shewed him the secrets of the times, and the end; and

commanded him, saying, [6] These words shalt thou declare, and these shalt thou hide. [7] And now I say unto thee, [8] That thou lay up in thy heart the signs that I have shewed, and the dreams that thou hast seen, and the interpretations which thou hast heard: [9] For thou shalt be taken away from all, and from henceforth thou shalt remain with my Son, and with such as be like thee, until the times be ended. [10] For the world hath lost his youth, and the times begin to wax old. [11] For the world is divided into twelve parts, and the ten parts of it are gone already, and half of a tenth part: [12] And there remaineth that which is after the half of the tenth part. [13] Now therefore set thine house in order, and reprove thy people, comfort such of them as be in trouble, and now renounce corruption, [14] Let go from thee mortal thoughts, cast away the burdens of man, put off now the weak nature, [15] And set aside the thoughts that are most heavy unto thee, and haste thee to flee from these times. [16] For yet greater evils than those which thou hast seen happen shall be done hereafter.

[17] For look how much the world shall be weaker through age, so much the more shall evils increase upon them that dwell therein. [18] For the time is fled far away, and leasing is hard at hand: for now hasteth the vision to come, which thou hast seen. [19] Then answered I before thee, and said, [20] Behold, Lord, I will go, as thou hast commanded me, and reprove the people which are present: but they that shall be born afterward, who shall admonish them? Thus the world is set in darkness, and they that dwell therein are without light. [21] For thy law is burnt, therefore no man knoweth the things that are done of thee, or the work that shall begin. [22] But if I have found grace before thee, send the Holy Ghost into me, and I shall write all that hath been done in the world since the beginning, which were written in thy law, that men may find thy path, and that they which will live in the latter days may live. [23] And he answered me, saying, Go thy way, gather the people together, and say unto them, that they seek thee not for forty days. [24] But look thou prepare thee many box trees, and take with thee Sarea, Dabria, Selemia, Ecanus, and Asiel, these five which are ready to write swiftly; [25] And come hither, and I shall light a candle of understanding in thine heart, which shall not be put out, till the things be performed which thou shalt begin to write. [26] And when thou hast done, some things shalt thou publish, and some things shalt thou shew secretly to the wise: to morrow this hour shalt thou begin to write. [27] Then went I forth, as he commanded, and gathered all the people together, and said, [28] Hear these words, O Israel. [29] Our fathers at the beginning were strangers in Egypt, from whence they were delivered: [30] And received the law of life, which they kept not, which ye also have transgressed after them. [31] Then was the land, even the land of Sion, parted among you by lot: but your fathers, and ye yourselves, have done unrighteousness, and have not kept the ways which the Highest commanded you. [32] And forasmuch as he is a righteous judge, he took from you in time the thing that he had given you. [33] And now are ye here, and your brethren among you. [34] Therefore if so be that ye will subdue your own understanding, and reform your hearts, ye shall be kept alive and after death ye shall obtain mercy. [35] For after death shall the judgment come, when we shall

live again: and then shall the names of the righteous be manifest, and the works of the ungodly shall be declared. [36] Let no man therefore come unto me now, nor seek after me these forty days. [37] So I took the five men, as he commanded me, and we went into the field, and remained there. [38] And the next day, behold, a voice called me, saying, Esdras, open thy mouth, and drink that I give thee to drink. [39] Then opened I my mouth, and, behold, he reached me a full cup, which was full as it were with water, but the colour of it was like fire. [40] And I took it, and drank: and when I had drunk of it, my heart uttered understanding, and wisdom grew in my breast, for my spirit strengthened my memory: [41] And my mouth was opened, and shut no more. [42] The Highest gave understanding unto the five men, and they wrote the wonderful visions of the night that were told, which they knew not: and they sat forty days, and they wrote in the day, and at night they ate bread. [43] As for me. I spake in the day, and I held not my tongue by night. [44] In forty days they wrote two hundred and four books. [45] And it came to pass, when the forty days were filled, that the Highest spake, saying, The first that thou hast written publish openly, that the worthy and unworthy may read it: [46] But keep the seventy last, that thou mayest deliver them only to such as be wise among the people: [47] For in them is the spring of understanding, the fountain of wisdom, and the stream of knowledge. [48] And I did so.

4Ezra.15

[1] Behold, speak thou in the ears of my people the words of prophecy, which I will put in thy mouth, saith the Lord: [2] And cause them to be written in paper: for they are faithful and true. [3] Fear not the imaginations against thee, let not the incredulity of them trouble thee, that speak against thee. [4] For all the unfaithful shall die in their unfaithfulness. [5] Behold, saith the Lord, I will bring plagues upon the world; the sword, famine, death, and destruction. [6] For wickedness hath exceedingly polluted the whole earth, and their hurtful works are fulfilled. [7] Therefore saith the Lord, [8] I will hold my tongue no more as touching their wickedness, which they profanely commit, neither will I suffer them in those things, in which they wickedly exercise themselves: behold, the innocent and righteous blood crieth unto me, and the souls of the just complain continually. [9] And therefore, saith the Lord, I will surely avenge them, and receive unto me all the innocent blood from among them. [10] Behold, my people is led as a flock to the slaughter: I will not suffer them now to dwell in the land of Egypt: [11] But I will bring them with a mighty hand and a stretched out arm, and smite Egypt with plagues, as before, and will destroy all the land thereof. [12] Egypt shall mourn, and the foundation of it shall be smitten with the plague and punishment that God shall bring upon it. [13] They that till the ground shall mourn: for their seeds shall fail through the blasting and hail, and with a fearful constellation. [14] Woe to the world and them that dwell therein! [15] For the sword and their destruction draweth nigh, and one people shall stand up and fight against another, and swords in their hands. [16] For there shall be sedition among men, and invading one another; they shall not regard their kings nor princes, and

the course of their actions shall stand in their power. [17] A man shall desire to go into a city, and shall not be able. [18] For because of their pride the cities shall be troubled, the houses shall be destroyed, and men shall be afraid. [19] A man shall have no pity upon his neighbour, but shall destroy their houses with the sword, and spoil their goods, because of the lack of bread, and for great tribulation. [20] Behold, saith God, I will call together all the kings of the earth to reverence me, which are from the rising of the sun, from the south, from the east, and Libanus; to turn themselves one against another, and repay the things that they have done to them. [21] Like as they do yet this day unto my chosen, so will I do also, and recompense in their bosom. Thus saith the Lord God; [22] My right hand shall not spare the sinners, and my sword shall not cease over them that shed innocent blood upon the earth. [23] The fire is gone forth from his wrath, and hath consumed the foundations of the earth, and the sinners, like the straw that is kindled. [24] Woe to them that sin, and keep not my commandments! saith the Lord. [25] I will not spare them: go your way, ye children, from the power, defile not my sanctuary. [26] For the Lord knoweth all them that sin against him, and therefore delivereth he them unto death and destruction. [27] For now are the plagues come upon the whole earth and ye shall remain in them: for God shall not deliver you, because ye have sinned against him. [28] Behold an horrible vision, and the appearance thereof from the east: [29] Where the nations of the dragons of Arabia shall come out with many chariots, and the multitude of them shall be carried as the wind upon earth, that all they which hear them may fear and tremble. [30] Also the Carmanians raging in wrath shall go forth as the wild boars of the wood, and with great power shall they come, and join battle with them, and shall waste a portion of the land of the Assyrians. [31] And then shall the dragons have the upper hand, remembering their nature; and if they shall turn themselves, conspiring together in great power to persecute them, [32] Then these shall be troubled bled, and keep silence through their power, and shall flee. [33] And from the land of the Assyrians shall the enemy besiege them, and consume some of them, and in their host shall be fear and dread, and strife among their kings. [34] Behold clouds from the east and from the north unto the south, and they are very horrible to look upon, full of wrath and storm. [35] They shall smite one upon another, and they shall smite down a great multitude of stars upon the earth, even their own star; and blood shall be from the sword unto the belly, [36] And dung of men unto the camel's hough. [37] And there shall be great fearfulness and trembling upon earth: and they that see the wrath shall be afraid, and trembling shall come upon them. [38] And then shall there come great storms from the south, and from the north, and another part from the west. [39] And strong winds shall arise from the east, and shall open it; and the cloud which he raised up in wrath, and the star stirred to cause fear toward the east and west wind, shall be destroyed. [40] The great and mighty clouds shall be puffed up full of wrath, and the star, that they may make all the earth afraid, and them that dwell therein; and they shall pour out over every high and eminent place an horrible star, [41] Fire, and hail, and flying swords, and many waters, that all fields may be full, and all rivers, with the abundance of great waters. [42] And they shall break down the cities and walls, mountains and hills, trees of the wood, and grass of the meadows, and their corn. [43] And they shall go stedfastly unto Babylon, and make her afraid. [44] They shall come to her, and besiege her, the star and all wrath shall they pour out upon her: then shall the dust and smoke go up unto the heaven, and all they that be about her shall bewail her. [45] And they that remain under her shall do service unto them that have put her in fear. [46] And thou, Asia, that art partaker of the hope of Babylon, and art the glory of her person: [47] Woe be unto thee, thou wretch, because thou hast made thyself like unto her; and hast decked thy daughters in whoredom, that they might please and glory in thy lovers, which have always desired to commit whoredom with thee. [48] Thou hast followed her that is hated in all her works and inventions: therefore saith God, [49] I will send plagues upon thee; widowhood, poverty, famine, sword, and pestilence, to waste thy houses with destruction and death. [50] And the glory of thy Power shall be dried up as a flower, the heat shall arise that is sent over thee. [51] Thou shalt be weakened as a poor woman with stripes, and as one chastised with wounds, so that the mighty and lovers shall not be able to receive thee. [52] Would I with jealousy have so proceeded against thee, saith the Lord, [53] If thou hadst not always slain my chosen, exalting the stroke of thine hands, and saying over their dead, when thou wast drunken, [54] Set forth the beauty of thy countenance? [55] The reward of thy whoredom shall be in thy bosom, therefore shalt thou receive recompence. [56] Like as thou hast done unto my chosen, saith the Lord, even so shall God do unto thee, and shall deliver thee into mischief [57] Thy children shall die of hunger, and thou shalt fall through the sword: thy cities shall be broken down, and all thine shall perish with the sword in the field. [58] They that be in the mountains shall die of hunger, and eat their own flesh, and drink their own blood, for very hunger of bread, and thirst of water. [59] Thou as unhappy shalt come through the sea, and receive plagues again. [60] And in the passage they shall rush on the idle city, and shall destroy some portion of thy land, and consume part of thy glory, and shall return to Babylon that was destroyed. [61] And thou shalt be cast down by them as stubble, and they shall be unto thee as fire; [62] And shall consume thee, and thy cities, thy land, and thy mountains; all thy woods and thy fruitful trees shall they burn up with fire. [63] Thy children shall they carry away captive, and, look, what thou hast, they shall spoil it, and mar the beauty of thy face.

4Ezra.16

[1] Woe be unto thee, Babylon, and Asia! Woe be unto thee, Egypt and Syria! [2] Gird up yourselves with cloths of sack and hair, bewail your children, and be sorry; for your destruction is at hand. [3] A sword is sent upon you, and who may turn it back? [4] A fire is sent among you, and who may quench it? [5] Plagues are sent unto you, and what is he that may drive them away? [6] May any man drive away an hungry lion in the wood? Or may any one quench the fire in stubble, when it hath begun to burn? [7] May one turn again the arrow that is shot of a strong archer? [8] The mighty Lord sendeth the plagues and who

is he that can drive them away? [9] A fire shall go forth from his wrath, and who is he that may quench it? [10] He shall cast lightnings, and who shall not fear? He shall thunder, and who shall not be afraid? [11] The Lord shall threaten, and who shall not be utterly beaten to powder at his presence? [12] The earth quaketh, and the foundations thereof; the sea ariseth up with waves from the deep, and the waves of it are troubled, and the fishes thereof also, before the Lord, and before the glory of his power: [13] For strong is his right hand that bendeth the bow, his arrows that he shooteth are sharp, and shall not miss, when they begin to be shot into the ends of the world. [14] Behold, the plagues are sent, and shall not return again, until they come upon the earth. [15] The fire is kindled, and shall not be put out, till it consume the foundation of the earth. [16] Like as an arrow which is shot of a mighty archer returneth not backward: even so the plagues that shall be sent upon earth shall not return again. [17] Woe is me! Woe is me! Who will deliver me in those days? [18] The beginning of sorrows and great mournings; the beginning of famine and great death; the beginning of wars, and the powers shall stand in fear; the beginning of evils! What shall I do when these evils shall come? [19] Behold, famine and plague, tribulation and anguish, are sent as scourges for amendment. [20] But for all these things they shall not turn from their wickedness, nor be always mindful of the scourges. [21] Behold, victuals shall be so good cheap upon earth, that they shall think themselves to be in good case, and even then shall evils grow upon earth, sword, famine, and great confusion. [22] For many of them that dwell upon earth shall perish of famine; and the other, that escape the hunger, shall the sword destroy. [23] And the dead shall be cast out as dung, and there shall be no man to comfort them: for the earth shall be wasted, and the cities shall be cast down. [24] There shall be no man left to till the earth, and to sow it [25] The trees shall give fruit, and who shall gather them? [26] The grapes shall ripen, and who shall tread them? For all places shall be desolate of men: [27] So that one man shall desire to see another, and to hear his voice. [28] For of a city there shall be ten left, and two of the field, which shall hide themselves in the thick groves, and in the clefts of the rocks. [29] As in an orchard of Olives upon every tree there are left three or four olives; [30] Or as when a vineyard is gathered, there are left some clusters of them that diligently seek through the vineyard: [31] Even so in those days there shall be three or four left by them that search their houses with the sword. [32] And the earth shall be laid waste, and the fields thereof shall wax old, and her ways and all her paths shall grow full of thorns, because no man shall travel therethrough. [33] The virgins shall mourn, having no bridegrooms; the women shall mourn, having no husbands; their daughters shall mourn, having no helpers. [34] In the wars shall their bridegrooms be destroyed, and their husbands shall perish of famine. [35] Hear now these things and understand them, ye servants of the Lord. [36] Behold, the word of the Lord, receive it: believe not the gods of whom the Lord spake. [37] Behold, the plagues draw nigh, and are not slack. [38] As when a woman with child in the ninth month bringeth forth her son, with two or three hours of her birth great pains compass her womb, which pains, when the child cometh forth, they slack not a moment: [39] Even so shall not the plagues be slack to come upon the earth, and the world shall mourn, and sorrows shall come upon it on every side. [40] O my people, hear my word: make you ready to thy battle, and in those evils be even as pilgrims upon the earth. [41] He that selleth, let him be as he that fleeth away: and he that buyeth, as one that will lose: [42] He that occupieth merchandise, as he that hath no profit by it: and he that buildeth, as he that shall not dwell therein: [43] He that soweth, as if he should not reap: so also he that planteth the vineyard, as he that shall not gather the grapes: [44] They that marry, as they that shall get no children; and they that marry not, as the widowers. [45] And therefore they that labour labour in vain: [46] For strangers shall reap their fruits, and spoil their goods, overthrow their houses, and take their children captives, for in captivity and famine shall they get children. [47] And they that occupy their merchandise with robbery, the more they deck their cities, their houses, their possessions, and their own persons: [48] The more will I be angry with them for their sin, saith the Lord. [49] Like as a whore envieth a right honest and virtuous woman: [50] So shall righteousness hate iniquity, when she decketh herself, and shall accuse her to her face, when he cometh that shall defend him that diligently searcheth out every sin upon earth. [51] And therefore be ye not like thereunto, nor to the works thereof. [52] For yet a little, and iniquity shall be taken away out of the earth, and righteousness shall reign among you. [53] Let not the sinner say that he hath not sinned: for God shall burn coals of fire upon his head, which saith before the Lord God and his glory, I have not sinned. [54] Behold, the Lord knoweth all the works of men, their imaginations, their thoughts, and their hearts: [55] Which spake but the word, Let the earth be made; and it was made: Let the heaven be made; and it was created. [56] In his word were the stars made, and he knoweth the number of them. [57] He searcheth the deep, and the treasures thereof; he hath measured the sea, and what it containeth. [58] He hath shut the sea in the midst of the waters, and with his word hath he hanged the earth upon the waters. [59] He spreadeth out the heavens like a vault; upon the waters hath he founded it. [60] In the desert hath he made springs of water, and pools upon the tops of the mountains, that the floods might pour down from the high rocks to water the earth. [61] He made man, and put his heart in the midst of the body, and gave him breath, life, and understanding. [62] Yea and the Spirit of Almighty God, which made all things, and searcheth out all hidden things in the secrets of the earth, [63] Surely he knoweth your inventions, and what ye think in your hearts, even them that sin, and would hide their sin. [64] Therefore hath the Lord exactly searched out all your works, and he will put you all to shame. [65] And when your sins are brought forth, ye shall be ashamed before men, and your own sins shall be your accusers in that day. [66] What will ye do? Or how will ye hide your sins before God and his angels? [67] Behold, God himself is the judge, fear him: leave off from your sins, and forget your iniquities, to meddle no more with them for ever: so shall God lead you forth, and deliver you from all trouble. [68] For, behold, the burning wrath of a great multitude is kindled over you, and they shall take away certain of you, and feed you, being idle, with things offered unto idols. [69] And they that consent unto them shall be had in derision and in reproach, and trodden under foot. [70] For there shall be in every place, and in the next cities, a great insurrection upon those that fear the Lord. [71] They shall be like mad men, sparing none, but still spoiling and destroying those that fear the Lord. [72] For they shall waste and take away their goods, and cast them out of their houses. [73] Then shall they be known, who are my chosen; and they shall be tried as the gold in the fire. [74] Hear, O ye my beloved, saith the Lord: behold, the days of trouble are at hand, but I will deliver you from the same. [75] Be ye not afraid neither doubt; for God is your guide, [76] And the guide of them who keep my commandments and precepts, saith the Lord God: let not your sins weigh you down, and let not your iniquities lift up themselves. [77] Woe be unto them that are bound with their sins, and covered with their iniquities like as a field is covered over with bushes, and the path thereof covered with thorns, that no man may travel through! [78] It is left undressed, and is cast into the fire to be consumed therewith.

TOBIT

Tob.1

[1] The book of the words of Tobit, son of Tobiel, the son of Ananiel, the son of Aduel, the son of Gabael, of the seed of Asael, of the tribe of Nephthali; [2] Who in the time of Enemessar king of the Assyrians was led captive out of Thisbe, which is at the right hand of that city, which is called properly Nephthali in Galilee above Aser. [3] I Tobit have walked all the days of my life in the ways of truth and justice, and I did many almsdeeds to my brethren, and my nation, who came with me to Nineve, into the land of the Assyrians. [4] And when I was in mine own country, in the land of Israel being but young, all the tribe of Nephthali my father fell from the house of Jerusalem, which was chosen out of all the tribes of Israel, that all the tribes should sacrifice there, where the temple of the habitation of the most High was consecrated and built for all ages. [5] Now all the tribes which together revolted, and the house of my father Nephthali, sacrificed unto the heifer Baal. [6] But I alone went often to Jerusalem at the feasts, as it was ordained unto all the people of Israel by an everlasting decree, having the firstfruits and tenths of increase, with that which was first shorn; and them gave I at the altar to the priests the children of Aaron. [7] The first tenth part of all increase I gave to the sons of Aaron, who ministered at Jerusalem: another tenth part I sold away, and went, and spent it every year at Jerusalem: [8] And the third I gave unto them to whom it was meet, as Debora my father's mother had commanded me, because I was left an orphan by my father. [9] Furthermore, when I was come to the age of a man, I married Anna of mine own kindred, and of her I begat Tobias. [10] And when we were carried away captives to Nineve, all my brethren and those that were of my kindred did eat of the bread of the Gentiles. [11] But I kept myself from eating; [12] Because I remembered God with all my heart. [13] And the most High gave me grace and favour before Enemessar, so that I was his purveyor. [14] And I went into Media, and left in trust with Gabael, the brother of Gabrias, at Rages a city of Media ten talents of silver. [15] Now when Enemessar was dead, Sennacherib his son reigned in his stead; whose estate was troubled, that I could not go into Media. [16] And in the time of Enemessar I gave many alms to my brethren, and gave my bread to the hungry, [17] And my clothes to the naked: and if I saw any of my nation dead, or cast about the walls of Nineve, I buried him. [18] And if the king Sennacherib had slain any, when he was come, and fled from Judea, I buried them privily; for in his wrath he killed many; but the bodies were not found, when they were sought for of the king. [19] And when one of the Ninevites went and complained of me to the king, that I buried them, and hid myself; understanding that I was sought for to be put to death, I withdrew myself for fear. [20] Then all my goods were forcibly taken away, neither was there any thing left me, beside my wife Anna and my son Tobias. [21] And there passed not five and fifty days, before two of his sons killed him, and they fled into the mountains of Ararath; and Sarchedonus his son reigned in his stead; who appointed over his father's accounts, and over all his affairs, Achiacharus my brother Anael's son. [22] And Achiacharus intreating for me, I returned to Nineve. Now Achiacharus was cupbearer, and keeper of the signet, and steward, and overseer of the accounts: and Sarchedonus appointed him next unto him: and he was my brother's son.

Tob.2

[1] Now when I was come home again, and my wife Anna was restored unto me, with my son Tobias, in the feast of Pentecost, which is the holy feast of the seven weeks, there was a good dinner prepared me, in the which I sat down to eat. [2] And when I saw abundance of meat, I said to my son, Go and bring what poor man soever thou shalt find out of our brethren, who is mindful of the Lord; and, lo, I tarry for thee. [3] But he came again, and said, Father, one of our nation is strangled, and is cast out in the marketplace. [4] Then before I had tasted of any meat, I started up, and took him up into a room until the going down of the sun. [5] Then I returned, and washed myself, and ate my meat in heaviness, [6] Remembering that prophecy of Amos, as he said, Your feasts shall be turned into mourning, and all your mirth into lamentation. [7] Therefore I wept: and after the going down of the sun I went and made a grave, and buried him. [8] But my neighbours mocked me, and said, This man is not yet afraid to be put to death for this matter: who fled away; and yet, lo, he burieth the dead again. [9] The same night also I returned from the burial, and slept by the wall of my courtyard, being polluted and my face was uncovered: [10] And I knew not that there were sparrows in the wall, and mine eyes being open, the sparrows muted warm dung into mine eyes, and a whiteness came in mine eyes: and I went to the physicians, but they helped me not: moreover Achiacharus did nourish me, until I went into Elymais. [11] And my wife Anna did take women's works to do. [12] And when she had sent them home to the owners, they paid her wages, and gave her also besides a kid. [13] And when it was in my house, and began to cry, I said unto her, From whence is this kid? Is it not stolen? Render it to the owners; for it is not lawful to eat any thing that is stolen. [14] But she replied upon me, It was given for a gift more than the wages. Howbeit I did not believe her, but bade her render it to the owners: and I was abashed at her. But she replied upon me, Where are thine alms and thy righteous deeds? Behold, thou and all thy works are known.

Tob.3

[1] Then I being grieved did weep, and in my sorrow prayed, saying, [2] O Lord, thou art just, and all thy works and all thy ways are mercy and truth, and thou judgest truly and justly for ever. [3] Remember me, and look on me, punish me not for my sins and ignorances, and the sins of mg fathers, who have sinned before thee: [4] For they obeyed not thy commandments: wherefore thou hast delivered us for a spoil, and unto captivity, and unto death, and for a proverb of reproach to all the nations among whom we are dispersed. [5] And now thy judgments are many and true: deal with me according to my sins and my fathers': because we have not kept thy commandments, neither have walked in truth before thee. [6] Now therefore deal with me as seemeth best unto thee, and

command my spirit to be taken from me, that I may be dissolved, and become earth: for it is profitable for me to die rather than to live, because I have heard false reproaches, and have much sorrow: command therefore that I may now be delivered out of this distress, and go into the everlasting place: turn not thy face away from me. [7] It came to pass the same day, that in Ecbatane a city of Media Sara the daughter of Raguel was also reproached by her father's maids; [8] Because that she had been married to seven husbands, whom Asmodeus the evil spirit had killed, before they had lain with her. Dost thou not know, said they, that thou hast strangled thine husbands? thou hast had already seven husbands, neither wast thou named after any of them. [9] Wherefore dost thou beat us for them? if they be dead, go thy ways after them, let us never see of thee either son or daughter. [10] Whe she heard these things, she was very sorrowful, so that she thought to have strangled herself; and she said, I am the only daughter of my father, and if I do this, it shall be a reproach unto him, and I shall bring his old age with sorrow unto the grave. [11] Then she prayed toward the window, and said, Blessed art thou, O Lord my God, and thine holy and glorious name is blessed and honourable for ever: let all thy works praise thee for ever. [12] And now, O Lord, I set I mine eyes and my face toward thee, [13] And say, Take me out of the earth, that I may hear no more the reproach. [14] Thou knowest, Lord, that I am pure from all sin with man,

[15] And that I never polluted my name, nor the name of my father, in the land of my captivity: I am the only daughter of my father, neither hath he any child to be his heir, neither any near kinsman, nor any son of his alive, to whom I may keep myself for a wife: my seven husbands are already dead; and why should I live? but if it please not thee that I should die, command some regard to be had of me, and pity taken of me, that I hear no more reproach. [16] So the prayers of them both were heard before the majesty of the great God. [17] And Raphael was sent to heal them both, that is, to scale away the whiteness of Tobit's eyes, and to give Sara the daughter of Raguel for a wife to Tobias the son of Tobit; and to bind Asmodeus the evil spirit; because she belonged to Tobias by right of inheritance. The selfsame time came Tobit home, and entered into his house, and Sara the daughter of Raguel came down from her upper chamber.

Tob.4

[1] In that day Tobit remembered the money which he had committed to Gabael in Rages of Media, [2] And said with himself, I have wished for death; wherefore do I not call for my son Tobias that I may signify to him of the money before I die? [3] And when he had called him, he said, My son, when I am dead, bury me; and despise not thy mother, but honour her all the days of thy life, and do that which shall please her, and grieve her not. [4] Remember, my son, that she saw many dangers for thee, when thou wast in her womb: and when she is dead, bury her by me in one grave. [5] My son, be mindful of the Lord our God all thy days, and let not thy will be set to sin, or to transgress his commandments: do uprightly all thy life long, and follow not the ways of unrighteousness. [6] For if thou deal truly, thy doings shall prosperously succeed to thee, and to all them that live justly. [7] Give alms of thy substance; and

when thou givest alms, let not thine eye be envious, neither turn thy face from any poor, and the face of God shall not be turned away from thee. [8] If thou hast abundance give alms accordingly: if thou have but a little, be not afraid to give according to that little: [9] For thou layest up a good treasure for thyself against the day of necessity. [10] Because that alms do deliver from death, and suffereth not to come into darkness. [11] For alms is a good gift unto all that give it in the sight of the most High. [12] Beware of all whoredom, my son, and chiefly take a wife of the seed of thy fathers, and take not a strange woman to wife, which is not of thy father's tribe: for we are the children of the prophets, Noe, Abraham, Isaac, and Jacob: remember, my son, that our fathers from the beginning, even that they all married wives of their own kindred, and were blessed in their children, and their seed shall inherit the land. [13] Now therefore, my son, love thy brethren, and despise not in thy heart thy brethren, the sons and daughters of thy people, in not taking a wife of them: for in pride is destruction and much trouble, and in lewdness is decay and great want: for lewdness is the mother of famine. [14] Let not the wages of any man, which hath wrought for thee, tarry with thee, but give him it out of hand: for if thou serve God, he will also repay thee: be circumspect my son, in all things thou doest, and be wise in all thy conversation.

[15] Do that to no man which thou hatest: drink not wine to make thee drunken: neither let drunkenness go with thee in thy journey. [16] Give of thy bread to the hungry, and of thy garments to them that are naked; and according to thine abundance give alms: and let not thine eye be envious, when thou givest alms. [17] Pour out thy bread on the burial of the just, but give nothing to the wicked. [18] Ask counsel of all that are wise, and despise not any counsel that is profitable. [19] Bless the Lord thy God alway, and desire of him that thy ways may be directed, and that all thy paths and counsels may prosper: for every nation hath not counsel; but the Lord himself giveth all good things, and he humbleth whom he will, as he will; now therefore, my son, remember my commandments, neither let them be put out of thy mind. [20] And now I signify this to they that I committed ten talents to Gabael the son of Gabrias at Rages in Media. [21] And fear not, my son, that we are made poor: for thou hast much wealth, if thou fear God, and depart from all sin, and do that which is pleasing in his sight.

Tob.5

[1] Tobias then answered and said, Father, I will do all things which thou hast commanded me: [2] But how can I receive the money, seeing I know him not? [3] Then he gave him the handwriting, and said unto him, Seek thee a man which may go with thee, whiles I yet live, and I will give him wages: and go and receive the money. [4] Therefore when he went to seek a man, he found Raphael that was an angel. [5] But he knew not; and he said unto him, Canst thou go with me to Rages? and knowest thou those places well? [6] To whom the angel said, I will go with thee, and I know the way well: for I have lodged with our brother Gabael. [7] Then Tobias said unto him, Tarry for me, till I tell my father. [8] Then he said unto him, Go and tarry not. So he went in and said to his father, Behold, I have found one which will go with me. Then he said, Call

him unto me, that I may know of what tribe he is, and whether he be a trusty man to go with thee. [9] So he called him, and he came in, and they saluted one another. [10] Then Tobit said unto him, Brother, shew me of what tribe and family thou art. [11] To whom he said, Dost thou seek for a tribe or family, or an hired man to go with thy son? Then Tobit said unto him, I would know, brother, thy kindred and name. [12] Then he said, I am Azarias, the son of Ananias the great, and of thy brethren. [13] Then Tobit said, Thou art welcome, brother; be not now angry with me, because I have enquired to know thy tribe and thy family; for thou art my brother, of an honest and good stock: for I know Ananias and Jonathas, sons of that great Samaias, as we went together to Jerusalem to worship, and offered the firstborn, and the tenths of the fruits; and they were not seduced with the error of our brethren: my brother, thou art of a good stock. [14] But tell me, what wages shall I give thee? wilt thou a drachm a day, and things necessary, as to mine own son? [15] Yea, moreover, if ye return safe, I will add something to thy wages. [16] So they were well pleased. Then said he to Tobias, Prepare thyself for the journey, and God send you a good journey. And when his son had prepared all things far the journey, his father said, Go thou with this man, and God, which dwelleth in heaven, prosper your journey, and the angel of God keep you company. So they went forth both, and the young man's dog with them. [17] But Anna his mother wept, and said to Tobit, Why hast thou sent away our son? is he not the staff of our hand, in going in and out before us? [18] Be not greedy to add money to money: but let it be as refuse in respect of our child. [19] For that which the Lord hath given us to live with doth suffice us. [20] Then said Tobit to her, Take no care, my sister; he shall return in safety, and thine eyes shall see him. [21] For the good angel will keep him company, and his journey shall be prosperous, and he shall return safe. [22] Then she made an end of weeping.

Tob.6

[1] And as they went on their journey, they came in the evening to the river Tigris, and they lodged there. [2] And when the young man went down to wash himself, a fish leaped out of the river, and would have devoured him. [3] Then the angel said unto him, Take the fish. And the young man laid hold of the fish, and drew it to land. [4] To whom the angel said, Open the fish, and take the heart and the liver and the gall, and put them up safely. [5] So the young man did as the angel commanded him; and when they had roasted the fish, they did eat it: then they both went on their way, till they drew near to Ecbatane. [6] Then the young man said to the angel, Brother Azarias, to what use is the heart and the liver and the gal of the fish? [7] And he said unto him, Touching the heart and the liver, if a devil or an evil spirit trouble any, we must make a smoke thereof before the man or the woman, and the party shall be no more vexed. [8] As for the gall, it is good to anoint a man that hath whiteness in his eyes, and he shall be healed. [9] And when they were come near to Rages, [10] The angel said to the young man, Brother, to day we shall lodge with Raguel, who is thy cousin; he also hath one only daughter, named Sara; I will speak for her, that she may be given thee

for a wife. [11] For to thee doth the right of her appertain, seeing thou only art of her kindred. [12] And the maid is fair and wise: now therefore hear me, and I will speak to her father; and when we return from Rages we will celebrate the marriage: for I know that Raguel cannot marry her to another according to the law of Moses, but he shall be guilty of death, because the right of inheritance doth rather appertain to thee than to any other. [13] Then the young man answered the angel, I have heard, brother Azarias that this maid hath been given to seven men, who all died in the marriage chamber. [14] And now I am the only son of my father, and I am afraid, lest if I go in unto her, I die, as the other before: for a wicked spirit loveth her, which hurteth no body, but those which come unto her; wherefore I also fear lest I die, and bring my father's and my mother's life because of me to the grave with sorrow: for they have no other son to bury them. [15] Then the angel said unto him, Dost thou not remember the precepts which thy father gave thee, that thou shouldest marry a wife of thine own kindred? wherefore hear me, O my brother; for she shall be given thee to wife; and make thou no reckoning of the evil spirit; for this same night shall she be given thee in marriage. [16] And when thou shalt come into the marriage chamber, thou shalt take the ashes of perfume, and shalt lay upon them some of the heart and liver of the fish, and shalt make a smoke with it: [17] And the devil shall smell it, and flee away, and never come again any more: but when thou shalt come to her, rise up both of you, and pray to God which is merciful, who will have pity on you, and save you: fear not, for she is appointed unto thee from the beginning; and thou shalt preserve her, and she shall go with thee. Moreover I suppose that she shall bear thee children. Now when Tobias had heard these things, he loved her, and his heart was effectually joined to her.

Tob.7

[1] And when they were come to Ecbatane, they came to the house of Raguel, and Sara met them: and after they had saluted one another, she brought them into the house. [2] Then said Raguel to Edna his wife, How like is this young man to Tobit my cousin! [3] And Raguel asked them, From whence are ye, brethren? To whom they said, We are of the sons of Nephthalim, which are captives in Nineve. [4] Then he said to them, Do ye know Tobit our kinsman? And they said, We know him. Then said he, Is he in good health? [5] And they said, He is both alive, and in good health: and Tobias said, He is my father. [6] Then Raguel leaped up, and kissed him, and wept, [7] And blessed him, and said unto him, Thou art the son of an honest and good man. But when he had heard that Tobit was blind, he was sorrowful, and wept. [8] And likewise Edna his wife and Sara his daughter wept. Moreover they entertained them cheerfully; and after that they had killed a ram of the flock, they set store of meat on the table. Then said Tobias to Raphael, Brother Azarias, speak of those things of which thou didst talk in the way, and let this business be dispatched. [9] So he communicated the matter with Raguel: and Raguel said to Tobias, Eat and drink, and make merry: [10] For it is meet that thou shouldest marry my daughter: nevertheless I will declare unto thee the truth. [11] I have given my daughter in marriage te seven men,

who died that night they came in unto her: nevertheless for the present be merry. But Tobias said, I will eat nothing here, till we agree and swear one to another. [12] Raguel said, Then take her from henceforth according to the manner, for thou art her cousin, and she is thine, and the merciful God give you good success in all things. [13] Then he called his daughter Sara, and she came to her father, and he took her by the hand, and gave her to be wife to Tobias, saying, Behold, take her after the law of Moses, and lead her away to thy father. And he blessed them; [14] And called Edna his wife, and took paper, and did write an instrument of covenants, and sealed it. [15] Then they began to eat. [16] After Raguel called his wife Edna, and said unto her, Sister, prepare another chamber, and bring her in thither. [17] Which when she had done as he had bidden her, she brought her thither: and she wept, and she received the tears of her daughter, and said unto her, [18] Be of good comfort, my daughter; the Lord of heaven and earth give thee joy for this thy sorrow: be of good comfort, my daughter.

Tob.8

[1] And when they had supped, they brought Tobias in unto her. [2] And as he went, he remembered the words of Raphael, and took the ashes of the perfumes, and put the heart and the liver of the fish thereupon, and made a smoke therewith. [3] The which smell when the evil spirit had smelled, he fled into the utmost parts of Egypt, and the angel bound him. [4] And after that they were both shut in together, Tobias rose out of the bed, and said, Sister, arise, and let us pray that God would have pity on us. [5] Then began Tobias to say, Blessed art thou, O God of our fathers, and blessed is thy holy and glorious name for ever; let the heavens bless thee, and all thy creatures. [6] Thou madest Adam, and gavest him Eve his wife for an helper and stay: of them came mankind: thou hast said, It is not good that man should be alone; let us make unto him an aid like unto himself. [7] And now, O Lord, I take not this my sister for lush but uprightly: therefore mercifully ordain that we may become aged together. [8] And she said with him, Amen. [9] So they slept both that night. And Raguel arose, and went and made a grave, [10] Saying, I fear lest he also be dead. [11] But when Raguel was come into his house, [12] He said unto his wife Edna. Send one of the maids, and let her see whether he be alive: if he be not, that we may bury him, and no man know it. [13] So the maid opened the door, and went in, and found them both asleep, [14] And came forth, and told them that he was alive. [15] Then Raguel praised God, and said, O God, thou art worthy to be praised with all pure and holy praise; therefore let thy saints praise thee with all thy creatures; and let all thine angels and thine elect praise thee for ever. [16] Thou art to be praised, for thou hast made me joyful; and that is not come to me which I suspected; but thou hast dealt with us according to thy great mercy. [17] Thou art to be praised because thou hast had mercy of two that were the only begotten children of their fathers: grant them mercy, O Lord, and finish their life in health with joy and mercy. [18] Then Raguel bade his servants to fill the grave. [19] And he kept the wedding feast fourteen days. [20] For before the days of the marriage were finished, Raguel had said unto him by an oath, that he should not depart till the fourteen days of the marriage were expired; [21] And then he should take the half of his goods, and go in safety to his father; and should have the rest when I and my wife be dead.

Tob.9

[1] Then Tobias called Raphael, and said unto him, [2] Brother Azarias, take with thee a servant, and two camels, and go to Rages of Media to Gabael, and bring me the money, and bring him to the wedding. [3] For Raguel hath sworn that I shall not depart. [4] But my father counteth the days; and if I tarry long, he will be very sorry. [5] So Raphael went out, and lodged with Gabael, and gave him the handwriting: who brought forth bags which were sealed up, and gave them to him. [6] And early in the morning they went forth both together, and came to the wedding: and Tobias blessed his wife.

Tob.10

[1] Now Tobit his father counted every day: and when the days of the journey were expired, and they came not, [2] Then Tobit said, Are they detained? or is Gabael dead, and there is no man to give him the money? [3] Therefore he was very sorry. [4] Then his wife said unto him, My son is dead, seeing he stayeth long; and she began to wail him, and said, [5] Now I care for nothing, my son, since I have let thee go, the light of mine eyes. [6] To whom Tobit said, Hold thy peace, take no care, for he is safe. [7] But she said, Hold thy peace, and deceive me not; my son is dead. And she went out every day into the way which they went, and did eat no meat on the daytime, and ceased not whole nights to bewail her son Tobias, until the fourteen days of the wedding were expired, which Raguel had sworn that he should spend there. Then Tobias said to Raguel, Let me go, for my father and my mother look no more to see me. [8] But his father in law said unto him, Tarry with me, and I will send to thy father, and they shall declare unto him how things go with thee. [9] But Tobias said, No; but let me go to my father. [10] Then Raguel arose, and gave him Sara his wife, and half his goods, servants, and cattle, and money: [11] And he blessed them, and sent them away, saying, The God of heaven give you a prosperous journey, my children. [12] And he said to his daughter, Honour thy father and thy mother in law, which are now thy parents, that I may hear good report of thee. And he kissed her. Edna also said to Tobias, The Lord of heaven restore thee, my dear brother, and grant that I may see thy children of my daughter Sara before I die, that I may rejoice before the Lord: behold, I commit my daughter unto thee of special trust; where are do not entreat her evil.

Tob.11

[1] After these things Tobias went his way, praising God that he had given him a prosperous journey, and blessed Raguel and Edna his wife, and went on his way till they drew near unto Nineve. [2] Then Raphael said to Tobias, Thou knowest, brother, how thou didst leave thy father: [3] Let us haste before thy wife, and prepare the house. [4] And take in thine hand the gall of the fish. So they went

their way, and the dog went after them. [5] Now Anna sat looking about toward the way for her son. [6] And when she espied him coming, she said to his father, Behold, thy son cometh, and the man that went with him. [7] Then said Raphael, I know, Tobias, that thy father will open his eyes. [8] Therefore anoint thou his eyes with the gall, and being pricked therewith, he shall rub, and the whiteness shall fall away, and he shall see thee. [9] Then Anna ran forth, and fell upon the neck of her son, and said unto him, Seeing I have seen thee, my son, from henceforth I am content to die. And they wept both. [10] Tobit also went forth toward the door, and stumbled: but his son ran unto him, [11] And took hold of his father: and he strake of the gall on his fathers' eyes, saying, Be of good hope, my father.

[12] And when his eyes began to smart, he rubbed them; [13] And the whiteness pilled away from the corners of his eyes: and when he saw his son, he fell upon his neck. [14] And he wept, and said, Blessed art thou, O God, and blessed is thy name for ever; and blessed are all thine holy angels: [15] For thou hast scourged, and hast taken pity on me: for, behold, I see my son Tobias. And his son went in rejoicing, and told his father the great things that had happened to him in Media. [16] Then Tobit went out to meet his daughter in law at the gate of Nineve, rejoicing and praising God: and they which saw him go marvelled, because he had received his sight. [17] But Tobias gave thanks before them, because God had mercy on him. And when he came near to Sara his daughter in law, he blessed her, saying, Thou art welcome, daughter: God be blessed, which hath brought thee unto us, and blessed be thy father and thy mother. And there was joy among all his brethren which were at Nineve. [18] And Achiacharus, and Nasbas his brother's son, came: [19] And Tobias' wedding was kept seven days with great joy.

Tob.12

[1] Then Tobit called his son Tobias, and said unto him, My son, see that the man have his wages, which went with thee, and thou must give him more. [2] And Tobias said unto him, O father, it is no harm to me to give him half of those things which I have brought: [3] For he hath brought me again to thee in safety, and made whole my wife, and brought me the money, and likewise healed thee. [4] Then the old man said, It is due unto him. [5] So he called the angel, and he said unto him, Take half of all that ye have brought and go away in safety. [6] Then he took them both apart, and said unto them, Bless God, praise him, and magnify him, and praise him for the things which he hath done unto you in the sight of all that live. It is good to praise God, and exalt his name, and honourably to shew forth the works of God; therefore be not slack to praise him. [7] It is good to keep close the secret of a king, but it is honourable to reveal the works of God. Do that which is good, and no evil shall touch you. [8] Prayer is good with fasting and alms and righteousness. A little with righteousness is better than much with unrighteousness. It is better to give alms than to lay up gold: [9] For alms doth deliver from death, and shall purge away all sin. Those that exercise alms and righteousness shall be filled with life: [10] But they that sin are enemies to their own life. [11] Surely I will keep close nothing from you. For I said, It was good to

keep close the secret of a king, but that it was honourable to reveal the works of God. [12] Now therefore, when thou didst pray, and Sara thy daughter in law, I did bring the remembrance of your prayers before the Holy One: and when thou didst bury the dead, I was with thee likewise. [13] And when thou didst not delay to rise up, and leave thy dinner, to go and cover the dead, thy good deed was not hid from me: but I was with thee. [14] And now God hath sent me to heal thee and Sara thy daughter in law. [15] I am Raphael, one of the seven holy angels, which present the prayers of the saints, and which go in and out before the glory of the Holy One. [16] Then they were both troubled, and fell upon their faces: for they feared. [17] But he said unto them, Fear not, for it shall go well with you; praise God therefore. [18] For not of any favour of mine, but by the will of our God I came; wherefore praise him for ever. [19] All these days I did appear unto you; but I did neither eat nor drink, but ye did see a vision. [20] Now therefore give God thanks: for I go up to him that sent me; but write all things which are done in a book. [21] And when they arose, they saw him no more. [22] Then they confessed the great and wonderful works of God, and how the angel of the Lord had appeared unto them.

Tob.13

[1] Then Tobit wrote a prayer of rejoicing, and said, Blessed be God that liveth for ever, and blessed be his kingdom. [2] For he doth scourge, and hath mercy: he leadeth down to hell, and bringeth up again: neither is there any that can avoid his hand. [3] Confess him before the Gentiles, ye children of Israel: for he hath scattered us among them. [4] There declare his greatness, and extol him before all the living: for he is our Lord, and he is the God our Father for ever. [5] And he will scourge us for our iniquities, and will have mercy again, and will gather us out of all nations, among whom he hath scattered us. [6] If ye turn to him with your whole heart, and with your whole mind, and deal uprightly before him, then will he turn unto you, and will not hide his face from you. Therefore see what he will do with you, and confess him with your whole mouth, and praise the Lord of might, and extol the everlasting King. In the land of my captivity do I praise him, and declare his might and majesty to a sinful nation. O ye sinners, turn and do justice before him: who can tell if he will accept you, and have mercy on you? [7] I will extol my God, and my soul shall praise the King of heaven, and shall rejoice in his greatness. [8] Let all men speak, and let all praise him for his righteousness. [9] O Jerusalem, the holy city, he will scourge thee for thy children's works, and will have mercy again on the sons of the righteous. [10] Give praise to the Lord, for he is good: and praise the everlasting King, that his tabernacle may be builded in thee again with joy, and let him make joyful there in thee those that are captives, and love in thee for ever those that are miserable. [11] Many nations shall come from far to the name of the Lord God with gifts in their hands, even gifts to the King of heaven; all generations shall praise thee with great joy. [12] Cursed are all they which hate thee, and blessed shall all be which love thee for ever. [13] Rejoice and be glad for the children of the just: for they shall be gathered together, and shall bless the Lord of the just. [14] O blessed are they which

love thee, for they shall rejoice in thy peace: blessed are they which have been sorrowful for all thy scourges; for they shall rejoice for thee, when they have seen all thy glory, and shall be glad for ever. [15] Let my soul bless God the great King. [16] For Jerusalem shall be built up with sapphires and emeralds, and precious stone: thy walls and towers and battlements with pure gold. [17] And the streets of Jerusalem shall be paved with beryl and carbuncle and stones of Ophir. [18] And all her streets shall say, Alleluia; and they shall praise him, saying, Blessed be God, which hath extolled it for ever.

Tob.14

[1] So Tobit made an end of praising God. [2] And he was eight and fifty years old when he lost his sight, which was restored to him after eight years: and he gave alms, and he increased in the fear of the Lord God, and praised him. [3] And when he was very aged he called his son, and the sons of his son, and said to him, My son, take thy children; for, behold, I am aged, and am ready to depart out of this life. [4] Go into Media my son, for I surely believe those things which Jonas the prophet spake of Nineve, that it shall be overthrown; and that for a time peace shall rather be in Media; and that our brethren shall lie scattered in the earth from that good land: and Jerusalem shall be desolate, and the house of God in it shall be burned, and shall be desolate for a time; [5] And that again God will have mercy on them, and bring them again into the land, where they shall build a temple, but not like to the first, until the time of that age be fulfilled; and afterward they shall return from all places of their captivity, and build up Jerusalem gloriously, and the house of God shall be built in it for ever with a glorious building, as the prophets have spoken thereof. [6] And all nations shall turn, and fear the Lord God truly, and shall bury their idols. [7] So shall all nations praise the Lord, and his people shall confess God, and the Lord shall exalt his people; and all those which love the Lord God in truth and justice shall rejoice, shewing mercy to our brethren. [8] And now, my son, depart out of Nineve, because that those things which the prophet Jonas spake shall surely come to pass. [9] But keep thou the law and the commandments, and shew thyself merciful and just, that it may go well with thee. [10] And bury me decently, and thy mother with me; but tarry no longer at Nineve. Remember, my son, how Aman handled Achiacharus that brought him up, how out of light he brought him into darkness, and how he rewarded him again: yet Achiacharus was saved, but the other had his reward: for he went down into darkness. Manasses gave alms, and escaped the snares of death which they had set for him: but Aman fell into the snare, and perished. [11] Wherefore now, my son, consider what alms doeth, and how righteousness doth deliver. When he had said these things, he gave up the ghost in the bed, being an hundred and eight and fifty years old; and he buried him honourably. [12] And when Anna his mother was dead, he buried her with his father. But Tobias departed with his wife and children to Ecbatane to Raguel his father in law, [13] Where he became old with honour, and he buried his father and mother in law honourably, and he inherited their substance, and his father Tobit's. [14] And he died at Ecbatane in Media, being an hundred and seven and twenty years old. [15] But before he died he heard of the destruction of Nineve, which was taken by Nabuchodonosor and Assuerus: and before his death he rejoiced over Nineve.

JUDITH

Jdt.1

[1] In the twelfth year of the reign of Nabuchodonosor, who reigned in Nineve, the great city; in the days of Arphaxad, which reigned over the Medes in Ecbatane, [2] And built in Ecbatane walls round about of stones hewn three cubits broad and six cubits long, and made the height of the wall seventy cubits, and the breadth thereof fifty cubits: [3] And set the towers thereof upon the gates of it an hundred cubits high, and the breadth thereof in the foundation threescore cubits: [4] And he made the gates thereof, even gates that were raised to the height of seventy cubits, and the breadth of them was forty cubits, for the going forth of his mighty armies, and for the setting in array of his footmen: [5] Even in those days king Nabuchodonosor made war with king Arphaxad in the great plain, which is the plain in the borders of Ragau. [6] And there came unto him all they that dwelt in the hill country, and all that dwelt by Euphrates, and Tigris and Hydaspes, and the plain of Arioch the king of the Elymeans, and very many nations of the sons of Chelod, assembled themselves to the battle. [7] Then Nabuchodonosor king of the Assyrians sent unto all that dwelt in Persia, and to all that dwelt westward, and to those that dwelt in Cilicia, and Damascus, and Libanus, and Antilibanus, and to all that dwelt upon the sea coast, [8] And to those among the nations that were of Carmel, and Galaad, and the higher Galilee, and the great plain of Esdrelom, [9] And to all that were in Samaria and the cities thereof, and beyond Jordan unto Jerusalem, and Betane, and Chelus, and Kades, and the river of Egypt, and Taphnes, and Ramesse, and all the land of Gesem, [10] Until ye come beyond Tanis and Memphis, and to all the inhabitants of Egypt, until ye come to the borders of Ethiopia. [11] But all the inhabitants of the land made light of the commandment of Nabuchodonosor king of the Assyrians, neither went they with him to the battle; for they were not afraid of him: yea, he was before them as one man, and they sent away his ambassadors from them without effect, and with disgrace. [12] Therefore Nabuchodonosor was very angry with all this country, and sware by his throne and kingdom, that he would surely be avenged upon all those coasts of Cilicia, and Damascus, and Syria, and that he would slay with the sword all the inhabitants of the land of Moab, and the children of Ammon, and all Judea, and all that were in Egypt, till ye come to the borders of the two seas. [13] Then he marched in battle array with his power against king Arphaxad in the seventeenth year, and he prevailed in his battle: for he overthrew all the power of Arphaxad, and all his horsemen, and all his chariots, [14] And became lord of his cities, and came unto Ecbatane, and took the towers, and spoiled the streets thereof, and turned the beauty thereof into shame. [15] He took also Arphaxad in the mountains of Ragau, and smote him through with his darts, and destroyed him utterly that day. [16] So he returned afterward to Nineve, both he and all his company of sundry nations being a very great multitude of men of war, and there he took his ease, and banqueted, both he and his army, an hundred and twenty days.

Jdt.2

[1] And in the eighteenth year, the two and twentieth day of the first month, there was talk in the house of Nabuchodonosor king of the Assyrians that he should, as he said, avenge himself on all the earth. [2] So he called unto him all his officers, and all his nobles, and communicated with them his secret counsel, and concluded the afflicting of the whole earth out of his own mouth. [3] Then they decreed to destroy all flesh, that did not obey the commandment of his mouth. [4] And when he had ended his counsel, Nabuchodonosor king of the Assyrians called Holofernes the chief captain of his army, which was next unto him, and said unto him. [5] Thus saith the great king, the lord of the whole earth, Behold, thou shalt go forth from my presence, and take with thee men that trust in their own strength, of footmen an hundred and twenty thousand; and the number of horses with their riders twelve thousand. [6] And thou shalt go against all the west country, because they disobeyed my commandment. [7] And thou shalt declare unto that they prepare for me earth and water: for I will go forth in my wrath against them and will cover the whole face of the earth with the feet of mine army, and I will give them for a spoil unto them: [8] So that their slain shall fill their valleys and brooks and the river shall be filled with their dead, till it overflow: [9] And I will lead them captives to the utmost parts of all the earth. [10] Thou therefore shalt go forth. and take beforehand for me all their coasts: and if they will yield themselves unto thee, thou shalt reserve them for me till the day of their punishment. [11] But concerning them that rebel, let not thine eye spare them; but put them to the slaughter, and spoil them wheresoever thou goest. [12] For as I live, and by the power of my kingdom, whatsoever I have spoken, that will I do by mine hand. [13] And take thou heed that thou transgress none of the commandments of thy lord, but accomplish them fully, as I have commanded thee, and defer not to do them. [14] Then Holofernes went forth from the presence of his lord, and called all the governors and captains, and the officers of the army of Assur; [15] And he mustered the chosen men for the battle, as his lord had commanded him, unto an hundred and twenty thousand, and twelve thousand archers on horseback; [16] And he ranged them, as a great army is ordered for the war. [17] And he took camels and asses for their carriages, a very great number; and sheep and oxen and goats without number for their provision: [18] And plenty of victual for every man of the army, and very much gold and silver out of the king's house. [19] Then he went forth and all his power to go before king Nabuchodonosor in the voyage, and to cover all the face of the earth westward with their chariots, and horsemen, and their chosen footmen. [20] A great number also sundry countries came with them like locusts, and like the sand of the earth: for the multitude was without number. [21] And they went forth of Nineve three days' journey toward the plain of Bectileth, and pitched from Bectileth near the mountain which is at the left hand of the upper Cilicia. [22] Then he took all his army, his footmen, and horsemen and chariots, and went from thence into the hill country; [23] And destroyed Phud and Lud, and spoiled all the children of Rasses, and the children of Israel, which were toward the wilderness at the south of

the land of the Chellians. [24] Then he went over Euphrates, and went through Mesopotamia, and destroyed all the high cities that were upon the river Arbonai, till ye come to the sea. [25] And he took the borders of Cilicia, and killed all that resisted him, and came to the borders of Japheth, which were toward the south, over against Arabia.

[26] He compassed also all the children of Madian, and burned up their tabernacles, and spoiled their sheepcotes. [27] Then he went down into the plain of Damascus in the time of wheat harvest, and burnt up all their fields, and destroyed their flocks and herds, also he spoiled their cities, and utterly wasted their countries, and smote all their young men with the edge of the sword. [28] Therefore the fear and dread of him fell upon all the inhabitants of the sea coasts, which were in Sidon and Tyrus, and them that dwelt in Sur and Ocina, and all that dwelt in Jemnaan; and they that dwelt in Azotus and Ascalon feared him greatly.

Jdt.3

[1] So they sent ambassadors unto him to treat of peace, saying, [2] Behold, we the servants of Nabuchodonosor the great king lie before thee; use us as shall be good in thy sight. [3] Behold, our houses, and all our places, and all our fields of wheat, and flocks, and herds, and all the lodges of our tents lie before thy face; use them as it pleaseth thee. [4] Behold, even our cities and the inhabitants thereof are thy servants; come and deal with them as seemeth good unto thee. [5] So the men came to Holofernes, and declared unto him after this manner. [6] Then came he down toward the sea coast, both he and his army, and set garrisons in the high cities, and took out of them chosen men for aid. [7] So they and all the country round about received them with garlands, with dances, and with timbrels. [8] Yet he did cast down their frontiers, and cut down their groves: for he had decreed to destroy all the gods of the land, that all nations should worship Nabuchodonosor only, and that all tongues and tribes should call upon him as god. [9] Also he came over against Esdraelon near unto Judea, over against the great strait of Judea. [10] And he pitched between Geba and Scythopolis, and there he tarried a whole month, that he might gather together all the carriages of his army.

Jdt.4

[1] Now the children of Israel, that dwelt in Judea, heard all that Holofernes the chief captain of Nabuchodonosor king of the Assyrians had done to the nations, and after what manner he had spoiled all their temples, and brought them to nought. [2] Therefore they were exceedingly afraid of him, and were troubled for Jerusalem, and for the temple of the Lord their God: [3] For they were newly returned from the captivity, and all the people of Judea were lately gathered together: and the vessels, and the altar, and the house, were sanctified after the profanation. [4] Therefore they sent into all the coasts of Samaria, and the villages and to Bethoron, and Belmen, and Jericho, and to Choba, and Esora, and to the valley of Salem: [5] And possessed themselves beforehand of all the tops of the high mountains, and fortified the villages that were in them, and laid up victuals for the provision of war: for their fields were of late reaped. [6] Also Joacim the high priest, which

was in those days in Jerusalem, wrote to them that dwelt in Bethulia, and Betomestham, which is over against Esdraelon toward the open country, near to Dothaim, [7] Charging them to keep the passages of the hill country: for by them there was an entrance into Judea, and it was easy to stop them that would come up, because the passage was straight, for two men at the most. [8] And the children of Israel did as Joacim the high priest had commanded them, with the ancients of all the people of Israel, which dwelt at Jerusalem. [9] Then every man of Israel cried to God with great fervency, and with great vehemency did they humble their souls: [10] Both they, and their wives and their children, and their cattle, and every stranger and hireling, and their servants bought with money, put sackcloth upon their loins. [11] Thus every man and women, and the little children, and the inhabitants of Jerusalem, fell before the temple, and cast ashes upon their heads, and spread out their sackcloth before the face of the Lord: also they put sackcloth about the altar, [12] And cried to the God of Israel all with one consent earnestly, that he would not give their children for a prey, and their wives for a spoil, and the cities of their inheritance to destruction, and the sanctuary to profanation and reproach, and for the nations to rejoice at. [13] So God heard their prayers, and looked upon their afflictions: for the people fasted many days in all Judea and Jerusalem before the sanctuary of the Lord Almighty. [14] And Joacim the high priest, and all the priests that stood before the Lord, and they which ministered unto the Lord, had their loins girt with sackcloth, and offered the daily burnt offerings, with the vows and free gifts of the people, [15] And had ashes on their mitres, and cried unto the Lord with all their power, that he would look upon all the house of Israel graciously.

Jdt.5

[1] Then was it declared to Holofernes, the chief captain of the army of Assur, that the children of Israel had prepared for war, and had shut up the passages of the hill country, and had fortified all the tops of the high hills and had laid impediments in the champaign countries: [2] Wherewith he was very angry, and called all the princes of Moab, and the captains of Ammon, and all the governors of the sea coast, [3] And he said unto them, Tell me now, ye sons of Chanaan, who this people is, that dwelleth in the hill country, and what are the cities that they inhabit, and what is the multitude of their army, and wherein is their power and strength, and what king is set over them, or captain of their army; [4] And why have they determined not to come and meet me, more than all the inhabitants of the west. [5] Then said Achior, the captain of all the sons of Ammon, Let my lord now hear a word from the mouth of thy servant, and I will declare unto thee the truth concerning this people, which dwelleth near thee, and inhabiteth the hill countries: and there shall no lie come out of the mouth of thy servant. [6] This people are descended of the Chaldeans: [7] And they sojourned heretofore in Mesopotamia, because they would not follow the gods of their fathers, which were in the land of Chaldea. [8] For they left the way of their ancestors, and worshipped the God of heaven, the God whom they knew: so they cast them out from the face of their gods, and they fled into Mesopotamia, and sojourned there many days. [9] Then

their God commanded them to depart from the place where they sojourned, and to go into the land of Chanaan: where they dwelt, and were increased with gold and silver, and with very much cattle. [10] But when a famine covered all the land of Chanaan, they went down into Egypt, and sojourned there, while they were nourished, and became there a great multitude, so that one could not number their nation. [11] Therefore the king of Egypt rose up against them, and dealt subtilly with them, and brought them low with labouring in brick, and made them slaves. [12] Then they cried unto their God, and he smote all the land of Egypt with incurable plagues: so the Egyptians cast them out of their sight. [13] And God dried the Red sea before them, [14] And brought them to mount Sina, and Cades-Barne, and cast forth all that dwelt in the wilderness. [15] So they dwelt in the land of the Amorites, and they destroyed by their strength all them of Esebon, and passing over Jordan they possessed all the hill country. [16] And they cast forth before them the Chanaanite, the Pherezite, the Jebusite, and the Sychemite, and all the Gergesites, and they dwelt in that country many days. [17] And whilst they sinned not before their God, they prospered, because the God that hateth iniquity was with them. [18] But when they departed from the way which he appointed them, they were destroyed in many battles very sore, and were led captives into a land that was not their's, and the temple of their God was cast to the ground, and their cities were taken by the enemies. [19] But now are they returned to their God, and are come up from the places where they were scattered, and have possessed Jerusalem, where their sanctuary is, and are seated in the hill country; for it was desolate. [20] Now therefore, my lord and governor, if there be any error against this people, and they sin against their God, let us consider that this shall be their ruin, and let us go up, and we shall overcome them. [21] But if there be no iniquity in their nation, let my lord now pass by, lest their Lord defend them, and their God be for them, and we become a reproach before all the world. [22] And when Achior had finished these sayings, all the people standing round about the tent murmured, and the chief men of Holofernes, and all that dwelt by the sea side, and in Moab, spake that he should kill him. [23] For, say they, we will not be afraid of the face of the children of Israel: for, lo, it is a people that have no strength nor power for a strong battle [24] Now therefore, lord Holofernes, we will go up, and they shall be a prey to be devoured of all thine army.

Jdt.6

[1] And when the tumult of men that were about the council was ceased, Holofernes the chief captain of the army of Assur said unto Achior and all the Moabites before all the company of other nations, [2] And who art thou, Achior, and the hirelings of Ephraim, that thou hast prophesied against us as to day, and hast said, that we should not make war with the people of Israel, because their God will defend them? and who is God but Nabuchodonosor? [3] He will send his power, and will destroy them from the face of the earth, and their God shall not deliver them: but we his servants will destroy them as one man; for they are not able to sustain the power of our horses. [4] For with them we will tread them under foot, and their mountains shall be drunken with their

blood, and their fields shall be filled with their dead bodies, and their footsteps shall not be able to stand before us, for they shall utterly perish, saith king Nabuchodonosor, lord of all the earth: for he said, None of my words shall be in vain. [5] And thou, Achior, an hireling of Ammon, which hast spoken these words in the day of thine iniquity, shalt see my face no more from this day, until I take vengeance of this nation that came out of Egypt. [6] And then shall the sword of mine army, and the multitude of them that serve me, pass through thy sides, and thou shalt fall among their slain, when I return. [7] Now therefore my servants shall bring thee back into the hill country, and shall set thee in one of the cities of the passages: [8] And thou shalt not perish, till thou be destroyed with them. [9] And if thou persuade thyself in thy mind that they shall be taken, let not thy countenance fall: I have spoken it, and none of my words shall be in vain. [10] Then Holofernes commanded his servants, that waited in his tent, to take Achior, and bring him to Bethulia, and deliver him into the hands of the children of Israel. [11] So his servants took him, and brought him out of the camp into the plain, and they went from the midst of the plain into the hill country, and came unto the fountains that were under Bethulia. [12] And when the men of the city saw them, they took up their weapons, and went out of the city to the top of the hill: and every man that used a sling kept them from coming up by casting of stones against them. [13] Nevertheless having gotten privily under the hill, they bound Achior, and cast him down, and left him at the foot of the hill, and returned to their lord. [14] But the Israelites descended from their city, and came unto him, and loosed him, and brought him to Bethulia, and presented him to the governors of the city:

[15] Which were in those days Ozias the son of Micha, of the tribe of Simeon, and Chabris the son of Gothoniel, and Charmis the son of Melchiel. [16] And they called together all the ancients of the city, and all their youth ran together, and their women, to the assembly, and they set Achior in the midst of all their people. Then Ozias asked him of that which was done. [17] And he answered and declared unto them the words of the council of Holofernes, and all the words that he had spoken in the midst of the princes of Assur, and whatsoever Holofernes had spoken proudly against the house of Israel. [18] Then the people fell down and worshipped God, and cried unto God. saying, [19] O Lord God of heaven, behold their pride, and pity the low estate of our nation, and look upon the face of those that are sanctified unto thee this day. [20] Then they comforted Achior, and praised him greatly. [21] And Ozias took him out of the assembly unto his house, and made a feast to the elders; and they called on the God of Israel all that night for help.

Jdt.7

[1] The next day Holofernes commanded all his army, and all his people which were come to take his part, that they should remove their camp against Bethulia, to take aforehand the ascents of the hill country, and to make war against the children of Israel. [2] Then their strong men removed their camps in that day, and the army of the men of war was an hundred and seventy thousand footmen, and twelve thousand horsemen, beside the baggage, and other men that were afoot among them, a very great multitude.

[3] And they camped in the valley near unto Bethulia, by the fountain, and they spread themselves in breadth over Dothaim even to Belmaim, and in length from Bethulia unto Cynamon, which is over against Esdraelon. [4] Now the children of Israel, when they saw the multitude of them, were greatly troubled, and said every one to his neighbour, Now will these men lick up the face of the earth; for neither the high mountains, nor the valleys, nor the hills, are able to bear their weight. [5] Then every man took up his weapons of war, and when they had kindled fires upon their towers, they remained and watched all that night. [6] But in the second day Holofernes brought forth all his horsemen in the sight of the children of Israel which were in Bethulia, [7] And viewed the passages up to the city, and came to the fountains of their waters, and took them, and set garrisons of men of war over them, and he himself removed toward his people. [8] Then came unto him all the chief of the children of Esau, and all the governors of the people of Moab, and the captains of the sea coast, and said, [9] Let our lord now hear a word, that there be not an overthrow in thine army. [10] For this people of the children of Israel do not trust in their spears, but in the height of the mountains wherein they dwell, because it is not easy to come up to the tops of their mountains. [11] Now therefore, my lord, fight not against them in battle array, and there shall not so much as one man of thy people perish. [12] Remain in thy camp, and keep all the men of thine army, and let thy servants get into their hands the fountain of water, which issueth forth of the foot of the mountain: [13] For all the inhabitants of Bethulia have their water thence; so shall thirst kill them, and they shall give up their city, and we and our people shall go up to the tops of the mountains that are near, and will camp upon them, to watch that none go out of the city. [14] So they and their wives and their children shall be consumed with fire, and before the sword come against them, they shall be overthrown in the streets where they dwell. [15] Thus shalt thou render them an evil reward; because they rebelled, and met not thy person peaceably. [16] And these words pleased Holofernes and all his servants, and he appointed to do as they had spoken. [17] So the camp of the children of Ammon departed, and with them five thousand of the Assyrians, and they pitched in the valley, and took the waters, and the fountains of the waters of the children of Israel. [18] Then the children of Esau went up with the children of Ammon, and camped in the hill country over against Dothaim: and they sent some of them toward the south, and toward the east over against Ekrebel, which is near unto Chusi, that is upon the brook Mochmur; and the rest of the army of the Assyrians camped in the plain, and covered the face of the whole land; and their tents and carriages were pitched to a very great multitude. [19] Then the children of Israel cried unto the Lord their God, because their heart failed, for all their enemies had compassed them round about, and there was no way to escape out from among them. [20] Thus all the company of Assur remained about them, both their footmen, chariots, and horsemen, four and thirty days, so that all their vessels of water failed all the inhabitants of Bethulia. [21] And the cisterns were emptied, and they had not water to drink their fill for one day; for they gave them drink by measure. [22] Therefore their young children were out of heart, and their women and young men fainted for thirst,

and fell down in the streets of the city, and by the passages of the gates, and there was no longer any strength in them. [23] Then all the people assembled to Ozias, and to the chief of the city, both young men, and women, and children, and cried with a loud voice, and said before all the elders, [24] God be judge between us and you: for ye have done us great injury, in that ye have not required peace of the children of Assur. [25] For now we have no helper: but God hath sold us into their hands, that we should be thrown down before them with thirst and great destruction. [26] Now therefore call them unto you, and deliver the whole city for a spoil to the people of Holofernes, and to all his army. [27] For it is better for us to be made a spoil unto them, than to die for thirst: for we will be his servants, that our souls may live, and not see the death of our infants before our eyes, nor our wives nor our children to die. [28] We take to witness against you the heaven and the earth, and our God and Lord of our fathers, which punisheth us according to our sins and the sins of our fathers, that he do not according as we have said this day. [29] Then there was great weeping with one consent in the midst of the assembly; and they cried unto the Lord God with a loud voice. [30] Then said Ozias to them, Brethren, be of good courage, let us yet endure five days, in the which space the Lord our God may turn his mercy toward us; for he will not forsake us utterly. [31] And if these days pass, and there come no help unto us, I will do according to your word. [32] And he dispersed the people, every one to their own charge; and they went unto the walls and towers of their city, and sent the women and children into their houses: and they were very low brought in the city.

Jdt.8

[1] Now at that time Judith heard thereof, which was the daughter of Merari, the son of Ox, the son of Joseph, the son of Ozel, the son of Elcia, the son of Ananias, the son of Gedeon, the son of Raphaim, the son of Acitho, the son of Eliu, the son of Eliab, the son of Nathanael, the son of Samael, the son of Salasadal, the son of Israel. [2] And Manasses was her husband, of her tribe and kindred, who died in the barley harvest. [3] For as he stood overseeing them that bound sheaves in the field, the heat came upon his head, and he fell on his bed, and died in the city of Bethulia: and they buried him with his fathers in the field between Dothaim and Balamo. [4] So Judith was a widow in her house three years and four months. [5] And she made her a tent upon the top of her house, and put on sackcloth upon her loins and ware her widow's apparel. [6] And she fasted all the days of her widowhood, save the eves of the sabbaths, and the sabbaths, and the eves of the new moons, and the new moons and the feasts and solemn days of the house of Israel. [7] She was also of a goodly countenance, and very beautiful to behold: and her husband Manasses had left her gold, and silver, and menservants and maidservants, and cattle, and lands; and she remained upon them. [8] And there was none that gave her an ill word; ar she feared God greatly. [9] Now when she heard the evil words of the people against the governor, that they fainted for lack of water; for Judith had heard all the words that Ozias had spoken unto them, and that he had sworn to deliver the city unto the Assyrians after five days; [10] Then she sent her waitingwoman, that had the

government of all things that she had, to call Ozias and Chabris and Charmis, the ancients of the city. [11] And they came unto her, and she said unto them, Hear me now, O ye governors of the inhabitants of Bethulia: for your words that ye have spoken before the people this day are not right, touching this oath which ye made and pronounced between God and you, and have promised to deliver the city to our enemies, unless within these days the Lord turn to help you. [12] And now who are ye that have tempted God this day, and stand instead of God among the children of men? [13] And now try the Lord Almighty, but ye shall never know any thing. [14] For ye cannot find the depth of the heart of man, neither can ye perceive the things that he thinketh: then how can ye search out God, that hath made all these things, and know his mind, or comprehend his purpose? Nay, my brethren, provoke not the Lord our God to anger. [15] For if he will not help us within these five days, he hath power to defend us when he will, even every day, or to destroy us before our enemies. [16] Do not bind the counsels of the Lord our God: for God is not as man, that he may be threatened; neither is he as the son of man, that he should be wavering. [17] Therefore let us wait for salvation of him, and call upon him to help us, and he will hear our voice, if it please him. [18] For there arose none in our age, neither is there any now in these days neither tribe, nor family, nor people, nor city among us, which worship gods made with hands, as hath been aforetime. [19] For the which cause our fathers were given to the sword, and for a spoil, and had a great fall before our enemies. [20] But we know none other god, therefore we trust that he will not dispise us, nor any of our nation. [21] For if we be taken so, all Judea shall lie waste, and our sanctuary shall be spoiled; and he will require the profanation thereof at our mouth. [22] And the slaughter of our brethren, and the captivity of the country, and the desolation of our inheritance, will he turn upon our heads among the Gentiles, wheresoever we shall be in bondage; and we shall be an offence and a reproach to all them that possess us. [23] For our servitude shall not be directed to favour: but the Lord our God shall turn it to dishonour. [24] Now therefore, O brethren, let us shew an example to our brethren, because their hearts depend upon us, and the sanctuary, and the house, and the altar, rest upon us. [25] Moreover let us give thanks to the Lord our God, which trieth us, even as he did our fathers. [26] Remember what things he did to Abraham, and how he tried Isaac, and what happened to Jacob in Mesopotamia of Syria, when he kept the sheep of Laban his mother's brother. [27] For he hath not tried us in the fire, as he did them, for the examination of their hearts, neither hath he taken vengeance on us: but the Lord doth scourge them that come near unto him, to admonish them. [28] Then said Ozias to her, All that thou hast spoken hast thou spoken with a good heart, and there is none that may gainsay thy words. [29] For this is not the first day wherein thy wisdom is manifested; but from the beginning of thy days all the people have known thy understanding, because the disposition of thine heart is good. [30] But the people were very thirsty, and compelled us to do unto them as we have spoken, and to bring an oath upon ourselves, which we will not break. [31] Therefore now pray thou for us, because thou art a godly woman, and the Lord will send us rain to fill our cisterns, and we shall faint no more. [32] Then said Judith unto them, Hear me, and I will do a thing, which shall go throughout all generations to the children of our nation. [33] Ye shall stand this night in the gate, and I will go forth with my waitingwoman: and within the days that ye have promised to deliver the city to our enemies the Lord will visit Israel by mine hand. [34] But enquire not ye of mine act: for I will not declare it unto you, till the things be finished that I do. [35] Then said Ozias and the princes unto her, Go in peace, and the Lord God be before thee, to take vengeance on our enemies. [36] So they returned from the tent, and went to their wards.

Jdt.9

[1] Judith fell upon her face, and put ashes upon her head, and uncovered the sackcloth wherewith she was clothed; and about the time that the incense of that evening was offered in Jerusalem in the house of the Lord Judith cried with a loud voice, and said, [2] O Lord God of my father Simeon, to whom thou gavest a sword to take vengeance of the strangers, who loosened the girdle of a maid to defile her, and discovered the thigh to her shame, and polluted her virginity to her reproach; for thou saidst, It shall not be so; and yet they did so: [3] Wherefore thou gavest their rulers to be slain, so that they dyed their bed in blood, being deceived, and smotest the servants with their lords, and the lords upon their thrones; [4] And hast given their wives for a prey, and their daughters to be captives, and all their spoils to be divided among thy dear children; which were moved with thy zeal, and abhorred the pollution of their blood, and called upon thee for aid: O God, O my God, hear me also a widow. [5] For thou hast wrought not only those things, but also the things which fell out before, and which ensued after; thou hast thought upon the things which are now, and which are to come. [6] Yea, what things thou didst determine were ready at hand, and said, Lo, we are here: for all thy ways are prepared, and thy judgments are in thy foreknowledge. [7] For, behold, the Assyrians are multiplied in their power; they are exalted with horse and man; they glory in the strength of their footmen; they trust in shield, and spear, and bow, and sling; and know not that thou art the Lord that breakest the battles: the Lord is thy name. [8] Throw down their strength in thy power, and bring down their force in thy wrath: for they have purposed to defile thy sanctuary, and to pollute the tabernacle where thy glorious name resteth and to cast down with sword the horn of thy altar. [9] Behold their pride, and send thy wrath upon their heads: give into mine hand, which am a widow, the power that I have conceived. [10] Smite by the deceit of my lips the servant with the prince, and the prince with the servant: break down their stateliness by the hand of a woman. [11] For thy power standeth not in multitude nor thy might in strong men: for thou art a God of the afflicted, an helper of the oppressed, an upholder of the weak, a protector of the forlorn, a saviour of them that are without hope. [12] I pray thee, I pray thee, O God of my father, and God of the inheritance of Israel, Lord of the heavens and earth, Creator of the waters, king of every creature, hear thou my prayer: [13] And make my speech and deceit to be their wound and stripe, who have purposed cruel things against thy covenant, and thy hallowed house, and against the top of Sion, and against the house of the possession of thy

children. [14] And make every nation and tribe to acknowledge that thou art the God of all power and might, and that there is none other that protecteth the people of Israel but thou.

Jdt.10

[1] Now after that she had ceased to cry unto the God of Israel, and had made an end of all these words. [2] She rose where she had fallen down, and called her maid, and went down into the house in the which she abode in the sabbath days, and in her feast days, [3] And pulled off the sackcloth which she had on, and put off the garments of her widowhood, and washed her body all over with water, and anointed herself with precious ointment, and braided the hair of her head, and put on a tire upon it, and put on her garments of gladness, wherewith she was clad during the life of Manasses her husband. [4] And she took sandals upon her feet, and put about her her bracelets, and her chains, and her rings, and her earrings, and all her ornaments, and decked herself bravely, to allure the eyes of all men that should see her. [5] Then she gave her maid a bottle of wine, and a cruse of oil, and filled a bag with parched corn, and lumps of figs, and with fine bread; so she folded all these things together, and laid them upon her. [6] Thus they went forth to the gate of the city of Bethulia, and found standing there Ozias and the ancients of the city, Chabris and Charmis. [7] And when they saw her, that her countenance was altered, and her apparel was changed, they wondered at her beauty very greatly, and said unto her. [8] The God, the God of our fathers give thee favour, and accomplish thine enterprizes to the glory of the children of Israel, and to the exaltation of Jerusalem. Then they worshipped God. [9] And she said unto them, Command the gates of the city to be opened unto me, that I may go forth to accomplish the things whereof ye have spoken with me. So they commanded the young men to open unto her, as she had spoken. [10] And when they had done so, Judith went out, she, and her maid with her; and the men of the city looked after her, until she was gone down the mountain, and till she had passed the valley, and could see her no more. [11] Thus they went straight forth in the valley: and the first watch of the Assyrians met her, [12] And took her, and asked her, Of what people art thou? and whence comest thou? and whither goest thou? And she said, I am a woman of the Hebrews, and am fled from them: for they shall be given you to be consumed: [13] And I am coming before Holofernes the chief captain of your army, to declare words of truth; and I will shew him a way, whereby he shall go, and win all the hill country, without losing the body or life of any one of his men. [14] Now when the men heard her words, and beheld her countenance, they wondered greatly at her beauty, and said unto her, [15] Thou hast saved thy life, in that thou hast hasted to come down to the presence of our lord: now therefore come to his tent, and some of us shall conduct thee, until they have delivered thee to his hands. [16] And when thou standest before him, be not afraid in thine heart, but shew unto him according to thy word; and he will entreat thee well. [17] Then they chose out of them an hundred men to accompany her and her maid; and they brought her to the tent of Holofernes. [18] Then was there a concourse throughout all the camp: for her coming was noised among the tents, and they came about her, as she stood without the tent of Holofernes, till they told him of her. [19] And they wondered at her beauty, and admired the children of Israel because of her, and every one said to his neighbour, Who would despise this people, that have among them such women? surely it is not good that one man of them be left who being let go might deceive the whole earth. [20] And they that lay near Holofernes went out, and all his servants and they brought her into the tent.

[21] Now Holofernes rested upon his bed under a canopy, which was woven with purple, and gold, and emeralds, and precious stones. [22] So they shewed him of her; and he came out before his tent with silver lamps going before him. [23] And when Judith was come before him and his servants they all marvelled at the beauty of her countenance; and she fell down upon her face, and did reverence unto him: and his servants took her up.

Jdt.11

[1] Then said Holofernes unto her, Woman, be of good comfort, fear not in thine heart: for I never hurt any that was willing to serve Nabuchodonosor, the king of all the earth. [2] Now therefore, if thy people that dwelleth in the mountains had not set light by me, I would not have lifted up my spear against them: but they have done these things to themselves. [3] But now tell me wherefore thou art fled from them, and art come unto us: for thou art come for safeguard; be of good comfort, thou shalt live this night, and hereafter: [4] For none shall hurt thee, but entreat thee well, as they do the servants of king Nabuchodonosor my lord. [5] Then Judith said unto him, Receive the words of thy servant, and suffer thine handmaid to speak in thy presence, and I will declare no lie to my lord this night. [6] And if thou wilt follow the words of thine handmaid, God will bring the thing perfectly to pass by thee; and my lord shall not fail of his purposes. [7] As Nabuchodonosor king of all the earth liveth, and as his power liveth, who hath sent thee for the upholding of every living thing: for not only men shall serve him by thee, but also the beasts of the field, and the cattle, and the fowls of the air, shall live by thy power under Nabuchodonosor and all his house. [8] For we have heard of thy wisdom and thy policies, and it is reported in all the earth, that thou only art excellent in all the kingdom, and mighty in knowledge, and wonderful in feats of war. [9] Now as concerning the matter, which Achior did speak in thy council, we have heard his words; for the men of Bethulia saved him, and he declared unto them all that he had spoken unto thee. [10] Therefore, O lord and governor, respect not his word; but lay it up in thine heart, for it is true: for our nation shall not be punished, neither can sword prevail against them, except they sin against their God. [11] And now, that my lord be not defeated and frustrate of his purpose, even death is now fallen upon them, and their sin hath overtaken them, wherewith they will provoke their God to anger whensoever they shall do that which is not fit to be done: [12] For their victuals fail them, and all their water is scant, and they have determined to lay hands upon their cattle, and purposed to consume all those things, that God hath forbidden them to eat by his laws: [13] And are resolved to spend the firstfruits of the the tenths of wine and oil, which they had sanctified, and reserved for the priests that serve

in Jerusalem before the face of our God; the which things it is not lawful for any of the people so much as to touch with their hands. [14] For they have sent some to Jerusalem, because they also that dwell there have done the like, to bring them a licence from the senate. [15] Now when they shall bring them word, they will forthwith do it, and they shall be given to thee to be destroyed the same day. [16] Wherefore I thine handmaid, knowing all this, am fled from their presence; and God hath sent me to work things with thee, whereat all the earth shall be astonished, and whosoever shall hear it. [17] For thy servant is religious, and serveth the God of heaven day and night: now therefore, my lord, I will remain with thee, and thy servant will go out by night into the valley, and I will pray unto God, and he will tell me when they have committed their sins: [18] And I will come and shew it unto thee: then thou shalt go forth with all thine army, and there shall be none of them that shall resist thee. [19] And I will lead thee through the midst of Judea, until thou come before Jerusalem; and I will set thy throne in the midst thereof; and thou shalt drive them as sheep that have no shepherd, and a dog shall not so much as open his mouth at thee: for these things were told me according to my foreknowledge, and they were declared unto me, and I am sent to tell thee. [20] Then her words pleased Holofernes and all his servants; and they marvelled at her wisdom, and said, [21] There is not such a woman from one end of the earth to the other, both for beauty of face, and wisdom of words. [22] Likewise Holofernes said unto her. God hath done well to send thee before the people, that strength might be in our hands and destruction upon them that lightly regard my lord. [23] And now thou art both beautiful in thy countenance, and witty in thy words: surely if thou do as thou hast spoken thy God shall be my God, and thou shalt dwell in the house of king Nabuchodonosor, and shalt be renowned through the whole earth.

Jdt.12

[1] Then he commanded to bring her in where his plate was set; and bade that they should prepare for her of his own meats, and that she should drink of his own wine. [2] And Judith said, I will not eat thereof, lest there be an offence: but provision shall be made for me of the things that I have brought. [3] Then Holofernes said unto her, If thy provision should fail, how should we give thee the like? for there be none with us of thy nation. [4] Then said Judith unto him As thy soul liveth, my lord, thine handmaid shall not spend those things that I have, before the Lord work by mine hand the things that he hath determined. [5] Then the servants of Holofernes brought her into the tent, and she slept till midnight, and she arose when it was toward the morning watch, [6] And sent to Holofernes, saying, Let my lord now command that thine handmaid may go forth unto prayer. [7] Then Holofernes commanded his guard that they should not stay her: thus she abode in the camp three days, and went out in the night into the valley of Bethulia, and washed herself in a fountain of water by the camp. [8] And when she came out, she besought the Lord God of Israel to direct her way to the raising up of the children of her people. [9] So she came in clean, and remained in the tent, until she did eat her meat at evening. [10] And in the fourth day Holofernes made a feast to his

own servants only, and called none of the officers to the banquet. [11] Then said he to Bagoas the eunuch, who had charge over all that he had, Go now, and persuade this Hebrew woman which is with thee, that she come unto us, and eat and drink with us. [12] For, lo, it will be a shame for our person, if we shall let such a woman go, not having had her company; for if we draw her not unto us, she will laugh us to scorn. [13] Then went Bagoas from the presence of Holofernes, and came to her, and he said, Let not this fair damsel fear to come to my lord, and to be honoured in his presence, and drink wine, and be merry with us and be made this day as one of the daughters of the Assyrians, which serve in the house of Nabuchodonosor. [14] Then said Judith unto him, Who am I now, that I should gainsay my lord? surely whatsoever pleaseth him I will do speedily, and it shall be my joy unto the day of my death. [15] So she arose, and decked herself with her apparel and all her woman's attire, and her maid went and laid soft skins on the ground for her over against Holofernes, which she had received of Bagoas far her daily use, that she might sit and eat upon them. [16] Now when Judith came in and sat down, Holofernes his heart was ravished with her, and his mind was moved, and he desired greatly her company; for he waited a time to deceive her, from the day that he had seen her. [17] Then said Holofernes unto her, Drink now, and be merry with us. [18] So Judith said, I will drink now, my lord, because my life is magnified in me this day more than all the days since I was born. [19] Then she took and ate and drank before him what her maid had prepared. [20] And Holofernes took great delight in her, and drank more wine than he had drunk at any time in one day since he was born.

Jdt.13

[1] Now when the evening was come, his servants made haste to depart, and Bagoas shut his tent without, and dismissed the waiters from the presence of his lord; and they went to their beds: for they were all weary, because the feast had been long. [2] And Judith was left along in the tent, and Holofernes lying along upon his bed: for he was filled with wine. [3] Now Judith had commanded her maid to stand without her bedchamber, and to wait for her. coming forth, as she did daily: for she said she would go forth to her prayers, and she spake to Bagoas according to the same purpose. [4] So all went forth and none was left in the bedchamber, neither little nor great. Then Judith, standing by his bed, said in her heart, O Lord God of all power, look at this present upon the works of mine hands for the exaltation of Jerusalem. [5] For now is the time to help thine inheritance, and to execute thine enterprizes to the destruction of the enemies which are risen against us. [6] Then she came to the pillar of the bed, which was at Holofernes' head, and took down his fauchion from thence, [7] And approached to his bed, and took hold of the hair of his head, and said, Strengthen me, O Lord God of Israel, this day. [8] And she smote twice upon his neck with all her might, and she took away his head from him. [9] And tumbled his body down from the bed, and pulled down the canopy from the pillars; and anon after she went forth, and gave Holofernes his head to her maid; [10] And she put it in her bag of meat: so they twain went together according to their custom unto prayer: and when they

passed the camp, they compassed the valley, and went up the mountain of Bethulia, and came to the gates thereof. [11] Then said Judith afar off, to the watchmen at the gate, Open, open now the gate: God, even our God, is with us, to shew his power yet in Jerusalem, and his forces against the enemy, as he hath even done this day. [12] Now when the men of her city heard her voice, they made haste to go down to the gate of their city, and they called the elders of the city. [13] And then they ran all together, both small and great, for it was strange unto them that she was come: so they opened the gate, and received them, and made a fire for a light, and stood round about them. [14] Then she said to them with a loud voice, Praise, praise God, praise God, I say, for he hath not taken away his mercy from the house of Israel, but hath destroyed our enemies by mine hands this night. [15] So she took the head out of the bag, and shewed it, and said unto them, behold the head of Holofernes, the chief captain of the army of Assur, and behold the canopy, wherein he did lie in his drunkenness; and the Lord hath smitten him by the hand of a woman. [16] As the Lord liveth, who hath kept me in my way that I went, my countenance hath deceived him to his destruction, and yet hath he not committed sin with me, to defile and shame me. [17] Then all the people were wonderfully astonished, and bowed themselves and worshipped God, and said with one accord, Blessed be thou, O our God, which hast this day brought to nought the enemies of thy people. [18] Then said Ozias unto her, O daughter, blessed art thou of the most high God above all the women upon the earth; and blessed be the Lord God, which hath created the heavens and the earth, which hath directed thee to the cutting off of the head of the chief of our enemies. [19] For this thy confidence shall not depart from the heart of men, which remember the power of God for ever. [20] And God turn these things to thee for a perpetual praise, to visit thee in good things because thou hast not spared thy life for the affliction of our nation, but hast revenged our ruin, walking a straight way before our God. And all the people said; So be it, so be it.

Jdt.14

[1] Then said Judith unto them, Hear me now, my brethren, and take this head, and hang it upon the highest place of your walls. [2] And so soon as the morning shall appear, and the sun shall come forth upon the earth, take ye every one his weapons, and go forth every valiant man out of the city, and set ye a captain over them, as though ye would go down into the field toward the watch of the Assyrians; but go not down. [3] Then they shall take their armour, and shall go into their camp, and raise up the captains of the army of Assur, and shall run to the tent of Holofernes, but shall not find him: then fear shall fall upon them, and they shall flee before your face. [4] So ye, and all that inhabit the coast of Israel, shall pursue them, and overthrow them as they go. [5] But before ye do these things, call me Achior the Ammonite, that he may see and know him that despised the house of Israel, and that sent him to us as it were to his death. [6] Then they called Achior out of the house of Ozias; and when he was come, and saw the head of Holofernes in a man's hand in the assembly of the people, he fell down on his face, and his spirit failed. [7] But when they had recovered him, he fell at Judith's feet,

and reverenced her, and said, Blessed art thou in all the tabernacles of Juda, and in all nations, which hearing thy name shall be astonished. [8] Now therefore tell me all the things that thou hast done in these days. Then Judith declared unto him in the midst of the people all that she had done, from the day that she went forth until that hour she spake unto them. [9] And when she had left off speaking, the people shouted with a loud voice, and made a joyful noise in their city. [10] And when Achior had seen all that the God of Israel had done, he believed in God greatly, and circumcised the flesh of his foreskin, and was joined unto the house of Israel unto this day. [11] And as soon as the morning arose, they hanged the head of Holofernes upon the wall, and every man took his weapons, and they went forth by bands unto the straits of the mountain. [12] But when the Assyrians saw them, they sent to their leaders, which came to their captains and tribunes, and to every one of their rulers. [13] So they came to Holofernes' tent, and said to him that had the charge of all his things, Waken now our lord: for the slaves have been bold to come down against us to battle, that they may be utterly destroyed. [14] Then went in Bagoas, and knocked at the door of the tent; for he thought that he had slept with Judith. [15] But because none answered, he opened it, and went into the bedchamber, and found him cast upon the floor dead, and his head was taken from him. [16] Therefore he cried with a loud voice, with weeping, and sighing, and a mighty cry, and rent his garments. [17] After he went into the tent where Judith lodged: and when he found her not, he leaped out to the people, and cried, [18] These slaves have dealt treacherously; one woman of the Hebrews hath brought shame upon the house of king Nabuchodonosor: for, behold, Holofernes lieth upon the ground without a head. [19] When the captains of the Assyrians' army heard these words, they rent their coats and their minds were wonderfully troubled, and there was a cry and a very great noise throughout the camp.

Jdt.15

[1] And when they that were in the tents heard, they were astonished at the thing that was done. [2] And fear and trembling fell upon them, so that there was no man that durst abide in the sight of his neighbour, but rushing out all together, they fled into every way of the plain, and of the hill country. [3] They also that had camped in the mountains round about Bethulia fled away. Then the children of Israel, every one that was a warrior among them, rushed out upon them. [4] Then sent Ozias to Betomasthem, and to Bebai, and Chobai, and Cola and to all the coasts of Israel, such as should tell the things that were done, and that all should rush forth upon their enemies to destroy them. [5] Now when the children of Israel heard it, they all fell upon them with one consent, and slew them unto Chobai: likewise also they that came from Jerusalem, and from all the hill country, (for men had told them what things were done in the camp of their enemies) and they that were in Galaad, and in Galilee, chased them with a great slaughter, until they were past Damascus and the borders thereof. [6] And the residue that dwelt at Bethulia, fell upon the camp of Assur, and spoiled them, and were greatly enriched. [7] And the children of Israel that returned from the slaughter had that

which remained; and the villages and the cities, that were in the mountains and in the plain, gat many spoils: for the multitude was very great. [8] Then Joacim the high priest, and the ancients of the children of Israel that dwelt in Jerusalem, came to behold the good things that God had shewed to Israel, and to see Judith, and to salute her. [9] And when they came unto her, they blessed her with one accord, and said unto her, Thou art the exaltation of Jerusalem, thou art the great glory of Israel, thou art the great rejoicing of our nation: [10] Thou hast done all these things by thine hand: thou hast done much good to Israel, and God is pleased therewith: blessed be thou of the Almighty Lord for evermore. And all the people said, So be it. [11] And the people spoiled the camp the space of thirty days: and they gave unto Judith Holofernes his tent, and all his plate, and beds, and vessels, and all his stuff: and she took it and laid it on her mule; and made ready her carts, and laid them thereon. [12] Then all the women of Israel ran together to see her, and blessed her, and made a dance among them for her: and she took branches in her hand, and gave also to the women that were with her. [13] And they put a garland of olive upon her and her maid that was with her, and she went before all the people in the dance, leading all the women: and all the men of Israel followed in their armour with garlands, and with songs in their mouths.

Jdt.16

[1] Then Judith began to sing this thanksgiving in all Israel, and all the people sang after her this song of praise. [2] And Judith said, Begin unto my God with timbrels, sing unto my Lord with cymbals: tune unto him a new psalm: exalt him, and call upon his name. [3] For God breaketh the battles: for among the camps in the midst of the people he hath delivered me out of the hands of them that persecuted me. [4] Assur came out of the mountains from the north, he came with ten thousands of his army, the multitude whereof stopped the torrents, and their horsemen have covered the hills. [5] He bragged that he would burn up my borders, and kill my young men with the sword, and dash the sucking children against the ground, and make mine infants as a prey, and my virgins as a spoil. [6] But the Almighty Lord hath disappointed them by the hand of a woman. [7] For the mighty one did not fall by the young men, neither did the sons of the Titans smite him, nor high giants set upon him: but Judith the daughter of Merari weakened him with the beauty of her countenance. [8] For she put off the garment of her widowhood for the exaltation of those that were oppressed in Israel, and anointed her face with ointment, and bound her hair in a tire, and took a linen garment to deceive him. [9] Her sandals ravished his eyes, her beauty took his mind prisoner, and the fauchion passed through his neck. [10] The Persians quaked at her boldness, and the Medes were daunted at her hardiness. [11] Then my afflicted shouted for joy, and my weak ones cried aloud; but they were astonished: these lifted up their voices, but they were overthrown. [12] The sons of the damsels have pierced them through, and wounded them as fugatives' children: they perished by the battle of the Lord. [13] I will sing unto the Lord a new song: O Lord, thou art great and glorious, wonderful in strength, and invincible. [14] Let all creatures serve thee: for thou spakest, and they were made, thou

didst send forth thy spirit, and it created them, and there is none that can resist thy voice. [15] For the mountains shall be moved from their foundations with the waters, the rocks shall melt as wax at thy presence: yet thou art merciful to them that fear thee. [16] For all sacrifice is too little for a sweet savour unto thee, and all the fat is not sufficient for thy burnt offering: but he that feareth the Lord is great at all times. [17] Woe to the nations that rise up against my kindred! the Lord Almighty will take vengeance of them in the day of judgment, in putting fire and worms in their flesh; and they shall feel them, and weep for ever. [18] Now as soon as they entered into Jerusalem, they worshipped the Lord; and as soon as the people were purified, they offered their burnt offerings, and their free offerings, and their gifts. [19] Judith also dedicated all the stuff of Holofernes, which the people had given her, and gave the canopy, which she had taken out of his bedchamber, for a gift unto the Lord. [20] So the people continued feasting in Jerusalem before the sanctuary for the space of three months and Judith remained with them. [21] After this time every one returned to his own inheritance, and Judith went to Bethulia, and remained in her own possession, and was in her time honourable in all the country. [22] And many desired her, but none knew her all the days of her life, after that Manasses her husband was dead, and was gathered to his people. [23] But she increased more and more in honour, and waxed old in her husband's house, being an hundred and five years old, and made her maid free; so she died in Bethulia: and they buried her in the cave of her husband Manasses. [24] And the house of Israel lamented her seven days: and before she died, she did distribute her goods to all them that were nearest of kindred to Manasses her husband, and to them that were the nearest of her kindred. [25] And there was none that made the children of Israel any more afraid in the days of Judith, nor a long time after her death.

ADDITIONS TO THE BOOK OF ESTHER

AddEsth.1

[1] Then Mardocheus said, God hath done these things. [2] For I remember a dream which I saw concerning these matters, and nothing thereof hath failed. [3] A little fountain became a river, and there was light, and the sun, and much water: this river is Esther, whom the king married, and made queen: [4] And the two dragons are I and Aman. [5] And the nations were those that were assembled to destroy the name of the Jews: [6] And my nation is this Israel, which cried to God, and were saved: for the Lord hath saved his people, and the Lord hath delivered us from all those evils, and God hath wrought signs and great wonders, which have not been done among the Gentiles. [7] Therefore hath he made two lots, one for the people of God, and another for all the Gentiles. [8] And these two lots came at the hour, and time, and day of judgment, before God among all nations. [9] So God remembered his people, and justified his inheritance. [10] Therefore those days shall be unto them in the month Adar, the fourteenth and fifteenth day of the same month, with an assembly, and joy, and with gladness before God, according to the generations for ever among his people.

AddEsth.2

[1] In the fourth year of the reign of Ptolemeus and Cleopatra, Dositheus, who said he was a priest and Levite, and Ptolemeus his son, brought this epistle of Phurim, which they said was the same, and that Lysimachus the son of Ptolemeus, that was in Jerusalem, had interpreted it. [2] In the second year of the reign of Artexerxes the great, in the first day of the month Nisan, Mardocheus the son of Jairus, the son of Semei, the son of Cisai, of the tribe of Benjamin, had a dream; [3] Who was a Jew, and dwelt in the city of Susa, a great man, being a servitor in the king's court. [4] He was also one of the captives, which Nabuchodonosor the king of Babylon carried from Jerusalem with Jechonias king of Judea; and this was his dream: [5] Behold a noise of a tumult, with thunder, and earthquakes, and uproar in the land: [6] And, behold, two great dragons came forth ready to fight, and their cry was great. [7] And at their cry all nations were prepared to battle, that they might fight against the righteous people. [8] And lo a day of darkness and obscurity, tribulation and anguish, affliction and great uproar, upon earth. [9] And the whole righteous nation was troubled, fearing their own evils, and were ready to perish. [10] Then they cried unto God, and upon their cry, as it were from a little fountain, was made a great flood, even much water. [11] The light and the sun rose up, and the lowly were exalted, and devoured the glorious. [12] Now when Mardocheus, who had seen this dream, and what God had determined to do, was awake, he bare this dream in mind, and until night by all means was desirous to know it.

AddEsth.3

[1] And Mardocheus took his rest in the court with Gabatha and Tharra, the two eunuchs of the king, and keepers of the palace. [2] And he heard their devices, and searched out their purposes, and learned that they were about to lay hands upon Artexerxes the king; and so he certified the king of them. [3] Then the king examined the two eunuchs, and after that they had confessed it, they were strangled. [4] And the king made a record of these things, and Mardocheus also wrote thereof. [5] So the king commanded, Mardocheus to serve in the court, and for this he rewarded him. [6] Howbeit Aman the son of Amadathus the Agagite, who was in great honour with the king, sought to molest Mardocheus and his people because of the two eunuchs of the king.

AddEsth.4

[1] The copy of the letters was this: The great king Artexerxes writeth these things to the princes and governours that are under him from India unto Ethiopia in an hundred and seven and twenty provinces. [2] After that I became lord over many nations and had dominion over the whole world, not lifted up with presumption of my authority, but carrying myself always with equity and mildness, I purposed to settle my subjects continually in a quiet life, and making my kingdom peaceable, and open for passage to the utmost coasts, to renew peace, which is desired of all men. [3] Now when I asked my counsellors how this might be brought to pass, Aman, that excelled in wisdom among us, and was approved for his constant good will and steadfast fidelity, and had the honour of the second place in the kingdom, [4] Declared unto us, that in all nations throughout the world there was scattered a certain malicious people, that had laws contrary to all nations, and continually despised the commandments of kings, so as the uniting of our kingdoms, honourably intended by us cannot go forward. [5] Seeing then we understand that this people alone is continually in opposition unto all men, differing in the strange manner of their laws, and evil affected to our state, working all the mischief they can that our kingdom may not be firmly established: [6] Therefore have we commanded, that all they that are signified in writing unto you by Aman, who is ordained over the affairs, and is next unto us, shall all, with their wives and children, be utterly destroyed by the sword of their enemies, without all mercy and pity, the fourteenth day of the twelfth month Adar of this present year: [7] That they, who of old and now also are malicious, may in one day with violence go into the grave, and so ever hereafter cause our affairs to be well settled, and without trouble. [8] Then Mardocheus thought upon all the works of the Lord, and made his prayer unto him, [9] Saying, O Lord, Lord, the King Almighty: for the whole world is in thy power, and if thou hast appointed to save Israel, there is no man that can gainsay thee: [10] For thou hast made heaven and earth, and all the wondrous things under the heaven. [11] Thou art Lord of all things, and and there is no man that can resist thee, which art the Lord. [12] Thou knowest all things, and thou knowest, Lord, that it was neither in contempt nor pride, nor for any desire of glory, that I did not bow down to proud Aman. [13] For I could have been content with good will for the

salvation of Israel to kiss the soles of his feet. [14] But I did this, that I might not prefer the glory of man above the glory of God: neither will I worship any but thee, O God, neither will I do it in pride. [15] And now, O Lord God and King, spare thy people: for their eyes are upon us to bring us to nought; yea, they desire to destroy the inheritance, that hath been thine from the beginning. [16] Despise not the portion, which thou hast delivered out of Egypt for thine own self. [17] Hear my prayer, and be merciful unto thine inheritance: turn our sorrow into joy, that we may live, O Lord, and praise thy name: and destroy not the mouths of them that praise thee, O Lord. [18] All Israel in like manner cried most earnestly unto the Lord, because their death was before their eyes.

AddEsth.5

[1] Queen Esther also, being in fear of death, resorted unto the Lord: [2] And laid away her glorious apparel, and put on the garments of anguish and mourning: and instead of precious ointments, she covered her head with ashes and dung, and she humbled her body greatly, and all the places of her joy she filled with her torn hair. [3] And she prayed unto the Lord God of Israel, saying, O my Lord, thou only art our King: help me, desolate woman, which have no helper but thee: [4] For my danger is in mine hand. [5] From my youth up I have heard in the tribe of my family that thou, O Lord, tookest Israel from among all people, and our fathers from all their predecessors, for a perpetual inheritance, and thou hast performed whatsoever thou didst promise them. [6] And now we have sinned before thee: therefore hast thou given us into the hands of our enemies, [7] Because we worshipped their gods: O Lord, thou art righteous. [8] Nevertheless it satisfieth them not, that we are in bitter captivity: but they have stricken hands with their idols, [9] That they will abolish the thing that thou with thy mouth hast ordained, and destroy thine inheritance, and stop the mouth of them that praise thee, and quench the glory of thy house, and of thine altar, [10] And open the mouths of the heathen to set forth the praises of the idols, and to magnify a fleshly king for ever. [11] O Lord, give not thy sceptre unto them that be nothing, and let them not laugh at our fall; but turn their device upon themselves, and make him an example, that hath begun this against us. [12] Remember, O Lord, make thyself known in time of our affliction, and give me boldness, O King of the nations, and Lord of all power. [13] Give me eloquent speech in my mouth before the lion: turn his heart to hate him that fighteth against us, that there may be an end of him, and of all that are likeminded to him: [14] But deliver us with thine hand, and help me that am desolate, and which have no other help but thee: [15] Thou knowest all things, O Lord; thou knowest that I hate the glory of the unrighteous, and abhor the bed of the uncircumcised, and of all the heathen. [16] Thou knowest my necessity: for I abhor the sign of my high estate, which is upon mine head in the days wherein I shew myself, and that I abhor it as a menstruous rag, and that I wear it not when I am private by myself. [17] And that thine handmaid hath not eaten at Aman's table, and that I have not greatly esteemed the king's feast, nor drunk the wine of the drink offerings. [18] Neither had thine handmaid any joy since the day that I was brought hither to this present, but in

thee, O Lord God of Abraham. [19] O thou mighty God above all, hear the voice of the forlorn and deliver us out of the hands of the mischievous, and deliver me out of my fear.

AddEsth.6

[1] And upon the third day, when she had ended her prayers, she laid away her mourning garments, and put on her glorious apparel. [2] And being gloriously adorned, after she had called upon God, who is the beholder and saviour of all things, she took two maids with her: [3] And upon the one she leaned, as carrying herself daintily; [4] And the other followed, bearing up her train. [5] And she was ruddy through the perfection of her beauty, and her countenance was cheerful and very amiable: but her heart was in anguish for fear. [6] Then having passed through all the doors, she stood before the king, who sat upon his royal throne, and was clothed with all his robes of majesty, all glittering with gold and precious stones; and he was very dreadful. [7] Then lifting up his countenance that shone with majesty, he looked very fiercely upon her: and the queen fell down, and was pale, and fainted, and bowed herself upon the head of the maid that went before her. [8] Then God changed the spirit of the king into mildness, who in a fear leaped from his throne, and took her in his arms, till she came to herself again, and comforted her with loving words and said unto her, [9] Esther, what is the matter? I am thy brother, be of good cheer: [10] Thou shalt not die, though our our commandment be general: come near. [11] And so be held up his golden sceptre, and laid it upon her neck, [12] And embraced her, and said, Speak unto me. [13] Then said she unto him, I saw thee, my lord, as an angel of God, and my heart was troubled for fear of thy majesty. [14] For wonderful art thou, lord, and thy countenance is full of grace. [15] And as she was speaking, she fell down for faintness. [16] Then the king was troubled, and all his servants comforted her.

AddEsth.7

[1] The great king Artexerxes unto the princes and governors of an hundred and seven and twenty provinces from India unto Ethiopia, and unto all our faithful subjects, greeting. [2] Many, the more often they are honoured with the great bounty of their gracious princes, the more proud they are waxen, [3] And endeavour to hurt not our subjects only, but not being able to bear abundance, do take in hand to practise also against those that do them good: [4] And take not only thankfulness away from among men, but also lifted up with the glorious words of lewd persons, that were never good, they think to escape the justice of God, that seeth all things and hateth evil. [5] Oftentimes also fair speech of those, that are put in trust to manage their friends' affairs, hath caused many that are in authority to be partakers of innocent blood, and hath enwrapped them in remediless calamities: [6] Beguiling with the falsehood and deceit of their lewd disposition the innocency and goodness of princes. [7] Now ye may see this, as we have declared, not so much by ancient histories, as ye may, if ye search what hath been wickedly done of late through the pestilent behaviour of them that are unworthily placed in authority.

[8] And we must take care for the time to come, that our kingdom may be quiet and peaceable for all men, [9] Both by changing our purposes, and always judging things that are evident with more equal proceeding. [10] For Aman, a Macedonian, the son of Amadatha, being indeed a stranger from the Persian blood, and far distant from our goodness, and as a stranger received of us, [11] Had so far forth obtained the favour that we shew toward every nation, as that he was called our father, and was continually honoured of all the next person unto the king. [12] But he, not bearing his great dignity, went about to deprive us of our kingdom and life: [13] Having by manifold and cunning deceits sought of us the destruction, as well of Mardocheus, who saved our life, and continually procured our good, as also of blameless Esther, partaker of our kingdom, with their whole nation. [14] For by these means he thought, finding us destitute of friends to have translated the kingdom of the Persians to the Macedonians. [15] But we find that the Jews, whom this wicked wretch hath delivered to utter destruction, are no evildoers, but live by most just laws: [16] And that they be children of the most high and most mighty, living God, who hath ordered the kingdom both unto us and to our progenitors in the most excellent manner. [17] Wherefore ye shall do well not to put in execution the letters sent unto you by Aman the son of Amadatha. [18] For he that was the worker of these things, is hanged at the gates of Susa with all his family: God, who ruleth all things, speedily rendering vengeance to him according to his deserts. [19] Therefore ye shall publish the copy of this letter in all places, that the Jews may freely live after their own laws. [20] And ye shall aid them, that even the same day, being the thirteenth day of the twelfth month Adar, they may be avenged on them, who in the time of their affliction shall set upon them. [21] For Almighty God hath turned to joy unto them the day, wherein the chosen people should have perished. [22] Ye shall therefore among your solemn feasts keep it an high day with all feasting: [23] That both now and hereafter there may be safety to us and the well affected Persians; but to those which do conspire against us a memorial of destruction. [24] Therefore every city and country whatsoever, which shall not do according to these things, shall be destroyed without mercy with fire and sword, and shall be made not only unpassable for men, but also most hateful to wild beasts and fowls for ever.

WISDOM OF SOLOMON

Wis.1

[1] Love righteousness, ye that be judges of the earth: think of the Lord with a good (heart,) and in simplicity of heart seek him. [2] For he will be found of them that tempt him not; and sheweth himself unto such as do not distrust him.

[3] For froward thoughts separate from God: and his power, when it is tried, reproveth the unwise. [4] For into a malicious soul wisdom shall not enter; nor dwell in the body that is subject unto sin. [5] For the holy spirit of discipline will flee deceit, and remove from thoughts that are without understanding, and will not abide when unrighteousness cometh in. [6] For wisdom is a loving spirit; and will not acquit a blasphemer of his words: for God is witness of his reins, and a true beholder of his heart, and a hearer of his tongue. [7] For the Spirit of the Lord filleth the world: and that which containeth all things hath knowledge of the voice. [8] Therefore he that speaketh unrighteous things cannot be hid: neither shall vengeance, when it punisheth, pass by him. [9] For inquisition shall be made into the counsels of the ungodly: and the sound of his words shall come unto the Lord for the manifestation of his wicked deeds. [10] For the ear of jealousy heareth all things: and the noise of murmurings is not hid. [11] Therefore beware of murmuring, which is unprofitable; and refrain your tongue from backbiting: for there is no word so secret, that shall go for nought: and the mouth that belieth slayeth the soul. [12] Seek not death in the error of your life: and pull not upon yourselves destruction with the works of your hands. [13] For God made not death: neither hath he pleasure in the destruction of the living. [14] For he created all things, that they might have their being: and the generations of the world were healthful; and there is no poison of destruction in them, nor the kingdom of death upon the earth: [15] (For righteousness is immortal:) [16] But ungodly men with their works and words called it to them: for when they thought to have it their friend, they consumed to nought, and made a covenant with it, because they are worthy to take part with it.

Wis.2

[1] For the ungodly said, reasoning with themselves, but not aright, Our life is short and tedious, and in the death of a man there is no remedy: neither was there any man known to have returned from the grave. [2] For we are born at all adventure: and we shall be hereafter as though we had never been: for the breath in our nostrils is as smoke, and a little spark in the moving of our heart: [3] Which being extinguished, our body shall be turned into ashes, and our spirit shall vanish as the soft air, [4] And our name shall be forgotten in time, and no man shall have our works in remembrance, and our life shall pass away as the trace of a cloud, and shall be dispersed as a mist, that is driven away with the beams of the sun, and overcome with the heat thereof. [5] For our time is a very shadow that passeth away; and after our end there is no returning: for it is fast sealed, so that no man cometh again. [6] Come on therefore, let us enjoy the good things that are present: and

let us speedily use the creatures like as in youth. [7] Let us fill ourselves with costly wine and ointments: and let no flower of the spring pass by us: [8] Let us crown ourselves with rosebuds, before they be withered: [9] Let none of us go without his part of our voluptuousness: let us leave tokens of our joyfulness in every place: for this is our portion, and our lot is this. [10] Let us oppress the poor righteous man, let us not spare the widow, nor reverence the ancient gray hairs of the aged. [11] Let our strength be the law of justice: for that which is feeble is found to be nothing worth. [12] Therefore let us lie in wait for the righteous; because he is not for our turn, and he is clean contrary to our doings: he upbraideth us with our offending the law, and objecteth to our infamy the transgressings of our education. [13] He professeth to have the knowledge of God: and he calleth himself the child of the Lord. [14] He was made to reprove our thoughts. [15] He is grievous unto us even to behold: for his life is not like other men's, his ways are of another fashion. [16] We are esteemed of him as counterfeits: he abstaineth from our ways as from filthiness: he pronounceth the end of the just to be blessed, and maketh his boast that God is his father. [17] Let us see if his words be true: and let us prove what shall happen in the end of him. [18] For if the just man be the son of God, he will help him, and deliver him from the hand of his enemies. [19] Let us examine him with despitefulness and torture, that we may know his meekness, and prove his patience. [20] Let us condemn him with a shameful death: for by his own saying he shall be respected. [21] Such things they did imagine, and were deceived: for their own wickedness hath blinded them. [22] As for the mysteries of God, they kn ew them not: neither hoped they for the wages of righteousness, nor discerned a reward for blameless souls. [23] For God created man to be immortal, and made him to be an image of his own eternity. [24] Nevertheless through envy of the devil came death into the world: and they that do hold of his side do find it.

Wis.3

[1] But the souls of the righteous are in the hand of God, and there shall no torment touch them. [2] In the sight of the unwise they seemed to die: and their departure is taken for misery, [3] And their going from us to be utter destruction: but they are in peace. [4] For though they be punished in the sight of men, yet is their hope full of immortality. [5] And having been a little chastised, they shall be greatly rewarded: for God proved them, and found them worthy for himself. [6] As gold in the furnace hath he tried them, and received them as a burnt offering. [7] And in the time of their visitation they shall shine, and run to and fro like sparks among the stubble. [8] They shall judge the nations, and have dominion over the people, and their Lord shall reign for ever. [9] They that put their trust in him shall understand the truth: and such as be faithful in love shall abide with him: for grace and mercy is to his saints, and he hath care for his elect. [10] But the ungodly shall be punished according to their own imaginations, which have neglected the righteous, and forsaken the Lord.

[11] For whoso despiseth wisdom and nurture, he is miserable, and their hope is vain, their labours unfruitful,

and their works unprofitable: [12] Their wives are foolish, and their children wicked: [13] Their offspring is cursed. Wherefore blessed is the barren that is undefiled, which hath not known the sinful bed: she shall have fruit in the visitation of souls. [14] And blessed is the eunuch, which with his hands hath wrought no iniquity, nor imagined wicked things against God: for unto him shall be given the special gift of faith, and an inheritance in the temple of the Lord more acceptable to his mind. [15] For glorious is the fruit of good labours: and the root of wisdom shall never fall away. [16] As for the children of adulterers, they shall not come to their perfection, and the seed of an unrighteous bed shall be rooted out. [17] For though they live long, yet shall they be nothing regarded: and their last age shall be without honour. [18] Or, if they die quickly, they have no hope, neither comfort in the day of trial. [19] For horrible is the end of the unrighteous generation.

Wis.4

[1] Better it is to have no children, and to have virtue: for the memorial thereof is immortal: because it is known with God, and with men. [2] When it is present, men take example at it; and when it is gone, they desire it: it weareth a crown, and triumpheth for ever, having gotten the victory, striving for undefiled rewards. [3] But the multiplying brood of the ungodly shall not thrive, nor take deep rooting from bastard slips, nor lay any fast foundation. [4] For though they flourish in branches for a time; yet standing not last, they shall be shaken with the wind, and through the force of winds they shall be rooted out. [5] The imperfect branches shall be broken off, their fruit unprofitable, not ripe to eat, yea, meet for nothing. [6] For children begotten of unlawful beds are witnesses of wickedness against their parents in their trial. [7] But though the righteous be prevented with death, yet shall he be in rest. [8] For honourable age is not that which standeth in length of time, nor that is measured by number of years. [9] But wisdom is the gray hair unto men, and an unspotted life is old age. [10] He pleased God, and was beloved of him: so that living among sinners he was translated. [11] Yea speedily was he taken away, lest that wickedness should alter his understanding, or deceit beguile his soul. [12] For the bewitching of naughtiness doth obscure things that are honest; and the wandering of concupiscence doth undermine the simple mind. [13] He, being made perfect in a short time, fulfilled a long time: [14] For his soul pleased the Lord: therefore hasted he to take him away from among the wicked. [15] This the people saw, and understood it not, neither laid they up this in their minds, That his grace and mercy is with his saints, and that he hath respect unto his chosen. [16] Thus the righteous that is dead shall condemn the ungodly which are living; and youth that is soon perfected the many years and old age of the unrighteous. [17] For they shall see the end of the wise, and shall not understand what God in his counsel hath decreed of him, and to what end the Lord hath set him in safety. [18] They shall see him, and despise him; but God shall laugh them to scorn: and they shall hereafter be a vile carcase, and a reproach among the dead for evermore. [19] For he shall rend them, and cast them down headlong, that they shall be speechless; and he shall

shake them from the foundation; and they shall be utterly laid waste, and be in sorrow; and their memorial shall perish. [20] And when they cast up the accounts of their sins, they shall come with fear: and their own iniquities shall convince them to their face.

Wis.5

[1] Then shall the righteous man stand in great boldness before the face of such as have afflicted him, and made no account of his labours. [2] When they see it, they shall be troubled with terrible fear, and shall be amazed at the strangeness of his salvation, so far beyond all that they looked for. [3] And they repenting and groaning for anguish of spirit shall say within themselves, This was he, whom we had sometimes in derision, and a proverb of reproach: [4] We fools accounted his life madness, and his end to be without honour: [5] How is he numbered among the children of God, and his lot is among the saints! [6] Therefore have we erred from the way of truth, and the light of righteousness hath not shined unto us, and the sun of righteousness rose not upon us. [7] We wearied ourselves in the way of wickedness and destruction: yea, we have gone through deserts, where there lay no way: but as for the way of the Lord, we have not known it. [8] What hath pride profited us? or what good hath riches with our vaunting brought us? [9] All those things are passed away like a shadow, and as a post that hasted by; [10] And as a ship that passeth over the waves of the water, which when it is gone by, the trace thereof cannot be found, neither the pathway of the keel in the waves; [11] Or as when a bird hath flown through the air, there is no token of her way to be found, but the light air being beaten with the stroke of her wings and parted with the violent noise and motion of them, is passed through, and therein afterwards no sign where she went is to be found; [12] Or like as when an arrow is shot at a mark, it parteth the air, which immediately cometh together again, so that a man cannot know where it went through: [13] Even so we in like manner, as soon as we were born, began to draw to our end, and had no sign of virtue to shew; but were consumed in our own wickedness. [14] For the hope of the Godly is like dust that is blown away with the wind; like a thin froth that is driven away with the storm; like as the smoke which is dispersed here and there with a tempest, and passeth away as the remembrance of a guest that tarrieth but a day. [15] But the righteous live for evermore; their reward also is with the Lord, and the care of them is with the most High. [16] Therefore shall they receive a glorious kingdom, and a beautiful crown from the Lord's hand: for with his right hand shall he cover them, and with his arm shall he protect them. [17] He shall take to him his jealousy for complete armour, and make the creature his weapon for the revenge of his enemies. [18] He shall put on righteousness as a breastplate, and true judgment instead of an helmet. [19] He shall take holiness for an invincible shield. [20] His severe wrath shall he sharpen for a sword, and the world shall fight with him against the unwise. [21] Then shall the right aiming thunderbolts go abroad; and from the clouds, as from a well drawn bow, shall they fly to the mark. [22] And hailstones full of wrath shall be cast as out of a stone bow, and the water of the sea shall rage against them, and

the floods shall cruelly drown them. [23] Yea, a mighty wind shall stand up against them, and like a storm shall blow them away: thus iniquity shall lay waste the whole earth, and ill dealing shall overthrow the thrones of the mighty.

Wis.6

[1] Hear therefore, O ye kings, and understand; learn, ye that be judges of the ends of the earth. [2] Give ear, ye that rule the people, and glory in the multitude of nations. [3] For power is given you of the Lord, and sovereignty from the Highest, who shall try your works, and search out your counsels. [4] Because, being ministers of his kingdom, ye have not judged aright, nor kept the law, nor walked after the counsel of God; [5] Horribly and speedily shall he come upon you: for a sharp judgment shall be to them that be in high places. [6] For mercy will soon pardon the meanest: but mighty men shall be mightily tormented. [7] For he which is Lord over all shall fear no man's person, neither shall he stand in awe of any man's greatness: for he hath made the small and great, and careth for all alike. [8] But a sore trial shall come upon the mighty. [9] Unto you therefore, O kings, do I speak, that ye may learn wisdom, and not fall away. [10] For they that keep holiness holily shall be judged holy: and they that have learned such things shall find what to answer. [11] Wherefore set your affection upon my words; desire them, and ye shall be instructed. [12] Wisdom is glorious, and never fadeth away: yea, she is easily seen of them that love her, and found of such as seek her. [13] She preventeth them that desire her, in making herself first known unto them. [14] Whoso seeketh her early shall have no great travail: for he shall find her sitting at his doors. [15] To think therefore upon her is perfection of wisdom: and whoso watcheth for her shall quickly be without care. [16] For she goeth about seeking such as are worthy of her, sheweth herself favourably unto them in the ways, and meeteth them in every thought. [17] For the very true beginning of her is the desire of discipline; and the care of discipline is love; [18] And love is the keeping of her laws; and the giving heed unto her laws is the assurance of incorruption; [19] And incorruption maketh us near unto God: [20] Therefore the desire of wisdom bringeth to a kingdom. [21] If your delight be then in thrones and sceptres, O ye kings of the people, honour wisdom, that ye may reign for evermore. [22] As for wisdom, what she is, and how she came up, I will tell you, and will not hide mysteries from you: but will seek her out from the beginning of her nativity, and bring the knowledge of her into light, and will not pass over the truth. [23] Neither will I go with consuming envy; for such a man shall have no fellowship with wisdom. [24] But the multitude of the wise is the welfare of the world: and a wise king is the upholding of the people. [25] Receive therefore instruction through my words, and it shall do you good.

Wis.7

[1] I myself also am a mortal man, like to all, and the offspring of him that was first made of the earth, [2] And in my mother's womb was fashioned to be flesh in the time of ten months, being compacted in blood, of the seed of man, and the pleasure that came with sleep. [3] And when I was born, I drew in the common air, and fell upon the earth, which is of like nature, and the first voice which I uttered was crying, as all others do. [4] I was nursed in swaddling clothes, and that with cares. [5] For there is no king that had any other beginning of birth. [6] For all men have one entrance into life, and the like going out. [7] Wherefore I prayed, and understanding was given me: I called upon God, and the spirit of wisdom came to me. [8] I preferred her before sceptres and thrones, and esteemed riches nothing in comparison of her. [9] Neither compared I unto her any precious stone, because all gold in respect of her is as a little sand, and silver shall be counted as clay before her. [10] I loved her above health and beauty, and chose to have her instead of light: for the light that cometh from her never goeth out. [11] All good things together came to me with her, and innumerable riches in her hands.

[12] And I rejoiced in them all, because wisdom goeth before them: and I knew not that she was the mother of them. [13] I learned diligently, and do communicate her liberally: I do not hide her riches. [14] For she is a treasure unto men that never faileth: which they that use become the friends of God, being commended for the gifts that come from learning. [15] God hath granted me to speak as I would, and to conceive as is meet for the things that are given me: because it is he that leadeth unto wisdom, and directeth the wise. [16] For in his hand are both we and our words; all wisdom also, and knowledge of workmanship. [17] For he hath given me certain knowledge of the things that are, namely, to know how the world was made, and the operation of the elements: [18] The beginning, ending, and midst of the times: the alterations of the turning of the sun, and the change of seasons: [19] The circuits of years, and the positions of stars: [20] The natures of living creatures, and the furies of wild beasts: the violence of winds, and the reasonings of men: the diversities of plants and the virtues of roots: [21] And all such things as are either secret or manifest, them I know. [22] For wisdom, which is the worker of all things, taught me: for in her is an understanding spirit holy, one only, manifold, subtil, lively, clear, undefiled, plain, not subject to hurt, loving the thing that is good quick, which cannot be letted, ready to do good, [23] Kind to man, steadfast, sure, free from care, having all power, overseeing all things, and going through all understanding, pure, and most subtil, spirits. [24] For wisdom is more moving than any motion: she passeth and goeth through all things by reason of her pureness. [25] For she is the breath of the power of God, and a pure influence flowing from the glory of the Almighty: therefore can no defiled thing fall into her.

[26] For she is the brightness of the everlasting light, the unspotted mirror of the power of God, and the image of his goodness. [27] And being but one, she can do all things: and remaining in herself, she maketh all things new: and in all ages entering into holy souls, she maketh them friends of God, and prophets. [28] For God loveth none but him that dwelleth with wisdom. [29] For she is more beautiful than the sun, and above all the order of stars: being compared with the light, she is found before it. [30] For after this cometh night: but vice shall not prevail against wisdom.

Wis.8

[1] Wisdom reacheth from one end to another mightily: and sweetly doth she order all things. [2] I loved her, and sought her out from my youth, I desired to make her my spouse, and I was a lover of her beauty. [3] In that she is conversant with God, she magnifieth her nobility: yea, the Lord of all things himself loved her. [4] For she is privy to the mysteries of the knowledge of God, and a lover of his works. [5] If riches be a possession to be desired in this life; what is richer than wisdom, that worketh all things? [6] And if prudence work; who of all that are is a more cunning workman than she? [7] And if a man love righteousness her labours are virtues: for she teacheth temperance and prudence, justice and fortitude: which are such things, as en can have nothing more profitable in their life. [8] If a man desire much experience, she knoweth things of old, and conjectureth aright what is to come: she knoweth the subtilties of speeches, and can expound dark sentences: she foreseeth signs and wonders, and the events of seasons and times. [9] Therefore I purposed to take her to me to live with me, knowing that she would be a counsellor of good things, and a comfort in cares and grief.

[10] For her sake I shall have estimation among the multitude, and honour with the elders, though I be young. [11] I shall be found of a quick conceit in judgment, and shall be admired in the sight of great men. [12] When I hold my tongue, they shall bide my leisure, and when I speak, they shall give good ear unto me: if I talk much, they shall lay their hands upon their mouth. [13] Moreover by the means of her I shall obtain immortality, and leave behind me an everlasting memorial to them that come after me. [14] I shall set the people in order, and the nations shall be subject unto me. [15] Horrible tyrants shall be afraid, when they do but hear of me; I shall be found good among the multitude, and valiant in war. [16] After I am come into mine house, I will repose myself with her: for her conversation hath no bitterness; and to live with her hath no sorrow, but mirth and joy. [17] Now when I considered these things in myself, and pondered them in my heart, how that to be allied unto wisdom is immortality;

[18] And great pleasure it is to have her friendship; and in the works of her hands are infinite riches; and in the exercise of conference with her, prudence; and in talking with her, a good report; I went about seeking how to take her to me. [19] For I was a witty child, and had a good spirit. [20] Yea rather, being good, I came into a body undefiled. [21] Nevertheless, when I perceived that I could not otherwise obtain her, except God gave her me; and that was a point of wisdom also to know whose gift she was; I prayed unto the Lord, and besought him, and with my whole heart I said,

Wis.9

[1] O God of my fathers, and Lord of mercy, who hast made all things with thy word, [2] And ordained man through thy wisdom, that he should have dominion over the creatures which thou hast made, [3] And order the world according to equity and righteousness, and execute judgment with an upright heart: [4] Give me wisdom, that sitteth by thy throne; and reject me not from among thy children: [5] For I thy servant and son of thine handmaid am a feeble person, and of a short time, and too young for the understanding of judgment and laws. [6] For though a man be never so perfect among the children of men, yet if thy wisdom be not with him, he shall be nothing regarded. [7] Thou hast chosen me to be a king of thy people, and a judge of thy sons and daughters: [8] Thou hast commanded me to build a temple upon thy holy mount, and an altar in the city wherein thou dwellest, a resemblance of the holy tabernacle, which thou hast prepared from the beginning. [9] And wisdom was with thee: which knoweth thy works, and was present when thou madest the world, and knew what was acceptable in thy sight, and right in thy commandments. [10] O send her out of thy holy heavens, and from the throne of thy glory, that being present she may labour with me, that I may know what is pleasing unto thee. [11] For she knoweth and understandeth all things, and she shall lead me soberly in my doings, and preserve me in her power. [12] So shall my works be acceptable, and then shall I judge thy people righteously, and be worthy to sit in my father's seat. [13] For what man is he that can know the counsel of God? or who can think what the will of the Lord is? [14] For the thoughts of mortal men are miserable, and our devices are but uncertain. [15] For the corruptible body presseth down the soul, and the earthy tabernacle weigheth down the mind that museth upon many things. [16] And hardly do we guess aright at things that are upon earth, and with labour do we find the things that are before us: but the things that are in heaven who hath searched out? [17] And thy counsel who hath known, except thou give wisdom, and send thy Holy Spirit from above? [18] For so the ways of them which lived on the earth were reformed, and men were taught the things that are pleasing unto thee, and were saved through wisdom.

Wis.10

[1] She preserved the first formed father of the world, that was created alone, and brought him out of his fall, [2] And gave him power to rule all things. [3] But when the unrighteous went away from her in his anger, he perished also in the fury wherewith he murdered his brother. [4] For whose cause the earth being drowned with the flood, wisdom again preserved it, and directed the course of the righteous in a piece of wood of small value. [5] Moreover, the nations in their wicked conspiracy being confounded, she found out the righteous, and preserved him blameless unto God, and kept him strong against his tender compassion toward his son. [6] When the ungodly perished, she delivered the righteous man, who fled from the fire which fell down upon the five cities. [7] Of whose wickedness even to this day the waste land that smoketh is a testimony, and plants bearing fruit that never come to ripeness: and a standing pillar of salt is a monument of an unbelieving soul. [8] For regarding not wisdom, they gat not only this hurt, that they knew not the things which were good; but also left behind them to the world a memorial of their foolishness: so that in the things wherein they offended they could not so much as be hid. [9] Rut wisdom delivered from pain those that attended upon her. [10] When the righteous fled from his brother's wrath she

guided him in right paths, shewed him the kingdom of God, and gave him knowledge of holy things, made him rich in his travels, and multiplied the fruit of his labours. [11] In the covetousness of such as oppressed him she stood by him, and made him rich. [12] She defended him from his enemies, and kept him safe from those that lay in wait, and in a sore conflict she gave him the victory; that he might know that goodness is stronger than all. [13] When the righteous was sold, she forsook him not, but delivered him from sin: she went down with him into the pit, [14] And left him not in bonds, till she brought him the sceptre of the kingdom, and power against those that oppressed him: as for them that had accused him, she shewed them to be liars, and gave him perpetual glory. [15] She delivered the righteous people and blameless seed from the nation that oppressed them. [16] She entered into the soul of the servant of the Lord, and withstood dreadful kings in wonders and signs; [17] Rendered to the righteous a reward of their labours, guided them in a marvellous way, and was unto them for a cover by day, and a light of stars in the night season; [18] Brought them through the Red sea, and led them through much water: [19] But she drowned their enemies, and cast them up out of the bottom of the deep. [20] Therefore the righteous spoiled the ungodly, and praised thy holy name, O Lord, and magnified with one accord thine hand, that fought for them. [21] For wisdom opened the mouth of the dumb, and made the tongues of them that cannot speak eloquent.

Wis.11

[1] She prospered their works in the hand of the holy prophet. [2] They went through the wilderness that was not inhabited, and pitched tents in places where there lay no way. [3] They stood against their enemies, and were avenged of their adversaries. [4] When they were thirsty, they called upon thee, and water was given them out of the flinty rock, and their thirst was quenched out of the hard stone. [5] For by what things their enemies were punished, by the same they in their need were benefited. [6] For instead of of a perpetual running river troubled with foul blood, [7] For a manifest reproof of that commandment, whereby the infants were slain, thou gavest unto them abundance of water by a means which they hoped not for: [8] Declaring by that thirst then how thou hadst punished their adversaries. [9] For when they were tried albeit but in mercy chastised, they knew how the ungodly were judged in wrath and tormented, thirsting in another manner than the just. [10] For these thou didst admonish and try, as a father: but the other, as a severe king, thou didst condemn and punish. [11] Whether they were absent or present, they were vexed alike. [12] For a double grief came upon them, and a groaning for the remembrance of things past. [13] For when they heard by their own punishments the other to be benefited, they had some feeling of the Lord. [14] For whom they respected with scorn, when he was long before thrown out at the casting forth of the infants, him in the end, when they saw what came to pass, they admired. [15] But for the foolish devices of their wickedness, wherewith being deceived they worshipped serpents void of reason, and vile beasts, thou didst send a multitude of unreasonable beasts upon them for vengeance; [16] That

they might know, that wherewithal a man sinneth, by the same also shall he be punished. [17] For thy Almighty hand, that made the world of matter without form, wanted not means to send among them a multitude of bears or fierce lions, [18] Or unknown wild beasts, full of rage, newly created, breathing out either a fiery vapour, or filthy scents of scattered smoke, or shooting horrible sparkles out of their eyes: [19] Whereof not only the harm might dispatch them at once, but also the terrible sight utterly destroy them. [20] Yea, and without these might they have fallen down with one blast, being persecuted of vengeance, and scattered abroad through the breath of thy power: but thou hast ordered all things in measure and number and weight. [21] For thou canst shew thy great strength at all times when thou wilt; and who may withstand the power of thine arm? [22] For the whole world before thee is as a little grain of the balance, yea, as a drop of the morning dew that falleth down upon the earth. [23] But thou hast mercy upon all; for thou canst do all things, and winkest at the sins of men, because they should amend. [24] For thou lovest all the things that are, and abhorrest nothing which thou hast made: for never wouldest thou have made any thing, if thou hadst hated it. [25] And how could any thing have endured, if it had not been thy will? or been preserved, if not called by thee? [26] But thou sparest all: for they are thine, O Lord, thou lover of souls.

Wis.12

[1] For thine incorruptible Spirit is in all things. [2] Therefore chastenest thou them by little and little that offend, and warnest them by putting them in remembrance wherein they have offended, that leaving their wickedness they may believe on thee, O Lord. [3] For it was thy will to destroy by the hands of our fathers both those old inhabitants of thy holy land, [4] Whom thou hatedst for doing most odious works of witchcrafts, and wicked sacrifices; [5] And also those merciless murderers of children, and devourers of man's flesh, and the feasts of blood, [6] With their priests out of the midst of their idolatrous crew, and the parents, that killed with their own hands souls destitute of help: [7] That the land, which thou esteemedst above all other, might receive a worthy colony of God's children. [8] Nevertheless even those thou sparedst as men, and didst send wasps, forerunners of thine host, to destroy them by little and little. [9] Not that thou wast unable to bring the ungodly under the hand of the righteous in battle, or to destroy them at once with cruel beasts, or with one rough word: [10] But executing thy judgments upon them by little and little, thou gavest them place of repentance, not being ignorant that they were a naughty generation, and that their malice was bred in them, and that their cogitation would never be changed. [11] For it was a cursed seed from the beginning; neither didst thou for fear of any man give them pardon for those things wherein they sinned. [12] For who shall say, What hast thou done? or who shall withstand thy judgment? or who shall accuse thee for the nations that perish, whom thou made? or who shall come to stand against thee, to be revenged for the unrighteous men? [13] For neither is there any God but thou that careth for all, to whom thou mightest shew that thy judgment is not unright. [14]

Neither shall king or tyrant be able to set his face against thee for any whom thou hast punished. [15] Forsomuch then as thou art righteous thyself, thou orderest all things righteously: thinking it not agreeable with thy power to condemn him that hath not deserved to be punished. [16] For thy power is the beginning of righteousness, and because thou art the Lord of all, it maketh thee to be gracious unto all. [17] For when men will not believe that thou art of a full power, thou shewest thy strength, and among them that know it thou makest their boldness manifest. [18] But thou, mastering thy power, judgest with equity, and orderest us with great favour: for thou mayest use power when thou wilt. [19] But by such works hast thou taught thy people that the just man should be merciful, and hast made thy children to be of a good hope that thou givest repentance for sins. [20] For if thou didst punish the enemies of thy children, and the condemned to death, with such deliberation, giving them time and place, whereby they might be delivered from their malice: [21] With how great circumspection didst thou judge thine own sons, unto whose fathers thou hast sworn, and made covenants of good promises? [22] Therefore, whereas thou dost chasten us, thou scourgest our enemies a thousand times more, to the intent that, when we judge, we should carefully think of thy goodness, and when we ourselves are judged, we should look for mercy. [23] Wherefore, whereas men have lived dissolutely and unrighteously, thou hast tormented them with their own abominations. [24] For they went astray very far in the ways of error, and held them for gods, which even among the beasts of their enemies were despised, being deceived, as children of no understanding. [25] Therefore unto them, as to children without the use of reason, thou didst send a judgment to mock them. [26] But they that would not be reformed by that correction, wherein he dallied with them, shall feel a judgment worthy of God. [27] For, look, for what things they grudged, when they were punished, that is, for them whom they thought to be gods; [now] being punished in them, when they saw it, they acknowledged him to be the true God, whom before they denied to know: and therefore came extreme damnation upon them.

Wis.13

[1] Surely vain are all men by nature, who are ignorant of God, and could not out of the good things that are seen know him that is: neither by considering the works did they acknowledge the workmaster; [2] But deemed either fire, or wind, or the swift air, or the circle of the stars, or the violent water, or the lights of heaven, to be the gods which govern the world. [3] With whose beauty if they being delighted took them to be gods; let them know how much better the Lord of them is: for the first author of beauty hath created them. [4] But if they were astonished at their power and virtue, let them understand by them, how much mightier he is that made them. [5] For by the greatness and beauty of the creatures proportionably the maker of them is seen. [6] But yet for this they are the less to be blamed: for they peradventure err, seeking God, and desirous to find him. [7] For being conversant in his works they search him diligently, and believe their sight: because the things are beautiful that are seen. [8] Howbeit neither are they to be pardoned. [9] For if they were able to know so much, that

they could aim at the world; how did they not sooner find out the Lord thereof? [10] But miserable are they, and in dead things is their hope, who call them gods, which are the works of men's hands, gold and silver, to shew art in, and resemblances of beasts, or a stone good for nothing, the work of an ancient hand. [11] Now a carpenter that felleth timber, after he hath sawn down a tree meet for the purpose, and taken off all the bark skilfully round about, and hath wrought it handsomely, and made a vessel thereof fit for the service of man's life; [12] And after spending the refuse of his work to dress his meat, hath filled himself; [13] And taking the very refuse among those which served to no use, being a crooked piece of wood, and full of knots, hath carved it diligently, when he had nothing else to do, and formed it by the skill of his understanding, and fashioned it to the image of a man; [14] Or made it like some vile beast, laying it over with vermilion, and with paint colouring it red, and covering every spot therein; [15] And when he had made a convenient room for it, set it in a wall, and made it fast with iron: [16] For he provided for it that it might not fall, knowing that it was unable to help itself; for it is an image, and hath need of help: [17] Then maketh he prayer for his goods, for his wife and children, and is not ashamed to speak to that which hath no life. [18] For health he calleth upon that which is weak: for life prayeth to that which is dead; for aid humbly beseecheth that which hath least means to help: and for a good journey he asketh of that which cannot set a foot forward: [19] And for gaining and getting, and for good success of his hands, asketh ability to do of him, that is most unable to do any thing.

Wis.14

[1] Again, one preparing himself to sail, and about to pass through the raging waves, calleth upon a piece of wood more rotten than the vessel that carrieth him. [2] For verily desire of gain devised that, and the workman built it by his skill. [3] But thy providence, O Father, governeth it: for thou hast made a way in the sea, and a safe path in the waves; [4] Shewing that thou canst save from all danger: yea, though a man went to sea without art. [5] Nevertheless thou wouldest not that the works of thy wisdom should be idle, and therefore do men commit their lives to a small piece of wood, and passing the rough sea in a weak vessel are saved. [6] For in the old time also, when the proud giants perished, the hope of the world governed by thy hand escaped in a weak vessel, and left to all ages a seed of generation. [7] For blessed is the wood whereby righteousness cometh. [8] But that which is made with hands is cursed, as well it, as he that made it: he, because he made it; and it, because, being corruptible, it was called god. [9] For the ungodly and his ungodliness are both alike hateful unto God. [10] For that which is made shall be punished together with him that made it. [11] Therefore even upon the idols of the Gentiles shall there be a visitation: because in the creature of God they are become an abomination, and stumblingblocks to the souls of men, and a snare to the feet of the unwise. [12] For the devising of idols was the beginning of spiritual fornication, and the invention of them the corruption of life. [13] For neither were they from the beginning, neither shall they be for ever.

[14] For by the vain glory of men they entered into the world, and therefore shall they come shortly to an end. [15] For a father afflicted with untimely mourning, when he hath made an image of his child soon taken away, now honoured him as a god, which was then a dead man, and delivered to those that were under him ceremonies and sacrifices. [16] Thus in process of time an ungodly custom grown strong was kept as a law, and graven images were worshipped by the commandments of kings. [17] Whom men could not honour in presence, because they dwelt far off, they took the counterfeit of his visage from far, and made an express image of a king whom they honoured, to the end that by this their forwardness they might flatter him that was absent, as if he were present. [18] Also the singular diligence of the artificer did help to set forward the ignorant to more superstition. [19] For he, peradventure willing to please one in authority, forced all his skill to make the resemblance of the best fashion. [20] And so the multitude, allured by the grace of the work, took him now for a god, which a little before was but honoured. [21] And this was an occasion to deceive the world: for men, serving either calamity or tyranny, did ascribe unto stones and stocks the incommunicable name. [22] Moreover this was not enough for them, that they erred in the knowledge of God; but whereas they lived in the great war of ignorance, those so great plagues called they peace. [23] For whilst they slew their children in sacrifices, or used secret ceremonies, or made revellings of strange rites; [24] They kept neither lives nor marriages any longer undefiled: but either one slew another traiterously, or grieved him by adultery. [25] So that there reigned in all men without exception blood, manslaughter, theft, and dissimulation, corruption, unfaithfulness, tumults, perjury, [26] Disquieting of good men, forgetfulness of good turns, defiling of souls, changing of kind, disorder in marriages, adultery, and shameless uncleanness. [27] For the worshipping of idols not to be named is the beginning, the cause, and the end, of all evil. [28] For either they are mad when they be merry, or prophesy lies, or live unjustly, or else lightly forswear themselves. [29] For insomuch as their trust is in idols, which have no life; though they swear falsely, yet they look not to be hurt. [30] Howbeit for both causes shall they be justly punished: both because they thought not well of God, giving heed unto idols, and also unjustly swore in deceit, despising holiness. [31] For it is not the power of them by whom they swear: but it is the just vengeance of sinners, that punisheth always the offence of the ungodly.

Wis.15

[1] But thou, O God, art gracious and true, longsuffering, and in mercy ordering all things, [2] For if we sin, we are thine, knowing thy power: but we will not sin, knowing that we are counted thine. [3] For to know thee is perfect righteousness: yea, to know thy power is the root of immortality. [4] For neither did the mischievous invention of men deceive us, nor an image spotted with divers colours, the painter's fruitless labour; [5] The sight whereof enticeth fools to lust after it, and so they desire the form of a dead image, that hath no breath. [6] Both they that make them, they that desire them, and they that worship them,

are lovers of evil things, and are worthy to have such things to trust upon. [7] For the potter, tempering soft earth, fashioneth every vessel with much labour for our service: yea, of the same clay he maketh both the vessels that serve for clean uses, and likewise also all such as serve to the contrary: but what is the use of either sort, the potter himself is the judge. [8] And employing his labours lewdly, he maketh a vain god of the same clay, even he which a little before was made of earth himself, and within a little while after returneth to the same, out when his life which was lent him shall be demanded. [9] Notwithstanding his care is, not that he shall have much labour, nor that his life is short: but striveth to excel goldsmiths and silversmiths, and endeavoureth to do like the workers in brass, and counteth it his glory to make counterfeit things. [10] His heart is ashes, his hope is more vile than earth, and his life of less value than clay: [11] Forasmuch as he knew not his Maker, and him that inspired into him an active soul, and breathed in a living spirit. [12] But they counted our life a pastime, and our time here a market for gain: for, say they, we must be getting every way, though it be by evil means. [13] For this man, that of earthly matter maketh brittle vessels and graven images, knoweth himself to offend above all others. [14] And all the enemies of thy people, that hold them in subjection, are most foolish, and are more miserable than very babes. [15] For they counted all the idols of the heathen to be gods: which neither have the use of eyes to see, nor noses to draw breath, nor ears to hear, nor fingers of hands to handle; and as for their feet, they are slow to go. [16] For man made them, and he that borrowed his own spirit fashioned them: but no man can make a god like unto himself. [17] For being mortal, he worketh a dead thing with wicked hands: for he himself is better than the things which he worshippeth: whereas he lived once, but they never. [18] Yea, they worshipped those beasts also that are most hateful: for being compared together, some are worse than others. [19] Neither are they beautiful, so much as to be desired in respect of beasts: but they went without the praise of God and his blessing.

Wis.16

[1] Therefore by the like were they punished worthily, and by the multitude of beasts tormented. [2] Instead of which punishment, dealing graciously with thine own people, thou preparedst for them meat of a strange taste, even quails to stir up their appetite: [3] To the end that they, desiring food, might for the ugly sight of the beasts sent among them lothe even that, which they must needs desire; but these, suffering penury for a short space, might be made partakers of a strange taste. [4] For it was requisite, that upon them exercising tyranny should come penury, which they could not avoid: but to these it should only be shewed how their enemies were tormented. [5] For when the horrible fierceness of beasts came upon these, and they perished with the stings of crooked serpents, thy wrath endured not for ever: [6] But they were troubled for a small season, that they might be admonished, having a sign of salvation, to put them in remembrance of the commandment of thy law. [7] For he that turned himself toward it was not saved by the thing that he saw, but by thee, that art the Saviour of all. [8] And in this thou madest thine enemies confess, that it is thou who deliverest from

all evil: [9] For them the bitings of grasshoppers and flies killed, neither was there found any remedy for their life: for they were worthy to be punished by such. [10] But thy sons not the very teeth of venomous dragons overcame: for thy mercy was ever by them, and healed them. [11] For they were pricked, that they should remember thy words; and were quickly saved, that not falling into deep forgetfulness, they might be continually mindful of thy goodness. [12] For it was neither herb, nor mollifying plaister, that restored them to health: but thy word, O Lord, which healeth all things. [13] For thou hast power of life and death: thou leadest to the gates of hell, and bringest up again. [14] A man indeed killeth through his malice: and the spirit, when it is gone forth, returneth not; neither the soul received up cometh again. [15] But it is not possible to escape thine hand. [16] For the ungodly, that denied to know thee, were scourged by the strength of thine arm: with strange rains, hails, and showers, were they persecuted, that they could not avoid, and through fire were they consumed. [17] For, which is most to be wondered at, the fire had more force in the water, that quencheth all things: for the world fighteth for the righteous. [18] For sometime the flame was mitigated, that it might not burn up the beasts that were sent against the ungodly; but themselves might see and perceive that they were persecuted with the judgment of God. [19] And at another time it burneth even in the midst of water above the power of fire, that it might destroy the fruits of an unjust land. [20] Instead whereof thou feddest thine own people with angels' food, and didst send them from heaven bread prepared without their labour, able to content every man's delight, and agreeing to every taste. [21] For thy sustenance declared thy sweetness unto thy children, and serving to the appetite of the eater, tempered itself to every man's liking. [22] But snow and ice endured the fire, and melted not, that they might know that fire burning in the hail, and sparkling in the rain, did destroy the fruits of the enemies. [23] But this again did even forget his own strength, that the righteous might be nourished. [24] For the creature that serveth thee, who art the Maker increaseth his strength against the unrighteous for their punishment, and abateth his strength for the benefit of such as put their trust in thee. [25] Therefore even then was it altered into all fashions, and was obedient to thy grace, that nourisheth all things, according to the desire of them that had need: [26] That thy children, O Lord, whom thou lovest, might know, that it is not the growing of fruits that nourisheth man: but that it is thy word, which preserveth them that put their trust in thee. [27] For that which was not destroyed of the fire, being warmed with a little sunbeam, soon melted away: [28] That it might be known, that we must prevent the sun to give thee thanks, and at the dayspring pray unto thee. [29] For the hope of the unthankful shall melt away as the winter's hoar frost, and shall run away as unprofitable water.

Wis.17

[1] For great are thy judgments, and cannot be expressed: therefore unnurtured souls have erred. [2] For when unrighteous men thought to oppress the holy nation; they being shut up in their houses, the prisoners of darkness, and fettered with the bonds of a long night, lay [there]

exiled from the eternal providence. [3] For while they supposed to lie hid in their secret sins, they were scattered under a dark veil of forgetfulness, being horribly astonished, and troubled with [strange] apparitions. [4] For neither might the corner that held them keep them from fear: but noises [as of waters] falling down sounded about them, and sad visions appeared unto them with heavy countenances. [5] No power of the fire might give them light: neither could the bright flames of the stars endure to lighten that horrible night. [6] Only there appeared unto them a fire kindled of itself, very dreadful: for being much terrified, they thought the things which they saw to be worse than the sight they saw not. [7] As for the illusions of art magick, they were put down, and their vaunting in wisdom was reproved with disgrace. [8] For they, that promised to drive away terrors and troubles from a sick soul, were sick themselves of fear, worthy to be laughed at.

[9] For though no terrible thing did fear them; yet being scared with beasts that passed by, and hissing of serpents, [10] They died for fear, denying that they saw the air, which could of no side be avoided. [11] For wickedness, condemned by her own witness, is very timorous, and being pressed with conscience, always forecasteth grievous things. [12] For fear is nothing else but a betraying of the succours which reason offereth. [13] And the expectation from within, being less, counteth the ignorance more than the cause which bringeth the torment. [14] But they sleeping the same sleep that night, which was indeed intolerable, and which came upon them out of the bottoms of inevitable hell, [15] Were partly vexed with monstrous apparitions, and partly fainted, their heart failing them: for a sudden fear, and not looked for, came upon them. [16] So then whosoever there fell down was straitly kept, shut up in a prison without iron bars, [17] For whether he were husbandman, or shepherd, or a labourer in the field, he was overtaken, and endured that necessity, which could not be avoided: for they were all bound with one chain of darkness. [18] Whether it were a whistling wind, or a melodious noise of birds among the spreading branches, or a pleasing fall of water running violently, [19] Or a terrible sound of stones cast down, or a running that could not be seen of skipping beasts, or a roaring voice of most savage wild beasts, or a rebounding echo from the hollow mountains; these things made them to swoon for fear. [20] For the whole world shined with clear light, and none were hindered in their labour: [21] Over them only was spread an heavy night, an image of that darkness which should afterward receive them: but yet were they unto themselves more grievous than the darkness.

Wis.18

[1] Nevertheless thy saints had a very great light, whose voice they hearing, and not seeing their shape, because they also had not suffered the same things, they counted them happy. [2] But for that they did not hurt them now, of whom they had been wronged before, they thanked them, and besought them pardon for that they had been enemies.

[3] Instead whereof thou gavest them a burning pillar of fire, both to be a guide of the unknown journey, and an harmless sun to entertain them honourably. [4] For they were worthy to be deprived of light and imprisoned in darkness, who had kept thy sons shut up, by whom the

uncorrupt light of the law was to be given unto the world. [5] And when they had determined to slay the babes of the saints, one child being cast forth, and saved, to reprove them, thou tookest away the multitude of their children, and destroyedst them altogether in a mighty water. [6] Of that night were our fathers certified afore, that assuredly knowing unto what oaths they had given credence, they might afterwards be of good cheer. [7] So of thy people was accepted both the salvation of the righteous, and destruction of the enemies. [8] For wherewith thou didst punish our adversaries, by the same thou didst glorify us, whom thou hadst called. [9] For the righteous children of good men did sacrifice secretly, and with one consent made a holy law, that the saints should be like partakers of the same good and evil, the fathers now singing out the songs of praise. [10] But on the other side there sounded an ill according cry of the enemies, and a lamentable noise was carried abroad for children that were bewailed. [11] The master and the servant were punished after one manner; and like as the king, so suffered the common person. [12] So they all together had innumerable dead with one kind of death; neither were the living sufficient to bury them: for in one moment the noblest offspring of them was destroyed. [13] For whereas they would not believe any thing by reason of the enchantments; upon the destruction of the firstborn, they acknowledged this people to be the sons of God. [14] For while all things were in quiet silence, and that night was in the midst of her swift course, [15] Thine Almighty word leaped down from heaven out of thy royal throne, as a fierce man of war into the midst of a land of destruction, [16] And brought thine unfeigned commandment as a sharp sword, and standing up filled all things with death; and it touched the heaven, but it stood upon the earth. [17] Then suddenly visions of horrible dreams troubled them sore, and terrors came upon them unlooked for. [18] And one thrown here, and another there, half dead, shewed the cause of his death. [19] For the dreams that troubled them did foreshew this, lest they should perish, and not know why they were afflicted. [20] Yea, the tasting of death touched the righteous also, and there was a destruction of the multitude in the wilderness: but the wrath endured not long. [21] For then the blameless man made haste, and stood forth to defend them; and bringing the shield of his proper ministry, even prayer, and the propitiation of incense, set himself against the wrath, and so brought the calamity to an end, declaring that he was thy servant. [22] So he overcame the destroyer, not with strength of body, nor force of arms, but with a word subdued him that punished, alleging the oaths and covenants made with the fathers. [23] For when the dead were now fallen down by heaps one upon another, standing between, he stayed the wrath, and parted the way to the living. [24] For in the long garment was the whole world, and in the four rows of the stones was the glory of the fathers graven, and thy Majesty upon the daidem of his head. [25] Unto these the destroyer gave place, and was afraid of them: for it was enough that they only tasted of the wrath.

Wis.19

[1] As for the ungodly, wrath came upon them without mercy unto the end: for he knew before what they would do; [2] How that having given them leave to depart, and sent them hastily away, they would repent and pursue them.

[3] For whilst they were yet mourning and making lamentation at the graves of the dead, they added another foolish device, and pursued them as fugitives, whom they had intreated to be gone. [4] For the destiny, whereof they were worthy, drew them unto this end, and made them forget the things that had already happened, that they might fulfil the punishment which was wanting to their torments:

[5] And that thy people might pass a wonderful way: but they might find a strange death. [6] For the whole creature in his proper kind was fashioned again anew, serving the peculiar commandments that were given unto them, that thy children might be kept without hurt: [7] As namely, a cloud shadowing the camp; and where water stood before, dry land appeared; and out of the Red sea a way without impediment; and out of the violent stream a green field: [8] Wherethrough all the people went that were defended with thy hand, seeing thy marvellous strange wonders. [9] For they went at large like horses, and leaped like lambs, praising thee, O Lord, who hadst delivered them. [10] For they were yet mindful of the things that were done while they sojourned in the strange land, how the ground brought forth flies instead of cattle, and how the river cast up a multitude of frogs instead of fishes. [11] But afterwards they saw a new generation of fowls, when, being led with their appetite, they asked delicate meats. [12] For quails came up unto them from the sea for their contentment. [13] And punishments came upon the sinners not without former signs by the force of thunders: for they suffered justly according to their own wickedness, insomuch as they used a more hard and hateful behaviour toward strangers. [14] For the Sodomites did not receive those, whom they knew not when they came: but these brought friends into bondage, that had well deserved of them. [15] And not only so, but peradventure some respect shall be had of those, because they used strangers not friendly: [16] But these very grievously afflicted them, whom they had received with feastings, and were already made partakers of the same laws with them. [17] Therefore even with blindness were these stricken, as those were at the doors of the righteous man: when, being compassed about with horrible great darkness, every one sought the passage of his own doors. [18] For the elements were changed in themselves by a kind of harmony, like as in a psaltery notes change the name of the tune, and yet are always sounds; which may well be perceived by the sight of the things that have been done. [19] For earthly things were turned into watery, and the things, that before swam in the water, now went upon the ground. [20] The fire had power in the water, forgetting his own virtue: and the water forgat his own quenching nature. [21] On the other side, the flames wasted not the flesh of the corruptible living things, though they walked therein; neither melted they the icy kind of heavenly meat that was of nature apt to melt. [22] For in all things, O Lord, thou didst magnify thy people, and glorify them, neither didst thou lightly regard them: but didst assist them in every time and place.

PROLOGUE TO WISDOM OF JESUS SON OF SIRACH

before in manners to live after the law.

[A Prologue made by an uncertain Author]

This Jesus was the son of Sirach, and grandchild to Jesus of the same name with him: this man therefore lived in the latter times, after the people had been led away captive, and called home a again, and almost after all the prophets. Now his grandfather Jesus, as he himself witnesseth, was a man of great diligence and wisdom among the Hebrews, who did not only gather the grave and short sentences of wise men, that had been before him, but himself also uttered some of his own, full of much understanding and wisdom. When as therefore the first Jesus died, leaving this book almost perfected, Sirach his son receiving it after him left it to his own son Jesus, who, having gotten it into his hands, compiled it all orderly into one volume, and called it Wisdom, intituling it both by his own name, his father's name, and his grandfather's; alluring the hearer by the very name of Wisdom to have a greater love to the study of this book. It containeth therefore wise sayings, dark sentences, and parables, and certain particular ancient godly stories of men that pleased God; also his prayer and song; moreover, what benefits God had vouchsafed his people, and what plagues he had heaped upon their enemies. This Jesus did imitate Solomon, and was no less famous for wisdom and learning, both being indeed a man of great learning, and so reputed also

Whereas many and great things have been delivered unto us by the law and the prophets, and by others that have followed their steps, for the which things Israel ought to be commended for learning and wisdom; and whereof not only the readers must needs become skilful themselves, but also they that desire to learn be able to profit them which are without, both by speaking and writing: my grandfather Jesus, when he had much given himself to the reading of the law, and the prophets, and other books of our fathers, and had gotten therein good judgment, was drawn on also himself to write something pertaining to learning and wisdom; to the intent that those which are desirous to learn, and are addicted to these things, might profit much more in living according to the law. Wherefore let me intreat you to read it with favour and attention, and to pardon us, wherein we may seem to come short of some words, which we have laboured to interpret. For the same things uttered in Hebrew, and translated into another tongue, have not the same force in them: and not only these things, but the law itself, and the prophets, and the rest of the books, have no small difference, when they are spoken in their own language. For in the eight and thirtieth year coming into Egypt, when Euergetes was king, and continuing there some time, I found a book of no small learning: therefore I thought it most necessary for me to bestow some diligence and travail to interpret it; using great watchfulness and skill in that space to bring the book to an end, and set it forth for them also, which in a strange country are willing to learn, being prepared

WISDOM OF JESUS SON OF SIRACH

Sir.1

[1] All wisdom cometh from the Lord, and is with him for ever. [2] Who can number the sand of the sea, and the drops of rain, and the days of eternity? [3] Who can find out the height of heaven, and the breadth of the earth, and the deep, and wisdom? [4] Wisdom hath been created before all things, and the understanding of prudence from everlasting. [5] The word of God most high is the fountain of wisdom; and her ways are everlasting commandments. [6] To whom hath the root of wisdom been revealed? or who hath known her wise counsels? [7] [Unto whom hath the knowledge of wisdom been made manifest? and who hath understood her great experience?] [8] There is one wise and greatly to be feared, the Lord sitting upon his throne. [9] He created her, and saw her, and numbered her, and poured her out upon all his works. [10] She is with all flesh according to his gift, and he hath given her to them that love him. [11] The fear of the Lord is honour, and glory, and gladness, and a crown of rejoicing. [12] The fear of the Lord maketh a merry heart, and giveth joy, and gladness, and a long life. [13] Whoso feareth the Lord, it shall go well with him at the last, and he shall find favour in the day of his death. [14] To fear the Lord is the beginning of wisdom: and it was created with the faithful in the womb. [15] She hath built an everlasting foundation with men, and she shall continue with their seed. [16] To fear the Lord is fulness of wisdom, and filleth men with her fruits. [17] She filleth all their house with things desirable, and the garners with her increase. [18] The fear of the Lord is a crown of wisdom, making peace and perfect health to flourish; both which are the gifts of God: and it enlargeth their rejoicing that love him. [19] Wisdom raineth down skill and knowledge of understanding standing, and exalteth them to honour that hold her fast. [20] The root of wisdom is to fear the Lord, and the branches thereof are long life. [21] The fear of the Lord driveth away sins: and where it is present, it turneth away wrath. [22] A furious man cannot be justified; for the sway of his fury shall be his destruction. [23] A patient man will tear for a time, and afterward joy shall spring up unto him. [24] He will hide his words for a time, and the lips of many shall declare his wisdom. [25] The parables of knowledge are in the treasures of wisdom: but godliness is an abomination to a sinner. [26] If thou desire wisdom, keep the commandments, and the Lord shall give her unto thee. [27] For the fear of the Lord is wisdom and instruction: and faith and meekness are his delight. [28] Distrust not the fear of the Lord when thou art poor: and come not unto him with a double heart. [29] Be not an hypocrite in the sight of men, and take good heed what thou speakest. [30] Exalt not thyself, lest thou fall, and bring dishonour upon thy soul, and so God discover thy secrets, and cast thee down in the midst of the congregation, because thou camest not in truth to the fear of the Lord, but thy heart is full of deceit.

Sir.2

[1] My son, if thou come to serve the Lord, prepare thy soul for temptation. [2] Set thy heart aright, and constantly endure, and make not haste in time of trouble. [3] Cleave unto him, and depart not away, that thou mayest be increased at thy last end. [4] Whatsoever is brought upon thee take cheerfully, and be patient when thou art changed to a low estate. [5] For gold is tried in the fire, and acceptable men in the furnace of adversity. [6] Believe in him, and he will help thee; order thy way aright, and trust in him. [7] Ye that fear the Lord, wait for his mercy; and go not aside, lest ye fall. [8] Ye that fear the Lord, believe him; and your reward shall not fail. [9] Ye that fear the Lord, hope for good, and for everlasting joy and mercy. [10] Look at the generations of old, and see; did ever any trust in the Lord, and was confounded? or did any abide in his fear, and was forsaken? or whom did he ever despise, that called upon him? [11] For the Lord is full of compassion and mercy, longsuffering, and very pitiful, and forgiveth sins, and saveth in time of affliction. [12] Woe be to fearful hearts, and faint hands, and the sinner that goeth two ways!

[13] Woe unto him that is fainthearted! for he believeth not; therefore shall he not be defended. [14] Woe unto you that have lost patience! and what will ye do when the Lord shall visit you? [15] They that fear the Lord will not disobey his Word; and they that love him will keep his ways. [16] They that fear the Lord will seek that which is well, pleasing unto him; and they that love him shall be filled with the law. [17] They that fear the Lord will prepare their hearts, and humble their souls in his sight, [18] Saying, We will fall into the hands of the Lord, and not into the hands of men: for as his majesty is, so is his mercy.

Sir.3

[1] Hear me your father, O children, and do thereafter, that ye may be safe. [2] For the Lord hath given the father honour over the children, and hath confirmed the authority of the mother over the sons. [3] Whoso honoureth his father maketh an atonement for his sins: [4] And he that honoureth his mother is as one that layeth up treasure. [5] Whoso honoureth his father shall have joy of his own children; and when he maketh his prayer, he shall be heard.

[6] He that honoureth his father shall have a long life; and he that is obedient unto the Lord shall be a comfort to his mother. [7] He that feareth the Lord will honour his father, and will do service unto his parents, as to his masters. [8] Honour thy father and mother both in word and deed, that a blessing may come upon thee from them. [9] For the blessing of the father establisheth the houses of children; but the curse of the mother rooteth out foundations. [10] Glory not in the dishonour of thy father; for thy father's dishonour is no glory unto thee. [11] For the glory of a man is from the honour of his father; and a mother in dishonour is a reproach to the children. [12] My son, help thy father in his age, and grieve him not as long as he liveth.

[13] And if his understanding fail, have patience with him; and despise him not when thou art in thy full strength. [14] For the relieving of thy father shall not be forgotten: and instead of sins it shall be added to build thee up. [15] In

the day of thine affliction it shall be remembered; thy sins also shall melt away, as the ice in the fair warm weather. [16] He that forsaketh his father is as a blasphemer; and he that angereth his mother is cursed: of God. [17] My son, go on with thy business in meekness; so shalt thou be beloved of him that is approved. [18] The greater thou art, the more humble thyself, and thou shalt find favour before the Lord. [19] Many are in high place, and of renown: but mysteries are revealed unto the meek. [20] For the power of the Lord is great, and he is honoured of the lowly. [21] Seek not out things that are too hard for thee, neither search the things that are above thy strength. [22] But what is commanded thee, think thereupon with reverence, for it is not needful for thee to see with thine eyes the things that are in secret. [23] Be not curious in unnecessary matters: for more things are shewed unto thee than men understand. [24] For many are deceived by their own vain opinion; and an evil suspicion hath overthrown their judgment. [25] Without eyes thou shalt want light: profess not the knowledge therefore that thou hast not. [26] A stubborn heart shall fare evil at the last; and he that loveth danger shall perish therein. [27] An obstinate heart shall be laden with sorrows; and the wicked man shall heap sin upon sin. [28] In the punishment of the proud there is no remedy; for the plant of wickedness hath taken root in him.

[29] The heart of the prudent will understand a parable; and an attentive ear is the desire of a wise man. [30] Water will quench a flaming fire; and alms maketh an atonement for sins. [31] And he that requiteth good turns is mindful of that which may come hereafter; and when he falleth, he shall find a stay.

Sir.4

[1] My son, defraud not the poor of his living, and make not the needy eyes to wait long. [2] Make not an hungry soul sorrowful; neither provoke a man in his distress. [3] Add not more trouble to an heart that is vexed; and defer not to give to him that is in need. [4] Reject not the supplication of the afflicted; neither turn away thy face from a poor man. [5] Turn not away thine eye from the needy, and give him none occasion to curse thee: [6] For if he curse thee in the bitterness of his soul, his prayer shall be heard of him that made him. [7] Get thyself the love of the congregation, and bow thy head to a great man. [8] Let it not grieve thee to bow down thine ear to the poor, and give him a friendly answer with meekness. [9] Deliver him that suffereth wrong from the hand of the oppressor; and be not fainthearted when thou sittest in judgment. [10] Be as a father unto the fatherless, and instead of an husband unto their mother: so shalt thou be as the son of the most High, and he shall love thee more than thy mother doth. [11] Wisdom exalteth her children, and layeth hold of them that seek her. [12] He that loveth her loveth life; and they that seek to her early shall be filled with joy. [13] He that holdeth her fast shall inherit glory; and wheresoever she entereth, the Lord will bless. [14] They that serve her shall minister to the Holy One: and them that love her the Lord doth love. [15] Whoso giveth ear unto her shall judge the nations: and he that attendeth unto her shall dwell securely.

[16] If a man commit himself unto her, he shall inherit her; and his generation shall hold her in possession. [17] For at the first she will walk with him by crooked ways, and bring fear and dread upon him, and torment him with her discipline, until she may trust his soul, and try him by her laws. [18] Then will she return the straight way unto him, and comfort him, and shew him her secrets. [19] But if he go wrong, she will forsake him, and give him over to his own ruin. [20] Observe the opportunity, and beware of evil; and be not ashamed when it concerneth thy soul. [21] For there is a shame that bringeth sin; and there is a shame which is glory and grace. [22] Accept no person against thy soul, and let not the reverence of any man cause thee to fall. [23] And refrain not to speak, when there is occasion to do good, and hide not thy wisdom in her beauty. [24] For by speech wisdom shall be known: and learning by the word of the tongue. [25] In no wise speak against the truth; but be abashed of the error of thine ignorance. [26] Be not ashamed to confess thy sins; and force not the course of the river. [27] Make not thyself an underling to a foolish man; neither accept the person of the mighty. [28] Strive for the truth unto death, and the Lord shall fight for thee. [29] Be not hasty in thy tongue, and in thy deeds slack and remiss. [30] Be not as a lion in thy house, nor frantick among thy servants. [31] Let not thine hand be stretched out to receive, and shut when thou shouldest repay.

Sir.5

[1] Set thy heart upon thy goods; and say not, I have enough for my life. [2] Follow not thine own mind and thy strength, to walk in the ways of thy heart: [3] And say not, Who shall controul me for my works? for the Lord will surely revenge thy pride. [4] Say not, I have sinned, and what harm hath happened unto me? for the Lord is longsuffering, he will in no wise let thee go. [5] Concerning propitiation, be not without fear to add sin unto sin: [6] And say not His mercy is great; he will be pacified for the multitude of my sins: for mercy and wrath come from him, and his indignation resteth upon sinners. [7] Make no tarrying to turn to the Lord, and put not off from day to day: for suddenly shall the wrath of the Lord come forth, and in thy security thou shalt be destroyed, and perish in the day of vengeance. [8] Set not thine heart upon goods unjustly gotten, for they shall not profit thee in the day of calamity. [9] Winnow not with every wind, and go not into every way: for so doth the sinner that hath a double tongue.

[10] Be stedfast in thy understanding; and let thy word be the same. [11] Be swift to hear; and let thy life be sincere; and with patience give answer. [12] If thou hast understanding, answer thy neighbour; if not, lay thy hand upon thy mouth. [13] Honour and shame is in talk: and the tongue of man is his fall. [14] Be not called a whisperer, and lie not in wait with thy tongue: for a foul shame is upon the thief, and an evil condemnation upon the double tongue. [15] Be not ignorant of any thing in a great matter or a small.

Sir.6

[1] Instead of a friend become not an enemy; for [thereby] thou shalt inherit an ill name, shame, and reproach: even so

shall a sinner that hath a double tongue. [2] Extol not thyself in the counsel of thine own heart; that thy soul be not torn in pieces as a bull [straying alone.] [3] Thou shalt eat up thy leaves, and lose thy fruit, and leave thyself as a dry tree. [4] A wicked soul shall destroy him that hath it, and shall make him to be laughed to scorn of his enemies. [5] Sweet language will multiply friends: and a fairspeaking tongue will increase kind greetings. [6] Be in peace with many: nevertheless have but one counsellor of a thousand. [7] If thou wouldest get a friend, prove him first and be not hasty to credit him. [8] For some man is a friend for his own occasion, and will not abide in the day of thy trouble. [9] And there is a friend, who being turned to enmity, and strife will discover thy reproach. [10] Again, some friend is a companion at the table, and will not continue in the day of thy affliction. [11] But in thy prosperity he will be as thyself, and will be bold over thy servants. [12] If thou be brought low, he will be against thee, and will hide himself from thy face. [13] Separate thyself from thine enemies, and take heed of thy friends. [14] A faithfull friend is a strong defence: and he that hath found such an one hath found a treasure. [15] Nothing doth countervail a faithful friend, and his excellency is invaluable. [16] A faithful friend is the medicine of life; and they that fear the Lord shall find him. [17] Whoso feareth the Lord shall direct his friendship aright: for as he is, so shall his neighbour be also.

[18] My son, gather instruction from thy youth up: so shalt thou find wisdom till thine old age. [19] Come unto her as one that ploweth and soweth, and wait for her good fruits: for thou shalt not toil much in labouring about her, but thou shalt eat of her fruits right soon. [20] She is very unpleasant to the unlearned: he that is without understanding will not remain with her. [21] She will lie upon him as a mighty stone of trial; and he will cast her from him ere it be long. [22] For wisdom is according to her name, and she is not manifest unto many. [23] Give ear, my son, receive my advice, and refuse not my counsel, [24] And put thy feet into her fetters, and thy neck into her chain. [25] Bow down thy shoulder, and bear her, and be not grieved with her bonds. [26] Come unto her with thy whole heart, and keep her ways with all thy power. [27] Search, and seek, and she shall be made known unto thee: and when thou hast got hold of her, let her not go. [28] For at the last thou shalt find her rest, and that shall be turned to thy joy. [29] Then shall her fetters be a strong defence for thee, and her chains a robe of glory. [30] For there is a golden ornament upon her, and her bands are purple lace. [31] Thou shalt put her on as a robe of honour, and shalt put her about thee as a crown of joy. [32] My son, if thou wilt, thou shalt be taught: and if thou wilt apply thy mind, thou shalt be prudent. [33] If thou love to hear, thou shalt receive understanding: and if thou bow thine ear, thou shalt be wise, [34] Stand in the multitude of the elders; and cleave unto him that is wise. [35] Be willing to hear every godly discourse; and let not the parables of understanding escape thee. [36] And if thou seest a man of understanding, get thee betimes unto him, and let thy foot wear the steps of his door. [37] Let thy mind be upon the ordinances of the Lord and meditate continually in his commandments: he shall establish thine

heart, and give thee wisdom at thine owns desire.

Sir.7

[1] Do no evil, so shall no harm come unto thee. [2] Depart from the unjust, and iniquity shall turn away from thee. [3] My son, sow not upon the furrows of unrighteousness, and thou shalt not reap them sevenfold. [4] Seek not of the Lord preeminence, neither of the king the seat of honour. [5] justify not thyself before the Lord; and boast not of thy wisdom before the king. [6] Seek not to be judge, being not able to take away iniquity; lest at any time thou fear the person of the mighty, an stumblingblock in the way of thy uprightness. [7] Offend not against the multitude of a city, and then thou shalt not cast thyself down among the people. [8] Bind not one sin upon another; for in one thou shalt not be unpunished. [9] Say not, God will look upon the multitude of my oblations, and when I offer to the most high God, he will accept it. [10] Be not fainthearted when thou makest thy prayer, and neglect not to give alms. [11] Laugh no man to scorn in the bitterness of his soul: for there is one which humbleth and exalteth. [12] Devise not a lie against thy brother; neither do the like to thy friend. [13] Use not to make any manner of lie: for the custom thereof is not good. [14] Use not many words in a multitude of elders, and make not much babbling when thou prayest. [15] Hate not laborious work, neither husbandry, which the most High hath ordained. [16] Number not thyself among the multitude of sinners, but remember that wrath will not tarry long. [17] Humble thyself greatly: for the vengeance of the ungodly is fire and worms. [18] Change not a friend for any good by no means; neither a faithful brother for the gold of Ophir. [19] Forego not a wise and good woman: for her grace is above gold. [20] Whereas thy servant worketh truly, entreat him not evil. nor the hireling that bestoweth himself wholly for thee. [21] Let thy soul love a good servant, and defraud him not of liberty. [22] Hast thou cattle? have an eye to them: and if they be for thy profit, keep them with thee. [23] Hast thou children? instruct them, and bow down their neck from their youth. [24] Hast thou daughters? have a care of their body, and shew not thyself cheerful toward them. [25] Marry thy daughter, and so shalt thou have performed a weighty matter: but give her to a man of understanding. [26] Hast thou a wife after thy mind? forsake her not: but give not thyself over to a light woman.

[27] Honour thy father with thy whole heart, and forget not the sorrows of thy mother. [28] Remember that thou wast begotten of them; and how canst thou recompense them the things that they have done for thee? [29] Fear the Lord with all thy soul, and reverence his priests. [30] Love him that made thee with all thy strength, and forsake not his ministers. [31] Fear the Lord, and honor the priest; and give him his portion, as it is commanded thee; the firstfruits, and the trespass offering, and the gift of the shoulders, and the sacrifice of sanctification, and the firstfruits of the holy things. [32] And stretch thine hand unto the poor, that thy blessing may be perfected. [33] A gift hath grace in the sight of every man living; and for the dead detain it not. [34] Fail not to be with them that weep, and mourn with them that mourn. [35] Be not slow to visit

the sick: fir that shall make thee to be beloved. [36] Whatsoever thou takest in hand, remember the end, and thou shalt never do amiss.

Sir.8

[1] Strive not with a mighty man' lest thou fall into his hands. [2] Be not at variance with a rich man, lest he overweigh thee: for gold hath destroyed many, and perverted the hearts of kings. [3] Strive not with a man that is full of tongue, and heap not wood upon his fire. [4] Jest not with a rude man, lest thy ancestors be disgraced. [5] Reproach not a man that turneth from sin, but remember that we are all worthy of punishment. [6] Dishonour not a man in his old age: for even some of us wax old. [7] Rejoice not over thy greatest enemy being dead, but remember that we die all. [8] Despise not the discourse of the wise, but acquaint thyself with their proverbs: for of them thou shalt learn instruction, and how to serve great men with ease. [9] Miss not the discourse of the elders: for they also learned of their fathers, and of them thou shalt learn understanding, and to give answer as need requireth. [10] Kindle not the coals of a sinner, lest thou be burnt with the flame of his fire. [11] Rise not up [in anger] at the presence of an injurious person, lest he lie in wait to entrap thee in thy words [12] Lend not unto him that is mightier than thyself; for if thou lendest him, count it but lost. [13] Be not surety above thy power: for if thou be surety, take care to pay it. [14] Go not to law with a judge; for they will judge for him according to his honour. [15] Travel not by the way with a bold fellow, lest he become grievous unto thee: for he will do according to his own will, and thou shalt perish with him through his folly. [16] Strive not with an angry man, and go not with him into a solitary place: for blood is as nothing in his sight, and where there is no help, he will overthrow thee. [17] Consult not with a fool; for he cannot keep counsel. [18] Do no secret thing before a stranger; for thou knowest not what he will bring forth. [19] Open not thine heart to every man, lest he requite thee with a shrewd turn.

Sir.9

[1] Be not jealous over the wife of thy bosom, and teach her not an evil lesson against thyself. [2] Give not thy soul unto a woman to set her foot upon thy substance. [3] Meet not with an harlot, lest thou fall into her snares. [4] Use not much the company of a woman that is a singer, lest thou be taken with her attempts. [5] Gaze not on a maid, that thou fall not by those things that are precious in her. [6] Give not thy soul unto harlots, that thou lose not thine inheritance. [7] Look not round about thee in the streets of the city, neither wander thou in the solitary place thereof. [8] Turn away thine eye from a beautiful woman, and look not upon another's beauty; for many have been deceived by the beauty of a woman; for herewith love is kindled as a fire. [9] Sit not at all with another man's wife, nor sit down with her in thine arms, and spend not thy money with her at the wine; lest thine heart incline unto her, and so through thy desire thou fall into destruction. [10] Forsake not an old friend; for the new is not comparable to him: a new friend is as new wine; when it is old, thou shalt drink it with

pleasure. [11] Envy not the glory of a sinner: for thou knowest not what shall be his end. [12] Delight not in the thing that the ungodly have pleasure in; but remember they shall not go unpunished unto their grave. [13] Keep thee far from the man that hath power to kill; so shalt thou not doubt the fear of death: and if thou come unto him, make no fault, lest he take away thy life presently: remember that thou goest in the midst of snares, and that thou walkest upon the battlements of the city. [14] As near as thou canst, guess at thy neighbour, and consult with the wise. [15] Let thy talk be with the wise, and all thy communication in the law of the most High. [16] And let just men eat and drink with thee; and let thy glorying be in the fear of the Lord. [17] For the hand of the artificer the work shall be commended: and the wise ruler of the people for his speech. [18] A man of an ill tongue is dangerous in his city; and he that is rash in his talk shall be hated.

Sir.10

[1] A wise judge will instruct his people; and the government of a prudent man is well ordered. [2] As the judge of the people is himself, so are his officers; and what manner of man the ruler of the city is, such are all they that dwell therein. [3] An unwise king destroyeth his people; but through the prudence of them which are in authority the city shall be inhabited. [4] The power of the earth is in the hand of the Lord, and in due time he will set over it one that is profitable. [5] In the hand of God is the prosperity of man: and upon the person of the scribe shall he lay his honour. [6] Bear not hatred to thy neighbour for every wrong; and do nothing at all by injurious practices. [7] Pride is hateful before God and man: and by both doth one commit iniquity. [8] Because of unrighteous dealings, injuries, and riches got by deceit, the kingdom is translated from one people to another. [9] Why is earth and ashes proud? There is not a more wicked thing than a covetous man: for such an one setteth his own soul to sale; because while he liveth he casteth away his bowels. [10] The physician cutteth off a long disease; and he that is to day a king to morrow shall die. [11] For when a man is dead, he shall inherit creeping things, beasts, and worms. [12] The beginning of pride is when one departeth from God, and his heart is turned away from his Maker. [13] For pride is the beginning of sin, and he that hath it shall pour out abomination: and therefore the Lord brought upon them strange calamities, and overthrew them utterly. [14] The Lord hath cast down the thrones of proud princes, and set up the meek in their stead. [15] The Lord hath plucked up the roots of the proud nations, and planted the lowly in their place. [16] The Lord overthrew countries of the heathen, and destroyed them to the foundations of the earth. [17] He took some of them away, and destroyed them, and hath made their memorial to cease from the earth. [18] Pride was not made for men, nor furious anger for them that are born of a woman. [19] They that fear the Lord are a sure seed, and they that love him an honourable plant: they that regard not the law are a dishonourable seed; they that transgress the commandments are a deceivable seed. [20] Among brethren he that is chief is honorable; so are they that fear the Lord in his eyes. [21] The fear of the Lord goeth before the obtaining of authority: but

roughness and pride is the losing thereof. [22] Whether he be rich, noble, or poor, their glory is the fear of the Lord. [23] It is not meet to despise the poor man that hath understanding; neither is it convenient to magnify a sinful man. [24] Great men, and judges, and potentates, shall be honoured; yet is there none of them greater than he that feareth the Lord. [25] Unto the servant that is wise shall they that are free do service: and he that hath knowledge will not grudge when he is reformed. [26] Be not overwise in doing thy business; and boast not thyself in the time of thy distress. [27] Better is he that laboureth, and aboundeth in all things, than he that boasteth himself, and wanteth bread. [28] My son, glorify thy soul in meekness, and give it honour according to the dignity thereof. [29] Who will justify him that sinneth against his own soul? and who will honour him that dishonoureth his own life? [30] The poor man is honoured for his skill, and the rich man is honoured for his riches. [31] He that is honoured in poverty, how much more in riches? and he that is dishonourable in riches, how much more in poverty?

Sir.11

[1] Wisdom lifteth up the head of him that is of low degree, and maketh him to sit among great men. [2] Commend not a man for his beauty; neither abhor a man for his outward appearance. [3] The bee is little among such as fly; but her fruit is the chief of sweet things. [4] Boast not of thy clothing and raiment, and exalt not thyself in the day of honour: for the works of the Lord are wonderful, and his works among men are hidden. [5] Many kings have sat down upon the ground; and one that was never thought of hath worn the crown. [6] Many mighty men have been greatly disgraced; and the honourable delivered into other men's hands. [7] Blame not before thou hast examined the truth: understand first, and then rebuke. [8] Answer not before thou hast heard the cause: neither interrupt men in the midst of their talk. [9] Strive not in a matter that concerneth thee not; and sit not in judgment with sinners. [10] My son, meddle not with many matters: for if thou meddle much, thou shalt not be innocent; and if thou follow after, thou shalt not obtain, neither shalt thou escape by fleeing. [11] There is one that laboureth, and taketh pains, and maketh haste, and is so much the more behind. [12] Again, there is another that is slow, and hath need of help, wanting ability, and full of poverty; yet the eye of the Lord looked upon him for good, and set him up from his low estate, [13] And lifted up his head from misery; so that many that saw from him is peace over all the [14] Prosperity and adversity, life and death, poverty and riches, come of the Lord. [15] Wisdom, knowledge, and understanding of the law, are of the Lord: love, and the way of good works, are from him. [16] Error and darkness had their beginning together with sinners: and evil shall wax old with them that glory therein. [17] The gift of the Lord remaineth with the ungodly, and his favour bringeth prosperity for ever. [18] There is that waxeth rich by his wariness and pinching, and this his the portion of his reward: [19] Whereas he saith, I have found rest, and now will eat continually of my goods; and yet he knoweth not what time shall come upon him, and that he must leave

those things to others, and die. [20] Be stedfast in thy covenant, and be conversant therein, and wax old in thy work. [21] Marvel not at the works of sinners; but trust in the Lord, and abide in thy labour: for it is an easy thing in the sight of the Lord on the sudden to make a poor man rich. [22] The blessing of the Lord is in the reward of the godly, and suddenly he maketh his blessing flourish. [23] Say not, What profit is there of my service? and what good things shall I have hereafter? [24] Again, say not, I have enough, and possess many things, and what evil shall I have hereafter? [25] In the day of prosperity there is a forgetfulness of affliction: and in the day of affliction there is no more remembrance of prosperity. [26] For it is an easy thing unto the Lord in the day of death to reward a man according to his ways. [27] The affliction of an hour maketh a man forget pleasure: and in his end his deeds shall be discovered. [28] Judge none blessed before his death: for a man shall be known in his children. [29] Bring not every man into thine house: for the deceitful man hath many trains. [30] Like as a partridge taken [and kept] in a cage, so is the heart of the proud; and like as a spy, watcheth he for thy fall: [31] For he lieth in wait, and turneth good into evil, and in things worthy praise will lay blame upon thee. [32] Of a spark of fire a heap of coals is kindled: and a sinful man layeth wait for blood. [33] Take heed of a mischievous man, for he worketh wickedness; lest he bring upon thee a perpetual blot. [34] Receive a stranger into thine house, and he will disturb thee, and turn thee out of thine own.

Sir.12

[1] When thou wilt do good know to whom thou doest it; so shalt thou be thanked for thy benefits. [2] Do good to the godly man, and thou shalt find a recompence; and if not from him, yet from the most High. [3] There can no good come to him that is always occupied in evil, nor to him that giveth no alms. [4] Give to the godly man, and help not a sinner. [5] Do well unto him that is lowly, but give not to the ungodly: hold back thy bread, and give it not unto him, lest he overmaster thee thereby: for [else] thou shalt receive twice as much evil for all the good thou shalt have done unto him. [6] For the most High hateth sinners, and will repay vengeance unto the ungodly, and keepeth them against the mighty day of their punishment. [7] Give unto the good, and help not the sinner. [8] A friend cannot be known in prosperity: and an enemy cannot be hidden in adversity. [9] In the prosperity of a man enemies will be grieved: but in his adversity even a friend will depart. [10] Never trust thine enemy: for like as iron rusteth, so is his wickedness. [11] Though he humble himself, and go crouching, yet take good heed and beware of him, and thou shalt be unto him as if thou hadst wiped a lookingglass, and thou shalt know that his rust hath not been altogether wiped away. [12] Set him not by thee, lest, when he hath overthrown thee, he stand up in thy place; neither let him sit at thy right hand, lest he seek to take thy seat, and thou at the last remember my words, and be pricked therewith. [13] Who will pity a charmer that is bitten with a serpent, or any such as come nigh wild beasts? [14] So one that goeth to a sinner, and is defiled with him in his sins, who will

pity? [15] For a while he will abide with thee, but if thou begin to fall, he will not tarry. [16] An enemy speaketh sweetly with his lips, but in his heart he imagineth how to throw thee into a pit: he will weep with his eyes, but if he find opportunity, he will not be satisfied with blood. [17] If adversity come upon thee, thou shalt find him there first; and though he pretend to help thee, yet shall he undermine thee. [18] He will shake his head, and clap his hands, and whisper much, and change his countenance.

Sir.13

[1] He that toucheth pitch shall be defiled therewith; and he that hath fellowship with a proud man shall be like unto him. [2] Burden not thyself above thy power while thou livest; and have no fellowship with one that is mightier and richer than thyself: for how agree the kettle and the earthen pot together? for if the one be smitten against the other, it shall be broken. [3] The rich man hath done wrong, and yet he threateneth withal: the poor is wronged, and he must intreat also. [4] If thou be for his profit, he will use thee: but if thou have nothing, he will forsake thee. [5] If thou have any thing, he will live with thee: yea, he will make thee bare, and will not be sorry for it. [6] If he have need of thee, he will deceive thee, and smile upon thee, and put thee in hope; he will speak thee fair, and say, What wantest thou? [7] And he will shame thee by his meats, until he have drawn thee dry twice or thrice, and at the last he will laugh thee to scorn afterward, when he seeth thee, he will forsake thee, and shake his head at thee. [8] Beware that thou be not deceived and brought down in thy jollity. [9] If thou be invited of a mighty man, withdraw thyself, and so much the more will he invite thee. [10] Press thou not upon him, lest thou be put back; stand not far off, lest thou be forgotten. [11] Affect not to be made equal unto him in talk, and believe not his many words: for with much communication will he tempt thee, and smiling upon thee will get out thy secrets: [12] But cruelly he will lay up thy words, and will not spare to do thee hurt, and to put thee in prison. [13] Observe, and take good heed, for thou walkest in peril of thy overthrowing: when thou hearest these things, awake in thy sleep. [14] Love the Lord all thy life, and call upon him for thy salvation. [15] Every beast loveth his like, and every man loveth his neighbor. [16] All flesh consorteth according to kind, and a man will cleave to his like. [17] What fellowship hath the wolf with the lamb? so the sinner with the godly. [18] What agreement is there between the hyena and a dog? and what peace between the rich and the poor? [19] As the wild ass is the lion's prey in the wilderness: so the rich eat up the poor. [20] As the proud hate humility: so doth the rich abhor the poor. [21] A rich man beginning to fall is held up of his friends: but a poor man being down is thrust away by his friends. [22] When a rich man is fallen, he hath many helpers: he speaketh things not to be spoken, and yet men justify him: the poor man slipped, and yet they rebuked him too; he spake wisely, and could have no place. [23] When a rich man speaketh, every man holdeth his tongue, and, look, what he saith, they extol it to the clouds: but if the poor man speak, they say, What fellow is this? and if he stumble, they will help to overthrow him. [24] Riches are good unto him that hath no sin, and poverty is evil in the mouth of the ungodly. [25] The heart of a man changeth his countenance, whether it be for good or evil: and a merry heart maketh a cheerful countenance. [26] A cheerful countenance is a token of a heart that is in prosperity; and the finding out of parables is a wearisome labour of the mind.

Sir.14

[1] Blessed is the man that hath not slipped with his mouth, and is not pricked with the multitude of sins. [2] Blessed is he whose conscience hath not condemned him, and who is not fallen from his hope in the Lord. [3] Riches are not comely for a niggard: and what should an envious man do with money? [4] He that gathereth by defrauding his own soul gathereth for others, that shall spend his goods riotously. [5] He that is evil to himself, to whom will he be good? he shall not take pleasure in his goods. [6] There is none worse than he that envieth himself; and this is a recompence of his wickedness. [7] And if he doeth good, he doeth it unwillingly; and at the last he will declare his wickedness. [8] The envious man hath a wicked eye; he turneth away his face, and despiseth men. [9] A covetous man's eye is not satisfied with his portion; and the iniquity of the wicked drieth up his soul. [10] A wicked eye envieth [his] bread, and he is a niggard at his table. [11] My son, according to thy ability do good to thyself, and give the Lord his due offering. [12] Remember that death will not be long in coming, and that the covenant of the grave is not shewed unto thee. [13] Do good unto thy friend before thou die, and according to thy ability stretch out thy hand and give to him. [14] Defraud not thyself of the good day, and let not the part of a good desire overpass thee. [15] Shalt thou not leave thy travails unto another? and thy labours to be divided by lot? [16] Give, and take, and sanctify thy soul; for there is no seeking of dainties in the grave. [17] All flesh waxeth old as a garment: for the covenant from the beginning is, Thou shalt die the death. [18] As of the green leaves on a thick tree, some fall, and some grow; so is the generation of flesh and blood, one cometh to an end, and another is born. [19] Every work rotteth and consumeth away, and the worker thereof shall go withal. [20] Blessed is the man that doth meditate good things in wisdom, and that reasoneth of holy things by his understanding. ing. [21] He that considereth her ways in his heart shall also have understanding in her secrets. [22] Go after her as one that traceth, and lie in wait in her ways.

[23] He that prieth in at her windows shall also hearken at her doors. [24] He that doth lodge near her house shall also fasten a pin in her walls. [25] He shall pitch his tent nigh unto her, and shall lodge in a lodging where good things are. [26] He shall set his children under her shelter, and shall lodge under her branches. [27] By her he shall be covered from heat, and in her glory shall he dwell.

Sir.15

[1] He that feareth the Lord will do good, and he that hath the knowledge of the law shall obtain her. [2] And as a mother shall she meet him, and receive him as a wife married of a virgin. [3] With the bread of understanding

shall she feed him, and give him the water of wisdom to drink. [4] He shall be stayed upon her, and shall not be moved; and shall rely upon her, and shall not be confounded. [5] She shall exalt him above his neighbours, and in the midst of the congregation shall she open his mouth. [6] He shall find joy and a crown of gladness, and she shall cause him to inherit an everlasting name. [7] But foolish men shall not attain unto her, and sinners shall not see her. [8] For she is far from pride, and men that are liars cannot remember her. [9] Praise is not seemly in the mouth of a sinner, for it was not sent him of the Lord. [10] For praise shall be uttered in wisdom, and the Lord will prosper it. [11] Say not thou, It is through the Lord that I fell away: for thou oughtest not to do the things that he hateth. [12] Say not thou, He hath caused me to err: for he hath no need of the sinful man. [13] The Lord hateth all abomination; and they that fear God love it not. [14] He himself made man from the beginning, and left him in the hand of his counsel; [15] If thou wilt, to keep the commandments, and to perform acceptable faithfulness. [16] He hath set fire and water before thee: stretch forth thy hand unto whether thou wilt. [17] Before man is life and death; and whether him liketh shall be given him. [18] For the wisdom of the Lord is great, and he is mighty in power, and beholdeth all things: [19] And his eyes are upon them that fear him, and he knoweth every work of man. [20] He hath commanded no man to do wickedly, neither hath he given any man licence to sin.

Sir.16

[1] Desire not a multitude of unprofitable children, neither delight in ungodly sons. [2] Though they multiply, rejoice not in them, except the fear of the Lord be with them. [3] Trust not thou in their life, neither respect their multitude: for one that is just is better than a thousand; and better it is to die without children, than to have them that are ungodly.

[4] For by one that hath understanding shall the city be replenished: but the kindred of the wicked shall speedily become desolate. [5] Many such things have I seen with mine eyes, and mine ear hath heard greater things than these. [6] In the congregation of the ungodly shall a fire be kindled; and in a rebellious nation wrath is set on fire. [7] He was not pacified toward the old giants, who fell away in the strength of their foolishness. [8] Neither spared he the place where Lot sojourned, but abhorred them for their pride. [9] He pitied not the people of perdition, who were taken away in their sins: [10] Nor the six hundred thousand footmen, who were gathered together in the hardness of their hearts. [11] And if there be one stiffnecked among the people, it is marvel if he escape unpunished: for mercy and wrath are with him; he is mighty to forgive, and to pour out displeasure. [12] As his mercy is great, so is his correction also: he judgeth a man according to his works [13] The sinner shall not escape with his spoils: and the patience of the godly shall not be frustrate. [14] Make way for every work of mercy: for every man shall find according to his works. [15] The Lord hardened Pharaoh, that he should not know him, that his powerful works might be known to the world. [16] His mercy is manifest to every creature; and he hath separated his light from the darkness

with an adamant. [17] Say not thou, I will hide myself from the Lord: shall any remember me from above? I shall not be remembered among so many people: for what is my soul among such an infinite number of creatures? [18] Behold, the heaven, and the heaven of heavens, the deep, and the earth, and all that therein is, shall be moved when he shall visit. [19] The mountains also and foundations of the earth be shaken with trembling, when the Lord looketh upon them. [20] No heart can think upon these things worthily: and who is able to conceive his ways? [21] It is a tempest which no man can see: for the most part of his works are hid. [22] Who can declare the works of his justice? or who can endure them? for his covenant is afar off, and the trial of all things is in the end. [23] He that wanteth understanding will think upon vain things: and a foolish man erring imagineth follies. [24] by son, hearken unto me, and learn knowledge, and mark my words with thy heart. [25] I will shew forth doctrine in weight, and declare his knowledge exactly. [26] The works of the Lord are done in judgment from the beginning: and from the time he made them he disposed the parts thereof. [27] He garnished his works for ever, and in his hand are the chief of them unto all generations: they neither labour, nor are weary, nor cease from their works. [28] None of them hindereth another, and they shall never disobey his word. [29] After this the Lord looked upon the earth, and filled it with his blessings.

[30] With all manner of living things hath he covered the face thereof; and they shall return into it again.

Sir.17

[1] The Lord created man of the earth, and turned him into it again. [2] He gave them few days, and a short time, and power also over the things therein. [3] He endued them with strength by themselves, and made them according to his image, [4] And put the fear of man upon all flesh, and gave him dominion over beasts and fowls. [5] They received the use of the five operations of the Lord, and in the sixth place he imparted them understanding, and in the seventh speech, an interpreter of the cogitations thereof.] [6] Counsel, and a tongue, and eyes, ears, and a heart, gave he them to understand. [7] Withal he filled them with the knowledge of understanding, and shewed them good and evil. [8] He set his eye upon their hearts, that he might shew them the greatness of his works. [9] He gave them to glory in his marvellous acts for ever, that they might declare his works with understanding. [10] And the elect shall praise his holy name. [11] Beside this he gave them knowledge, and the law of life for an heritage. [12] He made an everlasting covenant with them, and shewed them his judgments. [13] Their eyes saw the majesty of his glory, and their ears heard his glorious voice. [14] And he said unto them, Beware of all unrighteousness; and he gave every man commandment concerning his neighbour. [15] Their ways are ever before him, and shall not be hid from his eyes. [16] Every man from his youth is given to evil; neither could they make to themselves fleshy hearts for stony. [17] For in the division of the nations of the whole earth he set a ruler over every people; but Israel is the Lord's portion: [18] Whom, being his firstborn, he nourisheth with discipline, and giving him the light of his

love doth not forsake him. [19] Therefore all their works are as the sun before him, and his eyes are continually upon their ways. [20] None of their unrighteous deeds are hid from him, but all their sins are before the Lord [21] But the Lord being gracious and knowing his workmanship, neither left nor forsook them, but spared them. [22] The alms of a man is as a signet with him, and he will keep the good deeds of man as the apple of the eye, and give repentance to his sons and daughters. [23] Afterwards he will rise up and reward them, and render their recompence upon their heads. [24] But unto them that repent, he granted them return, and comforted those that failed in patience. [25] Return unto the Lord, and forsake thy sins, make thy prayer before his face, and offend less. [26] Turn again to the most High, and turn away from iniquity: for he will lead thee out of darkness into the light of health, and hate thou abomination vehemently. [27] Who shall praise the most High in the grave, instead of them which live and give thanks? [28] Thanksgiving perisheth from the dead, as from one that is not: the living and sound in heart shall praise the Lord. [29] How great is the lovingkindness of the Lord our God, and his compassion unto such as turn unto him in holiness! [30] For all things cannot be in men, because the son of man is not immortal. [31] What is brighter than the sun? yet the light thereof faileth; and flesh and blood will imagine evil. [32] He vieweth the power of the height of heaven; and all men are but earth and ashes.

Sir.18

[1] He that liveth for ever Hath created all things in general. [2] The Lord only is righteous, and there is none other but he, [3] Who governeth the world with the palm of his hand, and all things obey his will: for he is the King of all, by his power dividing holy things among them from profane. [4] To whom hath he given power to declare his works? and who shall find out his noble acts? [5] Who shall number the strength of his majesty? and who shall also tell out his mercies? [6] As for the wondrous works of the Lord, there may nothing be taken from them, neither may any thing be put unto them, neither can the ground of them be found out. [7] When a man hath done, then he beginneth; and when he leaveth off, then he shall be doubtful. [8] What is man, and whereto serveth he? what is his good, and what is his evil? [9] The number of a man's days at the most are an hundred years. [10] As a drop of water unto the sea, and a gravelstone in comparison of the sand; so are a thousand years to the days of eternity. [11] Therefore is God patient with them, and poureth forth his mercy upon them. [12] He saw and perceived their end to be evil; therefore he multiplied his compassion. [13] The mercy of man is toward his neighbour; but the mercy of the Lord is upon all flesh: he reproveth, and nurtureth, and teacheth and bringeth again, as a shepherd his flock. [14] He hath mercy on them that receive discipline, and that diligently seek after his judgments. [15] My son, blemish not thy good deeds, neither use uncomfortable words when thou givest any thing. [16] Shall not the dew asswage the heat? so is a word better than a gift. [17] Lo, is not a word better than a gift? but both are with a gracious man. [18] A fool will upbraid churlishly, and a gift of the envious

consumeth the eyes. [19] Learn before thou speak, and use physick or ever thou be sick. [20] Before judgment examine thyself, and in the day of visitation thou shalt find mercy. [21] Humble thyself before thou be sick, and in the time of sins shew repentance. [22] Let nothing hinder thee to pay thy vow in due time, and defer not until death to be justified. [23] Before thou prayest, prepare thyself; and be not as one that tempteth the Lord. [24] Think upon the wrath that shall be at the end, and the time of vengeance, when he shall turn away his face. [25] When thou hast enough, remember the time of hunger: and when thou art rich, think upon poverty and need. [26] From the morning until the evening the time is changed, and all things are soon done before the Lord. [27] A wise man will fear in every thing, and in the day of sinning he will beware of offence: but a fool will not observe time. [28] Every man of understanding knoweth wisdom, and will give praise unto him that found her. [29] They that were of understanding in sayings became also wise themselves, and poured forth exquisite parables. [30] Go not after thy lusts, but refrain thyself from thine appetites. [31] If thou givest thy soul the desires that please her, she will make thee a laughingstock to thine enemies that malign thee. [32] Take not pleasure in much good cheer, neither be tied to the expence thereof. [33] Be not made a beggar by banqueting upon borrowing, when thou hast nothing in thy purse: for thou shalt lie in wait for thine own life, and be talked on.

Sir.19

[1] A labouring man that A is given to drunkenness shall not be rich: and he that contemneth small things shall fall by little and little. [2] Wine and women will make men of understanding to fall away: and he that cleaveth to harlots will become impudent. [3] Moths and worms shall have him to heritage, and a bold man shall be taken away. [4] He that is hasty to give credit is lightminded; and he that sinneth shall offend against his own soul. [5] Whoso taketh pleasure in wickedness shall be condemned: but he that resisteth pleasures crowneth his life. [6] He that can rule his tongue shall live without strife; and he that hateth babbling shall have less evil. [7] Rehearse not unto another that which is told unto thee, and thou shalt fare never the worse. [8] Whether it be to friend or foe, talk not of other men's lives; and if thou canst without offence, reveal them not. [9] For he heard and observed thee, and when time cometh he will hate thee. [10] If thou hast heard a word, let it die with thee; and be bold, it will not burst thee. [11] A fool travaileth with a word, as a woman in labour of a child. [12] As an arrow that sticketh in a man's thigh, so is a word within a fool's belly. [13] Admonish a friend, it may be he hath not done it: and if he have done it, that he do it no more. [14] Admonish thy friend, it may be he hath not said it: and if he have, that he speak it not again. [15] Admonish a friend: for many times it is a slander, and believe not every tale. [16] There is one that slippeth in his speech, but not from his heart; and who is he that hath not offended with his tongue? [17] Admonish thy neighbour before thou threaten him; and not being angry, give place to the law of the most High. [18] The fear of the Lord is the first step to be accepted [of him,] and wisdom obtaineth

his love. [19] The knowledge of the commandments of the Lord is the doctrine of life: and they that do things that please him shall receive the fruit of the tree of immortality.

[20] The fear of the Lord is all wisdom; and in all wisdom is the performance of the law, and the knowledge of his omnipotency. [21] If a servant say to his master, I will not do as it pleaseth thee; though afterward he do it, he angereth him that nourisheth him. [22] The knowledge of wickedness is not wisdom, neither at any time the counsel of sinners prudence. [23] There is a wickedness, and the same an abomination; and there is a fool wanting in wisdom. [24] He that hath small understanding, and feareth God, is better than one that hath much wisdom, and transgresseth the law of the most High. [25] There is an exquisite subtilty, and the same is unjust; and there is one that turneth aside to make judgment appear; and there is a wise man that justifieth in judgment. [26] There is a wicked man that hangeth down his head sadly; but inwardly he is full of deceit, [27] Casting down his countenance, and making as if he heard not: where he is not known, he will do thee a mischief before thou be aware. [28] And if for want of power he be hindered from sinning, yet when he findeth opportunity he will do evil. [29] A man may be known by his look, and one that hath understanding by his countenance, when thou meetest him. [30] A man's attire, and excessive laughter, and gait, shew what he is.

Sir.20

[1] There is a reproof that is not comely: again, some man holdeth his tongue, and he is wise. [2] It is much better to reprove, than to be angry secretly: and he that confesseth his fault shall be preserved from hurt. [3] How good is it, when thou art reproved, to shew repentance! for so shalt thou escape wilful sin. [4] As is the lust of an eunuch to deflower a virgin; so is he that executeth judgment with violence. [5] There is one that keepeth silence, and is found wise: and another by much babbling becometh hateful. [6] Some man holdeth his tongue, because he hath not to answer: and some keepeth silence, knowing his time. [7] A wise man will hold his tongue till he see opportunity: but a babbler and a fool will regard no time. [8] He that useth many words shall be abhorred; and he that taketh to himself authority therein shall be hated. [9] There is a sinner that hath good success in evil things; and there is a gain that turneth to loss. [10] There is a gift that shall not profit thee; and there is a gift whose recompence is double. [11] There is an abasement because of glory; and there is that lifteth up his head from a low estate. [12] There is that buyeth much for a little, and repayeth it sevenfold. [13] A wise man by his words maketh him beloved: but the graces of fools shall be poured out. [14] The gift of a fool shall do thee no good when thou hast it; neither yet of the envious for his necessity: for he looketh to receive many things for one. [15] He giveth little, and upbraideth much; he openeth his mouth like a crier; to day he lendeth, and to morrow will he ask it again: such an one is to be hated of God and man. [16] The fool saith, I have no friends, I have no thank for all my good deeds, and they that eat my bread speak evil of me. [17] How oft, and of how many shall he be laughed to scorn! for he knoweth not aright what it is to have; and it is all one unto him as if he had it

not. [18] To slip upon a pavement is better than to slip with the tongue: so the fall of the wicked shall come speedily. [19] An unseasonable tale will always be in the mouth of the unwise. [20] A wise sentence shall be rejected when it cometh out of a fool's mouth; for he will not speak it in due season. [21] There is that is hindered from sinning through want: and when he taketh rest, he shall not be troubled. [22] There is that destroyeth his own soul through bashfulness, and by accepting of persons overthroweth himself. [23] There is that for bashfulness promiseth to his friend, and maketh him his enemy for nothing. [24] A lie is a foul blot in a man, yet it is continually in the mouth of the untaught. [25] A thief is better than a man that is accustomed to lie: but they both shall have destruction to heritage. [26] The disposition of a liar is dishonourable, and his shame is ever with him. [27] A wise man shall promote himself to honour with his words: and he that hath understanding will please great men. [28] He that tilleth his land shall increase his heap: and he that pleaseth great men shall get pardon for iniquity.

[29] Presents and gifts blind the eyes of the wise, and stop up his mouth that he cannot reprove. [30] Wisdom that is hid, and treasure that is hoarded up, what profit is in them both? [31] Better is he that hideth his folly than a man that hideth his wisdom. [32] Necessary patience in seeking ing the Lord is better than he that leadeth his life without a guide.

Sir.21

[1] My son, hast thou sinned? do so no more, but ask pardon for thy former sins. [2] Flee from sin as from the face of a serpent: for if thou comest too near it, it will bite thee: the teeth thereof are as the teeth of a lion, slaying the souls of men. [3] All iniquity is as a two edged sword, the wounds whereof cannot be healed. [4] To terrify and do wrong will waste riches: thus the house of proud men shall be made desolate. [5] A prayer out of a poor man's mouth reacheth to the ears of God, and his judgment cometh speedily. [6] He that hateth to be reproved is in the way of sinners: but he that feareth the Lord will repent from his heart. [7] An eloquent man is known far and near; but a man of understanding knoweth when he slippeth. [8] He that buildeth his house with other men's money is like one that gathereth himself stones for the tomb of his burial. [9] The congregation of the wicked is like tow wrapped together: and the end of them is a flame of fire to destroy them. [10] The way of sinners is made plain with stones, but at the end thereof is the pit of hell. [11] He that keepeth the law of the Lord getteth the understanding thereof: and the perfection of the fear of the Lord is wisdom. [12] He that is not wise will not be taught: but there is a wisdom which multiplieth bitterness. [13] The knowledge of a wise man shall abound like a flood: and his counsel is like a pure fountain of life. [14] The inner parts of a fool are like a broken vessel, and he will hold no knowledge as long as he liveth. [15] If a skilful man hear a wise word, he will commend it, and add unto it: but as soon as one of no understanding heareth it, it displeaseth him, and he casteth it behind his back. [16] The talking of a fool is like a burden in the way: but grace shall be found in the

lips of the wise. [17] They enquire at the mouth of the wise man in the congregation, and they shall ponder his words in their heart. [18] As is a house that is destroyed, so is wisdom to a fool: and the knowledge of the unwise is as talk without sense. [19] Doctrine unto fools is as fetters on the feet, and like manacles on the right hand. [20] A fool lifteth up his voice with laughter; but a wise man doth scarce smile a little. [21] Learning is unto a wise man as an ornament of gold, and like a bracelet upon his right arm. [22] A foolish man's foot is soon in his [neighbour's] house: but a man of experience is ashamed of him. [23] A fool will peep in at the door into the house: but he that is well nurtured will stand without. [24] It is the rudeness of a man to hearken at the door: but a wise man will be grieved with the disgrace. [25] The lips of talkers will be telling such things as pertain not unto them: but the words of such as have understanding are weighed in the balance. [26] The heart of fools is in their mouth: but the mouth of the wise is in their heart. [27] When the ungodly curseth Satan, he curseth his own soul. [28] A whisperer defileth his own soul, and is hated wheresoever he dwelleth.

Sir.22

[1] A slothful man is compared to a filthy stone, and every one will hiss him out to his disgrace. [2] A slothful man is compared to the filth of a dunghill: every man that takes it up will shake his hand. [3] An evilnurtured man is the dishonour of his father that begat him: and a [foolish] daughter is born to his loss. [4] A wise daughter shall bring an inheritance to her husband: but she that liveth dishonestly is her father's heaviness. [5] She that is bold dishonoureth both her father and her husband, but they both shall despise her. [6] A tale out of season [is as] musick in mourning: but stripes and correction of wisdom are never out of time. [7] Whoso teacheth a fool is as one that glueth a potsherd together, and as he that waketh one from a sound sleep. [8] He that telleth a tale to a fool speaketh to one in a slumber: when he hath told his tale, he will say, What is the matter? [9] If children live honestly, and have wherewithal, they shall cover the baseness of their parents. [10] But children, being haughty, through disdain and want of nurture do stain the nobility of their kindred. [11] Weep for the dead, for he hath lost the light: and weep for the fool, for he wanteth understanding: make little weeping for the dead, for he is at rest: but the life of the fool is worse than death. [12] Seven days do men mourn for him that is dead; but for a fool and an ungodly man all the days of his life. [13] Talk not much with a fool, and go not to him that hath no understanding: beware of him, lest thou have trouble, and thou shalt never be defiled with his fooleries: depart from him, and thou shalt find rest, and never be disquieted with madness. [14] What is heavier than lead? and what is the name thereof, but a fool? [15] Sand, and salt, and a mass of iron, is easier to bear, than a man without understanding. [16] As timber girt and bound together in a building cannot be loosed with shaking: so the heart that is stablished by advised counsel shall fear at no time. [17] A heart settled upon a thought of understanding is as a fair plaistering on the wall of a gallery. [18] Pales set on an high place will never stand against the wind: so a

fearful heart in the imagination of a fool cannot stand against any fear. [19] He that pricketh the eye will make tears to fall: and he that pricketh the heart maketh it to shew her knowledge. [20] Whoso casteth a stone at the birds frayeth them away: and he that upbraideth his friend breaketh friendship. [21] Though thou drewest a sword at thy friend, yet despair not: for there may be a returning [to favour.] [22] If thou hast opened thy mouth against thy friend, fear not; for there may be a reconciliation: except for upbraiding, or pride, or disclosing of secrets, or a treacherous wound: for for these things every friend will depart. [23] Be faithful to thy neighbour in his poverty, that thou mayest rejoice in his prosperity: abide stedfast unto him in the time of his trouble, that thou mayest be heir with him in his heritage: for a mean estate is not always to be contemned: nor the rich that is foolish to be had in admiration. [24] As the vapour and smoke of a furnace goeth before the fire; so reviling before blood. [25] I will not be ashamed to defend a friend; neither will I hide myself from him. [26] And if any evil happen unto me by him, every one that heareth it will beware of him. [27] Who shall set a watch before my mouth, and a seal of wisdom upon my lips, that I fall not suddenly by them, and that my tongue destroy me not?

Sir.23

[1] O Lord, Father and Governor of all my whole life, leave me not to their counsels, and let me not fall by them. [2] Who will set scourges over my thoughts, and the discipline of wisdom over mine heart? that they spare me not for mine ignorances, and it pass not by my sins: [3] Lest mine ignorances increase, and my sins abound to my destruction, and I fall before mine adversaries, and mine enemy rejoice over me, whose hope is far from thy mercy. [4] O Lord, Father and God of my life, give me not a proud look, but turn away from thy servants always a haughty mind. [5] Turn away from me vain hopes and concupiscence, and thou shalt hold him up that is desirous always to serve thee.

[6] Let not the greediness of the belly nor lust of the flesh take hold of me; and give not over me thy servant into an impudent mind. [7] Hear, O ye children, the discipline of the mouth: he that keepeth it shall never be taken in his lips. [8] The sinner shall be left in his foolishness: both the evil speaker and the proud shall fall thereby. [9] Accustom not thy mouth to swearing; neither use thyself to the naming of the Holy One. [10] For as a servant that is continually beaten shall not be without a blue mark: so he that sweareth and nameth God continually shall not be faultless. [11] A man that useth much swearing shall be filled with iniquity, and the plague shall never depart from his house: if he shall offend, his sin shall be upon him: and if he acknowledge not his sin, he maketh a double offence: and if he swear in vain, he shall not be innocent, but his house shall be full of calamities. [12] There is a word that is clothed about with death: God grant that it be not found in the heritage of Jacob; for all such things shall be far from the godly, and they shall not wallow in their sins. [13] Use not thy mouth to intemperate swearing, for therein is the word of sin. [14] Remember thy father and thy mother, when thou sittest among great men. Be not forgetful before them, and so thou by thy custom become a fool, and wish that thou hadst not been born, and curse they day of thy

nativity. [15] The man that is accustomed to opprobrious words will never be reformed all the days of his life. [16] Two sorts of men multiply sin, and the third will bring wrath: a hot mind is as a burning fire, it will never be quenched till it be consumed: a fornicator in the body of his flesh will never cease till he hath kindled a fire. [17] All bread is sweet to a whoremonger, he will not leave off till he die. [18] A man that breaketh wedlock, saying thus in his heart, Who seeth me? I am compassed about with darkness, the walls cover me, and no body seeth me; what need I to fear? the most High will not remember my sins: [19] Such a man only feareth the eyes of men, and knoweth not that the eyes of the Lord are ten thousand times brighter than the sun, beholding all the ways of men, and considering the most secret parts. [20] He knew all things ere ever they were created; so also after they were perfected he looked upon them all. [21] This man shall be punished in the streets of the city, and where he suspecteth not he shall be taken. [22] Thus shall it go also with the wife that leaveth her husband, and bringeth in an heir by another. [23] For first, she hath disobeyed the law of the most High; and secondly, she hath trespassed against her own husband; and thirdly, she hath played the whore in adultery, and brought children by another man. [24] She shall be brought out into the congregation, and inquisition shall be made of her children. [25] Her children shall not take root, and her branches shall bring forth no fruit. [26] She shall leave her memory to be cursed, and her reproach shall not be blotted out. [27] And they that remain shall know that there is nothing better than the fear of the Lord, and that there is nothing sweeter than to take heed unto the commandments of the Lord. [28] It is great glory to follow the Lord, and to be received of him is long life.

Sir.24

[1] Wisdom shall praise herself, and shall glory in the midst of her people. [2] In the congregation of the most High shall she open her mouth, and triumph before his power. [3] I came out of the mouth of the most High, and covered the earth as a cloud. [4] I dwelt in high places, and my throne is in a cloudy pillar. [5] I alone compassed the circuit of heaven, and walked in the bottom of the deep. [6] In the waves of the sea and in all the earth, and in every people and nation, I got a possession. [7] With all these I sought rest: and in whose inheritance shall I abide? [8] So the Creator of all things gave me a commandment, and he that made me caused my tabernacle to rest, and said, Let thy dwelling be in Jacob, and thine inheritance in Israel. [9] He created me from the beginning before the world, and I shall never fail. [10] In the holy tabernacle I served before him; and so was I established in Sion. [11] Likewise in the beloved city he gave me rest, and in Jerusalem was my power. [12] And I took root in an honourable people, even in the portion of the Lord's inheritance. [13] I was exalted like a cedar in Libanus, and as a cypress tree upon the mountains of Hermon. [14] I was exalted like a palm tree in En-gaddi, and as a rose plant in Jericho, as a fair olive tree in a pleasant field, and grew up as a plane tree by the water. [15] I gave a sweet smell like cinnamon and aspalathus, and I yielded a pleasant odour like the best myrrh, as galbanum, and onyx, and sweet storax, and as the fume of frankincense in the tabernacle. [16] As the turpentine tree I stretched out my branches, and my branches are the branches of honour and grace. [17] As the vine brought I forth pleasant savour, and my flowers are the fruit of honour and riches. [18] I am the mother of fair love, and fear, and knowledge, and holy hope: I therefore, being eternal, am given to all my children which are named of him. [19] Come unto me, all ye that be desirous of me, and fill yourselves with my fruits. [20] For my memorial is sweeter than honey, and mine inheritance than the honeycomb. [21] They that eat me shall yet be hungry, and they that drink me shall yet be thirsty. [22] He that obeyeth me shall never be confounded, and they that work by me shall not do amiss. [23] All these things are the book of the covenant of the most high God, even the law which Moses commanded for an heritage unto the congregations of Jacob. [24] Faint not to be strong in the Lord; that he may confirm you, cleave unto him: for the Lord Almighty is God alone, and beside him there is no other Saviour. [25] He filleth all things with his wisdom, as Phison and as Tigris in the time of the new fruits. [26] He maketh the understanding to abound like Euphrates, and as Jordan in the time of the harvest. [27] He maketh the doctrine of knowledge appear as the light, and as Geon in the time of vintage. [28] The first man knew her not perfectly: no more shall the last find her out. [29] For her thoughts are more than the sea, and her counsels profounder than the great deep. [30] I also came out as a brook from a river, and as a conduit into a garden. [31] I said, I will water my best garden, and will water abundantly my garden bed: and, lo, my brook became a river, and my river became a sea. [32] I will yet make doctrine to shine as the morning, and will send forth her light afar off. [33] I will yet pour out doctrine as prophecy, and leave it to all ages for ever. [34] Behold that I have not laboured for myself only, but for all them that seek wisdom.

Sir.25

[1] In three things I was beautified, and stood up beautiful both before God and men: the unity of brethren, the love of neighbours, a man and a wife that agree together. [2] Three sorts of men my soul hateth, and I am greatly offended at their life: a poor man that is proud, a rich man that is a liar, and an old adulterer that doateth. [3] If thou hast gathered nothing in thy youth, how canst thou find any thing in thine age? [4] O how comely a thing is judgment for gray hairs, and for ancient men to know counsel! [5] O how comely is the wisdom of old men, and understanding and counsel to men of honour. [6] Much experience is the crown of old men, and the fear of God is their glory. [7] There be nine things which I have judged in mine heart to be happy, and the tenth I will utter with my tongue: A man that hath joy of his children; and he that liveth to see the fall of his enemy: [8] Well is him that dwelleth with a wife of understanding, and that hath not slipped with his tongue, and that hath not served a man more unworthy than himself: [9] Well is him that hath found prudence, and he that speaketh in the ears of them that will hear: [10] O how great is he that findeth wisdom! yet is there none above him that feareth the Lord. [11] But the love of the

Lord passeth all things for illumination: he that holdeth it, whereto shall he be likened? [12] The fear of the Lord is the beginning of his love: and faith is the beginning of cleaving unto him. [13] [Give me] any plague, but the plague of the heart: and any wickedness, but the wickedness of a woman: [14] And any affliction, but the affliction from them that hate me: and any revenge, but the revenge of enemies. [15] There is no head above the head of a serpent; and there is no wrath above the wrath of an enemy. [16] I had rather dwell with a lion and a dragon, than to keep house with a wicked woman. [17] The wickedness of a woman changeth her face, and darkeneth her countenance like sackcloth. [18] Her husband shall sit among his neighbours; and when he heareth it shall sigh bitterly. [19] All wickedness is but little to the wickedness of a woman: let the portion of a sinner fall upon her. [20] As the climbing up a sandy way is to the feet of the aged, so is a wife full of words to a quiet man. [21] Stumble not at the beauty of a woman, and desire her not for pleasure. [22] A woman, if she maintain her husband, is full of anger, impudence, and much reproach. [23] A wicked woman abateth the courage, maketh an heavy countenance and a wounded heart: a woman that will not comfort her husband in distress maketh weak hands and feeble knees. [24] Of the woman came the beginning of sin, and through her we all die. [25] Give the water no passage; neither a wicked woman liberty to gad abroad. [26] If she go not as thou wouldest have her, cut her off from thy flesh, and give her a bill of divorce, and let her go.

Sir.26

[1] Blessed is the man that hath a virtuous wife, for the number of his days shall be double. [2] A virtuous woman rejoiceth her husband, and he shall fulfil the years of his life in peace. [3] A good wife is a good portion, which shall be given in the portion of them that fear the Lord. [4] Whether a man be rich or poor, if he have a good heart toward the Lord, he shall at all times rejoice with a cheerful countenance. [5] There be three things that mine heart feareth; and for the fourth I was sore afraid: the slander of a city, the gathering together of an unruly multitude, and a false accusation: all these are worse than death. [6] But a grief of heart and sorrow is a woman that is jealous over another woman, and a scourge of the tongue which communicateth with all. [7] An evil wife is a yoke shaken to and fro: he that hath hold of her is as though he held a scorpion. [8] A drunken woman and a gadder abroad causeth great anger, and she will not cover her own shame. [9] The whoredom of a woman may be known in her haughty looks and eyelids. [10] If thy daughter be shameless, keep her in straitly, lest she abuse herself through overmuch liberty. [11] Watch over an impudent eye: and marvel not if she trespass against thee. [12] She will open her mouth, as a thirsty traveller when he hath found a fountain, and drink of every water near her: by every hedge will she sit down, and open her quiver against every arrow. [13] The grace of a wife delighteth her husband, and her discretion will fatten his bones. [14] A silent and loving woman is a gift of the Lord; and there is nothing so much worth as a mind well instructed. [15] A

shamefaced and faithful woman is a double grace, and her continent mind cannot be valued. [16] As the sun when it ariseth in the high heaven; so is the beauty of a good wife in the ordering of her house. [17] As the clear light is upon the holy candlestick; so is the beauty of the face in ripe age. [18] As the golden pillars are upon the sockets of silver; so are the fair feet with a constant heart. [19] My son, keep the flower of thine age sound; and give not thy strength to strangers. [20] When thou hast gotten a fruitful possession through all the field, sow it with thine own seed, trusting in the goodness of thy stock. [21] So thy race which thou leavest shall be magnified, having the confidence of their good descent. [22] An harlot shall be accounted as spittle; but a married woman is a tower against death to her husband. [23] A wicked woman is given as a portion to a wicked man: but a godly woman is given to him that feareth the Lord. [24] A dishonest woman contemneth shame: but an honest woman will reverence her husband. [25] A shameless woman shall be counted as a dog; but she that is shamefaced will fear the Lord. [26] A woman that honoureth her husband shall be judged wise of all; but she that dishonoureth him in her pride shall be counted ungodly of all. [27] A loud crying woman and a scold shall be sought out to drive away the enemies. [28] There be two things that grieve my heart; and the third maketh me angry: a man of war that suffereth poverty; and men of understanding that are not set by; and one that returneth from righteousness to sin; the Lord prepareth such an one for the sword. [29] A merchant shall hardly keep himself from doing wrong; and an huckster shall not be freed from sin.

Sir.27

[1] Many have sinned for a small matter; and he that seeketh for abundance will turn his eyes away. [2] As a nail sticketh fast between the joinings of the stones; so doth sin stick close between buying and selling. [3] Unless a man hold himself diligently in the fear of the Lord, his house shall soon be overthrown. [4] As when one sifteth with a sieve, the refuse remaineth; so the filth of man in his talk. [5] The furnace proveth the potter's vessels; so the trial of man is in his reasoning. [6] The fruit declareth if the tree have been dressed; so is the utterance of a conceit in the heart of man. [7] Praise no man before thou hearest him speak; for this is the trial of men. [8] If thou followest righteousness, thou shalt obtain her, and put her on, as a glorious long robe. [9] The birds will resort unto their like; so will truth return unto them that practise in her. [10] As the lion lieth in wait for the prey; so sin for them that work iniquity. [11] The discourse of a godly man is always with wisdom; but a fool changeth as the moon. [12] If thou be among the indiscreet, observe the time; but be continually among men of understanding. [13] The discourse of fools is irksome, and their sport is the wantonness of sin. [14] The talk of him that sweareth much maketh the hair stand upright; and their brawls make one stop his ears. [15] The strife of the proud is bloodshedding, and their revilings are grievous to the ear. [16] Whoso discovereth secrets loseth his credit; and shall never find friend to his mind. [17] Love thy friend, and be faithful unto him: but if thou

betrayest his secrets, follow no more after him. [18] For as a man hath destroyed his enemy; so hast thou lost the love of thy neighbor. [19] As one that letteth a bird go out of his hand, so hast thou let thy neighbour go, and shalt not get him again [20] Follow after him no more, for he is too far off; he is as a roe escaped out of the snare. [21] As for a wound, it may be bound up; and after reviling there may be reconcilement: but he that betrayeth secrets is without hope. [22] He that winketh with the eyes worketh evil: and he that knoweth him will depart from him. [23] When thou art present, he will speak sweetly, and will admire thy words: but at the last he will writhe his mouth, and slander thy sayings. [24] I have hated many things, but nothing like him; for the Lord will hate him. [25] Whoso casteth a stone on high casteth it on his own head; and a deceitful stroke shall make wounds. [26] Whoso diggeth a pit shall fall therein: and he that setteth a trap shall be taken therein.

[27] He that worketh mischief, it shall fall upon him, and he shall not know whence it cometh. [28] Mockery and reproach are from the proud; but vengeance, as a lion, shall lie in wait for them. [29] They that rejoice at the fall of the righteous shall be taken in the snare; and anguish shall consume them before they die. [30] Malice and wrath, even these are abominations; and the sinful man shall have them both.

Sir.28

[1] He that revengeth shall find vengeance from the Lord, and he will surely keep his sins [in remembrance.] [2] Forgive thy neighbour the hurt that he hath done unto thee, so shall thy sins also be forgiven when thou prayest. [3] One man beareth hatred against another, and doth he seek pardon from the Lord? [4] He sheweth no mercy to a man, which is like himself: and doth he ask forgiveness of his own sins? [5] If he that is but flesh nourish hatred, who will intreat for pardon of his sins? [6] Remember thy end, and let enmity cease; [remember] corruption and death, and abide in the commandments. [7] Remember the commandments, and bear no malice to thy neighbour: [remember] the covenant of the Highest, and wink at ignorance. [8] Abstain from strife, and thou shalt diminish thy sins: for a furious man will kindle strife, [9] A sinful man disquieteth friends, and maketh debate among them that be at peace. [10] As the matter of the fire is, so it burneth: and as a man's strength is, so is his wrath; and according to his riches his anger riseth; and the stronger they are which contend, the more they will be inflamed. [11] An hasty contention kindleth a fire: and an hasty fighting sheddeth blood. [12] If thou blow the spark, it shall burn: if thou spit upon it, it shall be quenched: and both these come out of thy mouth. [13] Curse the whisperer and doubletongued: for such have destroyed many that were at peace. [14] A backbiting tongue hath disquieted many, and driven them from nation to nation: strong cities hath it pulled down, and overthrown the houses of great men. [15] A backbiting tongue hath cast out virtuous women, and deprived them of their labours. [16] Whoso hearkeneth unto it shall never find rest, and never dwell quietly. [17] The stroke of the whip maketh marks in the flesh: but the stroke of the tongue breaketh

the bones. [18] Many have fallen by the edge of the sword: but not so many as have fallen by the tongue. [19] Well is he that is defended through the venom thereof; who hath not drawn the yoke thereof, nor hath been bound in her bands. [20] For the yoke thereof is a yoke of iron, and the bands thereof are bands of brass. [21] The death thereof is an evil death, the grave were better than it. [22] It shall not have rule over them that fear God, neither shall they be burned with the flame thereof. [23] Such as forsake the Lord shall fall into it; and it shall burn in them, and not be quenched; it shall be sent upon them as a lion, and devour them as a leopard. [24] Look that thou hedge thy possession about with thorns, and bind up thy silver and gold, [25] And weigh thy words in a balance, and make a door and bar for thy mouth. [26] Beware thou slide not by it, lest thou fall before him that lieth in wait.

Sir.29

[1] He that is merciful will lend unto his neighbour; and he that strengtheneth his hand keepeth the commandments. [2] Lend to thy neighbour in time of his need, and pay thou thy neighbour again in due season. [3] Keep thy word, and deal faithfully with him, and thou shalt always find the thing that is necessary for thee. [4] Many, when a thing was lent them, reckoned it to be found, and put them to trouble that helped them. [5] Till he hath received, he will kiss a man's hand; and for his neighbour's money he will speak submissly: but when he should repay, he will prolong the time, and return words of grief, and complain of the time. [6] If he prevail, he shall hardly receive the half, and he will count as if he had found it: if not, he hath deprived him of his money, and he hath gotten him an enemy without cause: he payeth him with cursings and railings; and for honour he will pay him disgrace. [7] Many therefore have refused to lend for other men's ill dealing, fearing to be defrauded. [8] Yet have thou patience with a man in poor estate, and delay not to shew him mercy. [9] Help the poor for the commandment's sake, and turn him not away because of his poverty. [10] Lose thy money for thy brother and thy friend, and let it not rust under a stone to be lost. [11] Lay up thy treasure according to the commandments of the most High, and it shall bring thee more profit than gold. [12] Shut up alms in thy storehouses: and it shall deliver thee from all affliction. [13] It shall fight for thee against thine enemies better than a mighty shield and strong spear. [14] An honest man is surety for his neighbour: but he that is impudent will forsake him. [15] Forget not the friendship of thy surety, for he hath given his life for thee. [16] A sinner will overthrow the good estate of his surety: [17] And he that is of an unthankful mind will leave him [in danger] that delivered him. [18] Suretiship hath undone many of good estate, and shaken them as a wave of the sea: mighty men hath it driven from their houses, so that they wandered among strange nations. [19] A wicked man transgressing the commandments of the Lord shall fall into suretiship: and he that undertaketh and followeth other men's business for gain shall fall into suits. [20] Help thy neighbour according to thy power, and beware that thou thyself fall not into the same. [21] The chief thing for life is water, and

bread, and clothing, and an house to cover shame. [22] Better is the life of a poor man in a mean cottage, than delicate fare in another man's house. [23] Be it little or much, hold thee contented, that thou hear not the reproach of thy house. [24] For it is a miserable life to go from house to house: for where thou art a stranger, thou darest not open thy mouth. [25] Thou shalt entertain, and feast, and have no thanks: moreover thou shalt hear bitter words:

[26] Come, thou stranger, and furnish a table, and feed me of that thou hast ready. [27] Give place, thou stranger, to an honourable man; my brother cometh to be lodged, and I have need of mine house. [28] These things are grievous to a man of understanding; the upbraiding of houseroom, and reproaching of the lender.

Sir.30

[1] He that loveth his son causeth him oft to feel the rod, that he may have joy of him in the end. [2] He that chastiseth his son shall have joy in him, and shall rejoice of him among his acquaintance. [3] He that teacheth his son grieveth the enemy: and before his friends he shall rejoice of him. [4] Though his father die, yet he is as though he were not dead: for he hath left one behind him that is like himself. [5] While he lived, he saw and rejoiced in him: and when he died, he was not sorrowful. [6] He left behind him an avenger against his enemies, and one that shall requite kindness to his friends. [7] He that maketh too much of his son shall bind up his wounds; and his bowels will be troubled at every cry. [8] An horse not broken becometh headstrong: and a child left to himself will be wilful. [9] Cocker thy child, and he shall make thee afraid: play with him, and he will bring thee to heaviness. [10] Laugh not with him, lest thou have sorrow with him, and lest thou gnash thy teeth in the end. [11] Give him no liberty in his youth, and wink not at his follies. [12] Bow down his neck while he is young, and beat him on the sides while he is a child, lest he wax stubborn, and be disobedient unto thee, and so bring sorrow to thine heart. [13] Chastise thy son, and hold him to labour, lest his lewd behaviour be an offence unto thee. [14] Better is the poor, being sound and strong of constitution, than a rich man that is afflicted in his body. [15] Health and good estate of body are above all gold, and a strong body above infinite wealth. [16] There is no riches above a sound body, and no joy above the joy of the heart. [17] Death is better than a bitter life or continual sickness. [18] Delicates poured upon a mouth shut up are as messes of meat set upon a grave. [19] What good doeth the offering unto an idol? for neither can it eat nor smell: so is he that is persecuted of the Lord. [20] He seeth with his eyes and groaneth, as an eunuch that embraceth a virgin and sigheth. [21] Give not over thy mind to heaviness, and afflict not thyself in thine own counsel. [22] The gladness of the heart is the life of man, and the joyfulness of a man prolongeth his days. [23] Love thine own soul, and comfort thy heart, remove sorrow far from thee: for sorrow hath killed many, and there is no profit therein. [24] Envy and wrath shorten the life, and carefulness bringeth age before the time. [25] A cheerful and good heart will have a care of his meat and diet.

Sir.31

[1] Watching for riches consumeth the flesh, and the care thereof driveth away sleep. [2] Watching care will not let a man slumber, as a sore disease breaketh sleep, [3] The rich hath great labour in gathering riches together; and when he resteth, he is filled with his delicates. [4] The poor laboureth in his poor estate; and when he leaveth off, he is still needy. [5] He that loveth gold shall not be justified, and he that followeth corruption shall have enough thereof.

[6] Gold hath been the ruin of many, and their destruction was present. [7] It is a stumblingblock unto them that sacrifice unto it, and every fool shall be taken therewith. [8] Blessed is the rich that is found without blemish, and hath not gone after gold. [9] Who is he? and we will call him blessed: for wonderful things hath he done among his people. [10] Who hath been tried thereby, and found perfect? then let him glory. Who might offend, and hath not offended? or done evil, and hath not done it? [11] His goods shall be established, and the congregation shall declare his alms. [12] If thou sit at a bountiful table, be not greedy upon it, and say not, There is much meat on it. [13] Remember that a wicked eye is an evil thing: and what is created more wicked than an eye? therefore it weepeth upon every occasion. [14] Stretch not thine hand whithersoever it looketh, and thrust it not with him into the dish. [15] Judge not thy neighbour by thyself: and be discreet in every point. [16] Eat as it becometh a man, those things which are set before thee; and devour note, lest thou be hated. [17] Leave off first for manners' sake; and be not unsatiable, lest thou offend. [18] When thou sittest among many, reach not thine hand out first of all. [19] A very little is sufficient for a man well nurtured, and he fetcheth not his wind short upon his bed. [20] Sound sleep cometh of moderate eating: he riseth early, and his wits are with him: but the pain of watching, and choler, and pangs of the belly, are with an unsatiable man. [21] And if thou hast been forced to eat, arise, go forth, vomit, and thou shalt have rest. [22] My son, hear me, and despise me not, and at the last thou shalt find as I told thee: in all thy works be quick, so shall there no sickness come unto thee. [23] Whoso is liberal of his meat, men shall speak well of him; and the report of his good housekeeping will be believed. [24] But against him that is a niggard of his meat the whole city shall murmur; and the testimonies of his niggardness shall not be doubted of. [25] Shew not thy valiantness in wine; for wine hath destroyed many. [26] The furnace proveth the edge by dipping: so doth wine the hearts of the proud by drunkeness. [27] Wine is as good as life to a man, if it be drunk moderately: what life is then to a man that is without wine? for it was made to make men glad. [28] Wine measurably drunk and in season bringeth gladness of the heart, and cheerfulness of the mind: [29] But wine drunken with excess maketh bitterness of the mind, with brawling and quarrelling. [30] Drunkenness increaseth the rage of a fool till he offend: it diminisheth strength, and maketh wounds. [31] Rebuke not thy neighbour at the wine, and despise him not in his mirth: give him no despiteful words, and press not upon him with urging him [to drink.]

Sir.32

[1] If thou be made the master [of a feast,] lift not thyself up, but be among them as one of the rest; take diligent care for them, and so sit down. [2] And when thou hast done all thy office, take thy place, that thou mayest be merry with them, and receive a crown for thy well ordering of the feast. [3] Speak, thou that art the elder, for it becometh thee, but with sound judgment; and hinder not musick. [4] Pour not out words where there is a musician, and shew not forth wisdom out of time. [5] A concert of musick in a banquet of wine is as a signet of carbuncle set in gold. [6] As a signet of an emerald set in a work of gold, so is the melody of musick with pleasant wine. [7] Speak, young man, if there be need of thee: and yet scarcely when thou art twice asked. [8] Let thy speech be short, comprehending much in few words; be as one that knoweth and yet holdeth his tongue. [9] If thou be among great men, make not thyself equal with them; and when ancient men are in place, use not many words. [10] Before the thunder goeth lightning; and before a shamefaced man shall go favour. [11] Rise up betimes, and be not the last; but get thee home without delay. [12] There take thy pastime, and do what thou wilt: but sin not by proud speech. [13] And for these things bless him that made thee, and hath replenished thee with his good things. [14] Whoso feareth the Lord will receive his discipline; and they that seek him early shall find favour. [15] He that seeketh the law shall be filled therewith: but the hypocrite will be offended thereat. [16] They that fear the Lord shall find judgment, and shall kindle justice as a light. [17] A sinful man will not be reproved, but findeth an excuse according to his will. [18] A man of counsel will be considerate; but a strange and proud man is not daunted with fear, even when of himself he hath done without counsel. [19] Do nothing without advice; and when thou hast once done, repent not.

[20] Go not in a way wherein thou mayest fall, and stumble not among the stones. [21] Be not confident in a plain way. [22] And beware of thine own children. [23] In every good work trust thy own soul; for this is the keeping of the commandments. [24] He that believeth in the Lord taketh heed to the commandment; and he that trusteth in him shall fare never the worse.

Sir.33

[1] There shall no evil happen unto him that feareth the Lord; but in temptation even again he will deliver him. [2] A wise man hateth not the law; but he that is an hypocrite therein is as a ship in a storm. [3] A man of understanding trusteth in the law; and the law is faithful unto him, as an oracle. [4] Prepare what to say, and so thou shalt be heard: and bind up instruction, and then make answer. [5] The heart of the foolish is like a cartwheel; and his thoughts are like a rolling axletree. [6] A stallion horse is as a mocking friend, he neigheth under every one that sitteth upon him. [7] Why doth one day excel another, when as all the light of every day in the year is of the sun? [8] By the knowledge of the Lord they were distinguished: and he altered seasons and feasts. [9] Some of them hath he made high days, and hallowed them, and some of them hath he made ordinary

days. [10] And all men are from the ground, and Adam was created of earth: [11] In much knowledge the Lord hath divided them, and made their ways diverse. [12] Some of them hath he blessed and exalted and some of them he sanctified, and set near himself: but some of them hath he cursed and brought low, and turned out of their places. [13] As the clay is in the potter's hand, to fashion it at his pleasure: so man is in the hand of him that made him, to render to them as liketh him best. [14] Good is set against evil, and life against death: so is the godly against the sinner, and the sinner against the godly. [15] So look upon all the works of the most High; and there are two and two, one against another. [16] I awaked up last of all, as one that gathereth after the grapegatherers: by the blessing of the Lord I profited, and tred my winepress like a gatherer of grapes. [17] Consider that I laboured not for myself only, but for all them that seek learning. [18] Hear me, O ye great men of the people, and hearken with your ears, ye rulers of the congregation. [19] Give not thy son and wife, thy brother and friend, power over thee while thou livest, and give not thy goods to another: lest it repent thee, and thou intreat for the same again. [20] As long as thou livest and hast breath in thee, give not thyself over to any. [21] For better it is that thy children should seek to thee, than that thou shouldest stand to their courtesy. [22] In all thy works keep to thyself the preeminence; leave not a stain in thine honour. [23] At the time when thou shalt end thy days, and finish thy life, distribute thine inheritance. [24] Fodder, a wand, and burdens, are for the ass; and bread, correction, and work, for a servant. . [25] If thou set thy servant to labour, thou shalt find rest: but if thou let him go idle, he shall seek liberty. [26] A yoke and a collar do bow the neck: so are tortures and torments for an evil servant. [27] Send him to labour, that he be not idle; for idleness teacheth much evil. [28] Set him to work, as is fit for him: if he be not obedient, put on more heavy fetters. [29] But be not excessive toward any; and without discretion do nothing. [30] If thou have a servant, let him be unto thee as thyself, because thou hast bought him with a price. [31] If thou have a servant, entreat him as a brother: for thou hast need of him, as of thine own soul: if thou entreat him evil, and he run from thee, which way wilt thou go to seek him?

Sir.34

[1] The hopes of a man void of understanding are vain and false: and dreams lift up fools. [2] Whoso regardeth dreams is like him that catcheth at a shadow, and followeth after the wind. [3] The vision of dreams is the resemblance of one thing to another, even as the likeness of a face to a face. [4] Of an unclean thing what can be cleansed? and from that thing which is false what truth can come? [5] Divinations, and soothsayings, and dreams, are vain: and the heart fancieth, as a woman's heart in travail. [6] If they be not sent from the most High in thy visitation, set not thy heart upon them. [7] For dreams have deceived many, and they have failed that put their trust in them. [8] The law shall be found perfect without lies: and wisdom is perfection to a faithful mouth. [9] A man that hath travelled knoweth many things; and he that hath much

experience will declare wisdom. [10] He that hath no experience knoweth little: but he that hath travelled is full of prudence. [11] When I travelled, I saw many things; and I understand more than I can express. [12] I was ofttimes in danger of death: yet I was delivered because of these things. [13] The spirit of those that fear the Lord shall live; for their hope is in him that saveth them. [14] Whoso feareth the Lord shall not fear nor be afraid; for he is his hope. [15] Blessed is the soul of him that feareth the Lord: to whom doth he look? and who is his strength? [16] For the eyes of the Lord are upon them that love him, he is their mighty protection and strong stay, a defence from heat, and a cover from the sun at noon, a preservation from stumbling, and an help from falling. [17] He raiseth up the soul, and lighteneth the eyes: he giveth health, life, and blessing. [18] He that sacrificeth of a thing wrongfully gotten, his offering is ridiculous; and the gifts of unjust men are not accepted. [19] The most High is not pleased with the offerings of the wicked; neither is he pacified for sin by the multitude of sacrifices. [20] Whoso bringeth an offering of the goods of the poor doeth as one that killeth the son before his father's eyes. [21] The bread of the needy is their life: he that defraudeth him thereof is a man of blood. [22] He that taketh away his neighbour's living slayeth him; and he that defraudeth the labourer of his hire is a bloodshedder. [23] When one buildeth, and another pulleth down, what profit have they then but labour? [24] When one prayeth, and another curseth, whose voice will the Lord hear? [25] He that washeth himself after the touching of a dead body, if he touch it again, what availeth his washing? [26] So is it with a man that fasteth for his sins, and goeth again, and doeth the same: who will hear his prayer? or what doth his humbling profit him?

Sir.35

[1] He that keepeth the law bringeth offerings enough: he that taketh heed to the commandment offereth a peace offering. [2] He that requiteth a goodturn offereth fine flour; and he that giveth alms sacrificeth praise. [3] To depart from wickedness is a thing pleasing to the Lord; and to forsake unrighteousness is a propitiation. [4] Thou shalt not appear empty before the Lord. [5] For all these things [are to be done] because of the commandment. [6] The offering of the righteous maketh the altar fat, and the sweet savour thereof is before the most High. [7] The sacrifice of a just man is acceptable. and the memorial thereof shall never be forgotten. [8] Give the Lord his honour with a good eye, and diminish not the firstfruits of thine hands. [9] In all thy gifts shew a cheerful countenance, and dedicate thy tithes with gladness. [10] Give unto the most High according as he hath enriched thee; and as thou hast gotten, give with a cheerful eye. [11] For the Lord recompenseth, and will give thee seven times as much. [12] Do not think to corrupt with gifts; for such he will not receive: and trust not to unrighteous sacrifices; for the Lord is judge, and with him is no respect of persons. [13] He will not accept any person against a poor man, but will hear the prayer of the oppressed. [14] He will not despise the supplication of the fatherless; nor the widow, when she poureth out her complaint. [15] Do not the tears run down

the widow's cheeks? and is not her cry against him that causeth them to fall? [16] He that serveth the Lord shall be accepted with favour, and his prayer shall reach unto the clouds. [17] The prayer of the humble pierceth the clouds: and till it come nigh, he will not be comforted; and will not depart, till the most High shall behold to judge righteously, and execute judgment. [18] For the Lord will not be slack, neither will the Mighty be patient toward them, till he have smitten in sunder the loins of the unmerciful, and repayed vengeance to the heathen; till he have taken away the multitude of the proud, and broken the sceptre of the unrighteous; [19] Till he have rendered to every man according to his deeds, and to the works of men according to their devices; till he have judged the cause of his people, and made them to rejoice in his mercy. [20] Mercy is seasonable in the time of affliction, as clouds of rain in the time of drought.

Sir.36

[1] Have mercy upon us, O Lord God of all, and behold us: [2] And send thy fear upon all the nations that seek not after thee. [3] Lift up thy hand against the strange nations, and let them see thy power. [4] As thou wast sanctified in us before them: so be thou magnified among them before us. [5] And let them know thee, as we have known thee, that there is no God but only thou, O God. [6] Shew new signs, and make other strange wonders: glorify thy hand and thy right arm, that they may set forth thy wondrous works. [7] Raise up indignation, and pour out wrath: take away the adversary, and destroy the enemy. [8] Sake the time short, remember the covenant, and let them declare thy wonderful works. [9] Let him that escapeth be consumed by the rage of the fire; and let them perish that oppress the people. [10] Smite in sunder the heads of the rulers of the heathen, that say, There is none other but we. [11] Gather all the tribes of Jacob together, and inherit thou them, as from the beginning. [12] O Lord, have mercy upon the people that is called by thy name, and upon Israel, whom thou hast named thy firstborn. [13] O be merciful unto Jerusalem, thy holy city, the place of thy rest. [14] Fill Sion with thine unspeakable oracles, and thy people with thy glory: [15] Give testimony unto those that thou hast possessed from the beginning, and raise up prophets that have been in thy name. [16] Reward them that wait for thee, and let thy prophets be found faithful. [17] O Lord, hear the prayer of thy servants, according to the blessing of Aaron over thy people, that all they which dwell upon the earth may know that thou art the Lord, the eternal God. [18] The belly devoureth all meats, yet is one meat better than another. [19] As the palate tasteth divers kinds of venison: so doth an heart of understanding false speeches. [20] A froward heart causeth heaviness: but a man of experience will recompense him. [21] A woman will receive every man, yet is one daughter better than another. [22] The beauty of a woman cheereth the countenance, and a man loveth nothing better. [23] If there be kindness, meekness, and comfort, in her tongue, then is not her husband like other men. [24] He that getteth a wife beginneth a possession, a help like unto himself, and a pillar of rest. [25] Where no hedge is, there the possession is

spoiled: and he that hath no wife will wander up and down mourning. [26] Who will trust a thief well appointed, that skippeth from city to city? so [who will believe] a man that hath no house, and lodgeth wheresoever the night taketh him?

Sir.37

[1] Every friend saith, I am his friend also: but there is a friend, which is only a friend in name. [2] Is it not a grief unto death, when a companion and friend is turned to an enemy? [3] O wicked imagination, whence camest thou in to cover the earth with deceit? [4] There is a companion, which rejoiceth in the prosperity of a friend, but in the time of trouble will be against him. [5] There is a companion, which helpeth his friend for the belly, and taketh up the buckler against the enemy. [6] Forget not thy friend in thy mind, and be not unmindful of him in thy riches. [7] Every counsellor extolleth counsel; but there is some that counselleth for himself. [8] Beware of a counsellor, and know before what need he hath; for he will counsel for himself; lest he cast the lot upon thee, [9] And say unto thee, Thy way is good: and afterward he stand on the other side, to see what shall befall thee. [10] Consult not with one that suspecteth thee: and hide thy counsel from such as envy thee. [11] Neither consult with a woman touching her of whom she is jealous; neither with a coward in matters of war; nor with a merchant concerning exchange; nor with a buyer of selling; nor with an envious man of thankfulness; nor with an unmerciful man touching kindness; nor with the slothful for any work; nor with an hireling for a year of finishing work; nor with an idle servant of much business: hearken not unto these in any matter of counsel. [12] But be continually with a godly man, whom thou knowest to keep the commandments of the Lord, whose, mind is according to thy mind, and will sorrow with thee, if thou shalt miscarry. [13] And let the counsel of thine own heart stand: for there is no man more faithful unto thee than it. [14] For a man's mind is sometime wont to tell him more than seven watchmen, that sit above in an high tower. [15] And above all this pray to the most High, that he will direct thy way in truth. [16] Let reason go before every enterprize, and counsel before every action. [17] The countenance is a sign of changing of the heart. [18] Four manner of things appear: good and evil, life and death: but the tongue ruleth over them continually. [19] There is one that is wise and teacheth many, and yet is unprofitable to himself. [20] There is one that sheweth wisdom in words, and is hated: he shall be destitute of all food. [21] For grace is not given, him from the Lord, because he is deprived of all wisdom. [22] Another is wise to himself; and the fruits of understanding are commendable in his mouth. [23] A wise man instructeth his people; and the fruits of his understanding fail not. [24] A wise man shall be filled with blessing; and all they that see him shall count him happy. [25] The days of the life of man may be numbered: but the days of Israel are innumerable. [26] A wise man shall inherit glory among his people, and his name shall be perpetual. [27] My son, prove thy soul in thy life, and see what is evil for it, and give not that unto it. [28] For all things are not profitable for all men, neither hath every soul

pleasure in every thing. [29] Be not unsatiable in any dainty thing, nor too greedy upon meats: [30] For excess of meats bringeth sickness, and surfeiting will turn into choler. [31] By surfeiting have many perished; but he that taketh heed prolongeth his life.

Sir.38

[1] Honour a physician with the honour due unto him for the uses which ye may have of him: for the Lord hath created him. [2] For of the most High cometh healing, and he shall receive honour of the king. [3] The skill of the physician shall lift up his head: and in the sight of great men he shall be in admiration. [4] The Lord hath created medicines out of the earth; and he that is wise will not abhor them. [5] Was not the water made sweet with wood, that the virtue thereof might be known? [6] And he hath given men skill, that he might be honoured in his marvellous works. [7] With such doth he heal [men,] and taketh away their pains. [8] Of such doth the apothecary make a confection; and of his works there is no end; and from him is peace over all the earth, [9] My son, in thy sickness be not negligent: but pray unto the Lord, and he will make thee whole. [10] Leave off from sin, and order thine hands aright, and cleanse thy heart from all wickedness. [11] Give a sweet savour, and a memorial of fine flour; and make a fat offering, as not being. [12] Then give place to the physician, for the Lord hath created him: let him not go from thee, for thou hast need of him. [13] There is a time when in their hands there is good success. [14] For they shall also pray unto the Lord, that he would prosper that, which they give for ease and remedy to prolong life. [15] He that sinneth before his Maker, let him fall into the hand of the physician. [16] My son, let tears fall down over the dead, and begin to lament, as if thou hadst suffered great harm thyself; and then cover his body according to the custom, and neglect not his burial. [17] Weep bitterly, and make great moan, and use lamentation, as he is worthy, and that a day or two, lest thou be evil spoken of: and then comfort thyself for thy heaviness. [18] For of heaviness cometh death, and the heaviness of the heart breaketh strength. [19] In affliction also sorrow remaineth: and the life of the poor is the curse of the heart. [20] Take no heaviness to heart: drive it away, and member the last end. [21] Forget it not, for there is no turning again: thou shalt not do him good, but hurt thyself. [22] Remember my judgment: for thine also shall be so; yesterday for me, and to day for thee. [23] When the dead is at rest, let his remembrance rest; and be comforted for him, when his Spirit is departed from him. [24] The wisdom of a learned man cometh by opportunity of leisure: and he that hath little business shall become wise. [25] How can he get wisdom that holdeth the plough, and that glorieth in the goad, that driveth oxen, and is occupied in their labours, and whose talk is of bullocks? [26] He giveth his mind to make furrows; and is diligent to give the kine fodder. [27] So every carpenter and workmaster, that laboureth night and day: and they that cut and grave seals, and are diligent to make great variety, and give themselves to counterfeit imagery, and watch to finish a work: [28] The smith also sitting by the anvil, and considering the iron

work, the vapour of the fire wasteth his flesh, and he fighteth with the heat of the furnace: the noise of the hammer and the anvil is ever in his ears, and his eyes look still upon the pattern of the thing that he maketh; he setteth his mind to finish his work, and watcheth to polish it perfectly: [29] So doth the potter sitting at his work, and turning the wheel about with his feet, who is alway carefully set at his work, and maketh all his work by number; [30] He fashioneth the clay with his arm, and boweth down his strength before his feet; he applieth himself to lead it over; and he is diligent to make clean the furnace: [31] All these trust to their hands: and every one is wise in his work. [32] Without these cannot a city be inhabited: and they shall not dwell where they will, nor go up and down: [33] They shall not be sought for in publick counsel, nor sit high in the congregation: they shall not sit on the judges' seat, nor understand the sentence of judgment: they cannot declare justice and judgment; and they shall not be found where parables are spoken. [34] But they will maintain the state of the world, and [all] their desire is in the work of their craft.

Sir.39

[1] But he that giveth his mind to the law of the most High, and is occupied in the meditation thereof, will seek out the wisdom of all the ancient, and be occupied in prophecies. [2] He will keep the sayings of the renowned men: and where subtil parables are, he will be there also. [3] He will seek out the secrets of grave sentences, and be conversant in dark parables. [4] He shall serve among great men, and appear before princes: he will travel through strange countries; for he hath tried the good and the evil among men. [5] He will give his heart to resort early to the Lord that made him, and will pray before the most High, and will open his mouth in prayer, and make supplication for his sins. [6] When the great Lord will, he shall be filled with the spirit of understanding: he shall pour out wise sentences, and give thanks unto the Lord in his prayer. [7] He shall direct his counsel and knowledge, and in his secrets shall he meditate. [8] He shall shew forth that which he hath learned, and shall glory in the law of the covenant of the Lord. [9] Many shall commend his understanding; and so long as the world endureth, it shall not be blotted out; his memorial shall not depart away, and his name shall live from generation to generation. [10] Nations shall shew forth his wisdom, and the congregation shall declare his praise. [11] If he die, he shall leave a greater name than a thousand: and if he live, he shall increase it. [12] Yet have I more to say, which I have thought upon; for I am filled as the moon at the full. [13] Hearken unto me, ye holy children, and bud forth as a rose growing by the brook of the field: [14] And give ye a sweet savour as frankincense, and flourish as a lily, send forth a smell, and sing a song of praise, bless the Lord in all his works. [15] Magnify his name, and shew forth his praise with the songs of your lips, and with harps, and in praising him ye shall say after this manner: [16] All the works of the Lord are exceeding good, and whatsoever he commandeth shall be accomplished in due season. [17] And none may say, What is this? wherefore is that? for at time convenient they shall all be sought out: at his commandment the waters stood as an heap, and at the words of his mouth the

receptacles of waters. [18] At his commandment is done whatsoever pleaseth him; and none can hinder, when he will save. [19] The works of all flesh are before him, and nothing can be hid from his eyes. [20] He seeth from everlasting to everlasting; and there is nothing wonderful before him. [21] A man need not to say, What is this? wherefore is that? for he hath made all things for their uses.

[22] His blessing covered the dry land as a river, and watered it as a flood. [23] As he hath turned the waters into saltness: so shall the heathen inherit his wrath. [24] As his ways are plain unto the holy; so are they stumblingblocks unto the wicked. [25] For the good are good things created from the beginning: so evil things for sinners. [26] The principal things for the whole use of man's life are water, fire, iron, and salt, flour of wheat, honey, milk, and the blood of the grape, and oil, and clothing. [27] All these things are for good to the godly: so to the sinners they are turned into evil. [28] There be spirits that are created for vengeance, which in their fury lay on sore strokes; in the time of destruction they pour out their force, and appease the wrath of him that made them. [29] Fire, and hail, and famine, and death, all these were created for vengeance; [30] Teeth of wild beasts, and scorpions, serpents, and the sword punishing the wicked to destruction. [31] They shall rejoice in his commandment, and they shall be ready upon earth, when need is; and when their time is come, they shall not transgress his word. [32] Therefore from the beginning I was resolved, and thought upon these things, and have left them in writing. [33] All the works of the Lord are good: and he will give every needful thing in due season. [34] So that a man cannot say, This is worse than that: for in time they shall all be well approved. [35] And therefore praise ye the Lord with the whole heart and mouth, and bless the name of the Lord.

Sir.40

[1] Great travail is created for every man, and an heavy yoke is upon the sons of Adam, from the day that they go out of their mother's womb, till the day that they return to the mother of all things. [2] Their imagination of things to come, and the day of death, [trouble] their thoughts, and [cause] fear of heart; [3] From him that sitteth on a throne of glory, unto him that is humbled in earth and ashes; [4] From him that weareth purple and a crown, unto him that is clothed with a linen frock. [5] Wrath, and envy, trouble, and unquietness, fear of death, and anger, and strife, and in the time of rest upon his bed his night sleep, do change his knowledge. [6] A little or nothing is his rest, and afterward he is in his sleep, as in a day of keeping watch, troubled in the vision of his heart, as if he were escaped out of a battle.

[7] When all is safe, he awaketh, and marvelleth that the fear was nothing. [8] [Such things happen] unto all flesh, both man and beast, and that is sevenfold more upon sinners. [9] Death, and bloodshed, strife, and sword, calamities, famine, tribulation, and the scourge; [10] These things are created for the wicked, and for their sakes came the flood. [11] All things that are of the earth shall turn to the earth again: and that which is of the waters doth return into the sea. [12] All bribery and injustice shall be blotted out: but true dealing shall endure for ever. [13] The goods

of the unjust shall be dried up like a river, and shall vanish with noise, like a great thunder in rain. [14] While he openeth his hand he shall rejoice: so shall transgressors come to nought. [15] The children of the ungodly shall not bring forth many branches: but are as unclean roots upon a hard rock. [16] The weed growing upon every water and bank of a river shall be pulled up before all grass. [17] Bountifulness is as a most fruitful garden, and mercifulness endureth for ever. [18] To labour, and to be content with that a man hath, is a sweet life: but he that findeth a treasure is above them both. [19] Children and the building of a city continue a man's name: but a blameless wife is counted above them both. [20] Wine and musick rejoice the heart: but the love of wisdom is above them both. [21] The pipe and the psaltery make sweet melody: but a pleasant tongue is above them both. [22] Thine eye desireth favour and beauty: but more than both corn while it is green. [23] A friend and companion never meet amiss: but above both is a wife with her husband. [24] Brethren and help are against time of trouble: but alms shall deliver more than them both. [25] Gold and silver make the foot stand sure: but counsel is esteemed above them both. [26] Riches and strength lift up the heart: but the fear of the Lord is above them both: there is no want in the fear of the Lord, and it needeth not to seek help. [27] The fear of the Lord is a fruitful garden, and covereth him above all glory. [28] My son, lead not a beggar's life; for better it is to die than to beg. [29] The life of him that dependeth on another man's table is not to be counted for a life; for he polluteth himself with other men's meat: but a wise man well nurtured will beware thereof. [30] Begging is sweet in the mouth of the shameless: but in his belly there shall burn a fire.

Sir.41

[1] O death, how bitter is the remembrance of thee to a man that liveth at rest in his possessions, unto the man that hath nothing to vex him, and that hath prosperity in all things: yea, unto him that is yet able to receive meat! [2] O death, acceptable is thy sentence unto the needy, and unto him whose strength faileth, that is now in the last age, and is vexed with all things, and to him that despaireth, and hath lost patience! [3] Fear not the sentence of death, remember them that have been before thee, and that come after; for this is the sentence of the Lord over all flesh. [4] And why art thou against the pleasure of the most High? there is no inquisition in the grave, whether thou have lived ten, or an hundred, or a thousand years. [5] The children of sinners are abominable children, and they that are conversant in the dwelling of the ungodly. [6] The inheritance of sinners' children shall perish, and their posterity shall have a perpetual reproach. [7] The children will complain of an ungodly father, because they shall be reproached for his sake. [8] Woe be unto you, ungodly men, which have forsaken the law of the most high God! for if ye increase, it shall be to your destruction: [9] And if ye be born, ye shall be born to a curse: and if ye die, a curse shall be your portion. [10] All that are of the earth shall turn to earth again: so the ungodly shall go from a curse to destruction. [11] The mourning of men is about their bodies: but an ill name of sinners shall be blotted out. [12]

Have regard to thy name; for that shall continue with thee above a thousand great treasures of gold. [13] A good life hath but few days: but a good name endureth for ever. [14] My children, keep discipline in peace: for wisdom that is hid, and a treasure that is not seen, what profit is in them both? [15] A man that hideth his foolishness is better than a man that hideth his wisdom. [16] Therefore be shamefaced according to my word: for it is not good to retain all shamefacedness; neither is it altogether approved in every thing. [17] Be ashamed of whoredom before father and mother: and of a lie before a prince and a mighty man; [18] Of an offence before a judge and ruler; of iniquity before a congregation and people; of unjust dealing before thy partner and friend; [19] And of theft in regard of the place where thou sojournest, and in regard of the truth of God and his covenant; and to lean with thine elbow upon the meat; and of scorning to give and take; [20] And of silence before them that salute thee; and to look upon an harlot; [21] And to turn away thy face from thy kinsman; or to take away a portion or a gift; or to gaze upon another man's wife. [22] Or to be overbusy with his maid, and come not near her bed; or of upbraiding speeches before friends; and after thou hast given, upbraid not; [23] Or of iterating and speaking again that which thou hast heard; and of revealing of secrets. [24] So shalt thou be truly shamefaced and find favour before all men.

Sir.42

[1] Of these things be not thou ashamed, and accept no person to sin thereby: [2] Of the law of the most High, and his covenant; and of judgment to justify the ungodly; [3] Of reckoning with thy partners and travellers; or of the gift of the heritage of friends; [4] Of exactness of balance and weights; or of getting much or little; [5] And of merchants' indifferent selling; of much correction of children; and to make the side of an evil servant to bleed. [6] Sure keeping is good, where an evil wife is; and shut up, where many hands are. [7] Deliver all things in number and weight; and put all in writing that thou givest out, or receivest in. [8] Be not ashamed to inform the unwise and foolish, and the extreme aged that contendeth with those that are young: thus shalt thou be truly learned, and approved of all men living. [9] The father waketh for the daughter, when no man knoweth; and the care for her taketh away sleep: when she is young, lest she pass away the flower of her age; and being married, lest she should be hated: [10] In her virginity, lest she should be defiled and gotten with child in her father's house; and having an husband, lest she should misbehave herself; and when she is married, lest she should be barren. [11] Keep a sure watch over a shameless daughter, lest she make thee a laughingstock to thine enemies, and a byword in the city, and a reproach among the people, and make thee ashamed before the multitude. [12] Behold not every body's beauty, and sit not in the midst of women. [13] For from garments cometh a moth, and from women wickedness. [14] Better is the churlishness of a man than a courteous woman, a woman, I say, which bringeth shame and reproach. [15] I will now remember the works of the Lord, and declare the things that I have seen: In the words of the Lord are his works. [16] The sun that giveth light looketh upon all things, and

the work thereof is full of the glory of the Lord. [17] The Lord hath not given power to the saints to declare all his marvellous works, which the Almighty Lord firmly settled, that whatsoever is might be established for his glory. [18] He seeketh out the deep, and the heart, and considereth their crafty devices: for the Lord knoweth all that may be known, and he beholdeth the signs of the world. [19] He declareth the things that are past, and for to come, and revealeth the steps of hidden things. [20] No thought escapeth him, neither any word is hidden from him. [21] He hath garnished the excellent works of his wisdom, and he is from everlasting to everlasting: unto him may nothing be added, neither can he be diminished, and he hath no need of any counsellor. [22] Oh how desirable are all his works! and that a man may see even to a spark. [23] All these things live and remain for ever for all uses, and they are all obedient. [24] All things are double one against another: and he hath made nothing imperfect. [25] One thing establisheth the good or another: and who shall be filled with beholding his glory?

Sir.43

[1] The pride of the height, the clear firmament, the beauty of heaven, with his glorious shew; [2] The sun when it appeareth, declaring at his rising a marvellous instrument, the work of the most High: [3] At noon it parcheth the country, and who can abide the burning heat thereof? [4] A man blowing a furnace is in works of heat, but the sun burneth the mountains three times more; breathing out fiery vapours, and sending forth bright beams, it dimmeth the eyes. [5] Great is the Lord that made it; and at his commandment runneth hastily. [6] He made the moon also to serve in her season for a declaration of times, and a sign of the world. [7] From the moon is the sign of feasts, a light that decreaseth in her perfection. [8] The month is called after her name, increasing wonderfully in her changing, being an instrument of the armies above, shining in the firmament of heaven; [9] The beauty of heaven, the glory of the stars, an ornament giving light in the highest places of the Lord. [10] At the commandment of the Holy One they will stand in their order, and never faint in their watches. [11] Look upon the rainbow, and praise him that made it; very beautiful it is in the brightness thereof. [12] It compasseth the heaven about with a glorious circle, and the hands of the most High have bended it. [13] By his commandment he maketh the snow to fall aplace, and sendeth swiftly the lightnings of his judgment. [14] Through this the treasures are opened: and clouds fly forth as fowls. [15] By his great power he maketh the clouds firm, and the hailstones are broken small. [16] At his sight the mountains are shaken, and at his will the south wind bloweth. [17] The noise of the thunder maketh the earth to tremble: so doth the northern storm and the whirlwind: as birds flying he scattereth the snow, and the falling down thereof is as the lighting of grasshoppers: [18] The eye marvelleth at the beauty of the whiteness thereof, and the heart is astonished at the raining of it. [19] The hoarfrost also as salt he poureth on the earth, and being congealed, it lieth on the top of sharp stakes. [20] When the cold north wind bloweth, and the water is congealed into ice, it abideth upon every gathering together of water, and clotheth the

water as with a breastplate. [21] It devoureth the mountains, and burneth the wilderness, and consumeth the grass as fire. [22] A present remedy of all is a mist coming speedily, a dew coming after heat refresheth. [23] By his counsel he appeaseth the deep, and planteth islands therein.

[24] They that sail on the sea tell of the danger thereof; and when we hear it with our ears, we marvel thereat. [25] For therein be strange and wondrous works, variety of all kinds of beasts and whales created. [26] By him the end of them hath prosperous success, and by his word all things consist. [27] We may speak much, and yet come short: wherefore in sum, he is all. [28] How shall we be able to magnify him? for he is great above all his works. [29] The Lord is terrible and very great, and marvellous is his power.

[30] When ye glorify the Lord, exalt him as much as ye can; for even yet will he far exceed: and when ye exalt him, put forth all your strength, and be not weary; for ye can never go far enough. [31] Who hath seen him, that he might tell us? and who can magnify him as he is? [32] There are yet hid greater things than these be, for we have seen but a few of his works. [33] For the Lord hath made all things; and to the godly hath he given wisdom.

Sir.44

[1] Let us now praise famous men, and our fathers that begat us. [2] The Lord hath wrought great glory by them through his great power from the beginning. [3] Such as did bear rule in their kingdoms, men renowned for their power, giving counsel by their understanding, and declaring prophecies: [4] Leaders of the people by their counsels, and by their knowledge of learning meet for the people, wise and eloquent are their instructions: [5] Such as found out musical tunes, and recited verses in writing: [6] Rich men furnished with ability, living peaceably in their habitations: [7] All these were honoured in their generations, and were the glory of their times. [8] There be of them, that have left a name behind them, that their praises might be reported. [9] And some there be, which have no memorial; who are perished, as though they had never been; and are become as though they had never been born; and their children after them. [10] But these were merciful men, whose righteousness hath not been forgotten. [11] With their seed shall continually remain a good inheritance, and their children are within the covenant. [12] Their seed standeth fast, and their children for their sakes. [13] Their seed shall remain for ever, and their glory shall not be blotted out. [14] Their bodies are buried in peace; but their name liveth for evermore. [15] The people will tell of their wisdom, and the congregation will shew forth their praise. [16] Enoch pleased the Lord, and was translated, being an example of repentance to all generations. [17] Noah was found perfect and righteous; in the time of wrath he was taken in exchange [for the world;] therefore was he left as a remnant unto the earth, when the flood came. [18] An everlasting covenant was made with him, that all flesh should perish no more by the flood. [19] Abraham was a great father of many people: in glory was there none like unto him; [20] Who kept the law of the most High, and was in covenant with him: he established the covenant in his flesh; and when he was proved, he was

found faithful. [21] Therefore he assured him by an oath, that he would bless the nations in his seed, and that he would multiply him as the dust of the earth, and exalt his seed as the stars, and cause them to inherit from sea to sea, and from the river unto the utmost part of the land. [22] With Isaac did he establish likewise [for Abraham his father's sake] the blessing of all men, and the covenant, And made it rest upon the head of Jacob. He acknowledged him in his blessing, and gave him an heritage, and divided his portions; among the twelve tribes did he part them.

Sir.45

[1] And he brought out of him a merciful man, which found favour in the sight of all flesh, even Moses, beloved of God and men, whose memorial is blessed. [2] He made him like to the glorious saints, and magnified him, so that his enemies stood in fear of him. [3] By his words he caused the wonders to cease, and he made him glorious in the sight of kings, and gave him a commandment for his people, and shewed him part of his glory. [4] He sanctified him in his faithfuless and meekness, and chose him out of all men. [5] He made him to hear his voice, and brought him into the dark cloud, and gave him commandments before his face, even the law of life and knowledge, that he might teach Jacob his covenants, and Israel his judgments. [6] He exalted Aaron, an holy man like unto him, even his brother, of the tribe of Levi. [7] An everlasting covenant he made with him and gave him the priesthood among the people; he beautified him with comely ornaments, and clothed him with a robe of glory. [8] He put upon him perfect glory; and strengthened him with rich garments, with breeches, with a long robe, and the ephod. [9] And he compassed him with pomegranates, and with many golden bells round about, that as he went there might be a sound, and a noise made that might be heard in the temple, for a memorial to the children of his people; [10] With an holy garment, with gold, and blue silk, and purple, the work of the embroidere, with a breastplate of judgment, and with Urim and Thummim; [11] With twisted scarlet, the work of the cunning workman, with precious stones graven like seals, and set in gold, the work of the jeweller, with a writing engraved for a memorial, after the number of the tribes of Israel. [12] He set a crown of gold upon the mitre, wherein was engraved Holiness, an ornament of honour, a costly work, the desires of the eyes, goodly and beautiful. [13] Before him there were none such, neither did ever any stranger put them on, but only his children and his children's children perpetually. [14] Their sacrifices shall be wholly consumed every day twice continually. [15] Moses consecrated him, and anointed him with holy oil: this was appointed unto him by an everlasting covenant, and to his seed, so long as the heavens should remain, that they should minister unto him, and execute the office of the priesthood, and bless the people in his name. [16] He chose him out of all men living to offer sacrifices to the Lord, incense, and a sweet savour, for a memorial, to make reconciliation for his people. [17] He gave unto him his commandments, and authority in the statutes of judgments, that he should teach Jacob the testimonies, and inform Israel in his laws. [18] Strangers conspired together against him, and maligned him in the wilderness, even the men that were of Dathan's and Abiron's side, and the congregation

of Core, with fury and wrath. [19] This the Lord saw, and it displeased him, and in his wrathful indignation were they consumed: he did wonders upon them, to consume them with the fiery flame. [20] But he made Aaron more honourable, and gave him an heritage, and divided unto him the firstfruits of the increase; especially he prepared bread in abundance: [21] For they eat of the sacrifices of the Lord, which he gave unto him and his seed. [22] Howbeit in the land of the people he had no inheritance, neither had he any portion among the people: for the Lord himself is his portion and inheritance. [23] The third in glory is Phinees the son of Eleazar, because he had zeal in the fear of the Lord, and stood up with good courage of heart: when the people were turned back, and made reconciliation for Israel. [24] Therefore was there a covenant of peace made with him, that he should be the chief of the sanctuary and of his people, and that he and his posterity should have the dignity of the priesthood for ever: [25] According to the covenant made with David son of Jesse, of the tribe of Juda, that the inheritance of the king should be to his posterity alone: so the inheritance of Aaron should also be unto his seed. [26] God give you wisdom in your heart to judge his people in righteousness, that their good things be not abolished, and that their glory may endure for ever.

Sir.46

[1] Jesus the son a Nave was valiant in the wars, and was the successor of Moses in prophecies, who according to his name was made great for the saving of the elect of God, and taking vengeance of the enemies that rose up against them, that he might set Israel in their inheritance. [2] How great glory gat he, when he did lift up his hands, and stretched out his sword against the cities! [3] Who before him so stood to it? for the Lord himself brought his enemies unto him. [4] Did not the sun go back by his means? and was not one day as long as two? [5] He called upon the most high Lord, when the enemies pressed upon him on every side; and the great Lord heard him. [6] And with hailstones of mighty power he made the battle to fall violently upon the nations, and in the descent [of Beth-horon] he destroyed them that resisted, that the nations might know all their strength, because he fought in the sight of the Lord, and he followed the Mighty One. [7] In the time of Moses also he did a work of mercy, he and Caleb the son of Jephunne, in that they withstood the congregation, and withheld the people from sin, and appeased the wicked murmuring. [8] And of six hundred thousand people on foot, they two were preserved to bring them in to the heritage, even unto the land that floweth with milk and honey. [9] The Lord gave strength also unto Caleb, which remained with him unto his old age: so that he entered upon the high places of the land, and his seed obtained it for an heritage: [10] That all the children of Israel might see that it is good to follow the Lord. [11] And concerning the judges, every one by name, whose heart went not a whoring, nor departed from the Lord, let their memory be blessed. [12] Let their bones flourish out of their place, and let the name of them that were honoured be continued upon their children. [13] Samuel, the prophet of the Lord, beloved of his Lord, established a kingdom, and anointed princes over his people. [14] By the law of

the Lord he judged the congregation, and the Lord had respect unto Jacob. [15] By his faithfulness he was found a true prophet, and by his word he was known to be faithful in vision. [16] He called upon the mighty Lord, when his enemies pressed upon him on every side, when he offered the sucking lamb. [17] And the Lord thundered from heaven, and with a great noise made his voice to be heard. [18] And he destroyed the rulers of the Tyrians, and all the princes cf the Philistines. [19] And before his long sleep he made protestations in the sight of the Lord and his anointed, I have not taken any man's goods, so much as a shoe: and no man did accuse him. [20] And after his death he prophesied, and shewed the king his end, and lifted up his voice from the earth in prophecy, to blot out the wickedness of the people.

Sir.47

[1] And after him rose up Nathan to prophesy in the time of David. [2] As is the fat taken away from the peace offering, so was David chosen out of the children of Israel. [3] He played with lions as with kids, and with bears as with lambs. [4] Slew he not a giant, when he was yet but young? and did he not take away reproach from the people, when he lifted up his hand with the stone in the sling, and beat down the boasting of Goliath? [5] For he called upon the most high Lord; and he gave him strength in his right hand to slay that mighty warrior, and set up the horn of his people. [6] So the people honoured him with ten thousands, and praised him in the blessings of the Lord, in that he gave him a crown of glory. [7] For he destroyed the enemies on every side, and brought to nought the Philistines his adversaries, and brake their horn in sunder unto this day. [8] In all his works he praised the Holy One most high with words of glory; with his whole heart he sung songs, and loved him that made him. [9] He set singers also before the altar, that by their voices they might make sweet melody, and daily sing praises in their songs. [10] He beautified their feasts, and set in order the solemn times until the end, that they might praise his holy name, and that the temple might sound from morning. [11] The Lord took away his sins, and exalted his horn for ever: he gave him a covenant of kings, and a throne of glory in Israel. [12] After him rose up a wise son, and for his sake he dwelt at large. [13] Solomon reigned in a peaceable time, and was honoured; for God made all quiet round about him, that he might build an house in his name, and prepare his sanctuary for ever. [14] How wise wast thou in thy youth and, as a flood, filled with understanding! [15] Thy soul covered the whole earth, and thou filledst it with dark parables. [16] Thy name went far unto the islands; and for thy peace thou wast beloved. [17] The countries marvelled at thee for thy songs, and proverbs, and parables, and interpretations. [18] By the name of the Lord God, which is called the Lord God of Israel, thou didst gather gold as tin and didst multiply silver as lead. [19] Thou didst bow thy loins unto women, and by thy body thou wast brought into subjection. [20] Thou didst stain thy honour, and pollute thy seed: so that thou broughtest wrath upon thy children, and wast grieved for thy folly. [21] So the kingdom was divided, and out of Ephraim ruled a rebellious kingdom. [22] But the Lord will never leave off

his mercy, neither shall any of his works perish, neither will he abolish the posterity of his elect, and the seed of him that loveth him he will not take away: wherefore he gave a remnant unto Jacob, and out of him a root unto David. [23] Thus rested Solomon with his fathers, and of his seed he left behind him Roboam, even the foolishness of the people, and one that had no understanding, who turned away the people through his counsel. There was also Jeroboam the son of Nebat, who caused Israel to sin, and shewed Ephraim the way of sin: [24] And their sins were multiplied exceedingly, that they were driven out of the land. [25] For they sought out all wickedness, till the vengeance came upon them.

Sir.48

[1] Then stood up Elias the prophet as fire, and his word burned like a lamp. [2] He brought a sore famine upon them, and by his zeal he diminished their number. [3] By the word of the Lord he shut up the heaven, and also three times brought down fire. [4] O Elias, how wast thou honoured in thy wondrous deeds! and who may glory like unto thee! [5] Who didst raise up a dead man from death, and his soul from the place of the dead, by the word of the most High: [6] Who broughtest kings to destruction, and honorable men from their bed: [7] Who heardest the rebuke of the Lord in Sinai, and in Horeb the judgment of vengeance: [8] Who annointedst kings to take revenge, and prophets to succeed after him: [9] Who was taken up in a whirlwind of fire, and in a chariot of fiery horses: [10] Who wast ordained for reproofs in their times, to pacify the wrath of the Lord's judgment, before it brake forth into fury, and to turn the heart of the father unto the son, and to restore the tribes of Jacob. [11] Blessed are they that saw thee, and slept in love; for we shall surely live. [12] Elias it was, who was covered with a whirlwind: and Eliseus was filled with his spirit: whilst he lived, he was not moved with the presence of any prince, neither could any bring him into subjection. [13] No word could overcome him; and after his death his body prophesied. [14] He did wonders in his life, and at his death were his works marvellous. [15] For all this the people repented not, neither departed they from their sins, till they were spoiled and carried out of their land, and were scattered through all the earth: yet there remained a small people, and a ruler in the house of David: [16] Of whom some did that which was pleasing to God, and some multiplied sins. [17] Ezekias fortified his city, and brought in water into the midst thereof: he digged the hard rock with iron, and made wells for waters. [18] In his time Sennacherib came up, and sent Rabsaces, and lifted up his hand against Sion, and boasted proudly. [19] Then trembled their hearts and hands, and they were in pain, as women in travail. [20] But they called upon the Lord which is merciful, and stretched out their hands toward him: and immediately the Holy One heard them out of heaven, and delivered them by the ministry of Esay. [21] He smote the host of the Assyrians, and his angel destroyed them. [22] For Ezekias had done the thing that pleased the Lord, and was strong in the ways of David his father, as Esay the prophet, who was great and faithful in his vision, had commanded him. [23] In his time the sun went backward, and he lengthened the king's life. [24] He saw by an

excellent spirit what should come to pass at the last, and he comforted them that mourned in Sion. [25] He shewed what should come to pass for ever, and secret things or ever they came.

Sir.49

[1] The remembrance of Josias is like the composition of the perfume that is made by the art of the apothecary: it is sweet as honey in all mouths, and as musick at a banquet of wine. [2] He behaved himself uprightly in the conversion of the people, and took away the abominations of iniquity. [3] He directed his heart unto the Lord, and in the time of the ungodly he established the worship of God. [4] All, except David and Ezekias and Josias, were defective: for they forsook the law of the most High, even the kings of Juda failed. [5] Therefore he gave their power unto others, and their glory to a strange nation. [6] They burnt the chosen city of the sanctuary, and made the streets desolate, according to the prophecy of Jeremias. [7] For they entreated him evil, who nevertheless was a prophet, sanctified in his mother's womb, that he might root out, and afflict, and destroy; and that he might build up also, and plant. [8] It was Ezekiel who saw the glorious vision, which was shewed him upon the chariot of the cherubims. [9] For he made mention of the enemies under the figure of the rain, and directed them that went right. [10] And of the twelve prophets let the memorial be blessed, and let their bones flourish again out of their place: for they comforted Jacob, and delivered them by assured hope. [11] How shall we magnify Zorobabel? even he was as a signet on the right hand: [12] So was Jesus the son of Josedec: who in their time builded the house, and set up an holy temple to the Lord, which was prepared for everlasting glory. [13] And among the elect was Neemias, whose renown is great, who raised up for us the walls that were fallen, and set up the gates and the bars, and raised up our ruins again. [14] But upon the earth was no man created like Enoch; for he was taken from the earth. [15] Neither was there a young man born like Joseph, a governor of his brethren, a stay of the people, whose bones were regarded of the Lord. [16] Sem and Seth were in great honour among men, and so was Adam above every living thing in creation.

Sir.50

[1] Simon the high priest, the son of Onias, who in his life repaired the house again, and in his days fortified the temple: [2] And by him was built from the foundation the double height, the high fortress of the wall about the temple: [3] In his days the cistern to receive water, being in compass as the sea, was covered with plates of brass: [4] He took care of the temple that it should not fall, and fortified the city against besieging: [5] How was he honoured in the midst of the people in his coming out of the sanctuary! [6] He was as the morning star in the midst of a cloud, and as the moon at the full: [7] As the sun shining upon the temple of the most High, and as the rainbow giving light in the bright clouds: [8] And as the flower of roses in the spring of the year, as lilies by the rivers of waters, and as the branches of the frankincense tree in the time of summer: [9] As fire and incense in the censer, and as a vessel of beaten gold set with all manner of precious stones: [10] And as a fair olive tree budding forth fruit, and as a cypress tree which groweth up to the clouds.

[11] When he put on the robe of honour, and was clothed with the perfection of glory, when he went up to the holy altar, he made the garment of holiness honourable. [12] When he took the portions out of the priests' hands, he himself stood by the hearth of the altar, compassed about, as a young cedar in Libanus; and as palm trees compassed they him round about. [13] So were all the sons of Aaron in their glory, and the oblations of the Lord in their hands, before all the congregation of Israel. [14] And finishing the service at the altar, that he might adorn the offering of the most high Almighty, [15] He stretched out his hand to the cup, and poured of the blood of the grape, he poured out at the foot of the altar a sweetsmelling savour unto the most high King of all. [16] Then shouted the sons of Aaron, and sounded the silver trumpets, and made a great noise to be heard, for a remembrance before the most High. [17] Then all the people together hasted, and fell down to the earth upon their faces to worship their Lord God Almighty, the most High. [18] The singers also sang praises with their voices, with great variety of sounds was there made sweet melody. [19] And the people besought the Lord, the most High, by prayer before him that is merciful, till the solemnity of the Lord was ended, and they had finished his service. [20] Then he went down, and lifted up his hands over the whole congregation of the children of Israel, to give the blessing of the Lord with his lips, and to rejoice in his name. [21] And they bowed themselves down to worship the second time, that they might receive a blessing from the most High. [22] Now therefore bless ye the God of all, which only doeth wondrous things every where, which exalteth our days from the womb, and dealeth with us according to his mercy. [23] He grant us joyfulness of heart, and that peace may be in our days in Israel for ever: [24] That he would confirm his mercy with us, and deliver us at his time! [25] There be two manner of nations which my heart abhorreth, and the third is no nation: [26] They that sit upon the mountain of Samaria, and they that dwell among the Philistines, and that foolish people that dwell in Sichem. [27] Jesus the son of Sirach of Jerusalem hath written in this book the instruction of understanding and knowledge, who out of his heart poured forth wisdom. [28] Blessed is he that shall be exercised in these things; and he that layeth them up in his heart shall become wise. [29] For if he do them, he shall be strong to all things: for the light of the Lord leadeth him, who giveth wisdom to the godly. Blessed be the name of the Lord for ever. Amen, Amen.

Sir.51

[A Prayer of Jesus the son of Sirach.][1] I will thank thee, O Lord and King, and praise thee, O God my Saviour: I do give praise unto thy name: [2] For thou art my defender and helper, and has preserved my body from destruction, and from the snare of the slanderous tongue, and from the lips that forge lies, and has been mine helper against mine adversaries: [3] And hast delivered me, according to the multitude of they mercies and greatness of thy name, from the teeth of them that were ready to devour me, and out of the hands of such as sought after my life, and from the

manifold afflictions which I had; [4] From the choking of
fire on every side, and from the midst of the fire which I
kindled not; [5] From the depth of the belly of hell, from
an unclean tongue, and from lying words. [6] By an
accusation to the king from an unrighteous tongue my soul
drew near even unto death, my life was near to the hell
beneath. [7] They compassed me on every side, and there
was no man to help me: I looked for the succour of men,
but there was none. [8] Then thought I upon thy mercy, O
Lord, and upon thy acts of old, how thou deliverest such as
wait for thee, and savest them out of the hands of the
enemies. [9] Then lifted I up my supplications from the
earth, and prayed for deliverance from death. [10] I called
upon the Lord, the Father of my Lord, that he would not
leave me in the days of my trouble, and in the time of the
proud, when there was no help. [11] I will praise thy name
continually, and will sing praises with thanksgiving; and so
my prayer was heard: [12] For thou savedst me from
destruction, and deliveredst me from the evil time:
therefore will I give thanks, and praise thee, and bless they
name, O Lord. [13] When I was yet young, or ever I went
abroad, I desired wisdom openly in my prayer. [14] I
prayed for her before the temple, and will seek her out even
to the end. [15] Even from the flower till the grape was
ripe hath my heart delighted in her: my foot went the right
way, from my youth up sought I after her. [16] I bowed
down mine ear a little, and received her, and gat much
learning. [17] I profited therein, therefore will I ascribe
glory unto him that giveth me wisdom. [18] For I purposed
to do after her, and earnestly I followed that which is good;
so shall I not be confounded. [19] My soul hath wrestled
with her, and in my doings I was exact: I stretched forth my
hands to the heaven above, and bewailed my ignorances of
her. [20] I directed my soul unto her, and I found her in
pureness: I have had my heart joined with her from the
beginning, therefore shall I not be foresaken. [21] My heart
was troubled in seeking her: therefore have I gotten a good
possession. [22] The Lord hath given me a tongue for my
reward, and I will praise him therewith. [23] Draw near
unto me, ye unlearned, and dwell in the house of learning.
[24] Wherefore are ye slow, and what say ye to these things,
seeing your souls are very thirsty? [25] I opened my mouth,
and said, Buy her for yourselves without money. [26] Put
your neck under the yoke, and let your soul receive
instruction: she is hard at hand to find. [27] Behold with
your eyes, how that I have but little labour, and have gotten
unto me much rest. [28] Get learning with a great sum of
money, and get much gold by her. [29] Let your soul
rejoice in his mercy, and be not ashamed of his praise. [30]
Work your work betimes, and in his time he will give you
your reward.

BARUCH

Bar.1

[1] And these are the words of the book, which Baruch the son of Nerias, the son of Maasias, the son of Sedecias, the son of Asadias, the son of Chelcias, wrote in Babylon, [2] In the fifth year, and in the seventh day of the month, what time as the Chaldeans took Jerusalem, and burnt it with fire. [3] And Baruch did read the words of this book in the hearing of Jechonias the son of Joachim king of Juda, and in the ears of all the people that came to hear the book, [4] And in the hearing of the nobles, and of the king's sons, and in the hearing of the elders, and of all the people, from the lowest unto the highest, even of all them that dwelt at Babylon by the river Sud. [5] Whereupon they wept, fasted, and prayed before the Lord. [6] They made also a collection of money according to every man's power: [7] And they sent it to Jerusalem unto Joachim the high priest, the son of Chelcias, son of Salom, and to the priests, and to all the people which were found with him at Jerusalem, [8] At the same time when he received the vessels of the house of the Lord, that were carried out of the temple, to return them into the land of Juda, the tenth day of the month Sivan, namely, silver vessels, which Sedecias the son of Josias king of Jada had made, [9] After that Nabuchodonosor king of Babylon had carried away Jechonias, and the princes, and the captives, and the mighty men, and the people of the land, from Jerusalem, and brought them unto Babylon. [10] And they said, Behold, we have sent you money to buy you burnt offerings, and sin offerings, and incense, and prepare ye manna, and offer upon the altar of the Lord our God; [11] And pray for the life of Nabuchodonosor king of Babylon, and for the life of Balthasar his son, that their days may be upon earth as the days of heaven: [12] And the Lord will give us strength, and lighten our eyes, and we shall live under the shadow of Nabuchodonosor king of Babylon, and under the shadow of Balthasar his son, and we shall serve them many days, and find favour in their sight. [13] Pray for us also unto the Lord our God, for we have sinned against the Lord our God; and unto this day the fury of the Lord and his wrath is not turned from us. [14] And ye shall read this book which we have sent unto you, to make confession in the house of the Lord, upon the feasts and solemn days. [15] And ye shall say, To the Lord our God belongeth righteousness, but unto us the confusion of faces, as it is come to pass this day, unto them of Juda, and to the inhabitants of Jerusalem, [16] And to our kings, and to our princes, and to our priests, and to our prophets, and to our fathers: [17] For we have sinned before the Lord, [18] And disobeyed him, and have not hearkened unto the voice of the Lord our God, to walk in the commandments that he gave us openly: [19] Since the day that the Lord brought our forefathers out of the land of Egypt, unto this present day, we have been disobedient unto the Lord our God, and we have been negligent in not hearing his voice. [20] Wherefore the evils cleaved unto us, and the curse, which the Lord appointed by Moses his servant at the time that he brought our fathers out of the land of Egypt, to give us a land that floweth with milk and honey, like as it is to see this day. [21] Nevertheless we have not hearkened unto the voice of the Lord our God, according unto all the words of the prophets, whom he sent unto us: [22] But every man followed the imagination of his own wicked heart, to serve strange gods, and to do evil in the sight of the Lord our God.

Bar.2

[1] Therefore the Lord hath made good his word, which he pronounced against us, and against our judges that judged Israel, and against our kings, and against our princes, and against the men of Israel and Juda, [2] To bring upon us great plagues, such as never happened under the whole heaven, as it came to pass in Jerusalem, according to the things that were written in the law of Moses; [3] That a man should eat the flesh of his own son, and the flesh of his own daughter. [4] Moreover he hath delivered them to be in subjection to all the kingdoms that are round about us, to be as a reproach and desolation among all the people round about, where the Lord hath scattered them. [5] Thus we were cast down, and not exalted, because we have sinned against the Lord our God, and have not been obedient unto his voice. [6] To the Lord our God appertaineth righteousness: but unto us and to our fathers open shame, as appeareth this day. [7] For all these plagues are come upon us, which the Lord hath pronounced against us [8] Yet have we not prayed before the Lord, that we might turn every one from the imaginations of his wicked heart. [9] Wherefore the Lord watched over us for evil, and the Lord hath brought it upon us: for the Lord is righteous in all his works which he hath commanded us. [10] Yet we have not hearkened unto his voice, to walk in the commandments of the Lord, that he hath set before us. [11] And now, O Lord God of Israel, that hast brought thy people out of the land of Egypt with a mighty hand, and high arm, and with signs, and with wonders, and with great power, and hast gotten thyself a name, as appeareth this day: [12] O Lord our God, we have sinned, we have done ungodly, we have dealt unrighteously in all thine ordinances. [13] Let thy wrath turn from us: for we are but a few left among the heathen, where thou hast scattered us.

[14] Hear our prayers, O Lord, and our petitions, and deliver us for thine own sake, and give us favour in the sight of them which have led us away: [15] That all the earth may know that thou art the Lord our God, because Israel and his posterity is called by thy name. [16] O Lord, look down from thine holy house, and consider us: bow down thine ear, O Lord, to hear us. [17] Open thine eyes, and behold; for the dead that are in the graves, whose souls are taken from their bodies, will give unto the Lord neither praise nor righteousness: [18] But the soul that is greatly vexed, which goeth stooping and feeble, and the eyes that fail, and the hungry soul, will give thee praise and righteousness, O Lord. [19] Therefore we do not make our humble supplication before thee, O Lord our God, for the righteousness of our fathers, and of our kings. [20] For thou hast sent out thy wrath and indignation upon us, as thou hast spoken by thy servants the prophets, saying, [21] Thus saith the Lord, Bow down your shoulders to serve the king of Babylon: so shall ye remain in the land that I gave unto your fathers. [22] But if ye will not hear the voice of the Lord, to serve the king of Babylon, [23] I will cause to

cease out of the cites of Judah, and from without Jerusalem, the voice of mirth, and the voice of joy, the voice of the bridegroom, and the voice of the bride: and the whole land shall be desolate of inhabitants. [24] But we would not hearken unto thy voice, to serve the king of Babylon: therefore hast thou made good the words that thou spakest by thy servants the prophets, namely, that the bones of our kings, and the bones of our fathers, should be taken out of their place. [25] And, lo, they are cast out to the heat of the day, and to the frost of the night, and they died in great miseries by famine, by sword, and by pestilence. [26] And the house which is called by thy name hast thou laid waste, as it is to be seen this day, for the wickedness of the house of Israel and the house of Juda. [27] O Lord our God, thou hast dealt with us after all thy goodness, and according to all that great mercy of thine, [28] As thou spakest by thy servant Moses in the day when thou didst command him to write the law before the children of Israel, saying, [29] If ye will not hear my voice, surely this very great multitude shall be turned into a small number among the nations, where I will scatter them. [30] For I knew that they would not hear me, because it is a stiffnecked people: but in the land of their captivities they shall remember themselves. [31] And shall know that I am the Lord their God: for I will give them an heart, and ears to hear: [32] And they shall praise me in the land of their captivity, and think upon my name, [33] And return from their stiff neck, and from their wicked deeds: for they shall remember the way of their fathers, which sinned before the Lord. [34] And I will bring them again into the land which I promised with an oath unto their fathers, Abraham, Isaac, and Jacob, and they shall be lords of it: and I will increase them, and they shall not be diminished. [35] And I will make an everlasting covenant with them to be their God, and they shall be my people: and I will no more drive my people of Israel out of the land that I have given them.

Bar.3

[1] O Lord Almighty, God of Israel, the soul in anguish the troubled spirit, crieth unto thee. [2] Hear, O Lord, and have mercy; ar thou art merciful: and have pity upon us, because we have sinned before thee. [3] For thou endurest for ever, and we perish utterly. [4] O Lord Almighty, thou God of Israel, hear now the prayers of the dead Israelites, and of their children, which have sinned before thee, and not hearkened unto the voice of thee their God: for the which cause these plagues cleave unto us. [5] Remember not the iniquities of our forefathers: but think upon thy power and thy name now at this time. [6] For thou art the Lord our God, and thee, O Lord, will we praise. [7] And for this cause thou hast put thy fear in our hearts, to the intent that we should call upon thy name, and praise thee in our captivity: for we have called to mind all the iniquity of our forefathers, that sinned before thee. [8] Behold, we are yet this day in our captivity, where thou hast scattered us, for a reproach and a curse, and to be subject to payments, according to all the iniquities of our fathers, which departed from the Lord our God. [9] Hear, Israel, the commandments of life: give ear to understand wisdom. [10] How happeneth it Israel, that thou art in thine enemies' land, that thou art waxen old in a strange country, that thou art defiled with the dead, [11] That thou art counted with

them that go down into the grave? [12] Thou hast forsaken the fountain of wisdom. [13] For if thou hadst walked in the way of God, thou shouldest have dwelled in peace for ever. [14] Learn where is wisdom, where is strength, where is understanding; that thou mayest know also where is length of days, and life, where is the light of the eyes, and peace. [15] Who hath found out her place? or who hath come into her treasures ? [16] Where are the princes of the heathen become, and such as ruled the beasts upon the earth; [17] They that had their pastime with the fowls of the air, and they that hoarded up silver and gold, wherein men trust, and made no end of their getting? [18] For they that wrought in silver, and were so careful, and whose works are unsearchable, [19] They are vanished and gone down to the grave, and others are come up in their steads. [20] Young men have seen light, and dwelt upon the earth: but the way of knowledge have they not known, [21] Nor understood the paths thereof, nor laid hold of it: their children were far off from that way. [22] It hath not been heard of in Chanaan, neither hath it been seen in Theman. [23] The Agarenes that seek wisdom upon earth, the merchants of Meran and of Theman, the authors of fables, and searchers out of understanding; none of these have known the way of wisdom, or remember her paths. [24] O Israel, how great is the house of God! and how large is the place of his possession! [25] Great, and hath none end; high, and unmeasurable. [26] There were the giants famous from the beginning, that were of so great stature, and so expert in war. [27] Those did not the Lord choose, neither gave he the way of knowledge unto them: [28] But they were destroyed, because they had no wisdom, and perished through their own foolishness. [29] Who hath gone up into heaven, and taken her, and brought her down from the clouds? [30] Who hath gone over the sea, and found her, and will bring her for pure gold? [31] No man knoweth her way, nor thinketh of her path. [32] But he that knoweth all things knoweth her, and hath found her out with his understanding: he that prepared the earth for evermore hath filled it with fourfooted beasts: [33] He that sendeth forth light, and it goeth, calleth it again, and it obeyeth him with fear. [34] The stars shined in their watches, and rejoiced: when he calleth them, they say, Here we be; and so with cheerfulness they shewed light unto him that made them. [35] This is our God, and there shall none other be accounted of in comparison of him [36] He hath found out all the way of knowledge, and hath given it unto Jacob his servant, and to Israel his beloved. [37] Afterward did he shew himself upon earth, and conversed with men.

Bar.4

[1] This is the book of the commandments of God, and the law that endureth for ever: all they that keep it shall come to life; but such as leave it shall die. [2] Turn thee, O Jacob, and take hold of it: walk in the presence of the light thereof, that thou mayest be illuminated. [3] Give not thine honour to another, nor the things that are profitable unto thee to a strange nation. [4] O Israel, happy are we: for things that are pleasing to God are made known unto us. [5] Be of good cheer, my people, the memorial of Israel. [6] Ye were sold to the nations, not for [your] destruction:

but because ye moved God to wrath, ye were delivered unto the enemies. [7] For ye provoked him that made you by sacrificing unto devils, and not to God. [8] Ye have forgotten the everlasting God, that brought you up; and ye have grieved Jerusalem, that nursed you. [9] For when she saw the wrath of God coming upon you, she said, Hearken, O ye that dwell about Sion: God hath brought upon me great mourning; [10] For I saw the captivity of my sons and daughters, which the Everlasting brought upon them. [11] With joy did I nourish them; but sent them away with weeping and mourning. [12] Let no man rejoice over me, a widow, and forsaken of many, who for the sins of my children am left desolate; because they departed from the law of God. [13] They knew not his statutes, nor walked in the ways of his commandments, nor trod in the paths of discipline in his righteousness. [14] Let them that dwell about Sion come, and remember ye the captivity of my sons and daughters, which the Everlasting hath brought upon them. [15] For he hath brought a nation upon them from far, a shameless nation, and of a strange language, who neither reverenced old man, nor pitied child. [16] These have carried away the dear beloved children of the widow, and left her that was alone desolate without daughters. [17] But what can I help you? [18] For he that brought these plagues upon you will deliver you from the hands of your enemies. [19] Go your way, O my children, go your way: for I am left desolate. [20] I have put off the clothing of peace, and put upon me the sackcloth of my prayer: I will cry unto the Everlasting in my days. [21] Be of good cheer, O my children, cry unto the Lord, and he will deliver you from the power and hand of the enemies. [22] For my hope is in the Everlasting, that he will save you; and joy is come unto me from the Holy One, because of the mercy which shall soon come unto you from the Everlasting our Saviour. [23] For I sent you out with mourning and weeping: but God will give you to me again with joy and gladness for ever. [24] Like as now the neighbours of Sion have seen your captivity: so shall they see shortly your salvation from our God which shall come upon you with great glory, and brightness of the Everlasting. [25] My children, suffer patiently the wrath that is come upon you from God: for thine enemy hath persecuted thee; but shortly thou shalt see his destruction, and shalt tread upon his neck. [26] My delicate ones have gone rough ways, and were taken away as a flock caught of the enemies. [27] Be of good comfort, O my children, and cry unto God: for ye shall be remembered of him that brought these things upon you. [28] For as it was your mind to go astray from God: so, being returned, seek him ten times more. [29] For he that hath brought these plagues upon you shall bring you everlasting joy with your salvation. [30] Take a good heart, O Jerusalem: for he that gave thee that name will comfort thee. [31] Miserable are they that afflicted thee, and rejoiced at thy fall. [32] Miserable are the cities which thy children served: miserable is she that received thy sons. [33] For as she rejoiced at thy ruin, and was glad of thy fall: so shall she be grieved for her own desolation. [34] For I will take away the rejoicing of her great multitude, and her pride shall be turned into mourning. [35] For fire shall come upon her from the Everlasting, long to endure; and she shall be inhabited of devils for a great time. [36] O Jerusalem, look about thee toward the east, and behold the joy that cometh unto thee from God. [37] Lo, thy sons come, whom thou sentest away, they come gathered together from the east to the west by the word of the Holy One, rejoicing in the glory of God.

Bar.5

[1] Put off, O Jerusalem, the garment of mourning and affliction, and put on the comeliness of the glory that cometh from God for ever. [2] Cast about thee a double garment of the righteousness which cometh from God; and set a diadem on thine head of the glory of the Everlasting. [3] For God will shew thy brightness unto every country under heaven. [4] For thy name shall be called of God for ever The peace of righteousness, and The glory of God's worship. [5] Arise, O Jerusalem, and stand on high, and look about toward the east, and behold thy children gathered from the west unto the east by the word of the Holy One, rejoicing in the remembrance of God. [6] For they departed from thee on foot, and were led away of their enemies: but God bringeth them unto thee exalted with glory, as children of the kingdom. [7] For God hath appointed that every high hill, and banks of long continuance, should be cast down, and valleys filled up, to make even the ground, that Israel may go safely in the glory of God, [8] Moreover even the woods and every sweetsmelling tree shall overshadow Israel by the commandment of God. [9] For God shall lead Israel with joy in the light of his glory with the mercy and righteousness that cometh from him.

LETTER OF JEREMIAH

EpJer.1

A copy of an epistle, which Jeremy sent unto them which were to be led captives into Babylon by the king of the Babylonians, to certify them, as it was commanded him of God.[1] Because of the sins which ye have committed before God, ye shall be led away captives into Babylon by Nabuchodonosor king of the Babylonians. [2] So when ye be come unto Babylon, ye shall remain there many years, and for a long season, namely, seven generations: and after that I will bring you away peaceably from thence. [3] Now shall ye see in Babylon gods of silver, and of gold, and of wood, borne upon shoulders, which cause the nations to fear. [4] Beware therefore that ye in no wise be like to strangers, neither be ye and of them, when ye see the multitude before them and behind them, worshipping them. [5] But say ye in your hearts, O Lord, we must worship thee.

[6] For mine angel is with you, and I myself caring for your souls. [7] As for their tongue, it is polished by the workman, and they themselves are gilded and laid over with silver; yet are they but false, and cannot speak. [8] And taking gold, as it were for a virgin that loveth to go gay, they make crowns for the heads of their gods. [9] Sometimes also the priests convey from their gods gold and silver, and bestow it upon themselves. [10] Yea, they will give thereof to the common harlots, and deck them as men with garments, [being] gods of silver, and gods of gold, and wood. [11] Yet cannot these gods save themselves from rust and moth, though they be covered with purple raiment. [12] They wipe their faces because of the dust of the temple, when there is much upon them. [13] And he that cannot put to death one that offendeth him holdeth a sceptre, as though he were a judge of the country. [14] He hath also in his right hand a dagger and an ax: but cannot deliver himself from war and thieves. [15] Whereby they are known not to be gods: therefore fear them not. [16] For like as a vessel that a man useth is nothing worth when it is broken; even so it is with their gods: when they be set up in the temple, their eyes be full of dust through the feet of them that come in. [17] And as the doors are made sure on every side upon him that offendeth the king, as being committed to suffer death: even so the priests make fast their temples with doors, with locks, and bars, lest their gods be spoiled with robbers. [18] They light them candles, yea, more than for themselves, whereof they cannot see one. [19] They are as one of the beams of the temple, yet they say their hearts are gnawed upon by things creeping out of the earth; and when they eat them and their clothes, they feel it not. [20] Their faces are blacked through the smoke that cometh out of the temple. [21] Upon their bodies and heads sit bats, swallows, and birds, and the cats also. [22] By this ye may know that they are no gods: therefore fear them not. [23] Notwithstanding the gold that is about them to make them beautiful, except they wipe off the rust, they will not shine: for neither when they were molten did they feel it. [24] The things wherein there is no breath are bought for a most high price. [25] They are borne upon shoulders, having no feet whereby they declare unto men that they be nothing worth. [26] They also that serve them are ashamed: for if they fall to the ground at any time, they cannot rise up again of themselves: neither, if one set them upright, can they move of themselves: neither, if they be bowed down, can they make themselves straight: but they set gifts before them as unto dead men. [27] As for the things that are sacrificed unto them, their priests sell and abuse; in like manner their wives lay up part thereof in salt; but unto the poor and impotent they give nothing of it. [28] Menstruous women and women in childbed eat their sacrifices: by these things ye may know that they are no gods: fear them not. [29] For how can they be called gods? because women set meat before the gods of silver, gold, and wood. [30] And the priests sit in their temples, having their clothes rent, and their heads and beards shaven, and nothing upon their heads. [31] They roar and cry before their gods, as men do at the feast when one is dead. [32] The priests also take off their garments, and clothe their wives and children. [33] Whether it be evil that one doeth unto them, or good, they are not able to recompense it: they can neither set up a king, nor put him down. [34] In like manner, they can neither give riches nor money: though a man make a vow unto them, and keep it not, they will not require it. [35] They can save no man from death, neither deliver the weak from the mighty. [36] They cannot restore a blind man to his sight, nor help any man in his distress. [37] They can shew no mercy to the widow, nor do good to the fatherless. [38] Their gods of wood, and which are overlaid with gold and silver, are like the stones that be hewn out of the mountain: they that worship them shall be confounded. [39] How should a man then think and say that they are gods, when even the Chaldeans themselves dishonour them? [40] Who if they shall see one dumb that cannot speak, they bring him, and intreat Bel that he may speak, as though he were able to understand. [41] Yet they cannot understand this themselves, and leave them: for they have no knowledge. [42] The women also with cords about them, sitting in the ways, burn bran for perfume: but if any of them, drawn by some that passeth by, lie with him, she reproacheth her fellow, that she was not thought as worthy as herself, nor her cord broken. [43] Whatsoever is done among them is false: how may it then be thought or said that they are gods? [44] They are made of carpenters and goldsmiths: they can be nothing else than the workmen will have them to be. [45] And they themselves that made them can never continue long; how should then the things that are made of them be gods? [46] For they left lies and reproaches to them that come after. [47] For when there cometh any war or plague upon them, the priests consult with themselves, where they may be hidden with them. [48] How then

cannot men perceive that they be no gods, which can
neither save themselves from war, nor from plague? [49]
For seeing they be but of wood, and overlaid with silver
and gold, it shall be known hereafter that they are false:
[50] And it shall manifestly appear to all nations and
kings that they are no gods, but the works of men's
hands, and that there is no work of God in them. [51]
Who then may not know that they are no gods? [52] For
neither can they set up a king in the land, nor give rain
unto men. [53] Neither can they judge their own cause,
nor redress a wrong, being unable: for they are as crows
between heaven and earth. [54] Whereupon when fire
falleth upon the house of gods of wood, or laid over
with gold or silver, their priests will flee away, and
escape; but they themselves shall be burned asunder like
beams. [55] Moreover they cannot withstand any king or
enemies: how can it then be thought or said that they be
gods? [56] Neither are those gods of wood, and laid
over with silver or gold, able to escape either from
thieves or robbers. [57] Whose gold, and silver, and
garments wherewith they are clothed, they that are
strong take, and go away withal: neither are they able to
help themselves. [58] Therefore it is better to be a king
that sheweth his power, or else a profitable vessel in an
house, which the owner shall have use of, than such false
gods; or to be a door in an house, to keep such things
therein, than such false gods. or a pillar of wood in a a
palace, than such false gods. [59] For sun, moon, and
stars, being bright and sent to do their offices, are
obedient. [60] In like manner the lightning when it
breaketh forth is easy to be seen; and after the same
manner the wind bloweth in every country. [61] And
when God commandeth the clouds to go over the whole
world, they do as they are bidden. [62] And the fire sent
from above to consume hills and woods doeth as it is
commanded: but these are like unto them neither in
shew nor power. [63] Wherefore it is neither to be
supposed nor said that they are gods, seeing, they are
able neither to judge causes, nor to do good unto men.
[64] Knowing therefore that they are no gods, fear them
not, [65] For they can neither curse nor bless kings: [66]
Neither can they shew signs in the heavens among the
heathen, nor shine as the sun, nor give light as the moon.

[67] The beasts are better than they: for they can get
under a cover and help themselves. [68] It is then by no
means manifest unto us that they are gods: therefore fear
them not. [69] For as a scarecrow in a garden of
cucumbers keepeth nothing: so are their gods of wood,
and laid over with silver and gold. [70] And likewise
their gods of wood, and laid over with silver and gold,
are like to a white thorn in an orchard, that every bird
sitteth upon; as also to a dead body, that is east into the
dark. [71] And ye shall know them to be no gods by the
bright purple that rotteth upon then1: and they
themselves afterward shall be eaten, and shall be a
reproach in the country. [72] Better therefore is the just
man that hath none idols: for he shall be far from
reproach.

PRAYER OF AZARIAH

[1] And they walked in the midst of the fire, praising God, and blessing the Lord. [2] Then Azarias stood up, and prayed on this manner; and opening his mouth in the midst of the fire said, [3] Blessed art thou, O Lord God of our fathers: thy name is worthy to be praised and glorified for evermore: [4] For thou art righteous in all the things that thou hast done to us: yea, true are all thy works, thy ways are right, and all thy judgments truth. [5] In all the things that thou hast brought upon us, and upon the holy city of our fathers, even Jerusalem, thou hast executed true judgment: for according to truth and judgment didst thou bring all these things upon us because of our sins. [6] For we have sinned and committed iniquity, departing from thee. [7] In all things have we trespassed, and not obeyed thy commandments, nor kept them, neither done as thou hast commanded us, that it might go well with us. [8] Wherefore all that thou hast brought upon us, and every thing that thou hast done to us, thou hast done in true judgment. [9] And thou didst deliver us into the hands of lawless enemies, most hateful forsakers of God, and to an unjust king, and the most wicked in all the world. [10] And now we cannot open our mouths, we are become a shame and reproach to thy servants; and to them that worship thee. [11] Yet deliver us not up wholly, for thy name's sake, neither disannul thou thy covenant: [12] And cause not thy mercy to depart from us, for thy beloved Abraham's sake, for thy servant Issac's sake, and for thy holy Israel's sake; [13] To whom thou hast spoken and promised, that thou wouldest multiply their seed as the stars of heaven, and as the sand that lieth upon the seashore. [14] For we, O Lord, are become less than any nation, and be kept under this day in all the world because of our sins. [15] Neither is there at this time prince, or prophet, or leader, or burnt offering, or sacrifice, or oblation, or incense, or place to sacrifice before thee, and to find mercy. [16] Nevertheless in a contrite heart and an humble spirit let us be accepted. [17] Like as in the burnt offerings of rams and bullocks, and like as in ten thousands of fat lambs: so let our sacrifice be in thy sight this day, and grant that we may wholly go after thee: for they shall not be confounded that put their trust in thee. [18] And now we follow thee with all our heart, we fear thee, and seek thy face. [19] Put us not to shame: but deal with us after thy lovingkindness, and according to the multitude of thy mercies. [20] Deliver us also according to thy marvellous works, and give glory to thy name, O Lord: and let all them that do thy servants hurt be ashamed; [21] And let them be confounded in all their power and might, and let their strength be broken; [22] And let them know that thou art God, the only God, and glorious over the whole world. [23] And the king's servants, that put them in, ceased not to make the oven hot with rosin, pitch, tow, and small wood; [24] So that the flame streamed forth above the furnace forty and nine cubits. [25] And

it passed through, and burned those Chaldeans it found about the furnace. [26] But the angel of the Lord came down into the oven together with Azarias and his fellows, and smote the flame of the fire out of the oven; [27] And made the midst of the furnace as it had been a moist whistling wind, so that the fire touched them not at all, neither hurt nor troubled them. [28] Then the three, as out of one mouth, praised, glorified, and blessed, God in the furnace, saying, [29] Blessed art thou, O Lord God of our fathers: and to be praised and exalted above all for ever. [30] And blessed is thy glorious and holy name: and to be praised and exalted above all for ever. [31] Blessed art thou in the temple of thine holy glory: and to be praised and glorified above all for ever. [32] Blessed art thou that beholdest the depths, and sittest upon the cherubims: and to be praised and exalted above all for ever. [33] Blessed art thou on the glorious throne of thy kingdom: and to be praised and glorified above all for ever. [34] Blessed art thou in the firmament of heaven: and above ail to be praised and glorified for ever. [35] O all ye works of the Lord, bless ye the Lord : praise and exalt him above all for ever, [36] O ye heavens, bless ye the Lord : praise and exalt him above all for ever. [37] O ye angels of the Lord, bless ye the Lord: praise and exalt him above all for ever. [38] O all ye waters that be above the heaven, bless ye the Lord: praise and exalt him above all for ever. [39] O all ye powers of the Lord, bless ye the Lord: praise and exalt him above all for ever. [40] O ye sun and moon, bless ye the Lord: praise and exalt him above all for ever. [41] O ye stars of heaven, bless ye the Lord: praise and exalt him above all for ever. [42] O every shower and dew, bless ye the Lord: praise and exalt him above all for ever.

[43] O all ye winds, bless ye the Lord: praise and exalt him above all for ever, [44] O ye fire and heat, bless ye the Lord: praise and exalt him above all for ever. [45] O ye winter and summer, bless ye the Lord: praise and exalt him above all for ever. [46] 0 ye dews and storms of snow, bless ye the Lord: praise and exalt him above all for ever. [47] O ye nights and days, bless ye the Lord: bless and exalt him above all for ever. [48] O ye light and darkness, bless ye the Lord: praise and exalt him above all for ever. [49] O ye ice and cold, bless ye the Lord: praise and exalt him above all for ever. [50] O ye frost and snow, bless ye the Lord: praise and exalt him above all for ever. [51] O ye lightnings and clouds, bless ye the Lord: praise and exalt him above all for ever. [52] O let the earth bless the Lord: praise and exalt him above all for ever. [53] O ye mountains and little hills, bless ye the Lord: praise and exalt him above all for ever.

[54] O all ye things that grow in the earth, bless ye the Lord: praise and exalt him above all for ever. [55] O ye mountains, bless ye the Lord: Praise and exalt him above all for ever. [56] O ye seas and rivers, bless ye the Lord: praise and exalt him above all for ever. [57] O ye whales, and all that move in the waters, bless ye the Lord: praise and exalt him above all for ever. [58] O all ye fowls of the air, bless ye the Lord: praise and exalt him above all

for ever. [59] O all ye beasts and cattle, bless ye the Lord: praise and exalt him above all for ever. [60] O ye children of men, bless ye the Lord: praise and exalt him above all for ever. [61] O Israel, bless ye the Lord: praise and exalt him above all for ever. [62] O ye priests of the Lord, bless ye the Lord: praise and exalt him above all for ever. [63] O ye servants of the Lord, bless ye the Lord: praise and exalt him above all for ever. [64] O ye spirits and souls of the righteous, bless ye the Lord: praise and exalt him above all for ever. [65] O ye holy and humble men of heart, bless ye the Lord: praise and exalt him above all for ever. [66] O Ananias, Azarias, and Misael, bless ye the Lord: praise and exalt him above all for ever: far he hath delivered us from hell, and saved us from the hand of death, and delivered us out of the midst of the furnace and burning flame: even out of the midst of the fire hath he delivered us. [67] O give thanks unto the Lord, because he is gracious: for his mercy endureth for ever. [68] O all ye that worship the Lord, bless the God of gods, praise him, and give him thanks: for his mercy endureth for ever.

SUSANNA

Sus.1

Set apart from the beginning of Daniel, because it is not in the Hebrew, as neither the Narration of Bel and the Dragon.[1] There dwelt a man in Babylon, called Joacim:

[2] And he took a wife, whose name was Susanna, the daughter of Chelcias, a very fair woman, and one that feared the Lord. [3] Her parents also were righteous, and taught their daughter according to the law of Moses. [4] Now Joacim was a great rich man, and had a fair garden joining unto his house: and to him resorted the Jews; because he was more honourable than all others. [5] The same year were appointed two of the ancients of the people to be judges, such as the Lord spake of, that wickedness came from Babylon from ancient judges, who seemed to govern the people. [6] These kept much at Joacim's house: and all that had any suits in law came unto them. [7] Now when the people departed away at noon, Susanna went into her husband's garden to walk. [8] And the two elders saw her going in every day, and walking; so that their lust was inflamed toward her. [9] And they perverted their own mind, and turned away their eyes, that they might not look unto heaven, nor remember just judgments. [10] And albeit they both were wounded with her love, yet durst not one shew another his grief. [11] For they were ashamed to declare their lust, that they desired to have to do with her. [12] Yet they watched diligently from day to day to see her. [13] And the one said to the other, Let us now go home: for it is dinner time. [14] So when they were gone out, they parted the one from the other, and turning back again they came to the same place; and after that they had asked one another the cause, they acknowledged their lust: then appointed they a time both together, when they might find her alone. [15] And it fell out, as they watched a fit time, she went in as before with two maids only, and she was desirous to wash herself in the garden: for it was hot. [16] And there was no body there save the two elders, that had hid themselves, and watched her. [17] Then she said to her maids, Bring me oil and washing balls, and shut the garden doors, that I may wash me. [18] And they did as she bade them, and shut the garden doors, and went out themselves at privy doors to fetch the things that she had commanded them: but they saw not the elders, because they were hid. [19] Now when the maids were gone forth, the two elders rose up, and ran unto her, saying, [20] Behold, the garden doors are shut, that no man can see us, and we are in love with thee; therefore consent unto us, and lie with us. [21] If thou wilt not, we will bear witness against thee, that a young man was with thee: and therefore thou didst send away thy maids from thee. [22] Then Susanna sighed, and said, I am straitened on every side: for if I do this thing, it is death unto me: and if I do it not I cannot escape your hands. [23] It is better for me to fall into your hands, and not do it, than to sin

in the sight of the Lord. [24] With that Susanna cried with a loud voice: and the two elders cried out against her. [25] Then ran the one, and opened the garden door. [26] So when the servants of the house heard the cry in the garden, they rushed in at the privy door, to see what was done unto her. [27] But when the elders had declared their matter, the servants were greatly ashamed: for there was never such a report made of Susanna. [28] And it came to pass the next day, when the people were assembled to her husband Joacim, the two elders came also full of mischievous imagination against Susanna to put her to death; [29] And said before the people, Send for Susanna, the daughter of Chelcias, Joacim's wife. And so they sent. [30] So she came with her father and mother, her children, and all her kindred. [31] Now Susanna was a very delicate woman, and beauteous to behold. [32] And these wicked men commanded to uncover her face, (for she was covered) that they might be filled with her beauty. [33] Therefore her friends and all that saw her wept. [34] Then the two elders stood up in the midst of the people, and laid their hands upon her head. [35] And she weeping looked up toward heaven: for her heart trusted in the Lord. [36] And the elders said, As we walked in the garden alone, this woman came in with two maids, and shut the garden doors, and sent the maids away. [37] Then a young man, who there was hid, came unto her, and lay with her. [38] Then we that stood in a corner of the garden, seeing this wickedness, ran unto them. [39] And when we saw them together, the man we could not hold: for he was stronger than we, and opened the door, and leaped out. [40] But having taken this woman, we asked who the young man was, but she would not tell us: these things do we testify.

[41] Then the assembly believed them as those that were the elders and judges of the people: so they condemned her to death. [42] Then Susanna cried out with a loud voice, and said, O everlasting God, that knowest the secrets, and knowest all things before they be: [43] Thou knowest that they have borne false witness against me, and, behold, I must die; whereas I never did such things as these men have maliciously invented against me. [44] And the Lord heard her voice.

[45] Therefore when she was led to be put to death, the Lord raised up the holy spirit of a young youth whose name was Daniel: [46] Who cried with a loud voice, I am clear from the blood of this woman. [47] Then all the people turned them toward him, and said, What mean these words that thou hast spoken? [48] So he standing in the midst of them said, Are ye such fools, ye sons of Israel, that without examination or knowledge of the truth ye have condemned a daughter of Israel? [49] Return again to the place of judgment: for they have borne false witness against her. [50] Wherefore all the people turned again in haste, and the elders said unto him, Come, sit down among us, and shew it us, seeing God hath given thee the honour of an elder. [51] Then said Daniel unto them, Put these two aside one far from another, and I will examine them. [52] So when they

were put asunder one from another, he called one of
them, and said unto him, O thou that art waxen old in
wickedness, now thy sins which thou hast committed
aforetime are come to light. [53] For thou hast
pronounced false judgment and hast condemned the
innocent and hast let the guilty go free; albeit the Lord
saith, The innocent and righteous shalt thou not slay.
[54] Now then, if thou hast seen her, tell me, Under
what tree sawest thou them companying together? Who
answered, Under a mastick tree. [55] And Daniel said,
Very well; thou hast lied against thine own head; for
even now the angel of God hath received the sentence
of God to cut thee in two. [56] So he put him aside, and
commanded to bring the other, and said unto him, O
thou seed of Chanaan, and not of Juda, beauty hath
deceived thee, and lust hath perverted thine heart. [57]
Thus have ye dealt with the daughters of Israel, and they
for fear companied with you: but the daughter of Juda
would not abide your wickedness. [58] Now therefore
tell me, Under what tree didst thou take them
companying together? Who answered, Under an holm
tree. [59] Then said Daniel unto him, Well; thou hast
also lied against thine own head: for the angel of God
waiteth with the sword to cut thee in two, that he may
destroy you. [60] With that all the assembly cried out
with a loud voice, and praised God, who saveth them
that trust in him. [61] And they arose against the two
elders, for Daniel had convicted them of false witness by
their own mouth: [62] And according to the law of
Moses they did unto them in such sort as they
maliciously intended to do to their neighbour: and they
put them to death. Thus the innocent blood was saved
the same day. [63] Therefore Chelcias and his wife
praised God for their daughter Susanna, with Joacim her
husband, and all the kindred, because there was no
dishonesty found in her. [64] From that day forth was
Daniel had in great reputation in the sight of the people.

BEL AND THE DRAGON

The History of the Destruction of Bel and the Dragon, Cut off from the end of Daniel.

Bel.1

[1] And king Astyages was gathered to his fathers, and Cyrus of Persia received his kingdom. [2] And Daniel conversed with the king, and was honoured above all his friends. [3] Now the Babylons had an idol, called Bel, and there were spent upon him every day twelve great measures of fine flour, and forty sheep, and six vessels of wine. [4] And the king worshipped it and went daily to adore it: but Daniel worshipped his own God. And the king said unto him, Why dost not thou worship Bel? [5] Who answered and said, Because I may not worship idols made with hands, but the living God, who hath created the heaven and the earth, and hath sovereignty over all flesh. [6] Then said the king unto him, Thinkest thou not that Bel is a living God? seest thou not how much he eateth and drinketh every day? [7] Then Daniel smiled, and said, O king, be not deceived: for this is but clay within, and brass without, and did never eat or drink any thing. [8] So the king was wroth, and called for his priests, and said unto them, If ye tell me not who this is that devoureth these expences, ye shall die. [9] But if ye can certify me that Bel devoureth them, then Daniel shall die: for he hath spoken blasphemy against Bel. And Daniel said unto the king, Let it be according to thy word. [10] Now the priests of Bel were threescore and ten, beside their wives and children. And the king went with Daniel into the temple of Bel. [11] So Bel's priests said, Lo, we go out: but thou, O king, set on the meat, and make ready the wine, and shut the door fast and seal it with thine own signet; [12] And to morrow when thou comest in, if thou findest not that Bel hath eaten up all, we will suffer death: or else Daniel, that speaketh falsely against us. [13] And they little regarded it: for under the table they had made a privy entrance, whereby they entered in continually, and consumed those things. [14] So when they were gone forth, the king set meats before Bel. Now Daniel had commanded his servants to bring ashes, and those they strewed throughout all the temple in the presence of the king alone: then went they out, and shut the door, and sealed it with the king's signet, and so departed. [15] Now in the night came the priests with their wives and children, as they were wont to do, and did eat and drink up all. [16] In the morning betime the king arose, and Daniel with him. [17] And the king said, Daniel, are the seals whole? And he said, Yea, O king, they be whole. [18] And as soon as he had opened the dour, the king looked upon the table, and cried with a loud voice, Great art thou, O Bel, and with thee is no deceit at all. [19] Then laughed Daniel, and held the king that he should not go in, and said, Behold now the pavement, and mark well whose footsteps are these. [20] And the king said, I see the footsteps of men, women, and children. And then the king was angry, [21] And took the priests with their wives and children, who shewed him the privy doors, where they came in, and consumed such things as were upon the table. [22] Therefore the king slew them, and delivered Bel into Daniel's power, who destroyed him and his temple. [23] And in that same place there was a great dragon, which they of Babylon worshipped. [24] And the king said unto Daniel, Wilt thou also say that this is of brass? lo, he liveth, he eateth and drinketh; thou canst not say that he is no living god: therefore worship him. [25] Then said Daniel unto the king, I will worship the Lord my God: for he is the living God. [26] But give me leave, O king, and I shall slay this dragon without sword or staff. The king said, I give thee leave. [27] Then Daniel took pitch, and fat, and hair, and did seethe them together, and made lumps thereof: this he put in the dragon's mouth, and so the dragon burst in sunder : and Daniel said, Lo, these are the gods ye worship. [28] When they of Babylon heard that, they took great indignation, and conspired against the king, saying, The king is become a Jew, and he hath destroyed Bel, he hath slain the dragon, and put the priests to death. [29] So they came to the king, and said, Deliver us Daniel, or else we will destroy thee and thine house. [30] Now when the king saw that they pressed him sore, being constrained, he delivered Daniel unto them: [31] Who cast him into the lions' den: where he was six days. [32] And in the den there were seven lions, and they had given them every day two carcases, and two sheep: which then were not given to them, to the intent they might devour Daniel. [33] Now there was in Jewry a prophet, called Habbacuc, who had made pottage, and had broken bread in a bowl, and was going into the field, for to bring it to the reapers. [34] But the angel of the Lord said unto Habbacuc, Go, carry the dinner that thou hast into Babylon unto Daniel, who is in the lions' den. [35] And Habbacuc said, Lord, I never saw Babylon; neither do I know where the den is. [36] Then the angel of the Lord took him by the crown, and bare him by the hair of his head, and through the vehemency of his spirit set him in Babylon over the den.

[37] And Habbacuc cried, saying, O Daniel, Daniel, take the dinner which God hath sent thee. [38] And Daniel said, Thou hast remembered me, O God: neither hast thou forsaken them that seek thee and love thee. [39] So Daniel arose, and did eat: and the angel of the Lord set Habbacuc in his own place again immediately. [40] Upon the seventh day the king went to bewail Daniel: and when he came to the den, he looked in, and behold, Daniel was sitting. [41] Then cried the king with a loud voice, saying, Great art Lord God of Daniel, and there is none other beside thee. [42] And he drew him out, and cast those that were the cause of his destruction into the den: and they were devoured in a moment before his face.

PRAYER OF MANASSE

O Lord, Almighty God of our fathers, Abraham, Isaac, and Jacob, and of their righteous seed; who hast made heaven and earth, with all the ornament thereof; who hast bound the sea by the word of thy commandment; who hast shut up the deep, and sealed it by thy terrible and glorious name; whom all men fear, and tremble before thy power; for the majesty of thy glory cannot be borne, and thine angry threatening toward sinners is importable: but thy merciful promise is unmeasurable and unsearchable; for thou art the most high Lord, of great compassion, longsuffering, very merciful, and repentest of the evils of men. Thou, O Lord, according to thy great goodness hast promised repentance and forgiveness to them that have sinned against thee: and of thine infinite mercies hast appointed repentance unto sinners, that they may be saved. Thou therefore, O Lord, that art the God of the just, hast not appointed repentance to the just, as to Abraham, and Isaac, and Jacob, which have not sinned against thee; but thou hast appointed repentance unto me that am a sinner: for I have sinned above the number of the sands of the sea. My transgressions, O Lord, are multiplied: my transgressions are multiplied, and I am not worthy to behold and see the height of heaven for the multitude of mine iniquities. I am bowed down with many iron bands, that I cannot life up mine head, neither have any release: for I have provoked thy wrath, and done evil before thee: I did not thy will, neither kept I thy commandments: I have set up abominations, and have multiplied offences. Now therefore I bow the knee of mine heart, beseeching thee of grace. I have sinned, O Lord, I have sinned, and I acknowledge mine iniquities: wherefore, I humbly beseech thee, forgive me, O Lord, forgive me, and destroy me not with mine iniquites. Be not angry with me for ever, by reserving evil for me; neither condemn me to the lower parts of the earth. For thou art the God, even the God of them that repent; and in me thou wilt shew all thy goodness: for thou wilt save me, that am unworthy, according to thy great mercy. Therefore I will praise thee for ever all the days of my life: for all the powers of the heavens do praise thee, and thine is the glory for ever and ever. Amen.

1 MACCABEES

1Mac.1

[1] And it happened, after that Alexander son of Philip, the Macedonian, who came out of the land of Chettiim, had smitten Darius king of the Persians and Medes, that he reigned in his stead, the first over Greece, [2] And made many wars, and won many strong holds, and slew the kings of the earth, [3] And went through to the ends of the earth, and took spoils of many nations, insomuch that the earth was quiet before him; whereupon he was exalted and his heart was lifted up. [4] And he gathered a mighty strong host and ruled over countries, and nations, and kings, who became tributaries unto him. [5] And after these things he fell sick, and perceived that he should die. [6] Wherefore he called his servants, such as were honourable, and had been brought up with him from his youth, and parted his kingdom among them, while he was yet alive. [7] So Alexander reigned twelves years, and then died. [8] And his servants bare rule every one in his place. [9] And after his death they all put crowns upon themselves; so did their sons after them many years: and evils were multiplied in the earth. [10] And there came out of them a wicked root Antiochus surnamed Epiphanes, son of Antiochus the king, who had been an hostage at Rome, and he reigned in the hundred and thirty and seventh year of the kingdom of the Greeks. [11] In those days went there out of Israel wicked men, who persuaded many, saying, Let us go and make a covenant with the heathen that are round about us: for since we departed from them we have had much sorrow. [12] So this device pleased them well. [13] Then certain of the people were so forward herein, that they went to the king, who gave them licence to do after the ordinances of the heathen: [14] Whereupon they built a place of exercise at Jerusalem according to the customs of the heathen: [15] And made themselves uncircumcised, and forsook the holy covenant, and joined themselves to the heathen, and were sold to do mischief. [16] Now when the kingdom was established before Antiochus, he thought to reign over Egypt that he might have the dominion of two realms. [17] Wherefore he entered into Egypt with a great multitude, with chariots, and elephants, and horsemen, and a great navy, [18] And made war against Ptolemee king of Egypt: but Ptolemee was afraid of him, and fled; and many were wounded to death. [19] Thus they got the strong cities in the land of Egypt and he took the spoils thereof. [20] And after that Antiochus had smitten Egypt, he returned again in the hundred forty and third year, and went up against Israel and Jerusalem with a great multitude, [21] And entered proudly into the sanctuary, and took away the golden altar, and the candlestick of light, and all the vessels thereof, [22] And the table of the shewbread, and the pouring vessels, and the vials. and the censers of gold, and the veil, and the crown, and the golden ornaments that were before the temple, all which he pulled off. [23] He took also the silver and the gold, and the precious vessels: also he took the hidden treasures which he found. [24] And when he had taken all away, he went into his own land, having made a great massacre, and spoken very proudly. [25] Therefore there was a great mourning in Israel, in every place where they were; [26] So that the princes and elders mourned, the virgins and young men were made feeble, and the beauty of women was changed. [27] Every bridegroom took up lamentation, and she that sat in the marriage chamber was in heaviness, [28] The land also was moved for the inhabitants thereof, and all the house of Jacob was covered with confusion. [29] And after two years fully expired the king sent his chief collector of tribute unto the cities of Juda, who came unto Jerusalem with a great multitude, [30] And spake peaceable words unto them, but all was deceit: for when they had given him credence, he fell suddenly upon the city, and smote it very sore, and destroyed much people of Israel. [31] And when he had taken the spoils of the city, he set it on fire, and pulled down the houses and walls thereof on every side. [32] But the women and children took they captive, and possessed the cattle. [33] Then builded they the city of David with a great and strong wall, and with mighty towers, and made it a strong hold for them. [34] And they put therein a sinful nation, wicked men, and fortified themselves therein. [35] They stored it also with armour and victuals, and when they had gathered together the spoils of Jerusalem, they laid them up there, and so they became a sore snare: [36] For it was a place to lie in wait against the sanctuary, and an evil adversary to Israel. [37] Thus they shed innocent blood on every side of the sanctuary, and defiled it: [38] Insomuch that the inhabitants of Jerusalem fled because of them: whereupon the city was made an habitation of strangers, and became strange to those that were born in her; and her own children left her. [39] Her sanctuary was laid waste like a wilderness, her feasts were turned into mourning, her sabbaths into reproach her honour into contempt. [40] As had been her glory, so was her dishonour increased, and her excellency was turned into mourning. [41] Moreover king Antiochus wrote to his whole kingdom, that all should be one people, [42] And every one should leave his laws: so all the heathen agreed according to the commandment of the king. [43] Yea, many also of the Israelites consented to his religion, and sacrificed unto idols, and profaned the sabbath. [44] For the king had sent letters by messengers unto Jerusalem and the cities of Juda that they should follow the strange laws of the land, [45] And forbid burnt offerings, and sacrifice, and drink offerings, in the temple; and that they should profane the sabbaths and festival days: [46] And pollute the sanctuary and holy people: [47] Set up altars, and groves, and chapels of idols, and sacrifice swine's flesh, and unclean beasts: [48] That they should also leave their children uncircumcised, and make their souls abominable with all manner of uncleanness and profanation: [49] To the end they might forget the law, and change all the ordinances. [50] And whosoever would not do according to the commandment of the king, he said, he should die. [51] In the selfsame manner wrote he to his whole kingdom, and appointed overseers over all the people, commanding the cities of Juda to sacrifice, city by city. [52] Then many of the people were gathered unto them, to wit every one that forsook the law; and so they committed evils in the land; [53] And drove the Israelites into secret places, even wheresoever they could flee for succour. [54] Now the fifteenth day of the month Casleu, in the hundred forty and fifth year, they set up the

abomination of desolation upon the altar, and builded idol altars throughout the cities of Juda on every side; [55] And burnt incense at the doors of their houses, and in the streets. [56] And when they had rent in pieces the books of the law which they found, they burnt them with fire. [57] And whosoever was found with any the book of the testament, or if any committed to the law, the king's commandment was, that they should put him to death. [58] Thus did they by their authority unto the Israelites every month, to as many as were found in the cities. [59] Now the five and twentieth day of the month they did sacrifice upon the idol altar, which was upon the altar of God. [60] At which time according to the commandment they put to death certain women, that had caused their children to be circumcised. [61] And they hanged the infants about their necks, and rifled their houses, and slew them that had circumcised them. [62] Howbeit many in Israel were fully resolved and confirmed in themselves not to eat any unclean thing. [63] Wherefore the rather to die, that they might not be defiled with meats, and that they might not profane the holy covenant: so then they died. [64] And there was very great wrath upon Israel.

1Mac.2

[1] In those days arose Mattathias the son of John, the son of Simeon, a priest of the sons of Joarib, from Jerusalem, and dwelt in Modin. [2] And he had five sons, Joannan, called Caddis: [3] Simon; called Thassi: [4] Judas, who was called Maccabeus: [5] Eleazar, called Avaran: and Jonathan, whose surname was Apphus. [6] And when he saw the blasphemies that were committed in Juda and Jerusalem, [7] He said, Woe is me! wherefore was I born to see this misery of my people, and of the holy city, and to dwell there, when it was delivered into the hand of the enemy, and the sanctuary into the hand of strangers? [8] Her temple is become as a man without glory. [9] Her glorious vessels are carried away into captivity, her infants are slain in the streets, her young men with the sword of the enemy. [10] What nation hath not had a part in her kingdom and gotten of her spoils? [11] All her ornaments are taken away; of a free woman she is become a bondslave. [12] And, behold, our sanctuary, even our beauty and our glory, is laid waste, and the Gentiles have profaned it. [13] To what end therefore shall we live any longer? [14] Then Mattathias and his sons rent their clothes, and put on sackcloth, and mourned very sore. [15] In the mean while the king's officers, such as compelled the people to revolt, came into the city Modin, to make them sacrifice. [16] And when many of Israel came unto them, Mattathias also and his sons came together. [17] Then answered the king's officers, and said to Mattathias on this wise, Thou art a ruler, and an honourable and great man in this city, and strengthened with sons and brethren: [18] Now therefore come thou first, and fulfil the king's commandment, like as all the heathen have done, yea, and the men of Juda also, and such as remain at Jerusalem: so shalt thou and thy house be in the number of the king's friends, and thou and thy children shall be honoured with silver and gold, and many rewards. [19] Then Mattathias answered and spake with a loud voice, Though all the nations that are under the king's dominion obey him, and fall away every one from

the religion of their fathers, and give consent to his commandments: [20] Yet will I and my sons and my brethren walk in the covenant of our fathers. [21] God forbid that we should forsake the law and the ordinances. [22] We will not hearken to the king's words, to go from our religion, either on the right hand, or the left. [23] Now when he had left speaking these words, there came one of the Jews in the sight of all to sacrifice on the altar which was at Modin, according to the king's commandment. [24] Which thing when Mattathias saw, he was inflamed with zeal, and his reins trembled, neither could he forbear to shew his anger according to judgment: wherefore he ran, and slew him upon the altar. [25] Also the king's commissioner, who compelled men to sacrifice, he killed at that time, and the altar he pulled down. [26] Thus dealt he zealously for the law of God like as Phinees did unto Zambri the son of Salom. [27] And Mattathias cried throughout the city with a loud voice, saying, Whosoever is zealous of the law, and maintaineth the covenant, let him follow me. [28] So he and his sons fled into the mountains, and left all that ever they had in the city. [29] Then many that sought after justice and judgment went down into the wilderness, to dwell there: [30] Both they, and their children, and their wives; and their cattle; because afflictions increased sore upon them. [31] Now when it was told the king's servants, and the host that was at Jerusalem, in the city of David, that certain men, who had broken the king's commandment, were gone down into the secret places in the wilderness, [32] They pursued after them a great number, and having overtaken them, they camped against them, and made war against them on the sabbath day. [33] And they said unto them, Let that which ye have done hitherto suffice; come forth, and do according to the commandment of the king, and ye shall live. [34] But they said, We will not come forth, neither will we do the king's commandment, to profane the sabbath day. [35] So then they gave them the battle with all speed. [36] Howbeit they answered them not, neither cast they a stone at them, nor stopped the places where they lay hid; [37] But said, Let us die all in our innocency: heaven and earth will testify for us, that ye put us to death wrongfully. [38] So they rose up against them in battle on the sabbath, and they slew them, with their wives and children and their cattle, to the number of a thousand people. [39] Now when Mattathias and his friends understood hereof, they mourned for them right sore. [40] And one of them said to another, If we all do as our brethren have done, and fight not for our lives and laws against the heathen, they will now quickly root us out of the earth. [41] At that time therefore they decreed, saying, Whosoever shall come to make battle with us on the sabbath day, we will fight against him; neither will we die all, as our brethren that were murdered im the secret places. [42] Then came there unto him a company of Assideans who were mighty men of Israel, even all such as were voluntarily devoted unto the law. [43] Also all they that fled for persecution joined themselves unto them, and were a stay unto them. [44] So they joined their forces, and smote sinful men in their anger, and wicked men in their wrath: but the rest fled to the heathen for succour. [45] Then Mattathias and his friends went round about, and pulled down the altars: [46] And what children soever they found within the coast of Israel uncircumcised, those they circumcised valiantly. [47] They pursued also after the proud men, and the work prospered in their hand. [48] So they recovered the law out of the hand of the Gentiles, and out of the hand of kings, neither suffered they the sinner to triumph. [49] Now when the time drew near that Mattathias should die, he said unto his sons, Now hath pride and rebuke gotten strength, and the time of destruction, and the wrath of indignation: [50] Now therefore, my sons, be ye zealous for the law, and give your lives for the covenant of your fathers. [51] Call to remembrance what acts our fathers did in their time; so shall ye receive great honour and an everlasting name. [52] Was not Abraham found faithful in temptation, and it was imputed unto him for righteousness? [53] Joseph in the time of his distress kept the commandment and was made lord of Egypt. [54] Phinees our father in being zealous and fervent obtained the covenant of an everlasting priesthood. [55] Jesus for fulfilling the word was made a judge in Israel. [56] Caleb for bearing witness before the congregation received the heritage of the land. [57] David for being merciful possessed the throne of an everlasting kingdom. [58] Elias for being zealous and fervent for the law was taken up into heaven. [59] Ananias, Azarias, and Misael, by believing were saved out of the flame. [60] Daniel for his innocency was delivered from the mouth of lions. [61] And thus consider ye throughout all ages, that none that put their trust in him shall be overcome. [62] Fear not then the words of a sinful man: for his glory shall be dung and worms. [63] To day he shall be lifted up and to morrow he shall not be found, because he is returned into his dust, and his thought is come to nothing. [64] Wherefore, ye my sons, be valiant and shew yourselves men in the behalf of the law; for by it shall ye obtain glory. [65] And behold, I know that your brother Simon is a man of counsel, give ear unto him alway: he shall be a father unto you. [66] As for Judas Maccabeus, he hath been mighty and strong, even from his youth up: let him be your captain, and fight the battle of the people. [67] Take also unto you all those that observe the law, and avenge ye the wrong of your people. [68] Recompense fully the heathen, and take heed to the commandments of the law. [69] So he blessed them, and was gathered to his fathers. [70] And he died in the hundred forty and sixth year, and his sons buried him in the sepulchres of his fathers at Modin, and all Israel made great lamentation for him.

1Mac.3

[1] Then his son Judas, called Maccabeus, rose up in his stead. [2] And all his brethren helped him, and so did all they that held with his father, and they fought with cheerfulness the battle of Israel. [3] So he gat his people great honour, and put on a breastplate as a giant, and girt his warlike harness about him, and he made battles, protecting the host with his sword. [4] In his acts he was like a lion, and like a lion's whelp roaring for his prey. [5] For He pursued the wicked, and sought them out, and burnt up those that vexed his people. [6] Wherefore the wicked shrunk for fear of him, and all the workers of iniquity were troubled, because salvation prospered in his hand. [7] He grieved also many kings, and made Jacob glad

with his acts, and his memorial is blessed for ever. [8] Moreover he went through the cities of Juda, destroying the ungodly out of them, and turning away wrath from Israel: [9] So that he was renowned unto the utmost part of the earth, and he received unto him such as were ready to perish. [10] Then Apollonius gathered the Gentiles together, and a great host out of Samaria, to fight against Israel. [11] Which thing when Judas perceived, he went forth to meet him, and so he smote him, and slew him: many also fell down slain, but the rest fled. [12] Wherefore Judas took their spoils, and Apollonius' sword also, and therewith he fought all his life long. [13] Now when Seron, a prince of the army of Syria, heard say that Judas had gathered unto him a multitude and company of the faithful to go out with him to war; [14] He said, I will get me a name and honour in the kingdom; for I will go fight with Judas and them that are with him, who despise the king's commandment. [15] So he made him ready to go up, and there went with him a mighty host of the ungodly to help him, and to be avenged of the children of Israel. [16] And when he came near to the going up of Bethhoron, Judas went forth to meet him with a small company: [17] Who, when they saw the host coming to meet them, said unto Judas, How shall we be able, being so few, to fight against so great a multitude and so strong, seeing we are ready to faint with fasting all this day? [18] Unto whom Judas answered, It is no hard matter for many to be shut up in the hands of a few; and with the God of heaven it is all one, to deliver with a great multitude, or a small company: [19] For the victory of battle standeth not in the multitude of an host; but strength cometh from heaven. [20] They come against us in much pride and iniquity to destroy us, and our wives and children, and to spoil us: [21] But we fight for our lives and our laws. [22] Wherefore the Lord himself will overthrow them before our face: and as for you, be ye not afraid of them. [23] Now as soon as he had left off speaking, he leapt suddenly upon them, and so Seron and his host was overthrown before him. [24] And they pursued them from the going down of Bethhoron unto the plain, where were slain about eight hundred men of them; and the residue fled into the land of the Philistines. [25] Then began the fear of Judas and his brethren, and an exceeding great dread, to fall upon the nations round about them: [26] Insomuch as his fame came unto the king, and all nations talked of the battles of Judas. [27] Now when king Antiochus heard these things, he was full of indignation: wherefore he sent and gathered together all the forces of his realm, even a very strong army. [28] He opened also his treasure, and gave his soldiers pay for a year, commanding them to be ready whensoever he should need them. [29] Nevertheless, when he saw that the money of his treasures failed and that the tributes in the country were small, because of the dissension and plague, which he had brought upon the land in taking away the laws which had been of old time; [30] He feared that he should not be able to bear the charges any longer, nor to have such gifts to give so liberally as he did before: for he had abounded above the kings that were before him. [31] Wherefore, being greatly perplexed in his mind, he determined to go into Persia, there to take the tributes of the countries, and to gather much money. [32] So he left Lysias, a nobleman, and one of the blood royal, to oversee the affairs of the king from the river Euphrates unto the borders of Egypt: [33] And to bring up his son Antiochus, until he came again. [34] Moreover he delivered unto him the half of his forces, and the elephants, and gave him charge of all things that he would have done, as also concerning them that dwelt in Juda and Jerusalem: [35] To wit, that he should send an army against them, to destroy and root out the strength of Israel, and the remnant of Jerusalem, and to take away their memorial from that place; [36] And that he should place strangers in all their quarters, and divide their land by lot. [37] So the king took the half of the forces that remained, and departed from Antioch, his royal city, the hundred forty and seventh year; and having passed the river Euphrates, he went through the high countries. [38] Then Lysias chose Ptolemee the son of Dorymenes, Nicanor, and Gorgias, mighty men of the king's friends: [39] And with them he sent forty thousand footmen, and seven thousand horsemen, to go into the land of Juda, and to destroy it, as the king commanded. [40] So they went forth with all their power, and came and pitched by Emmaus in the plain country. [41] And the merchants of the country, hearing the fame of them, took silver and gold very much, with servants, and came into the camp to buy the children of Israel for slaves: a power also of Syria and of the land of the Philistines joined themselves unto them. [42] Now when Judas and his brethren saw that miseries were multiplied, and that the forces did encamp themselves in their borders: for they knew how the king had given commandment to destroy the people, and utterly abolish them; [43] They said one to another, Let us restore the decayed fortune of our people, and let us fight for our people and the sanctuary. [44] Then was the congregation gathered together, that they might be ready for battle, and that they might pray, and ask mercy and compassion. [45] Now Jerusalem lay void as a wilderness, there was none of her children that went in or out: the sanctuary also was trodden down, and aliens kept the strong hold; the heathen had their habitation in that place; and joy was taken from Jacob, and the pipe with the harp ceased. [46] Wherefore the Israelites assembled themselves together, and came to Maspha, over against Jerusalem; for in Maspha was the place where they prayed aforetime in Israel. [47] Then they fasted that day, and put on sackcloth, and cast ashes upon their heads, and rent their clothes, [48] And laid open the book of the law, wherein the heathen had sought to paint the likeness of their images. [49] They brought also the priests' garments, and the firstfruits, and the tithes: and the Nazarites they stirred up, who had accomplished their days. [50] Then cried they with a loud voice toward heaven, saying, What shall we do with these, and whither shall we carry them away? [51] For thy sanctuary is trodden down and profaned, and thy priests are in heaviness, and brought low. [52] And lo, the heathen are assembled together against us to destroy us: what things they imagine against us, thou knowest. [53] How shall we be able to stand against them, except thou, O God, be our help? [54] Then sounded they with trumpets, and cried with a loud voice. [55] And after this Judas ordained captains over the people, even captains over thousands, and over hundreds, and over fifties, and over tens. [56] But as for such as were building houses, or had betrothed wives, or were planting vineyards, or were fearful, those he commanded that they should

return, every man to his own house, according to the law. [57] So the camp removed, and pitched upon the south side of Emmaus. [58] And Judas said, arm yourselves, and be valiant men, and see that ye be in readiness against the morning, that ye may fight with these nations, that are assembled together against us to destroy us and our sanctuary: [59] For it is better for us to die in battle, than to behold the calamities of our people and our sanctuary. [60] Nevertheless, as the will of God is in heaven, so let him do.

1Mac.4

[1] Then took Gorgias five thousand footmen, and a thousand of the best horsemen, and removed out of the camp by night; [2] To the end he might rush in upon the camp of the Jews, and smite them suddenly. And the men of the fortress were his guides. [3] Now when Judas heard thereof he himself removed, and the valiant men with him, that he might smite the king's army which was at Emmaus,

[4] While as yet the forces were dispersed from the camp.

[5] In the mean season came Gorgias by night into the camp of Judas: and when he found no man there, he sought them in the mountains: for said he, These fellows flee from us [6] But as soon as it was day, Judas shewed himself in the plain with three thousand men, who nevertheless had neither armour nor swords to their minds.

[7] And they saw the camp of the heathen, that it was strong and well harnessed, and compassed round about with horsemen; and these were expert of war. [8] Then said Judas to the men that were with him, Fear ye not their multitude, neither be ye afraid of their assault. [9] Remember how our fathers were delivered in the Red sea, when Pharaoh pursued them with an army. [10] Now therefore let us cry unto heaven, if peradventure the Lord will have mercy upon us, and remember the covenant of our fathers, and destroy this host before our face this day: [11] That so all the heathen may know that there is one who delivereth and saveth Israel. [12] Then the strangers lifted up their eyes, and saw them coming over against them. [13] Wherefore they went out of the camp to battle; but they that were with Judas sounded their trumpets. [14] So they joined battle, and the heathen being discomfited fled into the plain. [15] Howbeit all the hindmost of them were slain with the sword: for they pursued them unto Gazera, and unto the plains of Idumea, and Azotus, and Jamnia, so that there were slain of them upon a three thousand men. [16] This done, Judas returned again with his host from pursuing them, [17] And said to the people, Be not greedy of the spoil inasmuch as there is a battle before us, [18] And Gorgias and his host are here by us in the mountain: but stand ye now against our enemies, and overcome them, and after this ye may boldly take the spoils. [19] As Judas was yet speaking these words, there appeared a part of them looking out of the mountain: [20] Who when they perceived that the Jews had put their host to flight and were burning the tents; for the smoke that was seen declared what was done: [21] When therefore they perceived these things, they were sore afraid, and seeing also the host of Judas in the plain ready to fight, [22] They fled every one into the land of strangers. [23] Then Judas returned to spoil the tents, where they got much gold, and

silver, and blue silk, and purple of the sea, and great riches.

[24] After this they went home, and sung a song of thanksgiving, and praised the Lord in heaven: because it is good, because his mercy endureth forever. [25] Thus Israel had a great deliverance that day. [26] Now all the strangers that had escaped came and told Lysias what had happened: [27] Who, when he heard thereof, was confounded and discouraged, because neither such things as he would were done unto Israel, nor such things as the king commanded him were come to pass. [28] The next year therefore following Lysias gathered together threescore thousand choice men of foot, and five thousand horsemen, that he might subdue them. [29] So they came into Idumea, and pitched their tents at Bethsura, and Judas met them with ten thousand men. [30] And when he saw that mighty army, he prayed and said, Blessed art thou, O Saviour of Israel, who didst quell the violence of the mighty man by the hand of thy servant David, and gavest the host of strangers into the hands of Jonathan the son of Saul, and his armourbearer; [31] Shut up this army in the hand of thy people Israel, and let them be confounded in their power and horsemen: [32] Make them to be of no courage, and cause the boldness of their strength to fall away, and let them quake at their destruction: [33] Cast them down with the sword of them that love thee, and let all those that know thy name praise thee with thanksgiving. [34] So they joined battle; and there were slain of the host of Lysias about five thousand men, even before them were they slain.

[35] Now when Lysias saw his army put to flight, and the manliness of Judas' soldiers, and how they were ready either to live or die valiantly, he went into Antiochia, and gathered together a company of strangers, and having made his army greater than it was, he purposed to come again into Judea. [36] Then said Judas and his brethren, Behold, our enemies are discomfited: let us go up to cleanse and dedicate the sanctuary. [37] Upon this all the host assembled themselves together, and went up into mount Sion. [38] And when they saw the sanctuary desolate, and the altar profaned, and the gates burned up, and shrubs growing in the courts as in a forest, or in one of the mountains, yea, and the priests' chambers pulled down; [39] They rent their clothes, and made great lamentation, and cast ashes upon their heads, [40] And fell down flat to the ground upon their faces, and blew an alarm with the trumpets, and cried toward heaven. [41] Then Judas appointed certain men to fight against those that were in the fortress, until he had cleansed the sanctuary. [42] So he chose priests of blameless conversation, such as had pleasure in the law: [43] Who cleansed the sanctuary, and bare out the defiled stones into an unclean place. [44] And when as they consulted what to do with the altar of burnt offerings, which was profaned; [45] They thought it best to pull it down, lest it should be a reproach to them, because the heathen had defiled it: wherefore they pulled it down, [46] And laid up the stones in the mountain of the temple in a convenient place, until there should come a prophet to shew what should be done with them. [47] Then they took whole stones according to the law, and built a new altar according to the former; [48] And made up the sanctuary, and the things that were within the temple, and hallowed the courts. [49] They made also new holy vessels, and into the temple they brought the candlestick, and the altar of

burnt offerings, and of incense, and the table. [50] And upon the altar they burned incense, and the lamps that were upon the candlestick they lighted, that they might give light in the temple. [51] Furthermore they set the loaves upon the table, and spread out the veils, and finished all the works which they had begun to make. [52] Now on the five and twentieth day of the ninth month, which is called the month Casleu, in the hundred forty and eighth year, they rose up betimes in the morning, [53] And offered sacrifice according to the law upon the new altar of burnt offerings, which they had made. [54] Look, at what time and what day the heathen had profaned it, even in that was it dedicated with songs, and citherns, and harps, and cymbals. [55] Then all the people fell upon their faces, worshipping and praising the God of heaven, who had given them good success. [56] And so they kept the dedication of the altar eight days and offered burnt offerings with gladness, and sacrificed the sacrifice of deliverance and praise. [57] They decked also the forefront of the temple with crowns of gold, and with shields; and the gates and the chambers they renewed, and hanged doors upon them. [58] Thus was there very great gladness among the people, for that the reproach of the heathen was put away. [59] Moreover Judas and his brethren with the whole congregation of Israel ordained, that the days of the dedication of the altar should be kept in their season from year to year by the space of eight days, from the five and twentieth day of the month Casleu, with mirth and gladness. [60] At that time also they builded up the mount Sion with high walls and strong towers round about, lest the Gentiles should come and tread it down as they had done before. [61] And they set there a garrison to keep it, and fortified Bethsura to preserve it; that the people might have a defence against Idumea.

1Mac.5

[1] Now when the nations round about heard that the altar was built and the sanctuary renewed as before, it displeased them very much. [2] Wherefore they thought to destroy the generation of Jacob that was among them, and thereupon they began to slay and destroy the people. [3] Then Judas fought against the children of Esau in Idumea at Arabattine, because they besieged Gael: and he gave them a great overthrow, and abated their courage, and took their spoils. [4] Also he remembered the injury of the children of Bean, who had been a snare and an offence unto the people, in that they lay in wait for them in the ways. [5] He shut them up therefore in the towers, and encamped against them, and destroyed them utterly, and burned the towers of that place with fire, and all that were therein. [6] Afterward he passed over to the children of Ammon, where he found a mighty power, and much people, with Timotheus their captain. [7] So he fought many battles with them, till at length they were discomfited before him; and he smote them. [8] And when he had taken Jazar, with the towns belonging thereto, he returned into Judea. [9] Then the heathen that were at Galaad assembled themselves together against the Israelites that were in their quarters, to destroy them; but they fled to the fortress of Dathema. [10] And sent letters unto Judas and his brethren, The heathen that are round about us are assembled together against us to destroy us: [11] And they

are preparing to come and take the fortress whereunto we are fled, Timotheus being captain of their host. [12] Come now therefore, and deliver us from their hands, for many of us are slain: [13] Yea, all our brethren that were in the places of Tobie are put to death: their wives and their children also they have carried away captives, and borne away their stuff; and they have destroyed there about a thousand men. [14] While these letters were yet reading, behold, there came other messengers from Galilee with their clothes rent, who reported on this wise, [15] And said, They of Ptolemais, and of Tyrus, and Sidon, and all Galilee of the Gentiles, are assembled together against us to consume us. [16] Now when Judas and the people heard these words, there assembled a great congregation together, to consult what they should do for their brethren, that were in trouble, and assaulted of them. [17] Then said Judas unto Simon his brother, Choose thee out men, and go and deliver thy brethren that are in Galilee, for I and Jonathan my brother will go into the country of Galaad. [18] So he left Joseph the son of Zacharias, and Azarias, captains of the people, with the remnant of the host in Judea to keep it. [19] Unto whom he gave commandment, saying, Take ye the charge of this people, and see that ye make not war against the heathen until the time that we come again. [20] Now unto Simon were given three thousand men to go into Galilee, and unto Judas eight thousand men for the country of Galaad. [21] Then went Simon into Galilee, where he fought many battles with the heathen, so that the heathen were discomfited by him. [22] And he pursued them unto the gate of Ptolemais; and there were slain of the heathen about three thousand men, whose spoils he took. [23] And those that were in Galilee, and in Arbattis, with their wives and their children, and all that they had, took he away with him, and brought them into Judea with great joy.

[24] Judas Maccabeus also and his brother Jonathan went over Jordan, and travelled three days' journey in the wilderness, [25] Where they met with the Nabathites, who came unto them in a peaceable manner, and told them every thing that had happened to their brethren in the land of Galaad: [26] And how that many of them were shut up in Bosora, and Bosor, and Alema, Casphor, Maked, and Carnaim; all these cities are strong and great: [27] And that they were shut up in the rest of the cities of the country of Galaad, and that against to morrow they had appointed to bring their host against the forts, and to take them, and to destroy them all in one day. [28] Hereupon Judas and his host turned suddenly by the way of the wilderness unto Bosora; and when he had won the city, he slew all the males with the edge of the sword, and took all their spoils, and burned the city with fire, [29] From whence he removed by night, and went till he came to the fortress. [30] And betimes in the morning they looked up, and, behold, there was an innumerable people bearing ladders and other engines of war, to take the fortress: for they assaulted them. [31] When Judas therefore saw that the battle was begun, and that the cry of the city went up to heaven, with trumpets, and a great sound, [32] He said unto his host, Fight this day for your brethren. [33] So he went forth behind them in three companies, who sounded their trumpets, and cried with prayer. [34] Then the host of Timotheus, knowing that it was Maccabeus, fled from him: wherefore he smote them with a great slaughter; so that

there were killed of them that day about eight thousand men. [35] This done, Judas turned aside to Maspha; and after he had assaulted it he took and slew all the males therein, and received the spoils thereof and and burnt it with fire. [36] From thence went he, and took Casphon, Maged, Bosor, and the other cities of the country of Galaad. [37] After these things gathered Timotheus another host and encamped against Raphon beyond the brook. [38] So Judas sent men to espy the host, who brought him word, saying, All the heathen that be round about us are assembled unto them, even a very great host. [39] He hath also hired the Arabians to help them and they have pitched their tents beyond the brook, ready to come and fight against thee. Upon this Judas went to meet them. [40] Then Timotheus said unto the captains of his host, When Judas and his host come near the brook, if he pass over first unto us, we shall not be able to withstand him; for he will mightily prevail against us: [41] But if he be afraid, and camp beyond the river, we shall go over unto him, and prevail against him. [42] Now when Judas came near the brook, he caused the scribes of the people to remain by the brook: unto whom he gave commandment, saying, Suffer no man to remain in the camp, but let all come to the battle. [43] So he went first over unto them, and all the people after him: then all the heathen, being discomfited before him, cast away their weapons, and fled unto the temple that was at Carnaim. [44] But they took the city, and burned the temple with all that were therein. Thus was Carnaim subdued, neither could they stand any longer before Judas. [45] Then Judas gathered together all the Israelites that were in the country of Galaad, from the least unto the greatest, even their wives, and their children, and their stuff, a very great host, to the end they might come into the land of Judea. [46] Now when they came unto Ephron, (this was a great city in the way as they should go, very well fortified) they could not turn from it, either on the right hand or the left, but must needs pass through the midst of it. [47] Then they of the city shut them out, and stopped up the gates with stones. [48] Whereupon Judas sent unto them in peaceable manner, saying, Let us pass through your land to go into our own country, and none shall do you any hurt; we will only pass through on foot: howbeit they would not open unto him. [49] Wherefore Judas commanded a proclamation to be made throughout the host, that every man should pitch his tent in the place where he was. [50] So the soldiers pitched, and assaulted the city all that day and all that night, till at the length the city was delivered into his hands: [51] Who then slew all the males with the edge of the sword, and rased the city, and took the spoils thereof, and passed through the city over them that were slain. [52] After this went they over Jordan into the great plain before Bethsan. [53] And Judas gathered together those that came behind, and exhorted the people all the way through, till they came into the land of Judea. [54] So they went up to mount Sion with joy and gladness, where they offered burnt offerings, because not one of them were slain until they had returned in peace. [55] Now what time as Judas and Jonathan were in the land of Galaad, and Simon his brother in Galilee before Ptolemais, [56] Joseph the son of Zacharias, and Azarias, captains of the garrisons, heard of the valiant acts and warlike deeds which they had done. [57] Wherefore they said, Let us also get us a name, and go fight against the heathen that are round about us. [58] So when they had given charge unto the garrison that was with them, they went toward Jamnia. [59] Then came Gorgias and his men out of the city to fight against them. [60] And so it was, that Joseph and Azaras were put to flight, and pursued unto the borders of Judea: and there were slain that day of the people of Israel about two thousand men. [61] Thus was there a great overthrow among the children of Israel, because they were not obedient unto Judas and his brethren, but thought to do some valiant act. [62] Moreover these men came not of the seed of those, by whose hand deliverance was given unto Israel. [63] Howbeit the man Judas and his brethren were greatly renowned in the sight of all Israel, and of all the heathen, wheresoever their name was heard of; [64] Insomuch as the the people assembled unto them with joyful acclamations. [65] Afterward went Judas forth with his brethren, and fought against the children of Esau in the land toward the south, where he smote Hebron, and the towns thereof, and pulled down the fortress of it, and burned the towers thereof round about. [66] From thence he removed to go into the land of the Philistines, and passed through Samaria. [67] At that time certain priests, desirous to shew their valour, were slain in battle, for that they went out to fight unadvisedly. [68] So Judas turned to Azotus in the land of the Philistines, and when he had pulled down their altars, and burned their carved images with fire, and spoiled their cities, he returned into the land of Judea.

1Mac.6

[1] About that time king Antiochus travelling through the high countries heard say, that Elymais in the country of Persia was a city greatly renowned for riches, silver, and gold; [2] And that there was in it a very rich temple, wherein were coverings of gold, and breastplates, and shields, which Alexander, son of Philip, the Macedonian king, who reigned first among the Grecians, had left there. [3] Wherefore he came and sought to take the city, and to spoil it; but he was not able, because they of the city, having had warning thereof, [4] Rose up against him in battle: so he fled, and departed thence with great heaviness, and returned to Babylon. [5] Moreover there came one who brought him tidings into Persia, that the armies, which went against the land of Judea, were put to flight: [6] And that Lysias, who went forth first with a great power was driven away of the Jews; and that they were made strong by the armour, and power, and store of spoils, which they had gotten of the armies, whom they had destroyed: [7] Also that they had pulled down the abomination, which he had set up upon the altar in Jerusalem, and that they had compassed about the sanctuary with high walls, as before, and his city Bethsura. [8] Now when the king heard these words, he was astonished and sore moved: whereupon he laid him down upon his bed, and fell sick for grief, because it had not befallen him as he looked for. [9] And there he continued many days: for his grief was ever more and more, and he made account that he should die. [10] Wherefore he called for all his friends, and said unto them, The sleep is gone from mine eyes, and my heart faileth for very care. [11] And I thought with myself, Into what tribulation am I

come, and how great a flood of misery is it, wherein now I am! for I was bountiful and beloved in my power. [12] But now I remember the evils that I did at Jerusalem, and that I took all the vessels of gold and silver that were therein, and sent to destroy the inhabitants of Judea without a cause. [13] I perceive therefore that for this cause these troubles are come upon me, and, behold, I perish through great grief in a strange land. [14] Then called he for Philip, one of his friends, who he made ruler over all his realm, [15] And gave him the crown, and his robe, and his signet, to the end he should bring up his son Antiochus, and nourish him up for the kingdom. [16] So king Antiochus died there in the hundred forty and ninth year. [17] Now when Lysias knew that the king was dead, he set up Antiochus his son, whom he had brought up being young, to reign in his stead, and his name he called Eupator. [18] About this time they that were in the tower shut up the Israelites round about the sanctuary, and sought always their hurt, and the strengthening of the heathen. [19] Wherefore Judas, purposing to destroy them, called all the people together to besiege them. [20] So they came together, and besieged them in the hundred and fiftieth year, and he made mounts for shot against them, and other engines. [21] Howbeit certain of them that were besieged got forth, unto whom some ungodly men of Israel joined themselves: [22] And they went unto the king, and said, How long will it be ere thou execute judgment, and avenge our brethren? [23] We have been willing to serve thy father, and to do as he would have us, and to obey his commandments; [24] For which cause they of our nation besiege the tower, and are alienated from us: moreover as many of us as they could light on they slew, and spoiled our inheritance. [25] Neither have they stretched out their hand against us only, but also against their borders. [26] And, behold, this day are they besieging the tower at Jerusalem, to take it: the sanctuary also and Bethsura have they fortified. [27] Wherefore if thou dost not prevent them quickly, they will do the greater things than these, neither shalt thou be able to rule them. [28] Now when the king heard this, he was angry, and gathered together all his friends, and the captains of his army, and those that had charge of the horse. [29] There came also unto him from other kingdoms, and from isles of the sea, bands of hired soldiers. [30] So that the number of his army was an hundred thousand footmen, and twenty thousand horsemen, and two and thirty elephants exercised in battle. [31] These went through Idumea, and pitched against Bethsura, which they assaulted many days, making engines of war; but they of Bethsura came out, and burned them with fire, and fought valiantly. [32] Upon this Judas removed from the tower, and pitched in Bathzacharias, over against the king's camp. [33] Then the king rising very early marched fiercely with his host toward Bathzacharias, where his armies made them ready to battle, and sounded the trumpets. [34] And to the end they might provoke the elephants to fight, they shewed them the blood of grapes and mulberries. [35] Moreover they divided the beasts among the armies, and for every elephant they appointed a thousand men, armed with coats of mail, and with helmets of brass on their heads; and beside this, for every beast were ordained five hundred horsemen of the best. [36] These were ready at every occasion: wheresoever the beast was, and whithersoever the beast went, they went also, neither departed they from him. [37] And upon the beasts were there strong towers of wood, which covered every one of them, and were girt fast unto them with devices: there were also upon every one two and thirty strong men, that fought upon them, beside the Indian that ruled him. [38] As for the remnant of the horsemen, they set them on this side and that side at the two parts of the host giving them signs what to do, and being harnessed all over amidst the ranks. [39] Now when the sun shone upon the shields of gold and brass, the mountains glistered therewith, and shined like lamps of fire. [40] So part of the king's army being spread upon the high mountains, and part on the valleys below, they marched on safely and in order. [41] Wherefore all that heard the noise of their multitude, and the marching of the company, and the rattling of the harness, were moved: for the army was very great and mighty. [42] Then Judas and his host drew near, and entered into battle, and there were slain of the king's army six hundred men. [43] Eleazar also, surnamed Savaran, perceiving that one of the beasts, armed with royal harness, was higher than all the rest, and supposing that the king was upon him, [44] Put himself in jeopardy, to the end he might deliver his people, and get him a perpetual name: [45] Wherefore he ran upon him courageously through the midst of the battle, slaying on the right hand and on the left, so that they were divided from him on both sides. [46] Which done, he crept under the elephant, and thrust him under, and slew him: whereupon the elephant fell down upon him, and there he died. [47] Howbeit the rest of the Jews seeing the strength of the king, and the violence of his forces, turned away from them. [48] Then the king's army went up to Jerusalem to meet them, and the king pitched his tents against Judea, and against mount Sion. [49] But with them that were in Bethsura he made peace: for they came out of the city, because they had no victuals there to endure the siege, it being a year of rest to the land. [50] So the king took Bethsura, and set a garrison there to keep it. [51] As for the sanctuary, he besieged it many days: and set there artillery with engines and instruments to cast fire and stones, and pieces to cast darts and slings. [52] Whereupon they also made engines against their engines, and held them battle a long season. [53] Yet at the last, their vessels being without victuals, (for that it was the seventh year, and they in Judea that were delivered from the Gentiles, had eaten up the residue of the store;) [54] There were but a few left in the sanctuary, because the famine did so prevail against them, that they were fain to disperse themselves, every man to his own place. [55] At that time Lysias heard say, that Philip, whom Antiochus the king, whiles he lived, had appointed to bring up his son Antiochus, that he might be king, [56] Was returned out of Persia and Media, and the king's host also that went with him, and that he sought to take unto him the ruling of the affairs. [57] Wherefore he went in all haste, and said to the king and the captains of the host and the company, We decay daily, and our victuals are but small, and the place we lay siege unto is strong, and the affairs of the kingdom lie upon us: [58] Now therefore let us be friends with these men, and make peace with them, and with all their nation; [59] And covenant with them, that they shall live after their laws, as they did before: for they are therefore displeased, and have done all these things, because we abolished their laws. [60] So the king and the princes were content: wherefore he sent unto them to make peace; and they accepted thereof. [61] Also the king and the princes made an oath unto them: whereupon they went out of the strong hold. [62] Then the king entered into mount Sion; but when he saw the strength of the place, he broke his oath that he had made, and gave commandment to pull down the wall round about. [63] Afterward departed he in all haste, and returned unto Antiochia, where he found Philip to be master of the city: so he fought against him, and took the city by force.

1Mac.7

[1] In the hundred and one and fiftieth year Demetrius the son of Seleucus departed from Rome, and came up with a few men unto a city of the sea coast, and reigned there. [2] And as he entered into the palace of his ancestors, so it was, that his forces had taken Antiochus and Lysias, to bring them unto him. [3] Wherefore, when he knew it, he said, Let me not see their faces. [4] So his host slew them. Now when Demetrius was set upon the throne of his kingdom, [5] There came unto him all the wicked and ungodly men of Israel, having Alcimus, who was desirous to be high priest, for their captain: [6] And they accused the people to the king, saying, Judas and his brethren have slain all thy friends, and driven us out of our own land. [7] Now therefore send some man whom thou trustest, and let him go and see what havock he hath made among us, and in the king's land, and let him punish them with all them that aid them. [8] Then the king chose Bacchides, a friend of the king, who ruled beyond the flood, and was a great man in the kingdom, and faithful to the king, [9] And him he sent with that wicked Alcimus, whom he made high priest, and commanded that he should take vengeance of the children of Israel. [10] So they departed, and came with a great power into the land of Judea, where they sent messengers to Judas and his brethren with peaceable words deceitfully. [11] But they gave no heed to their words; for they saw that they were come with a great power. [12] Then did there assemble unto Alcimus and Bacchides a company of scribes, to require justice. [13] Now the Assideans were the first among the children of Israel that sought peace of them: [14] For said they, One that is a priest of the seed of Aaron is come with this army, and he will do us no wrong. [15] So he spake unto them, peaceably, and sware unto them, saying, we will procure the harm neither of you nor your friends. [16] Whereupon they believed him: howbeit he took of them threescore men, and slew them in one day, according to the words which he wrote, [17] The flesh of thy saints have they cast out, and their blood have they shed round about Jerusalem, and there was none to bury them. [18] Wherefore the fear and dread of them fell upon all the people, who said, There is neither truth nor righteousness in them; for they have broken the covenant and oath that they made. [19] After this, removed Bacchides from Jerusalem, and pitched his tents in Bezeth, where he sent and took many of the men that had forsaken him, and certain of the people also, and when he had slain them, he cast them into the great pit. [20] Then committed he the country to Alcimus, and left with him a power to aid him: so Bacchides went to the

king. [21] But Alcimus contended for the high priesthood.

[22] And unto him resorted all such as troubled the people, who, after they had gotten the land of Juda into their power, did much hurt in Israel. [23] Now when Judas saw all the mischief that Alcimus and his company had done among the Israelites, even above the heathen, [24] He went out into all the coasts of Judea round about, and took vengeance of them that had revolted from him, so that they durst no more go forth into the country. [25] On the other side, when Alcimus saw that Judas and his company had gotten the upper hand, and knew that he was not able to abide their force, he went again to the king, and said all the worst of them that he could. [26] Then the king sent Nicanor, one of his honourable princes, a man that bare deadly hate unto Israel, with commandment to destroy the people. [27] So Nicanor came to Jerusalem with a great force; and sent unto Judas and his brethren deceitfully with friendly words, saying, [28] Let there be no battle between me and you; I will come with a few men, that I may see you in peace. [29] He came therefore to Judas, and they saluted one another peaceably. Howbeit the enemies were prepared to take away Judas by violence. [30] Which thing after it was known to Judas, to wit, that he came unto him with deceit, he was sore afraid of him, and would see his face no more. [31] Nicanor also, when he saw that his counsel was discovered, went out to fight against Judas beside Capharsalama: [32] Where there were slain of Nicanor's side about five thousand men, and the rest fled into the city of David. [33] After this went Nicanor up to mount Sion, and there came out of the sanctuary certain of the priests and certain of the elders of the people, to salute him peaceably, and to shew him the burnt sacrifice that was offered for the king. [34] But he mocked them, and laughed at them, and abused them shamefully, and spake proudly, [35] And sware in his wrath, saying, Unless Judas and his host be now delivered into my hands, if ever I come again in safety, I will burn up this house: and with that he went out in a great rage. [36] Then the priests entered in, and stood before the altar and the temple, weeping, and saying, [37] Thou, O Lord, didst choose this house to be called by thy name, and to be a house of prayer and petition for thy people: [38] Be avenged of this man and his host, and let them fall by the sword: remember their blasphemies, and suffer them not to continue any longer. [39] So Nicanor went out of Jerusalem, and pitched his tents in Bethhoron, where an host out of Syria met him. [40] But Judas pitched in Adasa with three thousand men, and there he prayed, saying, [41] O Lord, when they that were sent from the king of the Assyrians blasphemed, thine angel went out, and smote an hundred fourscore and five thousand of them. [42] Even so destroy thou this host before us this day, that the rest may know that he hath spoken blasphemously against thy sanctuary, and judge thou him according to his wickedness. [43] So the thirteenth day of the month Adar the hosts joined battle: but Nicanor's host was discomfited, and he himself was first slain in the battle. [44] Now when Nicanor's host saw that he was slain, they cast away their weapons, and fled. [45] Then they pursued after them a day's journey, from Adasa unto Gazera, sounding an alarm after them with their trumpets. [46] Whereupon they came forth out of all the towns of Judea round about, and closed them in; so that they, turning back upon them that pursued them, were all slain with the sword, and not one of them was left. [47] Afterwards they took the spoils, and the prey, and smote off Nicanors head, and his right hand, which he stretched out so proudly, and brought them away, and hanged them up toward Jerusalem. [48] For this cause the people rejoiced greatly, and they kept that day a day of great gladness. [49] Moreover they ordained to keep yearly this day, being the thirteenth of Adar. [50] Thus the land of Juda was in rest a little while.

1Mac.8

[1] Now Judas had heard of the the Romans, that they were mighty and valiant men, and such as would lovingly accept all that joined themselves unto them, and make a league of amity with all that came unto them; [2] And that they were men of great valour. It was told him also of their wars and noble acts which they had done among the Galatians, and how they had conquered them, and brought them under tribute; [3] And what they had done in the country of Spain, for the winning of the mines of the silver and gold which is there; [4] And that by their policy and patience they had conquered all the place, though it were very far from them; and the kings also that came against them from the uttermost part of the earth, till they had discomfited them, and given them a great overthrow, so that the rest did give them tribute every year: [5] Beside this, how they had discomfited in battle Philip, and Perseus, king of the Citims, with others that lifted up themselves against them, and had overcome them: [6] How also Antiochus the great king of Asia, that came against them in battle, having an hundred and twenty elephants, with horsemen, and chariots, and a very great army, was discomfited by them; [7] And how they took him alive, and covenanted that he and such as reigned after him should pay a great tribute, and give hostages, and that which was agreed upon, [8] And the country of India, and Media and Lydia and of the goodliest countries, which they took of him, and gave to king Eumenes: [9] Moreover how the Grecians had determined to come and destroy them; [10] And that they, having knowledge thereof sent against them a certain captain, and fighting with them slew many of them, and carried away captives their wives and their children, and spoiled them, and took possession of their lands, and pulled down their strong holds, and brought them to be their servants unto this day: [11] It was told him besides, how they destroyed and brought under their dominion all other kingdoms and isles that at any time resisted them; [12] But with their friends and such as relied upon them they kept amity: and that they had conquered kingdoms both far and nigh, insomuch as all that heard of their name were afraid of them: [13] Also that, whom they would help to a kingdom, those reign; and whom again they would, they displace: finally, that they were greatly exalted: [14] Yet for all this none of them wore a crown or was clothed in purple, to be magnified thereby: [15] Moreover how they had made for themselves a senate house, wherein three hundred and twenty men sat in council daily, consulting alway for the people, to the end they might be well ordered: [16] And that they committed their government to one man every year, who ruled over all their country, and that all were obedient to that one, and that there was neither

envy nor emmulation among them. [17] In consideration
of these things, Judas chose Eupolemus the son of John,
the son of Accos, and Jason the son of Eleazar, and sent
them to Rome, to make a league of amity and confederacy
with them, [18] And to intreat them that they would take
the yoke from them; for they saw that the kingdom of the
Grecians did oppress Israel with servitude. [19] They went
therefore to Rome, which was a very great journey, and
came into the senate, where they spake and said. [20] Judas
Maccabeus with his brethren, and the people of the Jews,
have sent us unto you, to make a confederacy and peace
with you, and that we might be registered your confederates
and friends. [21] So that matter pleased the Romans well.
[22] And this is the copy of the epistle which the senate
wrote back again in tables of brass, and sent to Jerusalem,
that there they might have by them a memorial of peace
and confederacy: [23] Good success be to the Romans, and
to the people of the Jews, by sea and by land for ever: the
sword also and enemy be far from them, [24] If there
come first any war upon the Romans or any of their
confederates throughout all their dominion, [25] The
people of the Jews shall help them, as the time shall be
appointed, with all their heart: [26] Neither shall they give
any thing unto them that make war upon them, or aid them
with victuals, weapons, money, or ships, as it hath seemed
good unto the Romans; but they shall keep their covenants
without taking any thing therefore. [27] In the same
manner also, if war come first upon the nation of the Jews,
the Romans shall help them with all their heart, according
as the time shall be appointed them: [28] Neither shall
victuals be given to them that take part against them, or
weapons, or money, or ships, as it hath seemed good to the
Romans; but they shall keep their covenants, and that
without deceit. [29] According to these articles did the
Romans make a covenant with the people of the Jews. [30]
Howbeit if hereafter the one party or the other shall think
to meet to add or diminish any thing, they may do it at their
pleasures, and whatsoever they shall add or take away shall
be ratified. [31] And as touching the evils that Demetrius
doeth to the Jews, we have written unto him, saying,
Wherefore thou made thy yoke heavy upon our friends and
confederates the Jews? [32] If therefore they complain any
more against thee, we will do them justice, and fight with
thee by sea and by land.

1Mac.9

[1] Furthermore, when Demetrius heard the Nicanor and
his host were slain in battle, he sent Bacchides and Alcimus
into the land of Judea the second time, and with them the
chief strength of his host: [2] Who went forth by the way
that leadeth to Galgala, and pitched their tents before
Masaloth, which is in Arbela, and after they had won it,
they slew much people. [3] Also the first month of the
hundred fifty and second year they encamped before
Jerusalem: [4] From whence they removed, and went to
Berea, with twenty thousand footmen and two thousand
horsemen. [5] Now Judas had pitched his tents at Eleasa,
and three thousand chosen men with him: [6] Who seeing
the multitude of the other army to he so great were sore
afraid; whereupon many conveyed themselves out of the
host, insomuch as abode of them no more but eight
hundred men. [7] When Judas therefore saw that his host

slipt away, and that the battle pressed upon him, he was
sore troubled in mind, and much distressed, for that he had
no time to gather them together. [8] Nevertheless unto
them that remained he said, Let us arise and go up against
our enemies, if peradventure we may be able to fight with
them. [9] But they dehorted him, saying, We shall never be
able: let us now rather save our lives, and hereafter we will
return with our brethren, and fight against them: for we are
but few. [10] Then Judas said, God forbid that I should do
this thing, and flee away from them: if our time be come,
let us die manfully for our brethren, and let us not stain our
honour. [11] With that the host of Bacchides removed out
of their tents, and stood over against them, their horsemen
being divided into two troops, and their slingers and
archers going before the host and they that marched in the
foreward were all mighty men. [12] As for Bacchides, he
was in the right wing: so the host drew near on the two
parts, and sounded their trumpets. [13] They also of Judas'
side, even they sounded their trumpets also, so that the
earth shook at the noise of the armies, and the battle
continued from morning till night. [14] Now when Judas
perceived that Bacchides and the strength of his army were
on the right side, he took with him all the hardy men, [15]
Who discomfited the right wing, and pursued them unto
the mount Azotus. [16] But when they of the left wing saw
that they of the right wing were discomfited, they followed
upon Judas and those that were with him hard at the heels
from behind: [17] Whereupon there was a sore battle,
insomuch as many were slain on both parts. [18] Judas also
was killed, and the remnant fled. [19] THen Jonathan and
Simon took Judas their brother, and buried him in the
sepulchre of his fathers in Modin. [20] Moreover they
bewailed him, and all Israel made great lamentation for
him, and mourned many days, saying, [21] How is the
valiant man fallen, that delivered Israel! [22] As for the
other things concerning Judas and his wars, and the noble
acts which he did, and his greatness, they are not written:
for they were very many. [23] Now after the death of Judas
the wicked began to put forth their heads in all the coasts
of Israel, and there arose up all such as wrought iniquity.
[24] In those days also was there a very great famine, by
reason whereof the country revolted, and went with them.
[25] Then Bacchides chose the wicked men, and made
them lords of the country. [26] And they made enquiry and
search for Judas' friends, and brought them unto Bacchides,
who took vengeance of them, and used them despitefully.
[27] So was there a great affliction in Israel, the like
whereof was not since the time that a prophet was not seen
among them. [28] For this cause all Judas' friends came
together, and said unto Jonathan, [29] Since thy brother
Judas died, we have no man like him to go forth against our
enemies, and Bacchides, and against them of our nation
that are adversaries to us. [30] Now therefore we have
chosen thee this day to be our prince and captain in his
stead, that thou mayest fight our battles. [31] Upon this
Jonathan took the governance upon him at that time, and
rose up instead of his brother Judas. [32] But when
Bacchides gat knowledge thereof, he sought for to slay him
[33] Then Jonathan, and Simon his brother, and all that
were with him, perceiving that, fled into the wilderness of
Thecoe, and pitched their tents by the water of the pool
Asphar. [34] Which when Bacchides understood, he came

near to Jordan with all his host upon the sabbath day. [35] Now Jonathan had sent his brother John, a captain of the people, to pray his friends the Nabathites, that they might leave with them their carriage, which was much. [36] But the children of Jambri came out of Medaba, and took John, and all that he had, and went their way with it. [37] After this came word to Jonathan and Simon his brother, that the children of Jambri made a great marriage, and were bringing the bride from Nadabatha with a great train, as being the daughter of one of the great princes of Chanaan. [38] Therefore they remembered John their brother, and went up, and hid themselves under the covert of the mountain: [39] Where they lifted up their eyes, and looked, and, behold, there was much ado and great carriage: and the bridegroom came forth, and his friends and brethren, to meet them with drums, and instruments of musick, and many weapons. [40] Then Jonathan and they that were with him rose up against them from the place where they lay in ambush, and made a slaughter of them in such sort, as many fell down dead, and the remnant fled into the mountain, and they took all their spoils. [41] Thus was the marriage turned into mourning, and the noise of their melody into lamentation. [42] So when they had avenged fully the blood of their brother, they turned again to the marsh of Jordan. [43] Now when Bacchides heard hereof, he came on the sabbath day unto the banks of Jordan with a great power. [44] Then Jonathan said to his company, Let us go up now and fight for our lives, for it standeth not with us to day, as in time past: [45] For, behold, the battle is before us and behind us, and the water of Jordan on this side and that side, the marsh likewise and wood, neither is there place for us to turn aside. [46] Wherefore cry ye now unto heaven, that ye may be delivered from the hand of your enemies. [47] With that they joined battle, and Jonathan stretched forth his hand to smite Bacchides, but he turned back from him. [48] Then Jonathan and they that were with him leapt into Jordan, and swam over unto the other bank: howbeit the other passed not over Jordan unto them. [49] So there were slain of Bacchides' side that day about a thousand men. [50] Afterward returned Bacchides to Jerusalem and repaired the strong cites in Judea; the fort in Jericho, and Emmaus, and Bethhoron, and Bethel, and Thamnatha, Pharathoni, and Taphon, these did he strengthen with high walls, with gates and with bars. [51] And in them he set a garrison, that they might work malice upon Israel. [52] He fortified also the city Bethsura, and Gazera, and the tower, and put forces in them, and provision of victuals. [53] Besides, he took the chief men's sons in the country for hostages, and put them into the tower at Jerusalem to be kept. [54] Moreover in the hundred fifty and third year, in the second month, Alcimus commanded that the wall of the inner court of the sanctuary should be pulled down; he pulled down also the works of the prophets [55] And as he began to pull down, even at that time was Alcimus plagued, and his enterprizes hindered: for his mouth was stopped, and he was taken with a palsy, so that he could no more speak any thing, nor give order concerning his house. [56] So Alcimus died at that time with great torment. [57] Now when Bacchides saw that Alcimus was dead, he returned to the king: whereupon the land of Judea was in rest two years. [58] Then all the ungodly men held a council, saying, Behold,

Jonathan and his company are at ease, and dwell without care: now therefore we will bring Bacchides hither, who shall take them all in one night. [59] So they went and consulted with him. [60] Then removed he, and came with a great host, and sent letters privily to his adherents in Judea, that they should take Jonathan and those that were with him: howbeit they could not, because their counsel was known unto them. [61] Wherefore they took of the men of the country, that were authors of that mischief, about fifty persons, and slew them. [62] Afterward Jonathan, and Simon, and they that were with him, got them away to Bethbasi, which is in the wilderness, and they repaired the decays thereof, and made it strong. [63] Which thing when Bacchides knew, he gathered together all his host, and sent word to them that were of Judea. [64] Then went he and laid siege against Bethbasi; and they fought against it a long season and made engines of war. [65] But Jonathan left his brother Simon in the city, and went forth himself into the country, and with a certain number went he forth. [66] And he smote Odonarkes and his brethren, and the children of Phasiron in their tent. [67] And when he began to smite them, and came up with his forces, Simon and his company went out of the city, and burned up the engines of war, [68] And fought against Bacchides, who was discomfited by them, and they afflicted him sore: for his counsel and travail was in vain. [69] Wherefore he was very wroth at the wicked men that gave him counsel to come into the country, inasmuch as he slew many of them, and purposed to return into his own country. [70] Whereof when Jonathan had knowledge, he sent ambassadors unto him, to the end he should make peace with him, and deliver them the prisoners. [71] Which thing he accepted, and did according to his demands, and sware unto him that he would never do him harm all the days of his life. [72] When therefore he had restored unto him the prisoners that he had taken aforetime out of the land of Judea, he returned and went his way into his own land, neither came he any more into their borders. [73] Thus the sword ceased from Israel: but Jonathan dwelt at Machmas, and began to govern the people; and he destroyed the ungodly men out of Israel.

1Mac.10

[1] In the hundred and sixtieth year Alexander, the son of Antiochus surnamed Epiphanes, went up and took Ptolemais: for the people had received him, by means whereof he reigned there, [2] Now when king Demetrius heard thereof, he gathered together an exceeding great host, and went forth against him to fight. [3] Moreover Demetrius sent letters unto Jonathan with loving words, so as he magnified him. [4] For said he, Let us first make peace with him, before he join with Alexander against us: [5] Else he will remember all the evils that we have done against him, and against his brethren and his people. [6] Wherefore he gave him authority to gather together an host, and to provide weapons, that he might aid him in battle: he commanded also that the hostages that were in the tower should be delivered him. [7] Then came Jonathan to Jerusalem, and read the letters in the audience of all the people, and of them that were in the tower: [8] Who were sore afraid, when they heard that the king had

given him authority to gather together an host. [9] Whereupon they of the tower delivered their hostages unto Jonathan, and he delivered them unto their parents. [10] This done, Jonathan settled himself in Jerusalem, and began to build and repair the city. [11] And he commanded the workmen to build the walls and the mount Sion and about with square stones for fortification; and they did so. [12] Then the strangers, that were in the fortresses which Bacchides had built, fled away; [13] Insomuch as every man left his place, and went into his own country. [14] Only at Bethsura certain of those that had forsaken the law and the commandments remained still: for it was their place of refuge. [15] Now when king Alexander had heard what promises Demetrius had sent unto Jonathan: when also it was told him of the battles and noble acts which he and his brethren had done, and of the pains that they had endured,

[16] He said, Shall we find such another man? now therefore we will make him our friend and confederate. [17] Upon this he wrote a letter, and sent it unto him, according to these words, saying, [18] King Alexander to his brother Jonathan sendeth greeting: [19] We have heard of thee, that thou art a man of great power, and meet to be our friend. [20] Wherefore now this day we ordain thee to be the high priest of thy nation, and to be called the king's friend; (and therewithal he sent him a purple robe and a crown of gold:) and require thee to take our part, and keep friendship with us. [21] So in the seventh month of the hundred and sixtieth year, at the feast of the tabernacles, Jonathan put on the holy robe, and gathered together forces, and provided much armour. [22] Whereof when Demetrius heard, he was very sorry, and said, [23] What have we done, that Alexander hath prevented us in making amity with the Jews to strengthen himself? [24] I also will write unto them words of encouragement, and promise them dignities and gifts, that I may have their aid. [25] He sent unto them therefore to this effect: King Demetrius unto the people of the Jews sendeth greeting: [26] Whereas ye have kept covenants with us, and continued in our friendship, not joining yourselves with our enemies, we have heard hereof, and are glad. [27] Wherefore now continue ye still to be faithful unto us, and we will well recompense you for the things ye do in our behalf, [28] And will grant you many immunities, and give you rewards.

[29] And now do I free you, and for your sake I release all the Jews, from tributes, and from the customs of salt, and from crown taxes, [30] And from that which appertaineth unto me to receive for the third part or the seed, and the half of the fruit of the trees, I release it from this day forth, so that they shall not be taken of the land of Judea, nor of the three governments which are added thereunto out of the country of Samaria and Galilee, from this day forth for evermore. [31] Let Jerusalem also be holy and free, with the borders thereof, both from tenths and tributes. [32] And as for the tower which is at Jerusalem, I yield up authority over it, and give the high priest, that he may set in it such men as he shall choose to keep it. [33] Moreover I freely set at liberty every one of the Jews, that were carried captives out of the land of Judea into any part of my kingdom, and I will that all my officers remit the tributes even of their cattle. [34] Furthermore I will that all the feasts, and sabbaths, and new moons, and solemn days, and the three days before the feast, and the three days after the

feast shall be all of immunity and freedom for all the Jews in my realm. [35] Also no man shall have authority to meddle with or to molest any of them in any matter. [36] I will further, that there be enrolled among the king's forces about thirty thousand men of the Jews, unto whom pay shall be given, as belongeth to all king's forces. [37] And of them some shall be placed in the king's strong holds, of whom also some shall be set over the affairs of the kingdom, which are of trust: and I will that their overseers and governors be of themselves, and that they live after their own laws, even as the king hath commanded in the land of Judea. [38] And concerning the three governments that are added to Judea from the country of Samaria, let them be joined with Judea, that they may be reckoned to be under one, nor bound to obey other authority than the high priest's. [39] As for Ptolemais, and the land pertaining thereto, I give it as a free gift to the sanctuary at Jerusalem for the necessary expences of the sanctuary. [40] Moreover I give every year fifteen thousand shekels of silver out of the king's accounts from the places appertaining. [41] And all the overplus, which the officers payed not in as in former time, from henceforth shall be given toward the works of the temple. [42] And beside this, the five thousand shekels of silver, which they took from the uses of the temple out of the accounts year by year, even those things shall be released, because they appertain to the priests that minister. [43] And whosoever they be that flee unto the temple at Jerusalem, or be within the liberties hereof, being indebted unto the king, or for any other matter, let them be at liberty, and all that they have in my realm. [44] For the building also and repairing of the works of the sanctuary expences shall be given of the king's accounts. [45] Yea, and for the building of the walls of Jerusalem, and the fortifying thereof round about, expences shall be given out of the king's accounts, as also for the building of the walls in Judea. [46] Now when Jonathan and the people heard these words, they gave no credit unto them, nor received them, because they remembered the great evil that he had done in Israel; for he had afflicted them very sore. [47] But with Alexander they were well pleased, because he was the first that entreated of true peace with them, and they were confederate with him always. [48] Then gathered king Alexander great forces, and camped over against Demetrius. [49] And after the two kings had joined battle, Demetrius' host fled: but Alexander followed after him, and prevailed against them. [50] And he continued the battle very sore until the sun went down: and that day was Demetrius slain. [51] Afterward Alexander sent ambassadors to Ptolemee king of Egypt with a message to this effect: [52] Forasmuch as I am come again to my realm, and am set in the throne of my progenitors, and have gotten the dominion, and overthrown Demetrius, and recovered our country; [53] For after I had joined battle with him, both he and his host was discomfited by us, so that we sit in the throne of his kingdom: [54] Now therefore let us make a league of amity together, and give me now thy daughter to wife: and I will be thy son in law, and will give both thee and her as according to thy dignity. [55] Then Ptolemee the king gave answer, saying, Happy be the day wherein thou didst return into the land of thy fathers, and satest in the throne of their kingdom. [56] And now will I do to thee, as thou hast written: meet me therefore at Ptolemais, that we may see one another; for I will marry my daughter to thee according to thy desire. [57] So Ptolemee went out of Egypt with his daughter Cleopatra, and they came unto Ptolemais in the hundred threescore and second year: [58] Where king Alexander meeting him, he gave unto him his daughter Cleopatra, and celebrated her marriage at Ptolemais with great glory, as the manner of kings is. [59] Now king Alexander had written unto Jonathan, that he should come and meet him. [60] Who thereupon went honourably to Ptolemais, where he met the two kings, and gave them and their friends silver and gold, and many presents, and found favour in their sight. [61] At that time certain pestilent fellows of Israel, men of a wicked life, assembled themselves against him, to accuse him: but the king would not hear them. [62] Yea more than that, the king commanded to take off his garments, and clothe him in purple: and they did so. [63] And he made him sit by himself, and said into his princes, Go with him into the midst of the city, and make proclamation, that no man complain against him of any matter, and that no man trouble him for any manner of cause. [64] Now when his accusers saw that he was honored according to the proclamation, and clothed in purple, they fled all away. [65] So the king honoured him, and wrote him among his chief friends, and made him a duke, and partaker of his dominion. [66] Afterward Jonathan returned to Jerusalem with peace and gladness. [67] Furthermore in the; hundred threescore and fifth year came Demetrius son of Demetrius out of Crete into the land of his fathers: [68] Whereof when king Alexander heard tell, he was right sorry, and returned into Antioch. [69] Then Demetrius made Apollonius the governor of Celosyria his general, who gathered together a great host, and camped in Jamnia, and sent unto Jonathan the high priest, saying, [70] Thou alone liftest up thyself against us, and I am laughed to scorn for thy sake, and reproached: and why dost thou vaunt thy power against us in the mountains? [71] Now therefore, if thou trustest in thine own strength, come down to us into the plain field, and there let us try the matter together: for with me is the power of the cities. [72] Ask and learn who I am, and the rest that take our part, and they shall tell thee that thy foot is not able to to flight in their own land. [73] Wherefore now thou shalt not be able to abide the horsemen and so great a power in the plain, where is neither stone nor flint, nor place to flee unto. [74] So when Jonathan heard these words of Apollonius, he was moved in his mind, and choosing ten thousand men he went out of Jerusalem, where Simon his brother met him for to help him. [75] And he pitched his tents against Joppa: but; they of Joppa shut him out of the city, because Apollonius had a garrison there. [76] Then Jonathan laid siege unto it: whereupon they of the city let him in for fear: and so Jonathan won Joppa. [77] Whereof when Apollonius heard, he took three thousand horsemen, with a great host of footmen, and went to Azotus as one that journeyed, and therewithal drew him forth into the plain. because he had a great number of horsemen, in whom he put his trust. [78] Then Jonathan followed after him to Azotus, where the armies joined battle. [79] Now Apollonius had left a thousand horsemen in ambush. [80] And Jonathan knew that there was an ambushment behind him; for they had compassed in his host, and cast darts at the people, from morning till evening. [81] But the people stood still, as Jonathan had commanded them: and so the enemies' horses were tired. [82] Then brought Simon forth his host, and set them against the footmen, (for the horsemen were spent) who were discomfited by him, and fled. [83] The horsemen also, being scattered in the field, fled to Azotus, and went into Bethdagon, their idol's temple, for safety. [84] But Jonathan set fire on Azotus, and the cities round about it, and took their spoils; and the temple of Dagon, with them that were fled into it, he burned with fire. [85] Thus there were burned and slain with the sword well nigh eight thousand men. [86] And from thence Jonathan removed his host, and camped against Ascalon, where the men of the city came forth, and met him with great pomp. [87] After this returned Jonathan and his host unto Jerusalem, having any spoils. [88] Now when king ALexander heard these things, he honoured Jonathan yet more. [89] And sent him a buckle of gold, as the use is to be given to such as are of the king's blood: he gave him also Accaron with the borders thereof in possession.

1Mac.11

[1] And the king of Egypt gathered together a great host, like the sand that lieth upon the sea shore, and many ships, and went about through deceit to get Alexander's kingdom, and join it to his own. [2] Whereupon he took his journey into Spain in peaceable manner, so as they of the cities opened unto him, and met him: for king Alexander had commanded them so to do, because he was his brother in law. [3] Now as Ptolemee entered into the cities, he set in every one of them a garrison of soldiers to keep it. [4] And when he came near to Azotus, they shewed him the temple of Dagon that was burnt, and Azotus and the suburbs thereof that were destroyed, and the bodies that were cast abroad and them that he had burnt in the battle; for they had made heaps of them by the way where he should pass. [5] Also they told the king whatsoever Jonathan had done, to the intent he might blame him: but the king held his peace. [6] Then Jonathan met the king with great pomp at Joppa, where they saluted one another, and lodged. [7] Afterward Jonathan, when he had gone with the king to the river called Eleutherus, returned again to Jerusalem. [8] King Ptolemee therefore, having gotten the dominion of the cities by the sea unto Seleucia upon the sea coast, imagined wicked counsels against Alexander. [9] Whereupon he sent ambasadors unto king Demetrius, saying, Come, let us make a league betwixt us, and I will give thee my daughter whom Alexander hath, and thou shalt reign in thy father's kingdom: [10] For I repent that I gave my daughter unto him, for he sought to slay me. [11] Thus did he slander him, because he was desirous of his kingdom. [12] Wherefore he took his daughter from him, and gave her to Demetrius, and forsook Alexander, so that their hatred was openly known. [13] Then Ptolemee entered into Antioch, where he set two crowns upon his head, the crown of Asia, and of Egypt. [14] In the mean season was king Alexander in Cilicia, because those that dwelt in those parts had revolted from him. [15] But when Alexander heard of this, he came to war against him: whereupon king Ptolemee brought forth his host, and met him with a mighty power, and put him to flight. [16] So

Alexander fled into Arabia there to be defended; but king Ptolemee was exalted: [17] For Zabdiel the Arabian took off Alexander's head, and sent it unto Ptolemee. [18] King Ptolemee also died the third day after, and they that were in the strong holds were slain one of another. [19] By this means Demetrius reigned in the hundred threescore and seventh year. [20] At the same time Jonathan gathered together them that were in Judea to take the tower that was in Jerusalem: and he made many engines of war against it. [21] Then came ungodly persons, who hated their own people, went unto the king, and told him that Jonathan besieged the tower, [22] Whereof when he heard, he was angry, and immediately removing, he came to Ptolemais, and wrote unto Jonathan, that he should not lay siege to the tower, but come and speak with him at Ptolemais in great haste. [23] Nevertheless Jonathan, when he heard this, commanded to besiege it still: and he chose certain of the elders of Israel and the priests, and put himself in peril; [24] And took silver and gold, and raiment, and divers presents besides, and went to Ptolemais unto the king, where he found favour in his sight. [25] And though certain ungodly men of the people had made complaints against him, [26] Yet the king entreated him as his predecessors had done before, and promoted him in the sight of all his friends, [27] And confirmed him in the high priesthood, and in all the honours that he had before, and gave him preeminence among his chief friends. [28] Then Jonathan desired the king, that he would make Judea free from tribute, as also the three governments, with the country of Samaria; and he promised him three hundred talents. [29] So the king consented, and wrote letters unto Jonathan of all these things after this manner: [30] King Demetrius unto his brother Jonathan, and unto the nation of the Jews, sendeth greeting: [31] We send you here a copy of the letter which we did write unto our cousin Lasthenes concerning you, that ye might see it. [32] King Demetrius unto his father Lasthenes sendeth greeting: [33] We are determined to do good to the people of the Jews, who are our friends, and keep covenants with us, because of their good will toward us. [34] Wherefore we have ratified unto them the borders of Judea, with the three governments of Apherema and Lydda and Ramathem, that are added unto Judea from the country of Samaria, and all things appertaining unto them, for all such as do sacrifice in Jerusalem, instead of the payments which the king received of them yearly aforetime out of the fruits of the earth and of trees. [35] And as for other things that belong unto us, of the tithes and customs pertaining unto us, as also the saltpits, and the crown taxes, which are due unto us, we discharge them of them all for their relief. [36] And nothing hereof shall be revoked from this time forth for ever. [37] Now therefore see that thou make a copy of these things, and let it be delivered unto Jonathan, and set upon the holy mount in a conspicuous place. [38] After this, when king Demetrius saw that the land was quiet before him, and that no resistance was made against him, he sent away all his forces, every one to his own place, except certain bands of strangers, whom he had gathered from the isles of the heathen: wherefore all the forces of his fathers hated him. [39] Moreover there was one Tryphon, that had been of Alexander's part afore, who, seeing that all the host murmured against Demetrius, went to Simalcue

the Arabian that brought up Antiochus the young son of Alexander, [40] And lay sore upon him to deliver him this young Antiochus, that he might reign in his father's stead: he told him therefore all that Demetrius had done, and how his men of war were at enmity with him, and there he remained a long season. [41] In the mean time Jonathan sent unto king Demetrius, that he would cast those of the tower out of Jerusalem, and those also in the fortresses: for they fought against Israel. [42] So Demetrius sent unto Jonathan, saying, I will not only do this for thee and thy people, but I will greatly honour thee and thy nation, if opportunity serve. [43] Now therefore thou shalt do well, if thou send me men to help me; for all my forces are gone from me. [44] Upon this Jonathan sent him three thousand strong men unto Antioch: and when they came to the king, the king was very glad of their coming. [45] Howbeit they that were of the city gathered themselves together into the midst of the city, to the number of an hundred and twenty thousand men, and would have slain the king. [46] Wherefore the king fled into the court, but they of the city kept the passages of the city, and began to fight. [47] Then the king called to the Jews for help, who came unto him all at once, and dispersing themselves through the city slew that day in the city to the number of an hundred thousand. [48] Also they set fire on the city, and gat many spoils that day, and delivered the king. [49] So when they of the city saw that the Jews had got the city as they would, their courage was abated: wherefore they made supplication to the king, and cried, saying, [50] Grant us peace, and let the Jews cease from assaulting us and the city. [51] With that they cast away their weapons, and made peace; and the Jews were honoured in the sight of the king, and in the sight of all that were in his realm; and they returned to Jerusalem, having great spoils. [52] So king Demetrius sat on the throne of his kingdom, and the land was quiet before him. [53] Nevertheless he dissembled in all that ever he spake, and estranged himself from Jonathan, neither rewarded he him according to the benefits which he had received of him, but troubled him very sore. [54] After this returned Tryphon, and with him the young child Antiochus, who reigned, and was crowned. [55] Then there gathered unto him all the men of war, whom Demetrius had put away, and they fought against Demetrius, who turned his back and fled. [56] Moreover Tryphon took the elephants, and won Antioch. [57] At that time young Antiochus wrote unto Jonathan, saying, I confirm thee in the high priesthood, and appoint thee ruler over the four governments, and to be one of the king's friends. [58] Upon this he sent him golden vessels to be served in, and gave him leave to drink in gold, and to be clothed in purple, and to wear a golden buckle. [59] His brother Simon also he made captain from the place called The ladder of Tyrus unto the borders of Egypt. [60] Then Jonathan went forth, and passed through the cities beyond the water, and all the forces of Syria gathered themselves unto him for to help him: and when he came to Ascalon, they of the city met him honourably. [61] From whence he went to Gaza, but they of Gaza shut him out; wherefore he laid siege unto it, and burned the suburbs thereof with fire, and spoiled them. [62] Afterward, when they of Gaza made supplication unto Jonathan, he made peace with them, and took the sons of their chief men for hostages, and sent them to

Jerusalem, and passed through the country unto Damascus.

[63] Now when Jonathan heard that Demetrius' princes were come to Cades, which is in Galilee, with a great power, purposing to remove him out of the country, [64] He went to meet them, and left Simon his brother in the country. [65] Then Simon encamped against Bethsura and fought against it a long season, and shut it up: [66] But they desired to have peace with him, which he granted them, and then put them out from thence, and took the city, and set a garrison in it. [67] As for Jonathan and his host, they pitched at the water of Gennesar, from whence betimes in the morning they gat them to the plain of Nasor. [68] And, behold, the host of strangers met them in the plain, who, having laid men in ambush for him in the mountains, came themselves over against him. [69] So when they that lay in ambush rose out of their places and joined battle, all that were of Jonathan's side fled; [70] Insomuch as there was not one of them left, except Mattathias the son of Absalom, and Judas the son of Calphi, the captains of the host. [71] Then Jonathan rent his clothes, and cast earth upon his head, and prayed. [72] Afterwards turning again to battle, he put them to flight, and so they ran away. [73] Now when his own men that were fled saw this, they turned again unto him, and with him pursued them to Cades, even unto their own tents, and there they camped. [74] So there were slain of the heathen that day about three thousand men: but Jonathan returned to Jerusalem.

1Mac.12

[1] Now when Jonathan saw that time served him, he chose certain men, and sent them to Rome, for to confirm and renew the friendship that they had with them. [2] He sent letters also to the Lacedemonians, and to other places, for the same purpose. [3] So they went unto Rome, and entered into the senate, and said, Jonathan the high priest, and the people of the Jews, sent us unto you, to the end ye should renew the friendship, which ye had with them, and league, as in former time. [4] Upon this the Romans gave them letters unto the governors of every place that they should bring them into the land of Judea peaceably. [5] And this is the copy of the letters which Jonathan wrote to the Lacedemonians: [6] Jonathan the high priest, and the elders of the nation, and the priests, and the other of the Jews, unto the Lacedemonians their brethren send greeting: [7] There were letters sent in times past unto Onias the high priest from Darius, who reigned then among you, to signify that ye are our brethren, as the copy here underwritten doth specify. [8] At which time Onias entreated the ambassador that was sent honourably, and received the letters, wherein declaration was made of the league and friendship. [9] Therefore we also, albeit we need none of these things, that we have the holy books of scripture in our hands to comfort us, [10] Have nevertheless attempted to send unto you for the renewing of brotherhood and friendship, lest we should become strangers unto you altogether: for there is a long time passed since ye sent unto us. [11] We therefore at all times without ceasing, both in our feasts, and other convenient days, do remember you in the sacrifices which we offer, and in our prayers, as reason is, and as it becometh us to think upon our brethren: [12] And we are right glad of your honour. [13] As for ourselves, we have had great troubles and wars on every side, forsomuch as the kings that are round about us have fought against us. [14] Howbeit we would not be troublesome unto you, nor to others of our confederates and friends, in these wars: [15] For we have help from heaven that succoureth us, so as we are delivered from our enemies, and our enemies are brought under foot. [16] For this cause we chose Numenius the son of Antiochus, and Antipater he son of Jason, and sent them unto the Romans, to renew the amity that we had with them, and the former league. [17] We commanded them also to go unto you, and to salute and to deliver you our letters concerning the renewing of our brotherhood. [18] Wherefore now ye shall do well to give us an answer thereto. [19] And this is the copy of the letters which Oniares sent. [20] Areus king of the Lacedemonians to Onias the high priest, greeting: [21] It is found in writing, that the Lacedemonians and Jews are brethren, and that they are of the stock of Abraham: [22] Now therefore, since this is come to our knowledge, ye shall do well to write unto us of your prosperity. [23] We do write back again to you, that your cattle and goods are our's, and our's are your's We do command therefore our ambassadors to make report unto you on this wise. [24] Now when Jonathan heard that Demebius' princes were come to fight against him with a greater host than afore, [25] He removed from Jerusalem, and met them in the land of Amathis: for he gave them no respite to enter his country. [26] He sent spies also unto their tents, who came again, and told him that they were appointed to come upon them in the night season. [27] Wherefore so soon as the sun was down, Jonathan commanded his men to watch, and to be in arms, that all the night long they might be ready to fight: also he sent forth centinels round about the host. [28] But when the adversaries heard that Jonathan and his men were ready for battle, they feared, and trembled in their hearts, and they kindled fires in their camp. [29] Howbeit Jonathan and his company knew it not till the morning: for they saw the lights burning. [30] Then Jonathan pursued after them, but overtook them not: for they were gone over the river Eleutherus. [31] Wherefore Jonathan turned to the Arabians, who were called Zabadeans, and smote them, and took their spoils. [32] And removing thence, he came to Damascus, and so passed through all the country, [33] Simon also went forth, and passed through the country unto Ascalon, and the holds there adjoining, from whence he turned aside to Joppa, and won it. [34] For he had heard that they would deliver the hold unto them that took Demetrius' part; wherefore he set a garrison there to keep it. [35] After this came Jonathan home again, and calling the elders of the people together, he consulted with them about building strong holds in Judea, [36] And making the walls of Jerusalem higher, and raising a great mount between the tower and the city, for to separate it from the city, that so it might be alone, that men might neither sell nor buy in it. [37] Upon this they came together to build up the city, forasmuch as part of the wall toward the brook on the east side was fallen down, and they repaired that which was called Caphenatha. [38] Simon also set up Adida in Sephela, and made it strong with gates and bars. [39] Now

Tryphon went about to get the kingdom of Asia, and to kill Antiochus the king, that he might set the crown upon his own head. [40] Howbeit he was afraid that Jonathan would not suffer him, and that he would fight against him; wherefore he sought a way how to take Jonathan, that he might kill him. So he removed, and came to Bethsan. [41] Then Jonathan went out to meet him with forty thousand men chosen for the battle, and came to Bethsan. [42] Now when Tryphon saw Jonathan came with so great a force, he durst not stretch his hand against him; [43] But received him honourably, and commended him unto all his friends, and gave him gifts, and commanded his men of war to be as obedient unto him, as to himself. [44] Unto Jonathan also he said, Why hast thou brought all this people to so great trouble, seeing there is no war betwixt us? [45] Therefore send them now home again, and choose a few men to wait on thee, and come thou with me to Ptolemais, for I will give it thee, and the rest of the strong holds and forces, and all that have any charge: as for me, I will return and depart: for this is the cause of my coming. [46] So Jonathan believing him did as he bade him, and sent away his host, who went into the land of Judea. [47] And with himself he retained but three thousand men, of whom he sent two thousand into Galilee, and one thousand went with him. [48] Now as soon as Jonathan entered into Ptolemais, they of Ptolemais shut the gates and took him, and all them that came with him they slew with the sword. [49] Then sent Tryphon an host of footmen and horsemen into Galilee, and into the great plain, to destroy all Jonathan's company. [50] But when they knew that Jonathan and they that were with him were taken and slain, they encouraged one another; and went close together, prepared to fight. [51] They therefore that followed upon them, perceiving that they were ready to fight for their lives, turned back again. [52] Whereupon they all came into the land of Judea peaceably, and there they bewailed Jonathan, and them that were with him, and they were sore afraid; wherefore all Israel made great lamentation. [53] Then all the heathen that were round about then sought to destroy them: for said they, They have no captain, nor any to help them: now therefore let us make war upon them, and take away their memorial from among men.

1Mac.13

[1] Now when Simon heard that Tryphon had gathered together a great host to invade the land of Judea, and destroy it, [2] And saw that the people was in great trembling and fear, he went up to Jerusalem, and gathered the people together, [3] And gave them exhortation, saying, Ye yourselves know what great things I, and my brethren, and my father's house, have done for the laws and the sanctuary, the battles also and troubles which we have seen. [4] By reason whereof all my brethren are slain for Israel's sake, and I am left alone. [5] Now therefore be it far from me, that I should spare mine own life in any time of trouble: for I am no better than my brethren. [6] Doubtless I will avenge my nation, and the sanctuary, and our wives, and our children: for all the heathen are gathered to destroy us of very malice. [7] Now as soon as the people heard these words, their spirit revived. [8] And they answered with a loud voice, saying, Thou shalt be our ʰⁿᵈᵉʳ instead of Judas and Jonathan thy brother. [9] Fight

thou our battles, and whatsoever, thou commandest us, that will we do. [10] So then he gathered together all the men of war, and made haste to finish the walls of Jerusalem, and he fortified it round about. [11] Also he sent Jonathan the son of Absolom, and with him a great power, to Joppa: who casting out them that were therein remained there in it. [12] So Tryphon removed from Ptolemaus with a great power to invade the land of Judea, and Jonathan was with him in ward. [13] But Simon pitched his tents at Adida, over against the plain. [14] Now when Tryphon knew that Simon was risen up instead of his brother Jonathan, and meant to join battle with him, he sent messengers unto him, saying, [15] Whereas we have Jonathan thy brother in hold, it is for money that he is owing unto the king's treasure, concerning the business that was committed unto him. [16] Wherefore now send an hundred talents of silver, and two of his sons for hostages, that when he is at liberty he may not revolt from us, and we will let him go. [17] Hereupon Simon, albeit he perceived that they spake deceitfully unto him yet sent he the money and the children, lest peradventure he should procure to himself great hatred of the people: [18] Who might have said, Because I sent him not the money and the children, therefore is Jonathan dead. [19] So he sent them the children and the hundred talents: howbeit Tryphon dissembled neither would he let Jonathan go. [20] And after this came Tryphon to invade the land, and destroy it, going round about by the way that leadeth unto Adora: but Simon and his host marched against him in every place, wheresoever he went. [21] Now they that were in the tower sent messengers unto Tryphon, to the end that he should hasten his coming unto them by the wilderness, and send them victuals. [22] Wherefore Tryphon made ready all his horsemen to come that night: but there fell a very great snow, by reason whereof he came not. So he departed, and came into the country of Galaad. [23] And when he came near to Bascama he slew Jonathan, who was buried there. [24] Afterward Tryphon returned and went into his own land. [25] Then sent Simon, and took the bones of Jonathan his brother, and buried them in Modin, the city of his fathers. [26] And all Israel made great lamentation for him, and bewailed him many days. [27] Simon also built a monument upon the sepulchre of his father and his brethren, and raised it aloft to the sight, with hewn stone behind and before. [28] Moreover he set up seven pyramids, one against another, for his father, and his mother, and his four brethren. [29] And in these he made cunning devices, about the which he set great pillars, and upon the pillars he made all their armour for a perpetual memory, and by the armour ships carved, that they might be seen of all that sail on the sea. [30] This is the sepulchre which he made at Modin, and it standeth yet unto this day.

[31] Now Tryphon dealt deceitfully with the young king Antiochus, and slew him. [32] And he reigned in his stead, and crowned himself king of Asia, and brought a great calamity upon the land. [33] Then Simon built up the strong holds in Judea, and fenced them about with high towers, and great walls, and gates, and bars, and laid up victuals therein. [34] Moreover Simon chose men, and sent to king Demetrius, to the end he should give the land an immunity, because all that Tryphon did was to spoil. [35] Unto whom king Demetrius answered and wrote after this

manner: [36] King Demetrius unto Simon the high priest, and friend of kings, as also unto the elders and nation of the Jews, sendeth greeting: [37] The golden crown, and the scarlet robe, which ye sent unto us, we have received: and we are ready to make a stedfast peace with you, yea, and to write unto our officers, to confirm the immunities which we have granted. [38] And whatsoever covenants we have made with you shall stand; and the strong holds, which ye have builded, shall be your own. [39] As for any oversight or fault committed unto this day, we forgive it, and the crown tax also, which ye owe us: and if there were any other tribute paid in Jerusalem, it shall no more be paid. [40] And look who are meet among you to be in our court, let then be enrolled, and let there be peace betwixt us. [41] Thus the yoke of the heathen was taken away from Israel in the hundred and seventieth year. [42] Then the people of Israel began to write in their instruments and contracts, In the first year of Simon the high priest, the governor and leader of the Jews. [43] In those days Simon camped against Gaza and besieged it round about; he made also an engine of war, and set it by the city, and battered a certain tower, and took it. [44] And they that were in the engine leaped into the city; whereupon there was a great uproar in the city: [45] Insomuch as the people of the city rent their clothes, and climbed upon the walls with their wives and children, and cried with a loud voice, beseeching Simon to grant them peace. [46] And they said, Deal not with us according to our wickedness, but according to thy mercy. [47] So Simon was appeased toward them, and fought no more against them, but put them out of the city, and cleansed the houses wherein the idols were, and so entered into it with songs and thanksgiving. [48] Yea, he put all uncleanness out of it, and placed such men there as would keep the law, and made it stronger than it was before, and built therein a dwellingplace for himself. [49] They also of the tower in Jerusalem were kept so strait, that they could neither come forth, nor go into the country, nor buy, nor sell: wherefore they were in great distress for want of victuals, and a great number of them perished through famine. [50] Then cried they to Simon, beseeching him to be at one with them: which thing he granted them; and when he had put them out from thence, he cleansed the tower from pollutions: [51] And entered into it the three and twentieth day of the second month in the hundred seventy and first year, with thanksgiving, and branches of palm trees, and with harps, and cymbals, and with viols, and hymns, and songs: because there was destroyed a great enemy out of Israel. [52] He ordained also that that day should be kept every year with gladness. Moreover the hill of the temple that was by the tower he made stronger than it was, and there he dwelt himself with his company. [53] And when Simon saw that John his son was a valiant man, he made him captain of all the hosts; and he dwelt in Gazera.

1Mac.14

[1] Now in the hundred threescore and twelfth year king Demetrius gathered his forces together, and went into Media to get him help to fight against Tryphone. [2] But when Arsaces, the king of Persia and Media, heard that Demetrius was entered within his borders, he sent one of his princes to take him alive: [3] Who went and smote the host of Demetrius, and took him, and brought him to Arsaces, by whom he was put in ward. [4] As for the land of Judea, that was quiet all the days of Simon; for he sought the good of his nation in such wise, as that evermore his authority and honour pleased them well. [5] And as he was honourable in all his acts, so in this, that he took Joppa for an haven, and made an entrance to the isles of the sea, [6] And enlarged the bounds of his nation, and recovered the country, [7] And gathered together a great number of captives, and had the dominion of Gazera, and Bethsura, and the tower, out of the which he took all uncleaness, neither was there any that resisted him. [8] Then did they till their ground in peace, and the earth gave her increase, and the trees of the field their fruit. [9] The ancient men sat all in the streets, communing together of good things, and the young men put on glorious and warlike apparel. [10] He provided victuals for the cities, and set in them all manner of munition, so that his honourable name was renowned unto the end of the world. [11] He made peace in the land, and Israel rejoiced with great joy: [12] For every man sat under his vine and his fig tree, and there was none to fray them: [13] Neither was there any left in the land to fight against them: yea, the kings themselves were overthrown in those days. [14] Moreover he strengthened all those of his people that were brought low: the law he searched out; and every contemner of the law and wicked person he took away. [15] He beautified the sanctuary, and multiplied vessels of the temple. [16] Now when it was heard at Rome, and as far as Sparta, that Jonathan was dead, they were very sorry. [17] But as soon as they heard that his brother Simon was made high priest in his stead, and ruled the country, and the cities therein: [18] They wrote unto him in tables of brass, to renew the friendship and league which they had made with Judas and Jonathan his brethren: [19] Which writings were read before the congregation at Jerusalem. [20] And this is the copy of the letters that the Lacedemonians sent; The rulers of the Lacedemonians, with the city, unto Simon the high priest, and the elders, and priests, and residue of the people of the Jews, our brethren, send greeting: [21] The ambassadors that were sent unto our people certified us of your glory and honour: wherefore we were glad of their coming, [22] And did register the things that they spake in the council of the people in this manner; Numenius son of Antiochus, and Antipater son of Jason, the Jews' ambassadors, came unto us to renew the friendship they had with us. [23] And it pleased the people to entertain the men honourably, and to put the copy of their ambassage in publick records, to the end the people of the Lacedemonians might have a memorial thereof: furthermore we have written a copy thereof unto Simon the high priest. [24] After this Simon sent Numenius to Rome with a great shield of gold of a thousand pound weight to confirm the league with them. [25] Whereof when the people heard, they said, What thanks shall we give to Simon and his sons? [26] For he and his brethren and the house of his father have established Israel, and chased away in fight their enemies from them, and confirmed their liberty. [27] So then they wrote it in tables of brass, which they set upon pillars in mount Sion: and this is the copy of the writing; The eighteenth day of the month Elul, in the hundred threescore and twelfth year, being the third year of Simon

the high priest, [28] At Saramel in the great congregation of the priests, and people, and rulers of the nation, and elders of the country, were these things notified unto us. [29] Forasmuch as oftentimes there have been wars in the country, wherein for the maintenance of their sanctuary, and the law, Simon the son of Mattathias, of the posterity of Jarib, together with his brethren, put themselves in jeopardy, and resisting the enemies of their nation did their nation great honour: [30] (For after that Jonathan, having gathered his nation together, and been their high priest, was added to his people, [31] Their enemies prepared to invade their country, that they might destroy it, and lay hands on the sanctuary: [32] At which time Simon rose up, and fought for his nation, and spent much of his own substance, and armed the valiant men of his nation and gave them wages, [33] And fortified the cities of Judea, together with Bethsura, that lieth upon the borders of Judea, where the armour of the enemies had been before; but he set a garrison of Jews there: [34] Moreover he fortified Joppa, which lieth upon the sea, and Gazera, that bordereth upon Azotus, where the enemies had dwelt before: but he placed Jews there, and furnished them with all things convenient for the reparation thereof.) [35] The people therefore sang the acts of Simon, and unto what glory he thought to bring his nation, made him their governor and chief priest, because he had done all these things, and for the justice and faith which he kept to his nation, and for that he sought by all means to exalt his people. [36] For in his time things prospered in his hands, so that the heathen were taken out of their country, and they also that were in the city of David in Jerusalem, who had made themselves a tower, out of which they issued, and polluted all about the sanctuary, and did much hurt in the holy place: [37] But he placed Jews therein. and fortified it for the safety of the country and the city, and raised up the walls of Jerusalem. [38] King Demetrius also confirmed him in the high priesthood according to those things, [39] And made him one of his friends, and honoured him with great honour. [40] For he had heard say, that the Romans had called the Jews their friends and confederates and brethren; and that they had entertained the ambassadors of Simon honourably; [41] Also that the Jews and priests were well pleased that Simon should be their governor and high priest for ever, until there should arise a faithful prophet; [42] Moreover that he should be their captain, and should take charge of the sanctuary, to set them over their works, and over the country, and over the armour, and over the fortresses, that, I say, he should take charge of the sanctuary; [43] Beside this, that he should be obeyed of every man, and that all the writings in the country should be made in his name, and that he should be clothed in purple, and wear gold: [44] Also that it should be lawful for none of the people or priests to break any of these things, or to gainsay his words, or to gather an assembly in the country without him, or to be clothed in purple, or wear a buckle of gold; [45] And whosoever should do otherwise, or break any of these things, he should be punished. [46] Thus it liked all the people to deal with Simon, and to do as hath been said. [47] Then Simon accepted hereof, and was well pleased to be high priest, and captain and governor of the Jews and priests, and to defend them all. [48] So they commanded that this writing should ˌ ˌ put in tables of brass, and that they should be set up

within the compass of the sanctuary in a conspicuous place; [49] Also that the copies thereof should be laid up in the treasury, to the end that Simon and his sons might have them.

1Mac.15

[1] Moreover Antiochus son of Demetrius the king sent letters from the isles of the sea unto Simon the priest and prince of the Jews, and to all the people; [2] The contents whereof were these: King Antiochus to Simon the high priest and prince of his nation, and to the people of the Jews, greeting: [3] Forasmuch as certain pestilent men have usurped the kingdom of our fathers, and my purpose is to challenge it again, that I may restore it to the old estate, and to that end have gathered a multitude of foreign soldiers together, and prepared ships of war; [4] My meaning also being to go through the country, that I may be avenged of them that have destroyed it, and made many cities in the kingdom desolate: [5] Now therefore I confirm unto thee all the oblations which the kings before me granted thee, and whatsoever gifts besides they granted. [6] I give thee leave also to coin money for thy country with thine own stamp. [7] And as concerning Jerusalem and the sanctuary, let them be free; and all the armour that thou hast made, and fortresses that thou hast built, and keepest in thine hands, let them remain unto thee. [8] And if anything be, or shall be, owing to the king, let it be forgiven thee from this time forth for evermore. [9] Furthermore, when we have obtained our kingdom, we will honour thee, and thy nation, and thy temple, with great honour, so that your honour shall be known throughout the world. [10] In the hundred threescore and fourteenth year went Antiochus into the land of his fathers: at which time all the forces came together unto him, so that few were left with Tryphon. [11] Wherefore being pursued by king Antiochus, he fled unto Dora, which lieth by the sea side: [12] For he saw that troubles came upon him all at once, and that his forces had forsaken him. [13] Then camped Antiochus against Dora, having with him an hundred and twenty thousand men of war, and eight thousand horsemen. [14] And when he had compassed the city round about, and joined ships close to the town on the sea side, he vexed the city by land and by sea, neither suffered he any to go out or in. [15] In the mean season came Numenius and his company from Rome, having letters to the kings and countries; wherein were written these things: [16] Lucius, consul of the Romans unto king Ptolemee, greeting: [17] The Jews' ambassadors, our friends and confederates, came unto us to renew the old friendship and league, being sent from Simon the high priest, and from the people of the Jews: [18] And they brought a shield of gold of a thousand pound. [19] We thought it good therefore to write unto the kings and countries, that they should do them no harm, nor fight against them, their cities, or countries, nor yet aid their enemies against them. [20] It seemed also good to us to receive the shield of them. [21] If therefore there be any pestilent fellows, that have fled from their country unto you, deliver them unto Simon the high priest, that he may punish them according to their own law. [22] The same things wrote he likewise unto Demetrius the king, and Attalus, to Ariarathes, and Arsaces,

[23] And to all the countries and to Sampsames, and the Lacedemonians, and to Delus, and Myndus, and Sicyon, and Caria, and Samos, and Pamphylia, and Lycia, and Halicarnassus, and Rhodus, and Aradus, and Cos, and Side, and Aradus, and Gortyna, and Cnidus, and Cyprus, and Cyrene. [24] And the copy hereof they wrote to Simon the high priest. [25] So Antiochus the king camped against Dora the second day, assaulting it continually, and making engines, by which means he shut up Tryphon, that he could neither go out nor in. [26] At that time Simon sent him two thousand chosen men to aid him; silver also, and gold, and much armour. [27] Nevertheless he would not receive them, but brake all the covenants which he had made with him afore, and became strange unto him. [28] Furthermore he sent unto him Athenobius, one of his friends, to commune with him, and say, Ye withhold Joppa and Gazera; with the tower that is in Jerusalem, which are cities of my realm. [29] The borders thereof ye have wasted, and done great hurt in the land, and got the dominion of many places within my kingdom. [30] Now therefore deliver the cities which ye have taken, and the tributes of the places, whereof ye have gotten dominion without the borders of Judea: [31] Or else give me for them five hundred talents of silver; and for the harm that ye have done, and the tributes of the cities, other five hundred talents: if not, we will come and fight against you [32] So Athenobius the king's friend came to Jerusalem: and when he saw the glory of Simon, and the cupboard of gold and silver plate, and his great attendance, he was astonished, and told him the king's message. [33] Then answered Simon, and said unto him, We have neither taken other men's land, nor holden that which appertaineth to others, but the inheritance of our fathers, which our enemies had wrongfully in possession a certain time. [34] Wherefore we, having opportunity, hold the inheritance of our fathers. [35] And whereas thou demandest Joppa and Gazera, albeit they did great harm unto the people in our country, yet will we give thee an hundred talents for them. Hereunto Athenobius answered him not a word; [36] But returned in a rage to the king, and made report unto him of these speeches, and of the glory of Simon, and of all that he had seen: whereupon the king was exceeding wroth. [37] In the mean time fled Tryphon by ship unto Orthosias. [38] Then the king made Cendebeus captain of the sea coast, and gave him an host of footmen and horsemen, [39] And commanded him to remove his host toward Judea; also he commanded him to build up Cedron, and to fortify the gates, and to war against the people; but as for the king himself, he pursued Tryphon. [40] So Cendebeus came to Jamnia and began to provoke the people and to invade Judea, and to take the people prisoners, and slay them. [41] And when he had built up Cedrou, he set horsemen there, and an host of footmen, to the end that issuing out they might make outroads upon the ways of Judea, as the king had commanded him.

1Mac.16

[1] Then came up John from Gazera, and told Simon his father what Cendebeus had done. [2] Wherefore Simon called his two eldest sons, Judas and John, and said unto them, I, and my brethren, and my father's house, have ever from my youth unto this day fought against the enemies of Israel; and things have prospered so well in our hands, that we have delivered Israel oftentimes. [3] But now I am old, and ye, by God's mercy, are of a sufficient age: be ye instead of me and my brother, and go and fight for our nation, and the help from heaven be with you. [4] So he chose out of the country twenty thousand men of war with horsemen, who went out against Cendebeus, and rested that night at Modin. [5] And when as they rose in the morning, and went into the plain, behold, a mighty great host both of footmen and horsemen came against them: howbeit there was a water brook betwixt them. [6] So he and his people pitched over against them: and when he saw that the people were afraid to go over the water brook, he went first over himself, and then the men seeing him passed through after him. [7] That done, he divided his men, and set the horsemen in the midst of the footmen: for the enemies' horsemen were very many. [8] Then sounded they with the holy trumpets: whereupon Cendebeus and his host were put to flight, so that many of them were slain, and the remnant gat them to the strong hold. [9] At that time was Judas John's brother wounded; but John still followed after them, until he came to Cedron, which Cendebeus had built. [10] So they fled even unto the towers in the fields of Azotus; wherefore he burned it with fire: so that there were slain of them about two thousand men. Afterward he returned into the land of Judea in peace. [11] Moreover in the plain of Jericho was Ptolemeus the son of Abubus made captain, and he had abundance of silver and gold: [12] For he was the high priest's son in law. [13] Wherefore his heart being lifted up, he thought to get the country to himself, and thereupon consulted deceitfully against Simon and his sons to destroy them. [14] Now Simon was visiting the cities that were in the country, and taking care for the good ordering of them; at which time he came down himself to Jericho with his sons, Mattathias and Judas, in the hundred threescore and seventeenth year, in the eleventh month, called Sabat: [15] Where the son of Abubus receiving them deceitfully into a little hold, called Docus, which he had built, made them a great banquet: howbeit he had hid men there. [16] So when Simon and his sons had drunk largely, Ptolemee and his men rose up, and took their weapons, and came upon Simon into the banqueting place, and slew him, and his two sons, and certain of his servants. [17] In which doing he committed a great treachery, and recompensed evil for good. [18] Then Ptolemee wrote these things, and sent to the king, that he should send him an host to aid him, and he would deliver him the country and cities. [19] He sent others also to Gazera to kill John: and unto the tribunes he sent letters to come unto him, that he might give them silver, and gold, and rewards. [20] And others he sent to take Jerusalem, and the mountain of the temple. [21] Now one had run afore to Gazera and told John that his father and brethren were slain, and, quoth he, Ptolemee hath sent to slay thee also. [22] Hereof when he heard, he was sore astonished: so he laid hands on them that were come to destroy him, and slew them; for he knew that they sought to make him away. [23] As concerning the rest of the acts of John, and his wars, and worthy deeds which he did, and the building of the walls which he made, and his doings, [24] Behold, these are written in the chronicles of his priesthood, from the time he was made high priest after his father.

2 MACCABEES

2Mac.1

[1] The brethren, the Jews that be at Jerusalem and in the land of Judea, wish unto the brethren, the Jews that are throughout Egypt health and peace: [2] God be gracious unto you, and remember his covenant that he made with Abraham, Isaac, and Jacob, his faithful servants; [3] And give you all an heart to serve him, and to do his will, with a good courage and a willing mind; [4] And open your hearts in his law and commandments, and send you peace, [5] And hear your prayers, and be at one with you, and never forsake you in time of trouble. [6] And now we be here praying for you. [7] What time as Demetrius reigned, in the hundred threescore and ninth year, we the Jews wrote unto you in the extremity of trouble that came upon us in those years, from the time that Jason and his company revolted from the holy land and kingdom, [8] And burned the porch, and shed innocent blood: then we prayed unto the Lord, and were heard; we offered also sacrifices and fine flour, and lighted the lamps, and set forth the loaves. [9] And now see that ye keep the feast of tabernacles in the month Casleu. [10] In the hundred fourscore and eighth year, the people that were at Jerusalem and in Judea, and the council, and Judas, sent greeting and health unto Aristobulus, king Ptolemeus' master, who was of the stock of the anointed priests, and to the Jews that were in Egypt:

[11] Insomuch as God hath delivered us from great perils, we thank him highly, as having been in battle against a king. [12] For he cast them out that fought within the holy city. [13] For when the leader was come into Persia, and the army with him that seemed invincible, they were slain in the temple of Nanea by the deceit of Nanea's priests. [14] For Antiochus, as though he would marry her, came into the place, and his friends that were with him, to receive money in name of a dowry. [15] Which when the priests of Nanea had set forth, and he was entered with a small company into the compass of the temple, they shut the temple as soon as Antiochus was come in: [16] And opening a privy door of the roof, they threw stones like thunderbolts, and struck down the captain, hewed them in pieces, smote off their heads and cast them to those that were without. [17] Blessed be our God in all things, who hath delivered up the ungodly. [18] Therefore whereas we are now purposed to keep the purification of the temple upon the five and twentieth day of the month Casleu, we thought it necessary to certify you thereof, that ye also might keep it, as the feast of the tabernacles, and of the fire, which was given us when Neemias offered sacrifice, after that he had builded the temple and the altar. [19] For when our fathers were led into Persia, the priests that were then devout took the fire of the altar privily, and hid it in an hollow place of a pit without water, where they kept it sure, so that the place was unknown to all men. [20] Now after many years, when it pleased God, Neemias, being sent from the king of Persia, did send of the posterity of those priests that had hid it to the fire: but when they told us they found no fire, but thick water; [21] Then commanded he them to draw it up, and to bring it; and when the sacrifices were laid on, Neemias commanded the priests to sprinkle the wood and the things

laid thereupon with the water. [22] When this was done, and the time came that the sun shone, which afore was hid in the cloud, there was a great fire kindled, so that every man marvelled. [23] And the priests made a prayer whilst the sacrifice was consuming, I say, both the priests, and all the rest, Jonathan beginning, and the rest answering thereunto, as Neemias did. [24] And the prayer was after this manner; O Lord, Lord God, Creator of all things, who art fearful and strong, and righteous, and merciful, and the only and gracious King, [25] The only giver of all things, the only just, almighty, and everlasting, thou that deliverest Israel from all trouble, and didst choose the fathers, and sanctify them: [26] Receive the sacrifice for thy whole people Israel, and preserve thine own portion, and sanctify it. [27] Gather those together that are scattered from us, deliver them that serve among the heathen, look upon them that are despised and abhorred, and let the heathen know that thou art our God. [28] Punish them that oppress us, and with pride do us wrong. [29] Plant thy people again in thy holy place, as Moses hath spoken. [30] And the priests sung psalms of thanksgiving. [31] Now when the sacrifice was consumed, Neemias commanded the water that was left to be poured on the great stones. [32] When this was done, there was kindled a flame: but it was consumed by the light that shined from the altar. [33] So when this matter was known, it was told the king of Persia, that in the place, where the priests that were led away had hid the fire, there appeared water, and that Neemias had purified the sacrifices therewith. [34] Then the king, inclosing the place, made it holy, after he had tried the matter. [35] And the king took many gifts, and bestowed thereof on those whom he would gratify. [36] And Neemias called this thing Naphthar, which is as much as to say, a cleansing: but many men call it Nephi.

2Mac.2

[1] It is also found in the records, that Jeremy the prophet commanded them that were carried away to take of the fire, as it hath been signified: [2] And how that the prophet, having given them the law, charged them not to forget the commandments of the Lord, and that they should not err in their minds, when they see images of silver and gold, with their ornaments. [3] And with other such speeches exhorted he them, that the law should not depart from their hearts. [4] It was also contained in the same writing, that the prophet, being warned of God, commanded the tabernacle and the ark to go with him, as he went forth into the mountain, where Moses climbed up, and saw the heritage of God. [5] And when Jeremy came thither, he found an hollow cave, wherein he laid the tabernacle, and the ark, and the altar of incense, and so stopped the door. [6] And some of those that followed him came to mark the way, but they could not find it. [7] Which when Jeremy perceived, he blamed them, saying, As for that place, it shall be unknown until the time that God gather his people again together, and receive them unto mercy. [8] Then shall the Lord shew them these things, and the glory of the Lord shall appear, and the cloud also, as it was shewed under Moses, and as when Solomon desired that the place might be honourably sanctified. [9] It was also declared, that he being wise offered the sacrifice of dedication, and of the

finishing of the temple. [10] And as when Moses prayed unto the Lord, the fire came down from heaven, and consumed the sacrifices: even so prayed Solomon also, and the fire came down from heaven, and consumed the burnt offerings. [11] And Moses said, Because the sin offering was not to be eaten, it was consumed. [12] So Solomon kept those eight days. [13] The same things also were reported in the writings and commentaries of Neemias; and how he founding a library gathered together the acts of the kings, and the prophets, and of David, and the epistles of the kings concerning the holy gifts. [14] In like manner also Judas gathered together all those things that were lost by reason of the war we had, and they remain with us, [15] Wherefore if ye have need thereof, send some to fetch them unto you. [16] Whereas we then are about to celebrate the purification, we have written unto you, and ye shall do well, if ye keep the same days. [17] We hope also, that the God, that delivered all his people, and gave them all an heritage, and the kingdom, and the priesthood, and the sanctuary, [18] As he promised in the law, will shortly have mercy upon us, and gather us together out of every land under heaven into the holy place: for he hath delivered us out of great troubles, and hath purified the place. [19] Now as concerning Judas Maccabeus, and his brethren, and the purification of the great temple, and the dedication of the altar, [20] And the wars against Antiochus Epiphanes, and Eupator his son, [21] And the manifest signs that came from heaven unto those that behaved themselves manfully to their honour for Judaism: so that, being but a few, they overcame the whole country, and chased barbarous multitudes, [22] And recovered again the temple renowned all the world over, and freed the city, and upheld the laws which were going down, the Lord being gracious unto them with all favour: [23] All these things, I say, being declared by Jason of Cyrene in five books, we will assay to abridge in one volume. [24] For considering the infinite number, and the difficulty which they find that desire to look into the narrations of the story, for the variety of the matter, [25] We have been careful, that they that will read may have delight, and that they that are desirous to commit to memory might have ease, and that all into whose hands it comes might have profit. [26] Therefore to us, that have taken upon us this painful labour of abridging, it was not easy, but a matter of sweat and watching; [27] Even as it is no ease unto him that prepareth a banquet, and seeketh the benefit of others: yet for the pleasuring of many we will undertake gladly this great pains; [28] Leaving to the author the exact handling of every particular, and labouring to follow the rules of an abridgement. [29] For as the master builder of a new house must care for the whole building; but he that undertaketh to set it out, and paint it, must seek out fit things for the adorning thereof: even so I think it is with us. [30] To stand upon every point, and go over things at large, and to be curious in particulars, belongeth to the first author of the story: [31] But to use brevity, and avoid much labouring of the work, is to be granted to him that will make an abridgment. [32] Here then will we begin the story: only adding thus much to that which hath been said, that it is a foolish thing to make a long prologue, and to be short in the story itself.

2Mac.3

[1] Now when the holy city was inhabited with all peace, and the laws were kept very well, because of the godliness of Onias the high priest, and his hatred of wickedness, [2] It came to pass that even the kings themselves did honour the place, and magnify the temple with their best gifts; [3] Insomuch that Seleucus of Asia of his own revenues bare all the costs belonging to the service of the sacrifices. [4] But one Simon of the tribe of Benjamin, who was made governor of the temple, fell out with the high priest about disorder in the city. [5] And when he could not overcome Onias, he gat him to Apollonius the son of Thraseas, who then was governor of Celosyria and Phenice, [6] And told him that the treasury in Jerusalem was full of infinite sums of money, so that the multitude of their riches, which did not pertain to the account of the sacrifices, was innumerable, and that it was possible to bring all into the king's hand. [7] Now when Apollonius came to the king, and had shewed him of the money whereof he was told, the king chose out Heliodorus his treasurer, and sent him with a commandment to bring him the foresaid money. [8] So forthwith Heliodorus took his journey; under a colour of visiting the cities of Celosyria and Phenice, but indeed to fulfil the king's purpose. [9] And when he was come to Jerusalem, and had been courteously received of the high priest of the city, he told him what intelligence was given of the money, and declared wherefore he came, and asked if these things were so indeed. [10] Then the high priest told him that there was such money laid up for the relief of widows and fatherless children: [11] And that some of it belonged to Hircanus son of Tobias, a man of great dignity, and not as that wicked Simon had misinformed: the sum whereof in all was four hundred talents of silver, and two hundred of gold: [12] And that it was altogether impossible that such wrongs should be done unto them, that had committed it to the holiness of the place, and to the majesty and inviolable sanctity of the temple, honoured over all the world. [13] But Heliodorus, because of the king's commandment given him, said, That in any wise it must be brought into the king's treasury. [14] So at the day which he appointed he entered in to order this matter: wherefore there was no small agony throughout the whole city. [15] But the priests, prostrating themselves before the altar in their priests' vestments, called unto heaven upon him that made a law concerning things given to he kept, that they should safely be preserved for such as had committed them to be kept. [16] Then whoso had looked the high priest in the face, it would have wounded his heart: for his countenance and the changing of his colour declared the inward agony of his mind. [17] For the man was so compassed with fear and horror of the body, that it was manifest to them that looked upon him, what sorrow he had now in his heart. [18] Others ran flocking out of their houses to the general supplication, because the place was like to come into contempt. [19] And the women, girt with sackcloth under their breasts, abounded in the streets, and the virgins that were kept in ran, some to the gates, and some to the walls, and others looked out of the windows. [20] And all, holding their hands toward heaven, made supplication. [21] Then it would have pitied a man to see the falling down of the multitude of all sorts, and the fear of the high priest being in such an agony. [22] They then

called upon the Almighty Lord to keep the things committed of trust safe and sure for those that had committed them. [23] Nevertheless Heliodorus executed that which was decreed. [24] Now as he was there present himself with his guard about the treasury, the Lord of spirits, and the Prince of all power, caused a great apparition, so that all that presumed to come in with him were astonished at the power of God, and fainted, and were sore afraid. [25] For there appeared unto them an horse with a terrible rider upon him, and adorned with a very fair covering, and he ran fiercely, and smote at Heliodorus with his forefeet, and it seemed that he that sat upon the horse had complete harness of gold. [26] Moreover two other young men appeared before him, notable in strength, excellent in beauty, and comely in apparel, who stood by him on either side; and scourged him continually, and gave him many sore stripes. [27] And Heliodorus fell suddenly unto the ground, and was compassed with great darkness: but they that were with him took him up, and put him into a litter. [28] Thus him, that lately came with a great train and with all his guard into the said treasury, they carried out, being unable to help himself with his weapons: and manifestly they acknowledged the power of God. [29] For he by the hand of God was cast down, and lay speechless without all hope of life. [30] But they praised the Lord, that had miraculously honoured his own place: for the temple; which a little afore was full of fear and trouble, when the Almighty Lord appeared, was filled with joy and gladness. [31] Then straightways certain of Heliodorus' friends prayed Onias, that he would call upon the most High to grant him his life, who lay ready to give up the ghost. [32] So the high priest, suspecting lest the king should misconceive that some treachery had been done to Heliodorus by the Jews, offered a sacrifice for the health of the man. [33] Now as the high priest was making an atonement, the same young men in the same clothing appeared and stood beside Heliodorus, saying, Give Onias the high priest great thanks, insomuch as for his sake the Lord hath granted thee life: [34] And seeing that thou hast been scourged from heaven, declare unto all men the mighty power of God. And when they had spoken these words, they appeared no more. [35] So Heliodorus, after he had offered sacrifice unto the Lord, and made great vows unto him that had saved his life, and saluted Onias, returned with his host to the king. [36] Then testified he to all men the works of the great God, which he had seen with his eyes. [37] And when the king Heliodorus, who might be a fit man to be sent yet once again to Jerusalem, he said, [38] If thou hast any enemy or traitor, send him thither, and thou shalt receive him well scourged, if he escape with his life: for in that place, no doubt; there is an especial power of God. [39] For he that dwelleth in heaven hath his eye on that place, and defendeth it; and he beateth and destroyeth them that come to hurt it. [40] And the things concerning Heliodorus, and the keeping of the treasury, fell out on this sort.

2Mac.4

[1] This Simon now, of whom we spake afore, having been a betrayer of the money, and of his country, slandered Onias, as if he ha terrified Heliodorus, and been the worker ʿthese evils. [2] Thus was he bold to call him a traitor,

that had deserved well of the city, and tendered his own nation, and was so zealous of the laws. [3] But when their hatred went so far, that by one of Simon's faction murders were committed, [4] Onias seeing the danger of this contention, and that Apollonius, as being the governor of Celosyria and Phenice, did rage, and increase Simon's malice, [5] He went to the king, not to be an accuser of his countrymen, but seeking the good of all, both publick and private: [6] For he saw that it was impossible that the state should continue quiet, and Simon leave his folly, unless the king did look thereunto. [7] But after the death of Seleucus, when Antiochus, called Epiphanes, took the kingdom, Jason the brother of Onias laboured underhand to be high priest, [8] Promising unto the king by intercession three hundred and threescore talents of silver, and of another revenue eighty talents: [9] Beside this, he promised to assign an hundred and fifty more, if he might have licence to set him up a place for exercise, and for the training up of youth in the fashions of the heathen, and to write them of Jerusalem by the name of Antiochians. [10] Which when the king had granted, and he had gotten into his hand the rule he forthwith brought his own nation to Greekish fashion. [11] And the royal privileges granted of special favour to the Jews by the means of John the father of Eupolemus, who went ambassador to Rome for amity and aid, he took away; and putting down the governments which were according to the law, he brought up new customs against the law: [12] For he built gladly a place of exercise under the tower itself, and brought the chief young men under his subjection, and made them wear a hat. [13] Now such was the height of Greek fashions, and increase of heathenish manners, through the exceeding profaneness of Jason, that ungodly wretch, and no high priest; [14] That the priests had no courage to serve any more at the altar, but despising the temple, and neglecting the sacrifices, hastened to be partakers of the unlawful allowance in the place of exercise, after the game of Discus called them forth; [15] Not setting by the honours of their fathers, but liking the glory of the Grecians best of all. [16] By reason whereof sore calamity came upon them: for they had them to be their enemies and avengers, whose custom they followed so earnestly, and unto whom they desired to be like in all things. [17] For it is not a light thing to do wickedly against the laws of God: but the time following shall declare these things. [18] Now when the game that was used every faith year was kept at Tyrus, the king being present, [19] This ungracious Jason sent special messengers from Jerusalem, who were Antiochians, to carry three hundred drachms of silver to the sacrifice of Hercules, which even the bearers thereof thought fit not to bestow upon the sacrifice, because it was not convenient, but to be reserved for other charges. [20] This money then, in regard of the sender, was appointed to Hercules' sacrifice; but because of the bearers thereof, it was employed to the making of gallies. [21] Now when Apollonius the son of Menestheus was sent into Egypt for the coronation of king Ptolemeus Philometor, Antiochus, understanding him not to be well affected to his affairs, provided for his own safety: whereupon he came to Joppa, and from thence to Jerusalem: [22] Where he was honourably received of Jason, and of the city, and was brought in with torch alight, and with great shoutings: and so afterward went with his host unto Phenice. [23] Three years afterward Jason sent

Menelans, the aforesaid Simon's brother, to bear the money unto the king, and to put him in mind of certain necessary matters. [24] But he being brought to the presence of the king, when he had magnified him for the glorious appearance of his power, got the priesthood to himself, offering more than Jason by three hundred talents of silver.

[25] So he came with the king's mandate, bringing nothing worthy the high priesthood, but having the fury of a cruel tyrant, and the rage of a savage beast. [26] Then Jason, who had undermined his own brother, being undermined by another, was compelled to flee into the country of the Ammonites. [27] So Menelans got the principality: but as for the money that he had promised unto the king, he took no good order for it, albeit Sostratis the ruler of the castle required it: [28] For unto him appertained the gathering of the customs. Wherefore they were both called before the king. [29] Now Menelans left his brother Lysimachus in his stead in the priesthood; and Sostratus left Crates, who was governor of the Cyprians. [30] While those things were in doing, they of Tarsus and Mallos made insurrection, because they were given to the king's concubine, called Antiochus. [31] Then came the king in all haste to appease matters, leaving Andronicus, a man in authority, for his deputy. [32] Now Menelans, supposing that he had gotten a convenient time, stole certain vessels of gold out of the temple, and gave some of them to Andronicus, and some he sold into Tyrus and the cities round about. [33] Which when Onias knew of a surety, he reproved him, and withdrew himself into a sanctuary at Daphne, that lieth by Antiochia. [34] Wherefore Menelans, taking Andronicus apart, prayed, him to get Onias into his hands; who being persuaded thereunto, and coming to Onias in deceit, gave him his right hand with oaths; and though he were suspected by him, yet persuaded he him to come forth of the sanctuary: whom forthwith he shut up without regard of justice. [35] For the which cause not only the Jews, but many also of other nations, took great indignation, and were much grieved for the unjust murder of the man. [36] And when the king was come again from the places about Cilicia, the Jews that were in the city, and certain of the Greeks that abhorred the fact also, complained because Onias was slain without cause. [37] Therefore Antiochus was heartily sorry, and moved to pity, and wept, because of the sober and modest behaviour of him that was dead. [38] And being kindled with anger, forthwith he took away Andronicus his purple, and rent off his clothes, and leading him through the whole city unto that very place, where he had committed impiety against Onias, there slew he the cursed murderer. Thus the Lord rewarded him his punishment, as he had deserved. [39] Now when many sacrileges had been committed in the city by Lysimachus with the consent of Menelans, and the fruit thereof was spread abroad, the multitude gathered themselves together against Lysimachus, many vessels of gold being already carried away. [40] Whereupon the common people rising, and being filled with rage, Lysimachus armed about three thousand men, and began first to offer violence; one Auranus being the leader, a man far gone in years, and no less in folly. [41] They then seeing the attempt of Lysimachus, some of them caught stones, some clubs, others taking handfuls of dust, that was next at hand, cast them all together upon Lysimachus, and those that set upon them. [42] Thus many of them they wounded, and

some they struck to the ground, and all of them they forced to flee: but as for the churchrobber himself, him they killed beside the treasury. [43] Of these matters therefore there was an accusation laid against Menelans. [44] Now when the king came to Tyrus, three men that were sent from the senate pleaded the cause before him: [45] But Menelans, being now convicted, promised Ptolemee the son of Dorymenes to give him much money, if he would pacify the king toward him. [46] Whereupon Ptolemee taking the king aside into a certain gallery, as it were to take the air, brought him to be of another mind: [47] Insomuch that he discharged Menelans from the accusations, who notwithstanding was cause of all the mischief: and those poor men, who, if they had told their cause, yea, before the Scythians, should have been judged innocent, them he condemned to death. [48] Thus they that followed the matter for the city, and for the people, and for the holy vessels, did soon suffer unjust punishment. [49] Wherefore even they of Tyrus, moved with hatred of that wicked deed, caused them to be honourably buried. [50] And so through the covetousness of them that were of power Menelans remained still in authority, increasing in malice, and being a great traitor to the citizens.

2Mac.5

[1] About the same time Antiochus prepared his second voyage into Egypt: [2] And then it happened, that through all the city, for the space almost of forty days, there were seen horsemen running in the air, in cloth of gold, and armed with lances, like a band of soldiers, [3] And troops of horsemen in array, encountering and running one against another, with shaking of shields, and multitude of pikes, and drawing of swords, and casting of darts, and glittering of golden ornaments, and harness of all sorts. [4] Wherefore every man prayed that that apparition might turn to good. [5] Now when there was gone forth a false rumour, as though Antiochus had been dead, Jason took at the least a thousand men, and suddenly made an assault upon the city; and they that were upon the walls being put back, and the city at length taken, Menelans fled into the castle: [6] But Jason slew his own citizens without mercy, not considering that to get the day of them of his own nation would be a most unhappy day for him; but thinking they had been his enemies, and not his countrymen, whom he conquered. [7] Howbeit for all this he obtained not the principality, but at the last received shame for the reward of his treason, and fled again into the country of the Ammonites. [8] In the end therefore he had an unhappy return, being accused before Aretas the king of the Arabians, fleeing from city to city, pursued of all men, hated as a forsaker of the laws, and being had in abomination as an open enemy of his country and countrymen, he was cast out into Egypt. [9] Thus he that had driven many out of their country perished in a strange land, retiring to the Lacedemonians, and thinking there to find succour by reason of his kindred: [10] And he that had cast out many unburied had none to mourn for him, nor any solemn funerals at all, nor sepulchre with his fathers. [11] Now when this that was done came to the king's ear, he thought that Judea had revolted: whereupon removing out of Egypt in a furious mind, he took the city by force of arms, [12] And commanded his men of war not to spare

such as they met, and to slay such as went up upon the houses. [13] Thus there was killing of young and old, making away of men, women, and children, slaying of virgins and infants. [14] And there were destroyed within the space of three whole days fourscore thousand, whereof forty thousand were slain in the conflict; and no fewer sold than slain. [15] Yet was he not content with this, but presumed to go into the most holy temple of all the world; Menelans, that traitor to the laws, and to his own country, being his guide: [16] And taking the holy vessels with polluted hands, and with profane hands pulling down the things that were dedicated by other kings to the augmentation and glory and honour of the place, he gave them away. [17] And so haughty was Antiochus in mind, that he considered not that the Lord was angry for a while for the sins of them that dwelt in the city, and therefore his eye was not upon the place. [18] For had they not been formerly wrapped in many sins, this man, as soon as he had come, had forthwith been scourged, and put back from his presumption, as Heliodorus was, whom Seleucus the king sent to view the treasury. [19] Nevertheless God did not choose the people for the place's sake, but the place far the people's sake. [20] And therefore the place itself, that was partaker with them of the adversity that happened to the nation, did afterward communicate in the benefits sent from the Lord: and as it was forsaken in the wrath of the Almighty, so again, the great Lord being reconciled, it was set up with all glory. [21] So when Antiochus had carried out of the temple a thousand and eight hundred talents, he departed in all haste unto Antiochia, weening in his pride to make the land navigable, and the sea passable by foot: such was the haughtiness of his mind. [22] And he left governors to vex the nation: at Jerusalem, Philip, for his country a Phrygian, and for manners more barbarous than he that set him there; [23] And at Garizim, Andronicus; and besides, Menelans, who worse than all the rest bare an heavy hand over the citizens, having a malicious mind against his countrymen the Jews. [24] He sent also that detestable ringleader Apollonius with an army of two and twenty thousand, commanding him to slay all those that were in their best age, and to sell the women and the younger sort: [25] Who coming to Jerusalem, and pretending peace, did forbear till the holy day of the sabbath, when taking the Jews keeping holy day, he commanded his men to arm themselves. [26] And so he slew all them that were gone to the celebrating of the sabbath, and running through the city with weapons slew great multitudes. [27] But Judas Maccabeus with nine others, or thereabout, withdrew himself into the wilderness, and lived in the mountains after the manner of beasts, with his company, who fed on herbs continually, lest they should be partakers of the pollution.

2Mac.6

[1] Not long after this the king sent an old man of Athens to compel the Jews to depart from the laws of their fathers, and not to live after the laws of God: [2] And to pollute also the temple in Jerusalem, and to call it the temple of Jupiter Olympius; and that in Garizim, of Jupiter the Defender of strangers, as they did desire that dwelt in the place. [3] The coming in of this mischief was sore and grievous to the people: [4] For the temple was filled with riot and revelling by the Gentiles, who dallied with harlots, and had to do with women within the circuit of the holy places, and besides that brought in things that were not lawful. [5] The altar also was filled with profane things, which the law forbiddeth. [6] Neither was it lawful for a man to keep sabbath days or ancient fasts, or to profess himself at all to be a Jew. [7] And in the day of the king's birth every month they were brought by bitter constraint to eat of the sacrifices; and when the fast of Bacchus was kept, the Jews were compelled to go in procession to Bacchus, carrying ivy. [8] Moreover there went out a decree to the neighbour cities of the heathen, by the suggestion of Ptolemee, against the Jews, that they should observe the same fashions, and be partakers of their sacrifices: [9] And whoso would not conform themselves to the manners of the Gentiles should be put to death. Then might a man have seen the present misery. [10] For there were two women brought, who had circumcised their children; whom when they had openly led round about the city, the babes handing at their breasts, they cast them down headlong from the wall. [11] And others, that had run together into caves near by, to keep the sabbath day secretly, being discovered by Philip, were all burnt together, because they made a conscience to help themselves for the honour of the most sacred day. [12] Now I beseech those that read this book, that they be not discouraged for these calamities, but that they judge those punishments not to be for destruction, but for a chastening of our nation. [13] For it is a token of his great goodness, when wicked doers are not suffered any long time, but forthwith punished. [14] For not as with other nations, whom the Lord patiently forbeareth to punish, till they be come to the fulness of their sins, so dealeth he with us, [15] Lest that, being come to the height of sin, afterwards he should take vengeance of us. [16] And therefore he never withdraweth his mercy from us: and though he punish with adversity, yet doth he never forsake his people. [17] But let this that we at spoken be for a warning unto us. And now will we come to the declaring of the matter in a few words. [18] Eleazar, one of the principal scribes, an aged man, and of a well favoured countenance, was constrained to open his mouth, and to eat swine's flesh. [19] But he, choosing rather to die gloriously, than to live stained with such an abomination, spit it forth, and came of his own accord to the torment, [20] As it behoved them to come, that are resolute to stand out against such things, as are not lawful for love of life to be tasted. [21] But they that had the charge of that wicked feast, for the old acquaintance they had with the man, taking him aside, besought him to bring flesh of his own provision, such as was lawful for him to use, and make as if he did eat of the flesh taken from the sacrifice commanded by the king; [22] That in so doing he might be delivered from death, and for the old friendship with them find favour. [23] But he began to consider discreetly, and as became his age, and the excellency of his ancient years, and the honour of his gray head, whereon was come, and his most honest education from a child, or rather the holy law made and given by God: therefore he answered accordingly, and willed them straightways to send him to the grave. [24] For it becometh not our age, said he, in any wise to dissemble, whereby many young persons might think that Eleazar, being fourscore years old and ten, were now gone to a strange religion; [25] And so they through

mine hypocrisy, and desire to live a little time and a moment longer, should be deceived by me, and I get a stain to mine old age, and make it abominable. [26] For though for the present time I should be delivered from the punishment of men: yet should I not escape the hand of the Almighty, neither alive, nor dead. [27] Wherefore now, manfully changing this life, I will shew myself such an one as mine age requireth, [28] And leave a notable example to such as be young to die willingly and courageously for the honourable and holy laws. And when he had said these words, immediately he went to the torment: [29] They that led him changing the good will they bare him a little before into hatred, because the foresaid speeches proceeded, as they thought, from a desperate mind. [30] But when he was ready to die with stripes, he groaned, and said, It is manifest unto the Lord, that hath the holy knowledge, that whereas I might have been delivered from death, I now endure sore pains in body by being beaten: but in soul am well content to suffer these things, because I fear him. [31] And thus this man died, leaving his death for an example of a noble courage, and a memorial of virtue, not only unto young men, but unto all his nation.

2Mac.7

[1] It came to pass also, that seven brethren with their mother were taken, and compelled by the king against the law to taste swine's flesh, and were tormented with scourges and whips. [2] But one of them that spake first said thus, What wouldest thou ask or learn of us? we are ready to die, rather than to transgress the laws of our fathers. [3] Then the king, being in a rage, commanded pans and caldrons to be made hot: [4] Which forthwith being heated, he commanded to cut out the tongue of him that spake first, and to cut off the utmost parts of his body, the rest of his brethren and his mother looking on. [5] Now when he was thus maimed in all his members, he commanded him being yet alive to be brought to the fire, and to be fried in the pan: and as the vapour of the pan was for a good space dispersed, they exhorted one another with the mother to die manfully, saying thus, [6] The Lord God looketh upon us, and in truth hath comfort in us, as Moses in his song, which witnessed to their faces, declared, saying, And he shall be comforted in his servants. [7] So when the first was dead after this number, they brought the second to make him a mocking stock: and when they had pulled off the skin of his head with the hair, they asked him, Wilt thou eat, before thou be punished throughout every member of thy body? [8] But he answered in his own language, and said, No. Wherefore he also received the next torment in order, as the former did. [9] And when he was at the last gasp, he said, Thou like a fury takest us out of this present life, but the King of the world shall raise us up, who have died for his laws, unto everlasting life. [10] After him was the third made a mocking stock: and when he was required, he put out his tongue, and that right soon, holding forth his hands manfully. [11] And said courageously, These I had from heaven; and for his laws I despise them; and from him I hope to receive them again. [12] Insomuch that the king, and they that were with him, marvelled at the young man's courage, for that he nothing regarded the pains. [13] Now when this man was dead also, they tormented and mangled the fourth in like manner. [14] So when he was

ready to die he said thus, It is good, being put to death by men, to look for hope from God to be raised up again by him: as for thee, thou shalt have no resurrection to life. [15] Afterward they brought the fifth also, and mangled him. [16] Then looked he unto the king, and said, Thou hast power over men, thou art corruptible, thou doest what thou wilt; yet think not that our nation is forsaken of God; [17] But abide a while, and behold his great power, how he will torment thee and thy seed. [18] After him also they brought the sixth, who being ready to die said, Be not deceived without cause: for we suffer these things for ourselves, having sinned against our God: therefore marvellous things are done unto us. [19] But think not thou, that takest in hand to strive against God, that thou shalt escape unpunished. [20] But the mother was marvellous above all, and worthy of honourable memory: for when she saw her seven sons slain within the space of one day, she bare it with a good courage, because of the hope that she had in the Lord. [21] Yea, she exhorted every one of them in her own language, filled with courageous spirits; and stirring up her womanish thoughts with a manly stomach, she said unto them, [22] I cannot tell how ye came into my womb: for I neither gave you breath nor life, neither was it I that formed the members of every one of you; [23] But doubtless the Creator of the world, who formed the generation of man, and found out the beginning of all things, will also of his own mercy give you breath and life again, as ye now regard not your own selves for his laws' sake. [24] Now Antiochus, thinking himself despised, and suspecting it to be a reproachful speech, whilst the youngest was yet alive, did not only exhort him by words, but also assured him with oaths, that he would make him both a rich and a happy man, if he would turn from the laws of his fathers; and that also he would take him for his friend, and trust him with affairs. [25] But when the young man would in no case hearken unto him, the king called his mother, and exhorted her that she would counsel the young man to save his life. [26] And when he had exhorted her with many words, she promised him that she would counsel her son. [27] But she bowing herself toward him, laughing the cruel tyrant to scorn, spake in her country language on this manner; O my son, have pity upon me that bare thee nine months in my womb, and gave thee such three years, and nourished thee, and brought thee up unto this age, and endured the troubles of education. [28] I beseech thee, my son, look upon the heaven and the earth, and all that is therein, and consider that God made them of things that were not; and so was mankind made likewise. [29] Fear not this tormentor, but, being worthy of thy brethren, take thy death that I may receive thee again in mercy with thy brethren. [30] Whiles she was yet speaking these words, the young man said, Whom wait ye for? I will not obey the king's commandment: but I will obey the commandment of the law that was given unto our fathers by Moses. [31] And thou, that hast been the author of all mischief against the Hebrews, shalt not escape the hands of God. [32] For we suffer because of our sins. [33] And though the living Lord be angry with us a little while for our chastening and correction, yet shall he be at one again with his servants. [34] But thou, O godless man, and of all other most wicked, be not lifted up without a cause, nor puffed up with uncertain hopes, lifting up thy hand against the servants of God: [35] For thou hast not yet escaped the judgment of Almighty God, who seeth all things. [36] For our brethren, who now have suffered a short pain, are dead under God's covenant of everlasting life: but thou, through the judgment of God, shalt receive just punishment for thy pride. [37] But I, as my brethren, offer up my body and life for the laws of our fathers, beseeching God that he would speedily be merciful unto our nation; and that thou by torments and plagues mayest confess, that he alone is God; [38] And that in me and my brethren the wrath of the Almighty, which is justly brought upon our nation, may cease. [39] Than the king' being in a rage, handed him worse than all the rest, and took it grievously that he was mocked. [40] So this man died undefiled, and put his whole trust in the Lord. [41] Last of all after the sons the mother died. [42] Let this be enough now to have spoken concerning the idolatrous feasts, and the extreme tortures.

2Mac.8

[1] Then Judas Maccabeus, and they that were with him, went privily into the towns, and called their kinsfolks together, and took unto them all such as continued in the Jews' religion, and assembled about six thousand men. [2] And they called upon the Lord, that he would look upon the people that was trodden down of all; and also pity the temple profaned of ungodly men; [3] And that he would have compassion upon the city, sore defaced, and ready to be made even with the ground; and hear the blood that cried unto him, [4] And remember the wicked slaughter of harmless infants, and the blasphemies committed against his name; and that he would shew his hatred against the wicked. [5] Now when Maccabeis had his company about him, he could not be withstood by the heathen: for the wrath of the Lord was turned into mercy. [6] Therefore he came at unawares, and burnt up towns and cities, and got into his hands the most commodious places, and overcame and put to flight no small number of his enemies. [7] But specially took he advantage of the night for such privy attempts, insomuch that the fruit of his holiness was spread every where. [8] So when Philip saw that this man increased by little and little, and that things prospered with him still more and more, he wrote unto Ptolemeus, the governor of Celosyria and Phenice, to yield more aid to the king's affairs. [9] Then forthwith choosing Nicanor the son of Patroclus, one of his special friends, he sent him with no fewer than twenty thousand of all nations under him, to root out the whole generation of the Jews; and with him he joined also Gorgias a captain, who in matters of war had great experience. [10] So Nicanor undertook to make so much money of the captive Jews, as should defray the tribute of two thousand talents, which the king was to pay to the Romans. [11] Wherefore immediately he sent to the cities upon the sea coast, proclaiming a sale of the captive Jews, and promising that they should have fourscore and ten bodies for one talent, not expecting the vengeance that was to follow upon him from the Almighty God. [12] Now when word was brought unto Judas of Nicanor's coming, and he had imparted unto those that were with him that the army was at hand, [13] They that were fearful, and distrusted the justice of God, fled, and conveyed themselves away. [14] Others sold all that they had left, vithal besought the Lord to deliver them, sold by the

wicked Nicanor before they met together: [15] And if not for their own sakes, yet for the covenants he had made with their fathers, and for his holy and glorious name's sake, by which they were called. [16] So Maccabeus called his men together unto the number of six thousand, and exhorted them not to be stricken with terror of the enemy, nor to fear the great multitude of the heathen, who came wrongly against them; but to fight manfully, [17] And to set before their eyes the injury that they had unjustly done to the holy place, and the cruel handling of the city, whereof they made a mockery, and also the taking away of the government of their forefathers: [18] For they, said he, trust in their weapons and boldness; but our confidence is in the Almighty who at a beck can cast down both them that come against us, and also all the world. [19] Moreover, he recounted unto them what helps their forefathers had found, and how they were delivered, when under Sennacherib an hundred fourscore and five thousand perished. [20] And he told them of the battle that they had in Babylon with the Galatians, how they came but eight thousand in all to the business, with four thousand Macedonians, and that the Macedonians being perplexed, the eight thousand destroyed an hundred and twenty thousand because of the help that they had from heaven, and so received a great booty. [21] Thus when he had made them bold with these words, and ready to die for the law and the country, he divided his army into four parts; [22] And joined with himself his own brethren, leaders of each band, to wit Simon, and Joseph, and Jonathan, giving each one fifteen hundred men. [23] Also he appointed Eleazar to read the holy book: and when he had given them this watchword, The help of God; himself leading the first band, [24] And by the help of the Almighty they slew above nine thousand of their enemies, and wounded and maimed the most part of Nicanor's host, and so put all to flight; [25] And took their money that came to buy them, and pursued them far: but lacking time they returned: [26] For it was the day before the sabbath, and therefore they would no longer pursue them. [27] So when they had gathered their armour together, and spoiled their enemies, they occupied themselves about the sabbath, yielding exceeding praise and thanks to the Lord, who had preserved them unto that day, which was the beginning of mercy distilling upon them. [28] And after the sabbath, when they had given part of the spoils to the maimed, and the widows, and orphans, the residue they divided among themselves and their servants. [29] When this was done, and they had made a common supplication, they besought the merciful Lord to be reconciled with his servants for ever. [30] Moreover of those that were with Timotheus and Bacchides, who fought against them, they slew above twenty thousand, and very easily got high and strong holds, and divided among themselves many spoils more, and made the maimed, orphans, widows, yea, and the aged also, equal in spoils with themselves. [31] And when they had gathered their armour together, they laid them up all carefully in convenient places, and the remnant of the spoils they brought to Jerusalem. [32] They slew also Philarches, that wicked person, who was with Timotheus, and had annoyed the Jews many ways. [33] Furthermore at such time as they kept the feast for the victory in their country they burnt Callisthenes, that had set fire upon the holy gates, who had fled into a little house; and so he received a reward meet for his wickedness. [34] As for that most ungracious Nicanor, who had brought a thousand merchants to buy the Jews, [35] He was through the help of the Lord brought down by them, of whom he made least account; and putting off his glorious apparel, and discharging his company, he came like a fugitive servant through the midland unto Antioch having very great dishonour, for that his host was destroyed. [36] Thus he, that took upon him to make good to the Romans their tribute by means of captives in Jerusalem, told abroad, that the Jews had God to fight for them, and therefore they could not be hurt, because they followed the laws that he gave them.

2Mac.9

[1] About that time came Antiochus with dishonour out of the country of Persia [2] For he had entered the city called Persepolis, and went about to rob the temple, and to hold the city; whereupon the multitude running to defend themselves with their weapons put them to flight; and so it happened, that Antiochus being put to flight of the inhabitants returned with shame. [3] Now when he came to Ecbatane, news was brought him what had happened unto Nicanor and Timotheus. [4] Then swelling with anger. he thought to avenge upon the Jews the disgrace done unto him by those that made him flee. Therefore commanded he his chariotman to drive without ceasing, and to dispatch the journey, the judgment of GOd now following him. For he had spoken proudly in this sort, That he would come to Jerusalem and make it a common burying place of the Jews. [5] But the Lord Almighty, the God of Isreal, smote him with an incurable and invisible plague: or as soon as he had spoken these words, a pain of the bowels that was remediless came upon him, and sore torments of the inner parts; [6] And that most justly: for he had tormented other men's bowels with many and strange torments. [7] Howbeit he nothing at all ceased from his bragging, but still was filled with pride, breathing out fire in his rage against the Jews, and commanding to haste the journey: but it came to pass that he fell down from his chariot, carried violently; so that having a sore fall, all the members of his body were much pained. [8] And thus he that a little afore thought he might command the waves of the sea, (so proud was he beyond the condition of man) and weigh the high mountains in a balance, was now cast on the ground, and carried in an horselitter, shewing forth unto all the manifest power of God. [9] So that the worms rose up out of the body of this wicked man, and whiles he lived in sorrow and pain, his flesh fell away, and the filthiness of his smell was noisome to all his army. [10] And the man, that thought a little afore he could reach to the stars of heaven, no man could endure to carry for his intolerable stink. [11] Here therefore, being plagued, he began to leave off his great pride, and to come to the knowledge of himself by the scourge of God, his pain increasing every moment. [12] And when he himself could not abide his own smell, he said these words, It is meet to be subject unto God, and that a man that is mortal should not proudly think of himself if he were God. [13] This wicked person vowed also unto the Lord, who now no more would have mercy upon him, saying thus, [14] That the holy city (to the which he was going in haste to lay it

even with the ground, and to make it a common buryingplace,) he would set at liberty: [15] And as touching the Jews, whom he had judged not worthy so much as to be buried, but to be cast out with their children to be devoured of the fowls and wild beasts, he would make them all equals to the citizens of Athens: [16] And the holy temple, which before he had spoiled, he would garnish with goodly gifts, and restore all the holy vessels with many more, and out of his own revenue defray the charges belonging to the sacrifices: [17] Yea, and that also he would become a Jew himself, and go through all the world that was inhabited, and declare the power of God. [18] But for all this his pains would not cease: for the just judgment of God was come upon him: therefore despairing of his health, he wrote unto the Jews the letter underwritten, containing the form of a supplication, after this manner: [19] Antiochus, king and governor, to the good Jews his citizens wisheth much joy, health, and prosperity: [20] If ye and your children fare well, and your affairs be to your contentment, I give very great thanks to God, having my hope in heaven. [21] As for me, I was weak, or else I would have remembered kindly your honour and good will returning out of Persia, and being taken with a grievous disease, I thought it necessary to care for the common safety of all: [22] Not distrusting mine health, but having great hope to escape this sickness. [23] But considering that even my father, at what time he led an army into the high countries. appointed a successor, [24] To the end that, if any thing fell out contrary to expectation, or if any tidings were brought that were grievous, they of the land, knowing to whom the state was left, might not be troubled: [25] Again, considering how that the princes that are borderers and neighbours unto my kingdom wait for opportunities, and expect what shall be the event. I have appointed my son Antiochus king, whom I often committed and commended unto many of you, when I went up into the high provinces; to whom I have written as followeth: [26] Therefore I pray and request you to remember the benefits that I have done unto you generally, and in special, and that every man will be still faithful to me and my son. [27] For I am persuaded that he understanding my mind will favourably and graciously yield to your desires. [28] Thus the murderer and blasphemer having suffered most grievously, as he entreated other men, so died he a miserable death in a strange country in the mountains. [29] And Philip, that was brought up with him, carried away his body, who also fearing the son of Antiochus went into Egypt to Ptolemeus Philometor.

2Mac.10

[1] Now Maccabeus and his company, the Lord guiding them, recovered the temple and the city: [2] But the altars which the heathen had built in the open street, and also the chapels, they pulled down. [3] And having cleansed the temple they made another altar, and striking stones they took fire out of them, and offered a sacrifice after two years, and set forth incense, and lights, and shewbread. [4] When that was done, they fell flat down, and besought the Lord that they might come no more into such troubles; but if they sinned any more against him, that he himself would chasten them with mercy, and that they might not be delivered unto the blasphemous and barbarous nations. [5]

Now upon the same day that the strangers profaned the temple, on the very same day it was cleansed again, even the five and twentieth day of the same month, which is Casleu. [6] And they kept the eight days with gladness, as in the feast of the tabernacles, remembering that not long afore they had held the feast of the tabernacles, when as they wandered in the mountains and dens like beasts. [7] Therefore they bare branches, and fair boughs, and palms also, and sang psalms unto him that had given them good success in cleansing his place. [8] They ordained also by a common statute and decree, That every year those days should be kept of the whole nation of the Jews. [9] And this was the end of Antiochus, called Epiphanes. [10] Now will we declare the acts of Antiochus Eupator, who was the son of this wicked man, gathering briefly the calamities of the wars. [11] So when he was come to the crown, he set one Lysias over the affairs of his realm, and appointed him his chief governor of Celosyria and Phenice. [12] For Ptolemeus, that was called Macron, choosing rather to do justice unto the Jews for the wrong that had been done unto them, endeavoured to continue peace with them. [13] Whereupon being accused of the king's friends before Eupator, and called traitor at every word because he had left Cyprus, that Philometor had committed unto him, and departed to Antiochus Epiphanes, and seeing that he was in no honourable place, he was so discouraged, that he poisoned himself and died. [14] But when Gorgias was governor of the holds, he hired soldiers, and nourished war continually with the Jews: [15] And therewithall the Idumeans, having gotten into their hands the most commodious holds, kept the Jews occupied, and receiving those that were banished from Jerusalem, they went about to nourish war. [16] Then they that were with Maccabeus made supplication, and besought God that he would be their helper; and so they ran with violence upon the strong holds of the Idumeans, [17] And assaulting them strongly, they won the holds, and kept off all that fought upon the wall, and slew all that fell into their hands, and killed no fewer than twenty thousand. [18] And because certain, who were no less than nine thousand, were fled together into two very strong castles, having all manner of things convenient to sustain the siege, [19] Maccabeus left Simon and Joseph, and Zaccheus also, and them that were with him, who were enough to besiege them, and departed himself unto those places which more needed his help. [20] Now they that were with Simon, being led with covetousness, were persuaded for money through certain of those that were in the castle, and took seventy thousand drachms, and let some of them escape. [21] But when it was told Maccabeus what was done, he called the governors of the people together, and accused those men, that they had sold their brethren for money, and set their enemies free to fight against them. [22] So he slew those that were found traitors, and immediately took the two castles. [23] And having good success with his weapons in all things he took in hand, he slew in the two holds more than twenty thousand. [24] Now Timotheus, whom the Jews had overcome before, when he had gathered a great multitude of foreign forces, and horses out of Asia not a few, came as though he would take Jewry by force of arms. [25] But when he drew near, they that were with Maccabeus turned themselves to pray unto God, and sprinkled earth upon their heads, and girded their loins with sackcloth, [26] And

fell down at the foot of the altar, and besought him to be merciful to them, and to be an enemy to their enemies, and an adversary to their adversaries, as the law declareth. [27] So after the prayer they took their weapons, and went on further from the city: and when they drew near to their enemies, they kept by themselves. [28] Now the sun being newly risen, they joined both together; the one part having together with their virtue their refuge also unto the Lord for a pledge of their success and victory: the other side making their rage leader of their battle [29] But when the battle waxed strong, there appeared unto the enemies from heaven five comely men upon horses, with bridles of gold, and two of them led the Jews, [30] And took Maccabeus betwixt them, and covered him on every side weapons, and kept him safe, but shot arrows and lightnings against the enemies: so that being confounded with blindness, and full of trouble, they were killed. [31] And there were slain of footmen twenty thousand and five hundred, and six hundred horsemen. [32] As for Timotheus himself, he fled into a very strong hold, called Gawra, where Chereas was governor. [33] But they that were with Maccabeus laid siege against the fortress courageously four days. [34] And they that were within, trusting to the strength of the place, blasphemed exceedingly, and uttered wicked words. [35] Nevertheless upon the fifth day early twenty young men of Maccabeus' company, inflamed with anger because of the blasphemies, assaulted the wall manly, and with a fierce courage killed all that they met withal. [36] Others likewise ascending after them, whiles they were busied with them that were within, burnt the towers, and kindling fires burnt the blasphemers alive; and others broke open the gates, and, having received in the rest of the army, took the city, [37] And killed Timotheus, that was hid in a certain pit, and Chereas his brother, with Apollophanes. [38] When this was done, they praised the Lord with psalms and thanksgiving, who had done so great things for Israel, and given them the victory.

2Mac.11

[1] Not long after the, Lysias the king's protector and cousin, who also managed the affairs, took sore displeasure for the things that were done. [2] And when he had gathered about fourscore thousand with all the horsemen, he came against the Jews, thinking to make the city an habitation of the Gentiles, [3] And to make a gain of the temple, as of the other chapels of the heathen, and to set the high priesthood to sale every year: [4] Not at all considering the power of God but puffed up with his ten thousands of footmen, and his thousands of horsemen, and his fourscore elephants. [5] So he came to Judea, and drew near to Bethsura, which was a strong town, but distant from Jerusalem about five furlongs, and he laid sore siege unto it. [6] Now when they that were with Maccabeus heard that he besieged the holds, they and all the people with lamentation and tears besought the Lord that he would send a good angel to deliver Israel. [7] Then Maccabeus himself first of all took weapons, exhorting the other that they would jeopard themselves together with him to help their brethren: so they went forth together with a willing mind. [8] And as they were at Jerusalem, there appeared before them on horseback one in white clothing, shaking his armour of gold. [9] Then they praised the

merciful God all together, and took heart, insomuch that they were ready not only to fight with men, but with most cruel beasts, and to pierce through walls of iron. [10] Thus they marched forward in their armour, having an helper from heaven: for the Lord was merciful unto them [11] And giving a charge upon their enemies like lions, they slew eleven thousand footmen, and sixteen hundred horsemen, and put all the other to flight. [12] Many of them also being wounded escaped naked; and Lysias himself fled away shamefully, and so escaped. [13] Who, as he was a man of understanding, casting with himself what loss he had had, and considering that the Hebrews could not be overcome, because the Almighty God helped them, he sent unto them, [14] And persuaded them to agree to all reasonable conditions, and promised that he would persuade the king that he must needs be a friend unto them. [15] Then Maccabeus consented to all that Lysias desired, being careful of the common good; and whatsoever Maccabeus wrote unto Lysias concerning the Jews, the king granted it. [16] For there were letters written unto the Jews from Lysias to this effect: Lysias unto the people of the Jews sendeth greeting: [17] John and Absolom, who were sent from you, delivered me the petition subscribed, and made request for the performance of the contents thereof. [18] Therefore what things soever were meet to be reported to the king, I have declared them, and he hath granted as much as might be. [19] And if then ye will keep yourselves loyal to the state, hereafter also will I endeavour to be a means of your good. [20] But of the particulars I have given order both to these and the other that came from me, to commune with you. [21] Fare ye well. The hundred and eight and fortieth year, the four and twentieth day of the month Dioscorinthius. [22] Now the king's letter contained these words: King Antiochus unto his brother Lysias sendeth greeting: [23] Since our father is translated unto the gods, our will is, that they that are in our realm live quietly, that every one may attend upon his own affairs. [24] We understand also that the Jews would not consent to our father, for to be brought unto the custom of the Gentiles, but had rather keep their own manner of living: for the which cause they require of us, that we should suffer them to live after their own laws. [25] Wherefore our mind is, that this nation shall be in rest, and we have determined to restore them their temple, that they may live according to the customs of their forefathers. [26] Thou shalt do well therefore to send unto them, and grant them peace, that when they are certified of our mind, they may be of good comfort, and ever go cheerfully about their own affairs. [27] And the letter of the king unto the nation of the Jews was after this manner: King Antiochus sendeth greeting unto the council, and the rest of the Jews: [28] If ye fare well, we have our desire; we are also in good health. [29] Menelaus declared unto us, that your desire was to return home, and to follow your own business: [30] Wherefore they that will depart shall have safe conduct till the thirtieth day of Xanthicus with security. [31] And the Jews shall use their own kind of meats and laws, as before; and none of them any manner of ways shall be molested for things ignorantly done. [32] I have sent also Menelaus, that he may comfort you. [33] Fare ye well. In the hundred forty and eighth year, and the fifteenth day of the month Xanthicus. [34] The Romans also sent unto them a letter containing these words: Quintus Memmius and Titus Manlius, ambassadors of the Romans, send greeting unto the people of the Jews. [35] Whatsoever Lysias the king's cousin hath granted, therewith we also are well pleased. [36] But touching such things as he judged to be referred to the king, after ye have advised thereof, send one forthwith, that we may declare as it is convenient for you: for we are now going to Antioch. [37] Therefore send some with speed, that we may know what is your mind. [38] Farewell. This hundred and eight and fortieth year, the fifteenth day of the month Xanthicus.

2Mac.12

[1] When these covenants were made, Lysias went unto the king, and the Jews were about their husbandry. [2] But of the governours of several places, Timotheus, and Apollonius the son of Genneus, also Hieronymus, and Demophon, and beside them Nicanor the governor of Cyprus, would not suffer them to be quiet and live in peace. [3] The men of Joppa also did such an ungodly deed: they prayed the Jews that dwelt among them to go with their wives and children into the boats which they had prepared, as though they had meant them no hurt. [4] Who accepted of it according to the common decree of the city, as being desirous to live in peace, and suspecting nothing: but when they were gone forth into the deep, they drowned no less than two hundred of them. [5] When Judas heard of this cruelty done unto his countrymen, he commanded those that were with him to make them ready. [6] And calling upon God the righteous Judge, he came against those murderers of his brethren, and burnt the haven by night, and set the boats on fire, and those that fled thither he slew. [7] And when the town was shut up, he went backward, as if he would return to root out all them of the city of Joppa. [8] But when he heard that the Jamnites were minded to do in like manner unto the Jews that dwelt among them, [9] He came upon the Jamnites also by night, and set fire on the haven and the navy, so that the light of the fire was seen at Jerusalem two hundred and forty furlongs off. [10] Now when they were gone from thence nine furlongs in their journey toward Timotheus, no fewer than five thousand men on foot and five hundred horsemen of the Arabians set upon him. [11] Whereupon there was a very sore battle; but Judas' side by the help of God got the victory; so that the Nomades of Arabia, being overcome, besought Judas for peace, promising both to give him cattle, and to pleasure him otherwise. [12] Then Judas, thinking indeed that they would be profitable in many things, granted them peace: whereupon they shook hands, and so they departed to their tents. [13] He went also about to make a bridge to a certain strong city, which was fenced about with walls, and inhabited by people of divers countries; and the name of it was Caspis. [14] But they that were within it put such trust in the strength of the walls and provision of victuals, that they behaved themselves rudely toward them that were with Judas, railing and blaspheming, and uttering such words as were not to be spoken. [15] Wherefore Judas with his company, calling upon the great Lord of the world, who without rams or engines of war did cast down Jericho in the time of Joshua, gave a fierce assault against the walls, [16] And took the city by the will of God, and made unspeakable slaughters,

insomuch that a lake two furlongs broad near adjoining thereunto, being filled full, was seen running with blood. [17] Then departed they from thence seven hundred and fifty furlongs, and came to Characa unto the Jews that are called Tubieni. [18] But as for Timotheus, they found him not in the places: for before he had dispatched any thing, he departed from thence, having left a very strong garrison in a certain hold. [19] Howbeit Dositheus and Sosipater, who were of Maccabeus' captains, went forth, and slew those that Timotheus had left in the fortress, above ten thousand men. [20] And Maccabeus ranged his army by bands, and set them over the bands, and went against Timotheus, who had about him an hundred and twenty thousand men of foot, and two thousand and five hundred horsemen. [21] Now when Timotheus had knowledge of Judas' coming, he sent the women and children and the other baggage unto a fortress called Carnion: for the town was hard to besiege, and uneasy to come unto, by reason of the straitness of all the places. [22] But when Judas his first band came in sight, the enemies, being smitten with fear and terror through the appearing of him who seeth all things, fled amain, one running into this way, another that way, so as that they were often hurt of their own men, and wounded with the points of their own swords. [23] Judas also was very earnest in pursuing them, killing those wicked wretches, of whom he slew about thirty thousand men. [24] Moreover Timotheus himself fell into the hands of Dositheus and Sosipater, whom he besought with much craft to let him go with his life, because he had many of the Jews' parents, and the brethren of some of them, who, if they put him to death, should not be regarded. [25] So when he had assured them with many words that he would restore them without hurt, according to the agreement, they let him go for the saving of their brethren. [26] Then Maccabeus marched forth to Carnion, and to the temple of Atargatis, and there he slew five and twenty thousand persons. [27] And after he had put to flight and destroyed them, Judas removed the host toward Ephron, a strong city, wherein Lysias abode, and a great multitude of divers nations, and the strong young men kept the walls, and defended them mightily: wherein also was great provision of engines and darts. [28] But when Judas and his company had called upon Almighty God, who with his power breaketh the strength of his enemies, they won the city, and slew twenty and five thousand of them that were within, [29] From thence they departed to Scythopolis, which lieth six hundred furlongs from Jerusalem, [30] But when the Jews that dwelt there had testified that the Scythopolitans dealt lovingly with them, and entreated them kindly in the time of their adversity; [31] They gave them thanks, desiring them to be friendly still unto them: and so they came to Jerusalem, the feast of the weeks approaching. [32] And after the feast, called Pentecost, they went forth against Gorgias the governor of Idumea, [33] Who came out with three thousand men of foot and four hundred horsemen. [34] And it happened that in their fighting together a few of the Jews were slain. [35] At which time Dositheus, one of Bacenor's company, who was on horseback, and a strong man, was still upon Gorgias, and taking hold of his coat drew him by force; and when he would have taken that cursed man alive, a horseman of Thracia coming upon him smote off his shoulder, so that ͏ias fled unto Marisa. [36] Now when they that were

with Gorgias had fought long, and were weary, Judas called upon the Lord, that he would shew himself to be their helper and leader of the battle. [37] And with that he began in his own language, and sung psalms with a loud voice, and rushing unawares upon Gorgias' men, he put them to flight. [38] So Judas gathered his host, and came into the city of Odollam, And when the seventh day came, they purified themselves, as the custom was, and kept the sabbath in the same place. [39] And upon the day following, as the use had been, Judas and his company came to take up the bodies of them that were slain, and to bury them with their kinsmen in their fathers' graves. [40] Now under the coats of every one that was slain they found things consecrated to the idols of the Jamnites, which is forbidden the Jews by the law. Then every man saw that this was the cause wherefore they were slain. [41] All men therefore praising the Lord, the righteous Judge, who had opened the things that were hid, [42] Betook themselves unto prayer, and besought him that the sin committed might wholly be put out of remembrance. Besides, that noble Judas exhorted the people to keep themselves from sin, forsomuch as they saw before their eyes the things that came to pass for the sins of those that were slain. [43] And when he had made a gathering throughout the company to the sum of two thousand drachms of silver, he sent it to Jerusalem to offer a sin offering, doing therein very well and honestly, in that he was mindful of the resurrection: [44] For if he had not hoped that they that were slain should have risen again, it had been superfluous and vain to pray for the dead. [45] And also in that he perceived that there was great favour laid up for those that died godly, it was an holy and good thought. Whereupon he made a reconciliation for the dead, that they might be delivered from sin.

2Mac.13

[1] In the hundred forty and ninth year it was told Judas, that Antiochus Eupator was coming with a great power into Judea, [2] And with him Lysias his protector, and ruler of his affairs, having either of them a Grecian power of footmen, an hundred and ten thousand, and horsemen five thousand and three hundred, and elephants two and twenty, and three hundred chariots armed with hooks. [3] Menelaus also joined himself with them, and with great dissimulation encouraged Antiochus, not for the safeguard of the country, but because he thought to have been made governor. [4] But the King of kings moved Antiochus' mind against this wicked wretch, and Lysias informed the king that this man was the cause of all mischief, so that the king commanded to bring him unto Berea, and to put him to death, as the manner is in that place. [5] Now there was in that place a tower of fifty cubits high, full of ashes, and it had a round instrument which on every side hanged down into the ashes. [6] And whosoever was condemned of sacrilege, or had committed any other grievous crime, there did all men thrust him unto death. [7] Such a death it happened that wicked man to die, not having so much as burial in the earth; and that most justly: [8] For inasmuch as he had committed many sins about the altar, whose fire and ashes were holy, he received his death in ashes. [9] Now the king came with a barbarous and haughty mind to do far worse to the Jews, than had been done in his father's

time. [10] Which things when Judas perceived, he commanded the multitude to call upon the Lord night and day, that if ever at any other time, he would now also help them, being at the point to be put from their law, from their country, and from the holy temple: [11] And that he would not suffer the people, that had even now been but a little refreshed, to be in subjection to the blasphemous nations. [12] So when they had all done this together, and besought the merciful Lord with weeping and fasting, and lying flat upon the ground three days long, Judas, having exhorted them, commanded they should be in a readiness. [13] And Judas, being apart with the elders, determined, before the king's host should enter into Judea, and get the city, to go forth and try the matter in fight by the help of the Lord. [14] So when he had committed all to the Creator of the world, and exhorted his soldiers to fight manfully, even unto death, for the laws, the temple, the city, the country, and the commonwealth, he camped by Modin:

[15] And having given the watchword to them that were about him, Victory is of God; with the most valiant and choice young men he went in into the king's tent by night, and slew in the camp about four thousand men, and the chiefest of the elephants, with all that were upon him. [16] And at last they filled the camp with fear and tumult, and departed with good success. [17] This was done in the break of the day, because the protection of the Lord did help him. [18] Now when the king had taken a taste of the manliness of the Jews, he went about to take the holds by policy, [19] And marched toward Bethsura, which was a strong hold of the Jews: but he was put to flight, failed, and lost of his men: [20] For Judas had conveyed unto them that were in it such things as were necessary. [21] But Rhodocus, who was in the Jews' host, disclosed the secrets to the enemies; therefore he was sought out, and when they had gotten him, they put him in prison. [22] The king treated with them in Bethsum the second time, gave his hand, took their's, departed, fought with Judas, was overcome; [23] Heard that Philip, who was left over the affairs in Antioch, was desperately bent, confounded, intreated the Jews, submitted himself, and sware to all equal conditions, agreed with them, and offered sacrifice, honoured the temple, and dealt kindly with the place, [24] And accepted well of Maccabeus, made him principal governor from Ptolemais unto the Gerrhenians; [25] Came to Ptolemais: the people there were grieved for the covenants; for they stormed, because they would make their covenants void: [26] Lysias went up to the judgment seat, said as much as could be in defence of the cause, persuaded, pacified, made them well affected, returned to Antioch. Thus it went touching the king's coming and departing.

2Mac.14

[1] After three years was Judas informed, that Demetrius the son of Seleucus, having entered by the haven of Tripolis with a great power and navy, [2] Had taken the country, and killed Antiochus, and Lysias his protector. [3] Now one Alcimus, who had been high priest, and had defiled himself wilfully in the times of their mingling with the Gentiles, seeing that by no means he could save himself, nor have any more access to the holy altar, [4] Came to king Demetrius in the hundred and one and fiftieth year, presenting unto him a crown of gold, and a palm, and also of the boughs which were used solemnly in the temple: and so that day he held his peace. [5] Howbeit having gotten opportunity to further his foolish enterprize, and being called into counsel by Demetrius, and asked how the Jews stood affected, and what they intended, he answered thereunto: [6] Those of the Jews that he called Assideans, whose captain is Judas Maccabeus, nourish war and are seditious, and will not let the rest be in peace. [7] Therefore I, being deprived of mine ancestors' honour, I mean the high priesthood, am now come hither: [8] First, verily for the unfeigned care I have of things pertaining to the king; and secondly, even for that I intend the good of mine own countrymen: for all our nation is in no small misery through the unadvised dealing of them aforersaid. [9] Wherefore, O king, seeing knowest all these things, be careful for the country, and our nation, which is pressed on every side, according to the clemency that thou readily shewest unto all. [10] For as long as Judas liveth, it is not possible that the state should be quiet. [11] This was no sooner spoken of him, but others of the king's friends, being maliciously set against Judas, did more incense Demetrius. [12] And forthwith calling Nicanor, who had been master of the elephants, and making him governor over Judea, he sent him forth, [13] Commanding him to slay Judas, and to scatter them that were with him, and to make Alcimus high priest of the great temple. [14] Then the heathen, that had fled out of Judea from Judas, came to Nicanor by flocks, thinking the harm and calamities ot the Jews to be their welfare. [15] Now when the Jews heard of Nicanor's coming, and that the heathen were up against them, they cast earth upon their heads, and made supplication to him that had established his people for ever, and who always helpeth his portion with manifestation of his presence. [16] So at the commandment of the captain they removed straightways from thence, and came near unto them at the town of Dessau. [17] Now Simon, Judas' brother, had joined battle with Nicanor, but was somewhat discomfited through the sudden silence of his enemies. [18] Nevertheless Nicanor, hearing of the manliness of them that were with Judas, and the courageousness that they had to fight for their country, durst not try the matter by the sword. [19] Wherefore he sent Posidonius, and Theodotus, and Mattathias, to make peace. [20] So when they had taken long advisement thereupon, and the captain had made the multitude acquainted therewith, and it appeared that they were all of one mind, they consented to the covenants, [21] And appointed a day to meet in together by themselves: and when the day came, and stools were set for either of them, [22] Ludas placed armed men ready in convenient places, lest some treachery should be suddenly practised by the enemies: so they made a peaceable conference. [23] Now Nicanor abode in Jerusalem, and did no hurt, but sent away the people that came flocking unto him. [24] And he would not willingly have Judas out of his sight: for he love the man from his heart [25] He prayed him also to take a wife, and to beget children: so he married, was quiet, and took part of this life.

[26] But Alcimus, perceiving the love that was betwixt them, and considering the covenants that were made, came to Demetrius, and told him that Nicanor was not well affected toward the state; for that he had ordained Judas, a

traitor to his realm, to be the king's successor. [27] Then
the king being in a rage, and provoked with the accusations
of the most wicked man, wrote to Nicanor, signifying that
he was much displeased with the covenants, and
commanding him that he should send Maccabeus prisoner
in all haste unto Antioch. [28] When this came to
Nicanor's hearing, he was much confounded in himself,
and took it grievously that he should make void the articles
which were agreed upon, the man being in no fault. [29]
But because there was no dealing against the king, he
watched his time to accomplish this thing by policy. [30]
Notwithstanding, when Maccabeus saw that Nicanor began
to be churlish unto him, and that he entreated him more
roughly than he was wont, perceiving that such sour
behaviour came not of good, he gathered together not a
few of his men, and withdrew himself from Nicanor. [31]
But the other, knowing that he was notably prevented by
Judas' policy, came into the great and holy temple, and
commanded the priests, that were offering their usual
sacrifices, to deliver him the man. [32] And when they
sware that they could not tell where the man was whom he
sought, [33] He stretched out his right hand toward the
temple, and made an oath in this manner: If ye will not
deliver me Judas as a prisoner, I will lay this temple of God
even with the ground, and I will break down the altar, and
erect a notable temple unto Bacchus. [34] After these
words he departed. Then the priests lifted up their hands
toward heaven, and besought him that was ever a defender
of their nation, saying in this manner; [35] Thou, O Lord
of all things, who hast need of nothing, wast pleased that
the temple of thine habitation should be among us: [36]
Therefore now, O holy Lord of all holiness, keep this
house ever undefiled, which lately was cleansed, and stop
every unrighteous mouth. [37] Now was there accused
unto Nicanor one Razis, one of the elders of Jerusalem, a
lover of his countrymen, and a man of very good report,
who for his kindness was called a father of the Jews. [38]
For in the former times, when they mingled not themselves
with the Gentiles, he had been accused of Judaism, and did
boldly jeopard his body and life with all vehemency for the
religion of the Jews. [39] So Nicanor, willing to declare the
hate that he bare unto the Jews, sent above five hundred
men of war to take him: [40] For he thought by taking him
to do the Jews much hurt. [41] Now when the multitude
would have taken the tower, and violently broken into the
outer door, and bade that fire should be brought to burn it,
he being ready to be taken on every side fell upon his
sword; [42] Choosing rather to die manfully, than to come
into the hands of the wicked, to be abused otherwise than
beseemed his noble birth: [43] But missing his stroke
through haste, the multitude also rushing within the doors,
he ran boldly up to the wall, and cast himself down
manfully among the thickest of them. [44] But they quickly
giving back, and a space being made, he fell down into the
midst of the void place. [45] Nevertheless, while there was
yet breath within him, being inflamed with anger, he rose
up; and though his blood gushed out like spouts of water,
and his wounds were grievous, yet he ran through the midst
of the throng; and standing upon a steep rock, [46] When
as his blood was now quite gone, he plucked out his
bowels, and taking them in both his hands, he cast them
upon the throng, and calling upon the Lord of life and
spirit to restore him those again, he thus died.

2Mac.15

[1] But Nicanor, hearing that Judas and his company were
in the strong places about Samaria, resolved without any
danger to set upon them on the sabbath day. [2]
Nevertheless the Jews that were compelled to go with him
said, O destroy not so cruelly and barbarously, but give
honour to that day, which he, that seeth all things, hath
honoured with holiness above all other days. [3] Then the
most ungracious wretch demanded, if there were a Mighty
one in heaven, that had commanded the sabbath day to be
kept. [4] And when they said, There is in heaven a living
Lord, and mighty, who commanded the seventh day to be
kept: [5] Then said the other, And I also am mighty upon
earth, and I command to take arms, and to do the king's
business. Yet he obtained not to have his wicked will done.
[6] So Nicanor in exceeding pride and haughtiness
determined to set up a publick monument of his victory
over Judas and them that were with him. [7] But
Maccabeus had ever sure confidence that the Lord would
help him: [8] Wherefore he exhorted his people not to fear
the coming of the heathen against them, but to remember
the help which in former times they had received from
heaven, and now to expect the victory and aid, which
should come unto them from the Almighty. [9] And so
comforting them out of the law and the prophets, and
withal putting them in mind of the battles that they won
afore, he made them more cheerful. [10] And when he had
stirred up their minds, he gave them their charge, shewing
them therewithall the falsehood of the heathen, and the
breach of oaths. [11] Thus he armed every one of them,
not so much with defence of shields and spears, as with
comfortable and good words: and beside that, he told them
a dream worthy to be believed, as if it had been so indeed,
which did not a little rejoice them. [12] And this was his
vision: That Onias, who had been high priest, a virtuous
and a good man, reverend in conversation, gentle in
condition, well spoken also, and exercised from a child in
all points of virtue, holding up his hands prayed for the
whole body of the Jews. [13] This done, in like manner
there appeared a man with gray hairs, and exceeding
glorious, who was of a wonderful and excellent majesty.
[14] Then Onias answered, saying, This is a lover of the
brethren, who prayeth much for the people, and for the
holy city, to wit, Jeremias the prophet of God. [15]
Whereupon Jeremias holding forth his right hand gave to
Judas a sword of gold, and in giving it spake thus, [16]
Take this holy sword, a gift from God, with the which thou
shalt wound the adversaries. [17] Thus being well
comforted by the words of Judas, which were very good,
and able to stir them up to valour, and to encourage the
hearts of the young men, they determined not to pitch
camp, but courageously to set upon them, and manfully to
try the matter by conflict, because the city and the
sanctuary and the temple were in danger. [18] For the care
that they took for their wives, and their children, their
brethren, and folks, was in least account with them: but the
greatest and principal fear was for the holy temple. [19]
Also they that were in the city took not the least care, being
troubled for the conflict abroad. [20] And now, when as all
looked what should be the trial, and the enemies were
already come near, and the army was set in array, and the
beasts conveniently placed, and the horsemen set in wings,

[21] Maccabeus seeing the coming of the multitude, and the divers preparations of armour, and the fierceness of the beasts, stretched out his hands toward heaven, and called upon the Lord that worketh wonders, knowing that victory cometh not by arms, but even as it seemeth good to him, he giveth it to such as are worthy: [22] Therefore in his prayer he said after this manner; O Lord, thou didst send thine angel in the time of Ezekias king of Judea, and didst slay in the host of Sennacherib an hundred fourscore and five thousand: [23] Wherefore now also, O Lord of heaven, send a good angel before us for a fear and dread unto them; [24] And through the might of thine arm let those be stricken with terror, that come against thy holy people to blaspheme. And he ended thus. [25] Then Nicanor and they that were with him came forward with trumpets and songs. [26] But Judas and his company encountered the enemies with invocation and prayer. [27] So that fighting with their hands, and praying unto God with their hearts, they slew no less than thirty and five thousand men: for through the appearance of God they were greatly cheered. [28] Now when the battle was done, returning again with joy, they knew that Nicanor lay dead in his harness. [29] Then they made a great shout and a noise, praising the Almighty in their own language. [30] And Judas, who was ever the chief defender of the citizens both in body and mind, and who continued his love toward his countrymen all his life, commanded to strike off Nicanor's head, and his hand with his shoulder, and bring them to Jerusalem. [31] So when he was there, and called them of his nation together, and set the priests before the altar, he sent for them that were of the tower, [32] And shewed them vile Nicanor's head, and the hand of that blasphemer, which with proud brags he had stretched out against the holy temple of the Almighty. [33] And when he had cut out the tongue of that ungodly Nicanor, he commanded that they should give it by pieces unto the fowls, and hang up the reward of his madness before the temple. [34] So every man praised toward the heaven the glorious Lord, saying, Blessed be he that hath kept his own place undefiled. [35] He hanged also Nicanor's head upon the tower, an evident and manifest sign unto all of the help of the Lord. [36] And they ordained all with a common decree in no case to let that day pass without solemnity, but to celebrate the thirtieth day of the twelfth month, which in the Syrian tongue is called Adar, the day before Mardocheus' day. [37] Thus went it with Nicanor: and from that time forth the Hebrews had the city in their power. And here will I make an end. [38] And if I have done well, and as is fitting the story, it is that which I desired: but if slenderly and meanly, it is that which I could attain unto. [39] For as it is hurtful to drink wine or water alone; and as wine mingled with water is pleasant, and delighteth the taste: even so speech finely framed delighteth the ears of them that read the story.

And here shall be an end.

Gustave Dorè - War in Heaven

REFERENCES

-THE BOOK OF ENOCH
Translated by R. H. Charles, D.Litt., D.D.
London Society for Promoting Christian Knowledge [1917]

-THE ANTE NICENE FAHTHER
The Writings of the Fathers down to A.D. 325 (1885)
Alexander Roberts and James Donaldson, Volume VIII and IX.

-THE APOCRYPHAL NEW TESTAMENT
Being the Apocryphal Gospels, Acts, Epistles, and Apocalypses
With Other Narratives and Fragments
Newly Translated by Montague Rhodes James
Litt.D., F.B.A., F.S.A. Provost of Eton; Sometime Provost of King's College,
Cambridge Oxford At the Clarendon Press 1924.

-THE FORGOTTEN BOOKS OF EDEN
Edited by Rutherford H. Platt, Jr.
New York, N.Y.; Alpha House
[1926]

-THE LOST BOOKS OF THE BIBLE
Edited by Rutherford H. Platt, Jr.
New York, N.Y.; Alpha House
[1926]

-THE DIDACHE or Teaching of the Twelve Apostles
Translation by Charles H. Hoole, M.A. student of Christ Church,
Oxford London David Nutt, 270–71 Strand [1894]

-GOSPEL.NET
Mark M. Mattison, Andrew Bernhard

-THE BOOK OF JUBILEES or The Little Genesis
Translated from the Ethiopic text by R. H. Charles, D.Litt., D.D.
Society for Promoting Christian Knowledge London 68, Haymarket, S.W. 1.
New York: The Macmillan Company 1917

-THE BOOK OF JASHER
Faithfully Translated from the original Hebrew into English.
Salt Lake City: published by J.H. Parry & Company 1887.

-THE APOCRYPHA AND PSEUDEPIGRAPHA
OF THE OLD TESTAMENT IN ENGLISH
R.H. Charles, D.Litt., D.D. Fellow of Merton College
Clarendon Press, Oxford, 1913

TimelessTruth Editions

2024

Made in United States
Troutdale, OR
06/28/2024

20885589R00423